THE HAMLYN
WORD GAME
DICTIONARY

TOM PULLIAM & GORTON CARRUTH

BCA
LONDON · NEW YORK · SYDNEY · TORONTO

Scrabble® is a Registered Trade Mark owned in
the United Kingdom and most of the world by
J. W. Spear & Sons plc, Enfield, Middlesex.
Scrabble® is a Registered Trade Mark owned in the USA
and Canada by Selchow and Righter Co., New York.
Reference to Scrabble® is printed with the permission of
Murfett Pty Ltd, 7-13 Keys Rd (PO Box 152), Moorabbin,
Victoria SU. 3189, the Australian owners of Scrabble®.
Hangman® is a Registered Trade Mark owned in the USA by
Hangman Games.
Anagram® is a Registered Trade Mark owned in the USA by
Airtime Mfg. Inc.

Previously published in 1985
under the title
Newnes Complete Word Game Dictionary

This edition published in 1992
by BCA by arrangement with
Octopus Illustrated Publishing
part of Reed International Books
Michelin House
81 Fulham Road, London SW3 6RB

First published 1984 in the USA and the United Kingdom as
The Complete Word Game Dictionary
by Facts on File Publications, New York and Bicester

© Copyright 1984 Tom Pulliam
and Gorton Carruth

CN 8127

Printed and bound in the United Kingdom
by The Bath Press

Contents

Preface

The *Hamlyn Word Game Dictionary* is a unique dictionary. Its size and comprehensiveness put it in a class by itself. It is equally useful for tournament play and for family fun at home. It contains nearly 230,000 words specially selected to help players of most word games, both those available in shops, and the kind that involve nothing more elaborate than a pencil and paper. It is designed to be used during play as the standard arbiter of the ever-present "challenge" which occurs in nearly every parlour word game: does your word exist or have you made it up? But the *Hamlyn Word Game Dictionary* is also designed to be studied before and after play to increase one's knowledge of those words that help to make a player a winner.

Millions play word games. Of all parlour games, word games are perhaps the first that children develop an interest in. Whole families play word games together, not only because of their sharp competitiveness, but also because of their educational value. We know of no survey or indepth study that has been conducted on such matters, but we venture to say that in the average home of today, one or more of the following are played: crossword puzzles, hangman, word-squares, anagrams, ghost, the word games sold under the Scrabble® brand, and other similar commercially available games.

Of all modern word games, none can rival the acknowledged stature of the Scrabble® brand crossword games. Since it was first invented more than 40 years ago, it captured interest year by year until it has now become an international classic among today's gamesters. The Scrabble® set rests alongside the Monopoly® set in most family rooms. Because it challenges personal aptitudes ranging from structural visualisation to "knowing how to spell", Scrabble® contains some inherent complexities not present in most other word games. In recognition of this fact, the *Hamlyn Word Game Dictionary* has been organised in such a way that its greatest value will be for the Scrabble® player, whether neophyte or of tournament calibre.

Some commercial word games depend on using lettered cards to form words, with graduated rewards to the players for his skill in doing so. These games often require a good deal of guile and bluff as the player has to try to deduce the concealed words formed by his opponents.

Other games use a number of lettered dice. After the player has thrown these dice at random, there is a strictly measured time period during which bona-fide words must be formed from the letters that have been turned up. In some, the score depends on the number of words of different lengths that the player can construct; in others, the words formed must intersect, much in the style of crossword puzzles or the Scrabble® brand games.

Traditional word games have rules and procedures that are almost universally recognised and accepted, even though the games themselves have many forms and variations. We will briefly describe a few of our own favourites:

Anagrams is played with lettered cards or tiles. These are normally exposed one at a time in the centre of the playing area. Within a specified time any player may form acceptable words by withdrawing the required letters from the pile in the centre. Words formed by any player are liable to capture by any other player, to form a new word, incorporating the original word and adding on to it one or more other letters from the pile. Generally some basic change in the form and meaning of the word is a prerequisite for a capture.

In **Guggenheim**, or **Categories**, each player in turn names aloud one category (colour, country, tree, sport, etc.) and these categories are listed by each player in a vertical column on a piece of paper. Another word is then selected, either at random or by agreement. This word is not normally very long, contains no unusual letters and no repeated letters. Each player then writes the letters of this word by each vertical heading, and then attempts to find acceptable words for that category that begin with each letter in turn of the key-word. Thus, if the keyword is *table* and one of the categories is "colour", the player might enter the words *tan, azure, blue, lilac, emerald.*

In **Ghost**, each player in turn names a letter aloud. Letters thus announced are mentally visualised by all players as being written in the order in which they are announced. From the fourth letter onwards, each player attempts to continue the process by adding another letter while taking care not to form a complete word. He cannot, however, name any letter at random; he has to be prepared to face a challenge and state what word he has in mind that contains the letter-chain he has made. Thus, if the letters BEA are presented to a player, he obviously wishes to avoid ending a word by choosing D M N R T or U. Instead, he will perhaps add a G, forming BEAG, with the word *beagle* in mind. The succeeding players will look out for this and try somehow to avoid the trap.

Normally, a player ending a word or caught in a bluff becomes "one-third of a ghost" and begins a new word. The next time he falls into error he becomes "two-thirds of a ghost". After three such losses, the player is eliminated, while the game continues among the survivors until only one remains.

Superghost is an embellishment of Ghost. Here the player may add his letter before or after the letter-chain with which he has been faced. For example, if presented with STABL, he might choose to prefix N to form NSTABL, with the word *unstable* in mind. The trap may not work, however, as the next player then might prefix an O, thinking of the word constable. The game calls for an agile mind and an ample vocabulary, and no-one should be over-hasty in challenging without weighing the calibre of the opponent.

Hangman is relatively simple, and a game for two. One player thinks of a word and represents it on paper by a series of dashes, one for each letter. The other player simply tries to guess the word by naming letters of the alphabet. If he "hits" a letter in the concealed word, it is written into its appropriate position. If not, his opponent draws a piece of a gallows. The object is to guess the word before you have been "hanged" for your number of wrong guesses.

The *Hamlyn Word Game Dictionary* has been developed as an aid and a wit-sharpener for the countless people who indulge in these and similar word games.

Part 1: The Comprehensive Word List

In practically all competitive word games there arises what is known as the "challenge". Most such games would be mild and placid were it not for this device. The word is self-explanatory: one player has made use of a word, another disagrees with its spelling or its validity, and issues a challenge to the first player to justify his word. Though the rules of many board games are not explicit about the steps to be taken after a challenge, most games agree in permitting the use of practically any word "found in a standard dictionary".

Modern desk dictionaries, though valuable for normal day-to-day uses, are not adequate as mediators for word games, which are becoming increasingly complex. The home dictionary will usually contain something under 60,000 words. And it may well not include words of recent origin, especially technical or scientific terms, or the many words that are flooding into English from other languages. It may serve to clarify your game query to the satisfaction of all – or it may not.

Even after a dictionary has been selected, lesser questions still hinder the progress of the game. Are proper nouns permitted? How about foreign words? Abbreviations? Past tenses? Illogical plurals? Irregular endings? And so it goes on.

These problems lead us to the underlying premise and purpose of the *Hamlyn Word Game Dictionary*. The greater part of it is devoted to a Comprehensive Word List, which serves, in the speediest way possible, to decide the acceptability of any word that arises during your game.

Does it have advantages over a dictionary that is mutually acceptable to all players? We believe it does.

In looking up any word in this Comprehensive Word List at the time of a challenge, you only have to skim through a single alphabetical list of 185,000 words to the exact word in question, be it commonplace or esoteric. Not so with a normal dictionary. The major objective of a dictionary is to define and clarify the meaning of words, and the bulk of its space is occupied by definitive and descriptive text. Valuable though such information may be, the impatient player must wade through it to arrive at the word under challenge – all in the interests of a word game in which meanings play no role. So the Comprehensive Word List is, first of all, the easiest, quickest source for deciding on the acceptability of a questionable word. What's more, the Comprehensive Word List is not based on any single dictionary and, with its grand total of 185,000 words, goes well beyond the scope of any desktop dictionary.

Let us further examine this Comprehensive Word List to discover what it does and does not contain.

Proper Names

Consider, for example, the use of proper nouns. It is up to you, the user, to determine whether your word game permits the use of proper names. Most do not. A certain game, for instance, specifies that "capitalised" words are not acceptable. This immediately throws us on the mercy of the "dictionary of your choice". If this should happen to be the *Oxford English Dictionary*, the whole game must immediately end – because *each* word listed therein is capitalised! At the other extreme, you may have agreed upon the *Merriam-Webster International Dictionary*, 3rd Edition, an equally reputable tome. You are now overwhelmed to find that "the sky's the limit": with very rare exceptions, no main entry is capitalised. You have to pore through the descriptive text to discover that a given word is "usually capitalised", "sometimes capitalised", etc.

So, to relieve you of this dilemma, we have established our own editorial criterion. Because most word games prohibit their use, we have excluded from the List all words that are always capitalised. You may find, on thumbing through the List, some words that seem to be proper names: Argentine, Inverness, Telamon, for example. But note that we have stated that we have omitted only words that are *always* capitalised. You will be well aware that "china" need not be capitalised when it is referring to porcelain; "argentine" is included here in its meaning of silvery, "inverness" is an overcoat, and "telamon" is an architectural figure.

To sum up, a word appears in the List only if we have found it as a common, or uncapitalised, word, in at least one source. As such, it deserves inclusion and warrants your using it freely in word games.

Foreign words

Most word games have some stated prohibition against the use of words "designated as foreign words". But one has only to scan representative dictionaries to see that they differ in their manner of designating foreign words. Some use special symbols antecedent to the main entry; others place the burden solely on the etymology to indicate the degree of "foreignness".

In the heat of a hotly contested word game you should not have to be concerned with such interpretations and decisions. The foreign word of yesterday is the English word of today. Such words as *confetti, junta, dirndl* and *houri* are commonplace to most game players, now, without thought as to their being foreign in the recent past. So we have taken the view that the only foreign words are those that are *solely* foreign in their use. If a word appears in an authoritative English dictionary, regardless of foreign designation by either symbol or text, we have included it in the Comprehensive Word List and consider it acceptable for word play.

Variant and Archaic Forms

The same can be said for variant spellings, and archaic and obsolete words. Eventually many of these words will fade from current usage completely and will be, undoubtedly, dropped from reputable dictionaries. Until that time, we have included archaic and variant spellings. Indeed, in our experience they add spice to the game and often present an escape outlet just when we are being painted into a corner in a tight crossword game.

Long Words

You will quickly note many long words in the Comprehensive Word List. Remembering that in a game such as Scrabble® you have only seven letters to play with, you may doubt the value of, say, the twelve-letter words.

Yet, as top players know, the best scores are made by interconnecting one or more letters with those already on the board. So while they are uncommon in normal social games, words of twelve letters or more are conceivable and actually occur in Scrabble® game patterns.

This does not mean we have included willy-nilly all long words that exist in reputable sources. We have exercised editorial prerogative here. If a long word is based upon an internal "root" word of common vintage, the chances are we have included it. The expert player closely inspects all existing words on the board to find a chance of adding letters to it fore or aft, or both. So we have chosen long words whose roots may easily be played in a normal game.

Verb Endings, Plurals and Adverbial Forms

These present a problem in all word games where the challenge is a factor. The rules of most word games are not sufficiently explicit to be certain of the permissibility of words in these categories. In Superghost, in particular, players are tempted to weasel out of a tight spot by means of a hastily contrived gerundive or participial form. In Scrabble®, the normal inflected forms are acceptable, whether or not they are specifically printed in standard dictionaries. These normal forms include past tense, past participle and present participle of verbs, and the plural of nouns. This gives free licence for the use of *-s, -es, -ed* and *-ing*. In most dictionaries such forms are entered only where there is an irregularity in spelling or form.

Comparative *(-er)* and superlative *(-est)* forms of adjectives are a somewhat different matter. One-syllable adjectives and their comparative and superlative forms *(strong, stronger, strongest)* are presumed to be acceptable, whether listed or not. Multisyllable adjectives are only permissible if the comparative and superlative forms actually appear in the agreed-upon authority.

The Comprehensive Word List frees you from the need for personal interpretation and judgement. It does not list *all* simple plurals that can be formed merely by adding *-s* or *-es*, though a great many are included. But it liberally includes inflected forms and unusual plurals, including those you might have trouble ferreting out of the dictionary. For instance, you might have trouble checking these plural forms in a normal dictionary: *feis – plural feiseanna; os – ora; drostdy – drostden.*

Definitions

One instantly apparent characteristic of the List is the absence of definitions. This is because we see no significant value or need for definitions in most word games. The basic consideration is simply whether the challenged word exists or not.

Some excellent books that serve as arbiters for word-game play do include definitions. But their users, in our experience, do not employ these definitions to edify the mind. The expressed purpose of the definitions is no more than to clarify the part of speech, and consequently the admissibility of plurals and inflected forms. The Comprehensive Word List already contains most inflected forms as well as unusual plurals. Including definitions as well would have been a labour of love without a corresponding benefit for the user.

Part 2: The High Scoring Word Lists

In recognition of the more complex play found in Scrabble® over other word games, the *Hamlyn Word Game Dictionary* contains a number of specialised lists. These are intended for the Scrabble® player, though their value extends to other word games as well.

Success in Scrabble® of course depends in large degree on the opportune placement of the high-scoring letters Z (ten points), Q (ten points), J (eight points) and X (eight points). Thus the high-scoring lists of Part 2 have been framed around words containing these four key letters. Each of these letters has a section, within which words are arranged first by word length, and then by type of list. There are three types of list: alphabetical, positional and scoring.

Alphabetical Lists

For any one of these key letters there first appear the Alphabetical Lists, arranged by word length, of acceptable words containing that letter. You should use these lists to become familiar with as many of the two and three-letter words as you can. Most experts agree that familiarity with these words is a key factor in top-quality play, since they represent the essential links in the interlocking process of forming new words in conjunction with those already appearing on the board.

Positional Lists

We have also prepared Positional Lists, by word length, for each of the key letters. These have a value far beyond the Scrabble® board; for instance for the crossword player who may be seeking a six-letter word with a Z in the fifth position.

Scoring Order Lists

Finally we have included for each of the key letters a Scoring Order List, in which the words are listed in order of the total Scrabble® score of all letters, arranged by word length.

This may require some clarification. We cannot, of course, allow for the variations in score brought about by double- or triple-letter scores. And you may come across some words, such as *jazz*, which seem to need more than the single Z tile that the Scrabble® set contains. In such cases we have assumed that the "extra" letter is formed by a blank or wild tile and its value has been computed as zero.

The *Hamlyn Word Game Dictionary* is intended to be used. In any word game in which the challenge arises, it is meant to be a handy arbiter. If you familiarise yourself with the contents of this volume and actually use it for its intended purposes, it cannot help but promote your progress as a gamester – without diluting the fun!

Tom Pulliam
Gorton Carruth

PART I

Comprehensive Word List

AA
AABEC
AAL
AALII
AAM
AAR
AARDVARK
AARDWOLF
AASVOGEL
ABA
ABACA
ABACATE
ABACAXI
ABACAY
ABACI
ABACINATE
ABACINATION
ABACISCUS
ABACIST
ABACK
ABACOT
ABACTINAL
ABACTINALLY
ABACTION
ABACTOR
ABACULI
ABACULUS
ABACUS
ABACUSES
ABAD
ABADA
ABADEJO
ABADENGO
ABADI
ABADIA
ABAFF
ABAFT
ABAISANCE
ABAISER
ABAISSE
ABAISSED
ABAKA
ABALIENATE
ABALIENATED
ABALIENATION
ABALONE
ABAMPERE
ABAND
ABANDON
ABANDONED
ABANDONEDLY
ABANDONER
ABANDONMENT
ABANDUM
ABANGA
ABAPTISTON
ABAPTISTUM
ABARTICULAR
ABARTICULATION
ABAS
ABASE
ABASED
ABASEDLY
ABASEDNESS
ABASEMENT
ABASER
ABASH

ABASHED
ABASHEDLY
ABASHING
ABASHLESS
ABASHLESSLY
ABASHMENT
ABASIA
ABASING
ABASIO
ABASK
ABASSI
ABASTARDIZE
ABATA
ABATABLE
ABATE
ABATED
ABATEMENT
ABATER
ABATI
ABATING
ABATIS
ABATON
ABATOR
ABATTIS
ABATTISED
ABATTOIR
ABATTOIRS
ABATTU
ABATTUE
ABATURE
ABAVE
ABAWE
ABAXIAL
ABAXILE
ABAYAH
ABAZE
ABB
ABBA
ABBACIES
ABBACY
ABBAS
ABBASI
ABBASSI
ABBATE
ABBATIAL
ABBATICAL
ABBAYE
ABBE
ABBESS
ABBEST
ABBEY
ABBEYS
ABBEYSTEDE
ABBOGADA
ABBOT
ABBOTCIES
ABBOTCY
ABBOTSHIP
ABBOZZO
ABBREVIATE
ABBREVIATED
ABBREVIATELY
ABBREVIATING
ABBREVIATION
ABBREVIATOR
ABBREVIATORY
ABBREVIATURE
ABCOULOMB
ABDAL
ABDALI
ABDAT
ABDEST
ABDICABLE
ABDICANT
ABDICATE
ABDICATED
ABDICATING

ABDICATION
ABDICATIVE
ABDICATOR
ABDITIVE
ABDITORY
ABDOMEN
ABDOMINAL
ABDOMINALES
ABDOMINALIAN
ABDOMINALLY
ABDOMINALS
ABDOMINOUS
ABDUCE
ABDUCENS
ABDUCENT
ABDUCT
ABDUCTED
ABDUCTION
ABDUCTOR
ABE
ABEAM
ABEAR
ABEARANCE
ABECEDAIRE
ABECEDARIA
ABECEDARIAN
ABECEDARIES
ABECEDARIUM
ABECEDARIUS
ABECEDARY
ABED
ABEEN
ABEGGE
ABEIGH
ABELE
ABELITE
ABELMOSK
ABELMUSK
ABELTREE
ABENTERIC
ABEPITHYMIA
ABERDAVINE
ABERDEVINE
ABERDUVINE
ABERR
ABERRANCE
ABERRANCY
ABERRANT
ABERRATE
ABERRATED
ABERRATING
ABERRATION
ABERRATIONAL
ABERRATOR
ABERROMETER
ABERROSCOPE
ABESSIVE
ABET
ABETMENT
ABETO
ABETTAL
ABETTED
ABETTER
ABETTING
ABETTOR
ABEVACUATION
ABEY
ABEYANCE
ABEYANCY
ABEYANT
ABFARAD
ABHAL
ABHENRY
ABHINAYA
ABHISEKA
ABHOMINABLE
ABHOR

ABHORRED
ABHORRENCE
ABHORRENCY
ABHORRENT
ABHORRENTLY
ABHORRER
ABHORRIBLE
ABHORRING
ABIDAL
ABIDANCE
ABIDDEN
ABIDE
ABIDED
ABIDER
ABIDING
ABIDINGLY
ABIDINGNESS
ABIEGH
ABIENCE
ABIETATE
ABIETENE
ABIETIC
ABIETINEOUS
ABIETINIC
ABIGAIL
ABIGAILSHIP
ABIGEI
ABIGEUS
ABILAO
ABILITIES
ABILITY
ABILLA
ABILO
ABIME
ABINTESTATE
ABIOGENESIS
ABIOGENETIC
ABIOGENIST
ABIOLOGICAL
ABIOLOGY
ABIOSIS
ABIOTIC
ABIOTROPHIC
ABIOTROPHY
ABIR
ABIRRITANT
ABIRRITATE
ABIRRITATED
ABIRRITATING
ABIRRITATION
ABIRRITATIVE
ABISTON
ABIURET
ABJECT
ABJECTEDNESS
ABJECTION
ABJECTIVE
ABJECTLY
ABJECTNESS
ABJOINT
ABJUDGE
ABJUDICATE
ABJUDICATION
ABJUDICATOR
ABJUNCTIVE
ABJURATION
ABJURATORY
ABJURE
ABJURED
ABJUREMENT
ABJURER
ABJURING
ABKAR
ABKARI
ABKARY
ABLACH
ABLACTATE

ABLACTATION
ABLARE
ABLASTEMIC
ABLASTIN
ABLASTOUS
ABLATE
ABLATION
ABLATITIOUS
ABLATIVAL
ABLATIVE
ABLATOR
ABLAUT
ABLAZE
ABLE
ABLEEZE
ABLEGATE
ABLEGATION
ABLENESS
ABLEPHARIA
ABLEPHAROUS
ABLEPSIA
ABLEPSY
ABLEPTICAL
ABLEPTICALLY
ABLER
ABLEST
ABLEWHACKETS
ABLINGS
ABLINS
ABLOOM
ABLOW
ABLUDE
ABLUENT
ABLUSH
ABLUTION
ABLUTIONARY
ABLY
ABNEGATE
ABNEGATED
ABNEGATING
ABNEGATION
ABNEGATIVE
ABNEGATOR
ABNERVAL
ABNET
ABNEURAL
ABNORMAL
ABNORMALITIES
ABNORMALITY
ABNORMALIZE
ABNORMALLY
ABNORMALNESS
ABNORMITIES
ABNORMITY
ABNORMOUS
ABOARD
ABOCOCKET
ABODAH
ABODE
ABODED
ABODEMENT
ABODING
ABOGADO
ABOGADOS
ABOHM
ABOIDEAU
ABOIDEAUS
ABOIDEAUX
ABOIL
ABOITEAU
ABOLETE
ABOLISH
ABOLISHABLE
ABOLISHED
ABOLISHER
ABOLISHING
ABOLISHMENT

ABOLITION	ABRASING	ABSCONDER	ABSTERGENT	ABUTTER
ABOLITIONARY	ABRASIOMETER	ABSEIL	ABSTERGING	ABUTTING
ABOLITIONISM	ABRASION	ABSENCE	ABSTERSION	ABUZZ
ABOLITIONIST	ABRASIVE	ABSENT	ABSTERSIVE	ABVOLT
ABOLITIONIZE	ABRASIVES	ABSENTATION	ABSTINENCE	ABWAB
ABOLLA	ABRASTOL	ABSENTEE	ABSTINENCY	ABWATT
ABOLLAE	ABRAUM	ABSENTEEISM	ABSTINENT	ABY
ABOMA	ABRAXAS	ABSENTER	ABSTINENTIAL	ABYE
ABOMASUM	ABRAZO	ABSENTLY	ABSTINENTLY	ABYSM
ABOMASUS	ABREACT	ABSENTMENT	ABSTORT	ABYSMAL
ABOMINABLE	ABREACTION	ABSENTMINDED	ABSTRACT	ABYSMALLY
ABOMINABLY	ABREAST	ABSENTMINDEDNESS	ABSTRACTED	ABYSS
ABOMINATE	ABREED	ABSENTNESS	ABSTRACTEDLY	ABYSSAL
ABOMINATED	ABREGE	ABSINTH	ABSTRACTEDNESS	ACACATECHIN
ABOMINATING	ABREID	ABSINTHE	ABSTRACTER	ACACATECHOL
ABOMINATION	ABRENOUNCE	ABSINTHIAL	ABSTRACTION	ACACETIN
ABOMINATOR	ABRENUNCIATE	ABSINTHIAN	ABSTRACTIVE	ACACIA
ABONDANCE	ABRET	ABSINTHIATE	ABSTRACTIVELY	ACACIIN
ABONNE	ABREUVOIR	ABSINTHIATED	ABSTRACTIVENESS	ACACIN
ABONNEMENT	ABRI	ABSINTHIATING	ABSTRACTLY	ACACINE
ABOO	ABRICO	ABSINTHIC	ABSTRACTNESS	ACADEME
ABOON	ABRICOT	ABSINTHIIN	ABSTRACTS	ACADEMIA
ABORAD	ABRIDGABLE	ABSINTHIN	ABSTRAHENT	ACADEMIAL
ABORAL	ABRIDGE	ABSINTHINE	ABSTRICT	ACADEMIAN
ABORALLY	ABRIDGEABLE	ABSINTHISM	ABSTRICTED	ACADEMIC
ABORD	ABRIDGED	ABSINTHISMIC	ABSTRICTION	ACADEMICAL
ABORIGINAL	ABRIDGEDLY	ABSINTHIUM	ABSTRUDE	ACADEMICALLY
ABORIGINALLY	ABRIDGEMENT	ABSISTOS	ABSTRUSE	ACADEMICALS
ABORIGINARY	ABRIDGER	ABSIT	ABSTRUSELY	ACADEMICIAN
ABORIGINE	ABRIDGING	ABSOLUTE	ABSTRUSENESS	ACADEMICISM
ABORIGINES	ABRIDGMENT	ABSOLUTELY	ABSTRUSION	ACADEMIE
ABORT	ABRIM	ABSOLUTENESS	ABSTRUSITIES	ACADEMIES
ABORTED	ABRIN	ABSOLUTION	ABSTRUSITY	ACADEMISM
ABORTICIDE	ABRINE	ABSOLUTISM	ABSUME	ACADEMIST
ABORTIENT	ABRIS	ABSOLUTIST	ABSUMPTION	ACADEMITE
ABORTIN	ABRISTLE	ABSOLUTISTA	ABSURD	ACADEMIZE
ABORTION	ABROACH	ABSOLUTISTIC	ABSURDITIES	ACADEMIZED
ABORTIONAL	ABROAD	ABSOLUTIVE	ABSURDITY	ACADEMIZING
ABORTIONIST	ABROCOME	ABSOLUTORY	ABSURDLY	ACADEMY
ABORTIVE	ABROGABLE	ABSOLVABLE	ABSURDNESS	ACADIALITE
ABORTIVELY	ABROGATE	ABSOLVATORY	ABSURDUM	ACAENA
ABORTIVENESS	ABROGATED	ABSOLVE	ABTERMINAL	ACALE
ABORTUS	ABROGATING	ABSOLVED	ABTHANAGE	ACALEPH
ABOUCHEMENT	ABROGATION	ABSOLVENT	ABU	ACALEPHAN
ABOUGHT	ABROGATIVE	ABSOLVER	ABUCCO	ACALEPHE
ABOULIA	ABROGATOR	ABSOLVING	ABULEIA	ACALEPHOID
ABOULIC	ABRONIA	ABSOLVITOR	ABULIA	ACALYCAL
ABOUND	ABROOD	ABSOLVITORY	ABULIC	ACALYCINE
ABOUNDING	ABROOK	ABSONANT	ABULOMANIA	ACALYCINOUS
ABOUNDINGLY	ABROTANUM	ABSORB	ABULYEIT	ACALYCULATE
ABOUT	ABROTIN	ABSORBABILITY	ABUNA	ACALYPTRATE
ABOUTS	ABROTINE	ABSORBABLE	ABUNDANCE	ACAMPSIA
ABOVE	ABRUPT	ABSORBANCY	ABUNDANCY	ACANA
ABOVEBOARD	ABRUPTEDLY	ABSORBED	ABUNDANT	ACANACEOUS
ABOVEDECK	ABRUPTION	ABSORBEDLY	ABUNDANTLY	ACANTH
ABOVEGROUND	ABRUPTLY	ABSORBEDNESS	ABUNE	ACANTHA
ABOVEPROOF	ABRUPTNESS	ABSORBENCY	ABURA	ACANTHACEOUS
ABOVESTAIRS	ABSAROKITE	ABSORBENT	ABURABOZU	ACANTHAD
ABOW	ABSCESS	ABSORBER	ABURAGIRI	ACANTHI
ABOX	ABSCESSED	ABSORBING	ABURST	ACANTHIAL
ABRA	ABSCESSES	ABSORBINGLY	ABURTON	ACANTHIN
ABRACADABRA	ABSCESSION	ABSORBITION	ABUSABLE	ACANTHINE
ABRACHIA	ABSCESSROOT	ABSORPT	ABUSAGE	ACANTHION
ABRADANT	ABSCIND	ABSORPTANCE	ABUSE	ACANTHITE
ABRADE	ABSCISE	ABSORPTION	ABUSED	ACANTHODEAN
ABRADED	ABSCISED	ABSORPTIVE	ABUSEE	ACANTHODIAN
ABRADER	ABSCISING	ABSORPTIVITY	ABUSER	ACANTHOLOGY
ABRADING	ABSCISS	ABSQUATULATE	ABUSING	ACANTHOLYSIS
ABRAID	ABSCISSA	ABSTAIN	ABUSION	ACANTHOMA
ABRANCHIAL	ABSCISSAE	ABSTAINER	ABUSIOUS	ACANTHON
ABRANCHIAN	ABSCISSAS	ABSTAINMENT	ABUSIVE	ACANTHOPOD
ABRANCHIATE	ABSCISSION	ABSTEMIOUS	ABUSIVELY	ACANTHOPORE
ABRANCHIOUS	ABSCONCE	ABSTEMIOUSLY	ABUSIVENESS	ACANTHOSIS
ABRASAX	ABSCOND	ABSTENTION	ABUT	ACANTHOUS
ABRASE	ABSCONDED	ABSTENTIOUS	ABUTTAL	ACANTHUS
ABRASED	ABSCONDEDLY	ABSTERGE	ABUTTALS	ACANTHUSES
ABRASH	ABSCONDENCE	ABSTERGED	ABUTTED	

ACAPNIA
ACAPNIAL
ACAPSULAR
ACAPU
ACAPULCO
ACARA
ACARDIA
ACARDIAC
ACARDITE
ACARI
ACARIAN
ACARIASIS
ACARIATRE
ACARICIDAL
ACARICIDE
ACARID
ACARIDOMATIA
ACARIFORM
ACARINE
ACAROCECIDIA
ACAROID
ACAROL
ACAROLOGIST
ACAROLOGY
ACAROPHILOUS
ACAROPHOBIA
ACAROTOXIC
ACARPELLOUS
ACARPELOUS
ACARPOUS
ACATALECTIC
ACATALEPSIA
ACATALEPSY
ACATALEPTIC
ACATAPHASIA
ACATAPOSIS
ACATASTASIA
ACATASTATIC
ACATE
ACATER
ACATERY
ACATES
ACATHARSIA
ACATHARSY
ACATHOLIC
ACAUDAL
ACAUDATE
ACAULESCENCE
ACAULESCENT
ACAULINE
ACAULOSE
ACAULOUS
ACCA
ACCABLE
ACCADEMIA
ACCEDE
ACCEDED
ACCEDENCE
ACCEDER
ACCEDING
ACCELERABLE
ACCELERANDO
ACCELERANT
ACCELERATE
ACCELERATED
ACCELERATEDLY
ACCELERATING
ACCELERATION
ACCELERATIVE
ACCELERATOR
ACCELERATORY
ACCEND
ACCENDIBLE
ACCENSION
ACCENSOR
ACCENT
ACCENTED

ACCENTOR
ACCENTUABLE
ACCENTUAL
ACCENTUALITY
ACCENTUALLY
ACCENTUATE
ACCENTUATED
ACCENTUATING
ACCENTUATION
ACCENTUATOR
ACCENTUS
ACCEPT
ACCEPTABILITY
ACCEPTABLE
ACCEPTABLENESS
ACCEPTABLY
ACCEPTANCE
ACCEPTANCY
ACCEPTANT
ACCEPTATION
ACCEPTED
ACCEPTEDLY
ACCEPTER
ACCEPTILATE
ACCEPTILATED
ACCEPTILATING
ACCEPTILATION
ACCEPTION
ACCEPTIVE
ACCEPTOR
ACCERSE
ACCERSITION
ACCERSITOR
ACCESS
ACCESSARILY
ACCESSARY
ACCESSIBILITY
ACCESSIBLE
ACCESSIBLY
ACCESSION
ACCESSIONAL
ACCESSIONED
ACCESSIONING
ACCESSIT
ACCESSIVE
ACCESSIVELY
ACCESSLESS
ACCESSORIAL
ACCESSORIES
ACCESSORII
ACCESSORILY
ACCESSORIUS
ACCESSORY
ACCIACCATURA
ACCIDENCE
ACCIDENCIES
ACCIDENCY
ACCIDENT
ACCIDENTAL
ACCIDENTALITY
ACCIDENTALLY
ACCIDENTARILY
ACCIDENTARY
ACCIDENTED
ACCIDENTIAL
ACCIDENTLY
ACCIDIA
ACCIDIE
ACCINGE
ACCINGED
ACCINGING
ACCIPITER
ACCIPITRAL
ACCIPITRARY
ACCIPITRINE
ACCIPTER
ACCISMUS

ACCITE
ACCLAIM
ACCLAIMABLE
ACCLAIMER
ACCLAMATION
ACCLAMATOR
ACCLAMATORY
ACCLIMATABLE
ACCLIMATE
ACCLIMATED
ACCLIMATING
ACCLIMATION
ACCLIMATIZE
ACCLIMATIZED
ACCLIMATIZER
ACCLIMATIZING
ACCLIMATURE
ACCLINAL
ACCLINATE
ACCLIVITIES
ACCLIVITOUS
ACCLIVITY
ACCLIVOUS
ACCLOY
ACCOAST
ACCOIL
ACCOLADE
ACCOLADED
ACCOLENT
ACCOLL
ACCOLLE
ACCOLLEE
ACCOMBINATION
ACCOMMODABLE
ACCOMMODATE
ACCOMMODATED
ACCOMMODATING
ACCOMMODATION
ACCOMMODATIVE
ACCOMMODATOR
ACCOMPANIED
ACCOMPANIER
ACCOMPANIMENT
ACCOMPANIST
ACCOMPANY
ACCOMPANYING
ACCOMPANYIST
ACCOMPLETIVE
ACCOMPLICE
ACCOMPLICITY
ACCOMPLISH
ACCOMPLISHED
ACCOMPLISHER
ACCOMPLISHING
ACCOMPLISHMENT
ACCOMPT
ACCON
ACCORD
ACCORDABLE
ACCORDANCE
ACCORDANCY
ACCORDANT
ACCORDANTLY
ACCORDATURA
ACCORDER
ACCORDING
ACCORDINGLY
ACCORDION
ACCORDIONIST
ACCORPORATE
ACCOST
ACCOSTABLE
ACCOSTED
ACCOUCHE
ACCOUCHEMENT
ACCOUCHEUR
ACCOUCHEUSE

ACCOUNT
ACCOUNTABILITY
ACCOUNTABLE
ACCOUNTABLY
ACCOUNTANCY
ACCOUNTANT
ACCOUNTING
ACCOUNTS
ACCOUPLE
ACCOUTER
ACCOUTERED
ACCOUTERING
ACCOUTERMENT
ACCOUTERMENTS
ACCOUTRE
ACCOUTRED
ACCOUTREMENT
ACCOUTRING
ACCOY
ACCOYED
ACCOYING
ACCREDIT
ACCREDITATION
ACCREDITED
ACCREDITING
ACCRESCE
ACCRESCENCE
ACCRESCENT
ACCRETE
ACCRETED
ACCRETING
ACCRETION
ACCRETIONARY
ACCRETIVE
ACCROACH
ACCROACHED
ACCROACHING
ACCRUAL
ACCRUE
ACCRUED
ACCRUEMENT
ACCRUER
ACCRUING
ACCUBATION
ACCUBITA
ACCUBITUM
ACCUBITUS
ACCUEIL
ACCULTURAL
ACCULTURATE
ACCULTURATION
ACCULTURIZE
ACCUMB
ACCUMBENCY
ACCUMBENT
ACCUMBER
ACCUMULABLE
ACCUMULATE
ACCUMULATED
ACCUMULATING
ACCUMULATION
ACCUMULATIVE
ACCUMULATIVELY
ACCUMULATIVENESS
ACCUMULATOR
ACCURACY
ACCURATE
ACCURATELY
ACCURATENESS
ACCURRE
ACCURSE
ACCURSED
ACCURSEDLY
ACCURSEDNESS
ACCURSING
ACCURST
ACCUSABLE

ACCUSABLY
ACCUSAL
ACCUSANT
ACCUSATION
ACCUSATIVAL
ACCUSATIVE
ACCUSATIVELY
ACCUSATORIAL
ACCUSATORY
ACCUSATRIX
ACCUSE
ACCUSED
ACCUSER
ACCUSING
ACCUSINGLY
ACCUSIVE
ACCUSTOM
ACCUSTOMED
ACCUSTOMEDLY
ACCUSTOMING
ACCUSTOMIZE
ACCUSTOMIZED
ACCUSTOMIZING
ACE
ACEANTHRENE
ACECAFFIN
ACECAFFINE
ACECONITIC
ACED
ACEDIA
ACEDIAMIN
ACEDIAMINE
ACEDIAST
ACEITE
ACEITUNA
ACELDAMA
ACEMILA
ACENAPHTHENE
ACENSUADA
ACENSUADOR
ACENTRIC
ACENTROUS
ACEOLOGIC
ACEOLOGY
ACEPHAL
ACEPHALINE
ACEPHALIST
ACEPHALOCYST
ACEPHALOUS
ACEPHALUS
ACEPOTS
ACEQUIA
ACEQUIADOR
ACERACEOUS
ACERATE
ACERATED
ACERATHERE
ACERATOSIS
ACERB
ACERBATE
ACERBATED
ACERBATING
ACERBIC
ACERBITIES
ACERBITUDE
ACERBITY
ACERDOL
ACERIN
ACEROLA
ACEROSE
ACEROUS
ACERRA
ACERTANNIN
ACERVAL
ACERVATE
ACERVATELY
ACERVATIM

ACERVATION
ACERVATIVE
ACERVOSE
ACERVULI
ACERVULINE
ACERVULUS
ACES
ACESCENCE
ACESCENCY
ACESCENT
ACESODYNE
ACETA
ACETABLE
ACETABULA
ACETABULAR
ACETABULUM
ACETAL
ACETALDEHYDE
ACETALDOL
ACETALIZE
ACETAMID
ACETAMIDE
ACETAMIDINE
ACETAMIDO
ACETAMINOL
ACETANILID
ACETANILIDE
ACETANION
ACETANISIDE
ACETARIOUS
ACETARSONE
ACETATE
ACETATED
ACETATION
ACETENYL
ACETIAM
ACETIC
ACETIFICATION
ACETIFIED
ACETIFIER
ACETIFY
ACETIFYING
ACETIMETER
ACETIMETRY
ACETIN
ACETINE
ACETOACETATE
ACETOACETIC
ACETOBENZOIC
ACETOCHLORAL
ACETOIN
ACETOL
ACETOLYSIS
ACETOLYTIC
ACETOMETER
ACETOMETRY
ACETOMORPHIN
ACETONAEMIA
ACETONAEMIC
ACETONATE
ACETONATION
ACETONE
ACETONEMIA
ACETONEMIC
ACETONIC
ACETONITRILE
ACETONIZATION
ACETONIZE
ACETONURIA
ACETONYL
ACETOPHENIN
ACETOPHENINE
ACETOPHENONE
ACETOPYRIN
ACETOPYRINE
ACETOSE
ACETOSITY

ACETOSOLUBLE
ACETOTOLUID
ACETOTOLUIDE
ACETOUS
ACETOXIM
ACETOXIME
ACETOXYL
ACETRACT
ACETTOLUIDE
ACETUM
ACETURIC
ACETYL
ACETYLAMINE
ACETYLATE
ACETYLATED
ACETYLATING
ACETYLATION
ACETYLATOR
ACETYLBIURET
ACETYLENE
ACETYLENIC
ACETYLENYL
ACETYLGLYCIN
ACETYLIC
ACETYLID
ACETYLIDE
ACETYLIODIDE
ACETYLIZABLE
ACETYLIZATION
ACETYLIZE
ACETYLIZER
ACETYLSALOL
ACETYLTHYMOL
ACETYLUREA
ACH
ACHAETOUS
ACHAFE
ACHAGE
ACHALASIA
ACHAR
ACHARNE
ACHARNEMENT
ACHARYA
ACHATE
ACHATES
ACHATOUR
ACHE
ACHED
ACHEILIA
ACHEILOUS
ACHEIRIA
ACHEIROUS
ACHEIRUS
ACHENE
ACHENIA
ACHENIAL
ACHENIUM
ACHENOCARP
ACHENODIA
ACHENODIUM
ACHER
ACHETE
ACHEWEED
ACHIEVABLE
ACHIEVE
ACHIEVED
ACHIEVEMENT
ACHIEVEMENTS
ACHIEVER
ACHIEVING
ACHIGAN
ACHILARY
ACHILL
ACHILLEIN
ACHILLEINE
ACHILLODYNIA
ACHIME

ACHING
ACHINGLY
ACHIOTE
ACHIR
ACHIRA
ACHLAMYDATE
ACHLAMYDEOUS
ACHLORHYDRIA
ACHLOROPSIA
ACHOLIA
ACHOLIC
ACHOLOUS
ACHOLURIA
ACHOLURIC
ACHONDRITE
ACHONDRITIC
ACHOR
ACHORDAL
ACHORDATE
ACHRAS
ACHREE
ACHROACYTE
ACHROGLOBIN
ACHROITE
ACHROMA
ACHROMACYTE
ACHROMASIA
ACHROMAT
ACHROMATE
ACHROMATIC
ACHROMATIN
ACHROMATINIC
ACHROMATISM
ACHROMATIZE
ACHROMATIZED
ACHROMATOPE
ACHROMATOSIS
ACHROMATOUS
ACHROMATURIA
ACHROMIA
ACHROMIC
ACHROMOUS
ACHROOUS
ACHROPSIA
ACHT
ACHTEHALBER
ACHTEL
ACHTELTHALER
ACHTER
ACHTERVELD
ACHUETE
ACHY
ACHYLIA
ACHYLOUS
ACHYMIA
ACHYMOUS
ACICHLORID
ACICHLORIDE
ACICULA
ACICULAE
ACICULAR
ACICULARLY
ACICULATE
ACICULATED
ACICULUM
ACICULUMS
ACID
ACIDAEMIA
ACIDEMIA
ACIDER
ACIDIC
ACIDIFEROUS
ACIDIFIABLE
ACIDIFIANT
ACIDIFIC
ACIDIFIED
ACIDIFIER

ACIDIFY
ACIDIFYING
ACIDIMETER
ACIDIMETRIC
ACIDIMETRY
ACIDITE
ACIDITIES
ACIDITY
ACIDIZE
ACIDLY
ACIDNESS
ACIDOLOGY
ACIDOPHIL
ACIDOPHILE
ACIDOPHILIC
ACIDOPHILOUS
ACIDOPHILUS
ACIDOSIS
ACIDOTIC
ACIDPROOF
ACIDULATE
ACIDULATED
ACIDULATING
ACIDULATION
ACIDULENT
ACIDULOUS
ACIER
ACIERAGE
ACIERATE
ACIERATED
ACIERATING
ACIERATION
ACIES
ACIFORM
ACINACEOUS
ACINACES
ACINACIFORM
ACINARIOUS
ACINETAE
ACING
ACINI
ACINIC
ACINIFORM
ACINOSE
ACINOTUBULAR
ACINOUS
ACINUS
ACIPENSERID
ACIPENSERINE
ACIPENSEROID
ACIURGY
ACKEE
ACKER
ACKEY
ACKMAN
ACKMEN
ACKNEW
ACKNOW
ACKNOWING
ACKNOWLEDGE
ACKNOWLEDGEABLE
ACKNOWLEDGED
ACKNOWLEDGEMENT
ACKNOWLEDGER
ACKNOWLEDGING
ACKNOWLEDGMENT
ACKNOWN
ACLASTIC
ACLE
ACLEIDIAN
ACLEISTOUS
ACLIDIAN
ACLINAL
ACLINIC
ACLOUD
ACLYDES
ACMAESTHESIA

ACMATIC
ACME
ACMESTHESIA
ACMIC
ACMITE
ACNE
ACNEFORM
ACNEIFORM
ACNEMIA
ACNODAL
ACNODE
ACOASMA
ACOCANTHERIN
ACOCK
ACOCKBILL
ACOCOTL
ACOEL
ACOELOMATE
ACOELOUS
ACOIN
ACOINE
ACOLD
ACOLOGIC
ACOLOGY
ACOLOUS
ACOLUTHIC
ACOLYTE
ACOLYTH
ACOLYTHATE
ACOMIA
ACOMOUS
ACON
ACONDYLOSE
ACONDYLOUS
ACONE
ACONIC
ACONIN
ACONINE
ACONITAL
ACONITE
ACONITIA
ACONITIC
ACONITIN
ACONITINE
ACONITUM
ACONTIA
ACONTIUM
ACONURESIS
ACOPIC
ACOPON
ACOR
ACOREA
ACORIA
ACORN
ACORNED
ACOSMIC
ACOSMISM
ACOSMIST
ACOSMISTIC
ACOST
ACOTYLEDON
ACOUASM
ACOUCHI
ACOUCHY
ACOUMETER
ACOUMETRY
ACOUOPHONIA
ACOUP
ACOUPA
ACOUPE
ACOUSMA
ACOUSMATA
ACOUSMATIC
ACOUSTIC
ACOUSTICAL
ACOUSTICALLY
ACOUSTICIAN

ACOUSTICS
ACQUAINT
ACQUAINTANCE
ACQUAINTANT
ACQUAINTED
ACQUENT
ACQUEREUR
ACQUEST
ACQUIESCE
ACQUIESCED
ACQUIESCENCE
ACQUIESCENT
ACQUIESCER
ACQUIESCING
ACQUIRABLE
ACQUIRE
ACQUIRED
ACQUIREMENT
ACQUIRENDA
ACQUIRER
ACQUIRING
ACQUISIBLE
ACQUISITA
ACQUISITE
ACQUISITED
ACQUISITION
ACQUISITIVE
ACQUISITIVELY
ACQUISITIVENESS
ACQUISITOR
ACQUISITUM
ACQUIST
ACQUIT
ACQUITAL
ACQUITMENT
ACQUITTAL
ACQUITTANCE
ACQUITTED
ACQUITTER
ACQUITTING
ACRACY
ACRAEIN
ACRALDEHYDE
ACRANIA
ACRANIAL
ACRANIATE
ACRASIA
ACRASPEDOTE
ACRASY
ACRATIA
ACRATURESIS
ACRAWL
ACRAZE
ACRE
ACREABLE
ACREAGE
ACREAK
ACREAM
ACRED
ACREMAN
ACREMEN
ACRES
ACRESTAFF
ACRID
ACRIDAN
ACRIDANE
ACRIDIAN
ACRIDIC
ACRIDID
ACRIDIN
ACRIDINE
ACRIDINIC
ACRIDINIUM
ACRIDITY
ACRIDLY
ACRIDNESS
ACRIDONE

ACRIDONIUM
ACRIDOPHAGUS
ACRIDYL
ACRIFLAVIN
ACRIFLAVINE
ACRIMONIES
ACRIMONIOUS
ACRIMONIOUSLY
ACRIMONY
ACRINDOLIN
ACRINDOLINE
ACRINYL
ACRISIA
ACRISY
ACRITAN
ACRITE
ACRITICAL
ACRITOL
ACRITY
ACROAMA
ACROAMATA
ACROAMATIC
ACROAMATICS
ACROASPHYXIA
ACROATAXIA
ACROATIC
ACROBACY
ACROBAT
ACROBATIC
ACROBATICAL
ACROBATICALLY
ACROBATICS
ACROBATISM
ACROBLAST
ACROBRYOUS
ACROBYSTITIS
ACROCARPOUS
ACROCEPHALIA
ACROCEPHALIC
ACROCEPHALY
ACROCHORDON
ACROCONIDIUM
ACROCORACOID
ACROCYANOSIS
ACROCYST
ACRODACTYLA
ACRODACTYLUM
ACRODONT
ACRODONTISM
ACRODROME
ACRODROMOUS
ACRODYNIA
ACROESTHESIA
ACROGAMOUS
ACROGAMY
ACROGEN
ACROGENIC
ACROGENOUS
ACROGENOUSLY
ACROGRAPHY
ACROGYNOUS
ACROLEIN
ACROLITH
ACROLITHAN
ACROLITHIC
ACROLOGIC
ACROLOGISM
ACROLOGUE
ACROLOGY
ACROMANIA
ACROMEGALIA
ACROMEGALIC
ACROMEGALY
ACROMELALGIA
ACROMETER
ACROMIA
ACROMIAL

ACROMICRIA
ACROMION
ACROMPHALUS
ACROMYODIAN
ACROMYODIC
ACROMYODOUS
ACROMYOTONIA
ACROMYOTONUS
ACRON
ACRONARCOTIC
ACRONEUROSIS
ACRONIC
ACRONICAL
ACRONICALLY
ACRONICHAL
ACRONICHALLY
ACRONYC
ACRONYCAL
ACRONYCALLY
ACRONYCH
ACRONYCHAL
ACRONYCHALLY
ACRONYCTOUS
ACRONYM
ACRONYX
ACROOK
ACROPATHY
ACROPETAL
ACROPETALLY
ACROPHOBIA
ACROPHONETIC
ACROPHONIC
ACROPHONY
ACROPODIA
ACROPODIUM
ACROPOLIS
ACROPOLISES
ACROPOLITAN
ACROPORE
ACRORHAGUS
ACRORRHEUMA
ACROSARC
ACROSARCA
ACROSARCUM
ACROSCOPIC
ACROSE
ACROSOME
ACROSPIRE
ACROSPIRED
ACROSPIRING
ACROSPORE
ACROSPOROUS
ACROSS
ACROSTIC
ACROSTICAL
ACROSTICALLY
ACROSTICHAL
ACROSTICHIC
ACROSTICHOID
ACROSTICISM
ACROTARSIAL
ACROTARSIUM
ACROTELEUTIC
ACROTER
ACROTERIAL
ACROTERIC
ACROTERIUM
ACROTIC
ACROTISM
ACROTOMOUS
ACROTROPHIC
ACRYL
ACRYLATE
ACRYLIC
ACRYLYL
ACT
ACTA

ACTABILITY
ACTABLE
ACTED
ACTIFICATION
ACTIFIER
ACTIFY
ACTIN
ACTINAL
ACTINALLY
ACTINE
ACTINENCHYMA
ACTING
ACTINIA
ACTINIAN
ACTINIARIAN
ACTINIC
ACTINICAL
ACTINICALLY
ACTINIDE
ACTINIFEROUS
ACTINIFORM
ACTININE
ACTINISM
ACTINIUM
ACTINOBRANCH
ACTINOCARP
ACTINOCARPIC
ACTINOCRINID
ACTINODROME
ACTINOGRAM
ACTINOGRAPH
ACTINOGRAPHY
ACTINOID
ACTINOLITE
ACTINOLITIC
ACTINOLOGOUS
ACTINOLOGUE
ACTINOLOGY
ACTINOMERE
ACTINOMERIC
ACTINOMETER
ACTINOMETRIC
ACTINOMETRY
ACTINOMORPHIC
ACTINOMORPHY
ACTINOMYCETE
ACTINOMYCOMA
ACTINON
ACTINOPHONE
ACTINOPHONIC
ACTINOPHORE
ACTINOPHRYAN
ACTINOPRAXIS
ACTINOSCOPY
ACTINOSOMA
ACTINOSOME
ACTINOST
ACTINOSTOMAL
ACTINOSTOME
ACTINOTROCHA
ACTINOZOAL
ACTINOZOAN
ACTINULA
ACTINULAE
ACTIO
ACTION
ACTIONABLE
ACTIONABLY
ACTIONAL
ACTIONARY
ACTIONER
ACTIONES
ACTIONIZE
ACTIONIZED
ACTIONIZING
ACTIONS
ACTIOUS

ACTIVATE
ACTIVATED
ACTIVATING
ACTIVATION
ACTIVATOR
ACTIVE
ACTIVELY
ACTIVENESS
ACTIVISM
ACTIVIST
ACTIVITAL
ACTIVITIES
ACTIVITY
ACTIVIZE
ACTLESS
ACTO
ACTON
ACTOR
ACTORISH
ACTORS
ACTORY
ACTOS
ACTRESS
ACTRESSY
ACTS
ACTU
ACTUAL
ACTUALISM
ACTUALIST
ACTUALISTIC
ACTUALITIES
ACTUALITY
ACTUALIZATION
ACTUALIZE
ACTUALIZED
ACTUALIZING
ACTUALLY
ACTUALNESS
ACTUARIAL
ACTUARIALLY
ACTUARIAN
ACTUARIES
ACTUARY
ACTUATE
ACTUATED
ACTUATES
ACTUATING
ACTUATION
ACTUATOR
ACTURE
ACTURIENCE
ACTUS
ACUATE
ACUATING
ACUATION
ACUCHI
ACUCLOSURE
ACUDUCTOR
ACUERDO
ACUERDOS
ACUITY
ACULEA
ACULEAE
ACULEATE
ACULEATED
ACULEI
ACULEIFORM
ACULEOLATE
ACULEUS
ACUMEN
ACUMINATE
ACUMINATED
ACUMINATING
ACUMINATION
ACUMINOSE
ACUMINOUS
ACUMINULATE

ACUPRESS	ADAPTITUDE	ADDLINS	ADENOMYXOMA	ADIAPHORESIS
ACUPRESSURE	ADAPTIVE	ADDORSED	ADENONCUS	ADIAPHORETIC
ACUPUNCTUATE	ADAPTIVELY	ADDOSSED	ADENONEURAL	ADIAPHORISM
ACUPUNCTURATOR	ADAPTIVENESS	ADDRESS	ADENONEURE	ADIAPHORIST
ACUPUNCTURE	ADAPTOMETER	ADDRESSED	ADENOPATHY	ADIAPHORITE
ACUPUNCTURED	ADAPTOR	ADDRESSEE	ADENOPHORE	ADIAPHORON
ACUS	ADAPTORIAL	ADDRESSER	ADENOPHOREUS	ADIAPHOROUS
ACUSHLA	ADARME	ADDRESSFUL	ADENOPHYLLOUS	ADIATE
ACUTA	ADARO	ADDRESSING	ADENOPHYMA	ADIATED
ACUTANGULAR	ADAT	ADDRESSOR	ADENOPODOUS	ADIATHERMAL
ACUTATE	ADATI	ADDREST	ADENOSARCOMA	ADIATHERMIC
ACUTE	ADATIS	ADDUCE	ADENOSE	ADIATHETIC
ACUTELY	ADATOM	ADDUCEABLE	ADENOSINE	ADIATING
ACUTENESS	ADATY	ADDUCED	ADENOSIS	ADIATION
ACUTIATOR	ADAUNT	ADDUCENT	ADENOTOME	ADIBASI
ACUTIFOLIATE	ADAW	ADDUCER	ADENOTOMIC	ADICITY
ACUTILINGUAL	ADAWE	ADDUCIBLE	ADENOTOMY	ADIENCE
ACUTILOBATE	ADAWLUT	ADDUCING	ADENOTYPHOID	ADIEU
ACUTIPLANTAR	ADAWN	ADDUCT	ADENOTYPHUS	ADIEUS
ACUTOGRAVE	ADAXIAL	ADDUCTION	ADENOUS	ADIEUX
ACUTONODOSE	ADAY	ADDUCTIVE	ADENYLIC	ADIGHE
ACUTORSION	ADAYS	ADDUCTOR	ADEPHAGAN	ADIGHT
ACXOYATL	ADAZZLE	ADDULCE	ADEPHAGOUS	ADINIDAN
ACYANOPSIA	ADCRAFT	ADE	ADEPS	ADINOLE
ACYCLIC	ADD	ADEAD	ADEPT	ADION
ACYESIS	ADDA	ADEEM	ADEPTION	ADIOS
ACYETIC	ADDABLE	ADEEP	ADEPTLY	ADIPATE
ACYL	ADDAX	ADELANTADO	ADEPTNESS	ADIPESCENT
ACYLAL	ADDEBTED	ADELANTE	ADEQUACY	ADIPIC
ACYLASE	ADDED	ADELING	ADEQUATE	ADIPINIC
ACYLATE	ADDEEM	ADELITE	ADEQUATELY	ADIPOCELE
ACYLATION	ADDEND	ADELOCODONIC	ADEQUATENESS	ADIPOCERE
ACYLOGEN	ADDENDA	ADELOMORPHIC	ADEQUATION	ADIPOCEROUS
ACYLOIN	ADDENDUM	ADELOPOD	ADEQUATIVE	ADIPOFIBROMA
ACYROLOGICAL	ADDER	ADELPHOGAMY	ADERMIA	ADIPOGENIC
ACYROLOGY	ADDERBOLT	ADELPHOLITE	ADERMIN	ADIPOGENOUS
ACYSTIA	ADDERSPIT	ADELPHOPHAGY	ADESPOTA	ADIPOID
AD	ADDERWORT	ADEMONIST	ADESPOTON	ADIPOLYSIS
ADACTYLIA	ADDIBILITY	ADEMPT	ADEVISM	ADIPOLYTIC
ADACTYLOUS	ADDIBLE	ADEMPTED	ADEW	ADIPOMA
ADAD	ADDICE	ADEMPTION	ADFIX	ADIPOMATA
ADAGA	ADDICENT	ADENALGY	ADHAKA	ADIPOMATOUS
ADAGE	ADDICT	ADENASE	ADHAMANT	ADIPOMETER
ADAGIAL	ADDICTED	ADENASTHENIA	ADHARMA	ADIPOPEXIA
ADAGIETTO	ADDICTEDNESS	ADENECTOMIES	ADHERE	ADIPOPEXIS
ADAGIO	ADDICTION	ADENECTOMY	ADHERED	ADIPOSE
ADAGIOS	ADDICTIVE	ADENECTOPIA	ADHERENCE	ADIPOSENESS
ADALAT	ADDIMENT	ADENECTOPIC	ADHERENCY	ADIPOSIS
ADALID	ADDING	ADENIA	ADHEREND	ADIPOSITY
ADAMANCY	ADDIO	ADENIFORM	ADHERENT	ADIPOSURIA
ADAMANT	ADDIS	ADENIN	ADHERENTLY	ADIPOUS
ADAMANTEAN	ADDITA	ADENINE	ADHERER	ADIPSIA
ADAMANTINE	ADDITAMENT	ADENITIS	ADHERESCENCE	ADIPSIC
ADAMANTINOMA	ADDITIMENT	ADENIZATION	ADHERESCENT	ADIPSOUS
ADAMANTOID	ADDITION	ADENOBLAST	ADHERING	ADIPYL
ADAMANTOMA	ADDITIONAL	ADENOCELE	ADHESION	ADIT
ADAMAS	ADDITIONALLY	ADENOCHROME	ADHESIONAL	ADITAL
ADAMELLITE	ADDITIONARY	ADENOCYST	ADHESIVE	ADITIO
ADAMINE	ADDITIONS	ADENODERMIA	ADHESIVELY	ADITUS
ADAMITE	ADDITITIOUS	ADENODYNIA	ADHESIVENESS	ADIVE
ADAMSITE	ADDITIVE	ADENOFIBROMA	ADHI	ADJAB
ADAN	ADDITIVELY	ADENOFIBROSIS	ADHIBIT	ADJACENCY
ADANCE	ADDITIVITY	ADENOGENESIS	ADHIBITED	ADJACENT
ADANGLE	ADDITORY	ADENOGENOUS	ADHIBITING	ADJACENTLY
ADAPID	ADDITUM	ADENOGRAPHY	ADHIBITION	ADJAG
ADAPT	ADDLE	ADENOID	ADHORT	ADJECT
ADAPTABILITY	ADDLEBRAIN	ADENOIDAL	ADIABAT	ADJECTION
ADAPTABLE	ADDLEBRAINED	ADENOIDISM	ADIABATIC	ADJECTIONAL
ADAPTABLENESS	ADDLED	ADENOLIPOMA	ADIABOLIST	ADJECTIVAL
ADAPTATION	ADDLEHEAD	ADENOLOGICAL	ADIACTINIC	ADJECTIVALLY
ADAPTATIONAL	ADDLEHEADED	ADENOLOGY	ADIAGNOSTIC	ADJECTIVE
ADAPTATIVE	ADDLEHEADEDLY	ADENOMA	ADIANTIFORM	ADJECTIVELY
ADAPTED	ADDLEPATE	ADENOMALACIA	ADIANTUM	ADJIGA
ADAPTEDNESS	ADDLEPATED	ADENOMATA	ADIAPHON	ADJIGER
ADAPTER	ADDLEPLOT	ADENOMATOUS	ADIAPHONON	ADJOIN
ADAPTION	ADDLING	ADENOMYCOSIS	ADIAPHORA	ADJOINED
ADAPTIONISM	ADDLINGS	ADENOMYOMA	ADIAPHORAL	ADJOINEDLY

ADJOINING
ADJOINT
ADJOURN
ADJOURNAL
ADJOURNMENT
ADJOUST
ADJUDGE
ADJUDGED
ADJUDGER
ADJUDGING
ADJUDICATE
ADJUDICATED
ADJUDICATING
ADJUDICATION
ADJUDICATIVE
ADJUDICATOR
ADJUDICATURE
ADJUGATE
ADJUMENT
ADJUNCT
ADJUNCTION
ADJUNCTIVE
ADJUNCTIVELY
ADJUNCTLY
ADJURATION
ADJURATORY
ADJURE
ADJURED
ADJURER
ADJURING
ADJUROR
ADJUST
ADJUSTABLE
ADJUSTAGE
ADJUSTED
ADJUSTER
ADJUSTIVE
ADJUSTMENT
ADJUSTOR
ADJUTAGE
ADJUTANCIES
ADJUTANCY
ADJUTANT
ADJUTANTSHIP
ADJUTOR
ADJUTORIOUS
ADJUTORY
ADJUTRICE
ADJUTRIX
ADJUVANT
ADJUVATE
ADLAY
ADLUMIDIN
ADLUMIDINE
ADLUMIN
ADLUMINE
ADMAN
ADMARGINATE
ADMAXILLARY
ADMEASURE
ADMEASURED
ADMEASURER
ADMEASURING
ADMEDIAL
ADMEDIAN
ADMEN
ADMI
ADMINICLE
ADMINICULAR
ADMINICULARY
ADMINICULATE
ADMINICULUM
ADMINISTER
ADMINISTERED
ADMINISTERIAL
ADMINISTRABLE
ADMINISTRANT

ADMINISTRATE
ADMINISTRATED
ADMINISTRATING
ADMINISTRATION
ADMINISTRATIONAL
ADMINISTRATIVE
ADMINISTRATOR
ADMIRABLE
ADMIRABLY
ADMIRAL
ADMIRALSHIP
ADMIRALTIES
ADMIRALTY
ADMIRATION
ADMIRATIVE
ADMIRATOR
ADMIRE
ADMIRED
ADMIREDLY
ADMIRER
ADMIRING
ADMIRINGLY
ADMISSIBLE
ADMISSIBLY
ADMISSION
ADMISSIVE
ADMISSORY
ADMIT
ADMITTABLE
ADMITTANCE
ADMITTATUR
ADMITTED
ADMITTEDLY
ADMITTEE
ADMITTER
ADMITTING
ADMITTY
ADMIX
ADMIXED
ADMIXING
ADMIXT
ADMIXTION
ADMIXTURE
ADMONISH
ADMONISHER
ADMONISHMENT
ADMONITION
ADMONITIVE
ADMONITIVELY
ADMONITOR
ADMONITORIAL
ADMONITORILY
ADMONITORY
ADMOVE
ADNASCENCE
ADNATE
ADNATION
ADNERVAL
ADNESCENT
ADNEURAL
ADNEX
ADNEXA
ADNEXAL
ADNEXED
ADNEXITIS
ADNEXOPEXY
ADNOMINAL
ADNOMINALLY
ADNOMINATION
ADNOUN
ADNUL
ADNUMBER
ADO
ADOBE
ADOLESCE
ADOLESCED
ADOLESCENCE

ADOLESCENCY
ADOLESCENT
ADOLESCENTLY
ADOLESCING
ADON
ADONIDIN
ADONIN
ADONIS
ADONITE
ADONITOL
ADONIZE
ADONIZED
ADONIZING
ADOORS
ADOPERATE
ADOPERATION
ADOPT
ADOPTABLE
ADOPTANT
ADOPTATIVE
ADOPTED
ADOPTEDLY
ADOPTEE
ADOPTER
ADOPTIAN
ADOPTIANISM
ADOPTIANIST
ADOPTION
ADOPTIONAL
ADOPTIONISM
ADOPTIONIST
ADOPTIOUS
ADOPTIVE
ADOPTIVELY
ADOR
ADORABILITY
ADORABLE
ADORABLENESS
ADORABLY
ADORAL
ADORALLY
ADORANT
ADORATION
ADORATORY
ADORE
ADORED
ADORER
ADORING
ADORN
ADORNED
ADORNER
ADORNMENT
ADOSCULATION
ADOULIE
ADOWN
ADOXACEOUS
ADOXIES
ADOXOGRAPHY
ADOXY
ADOZE
ADPRESS
ADPROMISSION
ADRAD
ADRADIAL
ADRADIALLY
ADRADIUS
ADREAD
ADREAM
ADREAMED
ADREAMT
ADRECTAL
ADRENAL
ADRENALIN
ADRENALINE
ADRENALIZE
ADRENALONE
ADRENCH

ADRENIN
ADRENINE
ADRENT
ADRIFT
ADRIP
ADROGATE
ADROIT
ADROITLY
ADROITNESS
ADROOP
ADROP
ADROSTRAL
ADROWSE
ADRUE
ADRY
ADSBUD
ADSCITITIOUS
ADSCRIPT
ADSCRIPTION
ADSCRIPTIVE
ADSIGNIFY
ADSMITH
ADSMITHING
ADSORB
ADSORBABLE
ADSORBATE
ADSORBENT
ADSORPTION
ADSORPTIVE
ADSORPTIVELY
ADSTIPULATE
ADSTIPULATED
ADSTIPULATOR
ADSUM
ADTERMINAL
ADUANA
ADUB
ADULAR
ADULARIA
ADULATE
ADULATED
ADULATING
ADULATION
ADULATOR
ADULATORY
ADULATRESS
ADULCE
ADULT
ADULTER
ADULTERANT
ADULTERATE
ADULTERATED
ADULTERATING
ADULTERATION
ADULTERATOR
ADULTERER
ADULTERESS
ADULTERIES
ADULTERINE
ADULTERIZE
ADULTEROUS
ADULTEROUSLY
ADULTERY
ADULTHOOD
ADULTNESS
ADULTOID
ADULTRESS
ADUMBRAL
ADUMBRANT
ADUMBRATE
ADUMBRATED
ADUMBRATING
ADUMBRATION
ADUMBRATIVE
ADUNC
ADUNCATE

ADUNCITY
ADUNCOUS
ADURE
ADURENT
ADUSK
ADUST
ADUSTIOSIS
ADUSTIVE
ADVANCE
ADVANCED
ADVANCEMENT
ADVANCER
ADVANCES
ADVANCING
ADVANCIVE
ADVANTAGE
ADVANTAGED
ADVANTAGEOUS
ADVANTAGEOUSLY
ADVANTAGEOUSNESS
ADVANTAGING
ADVECTION
ADVECTITIOUS
ADVECTIVE
ADVEHENT
ADVENE
ADVENIENCE
ADVENIENT
ADVENT
ADVENTIAL
ADVENTITIA
ADVENTITIOUS
ADVENTIVE
ADVENTUAL
ADVENTURE
ADVENTURED
ADVENTURER
ADVENTURESOME
ADVENTURESS
ADVENTURING
ADVENTUROUS
ADVENTUROUSLY
ADVENTUROUSNES
ADVERB
ADVERBIAL
ADVERBIALIZE
ADVERBIALLY
ADVERBIATION
ADVERSARIA
ADVERSARIES
ADVERSARY
ADVERSATIVE
ADVERSE
ADVERSED
ADVERSELY
ADVERSENESS
ADVERSING
ADVERSITIES
ADVERSITY
ADVERSUS
ADVERT
ADVERTENCE
ADVERTENCY
ADVERTENT
ADVERTENTLY
ADVERTISE
ADVERTISED
ADVERTISEMENT
ADVERTISER
ADVERTISING
ADVERTIZE
ADVERTIZEMENT
ADVERTIZING
ADVICE
ADVICEFUL
ADVISABILITY

ADVISABLE
ADVISABLENESS
ADVISABLY
ADVISAL
ADVISATORY
ADVISE
ADVISED
ADVISEDLY
ADVISEDNESS
ADVISEE
ADVISEMENT
ADVISER
ADVISING
ADVISIVE
ADVISIVENESS
ADVISO
ADVISOR
ADVISORILY
ADVISORY
ADVITANT
ADVOCAAT
ADVOCACY
ADVOCATE
ADVOCATED
ADVOCATES
ADVOCATING
ADVOCATION
ADVOCATOR
ADVOCATORY
ADVOCATRESS
ADVOKE
ADVOLUTION
ADVOWEE
ADVOWSON
ADY
ADYNAMIA
ADYNAMIC
ADYNAMY
ADYT
ADYTA
ADYTON
ADYTUM
ADZ
ADZE
ADZER
ADZES
AE
AEA
AECIA
AECIAL
AECIDIA
AECIDIUM
AECIOSPORE
AECIOSTAGE
AECIOTELIA
AECIOTELIUM
AECIUM
AEDEAGI
AEDEAGUS
AEDES
AEDICULA
AEDICULAE
AEDILE
AEDILESHIP
AEDILIAN
AEDILIC
AEDILITIAN
AEDILITIES
AEDILITY
AEDOEOLOGY
AEGAGRI
AEGAGROPILA
AEGAGROPILAE
AEGAGROPILE
AEGAGROPILES
AEGAGRUS
AEGER

AEGERIAN
AEGERIID
AEGICRANIA
AEGILOPS
AEGIRINE
AEGIRINOLITE
AEGIRITE
AEGIS
AEGROTANT
AEGROTAT
AEGYPTILLA
AEGYRITE
AELODICON
AELUROPHOBE
AELUROPHOBIA
AELUROPODOUS
AENACH
AENEAN
AENEOLITHIC
AENEOUS
AENIGMATITE
AEOLIAN
AEOLID
AEOLIGHT
AEOLINE
AEOLIPILE
AEOLIPYLE
AEOLISTIC
AEOLODICON
AEOLOTROPIC
AEOLOTROPISM
AEOLOTROPY
AEOLSKLAVIER
AEON
AEONIAL
AEONIAN
AEONIC
AEQUOR
AEQUOREAL
AER
AERAGE
AERARIAN
AERARIUM
AERATE
AERATED
AERATING
AERATION
AERATOR
AERENCHYMA
AERIAL
AERIALIST
AERIALITY
AERIALLY
AERIALNESS
AERIC
AERICAL
AERIDES
AERIE
AERIED
AERIFACTION
AERIFEROUS
AERIFICATION
AERIFIED
AERIFORM
AERIFY
AERIFYING
AERO
AEROBATE
AEROBATED
AEROBATICS
AEROBATING
AEROBE
AEROBIAN
AEROBIC
AEROBICALLY
AEROBIOLOGY
AEROBIOSCOPE

AEROBIOSIS
AEROBIOTIC
AEROBIOUS
AEROBIUM
AEROBOAT
AEROBUS
AEROCAMERA
AEROCOLPOS
AEROCURVE
AEROCYST
AERODONE
AERODONETIC
AERODONETICS
AERODROME
AERODROMICS
AERODUCT
AERODYNAMIC
AERODYNAMICS
AERODYNE
AEROEMBOLISM
AEROFOIL
AEROGEL
AEROGEN
AEROGENES
AEROGENIC
AEROGEOLOGY
AEROGNOSY
AEROGRAM
AEROGRAMME
AEROGRAPH
AEROGRAPHER
AEROGRAPHIC
AEROGRAPHICS
AEROGRAPHIES
AEROGRAPHY
AEROGUN
AEROHYDROUS
AEROIDES
AEROLITE
AEROLITH
AEROLITIC
AEROLITICS
AEROLOGIC
AEROLOGICAL
AEROLOGIES
AEROLOGIST
AEROLOGY
AEROMANCY
AEROMARINE
AEROMECHANIC
AEROMEDICAL
AEROMEDICINE
AEROMETER
AEROMETRIC
AEROMETRY
AEROMOTOR
AERONAT
AERONAUT
AERONAUTIC
AERONAUTICAL
AERONAUTICS
AERONAUTISM
AERONEF
AERONEUROSIS
AEROPATHY
AEROPAUSE
AEROPHAGIA
AEROPHAGIST
AEROPHANE
AEROPHILE
AEROPHILOUS
AEROPHOBIA
AEROPHOBIC
AEROPHONE
AEROPHOR
AEROPHORE
AEROPHYSICAL

AEROPHYSICS
AEROPHYTE
AEROPLANE
AEROPLANER
AEROPLANIST
AEROPLEUSTIC
AEROPOROTOMY
AEROSCEPSIS
AEROSCEPSY
AEROSCOPE
AEROSCOPIC
AEROSCOPY
AEROSE
AEROSIDERITE
AEROSOL
AEROSPACE
AEROSPHERE
AEROSTAT
AEROSTATIC
AEROSTATICAL
AEROSTATICS
AEROSTATION
AEROSTEAM
AEROTAXIS
AEROTHERAPY
AEROTROPIC
AEROTROPISM
AEROVIEW
AEROYACHT
AERUGINOUS
AERUGO
AERY
AES
AESC
AESCULACEOUS
AESTHESIA
AESTHESIS
AESTHETE
AESTHETIC
AESTHETICAL
AESTHETICALLY
AESTHETICIAN
AESTHETICISM
AESTHETICIZE
AESTHETICS
AESTIVAL
AESTIVATE
AESTIVATED
AESTIVATING
AESTIVATION
AESTIVATOR
AESTUATE
AESTUATION
AESTUOUS
AESTURE
AESTUS
AETHALIA
AETHALIUM
AETHELING
AETHEOGAM
AETHEOGAMIC
AETHEOGAMOUS
AETHER
AETHERED
AETHOGEN
AETHRIOSCOPE
AETIOGENIC
AETIOLOGICAL
AETIOLOGUE
AETIOLOGY
AETIOPHYLLIN
AETIOTROPIC
AETITES
AETOSAUR
AEVIA
AEVUM
AFACE

AFAINT
AFALD
AFAR
AFARA
AFEAR
AFEARD
AFEARED
AFERNAN
AFETAL
AFF
AFFA
AFFABILITY
AFFABLE
AFFABLENESS
AFFABLY
AFFABROUS
AFFAIR
AFFAIRE
AFFAIRS
AFFAITE
AFFAMISH
AFFECT
AFFECTATION
AFFECTED
AFFECTEDLY
AFFECTEDNESS
AFFECTER
AFFECTIBILITY
AFFECTIBLE
AFFECTING
AFFECTINGLY
AFFECTION
AFFECTIONAL
AFFECTIONALLY
AFFECTIONATE
AFFECTIONATELY
AFFECTIONATENESS
AFFECTIONED
AFFECTIVE
AFFECTIVELY
AFFECTIVITY
AFFEEBLE
AFFEER
AFFEERER
AFFEERMENT
AFFEEROR
AFFEIR
AFFERE
AFFERENT
AFFETTUOSO
AFFIANCE
AFFIANCED
AFFIANCER
AFFIANCING
AFFIANT
AFFICHE
AFFIDATION
AFFIDAVIT
AFFIDAVY
AFFIED
AFFILE
AFFILIABLE
AFFILIATE
AFFILIATED
AFFILIATING
AFFILIATION
AFFINAGE
AFFINAL
AFFINATION
AFFINE
AFFINED
AFFINELY
AFFINITATIVE
AFFINITATIVELY
AFFINITE
AFFINITIES
AFFINITION

AFFINITIVE
AFFINITY
AFFIRM
AFFIRMABLE
AFFIRMABLY
AFFIRMANCE
AFFIRMANT
AFFIRMATION
AFFIRMATIVE
AFFIRMATIVELY
AFFIRMATORY
AFFIRMER
AFFIX
AFFIXAL
AFFIXATION
AFFIXED
AFFIXER
AFFIXING
AFFIXION
AFFIXT
AFFIXTURE
AFFLATE
AFFLATED
AFFLATION
AFFLATUS
AFFLICT
AFFLICTED
AFFLICTER
AFFLICTING
AFFLICTINGLY
AFFLICTION
AFFLICTIVE
AFFLICTIVELY
AFFLOOF
AFFLUENCE
AFFLUENT
AFFLUENTLY
AFFLUENTNESS
AFFLUX
AFFLUXION
AFFODILL
AFFORCE
AFFORCED
AFFORCEMENT
AFFORCING
AFFORD
AFFORDABLE
AFFOREST
AFFORESTMENT
AFFORMATIVE
AFFRANCHISE
AFFRANCHISED
AFFRAP
AFFRAY
AFFRAYED
AFFRAYER
AFFRAYING
AFFREIGHT
AFFREIGHTER
AFFRET
AFFRETTANDO
AFFREUX
AFFRICATE
AFFRICATED
AFFRICATION
AFFRICATIVE
AFFRIGHT
AFFRIGHTED
AFFRIGHTEDLY
AFFRIGHTER
AFFRIGHTFUL
AFFRIGHTMENT
AFFRONT
AFFRONTE
AFFRONTED
AFFRONTEDLY
AFFRONTEE

AFFRONTER
AFFRONTIVE
AFFRONTY
AFFUSE
AFFUSED
AFFUSING
AFFUSION
AFFY
AFFYDAVY
AFFYING
AFGHAN
AFGHANI
AFGHANIS
AFICIONADO
AFIELD
AFIKOMEN
AFIND
AFINE
AFIRE
AFLAGELLAR
AFLAME
AFLARE
AFLAT
AFLAUNT
AFLEY
AFLICKER
AFLIGHT
AFLOAT
AFLOW
AFLOWER
AFLUKING
AFLUSH
AFLUTTER
AFOAM
AFONG
AFOOT
AFORE
AFOREHAND
AFOREMENTIONED
AFORENAMED
AFORESAID
AFORETHOUGHT
AFORETIME
AFOUL
AFOUNDE
AFRAID
AFREET
AFRESCA
AFRESH
AFRET
AFRETE
AFRIT
AFRITE
AFRONT
AFROWN
AFT
AFTABA
AFTEN
AFTER
AFTERBAY
AFTERBEAT
AFTERBIRTH
AFTERBODY
AFTERBRAIN
AFTERBREAST
AFTERBURNER
AFTERBURNING
AFTERCARE
AFTERCAST
AFTERCHROME
AFTERCLAP
AFTERCOME
AFTERCOMER
AFTERCOOLER
AFTERCROP
AFTERDAMP
AFTERDATE

AFTERDATED
AFTERDECK
AFTERDINNER
AFTEREFFECT
AFTEREYE
AFTERFEED
AFTERFORM
AFTERFUTURE
AFTERGAME
AFTERGAS
AFTERGLOW
AFTERGRASS
AFTERGROWTH
AFTERGUARD
AFTERHAND
AFTERHATCH
AFTERHEND
AFTERHOLD
AFTERIMAGE
AFTERINGS
AFTERLIFE
AFTERLIGHT
AFTERMAST
AFTERMATH
AFTERMILK
AFTERMOST
AFTERNIGHT
AFTERNOON
AFTERNOONS
AFTERNOTE
AFTERPAIN
AFTERPAINS
AFTERPART
AFTERPEAK
AFTERPIECE
AFTERPLAY
AFTERRAKE
AFTERRIDER
AFTERS
AFTERSHAFT
AFTERSHAFTED
AFTERSHINE
AFTERSHOCK
AFTERSONG
AFTERSOUND
AFTERSPRING
AFTERSTORM
AFTERSUPPER
AFTERSWARM
AFTERTASTE
AFTERTHOUGHT
AFTERTIME
AFTERTOUCH
AFTERTURN
AFTERVISION
AFTERWALE
AFTERWARD
AFTERWARDS
AFTERWASH
AFTERWHILE
AFTERWISE
AFTERWIT
AFTERWITTED
AFTERWORLD
AFTERWRIST
AFTERYEARS
AFTMOST
AFTOSA
AFTWARD
AFTWARDS
AFUNCTION
AFUNCTIONAL
AFWILLITE
AGA
AGABANEE
AGACANT
AGACANTE

AGACELLA
AGACERIE
AGAIN
AGAINBUY
AGAINSAY
AGAINST
AGAL
AGALACTIC
AGALACTOUS
AGALAXIA
AGALAXY
AGALITE
AGALLOCH
AGALLOCHUM
AGALMA
AGALMATOLITE
AGALWOOD
AGAMA
AGAME
AGAMETE
AGAMI
AGAMIAN
AGAMIC
AGAMICALLY
AGAMID
AGAMIS
AGAMIST
AGAMOBIA
AGAMOBIUM
AGAMOGENESIS
AGAMOGENETIC
AGAMOID
AGAMONT
AGAMOSPORE
AGAMOUS
AGAMY
AGANGLIONIC
AGAPAE
AGAPANTHUS
AGAPE
AGAPETAE
AGAPETI
AGAPETID
AGAR
AGARIC
AGARICACEOUS
AGARICIC
AGARICIFORM
AGARICIN
AGARICINE
AGARICINIC
AGARICOID
AGARITA
AGAROID
AGARWAL
AGASP
AGAST
AGASTRIC
AGATA
AGATE
AGATEWARE
AGATHIN
AGATHISM
AGATHIST
AGATHODAEMON
AGATHODEMON
AGATHOLOGY
AGATIFEROUS
AGATIFORM
AGATINE
AGATIZE
AGATIZED
AGATIZING
AGATOID
AGATY
AGAVE
AGAVOSE

AGAZE
AGAZED
AGBA
AGE
AGEABLE
AGED
AGEDLY
AGEDNESS
AGEE
AGEING
AGELESS
AGELONG
AGEN
AGENCIES
AGENCY
AGENDA
AGENDUM
AGENESIA
AGENESIC
AGENESIS
AGENIZE
AGENNESIS
AGENNETIC
AGENT
AGENTESS
AGENTIAL
AGENTING
AGENTIVAL
AGENTIVE
AGENTRY
AGEOMETRICAL
AGER
AGERASIA
AGERATUM
AGEUSIA
AGEUSIC
AGGER
AGGERATE
AGGEROSE
AGGEST
AGGLOMERANT
AGGLOMERATE
AGGLOMERATED
AGGLOMERATIC
AGGLOMERATING
AGGLOMERATION
AGGLOMERATIVE
AGGLOMERATOR
AGGLUTINABLE
AGGLUTINANT
AGGLUTINATE
AGGLUTINATED
AGGLUTINATION
AGGLUTINATIVE
AGGLUTINATOR
AGGLUTININ
AGGLUTINIZE
AGGLUTINOGEN
AGGLUTINOID
AGGRACE
AGGRADATION
AGGRADATIONAL
AGGRADE
AGGRADED
AGGRADING
AGGRANDIZE
AGGRANDIZED
AGGRANDIZEMENT
AGGRANDIZER
AGGRANDIZING
AGGRATE
AGGRAVATE
AGGRAVATED
AGGRAVATING
AGGRAVATINGLY
AGGRAVATION
AGGRAVATIVE

AGGRAVATOR
AGGREGABLE
AGGREGANT
AGGREGATE
AGGREGATED
AGGREGATELY
AGGREGATENESS
AGGREGATING
AGGREGATION
AGGREGATIVE
AGGREGATOR
AGGREGATORY
AGGREGE
AGGRESS
AGGRESSED
AGGRESSIN
AGGRESSING
AGGRESSION
AGGRESSIVE
AGGRESSIVELY
AGGRESSIVENESS
AGGRESSOR
AGGRI
AGGRIEVANCE
AGGRIEVE
AGGRIEVED
AGGRIEVEDLY
AGGRIEVING
AGGROUP
AGGRY
AGGUR
AGHA
AGHANEE
AGHAST
AGHASTNESS
AGIBLE
AGILAWOOD
AGILE
AGILELY
AGILENESS
AGILITY
AGIN
AGING
AGIO
AGIOS
AGIOTAGE
AGIST
AGISTER
AGISTMENT
AGISTOR
AGITABLE
AGITANT
AGITATE
AGITATED
AGITATEDLY
AGITATING
AGITATION
AGITATIONAL
AGITATIVE
AGITATO
AGITATOR
AGITATORIAL
AGITATRIX
AGITPROP
AGITPUNKT
AGLA
AGLANCE
AGLAOZONIA
AGLARE
AGLEAF
AGLEAM
AGLEE
AGLET
AGLETHEAD
AGLEY
AGLIMMER
AGLINT

AGLISTEN
AGLITTER
AGLOBULIA
AGLOBULISM
AGLOSSAL
AGLOSSATE
AGLOSSIA
AGLOW
AGLUCON
AGLUCONE
AGLUTITION
AGLYCON
AGLYCONE
AGLYPHOUS
AGMA
AGMATINE
AGMATOLOGY
AGMINATE
AGMINATED
AGNAIL
AGNAME
AGNAMED
AGNAT
AGNATE
AGNATHIA
AGNATHIC
AGNATHOUS
AGNATIC
AGNATICAL
AGNATICALLY
AGNATION
AGNEAU
AGNEAUX
AGNEL
AGNI
AGNIFICATION
AGNITION
AGNIZE
AGNIZED
AGNIZING
AGNOIOLOGY
AGNOMEN
AGNOMICAL
AGNOMINA
AGNOMINAL
AGNOMINATION
AGNOSIA
AGNOSTIC
AGNOSTICAL
AGNOSTICALLY
AGNOSTICISM
AGNOSY
AGNUS
AGNUSES
AGO
AGOG
AGOGE
AGOGIC
AGOGICS
AGOHO
AGOING
AGOJO
AGOMENSIN
AGOMPHIASIS
AGOMPHIOUS
AGON
AGONAL
AGONE
AGONES
AGONIA
AGONIADA
AGONIADIN
AGONIATITE
AGONIC
AGONIED
AGONIES
AGONIST

AGONISTARCH
AGONISTIC
AGONISTICAL
AGONISTICS
AGONIUM
AGONIZE
AGONIZED
AGONIZER
AGONIZING
AGONOTHETE
AGONOTHETIC
AGONY
AGOOD
AGORA
AGORAE
AGORAMANIA
AGORANOME
AGORANOMUS
AGORAPHOBIA
AGORAS
AGOS
AGOSTADERO
AGOUARA
AGOUTA
AGOUTI
AGOUTIES
AGOUTIS
AGOUTY
AGPAITE
AGPAITIC
AGRAFE
AGRAFFE
AGRAH
AGRAL
AGRAMED
AGRAMMATISM
AGRAPHA
AGRAPHIA
AGRAPHIC
AGRARIAN
AGRARIANISM
AGRARIANIZE
AGRARIANLY
AGREAT
AGREE
AGREEABILITY
AGREEABLE
AGREEABLENESS
AGREEABLY
AGREED
AGREEING
AGREEINGLY
AGREEMENT
AGREER
AGREGATION
AGREGE
AGREMENS
AGREMENT
AGREMENTS
AGREST
AGRESTAL
AGRESTIAL
AGRESTIAN
AGRESTIC
AGRESTICAL
AGRI
AGRIA
AGRICERE
AGRICOLE
AGRICOLIST
AGRICOLITE
AGRICOLOUS
AGRICULTOR
AGRICULTURAL
AGRICULTURALLY
AGRICULTURE
AGRICULTURER

AGRICULTURIST
AGRIEF
AGRIMONIES
AGRIMONY
AGRIMOTOR
AGRIN
AGRIOLOGIST
AGRIOLOGY
AGRIONID
AGRIOTYPE
AGRISE
AGRISED
AGRISING
AGRITO
AGRITOS
AGROAN
AGROBIOLOGIC
AGROBIOLOGY
AGRODOLCE
AGROGEOLOGY
AGROLOGIC
AGROLOGICAL
AGROLOGY
AGROM
AGROMYZID
AGRONOME
AGRONOMIC
AGRONOMICAL
AGRONOMICS
AGRONOMIST
AGRONOMY
AGROOF
AGROPE
AGROSTEROL
AGROSTOLOGIC
AGROSTOLOGY
AGROTE
AGROTECHNY
AGROTYPE
AGROUND
AGRUFE
AGRUIF
AGRYPNIA
AGRYPNIAI
AGRYPNOTIC
AGSAM
AGUA
AGUACATE
AGUADA
AGUADOR
AGUAJI
AGUAMAS
AGUAMIEL
AGUARA
AGUARDIENTE
AGUAVINA
AGUE
AGUEPROOF
AGUEWEED
AGUEY
AGUGLIA
AGUILARITE
AGUILT
AGUINALDO
AGUINALDOS
AGUIRAGE
AGUISE
AGUISH
AGUISHLY
AGUISHNESS
AGUJA
AGUJON
AGUNAH
AGUSH
AGUST
AGY
AGYE

AGYIOMANIA
AGYNARIOUS
AGYNARY
AGYNOUS
AGYRATE
AGYRIA
AH
AHA
AHAAINA
AHAMKARA
AHANKARA
AHARTALAV
AHAU
AHAUNCH
AHEAD
AHEAP
AHEIGHT
AHEM
AHEY
AHIGH
AHIMSA
AHIND
AHL
AHLUWALIA
AHM
AHMADI
AHMAR
AHMEDI
AHOLD
AHOLE
AHOLT
AHONG
AHOO
AHORSEBACK
AHOY
AHSAN
AHU
AHUACA
AHUATLE
AHUEHUETE
AHULL
AHUM
AHUNG
AHUNGERED
AHUNGRY
AHUNT
AHURA
AHUREWA
AHUSH
AHUULA
AHWAL
AHYPNIA
AI
AIBLINS
AICHMOPHOBIA
AID
AIDANCE
AIDANT
AIDE
AIDED
AIDER
AIDFUL
AIDING
AIDLESS
AIDMAN
AIE
AIEL
AIERY
AIGIALOSAUR
AIGLET
AIGREMORE
AIGRET
AIGRETTE
AIGUIERE
AIGUILLE
AIGUILLETTE
AIKANE

IKEN	AIRILY	AJAJA	AKONGE	ALANIN
IKINITE	AIRINESS	AJANGLE	AKORI	ALANINE
IL	AIRING	AJAR	AKOV	ALANNAH
ILANTERY	AIRISH	AJARI	AKPEK	ALANT
ILANTHIC	AIRLESS	AJAVA	AKRA	ALANTIC
ILANTHUS	AIRLIFT	AJAX	AKROCHORDITE	ALANTIN
ILANTINE	AIRLIKE	AJEE	AKROTER	ALANTOL
ILANTO	AIRLINE	AJENJO	AKROTERIA	ALANTOLIC
ILD	AIRLINER	AJHAR	AKROTERIAL	ALANYL
ILE	AIRLING	AJI	AKROTERION	ALAR
ILED	AIRMAIL	AJIMEZ	AKU	ALARE
ILERON	AIRMAN	AJITTER	AKUA	ALARES
ILETTE	AIRMANSHIP	AJIVA	AKUAMMIN	ALARM
ILING	AIRMARK	AJIVIKA	AKUAMMINE	ALARMABLE
ILLT	AIRMONGER	AJO	AKULE	ALARMED
ILMENT	AIROHYDROGEN	AJOG	AKUND	ALARMEDLY
ILSYTE	AIROMETER	AJOINT	AKVAVIT	ALARMING
ILUROID	AIRPARK	AJONJOLI	AL	ALARMINGLY
ILUROMANIA	AIRPLANE	AJOUR	ALA	ALARMISM
ILWEED	AIRPLANED	AJOURE	ALABAMIDE	ALARMIST
IM	AIRPLANING	AJOURISE	ALABAMINE	ALARUM
IMARA	AIRPLANIST	AJOWAN	ALABANDITE	ALARY
IMED	AIRPORT	AJUTMENT	ALABARCH	ALAS
IMER	AIRPROOF	AK	ALABASTER	ALASAS
IMFUL	AIRS	AKA	ALABASTRA	ALASKAITE
IMFULLY	AIRSCAPE	AKAAKAI	ALABASTRIAN	ALASKITE
IMING	AIRSCREW	AKABO	ALABASTRINE	ALASTRIM
IMLESS	AIRSHEET	AKALA	ALABASTRUM	ALATE
IMLESSLY	AIRSHIP	AKALIMBA	ALACHA	ALATED
IMLESSNESS	AIRSICK	AKAMAI	ALACHAH	ALATERN
IN	AIRSICKNESS	AKAMATSU	ALACK	ALATERNUS
INALEH	AIRSOME	AKAROA	ALACKADAY	ALATION
INCE	AIRSPACE	AKASA	ALACRAN	ALAUDINE
INE	AIRSPEED	AKAZGA	ALACREATINE	ALAUND
INEE	AIRSTREAM	AKAZGIN	ALACREATININ	ALAUNT
INHUM	AIRSTRIP	AKAZGINE	ALACRIFY	ALAY
INI	AIRT	AKCHA	ALACRIOUS	ALAZOR
INOI	AIRTH	AKCHEH	ALACRIOUSLY	ALB
INSELL	AIRTIGHT	AKE	ALACRITOUS	ALBA
ION	AIRTIGHTLY	AKEAKE	ALACRITY	ALBACEA
IPI	AIRTIGHTNESS	AKEBI	ALADA	ALBACORA
IPIM	AIRVIEW	AKED	ALAE	ALBACORE
IR	AIRWARD	AKEE	ALAGAO	ALBACORES
IRABLE	AIRWARDS	AKEKI	ALAGARTO	ALBAE
IRAMPO	AIRWAVE	AKELA	ALAGAU	ALBAHACA
IRAN	AIRWAY	AKELE	ALAHEE	ALBAM
IRBOAT	AIRWAYMAN	AKELEY	ALAI	ALBAN
IRBORNE	AIRWISE	AKEMBOLL	ALAIHI	ALBANITE
IRBOUND	AIRWOMAN	AKENBOLD	ALAITE	ALBARCO
IRBRUSH	AIRWOMEN	AKENE	ALAKE	ALBARDINE
IRBURST	AIRWORTHY	AKENOBEITE	ALAL	ALBARELLO
IRCRAFT	AIRY	AKEPIRO	ALALA	ALBARIUM
IRCRAFTMAN	AIS	AKEPIROS	ALALI	ALBASPIDIN
IRCRAFTMEN	AISEWEED	AKER	ALALIA	ALBATA
IRCRAFTSMAN	AISLE	AKERITE	ALALITE	ALBATROSS
IRCREW	AISLED	AKEY	ALALOI	ALBATROSSES
IRCREWMAN	AISLING	AKH	ALALONGA	ALBE
IRDOCK	AISTEOIR	AKHOOND	ALALUNGA	ALBEDO
IRDROME	AISTOPOD	AKHROT	ALALUS	ALBEDOGRAPH
IRDROP	AIT	AKHUN	ALAMBIQUE	ALBEE
IRDROPPED	AITCH	AKHUND	ALAMEDA	ALBEIT
IRDROPPING	AITCHBONE	AKHUNDZADA	ALAMIQUI	ALBERCA
IRE	AITCHES	AKIA	ALAMIRE	ALBERGATRICE
IRED	AITCHLESS	AKIMBO	ALAMO	ALBERGE
IRER	AITEN	AKIN	ALAMODALITY	ALBERGO
IRFIELD	AITESIS	AKINDLE	ALAMODE	ALBERTIN
IRFLOW	AITHOCHROI	AKINESIA	ALAMORT	ALBERTITE
IRFOIL	AITION	AKINESIC	ALAMOS	ALBERTTYPE
IRFRAME	AITIOTROPIC	AKINESIS	ALAMOSITE	ALBERTYPE
IRGLOW	AITIS	AKINETE	ALAN	ALBESCENCE
IRGRAPH	AITS	AKING	ALAND	ALBESCENT
IRHEAD	AITU	AKKUM	ALANE	ALBESPINE
IRIER	AIVER	AKLE	ALANG	ALBESTON
IRIEST	AIWAIN	AKMUDDAR	ALANGE	ALBETAD
IRIFEROUS	AIWAN	AKO	ALANGIN	ALBICANT
IRIFIED	AIZLE	AKOLOUTHIA	ALANGINE	ALBICATION
IRIG	AIZOACEOUS	AKOLUTHIA	ALANI	ALBICORE

ALBICULI	ALCARRAZA	ALDERMANESS	ALESE	ALGEBRAIC
ALBIFICATION	ALCATRAS	ALDERMANIC	ALESHOT	ALGEBRAICAL
ALBIFICATIVE	ALCAVALA	ALDERMANITY	ALESTAKE	ALGEBRAIST
ALBIFIED	ALCAYDE	ALDERMANLIKE	ALETAP	ALGEBRAIZE
ALBIFLOROUS	ALCAZABA	ALDERMANLY	ALETHIC	ALGEBRAIZED
ALBIFY	ALCAZAR	ALDERMANRY	ALETHIOLOGY	ALGEBRAIZING
ALBIFYING	ALCAZAVA	ALDERMANSHIP	ALETHOSCOPE	ALGEBRIZATION
ALBINAL	ALCE	ALDERMEN	ALETTE	ALGEDO
ALBINESS	ALCELAPHINE	ALDERN	ALEUCAEMIC	ALGEDONIC
ALBINIC	ALCHEMIC	ALDERS	ALEUCEMIC	ALGEDONICS
ALBINISM	ALCHEMICAL	ALDERWOMAN	ALEUKAEMIC	ALGEFACIENT
ALBINISTIC	ALCHEMICALLY	ALDERWOMEN	ALEUKEMIC	ALGERINE
ALBINO	ALCHEMIST	ALDIMIN	ALEURITIC	ALGESIA
ALBINOISM	ALCHEMISTER	ALDIMINE	ALEUROMANCY	ALGESIC
ALBINOS	ALCHEMISTIC	ALDINE	ALEUROMETER	ALGESIS
ALBINOTIC	ALCHEMISTRY	ALDITOL	ALEURONAT	ALGESTHESIS
ALBINURIA	ALCHEMIZE	ALDOL	ALEURONE	ALGETIC
ALBITE	ALCHEMIZED	ALDOLIZATION	ALEURONIC	ALGIC
ALBITIC	ALCHEMIZING	ALDOLIZE	ALEUROSCOPE	ALGICIDE
ALBITICAL	ALCHEMY	ALDOLIZED	ALEUTITE	ALGID
ALBITITE	ALCHERA	ALDOLIZING	ALEVIN	ALGIDITY
ALBITIZATION	ALCHERINGA	ALDOSE	ALEW	ALGIDNESS
ALBITOPHYRE	ALCHITRAN	ALDOXIME	ALEWHAP	ALGIFIC
ALBIZZIA	ALCHOCHODEN	ALDRIN	ALEWIFE	ALGIN
ALBOCRACY	ALCHORNEA	ALE	ALEWIVES	ALGINATE
ALBOLITE	ALCHYMY	ALEAK	ALEXANDERS	ALGINE
ALBOLITH	ALCIDINE	ALEATORY	ALEXANDRITE	ALGINIC
ALBOPANNIN	ALCINE	ALEBENCH	ALEXIA	ALGINURESIS
ALBOPRUINOSE	ALCLAD	ALEBERRY	ALEXIN	ALGIST
ALBORADA	ALCO	ALEBUSH	ALEXINE	ALGIVOROUS
ALBORANITE	ALCOGEL	ALEC	ALEXINIC	ALGOCYAN
ALBRICIAS	ALCOGENE	ALECITHAL	ALEXIPHARMIC	ALGODON
ALBRONZE	ALCOHOL	ALECIZE	ALEXIPYRETIC	ALGODONITE
ALBUGINEOUS	ALCOHOLATE	ALECONNER	ALEXITERIC	ALGOGENIC
ALBUGINES	ALCOHOLATURE	ALECOST	ALEY	ALGOID
ALBUGINITIS	ALCOHOLIC	ALECTORIA	ALEYARD	ALGOLAGNIA
ALBUGO	ALCOHOLICALLY	ALECTORIAE	ALEYRODID	ALGOLAGNIC
ALBUM	ALCOHOLICITY	ALECTORIDINE	ALEZAN	ALGOLAGNIST
ALBUMEAN	ALCOHOLISM	ALECTORIOID	ALEZE	ALGOLAGNY
ALBUMEN	ALCOHOLIST	ALECUP	ALFA	ALGOLOGICAL
ALBUMENIZE	ALCOHOLIZATION	ALEE	ALFAJE	ALGOLOGIST
ALBUMENIZED	ALCOHOLIZE	ALEF	ALFAKI	ALGOLOGY
ALBUMENIZER	ALCOHOLIZED	ALEFNULL	ALFALFA	ALGOMETER
ALBUMENIZING	ALCOHOLIZING	ALEFT	ALFAQUI	ALGOMETRIC
ALBUMENOID	ALCOHOLOMETER	ALEFZERO	ALFAQUIN	ALGOMETRICAL
ALBUMIMETER	ALCOHOLURIA	ALEGAR	ALFARGA	ALGOMETRY
ALBUMIN	ALCOHOLYSIS	ALEGER	ALFENIDE	ALGOPHILIA
ALBUMINATE	ALCOHOLYTIC	ALEHOOF	ALFEREZ	ALGOPHOBIA
ALBUMINIFORM	ALCORNOQUE	ALEHOUSE	ALFET	ALGOR
ALBUMINIZE	ALCOSOL	ALEIKOUM	ALFILARIA	ALGORISM
ALBUMINIZED	ALCOVE	ALEIKUM	ALFILERIA	ALGORISMIC
ALBUMINIZING	ALCUMY	ALEIPTES	ALFILERILLO	ALGORIST
ALBUMINOID	ALCYON	ALEKNIGHT	ALFIN	ALGORITHM
ALBUMINOIDAL	ALCYONACEAN	ALEM	ALFIONA	ALGORITHMIC
ALBUMINOSE	ALCYONARIAN	ALEMBIC	ALFIONE	ALGOSIS
ALBUMINOSIS	ALCYONIC	ALEMBICATE	ALFONCINO	ALGOUS
ALBUMINOUS	ALCYONIFORM	ALEMBROTH	ALFONSIN	ALGOVITE
ALBUMINURIA	ALCYONOID	ALEMITE	ALFONSO	ALGUACIL
ALBUMINURIC	ALD	ALEMMAL	ALFORGE	ALGUAZIL
ALBUMOSCOPE	ALDAMIN	ALEMONGER	ALFORJA	ALGUM
ALBUMOSE	ALDAMINE	ALEN	ALFRESCO	ALHACENA
ALBUMOSURIA	ALDANE	ALENGE	ALFRIDARIC	ALHENNA
ALBURN	ALDAY	ALENGTH	ALFRIDARY	ALHET
ALBURNOUS	ALDEA	ALENU	ALGA	ALIAS
ALBURNUM	ALDEAMENT	ALEPH	ALGAE	ALIASES
ALBUS	ALDEHOL	ALEPHS	ALGAECIDE	ALIBANGBANG
ALBUTANNIN	ALDEHYDASE	ALEPIDOTE	ALGAESTHESIS	ALIBI
ALCABALA	ALDEHYDE	ALEPINE	ALGAL	ALIBIED
ALCADE	ALDEHYDIC	ALEPOLE	ALGALIA	ALIBIING
ALCAICERIA	ALDEHYDINE	ALEPOT	ALGAROBA	ALIBILITY
ALCAIDE	ALDEIA	ALERCE	ALGARROBA	ALIBIS
ALCALDE	ALDER	ALERSE	ALGARROBILLA	ALIBLE
ALCALDIA	ALDERFLY	ALERT	ALGARROBIN	ALICHEL
ALCALIZATE	ALDERLIEFEST	ALERTA	ALGATE	ALICOCHE
ALCAMINE	ALDERMAN	ALERTLY	ALGATES	ALICTISAL
ALCANNA	ALDERMANATE	ALERTNESS	ALGAZEL	ALICULA
ALCANTARA	ALDERMANCY	ALESAN	ALGEBRA	ALICULAE

ALICYCLIC	ALIPTES	ALKALOIDS	ALLECRET	ALLIANCED
ALIDAD	ALIPTIC	ALKALOMETRY	ALLECT	ALLIANCER
ALIDADA	ALIQUANT	ALKALOSIS	ALLEE	ALLIANCING
ALIDADE	ALIQUID	ALKANAL	ALLEGATE	ALLIANT
ALIEN	ALIQUOT	ALKANET	ALLEGATION	ALLICHOLLY
ALIENABILITY	ALISANDERS	ALKANNA	ALLEGATOR	ALLICIENCY
ALIENABLE	ALISEPTAL	ALKANNIN	ALLEGE	ALLICIENT
ALIENAGE	ALISH	ALKANOL	ALLEGEABLE	ALLICIN
ALIENATE	ALISIER	ALKAPTON	ALLEGED	ALLIED
ALIENATED	ALISMA	ALKAPTONE	ALLEGEDLY	ALLIES
ALIENATING	ALISMACEOUS	ALKAPTONURIA	ALLEGEMENT	ALLIGATE
ALIENATION	ALISMAD	ALKAPTONURIC	ALLEGER	ALLIGATION
ALIENATOR	ALISMAL	ALKARSIN	ALLEGIANCE	ALLIGATOR
ALIENE	ALISMOID	ALKARSINE	ALLEGIANT	ALLIGATORED
ALIENED	ALISO	ALKEKENGI	ALLEGING	ALLIGATORING
ALIENEE	ALISON	ALKENE	ALLEGORIC	ALLINEATE
ALIENER	ALISONITE	ALKENYL	ALLEGORICAL	ALLINEATION
ALIENICOLA	ALISOS	ALKERMES	ALLEGORICALLY	ALLIS
ALIENICOLAE	ALISP	ALKID	ALLEGORIES	ALLISION
ALIENIGENATE	ALISPHENOID	ALKIDE	ALLEGORISM	ALLITERAL
ALIENING	ALIST	ALKIN	ALLEGORIST	ALLITERATE
ALIENISM	ALIT	ALKINE	ALLEGORISTER	ALLITERATED
ALIENIST	ALITE	ALKITRAN	ALLEGORISTIC	ALLITERATING
ALIENOR	ALITER	ALKOOL	ALLEGORIZATION	ALLITERATION
ALIETHMOID	ALITRUNK	ALKOXID	ALLEGORIZE	ALLITERATIVE
ALIETHMOIDAL	ALITURGIC	ALKOXIDE	ALLEGORIZED	ALLITERATOR
ALIF	ALITURGICAL	ALKOXY	ALLEGORIZER	ALLIUM
ALIFE	ALIUD	ALKOXYL	ALLEGORIZING	ALLIVALITE
ALIFEROUS	ALIUNDE	ALKY	ALLEGORY	ALLMOUTH
ALIFORM	ALIVE	ALKYD	ALLEGRESSE	ALLNESS
ALIGEROUS	ALIVENESS	ALKYL	ALLEGRETTO	ALLO
ALIGHT	ALIVINCULAR	ALKYLAMINE	ALLEGRETTOS	ALLOBAR
ALIGHTED	ALIYAH	ALKYLAMINO	ALLEGRO	ALLOBARIC
ALIGHTEN	ALIZARATE	ALKYLATE	ALLEGROS	ALLOCABLE
ALIGHTING	ALIZARI	ALKYLATED	ALLEL	ALLOCAFFEINE
ALIGN	ALIZARIN	ALKYLATING	ALLELE	ALLOCATABLE
ALIGNED	ALIZARINE	ALKYLATION	ALLELOMORPH	ALLOCATE
ALIGNER	ALJAMA	ALKYLENE	ALLELOTROPY	ALLOCATED
ALIGNING	ALJAMADO	ALKYLIC	ALLELUIA	ALLOCATING
ALIGNMENT	ALJAMIA	ALKYLIDENE	ALLELUIAH	ALLOCATION
ALIGREEK	ALJAMIADO	ALKYLIZE	ALLELUIATIC	ALLOCATUR
ALII	ALJAMIAH	ALKYLOGEN	ALLELUJA	ALLOCHEIRIA
ALIIPOE	ALJOFAINA	ALKYLOL	ALLEMAND	ALLOCHETITE
ALIKE	ALK	ALKYNE	ALLEMANDE	ALLOCHEZIA
ALIKENESS	ALKAHEST	ALL	ALLEMONTITE	ALLOCHIRAL
ALILA	ALKAHESTIC	ALLA	ALLENARLY	ALLOCHIRALLY
ALILONGHI	ALKAHESTICAL	ALLABUTA	ALLENE	ALLOCHIRIA
ALIM	ALKALAMIDE	ALLACTITE	ALLENTANDO	ALLOCHROIC
ALIMA	ALKALEMIA	ALLAEANTHUS	ALLENTATO	ALLOCHROITE
ALIMENT	ALKALESCENCE	ALLAGITE	ALLER	ALLOCHROOUS
ALIMENTAL	ALKALESCENCY	ALLALINITE	ALLERGEN	ALLOCLASE
ALIMENTALLY	ALKALESCENT	ALLAMONTI	ALLERGENIC	ALLOCLASITE
ALIMENTARY	ALKALI	ALLAMOTH	ALLERGIC	ALLOCOCHICK
ALIMENTATION	ALKALIC	ALLAMOTTI	ALLERGIES	ALLOCROTONIC
ALIMENTATIVE	ALKALIES	ALLAN	ALLERGIN	ALLOCRYPTIC
ALIMENTER	ALKALIFIABLE	ALLANITE	ALLERGIST	ALLOCTHONOUS
ALIMENTIC	ALKALIFIED	ALLANITIC	ALLERGY	ALLOCUTE
ALIMENTIVE	ALKALIFY	ALLANTIASIS	ALLERION	ALLOCUTION
ALIMONIED	ALKALIFYING	ALLANTOIC	ALLEVIATE	ALLOCUTIVE
ALIMONY	ALKALIGEN	ALLANTOID	ALLEVIATED	ALLOCYANINE
ALIN	ALKALIMETER	ALLANTOIDAL	ALLEVIATING	ALLOD
ALINASAL	ALKALIMETRIC	ALLANTOIDEAN	ALLEVIATION	ALLODELPHITE
ALINE	ALKALIMETRY	ALLANTOIDIAN	ALLEVIATIVE	ALLODESMISM
ALINEATION	ALKALINE	ALLANTOIN	ALLEVIATOR	ALLODGE
ALINED	ALKALINITY	ALLANTOIS	ALLEVIATORY	ALLODIA
ALINEMENT	ALKALINIZE	ALLANTURIC	ALLEY	ALLODIAL
ALINER	ALKALINIZED	ALLARGANDO	ALLEYED	ALLODIALISM
ALINING	ALKALINIZING	ALLASSOTONIC	ALLEYITE	ALLODIALIST
ALINIT	ALKALINURIA	ALLATIVE	ALLEYS	ALLODIALITY
ALINOTUM	ALKALIS	ALLATRATE	ALLEYWAY	ALLODIALLY
ALINTATAO	ALKALIZABLE	ALLAY	ALLGOOD	ALLODIAN
ALIOFAR	ALKALIZATE	ALLAYED	ALLGOVITE	ALLODIARIES
ALIPATA	ALKALIZATION	ALLAYER	ALLHEAL	ALLODIARY
ALIPED	ALKALIZE	ALLAYING	ALLIABLE	ALLODIES
ALIPHATIC	ALKALIZER	ALLAYMENT	ALLIABLY	ALLODIUM
ALIPIN	ALKALOID	ALLBE	ALLIACEOUS	ALLODY
ALIPTAE	ALKALOIDAL	ALLBONE	ALLIANCE	ALLOEOSIS

ALLOEOTIC
ALLOEROTIC
ALLOEROTISM
ALLOGAMOUS
ALLOGAMY
ALLOGENEITY
ALLOGENEOUS
ALLOGENIC
ALLOGRAPH
ALLOKINESIS
ALLOKINETIC
ALLOKURTIC
ALLOLALIA
ALLOLALIC
ALLOMERISM
ALLOMEROUS
ALLOMORPH
ALLOMORPHIC
ALLOMORPHISM
ALLOMORPHITE
ALLOMUCIC
ALLONGE
ALLONOMOUS
ALLONYM
ALLONYMOUS
ALLOPATH
ALLOPATHETIC
ALLOPATHIC
ALLOPATHIST
ALLOPATHY
ALLOPELAGIC
ALLOPHANAMID
ALLOPHANATES
ALLOPHANE
ALLOPHANIC
ALLOPHONE
ALLOPHORE
ALLOPHYLIAN
ALLOPHYTOID
ALLOPLASM
ALLOPLASMIC
ALLOPLAST
ALLOPLASTIC
ALLOPLASTY
ALLOPSYCHIC
ALLOQUIAL
ALLOQUIALISM
ALLOQUY
ALLOSAUR
ALLOSE
ALLOSEMATIC
ALLOSOME
ALLOT
ALLOTED
ALLOTELLURIC
ALLOTHEISM
ALLOTHIMORPH
ALLOTHOGENIC
ALLOTMENT
ALLOTRIURIA
ALLOTROPE
ALLOTROPIC
ALLOTROPICAL
ALLOTROPISM
ALLOTROPIZE
ALLOTROPOUS
ALLOTROPY
ALLOTRYLIC
ALLOTTED
ALLOTTEE
ALLOTTER
ALLOTTERY
ALLOTTING
ALLOTYPE
ALLOTYPICAL
ALLOVER
ALLOW

ALLOWABLE
ALLOWABLENESS
ALLOWABLY
ALLOWANCE
ALLOWANCED
ALLOWANCING
ALLOWED
ALLOWEDLY
ALLOWER
ALLOWING
ALLOXAN
ALLOXANATE
ALLOXANIC
ALLOXANTIN
ALLOXURIC
ALLOXY
ALLOY
ALLOYAGE
ALLOYED
ALLOYING
ALLOZOOID
ALLS
ALLSEED
ALLSPICE
ALLTHING
ALLTHORN
ALLTUD
ALLUDE
ALLUDED
ALLUDING
ALLUMETTE
ALLURE
ALLURED
ALLUREMENT
ALLURER
ALLURING
ALLURINGLY
ALLURINGNESS
ALLUSION
ALLUSIVE
ALLUSIVELY
ALLUSIVENESS
ALLUVIA
ALLUVIAL
ALLUVIATE
ALLUVIATION
ALLUVIO
ALLUVION
ALLUVIOUS
ALLUVIUM
ALLUVIUMS
ALLWHERE
ALLWHITHER
ALLWORK
ALLY
ALLYING
ALLYL
ALLYLAMINE
ALLYLATE
ALLYLATION
ALLYLENE
ALLYLIC
ALMA
ALMACEN
ALMACENISTA
ALMACIGA
ALMACIGO
ALMADIA
ALMADIE
ALMAGEST
ALMAGRA
ALMAH
ALMANAC
ALMANDER
ALMANDINE
ALMANDITE
ALME

ALMEH
ALMEIDINA
ALMEMAR
ALMEMOR
ALMENDRO
ALMENDRON
ALMERIITE
ALMICORE
ALMIGHTILY
ALMIGHTINESS
ALMIGHTY
ALMIQUE
ALMIRAH
ALMOCREBE
ALMOGAVAR
ALMOHAD
ALMOIGN
ALMOIN
ALMON
ALMOND
ALMONDY
ALMONER
ALMONING
ALMONRIES
ALMONRY
ALMOST
ALMOUS
ALMS
ALMSDEED
ALMSFOLK
ALMSGIVER
ALMSGIVING
ALMSHOUSE
ALMSMAN
ALMSMEN
ALMSMONEY
ALMSWOMAN
ALMSWOMEN
ALMUCANTAR
ALMUCE
ALMUD
ALMUDE
ALMUERZO
ALMUG
ALMURY
ALMUTEN
ALN
ALNAGE
ALNAGER
ALNAGERSHIP
ALNEIN
ALNICO
ALNIRESINOL
ALNOITE
ALNUIN
ALNUS
ALOCASIA
ALOCHIA
ALOD
ALODIAL
ALODIALISM
ALODIALIST
ALODIALITY
ALODIALLY
ALODIAN
ALODIARIES
ALODIARY
ALODIES
ALODIUM
ALODY
ALOE
ALOED
ALOEDARY
ALOEMODIN
ALOEROOT
ALOES
ALOESOL

ALOESWOOD
ALOETIC
ALOETICAL
ALOEWOOD
ALOFT
ALOGIA
ALOGICAL
ALOGICALLY
ALOGISM
ALOGY
ALOHA
ALOID
ALOIN
ALOISIITE
ALOJA
ALOMA
ALONE
ALONELY
ALONG
ALONGSHORE
ALONGSHOREMAN
ALONGSIDE
ALONGST
ALOOF
ALOOFE
ALOOFLY
ALOOFNESS
ALOOSE
ALOP
ALOPECIA
ALOPECIST
ALOPECOID
ALOPEKAI
ALOPEKE
ALOPHAS
ALOSE
ALOUATTE
ALOUD
ALOUT
ALOW
ALOWE
ALOYAU
ALOYSIA
ALP
ALPACA
ALPARGATA
ALPASOTES
ALPAX
ALPEEN
ALPENGLOW
ALPENHORN
ALPENSTOCK
ALPENSTOCKER
ALPESTRAL
ALPESTRIAN
ALPESTRINE
ALPHA
ALPHABET
ALPHABETARY
ALPHABETED
ALPHABETIC
ALPHABETICAL
ALPHABETICALLY
ALPHABETICS
ALPHABETIFORM
ALPHABETING
ALPHABETISM
ALPHABETIST
ALPHABETIZATION
ALPHABETIZE
ALPHABETIZED
ALPHABETIZER
ALPHABETIZING
ALPHATOLUIC
ALPHENIC
ALPHIN
ALPHOL

ALPHORN
ALPHOS
ALPHOSIS
ALPHYL
ALPHYN
ALPIEU
ALPIGENE
ALPINE
ALPINELY
ALPINERY
ALPINIA
ALPINISM
ALPINIST
ALPIST
ALPISTE
ALQUEIRE
ALQUIER
ALQUIFOU
ALRAUN
ALREADINESS
ALREADY
ALRIGHT
ALRIGHTY
ALROOT
ALRUNA
ALRUNE
ALS
ALSBACHITE
ALSIFILM
ALSIKE
ALSINACEOUS
ALSMEKILL
ALSO
ALSOON
ALSTONIDINE
ALSTONINE
ALSWEILL
ALSWITH
ALT
ALTAR
ALTARAGE
ALTARED
ALTARIST
ALTARLET
ALTARPIECE
ALTARWISE
ALTAZIMUTH
ALTEA
ALTER
ALTERABILITY
ALTERABLE
ALTERABLENESS
ALTERABLY
ALTERANT
ALTERATION
ALTERATIVE
ALTERCATE
ALTERCATED
ALTERCATING
ALTERCATION
ALTERCATIVE
ALTERED
ALTEREGOISM
ALTERER
ALTERING
ALTERITY
ALTERN
ALTERNACY
ALTERNAMENTE
ALTERNANCE
ALTERNANT
ALTERNARIOSE
ALTERNAT
ALTERNATE
ALTERNATED
ALTERNATELY
ALTERNATER

ALTERNATING	ALUMINIFORM	AMADOU	AMATIVENESS	AMBIPAROUS
ALTERNATION	ALUMINITE	AMAGA	AMATOL	AMBISINISTER
ALTERNATIVE	ALUMINIUM	AMAH	AMATORIAL	AMBIT
ALTERNATIVELY	ALUMINIZE	AMAIN	AMATORIALLY	AMBITAL
ALTERNATIVENESS	ALUMINIZED	AMAINE	AMATORIAN	AMBITENDENCY
ALTERNATIVITY	ALUMINIZING	AMAIST	AMATORIES	AMBITION
ALTERNATIVO	ALUMINOSE	AMAISTER	AMATORIO	AMBITIONIST
ALTERNATOR	ALUMINOSIS	AMAKEBE	AMATORIOUS	AMBITIONLESS
ALTERNE	ALUMINOSITY	AMALA	AMATORY	AMBITIOUS
ALTERNIZE	ALUMINOTYPE	AMALAITA	AMATRICE	AMBITIOUSLY
ALTERUM	ALUMINOUS	AMALAKA	AMATUNGULA	AMBITIOUSNESS
ALTESSE	ALUMINUM	AMALETT	AMAUROSIS	AMBITTY
ALTEZA	ALUMINYL	AMALGAM	AMAUROTIC	AMBITUS
ALTEZZA	ALUMITE	AMALGAMABLE	AMAXOMANIA	AMBIVALENCE
ALTHAEA	ALUMNA	AMALGAMATE	AMAY	AMBIVALENCY
ALTHAEIN	ALUMNAE	AMALGAMATED	AMAZE	AMBIVALENT
ALTHEA	ALUMNAL	AMALGAMATER	AMAZED	AMBIVERSION
ALTHEIN	ALUMNI	AMALGAMATING	AMAZEFUL	AMBIVERT
ALTHEINE	ALUMNIATE	AMALGAMATION	AMAZEMENT	AMBLE
ALTHIONIC	ALUMNUS	AMALGAMATIVE	AMAZING	AMBLED
ALTHO	ALUMROOT	AMALGAMATOR	AMAZON	AMBLER
ALTHORN	ALUMSTONE	AMALGAMIST	AMAZONITE	AMBLING
ALTHOUGH	ALUNITE	AMALGAMIZE	AMBA	AMBLINGLY
ALTI	ALUNOGEN	AMALTAS	AMBACH	AMBLOTIC
ALTIFY	ALUPAG	AMAMAU	AMBAGE	AMBLYGON
ALTIGRAPH	ALURE	AMAND	AMBAGES	AMBLYGONITE
ALTILIK	ALURGITE	AMANDIN	AMBAGIOSITY	AMBLYOPE
ALTILOQUENCE	ALUSHTITE	AMANG	AMBAGIOUS	AMBLYOPIA
ALTILOQUENT	ALUTA	AMANI	AMBAGIOUSLY	AMBLYOPIC
ALTIMETER	ALUTACEOUS	AMANIA	AMBAGITORY	AMBLYOSCOPE
ALTIMETRICAL	ALVAR	AMANITIN	AMBAK	AMBLYPOD
ALTIMETRY	ALVEARIES	AMANITINE	AMBALAM	AMBLYSTEGITE
ALTIN	ALVEARIUM	AMANORI	AMBAN	AMBO
ALTINCAR	ALVEARY	AMANOUS	AMBAR	AMBOCEPTOR
ALTININCK	ALVEI	AMANT	AMBAREE	AMBOMALLEAL
ALTIPLANICIE	ALVELOS	AMANTE	AMBARELLA	AMBON
ALTIPLANO	ALVELOZ	AMANUENSES	AMBARI	AMBONES
ALTISCOPE	ALVEOLA	AMANUENSIS	AMBARY	AMBONITE
ALTISONANT	ALVEOLAE	AMAPA	AMBAS	AMBOS
ALTISSIMO	ALVEOLAR	AMAR	AMBASH	AMBOSEXOUS
ALTITUDE	ALVEOLARY	AMARANTH	AMBASSADE	AMBRACAN
ALTITUDES	ALVEOLATE	AMARANTHINE	AMBASSADOR	AMBRAIN
ALTITUDINAL	ALVEOLATED	AMARANTHOID	AMBASSADRESS	AMBRETTE
ALTO	ALVEOLATION	AMARANTITE	AMBASSY	AMBRIES
ALTOCUMULUS	ALVEOLE	AMARELLE	AMBATCH	AMBRITE
ALTOGETHER	ALVEOLI	AMAREVOLE	AMBAY	AMBROID
ALTOIST	ALVEOLIFORM	AMARGOSA	AMBE	AMBROLOGY
ALTOMETER	ALVEOLITE	AMARGOSO	AMBEER	AMBROSE
ALTOS	ALVEOLONASAL	AMARGOSOS	AMBER	AMBROSIA
ALTOSTRATUS	ALVEOLOTOMY	AMARILLO	AMBERFISH	AMBROSIAC
ALTOUN	ALVEOLUS	AMARILLOS	AMBERGRIS	AMBROSIAL
ALTRICES	ALVEUS	AMARIN	AMBERIFEROUS	AMBROSIALLY
ALTRICIAL	ALVIDUCOUS	AMARINE	AMBERINA	AMBROSIAN
ALTROSE	ALVIN	AMARITY	AMBERITE	AMBROSIATE
ALTRUISM	ALVINE	AMAROID	AMBERJACK	AMBROSIN
ALTRUIST	ALVITE	AMAROIDAL	AMBEROID	AMBROSINE
ALTRUISTIC	ALVUS	AMARTHRITIS	AMBEROUS	AMBROSTEROL
ALTRUISTICALLY	ALWAY	AMARYLLID	AMBERY	AMBROTYPE
ALTSCHIN	ALWAYS	AMASESIS	AMBIANCE	AMBRY
ALTUN	ALWISE	AMASS	AMBIDEXTER	AMBSACE
ALTURE	ALY	AMASSED	AMBIDEXTERITY	AMBULACRA
ALTUS	ALYMPHIA	AMASSER	AMBIDEXTRAL	AMBULACRAL
ALUDEL	ALYPIN	AMASSETTE	AMBIDEXTROUS	AMBULACRUM
ALULA	ALYPINE	AMASSING	AMBIENCE	AMBULANCE
ALULAE	ALYSSON	AMASSMENT	AMBIENS	AMBULANCED
ALULAR	ALYSSUM	AMASTHENIC	AMBIENT	AMBULANCER
ALULET	ALYTARCH	AMASTIA	AMBIER	AMBULANCING
ALUM	AM	AMASTY	AMBIGENOUS	AMBULANT
ALUMBLOOM	AMA	AMATE	AMBIGUITIES	AMBULATE
ALUMEN	AMAAS	AMATEUR	AMBIGUITY	AMBULATED
ALUMETIZE	AMABILE	AMATEURISH	AMBIGUOUS	AMBULATING
ALUMINA	AMABILITY	AMATEURISHLY	AMBIGUOUSLY	AMBULATION
ALUMINAPHONE	AMACRATIC	AMATEURISHNESS	AMBIGUOUSNESS	AMBULATIVE
ALUMINATE	AMACRINAL	AMATEURISM	AMBILATERAL	AMBULATOR
ALUMINE	AMACRINE	AMATITO	AMBILEVOUS	AMBULATORIA
ALUMINIC	AMADAVAT	AMATIVE	AMBILIAN	AMBULATORIAL
ALUMINIDE	AMADELPHOUS	AMATIVELY	AMBIOPIA	AMBULATORIES

AMBULATORIUM	AMENORRHOEA	AMIDE	AMLIKAR	AMNIORRHEA
AMBULATORIUMS	AMENORRHOEAL	AMIDIC	AMLONG	AMNIOS
AMBULATORY	AMENORRHOEIC	AMIDIN	AMMA	AMNIOTE
AMBULIA	AMENT	AMIDINE	AMMAN	AMNIOTIC
AMBULING	AMENTA	AMIDO	AMMELINE	AMNIOTITIS
AMBULOMANCY	AMENTACEOUS	AMIDOACETAL	AMMEOS	AMNIOTOME
AMBURBIAL	AMENTAL	AMIDOACETIC	AMMER	AMOBARBITAL
AMBURY	AMENTIA	AMIDOCAPRIC	AMMETER	AMOBER
AMBUSCADE	AMENTIFEROUS	AMIDOGEN	AMMIACEOUS	AMOEBA
AMBUSCADED	AMENTIFORM	AMIDOHEXOSE	AMMINE	AMOEBAE
AMBUSCADER	AMENTULA	AMIDOKETONE	AMMINOLYSIS	AMOEBAEA
AMBUSCADING	AMENTULUM	AMIDOL	AMMINOLYTIC	AMOEBAEAN
AMBUSCADO	AMENTUM	AMIDOMYELIN	AMMIOLITE	AMOEBAEUM
AMBUSCADOED	AMENUSE	AMIDONE	AMMO	AMOEBAN
AMBUSH	AMER	AMIDOPHENOL	AMMOBIUM	AMOEBEAN
AMBUSHER	AMERCE	AMIDOPYRINE	AMMOCETE	AMOEBEUM
AMBUSHMENT	AMERCEABLE	AMIDOXIME	AMMOCHAETA	AMOEBIAN
AMCHOOR	AMERCED	AMIDOXYL	AMMOCHAETAE	AMOEBIASIS
AME	AMERCEMENT	AMIDRAZONE	AMMOCHRYSE	AMOEBIC
AMEBA	AMERCER	AMIDSHIP	AMMOCOETE	AMOEBICIDAL
AMEBAE	AMERCIAMENT	AMIDSHIPS	AMMOCOETES	AMOEBICIDE
AMEBAN	AMERCING	AMIDST	AMMOCOETID	AMOEBID
AMEBAS	AMERICIUM	AMIDSTREAM	AMMOCOETOID	AMOEBIFORM
AMEBIAN	AMERIKANI	AMIDULIN	AMMODYTE	AMOEBOCYTE
AMEBIASIS	AMERISM	AMIE	AMMODYTOID	AMOEBOID
AMEBIC	AMERISTIC	AMIGA	AMMONAL	AMOEBOIDISM
AMEBICIDAL	AMERVEIL	AMIGO	AMMONATE	AMOEBOUS
AMEBICIDE	AMESACE	AMIGOS	AMMONATION	AMOEBULA
AMEBID	AMESE	AMIL	AMMONIA	AMOINDER
AMEBIFORM	AMESITE	AMIMIA	AMMONIAC	AMOK
AMEBOBACTER	AMETABOLE	AMIN	AMMONIACAL	AMOKE
AMEBOCYTE	AMETABOLIC	AMINASE	AMMONIACUM	AMOLE
AMEBOID	AMETABOLISM	AMINATE	AMMONIAEMIA	AMOLILLA
AMEBOIDISM	AMETABOLOUS	AMINATION	AMMONIATE	AMOLISH
AMEBOUS	AMETALLOUS	AMINE	AMMONIATED	AMOLLISH
AMEBULA	AMETHODICAL	AMINI	AMMONIATING	AMOMAL
AMEED	AMETHYST	AMINIC	AMMONIATION	AMOMUM
AMEEN	AMETHYSTINE	AMINITY	AMMONIC	AMONG
AMEER	AMETRIA	AMINO	AMMONICAL	AMONGST
AMEIOSIS	AMETROMETER	AMINOACETAL	AMMONIEMIA	AMONTILLADO
AMEL	AMETROPE	AMINOACETONE	AMMONIFIER	AMOR
AMELAND	AMETROPIA	AMINOAZO	AMMONIFY	AMORA
AMELCORN	AMETROPIC	AMINOBENZENE	AMMONION	AMORADO
AMELET	AMETROUS	AMINOBENZOIC	AMMONITE	AMORAIC
AMELIORABLE	AMGARN	AMINOCAPROIC	AMMONITIC	AMORAIM
AMELIORANT	AMHAR	AMINOFORMIC	AMMONITOID	AMORAL
AMELIORATE	AMHERSTITE	AMINOGEN	AMMONIUM	AMORALISM
AMELIORATED	AMHRAN	AMINOKETONE	AMMONIURET	AMORALITY
AMELIORATING	AMI	AMINOLIPIN	AMMONIURETED	AMORALLY
AMELIORATION	AMIA	AMINOLYSIS	AMMONIURIA	AMORET
AMELIORATIVE	AMIABILITY	AMINOLYTIC	AMMONIZATION	AMORETTI
AMELIORATOR	AMIABLE	AMINOMYELIN	AMMONOBASIC	AMORETTO
AMELL	AMIABLENESS	AMINOPHENOL	AMMONOID	AMORINI
AMELLUS	AMIABLY	AMINOPURINE	AMMONOIDEAN	AMORINO
AMELU	AMIANTH	AMINOSIS	AMMONOLYSIS	AMORISM
AMELUS	AMIANTHINE	AMINOVALERIC	AMMONOLYTIC	AMORIST
AMEN	AMIANTHOID	AMINOXYLOL	AMMONOLYZE	AMORISTIC
AMENABILITY	AMIANTHOIDAL	AMIR	AMMOPHILOUS	AMOROSA
AMENABLE	AMIANTHUS	AMIRAY	AMMORESLINOL	AMOROSITY
AMENABLENESS	AMIANTUS	AMIS	AMMOTHERAPY	AMOROSO
AMENABLY	AMIC	AMISS	AMMU	AMOROUS
AMENAGE	AMICABILITY	AMISSIBILITY	AMMUNITION	AMOROUSLY
AMENANCE	AMICABLE	AMISSIBLE	AMNEMONIC	AMOROUSNESS
AMEND	AMICABLENESS	AMISSION	AMNESIA	AMORPH
AMENDABLE	AMICABLY	AMIT	AMNESIC	AMORPHA
AMENDATORY	AMICAL	AMITATE	AMNESTIC	AMORPHI
AMENDE	AMICE	AMITIE	AMNESTIES	AMORPHIA
AMENDER	AMICED	AMITIES	AMNESTY	AMORPHIC
AMENDING	AMICICIDE	AMITOSIS	AMNIA	AMORPHINISM
AMENDMENT	AMICOUS	AMITOTIC	AMNIAC	AMORPHISM
AMENDS	AMICROBIC	AMITOTICALLY	AMNIC	AMORPHOPHYTE
AMENE	AMICRON	AMITY	AMNIOCHORIAL	AMORPHOTAE
AMENITIES	AMICTUS	AMIXIA	AMNIOCLEPSIS	AMORPHOUS
AMENITY	AMID	AMLA	AMNIOMANCY	AMORPHOUSLY
AMENORRHEA	AMIDASE	AMLAH	AMNION	AMORPHUS
AMENORRHEAL	AMIDATE	AMLET	AMNIONIC	AMORPHY
AMENORRHEIC	AMIDATION	AMLI	AMNIONS	AMORT

AMORTISE	AMPHICHROMY	AMPHITHYRON	AMREL	AMYLATE
AMORTISSEUR	AMPHICOELOUS	AMPHITOKAL	AMRELLE	AMYLEMIA
AMORTIZABLE	AMPHICRANIA	AMPHITOKOUS	AMRIT	AMYLENE
AMORTIZATION	AMPHICRIBRAL	AMPHITOKY	AMRITA	AMYLIC
AMORTIZE	AMPHICTYON	AMPHITRIAENE	AMSATH	AMYLIDENE
AMORTIZED	AMPHICTYONIC	AMPHITRICHA	AMSEL	AMYLIFEROUS
AMORTIZEMENT	AMPHICTYONY	AMPHITROPAL	AMSONIA	AMYLIN
AMORTIZING	AMPHICYRTIC	AMPHITROPOUS	AMT	AMYLO
AMOSITE	AMPHICYTULA	AMPHIVASAL	AMTER	AMYLOCLASTIC
AMOTION	AMPHID	AMPHIVOROUS	AMTMAN	AMYLODEXTRIN
AMOTUS	AMPHIDE	AMPHODARCH	AMTMEN	AMYLOGEN
AMOULI	AMPHIDESMOUS	AMPHODELITE	AMTS	AMYLOGENESIS
AMOUNT	AMPHIDETIC	AMPHOGENOUS	AMU	AMYLOGENIC
AMOUR	AMPHIDIPLOID	AMPHOLYTE	AMUCK	AMYLOID
AMOURET	AMPHIDISC	AMPHOPEPTONE	AMUGIS	AMYLOIDAL
AMOURETTE	AMPHIDISK	AMPHOPHILIC	AMUGUIS	AMYLOIDOSIS
AMOURIST	AMPHIEROTIC	AMPHOPHILOUS	AMULA	AMYLOLEUCITE
AMOVABILITY	AMPHIEROTISM	AMPHORA	AMULAE	AMYLOLYSIS
AMOVABLE	AMPHIGAEAN	AMPHORAE	AMULAS	AMYLOLYTIC
AMOVE	AMPHIGAM	AMPHORAL	AMULET	AMYLOM
AMOVED	AMPHIGAMOUS	AMPHORE	AMULETIC	AMYLOME
AMOVING	AMPHIGEAN	AMPHORIC	AMULLA	AMYLOMETER
AMPALAYA	AMPHIGEN	AMPHORICITY	AMUNAM	AMYLON
AMPALEA	AMPHIGENE	AMPHORILOQUY	AMURCA	AMYLOPECTIN
AMPANGABEITE	AMPHIGENESIS	AMPHOROPHONY	AMURCOSITY	AMYLOPHAGIA
AMPARO	AMPHIGENETIC	AMPHOROUS	AMURCOUS	AMYLOPLAST
AMPASIMENITE	AMPHIGENOUS	AMPHOTERIC	AMUSABLE	AMYLOPLASTIC
AMPASSY	AMPHIGONIA	AMPLE	AMUSE	AMYLOPLASTID
AMPELITE	AMPHIGONIC	AMPLECT	AMUSED	AMYLOPSASE
AMPELITIC	AMPHIGONIUM	AMPLECTANT	AMUSEDLY	AMYLOPSIN
AMPELOGRAPHY	AMPHIGONOUS	AMPLENESS	AMUSEMENT	AMYLOSE
AMPELOPSIDIN	AMPHIGONY	AMPLEX	AMUSEMENTS	AMYLOSIS
AMPELOPSIN	AMPHIGORIC	AMPLEXATION	AMUSER	AMYLUM
AMPELOPSIS	AMPHIGORIES	AMPLEXICAUL	AMUSETTE	AMYLURIA
AMPER	AMPHIGORY	AMPLEXUS	AMUSIA	AMYNODONT
AMPERAGE	AMPHIGOURI	AMPLIATE	AMUSING	AMYOSTHENIA
AMPERE	AMPHIGOURIS	AMPLIATION	AMUSINGLY	AMYOSTHENIC
AMPEREMETER	AMPHIKARYON	AMPLIATIVE	AMUSINGNESS	AMYOTAXIA
AMPEROMETER	AMPHILOGISM	AMPLICATIVE	AMUSIVE	AMYOTONIA
AMPERSAND	AMPHILOGY	AMPLIFICATE	AMUSIVELY	AMYOTROPHIA
AMPERY	AMPHIMACER	AMPLIFICATION	AMUSIVENESS	AMYOTROPHIC
AMPHANTHIA	AMPHIMIXIS	AMPLIFICATIVE	AMUTTER	AMYOTROPHY
AMPHANTHIUM	AMPHIMORULA	AMPLIFICATOR	AMUYON	AMYOUS
AMPHEROTOKY	AMPHIMORULAE	AMPLIFIED	AMUYONG	AMYRIN
AMPHETAMINE	AMPHINEUROUS	AMPLIFIER	AMUZE	AMYROL
AMPHIASTER	AMPHINUCLEUS	AMPLIFY	AMVIS	AMYROOT
AMPHIB	AMPHIOXUS	AMPLIFYING	AMY	AN
AMPHIBALI	AMPHIPHLOIC	AMPLITUDE	AMYDON	ANA
AMPHIBALUS	AMPHIPLATYAN	AMPLY	AMYELIA	ANABAENA
AMPHIBIA	AMPHIPNEUST	AMPOLLOSITY	AMYELIC	ANABAENAS
AMPHIBIAL	AMPHIPNEUSTIC	AMPONGUE	AMYELINIC	ANABAPTIZED
AMPHIBIAN	AMPHIPOD	AMPOULE	AMYELONIC	ANABAPTIZING
AMPHIBIETY	AMPHIPODAL	AMPTE	AMYELOUS	ANABAS
AMPHIBIOLOGY	AMPHIPODAN	AMPUL	AMYGDAL	ANABASES
AMPHIBION	AMPHIPODOUS	AMPULE	AMYGDALA	ANABASIN
AMPHIBIOTIC	AMPHIPYRENIN	AMPULLA	AMYGDALAE	ANABASINE
AMPHIBIOUS	AMPHIRHINAL	AMPULLACEOUS	AMYGDALASE	ANABASIS
AMPHIBIOUSLY	AMPHIRHINE	AMPULLAE	AMYGDALATE	ANABASSE
AMPHIBIUM	AMPHISARCA	AMPULLAR	AMYGDALE	ANABATA
AMPHIBLASTIC	AMPHISBAENA	AMPULLARY	AMYGDALIC	ANABATHMOI
AMPHIBOLE	AMPHISBAENIC	AMPULLATE	AMYGDALIFORM	ANABATHMOS
AMPHIBOLIA	AMPHISCIANS	AMPULLATED	AMYGDALIN	ANABATIC
AMPHIBOLIC	AMPHISCII	AMPULLIFORM	AMYGDALINE	ANABEROGA
AMPHIBOLITE	AMPHISPORE	AMPULLITIS	AMYGDALITIS	ANABIBAZON
AMPHIBOLITIC	AMPHISTOME	AMPULLULA	AMYGDALOID	ANABIOSIS
AMPHIBOLOGY	AMPHISTOMOID	AMPUTATE	AMYGDALOIDAL	ANABIOTIC
AMPHIBOLOUS	AMPHISTOMOUS	AMPUTATED	AMYGDALOLITH	ANABLEPS
AMPHIBOLY	AMPHISTYLAR	AMPUTATING	AMYGDALONCUS	ANABO
AMPHIBRACH	AMPHISTYLIC	AMPUTATION	AMYGDALOTOME	ANABOHITSITE
AMPHIBRACHIC	AMPHISTYLY	AMPUTATIVE	AMYGDALOTOMY	ANABOLIC
AMPHIBRYOUS	AMPHITENE	AMPUTATOR	AMYGDOPHENIN	ANABOLIN
AMPHICARPIA	AMPHITHEATER	AMPUTEE	AMYGDULE	ANABOLISM
AMPHICARPIC	AMPHITHEATRE	AMPYCES	AMYL	ANABOLITE
AMPHICARPIUM	AMPHITHECIA	AMPYX	AMYLACEOUS	ANABOLIZE
AMPHICENTRIC	AMPHITHECIAL	AMPYXES	AMYLAMINE	ANABOLY
AMPHICHROIC	AMPHITHECIUM	AMRA	AMYLAN	ANABONG
AMPHICHROME	AMPHITHECT	AMREETA	AMYLASE	ANABRANCH

ANABROSIS	ANAEROPLASTY	ANALOGICALLY	ANAPESTIC	ANASTOMOSE
ANABROTIC	ANAESTHESIA	ANALOGICE	ANAPHASE	ANASTOMOSED
ANAC	ANAESTHESIS	ANALOGIES	ANAPHIA	ANASTOMOSES
ANACAHUITA	ANAESTHETIC	ANALOGION	ANAPHORA	ANASTOMOSING
ANACAHUITE	ANAESTHETIST	ANALOGISM	ANAPHORAL	ANASTOMOSIS
ANACALYPSIS	ANAESTHETIZE	ANALOGIST	ANAPHORIA	ANASTOMOTIC
ANACAMPSIS	ANAESTHETIZED	ANALOGISTIC	ANAPHORIC	ANASTROPHE
ANACAMPTIC	ANAESTHETIZER	ANALOGIZE	ANAPHORICAL	ANASTROPHY
ANACAMPTICS	ANAESTHETIZING	ANALOGIZED	ANAPHRODISIA	ANATASE
ANACANTH	ANAESTHYL	ANALOGIZING	ANAPHRODITIC	ANATEXIS
ANACANTHINE	ANAGALACTIC	ANALOGON	ANAPHYLACTIC	ANATHEMA
ANACANTHOUS	ANAGAP	ANALOGOUS	ANAPHYLACTIN	ANATHEMAS
ANACARA	ANAGENESIS	ANALOGOUSLY	ANAPHYLACTOID	ANATHEMATA
ANACARD	ANAGENETIC	ANALOGUE	ANAPHYLAXIS	ANATHEMATIC
ANACARDIC	ANAGEP	ANALOGY	ANAPHYTE	ANATHEMATISM
ANACATHARSIS	ANAGLYPH	ANALPHABET	ANAPLASIA	ANATHEMATIZE
ANACATHARTIC	ANAGLYPHIC	ANALPHABETE	ANAPLASIS	ANATHEMIZE
ANACEPHALIZE	ANAGLYPHICAL	ANALPHABETIC	ANAPLASM	ANATIFA
ANACHORISM	ANAGLYPHY	ANALYSAND	ANAPLASMOSIS	ANATIFAE
ANACHROMASIS	ANAGLYPTIC	ANALYSATION	ANAPLASTIC	ANATIFER
ANACHRONIC	ANAGLYPTICS	ANALYSE	ANAPLASTY	ANATIFEROUS
ANACHRONICAL	ANAGLYPTON	ANALYSED	ANAPLEROSIS	ANATINE
ANACHRONICALLY	ANAGNORISIS	ANALYSER	ANAPLEROTIC	ANATIRA
ANACHRONISM	ANAGNOST	ANALYSES	ANAPNEA	ANATMAN
ANACHRONIST	ANAGNOSTES	ANALYSING	ANAPNOGRAPH	ANATOCISM
ANACHRONISTIC	ANAGOGE	ANALYSIS	ANAPNOIC	ANATOMIC
ANACHRONIZE	ANAGOGIC	ANALYST	ANAPNOMETER	ANATOMICAL
ANACHRONOUS	ANAGOGICAL	ANALYTIC	ANAPODEICTIC	ANATOMICALLY
ANACID	ANAGOGICALLY	ANALYTICAL	ANAPOPHYSIAL	ANATOMIES
ANACIDITY	ANAGOGICS	ANALYTICALLY	ANAPOPHYSIS	ANATOMISM
ANACK	ANAGOGY	ANALYTICS	ANAPSID	ANATOMIST
ANACLASIS	ANAGRAM	ANALYZABLE	ANAPSIDAN	ANATOMIZE
ANACLASTIC	ANAGRAMMATIC	ANALYZATION	ANAPTERYGOTE	ANATOMIZED
ANACLASTICS	ANAGRAMS	ANALYZE	ANAPTOTIC	ANATOMIZER
ANACLETICA	ANAGRAPH	ANALYZED	ANAPTYCHI	ANATOMIZING
ANACLETICUM	ANAGUA	ANALYZER	ANAPTYCHUS	ANATOMY
ANACLINAL	ANAGYRINE	ANALYZING	ANAPTYCTIC	ANATOPISM
ANACLISIS	ANAHAO	ANAM	ANAPTYCTICAL	ANATOXIN
ANACLITIC	ANAHAU	ANAMA	ANAPTYXIS	ANATREPTIC
ANACOENOSIS	ANAI	ANAMESITE	ANAQUA	ANATRIPSIS
ANACOLUTHA	ANAKINESIS	ANAMIRTIN	ANARCESTEAN	ANATRIPTIC
ANACOLUTHIC	ANAKINETIC	ANAMMONIDE	ANARCH	ANATRON
ANACOLUTHON	ANAKTORON	ANAMNESIS	ANARCHIC	ANATROPAL
ANACOLUTHONS	ANAL	ANAMNESTIC	ANARCHICAL	ANATROPOUS
ANACONDA	ANALABOS	ANAMNIONIC	ANARCHICALLY	ANATTA
ANACOUSTIC	ANALAV	ANAMNIOTE	ANARCHISM	ANATTO
ANACROGYNOUS	ANALCIME	ANAMNIOTIC	ANARCHIST	ANAUDIA
ANACROTIC	ANALCIMITE	ANAMORPHIC	ANARCHISTIC	ANAUNTER
ANACROTISM	ANALCITE	ANAMORPHISM	ANARCHIZE	ANAUNTERS
ANACRUSIS	ANALCITITE	ANAMORPHOSE	ANARCHY	ANAUXITE
ANACRUSTIC	ANALECTA	ANAMORPHOSES	ANARETA	ANAXIAL
ANACUSIA	ANALECTIC	ANAMORPHOSIS	ANARETIC	ANAXON
ANACUSIC	ANALECTS	ANAMORPHOTE	ANARETICAL	ANAXONE
ANACUSIS	ANALEMMA	ANAMORPHOUS	ANARGYROI	ANAY
ANADEM	ANALEMMATIC	ANAN	ANARGYROS	ANAZOTURIA
ANADENIA	ANALEPSES	ANANA	ANARTHRIA	ANBA
ANADICROTIC	ANALEPSIS	ANANAS	ANARTHRIC	ANBURY
ANADICROTISM	ANALEPSY	ANANDA	ANARTHROSIS	ANCESTOR
ANADIDYMUS	ANALEPTIC	ANANDRARIOUS	ANARTHROUS	ANCESTORIAL
ANADIPLOSIS	ANALGEN	ANANDRIA	ANARTHROUSLY	ANCESTORS
ANADIPSIA	ANALGENE	ANANDROUS	ANARTISMOS	ANCESTRAL
ANADIPSIC	ANALGESIA	ANANEPIONIC	ANARYA	ANCESTRALLY
ANADROM	ANALGESIC	ANANGIOID	ANASARCA	ANCESTRESS
ANADROMOUS	ANALGESIS	ANANKE	ANASARCOUS	ANCESTRIES
ANAEMATOSIS	ANALGESIST	ANANTER	ANASCHISTIC	ANCESTRY
ANAEMIA	ANALGETIC	ANANTHERATE	ANASEISMIC	ANCHIETIN
ANAEMIC	ANALGIA	ANANTHEROUS	ANASPADIAS	ANCHIETINE
ANAERETIC	ANALGIC	ANANTHOUS	ANASPALIN	ANCHITHERE
ANAEROBATION	ANALGIZE	ANANYM	ANASTALSIS	ANCHITHERIOID
ANAEROBE	ANALLAGMATIC	ANAPAEST	ANASTALTIC	ANCHOR
ANAEROBIA	ANALLANTOIC	ANAPAESTIC	ANASTASIMON	ANCHORABLE
ANAEROBIC	ANALLERGIC	ANAPAESTICAL	ANASTASIMOS	ANCHORAGE
ANAEROBIOSIS	ANALLY	ANAPAGANIZE	ANASTASIS	ANCHORATE
ANAEROBIOTIC	ANALOG	ANAPAITE	ANASTATE	ANCHORED
ANAEROBIUM	ANALOGA	ANAPANAPA	ANASTATIC	ANCHORER
ANAEROPHYTE	ANALOGIC	ANAPEIRATIC	ANASTIGMAT	ANCHORESS
ANAEROPLASTIC	ANALOGICAL	ANAPEST	ANASTIGMATIC	ANCHORET

ANCHORETISM
ANCHORHOLD
ANCHORING
ANCHORITE
ANCHORITESS
ANCHORITIC
ANCHORITICAL
ANCHORITISM
ANCHORLESS
ANCHOVIES
ANCHOVY
ANCHUSA
ANCHUSIN
ANCHYLOSE
ANCHYLOSIS
ANCIENCE
ANCIENCY
ANCIENNETE
ANCIENT
ANCIENTISM
ANCIENTLY
ANCIENTNESS
ANCIENTRY
ANCIENTY
ANCILE
ANCILIA
ANCILLA
ANCILLARY
ANCIPITAL
ANCIPITOUS
ANCISTROID
ANCLE
ANCODONT
ANCOME
ANCON
ANCONA
ANCONAD
ANCONAGRA
ANCONAL
ANCONE
ANCONEAL
ANCONEI
ANCONES
ANCONEUS
ANCONITIS
ANCONOID
ANCONY
ANCORA
ANCYLOPOD
ANCYLOSE
ANCYLOSTOME
AND
ANDA
ANDABATA
ANDABATARIAN
ANDABATISM
ANDALUSITE
ANDANTE
ANDANTINO
ANDE
ANDERUN
ANDESINE
ANDESINITE
ANDESITE
ANDESITIC
ANDESYTE
ANDIRINE
ANDIROBA
ANDIRON
ANDORITE
ANDOUILLE
ANDOUILLET
ANDOUILLETTE
ANDRADITE
ANDRANATOMY
ANDRARCHY
ANDRENA

ANDRENID
ANDREWSITE
ANDRITE
ANDROCENTRIC
ANDROCLINIUM
ANDROCONIA
ANDROCONIUM
ANDROCRACY
ANDROCRATIC
ANDROCYTE
ANDROECIA
ANDROECIAL
ANDROECIUM
ANDROGEN
ANDROGENESIS
ANDROGENETIC
ANDROGENIC
ANDROGENOUS
ANDROGONIA
ANDROGONIAL
ANDROGYN
ANDROGYNAL
ANDROGYNARY
ANDROGYNE
ANDROGYNEITY
ANDROGYNIC
ANDROGYNISM
ANDROGYNOUS
ANDROGYNUS
ANDROGYNY
ANDROID
ANDROIDAL
ANDROIDES
ANDROKININ
ANDROL
ANDROLEPSIA
ANDROLEPSY
ANDROMANIA
ANDRON
ANDRONITIS
ANDROPETALAR
ANDROPHAGOUS
ANDROPHOBIA
ANDROPHORE
ANDROPHOROUS
ANDROPHORUM
ANDROPHYLL
ANDROSEME
ANDROSIN
ANDROSPHINX
ANDROSPORE
ANDROSTERONE
ANDROTAURIC
ANDS
ANE
ANEAR
ANEATH
ANECDOTA
ANECDOTAGE
ANECDOTAL
ANECDOTALISM
ANECDOTE
ANECDOTIC
ANECDOTICAL
ANECDOTIST
ANECHOIC
ANELE
ANELECTRIC
ANELED
ANELING
ANELYTROUS
ANEMATOSIS
ANEMI
ANEMIA
ANEMIC
ANEMOCHORD
ANEMOCHORE

ANEMOCLASTIC
ANEMOGRAM
ANEMOGRAPH
ANEMOGRAPHIC
ANEMOGRAPHY
ANEMOLOGIC
ANEMOLOGICAL
ANEMOLOGY
ANEMOMETER
ANEMOMETRIC
ANEMOMETRY
ANEMONAL
ANEMONE
ANEMONIN
ANEMONOL
ANEMOPATHY
ANEMOPHILE
ANEMOPHILOUS
ANEMOPHILY
ANEMOSCOPE
ANEMOSIS
ANEMOTAXIS
ANEMOTROPIC
ANEMOTROPISM
ANENCEPHALIA
ANENCEPHALIC
ANENCEPHALUS
ANENCEPHALY
ANEND
ANENERGIA
ANENST
ANENT
ANENTEROUS
ANEPIA
ANEPIGRAPHIC
ANEPIPLOIC
ANEPITHYMIA
ANERETHISIA
ANERETIC
ANERGIA
ANERGIC
ANERGY
ANERLY
ANEROID
ANEROTIC
ANESIS
ANESONE
ANESTHESIA
ANESTHESIANT
ANESTHESIOLOGIST
ANESTHESIOLOGY
ANESTHESIS
ANESTHETIC
ANESTHETIST
ANESTHETIZE
ANESTHETIZER
ANESTHYL
ANET
ANETH
ANETHOL
ANETHOLE
ANEUCH
ANEUPLOID
ANEUPLOIDY
ANEURIA
ANEURIC
ANEURILEMMIC
ANEURIN
ANEURISM
ANEURISMAL
ANEURISMALLY
ANEURISMATIC
ANEURYSM
ANEURYSMAL
ANEURYSMALLY
ANEURYSMATIC
ANEW

ANFEELD
ANFRACT
ANFRACTUOSE
ANFRACTUOUS
ANFRACTURE
ANGAKOK
ANGAKUT
ANGARALITE
ANGAREB
ANGAREEB
ANGAREP
ANGARIA
ANGARIATION
ANGARY
ANGEKKOK
ANGEKOK
ANGEKUT
ANGEL
ANGELATE
ANGELDOM
ANGELEEN
ANGELET
ANGELEYES
ANGELFISH
ANGELFISHES
ANGELHOOD
ANGELIC
ANGELICA
ANGELICAL
ANGELICALLY
ANGELICALNESS
ANGELICIZE
ANGELICO
ANGELIM
ANGELIN
ANGELINE
ANGELIQUE
ANGELITO
ANGELIZE
ANGELIZED
ANGELIZING
ANGELOCRACY
ANGELOGRAPHER
ANGELOLATER
ANGELOLATRY
ANGELOLOGIC
ANGELOLOGICAL
ANGELOLOGY
ANGELOMACHY
ANGELON
ANGELOPHANY
ANGELOT
ANGELS
ANGELUS
ANGER
ANGERED
ANGERING
ANGERLY
ANGERS
ANGEYOK
ANGIASTHENIA
ANGICO
ANGIECTASIS
ANGIECTOPIA
ANGIITIS
ANGILD
ANGILI
ANGINA
ANGINAL
ANGINIFORM
ANGINOID
ANGINOSE
ANGINOUS
ANGIOATAXIA
ANGIOBLAST
ANGIOBLASTIC
ANGIOCARP

ANGIOCARPIAN
ANGIOCARPIC
ANGIOCARPOUS
ANGIOCLAST
ANGIOCYST
ANGIOFIBROMA
ANGIOGENESIS
ANGIOGENIC
ANGIOGENY
ANGIOGLIOMA
ANGIOGRAPH
ANGIOGRAPHY
ANGIOID
ANGIOKINESIS
ANGIOKINETIC
ANGIOLIPOMA
ANGIOLITH
ANGIOLOGY
ANGIOMA
ANGIOMALACIA
ANGIOMAS
ANGIOMATA
ANGIOMATOSIS
ANGIOMATOUS
ANGIOMEGALY
ANGIOMETER
ANGIOMYOMA
ANGIONOMA
ANGIONOSIS
ANGIOPARESIS
ANGIOPATHY
ANGIOPHOROUS
ANGIOPLANY
ANGIOPLASTY
ANGIOPLEROSIS
ANGIOPOIETIC
ANGIORRHAGIA
ANGIORRHAPHY
ANGIORRHEA
ANGIORRHEXIS
ANGIOSARCOMA
ANGIOSCOPE
ANGIOSIS
ANGIOSPASM
ANGIOSPASTIC
ANGIOSPERM
ANGIOSPERMAL
ANGIOSPERMIC
ANGIOSPOROUS
ANGIOSTEOSIS
ANGIOSTOMIZE
ANGIOSTOMY
ANGIOSTROPHY
ANGIOTASIS
ANGIOTENOSIS
ANGIOTOME
ANGIOTOMY
ANGIOTONIC
ANGIOTRIBE
ANGIOTRIPSY
ANGIOTROPHIC
ANGKHAK
ANGLAISE
ANGLE
ANGLEBERRY
ANGLED
ANGLEDOG
ANGLEHOOK
ANGLEMETER
ANGLEPOD
ANGLER
ANGLES
ANGLESITE
ANGLESMITH
ANGLETOUCH
ANGLETWITCH
ANGLEWING

ANGLEWISE	ANHELOSE	ANIMALISM	ANISODACTYLE	ANKYROID
ANGLEWORM	ANHELOUS	ANIMALIST	ANISODONT	ANLACE
ANGLICIZE	ANHEMATOSIS	ANIMALISTIC	ANISOGAMETE	ANLAGE
ANGLICIZED	ANHEMOLYTIC	ANIMALITY	ANISOGAMETES	ANLAGEN
ANGLICIZING	ANHIDROSIS	ANIMALIZATION	ANISOGAMOUS	ANLAGES
ANGLIMANIAC	ANHIDROTIC	ANIMALIZE	ANISOGAMY	ANLAS
ANGLING	ANHIMA	ANIMALIZED	ANISOGENOUS	ANLAUT
ANGO	ANHINGA	ANIMALIZING	ANISOGENY	ANLAUTE
ANGOISE	ANHISTIC	ANIMALLY	ANISOGYNOUS	ANLET
ANGOLAR	ANHISTOUS	ANIMALS	ANISOIN	ANN
ANGOR	ANHUNGERED	ANIMANDO	ANISOL	ANNA
ANGOSTURA	ANHUNGRY	ANIMASTIC	ANISOLE	ANNABERGITE
ANGRIER	ANHYDRAEMIA	ANIMASTICAL	ANISOMELIA	ANNAL
ANGRIEST	ANHYDRAEMIC	ANIMATE	ANISOMELUS	ANNALE
ANGRILY	ANHYDRATE	ANIMATED	ANISOMERIC	ANNALIA
ANGRINESS	ANHYDRATED	ANIMATEDLY	ANISOMEROUS	ANNALINE
ANGRITE	ANHYDRATING	ANIMATELY	ANISOMETRIC	ANNALISM
ANGRY	ANHYDRATION	ANIMATENESS	ANISOMETROPE	ANNALIST
ANGST	ANHYDREMIA	ANIMATER	ANISOMYARIAN	ANNALISTIC
ANGSTER	ANHYDREMIC	ANIMATING	ANISOMYODIAN	ANNALIZE
ANGSTROM	ANHYDRIDE	ANIMATINGLY	ANISOMYODOUS	ANNALS
ANGUID	ANHYDRIDIZE	ANIMATION	ANISOPHYLLY	ANNALY
ANGUIFORM	ANHYDRITE	ANIMATISM	ANISOPIA	ANNAT
ANGUILLIFORM	ANHYDRIZE	ANIMATISTIC	ANISOPLEURAL	ANNATES
ANGUILLOID	ANHYDROUS	ANIMATIVE	ANISOPTEROUS	ANNATTO
ANGUINE	ANHYDROXIME	ANIMATO	ANISOSPORE	ANNEAL
ANGUINEOUS	ANI	ANIMATOGRAPH	ANISOSTHENIC	ANNEALED
ANGUIPED	ANICCA	ANIMATOR	ANISOSTOMOUS	ANNEALER
ANGUISH	ANICONIC	ANIME	ANISOTONIC	ANNEALING
ANGUISHED	ANICONISM	ANIMETTA	ANISOTROPAL	ANNECT
ANGUISHOUS	ANICULAR	ANIMIKITE	ANISOTROPE	ANNECTANT
ANGUISHOUSLY	ANICUT	ANIMISM	ANISOTROPIC	ANNECTENT
ANGULA	ANIDIAN	ANIMIST	ANISOTROPISM	ANNELID
ANGULAR	ANIDROSIS	ANIMISTIC	ANISOTROPOUS	ANNELIDAN
ANGULARE	ANIENTE	ANIMIZE	ANISOTROPY	ANNELIDIAN
ANGULARIA	ANIGH	ANIMO	ANISOYL	ANNELIDOUS
ANGULARITIES	ANIGHT	ANIMOSE	ANISUM	ANNELISM
ANGULARITY	ANIGHTS	ANIMOSENESS	ANISURIA	ANNELOID
ANGULARIZATION	ANIL	ANIMOSITIES	ANISYL	ANNERODITE
ANGULARIZE	ANILAO	ANIMOSITY	ANISYLIDENE	ANNERRE
ANGULARLY	ANILAU	ANIMOSO	ANITHER	ANNET
ANGULARNESS	ANILE	ANIMOUS	ANITO	ANNEX
ANGULATE	ANILENESS	ANIMUS	ANITOS	ANNEXA
ANGULATED	ANILIC	ANION	ANITROGENOUS	ANNEXABLE
ANGULATELY	ANILID	ANIONIC	ANJAN	ANNEXATION
ANGULATENESS	ANILIDE	ANIRIDIA	ANKARAMITE	ANNEXATIONAL
ANGULATING	ANILIDIC	ANIS	ANKARATRITE	ANNEXATIONIST
ANGULATION	ANILIDOXIME	ANISADO	ANKEE	ANNEXE
ANGULE	ANILIID	ANISAL	ANKER	ANNEXED
ANGULIFEROUS	ANILIN	ANISALCOHOL	ANKERHOLD	ANNEXER
ANGULINERVED	ANILINE	ANISALDEHYDE	ANKERITE	ANNEXING
ANGULOMETER	ANILINISM	ANISALDOXIME	ANKH	ANNEXION
ANGULOSE	ANILINO	ANISAMIDE	ANKLE	ANNEXIONIST
ANGULOSITY	ANILITY	ANISANDROUS	ANKLEBONE	ANNEXIVE
ANGULOUS	ANILLA	ANISANILIDE	ANKLEJACK	ANNEXMENT
ANGULUS	ANILOPYRIN	ANISATE	ANKLES	ANNEXURE
ANGURIA	ANILOPYRINE	ANISE	ANKLET	ANNICUT
ANGUS	ANIMA	ANISEED	ANKLONG	ANNIDALIN
ANGUST	ANIMABILITY	ANISEIKONIA	ANKUS	ANNIHILABLE
ANGUSTATE	ANIMABLE	ANISEIKONIC	ANKUSH	ANNIHILATE
ANGUSTICLAVE	ANIMABLENESS	ANISEROOT	ANKUSHA	ANNIHILATED
ANGWANTIBO	ANIMADVERSION	ANISETTE	ANKYLENTERON	ANNIHILATING
ANGWICH	ANIMADVERT	ANISIC	ANKYLODONTIA	ANNIHILATION
ANHAEMATOSIS	ANIMADVERTER	ANISIDINE	ANKYLOMELE	ANNIHILATIVE
ANHAEMOLYTIC	ANIMAL	ANISIDINO	ANKYLOMERISM	ANNIHILATOR
ANHALAMINE	ANIMALCULA	ANISIL	ANKYLOPHOBIA	ANNIHILATORY
ANHALINE	ANIMALCULAE	ANISILIC	ANKYLOPODIA	ANNITE
ANHALONIDINE	ANIMALCULAR	ANISOCARPIC	ANKYLOPOIETIC	ANNIVERSARIES
ANHALONIN	ANIMALCULE	ANISOCARPOUS	ANKYLOSE	ANNIVERSARY
ANHALONINE	ANIMALCULINE	ANISOCERCAL	ANKYLOSED	ANNIVERSE
ANHANG	ANIMALCULISM	ANISOCHROMIA	ANKYLOSING	ANNODATED
ANHARMONIC	ANIMALCULIST	ANISOCORIA	ANKYLOSIS	ANNONA
ANHEDONIA	ANIMALCULOUS	ANISOCOTYLY	ANKYLOSTOMA	ANNONACEOUS
ANHEDRAL	ANIMALCULUM	ANISOCRATIC	ANKYLOTIA	ANNONCE
ANHEDRON	ANIMALIAN	ANISOCYCLE	ANKYLOTIC	ANNOTATE
ANHELATION	ANIMALIC	ANISOCYTOSIS	ANKYLOTOME	ANNOTATED
ANHELE	ANIMALISH	ANISODACTYL	ANKYLOTOMY	ANNOTATING

ANNOTATION	ANODIC	ANOPLOTHERE	ANSWERED	ANTEDONIN
ANNOTATIVE	ANODICALLY	ANOPLOTHEROID	ANSWERER	ANTEED
ANNOTATOR	ANODINE	ANOPLURIFORM	ANSWERINGLY	ANTEFIX
ANNOTATORY	ANODIZE	ANOPSIA	ANSWERLESS	ANTEFIXA
ANNOTINE	ANODIZED	ANOPUBIC	ANSWERLESSLY	ANTEFIXAL
ANNOTINOUS	ANODIZING	ANORAK	ANT	ANTEFIXES
ANNOTTO	ANODONTIA	ANORCHI	ANTA	ANTEFLEXED
ANNOUNCE	ANODOS	ANORCHIA	ANTACID	ANTEFLEXION
ANNOUNCED	ANODYNE	ANORCHISM	ANTACRID	ANTEFURCA
ANNOUNCEMENT	ANODYNIA	ANORCHOUS	ANTADIFORM	ANTEFURCAE
ANNOUNCER	ANODYNIC	ANORCHUS	ANTAE	ANTEFURCAL
ANNOUNCING	ANODYNOUS	ANORECTAL	ANTAGONISM	ANTEGRADE
ANNOY	ANOEGENETIC	ANORECTIC	ANTAGONIST	ANTEING
ANNOYANCE	ANOESIA	ANORECTOUS	ANTAGONISTIC	ANTELABIUM
ANNOYANCER	ANOESIS	ANOREXIA	ANTAGONISTICAL	ANTELOCATION
ANNOYED	ANOESTROUS	ANOREXY	ANTAGONISTICALLY	ANTELOPE
ANNOYER	ANOESTRUM	ANORGANA	ANTAGONIZATION	ANTELOPES
ANNOYFUL	ANOESTRUS	ANORGANISM	ANTAGONIZE	ANTELOPIAN
ANNOYING	ANOETIC	ANORGANOLOGY	ANTAGONIZED	ANTELOPINE
ANNOYINGLY	ANOGENIC	ANORMAL	ANTAGONIZER	ANTELUCAN
ANNOYINGNESS	ANOGENITAL	ANORMALITY	ANTAGONIZING	ANTELUDE
ANNOYMENT	ANOIA	ANORN	ANTAGONY	ANTEMARGINAL
ANNOYOUS	ANOIL	ANOROGENIC	ANTAL	ANTEMASK
ANNOYOUSLY	ANOINE	ANORTH	ANTALGESIC	ANTEMERIDIAN
ANNUAL	ANOINT	ANORTHIC	ANTALGIC	ANTEMETIC
ANNUALIST	ANOINTER	ANORTHITE	ANTALGOL	ANTEMINGENT
ANNUALIZE	ANOINTMENT	ANORTHITIC	ANTALKALI	ANTEMUNDANE
ANNUALLY	ANOLE	ANORTHITITE	ANTALKALIES	ANTEMURAL
ANNUARY	ANOLI	ANORTHOCLASE	ANTALKALINE	ANTENATAL
ANNUATION	ANOLIAN	ANORTHOPHYRE	ANTALKALIS	ANTENATI
ANNUELER	ANOLYTE	ANORTHOPIA	ANTANACLASIS	ANTENATUS
ANNUELLER	ANOMALIES	ANORTHOSCOPE	ANTANEMIC	ANTENAVE
ANNUENT	ANOMALIPED	ANORTHOSE	ANTAPEX	ANTENNA
ANNUITANT	ANOMALIPOD	ANORTHOSITE	ANTAPODOSIS	ANTENNAE
ANNUITIES	ANOMALISM	ANOSCOPE	ANTAPOLOGY	ANTENNAL
ANNUITY	ANOMALIST	ANOSCOPY	ANTARCHISM	ANTENNARIID
ANNUL	ANOMALISTIC	ANOSMATIC	ANTARCHIST	ANTENNARY
ANNULAR	ANOMALONOMY	ANOSMIA	ANTARCHISTIC	ANTENNAS
ANNULARITY	ANOMALOSCOPE	ANOSMIC	ANTARCHY	ANTENNATE
ANNULARLY	ANOMALOUS	ANOSPHRASIA	ANTARCTICA	ANTENNIFORM
ANNULARY	ANOMALOUSLY	ANOSPHRESIA	ANTARCTICAL	ANTENNULA
ANNULATE	ANOMALURE	ANOSPINAL	ANTARCTICALLY	ANTENNULAR
ANNULATED	ANOMALY	ANOSTOSIS	ANTARTHRITIC	ANTENNULARY
ANNULATION	ANOMER	ANOTERITE	ANTASPHYCTIC	ANTENNULE
ANNULE	ANOMIA	ANOTHER	ANTASTHENIC	ANTENUMBER
ANNULET	ANOMIC	ANOTHERKINS	ANTASTHMATIC	ANTENUPTIAL
ANNULETTEE	ANOMIE	ANOTIA	ANTATROPHIC	ANTEOPERCLE
ANNULI	ANOMIES	ANOTUS	ANTBIRD	ANTEPAGMENTA
ANNULISM	ANOMITE	ANOUNOU	ANTE	ANTEPAGMENTS
ANNULLABLE	ANOMOCARPOUS	ANOVESICAL	ANTEAL	ANTEPALATAL
ANNULLATE	ANOMODONT	ANOXAEMIA	ANTEATER	ANTEPASCHAL
ANNULLATION	ANOMPHALOUS	ANOXAEMIC	ANTEBRACHIA	ANTEPAST
ANNULLED	ANOMURAL	ANOXEMIA	ANTEBRACHIAL	ANTEPECTORAL
ANNULLER	ANOMURAN	ANOXEMIC	ANTEBRACHIUM	ANTEPECTUS
ANNULLING	ANOMUROUS	ANOXIA	ANTECABINET	ANTEPENDIA
ANNULMENT	ANOMY	ANOXIC	ANTECEDE	ANTEPENDIUM
ANNULOID	ANON	ANOXIDATIVE	ANTECEDED	ANTEPENUIT
ANNULOSE	ANONANG	ANOXYBIOSIS	ANTECEDENCE	ANTEPHIALTIC
ANNULUS	ANONCILLO	ANOXYBIOTIC	ANTECEDENCY	ANTEPILEPTIC
ANNULUSES	ANONOL	ANOXYSCOPE	ANTECEDENT	ANTEPIRRHEMA
ANNUNCIABLE	ANONYCHIA	ANQUERA	ANTECEDENTAL	ANTEPONE
ANNUNCIATE	ANONYM	ANSA	ANTECEDENTALLY	ANTEPORT
ANNUNCIATED	ANONYMA	ANSAE	ANTECEDENTLY	ANTEPOSITION
ANNUNCIATING	ANONYME	ANSAR	ANTECEDING	ANTER
ANNUNCIATION	ANONYMITY	ANSARIAN	ANTECESSOR	ANTERETHIC
ANNUNCIATIVE	ANONYMOUS	ANSATE	ANTECHAMBER	ANTERGIC
ANNUNCIATOR	ANONYMOUSLY	ANSATED	ANTECHAPEL	ANTERI
ANNUNCIATORY	ANONYMOUSNESS	ANSATION	ANTECHOIR	ANTERIAD
ANNUS	ANONYMUNCULE	ANSERATED	ANTECHURCH	ANTERIN
ANOA	ANOOPSIA	ANSERIN	ANTECOLIC	ANTERIOR
ANOBING	ANOPERINEAL	ANSERINE	ANTECORNU	ANTERIORITY
ANOCARPOUS	ANOPHELE	ANSEROUS	ANTECOXAL	ANTERIORLY
ANOCIATION	ANOPHELES	ANSU	ANTED	ANTERIORNESS
ANOCOCCYGEAL	ANOPHELINE	ANSULATE	ANTEDATE	ANTERODORSAL
ANODAL	ANOPHTHALMOS	ANSWER	ANTEDATED	ANTEROGRADE
ANODE	ANOPHYTE	ANSWERABLE	ANTEDATING	ANTEROMEDIAL
ANODENDRON	ANOPIA	ANSWERABLY	ANTEDILUVIAL	ANTEROMEDIAN
			ANTEDILUVIAN	

ANTEROOM
ANTEROPYGAL
ANTEROSPINAL
ANTESCRIPT
ANTESIGNANI
ANTESTATURE
ANTESTERNAL
ANTESTERNUM
ANTETEMPLE
ANTETHEM
ANTETYPE
ANTEVENIENT
ANTEVERSION
ANTEVERT
ANTEVERTED
ANTEVERTING
ANTEVOCALIC
ANTEWAR
ANTHECOLOGY
ANTHELA
ANTHELAE
ANTHELIA
ANTHELICES
ANTHELION
ANTHELIONS
ANTHELIX
ANTHELMINTHIC
ANTHELMINTIC
ANTHEM
ANTHEMA
ANTHEMENE
ANTHEMIA
ANTHEMION
ANTHEMIS
ANTHEMWISE
ANTHEMY
ANTHER
ANTHERAL
ANTHERID
ANTHERIDIA
ANTHERIDIAL
ANTHERIDIUM
ANTHEROID
ANTHEROZOID
ANTHEROZOOID
ANTHESIS
ANTHESTERIN
ANTHESTEROL
ANTHEXIMETER
ANTHILL
ANTHINE
ANTHOBIOLOGY
ANTHOCARP
ANTHOCARPOUS
ANTHOCEROTE
ANTHOCHLOR
ANTHOCLINIUM
ANTHOCYAN
ANTHOCYANIN
ANTHODIA
ANTHODIUM
ANTHOECOLOGY
ANTHOGENESIS
ANTHOGENETIC
ANTHOGENOUS
ANTHOGRAPHY
ANTHOID
ANTHOLITE
ANTHOLOGICAL
ANTHOLOGIES
ANTHOLOGIST
ANTHOLOGIZE
ANTHOLOGIZED
ANTHOLOGIZING
ANTHOLOGY
ANTHOLYSIS
ANTHOMANIA

ANTHOMANIAC
ANTHOMEDUSAN
ANTHOMYIID
ANTHOPHAGOUS
ANTHOPHILE
ANTHOPHILIAN
ANTHOPHILOUS
ANTHOPHOBIA
ANTHOPHORE
ANTHOPHOROUS
ANTHOPHYTE
ANTHORINE
ANTHOTAXIS
ANTHOTAXY
ANTHOTROPIC
ANTHOTROPISM
ANTHOXANTHIN
ANTHOZOAN
ANTHOZOIC
ANTHOZOOID
ANTHOZOON
ANTHRACAEMIA
ANTHRACEMIA
ANTHRACENE
ANTHRACES
ANTHRACIA
ANTHRACIC
ANTHRACIN
ANTHRACITE
ANTHRACITIC
ANTHRACITISM
ANTHRACITOUS
ANTHRACNOSE
ANTHRACNOSIS
ANTHRACOCIDE
ANTHRACOID
ANTHRACONITE
ANTHRACOSIS
ANTHRACOTIC
ANTHRACYL
ANTHRADIOL
ANTHRAFLAVIC
ANTHRAGALLOL
ANTHRAMIN
ANTHRAMINE
ANTHRANIL
ANTHRANILATE
ANTHRANILIC
ANTHRANOL
ANTHRANONE
ANTHRANOYL
ANTHRANYL
ANTHRAQUINOL
ANTHRARUFIN
ANTHRATETROL
ANTHRATRIOL
ANTHRAX
ANTHRAXOLITE
ANTHRAXYLON
ANTHROIC
ANTHROL
ANTHRONE
ANTHROPIC
ANTHROPICAL
ANTHROPOGENY
ANTHROPOGLOT
ANTHROPOGONY
ANTHROPOID
ANTHROPOIDAL
ANTHROPOLITE
ANTHROPOLITH
ANTHROPOLOGIC
ANTHROPOLOGICAL
ANTHROPOLOGICALLY
ANTHROPOLOGIST
ANTHROPOLOGY
ANTHROPONOMY

ANTHROPOPHAGIT
ANTHROPOTOMY
ANTHROPOZOIC
ANTHROPURGIC
ANTHROXAN
ANTHROXANIC
ANTHRYL
ANTHRYLENE
ANTHURIUM
ANTI
ANTIABRIN
ANTIACID
ANTIADITIS
ANTIAE
ANTIAIRCRAFT
ANTIALBUMID
ANTIAR
ANTIARIN
ANTIBACCHIC
ANTIBACCHII
ANTIBACCHIUS
ANTIBACTERIAL
ANTIBARYON
ANTIBIONT
ANTIBIOSIS
ANTIBIOTIC
ANTIBLASTIC
ANTIBODIES
ANTIBODY
ANTIBROMIC
ANTIC
ANTICAL
ANTICARDIUM
ANTICATALASE
ANTICATALYST
ANTICATHODE
ANTICHANCE
ANTICHLOR
ANTICHLORINE
ANTICHRESES
ANTICHRESIS
ANTICHRETIC
ANTICHRIST
ANTICHTHON
ANTICIPANT
ANTICIPATE
ANTICIPATED
ANTICIPATING
ANTICIPATION
ANTICIPATIVE
ANTICIPATIVELY
ANTICIPATOR
ANTICIPATORY
ANTICIZE
ANTICK
ANTICKED
ANTICKER
ANTICKING
ANTICKT
ANTICLASTIC
ANTICLERICAL
ANTICLIMACTIC
ANTICLIMAX
ANTICLINAL
ANTICLINE
ANTICLINORIA
ANTICLY
ANTICNEMION
ANTICNESS
ANTICOAGULANT
ANTICOAGULIN
ANTICOR
ANTICOUS
ANTICREEP
ANTICREEPER
ANTICREEPING
ANTICROTALIC

ANTICRYPTIC
ANTICULARIA
ANTICUM
ANTICUS
ANTICYCLONE
ANTICYCLONIC
ANTIDACTYL
ANTIDETONANT
ANTIDORON
ANTIDOTAL
ANTIDOTALLY
ANTIDOTARY
ANTIDOTE
ANTIDOTED
ANTIDOTICAL
ANTIDOTING
ANTIDOTISM
ANTIDROMAL
ANTIDROMIC
ANTIDROMOUS
ANTIDROMY
ANTIENT
ANTIETHNIC
ANTIFEBRILE
ANTIFEDERAL
ANTIFOAM
ANTIFOGMATIC
ANTIFORMIN
ANTIFREEZE
ANTIFREEZING
ANTIFRICTION
ANTIGEN
ANTIGENE
ANTIGENIC
ANTIGLARE
ANTIGOD
ANTIGORITE
ANTIGRAPH
ANTIGRAVITY
ANTIGROPELOS
ANTIGUGGLER
ANTIHELICES
ANTIHELIX
ANTIHERO
ANTIHISTAMINE
ANTIHYDROPIN
ANTIKETOGEN
ANTIKETOGENIC
ANTIKNOCK
ANTILABORIST
ANTILEGALIST
ANTILEPSIS
ANTILEPTIC
ANTILIPOID
ANTILOBIUM
ANTILOG
ANTILOGIC
ANTILOGICAL
ANTILOGIES
ANTILOGISM
ANTILOGOUS
ANTILOGY
ANTILOQUY
ANTILUETIN
ANTILYSIN
ANTILYSIS
ANTILYSSIC
ANTILYTIC
ANTIMACASSAR
ANTIMASK
ANTIMASKER
ANTIMASQUE
ANTIMASQUER
ANTIMATTER
ANTIMELLIN
ANTIMENSIA
ANTIMENSION

ANTIMERE
ANTIMERIC
ANTIMERISM
ANTIMETABOLE
ANTIMETER
ANTIMINSIA
ANTIMINSION
ANTIMISSION
ANTIMNEMONIC
ANTIMONATE
ANTIMONIAL
ANTIMONIATED
ANTIMONIC
ANTIMONID
ANTIMONIDE
ANTIMONIOUS
ANTIMONITE
ANTIMONIUM
ANTIMONIURET
ANTIMONOUS
ANTIMONSOON
ANTIMONY
ANTIMONYL
ANTINEURITIC
ANTINEUTRINO
ANTINEUTRON
ANTINGANTING
ANTINIAL
ANTINION
ANTINODE
ANTINOME
ANTINOMIAN
ANTINOMIC
ANTINOMICAL
ANTINOMIES
ANTINOMIST
ANTINOMY
ANTIODONT
ANTIOPELMOUS
ANTIOXIDANT
ANTIOXYGEN
ANTIOXYGENIC
ANTIPARABEMA
ANTIPARALLEL
ANTIPART
ANTIPARTICLE
ANTIPASTIC
ANTIPASTO
ANTIPATHETIC
ANTIPATHIC
ANTIPATHIES
ANTIPATHIST
ANTIPATHIZE
ANTIPATHY
ANTIPEDAL
ANTIPEPSIN
ANTIPEPTONE
ANTIPERIODIC
ANTIPERTHITE
ANTIPETALOUS
ANTIPHARMIC
ANTIPHON
ANTIPHONA
ANTIPHONAL
ANTIPHONALLY
ANTIPHONARIES
ANTIPHONARY
ANTIPHONETIC
ANTIPHONIC
ANTIPHONICAL
ANTIPHONIES
ANTIPHONON
ANTIPHONY
ANTIPHRASES
ANTIPHRASIS
ANTIPHRASTIC
ANTIPLANET

ANTIPLASTIC
ANTIPLEION
ANTIPODAGRON
ANTIPODAL
ANTIPODE
ANTIPODEAN
ANTIPODES
ANTIPODIC
ANTIPODIST
ANTIPOINTS
ANTIPOLE
ANTIPOLEMIST
ANTIPOLO
ANTIPOPE
ANTIPRISM
ANTIPROTON
ANTIPTOSIS
ANTIPUDIC
ANTIPUTRID
ANTIPYIC
ANTIPYONIN
ANTIPYRESIS
ANTIPYRETIC
ANTIPYRIN
ANTIPYRINE
ANTIPYROTIC
ANTIPYRYL
ANTIQUA
ANTIQUARIAN
ANTIQUARIES
ANTIQUARISM
ANTIQUARY
ANTIQUATE
ANTIQUATED
ANTIQUATING
ANTIQUATION
ANTIQUE
ANTIQUED
ANTIQUELY
ANTIQUENESS
ANTIQUER
ANTIQUING
ANTIQUIST
ANTIQUITIES
ANTIQUITY
ANTIRACER
ANTIRACHITIC
ANTIRATTLER
ANTIRED
ANTIRENT
ANTIRENTER
ANTIRENTISM
ANTIRICIN
ANTIRRHINUM
ANTIS
ANTISALOON
ANTISCIA
ANTISCIANS
ANTISCII
ANTISCION
ANTISCOLIC
ANTISELENE
ANTISEPALOUS
ANTISEPSIS
ANTISEPTIC
ANTISEPTICAL
ANTISEPTICALLY
ANTISEPTICISM
ANTISEPTICIST
ANTISEPTICIZE
ANTISEPTION
ANTISERUM
ANTISIDERIC
ANTISIPHON
ANTISIPHONAL
ANTISLAVERY
ANTISNAPPER

ANTISOCIAL
ANTISOCIALIST
ANTISOCIALITY
ANTISOLAR
ANTISPACE
ANTISPADIX
ANTISPASMODIC
ANTISPAST
ANTISPASTIC
ANTISQUAMA
ANTISTES
ANTISTROPHAL
ANTISTROPHE
ANTISTROPHIC
ANTISTROPHON
ANTISUN
ANTITANK
ANTITHALIAN
ANTITHEFT
ANTITHEISM
ANTITHEIST
ANTITHEISTIC
ANTITHENAR
ANTITHERMIN
ANTITHESES
ANTITHESIS
ANTITHESISM
ANTITHESIZE
ANTITHET
ANTITHETIC
ANTITHETICAL
ANTITHETICS
ANTITOXIN
ANTITOXINE
ANTITRADE
ANTITRADES
ANTITRAGAL
ANTITRAGI
ANTITRAGIC
ANTITRAGICUS
ANTITRAGUS
ANTITROPE
ANTITROPIC
ANTITROPICAL
ANTITROPY
ANTITRUST
ANTITRYPSIN
ANTITRYPTIC
ANTITWILIGHT
ANTITYPAL
ANTITYPE
ANTITYPIC
ANTITYPICAL
ANTITYPY
ANTIVENENE
ANTIVENIN
ANTIVENINE
ANTIVIRAL
ANTIVIROTIC
ANTIWORLD
ANTIZOEA
ANTJAR
ANTLER
ANTLERED
ANTLERITE
ANTLERS
ANTLIA
ANTLIATE
ANTLING
ANTOECI
ANTOECIAN
ANTOECIANS
ANTONINIANI
ANTONINIANUS
ANTONOMASIA
ANTONOMASTIC
ANTONYM

ANTONYMOUS
ANTONYMY
ANTORBITAL
ANTRA
ANTRAL
ANTRALGIA
ANTRE
ANTRECTOMY
ANTRIN
ANTRITIS
ANTROCELE
ANTRONASAL
ANTROPHORE
ANTROPHOSE
ANTRORSE
ANTRORSELY
ANTROSCOPE
ANTROSCOPY
ANTROTOME
ANTROTOMY
ANTRUM
ANTRUSTION
ANTSHRIKE
ANTSY
ANUBIN
ANUBING
ANUKABIET
ANULOMA
ANUNDER
ANURAN
ANURESIS
ANURETIC
ANURIA
ANURIC
ANUROUS
ANURY
ANUS
ANUSIM
ANUSVARA
ANVIL
ANVILED
ANVILING
ANVILLED
ANVILLING
ANVILSMITH
ANVILTOP
ANXIETIES
ANXIETUDE
ANXIETY
ANXIOUS
ANXIOUSLY
ANXIOUSNESS
ANY
ANYBODIES
ANYBODY
ANYHOW
ANYMORE
ANYONE
ANYPLACE
ANYTHING
ANYWAY
ANYWAYS
ANYWHEN
ANYWHERE
ANYWHERENESS
ANYWHERES
ANYWHITHER
ANYWHY
ANYWISE
AO
AOGIRI
AONACH
AORIST
AORISTIC
AORISTICALLY
AORTA
AORTAE

AORTAL
AORTARCTIA
AORTAS
AORTECTASIA
AORTECTASIS
AORTIC
AORTICORENAL
AORTISM
AORTITIS
AORTOCLASIA
AORTOCLASIS
AORTOLITH
AORTOMALACIA
AORTOMALAXIS
AORTOPATHY
AORTOPTOSIA
AORTOPTOSIS
AORTORRHAPHY
AORTOTOMY
AOSMIC
AOUDAD
APA
APABHRAMSA
APACE
APACHE
APACHES
APACHISM
APACHITE
APADANA
APAESTHESIA
APAESTHETIC
APAESTHETIZE
APAESTICALLY
APAGOGE
APAGOGIC
APAGOGICAL
APAGOGICALLY
APAID
APALIT
APANAGE
APANAGED
APANAGING
APANDRY
APANG
APAR
APARA
APARAPHYSATE
APARDON
APAREJO
APAREJOS
APARITHMESIS
APART
APARTADO
APARTHEID
APARTHROSIS
APARTMENT
APARTMENTAL
APASOTE
APASS
APAST
APASTRON
APATAN
APATETIC
APATHETIC
APATHETICAL
APATHIA
APATHIC
APATHIES
APATHISM
APATHIST
APATHISTICAL
APATHOGENIC
APATHY
APATITE
APE
APEAK
APED

APEIRON
APELET
APELING
APELLOUS
APEPSIA
APEPSINIA
APEPSY
APEPTIC
APER
APERCH
APERCU
APERCUS
APEREA
APERIENT
APERIES
APERIODIC
APERISPERMIC
APERISTALSIS
APERITIF
APERITIVE
APERSEE
APERT
APERTION
APERTLY
APERTNESS
APERTOMETER
APERTURAL
APERTURE
APERTURED
APERULOSID
APERY
APESTHESIA
APESTHETIC
APESTHETIZE
APETALOID
APETALOSE
APETALOUS
APETALY
APEX
APEXED
APEXES
APEXING
APHAERESIS
APHAERETIC
APHAGIA
APHAKIA
APHAKIAL
APHAKIC
APHANESITE
APHANISIA
APHANISIS
APHANITE
APHANITIC
APHANITISM
APHANOPHYRE
APHASIA
APHASIAC
APHASIC
APHELIAN
APHELION
APHEMIA
APHEMIC
APHENGESCOPE
APHENGOSCOPE
APHENOSCOPE
APHERESIS
APHERETIC
APHESIS
APHETA
APHETIC
APHETICALLY
APHETISM
APHETIZE
APHID
APHIDES
APHIDIAN
APHIDICOLOUS

APHIDID	APICULA	APOBLAST	APOHYAL	APOQUININE
APHIDIOUS	APICULATE	APOCAFFEINE	APOIKIA	APORETIC
APHIDIVOROUS	APICULATED	APOCALYPSE	APOISE	APORETICAL
APHIDOLYSIN	APICULATION	APOCALYPST	APOJOVE	APORHYOLITE
APHIDOZER	APICULI	APOCALYPT	APOKREA	APORIA
APHIS	APICULTURAL	APOCALYPTIC	APOKREOS	APOROSE
APHLEBIA	APICULTURE	APOCALYPTIST	APOLAR	APORPHIN
APHLOGISTIC	APICULTURIST	APOCAMPHORIC	APOLARITY	APORPHINE
APHNOLOGY	APICULUS	APOCARP	APOLAUSTIC	APORRHAOID
APHODAL	APIECE	APOCARPOUS	APOLEGAMIC	APORRHEA
APHODI	APIECES	APOCARPY	APOLLONICON	APORRHEGMA
APHODIAN	APIGENIN	APOCATHARSIS	APOLOG	APORT
APHODUS	APII	APOCENTER	APOLOGAL	APORTOISE
APHONIA	APIIN	APOCENTRE	APOLOGETE	APOSAFRANINE
APHONIC	APIKORES	APOCENTRIC	APOLOGETIC	APOSATURN
APHONOUS	APIKOROS	APOCHA	APOLOGETICAL	APOSATURNIUM
APHORIA	APIKORSIM	APOCHAE	APOLOGETICALLY	APOSEMATIC
APHORISM	APILARY	APOCHOLIC	APOLOGETICS	APOSEPALOUS
APHORISMATIC	APIMANIA	APOCHROMAT	APOLOGIA	APOSIA
APHORISMER	APINCH	APOCHROMATIC	APOLOGIES	APOSIOPESIS
APHORISMIC	APING	APOCODEINE	APOLOGIST	APOSIOPETIC
APHORISMICAL	APINOID	APOCOPATE	APOLOGIZE	APOSITIA
APHORISMOS	APIO	APOCOPATED	APOLOGIZED	APOSITIC
APHORIST	APIOID	APOCOPATING	APOLOGIZER	APOSORO
APHORISTIC	APIOIDAL	APOCOPATION	APOLOGIZING	APOSPOROGONY
APHORISTICAL	APIOL	APOCOPE	APOLOGUE	APOSPOROUS
APHORIZE	APIOLE	APOCOPIC	APOLOGY	APOSPORY
APHORIZED	APIOLIN	APOCRENIC	APOLOUSIS	APOSTACY
APHORIZER	APIOLOGIST	APOCRISIARY	APOLUNE	APOSTASIES
APHORIZING	APIOLOGY	APOCRUSTIC	APOLUSIS	APOSTASIS
APHOTIC	APIONOL	APOCRYPH	APOLYSIS	APOSTASY
APHOTOTACTIC	APIOSE	APOCRYPHAL	APOLYTIKION	APOSTATE
APHOTOTAXIS	APIPHOBIA	APOCRYPHALLY	APOMECOMETER	APOSTATIC
APHOTOTROPIC	APISH	APOCRYPHATE	APOMECOMETRY	APOSTATICAL
APHRASIA	APISHAMORE	APOCYNACEOUS	APOMETABOLIC	APOSTATISM
APHRITE	APISHLY	APOCYNEOUS	APOMICT	APOSTATIZE
APHRIZITE	APISHNESS	APOCYTE	APOMICTIC	APOSTATIZED
APHRODISIA	APISM	APOD	APOMICTICAL	APOSTATIZING
APHRODISIAC	APITONG	APODAN	APOMIXIS	APOSTAXIS
APHRODISIAN	APITPAT	APODE	APOMORPHIA	APOSTEMATE
APHRODITE	APIVOROUS	APODEICTIC	APOMORPHIN	APOSTEMATIC
APHRODITIC	APJOHNITE	APODEICTICAL	APOMORPHINE	APOSTEMATION
APHRODITOUS	APLACENTAL	APODEIPNON	APONEUROLOGY	APOSTEMATOUS
APHROLITE	APLACOPHORAN	APODEMA	APONEUROSES	APOSTEME
APHRONIA	APLANAT	APODEMAL	APONEUROSIS	APOSTHIA
APHTHA	APLANATIC	APODEMATAL	APONEUROTIC	APOSTIL
APHTHAE	APLANATISM	APODEME	APONEUROTOME	APOSTILLE
APHTHIC	APLANOGAMETE	APODIA	APONEUROTOMY	APOSTLE
APHTHITALITE	APLANOSPORE	APODICTIC	APONIA	APOSTLES
APHTHOID	APLASIA	APODICTICAL	APONIC	APOSTLESHIP
APHTHONG	APLASTIC	APODICTIVE	APOOP	APOSTOLATE
APHTHONGAL	APLENTY	APODIXIS	APOPEMPTIC	APOSTOLESS
APHTHONGIA	APLITE	APODOSES	APOPETALOUS	APOSTOLI
APHTHOUS	APLITIC	APODOSIS	APOPHASIS	APOSTOLIC
APHYLLOSE	APLOBASALT	APODOUS	APOPHATIC	APOSTOLICAL
APHYLLOUS	APLODIORITE	APODYTERIA	APOPHONIA	APOSTOLICISM
APHYLLY	APLOMB	APODYTERIUM	APOPHONIC	APOSTOLICITY
APHYRIC	APLOME	APOEMBRYONY	APOPHONY	APOSTOLIZE
APIAN	APLOTAXENE	APOFENCHENE	APOPHTHEGM	APOSTROPHAL
APIARIAN	APLOTOMY	APOGAEIC	APOPHYGE	APOSTROPHE
APIARIES	APLUSTRA	APOGAIC	APOPHYLACTIC	APOSTROPHI
APIARIST	APLUSTRE	APOGALACTEUM	APOPHYLAXIS	APOSTROPHIC
APIARY	APLUSTRIA	APOGAMIC	APOPHYLLITE	APOSTROPHIED
APIATOR	APNEA	APOGAMICALLY	APOPHYLLOUS	APOSTROPHIZE
APICAD	APNEAL	APOGAMOUS	APOPHYSARY	APOSTROPHUS
APICAL	APNEIC	APOGAMOUSLY	APOPHYSATE	APOTELESM
APICALLY	APNEUMATIC	APOGAMY	APOPHYSEAL	APOTHEC
APICES	APNEUMATOSIS	APOGEAL	APOPHYSES	APOTHECAL
APICIFIXED	APNEUMONOUS	APOGEAN	APOPHYSIAL	APOTHECARIES
APICILAR	APNEUSIS	APOGEE	APOPHYSIS	APOTHECARY
APICILLARY	APNEUSTIC	APOGENOUS	APOPHYSITIS	APOTHECE
APICITIS	APNOEA	APOGENY	APOPLECTIC	APOTHECIA
APICKABACK	APNOEAL	APOGEOTROPIC	APOPLECTICAL	APOTHECIAL
APICKBACK	APNOEIC	APOGONID	APOPLEX	APOTHECIUM
APICKPACK	APOACONITINE	APOGRAPH	APOPLEXIOUS	APOTHEGM
APICOECTOMY	APOATROPINE	APOGRAPHAL	APOPLEXY	APOTHEGMATIC
APICOLYSIS	APOBIOTIC	APOHARMINE	APOPYLE	APOTHEM

APOTHEOSE
APOTHEOSES
APOTHEOSIS
APOTHEOSIZE
APOTHEOSIZED
APOTHESINE
APOTHESIS
APOTOME
APOTROPAIC
APOTROPAION
APOTROPAISM
APOTROPOUS
APOTURMERIC
APOTYPE
APOTYPIC
APOUT
APOXESIS
APOY
APOZEM
APOZEMA
APOZEMICAL
APPAIR
APPAL
APPALL
APPALLED
APPALLING
APPALLINGLY
APPALTO
APPANAGE
APPANAGED
APPANAGING
APPANAGIST
APPARATUS
APPARATUSES
APPAREL
APPARELED
APPARELING
APPARELLED
APPARELLING
APPARELMENT
APPARENCE
APPARENCY
APPARENT
APPARENTLY
APPARENTNESS
APPARITION
APPARITIONAL
APPARITOR
APPARTEMENT
APPASSIONATA
APPASSIONATO
APPAST
APPAUME
APPAUMEE
APPAY
APPEACH
APPEACHER
APPEACHMENT
APPEAL
APPEALABLE
APPEALED
APPEALER
APPEALING
APPEALINGLY
APPEALINGNESS
APPEAR
APPEARANCE
APPEARANCED
APPEARED
APPEARER
APPEARING
APPEASABLE
APPEASABLY
APPEASE
APPEASED
APPEASEMENT
APPEASER

APPEASING
APPEASINGLY
APPEASIVE
APPEL
APPELLABLE
APPELLANCY
APPELLANT
APPELLATION
APPELLATIVE
APPELLATIVED
APPELLATORY
APPELLEE
APPELLOR
APPENAGE
APPEND
APPENDAGE
APPENDAGED
APPENDALGIA
APPENDANCE
APPENDANCY
APPENDANT
APPENDECTOMIES
APPENDECTOMY
APPENDED
APPENDENT
APPENDICAL
APPENDICE
APPENDICEAL
APPENDICES
APPENDICITIS
APPENDICLE
APPENDICULAR
APPENDIX
APPENDIXED
APPENDIXES
APPENDIXING
APPENTICE
APPERCEIVE
APPERCEIVED
APPERCEIVING
APPERCEPTION
APPERCEPTIVE
APPERCIPIENT
APPERE
APPERIL
APPERT
APPERTAIN
APPERTISE
APPESTAT
APPET
APPETE
APPETENCE
APPETENCIES
APPETENCY
APPETENT
APPETENTLY
APPETIBILITY
APPETIBLE
APPETISER
APPETISING
APPETITE
APPETITION
APPETITIONAL
APPETITIOUS
APPETITIVE
APPETIZE
APPETIZED
APPETIZER
APPETIZING
APPETIZINGLY
APPINITE
APPLANATE
APPLANATION
APPLAUD
APPLAUDABLE
APPLAUDABLY
APPLAUDER

APPLAUDINGLY
APPLAUSE
APPLAUSIVE
APPLAUSIVELY
APPLE
APPLEBERRY
APPLEBLOSSOM
APPLECART
APPLED
APPLEDRANE
APPLEDRONE
APPLEGROWER
APPLEJACK
APPLEJOHN
APPLEMONGER
APPLENUT
APPLERINGIE
APPLERINGY
APPLEROOT
APPLES
APPLESAUCE
APPLEWIFE
APPLEWOMAN
APPLIABLE
APPLIABLENESS
APPLIABLY
APPLIANCE
APPLIANT
APPLICABLE
APPLICABLY
APPLICANCY
APPLICANT
APPLICATE
APPLICATION
APPLICATIVE
APPLICATOR
APPLICATORY
APPLIED
APPLIEDLY
APPLIER
APPLING
APPLIQUE
APPLIQUED
APPLIQUEING
APPLOSION
APPLOSIVE
APPLOT
APPLOTMENT
APPLY
APPLYING
APPLYINGLY
APPLYMENT
APPOGGIATURA
APPOGGIATURE
APPOINT
APPOINTE
APPOINTEE
APPOINTER
APPOINTIVE
APPOINTMENT
APPOINTOR
APPORT
APPORTION
APPORTIONER
APPORTIONMENT
APPOSABLE
APPOSE
APPOSED
APPOSER
APPOSING
APPOSITE
APPOSITELY
APPOSITENESS
APPOSITION
APPOSITIONAL
APPOSITIVE
APPOSITIVELY

APPRAISABLE
APPRAISAL
APPRAISE
APPRAISED
APPRAISEMENT
APPRAISER
APPRAISING
APPRAISIVE
APPRECIABLE
APPRECIABLY
APPRECIANT
APPRECIATE
APPRECIATED
APPRECIATING
APPRECIATION
APPRECIATIVE
APPRECIATIVELY
APPRECIATIVENESS
APPRECIATOR
APPRECIATORY
APPREHEND
APPREHENDED
APPREHENDER
APPREHENSIBLE
APPREHENSIBLY
APPREHENSION
APPREHENSIVE
APPREHENSIVELY
APPREHENSIVENESS
APPREND
APPRENTICE
APPRENTICED
APPRENTICESHIP
APPRENTICING
APPRESSED
APPRESSOR
APPRESSORIA
APPRESSORIAL
APPRESSORIUM
APPREST
APPRETEUR
APPRISE
APPRISED
APPRISING
APPRIZAL
APPRIZE
APPRIZEMENT
APPRIZER
APPRIZING
APPROACH
APPROACHABILITY
APPROACHABLE
APPROACHABLENESS
APPROACHER
APPROACHES
APPROACHING
APPROACHLESS
APPROACHMENT
APPROBATE
APPROBATED
APPROBATING
APPROBATION
APPROBATIVE
APPROBATOR
APPROBATORY
APPROOF
APPROPRE
APPROPRIABLE
APPROPRIATE
APPROPRIATED
APPROPRIATELY
APPROPRIATENES
APPROPRIATING
APPROPRIATION
APPROPRIATIVE
APPROPRIATOR
APPROVABLE

APPROVAL
APPROVANCE
APPROVE
APPROVED
APPROVEDLY
APPROVEMENT
APPROVER
APPROVING
APPROVINGLY
APPROXIMAL
APPROXIMATE
APPROXIMATED
APPROXIMATELY
APPROXIMATING
APPROXIMATION
APPROXIMATIVE
APPROXIMATOR
APPUI
APPULSE
APPULSION
APPULSIVE
APPULSIVELY
APPURTENANCE
APPURTENANT
APRAXIA
APRAXIC
APRENDIZ
APRES
APREYNTE
APRICATE
APRICATION
APRICKLE
APRICOT
APRIORISM
APRIORIST
APRIORISTIC
APRIORITY
APROCTIA
APROCTOUS
APRON
APRONEER
APRONLIKE
APROPOS
APROSEXIA
APROSOPIA
APROSOPOUS
APROTERODONT
APS
APSE
APSELAPHESIA
APSELAPHESIS
APSES
APSIDAL
APSIDALLY
APSIDES
APSIDIOLE
APSINTHION
APSIS
APSYCHIA
APSYCHICAL
APT
APTATE
APTERAL
APTERIA
APTERIAL
APTERIUM
APTEROID
APTEROUS
APTERYGIAL
APTERYGOTE
APTERYGOTOUS
APTERYLA
APTERYX
APTHA
APTITUDE
APTITUDINAL
APTITUDINALLY

APTLY
APTNESS
APTOTE
APTOTIC
APTYALIA
APTYALISM
APTYCHUS
APULMONIC
APULSE
APURPOSE
APUS
APYONIN
APYRASE
APYRENE
APYRETIC
APYREXIA
APYREXIAL
APYREXY
APYROTYPE
APYROUS
AQUA
AQUABIB
AQUACADE
AQUACULTURAL
AQUACULTURE
AQUAE
AQUAEMANALE
AQUAEMANALIA
AQUAFER
AQUAFORTIS
AQUAFORTIST
AQUAGE
AQUAGREEN
AQUALUNG
AQUAMARINE
AQUAMETER
AQUANAUT
AQUAPLANE
AQUAPLANED
AQUAPLANING
AQUAPUNCTURE
AQUARELLE
AQUARELLIST
AQUARIA
AQUARIAL
AQUARIAN
AQUARIIST
AQUARIST
AQUARIUM
AQUARIUMS
AQUARTER
AQUAS
AQUASCUTUM
AQUATE
AQUATIC
AQUATICAL
AQUATICALLY
AQUATICS
AQUATILE
AQUATINT
AQUATINTER
AQUATION
AQUATIVENESS
AQUATONE
AQUAVALENT
AQUAVIT
AQUEDUCT
AQUEITY
AQUEOGLACIAL
AQUEOIGNEOUS
AQUEOUS
AQUEOUSLY
AQUEOUSNESS
AQUICOLOUS
AQUICULTURAL
AQUICULTURE
AQUIFER

AQUIFEROUS
AQUIFORM
AQUIFUGE
AQUILA
AQUILAWOOD
AQUILEGE
AQUILEGIA
AQUILINE
AQUILINO
AQUIPAROUS
AQUIVER
AQUO
AQUOSE
AQUOSITY
AQUOTIZATION
AQUOTIZE
AR
ARA
ARABA
ARABAN
ARABESK
ARABESQUE
ARABESQUELY
ARABESQUERIE
ARABICA
ARABILITY
ARABIN
ARABINE
ARABINOSE
ARABINOSIC
ARABITE
ARABITOL
ARABLE
ARACA
ARACANGA
ARACARI
ARACE
ARACEOUS
ARACHE
ARACHIC
ARACHIDE
ARACHIDIC
ARACHIN
ARACHIS
ARACHNACTIS
ARACHNID
ARACHNIDAN
ARACHNIDIAL
ARACHNIDISM
ARACHNIDIUM
ARACHNISM
ARACHNITIS
ARACHNOID
ARACHNOIDAL
ARACHNOIDEA
ARACHNOIDEAN
ARACHNOLOGY
ARAD
ARADA
ARADID
ARADO
ARAGONITE
ARAGUANE
ARAGUATO
ARAH
ARAIN
ARAIRE
ARAK
ARAKE
ARAKI
ARALIA
ARALIACEOUS
ARALIAD
ARALIE
ARALKYL
ARALKYLATED
ARAMAYOITE

ARAMINA
ARANA
ARANEID
ARANEIDAN
ARANEIFORM
ARANEIN
ARANEOLOGIST
ARANEOLOGY
ARANEOSE
ARANEOUS
ARANGA
ARANGO
ARANGOES
ARANZADA
ARAPAHITE
ARAPAIMA
ARAPHOROSTIC
ARAPHOSTIC
ARAPONGA
ARAPUNGA
ARAR
ARARA
ARARAO
ARARAUNA
ARARIBA
ARAROBA
ARARU
ARAS
ARASE
ARATI
ARATINGA
ARATION
ARATORY
ARAUCARIA
ARAUCARIAN
ARAYNE
ARBA
ARBACIA
ARBACIN
ARBALEST
ARBALESTER
ARBALESTRE
ARBALIST
ARBALO
ARBALOS
ARBER
ARBITER
ARBITH
ARBITRABLE
ARBITRAGE
ARBITRAGER
ARBITRAGEUR
ARBITRAGIST
ARBITRAL
ARBITRAMENT
ARBITRARILY
ARBITRARINESS
ARBITRARY
ARBITRATE
ARBITRATED
ARBITRATING
ARBITRATION
ARBITRATIONAL
ARBITRATIVE
ARBITRATOR
ARBITREMENT
ARBITRER
ARBITRESS
ARBOLOCO
ARBOR
ARBORACEOUS
ARBORAL
ARBORARY
ARBORATOR
ARBOREAL
ARBOREALLY
ARBOREAN

ARBORED
ARBOREOUS
ARBORER
ARBORES
ARBORESCENCE
ARBORESCENT
ARBORESQUE
ARBORET
ARBORETA
ARBORETUM
ARBORETUMS
ARBORICAL
ARBORICOLE
ARBORICOLINE
ARBORICOLOUS
ARBORIFORM
ARBORISE
ARBORIST
ARBORIZATION
ARBORIZE
ARBORIZED
ARBORIZING
ARBOROID
ARBOROLATRY
ARBOROUS
ARBORS
ARBORVITAE
ARBORWAY
ARBOUR
ARBOURED
ARBUSCLE
ARBUSCULA
ARBUSCULAR
ARBUSCULE
ARBUSTA
ARBUSTERIN
ARBUSTEROL
ARBUSTUM
ARBUTE
ARBUTEAN
ARBUTIN
ARBUTUS
ARC
ARCA
ARCABUCERO
ARCADE
ARCADED
ARCADIAN
ARCADING
ARCAE
ARCANA
ARCANAL
ARCANE
ARCANUM
ARCATE
ARCATO
ARCATURE
ARCED
ARCELLA
ARCES
ARCH
ARCHA
ARCHAEOCYTE
ARCHAEOLATRY
ARCHAEOLOGER
ARCHAEOLOGIC
ARCHAEOLOGICAL
ARCHAEOLOGIST
ARCHAEOLOGY
ARCHAEUS
ARCHAI
ARCHAIC
ARCHAICAL
ARCHAICALLY
ARCHAICISM
ARCHAISE
ARCHAISM

ARCHAIST
ARCHAISTIC
ARCHAIZE
ARCHAIZED
ARCHAIZER
ARCHAIZING
ARCHANGEL
ARCHANGELIC
ARCHARIOS
ARCHBAND
ARCHBISHOP
ARCHBISHOPRIC
ARCHCHEMIC
ARCHDEACON
ARCHDEACONRY
ARCHDEAN
ARCHDIOCESAN
ARCHDIOCESE
ARCHDUCAL
ARCHDUCHESS
ARCHDUCHIES
ARCHDUCHY
ARCHDUKE
ARCHDUKEDOM
ARCHE
ARCHEAL
ARCHEBIOSIS
ARCHECENTRIC
ARCHED
ARCHEGONE
ARCHEGONIA
ARCHEGONIAL
ARCHEGONIATE
ARCHEGONIUM
ARCHEION
ARCHELOGY
ARCHENEMIES
ARCHENEMY
ARCHENTERIC
ARCHENTERON
ARCHEOCYTE
ARCHEOLITHIC
ARCHEOLOGIAN
ARCHEOLOGIC
ARCHEOLOGICAL
ARCHEOLOGIST
ARCHEOLOGY
ARCHEOPTERYX
ARCHEOSTOME
ARCHER
ARCHERFISH
ARCHERFISHES
ARCHERS
ARCHERY
ARCHES
ARCHESPORE
ARCHESPORIAL
ARCHESPORIUM
ARCHETYPAL
ARCHETYPALLY
ARCHETYPE
ARCHETYPIC
ARCHETYPICAL
ARCHETYPIST
ARCHEUS
ARCHFIEND
ARCHIATER
ARCHIBENTHAL
ARCHIBENTHIC
ARCHIBENTHOS
ARCHIBLAST
ARCHIBLASTIC
ARCHICAL
ARCHICARP
ARCHICEREBRA
ARCHICOELE
ARCHICYTE

ARCHICYTULA
ARCHIDOME
ARCHIE
ARCHIEREUS
ARCHIGENESIS
ARCHIKARYON
ARCHIL
ARCHILITHIC
ARCHILLA
ARCHILOWE
ARCHILUTE
ARCHIMAGE
ARCHIMAGUS
ARCHIMIME
ARCHIMORPHIC
ARCHIMORULA
ARCHIN
ARCHINE
ARCHINEURON
ARCHING
ARCHIPALLIAL
ARCHIPALLIUM
ARCHIPELAGIC
ARCHIPELAGO
ARCHIPELAGOES
ARCHIPELAGOS
ARCHIPHONEME
ARCHIPIN
ARCHIPLASM
ARCHIPLASMIC
ARCHISPERM
ARCHISPHERE
ARCHISPORE
ARCHISTOME
ARCHITECT
ARCHITECTIVE
ARCHITECTRESS
ARCHITECTURAL
ARCHITECTURALLY
ARCHITECTURE
ARCHITIS
ARCHITRAVAL
ARCHITRAVE
ARCHITRAVED
ARCHIVAL
ARCHIVAULT
ARCHIVE
ARCHIVED
ARCHIVES
ARCHIVING
ARCHIVIST
ARCHIVOLT
ARCHIZOIC
ARCHLUTE
ARCHLY
ARCHNESS
ARCHOCELE
ARCHOLOGY
ARCHON
ARCHONT
ARCHONTATE
ARCHONTIC
ARCHOPLASM
ARCHOPLASMA
ARCHOPLASMIC
ARCHOPTOMA
ARCHOPTOSIS
ARCHORRHAGIA
ARCHORRHEA
ARCHOSYRINX
ARCHPRIEST
ARCHPRIESTHOOD
ARCHPRIESTSHIP
ARCHSEE
ARCHWAY
ARCHWISE
ARCHY

ARCIFEROUS
ARCIFINIOUS
ARCIFORM
ARCING
ARCKED
ARCKING
ARCOCENTROUS
ARCOCENTRUM
ARCOGRAPH
ARCOSE
ARCOSOLIA
ARCOSOLIUM
ARCS
ARCT
ARCTATION
ARCTIAN
ARCTIC
ARCTICALLY
ARCTICIAN
ARCTICIZE
ARCTICIZED
ARCTICIZING
ARCTIID
ARCTOID
ARCTOIDEAN
ARCUAL
ARCUALE
ARCUALIA
ARCUATE
ARCUATED
ARCUATELY
ARCUATION
ARCULA
ARCULITE
ARCUS
ARD
ARDAB
ARDASSINE
ARDEB
ARDELIO
ARDELLA
ARDELLAE
ARDEN
ARDENCY
ARDENNITE
ARDENT
ARDENTLY
ARDENTNESS
ARDER
ARDILLA
ARDISH
ARDISIA
ARDITI
ARDITO
ARDOISE
ARDOO
ARDOR
ARDORS
ARDOUR
ARDRI
ARDRIGH
ARDU
ARDUINITE
ARDUOUS
ARDUOUSLY
ARDUOUSNESS
ARDURE
ARDUROUS
ARE
AREA
AREACH
AREAD
AREAE
AREAL
AREALITY
AREAR
AREAS

AREASON
AREAWAY
ARECA
ARECACEOUS
ARECHE
ARED
AREED
AREEK
AREEL
AREFACT
AREFACTION
AREFY
AREG
AREIC
AREITO
ARENA
ARENACEOUS
ARENAE
ARENARIAE
ARENARIOUS
ARENAS
ARENATION
AREND
ARENDALITE
ARENE
ARENG
ARENICOLITE
ARENICOLOUS
ARENILITIC
ARENITE
ARENOID
ARENOSE
ARENOSITY
AREOCENTRIC
AREOGRAPHER
AREOGRAPHIC
AREOGRAPHY
AREOLA
AREOLAE
AREOLAR
AREOLAS
AREOLATE
AREOLATED
AREOLATION
AREOLE
AREOLET
AREOLOGIC
AREOLOGICAL
AREOLOGIST
AREOLOGY
AREOMETER
AREOMETRIC
AREOMETRICAL
AREOMETRY
AREOPAGY
AREPA
ARERE
ARET
ARETAICS
ARETALOGY
ARETE
ARETHUSA
ARETTE
ARF
ARFVEDSONITE
ARGAL
ARGALA
ARGALI
ARGALIS
ARGASID
ARGEERS
ARGEL
ARGEMONE
ARGENOL
ARGENT
ARGENTAL
ARGENTAMID

ARGENTAMIDE
ARGENTAMIN
ARGENTAMINE
ARGENTARII
ARGENTARIUS
ARGENTATION
ARGENTEOUS
ARGENTER
ARGENTEUM
ARGENTIC
ARGENTIDE
ARGENTIN
ARGENTINE
ARGENTINO
ARGENTION
ARGENTITE
ARGENTOL
ARGENTOMETRY
ARGENTON
ARGENTOSE
ARGENTOUS
ARGENTUM
ARGH
ARGHAN
ARGHE
ARGHEL
ARGHOOL
ARGHOUL
ARGIFY
ARGIL
ARGILLACEOUS
ARGILLIC
ARGILLITE
ARGILLITIC
ARGILLOID
ARGILLOUS
ARGIN
ARGINASE
ARGINE
ARGININE
ARGLE
ARGO
ARGOL
ARGOLET
ARGOLETIER
ARGON
ARGONAUT
ARGONAUTIC
ARGONAUTID
ARGONAUTS
ARGOSIES
ARGOSY
ARGOT
ARGOTIC
ARGUABLE
ARGUE
ARGUED
ARGUENDO
ARGUER
ARGUFIED
ARGUFIER
ARGUFY
ARGUFYING
ARGUING
ARGUL
ARGUMENT
ARGUMENTA
ARGUMENTAL
ARGUMENTATION
ARGUMENTATIOUS
ARGUMENTATIVE
ARGUMENTATIVELY
ARGUMENTATIVENESS
ARGUMENTATOR
ARGUMENTATORY
ARGUMENTS
ARGUMENTUM

ARGUS
ARGUSFISH
ARGUSFISHES
ARGUTE
ARGUTELY
ARGUTENESS
ARGY
ARGYRANTHOUS
ARGYRIA
ARGYRIC
ARGYRITE
ARGYRODITE
ARGYROSE
ARGYRYTHROSE
ARHAR
ARHAT
ARIA
ARIBIN
ARIBINE
ARICIN
ARICINE
ARID
ARIDGE
ARIDIAN
ARIDITIES
ARIDITY
ARIDLY
ARIDNESS
ARIEGITE
ARIEL
ARIENZO
ARIES
ARIETATE
ARIETATION
ARIETINOUS
ARIETTA
ARIETTE
ARIGHT
ARIGHTLY
ARIGUE
ARIKI
ARIL
ARILED
ARILLARY
ARILLATE
ARILLATED
ARILLED
ARILLI
ARILLIFORM
ARILLODE
ARILLODIUM
ARILLOID
ARILLUS
ARIOLATE
ARIOLE
ARIOSE
ARIOSO
ARIOT
ARIPPLE
ARIS
ARISAID
ARISARD
ARISE
ARISEN
ARISING
ARISINGS
ARIST
ARISTA
ARISTAE
ARISTARCHIES
ARISTARCHY
ARISTATE
ARISTE
ARISTO
ARISTOCRACIES
ARISTOCRACY
ARISTOCRAT

ARISTOCRATIC
ARISTOCRATICAL
ARISTOCRATICALLY
ARISTOGENIC
ARISTOGENICS
ARISTOI
ARISTOLOGICAL
ARISTOLOGIST
ARISTOLOGY
ARISTOS
ARISTOTYPE
ARISTULATE
ARITE
ARITHMETIC
ARITHMETICAL
ARITHMETICALLY
ARITHMETICIAN
ARITHMETIZE
ARITHMOCRACY
ARITHMOGRAM
ARITHMOGRAPH
ARITHMOMANIA
ARITHMOMETER
ARITHROMANIA
ARIZONITE
ARJAN
ARJUN
ARK
ARKANSITE
ARKAR
ARKITE
ARKOSE
ARKOSIC
ARKSUTITE
ARLES
ARLING
ARLOUP
ARM
ARMADA
ARMADILLA
ARMADILLO
ARMADILLOS
ARMAGNAC
ARMAMENT
ARMAMENTARIA
ARMAMENTARY
ARMANGITE
ARMARIA
ARMARIUM
ARMATURE
ARMBAND
ARMBONE
ARMCHAIR
ARMCHAIRED
ARME
ARMED
ARMENIACEOUS
ARMENITE
ARMER
ARMET
ARMFUL
ARMFULS
ARMGAUNT
ARMGUARD
ARMHOLE
ARMHOOP
ARMIED
ARMIES
ARMIFEROUS
ARMIGER
ARMIGERAL
ARMIGERI
ARMIGEROUS
ARMIL
ARMILL
ARMILLA
ARMILLAE

ARMILLARY
ARMILLATE
ARMILLATED
ARMINE
ARMING
ARMIPOTENCE
ARMIPOTENT
ARMISONANT
ARMISONOUS
ARMISTICE
ARMITAS
ARMLET
ARMLOAD
ARMLOCK
ARMOIRE
ARMONICA
ARMOR
ARMORBEARER
ARMORED
ARMORER
ARMORIAL
ARMORIED
ARMORIES
ARMORIST
ARMORY
ARMOUR
ARMOURED
ARMOURER
ARMOURIES
ARMOURY
ARMOZEEN
ARMOZINE
ARMPIECE
ARMPIT
ARMPLATE
ARMRACK
ARMREST
ARMS
ARMSCYE
ARMSEYE
ARMSIZE
ARMURE
ARMY
ARMYWORM
ARN
ARNA
ARNATTA
ARNATTO
ARNBERRY
ARNEE
ARNEMENT
ARNI
ARNICA
ARNOTTO
ARNUT
AROAR
AROAST
AROCK
AROEIRA
AROID
AROIDEOUS
AROINT
AROLIA
AROLIUM
AROLLA
AROMA
AROMACITY
AROMADENDRIN
AROMAS
AROMATA
AROMATIC
AROMATICAL
AROMATICALLY
AROMATICITY
AROMATITAE
AROMATITE
AROMATITES

AROMATIZE
AROMATIZED
AROMATIZER
AROMATIZING
AROMATOUS
AROMO
AROOM
AROON
AROSE
AROUND
AROUSAL
AROUSE
AROUSED
AROUSER
AROUSING
AROW
AROXYL
AROYNT
ARPA
ARPEGGIANDO
ARPEGGIATION
ARPEGGIO
ARPEGGIOED
ARPEN
ARPENT
ARPENTEUR
ARQUEBUS
ARQUERITE
ARR
ARRA
ARRACACH
ARRACACHA
ARRACE
ARRACK
ARRAGE
ARRAH
ARRAIGN
ARRAIGNED
ARRAIGNER
ARRAIGNING
ARRAIGNMENT
ARRAME
ARRAND
ARRANGE
ARRANGED
ARRANGEMENT
ARRANGER
ARRANGING
ARRANT
ARRANTLY
ARRAS
ARRASED
ARRASENE
ARRASTRA
ARRASTRE
ARRATEL
ARRAU
ARRAY
ARRAYAL
ARRAYAN
ARRAYED
ARRAYER
ARRAYING
ARRAYMENT
ARREAR
ARREARAGE
ARREARS
ARRECT
ARRECTOR
ARRENT
ARRENTATION
ARREPTITIOUS
ARREST
ARRESTATION
ARRESTEE
ARRESTER
ARRESTING

ARRESTINGLY
ARRESTIVE
ARRESTMENT
ARRESTOR
ARRET
ARRHA
ARRHAL
ARRHENAL
ARRHENOTOKY
ARRHINIA
ARRHIZAL
ARRHIZOUS
ARRHYTHMIA
ARRHYTHMIC
ARRHYTHMICAL
ARRHYTHMICALLY
ARRHYTHMOUS
ARRHYTHMY
ARRIAGE
ARRIBA
ARRICCIO
ARRIDE
ARRIDGE
ARRIE
ARRIERE
ARRIERO
ARRIMBY
ARRIS
ARRISH
ARRISWAYS
ARRISWISE
ARRIVAGE
ARRIVAL
ARRIVE
ARRIVED
ARRIVER
ARRIVING
ARRIVISM
ARRIVIST
ARRIVISTE
ARROBA
ARRODE
ARROGANCE
ARROGANCY
ARROGANT
ARROGANTLY
ARROGANTNESS
ARROGATE
ARROGATED
ARROGATING
ARROGATION
ARROGATIVE
ARROGATOR
ARROJADITE
ARRONDI
ARROPE
ARROSION
ARROSIVE
ARROUND
ARROUSE
ARROW
ARROWBUSH
ARROWED
ARROWHEAD
ARROWHEADED
ARROWLEAF
ARROWLET
ARROWPLATE
ARROWROOT
ARROWS
ARROWSTONE
ARROWWEED
ARROWWOOD
ARROWWORM
ARROWY
ARROYA
ARROYO

ARROYOS
ARROYUELO
ARROZ
ARS
ARSANILIC
ARSE
ARSEDINE
ARSEFOOT
ARSENAL
ARSENATE
ARSENATION
ARSENETED
ARSENETTED
ARSENFAST
ARSENHEMOL
ARSENIASIS
ARSENIATE
ARSENIC
ARSENICAL
ARSENICALISM
ARSENICATE
ARSENICATED
ARSENICATING
ARSENICISM
ARSENICIZE
ARSENICKED
ARSENICKING
ARSENIDE
ARSENIDES
ARSENIFEROUS
ARSENILLO
ARSENIOUS
ARSENISM
ARSENITE
ARSENIUM
ARSENIURET
ARSENIURETED
ARSENIZATION
ARSENOFURAN
ARSENOLITE
ARSENOPHEN
ARSENOPHENOL
ARSENOPYRITE
ARSENOUS
ARSENOXIDE
ARSENYL
ARSES
ARSESMART
ARSHEEN
ARSHIN
ARSHINE
ARSHINS
ARSINE
ARSINIC
ARSINO
ARSIS
ARSLE
ARSNICKER
ARSOITE
ARSON
ARSONATE
ARSONATION
ARSONIC
ARSONIST
ARSONITE
ARSONIUM
ARSONO
ARSPHENAMINE
ARSYL
ARSYLENE
ART
ARTABA
ARTAL
ARTAR
ARTARIN
ARTARINE
ARTCRAFT

ARTEFAC
ARTEFACT
ARTEL
ARTEMIA
ARTEMISIA
ARTEMISIC
ARTEMISIN
ARTEMON
ARTER
ARTERIA
ARTERIAE
ARTERIAGRA
ARTERIAL
ARTERIALIZE
ARTERIALIZED
ARTERIALLY
ARTERIARCTIA
ARTERIASIS
ARTERIED
ARTERIES
ARTERIN
ARTERIOGRAM
ARTERIOGRAPH
ARTERIOLE
ARTERIOLITH
ARTERIOLOGY
ARTERIOMETER
ARTERIOMOTOR
ARTERIORENAL
ARTERIOSPASM
ARTERIOTOME
ARTERIOTOMY
ARTERIOUS
ARTERITIS
ARTERY
ARTERYING
ARTFUL
ARTFULLY
ARTFULNESS
ARTHA
ARTHEL
ARTHEMIS
ARTHRA
ARTHRAGRA
ARTHRAL
ARTHRALGIA
ARTHRALGIC
ARTHRECTOMY
ARTHREDEMA
ARTHRITIC
ARTHRITICAL
ARTHRITICINE
ARTHRITIDES
ARTHRITIS
ARTHRITISM
ARTHROBRANCH
ARTHROCACE
ARTHROCELE
ARTHROCLASIA
ARTHROCLISIS
ARTHRODERM
ARTHRODESIS
ARTHRODIA
ARTHRODIAE
ARTHRODIAL
ARTHRODIC
ARTHRODIRAN
ARTHRODIRE
ARTHRODIROUS
ARTHRODYMIC
ARTHRODYNIA
ARTHROGENOUS
ARTHROGRAPHY
ARTHROLITE
ARTHROLITH
ARTHROLOGY
ARTHROMERE

ARTHROMERIC
ARTHROMETER
ARTHROMETRY
ARTHRON
ARTHRONCUS
ARTHROPATHIC
ARTHROPATHY
ARTHROPHYMA
ARTHROPLASTY
ARTHROPLEURA
ARTHROPLEURE
ARTHROPOD
ARTHROPODAL
ARTHROPODAN
ARTHROPODOUS
ARTHROPYOSIS
ARTHROSES
ARTHROSIA
ARTHROSIS
ARTHROSPORE
ARTHROSPORIC
ARTHROSPOROUS
ARTHROSTOME
ARTHROSTOMY
ARTHROSYRINX
ARTHROTOME
ARTHROTOMIES
ARTHROTOMY
ARTHROTRAUMA
ARTHROTROPIC
ARTHROUS
ARTHROZOAN
ARTHROZOIC
ARTIAD
ARTICHOKE
ARTICLE
ARTICLED
ARTICLES
ARTICLING
ARTICULACY
ARTICULANT
ARTICULAR
ARTICULARE
ARTICULARLY
ARTICULARS
ARTICULATE
ARTICULATED
ARTICULATELY
ARTICULATENESS
ARTICULATING
ARTICULATION
ARTICULATIVE
ARTICULATOR
ARTICULATORY
ARTICULITE
ARTICULUS
ARTIFACT
ARTIFACTS
ARTIFEX
ARTIFICE
ARTIFICER
ARTIFICES
ARTIFICIAL
ARTIFICIALITIES
ARTIFICIALITY
ARTIFICIALLY
ARTIFICIALNESS
ARTILLER
ARTILLERIST
ARTILLERY
ARTILLERYMAN
ARTILLERYMEN
ARTILLERYSHIP
ARTINESS
ARTINITE
ARTIODACTYL
ARTIPHYLLOUS

ARTISAN
ARTISANRY
ARTISANSHIP
ARTIST
ARTISTE
ARTISTIC
ARTISTICAL
ARTISTICALLY
ARTISTRY
ARTLESS
ARTLESSLY
ARTLESSNESS
ARTLET
ARTLY
ARTOCARPAD
ARTOCARPEOUS
ARTOCARPOUS
ARTOLATER
ARTOPHAGOUS
ARTOPHORIA
ARTOPHORION
ARTOTYPE
ARTOTYPY
ARTS
ARTSMAN
ARTUS
ARTWARE
ARTWORK
ARTY
ARUI
ARUIN
ARUKE
ARUM
ARUMIN
ARUNDIFEROUS
ARUNDINEOUS
ARUPA
ARURA
ARUSA
ARUSHA
ARUSPEX
ARUSPICE
ARUSTLE
ARVAL
ARVEJON
ARVEL
ARVICOLE
ARVICOLINE
ARVICULTURE
ARX
ARY
ARYBALLOID
ARYBALLOS
ARYBALLUS
ARYL
ARYLAMINE
ARYLAMINO
ARYLATE
ARYLIDE
ARYTENOID
ARYTENOIDAL
ARZRUNITE
ARZUN
AS
ASADDLE
ASADO
ASAFETIDA
ASAFOETIDA
ASAK
ASAL
ASALE
ASAMBLEA
ASANA
ASAPHIA
ASAPHID
ASAR
ASARABACCA

ASARITE
ASARON
ASARONE
ASAROTUM
ASARUM
ASBEST
ASBESTIC
ASBESTIFORM
ASBESTINE
ASBESTINIZE
ASBESTOID
ASBESTOIDAL
ASBESTOS
ASBESTOSIS
ASBESTOUS
ASBESTUS
ASBOLAN
ASBOLANE
ASBOLIN
ASBOLITE
ASCAN
ASCARE
ASCARED
ASCARIASIS
ASCARICIDAL
ASCARICIDE
ASCARID
ASCARIDES
ASCARIDIASIS
ASCARIDOL
ASCARIDOLE
ASCARIS
ASCARON
ASCELLI
ASCELLUS
ASCEND
ASCENDABLE
ASCENDANCE
ASCENDANCY
ASCENDANT
ASCENDENCE
ASCENDENCY
ASCENDENT
ASCENDER
ASCENDIBLE
ASCENDING
ASCENDINGLY
ASCENSEUR
ASCENSION
ASCENSIONAL
ASCENSIVE
ASCENSOR
ASCENT
ASCERTAIN
ASCERTAINABLE
ASCERTAINABLY
ASCERTAINER
ASCERTAINMENT
ASCESIS
ASCETIC
ASCETICAL
ASCETICALLY
ASCETICISM
ASCHAFFITE
ASCHAM
ASCHER
ASCHISTIC
ASCI
ASCIAN
ASCIDIA
ASCIDIAN
ASCIDIATE
ASCIDICOLOUS
ASCIDIFEROUS
ASCiDIFORM
ASCIDIOID
ASCIDIOZOOID

ASCIDIUM
ASCIFEROUS
ASCIGEROUS
ASCII
ASCILL
ASCITES
ASCITIC
ASCITICAL
ASCITITIOUS
ASCLEPIAD
ASCLEPIDIN
ASCLEPIDOID
ASCLEPIN
ASCOCARP
ASCOCARPOUS
ASCOGENOUS
ASCOGONE
ASCOGONIAL
ASCOGONIDIA
ASCOGONIDIUM
ASCOGONIUM
ASCOLICHEN
ASCOMA
ASCOMATA
ASCOMYCETE
ASCOMYCETES
ASCOMYCETOUS
ASCON
ASCOPHORE
ASCOPHOROUS
ASCORBIC
ASCOSPORE
ASCOSPORIC
ASCOSPOROUS
ASCOT
ASCRIBABLE
ASCRIBE
ASCRIBED
ASCRIBING
ASCRIPT
ASCRIPTION
ASCRIPTITIOUS
ASCRIVE
ASCRY
ASCULA
ASCULAE
ASCUS
ASCYPHOUS
ASDIC
ASE
ASEA
ASEARCH
ASECRETORY
ASEETHE
ASEISMATIC
ASEISMIC
ASEISMICITY
ASEITAS
ASEITY
ASELAR
ASELGEIA
ASELLATE
ASELLUS
ASEM
ASEPSIS
ASEPTATE
ASEPTIC
ASEPTICALLY
ASEPTICISM
ASEPTICIZE
ASEPTICIZED
ASEPTICIZING
ASEPTIFY
ASEPTOL
ASEPTOLIN
ASEXUAL
ASEXUALITY

ASEXUALIZE
ASEXUALIZED
ASEXUALIZING
ASEXUALLY
ASH
ASHAKE
ASHAME
ASHAMED
ASHAMEDLY
ASHAMEDNESS
ASHAMNU
ASHBERRY
ASHCAKE
ASHCAN
ASHEN
ASHERAH
ASHERAHS
ASHERIES
ASHERIM
ASHERY
ASHES
ASHET
ASHFALL
ASHIER
ASHIEST
ASHILY
ASHIMMER
ASHINE
ASHINESS
ASHIPBOARD
ASHIVER
ASHKOKO
ASHLAR
ASHLARED
ASHLARING
ASHLER
ASHLERED
ASHLERING
ASHLING
ASHMAN
ASHMEN
ASHORE
ASHOT
ASHPAN
ASHPIT
ASHPLANT
ASHRAF
ASHRAFI
ASHRAM
ASHRAMA
ASHRE
ASHSTONE
ASHTRAY
ASHVAMEDHA
ASHWEED
ASHWORT
ASHY
ASIALIA
ASIDE
ASIDEHAND
ASIDEN
ASIENTO
ASIL
ASILID
ASIM
ASIMEN
ASIMMER
ASINEGO
ASINEGOES
ASININE
ASININELY
ASININITIES
ASININITY
ASIPHONATE
ASIS
ASITIA
ASK

ASKANCE
ASKANT
ASKAR
ASKAREL
ASKARI
ASKARIS
ASKER
ASKESIS
ASKEW
ASKI
ASKILE
ASKING
ASKINGLY
ASKIP
ASKOS
ASLAKE
ASLANT
ASLANTWISE
ASLAVER
ASLEEP
ASLOP
ASLOPE
ASLUMBER
ASMACK
ASMALTE
ASMEAR
ASMILE
ASMOKE
ASMOLDER
ASNIFFLE
ASNORT
ASOAK
ASOCIAL
ASOK
ASOKA
ASOMATOPHYTE
ASOMATOUS
ASONANT
ASONIA
ASOP
ASOR
ASOTE
ASOUTH
ASP
ASPACE
ASPALATHUS
ASPAR
ASPARAGIC
ASPARAGIN
ASPARAGINE
ASPARAGINIC
ASPARAGINOUS
ASPARAGUS
ASPARAGYL
ASPARKLE
ASPARTATE
ASPARTIC
ASPARTYL
ASPECT
ASPECTABLE
ASPECTANT
ASPECTION
ASPECTS
ASPEN
ASPER
ASPERATE
ASPERATED
ASPERATING
ASPERATION
ASPERGATION
ASPERGE
ASPERGER
ASPERGES
ASPERGILL
ASPERGILLA
ASPERGILLI
ASPERGILLIN

ASPERGILLUM
ASPERGILLUMS
ASPERGILLUS
ASPERITE
ASPERITIES
ASPERITY
ASPERMATIC
ASPERMATISM
ASPERMIA
ASPERMOUS
ASPEROUS
ASPEROUSLY
ASPERSE
ASPERSED
ASPERSER
ASPERSING
ASPERSION
ASPERSIONS
ASPERSIVE
ASPERSIVELY
ASPERSOR
ASPERSORIA
ASPERSORIUM
ASPERSORIUMS
ASPERSORY
ASPERULOSIDE
ASPERULOUS
ASPHALT
ASPHALTENE
ASPHALTER
ASPHALTIC
ASPHALTITE
ASPHALTUM
ASPHALTUS
ASPHETERISM
ASPHETERIZE
ASPHODEL
ASPHYCTIC
ASPHYCTOUS
ASPHYXIA
ASPHYXIAL
ASPHYXIANT
ASPHYXIATE
ASPHYXIATED
ASPHYXIATING
ASPHYXIATION
ASPHYXIATOR
ASPHYXIED
ASPHYXY
ASPIC
ASPIDATE
ASPIDE
ASPIDIARIA
ASPIDINOL
ASPIDISTRA
ASPIDIUM
ASPIDOMANCY
ASPIQUEE
ASPIRANT
ASPIRATA
ASPIRATAE
ASPIRATE
ASPIRATED
ASPIRATING
ASPIRATION
ASPIRATOR
ASPIRATORY
ASPIRE
ASPIRED
ASPIREE
ASPIRER
ASPIRIN
ASPIRING
ASPIRINGLY
ASPISH
ASPLANCHNIC
ASPLENIOID

ASPOROGENIC
ASPOROUS
ASPORT
ASPORTATION
ASPORULATE
ASPOUT
ASPRAWL
ASPREAD
ASPRING
ASPROUT
ASPY
ASQUARE
ASQUAT
ASQUEAL
ASQUINT
ASQUIRM
ASRAM
ASRAMA
ASS
ASSACU
ASSAFETIDA
ASSAFOETIDA
ASSAGAI
ASSAGAIED
ASSAGAIING
ASSAHY
ASSAI
ASSAIL
ASSAILABLE
ASSAILANT
ASSAILER
ASSAILMENT
ASSALTO
ASSAPAN
ASSAPANIC
ASSARION
ASSART
ASSARY
ASSASSIN
ASSASSINATE
ASSASSINATED
ASSASSINATING
ASSASSINATION
ASSASSINATIVE
ASSASSINATOR
ASSASSINATRESS
ASSASSINIST
ASSATE
ASSATION
ASSAULT
ASSAULTER
ASSAULTING
ASSAUT
ASSAY
ASSAYED
ASSAYER
ASSAYING
ASSBAA
ASSE
ASSEAL
ASSECURATION
ASSECURATOR
ASSEDAT
ASSEGAI
ASSEIZE
ASSELF
ASSEMBLABLE
ASSEMBLAGE
ASSEMBLE
ASSEMBLED
ASSEMBLEE
ASSEMBLER
ASSEMBLIES
ASSEMBLING
ASSEMBLY
ASSEMBLYMAN
ASSEMBLYMEN

ASSENT
ASSENTANEOUS
ASSENTATION
ASSENTATIOUS
ASSENTATORY
ASSENTED
ASSENTER
ASSENTIENT
ASSENTING
ASSENTIVE
ASSENTIVENESS
ASSENTOR
ASSERT
ASSERTA
ASSERTABLE
ASSERTATIVE
ASSERTER
ASSERTIBLE
ASSERTION
ASSERTIONAL
ASSERTIVE
ASSERTIVELY
ASSERTIVENESS
ASSERTOR
ASSERTORIAL
ASSERTORIC
ASSERTORICAL
ASSERTORILY
ASSERTORY
ASSERTRESS
ASSERTRIX
ASSERTUM
ASSERVE
ASSES
ASSESS
ASSESSABLE
ASSESSED
ASSESSEE
ASSESSING
ASSESSION
ASSESSIONARY
ASSESSMENT
ASSESSOR
ASSESSORIAL
ASSESSORY
ASSET
ASSETH
ASSETS
ASSEVER
ASSEVERATE
ASSEVERATED
ASSEVERATION
ASSEVERATIVE
ASSEVERATORY
ASSHEAD
ASSI
ASSIBILATE
ASSIBILATED
ASSIBILATING
ASSIBILATION
ASSIDENT
ASSIDUAL
ASSIDUALLY
ASSIDUITIES
ASSIDUITY
ASSIDUOUS
ASSIDUOUSLY
ASSIDUOUSNESS
ASSIEGE
ASSIENTIST
ASSIENTO
ASSIETTE
ASSIFY
ASSIGN
ASSIGNABLE
ASSIGNABLY
ASSIGNAT

ASSIGNATION	ASSUMING	ASTHMATICAL	ASTRINGENT	ASUDDEN
ASSIGNED	ASSUMINGLY	ASTHMATICALLY	ASTRINGENTLY	ASUNDER
ASSIGNEE	ASSUMINGNESS	ASTHMATOID	ASTRINGER	ASURA
ASSIGNER	ASSUMMON	ASTHMOGENIC	ASTRINGING	ASWAIL
ASSIGNMENT	ASSUMPSIT	ASTHORE	ASTRION	ASWARM
ASSIGNOR	ASSUMPT	ASTHORIN	ASTROBIOLOGY	ASWASH
ASSILAG	ASSUMPTION	ASTICHOUS	ASTROBLAST	ASWAY
ASSIMILABLE	ASSUMPTIOUS	ASTIGMATIC	ASTROBOTANY	ASWEAT
ASSIMILATE	ASSUMPTIVE	ASTIGMATICAL	ASTROCHEMIST	ASWELL
ASSIMILATED	ASSUMPTIVELY	ASTIGMATISM	ASTROCYTE	ASWEVE
ASSIMILATING	ASSURABLE	ASTIGMATIZER	ASTROCYTOMA	ASWIM
ASSIMILATION	ASSURANCE	ASTIGMIA	ASTROCYTOMAS	ASWING
ASSIMILATIVE	ASSURATE	ASTIGMISM	ASTROCYTOMATA	ASWIRL
ASSIMILATOR	ASSURD	ASTIGMOMETER	ASTRODOME	ASWOON
ASSIMILATORY	ASSURE	ASTIGMOMETRY	ASTROFEL	ASWOONED
ASSIS	ASSURED	ASTILBE	ASTROFELL	ASYLA
ASSISE	ASSUREDLY	ASTINT	ASTROGATE	ASYLLABIA
ASSISH	ASSUREDNESS	ASTIPULATE	ASTROGATED	ASYLLABIC
ASSISHLY	ASSURER	ASTIPULATION	ASTROGATING	ASYLLABICAL
ASSISHNESS	ASSURGE	ASTIR	ASTROGENY	ASYLUM
ASSIST	ASSURGENCY	ASTITE	ASTROGLIA	ASYLUMS
ASSISTANCE	ASSURGENT	ASTOGENY	ASTROGNOSY	ASYMBOLIA
ASSISTANT	ASSURING	ASTOMATAL	ASTROGONIC	ASYMBOLIC
ASSISTANTED	ASSURINGLY	ASTOMATOUS	ASTROGONY	ASYMBOLICAL
ASSISTER	ASSWAGE	ASTOMIA	ASTROGRAPH	ASYMMETRIC
ASSISTFUL	ASSYNTITE	ASTOMOUS	ASTROGRAPHIC	ASYMMETRICAL
ASSISTIVE	ASSYTH	ASTON	ASTROGRAPHY	ASYMMETRICALLY
ASSISTLESS	ASSYTHMENT	ASTOND	ASTROID	ASYMMETRY
ASSISTOR	ASTALK	ASTONE	ASTROITE	ASYMPTOTE
ASSIZE	ASTARBOARD	ASTONED	ASTROLABE	ASYMPTOTIC
ASSIZED	ASTARE	ASTONIED	ASTROLABICAL	ASYMPTOTICAL
ASSIZEMENT	ASTART	ASTONISH	ASTROLATER	ASYNARTETE
ASSIZER	ASTASIA	ASTONISHEDLY	ASTROLATRY	ASYNARTETIC
ASSIZES	ASTATIC	ASTONISHER	ASTROLOG	ASYNCHRONISM
ASSIZING	ASTATICALLY	ASTONISHING	ASTROLOGE	ASYNCHRONOUS
ASSMAN	ASTATICISM	ASTONISHINGLY	ASTROLOGER	ASYNDETIC
ASSMANSHIP	ASTATINE	ASTONISHMENT	ASTROLOGIAN	ASYNDETON
ASSOCIABLE	ASTATIZE	ASTONY	ASTROLOGIC	ASYNERGIA
ASSOCIATE	ASTATIZED	ASTONYING	ASTROLOGICAL	ASYNERGY
ASSOCIATED	ASTATIZER	ASTOOP	ASTROLOGICALLY	ASYNGAMIC
ASSOCIATING	ASTATIZING	ASTORE	ASTROLOGISTIC	ASYNGAMY
ASSOCIATION	ASTAY	ASTOUND	ASTROLOGIZE	ASYNTACTIC
ASSOCIATIVE	ASTEAM	ASTOUNDED	ASTROLOGOUS	ASYNTROPHY
ASSOCIATIVELY	ASTEATOSIS	ASTOUNDING	ASTROLOGY	ASYSTOLE
ASSOCIATIVENESS	ASTEEP	ASTOUNDINGLY	ASTROMANCER	ASYSTOLIC
ASSOCIATOR	ASTEER	ASTOUNDMENT	ASTROMANCY	ASYSTOLISM
ASSOCIE	ASTEISM	ASTRACHAN	ASTROMANTIC	ASYZYGETIC
ASSOIL	ASTELY	ASTRADDLE	ASTROMEDA	AT
ASSOILMENT	ASTER	ASTRAEAN	ASTROMETER	ATA
ASSOILZIE	ASTERACEOUS	ASTRAEID	ASTROMETRY	ATABAL
ASSOLUTO	ASTERIA	ASTRAEIFORM	ASTRONAUT	ATABEG
ASSONANCE	ASTERIAE	ASTRAGAL	ASTRONAUTIC	ATABEK
ASSONANCED	ASTERIAL	ASTRAGALAR	ASTRONAUTICS	ATABRINE
ASSONANT	ASTERIATED	ASTRAGALI	ASTRONOMER	ATACAMITE
ASSONANTAL	ASTERIN	ASTRAGALUS	ASTRONOMIC	ATACTIC
ASSONANTIC	ASTERION	ASTRAIN	ASTRONOMICAL	ATACTIFORM
ASSONATE	ASTERISK	ASTRAKANITE	ASTRONOMICALLY	ATAGHAN
ASSORT	ASTERISKOS	ASTRAKHAN	ASTRONOMICS	ATAJO
ASSORTATIVE	ASTERISM	ASTRAL	ASTRONOMIZE	ATAKE
ASSORTED	ASTERISMAL	ASTRALLY	ASTRONOMY	ATALAYA
ASSORTER	ASTERN	ASTRAND	ASTROPHIL	ATAMAN
ASSORTIVE	ASTERNAL	ASTRAPHOBIA	ASTROPHOBIA	ATAMASCO
ASSORTMENT	ASTERNIA	ASTRAY	ASTROPHYSICS	ATAME
ASSOT	ASTEROID	ASTRE	ASTROSCOPE	ATANGLE
ASSUADE	ASTEROIDAL	ASTREAM	ASTROSCOPY	ATAP
ASSUAGE	ASTEROIDEAN	ASTRER	ASTROSE	ATAR
ASSUAGED	ASTERT	ASTRICT	ASTROSPHERE	ATARACTIC
ASSUAGEMENT	ASTERWORT	ASTRICTION	ASTRUT	ATARAXIA
ASSUAGER	ASTHENIA	ASTRICTIVE	ASTUCIOUS	ATARAXIC
ASSUAGING	ASTHENIC	ASTRICTIVELY	ASTUCIOUSLY	ATARAXY
ASSUASIVE	ASTHENICAL	ASTRIDE	ASTUCITY	ATATSCHITE
ASSUETUDE	ASTHENOLOGY	ASTRIER	ASTUTE	ATAUNT
ASSUMABLE	ASTHENOPIA	ASTRIFEROUS	ASTUTELY	ATAUNTO
ASSUME	ASTHENOPIC	ASTRILD	ASTUTENESS	ATAVI
ASSUMED	ASTHENY	ASTRINGE	ASTUTIOUS	ATAVIC
ASSUMEDLY	ASTHMA	ASTRINGED	ASTYLAR	ATAVISM
ASSUMER	ASTHMATIC	ASTRINGENCY	ASUANG	ATAVIST

ATAVISTIC	ATHEROMATOUS	ATMOLOGIC	ATOPITE	ATTACCA
ATAVUS	ATHETESIS	ATMOLOGICAL	ATOPY	ATTACCO
ATAXAPHASIA	ATHETIZE	ATMOLOGIST	ATOUR	ATTACH
ATAXIA	ATHETIZED	ATMOLOGY	ATRABILAIRE	ATTACHABLE
ATAXIAGRAM	ATHETIZING	ATMOLYSIS	ATRABILAR	ATTACHE
ATAXIAGRAPH	ATHETOID	ATMOLYZATION	ATRABILARIAN	ATTACHED
ATAXIAMETER	ATHETOSIC	ATMOLYZE	ATRABILE	ATTACHEDLY
ATAXIAPHASIA	ATHETOSIS	ATMOLYZER	ATRABILIAR	ATTACHER
ATAXIC	ATHIN	ATMOMETER	ATRABILIARY	ATTACHING
ATAXINOMIC	ATHING	ATMOMETRIC	ATRABILIOUS	ATTACHMENT
ATAXITE	ATHINK	ATMOMETRY	ATRACHEATE	ATTACK
ATAXONOMIC	ATHIRST	ATMOSPHERE	ATRAGENE	ATTACKABLE
ATAXOPHEMIA	ATHLETE	ATMOSPHERIC	ATRAIL	ATTACKER
ATAXY	ATHLETIC	ATMOSPHERICAL	ATRAMENT	ATTACKS
ATAZIR	ATHLETICAL	ATMOSPHERICALLY	ATRAMENTAL	ATTACOLITE
ATBASH	ATHLETICALLY	ATMOSPHERICS	ATRAMENTARY	ATTACUS
ATE	ATHLETICISM	ATMOSTEA	ATRAMENTOUS	ATTAGEN
ATECHNIC	ATHLETICS	ATMOSTEAL	ATRAUMATIC	ATTAIN
ATECHNICAL	ATHLETISM	ATMOSTEON	ATREDE	ATTAINABILITY
ATECHNY	ATHODYD	ATO	ATREMATE	ATTAINABLE
ATEES	ATHOLD	ATOCHA	ATREMATOUS	ATTAINABLENESS
ATEETER	ATHONITE	ATOCIA	ATREMBLE	ATTAINDER
ATEF	ATHREPSIA	ATOKAL	ATRENNE	ATTAINED
ATELECTASIS	ATHREPTIC	ATOKE	ATREPSY	ATTAINER
ATELECTATIC	ATHRILL	ATOKOUS	ATREPTIC	ATTAINING
ATELESTITE	ATHRIVE	ATOLE	ATRESIA	ATTAINMENT
ATELIC	ATHROB	ATOLL	ATRESIC	ATTAINT
ATELIER	ATHROGENIC	ATOM	ATRETIC	ATTAINTED
ATELIOSIS	ATHRONG	ATOMATIC	ATRIA	ATTAINTING
ATELOCARDIA	ATHUMIA	ATOMECHANICS	ATRIAL	ATTAINTMENT
ATELOGLOSSIA	ATHWART	ATOMERG	ATRICHIA	ATTAINTURE
ATELOGNATHIA	ATHWARTHAWSE	ATOMIC	ATRICHIC	ATTALEH
ATELOMITIC	ATHWARTSHIP	ATOMICAL	ATRICHOUS	ATTAME
ATELOMYELIA	ATHWARTSHIPS	ATOMICALLY	ATRICKLE	ATTAP
ATELOPODIA	ATHWARTWISE	ATOMICIAN	ATRIENSES	ATTAR
ATELOSTOMIA	ATHYMIA	ATOMICISM	ATRIENSIS	ATTARGUL
ATEMOYA	ATHYMIC	ATOMICITY	ATRIO	ATTASK
ATEMPORAL	ATHYMY	ATOMICS	ATRIOPORAL	ATTASTE
ATES	ATHYREOSIS	ATOMIES	ATRIOPORE	ATTE
ATEUCHI	ATHYRIA	ATOMIFEROUS	ATRIP	ATTEMPER
ATEUCHUS	ATHYRID	ATOMISE	ATRIUM	ATTEMPERANCE
ATHALAMOUS	ATHYROID	ATOMISM	ATROCE	ATTEMPERATE
ATHALLINE	ATHYROIDISM	ATOMIST	ATROCHA	ATTEMPERATOR
ATHANASIA	ATI	ATOMISTIC	ATROCHAL	ATTEMPERED
ATHANASY	ATILT	ATOMISTICAL	ATROCHOUS	ATTEMPERING
ATHANOR	ATIMON	ATOMISTICALLY	ATROCIOUS	ATTEMPT
ATHBASH	ATINGA	ATOMISTICS	ATROCIOUSLY	ATTEMPTABILITY
ATHECATE	ATINGLE	ATOMITY	ATROCIOUSNESS	ATTEMPTABLE
ATHEISM	ATINKLE	ATOMIZATION	ATROCITIES	ATTEMPTER
ATHEIST	ATIP	ATOMIZE	ATROCITY	ATTEND
ATHEISTIC	ATIPTOE	ATOMIZED	ATROLACTIC	ATTENDANCE
ATHEISTICAL	ATIS	ATOMIZER	ATROPACEOUS	ATTENDANCY
ATHEISTICALLY	ATLANTAD	ATOMIZING	ATROPAL	ATTENDANT
ATHEIZE	ATLANTAL	ATOMOLOGY	ATROPHIA	ATTENDANTLY
ATHEIZER	ATLANTES	ATOMS	ATROPHIATED	ATTENDANTS
ATHEL	ATLANTITE	ATOMY	ATROPHIC	ATTENDED
ATHELIA	ATLANTOAXIAL	ATONABLE	ATROPHIED	ATTENDEE
ATHELING	ATLAS	ATONAL	ATROPHIES	ATTENDING
ATHEMATIC	ATLATL	ATONALISM	ATROPHODERMA	ATTENDINGLY
ATHENAEUM	ATLE	ATONALISTIC	ATROPHOUS	ATTENDMENT
ATHENEUM	ATLEE	ATONALITY	ATROPHY	ATTENDRESS
ATHENOR	ATLOAXOID	ATONALLY	ATROPHYING	ATTENSITY
ATHEOLOGICAL	ATLOID	ATONE	ATROPIA	ATTENT
ATHEOLOGY	ATLOIDEAN	ATONEABLE	ATROPIC	ATTENTAT
ATHEOUS	ATLOIDOAXOID	ATONED	ATROPIN	ATTENTATE
ATHER	ATMA	ATONEMENT	ATROPINE	ATTENTION
ATHERICERAN	ATMAN	ATONENESS	ATROPINIZE	ATTENTIONAL
ATHERICEROUS	ATMIATRY	ATONER	ATROPISM	ATTENTIVE
ATHERINE	ATMID	ATONIA	ATROPOUS	ATTENTIVELY
ATHERMANCY	ATMIDALBUMIN	ATONIC	ATRORUBENT	ATTENTIVENESS
ATHERMANOUS	ATMIDOMETER	ATONICITY	ATROUS	ATTENTLY
ATHERMIC	ATMIDOMETRY	ATONING	ATRY	ATTENUABLE
ATHERMOUS	ATMOCAUSIS	ATONINGLY	ATRYPOID	ATTENUANT
ATHEROMA	ATMOCAUTERY	ATONY	ATSARA	ATTENUATE
ATHEROMAS	ATMOCLASTIC	ATOP	ATT	ATTENUATED
ATHEROMASIA	ATMOGENIC	ATOPEN	ATTA	ATTENUATING
ATHEROMATA	ATMOGRAPH	ATOPIC	ATTABAL	ATTENUATION

ATTENUATOR
ATTER
ATTERCOP
ATTERMINE
ATTERN
ATTERR
ATTERY
ATTEST
ATTESTANT
ATTESTATION
ATTESTATIVE
ATTESTATOR
ATTESTED
ATTESTER
ATTESTIVE
ATTESTOR
ATTIC
ATTICE
ATTICISM
ATTICIST
ATTICIZE
ATTICIZED
ATTICIZING
ATTID
ATTIDAE
ATTINGE
ATTINGENCE
ATTINGENCY
ATTINGENT
ATTIRE
ATTIRED
ATTIREMENT
ATTIRER
ATTIRING
ATTITUDE
ATTITUDINAL
ATTITUDINISE
ATTITUDINIZE
ATTLE
ATTORN
ATTORNEY
ATTORNEYISM
ATTORNEYS
ATTORNEYSHIP
ATTORNMENT
ATTOUR
ATTOURNE
ATTRACT
ATTRACTABLE
ATTRACTANT
ATTRACTER
ATTRACTILE
ATTRACTINGLY
ATTRACTION
ATTRACTIVE
ATTRACTIVELY
ATTRACTIVENESS
ATTRACTIVITY
ATTRACTOR
ATTRAHENT
ATTRAP
ATTRIBUTABLE
ATTRIBUTAL
ATTRIBUTE
ATTRIBUTED
ATTRIBUTER
ATTRIBUTING
ATTRIBUTION
ATTRIBUTIVE
ATTRIBUTOR
ATTRIST
ATTRITE
ATTRITED
ATTRITION
ATTRITIVE
ATTRITUS
ATTRY

ATTUNE
ATTUNED
ATTUNELY
ATTUNEMENT
ATTUNING
ATTURN
ATU
ATUA
ATULE
ATUMBLE
ATUN
ATUNE
ATURN
ATWAIN
ATWEEL
ATWEEN
ATWIN
ATWIRL
ATWIST
ATWITCH
ATWITTER
ATWIXT
ATWO
ATYPIC
ATYPICAL
ATYPICALLY
ATYPY
AU
AUA
AUANTIC
AUBADE
AUBAIN
AUBAINE
AUBE
AUBERGE
AUBERGINE
AUBERGISTE
AUBIN
AUBRITE
AUBURN
AUCA
AUCHENIA
AUCHENIUM
AUCHLET
AUCHT
AUCTARY
AUCTION
AUCTIONARY
AUCTIONEER
AUCTIONING
AUCTOR
AUCTORIAL
AUCUBA
AUCUPATE
AUDACE
AUDACIOUS
AUDACIOUSLY
AUDACIOUSNESS
AUDACITY
AUDAD
AUDIBILITY
AUDIBLE
AUDIBLENESS
AUDIBLY
AUDIENCE
AUDIENCIA
AUDIENCIER
AUDIENT
AUDILE
AUDIO
AUDIOGRAM
AUDIOLOGICAL
AUDIOLOGY
AUDIOMETER
AUDIOMETRY
AUDION
AUDIOPHILE

AUDIPHONE
AUDIT
AUDITION
AUDITIVE
AUDITOR
AUDITORIA
AUDITORIAL
AUDITORIALLY
AUDITORILY
AUDITORIUM
AUDITORIUMS
AUDITORY
AUDITRESS
AUDITUAL
AUDIVISE
AUDIVISER
AUDIVISION
AUE
AUF
AUFAIT
AUFER
AUFGABE
AUFTAKT
AUGANITE
AUGE
AUGELITE
AUGEND
AUGER
AUGERER
AUGH
AUGHT
AUGHTLINS
AUGITE
AUGITIC
AUGITITE
AUGITOPHYRE
AUGMENT
AUGMENTABLE
AUGMENTATION
AUGMENTATIVE
AUGMENTED
AUGMENTEDLY
AUGMENTER
AUGMENTIVE
AUGRIM
AUGUR
AUGURAL
AUGURATE
AUGURATION
AUGURER
AUGURIES
AUGUROUS
AUGURY
AUGUST
AUGUSTAL
AUGUSTE
AUGUSTLY
AUGUSTNESS
AUH
AUHUHU
AUK
AUKLET
AUKSINAI
AUKSINAS
AUKSINU
AUL
AULA
AULARIAN
AULD
AULETE
AULETIC
AULETRIDES
AULETRIS
AULIC
AULICAL
AULICISM
AULLAY

AULOPHYTE
AULOS
AULOSTOMID
AULU
AUM
AUMAGA
AUMAIL
AUMAKUA
AUMIL
AUMILDAR
AUMONIERE
AUMOUS
AUMRIE
AUNCEL
AUNE
AUNT
AUNTER
AUNTERS
AUNTIE
AUNTRE
AUNTROUS
AUNTSARY
AUNTY
AUPAKA
AURA
AURAE
AURAL
AURALLY
AURAMIN
AURAMINE
AURANG
AURANTIA
AURANTIUM
AURAR
AURAS
AURATE
AURATED
AUREAL
AUREATE
AUREATELY
AUREATENESS
AUREATION
AUREI
AUREITY
AURELIA
AURELIAN
AURENE
AUREOLA
AUREOLE
AUREOLIN
AUREOLINE
AUREOMYCIN
AUREOUS
AUREOUSLY
AURES
AURESCA
AUREUS
AURIC
AURICHALCITE
AURICLE
AURICLED
AURICOMOUS
AURICULA
AURICULAE
AURICULAR
AURICULARE
AURICULARES
AURICULARIA
AURICULARIAE
AURICULARIAN
AURICULARIS
AURICULARLY
AURICULAS
AURICULATE
AURICULATED
AURICULATELY
AURIDE

AURIFEROUS
AURIFEX
AURIFIC
AURIFICATION
AURIFLAMME
AURIFORM
AURIFY
AURIGAL
AURIGATION
AURIGEROUS
AURIGO
AURILAVE
AURIN
AURINASAL
AURINE
AURIPHONE
AURIPHRYGIA
AURIPUNCTURE
AURIS
AURISCALP
AURISCOPE
AURISCOPY
AURIST
AURITE
AURIVOROUS
AUROAURIC
AUROBROMIDE
AUROCH
AUROCHS
AUROCYANIDE
AURODIAMINE
AUROPHOBIA
AUROPHORE
AURORA
AURORAL
AURORALLY
AURORE
AUROREAN
AURORIUM
AUROUS
AURRESCU
AURULENT
AURUM
AURUNG
AURURE
AURYL
AUSCULT
AUSCULTATE
AUSCULTATED
AUSCULTATING
AUSCULTATION
AUSCULTATOR
AUSCULTATORY
AUSLAUT
AUSPEX
AUSPICATE
AUSPICATED
AUSPICATING
AUSPICE
AUSPICES
AUSPICIAL
AUSPICIOUS
AUSPICIOUSLY
AUSPICIOUSNESS
AUSPICY
AUSTAUSCH
AUSTEMPER
AUSTENITE
AUSTENITIC
AUSTERE
AUSTERELY
AUSTERENESS
AUSTERITIES
AUSTERITY
AUSTRAL
AUSTRALENE
AUSTRALITE

AUSTRINE	AUTOBLAST	AUTOGRAPH	AUTOPHAGOUS	AUTUMNALLY
AUSTRINGER	AUTOBOAT	AUTOGRAPHER	AUTOPHAGY	AUTUMNIAN
AUSTRIUM	AUTOBOATING	AUTOGRAPHIC	AUTOPHOBIA	AUTUMNITY
AUSTROMANCY	AUTOBOLIDE	AUTOGRAPHICAL	AUTOPHOBY	AUTUNITE
AUSU	AUTOBUS	AUTOGRAPHISM	AUTOPHON	AUWAI
AUSUBO	AUTOCAB	AUTOGRAPHIST	AUTOPHONE	AUX
AUTACOID	AUTOCAMP	AUTOGRAPHY	AUTOPHONOUS	AUXANOGRAM
AUTACOIDAL	AUTOCAMPER	AUTOGRAVURE	AUTOPHONY	AUXANOLOGY
AUTANTITYPY	AUTOCAMPING	AUTOGYRO	AUTOPHYTE	AUXANOMETER
AUTARCH	AUTOCAR	AUTOHEADER	AUTOPHYTIC	AUXESIS
AUTARCHIC	AUTOCARIST	AUTOHYPNOSIS	AUTOPLASTIC	AUXETIC
AUTARCHICAL	AUTOCARP	AUTOICOUS	AUTOPLASTIES	AUXETICAL
AUTARCHIES	AUTOCARPIAN	AUTOIGNITION	AUTOPLASTY	AUXETICALLY
AUTARCHY	AUTOCARPIC	AUTOING	AUTOPOLO	AUXILIAR
AUTARKIC	AUTOCARPOUS	AUTOIST	AUTOPOLOIST	AUXILIARIES
AUTARKIK	AUTOCATALYZE	AUTOKINESIS	AUTOPORE	AUXILIARLY
AUTARKIKAL	AUTOCEPHALIA	AUTOKINETIC	AUTOPSIC	AUXILIARY
AUTARKY	AUTOCEPHALIC	AUTOKRATOR	AUTOPSICAL	AUXILIATE
AUTE	AUTOCEPHALITY	AUTOLITH	AUTOPSIES	AUXILIATION
AUTECHOSCOPE	AUTOCEPHALOUS	AUTOLOADING	AUTOPSY	AUXILIATOR
AUTECOLOGY	AUTOCEPHALY	AUTOLYSATE	AUTOPSYCHIC	AUXILIATORY
AUTEM	AUTOCEPTIVE	AUTOLYSIN	AUTOPTIC	AUXILIUM
AUTERE	AUTOCHROME	AUTOLYSIS	AUTOPTICAL	AUXIMONE
AUTHENTIC	AUTOCHROMY	AUTOLYTIC	AUTOPTICALLY	AUXIN
AUTHENTICAL	AUTOCHTHON	AUTOLYZATE	AUTOPTICITY	AUXOACTION
AUTHENTICALLY	AUTOCHTHONAL	AUTOLYZE	AUTORAIL	AUXOAMYLASE
AUTHENTICATE	AUTOCHTHONES	AUTOMA	AUTORISER	AUXOBLAST
AUTHENTICATED	AUTOCHTHONIC	AUTOMACY	AUTOROTATION	AUXOBODY
AUTHENTICATING	AUTOCHTHONOUS	AUTOMANIA	AUTORRHAPHY	AUXOCARDIA
AUTHENTICATION	AUTOCHTHONS	AUTOMANUAL	AUTOSCOPE	AUXOCHROME
AUTHENTICATOR	AUTOCHTHONY	AUTOMAT	AUTOSCOPIC	AUXOCHROMIC
AUTHENTICITY	AUTOCIDE	AUTOMATA	AUTOSCOPY	AUXOCHROMISM
AUTHENTICLY	AUTOCLASTIC	AUTOMATE	AUTOSERUM	AUXOCHROMOUS
AUTHENTICNESS	AUTOCLAVE	AUTOMATED	AUTOSIGHT	AUXOCYTE
AUTHIGENIC	AUTOCOHERER	AUTOMATIC	AUTOSITE	AUXOFLORE
AUTHIGENOUS	AUTOCOPIST	AUTOMATICAL	AUTOSITIC	AUXOFLUOR
AUTHOR	AUTOCOSM	AUTOMATICALLY	AUTOSKELETON	AUXOGRAPH
AUTHORCRAFT	AUTOCRACIES	AUTOMATICITY	AUTOSLED	AUXOGRAPHIC
AUTHORESS	AUTOCRACY	AUTOMATIN	AUTOSOMAL	AUXOHORMONE
AUTHORIAL	AUTOCRAT	AUTOMATING	AUTOSOME	AUXOLOGY
AUTHORIALLY	AUTOCRATIC	AUTOMATISM	AUTOSOTERIC	AUXOMETER
AUTHORITARIAN	AUTOCRATICAL	AUTOMATIST	AUTOSOTERISM	AUXOSPORE
AUTHORITATIVE	AUTOCRATICALLY	AUTOMATIVE	AUTOSPORE	AUXOTONIC
AUTHORITATIVELY	AUTOCRATOR	AUTOMATIZATION	AUTOSPORIC	AUXOTOX
AUTHORITATIVENESS	AUTOCRATORIC	AUTOMATIZE	AUTOSPRAY	AVA
AUTHORITIES	AUTOCRATRIX	AUTOMATON	AUTOSTAGE	AVADANA
AUTHORITY	AUTODIDACT	AUTOMATONS	AUTOSTYLIC	AVADAVAT
AUTHORIZATION	AUTODIDACTIC	AUTOMATOUS	AUTOSTYLISM	AVADHUTA
AUTHORIZE	AUTODROME	AUTOMETRIC	AUTOSTYLY	AVAHI
AUTHORIZED	AUTODYNAMIC	AUTOMETRY	AUTOTELIC	AVAIL
AUTHORIZER	AUTODYNE	AUTOMOBILE	AUTOTHEISM	AVAILABILITIES
AUTHORIZING	AUTOECIC	AUTOMOBILED	AUTOTHEIST	AVAILABILITY
AUTHORLESS	AUTOECIOUS	AUTOMOBILING	AUTOTHERAPY	AVAILABLE
AUTHORLING	AUTOECIOUSLY	AUTOMOBILISM	AUTOTOMIC	AVAILABLENESS
AUTHORLY	AUTOECISM	AUTOMOBILIST	AUTOTOMIZE	AVAILABLY
AUTHORS	AUTOED	AUTOMOBILITY	AUTOTOMY	AVAILED
AUTHORSHIP	AUTOEROTIC	AUTOMOLITE	AUTOTOXAEMIA	AVAILING
AUTHOTYPE	AUTOEROTISM	AUTOMORPH	AUTOTOXEMIA	AVAILINGLY
AUTISM	AUTOETTE	AUTOMORPHIC	AUTOTOXIC	AVAILS
AUTIST	AUTOFRETTAGE	AUTOMORPHISM	AUTOTOXIN	AVAL
AUTISTIC	AUTOGAMIC	AUTOMOTIVE	AUTOTRACTOR	AVALANCHE
AUTO	AUTOGAMOUS	AUTOMOWER	AUTOTROPHIC	AVALANCHED
AUTOALARM	AUTOGAMY	AUTOMPNE	AUTOTROPIC	AVALANCHING
AUTOALLOGAMY	AUTOGAUGE	AUTONOMIC	AUTOTROPISM	AVALE
AUTOBAHN	AUTOGENEAL	AUTONOMICAL	AUTOTRUCK	AVALENT
AUTOBAHNEN	AUTOGENESIS	AUTONOMIES	AUTOTYPE	AVALVULAR
AUTOBAHNS	AUTOGENETIC	AUTONOMIST	AUTOTYPIC	AVANIA
AUTOBASIDIA	AUTOGENIC	AUTONOMIZE	AUTOTYPY	AVANIOUS
AUTOBASIDIUM	AUTOGENOUS	AUTONOMOUS	AUTOVACCINE	AVANT
AUTOBIOGRAPHAL	AUTOGENOUSLY	AUTONOMOUSLY	AUTOVALVE	AVANTLAY
AUTOBIOGRAPHER	AUTOGENY	AUTONOMY	AUTOXIDATION	AVANYU
AUTOBIOGRAPHIC	AUTOGIRO	AUTONYM	AUTOXIDATOR	AVARAM
AUTOBIOGRAPHICAL	AUTOGIROS	AUTOPATHIC	AUTOXIDIZE	AVAREMOTEMO
AUTOBIOGRAPHICALLY	AUTOGNOSIS	AUTOPATHY	AUTOZOOID	AVARICE
AUTOBIOGRAPHIES	AUTOGNOSTIC	AUTOPELAGIC	AUTREFOIS	AVARICIOUS
AUTOBIOGRAPHIST	AUTOGRAFT	AUTOPHAGI	AUTUMN	AVARICIOUSLY
AUTOBIOGRAPHY	AUTOGRAFTING	AUTOPHAGIA	AUTUMNAL	AVAST

AVATAR	AVIATE	AVONDBLOEM	AWED	AXIFUGAL
AVATARA	AVIATED	AVOSET	AWEDE	AXIL
AVAUNT	AVIATIC	AVOUCH	AWEDNESS	AXILE
AVE	AVIATING	AVOUCHER	AWEE	AXILEMMA
AVEL	AVIATION	AVOUCHMENT	AWEEK	AXILEMMAS
AVELL	AVIATOR	AVOUE	AWEEL	AXILEMMATA
AVELLAN	AVIATORIAL	AVOURE	AWEIGH	AXILLA
AVELLANE	AVIATORY	AVOURNEEN	AWEING	AXILLAE
AVELLANEOUS	AVIATRESS	AVOUTRY	AWELESS	AXILLANT
AVELLANO	AVIATRICE	AVOW	AWESOME	AXILLAR
AVELONGE	AVIATRIX	AVOWABLE	AWESOMELY	AXILLARIES
AVELOZ	AVICHI	AVOWABLENESS	AWESOMENESS	AXILLARY
AVENACEOUS	AVICI	AVOWABLY	AWEST	AXINE
AVENAGE	AVICIDE	AVOWAL	AWESTRUCK	AXINITE
AVENALIN	AVICK	AVOWANCE	AWETO	AXINOMANCY
AVENANT	AVICOLOUS	AVOWANT	AWF	AXIOLITE
AVENARY	AVICULAR	AVOWED	AWFUL	AXIOLITIC
AVENER	AVICULARIA	AVOWEDLY	AWFULLY	AXIOLOGICAL
AVENERY	AVICULARIAN	AVOWEDNESS	AWFULNESS	AXIOLOGIST
AVENGE	AVICULARIUM	AVOWER	AWHAPE	AXIOLOGY
AVENGED	AVICULTURE	AVOWRIES	AWHEEL	AXIOM
AVENGEFUL	AVICULTURIST	AVOWRY	AWHEFT	AXIOMATIC
AVENGEMENT	AVID	AVOY	AWHET	AXIOMATICAL
AVENGER	AVIDIN	AVOYER	AWHILE	AXIOMATIZE
AVENGERESS	AVIDIOUS	AVOYERSHIP	AWHIR	AXION
AVENGING	AVIDIOUSLY	AVULSE	AWHIRL	AXIOPISTY
AVENGINGLY	AVIDITY	AVULSION	AWIDE	AXIS
AVENIDA	AVIDLY	AVUNCULAR	AWIGGLE	AXISYMMETRIC
AVENIN	AVIDOUS	AVUNCULATE	AWIKIWIKI	AXITE
AVENINE	AVIDYA	AVYS	AWING	AXLE
AVENOLITH	AVIE	AVYSE	AWINK	AXLED
AVENOUS	AVIEW	AW	AWIWI	AXLESMITH
AVENS	AVIFAUNA	AWA	AWK	AXLETREE
AVENTAIL	AVIFAUNAL	AWABI	AWKLY	AXLIKE
AVENTAYLE	AVIGATE	AWAFT	AWKWARD	AXMAKER
AVENTRE	AVIGATION	AWAG	AWKWARDLY	AXMAKING
AVENTURIN	AVIGATOR	AWAIT	AWKWARDNESS	AXMAN
AVENTURINE	AVIJJA	AWAITER	AWL	AXMANSHIP
AVENUE	AVILE	AWAITING	AWLESS	AXMASTER
AVER	AVILEMENT	AWAKE	AWLWORT	AXMEN
AVERA	AVINE	AWAKED	AWMER	AXODENDRITE
AVERAGE	AVIOLITE	AWAKEN	AWMOUS	AXOFUGAL
AVERAGED	AVION	AWAKENER	AWN	AXOGAMY
AVERAGELY	AVIONICS	AWAKENING	AWNED	AXOID
AVERAGER	AVIRULENCE	AWAKENINGLY	AWNER	AXOIDEAN
AVERAGING	AVIRULENT	AWAKENMENT	AWNIE	AXOLOTL
AVERAH	AVISION	AWAKING	AWNING	AXOLYSIS
AVERIL	AVISO	AWALD	AWNINGED	AXOMETER
AVERIN	AVISOS	AWALE	AWNLESS	AXON
AVERMENT	AVITAL	AWALT	AWNY	AXONAL
AVERRABLE	AVITAMINOSIS	AWANE	AWOKE	AXONE
AVERRAL	AVITAMINOTIC	AWANTING	AWOKEN	AXONEME
AVERRED	AVITIC	AWANYU	AWONDER	AXONEURE
AVERRING	AVIVES	AWAPUHI	AWORK	AXONEURON
AVERRUNCATE	AVIZANDUM	AWARD	AWREAK	AXONOLIPOUS
AVERRUNCATOR	AVO	AWARDABLE	AWRIST	AXONOMETRIC
AVERSANT	AVOCADO	AWARDER	AWRONG	AXONOMETRY
AVERSATION	AVOCADOS	AWARDMENT	AWRY	AXONOPHOROUS
AVERSE	AVOCATE	AWARE	AX	AXONOST
AVERSELY	AVOCATION	AWARENESS	AXAL	AXOPETAL
AVERSENESS	AVOCATIVE	AWARP	AXAN	AXOPHYTE
AVERSION	AVOCATORY	AWARRANT	AXBREAKER	AXOPLASM
AVERSIVE	AVOCET	AWARUITE	AXE	AXOPODIUM
AVERT	AVODIRE	AWASH	AXEBREAKER	AXOSPERMOUS
AVERTABLE	AVOGADRITE	AWASTE	AXED	AXOSTYLE
AVERTED	AVOGRAM	AWAT	AXEL	AXSEED
AVERTEDLY	AVOID	AWATCH	AXEMAN	AXSTONE
AVERTER	AVOIDABLE	AWATER	AXEMASTER	AXTREE
AVERTIBLE	AVOIDABLY	AWAVE	AXENIC	AXUNGE
AVESTRUZ	AVOIDANCE	AWAY	AXES	AXWEED
AVEUGLE	AVOIDER	AWAYNESS	AXHAMMER	AY
AVGAS	AVOIDLESS	AWBER	AXHAMMERED	AYA
AVIADOR	AVOIDMENT	AWE	AXIAL	AYACAHUITE
AVIAN	AVOIDS	AWEARIED	AXIALITY	AYAH
AVIANIZE	AVOIRDUPOIS	AWEARY	AXIALLY	AYAHUASCA
AVIARIST	AVOLATE	AWEATHER	AXIATE	AYAPANA
AVIARY	AVOLATION	AWEBAND	AXIFORM	AYE

AYEGREEN
AYEL
AYELP
AYEN
AYENBITE
AYENS
AYENST
AYIN
AYLESS
AYLET
AYLLU
AYN
AYNE
AYOND
AYONT
AYOUS
AYRE
AYU
AYUDANTE
AYUNTAMIENTO
AYUNTAMIENTOS
AYUYU
AYWHERE
AZADIRACHTA
AZAFRAN
AZAFRIN
AZALEA
AZALEAMUM
AZAM
AZAN
AZAROLE
AZEDARACH
AZELAIC
AZELATE
AZEOTROPE
AZEOTROPIC
AZEOTROPISM
AZEOTROPY
AZEW
AZIDE
AZIETHANE
AZILUT
AZIMENE
AZIMETHYLENE
AZIMIN
AZIMINE
AZIMINO
AZIMUTH
AZIMUTHAL
AZIMUTHALLY
AZINE
AZIOLA
AZLACTONE
AZLON
AZO
AZOBENZENE
AZOBENZIL
AZOBENZOIC
AZOBENZOL
AZOBLACK
AZOCH
AZOCOCHINEAL
AZOCORALLINE
AZOCORINTH
AZOCYANIDE
AZOCYCLIC
AZODIPHENYL
AZOERYTHRIN
AZOFICATION
AZOFIER
AZOFORMIC
AZOFY
AZOGALLEIN
AZOGREEN
AZOHUMIC
AZOIC
AZOIMIDE

AZOLE
AZOLITMIN
AZOMETHINE
AZON
AZONAL
AZONIC
AZONIUM
AZOOSPERMIA
AZOPARAFFIN
AZOPHEN
AZOPHENETOLE
AZOPHENINE
AZOPHENOL
AZOPHENYL
AZOPHENYLENE
AZOPHOSPHIN
AZOPHOSPHORE
AZOPROTEIN
AZORITE
AZOSULPHINE
AZOSULPHONIC
AZOTATE
AZOTE
AZOTEA
AZOTED
AZOTEMIA
AZOTENESIS
AZOTETRAZOLE
AZOTH
AZOTHIONIUM
AZOTIC
AZOTIN
AZOTINE
AZOTITE
AZOTIZED
AZOTIZING
AZOTOBACTER
AZOTOLUENE
AZOTOMETER
AZOTORRHEA
AZOTORRHOEA
AZOTOUS
AZOTURIA
AZOVERNINE
AZOXINE
AZOXONIUM
AZOXY
AZOXYBENZENE
AZTECA
AZTHIONIUM
AZULEJO
AZULENE
AZULITE
AZUMBRE
AZURE
AZUREAN
AZURED
AZURINE
AZURITE
AZUROUS
AZURY
AZYGOMATOUS
AZYGOS
AZYGOSPERM
AZYGOSPORE
AZYGOTE
AZYGOUS
AZYM
AZYME
AZYMITE
AZYMOUS

BA
BAA
BAAED
BAAHLING
BAAING
BAAL
BAAN
BAAS
BABA
BABACOOTE
BABAI
BABAJAGA
BABAKOTO
BABASCO
BABASSU
BABAYLAN
BABAYLANES
BABBISHLY
BABBITT
BABBITTED
BABBITTER
BABBITTING
BABBLATIVE
BABBLE
BABBLED
BABBLEMENT
BABBLER
BABBLESOME
BABBLING
BABBLISH
BABBLY
BABBO
BABBY
BABE
BABERY
BABESHIP
BABESIASIS
BABICHE
BABIED
BABIES
BABIL
BABILLARD
BABINGTONITE
BABIROUSSA
BABIRUSA
BABIRUSSA
BABISH
BABISHED
BABISHLY
BABISHNESS
BABLAH
BABLOH
BABOEN
BABOO
BABOODOM
BABOOISM
BABOOL
BABOON
BABOONERY
BABOONROOT
BABOOS
BABOOSH
BABOUCHE
BABRACOT
BABROOT
BABU
BABUDOM

BABUINA
BABUISM
BABUL
BABURD
BABUS
BABUSHKA
BABY
BABYFIED
BABYHOOD
BABYHOUSE
BABYING
BABYISH
BABYISHLY
BABYISHNESS
BABYLIKE
BAC
BACABA
BACACH
BACALAO
BACALAOS
BACAO
BACAUAN
BACBAKIRI
BACCA
BACCACEOUS
BACCAE
BACCALAUREAN
BACCAR
BACCARA
BACCARAT
BACCARE
BACCATE
BACCATED
BACCHANAL
BACCHANALIA
BACCHANALIAN
BACCHANALIZE
BACCHANALS
BACCHANT
BACCHANTE
BACCHANTES
BACCHANTIC
BACCHANTS
BACCHAR
BACCHARIS
BACCHAROID
BACCHEION
BACCHIAC
BACCHIAN
BACCHIC
BACCHII
BACCHIUS
BACCIFEROUS
BACCIFORM
BACCIVOROUS
BACCO
BACCY
BACH
BACHE
BACHEL
BACHELOR
BACHELORHOOD
BACHELORIZE
BACHELORLY
BACHELORSHIP
BACHELORWISE
BACHELRY
BACILE
BACILLAR
BACILLARY
BACILLI
BACILLICIDAL
BACILLICIDE
BACILLICIDIC
BACILLIFORM
BACILLIGENIC
BACILLITE

BACILLOGENIC
BACILLOSIS
BACILLURIA
BACILLUS
BACK
BACKACHE
BACKACHY
BACKARE
BACKBAND
BACKBAR
BACKBEAR
BACKBEARING
BACKBENCHER
BACKBEND
BACKBERAND
BACKBEREND
BACKBIT
BACKBITE
BACKBITER
BACKBITING
BACKBITTEN
BACKBLOCKS
BACKBOARD
BACKBONE
BACKBONED
BACKBONELESS
BACKBRAND
BACKBREAKER
BACKBREAKING
BACKCAP
BACKCAST
BACKCHAIN
BACKCHAT
BACKCOUNTRY
BACKCOURT
BACKCROSS
BACKDOOR
BACKDOWN
BACKDROP
BACKED
BACKEN
BACKENED
BACKENING
BACKER
BACKET
BACKFALL
BACKFATTER
BACKFIELD
BACKFILL
BACKFILLER
BACKFILLING
BACKFIRE
BACKFIRED
BACKFIRING
BACKFLAP
BACKFLASH
BACKFLIP
BACKFLOW
BACKFOLD
BACKFRAME
BACKFRIEND
BACKFURROW
BACKGAME
BACKGAMMON
BACKGROUND
BACKHAND
BACKHANDED
BACKHANDEDLY
BACKHANDER
BACKHATCH
BACKHAUL
BACKHEEL
BACKHOE
BACKHOOKER
BACKHOUSE
BACKIE
BACKIEBIRD

BACKING
BACKINGS
BACKJAW
BACKJOINT
BACKLAND
BACKLANDS
BACKLASH
BACKLASHING
BACKLESS
BACKLET
BACKLIST
BACKLOG
BACKLOTTER
BACKMOST
BACKPACK
BACKPEDAL
BACKPIECE
BACKPLATE
BACKREST
BACKROPE
BACKRUN
BACKSAW
BACKSEAT
BACKSET
BACKSETTING
BACKSETTLER
BACKSEY
BACKSHEESH
BACKSHIFT
BACKSHISH
BACKSIDE
BACKSIGHT
BACKSLAP
BACKSLAPPER
BACKSLAPPING
BACKSLID
BACKSLIDDEN
BACKSLIDE
BACKSLIDER
BACKSLIDING
BACKSPACE
BACKSPACER
BACKSPANG
BACKSPEAR
BACKSPEER
BACKSPEIR
BACKSPIER
BACKSPIERER
BACKSPIN
BACKSPREAD
BACKSPRINGING
BACKSTAFF
BACKSTAGE
BACKSTAIR
BACKSTAIRS
BACKSTAMP
BACKSTAY
BACKSTER
BACKSTICK
BACKSTITCH
BACKSTOP
BACKSTRAP
BACKSTRETCH
BACKSTRING
BACKSTRIP
BACKSTROKE
BACKSTROKED
BACKSTROKING
BACKSTROMITE
BACKSWEPT
BACKSWING
BACKSWORD
BACKSWORDING
BACKSWORDMAN
BACKSWORDSMAN
BACKTACK
BACKTENTER

BACKTRACK
BACKTRACKER
BACKTRICK
BACKUP
BACKVELD
BACKVELDER
BACKWALL
BACKWARD
BACKWARDLY
BACKWARDNESS
BACKWARDS
BACKWASH
BACKWASHER
BACKWASHING
BACKWATER
BACKWATERED
BACKWAY
BACKWIND
BACKWOOD
BACKWOODS
BACKWOODSMAN
BACKWOODSY
BACKWORD
BACKWORM
BACKWORT
BACKY
BACKYARD
BACKYARDER
BACLIN
BACON
BACONER
BACONIZE
BACONWEED
BACONY
BACTERIA
BACTERIACEOUS
BACTERIAEMIA
BACTERIAL
BACTERIALLY
BACTERIAN
BACTERIC
BACTERICIDAL
BACTERICIDE
BACTERICIDIN
BACTERIEMIA
BACTERIFORM
BACTERIN
BACTERIOBLAST
BACTERIOCYTE
BACTERIOID
BACTERIOLOGIC
BACTERIOLOGICAL
BACTERIOLOGY
BACTERIOLYZE
BACTERIOSIS
BACTERIOSTAT
BACTERIOTOXIC
BACTERIOUS
BACTERITIC
BACTERIUM
BACTERIURIA
BACTERIZE
BACTERIZED
BACTERIZING
BACTEROID
BACTEROIDAL
BACTRITICONE
BACTRITOID
BACUBERT
BACULA
BACULE
BACULERE
BACULI
BACULIFEROUS
BACULIFORM
BACULINE
BACULITE

BACULITIC
BACULITICONE
BACULOID
BACULUS
BACURY
BAD
BADAK
BADAM
BADAN
BADAUD
BADAXE
BADCHAN
BADDELEYITE
BADDERLOCKS
BADDIE
BADDISH
BADDISHLY
BADDISHNESS
BADDOCK
BADDY
BADE
BADENITE
BADGE
BADGED
BADGEMAN
BADGEMEN
BADGER
BADGERER
BADGERLY
BADGERS
BADGERWEED
BADGING
BADGIR
BADHAN
BADIA
BADIAGA
BADIAN
BADIGEON
BADINAGE
BADINAGED
BADINAGING
BADINER
BADINERIE
BADINEUR
BADIOUS
BADJU
BADLAND
BADLANDS
BADLING
BADLY
BADMAN
BADMEN
BADMINTON
BADNESS
BADRANS
BAEL
BAETULI
BAETULUS
BAETYL
BAETYLIC
BAETYLUS
BAETZNER
BAFARO
BAFF
BAFFIES
BAFFLE
BAFFLED
BAFFLEPLATE
BAFFLER
BAFFLING
BAFFLINGLY
BAFFY
BAFT
BAFTA
BAFTAH
BAG
BAGA

BAGANI
BAGASS
BAGASSE
BAGATAWAY
BAGATELLE
BAGATINE
BAGATTINI
BAGATTINO
BAGEL
BAGFUL
BAGGAGE
BAGGAGEMAN
BAGGAGEMASTER
BAGGAGER
BAGGALA
BAGGE
BAGGED
BAGGER
BAGGIE
BAGGIER
BAGGIEST
BAGGILY
BAGGINESS
BAGGING
BAGGIT
BAGGY
BAGHOUSE
BAGLE
BAGLEAVES
BAGLIKE
BAGMAN
BAGMEN
BAGNE
BAGNES
BAGNET
BAGNIO
BAGNUT
BAGO
BAGONG
BAGOONG
BAGPIPE
BAGPIPER
BAGPIPES
BAGPOD
BAGRATIONITE
BAGRE
BAGREEF
BAGROOM
BAGS
BAGTIKAN
BAGUE
BAGUET
BAGUETTE
BAGUIO
BAGUIOS
BAGWIG
BAGWIGGED
BAGWORM
BAGWYN
BAH
BAHADA
BAHADUR
BAHAN
BAHAR
BAHAY
BAHERA
BAHI
BAHIA
BAHIAITE
BAHNUNG
BAHO
BAHOE
BAHR
BAHT
BAHTS
BAHU
BAHUR

BAHUT
BAHUVRIHI
BAIDAK
BAIDAR
BAIGNOIRE
BAIKALITE
BAIKERINITE
BAIKERITE
BAIKIE
BAIL
BAILABLE
BAILE
BAILEE
BAILER
BAILEY
BAILEYS
BAILIARIES
BAILIARY
BAILIE
BAILIERIES
BAILIERY
BAILIFF
BAILIFFRY
BAILIWICK
BAILLI
BAILLIAGE
BAILLONE
BAILMENT
BAILO
BAILOR
BAILOUT
BAILPIECE
BAILSMAN
BAILSMEN
BAILWOOD
BAIN
BAINITE
BAIOC
BAIOCCO
BAIRA
BAIRAGI
BAIRN
BAIRNIE
BAIRNISH
BAIRNISHNESS
BAIRNLINESS
BAIRNLY
BAIRNTEAM
BAIRNTEEM
BAIRNTIME
BAIT
BAITER
BAITFISH
BAITH
BAITING
BAITTLE
BAIZA
BAIZE
BAIZED
BAIZING
BAJADA
BAJOCCO
BAJOCHI
BAJOIRE
BAJONADO
BAJRA
BAJREE
BAJU
BAJULATE
BAK
BAKA
BAKAL
BAKE
BAKEAPPLE
BAKEBOARD
BAKED
BAKEHEAD

BAKEHOUSE
BAKELITE
BAKELIZE
BAKEMEAT
BAKEN
BAKEOUT
BAKEPAN
BAKER
BAKERIES
BAKERITE
BAKERLY
BAKERY
BAKESHOP
BAKESTONE
BAKEWARE
BAKIE
BAKING
BAKLAVA
BAKSHEESH
BAKSHI
BAKSHISH
BAKTUN
BAKU
BAKULA
BAKUPARI
BAL
BALABOS
BALACHAN
BALACHONG
BALADINE
BALAENID
BALAFO
BALAGAN
BALAGHAT
BALAGHAUT
BALAI
BALALAIKA
BALAM
BALANCE
BALANCEABLE
BALANCED
BALANCELLE
BALANCER
BALANCING
BALANDRA
BALANDRANA
BALANEUTICS
BALANGAY
BALANIC
BALANID
BALANIFEROUS
BALANISM
BALANITE
BALANITIS
BALANOCELE
BALANOID
BALANOPHORE
BALANOPHORIN
BALANOPLASTY
BALANOPS
BALANT
BALANTIDIAL
BALANTIDIC
BALAO
BALAPHON
BALARAO
BALAS
BALAT
BALATA
BALATE
BALATONG
BALATRON
BALATRONIC
BALATTE
BALAU
BALAUSTA
BALAUSTINE

BALAUSTRE
BALAYEUSE
BALBOA
BALBRIGGAN
BALBUSARD
BALBUTIATE
BALBUTIENT
BALBUTIES
BALCHE
BALCONE
BALCONET
BALCONETTE
BALCONIED
BALCONIES
BALCONY
BALD
BALDACCHINI
BALDACCHINO
BALDACHIN
BALDACHINED
BALDACHINO
BALDACHINOS
BALDAKIN
BALDAQUIN
BALDBERRY
BALDCROWN
BALDEN
BALDER
BALDERDASH
BALDFACED
BALDHEAD
BALDHEADED
BALDICOOT
BALDING
BALDISH
BALDLING
BALDLY
BALDMONEY
BALDMONEYS
BALDNESS
BALDPATE
BALDPATED
BALDRIB
BALDRIC
BALDRICK
BALDRICKED
BALDUCTA
BALDUCTUM
BALDY
BALE
BALEBOS
BALED
BALEEN
BALEFIRE
BALEFUL
BALEFULLY
BALEFULNESS
BALEI
BALEISE
BALER
BALESTRA
BALETE
BALEWORT
BALEYS
BALI
BALIAN
BALIBAGO
BALIMBING
BALINE
BALING
BALINGER
BALINGHASAY
BALISAUR
BALISIER
BALISTARII
BALISTARIUS
BALISTID

BALISTRARIA
BALITA
BALITAO
BALITI
BALK
BALKANIZE
BALKANIZED
BALKANIZING
BALKER
BALKIER
BALKIEST
BALKINGLY
BALKLINE
BALKY
BALL
BALLAD
BALLADE
BALLADEER
BALLADER
BALLADIC
BALLADICAL
BALLADIER
BALLADMONGER
BALLADROMIC
BALLADRY
BALLAHOO
BALLAHOU
BALLAM
BALLAN
BALLANT
BALLARAG
BALLARD
BALLAS
BALLAST
BALLASTAGE
BALLASTER
BALLASTING
BALLATA
BALLATOON
BALLCARRIER
BALLDRESS
BALLED
BALLER
BALLERINA
BALLERINAS
BALLERINE
BALLET
BALLETOMANE
BALLFLOWER
BALLHOOTER
BALLIAGE
BALLING
BALLISM
BALLIST
BALLISTA
BALLISTAE
BALLISTIC
BALLISTICALLY
BALLISTICIAN
BALLISTICS
BALLIUM
BALLMINE
BALLOCK
BALLOEN
BALLOGAN
BALLON
BALLONET
BALLONETTE
BALLONNE
BALLOON
BALLOONATION
BALLOONER
BALLOONERY
BALLOONET
BALLOONING
BALLOONIST
BALLOT

BALLOTADE
BALLOTAGE
BALLOTE
BALLOTED
BALLOTER
BALLOTING
BALLOTTEMENT
BALLOW
BALLPLAYER
BALLPROOF
BALLROOM
BALLS
BALLUP
BALLWEED
BALLY
BALLYHACK
BALLYHOO
BALLYHOOED
BALLYHOOER
BALLYHOOING
BALLYRAG
BALLYWACK
BALLYWRACK
BALM
BALMACAAN
BALMIER
BALMIEST
BALMILY
BALMINESS
BALMONIES
BALMONY
BALMORAL
BALMY
BALNEA
BALNEAE
BALNEAL
BALNEARY
BALNEATION
BALNEATORY
BALNEOGRAPHY
BALNEOLOGIC
BALNEOLOGY
BALNEUM
BALO
BALON
BALONEY
BALOO
BALOP
BALOTADE
BALOW
BALSA
BALSAM
BALSAMIC
BALSAMICAL
BALSAMICALLY
BALSAMINE
BALSAMITIC
BALSAMIZE
BALSAMO
BALSAMOUS
BALSAMROOT
BALSAMWEED
BALSAMY
BALSAS
BALTEI
BALTER
BALTEUS
BALTHEUS
BALTIMORITE
BALU
BALUSHAI
BALUSTER
BALUSTERED
BALUSTRADE
BALUSTRADED
BALUT
BALWARRA

BALZARINE
BAM
BAMAH
BAMBA
BAMBAN
BAMBINI
BAMBINO
BAMBINOS
BAMBOCCIADE
BAMBOCHE
BAMBOO
BAMBOOZLE
BAMBOOZLED
BAMBOOZLEMENT
BAMBOOZLER
BAMBOOZLING
BAMBOULA
BAMBUCO
BAMBUK
BAMIA
BAN
BANABA
BANAGO
BANAGOS
BANAK
BANAKITE
BANAL
BANALITIES
BANALITY
BANALLY
BANANA
BANANAS
BANANIST
BANANIVOROUS
BANAT
BANATE
BANATITE
BANAUSIC
BANC
BANCA
BANCAL
BANCALES
BANCHA
BANCO
BANCOS
BANCUS
BAND
BANDAGE
BANDAGED
BANDAGER
BANDAGING
BANDAGIST
BANDAITE
BANDAKA
BANDALA
BANDALORE
BANDANA
BANDANNA
BANDANNAED
BANDAR
BANDARLOG
BANDBOX
BANDBOXICAL
BANDBOXY
BANDCUTTER
BANDE
BANDEAU
BANDEAUX
BANDED
BANDELET
BANDELETTE
BANDENG
BANDER
BANDERILLA
BANDERILLAS
BANDERILLERO
BANDERILLEROS

BANDERLOG
BANDEROL
BANDEROLE
BANDEROLED
BANDEROLING
BANDERSNATCH
BANDFISH
BANDHAVA
BANDHOOK
BANDHU
BANDI
BANDICOOT
BANDICOY
BANDIDO
BANDIDOS
BANDIE
BANDIED
BANDIES
BANDIKAI
BANDING
BANDIT
BANDITRY
BANDITS
BANDITTI
BANDLE
BANDLEADER
BANDMAN
BANDMASTER
BANDO
BANDOG
BANDOLEER
BANDOLEERED
BANDOLERISMO
BANDOLERO
BANDOLEROS
BANDOLIER
BANDOLINE
BANDON
BANDONION
BANDORE
BANDOS
BANDS
BANDSMAN
BANDSMEN
BANDSTAND
BANDSTER
BANDSTRING
BANDURA
BANDURRIA
BANDURRIAS
BANDWAGON
BANDWORK
BANDWORM
BANDY
BANDYBALL
BANDYING
BANDYMAN
BANE
BANEBERRIES
BANEBERRY
BANED
BANEFUL
BANEFULLY
BANEFULNESS
BANEWORT
BANG
BANGA
BANGALAY
BANGALOW
BANGE
BANGER
BANGHY
BANGIACEOUS
BANGING
BANGKOK
BANGLE
BANGLED

BANGLING
BANGO
BANGOS
BANGS
BANGSTER
BANGTAIL
BANGTAILED
BANGY
BANI
BANIA
BANIAN
BANIG
BANILAD
BANING
BANISH
BANISHED
BANISHER
BANISHMENT
BANISTER
BANISTERINE
BANIYA
BANJARA
BANJO
BANJOES
BANJORE
BANJORINE
BANJOS
BANK
BANKABLE
BANKBOOK
BANKED
BANKER
BANKERA
BANKET
BANKFULL
BANKING
BANKMAN
BANKMEN
BANKRIDER
BANKROLL
BANKRUPT
BANKRUPTCIES
BANKRUPTCY
BANKRUPTISM
BANKRUPTLY
BANKRUPTURE
BANKS
BANKSHALL
BANKSIA
BANKSIDE
BANKSMAN
BANKSMEN
BANKWEED
BANKY
BANLIEU
BANLIEUE
BANNACK
BANNAT
BANNED
BANNER
BANNERED
BANNERER
BANNERET
BANNERETTE
BANNERFISH
BANNERMAN
BANNERMEN
BANNEROL
BANNEROLE
BANNET
BANNIMUS
BANNING
BANNISTER
BANNOCK
BANNS
BANNUT
BANOVINA

BANQUE
BANQUET
BANQUETED
BANQUETEER
BANQUETEERING
BANQUETER
BANQUETING
BANQUETTE
BANS
BANSALAGUE
BANSHEE
BANSHIE
BANSTICKLE
BANT
BANTAM
BANTAMIZE
BANTAMWEIGHT
BANTAY
BANTAYAN
BANTENG
BANTER
BANTERED
BANTERER
BANTERING
BANTERINGLY
BANTERY
BANTIN
BANTING
BANTINGIZE
BANTLING
BANTU
BANTY
BANUS
BANUYO
BANXRING
BANYA
BANYAN
BANZAI
BAOBAB
BAP
BAPISTERY
BAPTISIN
BAPTISM
BAPTISMAL
BAPTISMALLY
BAPTISTERIES
BAPTISTERY
BAPTISTIC
BAPTISTRIES
BAPTISTRY
BAPTIZE
BAPTIZED
BAPTIZEE
BAPTIZEMENT
BAPTIZER
BAPTIZING
BAPU
BAR
BARABARA
BARABORA
BARAD
BARADARI
BARAGNOSIS
BARAGOUIN
BARAITA
BARAJILLO
BARAMIN
BARANDOS
BARANGAY
BARANI
BARARITE
BARASINGHA
BARAT
BARATHEA
BARATHRA
BARATHRON
BARATHRUM

BARATO
BARATTE
BARB
BARBACOU
BARBAL
BARBARESQUE
BARBARIAN
BARBARIC
BARBARICAL
BARBARICALLY
BARBARIOUS
BARBARISM
BARBARITIES
BARBARITY
BARBARIZE
BARBARIZED
BARBARIZING
BARBAROUS
BARBAROUSLY
BARBARY
BARBAS
BARBASCO
BARBASTEL
BARBASTELLE
BARBATE
BARBATED
BARBATIMAO
BARBE
BARBEAU
BARBECUE
BARBECUED
BARBECUING
BARBED
BARBEIRO
BARBEL
BARBELL
BARBELLATE
BARBELLULA
BARBELLULAE
BARBELLULATE
BARBEQUE
BARBER
BARBERA
BARBERMONGER
BARBERO
BARBERRIES
BARBERRY
BARBERSHOP
BARBERY
BARBET
BARBETTE
BARBICAN
BARBICEL
BARBIGEROUS
BARBING
BARBION
BARBITA
BARBITAL
BARBITALISM
BARBITON
BARBITONE
BARBITURATE
BARBITURIC
BARBLESS
BARBLET
BARBOLA
BARBONE
BARBOTINE
BARBOTTE
BARBOY
BARBUDO
BARBUDOS
BARBULA
BARBULATE
BARBULE
BARBULYIE
BARBWIRE

BARCA
BARCAROLE
BARCAROLLE
BARCAS
BARCELLA
BARCELONA
BARCELONAS
BARCHAN
BARCHE
BARCOLONGO
BARD
BARDANE
BARDASH
BARDE
BARDEE
BARDEL
BARDELLE
BARDESS
BARDIC
BARDIE
BARDIGLIO
BARDILY
BARDINESS
BARDING
BARDINGS
BARDISH
BARDISM
BARDLET
BARDLING
BARDO
BARDS
BARDY
BARE
BAREBACK
BAREBACKED
BAREBONE
BARECA
BARED
BAREFACED
BAREFACEDLY
BAREFIT
BAREFOOT
BAREFOOTED
BAREGE
BAREHANDED
BAREHEAD
BAREHEADED
BAREKA
BARELEGGED
BARELY
BARENECKED
BARER
BARES
BARESARK
BARESMA
BARETTA
BARFF
BARFISH
BARFLIES
BARFLY
BARFUL
BARGAIN
BARGAINEE
BARGAINER
BARGAINING
BARGAINOR
BARGE
BARGEBOARD
BARGED
BARGEE
BARGEER
BARGEESE
BARGEHOUSE
BARGELIKE
BARGELLI
BARGELLO
BARGELOAD

BARGEMAN
BARGEMASTER
BARGEMEN
BARGER
BARGH
BARGHAM
BARGHEST
BARGING
BARGIR
BARGOOSE
BARHAL
BARHOP
BARI
BARIA
BARIC
BARID
BARIE
BARIL
BARILLA
BARIN
BARING
BARIOLAGE
BARIS
BARISH
BARIT
BARITE
BARITONE
BARIUM
BARK
BARKAN
BARKARY
BARKBOUND
BARKEEP
BARKEEPER
BARKEN
BARKENED
BARKENING
BARKENTINE
BARKER
BARKERY
BARKEVIKITE
BARKEVIKITIC
BARKEY
BARKHAN
BARKIER
BARKIEST
BARKING
BARKINGLY
BARKLE
BARKLYITE
BARKOMETER
BARKPEEL
BARKPEELER
BARKPEELING
BARKS
BARKSOME
BARKSTONE
BARKY
BARLA
BARLEY
BARLEYBIRD
BARLEYBRAKE
BARLEYBREAK
BARLEYCORN
BARLEYHOOD
BARLEYMOW
BARLEYSICK
BARLING
BARLOW
BARLY
BARM
BARMAID
BARMAN
BARMASTER
BARMBRACK
BARMCLOTH
BARMEN

BARMFEL
BARMIE
BARMIER
BARMIEST
BARMKIN
BARMOTE
BARMSKIN
BARMY
BARMYBRAINED
BARN
BARNACLE
BARNACLED
BARNACLING
BARNARD
BARNEY
BARNHARDTITE
BARNMAN
BARNMEN
BARNS
BARNSTORM
BARNSTORMER
BARNSTORMING
BARNY
BARNYARD
BARO
BAROCCO
BAROGNOSIS
BAROGRAM
BAROGRAPH
BAROGRAPHIC
BAROI
BAROLO
BAROLOGY
BAROMETER
BAROMETRIC
BAROMETRICAL
BAROMETRY
BAROMETZ
BAROMOTOR
BARON
BARONAGE
BARONESS
BARONET
BARONETAGE
BARONETCIES
BARONETCY
BARONETED
BARONETICAL
BARONETING
BARONG
BARONI
BARONIAL
BARONIES
BARONNE
BARONRIES
BARONRY
BARONY
BAROQUE
BAROSCOPE
BAROSCOPIC
BAROSCOPICAL
BAROSMIN
BAROSTAT
BAROTACTIC
BAROTAXIS
BAROTAXY
BAROTO
BAROUCHE
BAROUCHET
BAROUCHETTE
BAROXYTON
BARPOST
BARQUE
BARQUENTINE
BARQUEST
BARR
BARRA

BARRABLE	BARRIO	BASE	BASILICAL	BASSIST
BARRABORA	BARRIOS	BASEBALL	BASILICAN	BASSO
BARRACAN	BARRISTER	BASEBALLER	BASILICAS	BASSON
BARRACE	BARRISTERIAL	BASEBOARD	BASILICON	BASSOON
BARRACK	BARRISTRESS	BASEBORN	BASILINNA	BASSOONIST
BARRACKER	BARROOM	BASEBRED	BASILISCAN	BASSORIN
BARRACKS	BARROW	BASEBURNER	BASILISCINE	BASSOS
BARRACLADE	BARROWCOAT	BASED	BASILISK	BASSUS
BARRACOON	BARROWMAN	BASELARD	BASILISSA	BASSWOOD
BARRACOUTA	BARRULET	BASELESS	BASILWEED	BAST
BARRACOUTAS	BARRULY	BASELESSLY	BASILYSIS	BASTA
BARRACUDA	BARRY	BASELESSNESS	BASILYST	BASTANT
BARRACUDAS	BARS	BASELINER	BASIN	BASTARD
BARRAD	BARSE	BASELLACEOUS	BASINASAL	BASTARDA
BARRAGAN	BARSOM	BASELY	BASINASIAL	BASTARDISM
BARRAGE	BARSPOON	BASEMAN	BASINED	BASTARDIZE
BARRAGED	BARSTOOL	BASEMEN	BASINET	BASTARDIZED
BARRAGING	BARTENDER	BASEMENT	BASING	BASTARDIZING
BARRAGON	BARTENDING	BASENESS	BASION	BASTARDLY
BARRAMUNDA	BARTER	BASENJI	BASIOPHITIC	BASTARDY
BARRAMUNDAS	BARTERED	BASEPLUG	BASIOTRIBE	BASTE
BARRAMUNDI	BARTERER	BASER	BASIOTRIPSY	BASTED
BARRAMUNDIES	BARTERING	BASES	BASIPETAL	BASTEN
BARRAMUNDIS	BARTH	BASEST	BASIPHOBIA	BASTER
BARRANCA	BARTHITE	BASH	BASIPODITE	BASTIDE
BARRANCO	BARTHOLINITIS	BASHA	BASIPODITIC	BASTILE
BARRANDITE	BARTIZAN	BASHAW	BASIRADIAL	BASTILLE
BARRAS	BARTIZANED	BASHED	BASIRHINAL	BASTINADE
BARRAT	BARTON	BASHER	BASIROSTRAL	BASTINADO
BARRATER	BARTREE	BASHFUL	BASIS	BASTINADOED
BARRATOR	BARU	BASHFULLY	BASISCOPIC	BASTINADOES
BARRATRIES	BARUKHZY	BASHFULNESS	BASISPHENOID	BASTINADOING
BARRATROUS	BARURIA	BASHING	BASITEMPORAL	BASTING
BARRATROUSLY	BARVEL	BASHLESS	BASIVENTRAL	BASTION
BARRATRY	BARVELL	BASHLIK	BASK	BASTIONARY
BARRE	BARWAY	BASHLYK	BASKER	BASTIONED
BARRED	BARWAYS	BASI	BASKET	BASTIONET
BARREL	BARWIN	BASIAL	BASKETBALL	BASTITE
BARRELAGE	BARWING	BASIATE	BASKETBALLER	BASTNASITE
BARRELED	BARWISE	BASIATION	BASKETING	BASTO
BARRELER	BARWOOD	BASIC	BASKETMAKER	BASTON
BARRELET	BARYCENTER	BASICALLY	BASKETMAKING	BASTONET
BARRELFUL	BARYCENTRE	BASICITY	BASKETRY	BASURAL
BARRELFULS	BARYCENTRIC	BASICRANIAL	BASKETWARE	BASURALE
BARRELHEAD	BARYE	BASIDIA	BASKETWOMAN	BAT
BARRELHOUSE	BARYECOIA	BASIDIAL	BASKETWOOD	BATA
BARRELING	BARYLITE	BASIDIGITALE	BASKETWORK	BATAAN
BARRELLED	BARYON	BASIDIGITALIA	BASOCYTE	BATAD
BARRELLING	BARYPHONIA	BASIDIOMYCETE	BASON	BATAK
BARRELMAKER	BARYPHONIC	BASIDIOMYCETES	BASOPHIL	BATAKAN
BARRELMAKING	BARYPHONY	BASIDIOPHORE	BASOPHILE	BATALEUR
BARRELS	BARYSILITE	BASIDIOSPORE	BASOPHILIA	BATAMOTE
BARREN	BARYSPHERE	BASIDIUM	BASOPHILIC	BATARA
BARRENER	BARYTA	BASIDORSAL	BASOPHILOUS	BATARDE
BARRENLY	BARYTE	BASIFACIAL	BASOTE	BATARDEAU
BARRENNESS	BARYTES	BASIFICATION	BASOTHO	BATATA
BARRENWORT	BARYTHYMIA	BASIFIED	BASQUE	BATATILLA
BARRER	BARYTIC	BASIFIER	BASQUED	BATCH
BARRERA	BARYTINE	BASIFIXED	BASQUINE	BATCHER
BARRET	BARYTONE	BASIFUGAL	BASS	BATE
BARRETRY	BAS	BASIFY	BASSANELLO	BATEA
BARRETTE	BASAL	BASIFYING	BASSANITE	BATEAU
BARRETTER	BASALE	BASIG	BASSARA	BATEAUX
BARRICADE	BASALIA	BASIGAMOUS	BASSARID	BATED
BARRICADED	BASALLY	BASIGAMY	BASSARISK	BATEFUL
BARRICADER	BASALT	BASIGENIC	BASSES	BATEL
BARRICADING	BASALTES	BASIGENOUS	BASSET	BATELEUR
BARRICO	BASALTIC	BASIHYAL	BASSETED	BATEMAN
BARRICOES	BASALTIFORM	BASIL	BASSETING	BATEMENT
BARRICOS	BASALTINE	BASILAR	BASSETITE	BATER
BARRIER	BASALTOID	BASILARY	BASSETTA	BATES
BARRIERS	BASALTWARE	BASILATERAL	BASSETTE	BATETE
BARRIGUDA	BASAN	BASILEIS	BASSI	BATFISH
BARRIGUDO	BASANITE	BASILEMMA	BASSIE	BATFOWL
BARRIGUDOS	BASAREE	BASILEUS	BASSINE	BATFOWLER
BARRIKIN	BASCULE	BASILIC	BASSINET	BATFOWLING
BARRING	BASCUNAN	BASILICA	BASSING	BATFUL

BATH	BATONIST	BATUKITE	BAYADERE	BEADSWOMAN
BATHE	BATONISTIC	BATULE	BAYAL	BEADWORK
BATHEABLE	BATONNE	BATUQUE	BAYAMO	BEADY
BATHED	BATONNIER	BATWING	BAYAN	BEAGLE
BATHER	BATOPHOBIA	BATYPHONE	BAYANO	BEAGLING
BATHETIC	BATRACHIAN	BATZ	BAYARD	BEAK
BATHFLOWER	BATRACHIATE	BATZEN	BAYARDLY	BEAKED
BATHHOUSE	BATRACHITE	BAUBEE	BAYBERRIES	BEAKER
BATHIC	BATRACHOID	BAUBLE	BAYBERRY	BEAKERMAN
BATHING	BATS	BAUBLERY	BAYBOLT	BEAKERMEN
BATHKOL	BATSMAN	BAUBLING	BAYBUSH	BEAKHEAD
BATHMAN	BATSMANSHIP	BAUCH	BAYED	BEAKIRON
BATHMIC	BATSMEN	BAUCHLE	BAYETA	BEAKLESS
BATHMISM	BATSWING	BAUCKIE	BAYETE	BEAKLIKE
BATHMOTROPIC	BATT	BAUD	BAYGALL	BEAKY
BATHOCHROME	BATTA	BAUDEKIN	BAYLET	BEAL
BATHOCHROMIC	BATTABLE	BAUDERY	BAYMAN	BEALA
BATHOCHROMY	BATTAILOUS	BAUDRONS	BAYMEN	BEALACH
BATHOFLORE	BATTALIA	BAUGH	BAYOG	BEALING
BATHOFLORIC	BATTALION	BAUHINIA	BAYOK	BEALLACH
BATHOLITE	BATTE	BAUK	BAYON	BEAM
BATHOLITH	BATTED	BAUL	BAYONET	BEAMAGE
BATHOLITHIC	BATTEL	BAULEA	BAYONETED	BEAMBIRD
BATHOLITIC	BATTELER	BAULEAH	BAYONETEER	BEAMED
BATHOMANIA	BATTEMENT	BAULK	BAYONETING	BEAMER
BATHOMETER	BATTEN	BAULKY	BAYONG	BEAMFILLING
BATHOPHOBIA	BATTENED	BAUMHAUERITE	BAYOU	BEAMFUL
BATHORSE	BATTENER	BAUMIER	BAYOUS	BEAMHOUSE
BATHOS	BATTENING	BAUNO	BAYWOOD	BEAMIER
BATHQOL	BATTENS	BAUR	BAZAAR	BEAMIEST
BATHROBE	BATTER	BAUSON	BAZAR	BEAMILY
BATHROOM	BATTERCAKE	BAUSOND	BAZE	BEAMINESS
BATHROOMED	BATTERDOCK	BAUTA	BAZOO	BEAMING
BATHROOT	BATTERED	BAUTTA	BAZOOKA	BEAMINGLY
BATHS	BATTERER	BAUXITE	BAZZITE	BEAMISH
BATHTUB	BATTERFANG	BAUXITITE	BB	BEAMLESS
BATHUKOLPIAN	BATTERIE	BAVARDAGE	BDELLID	BEAMLIKE
BATHVILLITE	BATTERIES	BAVAROISE	BDELLIUM	BEAMROOM
BATHWORT	BATTERING	BAVAROY	BDELLOID	BEAMSMAN
BATHYAL	BATTERMAN	BAVARY	BDELLOTOMY	BEAMSMEN
BATHYBIAN	BATTERY	BAVE	BE	BEAMSTER
BATHYBIC	BATTEUSE	BAVENITE	BEACH	BEAMY
BATHYBIUS	BATTIER	BAVETTE	BEACHBOY	BEAN
BATHYCOLPIAN	BATTIES	BAVIAN	BEACHCOMB	BEANBAG
BATHYCOLPIC	BATTIEST	BAVIN	BEACHCOMBER	BEANBAGS
BATHYL	BATTIK	BAVOSO	BEACHCOMBING	BEANBALL
BATHYMETER	BATTING	BAW	BEACHDROPS	BEANCOD
BATHYMETRIC	BATTISH	BAWARCHI	BEACHED	BEANERIES
BATHYMETRY	BATTLE	BAWBEE	BEACHHEAD	BEANERY
BATHYPELAGIC	BATTLED	BAWCOCK	BEACHIER	BEANFEAST
BATHYSCAPH	BATTLEDORE	BAWD	BEACHIEST	BEANFEASTER
BATHYSCAPHE	BATTLEDORED	BAWDIER	BEACHMAN	BEANFIELD
BATHYSEISM	BATTLEDORING	BAWDIEST	BEACHMASTER	BEANIE
BATHYSMAL	BATTLEFIELD	BAWDILY	BEACHMEN	BEANIER
BATHYSPHERE	BATTLEFUL	BAWDINESS	BEACHY	BEANIEST
BATIDACEOUS	BATTLEGROUND	BAWDRIC	BEACON	BEANO
BATIK	BATTLEMENT	BAWDRICK	BEACONAGE	BEANPOLE
BATIKED	BATTLEMENTED	BAWDRY	BEACONED	BEANS
BATIKER	BATTLEPLANE	BAWDSTROT	BEACONING	BEANSETTER
BATIKING	BATTLER	BAWDY	BEAD	BEANSHOOTER
BATIKULIN	BATTLESHIP	BAWDYHOUSE	BEADED	BEANSTALK
BATIKULING	BATTLESTEAD	BAWL	BEADER	BEANWEED
BATING	BATTLEWAGON	BAWLER	BEADFLUSH	BEANY
BATINO	BATTLING	BAWLEY	BEADHOUSE	BEAR
BATISTE	BATTOLOGICAL	BAWLING	BEADIER	BEARABLE
BATITINAN	BATTOLOGIST	BAWLY	BEADIEST	BEARABLENESS
BATLAN	BATTOLOGIZE	BAWN	BEADILY	BEARABLY
BATLER	BATTOLOGY	BAWNEEN	BEADINESS	BEARANCE
BATLET	BATTON	BAWREL	BEADING	BEARBAITER
BATLIKE	BATTS	BAWSUNT	BEADLE	BEARBAITING
BATLING	BATTU	BAWTIE	BEADLEDOM	BEARBANE
BATLON	BATTUE	BAWTY	BEADLERY	BEARBERRIES
BATMAN	BATTURE	BAXA	BEADMAN	BEARBERRY
BATMEN	BATTUTA	BAXTER	BEADROLL	BEARBIND
BATOID	BATTY	BAY	BEADROW	BEARBINE
BATON	BATTYCAKE	BAYA	BEADS	BEARCAT
BATONEER	BATU	BAYADEER	BEADSMAN	BEARCOOT

BEARD
BEARDED
BEARDER
BEARDIE
BEARDING
BEARDLESS
BEARDLIKE
BEARDTONGUE
BEARDY
BEARER
BEARERS
BEARFOOT
BEARFOOTS
BEARHERD
BEARHOUND
BEARING
BEARINGS
BEARISH
BEARISHLY
BEARISHNESS
BEARLET
BEARM
BEARS
BEARSKIN
BEARWARD
BEARWOOD
BEARWORT
BEAST
BEASTIE
BEASTILY
BEASTLIER
BEASTLIEST
BEASTLIKE
BEASTLILY
BEASTLINESS
BEASTLINGS
BEASTLY
BEASTMAN
BEASTS
BEAT
BEATA
BEATAE
BEATEE
BEATEN
BEATER
BEATERMAN
BEATERMEN
BEATH
BEATI
BEATIFIC
BEATIFICAL
BEATIFICALLY
BEATIFICATE
BEATIFIED
BEATIFY
BEATIFYING
BEATILLE
BEATING
BEATITUDE
BEATNIK
BEATSTER
BEATUS
BEAU
BEAUED
BEAUETRY
BEAUFIN
BEAUING
BEAUISH
BEAUISM
BEAUPERE
BEAUS
BEAUSEANT
BEAUT
BEAUTEOUS
BEAUTEOUSLY
BEAUTEOUSNESS
BEAUTICIAN

BEAUTIED
BEAUTIES
BEAUTIFIED
BEAUTIFIER
BEAUTIFUL
BEAUTIFULLY
BEAUTIFY
BEAUTIFYING
BEAUTY
BEAUX
BEAVER
BEAVERBOARD
BEAVERED
BEAVERETTE
BEAVERIES
BEAVERITE
BEAVERIZE
BEAVERKIN
BEAVERPELT
BEAVERROOT
BEAVERTEEN
BEAVERWOOD
BEAVERY
BEBAY
BEBEERIN
BEBEERINE
BEBEERU
BEBILYA
BEBIZATION
BEBLED
BEBOG
BEBOP
BECAFICO
BECALL
BECALM
BECALMED
BECALMING
BECAME
BECARD
BECARVE
BECASSE
BECASSINE
BECAUSE
BECCAFICO
BECCAFICOS
BECCHI
BECCO
BECHAMEL
BECHANCE
BECHANCED
BECHANCING
BECHER
BECK
BECKELITE
BECKER
BECKET
BECKETT
BECKIRON
BECKON
BECKONED
BECKONER
BECKONING
BECKONINGLY
BECLAD
BECLAP
BECLIP
BECLOUD
BECLOUDED
BECLOUT
BECOME
BECOMED
BECOMES
BECOMING
BECOMINGLY
BECON
BECOOM
BECORESH

BECOUSINED
BECQUERELITE
BECREEP
BECROSS
BECRUSH
BECUIBA
BECUNA
BED
BEDA
BEDABBLE
BEDAD
BEDAFF
BEDAGGLE
BEDAMN
BEDANGLED
BEDASH
BEDAUB
BEDAWN
BEDAY
BEDAZE
BEDAZZLE
BEDAZZLED
BEDAZZLING
BEDAZZLINGLY
BEDBUG
BEDCHAIR
BEDCHAMBER
BEDCLOTHES
BEDCORD
BEDCOVER
BEDDED
BEDDER
BEDDING
BEDE
BEDECK
BEDECKED
BEDEEN
BEDEGAR
BEDEGUAR
BEDEHOUSE
BEDEL
BEDELL
BEDELVE
BEDEMAN
BEDEN
BEDENE
BEDESMAN
BEDESMEN
BEDEVIL
BEDEVILED
BEDEVILING
BEDEVILLED
BEDEVILLING
BEDEVILMENT
BEDEW
BEDEWED
BEDEWER
BEDFAST
BEDFELLOW
BEDFLOWER
BEDFRAME
BEDGERY
BEDGOWN
BEDIGHT
BEDIGHTED
BEDIGHTING
BEDIKAH
BEDIM
BEDIMMED
BEDIMMING
BEDIZEN
BEDIZENED
BEDIZENING
BEDIZENMENT
BEDKEY
BEDLAM
BEDLAMER

BEDLAMISM
BEDLAMITE
BEDLAMIZE
BEDLAR
BEDLIDS
BEDMAN
BEDMATE
BEDO
BEDOG
BEDOWN
BEDOYO
BEDPAN
BEDPLATE
BEDPOST
BEDPOSTS
BEDQUILT
BEDRABBLE
BEDRAGGLE
BEDRAGGLED
BEDRAIL
BEDRAL
BEDRAPE
BEDREAD
BEDREL
BEDRESS
BEDRID
BEDRIDDEN
BEDRIGHT
BEDRIP
BEDRITE
BEDROCK
BEDROLL
BEDROOM
BEDROP
BEDS
BEDSIDE
BEDSITE
BEDSORE
BEDSPREAD
BEDSPRING
BEDSTAFF
BEDSTAND
BEDSTAVES
BEDSTEAD
BEDSTOCK
BEDSTRAW
BEDSWERVER
BEDTICK
BEDTIME
BEDU
BEDUB
BEDWARD
BEDWARDS
BEDWARMER
BEDWAY
BEDWELL
BEE
BEEBALL
BEEBEE
BEEBREAD
BEECH
BEECHDROPS
BEECHEN
BEECHES
BEECHNUT
BEECHNUTS
BEECHY
BEEF
BEEFCAKE
BEEFEATER
BEEFHEAD
BEEFHEADED
BEEFIER
BEEFIEST
BEEFILY
BEEFIN

BEEFINESS
BEEFISH
BEEFISHNESS
BEEFLESS
BEEFS
BEEFSTEAK
BEEFTONGUE
BEEFWOOD
BEEFY
BEEGERITE
BEEHEAD
BEEHEADED
BEEHERD
BEEHIVE
BEEHOUSE
BEEK
BEEKEEPER
BEEKEEPING
BEEKITE
BEELE
BEELINE
BEEMAN
BEEMASTER
BEEMEN
BEEN
BEENNUT
BEEP
BEEPER
BEER
BEERAGE
BEERBACHITE
BEERBIBBER
BEEREGAR
BEERHOUSE
BEERIER
BEERIEST
BEERILY
BEERINESS
BEERISH
BEERISHLY
BEERMAKER
BEERMAKING
BEERMONGER
BEEROCRACY
BEERPULL
BEERY
BEES
BEESTING
BEESTINGS
BEESWAX
BEESWING
BEET
BEETE
BEETEWK
BEETH
BEETIEST
BEETLE
BEETLED
BEETLEHEAD
BEETLEHEADED
BEETLER
BEETLESTOCK
BEETLESTONE
BEETLEWEED
BEETLING
BEETMISTER
BEETRAVE
BEETROOT
BEETROOTY
BEETS
BEETY
BEEVE
BEEVES
BEEVISH
BEEWARE
BEEWAY
BEEWEED

BEEWINGED	BEGINNING	BEHEST	BELATEDLY	BELLHANGING
BEEWORT	BEGIRD	BEHEW	BELATEDNESS	BELLHOP
BEEYARD	BEGIRDED	BEHIGHT	BELATING	BELLHOUSE
BEEZER	BEGIRDING	BEHIND	BELAUD	BELLIC
BEFALL	BEGIRT	BEHINDHAND	BELAY	BELLICAL
BEFALLEN	BEGLERBEG	BEHINDSIGHT	BELAYED	BELLICISM
BEFALLING	BEGLERBEGLIC	BEHN	BELAYING	BELLICOSE
BEFELL	BEGLERBEGLIK	BEHOLD	BELCH	BELLICOSELY
BEFFROY	BEGLERBEGLUC	BEHOLDEN	BELCHER	BELLICOSITY
BEFILE	BEGLEW	BEHOLDER	BELDAM	BELLIED
BEFIT	BEGNA	BEHOLDING	BELDAME	BELLIES
BEFITTED	BEGNAW	BEHOOF	BELDER	BELLIFEROUS
BEFITTING	BEGNAWED	BEHOOVE	BELDERROOT	BELLIGERENCE
BEFITTINGLY	BEGNAWN	BEHOOVED	BELDUQUE	BELLIGERENCY
BEFLOUR	BEGO	BEHOOVEFUL	BELE	BELLIGERENT
BEFLUM	BEGOB	BEHOOVEFULLY	BELEAGUER	BELLING
BEFOG	BEGOBS	BEHOOVES	BELEAGUERED	BELLIPOTENT
BEFOGGED	BEGOD	BEHOOVING	BELEAGUERER	BELLITE
BEFOGGING	BEGOHM	BEHOVE	BELEAGUERING	BELLMAKER
BEFOOL	BEGONE	BEHOVED	BELEAVE	BELLMAKING
BEFOOLED	BEGONIA	BEHOVELY	BELEE	BELLMAN
BEFOOLING	BEGONIACEOUS	BEHOVING	BELEED	BELLMASTER
BEFORE	BEGORRA	BEHOWL	BELEFT	BELLMEN
BEFOREHAND	BEGORRY	BEHUNG	BELEMNID	BELLMOUTH
BEFORETIME	BEGOT	BEIGE	BELEMNITE	BELLMOUTHED
BEFORTUNE	BEGOTTEN	BEIGNET	BELEMNITIC	BELLONION
BEFOUL	BEGOWK	BEIN	BELEMNOID	BELLOTA
BEFOULED	BEGRACE	BEING	BELETTER	BELLOTE
BEFOULER	BEGRIME	BEINGS	BELEVE	BELLOW
BEFOULING	BEGRIMED	BEINLY	BELFRIED	BELLOWER
BEFOULMENT	BEGRIMER	BEINNESS	BELFRIES	BELLOWING
BEFRET	BEGRIMING	BEIRA	BELFRY	BELLOWS
BEFRIEND	BEGRIPE	BEISA	BELGA	BELLOWSMAKER
BEFRIENDER	BEGRUDGE	BEJABBERS	BELGARD	BELLOWSMAN
BEFUDDLE	BEGRUDGED	BEJABERS	BELIBEL	BELLPULL
BEFUDDLED	BEGRUDGING	BEJADE	BELIE	BELLS
BEFUDDLEMENT	BEGRUDGINGLY	BEJAN	BELIED	BELLTAIL
BEFUDDLER	BEGRUNTLE	BEJANT	BELIEF	BELLTOPPER
BEFUDDLING	BEGRUTTEN	BEJAPE	BELIEFFUL	BELLUINE
BEG	BEGSTER	BEJEL	BELIEFFULNESS	BELLUM
BEGA	BEGTI	BEJESUS	BELIEFS	BELLWARE
BEGAD	BEGUESS	BEJEWEL	BELIER	BELLWAVER
BEGAN	BEGUILE	BEJEWELED	BELIEVABLE	BELLWEED
BEGANI	BEGUILED	BEJEWELING	BELIEVE	BELLWETHER
BEGAR	BEGUILEMENT	BEJEWELLED	BELIEVED	BELLWIND
BEGARI	BEGUILER	BEJEWELLING	BELIEVER	BELLWINE
BEGARIE	BEGUILING	BEJUCO	BELIEVERS	BELLWOOD
BEGARY	BEGUIN	BEJUGGLE	BELIEVING	BELLWORT
BEGASS	BEGUINE	BEKA	BELIEVINGLY	BELLY
BEGAT	BEGUM	BEKAH	BELIGHT	BELLYACHE
BEGATS	BEGUMMED	BEKEN	BELIKE	BELLYACHED
BEGATTAL	BEGUN	BEKING	BELIKELY	BELLYACHING
BEGEM	BEGUNK	BEKINKINITE	BELIME	BELLYBAND
BEGEMMED	BEHALF	BEKISS	BELITE	BELLYBUTTON
BEGEMMING	BEHALVES	BEKKO	BELITTLE	BELLYER
BEGET	BEHAR	BEKNAVE	BELITTLED	BELLYFISH
BEGETTER	BEHAVE	BEKNIGHT	BELITTLER	BELLYFUL
BEGETTING	BEHAVED	BEKNOW	BELITTLING	BELLYFULS
BEGGAR	BEHAVING	BEKNOWN	BELIVE	BELLYING
BEGGARDOM	BEHAVIOR	BEKRA	BELK	BELLYMAN
BEGGARED	BEHAVIORAL	BEKTI	BELKNAP	BELOEILITE
BEGGARER	BEHAVIORISM	BEL	BELL	BELOID
BEGGARHOOD	BEHAVIORIST	BELA	BELLADONNA	BELOMANCY
BEGGARIES	BEHAVIOUR	BELABOR	BELLARMINE	BELONG
BEGGARING	BEHEAD	BELABOUR	BELLBIND	BELONGED
BEGGARLINESS	BEHEADAL	BELACED	BELLBINDER	BELONGER
BEGGARLY	BEHEADED	BELAGE	BELLBINE	BELONGING
BEGGARMAN	BEHEADER	BELAH	BELLBIRD	BELONGINGS
BEGGARWEED	BEHEADING	BELAM	BELLBOY	BELONID
BEGGARWOMAN	BEHEAR	BELAMOUR	BELLE	BELONITE
BEGGARY	BEHEARS	BELAMY	BELLED	BELONOID
BEGGED	BEHEIRA	BELANDA	BELLEEK	BELOOK
BEGGER	BEHELD	BELANDER	BELLERIC	BELORD
BEGGING	BEHEMOTH	BELAR	BELLETER	BELOTTE
BEGILD	BEHEN	BELAST	BELLETRIST	BELOUKE
BEGIN	BEHENATE	BELATE	BELLETRISTIC	BELOVE
BEGINNER	BEHENIC	BELATED	BELLFLOWER	BELOVED

BELOW
BELOWSTAIRS
BELSIRE
BELT
BELTED
BELTER
BELTIE
BELTING
BELTMAKER
BELTMAKING
BELTMAN
BELTMEN
BELTON
BELTWAY
BELUE
BELUGA
BELUGITE
BELUTE
BELVE
BELVEDERE
BELVEDERED
BELY
BELYING
BELZEBUTH
BEMA
BEMASTER
BEMATA
BEMAUL
BEMAZED
BEME
BEMEAN
BEMEET
BEMENTITE
BEMETE
BEMIRE
BEMIRED
BEMIREMENT
BEMIRING
BEMIST
BEMOAN
BEMOANABLE
BEMOANER
BEMOCK
BEMOIL
BEMOL
BEMOON
BEMOURN
BEMOUTH
BEMUD
BEMUDDLE
BEMUDDLEMENT
BEMUSE
BEMUSED
BEMUSEDLY
BEMUSING
BEN
BENA
BENAB
BENADRYL
BENAME
BENAMED
BENAMEE
BENAMI
BENAMIDAR
BENAMING
BENASTY
BENBEN
BENCH
BENCHBOARD
BENCHER
BENCHES
BENCHFELLOW
BENCHING
BENCHLAND
BENCHMAN
BENCHMEN
BENCHWORK

BEND
BENDA
BENDAY
BENDED
BENDEE
BENDEL
BENDER
BENDERS
BENDING
BENDS
BENDSOME
BENDWAYS
BENDWISE
BENDY
BENE
BENEATH
BENECEPTION
BENECEPTIVE
BENECEPTOR
BENEDICITE
BENEDICK
BENEDICT
BENEDICTION
BENEDICTIVE
BENEDICTORY
BENEDIGHT
BENEFACTION
BENEFACTIVE
BENEFACTOR
BENEFACTORY
BENEFACTRESS
BENEFIC
BENEFICE
BENEFICED
BENEFICENCE
BENEFICENT
BENEFICENTLY
BENEFICIAIRE
BENEFICIAL
BENEFICIALLY
BENEFICIARIES
BENEFICIARY
BENEFICIATE
BENEFICING
BENEFICIUM
BENEFIT
BENEFITED
BENEFITER
BENEFITING
BENEGRO
BENEMPT
BENEMPTED
BENEPLACIT
BENEPLACITO
BENEPLACITY
BENET
BENETTED
BENETTING
BENEVOLENCE
BENEVOLENT
BENEVOLENTLY
BENEVOLIST
BENG
BENGALINE
BENIGHT
BENIGHTED
BENIGHTEDNESS
BENIGHTEN
BENIGHTER
BENIGHTING
BENIGN
BENIGNANCY
BENIGNANT
BENIGNANTLY
BENIGNITIES
BENIGNITY
BENIGNLY

BENISEED
BENISON
BENITIER
BENITOITE
BENJ
BENJAMIN
BENJAMINITE
BENJOIN
BENJY
BENK
BENMOST
BENN
BENNE
BENNEL
BENNET
BENNETWEED
BENNI
BENNIES
BENNISEED
BENNY
BENORTH
BENOTE
BENSAIL
BENSALL
BENSEL
BENSELL
BENSH
BENSIL
BENT
BENTANG
BENTHAL
BENTHIC
BENTHON
BENTHONIC
BENTHOS
BENTING
BENTLET
BENTONITE
BENTSTAR
BENTWOOD
BENTY
BENUMB
BENUMBED
BENUMBEDNESS
BENUMBING
BENUMBINGLY
BENUMBMENT
BENVENUTO
BENWARD
BENWEED
BENZAL
BENZALDEHYDE
BENZALDOXIME
BENZAMIDE
BENZAMIDO
BENZEDRINE
BENZEIN
BENZENE
BENZENOID
BENZENYL
BENZIDIN
BENZIDINE
BENZIDINO
BENZIL
BENZILIC
BENZIN
BENZINDULINE
BENZINE
BENZOATE
BENZOATED
BENZOBIS
BENZOCAINE
BENZOHYDROL
BENZOIC
BENZOIN
BENZOINATED
BENZOL

BENZOLATE
BENZOLE
BENZOLINE
BENZOLIZE
BENZONITRILE
BENZONITROL
BENZOPHENONE
BENZOPYRAN
BENZOXY
BENZOYL
BENZOYLATE
BENZOYLATION
BENZYL
BENZYLAMINE
BENZYLIC
BEO
BEPAINT
BEPAPER
BEPART
BEPRANKED
BEPRESS
BEPROSE
BEPUFFED
BEQAA
BEQUEATH
BEQUEATHAL
BEQUEATHER
BEQUEST
BEQUIRTLE
BER
BERAIN
BERAIROU
BERAKAH
BERAKOT
BERAKOTH
BERAT
BERATE
BERATED
BERATING
BERATTLE
BERAUNITE
BERAY
BERBAMINE
BERBE
BERBERID
BERBERIN
BERBERINE
BERBERRY
BERBERY
BERCEAU
BERCEUSE
BERCEUSES
BERDACHE
BERE
BEREAVE
BEREAVED
BEREAVEMENT
BEREAVEN
BEREAVER
BEREAVING
BEREDE
BEREFT
BERENDO
BERENGELITE
BERENGENA
BERESITE
BERG
BERGALITH
BERGAMIOL
BERGAMOT
BERGAPTENE
BERGER
BERGERE
BERGERETTE
BERGGYLT
BERGHAAN
BERGINIZATION

BERGINIZE
BERGSCHRUND
BERGUT
BERGY
BERGYLT
BERHYME
BERHYMED
BERHYMING
BERIBERI
BERIBERIC
BERIGORA
BERIME
BERIMED
BERIMING
BERINGITE
BERITH
BERKELIUM
BERLEY
BERLIN
BERLINE
BERLINITE
BERLOQUE
BERM
BERME
BERMUDITE
BERNICLE
BEROK
BERRENDO
BERRETTA
BERRETTINO
BERRI
BERRICHON
BERRICHONNE
BERRIED
BERRIES
BERRIGAN
BERRUGATE
BERRY
BERRYING
BERRYLIKE
BERSEEM
BERSERK
BERSERKER
BERSIM
BERTH
BERTHA
BERTHAGE
BERTHED
BERTHER
BERTHIERITE
BERTHING
BERTHS
BERTRANDITE
BERTRUM
BERUN
BERVIE
BERWICK
BERYCID
BERYCIFORM
BERYCINE
BERYCOID
BERYCOIDEAN
BERYL
BERYLLATE
BERYLLIA
BERYLLINE
BERYLLIUM
BERYLLOID
BERYLLONITE
BERYX
BERZELIANITE
BERZELIITE
BES
BESA
BESAGNE
BESAGUE
BESAIEL

BESAILE
BESAN
BESANT
BESAYLE
BESCREEN
BESEE
BESEECH
BESEECHED
BESEECHER
BESEECHING
BESEECHINGLY
BESEEM
BESEEMED
BESEEMING
BESEEMINGLY
BESEEMLINESS
BESEEMLY
BESEEN
BESEIGE
BESET
BESETMENT
BESETTER
BESETTING
BESHADE
BESHAG
BESHEAR
BESHINE
BESHLIK
BESHOW
BESHREW
BESICLOMETER
BESIDE
BESIDES
BESIEGE
BESIEGED
BESIEGEMENT
BESIEGER
BESIEGING
BESIEGINGLY
BESIN
BESING
BESIT
BESLAB
BESLAVER
BESLIME
BESLUBBER
BESLUIT
BESMEAR
BESMEARER
BESMIRCH
BESMIRCHER
BESMIRCHMENT
BESMOKE
BESMOTTERED
BESMUT
BESMUTTED
BESMUTTING
BESNOW
BESOIN
BESOM
BESOMER
BESOOTHE
BESOOTHEMENT
BESORT
BESOT
BESOTTED
BESOTTEDLY
BESOTTEDNESS
BESOTTING
BESOTTINGLY
BESOUGHT
BESPAKE
BESPANGLE
BESPANGLED
BESPANGLING
BESPATTER
BESPATTERED

BESPATTERER
BESPATTERING
BESPAWL
BESPEAK
BESPEAKER
BESPEAKING
BESPECKLE
BESPECTACLED
BESPELL
BESPETE
BESPIT
BESPOKE
BESPOKEN
BESPOT
BESPOTTED
BESPOTTING
BESPREAD
BESPREADING
BESPRENT
BESPRING
BESPRINKLE
BESPRINKLED
BESPRINKLER
BESPRINKLING
BESPRIZORNI
BESQUIRT
BESRA
BESSEMER
BESSEMERIZE
BESSEMERIZED
BESSEMERIZING
BESSES
BEST
BESTAIN
BESTAND
BESTEAD
BESTEAL
BESTED
BESTEER
BESTER
BESTIAL
BESTIALITIES
BESTIALITY
BESTIALIZE
BESTIALIZED
BESTIALIZING
BESTIALLY
BESTIALS
BESTIARIAN
BESTIARIES
BESTIARY
BESTICK
BESTICKING
BESTILL
BESTIR
BESTIRRED
BESTIRRING
BESTORM
BESTOW
BESTOWABLE
BESTOWAGE
BESTOWAL
BESTOWED
BESTOWER
BESTOWING
BESTOWMENT
BESTRADDLE
BESTRADDLED
BESTRADDLING
BESTRAUGHT
BESTREW
BESTREWED
BESTREWING
BESTREWN
BESTRID
BESTRIDDEN
BESTRIDE

BESTRIDING
BESTRODE
BESTRUT
BESTUCK
BESUGO
BESWINK
BET
BETA
BETACISM
BETACISMUS
BETAFITE
BETAINE
BETAINOGEN
BETAKE
BETAKEN
BETAKING
BETANAPHTHOL
BETEELA
BETEEM
BETEL
BETELNUT
BETERSCHAP
BETH
BETHABARA
BETHANKIT
BETHEL
BETHFLOWER
BETHINK
BETHINKING
BETHOUGHT
BETHROOT
BETHUMB
BETHUMP
BETHWACK
BETHYLID
BETID
BETIDE
BETIDED
BETIDING
BETIME
BETIMES
BETIS
BETISE
BETITLE
BETLE
BETOIL
BETOKEN
BETOKENED
BETOKENER
BETOKENING
BETON
BETONE
BETONGUE
BETONICA
BETONIES
BETONY
BETOOK
BETOSS
BETRAP
BETRAY
BETRAYAL
BETRAYED
BETRAYER
BETRAYING
BETRAYMENT
BETREND
BETRIM
BETROTH
BETROTHAL
BETROTHED
BETROTHING
BETROTHMENT
BETRUNK
BETRUST
BETS
BETSO
BETTED

BETTER
BETTERED
BETTERER
BETTERGATES
BETTERING
BETTERLY
BETTERMENT
BETTERMOST
BETTERNESS
BETTIES
BETTONG
BETTONGA
BETTOR
BETTY
BETULACEOUS
BETULIN
BETULINIC
BETULINOL
BETWEEN
BETWEENBRAIN
BETWEENITY
BETWEENMAID
BETWIXEN
BETWIXT
BEUDANITE
BEURRE
BEVARING
BEVATRON
BEVEL
BEVELED
BEVELER
BEVELING
BEVELLED
BEVELLER
BEVELLING
BEVER
BEVERAGE
BEVIES
BEVIL
BEVUE
BEVY
BEW
BEWAIL
BEWAILER
BEWAILING
BEWAILINGLY
BEWAKE
BEWARE
BEWARED
BEWARING
BEWED
BEWEEP
BEWEEPER
BEWEEPING
BEWEND
BEWEPT
BEWEST
BEWET
BEWHORE
BEWILDER
BEWILDERED
BEWILDEREDLY
BEWILDERING
BEWILDERMENT
BEWIT
BEWITCH
BEWITCHED
BEWITCHER
BEWITCHERY
BEWITCHING
BEWITCHINGLY
BEWITCHMENT
BEWITH
BEWONDER
BEWORK
BEWPERS
BEWRAP

BEWRAY
BEWRAYED
BEWRAYER
BEWRAYING
BEWRAYMENT
BEWREAK
BEY
BEYERITE
BEYLIC
BEYLICAL
BEYLIK
BEYOND
BEYRICHITE
BEZANT
BEZANTE
BEZANTEE
BEZANTY
BEZEL
BEZESTEEN
BEZETTA
BEZETTE
BEZIL
BEZIQUE
BEZOAR
BEZOARDIC
BEZONIAN
BEZZANT
BEZZLE
BEZZLED
BEZZLING
BEZZO
BHAGAT
BHAGAVAT
BHAGAVATA
BHAI
BHAIACHARA
BHAIYACHARA
BHAKTA
BHAKTI
BHALU
BHANDAR
BHANDARI
BHANG
BHANGI
BHARAL
BHARTI
BHAT
BHAVA
BHEESTIE
BHEESTY
BHIKSHU
BHISTI
BHISTIE
BHOKRA
BHOOSA
BHOY
BHUMIDAR
BHUNDER
BHUNGI
BHUNGINI
BHUSA
BHUT
BIABO
BIACETYL
BIACETYLENE
BIACUMINATE
BIACURU
BIAJAIBA
BIALATE
BIALLYL
BIALVEOLAR
BIALY
BIALYS
BIANCHITE
BIANCO
BIANGULAR
BIANGULATE

BIANGULATED
BIANGULOUS
BIANISIDINE
BIANNUAL
BIANNUALLY
BIARCHY
BIARCUATE
BIARCUATED
BIARTICULAR
BIARTICULATE
BIAS
BIASED
BIASES
BIASING
BIASSED
BIASSING
BIASTERIC
BIASWISE
BIATOMIC
BIAURICULAR
BIAURICULATE
BIAXAL
BIAXIAL
BIAXIALITY
BIAXIALLY
BIB
BIBACIOUS
BIBACITY
BIBASIC
BIBATION
BIBB
BIBBED
BIBBER
BIBBING
BIBBLE
BIBBLED
BIBBLER
BIBBLING
BIBBONS
BIBBY
BIBCOCK
BIBELOT
BIBENZYL
BIBERON
BIBI
BIBIONID
BIBIRI
BIBIRU
BIBITORY
BIBLE
BIBLICAL
BIBLIOCLASM
BIBLIOCLAST
BIBLIOFILM
BIBLIOGNOST
BIBLIOGONY
BIBLIOGRAPH
BIBLIOGRAPHIES
BIBLIOGRAPHY
BIBLIOKLEPT
BIBLIOLATER
BIBLIOLATRY
BIBLIOLOGIST
BIBLIOLOGY
BIBLIOMANCY
BIBLIOMANE
BIBLIOMANIA
BIBLIOMANIAC
BIBLIOMANIAN
BIBLIOPEGIC
BIBLIOPEGIST
BIBLIOPEGY
BIBLIOPHAGIC
BIBLIOPHIL
BIBLIOPHILE
BIBLIOPHILIC
BIBLIOPHOBIA

BIBLIOPOLAR
BIBLIOPOLE
BIBLIOPOLERY
BIBLIOPOLIC
BIBLIOPOLISM
BIBLIOPOLIST
BIBLIOPOLY
BIBLIOSOPH
BIBLIOTAPHIC
BIBLIOTHEC
BIBLIOTHECA
BIBLIOTHECAL
BIBLIOTHEKE
BIBLIOTHETIC
BIBLOS
BIBLUS
BIBULOSITY
BIBULOUS
BIBULOUSLY
BIBULOUSNESS
BICALCARATE
BICALVOUS
BICAMERAL
BICAMERIST
BICAPITATE
BICAPSULAR
BICARB
BICARBONATE
BICARBURETED
BICARBURETTED
BICARINATE
BICARPELLARY
BICARPELLATE
BICAUDAL
BICAUDATE
BICCHED
BICE
BICELLULAR
BICENTENARY
BICENTENNIAL
BICEPHALIC
BICEPHALOUS
BICEPS
BICEPSES
BICHLORIDE
BICHO
BICHORD
BICHOS
BICHROMATE
BICHROMATIC
BICHROME
BICHROMIC
BICHY
BICILIATE
BICILIATED
BICIPITAL
BICIPITOUS
BICIRCULAR
BICK
BICKER
BICKERED
BICKERER
BICKERING
BICKERN
BICKIRON
BICLINIA
BICLINIUM
BICOLLATERAL
BICOLLIGATE
BICOLOR
BICOLORED
BICOLOROUS
BICOLOUR
BICOLOURED
BICOLOUROUS
BICONCAVE
BICONCAVITY

BICONE
BICONIC
BICONICAL
BICONICALLY
BICONJUGATE
BICONVEX
BICORN
BICORNE
BICORNED
BICORNUATE
BICORNUOUS
BICORPORAL
BICORPORATE
BICORPOREAL
BICOSTATE
BICRENATE
BICROFARAD
BICRON
BICRURAL
BICULTURAL
BICURSAL
BICUSPID
BICUSPIDAL
BICUSPIDATE
BICYANIDE
BICYCLE
BICYCLED
BICYCLER
BICYCLIC
BICYCLICAL
BICYCLING
BICYCLISM
BICYCLIST
BICYCLO
BICYCULAR
BID
BIDAR
BIDARKA
BIDARKEE
BIDCOCK
BIDDABLE
BIDDABLENESS
BIDDABLY
BIDDANCE
BIDDEN
BIDDER
BIDDERY
BIDDIE
BIDDIES
BIDDING
BIDDY
BIDE
BIDED
BIDENE
BIDENT
BIDENTAL
BIDENTALIA
BIDENTATE
BIDER
BIDERY
BIDET
BIDI
BIDIGITATE
BIDING
BIDREE
BIDRI
BIDRY
BIDSTAND
BIDUOUS
BIEBERITE
BIEL
BIELBY
BIELD
BIELDY
BIELENITE
BIEN
BIENLY

BIENNE
BIENNESS
BIENNIA
BIENNIAL
BIENNIALLY
BIENNIUM
BIENSEANCE
BIENVENU
BIER
BIESTINGS
BIETLE
BIFACE
BIFACIAL
BIFANGED
BIFARA
BIFARIOUS
BIFARIOUSLY
BIFER
BIFEROUS
BIFF
BIFFIN
BIFFY
BIFID
BIFIDATE
BIFIDATED
BIFIDITY
BIFIDLY
BIFILAR
BIFILARLY
BIFISTULAR
BIFLABELLATE
BIFLAGELATE
BIFLECNODE
BIFLECTED
BIFLEX
BIFLORATE
BIFLOROUS
BIFLUORID
BIFLUORIDE
BIFOCAL
BIFOCALS
BIFOLD
BIFOLIA
BIFOLIATE
BIFOLIOLATE
BIFOLIUM
BIFOLLICULAR
BIFORATE
BIFORIN
BIFORINE
BIFORKED
BIFORM
BIFORMED
BIFORMITY
BIFRONT
BIFRONTAL
BIFRONTED
BIFURCAL
BIFURCATE
BIFURCATED
BIFURCATELY
BIFURCATING
BIFURCATION
BIFURCOUS
BIG
BIGA
BIGAMIC
BIGAMIST
BIGAMISTIC
BIGAMIZE
BIGAMOUS
BIGAMOUSLY
BIGAMY
BIGAN
BIGARADE
BIGAROON
BIGARREAU

BIGAS
BIGATE
BIGBLOOM
BIGBURY
BIGEMINAL
BIGEMINATE
BIGEMINATED
BIGENER
BIGENERIC
BIGENTIAL
BIGEYE
BIGG
BIGGED
BIGGEN
BIGGENED
BIGGENING
BIGGER
BIGGEST
BIGGETY
BIGGIE
BIGGIN
BIGGING
BIGGISH
BIGGITY
BIGGONET
BIGHA
BIGHEAD
BIGHEARTED
BIGHORN
BIGHORNS
BIGHT
BIGHTED
BIGHTING
BIGHTS
BIGLY
BIGMITT
BIGMOUTH
BIGMOUTHED
BIGNESS
BIGNONIA
BIGNONIAD
BIGNOU
BIGONIAC
BIGONIAL
BIGOT
BIGOTED
BIGOTEDLY
BIGOTHERO
BIGOTRIES
BIGOTRY
BIGOTTY
BIGRAM
BIGROOT
BIGTHATCH
BIGUANIDE
BIGUTTATE
BIGUTTULATE
BIGWIG
BIGWIGGED
BIGWIGGERY
BIGWIGGISM
BIHOURLY
BIJA
BIJASAL
BIJOU
BIJOUTERIE
BIJOUX
BIJUGATE
BIJUGOUS
BIJUGULAR
BIJWONER
BIKE
BIKER
BIKH
BIKIE
BIKINI
BIKKURIM

BILABE	BILKIS	BILSH	BINH	BIOGRAPH
BILABIAL	BILL	BILSTED	BINI	BIOGRAPHEE
BILABIATE	BILLABLE	BILTONG	BINIOU	BIOGRAPHER
BILALO	BILLABONG	BILTONGUE	BINIT	BIOGRAPHIC
BILAMINAR	BILLAGE	BIMA	BINK	BIOGRAPHICAL
BILAMINATE	BILLBACK	BIMACULATE	BINMAN	BIOGRAPHIES
BILAMINATED	BILLBOARD	BIMACULATED	BINMEN	BIOGRAPHIST
BILAN	BILLBROKING	BIMAH	BINNA	BIOGRAPHIZE
BILAND	BILLBUG	BIMANAL	BINNACLE	BIOGRAPHY
BILANDER	BILLED	BIMANE	BINNED	BIOHERM
BILATERAL	BILLER	BIMANOUS	BINNING	BIOLITE
BILATERALISM	BILLET	BIMANUAL	BINNITE	BIOLITH
BILATERALITY	BILLETED	BIMANUALLY	BINNOGUE	BIOLOGIC
BILATERALLY	BILLETER	BIMARINE	BINNY	BIOLOGICAL
BILBERRIES	BILLETHEAD	BIMASTIC	BINO	BIOLOGICALLY
BILBERRY	BILLETING	BIMASTISM	BINOCLE	BIOLOGIES
BILBI	BILLETTE	BIMASTOID	BINOCULAR	BIOLOGISM
BILBIE	BILLETTY	BIMAXILLARY	BINOCULARITY	BIOLOGIST
BILBO	BILLETY	BIMBASHI	BINOCULARLY	BIOLOGIZE
BILBOA	BILLFISH	BIMBIL	BINOCULARS	BIOLOGY
BILBOES	BILLFISHES	BIMBO	BINOCULATE	BIOLYSIS
BILBOQUET	BILLFOLD	BIMEBY	BINODAL	BIOLYTIC
BILBY	BILLHEAD	BIMENSAL	BINODE	BIOME
BILCH	BILLHEADING	BIMESTRIAL	BINOMEN	BIOMETER
BILCOCK	BILLHOLDER	BIMETAL	BINOMIAL	BIOMETRIC
BILDAR	BILLHOOK	BIMETALISM	BINOMIALISM	BIOMETRICAL
BILDER	BILLIAN	BIMETALLIC	BINOMIALLY	BIOMETRICIAN
BILDERS	BILLIARD	BIMETALLIST	BINOMINATED	BIOMETRICIST
BILE	BILLIARDIST	BIMILLENARY	BINOMINOUS	BIOMETRICS
BILECTION	BILLIARDLY	BIMILLENIUM	BINORMAL	BIOMETRY
BILECTIONED	BILLIARDS	BIMODAL	BINOTIC	BION
BILESTONE	BILLIE	BIMODALITY	BINOTONOUS	BIONERGY
BILEVE	BILLIES	BIMOLECULAR	BINOXALATE	BIONICS
BILGE	BILLIKIN	BIMONG	BINOXIDE	BIONOMIC
BILGED	BILLING	BIMONTHLY	BINT	BIONOMICAL
BILGING	BILLINGS	BIMORPH	BINTANGOR	BIONOMICS
BILGY	BILLINGSGATE	BIMOTORED	BINTURONG	BIONOMIST
BILHARZIAL	BILLION	BIMOTORS	BINUCLEAR	BIONOMY
BILHARZIASIS	BILLIONAIRE	BIMUSCULAR	BINUCLEATE	BIONT
BILHARZIC	BILLIONISM	BIN	BINUCLEATED	BIONTIC
BILHARZIOSIS	BILLIONTH	BINA	BINUCLEOLATE	BIOPHAGISM
BILIARY	BILLMAN	BINAL	BINUKAU	BIOPHAGOUS
BILIATE	BILLMEN	BINAPTHYL	BIOASSAY	BIOPHAGY
BILIATION	BILLON	BINARIES	BIOBLAST	BIOPHILOUS
BILIC	BILLOT	BINARY	BIOBLASTIC	BIOPHOR
BILICYANIN	BILLOW	BINATE	BIOCATALYST	BIOPHORE
BILIFACTION	BILLOWED	BINATELY	BIOCELLATE	BIOPHYSICAL
BILIFEROUS	BILLOWIER	BINATION	BIOCENTRIC	BIOPHYSICIST
BILIFICATION	BILLOWIEST	BINAURAL	BIOCHEMIC	BIOPHYSICS
BILIFUSCIN	BILLOWINESS	BINBASHI	BIOCHEMICAL	BIOPHYTE
BILIFY	BILLOWING	BIND	BIOCHEMICALLY	BIOPIC
BILIHUMIN	BILLOWY	BINDER	BIOCHEMICS	BIOPLASM
BILIMBI	BILLPOSTER	BINDERIES	BIOCHEMIST	BIOPLASMIC
BILIMBING	BILLPOSTING	BINDERY	BIOCHEMISTRY	BIOPLAST
BILIMBIS	BILLS	BINDHEIMITE	BIOCHEMY	BIOPLASTIC
BILIMENT	BILLSTICKER	BINDING	BIOCHORE	BIOPOESIS
BILINEAR	BILLSTICKING	BINDINGLY	BIOCHRON	BIOPOTENTIAL
BILINGUAL	BILLY	BINDINGNESS	BIOCIDE	BIOPSIC
BILINGUALISM	BILLYBOY	BINDLE	BIOCOENOSE	BIOPSIES
BILINGUALLY	BILLYCAN	BINDOREE	BIOCOENOSES	BIOPSY
BILINGUIST	BILLYCOCK	BINDWEB	BIOCOENOSIS	BIOPSYCHIC
BILINIGRIN	BILLYER	BINDWEED	BIOCOENOTIC	BIOPSYCHICAL
BILINITE	BILLYHOOD	BINDWITH	BIOCYCLE	BIOPYRIBOLE
BILIOUS	BILLYWIX	BINDWOOD	BIODYNAMIC	BIORDINAL
BILIOUSLY	BILO	BINE	BIODYNAMICAL	BIORGAN
BILIOUSNESS	BILOBATE	BINERVATE	BIODYNAMICS	BIOS
BILIPRASIN	BILOBATED	BINEWEED	BIOFLAVONOID	BIOSCOPE
BILIPYRRHIN	BILOBE	BING	BIOGEN	BIOSCOPIC
BILIRUBIN	BILOBED	BINGE	BIOGENASE	BIOSCOPY
BILIRUBINIC	BILOBULAR	BINGEE	BIOGENESIS	BIOSE
BILITERAL	BILOCATION	BINGEY	BIOGENESIST	BIOSESTON
BILITERALISM	BILOCELLATE	BINGEYS	BIOGENETIC	BIOSIS
BILITH	BILOCULAR	BINGHI	BIOGENETICAL	BIOSOCIAL
BILITHON	BILOCULATE	BINGIES	BIOGENOUS	BIOSOME
BILIVERDIN	BILOCULINE	BINGLE	BIOGENY	BIOSPHERE
BILK	BILOPHODONT	BINGO	BIOGEOGRAPHY	BIOSTATIC
BILKER	BILOS	BINGY	BIOGNOSIS	BIOSTATICAL

BIOSTATICS	BIQUARTZ	BIRSLE	BISMILLAH	BITER
BIOSTERIN	BIQUINTILE	BIRSY	BISMITE	BITERNATE
BIOSTEROL	BIRADIAL	BIRTH	BISMUTH	BITERNATELY
BIOSTROME	BIRADIATE	BIRTHBED	BISMUTHAL	BITEWING
BIOSYNTHESIS	BIRADIATED	BIRTHDAY	BISMUTHATE	BITHEISM
BIOSYNTHETIC	BIRAMOSE	BIRTHDOM	BISMUTHIC	BITI
BIOTA	BIRAMOUS	BIRTHING	BISMUTHIDE	BITING
BIOTAXY	BIRATIONAL	BIRTHLAND	BISMUTHINE	BITINGLY
BIOTIC	BIRCH	BIRTHLESS	BISMUTHINITE	BITINGNESS
BIOTICAL	BIRCHBARK	BIRTHMARK	BISMUTHITE	BITO
BIOTICS	BIRCHEN	BIRTHMATE	BISMUTHOUS	BITOLYL
BIOTIN	BIRCHES	BIRTHNIGHT	BISMUTHYL	BITONALITY
BIOTITE	BIRCHING	BIRTHPLACE	BISMUTITE	BITORE
BIOTITIC	BIRCHMAN	BIRTHRATE	BISNAGA	BITREADLE
BIOTOME	BIRCHWOOD	BIRTHRIGHT	BISON	BITRIPARTITE
BIOTOMY	BIRD	BIRTHROOT	BISONANT	BITRIPINNATIFID
BIOTOPE	BIRDBANDER	BIRTHSTONE	BISONTINE	BITRISEPTATE
BIOTRON	BIRDBANDING	BIRTHSTOOL	BISPINOSE	BITS
BIOTYPE	BIRDBATH	BIRTHWORT	BISPINOUS	BITSTALK
BIOTYPIC	BIRDBERRY	BIRTHY	BISPORE	BITSTOCK
BIOZONE	BIRDBRAIN	BIS	BISPOROUS	BITSY
BIPACK	BIRDCAGE	BISA	BISQUE	BITT
BIPALEOLATE	BIRDCALL	BISABOL	BISQUETTE	BITTACLE
BIPALMATE	BIRDCLAPPER	BISACROMIAL	BISSABOL	BITTE
BIPARASITIC	BIRDEEN	BISAGRE	BISSEXT	BITTED
BIPARENTAL	BIRDER	BISALT	BISSEXTILE	BITTEN
BIPARIETAL	BIRDEYE	BISAXILLARY	BISSON	BITTER
BIPAROUS	BIRDGLUE	BISBEEITE	BIST	BITTERBARK
BIPARTED	BIRDHOUSE	BISCAYEN	BISTER	BITTERBLAIN
BIPARTIBLE	BIRDIE	BISCHOFITE	BISTERED	BITTERBLOOM
BIPARTIENT	BIRDIKIN	BISCOTIN	BISTETRAZOLE	BITTERBUR
BIPARTILE	BIRDING	BISCUIT	BISTI	BITTERBUSH
BIPARTISAN	BIRDLIFE	BISCUITING	BISTIPULAR	BITTERER
BIPARTITE	BIRDLIME	BISCUITMAKER	BISTIPULATE	BITTEREST
BIPARTITELY	BIRDLIMED	BISCUITROOT	BISTIPULED	BITTERHEAD
BIPARTITION	BIRDLIMING	BISCUITS	BISTORT	BITTERISH
BIPECTINATE	BIRDLING	BISE	BISTOURIES	BITTERISHNESS
BIPECTINATED	BIRDMAN	BISECT	BISTOURNAGE	BITTERLESS
BIPED	BIRDMEN	BISECTION	BISTOURY	BITTERLING
BIPEDALITY	BIRDMOUTHED	BISECTIONAL	BISTRATAL	BITTERLY
BIPELTATE	BIRDNEST	BISECTOR	BISTRATOSE	BITTERN
BIPENNIFORM	BIRDS	BISECTRICES	BISTRE	BITTERNESS
BIPETALOUS	BIRDSEED	BISECTRIX	BISTRED	BITTERNS
BIPHASE	BIRDSNEST	BISEGMENT	BISTRIATE	BITTERNUT
BIPHASIC	BIRDSONG	BISERIAL	BISTRIAZOLE	BITTERROOT
BIPHENOL	BIRDSTONE	BISERIALLY	BISTRO	BITTERS
BIPHENYL	BIRDWEED	BISERRATE	BISUBSTITUTED	BITTERSWEET
BIPHENYLENE	BIRDWOMAN	BISETOSE	BISULCATE	BITTERWEED
BIPINNARIA	BIRDY	BISETOUS	BISULCATED	BITTERWORM
BIPINNATE	BIREFRINGENT	BISEXED	BISULFATE	BITTERWORT
BIPINNATED	BIREME	BISEXT	BISULFIDE	BITTHEAD
BIPINNATELY	BIRETTA	BISEXUAL	BISULFITE	BITTIE
BIPLANAR	BIRI	BISEXUALISM	BISULPHATE	BITTING
BIPLANE	BIRIBA	BISEXUALITY	BISULPHIDE	BITTOCK
BIPLICATE	BIRIMOSE	BISEXUALLY	BISULPHITE	BITTY
BIPLICITY	BIRK	BISEXUOUS	BISYLLABIC	BITUBERCULAR
BIPLOSION	BIRKEN	BISHOP	BISYLLABISM	BITULITHIC
BIPOD	BIRKIE	BISHOPDOM	BISYMMETRIC	BITUME
BIPOLAR	BIRKREMITE	BISHOPED	BISYMMETRY	BITUMED
BIPOLARITY	BIRKY	BISHOPESS	BIT	BITUMEN
BIPOROSE	BIRL	BISHOPING	BITABLE	BITUMINIZE
BIPOROUS	BIRLE	BISHOPRIC	BITANGENT	BITUMINIZED
BIPRISM	BIRLER	BISHOPSCAP	BITANGENTIAL	BITUMINIZING
BIPRONG	BIRLING	BISILIAC	BITANHOL	BITUMINOID
BIPROPELLANT	BIRLINN	BISILICATE	BITARTRATE	BITUMINOUS
BIPUNCTAL	BIRMA	BISIMINE	BITBRACE	BITWISE
BIPUNCTATE	BIRN	BISINUATE	BITCH	BITYITE
BIPUNCTUAL	BIRNE	BISINUATION	BITCHERY	BITYPIC
BIPUPILLATE	BIRODO	BISISCHIADIC	BITCHIER	BIUNE
BIPYRAMID	BIROTATION	BISISCHIATIC	BITCHIEST	BIUNIAL
BIPYRAMIDAL	BIROTATORY	BISK	BITCHY	BIUNITY
BIPYRIDINE	BIRR	BISKOP	BITE	BIURATE
BIPYRIDYL	BIRRED	BISMAR	BITEABLE	BIUREA
BIQUADRANTAL	BIRRING	BISMARINE	BITECHE	BIURET
BIQUADRATE	BIRRUS	BISME	BITED	BIVALENCE
BIQUADRATIC	BIRSE	BISMER	BITEMPORAL	BIVALENCY
BIQUARTERLY	BIRSIT	BISMERPUND	BITEN	BIVALENT

BIVALVE	BLACKFIRE	BLADYGRASS	BLASE	BLATJANG
BIVALVED	BLACKFISH	BLAE	BLASH	BLATTA
BIVALVES	BLACKFISHER	BLAEBERRY	BLASHY	BLATTED
BIVALVULAR	BLACKFISHES	BLAEWORT	BLASPHEME	BLATTER
BIVARIANT	BLACKFISHING	BLAFF	BLASPHEMED	BLATTERED
BIVASCULAR	BLACKFLY	BLAFFERT	BLASPHEMER	BLATTERER
BIVECTOR	BLACKGUARD	BLAFLUM	BLASPHEMIES	BLATTERING
BIVENTER	BLACKGUARDISM	BLAGGARD	BLASPHEMING	BLATTI
BIVENTRAL	BLACKGUARDLY	BLAGUE	BLASPHEMOUS	BLATTID
BIVERBAL	BLACKGUARDRY	BLAH	BLASPHEMY	BLATTING
BIVIOUS	BLACKGUM	BLAHLAUT	BLAST	BLATTOID
BIVITTATE	BLACKHEAD	BLAIK	BLASTAEA	BLAUBOK
BIVOCAL	BLACKHEADS	BLAIN	BLASTED	BLAUBOKS
BIVOCALIZED	BLACKHEART	BLAIR	BLASTEMA	BLAVER
BIVOLUMINOUS	BLACKHEARTED	BLAIRMORITE	BLASTEMAL	BLAW
BIVOUAC	BLACKIE	BLAKE	BLASTEMATA	BLAWORT
BIVOUACKED	BLACKIES	BLAKEBERYED	BLASTEMATIC	BLAY
BIVOUACKING	BLACKING	BLAKEITE	BLASTEMIC	BLAZE
BIWA	BLACKISH	BLAMABLE	BLASTER	BLAZED
BIWEEKLY	BLACKISHLY	BLAMABLENESS	BLASTHOLE	BLAZER
BIXACEOUS	BLACKISHNESS	BLAMABLY	BLASTID	BLAZES
BIXBYITE	BLACKJACK	BLAME	BLASTIE	BLAZING
BIXIN	BLACKLAND	BLAMEABLE	BLASTING	BLAZON
BIYEARLY	BLACKLEAD	BLAMED	BLASTMAN	BLAZONED
BIZ	BLACKLEG	BLAMEFUL	BLASTMENT	BLAZONER
BIZARDITE	BLACKLIST	BLAMEFULLY	BLASTOCELE	BLAZONING
BIZARRE	BLACKLY	BLAMEFULNESS	BLASTOCHEME	BLAZONMENT
BIZARRELY	BLACKMAIL	BLAMELESS	BLASTOCHYLE	BLAZONRY
BIZARRENESS	BLACKMAILER	BLAMELESSLY	BLASTOCOLLA	BLAZY
BIZARRERIE	BLACKMAN	BLAMER	BLASTOCYST	BLEA
BIZE	BLACKNEB	BLAMEWORTHY	BLASTOCYTE	BLEACH
BIZLE	BLACKNECK	BLAMING	BLASTODERM	BLEACHED
BIZYGOMATIC	BLACKNESS	BLAMINGLY	BLASTODERMIC	BLEACHER
BIZZARRO	BLACKNOB	BLANC	BLASTODISC	BLEACHERIES
BLAA	BLACKOUT	BLANCA	BLASTODISK	BLEACHERITE
BLAASOP	BLACKPOLL	BLANCARD	BLASTOFF	BLEACHERMAN
BLAB	BLACKPOT	BLANCH	BLASTOGENIC	BLEACHERS
BLABBED	BLACKPRINT	BLANCHED	BLASTOGENY	BLEACHERY
BLABBER	BLACKROOT	BLANCHER	BLASTOID	BLEACHFIELD
BLABBERER	BLACKS	BLANCHING	BLASTOMA	BLEACHHOUSE
BLABBERMOUTH	BLACKSHIRTED	BLANCHINGLY	BLASTOMATA	BLEACHING
BLABBING	BLACKSMITH	BLANCMANGE	BLASTOMERE	BLEACHMAN
BLACK	BLACKSNAKE	BLANCMANGER	BLASTOMERIC	BLEACHWORKS
BLACKACRE	BLACKSTICK	BLANCO	BLASTOMYCETE	BLEACHYARD
BLACKAMOOR	BLACKSTRAP	BLAND	BLASTOPHITIC	BLEAK
BLACKARM	BLACKTAIL	BLANDA	BLASTOPHORAL	BLEAKISH
BLACKBACK	BLACKTHORN	BLANDISH	BLASTOPHORE	BLEAKLY
BLACKBALL	BLACKTONGUE	BLANDISHER	BLASTOPHORIC	BLEAKNESS
BLACKBALLER	BLACKTOP	BLANDISHING	BLASTOPORAL	BLEAKS
BLACKBERRIES	BLACKTREE	BLANDISHMENT	BLASTOPORE	BLEAKY
BLACKBERRY	BLACKWASH	BLANDLY	BLASTOPORIC	BLEAR
BLACKBIRD	BLACKWASHER	BLANDNESS	BLASTOSPHERE	BLEARED
BLACKBIRDER	BLACKWATER	BLANK	BLASTOSTYLAR	BLEAREDNESS
BLACKBIRDING	BLACKWEED	BLANKBOOK	BLASTOSTYLE	BLEAREYE
BLACKBOARD	BLACKWOOD	BLANKED	BLASTOZOOID	BLEARIER
BLACKBOY	BLACKWORK	BLANKEEL	BLASTPLATE	BLEARIEST
BLACKBREAST	BLACKWORT	BLANKET	BLASTULA	BLEARILY
BLACKBRUSH	BLACKY	BLANKETED	BLASTULAE	BLEARINESS
BLACKBUSH	BLAD	BLANKETEER	BLASTULAR	BLEARY
BLACKBUTT	BLADDER	BLANKETING	BLASTULATION	BLEAT
BLACKCAP	BLADDERET	BLANKETRY	BLASTULE	BLEATER
BLACKCOAT	BLADDERNOSE	BLANKETY	BLASTY	BLEATING
BLACKCOCK	BLADDERNUT	BLANKING	BLAT	BLEATINGLY
BLACKDAMP	BLADDERSEED	BLANKISH	BLATANCY	BLEAUNT
BLACKEN	BLADDERWEED	BLANKLY	BLATANT	BLEB
BLACKENED	BLADDERWORT	BLANKNESS	BLATANTLY	BLEBBY
BLACKENER	BLADDERWRACK	BLANKS	BLATCH	BLECHNOID
BLACKENING	BLADDERY	BLANKY	BLATCHANG	BLECK
BLACKER	BLADE	BLANQUETTE	BLATE	BLED
BLACKEST	BLADEBONE	BLANQUILLO	BLATELY	BLEE
BLACKEY	BLADED	BLARE	BLATENESS	BLEED
BLACKEYE	BLADELET	BLARED	BLATEROON	BLEEDER
BLACKEYES	BLADER	BLARING	BLATHER	BLEEDING
BLACKFACE	BLADES	BLARNEY	BLATHERER	BLEEKBOK
BLACKFELLOW	BLADESMITH	BLARNEYER	BLATHERSKITE	BLEERY
BLACKFELLOWS	BLADING	BLART	BLATHERY	BLEEZE
BLACKFIN	BLADY	BLAS	BLATIFORM	BLEEZY

BLEIR
BLELLUM
BLEMISH
BLEMISHED
BLEMISHER
BLENCH
BLENCHER
BLENCHING
BLENCHINGLY
BLEND
BLENDCORN
BLENDE
BLENDED
BLENDER
BLENDING
BLENDURE
BLENK
BLENNIES
BLENNIID
BLENNIIFORM
BLENNIOID
BLENNORRHEA
BLENNORRHOEA
BLENNY
BLENS
BLENT
BLEO
BLEPHARA
BLEPHARAL
BLEPHARISM
BLEPHARITIS
BLEPHAROPLAST
BLESBOK
BLESBOKS
BLESBUCK
BLESMOL
BLESS
BLESSE
BLESSED
BLESSEDLY
BLESSEDNESS
BLESSER
BLESSING
BLESSINGLY
BLEST
BLET
BLETHE
BLETHER
BLETHERATION
BLETHERS
BLETTED
BLETTING
BLEU
BLEW
BLEWITS
BLIAUT
BLIBE
BLICK
BLICKEY
BLICKEYS
BLICKIE
BLICKIES
BLICKY
BLIGHT
BLIGHTBIRD
BLIGHTED
BLIGHTER
BLIGHTING
BLIGHTINGLY
BLIGHTY
BLIJVER
BLIMBING
BLIMP
BLIMY
BLIN
BLIND
BLINDAGE

BLINDBALL
BLINDED
BLINDEDLY
BLINDER
BLINDEST
BLINDEYES
BLINDFAST
BLINDFISH
BLINDFOLD
BLINDFOLDED
BLINDFOLDER
BLINDFOLDLY
BLINDING
BLINDINGLY
BLINDISM
BLINDLY
BLINDNESS
BLINDSTITCH
BLINDSTORIES
BLINDSTORY
BLINDWEED
BLINDWORM
BLINE
BLINGER
BLINK
BLINKARD
BLINKED
BLINKER
BLINKING
BLINKINGLY
BLINKS
BLINKY
BLINTER
BLINTZ
BLINTZE
BLIP
BLISS
BLISSFUL
BLISSFULLY
BLISSFULNESS
BLISSOM
BLIST
BLISTER
BLISTERED
BLISTERING
BLISTEROUS
BLISTERS
BLISTERWEED
BLISTERWORT
BLISTERY
BLITE
BLITHE
BLITHEFUL
BLITHEFULLY
BLITHELY
BLITHEMEAT
BLITHEN
BLITHENESS
BLITHER
BLITHERED
BLITHERING
BLITHESOME
BLITHESOMELY
BLITTER
BLITZ
BLIZZ
BLIZZARD
BLIZZARDLY
BLIZZARDOUS
BLIZZARDY
BLO
BLOAK
BLOAT
BLOATED
BLOATEDNESS
BLOATER
BLOATING

BLOB
BLOBBED
BLOBBER
BLOBBIER
BLOBBIEST
BLOBBING
BLOBBY
BLOC
BLOCAGE
BLOCK
BLOCKADE
BLOCKADED
BLOCKADER
BLOCKADING
BLOCKAGE
BLOCKBUSTER
BLOCKED
BLOCKER
BLOCKHEAD
BLOCKHEADED
BLOCKHEADISM
BLOCKHOLE
BLOCKHOLER
BLOCKHOUSE
BLOCKIER
BLOCKIEST
BLOCKING
BLOCKISH
BLOCKISHLY
BLOCKISHNESS
BLOCKLAYER
BLOCKLIKE
BLOCKLINE
BLOCKMAKER
BLOCKMAKING
BLOCKMAN
BLOCKOUT
BLOCKPATE
BLOCKS
BLOCKSHIP
BLOCKY
BLODE
BLODITE
BLOEDITE
BLOKE
BLOLLY
BLOND
BLONDE
BLONDENESS
BLONDINE
BLONDNESS
BLOO
BLOOD
BLOODALP
BLOODBERRY
BLOODBIRD
BLOODCURDLER
BLOODCURDLING
BLOODED
BLOODFIN
BLOODFLOWER
BLOODGUILT
BLOODGUILTY
BLOODHOUND
BLOODIED
BLOODIER
BLOODIEST
BLOODILY
BLOODINESS
BLOODING
BLOODLEAF
BLOODLESS
BLOODLESSLY
BLOODLETTER
BLOODLETTING
BLOODLINE
BLOODMOBILE

BLOODMONGER
BLOODNOUN
BLOODRIPE
BLOODROOT
BLOODSHED
BLOODSHEDDER
BLOODSHOT
BLOODSHOTTEN
BLOODSPILLER
BLOODSPILLING
BLOODSTAIN
BLOODSTAINED
BLOODSTANCH
BLOODSTOCK
BLOODSTONE
BLOODSUCK
BLOODSUCKER
BLOODSUCKING
BLOODTHIRST
BLOODTHIRSTER
BLOODTHIRSTY
BLOODWEED
BLOODWIT
BLOODWITE
BLOODWOOD
BLOODWORM
BLOODWORT
BLOODY
BLOODYBONES
BLOODYING
BLOOEY
BLOOIE
BLOOM
BLOOMAGE
BLOOMER
BLOOMERIES
BLOOMERS
BLOOMERY
BLOOMFELL
BLOOMING
BLOOMINGLY
BLOOMINGNESS
BLOOMY
BLOOP
BLOOPER
BLOOPING
BLOOTH
BLORE
BLOSMY
BLOSSOM
BLOSSOMBILL
BLOSSOMED
BLOSSOMING
BLOSSOMLESS
BLOSSOMRY
BLOSSOMS
BLOSSOMY
BLOT
BLOTCH
BLOTCHED
BLOTCHIER
BLOTCHIEST
BLOTCHINESS
BLOTCHING
BLOTCHY
BLOTE
BLOTLESS
BLOTTED
BLOTTER
BLOTTESQUE
BLOTTESQUELY
BLOTTING
BLOTTO
BLOTTY
BLOUSE
BLOUSED
BLOUSELIKE

BLOUSING
BLOUSY
BLOUT
BLOVIATE
BLOW
BLOWBACK
BLOWBALL
BLOWBY
BLOWBYS
BLOWCASE
BLOWDOWN
BLOWEN
BLOWER
BLOWFISH
BLOWFLIES
BLOWFLY
BLOWGUN
BLOWHARD
BLOWHOLE
BLOWIER
BLOWIEST
BLOWINESS
BLOWING
BLOWIRON
BLOWLAMP
BLOWLINE
BLOWN
BLOWOFF
BLOWOUT
BLOWPIPE
BLOWPIT
BLOWPOINT
BLOWPROOF
BLOWS
BLOWSPRAY
BLOWSY
BLOWTH
BLOWTORCH
BLOWTUBE
BLOWUP
BLOWY
BLOWZE
BLOWZED
BLOWZIER
BLOWZIEST
BLOWZING
BLOWZY
BLUB
BLUBBED
BLUBBER
BLUBBERED
BLUBBERER
BLUBBERING
BLUBBERMAN
BLUBBERY
BLUBBING
BLUCHER
BLUDE
BLUDGE
BLUDGEON
BLUDGEONED
BLUDGEONEER
BLUDGEONER
BLUDGER
BLUE
BLUEBACK
BLUEBALL
BLUEBEAD
BLUEBELL
BLUEBELLED
BLUEBERRIES
BLUEBERRY
BLUEBILL
BLUEBIRD
BLUEBLAW
BLUEBLOOD
BLUEBLOSSOM

BLUEBONNET
BLUEBOOK
BLUEBOTTLE
BLUEBREAST
BLUEBUCK
BLUEBUSH
BLUEBUTTON
BLUECAP
BLUECOAT
BLUECUP
BLUECURLS
BLUED
BLUEFIN
BLUEFISH
BLUEFISHES
BLUEGILL
BLUEGOWN
BLUEGRASS
BLUEGUM
BLUEHEARTS
BLUEING
BLUEISH
BLUEJACK
BLUEJACKET
BLUEJOINT
BLUELEGS
BLUELINE
BLUENESS
BLUENOSE
BLUENOSED
BLUEPOINT
BLUEPRINT
BLUEPRINTER
BLUER
BLUES
BLUESIDES
BLUEST
BLUESTEM
BLUESTOCKING
BLUESTONE
BLUESTONER
BLUET
BLUETICK
BLUETONGUE
BLUETOP
BLUETOPS
BLUEWEED
BLUEWING
BLUEWOOD
BLUEY
BLUEYS
BLUFF
BLUFFED
BLUFFER
BLUFFING
BLUFFLY
BLUFFNESS
BLUFFY
BLUFTER
BLUGGY
BLUID
BLUING
BLUISH
BLUISHNESS
BLUISNESS
BLUME
BLUMED
BLUMING
BLUNDER
BLUNDERBUSS
BLUNDERED
BLUNDERER
BLUNDERHEAD
BLUNDERING
BLUNDERINGLY
BLUNGE
BLUNGED

BLUNGER
BLUNGING
BLUNK
BLUNKER
BLUNKET
BLUNKS
BLUNT
BLUNTED
BLUNTER
BLUNTIE
BLUNTISH
BLUNTISHNESS
BLUNTLY
BLUNTNESS
BLUP
BLUR
BLURB
BLURBIST
BLURRED
BLURREDNESS
BLURRER
BLURRING
BLURRY
BLURT
BLUSH
BLUSHED
BLUSHER
BLUSHET
BLUSHFUL
BLUSHFULLY
BLUSHFULNESS
BLUSHINESS
BLUSHING
BLUSHINGLY
BLUSHT
BLUSHWORT
BLUSHY
BLUSTER
BLUSTERATION
BLUSTERED
BLUSTERER
BLUSTERING
BLUSTERINGLY
BLUSTEROUS
BLUSTEROUSLY
BLUSTERY
BLY
BLYPE
BO
BOA
BOAR
BOARD
BOARDED
BOARDER
BOARDING
BOARDINGHOUSE
BOARDLY
BOARDMAN
BOARDS
BOARDWALK
BOARDY
BOARFISH
BOARFISHES
BOARHOUND
BOARISH
BOARISHLY
BOARISHNESS
BOARS
BOART
BOARWOOD
BOAS
BOAST
BOASTER
BOASTFUL
BOASTFULLY
BOASTFULNESS
BOASTING

BOASTINGLY
BOAT
BOATABLE
BOATAGE
BOATBILL
BOATBUILDER
BOATBUILDING
BOATER
BOATHOOK
BOATHOUSE
BOATING
BOATION
BOATKEEPER
BOATLIP
BOATLOAD
BOATLOADER
BOATLOADING
BOATMAN
BOATMASTER
BOATMEN
BOATOWNER
BOATS
BOATSETTER
BOATSHOP
BOATSIDE
BOATSWAIN
BOATTAIL
BOATWRIGHT
BOB
BOBA
BOBAC
BOBACHE
BOBACHEE
BOBANCE
BOBBED
BOBBEJAAN
BOBBER
BOBBERIES
BOBBERY
BOBBIE
BOBBIES
BOBBIN
BOBBINER
BOBBINET
BOBBING
BOBBINS
BOBBISH
BOBBISHLY
BOBBLE
BOBBLED
BOBBLING
BOBBY
BOBBYSOXER
BOBCAT
BOBCATS
BOBCOAT
BOBECHE
BOBFLIES
BOBFLY
BOBIERRITE
BOBIZATION
BOBJEROM
BOBLET
BOBO
BOBOLINK
BOBOOTI
BOBOTEE
BOBOTIE
BOBSLED
BOBSLEDDED
BOBSLEDDING
BOBSLEIGH
BOBSTAY
BOBTAIL
BOBTAILED
BOBWHITE
BOBWOOD

BOCA
BOCACCIO
BOCAGE
BOCAL
BOCAN
BOCARDO
BOCASINE
BOCCA
BOCCALE
BOCCARELLA
BOCCARO
BOCCE
BOCCIE
BOCCONIA
BOCE
BOCHE
BOCHER
BOCHISM
BOCHUR
BOCK
BOCKEREL
BOCKERET
BOCKING
BOCO
BOCON
BOCOR
BOCOY
BOD
BODACH
BODACIOUS
BODACIOUSLY
BODAI
BODDAGH
BODDLE
BODE
BODED
BODEFUL
BODEGA
BODEGON
BODEMENT
BODEN
BODER
BODEWASH
BODEWORD
BODGE
BODGER
BODGERY
BODHI
BODHISAT
BODHISATTVA
BODHISATTWA
BODICE
BODICED
BODIED
BODIER
BODIERON
BODIES
BODIKIN
BODILESS
BODILESSNESS
BODILY
BODIMENT
BODING
BODINGLY
BODKIN
BODLE
BODOCK
BODONID
BODRAGE
BODSTICK
BODWORD
BODY
BODYBUILDER
BODYCHECK
BODYGUARD
BODYING
BODYKINS

BODYMAKER
BODYMAKING
BODYPLATE
BODYSHIRT
BODYWOOD
BODYWORK
BOE
BOEA
BOEG
BOEOTARCH
BOES
BOFF
BOFFIN
BOFFOLA
BOG
BOGA
BOGACH
BOGAN
BOGATYR
BOGBEAN
BOGBERRIES
BOGBERRY
BOGET
BOGEY
BOGEYMAN
BOGEYS
BOGFERN
BOGGARD
BOGGART
BOGGED
BOGGIER
BOGGIEST
BOGGIN
BOGGINESS
BOGGING
BOGGISH
BOGGISHNESS
BOGGLE
BOGGLEBO
BOGGLED
BOGGLER
BOGGLING
BOGGLISH
BOGGY
BOGHOLE
BOGIE
BOGIEMAN
BOGIER
BOGIES
BOGLAND
BOGLANDER
BOGLE
BOGLET
BOGMAN
BOGMIRE
BOGO
BOGONG
BOGOTANA
BOGSUCKER
BOGTROT
BOGTROTTER
BOGTROTTING
BOGUE
BOGUM
BOGUS
BOGWAY
BOGWOOD
BOGWORT
BOGY
BOH
BOHAWN
BOHEA
BOHIO
BOHMITE
BOHO
BOHOR
BOHORA

BOHUNK	BOLLER	BOMBASTICALLY	BONDSMAN	BONNINESS
BOID	BOLLIES	BOMBASTRY	BONDSMEN	BONNIVE
BOIGID	BOLLING	BOMBAZET	BONDSTONE	BONNOCK
BOIL	BOLLIX	BOMBAZETTE	BONDSWOMAN	BONNY
BOILDOWN	BOLLIXED	BOMBAZINE	BONDUC	BONNYCLABBER
BOILED	BOLLIXING	BOMBE	BONDUCNUT	BONNYVIS
BOILER	BOLLO	BOMBED	BONDWOMAN	BONSAI
BOILERMAKER	BOLLOCK	BOMBER	BONDWOMEN	BONSER
BOILERY	BOLLWORM	BOMBERNICKEL	BONE	BONSPELL
BOILING	BOLLY	BOMBICCITE	BONEACHE	BONSPIEL
BOILOVER	BOLNE	BOMBILATE	BONEBLACK	BONTE
BOILY	BOLO	BOMBILATION	BONEBREAKER	BONTEBOK
BOINA	BOLOED	BOMBILLA	BONED	BONTEBOKS
BOIS	BOLOGNA	BOMBINATE	BONEDOG	BONTEE
BOISSEAU	BOLOGRAPH	BOMBINATION	BONEEN	BONUM
BOISSEAUX	BOLOGRAPHIC	BOMBLE	BONEFISH	BONUS
BOIST	BOLOGRAPHY	BOMBLINE	BONEHEAD	BONUSES
BOISTEROUS	BOLOING	BOMBO	BONEHEADED	BONXIE
BOISTEROUSLY	BOLOISM	BOMBOLA	BONELESS	BONY
BOISTOUS	BOLOMAN	BOMBONNE	BONELESSLY	BONYFISH
BOISTOUSLY	BOLOMEN	BOMBOUS	BONELESSNESS	BONYTAIL
BOISTOUSNESS	BOLOMETER	BOMBPROOF	BONELET	BONZA
BOITE	BOLOMETRIC	BOMBS	BONER	BONZE
BOITHRIN	BOLONEY	BOMBSHELL	BONES	BONZER
BOJITE	BOLOROOT	BOMBSIGHT	BONESET	BONZERY
BOKADAM	BOLOS	BOMBYCID	BONESETTER	BONZIAN
BOKARD	BOLSA	BOMBYCIFORM	BONESETTING	BOO
BOKARK	BOLSHEVIK	BOMBYCINE	BONESHAKER	BOOB
BOKE	BOLSHEVISM	BOMBYX	BONESHAVE	BOOBERY
BOKO	BOLSHEVIST	BOMOS	BONESHAW	BOOBIES
BOKOM	BOLSHEVIZE	BON	BONETAIL	BOOBILY
BOLA	BOLSHEVIZED	BONA	BONETE	BOOBOO
BOLAR	BOLSHEVIZING	BONACE	BONEWOOD	BOOBOOK
BOLAS	BOLSHIE	BONACI	BONEWORK	BOOBOOS
BOLBONAC	BOLSON	BONAGH	BONEWORT	BOOBY
BOLD	BOLSTER	BONAGHT	BONEYARD	BOOBYALLA
BOLDEN	BOLSTERED	BONAILIE	BONFIRE	BOOD
BOLDER	BOLSTERER	BONAIR	BONG	BOODIE
BOLDEST	BOLSTERING	BONAIRE	BONGA	BOODLE
BOLDFACE	BOLSTERWORK	BONAIRLY	BONGAR	BOODLED
BOLDHEARTED	BOLT	BONAIRNESS	BONGO	BOODLER
BOLDIN	BOLTAGE	BONALLY	BONGOS	BOODLING
BOLDINE	BOLTANT	BONAMANO	BONGRACE	BOODY
BOLDLY	BOLTEL	BONANG	BONHOMIE	BOOED
BOLDNESS	BOLTER	BONANZA	BONHOMMIE	BOOER
BOLDO	BOLTHEAD	BONAO	BONIATA	BOOF
BOLDOINE	BOLTHEADER	BONASSUS	BONIER	BOOGER
BOLE	BOLTHEADING	BONASUS	BONIEST	BOOGERMAN
BOLECTION	BOLTI	BONAUGHT	BONIFACE	BOOGEYMAN
BOLECTIONED	BOLTIN	BONAV	BONIFICATION	BOOGIE
BOLED	BOLTING	BONAVIST	BONIFORM	BOOGUM
BOLEITE	BOLTINGS	BONBON	BONIFY	BOOH
BOLERO	BOLTONIA	BONBONNIERE	BONINESS	BOOHOO
BOLEROS	BOLTONITE	BONCE	BONING	BOOHOOED
BOLETACEOUS	BOLTROPE	BONCHIEF	BONINITE	BOOHOOING
BOLETE	BOLTSTRAKE	BOND	BONITA	BOOHOOS
BOLETIC	BOLTY	BONDAGE	BONITARIAN	BOOING
BOLETUS	BOLUS	BONDAGER	BONITARY	BOOJUM
BOLEWEED	BOLUSES	BONDAR	BONITO	BOOK
BOLEWORT	BOM	BONDED	BONITOES	BOOKBINDER
BOLIA	BOMA	BONDER	BONITOS	BOOKBINDERIES
BOLICHE	BOMB	BONDERMAN	BONITY	BOOKBINDERY
BOLIDE	BOMBARD	BONDFOLK	BONK	BOOKBINDING
BOLIMBA	BOMBARDE	BONDHOLDER	BONKA	BOOKBOARD
BOLIS	BOMBARDELLE	BONDHOLDING	BONNAZ	BOOKCASE
BOLITA	BOMBARDER	BONDIEUSERIE	BONNE	BOOKCASES
BOLIVAR	BOMBARDIER	BONDING	BONNET	BOOKCRAFT
BOLIVARES	BOMBARDMAN	BONDLAND	BONNETED	BOOKDEALER
BOLIVARS	BOMBARDMEN	BONDMAID	BONNETING	BOOKED
BOLIVIA	BOMBARDMENT	BONDMAN	BONNETMAN	BOOKEND
BOLIVIANO	BOMBARDON	BONDMEN	BONNETMEN	BOOKER
BOLIVIANOS	BOMBARDS	BONDMINDER	BONNETS	BOOKERY
BOLK	BOMBASINE	BONDOC	BONNIBEL	BOOKFAIR
BOLL	BOMBAST	BONDON	BONNIE	BOOKFOLD
BOLLARD	BOMBASTER	BONDSERVANT	BONNIER	BOOKHOLDER
BOLLED	BOMBASTIC	BONDSHIP	BONNIEST	BOOKIE
BOLLEN	BOMBASTICAL	BONDSLAVE	BONNILY	BOOKING

BOOKISH
BOOKISHLY
BOOKISHNESS
BOOKIT
BOOKKEEPER
BOOKKEEPING
BOOKLAND
BOOKLEAR
BOOKLESS
BOOKLET
BOOKLIFT
BOOKLORE
BOOKLOVER
BOOKMAKER
BOOKMAKING
BOOKMAN
BOOKMARK
BOOKMARKER
BOOKMATE
BOOKMEN
BOOKMOBILE
BOOKMONGER
BOOKPLATE
BOOKPRESS
BOOKRACK
BOOKREST
BOOKROOM
BOOKS
BOOKSELLER
BOOKSELLERISH
BOOKSELLERISM
BOOKSELLING
BOOKSHELF
BOOKSHELVES
BOOKSHOP
BOOKSTACK
BOOKSTALL
BOOKSTAND
BOOKSTORE
BOOKSY
BOOKWORK
BOOKWORM
BOOKWRIGHT
BOOKY
BOOL
BOOLEY
BOOLEYS
BOOLIES
BOOLY
BOOLYA
BOOM
BOOMAGE
BOOMAH
BOOMBOAT
BOOMDAS
BOOMER
BOOMERANG
BOOMINESS
BOOMING
BOOMINGLY
BOOMKIN
BOOMLET
BOOMORAH
BOOMSLANG
BOOMSLANGE
BOOMSTER
BOOMTOWN
BOOMY
BOON
BOONDOCK
BOONDOCKS
BOONDOGGLE
BOONDOGGLED
BOONDOGGLER
BOONDOGGLING
BOONG
BOONGARY

BOONK
BOOPIS
BOOR
BOORDLY
BOORISH
BOORISHLY
BOORISHNESS
BOORT
BOOS
BOOSE
BOOSIES
BOOST
BOOSTER
BOOSY
BOOT
BOOTBLACK
BOOTBOY
BOOTED
BOOTEE
BOOTER
BOOTERIES
BOOTERY
BOOTH
BOOTHAGE
BOOTHALE
BOOTHEEL
BOOTHER
BOOTHITE
BOOTHOLDER
BOOTHOSE
BOOTHS
BOOTIE
BOOTIED
BOOTIES
BOOTIKIN
BOOTING
BOOTJACK
BOOTJACKS
BOOTLACE
BOOTLE
BOOTLEG
BOOTLEGGED
BOOTLEGGER
BOOTLEGGING
BOOTLESS
BOOTLESSLY
BOOTLESSNESS
BOOTLICK
BOOTLICKER
BOOTMAKER
BOOTMAKING
BOOTMAN
BOOTS
BOOTSTRAP
BOOTY
BOOZE
BOOZED
BOOZER
BOOZILY
BOOZINESS
BOOZING
BOOZY
BOP
BOPEEP
BOPPED
BOPPER
BOPPING
BOPPIST
BOPSTER
BOPYRID
BOPYRIDIAN
BOR
BORA
BORACHIO
BORACIC
BORACIFEROUS
BORACITE

BORACOUS
BORAGE
BORAK
BORAL
BORANE
BORASCA
BORASCO
BORASQUE
BORATE
BORATED
BORAX
BORAZON
BORD
BORDAGE
BORDAR
BORDEL
BORDELLO
BORDER
BORDEREAU
BORDEREAUX
BORDERED
BORDERER
BORDERING
BORDERISM
BORDERLAND
BORDERLANDER
BORDERLINE
BORDRAG
BORDROOM
BORDUN
BORDURE
BORDURED
BORE
BOREAD
BOREAL
BOREALIS
BOREAN
BORECOLE
BORED
BOREDOM
BOREE
BOREEN
BOREGAT
BOREHOLE
BORELE
BORER
BORESOME
BORG
BORGH
BORGHI
BORGO
BORIC
BORICKITE
BORIDE
BORINE
BORING
BORINGLY
BORINGNESS
BORISH
BORISM
BORITH
BORITIES
BORITY
BORIZE
BORLASE
BORLEY
BORN
BORNANE
BORNE
BORNEOL
BORNING
BORNITE
BORNITIC
BORNYL
BORO
BOROCALCITE
BOROLANITE

BORON
BORONIC
BOROPHENOL
BOROSILICATE
BOROTUNGSTIC
BOROUGH
BORRACHA
BORRASCA
BORREL
BORRELIA
BORROW
BORROWED
BORROWER
BORROWING
BORSCH
BORSCHT
BORSHOLDER
BORSHT
BORSTAL
BORSTALL
BORT
BORTSCH
BORTZ
BORUN
BORWORT
BORYL
BORZOI
BOS
BOSA
BOSAL
BOSC
BOSCAGE
BOSCH
BOSCHBOK
BOSCHVARK
BOSCHVELD
BOSE
BOSER
BOSEY
BOSH
BOSHBOK
BOSHER
BOSHES
BOSHVARK
BOSK
BOSKAGE
BOSKER
BOSKET
BOSKINESS
BOSKY
BOSOM
BOSOMED
BOSOMER
BOSOMY
BOSON
BOSPORUS
BOSQUE
BOSQUET
BOSS
BOSSAGE
BOSSDOM
BOSSE
BOSSED
BOSSELATED
BOSSELATION
BOSSER
BOSSET
BOSSIER
BOSSIES
BOSSIEST
BOSSING
BOSSISM
BOSSY
BOST
BOSTAL
BOSTANGI
BOSTANJI

BOSTHOON
BOSTON
BOSTONITE
BOSTRYCHID
BOSTRYCHOID
BOSTRYX
BOSUN
BOT
BOTA
BOTANIC
BOTANICAL
BOTANICALLY
BOTANICS
BOTANIES
BOTANIST
BOTANIZE
BOTANIZED
BOTANIZER
BOTANIZING
BOTANY
BOTARGO
BOTARGOS
BOTCH
BOTCHED
BOTCHEDLY
BOTCHER
BOTCHERLY
BOTCHERY
BOTCHES
BOTCHIER
BOTCHIEST
BOTCHILY
BOTCHINESS
BOTCHING
BOTCHKA
BOTCHY
BOTE
BOTELER
BOTELLA
BOTEN
BOTEROL
BOTEROLL
BOTETE
BOTFLIES
BOTFLY
BOTH
BOTHER
BOTHERATION
BOTHERED
BOTHERER
BOTHERHEADED
BOTHERING
BOTHERMENT
BOTHERSOME
BOTHIE
BOTHIES
BOTHRENCHYMA
BOTHRIA
BOTHRIUM
BOTHROI
BOTHROPIC
BOTHROS
BOTHSIDED
BOTHWAY
BOTHY
BOTONE
BOTONEE
BOTONG
BOTONY
BOTOYAN
BOTRY
BOTRYOGEN
BOTRYOID
BOTRYOIDAL
BOTRYOIDALLY
BOTRYOLITE
BOTRYOMYCOMA

BOTRYOPTERID	BOUGHED	BOURGEON	BOWING	BOXY
BOTRYOSE	BOUGHPOT	BOURI	BOWINGLY	BOY
BOTS	BOUGHT	BOURN	BOWK	BOYANG
BOTT	BOUGHTEN	BOURNE	BOWKAIL	BOYAR
BOTTEGA	BOUGHY	BOURNONITE	BOWKNOT	BOYARD
BOTTEGHE	BOUGIE	BOUROCK	BOWL	BOYARDISM
BOTTEKIN	BOUILLI	BOURRAN	BOWLA	BOYARISM
BOTTIER	BOUILLON	BOURRE	BOWLDER	BOYAU
BOTTINE	BOUILLONE	BOURREAU	BOWLDERHEAD	BOYAUS
BOTTLE	BOUK	BOURREE	BOWLDERING	BOYAUX
BOTTLEBIRD	BOUKIT	BOURRELET	BOWLDERY	BOYCOTT
BOTTLED	BOUL	BOURSE	BOWLED	BOYCOTTAGE
BOTTLEFLOWER	BOULANGERITE	BOURTREE	BOWLEG	BOYCOTTER
BOTTLEHEAD	BOULDER	BOUSE	BOWLEGGED	BOYER
BOTTLEHOLDER	BOULDERHEAD	BOUSED	BOWLER	BOYFRIEND
BOTTLEMAKER	BOULDERING	BOUSER	BOWLIN	BOYHOOD
BOTTLEMAKING	BOULDERS	BOUSING	BOWLINE	BOYISH
BOTTLEMAN	BOULDERY	BOUSY	BOWLING	BOYISHLY
BOTTLENECK	BOULE	BOUT	BOWLMAKER	BOYISHNESS
BOTTLENEST	BOULEUTERIA	BOUTADE	BOWLS	BOYISM
BOTTLENOSE	BOULEUTERION	BOUTEFEU	BOWLY	BOYLA
BOTTLER	BOULEVARD	BOUTELL	BOWMAKER	BOYO
BOTTLESTONE	BOULEVARDIER	BOUTIQUE	BOWMAKING	BOYSENBERRIES
BOTTLING	BOULIMIA	BOUTO	BOWMAN	BOYSENBERRY
BOTTOM	BOULLE	BOUTON	BOWMEN	BOZA
BOTTOMED	BOULT	BOUTONNIERE	BOWN	BOZAH
BOTTOMER	BOULTEL	BOUTRE	BOWPIN	BOZAL
BOTTOMING	BOULTER	BOUTYLKA	BOWPOT	BOZINE
BOTTOMLAND	BOULTERER	BOUW	BOWRALITE	BOZO
BOTTOMLESS	BOUN	BOVARISM	BOWS	BOZZE
BOTTOMLESSLY	BOUNCE	BOVARYSM	BOWSE	BOZZETTO
BOTTOMMOST	BOUNCEABLE	BOVATE	BOWSER	BRA
BOTTOMRIED	BOUNCEABLY	BOVENLAND	BOWSERY	BRAB
BOTTOMRY	BOUNCED	BOVICIDE	BOWSHOT	BRABAGIOUS
BOTTOMRYING	BOUNCER	BOVICULTURE	BOWSIE	BRABANT
BOTTOMS	BOUNCIER	BOVID	BOWSMAN	BRABBLE
BOTTSTICK	BOUNCIEST	BOVIFORM	BOWSPRIT	BRABBLED
BOTTU	BOUNCILY	BOVINE	BOWSSEN	BRABBLEMENT
BOTULIFORM	BOUNCING	BOVINELY	BOWSTAVE	BRABBLER
BOTULIN	BOUNCINGLY	BOVINITY	BOWSTRING	BRABBLING
BOTULINUS	BOUNCY	BOVO	BOWSTRINGED	BRACA
BOTULISM	BOUND	BOVOID	BOWSTRINGING	BRACAE
BOTULISMUS	BOUNDARIES	BOVOVACCINE	BOWSTRUNG	BRACCAE
BOUBA	BOUNDARY	BOW	BOWTELL	BRACCATE
BOUBAS	BOUNDED	BOWABLE	BOWWOMAN	BRACCIALE
BOUBOU	BOUNDEN	BOWBACK	BOWWOOD	BRACCIANITE
BOUCAN	BOUNDER	BOWBELLS	BOWWORT	BRACCIO
BOUCH	BOUNDING	BOWBENT	BOWWOW	BRACE
BOUCHAL	BOUNDINGLY	BOWBOY	BOWWOWS	BRACED
BOUCHALEEN	BOUNDLESS	BOWDEN	BOWYANG	BRACELET
BOUCHARDE	BOUNDLESSLY	BOWDITCH	BOWYER	BRACELETED
BOUCHE	BOUNDLY	BOWDLERISM	BOX	BRACER
BOUCHEE	BOUNDS	BOWDLERIZE	BOXBERRIES	BRACERO
BOUCHER	BOUNTEOUS	BOWDLERIZED	BOXBERRY	BRACEROS
BOUCHERISM	BOUNTEOUSLY	BOWDLERIZING	BOXBOARD	BRACES
BOUCHERIZE	BOUNTIED	BOWED	BOXBUSH	BRACH
BOUCHETTE	BOUNTIES	BOWEL	BOXCAR	BRACHE
BOUCHON	BOUNTIFUL	BOWELED	BOXCARS	BRACHELYTROUS
BOUCHONS	BOUNTIFULLY	BOWELING	BOXEN	BRACHERER
BOUCLE	BOUNTITH	BOWELLED	BOXER	BRACHERING
BOUD	BOUNTREE	BOWELLING	BOXES	BRACHET
BOUDERIE	BOUNTY	BOWELS	BOXFISH	BRACHIA
BOUDIN	BOUQUET	BOWENITE	BOXHAUL	BRACHIAL
BOUDOIR	BOUQUETIERE	BOWER	BOXHEAD	BRACHIALIS
BOUDOIRESQUE	BOUQUINISTE	BOWERBIRD	BOXHOLDER	BRACHIATE
BOUET	BOURASQUE	BOWERIES	BOXING	BRACHIATED
BOUFFANCY	BOURBON	BOWERLY	BOXINGS	BRACHIATING
BOUFFANT	BOURBONIZE	BOWERMAIDEN	BOXKEEPER	BRACHIATION
BOUFFANTE	BOURD	BOWERMAY	BOXLIKE	BRACHIATOR
BOUFFE	BOURDER	BOWERWOMAN	BOXMAN	BRACHIOLARIA
BOUFFON	BOURDON	BOWERY	BOXROOM	BRACHIOPOD
BOUGAR	BOURETTE	BOWET	BOXTHORN	BRACHIOSAUR
BOUGE	BOURG	BOWFIN	BOXTREE	BRACHIUM
BOUGEE	BOURGADE	BOWGRACE	BOXTY	BRACHYAXIS
BOUGERON	BOURGEOIS	BOWHEAD	BOXWALLAH	BRACHYCEPHAL
BOUGET	BOURGEOISE	BOWIE	BOXWOOD	BRACHYCEPHALES
BOUGH	BOURGEOISIE	BOWIEFUL	BOXWORK	BRACHYCEPHALI

BRACHYCEROUS	BRAGGARTRY	BRAKY	BRANNIGAN	BRAVISSIMO
BRACHYCRANIC	BRAGGED	BRAMBLE	BRANNY	BRAVO
BRACHYDACTYL	BRAGGER	BRAMBLEBERRIES	BRANSLE	BRAVOES
BRACHYDONT	BRAGGERY	BRAMBLEBERRY	BRANT	BRAVOITE
BRACHYGRAPHY	BRAGGET	BRAMBLEBUSH	BRANTAIL	BRAVOS
BRACHYLOGY	BRAGGING	BRAMBLED	BRANTNESS	BRAVURA
BRACHYPODINE	BRAGGINGLY	BRAMBLIER	BRAROW	BRAW
BRACHYPODOUS	BRAGGISH	BRAMBLIEST	BRAS	BRAWL
BRACHYSKELIC	BRAGGISHLY	BRAMBLING	BRASERO	BRAWLER
BRACHYSM	BRAGGITE	BRAMBLY	BRASEROS	BRAWLING
BRACHYTIC	BRAGGLE	BRAME	BRASH	BRAWLINGLY
BRACHYTMEMA	BRAGGY	BRAN	BRASHIER	BRAWLY
BRACHYTYPOUS	BRAGITE	BRANCARD	BRASHIEST	BRAWN
BRACHYURAL	BRAGLY	BRANCARDIER	BRASHINESS	BRAWNED
BRACHYURAN	BRAGOZZO	BRANCH	BRASHLY	BRAWNEDNESS
BRACHYURE	BRAGUETTE	BRANCHAGE	BRASHNESS	BRAWNER
BRACHYUROUS	BRAGWORT	BRANCHED	BRASHY	BRAWNIER
BRACING	BRAHMA	BRANCHER	BRASIER	BRAWNIEST
BRACINGLY	BRAHMACHARI	BRANCHERY	BRASILETE	BRAWNINESS
BRACINGNESS	BRAID	BRANCHES	BRASILETTO	BRAWNY
BRACK	BRAIDED	BRANCHIA	BRASQUE	BRAWS
BRACKED	BRAIDER	BRANCHIAE	BRASQUED	BRAXIES
BRACKEN	BRAIDING	BRANCHIAL	BRASQUING	BRAXY
BRACKENED	BRAIES	BRANCHIATE	BRASS	BRAY
BRACKER	BRAIL	BRANCHIER	BRASSAGE	BRAYED
BRACKET	BRAILLE	BRANCHIER	BRASSARD	BRAYER
BRACKETING	BRAILLER	BRANCHIEST	BRASSART	BRAYERA
BRACKING	BRAILS	BRANCHIFORM	BRASSBOUND	BRAYERIN
BRACKISH	BRAIN	BRANCHIHYAL	BRASSBOUNDER	BRAYING
BRACKISHNESS	BRAINER	BRANCHING	BRASSE	BRAYSTONE
BRACKMARD	BRAINFAG	BRANCHIOMERE	BRASSER	BRAZA
BRACKY	BRAINGE	BRANCHIOPOD	BRASSERIE	BRAZE
BRACONID	BRAINIER	BRANCHIOSAUR	BRASSES	BRAZED
BRACONNIERE	BRAINIEST	BRANCHIREME	BRASSEY	BRAZEN
BRACOZZO	BRAINILY	BRANCHIUROUS	BRASSIDIC	BRAZENED
BRACT	BRAININESS	BRANCHLET	BRASSIE	BRAZENFACE
BRACTEA	BRAINISH	BRANCHLING	BRASSIER	BRAZENFACED
BRACTEAL	BRAINLESS	BRANCHMAN	BRASSIERE	BRAZENING
BRACTEATE	BRAINLESSLY	BRANCHSTAND	BRASSIES	BRAZENLY
BRACTED	BRAINPAN	BRANCHWAY	BRASSIEST	BRAZENNESS
BRACTEIFORM	BRAINPOWER	BRANCHY	BRASSILY	BRAZER
BRACTEOLATE	BRAINS	BRAND	BRASSINESS	BRAZERA
BRACTEOLE	BRAINSICK	BRANDED	BRASSY	BRAZIER
BRACTEOSE	BRAINSICKLY	BRANDER	BRAT	BRAZIERY
BRACTLET	BRAINSTEM	BRANDERING	BRATCHET	BRAZIL
BRAD	BRAINSTORM	BRANDIED	BRATLING	BRAZILEIN
BRADAWL	BRAINWASH	BRANDIES	BRATSTVA	BRAZILETTE
BRADDED	BRAINWASHING	BRANDING	BRATTACH	BRAZILITE
BRADDING	BRAINWOOD	BRANDISE	BRATTICE	BRAZILWOOD
BRADENHEAD	BRAINWORK	BRANDISH	BRATTICED	BRAZING
BRADOON	BRAINWORKER	BRANDISHER	BRATTICER	BREA
BRADSOT	BRAINY	BRANDISITE	BRATTICING	BREACH
BRADYCARDIA	BRAIRD	BRANDLE	BRATTISH	BREACHER
BRADYCARDIC	BRAIRDED	BRANDLIN	BRATTLE	BREACHY
BRADYCROTIC	BRAIRDING	BRANDLING	BRATTLED	BREAD
BRADYPOD	BRAIREAU	BRANDRETH	BRATTLING	BREADBASKET
BRADYPODE	BRAIRO	BRANDS	BRATWURST	BREADBERRY
BRADYPODOID	BRAISE	BRANDSOLDER	BRAUL	BREADBOARD
BRADYSEISM	BRAISED	BRANDY	BRAULA	BREADBOX
BRADYSEISMAL	BRAISING	BRANDYBALL	BRAUNA	BREADEARNER
BRADYSEISMIC	BRAIZE	BRANDYING	BRAUNITE	BREADEARNING
BRADYTELY	BRAK	BRANDYMAN	BRAVA	BREADED
BRAE	BRAKE	BRANDYWINE	BRAVADE	BREADEN
BRAEFACE	BRAKEAGE	BRANGLE	BRAVADO	BREADFRUIT
BRAEHEAD	BRAKED	BRANGLED	BRAVADOED	BREADMAKER
BRAEMAN	BRAKEHAND	BRANGLEMENT	BRAVADOES	BREADMAKING
BRAES	BRAKEHEAD	BRANGLER	BRAVADOING	BREADMAN
BRAESIDE	BRAKELESS	BRANGLING	BRAVADOS	BREADNUT
BRAG	BRAKEMAKER	BRANIAL	BRAVE	BREADROOT
BRAGAS	BRAKEMAN	BRANK	BRAVEHEARTED	BREADS
BRAGER	BRAKEMEN	BRANKIE	BRAVELY	BREADSELLER
BRAGGADOCIAN	BRAKER	BRANKS	BRAVENESS	BREADSTITCH
BRAGGADOCIO	BRAKESMAN	BRANKURSINE	BRAVER	BREADSTUFF
BRAGGADOCIOS	BRAKIE	BRANKY	BRAVERIES	BREADTH
BRAGGART	BRAKIER	BRANLE	BRAVERY	BREADTHRIDERS
BRAGGARTISM	BRAKIEST	BRANNER	BRAVEST	BREADTHWAYS
BRAGGARTLY	BRAKING	BRANNERITE	BRAVING	BREADTHWISE

BREADWINNER
BREADWINNING
BREAGHE
BREAK
BREAKABLE
BREAKABLY
BREAKAGE
BREAKAWAY
BREAKAX
BREAKAXE
BREAKBACK
BREAKBONE
BREAKBONES
BREAKDOWN
BREAKER
BREAKERMAN
BREAKERMEN
BREAKFAST
BREAKFASTER
BREAKFRONT
BREAKING
BREAKNECK
BREAKOFF
BREAKOUT
BREAKOVER
BREAKS
BREAKSTONE
BREAKTHROUGH
BREAKUP
BREAKWATER
BREAM
BREAMS
BREAN
BREARDS
BREAST
BREASTBAND
BREASTBEAM
BREASTBONE
BREASTED
BREASTER
BREASTHOOK
BREASTING
BREASTMARK
BREASTPIECE
BREASTPIN
BREASTPLATE
BREASTPLOUGH
BREASTPLOW
BREASTRAIL
BREASTROPE
BREASTS
BREASTSUMMER
BREASTWEED
BREASTWISE
BREASTWOOD
BREASTWORK
BREATH
BREATHABLE
BREATHE
BREATHED
BREATHER
BREATHIER
BREATHIEST
BREATHING
BREATHLESS
BREATHLESSLY
BREATHLESSNESS
BREATHSELLER
BREATHTAKING
BREATHY
BREBA
BRECCIA
BRECCIAL
BRECCIATED
BRECCIATION
BRECHAM
BRECHAN

BRECK
BRED
BREDBERGITE
BREDE
BREDESTITCH
BREDI
BREDSTITCH
BREE
BREECH
BREECHBLOCK
BREECHCLOTH
BREECHCLOUT
BREECHED
BREECHES
BREECHING
BREECHLOADER
BREECHLOADING
BREED
BREEDBATE
BREEDER
BREEDING
BREEDY
BREEKS
BREEKUMS
BREEM
BREENGE
BREER
BREEZE
BREEZED
BREEZEWAY
BREEZIER
BREEZIEST
BREEZILY
BREEZINESS
BREEZING
BREEZY
BREGMA
BREGMATA
BREGMATE
BREGMATIC
BREHON
BREI
BREIRD
BREISLAKITE
BREITHAUPTITE
BRELAN
BRELOQUE
BREME
BREMELY
BREMENESS
BREN
BRENNAGE
BRENNSCHLUSS
BRENT
BREPHIC
BRER
BREST
BRET
BRETELLE
BRETESSE
BRETH
BRETHEL
BRETHREN
BRETT
BREVA
BREVE
BREVET
BREVETCIES
BREVETCY
BREVETE
BREVETED
BREVETING
BREVETTED
BREVETTING
BREVIARIES
BREVIARY
BREVIATE

BREVIATURE
BREVICAUDATE
BREVICIPITID
BREVIER
BREVIFOLIATE
BREVIGER
BREVILINGUAL
BREVILOQUENT
BREVIPED
BREVIPEN
BREVIPENNATE
BREVIRADIATE
BREVIROSTRAL
BREVIT
BREVITIES
BREVITY
BREW
BREWAGE
BREWED
BREWER
BREWERIES
BREWERY
BREWHOUSE
BREWING
BREWIS
BREWMASTER
BREWSTER
BREWSTERITE
BREY
BRIAR
BRIARBERRY
BRIARED
BRIARROOT
BRIARWOOD
BRIARY
BRIBABLE
BRIBE
BRIBED
BRIBEE
BRIBEGIVER
BRIBEGIVING
BRIBEMONGER
BRIBER
BRIBERIES
BRIBERY
BRIBETAKER
BRIBETAKING
BRIBEWORTHY
BRIBING
BRICHETTE
BRICK
BRICKBAT
BRICKBATTED
BRICKBATTING
BRICKED
BRICKEN
BRICKFIELDER
BRICKIER
BRICKIEST
BRICKING
BRICKKILN
BRICKLAYING
BRICKLE
BRICKLENESS
BRICKLINER
BRICKLINING
BRICKLY
BRICKMAKER
BRICKMAKING
BRICKS
BRICKSET
BRICKSETTER
BRICKTIMBER
BRICKWORK
BRICKY
BRICKYARD
BRICOLE

BRIDAL
BRIDALE
BRIDALER
BRIDALLY
BRIDALTY
BRIDE
BRIDEBED
BRIDEBOWL
BRIDECAKE
BRIDECHAMBER
BRIDECUP
BRIDEGOD
BRIDEGROOM
BRIDEKNOT
BRIDELACE
BRIDELY
BRIDEMAIDEN
BRIDEMAN
BRIDESMAID
BRIDESMAIDING
BRIDESMAN
BRIDESMEN
BRIDESTAKE
BRIDEWAIN
BRIDEWEED
BRIDEWELL
BRIDEWORT
BRIDGE
BRIDGEABLE
BRIDGEBOARD
BRIDGEBUILDER
BRIDGEBUILDING
BRIDGED
BRIDGEHEAD
BRIDGEKEEPER
BRIDGEMAKER
BRIDGEMAKING
BRIDGEMAN
BRIDGEMASTER
BRIDGEMEN
BRIDGEPOT
BRIDGER
BRIDGETREE
BRIDGEWARD
BRIDGEWAY
BRIDGEWORK
BRIDGING
BRIDLE
BRIDLED
BRIDLEMAN
BRIDLER
BRIDLING
BRIDOON
BRIE
BRIEF
BRIEFCASE
BRIEFED
BRIEFING
BRIEFLESS
BRIEFLESSLY
BRIEFLY
BRIEFNESS
BRIEFS
BRIER
BRIERBERRY
BRIERED
BRIERROOT
BRIERS
BRIERWOOD
BRIERY
BRIEVE
BRIG
BRIGADE
BRIGADED
BRIGADIER
BRIGADING
BRIGALOW

BRIGAND
BRIGANDAGE
BRIGANDER
BRIGANDINE
BRIGANDISH
BRIGANDISHLY
BRIGANDISM
BRIGANTINE
BRIGBOTE
BRIGE
BRIGHT
BRIGHTEN
BRIGHTENER
BRIGHTER
BRIGHTEST
BRIGHTEYES
BRIGHTLY
BRIGHTNESS
BRIGHTS
BRIGHTSMITH
BRIGHTSOME
BRIGHTWORK
BRIGUE
BRIGUED
BRIGUER
BRIGUING
BRIKE
BRILL
BRILLANTE
BRILLIANCE
BRILLIANCY
BRILLIANDEER
BRILLIANT
BRILLIANTINE
BRILLIANTLY
BRILLS
BRIM
BRIMBORION
BRIMBORIUM
BRIMFUL
BRIMFULLY
BRIMFULNESS
BRIMING
BRIMLY
BRIMMED
BRIMMER
BRIMMERED
BRIMMERING
BRIMMING
BRIMMINGLY
BRIMSTONE
BRIMSTONY
BRIN
BRINCE
BRINDED
BRINDISI
BRINDLE
BRINDLED
BRINE
BRINED
BRINER
BRING
BRINGELA
BRINGER
BRINGING
BRINGS
BRINGSEL
BRINIE
BRINIER
BRINIEST
BRININESS
BRINING
BRINISH
BRINJAL
BRINJAREE
BRINJARRIES
BRINJARRY

BRINJAUL	BROADBILL	BROIDERED	BROMOPICRIN	BROOKFLOWER
BRINK	BROADBRIM	BROIDERER	BROMOPIKRIN	BROOKIE
BRINKMANSHIP	BROADCAST	BROIDERIES	BROMOPROTEIN	BROOKIER
BRINSELL	BROADCASTED	BROIDERING	BROMOTHYMOL	BROOKIEST
BRINSTON	BROADCASTER	BROIDERY	BROMOUS	BROOKING
BRINY	BROADCASTING	BROIGNE	BROMPICRIN	BROOKITE
BRIO	BROADCLOTH	BROIL	BROMTHYMOL	BROOKLET
BRIOCHE	BROADEN	BROILED	BROMURET	BROOKLIME
BRIOLET	BROADENED	BROILER	BROMVOEL	BROOKS
BRIOLETTE	BROADENING	BROILERY	BROMVOGEL	BROOKSIDE
BRIQUE	BROADEST	BROILING	BROMYRITE	BROOKWEED
BRIQUET	BROADGAGE	BROKAGE	BRON	BROOKY
BRIQUETTE	BROADHEAD	BROKE	BRONC	BROOL
BRIS	BROADHEARTED	BROKEN	BRONCHI	BROOM
BRISANCE	BROADHORN	BROKENHEARTED	BRONCHIA	BROOMBUSH
BRISANT	BROADLEAF	BROKENLY	BRONCHIAL	BROOMCORN
BRISCOLA	BROADLING	BROKENNESS	BRONCHIALLY	BROOMER
BRISE	BROADLINGS	BROKER	BRONCHILOQUY	BROOMMAKER
BRISEMENT	BROADLOOM	BROKERAGE	BRONCHIOCELE	BROOMMAKING
BRISK	BROADLY	BROKERY	BRONCHIOLAR	BROOMRAPE
BRISKED	BROADNESS	BROKES	BRONCHIOLE	BROOMROOT
BRISKEN	BROADPIECE	BROKING	BRONCHITIC	BROOMSHANK
BRISKENED	BROADSHARE	BROLETTI	BRONCHITIS	BROOMSTAFF
BRISKENING	BROADSHEET	BROLETTO	BRONCHO	BROOMSTICK
BRISKET	BROADSIDE	BROLGA	BRONCHOBUSTER	BROOMSTRAW
BRISKING	BROADSWORD	BROLL	BRONCHOGENIC	BROOMTAIL
BRISKLY	BROADTAIL	BROLLIES	BRONCHOS	BROOMWEED
BRISKNESS	BROADWAY	BROLLY	BRONCHOSCOPE	BROOMWOOD
BRISKY	BROADWAYS	BROMA	BRONCHOSCOPY	BROOMWORT
BRISLING	BROADWISE	BROMAL	BRONCHOTOMY	BROOMY
BRISQUE	BROB	BROMAMIDE	BRONCHUS	BROON
BRISS	BROCADE	BROMARGYRITE	BRONCO	BROOZLED
BRIST	BROCADED	BROMATE	BRONCOBUSTER	BROQUERY
BRISTLE	BROCADING	BROMATIUM	BRONCOS	BROQUINEER
BRISTLEBIRD	BROCARD	BROME	BRONGNIARDITE	BROSE
BRISTLECONE	BROCATEL	BROMEGRASS	BRONTEON	BROSOT
BRISTLED	BROCATELLE	BROMELIAD	BRONTEPHOBIA	BROSSE
BRISTLELIKE	BROCCOLI	BROMELIN	BRONTEUM	BROSY
BRISTLER	BROCH	BROMELLITE	BRONTIDE	BROT
BRISTLES	BROCHAN	BROMHIDROSIS	BRONTIDES	BROTCHEN
BRISTLETAIL	BROCHANT	BROMHYDRATE	BRONTOGRAM	BROTEL
BRISTLEWORT	BROCHANTITE	BROMHYDRIC	BRONTOGRAPH	BROTH
BRISTLIER	BROCHE	BROMIC	BRONTOLITE	BROTHE
BRISTLIEST	BROCHETTE	BROMID	BRONTOLITH	BROTHEL
BRISTLINESS	BROCHO	BROMIDE	BRONTOLOGY	BROTHER
BRISTLING	BROCHOPHONY	BROMIDIC	BRONTOMETER	BROTHERED
BRISTLY	BROCHT	BROMIDROSIS	BRONTOPHOBIA	BROTHERHOOD
BRISURE	BROCHURE	BROMIN	BRONTOSAUR	BROTHERING
BRIT	BROCK	BROMINATE	BRONTOSAURUS	BROTHERLY
BRITANNIA	BROCKAGE	BROMINATED	BRONTOSAURUSES	BROTHERS
BRITCHEL	BROCKED	BROMINATING	BRONTOSCOPY	BROTHERWORT
BRITCHES	BROCKET	BROMINATION	BRONZE	BROTHY
BRITE	BROCKLE	BROMINE	BRONZED	BROTOCRYSTAL
BRITH	BROD	BROMINISM	BRONZEN	BROTT
BRITSKA	BRODDER	BROMISM	BRONZER	BROTULID
BRITT	BRODE	BROMITE	BRONZESMITH	BROTULIFORM
BRITTEN	BRODEE	BROMIZATION	BRONZEWING	BROUD
BRITTLE	BRODEKIN	BROMIZE	BRONZIFY	BROUETTE
BRITTLEBUSH	BRODEQUIN	BROMIZER	BRONZINE	BROUGH
BRITTLELY	BRODERER	BROMLITE	BRONZING	BROUGHAM
BRITTLENESS	BRODERIE	BROMOACETONE	BRONZITE	BROUGHT
BRITTLESTEM	BRODIE	BROMOAURATES	BRONZITITE	BROUHAHA
BRITTLEWOOD	BRODYAGA	BROMOBENZENE	BRONZY	BROUILLON
BRITTLEWORT	BRODYAGI	BROMOCYANID	BROO	BROUZE
BRITTLING	BROG	BROMOCYANIDE	BROOCH	BROW
BRITZKA	BROGAN	BROMOFORM	BROOCHED	BROWACHE
BRITZSKA	BROGGER	BROMOHYDRATE	BROOCHING	BROWBAND
BRIZE	BROGGERITE	BROMOHYDRIN	BROOD	BROWBEAT
BRIZZ	BROGGLE	BROMOIL	BROODED	BROWBEATEN
BROACH	BROGUE	BROMOIODID	BROODER	BROWBEATER
BROACHED	BROGUED	BROMOIODIDE	BROODIER	BROWBEATING
BROACHER	BROGUENEER	BROMOIODISM	BROODIEST	BROWBOUND
BROACHING	BROGUER	BROMOIODIZED	BROODING	BROWDEN
BROAD	BROGUES	BROMOL	BROODSAC	BROWED
BROADACRE	BROGUING	BROMOMANIA	BROODY	BROWET
BROADAX	BROH	BROMOMETRIC	BROOK	BROWIS
BROADAXE	BROIDER	BROMOMETRY	BROOKED	BROWLESS

BROWMAN	BRUNNEOUS	BUBAL	BUCKETMAKING	BUDGERIGAR
BROWN	BRUNT	BUBALE	BUCKETMAN	BUDGERO
BROWNBACK	BRUSCUS	BUBALINE	BUCKETY	BUDGEROW
BROWNED	BRUSH	BUBALIS	BUCKEYE	BUDGERYGAH
BROWNER	BRUSHBALL	BUBAS	BUCKEYED	BUDGET
BROWNEST	BRUSHBIRD	BUBBER	BUCKHORN	BUDGETARY
BROWNIE	BRUSHBUSH	BUBBIES	BUCKHOUND	BUDGETED
BROWNING	BRUSHED	BUBBLE	BUCKIE	BUDGETEER
BROWNISH	BRUSHER	BUBBLEBOW	BUCKING	BUDGETER
BROWNNESS	BRUSHES	BUBBLED	BUCKISH	BUDGETING
BROWNNOSE	BRUSHET	BUBBLER	BUCKISHLY	BUDGIE
BROWNOUT	BRUSHIER	BUBBLES	BUCKISHNESS	BUDGING
BROWNPRINT	BRUSHIEST	BUBBLIER	BUCKISM	BUDLET
BROWNSTONE	BRUSHING	BUBBLIEST	BUCKJUMP	BUDLING
BROWNTAIL	BRUSHITE	BUBBLING	BUCKLE	BUDMASH
BROWNTOP	BRUSHLAND	BUBBLINGLY	BUCKLED	BUDTIME
BROWNWEED	BRUSHMAKER	BUBBLY	BUCKLER	BUDWOOD
BROWNWORT	BRUSHMAKING	BUBBY	BUCKLING	BUDWORM
BROWNY	BRUSHMAN	BUBBYBUSH	BUCKLUM	BUDZART
BROWPIECE	BRUSHMEN	BUBINGA	BUCKO	BUDZAT
BROWPOST	BRUSHOFF	BUBO	BUCKOES	BUF
BROWSE	BRUSHUP	BUBOED	BUCKONE	BUFAGIN
BROWSED	BRUSHWOOD	BUBOES	BUCKPLATE	BUFF
BROWSER	BRUSHWORK	BUBONALGIA	BUCKPOT	BUFFA
BROWSING	BRUSHY	BUBONIC	BUCKRA	BUFFABLE
BROWST	BRUSK	BUBONOCELE	BUCKRAM	BUFFALO
BROWZER	BRUSQUE	BUBU	BUCKRAMED	BUFFALOBACK
BRUANG	BRUSQUELY	BUBUD	BUCKRAMING	BUFFALOED
BRUBRU	BRUSQUENESS	BUBUKLE	BUCKS	BUFFALOES
BRUCELLOSIS	BRUSQUERIE	BUCAN	BUCKSAW	BUFFALOING
BRUCHID	BRUSSEL	BUCARE	BUCKSHEE	BUFFALOS
BRUCIA	BRUSTLE	BUCAYO	BUCKSHOT	BUFFBALL
BRUCIN	BRUSTLED	BUCCA	BUCKSKIN	BUFFBAR
BRUCINA	BRUSTLING	BUCCAL	BUCKSKINNED	BUFFCOAT
BRUCINE	BRUT	BUCCAN	BUCKSTALL	BUFFED
BRUCITE	BRUTAL	BUCCANED	BUCKSTAY	BUFFER
BRUCKLE	BRUTALITIES	BUCCANEER	BUCKSTONE	BUFFET
BRUCKLED	BRUTALITY	BUCCANING	BUCKTAIL	BUFFETED
BRUCKLENESS	BRUTALIZE	BUCCANNED	BUCKTHORN	BUFFETER
BRUET	BRUTALIZED	BUCCANNING	BUCKTOOTH	BUFFETING
BRUGH	BRUTALIZING	BUCCATE	BUCKTOOTHED	BUFFI
BRUH	BRUTALLY	BUCCHERO	BUCKU	BUFFIN
BRUIN	BRUTE	BUCCIN	BUCKWAGON	BUFFING
BRUISE	BRUTIFIED	BUCCINA	BUCKWASH	BUFFLE
BRUISED	BRUTIFY	BUCCINAE	BUCKWASHER	BUFFLEHEAD
BRUISER	BRUTIFYING	BUCCINAL	BUCKWASHING	BUFFLEHORN
BRUISEWORT	BRUTING	BUCCINATOR	BUCKWHEAT	BUFFO
BRUISING	BRUTISH	BUCCINATORY	BUCKWHEATER	BUFFONE
BRUIT	BRUTISHLY	BUCCINIFORM	BUCKY	BUFFONT
BRUITER	BRUTISHNESS	BUCCINOID	BUCOLIAST	BUFFOON
BRUJERIA	BRUTISM	BUCCO	BUCOLIC	BUFFOONERIES
BRUJO	BRUTTER	BUCCOLINGUAL	BUCOLICAL	BUFFOONERY
BRUKE	BRUXISM	BUCCULA	BUCOLICALLY	BUFFOONISH
BRULEE	BRUYERE	BUCCULAE	BUCRANE	BUFFOONISM
BRULOT	BRUZZ	BUCENTAUR	BUCRANIA	BUFFWARE
BRULYIE	BRYACEOUS	BUCHITE	BUCRANIUM	BUFFY
BRULYIEMENT	BRYNZA	BUCHNERITE	BUD	BUFIDIN
BRULZIE	BRYOGENIN	BUCHONITE	BUDA	BUFO
BRUM	BRYOLOGICAL	BUCHU	BUDBREAK	BUFONID
BRUMAL	BRYOLOGIST	BUCK	BUDDAGE	BUFONITE
BRUMBEE	BRYOLOGY	BUCKAROO	BUDDAH	BUFOTALIN
BRUMBIE	BRYONIA	BUCKASS	BUDDED	BUG
BRUMBIES	BRYONIDIN	BUCKAYRO	BUDDER	BUGA
BRUMBY	BRYONIES	BUCKBEAN	BUDDHI	BUGABOO
BRUME	BRYONIN	BUCKBERRY	BUDDIE	BUGALA
BRUMMAGEM	BRYONY	BUCKBOARD	BUDDIES	BUGAN
BRUMMER	BRYOPHYTE	BUCKBRUSH	BUDDING	BUGARA
BRUMMY	BRYOPHYTIC	BUCKBUSH	BUDDLE	BUGBANE
BRUMOUS	BRYOZOAN	BUCKED	BUDDLEIA	BUGBEAR
BRUNCH	BRYOZOON	BUCKEEN	BUDDLER	BUGBITE
BRUNE	BRYOZOUM	BUCKER	BUDDY	BUGEYE
BRUNET	BU	BUCKET	BUDGE	BUGFISH
BRUNETNESS	BUAL	BUCKETED	BUDGED	BUGGANE
BRUNETTE	BUAT	BUCKETEER	BUDGER	BUGGED
BRUNETTENESS	BUAZE	BUCKETER	BUDGEREE	BUGGER
BRUNISSURE	BUB	BUCKETING	BUDGEREEGAH	BUGGERY
BRUNIZEM	BUBA	BUCKETMAKER	BUDGERIGAH	BUGGIER

BUGGIES	BULCHIN	BULLFIST	BUMAREE	BUNCOING
BUGGIEST	BULDER	BULLFLOWER	BUMBAILIFF	BUNCOMBE
BUGGINESS	BULE	BULLFOOT	BUMBARD	BUNCOS
BUGGING	BULGE	BULLFROG	BUMBARGE	BUND
BUGGY	BULGED	BULLGINE	BUMBASS	BUNDER
BUGGYMAN	BULGER	BULLHEAD	BUMBASTE	BUNDIES
BUGGYMEN	BULGIER	BULLHEADED	BUMBAZE	BUNDLE
BUGHEAD	BULGIEST	BULLHEADEDLY	BUMBEE	BUNDLER
BUGHOUSE	BULGINESS	BULLHOOF	BUMBERSHOOT	BUNDLET
BUGHT	BULGING	BULLHORN	BUMBLE	BUNDOBUST
BUGHT	BULGUR	BULLIED	BUMBLEBEE	BUNDOC
BUGIA	BULGY	BULLIES	BUMBLEBERRY	BUNDOCKS
BUGLE	BULIES	BULLIFORM	BUMBLED	BUNDOOK
BUGLED	BULIMIA	BULLIMONG	BUMBLEFOOT	BUNDWEED
BUGLER	BULIMIAC	BULLING	BUMBLEKITE	BUNDY
BUGLET	BULIMIC	BULLION	BUMBLEPUPPY	BUNEMOST
BUGLEWEED	BULIMIFORM	BULLISH	BUMBLER	BUNG
BUGLING	BULIMOID	BULLISHLY	BUMBLING	BUNGALOID
BUGLOSS	BULIMY	BULLISHNESS	BUMBO	BUNGALOW
BUGLOSSES	BULK	BULLISM	BUMBOAT	BUNGARUM
BUGOLOGIST	BULKED	BULLNECK	BUMBOATMAN	BUNGED
BUGOLOGY	BULKER	BULLNECKED	BUMBOATWOMAN	BUNGEE
BUGOR	BULKHEAD	BULLNOSE	BUMCLOCK	BUNGERLY
BUGOUT	BULKHEADED	BULLNUT	BUMF	BUNGEY
BUGRE	BULKIER	BULLOCK	BUMFEG	BUNGFU
BUGS	BULKIEST	BULLOCKER	BUMICKY	BUNGFULL
BUGSEED	BULKILY	BULLOCKMAN	BUMKIN	BUNGHOLE
BUGWEED	BULKINESS	BULLOCKY	BUMMACK	BUNGING
BUGWORT	BULKING	BULLOSE	BUMMALO	BUNGLE
BUHL	BULKY	BULLOUS	BUMMALOS	BUNGLED
BUHLBUHL	BULL	BULLPATES	BUMMAREE	BUNGLER
BUHLWORK	BULLA	BULLPEN	BUMMED	BUNGLING
BUHR	BULLACE	BULLPOUT	BUMMEL	BUNGLINGLY
BUHRMILL	BULLAE	BULLPUP	BUMMER	BUNGMAKER
BUHRSTONE	BULLAMACOW	BULLRING	BUMMERY	BUNGO
BUILD	BULLAN	BULLROARER	BUMMIL	BUNGOS
BUILDER	BULLARIES	BULLS	BUMMING	BUNGS
BUILDING	BULLARY	BULLSTICKER	BUMMLE	BUNGTOWN
BUILDINGS	BULLATE	BULLSUCKER	BUMMLER	BUNGWALL
BUILDRESS	BULLATED	BULLTOAD	BUMMOCK	BUNGY
BUILDUP	BULLATION	BULLULE	BUMP	BUNION
BUILT	BULLBAITING	BULLWEED	BUMPER	BUNK
BUIRD	BULLBAT	BULLWHACK	BUMPERED	BUNKED
BUIRDLY	BULLBEGGAR	BULLWHACKER	BUMPERING	BUNKER
BUIRE	BULLBERRY	BULLWHIP	BUMPIER	BUNKERMAN
BUISSON	BULLBIRD	BULLWHIPPED	BUMPIEST	BUNKERMEN
BUIST	BULLBOAT	BULLWHIPPING	BUMPILY	BUNKHOUSE
BUKE	BULLCOMBER	BULLWORK	BUMPINESS	BUNKIE
BUKH	BULLDOG	BULLWORT	BUMPING	BUNKING
BUKID	BULLDOGGED	BULLY	BUMPINGLY	BUNKLOAD
BUKK	BULLDOGGER	BULLYBOY	BUMPITY	BUNKMATE
BUKSHEE	BULLDOGGING	BULLYHUFF	BUMPKIN	BUNKO
BUKSHI	BULLDOGGY	BULLYING	BUMPOLOGY	BUNKOED
BULAK	BULLDOZE	BULLYINGLY	BUMPSY	BUNKOING
BULAQ	BULLDOZED	BULLYRAG	BUMPTIOUS	BUNKOS
BULB	BULLDOZER	BULLYRAGGED	BUMPTIOUSLY	BUNKS
BULBACEOUS	BULLDOZING	BULLYRAGGER	BUMPY	BUNKUM
BULBAR	BULLDUST	BULLYRAGGING	BUMTRAP	BUNN
BULBED	BULLED	BULLYROCK	BUMWOOD	BUNNELL
BULBI	BULLER	BULLYROOK	BUN	BUNNIA
BULBIER	BULLET	BULREEDY	BUNA	BUNNIES
BULBIEST	BULLETED	BULRUSH	BUNCAL	BUNNING
BULBIFEROUS	BULLETHEAD	BULSE	BUNCE	BUNNY
BULBIFORM	BULLETIN	BULT	BUNCH	BUNNYMOUTH
BULBIL	BULLETINED	BULTEN	BUNCHBERRIES	BUNODONT
BULBILLA	BULLETINING	BULTER	BUNCHBERRY	BUNSENITE
BULBLET	BULLETMAKER	BULTEY	BUNCHED	BUNT
BULBLIKE	BULLETMAKING	BULTI	BUNCHER	BUNTAL
BULBOSE	BULLETPROOF	BULTO	BUNCHFLOWER	BUNTED
BULBOTUBER	BULLETS	BULTONG	BUNCHIER	BUNTER
BULBOUS	BULLETWOOD	BULTOW	BUNCHIEST	BUNTINE
BULBS	BULLETY	BULWAND	BUNCHILY	BUNTING
BULBUL	BULLFICE	BULWARK	BUNCHINESS	BUNTLINE
BULBULE	BULLFIGHT	BULWARKED	BUNCHING	BUNTON
BULBUS	BULLFIGHTER	BULWARKING	BUNCHY	BUNTS
BULBY	BULLFIGHTING	BULWARKS	BUNCO	BUNTY
BULCH	BULLFINCH	BUM	BUNCOED	BUNUELO

BUNYA
BUNYAH
BUNYIP
BUONAMANI
BUONAMANO
BUOY
BUOYAGE
BUOYANCE
BUOYANCIES
BUOYANCY
BUOYANT
BUOYANTLY
BUOYANTNESS
BUOYED
BUOYING
BUPHTHALMIA
BUPHTHALMIC
BUPHTHALMOS
BUPLEUROL
BUPLEVER
BUPRESTID
BUPRESTIDAN
BUR
BURA
BURAN
BURAO
BURBANKIAN
BURBARK
BURBLER
BURBLY
BURBOLT
BURBOT
BURBOTS
BURD
BURDASH
BURDEN
BURDENABLE
BURDENED
BURDENER
BURDENING
BURDENOUS
BURDENSOME
BURDENSOMELY
BURDIE
BURDOCK
BURDON
BURE
BUREAU
BUREAUCRACIES
BUREAUCRACY
BUREAUCRAT
BUREAUCRATIC
BUREAUS
BUREAUX
BUREL
BURELAGE
BURELE
BURELY
BUREO
BURET
BURETTE
BURFISH
BURG
BURGAGE
BURGALITY
BURGALL
BURGAMOT
BURGEE
BURGENSIC
BURGEON
BURGEONED
BURGEONING
BURGER
BURGESS
BURGH
BURGHAL
BURGHALPENNY

BURGHBOTE
BURGHER
BURGHMASTER
BURGHMOOT
BURGHMOTE
BURGI
BURGLAR
BURGLARIES
BURGLARIOUS
BURGLARIZE
BURGLARIZED
BURGLARIZING
BURGLARPROOF
BURGLARY
BURGLE
BURGLED
BURGLING
BURGOMASTER
BURGONET
BURGOO
BURGOOS
BURGOUT
BURGOYNE
BURGRAVE
BURGRAVIATE
BURGUL
BURGULLIAN
BURGUS
BURGWARE
BURGWERE
BURH
BURHEAD
BURHMOOT
BURI
BURIAL
BURIAN
BURIED
BURIER
BURIN
BURINIST
BURION
BURITI
BURK
BURKA
BURKE
BURKED
BURKER
BURKHA
BURKING
BURKITE
BURKUNDAUZE
BURKUNDAZ
BURL
BURLA
BURLAP
BURLAPS
BURLE
BURLED
BURLER
BURLESK
BURLESQUE
BURLESQUED
BURLESQUELY
BURLESQUER
BURLESQUING
BURLET
BURLETTA
BURLEY
BURLEYS
BURLIER
BURLIES
BURLIEST
BURLILY
BURLINESS
BURLING
BURLY
BURMITE

BURN
BURNABLE
BURNBEAT
BURNED
BURNER
BURNET
BURNETTIZE
BURNETTIZED
BURNETTIZING
BURNEWIN
BURNFIRE
BURNIE
BURNIEBEE
BURNING
BURNINGLY
BURNISH
BURNISHER
BURNISHING
BURNISHMENT
BURNOOSE
BURNOOSED
BURNOUS
BURNOUT
BURNOVER
BURNSIDE
BURNSIDES
BURNT
BURNUP
BURNUT
BURNWEED
BURNWOOD
BURNY
BURO
BURP
BURR
BURRA
BURRAH
BURRAWANG
BURRBARK
BURRED
BURREL
BURRER
BURRHEL
BURRIER
BURRIEST
BURRIO
BURRITO
BURRITOS
BURRKNOT
BURRO
BURROS
BURROW
BURROWED
BURROWEED
BURROWER
BURROWING
BURROWS
BURROWSTOWN
BURRSTONE
BURRY
BURSA
BURSAE
BURSAL
BURSAR
BURSARIAL
BURSARIES
BURSARY
BURSAS
BURSATE
BURSATI
BURSATTEE
BURSAUTEE
BURSE
BURSEED
BURSERACEOUS
BURSICLE
BURSICULATE

BURSIFORM
BURSITIS
BURST
BURSTED
BURSTER
BURSTING
BURSTONE
BURSTWORT
BURSULA
BURT
BURTHEN
BURTHENMAN
BURTON
BURTONIZATION
BURTONIZE
BURTREE
BURUCHA
BURWEED
BURY
BURYING
BUS
BUSBIES
BUSBOY
BUSBY
BUSCARL
BUSCARLE
BUSE
BUSED
BUSES
BUSH
BUSHBEATER
BUSHBOY
BUSHBUCK
BUSHED
BUSHEL
BUSHELED
BUSHELER
BUSHELING
BUSHELLED
BUSHELLER
BUSHELLING
BUSHELMAN
BUSHELS
BUSHELWOMAN
BUSHER
BUSHES
BUSHET
BUSHFIGHTER
BUSHFIGHTING
BUSHGOAT
BUSHGRASS
BUSHHAMMER
BUSHI
BUSHIDO
BUSHIER
BUSHIEST
BUSHILY
BUSHINESS
BUSHING
BUSHLAND
BUSHMAKER
BUSHMAKING
BUSHMASTER
BUSHMENT
BUSHPIG
BUSHRANGER
BUSHRANGING
BUSHROPE
BUSHTIT
BUSHVELD
BUSHWA
BUSHWACK
BUSHWAH
BUSHWHACK
BUSHWHACKER
BUSHWHACKING
BUSHWIFE

BUSHWOMAN
BUSHWOOD
BUSIED
BUSIER
BUSIEST
BUSILY
BUSINE
BUSINESS
BUSINESSES
BUSINESSLIKE
BUSINESSMAN
BUSINESSMEN
BUSINESSWOMAN
BUSING
BUSK
BUSKED
BUSKER
BUSKET
BUSKIN
BUSKINED
BUSKINS
BUSKLE
BUSMAN
BUSMEN
BUSS
BUSSE
BUSSED
BUSSER
BUSSES
BUSSING
BUSSOCK
BUSSU
BUSSY
BUST
BUSTARD
BUSTED
BUSTEE
BUSTER
BUSTHEAD
BUSTI
BUSTIAN
BUSTIC
BUSTICATE
BUSTING
BUSTLE
BUSTLED
BUSTLER
BUSTLING
BUSTLINGLY
BUSTO
BUSWAY
BUSY
BUSYBODIES
BUSYBODY
BUSYING
BUSYNESS
BUSYWORK
BUT
BUTADIENE
BUTANE
BUTANOL
BUTANONE
BUTCH
BUTCHA
BUTCHER
BUTCHERBIRD
BUTCHERBROOM
BUTCHERER
BUTCHERESS
BUTCHERIES
BUTCHERING
BUTCHERLY
BUTCHEROUS
BUTCHERY
BUTEIN
BUTENYL
BUTEONINE

BUTIN
BUTINE
BUTLER
BUTLERAGE
BUTLERIES
BUTLERY
BUTMENT
BUTOMACEOUS
BUTOR
BUTOXY
BUTOXYL
BUTS
BUTSUDAN
BUTT
BUTTAL
BUTTE
BUTTED
BUTTER
BUTTERACEOUS
BUTTERBACK
BUTTERBALL
BUTTERBILL
BUTTERBIRD
BUTTERBOUGH
BUTTERBOX
BUTTERBUMP
BUTTERBUR
BUTTERBURR
BUTTERBUSH
BUTTERCUP
BUTTERED
BUTTERFAT
BUTTERFISH
BUTTERFISHES
BUTTERFLIES
BUTTERFLOWER
BUTTERFLY
BUTTERHEAD
BUTTERIES
BUTTERINE
BUTTERIS
BUTTERJAGS
BUTTERMAN
BUTTERMILK
BUTTERMONGER
BUTTERNOSE
BUTTERNUT
BUTTERSCOTCH
BUTTERWEED
BUTTERWORKER
BUTTERWORT
BUTTERY
BUTTING
BUTTINSKY
BUTTLE
BUTTOCK
BUTTOCKED
BUTTOCKER
BUTTOCKS
BUTTON
BUTTONBALL
BUTTONBUR
BUTTONBUSH
BUTTONED
BUTTONER
BUTTONHOLD
BUTTONHOLDER
BUTTONHOLE
BUTTONHOLED
BUTTONHOLER
BUTTONHOLING
BUTTONHOOK
BUTTONING
BUTTONLIKE
BUTTONMOLD
BUTTONMOULD
BUTTONS

BUTTONWEED
BUTTONWOOD
BUTTONY
BUTTRESS
BUTTRESSED
BUTTRESSING
BUTTS
BUTTSTOCK
BUTTWOMAN
BUTTWOMEN
BUTTY
BUTTYMAN
BUTYL
BUTYLAMINE
BUTYLATION
BUTYLENE
BUTYLIC
BUTYNE
BUTYRACEOUS
BUTYRATE
BUTYRIC
BUTYRICALLY
BUTYRIN
BUTYRINASE
BUTYROMETER
BUTYROMETRIC
BUTYRONE
BUTYROUS
BUTYRYL
BUVETTE
BUXACEOUS
BUXERRIES
BUXERRY
BUXOM
BUXOMLY
BUXOMNESS
BUY
BUYABLE
BUYER
BUYING
BUYO
BUZANE
BUZZ
BUZZARD
BUZZARDLY
BUZZED
BUZZER
BUZZERPHONE
BUZZGLOAK
BUZZIER
BUZZIES
BUZZIEST
BUZZING
BUZZLE
BUZZWIG
BUZZY
BWANA
BWAZI
BY
BYARD
BYCOCKET
BYCOKET
BYE
BYEE
BYELAW
BYEMAN
BYERITE
BYERLITE
BYGO
BYGOING
BYGONE
BYHAND
BYLAND
BYLAW
BYLINA
BYLINER
BYLINY

BYNAME
BYNEDESTIN
BYON
BYOUS
BYOUSLY
BYPASS
BYPASSED
BYPASSER
BYPASSING
BYPAST
BYPATH
BYPLAY
BYRE
BYREMAN
BYREWOMAN
BYRL
BYRLADY
BYRLAW
BYRLAWMAN
BYRLAWMEN
BYRNIE
BYROAD
BYRRUS
BYRTHYNSAK
BYSEN
BYSMALITH
BYSPELL
BYSSACEOUS
BYSSAL
BYSSI
BYSSIFEROUS
BYSSIN
BYSSINE
BYSSOGENOUS
BYSSOID
BYSSOLITE
BYSSUS
BYSSUSES
BYSTANDER
BYSTREET
BYTH
BYTOWNITE
BYTOWNITITE
BYWALK
BYWALKER
BYWALKING
BYWAY
BYWONER
BYWORD
BYWORK
BYZANT
BYZEN

CAAM
CAAMA
CAAMING
CAAPEBA
CAAPI
CAATINGA
CAB
CABA
CABAAN
CABACK
CABAHO
CABAL
CABALA
CABALASSOU
CABALETTA
CABALIC
CABALISM
CABALIST
CABALISTIC
CABALISTICAL
CABALISTICALLY
CABALL
CABALLED
CABALLER
CABALLERIA
CABALLERO
CABALLEROS
CABALLINE
CABALLING
CABALLO
CABAN
CABANA
CABANE
CABARET
CABARETIER
CABAS
CABASA
CABASSET
CABASSOU
CABBAGE
CABBAGED
CABBAGEHEAD
CABBAGEWOOD
CABBAGING
CABBAGY
CABBALAH
CABBED
CABBER
CABBIES
CABBING
CABBLE
CABBLER
CABBY
CABDA
CABDRIVER
CABDRIVING
CABECERA
CABECUDO
CABELIAU
CABELLEROTE
CABER
CABERNET
CABESTRO
CABEZON
CABIE
CABILDO
CABILLIAU

CABIN
CABINED
CABINET
CABINETED
CABINETING
CABINETMAKER
CABINETMAKING
CABINETRY
CABINETTED
CABINETWORK
CABINETWORKER
CABINETWORKING
CABINING
CABINLIKE
CABIO
CABLE
CABLED
CABLEGRAM
CABLEMAN
CABLEMEN
CABLER
CABLES
CABLESE
CABLET
CABLEWAY
CABLING
CABMAN
CABOB
CABOCEER
CABOCHED
CABOCHON
CABOCLE
CABOCLO
CABOODLE
CABOOK
CABOOSE
CABOSHED
CABOT
CABOTAGE
CABOTIN
CABOTINAGE
CABOUCA
CABREE
CABRERITE
CABRESTA
CABRESTO
CABRET
CABRETTA
CABREUVA
CABRIE
CABRILLA
CABRIOLE
CABRIOLET
CABRIT
CABRITO
CABSTAND
CABUJA
CABULLA
CABURN
CABUYA
CACAESTHESIA
CACAFUEGO
CACAFUGO
CACAM
CACAO
CACAOS
CACAXTE
CACESTHESIA
CACESTHESIS
CACHACA
CACHAEMIA
CACHAEMIC
CACHALOT
CACHAZA
CACHE
CACHECTICAL
CACHED

CACHEMIA
CACHEMIC
CACHEPOT
CACHES
CACHET
CACHETIC
CACHEXIA
CACHEXIC
CACHEXY
CACHIBOU
CACHILA
CACHIMILLA
CACHINA
CACHING
CACHINNATE
CACHINNATION
CACHINNATOR
CACHINNATORY
CACHOEIRA
CACHOLONG
CACHOT
CACHOU
CACHRYS
CACHUA
CACHUCHA
CACHUCHO
CACHUNDE
CACIDROSIS
CACIOCAVALLO
CACIQUE
CACIQUISM
CACK
CACKEREL
CACKLE
CACKLED
CACKLER
CACKLING
CACO
CACOCHOLIA
CACOCHROIA
CACOCHYLIA
CACOCHYMIA
CACOCHYMIC
CACOCHYMICAL
CACOCHYMY
CACODAEMON
CACODEMON
CACODEMONIA
CACODEMONIAC
CACODEMONIAL
CACODEMONIC
CACODOXIAN
CACODOXICAL
CACODOXY
CACODYL
CACODYLIC
CACOECONOMY
CACOEPIST
CACOEPISTIC
CACOEPY
CACOETHES
CACOETHIC
CACOGALACTIA
CACOGASTRIC
CACOGENESIS
CACOGENIC
CACOGENICS
CACOGEUSIA
CACOGLOSSIA
CACOGRAPHER
CACOGRAPHIC
CACOGRAPHICAL
CACOGRAPHY
CACOLET
CACOLOGY
CACOMELIA
CACOMISTLE
CACOMIXL

CACOMIXLE
CACOMORPHIA
CACONYM
CACOON
CACOPATHY
CACOPHARYNGIA
CACOPHONIA
CACOPHONIC
CACOPHONICAL
CACOPHONICALLY
CACOPHONIST
CACOPHONIZE
CACOPHONOUS
CACOPHONOUSLY
CACOPHONY
CACOPLASIA
CACOPLASTIC
CACOPROCTIA
CACORHYTHMIC
CACORRHACHIS
CACORRHINIA
CACOSPERMIA
CACOSTOMIA
CACOTHELIN
CACOTHELINE
CACOTHYMIA
CACOTRICHIA
CACOTROPHIA
CACOTROPHY
CACOTYPE
CACOXENE
CACOXENITE
CACOZEAL
CACOZEALOUS
CACOZYME
CACTACEOUS
CACTAL
CACTI
CACTIFORM
CACTOID
CACTUS
CACTUSES
CACUMEN
CACUMINAL
CACUMINATE
CACUMINATION
CACUMINOUS
CACUR
CAD
CADALENE
CADAMBA
CADAR
CADASTER
CADASTRAL
CADASTRATION
CADASTRE
CADAVER
CADAVERIC
CADAVERIN
CADAVERINE
CADAVEROUS
CADAVEROUSLY
CADBAIT
CADBIT
CADBOTE
CADDED
CADDI
CADDICE
CADDICED
CADDIE
CADDIED
CADDIES
CADDING
CADDIS
CADDISED
CADDISH
CADDISHLY

CADDISHNESS
CADDLE
CADDOW
CADDY
CADDYING
CADE
CADEAU
CADELLE
CADENCE
CADENCED
CADENCIES
CADENCY
CADENETTE
CADENT
CADENTIAL
CADENZA
CADER
CADESSE
CADET
CADETCY
CADETSHIP
CADETTE
CADEW
CADGE
CADGED
CADGER
CADGILY
CADGINESS
CADGING
CADGY
CADI
CADIE
CADILESKER
CADILLO
CADINENE
CADIS
CADISH
CADJAN
CADLOCK
CADMIA
CADMIC
CADMIDE
CADMIFEROUS
CADMIUM
CADRANS
CADRE
CADUA
CADUAC
CADUCA
CADUCARY
CADUCE
CADUCEAN
CADUCEUS
CADUCIARY
CADUCIBRANCH
CADUCICORN
CADUCITY
CADUKE
CADUS
CADWEED
CADY
CAECA
CAECALLY
CAECECTOMY
CAECIFORM
CAECILIAN
CAECITIS
CAECOCOLIC
CAECOSTOMY
CAECOTOMY
CAECUM
CAELOMETER
CAENOSTYLIC
CAENOSTYLY
CAEOMA
CAESAREAN
CAESARIAN

CAESIOUS
CAESIUM
CAESPITOSE
CAESTUS
CAESURA
CAESURAE
CAESURAL
CAESURAS
CAESURIC
CAFARD
CAFARDISE
CAFE
CAFENEH
CAFENET
CAFETAL
CAFETERIA
CAFETIERE
CAFF
CAFFA
CAFFE
CAFFEATE
CAFFEIC
CAFFEIN
CAFFEINE
CAFFEINIC
CAFFEINISM
CAFFEISM
CAFFEOL
CAFFEONE
CAFFETANNIN
CAFFISO
CAFFLE
CAFFLED
CAFFLING
CAFFOLINE
CAFFOY
CAFILA
CAFIZ
CAFOY
CAFTA
CAFTAN
CAFTANED
CAFUSO
CAG
CAGE
CAGED
CAGELING
CAGEMAN
CAGEOT
CAGER
CAGESTER
CAGEWORK
CAGEY
CAGGY
CAGIER
CAGIEST
CAGIT
CAGMAG
CAHAR
CAHIER
CAHINCIC
CAHIZ
CAHOOT
CAHOOTS
CAHOT
CAHOW
CAHUITA
CAHUY
CAIARARA
CAID
CAILCEDRA
CAILLE
CAILLEACH
CAILLIACH
CAIMACAM
CAIMAKAM
CAIMAN

CAIMITILLO
CAIMITO
CAIN
CAINGIN
CAIQUE
CAIQUEJEE
CAIRD
CAIRN
CAIRNED
CAIRNGORM
CAIRNGORUM
CAIRNY
CAISSE
CAISSON
CAISSONED
CAITIF
CAITIFF
CAIXINHA
CAJA
CAJANG
CAJAPUT
CAJAVA
CAJEPUT
CAJETA
CAJI
CAJOLE
CAJOLED
CAJOLEMENT
CAJOLER
CAJOLERIES
CAJOLERY
CAJOLING
CAJOLINGLY
CAJON
CAJOO
CAJOU
CAJU
CAJUELA
CAJUN
CAJUPUT
CAJUPUTENE
CAJUPUTOL
CAKE
CAKEBOX
CAKEBREAD
CAKED
CAKEHOUSE
CAKEMAKER
CAKEMAKING
CAKER
CAKES
CAKETTE
CAKEWALK
CAKEY
CAKIER
CAKIEST
CAKING
CAKRA
CAKY
CAL
CALABA
CALABAR
CALABASH
CALABAZA
CALABAZILLA
CALABER
CALABOOSE
CALABOZO
CALABRASELLA
CALABRESE
CALABUR
CALADE
CALADIUM
CALAHAN
CALAITE
CALALU
CALAMANCOES

CALAMANCOS
CALAMANSI
CALAMARIAN
CALAMARIES
CALAMARIOID
CALAMAROID
CALAMARY
CALAMBAC
CALAMBOUR
CALAMI
CALAMIFORM
CALAMINE
CALAMINED
CALAMINING
CALAMINT
CALAMISTRAL
CALAMISTRUM
CALAMITE
CALAMITEAN
CALAMITIES
CALAMITOID
CALAMITOUS
CALAMITOUSLY
CALAMITY
CALAMONDIN
CALAMUS
CALAN
CALANDER
CALANDO
CALANDRE
CALANDRIA
CALANGAY
CALANID
CALANQUE
CALANTAS
CALANTHE
CALAO
CALAPITE
CALAPITTE
CALASCIONE
CALASH
CALATHEA
CALATHI
CALATHIDIA
CALATHIDIUM
CALATHISCI
CALATHISCUS
CALATHOS
CALATHUS
CALAVERITE
CALCAEMIA
CALCANEAL
CALCANEAN
CALCANEI
CALCANEUM
CALCANEUS
CALCAR
CALCARATE
CALCARATED
CALCAREOUS
CALCAREOUSLY
CALCARIA
CALCARIFORM
CALCARINE
CALCARIUM
CALCEATE
CALCED
CALCEDONY
CALCEIFORM
CALCEMIA
CALCEOLATE
CALCES
CALCEUS
CALCIC
CALCICLASE
CALCICOLOUS
CALCICOSIS

CALCIFEROL
CALCIFEROUS
CALCIFIC
CALCIFICATION
CALCIFIED
CALCIFORM
CALCIFUGAL
CALCIFUGE
CALCIFUGOUS
CALCIFY
CALCIFYING
CALCIGENOUS
CALCIGEROUS
CALCIMETER
CALCIMINE
CALCIMINED
CALCIMINER
CALCIMINING
CALCINATION
CALCINATORY
CALCINE
CALCINED
CALCINER
CALCINING
CALCINO
CALCIPEXY
CALCIPHILE
CALCIPHILIA
CALCIPHILOUS
CALCIPHYRE
CALCIPRIVIC
CALCITE
CALCITRANT
CALCITRATE
CALCITRATION
CALCIUM
CALCIVOROUS
CALCOGRAPHER
CALCOGRAPHIC
CALCOGRAPHY
CALCRETE
CALCSINTER
CALCSPAR
CALCTUFA
CALCTUFF
CALCULABLE
CALCULABLY
CALCULARY
CALCULATE
CALCULATED
CALCULATING
CALCULATION
CALCULATIONAL
CALCULATIVE
CALCULATOR
CALCULATORY
CALCULER
CALCULIFORM
CALCULIST
CALCULOUS
CALCULUS
CALCULUSES
CALDARIA
CALDARIUM
CALDEN
CALDERA
CALDRON
CALE
CALEAN
CALECHE
CALEDONITE
CALEFACIENT
CALEFACTION
CALEFACTIVE
CALEFACTOR
CALEFACTORY
CALELECTRIC

CALEMBOUR
CALENDAL
CALENDAR
CALENDARIAL
CALENDARIAN
CALENDARIC
CALENDER
CALENDERED
CALENDERER
CALENDERING
CALENDRIC
CALENDRICAL
CALENDRY
CALENDS
CALENDULA
CALENDULIN
CALENTURAL
CALENTURE
CALENTURED
CALENTURING
CALENTURIST
CALEPIN
CALESA
CALESCENCE
CALESCENT
CALESERO
CALESIN
CALF
CALFBOUND
CALFKILL
CALFLING
CALFSKIN
CALIBER
CALIBERED
CALIBOGUS
CALIBRATE
CALIBRATED
CALIBRATION
CALIBRATOR
CALIBRE
CALIBRED
CALICHE
CALICIFORM
CALICLE
CALICO
CALICOBACK
CALICOED
CALICOES
CALICOS
CALICULAR
CALID
CALIDITY
CALIDUCT
CALIF
CALIFORNITE
CALIFORNIUM
CALIGA
CALIGATED
CALIGINOSITY
CALIGINOUS
CALIGINOUSLY
CALIGO
CALIGRAPHY
CALIMANCO
CALIN
CALINDA
CALINE
CALINUT
CALIOLOGICAL
CALIOLOGIST
CALIOLOGY
CALIPASH
CALIPEE
CALIPER
CALIPERER
CALIPERS
CALIPH

CALIPHAL	CALMLY	CALVING	CAMBISTRY	CAMOUFLAGER
CALIPHATE	CALMNESS	CALVISH	CAMBIUM	CAMOUFLAGING
CALISAYA	CALMY	CALVITIES	CAMBLET	CAMOUFLET
CALISTHENEUM	CALO	CALVITY	CAMBOGIA	CAMOUFLEUR
CALISTHENIC	CALODAEMON	CALVOUS	CAMBOOSE	CAMP
CALISTHENICS	CALODEMON	CALX	CAMBOUIS	CAMPAGNA
CALIVER	CALODEMONIAL	CALXES	CAMBRESINE	CAMPAGNOL
CALIX	CALOMBA	CALYCANTH	CAMBRIC	CAMPAIGN
CALK	CALOMBIGAS	CALYCANTHEMY	CAMBUCA	CAMPAIGNER
CALKAGE	CALOMBO	CALYCANTHIN	CAME	CAMPANA
CALKER	CALOMEL	CALYCANTHINE	CAMEIST	CAMPANE
CALKING	CALOOL	CALYCATE	CAMEL	CAMPANELLA
CALL	CALOR	CALYCES	CAMELEER	CAMPANERO
CALLA	CALORESCENCE	CALYCIFEROUS	CAMELHAIR	CAMPANIFORM
CALLABLE	CALORESCENT	CALYCIFLORAL	CAMELINE	CAMPANILE
CALLAINITE	CALORIC	CALYCIFORM	CAMELISH	CAMPANILES
CALLAIS	CALORICITY	CALYCINE	CAMELISHNESS	CAMPANILLA
CALLAN	CALORIE	CALYCLE	CAMELKEEPER	CAMPANINI
CALLANT	CALORIFIC	CALYCLED	CAMELLIA	CAMPANIST
CALLATE	CALORIFICAL	CALYCOID	CAMELLIN	CAMPANISTIC
CALLBOY	CALORIFICS	CALYCOIDEOUS	CAMELMAN	CAMPANOLOGER
CALLE	CALORIFIER	CALYCOPHORAN	CAMELOID	CAMPANOLOGY
CALLED	CALORIFY	CALYCULAR	CAMELOPARD	CAMPANULAR
CALLER	CALORIGENIC	CALYCULATE	CAMELOT	CAMPANULATE
CALLES	CALORIMETER	CALYCULATED	CAMELRY	CAMPANULOUS
CALLET	CALORIMETRIC	CALYCULE	CAMEO	CAMPBELLITE
CALLI	CALORIMETRY	CALYCULUS	CAMEOGRAPH	CAMPCRAFT
CALLID	CALORIMOTOR	CALYMMA	CAMEOGRAPHY	CAMPECHE
CALLIDITY	CALORIS	CALYPHYOMY	CAMEOS	CAMPED
CALLIDNESS	CALORISATOR	CALYPSO	CAMERA	CAMPEPHAGINE
CALLIGRAPH	CALORIST	CALYPTER	CAMERAE	CAMPER
CALLIGRAPHER	CALORIZE	CALYPTRA	CAMERAL	CAMPESINO
CALLIGRAPHIC	CALORIZER	CALYPTRATE	CAMERALISM	CAMPESTRAL
CALLIGRAPHY	CALOSOMA	CALYPTRIFORM	CAMERALIST	CAMPFIGHT
CALLING	CALOTIN	CALYPTROGEN	CAMERALISTIC	CAMPFIRE
CALLIOPE	CALOTTE	CALYX	CAMERALISTICS	CAMPGROUND
CALLIOPHONE	CALOTYPE	CALZADA	CAMERAMAN	CAMPHANE
CALLIOPSIS	CALOTYPIC	CALZONERAS	CAMERAS	CAMPHANIC
CALLIPASH	CALOTYPIST	CALZOONS	CAMERATE	CAMPHANONE
CALLIPEE	CALOYER	CAM	CAMERATED	CAMPHANYL
CALLIPER	CALP	CAMACA	CAMERATION	CAMPHENE
CALLIPERER	CALPAC	CAMACEY	CAMERIER	CAMPHINE
CALLIPHORID	CALPACK	CAMACHILE	CAMERIERA	CAMPHIRE
CALLIPHORINE	CALPACKED	CAMAGON	CAMERIERI	CAMPHOID
CALLIPYGIAN	CALPOLLI	CAMAIEU	CAMERIST	CAMPHOL
CALLIPYGOUS	CALPUL	CAMAIL	CAMERLENGO	CAMPHOLIDE
CALLISECTION	CALPULLI	CAMAILE	CAMERLINGO	CAMPHOR
CALLISTEIA	CALQUE	CAMAILED	CAMIAS	CAMPHORATE
CALLISTHENIC	CALSOUNS	CAMALIG	CAMILLA	CAMPHORATED
CALLISTHENICS	CALTHROP	CAMALOTE	CAMINO	CAMPHORATING
CALLITHUMP	CALTRAP	CAMAN	CAMION	CAMPHORIC
CALLITYPE	CALTROP	CAMANAY	CAMIS	CAMPHOROYL
CALLITYPED	CALTROPS	CAMANSI	CAMISA	CAMPHORWOOD
CALLITYPING	CALUMBA	CAMARA	CAMISADE	CAMPHORYL
CALLOP	CALUMET	CAMARADA	CAMISADO	CAMPHYLENE
CALLOSAL	CALUMNIATE	CAMARADE	CAMISCIA	CAMPIER
CALLOSE	CALUMNIATED	CAMARADERIE	CAMISE	CAMPIEST
CALLOSITY	CALUMNIATION	CAMARERA	CAMISIA	CAMPILAN
CALLOSUM	CALUMNIATIVE	CAMARILLA	CAMISOLE	CAMPIMETER
CALLOUS	CALUMNIATOR	CAMARIN	CAMLET	CAMPIMETRY
CALLOUSED	CALUMNIATORY	CAMARON	CAMLETED	CAMPING
CALLOUSING	CALUMNIES	CAMAS	CAMLETEEN	CAMPIT
CALLOUSLY	CALUMNIOUS	CAMASS	CAMLETINE	CAMPLE
CALLOUSNESS	CALUMNIOUSLY	CAMATA	CAMLETING	CAMPMAN
CALLOW	CALUMNY	CAMATINA	CAMMED	CAMPMASTER
CALLOWER	CALUSAR	CAMAURO	CAMMOCK	CAMPO
CALLOWMAN	CALVA	CAMAY	CAMMOCKY	CAMPODEID
CALLUS	CALVAIRE	CAMBAYE	CAMOGIE	CAMPODEIFORM
CALLUSES	CALVARIA	CAMBER	CAMOIS	CAMPODEOID
CALM	CALVARIAL	CAMBERED	CAMOMILE	CAMPODY
CALMANT	CALVARIES	CAMBERING	CAMOOCH	CAMPONG
CALMATIVE	CALVARIUM	CAMBIAL	CAMOODI	CAMPOO
CALMATO	CALVARY	CAMBIATA	CAMOODIE	CAMPOODY
CALMECAC	CALVE	CAMBIFORM	CAMOTE	CAMPOREE
CALMER	CALVED	CAMBIO	CAMOUDIE	CAMPSHED
CALMEST	CALVER	CAMBISM	CAMOUFLAGE	CAMPSHEDDING
CALMIERER	CALVES	CAMBIST	CAMOUFLAGED	CAMPSHEETING

CAMPSHOT	CANCELATION	CANDIL	CANGIA	CANNILY
CAMPSITE	CANCELED	CANDIRU	CANGLE	CANNINESS
CAMPSTOOL	CANCELEER	CANDITE	CANGUE	CANNING
CAMPTODROME	CANCELER	CANDLE	CANGY	CANNON
CAMPTONITE	CANCELIER	CANDLEBALL	CANHOOP	CANNONADE
CAMPUS	CANCELING	CANDLEBEAM	CANI	CANNONADED
CAMPUSES	CANCELLARIAN	CANDLEBERRY	CANICULE	CANNONADING
CAMPWARD	CANCELLARIUS	CANDLEBOMB	CANID	CANNONED
CAMPY	CANCELLATE	CANDLEBOX	CANILLE	CANNONEER
CAMPYLITE	CANCELLATED	CANDLED	CANIN	CANNONEERING
CAMPYLODROME	CANCELLATION	CANDLEFISH	CANINAL	CANNONIER
CAMPYLOMETER	CANCELLED	CANDLEHOLDER	CANINE	CANNONPROOF
CAMSHACH	CANCELLER	CANDLELIGHT	CANING	CANNONRY
CAMSHACHLE	CANCELLI	CANDLELIGHTING	CANINIFORM	CANNOPHORI
CAMSHAFT	CANCELLING	CANDLELIT	CANINITY	CANNOT
CAMSTANE	CANCELLOUS	CANDLEMAKER	CANINUS	CANNULA
CAMSTEARY	CANCELS	CANDLEMAKING	CANIONED	CANNULAR
CAMSTEERY	CANCER	CANDLENUT	CANIONS	CANNULATE
CAMSTONE	CANCERATE	CANDLEPIN	CANISTEL	CANNULATED
CAMSTRARY	CANCERATED	CANDLEPOWER	CANISTER	CANNY
CAMUNING	CANCERATING	CANDLER	CANITIES	CANOE
CAMUS	CANCERATION	CANDLERENT	CANK	CANOEING
CAMUSE	CANCERDROPS	CANDLES	CANKER	CANOEIST
CAMUSED	CANCERED	CANDLESHINE	CANKERBERRY	CANOELOAD
CAMWOOD	CANCERIGENIC	CANDLESHRIFT	CANKERBIRD	CANOEMAN
CAN	CANCERISM	CANDLESNUFFER	CANKEREAT	CANOES
CANABA	CANCERITE	CANDLESTAND	CANKERED	CANOEWOOD
CANABAE	CANCEROPHOBE	CANDLESTICK	CANKEREDLY	CANON
CANACUAS	CANCEROUS	CANDLEWASTER	CANKEREDNESS	CANONCITO
CANADA	CANCEROUSLY	CANDLEWICK	CANKERFLOWER	CANONESS
CANADITE	CANCERROOT	CANDLEWICKING	CANKERFRET	CANONIC
CANADOL	CANCERWEED	CANDLEWOOD	CANKEROUS	CANONICAL
CANAFISTOLO	CANCERWORT	CANDLEWRIGHT	CANKERROOT	CANONICALLY
CANAFISTULA	CANCH	CANDLING	CANKERWEED	CANONICALS
CANAFISTULO	CANCHA	CANDOCK	CANKERWORM	CANONICATE
CANAGLIA	CANCHALAGUA	CANDOR	CANKERWORT	CANONICITY
CANAIGRE	CANCHITO	CANDOUR	CANKERY	CANONICS
CANAILLE	CANCION	CANDROY	CANMAN	CANONIST
CANAJONG	CANCIONERO	CANDROYS	CANN	CANONISTIC
CANAKIN	CANCIONES	CANDUC	CANNA	CANONISTICAL
CANAL	CANCRID	CANDY	CANNABIC	CANONIZANT
CANALBOAT	CANCRIFORM	CANDYING	CANNABIN	CANONIZATION
CANALE	CANCRINITE	CANDYMAKER	CANNABINE	CANONIZE
CANALER	CANCRISOCIAL	CANDYS	CANNABIS	CANONIZED
CANALETE	CANCRIVOROUS	CANDYSTICK	CANNABISM	CANONIZER
CANALI	CANCRIZANS	CANDYTUFT	CANNACEOUS	CANONIZING
CANALICULAR	CANCROID	CANDYWEED	CANNACH	CANONRY
CANALICULATE	CANCRUM	CANE	CANNAT	CANONS
CANALICULI	CANCRUMS	CANEBRAKE	CANNE	CANONSHIP
CANALICULUS	CAND	CANED	CANNED	CANOODLE
CANALIFEROUS	CANDAREEN	CANEL	CANNEL	CANOPID
CANALIFORM	CANDELABRA	CANELA	CANNELE	CANOPIED
CANALING	CANDELABRAS	CANELL	CANNELLATE	CANOPIES
CANALIS	CANDELABRUM	CANELLA	CANNELLATED	CANOPY
CANALIZATION	CANDELABRUMS	CANELLACEOUS	CANNELLE	CANOPYING
CANALIZE	CANDELILLA	CANELLE	CANNELLONI	CANOR
CANALIZED	CANDENCY	CANELO	CANNELON	CANOROUS
CANALIZING	CANDENT	CANEOLOGY	CANNELURE	CANOROUSLY
CANALLA	CANDESCENCE	CANEPHOR	CANNELURED	CANOROUSNESS
CANALLER	CANDESCENT	CANEPHORA	CANNEQUIN	CANOS
CANALLING	CANDESCENTLY	CANEPHORAE	CANNER	CANOTIER
CANAMO	CANDI	CANEPHORI	CANNERIES	CANROY
CANAO	CANDID	CANEPHOROE	CANNERY	CANROYER
CANAPE	CANDIDACIES	CANEPHOROI	CANNET	CANSH
CANAPINA	CANDIDACY	CANEPHOROS	CANNETILLE	CANSO
CANARD	CANDIDATE	CANEPHORUS	CANNIBAL	CANSOS
CANARI	CANDIDATED	CANEPIN	CANNIBALIC	CANST
CANARIES	CANDIDATES	CANER	CANNIBALISM	CANT
CANARIN	CANDIDATING	CANESCENT	CANNIBALISTIC	CANTABANK
CANARINE	CANDIDATURE	CANETON	CANNIBALITY	CANTABILE
CANARY	CANDIDLY	CANETTE	CANNIBALIZE	CANTADOR
CANASTER	CANDIDNESS	CANEWARE	CANNIBALIZED	CANTALA
CANAUT	CANDIED	CANEWORK	CANNIBALIZING	CANTALEVER
CANAVALIN	CANDIEL	CANEZOU	CANNIBALLY	CANTALITE
CANCAN	CANDIER	CANFIELDITE	CANNIER	CANTALOUP
CANCEL	CANDIES	CANG	CANNIEST	CANTALOUPE
CANCELABLE	CANDIFY	CANGAN	CANNIKIN	CANTANKEROUS

CANTAR	CANTUS	CAPEWEED	CAPON	CAPSIZAL
CANTARA	CANTUT	CAPFUL	CAPONIER	CAPSIZE
CANTARE	CANTUTA	CAPH	CAPONIERE	CAPSIZED
CANTARO	CANTY	CAPHAR	CAPONIZE	CAPSIZING
CANTATA	CANULA	CAPHITE	CAPONIZER	CAPSTAN
CANTATION	CANULATE	CAPIAS	CAPONNIERE	CAPSTONE
CANTATIVE	CANUN	CAPIASES	CAPORAL	CAPSULA
CANTATORY	CANVAS	CAPIBARA	CAPOT	CAPSULAR
CANTATRICE	CANVASBACK	CAPICHA	CAPOTASTO	CAPSULATE
CANTED	CANVASBACKS	CAPILACEOUS	CAPOTE	CAPSULATED
CANTEEN	CANVASMAN	CAPILLAIRE	CAPOUCH	CAPSULATION
CANTER	CANVASS	CAPILLAMENT	CAPPA	CAPSULE
CANTERED	CANVASSED	CAPILLARIES	CAPPADINE	CAPSULECTOMY
CANTERER	CANVASSER	CAPILLARITIES	CAPPAE	CAPSULED
CANTERING	CANVASSING	CAPILLARITY	CAPPED	CAPSULER
CANTHAL	CANY	CAPILLARY	CAPPELENITE	CAPSULING
CANTHARI	CANYON	CAPILLATION	CAPPER	CAPSULITIS
CANTHARIDAL	CANZON	CAPILLI	CAPPIE	CAPSULOTOME
CANTHARIDATE	CANZONA	CAPILLIFORM	CAPPING	CAPSULOTOMY
CANTHARIDEAN	CANZONE	CAPILLITIA	CAPPLE	CAPSUMIN
CANTHARIDES	CANZONET	CAPILLITIAL	CAPPO	CAPTACULA
CANTHARIDIAN	CANZONI	CAPILLITIUM	CAPPY	CAPTACULUM
CANTHARIDIN	CAOBA	CAPILLOSE	CAPRATE	CAPTAIN
CANTHARIDISM	CAOINE	CAPILLUS	CAPRELLINE	CAPTAINCIES
CANTHARIDIZE	CAOUTCHOUC	CAPILOTADE	CAPREOL	CAPTAINCY
CANTHARIS	CAP	CAPISTRATE	CAPREOLATE	CAPTAINESS
CANTHARUS	CAPA	CAPITA	CAPREOLINE	CAPTAINRIES
CANTHECTOMY	CAPABILITIES	CAPITAL	CAPRETTO	CAPTAINRY
CANTHI	CAPABILITY	CAPITALED	CAPRIC	CAPTAINSHIP
CANTHITIS	CAPABLE	CAPITALING	CAPRICCETTO	CAPTATION
CANTHOLYSIS	CAPABLENESS	CAPITALISM	CAPRICCETTOS	CAPTION
CANTHOPLASTY	CAPABLY	CAPITALIST	CAPRICCIO	CAPTIOUS
CANTHOTOMY	CAPACIOUS	CAPITALISTIC	CAPRICCIOS	CAPTIOUSLY
CANTHUS	CAPACIOUSLY	CAPITALIZE	CAPRICCIOSO	CAPTIOUSNESS
CANTIC	CAPACITANCE	CAPITALIZED	CAPRICE	CAPTIVATE
CANTICLE	CAPACITATE	CAPITALIZING	CAPRICIOUS	CAPTIVATED
CANTICLES	CAPACITATED	CAPITALLY	CAPRICIOUSLY	CAPTIVATELY
CANTICO	CAPACITATING	CAPITAN	CAPRICIOUSNESS	CAPTIVATING
CANTIGA	CAPACITATION	CAPITANA	CAPRID	CAPTIVATION
CANTIL	CAPACITATIVE	CAPITANO	CAPRIFICATE	CAPTIVATIVE
CANTILATED	CAPACITIES	CAPITATE	CAPRIFICATOR	CAPTIVATOR
CANTILATING	CAPACITIVE	CAPITATED	CAPRIFIG	CAPTIVE
CANTILENA	CAPACITOR	CAPITATIM	CAPRIFOIL	CAPTIVED
CANTILENE	CAPACITY	CAPITATION	CAPRIFOLE	CAPTIVING
CANTILENES	CAPANNA	CAPITATIVE	CAPRIFORM	CAPTIVITIES
CANTILEVER	CAPANNE	CAPITATUM	CAPRIGENOUS	CAPTIVITY
CANTILLATE	CAPARISON	CAPITE	CAPRIMULGINE	CAPTOR
CANTILLATION	CAPARISONED	CAPITELLA	CAPRIN	CAPTURE
CANTILY	CAPARISONING	CAPITELLAR	CAPRINE	CAPTURED
CANTINA	CAPATAZ	CAPITELLATE	CAPRINIC	CAPTURER
CANTING	CAPAX	CAPITELLUM	CAPRIOLE	CAPTURING
CANTINGLY	CAPCASE	CAPITOL	CAPRIOLED	CAPUCHE
CANTINGNESS	CAPE	CAPITOUL	CAPRIOLING	CAPUCHIN
CANTINO	CAPEADOR	CAPITOULATE	CAPRIPED	CAPUCINE
CANTION	CAPEL	CAPITULANT	CAPRIPEDE	CAPUL
CANTLE	CAPELET	CAPITULAR	CAPRIZANT	CAPULI
CANTLET	CAPELIN	CAPITULARIES	CAPROATE	CAPULIN
CANTLINE	CAPELINE	CAPITULARY	CAPROIC	CAPUT
CANTO	CAPELLET	CAPITULATE	CAPROIN	CAPUTIUM
CANTON	CAPER	CAPITULATED	CAPRONE	CAPYBARA
CANTONAL	CAPERBUSH	CAPITULATING	CAPRONIC	CAR
CANTONED	CAPERCAILLIE	CAPITULATION	CAPRONYL	CARA
CANTONER	CAPERCAILZIE	CAPITULATOR	CAPROYL	CARABAO
CANTONMENT	CAPERCUT	CAPITULATORY	CAPRYL	CARABAOS
CANTOON	CAPERED	CAPITULIFORM	CAPRYLATE	CARABEEN
CANTOR	CAPERER	CAPITULUM	CAPRYLIC	CARABID
CANTORAL	CAPERING	CAPLE	CAPRYLIN	CARABIDAN
CANTORIA	CAPERNOITED	CAPLIN	CAPRYLONE	CARABIDEOUS
CANTORIAL	CAPERNOITIE	CAPLING	CAPRYLYL	CARABIDOID
CANTORIS	CAPERNOITY	CAPLOCK	CAPS	CARABIN
CANTOROUS	CAPERNUTIE	CAPMAKER	CAPSA	CARABINE
CANTOS	CAPERS	CAPMAKING	CAPSAICIN	CARABINEER
CANTRAIP	CAPERSOME	CAPMAN	CAPSHEAF	CARABINERO
CANTRAP	CAPERWORT	CAPMINT	CAPSHORE	CARABINIER
CANTRED	CAPES	CAPNOMANCY	CAPSICIN	CARABINIERE
CANTREF	CAPESKIN	CAPOCCHIA	CAPSICUM	CARABINIERI
CANTRIP	CAPETTE	CAPOMO	CAPSID	CARABOID

CARABUS
CARAC
CARACAL
CARACARA
CARACK
CARACO
CARACOA
CARACOL
CARACOLE
CARACOLED
CARACOLER
CARACOLI
CARACOLING
CARACOLITE
CARACOLLER
CARACORA
CARACORE
CARACT
CARACTER
CARACUL
CARAFE
CARAFON
CARAGHEEN
CARAGUATA
CARAIBE
CARAIPE
CARAIPI
CARAJO
CARAJURA
CARAMBA
CARAMBOLA
CARAMBOLE
CARAMBOLED
CARAMBOLING
CARAMEL
CARAMELAN
CARAMELEN
CARAMELIN
CARAMELIZE
CARAMELIZED
CARAMELIZING
CARANCHA
CARANCHO
CARANDA
CARANDAY
CARANE
CARANGID
CARANGIN
CARANGOID
CARANNA
CARANX
CARAP
CARAPA
CARAPACE
CARAPACED
CARAPACIC
CARAPATO
CARAPAX
CARAPINE
CARAPO
CARAT
CARATCH
CARATS
CARAUNA
CARAUNDA
CARAVAN
CARAVANEER
CARAVANIST
CARAVANNER
CARAVANSARY
CARAVANSERAI
CARAVEL
CARAVELLE
CARAWAY
CARBAMATE
CARBAMIC
CARBAMIDE

CARBAMINE
CARBAMINO
CARBAMYL
CARBANIL
CARBANILIC
CARBANILID
CARBANILIDE
CARBARN
CARBASUS
CARBAZIC
CARBAZIDE
CARBAZIN
CARBAZINE
CARBAZOLE
CARBAZYLIC
CARBEEN
CARBENE
CARBERRY
CARBETHOXYL
CARBIDE
CARBIMIDE
CARBIN
CARBINE
CARBINEER
CARBINOL
CARBINYL
CARBO
CARBOAZOTINE
CARBOCER
CARBODIIMIDE
CARBOGELATIN
CARBOHYDRASE
CARBOHYDRATE
CARBOHYDRIDE
CARBOLATE
CARBOLATED
CARBOLIC
CARBOLINEATE
CARBOLIZE
CARBOLIZED
CARBOLIZING
CARBOLXYLOL
CARBON
CARBONA
CARBONACEOUS
CARBONADO
CARBONADOED
CARBONADOES
CARBONADOS
CARBONATE
CARBONATED
CARBONATING
CARBONATION
CARBONATOR
CARBONE
CARBONEMIA
CARBONERO
CARBONIC
CARBONIDE
CARBONIMETER
CARBONIMIDE
CARBONITE
CARBONITRIDE
CARBONIUM
CARBONIZE
CARBONIZED
CARBONIZER
CARBONIZING
CARBONOMETRY
CARBONOUS
CARBONURIA
CARBONYL
CARBONYLENE
CARBONYLIC
CARBOPHILOUS
CARBORA
CARBORUNDUM

CARBOSTYRIL
CARBOXIDE
CARBOXYL
CARBOXYLASE
CARBOXYLATE
CARBOXYLATED
CARBOXYLIC
CARBOY
CARBOYED
CARBOYS
CARBRO
CARBROMAL
CARBUNCLE
CARBUNCLED
CARBUNCULAR
CARBUNGI
CARBURAN
CARBURANT
CARBURATE
CARBURATED
CARBURATING
CARBURET
CARBURETANT
CARBURETED
CARBURETING
CARBURETION
CARBURETOR
CARBURETTED
CARBURETTER
CARBURETTING
CARBURETTOR
CARBURISE
CARBURIZE
CARBURIZED
CARBURIZER
CARBURIZING
CARBUROMETER
CARBYL
CARBYLAMINE
CARCAJOU
CARCAKE
CARCAN
CARCANET
CARCANETED
CARCANETTED
CARCASE
CARCASS
CARCASSED
CARCASSES
CARCASSING
CARCEAG
CARCEL
CARCER
CARCERAL
CARCERATE
CARCERATED
CARCERATING
CARCERATION
CARCHARIID
CARCHARIOID
CARCHARODONT
CARCINOGEN
CARCINOGENIC
CARCINOID
CARCINOLOGY
CARCINOLYSIN
CARCINOLYTIC
CARCINOMA
CARCINOMAS
CARCINOSIS
CARCINUS
CARCOON
CARD
CARDAISSIN
CARDAMOM
CARDAMUM
CARDANOL

CARDBOARD
CARDCASE
CARDE
CARDECU
CARDED
CARDEL
CARDER
CARDIA
CARDIAC
CARDIACAL
CARDIACEAN
CARDIAGRA
CARDIAGRAM
CARDIAGRAPH
CARDIAGRAPHY
CARDIAL
CARDIALGIA
CARDIALGIC
CARDIALGY
CARDIAMETER
CARDIANEURIA
CARDIANT
CARDIAPLEGIA
CARDIARCTIA
CARDIASTHMA
CARDIATAXIA
CARDIATOMY
CARDIAUXE
CARDIECTASIS
CARDIECTOMY
CARDIELCOSIS
CARDIFORM
CARDIN
CARDINAL
CARDINALATE
CARDINALATED
CARDINALIC
CARDINALIST
CARDINALLY
CARDINALS
CARDINES
CARDING
CARDIOBLAST
CARDIOCARPUM
CARDIOCELE
CARDIOCLASIA
CARDIODYNIA
CARDIOGENIC
CARDIOGRAM
CARDIOGRAPH
CARDIOGRAPHY
CARDIOID
CARDIOLITH
CARDIOLOGIST
CARDIOLOGY
CARDIOLYSIS
CARDIOMEGALY
CARDIOMETER
CARDIOMETRIC
CARDIOMETRY
CARDIONCUS
CARDIONEURAL
CARDIONOSUS
CARDIOPATHIC
CARDIOPATHY
CARDIOPHOBE
CARDIOPHOBIA
CARDIOPLASTY
CARDIOPLEGIA
CARDIOPTOSIS
CARDIORENAL
CARDIOSCOPE
CARDIOSPASM
CARDIOTOMY
CARDIOTONIC
CARDIOTOXIC
CARDITA

CARDITIC
CARDITIS
CARDMAKER
CARDMAKING
CARDO
CARDOL
CARDON
CARDONA
CARDONCILLO
CARDOOER
CARDOON
CARDOPHAGUS
CARDOSANTO
CARDPLAYER
CARDPLAYING
CARDS
CARDSHARP
CARDSHARPER
CARDSHARPING
CARDUACEOUS
CARE
CARECLOTH
CARED
CAREEN
CAREENAGE
CAREENED
CAREENER
CAREENING
CAREER
CAREERED
CAREERER
CAREERING
CAREERISM
CAREERIST
CAREFOX
CAREFREE
CAREFUL
CAREFULLY
CAREFULNESS
CARELESS
CARELESSLY
CARELESSNESS
CAREME
CARENE
CARER
CARESS
CARESSANT
CARESSED
CARESSER
CARESSING
CARESSINGLY
CARESSIVE
CARESSIVELY
CAREST
CARET
CARETAKER
CAREWORN
CAREX
CARF
CARFARE
CARFAX
CARFOUR
CARFUFFLE
CARFUFFLED
CARFUFFLING
CARGA
CARGADOR
CARGADORES
CARGASON
CARGO
CARGOES
CARGOOSE
CARGOS
CARHOP
CARHOUSE
CARIBE
CARIBOU

CARIBOUS
CARICACEOUS
CARICATURAL
CARICATURE
CARICATURED
CARICATURING
CARICATURIST
CARICETUM
CARICOGRAPHY
CARICOLOGIST
CARICOUS
CARID
CARIDEAN
CARIDEER
CARIDOID
CARIE
CARIEN
CARIES
CARILLON
CARILLONNED
CARILLONNEUR
CARILLONNING
CARINA
CARINAE
CARINAL
CARINATE
CARINATED
CARINATION
CARING
CARINIFORM
CARIOCA
CARIOLE
CARIOLING
CARIOSITY
CARIOUS
CARIOUSNESS
CARITAS
CARITATIVE
CARITIVE
CARK
CARKING
CARKINGLY
CARKLED
CARL
CARLAGE
CARLE
CARLET
CARLEY
CARLIN
CARLINA
CARLINE
CARLING
CARLINGS
CARLINO
CARLINS
CARLOAD
CARLOADING
CARLOADINGS
CARLOT
CARLS
CARMAGNOLE
CARMALUM
CARMAN
CARMELE
CARMELOITE
CARMEN
CARMETTA
CARMINATIVE
CARMINE
CARMINETTE
CARMINIC
CARMINITE
CARMOT
CARN
CARNAGE
CARNAL
CARNALITE

CARNALITIES
CARNALITY
CARNALIZE
CARNALIZED
CARNALIZING
CARNALLITE
CARNALLY
CARNAPTIOUS
CARNASSIAL
CARNATE
CARNATION
CARNATIONED
CARNATIONIST
CARNAUBA
CARNAUBYL
CARNEAU
CARNEL
CARNELIAN
CARNEOL
CARNEOUS
CARNET
CARNEY
CARNEYED
CARNIC
CARNIED
CARNIFEROUS
CARNIFERRIN
CARNIFEX
CARNIFEXES
CARNIFICES
CARNIFICIAL
CARNIFIED
CARNIFORM
CARNIFY
CARNIFYING
CARNIVAL
CARNIVALER
CARNIVALLER
CARNIVORAL
CARNIVORE
CARNIVORISM
CARNIVOROUS
CARNOSE
CARNOSIN
CARNOSINE
CARNOSITIES
CARNOSITY
CARNOTITE
CARNOUS
CARNY
CAROA
CAROACH
CAROB
CAROBA
CAROCH
CAROCHE
CAROL
CAROLE
CAROLED
CAROLER
CAROLIN
CAROLINE
CAROLING
CAROLLED
CAROLLER
CAROLLING
CAROLS
CAROLUS
CAROM
CAROMBOLETTE
CAROMS
CARONE
CAROOME
CAROON
CAROSELLA
CAROT
CAROTENE

CAROTENOID
CAROTIC
CAROTID
CAROTIDAL
CAROTIN
CAROTINAEMIA
CAROTINEMIA
CAROTINOID
CAROTOL
CAROTTE
CAROUBIER
CAROUSAL
CAROUSE
CAROUSED
CAROUSEL
CAROUSER
CAROUSING
CAROUSINGLY
CARP
CARPAINE
CARPAL
CARPALE
CARPALIA
CARPED
CARPEL
CARPELLARY
CARPELLATE
CARPELLUM
CARPELS
CARPENT
CARPENTER
CARPENTERING
CARPENTRY
CARPER
CARPET
CARPETBAG
CARPETBAGGER
CARPETBAGISM
CARPETBEATER
CARPETING
CARPETMAKING
CARPETMONGER
CARPETWEB
CARPETWEED
CARPETWORK
CARPETWOVEN
CARPHOLITE
CARPI
CARPID
CARPIDIUM
CARPINCHO
CARPING
CARPINGLY
CARPINTERO
CARPITIS
CARPOCACE
CARPOCARPAL
CARPOCERITE
CARPOGAM
CARPOGAMY
CARPOGENIC
CARPOGONE
CARPOGONIA
CARPOGONIUM
CARPOLITE
CARPOLITH
CARPOLOGICAL
CARPOLOGIST
CARPOLOGY
CARPOMANIA
CARPOPEDAL
CARPOPHORE
CARPOPHYL
CARPOPHYTE
CARPOPODITE
CARPOPTOSIS
CARPOS

CARPOSPERM
CARPOSPORE
CARPOSPORIC
CARPOSPOROUS
CARPOSTOME
CARPS
CARPSUCKER
CARPUS
CARQUAISE
CARR
CARRACK
CARRAGEEN
CARRAGEENIN
CARRAGHEEN
CARRE
CARREAU
CARREE
CARREFOUR
CARREL
CARRELL
CARRETA
CARRETELA
CARRETERA
CARRETON
CARRETTA
CARRIABLE
CARRIAGE
CARRIAGEABLE
CARRIAGEWAY
CARRICK
CARRIED
CARRIER
CARRIES
CARRIGEEN
CARRIOLE
CARRION
CARRITCH
CARRITCHES
CARRIWITCHET
CARRIZO
CARROCCI
CARROCCIO
CARROCH
CARROLLITE
CARROM
CARROMATA
CARRONADE
CARROON
CARROSSERIE
CARROT
CARROTAGE
CARROTER
CARROTIEST
CARROTIN
CARROTINESS
CARROTING
CARROTTOP
CARROTY
CARROUSEL
CARROW
CARROZZA
CARRY
CARRYABLE
CARRYALL
CARRYING
CARS
CARSE
CARSHOP
CARSICK
CARSMITH
CARSTONE
CART
CARTAGE
CARTE
CARTEL
CARTELISM
CARTELIST

CARTELIZE
CARTELLIST
CARTERLY
CARTHAME
CARTHAMIN
CARTIER
CARTIEST
CARTILAGE
CARTILAGINEAN
CARTILAGINEOUS
CARTILAGINOID
CARTILAGINOUS
CARTISANE
CARTLOAD
CARTMAKER
CARTMAKING
CARTMAN
CARTOGRAM
CARTOGRAPH
CARTOGRAPHER
CARTOGRAPHIC
CARTOGRAPHICAL
CARTOGRAPHY
CARTOMANCY
CARTON
CARTONER
CARTONNAGE
CARTOON
CARTOONED
CARTOONING
CARTOONIST
CARTOUCH
CARTOUCHE
CARTRIDGE
CARTSALE
CARTULARIES
CARTULARY
CARTWARE
CARTWAY
CARTWHEEL
CARTWHIP
CARTWRIGHT
CARTY
CARUAGE
CARUCAGE
CARUCAL
CARUCARIUS
CARUCATE
CARUCATED
CARUE
CARUNCLE
CARUNCULA
CARUNCULAR
CARUNCULATE
CARUNCULATED
CARUNCULOUS
CARUS
CARVACROL
CARVACRYL
CARVAL
CARVE
CARVED
CARVEL
CARVEN
CARVENE
CARVES
CARVESTRENE
CARVING
CARVOEIRA
CARVOL
CARVONE
CARVY
CARVYL
CARWITCHET
CARYATIC
CARYATID
CARYATIDAL

CARYATIDEAN
CARYL
CARYOPHYLLIN
CARYOPILITE
CARYOPSIS
CARYOTIN
CASA
CASABA
CASAL
CASALTY
CASAQUE
CASAQUIN
CASATE
CASAUN
CASCABEL
CASCABLE
CASCADE
CASCADED
CASCADING
CASCADITE
CASCADO
CASCALHO
CASCALOTE
CASCAN
CASCARA
CASCARILLA
CASCARON
CASCAVEL
CASCHROM
CASCO
CASCOL
CASCROM
CASCROME
CASE
CASEASE
CASEATE
CASEATED
CASEATING
CASEATION
CASEBOOK
CASEBOX
CASED
CASEFIED
CASEFY
CASEFYING
CASEHARDEN
CASEHARDENED
CASEIC
CASEIN
CASEINATE
CASEINE
CASEINOGEN
CASEKEEPER
CASELTY
CASEMAKER
CASEMAKING
CASEMATE
CASEMATED
CASEMENT
CASEMENTED
CASEOLYSIS
CASEOSE
CASEOUS
CASER
CASERIO
CASERIOS
CASERN
CASERNE
CASES
CASEWEED
CASEWOOD
CASEWORK
CASEWORKER
CASEWORM
CASH
CASHABLE
CASHAW

CASHBOOK
CASHBOX
CASHBOY
CASHED
CASHEL
CASHEW
CASHGIRL
CASHIER
CASHIERED
CASHIERER
CASHING
CASHKEEPER
CASHMERE
CASHMERETTE
CASHOO
CASIMERE
CASIMIRE
CASINA
CASINET
CASING
CASINO
CASINOS
CASIRI
CASITA
CASK
CASKET
CASKING
CASKS
CASQUE
CASQUED
CASQUET
CASQUETEL
CASQUETTE
CASS
CASSABA
CASSABANANA
CASSABULLY
CASSADA
CASSALTY
CASSAN
CASSARE
CASSAREEP
CASSATE
CASSATION
CASSAVA
CASSE
CASSELTY
CASSENA
CASSEROLE
CASSETTE
CASSIA
CASSICAN
CASSIDEOUS
CASSIDID
CASSIDONY
CASSIDULOID
CASSIE
CASSIMERE
CASSINA
CASSINE
CASSINETTE
CASSINO
CASSINOID
CASSIOBERRY
CASSIRI
CASSIS
CASSITERITE
CASSITES
CASSOCK
CASSOCKED
CASSOLETTE
CASSON
CASSONADE
CASSONE
CASSONS
CASSOON
CASSOWARIES

CASSOWARY
CASSUMUNAR
CASSUMUNIAR
CASSY
CAST
CASTAGNOLE
CASTANA
CASTANEAN
CASTANEOUS
CASTANET
CASTANIAN
CASTANO
CASTAWAY
CASTE
CASTELET
CASTELLAN
CASTELLANIES
CASTELLANO
CASTELLANY
CASTELLAR
CASTELLATE
CASTELLATED
CASTELLATION
CASTELLET
CASTEN
CASTER
CASTHOUSE
CASTICE
CASTIGABLE
CASTIGATE
CASTIGATED
CASTIGATING
CASTIGATION
CASTIGATIVE
CASTIGATOR
CASTIGATORIES
CASTIGATORY
CASTILE
CASTILIAN
CASTILLO
CASTING
CASTINGS
CASTLE
CASTLED
CASTLERY
CASTLET
CASTOCK
CASTOFF
CASTOR
CASTOREUM
CASTORIAL
CASTORIN
CASTORITE
CASTORIZED
CASTORY
CASTRAL
CASTRATE
CASTRATED
CASTRATER
CASTRATING
CASTRATION
CASTRATO
CASTRATOR
CASTRENSIAN
CASTRUM
CASTULI
CASUAL
CASUALISM
CASUALIST
CASUALLY
CASUALNESS
CASUALTY
CASUIST
CASUISTIC
CASUISTICAL
CASUISTICALLY
CASUISTRIES

CASUISTRY
CASULA
CASUS
CASWELLITE
CAT
CATABAPTIST
CATABASES
CATABASIS
CATABATIC
CATABIBAZON
CATABIOTIC
CATABOLIC
CATABOLICALLY
CATABOLIN
CATABOLISM
CATABOLITE
CATABOLIZE
CATABOLIZED
CATABOLIZING
CATACAUSTIC
CATACHRESES
CATACHRESIS
CATACHRESTIC
CATACHTHONIAN
CATACHTHONIC
CATACLASM
CATACLASMIC
CATACLASTIC
CATACLINAL
CATACLYSM
CATACLYSMAL
CATACLYSMIC
CATACLYSMIST
CATACOMB
CATACOROLLA
CATACOUSTICS
CATACROTIC
CATACUMBAL
CATADICROTIC
CATADIOPTRIC
CATADROMOUS
CATADUPE
CATAFALQUE
CATAGENESIS
CATAGENETIC
CATAGMATIC
CATAKINESIS
CATALASE
CATALECTA
CATALECTIC
CATALEPSY
CATALEPTIZE
CATALEXIS
CATALIN
CATALINA
CATALINETA
CATALINITE
CATALLACTIC
CATALLACTICS
CATALLUM
CATALO
CATALOES
CATALOG
CATALOGED
CATALOGER
CATALOGIC
CATALOGICAL
CATALOGING
CATALOGIST
CATALOGISTIC
CATALOGUE
CATALOGUED
CATALOGUER
CATALOGUING
CATALOGUIST
CATALOGUIZE
CATALOON

CATALOS
CATALOWNE
CATALPA
CATALUFA
CATALYSES
CATALYSIS
CATALYST
CATALYTE
CATALYTIC
CATALYZATOR
CATALYZE
CATALYZED
CATALYZER
CATALYZING
CATAMARAN
CATAMENIA
CATAMENIAL
CATAMITE
CATAMNESIS
CATAMOUNT
CATAMOUNTAIN
CATAN
CATAPAN
CATAPASM
CATAPETALOUS
CATAPHATIC
CATAPHORA
CATAPHORESIS
CATAPHORIA
CATAPHRACT
CATAPHRENIC
CATAPHYLL
CATAPHYLLARY
CATAPLASIA
CATAPLASIS
CATAPLASM
CATAPLEIITE
CATAPLEXY
CATAPULT
CATAPULTIC
CATAPULTIER
CATARACT
CATARACTAL
CATARACTED
CATARACTINE
CATARACTOUS
CATARIA
CATARINITE
CATARRH
CATARRHAL
CATARRHED
CATARRHINE
CATARRHINIAN
CATARRHOUS
CATASARKA
CATASTA
CATASTALTIC
CATASTASES
CATASTASIS
CATASTATE
CATASTATIC
CATASTERISM
CATASTROPHAL
CATASTROPHE
CATASTROPHIC
CATATHYMIC
CATATONIA
CATATONIAC
CATATONIC
CATAWAMPUS
CATBERRY
CATBIRD
CATBOAT
CATBRIER
CATCALL
CATCH
CATCHALL

CATCHCRY	CATERCOUSIN	CATLINE	CAUCUSSING	CAUSATUM
CATCHED	CATERED	CATLING	CAUDA	CAUSE
CATCHER	CATERER	CATLINITE	CAUDAD	CAUSED
CATCHFLY	CATERESS	CATMALISON	CAUDAL	CAUSER
CATCHIER	CATERING	CATMINT	CAUDALLY	CAUSERIE
CATCHIEST	CATERPILLAR	CATNACHE	CAUDATE	CAUSES
CATCHING	CATERPILLARS	CATNEP	CAUDATED	CAUSEUR
CATCHINGLY	CATERS	CATNIP	CAUDATION	CAUSEUSE
CATCHINGNESS	CATERVA	CATOBLEPAS	CAUDATORY	CAUSEWAY
CATCHLAND	CATERWAUL	CATOCALID	CAUDATUM	CAUSEWAYED
CATCHMENT	CATERWAULER	CATOCTIN	CAUDEX	CAUSEWAYING
CATCHPENNY	CATERWAULING	CATODONT	CAUDEXES	CAUSEWAYMAN
CATCHPLATE	CATES	CATOGENE	CAUDICES	CAUSEY
CATCHPOLE	CATFACE	CATOGENIC	CAUDICLE	CAUSEYS
CATCHPOLED	CATFACED	CATOPTRIC	CAUDIFORM	CAUSIDICAL
CATCHPOLERY	CATFALL	CATOPTRICAL	CAUDILLO	CAUSING
CATCHPOLING	CATFIGHT	CATOPTRICS	CAUDLE	CAUSINGNESS
CATCHPOLL	CATFISH	CATOPTRITE	CAUDODORSAL	CAUSSE
CATCHPOLLED	CATFISHES	CATOSTOMID	CAUDOFEMORAL	CAUSSON
CATCHPOLLERY	CATFOOT	CATOSTOMOID	CAUDOLATERAL	CAUSTIC
CATCHPOLLING	CATFOOTED	CATOUSE	CAUDOTIBIAL	CAUSTICAL
CATCHUP	CATGUT	CATPIECE	CAUFLE	CAUSTICALLY
CATCHWEED	CATHARIZE	CATPIPE	CAUGHT	CAUSTICISER
CATCHWEIGHT	CATHARIZED	CATS	CAUK	CAUSTICISM
CATCHWORD	CATHARIZING	CATSKIN	CAUKED	CAUSTICITY
CATCHWORK	CATHARPING	CATSKINNER	CAUKING	CAUSTICIZE
CATCHY	CATHARSIS	CATSLIDE	CAUL	CAUSTICIZED
CATE	CATHARTIC	CATSO	CAULD	CAUSTICIZER
CATECHESES	CATHARTICAL	CATSOS	CAULDRIFE	CAUSTICIZING
CATECHESIS	CATHEAD	CATSTANE	CAULES	CAUSTICLY
CATECHETIC	CATHECTIC	CATSTEP	CAULESCENT	CAUSTICNESS
CATECHETICAL	CATHEDRA	CATSTICK	CAULICLE	CAUSTIFIED
CATECHIN	CATHEDRAL	CATSTITCH	CAULICOLOUS	CAUSTIFY
CATECHISE	CATHEDRALIC	CATSTITCHER	CAULICULI	CAUSTIFYING
CATECHISED	CATHEDRATIC	CATSTONE	CAULICULUS	CAUTEL
CATECHISER	CATHEPSIN	CATSUP	CAULIFLOROUS	CAUTELA
CATECHISING	CATHETER	CATTABU	CAULIFLORY	CAUTELOUS
CATECHISM	CATHETERISM	CATTAIL	CAULIFLOWER	CAUTER
CATECHISMAL	CATHETERIZE	CATTALO	CAULIFORM	CAUTERANT
CATECHIST	CATHETERIZED	CATTAN	CAULIGENOUS	CAUTERIES
CATECHISTIC	CATHETOMETER	CATTED	CAULINE	CAUTERIZATION
CATECHISTICAL	CATHETUS	CATTER	CAULIS	CAUTERIZE
CATECHIZATION	CATHEXIS	CATTERIES	CAULOCARPIC	CAUTERIZED
CATECHIZE	CATHISMA	CATTERY	CAULOCARPOUS	CAUTERIZING
CATECHIZED	CATHODE	CATTIER	CAULOME	CAUTERY
CATECHIZER	CATHODEGRAPH	CATTIES	CAULOMER	CAUTIO
CATECHIZING	CATHODIC	CATTIEST	CAULOMIC	CAUTION
CATECHOL	CATHODICAL	CATTILY	CAULOTAXY	CAUTIONARIES
CATECHU	CATHODICALLY	CATTIMANDOO	CAULOTE	CAUTIONARY
CATECHUMEN	CATHODOGRAPH	CATTINESS	CAULP	CAUTIONER
CATECHUMENAL	CATHOLE	CATTISH	CAUM	CAUTIONES
CATEGOREM	CATHOLIC	CATTISHLY	CAUMA	CAUTIONRY
CATEGORIAL	CATHOLICAL	CATTISHNESS	CAUMATIC	CAUTIOUS
CATEGORIC	CATHOLICALLY	CATTLE	CAUP	CAUTIOUSLY
CATEGORICAL	CATHOLICATE	CATTLEBUSH	CAUPONATE	CAUTIOUSNESS
CATEGORIES	CATHOLICISM	CATTLEHIDE	CAUPONATION	CAVAL
CATEGORIST	CATHOLICITY	CATTLEMAN	CAUPONES	CAVALCADE
CATEGORIZE	CATHOLICIZE	CATTLEYA	CAUPONIZE	CAVALCADED
CATEGORIZED	CATHOLICIZED	CATTLEYAK	CAUR	CAVALCADING
CATEGORIZING	CATHOLICIZING	CATTY	CAURALE	CAVALIER
CATEGORY	CATHOLICLY	CATTYMAN	CAURE	CAVALIERE
CATELLA	CATHOLICNESS	CATUR	CAUSA	CAVALIERED
CATENA	CATHOLICON	CATVINE	CAUSABILITY	CAVALIERING
CATENAE	CATHOLICOS	CATWALK	CAUSABLE	CAVALIERISM
CATENARIAN	CATHOLICUS	CATWORT	CAUSAE	CAVALIERLY
CATENARIES	CATHOLYTE	CATYDID	CAUSAL	CAVALIERO
CATENARY	CATHOP	CATZERIE	CAUSALGIA	CAVALLA
CATENATE	CATHOUSE	CAUBEEN	CAUSALITIES	CAVALRIES
CATENATED	CATION	CAUBOGE	CAUSALITY	CAVALRY
CATENATING	CATIVO	CAUCH	CAUSALLY	CAVALRYMAN
CATENATION	CATJANG	CAUCHEMAR	CAUSATA	CAVASCOPE
CATENOID	CATKIN	CAUCHILLO	CAUSATE	CAVATE
CATENULATE	CATKINATE	CAUCHO	CAUSATION	CAVATINA
CATEPUCE	CATLA	CAUCUS	CAUSATIONAL	CAVAYARD
CATER	CATLAP	CAUCUSED	CAUSATIONIST	CAVE
CATERAN	CATLIKE	CAUCUSING	CAUSATIVE	CAVEA
CATERCAP	CATLIN	CAUCUSSED	CAUSATIVELY	CAVEAT

CAVEATEE	CAZIBI	CELARENT	CELLIST	CENOBIES
CAVEATOR	CAZIMI	CELATION	CELLO	CENOBITE
CAVEFISH	CAZIQUE	CELATIVE	CELLOBIOSE	CENOBITIC
CAVEFISHES	CAZY	CELATURE	CELLOCUT	CENOBITICAL
CAVEKEEPER	CE	CELEB	CELLOID	CENOBITISM
CAVEL	CEARIN	CELEBE	CELLOIDIN	CENOBIUM
CAVENDISH	CEASE	CELEBRANT	CELLOIST	CENOBY
CAVER	CEASED	CELEBRATE	CELLOPHANE	CENOGENESIS
CAVERN	CEASELESS	CELEBRATED	CELLOS	CENOGENETIC
CAVERNAL	CEASELESSLY	CELEBRATER	CELLOSE	CENOGONOUS
CAVERNED	CEASING	CELEBRATING	CELLS	CENOSITE
CAVERNITIS	CEASMIC	CELEBRATION	CELLULAR	CENOSITY
CAVERNOMA	CEBELL	CELEBRATIVE	CELLULARITY	CENOTAPH
CAVERNOUS	CEBID	CELEBRATOR	CELLULARLY	CENOTAPHIC
CAVERNOUSLY	CEBIL	CELEBRATORY	CELLULASE	CENOTAPHIES
CAVERNULOUS	CEBINE	CELEBRIOUS	CELLULATE	CENOTAPHY
CAVESON	CEBOID	CELEBRIOUSLY	CELLULATED	CENOTE
CAVESSON	CEBUR	CELEBRITIES	CELLULATION	CENOZOOLOGY
CAVETTO	CECA	CELEBRITY	CELLULE	CENS
CAVEY	CECCHINE	CELEMIN	CELLULIFUGAL	CENSE
CAVIAR	CECIDIOLOGY	CELEMINES	CELLULIN	CENSED
CAVIARE	CECIDIUM	CELEOMORPH	CELLULIPETAL	CENSER
CAVICORN	CECILITE	CELEOMORPHIC	CELLULITIS	CENSING
CAVIE	CECILS	CELER	CELLULOID	CENSITAIRE
CAVIES	CECITIS	CELERIAC	CELLULOIDED	CENSIVE
CAVIL	CECITY	CELERITY	CELLULOSE	CENSO
CAVILED	CECOGRAPH	CELERY	CELLULOSED	CENSOR
CAVILER	CECOMORPHIC	CELESTA	CELLULOSIC	CENSORATE
CAVILING	CECOTOMY	CELESTE	CELLULOSING	CENSORED
CAVILINGLY	CECUTIENCY	CELESTIAL	CELLULOSITIES	CENSORIAL
CAVILINGNESS	CEDAR	CELESTIALITY	CELLULOSITY	CENSORIAN
CAVILLATION	CEDARBIRD	CELESTIALIZE	CELLULOUS	CENSORING
CAVILLED	CEDARED	CELESTIALIZED	CELOM	CENSORIOUS
CAVILLINGLY	CEDARN	CELESTINA	CELOTOMIES	CENSORIOUSLY
CAVING	CEDARWARE	CELESTINE	CELOTOMY	CENSORSHIP
CAVINGS	CEDARWOOD	CELESTITE	CELSIAN	CENSUAL
CAVITARY	CEDE	CELIADELPHUS	CELSITUDE	CENSURABLE
CAVITATE	CEDED	CELIAGRA	CELT	CENSURABLY
CAVITATED	CEDENS	CELIBACY	CELTIFORM	CENSURE
CAVITATING	CEDENT	CELIBATAIRE	CELTIUM	CENSURED
CAVITATION	CEDILLA	CELIBATARIAN	CELTUCE	CENSURER
CAVITENO	CEDILLAS	CELIBATE	CELURE	CENSURESHIP
CAVITIED	CEDING	CELIBATIC	CEMBALIST	CENSURING
CAVITIES	CEDOR	CELIBATIST	CEMBALO	CENSUS
CAVITY	CEDRA	CELIBATORY	CEMBALON	CENSUSES
CAVIYA	CEDRAT	CELIDOGRAPHY	CEMBALOS	CENT
CAVORT	CEDRATE	CELIOCELE	CEMENT	CENTAGE
CAVORTED	CEDRE	CELIOCYESIS	CEMENTAL	CENTAL
CAVORTING	CEDRENE	CELIODYNIA	CEMENTATION	CENTAS
CAVUM	CEDRIN	CELIOLYMPH	CEMENTATORY	CENTAUR
CAVY	CEDRINE	CELIOMYALGIA	CEMENTER	CENTAURIAL
CAVYYARD	CEDRIRET	CELIORRHAPHY	CEMENTIN	CENTAURIAN
CAW	CEDRIUM	CELIORRHEA	CEMENTITE	CENTAURIC
CAWF	CEDROL	CELIOSCHISIS	CEMENTITIOUS	CENTAURIES
CAWK	CEDRON	CELIOSCOPE	CEMENTMAKER	CENTAURY
CAWKY	CEDRY	CELIOSCOPY	CEMENTMAKING	CENTAVO
CAWL	CEDULA	CELIOTOMY	CEMENTOBLAST	CENTAVOS
CAWNEY	CEDUOUS	CELITE	CEMENTOMA	CENTENA
CAWNIE	CEE	CELL	CEMENTUM	CENTENAR
CAWNY	CEEL	CELLA	CEMETERIAL	CENTENARIAN
CAWQUAW	CEIBA	CELLAE	CEMETERIES	CENTENARIES
CAXI	CEIBO	CELLAR	CEMETERY	CENTENARY
CAXIRI	CEIL	CELLARAGE	CENA	CENTENIER
CAXON	CEILE	CELLARED	CENACLE	CENTENNIAL
CAY	CEILED	CELLARER	CENACULUM	CENTENNIUM
CAYAR	CEILER	CELLARESS	CENANTHOUS	CENTER
CAYENNE	CEILIDH	CELLARET	CENANTHY	CENTERBOARD
CAYENNED	CEILIDHE	CELLARING	CENATION	CENTERED
CAYMAN	CEILING	CELLARMAN	CENATORY	CENTEREDNESS
CAYMANS	CEILINGED	CELLAROUS	CENCERRO	CENTERER
CAYNARD	CEILOMETER	CELLARWAY	CENCERROS	CENTERING
CAYO	CEINT	CELLARWOMAN	CENESTHESIA	CENTERLESS
CAYOS	CEINTURE	CELLATED	CENESTHESIS	CENTERMOST
CAYUCA	CEL	CELLED	CENESTHETIC	CENTERPIECE
CAYUCO	CELADONITE	CELLI	CENIZO	CENTESIMAL
CAYUSE	CELANDINE	CELLIFORM	CENOBE	CENTESIMALLY
CAZA		CELLIPETAL	CENOBIAN	CENTESIMATE

CENTESIMI
CENTESIMO
CENTESIMOS
CENTESIS
CENTESM
CENTETID
CENTGENER
CENTIARE
CENTIBAR
CENTIDAY
CENTIFOLIOUS
CENTIGRADE
CENTIGRAM
CENTIGRAMME
CENTILE
CENTILITER
CENTILITRE
CENTILLION
CENTILLIONTH
CENTIME
CENTIMETER
CENTIMETRE
CENTIMOLAR
CENTINORMAL
CENTIPEDAL
CENTIPEDE
CENTIPLUME
CENTIPOISE
CENTISTERE
CENTISTOKE
CENTNER
CENTO
CENTON
CENTONICAL
CENTONISM
CENTOS
CENTRA
CENTRAD
CENTRAL
CENTRALISM
CENTRALIST
CENTRALISTIC
CENTRALITY
CENTRALIZE
CENTRALIZED
CENTRALIZER
CENTRALIZING
CENTRANTH
CENTRARCHOID
CENTRE
CENTREBOARD
CENTRED
CENTRELESS
CENTREMOST
CENTREPIECE
CENTRER
CENTRIC
CENTRICAL
CENTRICALITY
CENTRICALLY
CENTRICIPUT
CENTRICITY
CENTRIFFED
CENTRIFUGAL
CENTRIFUGATE
CENTRIFUGE
CENTRIFUGED
CENTRIFUGING
CENTRING
CENTRIOLE
CENTRIPETAL
CENTRISCID
CENTRIST
CENTRO
CENTROACINAR
CENTROBARIC
CENTROCLINAL

CENTRODE
CENTRODORSAL
CENTROID
CENTROIDAL
CENTROLINEAD
CENTROLINEAL
CENTROPLASM
CENTROSOME
CENTROSOMIC
CENTROSPHERE
CENTRUM
CENTRUMS
CENTRY
CENTS
CENTUM
CENTUMVIR
CENTUMVIRAL
CENTUMVIRATE
CENTUPLE
CENTUPLICATE
CENTUPLY
CENTURE
CENTURIAL
CENTURIATE
CENTURIATION
CENTURIATOR
CENTURIED
CENTURIES
CENTURION
CENTURY
CEORL
CEP
CEPA
CEPACEOUS
CEPE
CEPHAELINE
CEPHALAD
CEPHALAGRA
CEPHALALGIA
CEPHALALGIC
CEPHALALGY
CEPHALATE
CEPHALEMIA
CEPHALETRON
CEPHALIC
CEPHALIN
CEPHALINE
CEPHALISM
CEPHALITIS
CEPHALOB
CEPHALOCELE
CEPHALOCHORD
CEPHALOCLAST
CEPHALOCONE
CEPHALOCONIC
CEPHALOCYST
CEPHALOGRAM
CEPHALOGRAPH
CEPHALOID
CEPHALOLOGY
CEPHALOMANCY
CEPHALOMANT
CEPHALOMELUS
CEPHALOMENIA
CEPHALOMERE
CEPHALOMETER
CEPHALOMETRIC
CEPHALOMETRY
CEPHALOMOTOR
CEPHALON
CEPHALONASAL
CEPHALOPAGUS
CEPHALOPATHY
CEPHALOPHINE
CEPHALOPHYMA
CEPHALOPOD
CEPHALOPODAN

CEPHALOPODIC
CEPHALOSOME
CEPHALOSTYLE
CEPHALOTHECA
CEPHALOTOME
CEPHALOTOMY
CEPHALOTRIBE
CEPHALOUS
CEPHID
CEPTER
CEPTOR
CEQUI
CERACEOUS
CERAGO
CERAL
CERAMAL
CERAMBYCID
CERAMIACEOUS
CERAMIC
CERAMICITE
CERAMICS
CERAMIDIUM
CERAMIST
CERAMOGRAPHY
CERARGYRITE
CERAS
CERASEIN
CERASIN
CERASTES
CERATA
CERATE
CERATECTOMY
CERATED
CERATIASIS
CERATIID
CERATIOID
CERATION
CERATITE
CERATITIC
CERATITOID
CERATOBRANCHIA
CERATOHYAL
CERATOID
CERATOMANIA
CERATOPHYTE
CERATOPSIAN
CERATOPSID
CERATORHINE
CERATOTHECA
CERATOTHECAE
CERATOTHECAL
CERAUNIA
CERAUNICS
CERAUNOGRAM
CERAUNOGRAPH
CERAUNOMANCY
CERAUNOPHONE
CERAUNOSCOPE
CERAUNOSCOPY
CERCAL
CERCARIA
CERCARIAE
CERCARIAL
CERCARIAN
CERCARIFORM
CERCIS
CERCLE
CERCOMONAD
CERCOPID
CERCOPOD
CERCUS
CERE
CEREAL
CEREALIAN
CEREALISM
CEREALIST
CEREALS

CEREBELLA
CEREBELLAR
CEREBELLUM
CEREBELLUMS
CEREBRAL
CEREBRALGIA
CEREBRALISM
CEREBRALIST
CEREBRATE
CEREBRATED
CEREBRATING
CEREBRATION
CEREBRIC
CEREBRICITY
CEREBRIFORM
CEREBRIFUGAL
CEREBRIN
CEREBRIPETAL
CEREBRITIS
CEREBRIZE
CEREBROID
CEREBROLOGY
CEREBROMA
CEREBROMETER
CEREBRON
CEREBRONIC
CEREBROPATHY
CEREBROPEDAL
CEREBROSCOPE
CEREBROSCOPY
CEREBROSE
CEREBROSIDE
CEREBROSIS
CEREBROSURIA
CEREBROTOMY
CEREBRUM
CERECLOTH
CERED
CEREMENT
CEREMONIAL
CEREMONIALLY
CEREMONIES
CEREMONIOUS
CEREMONY
CEREOUS
CERER
CERESIN
CERESINE
CEREUS
CEREVIS
CEREZA
CERFOIL
CERIA
CERIANTHID
CERIANTHOID
CERIC
CERID
CERIDE
CERIFEROUS
CERILLO
CERIMAN
CERIN
CERINE
CERING
CERIOPS
CERIPH
CERISE
CERITE
CERITHIOID
CERIUM
CERN
CERNED
CERNING
CERNITURE
CERNUOUS
CERO
CEROGRAPH

CEROGRAPHIC
CEROGRAPHICAL
CEROGRAPHIES
CEROGRAPHIST
CEROGRAPHY
CEROID
CEROLINE
CEROLITE
CEROMA
CEROMANCY
CEROPHILOUS
CEROPLAST
CEROPLASTIC
CEROPLASTICS
CEROS
CEROTATE
CEROTE
CEROTENE
CEROTIC
CEROTIN
CEROTYPE
CEROUS
CEROXYLE
CERRERO
CERRIAL
CERRIS
CERRO
CERT
CERTAIN
CERTAINLY
CERTAINTIES
CERTAINTY
CERTES
CERTIE
CERTIFIABLE
CERTIFICATE
CERTIFICATED
CERTIFICATING
CERTIFICATION
CERTIFICATIVE
CERTIFICATOR
CERTIFICATORY
CERTIFIED
CERTIFIER
CERTIFY
CERTIFYING
CERTIORARI
CERTIORATE
CERTIORATING
CERTITUDE
CERTOSA
CERTOSE
CERTOSINA
CERTOSINO
CERTY
CERULE
CERULEAN
CERULEITE
CERULEOUS
CERULEUM
CERULIGNOL
CERULIGNONE
CERUMEN
CERUMINOUS
CERUSE
CERUSITE
CERUSSITE
CERVALET
CERVANTITE
CERVELAT
CERVELIERE
CERVICAL
CERVICECTOMY
CERVICES
CERVICITIS
CERVICONASAL
CERVICORN

CERVID	CHABASIE	CHAINLET	CHALDER	CHAMM
CERVINE	CHABASITE	CHAINMAKER	CHALDESE	CHAMMA
CERVISIA	CHABAZITE	CHAINMAKING	CHALDRON	CHAMMY
CERVISIAL	CHABER	CHAINMAN	CHALET	CHAMOIS
CERVIX	CHABO	CHAINMEN	CHALICE	CHAMOISITE
CERVIXES	CHABOT	CHAINON	CHALICED	CHAMOLINE
CERVOID	CHABOUK	CHAINS	CHALICOSIS	CHAMOTTE
CERYL	CHABUK	CHAINWORK	CHALICOTHERE	CHAMP
CESAREAN	CHABUTRA	CHAIR	CHALININE	CHAMPAC
CESAREVITCH	CHACATE	CHAIRER	CHALK	CHAMPACA
CESARIAN	CHACCON	CHAIRMAKER	CHALKBOARD	CHAMPAGNE
CESAROLITE	CHACE	CHAIRMAKING	CHALKCUTTER	CHAMPAGNED
CESIOUS	CHACK	CHAIRMAN	CHALKED	CHAMPAGNING
CESIUM	CHACKER	CHAIRMEN	CHALKER	CHAMPAGNIZE
CESPITITIOUS	CHACKLE	CHAIRMENDER	CHALKIER	CHAMPAGNIZED
CESPITOSE	CHACMA	CHAIRMENDING	CHALKIEST	CHAMPAGNIZING
CESPITOSELY	CHACOLI	CHAIRWARMER	CHALKINESS	CHAMPAIGN
CESS	CHACONA	CHAIRWAY	CHALKING	CHAMPAIN
CESSANT	CHACONNE	CHAIRWOMAN	CHALKOGRAPHY	CHAMPAK
CESSATION	CHACRA	CHAIRWOMEN	CHALKONE	CHAMPART
CESSATIVE	CHACTE	CHAIS	CHALKOS	CHAMPE
CESSAVIT	CHADACRYST	CHAISE	CHALKOTHEKE	CHAMPED
CESSE	CHADELLE	CHAITRA	CHALKSTONE	CHAMPER
CESSED	CHADLOCK	CHAITYA	CHALKWORKER	CHAMPERTIES
CESSER	CHADOR	CHAITYAS	CHALKY	CHAMPERTOR
CESSING	CHAETA	CHAJA	CHALLAH	CHAMPERTOUS
CESSIO	CHAETAE	CHAK	CHALLENGE	CHAMPERTY
CESSION	CHAETIFEROUS	CHAKAR	CHALLENGED	CHAMPIAN
CESSIONAIRE	CHAETOGNATH	CHAKARI	CHALLENGEE	CHAMPIGNON
CESSIONARIES	CHAETOPOD	CHAKAZI	CHALLENGER	CHAMPION
CESSIONARY	CHAETOPODAN	CHAKDAR	CHALLENGING	CHAMPIONED
CESSOR	CHAETOPTERIN	CHAKOBU	CHALLIS	CHAMPIONESS
CESSPIPE	CHAETOSEMA	CHAKRA	CHALLOTE	CHAMPIONING
CESSPIT	CHAETOTAXY	CHAKRAVARTIN	CHALMER	CHAMPIONSHIP
CESSPOOL	CHAFE	CHAKSI	CHALON	CHAMPLEVE
CEST	CHAFED	CHAL	CHALONE	CHAMPY
CESTA	CHAFER	CHALACO	CHALOUPE	CHAMSIN
CESTODE	CHAFERY	CHALANA	CHALQUE	CHAN
CESTODES	CHAFEWAX	CHALASTIC	CHALTA	CHANCE
CESTOID	CHAFEWEED	CHALAZA	CHALUKA	CHANCEABLE
CESTON	CHAFF	CHALAZAE	CHALUMEAU	CHANCEABLY
CESTRUM	CHAFFCUTTER	CHALAZAL	CHALUMEAUX	CHANCED
CESTUI	CHAFFED	CHALAZAS	CHALYBEATE	CHANCEFUL
CESTUS	CHAFFER	CHALAZE	CHALYBEOUS	CHANCEFULLY
CESTUY	CHAFFERED	CHALAZIAN	CHALYBITE	CHANCEL
CETACEAN	CHAFFERER	CHALAZION	CHAM	CHANCELED
CETACEOUS	CHAFFERING	CHALAZIUM	CHAMADE	CHANCELLED
CETACEUM	CHAFFERY	CHALAZOGAM	CHAMAERRHINE	CHANCELLERY
CETE	CHAFFIER	CHALAZOGAMIC	CHAMAL	CHANCELLOR
CETENE	CHAFFIEST	CHALAZOGAMY	CHAMAR	CHANCELOR
CETERACH	CHAFFINCH	CHALAZOIDITE	CHAMBELLAN	CHANCELRY
CETIC	CHAFFING	CHALCANTHITE	CHAMBER	CHANCER
CETICIDE	CHAFFMAN	CHALCEDONIC	CHAMBERED	CHANCERIES
CETIN	CHAFFSEED	CHALCEDONIES	CHAMBERER	CHANCERY
CETIOSAURIAN	CHAFFWAX	CHALCEDONOUS	CHAMBERING	CHANCEY
CETOLOGICAL	CHAFFWEED	CHALCEDONY	CHAMBERLAIN	CHANCHE
CETOLOGIST	CHAFFY	CHALCEDONYX	CHAMBERLET	CHANCIER
CETOLOGY	CHAFING	CHALCHIHUITL	CHAMBERLETED	CHANCIEST
CETONIAN	CHAFT	CHALCHUITE	CHAMBERLETTED	CHANCILY
CETORHINID	CHAGIGAH	CHALCID	CHAMBERMAID	CHANCING
CETORHINOID	CHAGOMA	CHALCIDICUM	CHAMBERWOMAN	CHANCITO
CETOTOLITE	CHAGRIN	CHALCIDID	CHAMBRANLE	CHANCO
CETRARIN	CHAGRINED	CHALCIDIFORM	CHAMBRAY	CHANCRE
CETYL	CHAGRINING	CHALCITES	CHAMBUL	CHANCRIFORM
CETYLENE	CHAGRINS	CHALCOCITE	CHAMECEPHALY	CHANCROID
CETYLIC	CHAGUAR	CHALCOGRAPH	CHAMELEON	CHANCROIDAL
CEVADILLA	CHAGUL	CHALCOGRAPHY	CHAMELEONIC	CHANCROUS
CEVIAN	CHAHAR	CHALCOLITE	CHAMELEONIZE	CHANCY
CEVICHE	CHAI	CHALCOLITHIC	CHAMETZ	CHANDALA
CEVIN	CHAIN	CHALCOMANCY	CHAMFER	CHANDAM
CEVINE	CHAINAGE	CHALCOMENITE	CHAMFERER	CHANDELIER
CEYLANITE	CHAINBEARER	CHALCON	CHAMFRAIN	CHANDI
CEYLONITE	CHAINED	CHALCONE	CHAMFRON	CHANDLER
CHA	CHAINER	CHALCOPYRITE	CHAMISAL	CHANDLERIES
CHAA	CHAINETTE	CHALCOSINE	CHAMISE	CHANDLERING
CHAAC	CHAINING	CHALCOTRIPT	CHAMISO	CHANDLERLY
CHAB	CHAINLESS	CHALCUS	CHAMITE	CHANDLERY

CHANDOO
CHANDRAKANTA
CHANDRAKHI
CHANDU
CHANDUL
CHANFRIN
CHANG
CHANGA
CHANGAR
CHANGE
CHANGEABLE
CHANGEABLENESS
CHANGEABLY
CHANGED
CHANGEFUL
CHANGEFULLY
CHANGELESS
CHANGELESSLY
CHANGELING
CHANGEOVER
CHANGER
CHANGES
CHANGING
CHANK
CHANKINGS
CHANNEL
CHANNELBILL
CHANNELED
CHANNELING
CHANNELIZE
CHANNELIZED
CHANNELIZING
CHANNELLED
CHANNELLING
CHANNELS
CHANNER
CHANOYU
CHANSON
CHANSONNETTE
CHANSONNIER
CHANT
CHANTAGE
CHANTANT
CHANTECLER
CHANTEFABLE
CHANTEPLEURE
CHANTER
CHANTERELLE
CHANTEUR
CHANTEUSE
CHANTEY
CHANTEYMAN
CHANTICLEER
CHANTIER
CHANTING
CHANTINGLY
CHANTLATE
CHANTMENT
CHANTOR
CHANTRESS
CHANTRY
CHANTY
CHAOGENOUS
CHAOLOGY
CHAOS
CHAOTIC
CHAOTICAL
CHAOTICALLY
CHAOUA
CHAOUSH
CHAP
CHAPAH
CHAPAPOTE
CHAPARAJOS
CHAPAREJOS
CHAPARRAL
CHAPARRO

CHAPATTI
CHAPATTIES
CHAPATTY
CHAPBOOK
CHAPE
CHAPEAU
CHAPEAUS
CHAPEAUX
CHAPEL
CHAPELED
CHAPELET
CHAPELGOER
CHAPELGOING
CHAPELLANY
CHAPELLED
CHAPELLING
CHAPELMAN
CHAPELMASTER
CHAPELRIES
CHAPELRY
CHAPERNO
CHAPERON
CHAPERONAGE
CHAPERONED
CHAPERONING
CHAPFALLEN
CHAPFALLENLY
CHAPIN
CHAPITER
CHAPITRAL
CHAPLAIN
CHAPLAINCIES
CHAPLAINCY
CHAPLAINRY
CHAPLAINSHIP
CHAPLANRY
CHAPLESS
CHAPLET
CHAPLETED
CHAPMAN
CHAPON
CHAPOTE
CHAPOURNET
CHAPOURNETTED
CHAPPAUL
CHAPPE
CHAPPED
CHAPPER
CHAPPIE
CHAPPIES
CHAPPING
CHAPPOW
CHAPPY
CHAPRASI
CHAPS
CHAPT
CHAPTER
CHAPTERAL
CHAPTERED
CHAPTERING
CHAPTREL
CHAQUETA
CHAR
CHARABANC
CHARABANCER
CHARABANCS
CHARACEOUS
CHARACETUM
CHARACIN
CHARACINE
CHARACINID
CHARACINOID
CHARACT
CHARACTER
CHARACTERED
CHARACTERIAL

CHARACTERICAL
CHARACTERIES
CHARACTERING
CHARACTERISM
CHARACTERIST
CHARACTERISTIC
CHARACTERISTICALLY
CHARACTERIZATION
CHARACTERIZE
CHARACTERIZED
CHARACTERIZER
CHARACTERIZING
CHARACTERLESS
CHARACTERS
CHARACTERY
CHARADE
CHARADES
CHARADRINE
CHARADRIOID
CHARANGO
CHARAS
CHARBOCLE
CHARBON
CHARBONNIER
CHARCO
CHARCOAL
CHARCOALY
CHARCUTERIE
CHARCUTIER
CHARD
CHARDOCK
CHARE
CHARED
CHARELY
CHARER
CHARET
CHARETER
CHARETTE
CHARGE
CHARGEABLE
CHARGEABLY
CHARGED
CHARGEE
CHARGEFUL
CHARGEHOUSE
CHARGELING
CHARGEMAN
CHARGER
CHARGING
CHARIER
CHARIEST
CHARILY
CHARINESS
CHARIOT
CHARIOTED
CHARIOTEE
CHARIOTEER
CHARIOTEERS
CHARIOTMAN
CHARIOTRY
CHARISM
CHARISMATIC
CHARISTICARY
CHARITABLE
CHARITABLENESS
CHARITABLY
CHARITATIVE
CHARITIES
CHARITY
CHARIVARI
CHARIVARIS
CHARK
CHARKA
CHARKED
CHARKHA
CHARKHANA
CHARKING

CHARLADY
CHARLATAN
CHARLATANIC
CHARLATANISH
CHARLATANISM
CHARLATANRIES
CHARLATANRY
CHARLET
CHARLOCK
CHARLOTTE
CHARM
CHARMED
CHARMEDLY
CHARMER
CHARMEUSE
CHARMFUL
CHARMFULLY
CHARMING
CHARMINGLY
CHARNECO
CHARNEL
CHAROSES
CHARPIE
CHARPIT
CHARPOY
CHARQUE
CHARQUI
CHARR
CHARRE
CHARRED
CHARRIER
CHARRIEST
CHARRING
CHARRO
CHARRY
CHARS
CHARSHAF
CHART
CHARTA
CHARTACEOUS
CHARTER
CHARTERED
CHARTERER
CHARTERHOUSE
CHARTERING
CHARTERMASTER
CHARTHOUSE
CHARTLESS
CHARTOGRAPHY
CHARTOLOGY
CHARTOMETER
CHARTOPHYLAX
CHARTREUSE
CHARTROOM
CHARTS
CHARTULA
CHARTULAE
CHARTULARIES
CHARTULARY
CHARTULAS
CHARUK
CHARWOMAN
CHARWOMEN
CHARY
CHASE
CHASED
CHASER
CHASING
CHASM
CHASMA
CHASMAL
CHASMED
CHASMIC
CHASMOGAMIC
CHASMOGAMOUS
CHASMOGAMY
CHASMOPHYTE

CHASMY
CHASSE
CHASSED
CHASSEING
CHASSEPOT
CHASSEUR
CHASSIGNITE
CHASSIS
CHASTE
CHASTELY
CHASTEN
CHASTENER
CHASTENESS
CHASTISABLE
CHASTISE
CHASTISED
CHASTISEMENT
CHASTISER
CHASTISING
CHASTITY
CHASUBLE
CHASUBLED
CHAT
CHATAKA
CHATEAU
CHATEAUGRAY
CHATEAUX
CHATELAIN
CHATELAINE
CHATELAINRY
CHATHAMITE
CHATI
CHATON
CHATOYANCY
CHATOYANT
CHATS
CHATSOME
CHATTA
CHATTABLE
CHATTACK
CHATTAH
CHATTATION
CHATTED
CHATTEL
CHATTELISM
CHATTELIZE
CHATTELS
CHATTER
CHATTERATION
CHATTERBAG
CHATTERBOX
CHATTERED
CHATTERER
CHATTERING
CHATTERMAG
CHATTERY
CHATTIER
CHATTIES
CHATTIEST
CHATTILY
CHATTINESS
CHATTING
CHATTY
CHATWOOD
CHAUDRON
CHAUFER
CHAUFFAGE
CHAUFFER
CHAUFFEUR
CHAUFFEUSE
CHAUK
CHAUKIDARI
CHAULE
CHAULMAUGRA
CHAULMOOGRA
CHAULMOOGRIC
CHAULMUGRA

CHAUM
CHAUMER
CHAUMIERE
CHAUN
CHAURI
CHAUS
CHAUSSEE
CHAUSSEES
CHAUSSES
CHAUSSURE
CHAUTAUQUA
CHAUTE
CHAUTH
CHAUVE
CHAUVIN
CHAUVINISM
CHAUVINIST
CHAUVINISTIC
CHAVEL
CHAVENDER
CHAVER
CHAVIBETOL
CHAVICIN
CHAVICINE
CHAVICOL
CHAVISH
CHAVO
CHAW
CHAWAN
CHAWBACON
CHAWBONE
CHAWBUCK
CHAWDRON
CHAWER
CHAWK
CHAWL
CHAWLE
CHAWN
CHAWSTICK
CHAY
CHAYOTE
CHAZAN
CHAZANUT
CHAZZAN
CHAZZANUT
CHEAP
CHEAPEN
CHEAPENED
CHEAPENER
CHEAPENING
CHEAPER
CHEAPERY
CHEAPEST
CHEAPIE
CHEAPING
CHEAPISH
CHEAPLY
CHEAPNESS
CHEAPSKATE
CHEAT
CHEATED
CHEATEE
CHEATER
CHEATERS
CHEATERY
CHEATING
CHEATRIE
CHEATRY
CHEATS
CHEBEC
CHEBECK
CHEBEL
CHEBOG
CHEBULE
CHEBULIC
CHEBULINIC
CHECHAKO

CHECHEM
CHECHIA
CHECK
CHECKABLE
CHECKAGE
CHECKBIRD
CHECKBITE
CHECKBOOK
CHECKE
CHECKED
CHECKER
CHECKERBELLIES
CHECKERBELLY
CHECKERBERRIES
CHECKERBERRY
CHECKERBLOOM
CHECKERBOARD
CHECKERBREAST
CHECKERED
CHECKERING
CHECKERIST
CHECKERS
CHECKERWISE
CHECKERWORK
CHECKHOOK
CHECKING
CHECKLE
CHECKLESS
CHECKLINE
CHECKMAN
CHECKMATE
CHECKMATED
CHECKMATING
CHECKOFF
CHECKOUT
CHECKRACK
CHECKREIN
CHECKROLL
CHECKROOM
CHECKROPE
CHECKROW
CHECKROWER
CHECKS
CHECKSTONE
CHECKSTRAP
CHECKSTRING
CHECKWEIGHER
CHECKWORK
CHECKY
CHEDDAR
CHEDDARING
CHEDDITE
CHEDER
CHEDITE
CHEDLOCK
CHEE
CHEECHA
CHEECHACO
CHEECHAKO
CHEEK
CHEEKBONE
CHEEKER
CHEEKIER
CHEEKIEST
CHEEKILY
CHEEKINESS
CHEEKY
CHEENEY
CHEEP
CHEEPER
CHEEPIER
CHEEPIEST
CHEEPILY
CHEEPINESS
CHEER
CHEERED
CHEERER

CHEERFUL
CHEERFULIZE
CHEERFULLY
CHEERFULNESS
CHEERFULSOME
CHEERIER
CHEERIEST
CHEERILY
CHEERINESS
CHEERING
CHEERINGLY
CHEERIO
CHEERIOS
CHEERLEADER
CHEERLESS
CHEERLESSLY
CHEERLESSNESS
CHEERLY
CHEERO
CHEERS
CHEERY
CHEESE
CHEESEBURGER
CHEESECAKE
CHEESECLOTH
CHEESECURD
CHEESECUTTER
CHEESED
CHEESEFLOWER
CHEESELEP
CHEESELIP
CHEESEMONGER
CHEESEPARER
CHEESEPARING
CHEESER
CHEESERY
CHEESEWOOD
CHEESIER
CHEESIEST
CHEESINESS
CHEESING
CHEESY
CHEET
CHEETAH
CHEETAL
CHEETER
CHEEWINK
CHEF
CHEFE
CHEGOE
CHEGRE
CHEICERAL
CHEILION
CHEILITIS
CHEILOPLASTY
CHEIR
CHEIRAGRA
CHEIROGNOMY
CHEIROGRAPHY
CHEIROLIN
CHEIROLINE
CHEIROLOGY
CHEIROMANCY
CHEIROMEGALY
CHEIROPODIST
CHEIROPODY
CHEIROSOPHY
CHEIROSPASM
CHEK
CHEKAN
CHEKE
CHEKEN
CHEKI
CHEKKER
CHEKMAK
CHELA
CHELAE

CHELASHIP
CHELATE
CHELATED
CHELATION
CHELE
CHELEM
CHELERYTHRIN
CHELICERA
CHELICERATE
CHELIDON
CHELIDONATE
CHELIDONIAN
CHELIDONIC
CHELIDONIN
CHELIDONINE
CHELIFEROUS
CHELIFORM
CHELINGA
CHELINGAS
CHELINGO
CHELINGOS
CHELIPED
CHELODINE
CHELONE
CHELONIAN
CHELONID
CHELONIN
CHELOPHORE
CHELP
CHELYDROID
CHELYS
CHEMASTHENIA
CHEMAWINITE
CHEMESTHESIS
CHEMIATRIST
CHEMIATRY
CHEMIC
CHEMICAL
CHEMICALIZE
CHEMICALLY
CHEMICALS
CHEMICK
CHEMICKED
CHEMICKER
CHEMICKING
CHEMIGRAPH
CHEMIGRAPHIC
CHEMIGRAPHY
CHEMiLOON
CHEMIN
CHEMINEE
CHEMIOTACTIC
CHEMIOTAXIC
CHEMIOTAXIS
CHEMIOTROPIC
CHEMIPHOTIC
CHEMIS
CHEMISE
CHEMISETTE
CHEMISM
CHEMIST
CHEMISTRIES
CHEMISTRY
CHEMITYPE
CHEMITYPIES
CHEMITYPY
CHEMIZO
CHEMMY
CHEMOCEPTOR
CHEMOKINESIS
CHEMOKINETIC
CHEMOLYSIS
CHEMOLYTIC
CHEMOLYZE
CHEMOREFLEX
CHEMOSES
CHEMOSIS

CHEMOSMOSES
CHEMOSMOSIS
CHEMOSMOTIC
CHEMOSPHERE
CHEMOSPHERIC
CHEMOSTAT
CHEMOTACTIC
CHEMOTAXIS
CHEMOTAXY
CHEMOTHERAPY
CHEMOTIC
CHEMOTROPIC
CHEMOTROPISM
CHEMURGIC
CHEMURGICAL
CHEMURGY
CHENA
CHENDE
CHENEAU
CHENET
CHENEVIXITE
CHENFISH
CHENG
CHENGAL
CHENICA
CHENIER
CHENILLE
CHENOPOD
CHEOPLASTIC
CHEPSTER
CHEQUE
CHEQUEEN
CHEQUER
CHEQUERBOARD
CHEQUERED
CHEQUERING
CHEQUERS
CHEQUERWISE
CHEQUERWORK
CHEQUIN
CHERCOCK
CHERE
CHERELY
CHERI
CHERIE
CHERIMOYA
CHERIMOYER
CHERISH
CHERISHED
CHERISHER
CHERISHING
CHERISHINGLY
CHERISHMENT
CHERMES
CHERNA
CHERNOZEM
CHEROGRIL
CHEROOT
CHERRIED
CHERRIES
CHERRY
CHERRYING
CHERRYSTONE
CHERSONESE
CHERT
CHERTE
CHERTY
CHERUB
CHERUBIC
CHERUBICAL
CHERUBICALLY
CHERUBIM
CHERUBIMIC
CHERUBIN
CHERUBS
CHERVIL
CHERVONETS

CHERVONETZ	CHEWBARK	CHICKSTONE	CHILDISHNESS	CHIMERA
CHERVONTSI	CHEWED	CHICKWEED	CHILDKIND	CHIMERAL
CHESBOLL	CHEWELER	CHICKWIT	CHILDLESS	CHIMERAS
CHESIL	CHEWER	CHICKY	CHILDLIER	CHIMERIC
CHESON	CHEWET	CHICLE	CHILDLIEST	CHIMERICAL
CHESOUN	CHEWIER	CHICLERO	CHILDLIKE	CHIMERICALLY
CHESS	CHEWIEST	CHICNESS	CHILDLIKENESS	CHIMES
CHESSART	CHEWING	CHICO	CHILDLY	CHIMINAGE
CHESSBOARD	CHEWINK	CHICORIES	CHILDNESS	CHIMING
CHESSEL	CHEWSTICK	CHICORY	CHILDREN	CHIMLA
CHESSER	CHEWY	CHICOS	CHILDRENITE	CHIMLEY
CHESSET	CHEYNEY	CHICOT	CHILDRIDDEN	CHIMNEY
CHESSMAN	CHEYNEYS	CHICOTE	CHILDSHIP	CHIMNEYLESS
CHESSMEN	CHEZ	CHICQUED	CHILDWIFE	CHIMO
CHESSNER	CHHATRI	CHICQUER	CHILE	CHIMOPELAGIC
CHESSOM	CHI	CHICQUING	CHILENITE	CHIMP
CHESSTREE	CHIA	CHID	CHILI	CHIMPANZEE
CHESSYLITE	CHIACK	CHIDDEN	CHILIAD	CHIN
CHEST	CHIAROSCURIST	CHIDE	CHILIADAL	CHINA
CHESTER	CHIAROSCURO	CHIDED	CHILIADIC	CHINABERRIES
CHESTERBED	CHIAROSCUROS	CHIDER	CHILIAEDRON	CHINABERRY
CHESTERFIELD	CHIASM	CHIDING	CHILIAGON	CHINAFISH
CHESTERLITE	CHIASMA	CHIDINGLY	CHILIAHEDRON	CHINAFY
CHESTIER	CHIASMAL	CHIDINGNESS	CHILIARCH	CHINAMANIA
CHESTIEST	CHIASMATA	CHIDRA	CHILIARCHIA	CHINAMANIAC
CHESTILY	CHIASMATYPE	CHIEF	CHILIARCHY	CHINAMPA
CHESTINESS	CHIASMATYPY	CHIEFDOM	CHILIASM	CHINANTA
CHESTNUT	CHIASMIC	CHIEFERY	CHILIAST	CHINAPHTHOL
CHESTS	CHIASMUS	CHIEFLY	CHILIASTIC	CHINAR
CHESTY	CHIASTIC	CHIEFRY	CHILICOTE	CHINAROOT
CHETAH	CHIASTOLITE	CHIEFTAIN	CHILICOTHE	CHINAWARE
CHETH	CHIASTONEURY	CHIEFTAINCY	CHILIES	CHINCAPIN
CHETIF	CHIAUS	CHIEFTAINESS	CHILIOMB	CHINCH
CHETIVE	CHIAVE	CHIEFTAINRIES	CHILITIS	CHINCHA
CHETOPOD	CHIAVETTA	CHIEFTAINRY	CHILL	CHINCHAYOTE
CHETTIK	CHIB	CHIEFTAINSHIP	CHILLA	CHINCHE
CHETTY	CHIBINITE	CHIEFTESS	CHILLAGITE	CHINCHER
CHETVERT	CHIBOUK	CHIEFTY	CHILLED	CHINCHILLA
CHEUNG	CHIBOUQUE	CHIEL	CHILLER	CHINCHY
CHEVACHIE	CHIBRIT	CHIELD	CHILLI	CHINCOF
CHEVAGE	CHIC	CHIEN	CHILLIER	CHINCONA
CHEVAL	CHICA	CHIEVANCE	CHILLIEST	CHINCOUGH
CHEVALET	CHICADEE	CHIEVE	CHILLILY	CHINDEE
CHEVALINE	CHICALOTE	CHIFFCHAFF	CHILLINESS	CHINDI
CHEVANCE	CHICANE	CHIFFER	CHILLING	CHINE
CHEVE	CHICANED	CHIFFON	CHILLINGLY	CHINED
CHEVEE	CHICANER	CHIFFONADE	CHILLNESS	CHINELA
CHEVELURE	CHICANERIES	CHIFFONIER	CHILLO	CHINFEST
CHEVENER	CHICANERY	CHIFFONNIER	CHILLOES	CHING
CHEVEREL	CHICANING	CHIFFOROBE	CHILLROOM	CHINGMA
CHEVERIL	CHICARIC	CHIFFRE	CHILLSOME	CHINIK
CHEVESAILE	CHICAYOTE	CHIGETAI	CHILLUM	CHINIKS
CHEVESNE	CHICH	CHIGGA	CHILLUMCHEE	CHININ
CHEVET	CHICHA	CHIGGER	CHILLY	CHINING
CHEVEYS	CHICHARRA	CHIGNON	CHILODON	CHINIOFON
CHEVIED	CHICHICASTE	CHIGOE	CHILOGNATH	CHINK
CHEVIES	CHICHIMECAN	CHIH	CHILOGNATHAN	CHINKARA
CHEVILLE	CHICHIPATE	CHIKARA	CHILOMA	CHINKED
CHEVIN	CHICHIPE	CHIKEE	CHILOMATA	CHINKER
CHEVIOT	CHICHITUNA	CHIL	CHILONCUS	CHINKERS
CHEVISANCE	CHICK	CHILACAYOTE	CHILOPLASTY	CHINKING
CHEVISE	CHICKABIDDY	CHILALGIA	CHILOPOD	CHINKLE
CHEVON	CHICKADEE	CHILARIA	CHILOPODAN	CHINKS
CHEVRET	CHICKAREE	CHILARIUM	CHILOPODOUS	CHINKY
CHEVRETTE	CHICKASAW	CHILBLAIN	CHILOTOMY	CHINNED
CHEVREUIL	CHICKEE	CHILD	CHILTE	CHINNIER
CHEVRON	CHICKELL	CHILDAGE	CHILVER	CHINNIEST
CHEVRONE	CHICKEN	CHILDBEARING	CHIMACHIMA	CHINNING
CHEVRONEL	CHICKENBERRY	CHILDBED	CHIMAERA	CHINNY
CHEVRONELLY	CHICKENBILL	CHILDBIRTH	CHIMAERID	CHINOA
CHEVRONWISE	CHICKENS	CHILDCROWING	CHIMAEROID	CHINOISERIE
CHEVRONY	CHICKENWEED	CHILDE	CHIMANGO	CHINOL
CHEVROTAIN	CHICKENWORT	CHILDED	CHIMB	CHINOOK
CHEVVY	CHICKER	CHILDHOOD	CHIMBLE	CHINOS
CHEVY	CHICKERY	CHILDING	CHIME	CHINOTTI
CHEVYING	CHICKIES	CHILDISH	CHIMED	CHINOTTO
CHEW	CHICKPEA	CHILDISHLY	CHIMER	CHINOVNIK

CHINPIECE	CHIRONOMIC	CHITLIN	CHLORED	CHOBDAR
CHINQUAPIN	CHIRONOMID	CHITLING	CHLORELLA	CHOBIE
CHINSE	CHIRONOMY	CHITLINS	CHLOREMIA	CHOCA
CHINTS	CHIRONYM	CHITON	CHLORENCHYMA	CHOCALHO
CHINTZ	CHIROPLASTY	CHITOSAMINE	CHLORIC	CHOCARD
CHINTZE	CHIROPOD	CHITOSAN	CHLORIDATE	CHOCHO
CHINTZES	CHIROPODIAL	CHITOSE	CHLORIDATED	CHOCHOS
CHINTZIER	CHIROPODIC	CHITRA	CHLORIDE	CHOCK
CHINTZIEST	CHIROPODICAL	CHITS	CHLORIDIC	CHOCKABLOCK
CHINTZY	CHIROPODIST	CHITTACK	CHLORIDIZE	CHOCKER
CHINWOOD	CHIROPODISTRY	CHITTAK	CHLORIDIZED	CHOCKFUL
CHIOCOCCINE	CHIROPODOUS	CHITTAMWOOD	CHLORIDIZING	CHOCKS
CHIOLITE	CHIROPODY	CHITTED	CHLORIN	CHOCOLATE
CHIONABLEPSIA	CHIROPRACTIC	CHITTER	CHLORINATE	CHOCOLATIER
CHIP	CHIROPRACTOR	CHITTERLING	CHLORINATED	CHOCOLATIERE
CHIPCHOP	CHIROPRAXIS	CHITTING	CHLORINATING	CHOCOLATY
CHIPLET	CHIROPTER	CHITTY	CHLORINATION	CHOEL
CHIPLING	CHIROPTERAN	CHIURM	CHLORINATOR	CHOENIX
CHIPMUNK	CHIROPTERITE	CHIV	CHLORINE	CHOFFER
CHIPOLATA	CHIROS	CHIVAGE	CHLORINITY	CHOGA
CHIPPABLE	CHIROSOPHIST	CHIVALRESQUÉ	CHLORINOUS	CHOGAK
CHIPPAGE	CHIROTHERIAN	CHIVALRIC	CHLORIODIDE	CHOGSET
CHIPPED	CHIROTHESIA	CHIVALROUS	CHLORITE	CHOICE
CHIPPER	CHIROTONSOR	CHIVALROUSLY	CHLORITIC	CHOICEFUL
CHIPPERED	CHIROTONSORY	CHIVALRY	CHLORITIZE	CHOICELY
CHIPPERING	CHIROTONY	CHIVARI	CHLORITOID	CHOICENESS
CHIPPIER	CHIROTYPE	CHIVARRA	CHLOROACETIC	CHOICIER
CHIPPIES	CHIRP	CHIVARRO	CHLOROAMIDE	CHOICIEST
CHIPPIEST	CHIRPED	CHIVE	CHLOROAMINE	CHOICY
CHIPPING	CHIRPER	CHIVER	CHLOROAURATE	CHOIL
CHIPPINGS	CHIRPIER	CHIVERET	CHLOROAURIC	CHOILE
CHIPPY	CHIRPIEST	CHIVEY	CHLOROAURITE	CHOILER
CHIPS	CHIRPILY	CHIVIATITE	CHLOROCHROUS	CHOIR
CHIPWOOD	CHIRPING	CHIVIED	CHLOROCRESOL	CHOIRBOY
CHIPYARD	CHIRPINGLY	CHIVVY	CHLORODIZE	CHOIRMAN
CHIQUERO	CHIRPLING	CHIVY	CHLORODIZED	CHOIRMASTER
CHIQUEST	CHIRPY	CHIVYING	CHLORODIZING	CHOIRWISE
CHIR	CHIRR	CHIZZ	CHLOROFORM	CHOKAGE
CHIRAGRA	CHIRRE	CHIZZEL	CHLOROFORMED	CHOKE
CHIRAL	CHIRRED	CHKALIK	CHLOROFORMIC	CHOKEBERRIES
CHIRALGIA	CHIRRING	CHLADNITE	CHLOROGENIC	CHOKEBERRY
CHIRALITY	CHIRRUP	CHLAMYDATE	CHLOROGENINE	CHOKEBORE
CHIRAPSIA	CHIRRUPED	CHLAMYDEOUS	CHLOROHYDRIN	CHOKECHERRIES
CHIRATA	CHIRRUPER	CHLAMYDOZOAN	CHLOROIODIDE	CHOKECHERRY
CHIRIMEN	CHIRRUPING	CHLAMYPHORE	CHLOROMA	CHOKED
CHIRIMIA	CHIRRUPY	CHLAMYS	CHLOROMATA	CHOKEDAMP
CHIRIMOYA	CHIRT	CHLAMYSES	CHLOROMETER	CHOKER
CHIRIMOYER	CHIRU	CHLOANTHITE	CHLOROMETRIC	CHOKERED
CHIRIPA	CHIRURGEON	CHLOASMA	CHLOROMETRY	CHOKERMAN
CHIRIVITA	CHIRURGEONLY	CHLORAEMIA	CHLOROPAL	CHOKES
CHIRK	CHIRURGERY	CHLORAGEN	CHLOROPHANE	CHOKEWEED
CHIRKED	CHIRURGIC	CHLORAGOGEN	CHLOROPHENOL	CHOKEY
CHIRKING	CHIRURGICAL	CHLORAGOGUE	CHLOROPHYL	CHOKIDAR
CHIRL	CHISEL	CHLORAL	CHLOROPHYLL	CHOKIER
CHIRM	CHISELED	CHLORALIDE	CHLOROPICRIN	CHOKIEST
CHIRO	CHISELER	CHLORALISM	CHLOROPLAST	CHOKING
CHIROGALE	CHISELING	CHLORALIZATION	CHLOROPRENE	CHOKINGLY
CHIROGNOMIC	CHISELLED	CHLORALIZE	CHLOROPSIA	CHOKRA
CHIROGNOMY	CHISELLER	CHLORALIZED	CHLOROSIS	CHOKY
CHIROGNOSTIC	CHISELLING	CHLORALIZING	CHLOROSPINEL	CHOL
CHIROGRAPH	CHISELLY	CHLORALOSE	CHLOROTIC	CHOLAEMIA
CHIROGRAPHER	CHISELMOUTH	CHLORALUM	CHLOROUS	CHOLAGOGIC
CHIROGRAPHIC	CHISTERA	CHLORAMIDE	CHLORPIKRIN	CHOLAGOGUE
CHIROGRAPHICAL	CHISTKA	CHLORAMIN	CHLORSALOL	CHOLAM
CHIROGRAPHY	CHIT	CHLORAMINE	CHLORYL	CHOLANE
CHIROGYMNAST	CHITAL	CHLORANAEMIA	CHO	CHOLANGITIS
CHIROLOGICAL	CHITARRA	CHLORANEMIA	CHOACHYTE	CHOLATE
CHIROLOGIST	CHITARRINO	CHLORANEMIC	CHOANA	CHOLD
CHIROLOGY	CHITARRONE	CHLORANIL	CHOANATE	CHOLEATE
CHIROMANCE	CHITCHAT	CHLORANTHY	CHOANOCYTAL	CHOLECYANIN
CHIROMANCER	CHITCHATTY	CHLORAPATITE	CHOANOCYTE	CHOLECYANINE
CHIROMANCIST	CHITI	CHLORASTROLITE	CHOANOID	CHOLECYST
CHIROMANCY	CHITIN	CHLORATE	CHOANOSOME	CHOLECYSTIC
CHIROMANT	CHITINIZATION	CHLORAZIDE	CHOAR	CHOLECYSTIS
CHIROMANTIC	CHITINIZED	CHLORCOSANE	CHOATE	CHOLEDOCH
CHIROMEGALY	CHITINOID	CHLORDANE	CHOATY	CHOLEINE
CHIROMETER	CHITINOUS	CHLORE	CHOB	CHOLELITH

CHOLELITHIC	CHONDROID	CHORDS	CHOUCROUTE	CHROMATYPE
CHOLEMIA	CHONDROITIN	CHORE	CHOUETTE	CHROME
CHOLENT	CHONDROLOGY	CHOREA	CHOUFLEUR	CHROMED
CHOLEOKINASE	CHONDROMA	CHOREAL	CHOUGH	CHROMIC
CHOLEPOIETIC	CHONDROMAS	CHORED	CHOUKA	CHROMICIZE
CHOLER	CHONDROMATA	CHOREE	CHOULTRY	CHROMICIZING
CHOLERA	CHONDROMYOMA	CHOREGRAPHY	CHOUNCE	CHROMID
CHOLERAIC	CHONDROPHORE	CHOREI	CHOUP	CHROMIDE
CHOLERIC	CHONDROPHYTE	CHOREIC	CHOUPIC	CHROMIDIAL
CHOLERICLY	CHONDROSIN	CHOREIFORM	CHOUQUETTE	CHROMIDIUM
CHOLERICNESS	CHONDROSIS	CHOREOGRAPHY	CHOUS	CHROMIDROSIS
CHOLERINE	CHONDROSTEAN	CHOREOID	CHOUSE	CHROMIFEROUS
CHOLEROID	CHONDROTOME	CHOREOMANIA	CHOUSED	CHROMING
CHOLERRHAGIA	CHONDROTOMY	CHOREUS	CHOUSH	CHROMIOLE
CHOLESTANE	CHONDRULE	CHOREUTIC	CHOUSING	CHROMITE
CHOLESTANOL	CHONDRUS	CHORIAL	CHOUT	CHROMITITE
CHOLESTENE	CHONK	CHORIAMB	CHOUX	CHROMIUM
CHOLESTERATE	CHONOLITH	CHORIAMBI	CHOW	CHROMO
CHOLESTERIC	CHONTA	CHORIAMBIC	CHOWCHOW	CHROMOBLAST
CHOLESTERIN	CHOOCHOO	CHORIAMBIZE	CHOWDER	CHROMOCTYE
CHOLESTEROL	CHOOK	CHORIAMBUS	CHOWK	CHROMOGEN
CHOLESTERYL	CHOOKIE	CHORIAMBUSES	CHOWRIES	CHROMOGENIC
CHOLETELIN	CHOOP	CHORIC	CHOWRY	CHROMOGENOUS
CHOLETHERAPY	CHOOSABLE	CHORINE	CHOY	CHROMOGRAM
CHOLI	CHOOSE	CHORING	CHOZA	CHROMOGRAPH
CHOLIAMB	CHOOSEABLE	CHORIOCELE	CHREMATIST	CHROMOISOMER
CHOLIAMBIC	CHOOSER	CHORIOID	CHREMATISTIC	CHROMOLIPOID
CHOLIAMBIST	CHOOSEY	CHORIOMA	CHREOTECHNICS	CHROMOLITH
CHOLIC	CHOOSIER	CHORION	CHRESARD	CHROMOLITHIC
CHOLICK	CHOOSIEST	CHORIONIC	CHRESMOLOGY	CHROMOMERE
CHOLINE	CHOOSING	CHORIOPTIC	CHRESTOMATHY	CHROMOMETER
CHOLINIC	CHOOSINGLY	CHORISIS	CHRIA	CHROMONE
CHOLLA	CHOOSY	CHORISM	CHRIMSEL	CHROMOPAROUS
CHOLLER	CHOP	CHORIST	CHRISM	CHROMOPHANE
CHOLLERS	CHOPA	CHORISTATE	CHRISMA	CHROMOPHIL
CHOLO	CHOPBOAT	CHORISTER	CHRISMAL	CHROMOPHILE
CHOLOCHROME	CHOPDAR	CHORISTIC	CHRISMALE	CHROMOPHILIC
CHOLOGENETIC	CHOPFALLEN	CHORISTOMA	CHRISMARY	CHROMOPHOBE
CHOLOLITH	CHOPHOUSE	CHORISTRY	CHRISMATINE	CHROMOPHOBIC
CHOLOLITHIC	CHOPIN	CHORIZATION	CHRISMATION	CHROMOPHOR
CHOLOPHAEIN	CHOPINE	CHORIZONT	CHRISMATITE	CHROMOPHORE
CHOLOPHEIN	CHOPLOGIC	CHORIZONTES	CHRISMATORY	CHROMOPHORIC
CHOLORRHEA	CHOPPED	CHORIZONTIC	CHRISMON	CHROMOPHYL
CHOLOSCOPY	CHOPPER	CHORIZONTIST	CHRISOM	CHROMOPHYLL
CHOLUM	CHOPPERS	CHOROGI	CHRISROOT	CHROMOPLASM
CHOLURIA	CHOPPIER	CHOROGRAPH	CHRISTCROSS	CHROMOPLAST
CHOMAGE	CHOPPIEST	CHOROGRAPHER	CHRISTEN	CHROMOPSIA
CHOMER	CHOPPIN	CHOROGRAPHIC	CHRISTENER	CHROMOS
CHOMP	CHOPPINESS	CHOROGRAPHIES	CHRISTENING	CHROMOSCOPE
CHON	CHOPPING	CHOROGRAPHY	CHRISTIANITE	CHROMOSCOPIC
CHONDRAL	CHOPPY	CHOROID	CHROATOL	CHROMOSCOPY
CHONDRALGIA	CHOPS	CHOROIDITIS	CHROMA	CHROMOSOME
CHONDRECTOMY	CHOPSTICK	CHOROLOGICAL	CHROMAFFIN	CHROMOSPHERE
CHONDRIC	CHOPSTICKS	CHOROLOGIST	CHROMAFFINIC	CHROMOSPHERIC
CHONDRIFIED	CHOR	CHOROLOGY	CHROMAMAMIN	CHROMOTROPE
CHONDRIFY	CHORAGI	CHOROMANIA	CHROMAMMINE	CHROMOTROPIC
CHONDRIGEN	CHORAGIC	CHOROMANIC	CHROMATE	CHROMOTROPY
CHONDRIN	CHORAGION	CHOROMETRY	CHROMATIC	CHROMOTYPE
CHONDRINOUS	CHORAGIUM	CHOROOK	CHROMATICALLY	CHROMOTYPIC
CHONDRIOCONT	CHORAGUS	CHOROUS	CHROMATICISM	CHROMOTYPY
CHONDRIOMA	CHORAGY	CHORT	CHROMATICISM	CHROMOUS
CHONDRIOME	CHORAL	CHORTEN	CHROMATICITY	CHROMY
CHONDRIOMITE	CHORALCELO	CHORTLE	CHROMATICS	CHROMYL
CHONDRIOSOME	CHORALE	CHORTLED	CHROMATID	CHRONAL
CHONDRIOSOMES	CHORALIST	CHORTLER	CHROMATIN	CHRONANAGRAM
CHONDRITE	CHORALLY	CHORTLING	CHROMATINIC	CHRONAXIA
CHONDRITIC	CHORD	CHORTOSTEROL	CHROMATISM	CHRONAXIE
CHONDRITIS	CHORDA	CHORUS	CHROMATIST	CHRONAXIES
CHONDROBLAST	CHORDACEOUS	CHORUSED	CHROMATIZE	CHRONAXY
CHONDROCELE	CHORDAL	CHORUSING	CHROMATOCYTE	CHRONIC
CHONDROCLAST	CHORDATE	CHORUSSED	CHROMATOID	CHRONICA
CHONDROCYTE	CHORDED	CHORUSSING	CHROMATOLOGIES	CHRONICAL
CHONDRODITE	CHORDEE	CHORYOS	CHROMATOLOGY	CHRONICALLY
CHONDRODITIC	CHORDITIS	CHOSE	CHROMATOPHORE	CHRONICITY
CHONDRODYNIA	CHORDOID	CHOSEN	CHROMATOPSIA	CHRONICLE
CHONDROFETAL	CHORDOTOMY	CHOTT	CHROMATOSIS	CHRONICLED
CHONDROGENY	CHORDOTONAL	CHOU	CHROMATROPE	CHRONICLER

CHRONICLING
CHRONICON
CHRONIST
CHRONOCRATOR
CHRONODEIK
CHRONOGRAM
CHRONOGRAPH
CHRONOGRAPHIC
CHRONOGRAPHY
CHRONOLOGER
CHRONOLOGIC
CHRONOLOGICAL
CHRONOLOGIES
CHRONOLOGIST
CHRONOLOGIZE
CHRONOLOGIZED
CHRONOLOGIZING
CHRONOLOGY
CHRONOMANCY
CHRONOMANTIC
CHRONOMETER
CHRONOMETRIC
CHRONOMETRY
CHRONONOMY
CHRONOPHER
CHRONOSCOPIC
CHRONOSCOPY
CHRONOSEMIC
CHRONOTROPIC
CHROOCOCCOID
CHROTTA
CHRYSALID
CHRYSALIDA
CHRYSALIDES
CHRYSALIDIAN
CHRYSALINE
CHRYSALIS
CHRYSALISES
CHRYSALOID
CHRYSAMMIC
CHRYSANILIN
CHRYSANILINE
CHRYSANISIC
CHRYSANTHEMUM
CHRYSANTHOUS
CHRYSAROBIN
CHRYSAZIN
CHRYSAZOL
CHRYSENE
CHRYSIN
CHRYSOBERYL
CHRYSOBULL
CHRYSOCHLORE
CHRYSOCHROUS
CHRYSOCOLLA
CHRYSOCRACY
CHRYSOERIOL
CHRYSOGEN
CHRYSOGRAPH
CHRYSOGRAPHY
CHRYSOIDINE
CHRYSOLITE
CHRYSOLITIC
CHRYSOLOGY
CHRYSOME
CHRYSOMELID
CHRYSOMONAD
CHRYSOPAL
CHRYSOPEE
CHRYSOPHAN
CHRYSOPHANE
CHRYSOPHANIC
CHRYSOPOEIA
CHRYSOPOETIC
CHRYSOPRASE
CHRYSOPRASUS
CHRYSORIN

CHRYSOSPERM
CHRYSOTILE
CHRYSTOCRENE
CHTHONIAN
CHUANA
CHUB
CHUBA
CHUBBED
CHUBBEDNESS
CHUBBIER
CHUBBIEST
CHUBBILY
CHUBBINESS
CHUBBY
CHUBS
CHUCHO
CHUCK
CHUCKAWALLA
CHUCKED
CHUCKER
CHUCKHOLE
CHUCKIE
CHUCKIES
CHUCKING
CHUCKINGLY
CHUCKLE
CHUCKLED
CHUCKLEHEAD
CHUCKLEHEADED
CHUCKLER
CHUCKLING
CHUCKLINGLY
CHUCKRAM
CHUCKSTONE
CHUCKWALLA
CHUCKY
CHUD
CHUDDAH
CHUDDAR
CHUDDER
CHUET
CHUFA
CHUFF
CHUFFIER
CHUFFIEST
CHUG
CHUGGED
CHUGGER
CHUGGING
CHUGHOLE
CHUHRA
CHUKAR
CHUKKA
CHUKKAR
CHUKKER
CHUKOR
CHULAN
CHULHA
CHULLO
CHULLPA
CHULO
CHULPA
CHULTUN
CHUM
CHUMAR
CHUMBLE
CHUMMAGE
CHUMMER
CHUMMERY
CHUMMIER
CHUMMIES
CHUMMIEST
CHUMMILY
CHUMMY
CHUMP
CHUMPA
CHUMPISH

CHUMPY
CHUNAM
CHUNARI
CHUNDARI
CHUNGA
CHUNK
CHUNKED
CHUNKHEAD
CHUNKIER
CHUNKIEST
CHUNKINESS
CHUNKING
CHUNKY
CHUNNER
CHUNO
CHUNTER
CHUPA
CHUPAK
CHUPON
CHUPRASSIE
CHUPRASSY
CHURCH
CHURCHANITY
CHURCHCRAFT
CHURCHGOER
CHURCHGOING
CHURCHIANITY
CHURCHIER
CHURCHIEST
CHURCHIFIED
CHURCHING
CHURCHITE
CHURCHLESS
CHURCHLIKE
CHURCHLINESS
CHURCHLY
CHURCHMAN
CHURCHMANLY
CHURCHMANSHIP
CHURCHMASTER
CHURCHMEN
CHURCHREEVE
CHURCHSCOT
CHURCHSHOT
CHURCHWARD
CHURCHWARDEN
CHURCHWARDS
CHURCHWAY
CHURCHWOMAN
CHURCHWOMEN
CHURCHY
CHURCHYARD
CHUREL
CHURINGA
CHURL
CHURLED
CHURLIER
CHURLIEST
CHURLISH
CHURLISHLY
CHURLISHNESS
CHURLY
CHURN
CHURNABILITY
CHURNED
CHURNING
CHURNMILK
CHURNSTAFF
CHURR
CHURRASCO
CHURRED
CHURRING
CHURRO
CHURRUCK
CHURRUS
CHURRWORM
CHUSE

CHUSER
CHUT
CHUTE
CHUTER
CHUTNEE
CHUTNEY
CHUTNEYS
CHUTZPAH
CHUZWI
CHWAS
CHYACK
CHYAK
CHYLACEOUS
CHYLE
CHYLIFACTION
CHYLIFACTIVE
CHYLIFACTORY
CHYLIFEROUS
CHYLIFIC
CHYLIFIED
CHYLIFORM
CHYLIFY
CHYLIFYING
CHYLOCAULOUS
CHYLOCAULY
CHYLOCELE
CHYLOMICRON
CHYLOPHYLLY
CHYLOPOETIC
CHYLOPOIESIS
CHYLOPOIETIC
CHYLOTHORAX
CHYLOUS
CHYLURIA
CHYMAQUEOUS
CHYME
CHYMIA
CHYMIC
CHYMIFEROUS
CHYMIFIED
CHYMIFY
CHYMIFYING
CHYMIST
CHYMOSIN
CHYMOUS
CHYPRE
CHYTRA
CHYTRID
CHYTRIDIAL
CHYTRIDIOSE
CHYTRIDIOSIS
CIBARIAL
CIBARIAN
CIBARIOUS
CIBATION
CIBOL
CIBOLERO
CIBOPHOBIA
CIBORIA
CIBORIUM
CIBOULE
CICAD
CICADA
CICADAE
CICADAS
CICADID
CICALA
CICATRICE
CICATRICES
CICATRICIAL
CICATRICLE
CICATRICOSE
CICATRICULA
CICATRICULAE
CICATRISATE
CICATRISIVE
CICATRIX

CICATRIXES
CICATRIZANT
CICATRIZATE
CICATRIZE
CICATRIZED
CICATRIZER
CICATRIZING
CICATROSE
CICELIES
CICELY
CICER
CICERO
CICERONAGE
CICERONE
CICERONES
CICERONI
CICERONING
CICERONISM
CICERONIZE
CICHAR
CICHLID
CICHLIDAE
CICHLIDS
CICHLOID
CICINDELID
CICISBEISM
CICISBEO
CICLATOUN
CICONIFORM
CICONIID
CICONINE
CICOREE
CICURATE
CICUTOXIN
CIDARID
CIDARIS
CIDER
CIDERIST
CIEL
CIENAGA
CIERGE
CIG
CIGALA
CIGALE
CIGAR
CIGARESQUE
CIGARET
CIGARETTE
CIGARETTES
CIGARFISH
CIGARILLO
CIGARILLOS
CIGARITO
CIGARITOS
CIGUA
CIGUATERA
CILERY
CILIA
CILIARY
CILIATE
CILIATED
CILIATELY
CILIATION
CILICE
CILICIOUS
CILIECTOMY
CILIELLA
CILIFEROUS
CILIFORM
CILIIFORM
CILIOGRADE
CILIOLA
CILIOLATE
CILIOLUM
CILIORETINAL
CILIOSCLERAL
CILIOSPINAL

CILIUM	CINERATOR	CIRCS	CIRCUMLITIO	CISANDINE
CILLOSIS	CINEREA	CIRCUE	CIRCUMLOCUTE	CISATLANTIC
CIMA	CINEREAL	CIRCUIT	CIRCUMLOCUTION	CISCO
CIMAROON	CINEREOUS	CIRCUITAL	CIRCUMMURE	CISCOES
CIMBAL	CINERIN	CIRCUITEER	CIRCUMMURED	CISCOS
CIMBALOM	CINERITIOUS	CIRCUITER	CIRCUMMURING	CISE
CIMBIA	CINEROUS	CIRCUITIES	CIRCUMNATANT	CISEAUX
CIMBORIO	CINEVARIETY	CIRCUITION	CIRCUMNUTATE	CISELE
CIMELIA	CINGLE	CIRCUITMAN	CIRCUMOCULAR	CISELEUR
CIMETER	CINGULA	CIRCUITMEN	CIRCUMORAL	CISELURE
CIMEX	CINGULAR	CIRCUITOR	CIRCUMORBITAL	CISGANGETIC
CIMICID	CINGULATE	CIRCUITOUS	CIRCUMPOLAR	CISIUM
CIMICIDE	CINGULATED	CIRCUITOUSLY	CIRCUMPOSE	CISJURANE
CIMICIFORM	CINGULUM	CIRCUITRY	CIRCUMRENAL	CISLEITHAN
CIMICIFUGIN	CINNABAR	CIRCUITY	CIRCUMROTATE	CISLUNAR
CIMICOID	CINNABARIC	CIRCULABLE	CIRCUMSAIL	CISMARINE
CIMIER	CINNABARINE	CIRCULANT	CIRCUMSCRIBE	CISMONTANE
CIMINITE	CINNAMAL	CIRCULAR	CIRCUMSCRIBED	CISOCEANIC
CIMLINE	CINNAMATE	CIRCULARITIES	CIRCUMSCRIBER	CISPADANE
CIMMARON	CINNAMEIN	CIRCULARITY	CIRCUMSCRIPT	CISPLATINE
CIMOLITE	CINNAMIC	CIRCULARIZE	CIRCUMSOLAR	CISPONTINE
CINCH	CINNAMOL	CIRCULARIZED	CIRCUMSPECT	CISRHENANE
CINCHA	CINNAMON	CIRCULARIZING	CIRCUMSPECTION	CISSA
CINCHER	CINNAMONED	CIRCULARLY	CIRCUMSPECTLY	CISSING
CINCHOLOIPON	CINNAMONIC	CIRCULARNESS	CIRCUMSTANCE	CISSOID
CINCHONA	CINNAMONROOT	CIRCULATE	CIRCUMSTANCED	CISSOIDAL
CINCHONAMIN	CINNAMONWOOD	CIRCULATED	CIRCUMSTANCES	CIST
CINCHONAMINE	CINNAMYL	CIRCULATING	CIRCUMSTANTIAL	CISTACEOUS
CINCHONATE	CINNOLIN	CIRCULATION	CIRCUMSTANTIALLY	CISTED
CINCHONIA	CINNOLINE	CIRCULATIVE	CIRCUMSTANTIATE	CISTERN
CINCHONIC	CINQ	CIRCULATOR	CIRCUMSTANTIATED	CISTERNA
CINCHONICIN	CINQFOIL	CIRCULATORIES	CIRCUMSTANTIATING	CISTERNAL
CINCHONICINE	CINQUAIN	CIRCULATORY	CIRCUMVENT	CISTIC
CINCHONIDIA	CINQUE	CIRCULIN	CIRCUMVENTED	CISTOPHORIC
CINCHONIN	CINQUECENTO	CIRCULUS	CIRCUMVENTER	CISTOPHORUS
CINCHONINE	CINQUEFOIL	CIRCUMANAL	CIRCUMVENTING	CISTUS
CINCHONISM	CINQUEPACE	CIRCUMARCTIC	CIRCUMVENTION	CISTVAEN
CINCHONIZE	CINQUES	CIRCUMAVIATE	CIRCUMVIATE	CIT
CINCHONIZED	CINTER	CIRCUMAXIAL	CIRCUMVOLANT	CITABLE
CINCHONIZING	CINTRE	CIRCUMAXILE	CIRCUMVOLUTE	CITADEL
CINCHONOLOGY	CINURAN	CIRCUMAXILLARY	CIRCUMVOLVE	CITAL
CINCHOTINE	CINUROUS	CIRCUMBASAL	CIRCUMVOLVED	CITATION
CINCINNAL	CION	CIRCUMBOREAL	CIRCUMVOLVING	CITATOR
CINCINNI	CIONECTOMY	CIRCUMBUCCAL	CIRCUS	CITATORY
CINCINNUS	CIONITIS	CIRCUMBULBAR	CIRE	CITE
CINCLIDES	CIONOCRANIAL	CIRCUMCENTER	CIRL	CITEABLE
CINCLIS	CIONOCRANIAN	CIRCUMCINCT	CIRQUE	CITED
CINCT	CIONOPTOSIS	CIRCUMCIRCLE	CIRRATE	CITEE
CINCTURE	CIONOTOME	CIRCUMCISE	CIRRATED	CITER
CINCTURED	CIONOTOMY	CIRCUMCISED	CIRRHOSED	CITHARA
CINCTURING	CIOPPINO	CIRCUMCISER	CIRRHOSIS	CITHARIST
CINDER	CIPAYE	CIRCUMCISING	CIRRHOTIC	CITHAROEDIC
CINDERED	CIPHER	CIRCUMCISION	CIRRHOUS	CITHAROEDUS
CINDERING	CIPHERED	CIRCUMCLUDE	CIRRHUS	CITHER
CINDERMAN	CIPHERING	CIRCUMCLUSION	CIRRI	CITHERN
CINDERS	CIPO	CIRCUMCONE	CIRRIBRANCH	CITIED
CINDERY	CIPOLIN	CIRCUMCONIC	CIRRIFEROUS	CITIES
CINEAST	CIPPI	CIRCUMCORNEAL	CIRRIFORM	CITIFICATION
CINEFACTION	CIPPUS	CIRCUMDUCE	CIRRIGEROUS	CITIFIED
CINEL	CIRC	CIRCUMDUCING	CIRRIPED	CITIFY
CINEMA	CIRCA	CIRCUMDUCT	CIRRIPEDIAL	CITIGRADE
CINEMATIC	CIRCADIAN	CIRCUMDUCTED	CIRROCUMULUS	CITIZEN
CINEMATICAL	CIRCAR	CIRCUMFER	CIRROLITE	CITIZENESS
CINEMATOGRAPH	CIRCINAL	CIRCUMFERENCE	CIRROPODOUS	CITIZENISM
CINEMIZE	CIRCINATE	CIRCUMFERENT	CIRROSE	CITIZENIZE
CINEMOGRAPH	CIRCINATELY	CIRCUMFERENTOR	CIRROSTOME	CITIZENIZED
CINENCHYMA	CIRCINATION	CIRCUMFLECT	CIRROSTRATUS	CITIZENIZING
CINENE	CIRCITER	CIRCUMFLEX	CIRROUS	CITIZENLY
CINENEGATIVE	CIRCLE	CIRCUMFLUENT	CIRRUS	CITIZENRIES
CINEOL	CIRCLED	CIRCUMFLUOUS	CIRSECTOMY	CITIZENRY
CINEOLE	CIRCLER	CIRCUMFUSE	CIRSOID	CITIZENSHIP
CINEPHONE	CIRCLES	CIRCUMFUSILE	CIRSOMPHALOS	CITO
CINERACEOUS	CIRCLET	CIRCUMFUSING	CIRSOTOME	CITOLA
CINERARIA	CIRCLETING	CIRCUMFUSION	CIRSOTOMIES	CITOLE
CINERARIUM	CIRCLINE	CIRCUMGYRATE	CIRSOTOMY	CITOLER
CINERARY	CIRCLING	CIRCUMJACENT	CIRUELA	CITOYEN
CINERATION	CIRCOVARIAN	CIRCUMLENTAL	CISALPINE	CITOYENNE

CITRACONATE	CLACK	CLAMOROUSNESS	CLARIGOLD	CLATHRULATE
CITRACONIC	CLACKDISH	CLAMORSOME	CLARIN	CLATTER
CITRAL	CLACKED	CLAMOUR	CLARINA	CLATTERED
CITRAMIDE	CLACKER	CLAMOURED	CLARINET	CLATTERER
CITRANGE	CLACKET	CLAMOURER	CLARINETIST	CLATTERING
CITRANGEADE	CLACKETY	CLAMOURING	CLARINETTIST	CLATTERINGLY
CITRATE	CLACKING	CLAMOURIST	CLARINO	CLATTERTRAPS
CITRATED	CLACO	CLAMOUROUS	CLARION	CLATTERY
CITREAN	CLAD	CLAMOURSOME	CLARIONET	CLATTY
CITRENE	CLADANTHOUS	CLAMP	CLARISSIMO	CLAUBER
CITREOUS	CLADAUTOICOUS	CLAMPED	CLARITY	CLAUCHT
CITRIC	CLADDING	CLAMPER	CLARO	CLAUD
CITRICULTURE	CLADI	CLAMPING	CLAROS	CLAUDENT
CITRIL	CLADINE	CLAMSHELL	CLARSACH	CLAUDETITE
CITRIN	CLADOCARPOUS	CLAMWORM	CLART	CLAUDICANT
CITRINATION	CLADOCERAN	CLAN	CLARTIER	CLAUDICATE
CITRINE	CLADOCEROUS	CLANCULAR	CLARTIEST	CLAUDICATION
CITRININ	CLADODE	CLANCULARLY	CLARTY	CLAUGHT
CITROCOLA	CLADODIAL	CLANDESTINE	CLARY	CLAUSAL
CITROMETER	CLADODONT	CLANDESTINELY	CLASH	CLAUSE
CITRON	CLADODONTID	CLANFELLOW	CLASHED	CLAUSTHALITE
CITRONADE	CLADOGENOUS	CLANG	CLASHEE	CLAUSTRA
CITRONELLA	CLADONIOID	CLANGOR	CLASHER	CLAUSTRAL
CITRONELLAL	CLADOPHYLL	CLANGOROUS	CLASHES	CLAUSTRATION
CITRONELLE	CLADOPHYLLUM	CLANGOROUSLY	CLASHING	CLAUSTRUM
CITRONELLOL	CLADOPTOSIS	CLANGOUR	CLASHY	CLAUSULA
CITRONIN	CLADOSE	CLANK	CLASMATOCYTE	CLAUSULAR
CITRONIZE	CLADUS	CLANKED	CLASMATOSIS	CLAUSULE
CITRONWOOD	CLAG	CLANKETY	CLASP	CLAUSURE
CITROUS	CLAGGUM	CLANKING	CLASPED	CLAUT
CITRUL	CLAGGY	CLANKINGLY	CLASPER	CLAVA
CITRULLIN	CLAIK	CLANKINGNESS	CLASPING	CLAVACIN
CITRUS	CLAIM	CLANKUM	CLASPT	CLAVAE
CITTERN	CLAIMABLE	CLANNISH	CLASS	CLAVAL
CITTERNHEAD	CLAIMANT	CLANNISHLY	CLASSBOOK	CLAVATE
CITUA	CLAIMER	CLANNISHNESS	CLASSER	CLAVATED
CITY	CLAIMS	CLANSHIP	CLASSES	CLAVATELY
CITYCISM	CLAIRAUDIENT	CLANSMAN	CLASSFELLOW	CLAVATIN
CITYFIED	CLAIRCE	CLANSMEN	CLASSIC	CLAVATION
CITYSCAPE	CLAIRE	CLANSWOMAN	CLASSICAL	CLAVE
CITYWARD	CLAIRSCHACH	CLANSWOMEN	CLASSICALISM	CLAVECIN
CIUDAD	CLAIRVOYANCE	CLAP	CLASSICALIST	CLAVECINIST
CIVE	CLAIRVOYANT	CLAPBOARD	CLASSICALITIES	CLAVEL
CIVET	CLAITH	CLAPBOARDING	CLASSICALITY	CLAVELIZE
CIVETONE	CLAIVER	CLAPBREAD	CLASSICALLY	CLAVELLATED
CIVIC	CLAM	CLAPCAKE	CLASSICISM	CLAVER
CIVICAL	CLAMANT	CLAPDISH	CLASSICIST	CLAVES
CIVICALLY	CLAMAROO	CLAPHOLT	CLASSICISTIC	CLAVIAL
CIVICISM	CLAMATORIAL	CLAPMATCH	CLASSICIZE	CLAVIATURE
CIVICS	CLAMATORY	CLAPNEST	CLASSICIZED	CLAVICEMBALO
CIVIES	CLAMBAKE	CLAPNET	CLASSICIZING	CLAVICHORD
CIVIL	CLAMBER	CLAPPE	CLASSICS	CLAVICITHERN
CIVILIAN	CLAMBERER	CLAPPED	CLASSIER	CLAVICLE
CIVILISE	CLAMCRACKER	CLAPPER	CLASSIEST	CLAVICOR
CIVILIST	CLAME	CLAPPERCLAW	CLASSIFIABLE	CLAVICORN
CIVILITE	CLAMEHEWIT	CLAPPERED	CLASSIFIC	CLAVICORNATE
CIVILITIES	CLAMFLAT	CLAPPERING	CLASSIFICATION	CLAVICOTOMY
CIVILITY	CLAMJAMFERY	CLAPPERS	CLASSIFIED	CLAVICULAR
CIVILIZABLE	CLAMJAMFRY	CLAPPING	CLASSIFIER	CLAVICULATE
CIVILIZATION	CLAMJAMPHRIE	CLAPTRAP	CLASSIFY	CLAVICYMBAL
CIVILIZATORY	CLAMMED	CLAPWORT	CLASSIFYING	CLAVIER
CIVILIZE	CLAMMER	CLAQUE	CLASSIS	CLAVIERIST
CIVILIZED	CLAMMERSOME	CLAQUEUR	CLASSMAN	CLAVIFORM
CIVILIZEE	CLAMMIER	CLARABELLA	CLASSMATE	CLAVIGER
CIVILIZER	CLAMMIEST	CLARAIN	CLASSMEN	CLAVIHARP
CIVILIZING	CLAMMILY	CLARENCE	CLASSROOM	CLAVILUX
CIVISM	CLAMMINESS	CLARENDON	CLASSWORK	CLAVIOL
CIVITAS	CLAMMING	CLARET	CLASSY	CLAVIOLE
CIVITE	CLAMMISH	CLARIBELLA	CLASTIC	CLAVIS
CIVORY	CLAMMY	CLARIES	CLAT	CLAVISES
CIVVIES	CLAMOR	CLARIFIANT	CLATCH	CLAVODELTOID
CIVVY	CLAMORED	CLARIFICATION	CLATCHY	CLAVUS
CIXIID	CLAMORER	CLARIFIED	CLATHRACEOUS	CLAVY
CLABBER	CLAMORING	CLARIFIER	CLATHRARIAN	CLAW
CLABBERY	CLAMORIST	CLARIFY	CLATHRATE	CLAWBACK
CLACH	CLAMOROUS	CLARIFYING	CLATHROID	CLAWED
CLACHAN	CLAMOROUSLY	CLARIGATION	CLATHROSE	CLAWER

CLAWK
CLAWKER
CLAWS
CLAWSICK
CLAY
CLAYBANK
CLAYBRAINED
CLAYED
CLAYEN
CLAYER
CLAYEY
CLAYIER
CLAYIEST
CLAYING
CLAYISH
CLAYMAN
CLAYMORE
CLAYPAN
CLAYTONIA
CLAYWARE
CLAYWEED
CLEACH
CLEAD
CLEADED
CLEADING
CLEAM
CLEAMER
CLEAN
CLEANABLE
CLEANED
CLEANER
CLEANEST
CLEANHANDED
CLEANING
CLEANLIER
CLEANLIEST
CLEANLILY
CLEANLINESS
CLEANLY
CLEANNESS
CLEANOUT
CLEANSE
CLEANSED
CLEANSER
CLEANSING
CLEANUP
CLEAR
CLEARABLE
CLEARAGE
CLEARANCE
CLEARCOLE
CLEARCOLED
CLEARCOLING
CLEARED
CLEAREDNESS
CLEARER
CLEAREST
CLEARHEADED
CLEARING
CLEARINGHOUSE
CLEARLY
CLEARNESS
CLEARS
CLEARSKINS
CLEARSTARCH
CLEARSTORIED
CLEARSTORY
CLEARWEED
CLEARWING
CLEAT
CLEATED
CLEATING
CLEATS
CLEAVABILITY
CLEAVABLE
CLEAVAGE
CLEAVE

CLEAVED
CLEAVER
CLEAVERS
CLEAVERWORT
CLEAVING
CLEAVINGLY
CLECHE
CLECHEE
CLECHY
CLECK
CLEDDE
CLEDGE
CLEDGY
CLEDONISM
CLEE
CLEECH
CLEED
CLEEK
CLEEKED
CLEEKING
CLEEKS
CLEEKY
CLEEVE
CLEF
CLEFT
CLEFTED
CLEG
CLEGG
CLEIDAGRA
CLEIDOCOSTAL
CLEIDOHYOID
CLEIDOIC
CLEIDOMANCY
CLEIDOTOMY
CLEIDOTRIPSY
CLEISTOCARP
CLEISTOGAMIC
CLEISTOGAMY
CLEISTOGENE
CLEITHRA
CLEITHRAL
CLEITHRUM
CLEM
CLEMATIS
CLEMATITE
CLEMENCE
CLEMENCIES
CLEMENCY
CLEMENT
CLEMENTLY
CLENCH
CLENCHED
CLENCHING
CLENK
CLEOID
CLEOME
CLEP
CLEPE
CLEPED
CLEPING
CLEPSYDRA
CLEPSYDRAE
CLEPSYDRAS
CLEPTOBIOSIS
CLEPTOBIOTIC
CLEPTOMANIA
CLERESTOREY
CLERESTORIED
CLERESTORIES
CLERESTORY
CLERGEON
CLERGESS
CLERGIAL
CLERGIES
CLERGION
CLERGY
CLERGYABLE

CLERGYMAN
CLERGYMEN
CLERGYWOMAN
CLERGYWOMEN
CLERIC
CLERICAL
CLERICALISM
CLERICALIST
CLERICALITY
CLERICALLY
CLERICATE
CLERICATURE
CLERICISM
CLERICITY
CLERID
CLERIHEW
CLERISY
CLERK
CLERKAGE
CLERKED
CLERKERY
CLERKESS
CLERKING
CLERKISH
CLERKLESS
CLERKLIER
CLERKLIEST
CLERKLIKE
CLERKLINESS
CLERKLY
CLERKSHIP
CLEROMANCY
CLERONOMY
CLERUCH
CLERUCHIAL
CLERUCHIC
CLERUCHIES
CLERUCHY
CLETCH
CLEUCH
CLEUGH
CLEUK
CLEVE
CLEVEITE
CLEVER
CLEVERALITY
CLEVERER
CLEVEREST
CLEVERISH
CLEVERISHLY
CLEVERLY
CLEVERNESS
CLEVIS
CLEVY
CLEW
CLEWED
CLEWING
CLIACK
CLIANTHUS
CLICHE
CLICK
CLICKED
CLICKER
CLICKET
CLICKING
CLICKY
CLIENCY
CLIENT
CLIENTAGE
CLIENTAL
CLIENTED
CLIENTELE
CLIENTRY
CLIER
CLIFF
CLIFFED
CLIFFHANGER

CLIFFHANGING
CLIFFING
CLIFFS
CLIFFSIDE
CLIFFSMAN
CLIFFY
CLIFT
CLIFTONITE
CLIFTY
CLIMACTER
CLIMACTERIC
CLIMACTERICAL
CLIMACTIC
CLIMACUS
CLIMATAL
CLIMATE
CLIMATH
CLIMATIC
CLIMATICAL
CLIMATICALLY
CLIMATIZE
CLIMATOLOGIC
CLIMATOLOGY
CLIMATOMETER
CLIMATURE
CLIMAX
CLIMAXED
CLIMAXING
CLIMB
CLIMBABLE
CLIMBED
CLIMBER
CLIMBERS
CLIMBING
CLIME
CLIMOGRAPH
CLINAMEN
CLINANDRIA
CLINANDRIUM
CLINANTHIA
CLINANTHIUM
CLINCH
CLINCHER
CLINE
CLINER
CLING
CLINGER
CLINGFISH
CLINGFISHES
CLINGING
CLINGINGLY
CLINGINGNESS
CLINGSTONE
CLINGY
CLINIA
CLINIC
CLINICAL
CLINICIAN
CLINIQUE
CLINIUM
CLINK
CLINKED
CLINKER
CLINKERER
CLINKERMAN
CLINKING
CLINKSTONE
CLINKUM
CLINOCEPHALY
CLINOCHLORE
CLINOCLASE
CLINOCLASITE
CLINODOMATIC
CLINODOME
CLINOEDRITE
CLINOGRAPH
CLINOGRAPHIC

CLINOHEDRAL
CLINOHEDRITE
CLINOHUMITE
CLINOID
CLINOLOGIC
CLINOLOGY
CLINOMETER
CLINOMETRIC
CLINOMETRY
CLINOSTAT
CLINQUANT
CLINT
CLINTONIA
CLINTONITE
CLINTY
CLIP
CLIPBOARD
CLIPEUS
CLIPPABLE
CLIPPED
CLIPPER
CLIPPING
CLIPS
CLIPSE
CLIPSHEET
CLIPSOME
CLIQUE
CLIQUED
CLIQUIER
CLIQUIEST
CLIQUING
CLIQUISH
CLIQUISHLY
CLIQUISHNESS
CLIQUISM
CLIQUY
CLISEOMETER
CLISTOCARP
CLISTOGAMIC
CLISTOGAMOUS
CLISTOGAMY
CLISTOGENE
CLIT
CLITCH
CLITE
CLITELLAR
CLITELLINE
CLITELLUM
CLITELLUS
CLITES
CLITHE
CLITHRIDIATE
CLITION
CLITORAL
CLITORIDAUXE
CLITORIDEAN
CLITORIDITIS
CLITORIS
CLITORISM
CLITORITIS
CLITTER
CLIVAL
CLIVE
CLIVERS
CLIVIS
CLIVOSE
CLIVUS
CLOACA
CLOACAE
CLOACAL
CLOACITIS
CLOAK
CLOAKAGE
CLOAKED
CLOAKEDLY
CLOAKING
CLOAKMAKER

CLOAKMAKING	CLOISTERLY	CLOTURE	CLUBFELLOW	CLYER
CLOAKROOM	CLOISTRAL	CLOTWEED	CLUBFIST	CLYERS
CLOAM	CLOISTRESS	CLOU	CLUBFISTED	CLYFAKER
CLOAMEN	CLOIT	CLOUD	CLUBFOOT	CLYPE
CLOAMER	CLOKY	CLOUDAGE	CLUBFOOTED	CLYPEAL
CLOBBER	CLOMB	CLOUDBERRIES	CLUBHAUL	CLYPEASTROID
CLOBBERER	CLONAL	CLOUDBERRY	CLUBHOUSE	CLYPEATE
CLOCHAN	CLONE	CLOUDBURST	CLUBIONID	CLYPEATED
CLOCHE	CLONIC	CLOUDCAP	CLUBLAND	CLYPEI
CLOCHER	CLONICITY	CLOUDED	CLUBMAN	CLYPEIFORM
CLOCHETTE	CLONICOTONIC	CLOUDIER	CLUBMATE	CLYPEOLA
CLOCK	CLONISM	CLOUDIEST	CLUBMEN	CLYPEOLAR
CLOCKBIRD	CLONK	CLOUDILY	CLUBMONGER	CLYPEOLATE
CLOCKCASE	CLONOS	CLOUDINESS	CLUBRIDDEN	CLYPEOLE
CLOCKED	CLONUS	CLOUDING	CLUBROOM	CLYPEUS
CLOCKER	CLOOF	CLOUDLAND	CLUBROOT	CLYSIS
CLOCKFACE	CLOOK	CLOUDLESSLY	CLUBS	CLYSMA
CLOCKHOUSE	CLOOP	CLOUDS	CLUBSTART	CLYSMIAN
CLOCKING	CLOOT	CLOUDY	CLUBSTER	CLYSMIC
CLOCKKEEPER	CLOOTIE	CLOUE	CLUBWEED	CLYSSUS
CLOCKMAKER	CLOP	CLOUEE	CLUBWOMAN	CLYSTER
CLOCKMAKING	CLOPPED	CLOUGH	CLUBWOMEN	CLYTE
CLOCKMUTCH	CLOPPING	CLOUR	CLUBWOOD	CNAFE
CLOCKROOM	CLOQUE	CLOUT	CLUCK	CNEMIAL
CLOCKSMITH	CLOS	CLOUTED	CLUCKED	CNEMIDIUM
CLOCKWISE	CLOSE	CLOUTER	CLUCKING	CNEMIS
CLOCKWORK	CLOSED	CLOUTERLY	CLUE	CNICIN
CLOCKWORKED	CLOSEFISTED	CLOUTY	CLUED	CNIDA
CLOD	CLOSEHANDED	CLOVE	CLUF	CNIDARIAN
CLODBREAKER	CLOSELY	CLOVEN	CLUFE	CNIDOCELL
CLODDED	CLOSEMOUTH	CLOVENE	CLUFF	CNIDOCIL
CLODDER	CLOSEMOUTHED	CLOVER	CLUING	CNIDOPHORE
CLODDIER	CLOSEN	CLOVERLAY	CLUM	CNIDOPOD
CLODDIEST	CLOSENESS	CLOVERLEAF	CLUMBER	CNIDOSAC
CLODDILY	CLOSER	CLOVERLEAFS	CLUMP	CNIDOSIS
CLODDINESS	CLOSEST	CLOVERLEY	CLUMPER	CO
CLODDING	CLOSESTOOL	CLOVEROOT	CLUMPISH	COACERVATE
CLODDISH	CLOSET	CLOVERY	CLUMPS	COACERVATION
CLODDISHLY	CLOSEUP	CLOVES	CLUMPST	COACH
CLODDISHNESS	CLOSH	CLOVEWORT	CLUMPY	COACHABILITY
CLODDY	CLOSING	CLOW	CLUMSE	COACHABLE
CLODHEAD	CLOSISH	CLOWDER	CLUMSIER	COACHBUILDER
CLODHOPPER	CLOSTER	CLOWE	CLUMSIEST	COACHED
CLODHOPPING	CLOSTRIDIA	CLOWER	CLUMSILY	COACHEE
CLODPATE	CLOSTRIDIAL	CLOWN	CLUMSINESS	COACHER
CLODPATED	CLOSTRIDIUM	CLOWNADE	CLUMSY	COACHFELLOW
CLODPOLE	CLOSURE	CLOWNAGE	CLUNCH	COACHING
CLODPOLL	CLOSURED	CLOWNERIES	CLUNG	COACHMAKER
CLODS	CLOSURING	CLOWNERY	CLUNK	COACHMAKING
CLOES	CLOT	CLOWNHEAL	CLUNTER	COACHMAN
CLOFF	CLOTBUR	CLOWNISH	CLUPEID	COACHMASTER
CLOG	CLOTE	CLOWNISHLY	CLUPEIFORM	COACHMEN
CLOGDOGDO	CLOTH	CLOWNISHNESS	CLUPEIN	COACHSMITH
CLOGGED	CLOTHE	CLOWRE	CLUPEINE	COACHWAY
CLOGGER	CLOTHED	CLOWRING	CLUPEOID	COACHWHIP
CLOGGIER	CLOTHES	CLOY	CLUPIEN	COACHWOMAN
CLOGGIEST	CLOTHESBAG	CLOYED	CLUPPE	COACHWORK
CLOGGILY	CLOTHESBRUSH	CLOYEDNESS	CLURICAUNE	COACHWRIGHT
CLOGGINESS	CLOTHESHORSE	CLOYER	CLUSE	COACHY
CLOGGING	CLOTHESLINE	CLOYING	CLUSIACEOUS	COACT
CLOGGY	CLOTHESMAN	CLOYINGLY	CLUSTER	COACTED
CLOGHAD	CLOTHESPIN	CLOYINGNESS	CLUSTERBERRY	COACTING
CLOGHAUN	CLOTHESPRESS	CLOYMENT	CLUSTERED	COACTION
CLOGHEAD	CLOTHESYARD	CLOYSOME	CLUSTERFIST	COACTIVE
CLOGMAKER	CLOTHIER	CLUB	CLUSTERING	COACTIVELY
CLOGMAKING	CLOTHIFY	CLUBABLE	CLUSTERS	COACTIVITY
CLOGWHEEL	CLOTHING	CLUBBABILITY	CLUSTERY	COACTOR
CLOGWOOD	CLOTHMAKER	CLUBBED	CLUTCH	COADAMITE
CLOGWYN	CLOTHMAKING	CLUBBER	CLUTCHED	COADAPT
CLOINE	CLOTHS	CLUBBIER	CLUTCHING	COADJACENCE
CLOISON	CLOTHWORKER	CLUBBIEST	CLUTHER	COADJACENT
CLOISONNE	CLOTHY	CLUBBILY	CLUTTER	COADJACENTLY
CLOISTER	CLOTS	CLUBBING	CLUTTERED	COADJUMENT
CLOISTERAL	CLOTTAGE	CLUBBISH	CLUTTERER	COADJUST
CLOISTERED	CLOTTED	CLUBBIST	CLUTTERING	COADJUTANT
CLOISTERER	CLOTTER	CLUBBY	CLUTTERY	COADJUTATOR
CLOISTERING	CLOTTY	CLUBFEET	CLY	COADJUTE

COADJUTEMENT
COADJUTIVE
COADJUTOR
COADJUTRESS
COADJUTRICE
COADJUTRICES
COADJUTRIX
COADJUVANT
COADMIT
COADSORBENT
COADUNATE
COADUNATED
COADUNATING
COADUNATION
COADUNATIVE
COADUNATIVELY
COADVENTURE
COADVENTURER
COAEVAL
COAGED
COAGEL
COAGMENT
COAGULA
COAGULABLE
COAGULANT
COAGULASE
COAGULATE
COAGULATED
COAGULATING
COAGULATION
COAGULATIVE
COAGULATOR
COAGULATORY
COAGULIN
COAGULOMETER
COAGULUM
COAITA
COAK
COAKUM
COAL
COALBAG
COALBAGGER
COALBIN
COALBOX
COALDEALER
COALED
COALER
COALESCE
COALESCED
COALESCENCE
COALESCENCY
COALESCENT
COALESCING
COALFIELD
COALFISH
COALFISHES
COALHEUGH
COALHOLE
COALIFY
COALING
COALITE
COALITION
COALITIONAL
COALITIONER
COALITIONIST
COALIZE
COALIZED
COALIZING
COALMONGER
COALMOUSE
COALPIT
COALRAKE
COALS
COALSACK
COALSHED
COALTERNATE
COALTITUDE

COALY
COALYARD
COAMING
COAPT
COAPTATE
COAPTATION
COAPTED
COAPTING
COARB
COARCT
COARCTATE
COARCTATION
COARCTED
COARCTING
COARSE
COARSELY
COARSEN
COARSENESS
COARSER
COARSEST
COART
COAST
COASTAL
COASTER
COASTING
COASTLAND
COASTLINE
COASTMAN
COASTMEN
COASTSIDE
COASTWAITER
COASTWARD
COASTWAYS
COASTWISE
COAT
COATED
COATEE
COATER
COATH
COATI
COATING
COATIS
COATLESS
COATRACK
COATROOM
COATS
COATTAIL
COATTAILED
COAX
COAXAL
COAXATION
COAXED
COAXER
COAXIAL
COAXIALLY
COAXING
COAXINGLY
COAXY
COAZERVATE
COAZERVATION
COB
COBAEA
COBALAMIN
COBALT
COBALTAMINE
COBALTAMMINE
COBALTIC
COBALTOUS
COBANG
COBB
COBBE
COBBER
COBBERER
COBBIN
COBBLE
COBBLED
COBBLER

COBBLERFISH
COBBLERY
COBBLES
COBBLESTONE
COBBLING
COBBLY
COBBRA
COBBY
COBCAB
COBEGO
COBERGER
COBHEAD
COBHOUSE
COBIA
COBIRON
COBISHOP
COBLE
COBLEMAN
COBLOAF
COBNUT
COBOLA
COBOSS
COBRA
COBRIDGEHEAD
COBRIFORM
COBROTHER
COBS
COBSTONE
COBURG
COBWEB
COBWEBBED
COBWEBBERY
COBWEBBING
COBWEBBY
COBWEBS
COBWORK
COCA
COCAIN
COCAINE
COCAINISM
COCAINIZE
COCAINIZED
COCAINIZING
COCAINOMANIA
COCASH
COCASHWEED
COCCACEOUS
COCCAGEE
COCCAL
COCCERIN
COCCI
COCCID
COCCIDIA
COCCIDIAL
COCCIDIAN
COCCIDIOIDAL
COCCIDIOSIS
COCCIDIUM
COCCIDOLOGY
COCCIFEROUS
COCCIFORM
COCCIGENIC
COCCINELLA
COCCIONELLA
COCCO
COCCOGONE
COCCOGONIUM
COCCOID
COCCOLITE
COCCOLITH
COCCOSPHERE
COCCOSTEAN
COCCOSTEID
COCCOUS
COCCYGALGIA
COCCYGEAL
COCCYGEAN

COCCYGECTOMY
COCCYGES
COCCYGEUS
COCCYGINE
COCCYGODYNIA
COCCYGOMORPH
COCCYGOTOMY
COCCYX
COCHAL
COCHER
COCHERO
COCHINEAL
COCHLEA
COCHLEAE
COCHLEAR
COCHLEARE
COCHLEATE
COCHLEATED
COCHLEIFORM
COCHLEITIS
COCHLEOUS
COCHLIODONT
COCHLITIS
COCHON
COCHYLIS
COCILLANA
COCINERA
COCINERO
COCIRCULAR
COCK
COCKADE
COCKADED
COCKAL
COCKALAN
COCKALEEKIE
COCKALORUM
COCKAMAMIE
COCKAMAMY
COCKANDY
COCKARD
COCKAROUSE
COCKATEEL
COCKATIEL
COCKATOO
COCKATOOS
COCKATRICE
COCKAWEE
COCKBELL
COCKBILL
COCKBIRD
COCKBOAT
COCKBRAIN
COCKCHAFER
COCKCROW
COCKCROWER
COCKCROWING
COCKED
COCKER
COCKEREL
COCKERIE
COCKERING
COCKERNONNIE
COCKERNONY
COCKEROUSE
COCKET
COCKETED
COCKETING
COCKEYE
COCKEYED
COCKEYES
COCKFIGHT
COCKFIGHTING
COCKHEAD
COCKHORSE
COCKIE
COCKIELEEKIE
COCKIER

COCKIES
COCKIEST
COCKILY
COCKINESS
COCKING
COCKISH
COCKISHLY
COCKISHNESS
COCKLE
COCKLEBOAT
COCKLEBUR
COCKLED
COCKLER
COCKLESHELL
COCKLEWIFE
COCKLIGHT
COCKLING
COCKLOCHE
COCKLOFT
COCKLY
COCKMASTER
COCKMATCH
COCKMATE
COCKNEIAN
COCKNEITY
COCKNEY
COCKNEYBRED
COCKNEYDOM
COCKNEYESE
COCKNEYESS
COCKNEYFY
COCKNEYFYING
COCKNEYISH
COCKNEYISM
COCKNEYIZE
COCKNEYLAND
COCKPADDLE
COCKPIT
COCKROACH
COCKSCOMB
COCKSCOMBED
COCKSFOOT
COCKSHEAD
COCKSHIES
COCKSHOOT
COCKSHOT
COCKSHUT
COCKSHY
COCKSHYING
COCKSPUR
COCKSURE
COCKSURENESS
COCKSURETY
COCKSWAIN
COCKSY
COCKTAIL
COCKTHROWING
COCKUP
COCKWEED
COCKY
COCLEA
COCO
COCOA
COCOANUT
COCOAWOOD
COCOBOLO
COCOMAT
COCONA
COCONSCIOUS
COCONUT
COCOON
COCOONERIES
COCOONERY
COCOONS
COCOPAN
COCORICO
COCOROOT

COCOTTE
COCOWOOD
COCOWORT
COCOYAM
COCT
COCTILE
COCTION
COCTO
COCTOANTIGEN
COCUISA
COCUIZA
COCULLO
COCUM
COCUSWOOD
COCUYO
COD
CODA
CODAMIN
CODAMINE
CODBANK
CODDED
CODDER
CODDING
CODDLE
CODDLED
CODDLER
CODDLING
CODDY
CODE
CODED
CODEIA
CODEIN
CODEINE
CODEN
CODER
CODETTA
CODEX
CODFISH
CODFISHER
CODFISHERIES
CODFISHERY
CODFISHES
CODFISHING
CODGER
CODHEAD
CODHEADED
CODIACEOUS
CODICAL
CODICES
CODICIL
CODICILIC
CODIFICATION
CODIFIED
CODIFIER
CODIFYING
CODILLA
CODING
CODINIAC
CODIST
CODLIN
CODLING
CODLINGS
CODMAN
CODOL
CODOMINANT
CODON
CODPIECE
CODPITCHINGS
CODS
CODSHEAD
CODWORM
COE
COED
COEDUCATION
COEDUCATIONAL
COEFFECT

COEFFICIENT
COEHORN
COELACANTH
COELACANTHID
COELAR
COELARIUM
COELELMINTH
COELENTERATE
COELENTERIC
COELENTERON
COELESTINE
COELHO
COELIA
COELIAC
COELIALGIA
COELIGENOUS
COELIN
COELIORRHEA
COELIORRHOEA
COELIOSCOPY
COELIOTOMY
COELOBLASTIC
COELODONT
COELOM
COELOMA
COELOMATA
COELOMATE
COELOMATIC
COELOMATOUS
COELOME
COELOMIC
COELOMOPORE
COELOPLANULA
COELOSPERM
COELOSTAT
COELOZOIC
COEMPT
COEMPTIO
COEMPTION
COEMPTIONAL
COEMPTIVE
COEMPTOR
COENA
COENACULOUS
COENANTHIUM
COENENCHYMA
COENENCHYMAL
COENENCHYMATA
COENENCHYME
COENESTHESIA
COENESTHESIS
COENOBE
COENOBIAR
COENOBIC
COENOBIOD
COENOBITE
COENOBIUM
COENOBLAST
COENOBLASTIC
COENOBY
COENOCENTRUM
COENOCYTE
COENOCYTIC
COENOECIAL
COENOECIC
COENOECIUM
COENOGAMETE
COENOGENESIS
COENOSARC
COENOSARCAL
COENOSARCOUS
COENOSTEAL
COENOSTEUM
COENOTROPE
COENOTYPE
COENURE
COENURUS

COENZYME
COEQUAL
COEQUALITY
COEQUALLY
COEQUALNESS
COEQUATE
COEQUATED
COEQUATION
COERCE
COERCED
COERCER
COERCIBILITY
COERCIBLE
COERCIBLY
COERCING
COERCION
COERCIONARY
COERCIONIST
COERCITIVE
COERCIVE
COERCIVELY
COERCIVENESS
COERCIVITY
COESSENTIAL
COESTATE
COETANEITY
COETANEOUS
COETANEOUSLY
COETERNALLY
COETERNITY
COETUS
COEVAL
COEVALLY
COEXIST
COEXISTENCE
COEXISTENCY
COEXISTENT
COEXTEND
COEXTENSION
COEXTENSIVE
COFACTOR
COFEOFFEE
COFF
COFFE
COFFEE
COFFEEBERRIES
COFFEEBERRY
COFFEEBUSH
COFFEECAKE
COFFEEGROWER
COFFEEHOUSE
COFFEELEAF
COFFEEMAN
COFFEEPOT
COFFEEROOM
COFFEEWEED
COFFEEWOOD
COFFER
COFFERDAM
COFFERED
COFFERER
COFFERING
COFFERWORK
COFFIN
COFFINED
COFFING
COFFINING
COFFINMAKER
COFFINMAKING
COFFLE
COFFLED
COFFLING
COFFRET
COFT
COG
COGBOAT
COGENCE

COGENCY
COGENER
COGENT
COGGED
COGGER
COGGERS
COGGIE
COGGING
COGGLE
COGGLEDY
COGGLETY
COGGLY
COGHLE
COGIDA
COGITABILITY
COGITABLE
COGITABUND
COGITABUNDLY
COGITANT
COGITATE
COGITATED
COGITATING
COGITATION
COGITATIVE
COGITATIVELY
COGITATIVITY
COGITATOR
COGITO
COGMAN
COGNAC
COGNATE
COGNATIC
COGNATION
COGNATUS
COGNISE
COGNITION
COGNITIONAL
COGNITIVE
COGNITIVELY
COGNITUM
COGNIZABLE
COGNIZABLY
COGNIZANCE
COGNIZANT
COGNIZE
COGNIZED
COGNIZEE
COGNIZER
COGNIZING
COGNIZOR
COGNOMEN
COGNOMENS
COGNOMINA
COGNOMINAL
COGNOMINALLY
COGNOMINATE
COGNOMINATED
COGNOSCE
COGNOSCENTE
COGNOSCIBLE
COGNOSCITIVE
COGON
COGONAL
COGRAIL
COGREDIENCY
COGREDIENT
COGROAD
COGUE
COGWAY
COGWHEEL
COGWOOD
COHAB
COHABIT
COHABITANCY
COHABITANT
COHABITATION
COHABITED

COHABITER
COHABITING
COHEIR
COHEIRESS
COHENITE
COHERE
COHERED
COHERENCE
COHERENCY
COHERENT
COHERENTLY
COHERER
COHERING
COHERITAGE
COHERITOR
COHERT
COHESIBILITY
COHESIBLE
COHESION
COHESIVE
COHESIVELY
COHESIVENESS
COHIBIT
COHIBITION
COHIBITIVE
COHIBITOR
COHITRE
COHO
COHOBA
COHOBATE
COHOBATED
COHOBATING
COHOBATION
COHOBATOR
COHOE
COHOL
COHORT
COHORTATION
COHORTATIVE
COHOSH
COHOW
COHU
COHUE
COHUNE
COIF
COIFED
COIFFE
COIFFEUR
COIFFEUSE
COIFFURE
COIFFURED
COIFFURING
COIFING
COIGN
COIGNE
COIGNY
COIGUE
COIL
COILED
COILER
COILING
COILS
COILSMITH
COILYEAR
COIMPLICANT
COIN
COINABLE
COINAGE
COINCIDE
COINCIDENCE
COINCIDENCY
COINCIDENT
COINCIDENTAL
COINCIDENTALLY
COINCIDENTLY
COINCIDER
COINCIDING

COINDICANT	COLEOPTERAL	COLLEAGUED	COLLIMATING	COLLYRIE
COINDICATE	COLEOPTERAN	COLLEAGUING	COLLIMATION	COLLYRITE
COINDICATION	COLEOPTERIST	COLLECT	COLLIN	COLLYRIUM
COINED	COLEOPTEROID	COLLECTABLE	COLLINAL	COLLYRIUMS
COINER	COLEOPTERON	COLLECTANEA	COLLINE	COLLYWEST
COINHABIT	COLEOPTEROUS	COLLECTARIUM	COLLINEARITY	COLLYWESTON
COINHABITOR	COLEOPTILE	COLLECTED	COLLINEARLY	COLLYWOBBLES
COINHERITOR	COLEOPTILUM	COLLECTEDLY	COLLINEATE	COLMAR
COINING	COLEORHIZA	COLLECTIBLE	COLLINEATION	COLMOSE
COINMAKER	COLESEED	COLLECTION	COLLING	COLOBIN
COINMAKING	COLESLAW	COLLECTIONAL	COLLINGUAL	COLOBIUM
COINS	COLETIT	COLLECTIONER	COLLINSIA	COLOBOMA
COINSURANCE	COLEUR	COLLECTIVE	COLLINSITE	COLOCENTESIS
COINSURE	COLEUS	COLLECTIVELY	COLLIQUATE	COLOCLYSIS
COINSURED	COLEWORT	COLLECTIVISM	COLLIQUATION	COLOCOLA
COINSURER	COLF	COLLECTIVIST	COLLIQUATIVE	COLOCOLIC
COINSURING	COLFOX	COLLECTIVITY	COLLIS	COLOCOLO
COINTENSE	COLI	COLLECTIVIZE	COLLISION	COLOCYNTH
COINTENSITY	COLIBERT	COLLECTIVIZED	COLLISIONAL	COLOCYNTHIN
COINTISE	COLIBRI	COLLECTIVIZING	COLLISIVE	COLOGARITHM
COIR	COLIC	COLLECTOR	COLLOBLAST	COLOGNE
COISTREL	COLICAL	COLLECTORATE	COLLOCAL	COLOLITE
COISTRIL	COLICHEMARDE	COLLECTORSHIP	COLLOCATE	COLOMBIER
COITION	COLICIN	COLLEEN	COLLOCATED	COLOMBIN
COITURE	COLICKER	COLLEGATARY	COLLOCATING	COLOMETRIC
COITUS	COLICKY	COLLEGE	COLLOCATION	COLOMETRY
COIX	COLICROOT	COLLEGER	COLLOCK	COLON
COJONES	COLICWEED	COLLEGIA	COLLOCUTION	COLONATE
COJUROR	COLICWORT	COLLEGIAL	COLLOCUTOR	COLONEL
COKE	COLIES	COLLEGIALISM	COLLOCUTORY	COLONELCIES
COKEMAN	COLIFORM	COLLEGIALITY	COLLODION	COLONELCY
COKENEY	COLIMA	COLLEGIAN	COLLODIONIZE	COLONGITUDE
COKER	COLIN	COLLEGIANER	COLLODIOTYPE	COLONIAL
COKERNUT	COLINEAR	COLLEGIATE	COLLODIUM	COLONIALISM
COKERY	COLING	COLLEGIATELY	COLLOGEN	COLONIC
COKES	COLISEUM	COLLEGIATION	COLLOGUE	COLONIES
COKEWOLD	COLITIC	COLLEGIUM	COLLOGUED	COLONISE
COKEY	COLITIS	COLLEMBOLAN	COLLOGUING	COLONIST
COKIE	COLK	COLLEMBOLE	COLLOID	COLONITIS
COL	COLL	COLLEMBOLIC	COLLOIDAL	COLONIZATION
COLA	COLLABENT	COLLEMBOLOUS	COLLOIDALITY	COLONIZE
COLAGE	COLLABORATE	COLLEN	COLLOMIA	COLONIZED
COLALGIA	COLLABORATED	COLLENCHYMA	COLLOP	COLONIZER
COLANDER	COLLABORATING	COLLENCHYME	COLLOPED	COLONIZING
COLANE	COLLABORATOR	COLLENCYTAL	COLLOPHANITE	COLONNADE
COLATE	COLLAGEN	COLLENCYTE	COLLOPHORE	COLONNADED
COLATION	COLLAGENIC	COLLERY	COLLOQUE	COLONNETTE
COLATITUDE	COLLAGENOUS	COLLET	COLLOQUIAL	COLONOPATHY
COLATORIUM	COLLAPSABLE	COLLETER	COLLOQUIALLY	COLONOPEXY
COLATORY	COLLAPSE	COLLETERIA	COLLOQUIST	COLONOSCOPE
COLATURE	COLLAPSED	COLLETERIAL	COLLOQUIUM	COLONOSCOPY
COLAUXE	COLLAPSIBLE	COLLETERIUM	COLLOQUIZE	COLONS
COLAZIONE	COLLAPSING	COLLETIC	COLLOQUIZED	COLONUS
COLBERTER	COLLAR	COLLETIN	COLLOQUIZING	COLONY
COLBERTINE	COLLARBAND	COLLEY	COLLOQUY	COLOPEXIA
COLCANNON	COLLARBIRD	COLLIBERT	COLLOTYPE	COLOPEXOTOMY
COLCHICIA	COLLARBONE	COLLICLE	COLLOTYPIC	COLOPEXY
COLCHICIN	COLLARD	COLLICULATE	COLLOTYPY	COLOPHAN
COLCHICINE	COLLARED	COLLICULUS	COLLOXYLIN	COLOPHANE
COLCHICUM	COLLARET	COLLIDE	COLLUDE	COLOPHENE
COLCOTHAR	COLLARETTE	COLLIDED	COLLUDED	COLOPHON
COLD	COLLARMAN	COLLIDIN	COLLUDER	COLOPHONATE
COLDCOCK	COLLATE	COLLIDINE	COLLUDING	COLOPHONIST
COLDER	COLLATED	COLLIDING	COLLUM	COLOPHONITE
COLDFINCH	COLLATEE	COLLIE	COLLUSION	COLOPHONY
COLDHEARTED	COLLATERAL	COLLIED	COLLUSIVE	COLOPLICATION
COLDHEARTEDLY	COLLATERALLY	COLLIER	COLLUSIVELY	COLOPPE
COLDISH	COLLATING	COLLIERY	COLLUSORY	COLOQUIES
COLDLY	COLLATION	COLLIFORM	COLLUTORIES	COLOQUINTIDA
COLDONG	COLLATIONER	COLLIGATE	COLLUTORIUM	COLOR
COLE	COLLATITIOUS	COLLIGATED	COLLUTORY	COLORABILITY
COLECTOMIES	COLLATIVE	COLLIGATING	COLLUVIAL	COLORABLE
COLECTOMY	COLLATOR	COLLIGATION	COLLUVIES	COLORABLY
COLEGATEE	COLLATRESS	COLLIGATIVE	COLLY	COLORADO
COLEMANITE	COLLAUD	COLLIGIBLE	COLLYBA	COLORANT
COLEOPTER	COLLAUDATION	COLLIMATE	COLLYING	COLORATE
COLEOPTERA	COLLEAGUE	COLLIMATED	COLLYRIA	COLORATION

COLORATIONAL
COLORATIVE
COLORATURA
COLORCAST
COLORED
COLORER
COLORFAST
COLORFUL
COLORIFIC
COLORIFICS
COLORIMETER
COLORIMETRIC
COLORIMETRY
COLORIN
COLORING
COLORISM
COLORIST
COLORISTIC
COLORIZATION
COLORIZE
COLORLESS
COLORMAKER
COLORMAKING
COLORMAN
COLOROTO
COLORRHAPHY
COLORS
COLORTYPE
COLORY
COLOSSAL
COLOSSALITY
COLOSSALLY
COLOSSEAN
COLOSSEUM
COLOSSO
COLOSSUS
COLOSTOMIES
COLOSTOMY
COLOSTRAL
COLOSTRIC
COLOSTROUS
COLOSTRUM
COLOTOMIES
COLOTOMY
CCLOTYPHOID
COLOUR
COLOURABILITY
COLOURABLE
COLOURABLY
COLOURATION
COLOURATIVE
COLOURED
COLOURER
COLOURFUL
COLOURFULLY
COLOURFULNESS
COLOURIFIC
COLOURIFICS
COLOURING
COLOURIST
COLOURISTIC
COLOURIZE
COLOURLESS
COLOURLESSLY
COLOURMAN
COLOURTYPE
COLOURY
COLPENCHYMA
COLPEO
COLPEURYNTER
COLPEURYSIS
COLPHEG
COLPINDACH
COLPITIS
COLPOCELE
COLPOPLASTIC
COLPOPLASTY

COLPOPTOSIS
COLPORRHAGIA
COLPORRHAPHY
COLPORRHEA
COLPORRHEXIS
COLPORT
COLPORTAGE
COLPORTER
COLPORTEUR
COLPOSCOPE
COLPOSCOPY
COLPOSTAT
COLPOTOMY
COLT
COLTER
COLTISH
COLTPIXY
COLTS
COLTSFOOT
COLTSKIN
COLUBRID
COLUBRIFORM
COLUBRINE
COLUBROID
COLUGO
COLUGOS
COLUMBACEOUS
COLUMBARIA
COLUMBARIUM
COLUMBARY
COLUMBATE
COLUMBEION
COLUMBIAD
COLUMBIC
COLUMBIER
COLUMBIN
COLUMBINE
COLUMBITE
COLUMBIUM
COLUMBO
COLUMBOID
COLUMEL
COLUMELLA
COLUMELLAE
COLUMELLAR
COLUMELLATE
COLUMN
COLUMNAL
COLUMNAR
COLUMNATED
COLUMNEA
COLUMNED
COLUMNER
COLUMNIATION
COLUMNIFORM
COLUMNING
COLUMNIST
COLUMNS
COLUNAR
COLURE
COLUSITE
COLY
COLYBA
COLYMBIFORM
COLYMBION
COLYTIC
COLYUM
COLYUMIST
COLZA
COMA
COMACINE
COMAE
COMAL
COMALES
COMAMIE
COMARCA
COMART

COMAS
COMATE
COMATIC
COMATOSE
COMATOSELY
COMATOSENESS
COMATOSITY
COMATOUS
COMATULA
COMATULID
COMB
COMBARON
COMBASOU
COMBAT
COMBATABLE
COMBATANT
COMBATANTS
COMBATED
COMBATING
COMBATIVE
COMBATIVELY
COMBATIVITY
COMBATTED
COMBATTER
COMBATTING
COMBED
COMBER
COMBFISH
COMBFLOWER
COMBINABLE
COMBINANT
COMBINANTIVE
COMBINATE
COMBINATION
COMBINATIONS
COMBINATIVE
COMBINE
COMBINED
COMBINEDLY
COMBINEDNESS
COMBINEMENT
COMBINER
COMBING
COMBINGS
COMBINING
COMBITE
COMBLE
COMBMAKER
COMBMAKING
COMBO
COMBOLOIO
COMBOY
COMBURE
COMBURENT
COMBURGESS
COMBURIMETER
COMBURIMETRY
COMBUST
COMBUSTIBLE
COMBUSTIBLY
COMBUSTION
COMBUSTIOUS
COMBUSTIVE
COMBUSTOR
COMBWISE
COMBWRIGHT
COMBY
COME
COMEBACK
COMEDDLE
COMEDIA
COMEDIAL
COMEDIAN
COMEDIANT
COMEDIC
COMEDICAL
COMEDICALLY

COMEDIENNE
COMEDIES
COMEDIST
COMEDO
COMEDONES
COMEDOS
COMEDOWN
COMEDY
COMELIER
COMELIEST
COMELILY
COMELINESS
COMELING
COMELY
COMENDITE
COMEPHOROUS
COMER
COMES
COMESSATION
COMESTIBLE
COMESTION
COMET
COMETARIA
COMETARIUM
COMETARY
COMETHER
COMETIC
COMEUPANCE
COMEUPPANCE
COMFIT
COMFITURE
COMFORT
COMFORTABLE
COMFORTABLY
COMFORTED
COMFORTER
COMFORTING
COMFORTINGLY
COMFORTLESS
COMFREY
COMFREYS
COMFY
COMIC
COMICAL
COMICALITY
COMICALLY
COMICALNESS
COMICOCRATIC
COMICOGRAPHY
COMICRY
COMIDA
COMIFEROUS
COMING
COMINO
COMIQUE
COMISM
COMITAL
COMITANT
COMITATIVE
COMITATUS
COMITE
COMITES
COMITIA
COMITIAL
COMITIES
COMITIVA
COMITJE
COMITRAGEDY
COMITY
COMMA
COMMAES
COMMAING
COMMAND
COMMANDANT
COMMANDED
COMMANDEER
COMMANDER

COMMANDERY
COMMANDING
COMMANDINGLY
COMMANDMENT
COMMANDMENTS
COMMANDO
COMMANDOES
COMMANDOS
COMMANDRIES
COMMANDRY
COMMAS
COMMASSATION
COMMASSEE
COMMATA
COMMATIC
COMMATION
COMMATISM
COMMEASURE
COMMEASURED
COMMEASURING
COMMEM
COMMEMORABLE
COMMEMORATE
COMMEMORATED
COMMEMORATING
COMMEMORATION
COMMEMORATIVE
COMMEMORATOR
COMMEMORIZE
COMMEMORIZED
COMMEMORIZING
COMMENCE
COMMENCED
COMMENCEMENT
COMMENCER
COMMENCING
COMMEND
COMMENDA
COMMENDABLE
COMMENDABLY
COMMENDADOR
COMMENDAM
COMMENDATARY
COMMENDATION
COMMENDATOR
COMMENDATORIES
COMMENDATORY
COMMENDED
COMMENDER
COMMENDING
COMMENSAL
COMMENSALISM
COMMENSALIST
COMMENSALISTIC
COMMENSALITY
COMMENSALLY
COMMENSURABLE
COMMENSURABLY
COMMENSURATE
COMMENSURATED
COMMENSURATING
COMMENT
COMMENTARIAL
COMMENTARIES
COMMENTARY
COMMENTATE
COMMENTATION
COMMENTATOR
COMMENTER
COMMERCE
COMMERCED
COMMERCER
COMMERCIA
COMMERCIABLE
COMMERCIAL
COMMERCIALISM
COMMERCIALITY

COMMERCIALIZE	COMMODIOUSLY	COMMUNIZE	COMPARTMENT	COMPILED
COMMERCIALIZED	COMMODITIES	COMMUNIZED	COMPARTMENTS	COMPILEMENT
COMMERCIALIZING	COMMODITY	COMMUNIZING	COMPASS	COMPILER
COMMERCIALLY	COMMODORE	COMMUTABLE	COMPASSABLE	COMPILING
COMMERCING	COMMON	COMMUTANT	COMPASSED	COMPITAL
COMMERCIUM	COMMONABLE	COMMUTATE	COMPASSER	COMPITUM
COMMERGE	COMMONAGE	COMMUTATED	COMPASSES	COMPLACENCE
COMMERS	COMMONALITIES	COMMUTATING	COMPASSING	COMPLACENCIES
COMMESSO	COMMONALITY	COMMUTATION	COMPASSION	COMPLACENCY
COMMINATE	COMMONALTY	COMMUTATIVE	COMPASSIONATE	COMPLACENT
COMMINATED	COMMONED	COMMUTATOR	COMPASSIONATED	COMPLACENTLY
COMMINATING	COMMONER	COMMUTE	COMPASSIONATING	COMPLAIN
COMMINATION	COMMONEY	COMMUTED	COMPASSIVE	COMPLAINANT
COMMINATIVE	COMMONING	COMMUTER	COMPASSIVITY	COMPLAINED
COMMINATOR	COMMONLY	COMMUTING	COMPATERNITY	COMPLAINER
COMMINATORY	COMMONNESS	COMMUTUAL	COMPATIBLE	COMPLAINING
COMMINGLE	COMMONPLACE	COMMUTUALITY	COMPATIBLY	COMPLAINT
COMMINGLER	COMMONPLACELY	COMMY	COMPATIENCE	COMPLAINTIVE
COMMINISTER	COMMONPLACENES	COMODATO	COMPATIENT	COMPLAISANCE
COMMINUATE	COMMONS	COMODO	COMPATRIOT	COMPLAISANT
COMMINUTE	COMMONTY	COMOEDIA	COMPATRIOTIC	COMPLAISANTLY
COMMINUTED	COMMONWEAL	COMOEDUS	COMPEAR	COMPLANATE
COMMINUTING	COMMONWEALTH	COMOID	COMPEARANCE	COMPLANATION
COMMINUTION	COMMORANCY	COMOLECULE	COMPEARANT	COMPLANT
COMMINUTOR	COMMORANT	COMONTE	COMPEER	COMPLECT
COMMIS	COMMORIENT	COMOQUER	COMPEL	COMPLECTED
COMMISE	COMMORTH	COMORADO	COMPELLABLE	COMPLEMENT
COMMISERABLE	COMMOS	COMOSE	COMPELLABLY	COMPLEMENTAL
COMMISERATE	COMMOT	COMOUS	COMPELLATION	COMPLETE
COMMISERATED	COMMOTE	COMP	COMPELLATIVE	COMPLETED
COMMISERATING	COMMOTION	COMPACT	COMPELLED	COMPLETELY
COMMISERATION	COMMOTIONAL	COMPACTED	COMPELLENT	COMPLETENESS
COMMISERATIVE	COMMOVE	COMPACTEDLY	COMPELLER	COMPLETER
COMMISERATOR	COMMOVED	COMPACTER	COMPELLING	COMPLETING
COMMISSAR	COMMOVING	COMPACTING	COMPELLINGLY	COMPLETION
COMMISSARIAL	COMMUNAL	COMPACTION	COMPEND	COMPLETIVE
COMMISSARIAT	COMMUNALISM	COMPACTLY	COMPENDENCY	COMPLETIVELY
COMMISSARIES	COMMUNALIST	COMPACTNESS	COMPENDENT	COMPLETORIES
COMMISSARY	COMMUNALISTIC	COMPACTURE	COMPENDIA	COMPLETORY
COMMISSION	COMMUNALITY	COMPADRE	COMPENDIARY	COMPLEX
COMMISSIONAIRE	COMMUNALIZE	COMPAGE	COMPENDIATE	COMPLEXIFY
COMMISSIONAL	COMMUNALIZED	COMPAGES	COMPENDIOUS	COMPLEXION
COMMISSIONARY	COMMUNALIZER	COMPAGINATE	COMPENDIUM	COMPLEXIONAL
COMMISSIONATE	COMMUNALLY	COMPANIED	COMPENDIUMS	COMPLEXIONARY
COMMISSIONATED	COMMUNARD	COMPANIES	COMPENETRATE	COMPLEXIONED
COMMISSIONATING	COMMUNE	COMPANION	COMPENSABLE	COMPLEXITIES
COMMISSIONER	COMMUNED	COMPANIONABLE	COMPENSATE	COMPLEXITY
COMMISSIVE	COMMUNER	COMPANIONABLY	COMPENSATED	COMPLEXLY
COMMISSIVELY	COMMUNICABLE	COMPANIONAGE	COMPENSATING	COMPLEXNESS
COMMISSURAL	COMMUNICABLY	COMPANIONATE	COMPENSATION	COMPLEXUS
COMMISSURE	COMMUNICANT	COMPANIONED	COMPENSATIVE	COMPLIABLE
COMMIT	COMMUNICATE	COMPANIONING	COMPENSATOR	COMPLIABLY
COMMITMENT	COMMUNICATED	COMPANIONIZE	COMPENSATORY	COMPLIANCE
COMMITTABLE	COMMUNICATING	COMPANIONIZED	COMPENSE	COMPLIANCY
COMMITTAL	COMMUNICATION	COMPANIONIZING	COMPENSER	COMPLIANT
COMMITTED	COMMUNICATIVE	COMPANIONSHIP	COMPERE	COMPLIANTLY
COMMITTEE	COMMUNICATOR	COMPANIONWAY	COMPERT	COMPLICACIES
COMMITTEEMAN	COMMUNICATORY	COMPANY	COMPESCE	COMPLICACY
COMMITTEEMEN	COMMUNING	COMPANYING	COMPETE	COMPLICANT
COMMITTENT	COMMUNION	COMPARABLE	COMPETED	COMPLICATE
COMMITTER	COMMUNIONABLE	COMPARABLY	COMPETENCE	COMPLICATED
COMMITTIBLE	COMMUNIONAL	COMPARATE	COMPETENCY	COMPLICATING
COMMITTING	COMMUNIONIST	COMPARATIVAL	COMPETENT	COMPLICATION
COMMITTOR	COMMUNIQUE	COMPARATIVE	COMPETENTLY	COMPLICATIVE
COMMIX	COMMUNISM	COMPARATIVELY	COMPETIBLE	COMPLICE
COMMIXED	COMMUNIST	COMPARATOR	COMPETING	COMPLICITIES
COMMIXING	COMMUNISTERIES	COMPARE	COMPETITION	COMPLICITOUS
COMMIXT	COMMUNISTERY	COMPARED	COMPETITIVE	COMPLICITY
COMMIXTION	COMMUNISTIC	COMPARER	COMPETITIVELY	COMPLIER
COMMIXTURE	COMMUNISTICAL	COMPARING	COMPETITOR	COMPLIMENT
COMMODATA	COMMUNITAL	COMPARISON	COMPETITORY	COMPLIMENTAL
COMMODATARY	COMMUNITARIAN	COMPAROGRAPH	COMPETITRESS	COMPLIMENTARY
COMMODATE	COMMUNITARY	COMPARSA	COMPETITRIX	COMPLIMENTER
COMMODATION	COMMUNITIES	COMPART	COMPILATION	COMPLIMENTS
COMMODATUM	COMMUNITIVE	COMPARTED	COMPILATOR	COMPLIN
COMMODE	COMMUNITY	COMPARTING	COMPILATORY	COMPLINE
COMMODIOUS	COMMUNIZATION	COMPARTITION	COMPILE	COMPLINES

COMPLINS
COMPLISH
COMPLOT
COMPLOTTED
COMPLOTTER
COMPLOTTING
COMPLUVIUM
COMPLY
COMPLYING
COMPO
COMPOED
COMPOER
COMPOING
COMPONE
COMPONED
COMPONENCY
COMPONENDO
COMPONENT
COMPONENTAL
COMPONENTED
COMPONENTS
COMPONY
COMPORT
COMPORTABLE
COMPORTANCE
COMPORTMENT
COMPOS
COMPOSE
COMPOSED
COMPOSEDLY
COMPOSEDNESS
COMPOSER
COMPOSING
COMPOSIT
COMPOSITA
COMPOSITE
COMPOSITED
COMPOSITELY
COMPOSITING
COMPOSITION
COMPOSITIVE
COMPOSITOR
COMPOSITURE
COMPOSOGRAPH
COMPOSSIBLE
COMPOST
COMPOSTED
COMPOSTING
COMPOSTURE
COMPOSURE
COMPOT
COMPOTATION
COMPOTATOR
COMPOTATORY
COMPOTE
COMPOTOR
COMPOUND
COMPOUNDED
COMPOUNDER
COMPOUNDING
COMPRACHICO
COMPRACHICOS
COMPRADOR
COMPRADORE
COMPRECATION
COMPREHEND
COMPREHENDER
COMPREHENSE
COMPREHENSIBLE
COMPREHENSION
COMPREHENSIVE
COMPREHENSIVELY
COMPREHENSIVENESS
COMPREHENSOR
COMPRESBYTER
COMPRESENCE
COMPRESENT

COMPRESS
COMPRESSED
COMPRESSIBLE
COMPRESSING
COMPRESSION
COMPRESSIVE
COMPRESSIVELY
COMPRESSOR
COMPRESSURE
COMPREST
COMPRIEST
COMPRISABLE
COMPRISAL
COMPRISE
COMPRISED
COMPRISING
COMPRIZAL
COMPRIZE
COMPRIZED
COMPRIZING
COMPROBATE
COMPROBATION
COMPRODUCE
COMPROMISE
COMPROMISED
COMPROMISER
COMPROMISING
COMPROMIT
COMPROMITTED
COMPROMITTING
COMPT
COMPTER
COMPTIBLE
COMPTIE
COMPTLY
COMPTNESS
COMPTOIR
COMPTOMETER
COMPTROLLER
COMPULSATIVE
COMPULSATORY
COMPULSED
COMPULSION
COMPULSITOR
COMPULSIVE
COMPULSIVELY
COMPULSORILY
COMPULSORY
COMPUNCT
COMPUNCTION
COMPUNCTIOUS
COMPUNCTIVE
COMPURGATION
COMPURGATOR
COMPURGATORY
COMPURSION
COMPUTABLE
COMPUTABLY
COMPUTATION
COMPUTATIVE
COMPUTE
COMPUTED
COMPUTER
COMPUTING
COMPUTIST
COMPUTUS
COMRADE
COMRADELY
COMRADERY
COMRADESHIP
COMROGUE
COMSTOCKERIES
COMSTOCKERY
COMTE
COMTESSE
COMUNIDAD
CON

CONACASTE
CONACRE
CONAL
CONAMED
CONAND
CONARIAL
CONARIUM
CONATION
CONATIONAL
CONATIVE
CONATURAL
CONATUS
CONCAMERATE
CONCAMERATED
CONCANAVALIN
CONCAPTIVE
CONCASSATION
CONCATENARY
CONCATENATE
CONCATENATED
CONCATENATING
CONCATENATOR
CONCAUSE
CONCAVATION
CONCAVE
CONCAVED
CONCAVELY
CONCAVENESS
CONCAVER
CONCAVING
CONCAVITIES
CONCAVITY
CONCEAL
CONCEALED
CONCEALEDLY
CONCEALER
CONCEALING
CONCEALMENT
CONCEDE
CONCEDED
CONCEDEDLY
CONCEDER
CONCEDING
CONCEIT
CONCEITED
CONCEITEDLY
CONCEITING
CONCEITLESS
CONCEITY
CONCEIVABLE
CONCEIVABLY
CONCEIVE
CONCEIVED
CONCEIVER
CONCEIVING
CONCELEBRATE
CONCENT
CONCENTER
CONCENTERED
CONCENTERING
CONCENTIVE
CONCENTRATE
CONCENTRATED
CONCENTRATING
CONCENTRATION
CONCENTRATOR
CONCENTRE
CONCENTRED
CONCENTRIC
CONCENTRICAL
CONCENTRING
CONCENTUAL
CONCENTUS
CONCEPT
CONCEPTACLE
CONCEPTION
CONCEPTIONAL

CONCEPTISM
CONCEPTIVE
CONCEPTUAL
CONCEPTUALISM
CONCEPTUALITY
CONCEPTUALLY
CONCERN
CONCERNED
CONCERNEDLY
CONCERNING
CONCERNINGLY
CONCERNMENT
CONCERT
CONCERTATION
CONCERTED
CONCERTEDLY
CONCERTGOER
CONCERTI
CONCERTINA
CONCERTING
CONCERTINI
CONCERTINIST
CONCERTINO
CONCERTINOS
CONCERTION
CONCERTIST
CONCERTIZE
CONCERTIZED
CONCERTIZER
CONCERTIZING
CONCERTMASTER
CONCERTMEISTER
CONCERTO
CONCERTOS
CONCESSIBLE
CONCESSION
CONCESSIONAIRE
CONCESSIONAL
CONCESSIONER
CONCESSIVE
CONCESSIVELY
CONCESSOR
CONCESSORY
CONCETTI
CONCETTISM
CONCETTIST
CONCETTO
CONCH
CONCHA
CONCHAE
CONCHAL
CONCHATE
CONCHE
CONCHED
CONCHER
CONCHES
CONCHIES
CONCHIFEROUS
CONCHIFORM
CONCHININ
CONCHININE
CONCHIOLIN
CONCHITE
CONCHITIC
CONCHITIS
CONCHO
CONCHOID
CONCHOIDAL
CONCHOIDALLY
CONCHOLOGIST
CONCHOLOGIZE
CONCHOLOGY
CONCHOMETER
CONCHOMETRY
CONCHOTOME
CONCHS
CONCHY

CONCHYLIATED
CONCHYLIUM
CONCIERGE
CONCILE
CONCILIABLE
CONCILIABULE
CONCILIAR
CONCILIATE
CONCILIATED
CONCILIATING
CONCILIATION
CONCILIATIVE
CONCILIATOR
CONCILIATORY
CONCILIUM
CONCINNATE
CONCINNITIES
CONCINNITY
CONCINNOUS
CONCIO
CONCION
CONCIONAL
CONCIONARY
CONCIONATE
CONCIONATOR
CONCIONATORY
CONCIPIENCY
CONCIPIENT
CONCISE
CONCISELY
CONCISENESS
CONCISION
CONCITATION
CONCLAVE
CONCLAVIST
CONCLUDE
CONCLUDED
CONCLUDENCE
CONCLUDENCY
CONCLUDENT
CONCLUDENTLY
CONCLUDER
CONCLUDING
CONCLUDINGLY
CONCLUSION
CONCLUSIONAL
CONCLUSIVE
CONCLUSIVELY
CONCLUSORY
CONCOAGULATE
CONCOCT
CONCOCTER
CONCOCTION
CONCOCTIVE
CONCOCTOR
CONCOLOR
CONCOLOROUS
CONCOLOUR
CONCOMITANCE
CONCOMITANCY
CONCOMITANT
CONCOMITATE
CONCORD
CONCORDABLE
CONCORDABLY
CONCORDAL
CONCORDANCE
CONCORDANCER
CONCORDANCY
CONCORDANT
CONCORDANTLY
CONCORDAT
CONCORDATORY
CONCORDER
CONCORDIAL
CONCORDIST
CONCORDITY

CONCORDLY
CONCORPORATE
CONCORPORATED
CONCORPORATING
CONCOURS
CONCOURSE
CONCREATE
CONCREDIT
CONCREMATION
CONCREMENT
CONCRESCE
CONCRESCENCE
CONCRESCIBLE
CONCRESCIVE
CONCRETE
CONCRETED
CONCRETELY
CONCRETENESS
CONCRETER
CONCRETING
CONCRETION
CONCRETIONAL
CONCRETISM
CONCRETIVE
CONCRETIVELY
CONCRETIZE
CONCRETIZED
CONCRETIZING
CONCRETOR
CONCREW
CONCUBINAGE
CONCUBINAL
CONCUBINARY
CONCUBINE
CONCUBITANCY
CONCUBITANT
CONCUBITOUS
CONCUBITUS
CONCULCATE
CONCULCATION
CONCUMBENCY
CONCUPISCENCE
CONCUPISCENT
CONCUPY
CONCUR
CONCURRED
CONCURRENCE
CONCURRENCY
CONCURRENT
CONCURRENTLY
CONCURRING
CONCURRINGLY
CONCURSION
CONCURSO
CONCURSUS
CONCUSS
CONCUSSATION
CONCUSSED
CONCUSSING
CONCUSSION
CONCUSSIONAL
CONCUSSIVE
CONCUTIENT
CONCYCLIC
COND
CONDECENT
CONDEMN
CONDEMNATE
CONDEMNATION
CONDEMNATORY
CONDEMNED
CONDEMNER
CONDEMNING
CONDEMNINGLY
CONDEMNS
CONDENSABLE
CONDENSATE

CONDENSATION
CONDENSATIVE
CONDENSATOR
CONDENSE
CONDENSED
CONDENSER
CONDENSERY
CONDENSIBLE
CONDENSING
CONDENSITY
CONDER
CONDESCEND
CONDESCENDER
CONDESCENDING
CONDESCENSION
CONDESCENT
CONDICTION
CONDICTIOUS
CONDIDDLE
CONDIDDLED
CONDIDDLING
CONDIGN
CONDIGNITY
CONDIGNLY
CONDIGNNESS
CONDIMENT
CONDIMENTAL
CONDIMENTARY
CONDIMENTS
CONDISCIPLE
CONDITE
CONDITION
CONDITIONAL
CONDITIONALLY
CONDITIONATE
CONDITIONED
CONDITIONER
CONDITIONING
CONDIVISION
CONDOG
CONDOLATORY
CONDOLE
CONDOLED
CONDOLEMENT
CONDOLENCE
CONDOLENT
CONDOLER
CONDOLING
CONDOLINGLY
CONDOMINATE
CONDOMINIUM
CONDONANCE
CONDONATION
CONDONATIVE
CONDONE
CONDONED
CONDONER
CONDONING
CONDOR
CONDOTTIERE
CONDOTTIERI
CONDUCE
CONDUCED
CONDUCEMENT
CONDUCENT
CONDUCER
CONDUCIBLE
CONDUCIBLY
CONDUCING
CONDUCIVE
CONDUCT
CONDUCTA
CONDUCTANCE
CONDUCTED
CONDUCTIBLE
CONDUCTILITY
CONDUCTING

CONDUCTIO
CONDUCTION
CONDUCTIONAL
CONDUCTIVE
CONDUCTIVELY
CONDUCTIVITY
CONDUCTOR
CONDUCTORS
CONDUCTORY
CONDUCTRESS
CONDUCTUS
CONDUIT
CONDUPLICATE
CONDURANGIN
CONDYLAR
CONDYLARTH
CONDYLE
CONDYLION
CONDYLOID
CONDYLOMA
CONDYLOMATA
CONDYLOPOD
CONDYLOS
CONDYLURE
CONE
CONED
CONEEN
CONEFLOWER
CONEHEAD
CONEINE
CONELET
CONELRAD
CONEMAKER
CONEMAKING
CONENOSE
CONEPATE
CONEPATL
CONER
CONES
CONESSINE
CONEY
CONEYS
CONFAB
CONFABBED
CONFABBING
CONFABULAR
CONFABULATE
CONFABULATED
CONFABULATING
CONFACT
CONFARREATE
CONFARREATED
CONFATED
CONFECT
CONFECTION
CONFECTIONARIES
CONFECTIONARY
CONFECTIONER
CONFECTIONERIES
CONFECTIONERY
CONFECTORY
CONFECTURE
CONFEDER
CONFEDERACIES
CONFEDERACY
CONFEDERAL
CONFEDERALIST
CONFEDERATE
CONFEDERATED
CONFEDERATING
CONFEDERATIO
CONFEDERATION
CONFEDERATOR
CONFER
CONFEREE
CONFERENCE
CONFERENTIAL

CONFERMENT
CONFERRABLE
CONFERRED
CONFERREE
CONFERRER
CONFERRING
CONFERTED
CONFERVA
CONFERVAE
CONFERVAL
CONFERVAS
CONFERVOID
CONFERVOUS
CONFESS
CONFESSANT
CONFESSARIUS
CONFESSARY
CONFESSED
CONFESSEDLY
CONFESSER
CONFESSING
CONFESSION
CONFESSIONAL
CONFESSOR
CONFESSORY
CONFETTI
CONFIDANT
CONFIDANTE
CONFIDE
CONFIDED
CONFIDENCE
CONFIDENCES
CONFIDENCY
CONFIDENT
CONFIDENTIAL
CONFIDENTIALLY
CONFIDENTLY
CONFIDER
CONFIDING
CONFIDINGLY
CONFIGURAL
CONFIGURATE
CONFIGURATED
CONFIGURATING
CONFIGURATION
CONFIGURE
CONFIGURED
CONFIGURING
CONFINABLE
CONFINE
CONFINEABLE
CONFINED
CONFINEDLY
CONFINEDNESS
CONFINELESS
CONFINEMENT
CONFINER
CONFINES
CONFINING
CONFINITY
CONFIRM
CONFIRMABLE
CONFIRMAND
CONFIRMATION
CONFIRMATIVE
CONFIRMATORY
CONFIRMED
CONFIRMEDLY
CONFIRMEE
CONFIRMER
CONFIRMING
CONFIRMINGLY
CONFIRMITY
CONFIRMMENT
CONFIRMOR
CONFISCABLE
CONFISCATE

CONFISCATED
CONFISCATION
CONFISCATOR
CONFISCATORY
CONFISERIE
CONFISK
CONFISTICATING
CONFITENT
CONFITEOR
CONFITURE
CONFIX
CONFIXED
CONFIXING
CONFLAB
CONFLAGRANT
CONFLAGRATE
CONFLAGRATED
CONFLAGRATING
CONFLAGRATION
CONFLAGRATIVE
CONFLAGRATOR
CONFLATE
CONFLATED
CONFLATING
CONFLATION
CONFLICT
CONFLICTED
CONFLICTING
CONFLICTION
CONFLICTIVE
CONFLICTORY
CONFLICTS
CONFLOW
CONFLUENCE
CONFLUENT
CONFLUX
CONFLUXIBLE
CONFOCAL
CONFORM
CONFORMABLE
CONFORMABLY
CONFORMAL
CONFORMANCE
CONFORMANT
CONFORMATE
CONFORMATION
CONFORMATOR
CONFORMED
CONFORMER
CONFORMING
CONFORMIST
CONFORMITIES
CONFORMITY
CONFOUND
CONFOUNDED
CONFOUNDEDLY
CONFOUNDER
CONFOUNDING
CONFRATER
CONFRATERNAL
CONFRATERNITIES
CONFRATERNITY
CONFRERE
CONFRONT
CONFRONTAL
CONFRONTED
CONFRONTER
CONFRONTING
CONFRONTMENT
CONFUSABLE
CONFUSABLY
CONFUSE
CONFUSED
CONFUSEDLY
CONFUSEDNESS
CONFUSING
CONFUSINGLY

CONFUSION
CONFUSIONAL
CONFUSTICATE
CONFUTATION
CONFUTATIVE
CONFUTE
CONFUTED
CONFUTER
CONFUTING
CONGE
CONGEABLE
CONGEAL
CONGEALABLE
CONGEALED
CONGEALER
CONGEALING
CONGEALMENT
CONGED
CONGEE
CONGEING
CONGELATION
CONGENER
CONGENERACY
CONGENERIC
CONGENERICAL
CONGENEROUS
CONGENETIC
CONGENIAL
CONGENIALITY
CONGENIALIZE
CONGENIALLY
CONGENITAL
CONGENITALLY
CONGEON
CONGER
CONGEREE
CONGERIE
CONGERIES
CONGERY
CONGESSION
CONGEST
CONGESTED
CONGESTION
CONGESTIVE
CONGIARIES
CONGIARY
CONGIUS
CONGLACIATE
CONGLOBATE
CONGLOBATED
CONGLOBATELY
CONGLOBATING
CONGLOBATION
CONGLOBE
CONGLOBED
CONGLOBING
CONGLOBULATE
CONGLOMERATE
CONGLOMERATED
CONGLOMERATIC
CONGLOMERATING
CONGLOMERATION
CONGLUTIN
CONGLUTINANT
CONGLUTINATE
CONGLUTINATED
CONGLUTINATING
CONGO
CONGONI
CONGOU
CONGRATULANT
CONGRATULATE
CONGRATULATED
CONGRATULATING
CONGRATULATION
CONGREE
CONGREET

CONGREGABLE
CONGREGANIST
CONGREGANT
CONGREGATE
CONGREGATED
CONGREGATING
CONGREGATION
CONGREGATIVE
CONGREGATOR
CONGRESS
CONGRESSER
CONGRESSIONAL
CONGRESSIST
CONGRESSIVE
CONGRESSMAN
CONGRESSMEN
CONGRESSWOMAN
CONGRESSWOMEN
CONGRIO
CONGROID
CONGRUE
CONGRUENCE
CONGRUENCIES
CONGRUENCY
CONGRUENT
CONGRUENTIAL
CONGRUENTLY
CONGRUISM
CONGRUIST
CONGRUISTIC
CONGRUITIES
CONGRUITY
CONGRUOUS
CONGRUOUSLY
CONHYDRIN
CONHYDRINE
CONIC
CONICAL
CONICALITY
CONICALLY
CONICALNESS
CONICEIN
CONICEINE
CONICHALCITE
CONICINE
CONICITY
CONICLE
CONICOID
CONICOPOLY
CONICS
CONIDIA
CONIDIAL
CONIDIAN
CONIDIOID
CONIDIOPHORE
CONIDIOSPORE
CONIDIUM
CONIES
CONIFER
CONIFERIN
CONIFEROUS
CONIFERS
CONIFICATION
CONIFORM
CONIINE
CONIMA
CONIMENE
CONIN
CONING
CONIOLOGY
CONIROSTER
CONIROSTRAL
CONIUM
CONJECT
CONJECTIVE
CONJECTURAL
CONJECTURALLY

CONJECTURE
CONJECTURED
CONJECTURER
CONJECTURING
CONJEE
CONJOBBLE
CONJOIN
CONJOINED
CONJOINER
CONJOINING
CONJOINT
CONJOINTLY
CONJOINTNESS
CONJON
CONJUBILANT
CONJUGABLE
CONJUGACY
CONJUGAL
CONJUGALITY
CONJUGALLY
CONJUGANT
CONJUGATA
CONJUGATE
CONJUGATED
CONJUGATING
CONJUGATION
CONJUGATIVE
CONJUGATOR
CONJUGIAL
CONJUGIUM
CONJUNCT
CONJUNCTION
CONJUNCTIVAE
CONJUNCTIVAL
CONJUNCTIVAS
CONJUNCTIVE
CONJUNCTIVELY
CONJUNCTLY
CONJUNCTUR
CONJUNCTURAL
CONJUNCTURE
CONJURATION
CONJURATOR
CONJURE
CONJURED
CONJURER
CONJURING
CONJUROR
CONJURY
CONK
CONKER
CONKERS
CONKY
CONN
CONNACH
CONNARACEOUS
CONNARITE
CONNASCENCY
CONNASCENT
CONNATAL
CONNATE
CONNATELY
CONNATENESS
CONNATION
CONNATURAL
CONNATURALLY
CONNATURE
CONNECT
CONNECTED
CONNECTER
CONNECTING
CONNECTION
CONNECTIONAL
CONNECTIVAL
CONNECTIVE
CONNECTIVELY
CONNECTIVITY

CONNECTOR
CONNED
CONNELLITE
CONNER
CONNEX
CONNEXES
CONNEXION
CONNEXITIES
CONNEXITY
CONNEXIVA
CONNEXIVE
CONNEXIVUM
CONNEXUS
CONNING
CONNIPTION
CONNIVANCE
CONNIVANCY
CONNIVANT
CONNIVE
CONNIVED
CONNIVENCE
CONNIVENT
CONNIVER
CONNIVING
CONNOISSANCE
CONNOISSEUR
CONNOTATE
CONNOTATION
CONNOTATIVE
CONNOTE
CONNOTED
CONNOTING
CONNOTIVE
CONNOTIVELY
CONNU
CONNUBIAL
CONNUBIALITY
CONNUBIALLY
CONNUBIATE
CONNUBIUM
CONNUMERATE
CONOCLINIUM
CONOCUNEUS
CONODONT
CONOID
CONOIDAL
CONOIDALLY
CONOIDIC
CONOIDICAL
CONOIDICALLY
CONOPID
CONOPLAIN
CONOPODIUM
CONORMAL
CONOSCENTE
CONOSCENTI
CONOSCOPE
CONOURISH
CONPLANE
CONQUASSATE
CONQUEDLE
CONQUER
CONQUERABLE
CONQUERED
CONQUERING
CONQUERINGLY
CONQUEROR
CONQUEST
CONQUIAN
CONQUINAMINE
CONQUININE
CONQUISTADOR
CONQUISTADORES
CONRECTOR
CONRED
CONREY
CONS

CONSACRE
CONSANGUINE
CONSANGUINEOUS
CONSANGUINITY
CONSARCINATE
CONSARN
CONSARNED
CONSCIENCE
CONSCIENT
CONSCIENTIOUS
CONSCIENTIOUSLY
CONSCIENTIOUSNESS
CONSCIONABLE
CONSCIONABLY
CONSCIOUS
CONSCIOUSLY
CONSCIOUSNESS
CONSCIVE
CONSCRIBE
CONSCRIPT
CONSCRIPTION
CONSECRATE
CONSECRATED
CONSECRATER
CONSECRATING
CONSECRATION
CONSECRATIVE
CONSECRATOR
CONSECRATORY
CONSECTARY
CONSECUTE
CONSECUTION
CONSECUTIVE
CONSECUTIVELY
CONSECUTIVENESS
CONSECUTIVES
CONSENSION
CONSENSUAL
CONSENSUALLY
CONSENSUS
CONSENSUSES
CONSENT
CONSENTABLE
CONSENTANT
CONSENTED
CONSENTER
CONSENTFUL
CONSENTFULLY
CONSENTIENCE
CONSENTIENT
CONSENTIENTLY
CONSENTING
CONSENTINGLY
CONSENTIVE
CONSENTMENT
CONSEQUENCE
CONSEQUENT
CONSEQUENTIAL
CONSEQUENTLY
CONSERTAL
CONSERVABLE
CONSERVACY
CONSERVANCIES
CONSERVANCY
CONSERVANT
CONSERVATE
CONSERVATION
CONSERVATIONAL
CONSERVATISM
CONSERVATIST
CONSERVATIVE
CONSERVATIZE
CONSERVATOR
CONSERVATORIES
CONSERVATORY
CONSERVE
CONSERVED

CONSERVER	CONSORT	CONSTRICTED	CONTAGIOUS	CONTENU
CONSERVING	CONSORTABLE	CONSTRICTING	CONTAGIOUSLY	CONTERMINAL
CONSIDER	CONSORTED	CONSTRICTION	CONTAGIOUSNESS	CONTERMINANT
CONSIDERABLE	CONSORTER	CONSTRICTIVE	CONTAGIUM	CONTERMINATE
CONSIDERABLY	CONSORTIA	CONSTRICTOR	CONTAIN	CONTERMINE
CONSIDERANCE	CONSORTIAL	CONSTRINGE	CONTAINABLE	CONTERMINOUS
CONSIDERATE	CONSORTING	CONSTRINGED	CONTAINED	CONTESSA
CONSIDERATELY	CONSORTION	CONSTRINGENT	CONTAINER	CONTEST
CONSIDERATENESS	CONSORTISM	CONSTRINGING	CONTAINING	CONTESTABLE
CONSIDERATION	CONSORTIUM	CONSTRUABLE	CONTAINMENT	CONTESTANT
CONSIDERATOR	CONSOUND	CONSTRUCT	CONTAMINABLE	CONTESTANTS
CONSIDERED	CONSPECIES	CONSTRUCTED	CONTAMINANT	CONTESTATION
CONSIDERER	CONSPECIFIC	CONSTRUCTER	CONTAMINATE	CONTESTER
CONSIDERING	CONSPECT	CONSTRUCTION	CONTAMINATED	CONTEUR
CONSIGN	CONSPECTUS	CONSTRUCTIVE	CONTAMINATING	CONTEXT
CONSIGNABLE	CONSPECTUSES	CONSTRUCTIVELY	CONTAMINATION	CONTEXTUAL
CONSIGNATARY	CONSPERSE	CONSTRUCTIVENESS	CONTAMINATIVE	CONTEXTUALLY
CONSIGNATION	CONSPERSION	CONSTRUCTOR	CONTAMINATOR	CONTEXTURAL
CONSIGNED	CONSPICUITY	CONSTRUE	CONTAMINOUS	CONTEXTURE
CONSIGNEE	CONSPICUOUS	CONSTRUED	CONTANGO	CONTEXTURED
CONSIGNER	CONSPICUOUSLY	CONSTRUER	CONTE	CONTICENT
CONSIGNIFIED	CONSPIRACIES	CONSTRUING	CONTECK	CONTIGNATION
CONSIGNIFY	CONSPIRACY	CONSTUPRATE	CONTECT	CONTIGUITIES
CONSIGNIFYING	CONSPIRANT	CONSUETE	CONTECTION	CONTIGUITY
CONSIGNING	CONSPIRATIVE	CONSUETUDE	CONTEK	CONTIGUOUS
CONSIGNMENT	CONSPIRATOR	CONSUL	CONTEKE	CONTIGUOUSLY
CONSIGNOR	CONSPIRE	CONSULAGE	CONTEMN	CONTINENCE
CONSILIARY	CONSPIRED	CONSULAR	CONTEMNED	CONTINENCY
CONSILIENCE	CONSPIRER	CONSULARITY	CONTEMNER	CONTINENT
CONSILIENT	CONSPIRING	CONSULARY	CONTEMNING	CONTINENTAL
CONSIMILAR	CONSPIRINGLY	CONSULATE	CONTEMNINGLY	CONTINENTLY
CONSIMILATE	CONSPUE	CONSULSHIP	CONTEMNOR	CONTINEU
CONSIMILATED	CONSTABLE	CONSULT	CONTEMPER	CONTINGENCY
CONSIMILATING	CONSTABULAR	CONSULTANT	CONTEMPERATE	CONTINGENT
CONSIST	CONSTABULARIES	CONSULTARY	CONTEMPLABLE	CONTINGENTLY
CONSISTENCE	CONSTABULARY	CONSULTATION	CONTEMPLAMEN	CONTINUABLE
CONSISTENCIES	CONSTANCE	CONSULTATIVE	CONTEMPLANCE	CONTINUAL
CONSISTENCY	CONSTANCY	CONSULTATORY	CONTEMPLANT	CONTINUALITY
CONSISTENT	CONSTANT	CONSULTEE	CONTEMPLATE	CONTINUALLY
CONSISTENTLY	CONSTANTAN	CONSULTER	CONTEMPLATED	CONTINUANCE
CONSISTORIAL	CONSTANTLY	CONSULTING	CONTEMPLATING	CONTINUANDO
CONSISTORIAN	CONSTAT	CONSULTIVE	CONTEMPLATION	CONTINUANT
CONSISTORY	CONSTATATION	CONSULTOR	CONTEMPLATIST	CONTINUANTLY
CONSOCIATE	CONSTATE	CONSULTORY	CONTEMPLATIVE	CONTINUATE
CONSOCIATED	CONSTATORY	CONSUMABLE	CONTEMPLATIVELY	CONTINUATELY
CONSOCIATING	CONSTELLATE	CONSUME	CONTEMPLATOR	CONTINUATION
CONSOCIATION	CONSTELLATED	CONSUMED	CONTEMPORANEOUS	CONTINUATIVE
CONSOCIATIVE	CONSTELLATING	CONSUMEDLY	CONTEMPORARY	CONTINUATOR
CONSOCIES	CONSTELLATION	CONSUMELESS	CONTEMPORIZE	CONTINUE
CONSOL	CONSTELLATORY	CONSUMER	CONTEMPORIZED	CONTINUED
CONSOLABLE	CONSTER	CONSUMERS	CONTEMPORIZING	CONTINUEDLY
CONSOLATE	CONSTERNATE	CONSUMING	CONTEMPT	CONTINUER
CONSOLATION	CONSTERNATED	CONSUMINGLY	CONTEMPTFUL	CONTINUING
CONSOLATORY	CONSTERNATING	CONSUMMATE	CONTEMPTIBLE	CONTINUIST
CONSOLATRIX	CONSTERNATION	CONSUMMATED	CONTEMPTIBLENESS	CONTINUITY
CONSOLE	CONSTIPATE	CONSUMMATELY	CONTEMPTIBLY	CONTINUO
CONSOLED	CONSTIPATED	CONSUMMATING	CONTEMPTUOUS	CONTINUOUS
CONSOLER	CONSTIPATING	CONSUMMATION	CONTEMPTUOUSLY	CONTINUOUSLY
CONSOLIDANT	CONSTIPATION	CONSUMMATIVE	CONTEND	CONTINUUM
CONSOLIDATE	CONSTITUENCIES	CONSUMMATOR	CONTENDED	CONTISE
CONSOLIDATED	CONSTITUENCY	CONSUMMATORY	CONTENDER	CONTLINE
CONSOLIDATING	CONSTITUENT	CONSUMPT	CONTENDING	CONTO
CONSOLIDATOR	CONSTITUTE	CONSUMPTED	CONTENDINGLY	CONTOISE
CONSOLING	CONSTITUTED	CONSUMPTIBLE	CONTENT	CONTORNIATE
CONSOLS	CONSTITUTER	CONSUMPTION	CONTENTATION	CONTORNIATES
CONSOLUTE	CONSTITUTING	CONSUMPTIVE	CONTENTED	CONTORNO
CONSOMME	CONSTITUTION	CONSUTE	CONTENTEDLY	CONTORSIVE
CONSONANCE	CONSTITUTIONAL	CONTABESCENT	CONTENTFUL	CONTORT
CONSONANCY	CONSTITUTIVE	CONTACT	CONTENTING	CONTORTED
CONSONANT	CONSTITUTIVELY	CONTACTOR	CONTENTION	CONTORTEDLY
CONSONANTAL	CONSTITUTOR	CONTACTUAL	CONTENTIONAL	CONTORTING
CONSONANTIC	CONSTRAIN	CONTACTUALLY	CONTENTIOUS	CONTORTION
CONSONANTISM	CONSTRAINED	CONTAGIA	CONTENTLESS	CONTORTIONAL
CONSONANTIZE	CONSTRAINER	CONTAGION	CONTENTLY	CONTORTIONED
CONSONANTLY	CONSTRAINING	CONTAGIONED	CONTENTMENT	CONTORTIONIST
CONSONATE	CONSTRAINT	CONTAGIONIST	CONTENTNESS	CONTORTIVE
CONSONOUS	CONSTRICT	CONTAGIOSITY	CONTENTS	CONTOS

CONTOUR	CONTRIBUTIVE	CONVENER	CONVEYANCING	COOBA
CONTOURED	CONTRIBUTOR	CONVENERIES	CONVEYED	COOBAH
CONTOURING	CONTRIBUTORIES	CONVENERY	CONVEYER	COOCH
CONTRABAND	CONTRIBUTORY	CONVENIENCE	CONVEYING	COODLE
CONTRABASS	CONTRIST	CONVENIENCED	CONVEYOR	COOED
CONTRABASSO	CONTRITE	CONVENIENCY	CONVICINITY	COOEE
CONTRACIVIL	CONTRITELY	CONVENIENT	CONVICT	COOEED
CONTRACT	CONTRITENESS	CONVENIENTLY	CONVICTABLE	COOEEING
CONTRACTANT	CONTRITION	CONVENING	CONVICTED	COOER
CONTRACTED	CONTRITURATE	CONVENT	CONVICTIBLE	COOEY
CONTRACTEDLY	CONTRIVABLE	CONVENTICAL	CONVICTING	COOEYED
CONTRACTER	CONTRIVANCE	CONVENTICLE	CONVICTION	COOEYING
CONTRACTIBLE	CONTRIVANCY	CONVENTICLER	CONVICTIONAL	COOF
CONTRACTILE	CONTRIVE	CONVENTION	CONVICTISM	COOING
CONTRACTILITY	CONTRIVED	CONVENTIONAL	CONVICTIVE	COOINGLY
CONTRACTING	CONTRIVER	CONVENTIONALIST	CONVICTIVELY	COOJA
CONTRACTION	CONTRIVING	CONVENTIONALITY	CONVICTOR	COOK
CONTRACTIVE	CONTROL	CONVENTIONALIZE	CONVINCE	COOKABLE
CONTRACTOR	CONTROLLABLE	CONVENTIONALIZED	CONVINCED	COOKBOOK
CONTRACTUAL	CONTROLLED	CONVENTIONALIZING	CONVINCEMENT	COOKED
CONTRACTURE	CONTROLLER	CONVENTIONALLY	CONVINCER	COOKEE
CONTRACTURED	CONTROLLING	CONVENTIONER	CONVINCIBLE	COOKEITE
CONTRADA	CONTROVERSIAL	CONVENTO	CONVINCING	COOKER
CONTRADANCE	CONTROVERSIALIST	CONVENTUAL	CONVINCINGLY	COOKERIES
CONTRADE	CONTROVERSIALLY	CONVERGE	CONVITE	COOKERY
CONTRADICT	CONTROVERSIES	CONVERGED	CONVITO	COOKEY
CONTRADICTER	CONTROVERSY	CONVERGENCE	CONVIVAL	COOKHOUSE
CONTRADICTION	CONTROVERT	CONVERGENCY	CONVIVE	COOKIE
CONTRADICTIVE	CONTROVERTED	CONVERGENT	CONVIVIAL	COOKIES
CONTRADICTOR	CONTROVERTER	CONVERGING	CONVIVIALIST	COOKING
CONTRADICTORIES	CONTRUDE	CONVERSABLE	CONVIVIALITY	COOKMAID
CONTRADICTORY	CONTUBERNAL	CONVERSABLY	CONVIVIALLY	COOKROOM
CONTRADIVIDE	CONTUBERNIAL	CONVERSANCE	CONVIVIO	COOKSHACK
CONTRAFLOW	CONTUBERNIUM	CONVERSANCY	CONVOCANT	COOKSHOP
CONTRAFOCAL	CONTUMACIES	CONVERSANT	CONVOCATE	COOKSTOVE
CONTRAHENT	CONTUMACIOUS	CONVERSANTLY	CONVOCATED	COOKY
CONTRAIR	CONTUMACITIES	CONVERSATION	CONVOCATING	COOL
CONTRALTI	CONTUMACITY	CONVERSATIONAL	CONVOCATION	COOLABAH
CONTRALTO	CONTUMACY	CONVERSATIONALIST	CONVOCATIVE	COOLAMAN
CONTRALTOS	CONTUMAX	CONVERSATIONALLY	CONVOCATOR	COOLANT
CONTRAMARQUE	CONTUMELIES	CONVERSATIONIST	CONVOKE	COOLED
CONTRAOCTAVE	CONTUMELIOUS	CONVERSATIVE	CONVOKED	COOLEN
CONTRAPLEX	CONTUMELY	CONVERSE	CONVOKER	COOLER
CONTRAPONEND	CONTUND	CONVERSED	CONVOKING	COOLEST
CONTRAPOSE	CONTUNE	CONVERSELY	CONVOLUTE	COOLEY
CONTRAPOSITA	CONTURB	CONVERSER	CONVOLUTED	COOLHEADED
CONTRAPTION	CONTURBATION	CONVERSIBLE	CONVOLUTELY	COOLHEADEDLY
CONTRAPTIOUS	CONTUSE	CONVERSING	CONVOLUTING	COOLHOUSE
CONTRAPUNTAL	CONTUSED	CONVERSION	CONVOLUTION	COOLIBAH
CONTRARIANT	CONTUSING	CONVERSIONAL	CONVOLUTIVE	COOLIE
CONTRARIES	CONTUSION	CONVERSIVE	CONVOLVE	COOLIES
CONTRARIETY	CONTUSIONED	CONVERSO	CONVOLVED	COOLIMAN
CONTRARILY	CONTUSIVE	CONVERT	CONVOLVING	COOLING
CONTRARINESS	CONUBIUM	CONVERTED	CONVOLVULAD	COOLINGLY
CONTRARIOUS	CONULE	CONVERTEND	CONVOLVULIN	COOLINGNESS
CONTRARIOUSLY	CONUNDRUM	CONVERTER	CONVOLVULUS	COOLISH
CONTRARIWISE	CONURBATION	CONVERTIBLE	CONVOY	COOLLY
CONTRARY	CONURE	CONVERTIBLY	CONVOYED	COOLNESS
CONTRAST	CONUS	CONVERTING	CONVOYING	COOLTH
CONTRASTABLE	CONUSES	CONVERTISE	CONVULSANT	COOLUNG
CONTRASTED	CONVALESCE	CONVERTITE	CONVULSE	COOLWEED
CONTRASTING	CONVALESCED	CONVERTIVE	CONVULSED	COOLWORT
CONTRASTIVE	CONVALESCENT	CONVERTOR	CONVULSEDLY	COOLY
CONTRASTY	CONVALESCING	CONVETH	CONVULSING	COOM
CONTRATE	CONVALLARIN	CONVEX	CONVULSION	COOMB
CONTRAVENE	CONVECT	CONVEXED	CONVULSIONAL	COOMBE
CONTRAVENED	CONVECTION	CONVEXEDLY	CONVULSIVE	COOMY
CONTRAVENER	CONVECTIONAL	CONVEXEDNESS	CONVULSIVELY	COON
CONTRAVENING	CONVECTIVE	CONVEXITIES	CONVULSIVENESS	COONCAN
CONTRAVENTION	CONVECTIVELY	CONVEXITY	CONY	COONER
CONTRAYERVA	CONVECTOR	CONVEXLY	CONYCATCHER	COONIER
CONTREDANSE	CONVELL	CONVEXNESS	CONYGER	COONIEST
CONTRETEMPS	CONVENABLE	CONVEY	CONYNGE	COONILY
CONTRIBUTE	CONVENABLY	CONVEYABLE	CONYRIN	COONJINE
CONTRIBUTED	CONVENANCE	CONVEYAL	CONYRINE	COONROOT
CONTRIBUTING	CONVENE	CONVEYANCE	COO	COONSKIN
CONTRIBUTION	CONVENED	CONVEYANCER	COOB	COONTAIL

COONTIE
COONY
COOP
COOPED
COOPER
COOPERAGE
COOPERANCY
COOPERANT
COOPERATE
COOPERATED
COOPERATING
COOPERATION
COOPERATIVE
COOPERATIVELY
COOPERATOR
COOPERED
COOPERIES
COOPERING
COOPERY
COOPING
COOPT
COOPTATE
COOPTATION
COOPTATIVE
COOPTION
COOPTIVE
COORDAIN
COORDINAL
COORDINATE
COORDINATED
COORDINATELY
COORDINATING
COORDINATION
COORDINATIVE
COORDINATOR
COORDINATORY
COOREE
COORIE
COOSE
COOSER
COOSIFY
COOST
COOT
COOTCH
COOTER
COOTFOOT
COOTHAY
COOTIE
COOTY
COP
COPA
COPACETIC
COPAENE
COPAIBA
COPAIBIC
COPAIN
COPAIVA
COPAL
COPALCHE
COPALCHI
COPALCOCOTE
COPALINE
COPALITE
COPALJOCOTE
COPALM
COPARCENARY
COPARCENER
COPARCENY
COPART
COPARTNER
COPARTNERY
COPASETIC
COPATAIN
COPE
COPECK
COPED
COPEI

COPELIDINE
COPEMAN
COPEMATE
COPEN
COPEPOD
COPEPODAN
COPEPODOUS
COPER
COPEROSE
COPERTA
COPESETIC
COPESETTIC
COPESMATE
COPESTONE
COPHASAL
COPHOSIS
COPIA
COPIAPITE
COPIER
COPIHUE
COPING
COPIOSITY
COPIOUS
COPIOUSLY
COPIOUSNESS
COPIS
COPIST
COPLA
COPLANAR
COPLANARITY
COPOLYMER
COPOLYMERIZE
COPOLYMERIZED
COPOLYMERIZING
COPPA
COPPAELITE
COPPE
COPPED
COPPER
COPPERAH
COPPERAS
COPPERBOTTOM
COPPERED
COPPERHEAD
COPPERING
COPPERIZATION
COPPERIZE
COPPERLEAF
COPPERNOSE
COPPERNOSED
COPPERPLATE
COPPERPROOF
COPPERSKIN
COPPERSMITH
COPPERWING
COPPERWORKS
COPPERY
COPPET
COPPICE
COPPICED
COPPICING
COPPIN
COPPING
COPPLE
COPPLED
COPPRA
COPPY
COPRA
COPRAEMIA
COPRAEMIC
COPRAH
COPREMIA
COPREMIC
COPRODAEUM
COPROLAGNIA
COPROLAGNIST
COPROLALIA

COPROLALIAC
COPROLITE
COPROLITH
COPROLITIC
COPROLOGY
COPROPHAGAN
COPROPHAGIA
COPROPHAGIST
COPROPHAGOUS
COPROPHAGY
COPROPHILIA
COPROPHILIAC
COPROPHILIC
COPROPHILISM
COPROPHILOUS
COPROPHYTE
COPROSE
COPROSMA
COPROSTASIA
COPROSTASIS
COPROSTEROL
COPROZOIC
COPS
COPSE
COPSEWOOD
COPSEWOODED
COPSING
COPSY
COPTER
COPULA
COPULABLE
COPULAE
COPULAR
COPULARIUM
COPULAS
COPULATE
COPULATED
COPULATING
COPULATION
COPULATIVE
COPULATIVELY
COPULATORY
COPUNCTAL
COPUS
COPY
COPYBOOK
COPYCAT
COPYDESK
COPYGRAPH
COPYGRAPHED
COPYHOLD
COPYHOLDER
COPYHOLDING
COPYING
COPYIST
COPYMAN
COPYREAD
COPYREADER
COPYRIGHT
COPYRIGHTER
COPYWRITER
COQUE
COQUECIGRUE
COQUELICOT
COQUELUCHE
COQUET
COQUETOON
COQUETRIES
COQUETRY
COQUETTE
COQUETTED
COQUETTING
COQUETTISH
COQUETTISHLY
COQUILLE
COQUIMBITE
COQUIN

COQUINA
COQUITA
COQUITO
COR
CORACIIFORM
CORACINE
CORACLE
CORACLER
CORACOCOSTAL
CORACOHYOID
CORACOID
CORACOIDAL
CORADICATE
CORAGIO
CORAH
CORAL
CORALBERRY
CORALFLOWER
CORALIST
CORALITA
CORALLA
CORALLIC
CORALLIFORM
CORALLIN
CORALLINE
CORALLITE
CORALLOID
CORALLOIDAL
CORALLUM
CORALROOT
CORALWORT
CORAM
CORANCE
CORAVECA
CORB
CORBAN
CORBE
CORBEAU
CORBEIL
CORBEL
CORBELED
CORBELING
CORBELLED
CORBELLING
CORBET
CORBICULA
CORBICULAE
CORBICULATE
CORBIE
CORBINA
CORBLEU
CORBOVINUM
CORBULA
CORCASS
CORCHAT
CORCHORUS
CORCIR
CORCOPALI
CORD
CORDAGE
CORDAITALEAN
CORDAITEAN
CORDATE
CORDATELY
CORDAX
CORDE
CORDED
CORDEL
CORDELIERE
CORDELLE
CORDELLED
CORDELLING
CORDER
CORDIAL
CORDIALITIES
CORDIALITY
CORDIALLY

CORDIALNESS
CORDICEPS
CORDICOLE
CORDIFORM
CORDIGERI
CORDILLERA
CORDILLERAN
CORDING
CORDITE
CORDITIS
CORDLEAF
CORDMAKER
CORDOBA
CORDOBAN
CORDON
CORDONNET
CORDOVAN
CORDS
CORDUROY
CORDUROYED
CORDUROYING
CORDWAIN
CORDWAINER
CORDWAINERY
CORDWOOD
CORDY
CORE
COREBOX
CORED
COREDUCTASE
COREGONID
COREGONINE
COREGONOID
COREID
COREIGN
COREIGNER
CORELATION
CORELATIVE
CORELATIVELY
CORELESS
CORELIGIONIST
CORELLA
CORELYSIS
COREMAKER
COREMAKING
COREMIUM
COREOMETER
COREOPSIS
COREPLASTIC
COREPLASTY
CORER
CORESIDUAL
CORESPONDENT
CORETOMY
CORF
CORGE
CORIA
CORIACEOUS
CORIAL
CORIAMYRTIN
CORIANDER
CORIAUS
CORIIN
CORINDON
CORING
CORINNE
CORINTH
CORIUM
CORK
CORKAGE
CORKBOARD
CORKE
CORKED
CORKER
CORKIER
CORKIEST
CORKINESS

CORKING	CORNFLOOR	COROLLITIC	CORPUSCLE	CORROBOREE
CORKIR	CORNFLOWER	CORONA	CORPUSCULAR	CORROBOREED
CORKITE	CORNGROWER	CORONACH	CORPUSCULE	CORROBOREEING
CORKLINE	CORNHUSK	CORONAD	CORRADE	CORROBORI
CORKMAKER	CORNHUSKER	CORONADITE	CORRADED	CORRODE
CORKSCREW	CORNHUSKING	CORONAE	CORRADIAL	CORRODED
CORKSCREWY	CORNIC	CORONAGRAPH	CORRADIATE	CORRODENT
CORKWING	CORNICE	CORONAL	CORRADIATED	CORRODER
CORKWOOD	CORNICED	CORONALE	CORRADIATING	CORRODIARY
CORKY	CORNICING	CORONALED	CORRADIATION	CORRODIBLE
CORM	CORNICLE	CORONALLED	CORRADING	CORRODING
CORMEL	CORNICULATE	CORONALLY	CORRAL	CORROSIBLE
CORMI	CORNICULER	CORONAMEN	CORRALLED	CORROSION
CORMIDIUM	CORNICULUM	CORONARY	CORRALLING	CORROSIONAL
CORMOID	CORNIER	CORONAS	CORRASION	CORROSIVE
CORMOPHYTE	CORNIEST	CORONATE	CORRASIVE	CORROSIVED
CORMOPHYTIC	CORNIFIC	CORONATED	CORREAL	CORROSIVELY
CORMORANT	CORNIFIED	CORONATION	CORREALITY	CORROSIVING
CORMOUS	CORNIFORM	CORONATORIAL	CORRECT	CORROSIVITY
CORMUS	CORNIGEROUS	CORONENE	CORRECTABLE	CORRUGATE
CORN	CORNIN	CORONER	CORRECTANT	CORRUGATED
CORNACEOUS	CORNING	CORONERSHIP	CORRECTED	CORRUGATING
CORNADA	CORNIPLUME	CORONET	CORRECTEDNESS	CORRUGATION
CORNAGE	CORNLAND	CORONETED	CORRECTIBLE	CORRUGATOR
CORNAMUTE	CORNLOFT	CORONETTED	CORRECTIFY	CORRUMP
CORNBALL	CORNMASTER	CORONETTEE	CORRECTING	CORRUMPABLE
CORNBELL	CORNMEAL	CORONETTY	CORRECTINGLY	CORRUP
CORNBERRY	CORNMONGER	CORONIFORM	CORRECTION	CORRUPABLE
CORNBIN	CORNO	CORONILLIN	CORRECTIONAL	CORRUPT
CORNBIND	CORNOPEAN	CORONILLO	CORRECTIONER	CORRUPTED
CORNBINKS	CORNPIPE	CORONION	CORRECTITUDE	CORRUPTEDLY
CORNBIRD	CORNRICK	CORONITIS	CORRECTIVE	CORRUPTER
CORNBOLE	CORNROOT	CORONIUM	CORRECTIVELY	CORRUPTFUL
CORNBOTTLE	CORNSACK	CORONIZE	CORRECTLY	CORRUPTIBLE
CORNBRASH	CORNSTALK	CORONOFACIAL	CORRECTNESS	CORRUPTIBLY
CORNCOB	CORNSTALKS	CORONOID	CORRECTOR	CORRUPTING
CORNCOCKLE	CORNSTARCH	CORONULE	CORRECTRESS	CORRUPTINGLY
CORNCRACKER	CORNSTOOK	COROPLAST	CORRECTRICE	CORRUPTION
CORNCRAKE	CORNU	COROPLASTAE	CORREGIDOR	CORRUPTIVE
CORNCRIB	CORNUA	COROPLASTIC	CORRELATE	CORRUPTIVELY
CORNCRUSHER	CORNUAL	COROSCOPY	CORRELATED	CORRUPTLESS
CORNCUTTER	CORNUATE	COROTOMY	CORRELATING	CORRUPTLY
CORNCUTTING	CORNUATED	COROZO	CORRELATION	CORRUPTNESS
CORNDODGER	CORNUBIANITE	COROZOS	CORRELATIVE	CORRUPTOR
CORNEA	CORNUCOPIA	CORPORA	CORREO	CORRUPTRESS
CORNEAGEN	CORNUCOPIAN	CORPORAL	CORREPTION	CORSAC
CORNEAL	CORNUCOPIATE	CORPORALE	CORRESOL	CORSAGE
CORNEAS	CORNULE	CORPORALISM	CORRESPOND	CORSAINT
CORNED	CORNULITE	CORPORALITIES	CORRESPONDED	CORSAIR
CORNEIN	CORNUPETE	CORPORALITY	CORRESPONDENCE	CORSAK
CORNEL	CORNUS	CORPORALLY	CORRESPONDENT	CORSE
CORNELIAN	CORNUTE	CORPORALSHIP	CORRESPONDER	CORSELET
CORNEMUSE	CORNUTED	CORPORAS	CORRESPONDING	CORSELETED
CORNEOUS	CORNUTIN	CORPORATE	CORRESPONDINGLY	CORSELETING
CORNER	CORNUTINE	CORPORATELY	CORRIDA	CORSEQUE
CORNERBIND	CORNUTO	CORPORATION	CORRIDO	CORSER
CORNERCAP	CORNUTOS	CORPORATIVE	CORRIDOR	CORSET
CORNERED	CORNWALLIS	CORPORATIVELY	CORRIDORED	CORSETIER
CORNERER	CORNWALLITE	CORPORATOR	CORRIE	CORSETIERE
CORNERING	CORNY	CORPORATURE	CORRIGE	CORSETRY
CORNERPIECE	COROA	CORPOREAL	CORRIGENDUM	CORSETS
CORNERS	COROCLEISIS	CORPOREALIST	CORRIGENT	CORSIE
CORNERSTONE	CORODIARY	CORPOREALITY	CORRIGIBLE	CORSITE
CORNERWAYS	CORODIASTOLE	CORPOREALIZE	CORRIGIBLY	CORSLET
CORNERWISE	CORODIES	CORPOREITY	CORRIVAL	CORSO
CORNET	CORODY	CORPORIFY	CORRIVALITY	CORTA
CORNETCIES	COROJO	CORPOROSITY	CORRIVALRY	CORTARO
CORNETCY	COROL	CORPOSANT	CORRIVATE	CORTEGE
CORNETER	COROLLA	CORPS	CORRIVATION	CORTEISE
CORNETFISH	COROLLACEOUS	CORPSBRUDER	CORRIVE	CORTEX
CORNETIST	COROLLARIAL	CORPSE	CORROBBOREE	CORTICAL
CORNETTER	COROLLARIES	CORPSMEN	CORROBER	CORTICALLY
CORNETTINO	COROLLARY	CORPULENCE	CORROBORANT	CORTICATE
CORNETTIST	COROLLATE	CORPULENCY	CORROBORATE	CORTICATED
CORNETTO	COROLLATED	CORPULENT	CORROBORATED	CORTICATING
CORNEULE	COROLLIFORM	CORPULENTLY	CORROBORATING	CORTICATION
CORNFIELD	COROLLINE	CORPUS	CORROBORATOR	CORTICES

CORTICIFORM
CORTICIFUGAL
CORTICIPETAL
CORTICOLE
CORTICOLINE
CORTICOLOUS
CORTICOSE
CORTICOUS
CORTILE
CORTIN
CORTINA
CORTINAE
CORTINARIOUS
CORTINATE
CORTINE
CORTLANDTITE
CORUCO
CORUNDUM
CORUSCANT
CORUSCATE
CORUSCATED
CORUSCATING
CORUSCATION
CORVEE
CORVER
CORVES
CORVET
CORVETTE
CORVETTO
CORVIFORM
CORVILLOSUM
CORVINA
CORVINE
CORVISER
CORVISOR
CORVOID
CORVUS
CORYBANTIASM
CORYBANTIC
CORYDALIN
CORYDALINE
CORYDALIS
CORYDORA
CORYL
CORYLACEOUS
CORYLET
CORYLIN
CORYMB
CORYMBED
CORYMBIATE
CORYMBIATED
CORYMBIFORM
CORYMBOSE
CORYMBOSELY
CORYMBOUS
CORYPHAEI
CORYPHAENID
CORYPHAENOID
CORYPHAEUS
CORYPHEE
CORYPHENE
CORYPHODONT
CORYPHYLLY
CORYZA
COSALITE
COSAQUE
COSCET
COSCINOMANCY
COSCOROBA
COSEC
COSECANT
COSEISM
COSEISMAL
COSEISMIC
COSESSION
COSET
COSEY

COSH
COSHER
COSHERED
COSHERER
COSHERIES
COSHERING
COSHERY
COSIE
COSIER
COSIEST
COSIGNATORIES
COSIGNATORY
COSIGNER
COSILY
COSINAGE
COSINE
COSINESS
COSINGULAR
COSMECOLOGY
COSMESIS
COSMETIC
COSMETICAL
COSMETICALLY
COSMETICIAN
COSMETICS
COSMETISTE
COSMETOLOGY
COSMIC
COSMICAL
COSMICALITY
COSMICALLY
COSMINE
COSMISM
COSMIST
COSMOCRACY
COSMOCRAT
COSMOCRATIC
COSMOGENESIS
COSMOGENETIC
COSMOGONAL
COSMOGONIC
COSMOGONICAL
COSMOGONIES
COSMOGONIST
COSMOGONIZE
COSMOGONY
COSMOGRAPHER
COSMOGRAPHIC
COSMOGRAPHIES
COSMOGRAPHY
COSMOLABE
COSMOLATRY
COSMOLINE
COSMOLOGIC
COSMOLOGICAL
COSMOLOGICALLY
COSMOLOGIES
COSMOLOGIST
COSMOLOGY
COSMOMETRY
COSMONAUT
COSMOPATHIC
COSMOPLASTIC
COSMOPOIETIC
COSMOPOLICY
COSMOPOLIS
COSMOPOLITAN
COSMOPOLITE
COSMOPOLITIC
COSMORAMA
COSMORAMIC
COSMORGANIC
COSMOS
COSMOSCOPE
COSMOSOPHY
COSMOSPHERE
COSMOTHEISM

COSMOTHEIST
COSMOTHETIC
COSMOTRON
COSMOZOANS
COSMOZOIC
COSMOZOISM
COSO
COSPECIFIC
COSS
COSSAS
COSSET
COSSETTE
COSSETTED
COSSETTING
COSSHEN
COSSIC
COSSID
COSSNENT
COSSYRITE
COST
COSTA
COSTAE
COSTAGE
COSTAL
COSTALGIA
COSTALLY
COSTANDER
COSTAR
COSTARD
COSTARRED
COSTARRING
COSTATE
COSTATED
COSTEAN
COSTEANING
COSTECTOMY
COSTED
COSTEEN
COSTELLATE
COSTER
COSTERMONGER
COSTFUL
COSTIFEROUS
COSTIFORM
COSTING
COSTIVE
COSTIVELY
COSTIVENESS
COSTLESS
COSTLESSNESS
COSTLEW
COSTLIER
COSTLIEST
COSTLINESS
COSTLY
COSTMARY
COSTOAPICAL
COSTOCENTRAL
COSTOCHONDRAL
COSTOCOLIC
COSTOGENIC
COSTOINFERIOR
COSTOPHRENIC
COSTOPLEURAL
COSTOSTERNAL
COSTOTOME
COSTOTOMIES
COSTOTOMY
COSTOXIPHOID
COSTRAIGHT
COSTREL
COSTS
COSTULA
COSTULATION
COSTUME
COSTUMED
COSTUMER

COSTUMERY
COSTUMIC
COSTUMIER
COSTUMIERE
COSTUMING
COSTUMIST
COSTUSROOT
COSWEARER
COSY
COSYMMEDIAN
COT
COTANGENT
COTANGENTIAL
COTARIUS
COTARNIN
COTARNINE
COTBETTY
COTCH
COTE
COTEAU
COTED
COTEEN
COTELE
COTELINE
COTELLER
COTEMPORARY
COTENANCY
COTENANT
COTENURE
COTERELL
COTERIE
COTERMINOUS
COTH
COTHAMORE
COTHE
COTHISH
COTHON
COTHOUSE
COTHURN
COTHURNAL
COTHURNATE
COTHURNED
COTHURNI
COTHURNIAN
COTHURNUS
COTHY
COTICE
COTIDAL
COTILLAGE
COTILLION
COTILLON
COTING
COTINGA
COTINGID
COTINGOID
COTISE
COTISED
COTISING
COTITULAR
COTLAND
COTMAN
COTO
COTOIN
COTONIA
COTONIER
COTORO
COTOROS
COTQUEAN
COTRINE
COTRUSTEE
COTS
COTSET
COTSETLAND
COTSETLE
COTT
COTTA
COTTABUS

COTTAE
COTTAGE
COTTAGED
COTTAGER
COTTAGERS
COTTAR
COTTAS
COTTE
COTTED
COTTER
COTTERED
COTTEREL
COTTERING
COTTERITE
COTTERWAY
COTTID
COTTIER
COTTIFORM
COTTISE
COTTOID
COTTON
COTTONADE
COTTONED
COTTONEE
COTTONEER
COTTONER
COTTONING
COTTONIZE
COTTONMOUTH
COTTONOCRACY
COTTONSEED
COTTONTAIL
COTTONWEED
COTTONWOOD
COTTONY
COTTREL
COTTY
COTUIT
COTULA
COTUNNITE
COTYLA
COTYLAR
COTYLE
COTYLEDON
COTYLEDONAL
COTYLEDONAR
COTYLEDONARY
COTYLEDONOUS
COTYLIGEROUS
COTYLISCUS
COTYLOID
COTYLOIDAL
COTYLOPUBIC
COTYLOSACRAL
COTYLOSAUR
COTYLOSAURIAN
COTYPE
COUAC
COUCAL
COUCH
COUCHANCY
COUCHANT
COUCHE
COUCHED
COUCHEE
COUCHER
COUCHING
COUCHMAKER
COUCHMAKING
COUCHMATE
COUCHY
COUDE
COUDEE
COUGAR
COUGH
COUGHED
COUGHER

COUGHING
COUGHROOT
COUGHWEED
COUGNAR
COUHAGE
COUL
COULAGE
COULD
COULDNA
COULDST
COULE
COULEE
COULEUR
COULIE
COULIER
COULIS
COULISSE
COULOIR
COULOMB
COULOMETER
COULTER
COULTERNEB
COUMA
COUMALIN
COUMARAN
COUMARANE
COUMARATE
COUMARIC
COUMARIN
COUMARONE
COUMAROU
COUMBITE
COUNCIL
COUNCILLOR
COUNCILMAN
COUNCILMEN
COUNCILOR
COUNITE
COUNSEL
COUNSELED
COUNSELEE
COUNSELING
COUNSELLED
COUNSELLING
COUNSELLOR
COUNSELOR
COUNT
COUNTABLE
COUNTABLY
COUNTDOWN
COUNTED
COUNTENANCE
COUNTENANCED
COUNTENANCING
COUNTER
COUNTERACT
COUNTERACTANT
COUNTERACTED
COUNTERACTER
COUNTERACTING
COUNTERACTION
COUNTERACTIVE
COUNTERACTOR
COUNTERAPSE
COUNTERARCH
COUNTERBALANCE
COUNTERBALANCING
COUNTERBLAST
COUNTERBORE
COUNTERBRACE
COUNTERBRAND
COUNTERBUFF
COUNTERCHANGE
COUNTERCHANGED
COUNTERCHARGE
COUNTERCHARGED
COUNTERCHARGING

COUNTERCHECK
COUNTERCLAIM
COUNTERCLAIMING
COUNTERCLOCKWISE
COUNTERCOUPE
COUNTERCURRENT
COUNTERDIKE
COUNTERDRAIN
COUNTEREARTH
COUNTERFEIT
COUNTERFEITER
COUNTERFEITING
COUNTERFLORY
COUNTERFOIL
COUNTERFORT
COUNTERFUGUE
COUNTERGAGE
COUNTERGAGER
COUNTERGAUGE
COUNTERGLOW
COUNTERION
COUNTERIRRITANT
COUNTERLATH
COUNTERLATHED
COUNTERLODE
COUNTERMAN
COUNTERMAND
COUNTERMANDED
COUNTERMARCH
COUNTERMARK
COUNTERMINE
COUNTERMINED
COUNTERMINING
COUNTERMOVED
COUNTERMOVEMEN
COUNTERMOVING
COUNTERMURE
COUNTERPALY
COUNTERPANE
COUNTERPANED
COUNTERPART
COUNTERPLEA
COUNTERPLOT
COUNTERPLOTTED
COUNTERPLOTTING
COUNTERPOINT
COUNTERPOISE
COUNTERPOISED
COUNTERPOISING
COUNTERPOISON
COUNTERPOLE
COUNTERPROOF
COUNTERPROVE
COUNTERPUNCH
COUNTERRATE
COUNTERROLL
COUNTERROUND
COUNTERS
COUNTERSANK
COUNTERSCALE
COUNTERSEA
COUNTERSEAL
COUNTERSENSE
COUNTERSHADE
COUNTERSHAFT
COUNTERSIGN
COUNTERSIGNED
COUNTERSINK
COUNTERSINKING
COUNTERSLOPE
COUNTERSPY
COUNTERSTAIN
COUNTERSTAND
COUNTERSTOCK
COUNTERSTROKE
COUNTERSUN
COUNTERSUNK

COUNTERSUNKEN
COUNTERTAIL
COUNTERTALLY
COUNTERTENOR
COUNTERTERM
COUNTERTIME
COUNTERTURN
COUNTERTYPE
COUNTERVAIL
COUNTERVAILED
COUNTERVAILING
COUNTERVAIR
COUNTERVENE
COUNTERVIEW
COUNTERVOTE
COUNTERWALL
COUNTERWEIGH
COUNTERWEIGHED
COUNTERWEIGHING
COUNTERWEIGHT
COUNTERWHEEL
COUNTERWORD
COUNTERWORK
COUNTESS
COUNTIES
COUNTING
COUNTLESS
COUNTOR
COUNTOUR
COUNTRIES
COUNTRIFIED
COUNTRY
COUNTRYFIED
COUNTRYFOLK
COUNTRYMAN
COUNTRYMEN
COUNTRYSEAT
COUNTRYSIDE
COUNTRYWOMAN
COUNTRYWOMEN
COUNTS
COUNTY
COUP
COUPAGE
COUPE
COUPED
COUPEE
COUPELET
COUPER
COUPLE
COUPLED
COUPLER
COUPLERESS
COUPLET
COUPLETEER
COUPLING
COUPON
COUPS
COUPSTICK
COUPURE
COUR
COURAGE
COURAGEOUS
COURAGEOUSLY
COURAGER
COURANT
COURANTE
COURANTO
COURAP
COURATARI
COURB
COURBARIL
COURBE
COURE
COURGE
COURIDA
COURIE

COURIER
COURIL
COURLAN
COURONNE
COURSE
COURSED
COURSER
COURSES
COURSING
COURT
COURTAL
COURTBRED
COURTBY
COURTCRAFT
COURTEOUS
COURTEOUSLY
COURTEPY
COURTER
COURTESAN
COURTESIES
COURTESY
COURTEZAN
COURTHOUSE
COURTIER
COURTIERLY
COURTIERY
COURTIN
COURTING
COURTLET
COURTLIER
COURTLIEST
COURTLIKE
COURTLINESS
COURTLING
COURTLY
COURTMAN
COURTROOM
COURTS
COURTSHIP
COURTY
COURTYARD
COUS
COUSCOUS
COUSERANITE
COUSIN
COUSINAGE
COUSINHOOD
COUSINLY
COUSINRIES
COUSINRY
COUSINS
COUSINSHIP
COUSINY
COUTEAU
COUTEAUX
COUTEL
COUTELLE
COUTER
COUTH
COUTHE
COUTHIE
COUTHILY
COUTHINESS
COUTHLESS
COUTHLY
COUTHY
COUTIL
COUTILLE
COUTURE
COUTURIER
COUTURIERE
CCUVADE
COUVERT
COUVERTE
COUVEUSE
COUXIA
COUXIO

COVADO
COVALENCE
COVALENCY
COVALENT
COVARIANT
COVARIATION
COVE
COVED
COVELLINE
COVELLITE
COVEN
COVENABLE
COVENABLY
COVENANT
COVENANTAL
COVENANTALLY
COVENANTED
COVENANTEE
COVENANTER
COVENANTING
COVENANTOR
COVENT
COVER
COVERAGE
COVERALLS
COVERCHIEF
COVERCLE
COVERED
COVERER
COVERING
COVERLET
COVERLID
COVERSINE
COVERSLUT
COVERT
COVERTICAL
COVERTLY
COVERTNESS
COVERTURE
COVET
COVETABLE
COVETED
COVETER
COVETING
COVETINGLY
COVETISE
COVETIVENESS
COVETOUS
COVETOUSLY
COVETOUSNESS
COVEY
COVEYS
COVID
COVIDO
COVIN
COVINE
COVING
COVINOUS
COVITE
COVOLUME
COW
COWAGE
COWAL
COWAN
COWARD
COWARDICE
COWARDISH
COWARDLINESS
COWARDLY
COWARDNESS
COWARDY
COWBANE
COWBELL
COWBERRIES
COWBERRY
COWBIND
COWBIRD

COWBOY	COXALGY	CRABWEED	CRAIGMONTITE	CRANIOLOGIST
COWBRUTE	COXARTHRITIS	CRABWOOD	CRAIN	CRANIOLOGY
COWCATCHER	COXBONES	CRACCUS	CRAISEY	CRANIOMETER
COWD	COXCOMB	CRACHOIR	CRAIZEY	CRANIOMETRIC
COWDIE	COXCOMBESS	CRACK	CRAKE	CRANIOMETRY
COWED	COXCOMBICAL	CRACKAJACK	CRAKED	CRANIOPAGUS
COWEEN	COXCOMBRY	CRACKBRAIN	CRAKEFEET	CRANIOPATHIC
COWER	COXCOMBY	CRACKBRAINED	CRAKING	CRANIOPATHY
COWFISH	COXCOMICAL	CRACKDOWN	CRAKOW	CRANIOPHORE
COWFISHES	COXIER	CRACKED	CRAL	CRANIOPLASTY
COWGATE	COXIEST	CRACKER	CRAM	CRANIOSACRAL
COWGIRL	COXITE	CRACKERBERRY	CRAMASIE	CRANIOSCOPY
COWGRAM	COXITIS	CRACKERS	CRAMBAMBULEE	CRANIOSPINAL
COWGRASS	COXOCERITE	CRACKHEMP	CRAMBAMBULI	CRANIOSTOSIS
COWHAGE	COXOCERITIC	CRACKING	CRAMBE	CRANIOTABES
COWHEART	COXODYNIA	CRACKJAW	CRAMBID	CRANIOTOME
COWHEARTED	COXOFEMORAL	CRACKLE	CRAMBLE	CRANIOTOMIES
COWHEEL	COXOPODITE	CRACKLED	CRAMBLY	CRANIOTOMY
COWHERB	COXSWAIN	CRACKLEWARE	CRAMBO	CRANIUM
COWHERD	COXY	CRACKLING	CRAME	CRANIUMS
COWHIDE	COY	CRACKLY	CRAMMED	CRANK
COWHIDED	COYAN	CRACKNEL	CRAMMEL	CRANKBIRD
COWHIDING	COYDOG	CRACKPOT	CRAMMER	CRANKCASE
COWHOUSE	COYISH	CRACKROPE	CRAMMING	CRANKED
COWISH	COYLY	CRACKS	CRAMOISIE	CRANKER
COWITCH	COYNE	CRACKSMAN	CRAMOISY	CRANKERY
COWKEEPER	COYNESS	CRACKSMEN	CRAMP	CRANKIER
COWL	COYNYE	CRACKUP	CRAMPBIT	CRANKIEST
COWLE	COYO	CRACKY	CRAMPED	CRANKILY
COWLED	COYOL	CRACOVIENNE	CRAMPER	CRANKINESS
COWLEECH	COYOS	CRACOWE	CRAMPET	CRANKING
COWLEECHING	COYOTE	CRADDY	CRAMPETTE	CRANKISH
COWLICK	COYOTES	CRADGE	CRAMPFISH	CRANKLE
COWLICKS	COYOTING	CRADLE	CRAMPING	CRANKLED
COWLIKE	COYPOU	CRADLEBOARD	CRAMPIT	CRANKLING
COWLING	COYPU	CRADLECHILD	CRAMPON	CRANKMAN
COWLSTAFF	COYPUS	CRADLED	CRAMPONNEE	CRANKOUS
COWMAN	COYSTREL	CRADLEFELLOW	CRAMPOON	CRANKPIN
COWMEN	COYURE	CRADLELAND	CRAMPS	CRANKS
COWP	COZ	CRADLELIKE	CRAMPY	CRANKSHAFT
COWPATH	COZE	CRADLEMAKER	CRAN	CRANKUM
COWPEA	COZED	CRADLEMAKING	CRANAGE	CRANKY
COWPEN	COZEN	CRADLEMAN	CRANBERRIES	CRANNAGE
COWPER	COZENAGE	CRADLEMATE	CRANBERRY	CRANNEL
COWPERITIS	COZENER	CRADLEMEN	CRANCE	CRANNIED
COWPOX	COZENING	CRADLER	CRANCH	CRANNIES
COWPUNCHER	COZENINGLY	CRADLESIDE	CRANDALL	CRANNOCK
COWQUAKE	COZEY	CRADLESONG	CRANE	CRANNOG
COWR	COZIE	CRADLETIME	CRANEBILL	CRANNOGE
COWRIE	COZIER	CRADLING	CRANED	CRANNOGER
COWRIES	COZIEST	CRAER	CRANEMAN	CRANNY
COWROID	COZILY	CRAFT	CRANER	CRANNYING
COWRY	COZINESS	CRAFTIER	CRANES	CRANREUCH
COWS	COZING	CRAFTIEST	CRANESBILL	CRANSIER
COWSHARD	COZY	CRAFTILY	CRANET	CRANTARA
COWSHARN	CRAAL	CRAFTINESS	CRANEWAY	CRANTS
COWSHED	CRAB	CRAFTLY	CRANEY	CRANY
COWSHOT	CRABBED	CRAFTSMAN	CRANG	CRAP
COWSHUT	CRABBEDLY	CRAFTSMANSHIP	CRANIA	CRAPAUD
COWSKIN	CRABBEDNESS	CRAFTSMASTER	CRANIAD	CRAPAUDINE
COWSLIP	CRABBER	CRAFTSMEN	CRANIAL	CRAPE
COWSLIPPED	CRABBERY	CRAFTSWOMAN	CRANIALLY	CRAPEFISH
COWSON	CRABBIER	CRAFTWORK	CRANIAN	CRAPEHANGER
COWSUCKER	CRABBIEST	CRAFTWORKER	CRANIATE	CRAPETTE
COWTAIL	CRABBING	CRAFTY	CRANIC	CRAPON
COWTHWORT	CRABBISH	CRAG	CRANING	CRAPPER
COWTONGUE	CRABBIT	CRAGGAN	CRANIOCELE	CRAPPIE
COWWEED	CRABBY	CRAGGED	CRANIOCLASIS	CRAPPIES
COWWHEAT	CRABCATCHER	CRAGGEDNESS	CRANIOCLASM	CRAPPIN
COWY	CRABEATER	CRAGGIER	CRANIOCLAST	CRAPPLE
COWYARD	CRABER	CRAGGIEST	CRANIOFACIAL	CRAPPO
COX	CRABFISH	CRAGGINESS	CRANIOGNOMIC	CRAPPY
COXA	CRABHOLE	CRAGGY	CRANIOGNOMY	CRAPS
COXAE	CRABMILL	CRAGSMAN	CRANIOGNOSY	CRAPSHOOTER
COXAL	CRABS	CRAGSMEN	CRANIOGRAPH	CRAPULATE
COXALGIA	CRABSIDLE	CRAICHY	CRANIOGRAPHY	CRAPULENCE
COXALGIC	CRABSTICK	CRAIGHLE	CRANIOLOGICAL	CRAPULENCY

CRAPULENT	CRAYER	CREATIONIST	CREEPY	CREOSOTED
CRAPULOUS	CRAYFISH	CREATIVE	CREESE	CREOSOTER
CRAPULOUSLY	CRAYFISHES	CREATIVELY	CREESH	CREOSOTIC
CRAPWA	CRAYLET	CREATIVENESS	CREESHIE	CREOSOTING
CRAPY	CRAYON	CREATIVITY	CREESHY	CREPANCE
CRAQUELURE	CRAYTHUR	CREATOR	CREIRGIST	CREPE
CRARE	CRAZE	CREATORRHEA	CREMANT	CREPED
CRASES	CRAZED	CREATORSHIP	CREMASTER	CREPEY
CRASH	CRAZEDLY	CREATOTOXISM	CREMASTERIAL	CREPINE
CRASHED	CRAZEDNESS	CREATURAL	CREMASTERIC	CREPINESS
CRASHER	CRAZIER	CREATURE	CREMATE	CREPING
CRASHING	CRAZIES	CREATURELY	CREMATED	CREPITACULA
CRASIS	CRAZIEST	CREBRITY	CREMATING	CREPITACULUM
CRASPEDAL	CRAZILY	CREBROUS	CREMATION	CREPITANT
CRASPEDON	CRAZINESS	CRECHE	CREMATIONISM	CREPITATE
CRASPEDOTAL	CRAZING	CREDDOCK	CREMATIONIST	CREPITATED
CRASPEDOTE	CRAZY	CREDENCE	CREMATOR	CREPITATING
CRASPEDUM	CRAZYCAT	CREDENCIVE	CREMATORIAL	CREPITATION
CRASS	CRAZYWEED	CREDENDA	CREMATORIES	CREPITOUS
CRASSAMENTUM	CREA	CREDENDUM	CREMATORIUM	CREPITUS
CRASSIER	CREACH	CREDENS	CREMATORY	CREPON
CRASSITUDE	CREACHY	CREDENSIVE	CREMBALUM	CREPT
CRASSLY	CREAGH	CREDENT	CREME	CREPUSCLE
CRASSNESS	CREAGHT	CREDENTIAL	CREMERIE	CREPUSCULAR
CRASSULACEOUS	CREAK	CREDENZA	CREMNOPHOBIA	CREPUSCULINE
CRATCH	CREAKER	CREDIBILITY	CREMOCARP	CREPUSCULUM
CRATCHENS	CREAKIER	CREDIBLE	CREMOMETER	CREPY
CRATCHES	CREAKIEST	CREDIBLENESS	CREMOR	CRESAMINE
CRATCHINS	CREAKILY	CREDIBLY	CREMULE	CRESCENDO
CRATE	CREAKINESS	CREDIT	CRENA	CRESCENDOED
CRATED	CREAKING	CREDITABLE	CRENAE	CRESCENDOING
CRATEMAN	CREAKY	CREDITABLY	CRENATE	CRESCENDOS
CRATEMEN	CREAM	CREDITED	CRENATED	CRESCENT
CRATER	CREAMCUPS	CREDITIVE	CRENATELY	CRESCENTADE
CRATERAL	CREAMED	CREDITOR	CRENATION	CRESCENTED
CRATERIFORM	CREAMER	CREDNERITE	CRENATURE	CRESCENTIC
CRATERKIN	CREAMERIES	CREDO	CRENEL	CRESCENTING
CRATERLET	CREAMERY	CREDOS	CRENELATE	CRESCENTLIKE
CRATEROUS	CREAMERYMAN	CREDULITIES	CRENELATED	CRESCENTOID
CRATICULAR	CREAMERYMEN	CREDULITY	CRENELATING	CRESCIVE
CRATING	CREAMFRUIT	CREDULOUS	CRENELATION	CRESCOGRAPH
CRATOMETER	CREAMIER	CREDULOUSLY	CRENELE	CRESOLIN
CRATOMETRIC	CREAMIEST	CREE	CRENELED	CRESOLINE
CRATOMETRY	CREAMILY	CREED	CRENELEE	CRESORCIN
CRAUNCH	CREAMINESS	CREEDAL	CRENELET	CRESORCINOL
CRAVAT	CREAMING	CREEDALISM	CRENELING	CRESOTATE
CRAVATTED	CREAMMAKER	CREEDALIST	CRENELLATE	CRESOTIC
CRAVATTING	CREAMMAKING	CREEDED	CRENELLATED	CRESOTINATE
CRAVE	CREAMOMETER	CREEDITE	CRENELLATING	CRESOTINIC
CRAVED	CREAMSACS	CREEDMORE	CRENELLATION	CRESOXID
CRAVEN	CREAMWARE	CREEDSMAN	CRENELLE	CRESOXIDE
CRAVENETTE	CREAMY	CREEK	CRENELLED	CRESS
CRAVENLY	CREANCE	CREEKER	CRENELLING	CRESSED
CRAVENNESS	CREANCER	CREEKFISH	CRENIC	CRESSES
CRAVER	CREANT	CREEKFISHES	CRENITIC	CRESSET
CRAVING	CREASE	CREEKS	CRENOLOGY	CRESSWEED
CRAVINGLY	CREASED	CREEKSIDE	CRENOTHERAPY	CRESSWORT
CRAVINGNESS	CREASER	CREEKY	CRENULA	CRESSY
CRAVO	CREASHAKS	CREEL	CRENULATE	CREST
CRAW	CREASIER	CREELED	CRENULATED	CRESTED
CRAWDAD	CREASIEST	CREELER	CRENULATION	CRESTFALLEN
CRAWFISH	CREASING	CREELING	CREODONT	CRESTING
CRAWFISHES	CREASOL	CREEM	CREOLE	CRESTLESS
CRAWFOOT	CREASY	CREEN	CREOLEIZE	CRESTLINE
CRAWFOOTS	CREAT	CREEP	CREOLISM	CRESTMOREITE
CRAWK	CREATE	CREEPAGE	CREOLITE	CRESYL
CRAWL	CREATED	CREEPER	CREOLIZATION	CRESYLATE
CRAWLED	CREATIC	CREEPERS	CREOLIZE	CRESYLENE
CRAWLER	CREATIN	CREEPHOLE	CREOLIZED	CRESYLIC
CRAWLIE	CREATINE	CREEPIE	CREOLIZING	CRESYLITE
CRAWLIER	CREATING	CREEPIER	CREOPHAGIA	CRETA
CRAWLIEST	CREATININ	CREEPIEST	CREOPHAGISM	CRETACEOUS
CRAWLING	CREATININE	CREEPILY	CREOPHAGIST	CRETACEOUSLY
CRAWLINGLY	CREATION	CREEPINESS	CREOPHAGOUS	CRETEFACTION
CRAWLY	CREATIONAL	CREEPING	CREOPHAGY	CRETIC
CRAWM	CREATIONARY	CREEPMOUSE	CREOSOL	CRETIFY
CRAY	CREATIONISM	CREEPS	CREOSOTE	CRETIN

CRETINIC
CRETINISM
CRETINOID
CRETINOUS
CRETION
CRETIONARY
CRETONNE
CREVALLE
CREVASS
CREVASSE
CREVASSED
CREVASSING
CREVET
CREVETTE
CREVICE
CREVICED
CREVICES
CREW
CREWE
CREWEL
CREWELIST
CREWELLERY
CREWELWORK
CREWER
CREWET
CREWMAN
CRIANCE
CRIANT
CRIB
CRIBBAGE
CRIBBED
CRIBBER
CRIBBING
CRIBBLE
CRIBBLED
CRIBELLA
CRIBELLUM
CRIBO
CRIBRAL
CRIBRATE
CRIBRATELY
CRIBRATION
CRIBRIFORM
CRIBROSE
CRIBWORK
CRIC
CRICETID
CRICETINE
CRICK
CRICKE
CRICKET
CRICKETER
CRICKETERS
CRICKETING
CRICKETINGS
CRICKETY
CRICKEY
CRICKLE
CRICOID
CRICOTHYROID
CRICOTOMY
CRIDDLE
CRIED
CRIER
CRIERS
CRIES
CRIEY
CRIG
CRIKE
CRIKEY
CRILE
CRIMBLE
CRIME
CRIMEFUL
CRIMES
CRIMINAL
CRIMINALISM

CRIMINALIST
CRIMINALITIES
CRIMINALITY
CRIMINALLY
CRIMINALOID
CRIMINALS
CRIMINATE
CRIMINATED
CRIMINATING
CRIMINATION
CRIMINATIVE
CRIMINATOR
CRIMINATORY
CRIMINE
CRIMINI
CRIMINOGENIC
CRIMINOLOGIC
CRIMINOLOGY
CRIMINOUS
CRIMINOUSLY
CRIMMY
CRIMOGENIC
CRIMP
CRIMPAGE
CRIMPED
CRIMPER
CRIMPIER
CRIMPIEST
CRIMPING
CRIMPLE
CRIMPLED
CRIMPLING
CRIMPNESS
CRIMPY
CRIMSON
CRIMSONLY
CRIMSONNESS
CRIN
CRINAL
CRINANITE
CRINATED
CRINATORY
CRINCH
CRINE
CRINED
CRINET
CRINGE
CRINGED
CRINGELING
CRINGER
CRINGING
CRINGINGLY
CRINGINGNESS
CRINGLE
CRINICULTURE
CRINIERE
CRINIFEROUS
CRINIGEROUS
CRINION
CRINIPAROUS
CRINITE
CRINITORY
CRINIVOROUS
CRINK
CRINKLE
CRINKLED
CRINKLEROOT
CRINKLIER
CRINKLIEST
CRINKLING
CRINKLY
CRINKUM
CRINOID
CRINOIDAL
CRINOIDEAN
CRINOLINE
CRINOSE

CRINOSITY
CRINULA
CRINUM
CRIOBOLIUM
CRIOBOLY
CRIOCERATITE
CRIOLLA
CRIOLLO
CRIOPHORE
CRIOSPHINX
CRIP
CRIPES
CRIPPLE
CRIPPLED
CRIPPLER
CRIPPLES
CRIPPLING
CRIPPLY
CRIPS
CRISE
CRISES
CRISIC
CRISIS
CRISLE
CRISP
CRISPATE
CRISPATED
CRISPATION
CRISPATURE
CRISPED
CRISPER
CRISPEST
CRISPIER
CRISPIEST
CRISPILY
CRISPINESS
CRISPING
CRISPLY
CRISPNESS
CRISPY
CRISS
CRISSA
CRISSAL
CRISSCROSS
CRISSCROSSED
CRISSET
CRISSUM
CRISTA
CRISTAE
CRISTATE
CRISTATED
CRISTIFORM
CRISTOBALITE
CRISTY
CRITCH
CRITERIA
CRITERIOLOGY
CRITERION
CRITERIONAL
CRITERIONS
CRITH
CRITHMENE
CRITHOMANCY
CRITIC
CRITICAL
CRITICALITY
CRITICALLY
CRITICALNESS
CRITICASTER
CRITICASTRY
CRITICISED
CRITICISER
CRITICISING
CRITICISM
CRITICIZABLE
CRITICIZE
CRITICIZED

CRITICIZER
CRITICIZING
CRITICKIN
CRITICULE
CRITIQUE
CRITIZE
CRITLING
CRITTER
CRIZZEL
CRIZZLE
CRO
CROAK
CROAKED
CROAKER
CROAKIER
CROAKIEST
CROAKILY
CROAKINESS
CROAKING
CROAKS
CROAKY
CROAPE
CROC
CROCARD
CROCEIN
CROCEINE
CROCEOUS
CROCETIN
CROCEUS
CROCHE
CROCHET
CROCHETED
CROCHETING
CROCI
CROCIARY
CROCIATE
CROCIDOLITE
CROCIN
CROCINE
CROCK
CROCKARD
CROCKED
CROCKER
CROCKERY
CROCKERYWARE
CROCKET
CROCKETED
CROCKETING
CROCKING
CROCKY
CROCODILE
CROCODILEAN
CROCODILIAN
CROCODILINE
CROCODILITY
CROCODILOID
CROCOISITE
CROCOITE
CROCONATE
CROCONIC
CROCUS
CROCUSED
CROCUSES
CROCUTA
CROFT
CROFTER
CROFTERIZE
CROFTING
CROFTLAND
CROIGHLE
CROISADE
CROISE
CROISEE
CROISES
CROISSANT
CROISSANTE
CROJIK

CROMA
CROMALTITE
CROMB
CROMBEC
CROME
CROMFORDITE
CROMLECH
CROMME
CROMMEL
CROMORNA
CROMORNE
CROMSTER
CRONE
CRONEBERRY
CRONET
CRONIED
CRONIES
CRONISH
CRONK
CRONKNESS
CRONSTEDTITE
CRONY
CRONYING
CROO
CROOCH
CROOD
CROODLE
CROOK
CROOKBACK
CROOKBACKED
CROOKBILLED
CROOKED
CROOKEDLY
CROOKEDNESS
CROOKEN
CROOKESITE
CROOKFINGERED
CROOKHEADED
CROOKING
CROOKKNEED
CROOKLE
CROOKLEGGED
CROOKNECK
CROOKNECKED
CROOKNOSED
CROOKS
CROOKSIDED
CROOKSTERNED
CROOKTOOTHED
CROOL
CROOM
CROON
CROONED
CROONER
CROONING
CROOSE
CROP
CROPE
CROPHEAD
CROPLAND
CROPMAN
CROPPA
CROPPED
CROPPER
CROPPIE
CROPPING
CROPPY
CROPS
CROPSHIN
CROPSICK
CROPSICKNESS
CROPWEED
CROQUET
CROQUETED
CROQUETING
CROQUETTE
CROQUIGNOLE

CROQUIS
CRORE
CROSA
CROSET
CROSHABELL
CROSIER
CROSIERED
CROSNE
CROSNES
CROSS
CROSSABILITY
CROSSABLE
CROSSARM
CROSSBAND
CROSSBAR
CROSSBARRED
CROSSBARRING
CROSSBEAK
CROSSBEAM
CROSSBELT
CROSSBILL
CROSSBIRTH
CROSSBITE
CROSSBONES
CROSSBOW
CROSSBOWMAN
CROSSBOWMEN
CROSSBRED
CROSSBREED
CROSSBREEDING
CROSSCHECK
CROSSCURRENT
CROSSCUT
CROSSCUTTER
CROSSCUTTING
CROSSE
CROSSED
CROSSER
CROSSES
CROSSETTE
CROSSFALL
CROSSFIRE
CROSSFIRED
CROSSFIRING
CROSSFISH
CROSSFLOWER
CROSSFOOT
CROSSHACKLE
CROSSHAND
CROSSHATCH
CROSSHATCHED
CROSSHATCHER
CROSSHATCHING
CROSSHAUL
CROSSHEAD
CROSSING
CROSSITE
CROSSJACK
CROSSLEGS
CROSSLET
CROSSLETED
CROSSLIGHT
CROSSLIGHTED
CROSSLINE
CROSSLY
CROSSNESS
CROSSOPODIA
CROSSOPT
CROSSOVER
CROSSPATCH
CROSSPIECE
CROSSPOINT
CROSSPOST
CROSSRAIL
CROSSROAD
CROSSROW
CROSSRUFF

CROSSTALK
CROSSTIE
CROSSTIED
CROSSTOES
CROSSTREE
CROSSWALK
CROSSWAY
CROSSWAYS
CROSSWEB
CROSSWEED
CROSSWIND
CROSSWISE
CROSSWORD
CROSSWORDER
CROSSWORT
CROST
CROSTARIE
CROT
CROTAL
CROTALIC
CROTALID
CROTALIFORM
CROTALIN
CROTALINE
CROTALISM
CROTALO
CROTALOID
CROTALUM
CROTAPHIC
CROTAPHION
CROTAPHITE
CROTAPHITIC
CROTCH
CROTCHED
CROTCHET
CROTCHETED
CROTCHETEER
CROTCHETINESS
CROTCHETING
CROTCHETY
CROTCHING
CROTCHY
CROTESCO
CROTIN
CROTON
CROTONATE
CROTONIC
CROTONYL
CROTTAL
CROTTELS
CROTTLE
CROTYL
CROUCH
CROUCHANT
CROUCHE
CROUCHED
CROUCHER
CROUCHIE
CROUCHING
CROUD
CROUKE
CROUP
CROUPADE
CROUPAL
CROUPE
CROUPERBUSH
CROUPIER
CROUPIEST
CROUPILY
CROUPINESS
CROUPON
CROUPOUS
CROUPY
CROUSE
CROUSELY
CROUSTADE
CROUT

CROUTE
CROUTH
CROUTON
CROW
CROWBAIT
CROWBAR
CROWBELL
CROWBERRIES
CROWBERRY
CROWBILL
CROWD
CROWDED
CROWDEDLY
CROWDEDNESS
CROWDER
CROWDING
CROWDLE
CROWDWEED
CROWDY
CROWED
CROWER
CROWFEET
CROWFLOWER
CROWFOOT
CROWFOOTED
CROWHOP
CROWING
CROWKEEPER
CROWL
CROWN
CROWNAL
CROWNBEARD
CROWNED
CROWNER
CROWNET
CROWNING
CROWNLAND
CROWNLESS
CROWNLET
CROWNLING
CROWNMENT
CROWNPIECE
CROWNWORK
CROWNWORT
CROWSTEP
CROWSTONE
CROWTOE
CROY
CROYDON
CROZE
CROZED
CROZER
CROZIER
CROZING
CROZLE
CROZZLE
CROZZLY
CRU
CRUB
CRUBEEN
CRUCE
CRUCES
CRUCETHOUSE
CRUCHE
CRUCIAL
CRUCIALITY
CRUCIALLY
CRUCIAN
CRUCIATE
CRUCIATED
CRUCIATELY
CRUCIATING
CRUCIATION
CRUCIBLE
CRUCIFER
CRUCIFEROUS
CRUCIFICIAL

CRUCIFIED
CRUCIFIER
CRUCIFIX
CRUCIFIXION
CRUCIFORM
CRUCIFORMITY
CRUCIFORMLY
CRUCIFY
CRUCIFYING
CRUCIGEROUS
CRUCIS
CRUCK
CRUDDLE
CRUDE
CRUDELY
CRUDENESS
CRUDER
CRUDEST
CRUDITIES
CRUDITY
CRUDWORT
CRUDY
CRUE
CRUEL
CRUELER
CRUELEST
CRUELIZE
CRUELLY
CRUELNESS
CRUELS
CRUELTIES
CRUELTY
CRUENT
CRUENTOUS
CRUET
CRUETY
CRUISE
CRUISED
CRUISER
CRUISING
CRUISKEEN
CRUISKEN
CRUIVE
CRUL
CRULL
CRULLER
CRUM
CRUMB
CRUMBABLE
CRUMBCLOTH
CRUMBED
CRUMBER
CRUMBIER
CRUMBIEST
CRUMBING
CRUMBLE
CRUMBLED
CRUMBLIER
CRUMBLIEST
CRUMBLINESS
CRUMBLING
CRUMBLINGS
CRUMBLY
CRUMBS
CRUMBY
CRUMEN
CRUMENA
CRUMENAL
CRUMMABLE
CRUMMER
CRUMMIE
CRUMMIER
CRUMMIEST
CRUMMOCK
CRUMMY
CRUMP
CRUMPER

CRUMPET
CRUMPLE
CRUMPLED
CRUMPLER
CRUMPLING
CRUMPLY
CRUMPY
CRUMSTER
CRUNCH
CRUNCHED
CRUNCHILY
CRUNCHINESS
CRUNCHING
CRUNCHINGLY
CRUNCHWEED
CRUNCHY
CRUNK
CRUNKLE
CRUNODAL
CRUNODE
CRUNT
CRUOR
CRUP
CRUPPEN
CRUPPER
CRUPPERED
CRUPPERING
CRURA
CRURAL
CRUROGENITAL
CRUROTARSAL
CRUS
CRUSADE
CRUSADED
CRUSADER
CRUSADERS
CRUSADING
CRUSADO
CRUSADOES
CRUSADOS
CRUSE
CRUSET
CRUSH
CRUSHABILITY
CRUSHABLE
CRUSHED
CRUSHER
CRUSHING
CRUSIE
CRUSILE
CRUSILEE
CRUSILY
CRUST
CRUSTA
CRUSTACEAN
CRUSTACEOUS
CRUSTADE
CRUSTAL
CRUSTALOGIST
CRUSTALOGY
CRUSTATE
CRUSTATED
CRUSTATION
CRUSTED
CRUSTEDLY
CRUSTER
CRUSTIER
CRUSTIEST
CRUSTIFIC
CRUSTILY
CRUSTINESS
CRUSTING
CRUSTOSE
CRUSTOSIS
CRUSTS
CRUSTY
CRUT

CRUTCH	CRYPTOGRAPHY	CUARTILLO	CUCKQUEAN	CUIRASSIER
CRUTCHED	CRYPTOHERESY	CUARTINO	CUCKSTOOL	CUISH
CRUTCHER	CRYPTOLOGY	CUARTO	CUCOLINE	CUISINARY
CRUTCHING	CRYPTOMERE	CUB	CUCULARIS	CUISINE
CRUTCHLIKE	CRYPTOMEROUS	CUBA	CUCULE	CUISINIER
CRUTH	CRYPTOMNESIA	CUBAGE	CUCULIFORM	CUISSE
CRUTTER	CRYPTOMNESIC	CUBALAYA	CUCULINE	CUIT
CRUX	CRYPTOMONAD	CUBANGLE	CUCULLA	CUITLE
CRUXES	CRYPTONEMA	CUBANITE	CUCULLATE	CUITTLE
CRUZADO	CRYPTONYM	CUBATION	CUCULLATED	CUKE
CRUZEIRO	CRYPTONYMOUS	CUBATORY	CUCULLATELY	CUL
CRWTH	CRYPTOPAPIST	CUBATURE	CUCULLIFORM	CULBERT
CRY	CRYPTOPHYTE	CUBBIES	CUCULLUS	CULBUT
CRYABLE	CRYPTOPIN	CUBBING	CUCULOID	CULCH
CRYBABIES	CRYPTOPINE	CUBBISH	CUCUMBER	CULEBRA
CRYBABY	CRYPTORCHID	CUBBISHLY	CUCUMIFORM	CULERAGE
CRYER	CRYPTOSCOPE	CUBBISHNESS	CUCURB	CULET
CRYING	CRYPTOSCOPY	CUBBY	CUCURBIT	CULETT
CRYINGLY	CRYPTOSTOMA	CUBBYHOLE	CUCURBITE	CULGEE
CRYMODYNIA	CRYPTOSTOME	CUBBYHOUSE	CUCURBITINE	CULICID
CRYMOTHERAPY	CRYPTOUS	CUBBYYEW	CUCUYO	CULICIDE
CRYOCHORE	CRYPTOZOIC	CUBE	CUD	CULICIFORM
CRYOCHORIC	CRYPTOZONATE	CUBEB	CUDA	CULICIFUGAL
CRYOCONITE	CRYPTOZYGOUS	CUBED	CUDAVA	CULICIFUGE
CRYOGEN	CRYSTAL	CUBELET	CUDBEAR	CULICINE
CRYOGENIC	CRYSTALED	CUBER	CUDDEN	CULILAWAN
CRYOGENY	CRYSTALING	CUBERA	CUDDIE	CULINARILY
CRYOHYDRATE	CRYSTALITIC	CUBIC	CUDDIES	CULINARY
CRYOHYDRIC	CRYSTALLED	CUBICA	CUDDLE	CULL
CRYOLITE	CRYSTALLIC	CUBICAL	CUDDLED	CULLA
CRYOLOGY	CRYSTALLIKE	CUBICALLY	CUDDLESOME	CULLAGE
CRYOMETER	CRYSTALLIN	CUBICALNESS	CUDDLING	CULLAS
CRYOPHORIC	CRYSTALLINE	CUBICITY	CUDDLY	CULLAY
CRYOPHORUS	CRYSTALLING	CUBICLE	CUDDY	CULLE
CRYOPHYLLITE	CRYSTALLITE	CUBICONE	CUDDYHOLE	CULLED
CRYOPLANKTON	CRYSTALLIZE	CUBICULA	CUDEIGH	CULLENDER
CRYOSCOPE	CRYSTALLIZED	CUBICULAR	CUDGEL	CULLER
CRYOSCOPIC	CRYSTALLIZER	CUBICULARY	CUDGELED	CULLET
CRYOSCOPY	CRYSTALLIZING	CUBICULO	CUDGELER	CULLIBLE
CRYOSEL	CRYSTALLOGRAPH	CUBICULUM	CUDGELING	CULLIED
CRYOSTASE	CRYSTALLOID	CUBIFORM	CUDGELLED	CULLIES
CRYOSTAT	CRYSTALS	CUBING	CUDGELLER	CULLING
CRYOTHERAPY	CRYSTALWORT	CUBISM	CUDGELLING	CULLION
CRYPT	CRYSTE	CUBIST	CUDGERIE	CULLIONLY
CRYPTAL	CRYSTIC	CUBIT	CUDWEED	CULLIONRY
CRYPTAMNESIC	CRYSTOGRAPH	CUBITAL	CUE	CULLIONS
CRYPTANALYST	CRYSTOLEUM	CUBITALE	CUEBALL	CULLIS
CRYPTARCH	CRYSTOSPHENE	CUBITALIA	CUECA	CULLY
CRYPTARCHY	CSARDAS	CUBITED	CUED	CULLYING
CRYPTED	CTENE	CUBITIERE	CUEIST	CULM
CRYPTIC	CTENIDIA	CUBITO	CUEMAN	CULMEN
CRYPTICAL	CTENIDIAL	CUBITOCARPAL	CUEMANSHIP	CULMICOLOUS
CRYPTICALLY	CTENIDIUM	CUBITOPALMAR	CUEMEN	CULMIFEROUS
CRYPTOBRANCH	CTENIFORM	CUBITORADIAL	CUENA	CULMINAL
CRYPTOCARP	CTENII	CUBITUS	CUER	CULMINANT
CRYPTOCARPIC	CTENIZID	CUBMASTER	CUERDA	CULMINATE
CRYPTOCARPOUS	CTENOCYST	CUBOID	CUERPO	CULMINATED
CRYPTOCEROUS	CTENODACTYL	CUBOIDAL	CUESTA	CULMINATING
CRYPTOCOCCI	CTENODONT	CUBOIDES	CUFF	CULMINATION
CRYPTOCOCCIC	CTENOID	CUBOMEDUSAN	CUFFED	CULMS
CRYPTODEIST	CTENOIDEAN	CUCHIA	CUFFER	CULMY
CRYPTODIRAN	CTENOIDIAN	CUCK	CUFFIN	CULOT
CRYPTODIRE	CTENOLIUM	CUCKHOLD	CUFFING	CULOTTE
CRYPTODIROUS	CTENOPHORAL	CUCKING	CUFFLE	CULOTTES
CRYPTODOUBLE	CTENOPHORAN	CUCKOLD	CUFFY	CULOTTIC
CRYPTOGAM	CTENOPHORE	CUCKOLDED	CUFFYISM	CULOTTISM
CRYPTOGAMIAN	CTENOPHOROUS	CUCKOLDIZE	CUGGERMUGGER	CULP
CRYPTOGAMIC	CTENOSTOME	CUCKOLDLY	CUICA	CULPA
CRYPTOGAMIST	CTETOLOGY	CUCKOLDOM	CUIDADO	CULPABILITY
CRYPTOGAMOUS	CUADRA	CUCKOLDRY	CUIEJO	CULPABLE
CRYPTOGAMY	CUADRILLA	CUCKOO	CUIF	CULPABLENESS
CRYPTOGENIC	CUAPINOLE	CUCKOOFLOWER	CUINAGE	CULPABLY
CRYPTOGENOUS	CUARENTA	CUCKOOMAID	CUING	CULPATE
CRYPTOGLIOMA	CUARTA	CUCKOOMAIDEN	CUIR	CULPATORY
CRYPTOGRAM	CUARTEL	CUCKOOMATE	CUIRASS	CULPEO
CRYPTOGRAPH	CUARTERON	CUCKOOPINT	CUIRASSED	CULPON
CRYPTOGRAPHER	CUARTILLA	CUCKOOPINTLE	CUIRASSES	CULPOSE

CULPRIT
CULT
CULTCH
CULTELLATION
CULTELLUS
CULTI
CULTIC
CULTIGEN
CULTIROSTRAL
CULTISM
CULTIST
CULTIVABLE
CULTIVABLY
CULTIVAR
CULTIVATABLE
CULTIVATE
CULTIVATED
CULTIVATING
CULTIVATION
CULTIVATOR
CULTIVE
CULTRATE
CULTRATED
CULTURABLE
CULTURAL
CULTURALIST
CULTURALLY
CULTURE
CULTURED
CULTURINE
CULTURIST
CULTUS
CULTUSES
CULVER
CULVERFOOT
CULVERHOUSE
CULVERIN
CULVERINEER
CULVERINER
CULVERKEY
CULVERS
CULVERT
CULVERTAGE
CULVERWORT
CUM
CUMACEAN
CUMACEOUS
CUMAL
CUMALDEHYDE
CUMALIN
CUMAPHYTE
CUMAPHYTIC
CUMAPHYTISM
CUMARU
CUMAY
CUMBENT
CUMBER
CUMBERED
CUMBERING
CUMBERSOME
CUMBERSOMELY
CUMBERWORLD
CUMBHA
CUMBLE
CUMBLY
CUMBRAITE
CUMBRANCE
CUMBRE
CUMBROUS
CUMBROUSLY
CUMBROUSNESS
CUMBU
CUMENE
CUMENGITE
CUMENYL
CUMFLUTTER
CUMHAL

CUMIC
CUMIDIN
CUMIDINE
CUMIN
CUMINOIN
CUMINSEED
CUMLY
CUMMER
CUMMERBUND
CUMMIN
CUMMOCK
CUMOL
CUMQUAT
CUMSHA
CUMSHAW
CUMULANT
CUMULAR
CUMULATE
CUMULATED
CUMULATELY
CUMULATING
CUMULATION
CUMULATIST
CUMULATIVE
CUMULATIVELY
CUMULENE
CUMULI
CUMULIFORM
CUMULITE
CUMULOCIRRUS
CUMULONIMBUS
CUMULOSE
CUMULOUS
CUMULUS
CUMYL
CUNABULA
CUNABULAR
CUNCTATION
CUNCTATIOUS
CUNCTATIVE
CUNCTATOR
CUNCTATORY
CUNCTIPOTENT
CUNDITE
CUNDUM
CUNDY
CUNEAL
CUNEATE
CUNEATED
CUNEATELY
CUNEATIC
CUNEATOR
CUNEI
CUNEIFORM
CUNEIFORMIST
CUNEOCUBOID
CUNETTE
CUNEUS
CUNGEBOI
CUNGEVOI
CUNIC
CUNICULAR
CUNICULI
CUNICULUS
CUNIFORM
CUNIT
CUNJAH
CUNJER
CUNJEVOI
CUNNE
CUNNER
CUNNING
CUNNINGLY
CUNNINGNESS
CUNNY
CUNONIACEOUS
CUNYE

CUNYIE
CUNZIE
CUORIN
CUP
CUPAY
CUPBEARER
CUPBOARD
CUPCAKE
CUPEL
CUPELED
CUPELER
CUPELING
CUPELLATION
CUPELLED
CUPELLER
CUPELLING
CUPFLOWER
CUPFUL
CUPHEAD
CUPHOLDER
CUPIDINOUS
CUPIDITY
CUPIDON
CUPIDONE
CUPIUBA
CUPMAKER
CUPMAKING
CUPMAN
CUPMATE
CUPOLA
CUPOLAED
CUPOLAING
CUPOLAMAN
CUPOLAR
CUPOLAS
CUPOLATED
CUPPED
CUPPEN
CUPPER
CUPPIER
CUPPIEST
CUPPIN
CUPPING
CUPPY
CUPRAMMONIUM
CUPREIN
CUPREINE
CUPRENE
CUPREOUS
CUPRIC
CUPRIDE
CUPRIFEROUS
CUPRITE
CUPROCYANIDE
CUPROID
CUPRONICKEL
CUPROSILICON
CUPROUS
CUPRUM
CUPS
CUPSEED
CUPSTONE
CUPULA
CUPULAR
CUPULATE
CUPULE
CUPULIFEROUS
CUPULIFORM
CUR
CURA
CURABILITY
CURABLE
CURABLENESS
CURABLY
CURACAO
CURACE
CURACIES

CURACY
CURARE
CURARI
CURARINE
CURARIZATION
CURARIZE
CURARIZED
CURARIZING
CURASSOW
CURATAGE
CURATE
CURATEL
CURATESS
CURATIAL
CURATIC
CURATICAL
CURATION
CURATIVE
CURATIVELY
CURATIVENESS
CURATOLATRY
CURATOR
CURATORIAL
CURATORIUM
CURATORSHIP
CURATORY
CURB
CURBASH
CURBING
CURBLINE
CURBSTONE
CURBSTONER
CURBY
CURCAS
CURCH
CURCHY
CURCUDDOCH
CURCULIO
CURCULIONID
CURCULIONIST
CURCULIOS
CURCUMA
CURCUMIN
CURD
CURDED
CURDINESS
CURDING
CURDLE
CURDLED
CURDLER
CURDLING
CURDLY
CURDOO
CURDWORT
CURDY
CURE
CURED
CURELESS
CUREMASTER
CURER
CURET
CURETTAGE
CURETTE
CURETTED
CURETTEMENT
CURETTING
CURFEW
CURIA
CURIAE
CURIAL
CURIALISM
CURIALIST
CURIALISTIC
CURIALITIES
CURIALITY
CURIARA
CURIATE

CURIBOCA
CURIE
CURIEGRAM
CURIESCOPY
CURIET
CURIETHERAPY
CURINE
CURING
CURIO
CURIOLOGIC
CURIOLOGICAL
CURIOLOGICS
CURIOLOGY
CURIOMANIAC
CURIOS
CURIOSA
CURIOSI
CURIOSITIES
CURIOSITY
CURIOSO
CURIOSOS
CURIOUS
CURIOUSLY
CURIOUSNESS
CURIOUSNESSES
CURITE
CURIUM
CURL
CURLED
CURLEDLY
CURLEDNESS
CURLER
CURLEW
CURLEWS
CURLICUE
CURLIER
CURLIEST
CURLIEWURLIE
CURLIEWURLY
CURLINESS
CURLING
CURLINGLY
CURLPAPER
CURLS
CURLY
CURLYCUE
CURLYHEAD
CURLYLOCKS
CURMUDGEON
CURMUDGEONLY
CURMURGING
CURMURRING
CURN
CURNEY
CURNEYS
CURNIE
CURNIES
CURPEL
CURPIN
CURPLE
CURR
CURRACH
CURRACK
CURRAGH
CURRAJONG
CURRAN
CURRANCE
CURRANE
CURRANT
CURRATOW
CURRAWANG
CURRAWONG
CURRENCIES
CURRENCY
CURRENT
CURRENTLY
CURRENTNESS

CURRENTWISE
CURRICLE
CURRICLED
CURRICLING
CURRICULA
CURRICULAR
CURRICULUM
CURRICULUMS
CURRIED
CURRIER
CURRIERIES
CURRIERY
CURRIES
CURRISH
CURRISHLY
CURRISHNESS
CURROCK
CURRY
CURRYCOMB
CURRYFAVEL
CURRYFAVOUR
CURRYING
CURSAL
CURSARO
CURSE
CURSED
CURSEDLY
CURSEDNESS
CURSER
CURSING
CURSITOR
CURSIVE
CURSIVELY
CURSIVENESS
CURSOR
CURSORARY
CURSORIAL
CURSORILY
CURSORINESS
CURSORIOUS
CURSORY
CURST
CURSTFUL
CURSTFULLY
CURSTLY
CURSTNESS
CURSUS
CURT
CURTAIL
CURTAILED
CURTAILEDLY
CURTAILER
CURTAILING
CURTAILMENT
CURTAIN
CURTAINED
CURTAINING
CURTAL
CURTATE
CURTATION
CURTAXE
CURTED
CURTESIES
CURTESY
CURTILAGE
CURTLAX
CURTLY
CURTNESS
CURTSEY
CURTSEYED
CURTSEYING
CURTSEYS
CURTSIED
CURTSIES
CURTSY
CURTSYING
CURUA

CURUBA
CURUCUCU
CURULE
CURUPAY
CURUPAYS
CURUPEY
CURURO
CURUROS
CURVACEOUS
CURVANT
CURVATE
CURVATED
CURVATION
CURVATURE
CURVE
CURVED
CURVEDLY
CURVEDNESS
CURVER
CURVES
CURVET
CURVETED
CURVETING
CURVETTED
CURVETTING
CURVEY
CURVICAUDATE
CURVICOSTATE
CURVIDENTATE
CURVIFOLIATE
CURVIFORM
CURVILINEAL
CURVILINEAR
CURVINERVATE
CURVINERVED
CURVING
CURVIROSTRAL
CURVISERIAL
CURVITAL
CURVITIES
CURVITY
CURVOGRAPH
CURVOMETER
CURVOUS
CURVULATE
CURVY
CURWHIBBLE
CURY
CUSCOHYGRIN
CUSCOHYGRINE
CUSCONIN
CUSCONINE
CUSCUTACEOUS
CUSEC
CUSELITE
CUSH
CUSHA
CUSHAG
CUSHAT
CUSHAW
CUSHIE
CUSHIER
CUSHIEST
CUSHION
CUSHIONED
CUSHIONING
CUSHIONLIKE
CUSHIONY
CUSHY
CUSIE
CUSINERO
CUSK
CUSKS
CUSP
CUSPAL
CUSPATE
CUSPATED

CUSPED
CUSPID
CUSPIDAL
CUSPIDATE
CUSPIDATED
CUSPIDATION
CUSPIDES
CUSPIDOR
CUSPING
CUSPIS
CUSPULE
CUSS
CUSSED
CUSSEDLY
CUSSEDNESS
CUSSER
CUSTARD
CUSTERITE
CUSTODEE
CUSTODIA
CUSTODIAL
CUSTODIAN
CUSTODIER
CUSTODIES
CUSTODY
CUSTOM
CUSTOMABLE
CUSTOMABLY
CUSTOMANCE
CUSTOMARIES
CUSTOMARILY
CUSTOMARY
CUSTOMED
CUSTOMER
CUSTOMHOUSE
CUSTOMING
CUSTOMLY
CUSTOMS
CUSTOS
CUSTREL
CUSTRON
CUSTROUN
CUSTUMAL
CUT
CUTANEAL
CUTANEOUS
CUTAWAY
CUTBACK
CUTBANK
CUTCH
CUTCHA
CUTCHER
CUTCHERIES
CUTCHERRIES
CUTCHERRY
CUTCHERY
CUTDOWN
CUTE
CUTELY
CUTENESS
CUTER
CUTEST
CUTGRASS
CUTHEAL
CUTICLE
CUTICOLOR
CUTICULA
CUTICULAR
CUTICULARIZE
CUTICULATE
CUTIDURE
CUTIDURIS
CUTIE
CUTIES
CUTIFICATION
CUTIGERAL
CUTIKIN

CUTIN
CUTINIZATION
CUTINIZE
CUTINIZED
CUTINIZING
CUTIREACTION
CUTIS
CUTISECTOR
CUTITIS
CUTIZATION
CUTLAS
CUTLASH
CUTLASS
CUTLER
CUTLERESS
CUTLERY
CUTLET
CUTLING
CUTLINGS
CUTLIPS
CUTOFF
CUTOUT
CUTOVER
CUTPURSE
CUTS
CUTTABLE
CUTTAGE
CUTTAIL
CUTTANEE
CUTTED
CUTTER
CUTTERHEAD
CUTTHROAT
CUTTIES
CUTTIKIN
CUTTING
CUTTINGLY
CUTTINGNESS
CUTTINGS
CUTTLE
CUTTLEBONE
CUTTLEFISH
CUTTLEFISHES
CUTTLER
CUTTOO
CUTTOOS
CUTTY
CUTTYHUNK
CUTUP
CUTUPS
CUTWATER
CUTWEED
CUTWORK
CUTWORM
CUVAGE
CUVEE
CUVETTE
CUVIES
CUVY
CUYA
CUYAS
CUZCENO
CWIERC
CWM
CYAMELID
CYAMELIDE
CYANACETIC
CYANAMID
CYANAMIDE
CYANATE
CYANAURATE
CYANAURIC
CYANBENZYL
CYANEAN
CYANEMIA
CYANEOUS
CYANFORMATE

CYANFORMIC
CYANHYDRATE
CYANHYDRIC
CYANHYDRIN
CYANICIDE
CYANID
CYANIDATION
CYANIDE
CYANIDED
CYANIDIN
CYANIDINE
CYANIDING
CYANIDROSIS
CYANIMIDE
CYANIN
CYANINE
CYANITE
CYANIZE
CYANIZED
CYANIZING
CYANOACETATE
CYANOACETIC
CYANOAURATE
CYANOAURIC
CYANOBENZENE
CYANOCHROIA
CYANOCHROIC
CYANODERMA
CYANOGEN
CYANOGENESIS
CYANOGENETIC
CYANOHYDRIN
CYANOMETER
CYANOMETRIC
CYANOMETRIES
CYANOMETRY
CYANOPATHIC
CYANOPATHY
CYANOPHIL
CYANOPHILE
CYANOPHILOUS
CYANOPHORIC
CYANOPHOSE
CYANOPHYCEAN
CYANOPIA
CYANOPLASTID
CYANOPSIA
CYANOSE
CYANOSIS
CYANOSITE
CYANOTIC
CYANOTYPE
CYANURAMIDE
CYANURET
CYANURIC
CYANUS
CYAPHENINE
CYATH
CYATHIFORM
CYATHIUM
CYATHOLITH
CYATHOS
CYATHOZOOID
CYATHUS
CYBERNETIC
CYBERNETICS
CYCAD
CYCADACEOUS
CYCADEAN
CYCADEOID
CYCADEOUS
CYCADIFORM
CYCADITE
CYCLADES
CYCLAMEN
CYCLAMIN
CYCLAMINE

CYCLANE
CYCLAR
CYCLAS
CYCLE
CYCLECAR
CYCLED
CYCLENE
CYCLER
CYCLESMITH
CYCLIAN
CYCLIC
CYCLICAL
CYCLICALLY
CYCLIDE
CYCLINDROID
CYCLING
CYCLIST
CYCLISTIC
CYCLITIS
CYCLIZATION
CYCLIZE
CYCLOALKANE
CYCLOCOELIC
CYCLOCOELOUS
CYCLODIOLEFIN
CYCLODIOLEFINE
CYCLOGANOID
CYCLOGRAM
CYCLOGRAPH
CYCLOGRAPHER
CYCLOHEPTANE
CYCLOHEXANE
CYCLOHEXANOL
CYCLOHEXENE
CYCLOHEXYL
CYCLOID
CYCLOIDAL
CYCLOIDALLY
CYCLOIDEAN
CYCLOIDIAN
CYCLOLITH
CYCLOMANIA
CYCLOMETER
CYCLOMETRIC
CYCLOMETRIES
CYCLOMETRY
CYCLOMYARIAN
CYCLONAL
CYCLONE
CYCLONIC
CYCLONICAL
CYCLONICALLY
CYCLONIST
CYCLONOLOGY
CYCLONOMETER
CYCLONOSCOPE
CYCLOOLEFIN
CYCLOOLEFINE
CYCLOPAEDIA
CYCLOPAEDIAS
CYCLOPAEDIC
CYCLOPAEDIST
CYCLOPE
CYCLOPEAN
CYCLOPEDIA
CYCLOPEDIAS
CYCLOPEDIC
CYCLOPEDICAL
CYCLOPEDIST
CYCLOPENTANE
CYCLOPENTENE
CYCLOPHORIA
CYCLOPHORIC
CYCLOPIA
CYCLOPISM
CYCLOPITE
CYCLOPLEGIA

CYCLOPLEGIC
CYCLOPOID
CYCLOPROPANE
CYCLOPTEROID
CYCLOPY
CYCLORAMA
CYCLORAMAS
CYCLORAMIC
CYCLOSCOPE
CYCLOSE
CYCLOSIS
CYCLOSPOROUS
CYCLOSTOMATE
CYCLOSTOME
CYCLOSTYLE
CYCLOTHEM
CYCLOTHYME
CYCLOTHYMIA
CYCLOTHYMIAC
CYCLOTHYMIC
CYCLOTOME
CYCLOTOMIC
CYCLOTOMY
CYCLOTRON
CYCLUS
CYDIPPIAN
CYDIPPID
CYDONIUM
CYESIOLOGY
CYESIS
CYGNEOUS
CYGNET
CYGNINE
CYKE
CYLICES
CYLINDER
CYLINDERED
CYLINDERER
CYLINDERING
CYLINDERS
CYLINDRIC
CYLINDRICAL
CYLINDRICULE
CYLINDRIFORM
CYLINDRITE
CYLINDROID
CYLINDROIDAL
CYLINDROMA
CYLINDROMATA
CYLINDRURIA
CYLIX
CYLLOSES
CYLLOSIS
CYMA
CYMAE
CYMAPHEN
CYMAR
CYMARIN
CYMAROSE
CYMATIA
CYMATION
CYMATIUM
CYMBA
CYMBAL
CYMBALED
CYMBALEER
CYMBALIST
CYMBALLED
CYMBALLING
CYMBALOM
CYMBALS
CYMBATE
CYMBID
CYMBIFORM
CYMBLIN
CYMBLING
CYMBOCEPHALY

CYME
CYMENE
CYMIFEROUS
CYMLIN
CYMLING
CYMOGENE
CYMOGRAPH
CYMOGRAPHIC
CYMOID
CYMOMETER
CYMOPHANE
CYMOPHANOUS
CYMOPHENOL
CYMOSCOPE
CYMOSE
CYMOSELY
CYMOTRICHY
CYMOUS
CYMRITE
CYMULE
CYMULOSE
CYNANCHE
CYNANTHROPY
CYNARACEOUS
CYNAREOUS
CYNAROID
CYNEBOT
CYNEGETIC
CYNEGETICS
CYNEGILD
CYNHYENA
CYNIATRIA
CYNIATRICS
CYNIC
CYNICAL
CYNICALLY
CYNICALNESS
CYNICISM
CYNICIST
CYNIPID
CYNIPIDOUS
CYNIPOID
CYNISM
CYNOCEPHALIC
CYNOCEPHALUS
CYNOCLEPT
CYNODON
CYNODONT
CYNOID
CYNOLOGY
CYNOMORPHIC
CYNOMORPHOUS
CYNOPHILE
CYNOPHILIC
CYNOPHILIST
CYNOPHOBE
CYNOPHOBIA
CYNOPODOUS
CYNORRHODA
CYNORRHODON
CYNOSURAL
CYNOSURE
CYNOTHERAPY
CYP
CYPERACEOUS
CYPHELLA
CYPHELLAE
CYPHELLATE
CYPHER
CYPHONAUTES
CYPHONISM
CYPRAEA
CYPRAEID
CYPRAEIFORM
CYPRE
CYPRES
CYPRESS

CYPRESSED
CYPRESSES
CYPRESSROOT
CYPRID
CYPRIDINOID
CYPRINE
CYPRINID
CYPRINIFORM
CYPRININ
CYPRININE
CYPRINODONT
CYPRINODONTOID
CYPRINOID
CYPRINOIDEAN
CYPRIPEDIUM
CYPSELA
CYPSELAE
CYPSELINE
CYPSELOID
CYPSELOMORPH
CYPSELOUS
CYRTOLITE
CYRTOMETER
CYRTOPIA
CYRTOSIS
CYRTOSTYLE
CYRUS
CYST
CYSTADENOMA
CYSTAL
CYSTALGIA
CYSTATROPHIA
CYSTATROPHY
CYSTECTASIA
CYSTECTASY
CYSTECTOMIES
CYSTECTOMY
CYSTED
CYSTEIN
CYSTEINE
CYSTEINIC
CYSTELCOSIS
CYSTENCHYMA
CYSTENCHYME
CYSTENCYTE
CYSTERETHISM
CYSTIC
CYSTICARPIC
CYSTICARPIUM
CYSTICERCI
CYSTICERCOID
CYSTICERCUS
CYSTICOLOUS
CYSTID
CYSTIDIA
CYSTIDIUM
CYSTIDIUMS
CYSTIFEROUS
CYSTIFORM
CYSTIGEROUS
CYSTIN
CYSTINE
CYSTINURIA
CYSTIRRHEA
CYSTIS
CYSTITIS
CYSTITOME
CYSTOADENOMA
CYSTOCARP
CYSTOCARPIC
CYSTOCELE
CYSTOCYTE
CYSTODYNIA
CYSTOFIBROMA
CYSTOGENESIS
CYSTOGRAM
CYSTOID

CYSTOIDEAN
CYSTOLITH
CYSTOLITHIC
CYSTOMA
CYSTOMATA
CYSTOMYOMA
CYSTOMYXOMA
CYSTONECTOUS
CYSTOPHORE
CYSTOPLASTY
CYSTOPLEGIA
CYSTOPTOSIS
CYSTORRHAGIA
CYSTORRHAPHY
CYSTORRHEA
CYSTOSARCOMA
CYSTOSCHISIS
CYSTOSCOPE
CYSTOSCOPIC
CYSTOSCOPY
CYSTOSE
CYSTOSPASM
CYSTOSPASTIC
CYSTOSTOMIES
CYSTOSTOMY
CYSTOSYRINX
CYSTOTOME
CYSTOTOMY
CYSTOUS
CYTASE
CYTASIC
CYTASTER
CYTE
CYTHERA
CYTIDINE
CYTIODERM
CYTIODERMA
CYTISINE
CYTITIS
CYTOBLAST
CYTOBLASTEMA
CYTOCHROME
CYTOCHYLEMA
CYTOCIDE
CYTOCLASIS
CYTOCLASTIC
CYTOCOCCI
CYTOCOCCUS
CYTOCYST
CYTODE
CYTODENDRITE
CYTODERM
CYTODIERESIS
CYTOGAMY
CYTOGENE
CYTOGENESIS
CYTOGENETIC
CYTOGENETICS
CYTOGENIC
CYTOGENOUS
CYTOGENY
CYTOGLOBIN
CYTOID
CYTOKINESIS
CYTOLIST
CYTOLOGIC
CYTOLOGICAL
CYTOLOGICALLY
CYTOLOGIES
CYTOLOGIST
CYTOLOGY
CYTOLYMPH
CYTOLYSIN
CYTOLYSIS
CYTOLYTIC
CYTOME
CYTOMERE

CYTOMETER
CYTON
CYTONE
CYTOPHAGOUS
CYTOPHARYNX
CYTOPHIL
CYTOPHYSICS
CYTOPHYSIOLOGY
CYTOPLASM
CYTOPLASMIC
CYTOPLAST
CYTOPLASTIC
CYTOPROCT
CYTOPYGE
CYTORYCTES
CYTOSIN
CYTOSINE
CYTOSOME
CYTOST
CYTOSTOMAL
CYTOSTOME
CYTOSTROMA
CYTOSTROMATIC
CYTOTACTIC
CYTOTAXIS
CYTOTOXIC
CYTOTOXIN
CYTOTROPHY
CYTOTROPIC
CYTOTROPISM
CYTOZOIC
CYTOZOON
CYTOZYMASE
CYTOZYME
CYTULA
CYTULAE
CYWYDD
CZAR
CZARDOM
CZAREVITCH
CZAREVNA
CZARINA
CZARINIAN
CZARISH
CZARISM
CZARIST
CZARISTIC
CZARITZA
CZIGANY

DA
DAALDER
DAB
DABB
DABBA
DABBED
DABBER
DABBING
DABBLE
DABBLED
DABBLER
DABBLING
DABBLINGLY
DABBLINGNESS
DABBY
DABCHICK
DABOIA
DABOYA
DABSTER
DABUH
DACE
DACELONINE
DACES
DACHA
DACHS
DACHSHUND
DACITE
DACITIC
DACKER
DACOIT
DACOITAGE
DACOITED
DACOITIES
DACOITING
DACOITS
DACOITY
DACRYOCYST
DACRYOLITE
DACRYOLITH
DACRYOMA
DACRYON
DACRYOPS
DACTYLAR
DACTYLATE
DACTYLIC
DACTYLICALLY
DACTYLIOLOGY
DACTYLION
DACTYLIST
DACTYLITIC
DACTYLITIS
DACTYLOGRAM
DACTYLOGRAPH
DACTYLOID
DACTYLOLOGY
DACTYLONOMY
DACTYLOPORE
DACTYLORHIZA
DACTYLOSCOPY
DACTYLOSE
DACTYLOTHECA
DACTYLOUS
DACTYLOZOOID
DACTYLUS
DAD
DADA
DADAISM

DADAIST
DADAISTIC
DADAP
DADDER
DADDING
DADDLE
DADDLED
DADDLING
DADDOCK
DADDOCKY
DADDY
DADDYNUT
DADE
DADED
DADENHUDD
DADING
DADO
DADOED
DADOES
DADOING
DADOUCHOS
DADUCHUS
DAEDAL
DAEDALOID
DAEKON
DAEMON
DAEMONES
DAEMONIC
DAEMONIES
DAEMONS
DAEMONURGIST
DAEMONURGY
DAEMONY
DAENA
DAEVA
DAER
DAFF
DAFFADILLY
DAFFED
DAFFERY
DAFFIER
DAFFIEST
DAFFING
DAFFISH
DAFFLE
DAFFLED
DAFFLING
DAFFODIL
DAFFODILLY
DAFFY
DAFT
DAFTAR
DAFTARDAR
DAFTBERRY
DAFTLY
DAFTNESS
DAG
DAGABA
DAGAME
DAGASSA
DAGESH
DAGG
DAGGA
DAGGAR
DAGGE
DAGGED
DAGGER
DAGGERBUSH
DAGGERED
DAGGERING
DAGGERS
DAGGING
DAGGLE
DAGGLED
DAGGLETAIL
DAGGLETAILED
DAGGLING

DAGGLY
DAGGY
DAGH
DAGHESH
DAGLOCK
DAGO
DAGOBA
DAGOES
DAGON
DAGOS
DAGS
DAGSWAIN
DAGUE
DAGUILLA
DAH
DAHABEAH
DAHABEEYAH
DAHABIAH
DAHABIEH
DAHABIYEH
DAHI
DAHIL
DAHLIA
DAHOMEY
DAHOON
DAIDLE
DAIDLED
DAIDLIE
DAIDLING
DAIDLY
DAIGH
DAIKER
DAIKON
DAILIES
DAILINESS
DAILY
DAIM
DAIMEN
DAIMIATE
DAIMIEL
DAIMIO
DAIMIOATE
DAIMIOS
DAIMIOTE
DAIMON
DAIMONIC
DAIMONION
DAIMONISTIC
DAIMYO
DAIN
DAINCHA
DAINCHAS
DAINFUL
DAINT
DAINTETH
DAINTIER
DAINTIES
DAINTIEST
DAINTIFIED
DAINTIFY
DAINTIFYING
DAINTILY
DAINTINESS
DAINTITH
DAINTREL
DAINTY
DAIQUIRI
DAIRA
DAIRI
DAIRIES
DAIROUS
DAIRT
DAIRY
DAIRYING
DAIRYMAID
DAIRYMAN
DAIRYMEN

DAIRYWOMAN
DAIRYWOMEN
DAIS
DAISED
DAISEE
DAISES
DAISIED
DAISIES
DAISING
DAISY
DAISYBUSH
DAITYA
DAIVA
DAK
DAKER
DAKHMA
DAKOIT
DAKOO
DAKTYLOS
DAKU
DAL
DALAG
DALAGA
DALAR
DALE
DALER
DALES
DALESFOLK
DALESMAN
DALESMEN
DALESPEOPLE
DALESWOMAN
DALETH
DALIS
DALK
DALLACK
DALLE
DALLES
DALLI
DALLIANCE
DALLIED
DALLIER
DALLIS
DALLOP
DALLY
DALLYING
DALLYINGLY
DALLYMAN
DALMATIC
DALO
DALT
DALTEEN
DAM
DAMA
DAMAGE
DAMAGEABLE
DAMAGEABLY
DAMAGED
DAMAGEOUS
DAMAGER
DAMAGES
DAMAGING
DAMAN
DAMAR
DAMAS
DAMASCENE
DAMASCENED
DAMASCENER
DAMASCENINE
DAMASCENING
DAMASK
DAMASKEEN
DAMASKIN
DAMASKINE
DAMASSE
DAMASSIN
DAMBO

DAMBOARD
DAMBONITOL
DAMBOSE
DAMBROD
DAME
DAMENIZATION
DAMEWORT
DAMFOOL
DAMIANA
DAMIE
DAMIER
DAMINE
DAMKJERNITE
DAMMAR
DAMMARET
DAMME
DAMMED
DAMMER
DAMMING
DAMMISH
DAMMIT
DAMN
DAMNABILITY
DAMNABLE
DAMNABLENESS
DAMNABLY
DAMNATION
DAMNATORY
DAMNDEST
DAMNED
DAMNEDEST
DAMNER
DAMNIFIED
DAMNIFY
DAMNIFYING
DAMNING
DAMNINGLY
DAMNINGNESS
DAMNOUS
DAMNOUSLY
DAMNUM
DAMOISEAU
DAMOISELLE
DAMONICO
DAMOSEL
DAMOURITE
DAMOZEL
DAMP
DAMPANG
DAMPED
DAMPEN
DAMPENED
DAMPENER
DAMPENING
DAMPER
DAMPEST
DAMPING
DAMPISH
DAMPLY
DAMPNESS
DAMPPROOF
DAMPPROOFING
DAMSEL
DAMSELFISH
DAMSITE
DAMSON
DAMYANKEE
DAN
DANAIDE
DANAINE
DANAITE
DANALITE
DANARO
DANBURITE
DANCALITE
DANCE
DANCED

DANCER
DANCERESS
DANCERS
DANCERY
DANCES
DANCETTE
DANCETTEE
DANCETTY
DANCING
DAND
DANDA
DANDELION
DANDER
DANDI
DANDIACAL
DANDIACALLY
DANDIE
DANDIER
DANDIES
DANDIEST
DANDIFIED
DANDIFY
DANDIFYING
DANDILLY
DANDILY
DANDIPRAT
DANDIS
DANDISETTE
DANDIZETTE
DANDLE
DANDLED
DANDLER
DANDLING
DANDRUFF
DANDRUFFY
DANDY
DANDYISH
DANDYISM
DANDYIZE
DANDYPRAT
DANEWORT
DANG
DANGER
DANGEROUS
DANGEROUSLY
DANGERSOME
DANGLE
DANGLEBERRY
DANGLED
DANGLER
DANGLIN
DANGLING
DANGLINGLY
DANICISM
DANIO
DANK
DANKER
DANKEST
DANKISH
DANKISHNESS
DANKLY
DANKNESS
DANLI
DANNEMORITE
DANNER
DANNOCK
DANSANT
DANSEUR
DANSEUSE
DANSEUSES
DANSY
DANTA
DANTON
DANZA
DANZON
DAO
DAOINE

DAP
DAPHNE
DAPHNETIN
DAPHNI
DAPHNID
DAPHNIN
DAPHNITE
DAPICHO
DAPICO
DAPIFER
DAPPED
DAPPER
DAPPERLING
DAPPERLY
DAPPERNESS
DAPPING
DAPPLE
DAPPLED
DAPPLING
DAPS
DAR
DARABUKKA
DARAC
DARAF
DARAK
DARAT
DARB
DARBHA
DARBIES
DARBUKKA
DARBY
DARCY
DARDANARIUS
DARDANIUM
DARDAOL
DARE
DAREALL
DARED
DAREDEVIL
DAREDEVILRY
DAREDEVILTRY
DAREFUL
DARER
DARES
DARESAY
DARG
DARGAH
DARGER
DARGSMAN
DARGUE
DARI
DARIBAH
DARIC
DARING
DARINGLY
DARINGNESS
DARIOLE
DARK
DARKED
DARKEN
DARKENED
DARKENER
DARKENING
DARKER
DARKEST
DARKEY
DARKEYS
DARKFUL
DARKIE
DARKIES
DARKING
DARKISH
DARKISHNESS
DARKLE
DARKLED
DARKLING
DARKLINGS

DARKLY
DARKMANS
DARKNESS
DARKROOM
DARKS
DARKSKIN
DARKSOME
DARKSOMENESS
DARKSUM
DARKY
DARLING
DARLINGLY
DARLINGNESS
DARN
DARNDEST
DARNED
DARNEDEST
DARNEL
DARNER
DARNEX
DARNING
DAROGA
DAROGAH
DAROGHA
DAROO
DARR
DARREIN
DARSHAN
DARSHANA
DARSO
DARST
DART
DARTARS
DARTED
DARTER
DARTING
DARTINGLY
DARTINGNESS
DARTLE
DARTLIKE
DARTMAN
DARTOS
DARTRE
DARTROSE
DARTS
DARWAN
DARWESH
DARZEE
DARZI
DAS
DASEIN
DASH
DASHBOARD
DASHED
DASHEDLY
DASHEE
DASHEEN
DASHEL
DASHER
DASHIER
DASHIEST
DASHING
DASHINGLY
DASHMAKER
DASHPLATE
DASHPOT
DASHT
DASHWHEEL
DASHY
DASI
DASS
DASSENT
DASSIE
DASSY
DAST
DASTARD
DASTARDIZE

DASTARDLY
DASTARDY
DASTUR
DASTURI
DASWEN
DASYMETER
DASYPAEDAL
DASYPAEDES
DASYURE
DASYURID
DASYURINE
DASYUROID
DATA
DATABLE
DATANA
DATARIA
DATARIES
DATARY
DATCH
DATCHA
DATE
DATED
DATELESS
DATELINE
DATEMARK
DATER
DATIL
DATING
DATIO
DATION
DATISCETIN
DATISCIN
DATISCOSID
DATISCOSIDE
DATIVAL
DATIVE
DATIVELY
DATO
DATOLITE
DATOLITIC
DATTO
DATTOCK
DATTOS
DATU
DATUM
DATURISM
DAUB
DAUBE
DAUBED
DAUBER
DAUBERY
DAUBING
DAUBREEITE
DAUBREELITE
DAUBREITE
DAUBRY
DAUBSTER
DAUBY
DAUD
DAUDED
DAUDING
DAUDIT
DAUERLAUF
DAUGHTER
DAUGHTERLY
DAUGHTERS
DAUKIN
DAULT
DAUNCH
DAUNCY
DAUNDER
DAUNER
DAUNT
DAUNTED
DAUNTER
DAUNTING
DAUNTINGLY

DAUNTINGNESS
DAUNTLESS
DAUNTLESSLY
DAUPHIN
DAUPHINE
DAUPHINESS
DAURNA
DAUT
DAUTIE
DAUW
DAVACH
DAVAINEA
DAVEN
DAVENPORT
DAVER
DAVERDY
DAVIDSONITE
DAVIELY
DAVIES
DAVIESITE
DAVIT
DAVOCH
DAVY
DAVYNE
DAW
DAWCOCK
DAWDLE
DAWDLED
DAWDLER
DAWDLING
DAWISH
DAWK
DAWKIN
DAWN
DAWNED
DAWNING
DAWNY
DAWPATE
DAWSONITE
DAWT
DAWTIE
DAWUT
DAY
DAYABHAGA
DAYAL
DAYAN
DAYBEAM
DAYBED
DAYBERRY
DAYBLUSH
DAYBOOK
DAYBREAK
DAYDAWN
DAYDREAM
DAYDREAMED
DAYDREAMER
DAYDREAMY
DAYDRUDGE
DAYFLOWER
DAYFLY
DAYLIGHT
DAYLIGHTED
DAYLIGHTING
DAYLIGHTS
DAYLILIES
DAYLILY
DAYLIT
DAYLONG
DAYMAN
DAYMARE
DAYMARK
DAYMEN
DAYMENT
DAYNET
DAYROOM
DAYS
DAYSHINE

DAYSIDE
DAYSMAN
DAYSPRING
DAYSTAR
DAYSTREAK
DAYTALE
DAYTIDE
DAYTIME
DAYTIMES
DAYWORK
DAYWORKER
DAYWRIT
DAZE
DAZED
DAZEDLY
DAZEDNESS
DAZING
DAZY
DAZZLE
DAZZLED
DAZZLER
DAZZLING
DAZZLINGLY
DE
DEACETYLATE
DEACON
DEACONAL
DEACONATE
DEACONESS
DEACONRIES
DEACONRY
DEACONSHIP
DEACTIVATE
DEACTIVATED
DEACTIVATING
DEACTIVATION
DEAD
DEADBEAT
DEADBORN
DEADEN
DEADENED
DEADENER
DEADENING
DEADER
DEADEYE
DEADFALL
DEADHEAD
DEADHEARTED
DEADHOUSE
DEADING
DEADISH
DEADISHLY
DEADISHNESS
DEADLATCH
DEADLIER
DEADLIEST
DEADLIGHT
DEADLINE
DEADLINESS
DEADLOCK
DEADLY
DEADMAN
DEADMELT
DEADNESS
DEADPAN
DEADPANNED
DEADPANNING
DEADPAY
DEADS
DEADTONGUE
DEADWOOD
DEADWORKS
DEADWORT
DEAERATE
DEAERATION
DEAERATOR
DEAF

DEAFEN
DEAFENED
DEAFENING
DEAFENINGLY
DEAFISH
DEAFLY
DEAFNESS
DEAL
DEALATE
DEALATED
DEALATION
DEALBATE
DEALBATION
DEALER
DEALERS
DEALFISH
DEALFISHES
DEALING
DEALKALIZE
DEALKYLATE
DEALKYLATION
DEALT
DEAMBULATION
DEAMBULATORY
DEAMIDASE
DEAMIDATE
DEAMINASE
DEAMINATE
DEAMINATION
DEAN
DEANER
DEANERIES
DEANERY
DEANESS
DEANSHIP
DEAR
DEARBORN
DEARER
DEAREST
DEARIE
DEARIES
DEARLING
DEARLY
DEARN
DEARNESS
DEARSENICATE
DEARTH
DEARTHFU
DEARWORTH
DEARWORTHILY
DEARY
DEAS
DEASIL
DEASPIRATE
DEASPIRATION
DEATH
DEATHBED
DEATHBLOW
DEATHCUP
DEATHDAY
DEATHFUL
DEATHIFY
DEATHIN
DEATHINESS
DEATHLESS
DEATHLESSLY
DEATHLIKE
DEATHLINESS
DEATHLY
DEATHROOT
DEATHSMAN
DEATHSMEN
DEATHTRAP
DEATHWATCH
DEATHWEED
DEATHWORM
DEATHY

DEAURATE
DEAVE
DEAVED
DEAVELY
DEAVING
DEBACLE
DEBAG
DEBAR
DEBARK
DEBARKATION
DEBARKMENT
DEBARMENT
DEBARRANCE
DEBARRASS
DEBARRATION
DEBARRED
DEBARRING
DEBASE
DEBASED
DEBASEMENT
DEBASER
DEBASING
DEBAT
DEBATABLE
DEBATE
DEBATEFUL
DEBATEFULLY
DEBATEMENT
DEBATER
DEBATING
DEBATINGLY
DEBATTER
DEBAUCH
DEBAUCHED
DEBAUCHEDLY
DEBAUCHEDNESS
DEBAUCHEE
DEBAUCHER
DEBAUCHERIES
DEBAUCHERY
DEBAUCHING
DEBAUCHMENT
DEBBIES
DEBEL
DEBELL
DEBELLATE
DEBELLATION
DEBELLATOR
DEBEN
DEBENTURE
DEBENTURED
DEBENZOLIZE
DEBILE
DEBILISSIMA
DEBILITANT
DEBILITATE
DEBILITATED
DEBILITATING
DEBILITATION
DEBILITATIVE
DEBILITY
DEBIND
DEBIT
DEBITED
DEBITEUSE
DEBITING
DEBITOR
DEBITUM
DEBLAI
DEBLATERATE
DEBLOCK
DEBOISE
DEBOIST
DEBONAIR
DEBONAIRE
DEBONAIRITY
DEBONAIRLY

DEBONAIRNESS
DEBONNAIRE
DEBORD
DEBORDMENT
DEBOSH
DEBOSHED
DEBOSS
DEBOUCH
DEBOUCHE
DEBOUCHMENT
DEBOUCHURE
DEBOUT
DEBOWEL
DEBRIDE
DEBRIDEMENT
DEBRIEF
DEBRIS
DEBRUISE
DEBT
DEBTED
DEBTEE
DEBTFUL
DEBTOR
DEBTS
DEBUG
DEBUGGED
DEBUGGING
DEBUNK
DEBUNKER
DEBUNKMENT
DEBURSE
DEBUS
DEBUT
DEBUTANT
DEBUTANTE
DEBUTED
DEBUTING
DEBYE
DECACHORD
DECAD
DECADAL
DECADALLY
DECADARY
DECADATION
DECADE
DECADENCE
DECADENCY
DECADENT
DECADENZA
DECADESCENT
DECADIANOME
DECADIC
DECADIST
DECADRACHMA
DECADRACHMAE
DECAEDRON
DECAFFEINIZE
DECAFID
DECAGON
DECAGONAL
DECAGONALLY
DECAGRAM
DECAGRAMME
DECAHEDRA
DECAHEDRAL
DECAHEDRON
DECAHEDRONS
DECAHYDRATE
DECAHYDRATED
DECAL
DECALAGE
DECALCIFIED
DECALCIFIER
DECALCIFY
DECALCIFYING
DECALCOMANIA
DECALESCENCE

DECALESCENT
DECALITER
DECALITRE
DECALOBATE
DECALVANT
DECALVATION
DECAMERAL
DECAMEROUS
DECAMETER
DECAMETER
DECAMETRE
DECAMP
DECAMPED
DECAMPING
DECAMPMENT
DECAN
DECANAL
DECANALLY
DECANATE
DECANDENTLY
DECANDROUS
DECANE
DECANI
DECANICALLY
DECANOL
DECANOYL
DECANT
DECANTATE
DECANTATION
DECANTER
DECANTIST
DECAPITABLE
DECAPITATE
DECAPITATED
DECAPITATING
DECAPITATION
DECAPITATOR
DECAPOD
DECAPODAL
DECAPODAN
DECAPODIFORM
DECAPODOUS
DECAPPER
DECAPSULATE
DECARBONATE
DECARBONATED
DECARBONATING
DECARBONATOR
DECARBONIZE
DECARBONIZED
DECARBONIZER
DECARBURIZE
DECARBURIZED
DECARCH
DECARCHIES
DECARCHY
DECARD
DECARE
DECARHINUS
DECARNATE
DECARNATED
DECASEMIC
DECAST
DECASTELLATE
DECASTERE
DECASTICH
DECASUALIZE
DECASYLLABIC
DECASYLLABLE
DECATE
DECATHLON
DECATING
DECATIZE
DECATIZER
DECATOIC
DECATYL
DECAUDATE

DECAUDATION
DECAY
DECAYED
DECAYEDNESS
DECAYER
DECAYING
DECEASE
DECEASED
DECEASING
DECEDE
DECEDENT
DECEIT
DECEITFUL
DECEITFULLY
DECEITFULNESS
DECEIVABLE
DECEIVABLY
DECEIVE
DECEIVED
DECEIVER
DECEIVING
DECEIVINGLY
DECELERATE
DECELERATED
DECELERATING
DECELERATION
DECELERATOR
DECEMVIR
DECEMVIRAL
DECEMVIRATE
DECEMVIRI
DECEMVIRS
DECENARY
DECENCE
DECENCIES
DECENCY
DECENE
DECENNAL
DECENNARY
DECENNIA
DECENNIAL
DECENNIALLY
DECENNIUM
DECENNIUMS
DECENT
DECENTER
DECENTERED
DECENTERING
DECENTLY
DECENTNESS
DECENTRALISM
DECENTRALIST
DECENTRALIZE
DECENTRATION
DECENTRE
DECENTRED
DECENTRING
DECENYL
DECEPTIBLE
DECEPTION
DECEPTIOUS
DECEPTIOUSLY
DECEPTITIOUS
DECEPTIVE
DECEPTIVELY
DECEPTIVENESS
DECEPTIVITY
DECEREBRATE
DECEREBRATED
DECEREBRATING
DECEREBRIZE
DECERN
DECERNITURE
DECERP
DECESS
DECESSION
DECHENITE

DECHORALIZE
DECIARE
DECIBEL
DECICERONIZE
DECIDABLE
DECIDE
DECIDED
DECIDEDLY
DECIDEDNESS
DECIDER
DECIDING
DECIDINGLY
DECIDUA
DECIDUAL
DECIDUARY
DECIDUATE
DECIDUITIS
DECIDUOMA
DECIDUOUS
DECIDUOUSLY
DECIGRAM
DECIGRAMME
DECIL
DECILE
DECILITER
DECILITRE
DECILLION
DECILLIONTH
DECIMA
DECIMAL
DECIMALISM
DECIMALIST
DECIMALIZE
DECIMALIZED
DECIMALIZING
DECIMALLY
DECIMATE
DECIMATED
DECIMATING
DECIMATION
DECIMATOR
DECIME
DECIMESTRIAL
DECIMETER
DECIMETRE
DECIMOLAR
DECIMOLE
DECIMOSEXTO
DECINE
DECINORMAL
DECIPHER
DECIPHERED
DECIPHERER
DECIPHERING
DECIPHERMENT
DECIPIUM
DECIPOLAR
DECISE
DECISION
DECISIONAL
DECISIVE
DECISIVELY
DECISIVENESS
DECISTERE
DECIVILIZE
DECK
DECKE
DECKED
DECKEL
DECKEN
DECKER
DECKHAND
DECKHEAD
DECKHOUSE
DECKIE
DECKING
DECKLE

DECKLOAD
DECKMAN
DECKS
DECLAIM
DECLAIMANT
DECLAIMED
DECLAIMER
DECLAIMING
DECLAMANDO
DECLAMATION
DECLAMATORY
DECLARANT
DECLARATION
DECLARATIVE
DECLARATOR
DECLARATORY
DECLARE
DECLARED
DECLAREDLY
DECLAREDNESS
DECLARER
DECLARING
DECLASS
DECLASSE
DECLASSED
DECLASSEE
DECLASSING
DECLENSION
DECLENSIONAL
DECLINABLE
DECLINAL
DECLINATE
DECLINATION
DECLINATIONS
DECLINATORY
DECLINATURE
DECLINE
DECLINED
DECLINER
DECLINING
DECLINOGRAPH
DECLINOMETER
DECLIVATE
DECLIVE
DECLIVITIES
DECLIVITOUS
DECLIVITY
DECLIVOUS
DECLUTCH
DECOCT
DECOCTION
DECOCTIVE
DECOCTUM
DECODE
DECODED
DECODER
DECODING
DECOHERE
DECOHERER
DECOIC
DECOKE
DECOLL
DECOLLATE
DECOLLATED
DECOLLATING
DECOLLATION
DECOLLATOR
DECOLLETAGE
DECOLLETE
DECOLOR
DECOLORANT
DECOLORATE
DECOLORATION
DECOLORIZE
DECOLORIZED
DECOLORIZER
DECOLORIZING

DECOLOUR
DECOLOURISE
DECOLOURIZE
DECOMMISSION
DECOMPENSATE
DECOMPLEX
DECOMPONIBLE
DECOMPOSABLE
DECOMPOSE
DECOMPOSED
DECOMPOSER
DECOMPOSING
DECOMPOSITE
DECOMPOSITION
DECOMPOSURE
DECOMPOUND
DECOMPRESS
DECONGESTIVE
DECONSIDER
DECONTROL
DECONTROLLED
DECOPED
DECOR
DECORAMENT
DECORATE
DECORATED
DECORATING
DECORATION
DECORATIVE
DECORATOR
DECORATORY
DECORE
DECOREMENT
DECORIST
DECOROUS
DECOROUSLY
DECOROUSNESS
DECORTICATE
DECORTICATED
DECORUM
DECOUPAGE
DECOY
DECOYED
DECOYER
DECOYING
DECOYMAN
DECOYMEN
DECOYS
DECRASSIFIED
DECRASSIFY
DECREASE
DECREASED
DECREASELESS
DECREASING
DECREASINGLY
DECREATION
DECREATIVE
DECREE
DECREED
DECREEING
DECREEMENT
DECREER
DECREET
DECREMENT
DECREMETER
DECREPID
DECREPIT
DECREPITATE
DECREPITATED
DECREPITLY
DECREPITNESS
DECREPITUDE
DECREPITY
DECRESCENCE
DECRESCENDO
DECRESCENT
DECRETAL

DECRETALIST
DECRETE
DECRETIST
DECRETIVE
DECRETIVELY
DECRETORIAL
DECRETORILY
DECRETORY
DECRETUM
DECREW
DECRIAL
DECRIED
DECRIER
DECROWN
DECRUSTATION
DECRY
DECRYING
DECRYPT
DECUBITAL
DECUBITUS
DECULTURATE
DECULTURATED
DECUMAN
DECUMANA
DECUMANI
DECUMANUS
DECUMARY
DECUMBENCE
DECUMBENCY
DECUMBENT
DECUMBITURE
DECUPLE
DECUPLED
DECUPLET
DECUPLING
DECURIA
DECURIES
DECURION
DECURIONATE
DECURRENCE
DECURRENCES
DECURRENCIES
DECURRENCY
DECURRENT
DECURRENTLY
DECURSION
DECURSIVE
DECURSIVELY
DECURT
DECURTATE
DECURVATION
DECURVE
DECURVED
DECURVING
DECURY
DECUS
DECUSSATE
DECUSSATED
DECUSSATELY
DECUSSATING
DECUSSATION
DECUSSION
DECUSSIS
DECUSSORIA
DECUSSORIUM
DECYL
DECYLENE
DECYLENIC
DECYLIC
DECYNE
DED
DEDAL
DEDANS
DEDDY
DEDE
DEDECORATE
DEDECORATION

DEDECOROUS
DEDENDA
DEDENDUM
DEDENTITION
DEDICATE
DEDICATED
DEDICATEE
DEDICATING
DEDICATION
DEDICATIONAL
DEDICATIVE
DEDICATOR
DEDICATORIAL
DEDICATORILY
DEDICATORY
DEDICATURE
DEDIMUS
DEDIT
DEDITICIAN
DEDITION
DEDO
DEDOLATION
DEDOLENCE
DEDOLENCY
DEDOLENT
DEDUCE
DEDUCED
DEDUCEMENT
DEDUCIBILITY
DEDUCIBLE
DEDUCIBLY
DEDUCING
DEDUCIVE
DEDUCT
DEDUCTED
DEDUCTIBLE
DEDUCTILE
DEDUCTING
DEDUCTIO
DEDUCTION
DEDUCTIONS
DEDUCTIVE
DEDUCTIVELY
DEDUCTORY
DEDUIT
DEE
DEECE
DEED
DEEDBOX
DEEDED
DEEDEED
DEEDFUL
DEEDFULLY
DEEDILY
DEEDINESS
DEEDING
DEEDLESS
DEEDS
DEEDY
DEEJAY
DEEL
DEEM
DEEMED
DEEMER
DEEMIE
DEEMING
DEEMSTER
DEEMSTERSHIP
DEEN
DEENER
DEENY
DEEP
DEEPEN
DEEPENER
DEEPENING
DEEPER
DEEPEST

DEEPFREEZE
DEEPFREEZED
DEEPFREEZING
DEEPFROZE
DEEPFROZEN
DEEPING
DEEPLY
DEEPMOST
DEEPMOUTHED
DEEPNESS
DEEPSOME
DEEPWATER
DEEPWATERMAN
DEEPWATERMEN
DEER
DEERBERRY
DEERDOG
DEERDRIVE
DEERFLY
DEERFOOD
DEERGRASS
DEERHAIR
DEERHERD
DEERHORN
DEERHOUND
DEERKILL
DEERLET
DEERSKIN
DEERSTALKER
DEERSTALKING
DEERSTAND
DEERTONGUE
DEERVETCH
DEERWEED
DEERWOOD
DEERYARD
DEES
DEESCALATE
DEESCALATED
DEESCALATING
DEESCALATION
DEESE
DEESIS
DEESS
DEEVE
DEEVEY
DEEVILICK
DEEWAN
DEFACE
DEFACED
DEFACEMENT
DEFACER
DEFACING
DEFACINGLY
DEFADE
DEFAIL
DEFAILANCE
DEFAILLANCE
DEFAILMENT
DEFAITISME
DEFAITISTE
DEFALCATE
DEFALCATING
DEFALCATION
DEFALCATOR
DEFALK
DEFAMATION
DEFAMATORY
DEFAME
DEFAMED
DEFAMER
DEFAMING
DEFAMINGLY
DEFAMOUS
DEFAMY
DEFASSA

DEFAT
DEFATIGABLE
DEFATIGATE
DEFATIGATED
DEFATIGATION
DEFATTED
DEFATTING
DEFAULT
DEFAULTANT
DEFAULTER
DEFAULTURE
DEFEASANCE
DEFEASANCED
DEFEASE
DEFEASIBLE
DEFEAT
DEFEATED
DEFEATER
DEFEATISM
DEFEATIST
DEFEATMENT
DEFEATURE
DEFECANT
DEFECATE
DEFECATED
DEFECATING
DEFECATION
DEFECATOR
DEFECT
DEFECTIBLE
DEFECTION
DEFECTIONIST
DEFECTIOUS
DEFECTIVE
DEFECTIVELY
DEFECTOR
DEFECTOSCOPE
DEFECTS
DEFEDATION
DEFEISE
DEFEIT
DEFEMINIZE
DEFENCE
DEFENCELESS
DEFEND
DEFENDABLE
DEFENDANT
DEFENDED
DEFENDER
DEFENDRESS
DEFENSATIVE
DEFENSE
DEFENSELESS
DEFENSER
DEFENSIBLE
DEFENSIBLY
DEFENSION
DEFENSIVE
DEFENSIVELY
DEFENSOR
DEFENSORY
DEFER
DEFERENCE
DEFERENT
DEFERENTIAL
DEFERENTITIS
DEFERMENT
DEFERRABLE
DEFERRAL
DEFERRED
DEFERRER
DEFERRING
DEFERRIZE
DEFERRIZED
DEFERRIZING
DEFERVESCE
DEFERVESCENT

DEFET
DEFI
DEFIABLE
DEFIAL
DEFIANCE
DEFIANT
DEFIANTLY
DEFIANTNESS
DEFIBER
DEFIBRINATE
DEFIBRINIZE
DEFICIENCE
DEFICIENCY
DEFICIENT
DEFICIENTLY
DEFICIT
DEFIED
DEFIER
DEFIES
DEFIGURATION
DEFIGURE
DEFILADE
DEFILADED
DEFILADING
DEFILE
DEFILED
DEFILEMENT
DEFILER
DEFILIATION
DEFILING
DEFILINGLY
DEFINABILITY
DEFINABLE
DEFINABLY
DEFINE
DEFINED
DEFINEDLY
DEFINEMENT
DEFINER
DEFINING
DEFINITE
DEFINITELY
DEFINITENESS
DEFINITION
DEFINITIONAL
DEFINITIVE
DEFINITIVELY
DEFINITIZE
DEFINITIZED
DEFINITIZING
DEFINITOR
DEFINITUDE
DEFIX
DEFLAGRABLE
DEFLAGRATE
DEFLAGRATED
DEFLAGRATING
DEFLAGRATION
DEFLAGRATOR
DEFLATE
DEFLATED
DEFLATING
DEFLATION
DEFLATIONARY
DEFLATIONIST
DEFLATOR
DEFLECT
DEFLECTED
DEFLECTING
DEFLECTION
DEFLECTIVE
DEFLECTOR
DEFLEX
DEFLEXED
DEFLEXING
DEFLEXION
DEFLEXURE

DEFLOCCULANT
DEFLOCCULATE
DEFLOCCULENT
DEFLORATE
DEFLORATION
DEFLORE
DEFLOWER
DEFLOWERER
DEFLUENT
DEFLUVIUM
DEFLUX
DEFLUXION
DEFOIL
DEFOLIATE
DEFOLIATED
DEFOLIATING
DEFOLIATION
DEFOLIATOR
DEFORCE
DEFORCED
DEFORCEMENT
DEFORCER
DEFORCIANT
DEFORCING
DEFOREST
DEFORESTER
DEFORM
DEFORMABLE
DEFORMATION
DEFORMATIVE
DEFORMED
DEFORMEDLY
DEFORMEDNESS
DEFORMER
DEFORMETER
DEFORMING
DEFORMISM
DEFORMITIES
DEFORMITY
DEFOUL
DEFRAUD
DEFRAUDATION
DEFRAUDED
DEFRAUDER
DEFRAUDING
DEFRAUDMENT
DEFRAY
DEFRAYAL
DEFRAYED
DEFRAYER
DEFRAYING
DEFRAYMENT
DEFROCK
DEFROST
DEFROSTER
DEFT
DEFTER
DEFTERDAR
DEFTEST
DEFTLY
DEFTNESS
DEFUNCT
DEFUNCTION
DEFUSE
DEFUSION
DEFY
DEFYING
DEG
DEGAGE
DEGAME
DEGAS
DEGASES
DEGASSED
DEGASSER
DEGASSES
DEGASSING
DEGAUSS

DEGELATION
DEGEN
DEGENDER
DEGENER
DEGENERACY
DEGENERATE
DEGENERATED
DEGENERATELY
DEGENERATING
DEGENERATION
DEGENERATIVE
DEGERM
DEGERMINATE
DEGGED
DEGGER
DEGGING
DEGLAZE
DEGLAZED
DEGLAZING
DEGLUTINATE
DEGLUTINATED
DEGLUTITION
DEGLUTITIVE
DEGLUTITORY
DEGOMME
DEGRADAND
DEGRADATION
DEGRADATIVE
DEGRADE
DEGRADED
DEGRADEDLY
DEGRADEDNESS
DEGRADEMENT
DEGRADER
DEGRADING
DEGRADINGLY
DEGRAIN
DEGRAS
DEGREASE
DEGREASED
DEGREASER
DEGREASING
DEGREE
DEGREED
DEGREEING
DEGREES
DEGREEWISE
DEGRESSION
DEGRESSIVE
DEGRESSIVELY
DEGRINGOLADE
DEGU
DEGUELIN
DEGUM
DEGUMMED
DEGUMMING
DEGUST
DEGUSTATE
DEGUSTATION
DEHA
DEHAIR
DEHAIRER
DEHEMATIZE
DEHEPATIZE
DEHISCE
DEHISCED
DEHISCENCE
DEHISCENT
DEHISCING
DEHNSTUFE
DEHORN
DEHORNER
DEHORS
DEHORT
DEHORTATION
DEHORTATIVE
DEHORTATORY

DEHORTED
DEHORTER
DEHORTING
DEHULL
DEHUMANIZE
DEHUMANIZED
DEHUMANIZING
DEHUMIDIFIED
DEHUMIDIFIER
DEHUMIDIFY
DEHYDRANT
DEHYDRATE
DEHYDRATED
DEHYDRATING
DEHYDRATION
DEHYDRATOR
DEHYPNOTIZE
DEHYPNOTIZED
DEI
DEICE
DEICED
DEICER
DEICIDAL
DEICIDE
DEICING
DEICTIC
DEICTICALLY
DEIFIC
DEIFICAL
DEIFICATION
DEIFICATORY
DEIFIED
DEIFIER
DEIFORM
DEIFORMITY
DEIFY
DEIFYING
DEIGN
DEIGNED
DEIGNING
DEIGNOUS
DEIL
DEIN
DEINCRUSTANT
DEINOS
DEIONIZE
DEIPOTENT
DEIRID
DEISEAL
DEISM
DEIST
DEISTIC
DEISTICAL
DEISTICALLY
DEITIES
DEITY
DEJECT
DEJECTA
DEJECTED
DEJECTEDLY
DEJECTEDNESS
DEJECTILE
DEJECTION
DEJECTORY
DEJECTURE
DEJERATE
DEJEUNE
DEJEUNER
DEJUNKERIZE
DEKADRACHM
DEKAGRAM
DEKALITER
DEKALITRE
DEKAMETER
DEKAMETRE
DEKAN

DEKAPARSEC
DEKAPODE
DEKARCH
DEKASTERE
DEKE
DEKED
DEKING
DEKKO
DEL
DELACTATION
DELAINE
DELAMINATE
DELAMINATED
DELAMINATING
DELAMINATION
DELAPSE
DELAPSION
DELASSEMENT
DELATE
DELATED
DELATER
DELATING
DELATION
DELATOR
DELATORIAN
DELAVY
DELAWN
DELAY
DELAYAGE
DELAYED
DELAYER
DELAYING
DELAYINGLY
DELE
DELEAD
DELEATUR
DELECTABLE
DELECTABLY
DELECTATE
DELECTATED
DELECTATING
DELECTATION
DELECTUS
DELED
DELEERIT
DELEGABLE
DELEGACIES
DELEGACY
DELEGALIZE
DELEGANT
DELEGATE
DELEGATED
DELEGATEE
DELEGATING
DELEGATION
DELEGATIVE
DELEGATORY
DELEING
DELENDA
DELETE
DELETED
DELETERIOUS
DELETERY
DELETING
DELETION
DELETIVE
DELETORY
DELF
DELFT
DELFTWARE
DELIBATE
DELIBER
DELIBERANT
DELIBERATE
DELIBERATED
DELIBERATELY
DELIBERATENESS

DELIBERATING
DELIBERATION
DELIBERATIVE
DELIBERATOR
DELIBLE
DELICACIES
DELICACY
DELICATE
DELICATELY
DELICATENESS
DELICATESSEN
DELICE
DELICIAE
DELICIOSO
DELICIOUS
DELICIOUSLY
DELICIOUSNESS
DELICT
DELICTUM
DELIE
DELIERET
DELIGATED
DELIGATION
DELIGHT
DELIGHTABLE
DELIGHTED
DELIGHTEDLY
DELIGHTEDNESS
DELIGHTER
DELIGHTFUL
DELIGHTFULLY
DELIGHTFULNESS
DELIGHTING
DELIGHTINGLY
DELIGHTSOME
DELIGHTSOMELY
DELIGHTSOMENESS
DELIGNATE
DELIGNATED
DELIME
DELIMER
DELIMIT
DELIMITATE
DELIMITATED
DELIMITATING
DELIMITATION
DELIMITATIVE
DELIMITED
DELIMITER
DELIMITIZE
DELIMITIZED
DELIMITIZING
DELINE
DELINEABLE
DELINEATE
DELINEATED
DELINEATING
DELINEATION
DELINEATIVE
DELINEATOR
DELINEATORY
DELINEAVIT
DELINQUENCIES
DELINQUENCY
DELINQUENT
DELINQUENTLY
DELIQUESCE
DELIQUESCED
DELIQUESCENT
DELIQUESCING
DELIQUIUM
DELIRACY
DELIRAMENT
DELIRANT
DELIRATION
DELIRE
DELIRIA

DELIRIOUS
DELIRIOUSLY
DELIRIUM
DELIRIUMS
DELISK
DELITESCENCE
DELITESCENT
DELITOUS
DELIVER
DELIVERABLE
DELIVERANCE
DELIVERED
DELIVERER
DELIVERIES
DELIVERING
DELIVERLY
DELIVEROR
DELIVERY
DELIVERYMAN
DELIVERYMEN
DELK
DELL
DELLA
DELLENITE
DELLS
DELOCALIZE
DELOCALIZED
DELOCALIZING
DELOMORPHIC
DELOMORPHOUS
DELOUL
DELOUSE
DELOUSED
DELOUSING
DELPH
DELPHIN
DELPHINE
DELPHINIC
DELPHININ
DELPHININE
DELPHINITE
DELPHINIUM
DELPHINOID
DELT
DELTA
DELTAHEDRA
DELTAHEDRON
DELTAIC
DELTAITE
DELTAL
DELTATION
DELTHYRIA
DELTHYRIAL
DELTHYRIUM
DELTIC
DELTIDIA
DELTIDIAL
DELTIDIUM
DELTOHEDRA
DELTOHEDRON
DELTOID
DELTOIDAL
DELUBRUM
DELUDE
DELUDED
DELUDER
DELUDHER
DELUDING
DELUDINGLY
DELUGE
DELUGED
DELUGING
DELUL
DELUMINIZE
DELUNDUNG
DELUSION
DELUSIONAL

DELUSIONIST	DEMESNIAL	DEMIURGIC	DEMONSTRABLE	DENDRAXON
DELUSIVE	DEMETHYLATE	DEMIURGICAL	DEMONSTRABLY	DENDRIC
DELUSIVELY	DEMI	DEMIURGISM	DEMONSTRANCE	DENDRIFORM
DELUSIVENESS	DEMIBASTION	DEMIURGOS	DEMONSTRANT	DENDRITE
DELUSORY	DEMIBATH	DEMIURGUS	DEMONSTRATE	DENDRITIC
DELUSTER	DEMIBRIGADE	DEMIVIERGE	DEMONSTRATED	DENDRITICAL
DELUXE	DEMICADENCE	DEMIVOL	DEMONSTRATION	DENDRITIFORM
DELVE	DEMICANNON	DEMIVOLT	DEMONSTRATIVE	DENDROBE
DELVED	DEMICANTON	DEMIVOLTE	DEMONSTRATOR	DENDROCOELE
DELVER	DEMICAPONIER	DEMIWOLF	DEMOPHIL	DENDRODONT
DELVING	DEMICHAMFRON	DEMOB	DEMOPHILE	DENDROGRAPH
DEM	DEMICIRCLE	DEMOBBED	DEMOPHILISM	DENDROGRAPHY
DEMAGNETIZE	DEMICIRCULAR	DEMOBBING	DEMOPHOBE	DENDROID
DEMAGNETIZED	DEMICIVILIZED	DEMOBILIZE	DEMORALIZE	DENDROIDAL
DEMAGNETIZER	DEMICUIRASS	DEMOBILIZED	DEMORALIZED	DENDROLITE
DEMAGOG	DEMICULVERIN	DEMOBILIZING	DEMORALIZER	DENDROLOGIC
DEMAGOGIC	DEMIDITONE	DEMOCRACIES	DEMORALIZING	DENDROLOGIST
DEMAGOGICAL	DEMIDOLMEN	DEMOCRACY	DEMORPHISM	DENDROLOGY
DEMAGOGISM	DEMIES	DEMOCRAT	DEMOS	DENDROMETER
DEMAGOGUE	DEMIGAUNTLET	DEMOCRATIAN	DEMOTE	DENDRON
DEMAGOGUERY	DEMIGOD	DEMOCRATIC	DEMOTED	DENE
DEMAGOGUISM	DEMIGODDESS	DEMOCRATICAL	DEMOTIC	DENEGATE
DEMAGOGY	DEMIGORGE	DEMOCRATISM	DEMOTICS	DENEGATION
DEMAIN	DEMIHAG	DEMOCRATIZE	DEMOTING	DENEHOLE
DEMAL	DEMIHAGBUT	DEMOCRATIZED	DEMOTION	DENERVATE
DEMAND	DEMIHAGUE	DEMOCRAW	DEMOTIST	DENERVATION
DEMANDABLE	DEMIHAKE	DEMODE	DEMOUNT	DENGUE
DEMANDANT	DEMIHAQUE	DEMODED	DEMOUNTABLE	DENIABLE
DEMANDED	DEMIJAMBE	DEMODULATE	DEMPNE	DENIABLY
DEMANDER	DEMIJOHN	DEMODULATED	DEMPSTER	DENIAL
DEMANDING	DEMILANCE	DEMODULATING	DEMULCE	DENICOTINE
DEMANGANIZE	DEMILANCER	DEMODULATION	DEMULCEATE	DENICOTINIZE
DEMANTOID	DEMILEGATO	DEMODULATOR	DEMULCENT	DENIED
DEMARCATE	DEMILITARIZE	DEMOGENIC	DEMULSIFY	DENIER
DEMARCATED	DEMILITARIZED	DEMOGRAPHER	DEMULSION	DENIERAGE
DEMARCATING	DEMILUNE	DEMOGRAPHIC	DEMUR	DENIERER
DEMARCATION	DEMIMARK	DEMOGRAPHICAL	DEMURE	DENIGRATE
DEMARCH	DEMIMETOPE	DEMOGRAPHIST	DEMURELY	DENIGRATED
DEMARCHE	DEMIMONDAIN	DEMOGRAPHY	DEMURENESS	DENIGRATING
DEMARCHY	DEMIMONDAINE	DEMOID	DEMUREST	DENIGRATION
DEMAREE	DEMIMONDE	DEMOISELLE	DEMURITY	DENIGRATOR
DEMARK	DEMINERALIZE	DEMOLISH	DEMURRABLE	DENIM
DEMARKATION	DEMIOURGOI	DEMOLISHER	DEMURRAGE	DENIMS
DEMARKED	DEMIPARALLEL	DEMOLISHMENT	DEMURRAL	DENITRATE
DEMARKING	DEMIPAULDRON	DEMOLITION	DEMURRANT	DENITRATED
DEMAST	DEMIPIKE	DEMOLOGICAL	DEMURRED	DENITRATING
DEMATIACEOUS	DEMIPIQUE	DEMOLOGY	DEMURRER	DENITRATION
DEME	DEMIQUAVER	DEMON	DEMURRING	DENITRATOR
DEMEAN	DEMIRACLE	DEMONASTERY	DEMURRINGLY	DENITRIFIED
DEMEANED	DEMIRELIEF	DEMONETIZE	DEMUTIZATION	DENITRIFIER
DEMEANING	DEMIREP	DEMONETIZED	DEMY	DENITRIFY
DEMEANOR	DEMIRHUMB	DEMONETIZING	DEMYSHIP	DENITRIFYING
DEMEANOUR	DEMIRILIEVO	DEMONIAC	DEN	DENITRIZE
DEMEGORIC	DEMISABLE	DEMONIACAL	DENAR	DENIZATE
DEMELE	DEMISANG	DEMONIACALLY	DENARI	DENIZATION
DEMEMBRATION	DEMISE	DEMONIACISM	DENARIES	DENIZE
DEMENCY	DEMISEASON	DEMONIAL	DENARII	DENIZEN
DEMENT	DEMISED	DEMONIAN	DENARIUS	DENIZENATION
DEMENTATE	DEMISEMITONE	DEMONIANISM	DENARO	DENIZENIZE
DEMENTATION	DEMISING	DEMONIAST	DENARY	DENNED
DEMENTED	DEMISOLDE	DEMONIC	DENAT	DENNET
DEMENTEDLY	DEMISPHERE	DEMONICAL	DENATURALIZE	DENNING
DEMENTEDNESS	DEMISS	DEMONIFUGE	DENATURANT	DENOMINABLE
DEMENTHOLIZE	DEMISSION	DEMONIO	DENATURATE	DENOMINATE
DEMENTI	DEMISSIONARY	DEMONISM	DENATURATION	DENOMINATED
DEMENTIA	DEMISSLY	DEMONIST	DENATURE	DENOMINATING
DEMEORE	DEMISSNESS	DEMONIZE	DENATURED	DENOMINATION
DEMEPHITIZE	DEMISUIT	DEMONIZED	DENATURING	DENOMINATIONAL
DEMERGE	DEMIT	DEMONIZING	DENATURIZE	DENOMINATIVE
DEMERIT	DEMITASSE	DEMONOLATER	DENATURIZER	DENOMINATOR
DEMEROL	DEMITINT	DEMONOLATRY	DENAY	DENOTABLE
DEMERSAL	DEMITOILET	DEMONOLOGER	DENAZIFIED	DENOTATE
DEMERSE	DEMITONE	DEMONOLOGIC	DENAZIFY	DENOTATION
DEMERSED	DEMITTED	DEMONOLOGIST	DENAZIFYING	DENOTATIVE
DEMERSION	DEMITTING	DEMONOLOGY	DENDA	DENOTATIVELY
DEMESMAN	DEMIURGE	DEMONRY	DENDRACHATE	DENOTE
DEMESNE	DEMIURGEOUS	DEMONS	DENDRAL	DENOTED

DENOTEMENT
DENOTING
DENOTIVE
DENOUEMENT
DENOUNCE
DENOUNCED
DENOUNCEMENT
DENOUNCER
DENOUNCING
DENS
DENSATE
DENSATION
DENSE
DENSELY
DENSEN
DENSENESS
DENSER
DENSEST
DENSIFIED
DENSIFIER
DENSIFY
DENSIMETER
DENSIMETRIC
DENSIMETRY
DENSITIES
DENSITOMETER
DENSITY
DENT
DENTAGRA
DENTAL
DENTALE
DENTALISM
DENTALITY
DENTALIZE
DENTAPHONE
DENTARY
DENTATA
DENTATE
DENTATED
DENTATELY
DENTATION
DENTEL
DENTELATED
DENTELLATED
DENTELLE
DENTELLIERE
DENTELLO
DENTELURE
DENTEX
DENTICAL
DENTICATE
DENTICLE
DENTICULAR
DENTICULATE
DENTICULATED
DENTICULE
DENTIFORM
DENTIFRICE
DENTIGEROUS
DENTIL
DENTILABIAL
DENTILATED
DENTILATION
DENTILE
DENTILINGUAL
DENTILOGUY
DENTILOQUIST
DENTIMETER
DENTIN
DENTINAL
DENTINALGIA
DENTINASAL
DENTINE
DENTINITIS
DENTINOBLAST
DENTINOID
DENTINOMA

DENTIPAROUS
DENTIPHONE
DENTIPOSTER
DENTIROSTRAL
DENTISCALP
DENTIST
DENTISTIC
DENTISTICAL
DENTISTRY
DENTITION
DENTOID
DENTOLOLABIAL
DENTONASAL
DENTURAL
DENTURE
DENTY
DENUDANT
DENUDATE
DENUDATED
DENUDATING
DENUDATION
DENUDATIVE
DENUDE
DENUDED
DENUDER
DENUDING
DENUM
DENUMERABLE
DENUMERABLY
DENUMERAL
DENUMERANT
DENUMERATION
DENUMERATIVE
DENUNCIABLE
DENUNCIANT
DENUNCIATE
DENUNCIATED
DENUNCIATING
DENUNCIATION
DENUNCIATIVE
DENUNCIATOR
DENUNCIATORY
DENUTRITION
DENY
DENYING
DEOBSTRUENT
DEOCULATE
DEODAND
DEODAR
DEODATE
DEODORANT
DEODORIZE
DEODORIZED
DEODORIZER
DEODORIZING
DEONTOLOGIST
DEONTOLOGY
DEOPERCULATE
DEOPPILANT
DEOPPILATE
DEOPPILATION
DEOPPILATIVE
DEORDINATION
DEORSUM
DEOTA
DEOXIDIZE
DEOXIDIZED
DEOXIDIZER
DEOXIDIZING
DEOXYGENATE
DEOXYGENATED
DEOXYGENIZE
DEOZONIZE
DEOZONIZER
DEPA
DEPAINT
DEPAINTED

DEPAINTING
DEPAIR
DEPARLIAMENT
DEPART
DEPARTED
DEPARTEMENT
DEPARTER
DEPARTING
DEPARTITION
DEPARTMENT
DEPARTMENTAL
DEPARTURE
DEPAS
DEPASCENT
DEPASS
DEPASTURABLE
DEPASTURAGE
DEPASTURE
DEPASTURED
DEPASTURING
DEPATRIATE
DEPAUPERATE
DEPAUPERIZE
DEPAUPERIZED
DEPAYSE
DEPAYSEE
DEPE
DEPECHE
DEPEL
DEPENCIL
DEPEND
DEPENDABILITY
DEPENDABLE
DEPENDABLY
DEPENDANCY
DEPENDANT
DEPENDED
DEPENDENCE
DEPENDENCIES
DEPENDENCY
DEPENDENT
DEPENDER
DEPENDING
DEPENDINGLY
DEPEOPLE
DEPERDITE
DEPERDITELY
DEPERDITION
DEPERITION
DEPERM
DEPERSONIZE
DEPETALIZE
DEPETER
DEPETTICOAT
DEPHASE
DEPHASED
DEPHASING
DEPHLEGMATE
DEPHLEGMATED
DEPHLEGMATOR
DEPICT
DEPICTED
DEPICTER
DEPICTING
DEPICTION
DEPICTIVE
DEPICTOR
DEPICTURE
DEPICTURED
DEPICTURING
DEPIGMENT
DEPIGMENTATE
DEPIGMENTIZE
DEPILATE
DEPILATED
DEPILATING
DEPILATION

DEPILATOR
DEPILATORY
DEPILITANT
DEPILOUS
DEPIT
DEPLACE
DEPLANE
DEPLANED
DEPLANING
DEPLANT
DEPLANTATION
DEPLENISH
DEPLETE
DEPLETED
DEPLETHORIC
DEPLETING
DEPLETION
DEPLETIVE
DEPLETORY
DEPLORABILIA
DEPLORABLE
DEPLORABLY
DEPLORATION
DEPLORE
DEPLORED
DEPLORER
DEPLORING
DEPLOY
DEPLOYMENT
DEPLUMATE
DEPLUMATED
DEPLUMATION
DEPLUME
DEPLUMED
DEPLUMING
DEPOH
DEPOLARIZE
DEPOLARIZED
DEPOLARIZER
DEPOLARIZING
DEPOLISH
DEPOLISHING
DEPOLYMERIZE
DEPONE
DEPONED
DEPONENT
DEPONER
DEPONING
DEPOPULATE
DEPOPULATED
DEPOPULATING
DEPOPULATION
DEPOPULATIVE
DEPOPULATOR
DEPORT
DEPORTATION
DEPORTE
DEPORTED
DEPORTEE
DEPORTER
DEPORTING
DEPORTMENT
DEPOSABLE
DEPOSAL
DEPOSE
DEPOSED
DEPOSER
DEPOSING
DEPOSIT
DEPOSITA
DEPOSITARIES
DEPOSITARY
DEPOSITATION
DEPOSITED
DEPOSITEE
DEPOSITING
DEPOSITION

DEPOSITIONAL
DEPOSITIVE
DEPOSITO
DEPOSITOR
DEPOSITORIES
DEPOSITORY
DEPOSITS
DEPOSITUM
DEPOSITURE
DEPOSURE
DEPOT
DEPOTENTIATE
DEPRAVATE
DEPRAVATION
DEPRAVE
DEPRAVED
DEPRAVEDLY
DEPRAVEDNESS
DEPRAVER
DEPRAVING
DEPRAVITIES
DEPRAVITY
DEPRECABLE
DEPRECATE
DEPRECATED
DEPRECATING
DEPRECATION
DEPRECATIVE
DEPRECATOR
DEPRECATORY
DEPRECIABLE
DEPRECIANT
DEPRECIATE
DEPRECIATED
DEPRECIATING
DEPRECIATION
DEPRECIATIVE
DEPRECIATOR
DEPRECIATORY
DEPREDATE
DEPREDATED
DEPREDATING
DEPREDATION
DEPREDATOR
DEPREDATORY
DEPREHEND
DEPREHENSION
DEPRESS
DEPRESSANT
DEPRESSED
DEPRESSING
DEPRESSINGLY
DEPRESSION
DEPRESSIVE
DEPRESSIVELY
DEPRESSOR
DEPREST
DEPRETER
DEPRINT
DEPRIORIZE
DEPRIVABLE
DEPRIVAL
DEPRIVATE
DEPRIVATION
DEPRIVATIVE
DEPRIVE
DEPRIVED
DEPRIVEMENT
DEPRIVER
DEPRIVING
DEPROME
DEPSID
DEPSIDE
DEPTH
DEPTHEN
DEPTHING
DEPTHLESS

DEPTHOMETER	DERISIVE	DERMONEURAL	DESCENSION	DESIDERATION
DEPTHS	DERISIVELY	DERMOOSSEOUS	DESCENSIONAL	DESIDERATIVE
DEPULSE	DERISIVENESS	DERMOPATHIC	DESCENSIVE	DESIDERATUM
DEPURANT	DERISORY	DERMOPATHY	DESCENT	DESIDERIUM
DEPURATE	DERIVABILITY	DERMOPHOBE	DESCLOIZITE	DESIGHT
DEPURATED	DERIVABLE	DERMOPHYTE	DESCORT	DESIGHTMENT
DEPURATING	DERIVABLY	DERMOPHYTIC	DESCRIAL	DESIGN
DEPURATIVE	DERIVAL	DERMOPLASTY	DESCRIBABLE	DESIGNABLE
DEPURATOR	DERIVANT	DERMOPTERAN	DESCRIBABLY	DESIGNADO
DEPUTATION	DERIVATE	DERMOPTEROUS	DESCRIBE	DESIGNATE
DEPUTATIVE	DERIVATELY	DERMOSTOSIS	DESCRIBED	DESIGNATED
DEPUTATOR	DERIVATION	DERMOTROPIC	DESCRIBER	DESIGNATING
DEPUTE	DERIVATIONAL	DERMOVACCINE	DESCRIBING	DESIGNATION
DEPUTED	DERIVATIST	DERMUTATION	DESCRIED	DESIGNATIVE
DEPUTIES	DERIVATIVE	DERN	DESCRIER	DESIGNATOR
DEPUTING	DERIVE	DERNE	DESCRIPT	DESIGNATORY
DEPUTIZE	DERIVED	DERNED	DESCRIPTION	DESIGNED
DEPUTIZED	DERIVEDLY	DERNER	DESCRIPTIVE	DESIGNEDLY
DEPUTIZING	DERIVEDNESS	DERNFUL	DESCRIPTORY	DESIGNEDNESS
DEPUTY	DERIVER	DERNIER	DESCRIVE	DESIGNEE
DEQUEEN	DERIVING	DERNING	DESCRY	DESIGNER
DER	DERK	DERNLY	DESCRYING	DESIGNFUL
DERACIALIZE	DERM	DERODIDYMUS	DESCURE	DESIGNFULLY
DERACINATE	DERMA	DEROGATE	DESEAM	DESIGNING
DERACINATED	DERMAD	DEROGATED	DESECATE	DESIGNINGLY
DERACINATING	DERMAHEMIA	DEROGATELY	DESECRATE	DESILICATE
DERACINATION	DERMAL	DEROGATING	DESECRATED	DESILICATED
DERADELPHUS	DERMALITH	DEROGATION	DESECRATER	DESILICATING
DERADENITIS	DERMAMYIASIS	DEROGATIVE	DESECRATING	DESILICIFIED
DERADENONCUS	DERMAPTERAN	DEROGATIVELY	DESECRATION	DESILICIFY
DERAH	DERMAPTEROUS	DEROGATOR	DESECRATOR	DESILICONIZE
DERAIGN	DERMASURGERY	DEROGATORILY	DESEED	DESILVER
DERAIGNMENT	DERMATALGIA	DEROGATORY	DESEGREGATE	DESILVERIZE
DERAIL	DERMATAUXE	DEROUT	DESEGREGATED	DESILVERIZER
DERAILED	DERMATHEMIA	DERRICK	DESEMER	DESINENCE
DERAILER	DERMATIC	DERRICKING	DESENSITIZE	DESINENT
DERAILING	DERMATINE	DERRICKMAN	DESENSITIZER	DESINENTIAL
DERAILMENT	DERMATITIS	DERRICKMEN	DESERET	DESIPIENCE
DERANGE	DERMATOCELE	DERRID	DESERT	DESIPIENCY
DERANGED	DERMATOCYST	DERRIDE	DESERTED	DESIPIENT
DERANGEMENT	DERMATODYNIA	DERRIERE	DESERTEDLY	DESIRABILITY
DERANGER	DERMATOGEN	DERRIES	DESERTEDNESS	DESIRABLE
DERANGING	DERMATOGRAPH	DERRINGER	DESERTER	DESIRABLY
DERAT	DERMATOID	DERRY	DESERTFUL	DESIRE
DERATE	DERMATOLOGY	DERTRA	DESERTFULLY	DESIRED
DERATED	DERMATOLYSIS	DERTROTHECA	DESERTIC	DESIREDLY
DERATER	DERMATOMA	DERTRUM	DESERTION	DESIREDNESS
DERATING	DERMATOME	DERVISH	DESERTLESS	DESIREFUL
DERATIZATION	DERMATOMIC	DERVISHHOOD	DESERTLESSLY	DESIRER
DERAY	DERMATOMYOMA	DERVISHISM	DESERTNESS	DESIRING
DERBUKKA	DERMATONOSUS	DERVISHLIKE	DESERTS	DESIROUS
DERBY	DERMATOPHONE	DESA	DESERVE	DESIROUSLY
DERBYLITE	DERMATOPHONY	DESACRALIZE	DESERVED	DESIROUSNESS
DERE	DERMATOPHYTE	DESALT	DESERVEDLY	DESIST
DERECHO	DERMATOPLASM	DESAND	DESERVEDNESS	DESISTANCE
DERELICT	DERMATOPLAST	DESATURATE	DESERVER	DESISTENCE
DERELICTION	DERMATOPSY	DESAURIN	DESERVING	DESISTIVE
DERELICTLY	DERMATORRHEA	DESAURINE	DESERVINGLY	DESITION
DERELICTNESS	DERMATOSCOPY	DESCALE	DESEX	DESITIVE
DERELIGION	DERMATOSIS	DESCAMISADO	DESEXUALIZE	DESIZE
DERERE	DERMATOTHERAPY	DESCAMISADOS	DESEXUALIZED	DESK
DERESINATE	DERMATOTOMY	DESCANT	DESH	DESKILL
DERESINIFY	DERMATOZOON	DESCANTED	DESHABILLE	DESKMAN
DERESINIZE	DERMIC	DESCANTER	DESI	DESLIME
DERF	DERMIS	DESCANTING	DESIATIN	DESMA
DERFLY	DERMOBLAST	DESCEND	DESICCANT	DESMACHYME
DERFNESS	DERMOCHROME	DESCENDABLE	DESICCATE	DESMACYTE
DERHAM	DERMOCOCCUS	DESCENDANCE	DESICCATED	DESMAN
DERIC	DERMOGASTRIC	DESCENDANT	DESICCATING	DESMECTASIA
DERIDE	DERMOGRAPHIA	DESCENDED	DESICCATION	DESMIC
DERIDED	DERMOGRAPHIC	DESCENDENCE	DESICCATIVE	DESMID
DERIDER	DERMOHEMAL	DESCENDENT	DESICCATOR	DESMIDIAN
DERIDING	DERMOHEMIA	DESCENDENTAL	DESICCATORY	DESMIDIOLOGY
DERIDINGLY	DERMOID	DESCENDER	DESIDERANT	DESMINE
DERINGER	DERMOIDAL	DESCENDIBLE	DESIDERATE	DESMITIS
DERISIBLE	DERMOL	DESCENDING	DESIDERATED	DESMODONT
DERISION	DERMOLYSIS	DESCENDINGLY	DESIDERATING	DESMODYNIA

DESMOGEN
DESMOID
DESMOLOGY
DESMOMA
DESMON
DESMONEME
DESMOPELMOUS
DESMOSE
DESMOSIS
DESMOSITE
DESMOTOMY
DESMOTROPE
DESMOTROPIC
DESMOTROPISM
DESMOTROPY
DESOEUVRE
DESOLATE
DESOLATED
DESOLATELY
DESOLATENESS
DESOLATER
DESOLATING
DESOLATINGLY
DESOLATION
DESOLATIVE
DESOLATOR
DESONATION
DESORPTION
DESOXALATE
DESPAIR
DESPAIRED
DESPAIRER
DESPAIRFUL
DESPAIRFULLY
DESPAIRING
DESPAIRINGLY
DESPATCH
DESPATCHER
DESPECT
DESPERACY
DESPERADO
DESPERADOES
DESPERADOS
DESPERATE
DESPERATELY
DESPERATION
DESPERT
DESPICABLE
DESPICABLY
DESPISAL
DESPISE
DESPISED
DESPISEMENT
DESPISER
DESPISING
DESPITE
DESPITED
DESPITEFUL
DESPITEFULLY
DESPITEOUS
DESPITEOUSLY
DESPITING
DESPOIL
DESPOILER
DESPOILMENT
DESPOLIATION
DESPOND
DESPONDENCE
DESPONDENCY
DESPONDENT
DESPONDENTLY
DESPONDER
DESPONDING
DESPONDINGLY
DESPOT
DESPOTIC
DESPOTICAL

DESPOTICALLY
DESPOTISM
DESPOTIST
DESPOTIZE
DESPOUSE
DESPUMATE
DESPUMATED
DESPUMATING
DESPUMATION
DESPUME
DESQUAMATE
DESQUAMATED
DESQUAMATING
DESQUAMATION
DESQUAMATIVE
DESQUAMATORY
DESRAY
DESS
DESSA
DESSE
DESSERT
DESSERTSPOON
DESSIATINE
DESSIL
DESSOUS
DESSUS
DESTERILIZE
DESTINATE
DESTINATION
DESTINE
DESTINED
DESTINEZITE
DESTINIES
DESTINING
DESTINISM
DESTINIST
DESTINY
DESTITUTE
DESTITUTELY
DESTITUTION
DESTO
DESTOOL
DESTOUR
DESTRER
DESTRIER
DESTROY
DESTROYED
DESTROYER
DESTROYING
DESTRUCT
DESTRUCTIBLE
DESTRUCTION
DESTRUCTIVE
DESTRUCTOR
DESTRUDO
DESUCRATION
DESUETE
DESUETUDE
DESUGAR
DESUGARIZE
DESULFURATE
DESULFURIZE
DESULFURIZED
DESULFURIZER
DESULPHUR
DESULPHURATE
DESULPHURIZE
DESULTOR
DESULTORILY
DESULTORY
DESUME
DESYL
DESYNONYMIZE
DETACH
DETACHABLE
DETACHE
DETACHED

DETACHEDLY
DETACHEDNESS
DETACHER
DETACHING
DETACHMENT
DETAIL
DETAILED
DETAILEDLY
DETAILEDNESS
DETAILER
DETAILING
DETAIN
DETAINAL
DETAINED
DETAINEE
DETAINER
DETAINING
DETAINMENT
DETASSEL
DETECT
DETECTABLE
DETECTAPHONE
DETECTER
DETECTIBLE
DETECTING
DETECTION
DETECTIVE
DETECTIVES
DETECTOR
DETENT
DETENTE
DETENTION
DETENTIVE
DETENU
DETER
DETERGE
DETERGED
DETERGENCE
DETERGENCY
DETERGENT
DETERGING
DETERIORATE
DETERIORATED
DETERIORATING
DETERIORATION
DETERIORATOR
DETERIORISM
DETERIORITY
DETERM
DETERMA
DETERMENT
DETERMINABLE
DETERMINABLY
DETERMINACY
DETERMINANT
DETERMINANTS
DETERMINATE
DETERMINATION
DETERMINATIVE
DETERMINE
DETERMINED
DETERMINEDLY
DETERMINER
DETERMINING
DETERMINISM
DETERMINIST
DETERMINOID
DETERRED
DETERRENCE
DETERRENT
DETERRING
DETERSION
DETERSIVE
DETERSIVELY
DETEST
DETESTABLE
DETESTABLY

DETESTATION
DETESTED
DETESTER
DETESTING
DETHRONE
DETHRONED
DETHRONEMENT
DETHRONER
DETHRONING
DETHYROIDISM
DETIN
DETINET
DETINUE
DETINUIT
DETONABLE
DETONATE
DETONATED
DETONATING
DETONATION
DETONATIVE
DETONATOR
DETONIZE
DETORSION
DETORT
DETOUR
DETOXICANT
DETOXICATE
DETOXICATED
DETOXICATING
DETOXICATION
DETOXICATOR
DETOXIFY
DETRACT
DETRACTED
DETRACTER
DETRACTING
DETRACTION
DETRACTIVE
DETRACTIVELY
DETRACTOR
DETRACTORY
DETRAIN
DETRAINMENT
DETRAQUE
DETRAY
DETRECT
DETRIBALIZE
DETRIMENT
DETRIMENTAL
DETRITAL
DETRITED
DETRITION
DETRITUS
DETRUCK
DETRUDE
DETRUDED
DETRUDING
DETRUNCATE
DETRUNCATED
DETRUNCATING
DETRUNCATION
DETRUSION
DETRUSIVE
DETRUSOR
DETUBATION
DETUMESCENCE
DETUNE
DETUNED
DETUNING
DETUR
DETURB
DETURN
DEUCE
DEUCED
DEUCEDLY
DEUL
DEUNAM

DEURWAARDER
DEUS
DEUSAN
DEUTERANOMAL
DEUTERIC
DEUTERIDE
DEUTERIUM
DEUTEROCONE
DEUTEROCONID
DEUTERODOME
DEUTEROGAMY
DEUTEROGENIC
DEUTERON
DEUTEROPATHY
DEUTEROPLASM
DEUTEROSCOPY
DEUTEROSTOMA
DEUTEROTOKY
DEUTEROTYPE
DEUTEROZOOID
DEUTOBROMIDE
DEUTOMALA
DEUTOMALAL
DEUTOMALAR
DEUTOMERITE
DEUTON
DEUTONYMPH
DEUTONYMPHAL
DEUTOPLASM
DEUTOPLASMIC
DEUTOPLASTIC
DEUTOVUM
DEUTSCHEMARK
DEUZAN
DEVA
DEVACHAN
DEVADASI
DEVAL
DEVALL
DEVALOKA
DEVALUATE
DEVALUATED
DEVALUATING
DEVALUATION
DEVALUE
DEVANCE
DEVANT
DEVAPORATE
DEVAPORATION
DEVARAJA
DEVARSHI
DEVAST
DEVASTATE
DEVASTATED
DEVASTATING
DEVASTATION
DEVASTATIVE
DEVASTATOR
DEVASTAVIT
DEVASTER
DEVATA
DEVAUL
DEVAUNT
DEVEIN
DEVEL
DEVELIN
DEVELOP
DEVELOPABLE
DEVELOPE
DEVELOPED
DEVELOPEMENT
DEVELOPER
DEVELOPING
DEVELOPMENT
DEVELOPMENTAL
DEVELOPOID
DEVELOPS

DEVER	DEVOLVEMENT	DEXTEROUSLY	DHOTI	DIACTINISM
DEVEST	DEVOLVING	DEXTRAD	DHOTIS	DIACULUM
DEVEX	DEVONITE	DEXTRAL	DHOTY	DIAD
DEVIABILITY	DEVORATIVE	DEXTRALITY	DHOUL	DIADELPHIAN
DEVIABLE	DEVOT	DEXTRALLY	DHOURRA	DIADELPHOUS
DEVIANT	DEVOTARY	DEXTRAN	DHOW	DIADEM
DEVIATE	DEVOTE	DEXTRANE	DHU	DIADERM
DEVIATED	DEVOTED	DEXTRAURAL	DHURNA	DIADERMIC
DEVIATING	DEVOTEDLY	DEXTRIN	DHURRA	DIADOCHE
DEVIATION	DEVOTEDNESS	DEXTRINASE	DHURRIE	DIADOCHITE
DEVIATIONISM	DEVOTEE	DEXTRINATE	DHURRY	DIADOUMENOS
DEVIATIONIST	DEVOTEEISM	DEXTRINE	DHYAL	DIADROME
DEVIATIVE	DEVOTEMENT	DEXTRINIZE	DHYANA	DIADROMOUS
DEVIATOR	DEVOTER	DEXTRINOUS	DI	DIADUMENUS
DEVIATORY	DEVOTING	DEXTRO	DIA	DIAENE
DEVICE	DEVOTION	DEXTROCARDIA	DIABASE	DIAERESIS
DEVICEFUL	DEVOTIONAL	DEXTROCULAR	DIABASIC	DIAERETIC
DEVICEFULLY	DEVOTIONALLY	DEXTROGYRATE	DIABETES	DIAETETAE
DEVIL	DEVOTIONARY	DEXTROGYRE	DIABETIC	DIAGENESIS
DEVILBIRD	DEVOTIONATE	DEXTRORSAL	DIABETICAL	DIAGENETIC
DEVILDOM	DEVOTIONIST	DEXTRORSE	DIABETOGENIC	DIAGEOTROPIC
DEVILED	DEVOTIONS	DEXTROSAZONE	DIABETOMETER	DIAGLYPH
DEVILER	DEVOTO	DEXTROSE	DIABLE	DIAGLYPHIC
DEVILET	DEVOUR	DEXTROSURIA	DIABLERIE	DIAGLYPTIC
DEVILFISH	DEVOURED	DEXTROUS	DIABLERY	DIAGNOSE
DEVILFISHES	DEVOURER	DEXTROUSLY	DIABLO	DIAGNOSED
DEVILING	DEVOURING	DEXTROUSNESS	DIABLOTIN	DIAGNOSES
DEVILISH	DEVOURINGLY	DEY	DIABOLARCH	DIAGNOSING
DEVILISHLY	DEVOUT	DEYHOUSE	DIABOLEPSY	DIAGNOSIS
DEVILISHNESS	DEVOUTLY	DEYS	DIABOLEPTIC	DIAGNOSTIC
DEVILISM	DEVOUTNESS	DEYWOMAN	DIABOLIC	DIAGNOSTICS
DEVILIZE	DEVOVE	DEZINC	DIABOLICAL	DIAGOMETER
DEVILIZED	DEVOW	DEZINCATION	DIABOLICALLY	DIAGONAL
DEVILIZING	DEVULGARIZE	DEZINCIFIED	DIABOLIFY	DIAGONALITY
DEVILKIN	DEW	DEZINCIFY	DIABOLISM	DIAGONALIZE
DEVILLED	DEWA	DEZINCIFYING	DIABOLIST	DIAGONALLY
DEVILMENT	DEWAN	DEZINKIFY	DIABOLIZE	DIAGONIC
DEVILRIES	DEWANEE	DEZYMOTIZE	DIABOLIZED	DIAGRAM
DEVILRY	DEWANNY	DGHAISA	DIABOLIZING	DIAGRAMED
DEVILS	DEWAR	DHA	DIABOLO	DIAGRAMING
DEVILTRY	DEWATA	DHABB	DIABOLOLOGY	DIAGRAMMATIC
DEVILWOOD	DEWATER	DHAI	DIABOLUS	DIAGRAMMED
DEVILY	DEWATERER	DHAK	DIABROSIS	DIAGRAMMETER
DEVIOUS	DEWAX	DHAL	DIABROTIC	DIAGRAMMING
DEVIOUSLY	DEWBEAM	DHAMAN	DIACAUSTIC	DIAGRAPH
DEVIOUSNESS	DEWBERRIES	DHAMNOO	DIACETATE	DIAGRAPHIC
DEVIRGINATE	DEWBERRY	DHAN	DIACETIC	DIAGRAPHICAL
DEVIRGINATOR	DEWCAP	DHANGAR	DIACETURIA	DIAGRAPHICS
DEVIRILIZE	DEWCLAW	DHANUK	DIACETYL	DIAGREDIUM
DEVISABLE	DEWCLAWED	DHANUSH	DIACETYLENE	DIAGRYDIUM
DEVISAL	DEWCUP	DHAO	DIACHORETIC	DIAKINESIS
DEVISE	DEWDROP	DHARANA	DIACHRONIC	DIAL
DEVISED	DEWDROPPER	DHARANI	DIACHYLON	DIALCOHOL
DEVISEE	DEWER	DHARMA	DIACHYLUM	DIALDEHYDE
DEVISER	DEWEYLITE	DHARMSALA	DIACID	DIALECT
DEVISING	DEWFALL	DHARNA	DIACLASE	DIALECTAL
DEVISOR	DEWFLOWER	DHAURA	DIACLASIS	DIALECTALIZE
DEVITALIZE	DEWIER	DHAURI	DIACLE	DIALECTALLY
DEVITALIZED	DEWIEST	DHAVA	DIACLINAL	DIALECTIC
DEVITALIZING	DEWILY	DHAW	DIACODION	DIALECTICAL
DEVITAMINIZE	DEWINESS	DHER	DIACODIUM	DIALECTICALLY
DEVITRIFIED	DEWLAP	DHERI	DIACOELE	DIALECTICIAN
DEVITRIFY	DEWLAPPED	DHIKR	DIACOELIA	DIALECTICISM
DEVITRIFYING	DEWOOL	DHOBEE	DIACONAL	DIALECTICIZE
DEVOCALIZE	DEWORM	DHOBEY	DIACONATE	DIALECTICS
DEVOCALIZED	DEWRET	DHOBI	DIACONIA	DIALECTOLOGY
DEVOCALIZING	DEWROT	DHOBIE	DIACONICON	DIALECTOR
DEVOCATE	DEWTRY	DHOBIES	DIACOPE	DIALECTS
DEVOCATION	DEWY	DHOBIS	DIACRANTERIC	DIALED
DEVOICED	DEXIOTROPE	DHOBY	DIACRISIS	DIALER
DEVOID	DEXIOTROPIC	DHOLE	DIACRITIC	DIALIN
DEVOIR	DEXIOTROPISM	DHOLES	DIACRITICAL	DIALING
DEVOIRS	DEXIOTROPOUS	DHOLL	DIACT	DIALIST
DEVOLUTE	DEXTER	DHONI	DIACTIN	DIALKYL
DEVOLUTION	DEXTERICAL	DHOON	DIACTINAL	DIALKYLAMINE
DEVOLVE	DEXTERITY	DHOOTIE	DIACTINE	DIALKYLIC
DEVOLVED	DEXTEROUS	DHOTEE	DIACTINIC	DIALLAGE

DIALLAGIC	DIANODAL	DIASCHISMA	DIAZEUXIS	DICHASTIC
DIALLAGITE	DIANOETIC	DIASCHISTIC	DIAZID	DICHLONE
DIALLAGOID	DIANOETICAL	DIASCOPE	DIAZIDE	DICHLORAMIN
DIALLED	DIANOIA	DIASCORD	DIAZIN	DICHLORAMINE
DIALLEL	DIANTRE	DIASCORDIUM	DIAZINE	DICHLORIDE
DIALLELA	DIAPALMA	DIASENE	DIAZO	DICHOCARPOUS
DIALLELI	DIAPASE	DIASKEUASIS	DIAZOAMIN	DICHOGAMIC
DIALLELON	DIAPASM	DIASKEUAST	DIAZOAMINE	DICHOGAMOUS
DIALLELUS	DIAPASON	DIASPER	DIAZOATE	DICHOGAMY
DIALLER	DIAPASONAL	DIASPIDINE	DIAZOBENZENE	DICHONDRA
DIALLING	DIAPAUSE	DIASPIRIN	DIAZOIC	DICHOPTIC
DIALLIST	DIAPEDESIS	DIASPORE	DIAZOIMIDE	DICHORD
DIALOG	DIAPEDETIC	DIASTALSES	DIAZOLE	DICHOREE
DIALOGER	DIAPENTE	DIASTALTIC	DIAZOMA	DICHOTIC
DIALOGIC	DIAPER	DIASTASE	DIAZOMETHANE	DICHOTOMAL
DIALOGICAL	DIAPERED	DIASTASIC	DIAZONIUM	DICHOTOMIC
DIALOGICALLY	DIAPERING	DIASTASIS	DIAZOTATE	DICHOTOMIES
DIALOGISM	DIAPERY	DIASTATAXIC	DIAZOTIC	DICHOTOMIST
DIALOGIST	DIAPHANE	DIASTATAXY	DIAZOTIZE	DICHOTOMIZE
DIALOGISTIC	DIAPHANEITY	DIASTATIC	DIAZOTIZED	DICHOTOMIZED
DIALOGITE	DIAPHANIE	DIASTEM	DIAZOTIZING	DICHOTOMOUS
DIALOGIZE	DIAPHANOTYPE	DIASTEMA	DIAZOTYPE	DICHOTOMY
DIALOGIZED	DIAPHANOUS	DIASTEMATA	DIB	DICHROIC
DIALOGIZING	DIAPHANOUSLY	DIASTEMATIC	DIBASE	DICHROISM
DIALOGUE	DIAPHONE	DIASTER	DIBASIC	DICHROITE
DIALOGUED	DIAPHONIC	DIASTIMETER	DIBASICITY	DICHROITIC
DIALOGUER	DIAPHONICAL	DIASTOLE	DIBATAG	DICHROMASIA
DIALOGUING	DIAPHONIES	DIASTOLIC	DIBBED	DICHROMASY
DIALURIC	DIAPHONY	DIASTOMATIC	DIBBER	DICHROMAT
DIALYCARPOUS	DIAPHORESIS	DIASTRAL	DIBBING	DICHROMATE
DIALYSE	DIAPHORETIC	DIASTROPHE	DIBBLE	DICHROMATIC
DIALYSES	DIAPHORITE	DIASTROPHIC	DIBBLED	DICHROMATISM
DIALYSIS	DIAPHOTE	DIASTROPHISM	DIBBLER	DICHROMIC
DIALYSTELIC	DIAPHRAGM	DIASTYLE	DIBBLING	DICHROMISM
DIALYTIC	DIAPHRAGMAL	DIASYNTHESIS	DIBBUK	DICHRONOUS
DIALYTICALLY	DIAPHRAGMATIC	DIASYRM	DIBENZOYL	DICHROOSCOPE
DIALYZABLE	DIAPHRAGMED	DIATESSARON	DIBENZYL	DICHROOUS
DIALYZATE	DIAPHRAGMING	DIATHERMACY	DIBHOLE	DICHROSCOPE
DIALYZATION	DIAPHTHERIN	DIATHERMANCE	DIBLASTULA	DICHROSCOPIC
DIALYZATOR	DIAPHYSES	DIATHERMANCY	DIBRACH	DICHT
DIALYZE	DIAPHYSIAL	DIATHERMIA	DIBRANCH	DICING
DIALYZED	DIAPHYSIS	DIATHERMIC	DIBRANCHIATE	DICK
DIALYZER	DIAPIR	DIATHERMIES	DIBROMID	DICKCISSEL
DIALYZING	DIAPLASMA	DIATHERMY	DIBROMIDE	DICKENS
DIAMAGNETIC	DIAPLEXUS	DIATHESES	DIBS	DICKER
DIAMANTE	DIAPNOIC	DIATHESIS	DIBSTONE	DICKERED
DIAMANTINE	DIAPOPHYSES	DIATHETIC	DICACITY	DICKERING
DIAMANTOID	DIAPOPHYSIS	DIATOM	DICAEOLOGY	DICKEY
DIAMAT	DIAPOSITIVE	DIATOMACEAN	DICARBONATE	DICKEYBIRD
DIAMB	DIAPSID	DIATOMACEOID	DICARBOXYLIC	DICKEYS
DIAMBER	DIAPSIDAN	DIATOMACEOUS	DICAST	DICKIES
DIAMBIC	DIAPYESIS	DIATOMIC	DICASTERY	DICKINSONITE
DIAMETER	DIAPYETIC	DIATOMICITY	DICASTIC	DICKTY
DIAMETRAL	DIARCH	DIATOMIN	DICATALECTIC	DICKY
DIAMETRALLY	DIARCHIAL	DIATOMINE	DICATALEXIS	DICKYBIRD
DIAMETRIC	DIARCHIC	DIATOMITE	DICE	DICLINIC
DIAMETRICAL	DIARCHIES	DIATOMOUS	DICEBOARD	DICLINISM
DIAMICTON	DIARCHY	DIATONIC	DICEBOX	DICLINOUS
DIAMIDE	DIARIAL	DIATONICAL	DICECUP	DICLINY
DIAMIDO	DIARIAN	DIATONICALLY	DICED	DICOCCOUS
DIAMIDOGEN	DIARIST	DIATONICISM	DICELLATE	DICODEINE
DIAMIN	DIARISTIC	DIATONOUS	DICEMAN	DICOELIOUS
DIAMINE	DIARIZE	DIATORIC	DICENTRIN	DICOELOUS
DIAMMONIUM	DIARRHEA	DIATREME	DICENTRINE	DICOLIC
DIAMOND	DIARRHEAL	DIATRIBE	DICEPHALISM	DICOLON
DIAMONDBACK	DIARRHEIC	DIATROPIC	DICEPHALOUS	DICONDYLIAN
DIAMONDED	DIARRHETIC	DIATROPISM	DICEPHALUS	DICOPHANE
DIAMONDING	DIARRHOEA	DIAULI	DICEPLAY	DICOT
DIAMONDIZE	DIARRHOEAL	DIAULIC	DICER	DICOTYL
DIAMONDIZED	DIARRHOEIC	DIAULOS	DICERION	DICOTYLEDON
DIAMONDIZING	DIARRHOETIC	DIAVOLO	DICEROUS	DICROTAL
DIAMONDS	DIARSENIDE	DIAXIAL	DICETYL	DICROTIC
DIAMORPHINE	DIARTHRODIAL	DIAXON	DICH	DICROTISM
DIAMYLOSE	DIARTHROSIS	DIAXONE	DICHAS	DICROTOUS
DIAN	DIARTICULAR	DIAXONIC	DICHASIA	DICT
DIANDROUS	DIARY	DIAZENITHAL	DICHASIAL	DICTA
DIANITE	DIASCHISIS	DIAZEUTIC	DICHASIUM	DICTAMEN

DICTAMINA	DIDLER	DIETINE	DIGALLIC	DIGNIFIED
DICTAPHONE	DIDNA	DIETING	DIGAMETIC	DIGNIFIEDLY
DICTATE	DIDRACHM	DIETIST	DIGAMIST	DIGNIFY
DICTATED	DIDRACHMA	DIETITIAN	DIGAMMA	DIGNIFYING
DICTATING	DIDRACHMAL	DIETOTHERAPY	DIGAMMATE	DIGNITARIAL
DICTATINGLY	DIDRACHMAS	DIETOTOXIC	DIGAMMATED	DIGNITARIAN
DICTATION	DIDRIC	DIETRICHITE	DIGAMOUS	DIGNITARIES
DICTATIONAL	DIDROMIES	DIETTED	DIGAMY	DIGNITARY
DICTATIVE	DIDROMY	DIETZEITE	DIGASTRIC	DIGNITAS
DICTATOR	DIDST	DIEU	DIGENESIS	DIGNITIES
DICTATORIAL	DIDUCE	DIEUGARD	DIGENETIC	DIGNITY
DICTATORSHIP	DIDUCED	DIEWISE	DIGENITE	DIGNOSCE
DICTATORY	DIDUCING	DIEZEUGMENON	DIGENOUS	DIGONAL
DICTATRESS	DIDUCTION	DIFERRION	DIGENY	DIGONEUTIC
DICTATRIX	DIDUCTOR	DIFFA	DIGERENT	DIGONEUTISM
DICTATURE	DIDY	DIFFAME	DIGEST	DIGONOPOROUS
DICTERY	DIDYM	DIFFER	DIGESTANT	DIGONOUS
DICTIC	DIDYMATE	DIFFERED	DIGESTED	DIGOXIN
DICTION	DIDYMIA	DIFFERENCE	DIGESTEDLY	DIGRAM
DICTIONARIES	DIDYMIUM	DIFFERENCED	DIGESTEDNESS	DIGRAPH
DICTIONARY	DIDYMOID	DIFFERENCING	DIGESTER	DIGRAPHIC
DICTOGRAPH	DIDYMOLITE	DIFFERENCY	DIGESTIBLE	DIGREDIENCY
DICTUM	DIDYMOUS	DIFFERENT	DIGESTIBLY	DIGREDIENT
DICTUMS	DIDYMUS	DIFFERENTIA	DIGESTING	DIGRESS
DICTY	DIDYNAMOUS	DIFFERENTIAE	DIGESTION	DIGRESSED
DICTYNID	DIDYNAMY	DIFFERENTIAL	DIGESTIVE	DIGRESSING
DICTYOGEN	DIE	DIFFERENTIATE	DIGESTIVELY	DIGRESSION
DICTYOSOME	DIEB	DIFFERENTIATION	DIGESTOR	DIGRESSIONAL
DICTYOSTELE	DIEBACK	DIFFERENTLY	DIGGED	DIGRESSIVE
DICTYOSTELIC	DIECASE	DIFFERING	DIGGER	DIGRESSIVELY
DICTYOTIC	DIECIOUS	DIFFERINGLY	DIGGING	DIGRESSORY
DICYANID	DIECTASIS	DIFFICILE	DIGGINGS	DIGS
DICYANIDE	DIED	DIFFICULT	DIGHT	DIGUE
DICYANIN	DIEDRIC	DIFFICULTIES	DIGHTED	DIHALID
DICYANINE	DIEHARD	DIFFICULTY	DIGHTER	DIHALIDE
DICYCLE	DIEING	DIFFIDATION	DIGHTING	DIHALO
DICYCLIC	DIELDRIN	DIFFIDE	DIGIT	DIHALOGEN
DICYCLIST	DIELECTRIC	DIFFIDED	DIGITAL	DIHEDRAL
DICYEMID	DIELECTRICAL	DIFFIDENCE	DIGITALEIN	DIHEDRON
DID	DIEM	DIFFIDENT	DIGITALIN	DIHELIOS
DIDACTIC	DIEMAKING	DIFFIDENTLY	DIGITALIS	DIHELIUM
DIDACTICAL	DIENCEPHALIC	DIFFIDING	DIGITALISM	DIHELY
DIDACTICALLY	DIENCEPHALON	DIFFINITY	DIGITALIZE	DIHEXAGONAL
DIDACTICIAN	DIENE	DIFFLUENCE	DIGITALLY	DIHEXAHEDRAL
DIDACTICISM	DIENER	DIFFLUENT	DIGITATE	DIHEXAHEDRON
DIDACTICITY	DIER	DIFFORM	DIGITATED	DIHYBRID
DIDACTICS	DIERESES	DIFFORME	DIGITATELY	DIHYBRIDISM
DIDACTIVE	DIERESIS	DIFFORMED	DIGITATION	DIHYDRATE
DIDACTYL	DIERETIC	DIFFORMITY	DIGITIFORM	DIHYDRATED
DIDACTYLISM	DIES	DIFFRACT	DIGITIGRADE	DIHYDRIC
DIDACTYLOUS	DIESEL	DIFFRACTED	DIGITIZE	DIHYDRIDE
DIDAPPER	DIESELIZE	DIFFRACTING	DIGITIZED	DIHYDRITE
DIDASCALAR	DIESES	DIFFRACTION	DIGITIZER	DIHYDROGEN
DIDASCALIAE	DIESINKER	DIFFRACTIVE	DIGITIZING	DIHYDROXY
DIDASCALIC	DIESINKING	DIFFRANGIBLE	DIGITOGENIN	DII
DIDASCALOS	DIESIS	DIFFUGIENT	DIGITONIN	DIIAMB
DIDASCALY	DIESTOCK	DIFFUND	DIGITORIUM	DIIODID
DIDDER	DIESTRUM	DIFFUSATE	DIGITOXIN	DIIODIDE
DIDDERED	DIESTRUS	DIFFUSE	DIGITOXOSE	DIIODO
DIDDERING	DIET	DIFFUSED	DIGITULE	DIIODOFORM
DIDDEST	DIETAL	DIFFUSEDLY	DIGITUS	DIISATOGEN
DIDDIES	DIETARIAN	DIFFUSEDNESS	DIGLADIATE	DIJUDICATE
DIDDLE	DIETARIES	DIFFUSELY	DIGLADIATED	DIJUDICATION
DIDDLED	DIETARY	DIFFUSENESS	DIGLADIATING	DIK
DIDDLER	DIETER	DIFFUSER	DIGLADIATION	DIKA
DIDDLING	DIETETIC	DIFFUSIBLE	DIGLADIATOR	DIKAGE
DIDDY	DIETETICAL	DIFFUSIBLY	DIGLOSSIA	DIKAMALI
DIDELPH	DIETETICALLY	DIFFUSING	DIGLOT	DIKAMALLI
DIDELPHIAN	DIETETICS	DIFFUSION	DIGLOTTIC	DIKARYON
DIDELPHIC	DIETETIST	DIFFUSIONISM	DIGLOTTISM	DIKDIK
DIDELPHID	DIETHER	DIFFUSIONIST	DIGLOTTIST	DIKE
DIDELPHINE	DIETHYL	DIFFUSIVE	DIGLUCOSIDE	DIKED
DIDELPHOUS	DIETHYLAMINE	DIFFUSIVELY	DIGLYPH	DIKEGRAVE
DIDEST	DIETIC	DIFFUSIVITY	DIGLYPHIC	DIKELET
DIDIE	DIETICAL	DIFFUSOR	DIGMEAT	DIKER
DIDINE	DIETICIAN	DIG	DIGNATION	DIKEREEVE
DIDLE	DIETICS	DIGALLATE	DIGNE	DIKERIA

DIKERION
DIKETENE
DIKETO
DIKETONE
DIKING
DIKKOP
DIKSHA
DIKTAT
DIKTYONITE
DILACERATE
DILACERATED
DILACERATING
DILACERATION
DILACTONE
DILAMBDODONT
DILAPIDATE
DILAPIDATED
DILAPIDATING
DILAPIDATION
DILAPIDATOR
DILATABILITY
DILATABLY
DILATANCY
DILATANT
DILATATE
DILATATION
DILATATIVE
DILATATOR
DILATE
DILATED
DILATEDLY
DILATEDNESS
DILATEMENT
DILATER
DILATING
DILATION
DILATIVE
DILATOMETER
DILATOMETRIC
DILATOMETRY
DILATOR
DILATORILY
DILATORINESS
DILATORY
DILDO
DILDOES
DILDOS
DILECTION
DILEMMA
DILEMMATIC
DILEMMIC
DILETANT
DILETTANIST
DILETTANTE
DILETTANTES
DILETTANTI
DILETTANTISH
DILETTANTISM
DILIGENCE
DILIGENT
DILIGENTIA
DILIGENTLY
DILIGENTNESS
DILIS
DILKER
DILL
DILLENIAD
DILLESK
DILLI
DILLIER
DILLIES
DILLIGROUT
DILLING
DILLIS
DILLISK
DILLSEED
DILLUE

DILLUER
DILLWEED
DILLY
DILLYDALLIED
DILLYDALLIER
DILLYDALLY
DILLYMAN
DILLYMEN
DILO
DILOGY
DILOS
DILUCID
DILUENDO
DILUENT
DILUTE
DILUTED
DILUTEDLY
DILUTEDNESS
DILUTEE
DILUTELY
DILUTENESS
DILUTENT
DILUTER
DILUTING
DILUTION
DILUTIVE
DILUVIA
DILUVIAL
DILUVIALIST
DILUVIAN
DILUVIANISM
DILUVIUM
DILUVIUMS
DILUVY
DILVE
DIM
DIMANGANION
DIMASTIGATE
DIMBER
DIMBLE
DIME
DIMEDON
DIMEDONE
DIMENSIBLE
DIMENSION
DIMENSIONAL
DIMENSIONED
DIMENSIONING
DIMENSIVE
DIMENSUM
DIMER
DIMERAN
DIMERCAPROL
DIMERCURION
DIMERIC
DIMERISM
DIMERIZATION
DIMEROUS
DIMES
DIMETALLIC
DIMETER
DIMETHOXY
DIMETHYL
DIMETRIA
DIMETRIC
DIMICATION
DIMIDIATE
DIMIDIATED
DIMIDIATING
DIMIDIATION
DIMINISH
DIMINISHED
DIMINISHER
DIMINISHING
DIMINISHMENT
DIMINUE
DIMINUENDO

DIMINUENDOED
DIMINUTAL
DIMINUTE
DIMINUTED
DIMINUTELY
DIMINUTING
DIMINUTION
DIMINUTIVAL
DIMINUTIVE
DIMINUTIVELY
DIMISS
DIMISSION
DIMISSORY
DIMIT
DIMITIES
DIMITTED
DIMITTING
DIMITY
DIMLY
DIMMED
DIMMER
DIMMERS
DIMMEST
DIMMET
DIMMING
DIMMISH
DIMMIT
DIMMY
DIMNESS
DIMOLECULAR
DIMORIC
DIMORPH
DIMORPHIC
DIMORPHISM
DIMORPHOUS
DIMPLE
DIMPLED
DIMPLEMENT
DIMPLIER
DIMPLIEST
DIMPLING
DIMPLY
DIMPS
DIMPSY
DIMWIT
DIMWITTED
DIMWITTEDLY
DIMYARIAN
DIN
DINAMODE
DINANDERIE
DINAPHTHYL
DINAR
DINDER
DINDLE
DINDLED
DINDLING
DINE
DINED
DINER
DINERGATE
DINERIC
DINERO
DINEROS
DINES
DINETTE
DINEURIC
DINEUTRON
DING
DINGAR
DINGBAT
DINGDONG
DINGE
DINGED
DINGEING
DINGER
DINGEY

DINGEYS
DINGHIES
DINGHY
DINGIER
DINGIES
DINGIEST
DINGILY
DINGINESS
DINGLE
DINGLEBERRY
DINGLED
DINGLEDANGLE
DINGLING
DINGLY
DINGMAN
DINGMAUL
DINGO
DINGOES
DINGTHRIFT
DINGUS
DINGWALL
DINGY
DINHEIRO
DINIC
DINICAL
DINING
DINITRATE
DINK
DINKED
DINKEY
DINKEYS
DINKIER
DINKIES
DINKIEST
DINKING
DINKUM
DINKY
DINMAN
DINMONT
DINNA
DINNED
DINNER
DINNERLY
DINNERTIME
DINNERWARE
DINNERY
DINNING
DINOCERAS
DINOMIC
DINOS
DINOSAUR
DINOSAURIAN
DINOTHERE
DINSOME
DINT
DINTED
DINTING
DINUS
DIOBELY
DIOBOL
DIOBOLON
DIOCESAN
DIOCESE
DIOCOEL
DIOCTAHEDRAL
DIODE
DIODONT
DIOECIAN
DIOECIOUS
DIOECIOUSLY
DIOECISM
DIOESTROUS
DIOESTRUM
DIOESTRUS
DIOGENITE
DIOICOUS
DIOL

DIOLEFIN
DIOLEFINE
DIOLEFINIC
DIOMATE
DIONISE
DIONYM
DIONYMAL
DIOPSIDE
DIOPTASE
DIOPTER
DIOPTOGRAPH
DIOPTOMETER
DIOPTOMETRY
DIOPTRA
DIOPTRAL
DIOPTRATE
DIOPTRE
DIOPTRIC
DIOPTRICAL
DIOPTRICALLY
DIOPTRICS
DIOPTROSCOPY
DIOPTRY
DIORAMA
DIORAMIC
DIORDINAL
DIORITE
DIORITIC
DIORTHOSIS
DIORTHOTIC
DIOSCOREIN
DIOSCORINE
DIOSE
DIOSMIN
DIOSMOSE
DIOSPHENOL
DIOTA
DIOTIC
DIOVULAR
DIOXAN
DIOXANE
DIOXIDE
DIOXIME
DIOXY
DIP
DIPARTITE
DIPARTITION
DIPASCHAL
DIPCOAT
DIPENTENE
DIPENTINE
DIPETALOUS
DIPHASE
DIPHASER
DIPHASIC
DIPHEAD
DIPHENAN
DIPHENOL
DIPHENYL
DIPHENYLENE
DIPHOSGENE
DIPHOSPHATE
DIPHOSPHID
DIPHOSPHIDE
DIPHOSPHORIC
DIPHRELATIC
DIPHTHERIA
DIPHTHERIAL
DIPHTHERIAN
DIPHTHERIC
DIPHTHERITIC
DIPHTHERITIS
DIPHTHEROID
DIPHTHONG
DIPHTHONGAL
DIPHTHONGED
DIPHTHONGIC

DIPHTHONGING
DIPHTHONGIZE
DIPHTHONGIZED
DIPHYCERCAL
DIPHYCERCY
DIPHYGENIC
DIPHYLETIC
DIPHYLLOUS
DIPHYODONT
DIPHYOZOOID
DIPLACUSIS
DIPLANETIC
DIPLANETISM
DIPLANTIDIAN
DIPLARTHRISM
DIPLARTHROUS
DIPLASIASMUS
DIPLASIC
DIPLASION
DIPLEGIA
DIPLEURA
DIPLEURAL
DIPLEURIC
DIPLEX
DIPLEXER
DIPLOBLASTIC
DIPLOCARDIA
DIPLOCARDIAC
DIPLOCEPHALY
DIPLOCOCCAL
DIPLOCOCCI
DIPLOCOCCIC
DIPLOCOCCUS
DIPLOCONICAL
DIPLOCORIA
DIPLODOCUS
DIPLOE
DIPLOETIC
DIPLOGENESIS
DIPLOGENETIC
DIPLOGENIC
DIPLOGRAPH
DIPLOGRAPHY
DIPLOHEDRAL
DIPLOHEDRON
DIPLOIC
DIPLOID
DIPLOIDIC
DIPLOIDION
DIPLOIDIZE
DIPLOIDY
DIPLOIS
DIPLOKARYON
DIPLOMA
DIPLOMACIES
DIPLOMACY
DIPLOMAED
DIPLOMAING
DIPLOMAT
DIPLOMATE
DIPLOMATIC
DIPLOMATICAL
DIPLOMATICS
DIPLOMATISM
DIPLOMATIST
DIPLOMATIZE
DIPLOMATIZED
DIPLOMYELIA
DIPLONEMA
DIPLONEURAL
DIPLONT
DIPLOPHASE
DIPLOPHYTE
DIPLOPIA
DIPLOPIAS
DIPLOPIC
DIPLOPLACULA

DIPLOPOD
DIPLOPODIC
DIPLOPODOUS
DIPLOSIS
DIPLOSOME
DIPLOSPHENAL
DIPLOTEGIA
DIPLOTENE
DIPLUMBIC
DIPMETER
DIPNEUST
DIPNOAN
DIPNOID
DIPNOOUS
DIPODE
DIPODIC
DIPODID
DIPODIES
DIPODY
DIPOLAR
DIPOLARIZE
DIPOLE
DIPOLSPHENE
DIPORPA
DIPPED
DIPPER
DIPPIER
DIPPIEST
DIPPING
DIPPY
DIPRIMARY
DIPRISMATIC
DIPROPYL
DIPSADES
DIPSAS
DIPSETIC
DIPSEY
DIPSIE
DIPSO
DIPSOMANIA
DIPSOMANIAC
DIPSOSIS
DIPSTICK
DIPSY
DIPT
DIPTER
DIPTERAL
DIPTERAN
DIPTERIST
DIPTEROCARP
DIPTEROLOGY
DIPTERON
DIPTEROS
DIPTEROUS
DIPTOTE
DIPTYCA
DIPTYCH
DIPTYCHON
DIPWARE
DIPYGI
DIPYGUS
DIPYLON
DIPYRE
DIPYRENOUS
DIRD
DIRDUM
DIRE
DIRECT
DIRECTABLE
DIRECTED
DIRECTER
DIRECTING
DIRECTION
DIRECTIONAL
DIRECTIONS
DIRECTITUDE
DIRECTIVE

DIRECTIVELY
DIRECTIVITY
DIRECTLY
DIRECTNESS
DIRECTOR
DIRECTORAL
DIRECTORATE
DIRECTORIAL
DIRECTORIES
DIRECTORSHIP
DIRECTORY
DIRECTRESS
DIRECTRICES
DIRECTRIX
DIRECTRIXES
DIREFUL
DIREFULLY
DIREFULNESS
DIRELY
DIREMPT
DIREMPTION
DIRENESS
DIREPTION
DIRER
DIREST
DIRGE
DIRGED
DIRGEFUL
DIRGELIKE
DIRGEMAN
DIRGIE
DIRGING
DIRGLER
DIRGY
DIRHAM
DIRHEM
DIRIGENT
DIRIGIBILITY
DIRIGIBLE
DIRIGO
DIRIGOMOTOR
DIRIMENT
DIRK
DIRKED
DIRKING
DIRL
DIRNDL
DIRT
DIRTBIRD
DIRTBOARD
DIRTEN
DIRTIED
DIRTIER
DIRTIEST
DIRTILY
DIRTINESS
DIRTPLATE
DIRTY
DIRTYING
DIS
DISABILITIES
DISABILITY
DISABLE
DISABLED
DISABLEMENT
DISABLENESS
DISABLING
DISABUSAL
DISABUSE
DISABUSED
DISABUSING
DISACCHARID
DISACCHARIDE
DISACCORD
DISACCORDANT
DISACCUSTOM
DISACCUSTOMED

DISACIDIFIED
DISACIDIFY
DISACKNOWLEDGE
DISACQUAINT
DISADJUST
DISADVANCE
DISADVANCED
DISADVANCING
DISADVANTAGE
DISADVANTAGEOUS
DISADVENTURE
DISADVISE
DISADVISED
DISADVISING
DISAFFECT
DISAFFECTED
DISAFFECTING
DISAFFECTION
DISAFFILIATE
DISAFFIRM
DISAFFOREST
DISAGIO
DISAGREE
DISAGREEABLE
DISAGREEABLENESS
DISAGREEABLY
DISAGREED
DISAGREEING
DISAGREEMENT
DISAGREER
DISALIGN
DISALIGNED
DISALIGNING
DISALIGNMENT
DISALLIEGE
DISALLOW
DISALLOWABLE
DISALLOWANCE
DISALLOWED
DISALLOWING
DISALLY
DISANCHOR
DISANIMATE
DISANIMATED
DISANIMATING
DISANIMATION
DISANNEX
DISANNUL
DISANNULLER
DISANOINT
DISAPPAREL
DISAPPEAR
DISAPPEARANCE
DISAPPEARED
DISAPPEARER
DISAPPEARING
DISAPPOINT
DISAPPOINTED
DISAPPOINTER
DISAPPOINTING
DISAPPOINTMENT
DISAPPROBATION
DISAPPROVAL
DISAPPROVE
DISAPPROVED
DISAPPROVER
DISAPPROVING
DISAPPROVINGLY
DISARD
DISARM
DISARMAMENT
DISARMATURE
DISARMED
DISARMER
DISARMING
DISARMINGLY
DISARRANGE

DISARRANGED
DISARRANGEMENT
DISARRANGING
DISARRAY
DISARRAYED
DISASINIZE
DISASSEMBLE
DISASSEMBLED
DISASSEMBLY
DISASSENT
DISASSIDUITY
DISASSOCIATE
DISASTER
DISASTERLY
DISASTROUS
DISASTROUSLY
DISATTAINT
DISATTIRE
DISAVAIL
DISAVOUCH
DISAVOW
DISAVOWAL
DISAVOWANCE
DISAVOWER
DISAVOWMENT
DISAWA
DISBALANCE
DISBAND
DISBANDED
DISBANDING
DISBANDMENT
DISBAR
DISBARK
DISBARMENT
DISBARRED
DISBARRING
DISBASE
DISBECOME
DISBELIEF
DISBELIEVE
DISBELIEVED
DISBELIEVER
DISBELIEVING
DISBENCH
DISBENCHED
DISBENCHING
DISBEND
DISBLAME
DISBOARD
DISBODIED
DISBODY
DISBOSOM
DISBOWEL
DISBRANCH
DISBRANCHED
DISBRANCHING
DISBUD
DISBUDDED
DISBUDDER
DISBUDDING
DISBURDEN
DISBURDENED
DISBURDENING
DISBURSABLE
DISBURSE
DISBURSED
DISBURSEMENT
DISBURSER
DISBURSING
DISBURTHEN
DISBURY
DISBUTTON
DISC
DISCAL
DISCALCEATE
DISCALCED
DISCAMP

DISCANDY
DISCANONIZE
DISCANONIZED
DISCANT
DISCARD
DISCARDED
DISCARDER
DISCARDING
DISCARNATE
DISCARNATION
DISCASE
DISCEDE
DISCEPT
DISCEPTATION
DISCEPTATOR
DISCERN
DISCERNED
DISCERNER
DISCERNIBLE
DISCERNIBLY
DISCERNING
DISCERNINGLY
DISCERNMENT
DISCERP
DISCERPED
DISCERPING
DISCERPTIBLE
DISCERPTION
DISCHARGE
DISCHARGED
DISCHARGER
DISCHARGING
DISCHARM
DISCHASE
DISCHURCH
DISCI
DISCIDE
DISCIFLORAL
DISCIFLOROUS
DISCINCT
DISCIND
DISCIPLE
DISCIPLED
DISCIPLESHIP
DISCIPLINAL
DISCIPLINANT
DISCIPLINARIAN
DISCIPLINARY
DISCIPLINE
DISCIPLINED
DISCIPLINER
DISCIPLING
DISCIPLINING
DISCIPULAR
DISCISSION
DISCITIS
DISCLAIM
DISCLAIMANT
DISCLAIMED
DISCLAIMER
DISCLAIMING
DISCLAMATION
DISCLAMATORY
DISCLOISTER
DISCLOSE
DISCLOSED
DISCLOSER
DISCLOSING
DISCLOSIVE
DISCLOSURE
DISCLOUD
DISCOAST
DISCOBLASTIC
DISCOBOLOS
DISCOBOLUS
DISCODACTYL
DISCOGRAPHY

DISCOID
DISCOIDAL
DISCOLICHEN
DISCOLITH
DISCOLOR
DISCOLORATE
DISCOLORATED
DISCOLORATION
DISCOLORED
DISCOLORING
DISCOLORMENT
DISCOLOUR
DISCOLOURED
DISCOLOURING
DISCOMEDUSAN
DISCOMFIT
DISCOMFITER
DISCOMFITURE
DISCOMFORT
DISCOMFORTED
DISCOMMEND
DISCOMMENDER
DISCOMMODE
DISCOMMODED
DISCOMMODING
DISCOMMODITY
DISCOMMON
DISCOMMONED
DISCOMMONING
DISCOMMUNITY
DISCOMORULA
DISCOMPOSE
DISCOMPOSED
DISCOMPOSING
DISCOMPOSURE
DISCOMPT
DISCOMYCETE
DISCONCERT
DISCONCERTED
DISCONGRUITY
DISCONNECT
DISCONNECTED
DISCONNECTER
DISCONNECTOR
DISCONSIDER
DISCONSOLATE
DISCONTENT
DISCONTENTED
DISCONTINUANCE
DISCONTINUE
DISCONTINUED
DISCONTINUEE
DISCONTINUER
DISCONTINUITY
DISCONTINUOR
DISCONTINUOUS
DISCONULA
DISCOPHILE
DISCOPHOROUS
DISCOPLASM
DISCOPODOUS
DISCORD
DISCORDANCE
DISCORDANCY
DISCORDANT
DISCORDANTLY
DISCORDER
DISCORDING
DISCORPORATE
DISCOTHEQUE
DISCOUNT
DISCOUNTABLE
DISCOUNTED
DISCOUNTER
DISCOUNTING
DISCOURAGE
DISCOURAGED

DISCOURAGEMENT
DISCOURAGER
DISCOURAGING
DISCOURSE
DISCOURSED
DISCOURSER
DISCOURSING
DISCOURSIVE
DISCOURTEOUS
DISCOURTEOUSLY
DISCOURTESY
DISCOUS
DISCOVER
DISCOVERABLE
DISCOVERED
DISCOVERER
DISCOVERIES
DISCOVERING
DISCOVERT
DISCOVERTURE
DISCOVERY
DISCREATE
DISCREATION
DISCREDIT
DISCREDITABLE
DISCREDITED
DISCREDITING
DISCREET
DISCREETER
DISCREETEST
DISCREETLY
DISCREETNESS
DISCREPANCE
DISCREPANCY
DISCREPANT
DISCREPANTLY
DISCREPATE
DISCREPATED
DISCREPATING
DISCRETE
DISCRETELY
DISCRETENESS
DISCRETION
DISCRETIONAL
DISCRETIVE
DISCRIMINAL
DISCRIMINANT
DISCRIMINATE
DISCRIMINATED
DISCRIMINATING
DISCRIMINATINGLY
DISCRIMINATION
DISCROWN
DISCULPATE
DISCULPATION
DISCULPATORY
DISCUMB
DISCUMBER
DISCURE
DISCUREN
DISCURRE
DISCURSATIVE
DISCURSIFY
DISCURSION
DISCURSIVE
DISCURSIVELY
DISCURSORY
DISCURSUS
DISCURTAIN
DISCUS
DISCUSES
DISCUSS
DISCUSSANT
DISCUSSED
DISCUSSER
DISCUSSIBLE
DISCUSSING

DISCUSSION
DISCUSSIONAL
DISCUSSIVE
DISCUTABLE
DISCUTE
DISDAIN
DISDAINED
DISDAINER
DISDAINFUL
DISDAINFULLY
DISDAINING
DISDAINLY
DISDAINOUS
DISDAR
DISDECEIVE
DISDIACLAST
DISDIAPASON
DISDIAZO
DISEASE
DISEASED
DISEASEDLY
DISEASEDNESS
DISEASEFUL
DISEASES
DISEASING
DISEASY
DISECONDARY
DISEDGE
DISEDIFY
DISELENID
DISELENIDE
DISEMATISM
DISEMBARK
DISEMBARKED
DISEMBARKING
DISEMBARRASS
DISEMBODIED
DISEMBODIMENT
DISEMBODY
DISEMBODYING
DISEMBOGUE
DISEMBOGUED
DISEMBOGUING
DISEMBOSOM
DISEMBOWEL
DISEMBOWELED
DISEMBURDEN
DISEME
DISEMIC
DISEMPLANE
DISEMPLANED
DISEMPLOY
DISENABLE
DISENABLED
DISENABLING
DISENACT
DISENCHANT
DISENCHANTED
DISENCHANTER
DISENCUMBER
DISENCUMBER
DISENDOW
DISENDOWER
DISENDOWMENT
DISENGAGE
DISENGAGED
DISENGAGING
DISENSOUL
DISENTAIL
DISENTANGLE
DISENTANGLED
DISENTANGLEMENT
DISENTANGLER
DISENTANGLING
DISENTHRALL
DISENTHRALLED
DISENTHRONE

DISENTHRONED
DISENTITLE
DISENTITLED
DISENTITLING
DISENTOMB
DISENTRACED
DISENTRAIN
DISENTRAINMENT
DISENTRANCE
DISENTWINE
DISENTWINED
DISEPALOUS
DISEQUALIZE
DISERT
DISESTABLISH
DISESTEEM
DISESTEEMED
DISESTEEMER
DISESTEEMING
DISEUR
DISEUSE
DISFAITH
DISFAME
DISFASHION
DISFAVOR
DISFAVORED
DISFAVORER
DISFAVORING
DISFAVOUR
DISFAVOURED
DISFAVOURER
DISFAVOURING
DISFEATURE
DISFEATURED
DISFEATURING
DISFEN
DISFIGURE
DISFIGURED
DISFIGUREMENT
DISFIGURER
DISFIGURING
DISFLESH
DISFOREST
DISFORM
DISFRANCHISE
DISFROCK
DISFURNISH
DISFURNISHED
DISFURNITURE
DISGAGE
DISGARNISH
DISGAVEL
DISGAVELED
DISGAVELING
DISGAVELLED
DISGAVELLING
DISGENERIC
DISGENIC
DISGLORY
DISGOOD
DISGORGE
DISGORGED
DISGORGER
DISGORGING
DISGOSPELIZE
DISGOWN
DISGRACE
DISGRACED
DISGRACEFUL
DISGRACER
DISGRACING
DISGRACIOUS
DISGRADE
DISGRADED
DISGRADING
DISGREGATE
DISGREGATION

DISGRESS	DISHUMOR	DISKERY	DISMEMBERED	DISPARPLING
DISGRUNTLE	DISHWASH	DISKLESS	DISMEMBERER	DISPART
DISGRUNTLED	DISHWASHER	DISKLIKE	DISMEMBERING	DISPARTMENT
DISGRUNTLING	DISHWASHINGS	DISKOS	DISMEMBRATE	DISPASSION
DISGUISAL	DISHWATER	DISKS	DISMEMBRATED	DISPASSIONATE
DISGUISE	DISHWATERY	DISLEAF	DISMEMBRATOR	DISPASSIONED
DISGUISED	DISHWIPER	DISLEAFED	DISMISS	DISPATCH
DISGUISEDLY	DISIDENTIFY	DISLEAFING	DISMISSAL	DISPATCHED
DISGUISER	DISILICID	DISLEAL	DISMISSED	DISPATCHER
DISGUISING	DISILICIDE	DISLEAVE	DISMISSIBLE	DISPATCHFUL
DISGULF	DISILLUDE	DISLEAVED	DISMISSING	DISPATCHING
DISGUST	DISILLUDED	DISLEAVING	DISMISSION	DISPATRIATED
DISGUSTED	DISILLUSION	DISLEVELMENT	DISMISSIVE	DISPAUPER
DISGUSTEDLY	DISILLUSIVE	DISLIKABLE	DISMIT	DISPAUPERIZE
DISGUSTER	DISIMAGINE	DISLIKE	DISMODED	DISPEACE
DISGUSTFUL	DISIMITATE	DISLIKED	DISMOUNT	DISPEACEFUL
DISGUSTFULLY	DISIMITATION	DISLIKEFUL	DISMOUNTABLE	DISPEED
DISGUSTING	DISIMPRISON	DISLIKEN	DISMUTATION	DISPEL
DISGUSTINGLY	DISINCLINATION	DISLIKER	DISNA	DISPELLED
DISH	DISINCLINE	DISLIKING	DISNATURE	DISPELLER
DISHABILLE	DISINCLINED	DISLIMB	DISNATURED	DISPELLING
DISHABIT	DISINCLINING	DISLIMN	DISNATURING	DISPEND
DISHABITUATE	DISINFECT	DISLINK	DISOBEDIENCE	DISPENDER
DISHALLOW	DISINFECTANT	DISLOAD	DISOBEDIENT	DISPENDIOUS
DISHARMONIC	DISINFECTED	DISLOCATE	DISOBEY	DISPENDITURE
DISHARMONIES	DISINFECTING	DISLOCATED	DISOBEYAL	DISPENSABLE
DISHARMONIZE	DISINFECTION	DISLOCATING	DISOBEYED	DISPENSARIES
DISHARMONY	DISINFECTIVE	DISLOCATION	DISOBEYER	DISPENSARY
DISHBOARD	DISINFECTOR	DISLOCATOR	DISOBEYING	DISPENSATE
DISHCLOTH	DISINFEST	DISLOCATORY	DISOBLIGE	DISPENSATED
DISHCLOUT	DISINFLATION	DISLOCK	DISOBLIGED	DISPENSATING
DISHEART	DISINGENUITY	DISLODGE	DISOBLIGER	DISPENSATION
DISHEARTEN	DISINGENUOUS	DISLODGED	DISOBLIGING	DISPENSATIVE
DISHEARTENED	DISINHERISON	DISLODGEMENT	DISOCCUPIED	DISPENSATOR
DISHEARTENER	DISINHERIT	DISLODGING	DISOCCUPY	DISPENSATORY
DISHEARTENING	DISINHUME	DISLODGMENT	DISOCCUPYING	DISPENSATRIX
DISHEATHING	DISINTEGRANT	DISLOYAL	DISOMATIC	DISPENSE
DISHED	DISINTEGRATE	DISLOYALIST	DISOMATOUS	DISPENSED
DISHEIR	DISINTEGRATING	DISLOYALLY	DISOMATY	DISPENSER
DISHELM	DISINTEGRATION	DISLOYALTIES	DISOMUS	DISPENSING
DISHER	DISINTEGROUS	DISLOYALTY	DISORB	DISPEOPLE
DISHERENT	DISINTER	DISLUSTER	DISORDER	DISPEOPLED
DISHERISON	DISINTEREST	DISLUSTERED	DISORDERED	DISPEOPLER
DISHERIT	DISINTERESTED	DISLUSTERING	DISORDEREDLY	DISPEOPLING
DISHERITMENT	DISINTERMENT	DISLUSTRE	DISORDERING	DISPERATO
DISHES	DISINTERRED	DISLUSTRED	DISORDERLY	DISPERGATE
DISHEVEL	DISINTERRING	DISLUSTRING	DISORDERS	DISPERGATED
DISHEVELED	DISINTRENCH	DISMAIL	DISORDINATE	DISPERGATING
DISHEVELING	DISINVEST	DISMAIN	DISORDINATED	DISPERGATION
DISHEVELLED	DISINVITE	DISMAL	DISORGANIC	DISPERGATOR
DISHEVELLING	DISINVOLVE	DISMALITIES	DISORGANIZE	DISPERMIC
DISHFUL	DISJASKED	DISMALITY	DISORGANIZED	DISPERMOUS
DISHING	DISJASKIT	DISMALLY	DISORGANIZER	DISPERSAL
DISHLIKE	DISJECT	DISMALNESS	DISORIENT	DISPERSE
DISHMAKER	DISJECTED	DISMALS	DISORIENTATE	DISPERSED
DISHMAKING	DISJECTING	DISMANTLE	DISOUR	DISPERSEDLY
DISHMONGER	DISJECTION	DISMANTLED	DISOWN	DISPERSER
DISHMOP	DISJEUNE	DISMANTLER	DISOXYGENATE	DISPERSIBLE
DISHONEST	DISJOIN	DISMANTLING	DISPACE	DISPERSING
DISHONESTIES	DISJOINED	DISMARBLE	DISPAIR	DISPERSION
DISHONESTLY	DISJOINING	DISMARCH	DISPAND	DISPERSITY
DISHONESTY	DISJOINT	DISMARK	DISPAR	DISPERSIVE
DISHONOR	DISJOINTED	DISMARKET	DISPARAGE	DISPERSIVELY
DISHONORABLE	DISJOINTEDLY	DISMARKETED	DISPARAGED	DISPERSOID
DISHONORARY	DISJOINTING	DISMARKETING	DISPARAGEMENT	DISPHENOID
DISHONORED	DISJOINTLY	DISMASK	DISPARAGER	DISPIECE
DISHONORER	DISJOINTURE	DISMAST	DISPARAGING	DISPIREM
DISHONORING	DISJUNCT	DISMASTED	DISPARATE	DISPIREME
DISHONOUR	DISJUNCTION	DISMASTING	DISPARATELY	DISPIRIT
DISHONOURARY	DISJUNCTIVE	DISMAY	DISPARATION	DISPIRITED
DISHONOURED	DISJUNCTIVELY	DISMAYED	DISPARATUM	DISPIRITEDLY
DISHONOURER	DISJUNCTOR	DISMAYEDNESS	DISPARISH	DISPIRITING
DISHONOURING	DISJUNCTURE	DISMAYFUL	DISPARITIES	DISPITEOUS
DISHORSE	DISJUNE	DISMAYFULLY	DISPARITY	DISPITEOUSLY
DISHPAN	DISK	DISMAYING	DISPARK	DISPLACE
DISHRAG	DISKELION	DISME	DISPARPLE	DISPLACED
DISHTOWEL	DISKER	DISMEMBER	DISPARPLED	DISPLACEMENT

DISPLACENCY
DISPLACER
DISPLACING
DISPLANT
DISPLAY
DISPLAYED
DISPLAYER
DISPLAYING
DISPLAYS
DISPLE
DISPLEASE
DISPLEASED
DISPLEASER
DISPLEASING
DISPLEASURE
DISPLENISH
DISPLICENCY
DISPLODE
DISPLODED
DISPLODING
DISPLUME
DISPLUMED
DISPLUMING
DISPLUVIATE
DISPOINT
DISPONDAIC
DISPONDEE
DISPONE
DISPONENT
DISPOROUS
DISPORT
DISPORTIVE
DISPORTMENT
DISPOSABLE
DISPOSAL
DISPOSE
DISPOSED
DISPOSEDLY
DISPOSEDNESS
DISPOSER
DISPOSING
DISPOSITION
DISPOSITIVE
DISPOSSESS
DISPOSSESSED
DISPOSSESSOR
DISPOST
DISPOSURE
DISPRAISE
DISPRAISED
DISPRAISER
DISPRAISING
DISPREAD
DISPREADER
DISPREADING
DISPREPARE
DISPRIVACIED
DISPRIZE
DISPRIZED
DISPRIZING
DISPROBATIVE
DISPROFIT
DISPROOF
DISPROPORTIONATE
DISPROVABLE
DISPROVAL
DISPROVE
DISPROVED
DISPROVEMENT
DISPROVEN
DISPROVER
DISPROVING
DISPUNCT
DISPUNGE
DISPUTABLE
DISPUTABLY
DISPUTANT

DISPUTATION
DISPUTATIOUS
DISPUTATIVE
DISPUTATOR
DISPUTE
DISPUTED
DISPUTER
DISPUTING
DISQUALIFIED
DISQUALIFY
DISQUIET
DISQUIETED
DISQUIETEDLY
DISQUIETER
DISQUIETING
DISQUIETLY
DISQUIETUDE
DISQUIPARANT
DISQUISIT
DISQUISITE
DISQUISITED
DISQUISITING
DISQUISITION
DISQUISITIVE
DISQUISITOR
DISQUISITORY
DISQUIXOTE
DISRANK
DISRATE
DISRATED
DISRATING
DISRAY
DISREALIZE
DISREGARD
DISREGARDED
DISREGARDER
DISREGARDFUL
DISREGARDING
DISRELATED
DISRELATION
DISRELISH
DISREMEMBER
DISREPAIR
DISREPUTABLE
DISREPUTABLENESS
DISREPUTABLY
DISREPUTE
DISRESPECT
DISRESPECTFUL
DISREST
DISROBE
DISROBED
DISROBEMENT
DISROBER
DISROBING
DISROOF
DISROOT
DISRUMP
DISRUPT
DISRUPTED
DISRUPTER
DISRUPTION
DISRUPTIVE
DISRUPTIVELY
DISRUPTMENT
DISRUPTOR
DISRUPTURE
DISS
DISSAIT
DISSATISFACTION
DISSATISFIED
DISSATISFY
DISSATURATE
DISSAVA
DISSCEPTER
DISSCEPTERED
DISSCEPTRE

DISSCEPTRED
DISSCEPTRING
DISSEAT
DISSECT
DISSECTED
DISSECTING
DISSECTION
DISSECTIONAL
DISSECTIVE
DISSECTOR
DISSEISE
DISSEISED
DISSEISEE
DISSEISIN
DISSEISOR
DISSEISORESS
DISSEIZE
DISSEIZED
DISSEIZEE
DISSEIZIN
DISSEIZING
DISSEIZOR
DISSEIZORESS
DISSEIZURE
DISSELBOOM
DISSEMBLANCE
DISSEMBLE
DISSEMBLED
DISSEMBLER
DISSEMBLIES
DISSEMBLING
DISSEMBLY
DISSEMINATE
DISSEMINATED
DISSEMINATOR
DISSEMINULE
DISSENSION
DISSENT
DISSENTED
DISSENTER
DISSENTIENCE
DISSENTIENT
DISSENTING
DISSENTINGLY
DISSENTIOUS
DISSENTIVE
DISSEPIMENT
DISSERT
DISSERTATE
DISSERTATED
DISSERTATING
DISSERTATION
DISSERTATIVE
DISSERTATOR
DISSERVE
DISSERVED
DISSERVICE
DISSERVING
DISSEVER
DISSEVERANCE
DISSEVERED
DISSEVERING
DISSHEATHE
DISSHEATHED
DISSIDENCE
DISSIDENT
DISSIDENTLY
DISSIGHT
DISSIGHTLY
DISSILIENCY
DISSILIENT
DISSIMILAR
DISSIMILARLY
DISSIMILARS
DISSIMILATE
DISSIMULATE
DISSIMULATED

DISSIMULATION
DISSIMULATOR
DISSIMULE
DISSIPABLE
DISSIPATE
DISSIPATED
DISSIPATEDLY
DISSIPATER
DISSIPATING
DISSIPATION
DISSIPATIVE
DISSIPATOR
DISSITE
DISSOCIABLE
DISSOCIABLY
DISSOCIAL
DISSOCIALITY
DISSOCIALIZE
DISSOCIANT
DISSOCIATE
DISSOCIATED
DISSOCIATING
DISSOCIATION
DISSOCIATIVE
DISSOCONCH
DISSOGENY
DISSOLUBLE
DISSOLUTE
DISSOLUTELY
DISSOLUTION
DISSOLUTIVE
DISSOLVABLE
DISSOLVE
DISSOLVED
DISSOLVENT
DISSOLVER
DISSOLVING
DISSONANCE
DISSONANCY
DISSONANT
DISSONANTLY
DISSONATE
DISSONOUS
DISSOUR
DISSPREAD
DISSUADE
DISSUADED
DISSUADER
DISSUADING
DISSUASION
DISSUASIVE
DISSUASIVELY
DISSUASORY
DISSUIT
DISSUITABLE
DISSUITED
DISSYLLABIC
DISSYLLABIFY
DISSYLLABISM
DISSYLLABIZE
DISSYLLABLE
DISSYMMETRIC
DISSYMMETRY
DISTAD
DISTAFF
DISTAFFS
DISTAIN
DISTAL
DISTALE
DISTALIA
DISTALLY
DISTANCE
DISTANCED
DISTANCING
DISTANCY
DISTANT
DISTANTLY

DISTANTNESS
DISTASTE
DISTASTED
DISTASTEFUL
DISTASTING
DISTAVES
DISTELFINK
DISTEMPER
DISTEMPERED
DISTEMPERING
DISTEND
DISTENDED
DISTENDER
DISTENDING
DISTENSIBLE
DISTENSION
DISTENSIVE
DISTENT
DISTENTION
DISTER
DISTHENE
DISTHRONE
DISTHRONED
DISTHRONING
DISTICH
DISTICHOUS
DISTICHOUSLY
DISTICHS
DISTIL
DISTILL
DISTILLABLE
DISTILLAGE
DISTILLATE
DISTILLATION
DISTILLATORY
DISTILLED
DISTILLER
DISTILLERY
DISTILLING
DISTILMENT
DISTILMENT
DISTINCT
DISTINCTIFY
DISTINCTIO
DISTINCTION
DISTINCTIONAL
DISTINCTITY
DISTINCTIVE
DISTINCTIVENESS
DISTINCTLY
DISTINCTNESS
DISTINGUE
DISTINGUEE
DISTINGUISH
DISTINGUISHED
DISTINGUISHING
DISTOCLUSION
DISTOMATOUS
DISTOME
DISTOMIASIS
DISTORT
DISTORTED
DISTORTEDLY
DISTORTER
DISTORTING
DISTORTION
DISTORTIONAL
DISTORTIVE
DISTRACT
DISTRACTED
DISTRACTEDLY
DISTRACTER
DISTRACTIBLE
DISTRACTING
DISTRACTION
DISTRACTIVE
DISTRAIN

DISTRAINABLE	DISVALUE	DITTOGRAPH	DIVERT	DIVISIVELY
DISTRAINED	DISVALUED	DITTOGRAPHIC	DIVERTED	DIVISIVENESS
DISTRAINEE	DISVALUING	DITTOGRAPHY	DIVERTEDLY	DIVISOR
DISTRAINER	DISVELOP	DITTOING	DIVERTER	DIVISORIAL
DISTRAINING	DISVISAGE	DITTOLOGIES	DIVERTICLE	DIVISORY
DISTRAINMENT	DISVOUCH	DITTOLOGY	DIVERTICULAR	DIVISURAL
DISTRAINOR	DISWARREN	DITTON	DIVERTICULUM	DIVORCE
DISTRAINT	DISWARRENED	DITTOS	DIVERTIMENTO	DIVORCED
DISTRAIT	DISWARRENING	DITTY	DIVERTING	DIVORCEE
DISTRAITE	DISWASHING	DITTYING	DIVERTINGLY	DIVORCEMENT
DISTRAUGHT	DISWORSHIP	DIURANATE	DIVERTISE	DIVORCER
DISTRAUGHTED	DISYLLABLE	DIURESIS	DIVERTISSANT	DIVORCEUSE
DISTRESS	DISYOKE	DIURETIC	DIVERTIVE	DIVORCING
DISTRESSED	DISYOKED	DIURETICAL	DIVERTOR	DIVORCIVE
DISTRESSEDLY	DISYOKING	DIURETICALLY	DIVES	DIVORT
DISTRESSFUL	DIT	DIURN	DIVEST	DIVOT
DISTRESSING	DITA	DIURNAL	DIVESTED	DIVOTO
DISTREST	DITAL	DIURNALLY	DIVESTING	DIVULGATE
DISTRIBUTARY	DITALI	DIURNALNESS	DIVESTITIVE	DIVULGATED
DISTRIBUTE	DITALINI	DIURNATION	DIVESTITURE	DIVULGATER
DISTRIBUTED	DITATION	DIURNE	DIVESTMENT	DIVULGATING
DISTRIBUTEE	DITCH	DIURNULE	DIVESTURE	DIVULGATION
DISTRIBUTER	DITCHBANK	DIUTURNAL	DIVI	DIVULGATORY
DISTRIBUTING	DITCHBUR	DIUTURNITY	DIVIDABLE	DIVULGE
DISTRIBUTION	DITCHDIGGER	DIV	DIVIDANT	DIVULGED
DISTRIBUTIVE	DITCHDOWN	DIVA	DIVIDE	DIVULGEMENT
DISTRIBUTIVELY	DITCHED	DIVAGATE	DIVIDED	DIVULGENCE
DISTRIBUTOR	DITCHER	DIVAGATED	DIVIDEDLY	DIVULGER
DISTRICT	DITCHING	DIVAGATING	DIVIDEDNESS	DIVULGING
DISTRICTLY	DITCHSIDE	DIVAGATION	DIVIDEND	DIVULSE
DISTRICTS	DITE	DIVALENCE	DIVIDER	DIVULSED
DISTRINGAS	DITED	DIVALENT	DIVIDERS	DIVULSING
DISTRITO	DITER	DIVAN	DIVIDING	DIVULSION
DISTRITOS	DITERTIARY	DIVARICATE	DIVIDINGLY	DIVULSIVE
DISTRUSS	DITHECAL	DIVARICATED	DIVIDUAL	DIVULSOR
DISTRUST	DITHECOUS	DIVARICATELY	DIVIDUALLY	DIVUS
DISTRUSTED	DITHEISM	DIVARICATING	DIVIDUITY	DIVVIED
DISTRUSTER	DITHEIST	DIVARICATION	DIVIDUOUS	DIVVIES
DISTRUSTFUL	DITHEISTIC	DIVARICATOR	DIVINAIL	DIVVY
DISTRUSTING	DITHEISTICAL	DIVAS	DIVINATION	DIVVYING
DISTURB	DITHER	DIVATA	DIVINATOR	DIWAN
DISTURBANCE	DITHERED	DIVE	DIVINATORY	DIWANI
DISTURBANT	DITHERING	DIVED	DIVINE	DIWATA
DISTURBATIVE	DITHERY	DIVEKEEPER	DIVINED	DIX
DISTURBED	DITHION	DIVEL	DIVINELY	DIXAIN
DISTURBER	DITHIONATE	DIVELLED	DIVINENESS	DIXENITE
DISTURBING	DITHIONIC	DIVELLENT	DIVINER	DIXI
DISTURN	DITHYRAMB	DIVELLICATE	DIVINERESS	DIXIE
DISULFATE	DITHYRAMBIC	DIVELLING	DIVINESSE	DIXIT
DISULFID	DITING	DIVER	DIVINEST	DIXY
DISULFIDE	DITION	DIVERB	DIVING	DIZAIN
DISULFOXID	DITOKOUS	DIVERGE	DIVINIFIED	DIZAINE
DISULFOXIDE	DITOLYL	DIVERGED	DIVINIFY	DIZDAR
DISULFURET	DITONE	DIVERGENCE	DIVINIFYING	DIZEN
DISULPHATE	DITREMATOUS	DIVERGENCES	DIVINING	DIZENED
DISULPHID	DITREMID	DIVERGENCIES	DIVININGLY	DIZENING
DISULPHIDE	DITRIGLYPH	DIVERGENCY	DIVINISTRE	DIZENMENT
DISULPHONATE	DITRIGLYPHIC	DIVERGENT	DIVINITIES	DIZYGOTIC
DISULPHOXID	DITRIGONAL	DIVERGENTLY	DIVINITY	DIZZARD
DISULPHOXIDE	DITRIGONALLY	DIVERGING	DIVINIZATION	DIZZARDLY
DISULPHURET	DITROCHEAN	DIVERGINGLY	DIVINIZE	DIZZEN
DISUNIFORM	DITROCHEE	DIVERS	DIVINIZED	DIZZIED
DISUNIFY	DITROCHOUS	DIVERSE	DIVINIZING	DIZZIER
DISUNION	DITROITE	DIVERSELY	DIVINYL	DIZZIEST
DISUNIONISM	DITT	DIVERSENESS	DIVISA	DIZZILY
DISUNIONIST	DITTAMY	DIVERSIFIED	DIVISI	DIZZINESS
DISUNITE	DITTANDER	DIVERSIFIER	DIVISIBILITY	DIZZY
DISUNITED	DITTANIES	DIVERSIFORM	DIVISIBLE	DIZZYING
DISUNITER	DITTANY	DIVERSIFY	DIVISIBLENESS	DJAGOONG
DISUNITIES	DITTAY	DIVERSIFYING	DIVISIBLY	DJALMAITE
DISUNITING	DITTED	DIVERSION	DIVISION	DJATI
DISUNITY	DITTIED	DIVERSIONAL	DIVISIONAL	DJEBEL
DISUSAGE	DITTIES	DIVERSIONARY	DIVISIONALLY	DJELFA
DISUSE	DITTING	DIVERSITIES	DIVISIONARY	DJERIB
DISUSED	DITTO	DIVERSITY	DIVISIONISM	DJERSA
DISUSING	DITTOED	DIVERSLY	DIVISIONIST	DJIBBAH
DISUTILITY	DITTOGRAM	DIVERSORY	DIVISIVE	DJIN

DJINN
DJINNI
DJO
DO
DOAB
DOABLE
DOACH
DOARIUM
DOAT
DOATED
DOATER
DOATISH
DOATY
DOB
DOBBER
DOBBIE
DOBBIES
DOBBIN
DOBBY
DOBE
DOBIE
DOBLA
DOBLON
DOBLONES
DOBOS
DOBRA
DOBRAO
DOBRAS
DOBROES
DOBSON
DOBY
DOC
DOCENT
DOCENTSHIP
DOCETISM
DOCHMIAC
DOCHMIACAL
DOCHMIASIS
DOCHMII
DOCHMIUS
DOCHTER
DOCIBILITY
DOCIBLE
DOCIBLENESS
DOCILE
DOCILELY
DOCILITY
DOCIMASIES
DOCIMASTIC
DOCIMASTICAL
DOCIMASY
DOCIMOLOGY
DOCIOUS
DOCITY
DOCK
DOCKAGE
DOCKED
DOCKEN
DOCKER
DOCKET
DOCKHAND
DOCKHEAD
DOCKHOUSE
DOCKING
DOCKIZATION
DOCKIZE
DOCKMACKIE
DOCKMAN
DOCKMASTER
DOCKSIDE
DOCKYARD
DOCMAC
DOCOSANE
DOCTOR
DOCTORAL
DOCTORALLY
DOCTORATE

DOCTORBIRD
DOCTORED
DOCTORESS
DOCTORFISH
DOCTORIAL
DOCTORIALLY
DOCTORING
DOCTORIZE
DOCTORLY
DOCTORS
DOCTORSHIP
DOCTRESS
DOCTRINABLE
DOCTRINAIRE
DOCTRINAL
DOCTRINALISM
DOCTRINALIST
DOCTRINALITY
DOCTRINALLY
DOCTRINARIAN
DOCTRINARILY
DOCTRINARITY
DOCTRINARY
DOCTRINATE
DOCTRINE
DOCTRINES
DOCTRINISM
DOCTRINIST
DOCTRINIZE
DOCTRINIZED
DOCTRINIZING
DOCTUS
DOCUMENT
DOCUMENTAL
DOCUMENTARY
DOCUMENTIZE
DOD
DODA
DODAD
DODD
DODDARD
DODDART
DODDED
DODDER
DODDERED
DODDERER
DODDERING
DODDERY
DODDIE
DODDLE
DODDY
DODDYPOLL
DODECADE
DODECADRACHM
DODECAFID
DODECAGON
DODECAGONAL
DODECAHEDRA
DODECAHEDRAL
DODECAHEDRON
DODECAMEROUS
DODECANE
DODECANT
DODECAPHONIC
DODECARCH
DODECARCHY
DODECASEMIC
DODECASTYLE
DODECASTYLOS
DODECATEMORY
DODECATYL
DODECATYLIC
DODECUPLET
DODECYL
DODECYLENE
DODECYLIC
DODGASTED

DODGE
DODGED
DODGER
DODGERY
DODGILY
DODGINESS
DODGING
DODGY
DODKIN
DODLET
DODMAN
DODO
DODOES
DODOISM
DODOMA
DODOS
DODS
DODUNK
DOE
DOEBIRD
DOEGLING
DOELING
DOER
DOES
DOESKIN
DOEST
DOETH
DOFF
DOFFED
DOFFER
DOFFING
DOFTBERRY
DOFUNNY
DOG
DOGAL
DOGANA
DOGARESSA
DOGATE
DOGBANE
DOGBERRIES
DOGBERRY
DOGBITE
DOGBLOW
DOGBOAT
DOGBODY
DOGBOLT
DOGBUSH
DOGCART
DOGCATCHER
DOGDOM
DOGE
DOGEDOM
DOGELESS
DOGES
DOGESHIP
DOGFACE
DOGFALL
DOGFENNEL
DOGFIGHT
DOGFISH
DOGFISHES
DOGFOOT
DOGGED
DOGGEDLY
DOGGEDNESS
DOGGER
DOGGEREL
DOGGERELED
DOGGERELER
DOGGERELIZE
DOGGERELIZER
DOGGERELIZING
DOGGERELLED
DOGGERELLING
DOGGERIES
DOGGERY
DOGGESS

DOGGIE
DOGGIER
DOGGIES
DOGGIEST
DOGGING
DOGGISH
DOGGISHLY
DOGGISHNESS
DOGGLE
DOGGO
DOGGONE
DOGGONED
DOGGONING
DOGGREL
DOGGRELIZE
DOGGY
DOGHEAD
DOGHOLE
DOGHOUSE
DOGIE
DOGLEG
DOGLIKE
DOGLY
DOGMA
DOGMAN
DOGMAS
DOGMATA
DOGMATIC
DOGMATICAL
DOGMATICALLY
DOGMATICIAN
DOGMATICS
DOGMATISM
DOGMATIST
DOGMATIZE
DOGMATIZED
DOGMATIZER
DOGMATIZING
DOGMEAT
DOGMEN
DOGMOUTH
DOGPLATE
DOGS
DOGSHORE
DOGSKIN
DOGSLED
DOGSLEEP
DOGSTAIL
DOGSTONE
DOGTAIL
DOGTIE
DOGTOOTH
DOGTRICK
DOGTROT
DOGVANE
DOGWATCH
DOGWOOD
DOGY
DOH
DOHL
DOIGT
DOIGTE
DOILED
DOILIES
DOILY
DOINA
DOINE
DOING
DOINGS
DOIT
DOITED
DOITRIFIED
DOJO
DOKE
DOKHMA
DOL
DOLABRA

DOLABRATE
DOLABRIFORM
DOLCAN
DOLCE
DOLCIAN
DOLCINO
DOLCISSIMO
DOLD
DOLDRUM
DOLDRUMS
DOLE
DOLEANCE
DOLED
DOLEFISH
DOLEFUL
DOLEFULLY
DOLEFULNESS
DOLEFULS
DOLENT
DOLENTE
DOLENTISSIMO
DOLERITE
DOLERITIC
DOLESMAN
DOLESOME
DOLESS
DOLEY
DOLICHOBLOND
DOLICHURIC
DOLICHURUS
DOLINA
DOLINE
DOLING
DOLIOFORM
DOLISIE
DOLITE
DOLITTLE
DOLIUM
DOLL
DOLLAR
DOLLARBIRD
DOLLARDEE
DOLLARFISH
DOLLARFISHES
DOLLARLEAF
DOLLARS
DOLLBEER
DOLLEY
DOLLFACE
DOLLFISH
DOLLHOUSE
DOLLIE
DOLLIED
DOLLIER
DOLLIES
DOLLIN
DOLLINESS
DOLLISH
DOLLISHLY
DOLLISHNESS
DOLLMAKER
DOLLMAKING
DOLLOP
DOLLS
DOLLY
DOLLYING
DOLLYMAN
DOLLYWAY
DOLMAN
DOLMEN
DOLOMITE
DOLOMITIC
DOLOMITIZE
DOLOR
DOLORIFEROUS
DOLORIFIC
DOLORIFUGE

DOLORIMETRY
DOLOROSO
DOLOROUS
DOLOROUSLY
DOLOROUSNESS
DOLOS
DOLOSE
DOLOUR
DOLPHIN
DOLT
DOLTHEAD
DOLTISH
DOLTISHLY
DOLTISHNESS
DOLUS
DOM
DOMAIN
DOMAL
DOMANIAL
DOMATIUM
DOMBA
DOME
DOMED
DOMENT
DOMER
DOMESDAY
DOMESTIC
DOMESTICABLE
DOMESTICALLY
DOMESTICATE
DOMESTICATED
DOMESTICATOR
DOMESTICITY
DOMESTICIZE
DOMESTICIZED
DOMESTICS
DOMETT
DOMEYKITE
DOMIC
DOMICAL
DOMICALLY
DOMICIL
DOMICILE
DOMICILED
DOMICILIAR
DOMICILIARY
DOMICILIATE
DOMICILIATED
DOMICILING
DOMIFICATION
DOMIFY
DOMINA
DOMINAE
DOMINANCE
DOMINANCY
DOMINANT
DOMINANTLY
DOMINATE
DOMINATED
DOMINATING
DOMINATION
DOMINATIVE
DOMINATOR
DOMINE
DOMINEER
DOMINEERED
DOMINEERER
DOMINEERING
DOMING
DOMINI
DOMINIAL
DOMINICAL
DOMINIE
DOMINION
DOMINIONISM
DOMINIONIST
DOMINIONS

DOMINIUM
DOMINO
DOMINOES
DOMINOS
DOMINULE
DOMINUS
DOMITE
DOMITIC
DOMN
DOMNEI
DOMOID
DOMPT
DOMPTEUSE
DOMRA
DOMUS
DOMY
DON
DONA
DONABLE
DONACIFORM
DONACK
DONAH
DONARIES
DONARY
DONATARIES
DONATARY
DONATE
DONATED
DONATEE
DONATING
DONATIO
DONATION
DONATIVE
DONATIVELY
DONATOR
DONATORIES
DONATORY
DONATRESS
DONAX
DONCELLA
DONCY
DONDAINE
DONDINE
DONE
DONEE
DONEY
DONG
DONGA
DONGOLA
DONGON
DONI
DONICKER
DONJON
DONK
DONKEY
DONKEYBACK
DONKEYMAN
DONKEYMEN
DONKEYS
DONKEYWORK
DONNA
DONNE
DONNED
DONNEE
DONNERED
DONNERT
DONNICK
DONNING
DONNISH
DONNISHNESS
DONNISM
DONNOCK
DONNOT
DONNY
DONNYBROOK
DONOR
DONOUGHT

DONSHIP
DONSIE
DONSKY
DONSY
DONUM
DONUT
DONZEL
DONZELLA
DOO
DOOB
DOOCOT
DOODAB
DOODAD
DOODAH
DOODLE
DOODLEBUG
DOODLED
DOODLESACK
DOODLING
DOODSKOP
DOOHICKEY
DOOHICKEYS
DOOHICKUS
DOOHINKEY
DOOHINKUS
DOOK
DOOKET
DOOL
DOOLEE
DOOLEY
DOOLFU
DOOLI
DOOLIE
DOOLIES
DOOLY
DOOM
DOOMAGE
DOOMBOOK
DOOMED
DOOMER
DOOMFUL
DOOMING
DOOMLIKE
DOOMS
DOOMSDAY
DOOMSMAN
DOOMSTEAD
DOOMSTER
DOON
DOOPUTTY
DOOR
DOORBELL
DOORBOY
DOORBRAND
DOORCASE
DOORCHEEK
DOORED
DOORFRAME
DOORHAWK
DOORHEAD
DOORJAMB
DOORKEEPER
DOORKNOB
DOORMAID
DOORMAKER
DOORMAKING
DOORMAN
DOORMAT
DOORNAIL
DOORNBOOM
DOORPLATE
DOORPOST
DOORS
DOORSILL
DOORSTEAD
DOORSTEP
DOORSTONE

DOORSTOP
DOORWARD
DOORWAY
DOORWEED
DOORYARD
DOOSE
DOOZY
DOP
DOPA
DOPAMELANIN
DOPAOXIDASE
DOPATTA
DOPCHICK
DOPE
DOPEBOOK
DOPED
DOPEHEAD
DOPER
DOPESHEET
DOPESTER
DOPEY
DOPIER
DOPIEST
DOPING
DOPP
DOPPED
DOPPER
DOPPERBIRD
DOPPIA
DOPPING
DOPPIO
DOPPLERITE
DOPSTER
DOPY
DOR
DORAB
DORAD
DORADILLA
DORADO
DORALIUM
DORAY
DORBEETLE
DORBEL
DORBIE
DORBUG
DORCASTRY
DORE
DOREA
DOREE
DOREY
DORHAWK
DORIA
DORIES
DORIPPID
DORJE
DORLACH
DORLOT
DORM
DORMANCY
DORMANT
DORME
DORMER
DORMERED
DORMETTE
DORMEUSE
DORMICE
DORMIE
DORMIENT
DORMILONA
DORMITARY
DORMITION
DORMITIVE
DORMITORIES
DORMITORY
DORMOUSE
DORMY
DORN

DORNECK
DORNIC
DORNICK
DORNOCK
DORON
DOROSACRAL
DOROSCENTRAL
DOROSTERNAL
DORP
DORPER
DORR
DORRBEETLE
DORRE
DORSA
DORSAD
DORSAL
DORSALIS
DORSALLY
DORSALMOST
DORSE
DORSEL
DORSER
DORSICOLLAR
DORSICOLUMN
DORSICORNU
DORSIDUCT
DORSIFEROUS
DORSIFIXED
DORSIFLEX
DORSIFLEXION
DORSIFLEXOR
DORSIGRADE
DORSILATERAL
DORSILUMBAR
DORSIMEDIAN
DORSIMESAL
DORSIPAROUS
DORSIPINAL
DORSIVENTRAL
DORSO
DORSOCAUDAD
DORSOLATERAL
DORSOMEDIAL
DORSOMESAL
DORSONASAL
DORSONUCHAL
DORSOPLEURAL
DORSORADIAL
DORSOVENTRAD
DORSOVENTRAL
DORSULA
DORSULUM
DORSUM
DORSUMBONAL
DORT
DORTER
DORTINESS
DORTISHIP
DORTOUR
DORTS
DORTY
DORUCK
DORY
DORYLINE
DORYMAN
DORYPHOROS
DORYPHORUS
DOS
DOSA
DOSADH
DOSAGE
DOSAIN
DOSE
DOSED
DOSER
DOSES
DOSIMETER

DOSIMETRIC
DOSIMETRIST
DOSIMETRY
DOSING
DOSIOLOGY
DOSIS
DOSOLOGY
DOSS
DOSSAL
DOSSED
DOSSEL
DOSSENNUS
DOSSER
DOSSERET
DOSSETY
DOSSIER
DOSSIERE
DOSSIL
DOSSING
DOSSMAN
DOSSMEN
DOSSY
DOST
DOT
DOTAGE
DOTAL
DOTANT
DOTARD
DOTARDISM
DOTARDLY
DOTARDY
DOTATE
DOTATION
DOTCHIN
DOTE
DOTED
DOTER
DOTES
DOTH
DOTHER
DOTIER
DOTIEST
DOTINESS
DOTING
DOTINGLY
DOTINGNESS
DOTISH
DOTISHNESS
DOTKIN
DOTLET
DOTS
DOTTED
DOTTEL
DOTTER
DOTTEREL
DOTTERELS
DOTTI
DOTTIER
DOTTIEST
DOTTILY
DOTTINESS
DOTTING
DOTTLE
DOTTLED
DOTTLER
DOTTLING
DOTTREL
DOTTY
DOTY
DOUANE
DOUANIER
DOUAR
DOUBLE
DOUBLED
DOUBLEDAMN
DOUBLEGANGER
DOUBLELEAF

DOUBLENESS
DOUBLER
DOUBLES
DOUBLET
DOUBLETED
DOUBLETHINK
DOUBLETON
DOUBLETONE
DOUBLETREE
DOUBLETS
DOUBLETTE
DOUBLEYOU
DOUBLING
DOUBLOON
DOUBLURE
DOUBLY
DOUBT
DOUBTABLE
DOUBTANCE
DOUBTED
DOUBTEDLY
DOUBTER
DOUBTFUL
DOUBTFULLY
DOUBTFULNESS
DOUBTING
DOUBTINGLY
DOUBTINGNESS
DOUBTLESS
DOUBTLESSLY
DOUBTMONGER
DOUBTOUS
DOUBTSOME
DOUBTY
DOUC
DOUCE
DOUCELY
DOUCENESS
DOUCET
DOUCEUR
DOUCHE
DOUCHED
DOUCHING
DOUCIN
DOUCINE
DOUDLE
DOUF
DOUGH
DOUGHBOY
DOUGHFACE
DOUGHHEAD
DOUGHINESS
DOUGHMAKER
DOUGHMAKING
DOUGHMAN
DOUGHMEN
DOUGHNUT
DOUGHT
DOUGHTIER
DOUGHTIEST
DOUGHTILY
DOUGHTINESS
DOUGHTY
DOUGHY
DOULCE
DOULOCRACY
DOUM
DOUMA
DOUMAIST
DOUNDAKE
DOUP
DOUPER
DOUPING
DOUPION
DOUPIONI
DOUR
DOURA

DOURADE
DOURE
DOURICOULI
DOURINE
DOURLY
DOURNESS
DOUSE
DOUSED
DOUSER
DOUSING
DOUT
DOUTER
DOUTOUS
DOUX
DOUZAINE
DOUZAINIER
DOUZEPER
DOUZEPERS
DOVAP
DOVE
DOVECOT
DOVECOTE
DOVEFLOWER
DOVEFOOT
DOVEHOUSE
DOVEKEY
DOVEKIE
DOVELET
DOVELIKE
DOVELING
DOVER
DOVES
DOVETAIL
DOVETAILED
DOVETAILER
DOVETAILING
DOVEWEED
DOVEWOOD
DOVISH
DOW
DOWABLE
DOWAGE
DOWAGER
DOWCET
DOWCOTE
DOWD
DOWDIER
DOWDIES
DOWDIEST
DOWDILY
DOWDINESS
DOWDY
DOWDYISH
DOWDYISM
DOWED
DOWEL
DOWELED
DOWELING
DOWELLED
DOWELLING
DOWER
DOWERAL
DOWERED
DOWERESS
DOWERING
DOWERY
DOWF
DOWFART
DOWFF
DOWIE
DOWILY
DOWINESS
DOWING
DOWITCH
DOWITCHER
DOWITCHERS
DOWL

DOWLAS
DOWLE
DOWLESS
DOWLY
DOWN
DOWNA
DOWNBEAR
DOWNBEARD
DOWNBEAT
DOWNBEND
DOWNBENT
DOWNBY
DOWNBYE
DOWNCAST
DOWNCASTLY
DOWNCASTNESS
DOWNCOME
DOWNCOMER
DOWNCOMING
DOWNCRIED
DOWNCRY
DOWNCRYING
DOWNCURVED
DOWNCUT
DOWNDALE
DOWNDRAFT
DOWNDRAUGHT
DOWNED
DOWNER
DOWNFACE
DOWNFALL
DOWNFALLEN
DOWNFALLING
DOWNFEED
DOWNFLOW
DOWNFOLD
DOWNFOLDED
DOWNGATE
DOWNGONE
DOWNGRADE
DOWNGRADED
DOWNGRADING
DOWNGROWTH
DOWNGYVED
DOWNHANGING
DOWNHAUL
DOWNHEADED
DOWNHEARTED
DOWNHILL
DOWNIER
DOWNIEST
DOWNINESS
DOWNING
DOWNLAND
DOWNLIE
DOWNLIER
DOWNLIGGING
DOWNLINE
DOWNLOOKED
DOWNLOOKER
DOWNLYING
DOWNMOST
DOWNPIPE
DOWNPOUR
DOWNPOURING
DOWNRIGHT
DOWNRIGHTLY
DOWNRUSH
DOWNRUSHING
DOWNS
DOWNSET
DOWNSHORE
DOWNSIDE
DOWNSINKING
DOWNSITTING
DOWNSLIDING
DOWNSLIP

DOWNSLOPE
DOWNSMAN
DOWNSOME
DOWNSPOUT
DOWNSTAGE
DOWNSTAIR
DOWNSTAIRS
DOWNSTATE
DOWNSTATER
DOWNSTREAM
DOWNSTREET
DOWNSTROKE
DOWNSWING
DOWNTAKE
DOWNTHROW
DOWNTHROWN
DOWNTHRUST
DOWNTOWN
DOWNTREADING
DOWNTROD
DOWNTRODDEN
DOWNTURN
DOWNWARD
DOWNWARDLY
DOWNWARDNESS
DOWNWARDS
DOWNWARP
DOWNWASH
DOWNWAY
DOWNWEED
DOWNWEIGH
DOWNWEIGHT
DOWNWEIGHTED
DOWNWIND
DOWNWITH
DOWNY
DOWP
DOWRY
DOWSABEL
DOWSE
DOWSED
DOWSER
DOWSET
DOWSETS
DOWSING
DOWVE
DOWY
DOXASTIC
DOXASTICON
DOXIE
DOXIES
DOXOGRAPHER
DOXOGRAPHY
DOXOLOGICAL
DOXOLOGIES
DOXOLOGIZE
DOXOLOGIZED
DOXOLOGIZING
DOXOLOGY
DOXY
DOYEN
DOYENNE
DOYLEY
DOYLT
DOYLY
DOYST
DOZE
DOZED
DOZEN
DOZENED
DOZENER
DOZENS
DOZENT
DOZENTH
DOZER
DOZIER
DOZIEST

DOZILY	DRAGGLE	DRAMATICS	DRAWBAR	DREADLESSLY
DOZINESS	DRAGGLED	DRAMATICULE	DRAWBEAM	DREADLY
DOZING	DRAGGLETAIL	DRAMATISE	DRAWBENCH	DREADNAUGHT
DOZY	DRAGGLING	DRAMATISM	DRAWBOARD	DREADNESS
DOZZLE	DRAGGLY	DRAMATIST	DRAWBOLT	DREADNOUGHT
DOZZLED	DRAGGY	DRAMATIZATION	DRAWBORE	DREAM
DRA	DRAGHOUND	DRAMATIZE	DRAWBORED	DREAMED
DRAA	DRAGLINE	DRAMATIZED	DRAWBORING	DREAMER
DRAB	DRAGMAN	DRAMATIZER	DRAWBOY	DREAMERIES
DRABANT	DRAGNET	DRAMATIZING	DRAWBRIDGE	DREAMERY
DRABBED	DRAGO	DRAMATURGE	DRAWCARD	DREAMFUL
DRABBER	DRAGOMAN	DRAMATURGIC	DRAWCORD	DREAMFULLY
DRABBEST	DRAGOMANATE	DRAMATURGIST	DRAWCUT	DREAMFULNESS
DRABBET	DRAGOMANIC	DRAMATURGY	DRAWCUTTING	DREAMHOLE
DRABBING	DRAGOMANISH	DRAME	DRAWDOWN	DREAMIER
DRABBISH	DRAGOMANS	DRAMM	DRAWEE	DREAMIEST
DRABBLE	DRAGOMEN	DRAMMAGE	DRAWER	DREAMILY
DRABBLED	DRAGON	DRAMME	DRAWERS	DREAMINESS
DRABBLER	DRAGONESS	DRAMMED	DRAWFILE	DREAMING
DRABBLETAIL	DRAGONET	DRAMMER	DRAWFILED	DREAMINGLY
DRABBLING	DRAGONFISH	DRAMMING	DRAWFILING	DREAMLAND
DRABBY	DRAGONFISHES	DRAMMOCK	DRAWGATE	DREAMLESS
DRABI	DRAGONFLIES	DRAMSELLER	DRAWGEAR	DREAMLESSLY
DRABLER	DRAGONFLY	DRAMSHOP	DRAWGLOVE	DREAMLIKE
DRABLY	DRAGONHEAD	DRANE	DRAWGLOVES	DREAMLIT
DRABNESS	DRAGONISM	DRANG	DRAWHEAD	DREAMLORE
DRACHEN	DRAGONIZE	DRANK	DRAWHORSE	DREAMS
DRACHM	DRAGONKIND	DRANT	DRAWING	DREAMSILY
DRACHMA	DRAGONNADE	DRAP	DRAWK	DREAMSINESS
DRACHMAE	DRAGONNE	DRAPE	DRAWKNIFE	DREAMSY
DRACHMAI	DRAGONROOT	DRAPEAU	DRAWKNIVES	DREAMT
DRACHMAL	DRAGONTAIL	DRAPED	DRAWKNOT	DREAMTIDE
DRACHMAS	DRAGONWORT	DRAPER	DRAWL	DREAMTIME
DRACMA	DRAGOON	DRAPERESS	DRAWLATCH	DREAMWHILE
DRACONIAN	DRAGOONAGE	DRAPERIED	DRAWLED	DREAMWORLD
DRACONITES	DRAGOONED	DRAPERIES	DRAWLER	DREAMY
DRACONITIC	DRAGOONER	DRAPERY	DRAWLIER	DREAR
DRACONTIAN	DRAGOONING	DRAPET	DRAWLIEST	DREARIER
DRACONTIASIS	DRAGROPE	DRAPING	DRAWLING	DREARIEST
DRACONTIC	DRAGSAW	DRAPPIE	DRAWLINGLY	DREARIHEAD
DRACONTINE	DRAGSHOE	DRAPPY	DRAWLINGNESS	DREARIHOOD
DRACONTITES	DRAGSMAN	DRASH	DRAWLINK	DREARILY
DRACUNCULUS	DRAGSMEN	DRASHEL	DRAWLOOM	DREARIMENT
DRAD	DRAGSTAFF	DRASS	DRAWLY	DREARINESS
DRAFF	DRAGSTER	DRASSID	DRAWN	DREARING
DRAFFISH	DRAIL	DRAST	DRAWNET	DREARLY
DRAFFMAN	DRAILED	DRASTIC	DRAWOFF	DREARNESS
DRAFFSACK	DRAILING	DRASTICALLY	DRAWOUT	DREARY
DRAFFY	DRAIN	DRASTY	DRAWPLATE	DRECK
DRAFT	DRAINAGE	DRAT	DRAWPOINT	DREDDOUR
DRAFTAGE	DRAINAGEWAY	DRATCHELL	DRAWROD	DREDGE
DRAFTED	DRAINBOARD	DRATE	DRAWSHAVE	DREDGED
DRAFTEE	DRAINE	DRATTED	DRAWSHEET	DREDGEMAN
DRAFTER	DRAINED	DRATTING	DRAWSPAN	DREDGER
DRAFTIER	DRAINER	DRAUGHT	DRAWSPRING	DREDGIE
DRAFTILY	DRAINERMAN	DRAUGHTAGE	DRAWSTOP	DREDGING
DRAFTINESS	DRAINERMEN	DRAUGHTBOARD	DRAWSTRING	DREE
DRAFTING	DRAINING	DRAUGHTED	DRAWTONGS	DREECH
DRAFTS	DRAINLESS	DRAUGHTER	DRAWTUBE	DREED
DRAFTSMAN	DRAINMAN	DRAUGHTHOUSE	DRAY	DREEING
DRAFTY	DRAINPIPE	DRAUGHTIER	DRAYAGE	DREEL
DRAG	DRAINS	DRAUGHTIEST	DRAYED	DREELY
DRAGADE	DRAINTILE	DRAUGHTILY	DRAYING	DREEN
DRAGADED	DRAISENE	DRAUGHTINESS	DRAYMAN	DREEP
DRAGADING	DRAISINE	DRAUGHTING	DRAYMEN	DREEPINESS
DRAGBAR	DRAKE	DRAUGHTS	DRAZEL	DREEPY
DRAGBOAT	DRAKELET	DRAUGHTSMAN	DRAZIL	DREG
DRAGBOLT	DRAKESTONE	DRAUGHTSMEN	DREAD	DREGGIER
DRAGEE	DRAKONITE	DRAUGHTY	DREADABLE	DREGGIEST
DRAGEOIR	DRAM	DRAUNT	DREADED	DREGGILY
DRAGGED	DRAMA	DRAVE	DREADER	DREGGINESS
DRAGGER	DRAMALOGUE	DRAVITE	DREADFUL	DREGGISH
DRAGGIER	DRAMAMINE	DRAW	DREADFULLY	DREGGY
DRAGGIEST	DRAMATIC	DRAWABLE	DREADFULNESS	DREGS
DRAGGILY	DRAMATICAL	DRAWARM	DREADING	DREICH
DRAGGINESS	DRAMATICALLY	DRAWBACK	DREADINGLY	DREIDEL
DRAGGING	DRAMATICISM	DRAWBAND	DREADLESS	DREIE

DREIGH	DRIGHTIN	DROGHERMAN	DROPKICK	DROZE
DREILING	DRIKI	DROGHLIN	DROPLET	DRUB
DRENCH	DRILL	DROGUE	DROPLIGHT	DRUBBED
DRENCHED	DRILLED	DROGUET	DROPLINE	DRUBBER
DRENCHER	DRILLER	DROICH	DROPLING	DRUBBING
DRENCHING	DRILLET	DROIL	DROPMAN	DRUBBLE
DRENCHINGLY	DRILLING	DROIT	DROPMEAL	DRUBLY
DRENG	DRILLMAN	DROITS	DROPOUT	DRUCKEN
DRENGAGE	DRILLMASTER	DROITURAL	DROPPED	DRUDGE
DRENGH	DRILLSTOCK	DROKE	DROPPER	DRUDGED
DREPANE	DRILVIS	DROLE	DROPPING	DRUDGER
DREPANIA	DRILY	DROLERIE	DROPPY	DRUDGERIES
DREPANID	DRING	DROLL	DROPS	DRUDGERY
DREPANIFORM	DRINGLE	DROLLED	DROPSEED	DRUDGING
DREPANIUM	DRINK	DROLLER	DROPSICAL	DRUDGINGLY
DREPANOID	DRINKABILITY	DROLLERIES	DROPSICALLY	DRUDGISM
DREPE	DRINKABLE	DROLLERY	DROPSIED	DRUERY
DRESS	DRINKABLY	DROLLEST	DROPSIES	DRUG
DRESSAGE	DRINKER	DROLLING	DROPSY	DRUGGE
DRESSED	DRINKERY	DROLLISH	DROPT	DRUGGED
DRESSER	DRINKING	DROLLISHNESS	DROPVIE	DRUGGER
DRESSES	DRINKLESS	DROLLIST	DROPWISE	DRUGGERIES
DRESSIER	DRINKS	DROLLY	DROPWORM	DRUGGERY
DRESSIEST	DRINKY	DROME	DROPWORT	DRUGGET
DRESSILY	DRINN	DROMED	DROSHKIES	DRUGGIER
DRESSINESS	DRIP	DROMEDARIAN	DROSHKY	DRUGGIEST
DRESSING	DRIPOLATOR	DROMEDARIES	DROSKY	DRUGGING
DRESSMAKER	DRIPPED	DROMEDARIST	DROSOGRAPH	DRUGGIST
DRESSMAKERY	DRIPPER	DROMEDARY	DROSOMETER	DRUGGY
DRESSMAKING	DRIPPIER	DROMETER	DROSOPHILA	DRUGLESS
DRESSY	DRIPPIEST	DROMI	DROSS	DRUGMAN
DREST	DRIPPING	DROMIC	DROSSED	DRUGS
DRETCH	DRIPPLE	DROMICAL	DROSSEL	DRUGSHOP
DREW	DRIPPY	DROMOGRAPH	DROSSER	DRUGSTORE
DREWITE	DRIPSTICK	DROMOMANIA	DROSSIER	DRUID
DREY	DRIPSTONE	DROMOMETER	DROSSIEST	DRUIDESS
DRIAS	DRIPT	DROMON	DROSSINESS	DRUIDIC
DRIB	DRISHEEN	DROMOND	DROSSING	DRUIDICAL
DRIBBED	DRISK	DROMOS	DROSSY	DRUIDISM
DRIBBER	DRISSEL	DROMOTROPIC	DROSTDEN	DRUIDRY
DRIBBING	DRIVABLE	DRONA	DROSTDY	DRUK
DRIBBLE	DRIVAGE	DRONAGE	DROUD	DRUM
DRIBBLED	DRIVE	DRONE	DROUGHERMEN	DRUMBEAT
DRIBBLER	DRIVEABLE	DRONED	DROUGHT	DRUMBLE
DRIBBLET	DRIVEAWAY	DRONEL	DROUGHTINESS	DRUMBLED
DRIBBLING	DRIVEBOAT	DRONER	DROUGHTY	DRUMBLEDORE
DRIBLET	DRIVEBOLT	DRONET	DROUK	DRUMBLER
DRIDDER	DRIVECAP	DRONG	DROUKAN	DRUMBLING
DRIDDLE	DRIVEHEAD	DRONGO	DROUKED	DRUMFIRE
DRIECH	DRIVEL	DRONGOS	DROUKET	DRUMFISH
DRIED	DRIVELED	DRONING	DROUKING	DRUMFISHES
DRIEGH	DRIVELER	DRONISH	DROUKIT	DRUMHEAD
DRIER	DRIVELING	DRONISHLY	DROUMY	DRUMHEADS
DRIERMAN	DRIVELINGLY	DRONISHNESS	DROUTH	DRUMLER
DRIES	DRIVELLED	DRONKGRASS	DROUTHY	DRUMLIN
DRIEST	DRIVELLER	DRONY	DROVE	DRUMLINE
DRIFT	DRIVELLING	DROOK	DROVED	DRUMLINOID
DRIFTAGE	DRIVEN	DROOL	DROVER	DRUMLOID
DRIFTBOLT	DRIVEPIPE	DROOLED	DROVING	DRUMLOIDAL
DRIFTED	DRIVER	DROOP	DROVY	DRUMLY
DRIFTER	DRIVESCREW	DROOPED	DROW	DRUMMED
DRIFTIER	DRIVEWAY	DROOPER	DROWK	DRUMMER
DRIFTIEST	DRIVING	DROOPIER	DROWN	DRUMMING
DRIFTING	DRIVINGLY	DROOPIEST	DROWNED	DRUMMOCK
DRIFTINGLY	DRIZZLE	DROOPILY	DROWNER	DRUMMY
DRIFTLAND	DRIZZLED	DROOPINESS	DROWNING	DRUMS
DRIFTLESS	DRIZZLING	DROOPING	DROWSE	DRUMSKIN
DRIFTLET	DRIZZLY	DROOPINGLY	DROWSED	DRUMSLER
DRIFTMAN	DROB	DROOPINGNESS	DROWSIER	DRUMSTICK
DRIFTPIECE	DROCHUIL	DROOPT	DROWSIEST	DRUMWOOD
DRIFTPIN	DRODDUM	DROOPY	DROWSIHEAD	DRUN
DRIFTWAY	DROFLAND	DROP	DROWSIHOOD	DRUNG
DRIFTWEED	DROGER	DROPCLOTH	DROWSILY	DRUNGAR
DRIFTWIND	DROGERMAN	DROPFORGE	DROWSINESS	DRUNK
DRIFTWOOD	DROGERMEN	DROPFORGED	DROWSING	DRUNKARD
DRIFTY	DROGH	DROPFORGING	DROWSY	DRUNKELEW
DRIGHTEN	DROGHER	DROPHEAD	DROY	DRUNKEN

DRUNKENLY	DUARCH	DUCKTAIL	DUFRENOYSITE	DULLISH
DRUNKENNESS	DUARCHY	DUCKWEED	DUFTER	DULLITY
DRUNKER	DUB	DUCKWIFE	DUFTERDAR	DULLNESS
DRUNKERIES	DUBASH	DUCKWING	DUFTERY	DULLPATE
DRUNKERY	DUBB	DUCKY	DUFTITE	DULLSOME
DRUNKOMETER	DUBBA	DUCT	DUFTRY	DULLY
DRUNT	DUBBAH	DUCTIBILITY	DUG	DULNESS
DRUPACEOUS	DUBBED	DUCTIBLE	DUGAL	DULOCRACY
DRUPAL	DUBBEH	DUCTILE	DUGDUG	DULOSIS
DRUPE	DUBBELTJE	DUCTILELY	DUGGLER	DULOTIC
DRUPEL	DUBBER	DUCTILENESS	DUGON	DULSE
DRUPELET	DUBBIN	DUCTILIMETER	DUGONG	DULT
DRUPEOLE	DUBBING	DUCTILITY	DUGOUT	DULTIE
DRUPETUM	DUBBY	DUCTILIZE	DUGWAY	DULWILLY
DRUPIFEROUS	DUBIETIES	DUCTILIZED	DUHAT	DULY
DRURY	DUBIETY	DUCTILIZING	DUI	DUMA
DRUSE	DUBIOSITIES	DUCTION	DUIKER	DUMAIST
DRUSED	DUBIOSITY	DUCTOR	DUIKERBOK	DUMAL
DRUSH	DUBIOUS	DUCTULE	DUIKERBOKS	DUMB
DRUSY	DUBIOUSLY	DUCTURE	DUIKERBUCK	DUMBA
DRUTHER	DUBIOUSNESS	DUCTUS	DUIM	DUMBBELL
DRUTHERS	DUBITABLE	DUD	DUIME	DUMBBELLER
DRUTTLE	DUBITABLY	DUDAIM	DUINHEWASSEL	DUMBCOW
DRUVE	DUBITANT	DUDDER	DUIT	DUMBFISH
DRUVY	DUBITANTE	DUDDERY	DUJAN	DUMBFOUND
DRUXEY	DUBITATE	DUDDIE	DUKAN	DUMBFOUNDED
DRUXINESS	DUBITATION	DUDDLE	DUKE	DUMBHEAD
DRUXY	DUBITATIVE	DUDDY	DUKEDOM	DUMBLE
DRY	DUBITATIVELY	DUDE	DUKELING	DUMBLEDORE
DRYAD	DUBS	DUDEEN	DUKELY	DUMBLY
DRYADES	DUC	DUDGEN	DUKERY	DUMBNESS
DRYADIC	DUCAL	DUDGECN	DUKES	DUMBWAITER
DRYAS	DUCALLY	DUDINE	DUKHN	DUMBY
DRYASDUST	DUCAPE	DUDISH	DUKKER	DUMDUM
DRYBEARD	DUCAT	DUDLER	DUKKERIPEN	DUMFOUND
DRYER	DUCATO	DUDLEY	DUKU	DUMFOUNDED
DRYERMAN	DUCATON	DUDLEYITE	DUKUMA	DUMKA
DRYERMEN	DUCATOON	DUDMAN	DULBERT	DUMKY
DRYEST	DUCATUS	DUDS	DULCAMARA	DUMMEL
DRYFIST	DUCDAME	DUE	DULCARNON	DUMMERED
DRYFOOT	DUCE	DUEFUL	DULCE	DUMMERER
DRYGOODSMAN	DUCES	DUEL	DULCELY	DUMMIES
DRYHOUSE	DUCHAN	DUELED	DULCENESS	DUMMKOPF
DRYING	DUCHERY	DUELER	DULCET	DUMMY
DRYINID	DUCHESS	DUELING	DULCETLY	DUMONTITE
DRYISH	DUCHESSE	DUELIST	DULCETNESS	DUMORTIERITE
DRYLOT	DUCHIES	DUELISTIC	DULCIAN	DUMOSE
DRYLY	DUCHN	DUELLED	DULCIANA	DUMOSITY
DRYNESS	DUCHY	DUELLER	DULCID	DUMOUS
DRYOPTEROID	DUCK	DUELLING	DULCIFIED	DUMP
DRYPOINT	DUCKBILL	DUELLIST	DULCIFLUOUS	DUMPAGE
DRYS	DUCKBLIND	DUELLISTIC	DULCIFY	DUMPCART
DRYSALTER	DUCKBOARD	DUELLIZE	DULCIFYING	DUMPED
DRYSALTERIES	DUCKBOAT	DUELLO	DULCILOQUENT	DUMPER
DRYSALTERY	DUCKED	DUELLOS	DULCILOQUY	DUMPIER
DRYSNE	DUCKER	DUENA	DULCIMER	DUMPIES
DRYSTER	DUCKERIES	DUENAS	DULCITE	DUMPIEST
DRYTH	DUCKERY	DUENNA	DULCITOL	DUMPILY
DRYWORKER	DUCKFOOT	DUENNAS	DULCITUDE	DUMPING
DU	DUCKHEARTED	DUES	DULCITY	DUMPISH
DUAB	DUCKHOUSE	DUET	DULCOR	DUMPISHLY
DUAD	DUCKHUNTING	DUETTED	DULEDGE	DUMPISHNESS
DUADIC	DUCKIE	DUETTING	DULER	DUMPLE
DUAL	DUCKIER	DUETTINO	DULIA	DUMPLED
DUALI	DUCKIEST	DUETTIST	DULL	DUMPLER
DUALIN	DUCKING	DUETTO	DULLARD	DUMPLING
DUALISM	DUCKISH	DUFF	DULLARDISM	DUMPOKE
DUALIST	DUCKLAR	DUFFADAR	DULLARDNESS	DUMPS
DUALISTIC	DUCKLET	DUFFED	DULLBRAINED	DUMPTY
DUALITY	DUCKLING	DUFFEL	DULLED	DUMPY
DUALIZATION	DUCKMEAT	DUFFER	DULLER	DUN
DUALIZE	DUCKMOLE	DUFFIES	DULLERY	DUNAIR
DUALIZED	DUCKPIN	DUFFING	DULLEST	DUNAL
DUALIZING	DUCKPINS	DUFFLE	DULLHEAD	DUNAM
DUAN	DUCKPOND	DUFFY	DULLHEARTED	DUNAMIS
DUANT	DUCKS	DUFOIL	DULLIFY	DUNBIRD
DUAR	DUCKSTONE	DUFRENITE	DULLING	DUNCE

DUNCERY	DUODECIMOS	DURAL	DUSTED	DWARFISM
DUNCH	DUODECUPLE	DURAMEN	DUSTEE	DWARFLING
DUNCICAL	DUODENA	DURANCE	DUSTER	DWARFNESS
DUNCIFY	DUODENAL	DURANGITE	DUSTERMAN	DWARFS
DUNCIFYING	DUODENARY	DURANT	DUSTERMEN	DWARFY
DUNCISH	DUODENATE	DURANTE	DUSTFALL	DWARVES
DUNCISHLY	DUODENATION	DURAPLASTY	DUSTHEAP	DWAYBERRY
DUNCISHNESS	DUODENE	DURAQUARA	DUSTIER	DWEEBLE
DUNDASITE	DUODENITIS	DURATION	DUSTIEST	DWELL
DUNDER	DUODENUM	DURATIONAL	DUSTILY	DWELLED
DUNDERFUNK	DUODRAMA	DURATIVE	DUSTINESS	DWELLER
DUNDERHEAD	DUOGRAPH	DURAX	DUSTING	DWELLING
DUNDERHEADED	DUOLE	DURBACHITE	DUSTLESS	DWELT
DUNDERPATE	DUOLITERAL	DURBAR	DUSTLIKE	DWERE
DUNE	DUOLOG	DURDENITE	DUSTMAN	DWINDLE
DUNES	DUOLOGUE	DURDUM	DUSTOOR	DWINDLED
DUNFISH	DUOMACHY	DURE	DUSTOORI	DWINDLING
DUNG	DUOMI	DUREE	DUSTOUR	DWINE
DUNGA	DUOMO	DUREFUL	DUSTPAN	DWINED
DUNGANNONITE	DUOPOD	DURENOL	DUSTPOINT	DWINING
DUNGAREE	DUOS	DURESS	DUSTPROOF	DYAD
DUNGARI	DUOSECANT	DURESSOR	DUSTRAG	DYADIC
DUNGBECK	DUOTONED	DUREZZA	DUSTUCK	DYARCHIC
DUNGBIRD	DUOTYPE	DURGAH	DUSTUK	DYARCHICAL
DUNGED	DUOVIRI	DURGAN	DUSTUP	DYARCHY
DUNGEON	DUP	DURGEN	DUSTY	DYBBUK
DUNGEONER	DUPABILITY	DURIAN	DUSTYFOOT	DYCE
DUNGER	DUPABLE	DURICRUST	DUTCH	DYDE
DUNGHILL	DUPE	DURIDINE	DUTCHED	DYE
DUNGHILLY	DUPED	DURING	DUTCHESS	DYEABLE
DUNGING	DUPER	DURINGLY	DUTCHING	DYEBECK
DUNGON	DUPERIES	DURION	DUTCHMAN	DYED
DUNGY	DUPERY	DURITY	DUTCHMEN	DYEHOUSE
DUNIEWASSAL	DUPING	DURMAST	DUTEOUS	DYEING
DUNITE	DUPION	DURN	DUTEOUSLY	DYELEAVES
DUNK	DUPLATION	DURNED	DUTEOUSNESS	DYER
DUNKADOO	DUPLE	DURO	DUTIABILITY	DYESTER
DUNKER	DUPLET	DUROMETER	DUTIABLE	DYESTUFF
DUNKING	DUPLEX	DUROQUINONE	DUTIED	DYEWARE
DUNKLE	DUPLEXED	DUROS	DUTIES	DYEWEED
DUNKLED	DUPLEXER	DUROY	DUTIFUL	DYEWOOD
DUNKLING	DUPLEXES	DURR	DUTIFULLY	DYGOGRAM
DUNLIN	DUPLEXING	DURRA	DUTIFULNESS	DYING
DUNLINS	DUPLEXITY	DURRIE	DUTRA	DYKAGE
DUNNAGE	DUPLICABLE	DURRIES	DUTUBURI	DYKE
DUNNAGED	DUPLICAND	DURRIN	DUTY	DYKEHOPPER
DUNNAGING	DUPLICANDO	DURRY	DUUMVIR	DYKER
DUNNE	DUPLICATE	DURST	DUUMVIRAL	DYKEREEVE
DUNNED	DUPLICATED	DURUKULI	DUUMVIRATE	DYNAGRAPH
DUNNER	DUPLICATELY	DURUM	DUUMVIRI	DYNAM
DUNNESS	DUPLICATING	DURWAN	DUUMVIRS	DYNAMETER
DUNNIEWASSEL	DUPLICATION	DURWAUN	DUVEL	DYNAMETRIC
DUNNING	DUPLICATIVE	DURYL	DUVET	DYNAMETRICAL
DUNNISH	DUPLICATOR	DURZEE	DUVETINE	DYNAMIC
DUNNITE	DUPLICATURE	DUSACK	DUVETYN	DYNAMICAL
DUNNOCK	DUPLICIDENT	DUSCLE	DUVETYNE	DYNAMICALLY
DUNNY	DUPLICITAS	DUSE	DUX	DYNAMICS
DUNST	DUPLICITIES	DUSH	DUXELLES	DYNAMIS
DUNSTABLE	DUPLICITY	DUSIO	DUXES	DYNAMISM
DUNSTER	DUPLIFIED	DUSK	DUYKER	DYNAMIST
DUNT	DUPLIFY	DUSKEN	DVAITA	DYNAMISTIC
DUNTED	DUPLIFYING	DUSKIER	DVANDVA	DYNAMITARD
DUNTING	DUPLONE	DUSKIEST	DVORNIK	DYNAMITE
DUNTLE	DUPLY	DUSKILY	DWAIBLE	DYNAMITED
DUNUM	DUPONDIUS	DUSKINESS	DWAIBLY	DYNAMITER
DUNY	DUPPER	DUSKINGTIDE	DWAIN	DYNAMITIC
DUNZIEKTE	DUPPIES	DUSKISH	DWALE	DYNAMITICAL
DUO	DUPPY	DUSKLY	DWALL	DYNAMITING
DUOCOSANE	DUR	DUSKNESS	DWALM	DYNAMITISM
DUODECANE	DURA	DUSKY	DWAM	DYNAMITIST
DUODECENNIAL	DURABILITIES	DUST	DWANG	DYNAMIZATION
DUODECILLION	DURABILITY	DUSTBAND	DWARF	DYNAMIZE
DUODECIMAL	DURABLE	DUSTBIN	DWARFED	DYNAMO
DUODECIMALITY	DURABLENESS	DUSTBLU	DWARFING	DYNAMOGENIC
DUODECIMALLY	DURABLY	DUSTBOX	DWARFISH	DYNAMOGENOUS
DUODECIMO	DURACINE	DUSTCLOTH	DWARFISHLY	DYNAMOMETER
DUODECIMOLE	DURAIN	DUSTCOAT	DWARFISHNESS	DYNAMOMETRIC

DYNAMOMETRY
DYNAMONEURE
DYNAMOPHONE
DYNAMOSTATIC
DYNAMOTOR
DYNAST
DYNASTIC
DYNASTICAL
DYNASTICALLY
DYNASTID
DYNASTIDAN
DYNASTIES
DYNASTY
DYNATRON
DYNE
DYNODE
DYOPHONE
DYOTHEISM
DYPHONE
DYPNONE
DYSACOUSIA
DYSACOUSIS
DYSAESTHESIA
DYSANALYTE
DYSAPHIA
DYSARTHRIA
DYSARTHRIC
DYSARTHROSIS
DYSBULIA
DYSBULIC
DYSCHIRIA
DYSCHROA
DYSCHROIA
DYSCHRONOUS
DYSCRASE
DYSCRASED
DYSCRASIA
DYSCRASIC
DYSCRASING
DYSCRASITE
DYSCRATIC
DYSENTERIC
DYSENTERY
DYSERGASIA
DYSERGIA
DYSESTHESIA
DYSFUNCTION
DYSGENESIC
DYSGENESIS
DYSGENIC
DYSGENICS
DYSGEOGENOUS
DYSGNOSIA
DYSGRAPHIA
DYSIDROSIS
DYSKINESIA
DYSKINETIC
DYSLOGIA
DYSLOGISTIC
DYSLOGY
DYSLUITE
DYSLYSIN
DYSMENORRHEA
DYSMERISM
DYSMERISTIC
DYSMEROMORPH
DYSMNESIA
DYSMORPHISM
DYSNEURIA
DYSNOMY
DYSODILE
DYSOREXY
DYSOXIDATION
DYSOXIDIZE
DYSPATHETIC
DYSPATHY
DYSPEPSIA

DYSPEPSY
DYSPEPTIC
DYSPEPTICAL
DYSPHAGIA
DYSPHAGIC
DYSPHASIA
DYSPHASIC
DYSPHONIA
DYSPHONIC
DYSPHORIA
DYSPHORIC
DYSPHOTIC
DYSPHRASIA
DYSPHRENIA
DYSPNEA
DYSPNEAL
DYSPNEIC
DYSPNOEA
DYSPNOEAL
DYSPROSIA
DYSPROSIUM
DYSSNITE
DYSSYNERGIA
DYSSYNERGY
DYSSYSTOLE
DYSTAXIA
DYSTECTIC
DYSTELEOLOGY
DYSTHYMIA
DYSTOCIA
DYSTOCIAL
DYSTOME
DYSTOMIC
DYSTOMOUS
DYSTONIA
DYSTOPIA
DYSTROPHIA
DYSTROPHIC
DYSTROPHY
DYSURIA
DYSURIC
DYSYNTRIBITE
DYTE
DYTISCID
DYVOUR
DZEREN
DZERIN
DZERON
DZIGGETAI
DZO

EA
EACEWORM
EACH
EACHWHERE
EAGER
EAGERLY
EAGERNESS
EAGLE
EAGLESS
EAGLESTONE
EAGLET
EAGLEWOOD
EAGRASS
EAGRE
EALDERMAN
EALDORMAN
EAN
EANED
EANING
EANLING
EAR
EARABLE
EARACHE
EARBASH
EARBOB
EARCAP
EARCLIP
EARCOCKLE
EARD
EARDROP
EARDROPPER
EARDROPS
EARDRUM
EARED
EARFLAP
EARFLOWER
EARFUL
EARHEAD
EARHOLE
EARING
EARJEWEL
EARL
EARLAP
EARLDOM
EARLDUCK
EARLET
EARLIER
EARLIEST
EARLIKE
EARLINESS
EARLOBE
EARLOCK
EARLSHIP
EARLY
EARLYISH
EARMARK
EARMARKED
EARMARKING
EARMUFF
EARN
EARNED
EARNER
EARNEST
EARNESTLY
EARNESTNESS
EARNFUL
EARNING

EARNINGS
EAROCK
EARPHONE
EARPICK
EARPIECE
EARPLUG
EARREACH
EARRING
EARRINGED
EARS
EARSCREW
EARSHOT
EARSORE
EARSPLITTING
EARSPOOL
EARSTONE
EARTAB
EARTAG
EARTH
EARTHBOARD
EARTHBORN
EARTHBRED
EARTHDRAKE
EARTHED
EARTHEN
EARTHENHEARTED
EARTHENWARE
EARTHFALL
EARTHFAST
EARTHGALL
EARTHGRUBBER
EARTHIAN
EARTHIER
EARTHIEST
EARTHINESS
EARTHING
EARTHKIN
EARTHLESS
EARTHLIGHT
EARTHLIKE
EARTHLINESS
EARTHLING
EARTHLY
EARTHMAKER
EARTHMAKING
EARTHNUT
EARTHPEA
EARTHQUAKE
EARTHQUAKED
EARTHQUAKEN
EARTHQUAKING
EARTHQUAVE
EARTHS
EARTHSET
EARTHSHINE
EARTHSHOCK
EARTHSLIDE
EARTHSMOKE
EARTHSTAR
EARTHTONGUE
EARTHWARD
EARTHWARDS
EARTHWORK
EARTHWORM
EARTHY
EARWAX
EARWIG
EARWIGGED
EARWIGGINESS
EARWIGGING
EARWIGGY
EARWITNESS
EARWORM
EARWORT
EASE
EASED
EASEFUL

EASEFULLY
EASEFULNESS
EASEL
EASELED
EASELESS
EASEMENT
EASER
EASIER
EASIEST
EASILY
EASINESS
EASING
EASSEL
EAST
EASTABOUT
EASTBOUND
EASTED
EASTER
EASTERLING
EASTERLY
EASTERMOST
EASTERN
EASTERNER
EASTERNLY
EASTERNMOST
EASTING
EASTLAND
EASTLIN
EASTLING
EASTLINGS
EASTLINS
EASTMOST
EASTWARD
EASTWARDLY
EASTWARDS
EASY
EASYGOING
EASYLIKE
EAT
EATABILITY
EATABLE
EATABLENESS
EATABLES
EATAGE
EATBERRY
EATCHE
EATEN
EATER
EATERY
EATH
EATHLY
EATING
EATS
EAU
EAUX
EAVE
EAVEDROP
EAVEDROPPER
EAVEDROPPING
EAVER
EAVES
EAVESDRIP
EAVESDROP
EAVESDROPPER
EAVESING
EAWT
EBANO
EBAUCHE
EBB
EBBED
EBBET
EBBING
EBBMAN
EBENEOUS
EBO
EBOE
EBON

EBONIST
EBONITE
EBONIZE
EBONIZED
EBONIZING
EBONY
EBRACTEATE
EBRACTEOLATE
EBRIATE
EBRIATED
EBRIETY
EBRILLADE
EBRIOSE
EBRIOSITY
EBRIOUS
EBRIOUSLY
EBULLATE
EBULLIATE
EBULLIENCE
EBULLIENCY
EBULLIENT
EBULLIENTLY
EBULLIOMETER
EBULLIOSCOPE
EBULLIOSCOPIC
EBULLITION
EBULLITIVE
EBULUS
EBURATED
EBURE
EBURINE
EBURNATED
EBURNATION
EBURNEAN
EBURNEOID
EBURNEOUS
ECAD
ECALCARATE
ECANDA
ECARDINAL
ECARINATE
ECARTE
ECAUDATE
ECBASIS
ECBATIC
ECBLASTESIS
ECBOLE
ECBOLIC
ECCALEOBION
ECCE
ECCENTRATE
ECCENTRIC
ECCENTRICAL
ECCENTRICALLY
ECCENTRICITIES
ECCENTRICITY
ECCENTRING
ECCHONDROMA
ECCHYMOMA
ECCHYMOSE
ECCHYMOSES
ECCHYMOSIS
ECCHYMOTIC
ECCLE
ECCLESIA
ECCLESIAL
ECCLESIARCH
ECCLESIARCHY
ECCLESIAST
ECCLESIASTIC
ECCLESIASTICAL
ECCLESIASTICALLY
ECCLESIASTICIS
ECCLESIASTICS
ECCLESIASTRY
ECCLESIOLATER
ECCLESIOLOGIC

ECCOPROTIC
ECCRINOLOGY
ECCRISIS
ECCRITIC
ECCYCLEMA
ECCYESIS
ECDEMIC
ECDEMITE
ECDERON
ECDERONIC
ECDYSES
ECDYSIAST
ECDYSIS
ECE
ECESIC
ECESIS
ECGONIN
ECGONINE
ECHAPPE
ECHAPPEE
ECHARD
ECHE
ECHEA
ECHELETTE
ECHELLE
ECHELON
ECHENEID
ECHENEIDID
ECHEVIN
ECHIDNA
ECHIDNAE
ECHINACEA
ECHINAL
ECHINATE
ECHINATED
ECHINID
ECHINIDAN
ECHINIFORM
ECHINITAL
ECHINITE
ECHINOCHROME
ECHINOCOCCUS
ECHINODERM
ECHINODERMAL
ECHINODERMIC
ECHINOID
ECHINOLOGIST
ECHINOLOGY
ECHINOPSINE
ECHINULATE
ECHINULATION
ECHINULIFORM
ECHINUS
ECHITAMINE
ECHIUROID
ECHO
ECHOER
ECHOES
ECHOIC
ECHOISM
ECHOIZE
ECHOIZED
ECHOIZING
ECHOLALIA
ECHOLALIC
ECHOLOCATION
ECHOPRACTIC
ECHOPRAXIA
ECILIATE
ECIZE
ECKLE
ECLAIR
ECLAMPSIA
ECLAMPTIC
ECLAT
ECLATED
ECLATING

ECLECTIC
ECLECTICAL
ECLECTICALLY
ECLECTICISM
ECLEGM
ECLEGMA
ECLIPSAREON
ECLIPSE
ECLIPSED
ECLIPSER
ECLIPSING
ECLIPSIS
ECLIPTIC
ECLIPTICAL
ECLIPTICALLY
ECLOGITE
ECLOGUE
ECLOSION
ECMNESIA
ECOD
ECOID
ECOLE
ECOLOGIC
ECOLOGICAL
ECOLOGICALLY
ECOLOGIST
ECOLOGY
ECONOMETER
ECONOMETRIC
ECONOMETRICAL
ECONOMETRICS
ECONOMIC
ECONOMICAL
ECONOMICALLY
ECONOMICS
ECONOMIES
ECONOMISM
ECONOMIST
ECONOMIZATION
ECONOMIZE
ECONOMIZED
ECONOMIZER
ECONOMIZING
ECONOMY
ECOPHENE
ECOPHOBIA
ECORCHE
ECORTICATE
ECOSPECIES
ECOSTATE
ECOTIPICALLY
ECOTONE
ECOTYPE
ECOTYPIC
ECPHONESIS
ECPHORIA
ECPHORIAE
ECPHORIAS
ECPHORIZE
ECPHORY
ECPHRASIS
ECRASE
ECRASEUR
ECRASITE
ECRU
ECRUSTACEOUS
ECSTASIES
ECSTASY
ECSTATIC
ECSTATICA
ECSTATICAL
ECSTATICALLY
ECTAD
ECTAL
ECTALLY
ECTASIA
ECTASIS

ECTENE
ECTENTAL
ECTETHMOID
ECTETHMOIDAL
ECTHETICALLY
ECTHLIPSIS
ECTHYMA
ECTHYMATA
ECTIRIS
ECTOBATIC
ECTOBLAST
ECTOCARDIA
ECTOCARPOUS
ECTOCELIC
ECTOCINEREA
ECTOCINEREAL
ECTOCOELIC
ECTOCONDYLE
ECTOCONDYLOID
ECTOCORNEA
ECTOCRANIAL
ECTOCYST
ECTODERM
ECTODERMAL
ECTODERMIC
ECTODERMOSIS
ECTOENTAD
ECTOENZYM
ECTOENZYME
ECTOETHMOID
ECTOGENESIS
ECTOGENIC
ECTOGENOUS
ECTOGLIA
ECTOLECITHAL
ECTOLOPH
ECTOMERE
ECTOMERIC
ECTOMORPHIC
ECTOMORPHY
ECTOPARASITE
ECTOPATAGIA
ECTOPATAGIUM
ECTOPHLOIC
ECTOPHYTE
ECTOPHYTIC
ECTOPIA
ECTOPIC
ECTOPLACENTA
ECTOPLASM
ECTOPLASMIC
ECTOPLASY
ECTOPROCTAN
ECTOPROCTOUS
ECTORETINA
ECTORHINAL
ECTOSARC
ECTOSARCOUS
ECTOSKELETON
ECTOSOMAL
ECTOSOME
ECTOSPHERE
ECTOSTEAL
ECTOSTOSIS
ECTOTHECA
ECTOTHERM
ECTOTROPHIC
ECTOZOA
ECTOZOAN
ECTOZOIC
ECTRODACTYLY
ECTROGENIC
ECTROGENY
ECTROMELIA
ECTROMELIAN
ECTROMELIC
ECTROPION

ECTYPAL
ECTYPE
ECTYPOGRAPHY
ECU
ECUELLE
ECUELLING
ECUMENE
ECUMENIC
ECUMENICAL
ECUMENICALLY
ECUMENICITY
ECUMENISM
ECYPHELLATE
ECZEMA
ECZEMATOID
ECZEMATOSIS
ECZEMATOUS
EDACIOUS
EDACIOUSLY
EDACIOUSNESS
EDACITY
EDAPHIC
EDAPHOLOGY
EDAPHON
EDDER
EDDIED
EDDIES
EDDISH
EDDO
EDDY
EDDYING
EDDYROOT
EDEA
EDEAGRA
EDELWEISS
EDEMA
EDEMATA
EDEMATOUS
EDEMIC
EDENITE
EDENTAL
EDENTATE
EDENTULATE
EDENTULOUS
EDEODYNIA
EDEOLOGY
EDEOMANIA
EDEOSCOPY
EDEOTOMY
EDESTAN
EDESTIN
EDGE
EDGEBONE
EDGED
EDGELESS
EDGEMAKER
EDGEMAKING
EDGEMAN
EDGER
EDGERMAN
EDGES
EDGESHOT
EDGESTONE
EDGEWAYS
EDGEWEED
EDGEWISE
EDGINESS
EDGING
EDGINGLY
EDGREW
EDGROW
EDGY
EDH
EDI
EDIBILITY
EDIBLE
EDIBLENESS

EDICT
EDICTAL
EDICTALLY
EDICULE
EDIFICABLE
EDIFICATE
EDIFICATION
EDIFICATOR
EDIFICATORY
EDIFICE
EDIFICED
EDIFICES
EDIFICING
EDIFIED
EDIFY
EDIFYING
EDIFYINGLY
EDILE
EDILITY
EDINGTONITE
EDIT
EDITAL
EDITION
EDITOR
EDITORIAL
EDITORIALIZE
EDITORIALIZED
EDITORIALIZING
EDITORIALLY
EDITORSHIP
EDUCABILIAN
EDUCABILITY
EDUCABLE
EDUCAND
EDUCATABLE
EDUCATE
EDUCATED
EDUCATEE
EDUCATING
EDUCATION
EDUCATIONAL
EDUCATIONALLY
EDUCATIONARY
EDUCATIONIST
EDUCATIVE
EDUCATOR
EDUCATORY
EDUCE
EDUCED
EDUCIBLE
EDUCING
EDUCT
EDUCTION
EDUCTIVE
EDUCTOR
EDULCORATE
EDULCORATED
EDULCORATING
EDULCORATION
EDULCORATIVE
EDULCORATOR
EDULE
EE
EEBREE
EED
EEGRASS
EEL
EELBOAT
EELBOB
EELBOBBER
EELCAKE
EELCATCHER
EELED
EELER
EELERY
EELFARE
EELFISH

EELGRASS
EELING
EELPOT
EELPOUT
EELS
EELSHOP
EELSKIN
EELSPEAR
EELWARE
EELWORM
EELY
EEM
EEMIS
EEN
EENCE
EER
EERIE
EERILY
EERINESS
EERISOME
EEROCK
EERY
EES
EESOME
EF
EFECKS
EFF
EFFABLE
EFFACE
EFFACEABLE
EFFACED
EFFACEMENT
EFFACER
EFFACING
EFFATE
EFFATUM
EFFECT
EFFECTER
EFFECTFUL
EFFECTIBLE
EFFECTIVE
EFFECTIVELY
EFFECTIVENESS
EFFECTIVITY
EFFECTOR
EFFECTS
EFFECTUAL
EFFECTUALITY
EFFECTUALIZE
EFFECTUALLY
EFFECTUALNESS
EFFECTUATE
EFFECTUATED
EFFECTUATING
EFFECTUATION
EFFEIR
EFFEMINACY
EFFEMINATE
EFFEMINATED
EFFEMINATELY
EFFEMINATING
EFFEMINATION
EFFEMINATIZE
EFFEMINIZE
EFFEMINIZED
EFFEMINIZING
EFFENDI
EFFENDIS
EFFERENT
EFFERVESCE
EFFERVESCED
EFFERVESCENCE
EFFERVESCENCY
EFFERVESCENT
EFFERVESCENTLY
EFFERVESCING
EFFERVESCIVE

EFFET	EGAL	EGREGIOUSLY	EJACULATED	ELAPHURINE
EFFETE	EGALITARIAN	EGREGIOUSNESS	EJACULATING	ELAPID
EFFETMAN	EGALITARIANISM	EGRESS	EJACULATION	ELAPINE
EFFETMEN	EGALITE	EGRESSES	EJACULATIVE	ELAPOID
EFFICACIES	EGALITY	EGRESSION	EJACULATOR	ELAPSE
EFFICACIOUS	EGALLY	EGRESSOR	EJACULATORY	ELAPSED
EFFICACITY	EGENCE	EGRET	EJECT	ELAPSING
EFFICACY	EGENCY	EGRETS	EJECTA	ELASMOBRANCH
EFFICIENCE	EGER	EGRIMONY	EJECTAMENTA	ELASMOTHERE
EFFICIENCIES	EGERAN	EGROMANCY	EJECTED	ELASTANCE
EFFICIENCY	EGEST	EGUALMENTE	EJECTING	ELASTASE
EFFICIENT	EGESTA	EGUEIITE	EJECTION	ELASTIC
EFFICIENTLY	EGESTED	EGURGITATE	EJECTIVE	ELASTICA
EFFIGIAL	EGESTING	EGURGITATED	EJECTIVELY	ELASTICALLY
EFFIGIATE	EGESTION	EGURGITATING	EJECTIVITY	ELASTICIAN
EFFIGIATION	EGESTIVE	EH	EJECTMENT	ELASTICIN
EFFIGIES	EGG	EHEU	EJECTOR	ELASTICITY
EFFIGURATE	EGGAR	EHLITE	EJICIENT	ELASTICIZE
EFFIGURATION	EGGBERRIES	EHRWALDITE	EJIDAL	ELASTICIZER
EFFIGY	EGGBERRY	EHTANETHIAL	EJIDO	ELASTIN
EFFLATE	EGGCUP	EHUAWA	EJOO	ELASTIVITY
EFFLATION	EGGCUPFUL	EICHBERGITE	EJULATE	ELASTOMER
EFFLORESCE	EGGEATER	EICOSANE	EJURATE	ELASTOMETER
EFFLORESCED	EGGED	EIDE	EKABORON	ELASTOMETRY
EFFLORESCENCE	EGGER	EIDENT	EKACAESIUM	ELASTOSE
EFFLORESCENCY	EGGFISH	EIDENTLY	EKAHA	ELATE
EFFLORESCENT	EGGFRUIT	EIDER	EKAMANGANESE	ELATED
EFFLORESCING	EGGHEAD	EIDERDOWN	EKASILICON	ELATEDLY
EFFLOWER	EGGHOT	EIDETIC	EKATANTALUM	ELATEDNESS
EFFLUENCE	EGGING	EIDOGRAPH	EKE	ELATER
EFFLUENCY	EGGLER	EIDOLIC	EKEBERGITE	ELATERID
EFFLUENT	EGGMENT	EIDOLISM	EKED	ELATERIN
EFFLUVE	EGGNOG	EIDOLOLOGY	EKENAME	ELATERITE
EFFLUVIA	EGGPLANT	EIDOLON	EKER	ELATERIUM
EFFLUVIAL	EGGS	EIDOPTOMETRY	EKERITE	ELATINACEOUS
EFFLUVIOUS	EGGSHELL	EIDOS	EKHIMI	ELATING
EFFLUVIUM	EGGY	EIDOURANION	EKING	ELATION
EFFLUX	EGILOPS	EIE	EKKA	ELATIVE
EFFLUXES	EGIS	EIGHE	EKKI	ELATOR
EFFODIENT	EGLANDULAR	EIGHT	EKPHORE	ELATROMETER
EFFORM	EGLANDULOSE	EIGHTEEN	EKPHORIA	ELAYL
EFFORMATION	EGLANDULOUS	EIGHTEENMO	EKPHORIAS	ELB
EFFORT	EGLANTINE	EIGHTEENTH	EKPHORIZE	ELBOIC
EFFORTLESS	EGLATERE	EIGHTFOIL	EKPHORY	ELBOW
EFFORTLESSLY	EGLESTONITE	EIGHTFOLD	EKTENE	ELBOWBOARD
EFFORTLESSNESS	EGLING	EIGHTH	EL	ELBOWBUSH
EFFOSSION	EGMA	EIGHTHLY	ELABOR	ELBOWCHAIR
EFFRACTION	EGO	EIGHTIETH	ELABORATE	ELBOWED
EFFRANCHISE	EGOCENTRIC	EIGHTLING	ELABORATED	ELBOWER
EFFRAY	EGOCENTRICITY	EIGHTS	ELABORATELY	ELBOWPIECE
EFFRONT	EGOCENTRISM	EIGHTSCORE	ELABORATENESS	ELBOWROOM
EFFRONTERIES	EGOISM	EIGHTSMAN	ELABORATING	ELBOWS
EFFRONTERY	EGOIST	EIGHTSMEN	ELABORATION	ELBOWY
EFFULGE	EGOISTIC	EIGHTSOME	ELABORATIVE	ELBUCK
EFFULGED	EGOISTICAL	EIGHTVO	ELABORATOR	ELCAJA
EFFULGENCE	EGOISTICALLY	EIGHTY	ELABORATORY	ELCHEE
EFFULGENT	EGOITY	EIGNE	ELABRATE	ELCHI
EFFULGENTLY	EGOIZE	EIK	ELAENIA	ELD
EFFULGING	EGOL	EIKON	ELAEOBLAST	ELDER
EFFUME	EGOLATROUS	EILD	ELAEOBLASTIC	ELDERBERRY
EFFUND	EGOMANIA	EILE	ELAEODOCHON	ELDERBUSH
EFFUSE	EGOMANIAC	EIMER	ELAEOPTEN	ELDERLIES
EFFUSED	EGOMANIACAL	EIMERIA	ELAEOPTENE	ELDERLY
EFFUSING	EGOPHONIC	EINKORN	ELAEOTHESIUM	ELDERMAN
EFFUSION	EGOPHONY	EIRACK	ELAIDATE	ELDERMEN
EFFUSIVE	EGOS	EIRE	ELAIDIC	ELDERN
EFFUSIVENESS	EGOSYNTONIC	EIRESIONE	ELAIDIN	ELDERSHIP
EFFUVIATE	EGOTHEISM	EISEGESIS	ELAIOLEUCITE	ELDERWOMAN
EFOVEOLATE	EGOTISM	EISEL	ELAIOPLAST	ELDERWOMEN
EFREET	EGOTIST	EISELL	ELAIOSOME	ELDERWOOD
EFT	EGOTISTIC	EISTEDDFOD	ELAN	ELDERWORT
EFTER	EGOTISTICAL	EISTEDDFODAU	ELANCE	ELDEST
EFTEST	EGOTISTICALLY	EISTEDDFODIC	ELAND	ELDIN
EFTSOON	EGOTIZE	EISTEDDFODS	ELANDS	ELDING
EFTSOONS	EGOTIZED	EITH	ELANET	ELDMOTHER
EGAD	EGOTIZING	EITHER	ELAPHINE	ELDRICH
EGADI	EGREGIOUS	EJACULATE	ELAPHURE	ELDRITCH

ELE
ELEAN
ELECAMPANE
ELECT
ELECTANT
ELECTED
ELECTING
ELECTION
ELECTIONEER
ELECTIONEERER
ELECTIVE
ELECTIVELY
ELECTIVENESS
ELECTIVITY
ELECTO
ELECTOR
ELECTORATE
ELECTORIAL
ELECTRAGIST
ELECTRAL
ELECTRALIZE
ELECTRE
ELECTREPETER
ELECTRESS
ELECTRET
ELECTRIC
ELECTRICAL
ELECTRICALIZE
ELECTRICALLY
ELECTRICIAN
ELECTRICITY
ELECTRICIZE
ELECTRIFIED
ELECTRIFIER
ELECTRIFY
ELECTRIFYING
ELECTRIZE
ELECTRIZED
ELECTRIZER
ELECTRIZING
ELECTRO
ELECTROBATH
ELECTROBUS
ELECTROCUTE
ELECTROCUTED
ELECTROCUTING
ELECTROCUTION
ELECTRODE
ELECTRODEPOSIT
ELECTRODES
ELECTROED
ELECTROFORM
ELECTROFUSED
ELECTROGILT
ELECTROGRAPH
ELECTROING
ELECTROIONIC
ELECTROLIER
ELECTROLYSIS
ELECTROLYTE
ELECTROLYTIC
ELECTROLYZE
ELECTROLYZED
ELECTROLYZER
ELECTROLYZING
ELECTROMAGNET
ELECTROMAGNETIC
ELECTROMER
ELECTROMETER
ELECTROMETRY
ELECTROMOBILE
ELECTROMOTOR
ELECTRON
ELECTRONIC
ELECTRONICS
ELECTROPATHY
ELECTROPHONE

ELECTROPISM
ELECTROPLATE
ELECTROPLATED
ELECTROPLATING
ELECTROPOION
ELECTROPOLAR
ELECTROPOWER
ELECTROS
ELECTROSCOPE
ELECTROSHOCK
ELECTROSTATIC
ELECTROSTATICS
ELECTROSTEEL
ELECTROTAXIS
ELECTROTEST
ELECTROTONIC
ELECTROTONIZE
ELECTROTONUS
ELECTROTYPE
ELECTROTYPED
ELECTROTYPER
ELECTROTYPY
ELECTROVITAL
ELECTROWIN
ELECTRUM
ELECTUARY
ELEEMOSINAR
ELEEMOSYNAR
ELEEMOSYNARY
ELEGANCE
ELEGANCIES
ELEGANCY
ELEGANT
ELEGANTE
ELEGANTLY
ELEGIAC
ELEGIACAL
ELEGIAMBIC
ELEGIAMBUS
ELEGIAST
ELEGIES
ELEGIOUS
ELEGIST
ELEGIT
ELEGIZE
ELEGIZED
ELEGIZING
ELEGY
ELEIDIN
ELEME
ELEMENT
ELEMENTAL
ELEMENTALISM
ELEMENTALIST
ELEMENTALITY
ELEMENTARILY
ELEMENTARINESS
ELEMENTARITY
ELEMENTARY
ELEMENTOID
ELEMENTS
ELEMI
ELEMICIN
ELEMIN
ELEMOL
ELENCH
ELENCHI
ELENCHIZE
ELENCHUS
ELENCTIC
ELENCTICAL
ELENGE
ELENGELY
ELENGENESS
ELEOLITE
ELEOMARGARIC
ELEONORITE

ELEOPLAST
ELEOPTENE
ELEOTRID
ELEPAIO
ELEPHANT
ELEPHANTA
ELEPHANTIAC
ELEPHANTIASIS
ELEPHANTIC
ELEPHANTINE
ELEPHANTOID
ELEPHANTOIDAL
ELEPHANTOUS
ELEPHANTS
ELEUTHERISM
ELEVATE
ELEVATED
ELEVATEDLY
ELEVATEDNESS
ELEVATING
ELEVATINGLY
ELEVATIO
ELEVATION
ELEVATIONAL
ELEVATO
ELEVATOR
ELEVE
ELEVEN
ELEVENER
ELEVENS
ELEVENTH
ELEVON
ELF
ELFENFOLK
ELFIC
ELFIN
ELFISH
ELFISHLY
ELFISHNESS
ELFKIN
ELFLAND
ELFLIKE
ELFLOCK
ELFS
ELFT
ELFWORT
ELGER
ELIAD
ELIASITE
ELICIT
ELICITABLE
ELICITATE
ELICITATION
ELICITED
ELICITING
ELICITOR
ELICITORY
ELIDE
ELIDED
ELIDIBLE
ELIDING
ELIGENT
ELIGIBILITIES
ELIGIBILITY
ELIGIBLE
ELIMINABLE
ELIMINAND
ELIMINANT
ELIMINATE
ELIMINATED
ELIMINATING
ELIMINATION
ELIMINATIVE
ELIMINATOR
ELIMINATORY
ELIQUATE
ELIQUATED

ELIQUATING
ELIQUATION
ELISION
ELISOR
ELITE
ELIX
ELIXATE
ELIXATION
ELIXIR
ELK
ELKHOUND
ELKS
ELKSLIP
ELKWOOD
ELL
ELLACHICK
ELLAGATE
ELLAGIC
ELLAGITANNIN
ELLE
ELLECK
ELLER
ELLFISH
ELLIPSE
ELLIPSES
ELLIPSIS
ELLIPSOGRAPH
ELLIPSOID
ELLIPSOIDAL
ELLIPSONE
ELLIPTIC
ELLIPTICAL
ELLIPTICALLY
ELLIPTICALNESS
ELLIPTICITY
ELLIPTOID
ELLOPS
ELLWAND
ELM
ELMEN
ELMY
ELOCULAR
ELOCUTE
ELOCUTION
ELOCUTIONARY
ELOCUTIONER
ELOCUTIONIST
ELOD
ELOGE
ELOGIUM
ELOGY
ELOIGN
ELOIGNER
ELOIGNMENT
ELOINE
ELON
ELONG
ELONGATE
ELONGATED
ELONGATING
ELONGATION
ELONGATIVE
ELOPE
ELOPED
ELOPEMENT
ELOPER
ELOPING
ELOPS
ELOQUENCE
ELOQUENT
ELOQUENTIAL
ELOTILLO
ELPASOLITE
ELPIDITE
ELRITCH
ELS
ELSE

ELSEHOW
ELSEN
ELSEWARDS
ELSEWAYS
ELSEWHAT
ELSEWHEN
ELSEWHERE
ELSEWHERES
ELSEWHITHER
ELSEWISE
ELSHIN
ELSIN
ELSON
ELT
ELTROT
ELUATE
ELUCIDATE
ELUCIDATED
ELUCIDATING
ELUCIDATION
ELUCIDATIVE
ELUCIDATOR
ELUCIDATORY
ELUCTATE
ELUCUBRATE
ELUDE
ELUDED
ELUDER
ELUDING
ELUENT
ELUSION
ELUSIVE
ELUSIVELY
ELUSIVENESS
ELUSORINESS
ELUSORY
ELUTE
ELUTION
ELUTOR
ELUTRIATE
ELUTRIATED
ELUTRIATING
ELUTRIATION
ELUTRIATOR
ELUVIAL
ELUVIATION
ELUVIUM
ELVAN
ELVANITE
ELVANITIC
ELVEN
ELVER
ELVES
ELVISH
ELVISHLY
ELY
ELYDORIC
ELYNG
ELYTRA
ELYTRAL
ELYTRIFEROUS
ELYTRIFORM
ELYTRIGEROUS
ELYTRIN
ELYTROCELE
ELYTROCLASIA
ELYTROID
ELYTRON
ELYTROPLASTIC
ELYTROPTOSIS
ELYTRORHAGIA
ELYTROTOMY
ELYTROUS
ELYTRUM
EM
EMACIATE
EMACIATED

EMACIATING
EMACIATION
EMAGRAM
EMAIL
EMAJAGUA
EMANANT
EMANATE
EMANATED
EMANATING
EMANATION
EMANATIONAL
EMANATIONISM
EMANATIONIST
EMANATIVE
EMANATIVELY
EMANATOR
EMANATORY
EMANCIPATE
EMANCIPATED
EMANCIPATING
EMANCIPATIO
EMANCIPATION
EMANCIPATIONIST
EMANCIPATIVE
EMANCIPATOR
EMANCIPATORY
EMANCIPATRESS
EMANCIPIST
EMANDIBULATE
EMANE
EMANIUM
EMARCID
EMARGINATE
EMARGINATED
EMARGINATING
EMARGINATION
EMASCULATE
EMASCULATED
EMASCULATING
EMASCULATION
EMASCULATIVE
EMASCULATOR
EMASCULATORY
EMBAIN
EMBALE
EMBALL
EMBALM
EMBALMED
EMBALMER
EMBALMING
EMBALMMENT
EMBANK
EMBANKMENT
EMBAR
EMBARCATION
EMBARGO
EMBARGOED
EMBARGOES
EMBARGOING
EMBARK
EMBARKATION
EMBARKED
EMBARKING
EMBARKMENT
EMBARMENT
EMBARRAS
EMBARRASS
EMBARRASSED
EMBARRASSING
EMBARRASSINGLY
EMBARRASSMENT
EMBARRED
EMBARRING
EMBASE
EMBASSADOR
EMBASSAGE
EMBASSY

EMBATHE
EMBATTLE
EMBATTLED
EMBATTLING
EMBAY
EMBAYED
EMBAYING
EMBAYMENT
EMBED
EMBEDDED
EMBEDDING
EMBEDMENT
EMBELIF
EMBELIN
EMBELLISH
EMBELLISHED
EMBELLISHER
EMBELLISHING
EMBELLISHMENT
EMBER
EMBERGEESE
EMBERGOOSE
EMBERS
EMBEZZLE
EMBEZZLED
EMBEZZLEMENT
EMBEZZLER
EMBEZZLING
EMBIID
EMBIND
EMBIOTOCID
EMBIOTOCOID
EMBIRA
EMBITTER
EMBITTERED
EMBITTERER
EMBITTERING
EMBITTERMENT
EMBLANCH
EMBLAZE
EMBLAZED
EMBLAZER
EMBLAZING
EMBLAZON
EMBLAZONED
EMBLAZONER
EMBLAZONMENT
EMBLAZONRY
EMBLEM
EMBLEMA
EMBLEMATIC
EMBLEMATICAL
EMBLEMATICIZE
EMBLEMATIZE
EMBLEMATIST
EMBLEMATIZE
EMBLEMATIZED
EMBLEMATIZING
EMBLEMENT
EMBLEMENTS
EMBLEMIST
EMBLEMIZE
EMBLEMIZED
EMBLEMIZING
EMBLIC
EMBLISS
EMBLOSSOM
EMBODIED
EMBODIER
EMBODIMENT
EMBODY
EMBODYING
EMBOG
EMBOITE
EMBOITEMENT
EMBOLDEN
EMBOLDENER
EMBOLE

EMBOLECTOMIES
EMBOLECTOMY
EMBOLEMIA
EMBOLIC
EMBOLIFORM
EMBOLISM
EMBOLISMIC
EMBOLITE
EMBOLIUM
EMBOLIZE
EMBOLO
EMBOLOLALIA
EMBOLOMERISM
EMBOLOMEROUS
EMBOLOMYCOTIC
EMBOLON
EMBOLUM
EMBOLUS
EMBOLY
EMBONPOINT
EMBORDER
EMBOSK
EMBOSOM
EMBOSS
EMBOSSED
EMBOSSER
EMBOSSING
EMBOSSMAN
EMBOSSMEN
EMBOSSMENT
EMBOST
EMBOUCHURE
EMBOUND
EMBOW
EMBOWED
EMBOWEL
EMBOWELED
EMBOWELER
EMBOWELING
EMBOWELLED
EMBOWELLER
EMBOWELLING
EMBOWER
EMBOWERED
EMBOWERING
EMBOWING
EMBOWMENT
EMBOX
EMBRACE
EMBRACED
EMBRACEMENT
EMBRACEOR
EMBRACER
EMBRACERY
EMBRACING
EMBRACIVE
EMBRAID
EMBRAKE
EMBRANCHMENT
EMBRANGLE
EMBRANGLED
EMBRANGLEMENT
EMBRANGLING
EMBRASE
EMBRASURE
EMBRASURED
EMBRASURING
EMBRAVE
EMBRAWN
EMBREATHE
EMBREW
EMBRIGHT
EMBRIGHTEN
EMBRITTLE
EMBRITTLEMENT
EMBROADEN
EMBROCATE

EMBROCATED
EMBROCATING
EMBROCATION
EMBROCHE
EMBROIDER
EMBROIDERED
EMBROIDERER
EMBROIDERESS
EMBROIDERIES
EMBROIDERING
EMBROIDERY
EMBROIL
EMBROILED
EMBROILER
EMBROILING
EMBROILMENT
EMBRONZE
EMBROSCOPIC
EMBROWN
EMBRUE
EMBRYECTOMY
EMBRYO
EMBRYOCARDIA
EMBRYOCTONY
EMBRYOFEROUS
EMBRYOGENIC
EMBRYOGENY
EMBRYOGONY
EMBRYOGRAPHY
EMBRYOID
EMBRYOLOGIC
EMBRYOLOGICAL
EMBRYOLOGICALLY
EMBRYOLOGIST
EMBRYOLOGY
EMBRYOMA
EMBRYOMAS
EMBRYOMATA
EMBRYON
EMBRYONAL
EMBRYONARY
EMBRYONATE
EMBRYONATED
EMBRYONIC
EMBRYONICALLY
EMBRYONIFORM
EMBRYONY
EMBRYOPHAGOUS
EMBRYOPHORE
EMBRYOPLASTIC
EMBRYOS
EMBRYOSCOPE
EMBRYOTEGA
EMBRYOTEGAE
EMBRYOTIC
EMBRYOTOME
EMBRYOTOMY
EMBRYOTROPHY
EMBRYOUS
EMBUE
EMBUIA
EMBUS
EMBUSK
EMBUSQUE
EMBUSSED
EMBUSSING
EMCEE
EMCUMBERING
EME
EMEER
EMEND
EMENDABLE
EMENDATE
EMENDATED
EMENDATELY
EMENDATING
EMENDATION

EMENDATOR
EMENDATORY
EMENDER
EMERALD
EMERANT
EMERAUDE
EMERGE
EMERGED
EMERGENCE
EMERGENCIES
EMERGENCY
EMERGENT
EMERGENTLY
EMERGENTNESS
EMERGING
EMERIED
EMERIL
EMERITED
EMERITI
EMERITUS
EMERIZE
EMEROD
EMERODS
EMEROID
EMERSED
EMERSION
EMERY
EMERYING
EMESIS
EMETIC
EMETICAL
EMETIN
EMETINE
EMETOLOGY
EMEU
EMEUTE
EMFORTH
EMGALLA
EMICTION
EMICTORY
EMIGRANT
EMIGRATE
EMIGRATED
EMIGRATING
EMIGRATION
EMIGRATIONAL
EMIGRATIVE
EMIGRATOR
EMIGRATORY
EMIGRE
EMIGREE
EMIGRES
EMINENCE
EMINENCIES
EMINENCY
EMINENT
EMINENTLY
EMIR
EMIRATE
EMISSARIA
EMISSARIUM
EMISSARY
EMISSILE
EMISSION
EMISSIVE
EMISSIVITY
EMIT
EMITTED
EMITTENT
EMITTER
EMITTING
EMMA
EMMARBLE
EMMARVEL
EMMELEIA
EMMENAGOGUE
EMMENIC

EMMENIOPATHY
EMMENOLOGY
EMMENSITE
EMMER
EMMET
EMMETROPE
EMMETROPIA
EMMETROPIC
EMODIN
EMOL
EMOLLESCENCE
EMOLLIATE
EMOLLIENT
EMOLOA
EMOLUMENT
EMOLUMENTAL
EMONY
EMORY
EMOTE
EMOTION
EMOTIONABLE
EMOTIONAL
EMOTIONALISM
EMOTIONALIST
EMOTIONALITY
EMOTIONALIZE
EMOTIONALIZED
EMOTIONED
EMOTIONIZE
EMOTIONLESS
EMOTIONS
EMOTIVE
EMOTIVELY
EMOTIVENESS
EMOTIVITY
EMPACKET
EMPAESTIC
EMPAISTIC
EMPALE
EMPANADA
EMPANEL
EMPANELMENT
EMPANOPLY
EMPAPER
EMPARADISE
EMPARK
EMPARL
EMPASM
EMPASMA
EMPATHIC
EMPATHICALLY
EMPATHIZE
EMPATHIZED
EMPATHIZING
EMPATHY
EMPATRON
EMPEARL
EMPEINE
EMPEIREMA
EMPENNAGE
EMPERESS
EMPERIES
EMPERIL
EMPEROR
EMPERORSHIP
EMPERY
EMPEST
EMPETRACEOUS
EMPEXA
EMPHASES
EMPHASIS
EMPHASIZE
EMPHASIZED
EMPHASIZING
EMPHATIC
EMPHATICAL
EMPHATICALLY

EMPHATICALNESS
EMPHEMERALNESS
EMPHLYSIS
EMPHRACTIC
EMPHRAXIS
EMPHYSEMA
EMPHYTEUSIS
EMPHYTEUTA
EMPHYTEUTIC
EMPICTURE
EMPID
EMPIECEMENT
EMPIGHT
EMPIRE
EMPIREMA
EMPIRIC
EMPIRICAL
EMPIRICALLY
EMPIRICALNESS
EMPIRICISM
EMPIRICIST
EMPIRICS
EMPIRISM
EMPIRISTIC
EMPIRY
EMPLACE
EMPLACEMENT
EMPLANE
EMPLANED
EMPLANING
EMPLASTIC
EMPLASTRA
EMPLASTRATION
EMPLASTRUM
EMPLECTITE
EMPLEOMANIA
EMPLOY
EMPLOYE
EMPLOYED
EMPLOYEE
EMPLOYER
EMPLOYING
EMPLOYMENT
EMPODIA
EMPODIUM
EMPOISON
EMPOISONED
EMPOISONER
EMPOISONING
EMPOISONMENT
EMPOLDER
EMPORETIC
EMPOREUTIC
EMPORIA
EMPORIAL
EMPORIUM
EMPORIUMS
EMPORTE
EMPORY
EMPOVER
EMPOVERISH
EMPOWER
EMPRESA
EMPRESARIO
EMPRESS
EMPRESSE
EMPRESSEMENT
EMPRISE
EMPRIZE
EMPT
EMPTIED
EMPTIER
EMPTIES
EMPTIEST
EMPTILY
EMPTINESS
EMPTINGS

EMPTINS
EMPTIO
EMPTION
EMPTOR
EMPTY
EMPTYHEARTED
EMPTYING
EMPTYSIS
EMPURPLE
EMPURPLED
EMPURPLING
EMPYEMA
EMPYEMATA
EMPYEMIC
EMPYESIS
EMPYOCELE
EMPYREAL
EMPYREAN
EMPYREUM
EMPYREUMA
EMPYREUMATA
EMPYREUMATIC
EMPYROMANCY
EMRAUD
EMU
EMULABLE
EMULANT
EMULATE
EMULATED
EMULATING
EMULATION
EMULATIVE
EMULATOR
EMULATORY
EMULATRESS
EMULE
EMULGE
EMULGENCE
EMULGENT
EMULOUS
EMULOUSLY
EMULOUSNESS
EMULSIBILITY
EMULSIBLE
EMULSIFIABILITY
EMULSIFIABLE
EMULSIFIED
EMULSIFIER
EMULSIFY
EMULSIFYING
EMULSIN
EMULSION
EMULSIONIZE
EMULSIVE
EMULSOID
EMULSOR
EMUNCTORY
EMUNDATION
EMUNGE
EMURE
EMYD
EMYDIAN
EN
ENABLE
ENABLED
ENABLER
ENABLING
ENACH
ENACT
ENACTION
ENACTIVE
ENACTMENT
ENACTOR
ENACTORY
ENACTURE
ENAENA
ENAGE

ENALID
ENALIOSAUR
ENALIOSAURIAN
ENALITE
ENALLAGE
ENALURON
ENALYRON
ENAM
ENAMDAR
ENAMEL
ENAMELED
ENAMELER
ENAMELING
ENAMELIST
ENAMELLED
ENAMELLER
ENAMELLING
ENAMELLIST
ENAMELOMA
ENAMELWARE
ENAMOR
ENAMORATO
ENAMORED
ENAMOREDNESS
ENAMORING
ENAMOUR
ENAMOURED
ENAMOUREDNESS
ENAMOURING
ENANTHEM
ENANTHEMA
ENANTHEMATOUS
ENANTHESIS
ENANTIOMORPH
ENANTIOPATHY
ENANTIOSIS
ENANTIOTROPY
ENARCHED
ENARGITE
ENARM
ENARME
ENARRATION
ENARTHRODIA
ENARTHRODIAL
ENARTHROSIS
ENATE
ENATIC
ENATION
ENBUSSHE
ENCAENIA
ENCAGE
ENCAGED
ENCAGING
ENCAMP
ENCAMPMENT
ENCANTHIS
ENCAPSULATE
ENCAPSULATED
ENCAPSULATING
ENCAPSULATION
ENCARNALIZE
ENCARNALIZED
ENCARNALIZING
ENCARPIUM
ENCARPUS
ENCASE
ENCASED
ENCASEMENT
ENCASH
ENCASHABLE
ENCASHMENT
ENCASTAGE
ENCASTRE
ENCASTREMENT
ENCAUMA
ENCAUSTES
ENCAUSTIC

ENCAUSTICALLY
ENCAVE
ENCEINT
ENCEINTE
ENCEPHALA
ENCEPHALIC
ENCEPHALIN
ENCEPHALITIC
ENCEPHALITIS
ENCEPHALOGRAM
ENCEPHALOGRAPH
ENCEPHALOID
ENCEPHALOLOGY
ENCEPHALOMA
ENCEPHALOMAS
ENCEPHALOMATA
ENCEPHALON
ENCEPHALOUS
ENCHAFE
ENCHAIN
ENCHAINED
ENCHAINING
ENCHAINMENT
ENCHANNEL
ENCHANT
ENCHANTED
ENCHANTER
ENCHANTING
ENCHANTINGLY
ENCHANTINGNESS
ENCHANTMENT
ENCHANTRESS
ENCHARGE
ENCHARGED
ENCHARGING
ENCHASE
ENCHASED
ENCHASER
ENCHASING
ENCHASTEN
ENCHEASON
ENCHEER
ENCHEQUER
ENCHESON
ENCHILADA
ENCHILADAS
ENCHIRIDION
ENCHODONTID
ENCHODONTOID
ENCHONDROMA
ENCHONDROMAS
ENCHONDROMATA
ENCHONDROSIS
ENCHORIAL
ENCHORIC
ENCHURCH
ENCHYLEMA
ENCHYMATOUS
ENCHYTRAE
ENCHYTRAEID
ENCINA
ENCINAL
ENCINCTURE
ENCINILLO
ENCIPHER
ENCIPHERED
ENCIPHERING
ENCIRCLE
ENCIRCLED
ENCIRCLEMENT
ENCIRCLER
ENCIRCLING
ENCLARET
ENCLASP
ENCLASPED
ENCLASPING
ENCLAVE

ENCLAVED
ENCLAVEMENT
ENCLAVING
ENCLEAR
ENCLISIS
ENCLITIC
ENCLITICAL
ENCLITICALLY
ENCLOAK
ENCLOG
ENCLOISTER
ENCLOSE
ENCLOSED
ENCLOSER
ENCLOSING
ENCLOSURE
ENCLOTHE
ENCLOUD
ENCODE
ENCODED
ENCODER
ENCODING
ENCOIGNURE
ENCOLLAR
ENCOLOR
ENCOLOUR
ENCOLPIA
ENCOLPION
ENCOLURE
ENCOMENDERO
ENCOMIA
ENCOMIAST
ENCOMIASTIC
ENCOMIC
ENCOMIENDA
ENCOMIOLOGIC
ENCOMIUM
ENCOMIUMS
ENCOMPASS
ENCOMPASSED
ENCOMPASSER
ENCOMPASSING
ENCOMY
ENCORBELMENT
ENCORE
ENCORED
ENCORING
ENCOUNTER
ENCOUNTERABLE
ENCOUNTERED
ENCOUNTERER
ENCOUNTERING
ENCOUNTERS
ENCOURAGE
ENCOURAGED
ENCOURAGEMENT
ENCOURAGER
ENCOURAGING
ENCOURAGINGLY
ENCRANIAL
ENCRATIC
ENCRATY
ENCRIMSON
ENCRINAL
ENCRINIC
ENCRINITAL
ENCRINITE
ENCRINITIC
ENCRINITICAL
ENCRINOID
ENCRISP
ENCROACH
ENCROACHED
ENCROACHER
ENCROACHING
ENCROACHMENT
ENCROTCHET

ENCRUST
ENCRUSTED
ENCRUSTMENT
ENCRYPT
ENCULTURATION
ENCUMBER
ENCUMBERED
ENCUMBERMENT
ENCUMBRANCE
ENCUMBRANCER
ENCURTAIN
ENCYCLIC
ENCYCLICAL
ENCYCLOPAEDIA
ENCYCLOPAEDIAC
ENCYCLOPAEDIAL
ENCYCLOPAEDIAN
ENCYCLOPAEDIC
ENCYCLOPAEDICAL
ENCYCLOPAEDICALLY
ENCYCLOPAEDISM
ENCYCLOPAEDIST
ENCYCLOPAEDIZE
ENCYCLOPEDIA
ENCYCLOPEDIAC
ENCYCLOPEDIACAL
ENCYCLOPEDIAL
ENCYCLOPEDIAN
ENCYCLOPEDIAST
ENCYCLOPEDIC
ENCYCLOPEDICAL
ENCYCLOPEDICALLY
ENCYCLOPEDISM
ENCYCLOPEDIST
ENCYCLOPEDIZE
ENCYRTID
ENCYST
ENCYSTATION
ENCYSTED
ENCYSTING
ENCYSTMENT
END
ENDAMAGE
ENDAMAGEABLE
ENDAMAGED
ENDAMAGEMENT
ENDAMAGING
ENDAMASK
ENDAMEBA
ENDAMEBIASIS
ENDAMEBIC
ENDAMOEBIASIS
ENDAMOEBIC
ENDANGER
ENDANGERED
ENDANGERER
ENDANGERING
ENDANGERMENT
ENDANGIUM
ENDAORTIC
ENDAORTITIS
ENDARCH
ENDARCHY
ENDARK
ENDARTERIAL
ENDARTERITIS
ENDARTERIUM
ENDASEH
ENDASPIDEAN
ENDAZE
ENDBALL
ENDBOARD
ENDBRAIN
ENDEAR
ENDEARANCE
ENDEARED
ENDEAREDLY

ENDEARING
ENDEARINGLY
ENDEARINGNESS
ENDEARMENT
ENDEAVOR
ENDEAVORED
ENDEAVORER
ENDEAVORING
ENDEAVOUR
ENDEAVOURED
ENDEAVOURER
ENDEAVOURING
ENDECHA
ENDED
ENDEICTIC
ENDELLIONITE
ENDEMIC
ENDEMICAL
ENDEMICALLY
ENDEMICITY
ENDEMIOLOGICAL
ENDEMIOLOGY
ENDEMISM
ENDENIZEN
ENDER
ENDERMATIC
ENDERMIC
ENDERON
ENDEW
ENDGATE
ENDIMANCHE
ENDING
ENDITE
ENDIVE
ENDLESS
ENDLESSLY
ENDLESSNESS
ENDLONG
ENDMOST
ENDOBLAST
ENDOBLASTIC
ENDOCARDIAC
ENDOCARDIAL
ENDOCARDITIC
ENDOCARDITIS
ENDOCARDIUM
ENDOCARP
ENDOCARPAL
ENDOCARPIC
ENDOCARPOID
ENDOCENTRIC
ENDOCHROME
ENDOCHYLOUS
ENDOCLINAL
ENDOCLINE
ENDOCOELAR
ENDOCOELE
ENDOCONE
ENDOCONIDIA
ENDOCONIDIUM
ENDOCRANIAL
ENDOCRANIUM
ENDOCRIN
ENDOCRINAL
ENDOCRINE
ENDOCRINIC
ENDOCRINISM
ENDOCRINOLOGY
ENDOCRINOUS
ENDOCRITIC
ENDOCYCLE
ENDOCYCLIC
ENDOCYEMATE
ENDOCYST
ENDODERM
ENDODERMAL
ENDODERMIC

ENDODERMIS
ENDODONTIA
ENDODONTICS
ENDOENZYME
ENDOGAMIC
ENDOGAMOUS
ENDOGAMY
ENDOGASTRIC
ENDOGEN
ENDOGENESIS
ENDOGENETIC
ENDOGENIC
ENDOGENOUS
ENDOGENOUSLY
ENDOGENY
ENDOGLOBULAR
ENDOGNATH
ENDOGNATHAL
ENDOGNATHION
ENDOLEMMA
ENDOLYMPH
ENDOLYMPHIC
ENDOLYSIN
ENDOMETRIAL
ENDOMETRITIS
ENDOMETRIUM
ENDOMETRY
ENDOMIXIS
ENDOMORPH
ENDOMORPHIC
ENDOMORPHISM
ENDOMORPHY
ENDOMYSIAL
ENDOMYSIUM
ENDONEURIUM
ENDONUCLEOLUS
ENDOPARASITE
ENDOPATHIC
ENDOPERIDIAL
ENDOPERIDIUM
ENDOPHAGOUS
ENDOPHAGY
ENDOPHRAGM
ENDOPHRAGMAL
ENDOPHYTAL
ENDOPHYTE
ENDOPHYTOUS
ENDOPLASM
ENDOPLASMA
ENDOPLASMIC
ENDOPLAST
ENDOPLASTULAR
ENDOPLASTULE
ENDOPLEURA
ENDOPLEURAL
ENDOPLEURITE
ENDOPLEURITIC
ENDOPOD
ENDOPODITE
ENDOPODITIC
ENDOPROCT
ENDOPROCTOUS
ENDOPSYCHIC
ENDORACHIS
ENDORAL
ENDORE
ENDORSABLE
ENDORSATION
ENDORSE
ENDORSED
ENDORSEE
ENDORSEMENT
ENDORSER
ENDORSING
ENDORSOR
ENDOSARC
ENDOSARCOUS

ENDOSCLERITE
ENDOSCOPE
ENDOSCOPY
ENDOSEPSIS
ENDOSKELETAL
ENDOSKELETON
ENDOSMOMETER
ENDOSMOSIC
ENDOSMOSIS
ENDOSMOTIC
ENDOSMOTICALLY
ENDOSOME
ENDOSPERM
ENDOSPERMIC
ENDOSPORE
ENDOSPORIUM
ENDOSPOROUS
ENDOSS
ENDOSTEAL
ENDOSTEALLY
ENDOSTEITIS
ENDOSTEOMA
ENDOSTEOMAS
ENDOSTEOMATA
ENDOSTERNITE
ENDOSTEUM
ENDOSTITIS
ENDOSTOMA
ENDOSTOMATA
ENDOSTOME
ENDOSTOSIS
ENDOSTRACAL
ENDOSTRACUM
ENDOSTYLAR
ENDOSTYLE
ENDOSTYLIC
ENDOTHECA
ENDOTHECAL
ENDOTHECIA
ENDOTHECIAL
ENDOTHECIUM
ENDOTHELIA
ENDOTHELIAL
ENDOTHELIOMA
ENDOTHELIUM
ENDOTHELOID
ENDOTHERM
ENDOTHERMAL
ENDOTHERMIC
ENDOTHERMOUS
ENDOTHERMY
ENDOTHORAX
ENDOTHYS
ENDOTOXIC
ENDOTOXIN
ENDOTROPHIC
ENDOTYS
ENDOUTE
ENDOW
ENDOWED
ENDOWER
ENDOWING
ENDOWMENT
ENDPAPERS
ENDPIECE
ENDPLATE
ENDRIN
ENDRUMPF
ENDS
ENDSEAL
ENDSHIP
ENDUE
ENDUED
ENDUING
ENDUNGEON
ENDURA
ENDURABILITY

ENDURABLE	ENFLAGELLATE	ENGIRDLE	ENHANCER	ENLARGING
ENDURABLENESS	ENFLAGELLATION	ENGIRDLED	ENHANCING	ENLARGINGLY
ENDURABLY	ENFLAME	ENGIRT	ENHANCIVE	ENLIGHT
ENDURANCE	ENFLESH	ENGLACIAL	ENHARBOR	ENLIGHTEN
ENDURANT	ENFLEURAGE	ENGLEIM	ENHARDEN	ENLIGHTENED
ENDURE	ENFLOWER	ENGLISH	ENHARDY	ENLIGHTENER
ENDURED	ENFLOWERED	ENGLISHER	ENHARMONIC	ENLIGHTENING
ENDURER	ENFLOWERING	ENGLOBE	ENHARMONICAL	ENLIGHTENMENT
ENDURING	ENFOLD	ENGLUE	ENHARMONICALLY	ENLIMN
ENDURINGLY	ENFOLDED	ENGLUT	ENHAUNT	ENLINK
ENDURINGNESS	ENFOLDEN	ENGLUTE	ENHEART	ENLINKED
ENDWAYS	ENFOLDING	ENGLYN	ENHEARTEN	ENLINKING
ENDWISE	ENFONCE	ENGLYNS	ENHEDGE	ENLINKMENT
ENDYSIS	ENFONCED	ENGOBE	ENHEMOSPORE	ENLIST
ENECATE	ENFONCEE	ENGORE	ENHORROR	ENLISTED
ENEMA	ENFORCE	ENGORGE	ENHYDRITE	ENLISTER
ENEMAS	ENFORCEABLE	ENGORGED	ENHYDRITIC	ENLISTING
ENEMATA	ENFORCED	ENGORGEMENT	ENHYDROUS	ENLISTMENT
ENEMIED	ENFORCEDLY	ENGORGING	ENHYPOSTASIA	ENLIVEN
ENEMIES	ENFORCEMENT	ENGOUE	ENHYPOSTASIS	ENLIVENED
ENEMY	ENFORCER	ENGOUEE	ENHYPOSTATIC	ENLIVENER
ENEMYING	ENFORCING	ENGOUEMENT	ENHYPOSTATIZE	ENLIVENING
ENEPIDERMIC	ENFORCIVE	ENGOULED	ENIAC	ENLIVENINGLY
ENERGEIA	ENFORCIVELY	ENGOUMENT	ENIGMA	ENLIVENMENT
ENERGESIS	ENFORT	ENGRACE	ENIGMAS	ENLOCK
ENERGETIC	ENFORTH	ENGRACED	ENIGMATIC	ENLURE
ENERGETICALLY	ENFRAI	ENGRACING	ENIGMATICAL	ENLUTE
ENERGETICIST	ENFRAME	ENGRAFF	ENIGMATICALLY	ENMESH
ENERGETICS	ENFRAMED	ENGRAFFED	ENIGMATIST	ENMESHED
ENERGETISTIC	ENFRAMEMENT	ENGRAFFING	ENIGMATIZE	ENMESHING
ENERGIC	ENFRAMING	ENGRAFT	ENIGMATIZED	ENMESHMENT
ENERGICO	ENFRANCHISED	ENGRAFTATION	ENIGMATIZING	ENMITIES
ENERGID	ENFRANCHISEMENT	ENGRAFTED	ENIGMATOGRAPHER	ENMITY
ENERGIES	ENFRANCHISER	ENGRAFTER	ENIGMATOGRAPHY	ENMOVE
ENERGISM	ENFRANCHISING	ENGRAFTING	ENIGUA	ENMUFFLE
ENERGIST	ENFRENZY	ENGRAFTMENT	ENISLE	ENNEAD
ENERGIZE	ENFUME	ENGRAIL	ENISLED	ENNEADIC
ENERGIZED	ENG	ENGRAILED	ENISLING	ENNEAGON
ENERGIZER	ENGAGE	ENGRAILING	ENIUN	ENNEAGONAL
ENERGIZING	ENGAGED	ENGRAILMENT	ENJAIL	ENNEAGYNOUS
ENERGUMEN	ENGAGEDLY	ENGRAIN	ENJAMB	ENNEAHEDRA
ENERGY	ENGAGEDNESS	ENGRAINED	ENJAMBED	ENNEAHEDRAL
ENERVATE	ENGAGEMENT	ENGRAINEDLY	ENJAMBEMENT	ENNEAHEDRIA
ENERVATED	ENGAGER	ENGRAINER	ENJAMBMENT	ENNEAHEDRON
ENERVATING	ENGAGING	ENGRAINING	ENJEOPARD	ENNEAHEDRONS
ENERVATION	ENGAGINGLY	ENGRAM	ENJEOPARDY	ENNEASEMIC
ENERVATIVE	ENGAGINGNESS	ENGRAMMA	ENJEWEL	ENNEASTYLE
ENERVATOR	ENGARDE	ENGRAMMATIC	ENJOIN	ENNEASTYLOS
ENEW	ENGARLAND	ENGRAMME	ENJOINDER	ENNEASYLLABIC
ENFACE	ENGARRISON	ENGRAMMIC	ENJOINED	ENNEATIC
ENFACED	ENGASTRIMYTH	ENGRANDIZE	ENJOINER	ENNOBLE
ENFACEMENT	ENGASTRIMYTHIC	ENGRAPHIA	ENJOINING	ENNOBLED
ENFACING	ENGAZE	ENGRAPHIC	ENJOINMENT	ENNOBLEMENT
ENFAMISH	ENGENDER	ENGRAPHICALLY	ENJOY	ENNOBLER
ENFANT	ENGENDERED	ENGRAPHY	ENJOYABLE	ENNOBLING
ENFARCE	ENGENDERER	ENGRAVE	ENJOYABLENESS	ENNOMIC
ENFATICO	ENGENDERING	ENGRAVED	ENJOYABLY	ENNUE
ENFAVOR	ENGENDERMENT	ENGRAVEMENT	ENJOYED	ENNUI
ENFEEBLE	ENGENDRURE	ENGRAVER	ENJOYER	ENNUIED
ENFEEBLED	ENGENDURE	ENGRAVING	ENJOYING	ENNUIS
ENFEEBLEMENT	ENGHLE	ENGREGGE	ENJOYMENT	ENNUYANT
ENFEEBLER	ENGHOSTED	ENGRIEVE	ENKINDLE	ENNUYE
ENFEEBLING	ENGI	ENGROSS	ENKINDLED	ENNUYEE
ENFELON	ENGILD	ENGROSSED	ENKINDLER	ENNUYING
ENFEOFF	ENGINE	ENGROSSEDLY	ENKINDLING	ENODAL
ENFEOFFED	ENGINED	ENGROSSER	ENKO	ENODALLY
ENFEOFFING	ENGINEER	ENGROSSING	ENLACE	ENODATE
ENFEOFFMENT	ENGINEERED	ENGROSSINGLY	ENLACED	ENODATION
ENFETTER	ENGINEERING	ENGROSSINGNESS	ENLACEMENT	ENODE
ENFILADE	ENGINEMAN	ENGROSSMENT	ENLACING	ENOIL
ENFILADED	ENGINEMEN	ENGULF	ENLARD	ENOL
ENFILADING	ENGINERY	ENGYSCOPE	ENLARGE	ENOLASE
ENFILE	ENGINING	ENHAEMOSPORE	ENLARGED	ENOLATE
ENFILED	ENGINOUS	ENHALO	ENLARGEDLY	ENOLIC
ENFIN	ENGIRD	ENHANCE	ENLARGEDNESS	ENOLIZABLE
ENFIRE	ENGIRDED	ENHANCED	ENLARGEMENT	ENOLIZATION
ENFIRM	ENGIRDING	ENHANCEMENT	ENLARGER	ENOLIZE

ENOLOGY	ENROLLMENT	ENSNARING	ENTERA	ENTHRILL
ENOMANIA	ENROLMENT	ENSNARINGLY	ENTERADEN	ENTHRONE
ENOMOTARCH	ENROOT	ENSNARL	ENTERAL	ENTHRONED
ENOMOTY	ENROOTED	ENSNOW	ENTERALGIA	ENTHRONG
ENOPHTHALMOS	ENROOTING	ENSORCEL	ENTERATE	ENTHRONING
ENOPHTHALMUS	ENROUGH	ENSORCELIZE	ENTERAUXE	ENTHRONIZATION
ENOPLAN	ENROUND	ENSORCELL	ENTERCLOSE	ENTHRONIZE
ENOPLION	ENS	ENSORCERIZE	ENTERECTOMY	ENTHRONIZED
ENOPTROMANCY	ENSAINT	ENSOUL	ENTERED	ENTHRONIZING
ENORGANIC	ENSALADA	ENSPHERE	ENTERER	ENTHUSE
ENORM	ENSAMPLE	ENSPHERED	ENTERGOGENIC	ENTHUSIASM
ENORMITIES	ENSAMPLER	ENSPHERING	ENTERIC	ENTHUSIAST
ENORMITY	ENSANGUINE	ENSTAMP	ENTERICOID	ENTHUSIASTIC
ENORMOUS	ENSANGUINED	ENSTAR	ENTERING	ENTHUSIASTICAL
ENORMOUSLY	ENSANGUINING	ENSTATE	ENTERITIDIS	ENTHUSIASTICALLY
ENORMOUSNESS	ENSATE	ENSTATITE	ENTERITIS	ENTHUSIASTLY
ENOSIS	ENSCENE	ENSTATITIC	ENTERMETE	ENTHYMEMATIC
ENOSTOSIS	ENSCONCE	ENSTATITITE	ENTEROCELE	ENTHYMEME
ENOUGH	ENSCONCED	ENSTATOLITE	ENTEROCEPTOR	ENTIA
ENOUNCE	ENSCONCING	ENSTEEP	ENTEROCOELE	ENTICE
ENOUNCED	ENSCROLL	ENSTOOL	ENTEROCOELIC	ENTICED
ENOUNCEMENT	ENSE	ENSTORE	ENTEROCOELOUS	ENTICEMENT
ENOUNCING	ENSEAL	ENSTRANGED	ENTEROCYST	ENTICER
ENOW	ENSEALED	ENSTYLE	ENTERODYNIA	ENTICING
ENPHYTOTIC	ENSEALING	ENSUABLE	ENTEROGENOUS	ENTICINGLY
ENPLANE	ENSEAM	ENSUANCE	ENTEROGRAM	ENTICINGNESS
ENPLANED	ENSEAR	ENSUANT	ENTEROGRAPH	ENTIFICAL
ENPLANING	ENSEARCH	ENSUE	ENTEROGRAPHY	ENTIFICATION
ENQUIRE	ENSEARCHER	ENSUED	ENTEROID	ENTIFY
ENQUIRER	ENSEAT	ENSUER	ENTEROKINASE	ENTIRE
ENQUIRY	ENSEATED	ENSUING	ENTEROLITH	ENTIRELY
ENRACE	ENSEATING	ENSURE	ENTEROLOGY	ENTIRENESS
ENRAGE	ENSELLURE	ENSURED	ENTEROLYSIS	ENTIRETY
ENRAGED	ENSEMBLE	ENSURER	ENTEROMERE	ENTIRIS
ENRAGEDLY	ENSEPULCHER	ENSURING	ENTERON	ENTITATIVE
ENRAGEDNESS	ENSEPULCHERED	ENSWATHE	ENTEROPATHY	ENTITATIVELY
ENRAGING	ENSEPULCHERING	ENSWATHED	ENTEROPEXIA	ENTITLE
ENRAMADA	ENSEPULCHRE	ENSWATHEMENT	ENTEROPLASTY	ENTITLED
ENRANGE	ENSETE	ENSWATHING	ENTEROPLEGIA	ENTITLING
ENRANK	ENSHEATHE	ENSWEEP	ENTEROPTOSIS	ENTITY
ENRAPT	ENSHIELD	ENTABLATURE	ENTEROPTOTIC	ENTOBLAST
ENRAPTURE	ENSHIELDED	ENTABLATURED	ENTERORRHEA	ENTOBLASTIC
ENRAPTURED	ENSHIELDING	ENTABLEMENT	ENTEROSCOPE	ENTOCAROTID
ENRAPTURER	ENSHRINE	ENTACH	ENTEROSCOPY	ENTOCELE
ENRAPTURING	ENSHRINED	ENTAD	ENTEROSEPSIS	ENTOCNEMIAL
ENRAVISH	ENSHRINEMENT	ENTAIL	ENTEROSPASM	ENTOCOELE
ENRAVISHED	ENSHRINING	ENTAILED	ENTEROSTASIS	ENTOCOELIC
ENRAVISHING	ENSHROUD	ENTAILING	ENTEROSTOMY	ENTOCONDYLE
ENRAVISHINGLY	ENSIFORM	ENTAILMENT	ENTEROTOMY	ENTOCONE
ENREGIMENT	ENSIGN	ENTAL	ENTEROTOXEMIA	ENTOCONID
ENREGISTER	ENSIGNCY	ENTALENT	ENTERPILLAR	ENTOCRANIAL
ENREGISTERED	ENSIGNED	ENTAME	ENTERPRISE	ENTOCYEMATE
ENREGISTERING	ENSIGNING	ENTAMEBIC	ENTERPRISED	ENTODERM
ENREGISTRATION	ENSIGNMENT	ENTAMOEBA	ENTERPRISER	ENTODERMAL
ENREGISTRY	ENSIGNRY	ENTAMOEBIC	ENTERPRISING	ENTODERMIC
ENRICH	ENSIGNSHIP	ENTANGLE	ENTERPRISINGLY	ENTOGASTRIC
ENRICHED	ENSILAGE	ENTANGLED	ENTERTAIN	ENTOGENOUS
ENRICHER	ENSILATE	ENTANGLEDLY	ENTERTAINED	ENTOGLOSSAL
ENRICHING	ENSILATION	ENTANGLEDNESS	ENTERTAINER	ENTOIL
ENRICHINGLY	ENSILE	ENTANGLEMENT	ENTERTAINING	ENTOILED
ENRICHMENT	ENSILIST	ENTANGLER	ENTERTAININGLY	ENTOILING
ENRIDGED	ENSISTERNUM	ENTANGLING	ENTERTAININGNESS	ENTOIRE
ENRIGHT	ENSKIED	ENTAPOPHYSIAL	ENTERTAINMENT	ENTOMB
ENRING	ENSKY	ENTAPOPHYSIS	ENTHALPY	ENTOMBED
ENRINGED	ENSKYED	ENTARTHROTIC	ENTHEATE	ENTOMBING
ENRINGING	ENSLAVE	ENTASIA	ENTHELMINTHA	ENTOMBMENT
ENROBE	ENSLAVED	ENTASIS	ENTHELMINTHES	ENTOMERE
ENROBED	ENSLAVEDNESS	ENTASTIC	ENTHEOS	ENTOMERIC
ENROBEMENT	ENSLAVEMENT	ENTE	ENTHETIC	ENTOMICAL
ENROBER	ENSLAVER	ENTELAM	ENTHRAL	ENTOMION
ENROBING	ENSLAVING	ENTELECHIES	ENTHRALL	ENTOMOGENOUS
ENROCKMENT	ENSLUMBER	ENTELECHY	ENTHRALLED	ENTOMOID
ENROL	ENSMALL	ENTELLUS	ENTHRALLER	ENTOMOLITE
ENROLL	ENSNARE	ENTELODONT	ENTHRALLING	ENTOMOLOGIC
ENROLLED	ENSNARED	ENTEMPLE	ENTHRALLINGLY	ENTOMOLOGICAL
ENROLLER	ENSNAREMENT	ENTENTE	ENTHRALLMENT	ENTOMOLOGICALL
ENROLLING	ENSNARER	ENTER	ENTHRALMENT	ENTOMOLOGIES

ENTOMOLOGIZE	ENTREMES	ENVIABLY	EOSINOPHILIA	EPEXEGESIS
ENTOMOLOGIZED	ENTREMESS	ENVIED	EOSINOPHILIC	EPEXEGETIC
ENTOMOLOGIZING	ENTREMETS	ENVIER	EOSINOPHILOUS	EPEXEGETICAL
ENTOMOLOGY	ENTRENCH	ENVIES	EOSPHORITE	EPEXEGETICALLY
ENTOMOPHAGAN	ENTRENCHMENT	ENVINE	EOZOON	EPHA
ENTOMOPHILY	ENTREPAS	ENVIOUS	EOZOONAL	EPHAH
ENTOMOTAXY	ENTREPOT	ENVIOUSLY	EP	EPHAPSE
ENTOMOTOMIST	ENTREPRENANT	ENVIOUSNESS	EPACMAIC	EPHARMONIC
ENTOMOTOMY	ENTREPRENEUR	ENVIRE	EPACME	EPHARMONY
ENTOOLITIC	ENTREPRENEUSE	ENVIRON	EPACRID	EPHEBE
ENTOPHYTAL	ENTRER	ENVIRONAL	EPACRIDACEOUS	EPHEBEION
ENTOPHYTE	ENTRESALLE	ENVIRONED	EPACT	EPHEBEUM
ENTOPHYTIC	ENTRESOL	ENVIRONIC	EPACTAL	EPHEBIC
ENTOPHYTICALLY	ENTRESSE	ENVIRONING	EPAGOGE	EPHEBOS
ENTOPHYTOUS	ENTREZ	ENVIRONMENT	EPAGOGIC	EPHEBUS
ENTOPIC	ENTRIES	ENVIRONMENTAL	EPAGOMENAE	EPHECTIC
ENTOPICAL	ENTRIKE	ENVIRONMENTALI	EPAGOMENAL	EPHEDRIN
ENTOPLASM	ENTROCHITE	ENVIRONMENTALI	EPAGOMENIC	EPHEDRINE
ENTOPLASTIC	ENTROPIES	ENVIRONS	EPAGOMENOUS	EPHELCYSTIC
ENTOPLASTRAL	ENTROPION	ENVISAGE	EPALPATE	EPHELIS
ENTOPLASTRON	ENTROPY	ENVISAGED	EPANADIPLOSIS	EPHEMERA
ENTOPTICAL	ENTRUST	ENVISAGEMENT	EPANALEPSIS	EPHEMERAE
ENTOPTICALLY	ENTRY	ENVISAGING	EPANALEPTIC	EPHEMERAL
ENTOPTICS	ENTRYMAN	ENVISION	EPANAPHORA	EPHEMERALITY
ENTOPTOSCOPE	ENTRYMEN	ENVOI	EPANAPHORAL	EPHEMERALLY
ENTOPTOSCOPIC	ENTRYWAY	ENVOLUME	EPANASTROPHE	EPHEMERAN
ENTOPTOSCOPY	ENTUM	ENVOY	EPANODOS	EPHEMERAS
ENTORETINA	ENTUNE	ENVY	EPANODY	EPHEMERID
ENTORGANISM	ENTWINE	ENVYING	EPANORTHOSIS	EPHEMERIDES
ENTOSPHERE	ENTWINED	ENVYINGLY	EPANTHOUS	EPHEMERIS
ENTOSTERNA	ENTWINING	ENWHEEL	EPAPILLATE	EPHEMEROMORPHI
ENTOSTERNAL	ENTWIST	ENWIND	EPAPOPHYSIAL	EPHEMERON
ENTOSTERNITE	ENTWISTED	ENWOMB	EPAPOPHYSIS	EPHEMERONS
ENTOSTERNUM	ENTWISTING	ENWOMBED	EPAPPOSE	EPHEMEROUS
ENTOTIC	ENUCLEATE	ENWOMBING	EPARC	EPHERERIST
ENTOTYMPANIC	ENUCLEATED	ENWORTHY	EPARCH	EPHESTIA
ENTOURAGE	ENUCLEATING	ENWRAP	EPARCHATE	EPHETAE
ENTOZOA	ENUCLEATION	ENWRAPPED	EPARCHIAL	EPHETE
ENTOZOAL	ENUCLEATOR	ENWRAPPING	EPARCHIES	EPHETIC
ENTOZOAN	ENUMERABLE	ENWRAPT	EPARCHY	EPHIDROSIS
ENTOZOIC	ENUMERATE	ENWREATHE	EPARCUALE	EPHIPPIA
ENTOZOOLOGY	ENUMERATED	ENWROUGHT	EPARTERIAL	EPHIPPIAL
ENTOZOON	ENUMERATING	ENZOOTIC	EPAULE	EPHIPPIUM
ENTRADA	ENUMERATION	ENZYM	EPAULEMENT	EPHOD
ENTRAIL	ENUMERATIVE	ENZYMATIC	EPAULET	EPHOR
ENTRAILS	ENUMERATOR	ENZYME	EPAULETED	EPHORAL
ENTRAIN	ENUNCIABILITY	ENZYMICALLY	EPAULETTE	EPHORALTY
ENTRAINED	ENUNCIABLE	ENZYMOLOGY	EPAULETTED	EPHORATE
ENTRAINER	ENUNCIATE	ENZYMOLYSIS	EPAULIERE	EPHORI
ENTRAINING	ENUNCIATED	ENZYMOLYTIC	EPAXIAL	EPHORIC
ENTRANCE	ENUNCIATING	ENZYMOSIS	EPAXIALLY	EPHORS
ENTRANCED	ENUNCIATION	ENZYMOTIC	EPEDAPHIC	EPHORUS
ENTRANCEMENT	ENUNCIATIVE	EOAN	EPEE	EPHPHATHA
ENTRANCEWAY	ENUNCIATIVELY	EOBIONT	EPEEIST	EPHTHIANURE
ENTRANCING	ENUNCIATOR	EODISCID	EPEIRIC	EPHYDRIAD
ENTRANCINGLY	ENUNCIATORY	EOHIPPUS	EPEIROGENETIC	EPHYDRID
ENTRANT	ENURE	EOLATION	EPEIROGENIC	EPHYMNIUM
ENTRAP	ENURESIS	EOLIAN	EPEIROGENY	EPHYRA
ENTRAPMENT	ENURNY	EOLIENNE	EPEISODION	EPHYRAE
ENTRAPPED	ENVASSAL	EOLIPILE	EPEMBRYONIC	EPHYRULA
ENTRAPPER	ENVASSALAGE	EOLITH	EPENCEPHAL	EPI
ENTRAPPING	ENVAYE	EOLITHIC	EPENCEPHALIC	EPIBASAL
ENTREASURE	ENVEIL	EOLOTROPIC	EPENCEPHALON	EPIBATUS
ENTREAT	ENVELOP	EON	EPENDYMA	EPIBENTHIC
ENTREATABLE	ENVELOPE	EONIAN	EPENDYMAL	EPIBENTHOS
ENTREATED	ENVELOPED	EONISM	EPENDYMOMA	EPIBIOTIC
ENTREATER	ENVELOPER	EOPHYTE	EPENDYTES	EPIBLAST
ENTREATFUL	ENVELOPING	EOPHYTIC	EPENETIC	EPIBLASTIC
ENTREATIES	ENVELOPMENT	EORHYOLITE	EPENTHESES	EPIBLEMA
ENTREATING	ENVENOM	EORL	EPENTHESIS	EPIBLEMATA
ENTREATMENT	ENVENOMATION	EOSATE	EPENTHESIZE	EPIBOLE
ENTREATY	ENVENOMED	EOSIN	EPENTHETIC	EPIBOLISM
ENTRECHAT	ENVENOMING	EOSINE	EPERGNE	EPIBOLY
ENTRECOTE	ENVERGURE	EOSINIC	EPERLAN	EPIBRANCHIAL
ENTREDEUX	ENVERMEIL	EOSINOBLAST	EPEROTESIS	EPIC
ENTREE	ENVIABLE	EOSINOPHIL	EPERVA	EPICAL
ENTREFER	ENVIABLENESS	EOSINOPHILE	EPEUS	EPICALLY

EPICALYCES	EPICYESIS	EPIGONATION	EPINAOS	EPIPROCT
EPICALYX	EPICYSTOTOMY	EPIGONE	EPINARD	EPIPTERIC
EPICALYXES	EPICYTE	EPIGONIC	EPINASTIC	EPIPTEROUS
EPICANTHIC	EPIDEICTIC	EPIGONIUM	EPINASTICALLY	EPIPTERYGOID
EPICANTHUS	EPIDEICTICAL	EPIGONOUS	EPINASTY	EPIPUBES
EPICARDIA	EPIDEISTIC	EPIGRAM	EPINEPHRIN	EPIPUBIC
EPICARDIAC	EPIDEMIC	EPIGRAMMATIC	EPINEPHRINE	EPIPUBIS
EPICARDIAL	EPIDEMICAL	EPIGRAMMATICAL	EPINETTE	EPIRHIZOUS
EPICARDIUM	EPIDEMICALLY	EPIGRAMMATISM	EPINEURAL	EPIROGENIC
EPICARID	EPIDEMICALNESS	EPIGRAMMATIST	EPINEURIAL	EPIROGENY
EPICARIDAN	EPIDEMICITY	EPIGRAMMATIZE	EPINEURIUM	EPIROTULIAN
EPICARP	EPIDEMIOGRAPHY	EPIGRAMMATIZED	EPINGLE	EPIRRHEMA
EPICE	EPIDEMIOLOGY	EPIGRAMME	EPINGLETTE	EPIRRHEMATIC
EPICEDE	EPIDEMY	EPIGRAPH	EPINICIA	EPIRRHEME
EPICEDIAL	EPIDENDRAL	EPIGRAPHER	EPINICIAN	EPISARCINE
EPICEDIUM	EPIDENDRIC	EPIGRAPHIC	EPINICION	EPISARKINE
EPICENE	EPIDERM	EPIGRAPHICAL	EPINIKIA	EPISCENIA
EPICENISM	EPIDERMA	EPIGRAPHICALLY	EPINIKIAN	EPISCENIUM
EPICENITY	EPIDERMAL	EPIGRAPHIST	EPINIKION	EPISCIA
EPICENTER	EPIDERMATIC	EPIGRAPHY	EPININE	EPISCLERA
EPICENTRA	EPIDERMATOID	EPIGUANINE	EPIOPTICON	EPISCLERAL
EPICENTRAL	EPIDERMIC	EPIGYNE	EPIOTIC	EPISCLERITIS
EPICENTRE	EPIDERMICAL	EPIGYNOUS	EPIPALEOLITHIC	EPISCOPABLE
EPICENTRUM	EPIDERMICALLY	EPIGYNUM	EPIPARODOS	EPISCOPACIES
EPICHEIREMA	EPIDERMIS	EPIGYNY	EPIPASTIC	EPISCOPACY
EPICHEIREMATA	EPIDERMIZATION	EPIHYAL	EPIPERIPHERAL	EPISCOPAL
EPICHILE	EPIDERMOID	EPIKEIA	EPIPETALOUS	EPISCOPALIAN
EPICHILIA	EPIDERMOIDAL	EPIKIA	EPIPHANOUS	EPISCOPALISM
EPICHILIUM	EPIDERMOLYSIS	EPIKLESIS	EPIPHANY	EPISCOPALITY
EPICHIREMA	EPIDERMOSE	EPIKY	EPIPHARYNGEAL	EPISCOPALLY
EPICHONDROSIS	EPIDERMOUS	EPILABRA	EPIPHARYNX	EPISCOPATE
EPICHONDROTIC	EPIDESMINE	EPILABRUM	EPIPHLOEDAL	EPISCOPATION
EPICHORDAL	EPIDIALOGUE	EPILAMELLAR	EPIPHLOEDIC	EPISCOPATURE
EPICHORIAL	EPIDIASCOPE	EPILARYNGEAL	EPIPHONEMA	EPISCOPE
EPICHORIC	EPIDIDYMAL	EPILATE	EPIPHORA	EPISCOPICIDE
EPICHORION	EPIDIDYMIDES	EPILATED	EPIPHRAGM	EPISCOPIZATION
EPICHORISTIC	EPIDIDYMIS	EPILATING	EPIPHRAGMAL	EPISCOPIZE
EPICIER	EPIDIDYMITE	EPILATION	EPIPHYLL	EPISCOPIZED
EPICISM	EPIDIDYMITIS	EPILATOR	EPIPHYLLINE	EPISCOPIZING
EPICIST	EPIDIORITE	EPILEGOMENON	EPIPHYSARY	EPISCOPOLATRY
EPICLASTIC	EPIDOSITE	EPILEMMA	EPIPHYSEAL	EPISCOPY
EPICLEIDIAN	EPIDOTE	EPILEMMAL	EPIPHYSES	EPISCOTISTER
EPICLEIDIUM	EPIDOTIC	EPILEPSY	EPIPHYSIAL	EPISEMATIC
EPICLESIS	EPIDOTIZATION	EPILEPTIC	EPIPHYSIS	EPISEPALOUS
EPICLY	EPIDURAL	EPILEPTICAL	EPIPHYSITIS	EPISIOCELE
EPICNEMIAL	EPIFOCAL	EPILEPTICALLY	EPIPHYTAL	EPISIOPLASTY
EPICOELAR	EPIGAMIC	EPILEPTIFORM	EPIPHYTE	EPISIOTOMY
EPICOELE	EPIGASTER	EPILEPTOID	EPIPHYTIC	EPISKELETAL
EPICOELIA	EPIGASTRAL	EPILIMNION	EPIPHYTICAL	EPISODAL
EPICOELIAC	EPIGASTRIA	EPILOBE	EPIPHYTICALLY	EPISODE
EPICOELIAN	EPIGASTRIAL	EPILOG	EPIPHYTOTIC	EPISODIC
EPICOELOMA	EPIGASTRIC	EPILOGATION	EPIPHYTOUS	EPISODICAL
EPICOELOUS	EPIGASTRICAL	EPILOGIC	EPIPIAL	EPISODICALLY
EPICOLIC	EPIGASTRIUM	EPILOGICAL	EPIPLANKTON	EPISPADIA
EPICONDYLE	EPIGASTROCELE	EPILOGISM	EPIPLASM	EPISPADIAC
EPICONDYLIAN	EPIGEAL	EPILOGIST	EPIPLASMIC	EPISPADIAS
EPICONDYLIC	EPIGEAN	EPILOGIZE	EPIPLASTRAL	EPISPASTIC
EPICONTINENTAL	EPIGEE	EPILOGIZED	EPIPLASTRON	EPISPERM
EPICORACOID	EPIGEIC	EPILOGIZING	EPIPLECTIC	EPISPLENITIS
EPICORACOIDAL	EPIGENE	EPILOGUE	EPIPLEURA	EPISPORE
EPICORMIC	EPIGENESIS	EPILOIA	EPIPLEURAE	EPISTAPEDIAL
EPICOTYL	EPIGENESIST	EPIMACUS	EPIPLEURAL	EPISTASIS
EPICRANIAL	EPIGENETIC	EPIMANDIBULAR	EPIPLEXIS	EPISTATIC
EPICRANIUM	EPIGENETICALLY	EPIMANIKIA	EPIPLOCE	EPISTAXIS
EPICRISES	EPIGENIC	EPIMANIKION	EPIPLOCELE	EPISTEME
EPICRISIS	EPIGENIST	EPIMER	EPIPLOIC	EPISTEMIC
EPICRITIC	EPIGENOUS	EPIMERAL	EPIPLOITIS	EPISTEMOLOG
EPICRYSTALLINE	EPIGEOUS	EPIMERE	EPIPLOON	EPISTEMOLOGY
EPICURE	EPIGEUM	EPIMERITE	EPIPLOPEXY	EPISTEMONIC
EPICUREAN	EPIGLOTTAL	EPIMERITIC	EPIPODIA	EPISTEMONICAL
EPICUREANISM	EPIGLOTTIDEAN	EPIMERON	EPIPODIAL	EPISTERNA
EPICYCLE	EPIGLOTTIDITIS	EPIMORPHA	EPIPODIALE	EPISTERNAL
EPICYCLIC	EPIGLOTTIS	EPIMORPHIC	EPIPODIALIA	EPISTERNALIA
EPICYCLICAL	EPIGLOTTITIS	EPIMORPHOSIS	EPIPODITE	EPISTERNITE
EPICYCLOID	EPIGNATHOUS	EPIMYSIUM	EPIPODIUM	EPISTERNUM
EPICYCLOIDAL	EPIGNE	EPIMYTH	EPIPOLISM	EPISTILBITE
EPICYEMATE	EPIGONAL	EPINAOI	EPIPOLIZE	EPISTLE

EPISTLER
EPISTOLARIAN
EPISTOLARILY
EPISTOLATORY
EPISTOLER
EPISTOLET
EPISTOLIC
EPISTOLICAL
EPISTOLIST
EPISTOLIZABLE
EPISTOLIZATION
EPISTOLIZE
EPISTOLOGRAPHER
EPISTOLOGRAPHIST
EPISTOLOGRAPHY
EPISTOMA
EPISTOMAL
EPISTOMATA
EPISTOME
EPISTOMIAN
EPISTROPHE
EPISTROPHEAL
EPISTROPHEUS
EPISTROPHIC
EPISTROPHY
EPISTYLAR
EPISTYLE
EPISYLLOGISM
EPISYNALOEPHE
EPISYNTHETON
EPITACTIC
EPITAPH
EPITAPHER
EPITAPHIAL
EPITAPHIAN
EPITAPHIC
EPITAPHICAL
EPITAPHIZE
EPITASIS
EPITELA
EPITENDINEUM
EPITHALAMIA
EPITHALAMIC
EPITHALAMION
EPITHALAMIUM
EPITHALAMIUMS
EPITHALAMIZE
EPITHALAMUS
EPITHALAMY
EPITHALLINE
EPITHECA
EPITHECAL
EPITHECATE
EPITHECIA
EPITHECIUM
EPITHELIA
EPITHELIAL
EPITHELIOID
EPITHELIOMA
EPITHELIOMAS
EPITHELIOMATA
EPITHELIOSIS
EPITHELIUM
EPITHELIUMS
EPITHELIZATION
EPITHELIZE
EPITHELOID
EPITHEM
EPITHEMA
EPITHEME
EPITHESIS
EPITHET
EPITHETIC
EPITHETICAL
EPITHETICIAN
EPITHETON
EPITHYME

EPITHYMETIC
EPITIMESIS
EPITOKE
EPITOMATOR
EPITOMATORY
EPITOME
EPITOMES
EPITOMIC
EPITOMICAL
EPITOMICALLY
EPITOMISE
EPITOMIST
EPITOMIZATION
EPITOMIZE
EPITOMIZED
EPITOMIZER
EPITOMIZING
EPITONIC
EPITONION
EPITOXOID
EPITRICHIAL
EPITRICHIUM
EPITRITE
EPITRITIC
EPITROCHLEA
EPITROCHLEAR
EPITROCHOID
EPITROCHOIDAL
EPITROPE
EPITROPHIC
EPITROPHY
EPITYMPANIC
EPITYMPANUM
EPITYPHLITIS
EPITYPHLON
EPIURAL
EPIVALVE
EPIZEUXIS
EPIZOA
EPIZOAL
EPIZOAN
EPIZOIC
EPIZOON
EPIZOOTIC
EPIZOOTIOLOGY
EPIZOOTY
EPOCH
EPOCHA
EPOCHAL
EPOCHALLY
EPOCHE
EPOCHISM
EPOCHIST
EPODE
EPODIC
EPOLLICATE
EPONGE
EPONYCHIUM
EPONYM
EPONYMIC
EPONYMOUS
EPONYMY
EPOOPHORON
EPOPEE
EPOPOEAN
EPOPOEIA
EPOPOEIST
EPOPT
EPOPTAE
EPOPTIC
EPORNITIC
EPORNITICALLY
EPOS
EPOTE
EPOXIDE
EPOXY
EPRIS

EPRISE
EPRUINOSE
EPSILON
EPSOMITE
EPULARY
EPULATION
EPULIS
EPULO
EPULOID
EPULOSIS
EPULOTIC
EPUPILLATE
EPURAL
EPURATE
EPURATION
EPURE
EPYLLIA
EPYLLION
EQUABILITY
EQUABLE
EQUABLENESS
EQUABLY
EQUAEVAL
EQUAL
EQUALED
EQUALING
EQUALISE
EQUALIST
EQUALITARIAN
EQUALITARIANISM
EQUALITIES
EQUALITY
EQUALIZATION
EQUALIZE
EQUALIZED
EQUALIZER
EQUALIZING
EQUALLED
EQUALLING
EQUALLY
EQUALNESS
EQUANGULAR
EQUANIMITY
EQUANIMOUS
EQUANIMOUSLY
EQUANT
EQUATE
EQUATED
EQUATING
EQUATION
EQUATIONAL
EQUATIONALLY
EQUATIONISM
EQUATIONIST
EQUATIVE
EQUATOR
EQUATOREAL
EQUATORIAL
EQUATORIALLY
EQUERRIES
EQUERRY
EQUES
EQUESTRIAN
EQUESTRIENNE
EQUIANGULAR
EQUIAXED
EQUID
EQUIDISTANCE
EQUIDISTANT
EQUIDISTANTIAL
EQUIDISTANTLY
EQUIDIURNAL
EQUIFORM
EQUIFORMAL
EQUIFORMITY
EQUIGRANULAR
EQUIJACENT

EQUILATERAL
EQUILIBRANT
EQUILIBRATE
EQUILIBRATED
EQUILIBRATING
EQUILIBRATION
EQUILIBRATIVE
EQUILIBRATOR
EQUILIBRATORY
EQUILIBRIA
EQUILIBRIAL
EQUILIBRIATE
EQUILIBRIOUS
EQUILIBRIST
EQUILIBRISTAT
EQUILIBRISTIC
EQUILIBRITY
EQUILIBRIUM
EQUILIBRIUMS
EQUILIBRIZE
EQUILIN
EQUIMODAL
EQUIMOLAR
EQUIMOLECULAR
EQUIMOMENTAL
EQUIMULTIPLE
EQUINAL
EQUINATE
EQUINE
EQUINIA
EQUINITY
EQUINOCTIAL
EQUINOCTIALLY
EQUINOVARUS
EQUINOX
EQUINUS
EQUIP
EQUIPAGA
EQUIPAGE
EQUIPARANT
EQUIPARATE
EQUIPARATION
EQUIPARTILE
EQUIPARTITION
EQUIPEDAL
EQUIPLUVE
EQUIPMENT
EQUIPOISE
EQUIPOISED
EQUIPOISING
EQUIPOLLENCE
EQUIPOLLENCY
EQUIPOLLENT
EQUIPOLLENTLY
EQUIPONDERANT
EQUIPONDERATE
EQUIPONDERATED
EQUIPONDERATING
EQUIPOSTILE
EQUIPOTENTIAL
EQUIPPED
EQUIPPER
EQUIPPING
EQUIPROBABLE
EQUIPT
EQUISETA
EQUISETACEOUS
EQUISETIC
EQUISETUM
EQUISETUMS
EQUISIGNAL
EQUISON
EQUISONANCE
EQUISONANT
EQUITABLE
EQUITABLY
EQUITANT

EQUITATION
EQUITATIVE
EQUITES
EQUITIES
EQUITIST
EQUITY
EQUIVALENCE
EQUIVALENCED
EQUIVALENCY
EQUIVALENT
EQUIVALENTLY
EQUIVALVE
EQUIVOCACY
EQUIVOCAL
EQUIVOCALITY
EQUIVOCATE
EQUIVOCATED
EQUIVOCATING
EQUIVOCATION
EQUIVOCATOR
EQUIVOCATORY
EQUIVOKE
EQUIVOLUMINAL
EQUIVOQUE
EQUIVOROUS
EQUOID
EQUULEI
EQUULEUS
ER
ERA
ERADE
ERADIATE
ERADIATED
ERADIATING
ERADIATION
ERADICABLE
ERADICATE
ERADICATED
ERADICATING
ERADICATION
ERADICATIVE
ERADICATOR
ERADICATORY
ERADICULOSE
ERAL
ERANIST
ERASABLE
ERASE
ERASED
ERASER
ERASING
ERASION
ERASURE
ERBER
ERBIA
ERBIUM
ERD
ERDVARK
ERE
EREB
ERECT
ERECTED
ERECTER
ERECTILE
ERECTILITY
ERECTING
ERECTION
ERECTIVE
ERECTLY
ERECTNESS
ERECTOPATENT
ERECTOR
ERELONG
EREMACAUSIS
EREMIC
EREMITAL
EREMITE

EREMITIC
EREMITICAL
EREMITISH
EREMOLOGY
EREMOPHYTE
ERENACH
ERENOW
EREPSIN
EREPT
EREPTASE
EREPTIC
ERER
ERETHIC
ERETHISIA
ERETHISM
ERETHISMIC
ERETHISTIC
ERETHITIC
EREV
EREWHILE
ERF
ERG
ERGAL
ERGAMINE
ERGASIA
ERGASTERION
ERGASTIC
ERGASTOPLASM
ERGASTOPLASMIC
ERGASTULUM
ERGATANDROUS
ERGATANDRY
ERGATE
ERGATES
ERGATIVE
ERGATOCRACY
ERGATOGYNE
ERGATOGYNOUS
ERGATOGYNY
ERGATOID
ERGATOMORPH
ERGATOMORPHIC
ERGATOMORPHISM
ERGMETER
ERGO
ERGODIC
ERGOGRAM
ERGOGRAPH
ERGOISM
ERGOLOGY
ERGOMANIAC
ERGOMETER
ERGON
ERGOPHILE
ERGOPHOBIA
ERGOPHOBIAC
ERGOPLASM
ERGOSTAT
ERGOSTEROL
ERGOT
ERGOTAMINE
ERGOTAMININE
ERGOTED
ERGOTIC
ERGOTIN
ERGOTINE
ERGOTININE
ERGOTISM
ERGOTIST
ERGOTIZATION
ERGOTIZE
ERGOTIZED
ERGOTIZING
ERGOTOXINE
ERGUSIA
ERIA
ERIC

ERICACEOUS
ERICAD
ERICAL
ERICETAL
ERICHTHOID
ERICHTHUS
ERICINEOUS
ERICIUS
ERICOID
ERICOLIN
ERICOPHYTE
ERIGERON
ERIGIBLE
ERIGLOSSATE
ERIKA
ERIKITE
ERINACEOUS
ERINEUM
ERINGO
ERINITE
ERINOSE
ERIOMETER
ERIONITE
ERIOPHORUM
ERIOPHYLLOUS
ERISTIC
ERISTICAL
ERISTICALLY
ERIZO
ERK
ERLICHE
ERLKING
ERME
ERMELIN
ERMILINE
ERMIN
ERMINE
ERMINED
ERMINEE
ERMINES
ERMINING
ERMINITES
ERMINOIS
ERN
ERNE
ERODE
ERODED
ERODENT
ERODING
EROGATE
EROGENEITY
EROGENESIS
EROGENETIC
EROGENIC
EROGENOUS
EROSE
EROSIBLE
EROSION
EROSIONAL
EROSIONIST
EROSIVE
EROSTRATE
EROTEMA
EROTEME
EROTESIS
EROTETIC
EROTIC
EROTICA
EROTICAL
EROTICALLY
EROTICISM
EROTICOMANIA
EROTISM
EROTOGENIC
EROTOMANIA
EROTOMANIAC
EROTOPATH

EROTOPATHY
EROTYLID
ERR
ERRABILITY
ERRABLE
ERRABLENESS
ERRABUND
ERRANCY
ERRAND
ERRANT
ERRANTLY
ERRANTNESS
ERRANTRIES
ERRANTRY
ERRATA
ERRATIC
ERRATICAL
ERRATICALLY
ERRATICALNESS
ERRATUM
ERRED
ERRHINE
ERRING
ERRINGLY
ERRITE
ERRONEOUS
ERRONEOUSLY
ERRONEOUSNESS
ERROR
ERRORIST
ERS
ERSATZ
ERST
ERSTWHILE
ERSTWHILES
ERT
ERUB
ERUBESCENCE
ERUBESCENT
ERUC
ERUCA
ERUCIN
ERUCT
ERUCTATE
ERUCTATION
ERUCTATIVE
ERUDIT
ERUDITE
ERUDITELY
ERUDITENESS
ERUDITICAL
ERUDITION
ERUDITIONAL
ERUDITIONIST
ERUGATE
ERUGATION
ERUGATORY
ERUMPENT
ERUPT
ERUPTED
ERUPTING
ERUPTION
ERUPTIONAL
ERUPTIVE
ERUPTIVELY
ERUPTIVENESS
ERUPTIVITY
ERUPTURIENT
ERUV
ERVEN
ERVENHOLDER
ERVIL
ERYNGO
ERYOPID
ERYSIPELAS
ERYSIPELATOID
ERYSIPELOID

ERYTHEMA
ERYTHEMATIC
ERYTHEMATOUS
ERYTHEMIC
ERYTHRAEAN
ERYTHRAEMIA
ERYTHRASMA
ERYTHREAN
ERYTHREMIA
ERYTHRIN
ERYTHRINE
ERYTHRISM
ERYTHRISMAL
ERYTHRISTIC
ERYTHRITE
ERYTHRITIC
ERYTHRITOL
ERYTHROBLAST
ERYTHROCARPOUS
ERYTHROCYTOSIS
ERYTHRODERMIA
ERYTHROGENIC
ERYTHROGLUCIN
ERYTHROID
ERYTHROL
ERYTHROLEIN
ERYTHROLYSIN
ERYTHROLYSIS
ERYTHROLYTIC
ERYTHROMANIA
ERYTHRONIUM
ERYTHROPENIA
ERYTHROPHOBIA
ERYTHROPHORE
ERYTHROPHYLL
ERYTHROPIA
ERYTHROPSIA
ERYTHROPSIN
ERYTHROSCOPE
ERYTHROSE
ERYTHROSIN
ERYTHROSIS
ERYTHROZYME
ERYTHRULOSE
ERZAHLER
ES
ESAN
ESBAY
ESCA
ESCADRILLE
ESCALADE
ESCALADED
ESCALADER
ESCALADING
ESCALADO
ESCALAN
ESCALATE
ESCALATED
ESCALATING
ESCALATION
ESCALATOR
ESCALIER
ESCALLOP
ESCALLOPED
ESCALOP
ESCALOPED
ESCAMBIO
ESCAMBRON
ESCAMOTAGE
ESCAPABLE
ESCAPADE
ESCAPAGE
ESCAPE
ESCAPED
ESCAPEE
ESCAPEMENT
ESCAPER

ESCAPING
ESCAPISM
ESCAPIST
ESCARBUNCLE
ESCARGOT
ESCAROLE
ESCARP
ESCARPMENT
ESCHALOT
ESCHAR
ESCHARA
ESCHARINE
ESCHAROID
ESCHAROTIC
ESCHATOCOL
ESCHATOLOGY
ESCHAUFE
ESCHEAT
ESCHEATABLE
ESCHEATAGE
ESCHEATED
ESCHEATING
ESCHEATOR
ESCHEL
ESCHEW
ESCHEWAL
ESCHEWANCE
ESCHEWED
ESCHEWER
ESCHEWING
ESCHYNITE
ESCLANDRE
ESCLAVAGE
ESCOBA
ESCOBADURA
ESCOBILLA
ESCOBITA
ESCOLAR
ESCOLARS
ESCONSON
ESCOPET
ESCOPETA
ESCOPETTE
ESCORT
ESCORTED
ESCORTING
ESCOT
ESCRIBANO
ESCRIBE
ESCRIBED
ESCRIBIENTE
ESCRIBIENTES
ESCRIBING
ESCRIME
ESCRIPT
ESCRITOIRE
ESCRITORIAL
ESCROD
ESCROL
ESCROLL
ESCROW
ESCROWEE
ESCRY
ESCUAGE
ESCUDERO
ESCUDO
ESCUDOS
ESCULENT
ESCULETIN
ESCULIN
ESCUTCHEON
ESCUTCHEONED
ESCUTELLATE
ESEMPLASTIC
ESEMPLASY
ESEPTATE
ESERE

ESERIN
ESERINE
ESEXUAL
ESGUARD
ESHIN
ESILL
ESIPHONAL
ESK
ESKAR
ESKER
ESLABON
ESMERALDA
ESMERALDITE
ESNE
ESNECY
ESOANHYDRIDE
ESOCIFORM
ESODIC
ESOENTERITIS
ESOGASTRITIS
ESONARTHEX
ESONEURAL
ESOPHAGAL
ESOPHAGEAL
ESOPHAGEAN
ESOPHAGISM
ESOPHAGITIS
ESOPHAGOCELE
ESOPHAGOTOME
ESOPHAGOTOMY
ESOPHAGUS
ESOPHORIA
ESOTERIC
ESOTERICA
ESOTERICAL
ESOTERICALLY
ESOTERICISM
ESOTERICS
ESOTERISM
ESOTERIST
ESOTERIZE
ESOTERY
ESOTHYROPEXY
ESOTROPE
ESOTROPIA
ESOTROPIC
ESOX
ESP
ESPACEMENT
ESPADA
ESPADON
ESPADRILLE
ESPAGNOLETTE
ESPALIER
ESPALIERED
ESPALIERING
ESPANTOON
ESPARCET
ESPARTO
ESPATHATE
ESPAVE
ESPAVEL
ESPECE
ESPECIAL
ESPECIALLY
ESPECIALNESS
ESPEIRE
ESPERANCE
ESPHRESIS
ESPIAL
ESPIED
ESPIEGLE
ESPIEGLERIE
ESPIER
ESPINAL
ESPINEL
ESPINGOLE

ESPINO
ESPINOS
ESPIONAGE
ESPLANADE
ESPLEES
ESPOUSAL
ESPOUSE
ESPOUSED
ESPOUSER
ESPOUSING
ESPRESSIVO
ESPRESSOS
ESPRINGAL
ESPRISE
ESPRIT
ESPROVE
ESPUNDIA
ESPY
ESPYING
ESQUAMATE
ESQUAMULOSE
ESQUIRE
ESQUIRED
ESQUIRING
ESQUISSE
ESS
ESSANG
ESSART
ESSAY
ESSAYED
ESSAYER
ESSAYETTE
ESSAYICAL
ESSAYING
ESSAYIST
ESSAYISTIC
ESSAYISTICAL
ESSE
ESSED
ESSEDA
ESSEDE
ESSENCE
ESSENCED
ESSENCING
ESSENHOUT
ESSENTIA
ESSENTIAL
ESSENTIALITIES
ESSENTIALITY
ESSENTIALLY
ESSENTIATE
ESSENWOOD
ESSES
ESSEXITE
ESSIVE
ESSLING
ESSOIGN
ESSOIN
ESSOINED
ESSOINEE
ESSOINER
ESSOINING
ESSONITE
ESSORANT
EST
ESTABLISH
ESTABLISHED
ESTABLISHER
ESTABLISHING
ESTABLISHMENT
ESTACADE
ESTADAL
ESTADEL
ESTADIO
ESTADO
ESTAFA
ESTAFET

ESTAFETTE
ESTAFETTED
ESTAMENE
ESTAMIN
ESTAMINET
ESTAMP
ESTAMPAGE
ESTAMPEDE
ESTAMPEDERO
ESTAMPIE
ESTANCIA
ESTANCIERO
ESTANTION
ESTATE
ESTATED
ESTATES
ESTATESMAN
ESTATESMEN
ESTATING
ESTATS
ESTEEM
ESTEEMABLE
ESTEEMED
ESTEEMER
ESTEEMING
ESTER
ESTERASE
ESTERELLITE
ESTERIFEROUS
ESTERIFICATION
ESTERIFIED
ESTERIFY
ESTERIFYING
ESTERIZATION
ESTERIZE
ESTERIZING
ESTERLIN
ESTERO
ESTEROS
ESTEVIN
ESTHEMATOLOGY
ESTHERIAN
ESTHESIA
ESTHESIOGEN
ESTHESIOLOGY
ESTHESIS
ESTHETE
ESTHETIC
ESTHETICAL
ESTHETICALLY
ESTHETICIAN
ESTHETICISM
ESTHETICS
ESTHETOLOGY
ESTHETOPHORE
ESTHIOMENE
ESTHIOMENUS
ESTIMABLE
ESTIMABLY
ESTIMATE
ESTIMATED
ESTIMATING
ESTIMATINGLY
ESTIMATION
ESTIMATIVE
ESTIMATOR
ESTIPULATE
ESTIVAGE
ESTIVAL
ESTIVATE
ESTIVATED
ESTIVATING
ESTIVATION
ESTIVATOR
ESTIVE
ESTMARK
ESTOC

ESTOCADA
ESTOILE
ESTOLIDE
ESTOP
ESTOPPAGE
ESTOPPED
ESTOPPEL
ESTOPPING
ESTOQUE
ESTOVERS
ESTRADA
ESTRADAS
ESTRADE
ESTRADIOL
ESTRAGOL
ESTRAGOLE
ESTRAGON
ESTRANGE
ESTRANGED
ESTRANGEDNESS
ESTRANGEMENT
ESTRANGER
ESTRANGING
ESTRAPADE
ESTRAY
ESTRAYED
ESTRAYING
ESTRE
ESTREAT
ESTREATED
ESTREATING
ESTREPE
ESTREPEMENT
ESTRIATE
ESTRICHE
ESTRIF
ESTRIOL
ESTRO
ESTROGEN
ESTROGENIC
ESTRONE
ESTROUS
ESTRUAL
ESTRUM
ESTRUS
ESTUARIAL
ESTUARIAN
ESTUARIES
ESTUARINE
ESTUARY
ESTUATE
ESTUDY
ESTUFA
ESTUOUS
ESTURE
ESTUS
ESURIENCE
ESURIENCY
ESURIENT
ESURIENTLY
ESURINE
ET
ETA
ETAAC
ETABALLI
ETABELLI
ETACISM
ETAERIO
ETAGE
ETAGERE
ETALAGE
ETALON
ETAMINE
ETAPE
ETAS
ETATISM
ETATISME

ETCETERA
ETCETERAS
ETCH
ETCHANT
ETCHED
ETCHEMIN
ETCHER
ETCHING
ETEN
ETERN
ETERNAL
ETERNALIST
ETERNALIZATION
ETERNALIZE
ETERNALLY
ETERNALNESS
ETERNE
ETERNISH
ETERNITIES
ETERNITY
ETERNIZATION
ETERNIZE
ETERNIZED
ETERNIZING
ETESIAN
ETH
ETHAL
ETHALDEHYDE
ETHANAL
ETHANAMIDE
ETHANE
ETHANETHIOL
ETHANOL
ETHANOYL
ETHEL
ETHELING
ETHENE
ETHENOID
ETHENOIDAL
ETHENOL
ETHENYL
ETHEOSTOMOID
ETHER
ETHERATE
ETHEREAL
ETHEREALISM
ETHEREALITY
ETHEREALIZE
ETHEREALIZED
ETHEREALIZING
ETHEREALLY
ETHEREALNESS
ETHERED
ETHEREOUS
ETHERIC
ETHERICAL
ETHERIFIED
ETHERIFORM
ETHERIFY
ETHERIFYING
ETHERIN
ETHERION
ETHERISM
ETHERIZATION
ETHERIZE
ETHERIZED
ETHERIZER
ETHERIZING
ETHEROLATE
ETHEROUS
ETHIC
ETHICAL
ETHICALITY
ETHICALLY
ETHICALNESS
ETHICIAN
ETHICIST

ETHICIZE
ETHICIZED
ETHICIZING
ETHICS
ETHIDE
ETHIDENE
ETHINE
ETHINYL
ETHIODIDE
ETHIOPS
ETHIZE
ETHMOID
ETHMOIDAL
ETHMOIDITIS
ETHMOLITH
ETHMYPHITIS
ETHNARCH
ETHNARCHIES
ETHNARCHY
ETHNIC
ETHNICAL
ETHNICALLY
ETHNICISM
ETHNICIST
ETHNOBOTANY
ETHNOCENTRIC
ETHNOCENTRISM
ETHNOCRACY
ETHNODICY
ETHNOFLORA
ETHNOGENIC
ETHNOGENIES
ETHNOGENY
ETHNOGRAPHER
ETHNOGRAPHIC
ETHNOGRAPHIES
ETHNOGRAPHIST
ETHNOGRAPHY
ETHNOLOGER
ETHNOLOGIC
ETHNOLOGICAL
ETHNOLOGIST
ETHNOLOGY
ETHNOMANIAC
ETHNOPSYCHIC
ETHNOS
ETHNOZOOLOGY
ETHOGRAPHY
ETHOLIDE
ETHOLOGIC
ETHOLOGICAL
ETHOLOGY
ETHONOMIC
ETHONOMICS
ETHOPOEIA
ETHOS
ETHOXIDE
ETHOXYL
ETHROG
ETHYL
ETHYLAMIDE
ETHYLAMIME
ETHYLAMIN
ETHYLATE
ETHYLATED
ETHYLATING
ETHYLATION
ETHYLENE
ETHYLENIC
ETHYLIC
ETHYLIDENE
ETHYLIN
ETHYNE
ETHYNYL
ETHYSULPHURIC
ETIK
ETIOLATE

ETIOLATED
ETIOLATING
ETIOLATION
ETIOLIN
ETIOLIZE
ETIOLOGICAL
ETIOLOGICALLY
ETIOLOGIST
ETIOLOGUE
ETIOLOGY
ETIOPHYLLIN
ETIOTROPIC
ETIQUET
ETIQUETTE
ETIQUETTICAL
ETNA
ETOILE
ETOUFFE
ETOURDERIE
ETRENNE
ETROG
ETTERCAP
ETTLE
ETTLED
ETTLING
ETUDE
ETUI
ETWEE
ETWITE
ETYM
ETYMA
ETYMIC
ETYMOGRAPHY
ETYMOLOGER
ETYMOLOGIC
ETYMOLOGICAL
ETYMOLOGICON
ETYMOLOGIST
ETYMOLOGIZE
ETYMOLOGIZED
ETYMOLOGIZING
ETYMOLOGY
ETYMON
ETYMONS
ETYPIC
ETYPICAL
ETYPICALLY
EUANGIOTIC
EUASTER
EUBACTERIUM
EUCAINE
EUCAIRITE
EUCALYPT
EUCALYPTEOL
EUCALYPTI
EUCALYPTIAN
EUCALYPTIC
EUCALYPTOL
EUCALYPTOLE
EUCALYPTUS
EUCALYPTUSES
EUCATROPINE
EUCEPHALOUS
EUCHARIS
EUCHARIST
EUCHARISTIAL
EUCHARISTIC
EUCHARISTICAL
EUCHARISTIZE
EUCHARISTIZED
EUCHARISTIZING
EUCHLORHYDRIA
EUCHLORINE
EUCHOLOGION
EUCHOLOGY
EUCHRE
EUCHRED

EUCHRING
EUCHROITE
EUCHROME
EUCHROMOSOME
EUCLASE
EUCLEID
EUCOLITE
EUCONE
EUCONIC
EUCOSMID
EUCRASIA
EUCRASITE
EUCRASY
EUCRITE
EUCRYPTITE
EUCRYSTALLINE
EUCTICAL
EUCYCLIC
EUDAEMON
EUDAEMONIA
EUDAEMONIC
EUDAEMONICAL
EUDAEMONICS
EUDAEMONISM
EUDAEMONIST
EUDAEMONIZE
EUDAEMONY
EUDALENE
EUDEMON
EUDESMOL
EUDIAGNOSTIC
EUDIALYTE
EUDIDYMITE
EUDIOMETER
EUDIOMETRY
EUDIPLEURAL
EUGE
EUGENESIC
EUGENESIS
EUGENETIC
EUGENIC
EUGENICAL
EUGENICALLY
EUGENICIST
EUGENICS
EUGENISM
EUGENIST
EUGENOL
EUGENOLATE
EUGENY
EUGLENOID
EUGLOBULIN
EUGRANITIC
EUHARMONIC
EUHEDRAL
EUHEMERISM
EUHEMERIST
EUHEMERISTIC
EUHEMERIZE
EUHEMERIZED
EUHEMERIZING
EUHYOSTYLIC
EUHYOSTYLY
EUKTOLITE
EULACHAN
EULACHANS
EULACHON
EULACHONS
EULALIA
EULOGIA
EULOGIC
EULOGICAL
EULOGICALLY
EULOGIES
EULOGIOUS
EULOGISM
EULOGIST

EULOGISTIC
EULOGISTICAL
EULOGIUM
EULOGIUMS
EULOGIZATION
EULOGIZE
EULOGIZED
EULOGIZER
EULOGIZING
EULOGY
EULOPHID
EULYSITE
EULYTINE
EULYTITE
EUMEMORRHEA
EUMENID
EUMERISM
EUMERISTIC
EUMEROMORPH
EUMITOSIS
EUMITOTIC
EUMOIROUS
EUMOLPIQUE
EUMORPHOUS
EUMYCETE
EUMYCETIC
EUNICID
EUNOMY
EUNUCH
EUNUCHAL
EUNUCHOID
EUNUCHOIDISM
EUNUCHRY
EUOMPHALID
EUONYM
EUONYMIN
EUONYMOUS
EUONYMUS
EUONYMY
EUOSMITE
EUOUAE
EUPAD
EUPATHY
EUPATORIN
EUPATORIUM
EUPATORY
EUPATRID
EUPATRIDAE
EUPATRIDS
EUPEPSIA
EUPEPSY
EUPEPTIC
EUPEPTICISM
EUPEPTICITY
EUPHAUSID
EUPHEMIAN
EUPHEMIOUS
EUPHEMIOUSLY
EUPHEMISM
EUPHEMIST
EUPHEMISTIC
EUPHEMIZE
EUPHEMIZED
EUPHEMIZER
EUPHEMIZING
EUPHEMOUS
EUPHEMY
EUPHON
EUPHONE
EUPHONETIC
EUPHONETICS
EUPHONIA
EUPHONIC
EUPHONICAL
EUPHONICALLY
EUPHONIES
EUPHONIOUS

EUPHONIOUSLY
EUPHONISM
EUPHONIUM
EUPHONIZE
EUPHONIZED
EUPHONIZING
EUPHONON
EUPHONOUS
EUPHONY
EUPHONYM
EUPHORBIA
EUPHORBIAL
EUPHORBIUM
EUPHORIA
EUPHORIC
EUPHORY
EUPHRASY
EUPHROE
EUPHUISM
EUPHUIST
EUPHUISTIC
EUPHUISTICALLY
EUPHUIZE
EUPHUIZED
EUPHUIZING
EUPION
EUPIONE
EUPITTONE
EUPLASTIC
EUPLOID
EUPLOIDY
EUPNEA
EUPNOEA
EUPOLYZOAN
EUPRACTIC
EUPRAXIA
EUPSYCHICS
EUPYRCHROITE
EUPYRENE
EUPYRION
EURE
EUREKA
EURHODINE
EURHODOL
EURHYTHMIC
EURHYTHMICAL
EURHYTHMICS
EURHYTHMY
EURIPUS
EURITE
EURO
EUROBIN
EUROPIUM
EUROUS
EURYALIDAN
EURYBENTHIC
EURYCEPHALIC
EURYGNATHIC
EURYGNATHISM
EURYGNATHOUS
EURYHALINE
EURYLAIMOID
EURYON
EURYPROSOPIC
EURYPTERID
EURYPTEROID
EURYPYLOUS
EURYSCOPE
EURYTE
EURYTHERMAL
EURYTHERMIC
EURYTHMIC
EURYTHMICAL
EURYTHMICS
EURYTHMY
EURYTOMID
EURYZYGOUS

EUSOL	EVANGELIST	EVENTUALLY	EVINCE	EXACTER
EUSTACY	EVANGELISTARIES	EVENTUATE	EVINCED	EXACTING
EUSTATIC	EVANGELISTARY	EVENTUATED	EVINCEMENT	EXACTINGLY
EUSTELE	EVANGELISTIC	EVENTUATING	EVINCIBLE	EXACTINGNESS
EUSTOMATOUS	EVANGELIUM	EVENWISE	EVINCING	EXACTION
EUSTYLE	EVANGELIZE	EVEQUE	EVINCIVE	EXACTITUDE
EUSUCHIAN	EVANGELIZED	EVER	EVIRATE	EXACTIVE
EUSYNCHITE	EVANGELIZER	EVERBEARER	EVIRATO	EXACTIVENESS
EUTAXIC	EVANGELIZING	EVERBEARING	EVISCERATE	EXACTLY
EUTAXIE	EVANID	EVERBLOOMING	EVISCERATED	EXACTMENT
EUTAXITE	EVANISH	EVERDURING	EVISCERATING	EXACTNESS
EUTAXITIC	EVANISHED	EVERGLADE	EVISCERATION	EXACTOR
EUTAXY	EVANISHING	EVERGLADES	EVISITE	EXACUATE
EUTECHNIC	EVANISHMENT	EVERGREEN	EVITABLE	EXADVERSO
EUTECHNICS	EVANSITE	EVERGREENERY	EVITATE	EXADVERSUM
EUTECTIC	EVAPORABLE	EVERGREENITE	EVITATION	EXAGGERATE
EUTECTOID	EVAPORATE	EVERICH	EVITE	EXAGGERATED
EUTELEGENIC	EVAPORATED	EVERLASTING	EVITTATE	EXAGGERATING
EUTEXIA	EVAPORATING	EVERLASTINGLY	EVOCABLE	EXAGGERATION
EUTHANASIA	EVAPORATION	EVERLIVING	EVOCATE	EXAGGERATIVE
EUTHANASY	EVAPORATIVE	EVERLY	EVOCATED	EXAGGERATOR
EUTHENICS	EVAPORATIVITY	EVERMO	EVOCATING	EXAGGERATORY
EUTHENIST	EVAPORATOR	EVERMORE	EVOCATION	EXAGITATE
EUTHERMIC	EVAPORIMETER	EVERNIOID	EVOCATIVE	EXAIRESIS
EUTHYTROPIC	EVAPORIZE	EVERSE	EVOCATOR	EXALATE
EUTOCIA	EVASE	EVERSIBLE	EVOCATORY	EXALBUMINOSE
EUTOMOUS	EVASIBLE	EVERSION	EVOE	EXALBUMINOUS
EUTROPHIC	EVASION	EVERSIVE	EVOHE	EXALLOTRIOTE
EUTROPHY	EVASIONAL	EVERSPORTING	EVOID	EXALT
EUTROPIC	EVASIVE	EVERT	EVOKE	EXALTATE
EUTROPOUS	EVASIVELY	EVERTEBRAL	EVOKED	EXALTATION
EUXANTHATE	EVASIVENESS	EVERTEBRATE	EVOKER	EXALTATIVE
EUXANTHONE	EVE	EVERTED	EVOKING	EXALTE
EUXENITE	EVECHURR	EVERTILE	EVOLUTE	EXALTED
EVACUANT	EVECK	EVERTING	EVOLUTION	EXALTEDLY
EVACUATE	EVECTION	EVERTOR	EVOLUTIONAL	EXALTEDNESS
EVACUATED	EVECTIONAL	EVERWHICH	EVOLUTIONARY	EXALTEE
EVACUATING	EVEJAR	EVERWHO	EVOLUTIONISM	EXALTER
EVACUATION	EVEL	EVERY	EVOLUTIONIST	EXALTING
EVACUATOR	EVELIGHT	EVERYBODY	EVOLUTIONIZE	EXAM
EVACUE	EVELONG	EVERYDAY	EVOLUTIVE	EXAMEN
EVACUEE	EVEN	EVERYHOW	EVOLVABLE	EXAMINABLE
EVADABLE	EVENDOWN	EVERYLIKE	EVOLVE	EXAMINANT
EVADE	EVENE	EVERYONE	EVOLVEMENT	EXAMINATE
EVADED	EVENED	EVERYTHING	EVOLVENT	EXAMINATION
EVADER	EVENER	EVERYWHERE	EVOME	EXAMINATIONAL
EVADIBLE	EVENFALL	EVERYWHERES	EVOMIT	EXAMINATIVE
EVADING	EVENGLOME	EVERYWHITHER	EVONYMUS	EXAMINATOR
EVAGATION	EVENGLOW	EVESTAR	EVOVAE	EXAMINATORY
EVAGINABLE	EVENHAND	EVET	EVULGATE	EXAMINE
EVAGINATE	EVENHANDED	EVETIDE	EVULGATION	EXAMINED
EVAGINATED	EVENHANDEDLY	EVEWEED	EVULGE	EXAMINEE
EVAGINATING	EVENING	EVIBRATE	EVULSE	EXAMINER
EVAGINATION	EVENK	EVICKE	EVULSION	EXAMINING
EVALUABLE	EVENLONG	EVICT	EVZONE	EXAMPLE
EVALUATE	EVENLY	EVICTED	EVZONES	EXAMPLED
EVALUATED	EVENMETE	EVICTING	EWAGE	EXAMPLING
EVALUATING	EVENMINDED	EVICTION	EWDER	EXANIMATE
EVALUATION	EVENNESS	EVICTOR	EWE	EXANIMATION
EVALUATIVE	EVENOO	EVIDENCE	EWELEASE	EXANTHEM
EVALUE	EVENS	EVIDENCED	EWER	EXANTHEMA
EVANESCE	EVENSONG	EVIDENCING	EWERER	EXANTHEMAS
EVANESCED	EVENT	EVIDENCIVE	EWERIES	EXANTHEMATA
EVANESCENCE	EVENTAIL	EVIDENT	EWERY	EXANTHEMATIC
EVANESCENCY	EVENTFUL	EVIDENTIAL	EWEST	EXANTLATE
EVANESCENT	EVENTFULLY	EVIDENTIALLY	EWHOW	EXANTLATION
EVANESCENTLY	EVENTFULNESS	EVIDENTIARY	EWK	EXARATE
EVANESCIBLE	EVENTIDE	EVIDENTLY	EWRY	EXARATION
EVANESCING	EVENTLESS	EVIL	EX	EXARCH
EVANGEL	EVENTLESSLY	EVILDOER	EXACERBATE	EXARCHAL
EVANGELIAN	EVENTOGNATH	EVILHEARTED	EXACERBATED	EXARCHATE
EVANGELIC	EVENTRATION	EVILLY	EXACERBATING	EXARCHIST
EVANGELICAL	EVENTS	EVILNESS	EXACERBATION	EXARCHY
EVANGELICALLY	EVENTUAL	EVILSAYER	EXACT	EXARTERITIS
EVANGELICITY	EVENTUALITIES	EVILSPEAKER	EXACTA	EXARTICULATE
EVANGELION	EVENTUALITY	EVILSPEAKING	EXACTABLE	EXASPER
EVANGELISM	EVENTUALIZE	EVILWISHING	EXACTED	EXASPERATE

EXASPERATED
EXASPERATER
EXASPERATING
EXASPERATION
EXASPERATIVE
EXASPIDEAN
EXAUCTORATE
EXAUGURATE
EXAUGURATION
EXAUTHORIZE
EXCALATE
EXCALATION
EXCALCARATE
EXCALCEATE
EXCAMB
EXCAMBER
EXCAMBION
EXCANDESCENT
EXCANTATION
EXCARNATE
EXCARNATION
EXCATHEDRAL
EXCAUDATE
EXCAVATE
EXCAVATED
EXCAVATING
EXCAVATION
EXCAVATIONS
EXCAVATOR
EXCAVE
EXCECATE
EXCECATION
EXCEDENT
EXCEED
EXCEEDED
EXCEEDING
EXCEEDINGLY
EXCEL
EXCELENTE
EXCELLED
EXCELLENCE
EXCELLENCIES
EXCELLENCY
EXCELLENT
EXCELLENTLY
EXCELLING
EXCELS
EXCELSE
EXCELSIN
EXCELSIOR
EXCENTRAL
EXCENTRIC
EXCEPT
EXCEPTANT
EXCEPTED
EXCEPTER
EXCEPTING
EXCEPTIO
EXCEPTION
EXCEPTIONAL
EXCEPTIONALLY
EXCEPTIONARY
EXCEPTIONER
EXCEPTIOUS
EXCEPTIVE
EXCEPTIVELY
EXCERN
EXCERPT
EXCERPTA
EXCERPTED
EXCERPTIBLE
EXCERPTING
EXCERPTION
EXCERPTIVE
EXCERPTOR
EXCESS
EXCESSIVE

EXCESSIVELY
EXCESSIVENESS
EXCESSMAN
EXCESSMEN
EXCHANGE
EXCHANGEABLE
EXCHANGEABLY
EXCHANGED
EXCHANGER
EXCHANGING
EXCHEAT
EXCHEQUER
EXCIDE
EXCIDED
EXCIDING
EXCIPIENT
EXCIPLE
EXCIPULAR
EXCIPULE
EXCIPULIFORM
EXCIPULUM
EXCIRCLE
EXCISABLE
EXCISE
EXCISED
EXCISEMAN
EXCISEMEN
EXCISING
EXCISION
EXCISOR
EXCITABILITIES
EXCITABILITY
EXCITABLE
EXCITABLENESS
EXCITABLY
EXCITANCY
EXCITANT
EXCITATE
EXCITATION
EXCITATIVE
EXCITATOR
EXCITATORY
EXCITE
EXCITED
EXCITEDLY
EXCITEDNESS
EXCITEMENT
EXCITER
EXCITING
EXCITINGLY
EXCITIVE
EXCITOMOTOR
EXCITOMOTORY
EXCITON
EXCITOR
EXCITORY
EXCITRON
EXCLAIM
EXCLAIMED
EXCLAIMER
EXCLAIMING
EXCLAMATION
EXCLAMATIONAL
EXCLAMATIVE
EXCLAMATIVELY
EXCLAMATORILY
EXCLAMATORY
EXCLAVE
EXCLUDE
EXCLUDED
EXCLUDER
EXCLUDING
EXCLUSION
EXCLUSIONARY
EXCLUSIONER
EXCLUSIONISM
EXCLUSIONIST

EXCLUSIVE
EXCLUSIVELY
EXCLUSIVENESS
EXCLUSIVISM
EXCLUSIVITY
EXCLUSORY
EXCOCT
EXCOCTION
EXCOGITABLE
EXCOGITATE
EXCOGITATED
EXCOGITATING
EXCOGITATION
EXCOGITATIVE
EXCOGITATOR
EXCOMMUNICABLE
EXCOMMUNICANT
EXCOMMUNICATE
EXCOMMUNICATED
EXCOMMUNICATING
EXCOMMUNICATION
EXCOMMUNICATIVE
EXCOMMUNICATOR
EXCOMMUNICATORY
EXCOMMUNION
EXCONJUGANT
EXCORIABLE
EXCORIATE
EXCORIATED
EXCORIATING
EXCORIATION
EXCORIATOR
EXCORTICATE
EXCORTICATED
EXCORTICATING
EXCORTICATION
EXCREMENT
EXCREMENTAL
EXCREMENTARY
EXCREMENTIVE
EXCRESCE
EXCRESCENCE
EXCRESCENCES
EXCRESCENCIES
EXCRESCENCY
EXCRESCENT
EXCRESCENTIAL
EXCRETA
EXCRETAL
EXCRETE
EXCRETED
EXCRETER
EXCRETES
EXCRETING
EXCRETION
EXCRETIONARY
EXCRETIVE
EXCRETORY
EXCRIMINATE
EXCRUCIABLE
EXCRUCIATE
EXCRUCIATED
EXCRUCIATING
EXCRUCIATINGLY
EXCRUCIATION
EXCRUCIATOR
EXCUBANT
EXCUDATE
EXCUDERUNT
EXCUDIT
EXCULPABLE
EXCULPATE
EXCULPATED
EXCULPATING
EXCULPATION
EXCULPATIVE
EXCULPATORY

EXCUR
EXCURRENT
EXCURSE
EXCURSED
EXCURSING
EXCURSION
EXCURSIONAL
EXCURSIONARY
EXCURSIONER
EXCURSIONISM
EXCURSIONIST
EXCURSIONIZE
EXCURSIVE
EXCURSIVELY
EXCURSUS
EXCURVATE
EXCURVATED
EXCURVATURE
EXCURVED
EXCUSABILITY
EXCUSABLE
EXCUSABLENESS
EXCUSABLY
EXCUSAL
EXCUSATIVE
EXCUSATOR
EXCUSATORY
EXCUSE
EXCUSED
EXCUSER
EXCUSING
EXCUSIVE
EXCUSS
EXCUSSED
EXCUSSING
EXCYST
EXCYSTATION
EXCYSTED
EXCYSTMENT
EXEAT
EXEC
EXECRABLE
EXECRABLENESS
EXECRABLY
EXECRATE
EXECRATED
EXECRATING
EXECRATION
EXECRATIVE
EXECRATOR
EXECRATORY
EXECUTABLE
EXECUTANCY
EXECUTANT
EXECUTE
EXECUTED
EXECUTER
EXECUTING
EXECUTION
EXECUTIONAL
EXECUTIONEERING
EXECUTIONER
EXECUTIONERESS
EXECUTIONS
EXECUTIVE
EXECUTIVELY
EXECUTIVENESS
EXECUTOR
EXECUTORIAL
EXECUTORY
EXECUTRESS
EXECUTRICES
EXECUTRIX
EXECUTRIXES
EXECUTRY
EXEDE
EXEDENT

EXEDRA
EXEEM
EXEGESES
EXEGESIS
EXEGETE
EXEGETIC
EXEGETICAL
EXEGETICALLY
EXEGETICS
EXEGETIST
EXEME
EXEMPLA
EXEMPLAR
EXEMPLARIC
EXEMPLARILY
EXEMPLARINESS
EXEMPLARISM
EXEMPLARITY
EXEMPLARY
EXEMPLIFICATION
EXEMPLIFIED
EXEMPLIFIER
EXEMPLIFY
EXEMPLIFYING
EXEMPLUM
EXEMPT
EXEMPTIBLE
EXEMPTILE
EXEMPTION
EXEMPTIVE
EXENCEPHALIA
EXENCEPHALIC
EXENCEPHALUS
EXENTERATE
EXENTERATED
EXENTERATING
EXENTERATION
EXEQUATUR
EXEQUIAL
EXEQUIES
EXEQUY
EXERCE
EXERCENT
EXERCISABLE
EXERCISE
EXERCISED
EXERCISER
EXERCISES
EXERCISING
EXERCITANT
EXERCITATION
EXERCITOR
EXERCITORIAL
EXERESIS
EXERGUAL
EXERGUE
EXERT
EXERTED
EXERTING
EXERTION
EXERTIVE
EXES
EXESION
EXEUNT
EXFIGURATION
EXFIGURE
EXFILTRATION
EXFLAGELLATE
EXFLECT
EXFODIATE
EXFODIATION
EXFOLIATE
EXFOLIATED
EXFOLIATING
EXFOLIATION
EXFOLIATIVE
EXFOLIATORY

EXHALABLE
EXHALANT
EXHALATE
EXHALATION
EXHALATORY
EXHALE
EXHALED
EXHALING
EXHANCE
EXHAUST
EXHAUSTED
EXHAUSTEDLY
EXHAUSTEDNESS
EXHAUSTER
EXHAUSTIBLE
EXHAUSTING
EXHAUSTINGLY
EXHAUSTION
EXHAUSTIVE
EXHAUSTIVELY
EXHAUSTIVENESS
EXHAUSTLESS
EXHAUSTLESSLY
EXHEDRA
EXHIBIT
EXHIBITANT
EXHIBITED
EXHIBITING
EXHIBITION
EXHIBITIONAL
EXHIBITIONER
EXHIBITIONISM
EXHIBITIONIST
EXHIBITIONISTIC
EXHIBITIVE
EXHIBITIVELY
EXHIBITOR
EXHIBITORSHIP
EXHIBITORY
EXHIBITS
EXHILARANT
EXHILARATE
EXHILARATED
EXHILARATING
EXHILARATINGLY
EXHILARATION
EXHILARATIVE
EXHILARATOR
EXHILARATORY
EXHORT
EXHORTATION
EXHORTATIVE
EXHORTATIVELY
EXHORTATORY
EXHORTED
EXHORTER
EXHORTING
EXHUMATE
EXHUMATED
EXHUMATING
EXHUMATION
EXHUMATOR
EXHUMATORY
EXHUME
EXHUMED
EXHUMER
EXHUMING
EXIDO
EXIES
EXIGEANT
EXIGEANTE
EXIGENCE
EXIGENCIES
EXIGENCY
EXIGENT
EXIGENTER
EXIGENTLY

EXIGIBLE
EXIGUITY
EXIGUOUS
EXIGUOUSLY
EXIGUOUSNESS
EXILARCH
EXILARCHATE
EXILE
EXILED
EXILER
EXILIAN
EXILIC
EXILING
EXILITY
EXIMIOUS
EXIMIOUSLY
EXIMIOUSNESS
EXINANITE
EXINANITION
EXINE
EXINGUINAL
EXINITE
EXIST
EXISTED
EXISTENCE
EXISTENT
EXISTENTIAL
EXISTENTIALISM
EXISTENTIALIST
EXISTENTIALLY
EXISTENTLY
EXISTER
EXISTING
EXISTLESSNESS
EXIT
EXITE
EXITIAL
EXITION
EXITIOUS
EXITURE
EXITUS
EXLEX
EXOARTERITIS
EXOCARDIA
EXOCARDIAC
EXOCARDIAL
EXOCARP
EXOCCIPITAL
EXOCENTRIC
EXOCHORION
EXOCLINAL
EXOCLINE
EXOCOELAR
EXOCOELE
EXOCOELIC
EXOCOELOM
EXOCOELUM
EXOCOLITIS
EXOCONE
EXOCULATE
EXOCULATED
EXOCULATING
EXOCYCLIC
EXODE
EXODERM
EXODERMIS
EXODIC
EXODIST
EXODIUM
EXODONTIA
EXODROMIC
EXODROMY
EXODUS
EXODY
EXOENZYME
EXOGAMIC
EXOGAMOUS

EXOGAMY
EXOGASTRIC
EXOGASTRICALLY
EXOGASTRITIS
EXOGEN
EXOGENETIC
EXOGENIC
EXOGENOUS
EXOGENOUSLY
EXOGNATHION
EXOGNATHITE
EXOGRAPH
EXOLEMMA
EXOLETE
EXOLVE
EXOMETRITIS
EXOMION
EXOMIS
EXOMOLOGESIS
EXOMORPHIC
EXOMORPHISM
EXOMPHALOS
EXOMPHALOUS
EXOMPHALUS
EXON
EXONARTHEX
EXONER
EXONERATE
EXONERATED
EXONERATING
EXONERATION
EXONERATIVE
EXONERATOR
EXONERETUR
EXONEURAL
EXOPATHIC
EXOPERIDIUM
EXOPHAGOUS
EXOPHAGY
EXOPHORIA
EXOPHORIC
EXOPHTHALMIA
EXOPHTHALMIC
EXOPHTHALMOS
EXOPHTHALMUS
EXOPOD
EXOPODITE
EXOPODITIC
EXORABILITY
EXORABLE
EXORABLENESS
EXORATE
EXORBITAL
EXORBITANCE
EXORBITANCY
EXORBITANT
EXORBITANTLY
EXORBITATE
EXORBITATION
EXORCISATION
EXORCISE
EXORCISED
EXORCISEMENT
EXORCISER
EXORCISING
EXORCISM
EXORCISMAL
EXORCISORY
EXORCIST
EXORCISTIC
EXORCISTICAL
EXORCIZATION
EXORCIZE
EXORCIZED
EXORCIZEMENT
EXORCIZER
EXORCIZING

EXORDIAL
EXORDIUM
EXORDIUMS
EXORDIZE
EXORGANIC
EXORMIA
EXORN
EXORNATION
EXOSEPSIS
EXOSKELETAL
EXOSKELETON
EXOSMIC
EXOSMOSIS
EXOSMOTIC
EXOSPERM
EXOSPHERE
EXOSPHERIC
EXOSPORAL
EXOSPORE
EXOSPORIUM
EXOSPOROUS
EXOSTOME
EXOSTOSED
EXOSTOSES
EXOSTOSIS
EXOSTOTIC
EXOSTRA
EXOSTRACISM
EXOSTRACIZE
EXOSTRAE
EXOTERIC
EXOTERICAL
EXOTERICALLY
EXOTERICISM
EXOTERICS
EXOTHECA
EXOTHECAL
EXOTHECATE
EXOTHECIUM
EXOTHERMAL
EXOTHERMIC
EXOTHERMOUS
EXOTIC
EXOTICALLY
EXOTICALNESS
EXOTICISM
EXOTICIST
EXOTICITY
EXOTICNESS
EXOTISM
EXOTOSPORE
EXOTOXIC
EXOTOXIN
EXOTROPIA
EXOTROPISM
EXPALPATE
EXPAND
EXPANDED
EXPANDEDLY
EXPANDEDNESS
EXPANDER
EXPANDING
EXPANDINGLY
EXPANSE
EXPANSIBILITY
EXPANSIBLE
EXPANSIBLENESS
EXPANSIBLY
EXPANSILE
EXPANSION
EXPANSIONAL
EXPANSIONISM
EXPANSIONIST
EXPANSIVE
EXPANSIVELY
EXPANSIVENESS
EXPANSIVITY

EXPANSUM
EXPANSURE
EXPATIATE
EXPATIATED
EXPATIATER
EXPATIATING
EXPATIATION
EXPATIATIVE
EXPATIATOR
EXPATIATORY
EXPATRIATE
EXPATRIATED
EXPATRIATING
EXPATRIATION
EXPECT
EXPECTABLE
EXPECTANCE
EXPECTANCIES
EXPECTANCY
EXPECTANT
EXPECTANTLY
EXPECTATION
EXPECTATIVE
EXPECTED
EXPECTER
EXPECTING
EXPECTIVE
EXPECTORANT
EXPECTORATE
EXPECTORATED
EXPECTORATING
EXPECTORATION
EXPECTORATOR
EXPEDE
EXPEDED
EXPEDIATE
EXPEDIENCE
EXPEDIENCIES
EXPEDIENCY
EXPEDIENT
EXPEDIENTE
EXPEDIENTIAL
EXPEDIENTIALLY
EXPEDIENTIST
EXPEDIENTLY
EXPEDING
EXPEDITATE
EXPEDITATED
EXPEDITATING
EXPEDITATION
EXPEDITE
EXPEDITED
EXPEDITELY
EXPEDITENESS
EXPEDITER
EXPEDITING
EXPEDITION
EXPEDITIONARY
EXPEDITIONIST
EXPEDITIOUS
EXPEDITIOUSLY
EXPEDITIOUSNESS
EXPEDITOR
EXPEL
EXPELLABLE
EXPELLANT
EXPELLED
EXPELLEE
EXPELLENT
EXPELLER
EXPELLING
EXPEND
EXPENDABILITY
EXPENDABLE
EXPENDED
EXPENDER
EXPENDING

EXPENDITOR	EXPLAINER	EXPORTATION	EXPURGATE	EXTEMPORIZER
EXPENDITRIX	EXPLAINING	EXPORTED	EXPURGATED	EXTEMPORIZING
EXPENDITURE	EXPLANATE	EXPORTER	EXPURGATING	EXTEND
EXPENSE	EXPLANATION	EXPORTING	EXPURGATION	EXTENDED
EXPENSEFUL	EXPLANATIVE	EXPOSAL	EXPURGATIVE	EXTENDEDLY
EXPENSEFULNESS	EXPLANATIVELY	EXPOSE	EXPURGATOR	EXTENDEDNESS
EXPENSES	EXPLANATOR	EXPOSED	EXPURGATORIAL	EXTENDER
EXPENSILATION	EXPLANATORILY	EXPOSER	EXPURGATORY	EXTENDIBILITY
EXPENSIVE	EXPLANATORINES	EXPOSING	EXPURGE	EXTENDIBLE
EXPENSIVELY	EXPLANATORY	EXPOSIT	EXQUIRE	EXTENDING
EXPENSIVENESS	EXPLANT	EXPOSITION	EXQUISITE	EXTENSE
EXPENTHESIS	EXPLANTATION	EXPOSITIONAL	EXQUISITELY	EXTENSIBILITY
EXPERIENCE	EXPLAT	EXPOSITIONARY	EXQUISITENESS	EXTENSIBLE
EXPERIENCED	EXPLEMENT	EXPOSITIVE	EXQUISITISM	EXTENSIBLENESS
EXPERIENCER	EXPLEMENTAL	EXPOSITIVELY	EXQUISITIVELY	EXTENSILE
EXPERIENCES	EXPLETE	EXPOSITOR	EXQUISITIVENES	EXTENSIMETER
EXPERIENCING	EXPLETIVE	EXPOSITORIAL	EXRADIO	EXTENSION
EXPERIENT	EXPLETIVELY	EXPOSITORIALLY	EXRADIUS	EXTENSIONAL
EXPERIENTIAL	EXPLETIVENESS	EXPOSITORILY	EXRUPEAL	EXTENSIONIST
EXPERIENTIALLY	EXPLETORY	EXPOSITORINESS	EXSANGUINATE	EXTENSITY
EXPERIMENT	EXPLICABLE	EXPOSITORY	EXSANGUINE	EXTENSIVE
EXPERIMENTAL	EXPLICATE	EXPOSTULATE	EXSANGUINOUS	EXTENSIVELY
EXPERIMENTALISM	EXPLICATED	EXPOSTULATED	EXSANGUIOUS	EXTENSIVENESS
EXPERIMENTALIST	EXPLICATING	EXPOSTULATING	EXSCIND	EXTENSOMETER
EXPERIMENTALIZE	EXPLICATION	EXPOSTULATION	EXSCINDING	EXTENSOR
EXPERIMENTALLY	EXPLICATIVE	EXPOSTULATIVE	EXSCRIBE	EXTENSUM
EXPERIMENTARIAN	EXPLICATOR	EXPOSTULATIVELY	EXSCRIPT	EXTENT
EXPERIMENTATION	EXPLICATORY	EXPOSTULATOR	EXSCRIPTURAL	EXTENUATE
EXPERIMENTATIVE	EXPLICIT	EXPOSTULATORY	EXSCULPTATE	EXTENUATED
EXPERIMENTATOR	EXPLICITLY	EXPOSURE	EXSCUTELLATE	EXTENUATING
EXPERIMENTED	EXPLICITNESS	EXPOUND	EXSECANT	EXTENUATINGLY
EXPERIMENTEE	EXPLODE	EXPOUNDED	EXSECT	EXTENUATION
EXPERIMENTER	EXPLODED	EXPOUNDER	EXSECTILE	EXTENUATIVE
EXPERIMENTING	EXPLODENT	EXPOUNDING	EXSECTION	EXTENUATOR
EXPERIMENTIST	EXPLODER	EXPREME	EXSECTOR	EXTENUATORY
EXPERIMENTIZE	EXPLODING	EXPRESS	EXSERT	EXTER
EXPERIMENTLY	EXPLOIT	EXPRESSAGE	EXSERTED	EXTERIOR
EXPERMENTIZED	EXPLOITABLE	EXPRESSED	EXSERTILE	EXTERIORATE
EXPERT	EXPLOITAGE	EXPRESSER	EXSERTING	EXTERIORATION
EXPERTISE	EXPLOITATION	EXPRESSIBLE	EXSERTION	EXTERIORITY
EXPERTLY	EXPLOITATIONIST	EXPRESSING	EXSHEATH	EXTERIORIZATION
EXPERTNESS	EXPLOITATIVE	EXPRESSION	EXSIBILATE	EXTERIORIZE
EXPIABLE	EXPLOITED	EXPRESSIONAL	EXSICCATAE	EXTERIORIZED
EXPIATE	EXPLOITER	EXPRESSIONISM	EXSICCATE	EXTERIORIZING
EXPIATED	EXPLOITING	EXPRESSIONIST	EXSICCATED	EXTERIORLY
EXPIATING	EXPLOITIVE	EXPRESSIONISTIC	EXSICCATING	EXTERIORNESS
EXPIATION	EXPLOITURE	EXPRESSIONLESS	EXSICCATION	EXTERMINATE
EXPIATIONAL	EXPLORATION	EXPRESSIONLESSLY	EXSICCATIVE	EXTERMINATED
EXPIATIST	EXPLORATIONAL	EXPRESSIVE	EXSILIENCY	EXTERMINATING
EXPIATIVE	EXPLORATIVE	EXPRESSIVELY	EXSOLVE	EXTERMINATION
EXPIATOR	EXPLORATIVELY	EXPRESSIVENESS	EXSOMATIC	EXTERMINATIVE
EXPIATORINESS	EXPLORATIVENESS	EXPRESSLESS	EXSPUITION	EXTERMINATOR
EXPIATORY	EXPLORATOR	EXPRESSLY	EXSPUTORY	EXTERMINATORY
EXPILATE	EXPLORATORY	EXPRESSMAN	EXSTIPULATE	EXTERMINE
EXPILATION	EXPLORE	EXPRESSWAY	EXSTROPHY	EXTERN
EXPILATOR	EXPLORED	EXPROBATE	EXSUCCOUS	EXTERNA
EXPIRANT	EXPLOREMENT	EXPROBRATORY	EXSUCTION	EXTERNAL
EXPIRATE	EXPLORER	EXPROMISSION	EXSUFFLATE	EXTERNALISM
EXPIRATION	EXPLORING	EXPROPRIATE	EXSUFFLATION	EXTERNALIST
EXPIRATOR	EXPLOSIBILITY	EXPROPRIATED	EXSUFFLICATE	EXTERNALISTIC
EXPIRATORY	EXPLOSIBLE	EXPROPRIATING	EXSURGE	EXTERNALITIES
EXPIRE	EXPLOSION	EXPROPRIATION	EXSURGENT	EXTERNALITY
EXPIRED	EXPLOSIONIST	EXPROPRIATOR	EXTANCY	EXTERNALIZATION
EXPIREE	EXPLOSIVE	EXPUGN	EXTANT	EXTERNALIZE
EXPIRER	EXPLOSIVELY	EXPUGNABLE	EXTEMPORAL	EXTERNALLY
EXPIRIES	EXPLOSIVENESS	EXPUITION	EXTEMPORALLY	EXTERNAT
EXPIRING	EXPLOSIVES	EXPULSATORY	EXTEMPORALNESS	EXTERNATE
EXPIRY	EXPONE	EXPULSE	EXTEMPORANEOUS	EXTERNATION
EXPISCATE	EXPONENCE	EXPULSER	EXTEMPORANEOUSLY	EXTERNE
EXPISCATED	EXPONENT	EXPULSION	EXTEMPORANEOUSNESS	EXTERNIZATION
EXPISCATING	EXPONENTIAL	EXPULSIVE	EXTEMPORARILY	EXTERNIZE
EXPISCATION	EXPONENTIALLY	EXPULSORY	EXTEMPORARINESS	EXTERNUM
EXPISCATOR	EXPONENTS	EXPUNCTION	EXTEMPORARY	EXTEROCEPTIST
EXPISCATORY	EXPONIBLE	EXPUNGE	EXTEMPORE	EXTEROCEPTIVE
EXPLAIN	EXPORT	EXPUNGED	EXTEMPORIZE	EXTEROCEPTOR
EXPLAINABLE	EXPORTABILITY	EXPUNGER	EXTEMPORIZED	EXTERRANEOUS
EXPLAINED	EXPORTABLE	EXPUNGING	EXTEMPORIZED	EXTERRESTRIAL

EXTERRITORIAL
EXTILL
EXTIMA
EXTIME
EXTINCT
EXTINCTEUR
EXTINCTION
EXTINCTIVE
EXTINCTOR
EXTINE
EXTINGUISH
EXTINGUISHED
EXTINGUISHER
EXTIRP
EXTIRPATE
EXTIRPATED
EXTIRPATING
EXTIRPATION
EXTIRPATIVE
EXTIRPATOR
EXTIRPATORY
EXTISPEX
EXTISPICES
EXTISPICIOUS
EXTISPICY
EXTOGENOUS
EXTOL
EXTOLL
EXTOLLATION
EXTOLLED
EXTOLLER
EXTOLLING
EXTOLLMENT
EXTOLMENT
EXTOOLITIC
EXTORSIVE
EXTORSIVELY
EXTORT
EXTORTED
EXTORTER
EXTORTING
EXTORTION
EXTORTIONARY
EXTORTIONATE
EXTORTIONER
EXTORTIONIST
EXTORTIVE
EXTRA
EXTRABOLD
EXTRABULBAR
EXTRACAPSULAR
EXTRACARPAL
EXTRACOSTAL
EXTRACT
EXTRACTABLE
EXTRACTED
EXTRACTIBLE
EXTRACTIFORM
EXTRACTING
EXTRACTION
EXTRACTIVE
EXTRACTOR
EXTRACTS
EXTRACURRICULAR
EXTRACYSTIC
EXTRADITABLE
EXTRADITE
EXTRADITED
EXTRADITING
EXTRADITION
EXTRADOS
EXTRADOSED
EXTRADOTAL
EXTRADUCTION
EXTRAENTERIC
EXTRAFORMAL
EXTRAGALACTIC

EXTRAJUDICIAL
EXTRALATERAL
EXTRALITE
EXTRALITY
EXTRAMUNDANE
EXTRAMURAL
EXTRAMURALLY
EXTRANEAN
EXTRANEITY
EXTRANEOUS
EXTRANEOUSLY
EXTRANEOUSNESS
EXTRAORDINARIES
EXTRAORDINARILY
EXTRAORDINARY
EXTRAPHYSICAL
EXTRAPOLAR
EXTRAPOLATE
EXTRAPOLATED
EXTRAPOLATING
EXTRAPOLATION
EXTRAPOLATIVE
EXTRAPOLATOR
EXTRARED
EXTRAREGULAR
EXTRARETINAL
EXTRASENSORY
EXTRASEROUS
EXTRASOLAR
EXTRASTAPEDIAL
EXTRASYSTOLE
EXTRATARSAL
EXTRATERRESTRIAL
EXTRATRIBAL
EXTRATUBAL
EXTRAUTERINE
EXTRAVAGANCE
EXTRAVAGANCIES
EXTRAVAGANCY
EXTRAVAGANT
EXTRAVAGANTLY
EXTRAVAGANTNESS
EXTRAVAGANZA
EXTRAVAGATE
EXTRAVAGATED
EXTRAVAGATING
EXTRAVAGATION
EXTRAVAGINAL
EXTRAVASATE
EXTRAVASATED
EXTRAVASATING
EXTRAVASATION
EXTRAVASCULAR
EXTRAVENTRICULAR
EXTRAVERSION
EXTRAVERT
EXTRAVIOLET
EXTRE
EXTREAT
EXTREME
EXTREMELY
EXTREMENESS
EXTREMER
EXTREMES
EXTREMEST
EXTREMISM
EXTREMIST
EXTREMISTIC
EXTREMITAL
EXTREMITIES
EXTREMITY
EXTREMUM
EXTRICABLE
EXTRICABLY
EXTRICATE
EXTRICATED
EXTRICATING

EXTRICATION
EXTRINSIC
EXTRINSICAL
EXTRINSICALLY
EXTRINSICATE
EXTROITIVE
EXTROPICAL
EXTRORSAL
EXTRORSE
EXTRORSELY
EXTROSPECT
EXTROSPECTION
EXTROSPECTIVE
EXTROVERSION
EXTROVERSIVE
EXTROVERT
EXTRUCT
EXTRUDE
EXTRUDED
EXTRUDER
EXTRUDING
EXTRUSILE
EXTRUSION
EXTRUSIVE
EXTRUSORY
EXTUBATE
EXTUBATION
EXTUMESCENCE
EXTUND
EXTURB
EXTUSION
EXUBERANCE
EXUBERANCY
EXUBERANT
EXUBERANTLY
EXUBERANTNESS
EXUBERATE
EXUBERATED
EXUBERATING
EXUBERATION
EXUDATE
EXUDATION
EXUDATIVE
EXUDATORY
EXUDE
EXUDED
EXUDENCE
EXUDING
EXUL
EXULATE
EXULCERATE
EXULCERATED
EXULCERATING
EXULCERATION
EXULCERATIVE
EXULCERATORY
EXULT
EXULTANCY
EXULTANT
EXULTANTLY
EXULTATION
EXULTED
EXULTET
EXULTING
EXULTINGLY
EXULULATE
EXUMBRAL
EXUMBRELLA
EXUMBRELLAR
EXUNDATE
EXUNDATION
EXURB
EXURBANITE
EXURBIA
EXUST
EXUTE
EXUVIABILITY

EXUVIABLE
EXUVIAE
EXUVIAL
EXUVIATE
EXUVIATED
EXUVIATING
EXUVIATION
EXZODIACAL
EY
EYAH
EYALET
EYAS
EYDENT
EYE
EYEABLE
EYEBALL
EYEBALM
EYEBAR
EYEBEAM
EYEBERRY
EYEBLINK
EYEBOLT
EYEBREE
EYEBRIDLED
EYEBRIGHT
EYEBROW
EYECUP
EYED
EYEDNESS
EYEDOT
EYEDROP
EYEFLAP
EYEFUL
EYEGLANCE
EYEGLASS
EYEGLASSES
EYEGROUND
EYEHOLE
EYEHOOK
EYEING
EYELASH
EYELAST
EYELESS
EYELET
EYELETED
EYELETEER
EYELETING
EYELETTER
EYELID
EYELIDS
EYELIGHT
EYELINE
EYEMARK
EYEN
EYEPIECE
EYEPIT
EYEPOINT
EYER
EYEREACH
EYEROOT
EYES
EYESALVE
EYESEED
EYESERVANT
EYESERVER
EYESERVICE
EYESHADE
EYESHIELD
EYESHINE
EYESHOT
EYESIGHT
EYESOME
EYESORE
EYESPOT
EYESS
EYESTALK
EYESTONE

EYESTRAIN
EYESTRING
EYETEETH
EYETOOTH
EYEWAITER
EYEWASH
EYEWATER
EYEWEAR
EYEWINK
EYEWINKER
EYEWITNESS
EYEWORT
EYEY
EYING
EYLE
EYLIAD
EYNE
EYOT
EYRA
EYRE
EYREN
EYRIE
EYRIR
EYRY
EYSOGE
EZBA

FA
FABA
FABACEOUS
FABE
FABELLA
FABES
FABIFORM
FABLE
FABLED
FABLEDOM
FABLEIST
FABLELAND
FABLEMAKER
FABLEMONGER
FABLER
FABLIAU
FABLIAUX
FABLING
FABRIC
FABRICANT
FABRICATE
FABRICATED
FABRICATES
FABRICATING
FABRICATION
FABRICATIVE
FABRICATOR
FABRICATURE
FABRICS
FABRIKOID
FABRILE
FABRIQUE
FABULA
FABULAR
FABULIST
FABULIZE
FABULOSITY
FABULOUS
FABULOUSLY
FABULOUSNESS
FABURDEN
FAC
FACADAL
FACADE
FACE
FACEABLE
FACEBOW
FACED
FACELESS
FACEMAKER
FACEMAKING
FACEMAN
FACEMARK
FACEPIECE
FACEPLATE
FACER
FACES
FACET
FACETE
FACETED
FACETELY
FACETENESS
FACETIAE
FACETIATION
FACETING
FACETIOUS
FACETIOUSLY

FACETIOUSNESS
FACETTE
FACEWORK
FACIA
FACIAL
FACIEND
FACIENT
FACIER
FACIES
FACIEST
FACILE
FACILELY
FACILENESS
FACILITATE
FACILITATED
FACILITATING
FACILITATION
FACILITATIVE
FACILITATOR
FACILITIES
FACILITY
FACING
FACINGLY
FACINOROUS
FACIOCERVICAL
FACIOPLEGIA
FACK
FACKELTANZ
FACKINS
FACON
FACONNE
FACSIMILE
FACSIMILED
FACSIMILEING
FACSIMILES
FACSIMILIST
FACSIMILIZE
FACT
FACTA
FACTABLE
FACTICE
FACTICIDE
FACTION
FACTIONAL
FACTIONALISM
FACTIONARIES
FACTIONARY
FACTIONATE
FACTIONEER
FACTIONISM
FACTIONIST
FACTIOUS
FACTIOUSLY
FACTIOUSNESS
FACTISH
FACTITIAL
FACTITIOUS
FACTITIOUSLY
FACTITIOUSNESS
FACTITIVE
FACTITIVELY
FACTITUDE
FACTIVE
FACTO
FACTOR
FACTORABILITY
FACTORABLE
FACTORAGE
FACTORED
FACTORIAL
FACTORIALLY
FACTORIES
FACTORING
FACTORIST
FACTORIZATION
FACTORIZE
FACTORIZED

FACTORIZING
FACTORS
FACTORSHIP
FACTORY
FACTORYSHIP
FACTOTUM
FACTRIX
FACTS
FACTUAL
FACTUALITY
FACTUALLY
FACTUALNESS
FACTUM
FACTURE
FACTY
FACULA
FACULAE
FACULAR
FACULOUS
FACULTATE
FACULTATIVE
FACULTATIVELY
FACULTIED
FACULTIES
FACULTIZE
FACULTY
FACUND
FACUNDITY
FACY
FAD
FADAISE
FADDINESS
FADDING
FADDISH
FADDISHNESS
FADDISM
FADDIST
FADDLE
FADDY
FADE
FADEAWAY
FADED
FADEDLY
FADEDNESS
FADELESS
FADELESSLY
FADER
FADGE
FADGED
FADGING
FADING
FADINGLY
FADINGNESS
FADME
FADO
FADS
FADY
FAE
FAECAL
FAECALITH
FAECES
FAECULA
FAENA
FAENUS
FAERIE
FAERY
FAEX
FAFF
FAFFLE
FAFFY
FAG
FAGACEOUS
FAGALD
FAGARA
FAGE
FAGER
FAGGED

FAGGER
FAGGERY
FAGGING
FAGGOT
FAGGOTED
FAGGOTY
FAGGY
FAGINE
FAGOPYRISM
FAGOT
FAGOTED
FAGOTER
FAGOTING
FAGOTT
FAGOTTE
FAGOTTINO
FAGOTTIST
FAGOTTO
FAGOTTONE
FAGOTY
FAHAM
FAHLBAND
FAHLERZ
FAHLORE
FAHLUNITE
FAIENCE
FAIK
FAIL
FAILANCE
FAILED
FAILING
FAILINGLY
FAILINGNESS
FAILLE
FAILURE
FAIN
FAINAIGUE
FAINAIGUED
FAINAIGUER
FAINAIGUING
FAINEANCE
FAINEANCY
FAINEANT
FAINEANTISE
FAINLY
FAINNESS
FAINS
FAINT
FAINTED
FAINTER
FAINTEST
FAINTFUL
FAINTHEART
FAINTHEARTED
FAINTHEARTEDLY
FAINTHEARTEDNESS
FAINTING
FAINTINGLY
FAINTISH
FAINTLING
FAINTLY
FAINTNESS
FAINTS
FAINTY
FAIPULE
FAIR
FAIRD
FAIRED
FAIRER
FAIREST
FAIRFIELDITE
FAIRGROUND
FAIRHEAD
FAIRIES
FAIRILY
FAIRING
FAIRISH

FAIRISHLY
FAIRLY
FAIRNESS
FAIRSHIP
FAIRSOME
FAIRWATER
FAIRWAY
FAIRY
FAIRYDOM
FAIRYFOLK
FAIRYHOOD
FAIRYISM
FAIRYLAND
FAIRYLIKE
FAIRYOLOGY
FAISCEAU
FAIT
FAITERY
FAITH
FAITHBREACH
FAITHBREAKER
FAITHFUL
FAITHFULLY
FAITHFULNESS
FAITHLESS
FAITHLESSLY
FAITHLESSNESS
FAITHWORTHINESS
FAITHWORTHY
FAITOR
FAITOUR
FAIZE
FAJA
FAKE
FAKED
FAKEER
FAKEMENT
FAKER
FAKERY
FAKING
FAKIR
FAKY
FALANAKA
FALBALA
FALBELO
FALCADE
FALCATE
FALCATED
FALCATION
FALCES
FALCHION
FALCIAL
FALCIFORM
FALCON
FALCONBILL
FALCONER
FALCONET
FALCONINE
FALCONOID
FALCONRY
FALCOPERN
FALCULA
FALCULAR
FALCULATE
FALDA
FALDAGE
FALDERAL
FALDEROL
FALDETTA
FALDFEE
FALDING
FALDISTORY
FALDSTOOL
FALDWORTH
FALK
FALL
FALLACIA

FALLACIES
FALLACIOUS
FALLACIOUSLY
FALLACIOUSNESS
FALLACY
FALLAGE
FALLAL
FALLALERY
FALLATION
FALLAWAY
FALLBACK
FALLECTOMY
FALLEN
FALLENCY
FALLER
FALLFISH
FALLFISHES
FALLIBILITY
FALLIBLE
FALLIBLENESS
FALLIBLY
FALLING
FALLOFF
FALLOSTOMY
FALLOUT
FALLOW
FALLOWED
FALLOWING
FALLOWNESS
FALLS
FALLTIME
FALLWAY
FALLY
FALSARY
FALSE
FALSEDAD
FALSEHEARTED
FALSEHEARTEDLY
FALSEHEARTEDNESS
FALSEHOOD
FALSEHOODS
FALSELY
FALSEN
FALSENESS
FALSER
FALSEST
FALSETTIST
FALSETTO
FALSETTOS
FALSEWORK
FALSIDICAL
FALSIE
FALSIES
FALSIFICATE
FALSIFICATION
FALSIFICATOR
FALSIFIED
FALSIFIER
FALSIFY
FALSIFYING
FALSISM
FALSITEIT
FALSITIES
FALSITY
FALSUM
FALTBOAT
FALTER
FALTERED
FALTERER
FALTERING
FALTERINGLY
FALUN
FALUS
FALX
FAM
FAMATINITE
FAMBLE

FAME
FAMED
FAMEFLOWER
FAMELESS
FAMELIC
FAMILIA
FAMILIAL
FAMILIAR
FAMILIARISM
FAMILIARITY
FAMILIARIZATION
FAMILIARIZE
FAMILIARIZED
FAMILIARIZER
FAMILIARIZING
FAMILIARIZINGLY
FAMILIARLY
FAMILIES
FAMILISM
FAMILIST
FAMILISTERE
FAMILISTIC
FAMILISTICAL
FAMILY
FAMINE
FAMING
FAMISH
FAMISHED
FAMISHING
FAMISHMENT
FAMOSE
FAMOUS
FAMOUSLY
FAMOUSNESS
FAMULAR
FAMULARY
FAMULI
FAMULUS
FAN
FANA
FANAKALO
FANAL
FANALOKA
FANAM
FANATIC
FANATICAL
FANATICALLY
FANATICALNESS
FANATICISM
FANATICIZE
FANATICIZED
FANATICIZING
FANATICS
FANBACK
FANBEARER
FANCICAL
FANCIED
FANCIER
FANCIES
FANCIEST
FANCIFUL
FANCIFULLY
FANCIFULNESS
FANCIFY
FANCILESS
FANCILY
FANCY
FANCYING
FANCYMONGER
FANCYWORK
FAND
FANDANGLE
FANDANGO
FANE
FANEGA
FANEGADA
FANFARE

FANFARON
FANFARONADE
FANFARONADING
FANFLOWER
FANFOLD
FANFOOT
FANG
FANGA
FANGED
FANGER
FANGING
FANGLE
FANGLED
FANGLESS
FANGLIKE
FANGLOMERATE
FANGO
FANGOT
FANGS
FANGY
FANHOUSE
FANIENTE
FANION
FANIONED
FANIT
FANJET
FANK
FANKLE
FANLIGHT
FANLIKE
FANMAKER
FANMAKING
FANMAN
FANNED
FANNEL
FANNELING
FANNER
FANNIER
FANNIES
FANNING
FANNINGS
FANNON
FANO
FANON
FANS
FANTAD
FANTADDISH
FANTAIL
FANTAISIE
FANTASIA
FANTASIED
FANTASIST
FANTASIZE
FANTASIZED
FANTASIZING
FANTASM
FANTASMAL
FANTASQUE
FANTASSIN
FANTAST
FANTASTIC
FANTASTICAL
FANTASTICALITY
FANTASTICALLY
FANTASTICALNESS
FANTASTICATE
FANTASTICATION
FANTASTICLY
FANTASTICNESS
FANTASTICO
FANTASTRY
FANTASY
FANTASYING
FANTEAGUE
FANTEEG
FANTIGUE
FANTOCCINI

FANTOCINE
FANTOD
FANTODDISH
FANTOM
FANUM
FANWEED
FANWORK
FANWORT
FANWRIGHT
FANZINE
FAON
FAP
FAPE
FAPESMO
FAQIH
FAQUIR
FAR
FARAD
FARADAIC
FARADAY
FARADIC
FARADISM
FARADIZATION
FARADIZE
FARADIZED
FARADIZER
FARADMETER
FARAND
FARANDINE
FARANDMAN
FARANDMEN
FARANDOLA
FARANDOLE
FARAON
FARASULA
FARAWAY
FARAWAYNESS
FARCE
FARCED
FARCER
FARCETTA
FARCEUR
FARCEUSE
FARCI
FARCIALIZE
FARCICAL
FARCICALITY
FARCICALLY
FARCICALNESS
FARCIE
FARCIED
FARCIFY
FARCIN
FARCING
FARCIST
FARCTATE
FARCY
FARD
FARDA
FARDAGE
FARDEL
FARDELS
FARDH
FARDO
FARE
FARED
FARER
FAREWELL
FARFARA
FARFEL
FARFET
FARFETCH
FARFETCHED
FARFETCHEDNESS
FARGOING
FARGOOD
FARINA

FARINACEOUS
FARINE
FARING
FARINHA
FARINOMETER
FARINOSE
FARINOSELY
FARINULENT
FARISH
FARKLEBERRY
FARL
FARLE
FARLEU
FARLEY
FARM
FARMAGE
FARMED
FARMER
FARMERESS
FARMERETTE
FARMERLY
FARMERY
FARMHAND
FARMHOLD
FARMHOUSE
FARMING
FARMLAND
FARMOST
FARMOUT
FARMPLACE
FARMSTEAD
FARMSTEADING
FARMTOWN
FARMWIFE
FARMY
FARMYARD
FARMYARDY
FARNESOL
FARNESS
FARO
FAROEISH
FAROL
FAROLITO
FAROUCHE
FARRAGE
FARRAGINOUS
FARRAGO
FARRAGOES
FARRAND
FARRANDLY
FARRANT
FARRANTLY
FARREL
FARRIER
FARRIERIES
FARRIERY
FARRISITE
FARROW
FARRUCA
FARSAKH
FARSANG
FARSE
FARSEEING
FARSEEINGNESS
FARSEER
FARSET
FARSIGHTED
FARSIGHTEDLY
FARSIGHTEDNESS
FARSTEPPED
FART
FARTHER
FARTHERMOST
FARTHEST
FARTHING
FARTHINGALE
FARTHINGS

FARWELTERED
FASCES
FASCET
FASCIA
FASCIAL
FASCIATE
FASCIATED
FASCIATELY
FASCIATION
FASCICLE
FASCICLED
FASCICULAR
FASCICULARLY
FASCICULATE
FASCICULATED
FASCICULATELY
FASCICULATION
FASCICULE
FASCICULI
FASCICULUS
FASCINATE
FASCINATED
FASCINATING
FASCINATINGLY
FASCINATION
FASCINATIVE
FASCINATOR
FASCINATRESS
FASCINE
FASCINERY
FASCINES
FASCIOLA
FASCIOLAE
FASCIOLAR
FASCIOLE
FASCIOLET
FASCIOLIASIS
FASCIOLOID
FASCIS
FASCISM
FASCIST
FASCISTIC
FASCISTICIZE
FASCISTIZE
FASELS
FASH
FASHER
FASHERIE
FASHERY
FASHION
FASHIONABILITY
FASHIONABLE
FASHIONABLENESS
FASHIONABLY
FASHIONATIVE
FASHIONED
FASHIONER
FASHIONING
FASHIONIST
FASHIONIZE
FASHIONMONGER
FASHIOUS
FASHIOUSNESS
FASIBITIKITE
FASINITE
FASNACHT
FASOLA
FASSAITE
FAST
FASTEN
FASTENED
FASTENER
FASTENING
FASTENINGS
FASTENS
FASTER
FASTEST

FASTHOLD
FASTI
FASTIDIOSITY
FASTIDIOUS
FASTIDIOUSLY
FASTIDIOUSNESS
FASTIDIUM
FASTIGATE
FASTIGIA
FASTIGIATE
FASTIGIATED
FASTIGIUM
FASTING
FASTINGLY
FASTLAND
FASTLY
FASTNESS
FASTUOUS
FASTUOUSLY
FASTUOUSNESS
FAT
FATAL
FATALISM
FATALIST
FATALISTIC
FATALISTICALLY
FATALITY
FATALIZE
FATALLY
FATBACK
FATBIRD
FATCAKE
FATE
FATED
FATEFUL
FATEFULLY
FATEFULNESS
FATES
FATHEAD
FATHEADED
FATHEADEDNESS
FATHEARTED
FATHER
FATHERED
FATHERHOOD
FATHERING
FATHERLAND
FATHERLESS
FATHERLESSNESS
FATHERLINESS
FATHERLY
FATHOM
FATHOMABLE
FATHOMAGE
FATHOMED
FATHOMER
FATHOMING
FATHOMLESS
FATHOMLESSLY
FATHOMLESSNESS
FATHOMS
FATIDIC
FATIDICAL
FATIDICALLY
FATIFEROUS
FATIGABILITY
FATIGABLE
FATIGABLENESS
FATIGATE
FATIGATION
FATIGUE
FATIGUED
FATIGUES
FATIGUESOME
FATIGUING
FATIHA
FATIHAH

FATILOQUENT
FATING
FATISCENCE
FATISCENT
FATLESS
FATLIKE
FATLING
FATLY
FATNESS
FATSIA
FATSO
FATSTOCK
FATTED
FATTEN
FATTENED
FATTENER
FATTENING
FATTER
FATTEST
FATTIER
FATTIEST
FATTILY
FATTINESS
FATTING
FATTISH
FATTISHNESS
FATTRELS
FATTY
FATUITIES
FATUITOUS
FATUITY
FATUOID
FATUOUS
FATUOUSLY
FATUOUSNESS
FATWOOD
FAUBOURG
FAUCAL
FAUCALIZE
FAUCES
FAUCET
FAUCHARD
FAUCIAL
FAUCITIS
FAUCONNIER
FAUCRE
FAUD
FAUGH
FAUJASITE
FAUJDAR
FAULD
FAULT
FAULTAGE
FAULTED
FAULTER
FAULTFIND
FAULTFINDER
FAULTFINDING
FAULTFUL
FAULTIER
FAULTIEST
FAULTILY
FAULTINESS
FAULTING
FAULTLESS
FAULTLESSLY
FAULTLESSNESS
FAULTSMAN
FAULTY
FAULX
FAUN
FAUNA
FAUNAE
FAUNAL
FAUNALLY
FAUNAS
FAUNCH

FAUNIST
FAUNISTIC
FAUNISTICAL
FAUNOLOGICAL
FAUNOLOGY
FAUNULA
FAUNULE
FAUR
FAURD
FAURED
FAUS
FAUSANT
FAUSE
FAUSEN
FAUSSEBRAIE
FAUSSEBRAYE
FAUSSEBRAYED
FAUST
FAUSTER
FAUTERER
FAUTEUIL
FAUTOR
FAUTORSHIP
FAUVE
FAUVETTE
FAUX
FAVA
FAVAGINOUS
FAVEL
FAVELIDIUM
FAVELLA
FAVELLOID
FAVEOLATE
FAVEOLUS
FAVI
FAVIFORM
FAVILLA
FAVILLAE
FAVILLOUS
FAVISM
FAVISSA
FAVISSAE
FAVONIAN
FAVOR
FAVORABLE
FAVORABLY
FAVORED
FAVOREDLY
FAVOREDNESS
FAVORER
FAVORESS
FAVORING
FAVORINGLY
FAVORITE
FAVORITISM
FAVORLESS
FAVORS
FAVOSE
FAVOSELY
FAVOSITE
FAVOSITOID
FAVOUR
FAVOURABLE
FAVOURABLENESS
FAVOURED
FAVOUREDLY
FAVOUREDNESS
FAVOURER
FAVOURESS
FAVOURING
FAVOURINGLY
FAVOURITE
FAVOURITISM
FAVOURLESS
FAVOUS
FAVUS
FAW

FAWN
FAWNED
FAWNER
FAWNERY
FAWNING
FAWNINGLY
FAWNINGNESS
FAWNY
FAX
FAXED
FAY
FAYALITE
FAYED
FAYING
FAYLES
FAZE
FAZED
FAZENDA
FAZENDEIRO
FAZING
FEABERRY
FEAGUE
FEAK
FEAKED
FEAKING
FEAL
FEALTIES
FEALTY
FEAR
FEARBABE
FEARED
FEAREDLY
FEAREDNESS
FEARER
FEARFUL
FEARFULLY
FEARFULNESS
FEARING
FEARINGLY
FEARLESS
FEARLESSLY
FEARLESSNESS
FEARNAUGHT
FEARNOUGHT
FEARSOME
FEARSOMELY
FEARSOMENESS
FEASANCE
FEASE
FEASIBILITY
FEASIBLE
FEASIBLENESS
FEASIBLY
FEASOR
FEAST
FEASTED
FEASTEN
FEASTER
FEASTFUL
FEASTFULLY
FEASTING
FEASTLY
FEAT
FEATER
FEATEST
FEATHER
FEATHERBACK
FEATHERBEDDED
FEATHERBEDDING
FEATHERBIRD
FEATHERBONE
FEATHERBRAIN
FEATHERBRAINED
FEATHERCUT
FEATHERDOM
FEATHERED
FEATHEREDGE

FEATHEREDGED
FEATHERER
FEATHERFEW
FEATHERFOIL
FEATHERHEAD
FEATHERHEADED
FEATHERINESS
FEATHERING
FEATHERLEAF
FEATHERMAN
FEATHERMONGER
FEATHERS
FEATHERSTITCH
FEATHERTOP
FEATHERWAY
FEATHERWEED
FEATHERWEIGHT
FEATHERWING
FEATHERWOOD
FEATHERWORK
FEATHERWORKER
FEATHERY
FEATISH
FEATISHLY
FEATISHNESS
FEATLESS
FEATLINESS
FEATLY
FEATOUS
FEATURAL
FEATURALLY
FEATURE
FEATURED
FEATUREFUL
FEATURELESS
FEATURELINESS
FEATURELY
FEATURES
FEATURING
FEATY
FEAZE
FEAZED
FEAZING
FEAZINGS
FEBRICANT
FEBRICIDE
FEBRICITY
FEBRICULA
FEBRIFACIENT
FEBRIFIC
FEBRIFUGAL
FEBRIFUGE
FEBRILE
FEBRILITY
FEBRIS
FEBRUATION
FECAL
FECALITH
FECALOID
FECCHE
FECES
FECIAL
FECIT
FECK
FECKET
FECKFUL
FECKFULLY
FECKLESS
FECKLESSLY
FECKLESSNESS
FECKLY
FECULA
FECULAE
FECULENCE
FECULENCY
FECULENT
FECUND

FECUNDATE
FECUNDATED
FECUNDATING
FECUNDATION
FECUNDATIVE
FECUNDATOR
FECUNDATORY
FECUNDIFY
FECUNDITY
FECUNDIZE
FED
FEDAI
FEDARIE
FEDAYEE
FEDDAN
FEDELINI
FEDERACIES
FEDERACY
FEDERAL
FEDERALISM
FEDERALIST
FEDERALISTIC
FEDERALIZATION
FEDERALIZE
FEDERALIZED
FEDERALIZING
FEDERALLY
FEDERALNESS
FEDERARY
FEDERATE
FEDERATED
FEDERATING
FEDERATION
FEDERATIVE
FEDERATIVELY
FEDERATOR
FEDIFRAGOUS
FEDITY
FEDORA
FEE
FEEB
FEEBLE
FEEBLEBRAINED
FEEBLEHEARTED
FEEBLEHEARTEDLY
FEEBLEHEARTEDNESS
FEEBLEMINDED
FEEBLENESS
FEEBLER
FEEBLEST
FEEBLISH
FEEBLY
FEED
FEEDBACK
FEEDBAG
FEEDBIN
FEEDBOARD
FEEDBOX
FEEDER
FEEDHEAD
FEEDING
FEEDLOT
FEEDMAN
FEEDS
FEEDSMAN
FEEDSTUFF
FEEDWAY
FEEDY
FEEING
FEEK
FEEL
FEELABLE
FEELER
FEELING
FEELINGLY
FEELINGNESS
FEELINGS

FEER
FEERE
FEERIE
FEERING
FEES
FEEST
FEET
FEEZE
FEFNICUTE
FEGARY
FEGS
FEHME
FEI
FEID
FEIGH
FEIGHER
FEIGN
FEIGNED
FEIGNEDLY
FEIGNEDNESS
FEIGNER
FEIGNING
FEIL
FEINT
FEINTER
FEIRIE
FEIS
FEISEANNA
FEIST
FEISTIER
FEISTIEST
FEISTY
FEKE
FELAPTON
FELD
FELDSHER
FELDSPAR
FELDSPARPHYRE
FELDSPATH
FELDSPATHIC
FELDSPATHOID
FELDSPATHOSE
FELF
FELICIDE
FELICIFIC
FELICIFY
FELICITATE
FELICITATED
FELICITATING
FELICITATION
FELICITATOR
FELICITIES
FELICITOUS
FELICITOUSLY
FELICITOUSNESS
FELICITY
FELID
FELIFORM
FELINE
FELINELY
FELINENESS
FELINITY
FELINOPHILE
FELINOPHOBE
FELIS
FELL
FELLABLE
FELLAGE
FELLAGHA
FELLAH
FELLAHEEN
FELLAHIN
FELLAHS
FELLATA
FELLED
FELLEN
FELLER

FELLFARE
FELLIC
FELLIES
FELLIFLUOUS
FELLING
FELLMONGER
FELLNESS
FELLOE
FELLOW
FELLOWCRAFT
FELLOWED
FELLOWING
FELLOWLIKE
FELLOWLY
FELLOWMAN
FELLOWS
FELLOWSHIP
FELLOWSHIPED
FELLOWSHIPING
FELLOWSHIPPED
FELLOWSHIPPING
FELLSIDE
FELLY
FELO
FELOID
FELON
FELONIES
FELONIOUS
FELONIOUSLY
FELONIOUSNESS
FELONOUS
FELONRY
FELONSETTER
FELONWEED
FELONWOOD
FELONWORT
FELONY
FELS
FELSITE
FELSITIC
FELSOBANYITE
FELSOPHYRE
FELSOPHYRIC
FELSPAR
FELSPATH
FELSTONE
FELT
FELTED
FELTER
FELTING
FELTLIKE
FELTMAKER
FELTMAKING
FELTMAN
FELTMONGER
FELTWORK
FELTWORT
FELTY
FELTYFARE
FELTYFLIER
FELUCCA
FELWORT
FELZE
FEMALE
FEMALELY
FEMALENESS
FEMALIST
FEMALITY
FEMCEE
FEME
FEMEREIL
FEMERELL
FEMIC
FEMICIDE
FEMINACY
FEMINAL
FEMINALITY

FEMINATE
FEMINEITY
FEMINIE
FEMINILITY
FEMININ
FEMININE
FEMININELY
FEMININENESS
FEMININITY
FEMINISM
FEMINIST
FEMINISTIC
FEMINITY
FEMINIZATION
FEMINIZE
FEMME
FEMORA
FEMORAL
FEMUR
FEMURS
FEN
FENAGLE
FENBANK
FENBERRY
FENCE
FENCED
FENCEFUL
FENCELESS
FENCELESSNESS
FENCEPLAY
FENCER
FENCHENE
FENCHOL
FENCHONE
FENCHYL
FENCIBLE
FENCING
FEND
FENDABLE
FENDED
FENDER
FENDERING
FENDING
FENDY
FENERATION
FENESTELLA
FENESTER
FENESTRA
FENESTRAE
FENESTRAL
FENESTRATE
FENESTRATED
FENESTRATION
FENESTRATO
FENESTRONE
FENESTRULE
FENETRE
FENITE
FENKS
FENLAND
FENLANDER
FENMAN
FENMAN
FENNEC
FENNEL
FENNELFLOWER
FENNER
FENNIG
FENNISH
FENNY
FENOUILLET
FENOUILLETTE
FENS
FENSTER
FENT
FENTER
FENUGREEK

FEOD	FERMORITE	FERRUGINATING	FESTILOGIES	FETTER
FEODAL	FERN	FERRUGINEAN	FESTILOGY	FETTERBUSH
FEODALITY	FERNBIRD	FERRUGINEOUS	FESTINATE	FETTERED
FEODARY	FERNBRAKE	FERRUGINOUS	FESTINATED	FETTERER
FEODATORY	FERNED	FERRUGO	FESTINATELY	FETTERING
FEODUM	FERNENT	FERRULE	FESTINATING	FETTERLOCK
FEOFF	FERNERIES	FERRULED	FESTINATION	FETTERS
FEOFFED	FERNERY	FERRULER	FESTINE	FETTICUS
FEOFFEE	FERNGALE	FERRULING	FESTINO	FETTING
FEOFFEESHIP	FERNGROWER	FERRUM	FESTIVAL	FETTLE
FEOFFER	FERNINST	FERRUMINATE	FESTIVALLY	FETTLED
FEOFFING	FERNLAND	FERRUMINATED	FESTIVE	FETTLER
FEOFFMENT	FERNLEAF	FERRUMINATING	FESTIVELY	FETTLING
FEOFFOR	FERNLIKE	FERRY	FESTIVENESS	FETTUCINI
FER	FERNSHAW	FERRYAGE	FESTIVITIES	FETURE
FERACIOUS	FERNSICK	FERRYBOAT	FESTIVITY	FETUS
FERACITY	FERNTICKLE	FERRYHOUSE	FESTIVOUS	FETUSES
FERAL	FERNTICKLED	FERRYING	FESTOLOGY	FEU
FERASH	FERNWORT	FERRYMAN	FESTON	FEUAGE
FERBAM	FERNY	FERRYMEN	FESTOON	FEUAR
FERBERITE	FERNYEAR	FERRYWAY	FESTOONED	FEUCHT
FERDWIT	FEROCE	FERS	FESTOONERIES	FEUD
FERE	FEROCIOUS	FERSMITE	FESTOONERY	FEUDAL
FERETORIES	FEROCIOUSLY	FERTILE	FESTOONING	FEUDALISM
FERETORY	FEROCIOUSNESS	FERTILELY	FESTOONY	FEUDALIST
FERETRA	FEROCITIES	FERTILENESS	FESTUCA	FEUDALISTIC
FERETRUM	FEROCITY	FERTILITIES	FESTUCINE	FEUDALITY
FERFEL	FEROHER	FERTILITY	FESTY	FEUDALIZATION
FERGANITE	FERRAMENT	FERTILIZABLE	FET	FEUDALIZE
FERGUSITE	FERRASH	FERTILIZATION	FETA	FEUDALIZED
FERGUSONITE	FERRATE	FERTILIZATIONAL	FETAL	FEUDALIZING
FERIA	FERRATED	FERTILIZE	FETALISM	FEUDALLY
FERIAE	FERRATIN	FERTILIZED	FETATION	FEUDARIES
FERIAL	FERRE	FERTILIZER	FETCH	FEUDARY
FERIDJEE	FERREIRO	FERTILIZIN	FETCHED	FEUDATORIAL
FERIDJI	FERREL	FERTILIZING	FETCHER	FEUDATORIES
FERIE	FERREOUS	FERU	FETCHING	FEUDATORY
FERIGEE	FERRER	FERULA	FETCHINGLY	FEUDEE
FERIJEE	FERRET	FERULACEOUS	FETE	FEUDIST
FERINE	FERRETED	FERULAE	FETED	FEUDUM
FERINELY	FERRETER	FERULAS	FETERITA	FEUED
FERINENESS	FERRETING	FERULE	FETIAL	FEUILLAGE
FERIO	FERRETTO	FERULED	FETIALES	FEUILLE
FERISON	FERRETY	FERULIC	FETIALIS	FEUILLETON
FERITY	FERRI	FERULING	FETICH	FEUING
FERK	FERRIAGE	FERVANITE	FETICHIC	FEUTE
FERLIE	FERRIC	FERVENCIES	FETICHISM	FEUTER
FERLIED	FERRICYANIC	FERVENCY	FETICHIST	FEVER
FERLIES	FERRICYANIDE	FERVENT	FETICHISTIC	FEVERBERRIES
FERLING	FERRIED	FERVENTLY	FETICHIZE	FEVERBERRY
FERLY	FERRIER	FERVENTNESS	FETICHRY	FEVERBUSH
FERLYING	FERRIES	FERVESCENCE	FETICIDAL	FEVERCUP
FERM	FERRIFEROUS	FERVESCENT	FETICIDE	FEVERED
FERMAIL	FERRING	FERVID	FETID	FEVERET
FERMATA	FERRITE	FERVIDITY	FETIDLY	FEVERFEW
FERME	FERRITIN	FERVIDLY	FETIDNESS	FEVERGUM
FERMENT	FERRIVOROUS	FERVIDNESS	FETIFEROUS	FEVERING
FERMENTABILITY	FERROALLOY	FERVOR	FETII	FEVERISH
FERMENTABLE	FERROBORON	FERVOROUS	FETING	FEVERISHLY
FERMENTARIAN	FERROCALCITE	FERVOUR	FETIPAROUS	FEVERISHNESS
FERMENTATION	FERROCERIUM	FESAPO	FETIS	FEVERLESS
FERMENTATIVE	FERROCHROME	FESCENNINITY	FETISH	FEVEROUS
FERMENTATIVELY	FERROCONCRETE	FESCUE	FETISHEER	FEVEROUSLY
FERMENTATIVENESS	FERROCYANIC	FESH	FETISHER	FEVERROOT
FERMENTATORY	FERROCYANIDE	FESS	FETISHIC	FEVERTRAP
FERMENTED	FERROINCLAVE	FESSE	FETISHISM	FEVERTWIG
FERMENTER	FERROMAGNETIC	FESSEWISE	FETISHIST	FEVERWEED
FERMENTING	FERROMAGNETISM	FESSWAYS	FETISHISTIC	FEVERWORT
FERMENTIVE	FERRONATRITE	FESSWISE	FETISHIZE	FEVERY
FERMENTOLOGY	FERRONICKEL	FEST	FETISHRY	FEW
FERMENTOR	FERROPRINT	FESTA	FETLOCK	FEWER
FERMENTUM	FERROSILICON	FESTAL	FETLOCKED	FEWEST
FERMERER	FERROTYPE	FESTALLY	FETLOW	FEWMAND
FERMERY	FERROTYPER	FESTER	FETOGRAPHY	FEWMET
FERMI	FERROUS	FESTERED	FETOMETRY	FEWNESS
FERMION	FERRUGINATE	FESTERING	FETOR	FEWSOME
FERMIUM	FERRUGINATED	FESTERMENT	FETTED	FEWTER

FEWTERER
FEWTRILS
FEY
FEZ
FEZZED
FEZZES
FEZZY
FIACRE
FIADOR
FIANCAILLES
FIANCE
FIANCED
FIANCEE
FIANCHETTI
FIANCHETTO
FIANCING
FIANT
FIANTS
FIAR
FIARD
FIASCO
FIASCOES
FIASCOS
FIAT
FIB
FIBBED
FIBBER
FIBBERY
FIBBING
FIBER
FIBERBOARD
FIBERED
FIBERIZE
FIBERIZER
FIBERS
FIBRA
FIBRATION
FIBRE
FIBREBOARD
FIBRED
FIBRIFORM
FIBRIL
FIBRILLA
FIBRILLAE
FIBRILLAR
FIBRILLARY
FIBRILLATE
FIBRILLATED
FIBRILLATION
FIBRILLED
FIBRILLIFORM
FIBRILLOSE
FIBRILLOUS
FIBRILS
FIBRIN
FIBRINATE
FIBRINATION
FIBRINE
FIBRINOGEN
FIBRINOGENIC
FIBRINOLYSIN
FIBRINOLYSIS
FIBRINOLYTIC
FIBRINOSE
FIBRINOSIS
FIBRINOUS
FIBROADENIA
FIBROADENOMA
FIBROADIPOSE
FIBROAREOLAR
FIBROBLAST
FIBROBLASTIC
FIBROCARTILAGE
FIBROCASEOSE
FIBROCELLULAR
FIBROCYST
FIBROCYSTIC

FIBROCYSTOMA
FIBROCYTE
FIBROELASTIC
FIBROFATTY
FIBROFERRITE
FIBROGLIA
FIBROGLIOMA
FIBROID
FIBROIN
FIBROLIPOMA
FIBROLITIC
FIBROMA
FIBROMAS
FIBROMATA
FIBROMATOID
FIBROMATOSIS
FIBROMATOUS
FIBROMUCOUS
FIBROMYITIS
FIBROMYOMA
FIBROMYOTOMY
FIBROMYXOMA
FIBRONEUROMA
FIBRONUCLEAR
FIBROPLASIA
FIBROPLASTIC
FIBROPOLYPUS
FIBROSARCOMA
FIBROSE
FIBROSEROUS
FIBROSIS
FIBROSITIS
FIBROTIC
FIBROUS
FIBROUSLY
FIBROUSNESS
FIBROVASAL
FIBRY
FIBSTER
FIBULA
FIBULAE
FIBULAR
FIBULARE
FIBULARIA
FIBULAS
FICARIES
FICARY
FICCHE
FICE
FICELLE
FICHAT
FICHE
FICHTELITE
FICHU
FICIFORM
FICK
FICKLE
FICKLEHEARTED
FICKLENESS
FICKLETY
FICKLY
FICO
FICOES
FICOID
FICOIDAL
FICTATION
FICTIL
FICTILE
FICTILENESS
FICTILITY
FICTION
FICTIONAL
FICTIONALIZATION
FICTIONALIZED
FICTIONALIZING
FICTIONALLY
FICTIONARY

FICTIONEER
FICTIONER
FICTIONIST
FICTIONISTIC
FICTIONIZE
FICTIONIZED
FICTIONIZING
FICTIOUS
FICTITIOUS
FICTITIOUSLY
FICTITIOUSNESS
FICTIVE
FICTIVELY
FICTOR
FID
FIDAI
FIDALGO
FIDATE
FIDATION
FIDAWI
FIDDED
FIDDING
FIDDLE
FIDDLEBACK
FIDDLECOME
FIDDLED
FIDDLEDEEDEE
FIDDLEFACED
FIDDLEHEAD
FIDDLEHEADED
FIDDLENECK
FIDDLER
FIDDLERFISH
FIDDLERFISHES
FIDDLERY
FIDDLESTICK
FIDDLESTICKS
FIDDLESTRING
FIDDLEWOOD
FIDDLEY
FIDDLEYS
FIDDLIES
FIDDLING
FIDE
FIDEICOMMISS
FIDEISM
FIDEIST
FIDEJUSSION
FIDEJUSSOR
FIDEJUSSORY
FIDELITIES
FIDELITY
FIDEOS
FIDFAD
FIDGE
FIDGED
FIDGET
FIDGETATION
FIDGETED
FIDGETER
FIDGETILY
FIDGETINESS
FIDGETING
FIDGETINGLY
FIDGETY
FIDGING
FIDICINAL
FIDICINALES
FIDICULA
FIDICULAE
FIDUCIA
FIDUCIAL
FIDUCIALLY
FIDUCIARIES
FIDUCIARILY
FIDUCIARY
FIE

FIEDLERITE
FIEF
FIELD
FIELDBIRD
FIELDED
FIELDEN
FIELDER
FIELDFARE
FIELDFIGHT
FIELDIE
FIELDING
FIELDMAN
FIELDMEN
FIELDPIECE
FIELDS
FIELDSMAN
FIELDSMEN
FIELDSTONE
FIELDWORK
FIELDWORKER
FIELDWORT
FIELDY
FIEND
FIENDFUL
FIENDFULLY
FIENDHEAD
FIENDISH
FIENDISHLY
FIENDISHNESS
FIENDLIKE
FIENDLINESS
FIENDLY
FIENDSHIP
FIENT
FIER
FIERASFEROID
FIERCE
FIERCEHEARTED
FIERCELY
FIERCEN
FIERCENED
FIERCENESS
FIERCENING
FIERCER
FIERCEST
FIERDING
FIERIER
FIERIEST
FIERILY
FIERINESS
FIERY
FIESTA
FIFE
FIFED
FIFER
FIFIE
FIFING
FIFISH
FIFTEEN
FIFTEENER
FIFTEENTH
FIFTEENTHLY
FIFTH
FIFTHLY
FIFTIES
FIFTIETH
FIFTY
FIG
FIGARY
FIGBIRD
FIGBOY
FIGEATER
FIGENT
FIGGED
FIGGERY
FIGGING
FIGGLE

FIGGY
FIGHT
FIGHTABLE
FIGHTER
FIGHTING
FIGHTINGLY
FIGHTWITE
FIGMENT
FIGMENTAL
FIGO
FIGPECKER
FIGS
FIGSHELL
FIGULATE
FIGULATED
FIGULINE
FIGURA
FIGURABILITY
FIGURABLE
FIGURAE
FIGURAL
FIGURANT
FIGURANTE
FIGURATE
FIGURATELY
FIGURATION
FIGURATIVE
FIGURATIVELY
FIGURATIVENESS
FIGURATO
FIGURE
FIGURED
FIGUREDLY
FIGUREHEAD
FIGURER
FIGURES
FIGURESOME
FIGURETTE
FIGURIAL
FIGURINE
FIGURING
FIGURISM
FIGURIST
FIGURIZE
FIGURY
FIGWORM
FIGWORT
FIKE
FIKERY
FIKEY
FIKIE
FIKY
FIL
FILA
FILACE
FILACEOUS
FILACER
FILAGREE
FILAMENT
FILAMENTAR
FILAMENTARY
FILAMENTED
FILAMENTOID
FILAMENTOSE
FILAMENTOUS
FILAMENTS
FILAMENTULE
FILANDER
FILANDERS
FILAO
FILAR
FILAREE
FILARIA
FILARIAE
FILARIAL
FILARIAN
FILARIASIS

FILARICIDAL	FILIPPO	FILTRATABLE	FINER	FINITIVE
FILARIFORM	FILIPUNCTURE	FILTRATE	FINERIES	FINITUDE
FILARIID	FILITE	FILTRATED	FINERY	FINITY
FILARIOUS	FILIUS	FILTRATING	FINES	FINJAN
FILASSE	FILL	FILTRATION	FINESPUN	FINK
FILATE	FILLAGREE	FILUM	FINESSE	FINKEL
FILATOR	FILLE	FIMBLE	FINESSED	FINLAND
FILATURE	FILLED	FIMBRIA	FINESSER	FINLESS
FILAZER	FILLER	FIMBRIAE	FINESSING	FINLET
FILBERT	FILLERCAP	FIMBRIAL	FINEST	FINNAC
FILCH	FILLET	FIMBRIATE	FINESTILL	FINNACK
FILCHED	FILLETED	FIMBRIATED	FINESTILLER	FINNED
FILCHER	FILLETER	FIMBRIATING	FINETOP	FINNER
FILCHERY	FILLETING	FIMBRIATION	FINEW	FINNESKO
FILCHING	FILLETS	FIMBRICATE	FINEWED	FINNICK
FILCHINGLY	FILLIES	FIMBRICATED	FINFISH	FINNICKING
FILE	FILLING	FIMBRILLA	FINFOOTS	FINNICKY
FILED	FILLINGLY	FIMBRILLAE	FINGAN	FINNING
FILEFISH	FILLINGNESS	FIMBRILLATE	FINGENT	FINNIP
FILEFISHES	FILLIP	FIMBRILLOSE	FINGER	FINNOC
FILEMAKER	FILLIPED	FIME	FINGERBERRY	FINNY
FILEMAKING	FILLIPEEN	FIMETIC	FINGERBOARD	FINO
FILEMOT	FILLIPING	FIMICOLOUS	FINGERED	FINOCHIO
FILER	FILLISTER	FIN	FINGERER	FINTA
FILET	FILLMASS	FINABLE	FINGERFISH	FINTADORES
FILETED	FILLOCK	FINABLENESS	FINGERFISHES	FIORD
FILETING	FILLOWITE	FINAGLE	FINGERFLOWER	FIORDED
FILI	FILLY	FINAGLED	FINGERHOLD	FIORIN
FILIAL	FILM	FINAGLER	FINGERHOOK	FIORITE
FILIALITY	FILMED	FINAGLING	FINGERING	FIORITURA
FILIALLY	FILMGOER	FINAL	FINGERLEAF	FIORITURE
FILIALNESS	FILMGOING	FINALE	FINGERLING	FIP
FILIATE	FILMIC	FINALIS	FINGERNAIL	FIPENNY
FILIATED	FILMIER	FINALISM	FINGERNAILS	FIPPLE
FILIATING	FILMIEST	FINALIST	FINGERPARTED	FIQUE
FILIATION	FILMIFORM	FINALITIES	FINGERPRINT	FIR
FILIBEG	FILMILY	FINALITY	FINGERPRINTING	FIRCA
FILIBRANCH	FILMINESS	FINALIZE	FINGERROOT	FIRE
FILIBRANCHIATE	FILMING	FINALIZED	FINGERS	FIREARM
FILIBUSTER	FILMISH	FINALIZING	FINGERSMITH	FIREBACK
FILIBUSTERED	FILMIST	FINALLY	FINGERSPIN	FIREBALL
FILIBUSTERER	FILMIZE	FINANCE	FINGERSTALL	FIREBED
FILIBUSTERING	FILMIZED	FINANCED	FINGERSTONE	FIREBIRD
FILIBUSTERISM	FILMIZING	FINANCIAL	FINGERTIP	FIREBLENDE
FILIBUSTEROUS	FILMLAND	FINANCIALIST	FINGERWORK	FIREBOARD
FILIBUSTROUS	FILMLIKE	FINANCIALLY	FINGERY	FIREBOAT
FILICAL	FILMOGEN	FINANCIER	FINGIAN	FIREBOLT
FILICAULINE	FILMS	FINANCIERED	FINGRIGO	FIREBOLTED
FILICIDAL	FILMSLIDE	FINANCIERING	FINIAL	FIREBOOT
FILICIDE	FILMY	FINANCIERY	FINIALED	FIREBOTE
FILICIFORM	FILO	FINANCING	FINICAL	FIREBOX
FILICIN	FILOPLUME	FINANCIST	FINICALITY	FIREBOY
FILICINEAN	FILOPODIA	FINBACK	FINICALLY	FIREBRAND
FILICINIAN	FILOPODIUM	FINBONE	FINICALNESS	FIREBRAT
FILICITE	FILOSE	FINCA	FINICISM	FIREBREAK
FILICOID	FILOSELLE	FINCAS	FINICK	FIREBRICK
FILID	FILS	FINCH	FINICKILY	FIREBUG
FILIETY	FILTER	FINCHBACKED	FINICKING	FIRECLAY
FILIFEROUS	FILTERABILITY	FINCHED	FINICKINGLY	FIRECOAT
FILIFORM	FILTERABLE	FINCHERY	FINICKY	FIRECRACKER
FILIFORMED	FILTERABLENESS	FINCHES	FINIFIC	FIRECREST
FILIGEROUS	FILTERED	FIND	FINIFY	FIRED
FILIGRAIN	FILTERER	FINDAL	FINIKIN	FIREDAMP
FILIGRAINED	FILTERING	FINDER	FINIKING	FIREDOG
FILIGRANE	FILTERMAN	FINDFAULT	FINING	FIREDRAGON
FILIGRANED	FILTERMEN	FINDING	FINIS	FIREDRAKE
FILIGREE	FILTH	FINDJAN	FINISES	FIREFALL
FILIGREED	FILTHIER	FINE	FINISH	FIREFANG
FILIGREEING	FILTHIEST	FINEABLE	FINISHED	FIREFANGED
FILII	FILTHIFIED	FINEBENT	FINISHER	FIREFANGING
FILING	FILTHIFY	FINECOMB	FINISHES	FIREFIGHTER
FILINGS	FILTHIFYING	FINED	FINISHING	FIREFLAUGHT
FILIONYMIC	FILTHILY	FINELEAF	FINITE	FIREFLIES
FILIOQUE	FILTHINESS	FINELESS	FINITELY	FIREFLIRT
FILIP	FILTHY	FINELY	FINITENESS	FIREFLOWER
FILIPPI	FILTRABILITY	FINEMENT	FINITESIMAL	FIREFLY
FILIPPIC	FILTRABLE	FINENESS	FINITISM	FIREGUARD

FIREHALL	FIRST	FISHTAILS	FITCHERED	FIZGIG
FIREHOUSE	FIRSTBORN	FISHWAY	FITCHERING	FIZZ
FIRELESS	FIRSTCOMER	FISHWEED	FITCHERY	FIZZED
FIRELIGHT	FIRSTER	FISHWEIR	FITCHES	FIZZER
FIRELIT	FIRSTLING	FISHWIFE	FITCHET	FIZZIER
FIRELOCK	FIRSTLY	FISHWIVES	FITCHEW	FIZZIEST
FIREMAN	FIRTH	FISHWOMAN	FITE	FIZZING
FIREMASTER	FISC	FISHWOOD	FITFUL	FIZZLE
FIREMEN	FISCAL	FISHWORKER	FITFULLY	FIZZLED
FIREPAN	FISCALITY	FISHWORKS	FITFULNESS	FIZZLING
FIREPINK	FISCALIZATION	FISHWORM	FITIFIED	FIZZY
FIREPLACE	FISCALIZE	FISHY	FITLY	FJALL
FIREPLOUGH	FISCALIZED	FISHYARD	FITMENT	FJELD
FIREPLOW	FISCALIZING	FISK	FITMENTS	FJORD
FIREPLUG	FISCHERITE	FISNOGA	FITNESS	FJORDED
FIREPOT	FISCUS	FISSATE	FITOUT	FLAB
FIREPOWER	FISETIN	FISSILE	FITROOT	FLABBERGAST
FIREPROOF	FISH	FISSILINGUAL	FITS	FLABBERGASTED
FIREPROOFED	FISHABLE	FISSILITY	FITTABLE	FLABBERGASTING
FIREPROOFING	FISHBACK	FISSION	FITTAGE	FLABBIER
FIREPROOFNESS	FISHBED	FISSIONABLE	FITTED	FLABBIEST
FIRER	FISHBERRIES	FISSIPALMATE	FITTEDNESS	FLABBILY
FIREROOM	FISHBERRY	FISSIPARISM	FITTEN	FLABBINESS
FIRESAFE	FISHBOLT	FISSIPARITY	FITTER	FLABBY
FIRESAFENESS	FISHBONE	FISSIPAROUS	FITTERS	FLABEL
FIRESAFETY	FISHBOWL	FISSIPED	FITTEST	FLABELLA
FIRESHINE	FISHEATER	FISSIPEDAL	FITTIER	FLABELLATE
FIRESIDE	FISHED	FISSIPEDATE	FITTIEST	FLABELLATION
FIRESIDER	FISHER	FISSIPEDIAL	FITTILY	FLABELLIFORM
FIRESIDESHIP	FISHERBOAT	FISSIROSTRAL	FITTINESS	FLABELLUM
FIRESPOUT	FISHERBOY	FISSIVE	FITTING	FLABRA
FIRESTONE	FISHERFOLK	FISSLE	FITTINGLY	FLABRUM
FIRESTOPPING	FISHERGIRL	FISSURA	FITTINGNESS	FLACCID
FIRETAIL	FISHERIES	FISSURAL	FITTIT	FLACCIDITY
FIRETHORN	FISHERMAN	FISSURATION	FITTY	FLACCIDLY
FIRETOP	FISHERMEN	FISSURE	FITTYFIED	FLACCIDNESS
FIRETRAP	FISHERPEOPLE	FISSURED	FITTYWAYS	FLACHERIE
FIREWARD	FISHERS	FISSURIFORM	FITTYWISE	FLACHERY
FIREWARDEN	FISHERWOMAN	FISSURING	FITWEED	FLACK
FIREWATER	FISHERY	FISSURY	FIVE	FLACKED
FIREWEED	FISHES	FIST	FIVEBAR	FLACKER
FIREWOOD	FISHET	FISTED	FIVEFOLD	FLACKET
FIREWORK	FISHEYE	FISTER	FIVELING	FLACON
FIREWORKLESS	FISHFALL	FISTFIGHT	FIVEPENCE	FLAE
FIREWORKS	FISHGARTH	FISTFUL	FIVEPENNY	FLAFF
FIREWORKY	FISHGIG	FISTFULS	FIVEPINS	FLAFFER
FIREWORM	FISHGRASS	FISTIANA	FIVER	FLAG
FIRING	FISHHOLD	FISTIC	FIVES	FLAGARIE
FIRK	FISHHOOK	FISTICAL	FIVESCORE	FLAGBOAT
FIRKED	FISHHOOKS	FISTICUFF	FIVESOME	FLAGELLA
FIRKER	FISHHOUSE	FISTICUFFED	FIVESTONES	FLAGELLANT
FIRKIN	FISHIER	FISTICUFFER	FIX	FLAGELLAR
FIRKING	FISHIEST	FISTICUFFERY	FIXABLE	FLAGELLATE
FIRLOT	FISHIFIED	FISTICUFFING	FIXAGE	FLAGELLATED
FIRM	FISHIFY	FISTIFY	FIXATE	FLAGELLATING
FIRMA	FISHIFYING	FISTINESS	FIXATED	FLAGELLATION
FIRMAMENT	FISHILY	FISTING	FIXATIF	FLAGELLATIVE
FIRMAMENTAL	FISHINESS	FISTLE	FIXATING	FLAGELLATOR
FIRMAN	FISHING	FISTMELE	FIXATION	FLAGELLATORY
FIRMANS	FISHLIKE	FISTNOTE	FIXATIVE	FLAGELLIFORM
FIRMARII	FISHLINE	FISTUCA	FIXATOR	FLAGELLIST
FIRMARIUS	FISHMAN	FISTULA	FIXATURE	FLAGELLOSIS
FIRMED	FISHMEAL	FISTULAE	FIXED	FLAGELLULA
FIRMER	FISHMEN	FISTULAR	FIXEDLY	FLAGELLULAE
FIRMEST	FISHMONGER	FISTULAS	FIXEDNESS	FLAGELLUM
FIRMHEARTED	FISHMOUTH	FISTULATOME	FIXER	FLAGELLUMS
FIRMING	FISHNET	FISTULATOUS	FIXIDITY	FLAGEOLET
FIRMISTERNAL	FISHPLATE	FISTULIFORM	FIXING	FLAGFALL
FIRMISTERNIAL	FISHPOLE	FISTULIZE	FIXINGS	FLAGFISH
FIRMISTERNOUS	FISHPOND	FISTULOSE	FIXITIES	FLAGGED
FIRMLAND	FISHPOOL	FISTULOUS	FIXITY	FLAGGER
FIRMLY	FISHPOT	FISTY	FIXT	FLAGGERY
FIRMNESS	FISHPOTTER	FIT	FIXTURE	FLAGGIER
FIRMS	FISHPOUND	FITCH	FIXURE	FLAGGIEST
FIRN	FISHSKIN	FITCHE	FIXY	FLAGGILY
FIRRY	FISHSPEAR	FITCHEE	FIZ	FLAGGINESS
FIRS	FISHTAIL	FITCHER	FIZELYITE	FLAGGING

FLAGGINGLY
FLAGGISH
FLAGGY
FLAGITATE
FLAGITATION
FLAGITIOUS
FLAGITIOUSLY
FLAGLEAF
FLAGLESS
FLAGLIKE
FLAGMAKER
FLAGMAKING
FLAGMAN
FLAGON
FLAGONET
FLAGPOLE
FLAGRANCE
FLAGRANCY
FLAGRANT
FLAGRANTLY
FLAGRANTNESS
FLAGROOT
FLAGS
FLAGSHIP
FLAGSTAFF
FLAGSTAFFS
FLAGSTAVES
FLAGSTICK
FLAGSTONE
FLAGWORM
FLAIL
FLAILED
FLAILING
FLAIR
FLAITE
FLAITH
FLAITHSHIP
FLAJOLOTITE
FLAK
FLAKAGE
FLAKE
FLAKED
FLAKER
FLAKIER
FLAKIEST
FLAKILY
FLAKINESS
FLAKING
FLAKY
FLAM
FLAMANT
FLAMB
FLAMBAGE
FLAMBANT
FLAMBE
FLAMBEAU
FLAMBEAUS
FLAMBEAUX
FLAMBEE
FLAMBERG
FLAMBERGE
FLAMBOYANCE
FLAMBOYANCY
FLAMBOYANT
FLAMBOYANTISM
FLAMBOYANTIZE
FLAMBOYANTLY
FLAME
FLAMED
FLAMELET
FLAMEN
FLAMENCO
FLAMENS
FLAMEOUT
FLAMEPROOF
FLAMER
FLAMFEW

FLAMIER
FLAMIEST
FLAMINEOUS
FLAMINES
FLAMING
FLAMINGLY
FLAMINGO
FLAMINGOES
FLAMINGOS
FLAMINICA
FLAMINICAL
FLAMMABILITY
FLAMMABLE
FLAMMANT
FLAMMED
FLAMMEOUS
FLAMMING
FLAMMULATED
FLAMMULATION
FLAMMULE
FLAMY
FLAN
FLANCARD
FLANCH
FLANCHARD
FLANCHE
FLANCHED
FLANCONADE
FLANCONNADE
FLANDAN
FLANERIE
FLANEUR
FLANG
FLANGE
FLANGED
FLANGER
FLANGEWAY
FLANGING
FLANK
FLANKARD
FLANKED
FLANKER
FLANKING
FLANNED
FLANNEL
FLANNELBUSH
FLANNELED
FLANNELET
FLANNELETTE
FLANNELFLOWER
FLANNELLEAF
FLANNELLED
FLANNELLY
FLANNELMOUTH
FLANNELMOUTHED
FLANNELS
FLANNING
FLAP
FLAPCAKE
FLAPDOCK
FLAPDOODLE
FLAPDRAGON
FLAPJACK
FLAPMOUTHED
FLAPPED
FLAPPER
FLAPPERDOM
FLAPPERED
FLAPPERHOOD
FLAPPERING
FLAPPERISH
FLAPPERISM
FLAPPET
FLAPPING
FLAPPY
FLAPS
FLARE

FLAREBACK
FLAREBOARD
FLARED
FLARER
FLARING
FLARINGLY
FLARY
FLASER
FLASH
FLASHBACK
FLASHBOARD
FLASHED
FLASHER
FLASHET
FLASHGUN
FLASHIER
FLASHIEST
FLASHILY
FLASHINESS
FLASHING
FLASHINGLY
FLASHLIGHT
FLASHLIKE
FLASHLY
FLASHNESS
FLASHOVER
FLASHPAN
FLASHPROOF
FLASHTESTER
FLASHY
FLASK
FLASKER
FLASKET
FLASKLET
FLASQUE
FLAT
FLATBED
FLATBOAT
FLATBOTTOM
FLATBROD
FLATCAP
FLATCAR
FLATDOM
FLATED
FLATFISH
FLATFISHES
FLATFOOT
FLATH
FLATHE
FLATHEAD
FLATIRON
FLATLAND
FLATLET
FLATLING
FLATLINGS
FLATLONG
FLATLY
FLATMAN
FLATMEN
FLATNESS
FLATNOSE
FLATS
FLATTEN
FLATTENED
FLATTENER
FLATTENING
FLATTER
FLATTERABLE
FLATTERCAP
FLATTERDOCK
FLATTERED
FLATTERER
FLATTERESS
FLATTERIES
FLATTERING
FLATTERINGLY
FLATTERINGNESS

FLATTEROUS
FLATTERY
FLATTEST
FLATTIE
FLATTING
FLATTISH
FLATTOP
FLATTY
FLATULENCE
FLATULENCY
FLATULENT
FLATULENTLY
FLATULENTNESS
FLATUOUS
FLATUS
FLATUSES
FLATWARE
FLATWAY
FLATWAYS
FLATWEED
FLATWISE
FLATWOODS
FLATWORK
FLATWORM
FLAUCHT
FLAUGHT
FLAUGHTBRED
FLAUGHTER
FLAUGHTS
FLAUNT
FLAUNTED
FLAUNTER
FLAUNTIER
FLAUNTIEST
FLAUNTILY
FLAUNTINESS
FLAUNTING
FLAUNTINGLY
FLAUNTY
FLAUTATO
FLAUTINO
FLAUTIST
FLAUTO
FLAVANILIN
FLAVANILINE
FLAVANTHRENE
FLAVANTHRONE
FLAVE
FLAVEDO
FLAVESCENCE
FLAVESCENT
FLAVIC
FLAVICANT
FLAVID
FLAVIN
FLAVINE
FLAVONE
FLAVONOL
FLAVOPROTEIN
FLAVOR
FLAVORED
FLAVORER
FLAVORFUL
FLAVORING
FLAVORLESS
FLAVOROUS
FLAVORSOME
FLAVORY
FLAVOUR
FLAVOURED
FLAVOURER
FLAVOURING
FLAVOUROUS
FLAVOURSOME
FLAVOURY
FLAW
FLAWED

FLAWFLOWER
FLAWIER
FLAWIEST
FLAWING
FLAWLESS
FLAWLESSLY
FLAWLESSNESS
FLAWN
FLAWS
FLAWY
FLAX
FLAXBIRD
FLAXBOARD
FLAXBUSH
FLAXDROP
FLAXEN
FLAXIER
FLAXIEST
FLAXMAN
FLAXSEED
FLAXTAIL
FLAXWEED
FLAXWENCH
FLAXWIFE
FLAXWOMAN
FLAXWORT
FLAXY
FLAY
FLAYER
FLAYFLINT
FLEA
FLEABAG
FLEABANE
FLEABITE
FLEABITING
FLEADOCK
FLEAK
FLEAM
FLEAS
FLEASEED
FLEAWEED
FLEAWOOD
FLEAWORT
FLEAY
FLEBILE
FLECH
FLECHE
FLECHETTE
FLECHETTES
FLECK
FLECKED
FLECKER
FLECKERED
FLECKERING
FLECKIER
FLECKIEST
FLECKINESS
FLECKING
FLECKLED
FLECKY
FLECNODE
FLECTION
FLECTIONAL
FLECTOR
FLED
FLEDGE
FLEDGED
FLEDGELESS
FLEDGELING
FLEDGING
FLEDGLING
FLEDGY
FLEE
FLEECE
FLEECED
FLEECEFLOWER
FLEECER

FLEECH	FLEWIT	FLIMSIER	FLISKIER	FLOCK
FLEECHMENT	FLEWS	FLIMSIES	FLISKIEST	FLOCKED
FLEECIER	FLEX	FLIMSIEST	FLISKING	FLOCKER
FLEECIEST	FLEXANIMOUS	FLIMSILY	FLISKMAHOY	FLOCKET
FLEECILY	FLEXED	FLIMSINESS	FLISKY	FLOCKIER
FLEECINESS	FLEXIBILITY	FLIMSY	FLIT	FLOCKIEST
FLEECING	FLEXIBLE	FLINCH	FLITCH	FLOCKING
FLEECY	FLEXIBLENESS	FLINCHED	FLITCHED	FLOCKLING
FLEEING	FLEXIBLY	FLINCHER	FLITCHEN	FLOCKMAN
FLEEM	FLEXILE	FLINCHING	FLITCHING	FLOCKMASTER
FLEER	FLEXILITY	FLINCHINGLY	FLITE	FLOCKMEAL
FLEERED	FLEXING	FLINDER	FLITED	FLOCKMEN
FLEERER	FLEXION	FLINDERS	FLITFOLD	FLOCKOWNER
FLEERING	FLEXIONAL	FLINDOSA	FLITING	FLOCKS
FLEERINGLY	FLEXIVE	FLINDOSY	FLITTED	FLOCKWISE
FLEERISH	FLEXOR	FLING	FLITTER	FLOCKY
FLEET	FLEXUOSE	FLINGDUST	FLITTERBAT	FLOCOON
FLEETER	FLEXUOSITIES	FLINGER	FLITTERED	FLODGE
FLEETEST	FLEXUOSITY	FLINGING	FLITTERING	FLOE
FLEETING	FLEXUOUS	FLINGY	FLITTERMICE	FLOEBERG
FLEETINGLY	FLEXUOUSLY	FLINKITE	FLITTERMOUSE	FLOG
FLEETINGNESS	FLEXUOUSNESS	FLINT	FLITTERN	FLOGGABLE
FLEETINGS	FLEXURA	FLINTED	FLITTERS	FLOGGED
FLEETLY	FLEXURAL	FLINTER	FLITTINESS	FLOGGER
FLEETNESS	FLEXURE	FLINTHEAD	FLITTING	FLOGGING
FLEETWING	FLEXURED	FLINTHEARTED	FLITTINGLY	FLOGMASTER
FLEG	FLEY	FLINTIER	FLITTY	FLOGSTER
FLEME	FLEYEDLY	FLINTIEST	FLITWITE	FLOIT
FLEMER	FLEYEDNESS	FLINTIFIED	FLIVVER	FLOKITE
FLEMISH	FLEYLAND	FLINTIFY	FLIX	FLONG
FLENCH	FLEYSOME	FLINTIFYING	FLIXWEED	FLOOD
FLENSE	FLIC	FLINTILY	FLO	FLOODAGE
FLENSED	FLICFLAC	FLINTINESS	FLOAT	FLOODBOARD
FLENSER	FLICHTER	FLINTING	FLOATABILITY	FLOODCOCK
FLENSING	FLICHTERED	FLINTLOCK	FLOATABLE	FLOODED
FLENTES	FLICK	FLINTS	FLOATAGE	FLOODER
FLERRIED	FLICKED	FLINTWOOD	FLOATATION	FLOODGATE
FLERRY	FLICKER	FLINTWORK	FLOATATIVE	FLOODING
FLERRYING	FLICKERED	FLINTWORKER	FLOATBOARD	FLOODLIGHT
FLESH	FLICKERING	FLINTY	FLOATED	FLOODLIGHTED
FLESHBRUSH	FLICKERS	FLIOMA	FLOATER	FLOODLIGHTING
FLESHED	FLICKERTAIL	FLIP	FLOATERS	FLOODLIT
FLESHEN	FLICKERY	FLIPE	FLOATIER	FLOODMARK
FLESHER	FLICKING	FLIPED	FLOATIEST	FLOODOMETER
FLESHFUL	FLICKS	FLIPING	FLOATINESS	FLOODPLAIN
FLESHHOOK	FLICKY	FLIPJACK	FLOATING	FLOODTIME
FLESHIER	FLIDDER	FLIPPANCE	FLOATINGLY	FLOODWATER
FLESHIEST	FLIED	FLIPPANCIES	FLOATIVE	FLOODWAY
FLESHINESS	FLIER	FLIPPANCY	FLOATS	FLOODWOOD
FLESHING	FLIERS	FLIPPANT	FLOATSMAN	FLOODY
FLESHINGS	FLIES	FLIPPANTLY	FLOATSMEN	FLOOEY
FLESHLESS	FLIEST	FLIPPANTNESS	FLOATSTONE	FLOOKAN
FLESHLILY	FLIFFUS	FLIPPED	FLOATY	FLOOR
FLESHLINESS	FLIGGED	FLIPPER	FLOB	FLOORAGE
FLESHLY	FLIGGER	FLIPPERLING	FLOC	FLOORBOARD
FLESHMENT	FLIGHT	FLIPPERY	FLOCCI	FLOORCLOTH
FLESHPOT	FLIGHTED	FLIPPING	FLOCCILATION	FLOORED
FLESHQUAKE	FLIGHTER	FLIRD	FLOCCIPEND	FLOORER
FLESHY	FLIGHTFUL	FLIRE	FLOCCOSE	FLOORHEAD
FLET	FLIGHTHEAD	FLIRT	FLOCCOSELY	FLOORING
FLETCH	FLIGHTIER	FLIRTABLE	FLOCCULABLE	FLOORMAN
FLETCHED	FLIGHTIEST	FLIRTATION	FLOCCULAR	FLOORMEN
FLETCHER	FLIGHTILY	FLIRTATIONAL	FLOCCULATE	FLOORS
FLETCHING	FLIGHTINESS	FLIRTATIOUS	FLOCCULATED	FLOORWALKER
FLETHER	FLIGHTING	FLIRTATIOUSLY	FLOCCULATING	FLOORWAY
FLETTON	FLIGHTLESS	FLIRTATIOUSNESS	FLOCCULATION	FLOOSY
FLEUR	FLIGHTS	FLIRTED	FLOCCULATOR	FLOOZIES
FLEURET	FLIGHTSHOT	FLIRTER	FLOCCULE	FLOOZY
FLEURETTEE	FLIGHTWORTHY	FLIRTIER	FLOCCULENCE	FLOP
FLEURETTY	FLIGHTY	FLIRTIEST	FLOCCULENCY	FLOPEROO
FLEURON	FLIMFLAM	FLIRTIGIG	FLOCCULENT	FLOPHOUSE
FLEURONE	FLIMFLAMMED	FLIRTING	FLOCCULENTLY	FLOPOVER
FLEURONNE	FLIMFLAMMER	FLIRTISH	FLOCCULI	FLOPPED
FLEURONNEE	FLIMFLAMMERY	FLIRTISHNESS	FLOCCULOSE	FLOPPER
FLEURY	FLIMFLAMMING	FLIRTY	FLOCCULOUS	FLOPPERS
FLEW	FLIMMER	FLISK	FLOCCULUS	FLOPPIER
FLEWED	FLIMP	FLISKED	FLOCCUS	FLOPPIEST

FLOPPILY
FLOPPINESS
FLOPPING
FLOPPY
FLOPWING
FLOR
FLORA
FLORAE
FLORAISON
FLORAL
FLORALIZE
FLORALLY
FLORAMOR
FLORAMOUR
FLORAN
FLORAS
FLORATE
FLOREAL
FLOREATE
FLOREATED
FLOREATING
FLORENCE
FLORENT
FLORENTIUM
FLORES
FLORESCENCE
FLORESCENT
FLORESSENCE
FLORET
FLORETA
FLORETED
FLORETTY
FLORETUM
FLORIATE
FLORIATED
FLORIATION
FLORIBUNDA
FLORICAN
FLORICIN
FLORICULTURE
FLORID
FLORIDEAN
FLORIDEOUS
FLORIDITIES
FLORIDITY
FLORIDLY
FLORIDNESS
FLORIFEROUS
FLORIFEROUSLY
FLORIFEROUSNESS
FLORIFICATION
FLORIFORM
FLORIGEN
FLORIGRAPHY
FLORILEGE
FLORILEGIA
FLORILEGIUM
FLORIMANIA
FLORIMANIST
FLORIN
FLORIPAROUS
FLORIPONDIO
FLORISCOPE
FLORIST
FLORISTIC
FLORISTICALLY
FLORISTICS
FLORISTRY
FLORISUGENT
FLORIZINE
FLOROON
FLOROSCOPE
FLORUIT
FLORULA
FLORULAE
FLORULAS
FLORULENT

FLORY
FLOSCULAR
FLOSCULARIAN
FLOSCULE
FLOSCULOSE
FLOSCULOUS
FLOSH
FLOSS
FLOSSA
FLOSSER
FLOSSFLOWER
FLOSSIE
FLOSSIER
FLOSSIES
FLOSSIEST
FLOSSING
FLOSSY
FLOT
FLOTA
FLOTAGE
FLOTANT
FLOTATION
FLOTATIVE
FLOTE
FLOTILLA
FLOTS
FLOTSAM
FLOTSAN
FLOTSEN
FLOTSON
FLOTTER
FLOUNCE
FLOUNCED
FLOUNCING
FLOUNCY
FLOUNDER
FLOUNDERED
FLOUNDERING
FLOUNDERINGLY
FLOUNDERS
FLOUR
FLOURED
FLOURING
FLOURISH
FLOURISHED
FLOURISHER
FLOURISHES
FLOURISHING
FLOURISHINGLY
FLOURISHY
FLOURY
FLOUSE
FLOUSH
FLOUT
FLOUTED
FLOUTER
FLOUTING
FLOUTINGLY
FLOW
FLOWAGE
FLOWED
FLOWER
FLOWERAGE
FLOWERED
FLOWERER
FLOWERET
FLOWERFENCE
FLOWERFLY
FLOWERIER
FLOWERIEST
FLOWERILY
FLOWERINESS
FLOWERING
FLOWERIST
FLOWERLET
FLOWERPECKER
FLOWERPOT

FLOWERS
FLOWERWORK
FLOWERY
FLOWING
FLOWINGLY
FLOWINGNESS
FLOWMETER
FLOWN
FLOWOFF
FLU
FLUATE
FLUAVIL
FLUAVILE
FLUB
FLUBBED
FLUBBING
FLUBDUB
FLUBDUBBERIES
FLUBDUBBERY
FLUCAN
FLUCTUABILITY
FLUCTUABLE
FLUCTUANT
FLUCTUATE
FLUCTUATED
FLUCTUATING
FLUCTUATION
FLUCTUOSITY
FLUCTUOUS
FLUE
FLUED
FLUELLEN
FLUELLIN
FLUELLITE
FLUEMAN
FLUEMEN
FLUENCE
FLUENCIES
FLUENCY
FLUENT
FLUENTLY
FLUENTNESS
FLUER
FLUEWORK
FLUEY
FLUFF
FLUFFED
FLUFFER
FLUFFIER
FLUFFIEST
FLUFFILY
FLUFFINESS
FLUFFING
FLUFFY
FLUGEL
FLUGELHORN
FLUGELMAN
FLUGELMEN
FLUIBLE
FLUID
FLUIDAL
FLUIDALLY
FLUIDEXTRACT
FLUIDIC
FLUIDICS
FLUIDIFICATION
FLUIDIFIED
FLUIDIFIER
FLUIDIFY
FLUIDIFYING
FLUIDIMETER
FLUIDISM
FLUIDIST
FLUIDITY
FLUIDIZATION
FLUIDIZE
FLUIDIZED

FLUIDIZING
FLUIDLY
FLUIDNESS
FLUIDRACHM
FLUIDRAM
FLUIGRAM
FLUIGRAMME
FLUING
FLUITANT
FLUKE
FLUKED
FLUKES
FLUKEWORT
FLUKEY
FLUKIER
FLUKIEST
FLUKILY
FLUKINESS
FLUKING
FLUKY
FLUM
FLUMDIDDLE
FLUME
FLUMED
FLUMERIN
FLUMING
FLUMINOSE
FLUMINOUS
FLUMMER
FLUMMERIES
FLUMMERY
FLUMMOX
FLUMMOXED
FLUMMOXING
FLUMP
FLUMPED
FLUMPING
FLUNG
FLUNK
FLUNKED
FLUNKER
FLUNKEY
FLUNKEYISM
FLUNKEYISTIC
FLUNKEYITE
FLUNKEYS
FLUNKIES
FLUNKING
FLUNKY
FLUNKYISM
FLUNKYISTIC
FLUNKYITE
FLUOARSENATE
FLUOBORATE
FLUOBORIC
FLUOBORITE
FLUOCERINE
FLUOCERITE
FLUOHYDRIC
FLUOR
FLUORAN
FLUORANE
FLUORANTHENE
FLUORAPATITE
FLUORATE
FLUORENE
FLUORESAGE
FLUORESCE
FLUORESCED
FLUORESCEIN
FLUORESCEINE
FLUORESCENCE
FLUORESCENT
FLUORESCIN
FLUORESCING
FLUORHYDRIC
FLUORIC

FLUORID
FLUORIDATE
FLUORIDATED
FLUORIDATING
FLUORIDATION
FLUORIDE
FLUORIN
FLUORINATE
FLUORINATION
FLUORINDIN
FLUORINE
FLUORITE
FLUORMETER
FLUOROBORATE
FLUOROCARBON
FLUOROFORM
FLUOROFORMOL
FLUOROGEN
FLUOROGENIC
FLUOROGRAPHY
FLUOROID
FLUOROMETER
FLUOROSCOPE
FLUOROSCOPIC
FLUOROSCOPY
FLUOROTYPE
FLUORSPAR
FLUORYL
FLUOSILICATE
FLUOSILICIC
FLUOTANTALIC
FLURN
FLURR
FLURRIED
FLURRIEDLY
FLURRIES
FLURRIMENT
FLURRY
FLURRYING
FLUSH
FLUSHBOARD
FLUSHED
FLUSHER
FLUSHERMAN
FLUSHERMEN
FLUSHEST
FLUSHGATE
FLUSHING
FLUSHINGLY
FLUSHNESS
FLUSHY
FLUSK
FLUSKER
FLUSTER
FLUSTERATE
FLUSTERATION
FLUSTERED
FLUSTERER
FLUSTERING
FLUSTERY
FLUSTRATE
FLUSTRATION
FLUSTRINE
FLUSTROID
FLUSTRUM
FLUTE
FLUTEBIRD
FLUTED
FLUTEMOUTH
FLUTER
FLUTES
FLUTEWORK
FLUTHER
FLUTIER
FLUTIEST
FLUTINA
FLUTING

FLUTINGS	FLYTAIL	FOETICIDE	FOLDEDLY	FOLLICULATED
FLUTIST	FLYTE	FOETIFEROUS	FOLDEN	FOLLICULE
FLUTTER	FLYTED	FOETIPAROUS	FOLDER	FOLLICULITIS
FLUTTERATION	FLYTIER	FOETOR	FOLDEROL	FOLLICULOSE
FLUTTERED	FLYTIME	FOETURE	FOLDING	FOLLICULOSIS
FLUTTERER	FLYTING	FOETUS	FOLDOUT	FOLLICULOUS
FLUTTERING	FLYTRAP	FOETUSES	FOLDS	FOLLIED
FLUTTERINGLY	FLYWAY	FOFARRAW	FOLDSKIRT	FOLLIES
FLUTTERSOME	FLYWEIGHT	FOG	FOLDURE	FOLLIFUL
FLUTTERY	FLYWHEEL	FOGAS	FOLDY	FOLLILY
FLUTY	FLYWINCH	FOGBOUND	FOLEYE	FOLLIS
FLUVANNA	FLYWIRE	FOGBOW	FOLIA	FOLLOW
FLUVIAL	FLYWORT	FOGDOG	FOLIACEOUS	FOLLOWED
FLUVIALIST	FNESE	FOGE	FOLIAGE	FOLLOWER
FLUVIATIC	FOAL	FOGEATER	FOLIAGED	FOLLOWERSHIP
FLUVIATILE	FOALED	FOGEY	FOLIAGEOUS	FOLLOWING
FLUVICOLINE	FOALFOOT	FOGFRUIT	FOLIAGING	FOLLOWS
FLUVIOGRAPH	FOALFOOTS	FOGGAGE	FOLIAL	FOLLY
FLUVIOLOGY	FOALING	FOGGARA	FOLIAR	FOLLYER
FLUVIOMARINE	FOALY	FOGGED	FOLIARY	FOLLYING
FLUVIOSE	FOAM	FOGGER	FOLIATE	FOLO
FLUVIOUS	FOAMBOW	FOGGIER	FOLIATED	FOMENT
FLUX	FOAMED	FOGGIEST	FOLIATING	FOMENTATION
FLUXATION	FOAMER	FOGGILY	FOLIATION	FOMENTED
FLUXED	FOAMFLOWER	FOGGINESS	FOLIATURE	FOMENTER
FLUXER	FOAMIER	FOGGING	FOLIE	FOMENTING
FLUXIBILITY	FOAMIEST	FOGGY	FOLIICOLOUS	FOMENTO
FLUXIBLE	FOAMILY	FOGHORN	FOLIIFEROUS	FOMES
FLUXIBLENESS	FOAMINESS	FOGIE	FOLIIFORM	FOMITES
FLUXIBLY	FOAMING	FOGIES	FOLIO	FON
FLUXILE	FOAMY	FOGLE	FOLIOBRANCH	FOND
FLUXILITY	FOB	FOGLIETTO	FOLIOED	FONDA
FLUXING	FOBBED	FOGMAN	FOLIOING	FONDACO
FLUXION	FOBBING	FOGMEN	FOLIOLATE	FONDANT
FLUXIONAL	FOCAL	FOGO	FOLIOLE	FONDATEUR
FLUXIONALLY	FOCALIZATION	FOGON	FOLIOLOSE	FONDER
FLUXIONARY	FOCALIZE	FOGOU	FOLIOS	FONDEST
FLUXIONIST	FOCALIZED	FOGRAM	FOLIOSE	FONDISH
FLUXIVE	FOCALIZING	FOGRAMITE	FOLIOSITY	FONDLE
FLUXMETER	FOCALLY	FOGRAMITY	FOLIOT	FONDLED
FLUXROOT	FOCALOID	FOGRUM	FOLIOUS	FONDLER
FLUXURE	FOCI	FOGSCOFFER	FOLIOUSLY	FONDLING
FLUXWEED	FOCIMETER	FOGUS	FOLIUM	FONDLY
FLY	FOCIMETRY	FOGY	FOLIUMS	FONDNESS
FLYABLE	FOCKLE	FOGYDOM	FOLK	FONDOUK
FLYAWAY	FOCOIDS	FOGYISH	FOLKCRAFT	FONDU
FLYBACK	FOCOMETER	FOGYISM	FOLKFREE	FONDUE
FLYBALL	FOCOMETRY	FOH	FOLKLAND	FONDUK
FLYBANE	FOCSLE	FOHAT	FOLKLORE	FONIO
FLYBELT	FOCUS	FOHN	FOLKLORIC	FONO
FLYBLEW	FOCUSED	FOIBLE	FOLKLORISH	FONS
FLYBLOW	FOCUSER	FOIE	FOLKLORISM	FONT
FLYBLOWN	FOCUSES	FOIL	FOLKLORIST	FONTAL
FLYBOAT	FOCUSING	FOILED	FOLKLORISTIC	FONTALLY
FLYBOY	FOCUSSED	FOILER	FOLKMOOT	FONTANEL
FLYBRUSH	FOCUSSING	FOILING	FOLKMOOTER	FONTANELLE
FLYBY	FODDA	FOILSMAN	FOLKMOT	FONTANGE
FLYCATCHER	FODDER	FOILSMEN	FOLKMOTE	FONTED
FLYEATER	FODDERED	FOIN	FOLKMOTER	FONTES
FLYER	FODDERER	FOINED	FOLKRIGHT	FONTICULUS
FLYFLAP	FODDERING	FOINING	FOLKS	FONTINA
FLYFLAPPER	FODE	FOISON	FOLKSEY	FONTINAL
FLYFLOWER	FODGE	FOISONLESS	FOLKSIER	FOO
FLYING	FODGEL	FOISONS	FOLKSIEST	FOOD
FLYINGLY	FODIENT	FOIST	FOLKSINESS	FOODER
FLYINGS	FOE	FOISTED	FOLKSY	FOODLESS
FLYLEAF	FOEDERATI	FOISTER	FOLKWAY	FOODS
FLYLEAVES	FOEDERATUS	FOISTINESS	FOLKWAYS	FOODSTUFF
FLYMAN	FOEHN	FOISTING	FOLKY	FOODY
FLYMEN	FOEHOOD	FOISTY	FOLLE	FOOFARAW
FLYNESS	FOEMAN	FOITER	FOLLER	FOOL
FLYOVER	FOEMANSHIP	FOLCGEMOT	FOLLES	FOOLED
FLYPAPER	FOEMEN	FOLD	FOLLETTI	FOOLER
FLYPE	FOETAL	FOLDAGE	FOLLETTO	FOOLERIES
FLYPROOF	FOETALISM	FOLDBOAT	FOLLICLE	FOOLERY
FLYSPECK	FOETATION	FOLDCOURSE	FOLLICULAR	FOOLESS
FLYSWAT	FOETICIDAL	FOLDED	FOLLICULATE	FOOLFISH

FOOLFISHES
FOOLHARDIER
FOOLHARDIEST
FOOLHARDIHOOD
FOOLHARDILY
FOOLHARDINESS
FOOLHARDY
FOOLHEAD
FOOLIFY
FOOLING
FOOLISH
FOOLISHLY
FOOLISHNESS
FOOLMONGER
FOOLOCRACY
FOOLPROOF
FOOLPROOFNESS
FOOLSCAP
FOONER
FOOSTER
FOOSTERER
FOOT
FOOTAGE
FOOTBACK
FOOTBALL
FOOTBALLER
FOOTBALLIST
FOOTBAND
FOOTBEAT
FOOTBLOWER
FOOTBOARD
FOOTBOARDS
FOOTBOY
FOOTBREADTH
FOOTBRIDGE
FOOTCLOTH
FOOTCLOTHS
FOOTED
FOOTEITE
FOOTER
FOOTFALL
FOOTFARER
FOOTFAULT
FOOTFEED
FOOTFOLK
FOOTFUL
FOOTGANGER
FOOTGEAR
FOOTGELD
FOOTGLOVE
FOOTGRIP
FOOTH
FOOTHALT
FOOTHILL
FOOTHOLD
FOOTHOOK
FOOTHOT
FOOTIER
FOOTIEST
FOOTING
FOOTINGLY
FOOTINGS
FOOTLE
FOOTLED
FOOTLER
FOOTLESS
FOOTLICKER
FOOTLIGHT
FOOTLIGHTS
FOOTLIKE
FOOTLING
FOOTLINING
FOOTLOCK
FOOTLOCKER
FOOTLOG
FOOTLOOSE
FOOTMAKER

FOOTMAN
FOOTMANHOOD
FOOTMANRY
FOOTMANSHIP
FOOTMARK
FOOTMEN
FOOTNOTE
FOOTNOTED
FOOTNOTING
FOOTPACE
FOOTPAD
FOOTPADDERY
FOOTPATH
FOOTPICK
FOOTPLATE
FOOTPRINT
FOOTRAIL
FOOTREST
FOOTRILL
FOOTROOM
FOOTROPE
FOOTS
FOOTSCALD
FOOTSLOG
FOOTSLOGGER
FOOTSORE
FOOTSORENESS
FOOTSTALK
FOOTSTALL
FOOTSTEP
FOOTSTICK
FOOTSTOCK
FOOTSTONE
FOOTSTOOL
FOOTWALK
FOOTWALL
FOOTWAY
FOOTWEAR
FOOTWORK
FOOTWORN
FOOTY
FOOYOUNG
FOOYUNG
FOOZLE
FOOZLED
FOOZLER
FOOZLING
FOP
FOPDOODLE
FOPLING
FOPPERIES
FOPPERLY
FOPPERY
FOPPISH
FOPPISHLY
FOPPISHNESS
FOPPY
FOPSHIP
FOR
FORA
FORAGE
FORAGED
FORAGEMENT
FORAGER
FORAGERS
FORAGING
FORALITE
FORAM
FORAMEN
FORAMENS
FORAMINA
FORAMINATE
FORAMINATED
FORAMINATION
FORAMINIFER
FORAMINOSE
FORAMINOUS

FORAMINULATE
FORAMINULE
FORAMINULOSE
FORAMINULOUS
FORANE
FORANEOUS
FORASTERO
FORAY
FORAYED
FORAYER
FORAYING
FORB
FORBAD
FORBADE
FORBAR
FORBARE
FORBARRED
FORBEAR
FORBEARABLE
FORBEARANCE
FORBEARANT
FORBEARANTLY
FORBEARER
FORBEARING
FORBESITE
FORBID
FORBIDDAL
FORBIDDANCE
FORBIDDEN
FORBIDDENLY
FORBIDDENNESS
FORBIDDER
FORBIDDING
FORBIDDINGLY
FORBIDDiNGNESS
FORBITE
FORBLED
FORBLOW
FORBODE
FORBORE
FORBORNE
FORBREAK
FORBY
FORBYE
FORBYSEN
FORBYSENING
FORCAT
FORCE
FORCEABLE
FORCED
FORCEDLY
FORCEDNESS
FORCEFUL
FORCEFULLY
FORCEFULNESS
FORCELET
FORCEMEAT
FORCEMENT
FORCENE
FOHCEPS
FORCEPSES
FORCEPUT
FORCER
FORCET
FORCHASE
FORCHES
FORCIBILITY
FORCIBLE
FORCIBLENESS
FORCIBLY
FORCING
FORCIPATE
FORCIPATED
FORCIPES
FORCIPIFORM
FORCIPRESSURE
FORCIPULATE

FORCIVE
FORCUT
FORCY
FORD
FORDABLE
FORDEAL
FORDID
FORDING
FORDO
FORDOING
FORDONE
FORDULL
FORDWINE
FORDY
FORE
FOREARM
FOREBACKWARDLY
FOREBAR
FOREBAY
FOREBEAR
FOREBITT
FOREBITTER
FOREBOARD
FOREBODE
FOREBODED
FOREBODER
FOREBODING
FOREBODINGLY
FOREBODINGNESS
FOREBODY
FOREBOOM
FOREBOOT
FOREBOW
FOREBOWELS
FOREBOWS
FOREBRACE
FOREBRAIN
FOREBREAST
FOREBROADS
FOREBUSH
FOREBY
FOREBYE
FORECABIN
FORECAR
FORECARRIAGE
FORECAST
FORECASTED
FORECASTER
FORECASTING
FORECASTLE
FORECASTLEHEAD
FORECASTLEMAN
FORECASTLEMEN
FORECHASE
FORECHURCH
FORECLOSABLE
FORECLOSE
FORECLOSED
FORECLOSING
FORECLOSURE
FORECOME
FORECOMINGNESS
FORECOOL
FORECOOLER
FORECOURSE
FORECOURT
FOREDATE
FOREDATED
FOREDATING
FOREDAWN
FOREDAY
FOREDAYS
FOREDECK
FOREDEEM
FOREDEEP
FOREDESTINE
FOREDESTINED

FOREDESTINING
FOREDESTINY
FOREDO
FOREDONE
FOREDOOM
FOREDOOMED
FOREDOOMER
FOREDOOMING
FOREDOOR
FOREDUNE
FOREFACE
FOREFATHER
FOREFATHERLY
FOREFEEL
FOREFEELING
FOREFEELINGLY
FOREFEET
FOREFELT
FOREFEND
FOREFIELD
FOREFINGER
FOREFOOT
FOREFRONT
FOREGAME
FOREGANGER
FOREGATE
FOREGATHER
FOREGIFT
FOREGIRTH
FOREGLANCE
FOREGLEAM
FOREGLIMPSE
FOREGO
FOREGOER
FOREGOING
FOREGONE
FOREGONENESS
FOREGROUND
FOREGUT
FOREHALL
FOREHAMMER
FOREHAND
FOREHANDED
FOREHANDEDNESS
FOREHARD
FOREHEAD
FOREHEADED
FOREHEARTH
FOREHEATER
FOREHENT
FOREHOLD
FOREHOOF
FOREHOOK
FOREIGN
FOREIGNEERING
FOREIGNER
FOREIGNISM
FOREIGNNESS
FOREIRON
FOREJUDGE
FOREJUDGED
FOREJUDGER
FOREJUDGING
FOREKNEW
FOREKNOW
FOREKNOWER
FOREKNOWING
FOREKNOWLEDGE
FOREKNOWN
FOREL
FORELADIES
FORELADY
FORELAID
FORELAND
FORELAY
FORELAYING
FORELEECH

FORELEG
FORELIMB
FORELOCK
FORELOOK
FORELOOP
FORELOOPER
FORELOPER
FORELOUPER
FOREMAN
FOREMANSHIP
FOREMARCH
FOREMAST
FOREMASTHAND
FOREMASTMAN
FOREMASTMEN
FOREMEN
FOREMILK
FOREMIND
FOREMISTRESS
FOREMOST
FOREMOTHER
FORENAME
FORENAMED
FORENENT
FORENIGHT
FORENOON
FORENOTE
FORENSAL
FORENSIC
FORENSICAL
FORENSICALITY
FORENSICALLY
FOREORDAIN
FOREORDAINMENT
FOREORDINATE
FOREORDINATED
FOREORDINATING
FOREORDINATION
FOREPALE
FOREPALED
FOREPALING
FOREPARENT
FOREPARENTS
FOREPART
FOREPASS
FOREPASSED
FOREPAST
FOREPEAK
FOREPIECE
FOREPLOT
FOREPOINT
FOREPOINTER
FOREPOLE
FOREPOLED
FOREPOLING
FOREPOST
FOREPRISE
FOREPRIZE
FOREQUARTER
FORERAN
FORERANK
FOREREACH
FOREREACHING
FORERIBS
FORERIGHT
FOREROOM
FORERUN
FORERUNNER
FORERUNNING
FORERUNNINGS
FORES
FORESADDLE
FORESAID
FORESAIL
FORESAW
FORESAY
FORESAYING

FORESCENT
FORESCRIPT
FORESEE
FORESEEING
FORESEEINGLY
FORESEEN
FORESEER
FORESET
FORESEY
FORESHADOW
FORESHADOWER
FORESHAFT
FORESHEET
FORESHIFT
FORESHIP
FORESHOCK
FORESHORE
FORESHORTEN
FORESHORTENING
FORESHOT
FORESHOW
FORESHOWED
FORESHOWER
FORESHOWING
FORESHOWN
FORESIDE
FORESIGHT
FORESIGHTED
FORESIGHTEDLY
FORESIGHTEDNESS
FORESIGHTFUL
FORESIGN
FORESIGNIFY
FORESINGER
FORESKIN
FORESLEEVE
FORESLOW
FORESOUND
FORESPAKE
FORESPEAK
FORESPEAKER
FORESPEAKING
FORESPEECH
FORESPEED
FORESPOKE
FORESPOKEN
FOREST
FORESTAFF
FORESTAGE
FORESTAIR
FORESTAL
FORESTALL
FORESTALLED
FORESTALLER
FORESTALLING
FORESTARLING
FORESTATION
FORESTAY
FORESTAYSAIL
FORESTCRAFT
FORESTED
FORESTEM
FORESTEP
FORESTER
FORESTIAL
FORESTICK
FORESTINE
FORESTING
FORESTLESS
FORESTOLOGY
FORESTRAL
FORESTRESS
FORESTRY
FORESTS
FORESTSIDE
FORESTY
FORESWEAT

FORETACK
FORETACKLE
FORETAKE
FORETALK
FORETALKING
FORETASTE
FORETASTED
FORETASTER
FORETASTING
FORETEETH
FORETELL
FORETELLER
FORETELLING
FORETHINK
FORETHINKER
FORETHINKING
FORETHOUGHT
FORETHOUGHTED
FORETHOUGHTFUL
FORETHOUGHTFULLY
FORETHOUGHTFULNESS
FORETIME
FORETOKEN
FORETOKENED
FORETOKENING
FORETOLD
FORETOOTH
FORETOP
FORETOPMAN
FORETOPMAST
FORETOPMEN
FORETOPSAIL
FORETURN
FORETYPE
FOREVER
FOREVERMORE
FOREWARD
FOREWARM
FOREWARMER
FOREWARN
FOREWARNED
FOREWARNER
FOREWARNING
FOREWATERS
FOREWENT
FOREWING
FOREWINNING
FOREWISDOM
FOREWIT
FOREWOMAN
FOREWOMEN
FOREWORD
FOREWORLD
FOREWORN
FOREYARD
FORFAIRN
FORFAR
FORFARE
FORFARS
FORFAULT
FORFAULTURE
FORFEIT
FORFEITABLE
FORFEITED
FORFEITER
FORFEITING
FORFEITS
FORFEITURE
FORFEND
FORFENDED
FORFENDING
FORFEX
FORFICATE
FORFICATED
FORFICATION
FORFICIFORM
FORFICULATE

FORFOUCHTEN
FORFOUGHEN
FORFOUGHTEN
FORGAB
FORGAINST
FORGAT
FORGATHER
FORGATHERED
FORGATHERING
FORGAVE
FORGE
FORGED
FORGEFUL
FORGEMAN
FORGEMEN
FORGER
FORGERIES
FORGERY
FORGET
FORGETFUL
FORGETFULLY
FORGETFULNESS
FORGETIVE
FORGETNESS
FORGETT
FORGETTABLE
FORGETTE
FORGETTER
FORGETTING
FORGETTINGLY
FORGIFT
FORGING
FORGIVABLE
FORGIVE
FORGIVELESS
FORGIVEN
FORGIVENESS
FORGIVER
FORGIVING
FORGIVINGLY
FORGIVINGNESS
FORGO
FORGOER
FORGOING
FORGONE
FORGOT
FORGOTTEN
FORGROW
FORGROWN
FORHAILE
FORHEED
FORHOO
FORHOOIE
FORHOOY
FORHOW
FORINSEC
FORINT
FORJASKIT
FORJESKET
FORJUDGE
FORJUDGED
FORJUDGER
FORJUDGING
FORK
FORKBEARD
FORKED
FORKEDLY
FORKEDNESS
FORKER
FORKHEAD
FORKINESS
FORKING
FORKLIFT
FORKMAN
FORKMEN
FORKSMITH
FORKTAIL

FORKY
FORLAIN
FORLANA
FORLAY
FORLEAVE
FORLEAVING
FORLEFT
FORLEIT
FORLESE
FORLET
FORLETTING
FORLIE
FORLIVE
FORLOIN
FORLORN
FORLORNITY
FORLORNLY
FORLORNNESS
FORM
FORMA
FORMAL
FORMALAZINE
FORMALDEHYD
FORMALDEHYD
FORMALDOXIM
FORMALESQUE
FORMALISM
FORMALIST
FORMALISTIC
FORMALITER
FORMALITH
FORMALITIES
FORMALITY
FORMALIZATIO
FORMALIZE
FORMALIZED
FORMALIZER
FORMALIZING
FORMALLY
FORMAMIDE
FORMAMIDINE
FORMANILIDE
FORMANT
FORMAT
FORMATE
FORMATION
FORMATIONAL
FORMATIVE
FORMATIVELY
FORMATIVENES
FORMATURE
FORMAZAN
FORMAZYL
FORMBY
FORME
FORMED
FORMEDON
FORMEE
FORMEL
FORMELT
FORMENE
FORMENIC
FORMER
FORMERET
FORMERLY
FORMFUL
FORMIATE
FORMIC
FORMICA
FORMICARIAN
FORMICARIES
FORMICARY
FORMICATE
FORMICATED
FORMICATING
FORMICATION
FORMICATIVE

FORMICID
FORMICIDE
FORMICINE
FORMIDABILITY
FORMIDABLE
FORMIDABLENESS
FORMIDABLY
FORMIN
FORMING
FORMISM
FORMITY
FORMLESS
FORMLESSLY
FORMLESSNESS
FORMLY
FORMOLIT
FORMOLITE
FORMONITRILE
FORMOSE
FORMOSITY
FORMOUS
FORMS
FORMULA
FORMULABLE
FORMULAE
FORMULAIC
FORMULAR
FORMULARIES
FORMULARISM
FORMULARIST
FORMULARIZATION
FORMULARIZE
FORMULARIZED
FORMULARIZING
FORMULARY
FORMULAS
FORMULATE
FORMULATED
FORMULATING
FORMULATION
FORMULATOR
FORMULATORY
FORMULE
FORMULISM
FORMULIST
FORMULISTIC
FORMULIZATION
FORMULIZE
FORMULIZED
FORMULIZER
FORMULIZING
FORMWORK
FORMY
FORMYL
FORMYLATE
FORMYLATED
FORMYLATING
FORMYLATION
FORNACIC
FORNAXID
FORNCAST
FORNE
FORNENST
FORNENT
FORNICAL
FORNICATE
FORNICATED
FORNICATING
FORNICATION
FORNICATOR
FORNICATRICES
FORNICATRIX
FORNINST
FORNIX
FOROLD
FORPASS
FORPET

FORPINE
FORPINED
FORPINING
FORPIT
FORPRISE
FORREL
FORRIL
FORRIT
FORRITSOME
FORSADO
FORSAKE
FORSAKEN
FORSAKENLY
FORSAKENNESS
FORSAKER
FORSAKES
FORSAKING
FORSAR
FORSAY
FORSEEK
FORSET
FORSHAPE
FORSLACK
FORSLAKE
FORSLOW
FORSOOK
FORSOOTH
FORSPEAK
FORSPEAKING
FORSPEND
FORSPENT
FORSPOKE
FORSPOKEN
FORSTAND
FORSTEAL
FORSTERITE
FORSUNG
FORSWEAR
FORSWEARER
FORSWEARING
FORSWORE
FORSWORN
FORSWORNNESS
FORT
FORTAKE
FORTALICE
FORTE
FORTEMENTE
FORTEPIANO
FORTES
FORTESCUE
FORTESCURE
FORTH
FORTHBRING
FORTHBRINGER
FORTHBRINGING
FORTHBROUGHT
FORTHBY
FORTHCALL
FORTHCAME
FORTHCOME
FORTHCOMER
FORTHCOMING
FORTHFARE
FORTHGAZE
FORTHGO
FORTHGOING
FORTHINK
FORTHINKING
FORTHON
FORTHOUGHT
FORTHPUTTING
FORTHRIGHT
FORTHRIGHTLY
FORTHRIGHTNESS
FORTHRIGHTS
FORTHSET

FORTHTELL
FORTHTELLER
FORTHWARD
FORTHWITH
FORTHY
FORTIES
FORTIETH
FORTIFIABLE
FORTIFICATION
FORTIFICATIONS
FORTIFIED
FORTIFIER
FORTIFY
FORTIFYING
FORTIFYINGLY
FORTIN
FORTIS
FORTISSIMI
FORTISSIMO
FORTISSIMOS
FORTITUDE
FORTITUDINOUS
FORTLET
FORTNIGHT
FORTNIGHTLY
FORTO
FORTRAVAIL
FORTREAD
FORTRESS
FORTRESSED
FORTRESSING
FORTUITIES
FORTUITISM
FORTUITIST
FORTUITOUS
FORTUITOUSLY
FORTUITOUSNESS
FORTUITY
FORTUNATE
FORTUNATELY
FORTUNATENESS
FORTUNATION
FORTUNE
FORTUNED
FORTUNEL
FORTUNETELL
FORTUNETELLER
FORTUNETELLING
FORTUNING
FORTUNITE
FORTY
FORUM
FORUMIZE
FORUMS
FORVAY
FORWAKE
FORWAKED
FORWALK
FORWANDER
FORWARD
FORWARDAL
FORWARDATION
FORWARDED
FORWARDER
FORWARDING
FORWARDLY
FORWARDNESS
FORWARDS
FORWARN
FORWASTE
FORWEAN
FORWEAR
FORWEARIED
FORWEARY
FORWEARYING
FORWEEND
FORWELK

FORWENT
FORWHY
FORWODEN
FORWORDEN
FORWORE
FORWORK
FORWORN
FORWRAP
FORYIELD
FORZANDO
FORZATO
FOSH
FOSS
FOSSA
FOSSAE
FOSSAGE
FOSSANE
FOSSARIAN
FOSSE
FOSSES
FOSSETTE
FOSSICK
FOSSICKED
FOSSICKER
FOSSICKING
FOSSIFIED
FOSSIFORM
FOSSIL
FOSSILAGE
FOSSILATED
FOSSILATION
FOSSILED
FOSSILFYING
FOSSILIFEROUS
FOSSILIFICATION
FOSSILIFY
FOSSILIST
FOSSILIZATION
FOSSILIZE
FOSSILIZED
FOSSILIZING
FOSSILOGIST
FOSSILOGY
FOSSILOLOGIST
FOSSILOLOGY
FOSSILS
FOSSOR
FOSSORES
FOSSORIAL
FOSSORIOUS
FOSSORS
FOSSULA
FOSSULAE
FOSSULATE
FOSSULE
FOSSULET
FOSTELL
FOSTER
FOSTERAGE
FOSTERED
FOSTERER
FOSTERING
FOSTERINGLY
FOSTERITE
FOSTERLAND
FOSTERLING
FOSTRESS
FOT
FOTCH
FOTCHED
FOTHER
FOTHERED
FOTHERING
FOTMAL
FOTUI
FOU
FOUCH

FOUD
FOUDROYANT
FOUETTE
FOUETTEE
FOUGADE
FOUGASSE
FOUGHT
FOUGHTEN
FOUGHTY
FOUGUE
FOUJDAR
FOUJDARRY
FOUJDARY
FOUL
FOULAGE
FOULARD
FOULDRE
FOULE
FOULED
FOULER
FOULEST
FOULING
FOULLY
FOULMART
FOULMOUTHED
FOULMOUTHEDLY
FOULMOUTHEDNESS
FOULNESS
FOULSOME
FOUMART
FOUN
FOUNCE
FOUND
FOUNDATION
FOUNDATIONAL
FOUNDATIONALLY
FOUNDATIONARY
FOUNDATIONER
FOUNDED
FOUNDER
FOUNDERED
FOUNDERING
FOUNDEROUS
FOUNDING
FOUNDLING
FOUNDRIES
FOUNDRY
FOUNDRYMAN
FOUNDRYMEN
FOUNT
FOUNTAIN
FOUNTAINED
FOUNTAINEER
FOUNTAINHEAD
FOUNTAINOUS
FOUNTAINOUSLY
FOUNTE
FOUNTFUL
FOUR
FOURB
FOURBE
FOURBLE
FOURCHE
FOURCHEE
FOURCHER
FOURCHET
FOURCHETTE
FOURCHITE
FOURER
FOURFLUSHER
FOURFOLD
FOURGON
FOURHANDED
FOURLING
FOURPENCE
FOURPENNY
FOURPOUNDER

FOURQUINE
FOURRAGERE
FOURRE
FOURRIER
FOURS
FOURSCORE
FOURSCORTH
FOURSOME
FOURSQUARE
FOURSQUARELY
FOURSQUARENESS
FOURSTRAND
FOURTEEN
FOURTEENER
FOURTEENTH
FOURTEENTHLY
FOURTH
FOURTHER
FOURTHLY
FOUSSA
FOUTE
FOUTER
FOUTH
FOUTRA
FOUTRE
FOUTY
FOVEA
FOVEAE
FOVEAL
FOVEATE
FOVEATED
FOVEATION
FOVEIFORM
FOVENT
FOVEOLA
FOVEOLAE
FOVEOLARIOUS
FOVEOLATE
FOVEOLATED
FOVEOLE
FOVEOLET
FOW
FOWD
FOWL
FOWLED
FOWLER
FOWLERITE
FOWLERY
FOWLFOOT
FOWLING
FOWLS
FOX
FOXBANE
FOXBERRIES
FOXBERRY
FOXCHOP
FOXED
FOXER
FOXERY
FOXES
FOXFEET
FOXFIRE
FOXFISH
FOXGLOVE
FOXHOLE
FOXHOUND
FOXIER
FOXIEST
FOXILY
FOXINESS
FOXING
FOXISH
FOXLIKE
FOXSKIN
FOXTAIL
FOXTAILED
FOXTROT

FOXY
FOY
FOYAITE
FOYAITIC
FOYBOAT
FOYER
FOYLE
FOZE
FOZINESS
FOZY
FRA
FRAB
FRABBIT
FRABJOUS
FRABJOUSLY
FRABOUS
FRACAS
FRACASES
FRACEDINOUS
FRACHE
FRACID
FRACK
FRACT
FRACTABLE
FRACTABLING
FRACTED
FRACTILE
FRACTION
FRACTIONAL
FRACTIONALISM
FRACTIONALIZE
FRACTIONALLY
FRACTIONARY
FRACTIONATE
FRACTIONATED
FRACTIONATING
FRACTIONATION
FRACTIONATOR
FRACTIONED
FRACTIONING
FRACTIONIZATION
FRACTIONIZE
FRACTIONIZED
FRACTIONIZING
FRACTIOUS
FRACTIOUSLY
FRACTIOUSNESS
FRACTUOSITY
FRACTUR
FRACTURAL
FRACTURE
FRACTURED
FRACTURING
FRADICIN
FRAE
FRAENA
FRAENULAR
FRAENULUM
FRAENUM
FRAENUMS
FRAG
FRAGE
FRAGGING
FRAGHAN
FRAGILE
FRAGILELY
FRAGILENESS
FRAGILITIES
FRAGILITY
FRAGMENT
FRAGMENTAL
FRAGMENTALLY
FRAGMENTARILY
FRAGMENTARINESS
FRAGMENTARY
FRAGMENTATION
FRAGMENTED

FRAGMENTIST
FRAGMENTITIOUS
FRAGMENTIZE
FRAGMENTS
FRAGOR
FRAGRANCE
FRAGRANCIES
FRAGRANCY
FRAGRANT
FRAGRANTLY
FRAGRANTNESS
FRAICHEUR
FRAID
FRAIK
FRAIL
FRAILE
FRAILEJON
FRAILER
FRAILES
FRAILEST
FRAILLY
FRAILNESS
FRAILTIES
FRAILTY
FRAIM
FRAIN
FRAISE
FRAISED
FRAISING
FRAIST
FRAKE
FRAM
FRAMBESIA
FRAMBOESIA
FRAME
FRAMEA
FRAMEAE
FRAMED
FRAMER
FRAMES
FRAMESMITH
FRAMEWORK
FRAMING
FRAMMIT
FRAMPLER
FRAMPOLD
FRANC
FRANCHISE
FRANCHISEMENT
FRANCHISER
FRANCISC
FRANCISCA
FRANCIUM
FRANCO
FRANCOLIN
FRANCOLITE
FRANGENT
FRANGIBILITY
FRANGIBLE
FRANGIBLENESS
FRANGIPANE
FRANGIPANI
FRANGULA
FRANGULIC
FRANGULIN
FRANGULINIC
FRANION
FRANK
FRANKALMOIGN
FRANKALMOIGNE
FRANKALMOIN
FRANKED
FRANKENIACEOUS
FRANKER
FRANKEST
FRANKFORT
FRANKFORTER

FRANKFURT
FRANKFURTER
FRANKHEARTED
FRANKHEARTEDLY
FRANKHEARTNESS
FRANKINCENSE
FRANKINCENSED
FRANKING
FRANKLANDITE
FRANKLIN
FRANKLINITE
FRANKLY
FRANKMARRIAGE
FRANKNESS
FRANKPLEDGE
FRANSERIA
FRANTIC
FRANTICALLY
FRANTICLY
FRANTICNESS
FRAP
FRAPE
FRAPLE
FRAPLER
FRAPPE
FRAPPED
FRAPPEED
FRAPPEING
FRAPPING
FRARY
FRASE
FRASER
FRASIER
FRASS
FRAT
FRATCH
FRATCHED
FRATCHEOUS
FRATCHER
FRATCHETY
FRATCHY
FRATE
FRATER
FRATERIES
FRATERNAL
FRATERNALISM
FRATERNALIST
FRATERNALITY
FRATERNALLY
FRATERNATE
FRATERNATION
FRATERNISM
FRATERNITIES
FRATERNITY
FRATERNIZATION
FRATERNIZE
FRATERNIZED
FRATERNIZER
FRATERNIZING
FRATERY
FRATI
FRATRICIDAL
FRATRICIDE
FRATRIES
FRATRY
FRAUD
FRAUDER
FRAUDFUL
FRAUDFULLY
FRAUDLESS
FRAUDLESSLY
FRAUDLESSNESS
FRAUDULENCE
FRAUDULENCY
FRAUDULENT
FRAUDULENTLY
FRAUDULENTNESS

FRAUEN
FRAUGHT
FRAUGHTED
FRAUGHTING
FRAUNCH
FRAVASHI
FRAWN
FRAXETIN
FRAXIN
FRAXINELLA
FRAY
FRAYED
FRAYING
FRAYN
FRAYNE
FRAZE
FRAZER
FRAZIL
FRAZZLE
FRAZZLED
FRAZZLING
FREAK
FREAKED
FREAKERY
FREAKFUL
FREAKIER
FREAKIEST
FREAKILY
FREAKINESS
FREAKING
FREAKISH
FREAKISHLY
FREAKISHNESS
FREAKPOT
FREAKY
FREAM
FREATH
FRECK
FRECKEN
FRECKET
FRECKLE
FRECKLED
FRECKLEDNESS
FRECKLING
FRECKLY
FREDAINE
FREDDO
FREDERIK
FREDRICITE
FREE
FREEBOARD
FREEBOOT
FREEBOOTED
FREEBOOTER
FREEBOOTERY
FREEBOOTING
FREEBOOTY
FREEBORN
FREED
FREEDMAN
FREEDMEN
FREEDOM
FREEDWOMAN
FREEDWOMEN
FREEHAND
FREEHANDED
FREEHANDEDLY
FREEHANDEDNESS
FREEHEARTED
FREEHOLD
FREEHOLDER
FREEHOLDING
FREEING
FREELAGE
FREELOAD
FREELOADER
FREELY

FREEMAN	FREQUENCIES	FRIBBLER	FRIGIDLY	FRISSON
FREEMARTIN	FREQUENCY	FRIBBLERY	FRIGIDNESS	FRIST
FREEMASON	FREQUENT	FRIBBLING	FRIGIFEROUS	FRISURE
FREEMASONIC	FREQUENTABLE	FRIBBY	FRIGO	FRISZKA
FREEMASONICAL	FREQUENTAGE	FRIBORG	FRIGOLABILE	FRIT
FREEMASONISM	FREQUENTATION	FRIBOURG	FRIGOR	FRITH
FREEMASONS	FREQUENTATIVE	FRICACE	FRIGORIC	FRITHBORGH
FREEMEN	FREQUENTED	FRICANDEAU	FRIGORIFIC	FRITHBORH
FREENESS	FREQUENTER	FRICANDEAUX	FRIGORIFICAL	FRITHBOT
FREER	FREQUENTING	FRICANDEL	FRIGORIFICO	FRITHLES
FREESIA	FREQUENTLY	FRICANDELLE	FRIGORIFY	FRITHSOKEN
FREEST	FREQUENTNESS	FRICANDO	FRIGORIMETER	FRITHSTOOL
FREESTANDING	FRERE	FRICASSEE	FRIGOSTABLE	FRITHWORK
FREESTONE	FRERES	FRICASSEED	FRIGOTHERAPY	FRITHY
FREESTYLE	FRESCADE	FRICASSEEING	FRIJOL	FRITILLARIES
FREESTYLER	FRESCO	FRICATION	FRIJOLE	FRITILLARY
FREET	FRESCOED	FRICATIVE	FRIJOLES	FRITT
FREETHINKER	FRESCOER	FRICATRICE	FRIJOLILLO	FRITTATA
FREETHINKING	FRESCOES	FRICK	FRIKE	FRITTED
FREETRADER	FRESCOING	FRICTION	FRILAL	FRITTER
FREETY	FRESCOIST	FRICTIONAL	FRILL	FRITTERED
FREEWARD	FRESCOS	FRICTIONALLY	FRILLBACK	FRITTERER
FREEWAY	FRESE	FRICTIONIZE	FRILLED	FRITTERING
FREEWHEEL	FRESH	FRICTIONIZED	FRILLER	FRITTERS
FREEWHEELER	FRESHEN	FRICTIONIZING	FRILLERY	FRITTING
FREEWHEELING	FRESHENER	FRICTIONLESS	FRILLIER	FRIVOL
FREEWILL	FRESHER	FRIDGE	FRILLIES	FRIVOLED
FREEWOMAN	FRESHEST	FRIDSTOOL	FRILLIEST	FRIVOLER
FREEWOMEN	FRESHET	FRIE	FRILLILY	FRIVOLISM
FREEZABLE	FRESHHEARTED	FRIED	FRILLINESS	FRIVOLITIES
FREEZE	FRESHING	FRIEDCAKE	FRILLING	FRIVOLITY
FREEZER	FRESHLY	FRIEDELITE	FRILLY	FRIVOLIZE
FREEZING	FRESHMAN	FRIEND	FRIM	FRIVOLIZED
FREEZY	FRESHMANIC	FRIENDED	FRIMITTS	FRIVOLIZING
FREIBERGITE	FRESHMEN	FRIENDING	FRINGE	FRIVOLLED
FREIGHT	FRESHNESS	FRIENDLESS	FRINGED	FRIVOLLER
FREIGHTAGE	FRESNE	FRIENDLESSNESS	FRINGEFLOWER	FRIVOLOUS
FREIGHTED	FRESNEL	FRIENDLIER	FRINGEFOOT	FRIVOLOUSLY
FREIGHTER	FRET	FRIENDLIES	FRINGENT	FRIVOLOUSNESS
FREIGHTING	FRETA	FRIENDLIEST	FRINGEPOD	FRIZ
FREIJO	FRETFUL	FRIENDLILY	FRINGES	FRIZADO
FREINAGE	FRETFULLY	FRIENDLINESS	FRINGIER	FRIZE
FREIT	FRETFULNESS	FRIENDLY	FRINGIEST	FRIZEL
FREITH	FRETISH	FRIENDS	FRINGILLACEOUS	FRIZER
FREITY	FRETIZE	FRIENDSHIP	FRINGILLINE	FRIZETTE
FREKE	FRETSAW	FRIER	FRINGILLOID	FRIZZ
FREM	FRETSOME	FRIESEITE	FRINGING	FRIZZED
FREMD	FRETT	FRIEZE	FRINGY	FRIZZEN
FREMDLY	FRETTAGE	FRIEZED	FRIPPER	FRIZZER
FREMDNESS	FRETTATION	FRIEZER	FRIPPERER	FRIZZES
FREMESCENCE	FRETTE	FRIEZING	FRIPPERIES	FRIZZIER
FREMESCENT	FRETTED	FRIEZY	FRIPPERY	FRIZZIEST
FREMITUS	FRETTEN	FRIG	FRISADO	FRIZZILY
FREMT	FRETTER	FRIGATE	FRISCA	FRIZZINESS
FRENA	FRETTIER	FRIGATOON	FRISCAL	FRIZZING
FRENAL	FRETTIEST	FRIGGLE	FRISCH	FRIZZLE
FRENATE	FRETTING	FRIGHT	FRISCO	FRIZZLED
FRENCHED	FRETTINGLY	FRIGHTED	FRISE	FRIZZLER
FRENCHEN	FRETTY	FRIGHTEN	FRISETTE	FRIZZLING
FRENCHIFY	FRETUM	FRIGHTENED	FRISEUR	FRIZZLY
FRENCHING	FRETWORK	FRIGHTENEDLY	FRISK	FRIZZY
FRENETIC	FRETWORKED	FRIGHTENEDNESS	FRISKER	FRO
FRENETICAL	FREYALITE	FRIGHTENER	FRISKEST	FROCK
FRENETICALLY	FRIABILITY	FRIGHTENING	FRISKET	FROCKING
FRENNE	FRIABLE	FRIGHTENINGLY	FRISKFUL	FROCKMAKER
FRENULA	FRIABLENESS	FRIGHTER	FRISKIER	FROE
FRENULAR	FRIAND	FRIGHTFUL	FRISKIEST	FROEMAN
FRENULUM	FRIANDISE	FRIGHTFULLY	FRISKILY	FROG
FRENUM	FRIAR	FRIGHTFULNESS	FRISKIN	FROGBIT
FRENUMS	FRIARBIRD	FRIGHTING	FRISKINESS	FROGEATER
FRENZIED	FRIARIES	FRIGHTSOME	FRISKING	FROGEYE
FRENZIEDLY	FRIARLY	FRIGHTY	FRISKINGLY	FROGFACE
FRENZIES	FRIARY	FRIGID	FRISKLE	FROGFISH
FRENZILY	FRIATION	FRIGIDARIA	FRISKY	FROGFISHES
FRENZY	FRIB	FRIGIDARIUM	FRISOLEE	FROGFLOWER
FRENZYING	FRIBBLE	FRIGIDITIES	FRISON	FROGFOOT
FREQUENCE	FRIBBLED	FRIGIDITY	FRISS	FROGGED

FROGGER
FROGGERY
FROGGIER
FROGGIES
FROGGIEST
FROGGINESS
FROGGING
FROGGISH
FROGGY
FROGHOPPER
FROGLAND
FROGLEAF
FROGLET
FROGMAN
FROGMEN
FROGMOUTH
FROGNOSE
FROGS
FROGSKIN
FROGSTOOL
FROGTONGUE
FROGWORT
FROHLICH
FROIDEUR
FROISE
FROISSE
FROKIN
FROLIC
FROLICFUL
FROLICKED
FROLICKER
FROLICKING
FROLICKY
FROLICLY
FROLICNESS
FROLICSOME
FROLICSOMELY
FROLICSOMENESS
FROM
FROMAGE
FROMENTY
FROMWARD
FROMWARDS
FROND
FRONDAGE
FRONDED
FRONDENT
FRONDESCE
FRONDESCED
FRONDESCENCE
FRONDESCENT
FRONDESCING
FRONDIFEROUS
FRONDIFORM
FRONDIGEROUS
FRONDIVOROUS
FRONDLET
FRONDOSE
FRONDOSELY
FRONDOUS
FRONS
FRONT
FRONTAD
FRONTAGE
FRONTAGER
FRONTAL
FRONTALIS
FRONTALITY
FRONTED
FRONTER
FRONTES
FRONTIER
FRONTIERMAN
FRONTIERSMAN
FRONTIERSMEN
FRONTING
FRONTIS

FRONTISPIECE
FRONTISPIECED
FRONTISPIECING
FRONTLESS
FRONTLESSLY
FRONTLESSNESS
FRONTLET
FRONTOLYSIS
FRONTOMALAR
FRONTOMENTAL
FRONTON
FRONTONASAL
FRONTPIECE
FRONTSMAN
FRONTSTALL
FRONTURE
FROOM
FROPPISH
FRORE
FROREN
FRORY
FROSH
FROSK
FROST
FROSTATION
FROSTBIRD
FROSTBIT
FROSTBITE
FROSTBITING
FROSTBITTEN
FROSTBOW
FROSTED
FROSTER
FROSTFISH
FROSTFISHES
FROSTFLOWER
FROSTIER
FROSTIEST
FROSTILY
FROSTINESS
FROSTING
FROSTLESS
FROSTPROOFING
FROSTROOT
FROSTWEED
FROSTWORK
FROSTY
FROT
FROTH
FROTHED
FROTHER
FROTHIER
FROTHIEST
FROTHILY
FROTHINESS
FROTHING
FROTHY
FROTTAGE
FROTTED
FROTTING
FROTTOLA
FROTTON
FROUD
FROUFROU
FROUGH
FROUGHY
FROUNCE
FROUNCED
FROUNCING
FROUST
FROUSTY
FROUZE
FROUZY
FROW
FROWARD
FROWARDLY
FROWARDNESS

FROWER
FROWL
FROWN
FROWNED
FROWNER
FROWNING
FROWNY
FROWST
FROWSTIER
FROWSTIEST
FROWSTY
FROWSY
FROWY
FROWZE
FROWZIER
FROWZIEST
FROWZILY
FROWZINESS
FROWZLED
FROWZY
FROZE
FROZEN
FROZENLY
FROZENNESS
FRUB
FRUBBISH
FRUCTED
FRUCTESCENCE
FRUCTESCENT
FRUCTICULTURAL
FRUCTIFEROUS
FRUCTIFIED
FRUCTIFIER
FRUCTIFORM
FRUCTIFY
FRUCTIFYING
FRUCTIPAROUS
FRUCTIVOROUS
FRUCTOSE
FRUCTOSIDE
FRUCTUARIUS
FRUCTUOSE
FRUCTUOSITY
FRUCTUOUS
FRUCTUOUSLY
FRUCTUOUSNESS
FRUGAL
FRUGALISM
FRUGALIST
FRUGALITIES
FRUGALITY
FRUGALLY
FRUGALNESS
FRUGGAN
FRUGGIN
FRUGIFEROUS
FRUGIFEROUSNESS
FRUGIVOROUS
FRUIT
FRUITADE
FRUITAGE
FRUITARIAN
FRUITARIANISM
FRUITCAKE
FRUITED
FRUITER
FRUITERER
FRUITERESS
FRUITERIES
FRUITERY
FRUITFUL
FRUITFULLY
FRUITFULNESS
FRUITGROWER
FRUITGROWING
FRUITIER
FRUITIEST

FRUITINESS
FRUITING
FRUITION
FRUITIST
FRUITIVE
FRUITLESS
FRUITLESSLY
FRUITLESSNESS
FRUITLET
FRUITS
FRUITSTALK
FRUITTIME
FRUITWISE
FRUITWOMAN
FRUITWOMEN
FRUITWORM
FRUITY
FRUM
FRUMARYL
FRUMENT
FRUMENTATION
FRUMENTUM
FRUMENTY
FRUMETY
FRUMP
FRUMPERIES
FRUMPERY
FRUMPIER
FRUMPIEST
FRUMPILY
FRUMPINESS
FRUMPISH
FRUMPISHLY
FRUMPISHNESS
FRUMPLE
FRUMPLED
FRUMPLING
FRUMPS
FRUMPY
FRUNDEL
FRUSH
FRUST
FRUSTA
FRUSTRANEOUS
FRUSTRATE
FRUSTRATED
FRUSTRATELY
FRUSTRATER
FRUSTRATES
FRUSTRATING
FRUSTRATION
FRUSTRATIVE
FRUSTRATORY
FRUSTULE
FRUSTULENT
FRUSTULOSE
FRUSTUM
FRUSTUMS
FRUTESCENCE
FRUTESCENT
FRUTEX
FRUTICES
FRUTICETA
FRUTICETUM
FRUTICOSE
FRUTICOUS
FRUTICULOSE
FRUTICULTURE
FRUTIFY
FRUTILLA
FRY
FRYER
FRYING
FRYPAN
FU
FUANG
FUB

FUBBERY
FUBBY
FUBSIER
FUBSIEST
FUBSY
FUCACEOUS
FUCATE
FUCATION
FUCATIOUS
FUCHSIA
FUCHSIN
FUCHSINE
FUCHSINOPHIL
FUCHSITE
FUCHSONE
FUCI
FUCINITA
FUCIPHAGOUS
FUCIVOROUS
FUCOID
FUCOIDAL
FUCOIDIN
FUCOSAN
FUCOSE
FUCOUS
FUCOXANTHIN
FUCUS
FUCUSED
FUCUSES
FUD
FUDDLE
FUDDLED
FUDDLER
FUDDLING
FUDER
FUDGE
FUDGED
FUDGER
FUDGING
FUDGY
FUEL
FUELED
FUELER
FUELING
FUELIZER
FUELLED
FUELLER
FUELLING
FUERO
FUERTE
FUFF
FUFFIT
FUFFLE
FUFFY
FUG
FUGA
FUGACIOUS
FUGACIOUSLY
FUGACIOUSNESS
FUGACITIES
FUGACITY
FUGACY
FUGAL
FUGALLY
FUGARA
FUGATO
FUGGY
FUGI
FUGIE
FUGIENT
FUGITATE
FUGITATED
FUGITATING
FUGITATION
FUGITIVE
FUGITIVELY
FUGITIVENESS

FUGITIVITY	FULLNESS	FUMIGATED	FUNDITOR	FUNNEL
FUGLE	FULLOM	FUMIGATING	FUNDITORES	FUNNELED
FUGLED	FULLY	FUMIGATION	FUNDMONGER	FUNNELFORM
FUGLEMAN	FULMAR	FUMIGATOR	FUNDMONGERING	FUNNELING
FUGLEMEN	FULMEN	FUMIGATORIES	FUNDO	FUNNELLED
FUGLER	FULMINA	FUMIGATORY	FUNDS	FUNNELLIKE
FUGLING	FULMINANCY	FUMILY	FUNDUCK	FUNNELLING
FUGU	FULMINANT	FUMINESS	FUNDULINE	FUNNIER
FUGUE	FULMINATE	FUMING	FUNDUS	FUNNIES
FUGUIST	FULMINATED	FUMINGLY	FUNEBRE	FUNNIEST
FUIDHIR	FULMINATING	FUMISH	FUNEBRIAL	FUNNILY
FUIRDAYS	FULMINATION	FUMISHLY	FUNEBRIOUS	FUNNIMENT
FUJI	FULMINATOR	FUMISHNESS	FUNEBROUS	FUNNINESS
FULCIFORM	FULMINATORY	FUMISTERY	FUNERAL	FUNNING
FULCRA	FULMINE	FUMITORIES	FUNERALIZE	FUNNY
FULCRAL	FULMINED	FUMITORY	FUNERALLY	FUNNYMAN
FULCRATE	FULMINEOUS	FUMMEL	FUNERALS	FUNNYMEN
FULCRUM	FULMINING	FUMMLE	FUNERARY	FUNORI
FULCRUMAGE	FULMINOUS	FUMOSE	FUNERATE	FUNORIN
FULCRUMED	FULMINURATE	FUMOSITY	FUNERATION	FUNSTER
FULCRUMING	FULMINURIC	FUMOUS	FUNEREAL	FUNT
FULCRUMS	FULNESS	FUMOUSLY	FUNEREALLY	FUR
FULFIL	FULSOME	FUMULI	FUNEST	FURACANA
FULFILL	FULSOMELY	FUMULUS	FUNESTAL	FURACIOUS
FULFILLED	FULSOMENESS	FUMY	FUNFEST	FURACIOUSNESS
FULFILLER	FULTH	FUN	FUNGACEOUS	FURACITY
FULFILLING	FULTZ	FUNA	FUNGAL	FURAL
FULFILLMENT	FULVENE	FUNAMBULATE	FUNGATE	FURAN
FULFILMENT	FULVESCENT	FUNAMBULATED	FUNGATED	FURANE
FULGENCE	FULVID	FUNAMBULATING	FUNGATING	FURANOSE
FULGENCY	FULVIDNESS	FUNAMBULATION	FUNGE	FURBEARER
FULGENT	FULVOUS	FUNAMBULATORY	FUNGI	FURBELOW
FULGENTLY	FULWA	FUNAMBULIC	FUNGIAN	FURBELOWED
FULGENTNESS	FULYIE	FUNAMBULISM	FUNGIBILITY	FURBELOWING
FULGID	FULZIE	FUNAMBULIST	FUNGIBLE	FURBISH
FULGIDE	FUM	FUNAMBULO	FUNGIC	FURBISHED
FULGIDITY	FUMACIOUS	FUNAMBULOES	FUNGICIDAL	FURBISHER
FULGOR	FUMADO	FUNCTION	FUNGICIDE	FURBISHING
FULGORID	FUMADOS	FUNCTIONAL	FUNGID	FURCA
FULGOROUS	FUMAGE	FUNCTIONALISM	FUNGIFORM	FURCAE
FULGOUR	FUMAGINE	FUNCTIONALIST	FUNGIFY	FURCAL
FULGOUROUS	FUMARASE	FUNCTIONALITY	FUNGILLIFORM	FURCATE
FULGURAL	FUMARATE	FUNCTIONALIZE	FUNGIN	FURCATED
FULGURANT	FUMARIA	FUNCTIONALIZED	FUNGISTAT	FURCATELY
FULGURANTLY	FUMARIC	FUNCTIONALIZIN	FUNGISTATIC	FURCATING
FULGURATA	FUMARINE	FUNCTIONALLY	FUNGO	FURCATION
FULGURATE	FUMARIUM	FUNCTIONARIES	FUNGOES	FURCELLATE
FULGURATED	FUMAROID	FUNCTIONARISM	FUNGOID	FURCIFERINE
FULGURATING	FUMAROIDAL	FUNCTIONARY	FUNGOIDAL	FURCIFEROUS
FULGURATION	FUMAROLE	FUNCTIONATE	FUNGOLOGICAL	FURCIFORM
FULGURITE	FUMAROLIC	FUNCTIONATED	FUNGOLOGIST	FURCILIA
FULGUROUS	FUMATORIA	FUNCTIONATING	FUNGOLOGY	FURCRAEA
FULHAM	FUMATORIES	FUNCTIONATION	FUNGOSE	FURCULA
FULICINE	FUMATORIUM	FUNCTIONED	FUNGOSITY	FURCULAE
FULIGINOSITY	FUMATORIUMS	FUNCTIONING	FUNGOUS	FURCULAR
FULIGINOUS	FUMATORY	FUNCTIONIZE	FUNGUS	FURCULE
FULIGINOUSLY	FUMBA	FUNCTIONLESS	FUNGUSED	FURCULUM
FULIGINOUSNESS	FUMBLE	FUNCTOR	FUNGUSES	FURDEL
FULIGULINE	FUMBLED	FUND	FUNGUSY	FURDLE
FULK	FUMBLER	FUNDA	FUNICLE	FURE
FULL	FUMBLING	FUNDAL	FUNICULAR	FURFUR
FULLAM	FUMBULATOR	FUNDAMENT	FUNICULATE	FURFURACEOUS
FULLBACK	FUME	FUNDAMENTAL	FUNICULI	FURFURAL
FULLDO	FUMED	FUNDAMENTALISM	FUNICULITIS	FURFURAMID
FULLED	FUMER	FUNDAMENTALIST	FUNICULUS	FURFURAMIDE
FULLER	FUMEROOT	FUNDAMENTALITY	FUNIFORM	FURFURAN
FULLERBOARD	FUMET	FUNDAMENTALLY	FUNIS	FURFURATION
FULLERED	FUMETTE	FUNDATORIAL	FUNK	FURFURES
FULLERIES	FUMEWORT	FUNDATRICES	FUNKED	FURFURINE
FULLERING	FUMID	FUNDATRIX	FUNKER	FURFUROID
FULLERY	FUMIDITY	FUNDED	FUNKIER	FURFUROL
FULLFACE	FUMIDUCT	FUNDER	FUNKIEST	FURFUROLE
FULLHEARTED	FUMIER	FUNDHOLDER	FUNKINESS	FURFUROUS
FULLING	FUMIEST	FUNDI	FUNKING	FURFURYL
FULLMOUTH	FUMIFEROUS	FUNDIC	FUNKY	FURIAL
FULLMOUTHED	FUMIGANT	FUNDIFORM	FUNMAKER	FURIANT
FULLMOUTHEDLY	FUMIGATE	FUNDING	FUNNED	FURIBUND

FURICANE
FURIED
FURIES
FURIFY
FURIL
FURILE
FURILIC
FURIOSO
FURIOUS
FURIOUSITY
FURIOUSLY
FURIOUSNESS
FURISON
FURL
FURLANA
FURLED
FURLER
FURLING
FURLONG
FURLOUGH
FURLOUGHED
FURLOUGHING
FURMENTY
FURMETY
FURMITY
FURNACE
FURNACED
FURNACEMAN
FURNACEMEN
FURNACER
FURNACING
FURNACITE
FURNAGE
FURNER
FURNISH
FURNISHED
FURNISHER
FURNISHING
FURNISHINGS
FURNISHMENT
FURNISHNESS
FURNITURE
FUROATE
FUROID
FUROIN
FUROL
FUROLE
FUROMONAZOLE
FUROR
FURORE
FURPHY
FURR
FURRED
FURRIER
FURRIERED
FURRIERIES
FURRIERY
FURRIEST
FURRILY
FURRINESS
FURRING
FURROW
FURROWED
FURROWER
FURROWING
FURROWS
FURROWY
FURRURE
FURRY
FURS
FURTHER
FURTHERANCE
FURTHERED
FURTHERER
FURTHERING
FURTHERLY
FURTHERMORE

FURTHERMOST
FURTHERSOME
FURTHEST
FURTHY
FURTIVE
FURTIVELY
FURTIVENESS
FURTUM
FURUNCLE
FURUNCULAR
FURUNCULOID
FURUNCULOSIS
FURUNCULOUS
FURWA
FURY
FURYL
FURZE
FURZECHAT
FURZED
FURZERY
FURZETOP
FURZY
FUSAIN
FUSARIAL
FUSARIOSE
FUSARIOSIS
FUSAROLE
FUSATE
FUSC
FUSCESCENT
FUSCIN
FUSCOHYALINE
FUSCOUS
FUSE
FUSEAU
FUSEBOARD
FUSED
FUSEE
FUSEL
FUSELAGE
FUSEPLUG
FUSIBILITY
FUSIBLE
FUSIBLENESS
FUSIBLY
FUSIFORM
FUSIL
FUSILADED
FUSILADING
FUSILE
FUSILEER
FUSILIER
FUSILLADE
FUSILLY
FUSING
FUSINIST
FUSINITE
FUSION
FUSIONAL
FUSIONISM
FUSIONIST
FUSIONLESS
FUSOID
FUSS
FUSSED
FUSSER
FUSSIER
FUSSIEST
FUSSIFICATION
FUSSIFY
FUSSILY
FUSSINESS
FUSSING
FUSSLE
FUSSOCK
FUSSY
FUST

FUSTANELLA
FUSTANELLE
FUSTEE
FUSTER
FUSTERIC
FUSTET
FUSTIAN
FUSTIANIST
FUSTIC
FUSTIE
FUSTIER
FUSTIEST
FUSTIGATE
FUSTIGATED
FUSTIGATING
FUSTIGATION
FUSTIGATOR
FUSTIGATORY
FUSTILUGS
FUSTILY
FUSTIN
FUSTINESS
FUSTLE
FUSTOC
FUSTY
FUSULA
FUSUMA
FUSURE
FUT
FUTCHEL
FUTCHELL
FUTE
FUTHARC
FUTHARK
FUTHORC
FUTHORK
FUTILE
FUTILELY
FUTILENESS
FUTILITARIAN
FUTILITIES
FUTILITY
FUTILOUS
FUTTAH
FUTTER
FUTTERET
FUTTOCK
FUTURAL
FUTURAMA
FUTURE
FUTURELESS
FUTURELY
FUTURISM
FUTURIST
FUTURISTIC
FUTURITIES
FUTURITION
FUTURITY
FUTWA
FUYE
FUZE
FUZEE
FUZIL
FUZZ
FUZZBALL
FUZZIER
FUZZIEST
FUZZILY
FUZZINESS
FUZZLE
FUZZTAIL
FUZZY
FYCE
FYKE
FYLE
FYLFOT
FYLGJA

FYLGJUR
FYLKE
FYLKER
FYND
FYRD
FYRDUNG

GA
GAAL
GAATCH
GAB
GABARDINE
GABARI
GABARIT
GABBACK
GABBAI
GABBARD
GABBART
GABBED
GABBER
GABBIER
GABBIEST
GABBING
GABBLE
GABBLED
GABBLEMENT
GABBLER
GABBLING
GABBRO
GABBROIC
GABBROID
GABBROITIC
GABBROS
GABBY
GABE
GABELER
GABELLE
GABELLED
GABELLEMAN
GABELLER
GABERDINE
GABERLUNZIE
GABGAB
GABI
GABION
GABIONADE
GABIONAGE
GABIONED
GABLATORES
GABLE
GABLEBOARD
GABLET
GABLEWISE
GABLOCK
GABY
GACHUPIN
GAD
GADABOUT
GADBEE
GADBUSH
GADDED
GADDER
GADDI
GADDING
GADDINGLY
GADDISH
GADDISHNESS
GADE
GADES
GADFLY
GADGE
GADGER
GADGET
GADGETRY

GADHI
GADID
GADININE
GADLING
GADMAN
GADOID
GADOLINIA
GADOLINIC
GADOLINITE
GADOLINIUM
GADROON
GADROONAGE
GADSMAN
GADUIN
GADWALL
GADWELL
GAE
GAED
GAEDOWN
GAET
GAFF
GAFFE
GAFFED
GAFFER
GAFFING
GAFFLE
GAFFLET
GAFFSAIL
GAFFSMAN
GAG
GAGA
GAGATE
GAGE
GAGED
GAGEE
GAGEITE
GAGEL
GAGER
GAGES
GAGGED
GAGGER
GAGGERY
GAGGING
GAGGLE
GAGGLED
GAGGLER
GAGGLING
GAGING
GAGMAN
GAGOR
GAGROOT
GAGTOOTH
GAHE
GAHNITE
GAIAC
GAIASSA
GAIETY
GAIG
GAIL
GAILLARD
GAILY
GAIN
GAINAGE
GAINBIRTH
GAINCALL
GAINCOME
GAINCOPE
GAINE
GAINED
GAINER
GAINFUL
GAINFULLY
GAINFULNESS
GAINGIVING
GAINING
GAINLESS
GAINLINESS

GAINLY
GAINOR
GAINPAIN
GAINS
GAINSAY
GAINSAYER
GAINSET
GAINSOME
GAINSPEAKER
GAINSPEAKING
GAINST
GAINSTAND
GAINSTRIVE
GAINTURN
GAINTWIST
GAINWARD
GAINYIELD
GAIR
GAIRFISH
GAIRFOWL
GAIST
GAIT
GAITED
GAITER
GAITING
GAITT
GAIZE
GAJO
GAL
GALA
GALABEAH
GALABIA
GALABIEH
GALACTAGOG
GALACTAGOGUE
GALACTAN
GALACTASE
GALACTEMIA
GALACTIC
GALACTIN
GALACTITE
GALACTOCELE
GALACTOGOGUE
GALACTOHEMIA
GALACTOID
GALACTOLYSIS
GALACTOLYTIC
GALACTOMETER
GALACTONIC
GALACTOPATHY
GALACTOPHORE
GALACTOPYRA
GALACTOSCOPE
GALACTOSE
GALACTOSIDE
GALACTOSIS
GALACTOSURIA
GALACTURIA
GALAGALA
GALAH
GALANAS
GALANGAL
GALANGIN
GALANT
GALANTE
GALANTINE
GALAPAGO
GALATEA
GALAVANT
GALAXIAN
GALAXY
GALBAN
GALBANUM
GALBE
GALBULUS
GALD
GALE

GALEA
GALEAE
GALEAGE
GALEATE
GALEATED
GALECHE
GALEE
GALEENY
GALEGINE
GALEID
GALEIFORM
GALEMPONG
GALENA
GALENIC
GALENICAL
GALENITE
GALENOID
GALEOID
GALERA
GALERICULATE
GALERIE
GALERUM
GALERUS
GALESAUR
GALET
GALETTE
GALEWORT
GALGAL
GALI
GALIANES
GALILEE
GALIMATIAS
GALINGALE
GALIONGEE
GALIONJI
GALIOT
GALIPOT
GALIVANT
GALJOEN
GALL
GALLA
GALLACH
GALLAH
GALLANILIDE
GALLANT
GALLANTLY
GALLANTNESS
GALLANTRY
GALLATE
GALLATURE
GALLBERRY
GALLBUSH
GALLEASS
GALLED
GALLEIN
GALLEINE
GALLEON
GALLER
GALLERA
GALLERIAN
GALLERIES
GALLERY
GALLET
GALLETA
GALLEY
GALLEYMAN
GALLEYS
GALLEYWORM
GALLFLOWER
GALLFLY
GALLIAMBIC
GALLIAMBUS
GALLIARD
GALLIARDISE
GALLIARDLY
GALLIARDNESS
GALLIASS

GALLIC
GALLICIZER
GALLICOLA
GALLICOLOUS
GALLIFEROUS
GALLIFORM
GALLIGASKIN
GALLIGASKINS
GALLIMAUFRY
GALLINACEAN
GALLINACEOUS
GALLINAZO
GALLINE
GALLINEY
GALLING
GALLINGLY
GALLINGNESS
GALLINIPPER
GALLINULE
GALLINULINE
GALLIOT
GALLIPOT
GALLISH
GALLIUM
GALLIVANT
GALLIVANTER
GALLIVAT
GALLIVOROUS
GALLIWASP
GALLIZE
GALLNUT
GALLOFLAVIN
GALLOFLAVINE
GALLOGLASS
GALLON
GALLONAGE
GALLOON
GALLOONED
GALLOOT
GALLOP
GALLOPADE
GALLOPED
GALLOPER
GALLOPING
GALLOPTIOUS
GALLOTANNATE
GALLOTANNIN
GALLOUS
GALLOW
GALLOWAY
GALLOWGLASS
GALLOWS
GALLOWSNESS
GALLSTONE
GALLUSES
GALLWEED
GALLWORT
GALLY
GALLYBAGGER
GALLYBEGGAR
GALLYCROW
GALLYGASKINS
GALLYWASP
GALON
GALOOT
GALOP
GALOPADE
GALOPED
GALOPIN
GALOPING
GALORE
GALOSH
GALOSHE
GALOUBET
GALP
GALRAVAGE
GALRAVITCH

GALT
GALTRAP
GALUCHAT
GALUMPH
GALUMPTIOUS
GALUT
GALUTH
GALVANIC
GALVANICAL
GALVANICALLY
GALVANISE
GALVANISM
GALVANIST
GALVANIZATION
GALVANIZE
GALVANIZED
GALVANIZER
GALVANIZING
GALVANOGRAPH
GALVANOLOGY
GALVANOMETER
GALVANOMETRY
GALVANOSCOPE
GALVANOSCOPY
GALVANOTAXIS
GALVAYNE
GALVAYNED
GALVAYNING
GALYAC
GALYAK
GAM
GAMAHE
GAMARI
GAMASHES
GAMB
GAMBA
GAMBADE
GAMBADO
GAMBANG
GAMBE
GAMBEER
GAMBEERED
GAMBEERING
GAMBESON
GAMBET
GAMBETTE
GAMBIAE
GAMBIER
GAMBIR
GAMBIST
GAMBIT
GAMBLE
GAMBLED
GAMBLER
GAMBLERS
GAMBLING
GAMBO
GAMBOGE
GAMBOGIAN
GAMBOISED
GAMBOL
GAMBOLED
GAMBOLING
GAMBOLLED
GAMBOLLING
GAMBONE
GAMBREL
GAMBRELED
GAMBRELLED
GAMBROON
GAMDEBOO
GAME
GAMEBAG
GAMEBALL
GAMECOCK
GAMECRAFT
GAMED

GAMEFUL
GAMEKEEPER
GAMEKEEPING
GAMELAN
GAMELANG
GAMELIN
GAMELOTE
GAMELOTTE
GAMELY
GAMENE
GAMENESS
GAMER
GAMES
GAMESOME
GAMESOMELY
GAMESOMENESS
GAMEST
GAMESTER
GAMETAL
GAMETANGIUM
GAMETE
GAMETIC
GAMETICALLY
GAMETOCYST
GAMETOCYTE
GAMETOGENIC
GAMETOGENOUS
GAMETOGENY
GAMETOGONIUM
GAMETOID
GAMETOPHORE
GAMETOPHYLL
GAMETOPHYTE
GAMEY
GAMIC
GAMIE
GAMIER
GAMIEST
GAMILY
GAMIN
GAMINE
GAMINESS
GAMING
GAMLA
GAMMA
GAMMACISM
GAMMADION
GAMMARID
GAMMAROID
GAMMATION
GAMME
GAMMELOST
GAMMER
GAMMERSTANG
GAMMICK
GAMMOCK
GAMMON
GAMMONER
GAMMONING
GAMMY
GAMOBIUM
GAMODEME
GAMODESMIC
GAMODESMY
GAMOGAMY
GAMOGENESIS
GAMOGENETIC
GAMOGENY
GAMOND
GAMONT
GAMOPETALOUS
GAMOPHAGIA
GAMOPHYLLOUS
GAMORI
GAMOSEPALOUS
GAMOSTELE
GAMOSTELIC

GAMOSTELY
GAMP
GAMPHREL
GAMUT
GAMY
GAN
GANAM
GANANCIAL
GANANCIALES
GANANCIAS
GANCH
GANCHED
GANCHING
GANDER
GANDERESS
GANDERGOOSE
GANDERMOONER
GANDERTEETH
GANDI
GANDOURA
GANDUL
GANDUM
GANDURAH
GANE
GANEF
GANG
GANGA
GANGAVA
GANGBOARD
GANGE
GANGED
GANGER
GANGEREL
GANGFLOWER
GANGGANG
GANGING
GANGION
GANGLAND
GANGLANDER
GANGLIA
GANGLIAC
GANGLIAL
GANGLIAR
GANGLIATE
GANGLIATED
GANGLIFORM
GANGLING
GANGLIOBLAST
GANGLIOCYTE
GANGLIOFORM
GANGLIOMA
GANGLIOMAS
GANGLIOMATA
GANGLION
GANGLIONARY
GANGLIONATE
GANGLIONATED
GANGLIONIC
GANGLIONITIS
GANGLIONS
GANGLY
GANGMAN
GANGMASTER
GANGPLANK
GANGPLOW
GANGREL
GANGRENATE
GANGRENE
GANGRENED
GANGRENING
GANGRENOUS
GANGSA
GANGSMAN
GANGSTER
GANGSTERISM
GANGTIDE
GANGUE

GANGWA
GANGWAY
GANGWAYMAN
GANGWAYMEN
GANISTER
GANJA
GANNER
GANNET
GANNETRY
GANNETS
GANOF
GANOID
GANOIDAL
GANOIDEAN
GANOIDIAN
GANOIN
GANOMALITE
GANOPHYLLITE
GANOSIS
GANSEL
GANSEY
GANSH
GANSY
GANT
GANTA
GANTANG
GANTANGS
GANTLET
GANTLETED
GANTLETING
GANTLINE
GANTLOPE
GANTRIES
GANTRY
GANTRYMAN
GANYIE
GANZA
GANZIE
GAOL
GAOLAGE
GAOLBIRD
GAOLER
GAOLERING
GAOLERNESS
GAOLORING
GAP
GAPE
GAPED
GAPER
GAPES
GAPESEED
GAPEWORM
GAPING
GAPINGSTOCK
GAPO
GAPPED
GAPPER
GAPPIER
GAPPIEST
GAPPING
GAPPY
GAPS
GAPY
GAR
GARABATO
GARAD
GARAGE
GARAGED
GARAGEMAN
GARAGING
GARANCE
GARANCIN
GARAPATA
GARAPATO
GARAU
GARAVA
GARAVANCE

GARAWI
GARB
GARBAGE
GARBANZO
GARBILL
GARBLE
GARBLED
GARBLER
GARBLING
GARBLINGS
GARBOARD
GARBOIL
GARBURE
GARCE
GARCON
GARD
GARDANT
GARDE
GARDEBRAS
GARDEEN
GARDEN
GARDENED
GARDENER
GARDENIN
GARDENING
GARDENIZE
GARDENS
GARDENY
GARDEROBE
GARDEVIANCE
GARDEVIN
GARDEVISURE
GARDINOL
GARDNAP
GARDON
GARDY
GARDYLOO
GARE
GAREFOWL
GAREH
GARETTA
GAREWAITE
GARFISH
GARFISHES
GARGANEY
GARGET
GARGETY
GARGIL
GARGLE
GARGLED
GARGLING
GARGOYLE
GARGOYLEY
GARIAL
GARIBA
GARIBALDI
GARIGUE
GARISH
GARISHLY
GARISHNESS
GARLAND
GARLANDAGE
GARLANDED
GARLANDING
GARLANDRY
GARLE
GARLIC
GARLICKY
GARLION
GARLOPA
GARMENT
GARMENTED
GARMENTING
GARMENTMAKER
GARMENTS
GARMENTURE
GARN

GARNEL
GARNER
GARNERED
GARNERING
GARNET
GARNETBERRY
GARNETER
GARNETT
GARNETWORK
GARNETZ
GARNI
GARNIEC
GARNIERITE
GARNISH
GARNISHED
GARNISHEE
GARNISHEED
GARNISHEEING
GARNISHER
GARNISHING
GARNISHMENT
GARNISHRY
GARNITURE
GAROO
GAROOKUH
GAROTE
GAROTTE
GAROTTED
GAROTTER
GARPIKE
GARR
GARRAFA
GARRAN
GARRAT
GARRE
GARRETEER
GARRICK
GARRIDGE
GARRIGUE
GARRISON
GARRON
GARROO
GARROT
GARROTE
GARROTED
GARROTER
GARROTING
GARROTTE
GARROTTING
GARRULINE
GARRULITY
GARRULOUS
GARRULOUSLY
GARRUPA
GARSE
GARSIL
GARSTON
GARTEN
GARTER
GARTERED
GARTERING
GARTERS
GARTH
GARTHMAN
GARUM
GARVANCE
GARVANZO
GARVEY
GARVIE
GARVOCK
GAS
GASALIER
GASBAG
GASBOAT
GASCHECK
GASCON
GASCONADE

GASCONADED
GASCONADER
GASCONADING
GASCONISM
GASEITY
GASELIER
GASEOSITY
GASEOUS
GASEOUSNESS
GASH
GASHED
GASHES
GASHFUL
GASHING
GASHLINESS
GASHLY
GASHOLDER
GASHOUSE
GASHY
GASIFIABLE
GASIFICATION
GASIFIED
GASIFIER
GASIFORM
GASIFY
GASIFYING
GASKET
GASKIN
GASKING
GASKINS
GASLIGHT
GASLIGHTED
GASLIGHTING
GASLIT
GASLOCK
GASMAN
GASMEN
GASOGEN
GASOGENE
GASOLIER
GASOLIERY
GASOLINE
GASOLINER
GASOMETER
GASOMETRIC
GASOMETRICAL
GASOMETRY
GASP
GASPARILLO
GASPER
GASPEREAU
GASPERGOU
GASPING
GASPY
GASSER
GASSES
GASSING
GASSY
GAST
GASTALDITE
GASTALDO
GASTER
GASTERALGIA
GASTERIA
GASTEROPOD
GASTEROSTEID
GASTEROTHECA
GASTEROZOOID
GASTFUL
GASTIGHT
GASTIGHTNESS
GASTNESS
GASTRAEA
GASTRAEAL
GASTRAEUM
GASTRAL
GASTRALGIA

GASTRALGIC
GASTRECTOMY
GASTRELCOSIS
GASTRIC
GASTRICISM
GASTRIMARGY
GASTRIN
GASTRITIC
GASTRITIS
GASTROATONIA
GASTROCELE
GASTROCOEL
GASTROCOELE
GASTROCOLIC
GASTROCYSTIS
GASTRODISK
GASTRODYNIA
GASTROGRAPH
GASTROID
GASTROLATER
GASTROLIENAL
GASTROLITH
GASTROLOGER
GASTROLOGIST
GASTROLOGY
GASTROLYSIS
GASTROMANCY
GASTROMELUS
GASTROMENIA
GASTROMYCES
GASTRONOME
GASTRONOMER
GASTRONOMIC
GASTRONOMIST
GASTRONOMY
GASTRONOSUS
GASTROPEXY
GASTROPHILE
GASTROPLASTY
GASTROPOD
GASTROPODAN
GASTROPORE
GASTROPTOSIS
GASTRORRHEA
GASTROSCOPE
GASTROSCOPIC
GASTROSCOPY
GASTROSOPH
GASTROSOPHER
GASTROSOPHY
GASTROSPASM
GASTROSTEGAL
GASTROSTEGE
GASTROSTOMY
GASTROTAXIS
GASTROTHECA
GASTROTHECAL
GASTROTOME
GASTROTOMIC
GASTROTOMY
GASTROXYNSIS
GASTROZOOID
GASTRULA
GASTRULATE
GASTRULATION
GASWORKER
GASWORKS
GAT
GATA
GATCH
GATCHWORK
GATE
GATEADO
GATEAGE
GATEAU
GATED
GATEFOLD

GATEHOUSE
GATEKEEPER
GATEMAKER
GATEMAN
GATEPOST
GATER
GATES
GATETENDER
GATEWARD
GATEWAY
GATEWAYMAN
GATEWAYMEN
GATEWOMAN
GATEWORKS
GATEWRIGHT
GATHER
GATHERED
GATHERER
GATHERING
GATHERUM
GATING
GATO
GATOR
GATTER
GATTINE
GAU
GAUB
GAUCHE
GAUCHELY
GAUCHENESS
GAUCHERIE
GAUCIE
GAUCY
GAUD
GAUDEAMUS
GAUDERY
GAUDFUL
GAUDIER
GAUDIES
GAUDIEST
GAUDILY
GAUDINESS
GAUDISH
GAUDSMAN
GAUDY
GAUE
GAUFFER
GAUFFERED
GAUFFERER
GAUFFERING
GAUFFRE
GAUFFRED
GAUFRE
GAUFRETTE
GAUFRETTES
GAUG
GAUGE
GAUGEABLE
GAUGED
GAUGER
GAUGING
GAULDING
GAULE
GAULIN
GAULOISERIE
GAULSH
GAULT
GAULTER
GAULTHERASE
GAULTHERIA
GAULTHERIN
GAULTHERINE
GAUM
GAUMISH
GAUMLESS
GAUMLIKE
GAUMY

GAUN
GAUNCH
GAUNT
GAUNTED
GAUNTER
GAUNTEST
GAUNTLET
GAUNTLETED
GAUNTLY
GAUNTNESS
GAUNTRY
GAUNTY
GAUP
GAUPUS
GAUR
GAURIC
GAURIE
GAUS
GAUSS
GAUSSAGE
GAUSSBERGITE
GAUSTER
GAUSTERER
GAUT
GAUTEITE
GAUZE
GAUZELIKE
GAUZEWING
GAUZIER
GAUZIEST
GAUZILY
GAUZINESS
GAUZY
GAV
GAVAGE
GAVALL
GAVE
GAVEL
GAVELAGE
GAVELER
GAVELKIND
GAVELKINDER
GAVELLER
GAVELMAN
GAVELMEN
GAVELOCK
GAVIAL
GAVIALOID
GAVOT
GAVOTTE
GAVYUTI
GAW
GAWCEY
GAWD
GAWISH
GAWK
GAWKHAMMER
GAWKIER
GAWKIEST
GAWKILY
GAWKINESS
GAWKISH
GAWKY
GAWN
GAWNEY
GAWP
GAWSIE
GAWSY
GAY
GAYAL
GAYALS
GAYATRI
GAYBINE
GAYCAT
GAYDIANG
GAYER
GAYEST

GAYETY
GAYLIES
GAYLUSSITE
GAYLY
GAYMENT
GAYNESS
GAYSOME
GAYWAY
GAYWINGS
GAYYOU
GAZ
GAZABO
GAZABOES
GAZABOS
GAZANGABIN
GAZE
GAZEBO
GAZEBOES
GAZEBOS
GAZED
GAZEHOUND
GAZEL
GAZELESS
GAZELLE
GAZELLES
GAZEMENT
GAZER
GAZET
GAZETTAL
GAZETTE
GAZETTED
GAZETTEER
GAZETTEERAGE
GAZETTING
GAZI
GAZING
GAZINGLY
GAZINGSTOCK
GAZOGENE
GAZON
GAZOO
GAZOOK
GAZOZ
GAZPACHO
GAZY
GAZZETTA
GBO
GEAL
GEAN
GEANTICLINAL
GEANTICLINE
GEAR
GEARBOX
GEARCASE
GEARE
GEARED
GEARING
GEARKSUTITE
GEARLESS
GEARMAN
GEARS
GEARSET
GEARSHIFT
GEARWHEEL
GEASON
GEAST
GEBANG
GEBANGA
GEBBIE
GEBUR
GECK
GECKO
GECKOES
GECKOS
GED
GEDACT
GEDANITE

GEDD
GEDDA
GEDDER
GEDECKT
GEDECKTWORK
GEDRITE
GEDUNK
GEE
GEEBUNG
GEED
GEEING
GEEK
GEELBEC
GEELBECK
GEELBEK
GEELHOUT
GEEPOUND
GEERAH
GEES
GEESE
GEEST
GEET
GEEZER
GEFULLTEFISH
GEG
GEGENION
GEGENSCHEIN
GEGG
GEGGEE
GEGGER
GEGGERY
GEHLENITE
GEIG
GEIGE
GEIGER
GEIKIELITE
GEIN
GEIR
GEIRA
GEISHA
GEISHAS
GEISON
GEISOTHERM
GEISOTHERMAL
GEISTLICH
GEITJIE
GEITONOGAMY
GEKKONID
GEKKONOID
GEL
GELABLE
GELADA
GELANDESPRUNG
GELASTIC
GELATE
GELATIA
GELATIN
GELATINATE
GELATINATED
GELATINATING
GELATINATION
GELATINE
GELATINED
GELATINITY
GELATINIZE
GELATINIZED
GELATINIZER
GELATINIZING
GELATINOID
GELATINOTYPE
GELATINOUS
GELATINOUSLY
GELATION
GELATOSE
GELD
GELDANT
GELDED

GELDER
GELDING
GELEE
GELEEM
GELID
GELIDITY
GELIDLY
GELIDNESS
GELIGNITE
GELILAH
GELINOTTE
GELL
GELLED
GELLING
GELLY
GELOFER
GELOFRE
GELOGENIC
GELONG
GELOSCOPY
GELOSE
GELOSIN
GELOSINE
GELOTHERAPY
GELOTOSCOPY
GELSEMIN
GELSEMINE
GELSEMININE
GELSEMIUM
GELT
GEM
GEMATRIA
GEMATRICAL
GEMATRIOT
GEMAUVE
GEMEINDE
GEMEL
GEMELED
GEMELLED
GEMELLION
GEMELLUS
GEMELS
GEMINATE
GEMINATED
GEMINATELY
GEMINATING
GEMINATION
GEMINATIVE
GEMINIFORM
GEMINOUS
GEMLIKE
GEMMA
GEMMACEOUS
GEMMAE
GEMMAN
GEMMARY
GEMMATE
GEMMATED
GEMMATING
GEMMATION
GEMMATIVE
GEMMED
GEMMEL
GEMMEOUS
GEMMER
GEMMIFEROUS
GEMMIFORM
GEMMILY
GEMMINESS
GEMMING
GEMMIPARA
GEMMIPARES
GEMMIPARITY
GEMMIPAROUS
GEMMOID
GEMMOLOGY
GEMMULA

GEMMULATION
GEMMULE
GEMMY
GEMOLOGY
GEMOT
GEMOTE
GEMSBOK
GEMSBUCK
GEMSHORN
GEMSTONE
GEMUL
GEMUTLICH
GEMWORK
GEN
GENA
GENAE
GENAL
GENAPP
GENAPPE
GENAPPER
GENARCH
GENARCHA
GENDARME
GENDARMERIE
GENDARMERY
GENDERED
GENDERER
GENDERING
GENDERLESS
GENE
GENEAL
GENEALOGIC
GENEALOGICAL
GENEALOGIES
GENEALOGIST
GENEALOGIZE
GENEALOGIZER
GENEALOGY
GENEAT
GENEKI
GENEPI
GENER
GENERA
GENERABILITY
GENERABLE
GENERAL
GENERALATE
GENERALCIES
GENERALCY
GENERALE
GENERALIA
GENERALIFIC
GENERALISM
GENERALIST
GENERALISTIC
GENERALITER
GENERALITY
GENERALIZABLE
GENERALIZATION
GENERALIZE
GENERALIZED
GENERALIZER
GENERALL
GENERALLY
GENERALNESS
GENERALSHIP
GENERALTY
GENERANT
GENERATE
GENERATED
GENERATING
GENERATION
GENERATIONAL
GENERATIVE
GENERATOR
GENERATRICES
GENERATRIX

GENERIC
GENERICAL
GENERICALLY
GENEROSITIES
GENEROSITY
GENEROUS
GENEROUSLY
GENEROUSNESS
GENESERINE
GENESERINE
GENESES
GENESIAL
GENESIC
GENESIOLOGY
GENESIS
GENESIURGIC
GENET
GENETHLIAC
GENETHLIC
GENETIC
GENETICAL
GENETICALLY
GENETICISM
GENETICIST
GENETICS
GENETOR
GENETOUS
GENETRIX
GENETTE
GENEVOISE
GENIAL
GENIALITY
GENIALIZE
GENIALLY
GENIC
GENICULATE
GENICULATED
GENICULATELY
GENICULUM
GENIE
GENII
GENIN
GENIO
GENIOGLOSSAL
GENIOGLOSSUS
GENIOHYOID
GENIOLATRY
GENION
GENIOPLASTY
GENIP
GENIPAP
GENIPAPADA
GENISARO
GENISTEIN
GENISTIN
GENITAL
GENITALIA
GENITALS
GENITIVAL
GENITIVALLY
GENITIVE
GENITOCRURAL
GENITOR
GENITORIAL
GENITORY
GENITURE
GENIUS
GENIUSES
GENIZAH
GENOBLAST
GENOBLASTIC
GENOCIDE
GENOME
GENOS
GENOTYPE
GENOTYPIC
GENOTYPICAL

GENOUILLERE
GENOVINO
GENRE
GENRO
GENROS
GENS
GENSON
GENT
GENTE
GENTEEL
GENTEELISM
GENTEELLY
GENTEELNESS
GENTES
GENTHITE
GENTIAN
GENTIANELLA
GENTIANOSE
GENTIANWORT
GENTIL
GENTILE
GENTILES
GENTILESSE
GENTILIC
GENTILISH
GENTILISM
GENTILITIAL
GENTILITIAN
GENTILITIES
GENTILITIOUS
GENTILITY
GENTILIZE
GENTIOBIOSE
GENTIOPICRIN
GENTISEIN
GENTISIN
GENTLE
GENTLED
GENTLEFOLK
GENTLEFOLKS
GENTLEHOOD
GENTLEMAN
GENTLEMANLY
GENTLEMEN
GENTLENESS
GENTLER
GENTLESHIP
GENTLEST
GENTLEWOMAN
GENTLEWOMEN
GENTLING
GENTLY
GENTMAN
GENTRICE
GENTRY
GENTY
GENU
GENUA
GENUAL
GENUCLAST
GENUFLECT
GENUFLECTED
GENUFLECTING
GENUFLECTION
GENUFLECTOR
GENUFLECTORY
GENUFLEXION
GENUFLEXUOUS
GENUINE
GENUINELY
GENUINENESS
GENUS
GENUSES
GEO
GEOBIOLOGIC
GEOBIOLOGY
GEOBIONT

GEOBIOS
GEOBLAST
GEOBOTANY
GEOCARPIC
GEOCENTRIC
GEOCENTRICAL
GEOCERITE
GEOCHEMICAL
GEOCHEMIST
GEOCHEMISTRY
GEOCHRONIC
GEOCHRONY
GEOCLINE
GEOCORONIUM
GEOCRATIC
GEOCRONITE
GEOCYCLIC
GEODAESIA
GEODE
GEODESIA
GEODESIC
GEODESICAL
GEODESIST
GEODESY
GEODETE
GEODETIC
GEODETICAL
GEODETICALLY
GEODETICS
GEODIC
GEODIFEROUS
GEODIST
GEODUCK
GEODYNAMIC
GEODYNAMICAL
GEODYNAMICS
GEOETHNIC
GEOFORM
GEOGEN
GEOGENESIS
GEOGENETIC
GEOGENIC
GEOGENOUS
GEOGENY
GEOGLYPHIC
GEOGNOSIS
GEOGNOSIST
GEOGNOST
GEOGNOSTIC
GEOGNOSTICAL
GEOGNOSY
GEOGONIC
GEOGONICAL
GEOGONY
GEOGRAPHER
GEOGRAPHIC
GEOGRAPHICAL
GEOGRAPHICS
GEOGRAPHIES
GEOGRAPHIZED
GEOGRAPHY
GEOHYDROI OGY
GEOID
GEOIDAL
GEOLATRY
GEOLOGER
GEOLOGIAN
GEOLOGIC
GEOLOGICAL
GEOLOGICALLY
GEOLOGIES
GEOLOGIST
GEOLOGIZE
GEOLOGIZED
GEOLOGIZING
GEOLOGY
GEOM

GEOMAGNETIC
GEOMAGNETICS
GEOMAGNETISM
GEOMALIC
GEOMALISM
GEOMANCE
GEOMANCER
GEOMANCY
GEOMANT
GEOMANTIC
GEOMANTICAL
GEOMEDICINE
GEOMETER
GEOMETRIC
GEOMETRICAL
GEOMETRICIAN
GEOMETRICIZE
GEOMETRID
GEOMETRIES
GEOMETRIZE
GEOMETRIZED
GEOMETRIZING
GEOMETRY
GEOMOROI
GEOMORPHIC
GEOMORPHIST
GEOMORPHY
GEOMYID
GEONEGATIVE
GEOPHAGIA
GEOPHAGISM
GEOPHAGIST
GEOPHAGOUS
GEOPHAGY
GEOPHILID
GEOPHILOUS
GEOPHYSICAL
GEOPHYSICIST
GEOPHYSICS
GEOPHYTE
GEOPHYTIC
GEOPOLAR
GEOPOLITIC
GEOPOLITICAL
GEOPOLITICS
GEOPONIC
GEOPONICAL
GEOPONICS
GEOPONY
GEOPOSITIVE
GEORAMA
GEORG
GEORGIC
GEORGICAL
GEOSCOPIC
GEOSCOPY
GEOSELENIC
GEOSPHERE
GEOSTATIC
GEOSTATICS
GEOSTROPHIC
GEOSYNCLINAL
GEOSYNCLINE
GEOTACTIC
GEOTAXIS
GEOTAXY
GEOTECHNICS
GEOTECTOLOGY
GEOTECTONIC
GEOTHERM
GEOTHERMAL
GEOTHERMIC
GEOTONIC
GEOTONUS
GEOTROPIC
GEOTROPISM
GEOTROPY

GEPHYREAN
GER
GERA
GERAERA
GERAH
GERANIACEOUS
GERANIAL
GERANIOL
GERANIUM
GERANYL
GERARA
GERARDIA
GERASTIAN
GERATE
GERATED
GERATELY
GERATIC
GERATOLOGY
GERB
GERBE
GERBIL
GERBILLE
GERCROW
GERE
GEREAGLE
GEREFA
GERENDUM
GERENT
GERENUK
GERFALCON
GERFUL
GERHARDTITE
GERIATRIC
GERIATRICIAN
GERIATRICS
GERIATRIST
GERIP
GERKIN
GERM
GERMAL
GERMAN
GERMANDER
GERMANE
GERMANIC
GERMANITE
GERMANITY
GERMANIUM
GERMANIZE
GERMANOUS
GERMANYL
GERMARIUM
GERMEN
GERMENS
GERMFREE
GERMICIDAL
GERMICIDE
GERMIFUGE
GERMIN
GERMINABLE
GERMINAL
GERMINALLY
GERMINANCE
GERMINANCY
GERMINANT
GERMINATE
GEPMINATED
GERMINATING
GERMINATION
GERMINATIVE
GERMINATOR
GERMING
GERMINOGONY
GERMIPARITY
GERMLING
GERMON
GERMPROOF
GERMS

GERMULE
GEROCOMIA
GEROCOMICAL
GEROCOMY
GERODERMA
GERODERMIA
GEROMORPHISM
GERONTAL
GERONTES
GERONTIC
GERONTINE
GERONTISM
GERONTOCRACY
GERONTOGEOUS
GERONTOLOGY
GERONTOXON
GEROUSIA
GERRYMANDER
GERS
GERSDORFFITE
GERSUM
GERTRUDE
GERUND
GERUNDIAL
GERUNDIALLY
GERUNDIVAL
GERUNDIVE
GERUNDIVELY
GERUSIA
GERVAO
GERY
GERYONID
GESITH
GESITHCUND
GESNERAD
GESSERON
GESSO
GEST
GESTALT
GESTALTEN
GESTALTER
GESTALTIST
GESTALTS
GESTANT
GESTATE
GESTATED
GESTATING
GESTATION
GESTATIONAL
GESTATIVE
GESTATORIAL
GESTATORIUM
GESTATORY
GESTE
GESTED
GESTEN
GESTENING
GESTER
GESTIC
GESTICAL
GESTICULANT
GESTICULAR
GESTICULATE
GESTICULATED
GESTICULATOR
GESTIO
GESTION
GESTNING
GESTONIE
GESTURAL
GESTURE
GESTURED
GESTURER
GESTURES
GESTURING
GESWARP
GET

GETA
GETAN
GETAS
GETAWAY
GETHSEMANE
GETLING
GETPENNY
GETT
GETTABLE
GETTER
GETTING
GETUP
GEULAH
GEVE
GEWGAW
GEWGAWED
GEWGAWISH
GEWGAWRY
GEY
GEYAN
GEYERITE
GEYLIES
GEYSER
GEYSERAL
GEYSERIC
GEYSERINE
GEYSERITE
GEYZE
GEZ
GEZERAH
GHAFFIR
GHAFIR
GHALVA
GHARIAL
GHARNAO
GHARRI
GHARRIES
GHARRY
GHAST
GHASTFUL
GHASTFULLY
GHASTFULNESS
GHASTILY
GHASTLIER
GHASTLIEST
GHASTLILY
GHASTLINESS
GHASTLY
GHAT
GHATS
GHATWAL
GHAUT
GHAWAZEE
GHAWAZI
GHAZAL
GHAZEL
GHAZI
GHAZIES
GHEBETA
GHEE
GHELD
GHENTING
GHERKIN
GHETCHOO
GHETTO
GHI
GHILLIE
GHIZITE
GHOL
GHOOM
GHOR
GHORKHAR
GHOST
GHOSTCRAFT
GHOSTDOM
GHOSTED
GHOSTER

GHOSTFISH
GHOSTFLOWER
GHOSTIFIED
GHOSTILY
GHOSTING
GHOSTISM
GHOSTLAND
GHOSTLIER
GHOSTLIEST
GHOSTLIFY
GHOSTLIKE
GHOSTLY
GHOSTMONGER
GHOSTOLOGY
GHOSTS
GHOSTSHIP
GHOSTWEED
GHOSTWRITE
GHOSTWRITER
GHOSTWRITING
GHOSTWRITTEN
GHOSTWROTE
GHOSTY
GHOUL
GHOULIE
GHOULISH
GHOULISHLY
GHOULISHNESS
GHURRY
GHYLL
GI
GIALLOLINO
GIANSAR
GIANT
GIANTESS
GIANTISM
GIANTIZE
GIANTKIND
GIANTLY
GIANTRY
GIANTS
GIAOUR
GIARDIASIS
GIB
GIBARO
GIBBALS
GIBBAR
GIBBARTAS
GIBBED
GIBBER
GIBBERED
GIBBERELLIN
GIBBERGUNYAH
GIBBERING
GIBBERISH
GIBBEROSE
GIBBEROSITY
GIBBERT
GIBBET
GIBBETED
GIBBETING
GIBBLEGABLE
GIBBLES
GIBBOL
GIBBON
GIBBOSE
GIBBOSITIES
GIBBOSITY
GIBBOUS
GIBBOUSLY
GIBBOUSNESS
GIBBSITE
GIBBUS
GIBBY
GIBE
GIBED
GIBEL

GIBELITE
GIBER
GIBETTING
GIBING
GIBINGLY
GIBLEH
GIBLET
GIBLETS
GIBOIA
GIBSTAFF
GIBUS
GID
GIDDAP
GIDDIED
GIDDIER
GIDDIEST
GIDDIFY
GIDDILY
GIDDINESS
GIDDY
GIDDYBERRY
GIDDYBRAIN
GIDDYHEAD
GIDDYING
GIDE
GIDGEA
GIDGEE
GIDIA
GIDJEE
GIDYA
GIDYEA
GIE
GIER
GIESECKITE
GIF
GIFBLAAR
GIFFGAFF
GIFT
GIFTBOOK
GIFTED
GIFTEDLY
GIFTEDNESS
GIFTIE
GIFTING
GIFTS
GIFTURE
GIFTWARE
GIG
GIGA
GIGACYCLE
GIGANT
GIGANTAL
GIGANTEAN
GIGANTESQUE
GIGANTIC
GIGANTICAL
GIGANTICALLY
GIGANTICIDAL
GIGANTICIDE
GIGANTICNESS
GIGANTISM
GIGANTIZE
GIGANTOBLAST
GIGANTOCYTE
GIGANTOLITE
GIGANTOLOGY
GIGATON
GIGBACK
GIGELIRA
GIGERIUM
GIGGE
GIGGED
GIGGER
GIGGING
GIGGISH
GIGGIT
GIGGLE

GIGGLED
GIGGLER
GIGGLIER
GIGGLIEST
GIGGLING
GIGGLY
GIGLET
GIGLIATO
GIGLIO
GIGLOT
GIGMAN
GIGMANESS
GIGMANHOOD
GIGMANIA
GIGMANIC
GIGMANICALLY
GIGMANISM
GIGMANITY
GIGNATE
GIGNITIVE
GIGOLO
GIGOT
GIGSMAN
GIGSMEN
GIGSTER
GIGTREE
GIGUE
GIGUNU
GIKE
GIL
GILBERT
GILBERTAGE
GILBERTITE
GILD
GILDABLE
GILDED
GILDEN
GILDER
GILDING
GILDSHIP
GILDSMAN
GILENYER
GILENYIE
GILET
GILGAI
GILGAMES
GILGAMESH
GILGUL
GILGUY
GILIAK
GILL
GILLAR
GILLAROO
GILLED
GILLER
GILLFLIRT
GILLHOOTER
GILLIE
GILLIED
GILLIES
GILLING
GILLIVER
GILLNET
GILLOT
GILLOTAGE
GILLOTYPE
GILLS
GILLSTOUP
GILLY
GILLYFLOWER
GILLYGAUPUS
GILLYING
GILO
GILOE
GILP
GILPEY
GILPY

GILRAVAGE
GILRAVAGER
GILSONITE
GILT
GILTCUP
GILTEN
GILTHEAD
GILTTAIL
GILVER
GIM
GIMBAL
GIMBALED
GIMBALJAWED
GIMBALS
GIMBERJAWED
GIMBLE
GIMBRI
GIMCRACK
GIMCRACKERY
GIMCRACKY
GIME
GIMEL
GIMLET
GIMLETEYED
GIMLETY
GIMMAL
GIMMALED
GIMME
GIMMER
GIMMERINGLY
GIMMICK
GIMMICKRY
GIMMICKY
GIMMOR
GIMP
GIMPER
GIMPIER
GIMPIEST
GIMPING
GIMPY
GIN
GINEP
GINETE
GING
GINGAL
GINGALL
GINGE
GINGELEY
GINGELI
GINGELLY
GINGELY
GINGER
GINGERADE
GINGERBERRY
GINGERBREAD
GINGERBREADY
GINGERIN
GINGERLEAF
GINGERLINE
GINGERLY
GINGERNUT
GINGEROL
GINGEROUS
GINGERROOT
GINGERSNAP
GINGERSPICE
GINGERWORK
GINGERWORT
GINGERY
GINGHAM
GINGHAMED
GINGILI
GINGIVA
GINGIVAL
GINGIVALGIA
GINGIVECTOMY
GINGIVITIS

GINGKO
GINGLYFORM
GINGLYMOID
GINGLYMUS
GINGRAS
GINHOUSE
GINK
GINNED
GINNEL
GINNER
GINNERIES
GINNERS
GINNERY
GINNING
GINNLE
GINNY
GINORITE
GINSENG
GIO
GIOCOSO
GIOJOSO
GIORNATA
GIP
GIPON
GIPPED
GIPPER
GIPPING
GIPPO
GIPSEIAN
GIPSER
GIPSIES
GIPSIOLOGIST
GIPSIRE
GIPSOLOGY
GIPSY
GIPSYDOM
GIPSYFY
GIPSYHEAD
GIPSYRY
GIPSYWEED
GIPSYWORT
GIR
GIRAFFE
GIRAFFES
GIRAFFINE
GIRAFFOID
GIRANDOLE
GIRASOL
GIRASOLE
GIRBA
GIRD
GIRDED
GIRDER
GIRDERAGE
GIRDING
GIRDLE
GIRDLECAKE
GIRDLED
GIRDLER
GIRDLESTEAD
GIRDLING
GIRDLINGLY
GIREH
GIRG
GIRL
GIRLEEN
GIRLERY
GIRLFULLY
GIRLHOOD
GIRLIE
GIRLING
GIRLISH
GIRLISHLY
GIRLISHNESS
GIRLY
GIRN
GIRNAL

GIRNEL
GIRNIE
GIRNY
GIRO
GIRON
GIROSOL
GIROUETTE
GIROUETTISM
GIRR
GIRRIT
GIRSE
GIRSH
GIRT
GIRTED
GIRTH
GIRTING
GIRTLINE
GISANT
GISARME
GISE
GISH
GISLER
GISMO
GISMONDITE
GISMOS
GISPIN
GIST
GISTS
GIT
GITALIGENIN
GITALIN
GITANA
GITANEMUK
GITANO
GITANOS
GITE
GITERNE
GITH
GITONIN
GITOXIGENIN
GITOXIN
GITTER
GITTERN
GITTITH
GIULIO
GIUSTAMENTE
GIUSTINA
GIUSTO
GIVE
GIVEAWAY
GIVEN
GIVER
GIVEY
GIVING
GIZMO
GIZZ
GIZZARD
GIZZEN
GIZZENED
GIZZERN
GJEDOST
GJOLL
GLABELLA
GLABELLAE
GLABELLAR
GLABELLOUS
GLABRATE
GLABRESCENT
GLABROUS
GLACE
GLACIABLE
GLACIAL
GLACIALISM
GLACIALIST
GLACIALLY
GLACIARIUM
GLACIATE

GLACIATION
GLACIER
GLACIERED
GLACIERET
GLACIERIST
GLACIOLOGIC
GLACIOLOGIST
GLACIOLOGY
GLACIOMARINE
GLACIOMETER
GLACIONATANT
GLACIS
GLACK
GLACON
GLAD
GLADDED
GLADDEN
GLADDENED
GLADDENER
GLADDENING
GLADDER
GLADDEST
GLADDING
GLADDON
GLADDY
GLADE
GLADEN
GLADES
GLADEYE
GLADFUL
GLADFULLY
GLADFULNESS
GLADHEARTED
GLADIATE
GLADIATOR
GLADIATORIAL
GLADIFY
GLADIOLA
GLADIOLAR
GLADIOLI
GLADIOLUS
GLADIOLUSES
GLADITE
GLADIUS
GLADKAITE
GLADLESS
GLADLY
GLADNESS
GLADSHIP
GLADSOME
GLADSOMELY
GLADSOMENESS
GLADY
GLAGA
GLAGAH
GLAIEUL
GLAIK
GLAIKET
GLAIKETNESS
GLAIKIT
GLAIKITNESS
GLAIKS
GLAIR
GLAIRED
GLAIREOUS
GLAIRIER
GLAIRIEST
GLAIRINESS
GLAIRING
GLAIRY
GLAISTER
GLAISTIG
GLAIVE
GLAIZIE
GLAKED
GLAKY
GLAM

GLAMBERRY
GLAME
GLAMOR
GLAMORIZE
GLAMORIZED
GLAMORIZING
GLAMOROUS
GLAMOROUSLY
GLAMOUR
GLAMOURED
GLAMOURIE
GLAMOURING
GLAMOUROUS
GLAMOUROUS
GLAMOUROUSLY
GLAMOURY
GLAMP
GLANCE
GLANCED
GLANCER
GLANCING
GLANCINGLY
GLAND
GLANDACEOUS
GLANDERED
GLANDEROUS
GLANDERS
GLANDES
GLANDIFEROUS
GLANDIFORM
GLANDULA
GLANDULAR
GLANDULE
GLANDULOSE
GLANDULOUS
GLANIS
GLANS
GLAR
GLARE
GLAREOLE
GLAREOUS
GLAREWORM
GLARIER
GLARIEST
GLARILY
GLARINESS
GLARING
GLARINGLY
GLARINGNESS
GLARRY
GLARY
GLASHAN
GLASS
GLASSBLOWER
GLASSBLOWING
GLASSED
GLASSEN
GLASSER
GLASSES
GLASSEYE
GLASSFUL
GLASSHOUSE
GLASSIE
GLASSIER
GLASSIEST
GLASSILY
GLASSIN
GLASSINE
GLASSINESS
GLASSING
GLASSMAKER
GLASSMAKING
GLASSMAN
GLASSMEN
GLASSTEEL
GLASSWARE
GLASSWEED

GLASSWORK
GLASSWORKER
GLASSWORKERS
GLASSWORKING
GLASSWORKS
GLASSWORM
GLASSWORT
GLASSY
GLAUBERITE
GLAUCESCENCE
GLAUCESCENT
GLAUCINE
GLAUCODOT
GLAUCOLITE
GLAUCOMA
GLAUCOMATOUS
GLAUCONITE
GLAUCONITIC
GLAUCOPHANE
GLAUCOUS
GLAUM
GLAUMRIE
GLAUR
GLAVE
GLAVER
GLAVERED
GLAVERING
GLAZE
GLAZED
GLAZEN
GLAZER
GLAZEWORK
GLAZIER
GLAZIERS
GLAZIERY
GLAZIEST
GLAZILY
GLAZINESS
GLAZING
GLAZY
GLEAD
GLEAM
GLEAMED
GLEAMIER
GLEAMIEST
GLEAMILY
GLEAMINESS
GLEAMING
GLEAMY
GLEAN
GLEANER
GLEANING
GLEARY
GLEAVE
GLEBA
GLEBE
GLEBOUS
GLEBY
GLED
GLEDE
GLEDGE
GLEDY
GLEE
GLEED
GLEEDS
GLEEFUL
GLEEFULLY
GLEEFULNESS
GLEEK
GLEEMAIDEN
GLEEMAN
GLEEMEN
GLEEN
GLEESOME
GLEESOMELY
GLEESOMENESS
GLEET

GLEETY
GLEG
GLEGLY
GLEGNESS
GLEIT
GLEN
GLENE
GLENOHUMERAL
GLENOID
GLENOIDAL
GLENT
GLESSITE
GLET
GLETTY
GLEW
GLEY
GLEYD
GLEYDE
GLIA
GLIADIN
GLIAL
GLIB
GLIBBER
GLIBBERY
GLIBBEST
GLIBLY
GLIBNESS
GLIDDER
GLIDDERY
GLIDE
GLIDED
GLIDELESS
GLIDENESS
GLIDER
GLIDERPORT
GLIDEWORT
GLIDING
GLIDINGLY
GLIFF
GLIFFING
GLIFFY
GLIM
GLIMA
GLIME
GLIMMER
GLIMMERED
GLIMMERING
GLIMMERITE
GLIMMEROUS
GLIMMERS
GLIMMERY
GLIMPSE
GLIMPSED
GLIMPSER
GLIMPSING
GLIMS
GLIN
GLINK
GLINSE
GLINT
GLINTED
GLINTING
GLIOCYTE
GLIOMA
GLIOMAS
GLIOMATA
GLIOMATOUS
GLIOSA
GLIOSIS
GLIRIFORM
GLIRINE
GLISK
GLISKY
GLISS
GLISSADE
GLISSADED
GLISSADER

GLISSADING
GLISSANDO
GLISSETTE
GLIST
GLISTEN
GLISTENED
GLISTENING
GLISTER
GLISTERED
GLISTERING
GLIT
GLITTER
GLITTERANCE
GLITTERED
GLITTERING
GLITTERINGLY
GLITTERY
GLOAM
GLOAMING
GLOAT
GLOATED
GLOATER
GLOATING
GLOATINGLY
GLOB
GLOBAL
GLOBALLY
GLOBATE
GLOBATED
GLOBE
GLOBED
GLOBEFISH
GLOBEFLOWER
GLOBEHOLDER
GLOBETROTTER
GLOBICAL
GLOBIFEROUS
GLOBIGERINA
GLOBIN
GLOBING
GLOBOID
GLOBOSE
GLOBOSELY
GLOBOSENESS
GLOBOSITE
GLOBOSITY
GLOBOUS
GLOBOUSLY
GLOBOUSNESS
GLOBULAR
GLOBULARITY
GLOBULARLY
GLOBULARNESS
GLOBULE
GLOBULET
GLOBULICIDE
GLOBULIN
GLOBULITE
GLOBULITIC
GLOBULOID
GLOBULOSE
GLOBULOUS
GLOBULYSIS
GLOBY
GLOCHID
GLOCHIDEOUS
GLOCHIDIAL
GLOCHIDIATE
GLOCHIDIUM
GLOCHIS
GLOCK
GLOCKENSPIEL
GLODE
GLOEA
GLOEAL
GLOEOCAPSOID
GLOFF

GLOGG
GLOM
GLOME
GLOMERA
GLOMERATE
GLOMERATION
GLOMERULAR
GLOMERULATE
GLOMERULE
GLOMERULOSE
GLOMERULUS
GLOMMOX
GLOMUS
GLONOIN
GLONOINE
GLOOM
GLOOMED
GLOOMFUL
GLOOMFULLY
GLOOMIER
GLOOMIEST
GLOOMILY
GLOOMINESS
GLOOMING
GLOOMINGLY
GLOOMS
GLOOMTH
GLOOMY
GLOP
GLOPNEN
GLOPPEN
GLOR
GLORE
GLORIATION
GLORIED
GLORIETTE
GLORIFICATION
GLORIFIED
GLORIFIER
GLORIFY
GLORIFYING
GLORIOLE
GLORIOSO
GLORIOUS
GLORIOUSLY
GLORIOUSNESS
GLORY
GLORYFUL
GLORYLESS
GLOSE
GLOSS
GLOSSA
GLOSSAGRA
GLOSSAL
GLOSSALGIA
GLOSSALGY
GLOSSARIAL
GLOSSARIALLY
GLOSSARIAN
GLOSSARIES
GLOSSARIST
GLOSSARY
GLOSSATE
GLOSSATOR
GLOSSATORIAL
GLOSSECTOMY
GLOSSED
GLOSSER
GLOSSIC
GLOSSIER
GLOSSIEST
GLOSSILY
GLOSSINESS
GLOSSING
GLOSSIST
GLOSSITIC
GLOSSITIS

GLOSSMETER
GLOSSOCELE
GLOSSOCOMA
GLOSSOCOMON
GLOSSODYNIA
GLOSSOGRAPH
GLOSSOGRAPHER
GLOSSOGRAPHY
GLOSSOHYAL
GLOSSOID
GLOSSOLABIAL
GLOSSOLALIA
GLOSSOLALIST
GLOSSOLALY
GLOSSOLOGIST
GLOSSOLOGY
GLOSSOPATHY
GLOSSOPETRA
GLOSSOPHYTIA
GLOSSOPLASTY
GLOSSOPLEGIA
GLOSSOPODIUM
GLOSSOPTOSIS
GLOSSOSCOPIA
GLOSSOSCOPY
GLOSSOSPASM
GLOSSOTOMY
GLOSSOTYPE
GLOSSY
GLOST
GLOTTAL
GLOTTALITE
GLOTTALIZE
GLOTTIC
GLOTTID
GLOTTIDEAN
GLOTTIDES
GLOTTIS
GLOTTISCOPE
GLOTTISES
GLOTTOGONIC
GLOTTOGONIST
GLOTTOGONY
GLOTTOLOGIC
GLOTTOLOGICAL
GLOTTOLOGIST
GLOTTOLOGY
GLOTUM
GLOUP
GLOUT
GLOVE
GLOVEMAKER
GLOVEMAKING
GLOVEMAN
GLOVER
GLOVERESS
GLOVING
GLOW
GLOWBIRD
GLOWED
GLOWER
GLOWERER
GLOWERING
GLOWERINGLY
GLOWFLIES
GLOWFLY
GLOWING
GLOWINGLY
GLOWWORM
GLOX
GLOY
GLOZE
GLOZED
GLOZER
GLOZING
GLUB
GLUCAEMIA

GLUCASE
GLUCEMIA
GLUCIDE
GLUCINA
GLUCINE
GLUCINIC
GLUCINIUM
GLUCINUM
GLUCK
GLUCKE
GLUCOKININ
GLUCOSAMIN
GLUCOSAMINE
GLUCOSAN
GLUCOSAZONE
GLUCOSE
GLUCOSIC
GLUCOSIDAL
GLUCOSIDE
GLUCOSIDIC
GLUCOSINE
GLUCOSONE
GLUCOSURIA
GLUCURONIC
GLUE
GLUED
GLUEMAKER
GLUEMAKING
GLUEMAN
GLUEPOT
GLUER
GLUEY
GLUEYNESS
GLUG
GLUGGLUG
GLUHWEIN
GLUING
GLUISH
GLUISHNESS
GLUM
GLUMA
GLUMACEOUS
GLUMAL
GLUME
GLUMES
GLUMIFEROUS
GLUMLY
GLUMMER
GLUMMEST
GLUMMY
GLUMNESS
GLUMOSE
GLUMOSITY
GLUMOUS
GLUMP
GLUMPIER
GLUMPIEST
GLUMPILY
GLUMPINESS
GLUMPISH
GLUMPY
GLUNCH
GLUSIDE
GLUT
GLUTAMIC
GLUTAMINE
GLUTAMINIC
GLUTARIC
GLUTATHIONE
GLUTCH
GLUTEAL
GLUTELIN
GLUTEN
GLUTENIN
GLUTENOUS
GLUTEUS
GLUTIN

GLUTINATE
GLUTINATION
GLUTINATIVE
GLUTINIZE
GLUTINOSE
GLUTINOSITY
GLUTINOUS
GLUTINOUSLY
GLUTITION
GLUTOID
GLUTOSE
GLUTTED
GLUTTER
GLUTTERY
GLUTTING
GLUTTON
GLUTTONIES
GLUTTONIZE
GLUTTONIZED
GLUTTONIZING
GLUTTONOUS
GLUTTONOUSLY
GLUTTONY
GLY
GLYCAN
GLYCERATE
GLYCERIC
GLYCERIDE
GLYCERIN
GLYCERINATE
GLYCERINE
GLYCERINIZE
GLYCERITE
GLYCERIZE
GLYCEROGEL
GLYCEROL
GLYCEROLATE
GLYCEROSE
GLYCERYL
GLYCID
GLYCIDE
GLYCIDIC
GLYCIDOL
GLYCIN
GLYCININ
GLYCOCHOLATE
GLYCOCHOLIC
GLYCOCIN
GLYCOCOLL
GLYCOGELATIN
GLYCOGEN
GLYCOGENESIS
GLYCOGENETIC
GLYCOGENIC
GLYCOGENOUS
GLYCOGENY
GLYCOL
GLYCOLATE
GLYCOLIC
GLYCOLIDE
GLYCOLIPID
GLYCOLIPIDE
GLYCOLIPIN
GLYCOLIPINE
GLYCOLURIL
GLYCOLYL
GLYCOLYSIS
GLYCOLYTIC
GLYCOLYTICALLY
GLYCONIC
GLYCONIN
GLYCOPROTEIN
GLYCOSE
GLYCOSIDE
GLYCOSIN
GLYCOSINE
GLYCOSURIA

GLYCOSURIC
GLYCURESIS
GLYCYL
GLYCYPHYLLIN
GLYCYRRHIZIN
GLYDE
GLYN
GLYOXAL
GLYOXALASE
GLYOXALIC
GLYOXALINE
GLYOXIME
GLYOXYL
GLYOXYLIC
GLYPH
GLYPHIC
GLYPHOGRAPH
GLYPHOGRAPHY
GLYPTIC
GLYPTICAL
GLYPTICIAN
GLYPTICS
GLYPTODONT
GLYPTOGRAPH
GLYPTOGRAPHY
GLYPTOLOGY
GLYPTOTHECA
GMELINITE
GNABBLE
GNAP
GNAR
GNARE
GNARL
GNARLED
GNARLIER
GNARLIEST
GNARLINESS
GNARLING
GNARLY
GNARR
GNARRED
GNARRING
GNASH
GNASHED
GNASHING
GNAT
GNATCATCHER
GNATFLOWER
GNATHAL
GNATHIC
GNATHIDIUM
GNATHION
GNATHISM
GNATHITE
GNATHOBASE
GNATHOBASIC
GNATHOMETER
GNATHONIC
GNATHONICAL
GNATHONIZE
GNATHOPOD
GNATHOPODITE
GNATHOSTOME
GNATHOTHECA
GNATLING
GNATSNAP
GNATSNAPPER
GNATTER
GNATTY
GNAW
GNAWED
GNAWER
GNAWING
GNAWINGLY
GNAWINGS
GNAWN

GNEDE
GNEDELY
GNEISS
GNEISSIC
GNEISSITIC
GNEISSOID
GNEISSOSE
GNEISSY
GNIB
GNOCCHETTI
GNOCCHI
GNOF
GNOFF
GNOME
GNOMED
GNOMIC
GNOMICAL
GNOMICALLY
GNOMIDE
GNOMISH
GNOMIST
GNOMOLOGIC
GNOMOLOGICAL
GNOMOLOGIST
GNOMOLOGY
GNOMON
GNOMONIC
GNOMONICS
GNOMONOLOGY
GNOSIOLOGY
GNOSIS
GNOSTIC
GNOSTICAL
GNOSTICALLY
GNOSTICITY
GNU
GO
GOA
GOAD
GOADED
GOADING
GOADMAN
GOADSMAN
GOADSTER
GOAF
GOAI
GOAL
GOALAGE
GOALEE
GOALIE
GOALKEEPER
GOALKEEPING
GOALLESS
GOALMOUTH
GOALTENDER
GOAM
GOANA
GOANNA
GOAT
GOATBEARD
GOATBRUSH
GOATBUSH
GOATEE
GOATEED
GOATFISH
GOATFISHES
GOATHERD
GOATHERDESS
GOATISH
GOATISHLY
GOATISHNESS
GOATLAND
GOATLING
GOATLY
GOATROOT
GOATSBANE
GOATSBEARD

GOATSFOOT
GOATSFOOTS
GOATSKIN
GOATSTONE
GOATSUCKER
GOATWEED
GOATY
GOAVE
GOB
GOBACK
GOBAN
GOBANG
GOBBE
GOBBER
GOBBET
GOBBIN
GOBBING
GOBBLE
GOBBLED
GOBBLEDYGOOK
GOBBLER
GOBBLING
GOBBO
GOBBY
GOBELIN
GOBERNADOR
GOBERNADORA
GOBIERNO
GOBIES
GOBIID
GOBIIFORM
GOBIOID
GOBLET
GOBLETED
GOBLIN
GOBLINE
GOBLINRY
GOBMOUTHED
GOBO
GOBONATED
GOBONE
GOBONY
GOBOS
GOBSTICK
GOBURRA
GOBY
GOCART
GOD
GODCHILD
GODDAM
GODDAMN
GODDAMNED
GODDARD
GODDAUGHTER
GODDESS
GODDIZE
GODE
GODET
GODFATHER
GODFORSAKEN
GODHEAD
GODHOOD
GODIVEAU
GODKIN
GODLESS
GODLESSLY
GODLESSNESS
GODLET
GODLIER
GODLIEST
GODLIKE
GODLIKENESS
GODLILY
GODLINESS
GODLING
GODLY
GODMAMMA

GODMOTHER
GODOWN
GODPAPA
GODPARENT
GODPHERE
GODROON
GODS
GODSEND
GODSHIP
GODSON
GODSONSHIP
GODWIT
GOEL
GOELAND
GOELISM
GOER
GOES
GOETHITE
GOETIC
GOETY
GOFE
GOFER
GOFF
GOFFER
GOFFERED
GOFFERER
GOFFERING
GOFFLE
GOG
GOGA
GOGGA
GOGGAN
GOGGANS
GOGGLE
GOGGLED
GOGGLER
GOGGLES
GOGGLING
GOGGLY
GOGLET
GOGO
GOH
GOI
GOIABADA
GOING
GOINGS
GOITCHO
GOITER
GOITERED
GOITRE
GOITRED
GOITROUS
GOL
GOLA
GOLACH
GOLADAR
GOLAH
GOLANDAAS
GOLANDAUSE
GOLANDAUZE
GOLD
GOLDARN
GOLDBACK
GOLDBEATER
GOLDBEATING
GOLDBRICK
GOLDBUG
GOLDCREST
GOLDCUP
GOLDE
GOLDEN
GOLDENBACK
GOLDENEYE
GOLDENEYES
GOLDENFLEECE
GOLDENLOCKS
GOLDENLY

GOLDENNESS	GOME	GONOCOELE	GOOG	GORAL
GOLDENPERT	GOMER	GONOCYTE	GOOGLY	GORALOG
GOLDENROD	GOMERAL	GONOECIUM	GOOGOL	GORALS
GOLDENSEAL	GOMEREL	GONOF	GOOGOLPLEX	GORAN
GOLDENTOP	GOMERIL	GONOMERE	GOOGUL	GORB
GOLDENWING	GOMLAH	GONOMERY	GOOIER	GORBELLIES
GOLDER	GOMMIER	GONOPH	GOOIEST	GORBELLY
GOLDEYE	GOMPHODONT	GONOPHORE	GOOK	GORBET
GOLDFIELDER	GOMPHOSIS	GONOPHORIC	GOOL	GORBIT
GOLDFINCH	GOMUKHI	GONOPHOROUS	GOOLAH	GORBLE
GOLDFINNIES	GOMUTI	GONOPLASM	GOOLDE	GORBLIMY
GOLDFINNY	GON	GONOPOD	GOOLS	GORBLIN
GOLDFISH	GONAD	GONOPOIETIC	GOOM	GORCE
GOLDFISHES	GONADAL	GONORRHEA	GOOMA	GORCOCK
GOLDFLOWER	GONADIAL	GONORRHEAL	GOOMBAY	GORCROW
GOLDHAMMER	GONADIC	GONORRHEIC	GOON	GORDIID
GOLDHEAD	GONADUCT	GONORRHOEA	GOONCH	GORDIOID
GOLDIE	GONAGRA	GONORRHOEAL	GOONDA	GORDOLOBO
GOLDILOCKS	GONAKE	GONORRHOEIC	GOONDIE	GORDUNITE
GOLDIN	GONAKIE	GONOSOMAL	GOONEY	GORE
GOLDING	GONAL	GONOSOME	GOONIE	GORED
GOLDMIST	GONALGIA	GONOSPHERE	GOONY	GOREFISH
GOLDNEY	GONAPOD	GONOSTYLE	GOOR	GORER
GOLDSMITH	GONAPOPHYSAL	GONOTHECA	GOORAL	GOREVAN
GOLDSMITHERY	GONAPOPHYSIS	GONOTHECAL	GOORANUT	GORFLY
GOLDSMITHING	GONARTHRITIS	GONOTOCONT	GOOSANDER	GORGE
GOLDSMITHRY	GONCALO	GONOTOKONT	GOOSE	GORGED
GOLDSPINK	GONDANG	GONOTOME	GOOSEBEAK	GORGEDLY
GOLDSTONE	GONDITE	GONOTYL	GOOSEBERRY	GORGELET
GOLDTAIL	GONDOLA	GONOTYPE	GOOSEBILL	GORGEOUS
GOLDTHREAD	GONDOLET	GONOZOOID	GOOSEBIRD	GORGEOUSLY
GOLDTIT	GONDOLIER	GONY	GOOSEBONE	GORGEOUSNESS
GOLDURN	GONE	GONYALGIA	GOOSEBOY	GORGER
GOLDWATER	GONENESS	GONYDEAL	GOOSECAP	GORGERIN
GOLDWEED	GONEOCLINIC	GONYDIAL	GOOSED	GORGES
GOLDWORK	GONEPOIESIS	GONYOCELE	GOOSEFLESH	GORGET
GOLDWORKER	GONEPOIETIC	GONYONCUS	GOOSEFLOWER	GORGETED
GOLDY	GONER	GONYS	GOOSEFOOT	GORGIA
GOLE	GONESOME	GONYTHECA	GOOSEGIRL	GORGING
GOLEE	GONEY	GONZALO	GOOSEGOG	GORGIO
GOLEM	GONFALON	GOO	GOOSEGRASS	GORGON
GOLES	GONFALONIER	GOOBER	GOOSEHERD	GORGONACEAN
GOLF	GONFANON	GOOD	GOOSEHOUSE	GORGONESQUE
GOLFER	GONG	GOODHAP	GOOSEMOUTH	GORGONEUM
GOLFING	GONGMAN	GOODHEARTED	GOOSENECK	GORGONIAN
GOLI	GONGORISTIC	GOODIES	GOOSERIES	GORGONIN
GOLIAD	GONIAC	GOODING	GOOSERUMPED	GORGONIZE
GOLIARD	GONIAL	GOODISH	GOOSERY	GORGONIZED
GOLIARDERY	GONIALE	GOODISHNESS	GOOSES	GORHEN
GOLIARDIC	GONID	GOODLIER	GOOSESKIN	GORIC
GOLILLA	GONIDANGIUM	GOODLIEST	GOOSETONGUE	GORILLA
GOLKAKRA	GONIDIA	GOODLIHEAD	GOOSEWEED	GORILLAS
GOLL	GONIDIAL	GOODLIKE	GOOSEWING	GORILLIAN
GOLLAND	GONIDIOSE	GOODLINESS	GOOSEWINGED	GORILLOID
GOLLAR	GONIDIOSPORE	GOODLY	GOOSEY	GORILY
GOLLER	GONIDIUM	GOODMAN	GOOSIER	GORINESS
GOLLIWOG	GONIMIC	GOODNESS	GOOSIEST	GORING
GOLLIWOGG	GONIMOBLAST	GOODS	GOOSING	GORKUN
GOLLOP	GONIMOLOBE	GOODSIRE	GOOSISH	GORLIN
GOLLY	GONIMOUS	GOODWIFE	GOOSISHLY	GORLING
GOLOCH	GONIOMETER	GOODWILL	GOOSISHNESS	GORM
GOLOE	GONIOMETRIC	GOODWILLIT	GOOSY	GORMA
GOLOKA	GONIOMETRY	GOODWILLY	GOOTE	GORMAND
GOLOSH	GONION	GOODWIVES	GOOTEE	GORMANDIZE
GOLP	GONIOSTAT	GOODY	GOOZLE	GORMANDIZER
GOLPE	GONIOTHECA	GOODYEAR	GOPAK	GORMAW
GOLUNDAUZE	GONIOTROPOUS	GOOEY	GOPE	GORMED
GOM	GONITIS	GOOF	GOPHER	GORRAF
GOMARI	GONIUM	GOOFA	GOPHERBERRY	GORREL
GOMART	GONNARDITE	GOOFAH	GOPHERMAN	GORSE
GOMASHTA	GONOBLAST	GOOFBALL	GOPHERROOT	GORSEBIRD
GOMASTA	GONOBLASTIC	GOOFER	GOPHERWOOD	GORSECHAT
GOMAVEL	GONOCALYX	GOOFIER	GOPURA	GORSEDD
GOMBAY	GONOCHORISM	GOOFIEST	GOR	GORSEHATCH
GOMBEEN	GONOCOCCI	GOOFILY	GORA	GORSIER
GOMBO	GONOCOCCUS	GOOFINESS	GORACCO	GORSIEST
GOMBROON	GONOCOEL	GOOFY	GORAH	GORST

GORSY
GORY
GOS
GOSAIN
GOSCHENS
GOSH
GOSHAWK
GOSHENITE
GOSLARITE
GOSLET
GOSLING
GCSMORE
GOSPEL
GOSPELER
GOSPELIZE
GOSPELLER
GOSPELLIKE
GOSPELLY
GOSPODAR
GOSPODIN
GOSPORT
GOSSAMER
GOSSAMERED
GOSSAMERY
GOSSAMPINE
GOSSAN
GOSSARD
GOSSIP
GOSSIPED
GOSSIPER
GOSSIPHOOD
GOSSIPINESS
GOSSIPING
GOSSIPINGLY
GOSSIPMONGER
GOSSIPPED
GOSSIPPING
GOSSIPRED
GOSSIPRY
GOSSIPY
GOSSOON
GOSSY
GOSSYPIN
GOSSYPINE
GOSSYPOL
GOSTER
GOSTHER
GOT
GOTA
GOTCH
GOTCHED
GOTCHY
GOTE
GOTHIC
GOTHITE
GOTHS
GOTRA
GOTRAJA
GOTTEN
GOUACHE
GOUAREE
GOUFF
GOUGE
GOUGED
GOUGER
GOUGING
GOUJAT
GOUJON
GOUK
GOUL
GOULASH
GOULDIAN
GOUM
GOUMI
GOUMIER
GOUNAU
GOUND

GOUNDOU
GOUPEN
GOUPIN
GOUR
GOURA
GOURAMI
GOURD
GOURDE
GOURDED
GOURDHEAD
GOURDINESS
GOURDING
GOURDY
GOURMAND
GOURMANDER
GOURMANDERIE
GOURMANDISE
GOURMET
GOUROUNUT
GOURY
GOUSTIE
GOUSTROUS
GOUSTY
GOUT
GOUTER
GOUTIER
GOUTIEST
GOUTIFY
GOUTILY
GOUTINESS
GOUTISH
GOUTTE
GOUTWEED
GOUTWORT
GOUTY
GOUVERNANTE
GOVE
GOVERN
GOVERNABLE
GOVERNAIL
GOVERNANCE
GOVERNED
GOVERNESS
GOVERNING
GOVERNMENT
GOVERNMENTAL
GOVERNOR
GOVERNORATE
GOVERNORS
GOVERNORSHIP
GOW
GOWAN
GOWANED
GOWANY
GOWD
GOWDIE
GOWDNIE
GOWDNOOK
GOWDY
GOWF
GOWFF
GOWIDDIE
GOWK
GOWKED
GOWKEDLY
GOWKEDNESS
GOWKIT
GOWL
GOWLAN
GOWLAND
GOWN
GOWNED
GOWNING
GOWNSMAN
GOWP
GOWPEN
GOWPIN

GOWT
GOY
GOYAL
GOYAZITE
GOYIM
GOYIN
GOYISH
GOYLE
GOZELL
GOZILL
GOZZAN
GOZZARD
GRA
GRAAL
GRAAP
GRAB
GRABBED
GRABBER
GRABBING
GRABBLE
GRABBLER
GRABBLING
GRABBOTS
GRABBY
GRABEN
GRABHOOK
GRABMAN
GRABOUCHE
GRACE
GRACED
GRACEFUL
GRACEFULLY
GRACEFULNESS
GRACELESS
GRACELESSLY
GRACER
GRACES
GRACILARIID
GRACILE
GRACILENESS
GRACILESCENT
GRACILIS
GRACILITY
GRACING
GRACIOSITY
GRACIOSO
GRACIOUS
GRACIOUSLY
GRACIOUSNESS
GRACKLE
GRACY
GRAD
GRADAL
GRADATE
GRADATED
GRADATIM
GRADATING
GRADATION
GRADATIONAL
GRADATIVE
GRADATORY
GRADDAN
GRADE
GRADED
GRADEFINDER
GRADELY
GRADER
GRADES
GRADGRIND
GRADIENT
GRADIENTER
GRADIN
GRADINE
GRADING
GRADINO
GRADIOMETER
GRADIOMETRIC

GRADO
GRADOMETER
GRADUAL
GRADUALE
GRADUALISM
GRADUALIST
GRADUALISTIC
GRADUALITY
GRADUALLY
GRADUALNESS
GRADUAND
GRADUATE
GRADUATED
GRADUATICAL
GRADUATING
GRADUATION
GRADUS
GRAFF
GRAFFAGE
GRAFFER
GRAFFITO
GRAFT
GRAFTAGE
GRAFTED
GRAFTER
GRAFTING
GRAFTONITE
GRAGER
GRAHAM
GRAHAMITE
GRAIL
GRAILER
GRAILING
GRAILLE
GRAIN
GRAINAGE
GRAINE
GRAINED
GRAINER
GRAINERING
GRAINERY
GRAINFIELD
GRAINIER
GRAINIEST
GRAININESS
GRAINING
GRAINLAND
GRAINLESS
GRAINMAN
GRAINS
GRAINSICK
GRAINSICKNESS
GRAINSMAN
GRAINSMEN
GRAINY
GRAIP
GRAISSE
GRAITH
GRAITHLY
GRALLATORIAL
GRALLATORY
GRALLIC
GRALLINE
GRALLOCH
GRAM
GRAMA
GRAMARY
GRAMARYE
GRAME
GRAMENITE
GRAMERCY
GRAMINEAL
GRAMINEOUS
GRAMINIFORM
GRAMININ
GRAMINIVORE
GRAMINOLOGY

GRAMINOUS
GRAMMA
GRAMMALOGUE
GRAMMAR
GRAMMARIAN
GRAMMATES
GRAMMATICAL
GRAMMATICALLY
GRAMMATICISM
GRAMMATICIZE
GRAMMATICS
GRAMMATIST
GRAMME
GRAMMEL
GRAMOCHES
GRAMOPHONE
GRAMOPHONIC
GRAMP
GRAMPS
GRAMPUS
GRAMY
GRAN
GRANA
GRANADILLA
GRANADILLO
GRANAGE
GRANAM
GRANARY
GRANAT
GRANATE
GRANATUM
GRANCH
GRAND
GRANDAD
GRANDADA
GRANDADDY
GRANDAM
GRANDAME
GRANDAUNT
GRANDCHILD
GRANDDAD
GRANDDADA
GRANDDADDY
GRANDDAM
GRANDDAUGHTER
GRANDE
GRANDEE
GRANDER
GRANDESQUE
GRANDEST
GRANDEUR
GRANDEVAL
GRANDEVITY
GRANDEZA
GRANDFATHER
GRANDFER
GRANDFILIAL
GRANDGORE
GRANDILOQUENT
GRANDIOSE
GRANDIOSELY
GRANDIOSITY
GRANDIOSO
GRANDISONANT
GRANDISONOUS
GRANDITY
GRANDLY
GRANDMA
GRANDMAMA
GRANDMAMMA
GRANDMATERNAL
GRANDMOTHER
GRANDNEPHEW
GRANDNESS
GRANDNIECE
GRANDO
GRANDPA

GRANDPAPA
GRANDPARENT
GRANDPARENTS
GRANDPATERNAL
GRANDSIR
GRANDSIRE
GRANDSON
GRANDSTAND
GRANDSTANDER
GRANDUNCLE
GRANE
GRANES
GRANET
GRANGE
GRANGER
GRANGERISM
GRANGERITE
GRANGERIZE
GRANI
GRANIFEROUS
GRANIFORM
GRANILLA
GRANITA
GRANITE
GRANITEWARE
GRANITIC
GRANITICAL
GRANITITE
GRANITIZE
GRANITOID
GRANITOIDAL
GRANIVORE
GRANIVOROUS
GRANJENO
GRANK
GRANNAM
GRANNIE
GRANNOM
GRANNY
GRANNYBUSH
GRANNYKNOT
GRANO
GRANOBLASTIC
GRANODIORITE
GRANOGABBRO
GRANOLITH
GRANOLITHIC
GRANOMERITE
GRANOPHYRE
GRANOPHYRIC
GRANOSE
GRANOSPHERITE
GRANT
GRANTABLE
GRANTED
GRANTEE
GRANTER
GRANTHI
GRANTING
GRANTOR
GRANTS
GRANULA
GRANULAR
GRANULARITY
GRANULARLY
GRANULARY
GRANULATE
GRANULATED
GRANULATER
GRANULATING
GRANULATION
GRANULATIVE
GRANULATOR
GRANULE
GRANULET
GRANULITE
GRANULITIC

GRANULITIS
GRANULITIZE
GRANULIZE
GRANULOCYTE
GRANULOMA
GRANULOMAS
GRANULOMATA
GRANULOSE
GRANUM
GRANZA
GRAO
GRAPE
GRAPED
GRAPEFLOWER
GRAPEFRUIT
GRAPEFRUITS
GRAPELET
GRAPELIKE
GRAPENUTS
GRAPEROOT
GRAPERY
GRAPES
GRAPESHOT
GRAPESKIN
GRAPESTALK
GRAPESTONE
GRAPEVINE
GRAPEWORT
GRAPH
GRAPHALLOY
GRAPHIC
GRAPHICAL
GRAPHICALLY
GRAPHICLY
GRAPHICNESS
GRAPHICS
GRAPHIOLOGY
GRAPHITE
GRAPHITER
GRAPHITIC
GRAPHITIZE
GRAPHITIZED
GRAPHITOID
GRAPHITOIDAL
GRAPHOLOGIC
GRAPHOLOGIST
GRAPHOLOGY
GRAPHOMETER
GRAPHOMETRIC
GRAPHOMETRY
GRAPHOMOTOR
GRAPHOPHONE
GRAPHOPHONIC
GRAPHORRHEA
GRAPHOSCOPE
GRAPHOSPASM
GRAPHOSTATIC
GRAPHOTYPE
GRAPHY
GRAPIER
GRAPIEST
GRAPING
GRAPLIN
GRAPLINE
GRAPNEL
GRAPPA
GRAPPLE
GRAPPLED
GRAPPLER
GRAPPLING
GRAPSOID
GRAPTOLITE
GRAPTOLITIC
GRAPTOMANCY
GRAPY
GRASH
GRASNI

GRASO
GRASP
GRASPABLE
GRASPED
GRASPER
GRASPING
GRASPINGLY
GRASPINGNESS
GRASPLESS
GRASS
GRASSANT
GRASSATION
GRASSBIRD
GRASSCHAT
GRASSCUT
GRASSCUTTER
GRASSED
GRASSER
GRASSERIE
GRASSET
GRASSEYE
GRASSFLAT
GRASSFLOWER
GRASSHOP
GRASSHOPPER
GRASSHOUSE
GRASSIE
GRASSIER
GRASSIEST
GRASSILY
GRASSINESS
GRASSING
GRASSLAND
GRASSLESS
GRASSLIKE
GRASSMAN
GRASSMEN
GRASSNUT
GRASSPLAT
GRASSPLOT
GRASSQUIT
GRASSROOTS
GRASSWEED
GRASSWIDOW
GRASSWORK
GRASSWORM
GRASSY
GRAT
GRATE
GRATED
GRATEFUL
GRATEFULLY
GRATEFULNESS
GRATEMAN
GRATER
GRATHER
GRATICULATE
GRATICULE
GRATIFICATION
GRATIFIED
GRATIFIEDLY
GRATIFIER
GRATIFY
GRATIFYING
GRATIFYINGLY
GRATILITY
GRATILLITY
GRATIN
GRATINATE
GRATINATED
GRATINATING
GRATING
GRATINGLY
GRATINGS
GRATIOLIN
GRATIOSOLIN
GRATIS

GRATITUDE
GRATTEN
GRATTERS
GRATTOIR
GRATTON
GRATUITANT
GRATUITIES
GRATUITO
GRATUITOUS
GRATUITOUSLY
GRATUITY
GRATULANT
GRATULATE
GRATULATED
GRATULATION
GRATULATORY
GRAUPEL
GRAVAMEN
GRAVAMINA
GRAVAMINOUS
GRAVAT
GRAVATA
GRAVE
GRAVECLOD
GRAVECLOTH
GRAVECLOTHES
GRAVED
GRAVEDIGGER
GRAVEDO
GRAVEGARTH
GRAVEL
GRAVELED
GRAVELING
GRAVELLED
GRAVELLINESS
GRAVELLING
GRAVELLY
GRAVELSTONE
GRAVELWEED
GRAVELY
GRAVEMAKER
GRAVEMAKING
GRAVEMAN
GRAVEMASTER
GRAVEN
GRAVENESS
GRAVEOLENCE
GRAVEOLENCY
GRAVEOLENT
GRAVER
GRAVERY
GRAVES
GRAVESHIP
GRAVESIDE
GRAVEST
GRAVESTEAD
GRAVESTONE
GRAVETTE
GRAVEWARD
GRAVEWARDS
GRAVEYARD
GRAVIC
GRAVID
GRAVIDA
GRAVIDATE
GRAVIDATION
GRAVIDITY
GRAVIDLY
GRAVIDNESS
GRAVIERS
GRAVIFIC
GRAVIGRADE
GRAVILEA
GRAVIMETER
GRAVIMETRIC
GRAVIMETRY
GRAVING

GRAVIPAUSE
GRAVISPHERIC
GRAVITATE
GRAVITATED
GRAVITATER
GRAVITATING
GRAVITATION
GRAVITATIONAL
GRAVITATIVE
GRAVITIES
GRAVITY
GRAVURE
GRAVY
GRAWLS
GRAY
GRAYBACK
GRAYBEARD
GRAYCOAT
GRAYED
GRAYER
GRAYEST
GRAYFISH
GRAYFLY
GRAYHEAD
GRAYHOUND
GRAYISH
GRAYLAG
GRAYLAGS
GRAYLING
GRAYLINGS
GRAYLY
GRAYMILL
GRAYNESS
GRAYOUT
GRAYPATE
GRAYS
GRAYSBY
GRAYWACKE
GRAYWALL
GRAYWARE
GRAYWETHER
GRAZE
GRAZED
GRAZIER
GRAZIERY
GRAZING
GRAZINGLY
GRAZIOSO
GREABLE
GREABLY
GREASE
GREASEBUSH
GREASED
GREASEHORN
GREASER
GREASEWOOD
GREASIER
GREASIEST
GREASILY
GREASINESS
GREASING
GREASY
GREAT
GREATCOAT
GREATCOATED
GREATEN
GREATER
GREATEST
GREATHEAD
GREATHEART
GREATHEARTED
GREATLY
GREATMOUTHED
GREATNESS
GREAVE
GREAVES
GREBE

GREBES	GREENY	GREYS	GRIMACING	GRIPPOTOXIN
GRECE	GREENYARD	GREYSKIN	GRIMACINGLY	GRIPPY
GRECQUE	GREESAGH	GREYWACKE	GRIMALKIN	GRIPS
GREDE	GREESE	GREYWARE	GRIME	GRIPSACK
GREE	GREESHOCH	GREYWETHER	GRIMED	GRIPT
GREED	GREET	GRI	GRIMFUL	GRIPY
GREEDIER	GREETED	GRIBANE	GRIMGRIBBER	GRIQUAITE
GREEDIEST	GREETER	GRIBBLE	GRIMIER	GRIS
GREEDILY	GREETING	GRICE	GRIMIEST	GRISAILLE
GREEDINESS	GREETINGLY	GRID	GRIMILY	GRISARD
GREEDLESS	GREFFE	GRIDDER	GRIMINESS	GRISBET
GREEDSOME	GREFFIER	GRIDDLE	GRIMING	GRISE
GREEDY	GREFFOTOME	GRIDDLECAKE	GRIMLY	GRISEOUS
GREEDYGUT	GREGAL	GRIDDLED	GRIMME	GRISETTE
GREEDYGUTS	GREGALE	GRIDDLER	GRIMMER	GRISETTISH
GREEGREE	GREGALOID	GRIDDLING	GRIMMEST	GRISKIN
GREEN	GREGARIAN	GRIDE	GRIMNESS	GRISLIER
GREENALITE	GREGARIANISM	GRIDELIN	GRIMOIRE	GRISLIEST
GREENBACK	GREGARINE	GRIDING	GRIMP	GRISLINESS
GREENBELT	GREGARINIDAL	GRIDIRON	GRIMSIR	GRISLY
GREENBOARD	GREGARINOSIS	GRIEBEN	GRIMSIRE	GRISON
GREENBONE	GREGARINOUS	GRIECE	GRIMY	GRISONS
GREENBRIER	GREGARIOUS	GRIECED	GRIN	GRISOUNITE
GREENBUL	GREGARIOUSLY	GRIEF	GRINAGOG	GRISOUTINE
GREENCOAT	GREGARITIC	GRIEFFUL	GRINCH	GRISP
GREENED	GREGATIM	GRIEGE	GRINCOME	GRISPING
GREENER	GREGE	GRIEKO	GRIND	GRISSEN
GREENERIES	GREGGLE	GRIEN	GRINDAL	GRISSET
GREENERY	GREGO	GRIESHOCH	GRINDED	GRIST
GREENEY	GREIGE	GRIESHUCKLE	GRINDER	GRISTBITE
GREENFINCH	GREILLADE	GRIEVANCE	GRINDERMAN	GRISTER
GREENFISH	GREIN	GRIEVE	GRINDERS	GRISTLE
GREENFLY	GREISEN	GRIEVED	GRINDERY	GRISTLINESS
GREENGAGE	GREKING	GRIEVER	GRINDING	GRISTLY
GREENGILL	GRELOT	GRIEVESHIP	GRINDLE	GRISTMILL
GREENGROCER	GREMIAL	GRIEVING	GRINDSTONE	GRISTMILLER
GREENGROCERY	GREMIALE	GRIEVINGLY	GRINGO	GRISTMILLING
GREENHEAD	GREMIO	GRIEVOUS	GRINGOLE	GRISTY
GREENHEADED	GREMLIN	GRIEVOUSLY	GRINGOLEE	GRIT
GREENHEART	GRENADE	GRIEVOUSNESS	GRINNED	GRITH
GREENHEW	GRENADES	GRIFF	GRINNER	GRITHBREACH
GREENHIDE	GRENADIER	GRIFFADE	GRINNIE	GRITHMAN
GREENHORN	GRENADIERIAL	GRIFFADO	GRINNING	GRITROCK
GREENHOUSE	GRENADIERLY	GRIFFAUN	GRINNINGLY	GRITS
GREENIER	GRENADIN	GRIFFE	GRINNY	GRITTED
GREENIEST	GRENADINE	GRIFFIN	GRINT	GRITTEN
GREENING	GRENADO	GRIFFINAGE	GRINTER	GRITTER
GREENISH	GRENAT	GRIFFITHITE	GRINTERN	GRITTIE
GREENISHNESS	GRENIER	GRIFFON	GRIOTTE	GRITTIER
GREENKEEPER	GRES	GRIFFONAGE	GRIP	GRITTIEST
GREENKEEPING	GRESIL	GRIFT	GRIPE	GRITTILY
GREENLANDITE	GRESSORIAL	GRIFTER	GRIPED	GRITTINESS
GREENLEEK	GRESSORIOUS	GRIG	GRIPEFUL	GRITTING
GREENLET	GRETH	GRIGGLES	GRIPER	GRITTLE
GREENLING	GREUND	GRIGNET	GRIPES	GRITTY
GREENLY	GREW	GRIGRI	GRIPGRASS	GRIVE
GREENNESS	GREWHOUND	GRIGS	GRIPH	GRIVET
GREENOCKITE	GREWSOME	GRIHYASUTRA	GRIPHE	GRIVNA
GREENOVITE	GREWSOMELY	GRIKE	GRIPHITE	GRIVOIS
GREENROOM	GREWSOMENESS	GRIL	GRIPHUS	GRIVOISE
GREENS	GREWT	GRILL	GRIPIER	GRIZARD
GREENSAND	GREX	GRILLADE	GRIPIEST	GRIZZLE
GREENSAUCE	GREY	GRILLAGE	GRIPING	GRIZZLED
GREENSHANK	GREYBACK	GRILLE	GRIPINGLY	GRIZZLER
GREENSICK	GREYBEARD	GRILLED	GRIPLESS	GRIZZLIER
GREENSICKNESS	GREYCOAT	GRILLEE	GRIPMAN	GRIZZLIES
GREENSIDE	GREYER	GRILLER	GRIPPAL	GRIZZLIEST
GREENSTONE	GREYEST	GRILLING	GRIPPE	GRIZZLING
GREENSWARD	GREYFISH	GRILLROOM	GRIPPED	GRIZZLY
GREENSWARDED	GREYFLIES	GRILLWORK	GRIPPER	GRIZZLYMAN
GREENTH	GREYFLY	GRILLY	GRIPPERS	GROAK
GREENUK	GREYHOUND	GRILSE	GRIPPING	GROAN
GREENWAX	GREYHOUNDS	GRILSES	GRIPPINGLY	GROANED
GREENWEED	GREYLAG	GRIM	GRIPPINGNESS	GROANER
GREENWING	GREYLY	GRIMACE	GRIPPIT	GROANFUL
GREENWITHE	GREYNESS	GRIMACED	GRIPPLE	GROANING
GREENWOOD	GREYPATE	GRIMACER	GRIPPLENESS	GROANINGLY

GROAT
GROATS
GROATSWORTH
GROBIAN
GROBIANISM
GROCER
GROCERIES
GROCERLY
GROCERY
GROFF
GROG
GROGGED
GROGGER
GROGGERIES
GROGGERY
GROGGIER
GROGGIEST
GROGGILY
GROGGINESS
GROGGING
GROGGY
GROGNARD
GROGRAM
GROGSHOP
GROIN
GROINED
GROINERY
GROINING
GROM
GROMATIC
GROMATICAL
GROMATICS
GROMET
GROMMET
GROMWELL
GROMYL
GRONDWET
GRONT
GROOF
GROOM
GROOMED
GROOMER
GROOMING
GROOMLET
GROOMSMAN
GROOMSMEN
GROOMY
GROOP
GROOSE
GROOT
GROOTY
GROOVE
GROOVED
GROOVER
GROOVERHEAD
GROOVIER
GROOVIEST
GROOVING
GROOVY
GROPE
GROPED
GROPER
GROPING
GROPINGLY
GROPPLE
GRORUDITE
GROS
GROSBEAK
GROSCHEN
GROSER
GROSET
GROSGRAIN
GROSGRAINED
GROSS
GROSSEN
GROSSER
GROSSES

GROSSEST
GROSSIERETE
GROSSIFY
GROSSLY
GROSSO
GROSSULAR
GROSSULARITE
GROSZ
GROSZY
GROT
GROTE
GROTEN
GROTESCO
GROTESQUE
GROTESQUELY
GROTESQUERIE
GROTESQUERY
GROTHINE
GROTHITE
GROTTO
GROTTOED
GROTTOWORK
GROTZEN
GROUCH
GROUCHIER
GROUCHIEST
GROUCHILY
GROUCHINESS
GROUCHY
GROUF
GROUGH
GROUND
GROUNDABLE
GROUNDAGE
GROUNDBERRY
GROUNDBIRD
GROUNDED
GROUNDEDLY
GROUNDEDNESS
GROUNDEN
GROUNDENELL
GROUNDER
GROUNDHOG
GROUNDING
GROUNDLESS
GROUNDLESSLY
GROUNDLINE
GROUNDLINESS
GROUNDLING
GROUNDLY
GROUNDMAN
GROUNDMASS
GROUNDNEEDLE
GROUNDNUT
GROUNDS
GROUNDSEL
GROUNDSILL
GROUNDSMAN
GROUNDWALL
GROUNDWARD
GROUNDWARDS
GROUNDWOOD
GROUNDWORK
GROUNDY
GROUP
GROUPAGE
GROUPED
GROUPER
GROUPIE
GROUPING
GROUPMENT
GROUPS
GROUSE
GROUSED
GROUSER
GROUSING
GROUSY

GROUT
GROUTED
GROUTER
GROUTHEAD
GROUTIER
GROUTIEST
GROUTING
GROUTITE
GROUTS
GROUTY
GROUZE
GROVE
GROVED
GROVEL
GROVELED
GROVELER
GROVELING
GROVELINGLY
GROVELINGS
GROVELLED
GROVELLER
GROVELLING
GROVELLINGLY
GROVELLINGS
GROVET
GROVY
GROW
GROWAN
GROWER
GROWING
GROWL
GROWLED
GROWLER
GROWLERIES
GROWLERY
GROWLING
GROWLY
GROWN
GROWNUP
GROWS
GROWSE
GROWSOME
GROWTH
GROWTHINESS
GROWTHY
GROWZE
GROYNE
GROZART
GROZER
GRU
GRUB
GRUBBED
GRUBBER
GRUBBERIES
GRUBBERY
GRUBBIER
GRUBBIEST
GRUBBILY
GRUBBINESS
GRUBBING
GRUBBLE
GRUBBY
GRUBROOT
GRUBS
GRUBSTAKE
GRUBSTAKER
GRUBSTREET
GRUBWORM
GRUDGE
GRUDGED
GRUDGER
GRUDGERY
GRUDGING
GRUDGINGLY
GRUE
GRUEL
GRUELED

GRUELER
GRUELING
GRUELLED
GRUELLER
GRUELLING
GRUELLY
GRUESOME
GRUESOMELY
GRUESOMENESS
GRUF
GRUFF
GRUFFER
GRUFFEST
GRUFFILY
GRUFFINESS
GRUFFLY
GRUFFNESS
GRUFFS
GRUFFY
GRUFT
GRUFTED
GRUG
GRUGOUS
GRUGRU
GRUIFORM
GRUINE
GRULLA
GRUM
GRUMBLE
GRUMBLED
GRUMBLER
GRUMBLING
GRUMBLINGLY
GRUMBLY
GRUME
GRUMLY
GRUMMEL
GRUMMELS
GRUMMER
GRUMMEST
GRUMMET
GRUMMETER
GRUMNESS
GRUMOSE
GRUMOUS
GRUMOUSNESS
GRUMP
GRUMPH
GRUMPHIE
GRUMPHY
GRUMPIER
GRUMPIEST
GRUMPILY
GRUMPINESS
GRUMPISH
GRUMPS
GRUMPY
GRUN
GRUNCH
GRUNDY
GRUNERITE
GRUNION
GRUNT
GRUNTER
GRUNTING
GRUNTLE
GRUNTLED
GRUNTLING
GRUNZIE
GRUP
GRUPPETTO
GRUPPO
GRUSH
GRUSHIE
GRUSS
GRUTCH
GRY

GRYLLE
GRYLLI
GRYLLID
GRYLLOS
GRYLLUS
GRYPANIAN
GRYPHON
GRYPOSIS
GRYS
GRYSBOK
GUACA
GUACACOA
GUACHAMACA
GUACHARO
GUACHIPILIN
GUACIMO
GUACIN
GUACO
GUACONIZE
GUADUA
GUAGUANCHE
GUAHIVO
GUAIAC
GUAIACOL
GUAIACUM
GUAIASANOL
GUAICAN
GUAIOCUM
GUAIOL
GUAJILLO
GUAJIRA
GUAKO
GUALE
GUAMA
GUAN
GUANA
GUANABANA
GUANABANO
GUANACO
GUANAJUATITE
GUANAMINE
GUANARE
GUANASE
GUANAY
GUANEIDE
GUANGO
GUANIDINE
GUANIFEROUS
GUANINE
GUANIZE
GUANO
GUANOPHORE
GUANOSINE
GUANYL
GUAO
GUAPENA
GUAPILLA
GUAPINOL
GUAR
GUARA
GUARABU
GUARACHA
GUARACHE
GUARAGUAO
GUARANA
GUARAND
GUARANINE
GUARANTEE
GUARANTEED
GUARANTEES
GUARANTIED
GUARANTIES
GUARANTOR
GUARANTY
GUARANTYING
GUARAPO
GUARAPUCU

GUARD
GUARDAGE
GUARDANT
GUARDED
GUARDEDLY
GUARDEDNESS
GUARDEE
GUARDER
GUARDFUL
GUARDFULLY
GUARDHOUSE
GUARDIAN
GUARDIANCY
GUARDIANLY
GUARDIANSHIP
GUARDING
GUARDO
GUARDRAIL
GUARDROOM
GUARDS
GUARDSMAN
GUARDSMEN
GUARDSTONE
GUARIBA
GUARICO
GUARINITE
GUARISH
GUARRI
GUARY
GUASA
GUASO
GUATAMBU
GUATIBERO
GUATIVERE
GUAVA
GUAVABERRY
GUAVINA
GUAXIMA
GUAYABA
GUAYABI
GUAYABO
GUAYACAN
GUAYROTO
GUAYULE
GUAZA
GUAZUTI
GUB
GUBAT
GUBBERTUSH
GUBBIN
GUBBINGS
GUBBINS
GUBBO
GUBERNATION
GUBERNATIVE
GUBERNATOR
GUBERNATRIX
GUBERNIA
GUBERNIYA
GUCK
GUCKED
GUDAME
GUDDA
GUDDLE
GUDE
GUDEMOTHER
GUDESIRE
GUDEWIFE
GUDGE
GUDGEON
GUDGET
GUDOK
GUE
GUEBUCU
GUEJARITE
GUEMAL
GUEMUL

GUENON
GUEPARD
GUEPARDE
GUERDON
GUERDONER
GUEREBA
GUEREZA
GUERIDON
GUERILLA
GUERISON
GUERITE
GUERNSEYED
GUERNSEYS
GUERRILLA
GUESS
GUESSED
GUESSER
GUESSING
GUESSTIMATE
GUESSWORK
GUESSWORKER
GUEST
GUESTCHAMBER
GUESTED
GUESTEN
GUESTER
GUESTHOUSE
GUESTING
GUESTIVE
GUESTMASTER
GUETRE
GUF
GUFA
GUFF
GUFFAW
GUFFER
GUFFIN
GUFFY
GUGAL
GUGGLE
GUGGLET
GUGLET
GUGLIA
GUGLIO
GUGU
GUGUL
GUHR
GUIB
GUIBA
GUICHET
GUID
GUIDA
GUIDABLE
GUIDAGE
GUIDANCE
GUIDE
GUIDEBOARD
GUIDEBOOK
GUIDECRAFT
GUIDED
GUIDELINE
GUIDEPOST
GUIDER
GUIDERESS
GUIDESHIP
GUIDEWAY
GUIDING
GUIDMAN
GUIDON
GUIDSIRE
GUIDWIFE
GUIGE
GUIGNE
GUIJO
GUILD
GUILDER
GUILDHALL

GUILDIC
GUILDITE
GUILDRY
GUILDSHIP
GUILDSMAN
GUILDSMEN
GUILE
GUILEFUL
GUILEFULLY
GUILEFULNESS
GUILELESS
GUILELESSLY
GUILER
GUILERY
GUILLEMET
GUILLEMOT
GUILLEVAT
GUILLOCHE
GUILLOCHEE
GUILLOTINADE
GUILLOTINE
GUILLOTINED
GUILLOTINER
GUILLOTINING
GUILLOTINISM
GUILLOTINIST
GUILT
GUILTFUL
GUILTIER
GUILTIEST
GUILTILY
GUILTINESS
GUILTLESS
GUILTLESSLY
GUILTSICK
GUILTY
GUILY
GUIMBARD
GUIMPE
GUINEA
GUIPURE
GUIRO
GUISE
GUISED
GUISER
GUISING
GUITAR
GUITARFISH
GUITARIST
GUITERMANITE
GUITGUIT
GUJERAT
GUL
GULA
GULAMAN
GULANCHA
GULAR
GULARIS
GULASH
GULCH
GULDEN
GULE
GULES
GULF
GULFWEED
GULFY
GULGUL
GULINULA
GULINULAR
GULIX
GULL
GULLAGE
GULLED
GULLER
GULLERIES
GULLERY
GULLET

GULLEY
GULLIBILITY
GULLIBLE
GULLIBLY
GULLIED
GULLIES
GULLING
GULLION
GULLISH
GULLISHLY
GULLISHNESS
GULLY
GULLYGUT
GULLYHOLE
GULLYING
GULMOHAR
GULOC
GULOSE
GULOSITY
GULP
GULPED
GULPER
GULPH
GULPIN
GULPING
GULPINGLY
GULPS
GULPY
GULSACH
GULY
GUM
GUMBE
GUMBO
GUMBOIL
GUMBOTIL
GUMBY
GUMCHEWER
GUMDIGGER
GUMDIGGING
GUMDROP
GUME
GUMFIELD
GUMFLOWER
GUMHAR
GUMIHAN
GUMLAH
GUMLY
GUMMA
GUMMAGE
GUMMAKER
GUMMAS
GUMMATA
GUMMATOUS
GUMMED
GUMMER
GUMMIER
GUMMIEST
GUMMIFEROUS
GUMMINESS
GUMMING
GUMMITE
GUMMOSE
GUMMOSIS
GUMMOSITY
GUMMOUS
GUMMY
GUMP
GUMPHEON
GUMPHION
GUMPTION
GUMPUS
GUMS
GUMSHOE
GUMSHOED
GUMSHOEING
GUMTREE
GUMWEED

GUMWOOD
GUN
GUNA
GUNATE
GUNATED
GUNATING
GUNATION
GUNBOAT
GUNBOATS
GUNBUILDER
GUNCOTTON
GUNDA
GUNDALOW
GUNDECK
GUNDELOW
GUNDI
GUNDIE
GUNDOG
GUNDY
GUNDYGUT
GUNFIGHT
GUNFIRE
GUNFLINT
GUNGE
GUNHOUSE
GUNITER
GUNJ
GUNJA
GUNJAH
GUNK
GUNKHOLE
GUNLAYER
GUNLAYING
GUNLINE
GUNLOCK
GUNMAKER
GUNMAKING
GUNMAN
GUNMEN
GUNMETAL
GUNNAGE
GUNNED
GUNNEL
GUNNELS
GUNNER
GUNNERY
GUNNIES
GUNNING
GUNNUNG
GUNNY
GUNNYSACK
GUNOCRACY
GUNONG
GUNPAPER
GUNPLAY
GUNPORT
GUNPOWDER
GUNPOWDEROUS
GUNPOWER
GUNRACK
GUNREACH
GUNRUNNER
GUNRUNNING
GUNS
GUNSEL
GUNSHIP
GUNSHOP
GUNSHOT
GUNSMAN
GUNSMITH
GUNSMITHERY
GUNSMITHING
GUNSTER
GUNSTICK
GUNSTOCK
GUNSTOCKER
GUNSTOCKING

GUNSTONE	GUT	GWINIAD	GYNECIDE	GYRATORY
GUNTER	GUTBUCKET	GWYNIAD	GYNECIUM	GYRE
GUNTUB	GUTLESS	GYANI	GYNECOCRACY	GYRED
GUNUNG	GUTLING	GYASCUTUS	GYNECOCRAT	GYRENE
GUNWALE	GUTS	GYASSA	GYNECOCRATIC	GYRFALCON
GUNYAH	GUTSIER	GYBE	GYNECOID	GYRING
GUNYANG	GUTSIEST	GYLE	GYNECOLATRY	GYRINID
GUNYEH	GUTSY	GYM	GYNECOLOGIC	GYRO
GUP	GUTT	GYMEL	GYNECOLOGIST	GYROCAR
GUPPIES	GUTTA	GYMKHANA	GYNECOLOGY	GYROCERACONE
GUPPY	GUTTAE	GYMNANTHOUS	GYNECOMASTIA	GYROCERAN
GUPTAVIDYA	GUTTATE	GYMNASIA	GYNECOMASTY	GYROCHROME
GUR	GUTTATED	GYMNASIAL	GYNECOMAZIA	GYROCOMPASS
GURDFISH	GUTTATIM	GYMNASIARCH	GYNECONITIS	GYRODYNE
GURDWARA	GUTTE	GYMNASIARCHY	GYNECOPATHIC	GYROGONITE
GURDY	GUTTED	GYMNASIAST	GYNECOPATHY	GYROGRAPH
GURGE	GUTTEE	GYMNASIC	GYNECOTELIC	GYROHORIZON
GURGEONS	GUTTER	GYMNASIUM	GYNECRATIC	GYROIDAL
GURGES	GUTTERAL	GYMNAST	GYNEE	GYROIDALLY
GURGITATION	GUTTERBLOOD	GYMNASTIC	GYNEOCRACY	GYROLITE
GURGLE	GUTTERED	GYMNASTICAL	GYNEOLATER	GYROLITH
GURGLED	GUTTERING	GYMNASTICS	GYNEOLATRY	GYROMA
GURGLET	GUTTERLING	GYMNETROUS	GYNETHUSIA	GYROMAGNETIC
GURGLING	GUTTERMAN	GYMNIC	GYNETYPE	GYROMANCY
GURGLINGLY	GUTTERS	GYMNICAL	GYNIATRICS	GYROMELE
GURGLY	GUTTERSNIPE	GYMNICS	GYNICS	GYROMETER
GURGULATION	GUTTERY	GYMNITE	GYNOBASE	GYRON
GURGULIO	GUTTIDE	GYMNOBLASTIC	GYNOBASEOUS	GYRONNY
GURJAN	GUTTIE	GYMNOCARPIC	GYNOBASIC	GYROPIGEON
GURJUN	GUTTIFEROUS	GYMNOCARPOUS	GYNOCARDIC	GYROPLANE
GURK	GUTTIFORM	GYMNOCIDIUM	GYNOCRACY	GYROSCOPE
GURL	GUTTING	GYMNODONT	GYNOCRATIC	GYROSCOPIC
GURLET	GUTTLE	GYMNOGENOUS	GYNOECIUM	GYROSE
GURLY	GUTTLED	GYMNOGLOSSATE	GYNOGENESIS	GYROSTAT
GURNARD	GUTTLER	GYMNOGYNOUS	GYNOPARA	GYROSTATIC
GURNARDS	GUTTLING	GYMNOPAEDIC	GYNOPHAGITE	GYROSTATICS
GURNEY	GUTTULA	GYMNOPLAST	GYNOPHORE	GYROUS
GURR	GUTTULAR	GYMNORHINAL	GYNOPHORIC	GYROVAGUES
GURRAH	GUTTULATE	GYMNOSOPH	GYNOSTEGIUM	GYROWHEEL
GURRY	GUTTULE	GYMNOSOPHIST	GYOKURO	GYRTH
GURT	GUTTULOUS	GYMNOSOPHY	GYP	GYRUS
GURU	GUTTUR	GYMNOSPERM	GYPE	GYTE
GUSAIN	GUTTURAL	GYMNOSPERMY	GYPPED	GYTLING
GUSH	GUTTURALISM	GYMNOSPORE	GYPPERY	GYTRASH
GUSHED	GUTTURALITY	GYMNOSPOROUS	GYPPING	GYTTJA
GUSHER	GUTTURALIZE	GYMNOSTOMOUS	GYPS	GYVE
GUSHET	GUTTURALIZING	GYMNOTID	GYPSEIAN	GYVED
GUSHIER	GUTTURALLY	GYMNOTOKOUS	GYPSIED	GYVING
GUSHIEST	GUTTURALNESS	GYMNURE	GYPSIES	
GUSHILY	GUTTUS	GYMNURINE	GYPSIFEROUS	
GUSHINESS	GUTTY	GYMPIE	GYPSINE	
GUSHING	GUTWEED	GYN	GYPSIOLOGIST	
GUSHINGLY	GUTWORT	GYNAECEUM	GYPSITE	
GUSHINGNESS	GUV	GYNAECIUM	GYPSOGRAPHY	
GUSHY	GUY	GYNAECOCRACY	GYPSOLOGIST	
GUSLA	GUYED	GYNAECOCRAT	GYPSOLOGY	
GUSLE	GUYER	GYNAECOLOGIC	GYPSOPLAST	
GUSLEE	GUYING	GYNAECOLOGY	GYPSOUS	
GUSLI	GUYO	GYNAECONITIS	GYPSUM	
GUSS	GUYOT	GYNAEOCRACY	GYPSUMED	
GUSSET	GUYTRASH	GYNAEOLATER	GYPSUMING	
GUSSIE	GUYVER	GYNAEOLATRY	GYPSY	
GUST	GUZ	GYNANDER	GYPSYFY	
GUSTABLE	GUZE	GYNANDRARCHY	GYPSYHEAD	
GUSTATION	GUZERAT	GYNANDRIA	GYPSYING	
GUSTATIVE	GUZZLE	GYNANDRIAN	GYPSYRY	
GUSTATORY	GUZZLED	GYNANDRISM	GYPSYWEED	
GUSTFUL	GUZZLER	GYNANDROID	GYPSYWORT	
GUSTFULLY	GUZZLING	GYNANDROUS	GYRAL	
GUSTFULNESS	GWAG	GYNANDRY	GYRALLY	
GUSTIER	GWANTUS	GYNANTHEROUS	GYRANT	
GUSTIEST	GWEDUC	GYNARCHIC	GYRATE	
GUSTILY	GWEDUCK	GYNARCHIES	GYRATED	
GUSTINESS	GWEED	GYNARCHY	GYRATING	
GUSTO	GWEEON	GYNE	GYRATION	
GUSTOSO	GWELY	GYNECIC	GYRATIONAL	
GUSTY	GWERZIOU	GYNECIDAL	GYRATOR	

HA
HAAB
HAAF
HAAK
HAAR
HABBLE
HABDALAH
HABEAS
HABENA
HABENAL
HABENAR
HABENDUM
HABENULA
HABENULAR
HABERDASH
HABERDASHER
HABERDASHERY
HABERDINE
HABERGEON
HABI
HABIL
HABILABLE
HABILE
HABILIMENT
HABILIMENTAL
HABILIMENTARY
HABILIMENTATIO
HABILIMENTED
HABILITATE
HABILITATION
HABILITATOR
HABILITY
HABILLE
HABIT
HABITABLE
HABITABLY
HABITACLE
HABITACULE
HABITALLY
HABITAN
HABITANCE
HABITANT
HABITAT
HABITATAL
HABITATE
HABITATIO
HABITATION
HABITATIVE
HABITUAL
HABITUALITY
HABITUALLY
HABITUALNESS
HABITUATE
HABITUATED
HABITUATION
HABITUDE
HABITUE
HABITUS
HABNAB
HABOOB
HABRO
HABRONEMIC
HABROWNE
HABU
HABUKA
HABUTAI
HABUTAYE

HACCUCAL
HACEK
HACHE
HACHIS
HACHMENT
HACHT
HACHURE
HACIENDA
HACK
HACKAMORE
HACKBARROW
HACKBERRY
HACKBOLT
HACKBUSH
HACKBUT
HACKBUTEER
HACKBUTTER
HACKED
HACKEE
HACKEEM
HACKER
HACKERY
HACKEYMAL
HACKIA
HACKIE
HACKIN
HACKING
HACKINGLY
HACKLE
HACKLEBACK
HACKLER
HACKLES
HACKLET
HACKLOG
HACKLY
HACKMACK
HACKMALL
HACKMAN
HACKMATACK
HACKNEY
HACKNEYED
HACKNEYER
HACKNEYMAN
HACKSAW
HACKSILBER
HACKSTER
HACKTHORN
HACKTREE
HACKWOOD
HACKY
HAD
HADADA
HADBOT
HADBOTE
HADDEN
HADDER
HADDIE
HADDIN
HADDO
HADDOCK
HADDOCKER
HADE
HADES
HADING
HADIT
HADJ
HADJI
HADLAND
HADNA
HADROM
HADROME
HADROSAUR
HAE
HAEC
HAECCEITY
HAEM
HAEMAD

HAEMATHERM
HAEMATHERMAL
HAEMATHERMOUS
HAEMATID
HAEMATITE
HAEMONY
HAEMOPHILE
HAEMOPOD
HAEMOSTAT
HAEN
HAEREMAI
HAERES
HAET
HAFF
HAFFET
HAFFIT
HAFFLE
HAFFLINS
HAFIZ
HAFLIN
HAFNIUM
HAFNYL
HAFT
HAFTARAH
HAFTER
HAG
HAGADA
HAGADIST
HAGBERRY
HAGBOAT
HAGBOLT
HAGBORN
HAGBUSH
HAGBUT
HAGDEN
HAGDIN
HAGDON
HAGDOWN
HAGEEN
HAGEIN
HAGFISH
HAGG
HAGGADAL
HAGGADAY
HAGGADIC
HAGGADIST
HAGGARD
HAGGARDLY
HAGGARDNESS
HAGGED
HAGGEIS
HAGGIOGRAPHAL
HAGGIS
HAGGISH
HAGGISHLY
HAGGISHNESS
HAGGLE
HAGGLER
HAGGLING
HAGGLY
HAGGY
HAGI
HAGIA
HAGIARCHY
HAGIGAH
HAGIOCRACY
HAGIOGRAPHER
HAGIOGRAPHIC
HAGIOGRAPHIST
HAGIOGRAPHY
HAGIOLATER
HAGIOLATROUS
HAGIOLATRY
HAGIOLITH
HAGIOLOGIC
HAGIOLOGIST
HAGIOLOGY

HAGIOSCOPE
HAGLET
HAGLIKE
HAGLIN
HAGMALL
HAGMENA
HAGRIDDEN
HAGRIDE
HAGROPE
HAGSEED
HAGSTONE
HAGTAPER
HAGWEED
HAGWORM
HAH
HAHAM
HAHR
HAI
HAIARI
HAICK
HAIK
HAIKAI
HAIKAL
HAIKU
HAIKUN
HAIKWAN
HAIL
HAILER
HAILL
HAILPROOF
HAILSE
HAILSHOT
HAILSTONE
HAILSTORM
HAILWEED
HAIM
HAIMSUCKEN
HAIN
HAINBERRY
HAINCH
HAINE
HAINED
HAIR
HAIRBALL
HAIRBAND
HAIRBEARD
HAIRBELL
HAIRBIRD
HAIRBRAIN
HAIRBRAINED
HAIRBREADTH
HAIRBRUSH
HAIRCAP
HAIRCLOTH
HAIRCUT
HAIRDO
HAIRDRESS
HAIRDRESSER
HAIRDRESSING
HAIRE
HAIRED
HAIREN
HAIRHOOF
HAIRHOUND
HAIRIF
HAIRINESS
HAIRLACE
HAIRLESS
HAIRLIKE
HAIRLINE
HAIRLOCK
HAIRMONEERING
HAIRMONGER
HAIRN
HAIROF
HAIRPIECE
HAIRPIN

HAIRS
HAIRSBREADTH
HAIRSE
HAIRSPLITTER
HAIRSPLITTING
HAIRSPRING
HAIRST
HAIRSTANE
HAIRSTONE
HAIRSTREAK
HAIRTAIL
HAIRUP
HAIRWEAVE
HAIRWEAVING
HAIRWEED
HAIRWORK
HAIRWORM
HAIRY
HAIT
HAITH
HAITSAI
HAIVER
HAJ
HAJE
HAJI
HAJIB
HAJILIJ
HAJJ
HAJJI
HAK
HAKA
HAKAFOTH
HAKAM
HAKAMIM
HAKDAR
HAKE
HAKED
HAKEEM
HAKH
HAKIM
HAKO
HAKU
HAL
HALA
HALACHA
HALACHAH
HALACHIST
HALAKA
HALAKAH
HALAKIC
HALAKIST
HALAL
HALALCOR
HALAPEPE
HALAS
HALATION
HALAZONE
HALBE
HALBERD
HALBERDIER
HALBERDMAN
HALBERDS
HALBERT
HALCH
HALCYON
HALDI
HALDU
HALE
HALEBI
HALECRET
HALEDAY
HALELY
HALENESS
HALER
HALERZ
HALES
HALESOME

HALEWEED	HALLOW	HAMBO	HANAPER	HANDLOCK
HALF	HALLOWD	HAMBONE	HANASTER	HANDLOOM
HALFA	HALLOWED	HAMBURGER	HANCE	HANDMADE
HALFBACK	HALLOWEDLY	HAMDMAID	HANCED	HANDMAIDEN
HALFBEAK	HALLOWEDNESS	HAME	HANCH	HANDOUT
HALFCOCK	HALLOWER	HAMEIL	HANCOCKITE	HANDPOST
HALFCOCKED	HALLUCES	HAMEL	HAND	HANDPRINT
HALFEN	HALLUCINATE	HAMELT	HANDARM	HANDRAIL
HALFHEADED	HALLUCINATION	HAMESOKEN	HANDBAG	HANDRAILING
HALFHEARTED	HALLUCINED	HAMESUCKEN	HANDBALL	HANDREADER
HALFHEARTEDLY	HALLUX	HAMETZ	HANDBALLER	HANDREADING
HALFHEARTEDNESS	HALLWAY	HAMEWITH	HANDBANK	HANDREST
HALFLANG	HALM	HAMFARE	HANDBANKER	HANDS
HALFLIN	HALMA	HAMFAT	HANDBARROW	HANDSALE
HALFLING	HALMALILLE	HAMFATTER	HANDBELL	HANDSAW
HALFLINGS	HALO	HAMHUNG	HANDBILL	HANDSCRAPE
HALFLY	HALOBIOS	HAMI	HANDBLOW	HANDSEL
HALFMAN	HALOBIOTIC	HAMIFORM	HANDBOLT	HANDSELLER
HALFNESS	HALOESQUE	HAMILT	HANDBOOK	HANDSET
HALFPACE	HALOGEN	HAMINGJA	HANDBOW	HANDSHAKE
HALFPACED	HALOGENATION	HAMINOEA	HANDBREADTH	HANDSHAKER
HALFPENCE	HALOID	HAMLAH	HANDBREED	HANDSHAKING
HALFPENNIES	HALOLIKE	HAMLET	HANDCAR	HANDSLED
HALFPENNY	HALOMETER	HAMLETED	HANDCART	HANDSMOOTH
HALFWAY	HALOPHILE	HAMLETEER	HANDCLAP	HANDSOME
HALFWISE	HALOPHYTE	HAMLETIZE	HANDCLASP	HANDSOMELY
HALFY	HALOPHYTIC	HAMLINE	HANDCLOTH	HANDSOMENESS
HALIBIOS	HALOSCOPE	HAMLINITE	HANDCRAFT	HANDSPADE
HALIBIU	HALOSERE	HAMMAID	HANDCUFF	HANDSPAN
HALIBUT	HALPACE	HAMMAL	HANDED	HANDSPEC
HALIBUTER	HALPER	HAMMER	HANDEDNESS	HANDSPIKE
HALID	HALS	HAMMERABLE	HANDER	HANDSPOKE
HALIDE	HALSE	HAMMERBIRD	HANDERSOME	HANDSPRING
HALIDOM	HALSEN	HAMMERCLOTH	HANDFAST	HANDSTAFF
HALIDOME	HALSFANG	HAMMERDRESS	HANDFASTING	HANDSTAND
HALIEUTIC	HALSH	HAMMERED	HANDFASTLY	HANDSTONE
HALIEUTICAL	HALT	HAMMERER	HANDFASTNESS	HANDSTROKE
HALIEUTICALLY	HALTER	HAMMERFISH	HANDFISH	HANDTRAP
HALIEUTICS	HALTERBREAK	HAMMERHEAD	HANDFLAG	HANDWALED
HALIMOT	HALTERE	HAMMERHEADED	HANDFLOWER	HANDWHEEL
HALIMOUS	HALTERES	HAMMERING	HANDFUL	HANDWHILE
HALINOUS	HALTING	HAMMERKOP	HANDGRAVURE	HANDWORK
HALIOTOID	HALTINGLY	HAMMERLESS	HANDGRIP	HANDWORKMAN
HALIPLID	HALTINGNESS	HAMMERLIKE	HANDGRIPING	HANDWORM
HALITE	HALTLESS	HAMMERMAN	HANDGUN	HANDWRIST
HALITOSIS	HALUCKET	HAMMERSMITH	HANDHAVING	HANDWRIT
HALITUOUS	HALUKKAH	HAMMERSTONE	HANDHOLD	HANDWRITE
HALITUS	HALURGIST	HAMMERTOE	HANDHOLE	HANDWRITING
HALK	HALURGY	HAMMERWORT	HANDICAP	HANDY
HALKE	HALUTZ	HAMMOCK	HANDICAPPED	HANDYBLOW
HALL	HALUTZIM	HAMMY	HANDICAPPER	HANDYBOOK
HALLAGE	HALVANER	HAMOSE	HANDICRAFT	HANDYCUFF
HALLAH	HALVANS	HAMOTZI	HANDICRAFTSMAN	HANDYFIGHT
HALLALCOR	HALVE	HAMOUS	HANDICRAFTSWOMAN	HANDYFRAME
HALLALI	HALVED	HAMP	HANDICUFF	HANDYGRIP
HALLAN	HALVELINGS	HAMPER	HANDIER	HANDYGRIPE
HALLBOY	HALVER	HAMPERED	HANDIEST	HANDYMAN
HALLCIST	HALVERS	HAMPERER	HANDILY	HANG
HALLE	HALVES	HAMPERING	HANDINESS	HANGABLE
HALLEBARDIER	HALVING	HAMPERMAN	HANDING	HANGALAI
HALLECRET	HALWE	HAMRONGITE	HANDIRON	HANGAR
HALLEL	HALY	HAMSA	HANDISTROKE	HANGBIRD
HALLELUIAH	HALYARD	HAMSHACKLE	HANDIWORK	HANGBY
HALLIARD	HAM	HAMSTER	HANDJAR	HANGDOG
HALLICET	HAMADA	HAMSTRING	HANDKERCHER	HANGE
HALLIDOME	HAMADRYAD	HAMULAR	HANDLAID	HANGEE
HALLING	HAMAL	HAMULATE	HANDLE	HANGER
HALLION	HAMALD	HAMULE	HANDLEABLE	HANGFIRE
HALLMAN	HAMAMELIN	HAMULOSE	HANDLEBAR	HANGI
HALLMARK	HAMARTIA	HAMULOUS	HANDLED	HANGIE
HALLMARKER	HAMARTITE	HAMULUS	HANDLER	HANGING
HALLMOOT	HAMATE	HAMUS	HANDLES	HANGKANG
HALLMOTE	HAMATED	HAMZA	HANDLESS	HANGLE
HALLO	HAMATUM	HAMZAH	HANDLIKE	HANGMAN
HALLOA	HAMAUL	HAN	HANDLING	HANGMENT
HALLOCK	HAMBER	HANAHILL	HANDLOAD	HANGNAIL
HALLOO	HAMBLE	HANAP	HANDLOADING	HANGNEST

HANGOUT
HANGOVER
HANGTAG
HANGUL
HANGUP
HANGWORM
HANGWORTHY
HANIF
HANIFISM
HANIFITE
HANIFIYA
HANK
HANKER
HANKERER
HANKERING
HANKERINGLY
HANKIE
HANKING
HANKLE
HANKS
HANKSITE
HANKT
HANKUL
HANKY
HANNA
HANNAYITE
HANOLOGATE
HANSA
HANSE
HANSEL
HANSELIN
HANSGRAVE
HANSOM
HANT
HANTLE
HANUM
HANUMAN
HAO
HAOLE
HAOMA
HAP
HAPALOTE
HAPHAZARD
HAPHAZARDLY
HAPHAZARDNESS
HAPHTARAH
HAPITON
HAPLESS
HAPLESSLY
HAPLESSNESS
HAPLITE
HAPLITIC
HAPLODONT
HAPLODONTY
HAPLOID
HAPLOIDIC
HAPLOIDY
HAPLOLALY
HAPLOLOGIC
HAPLOLOGY
HAPLOMA
HAPLOME
HAPLOMID
HAPLONT
HAPLOPHASE
HAPLOSCOPE
HAPLOSIS
HAPLOTYPE
HAPLY
HAPPEN
HAPPENING
HAPPER
HAPPIER
HAPPIEST
HAPPIFY
HAPPILESS
HAPPILY

HAPPINESS
HAPPING
HAPPY
HAPS
HAPT
HAPTERA
HAPTERE
HAPTERON
HAPTIC
HAPTICS
HAPTOMETER
HAPTOR
HAPTOTROPIC
HAPU
HAPUKU
HAQUETON
HAR
HARACE
HARAKEKE
HARANG
HARANGUE
HARANGUEFUL
HARANGUER
HARAS
HARASS
HARASSED
HARASSEDLY
HARASSER
HARASSING
HARASSINGLY
HARASSMENT
HARAST
HARATCH
HARATEEN
HARAUCANA
HARBERGAGE
HARBI
HARBINGE
HARBINGER
HARBORAGE
HARBORER
HARBORLESS
HARBORMASTER
HARBORSIDE
HARBOUR
HARBOURAGE
HARBOURER
HARBOURSIDE
HARD
HARDANGER
HARDBACK
HARDBAKE
HARDBALL
HARDBEAM
HARDBERRY
HARDCASE
HARDEN
HARDENED
HARDENER
HARDENING
HARDENITE
HARDER
HARDEST
HARDFERN
HARDFIST
HARDFISTED
HARDHACK
HARDHANDED
HARDHEAD
HARDHEADED
HARDHEADEDLY
HARDHEADEDNESS
HARDHEARTED
HARDHEARTEDLY
HARDHEARTEDNESS
HARDHEWER
HARDIE

HARDIER
HARDIES
HARDIESSE
HARDIEST
HARDIHEAD
HARDIHOOD
HARDILY
HARDIM
HARDIMENT
HARDINESS
HARDISH
HARDLY
HARDMOUTH
HARDMOUTHED
HARDNESS
HARDOCK
HARDPAN
HARDS
HARDSALT
HARDSET
HARDSHIP
HARDSTAND
HARDTACK
HARDTAIL
HARDTOP
HARDWARE
HARDWAY
HARDWEED
HARDWOOD
HARDWORKING
HARDY
HARDYHEAD
HARE
HAREBELL
HAREBOTTLE
HAREBRAIN
HAREBRAINED
HAREBUR
HAREEM
HAREFOOT
HAREFOOTED
HAREHEARTED
HAREHOUND
HARELIKE
HARELIP
HARELIPPED
HAREM
HAREMISM
HAREMLIK
HARENUT
HARES
HAREWOOD
HARFANG
HARIANA
HARICO
HARICOT
HARIER
HARIF
HARIFFE
HARIGALDS
HARIOLATE
HARIOLATION
HARISH
HARK
HARKA
HARKEN
HARKENER
HARL
HARLE
HARLEQUIN
HARLEQUINA
HARLEQUINADE
HARLEQUINESQUE
HARLEQUINIC
HARLEQUINIZE
HARLING
HARLOCK

HARLOT
HARLOTRIES
HARLOTRY
HARM
HARMAL
HARMALA
HARMALIN
HARMALINE
HARMAN
HARMATTAN
HARMEL
HARMER
HARMFUL
HARMFULLY
HARMFULNESS
HARMIN
HARMINE
HARMLESS
HARMLESSLY
HARMLESSNESS
HARMONIA
HARMONIACAL
HARMONIC
HARMONICA
HARMONICAL
HARMONICALLY
HARMONICI
HARMONICON
HARMONICS
HARMONIES
HARMONIOUS
HARMONIOUSLY
HARMONIOUSNESS
HARMONIST
HARMONISTIC
HARMONISTICALLY
HARMONIUM
HARMONIZE
HARMONIZER
HARMONIZING
HARMONY
HARMOOT
HARMOST
HARMOTOME
HARMOUT
HARN
HARNESS
HARNESSED
HARNESSER
HARNESSRY
HARNPAN
HARO
HAROSET
HARP
HARPAGO
HARPAGON
HARPE
HARPER
HARPIER
HARPIES
HARPIN
HARPINGS
HARPINS
HARPIST
HARPLESS
HARPLIKE
HARPOON
HARPOONED
HARPOONEER
HARPOONER
HARPSICAL
HARPSICHON
HARPSICHORD
HARPULA
HARPWISE
HARPY
HARQUEBUS

HARQUEBUSS
HARR
HARRAGE
HARRATEEN
HARRID
HARRIDAN
HARRIED
HARRIER
HARRISITE
HARROW
HARROWED
HARROWER
HARROWING
HARROWINGLY
HARROWINGNESS
HARROWMENT
HARROWTRY
HARRUMPH
HARRY
HARRYCANE
HARSH
HARSHISH
HARSHLY
HARSHNESS
HARSK
HARSLET
HARST
HARSTIGITE
HARSTRANG
HARSTRONG
HART
HARTAIL
HARTAKE
HARTAL
HARTALL
HARTBERRY
HARTEBEEST
HARTEN
HARTH
HARTIN
HARTITE
HARTLY
HARTSHORN
HARTSTONGUE
HARTTITE
HARUSPEX
HARUSPICAL
HARUSPICE
HARUSPICES
HARVEST
HARVESTER
HARVESTING
HARVESTLESS
HARVESTMAN
HARVESTRY
HARVESTTIME
HARZBURGITE
HAS
HASAN
HASARD
HASEL
HASH
HASHAB
HASHABI
HASHEESH
HASHER
HASHISH
HASHT
HASHY
HASK
HASKARD
HASKNESS
HASKWORT
HASKY
HASLET
HASLOCK
HASP

HASPICOL
HASS
HASSAR
HASSEL
HASSING
HASSLE
HASSLET
HASSOCK
HASSOCKY
HASTA
HASTATE
HASTATED
HASTATELY
HASTATI
HASTE
HASTEFUL
HASTEFULLY
HASTEN
HASTENER
HASTER
HASTIER
HASTIEST
HASTIF
HASTIFLY
HASTIFNESS
HASTILUDE
HASTILY
HASTINESS
HASTINGS
HASTINGSITE
HASTISH
HASTIVE
HASTLER
HASTULA
HASTY
HAT
HATABLE
HATBAND
HATBOX
HATCH
HATCHABLE
HATCHED
HATCHEL
HATCHELER
HATCHELLER
HATCHER
HATCHERIES
HATCHERY
HATCHERYMAN
HATCHET
HATCHETBACK
HATCHETLIKE
HATCHETTINE
HATCHETTITE
HATCHETY
HATCHGATE
HATCHING
HATCHITE
HATCHLING
HATCHMAN
HATCHMENT
HATCHWAY
HATCHWAYMAN
HATE
HATEABLE
HATEFUL
HATEFULLY
HATEFULNESS
HATEL
HATEN
HATER
HATFUL
HATH
HATHERLITE
HATHI
HATLESS
HATLIKE

HATMAKER
HATMAKING
HATPIN
HATRACK
HATRAIL
HATRED
HATRESS
HATS
HATSTAND
HATT
HATTE
HATTED
HATTER
HATTERIA
HATTERY
HATTING
HATTOCK
HATTY
HAU
HAUBERGEON
HAUBERGET
HAUBERK
HAUD
HAUERITE
HAUF
HAUFLIN
HAUGH
HAUGHLAND
HAUGHT
HAUGHTILY
HAUGHTINESS
HAUGHTONITE
HAUGHTY
HAUL
HAULABOUT
HAULAGE
HAULAGEWAY
HAULAWAY
HAULBACK
HAULD
HAULE
HAULER
HAULIER
HAULING
HAULM
HAULMY
HAULSTER
HAULT
HAULYARD
HAUN
HAUNCH
HAUNCHED
HAUNCHER
HAUNCHES
HAUNCHING
HAUNCHLESS
HAUNCHY
HAUNT
HAUNTED
HAUNTER
HAUNTING
HAUNTINGLY
HAUNTY
HAUPIA
HAURIANT
HAURIENT
HAURN
HAUSE
HAUSEN
HAUSSE
HAUSTELLA
HAUSTELLATE
HAUSTELLATED
HAUSTELLUM
HAUSTORIUM
HAUSTRAL
HAUSTRUM

HAUSTUS
HAUT
HAUTAIN
HAUTBOIS
HAUTBOY
HAUTBOYIST
HAUTESSE
HAUTEUR
HAUYNE
HAUYNITE
HAVAGE
HAVANCE
HAVE
HAVEAGE
HAVEL
HAVELESS
HAVELOCK
HAVEN
HAVENAGE
HAVENER
HAVENET
HAVER
HAVERAL
HAVERCAKE
HAVEREL
HAVERER
HAVERGRASS
HAVERING
HAVERMEAL
HAVERS
HAVERSACK
HAVERSINE
HAVIER
HAVILDAR
HAVING
HAVINGNESS
HAVINGS
HAVIOR
HAVIORED
HAVIOUR
HAVIOURED
HAVLAGAH
HAVOC
HAVOCKER
HAW
HAWAIITE
HAWBUCK
HAWCUBITE
HAWEBAKE
HAWER
HAWFINCH
HAWK
HAWKBILL
HAWKBIT
HAWKED
HAWKER
HAWKERY
HAWKEY
HAWKIE
HAWKING
HAWKINS
HAWKISH
HAWKNOSE
HAWKNOSED
HAWKNUT
HAWKS
HAWKSBILL
HAWKSHAW
HAWKWEED
HAWKY
HAWM
HAWN
HAWOK
HAWSE
HAWSEHOLE
HAWSEMAN
HAWSEPIECE

HAWSEPIPE
HAWSER
HAWTHORN
HAWTHORNY
HAY
HAYA
HAYBAND
HAYBIRD
HAYBOTE
HAYBURNER
HAYCAP
HAYCOCK
HAYDENITE
HAYE
HAYEY
HAYFIELD
HAYFORK
HAYING
HAYLOFT
HAYMAKER
HAYMAKING
HAYMARKET
HAYMOW
HAYNE
HAYRACK
HAYRICK
HAYRIDE
HAYS
HAYSEED
HAYSEL
HAYSHOCK
HAYSTACK
HAYSUCK
HAYWARD
HAYWEED
HAYWIRE
HAYZ
HAZAN
HAZANUT
HAZARD
HAZARDER
HAZARDOUS
HAZARDOUSLY
HAZARDOUSNESS
HAZARDRY
HAZE
HAZEL
HAZELED
HAZELLY
HAZELNUT
HAZEN
HAZER
HAZIER
HAZIEST
HAZILY
HAZINESS
HAZING
HAZLE
HAZNADAR
HAZY
HAZZAN
HAZZANUT
HE
HEAD
HEADACHE
HEADACHY
HEADBAND
HEADBANDER
HEADBOARD
HEADBOROUGH
HEADBOX
HEADCAP
HEADCHAIR
HEADCHEESE
HEADCHUTE
HEADCLOTH
HEADDRESS

HEADED
HEADENDER
HEADER
HEADFAST
HEADFIRST
HEADFISH
HEADFOREMOST
HEADFRAME
HEADFUL
HEADGEAR
HEADHUNT
HEADHUNTER
HEADIER
HEADIEST
HEADILY
HEADINESS
HEADING
HEADINGS
HEADLAND
HEADLE
HEADLEDGE
HEADLESS
HEADLIGHT
HEADLIGHTING
HEADLINE
HEADLINER
HEADLING
HEADLOAD
HEADLOCK
HEADLONG
HEADLONGLY
HEADLONGNESS
HEADLY
HEADMAN
HEADMARK
HEADMASTER
HEADMASTERLY
HEADMISTRESS
HEADMOLD
HEADMOST
HEADMOULD
HEADNOTE
HEADPENNY
HEADPHONE
HEADPIECE
HEADPIN
HEADPLATE
HEADPOST
HEADQUARTER
HEADQUARTERS
HEADRAIL
HEADREACH
HEADRENT
HEADREST
HEADRIG
HEADRIGHT
HEADRING
HEADROOM
HEADROPE
HEADS
HEADSAIL
HEADSAW
HEADSET
HEADSHAKE
HEADSHIP
HEADSILL
HEADSKIN
HEADSMAN
HEADSPACE
HEADSPRING
HEADSTALL
HEADSTAND
HEADSTICK
HEADSTOCK
HEADSTONE
HEADSTREAM
HEADSTRONG

HEADSTRONGLY	HEARTENER	HEATHLIKE	HECTORLY	HEFTER
HEADSTRONGNESS	HEARTENING	HEATHWORT	HECTOSTERE	HEFTIER
HEADTIRE	HEARTFELT	HEATHY	HECTOWATT	HEFTIEST
HEADWAITER	HEARTFUL	HEATING	HED	HEFTILY
HEADWALL	HEARTFULLY	HEATINGLY	HEDDE	HEFTINESS
HEADWARD	HEARTFULNESS	HEATLESS	HEDDLE	HEFTY
HEADWARDS	HEARTGRIEF	HEATSMAN	HEDDLER	HEG
HEADWARK	HEARTH	HEATSTROKE	HEDDLES	HEGEMON
HEADWATER	HEARTHMAN	HEAUME	HEDEBO	HEGEMONIC
HEADWATERS	HEARTHPENNY	HEAUMER	HEDER	HEGEMONICAL
HEADWAY	HEARTHRUG	HEAUTARIT	HEDERACEOUS	HEGEMONIST
HEADWEAR	HEARTHS	HEAVE	HEDERATED	HEGEMONY
HEADWORK	HEARTHSTONE	HEAVEN	HEDERIC	HEGIRA
HEADWORKER	HEARTHWARD	HEAVENLY	HEDERIN	HEGUMEN
HEADWORKING	HEARTHWARMING	HEAVENS	HEDEROSE	HEGUMENESS
HEADY	HEARTIER	HEAVENWARD	HEDGE	HEGUMENOS
HEAF	HEARTIES	HEAVENWARDLY	HEDGEBERRY	HEGUMENY
HEAL	HEARTIEST	HEAVENWARDNESS	HEDGEBETTY	HEIAU
HEALD	HEARTIKIN	HEAVENWARDS	HEDGEBOTE	HEIFER
HEALDER	HEARTILY	HEAVER	HEDGEHOG	HEIGH
HEALED	HEARTINESS	HEAVES	HEDGEHOGGY	HEIGHT
HEALER	HEARTING	HEAVIER	HEDGEHOP	HEIGHTEN
HEALFUL	HEARTLEAF	HEAVIES	HEDGEPIG	HEIGHTENER
HEALING	HEARTLESS	HEAVIEST	HEDGER	HEIGHTH
HEALINGLY	HEARTLESSLY	HEAVILY	HEDGEROW	HEII
HEALLESS	HEARTLESSNESS	HEAVINESS	HEDGES	HEIL
HEALSOME	HEARTLY	HEAVING	HEDGESMITH	HEIMIN
HEALSOMENESS	HEARTNUT	HEAVISOME	HEDGESTRAW	HEIMLICH
HEALTH	HEARTPEA	HEAVITY	HEDGETAPER	HEIN
HEALTHCRAFT	HEARTQUAKE	HEAVY	HEDGING	HEINOUS
HEALTHFUL	HEARTROOT	HEAVYBACK	HEDGINGLY	HEINOUSLY
HEALTHFULLY	HEARTROT	HEAVYSET	HEDGY	HEINOUSNESS
HEALTHFULNESS	HEARTS	HEAVYWEIGHT	HEDONIC	HEIR
HEALTHGUARD	HEARTSCALD	HEAZY	HEDONICAL	HEIRDOM
HEALTHIER	HEARTSEASE	HEBAMIC	HEDONICALLY	HEIRESS
HEALTHIEST	HEARTSEED	HEBDOMAD	HEDONICS	HEIRLOOM
HEALTHLESS	HEARTSETTE	HEBDOMADAL	HEDONISM	HEIRMOS
HEALTHSOME	HEARTSICK	HEBDOMADALLY	HEDONIST	HEIRSHIP
HEALTHY	HEARTSOME	HEBDOMADARY	HEDONISTIC	HEIST
HEAM	HEARTSOMELY	HEBDOMADER	HEDONISTICALLY	HEISTER
HEAP	HEARTSORE	HEBEANTHOUS	HEDROCELE	HEITIKI
HEAPED	HEARTSTRING	HEBECARPOUS	HEDRUMITE	HEJIRA
HEAPER	HEARTSTRINGS	HEBECLADOUS	HEDYPHANE	HEKTEUS
HEAPING	HEARTTHROB	HEBENON	HEE	HEL
HEAPS	HEARTWATER	HEBEPHRENIC	HEED	HELAS
HEAPSTEAD	HEARTWEED	HEBETATE	HEEDER	HELBEH
HEAPY	HEARTWOOD	HEBETATION	HEEDFUL	HELCOID
HEAR	HEARTWORM	HEBETATIVE	HEEDFULLY	HELCOLOGY
HEARD	HEARTWORT	HEBETE	HEEDFULNESS	HELCOPLASTY
HEARER	HEARTY	HEBETIC	HEEDILY	HELCOSIS
HEARING	HEAT	HEBETUDE	HEEDINESS	HELCOTIC
HEARKEN	HEATDROPS	HECATOMB	HEEDLESS	HELD
HEARKENER	HEATED	HECATOMPED	HEEDLESSLY	HELDER
HEARSAY	HEATEDLY	HECCEITY	HEEDLESSNESS	HELENIN
HEARSE	HEATEN	HECCO	HEEDY	HELEPOLE
HEARSECLOTH	HEATER	HECH	HEEHAW	HELER
HEARST	HEATERMAN	HECHIMA	HEEL	HELIAC
HEART	HEATH	HECHSHER	HEELBALL	HELIACAL
HEARTACHE	HEATHBERRY	HECK	HEELCAP	HELIACALLY
HEARTACHING	HEATHBIRD	HECKIMAL	HEELD	HELIANTHUS
HEARTBEAT	HEATHEN	HECKLE	HEELED	HELIAST
HEARTBIRD	HEATHENDOM	HECKLER	HEELER	HELIASTIC
HEARTBLOCK	HEATHENESSE	HECTARE	HEELING	HELICAL
HEARTBLOOD	HEATHENISH	HECTE	HEELPATH	HELICALLY
HEARTBREAK	HEATHENISHLY	HECTIC	HEELPIECE	HELICED
HEARTBREAKER	HEATHENISHNESS	HECTICAL	HEELPLATE	HELICINE
HEARTBREAKING	HEATHENISM	HECTICALLY	HEELPOST	HELICITIC
HEARTBROKEN	HEATHENIST	HECTIVE	HEELS	HELICLINE
HEARTBROKENLY	HEATHENIZE	HECTOGRAM	HEELSTRAP	HELICOGRAPH
HEARTBROKENNESS	HEATHENLY	HECTOGRAMME	HEELTAP	HELICOGYRE
HEARTBURN	HEATHENRY	HECTOGRAPH	HEELTREE	HELICOID
HEARTBURNING	HEATHER	HECTOGRAPHIC	HEELWORK	HELICOIDAL
HEARTDEEP	HEATHERED	HECTOLITER	HEEMRAAD	HELICOIDALLY
HEARTEASE	HEATHERINESS	HECTOLITRE	HEEMRAAT	HELICOMETRY
HEARTED	HEATHERY	HECTOR	HEER	HELICON
HEARTEDLY	HEATHIER	HECTORED	HEEZE	HELICONIST
HEARTEN	HEATHIEST	HECTORING	HEFT	HELICOPROTEIN

HELICOPTER	HELLROOT	HEMATOSIN	HEMITONE	HENEQUEN
HELICORUBIN	HELLSHIP	HEMATOSIS	HEMITROPAL	HENFISH
HELICOTREMA	HELLUO	HEMATOZOON	HEMITROPE	HENHEARTED
HELICTITE	HELLVINE	HEMATURIA	HEMITROPIC	HENHUSSIES
HELID	HELLWEED	HEME	HEMITYPE	HENHUSSY
HELIDE	HELLY	HEMEL	HEMITYPIC	HENISM
HELIO	HELM	HEMEN	HEML	HENNA
HELIOCENTRIC	HELMAGE	HEMERA	HEMLOCK	HENNERIES
HELIOCENTRICAL	HELMED	HEMERALOPE	HEMMEL	HENNERY
HELIOCENTRICITY	HELMET	HEMERALOPIA	HEMMER	HENNIN
HELIOCHROME	HELMETED	HEMERALOPIC	HEMMING	HENNISH
HELIOCHROMIC	HELMETFLOWER	HEMIACETAL	HEMOBLAST	HENNY
HELIOCHROMY	HELMETLIKE	HEMIALGIA	HEMOCHROME	HENOTIC
HELIOCULTURE	HELMETPOD	HEMIAMB	HEMOCONIA	HENPECK
HELIODON	HELMINTH	HEMIAUXIN	HEMOCYTE	HENPECKED
HELIODOR	HELMINTHIC	HEMIBRANCH	HEMOFUSCIN	HENPEN
HELIOELECTRIC	HELMINTHISM	HEMIC	HEMOGASTRIC	HENRIES
HELIOFUGAL	HELMSMAN	HEMICARDIA	HEMOGLOBIN	HENRYS
HELIOGRAM	HELO	HEMICARP	HEMOGRAM	HENS
HELIOGRAPH	HELOBIOUS	HEMICENTRUM	HEMOID	HENT
HELIOGRAPHER	HELODES	HEMICHORDATE	HEMOL	HENWARE
HELIOGRAPHIC	HELOE	HEMICOLLIN	HEMOLYSIN	HENWILE
HELIOGRAPHY	HELOMA	HEMICRANE	HEMOLYSIS	HENWOODITE
HELIOGRAVURE	HELONIN	HEMICRANIA	HEMOLYZE	HEO
HELIOID	HELOSIS	HEMICYCLE	HEMOPHILE	HEP
HELIOLATER	HELOT	HEMICYCLIC	HEMOPHILIA	HEPAR
HELIOLATOR	HELOTISM	HEMIDITONE	HEMOPHILIAC	HEPARIN
HELIOLATROUS	HELOTOMY	HEMIDOME	HEMOPHILIC	HEPATIC
HELIOLATRY	HELOTRY	HEMIEPES	HEMOPTOE	HEPATICAE
HELIOLITE	HELP	HEMIFACIAL	HEMORRHAGE	HEPATICAL
HELIOMETER	HELPER	HEMIFORM	HEMORRHOID	HEPATITE
HELIOMETRIC	HELPFUL	HEMIGLYPH	HEMOSCOPE	HEPATITIS
HELIOMETRY	HELPFULLY	HEMIHEDRAL	HEMOSCOPY	HEPATIZE
HELIOSCOPE	HELPFULNESS	HEMIHEDRIC	HEMOSTASIA	HEPATOID
HELIOSIS	HELPING	HEMIKARYON	HEMOSTASIS	HEPATOMA
HELIOSTAT	HELPLESS	HEMIMELLITIC	HEMOSTAT	HEPPEN
HELIOTACTIC	HELPLESSLY	HEMIMELUS	HEMOSTATIC	HEPPER
HELIOTAXIS	HELPLESSNESS	HEMIMORPH	HEMOTHORAX	HEPTACHORD
HELIOTHERAPY	HELPLY	HEMIMORPHIC	HEMOTOXIC	HEPTACOLIC
HELIOTROPE	HELPMATE	HEMIMORPHITE	HEMOTOXIN	HEPTAD
HELIOTROPIC	HELPMEET	HEMIN	HEMOTROPHE	HEPTAGLOT
HELIOTROPISM	HELPSOME	HEMINA	HEMOTROPIC	HEPTAGON
HELIOTROPY	HELPWORTHY	HEMINE	HEMOZOON	HEPTAGONAL
HELIOTYPE	HELVE	HEMINEE	HEMP	HEPTAHEDRAL
HELIOZOAN	HELVELL	HEMIOLA	HEMPBUSH	HEPTAHEDRON
HELIPORT	HELVELLIC	HEMIOLIA	HEMPEN	HEPTAL
HELIUM	HELVIN	HEMIOLIC	HEMPHERDS	HEPTAMETER
HELIX	HELVINE	HEMIONUS	HEMPIE	HEPTANE
HELIXIN	HELVITE	HEMIOPE	HEMPIER	HEPTANGULAR
HELL	HELZEL	HEMIOPIA	HEMPIEST	HEPTANONE
HELLBENDER	HEM	HEMIOPIC	HEMPSEED	HEPTAPLOID
HELLBOX	HEMACHATE	HEMIOPSIA	HEMPSTRING	HEPTAPODY
HELLBROTH	HEMACHROME	HEMIPENIS	HEMPWEED	HEPTARCH
HELLCAT	HEMACITE	HEMIPHRASE	HEMPWORT	HEPTARCHAL
HELLDOG	HEMAD	HEMIPIC	HEMPY	HEPTARCHIC
HELLEBORE	HEMAGOG	HEMIPLEGIA	HEMSELF	HEPTARCHIES
HELLEBOREIN	HEMAGOGIC	HEMIPLEGIC	HEMSTITCH	HEPTARCHIST
HELLEBORIC	HEMAGOGUE	HEMIPLEGY	HEMSTITCHER	HEPTARCHY
HELLEBORIN	HEMAL	HEMIPOD	HEN	HEPTASTICH
HELLER	HEMAMEBA	HEMIPODE	HENAD	HEPTENE
HELLERI	HEMAPOD	HEMIPPE	HENBANE	HEPTERIS
HELLERY	HEMATAL	HEMIPRISM	HENBILL	HEPTITE
HELLFIRE	HEMATEIN	HEMIPROTEIN	HENBIT	HEPTITOL
HELLGRAMMITE	HEMATIC	HEMIPTER	HENCE	HEPTOIC
HELLHAG	HEMATID	HEMIPTERAL	HENCEFORTH	HEPTORITE
HELLHOLE	HEMATIN	HEMIPTERAN	HENCEFORWARDS	HEPTOSE
HELLHOUND	HEMATINE	HEMIPTERON	HENCH	HEPTOXIDE
HELLICAT	HEMATINIC	HEMIPTEROUS	HENCHBOY	HEPTYL
HELLICATE	HEMATITE	HEMISECT	HENCHMAN	HEPTYLENE
HELLIER	HEMATITIC	HEMISPHERAL	HENCOOP	HEPTYLIC
HELLIM	HEMATOCELE	HEMISPHERE	HEND	HEPTYNE
HELLION	HEMATOID	HEMISPHERED	HENDE	HER
HELLISH	HEMATOLIN	HEMISTATER	HENDECAGON	HERALD
HELLISHLY	HEMATOMA	HEMISTICH	HENDECANE	HERALDIC
HELLISHNESS	HEMATOMETER	HEMITERATA	HENDECOIC	HERALDICAL
HELLKITE	HEMATOSCOPE	HEMITERIA	HENDECYL	HERALDIST
HELLO	HEMATOSE	HEMITERY	HENDIADYS	HERALDIZE

HERALDRIES	HEREM	HERNIATED	HETERISM	HEURETIC
HERALDRY	HERENACH	HERNIATION	HETERIZE	HEURT
HERB	HERENIGING	HERO	HETEROCENTRIC	HEUVEL
HERBACEOUS	HEREOF	HERODIAN	HETEROCERC	HEVEN
HERBAGE	HEREON	HEROES	HETEROCERCAL	HEVER
HERBAGED	HEREOUT	HEROESS	HETEROCHIRAL	HEVI
HERBAGER	HERERIGHT	HEROIC	HETEROCHROME	HEW
HERBAGIOUS	HERES	HEROICAL	HETEROCLINE	HEWE
HERBAL	HERES'ARCH	HEROICITY	HETEROCLITE	HEWEL
HERBALIST	HERESIES	HEROICOMIC	HETEROCLITIC	HEWER
HERBALIZE	HERESIMACH	HEROICS	HETEROCYCLE	HEWGAG
HERBARISM	HERESIOLOGER	HEROID	HETEROCYCLIC	HEWHALL
HERBARIZE	HERESIOLOGY	HEROIFY	HETEROCYST	HEWHOLE
HERBARY	HERESY	HEROIN	HETERODONT	HEWN
HERBBANE	HERETIC	HEROINE	HETERODOX	HEWT
HERBER	HERETICAL	HEROISM	HETERODOXIES	HEX
HERBESCENT	HERETICALLY	HEROISTIC	HETERODOXY	HEXABASIC
HERBICIDE	HERETICALNESS	HEROLA	HETERODYNE	HEXABIOSE
HERBIFEROUS	HERETICATE	HERON	HETEROECY	HEXABROMID
HERBIVORE	HERETICATED	HERONBILL	HETEROEROTISM	HEXABROMIDE
HERBLET	HERETICATION	HERONER	HETEROGAMETE	HEXACHORD
HERBMAN	HERETICATOR	HERONITE	HETEROGAMIC	HEXACID
HERBORIST	HERETICIDE	HERONRY	HETEROGAMY	HEXACOLIC
HERBORIZE	HERETICIZE	HERONS	HETEROGENE	HEXACOSANE
HERBOSE	HERETO	HERONSEW	HETEROGENEOUS	HEXACTINAL
HERBS	HERETOFORE	HEROOGONY	HETEROGONY	HEXACYCLIC
HERBWIFE	HERETOGA	HEROOLOGY	HETEROGRAFT	HEXAD
HERBWOMAN	HEREUNDER	HERPES	HETEROGRAPHIES	HEXADE
HERBY	HEREUNTO	HERPESTINE	HETEROGRAPHY	HEXADECANE
HERCULEAN	HEREUPON	HERPETIC	HETEROGYNAL	HEXADECYL
HERCYNITE	HEREWITH	HERRING	HETEROLATERAL	HEXADIC
HERD	HEREWITHAL	HERRINGBONE	HETEROLITH	HEXADIENE
HERDBOOK	HEREZELD	HERRINGER	HETEROLOGICAL	HEXADIINE
HERDBOY	HERIF	HERRINGS	HETEROLOGIES	HEXADIYNE
HERDER	HERILE	HERRY	HETEROLOGY	HEXAEMERIC
HERDERITE	HERIOT	HERS	HETEROLYSIS	HEXAEMERON
HERDIC	HERIOTABLE	HERSALL	HETEROLYTIC	HEXAFOIL
HERDING	HERISSON	HERSCHELITE	HETEROMORPHIC	HEXAFOOS
HERDSMAN	HERITABLE	HERSE	HETERONOMOUS	HEXAGLOT
HERDSMEN	HERITABLY	HERSED	HETERONOMY	HEXAGON
HERDSWOMAN	HERITAGE	HERSELF	HETERONUCLEAR	HEXAGONAL
HERDWICK	HERITANCE	HERSHIP	HETERONYM	HEXAGONALLY
HERE	HERITOR	HERSIR	HETERONYMOUS	HEXAGRAM
HEREABOUT	HERITRIX	HERTZ	HETEROPATHIC	HEXAGYN
HEREABOUTS	HERL	HERTZIAN	HETEROPATHY	HEXAGYNOUS
HEREADAYS	HERLING	HERY	HETEROPLASM	HEXAHEDRA
HEREAFTER	HERM	HESH	HETEROPLASTIC	HEXAHEDRAL
HEREAFTERWARD	HERMA	HESITANCE	HETEROPLASTIES	HEXAHEDRON
HEREAGAIN	HERMAE	HESITANCY	HETEROPLASTY	HEXAHYDRIC
HEREAGAINST	HERMAEAN	HESITANT	HETEROPOLAR	HEXAMER
HEREAMONG	HERMAI	HESITANTLY	HETEROPTICS	HEXAMERAL
HEREANENT	HERMAIC	HESITATE	HETEROSCOPE	HEXAMERISM
HEREAT	HERMANDAD	HESITATER	HETEROSEXUAL	HEXAMERON
HEREAWAY	HERMAPHRODITE	HESITATING	HETEROSIS	HEXAMEROUS
HEREBEFORE	HERMAPHRODITIC	HESITATION	HETEROSPHERE	HEXAMETER
HEREBY	HERMAPHRODITISM	HESITATIVE	HETEROSTATIC	HEXAMETRAL
HEREDIA	HERME	HESITATOR	HETEROTACTIC	HEXAMETRIC
HEREDITABLE	HERMELE	HESPED	HETEROTAXIA	HEXAMINE
HEREDITAL	HERMENEUT	HESPEL	HETEROTAXIC	HEXAMMIN
HEREDITAMENT	HERMENEUTIC	HESPERIDATE	HETEROTAXIS	HEXAMMINE
HEREDITARY	HERMETIC	HESPERIDENE	HETEROTELIC	HEXANAL
HEREDITAS	HERMETICAL	HESPERIDIN	HETEROTOPIA	HEXANDRIC
HEREDITIES	HERMIDIN	HESSITE	HETEROTOPIC	HEXANDROUS
HEREDITISM	HERMIT	HESSONITE	HETEROTOPY	HEXANDRY
HEREDITIST	HERMITAGE	HEST	HETEROTROPAL	HEXANE
HEREDITY	HERMITARY	HET	HETEROTROPHIC	HEXANGULAR
HEREDOLUES	HERMITIC	HETAERA	HETEROTYPIC	HEXAPED
HEREFORE	HERMITICAL	HETAERIA	HETEROXENOUS	HEXAPLA
HEREFROM	HERMITRY	HETAERIO	HETEROZYGOTE	HEXAPLAR
HEREGELD	HERN	HETAERISM	HETEROZYGOUS	HEXAPLARIC
HEREGILD	HERNE	HETAERIST	HETHEN	HEXAPLOID
HEREHENCE	HERNIA	HETAERY	HETHING	HEXAPOD
HEREIN	HERNIAE	HETAIRIA	HETMAN	HEXAPODIES
HEREINABOVE	HERNIAL	HETAIRISM	HETTER	HEXAPODY
HEREINAFTER	HERNIARIN	HETAIRY	HEU	HEXARADIAL
HEREINBEFORE	HERNIARY	HETE	HEUCH	HEXARCHIES
HEREINTO	HERNIATE	HETERAKID	HEUGH	HEXARCHY

HEXASEME	HIDEBIND	HIGGAION	HILLSALE	HIPMOLD
HEXASEMIC	HIDEBOUND	HIGGLE	HILLSALESMAN	HIPPARCH
HEXASTER	HIDEBOUNDNESS	HIGGLEHAGGLE	HILLSIDE	HIPPED
HEXASTICH	HIDED	HIGGLER	HILLSMAN	HIPPEN
HEXASTICHIC	HIDEL	HIGGLERY	HILLTOP	HIPPIAN
HEXASTICHY	HIDELAND	HIGH	HILLTROT	HIPPIATER
HEXASTIGM	HIDELING	HIGHBALL	HILLWORT	HIPPIATRIC
HEXASTYLOS	HIDEOSITY	HIGHBINDER	HILLY	HIPPIATRY
HEXATHLON	HIDEOUS	HIGHBORN	HILSA	HIPPIC
HEXATOMIC	HIDEOUSLY	HIGHBOY	HILSAH	HIPPIE
HEXATRIOSE	HIDEOUSNESS	HIGHBRED	HILT	HIPPING
HEXAVALENT	HIDEOUT	HIGHBROW	HILUM	HIPPISH
HEXAXON	HIDER	HIGHBROWED	HILUS	HIPPLE
HEXENE	HIDES	HIGHBROWISM	HIM	HIPPO
HEXER	HIDING	HIGHCHAIR	HIMATIA	HIPPOBOSCID
HEXEREI	HIDLING	HIGHDAY	HIMATION	HIPPOCAMPAL
HEXERIS	HIDLINGS	HIGHER	HIMENE	HIPPOCAMPUS
HEXINE	HIDLINS	HIGHERMOST	HIMMING	HIPPOCAUST
HEXIS	HIDROSIS	HIGHEST	HIMP	HIPPOCERF
HEXITOL	HIDROTIC	HIGHFALUTIN	HIMPLE	HIPPOCRAS
HEXOBARBITAL	HIE	HIGHFALUTING	HIMSELF	HIPPODROME
HEXODE	HIEDER	HIGHFLIER	HIN	HIPPOGRIFF
HEXOIC	HIELAMAN	HIGHFLYER	HINAU	HIPPOGRYPH
HEXONE	HIELAMEN	HIGHFLYING	HINCH	HIPPOID
HEXONIC	HIELD	HIGHHANDED	HIND	HIPPOLITH
HEXOSAN	HIELMITE	HIGHHEARTED	HINDBERRY	HIPPOLOGY
HEXOSE	HIEMAL	HIGHHOLE	HINDBRAIN	HIPPOMANES
HEXPARTITE	HIEMATION	HIGHJACK	HINDCAST	HIPPONOUS
HEXT	HIEMS	HIGHJACKER	HINDDECK	HIPPOPHILE
HEXYL	HIEN	HIGHLAND	HINDER	HIPPOPOD
HEXYLENE	HIER	HIGHLANDER	HINDERANCE	HIPPOPOTAMIC
HEXYLIC	HIERA	HIGHLIGHT	HINDERED	HIPPOPOTAMUS
HEXYNE	HIERAPICRA	HIGHLINE	HINDERER	HIPPOTOMY
HEY	HIERARCH	HIGHLOW	HINDEREST	HIPPURATE
HEYDAY	HIERARCHAL	HIGHLY	HINDERFUL	HIPPURIC
HEYDEGUY	HIERARCHIC	HIGHMAN	HINDERFULLY	HIPPURID
HEYDEY	HIERARCHICAL	HIGHMOOR	HINDERLY	HIPPURITE
HEYRAT	HIERARCHICALLY	HIGHMOST	HINDERMENT	HIPPUS
HEYT	HIERARCHISM	HIGHNESS	HINDERMOST	HIPPY
HI	HIERARCHIST	HIGHROAD	HINDERSOME	HIPS
HIA	HIERARCHIZE	HIGHT	HINDGUT	HIPSHOT
HIANT	HIERARCHY	HIGHTAIL	HINDHAND	HIPSTER
HIATAL	HIERATIC	HIGHTIDE	HINDHEAD	HIRABLE
HIATE	HIERATICAL	HIGHTOBY	HINDMOST	HIRAGANA
HIATION	HIERATICALLY	HIGHTOP	HINDQUARTER	HIRCARRA
HIATUS	HIERATITE	HIGHVELD	HINDQUARTERS	HIRCH
HIBACHI	HIEROCRACIES	HIGHWAY	HINDRANCE	HIRCINE
HIBBIN	HIEROCRACY	HIGHWAYMAN	HINDS	HIRCINOUS
HIBERNAL	HIEROCRATIC	HIGRE	HINDSADDLE	HIRCUS
HIBERNATE	HIEROCRATICAL	HIGUERO	HINDSIGHT	HIRE
HIBERNATING	HIERODULE	HIJACK	HINE	HIRED
HIBERNATION	HIEROGAMY	HIJACKER	HING	HIRELING
HIC	HIEROGLYPH	HIJINKS	HINGE	HIRER
HICACO	HIEROGLYPHER	HIKE	HINGECORNER	HIRING
HICAN	HIEROGLYPHIC	HIKER	HINGED	HIRLING
HICATEE	HIEROGRAM	HIKU	HINGEFLOWER	HIRMOS
HICCAN	HIEROGRAPH	HIKULI	HINGLE	HIRO
HICCOUGH	HIEROGRAPHER	HILARIOUS	HINK	HIRONDELLE
HICCUP	HIEROGRAPHIC	HILARIOUSLY	HINNA	HIRPLE
HICHT	HIEROGRAPHY	HILARIOUSNESS	HINNER	HIRR
HICHU	HIEROLATRY	HILARITY	HINNIBLE	HIRRIENT
HICK	HIEROLOGIC	HILASMIC	HINNIES	HIRSE
HICKEY	HIEROLOGIST	HILCH	HINNY	HIRSEL
HICKORY	HIEROLOGY	HILDING	HINOID	HIRSELED
HICKWALL	HIEROMACHY	HILL	HINOIDEOUS	HIRSELING
HICKWAY	HIEROMANCY	HILLBILLIES	HINOKI	HIRSELLED
HICKY	HIEROMNEMON	HILLBILLY	HINSDALITE	HIRSELLING
HID	HIEROMONACH	HILLBIRD	HINT	HIRSH
HIDAGE	HIERON	HILLER	HINTERLAND	HIRSLE
HIDALGO	HIEROPATHIC	HILLET	HIODONT	HIRST
HIDATED	HIEROPHANCY	HILLMAN	HIP	HIRSUTE
HIDATION	HIEROPHANT	HILLO	HIPBERRY	HIRSUTENESS
HIDDELS	HIEROS	HILLOA	HIPBONE	HIRSUTIES
HIDDEN	HIEROSCOPY	HILLOCK	HIPE	HIRSUTISM
HIDDENITE	HIERURGY	HILLOCKED	HIPHALT	HIRTCH
HIDE	HIFALUTIN	HILLOCKY	HIPHAPE	HIRUDINEAN
HIDEAWAY	HIGDON	HILLS	HIPLINE	HIRUDINOID

HIRUNDINE	HITCHHIKE	HOBO	HOGSTEER	HOLLIN
HIS	HITCHHIKER	HOBOISM	HOGSUCKER	HOLLIPER
HISH	HITCHILY	HOBTHRUSH	HOGTON	HOLLO
HISINGERITE	HITCHING	HOC	HOGWARD	HOLLOA
HISLOPITE	HITCHY	HOCCO	HOGWASH	HOLLOCK
HISN	HITHE	HOCH	HOGWEED	HOLLONG
HISPID	HITHER	HOCK	HOGWORT	HOLLOW
HISPIDITY	HITHERMOST	HOCKELTY	HOI	HOLLOWED
HISPIDULATE	HITHERTILLS	HOCKER	HOICK	HOLLOWER
HISPIDULOUS	HITHERTO	HOCKET	HOICKS	HOLLOWFACED
HISS	HITHERTOWARD	HOCKEY	HOIDEN	HOLLOWFOOT
HISSEL	HITHERUNTO	HOCKING	HOIGH	HOLLOWHEARTED
HISSELF	HITHERWARD	HOCKSHIN	HOIHERE	HOLLOWLY
HISSER	HITTABLE	HOCKY	HOIN	HOLLOWNESS
HISSING	HITTER	HOCUS	HOISE	HOLLOWROOT
HISSY	HIVE	HOD	HOIST	HOLLUSCHICK
HIST	HIVER	HODAG	HOISTAWAY	HOLLY
HISTAMINE	HIVES	HODDEN	HOISTED	HOLLYHOCK
HISTAMINIC	HIYA	HODDER	HOISTER	HOLLYLEAF
HISTER	HIYAKKIN	HODDLE	HOISTING	HOLM
HISTIDINE	HIZ	HODDY	HOISTMAN	HOLMBERRY
HISTIE	HIZZ	HODENING	HOISTWAY	HOLMES
HISTOBLAST	HIZZIE	HODFUL	HOIT	HOLMGANG
HISTOCHEMIC	HO	HODGEPODGE	HOJA	HOLMIA
HISTOCHEMICAL	HOACTZIN	HODIERNAL	HOJU	HOLMIC
HISTOCLASTIC	HOAR	HODJA	HOK	HOLMIUM
HISTOGEN	HOARD	HODMAN	HOKE	HOLMOS
HISTOGENESIS	HOARDED	HODMANDOD	HOKER	HOLOBAPTIST
HISTOGENETIC	HOARDER	HODOGRAPH	HOKERER	HOLOBENTHIC
HISTOGENIC	HOARDING	HODOMETER	HOKERLY	HOLOBLASTIC
HISTOGENOUS	HOARDWARD	HODOMETRICAL	HOKEY	HOLOBRANCH
HISTOGENY	HOARFROST	HODOSCOPE	HOKKU	HOLOCAINE
HISTOGRAM	HOARHEAD	HODURE	HOKUM	HOLOCARPIC
HISTOGRAPHIC	HOARHEADED	HOE	HOL	HOLOCAUST
HISTOGRAPHY	HOARHOUND	HOECAKE	HOLA	HOLOCAUSTAL
HISTOID	HOARINESS	HOEDOWN	HOLARCTIC	HOLOCAUSTIC
HISTOLOGIC	HOARISH	HOER	HOLARD	HOLOCHORDATE
HISTOLOGICAL	HOARSE	HOERNESITE	HOLCAD	HOLOCHROAL
HISTOLOGIES	HOARSELY	HOG	HOLCODONT	HOLOCLASTIC
HISTOLOGIST	HOARSEN	HOGA	HOLD	HOLOGAMOUS
HISTOLOGY	HOARSENESS	HOGAN	HOLDALL	HOLOGAMY
HISTOLYSIS	HOARSTONE	HOGBACK	HOLDBACK	HOLOGRAM
HISTON	HOARWORT	HOGBUSH	HOLDE	HOLOGRAPH
HISTONAL	HOARY	HOGCHOKER	HOLDENITE	HOLOGRAPHIC
HISTONE	HOAST	HOGCOTE	HOLDER	HOLOGRAPHY
HISTONOMY	HOASTMAN	HOGFISH	HOLDFAST	HOLOHEDRAL
HISTORIAL	HOATZIN	HOGFRAME	HOLDING	HOLOHEDRIC
HISTORIAN	HOAX	HOGG	HOLDINGS	HOLOHEDRON
HISTORIC	HOAXEE	HOGGASTER	HOLDMAN	HOLOKU
HISTORICAL	HOAXER	HOGGED	HOLDOUT	HOLOMETER
HISTORICALNESS	HOAXPROOF	HOGGEE	HOLDOVER	HOLOMORPH
HISTORICS	HOB	HOGGER	HOLDSMAN	HOLOMORPHIC
HISTORIED	HOBB	HOGGEREL	HOLDUP	HOLOMORPHISM
HISTORIER	HOBBER	HOGGERY	HOLE	HOLOMORPHY
HISTORIES	HOBBET	HOGGET	HOLEABLE	HOLOPARASITE
HISTORIETTE	HOBBIL	HOGGIE	HOLEMAN	HOLOPHOTAL
HISTORIFY	HOBBINOLL	HOGGIN	HOLER	HOLOPHOTE
HISTORIOGRAPH	HOBBIT	HOGGING	HOLES	HOLOPHRASE
HISTORIOGRAPHER	HOBBLE	HOGGINS	HOLEWORT	HOLOPHRASM
HISTORIOUS	HOBBLEBUSH	HOGGISH	HOLEY	HOLOPHRASTIC
HISTORISM	HOBBLEDEHOY	HOGGISHLY	HOLIA	HOLOPHYTE
HISTORIZE	HOBBLER	HOGGISHNESS	HOLIDAY	HOLOPHYTIC
HISTORY	HOBBLES	HOGGLER	HOLIDAYER	HOLOPLEXIA
HISTOTOME	HOBBLING	HOGGY	HOLIES	HOLOPTIC
HISTOTOMY	HOBBLY	HOGHEAD	HOLILY	HOLORHINAL
HISTOTROPHIC	HOBBY	HOGHERD	HOLINESS	HOLOSIDE
HISTOTROPHY	HOBBYHORSE	HOGLING	HOLING	HOLOSIDERITE
HISTOTROPIC	HOBBYISM	HOGMACE	HOLISHKES	HOLOSTEAN
HISTRIO	HOBBYIST	HOGMANAY	HOLISM	HOLOSTERIC
HISTRION	HOBGOBLIN	HOGNOSE	HOLISTIC	HOLOSTOME
HISTRIONIC	HOBHOUCHIN	HOGNUT	HOLISTICALLY	HOLOSTYLIC
HISTRIONICAL	HOBLIKE	HOGO	HOLL	HOLOTHURIAN
HISTRIONICALLY	HOBLOB	HOGREEVE	HOLLA	HOLOTONY
HISTRIONICS	HOBNAIL	HOGS	HOLLAITE	HOLOTYPE
HIT	HOBNAILED	HOGSHEAD	HOLLANDAISE	HOLOTYPIC
HITCH	HOBNAILER	HOGSHOUTHER	HOLLEKE	HOLOUR
HITCHER	HOBNOB	HOGSKIN	HOLLER	HOLOZOIC

HOLP	HOMICIDALLY	HOMOLOGY	HONEYCOMBING	HOOFLET
HOLSOM	HOMICIDE	HOMOLOSINE	HONEYCUP	HOOFPRINT
HOLSTER	HOMICULTURE	HOMOMERAL	HONEYDEW	HOOFS
HOLSTERED	HOMILETE	HOMOMEROUS	HONEYDEWED	HOOFWORM
HOLSTERS	HOMILETIC	HOMOMORPH	HONEYED	HOOGAARS
HOLT	HOMILETICAL	HOMOMORPHIC	HONEYEDNESS	HOOK
HOLY	HOMILETICS	HOMOMORPHISM	HONEYFALL	HOOKA
HOLYDAY	HOMILIST	HOMOMORPHY	HONEYFLOWER	HOOKAH
HOLYSTONE	HOMILITE	HOMONID	HONEYFOGLE	HOOKAROON
HOLYTIDE	HOMILIZE	HOMONYM	HONEYFUGLE	HOOKED
HOMA	HOMILY	HOMONYMIC	HONEYLIPPED	HOOKEDNESS
HOMAGE	HOMINAL	HOMONYMOUS	HONEYMONTH	HOOKER
HOMAGEABLE	HOMINESS	HOMONYMY	HONEYMOON	HOOKERS
HOMAGER	HOMING	HOMOPATHY	HONEYMOONY	HOOKHEAL
HOMALOID	HOMINID	HOMOPHENE	HONEYMOUTHED	HOOKLAND
HOMARD	HOMININE	HOMOPHONE	HONEYPOD	HOOKLET
HOMATOMIC	HOMINOID	HOMOPHONIC	HONEYPOT	HOOKLIKE
HOMAXIAL	HOMINY	HOMOPHONY	HONEYS	HOOKMAN
HOME	HOMISH	HOMOPHYLIC	HONEYSUCK	HOOKNOSE
HOMEBODY	HOMISHNESS	HOMOPHYLY	HONEYSUCKER	HOOKS
HOMEBORN	HOMME	HOMOPLASIS	HONEYSUCKLE	HOOKSHOP
HOMEBOUND	HOMO	HOMOPLASMIC	HONEYSUCKLED	HOOKTIP
HOMEBRED	HOMOBARIC	HOMOPLASMY	HONEYSWEET	HOOKUM
HOMECOMING	HOMOBLASTIC	HOMOPLASSY	HONEYWARE	HOOKUP
HOMECRAFT	HOMOBLASTY	HOMOPLAST	HONEYWOOD	HOOKUPU
HOMECROFT	HOMOCENTRIC	HOMOPLASTIC	HONEYWORT	HOOKWEED
HOMEFELT	HOMOCENTRICAL	HOMOPLASY	HONG	HOOKWORM
HOMEKEEPER	HOMOCERC	HOMOPOLAR	HONIED	HOOKWORMER
HOMEKEEPING	HOMOCERCAL	HOMOPOLIC	HONK	HOOKWORMY
HOMELAND	HOMOCERCY	HOMOPTER	HONKER	HOOKY
HOMELESS	HOMOCEREBRIN	HOMORGANIC	HONKIE	HOOLAKIN
HOMELIFE	HOMOCHIRAL	HOMOSEXUAL	HONKIES	HOOLAULEA
HOMELIKE	HOMOCHROME	HOMOSEXUALITY	HONKY	HOOLEY
HOMELIKENESS	HOMOCHROMIC	HOMOSTYLED	HONOR	HOOLIE
HOMELILY	HOMOCHRONOUS	HOMOSTYLIC	HONORABILITY	HOOLIGAN
HOMELINESS	HOMOCLINE	HOMOSTYLY	HONORABLE	HOOLIHAN
HOMELING	HOMOCYCLIC	HOMOTACTIC	HONORABLENESS	HOOLOCK
HOMELY	HOMODERMIC	HOMOTATIC	HONORABLY	HOOLY
HOMELYN	HOMODERMY	HOMOTAXIS	HONORANCE	HOON
HOMEMADE	HOMODONT	HOMOTAXY	HONORARIUM	HOONDEE
HOMEMAKER	HOMODOX	HOMOTHALLIC	HONORARY	HOONDI
HOMEMAKING	HOMODROMAL	HOMOTHETIC	HONORED	HOOP
HOMEOID	HOMODROME	HOMOTHETY	HONORER	HOOPED
HOMEOIDAL	HOMODROMY	HOMOTONIC	HONORIFIC	HOOPER
HOMEOPATH	HOMODYNAMIC	HOMOTONY	HONORIFICALLY	HOOPING
HOMEOPOLAR	HOMODYNE	HOMOTOPIC	HONORS	HOOPLA
HOMEOSIS	HOMOEOMERIC	HOMOTROPAL	HONOUR	HOOPLE
HOMEOSTASIS	HOMOEOMERY	HOMOTYPAL	HONOURABILITY	HOOPLIKE
HOMEOSTATIC	HOMOGAMY	HOMOTYPE	HONOURABLE	HOOPMAKER
HOMEOTIC	HOMOGEN	HOMOTYPIC	HONOURABLY	HOOPMAN
HOMEOTYPE	HOMOGENE	HOMOTYPY	HONOURER	HOOPOE
HOMEOTYPIC	HOMOGENEAL	HOMOZYGOTE	HONOURS	HOOPS
HOMEOWNER	HOMOGENEITY	HOMOZYGOUS	HONTISH	HOOPSKIRT
HOMER	HOMOGENEOUS	HOMUNCIO	HONTOUS	HOOPSTER
HOMEROOM	HOMOGENESIS	HOMUNCLE	HOO	HOOPSTICK
HOMESEEKER	HOMOGENETIC	HOMY	HOOCH	HOOPWOOD
HOMESICK	HOMOGENIZE	HON	HOOD	HOORAH
HOMESICKLY	HOMOGENIZER	HONAN	HOODCAP	HOORAY
HOMESICKNESS	HOMOGENOUS	HONDA	HOODED	HOOROOSH
HOMESITE	HOMOGENY	HONDO	HOODIE	HOOSE
HOMESOME	HOMOGLOT	HONE	HOODING	HOOSEGOW
HOMESPUN	HOMOGONE	HONEST	HOODLUM	HOOSH
HOMESTALL	HOMOGONY	HONESTLY	HOODMAN	HOOT
HOMESTEAD	HOMOGRAPH	HONESTONE	HOODMOLD	HOOTAY
HOMESTEADER	HOMOGRAPHIC	HONESTY	HOODOO	HOOTER
HOMESTER	HOMOGRAPHY	HONEWORT	HOODSHY	HOOTS
HOMESTRETCH	HOMOHEDRAL	HONEY	HOODSHYNESS	HOOVE
HOMETOWN	HOMOLATERAL	HONEYBALLS	HOODWINK	HOOVEY
HOMEWARD	HOMOLOG	HONEYBEE	HOODWINKER	HOOZE
HOMEWARDLY	HOMOLOGATE	HONEYBEES	HOODWORT	HOP
HOMEWARDS	HOMOLOGIC	HONEYBERRY	HOODY	HOPBIND
HOMEWORK	HOMOLOGICAL	HONEYBIND	HOOEY	HOPBINE
HOMEWORKER	HOMOLOGIES	HONEYBLOB	HOOF	HOPBUSH
HOMEWORT	HOMOLOGIZE	HONEYBLOOM	HOOFBEAT	HOPCALITE
HOMEY	HOMOLOGON	HONEYBUN	HOOFBOUND	HOPCREASE
HOMEYNESS	HOMOLOGOUS	HONEYCOMB	HOOFED	HOPE
HOMICIDAL	HOMOLOGUE	HONEYCOMBED	HOOFER	HOPED

HOPEFUL
HOPEFULLY
HOPEFULNESS
HOPEITE
HOPELESS
HOPELESSLY
HOPELESSNESS
HOPER
HOPHEAD
HOPLITE
HOPLITIC
HOPLOLOGY
HOPLOMACHIC
HOPLOMACHY
HOPO
HOPOFF
HOPPE
HOPPED
HOPPER
HOPPERBURN
HOPPERDOZER
HOPPERETTE
HOPPERINGS
HOPPERMAN
HOPPERS
HOPPESTERE
HOPPET
HOPPING
HOPPITY
HOPPLE
HOPPO
HOPPY
HOPS
HOPSACK
HOPSACKING
HOPSAGE
HOPSCOTCH
HOPTOAD
HOPVINE
HOPYARD
HORA
HORAL
HORARY
HORBACHITE
HORDARIAN
HORDARY
HORDE
HORDEACEOUS
HORDEATE
HORDEIFORM
HORDEIN
HORDENINE
HORDEOLUM
HORDOCK
HORE
HOREHOUND
HORISMOLOGY
HORIZOMETER
HORIZON
HORIZONTAL
HORIZONTALITY
HORIZONTALIZE
HORIZONTALLY
HORIZONTIC
HORIZONTICAL
HORIZONTICALLY
HORKEY
HORME
HORMIC
HORMIGO
HORMION
HORMISM
HORMIST
HORMONE
HORMONES
HORMOS
HORN

HORNADA
HORNBEAM
HORNBILL
HORNBLENDE
HORNBLOWER
HORNBOOK
HORNED
HORNER
HORNERAH
HORNERO
HORNET
HORNETY
HORNFAIR
HORNFELS
HORNFISH
HORNGELD
HORNIFY
HORNING
HORNIST
HORNITO
HORNKECK
HORNLESS
HORNLIKE
HORNOTINE
HORNPIE
HORNPIPE
HORNPLANT
HORNS
HORNSLATE
HORNSMAN
HORNSTAY
HORNSTONE
HORNSWOGGLE
HORNTAIL
HORNTHUMB
HORNTIP
HORNWEED
HORNWOOD
HORNWORK
HORNWORM
HORNWORT
HORNY
HORNYHANDED
HORNYHEAD
HOROGRAPH
HOROGRAPHER
HOROGRAPHY
HOROKAKA
HOROLOGE
HOROLOGER
HOROLOGIC
HOROLOGICAL
HOROLOGICALLY
HOROLOGIST
HOROLOGIUM
HOROLOGUE
HOROLOGY
HOROMETRY
HOROPITO
HOROPTER
HOROPTERIC
HOROPTERY
HOROSCOPAL
HOROSCOPE
HOROSCOPER
HOROSCOPICAL
HOROSCOPIST
HOROSCOPY
HOROTELY
HORRAL
HORRENDOUS
HORRENDOUSLY
HORRENT
HORRESCENT
HORREUM
HORRIBLE
HORRIBLENESS

HORRIBLES
HORRIBLY
HORRID
HORRIDITY
HORRIDLY
HORRIFIC
HORRIFICATION
HORRIFIED
HORRIFY
HORRIFYING
HORRIPILANT
HORRIPILATE
HORRISONANT
HORROR
HORROROUS
HORRORS
HORRORSOME
HORRY
HORS
HORSE
HORSEBACK
HORSEBACKER
HORSEBANE
HORSEBLOCK
HORSEBOY
HORSEBREAKER
HORSEBUSH
HORSECAR
HORSECLOTH
HORSEDRAWING
HORSEFAIR
HORSEFIGHT
HORSEFISH
HORSEFLESH
HORSEFLIES
HORSEFLOWER
HORSEFLY
HORSEFOOT
HORSEGATE
HORSEHAIR
HORSEHAIRED
HORSEHEAD
HORSEHEAL
HORSEHEEL
HORSEHIDE
HORSEHOOF
HORSEKEEPER
HORSEKEEPING
HORSELAUGH
HORSELAUGHTER
HORSELEACH
HORSELEECH
HORSELESS
HORSELOAD
HORSELOCK
HORSELY
HORSEMAN
HORSEMANSHIP
HORSEMEN
HORSEMINT
HORSENAIL
HORSEPIPE
HORSEPOND
HORSEPOWER
HORSEPOX
HORSER
HORSERADISH
HORSES
HORSESHOE
HORSESHOER
HORSETAIL
HORSETONGUE
HORSETREE
HORSEWAY
HORSEWEED
HORSEWHIP
HORSEWHIPPER

HORSEWOMAN
HORSEWOMANSHIP
HORSEWOOD
HORSFORDITE
HORSIFY
HORSINESS
HORSING
HORST
HORSTE
HORSY
HORSYISM
HORTATION
HORTATIVE
HORTATOR
HORTATORILY
HORTATORY
HORTENSIAL
HORTESIAN
HORTICULTURAL
HORTICULTURALLY
HORTICULTURE
HORTITE
HORTONOLITE
HORTULAN
HORTYARD
HORY
HOSANNA
HOSE
HOSEBIRD
HOSED
HOSEL
HOSEMAN
HOSEN
HOSEPIPE
HOSIER
HOSIERY
HOSIOMARTYR
HOSPICE
HOSPITABLE
HOSPITABLENESS
HOSPITABLY
HOSPITAGE
HOSPITAL
HOSPITALARY
HOSPITALER
HOSPITALISM
HOSPITALITY
HOSPITALIZATION
HOSPITALIZE
HOSPITALLER
HOSPITANT
HOSPITATE
HOSPITIUM
HOSPODAR
HOSPODARIAT
HOSPODARIATE
HOSS
HOST
HOSTAGE
HOSTAGER
HOSTEL
HOSTELER
HOSTELRY
HOSTER
HOSTESS
HOSTILE
HOSTILELY
HOSTILENESS
HOSTILITIES
HOSTILITY
HOSTING
HOSTLE
HOSTLER
HOSTLERWIFE
HOSTLY
HOSTRY
HOT

HOTBED
HOTBLOOD
HOTBOX
HOTCH
HOTCHA
HOTCHPOT
HOTCHPOTCH
HOTCHPOTCHLY
HOTE
HOTEL
HOTELIER
HOTELKEEPER
HOTFOOT
HOTHEAD
HOTHEADED
HOTHEADEDLY
HOTHEADEDNESS
HOTHOUSE
HOTI
HOTLY
HOTMELT
HOTMOUTHED
HOTNESS
HOTPRESS
HOTSPUR
HOTSPURRED
HOTT
HOTTER
HOTTERY
HOTTLE
HOUBARA
HOUGH
HOUGHER
HOUGHITE
HOUGHMAGANDY
HOUGHSINEW
HOUHERE
HOUNCE
HOUND
HOUNDER
HOUNDFISH
HOUNDING
HOUNDMAN
HOUNDS
HOUNDSBANE
HOUNDSBERRY
HOUNDSHARK
HOUNDY
HOUPPELANDE
HOUR
HOURGLASS
HOURI
HOURLY
HOUSAGE
HOUSAL
HOUSE
HOUSEBALL
HOUSEBOAT
HOUSEBOATING
HOUSEBOTE
HOUSEBOUND
HOUSEBOY
HOUSEBREAK
HOUSEBREAKER
HOUSEBROKE
HOUSEBROKEN
HOUSEBUG
HOUSEBUILDER
HOUSECARL
HOUSECOAT
HOUSEDRESS
HOUSEFAST
HOUSEFATHER
HOUSEFLY
HOUSEFUL
HOUSEHOLD
HOUSEHOLDER

HOUSEHOLDING	HOWLER	HUERTA	HUMANITIES	HUMORIZE
HOUSEHOLDRY	HOWLET	HUFFCAP	HUMANITY	HUMOROUS
HOUSEKEEP	HOWLING	HUFFER	HUMANIZE	HUMOROUSLY
HOUSEKEEPER	HOWLINGLY	HUFFILY	HUMANIZER	HUMOROUSNESS
HOUSEKEEPERLY	HOWLITE	HUFFINESS	HUMANKIND	HUMORS
HOUSEKEEPING	HOWSO	HUFFINGLY	HUMANLY	HUMOUR
HOUSEL	HOWSOEVER	HUFFISH	HUMANOID	HUMOURAL
HOUSELEEK	HOWSOMEVER	HUFFISHLY	HUMATE	HUMOURIST
HOUSELESS	HOWSOUR	HUFFISHNESS	HUMATION	HUMOURIZE
HOUSELINE	HOX	HUFFLE	HUMBIRD	HUMOURS
HOUSELING	HOY	HUFFLER	HUMBLE	HUMOUS
HOUSEMAID	HOYDEN	HUFFY	HUMBLEBEE	HUMP
HOUSEMAIDENLY	HOYMAN	HUG	HUMBLED	HUMPBACK
HOUSEMAIDY	HSIEN	HUGE	HUMBLENESS	HUMPBACKED
HOUSEMAN	HSIN	HUGELITE	HUMBLER	HUMPED
HOUSEMASTER	HU	HUGELY	HUMBLESSO	HUMPH
HOUSEMATE	HUACA	HUGENESS	HUMBLIE	HUMPINESS
HOUSEMINDER	HUACO	HUGEOUS	HUMBLING	HUMPTY
HOUSEMISTRESS	HUAJILLO	HUGEOUSLY	HUMBLY	HUMPY
HOUSEMOTHER	HUAMUCHIL	HUGEOUSNESS	HUMBO	HUMSTRUM
HOUSER	HUAPANGO	HUGGABLE	HUMBOLDTITE	HUMULENE
HOUSERIDDEN	HUARACHE	HUGGER	HUMBUG	HUMULON
HOUSEROOM	HUARACHO	HUGGING	HUMBUGGER	HUMULONE
HOUSES	HUARIZO	HUGGLE	HUMBUZZ	HUMUS
HOUSESMITH	HUB	HUGMATEE	HUMDINGER	HUNCH
HOUSETOP	HUBAM	HUGONIS	HUMDRUM	HUNCHBACK
HOUSEWARES	HUBB	HUH	HUMECT	HUNCHBACKED
HOUSEWARM	HUBBA	HUHU	HUMECTANT	HUNCHET
HOUSEWARMING	HUBBABOO	HUI	HUMECTATE	HUNCHY
HOUSEWIFE	HUBBER	HUIA	HUMERAL	HUNDER
HOUSEWIFELY	HUBBLE	HUILA	HUMERUS	HUNDI
HOUSEWIFERY	HUBBLY	HUIPIL	HUMET	HUNDRED
HOUSEWIVES	HUBBUB	HUIPILLA	HUMETTEE	HUNDREDAL
HOUSEWORK	HUBBUBOO	HUISACHE	HUMETTY	HUNDREDER
HOUSEWRIGHT	HUBBY	HUISCOYOL	HUMHUM	HUNDREDFOLD
HOUSING	HUBCAP	HUISHER	HUMIC	HUNDREDPENNY
HOUSINGS	HUBNERITE	HUISQUIL	HUMID	HUNDREDTH
HOUSTONIA	HUBRIS	HUISSIER	HUMIDATE	HUNDREDWEIGHT
HOUSTY	HUBRISTIC	HUITAIN	HUMIDIFIER	HUNDREDWORK
HOUSY	HUBSHI	HUITRE	HUMIDIFY	HUNFYSH
HOUTING	HUCCATOON	HUKE	HUMIDITY	HUNG
HOUTOU	HUCH	HULA	HUMIDLY	HUNGARITE
HOUVARI	HUCHEN	HULCH	HUMIDNESS	HUNGER
HOUVE	HUCHO	HULCHY	HUMIDOR	HUNGERINGLY
HOVEDANCE	HUCK	HULDEE	HUMIFIC	HUNGERLY
HOVEL	HUCKABACK	HULDI	HUMIFUSE	HUNGERROOT
HOVELER	HUCKLE	HULK	HUMIFY	HUNGERWEED
HOVELLER	HUCKLEBACK	HULKAGE	HUMILIANT	HUNGRIER
HOVEN	HUCKLEBACKED	HULKING	HUMILIATE	HUNGRIEST
HOVER	HUCKLEBERRIES	HULKY	HUMILIATED	HUNGRIFY
HOVERCRAFT	HUCKLEBERRY	HULL	HUMILIATION	HUNGRILY
HOVERER	HUCKLEBONE	HULLABALOO	HUMILITIES	HUNGRINESS
HOVERING	HUCKMUCK	HULLED	HUMILITY	HUNGRY
HOVERINGLY	HUCKSTER	HULLER	HUMIN	HUNH
HOVERLY	HUCKSTERER	HULLING	HUMIT	HUNIA
HOW	HUCKSTERISM	HULLO	HUMITE	HUNK
HOWADJI	HUCKSTERY	HULLOCK	HUMLIE	HUNKER
HOWARDITE	HUD	HULLOO	HUMMAUL	HUNKEROUS
HOWBEIT	HUDDERON	HULLS	HUMMEL	HUNKERS
HOWD	HUDDLE	HULSITE	HUMMELER	HUNKIES
HOWDAH	HUDDLER	HULSTER	HUMMER	HUNKS
HOWDER	HUDDLING	HULU	HUMMIE	HUNKY
HOWDIE	HUDDOCK	HULVER	HUMMING	HUNNER
HOWDY	HUDDROUN	HULVERHEAD	HUMMINGBIRD	HUNT
HOWE	HUDDUP	HULVERHEADED	HUMMINGLY	HUNTER
HOWEL	HUDE	HULWORT	HUMMOCK	HUNTILITE
HOWEVER	HUDGE	HUM	HUMMOCKY	HUNTING
HOWF	HUDSONIA	HUMAN	HUMMUM	HUNTRESS
HOWFF	HUE	HUMANE	HUMOR	HUNTSMAN
HOWFING	HUED	HUMANELY	HUMORAL	HUNTSWOMAN
HOWGATES	HUEFUL	HUMANENESS	HUMORALISM	HUP
HOWISH	HUEHUETL	HUMANIFY	HUMORALIST	HUPP
HOWITZ	HUEL	HUMANISM	HUMORED	HURA
HOWITZER	HUELESS	HUMANIST	HUMORESQUE	HURCHEON
HOWK	HUELESSNESS	HUMANISTIC	HUMORISM	HURDIES
HOWKIT	HUEMUL	HUMANITARIAN	HUMORIST	HURDIS
HOWL	HUER	HUMANITARY	HUMORISTIC	HURDLE

HURDLEMAN
HURDLER
HURDLES
HURDS
HURE
HUREAULITE
HUREEK
HURGILA
HURKLE
HURL
HURLBARROW
HURLBAT
HURLED
HURLEMENT
HURLER
HURLEY
HURLEYHACKET
HURLEYHOUSE
HURLIES
HURLING
HURLOCK
HURLY
HURON
HURR
HURRAH
HURRAY
HURRER
HURRICANE
HURRICANIZE
HURRICANO
HURRIED
HURRIEDLY
HURRIEDNESS
HURRIER
HURRIES
HURRISOME
HURROCK
HURROO
HURROOSH
HURRY
HURSE
HURST
HURT
HURTER
HURTFUL
HURTFULLY
HURTFULNESS
HURTING
HURTINGEST
HURTLE
HURTLEBERRY
HURTLESS
HURTLESSLY
HURTLESSNESS
HURTLING
HURTSOME
HURTY
HUSBAND
HUSBANDAGE
HUSBANDED
HUSBANDER
HUSBANDFIELD
HUSBANDLAND
HUSBANDLY
HUSBANDMAN
HUSBANDRESS
HUSBANDRY
HUSCARL
HUSE
HUSH
HUSHABY
HUSHCLOTH
HUSHED
HUSHEEN
HUSHEL
HUSHER
HUSHFUL

HUSHING
HUSHION
HUSHPUPPIES
HUSHPUPPY
HUSI
HUSK
HUSKANAW
HUSKED
HUSKENED
HUSKER
HUSKIER
HUSKIEST
HUSKING
HUSKROOT
HUSKS
HUSKWORT
HUSKY
HUSO
HUSPEL
HUSPIL
HUSS
HUSSAR
HUSSIES
HUSSY
HUST
HUSTING
HUSTINGS
HUSTLE
HUSTLECAP
HUSTLEMENT
HUSTLER
HUSTLING
HUT
HUTCH
HUTCHER
HUTCHET
HUTHOLD
HUTIA
HUTKEEPER
HUTMENT
HUTS
HUTTONING
HUTTONWEED
HUTUKHTU
HUTUKTU
HUTUNG
HUTZPAH
HUURDER
HUVELYK
HUXEN
HUZ
HUZOOR
HUZZ
HUZZA
HUZZAH
HUZZARD
HUZZY
HWAN
HY
HYACINTH
HYACINTHINE
HYAENA
HYAENID
HYAHYA
HYALESCENCE
HYALESCENT
HYALIN
HYALINIZE
HYALITE
HYALITHE
HYALITIS
HYALOGEN
HYALOGRAPH
HYALOGRAPHER
HYALOGRAPHY
HYALOID

HYALOLIPARITE
HYALOLITH
HYALOMUCOID
HYALOPLASM
HYALOPLASMA
HYALOPLASMIC
HYALOPSITE
HYALOSIDERITE
HYALOTEKITE
HYALOTYPE
HYBODONT
HYBOSIS
HYBRID
HYBRIDAL
HYBRIDATION
HYBRIDISM
HYBRIDITY
HYBRIDIZABLE
HYBRIDIZATION
HYBRIDIZE
HYBRIDIZER
HYBRIDOUS
HYBRIS
HYDANTOIC
HYDANTOIN
HYDATHODE
HYDATID
HYDATIFORM
HYDATOGENESIS
HYDATOGENIC
HYDATOID
HYDATOMORPHIC
HYDNOID
HYDRA
HYDRACID
HYDRACORAL
HYDRACRYLATE
HYDRACRYLIC
HYDRAE
HYDRAGOG
HYDRAGOGUE
HYDRAGOGY
HYDRAMINE
HYDRANGEA
HYDRANT
HYDRANTH
HYDRARCH
HYDRASE
HYDRASTINE
HYDRATE
HYDRATED
HYDRATION
HYDRATOR
HYDRAULIC
HYDRAULICS
HYDRAZIN
HYDRAZINE
HYDRAZOATE
HYDRAZOIC
HYDRAZONE
HYDRIA
HYDRIC
HYDRIDE
HYDRIFORM
HYDRIODIC
HYDRION
HYDRO
HYDROA
HYDROAERIC
HYDROAROMATIC
HYDROBENZOIN
HYDROBIOLOGY
HYDROBIOSIS
HYDROBIPLANE
HYDROBROMATE
HYDROBROMIC
HYDROBROMID

HYDROBROMIDE
HYDROCARBON
HYDROCARBONATE
HYDROCARBONIC
HYDROCAULINE
HYDROCAULUS
HYDROCELE
HYDROCEPHALIC
HYDROCEPHALY
HYDROCERAMIC
HYDROCHLORATE
HYDROCHLORIC
HYDROCHLORID
HYDROCHLORIDE
HYDROCLADIUM
HYDROCLASTIC
HYDROCOELE
HYDROCONION
HYDROCYANIC
HYDROCYANIDE
HYDROCYCLE
HYDROCYCLIC
HYDROCYCLIST
HYDROCYST
HYDROCYSTIC
HYDRODYNAMIC
HYDRODYNAMICS
HYDROELECTRIC
HYDROEXTRACT
HYDROEXTRACTOR
HYDROFLUATE
HYDROFLUORIC
HYDROFOIL
HYDROFUGE
HYDROGEL
HYDROGEN
HYDROGENASE
HYDROGENATE
HYDROGENATOR
HYDROGENIC
HYDROGENIZE
HYDROGEOLOGY
HYDROGLIDER
HYDROGNOSY
HYDROGODE
HYDROGRAPH
HYDROGRAPHER
HYDROGRAPHIC
HYDROGRAPHY
HYDROHALID
HYDROHALIDE
HYDROHEMATITE
HYDROID
HYDROKINETIC
HYDROL
HYDROLASE
HYDROLATRY
HYDROLOGIC
HYDROLOGICAL
HYDROLOGICALLY
HYDROLOGIST
HYDROLYSIS
HYDROLYST
HYDROLYTE
HYDROLYTIC
HYDROLYZATE
HYDROLYZE
HYDROMANIA
HYDROMANIAC
HYDROMANTIC
HYDROME
HYDROMEL
HYDROMETER
HYDROMETRA
HYDROMETRIC
HYDROMETRID
HYDROMETRY

HYDROMICA
HYDROMOTOR
HYDROMYOMA
HYDRONE
HYDRONITRIC
HYDRONIUM
HYDROPATH
HYDROPATHIC
HYDROPATHY
HYDROPERIOD
HYDROPHANE
HYDROPHANOUS
HYDROPHID
HYDROPHIL
HYDROPHILE
HYDROPHILIC
HYDROPHILID
HYDROPHILY
HYDROPHOBE
HYDROPHOBIA
HYDROPHOBIC
HYDROPHOBICAL
HYDROPHOBIST
HYDROPHOBOUS
HYDROPHONE
HYDROPHORIA
HYDROPHYLL
HYDROPHYLLIUM
HYDROPHYTE
HYDROPHYTIC
HYDROPHYTON
HYDROPIC
HYDROPICAL
HYDROPLANE
HYDROPOLYP
HYDROPONIC
HYDROPONICS
HYDROPOT
HYDROPS
HYDROPSY
HYDROPTIC
HYDROPULT
HYDROQUININE
HYDROQUINONE
HYDRORHIZA
HYDRORHIZAL
HYDRORRHEA
HYDRORRHOEA
HYDRORUBBER
HYDROSALT
HYDROSCOPE
HYDROSCOPIC
HYDROSELENIDE
HYDROSOL
HYDROSOLE
HYDROSOMA
HYDROSOME
HYDROSORBIC
HYDROSPHERE
HYDROSPIRE
HYDROSPIRIC
HYDROSTAT
HYDROSTATIC
HYDROSTATICS
HYDROSTOME
HYDROSULFATE
HYDROTALCITE
HYDROTAXIS
HYDROTECHNIC
HYDROTECHNY
HYDROTERPENE
HYDROTHECA
HYDROTHECAL
HYDROTHERAPY
HYDROTHERMAL
HYDROTHORAX
HYDROTYPE

HYDROUS
HYDROVANE
HYDROXIDE
HYDROZINCITE
HYDROZOAL
HYDROZOAN
HYDROZOIC
HYDROZOON
HYDRULA
HYE
HYENA
HYENIA
HYENIC
HYENINE
HYENOID
HYETAL
HYETOGRAPH
HYETOGRAPHIC
HYETOGRAPHY
HYGEEN
HYGEIST
HYGEISTIC
HYGIEIST
HYGIENE
HYGIENIC
HYGIENICS
HYGIENIST
HYGIENIZE
HYGRE
HYGRIC
HYGRIN
HYGRINE
HYGRODEIK
HYGROGRAPH
HYGROMA
HYGROMETER
HYGROMETRIC
HYGROMETRY
HYGROPHOBIA
HYGROPHYTE
HYGROPLASM
HYGROSCOPE
HYGROSCOPIC
HYGROSCOPY
HYGROSTAT
HYGROSTATICS
HYGROSTOMIA
HYGROTHERMAL
HYINGLY
HYKE
HYLA
HYLACTIC
HYLE
HYLEAN
HYLEG
HYLEGIACAL
HYLIC
HYLICIST
HYLID
HYLISM
HYLOID
HYLOLOGY
HYLOTHEISM
HYLOTHEIST
HYLOZOIC
HYLOZOISM
HYLOZOIST
HYMEN
HYMENAL
HYMENEAL
HYMENEALS
HYMENEAN
HYMENIAL
HYMENIC
HYMENIUM
HYMENOID
HYMN

HYMNAL
HYMNARY
HYMNBOOK
HYMNER
HYMNIC
HYMNIST
HYMNODE
HYMNODIST
HYMNODY
HYMNOLOGY
HYNDE
HYNE
HYOID
HYOIDES
HYOMENTAL
HYOPLASTRAL
HYOPLASTRON
HYOSCINE
HYOSTERNAL
HYOSTERNUM
HYOSTYLIC
HYOSTYLY
HYOTHERE
HYP
HYPALGIA
HYPALLAGE
HYPANTRUM
HYPASPIST
HYPATE
HYPATON
HYPAXIAL
HYPE
HYPER
HYPERABELIAN
HYPERACUSIA
HYPERALGESIA
HYPERALGESIC
HYPERALGESIS
HYPERAPHIA
HYPERAPHIC
HYPERBARIC
HYPERBARISM
HYPERBATIC
HYPERBATON
HYPERBOLA
HYPERBOLAS
HYPERBOLE
HYPERBOLIC
HYPERBOLISM
HYPERBOLIZE
HYPERBOLIZED
HYPERBOLIZING
HYPERBOREAL
HYPERBOREAN
HYPERBULIA
HYPERCONE
HYPERCORACOID
HYPERCORRECT
HYPERCRITIC
HYPERCRITICAL
HYPERCUBE
HYPERCYCLE
HYPERCYLINDER
HYPERDACTYL
HYPERDIAPASON
HYPERDIAPENTE
HYPERDITONE
HYPERDULIA
HYPERDULIC
HYPERELLIPTIC
HYPEREMESIS
HYPEREMIA
HYPEREMIC
HYPERESSENCE
HYPERESTHESIA
HYPERESTHETIC
HYPEREUTECTIC

HYPERFOCAL
HYPERGAMY
HYPERGEOMETRY
HYPERGOLIC
HYPERIN
HYPERKINESIA
HYPERKINESIS
HYPERKINETIC
HYPERMETER
HYPERMETRIC
HYPERMETRICAL
HYPERMORPH
HYPERNIC
HYPERON
HYPEROON
HYPEROPIC
HYPEROSMIA
HYPEROSMIC
HYPEROSTOSIS
HYPEROSTOTIC
HYPEROTRETAN
HYPEROXIDE
HYPERPENCIL
HYPERPER
HYPERPHORIA
HYPERPHORIC
HYPERPIESIA
HYPERPIESIS
HYPERPIETIC
HYPERPLANE
HYPERPLASIA
HYPERPLASTIC
HYPERPLOID
HYPERPLOIDY
HYPERPNEA
HYPERPRISM
HYPERPYRAMID
HYPERPYRETIC
HYPERSOLID
HYPERSONIC
HYPERSONICS
HYPERSPACE
HYPERSPHERE
HYPERTELY
HYPERTHESIS
HYPERTHETIC
HYPERTHYROID
HYPERTONIA
HYPERTONIC
HYPERTONUS
HYPERTROPHY
HYPERTROPIA
HYPERTYPE
HYPERTYPIC
HYPERTYPICAL
HYPETHRAL
HYPHA
HYPHAE
HYPHAL
HYPHEMA
HYPHEMIA
HYPHEN
HYPHENATE
HYPHENATED
HYPHENED
HYPHO
HYPHODROME
HYPNALE
HYPNOBATE
HYPNOCYST
HYPNODY
HYPNOETIC
HYPNOID
HYPNOIDAL
HYPNOIDIZE
HYPNOLOGIC
HYPNOLOGY

HYPNOSIS
HYPNOSPORE
HYPNOSPORIC
HYPNOTIC
HYPNOTISM
HYPNOTIST
HYPNOTIZE
HYPNOTOID
HYPO
HYPOADENIA
HYPOADRENIA
HYPOBARIC
HYPOBARISM
HYPOBASAL
HYPOBLAST
HYPOBLASTIC
HYPOBOLE
HYPOBROMITES
HYPOBROMOUS
HYPOBULIA
HYPOBULIC
HYPOCARP
HYPOCAUST
HYPOCENTER
HYPOCENTRUM
HYPOCHIL
HYPOCHNOSE
HYPOCHONDRIA
HYPOCHONDRIAC
HYPOCHORDAL
HYPOCHROMIA
HYPOCHROSIS
HYPOCIST
HYPOCONE
HYPOCORISTIC
HYPOCOTYL
HYPOCRATER
HYPOCRISIS
HYPOCRISY
HYPOCRITAL
HYPOCRITE
HYPOCRITIC
HYPOCRITICAL
HYPOCRITICALLY
HYPOCRIZE
HYPOCYCLOID
HYPOCYTOSIS
HYPODERM
HYPODERMA
HYPODERMAL
HYPODERMIC
HYPODERMIS
HYPODITONE
HYPOEUTECTIC
HYPOGAMY
HYPOGASTRIC
HYPOGEAL
HYPOGEAN
HYPOGEE
HYPOGEIC
HYPOGENE
HYPOGENESIS
HYPOGENIC
HYPOGEOUS
HYPOGEUM
HYPOGLOSSAL
HYPOGLOSSUS
HYPOGLOTTIS
HYPOGYNIC
HYPOGYNIUM
HYPOHALOUS
HYPOHEMIA
HYPOHIDROSIS
HYPOHYAL
HYPOID
HYPOMANIA
HYPOMANIC

HYPOMERAL
HYPOMERE
HYPOMORPH
HYPONASTIC
HYPONASTY
HYPONITRITE
HYPONOIA
HYPONOME
HYPONYM
HYPOPHARE
HYPOPHARYNX
HYPOPHONIC
HYPOPHORA
HYPOPHORIA
HYPOPHRENIA
HYPOPHYGE
HYPOPHYLL
HYPOPHYSE
HYPOPLASIA
HYPOPLASTIC
HYPOPLASTRAL
HYPOPLASTRON
HYPOPLOID
HYPOPNEA
HYPOPODIUM
HYPOPRAXIA
HYPOPTERAL
HYPOPTERON
HYPOPTILUM
HYPOPUS
HYPOPYON
HYPORADIAL
HYPORADIUS
HYPORHINED
HYPORIT
HYPOSCLERAL
HYPOSCOPE
HYPOSKELETAL
HYPOSMIA
HYPOSPADIAC
HYPOSPADIAS
HYPOSPHENE
HYPOSTASIS
HYPOSTATIC
HYPOSTATICAL
HYPOSTATIZE
HYPOSTHENIA
HYPOSTIGMA
HYPOSTILBITE
HYPOSTOMA
HYPOSTOME
HYPOSTYLE
HYPOSTYPSIS
HYPOSTYPTIC
HYPOTARSAL
HYPOTARSUS
HYPOTAXIA
HYPOTAXIC
HYPOTAXIS
HYPOTENSION
HYPOTENSIVE
HYPOTENSOR
HYPOTENUSE
HYPOTHEC
HYPOTHECA
HYPOTHECARY
HYPOTHECATE
HYPOTHECIAL
HYPOTHENAL
HYPOTHENAR
HYPOTHENIC
HYPOTHERMAL
HYPOTHERMIA
HYPOTHERMIC
HYPOTHESIS
HYPOTHETICAL
HYPOTONIC

HYPOTOXICITY
HYPOTRACHELIUM
HYPOTROPHY
HYPOTYPE
HYPOTYPIC
HYPOVALVE
HYPOVANADATE
HYPOVANADIC
HYPOXANTHIC
HYPOXANTHINE
HYPOZEUGMA
HYPOZEUXIS
HYPOZOAN
HYPOZOIC
HYPPISH
HYPSIPYLE
HYPSOMETER
HYPSOMETRIC
HYPSOMETRY
HYPSOPHOBIA
HYPSOPHYLL
HYPURAL
HYRACEUM
HYRACID
HYRAX
HYRST
HYSON
HYSSOP
HYSTERIA
HYSTERIAC
HYSTERIC
HYSTERICAL
HYSTERICALLY
HYSTERICS
HYSTERIFORM
HYSTEROGEN
HYSTEROGENETIC
HYSTEROGENIC
HYSTEROID
HYSTEROLITH
HYSTEROLOGY
HYSTEROMANIA
HYSTEROMETER
HYSTEROMETRY
HYSTEROPATHY
HYSTEROSCOPE
HYSTEROTOME
HYTE

IAMATOLOGY
IAMB
IAMBELEGUS
IAMBIC
IAMBICAL
IAMBICALLY
IAMBIST
IAMBIZE
IAMBOGRAPHER
IAMBUS
IANTHINE
IANTHINITE
IAO
IATRALIPTIC
IATRALIPTICS
IATRIC
IATRICAL
IATROCHEMICAL
IATROCHEMISTRY
IATROGENIC
IATROLOGICAL
IATROLOGY
IATROPHYSICS
IATROTECHNICS
IBA
IBE
IBERITE
IBEX
IBEXES
IBICES
IBID
IBIDEM
IBIS
IBISBILL
IBISES
IBIT
IBOLIUM
IBOTA
ICACINACEOUS
ICACO
ICE
ICEBERG
ICEBLINK
ICEBOAT
ICEBONE
ICEBOUND
ICEBOX
ICEBREAKER
ICECAP
ICECRAFT
ICED
ICEFALL
ICEFISH
ICEFISHES
ICEHOUSE
ICELAND
ICELEAF
ICEMAN
ICEMEN
ICEQUAKE
ICER
ICEROOT
ICEWORK
ICH
ICHAM
ICHEBU
ICHIBU

ICHNEUMON
ICHNEUMONED
ICHNEUMOUS
ICHNEUTIC
ICHNITE
ICHNOGRAPHIC
ICHNOGRAPHY
ICHNOLITE
ICHNOLITIC
ICHNOLOGICAL
ICHNOLOGY
ICHNOMANCY
ICHO
ICHOGLAN
ICHOR
ICHOROUS
ICHORRHAEMIA
ICHORRHEA
ICHORRHEMIA
ICHORRHOEA
ICHTHULIN
ICHTHULINIC
ICHTHUS
ICHTHYAL
ICHTHYIC
ICHTHYISM
ICHTHYISMUS
ICHTHYIZATION
ICHTHYIZED
ICHTHYOCOL
ICHTHYOCOLLA
ICHTHYODIAN
ICHTHYODONT
ICHTHYOFAUNA
ICHTHYOID
ICHTHYOIDAL
ICHTHYOLATRY
ICHTHYOLITE
ICHTHYOLOGIC
ICHTHYOLOGY
ICHTHYOMANIA
ICHTHYOPHAGI
ICHTHYOPHAGY
ICHTHYOPSID
ICHTHYOSAUR
ICHTHYOSIS
ICHTHYOSISM
ICHTHYOTOMY
ICHTHYOTOXIN
ICHTHYS
ICHU
ICHULLE
ICICA
ICICLE
ICICLED
ICIER
ICIEST
ICILY
ICINESS
ICING
ICK
ICKER
ICKLE
ICKY
ICON
ICONES
ICONIC
ICONICAL
ICONISM
ICONOCLASM
ICONOCLAST
ICONOCLASTIC
ICONODULE
ICONODULIC
ICONODULIST
ICONODULY
ICONOGRAPH

ICONOGRAPHER
ICONOGRAPHIC
ICONOGRAPHIST
ICONOGRAPHY
ICONOLATER
ICONOLATROUS
ICONOLATRY
ICONOLOGICAL
ICONOLOGIST
ICONOLOGY
ICONOMACHAL
ICONOMACHIST
ICONOMACHY
ICONOMANIA
ICONOMATIC
ICONOMATICISM
ICONOMETER
ICONOMETRIC
ICONOMETRICAL
ICONOMETRY
ICONOPHILE
ICONOPHILISM
ICONOPHILIST
ICONOPHILY
ICONOPLAST
ICONOSCOPE
ICONOSTAS
ICONOSTASES
ICONOSTASION
ICONOSTASIS
ICONOTYPE
ICONS
ICOSAHEDRA
ICOSAHEDRAL
ICOSAHEDRON
ICOSASEMIC
ICOSIAN
ICOSTEID
ICOSTEINE
ICOTYPE
ICRE
ICTERIC
ICTERICAL
ICTERINE
ICTERITIOUS
ICTERITOUS
ICTERODE
ICTEROGENIC
ICTEROHEMATURIA
ICTEROID
ICTERUS
ICTIC
ICTUATE
ICTUS
ICTUSES
ICY
ID
IDAEIN
IDALIA
IDANT
IDDAT
IDE
IDEA
IDEAED
IDEAGENOUS
IDEAL
IDEALISM
IDEALIST
IDEALISTIC
IDEALISTICAL
IDEALISTICALLY
IDEALITIES
IDEALITY
IDEALIZATION
IDEALIZE
IDEALIZED
IDEALIZER

IDEALIZING
IDEALLY
IDEAS
IDEATE
IDEATED
IDEATING
IDEATION
IDEATIONAL
IDEATIONALLY
IDEATIVE
IDEATUM
IDEE
IDEIN
IDEIST
IDEM
IDEMPOTENT
IDENT
IDENTIC
IDENTICAL
IDENTICALISM
IDENTICALLY
IDENTIFICATION
IDENTIFIED
IDENTIFIER
IDENTIFY
IDENTIFYING
IDENTISM
IDENTITIES
IDENTITY
IDEOGENICAL
IDEOGENY
IDEOGLYPH
IDEOGRAM
IDEOGRAMMIC
IDEOGRAPH
IDEOGRAPHIC
IDEOGRAPHY
IDEOLOGIC
IDEOLOGICAL
IDEOLOGICALLY
IDEOLOGIES
IDEOLOGIST
IDEOLOGY
IDEOMANIA
IDEOMOTION
IDEOMOTOR
IDEOPHONE
IDEOPHONOUS
IDEOPLASTIA
IDEOPLASTIC
IDEOPLASTICS
IDEOPLASTY
IDEOPRAXIST
IDEOTYPE
IDES
IDESIA
IDGAH
IDIASM
IDIGBO
IDIOBLAST
IDIOBLASTIC
IDIOCRASIES
IDIOCRASIS
IDIOCRASY
IDIOCRATIC
IDIOCRATICAL
IDIOCY
IDIOELECTRIC
IDIOGENOUS
IDIOGLOSSIA
IDIOGLOTTIC
IDIOGRAM
IDIOGRAPH
IDIOGRAPHIC
IDIOGRAPHICAL
IDIOLATRY
IDIOLECT

IDIOLOGISM
IDIOM
IDIOMATIC
IDIOMATICAL
IDIOMATICALLY
IDIOMATICALNESS
IDIOMELON
IDIOMETER
IDIOMOGRAPHY
IDIOMOLOGY
IDIOMORPHIC
IDIOMORPHOUS
IDIOMUSCULAR
IDIOPATHETIC
IDIOPATHIC
IDIOPATHICAL
IDIOPATHICALLY
IDIOPATHIES
IDIOPATHY
IDIOPHANISM
IDIOPHANOUS
IDIOPHONE
IDIOPHONIC
IDIOPLASM
IDIOPLASMATIC
IDIOPLASMIC
IDIORETINAL
IDIOSOME
IDIOSPASM
IDIOSPASTIC
IDIOSTATIC
IDIOSYNCRASIES
IDIOSYNCRASY
IDIOSYNCRATIC
IDIOSYNCRATICA
IDIOT
IDIOTCIES
IDIOTCY
IDIOTHERMIC
IDIOTHERMOUS
IDIOTHERMY
IDIOTIC
IDIOTICAL
IDIOTICALLY
IDIOTICON
IDIOTISM
IDIOTROPIAN
IDIOTRY
IDIOTYPE
IDIOTYPIC
IDIOZOME
IDITE
IDITOL
IDLE
IDLEBY
IDLED
IDLEFUL
IDLEHEADED
IDLEHOOD
IDLEMAN
IDLEMEN
IDLENESS
IDLER
IDLESET
IDLESHIP
IDLESSE
IDLEST
IDLING
IDLY
IDOCRASE
IDOL
IDOLA
IDOLASTER
IDOLASTRE
IDOLATER
IDOLATRIC
IDOLATRICAL

IDOLATRIES
IDOLATRIZE
IDOLATRIZED
IDOLATRIZER
IDOLATRIZING
IDOLATROUS
IDOLATROUSLY
IDOLATRY
IDOLET
IDOLIFY
IDOLISH
IDOLISM
IDOLIST
IDOLISTIC
IDOLIZATION
IDOLIZE
IDOLIZED
IDOLIZER
IDOLIZING
IDOLOCLAST
IDOLOCLASTIC
IDOLODULIA
IDOLOMANCY
IDOLOMANIA
IDOLON
IDOLOTHYTE
IDOLOTHYTIC
IDOLOUS
IDOLUM
IDONEAL
IDONEITY
IDONEOUS
IDONEOUSNESS
IDORGAN
IDOSACCHARIC
IDOSE
IDRIALIN
IDRIALINE
IDRIALITE
IDROSIS
IDRYL
IDYL
IDYLER
IDYLIAN
IDYLIST
IDYLL
IDYLLER
IDYLLIA
IDYLLIAN
IDYLLIC
IDYLLICAL
IDYLLICALLY
IDYLLICISM
IDYLLION
IDYLLIST
IDYLLIUM
IE
IEROE
IF
IFE
IFFEN
IFFY
IFIL
IFRIT
IGAD
IGARAPE
IGELSTROMITE
IGITUR
IGLESIA
IGLOO
IGLU
IGNAME
IGNARO
IGNATIA
IGNAVIA
IGNAVY
IGNEOUS

IGNESCENT
IGNICOLIST
IGNIFEROUS
IGNIFIED
IGNIFORM
IGNIFUGE
IGNIFY
IGNIFYING
IGNIGENOUS
IGNIPOTENT
IGNIPUNCTURE
IGNITE
IGNITED
IGNITER
IGNITING
IGNITION
IGNITIVE
IGNITOR
IGNITRON
IGNIVOMOUS
IGNOBILITY
IGNOBLE
IGNOBLESSE
IGNOBLY
IGNOMINIES
IGNOMINIOUS
IGNOMINIOUSLY
IGNOMINY
IGNOMIOUS
IGNORAMUS
IGNORAMUSES
IGNORANCE
IGNORANT
IGNORANTISM
IGNORANTIST
IGNORANTLY
IGNORATION
IGNORE
IGNORED
IGNORER
IGNORING
IGNOTE
IGUANA
IGUANODONT
IGUANOID
IHI
IHLEITE
IHRAM
IIWI
IJMA
IJMAA
IJOLITE
IJUSSITE
IKARY
IKAT
IKBAL
IKEY
IKEYNESS
IKMO
IKON
IKONA
IL
ILD
ILE
ILEAC
ILEECTOMY
ILEITIS
ILEOCAECAL
ILEOCECAL
ILEOCOLIC
ILEOCOLITIS
ILEOSTOMIES
ILEOSTOMY
ILEOTOMY
ILESITE
ILEUM
ILEUS

ILEX
ILEXES
ILIAC
ILIACUS
ILIAHI
ILIAL
ILIAU
ILICACEOUS
ILICIC
ILICIN
ILIMA
ILIOCAUDALIS
ILION
ILIOPSOAS
ILIOPSOATIC
ILK
ILKA
ILKANE
ILL
ILLABORATE
ILLAPSABLE
ILLAPSE
ILLAPSED
ILLAPSING
ILLAPSIVE
ILLAQUEATE
ILLATION
ILLATIVE
ILLATIVELY
ILLAUDABLE
ILLAUDABLY
ILLAUDATION
ILLAUDATORY
ILLBRED
ILLE
ILLECEBROUS
ILLECK
ILLEGAL
ILLEGALITIES
ILLEGALITY
ILLEGALIZE
ILLEGALIZED
ILLEGALIZING
ILLEGALLY
ILLEGALNESS
ILLEGIBILITY
ILLEGIBLE
ILLEGIBLY
ILLEGITIMACIES
ILLEGITIMACY
ILLEGITIMATE
ILLEGITIMATED
ILLEGITIMATING
ILLEISM
ILLEIST
ILLER
ILLFARE
ILLGUIDE
ILLGUIDED
ILLGUIDING
ILLIBERAL
ILLIBERALITY
ILLIBERALLY
ILLICIT
ILLICITLY
ILLICITNESS
ILLIMITABLE
ILLIMITABLY
ILLIMITATE
ILLIMITATION
ILLIMITED
ILLINITION
ILLINIUM
ILLIPENE
ILLIQUATION
ILLIQUID
ILLIQUIDLY

ILLISH
ILLISION
ILLITE
ILLITERACIES
ILLITERACY
ILLITERAL
ILLITERATE
ILLITERATELY
ILLITERATURE
ILLIUM
ILLNESS
ILLOCAL
ILLOCALITY
ILLOCALLY
ILLOGIC
ILLOGICAL
ILLOGICALITY
ILLOGICIAN
ILLOGICITY
ILLORICATE
ILLOYAL
ILLTH
ILLUCIDATE
ILLUCIDATION
ILLUCIDATIVE
ILLUDE
ILLUDED
ILLUDER
ILLUDING
ILLUK
ILLUME
ILLUMED
ILLUMER
ILLUMINANCE
ILLUMINANT
ILLUMINATE
ILLUMINATED
ILLUMINATI
ILLUMINATING
ILLUMINATION
ILLUMINATISM
ILLUMINATIVE
ILLUMINATO
ILLUMINATOR
ILLUMINATORY
ILLUMINATUS
ILLUMINE
ILLUMINED
ILLUMINEE
ILLUMINER
ILLUMING
ILLUMINING
ILLUMINIST
ILLUMINOMETER
ILLUMINOUS
ILLUPI
ILLURE
ILLUREMENT
ILLUSIBLE
ILLUSION
ILLUSIONABLE
ILLUSIONAL
ILLUSIONARY
ILLUSIONED
ILLUSIONISM
ILLUSIONIST
ILLUSIVE
ILLUSIVELY
ILLUSIVENESS
ILLUSOR
ILLUSORILY
ILLUSORINESS
ILLUSORY
ILLUSTRABLE
ILLUSTRATE
ILLUSTRATED
ILLUSTRATING

ILLUSTRATION
ILLUSTRATIVE
ILLUSTRATOR
ILLUSTRATORY
ILLUSTRE
ILLUSTRICITY
ILLUSTRIOUS
ILLUTATE
ILLUTATION
ILLUVIAL
ILLUVIATION
ILLY
ILMENITE
ILMENORUTILE
ILOT
ILVAITE
ILYSIOID
IMAGE
IMAGED
IMAGER
IMAGERIAL
IMAGERIALLY
IMAGERY
IMAGES
IMAGINABLE
IMAGINAL
IMAGINANT
IMAGINARILY
IMAGINARY
IMAGINATE
IMAGINATED
IMAGINATING
IMAGINATION
IMAGINATIONAL
IMAGINATIVE
IMAGINATOR
IMAGINE
IMAGINED
IMAGINER
IMAGINES
IMAGING
IMAGINING
IMAGINIST
IMAGINOUS
IMAGISM
IMAGIST
IMAGISTIC
IMAGO
IMAGOES
IMAMAH
IMAMATE
IMAMBARA
IMAMBARAH
IMAMBARRA
IMAMIC
IMANLAUT
IMARET
IMAUM
IMAUMBARAH
IMBALANCE
IMBALM
IMBAN
IMBAND
IMBANNERED
IMBARGE
IMBARK
IMBARKATION
IMBARN
IMBASED
IMBASTARDIZE
IMBAT
IMBAUBA
IMBE
IMBECILE
IMBECILELY
IMBECILITATE
IMBECILITATED

IMBECILITIES	IMITANT	IMMENSITIES	IMMORALIST	IMPALER
IMBECILITY	IMITATE	IMMENSITY	IMMORALITIES	IMPALING
IMBED	IMITATED	IMMENSIVE	IMMORALITY	IMPALM
IMBEDDED	IMITATEE	IMMENSURABLE	IMMORIGEROUS	IMPALPABLE
IMBEDDING	IMITATING	IMMENSURATE	IMMORTABLE	IMPALPABLY
IMBELLIC	IMITATION	IMMERD	IMMORTAL	IMPALSY
IMBELLIOUS	IMITATIONAL	IMMERGE	IMMORTALISM	IMPALUDISM
IMBER	IMITATIONIST	IMMERGED	IMMORTALIST	IMPANATE
IMBERBE	IMITATIVE	IMMERGENCE	IMMORTALITY	IMPANATED
IMBIBE	IMITATIVELY	IMMERGENT	IMMORTALIZE	IMPANATION
IMBIBED	IMITATOR	IMMERGING	IMMORTALIZED	IMPANATOR
IMBIBER	IMMACULACY	IMMERIT	IMMORTALIZER	IMPANE
IMBIBING	IMMACULANCE	IMMERITED	IMMORTALIZING	IMPANEL
IMBIBITION	IMMACULATE	IMMERITORIOUS	IMMORTALLY	IMPANELED
IMBIBITIONAL	IMMACULATELY	IMMERSE	IMMORTELLE	IMPANELING
IMBIBITORY	IMMALLEABLE	IMMERSED	IMMORTIFIED	IMPANELLED
IMBIRUSSU	IMMANACLE	IMMERSIBLE	IMMOTE	IMPANELLING
IMBITTER	IMMANACLED	IMMERSING	IMMOTILE	IMPAPYRATE
IMBLAZE	IMMANACLING	IMMERSION	IMMOTIONED	IMPAPYRATED
IMBODY	IMMANATION	IMMERSIONISM	IMMOTIVE	IMPAR
IMBOLDEN	IMMANE	IMMERSIONIST	IMMOUND	IMPARADISE
IMBOLISH	IMMANELY	IMMERSIVE	IMMOVABILITY	IMPARALLELED
IMBONDO	IMMANENCE	IMMESH	IMMOVABLE	IMPARASITIC
IMBONITY	IMMANENCY	IMMETHODIC	IMMOVABLY	IMPARDONABLE
IMBORDURE	IMMANENESS	IMMETHODIZE	IMMOVED	IMPARITY
IMBORSATION	IMMANENT	IMMEW	IMMUND	IMPARK
IMBOSCATA	IMMANENTAL	IMMI	IMMUNDITY	IMPARKATION
IMBOSK	IMMANENTISM	IMMIE	IMMUNE	IMPARKED
IMBOSOM	IMMANENTIST	IMMIGRANT	IMMUNIST	IMPARKING
IMBOST	IMMANENTLY	IMMIGRANTS	IMMUNITIES	IMPARL
IMBOWER	IMMANIFEST	IMMIGRATE	IMMUNITY	IMPARLANCE
IMBREATHE	IMMANITY	IMMIGRATED	IMMUNIZATION	IMPARLED
IMBREVIATE	IMMANTLE	IMMIGRATING	IMMUNIZE	IMPARLING
IMBREVIATED	IMMANTLED	IMMIGRATION	IMMUNIZED	IMPARSONEE
IMBREVIATING	IMMANTLING	IMMIGRATOR	IMMUNOGENIC	IMPART
IMBREX	IMMARBLE	IMMIGRATORY	IMMUNOLOGY	IMPARTABLE
IMBRICATE	IMMARGINATE	IMMIND	IMMUNOREACTION	IMPARTANCE
IMBRICATED	IMMASK	IMMINENCE	IMMUNOTOXIN	IMPARTATION
IMBRICATELY	IMMATCHABLE	IMMINENCY	IMMURATION	IMPARTED
IMBRICATING	IMMATCHLESS	IMMINENT	IMMURE	IMPARTER
IMBRICATION	IMMATERIAL	IMMINENTLY	IMMURED	IMPARTIAL
IMBRICATIVE	IMMATERIALISM	IMMINGLE	IMMURING	IMPARTIALITY
IMBRICES	IMMATERIALIST	IMMINUTION	IMMUSICAL	IMPARTIALLY
IMBRIER	IMMATERIALITIES	IMMIS	IMMUSICALLY	IMPARTIBLE
IMBROGLIO	IMMATERIALITY	IMMISCIBLE	IMMUTABILITY	IMPARTIBLY
IMBROGLIOS	IMMATERIALIZE	IMMISCIBLY	IMMUTABLE	IMPARTICIPABLE
IMBROIN	IMMATERIALS	IMMISS	IMMUTABLY	IMPARTING
IMBROWN	IMMATERIATE	IMMISSION	IMMUTATION	IMPARTITE
IMBRUE	IMMATRICULATE	IMMIT	IMMUTE	IMPARTIVE
IMBRUED	IMMATURE	IMMITIGABLE	IMMUTILATE	IMPARTIVITY
IMBRUING	IMMATURED	IMMITIGABLY	IMMUTUAL	IMPARTMENT
IMBRUTE	IMMATURELY	IMMITTED	IMO	IMPASSABLE
IMBRUTED	IMMATURENESS	IMMITTING	IMONIUM	IMPASSABLY
IMBRUTING	IMMATURITIES	IMMIX	IMP	IMPASSE
IMBUE	IMMATURITY	IMMIXT	IMPACABLE	IMPASSES
IMBUED	IMMEABILITY	IMMIXTURE	IMPACK	IMPASSIBLE
IMBUIA	IMMEASURABLE	IMMOBILE	IMPACT	IMPASSIBLY
IMBUING	IMMEASURABLY	IMMOBILITY	IMPACTED	IMPASSION
IMBURSE	IMMEASURED	IMMOBILIZATION	IMPACTER	IMPASSIONATE
IMBURSED	IMMECHANICAL	IMMOBILIZE	IMPACTING	IMPASSIONED
IMBURSING	IMMEDIACY	IMMOBILIZED	IMPACTION	IMPASSIONING
IMELLE	IMMEDIAL	IMMOBILIZING	IMPACTIONIZE	IMPASSIVE
IMI	IMMEDIATE	IMMODERACY	IMPACTMENT	IMPASSIVELY
IMID	IMMEDIATELY	IMMODERATE	IMPACTOR	IMPASSIVENESS
IMIDAZOL	IMMEDIATENESS	IMMODERATENESS	IMPACTUAL	IMPASTATION
IMIDAZOLE	IMMEDIATISM	IMMODERATION	IMPAGES	IMPASTE
IMIDAZOLYL	IMMEDIATIST	IMMODEST	IMPAINT	IMPASTED
IMIDE	IMMEDICABLE	IMMODESTY	IMPAIR	IMPASTING
IMIDIC	IMMEDICABLY	IMMOLATE	IMPAIRED	IMPASTO
IMIDO	IMMELODIOUS	IMMOLATED	IMPAIRER	IMPASTURE
IMIDOGEN	IMMEMBER	IMMOLATING	IMPAIRING	IMPATERNATE
IMIN	IMMEMORABLE	IMMOLATION	IMPAIRMENT	IMPATIBLE
IMINE	IMMEMORIAL	IMMOLATOR	IMPALA	IMPATIENCE
IMINO	IMMENSE	IMMOMENT	IMPALACE	IMPATIENCY
IMITABILITY	IMMENSELY	IMMONASTERED	IMPALE	IMPATIENS
IMITABLE	IMMENSENESS	IMMORAL	IMPALED	IMPATIENT
IMITANCY	IMMENSIBLE	IMMORALISM	IMPALEMENT	IMPATIENTLY

IMPATRONIZE
IMPAVE
IMPAVID
IMPAVIDITY
IMPAVIDLY
IMPAWN
IMPAWNED
IMPAWNING
IMPAYABLE
IMPEACH
IMPEACHABLE
IMPEACHED
IMPEACHER
IMPEACHING
IMPEACHMENT
IMPEARL
IMPEARLED
IMPEARLING
IMPECCABLE
IMPECCABLY
IMPECCANCE
IMPECCANCY
IMPECCANT
IMPECTINATE
IMPECUNIARY
IMPECUNIOUS
IMPEDANCE
IMPEDE
IMPEDED
IMPEDER
IMPEDIBILITY
IMPEDIBLE
IMPEDIENT
IMPEDIMENT
IMPEDIMENTA
IMPEDIMENTAL
IMPEDIMENTARY
IMPEDING
IMPEDINGLY
IMPEDITE
IMPEDITION
IMPEDITIVE
IMPEDOMETER
IMPEDOR
IMPEEVISH
IMPEL
IMPELLED
IMPELLENT
IMPELLER
IMPELLING
IMPEN
IMPEND
IMPENDED
IMPENDENCE
IMPENDENCY
IMPENDENT
IMPENDING
IMPENETRABILITY
IMPENETRABLE
IMPENETRABLY
IMPENETRATE
IMPENITENCE
IMPENITENCY
IMPENITENT
IMPENITENTLY
IMPENITIBLE
IMPENNATE
IMPENT
IMPERANCE
IMPERANT
IMPERATE
IMPERATION
IMPERATIVE
IMPERATIVELY
IMPERATOR
IMPERATORIAL
IMPERATORY

IMPERATRICE
IMPERATRIX
IMPERCEIVED
IMPERCEPTIBLE
IMPERCEPTION
IMPERCEPTIVE
IMPERCIPIENT
IMPERENT
IMPERFECT
IMPERFECTED
IMPERFECTIBLE
IMPERFECTION
IMPERFECTIOUS
IMPERFECTIVE
IMPERFECTLY
IMPERFORABLE
IMPERFORATE
IMPERFORATED
IMPERFORATION
IMPERIA
IMPERIAL
IMPERIALIN
IMPERIALINE
IMPERIALISM
IMPERIALIST
IMPERIALISTIC
IMPERIALITIES
IMPERIALITY
IMPERIALIZE
IMPERIALIZED
IMPERIALIZING
IMPERIALTY
IMPERIL
IMPERILED
IMPERILING
IMPERILLED
IMPERILLING
IMPERIOUS
IMPERIOUSLY
IMPERISH
IMPERISHABLE
IMPERITE
IMPERIUM
IMPERMANENCE
IMPERMANENT
IMPERMEABLE
IMPERMEABLY
IMPERMEATOR
IMPERMISSIBLE
IMPERMIXT
IMPERMUTABLE
IMPERSONABLE
IMPERSONAL
IMPERSONALITIES
IMPERSONALITY
IMPERSONALIZE
IMPERSONALIZED
IMPERSONALIZING
IMPERSONATE
IMPERSONATED
IMPERSONATING
IMPERSONATION
IMPERSONATIVE
IMPERSONATOR
IMPERSUADABLE
IMPERSUASIBLE
IMPERTINACY
IMPERTINENCE
IMPERTINENCES
IMPERTINENCIES
IMPERTINENCY
IMPERTINENT
IMPERTRANSIBLE
IMPERTURBABILITY
IMPERTURBABLE
IMPERTURBABLY
IMPERTURBED

IMPERVERSE
IMPERVERTIBLE
IMPERVIABLE
IMPERVIAL
IMPERVIOUS
IMPERVIOUSLY
IMPEST
IMPESTATION
IMPESTER
IMPETICOS
IMPETIGINOUS
IMPETIGO
IMPETITION
IMPETRATE
IMPETRATED
IMPETRATING
IMPETRATION
IMPETRATIVE
IMPETRATOR
IMPETRATORY
IMPETRE
IMPETULANT
IMPETUOSITY
IMPETUOSO
IMPETUOUS
IMPETUOUSLY
IMPETUS
IMPETUSES
IMPHEE
IMPI
IMPICTURE
IMPIERCEABLE
IMPIETIES
IMPIETY
IMPIGNORATE
IMPIGNORATED
IMPIGNORATING
IMPING
IMPINGE
IMPINGED
IMPINGEMENT
IMPINGENCE
IMPINGENT
IMPINGER
IMPINGING
IMPINGUATE
IMPIOUS
IMPIOUSLY
IMPIOUSNESS
IMPISH
IMPISHLY
IMPISHNESS
IMPITEOUS
IMPITIABLY
IMPLACABLE
IMPLACABLY
IMPLACEMENT
IMPLACENTAL
IMPLACENTATE
IMPLANT
IMPLANTATION
IMPLANTED
IMPLANTER
IMPLANTING
IMPLASTIC
IMPLATE
IMPLAUSIBILITY
IMPLAUSIBLE
IMPLEACH
IMPLEAD
IMPLEADABLE
IMPLEADER
IMPLEDGE
IMPLEMENT
IMPLEMENTAL
IMPLETE
IMPLETION

IMPLETIVE
IMPLEX
IMPLIABLE
IMPLIAL
IMPLICANT
IMPLICATE
IMPLICATED
IMPLICATELY
IMPLICATING
IMPLICATION
IMPLICATIONAL
IMPLICATIVE
IMPLICATORY
IMPLICIT
IMPLICITLY
IMPLICITNESS
IMPLIED
IMPLIEDLY
IMPLODE
IMPLODED
IMPLODENT
IMPLODING
IMPLORATION
IMPLORATOR
IMPLORATORY
IMPLORE
IMPLORED
IMPLORER
IMPLORING
IMPLORINGLY
IMPLOSION
IMPLOSIVE
IMPLOSIVELY
IMPLUME
IMPLUNGE
IMPLUVIA
IMPLUVIUM
IMPLY
IMPLYING
IMPOCKET
IMPOFO
IMPOLICY
IMPOLISHED
IMPOLITE
IMPOLITELY
IMPOLITENESS
IMPOLITIC
IMPOLITICAL
IMPOLITICLY
IMPOLLUTE
IMPONDERABILIA
IMPONDERABLE
IMPONDERABLY
IMPONDEROUS
IMPONE
IMPONENT
IMPOOR
IMPOROSITY
IMPOROUS
IMPORT
IMPORTABLE
IMPORTABLY
IMPORTANCE
IMPORTANT
IMPORTATION
IMPORTED
IMPORTER
IMPORTING
IMPORTLESS
IMPORTMENT
IMPORTRAITURE
IMPORTRAY
IMPORTUNACY
IMPORTUNANCE
IMPORTUNATE
IMPORTUNATELY
IMPORTUNATOR

IMPORTUNE
IMPORTUNED
IMPORTUNELY
IMPORTUNEMENT
IMPORTUNER
IMPORTUNING
IMPORTUNITIES
IMPORTUNITY
IMPOSAL
IMPOSE
IMPOSED
IMPOSEMENT
IMPOSER
IMPOSING
IMPOSINGLY
IMPOSINGNESS
IMPOSITION
IMPOSITIONAL
IMPOSSIBILIST
IMPOSSIBILITIES
IMPOSSIBILITY
IMPOSSIBLE
IMPOSSIBLY
IMPOST
IMPOSTED
IMPOSTER
IMPOSTEROUS
IMPOSTHUMATE
IMPOSTHUME
IMPOSTING
IMPOSTOR
IMPOSTRIX
IMPOSTROUS
IMPOSTUMATE
IMPOSTUME
IMPOSTURE
IMPOSTUROUS
IMPOSURE
IMPOT
IMPOTENCE
IMPOTENCY
IMPOTENT
IMPOTENTLY
IMPOTENTNESS
IMPOUND
IMPOUNDAGE
IMPOUNDED
IMPOUNDER
IMPOUNDING
IMPOUNDMENT
IMPOVERISH
IMPOVERISHED
IMPOVERISHER
IMPOVERISHING
IMPOWER
IMPRACTICABLE
IMPRACTICAL
IMPRECANT
IMPRECATE
IMPRECATED
IMPRECATING
IMPRECATION
IMPRECATOR
IMPRECATORY
IMPRECISE
IMPRECISELY
IMPRECISION
IMPREDICABLE
IMPREGN
IMPREGNABILITY
IMPREGNABLE
IMPREGNABLY
IMPREGNANT
IMPREGNATE
IMPREGNATED
IMPREGNATING
IMPREGNATION

IMPREGNATIVE	IMPROPRIETIES	IN	INAPPOSITELY	INBYE
IMPREGNATOR	IMPROPRIETY	INA	INAPPRECIABLE	INCAGE
IMPREGNATORY	IMPROVABLE	INABILITY	INAPPROPRIATE	INCALCULABLE
IMPREJUDICE	IMPROVABLY	INABORDABLE	INAPT	INCALCULABLY
IMPREMEDITATE	IMPROVE	INACCEPTABLE	INAPTITUDE	INCALESCENT
IMPREPARATION	IMPROVED	INACCESSIBILITY	INAPTLY	INCALICULATE
IMPRESA	IMPROVEMENT	INACCESSIBLE	INAPTNESS	INCALVER
IMPRESARI	IMPROVER	INACCESSIBLY	INARCH	INCALVING
IMPRESARIO	IMPROVIDENCE	INACCURACIES	INARCHING	INCAMERATION
IMPRESARIOS	IMPROVIDENT	INACCURACY	INARCULUM	INCAMP
IMPRESCIENCE	IMPROVING	INACCURATE	INARM	INCANDENT
IMPRESE	IMPROVINGLY	INACCURATELY	INARTICULACY	INCANDESCE
IMPRESS	IMPROVISATE	INACHID	INARTICULATE	INCANDESCED
IMPRESSED	IMPROVISATION	INACHOID	INARTICULATED	INCANDESCENCE
IMPRESSEDLY	IMPROVISATOR	INACTION	INARTICULATELY	INCANDESCENT
IMPRESSER	IMPROVISATORY	INACTIONIST	INARTICULATION	INCANDESCING
IMPRESSIBLE	IMPROVISE	INACTIVATE	INARTIFICIAL	INCANOUS
IMPRESSIBLY	IMPROVISED	INACTIVATION	INARTISTIC	INCANT
IMPRESSING	IMPROVISER	INACTIVE	INASMUCH	INCANTATION
IMPRESSION	IMPROVISING	INACTIVELY	INASSIMILATION	INCANTATOR
IMPRESSIONABLE	IMPROVISO	INACTIVENESS	INATTENTION	INCANTATORY
IMPRESSIONARY	IMPRUDENCE	INACTIVITY	INATTENTIVE	INCANTON
IMPRESSIONISM	IMPRUDENT	INACTUATE	INAUDIBILITY	INCAPABILITY
IMPRESSIONIST	IMPRUDENTIAL	INACTUATION	INAUDIBLE	INCAPABLE
IMPRESSIONISTIC	IMPRUDENTLY	INADAPTABLE	INAUDIBLY	INCAPABLY
IMPRESSIVE	IMPUBERAL	INADAPTATION	INAUGUR	INCAPACIOUS
IMPRESSIVELY	IMPUBERATE	INADEQUACY	INAUGURAL	INCAPACITATE
IMPRESSMENT	IMPUBERTY	INADEQUATE	INAUGURATE	INCAPACITATED
IMPRESSOR	IMPUBIC	INADEQUATELY	INAUGURATED	INCAPACITATING
IMPRESSURE	IMPUDENCE	INADEQUATION	INAUGURATING	INCAPACITATION
IMPREST	IMPUDENCIES	INADMISSIBLE	INAUGURATION	INCAPACITIES
IMPRESTED	IMPUDENCY	INADVERTENCE	INAUGURATIVE	INCAPACITY
IMPRESTING	IMPUDENT	INADVERTENCES	INAUGURATOR	INCAPSULATE
IMPREVISION	IMPUDENTLY	INADVERTENCY	INAUGURATORY	INCAPSULATED
IMPREVU	IMPUDENTNESS	INADVERTENT	INAUGURER	INCAPSULATING
IMPRIMATUR	IMPUDICITY	INADVERTENTLY	INAURATE	INCAPSULATION
IMPRIME	IMPUGN	INADVISABLE	INAURATION	INCAPTIVATE
IMPRIMENT	IMPUGNABLE	INADVISEDLY	INAUSPICIOUS	INCARCERATE
IMPRIMERIE	IMPUGNATION	INAESTHETIC	INAUTHENTIC	INCARCERATED
IMPRIMERY	IMPUGNED	INAFFABILITY	INAXON	INCARCERATING
IMPRIMIS	IMPUGNER	INAFFABLE	INBASSAT	INCARCERATOR
IMPRIMITIVE	IMPUGNING	INAFFABLY	INBE	INCARDINATE
IMPRINT	IMPUISSANCE	INAGGLUTINABLE	INBEAMING	INCARMINED
IMPRINTED	IMPUISSANT	INAJA	INBEARING	INCARN
IMPRINTER	IMPULSE	INALACRITY	INBEING	INCARNADINE
IMPRINTING	IMPULSES	INALIENABLE	INBENDING	INCARNADINED
IMPRISON	IMPULSION	INALIENABLY	INBENT	INCARNADINING
IMPRISONED	IMPULSIVE	INALTERABLE	INBIRTH	INCARNANT
IMPRISONER	IMPULSIVELY	INALTERABLY	INBLOW	INCARNATE
IMPRISONING	IMPULSIVITY	INAM	INBLOWING	INCARNATED
IMPRISONMENT	IMPULSOR	INAMIA	INBLOWN	INCARNATING
IMPROBABILITIES	IMPULSORY	INAMISSIBLE	INBOARD	INCARNATION
IMPROBABILITY	IMPUNIBLE	INAMORATA	INBODY	INCARNATIONAL
IMPROBABILIZE	IMPUNITY	INAMORATE	INBOND	INCARNATIONIST
IMPROBABLE	IMPURE	INAMORATION	INBORN	INCARNATIVE
IMPROBABLY	IMPURELY	INAMORATO	INBOUND	INCASE
IMPROBATION	IMPURENESS	INAMORATOS	INBOW	INCASED
IMPROBATIVE	IMPURIFY	INAMOVABLE	INBREAD	INCASEMENT
IMPROBATORY	IMPURITAN	INANE	INBREAK	INCASING
IMPROBITY	IMPURITIES	INANELY	INBREAKING	INCASK
IMPROCREANT	IMPURITY	INANGA	INBREATHE	INCAST
IMPRODUCIBLE	IMPUT	INANIMATE	INBREATHED	INCASTELLATE
IMPROFICIENCY	IMPUTABILITY	INANIMATED	INBREATHER	INCATENATE
IMPROMPT	IMPUTABLE	INANIMATELY	INBREATHING	INCATENATION
IMPROMPTITUDE	IMPUTABLY	INANIMATION	INBRED	INCAUTION
IMPROMPTU	IMPUTATION	INANITIES	INBREED	INCAUTIOUS
IMPROOF	IMPUTATIVE	INANITION	INBREEDING	INCAUTIOUSLY
IMPROPER	IMPUTATIVELY	INANITY	INBRING	INCAVATE
IMPROPERATION	IMPUTE	INANTHERATE	INBRINGER	INCAVATED
IMPROPERLY	IMPUTED	INAPPEASABLE	INBRINGING	INCAVATION
IMPROPRIATE	IMPUTER	INAPPETENCE	INBROUGHT	INCAVERN
IMPROPRIATED	IMPUTING	INAPPETENCY	INBUILT	INCAVO
IMPROPRIATING	IMPUTRESCENCE	INAPPETENT	INBURNING	INCEDE
IMPROPRIATION	IMPY	INAPPLICABLE	INBURNT	INCEDINGLY
IMPROPRIATOR	IMSHI	INAPPLICABLY	INBURST	INCELEBRITY
IMPROPRIATRICE	IMSONIC	INAPPLICATION	INBUSH	INCEND
IMPROPRIATRIX	IMU	INAPPOSITE	INBY	INCENDIARIES

INCENDIARISM
INCENDIARY
INCENDIUM
INCENDIVITY
INCENSATION
INCENSE
INCENSED
INCENSER
INCENSING
INCENSION
INCENSOR
INCENSORIES
INCENSORY
INCENTER
INCENTIVE
INCENTIVELY
INCENTOR
INCENTRE
INCEPT
INCEPTED
INCEPTING
INCEPTION
INCEPTIVE
INCEPTIVELY
INCEPTOR
INCERATE
INCERATION
INCERTITUDE
INCESSABLE
INCESSABLY
INCESSANCY
INCESSANT
INCESSANTLY
INCESSION
INCEST
INCESTUOUS
INCESTUOUSLY
INCH
INCHAIN
INCHED
INCHER
INCHES
INCHLING
INCHMEAL
INCHOACY
INCHOANT
INCHOATE
INCHOATED
INCHOATELY
INCHOATENESS
INCHOATING
INCHOATION
INCHOATIVE
INCHPIN
INCHWORM
INCIDE
INCIDENCE
INCIDENT
INCIDENTAL
INCIDENTALLY
INCIENSO
INCINERABLE
INCINERATE
INCINERATED
INCINERATING
INCINERATION
INCINERATOR
INCIPIENCE
INCIPIENCY
INCIPIENT
INCIPIENTLY
INCIPIT
INCIRCLET
INCISAL
INCISE
INCISED
INCISELY

INCISIFORM
INCISING
INCISION
INCISIVE
INCISIVELY
INCISIVENESS
INCISOR
INCISORIAL
INCISORY
INCISURA
INCISURE
INCITABILITY
INCITABLE
INCITAMENTUM
INCITANT
INCITATE
INCITATION
INCITE
INCITED
INCITEMENT
INCITER
INCITING
INCITIVE
INCIVIL
INCIVILITIES
INCIVILITY
INCIVILIZATION
INCIVILLY
INCIVISM
INCLASP
INCLASPED
INCLASPING
INCLE
INCLEMENCIES
INCLEMENCY
INCLEMENT
INCLEMENTLY
INCLINABLE
INCLINABLENESS
INCLINATION
INCLINATOR
INCLINATORY
INCLINE
INCLINED
INCLINER
INCLINING
INCLINOGRAPH
INCLINOMETER
INCLIP
INCLOSE
INCLOSURE
INCLUDE
INCLUDED
INCLUDER
INCLUDING
INCLUSA
INCLUSE
INCLUSION
INCLUSIVE
INCLUSIVELY
INCLUSORY
INCLUSUS
INCOALESCENCE
INCOERCIBLE
INCOG
INCOGITABLE
INCOGITANCY
INCOGITANT
INCOGITANTLY
INCOGITATIVE
INCOGNITA
INCOGNITE
INCOGNITO
INCOGNITOS
INCOGNIZABLE
INCOGNIZANCE
INCOGNIZANT

INCOGNOSCENT
INCOGNOSCIBILITY
INCOHERENCE
INCOHERENCES
INCOHERENCIES
INCOHERENCY
INCOHERENT
INCOHERENTIFIC
INCOHERENTLY
INCOHERENTNESS
INCOHERING
INCOLANT
INCOMBUSTIBLE
INCOME
INCOMER
INCOMING
INCOMMENSURABILITY
INCOMMENSURABLE
INCOMMENSURABLENESS
INCOMMENSURABLY
INCOMMENSURATE
INCOMMISCIBLE
INCOMMODATE
INCOMMODATION
INCOMMODE
INCOMMODED
INCOMMODING
INCOMMODIOUS
INCOMMODITIES
INCOMMODITY
INCOMMUNICABLE
INCOMMUTABILITY
INCOMMUTABLE
INCOMPACT
INCOMPACTLY
INCOMPARABILITY
INCOMPARABLE
INCOMPARABLY
INCOMPARED
INCOMPATIBILITY
INCOMPATIBLE
INCOMPATIBLY
INCOMPENSATION
INCOMPETENCE
INCOMPETENCY
INCOMPETENT
INCOMPLETABLE
INCOMPLETE
INCOMPLETED
INCOMPLETELY
INCOMPLETENESS
INCOMPLETION
INCOMPLEX
INCOMPLIANCE
INCOMPLIANCY
INCOMPLIANT
INCOMPLIANTLY
INCOMPOSED
INCOMPOSEDLY
INCOMPOSEDNESS
INCOMPOSITE
INCOMPOSSIBLE
INCOMPREHENSIBLE
INCOMPREHENSIBLY
INCOMPRESSIBLE
INCOMPT
INCOMPUTABLE
INCONCEIVABILITY
INCONCEIVABLE
INCONCINNATE
INCONCINNITY
INCONCINNOUS
INCONCLUDENT
INCONCLUDING
INCONCLUSION
INCONCLUSIVE
INCONDENSABLE

INCONDENSIBLE
INCONDITE
INCONFORMITY
INCONFUSED
INCONFUSEDLY
INCONFUSION
INCONGEALABLE
INCONGRUENCE
INCONGRUENT
INCONGRUENTLY
INCONGRUITIES
INCONGRUITY
INCONGRUOUS
INCONJOINABLE
INCONJUNCT
INCONNU
INCONSCIENCE
INCONSCIENT
INCONSCIENTLY
INCONSCIOUS
INCONSEQUENCE
INCONSEQUENT
INCONSEQUENTIAL
INCONSEQUENTLY
INCONSEQUENTNESS
INCONSIDERABLE
INCONSIDERABLY
INCONSIDERATE
INCONSIDERATELY
INCONSIDERATION
INCONSIDERED
INCONSISTENCE
INCONSISTENCIES
INCONSISTENCY
INCONSISTENT
INCONSISTENTLY
INCONSOLABLE
INCONSOLABLY
INCONSOLATE
INCONSONANCE
INCONSONANT
INCONSPICUOUS
INCONSPICUOUSLY
INCONSPICUOUSNESS
INCONSTANCY
INCONSTANT
INCONSTANTLY
INCONSTANTNESS
INCONSUMABLE
INCONSUMABLY
INCONTAMINATE
INCONTESTABLE
INCONTESTABLY
INCONTINENCE
INCONTINENCY
INCONTINENT
INCONTINENTLY
INCONTINUITY
INCONTINUOUS
INCONTRACTILE
INCONTRACTION
INCONTROLLABLE
INCONTROLLABLY
INCONTROVERTIBLE
INCONVENIENCE
INCONVENIENCY
INCONVENIENT
INCONVERSABLE
INCONVERTIBLE
INCONVINCIBLE
INCONY
INCOORDINATION
INCORONATE
INCORONATED
INCORONATION
INCORPORABLE
INCORPORAL

INCORPORALITY
INCORPORALLY
INCORPORALNESS
INCORPORATE
INCORPORATED
INCORPORATING
INCORPORATION
INCORPORATIVE
INCORPORATOR
INCORPOREAL
INCORPOREITIES
INCORPOREITY
INCORPOREOUS
INCORPSE
INCORRECT
INCORRECTION
INCORRECTLY
INCORRECTNESS
INCORRIGIBLE
INCORRIGIBLENESS
INCORRIGIBLY
INCORRUPT
INCORRUPTED
INCORRUPTIBILITY
INCORRUPTIBLE
INCORRUPTION
INCORRUPTLY
INCOUP
INCOURSE
INCOURTEOUS
INCOURTEOUSLY
INCRASH
INCRASSATE
INCRASSATED
INCRASSATING
INCRASSATION
INCREASE
INCREASED
INCREASEMENT
INCREASER
INCREASING
INCREASINGLY
INCREATE
INCREATELY
INCREATIVE
INCREDIBILITIES
INCREDIBILITY
INCREDIBLE
INCREDIBLENESS
INCREDIBLY
INCREDULITY
INCREDULOUS
INCREDULOUSLY
INCREEP
INCREEPING
INCREMATE
INCREMATED
INCREMATING
INCREMATION
INCREMENT
INCREMENTAL
INCREPATION
INCREPT
INCRESCENCE
INCRESCENT
INCREST
INCRETION
INCRETIONARY
INCRETORY
INCRIMINATE
INCRIMINATED
INCRIMINATING
INCRIMINATION
INCRIMINATOR
INCRIMINATORY
INCROSS
INCROSSING

INCROTCHET	INCURRING	INDELIBILITY	INDICT	INDISCRETE
INCROYABLE	INCURSE	INDELIBLE	INDICTABLE	INDISCRETELY
INCRUENT	INCURSION	INDELIBLY	INDICTABLY	INDISCRETION
INCRUENTAL	INCURSIONIST	INDELICACIES	INDICTED	INDISCRIMINATE
INCRUENTOUS	INCURSIVE	INDELICACY	INDICTEE	INDISCRIMINATED
INCRUST	INCURVATE	INDELICATE	INDICTER	INDISCRIMINATELY
INCRUSTANT	INCURVATED	INDELICATELY	INDICTING	INDISCRIMINATING
INCRUSTATE	INCURVATING	INDEMNIFICATION	INDICTION	INDISCRIMINATION
INCRUSTATED	INCURVATION	INDEMNIFIED	INDICTIONAL	INDISCRIMINATIVE
INCRUSTATING	INCURVATURE	INDEMNIFIER	INDICTIVE	INDISPENSABLE
INCRUSTATION	INCURVE	INDEMNIFY	INDICTMENT	INDISPOSE
INCRUSTATOR	INCURVED	INDEMNIFYING	INDICTOR	INDISPOSED
INCRUSTED	INCUS	INDEMNITEE	INDIENNE	INDISPOSING
INCRUSTING	INCUSE	INDEMNITIES	INDIFEROUS	INDISPOSITION
INCRUSTIVE	INCUSED	INDEMNITOR	INDIFFERENCE	INDISPUTABLE
INCRUSTMENT	INCUSING	INDEMNITY	INDIFFERENCIES	INDISPUTABLY
INCRYSTAL	INCUSS	INDEMONIATE	INDIFFERENCY	INDISSOLUBLE
INCUBATE	INCUTE	INDEMONSTRABLE	INDIFFERENT	INDISSOLUBLY
INCUBATED	INCUTTING	INDENE	INDIFFERENTIAL	INDISSOLUTE
INCUBATING	INDABA	INDENIZE	INDIFFERENTISM	INDISSOLVABLE
INCUBATION	INDACONITIN	INDENT	INDIFFERENTIST	INDISTINCT
INCUBATIONAL	INDACONITINE	INDENTATION	INDIFFERENTLY	INDISTINCTION
INCUBATIVE	INDAGATE	INDENTED	INDIGENA	INDISTINCTIVE
INCUBATOR	INDAGATION	INDENTEDLY	INDIGENAE	INDISTINCTLY
INCUBATORIUM	INDAGATIVE	INDENTEE	INDIGENAL	INDISTINCTNESS
INCUBATORY	INDAGATOR	INDENTER	INDIGENATE	INDISTORTABLE
INCUBE	INDAGATORY	INDENTING	INDIGENCE	INDISTURBANCE
INCUBI	INDAMIN	INDENTION	INDIGENCY	INDITE
INCUBOUS	INDAMINE	INDENTMENT	INDIGENE	INDITED
INCUBUS	INDAN	INDENTOR	INDIGENEITY	INDITEMENT
INCUBUSES	INDANE	INDENTURE	INDIGENITY	INDITER
INCUDAL	INDART	INDENTURED	INDIGENOUS	INDITING
INCUDATE	INDAZOL	INDENTURING	INDIGENT	INDIUM
INCUDECTOMY	INDAZOLE	INDENTWISE	INDIGENTLY	INDIVERTIBLE
INCUDES	INDEBT	INDEPENDENCE	INDIGEST	INDIVERTIBLY
INCULCATE	INDEBTED	INDEPENDENCIES	INDIGESTED	INDIVIDUA
INCULCATED	INDEBTEDNESS	INDEPENDENCY	INDIGESTIBLE	INDIVIDUAL
INCULCATING	INDEBTING	INDEPENDENT	INDIGESTIBLY	INDIVIDUALISM
INCULCATION	INDEBTMENT	INDEPENDENTLY	INDIGESTION	INDIVIDUALIST
INCULCATIVE	INDECENCE	INDERITE	INDIGESTIVE	INDIVIDUALITIES
INCULCATOR	INDECENCIES	INDESCRIBABLE	INDIGITATE	INDIVIDUALITY
INCULCATORY	INDECENCY	INDESCRIPT	INDIGITATION	INDIVIDUALIZE
INCULK	INDECENT	INDESERT	INDIGN	INDIVIDUALIZED
INCULPABLE	INDECENTLY	INDESIGNATE	INDIGNANCE	INDIVIDUALIZING
INCULPABLY	INDECENTNESS	INDESTRUCTIBLE	INDIGNANCY	INDIVIDUALLY
INCULPATE	INDECIDUATE	INDETERMINACY	INDIGNANT	INDIVIDUATE
INCULPATED	INDECIDUOUS	INDETERMINATE	INDIGNANTLY	INDIVIDUATED
INCULPATING	INDECISION	INDEVOTION	INDIGNATION	INDIVIDUATING
INCULPATION	INDECISIVE	INDEX	INDIGNATORY	INDIVIDUATION
INCULPATIVE	INDECISIVELY	INDEXED	INDIGNIFIED	INDIVIDUATOR
INCULPATORY	INDECISIVENESS	INDEXER	INDIGNIFY	INDIVIDUITY
INCULT	INDECLINABLE	INDEXES	INDIGNIFYING	INDIVIDUUM
INCULTURE	INDECLINABLY	INDEXICAL	INDIGNITIES	INDIVIDUUMS
INCUMBENCE	INDECOROUS	INDEXICALLY	INDIGNITY	INDIVINABLE
INCUMBENCIES	INDECOROUSLY	INDEXING	INDIGNLY	INDIVISIBLE
INCUMBENCY	INDECORUM	INDEXTERITY	INDIGO	INDIVISIBLY
INCUMBENT	INDEED	INDIANAITE	INDIGOES	INDIVISIM
INCUMBENTLY	INDEFATIGABLE	INDICAN	INDIGOFEROUS	INDIVISION
INCUMBER	INDEFEASIBLE	INDICANT	INDIGOID	INDOCIBLE
INCUMBRANCE	INDEFEASIBLY	INDICANURIA	INDIGOS	INDOCILE
INCUNABLE	INDEFECTIBLE	INDICATE	INDIGOTIC	INDOCILITY
INCUNABULA	INDEFECTIBLY	INDICATED	INDIGOTIN	INDOCTRINATE
INCUNABULAR	INDEFECTIVE	INDICATING	INDIGOTINE	INDOCTRINATED
INCUNABULIST	INDEFENSIBLE	INDICATION	INDIMENSIBLE	INDOCTRINATING
INCUNABULUM	INDEFICIENCY	INDICATIVE	INDIMPLE	INDOCTRINE
INCUNEATION	INDEFICIENT	INDICATIVELY	INDIO	INDOCTRINIZE
INCUR	INDEFICIENTLY	INDICATOR	INDIRECT	INDOGEN
INCURABILITY	INDEFINABLE	INDICATORY	INDIRECTION	INDOGENIDE
INCURABLE	INDEFINABLY	INDICATRIX	INDIRECTLY	INDOL
INCURABLENESS	INDEFINITE	INDICAVIT	INDIRECTNESS	INDOLE
INCURABLY	INDEFINITELY	INDICE	INDIRUBIN	INDOLENCE
INCURIOSITY	INDEFINITY	INDICES	INDIRUBINE	INDOLENT
INCURIOUS	INDEFLECTIBLE	INDICIA	INDISCERNIBLE	INDOLENTLY
INCURIOUSLY	INDEHISCENCE	INDICIAL	INDISCERNIBLY	INDOLES
INCURRED	INDEHISCENT	INDICIBLE	INDISCIPLINE	INDOLIN
INCURRENCE	INDELECTABLE	INDICO	INDISCREET	INDOLINE
INCURRENT	INDELIBERATE	INDICOLITE	INDISCREETLY	INDOLOID

INDOMITABLE
INDONE
INDOOR
INDOORS
INDOPHENIN
INDOPHENOL
INDORSATION
INDORSE
INDORSED
INDORSING
INDOXYL
INDOXYLIC
INDRAFT
INDRAUGHT
INDRAWAL
INDRAWING
INDRAWN
INDRENCH
INDRI
INDUBIOUS
INDUBIOUSLY
INDUBITABLE
INDUBITABLY
INDUCE
INDUCED
INDUCEMENT
INDUCER
INDUCIAE
INDUCIBLE
INDUCING
INDUCIVE
INDUCT
INDUCTANCE
INDUCTED
INDUCTEE
INDUCTEOUS
INDUCTILE
INDUCTILITY
INDUCTING
INDUCTION
INDUCTIONAL
INDUCTIVE
INDUCTIVELY
INDUCTIVITY
INDUCTOMETER
INDUCTOPHONE
INDUCTOR
INDUCTORY
INDUCTOSCOPE
INDUE
INDUED
INDUING
INDULGE
INDULGED
INDULGENCE
INDULGENCED
INDULGENCY
INDULGENT
INDULGENTIAL
INDULGENTLY
INDULGENTNESS
INDULGER
INDULGING
INDULGINGLY
INDULIN
INDULINE
INDULT
INDULTO
INDULTS
INDUMENT
INDUMENTUM
INDUNA
INDUPLICATE
INDUPLICATION
INDUPLICATIVE
INDURATE

INDURATED
INDURATING
INDURATION
INDURATIVE
INDURE
INDURITE
INDUSIA
INDUSIAL
INDUSIATE
INDUSIATED
INDUSIFORM
INDUSIOID
INDUSIUM
INDUSTRIAL
INDUSTRIALLY
INDUSTRIES
INDUSTRIOUS
INDUSTRY
INDUVIAE
INDUVIAL
INDUVIATE
INDWELL
INDWELLER
INDWELLING
INDWELT
INDYL
INDYLIC
INEARTH
INEBRIACY
INEBRIANT
INEBRIATE
INEBRIATED
INEBRIATING
INEBRIATION
INEBRIATIVE
INEBRIETY
INEBRIOUS
INEDIBILITY
INEDIBLE
INEDITA
INEDITED
INEDUCATION
INEE
INEFFABILITY
INEFFABLE
INEFFABLY
INEFFACEABLE
INEFFACEABLY
INEFFECTIBLE
INEFFECTIBLY
INEFFECTIVE
INEFFECTIVELY
INEFFECTUAL
INEFFICACITY
INEFFICACY
INEFFICIENCE
INEFFICIENCY
INEFFICIENT
INELASTIC
INELASTICATE
INELASTICITY
INELEGANCE
INELEGANCES
INELEGANCIES
INELEGANCY
INELEGANT
INELEGANTLY
INELIGIBLE
INELIGIBLY
INELOQUENCE
INELOQUENT
INELUCTABLE
INELUCTABLY
INELUDIBLE
INENARRABLE
INENUBILABLE
INEPT

INEPTITUDE
INEPTLY
INEPTNESS
INEQUAL
INEQUALITARIAN
INEQUALITIES
INEQUALITY
INEQUALLY
INEQUALNESS
INEQUATION
INEQUITABLE
INEQUITABLY
INEQUITIES
INEQUITY
INEQUIVALVE
INERADICABLE
INERASABLE
INERASABLY
INERM
INERMOUS
INERRABLE
INERRANCY
INERRANT
INERRANTLY
INERRATIC
INERRING
INERRINGLY
INERT
INERTIA
INERTION
INERTLY
INERTNESS
INERUDITE
INERUDITELY
INERUDITION
INESCAPABLE
INESCATE
INESCATION
INESCULENT
INESCUTCHEON
INESITE
INESSENTIAL
INESTHETIC
INESTIMABLE
INESTIMABLY
INEUNT
INEVAPORABLE
INEVASIBLE
INEVIDENCE
INEVIDENT
INEVITABILITY
INEVITABLE
INEVITABLY
INEXACT
INEXACTITUDE
INEXACTLY
INEXACTNESS
INEXCUSABLE
INEXCUSABLY
INEXECUTION
INEXERTION
INEXHAUSTIBLE
INEXHAUSTIVE
INEXIST
INEXISTENCE
INEXISTENCY
INEXISTENT
INEXORABLE
INEXORABLY
INEXPECTED
INEXPECTEDLY
INEXPEDIENCY
INEXPEDIENT
INEXPENSIVE
INEXPERIENCE
INEXPERIENCED
INEXPERT

INEXPERTLY
INEXPERTNESS
INEXPIABLE
INEXPIABLENESS
INEXPIABLY
INEXPIATE
INEXPLICABLE
INEXPLICABLES
INEXPLICABLY
INEXPLICIT
INEXPLICITLY
INEXPRESS
INEXPRESSIBLE
INEXPRESSIVE
INEXPUGNABLE
INEXTENSIVE
INEXTERMINABLE
INEXTIRPABLE
INEXTRICABLE
INEXTRICABLY
INEYE
INFACE
INFAIR
INFALL
INFALLIBILIST
INFALLIBILITY
INFALLIBLE
INFALLIBLY
INFALLID
INFALLING
INFAME
INFAMED
INFAMIES
INFAMIZE
INFAMIZED
INFAMIZING
INFAMONIZE
INFAMOUS
INFAMOUSLY
INFAMOUSNESS
INFAMY
INFANCIES
INFANCY
INFAND
INFANDOUS
INFANG
INFANGLEMENT
INFANGTHEF
INFANGTHIEF
INFANS
INFANT
INFANTA
INFANTADO
INFANTE
INFANTICIDAL
INFANTICIDE
INFANTILE
INFANTILISM
INFANTILITY
INFANTINE
INFANTRIES
INFANTRY
INFANTRYMAN
INFANTS
INFARCT
INFARCTATE
INFARCTED
INFARCTION
INFARE
INFATUATE
INFATUATED
INFATUATEDLY
INFATUATING
INFATUATION
INFATUATOR
INFAUST
INFAUSTING

INFEASIBLE
INFECT
INFECTANT
INFECTED
INFECTEDNESS
INFECTING
INFECTION
INFECTIOUS
INFECTIVE
INFECTIVENESS
INFECTIVITY
INFECTOR
INFECTUM
INFECTUOUS
INFECUND
INFEED
INFEFT
INFEFTING
INFEFTMENT
INFELICIFIC
INFELICITIES
INFELICITOUS
INFELICITY
INFELT
INFEOFF
INFEOFFMENT
INFER
INFERABLE
INFERENCE
INFERENT
INFERENTIAL
INFERENTIALISM
INFERENTIALLY
INFERI
INFERIAE
INFERIAL
INFERIOR
INFERIORITY
INFERN
INFERNAL
INFERNALITY
INFERNALLY
INFERNALRY
INFERNO
INFERNOS
INFERRED
INFERRER
INFERRIBLE
INFERRING
INFERTILE
INFERTILELY
INFERTILITY
INFEST
INFESTANT
INFESTATION
INFESTED
INFESTER
INFESTING
INFESTIOUS
INFESTIVE
INFESTIVITY
INFESTMENT
INFEUDATION
INFIBULATE
INFIBULATION
INFICETE
INFIDEL
INFIDELIC
INFIDELICAL
INFIDELITIES
INFIDELITY
INFIELD
INFIELDER
INFIGHTER
INFIGHTING
INFILE
INFILL

INFILLING
INFILM
INFILTER
INFILTERED
INFILTERING
INFILTRATE
INFILTRATED
INFILTRATING
INFILTRATION
INFILTRATIVE
INFINITANT
INFINITARILY
INFINITARY
INFINITATE
INFINITATED
INFINITATING
INFINITATION
INFINITE
INFINITELY
INFINITENESS
INFINITESIMAL
INFINITETH
INFINITIES
INFINITIETH
INFINITIVAL
INFINITIVE
INFINITIVELY
INFINITO
INFINITUDE
INFINITUM
INFINITUPLE
INFINITY
INFIRM
INFIRMARER
INFIRMARESS
INFIRMARIAN
INFIRMARIES
INFIRMARY
INFIRMATE
INFIRMATION
INFIRMATIVE
INFIRMED
INFIRMING
INFIRMITIES
INFIRMITY
INFIT
INFITTER
INFIX
INFIXED
INFIXES
INFIXING
INFIXION
INFLAME
INFLAMED
INFLAMEDLY
INFLAMEDNESS
INFLAMER
INFLAMING
INFLAMINGLY
INFLAMMABILITY
INFLAMMABLE
INFLAMMABLENESS
INFLAMMABLY
INFLAMMATION
INFLAMMATIVE
INFLAMMATORY
INFLATE
INFLATED
INFLATEDLY
INFLATEDNESS
INFLATER
INFLATILE
INFLATING
INFLATION
INFLATIONARY
INFLATIONISM
INFLATIONIST

INFLATIVE
INFLATUS
INFLECT
INFLECTED
INFLECTING
INFLECTION
INFLECTIONAL
INFLECTIVE
INFLECTOR
INFLEX
INFLEXED
INFLEXIBILITY
INFLEXIBLE
INFLEXIBLY
INFLEXION
INFLEXIVE
INFLICT
INFLICTED
INFLICTER
INFLICTING
INFLICTION
INFLICTIVE
INFLOOD
INFLORESCENCE
INFLORESCENT
INFLOW
INFLUENCE
INFLUENCED
INFLUENCER
INFLUENCES
INFLUENCING
INFLUENCIVE
INFLUENT
INFLUENTIAL
INFLUENZA
INFLUENZAL
INFLUENZIC
INFLUX
INFLUXION
INFLUXIONISM
INFLUXIVE
INFO
INFOLD
INFOLDED
INFOLDER
INFOLDING
INFOLIATE
INFORM
INFORMAL
INFORMALITIES
INFORMALITY
INFORMALIZE
INFORMALLY
INFORMANT
INFORMATION
INFORMATIONAL
INFORMATIVE
INFORMATIVELY
INFORMATORY
INFORMED
INFORMEDLY
INFORMER
INFORMIDABLE
INFORMING
INFORMITY
INFORTIATE
INFORTITUDE
INFORTUNATE
INFORTUNE
INFOUND
INFRA
INFRABASAL
INFRACENTRAL
INFRACLUSION
INFRACOSTAL
INFRACT
INFRACTED

INFRACTING
INFRACTION
INFRACTOR
INFRADENTARY
INFRAGLACIAL
INFRAGLENOID
INFRAGULAR
INFRAHUMAN
INFRAHYOID
INFRALABIAL
INFRALITTORAL
INFRAMEDIAN
INFRANATURAL
INFRANGIBLE
INFRAPOSE
INFRAPOSED
INFRAPOSING
INFRAPROTEIN
INFRARED
INFRASONIC
INFRASPINAL
INFRASPINATUS
INFRASPINOUS
INFRATEMPORAL
INFRAVENTRAL
INFREQUENCE
INFREQUENCY
INFREQUENT
INFRIGIDATE
INFRINGE
INFRINGED
INFRINGEMENT
INFRINGER
INFRINGIBLE
INFRINGING
INFRUCTUOSE
INFRUCTUOUS
INFRUNITE
INFULA
INFULAE
INFUMATE
INFUMATED
INFUND
INFUNDIBULAR
INFUNDIBULUM
INFURIATE
INFURIATED
INFURIATELY
INFURIATING
INFURIATION
INFUSCATE
INFUSCATED
INFUSCATION
INFUSE
INFUSED
INFUSER
INFUSIBILITY
INFUSIBLE
INFUSING
INFUSION
INFUSIONISM
INFUSIONIST
INFUSIVE
INFUSORIAL
INFUSORIAN
INFUSORIES
INFUSORY
INGALLANTRY
INGANG
INGANGS
INGATE
INGATES
INGATHER
INGATHERED
INGATHERER
INGATHERING
INGE

INGEMINATE
INGEMINATED
INGEMINATING
INGENDER
INGENE
INGENERABLE
INGENERABLY
INGENERATE
INGENERATED
INGENERATING
INGENERATION
INGENIER
INGENIOSITY
INGENIOUS
INGENIOUSLY
INGENIT
INGENITAL
INGENITE
INGENT
INGENUE
INGENUITIES
INGENUITY
INGENUOUS
INGENUOUSLY
INGENUOUSNESS
INGENY
INGERMINATE
INGEST
INGESTA
INGESTED
INGESTER
INGESTIBLE
INGESTING
INGESTION
INGESTIVE
INGINE
INGIVER
INGIVING
INGLE
INGLENOOK
INGLES
INGLESA
INGLESIDE
INGLOBATE
INGLOBE
INGLOBED
INGLOBING
INGLORIOUS
INGLORIOUSLY
INGLORIOUSNESS
INGLUTITION
INGLUVIAL
INGLUVIES
INGLUVIITIS
INGOING
INGOT
INGOTED
INGOTING
INGOTMAN
INGOTMEN
INGOTS
INGRAFT
INGRAIN
INGRAINED
INGRAINEDLY
INGRAINING
INGRAMNESS
INGRANDIZE
INGRATE
INGRATEFUL
INGRATEFULNESS
INGRATELY
INGRATIATE
INGRATIATED
INGRATIATING
INGRATIATION
INGRATIATORY

INGRATITUDE
INGRAVESCENT
INGRAVIDATE
INGREAT
INGREDIENCE
INGREDIENT
INGRESS
INGRESSION
INGRESSIVE
INGROSS
INGROUP
INGROW
INGROWING
INGROWN
INGROWTH
INGRUENT
INGUEN
INGUINAL
INGULF
INGULFMENT
INGURGITATE
INGURGITATED
INGURGITATING
INGUSTABLE
INGYRE
INHABILE
INHABIT
INHABITABILITY
INHABITABLE
INHABITANCE
INHABITANCY
INHABITANT
INHABITATE
INHABITATION
INHABITATIVE
INHABITED
INHABITER
INHABITING
INHABITRESS
INHALANT
INHALATION
INHALE
INHALED
INHALENT
INHALER
INHALING
INHAME
INHARMONIC
INHARMONIOUS
INHARMONY
INHAUL
INHAULER
INHAUST
INHAUSTION
INHEARSE
INHEAVEN
INHELDE
INHERE
INHERED
INHERENCE
INHERENCIES
INHERENCY
INHERENT
INHERENTLY
INHERING
INHERIT
INHERITABLE
INHERITABLY
INHERITAGE
INHERITANCE
INHERITED
INHERITING
INHERITOR
INHESION
INHIATE
INHIBIT
INHIBITABLE

INHIBITED
INHIBITER
INHIBITION
INHIBITIONIST
INHIBITIONS
INHIBITIVE
INHIBITOR
INHIBITORY
INHOLDER
INHONEST
INHOOP
INHOSPITABLE
INHOSPITABLY
INHOSPITALITY
INHUMAN
INHUMANE
INHUMANELY
INHUMANITIES
INHUMANITY
INHUMANLY
INHUMANNESS
INHUMATE
INHUMATION
INHUMATIONIST
INHUME
INHUMED
INHUMER
INHUMING
INIAL
INIMICABLE
INIMICAL
INIMICALITY
INIMICALLY
INIMICALNESS
INIMICITIOUS
INIMICOUS
INIMITABILITY
INIMITABLE
INIMITABLY
INIOME
INIOMOUS
INION
INIQUITABLE
INIQUITIES
INIQUITOUS
INIQUITOUSLY
INIQUITY
INIRRITABILITY
INIRRITABLE
INISSUABLE
INITIAL
INITIALED
INITIALER
INITIALING
INITIALIST
INITIALLED
INITIALLY
INITIANT
INITIARY
INITIATE
INITIATED
INITIATING
INITIATION
INITIATIVE
INITIATIVELY
INITIATOR
INITIATORILY
INITIATORY
INITION
INJECT
INJECTED
INJECTING
INJECTION
INJECTOR
INJELLY
INJOINT
INJUDICIAL

INJUDICIALLY
INJUDICIOUS
INJUDICIOUSLY
INJUDICIOUSNESS
INJUNCT
INJUNCTION
INJUNCTIVE
INJUNCTIVELY
INJURE
INJURED
INJUREDLY
INJUREDNESS
INJURER
INJURIA
INJURIES
INJURING
INJURIOUS
INJURIOUSLY
INJURY
INJUST
INJUSTICE
INJUSTLY
INK
INKBERRIES
INKBERRY
INKBLOT
INKED
INKEN
INKER
INKET
INKFISH
INKHOLDER
INKHORN
INKHORNISM
INKHORNIST
INKHORNIZE
INKHORNIZER
INKIER
INKIEST
INKINDLE
INKING
INKLE
INKLING
INKMAN
INKNIT
INKNOT
INKOS
INKOSI
INKPOT
INKROOT
INKS
INKSHED
INKSLINGER
INKSLINGING
INKSTAND
INKSTANDISH
INKSTONE
INKWEED
INKWELL
INKWOOD
INKWRITER
INKY
INLAGATION
INLAID
INLAIK
INLAKE
INLAND
INLANDER
INLANDISH
INLAPIDATE
INLARD
INLAUT
INLAW
INLAWRY
INLAY
INLAYER
INLAYING

INLEAGUE
INLEAGUED
INLEAGUING
INLEAK
INLEAKAGE
INLESS
INLET
INLETTING
INLIER
INLIKE
INLOOK
INLOOKER
INLOOKING
INLY
INLYING
INMATE
INMEATS
INMESH
INMIXTURE
INMORE
INMOST
INN
INNAM
INNARDS
INNASCIBLE
INNATE
INNATELY
INNATENESS
INNATISM
INNATIVE
INNATURAL
INNATURALITY
INNATURALLY
INNEITY
INNER
INNERLY
INNERMORE
INNERMOST
INNERVATE
INNERVATED
INNERVATING
INNERVATION
INNERVATIONAL
INNERVE
INNERVED
INNERVING
INNESS
INNEST
INNET
INNHOLDER
INNING
INNINGS
INNINMORITE
INNITENCY
INNKEEPER
INNOCENCE
INNOCENCIES
INNOCENCY
INNOCENT
INNOCENTLY
INNOCENTNESS
INNOCUITY
INNOCUOUS
INNOCUOUSLY
INNOCUOUSNESS
INNODATE
INNOMINABLE
INNOMINABLES
INNOMINATA
INNOMINATE
INNOMINATUM
INNOVANT
INNOVATE
INNOVATED
INNOVATING
INNOVATION
INNOVATIVE

INNOVATOR
INNOVATORY
INNOXIOUS
INNOXIOUSLY
INNUATE
INNUENDO
INNUENDOED
INNUENDOES
INNUENDOING
INNUMERABLE
INNUMERABLY
INNUMEROUS
INNUTRIENT
INNUTRITION
INNUTRITIOUS
INNYARD
INOBEDIENCE
INOBEDIENT
INOBNOXIOUS
INOBSCURABLE
INOBSERVANCE
INOBSERVANCY
INOBSERVANT
INOBSERVANTLY
INOBSERVATION
INOBTAINABLE
INOBTRUSIVE
INOCCUPATION
INOCULABILITY
INOCULABLE
INOCULANT
INOCULAR
INOCULATE
INOCULATED
INOCULATING
INOCULATION
INOCULATIVE
INOCULATOR
INOCULUM
INODIATE
INODOROUS
INODOROUSLY
INODOROUSNESS
INOFFENSIVE
INOFFICIOSITY
INOFFICIOUS
INOFFICIOUSNESS
INOGEN
INOMA
INOMINOUS
INONE
INOPERABLE
INOPERATIVE
INOPERCULAR
INOPERCULATE
INOPINABLE
INOPINATE
INOPINATELY
INOPINE
INOPPORTUNE
INOPPORTUNELY
INOPPORTUNIST
INOPPORTUNITY
INOPULENT
INORB
INORDINACY
INORDINATE
INORDINATELY
INORDINATENESS
INORDINATION
INORGANIC
INORGANIZATION
INORIGINATE
INORNATE
INOSCULATED
INOSCULATING
INOSINE

INOSITE
INOSITOL
INOTROPIC
INOWER
INOXIDIZE
INOXIDIZED
INOXIDIZING
INPARFIT
INPATIENT
INPAYMENT
INPENSIONER
INPHASE
INPORT
INPOUR
INPOURING
INPUSH
INPUT
INQUAINTANCE
INQUARTATION
INQUEST
INQUESTUAL
INQUIET
INQUIETLY
INQUIETNESS
INQUIETUDE
INQUILINE
INQUILINISM
INQUILINITY
INQUILINOUS
INQUINATE
INQUINATED
INQUINATING
INQUINATION
INQUIRABLE
INQUIRATION
INQUIRE
INQUIRED
INQUIRENDO
INQUIRENT
INQUIRER
INQUIRIES
INQUIRING
INQUIRINGLY
INQUIRY
INQUISIT
INQUISITE
INQUISITION
INQUISITIONAL
INQUISITIONIST
INQUISITIVE
INQUISITOR
INQUISITORIAL
INQUISITORY
INRADIUS
INRIGGED
INRIGGER
INRIGHTED
INRING
INRO
INROAD
INROADER
INROLL
INROOTED
INRUB
INRUN
INRUNNING
INRUPTION
INRUSH
INS
INSACK
INSAGACITY
INSALIVATE
INSALIVATED
INSALIVATING
INSALIVATION
INSALUBRIOUS
INSALUBRITY

INSAME
INSANE
INSANELY
INSANENESS
INSANIFY
INSANITARY
INSANITATION
INSANITY
INSATIABLE
INSATIABLY
INSATIATE
INSATIATED
INSATIATELY
INSATIETY
INSATISFACTION
INSATURABLE
INSCENATION
INSCIENCE
INSCIENT
INSCIOUS
INSCRIBABLE
INSCRIBE
INSCRIBED
INSCRIBER
INSCRIBING
INSCRIPT
INSCRIPTIBLE
INSCRIPTION
INSCRIPTIONED
INSCRIPTIVE
INSCRIPTURED
INSCROLL
INSCROLLED
INSCROLLING
INSCRUTABLE
INSCRUTABLES
INSCRUTABLY
INSCULP
INSCULPTURE
INSEA
INSEAM
INSEAMER
INSECT
INSECTAN
INSECTARIA
INSECTARIES
INSECTARIUM
INSECTARIUMS
INSECTARY
INSECTEAN
INSECTED
INSECTICIDAL
INSECTICIDE
INSECTILE
INSECTION
INSECTIVAL
INSECTIVORE
INSECTIVOROUS
INSECTMONGER
INSECTOLOGER
INSECTOLOGY
INSECTS
INSECURE
INSECURELY
INSECURENESS
INSECURITIES
INSECURITY
INSEE
INSEEING
INSEER
INSELBERG
INSELBERGE
INSEMINATE
INSEMINATED
INSEMINATING
INSEMINATION
INSENESCIBLE

INSENSATE
INSENSATELY
INSENSE
INSENSED
INSENSIBILITY
INSENSIBILIZE
INSENSIBLE
INSENSIBLY
INSENSING
INSENSITIVE
INSENSUOUS
INSENTIENCE
INSENTIENCY
INSENTIENT
INSEPARABLE
INSEPARABLY
INSEPARATE
INSEPARATELY
INSEQUENT
INSERT
INSERTED
INSERTER
INSERTING
INSERTION
INSERTIONAL
INSERTIVE
INSERVIENT
INSESSION
INSESSOR
INSESSORIAL
INSET
INSETTER
INSEVERABLE
INSEVERABLY
INSHAVE
INSHEATHE
INSHEATHED
INSHEATHING
INSHELL
INSHINING
INSHIP
INSHOE
INSHOOT
INSHORE
INSHRINE
INSIDE
INSIDENT
INSIDER
INSIDES
INSIDIATE
INSIDIATION
INSIDIATOR
INSIDIOSITY
INSIDIOUS
INSIDIOUSLY
INSIGHT
INSIGHTED
INSIGHTFUL
INSIGNE
INSIGNIA
INSIGNIFICANCE
INSIGNIFICANCIES
INSIGNIFICANCY
INSIGNIFICANT
INSIGNIFICANTLY
INSIMPLICITY
INSINCERE
INSINCERELY
INSINCERITIES
INSINCERITY
INSINEW
INSINKING
INSINUANT
INSINUATE
INSINUATED
INSINUATING
INSINUATION

INSINUATIVE
INSINUATOR
INSINUATORY
INSINUENDO
INSIPID
INSIPIDITIES
INSIPIDITY
INSIPIDLY
INSIPIDNESS
INSIPIENCE
INSIPIENT
INSIPIENTLY
INSIST
INSISTED
INSISTENCE
INSISTENCY
INSISTENT
INSISTENTLY
INSISTER
INSISTING
INSISTIVE
INSISTURE
INSITE
INSITION
INSITITIOUS
INSNARE
INSNAREMENT
INSNARER
INSOBRIETY
INSOCIABILITY
INSOCIABLE
INSOCIABLY
INSOCIAL
INSOCIALLY
INSOLATE
INSOLATED
INSOLATING
INSOLATION
INSOLE
INSOLENCE
INSOLENCY
INSOLENT
INSOLENTLY
INSOLENTNESS
INSOLID
INSOLIDITY
INSOLITE
INSOLUBILITY
INSOLUBLE
INSOLUBLY
INSOLVABLE
INSOLVABLY
INSOLVENCE
INSOLVENCIES
INSOLVENCY
INSOLVENT
INSOMNIA
INSOMNIAC
INSOMNIOUS
INSOMNOLENCE
INSOMNOLENCY
INSOMNOLENT
INSOMUCH
INSOOTH
INSORB
INSORDID
INSOUCIANCE
INSOUCIANT
INSOUCIANTLY
INSOUL
INSPAKE
INSPAN
INSPANNED
INSPANNING
INSPEAK
INSPEAKING
INSPECT

INSPECTED
INSPECTING
INSPECTION
INSPECTIONAL
INSPECTIONEER
INSPECTIVE
INSPECTOR
INSPECTORAL
INSPECTORATE
INSPECTORIAL
INSPECTRESS
INSPECTRIX
INSPEXIMUS
INSPHERATION
INSPHERE
INSPIRABILITY
INSPIRABLE
INSPIRANT
INSPIRATION
INSPIRATIONAL
INSPIRATIVE
INSPIRATOR
INSPIRATORY
INSPIRE
INSPIRED
INSPIREDLY
INSPIRER
INSPIRING
INSPIRINGLY
INSPIRIT
INSPIRITED
INSPIRITER
INSPIRITING
INSPIRITINGLY
INSPIROMETER
INSPISSANT
INSPISSATE
INSPISSATED
INSPISSATING
INSPISSATION
INSPISSATOR
INSPISSOSIS
INSPOKE
INSPOKEN
INSPREITH
INSTABILITIES
INSTABILITY
INSTABLE
INSTAL
INSTALL
INSTALLANT
INSTALLATION
INSTALLED
INSTALLER
INSTALLING
INSTALLMENT
INSTANCE
INSTANCED
INSTANCING
INSTANCY
INSTANDING
INSTANT
INSTANTANEITY
INSTANTANEOUS
INSTANTER
INSTANTIAL
INSTANTLY
INSTAR
INSTARRED
INSTARRING
INSTATE
INSTATED
INSTATING
INSTAURATE
INSTAURATION
INSTAURATOR
INSTEAD

INSTEALING
INSTEAM
INSTEEP
INSTELLATION
INSTEP
INSTIGANT
INSTIGATE
INSTIGATED
INSTIGATING
INSTIGATION
INSTIGATIVE
INSTIGATOR
INSTIL
INSTILL
INSTILLATION
INSTILLATOR
INSTILLATORY
INSTILLED
INSTILLER
INSTILLING
INSTINCT
INSTINCTION
INSTINCTIVE
INSTINCTIVELY
INSTINCTIVIST
INSTINCTIVITY
INSTINCTUAL
INSTIPULATE
INSTITOR
INSTITORIAL
INSTITORY
INSTITUE
INSTITUTE
INSTITUTED
INSTITUTING
INSTITUTION
INSTITUTIONAL
INSTITUTIVE
INSTITUTOR
INSTONEMENT
INSTOP
INSTORE
INSTRATIFIED
INSTRENGTHEN
INSTRESSED
INSTROKE
INSTRUCT
INSTRUCTED
INSTRUCTING
INSTRUCTION
INSTRUCTIONAL
INSTRUCTIVE
INSTRUCTOR
INSTRUMENT
INSTRUMENTAL
INSTRUMENTALIST
INSTRUMENTALITIES
INSTRUMENTALITY
INSTRUMENTATE
INSTRUMENTED
INSTRUMENTS
INSTYLE
INSUAVITY
INSUBJECTION
INSUBMISSION
INSUBORDINATE
INSUBORDINATION
INSUBSTANTIAL
INSUBSTANTIALITY
INSUBSTANTIATE
INSUCCATION
INSUCCESS
INSUCCESSFUL
INSUCKEN
INSUETUDE
INSUFFERABLE
INSUFFERABLY

INSUFFICIENCE
INSUFFICIENCY
INSUFFICIENT
INSUFFICIENTLY
INSUFFLATE
INSUFFLATED
INSUFFLATION
INSUFFLATOR
INSULA
INSULAE
INSULANCE
INSULANT
INSULAR
INSULARITY
INSULARY
INSULATE
INSULATED
INSULATING
INSULATION
INSULATOR
INSULIN
INSULIZE
INSULPHURED
INSULSE
INSULSITY
INSULT
INSULTANT
INSULTATION
INSULTED
INSULTER
INSULTING
INSULTINGLY
INSUME
INSUNK
INSUPER
INSUPERABLE
INSUPERABLY
INSUPPORTABLE
INSUPPRESSIVE
INSURABILITY
INSURABLE
INSURANCE
INSURANT
INSURE
INSURED
INSUREDS
INSURER
INSURGE
INSURGENCE
INSURGENCY
INSURGENT
INSURGESCENCE
INSURING
INSURMOUNTABLE
INSURRECT
INSURRECTION
INSURRECTO
INSURRECTORY
INSUSCEPTIBLE
INSWARMING
INSWATHE
INSWATHEMENT
INSWEEPING
INSWELL
INSWEPT
INSWING
INSWINGER
INTABULATE
INTACT
INTACTILE
INTACTLY
INTACTNESS
INTAGLI
INTAGLIATED
INTAGLIO
INTAGLIOED
INTAGLIOING

INTAGLIOS
INTAKE
INTAKER
INTANGIBLE
INTANGIBLY
INTARISSABLE
INTARSIA
INTARSIATE
INTARSIST
INTEGER
INTEGERS
INTEGRABLE
INTEGRAL
INTEGRALITY
INTEGRANT
INTEGRAPH
INTEGRATE
INTEGRATED
INTEGRATING
INTEGRATION
INTEGRATIVE
INTEGRATOR
INTEGRIOUS
INTEGRIOUSLY
INTEGRITY
INTEGUMENT
INTEGUMENTAL
INTEIND
INTELLECT
INTELLECTATION
INTELLECTED
INTELLECTIBLE
INTELLECTION
INTELLECTIVE
INTELLECTUAL
INTELLIGENCE
INTELLIGENCY
INTELLIGENT
INTELLIGENTLY
INTELLIGENTSIA
INTELLIGIBLE
INTELLIGIBLY
INTELLIGIZE
INTEMERATE
INTEMERATELY
INTEMERATION
INTEMPERANCE
INTEMPERANCY
INTEMPERATE
INTEMPERATURE
INTEMPESTIVE
INTEMPORAL
INTEMPORALLY
INTEND
INTENDANCE
INTENDANCIES
INTENDANCY
INTENDANT
INTENDED
INTENDEDLY
INTENDEDNESS
INTENDENCE
INTENDENCIA
INTENDENTE
INTENDER
INTENDIBLE
INTENDING
INTENDINGLY
INTENDIT
INTENDMENT
INTENERATE
INTENERATED
INTENERATING
INTENERATION
INTENIBLE
INTENSATE
INTENSATION

INTENSATIVE
INTENSE
INTENSELY
INTENSIFIED
INTENSIFIER
INTENSIFY
INTENSIFYING
INTENSION
INTENSIONAL
INTENSIONALLY
INTENSITIES
INTENSITIVE
INTENSITY
INTENSIVE
INTENSIVELY
INTENSIVENESS
INTENT
INTENTED
INTENTION
INTENTIONAL
INTENTIONALITY
INTENTIONED
INTENTIVE
INTENTIVELY
INTENTLY
INTER
INTERACINOUS
INTERACT
INTERACTION
INTERACTIONISM
INTERACTIVE
INTERADDITIVE
INTERAGENT
INTERALLIED
INTERAMNIAN
INTERATOMIC
INTERAXAL
INTERAXIAL
INTERAXIS
INTERBANDED
INTERBED
INTERBEDDED
INTERBLEND
INTERBLENDED
INTERBLENDING
INTERBLENT
INTERBONDING
INTERBOROUGH
INTERBOURSE
INTERBRAIN
INTERBREED
INTERBREEDING
INTERCADENCE
INTERCADENT
INTERCALARE
INTERCALARIUM
INTERCALARY
INTERCALATE
INTERCALATED
INTERCALATING
INTERCALATION
INTERCANAL
INTERCARDINAL
INTERCAROTID
INTERCARPAL
INTERCEDE
INTERCEDED
INTERCEDER
INTERCEDING
INTERCENSAL
INTERCENTRA
INTERCENTRAL
INTERCENTRUM
INTERCEPT
INTERCEPTED
INTERCEPTER
INTERCEPTING

INTERCEPTION
INTERCEPTIVE
INTERCEPTOR
INTERCESS
INTERCESSION
INTERCESSIVE
INTERCESSOR
INTERCESSORY
INTERCHANGE
INTERCHANGEABLE
INTERCHANGED
INTERCHANGER
INTERCHANGING
INTERCHURCH
INTERCILIARY
INTERCILIUM
INTERCISION
INTERCIVIC
INTERCLAVICLE
INTERCLOUD
INTERCLUDE
INTERCLUSION
INTERCOASTAL
INTERCOLLEGE
INTERCOLLINE
INTERCOLONIAL
INTERCOLUMNIATION
INTERCOM
INTERCOMMON
INTERCOMMONED
INTERCOMMONING
INTERCOMMUNE
INTERCOMMUNED
INTERCOMMUNICATION
INTERCOMMUNING
INTERCONNECTED
INTERCONNECTING
INTERCONNECTION
INTERCOOLER
INTERCOOLING
INTERCOSMIC
INTERCOSTAL
INTERCOURSE
INTERCROP
INTERCROPPED
INTERCROPPING
INTERCROSS
INTERCROSSED
INTERCROSSING
INTERCUR
INTERCURRENT
INTERCUT
INTERDEAL
INTERDEALER
INTERDENTAL
INTERDENTIL
INTERDEPEND
INTERDEPENDENT
INTERDICT
INTERDICTION
INTERDICTIVE
INTERDICTOR
INTERDICTORY
INTERDIGITATE
INTERDIGITATED
INTERDIGITATING
INTERDOME
INTERESS
INTERESSE
INTERESSEE
INTEREST
INTERESTED
INTERESTER
INTERESTING
INTERESTINGLY
INTERESTS
INTERFACE

INTERFACIAL
INTERFECTOR
INTERFERANT
INTERFERE
INTERFERED
INTERFERENCE
INTERFERENT
INTERFERER
INTERFERING
INTERFEROMETER
INTERFERON
INTERFERRIC
INTERFERTILE
INTERFILAR
INTERFINGER
INTERFLANGE
INTERFLOW
INTERFLUENCE
INTERFLUENT
INTERFLUOUS
INTERFLUVE
INTERFLUVIAL
INTERFOLD
INTERFOLIATE
INTERFRET
INTERFRETTED
INTERFRONTAL
INTERFUSE
INTERFUSED
INTERFUSING
INTERFUSION
INTERGLACIAL
INTERGLYPH
INTERGRADE
INTERGRADED
INTERGRADING
INTERGRAFT
INTERGRAVE
INTERGROW
INTERGROWN
INTERGROWTH
INTERGULAR
INTERHAEMAL
INTERHEMAL
INTERHYAL
INTERIEUR
INTERIM
INTERIMIST
INTERIMISTIC
INTERIONIC
INTERIOR
INTERIORITY
INTERJACENCE
INTERJACENT
INTERJECT
INTERJECTED
INTERJECTING
INTERJECTION
INTERJECTOR
INTERJECTORY
INTERJOIN
INTERJOIST
INTERJUNCTION
INTERKINESIS
INTERKINETIC
INTERKNIT
INTERKNOT
INTERKNOW
INTERLACE
INTERLACED
INTERLACEDLY
INTERLACEMENT
INTERLACERY
INTERLACING
INTERLAID
INTERLAMINATE
INTERLAMINATED

INTERLAMINATING
INTERLAP
INTERLAPSE
INTERLARD
INTERLARDED
INTERLARDING
INTERLAY
INTERLAYING
INTERLEAF
INTERLEAGUE
INTERLEAVE
INTERLEAVED
INTERLEAVER
INTERLEAVES
INTERLEAVING
INTERLIBEL
INTERLINE
INTERLINEAL
INTERLINEAR
INTERLINEARLY
INTERLINEARY
INTERLINEATE
INTERLINED
INTERLINER
INTERLINGUAL
INTERLINING
INTERLINK
INTERLINKED
INTERLOCAL
INTERLOCATE
INTERLOCK
INTERLOCKED
INTERLOCKER
INTERLOCKING
INTERLOCULUS
INTERLOCUTION
INTERLOCUTIVE
INTERLOCUTOR
INTERLOCUTORY
INTERLOPE
INTERLOPED
INTERLOPER
INTERLOPING
INTERLOT
INTERLUCENT
INTERLUDE
INTERLUDER
INTERLUDIAL
INTERLUNAR
INTERLUNARY
INTERLUNATION
INTERMARRIED
INTERMARRY
INTERMARRYING
INTERMASTOID
INTERMEDDLE
INTERMEDDLED
INTERMEDDLER
INTERMEDDLING
INTERMEDE
INTERMEDIA
INTERMEDIACY
INTERMEDIAE
INTERMEDIAL
INTERMEDIARIES
INTERMEDIARY
INTERMEDIATE
INTERMEDIATED
INTERMEDIATING
INTERMEDIATOR
INTERMEDIUM
INTERMEDIUS
INTERMEMBRAL
INTERMENT
INTERMENTION
INTERMESH
INTERMESSAGE

INTERMEW
INTERMEWED
INTERMEWER
INTERMEZZI
INTERMEZZO
INTERMEZZOS
INTERMINABLE
INTERMINANT
INTERMINATE
INTERMINATED
INTERMINE
INTERMINED
INTERMINGLE
INTERMINGLED
INTERMINGLING
INTERMINING
INTERMISSION
INTERMISSIVE
INTERMIT
INTERMITTED
INTERMITTENT
INTERMITTENTLY
INTERMITTING
INTERMIX
INTERMIXED
INTERMIXEDLY
INTERMIXING
INTERMIXT
INTERMIXTLY
INTERMIXTURE
INTERMURAL
INTERMUTATION
INTERMUTUAL
INTERN
INTERNAL
INTERNALITIES
INTERNALITY
INTERNALIZE
INTERNALLY
INTERNALNESS
INTERNARIAL
INTERNASAL
INTERNATION
INTERNATIONAL
INTERNE
INTERNECINE
INTERNECION
INTERNECIVE
INTERNECT
INTERNECTION
INTERNED
INTERNEE
INTERNETTED
INTERNEURAL
INTERNEURON
INTERNING
INTERNIST
INTERNMENT
INTERNOBASAL
INTERNODAL
INTERNODE
INTERNODIA
INTERNODIAL
INTERNODIAN
INTERNODIUM
INTERNSHIP
INTERNUCLEAR
INTERNUNCIAL
INTERNUNCIO
INTERNUNCIOS
INTERNUPTIAL
INTERNUPTIALS
INTEROCEPTOR
INTEROCULAR
INTEROLIVARY
INTEROPERCLE
INTEROPTIC

INTEROSCULANT
INTEROSCULATE
INTEROSCULATED
INTEROSCULATING
INTEROSSEAL
INTEROSSEI
INTEROSSEOUS
INTEROSSEUS
INTERPAGE
INTERPASS
INTERPAUSE
INTERPEAL
INTERPEL
INTERPELLANT
INTERPELLATE
INTERPELLATED
INTERPELLATING
INTERPELLATION
INTERPELLED
INTERPELLING
INTERPENDENT
INTERPENETRATE
INTERPENETRATE
INTERPHASE
INTERPIECE
INTERPLACE
INTERPLAIT
INTERPLAY
INTERPLEA
INTERPLEAD
INTERPLEADER
INTERPLEURAL
INTERPLICATE
INTERPOINT
INTERPOLABLE
INTERPOLAR
INTERPOLARY
INTERPOLATE
INTERPOLATED
INTERPOLATER
INTERPOLATING
INTERPOLATION
INTERPOLATOR
INTERPOLE
INTERPOLISH
INTERPOLITY
INTERPONE
INTERPORTAL
INTERPOSAL
INTERPOSE
INTERPOSED
INTERPOSER
INTERPOSING
INTERPOSURE
INTERPRET
INTERPRETABLE
INTERPRETATE
INTERPRETATION
INTERPRETED
INTERPRETER
INTERPRETING
INTERPRETIVE
INTERPUBIC
INTERRACIAL
INTERRADIAL
INTERRADII
INTERRADIUM
INTERRADIUS
INTERRAMAL
INTERRED
INTERREGAL
INTERREGES
INTERREGNA
INTERREGNAL
INTERREGNUM
INTERREIGN
INTERRELATE

INTERRELATED
INTERRELATING
INTERRELATION
INTERRELATIONS
INTERRENAL
INTERRER
INTERREX
INTERRIGHT
INTERRING
INTERROGANT
INTERROGATE
INTERROGATED
INTERROGATEE
INTERROGATING
INTERROGATION
INTERROGATOR
INTERROGEE
INTERRUPT
INTERRUPTED
INTERRUPTER
INTERRUPTING
INTERRUPTION
INTERRUPTIVE
INTERRUPTOR
INTERSCRIBE
INTERSEAMED
INTERSECT
INTERSECTANT
INTERSECTED
INTERSECTING
INTERSECTION
INTERSEPTAL
INTERSERTAL
INTERSESSION
INTERSEX
INTERSEXUAL
INTERSEXUALITY
INTERSHOCK
INTERSHOOT
INTERSOCIAL
INTERSOMNIAL
INTERSOW
INTERSPACE
INTERSPATIAL
INTERSPEAKER
INTERSPERSAL
INTERSPERSE
INTERSPERSED
INTERSPERSING
INTERSPHERE
INTERSPINAL
INTERSPINOUS
INTERSPORAL
INTERSTADIAL
INTERSTAGE
INTERSTATE
INTERSTELLAR
INTERSTERILE
INTERSTERNAL
INTERSTICE
INTERSTICED
INTERSTICES
INTERSTITIAL
INTERSTRATIFY
INTERSTRIAL
INTERTALK
INTERTANGLE
INTERTEAR
INTERTERGAL
INTERTEX
INTERTEXTURE
INTERTIDAL
INTERTIE
INTERTILL
INTERTILLAGE
INTERTISSUED
INTERTONE

INTERTONGUE
INTERTONIC
INTERTRAGIAN
INTERTRIBAL
INTERTRIGO
INTERTROPIC
INTERTROPICS
INTERTRUDE
INTERTWINE
INTERTWINED
INTERTWINING
INTERTWIST
INTERTWISTED
INTERTWISTING
INTERURBAN
INTERVAL
INTERVALE
INTERVALED
INTERVALING
INTERVALLED
INTERVALLIC
INTERVALLING
INTERVALS
INTERVEIN
INTERVEINAL
INTERVEINED
INTERVEINING
INTERVENANT
INTERVENE
INTERVENED
INTERVENER
INTERVENIENT
INTERVENING
INTERVENIUM
INTERVENOR
INTERVENT
INTERVENTION
INTERVENTIVE
INTERVENTOR
INTERVENULAR
INTERVERBAL
INTERVERSION
INTERVERT
INTERVERTED
INTERVERTING
INTERVIEW
INTERVIEWED
INTERVIEWEE
INTERVIEWER
INTERVIEWING
INTERVILLOUS
INTERVISIT
INTERVITAL
INTERVOCAL
INTERVOCALIC
INTERVOLVE
INTERVOLVED
INTERVOLVING
INTERWEAVE
INTERWEAVED
INTERWEAVER
INTERWEAVING
INTERWED
INTERWIND
INTERWINDING
INTERWORK
INTERWORKED
INTERWORKING
INTERWOUND
INTERWOVE
INTERWOVEN
INTERWREATHE
INTERWREATHED
INTERWREATHING
INTERWROUGHT
INTERXYLARY
INTERZONAL

INTESTABLE	INTOOTHED	INTRIGANT	INTUBATE	INVALESCENCE
INTESTACIES	INTORSION	INTRIGANTE	INTUBATION	INVALID
INTESTACY	INTORT	INTRIGANTS	INTUBATOR	INVALIDATE
INTESTATE	INTORTED	INTRIGO	INTUBE	INVALIDATED
INTESTATION	INTORTILLAGE	INTRIGUE	INTUE	INVALIDATING
INTESTINAL	INTORTING	INTRIGUED	INTUENT	INVALIDATOR
INTESTINE	INTOWER	INTRIGUER	INTUICITY	INVALIDED
INTESTINES	INTOWN	INTRIGUERY	INTUIT	INVALIDING
INTEXINE	INTOXATION	INTRIGUING	INTUITABLE	INVALIDISM
INTEXT	INTOXICABLE	INTRIGUINGLY	INTUITION	INVALIDITY
INTEXTINE	INTOXICANT	INTRINE	INTUITIONAL	INVALUABLE
INTEXTURE	INTOXICATE	INTRINSE	INTUITIONISM	INVALUABLY
INTHRAL	INTOXICATED	INTRINSIC	INTUITIONIST	INVALUED
INTHRALL	INTOXICATING	INTRINSICAL	INTUITIVE	INVARIABLE
INTHRALLMENT	INTOXICATION	INTRINSICALLY	INTUITIVELY	INVARIABLENESS
INTHRALMENT	INTOXICATIVE	INTRINSICATE	INTUITIVISM	INVARIABLY
INTHRONE	INTOXICATOR	INTRO	INTUITIVIST	INVARIANCE
INTHRONG	INTRA	INTROCEPTIVE	INTUMESCE	INVARIANCY
INTHRONISTIC	INTRABIONTIC	INTRODDEN	INTUMESCED	INVARIANT
INTHRONIZATE	INTRABRED	INTRODUCE	INTUMESCENCE	INVARIANTIVE
INTHRONIZE	INTRACARDIAC	INTRODUCED	INTUMESCENT	INVARIANTLY
INTHROW	INTRACHORDAL	INTRODUCEE	INTUMESCING	INVARIED
INTHRUST	INTRACISTERN	INTRODUCER	INTURBIDATE	INVASION
INTIL	INTRACOASTAL	INTRODUCING	INTURN	INVASIVE
INTILL	INTRACTABLE	INTRODUCTION	INTURNED	INVECT
INTIMA	INTRACTABLY	INTRODUCTIVE	INTURNING	INVECTED
INTIMACIES	INTRACTILE	INTRODUCTOR	INTUSE	INVECTION
INTIMACY	INTRADA	INTRODUCTORY	INTUSSUSCEPT	INVECTIVE
INTIMADO	INTRADO	INTROFACTION	INTWINE	INVECTIVELY
INTIMADOS	INTRADOS	INTROFIED	INTWIST	INVEIGH
INTIMAE	INTRADURAL	INTROFIER	INUKSHUK	INVEIGHED
INTIMAL	INTRAFUSAL	INTROFLEX	INULA	INVEIGHER
INTIMATE	INTRAGANTES	INTROFLEXION	INULACEOUS	INVEIGHING
INTIMATED	INTRAGLACIAL	INTROFY	INULASE	INVEIGLE
INTIMATELY	INTRAGROUP	INTROFYING	INULIN	INVEIGLED
INTIMATENESS	INTRAGROUPAL	INTROIT	INULOID	INVEIGLER
INTIMATER	INTRAIL	INTROITUS	INUMBRATE	INVEIGLING
INTIMATING	INTRAIT	INTROJECTION	INUNCT	INVEIL
INTIMATION	INTRALOGICAL	INTROMISSION	INUNCTION	INVENIENT
INTIME	INTRAMENTAL	INTROMISSIVE	INUNCTUM	INVENIT
INTIMIDATE	INTRAMONTANE	INTROMIT	INUND	INVENT
INTIMIDATED	INTRAMUNDANE	INTROMITTED	INUNDABLE	INVENTARY
INTIMIDATING	INTRAMURAL	INTROMITTENT	INUNDANT	INVENTED
INTIMIDATION	INTRAMURALLY	INTROMITTER	INUNDATE	INVENTER
INTIMIDATOR	INTRANATAL	INTROMITTING	INUNDATED	INVENTIBLE
INTIMISM	INTRANEOUS	INTROPULSIVE	INUNDATING	INVENTING
INTIMITY	INTRANSIENT	INTRORSE	INUNDATION	INVENTION
INTINCT	INTRANSIGENT	INTRORSELY	INUNDATOR	INVENTIONAL
INTINCTION	INTRANSITABLE	INTROSPECT	INUNDATORY	INVENTIVE
INTINE	INTRANSITIVE	INTROSPECTED	INURBANE	INVENTIVELY
INTISY	INTRANT	INTROSPECTING	INURBANITY	INVENTIVENESS
INTITLE	INTRAPIAL	INTROSPECTION	INURE	INVENTOR
INTITULE	INTRAPOLAR	INTROSPECTOR	INURED	INVENTORIAL
INTITULED	INTRAPSYCHIC	INTROSUSCEPT	INUREDNESS	INVENTORIED
INTITULING	INTRASTATE	INTROVENIENT	INURING	INVENTORIES
INTO	INTRATE	INTROVERSE	INURN	INVENTORY
INTOED	INTRATHECAL	INTROVERSION	INURNED	INVENTORYING
INTOLERABLE	INTRATHYROID	INTROVERSIVE	INURNING	INVERACITY
INTOLERABLY	INTRAUTERINE	INTROVERT	INUSITATE	INVERITY
INTOLERANCE	INTRAVAGINAL	INTROVERTED	INUSITATION	INVERMINATE
INTOLERANCY	INTRAVENOUS	INTROVERTING	INUSTION	INVERSE
INTOLERANT	INTRAVITAL	INTROVERTIVE	INUTILE	INVERSED
INTOLERANTLY	INTRAXYLARY	INTRUDANCE	INUTILELY	INVERSEDLY
INTOLERATING	INTREAT	INTRUDE	INUTILITIES	INVERSELY
INTOLERATION	INTRENCH	INTRUDED	INUTILITY	INVERSION
INTOMB	INTRENCHANT	INTRUDER	INUTTERABLE	INVERSIVE
INTONABLE	INTRENCHED	INTRUDING	INVACCINATE	INVERT
INTONACO	INTRENCHER	INTRUDINGLY	INVADE	INVERTASE
INTONATE	INTRENCHING	INTRUS	INVADED	INVERTEBRAL
INTONATED	INTREPID	INTRUSE	INVADER	INVERTEBRATE
INTONATING	INTREPIDITY	INTRUSION	INVADERS	INVERTED
INTONATION	INTREPIDLY	INTRUSIONAL	INVADING	INVERTEDLY
INTONATOR	INTREPIDNESS	INTRUSIONIST	INVAGINABLE	INVERTEND
INTONE	INTRICACIES	INTRUSIVE	INVAGINATE	INVERTER
INTONED	INTRICACY	INTRUSIVELY	INVAGINATED	INVERTIBLE
INTONER	INTRICATE	INTRUSO	INVAGINATING	INVERTILE
INTONING	INTRICATELY	INTRUST	INVAGINATION	INVERTIN

INVERTING	INVOKE	IODIZATION	IRATE	IRONBOUND
INVERTOR	INVOKED	IODIZE	IRATELY	IRONBUSH
INVEST	INVOKER	IODIZED	IRBIS	IRONCLAD
INVESTED	INVOKING	IODIZER	IRCHIN	IRONE
INVESTIENT	INVOLUCEL	IODIZING	IRE	IRONED
INVESTIGABLE	INVOLUCRA	IODO	IREFUL	IRONER
INVESTIGATE	INVOLUCRAL	IODOBEHENATE	IREFULLY	IRONFISTED
INVESTIGATED	INVOLUCRATE	IODOBENZENE	IREFULNESS	IRONFLOWER
INVESTIGATING	INVOLUCRE	IODOBROMITE	IRENARCH	IRONHANDED
INVESTIGATION	INVOLUCRED	IODOCASEIN	IRENIC	IRONHARD
INVESTIGATOR	INVOLUCRUM	IODOCHLORID	IRENICA	IRONHEAD
INVESTING	INVOLUNTARY	IODOCHLORIDE	IRENICAL	IRONHEADED
INVESTITIVE	INVOLUTE	IODOCRESOL	IRENICALLY	IRONHEARTED
INVESTITOR	INVOLUTED	IODODERMA	IRENICISM	IRONIC
INVESTITURE	INVOLUTEDLY	IODOETHANE	IRENICIST	IRONICAL
INVESTMENT	INVOLUTION	IODOFORM	IRENICON	IRONICALLY
INVESTOR	INVOLUTIONAL	IODOGALLICIN	IRENICS	IRONICALNESS
INVETERACY	INVOLUTORIAL	IODOHYDRIN	IREOS	IRONICE
INVETERATE	INVOLUTORY	IODOL	IRIAN	IRONIES
INVETERATELY	INVOLVE	IODOMETHANE	IRID	IRONING
INVIABLE	INVOLVED	IODOMETRIC	IRIDACEOUS	IRONIOUSLY
INVIABLY	INVOLVEMENT	IODOMETRY	IRIDAL	IRONISH
INVICT	INVOLVENT	IODONIUM	IRIDATE	IRONISM
INVICTED	INVOLVER	IODOSO	IRIDECTOMIES	IRONIST
INVICTIVE	INVOLVING	IODOSPONGIN	IRIDECTOMY	IRONIZE
INVIDIOUS	INVULNERABLE	IODOTHERAPY	IRIDEOUS	IRONLESS
INVIDIOUSLY	INVULNERABLY	IODOTHYRIN	IRIDES	IRONLIKE
INVIGILATE	INVULTUATION	IODOUS	IRIDESCE	IRONLY
INVIGILATION	INWALE	IODOXY	IRIDESCENCE	IRONMAN
INVIGILATOR	INWALL	IODYRITE	IRIDESCENCY	IRONMASTER
INVIGORANT	INWANDERING	IOLITE	IRIDESCENT	IRONMEN
INVIGORATE	INWARD	ION	IRIDESCENTLY	IRONMONGER
INVIGORATED	INWARDLY	IONIC	IRIDIATE	IRONMONGERY
INVIGORATING	INWARDNESS	IONICAL	IRIDIC	IRONNESS
INVIGORATION	INWARDS	IONIUM	IRIDICAL	IRONS
INVIGORATIVE	INWEAVE	IONIZABLE	IRIDIN	IRONSHOD
INVIGORATOR	INWEDGED	IONIZATION	IRIDINE	IRONSHOT
INVINATE	INWEED	IONIZE	IRIDIOUS	IRONSIDE
INVINATION	INWEIGHT	IONIZER	IRIDITE	IRONSIDED
INVINCIBLE	INWICK	IONOGEN	IRIDIUM	IRONSIDES
INVINCIBLY	INWIND	IONOGENIC	IRIDIZATION	IRONSMITH
INVIOLABILITY	INWINDING	IONONE	IRIDIZE	IRONSTONE
INVIOLABLE	INWIT	IONOPAUSE	IRIDIZED	IRONWARE
INVIOLABLY	INWITH	IONOSPHERE	IRIDIZING	IRONWEED
INVIOLACY	INWORK	IOTA	IRIDOCYTE	IRONWOOD
INVIOLATE	INWORKS	IOTACISM	IRIDODESIS	IRONWORK
INVIOLATELY	INWORN	IOTACISMUS	IRIDODONESIS	IRONWORKED
INVIOUS	INWOUND	IOTACIST	IRIDOPHORE	IRONWORKER
INVIOUSNESS	INWOVEN	IOTAS	IRIDOPLEGIA	IRONWORKING
INVIRTUATE	INWRAP	IOTIZATION	IRIDOSMINE	IRONWORKS
INVISCATE	INWRAPPED	IOTIZE	IRIDOTASIS	IRONWORT
INVISED	INWRAPPING	IOTIZED	IRIDOTOMIES	IRONY
INVISIBILITY	INWRAPT	IOTIZING	IRIDOTOMY	IROUS
INVISIBLE	INWREATHE	IPECAC	IRIRI	IRPE
INVISIBLY	INWRIT	IPECACUANHA	IRIS	IRRADIANCE
INVITANT	INWRITTEN	IPECACUANHIC	IRISATED	IRRADIANCY
INVITATION	INWROUGHT	IPETE	IRISATION	IRRADIANT
INVITATIONAL	INYALA	IPI	IRISCOPE	IRRADIATE
INVITATORY	INYOITE	IPID	IRISED	IRRADIATED
INVITE	INYOKE	IPIL	IRISES	IRRADIATING
INVITED	IOA	IPILIPIL	IRISIN	IRRADIATION
INVITEE	IOD	IPITI	IRISING	IRRADIATIVE
INVITER	IODATE	IPO	IRISROOT	IRRADIATOR
INVITING	IODATED	IPOMEA	IRITIC	IRRADICABLE
INVITINGLY	IODATING	IPOMOEIN	IRITIS	IRRADICATE
INVITINGNESS	IODATION	IPSE	IRK	IRRAREFIABLE
INVIVID	IODIC	IPSEAND	IRKED	IRRATIONABLE
INVOCABLE	IODID	IPSEITY	IRKING	IRRATIONAL
INVOCANT	IODIDE	IR	IRKSOME	IRRATIONALLY
INVOCATE	IODIN	IRACUND	IRKSOMELY	IRREALITY
INVOCATION	IODINATE	IRACUNDITY	IRKSOMENESS	IRREALIZABLE
INVOCATIVE	IODINATION	IRACUNDULOUS	IRNE	IRREBUTTABLE
INVOCATOR	IODINE	IRADE	IROK	IRRECEPTIVE
INVOCATORY	IODINOPHIL	IRASCENT	IROKO	IRRECIPROCAL
INVOICE	IODINOPHILE	IRASCIBILITY	IRON	IRRECLAIMED
INVOICED	IODINOPHILIC	IRASCIBLE	IRONBACK	IRRECONCILE
INVOICING	IODISM	IRASCIBLY	IRONBARK	IRRECORDABLE

IRRECUSABLE	IRRESOLUTE	IRRUBRICAL	ISINGLASS	ISOCOLIC
IRREDEEMABLE	IRRESOLUTELY	IRRUGATE	ISLAND	ISOCOLON
IRREDEEMABLY	IRRESOLUTION	IRRUPT	ISLANDED	ISOCORIA
IRREDENTA	IRRESOLVABLE	IRRUPTED	ISLANDER	ISOCRACY
IRREDENTIAL	IRRESOLVED	IRRUPTIBLE	ISLANDIC	ISOCRAT
IRREDRESSIBLE	IRRESOLVEDLY	IRRUPTING	ISLANDING	ISOCRATIC
IRREDUCIBLE	IRRESONANCE	IRRUPTION	ISLANDMAN	ISOCRYMAL
IRREDUCIBLY	IRRESONANT	IRRUPTIVE	ISLANDMEN	ISOCRYME
IRREDUCTIBLE	IRRESPECTABLE	IRRUPTIVELY	ISLANDRY	ISOCRYMIC
IRREDUCTION	IRRESPECTFUL	IRUL	ISLANDS	ISOCYANATE
IRREFERABLE	IRRESPECTIVE	IRY	ISLANDY	ISOCYANIC
IRREFLECTION	IRRESPIRABLE	IS	ISLAY	ISOCYANID
IRREFLECTIVE	IRRESPONSIBLE	ISABELINA	ISLE	ISOCYANIDE
IRREFLEXIVE	IRRESPONSIVE	ISABELITA	ISLED	ISOCYANIN
IRREFORMABLE	IRRESTRICTIVE	ISABELITE	ISLEMAN	ISOCYANINE
IRREFRAGABLE	IRRESULTIVE	ISABNORMAL	ISLESMEN	ISOCYANO
IRREFRANGIBLE	IRRETENTION	ISACOUSTIC	ISLET	ISOCYTIC
IRREFUSABLE	IRRETENTIVE	ISADELPHOUS	ISLETED	ISODACTYLOUS
IRREFUTABLE	IRRETICENCE	ISAGOGE	ISLING	ISODIABATIC
IRREGARDLESS	IRRETICENT	ISAGOGIC	ISLOT	ISODIAMETRIC
IRREGENERACY	IRRETRACEABLE	ISAGOGICAL	ISM	ISODOMON
IRREGENERATE	IRRETRACTABLE	ISAGOGICALLY	ISMAL	ISODOMOUS
IRREGULAR	IRRETRACTILE	ISAGOGICS	ISMATIC	ISODOMUM
IRREGULARIST	IRRETRIEVABLE	ISAGON	ISMATICAL	ISODONT
IRREGULARITIES	IRRETURNABLE	ISALLOBAR	ISMY	ISODONTOUS
IRREGULARITY	IRREVEALABLE	ISALLOTHERM	ISNAD	ISODRIN
IRREGULARIZE	IRREVEALABLY	ISAMIN	ISO	ISODROME
IRREGULARLY	IRREVERENCE	ISAMINE	ISOAMID	ISODYNAMIA
IRREGULATE	IRREVEREND	ISANDROUS	ISOAMIDE	ISODYNAMIC
IRREGULATED	IRREVERENDLY	ISANEMONE	ISOAMYL	ISOELECTRIC
IRREGULOUS	IRREVERENT	ISANOMAL	ISOBAR	ISOENERGETIC
IRRELATE	IRREVERENTLY	ISANOMALOUS	ISOBARE	ISOEUGENOL
IRRELATED	IRREVERSIBLE	ISANTHOUS	ISOBARIC	ISOGAM
IRRELATION	IRREVERSIBLY	ISAPOSTOLIC	ISOBARISM	ISOGAMETE
IRRELATIVE	IRREVERTIBLE	ISARIOID	ISOBASE	ISOGAMETIC
IRRELATIVELY	IRREVISABLE	ISATATE	ISOBATH	ISOGAMETISM
IRRELEVANCE	IRREVOCABLE	ISATIC	ISOBATHIC	ISOGAMIC
IRRELEVANCIES	IRREVOCABLY	ISATID	ISOBORNEOL	ISOGAMOUS
IRRELEVANCY	IRREVOLUBLE	ISATIDE	ISOBRONT	ISOGAMY
IRRELEVANT	IRRIDE	ISATIN	ISOBRONTON	ISOGEN
IRRELEVANTLY	IRRIGABLE	ISATINE	ISOBUTYRIC	ISOGENESIS
IRRELIEVABLE	IRRIGABLY	ISATOGEN	ISOCARPIC	ISOGENETIC
IRRELIGION	IRRIGANT	ISATOGENIC	ISOCARPOUS	ISOGENIC
IRRELIGIOUS	IRRIGATE	ISBA	ISOCELLULAR	ISOGENOTYPE
IRRELUCTANT	IRRIGATED	ISCHAR	ISOCEPHALIC	ISOGENOUS
IRREMEABLE	IRRIGATING	ISCHEMIA	ISOCEPHALISM	ISOGENY
IRREMEABLY	IRRIGATION	ISCHIA	ISOCEPHALY	ISOGEOTHERM
IRREMEDIABLE	IRRIGATIONAL	ISCHIAC	ISOCERCAL	ISOGLOSS
IRREMEDIABLY	IRRIGATIVE	ISCHIADIC	ISOCERCY	ISOGLOSSAL
IRREMEDILESS	IRRIGATOR	ISCHIALGIA	ISOCHASM	ISOGLOSSES
IRREMISSIBLE	IRRIGATORY	ISCHIALGIC	ISOCHASMIC	ISOGNATHISM
IRREMISSIBLY	IRRIGUOUS	ISCHIATIC	ISOCHEIM	ISOGNATHOUS
IRREMISSIVE	IRRISION	ISCHIDROSIS	ISOCHEIMAL	ISOGON
IRREMOVABLE	IRRISOR	ISCHIOCERITE	ISOCHEIMENAL	ISOGONAL
IRREMOVABLY	IRRISORY	ISCHIOPODITE	ISOCHEIMIC	ISOGONALITY
IRRENDERABLE	IRRITABILITIES	ISCHIOPUBIS	ISOCHELA	ISOGONALLY
IRRENEWABLE	IRRITABILITY	ISCHIUM	ISOCHLOR	ISOGONIC
IRREPAIR	IRRITABLE	ISCHOCHOLIA	ISOCHOR	ISOGONIOSTAT
IRREPAIRABLE	IRRITABLY	ISCHURETIC	ISOCHORE	ISOGONISM
IRREPARABLE	IRRITAMENT	ISCHURIA	ISOCHORIC	ISOGRAFT
IRREPARABLY	IRRITANCIES	ISCHURY	ISOCHROMATIC	ISOGRAM
IRREPASSABLE	IRRITANCY	ISE	ISOCHRONAL	ISOGRAPH
IRREPEALABLE	IRRITANT	ISEL	ISOCHRONALLY	ISOGRAPHIC
IRREPEALABLY	IRRITATE	ISENERGIC	ISOCHRONE	ISOGRAPHY
IRREPENTANCE	IRRITATED	ISENTROPIC	ISOCHRONIC	ISOGRIV
IRREPENTANT	IRRITATING	ISEPIPTESIAL	ISOCHRONISM	ISOGYNOUS
IRREPORTABLE	IRRITATINGLY	ISEPIPTESIS	ISOCHRONIZE	ISOGYRE
IRREPRESSIVE	IRRITATION	ISERINE	ISOCHRONIZED	ISOHALSINE
IRREPROACHABLE	IRRITATIVE	ISERITE	ISOCHRONIZING	ISOHEL
IRREPROVABLE	IRRITATOR	ISETHIONATE	ISOCHRONON	ISOHYDRIC
IRREPROVABLY	IRRITATORY	ISH	ISOCHRONOUS	ISOHYET
IRREPTITIOUS	IRRITE	ISHPINGO	ISOCHROOUS	ISOHYETAL
IRRESILIENT	IRRITOMOTILE	ISIDIA	ISOCLASITE	ISOKERAUNIC
IRRESISTANCE	IRROGATE	ISIDIOID	ISOCLINAL	ISOKONTAN
IRRESISTIBLE	IRRORATE	ISIDIOSE	ISOCLINE	ISOLABILITY
IRRESISTIBLY	IRRORATION	ISIDIUM	ISOCLINIC	ISOLABLE
IRRESOLUBLE	IRROTATIONAL	ISING	ISOCOLA	ISOLATE

ISOLATED	ISOPODIFORM	ISSITE	ITINERANT
ISOLATING	ISOPODOUS	ISSUABLE	ITINERANTLY
ISOLATION	ISOPOGONOUS	ISSUANCE	ITINERARIAN
ISOLATIONISM	ISOPOLITE	ISSUANT	ITINERARIES
ISOLATIONIST	ISOPOLITICAL	ISSUE	ITINERARY
ISOLATIVE	ISOPOLITY	ISSUED	ITINERATE
ISOLATOR	ISOPOLY	ISSUER	ITINERATED
ISOLEAD	ISOPRENE	ISSUING	ITINERATING
ISOLETTE	ISOPROPENYL	IST	ITINERATION
ISOLEUCINE	ISOPROPYL	ISTHMI	ITMO
ISOLICHENIN	ISOPSEPHIC	ISTHMIAN	ITOUBOU
ISOLINE	ISOPSEPHISM	ISTHMIATE	ITR
ISOLOG	ISOPTEROUS	ISTHMIC	ITS
ISOLOGOUS	ISOPTIC	ISTHMOID	ITSELF
ISOLOGUE	ISOPYCNIC	ISTHMUS	ITZEBU
ISOLOGY	ISOPYRE	ISTHMUSES	IUS
ISOLYSIN	ISOQUINOLINE	ISTLE	IVA
ISOLYSIS	ISORHYTHM	ISURETINE	IVIED
ISOMAGNETIC	ISORITHM	ISUROID	IVIES
ISOMALTOSE	ISORRHYTHMIC	IT	IVIN
ISOMASTIGATE	ISORROPIC	ITABIRITE	IVORIED
ISOMER	ISOSCELE	ITAC	IVORIES
ISOMERE	ISOSCELES	ITACISM	IVORINE
ISOMERIC	ISOSCOPE	ITACIST	IVORINESS
ISOMERICAL	ISOSEISMAL	ITACISTIC	IVORIST
ISOMERICALLY	ISOSEISMIC	ITACOLUMITE	IVORY
ISOMERIDE	ISOSMOTIC	ITACONIC	IVORYTYPE
ISOMERISM	ISOSPORE	ITALIC	IVRAY
ISOMERIZE	ISOSPORIC	ITALICIZE	IVRESSE
ISOMEROUS	ISOSPOROUS	ITALICIZED	IVY
ISOMERY	ISOSPORY	ITALICIZING	IVYBELLS
ISOMETRIC	ISOSTASIST	ITALICS	IVYBERRY
ISOMETRICAL	ISOSTASY	ITALITE	IVYFLOWER
ISOMETROGRAPH	ISOSTATIC	ITAUBA	IVYING
ISOMETROPIA	ISOSTATICAL	ITCH	IVYWOOD
ISOMETRY	ISOSTEMONY	ITCHED	IVYWORT
ISOMORPH	ISOSTER	ITCHEOGLAN	IWA
ISOMORPHIC	ISOSTERE	ITCHIER	IWAIWA
ISOMORPHISM	ISOSTERIC	ITCHIEST	IWAN
ISOMORPHOUS	ISOSTERISM	ITCHING	IWEARTH
ISOMYARIAN	ISOTAC	ITCHINGLY	IWIS
ISONEPH	ISOTACH	ITCHLESS	IWORTH
ISONEPHELIC	ISOTE	ITCHREED	IWURCHE
ISONIAZID	ISOTELES	ITCHWEED	IWURTHEN
ISONITRIL	ISOTELY	ITCHWOOD	IXODIAN
ISONITRILE	ISOTHERAL	ITCHY	IXODIC
ISONITRO	ISOTHERE	ITCZE	IXODID
ISONITROSO	ISOTHERM	ITEM	IXTLE
ISONOMIC	ISOTHERMAL	ITEMING	IYA
ISONOMOUS	ISOTHERMIC	ITEMIZATION	IYO
ISONOMY	ISOTHERMICAL	ITEMIZE	IZAFAT
ISONUCLEAR	ISOTHERMOUS	ITEMIZED	IZAR
ISONYM	ISOTHIOCYANO	ITEMIZER	IZARD
ISONYMIC	ISOTOME	ITEMIZING	IZBA
ISONYMY	ISOTOMOUS	ITEMS	IZLE
ISOOCTANE	ISOTONE	ITEMY	IZOTE
ISOPACHOUS	ISOTONIA	ITER	IZTLE
ISOPAG	ISOTONIC	ITERABLE	IZTLI
ISOPARAFFIN	ISOTONICITY	ITERANCE	IZVOZCHIK
ISOPERIMETER	ISOTOPE	ITERANCY	IZZARD
ISOPERIMETRY	ISOTOPIC	ITERANT	IZZAT
ISOPETALOUS	ISOTOPISM	ITERATE	
ISOPHANAL	ISOTOPY	ITERATED	
ISOPHANE	ISOTRON	ITERATELY	
ISOPHASAL	ISOTROPE	ITERATING	
ISOPHENE	ISOTROPIC	ITERATION	
ISOPHORIA	ISOTROPISM	ITERATIVE	
ISOPHOTE	ISOTROPOUS	ITERATIVELY	
ISOPHTHALIC	ISOTROPY	ITERS	
ISOPHTHALYL	ISOTYPE	ITERUM	
ISOPHYLLOUS	ISOTYPIC	ITHAGINE	
ISOPHYLLY	ISOTYPICAL	ITHAND	
ISOPIESTIC	ISOVALERATE	ITHER	
ISOPLERE	ISOXAZOLE	ITHOMIID	
ISOPLETH	ISOZOOID	ITHYPHALLIC	
ISOPOD	ISPAGHUL	ITINERACY	
ISOPODAN	ISPRAYNIK	ITINERANCY	

JA
JAB
JABBED
JABBER
JABBERED
JABBERER
JABBERING
JABBERINGLY
JABBERMENT
JABBING
JABBLE
JABERS
JABIA
JABIRU
JABORANDI
JABORIN
JABORINE
JABOT
JABOTICABA
JABOTS
JABUL
JABULES
JACA
JACAL
JACALES
JACAMAR
JACAMEROPINE
JACAMIN
JACANA
JACARANDA
JACARE
JACATE
JACATOO
JACCHUS
JACCONET
JACCONOT
JACENT
JACINTH
JACINTHE
JACITARA
JACK
JACKAL
JACKALS
JACKANAPES
JACKAROO
JACKASH
JACKASS
JACKASSERY
JACKBIRD
JACKBOOT
JACKBOX
JACKBOY
JACKDAW
JACKED
JACKEEN
JACKER
JACKEROO
JACKEROOS
JACKET
JACKETED
JACKETING
JACKETY
JACKFISH
JACKFISHES
JACKFRUIT
JACKHAMMER
JACKHEAD

JACKING
JACKKNIFE
JACKKNIVES
JACKLEG
JACKLIGHT
JACKMAN
JACKMEN
JACKO
JACKPLANE
JACKPOT
JACKPOTS
JACKPUDDING
JACKROD
JACKROLL
JACKS
JACKSAW
JACKSCREW
JACKSHAFT
JACKSHAY
JACKSHEA
JACKSLAVE
JACKSMELT
JACKSMITH
JACKSNIPE
JACKSNIPES
JACKSTAY
JACKSTOCK
JACKSTONE
JACKSTRAW
JACKTAN
JACKWEED
JACKWOOD
JACKY
JACOBAEA
JACOBIN
JACOBSITE
JACOBUS
JACOBY
JACOLATT
JACONET
JACOUNCE
JACQUARD
JACQUERIE
JACTANCE
JACTANCY
JACTANT
JACTATION
JACTITATE
JACTITATED
JACTITATING
JACTITATION
JACTURE
JACU
JACUARU
JACULATE
JACULATED
JACULATING
JACULATION
JACULATIVE
JACULATOR
JACULATORIAL
JACULATORY
JACULIFEROUS
JACUTINGA
JAD
JADDED
JADDER
JADDING
JADE
JADED
JADEDLY
JADEDNESS
JADEITE
JADERY
JADING
JADISH
JADISHLY

JADISHNESS
JADOO
JADU
JADY
JAEGER
JAELA
JAG
JAGAT
JAGEER
JAGER
JAGG
JAGGAR
JAGGARY
JAGGED
JAGGEDLY
JAGGEDNESS
JAGGER
JAGGERY
JAGGHERY
JAGGIER
JAGGIEST
JAGGING
JAGGY
JAGHEER
JAGHEERDAR
JAGHIR
JAGHIRDAR
JAGHIRE
JAGHIREDAR
JAGIR
JAGIRDAR
JAGLA
JAGONG
JAGRA
JAGRATA
JAGS
JAGUA
JAGUAR
JAGUARETE
JAGUARONDI
JAGUARS
JAGUARUNDI
JAGUEY
JAIL
JAILAGE
JAILBIRD
JAILED
JAILER
JAILERESS
JAILERING
JAILHOUSE
JAILKEEPER
JAILMATE
JAILOR
JAILORING
JAILYARD
JAK
JAKE
JAKES
JAKEY
JAKFRUIT
JAKO
JAKOS
JALAP
JALAPA
JALAPENO
JALAPIC
JALAPIN
JALEO
JALET
JALKAR
JALLOPED
JALOP
JALOPIES
JALOPPY
JALOPY
JALOUSE

JALOUSED
JALOUSIE
JALOUSIED
JALOUSING
JALPAITE
JAM
JAMA
JAMAH
JAMAN
JAMB
JAMBA
JAMBALAYA
JAMBE
JAMBEAU
JAMBEAUX
JAMBEE
JAMBER
JAMBO
JAMBOLAN
JAMBOLANA
JAMBON
JAMBONE
JAMBOOL
JAMBOREE
JAMBOSA
JAMBSTONE
JAMBUL
JAMDANEE
JAMDANI
JAMESONITE
JAMI
JAMMED
JAMMER
JAMMING
JAMMY
JAMNUT
JAMOKE
JAMON
JAMPAN
JAMPANEE
JAMPANI
JAMROSADE
JAMTLAND
JAMWOOD
JAN
JANAPA
JANAPAN
JANAPUM
JANDERS
JANE
JANG
JANGADA
JANGAR
JANGKAR
JANGLE
JANGLED
JANGLER
JANGLING
JANGLY
JANICEPS
JANISARY
JANISSARY
JANITOR
JANITORIAL
JANITRESS
JANITRIX
JANIZARIES
JANIZARY
JANK
JANKER
JANKERS
JANN
JANNER
JANNOCK
JANTEE
JANTU
JANTY

JANUA
JAOB
JAOUR
JAP
JAPACONIN
JAPACONINE
JAPACONITIN
JAPACONITINE
JAPAN
JAPANNED
JAPANNER
JAPANNERY
JAPANNING
JAPE
JAPED
JAPER
JAPERIES
JAPERY
JAPING
JAPISH
JAPISHLY
JAPISHNESS
JAPONICA
JAPYGID
JAPYGOID
JAQUETTE
JAQUIMA
JAR
JARA
JARABE
JARAGUA
JARANA
JARARACA
JARARACUSSU
JARBIRD
JARBLE
JARBOT
JARDE
JARDINIERE
JAREED
JARFLY
JARFUL
JARG
JARGON
JARGONAL
JARGONED
JARGONEL
JARGONELLE
JARGONER
JARGONIC
JARGONING
JARGONISH
JARGONIST
JARGONIUM
JARGONIZE
JARGONIZED
JARGONIZING
JARGONNELLE
JARGOON
JARHEAD
JARINA
JARK
JARKMAN
JARL
JARLESS
JARLITE
JARNUT
JAROOL
JAROSITE
JAROVIZATION
JAROVIZE
JAROVIZED
JAROVIZING
JARRA
JARRAH
JARRED
JARRET

JARRING	JAVER	JEFFERISITE	JEREED	JETTED
JARRY	JAVVER	JEFFERSONITE	JEREMIAD	JETTER
JARVEY	JAW	JEHAD	JEREZ	JETTIED
JARVEYS	JAWAB	JEHUP	JERIB	JETTIES
JASEY	JAWBATION	JEJUNA	JERICAN	JETTINESS
JASEYED	JAWBONE	JEJUNAL	JERK	JETTING
JASEYS	JAWBREAKER	JEJUNATOR	JERKED	JETTISON
JASK	JAWBREAKING	JEJUNE	JERKER	JETTO
JASM	JAWBREAKINGLY	JEJUNELY	JERKIER	JETTON
JASMIN	JAWCRUSHER	JEJUNENESS	JERKIEST	JETTRU
JASMINE	JAWED	JEJUNITIS	JERKILY	JETTY
JASMINED	JAWFALL	JEJUNITY	JERKIN	JETTYHEAD
JASMINEWOOD	JAWFALLEN	JEJUNOSTOMY	JERKINED	JETWARE
JASMONE	JAWFEET	JEJUNOTOMY	JERKINESS	JEU
JASPACHATE	JAWFISH	JEJUNUM	JERKING	JEUNESSE
JASPAGATE	JAWFISHES	JELAB	JERKISH	JEUX
JASPE	JAWFOOT	JELERANG	JERKS	JEW
JASPER	JAWFOOTED	JELICK	JERKSOME	JEWBIRD
JASPERATED	JAWHOLE	JELL	JERKWATER	JEWBUSH
JASPERED	JAWING	JELLAB	JERKY	JEWEL
JASPERITE	JAWS	JELLICA	JERL	JEWELED
JASPERIZE	JAWSMITH	JELLICO	JERM	JEWELER
JASPERIZED	JAWY	JELLIED	JERMONAL	JEWELHOUSE
JASPERIZING	JAY	JELLIEDNESS	JERMOONAL	JEWELING
JASPEROID	JAYGEE	JELLIES	JERNIE	JEWELLED
JASPERY	JAYHAWK	JELLIFICATION	JEROBOAM	JEWELLER
JASPIDEAN	JAYHAWKER	JELLIFIED	JERQUE	JEWELLERY
JASPIDEOUS	JAYPIE	JELLIFY	JERQUED	JEWELLING
JASPILITE	JAYPIET	JELLIFYING	JERQUER	JEWELLY
JASPILYTE	JAYVEE	JELLILY	JERQUING	JEWELRY
JASPIS	JAYWALK	JELLO	JERRICAN	JEWELS
JASPOID	JAYWALKER	JELLOID	JERRID	JEWELSMITH
JASPONYX	JAYWALKING	JELLY	JERRIES	JEWELWEED
JASPOPAL	JAZEL	JELLYBEAN	JERRY	JEWELY
JASS	JAZERAN	JELLYFISH	JERRYBUILD	JEWFISH
JASSID	JAZERANT	JELLYFISHES	JERRYBUILDING	JEWFISHES
JATACO	JAZZ	JELLYING	JERRYBUILT	JEWING
JATAMANSI	JAZZBOW	JELLYLEAF	JERRYISM	JEZAIL
JATEORHIZIN	JAZZER	JELLYLIKE	JERSEY	JEZEKITE
JATEORHIZINE	JAZZIER	JELOTONG	JERSEYED	JEZIA
JATHA	JAZZIEST	JELUTONG	JERSEYS	JEZIAH
JATI	JAZZILY	JEMADAR	JERT	JHANA
JATO	JAZZINESS	JEMBLE	JERVIA	JHARAL
JATOBA	JAZZY	JEMIDAR	JERVIN	JHEEL
JATROPHIC	JEALOUS	JEMMIES	JERVINA	JHIL
JAUD	JEALOUSE	JEMMILY	JERVINE	JHOOL
JAUDIE	JEALOUSIES	JEMMINESS	JES	JHOOM
JAUG	JEALOUSLY	JEMMY	JESS	JHOW
JAUK	JEALOUSNESS	JEN	JESSAKEED	JHUM
JAUN	JEALOUSY	JENKIN	JESSAMIES	JIB
JAUNCE	JEAN	JENNA	JESSAMINE	JIBBA
JAUNDER	JEANS	JENNERIZE	JESSAMY	JIBBAH
JAUNDERS	JEBAT	JENNET	JESSANT	JIBBED
JAUNDICE	JEBEL	JENNETING	JESSED	JIBBEH
JAUNDICED	JECORAL	JENNIER	JESSING	JIBBER
JAUNDICEROOT	JECORIN	JENNIES	JESSUR	JIBBING
JAUNDICING	JECORIZE	JENNY	JEST	JIBBINGS
JAUNE	JED	JENOAR	JESTBOOK	JIBBOOM
JAUNER	JEDCOCK	JENTACULAR	JESTED	JIBE
JAUNT	JEDDOCK	JEOFAIL	JESTEE	JIBED
JAUNTED	JEDGE	JEOPARD	JESTER	JIBER
JAUNTIE	JEE	JEOPARDED	JESTING	JIBHEAD
JAUNTIER	JEEL	JEOPARDER	JESTINGLY	JIBI
JAUNTIEST	JEEP	JEOPARDIED	JESTINGSTOCK	JIBING
JAUNTILY	JEEPERS	JEOPARDING	JESTWORD	JIBMAN
JAUNTINESS	JEEPNEY	JEOPARDIOUS	JET	JIBMEN
JAUNTING	JEER	JEOPARDIZE	JETBEAD	JIBOA
JAUNTY	JEERED	JEOPARDIZED	JETE	JIBOYA
JAUP	JEERER	JEOPARDIZING	JETEE	JIBSTAY
JAUPS	JEERING	JEOPARDOUS	JETLINER	JICAMA
JAVA	JEERINGLY	JEOPARDOUSLY	JETON	JICARA
JAVALI	JEERS	JEOPARDY	JETPORT	JIFF
JAVEL	JEERY	JEOPARDYING	JETSAM	JIFFIES
JAVELIN	JEETEE	JEQUERITY	JETTAGE	JIFFLE
JAVELINA	JEEZ	JEQUIRITIES	JETTATORE	JIFFY
JAVELINEER	JEFE	JEQUIRITY	JETTATURA	JIG
JAVELOT	JEFF	JERBOA	JETTEAU	JIGAMAREE

JIGGED	JINJA	JOBBISH	JOGTROTTISM	JOLLITY
JIGGER	JINJILI	JOBBLE	JOHANNES	JOLLOP
JIGGERED	JINK	JOBE	JOHANNITE	JOLLOPED
JIGGERER	JINKED	JOBHOLDER	JOHN	JOLLY
JIGGERMAN	JINKER	JOBLESS	JOHNBOAT	JOLLYHEAD
JIGGERS	JINKET	JOBLESSNESS	JOHNIN	JOLLYING
JIGGET	JINKING	JOBMAN	JOHNNYCAKE	JOLT
JIGGETY	JINKLE	JOBMASTER	JOHNSTRUPITE	JOLTED
JIGGINESS	JINKS	JOBMEN	JOIN	JOLTER
JIGGING	JINN	JOBMISTRESS	JOINANT	JOLTERHEAD
JIGGISH	JINNEE	JOBMONGER	JOINDER	JOLTERHEADED
JIGGIT	JINNESTAN	JOBO	JOINED	JOLTHEAD
JIGGLE	JINNI	JOBS	JOINER	JOLTHEADED
JIGGLED	JINNIES	JOBSITE	JOINERED	JOLTINESS
JIGGLING	JINNIWINK	JOBSMITH	JOINERING	JOLTING
JIGGLY	JINNIYEH	JOBSON	JOINERY	JOLTY
JIGGUMBOB	JINNY	JOCANT	JOINHAND	JONDLA
JIGGY	JINNYWINK	JOCATORY	JOINING	JONG
JIGMAN	JINRICKSHA	JOCH	JOININGLY	JONGLERY
JIGMEN	JINRIKI	JOCK	JOINT	JONGLEUR
JIGOTE	JINRIKIMAN	JOCKER	JOINTAGE	JONK
JIGSAW	JINRIKIMEN	JOCKEY	JOINTED	JONQUIL
JIGUA	JINRIKISHA	JOCKEYED	JOINTEDLY	JONQUILLE
JIHAD	JINSHA	JOCKEYING	JOINTEDNESS	JOOKERIE
JIKUNGU	JINSHANG	JOCKEYISM	JOINTER	JOOLA
JILL	JINSING	JOCKEYS	JOINTING	JOOM
JILLET	JINX	JOCKO	JOINTIST	JOPY
JILLFLIRT	JIPIJAPA	JOCKOS	JOINTLY	JORAM
JILLING	JIPPER	JOCKS	JOINTRESS	JORDAN
JILLION	JIPPO	JOCKSTRAP	JOINTS	JORDANITE
JILT	JIQUE	JOCKTELEG	JOINTURE	JORDANON
JILTED	JIQUI	JOCO	JOINTURED	JORDEN
JILTEE	JIRBLE	JOCOQUE	JOINTURESS	JOREE
JILTER	JIRD	JOCOQUI	JOINTURING	JORNADA
JILTING	JIRGA	JOCOSE	JOINTWEED	JOROPO
JIMBANG	JIRGAH	JOCOSELY	JOINTWOOD	JORRAM
JIMBERJAW	JIRKINET	JOCOSENESS	JOINTWORM	JORUM
JIMBERJAWED	JIRT	JOCOSERIOUS	JOINTY	JOSEF
JIMCRACK	JITI	JOCOSITIES	JOISE	JOSEFITE
JIMJAM	JITNEUR	JOCOSITY	JOIST	JOSEITE
JIMJAMS	JITNEUSE	JOCOTE	JOISTED	JOSEPH
JIMMER	JITNEY	JOCTELEG	JOISTING	JOSEPHINITE
JIMMIED	JITNEYMAN	JOCU	JOJOBA	JOSEY
JIMMIES	JITNEYS	JOCULAR	JOKE	JOSH
JIMMY	JITTER	JOCULARITY	JOKED	JOSHER
JIMMYING	JITTERBUG	JOCULARLY	JOKELET	JOSHI
JIMMYWEED	JITTERS	JOCULARNESS	JOKER	JOSIE
JIMP	JITTERY	JOCULATOR	JOKESMITH	JOSKIN
JIMPLY	JIUJITSU	JOCULATORY	JOKESOME	JOSS
JIMPNESS	JIUJUTSU	JOCUM	JOKESOMENESS	JOSSA
JIMPRICUTE	JIVA	JOCUMA	JOKESTER	JOSSER
JIMPY	JIVATMA	JOCUND	JOKEY	JOSTLE
JIMSEDGE	JIVE	JOCUNDITIES	JOKIER	JOSTLED
JIMSON	JIXIE	JOCUNDITY	JOKIEST	JOSTLEMENT
JINA	JIZ	JOCUNDLY	JOKING	JOSTLER
JINETE	JIZYA	JOCUNDNESS	JOKINGLY	JOSTLING
JING	JIZYAH	JOCUNDRY	JOKISH	JOSUP
JINGAL	JIZZEN	JOD	JOKIST	JOT
JINGALL	JNANA	JODEL	JOKUL	JOTA
JINGBANG	JNANAMARGA	JODHPURS	JOKY	JOTATION
JINGLE	JNANASHAKTI	JOE	JOLE	JOTI
JINGLEBOB	JNANAYOGA	JOEBUSH	JOLI	JOTISARU
JINGLED	JNANENDRIYA	JOES	JOLIE	JOTISI
JINGLEJANGLE	JNANI	JOEWOOD	JOLL	JOTTED
JINGLER	JO	JOEY	JOLLIED	JOTTER
JINGLET	JOANNES	JOG	JOLLIER	JOTTING
JINGLING	JOAQUINITE	JOGGED	JOLLIES	JOTTY
JINGLINGLY	JOB	JOGGER	JOLLIEST	JOUBARB
JINGLY	JOBADE	JOGGING	JOLLIFICATION	JOUG
JINGO	JOBARBE	JOGGLE	JOLLIFIED	JOUGH
JINGOED	JOBATION	JOGGLED	JOLLIFY	JOUGS
JINGOES	JOBBED	JOGGLER	JOLLIFYING	JOUISSANCE
JINGOING	JOBBER	JOGGLETY	JOLLILY	JOUK
JINGOISH	JOBBERIES	JOGGLEWORK	JOLLIMENT	JOUKERY
JINGOISM	JOBBERNOWL	JOGGLING	JOLLINESS	JOULE
JINGOIST	JOBBERY	JOGGLY	JOLLITIES	JOULEAN
JINGOISTIC	JOBBING	JOGI	JOLLITRY	JOULEMETER

JOUNCE
JOUNCED
JOUNCING
JOURNAL
JOURNALED
JOURNALESE
JOURNALING
JOURNALISE
JOURNALISM
JOURNALIST
JOURNALISTIC
JOURNALIZE
JOURNALIZED
JOURNALIZER
JOURNALIZING
JOURNALLED
JOURNALLING
JOURNEY
JOURNEYCAKE
JOURNEYED
JOURNEYER
JOURNEYING
JOURNEYMAN
JOURNEYMEN
JOURNEYS
JOURNEYWOMAN
JOURNEYWOMEN
JOURNEYWORK
JOURS
JOUST
JOUSTER
JOUSTING
JOUSTS
JOUTES
JOVIAL
JOVIALIST
JOVIALISTIC
JOVIALITY
JOVIALIZE
JOVIALIZED
JOVIALIZING
JOVIALLY
JOVIALNESS
JOVIALTY
JOVILABE
JOVY
JOW
JOWAR
JOWARI
JOWEL
JOWER
JOWERY
JOWL
JOWLER
JOWLOP
JOWLY
JOWPY
JOWSER
JOWTER
JOY
JOYANCE
JOYANCY
JOYANT
JOYED
JOYFUL
JOYFULLY
JOYFULNESS
JOYHOP
JOYHOUSE
JOYING
JOYLEAF
JOYLESS
JOYLESSLY
JOYLESSNESS
JOYOUS
JOYOUSLY
JOYOUSNESS

JOYPOPPER
JOYRIDE
JOYSOME
JOYWEED
JUAMAVE
JUB
JUBA
JUBARB
JUBARTAS
JUBARTES
JUBATE
JUBBAH
JUBBE
JUBEROUS
JUBHAH
JUBILANCE
JUBILANCY
JUBILANT
JUBILANTLY
JUBILARIAN
JUBILATE
JUBILATED
JUBILATING
JUBILATIO
JUBILATION
JUBILATORY
JUBILE
JUBILEAN
JUBILEE
JUBILIST
JUBILIZATION
JUBILIZE
JUBILUS
JUBO
JUBUS
JUCHART
JUCK
JUCKIES
JUCUNDITY
JUD
JUDAIZER
JUDCOCK
JUDD
JUDDER
JUDDOCK
JUDEX
JUDGE
JUDGED
JUDGEMENT
JUDGER
JUDGING
JUDGMATIC
JUDGMATICAL
JUDGMENT
JUDGMENTS
JUDICABLE
JUDICATE
JUDICATION
JUDICATIVE
JUDICATOR
JUDICATORIAL
JUDICATORIES
JUDICATORY
JUDICATURE
JUDICES
JUDICIABLE
JUDICIAL
JUDICIALITY
JUDICIALIZE
JUDICIALLY
JUDICIARIES
JUDICIARILY
JUDICIARY
JUDICIOUS
JUDICIOUSLY
JUDICIOUSNESS

JUDICIUM
JUDKA
JUDO
JUDOPHOBIA
JUECES
JUEY
JUEZ
JUFFER
JUFTI
JUFTS
JUG
JUGA
JUGAL
JUGALE
JUGATE
JUGATED
JUGATION
JUGER
JUGFUL
JUGGED
JUGGER
JUGGERNAUT
JUGGING
JUGGINS
JUGGLE
JUGGLED
JUGGLEMENT
JUGGLER
JUGGLERIES
JUGGLERY
JUGGLING
JUGGLINGLY
JUGHEAD
JUGLANDIN
JUGLAR
JUGLONE
JUGULA
JUGULAR
JUGULATE
JUGULATED
JUGULATING
JUGULATION
JUGULUM
JUGUM
JUGUMS
JUICE
JUICER
JUICIER
JUICIEST
JUICILY
JUICINESS
JUICY
JUISE
JUJITSU
JUJU
JUJUBE
JUJUISM
JUJUIST
JUJUTSU
JUKE
JUKEBOX
JUKES
JULEP
JULID
JULIDAN
JULIENITE
JULIENNE
JULIETT
JULIO
JULOID
JULOIDIAN
JULOL
JULOLE
JULOLIDIN
JULOLIDINE
JULOLIN
JULOLINE

JUM
JUMART
JUMBA
JUMBIE
JUMBLE
JUMBLED
JUMBLEMENT
JUMBLER
JUMBLING
JUMBLY
JUMBO
JUMBOISM
JUMBOS
JUMBUCK
JUMBY
JUMELLE
JUMENT
JUMENTOUS
JUMFRU
JUMILLITE
JUMMA
JUMP
JUMPED
JUMPER
JUMPERS
JUMPIER
JUMPIEST
JUMPINESS
JUMPING
JUMPOFF
JUMPROCK
JUMPROCKS
JUMPS
JUMPSCRAPE
JUMPSEED
JUMPSOME
JUMPY
JUNCACEOUS
JUNCIFORM
JUNCITE
JUNCO
JUNCOS
JUNCOUS
JUNCTION
JUNCTIONAL
JUNCTIVE
JUNCTLY
JUNCTURE
JUNCUS
JUNDIE
JUNDY
JUNE
JUNECTOMY
JUNEFISH
JUNGLE
JUNGLED
JUNGLESIDE
JUNGLEWOOD
JUNGLI
JUNGLIER
JUNGLIEST
JUNGLY
JUNIATA
JUNIOR
JUNIORATE
JUNIORITY
JUNIPER
JUNK
JUNKBOARD
JUNKDEALER
JUNKER
JUNKERDOM
JUNKERISM
JUNKET
JUNKETED
JUNKETER
JUNKETING

JUNKIE
JUNKING
JUNKMAN
JUNKMEN
JUNKY
JUNKYARD
JUNT
JUNTA
JUNTAS
JUNTO
JUNTOS
JUPATI
JUPE
JUPES
JUPON
JUR
JURA
JURAL
JURALLY
JURAMENT
JURAMENTA
JURAMENTADO
JURAMENTAL
JURAMENTALLY
JURAMENTUM
JURANT
JURARA
JURAT
JURATA
JURATION
JURATIVE
JURATOR
JURATORIAL
JURATORY
JURE
JUREL
JURIDIC
JURIDICAL
JURIDICALLY
JURIDICIAL
JURIES
JURING
JURISCONSULT
JURISDICTION
JURISDICTIVE
JURISPRUDENCE
JURISPRUDENT
JURIST
JURISTIC
JURISTICAL
JURISTICALLY
JURM
JUROR
JURORS
JURR
JURT
JURUPAITE
JURY
JURYMAN
JURYMEN
JURYWOMAN
JUS
JUSI
JUSLIK
JUSSAL
JUSSEL
JUSSHELL
JUSSION
JUSSIVE
JUSSORY
JUST
JUSTAUCORPS
JUSTEN
JUSTER
JUSTICE
JUSTICED
JUSTICEHOOD

JUSTICER
JUSTICESHIP
JUSTICEWEED
JUSTICIABLE
JUSTICIAL
JUSTICIAR
JUSTICIARY
JUSTICIER
JUSTICIES
JUSTICING
JUSTICO
JUSTIFIABLE
JUSTIFIABLY
JUSTIFICATION
JUSTIFICATIVE
JUSTIFICATOR
JUSTIFIED
JUSTIFIER
JUSTIFY
JUSTIFYING
JUSTIFYINGLY
JUSTITIA
JUSTLE
JUSTLER
JUSTLY
JUSTMENT
JUSTMENTS
JUSTNESS
JUSTO
JUT
JUTE
JUTES
JUTIA
JUTKA
JUTTED
JUTTIES
JUTTING
JUTTINGLY
JUTTY
JUVENAL
JUVENATE
JUVENESCENCE
JUVENESCENT
JUVENILE
JUVENILELY
JUVENILENESS
JUVENILIA
JUVENILIFY
JUVENILISM
JUVENILITIES
JUVENILITY
JUVENT
JUVENTUDE
JUVIA
JUVITE
JUWISE
JUXTA
JUXTAMARINE
JUXTAPOSE
JUXTAPOSED
JUXTAPOSING
JUXTAPOSIT
JUXTAPOSITION
JUXTAPYLORIC
JUXTASPINAL
JUZAIL
JYNGINE
JYNX

KA
KAAMA
KAAS
KAB
KABAKA
KABALA
KABAR
KABAYA
KABBALA
KABEL
KABELJOU
KABERU
KABIET
KABOB
KABUKI
KACHIN
KACHINA
KADDER
KADE
KADEIN
KADI
KADIKANE
KADINE
KADISCHI
KADOS
KADSURA
KADY
KAE
KAEMPFEROL
KAFERITA
KAFFIR
KAFFIRS
KAFFIYEH
KAFIR
KAFIRIN
KAFIZ
KAFTAN
KAGO
KAGU
KAGURA
KAHA
KAHAL
KAHALA
KAHAR
KAHAU
KAHAWAI
KAHIKATEA
KAHILI
KAHU
KAHUNA
KAI
KAIAK
KAID
KAIF
KAIK
KAIKA
KAIKARA
KAIKAWAKA
KAIL
KAILS
KAILYARD
KAILYARDER
KAILYARDISM
KAIN
KAINGA
KAINGIN
KAINIT

KAINITE
KAINSI
KAIO
KAIR
KAIRI
KAIRIN
KAIRINE
KAIROLIN
KAIROLINE
KAIROS
KAISER
KAISERDOM
KAISERISM
KAITAKA
KAIVALYA
KAIWHIRIA
KAIWI
KAJAWAH
KAJEPUT
KAJUGARU
KAKA
KAKAPO
KAKAR
KAKARALI
KAKARALLI
KAKARIKI
KAKAWAHIE
KAKEL
KAKEMONO
KAKI
KAKIDROSIS
KAKISTOCRACY
KAKKAK
KAKKE
KAKORTOKITE
KAKU
KAKUR
KAL
KALA
KALAC
KALACH
KALADANA
KALAM
KALAMANSANAI
KALAMKARI
KALAN
KALASIE
KALE
KALEIDOPHON
KALEIDOPHONE
KALEIDOSCOPE
KALEMA
KALENDS
KALEWIFE
KALEWIVES
KALEYARD
KALI
KALIAN
KALIDIUM
KALIF
KALIFORM
KALIGENOUS
KALIJ
KALINITE
KALIOPHILITE
KALIPAYA
KALIPH
KALIUM
KALKVIS
KALLAH
KALLEGE
KALLILITE
KALLITYPE
KALMIA
KALMUCK
KALMUK
KALO

KALOKAGATHIA
KALON
KALONG
KALPAK
KALPIS
KALSOMINE
KALUA
KALUMPANG
KALUMPIT
KALUNTI
KALYMMOCYTE
KALYPTRA
KAM
KAMAAINA
KAMACHI
KAMACHILE
KAMACITE
KAMAHI
KAMALA
KAMALOKA
KAMANCHILE
KAMANI
KAMAO
KAMAREZITE
KAMARUPA
KAMARUPIC
KAMAS
KAMASS
KAMASSI
KAMAVACHARA
KAMBAL
KAMBOH
KAMBOU
KAME
KAMEEL
KAMEELDOORN
KAMEELTHORN
KAMELA
KAMELAUKION
KAMERAD
KAMI
KAMIAN
KAMIAS
KAMICHI
KAMIK
KAMIKA
KAMIKAZE
KAMIKS
KAMIS
KAMLEIKA
KAMMALAN
KAMMERERITE
KAMMEU
KAMPERITE
KAMPONG
KAMPTOMORPH
KAMSEEN
KAMSIN
KAN
KANA
KANAE
KANAF
KANAFF
KANAGI
KANAIMA
KANARA
KANARI
KANAT
KANCHIL
KANDE
KANDH
KANDJAR
KANE
KANEH
KANGA
KANGANI
KANGANY

KANGAROO
KANGAROOER
KANGAROOS
KANGAYAM
KANGLA
KANGRI
KANIN
KANKEDORT
KANKIE
KANKREJ
KANNA
KANNE
KANNEN
KANNU
KANNUME
KANONE
KANOON
KANS
KANT
KANTAR
KANTELA
KANTELE
KANTELETAR
KANTEN
KANTIARA
KANUKA
KANYAW
KANZU
KAOLIANG
KAOLIN
KAOLINATE
KAOLINE
KAOLINIC
KAOLINITE
KAOLINIZE
KAORI
KAPA
KAPAI
KAPEIKA
KAPH
KAPOK
KAPOR
KAPOTE
KAPP
KAPPA
KAPPARAH
KAPPE
KAPPIE
KAPPLAND
KAPU
KAPUKA
KAPUR
KAPUT
KAPUTT
KARABINER
KARAGAN
KARAKA
KARAKUL
KARAKULE
KARAKURT
KARAMU
KARAO
KARAT
KARATAS
KARATE
KARATTO
KARAYA
KARBI
KARCH
KAREAO
KAREAU
KAREETA
KARELA
KAREWA
KAREZ
KARI
KARINGHOTA

KARITE
KARITI
KARMA
KARMADHARAYA
KARMIC
KARMOUTH
KARN
KARO
KAROO
KAROOS
KAROSS
KAROU
KARPAS
KARREE
KARREN
KARRI
KARROO
KARROOS
KARRUSEL
KARSHA
KARST
KARSTIC
KARTEL
KARTOS
KARUNA
KARVAR
KARWAR
KARYOCHROME
KARYOGAMIC
KARYOGAMY
KARYOKINESIS
KARYOKINETIC
KARYOLYMPH
KARYOLYSIS
KARYOLYTIC
KARYOMERE
KARYOMERITE
KARYOMITOIC
KARYOMITOME
KARYOMITOSIS
KARYOMITOTIC
KARYON
KARYOPLASM
KARYOPLASMA
KARYOPLASMIC
KARYORRHEXIS
KARYOSOMA
KARYOSOME
KARYOTIN
KAS
KASA
KASBA
KASBEKE
KASCAMIOL
KASHA
KASHER
KASHGA
KASHI
KASHIM
KASHIMA
KASHMIR
KASHRUTH
KASIDA
KASM
KASOLITE
KASSABAH
KASSU
KASTURA
KASWA
KAT
KATA
KATABASES
KATABASIS
KATABATIC
KATABELLA
KATABOLIC
KATABOLISM

KATABOLITE	KAYO	KEESLIP	KENDO	KERATOMA
KATABOLIZE	KAYS	KEEST	KENDYR	KERATOME
KATABOTHRA	KAZAK	KEESTER	KENEMA	KERATOMETER
KATABOTHRON	KAZI	KEET	KENLORE	KERATOMETRY
KATACROTIC	KAZOO	KEETH	KENMARK	KERATONCUS
KATACROTISM	KAZY	KEEVE	KENNA	KERATONOSUS
KATAGENESIS	KEA	KEF	KENNEBUNKER	KERATONYXIS
KATAGENETIC	KEACH	KEFFEL	KENNED	KERATOPHYRE
KATAKANA	KEACORN	KEFIR	KENNEL	KERATOPLASTY
KATAKINESIS	KEAWE	KEFIRIC	KENNELED	KERATOSCOPE
KATAKINETIC	KEBAR	KEG	KENNELING	KERATOSCOPY
KATAKIRIBORI	KEBBIE	KEGLER	KENNELLED	KERATOSE
KATALASE	KEBBOCK	KEGLING	KENNELLING	KERATOSES
KATALYSIS	KEBBUCK	KEGMEG	KENNELLY	KERATOSIS
KATALYST	KEBBY	KEHAYA	KENNELMAN	KERATOTOME
KATALYTIC	KEBOB	KEHILLAH	KENNELMEN	KERATOTOMY
KATALYZE	KEBYAR	KEHILLOTH	KENNER	KERATTO
KATAMORPHISM	KECHEL	KEHOEITE	KENNET	KERAULOPHON
KATANA	KECHIL	KEIKI	KENNING	KERAULOPHONE
KATAPHORESIS	KECK	KEILHAUITE	KENNINGWORT	KERAUNIA
KATAPHORETIC	KECKLE	KEIR	KENNO	KERAUNION
KATAPHORIC	KECKLING	KEIRI	KENO	KERAUNOGRAPH
KATAPHRENIA	KECKSY	KEIST	KENOGENESIS	KERAUNOPHONE
KATAPLASIA	KECKY	KEISTER	KENOSIS	KERB
KATAPLECTIC	KED	KEITLOA	KENOTIC	KERBAU
KATAPLEXY	KEDDAH	KELCHIN	KENOTICISM	KERBSTONE
KATAR	KEDGE	KELCHYN	KENOTICIST	KERCHER
KATASTATE	KEDGER	KELD	KENOTISM	KERCHIEF
KATASTATIC	KEDGEREE	KELDER	KENOTIST	KERCHIEFED
KATATONIA	KEDGY	KELE	KENOTOXIN	KERCHIEFT
KATATONIC	KEDIRI	KELEBE	KENOTRON	KERCHOO
KATATYPE	KEDJAVE	KELECTOME	KENSCOFF	KERCHUG
KATCHUNG	KEDLOCK	KELEH	KENSINGTON	KERCHUNK
KATCINA	KEDUSHAH	KELEK	KENSPECK	KERE
KATE	KEECH	KELEP	KENSPECKLE	KEREL
KATEL	KEEF	KELK	KENT	KERF
KATH	KEEK	KELL	KENTALLENITE	KERFLAP
KATHA	KEEKER	KELLA	KENTIA	KERFLOP
KATHAK	KEEKERS	KELLECK	KENTLEDGE	KERFLUMMOX
KATHAKALI	KEEL	KELLEG	KENTROGON	KERI
KATHAL	KEELAGE	KELLIN	KENTROLITE	KERIAH
KATHAROMETER	KEELBACK	KELLION	KENYTE	KERION
KATHARSIS	KEELBILL	KELLUPWEED	KEOUT	KERITE
KATHARTIC	KEELBIRD	KELLY	KEP	KERLOCK
KATHODE	KEELBLOCK	KELOID	KEPE	KERMES
KATI	KEELBOAT	KELP	KEPHIR	KERMESITE
KATIN	KEELBOATMAN	KELPER	KEPI	KERMESS
KATION	KEELED	KELPFISH	KEPT	KERMIS
KATIPO	KEELER	KELPIE	KERALITE	KERN
KATJEPIERING	KEELFAT	KELPWARE	KERAMIC	KERNE
KATMON	KEELHALE	KELPWORT	KERAMICS	KERNEL
KATOGLE	KEELHAUL	KELPY	KERANA	KERNELED
KATONKEL	KEELIE	KELSON	KERAPHYLLOUS	KERNELLATE
KATSU	KEELING	KELT	KERASIN	KERNELLED
KATUKA	KEELIVINE	KELTER	KERASINE	KERNELLY
KATUN	KEELMAN	KELTIE	KERAT	KERNER
KATURAI	KEELS	KELTY	KERATALGIA	KERNETTY
KATYDID	KEELSON	KELVIN	KERATECTASIA	KERNISH
KATZENJAMMER	KEELVAT	KELYPHITE	KERATECTOMY	KERNITE
KAURI	KEEN	KEM	KERATIN	KERNOI
KAURY	KEENA	KEMANCHA	KERATINIZE	KERNOS
KAVA	KEENED	KEMB	KERATINOSE	KEROGEN
KAVAKAVA	KEENER	KEMIRI	KERATINOUS	KEROSENE
KAVASS	KEENLY	KEMP	KERATITIS	KEROSINE
KAVIKA	KEENNESS	KEMPAS	KERATOCELE	KERPLUNK
KAVVANAH	KEEP	KEMPER	KERATOCONUS	KERRANA
KAVYA	KEEPER	KEMPERYMAN	KERATODE	KERRIL
KAW	KEEPERING	KEMPITE	KERATODERMIA	KERRITE
KAWA	KEEPING	KEMPLE	KERATOGENIC	KERRY
KAWAKA	KEEPS	KEMPSTER	KERATOGENOUS	KERS
KAWAKAWA	KEEPSAKE	KEMPT	KERATOGLOBUS	KERSANNE
KAY	KEEPSAKY	KEMPY	KERATOHYAL	KERSANTITE
KAYA	KEEPWORTHY	KEN	KERATOID	KERSE
KAYAK	KEEROGUE	KENAF	KERATOIRITIS	KERSENNEH
KAYAKER	KEESH	KENCH	KERATOL	KERSEY
KAYLE	KEESHOND	KENDIR	KERATOLYSIS	KERSEYMERE
KAYLES	KEESHONDEN	KENDNA	KERATOLYTIC	KERSEYS

KERSLAM
KERSLOSH
KERSMASH
KERUGMA
KERUING
KERWHAM
KERYGMA
KERYGMATIC
KERYKEION
KERYSTIC
KESSLERMAN
KESTREL
KET
KETA
KETAL
KETAPANG
KETATE
KETCH·
KETCHCRAFT
KETCHUP
KETCHY
KETEMBILLA
KETEN
KETENE
KETHIB
KETHIBH
KETIB
KETIMID
KETIMIDE
KETIMIN
KETIMINE
KETIPATE
KETIPIC
KETMIE
KETOGEN
KETOGENESIS
KETOGENIC
KETOHEPTOSE
KETOL
KETOLE
KETOLYSIS
KETOLYTIC
KETONAEMIA
KETONE
KETONEMIA
KETONIC
KETONIZATION
KETONIZE
KETONURIA
KETOSE
KETOSIDE
KETOSIS
KETOXIME
KETTE
KETTLE
KETTLECASE
KETTLEDRUM
KETTLER
KETTRIN
KETTY
KETUBA
KETUBAH
KETUPA
KETYL
KEUP
KEURBOOM
KEVALIN
KEVAZINGO
KEVEL
KEVELHEAD
KEVUTZAH
KEVUTZOTH
KEWEENAWITE
KEWPIE
KEX
KEXY
KEY

KEYAKI
KEYBOARD
KEYED
KEYER
KEYHOLE
KEYLOCK
KEYMAN
KEYMOVE
KEYNOTE
KEYNOTER
KEYSEAT
KEYSEATER
KEYSERLICK
KEYSLOT
KEYSMITH
KEYSTER
KEYSTONE
KEYSTONED
KEYWAY
KHADDAR
KHADI
KHAGIARITE
KHAIKI
KHAIR
KHAJA
KHAJUR
KHAKAN
KHAKHAM
KHAKI
KHAKIED
KHAKIS
KHAL
KHALAL
KHALAT
KHALIF
KHALIFA
KHALIFAT
KHALSA
KHALSAH
KHAMAL
KHAMSEEN
KHAMSIN
KHAN
KHANATE
KHANDA
KHANDAIT
KHANJAR
KHANJEE
KHANKAH
KHANSAMA
KHANSAMAH
KHANSAMAN
KHANUM
KHAR
KHARAJ
KHARIF
KHAROUBA
KHARUA
KHARWA
KHAS
KHASS
KHAT
KHATIB
KHATIN
KHATRI
KHAUR
KHAYA
KHAZEN
KHEDAH
KHEDIVE
KHEDIVIAH
KHEDIVIAL
KHEDIVIATE
KHELLA
KHELLIN
KHEPESH
KHESARI

KHET
KHIDMATGAR
KHIDMUTGAR
KHILAT
KHIR
KHIRKA
KHIRKAH
KHOA
KHODJA
KHOJA
KHOJAH
KHOKA
KHOR
KHOT
KHUBBER
KHUD
KHULA
KHUR
KHUSKHUS
KHUTBA
KHUTBAH
KHVAT
KI
KIABOOCA
KIACK
KIAK
KIAKI
KIALEE
KIANG
KIAUGH
KIBBE
KIBBEH
KIBBER
KIBBLE
KIBBLER
KIBBLERMAN
KIBBUTZ
KIBBUTZIM
KIBE
KIBITKA
KIBITZ
KIBITZER
KIBLA
KIBLAH
KIBOSH
KIBSEY
KIBY
KICHEL
KICK
KICKBACK
KICKBALL
KICKDOWN
KICKER
KICKING
KICKISH
KICKOFF
KICKOUT
KICKS
KICKSEYS
KICKSHAW
KICKSIES
KICKUP
KICKXIA
KICKY
KID
KIDANG
KIDCOTE
KIDDED
KIDDER
KIDDIE
KIDDIER
KIDDIES
KIDDING
KIDDISH
KIDDLE
KIDDUSH
KIDDUSHIN

KIDDY
KIDLET
KIDNAP
KIDNAPER
KIDNAPING
KIDNAPPER
KIDNEY
KIDNEYLIPPED
KIDNEYROOT
KIDNEYS
KIDNEYWORT
KIDSKIN
KIDSMAN
KIEF
KIEFEKIL
KIEKIE
KIELBASA
KIER
KIESELGUHR
KIESELGUR
KIESERITE
KIESTER
KIESTLESS
KIEVE
KIF
KIKAR
KIKE
KIKEPA
KIKI
KIKORI
KIKU
KIKUEL
KIKUMON
KIL
KILADJA
KILAH
KILDEE
KILDERKIN
KILE
KILEH
KILERG
KILEY
KILHIG
KILIARE
KILIM
KILL
KILLABLE
KILLADAR
KILLAS
KILLBUCK
KILLCALF
KILLCROP
KILLCU
KILLDEE
KILLDEER
KILLED
KILLEEKILLEE
KILLEEN
KILLER
KILLICK
KILLIFISH
KILLIG
KILLIKINICK
KILLING
KILLINGLY
KILLINGNESS
KILLINITE
KILLJOY
KILLOCK
KILLOGIE
KILLOW
KILLWEED
KILLWORT
KILLY
KILN
KILNEYE
KILNHOLE

KILNRIB
KILNSTICK
KILNTREE
KILO
KILOAMPERE
KILOBAR
KILOCALORIE
KILOCYCLE
KILODYNE
KILOGAUSS
KILOGRAM
KILOGRAMME
KILOJOULE
KILOLITER
KILOLITRE
KILOLUMEN
KILOMETER
KILOMETRE
KILOMETRIC
KILOMETRICAL
KILOPARSEC
KILOS
KILOTON
KILOVAR
KILOVOLT
KILOWARE
KILOWATT
KILP
KILT
KILTED
KILTER
KILTIE
KILTIES
KILTING
KILTY
KIM
KIMBERLIN
KIMBERLITE
KIMBO
KIMCHI
KIMIGAYO
KIMMER
KIMNEL
KIMONO
KIMONOED
KIMRI
KIN
KINA
KINAESTHESIA
KINAESTHESIS
KINAH
KINASE
KINBOOT
KINBOT
KINBOTE
KINCH
KINCHIN
KINCHINMORT
KINCOB
KIND
KINDAL
KINDERGARTEN
KINDHEART
KINDHEARTED
KINDLE
KINDLER
KINDLESOME
KINDLESS
KINDLESSLY
KINDLIER
KINDLIEST
KINDLINESS
KINDLING
KINDLY
KINDNESS
KINDRED
KINDREDLY

KINDREDNESS
KINE
KINEMATIC
KINEMATICAL
KINEMATICS
KINEMOMETER
KINEPLASTY
KINEPOX
KINESALGIA
KINESCOPE
KINESIATRIC
KINESIATRICS
KINESIC
KINESIMETER
KINESIOMETER
KINESIS
KINESODIC
KINESTHESIA
KINESTHESIS
KINESTHETIC
KINETIC
KINETICAL
KINETICALLY
KINETICS
KINETOGENESIS
KINETOGENIC
KINETOGRAM
KINETOGRAPH
KINETOPHONE
KINETOSCOPE
KINETOSCOPIC
KINETOSIS
KINFOLK
KING
KINGBIRD
KINGBOLT
KINGCOB
KINGCRAFT
KINGCUP
KINGDOM
KINGDOMED
KINGDOMSHIP
KINGFISH
KINGFISHER
KINGHEAD
KINGHOOD
KINGHUNTER
KINGKLIP
KINGLESS
KINGLESSNESS
KINGLET
KINGLIER
KINGLIEST
KINGLIHOOD
KINGLIKE
KINGLILY
KINGLINESS
KINGLING
KINGLY
KINGMAKER
KINGMAKING
KINGPIECE
KINGPIN
KINGSHIP
KINGSMAN
KINGWEED
KINGWOOD
KINIC
KININ
KINK
KINKAJOU
KINKCOUGH
KINKER
KINKHAB
KINKHAUST
KINKHOST
KINKIER

KINKIEST
KINKILY
KINKINESS
KINKING
KINKLE
KINKLED
KINKSBUSH
KINKY
KINNERY
KINNIKINIC
KINNIKINNICK
KINNOR
KINO
KINOFLUOUS
KINOLOGY
KINOPLASM
KINOPLASMIC
KINOSPORE
KINOT
KINOTANNIC
KINSEN
KINSFOLK
KINSHIP
KINSMAN
KINSMANLY
KINSMEN
KINSPEOPLE
KINSWOMAN
KINTAR
KINTRA
KINTRY
KINURA
KIO
KIOEA
KIORE
KIOSK
KIOTOME
KIP
KIPE
KIPFEL
KIPP
KIPPAGE
KIPPEEN
KIPPER
KIPPERER
KIPPIN
KIPPY
KIPSEY
KIPSKIN
KIPUKA
KIRBY
KIRI
KIRIMON
KIRK
KIRKER
KIRKIFY
KIRKMAN
KIRKTON
KIRKTOWN
KIRKYARD
KIRMESS
KIRMEW
KIRN
KIROMBO
KIRPAN
KIRSCH
KIRSCHWASSER
KIRSEN
KIRTLE
KIRTLED
KIRVE
KIRVER
KIRVI
KISAENG
KISAN
KISANG
KISH

KISHEN
KISHKE
KISI
KISKADEE
KISKATOM
KISKATOMAS
KISKITOM
KISKITOMAS
KISM
KISMET
KISRA
KISS
KISSAGE
KISSAR
KISSER
KISSES
KISSING
KISSINGLY
KIST
KISTFUL
KISTVAEN
KISWA
KISWAH
KIT
KITAB
KITABI
KITAR
KITCAT
KITCHEN
KITCHENER
KITCHENET
KITCHENETTE
KITCHENMAID
KITCHENMAN
KITCHENRY
KITCHENWARE
KITCHENY
KITCHIE
KITE
KITEFLIER
KITEFLYING
KITES
KITH
KITHARA
KITHE
KITHOGUE
KITISH
KITLING
KITMAN
KITMUDGAR
KITT
KITTAR
KITTE
KITTEL
KITTEN
KITTENISH
KITTENISHLY
KITTER
KITTEREEN
KITTHOGE
KITTIE
KITTIWAKE
KITTLE
KITTLEPINS
KITTLES
KITTLISH
KITTLY
KITTOCK
KITTOOL
KITTUL
KITTY
KITTYSOL
KITUL
KIUTLE
KIVA
KIVER
KIVIKIVI

KIVU
KIVVER
KIWACH
KIWI
KIYAS
KIYI
KJELDAHLIZE
KLAFTER
KLAM
KLATSCH
KLAVERN
KLAXON
KLEENEBOC
KLEENEX
KLEG
KLEINITE
KLEPHT
KLEPHTIC
KLEPHTISM
KLEPTIC
KLEPTISTIC
KLEPTOMANIA
KLEPTOMANIAC
KLEPTOMANIST
KLEPTOPHOBIA
KLEZMER
KLICKET
KLINK
KLIP
KLIPBOK
KLIPDAS
KLIPFISH
KLIPHAAS
KLIPPE
KLIPPEN
KLIPSPRINGER
KLISMOS
KLISTER
KLOCKMANNITE
KLOM
KLOMP
KLONG
KLOOCH
KLOOF
KLOOTCHMAN
KLOP
KLOPS
KLOSH
KLOWET
KLUCKER
KLYSTRON
KMET
KNAB
KNABBLE
KNACK
KNACKAWAY
KNACKEBROD
KNACKER
KNACKERY
KNACKIER
KNACKIEST
KNACKWURST
KNACKY
KNAG
KNAGGED
KNAGGIER
KNAGGIEST
KNAGGY
KNAIDEL
KNAP
KNAPE
KNAPPAN
KNAPPE
KNAPPER
KNAPPISH
KNAPPISHLY
KNAPPLE

KNAPSACK
KNAPSACKED
KNAPSACKING
KNAPSCAP
KNAPSCULL
KNAPWEED
KNAR
KNARK
KNARL
KNARRED
KNARRY
KNASH
KNATCH
KNATTE
KNAUR
KNAVE
KNAVERY
KNAVESHIP
KNAVISH
KNAVISHLY
KNAVISHNESS
KNAW
KNAWEL
KNEAD
KNEADER
KNEADING
KNEADINGLY
KNEBELITE
KNECK
KNEE
KNEEBRUSH
KNEECAP
KNEED
KNEEHOLE
KNEEL
KNEELER
KNEELET
KNEELING
KNEELINGLY
KNEEPAD
KNEEPAN
KNEEPIECE
KNEESTONE
KNELL
KNELT
KNETCH
KNEVEL
KNEW
KNEZ
KNEZI
KNIAZ
KNICK
KNICKER
KNICKERED
KNICKERS
KNICKKNACK
KNICKKNACKED
KNICKKNACKET
KNICKKNACKY
KNICKPOINT
KNIFE
KNIFEBOARD
KNIFEFUL
KNIFELIKE
KNIFEMAN
KNIFER
KNIFESMITH
KNIFEWAY
KNIGHT
KNIGHTAGE
KNIGHTESS
KNIGHTHEAD
KNIGHTHOOD
KNIGHTLESS
KNIGHTLIKE
KNIGHTLINESS
KNIGHTLY

KNIP	KNOUT	KOFT	KOMONDOR	KORREL
KNISH	KNOW	KOFTGAR	KOMPENI	KORRIGAN
KNIT	KNOWABILITY	KOFTGARI	KOMPOW	KORRIGUM
KNITBACK	KNOWABLE	KOGASIN	KOMTOK	KORUMBURRA
KNITCH	KNOWABLENESS	KOGON	KON	KORUN
KNITTED	KNOWE	KOHEKOHE	KONA	KORUNA
KNITTER	KNOWER	KOHEMP	KONAK	KORUNY
KNITTING	KNOWING	KOHL	KONFYT	KORZEC
KNITTLE	KNOWINGLY	KOHLRABI	KONG	KOS
KNITWEAR	KNOWINGNESS	KOHLRABIES	KONGONI	KOSAM
KNITWEED	KNOWLEDGE	KOHUA	KONGSBERGITE	KOSHARE
KNITWORK	KNOWLEDGEABLE	KOI	KONGU	KOSHER
KNIVE	KNOWLEDGED	KOIL	KONIMETER	KOSIN
KNIVED	KNOWLEDGEMENT	KOILON	KONINCKITE	KOSMOKRATOR
KNIVES	KNOWLEDGING	KOIMESIS	KONINI	KOSO
KNIVEY	KNOWN	KOINE	KONIOLOGY	KOSONG
KNOB	KNUB	KOINON	KONISCOPE	KOSOTOXIN
KNOBBED	KNUBBIER	KOINONIA	KONJAK	KOSS
KNOBBER	KNUBBIEST	KOJI	KONK	KOSSO
KNOBBIER	KNUBBLY	KOK	KONOHIKI	KOSWITE
KNOBBIEST	KNUBBY	KOKAKO	KONSEAL	KOTAL
KNOBBLE	KNUCK	KOKAM	KONZE	KOTO
KNOBBLER	KNUCKLE	KOKAMA	KOODOO	KOTOITE
KNOBBLIER	KNUCKLEBONE	KOKAN	KOODOOS	KOTSCHUBEITE
KNOBBLIEST	KNUCKLED	KOKANEE	KOOKA	KOTTIGITE
KNOBBLY	KNUCKLER	KOKERBOOM	KOOKABURRA	KOTUKU
KNOBBY	KNUCKLESOME	KOKIL	KOOKIE	KOTUKUTUKU
KNOBKERRY	KNUCKLING	KOKILA	KOOKIER	KOTWAL
KNOBLIKE	KNUCKLY	KOKIO	KOOKIEST	KOTWALEE
KNOBSTICK	KNUCKS	KOKKO	KOOKINESS	KOTYLE
KNOBSTONE	KNULLING	KOKLA	KOOKY	KOU
KNOBULAR	KNUR	KOKLAS	KOOLAH	KOUBA
KNOBWEED	KNURL	KOKO	KOOLAU	KOULAN
KNOBWOOD	KNURLED	KOKOON	KOOLETAH	KOUMISS
KNOCK	KNURLIER	KOKOONA	KOOLIMAN	KOUMYS
KNOCKABOUT	KNURLIEST	KOKOPU	KOOLOKAMBA	KOUPREY
KNOCKAWAY	KNURLIN	KOKOWAI	KOOMBAR	KOUPROH
KNOCKDOWN	KNURLING	KOKRA	KOOMKIE	KOURBASH
KNOCKEMDOWN	KNURLY	KOKSTAD	KOONTI	KOUROS
KNOCKER	KNURR	KOKTAITE	KOOP	KOUS
KNOCKING	KNURRY	KOKU	KOOPBRIEF	KOUSE
KNOCKOFF	KNUT	KOKUM	KOORAJONG	KOUSIN
KNOCKOUT	KNYAZ	KOKUMIN	KOORHAAN	KOUSSIN
KNOCKSTONE	KNYSNA	KOLA	KOORKA	KOUSSO
KNOCKUP	KO	KOLACH	KOOSIN	KOUZA
KNOCKWURST	KOA	KOLAMI	KOOTCHA	KOVIL
KNOIT	KOAE	KOLATTAM	KOOTCHAR	KOWBIRD
KNOLL	KOALA	KOLEA	KOP	KOWHAI
KNOLLER	KOALI	KOLEK	KOPECK	KOWL
KNOLLY	KOAN	KOLEL	KOPEK	KOWTOW
KNOP	KOB	KOLEROGA	KOPH	KOWTOWER
KNOPITE	KOBA	KOLINSKI	KOPI	KOY
KNOPPED	KOBAN	KOLINSKY	KOPJE	KOYEMSHI
KNOPPER	KOBANG	KOLKHOS	KOPPA	KOZO
KNOPPIE	KOBELLITE	KOLKHOZ	KOPPEN	KRA
KNOPPY	KOBIL	KOLKOZ	KOPPIE	KRAAL
KNORHAAN	KOBIRD	KOLLER	KOPPITE	KRAFT
KNOSP	KOBOLD	KOLLERGANG	KOR	KRAGEROITE
KNOSPED	KOBONG	KOLM	KORA	KRAIT
KNOT	KOBU	KOLO	KORADJI	KRAKEN
KNOTBERRY	KOCHIA	KOLOBIA	KORAIT	KRAKOWIAK
KNOTGRASS	KODA	KOLOBION	KORAKAN	KRAL
KNOTHEAD	KODAK	KOLOKOLO	KORARI	KRAN
KNOTHOLE	KODAKED	KOLS	KORDAX	KRANG
KNOTHORN	KODAKER	KOLSKITE	KORE	KRANS
KNOTROOT	KODAKING	KOLSUN	KOREC	KRANTZ
KNOTS	KODAKIST	KOLTUNNA	KORERO	KRANTZITE
KNOTTED	KODAKKED	KOM	KORHAAN	KRAPFEN
KNOTTER	KODAKKING	KOMARCH	KORI	KRAS
KNOTTIER	KODAKRY	KOMATIK	KORIMAKO	KRASIS
KNOTTIEST	KODKOD	KOMBO	KORIN	KRATER
KNOTTINESS	KODRA	KOMBU	KORNERUPINE	KRATOGEN
KNOTTING	KODURITE	KOMINUTER	KORO	KRATOGENIC
KNOTTY	KOECHLINITE	KOMITADJI	KOROMIKA	KRAUSEN
KNOTWEED	KOEL	KOMITAJI	KOROMIKO	KRAUSITE
KNOTWORK	KOENENITE	KOMMETJE	KORONA	KRAUT
KNOTWORT	KOFF	KOMMOS	KOROVA	KRAUTHEAD

KRAUTWEED
KRAVERS
KREEF
KREESE
KREIS
KREISTLE
KREITONITE
KRELOS
KREMERSITE
KREMLIN
KREMS
KRENG
KRENNERITE
KREPLACH
KREPLECH
KREUTZER
KREUZER
KREX
KRIEGSPIEL
KRIEKER
KRIGIA
KRILL
KRIMMER
KRIS
KRISS
KRITARCHY
KRITRIMA
KROBYLOI
KROBYLOS
KROCKET
KROHNKITE
KROMESKI
KROMESKY
KROMOGRAM
KROMSKOP
KRONA
KRONE
KRONEN
KRONER
KRONOR
KRONOS
KRONUR
KROON
KROONI
KROONS
KROSA
KROUCHKA
KROUSHKA
KRUBI
KRUBUT
KRULLER
KRUMHORN
KRUMMHORN
KRYOKONITE
KRYOLITE
KRYOLITH
KRYPSIS
KRYPTIC
KRYPTICISM
KRYPTOL
KRYPTON
KTHIB
KTHIBH
KUAN
KUBA
KUBBA
KUBONG
KUBUKLION
KUCHEN
KUDIZE
KUDOS
KUDU
KUDZU
KUE
KUEI
KUERR
KUFA

KUGE
KUGEL
KUGELHOF
KUICHUA
KUJAWIAK
KUKERI
KUKRI
KUKU
KUKUI
KUKUPA
KULA
KULAH
KULAITE
KULAK
KULAKISM
KULAN
KULANG
KULKARNI
KULLAITE
KULM
KULMET
KULP
KUMARA
KUMBI
KUMBUK
KUMHAR
KUMISS
KUMKUM
KUMMEL
KUMMERBUND
KUMQUAT
KUMRAH
KUMYS
KUNAI
KUNG
KUNK
KUNKUR
KUNMIUT
KUNZITE
KUPFERNICKEL
KUPFFERITE
KUPHAR
KUPPER
KURBASH
KURCHICINE
KURCHINE
KURGAN
KURI
KURK
KURRAJONG
KURSI
KURTOSIS
KURUMA
KURUMAYA
KURUNG
KURUNJ
KURVEY
KURVEYOR
KUSA
KUSAM
KUSHA
KUSIMANSE
KUSIMANSEL
KUSKITE
KUSKUS
KUSSO
KUSTI
KUSU
KUSUM
KUTAI
KUTCH
KUTCHA
KUTTAB
KUTTAR
KUVASZ
KVARNER
KVAS

KVASS
KVINT
KVUTZA
KVUTZAH
KWAN
KWARTA
KWASHIORKOR
KWATUMA
KWAZOKU
KWEEK
KWEI
KWIEN
KWINTRA
KYAAK
KYACK
KYAH
KYANG
KYANISE
KYANITE
KYANIZATION
KYANIZE
KYAR
KYAT
KYATHOS
KYAUNG
KYE
KYKE
KYL
KYLE
KYLIE
KYLIKES
KYLIN
KYLITE
KYLIX
KYMATOLOGY
KYMBALON
KYMOGRAM
KYMOGRAPH
KYMOGRAPHIC
KYNURENIC
KYNURIN
KYNURINE
KYOODLE
KYPHOSIS
KYPHOTIC
KYPOO
KYRIAL
KYRIALE
KYRIELLE
KYRIN
KYRINE
KYRIOS
KYSCHTYMITE
KYTE
KYTHE

LA
LAAGER
LAAGTE
LAANG
LAAP
LAARP
LAB
LABARA
LABARIA
LABARUM
LABBA
LABBER
LABDACISM
LABDACISMUS
LABDANUM
LABEFACT
LABEFACTION
LABEFIED
LABEFY
LABEFYING
LABEL
LABELED
LABELER
LABELING
LABELLATE
LABELLED
LABELLER
LABELLING
LABELLOID
LABELLUM
LABIA
LABIAL
LABIALISM
LABIALISMUS
LABIALITY
LABIALIZE
LABIALIZED
LABIALIZING
LABIALLY
LABIATE
LABIATED
LABIE
LABIELLA
LABILE
LABILITY
LABILIZATION
LABILIZE
LABIODENTAL
LABIOGLOSSAL
LABIOGRAPH
LABIOLINGUAL
LABIOMANCY
LABIOMENTAL
LABIONASAL
LABIOPALATAL
LABIOPLASTY
LABIOSE
LABIOVELAR
LABIOVERSION
LABIS
LABITE
LABIUM
LABLAB
LABOR
LABORAGE
LABORANT
LABORATORIAL

LABORATORIAN
LABORATORIES
LABORATORY
LABORED
LABOREDLY
LABOREDNESS
LABORER
LABORES
LABORESS
LABORING
LABORINGLY
LABORIOUS
LABORIOUSLY
LABORIOUSNESS
LABORISM
LABORIST
LABORITE
LABOROUS
LABORSAVING
LABORSOME
LABORSOMELY
LABOUR
LABOURAGE
LABOURED
LABOUREDLY
LABOUREDNESS
LABOURER
LABOURESS
LABOURING
LABOURINGLY
LABOURISM
LABOURIST
LABOURITE
LABOURSAVING
LABOURSOME
LABOURSOMELY
LABRA
LABRADORITE
LABRADORITIC
LABRAL
LABRAS
LABRET
LABRETIFERY
LABRID
LABROID
LABROSAURID
LABROSAUROID
LABROSE
LABRUM
LABRUSCA
LABRYS
LABURNUM
LABYRINTH
LABYRINTHAL
LABYRINTHALLY
LABYRINTHED
LABYRINTHIAN
LABYRINTHIC
LABYRINTHICAL
LABYRINTHICALLY
LABYRINTHINE
LAC
LACATAN
LACCA
LACCASE
LACCOL
LACCOLITE
LACCOLITH
LACCOLITHIC
LACCOLITIC
LACE
LACEBARK
LACED
LACEFLOWER
LACELEAF
LACEMAKER
LACEMAKING

LACEMAN
LACEMEN
LACEPIECE
LACEPOD
LACER
LACERABILITY
LACERABLE
LACERANT
LACERATE
LACERATED
LACERATELY
LACERATING
LACERATION
LACERATIVE
LACERT
LACERTIAN
LACERTIFORM
LACERTILIAN
LACERTILOID
LACERTINE
LACERTOID
LACERY
LACET
LACEWING
LACEWOMAN
LACEWOMEN
LACEWOOD
LACEWORK
LACEWORKER
LACHE
LACHES
LACHRYMA
LACHRYMAL
LACHRYMALLY
LACHRYMARY
LACHRYMATION
LACHRYMATOR
LACHRYMATORY
LACHRYMIFORM
LACHRYMIST
LACHRYMOSAL
LACHRYMOSE
LACHRYMOSELY
LACHRYMOSITY
LACHRYMOUS
LACHSA
LACIER
LACIEST
LACILY
LACINESS
LACING
LACINIA
LACINIATE
LACINIATED
LACINIATION
LACINIFORM
LACINIOSE
LACINIOUS
LACINULA
LACINULAS
LACINULATE
LACINULOSE
LACIS
LACK
LACKADAISICAL
LACKADAISY
LACKADAY
LACKED
LACKER
LACKERER
LACKERING
LACKEY
LACKEYED
LACKEYING
LACKEYS
LACKIES
LACKING

LACKLAND
LACKLUSTER
LACKLUSTRE
LACKLUSTROUS
LACKWIT
LACKWITTEDLY
LACKWITTEDNESS
LACMOID
LACMUS
LACONIC
LACONICAL
LACONICALLY
LACONICISM
LACONICS
LACONICUM
LACONISM
LACONIZE
LACONIZED
LACONIZER
LACONIZING
LACQUER
LACQUERED
LACQUERER
LACQUERING
LACQUERIST
LACQUERWORK
LACQUEY
LACRIMAL
LACRIMATOR
LACROIXITE
LACROSSE
LACROSSER
LACTALBUMIN
LACTAM
LACTAMIDE
LACTANT
LACTARENE
LACTARINE
LACTARIUM
LACTARY
LACTASE
LACTATE
LACTATED
LACTATING
LACTATION
LACTEAL
LACTEAN
LACTENIN
LACTEOUS
LACTESCE
LACTESCENCE
LACTESCENCY
LACTESCENT
LACTIC
LACTICINIA
LACTID
LACTIDE
LACTIFEROUS
LACTIFIC
LACTIFICAL
LACTIFIED
LACTIFLOROUS
LACTIFLUOUS
LACTIFORM
LACTIFUGE
LACTIFY
LACTIFYING
LACTIGENIC
LACTIGENOUS
LACTIGEROUS
LACTIM
LACTIMIDE
LACTINATE
LACTIVOROUS
LACTO
LACTOCHROME
LACTOCITRATE

LACTOFLAVIN
LACTOGEN
LACTOGENIC
LACTOID
LACTOL
LACTOMETER
LACTONE
LACTONIC
LACTONIZE
LACTOPROTEID
LACTOPROTEIN
LACTOSCOPE
LACTOSE
LACTOSID
LACTOSIDE
LACTOSURIA
LACTOTOXIN
LACTUCARIUM
LACTUCERIN
LACTUCIN
LACTUCOL
LACTUCON
LACTYL
LACUNA
LACUNAE
LACUNAL
LACUNAR
LACUNARIA
LACUNARS
LACUNARY
LACUNAS
LACUNE
LACUNOME
LACUNOSE
LACUNOSITY
LACUNULE
LACUNULOSE
LACUSCULAR
LACUSTRAL
LACUSTRIAN
LACUSTRINE
LACWORK
LACY
LAD
LADANG
LADANIGEROUS
LADANUM
LADDER
LADDERED
LADDERING
LADDERWAY
LADDERY
LADDESS
LADDIE
LADDIKIE
LADDISH
LADDOCK
LADE
LADED
LADEMAN
LADEN
LADENED
LADENING
LADER
LADIES
LADIFIED
LADIFY
LADIFYING
LADING
LADKIN
LADLE
LADLED
LADLEFUL
LADLER
LADLEWOOD
LADLING
LADRONE

LADRONISM
LADRONIZE
LADY
LADYBIRD
LADYBUG
LADYCLOCK
LADYFINGER
LADYFISH
LADYFLIES
LADYFLY
LADYFY
LADYHOOD
LADYKIN
LADYKIND
LADYLIKE
LADYLIKELY
LADYLING
LADYLOVE
LADYPALM
LADYSFINGER
LADYSHIP
LADYSLIPPER
LAEMODIPOD
LAEMODIPODAN
LAEN
LAENDER
LAEOTROPIC
LAEOTROPISM
LAEOTROPOUS
LAET
LAETATION
LAETI
LAETIC
LAEVO
LAEVODUCTION
LAEVOGYRATE
LAEVOGYRE
LAEVOVERSION
LAFAYETTE
LAFE
LAFT
LAG
LAGAN
LAGE
LAGEN
LAGENA
LAGENAE
LAGEND
LAGER
LAGERED
LAGERING
LAGETTO
LAGGAR
LAGGARD
LAGGARDLY
LAGGARDNESS
LAGGED
LAGGEN
LAGGER
LAGGIN
LAGGING
LAGLAST
LAGNA
LAGNAPPE
LAGNIAPPE
LAGO
LAGOMORPH
LAGOMORPHIC
LAGOMORPHOUS
LAGONITE
LAGOON
LAGOONAL
LAGOPODE
LAGOPODOUS
LAGOPOUS
LAGOSTOMA
LAGS

LAGUNA
LAGUNE
LAGWORT
LAHAR
LAHN
LAI
LAIC
LAICAL
LAICALITY
LAICALLY
LAICH
LAICISM
LAICITY
LAICIZATION
LAICIZE
LAICIZED
LAICIZER
LAICIZING
LAID
LAIDE
LAIDLY
LAIGH
LAIN
LAINAGE
LAINE
LAINER
LAIOSE
LAIR
LAIRAGE
LAIRD
LAIRDESS
LAIRDIE
LAIRDLY
LAIRDOCRACY
LAIRDSHIP
LAIRED
LAIRING
LAIRMAN
LAIRMEN
LAIRSTONE
LAIRY
LAISSE
LAIT
LAITANCE
LAITH
LAITHE
LAITHLY
LAITIES
LAITY
LAK
LAKARPITE
LAKATAN
LAKATOI
LAKE
LAKED
LAKELAND
LAKELANDER
LAKELET
LAKEMANSHIP
LAKER
LAKES
LAKESHORE
LAKEWEED
LAKEY
LAKH
LAKIE
LAKIER
LAKIEST
LAKIN
LAKING
LAKISH
LAKISHNESS
LAKISM
LAKIST
LAKMUS
LAKY
LALA

LALANG
LALAPALOOZA
LALAQUI
LALI
LALLAPALOOZA
LALLATION
LALLING
LALLYGAG
LALO
LALONEUROSIS
LALOPATHY
LALOPHOBIA
LALOPLEGIA
LAM
LAMA
LAMAIC
LAMANTIN
LAMANY
LAMASERIES
LAMASERY
LAMB
LAMBA
LAMBACK
LAMBALE
LAMBAST
LAMBASTE
LAMBASTED
LAMBASTING
LAMBDA
LAMBDACISM
LAMBDOID
LAMBDOIDAL
LAMBEAU
LAMBENCIES
LAMBENCY
LAMBENT
LAMBENTLY
LAMBER
LAMBERT
LAMBIE
LAMBINESS
LAMBISH
LAMBITIVE
LAMBKILL
LAMBKIN
LAMBLIASIS
LAMBLIKE
LAMBLING
LAMBOYS
LAMBREQUIN
LAMBS
LAMBSDOWN
LAMBSKIN
LAMDAN
LAMDEN
LAME
LAMED
LAMEDH
LAMEL
LAMELLA
LAMELLAE
LAMELLAR
LAMELLARY
LAMELLAS
LAMELLATE
LAMELLATED
LAMELLATELY
LAMELLATION
LAMELLICORN
LAMELLIFORM
LAMELLOID
LAMELLOSE
LAMELLOSITY
LAMELLULE
LAMELY
LAMENESS
LAMENT

LAMENTABLE
LAMENTABLY
LAMENTATION
LAMENTATORY
LAMENTED
LAMENTEDLY
LAMENTER
LAMENTFUL
LAMENTING
LAMENTINGLY
LAMENTIVE
LAMENTORY
LAMER
LAMEST
LAMESTER
LAMETER
LAMETTA
LAMIA
LAMIACEOUS
LAMIAE
LAMIAS
LAMIGER
LAMIID
LAMIN
LAMINA
LAMINABILITY
LAMINABLE
LAMINAE
LAMINAL
LAMINAR
LAMINARIAN
LAMINARIN
LAMINARIOID
LAMINARITE
LAMINARY
LAMINAS
LAMINATE
LAMINATED
LAMINATING
LAMINATION
LAMINBOARD
LAMINECTOMY
LAMING
LAMINIFEROUS
LAMINIFORM
LAMINITIS
LAMINOSE
LAMINOUS
LAMISH
LAMITER
LAMM
LAMMAS
LAMMED
LAMMER
LAMMERGEIER
LAMMERGEIR
LAMMERGEYER
LAMMIE
LAMMING
LAMMOCK
LAMMY
LAMNID
LAMNOID
LAMP
LAMPAD
LAMPADARIES
LAMPADARY
LAMPADEDROMY
LAMPADEPHORE
LAMPADITE
LAMPARA
LAMPAS
LAMPATIA
LAMPBLACK
LAMPBLACKED
LAMPBLACKING
LAMPED

LAMPER
LAMPERN
LAMPERS
LAMPFLOWER
LAMPFLY
LAMPFUL
LAMPHOLE
LAMPING
LAMPION
LAMPIST
LAMPISTRY
LAMPLESS
LAMPLET
LAMPLIGHT
LAMPLIGHTED
LAMPLIGHTER
LAMPLIT
LAMPMAKER
LAMPMAKING
LAMPMAN
LAMPMEN
LAMPOON
LAMPOONED
LAMPOONER
LAMPOONERY
LAMPOONING
LAMPOONIST
LAMPPOST
LAMPREL
LAMPRET
LAMPREY
LAMPREYS
LAMPROPHONY
LAMPROPHYRE
LAMPROPHYRIC
LAMPROTYPE
LAMPS
LAMPSHADE
LAMPSTAND
LAMPWICK
LAMPYRID
LAMPYRINE
LAMSIEKTE
LAMSTER
LAMZIEKTE
LAN
LANA
LANAC
LANAI
LANAMETER
LANARKITE
LANAS
LANATE
LANATED
LANAZ
LANCE
LANCED
LANCEGAY
LANCEGAYE
LANCELET
LANCELY
LANCEMAN
LANCEMEN
LANCEOLATE
LANCEOLATED
LANCEOLATELY
LANCEOLATION
LANCEPESADE
LANCEPOD
LANCEPRISADO
LANCER
LANCERS
LANCES
LANCET
LANCETED
LANCETEER
LANCEWOOD

LANCHA	LANDRACE	LANGUIDLY	LANUGO	LAPSI
LANCHARA	LANDRAKER	LANGUIDNESS	LANUGOS	LAPSIBILITY
LANCIERS	LANDREEVE	LANGUISH	LANUM	LAPSIBLE
LANCIFEROUS	LANDRIGHT	LANGUISHED	LANX	LAPSING
LANCIFORM	LANDS	LANGUISHER	LANYARD	LAPSINGLY
LANCINATE	LANDSALE	LANGUISHING	LANZON	LAPSTONE
LANCINATED	LANDSCAPE	LANGUISHINGLY	LAODAH	LAPSTRAKE
LANCINATING	LANDSCAPED	LANGUISHMENT	LAP	LAPSTREAK
LANCINATION	LANDSCAPING	LANGUOR	LAPACHO	LAPSTREAKED
LANCING	LANDSCAPIST	LANGUORMENT	LAPACHOL	LAPSTREAKER
LAND	LANDSHARD	LANGUOROUS	LAPACTIC	LAPSUS
LANDAGE	LANDSHIP	LANGUOROUSLY	LAPAN	LAPULAPU
LANDAMMAN	LANDSICK	LANGUR	LAPARECTOMY	LAPWING
LANDAU	LANDSIDE	LANIA	LAPAROCELE	LAPWORK
LANDAULET	LANDSKIP	LANIARD	LAPAROMYITIS	LAQUEAR
LANDAULETTE	LANDSLIDE	LANIARIES	LAPAROSCOPY	LAQUEARIA
LANDBLINK	LANDSLIP	LANIARIFORM	LAPAROSTICT	LAQUEARIAN
LANDBOC	LANDSMAN	LANIARY	LAPAROTOME	LAQUEUS
LANDBOOK	LANDSMEN	LANIATE	LAPAROTOMIST	LAR
LANDDROST	LANDSPOUT	LANIFEROUS	LAPAROTOMIZE	LARARIUM
LANDDROSTEN	LANDSPRINGY	LANIFIC	LAPAROTOMY	LARB
LANDE	LANDSTORM	LANIFICE	LAPBOARD	LARBOARD
LANDED	LANDTROST	LANIFLOROUS	LAPCOCK	LARBOLINS
LANDER	LANDWAITER	LANIFORM	LAPDOG	LARBOWLINES
LANDESITE	LANDWARD	LANIGEROUS	LAPEL	LARCENER
LANDFALL	LANDWARDS	LANIIFORM	LAPELER	LARCENIC
LANDFANG	LANDWASH	LANISTA	LAPELLED	LARCENIES
LANDFAST	LANDWAY	LANISTAE	LAPFUL	LARCENISH
LANDFLOOD	LANDWAYS	LANITAL	LAPFULS	LARCENIST
LANDFOLK	LANDWHIN	LANK	LAPICIDE	LARCENOUS
LANDFORM	LANDWIRE	LANKER	LAPIDARIAN	LARCENOUSLY
LANDGAFOL	LANDWRACK	LANKEST	LAPIDARIES	LARCENY
LANDGATE	LANDWRECK	LANKET	LAPIDARIST	LARCH
LANDGATES	LANDYARD	LANKIER	LAPIDARY	LARCIN
LANDGRAVE	LANE	LANKIEST	LAPIDATE	LARCINRY
LANDGRAVESS	LANELY	LANKILY	LAPIDATED	LARD
LANDGRAVIATE	LANER	LANKINESS	LAPIDATING	LARDACEIN
LANDGRAVINE	LANESOME	LANKLY	LAPIDATION	LARDACEOUS
LANDHOLDER	LANETE	LANKNESS	LAPIDATOR	LARDED
LANDHOLDING	LANEWAY	LANKY	LAPIDEON	LARDER
LANDIMERE	LANEY	LANNER	LAPIDEOUS	LARDERELLITE
LANDING	LANG	LANNERET	LAPIDES	LARDERER
LANDIRON	LANGAHA	LANOLIN	LAPIDESCENCE	LARDIFORM
LANDLADIES	LANGARAI	LANOLINE	LAPIDESCENT	LARDINER
LANDLADY	LANGBANITE	LANOSE	LAPIDICOLOUS	LARDING
LANDLEAPER	LANGBEINITE	LANOSITY	LAPIDIFIC	LARDITE
LANDLER	LANGCA	LANSA	LAPIDIFICAL	LARDON
LANDLESS	LANGEL	LANSAT	LAPIDIFIED	LARDOON
LANDLESSNESS	LANGI	LANSDOWNE	LAPIDIFY	LARDRY
LANDLINE	LANGITE	LANSEH	LAPIDIFYING	LARDY
LANDLOCK	LANGKA	LANSFORDITE	LAPIDIST	LAREABELL
LANDLOCKED	LANGLAUF	LANSQUENET	LAPIDITY	LARES
LANDLOOK	LANGLAUFER	LANT	LAPIDOSE	LARGAMENTE
LANDLOOKER	LANGLE	LANTACA	LAPIES	LARGANDO
LANDLOPER	LANGOON	LANTAKA	LAPILLI	LARGE
LANDLOPING	LANGOOTY	LANTANA	LAPILLIFORM	LARGEBRAINED
LANDLORD	LANGOSTA	LANTCHA	LAPILLO	LARGEHEARTED
LANDLORDISM	LANGOUSTE	LANTERLOO	LAPILLUS	LARGEHEARTEDNES
LANDLORDLY	LANGRAGE	LANTERN	LAPIN	LARGELY
LANDLORDRY	LANGREL	LANTERNED	LAPIS	LARGEMOUTHED
LANDLORDSHIP	LANGRET	LANTERNING	LAPLING	LARGEN
LANDLOUPER	LANGRIDGE	LANTERNLEAF	LAPON	LARGENESS
LANDLOUPING	LANGSETTLE	LANTERNMAN	LAPPACEOUS	LARGEOUR
LANDLUBBER	LANGSHAN	LANTERNS	LAPPAGE	LARGEOUS
LANDLUBBERISH	LANGSPIEL	LANTHANA	LAPPED	LARGER
LANDLUBBERLY	LANGSPIL	LANTHANIA	LAPPER	LARGESS
LANDLUBBING	LANGSYNE	LANTHANID	LAPPET	LARGESSE
LANDMAN	LANGUAGE	LANTHANIDE	LAPPETED	LARGEST
LANDMARK	LANGUAGED	LANTHANITE	LAPPETHEAD	LARGHETTO
LANDMASS	LANGUAGES	LANTHANON	LAPPING	LARGHETTOS
LANDMEN	LANGUAGING	LANTHANUM	LAPPISH	LARGHISSIMO
LANDOCRACY	LANGUE	LANTHOPIN	LAPSABILITY	LARGHISSIMOS
LANDOCRAT	LANGUENT	LANTHOPINE	LAPSABLE	LARGIFICAL
LANDOWNER	LANGUESCENT	LANTHORN	LAPSATION	LARGISH
LANDOWNERSHIP	LANGUET	LANTUM	LAPSE	LARGITION
LANDOWNING	LANGUETTE	LANUGINOSE	LAPSED	LARGITIONAL
LANDPLANE	LANGUID	LANUGINOUS	LAPSER	LARGO

LARGY
LARI
LARIAT
LARIATED
LARIATING
LARICK
LARID
LARIDINE
LARIGO
LARIGOT
LARIID
LARIN
LARINE
LARIOT
LARIX
LARIXIN
LARK
LARKED
LARKER
LARKING
LARKINGLY
LARKISH
LARKISHNESS
LARKS
LARKSOME
LARKSPUR
LARKY
LARM
LARME
LARMIER
LARMOYANT
LARNAKES
LARNAX
LAROID
LARON
LARREE
LARRIES
LARRIGAN
LARRIKIN
LARRIKINESS
LARRIKINISM
LARRIMAN
LARRUP
LARRUPED
LARRUPING
LARRY
LARS
LARSENITE
LARUM
LARVA
LARVAE
LARVAL
LARVARIA
LARVARIUM
LARVARIUMS
LARVATE
LARVATED
LARVE
LARVICIDAL
LARVICIDE
LARVICOLOUS
LARVIFORM
LARVIGEROUS
LARVIPAROUS
LARVIPOSIT
LARVIPOSITION
LARVIVOROUS
LARVULE
LARY
LARYNGAL
LARYNGALGIA
LARYNGEAL
LARYNGEAN
LARYNGEATING
LARYNGECTOMY
LARYNGES
LARYNGIC

LARYNGISMAL
LARYNGISMUS
LARYNGITIC
LARYNGITIS
LARYNGOCELE
LARYNGOGRAPH
LARYNGOLOGY
LARYNGOMETRY
LARYNGOPATHY
LARYNGOPHONY
LARYNGORRHEA
LARYNGOSCOPE
LARYNGOSCOPY
LARYNGOSTOMY
LARYNGOTOME
LARYNGOTOMY
LARYNX
LARYNXES
LAS
LASAGNA
LASAGNE
LASCAR
LASCHETY
LASCIVIENT
LASCIVIENTLY
LASCIVIOUS
LASCIVIOUSLY
LASCIVIOUSNESS
LASER
LASERWORT
LASH
LASHED
LASHER
LASHES
LASHING
LASHINGS
LASHINS
LASHLESS
LASHLIGHT
LASHLITE
LASHNESS
LASHORN
LASIOCAMPID
LASIOCARPOUS
LASK
LASKE
LASKET
LASKING
LASPRING
LASQUE
LASS
LASSET
LASSIE
LASSIKY
LASSITUDE
LASSLORN
LASSO
LASSOCK
LASSOCKIE
LASSOED
LASSOER
LASSOES
LASSOING
LASSOS
LASSU
LAST
LASTAGE
LASTER
LASTEX
LASTING
LASTINGLY
LASTINGNESS
LASTLY
LASTRE
LASTY
LASYA
LAT

LATA
LATAH
LATANIER
LATCH
LATCHED
LATCHER
LATCHET
LATCHING
LATCHKEY
LATCHMAN
LATCHMEN
LATCHSTRING
LATE
LATEBRA
LATEBRICOLE
LATECOMER
LATECOMING
LATED
LATEEN
LATEENER
LATELINESS
LATELY
LATEMOST
LATEN
LATENCE
LATENCIES
LATENCY
LATENESS
LATENT
LATENTLY
LATER
LATERA
LATERAD
LATERAL
LATERALITY
LATERALIZE
LATERALIZED
LATERALIZING
LATERALLY
LATERAN
LATERIFLORAL
LATERIGRADE
LATERITE
LATERITIC
LATERIZATION
LATEROCAUDAL
LATERODORSAL
LATERONUCHAL
LATESCENCE
LATESCENT
LATESOME
LATEST
LATEWARD
LATEWHILE
LATEWHILES
LATEWOOD
LATEX
LATEXES
LATEXOSIS
LATH
LATHE
LATHED
LATHEE
LATHEMAN
LATHEN
LATHER
LATHERED
LATHEREEVE
LATHERER
LATHERIN
LATHERING
LATHERWORT
LATHERY
LATHESMAN
LATHESMEN
LATHI
LATHIE

LATHIER
LATHIEST
LATHING
LATHREEVE
LATHS
LATHWORK
LATHY
LATHYRIC
LATHYRISM
LATI
LATIBULIZE
LATICES
LATICIFEROUS
LATICLAVE
LATICOSTATE
LATIDENTATE
LATIFOLIATE
LATIFOLIOUS
LATIFUNDIA
LATIFUNDIAN
LATIFUNDIUM
LATIGO
LATINISM
LATINIZE
LATION
LATIPENNATE
LATIPENNINE
LATIPLANTAR
LATIROSTRAL
LATIROSTROUS
LATISEPT
LATISEPTAL
LATISEPTATE
LATISH
LATISTERNAL
LATITANCY
LATITANT
LATITAT
LATITE
LATITUDE
LATITUDINAL
LATITUDINALLY
LATITUDINARIAN
LATITUDINARY
LATITUDINOUS
LATIVE
LATKE
LATOMIA
LATOMY
LATOSOL
LATRANT
LATRATION
LATREDE
LATREUTIC
LATREUTICAL
LATRIA
LATRIAL
LATRIALLY
LATRIAN
LATRINE
LATRO
LATROBE
LATROBITE
LATROCINIUM
LATROCINY
LATRON
LATS
LATTEN
LATTENER
LATTENS
LATTER
LATTERLY
LATTERMATH
LATTERMOST
LATTICE
LATTICED
LATTICELEAF

LATTICEWORK
LATTICING
LATTICINIO
LATTIN
LATU
LATUS
LAUAN
LAUBANITE
LAUD
LAUDABILITY
LAUDABLE
LAUDABLENESS
LAUDABLY
LAUDANIDINE
LAUDANIN
LAUDANINE
LAUDANOSINE
LAUDANUM
LAUDATION
LAUDATIVE
LAUDATORILY
LAUDATORY
LAUDED
LAUDER
LAUDIFICATION
LAUDING
LAUDIST
LAUDS
LAUGH
LAUGHABLE
LAUGHABLENESS
LAUGHABLY
LAUGHED
LAUGHEE
LAUGHER
LAUGHFUL
LAUGHING
LAUGHINGLY
LAUGHINGSTOCK
LAUGHS
LAUGHSOME
LAUGHTER
LAUGHWORTHY
LAUGHY
LAUHALA
LAUIA
LAUK
LAULAU
LAUMONITE
LAUMONTITE
LAUN
LAUNCE
LAUNCH
LAUNCHED
LAUNCHER
LAUNCHING
LAUND
LAUNDER
LAUNDERED
LAUNDERER
LAUNDERETTE
LAUNDERING
LAUNDRESS
LAUNDRIES
LAUNDROMAT
LAUNDRY
LAUNDRYMAID
LAUNDRYMAN
LAUNDRYMEN
LAUNDRYOWNER
LAUNDRYWOMAN
LAUNDRYWOMEN
LAUNEDDAS
LAURA
LAURACEOUS
LAURAE
LAURALDEHYDE

LAURAS
LAURATE
LAURDALITE
LAURE
LAUREATE
LAUREATED
LAUREATESHIP
LAUREATING
LAUREATION
LAUREL
LAURELED
LAURELING
LAURELLED
LAURELLING
LAURELS
LAURELSHIP
LAURELWOOD
LAUREOLE
LAURIC
LAURIN
LAURINOXYLON
LAURIONITE
LAURITE
LAURONE
LAURUSTINE
LAURUSTINUS
LAURVIKITE
LAURY
LAURYL
LAUTARITE
LAUTER
LAUTITE
LAUTITIOUS
LAUTU
LAUWINE
LAVA
LAVABO
LAVABOES
LAVACRE
LAVADERO
LAVAGE
LAVALIER
LAVALIERE
LAVAMENT
LAVANDERA
LAVANDERAS
LAVANDERO
LAVANDEROS
LAVANDIN
LAVANGA
LAVANT
LAVARET
LAVASH
LAVATIC
LAVATION
LAVATIONAL
LAVATORIES
LAVATORY
LAVE
LAVED
LAVEER
LAVEMENT
LAVENDER
LAVENDERED
LAVENDERING
LAVENITE
LAVER
LAVEROCK
LAVETTE
LAVIALITE
LAVING
LAVISH
LAVISHED
LAVISHER
LAVISHING
LAVISHINGLY
LAVISHLY

LAVISHNESS
LAVOLTA
LAVROCK
LAVROFFITE
LAVROVITE
LAVY
LAW
LAWBOOK
LAWBREAKER
LAWBREAKERS
LAWBREAKING
LAWFUL
LAWFULLY
LAWFULNESS
LAWGIVER
LAWGIVING
LAWINE
LAWING
LAWISH
LAWK
LAWKS
LAWLANTS
LAWLESS
LAWLESSLY
LAWLESSNESS
LAWLIKE
LAWMAKER
LAWMAKING
LAWMAN
LAWMEN
LAWMONGER
LAWN
LAWNED
LAWNER
LAWNLEAF
LAWNLET
LAWNLIKE
LAWNY
LAWPROOF
LAWRENCITE
LAWRENCIUM
LAWRIGHTMAN
LAWRIGHTMEN
LAWS
LAWSONE
LAWSONITE
LAWSUIT
LAWSUITING
LAWTER
LAWYER
LAWYERLIKE
LAWYERLY
LAWYERY
LAX
LAXATE
LAXATION
LAXATIVE
LAXATIVELY
LAXATIVENESS
LAXER
LAXEST
LAXIFLOROUS
LAXIFOLIATE
LAXIFOLIOUS
LAXISM
LAXIST
LAXITY
LAXLY
LAXNESS
LAY
LAYAWAY
LAYBACK
LAYBOY
LAYER
LAYERAGE
LAYERED
LAYERING

LAYERS
LAYERY
LAYETTE
LAYFOLK
LAYING
LAYLAND
LAYLIGHT
LAYLOCK
LAYMAN
LAYMANSHIP
LAYMEN
LAYNE
LAYOFF
LAYOUT
LAYOVER
LAYROCK
LAYSTALL
LAYSTOW
LAYWOMAN
LAYWOMEN
LAZAR
LAZARET
LAZARETTE
LAZARETTO
LAZARETTOS
LAZARLY
LAZAROLE
LAZARONE
LAZAROUS
LAZARY
LAZE
LAZED
LAZIER
LAZIEST
LAZILY
LAZINESS
LAZING
LAZO
LAZULE
LAZULI
LAZULITE
LAZULITIC
LAZURITE
LAZY
LAZYBACK
LAZYBED
LAZYBIRD
LAZYBONE
LAZYBONES
LAZYBOOTS
LAZYLEGS
LAZZARONE
LAZZARONI
LAZZO
LE
LEA
LEACH
LEACHATE
LEACHED
LEACHER
LEACHIER
LEACHIEST
LEACHING
LEACHMAN
LEACHMEN
LEACHY
LEAD
LEADAGE
LEADBACK
LEADED
LEADEN
LEADENLY
LEADENNESS
LEADER
LEADERETTE
LEADERS
LEADERSHIP

LEADHILLITE
LEADIN
LEADING
LEADMAN
LEADOFF
LEADOFFS
LEADOUT
LEADPLANT
LEADS
LEADSMAN
LEADSMEN
LEADWAY
LEADWOOD
LEADWORK
LEADWORT
LEADY
LEAF
LEAFAGE
LEAFBIRD
LEAFBOY
LEAFCUP
LEAFDOM
LEAFED
LEAFEN
LEAFER
LEAFERY
LEAFGIRL
LEAFHOPPER
LEAFIER
LEAFIEST
LEAFINESS
LEAFING
LEAFIT
LEAFLESS
LEAFLET
LEAFLETEER
LEAFLIKE
LEAFMOLD
LEAFSTALK
LEAFWOOD
LEAFWORK
LEAFWORM
LEAFY
LEAG
LEAGUE
LEAGUED
LEAGUER
LEAGUERER
LEAGUING
LEAK
LEAKAGE
LEAKANCE
LEAKED
LEAKER
LEAKIER
LEAKIEST
LEAKINESS
LEAKING
LEAKY
LEAL
LEALAND
LEALLY
LEALNESS
LEALTY
LEAM
LEAMER
LEAN
LEANED
LEANER
LEANING
LEANLY
LEANNESS
LEANT
LEANY
LEAP
LEAPED
LEAPER

LEAPFROG
LEAPFROGGER
LEAPFROGGING
LEAPING
LEAPINGLY
LEAPS
LEAPT
LEAR
LEARN
LEARNED
LEARNEDLY
LEARNEDNESS
LEARNER
LEARNING
LEARNT
LEARY
LEASE
LEASEBACK
LEASED
LEASEHOLD
LEASEHOLDER
LEASEHOLDING
LEASEMONGER
LEASER
LEASH
LEASING
LEASOW
LEAST
LEASTWAYS
LEASTWISE
LEAT
LEATH
LEATHER
LEATHERBACK
LEATHERBARK
LEATHERBOARD
LEATHERCOAT
LEATHERER
LEATHERETTE
LEATHERFISH
LEATHERFISHES
LEATHERFLOWER
LEATHERHEAD
LEATHERINE
LEATHERINESS
LEATHERING
LEATHERIZE
LEATHERJACKET
LEATHERLEAF
LEATHERN
LEATHERNECK
LEATHEROID
LEATHERS
LEATHERSIDE
LEATHERWARE
LEATHERWING
LEATHERWOOD
LEATHERWORK
LEATHERWORKER
LEATHERWORKING
LEATHERY
LEATHWAKE
LEATMAN
LEATMEN
LEAVE
LEAVED
LEAVELESS
LEAVELOOKER
LEAVEN
LEAVENED
LEAVENING
LEAVENOUS
LEAVER
LEAVES
LEAVIER
LEAVIEST
LEAVING

LEAVINGS	LEDGEMAN	LEFTWARDLY	LEGISLATION	LEIOTRICHY
LEAVY	LEDGEMENT	LEFTWARDS	LEGISLATIONAL	LEIOTROPIC
LEAWILL	LEDGER	LEFTY	LEGISLATIVE	LEIR
LEAZE	LEDGERED	LEG	LEGISLATIVELY	LEIS
LEBAN	LEDGERING	LEGACIES	LEGISLATOR	LEISHMANIA
LEBBAN	LEDGES	LEGACY	LEGISLATORIAL	LEISHMANIASIS
LEBBEK	LEDGIER	LEGAL	LEGISLATRESS	LEISS
LEBEN	LEDGIEST	LEGALESE	LEGISLATRIX	LEISTER
LEBHAFT	LEDGING	LEGALISE	LEGISLATURE	LEISTERER
LEBO	LEDGMENT	LEGALISM	LEGIST	LEISURABLE
LEBRANCHO	LEDGY	LEGALIST	LEGISTER	LEISURABLY
LEBU	LEDOL	LEGALISTIC	LEGIT	LEISURE
LECAMA	LEE	LEGALISTICALLY	LEGITIM	LEISURED
LECANIID	LEEANGLE	LEGALITIES	LEGITIMACY	LEISURELINESS
LECANINE	LEEBOARD	LEGALITY	LEGITIMATE	LEISURELY
LECANOMANCER	LEECH	LEGALIZATION	LEGITIMATED	LEITMOTIF
LECANOMANCY	LEECHCRAFT	LEGALIZE	LEGITIMATELY	LEITMOTIV
LECANOMANTIC	LEECHDOM	LEGALIZED	LEGITIMATENESS	LEK
LECANORINE	LEECHEATER	LEGALIZING	LEGITIMATING	LEKACH
LECANOROID	LEECHED	LEGALLY	LEGITIMATION	LEKANAI
LECANOSCOPIC	LEECHER	LEGANTINE	LEGITIMATIST	LEKANE
LECANOSCOPY	LEECHERY	LEGATARY	LEGITIMATIZE	LEKIN
LECCE	LEECHES	LEGATE	LEGITIMATIZED	LEKYTHOS
LECH	LEECHING	LEGATEE	LEGITIMATIZING	LELWEL
LECHER	LEECHMAN	LEGATESHIP	LEGITIME	LEMAN
LECHERER	LEECHWORT	LEGATI	LEGITIMISM	LEMANRY
LECHERIES	LEED	LEGATINE	LEGITIMIST	LEMANS
LECHEROUS	LEEFANG	LEGATION	LEGITIMISTIC	LEMEL
LECHEROUSLY	LEEFANGE	LEGATIONARY	LEGITIMITY	LEMMA
LECHEROUSNESS	LEEFTAIL	LEGATIVE	LEGITIMIZATION	LEMMAS
LECHERY	LEEFUL	LEGATO	LEGITIMIZE	LEMMATA
LECHOSA	LEEFULLY	LEGATOR	LEGITIMIZED	LEMMING
LECHRIODONT	LEEFULNESS	LEGATORIAL	LEGITIMIZING	LEMMINGS
LECHUGUILLA	LEEGTE	LEGATOS	LEGLEN	LEMMOBLASTIC
LECHWE	LEEK	LEGATUS	LEGLESS	LEMMOCYTE
LECIDEIFORM	LEEKY	LEGBAR	LEGLET	LEMMON
LECIDEINE	LEELANE	LEGEND	LEGMAN	LEMNACEOUS
LECIDIOID	LEELANG	LEGENDA	LEGOA	LEMNAD
LECITHAL	LEEM	LEGENDARIAN	LEGONG	LEMNISCATA
LECITHALITY	LEEN	LEGENDARY	LEGPIECE	LEMNISCATE
LECITHIN	LEEP	LEGENDIC	LEGPULL	LEMNISCATIC
LECITHOBLAST	LEEPIT	LEGENDRY	LEGPULLER	LEMNISCI
LECK	LEER	LEGENDS	LEGPULLING	LEMNISCUS
LECKER	LEERED	LEGER	LEGROOM	LEMOGRAPHY
LECONTITE	LEERFISH	LEGERDEMAIN	LEGS	LEMOLOGY
LECOTROPAL	LEERIER	LEGERDEMAINIST	LEGUA	LEMON
LECTERN	LEERIEST	LEGERETE	LEGUAN	LEMONADE
LECTION	LEERING	LEGERITY	LEGULEIAN	LEMONADO
LECTIONARIES	LEERISH	LEGES	LEGULEIOUS	LEMONGRASS
LECTIONARY	LEERNESS	LEGGE	LEGUME	LEMONWEED
LECTOR	LEERY	LEGGED	LEGUMELIN	LEMONWOOD
LECTORATE	LEES	LEGGER	LEGUMEN	LEMONY
LECTORIAL	LEESE	LEGGIER	LEGUMIN	LEMPIRA
LECTOTYPE	LEESER	LEGGIERO	LEGUMINIFORM	LEMUR
LECTRESS	LEESING	LEGGIEST	LEGUMINOSE	LEMURES
LECTRICE	LEESOME	LEGGINESS	LEGUMINOUS	LEMURIFORM
LECTUAL	LEESOMELY	LEGGING	LEGWORK	LEMURINE
LECTUARY	LEET	LEGGINGED	LEHAYIM	LEMUROID
LECTURE	LEETLE	LEGGINGS	LEHIITE	LEMURS
LECTURED	LEETMAN	LEGGY	LEHR	LENA
LECTURER	LEETMEN	LEGHORN	LEHRBACHITE	LENAD
LECTURESHIP	LEEVE	LEGIBILITY	LEHRMAN	LENARD
LECTURETTE	LEEWAN	LEGIBLE	LEHRMEN	LENCH
LECTURING	LEEWARD	LEGIBLENESS	LEHRSMAN	LENCHEON
LECYTH	LEEWARDLY	LEGIBLY	LEHRSMEN	LEND
LECYTHI	LEEWARDMOST	LEGIFER	LEHUA	LENDE
LECYTHID	LEEWAY	LEGIFIC	LEI	LENDER
LECYTHOI	LEEWILL	LEGION	LEIE	LENDING
LECYTHOID	LEFSE	LEGIONARIES	LEIF	LENE
LECYTHUS	LEFSEL	LEGIONARY	LEIFITE	LENES
LED	LEFSEN	LEGIONED	LEIGHTON	LENG
LEDE	LEFT	LEGIONER	LEIMTYPE	LENGTH
LEDEN	LEFTISM	LEGIONNAIRE	LEIOCOME	LENGTHEN
LEDERHOSEN	LEFTIST	LEGIONRY	LEIOMYOMA	LENGTHENED
LEDERITE	LEFTMENTS	LEGISLATE	LEIOMYOMATA	LENGTHENING
LEDGE	LEFTOVER	LEGISLATED	LEIOTRICHINE	LENGTHER
LEDGED	LEFTWARD	LEGISLATING	LEIOTRICHOUS	LENGTHIER

LENGTHIEST
LENGTHILY
LENGTHINESS
LENGTHS
LENGTHSMAN
LENGTHSMEN
LENGTHWAYS
LENGTHWISE
LENGTHY
LENIATE
LENIENCE
LENIENCY
LENIENT
LENIENTLY
LENIFY
LENIS
LENITIC
LENITIES
LENITION
LENITIVE
LENITIVELY
LENITIVENESS
LENITUDE
LENITY
LENNILITE
LENNOACEOUS
LENNOW
LENO
LENOS
LENS
LENSED
LENSES
LENSLESS
LENSMAN
LENT
LENTAMENTE
LENTANDO
LENTEN
LENTICEL
LENTICELLATE
LENTICLE
LENTICONUS
LENTICULA
LENTICULAE
LENTICULAR
LENTICULARE
LENTICULARIS
LENTICULARLY
LENTICULAS
LENTICULATE
LENTICULE
LENTIFORM
LENTIGEROUS
LENTIGINES
LENTIGINOSE
LENTIGINOUS
LENTIGO
LENTIL
LENTILE
LENTINER
LENTISCINE
LENTISCUS
LENTISSIMO
LENTITUDE
LENTNER
LENTO
LENTOID
LENTOR
LENTOUS
LENVOY
LEODICID
LEONCITO
LEONHARDITE
LEONINE
LEONINELY
LEONINES
LEONITE

LEONTIASIS
LEOPARD
LEOPARDE
LEOPARDESS
LEOPARDITE
LEOTARD
LEOTARDS
LEP
LEPADID
LEPADOID
LEPER
LEPERED
LEPERO
LEPID
LEPIDIN
LEPIDINE
LEPIDITY
LEPIDLY
LEPIDOBLASTIC
LEPIDOID
LEPIDOLITE
LEPIDOMELANE
LEPIDOPHYTE
LEPIDOPHYTIC
LEPIDOPTER
LEPIDOPTERA
LEPIDOPTERAL
LEPIDOPTERAN
LEPIDOPTERID
LEPIDOPTERIST
LEPIDOPTERON
LEPIDOPTEROUS
LEPIDOSIREN
LEPIDOSIS
LEPIDOSTEOID
LEPIDOTE
LEPOCYTA
LEPOCYTE
LEPORID
LEPORIDE
LEPORIFORM
LEPORINE
LEPOTHRIX
LEPPER
LEPPY
LEPRA
LEPRECHAUN
LEPRIC
LEPRID
LEPROID
LEPROLOGIC
LEPROLOGIST
LEPROLOGY
LEPROMA
LEPROMATOUS
LEPROSARIA
LEPROSARIUM
LEPROSARIUMS
LEPROSE
LEPROSED
LEPROSERIES
LEPROSERY
LEPROSIED
LEPROSIS
LEPROSITY
LEPROSY
LEPROUS
LEPROUSLY
LEPROUSNESS
LEPRY
LEPTA
LEPTANDRIN
LEPTENE
LEPTID
LEPTINOLITE
LEPTITE
LEPTOBOS

LEPTOCARDIAN
LEPTOCENTRIC
LEPTOCERCAL
LEPTOCHROA
LEPTOCHROUS
LEPTOCLASE
LEPTODACTYL
LEPTODERMOUS
LEPTOFORM
LEPTOLOGY
LEPTOMATIC
LEPTOME
LEPTOMEDUSAN
LEPTOMETER
LEPTOMONAD
LEPTON
LEPTONEMA
LEPTONS
LEPTOPELLIC
LEPTOPROSOPE
LEPTOPROSOPY
LEPTORRHIN
LEPTORRHINE
LEPTOSOME
LEPTOSPERM
LEPTOSPIROSIS
LEPTOSTRACAN
LEPTOTENE
LEPTUS
LEPTYNITE
LERE
LERED
LERER
LERNAEAN
LEROT
LERP
LERRET
LES
LESBIAN
LESBIANISM
LESCHE
LESE
LESED
LESHEY
LESHY
LESION
LESIY
LESKEACEOUS
LESS
LESSE
LESSEE
LESSEN
LESSENED
LESSENER
LESSENING
LESSER
LESSES
LESSEST
LESSIVE
LESSNESS
LESSON
LESSONED
LESSONING
LESSOR
LEST
LESTIWARITE
LESTOBIOSIS
LESTOBIOTIC
LESTRAD
LET
LETCH
LETCHY
LETDOWN
LETGAME
LETHAL
LETHALITY
LETHARGIC

LETHARGICAL
LETHARGICALLY
LETHARGIZE
LETHARGIZED
LETHARGIZING
LETHARGUS
LETHARGY
LETHIED
LETHIFEROUS
LETHOLOGICA
LETOFF
LETON
LETTED
LETTEN
LETTER
LETTERED
LETTERER
LETTERET
LETTERGAE
LETTERGRAM
LETTERHEAD
LETTERING
LETTERLEAF
LETTERMAN
LETTERMEN
LETTERPRESS
LETTERS
LETTERSPACE
LETTERWEIGHT
LETTICE
LETTIGA
LETTING
LETTRURE
LETTUCE
LETUP
LEU
LEUCAETHIOP
LEUCAETHIOPES
LEUCAETHIOPIC
LEUCANILINE
LEUCANTHOUS
LEUCAUGITE
LEUCAURIN
LEUCIN
LEUCINE
LEUCITE
LEUCITIC
LEUCITIS
LEUCITITE
LEUCITOID
LEUCITOPHYRE
LEUCO
LEUCOBASALT
LEUCOBLAST
LEUCOBLASTIC
LEUCOCARPOUS
LEUCOCHOLIC
LEUCOCHOLY
LEUCOCHROIC
LEUCOCIDIC
LEUCOCIDIN
LEUCOCRATE
LEUCOCRATIC
LEUCOCYAN
LEUCOCYTE
LEUCOCYTIC
LEUCOCYTOID
LEUCOCYTOSIS
LEUCOCYTOTIC
LEUCODERMA
LEUCODERMIA
LEUCODERMIC
LEUCOGENIC
LEUCOID
LEUCOMA
LEUCOMAINE
LEUCOMATOUS

LEUCOMELANIC
LEUCON
LEUCONES
LEUCOPENIA
LEUCOPENIC
LEUCOPHANE
LEUCOPHANITE
LEUCOPHORE
LEUCOPHYRE
LEUCOPLAKIA
LEUCOPLAKIAL
LEUCOPLAST
LEUCOPLASTID
LEUCOPOIESIS
LEUCOPYRITE
LEUCORRHEA
LEUCORRHEAL
LEUCORRHOEA
LEUCORRHOEAL
LEUCORYX
LEUCOSPHERE
LEUCOSPHERIC
LEUCOSTASIS
LEUCOSYENITE
LEUCOTOME
LEUCOTOXIC
LEUCOUS
LEUCOXENE
LEUCYL
LEUD
LEUDES
LEUDS
LEUGH
LEUKAEMIA
LEUKAEMIC
LEUKEMIA
LEUKEMIC
LEUKEMID
LEUKOCIDIC
LEUKOCIDIN
LEUKOCYTE
LEUKOCYTOSIS
LEUKOCYTOTIC
LEUKODERMA
LEUKODERMIC
LEUKOMA
LEUKOPENIA
LEUKOPENIC
LEUKORRHEA
LEUKOSIS
LEUMA
LEV
LEVA
LEVADE
LEVAN
LEVANCE
LEVANCY
LEVANT
LEVANTER
LEVANTINE
LEVATION
LEVATOR
LEVATORES
LEVATORS
LEVE
LEVEE
LEVEED
LEVEEING
LEVEL
LEVELED
LEVELER
LEVELHEADED
LEVELHEADEDLY
LEVELHEADEDNESS
LEVELING
LEVELISM
LEVELLED

LEVELLER	LEXICOLOGIST	LIBERALLY	LICENTIOUSNESS	LIENCULI
LEVELLING	LEXICOLOGY	LIBERALNESS	LICET	LIENCULUS
LEVELLY	LEXICON	LIBERATE	LICH	LIENEE
LEVELMAN	LEXICONIST	LIBERATED	LICHAM	LIENIC
LEVELNESS	LEXICONIZE	LIBERATING	LICHANOS	LIENITIS
LEVER	LEXIGRAPHIC	LIBERATION	LICHEE	LIENOCELE
LEVERAGE	LEXIGRAPHICAL	LIBERATIONISM	LICHEN	LIENOGASTRIC
LEVERED	LEXIGRAPHY	LIBERATIONIST	LICHENACEOUS	LIENOR
LEVERER	LEXIPHANIC	LIBERATIVE	LICHENED	LIENORENAL
LEVERET	LEY	LIBERATOR	LICHENIAN	LIENOTOXIN
LEVERING	LEYE	LIBERATORY	LICHENIASIS	LIENTERIC
LEVERMAN	LEYLAND	LIBERATRESS	LICHENIC	LIENTERY
LEVERS	LEYSING	LIBERATRICE	LICHENIFORM	LIEPOT
LEVESEL	LEZA	LIBERATRIX	LICHENIN	LIER
LEVET	LHERZITE	LIBEROMOTOR	LICHENISM	LIERNE
LEVIABLE	LI	LIBERTARIAN	LICHENIST	LIERRE
LEVIATHAN	LIABILITIES	LIBERTARIANISM	LICHENIZATION	LIES
LEVIED	LIABILITY	LIBERTICIDAL	LICHENIZE	LIESPFUND
LEVIER	LIABLE	LIBERTICIDE	LICHENOID	LIEU
LEVIES	LIABLENESS	LIBERTIES	LICHENOLOGY	LIEUE
LEVIGABLE	LIAISON	LIBERTINAGE	LICHENOSE	LIEUTENANCY
LEVIGATE	LIAMBA	LIBERTINE	LICHENOUS	LIEUTENANT
LEVIGATION	LIANA	LIBERTINISM	LICHENS	LIEVE
LEVIGATOR	LIANE	LIBERTY	LICHI	LIEVER
LEVIN	LIANG	LIBETHENITE	LICHT	LIEVEST
LEVINING	LIANGLE	LIBIDIBI	LICHWAKE	LIEVRITE
LEVIR	LIAR	LIBIDINAL	LICIT	LIFE
LEVIRATE	LIARD	LIBIDINALLY	LICITATION	LIFEBLOOD
LEVIRATIC	LIB	LIBIDINOSITY	LICITLY	LIFEBOAT
LEVIRATICAL	LIBAMENT	LIBIDINOUS	LICITNESS	LIFEBOATMAN
LEVIRATION	LIBANIFEROUS	LIBIDINOUSLY	LICK	LIFEBOATMEN
LEVITANT	LIBANT	LIBIDINOUSNESS	LICKED	LIFEDAY
LEVITATE	LIBATE	LIBIDO	LICKER	LIFEDROP
LEVITATED	LIBATED	LIBKEN	LICKERISH	LIFEFUL
LEVITATING	LIBATING	LIBKIN	LICKERISHLY	LIFEFULLY
LEVITATION	LIBATION	LIBRA	LICKERISHNESS	LIFEFULNESS
LEVITATIONAL	LIBATIONARY	LIBRAE	LICKING	LIFEGUARD
LEVITATIVE	LIBATIONER	LIBRAL	LICKPENNY	LIFEHOLD
LEVITATOR	LIBATORY	LIBRARIAN	LICKSPIT	LIFEHOLDER
LEVITIES	LIBBARD	LIBRARIANESS	LICKSPITTLE	LIFEHOOD
LEVITY	LIBBER	LIBRARIANSHIP	LICORICE	LIFELEAF
LEVODUCTION	LIBBET	LIBRARIES	LICORN	LIFELESS
LEVOGYRATE	LIBBRA	LIBRARII	LICORNE	LIFELESSLY
LEVOGYRE	LIBECCIO	LIBRARIOUS	LICTOR	LIFELESSNESS
LEVOROTATION	LIBEL	LIBRARIUS	LICTORIAN	LIFELET
LEVOROTATORY	LIBELANT	LIBRARY	LICURI	LIFELIKE
LEVOVERSION	LIBELED	LIBRAS	LICURY	LIFELIKENESS
LEVULIN	LIBELEE	LIBRATE	LID	LIFELINE
LEVULINIC	LIBELER	LIBRATED	LIDDED	LIFELONG
LEVULOSE	LIBELING	LIBRATING	LIDDER	LIFER
LEVULOSURIA	LIBELIST	LIBRATION	LIDDERON	LIFERENT
LEVY	LIBELLANT	LIBRATORY	LIDFLOWER	LIFERENTED
LEVYING	LIBELLARY	LIBRETTI	LIDGATE	LIFERENTER
LEVYIST	LIBELLATE	LIBRETTIST	LIDLESS	LIFERENTING
LEVYNE	LIBELLED	LIBRETTO	LIE	LIFERENTRIX
LEVYNITE	LIBELLEE	LIBRETTOS	LIEBENERITE	LIFEROOT
LEW	LIBELLER	LIBRIFORM	LIEBIGITE	LIFESAVER
LEWAN	LIBELLING	LIBROPLAST	LIEBLICH	LIFESAVING
LEWD	LIBELLIST	LICAREOL	LIED	LIFESOME
LEWDER	LIBELLOUS	LICCA	LIEDER	LIFESOMELY
LEWDEST	LIBELLOUSLY	LICE	LIEDERKRANZ	LIFESOMENESS
LEWDLY	LIBELLULID	LICENCE	LIEF	LIFESPRING
LEWDNESS	LIBELLULOID	LICENCED	LIEFER	LIFETIME
LEWIS	LIBELOUS	LICENCEE	LIEFEST	LIFEWAY
LEWISITE	LIBELOUSLY	LICENCER	LIEFLY	LIFEWORK
LEWISSON	LIBER	LICENSABLE	LIEFSOME	LIFEY
LEWTH	LIBERAL	LICENSE	LIEGE	LIFT
LEWTY	LIBERALISM	LICENSED	LIEGEFUL	LIFTED
LEX	LIBERALIST	LICENSEE	LIEGEFULLY	LIFTER
LEXIA	LIBERALISTIC	LICENSER	LIEGELESS	LIFTING
LEXIC	LIBERALITES	LICENSING	LIEGELY	LIFTMAN
LEXICAL	LIBERALITY	LICENSOR	LIEGEMAN	LIFTMEN
LEXICALIC	LIBERALIZATION	LICENSURE	LIEGEMEN	LIFTOFF
LEXICALITY	LIBERALIZE	LICENTIATE	LIEGER	LIG
LEXICOGRAPHY	LIBERALIZED	LICENTIATION	LIEGEWOMAN	LIGABLE
LEXICOLOGIC	LIBERALIZER	LICENTIOUS	LIEN	LIGAMENT
LEXICOLOGICAL	LIBERALIZING	LICENTIOUSLY	LIENAL	LIGAMENTA

LIGAMENTAL
LIGAMENTARY
LIGAMENTOUS
LIGAMENTOUSLY
LIGAMENTS
LIGAMENTUM
LIGAN
LIGAND
LIGAS
LIGATE
LIGATED
LIGATING
LIGATION
LIGATIVE
LIGATOR
LIGATORY
LIGATURE
LIGATURED
LIGATURING
LIGE
LIGEANCE
LIGER
LIGG
LIGGAT
LIGGER
LIGHT
LIGHTBOAT
LIGHTED
LIGHTEN
LIGHTENED
LIGHTENER
LIGHTENING
LIGHTER
LIGHTERAGE
LIGHTERMAN
LIGHTERMEN
LIGHTEST
LIGHTFACE
LIGHTFOOT
LIGHTFUL
LIGHTHEADED
LIGHTHEADEDLY
LIGHTHEADEDNESS
LIGHTHEARTEDLY
LIGHTHEARTEDNESS
LIGHTHOUSE
LIGHTHOUSES
LIGHTING
LIGHTISH
LIGHTKEEPER
LIGHTLESS
LIGHTLY
LIGHTMAN
LIGHTMANSHIP
LIGHTMEN
LIGHTMOUTHED
LIGHTNESS
LIGHTNING
LIGHTPROOF
LIGHTROOM
LIGHTS
LIGHTSCOT
LIGHTSHIP
LIGHTSMAN
LIGHTSMEN
LIGHTSOME
LIGHTSOMELY
LIGHTSOMENESS
LIGHTWEIGHT
LIGHTWOOD
LIGNALOES
LIGNE
LIGNEOUS
LIGNESCENT
LIGNICOLE
LIGNICOLINE
LIGNICOLOUS

LIGNIFEROUS
LIGNIFICATION
LIGNIFIED
LIGNIFORM
LIGNIFY
LIGNIFYING
LIGNIN
LIGNIPERDOUS
LIGNITE
LIGNITIC
LIGNITIZE
LIGNIVOROUS
LIGNOCERIC
LIGNOGRAPHY
LIGNONE
LIGNOSE
LIGNOSITY
LIGNOUS
LIGNUM
LIGROIN
LIGROINE
LIGULA
LIGULAE
LIGULAR
LIGULAS
LIGULATE
LIGULE
LIGULIFORM
LIGULIN
LIGULOID
LIGURE
LIGURITE
LIGURITION
LIGURRITION
LIIN
LIJA
LIKABILITY
LIKABLE
LIKABLENESS
LIKE
LIKEABILITY
LIKEABLE
LIKEABLENESS
LIKED
LIKEFUL
LIKELIER
LIKELIEST
LIKELIHEAD
LIKELIHOOD
LIKELY
LIKEN
LIKENED
LIKENESS
LIKENING
LIKER
LIKEROUS
LIKES
LIKESOME
LIKEST
LIKEWAYS
LIKEWISE
LIKEWISELY
LIKEWISENESS
LIKIN
LIKING
LIKINGLY
LIKNA
LIKNON
LIL
LILAC
LILACEOUS
LILACIN
LILACKY
LILACTHROAT
LILACTIDE
LILAS
LILBURNE

LILE
LILES
LILIACEOUS
LILIAL
LILIATED
LILIED
LILIES
LILIFORM
LILIUM
LILL
LILLIANITE
LILLIBULLERO
LILT
LILTED
LILTING
LILY
LILYFY
LILYWORT
LIM
LIMA
LIMACEL
LIMACELLE
LIMACEOUS
LIMACIFORM
LIMACINE
LIMACINID
LIMACOID
LIMACON
LIMAIL
LIMAILLE
LIMAN
LIMATION
LIMB
LIMBA
LIMBATE
LIMBATION
LIMBEC
LIMBECK
LIMBED
LIMBER
LIMBERED
LIMBERER
LIMBEREST
LIMBERHAM
LIMBERING
LIMBERLY
LIMBERNESS
LIMBERS
LIMBIC
LIMBIFEROUS
LIMBING
LIMBMEAL
LIMBO
LIMBOS
LIMBOUS
LIMBURGER
LIMBURGITE
LIMBUS
LIMBY
LIME
LIMEADE
LIMEBERRIES
LIMEBERRY
LIMEBUSH
LIMED
LIMEHOUSE
LIMEKILN
LIMELIGHT
LIMELIGHTER
LIMEMAN
LIMEN
LIMENS
LIMEQUAT
LIMER
LIMERICK
LIMES
LIMESTONE

LIMETTIN
LIMEWASH
LIMEWATER
LIMEWORT
LIMEY
LIMEYS
LIMICOLINE
LIMICOLOUS
LIMIER
LIMIEST
LIMINA
LIMINAL
LIMINARY
LIMING
LIMIT
LIMITABLE
LIMITAL
LIMITARIAN
LIMITARIES
LIMITARY
LIMITATE
LIMITATION
LIMITATIVE
LIMITATIVELY
LIMITED
LIMITEDLY
LIMITEDNESS
LIMITER
LIMITES
LIMITING
LIMITIVE
LIMITLESS
LIMITLESSLY
LIMITLESSNESS
LIMITROPHE
LIMITS
LIMITY
LIMIVOROUS
LIMMA
LIMMATA
LIMMER
LIMMOCK
LIMMU
LIMN
LIMNAL
LIMNANTH
LIMNED
LIMNER
LIMNERY
LIMNETIC
LIMNIAD
LIMNIMETER
LIMNIMETRIC
LIMNING
LIMNITE
LIMNOBIOLOGY
LIMNOBIOS
LIMNOGRAPH
LIMNOLOGIC
LIMNOLOGICAL
LIMNOLOGIST
LIMNOLOGY
LIMNOMETER
LIMNOPHIL
LIMNOPHILE
LIMNOPHILID
LIMNOPHILOUS
LIMNORIOID
LIMON
LIMONCILLO
LIMONCITO
LIMONENE
LIMONIAD
LIMONIN
LIMONITE
LIMONITIC
LIMONIUM

LIMOSE
LIMOUS
LIMOUSINE
LIMP
LIMPA
LIMPED
LIMPER
LIMPEST
LIMPET
LIMPHAULT
LIMPID
LIMPIDITY
LIMPIDLY
LIMPIDNESS
LIMPIN
LIMPING
LIMPINGLY
LIMPINGNESS
LIMPKIN
LIMPLY
LIMPNESS
LIMPSY
LIMPY
LIMSY
LIMU
LIMULID
LIMULOID
LIMULUS
LIMURITE
LIMY
LIN
LINA
LINABLE
LINACEOUS
LINAGA
LINAGE
LINALOA
LINALOE
LINALOOL
LINALYL
LINAMARIN
LINARITE
LINCH
LINCHBOLT
LINCHET
LINCHPIN
LINCHPINNED
LINCLOTH
LINCTUS
LIND
LINDACKERITE
LINDANE
LINDEN
LINDER
LINDO
LINDOITE
LINDWORM
LINE
LINEA
LINEABLE
LINEAGE
LINEAGED
LINEAL
LINEALITY
LINEALLY
LINEAMENT
LINEAMENTAL
LINEAMETER
LINEAR
LINEARITY
LINEARIZATION
LINEARIZE
LINEARLY
LINEARY
LINEAS
LINEATE
LINEATED

LINEATION
LINEATURE
LINEBACKER
LINEBACKING
LINECUT
LINED
LINEIFORM
LINELESS
LINELET
LINEMAN
LINEMEN
LINEN
LINENER
LINENETTE
LINENIZE
LINENIZER
LINENMAN
LINENS
LINEOGRAPH
LINEOLATE
LINEOLATED
LINER
LINES
LINESIDES
LINESMAN
LINESMEN
LINEUP
LINEWALKER
LINEWORK
LINEY
LING
LINGA
LINGAM
LINGBERRIES
LINGBERRY
LINGBIRD
LINGCOD
LINGE
LINGEL
LINGENBERRY
LINGER
LINGERED
LINGERER
LINGERIE
LINGERING
LINGERINGLY
LINGET
LINGLE
LINGO
LINGOE
LINGOES
LINGONBERRIES
LINGONBERRY
LINGOT
LINGS
LINGSTER
LINGTOW
LINGTOWMAN
LINGUA
LINGUACIOUS
LINGUADENTAL
LINGUAE
LINGUAL
LINGUALE
LINGUALIS
LINGUALITY
LINGUALIZE
LINGUANASAL
LINGUATULOID
LINGUET
LINGUIDENTAL
LINGUIFORM
LINGUISHED
LINGUIST
LINGUISTER
LINGUISTIC
LINGUISTICAL

LINGUISTICALLY
LINGUISTICIAN
LINGUISTICS
LINGUISTRY
LINGULA
LINGULAE
LINGULATE
LINGULATED
LINGULID
LINGULIFORM
LINGULOID
LINGUODENTAL
LINGUODISTAL
LINGWORT
LINGY
LINHA
LINHAY
LINIE
LINIER
LINIEST
LINIMENT
LININ
LINING
LININGS
LINITIS
LINIYA
LINJA
LINJE
LINK
LINKAGE
LINKBOY
LINKED
LINKER
LINKIER
LINKIEST
LINKING
LINKMAN
LINKMEN
LINKS
LINKSMITH
LINKSTER
LINKWORK
LINKY
LINN
LINNAEITE
LINNEON
LINNET
LINO
LINOLATE
LINOLEATE
LINOLEIC
LINOLEIN
LINOLENATE
LINOLENIC
LINOLENIN
LINOLEUM
LINOMETER
LINON
LINOTYPE
LINOTYPED
LINOTYPER
LINOTYPING
LINOTYPIST
LINQUISH
LINS
LINSANG
LINSEED
LINSEY
LINSTOCK
LINT
LINTEL
LINTELED
LINTELING
LINTELLED
LINTELLING
LINTEN
LINTER

LINTERN
LINTERS
LINTIE
LINTIER
LINTIEST
LINTONITE
LINTSEED
LINTWHITE
LINTY
LINWOOD
LINY
LIODERMIA
LIOMYOMA
LION
LIONCEL
LIONESS
LIONET
LIONHEART
LIONHEARTED
LIONHEARTEDNESS
LIONISM
LIONIZABLE
LIONIZATION
LIONIZE
LIONIZED
LIONIZER
LIONIZING
LIONLIKE
LIONLY
LIONS
LIOS
LIP
LIPA
LIPARIAN
LIPAROCELE
LIPAROID
LIPAROUS
LIPASE
LIPE
LIPID
LIPIDE
LIPIN
LIPOBLAST
LIPOBLASTOMA
LIPOCELE
LIPOCERATOUS
LIPOCERE
LIPOCHROME
LIPOCLASIS
LIPOCLASTIC
LIPOCYTE
LIPOFEROUS
LIPOFIBROMA
LIPOGENESIS
LIPOGENETIC
LIPOGENIC
LIPOGENOUS
LIPOGRAM
LIPOGRAPHY
LIPOHEMIA
LIPOID
LIPOIDAEMIA
LIPOIDAL
LIPOIDEMIA
LIPOIDIC
LIPOLYSIS
LIPOLYTIC
LIPOMA
LIPOMAS
LIPOMATA
LIPOMATOSIS
LIPOMATOUS
LIPOMYOMA
LIPOMYXOMA
LIPOPEXIA
LIPOPHAGIC
LIPOPHORE

LIPOPOD
LIPOPROTEIN
LIPOSARCOMA
LIPOSIS
LIPOSOME
LIPOSTOMY
LIPOTHYMIA
LIPOTHYMIAL
LIPOTHYMIC
LIPOTHYMY
LIPOTROPHIC
LIPOTROPHY
LIPOTROPIC
LIPOTROPY
LIPOTYPE
LIPOVACCINE
LIPOXENOUS
LIPOXENY
LIPPED
LIPPEN
LIPPER
LIPPIE
LIPPIER
LIPPIEST
LIPPINESS
LIPPING
LIPPITUDE
LIPPITUDO
LIPPY
LIPS
LIPSANOTHECA
LIPSTICK
LIPURIA
LIPWORK
LIQUABLE
LIQUAMEN
LIQUATE
LIQUATED
LIQUATING
LIQUATION
LIQUEFACIENT
LIQUEFACTION
LIQUEFACTIVE
LIQUEFIABLE
LIQUEFIED
LIQUEFIER
LIQUEFY
LIQUEFYING
LIQUESCE
LIQUESCENCE
LIQUESCENCY
LIQUESCENT
LIQUET
LIQUEUR
LIQUEURED
LIQUEURING
LIQUID
LIQUIDABLE
LIQUIDAMBAR
LIQUIDAMBER
LIQUIDATE
LIQUIDATED
LIQUIDATING
LIQUIDATION
LIQUIDATOR
LIQUIDITY
LIQUIDIZE
LIQUIDIZED
LIQUIDIZING
LIQUIDLY
LIQUIDNESS
LIQUIDOGENIC
LIQUIDS
LIQUIDUS
LIQUIDY
LIQUIFORM
LIQUIFY

LIQUOR
LIQUORED
LIQUORER
LIQUORICE
LIQUORING
LIQUORISH
LIQUORISHLY
LIQUORISHNESS
LIQUORIST
LIQUORS
LIQUORY
LIRA
LIRAS
LIRATE
LIRATION
LIRE
LIRELLA
LIRELLATE
LIRELLIFORM
LIRELLINE
LIRELLOUS
LIRIODENDRON
LIRIPIPE
LIRIPOOP
LIRK
LIROCONITE
LIRP
LIS
LISERE
LISETTE
LISH
LISI
LISIERE
LISK
LISLE
LISP
LISPED
LISPER
LISPING
LISPOUND
LISPUND
LISS
LISSE
LISSES
LISSOM
LISSOME
LISSOMELY
LISSOMENESS
LISSOTRICHAN
LISSOTRICHY
LIST
LISTABLE
LISTED
LISTEDNESS
LISTEL
LISTEN
LISTENED
LISTENER
LISTENERS
LISTENING
LISTER
LISTERIA
LISTFUL
LISTING
LISTLESS
LISTLESSLY
LISTLESSNESS
LISTRED
LISTS
LISTWORK
LISTY
LIT
LITAI
LITANEUTICAL
LITANIES
LITANY
LITAS

LITATION	LITHOCHROMY	LITHOTOMICAL	LITURGIC	LLANERO
LITCH	LITHOCLASE	LITHOTOMIES	LITURGICAL	LLANO
LITCHI	LITHOCLAST	LITHOTOMIST	LITURGICALLY	LLANOS
LITE	LITHOCULTURE	LITHOTOMIZE	LITURGICIAN	LLARETA
LITER	LITHOCYST	LITHOTOMOUS	LITURGICS	LLAUTU
LITERACY	LITHODESMA	LITHOTOMY	LITURGIES	LLYN
LITERAL	LITHODID	LITHOTONY	LITURGIOLOGY	LO
LITERALISM	LITHODOMOUS	LITHOTRESIS	LITURGISM	LOA
LITERALIST	LITHOFELLIC	LITHOTRIPSY	LITURGIST	LOACH
LITERALISTIC	LITHOFELLINIC	LITHOTRITE	LITURGIZE	LOACHES
LITERALITIES	LITHOFRACTEUR	LITHOTRITIC	LITURGY	LOAD
LITERALITY	LITHOFRACTOR	LITHOTRITIES	LITUS	LOADED
LITERALIZATION	LITHOGENESIS	LITHOTRITIST	LITUUS	LOADEN
LITERALIZE	LITHOGENESY	LITHOTRITOR	LITZ	LOADER
LITERALIZED	LITHOGENETIC	LITHOTRITY	LIVABILITY	LOADING
LITERALIZER	LITHOGENOUS	LITHOTYPE	LIVABLE	LOADPENNY
LITERALIZING	LITHOGENY	LITHOTYPED	LIVABLENESS	LOADS
LITERALLY	LITHOGLYPH	LITHOTYPIC	LIVE	LOADSOME
LITERALNESS	LITHOGLYPHER	LITHOTYPING	LIVEABLE	LOADSTAR
LITERARIAN	LITHOGLYPHIC	LITHOTYPY	LIVED	LOADSTONE
LITERARILY	LITHOGLYPTIC	LITHOUS	LIVEDO	LOADUM
LITERARINESS	LITHOGLYPTICS	LITHOXYL	LIVELIER	LOAF
LITERARY	LITHOGRAPH	LITHOXYLE	LIVELIEST	LOAFER
LITERATE	LITHOGRAPHED	LITHOXYLITE	LIVELIHOOD	LOAFING
LITERATED	LITHOGRAPHER	LITHSMAN	LIVELINESS	LOAFINGLY
LITERATI	LITHOGRAPHIC	LITHURESIS	LIVELONG	LOAGHTAN
LITERATIM	LITHOGRAPHING	LITHURIA	LIVELY	LOAIASIS
LITERATION	LITHOGRAPHY	LITHY	LIVEN	LOAM
LITERATIST	LITHOGRAVURE	LITI	LIVENER	LOAMIER
LITERATO	LITHOID	LITIGABLE	LIVER	LOAMIEST
LITERATOR	LITHOIDAL	LITIGANT	LIVERANCE	LOAMILY
LITERATOS	LITHOIDITE	LITIGATE	LIVERBERRY	LOAMINESS
LITERATURE	LITHOLABE	LITIGATED	LIVERED	LOAMING
LITERATURED	LITHOLAPAXY	LITIGATING	LIVERIED	LOAMY
LITERATUS	LITHOLATROUS	LITIGATION	LIVERIES	LOAN
LITEROSE	LITHOLATRY	LITIGATOR	LIVERING	LOANABLE
LITEROSITY	LITHOLOGIC	LITIGATORY	LIVERISH	LOANBLEND
LITH	LITHOLOGICAL	LITIGIOSITY	LIVERISHNESS	LOANED
LITHAEMIA	LITHOLOGIST	LITIGIOUS	LIVERLEAF	LOANER
LITHAEMIC	LITHOLOGY	LITIGIOUSLY	LIVERWORT	LOANGE
LITHAGOGUE	LITHOLYSIS	LITIGIOUSNESS	LIVERWURST	LOANIN
LITHANGIURIA	LITHOLYTE	LITISCONTEST	LIVERY	LOANING
LITHANTHRAX	LITHOLYTIC	LITMUS	LIVERYMAN	LOANMONGER
LITHARGE	LITHOMANCY	LITORINOID	LIVERYMEN	LOANSHIFT
LITHATE	LITHOMARGE	LITOTES	LIVES	LOANWORD
LITHATIC	LITHOMETER	LITRA	LIVESTOCK	LOASACEOUS
LITHE	LITHONEPHRIA	LITRE	LIVETIN	LOATH
LITHECTASY	LITHONTRIPTIC	LITRO	LIVEYER	LOATHE
LITHECTOMY	LITHOPAEDION	LITS	LIVID	LOATHED
LITHELY	LITHOPAEDIUM	LITTEN	LIVIDITY	LOATHER
LITHEMIA	LITHOPEDION	LITTER	LIVIDLY	LOATHFUL
LITHEMIC	LITHOPEDIUM	LITTERATEUR	LIVIDNESS	LOATHFULLY
LITHENESS	LITHOPHAGOUS	LITTERATIM	LIVIER	LOATHFULNESS
LITHER	LITHOPHANE	LITTERBUG	LIVING	LOATHING
LITHERLY	LITHOPHANIC	LITTERED	LIVINGS	LOATHINGLY
LITHERNESS	LITHOPHANY	LITTERER	LIVISH	LOATHLINESS
LITHESOME	LITHOPHILOUS	LITTERING	LIVISHLY	LOATHLY
LITHESOMENESS	LITHOPHONE	LITTERY	LIVOR	LOATHSOME
LITHEST	LITHOPHYL	LITTLE	LIVRE	LOATHSOMELY
LITHI	LITHOPHYLL	LITTLENECK	LIVRES	LOATHSOMENESS
LITHIA	LITHOPHYSA	LITTLENESS	LIVYER	LOATHY
LITHIASIS	LITHOPHYSAE	LITTLER	LIWA	LOAVE
LITHIASTIC	LITHOPHYSAL	LITTLEST	LIWAN	LOAVES
LITHIATE	LITHOPHYTE	LITTLEWALE	LIXIVIAL	LOB
LITHIC	LITHOPHYTIC	LITTLIN	LIXIVIATE	LOBA
LITHIFICATION	LITHOPHYTOUS	LITTLING	LIXIVIATED	LOBAL
LITHIFIED	LITHOPONE	LITTORAL	LIXIVIATING	LOBAR
LITHIFY	LITHOSCOPE	LITTRESS	LIXIVIATION	LOBATE
LITHIFYING	LITHOSIAN	LITU	LIXIVIATOR	LOBATED
LITHITE	LITHOSIID	LITUATE	LIXIVIOUS	LOBATION
LITHIUM	LITHOSIS	LITUI	LIXIVIUM	LOBBED
LITHLESS	LITHOSPERM	LITUIFORM	LIZA	LOBBER
LITHO	LITHOSPERMON	LITUITE	LIZARD	LOBBIED
LITHOBIID	LITHOSPHERE	LITUITOID	LIZARDTAIL	LOBBIES
LITHOBIOID	LITHOTINT	LITUOLINE	LIZARY	LOBBING
LITHOCENOSIS	LITHOTOME	LITUOLOID	LLAMA	LOBBISH
LITHOCHROMIC	LITHOTOMIC	LITURATE	LLAMAS	LOBBY

LOBBYER	LOCALNESS	LOCOMOTIVEMAN	LOGANBERRIES	LOGOMACHIST
LOBBYGOW	LOCANDA	LOCOMOTIVEMEN	LOGANBERRY	LOGOMACHIZE
LOBBYING	LOCATABLE	LOCOMOTIVITY	LOGANIACEOUS	LOGOMACHY
LOBBYISM	LOCATE	LOCOMOTOR	LOGANIN	LOGOMANCY
LOBBYIST	LOCATED	LOCOMOTORY	LOGAOEDIC	LOGOMANIAC
LOBBYMAN	LOCATER	LOCOMUTATION	LOGARITHM	LOGOMETER
LOBBYMEN	LOCATING	LOCOS	LOGARITHMAL	LOGOMETRIC
LOBCOCK	LOCATIO	LOCOWEED	LOGARITHMIC	LOGOMETRICAL
LOBCOKT	LOCATION	LOCULAMENT	LOGARITHMICAL	LOGOPEDIA
LOBE	LOCATIONAL	LOCULAR	LOGARITHMICALLY	LOGOPEDICS
LOBECTOMY	LOCATIONS	LOCULATE	LOGBOOK	LOGORRHEA
LOBED	LOCATIVE	LOCULATED	LOGCOCK	LOGORRHOEA
LOBEFOOT	LOCATOR	LOCULATION	LOGE	LOGOS
LOBEFOOTED	LOCELLATE	LOCULE	LOGEIA	LOGOTHETE
LOBEFOOTS	LOCELLUS	LOCULI	LOGEION	LOGOTYPE
LOBELIA	LOCH	LOCULICIDAL	LOGGAT	LOGOTYPY
LOBELIACEOUS	LOCHAGUS	LOCULOSE	LOGGATS	LOGROLL
LOBELIN	LOCHAN	LOCULOUS	LOGGED	LOGROLLER
LOBELINE	LOCHE	LOCULUS	LOGGER	LOGROLLING
LOBELLATED	LOCHETIC	LOCUM	LOGGERHEAD	LOGS
LOBFIG	LOCHI	LOCUPLETE	LOGGERHEADED	LOGWAY
LOBI	LOCHIA	LOCUPLETELY	LOGGERHEADS	LOGWOOD
LOBIFORM	LOCHIAL	LOCUS	LOGGET	LOGWORK
LOBIGEROUS	LOCHIOCOLPOS	LOCUST	LOGGIA	LOGY
LOBING	LOCHIOCYTE	LOCUSTA	LOGGIAS	LOHAN
LOBIPED	LOCHIOMETRA	LOCUSTBERRY	LOGGIN	LOHOCH
LOBLOLLIES	LOCHIOPYRA	LOCUSTELLE	LOGGING	LOHOCK
LOBLOLLY	LOCHIORRHEA	LOCUSTID	LOGGY	LOI
LOBO	LOCHOPYRA	LOCUSTING	LOGHE	LOIMIC
LOBOLA	LOCHUS	LOCUTION	LOGHEAD	LOIMOGRAPHY
LOBOPODIUM	LOCHY	LOCUTOR	LOGHEADED	LOIMOLOGY
LOBOS	LOCI	LOCUTORIES	LOGIA	LOIN
LOBOSE	LOCK	LOCUTORSHIP	LOGIC	LOINCLOTH
LOBOTOMIES	LOCKABLE	LOCUTORY	LOGICAL	LOINED
LOBOTOMY	LOCKAGE	LOD	LOGICALIST	LOINS
LOBSCOURSE	LOCKBOX	LODE	LOGICALITY	LOIR
LOBSCOUSE	LOCKED	LODEMAN	LOGICALIZATION	LOITER
LOBSCOUSER	LOCKER	LODEMANAGE	LOGICALIZE	LOITERED
LOBSTER	LOCKERMAN	LODEN	LOGICALLY	LOITERER
LOBSTERING	LOCKERMEN	LODESMAN	LOGICALNESS	LOITERING
LOBSTERPROOF	LOCKET	LODESMEN	LOGICASTER	LOKA
LOBSTERS	LOCKFAST	LODESTAR	LOGICIAN	LOKAO
LOBSTICK	LOCKFUL	LODESTONE	LOGICIANER	LOKAPALA
LOBTAIL	LOCKHOLE	LODESTUFF	LOGICISM	LOKE
LOBULAR	LOCKING	LODGE	LOGICITY	LOKELANI
LOBULARLY	LOCKJAW	LODGED	LOGICIZE	LOKIEC
LOBULATE	LOCKLESS	LODGEMAN	LOGICS	LOKSHEN
LOBULATED	LOCKLET	LODGEMENT	LOGIE	LOLL
LOBULATION	LOCKMAKER	LODGEPOLE	LOGIER	LOLLAPALOOSA
LOBULE	LOCKMAN	LODGER	LOGIEST	LOLLAPALOOZA
LOBULETTE	LOCKNUT	LODGING	LOGIN	LOLLED
LOBULI	LOCKOUT	LODGINGHOUSE	LOGION	LOLLER
LOBULOSE	LOCKPIN	LODGMENT	LOGIS	LOLLIES
LOBULOUS	LOCKRAM	LODICULA	LOGISTIC	LOLLING
LOBULUS	LOCKRUM	LODICULE	LOGISTICAL	LOLLINGITE
LOBUS	LOCKSMAN	LOESS	LOGISTICIAN	LOLLIPOP
LOBWORM	LOCKSMITH	LOESSAL	LOGISTICS	LOLLOP
LOCA	LOCKSMITHERY	LOESSIAL	LOGJAM	LOLLOPY
LOCABLE	LOCKSMITHING	LOESSIC	LOGMAN	LOLLUP
LOCAL	LOCKSPIT	LOESSLAND	LOGOCRACY	LOLLY
LOCALE	LOCKUP	LOESSOID	LOGODAEDALY	LOLLYGAG
LOCALED	LOCKWORK	LOF	LOGOGOGUE	LOLLYPOP
LOCALING	LOCKY	LOFT	LOGOGRAM	LOMA
LOCALISM	LOCKYER	LOFTED	LOGOGRAPH	LOMASTOME
LOCALIST	LOCO	LOFTER	LOGOGRAPHER	LOMATA
LOCALISTIC	LOCOED	LOFTIER	LOGOGRAPHIC	LOMATINE
LOCALITIES	LOCOFOCO	LOFTIEST	LOGOGRAPHICAL	LOMATINOUS
LOCALITY	LOCOFOCOS	LOFTILY	LOGOGRAPHY	LOMBOY
LOCALIZABLE	LOCOING	LOFTINESS	LOGOGRIPH	LOMENT
LOCALIZATION	LOCOISM	LOFTING	LOGOGRIPHIC	LOMENTACEOUS
LOCALIZE	LOCOMOBILE	LOFTMAN	LOGOLATRY	LOMENTUM
LOCALIZED	LOCOMOBILITY	LOFTMEN	LOGOLOGY	LOMILOMI
LOCALIZER	LOCOMOTE	LOFTSMAN	LOGOMACH	LOMITA
LOCALIZING	LOCOMOTILITY	LOFTSMEN	LOGOMACHER	LOMONITE
LOCALLED	LOCOMOTION	LOFTY	LOGOMACHIC	LONE
LOCALLING	LOCOMOTIVE	LOG	LOGOMACHICAL	LONEFUL
LOCALLY	LOCOMOTIVELY	LOGAN	LOGOMACHIES	LONELIER

LONELIEST
LONELIHOOD
LONELILY
LONELINESS
LONELY
LONENESS
LONER
LONESOME
LONESOMELY
LONESOMENESS
LONG
LONGA
LONGACRE
LONGAN
LONGANIMITIES
LONGANIMITY
LONGANIMOUS
LONGBEAK
LONGBEARD
LONGBILL
LONGBOAT
LONGBOW
LONGCLOTH
LONGE
LONGEAR
LONGED
LONGER
LONGERON
LONGEST
LONGEVAL
LONGEVE
LONGEVITY
LONGEVOUS
LONGFIN
LONGFUL
LONGHAIR
LONGHAND
LONGHEAD
LONGHEADED
LONGHEADEDLY
LONGHEADEDNESS
LONGHORN
LONGICAUDAL
LONGICAUDATE
LONGICONE
LONGICORN
LONGILATERAL
LONGILINGUAL
LONGIMANOUS
LONGIMETRIC
LONGIMETRY
LONGING
LONGINGLY
LONGINQUITY
LONGIPENNATE
LONGIPENNINE
LONGIROSTRAL
LONGIROSTRATE
LONGISH
LONGITUDE
LONGITUDINAL
LONGITUDINALLY
LONGJAW
LONGJAWS
LONGLEAF
LONGLEGS
LONGLICK
LONGLINE
LONGLINER
LONGLINERMAN
LONGLINERMEN
LONGNECK
LONGNOSE
LONGPOD
LONGROOT
LONGS
LONGSHANKS

LONGSHORE
LONGSHOREMAN
LONGSHOREMEN
LONGSHUCKS
LONGSOME
LONGSOMELY
LONGSOMENESS
LONGSPUR
LONGTAIL
LONGTIMER
LONGUE
LONGUEUR
LONGULITE
LONGUS
LONGWALL
LONGWAYS
LONGWISE
LONGWOOD
LONGWOOL
LONGWORK
LONGYI
LONQUHARD
LONTAR
LOO
LOOBIES
LOOBILY
LOOBY
LOOCH
LOOD
LOOED
LOOF
LOOFA
LOOFAH
LOOFIE
LOOING
LOOK
LOOKED
LOOKER
LOOKING
LOOKOUT
LOOKOUTS
LOOKUM
LOOL
LOOM
LOOMED
LOOMER
LOOMERY
LOOMFIXER
LOOMING
LOOMS
LOON
LOONERY
LOONEY
LOONIER
LOONIES
LOONIEST
LOONY
LOOP
LOOPED
LOOPER
LOOPFUL
LOOPHOLE
LOOPHOLED
LOOPHOLING
LOOPIER
LOOPIEST
LOOPING
LOOPIST
LOOPS
LOOPY
LOORY
LOOS
LOOSE
LOOSED
LOOSELY
LOOSEN
LOOSENED

LOOSENER
LOOSENESS
LOOSENING
LOOSER
LOOSEST
LOOSESTRIFE
LOOSING
LOOT
LOOTED
LOOTER
LOOTIE
LOOTIEWALLAH
LOOTING
LOOTSMAN
LOOTSMANS
LOP
LOPE
LOPED
LOPER
LOPESKONCE
LOPHEAVY
LOPHIID
LOPHIN
LOPHINE
LOPHIODONT
LOPHOBRANCH
LOPHOCERCAL
LOPHODONT
LOPHOPHORAL
LOPHOPHORE
LOPHOPHORINE
LOPHOSTEA
LOPHOSTEON
LOPHOSTEONS
LOPHOTRIAENE
LOPING
LOPOLITH
LOPPARD
LOPPE
LOPPED
LOPPER
LOPPET
LOPPIER
LOPPIEST
LOPPING
LOPPY
LOPSEED
LOPSIDED
LOPSIDEDLY
LOPSIDEDNESS
LOPSTICK
LOQUACIOUS
LOQUACIOUSLY
LOQUACIOUSNESS
LOQUACITY
LOQUAT
LOQUENCE
LOQUENCY
LOQUENT
LOQUENTLY
LOQUITUR
LOR
LORA
LORAE
LORAL
LORAN
LORANDITE
LORANSKITE
LORARII
LORARIUS
LORATE
LORCHA
LORD
LORDAN
LORDED
LORDING
LORDINGS

LORDLESS
LORDLIER
LORDLIEST
LORDLIKE
LORDLINESS
LORDLING
LORDLY
LORDOLATRY
LORDOMA
LORDOSIS
LORDOTIC
LORDSHIP
LORDSWIKE
LORDWOOD
LORE
LOREAL
LORED
LOREL
LORENZENITE
LORETIN
LORETTOITE
LORGNETTE
LORGNON
LORIC
LORICA
LORICAE
LORICARIAN
LORICARIOID
LORICATE
LORICATED
LORICATING
LORICATION
LORICOID
LORIES
LORIKEET
LORILET
LORIMER
LORINER
LORING
LORIOT
LORIS
LORISES
LORMERY
LORN
LORO
LOROS
LORRE
LORRIES
LORRIKER
LORRY
LORS
LORUM
LORY
LOSABLE
LOSE
LOSEL
LOSELRY
LOSENGER
LOSER
LOSH
LOSING
LOSINGLY
LOSS
LOSSE
LOSSENITE
LOSSER
LOSSFUL
LOST
LOT
LOTA
LOTAH
LOTASE
LOTE
LOTEBUSH
LOTEWOOD
LOTH
LOTHE

LOTIC
LOTIFORM
LOTION
LOTIUM
LOTMENT
LOTONG
LOTOPHAGOUS
LOTOS
LOTRITE
LOTS
LOTTED
LOTTER
LOTTERIES
LOTTERY
LOTTING
LOTTO
LOTUS
LOTUSIN
LOUCH
LOUCHE
LOUCHETTES
LOUD
LOUDEN
LOUDERING
LOUDISH
LOUDLY
LOUDMOUTHED
LOUDNESS
LOUDSPEAKER
LOUEY
LOUGH
LOUGHEEN
LOUIS
LOUISINE
LOUK
LOUKE
LOUKOUM
LOUKOUMI
LOULU
LOUN
LOUND
LOUNDER
LOUNDERER
LOUNGE
LOUNGED
LOUNGER
LOUNGING
LOUNGY
LOUP
LOUPE
LOUR
LOURD
LOURDISH
LOURDY
LOURE
LOURED
LOURIE
LOURING
LOURINGLY
LOURINGNESS
LOURY
LOUSE
LOUSEBERRIES
LOUSEBERRY
LOUSED
LOUSEWORT
LOUSIER
LOUSIEST
LOUSILY
LOUSINESS
LOUSING
LOUSTER
LOUSY
LOUT
LOUTER
LOUTHER
LOUTISH

LOUTISHLY
LOUTISHNESS
LOUTRE
LOUTROPHOROS
LOUTY
LOUVAR
LOUVER
LOUVERED
LOUVERWORK
LOVABILITY
LOVABLE
LOVABLENESS
LOVABLY
LOVAGE
LOVANENTY
LOVAT
LOVE
LOVEABLE
LOVEBIRD
LOVED
LOVEFLOWER
LOVEHOOD
LOVELASS
LOVELESS
LOVELESSLY
LOVELESSNESS
LOVELIER
LOVELIEST
LOVELIHEAD
LOVELILY
LOVELINESS
LOVELING
LOVELOCK
LOVELORN
LOVELORNNESS
LOVELY
LOVEMAKING
LOVEMAN
LOVEMANS
LOVEMATE
LOVEMONGER
LOVER
LOVERED
LOVERING
LOVERLINESS
LOVERLY
LOVESICK
LOVESICKNESS
LOVESOME
LOVESOMELY
LOVESOMENESS
LOVEVINE
LOVING
LOVINGLY
LOVINGNESS
LOW
LOWA
LOWABLE
LOWAN
LOWANCE
LOWBALL
LOWBELL
LOWBORN
LOWBOY
LOWBRED
LOWBROW
LOWBROWISM
LOWDAH
LOWDER
LOWDOWN
LOWE
LOWED
LOWEITE
LOWER
LOWERCLASSMAN
LOWERCLASSMEN
LOWERED

LOWERER
LOWERING
LOWERINGLY
LOWERINGNESS
LOWERMOST
LOWERY
LOWEST
LOWIGITE
LOWING
LOWLAND
LOWLANDER
LOWLIER
LOWLIEST
LOWLIHEAD
LOWLY
LOWMEN
LOWMOST
LOWN
LOWNESS
LOWRIE
LOWRY
LOWSE
LOWSIN
LOWTH
LOWWOOD
LOWY
LOX
LOXIA
LOXOCLASE
LOXOCOSM
LOXODOGRAPH
LOXODONT
LOXODROME
LOXODROMIC
LOXODROMICS
LOXODROMISM
LOXODROMY
LOXOSOMA
LOXOTIC
LOXOTOMY
LOY
LOYAL
LOYALISM
LOYALIST
LOYALLY
LOYALNESS
LOYALTIES
LOYALTY
LOYN
LOZEN
LOZENGE
LOZENGED
LOZENGER
LOZENGY
LUAU
LUBBER
LUBBERCOCK
LUBBERLINESS
LUBBERLY
LUBRA
LUBRIC
LUBRICAL
LUBRICANT
LUBRICATE
LUBRICATED
LUBRICATING
LUBRICATION
LUBRICATIONAL
LUBRICATIVE
LUBRICATOR
LUBRICATORY
LUBRICIOUS
LUBRICITIES
LUBRICITY
LUBRICOUS
LUBRIFY
LUBRITORIAN

LUBRITORIUM
LUBRITORY
LUCANID
LUCARNE
LUCBAN
LUCE
LUCENCE
LUCENCY
LUCENT
LUCENTLY
LUCERN
LUCERNAL
LUCERNE
LUCES
LUCET
LUCIBLE
LUCID
LUCIDA
LUCIDITY
LUCIDLY
LUCIDNESS
LUCIFER
LUCIFERASE
LUCIFERIN
LUCIFEROID
LUCIFEROUS
LUCIFEROUSLY
LUCIFIC
LUCIFORM
LUCIFUGAL
LUCIFUGOUS
LUCIGEN
LUCIMETER
LUCINOID
LUCIVEE
LUCK
LUCKEN
LUCKFUL
LUCKIE
LUCKIER
LUCKIES
LUCKIEST
LUCKILY
LUCKINESS
LUCKLESS
LUCKLESSLY
LUCKLESSNESS
LUCKLY
LUCKY
LUCOMBE
LUCRATION
LUCRATIVE
LUCRATIVELY
LUCRATIVENESS
LUCRE
LUCRIFEROUS
LUCRIFIC
LUCRIFY
LUCROUS
LUCTATION
LUCTIFEROUS
LUCTUAL
LUCUBRATE
LUCUBRATED
LUCUBRATING
LUCUBRATION
LUCUBRATOR
LUCUBRATORY
LUCULE
LUCULENT
LUCULENTLY
LUCULLITE
LUCUMIA
LUCUMONY
LUCY
LUD
LUDDEN

LUDDY
LUDI
LUDIBRIOUS
LUDIBRY
LUDICROSITIES
LUDICROSITY
LUDICROUS
LUDICROUSLY
LUDICROUSNESS
LUDIFICATION
LUDLAMITE
LUDO
LUDWIGITE
LUE
LUES
LUETIC
LUETICALLY
LUFF
LUFFA
LUFFED
LUFFER
LUFFING
LUG
LUGE
LUGER
LUGGAGE
LUGGAR
LUGGARD
LUGGED
LUGGER
LUGGIE
LUGGING
LUGHDOAN
LUGMARK
LUGS
LUGSAIL
LUGSOME
LUGUBRIOSITY
LUGUBRIOUS
LUGUBRIOUSLY
LUGUBRIOUSNESS
LUGUBROUS
LUGWORM
LUHINGA
LUIGINI
LUIGINO
LUJAURITE
LUJAVRITE
LUJULA
LUKE
LUKET
LUKEWARD
LUKEWARM
LUKEWARMLY
LUKEWARMNESS
LUKEWARMTH
LULAB
LULL
LULLABIES
LULLABY
LULLAY
LULLED
LULLER
LULLILOO
LULLILOOED
LULLILOOING
LULLING
LULLY
LULU
LULUAI
LUM
LUMACHEL
LUMACHELLA
LUMACHELLE
LUMBAGINOUS
LUMBAGO
LUMBANG

LUMBAR
LUMBAYAO
LUMBER
LUMBERDAR
LUMBERED
LUMBERER
LUMBERING
LUMBERINGLY
LUMBERJACK
LUMBERJACKET
LUMBERLY
LUMBERMAN
LUMBERMEN
LUMBERYARD
LUMBODYNIA
LUMBOSACRAL
LUMBRICAL
LUMBRICALES
LUMBRICALIS
LUMBRICID
LUMBRICIFORM
LUMBRICINE
LUMBRICOID
LUMBRICOSIS
LUMBROUS
LUMEN
LUMENS
LUMINA
LUMINAIRE
LUMINAL
LUMINANCE
LUMINANT
LUMINARIES
LUMINARIOUS
LUMINARISM
LUMINARIST
LUMINARY
LUMINATE
LUMINATION
LUMINATIVE
LUMINATOR
LUMINE
LUMINESCE
LUMINESCED
LUMINESCENCE
LUMINESCENT
LUMINESCING
LUMINIFEROUS
LUMINIFICENT
LUMINISM
LUMINIST
LUMINISTE
LUMINOSITIES
LUMINOSITY
LUMINOUS
LUMINOUSLY
LUMINOUSNESS
LUMM
LUMMOX
LUMMY
LUMP
LUMPED
LUMPEN
LUMPER
LUMPET
LUMPFISH
LUMPFISHES
LUMPIER
LUMPIEST
LUMPILY
LUMPINESS
LUMPING
LUMPINGLY
LUMPISH
LUMPISHLY
LUMPISHNESS
LUMPKIN

LUMPMAN
LUMPMEN
LUMPS
LUMPSUCKER
LUMPY
LUMUT
LUNA
LUNACIES
LUNACY
LUNAMBULISM
LUNAR
LUNARE
LUNARIA
LUNARIAN
LUNARIST
LUNARIUM
LUNARY
LUNATA
LUNATE
LUNATED
LUNATELLUS
LUNATELY
LUNATIC
LUNATICAL
LUNATICALLY
LUNATION
LUNATIZE
LUNATUM
LUNCH
LUNCHEON
LUNCHEONER
LUNCHEONETTE
LUNCHER
LUNCHROOM
LUNDYFOOT
LUNE
LUNES
LUNET
LUNETS
LUNETTE
LUNETTES
LUNG
LUNGE
LUNGED
LUNGEE
LUNGEOUS
LUNGER
LUNGFISH
LUNGFISHES
LUNGFLOWER
LUNGI
LUNGIE
LUNGING
LUNGIS
LUNGMOTOR
LUNGOOR
LUNGS
LUNGSICK
LUNGWORM
LUNGWORT
LUNGY
LUNICURRENT
LUNIES
LUNIFORM
LUNISOLAR
LUNISTICE
LUNISTITIAL
LUNITIDAL
LUNKER
LUNKHEAD
LUNKHEADED
LUNN
LUNOID
LUNT
LUNULA
LUNULAE
LUNULAR

LUNULATE
LUNULATED
LUNULE
LUNULET
LUNULITE
LUNY
LUNYIE
LUPANAR
LUPANARIAN
LUPANIN
LUPANINE
LUPE
LUPEOL
LUPEOSE
LUPETIDIN
LUPETIDINE
LUPICIDE
LUPIFORM
LUPIN
LUPINASTER
LUPINE
LUPININ
LUPININE
LUPINOSIS
LUPINOUS
LUPIS
LUPOID
LUPOUS
LUPULIN
LUPULINE
LUPULINIC
LUPULINOUS
LUPULUS
LUPUS
LUR
LURA
LURACAN
LURCH
LURCHER
LURCHING
LURDAN
LURDANE
LURE
LURED
LUREMENT
LURER
LURG
LURGWORM
LURID
LURIDITY
LURIDLY
LURIDNESS
LURING
LURK
LURKED
LURKER
LURKING
LURKINGLY
LURKY
LURRIER
LURRIES
LURRY
LUSCIOUS
LUSCIOUSLY
LUSCIOUSNESS
LUSH
LUSHBURG
LUSHER
LUSHLY
LUSHNESS
LUSHY
LUSK
LUSKISH
LUSKY
LUSORY
LUST
LUSTED

LUSTER
LUSTERED
LUSTERER
LUSTERING
LUSTERLESS
LUSTERWARE
LUSTFUL
LUSTFULLY
LUSTFULNESS
LUSTICK
LUSTIER
LUSTIEST
LUSTIHOOD
LUSTILY
LUSTING
LUSTLESS
LUSTLY
LUSTRA
LUSTRAL
LUSTRANT
LUSTRATE
LUSTRATED
LUSTRATING
LUSTRATION
LUSTRATIVE
LUSTRATORY
LUSTRE
LUSTRED
LUSTREWARE
LUSTRICAL
LUSTRIFY
LUSTRINE
LUSTRING
LUSTROUS
LUSTROUSLY
LUSTROUSNESS
LUSTRUM
LUSTRUMS
LUSTY
LUSUS
LUTACEOUS
LUTANIST
LUTANY
LUTATION
LUTE
LUTEAL
LUTECIA
LUTECIUM
LUTED
LUTEIN
LUTENIST
LUTEOFULVOUS
LUTEOFUSCOUS
LUTEOLIN
LUTEOLOUS
LUTEOMA
LUTEOUS
LUTER
LUTESCENT
LUTETIUM
LUTEUM
LUTFISK
LUTH
LUTHERN
LUTHIER
LUTIANID
LUTIANOID
LUTIDIN
LUTIDINE
LUTIDINIC
LUTING
LUTIST
LUTJANID
LUTONG
LUTOSE
LUTRIN
LUTRINE

LUTULENCE
LUTULENT
LUTZ
LUX
LUXATE
LUXATED
LUXATING
LUXATION
LUXE
LUXES
LUXIVE
LUXULLIANITE
LUXUR
LUXURIANCE
LUXURIANCY
LUXURIANT
LUXURIANTLY
LUXURIANTNESS
LUXURIATE
LUXURIATED
LUXURIATING
LUXURIATION
LUXURIES
LUXURIOUS
LUXURIOUSLY
LUXURIOUSNESS
LUXURIST
LUXURITY
LUXURY
LUXUS
LY
LYAM
LYANCE
LYARD
LYART
LYCAENID
LYCANTHROPE
LYCANTHROPIC
LYCANTHROPY
LYCEA
LYCEAL
LYCEE
LYCEUM
LYCEUMS
LYCHEE
LYCHNIS
LYCHNOMANCY
LYCHNOSCOPE
LYCHNOSCOPIC
LYCID
LYCODOID
LYCOPENE
LYCOPERDOID
LYCOPIN
LYCOPOD
LYCOPODE
LYCOPODIUM
LYCORINE
LYCOSID
LYCTID
LYDDITE
LYDITE
LYE
LYED
LYERY
LYFKIE
LYGAEID
LYGUS
LYING
LYINGLY
LYKEWAKE
LYM
LYMANTRIID
LYME
LYMNAEAN
LYMNAEID
LYMPH

LYMPHAD
LYMPHADENIA
LYMPHADENOID
LYMPHADENOMA
LYMPHAEMIA
LYMPHAGOGUE
LYMPHANGIAL
LYMPHANGIOMA
LYMPHANGIOMATA
LYMPHANGITIC
LYMPHANGITIS
LYMPHATIC
LYMPHATICAL
LYMPHATION
LYMPHATISM
LYMPHATITIS
LYMPHECTASIA
LYMPHEDEMA
LYMPHEMIA
LYMPHOBLAST
LYMPHOBLASTIC
LYMPHOCELE
LYMPHOCYST
LYMPHOCYTE
LYMPHOCYTIC
LYMPHOCYTOSIS
LYMPHOCYTOTIC
LYMPHODERMIA
LYMPHODUCT
LYMPHOEDEMA
LYMPHOGENIC
LYMPHOID
LYMPHOLOGY
LYMPHOMA
LYMPHOMATOUS
LYMPHOPATHY
LYMPHOPENIAL
LYMPHORRHAGE
LYMPHORRHEA
LYMPHOSTASIS
LYMPHOTOME
LYMPHOTOMY
LYMPHOTOXIN
LYMPHOTROPHY
LYMPHOUS
LYMPHURIA
LYMPHY
LYN
LYNCEAN
LYNCH
LYNCHED
LYNCHER
LYNCHET
LYNCHING
LYNCINE
LYNE
LYNNHAVEN
LYNX
LYNXES
LYOMEROUS
LYONETIID
LYONNAISE
LYOPHIL
LYOPHILE
LYOPHILIC
LYOPHOBE
LYOPHOBIC
LYOTROPE
LYOTROPIC
LYPEMANIA
LYPOTHYMIA
LYRA
LYRATE
LYRATED
LYRATELY
LYRAWAY
LYRE

LYREBIRD
LYREMAN
LYRETAIL
LYRIC
LYRICAL
LYRICALLY
LYRICALNESS
LYRICHORD
LYRICISM
LYRICIST
LYRICKED
LYRICKING
LYRIFORM
LYRISM
LYRIST
LYSATE
LYSE
LYSED
LYSIDIN
LYSIDINE
LYSIGENIC
LYSIGENOUS
LYSIGENOUSLY
LYSIMETER
LYSIN
LYSINE
LYSING
LYSIS
LYSOGEN
LYSOGENESIS
LYSOGENETIC
LYSOGENIC
LYSSA
LYSSIC
LYTERIAN
LYTHE
LYTHRACEOUS
LYTIC
LYTTA
LYTTAE
LYXOSE

MA
MAA
MAABARA
MAAL
MAAR
MAARAD
MAARIB
MAASS
MAATJE
MAB
MABE
MABI
MABOLO
MABUTI
MABYER
MAC
MACAASIM
MACABER
MACABI
MACABRE
MACAC
MACACO
MACACOS
MACADAM
MACADAMER
MACADAMIA
MACADAMITE
MACADAMIZE
MACADAMIZED
MACADAMIZER
MACADAMIZING
MACAN
MACANA
MACAO
MACAQUE
MACARISM
MACARIZE
MACARIZED
MACARIZING
MACARON
MACARONI
MACARONIC
MACARONICAL
MACARONICALLY
MACARONICISM
MACARONIES
MACARONIS
MACARONISM
MACAROON
MACAW
MACCABOY
MACCHIA
MACCHIE
MACCO
MACCOBOY
MACCUS
MACE
MACEBEARER
MACEDOINE
MACEHEAD
MACELLUM
MACEMAN
MACER
MACERABLE
MACERAL
MACERATE
MACERATED

MACERATER
MACERATING
MACERATION
MACERATOR
MACH
MACHAIR
MACHAIRODONT
MACHAN
MACHAON
MACHAR
MACHEER
MACHETE
MACHI
MACHICOLATE
MACHICOLATED
MACHILA
MACHIN
MACHINA
MACHINABLE
MACHINAL
MACHINAMENT
MACHINATE
MACHINATED
MACHINATING
MACHINATION
MACHINATOR
MACHINE
MACHINED
MACHINELY
MACHINEMAN
MACHINEMEN
MACHINER
MACHINERY
MACHINING
MACHINISM
MACHINIST
MACHINULE
MACHISMO
MACHMETER
MACHOPOLYP
MACHREE
MACIES
MACILENCE
MACILENCY
MACILENT
MACINTOSH
MACK
MACKALLOW
MACKAYBEAN
MACKENBOY
MACKEREL
MACKERELER
MACKERELING
MACKERELS
MACKINAW
MACKINBOY
MACKINS
MACKINTOSH
MACKINTOSHITE
MACKLE
MACKLED
MACKLIKE
MACKLING
MACLE
MACLED
MACLURIN
MACO
MACONITE
MACONNE
MACRADENOUS
MACRAME
MACRANDER
MACRANDRE
MACRANDROUS
MACRIO
MACROANALYST
MACROBIAN

MACROBIOSIS
MACROBIOTE
MACROBIOTICS
MACROCEPHALY
MACROCHAETA
MACROCHAETAE
MACROCHIRAN
MACROCLIMATE
MACROCOSM
MACROCOSMIC
MACROCOSMOS
MACROCYST
MACROCYTE
MACROCYTIC
MACROCYTOSIS
MACRODONT
MACRODONTIA
MACRODONTISM
MACROGAMETE
MACROGAMY
MACROGRAPH
MACROGRAPHIC
MACROGRAPHY
MACROLOGY
MACROMANIA
MACROMERAL
MACROMERE
MACROMERIC
MACROMERITE
MACROMERITIC
MACROMETER
MACROMETHOD
MACROMYELON
MACRON
MACRONUCLEAR
MACRONUCLEUS
MACROPHAGE
MACROPHAGUS
MACROPHYSICS
MACROPODIAN
MACROPODINE
MACROPODOUS
MACROPSIA
MACROPSY
MACROPTEROUS
MACROSCIAN
MACROSCOPIC
MACROSEISM
MACROSEISMIC
MACROSMATIC
MACROSPECIES
MACROSPORE
MACROSPORIC
MACROSTRUCTURE
MACROSTYLE
MACROSTYLOUS
MACROTHERE
MACROTHERM
MACROTIA
MACROTIN
MACROTOME
MACROTOUS
MACROURID
MACRURAL
MACRURAN
MACRUROID
MACRUROUS
MACTATION
MACTROID
MACUCA
MACULA
MACULAE
MACULAR
MACULATE
MACULATED
MACULATING
MACULATION

MACULE
MACULED
MACULICOLE
MACULICOLOUS
MACULIFEROUS
MACULING
MACULOSE
MACUPA
MACUPI
MACUSHLA
MACUTA
MACUTE
MAD
MADAM
MADAME
MADAMS
MADAPOLAM
MADAPOLAN
MADAPOLLAM
MADAR
MADAROSIS
MADAROTIC
MADBRAIN
MADBRAINED
MADCAP
MADDED
MADDEN
MADDENED
MADDENING
MADDENINGLY
MADDER
MADDERISH
MADDERWORT
MADDEST
MADDING
MADDINGLY
MADDISH
MADDLE
MADDOCK
MADE
MADEFACTION
MADEFY
MADELEINE
MADELINE
MADEMOISELLE
MADESCENT
MADHAB
MADHOUSE
MADHUCA
MADID
MADIDANS
MADISTERIUM
MADLING
MADLY
MADMAN
MADMEN
MADNEP
MADNESS
MADO
MADONNA
MADOQUA
MADOR
MADRAGUE
MADRAS
MADRASA
MADRASAH
MADRASSAH
MADRASSEH
MADRE
MADREPERL
MADREPORAL
MADREPORE
MADREPORIAN
MADREPORIC
MADREPORITE
MADREPORITIC
MADRIER

MADRIGAL
MADRIGALER
MADRIGALETTO
MADRIGALIAN
MADRIGALIST
MADRIH
MADRILENE
MADRONA
MADRONO
MADSTONE
MADURO
MADWEED
MADWOMAN
MADWOMEN
MADWORT
MAE
MAEANDER
MAEANDRINE
MAEANDRINOID
MAEANDROID
MAEGBOT
MAEGBOTE
MAELSTROM
MAENAD
MAENADES
MAENADIC
MAENADICALLY
MAENADISM
MAENADS
MAENAITE
MAESTIVE
MAESTOSO
MAESTRA
MAESTRO
MAESTROS
MAFEY
MAFFIA
MAFFICK
MAFFICKED
MAFFICKER
MAFFICKING
MAFFIOSO
MAFFLE
MAFFLER
MAFFLIN
MAFIA
MAFIC
MAFIOSO
MAFOO
MAFTIR
MAFU
MAFURA
MAFURRA
MAG
MAGADIS
MAGADIZE
MAGANI
MAGAS
MAGAZINABLE
MAGAZINAGE
MAGAZINE
MAGAZINED
MAGAZINER
MAGAZINING
MAGAZINISM
MAGAZINIST
MAGAZINY
MAGBOTE
MAGDALEN
MAGE
MAGENTA
MAGERFUL
MAGG
MAGGED
MAGGID
MAGGIORE
MAGGLE

MAGGOT	MAGNETO	MAHIMAHI	MAIMING	MAJOR
MAGGOTINESS	MAGNETOBELL	MAHJONG	MAIMON	MAJORAT
MAGGOTPIE	MAGNETOGRAM	MAHJONGG	MAIMUL	MAJORATE
MAGGOTRY	MAGNETOGRAPH	MAHLSTICK	MAIN	MAJORATION
MAGGOTY	MAGNETOID	MAHMAL	MAINE	MAJORDOMO
MAGHZEN	MAGNETOLYSIS	MAHMUDI	MAINFERRE	MAJORETTE
MAGI	MAGNETOMETER	MAHO	MAINLAND	MAJORITIES
MAGIC	MAGNETOMETRY	MAHOE	MAINLANDER	MAJORITY
MAGICAL	MAGNETOMOTOR	MAHOGANIES	MAINLINE	MAJORIZE
MAGICALLY	MAGNETON	MAHOGANIZE	MAINLINED	MAJOS
MAGICIAN	MAGNETOOPTIC	MAHOGANY	MAINLINER	MAJUSCULAE
MAGICKED	MAGNETOPHONE	MAHOITRE	MAINLINING	MAJUSCULAR
MAGICKING	MAGNETOS	MAHOLI	MAINLY	MAJUSCULE
MAGILP	MAGNETOSCOPE	MAHOLTINE	MAINMAST	MAK
MAGIRIC	MAGNETRON	MAHONE	MAINMORTABLE	MAKADOO
MAGIRICS	MAGNETS	MAHOUT	MAINOR	MAKAHIKI
MAGIRIST	MAGNICAUDATE	MAHR	MAINOUR	MAKAI
MAGIRISTIC	MAGNIFIABLE	MAHSEER	MAINPAST	MAKALE
MAGIROLOGIST	MAGNIFIC	MAHSIR	MAINPERNABLE	MAKAR
MAGIROLOGY	MAGNIFICAL	MAHSUR	MAINPERNOR	MAKARA
MAGISTER	MAGNIFICALLY	MAHUA	MAINPIN	MAKATEA
MAGISTERIAL	MAGNIFICATE	MAHUANG	MAINPORT	MAKE
MAGISTERIES	MAGNIFICATION	MAHWA	MAINPOST	MAKEBATE
MAGISTERIUM	MAGNIFICE	MAHZOR	MAINPRISE	MAKEDOM
MAGISTERY	MAGNIFICENCE	MAI	MAINPRIZE	MAKEFAST
MAGISTRACIES	MAGNIFICENT	MAIAN	MAINPRIZER	MAKELESS
MAGISTRACY	MAGNIFICENTLY	MAID	MAINS	MAKER
MAGISTRAL	MAGNIFICO	MAIDAN	MAINSAIL	MAKEREADY
MAGISTRALITY	MAGNIFICOES	MAIDCHILD	MAINSHEET	MAKERESS
MAGISTRALLY	MAGNIFIED	MAIDEN	MAINSPRING	MAKERS
MAGISTRAND	MAGNIFIER	MAIDENCHILD	MAINSTAY	MAKES
MAGISTRANT	MAGNIFIQUE	MAIDENHAIR	MAINSTREAM	MAKESHIFT
MAGISTRATE	MAGNIFY	MAIDENHEAD	MAINT	MAKESHIFTY
MAGISTRATIVE	MAGNIFYING	MAIDENHOOD	MAINTAIN	MAKEWEIGHT
MAGISTRATURE	MAGNILOQUENT	MAIDENLINESS	MAINTAINED	MAKHORKA
MAGMA	MAGNIPOTENCE	MAIDENLY	MAINTAINER	MAKHZAN
MAGMAS	MAGNIPOTENT	MAIDENWEED	MAINTAINING	MAKHZEN
MAGMATA	MAGNISONANT	MAIDHEAD	MAINTAINOR	MAKI
MAGMATIC	MAGNITUDE	MAIDHOOD	MAINTENANCE	MAKIMONO
MAGNA	MAGNITUDES	MAIDIN	MAINTOP	MAKIN
MAGNALE	MAGNITUDINOUS	MAIDISM	MAINTOPMAN	MAKING
MAGNANERIE	MAGNOLIA	MAIDKIN	MAINTOPMAST	MAKINGS
MAGNANIME	MAGNUM	MAIDLY	MAINTOPMEN	MAKLUK
MAGNANIMITY	MAGOT	MAIDSERVANT	MAINTOPSAIL	MAKO
MAGNANIMOUS	MAGPIE	MAIDY	MAINWARD	MAKOMAKO
MAGNANIMOUSLY	MAGPIED	MAIEUTIC	MAIOLICA	MAKOPA
MAGNASCOPE	MAGRIM	MAIEUTICAL	MAIPO	MAKOUA
MAGNASCOPIC	MAGSMAN	MAIEUTICS	MAIRATOUR	MAKRAN
MAGNATE	MAGUARI	MAIG	MAIRE	MAKROSKELIC
MAGNELECTRIC	MAGUEY	MAIGRE	MAIRIE	MAKUK
MAGNEOPTIC	MAHA	MAIHEM	MAISON	MAKUTU
MAGNES	MAHAJAN	MAIID	MAISONETTE	MAL
MAGNESIA	MAHAJUN	MAIL	MAIST	MALA
MAGNESIAL	MAHAL	MAILABLE	MAISTRY	MALAANONANG
MAGNESIAN	MAHALA	MAILBAG	MAITLANDITE	MALABATHRUM
MAGNESIC	MAHALAMAT	MAILBOX	MAITRE	MALACANTHID
MAGNESITE	MAHALEB	MAILCATCHER	MAITRESSE	MALACEOUS
MAGNESIUM	MAHALLA	MAILCLAD	MAITRISE	MALACHITE
MAGNET	MAHALY	MAILE	MAIZE	MALACIA
MAGNETA	MAHAN	MAILED	MAIZEBIRD	MALACODERM
MAGNETIC	MAHANT	MAILER	MAIZER	MALACOID
MAGNETICAL	MAHAR	MAILGUARD	MAJA	MALACOLITE
MAGNETICALLY	MAHARAJA	MAILIE	MAJAGUA	MALACOLOGIST
MAGNETICIAN	MAHARAJAH	MAILING	MAJAS	MALACOLOGY
MAGNETICS	MAHARAJRANA	MAILL	MAJESTIC	MALACON
MAGNETIFY	MAHARANA	MAILLE	MAJESTICAL	MALACONE
MAGNETIMETER	MAHARANEE	MAILLECHORT	MAJESTICALLY	MALACTIC
MAGNETISM	MAHARANI	MAILLOT	MAJESTIES	MALADAPTATION
MAGNETIST	MAHARAO	MAILMAN	MAJESTIOUS	MALADDRESS
MAGNETITE	MAHARAWAL	MAILMEN	MAJESTY	MALADE
MAGNETITIC	MAHARAWAT	MAILPLANE	MAJID	MALADIES
MAGNETIZABLE	MAHARMAH	MAILPOUCH	MAJIDIEH	MALADIVE
MAGNETIZATION	MAHARSHI	MAIM	MAJO	MALADJUSTED
MAGNETIZE	MAHAT	MAIMED	MAJOE	MALADJUSTMENT
MAGNETIZED	MAHATMA	MAIMEDLY	MAJOLICA	MALADROIT
MAGNETIZER	MAHATMAISM	MAIMEDNESS	MAJOLIST	MALADROITLY
MAGNETIZING	MAHBUB	MAIMER	MAJOON	MALADVENTURE

MALADY
MALAGMA
MALAHACK
MALAISE
MALAKIN
MALAKON
MALAMBO
MALAMUTE
MALANDERED
MALANDERS
MALANDROUS
MALANGA
MALAPAHO
MALAPERT
MALAPERTLY
MALAPERTNESS
MALAPROP
MALAPROPIAN
MALAPROPISM
MALAPROPOS
MALAR
MALARIA
MALARIAL
MALARIAN
MALARIN
MALARIOID
MALARIOLOGY
MALARIOUS
MALARKEY
MALARKY
MALATE
MALATI
MALAX
MALAXABLE
MALAXAGE
MALAXATE
MALAXATION
MALAXATOR
MALAXED
MALAXERMAN
MALAXERMEN
MALAXING
MALBROUCK
MALCHITE
MALCONDUCT
MALCONTENT
MALCONTENTED
MALCONTENTEDLY
MALCONTENTISM
MALCONTENTLY
MALCONTENTMENT
MALDOCCHIO
MALDONITE
MALDUCK
MALE
MALEABILITY
MALEASE
MALEATE
MALEDICENT
MALEDICT
MALEDICTION
MALEDICTIVE
MALEDICTORY
MALEFACTION
MALEFACTOR
MALEFACTORY
MALEFACTRESS
MALEFIC
MALEFICAL
MALEFICALLY
MALEFICE
MALEFICENCE
MALEFICENT
MALEFICIAL
MALEFICIATE
MALEIC
MALEINOID

MALEINOIDAL
MALELLA
MALELLAE
MALEMIUT
MALEMUTE
MALENESS
MALENGINE
MALENTENDU
MALEO
MALEOS
MALETOTE
MALEVOLENCE
MALEVOLENCY
MALEVOLENT
MALEVOLENTLY
MALEVOLOUS
MALFEASANCE
MALFEASANT
MALFEASOR
MALFORMATION
MALFORMED
MALFUNCTION
MALGRACE
MALGRADO
MALGRE
MALGUZAR
MALGUZARI
MALHEUR
MALI
MALIC
MALICE
MALICEFUL
MALICIOUS
MALICIOUSLY
MALICORIUM
MALIFEROUS
MALIFORM
MALIGN
MALIGNANCE
MALIGNANCIES
MALIGNANCY
MALIGNANT
MALIGNANTLY
MALIGNATION
MALIGNED
MALIGNER
MALIGNIFIED
MALIGNIFY
MALIGNIFYING
MALIGNING
MALIGNITIES
MALIGNITY
MALIGNLY
MALIGNMENT
MALIHINI
MALIK
MALIKANA
MALINCHE
MALINE
MALINES
MALINGER
MALINGERED
MALINGERER
MALINGERING
MALINGERY
MALINOWSKITE
MALINTENT
MALISM
MALISON
MALIST
MALISTIC
MALKIN
MALL
MALLADRITE
MALLANGONG
MALLARD
MALLARDITE

MALLARDS
MALLEABLE
MALLEABLEIZE
MALLEABLEIZED
MALLEABLEIZING
MALLEABLIZE
MALLEABLY
MALLEAL
MALLEATE
MALLEATED
MALLEATING
MALLEATION
MALLED
MALLEE
MALLEI
MALLEIFEROUS
MALLEIFORM
MALLEIN
MALLEINIZE
MALLEMUCK
MALLENDERS
MALLEOINCUDAL
MALLEOLABLE
MALLEOLAR
MALLEOLI
MALLEOLUS
MALLET
MALLETED
MALLETING
MALLEUS
MALLING
MALLOPHAGAN
MALLOPHAGOUS
MALLOSEISMIC
MALLOW
MALLOWWORT
MALLUM
MALLUS
MALM
MALMARSH
MALMED
MALMIGNATTE
MALMING
MALMOCK
MALMSEY
MALMSEYS
MALMSTONE
MALMY
MALNUTRITE
MALNUTRITION
MALO
MALOCA
MALOCCHIO
MALOCCLUDED
MALOCCLUSION
MALODOR
MALODOROUS
MALODOROUSLY
MALODOUR
MALONATE
MALONIC
MALONYL
MALONYLUREA
MALOUAH
MALPAIS
MALPOSED
MALPOSITION
MALPRACTICE
MALPRACTITIONER
MALPRAXIS
MALPROPRIETY
MALT
MALTASE
MALTED
MALTER
MALTHA
MALTHOUSE

MALTIER
MALTIEST
MALTING
MALTMAN
MALTOLTE
MALTOSE
MALTREAT
MALTREATED
MALTREATING
MALTREATMENT
MALTREATOR
MALTSTER
MALTWORM
MALTY
MALUM
MALURINE
MALVACEOUS
MALVASIA
MALVASIAN
MALVERSATION
MALVERSE
MALVIN
MALVOISIE
MAMA
MAMALOI
MAMAMU
MAMBA
MAMBO
MAMBOS
MAMBU
MAMELIERE
MAMELON
MAMELUCO
MAMEYES
MAMEYS
MAMILLA
MAMLATDAR
MAMLUTDAR
MAMMA
MAMMAE
MAMMAL
MAMMALGIA
MAMMALIAN
MAMMALITY
MAMMALOGICAL
MAMMALOGIST
MAMMALOGY
MAMMARY
MAMMATE
MAMMATUS
MAMME
MAMMEE
MAMMER
MAMMET
MAMMEY
MAMMIE
MAMMIES
MAMMIFER
MAMMIFEROUS
MAMMIFORM
MAMMILATE
MAMMILATED
MAMMILLA
MAMMILLAE
MAMMILLAR
MAMMILLARY
MAMMILLATION
MAMMILLIFORM
MAMMILLOID
MAMMITIS
MAMMOCK
MAMMOCKED
MAMMOCKING
MAMMON
MAMMONI
MAMMONIACAL
MAMMONISH

MAMMONISM
MAMMONIST
MAMMONISTIC
MAMMONITE
MAMMONITISH
MAMMONIZATION
MAMMONIZE
MAMMONOLATRY
MAMMOSE
MAMMOTH
MAMMOTHREPT
MAMMULA
MAMMULAE
MAMMULAR
MAMMY
MAMO
MAMONA
MAMOTY
MAMPALON
MAMPUS
MAMRY
MAMUSHI
MAMZER
MAN
MANA
MANACLE
MANACLED
MANACLES
MANACLING
MANADA
MANAGE
MANAGEABILITY
MANAGEABLE
MANAGEABLENESS
MANAGEABLY
MANAGED
MANAGELESS
MANAGEMENT
MANAGEMENTAL
MANAGER
MANAGERESS
MANAGERIAL
MANAGERIALLY
MANAGERSHIP
MANAGERY
MANAGES
MANAGING
MANAI
MANAKIN
MANAL
MANANA
MANARVEL
MANAS
MANATEE
MANATI
MANATINE
MANATION
MANATOID
MANAVEL
MANAVELINS
MANAVILINS
MANBARKLAK
MANBIRD
MANBOT
MANBOTE
MANCALA
MANCANDO
MANCHE
MANCHET
MANCHINEEL
MANCINISM
MANCIPABLE
MANCIPANT
MANCIPATE
MANCIPATION
MANCIPATIVE
MANCIPATORY

MANCIPEE
MANCIPIA
MANCIPIUM
MANCIPLE
MANCIPULAR
MANCO
MANCONO
MANCUS
MAND
MANDALA
MANDAMENT
MANDAMUS
MANDAMUSED
MANDAMUSING
MANDAPA
MANDAR
MANDARAH
MANDARIN
MANDARINATE
MANDARINED
MANDARINESS
MANDARINIC
MANDARINING
MANDARINISM
MANDAT
MANDATARIES
MANDATARY
MANDATE
MANDATED
MANDATEE
MANDATING
MANDATION
MANDATIVE
MANDATOR
MANDATORIES
MANDATORILY
MANDATORY
MANDATS
MANDATUM
MANDELATE
MANDELIC
MANDIBLE
MANDIBULAR
MANDIBULARY
MANDIBULATE
MANDIBULATED
MANDIL
MANDILION
MANDIR
MANDLEN
MANDOER
MANDOLA
MANDOLIN
MANDOLINIST
MANDOLUTE
MANDORA
MANDORE
MANDORLA
MANDORLE
MANDRA
MANDRAGON
MANDRAGORA
MANDRAKE
MANDREL
MANDRIARCH
MANDRIL
MANDRILL
MANDRIN
MANDRITTA
MANDRUKA
MANDS
MANDUA
MANDUCABLE
MANDUCATE
MANDUCATED
MANDUCATING
MANDUCATION

MANDUCATORY
MANDYAS
MANE
MANED
MANEGE
MANEH
MANEI
MANELESS
MANENT
MANERIAL
MANES
MANESHEET
MANESS
MANET
MANEUVER
MANEUVERABLE
MANEUVERED
MANEUVERER
MANEUVERING
MANEUVRABLE
MANEUVRE
MANEUVRED
MANEUVRING
MANEY
MANFISH
MANFUL
MANFULLY
MANFULNESS
MANG
MANGA
MANGABEIRA
MANGABEY
MANGABY
MANGANA
MANGANATE
MANGANBLENDE
MANGANEISEN
MANGANESE
MANGANESIAN
MANGANESIC
MANGANETIC
MANGANIC
MANGANITE
MANGANIUM
MANGANIZE
MANGANOSITE
MANGANOUS
MANGE
MANGEAO
MANGEL
MANGELIN
MANGER
MANGERITE
MANGERY
MANGI
MANGIER
MANGIEST
MANGILY
MANGINESS
MANGLE
MANGLED
MANGLEMAN
MANGLER
MANGLING
MANGLINGLY
MANGO
MANGOES
MANGOLD
MANGONA
MANGONEL
MANGONISM
MANGONIZE
MANGORO
MANGOS
MANGOSTEEN
MANGOUR
MANGRASS

MANGRATE
MANGROVE
MANGUE
MANGWE
MANGY
MANHANDLE
MANHANDLED
MANHANDLING
MANHEAD
MANHOLE
MANHOOD
MANHUNT
MANHUNTER
MANHUNTING
MANI
MANIA
MANIABLE
MANIAC
MANIACAL
MANIACALLY
MANIC
MANICATE
MANICHORDON
MANICOLE
MANICON
MANICORD
MANICURE
MANICURED
MANICURING
MANICURIST
MANID
MANIFEST
MANIFESTABLE
MANIFESTANT
MANIFESTATION
MANIFESTED
MANIFESTER
MANIFESTING
MANIFESTIVE
MANIFESTLY
MANIFESTO
MANIFESTOES
MANIFESTOS
MANIFOLD
MANIFOLDED
MANIFOLDER
MANIFOLDING
MANIFOLDLY
MANIFOLDNESS
MANIFORM
MANIFY
MANIHOT
MANIKIN
MANIKINISM
MANILA
MANILLA
MANILLE
MANINI
MANIOC
MANIPLE
MANIPULABLE
MANIPULAR
MANIPULARY
MANIPULATE
MANIPULATED
MANIPULATING
MANIPULATION
MANIPULATIVE
MANIPULATOR
MANIPULATORY
MANISM
MANIST
MANISTIC
MANITO
MANITOU
MANITRUNK
MANITU

MANIU
MANJACK
MANJAK
MANJEET
MANJEL
MANK
MANKEEPER
MANKIE
MANKILLER
MANKILLING
MANKIN
MANKIND
MANKINDLY
MANKY
MANLESS
MANLESSLY
MANLESSNESS
MANLIER
MANLIEST
MANLIHOOD
MANLIKE
MANLIKELY
MANLIKENESS
MANLILY
MANLINESS
MANLY
MANMADE
MANNA
MANNAIA
MANNAN
MANNED
MANNEQUIN
MANNER
MANNERABLE
MANNERED
MANNERING
MANNERISM
MANNERIST
MANNERISTIC
MANNERIZE
MANNERLESS
MANNERLINESS
MANNERLY
MANNERS
MANNERSOME
MANNESS
MANNET
MANNIE
MANNIFEROUS
MANNIFY
MANNIKIN
MANNIKINISM
MANNING
MANNISH
MANNISHLY
MANNISHNESS
MANNITAN
MANNITE
MANNITIC
MANNITOL
MANNITOSE
MANNOHEPTITE
MANNOHEPTITOL
MANNOHEPTOSE
MANNONIC
MANNOSAN
MANNOSE
MANNY
MANO
MANOC
MANOEUVER
MANOEUVRE
MANOEUVRER
MANOGRAPH
MANOIR
MANOMETER
MANOMETRIC

MANOMETRICAL
MANOMETRY
MANOMIN
MANOR
MANORIAL
MANORIALISM
MANORIALIZE
MANOSCOPE
MANPOWER
MANQUE
MANQUEE
MANRED
MANRENT
MANROOT
MANROPE
MANSARD
MANSARDED
MANSE
MANSERVANT
MANSHIP
MANSION
MANSIONAL
MANSIONARY
MANSIONED
MANSIONRY
MANSLAUGHTER
MANSLAUGHTERER
MANSLAUGHTERING
MANSLAYER
MANSLAYING
MANSO
MANSTEALER
MANSTEALING
MANSTOPPER
MANSTOPPING
MANSUETE
MANSUETELY
MANSUETUDE
MANSWEAR
MANSWORN
MANT
MANTA
MANTAL
MANTEAU
MANTEAUS
MANTEAUX
MANTEEL
MANTEGAR
MANTEL
MANTELET
MANTELLETTA
MANTELLONE
MANTELPIECE
MANTELSHELF
MANTELTREE
MANTER
MANTES
MANTEVIL
MANTIC
MANTICISM
MANTICORA
MANTICORE
MANTID
MANTILLA
MANTIS
MANTISES
MANTISPID
MANTISSA
MANTISTIC
MANTLE
MANTLED
MANTLEROCK
MANTLET
MANTLING
MANTO
MANTOID
MANTOLOGIST

MANTOLOGY	MANWISE	MARBLEHEADER	MARGAY	MARITIMAL
MANTRA	MANY	MARBLEIZE	MARGE	MARITIMATE
MANTRAM	MANYATTA	MARBLEIZED	MARGELINE	MARITIME
MANTRAP	MANYBERRY	MARBLEIZER	MARGENT	MARITIMES
MANTUA	MANYFOLD	MARBLEIZING	MARGIN	MARITORIOUS
MANTUAMAKER	MANYPLIES	MARBLER	MARGINAL	MARIUPOLITE
MANTUAMAKING	MANYROOT	MARBLES	MARGINALIA	MARJORAM
MANTY	MANYWHERE	MARBLEWOOD	MARGINALITY	MARK
MANU	MANZANA	MARBLING	MARGINALIZE	MARKA
MANUAL	MANZANILLA	MARBLY	MARGINALLY	MARKABLE
MANUALII	MANZANILLO	MARBRINUS	MARGINATE	MARKAZ
MANUALIST	MANZANITA	MARC	MARGINATED	MARKAZES
MANUALITER	MANZIL	MARCANDO	MARGINATING	MARKDOWN
MANUALLY	MAO	MARCANTANT	MARGINATION	MARKED
MANUAO	MAOMAO	MARCASITE	MARGINED	MARKEDLY
MANUARY	MAORMOR	MARCASITIC	MARGINIFORM	MARKEDNESS
MANUBALISTE	MAP	MARCASITICAL	MARGINING	MARKER
MANUBRIA	MAPACH	MARCATISSIMO	MARGINOPLASTY	MARKERY
MANUBRIAL	MAPACHE	MARCATO	MARGINS	MARKET
MANUBRIATED	MAPAU	MARCEL	MARGOSA	MARKETABILITY
MANUBRIUM	MAPLAND	MARCELINE	MARGRAVATE	MARKETABLE
MANUBRIUMS	MAPLE	MARCELLA	MARGRAVE	MARKETABLY
MANUCAPTION	MAPLEFACE	MARCELLED	MARGRAVELY	MARKETED
MANUCAPTOR	MAPLES	MARCELLER	MARGRAVIAL	MARKETEER
MANUCAPTURE	MAPO	MARCELLING	MARGRAVIATE	MARKETER
MANUCODE	MAPPED	MARCELLO	MARGRAVINE	MARKETING
MANUCODIATA	MAPPEMONDE	MARCESCENCE	MARGUERITE	MARKETMAN
MANUDUCE	MAPPEN	MARCESCENT	MARGULLIE	MARKETPLACE
MANUDUCT	MAPPER	MARCH	MARHALA	MARKETSTEAD
MANUDUCTION	MAPPING	MARCHAND	MARIA	MARKFIELDITE
MANUDUCTIVE	MAPPIST	MARCHED	MARIACHI	MARKHOOR
MANUDUCTOR	MAPPY	MARCHER	MARIALITE	MARKHOR
MANUDUCTORY	MAPS	MARCHESA	MARIANA	MARKING
MANUFACT	MAPWISE	MARCHESE	MARIANNA	MARKINGLY
MANUFACTION	MAQUAHUITL	MARCHESI	MARIANNE	MARKINGS
MANUFACTOR	MAQUETTE	MARCHET	MARICA	MARKKA
MANUFACTORY	MAQUI	MARCHETTI	MARICOLOUS	MARKKAA
MANUFACTURAL	MAQUIS	MARCHETTO	MARID	MARKLAND
MANUFACTURE	MAR	MARCHING	MARIGENOUS	MARKMAN
MANUFACTURED	MARABOTIN	MARCHIONESS	MARIGOLD	MARKMEN
MANUFACTURER	MARABOU	MARCHITE	MARIGRAM	MARKMOOT
MANUFACTURING	MARABOUT	MARCHLAND	MARIGRAPH	MARKMOTE
MANUKA	MARABUTO	MARCHMAN	MARIGRAPHIC	MARKS
MANUL	MARACA	MARCHMEN	MARIHUANA	MARKSHOT
MANUMA	MARACAN	MARCHPANE	MARIJUANA	MARKSMAN
MANUMEA	MARACOCK	MARCID	MARIKINA	MARKSMANLY
MANUMISABLE	MARAE	MARCO	MARIMBA	MARKSMANSHIP
MANUMISE	MARAI	MARCONI	MARIMONDA	MARKSMEN
MANUMISSION	MARAKAPAS	MARCONIGRAM	MARINA	MARKSTONE
MANUMISSIVE	MARAL	MARCONIGRAPH	MARINADE	MARKSWOMAN
MANUMIT	MARAN	MARCOR	MARINADED	MARKSWOMEN
MANUMITTED	MARANAO	MARCOT	MARINADING	MARKUP
MANUMITTER	MARANG	MARCOTTAGE	MARINAL	MARKWEED
MANUMITTING	MARANON	MARDY	MARINATE	MARKWORTHY
MANUMOTIVE	MARANTACEOUS	MARE	MARINATED	MARL
MANUPRISOR	MARANTIC	MAREBLOB	MARINATING	MARLACEOUS
MANURABLE	MARARA	MARECHAL	MARINE	MARLBERRY
MANURAGE	MARARIE	MARECHALE	MARINER	MARLED
MANURANCE	MARAS	MAREKANITE	MARINERSHIP	MARLER
MANURE	MARASCA	MAREMMA	MARINHEIRO	MARLET
MANURED	MARASCHINO	MAREMMATIC	MARINIST	MARLI
MANUREMENT	MARASMIC	MAREMME	MARINORAMA	MARLIN
MANURER	MARASMOID	MAREMMESE	MARIONET	MARLINE
MANURIAL	MARASMOUS	MARENGO	MARIONETTE	MARLINESPIKE
MANURIALLY	MARASMUS	MARENNIN	MARIPOSITE	MARLING
MANURING	MARATHON	MARES	MARIS	MARLINGSPIKE
MANUS	MARATHONER	MARFIRE	MARISH	MARLINSPIKE
MANUSCRIPT	MARAUD	MARGA	MARISHNESS	MARLITE
MANUSCRIPTAL	MARAUDED	MARGARATE	MARISHY	MARLITIC
MANUSCRIPTION	MARAUDER	MARGARIC	MARITA	MARLOCK
MANUSINA	MARAUDING	MARGARIN	MARITAGE	MARLPIT
MANUTAGI	MARAVEDI	MARGARINE	MARITAGIUM	MARLY
MANUTERGIUM	MARAY	MARGARITA	MARITAL	MARM
MANWARD	MARBELIZE	MARGARITAE	MARITALITY	MARMALADE
MANWARDS	MARBLE	MARGARITE	MARITALLY	MARMALADY
MANWAY	MARBLED	MARGARITIC	MARITICIDAL	MARMARITIN
MANWEED	MARBLEHEAD	MARGARODITE	MARITICIDE	MARMARIZE

MARMARIZED
MARMARIZING
MARMAROSIS
MARMATITE
MARMELOS
MARMENNILL
MARMION
MARMIT
MARMITE
MARMOLITE
MARMOR
MARMORACEOUS
MARMORATE
MARMOREAL
MARMOREALLY
MARMOREAN
MARMORIC
MARMOSE
MARMOSET
MARMOT
MARO
MAROCAIN
MAROK
MAROON
MAROONED
MAROONER
MAROONING
MAROQUIN
MAROR
MAROS
MAROTTE
MARPLOT
MARPLOTRY
MARQUE
MARQUEE
MARQUESS
MARQUETERIE
MARQUETRY
MARQUIS
MARQUISAL
MARQUISATE
MARQUISDOM
MARQUISE
MARQUISESS
MARQUISETTE
MARQUISINA
MARQUISOTTE
MARQUITO
MARRAINE
MARRAM
MARRANISM
MARRANIZE
MARRANO
MARRED
MARREE
MARRER
MARRIABLE
MARRIAGE
MARRIAGEABLE
MARRIED
MARRIER
MARRING
MARROCK
MARRON
MARROT
MARROW
MARROWBONE
MARROWED
MARROWFAT
MARROWING
MARROWSKY
MARROWSKYER
MARROWY
MARRUBE
MARRY
MARRYER
MARRYING

MARRYMUFFE
MARSE
MARSEILLE
MARSEILLES
MARSH
MARSHAL
MARSHALATE
MARSHALCY
MARSHALED
MARSHALER
MARSHALESS
MARSHALING
MARSHALLED
MARSHALLER
MARSHALLING
MARSHALMAN
MARSHALSHIP
MARSHBERRIES
MARSHBERRY
MARSHBUCK
MARSHFIRE
MARSHFLOWER
MARSHIER
MARSHIEST
MARSHINESS
MARSHITE
MARSHLAND
MARSHLANDER
MARSHLOCKS
MARSHMALLOW
MARSHMAN
MARSHMEN
MARSHWORT
MARSHY
MARSOON
MARSUPIA
MARSUPIAL
MARSUPIALIAN
MARSUPIALIZE
MARSUPIAN
MARSUPIATE
MARSUPIUM
MART
MARTAGON
MARTEL
MARTELINE
MARTELLATE
MARTELLATO
MARTELLEMENT
MARTELLO
MARTEN
MARTENIKO
MARTENOT
MARTENS
MARTENSITE
MARTENSITIC
MARTEXT
MARTIAL
MARTIALISM
MARTIALIST
MARTIALITY
MARTIALIZE
MARTIALLY
MARTIALNESS
MARTILOGE
MARTIN
MARTINET
MARTINETA
MARTINETISM
MARTINGAL
MARTINGALE
MARTINI
MARTINICO
MARTINIS
MARTINOE
MARTITE
MARTLET

MARTRIX
MARTYR
MARTYRDOM
MARTYRED
MARTYRER
MARTYRESS
MARTYRIES
MARTYRING
MARTYRIUM
MARTYRIZE
MARTYRIZED
MARTYRIZER
MARTYRIZING
MARTYRLY
MARTYROLATRY
MARTYROLOGE
MARTYROLOGIC
MARTYROLOGICAL
MARTYROLOGY
MARTYRY
MARU
MARUA
MARUM
MARVEL
MARVELED
MARVELING
MARVELLED
MARVELLING
MARVELLOUS
MARVELLOUSLY
MARVELOUS
MARVELOUSLY
MARVELRY
MARVER
MARY
MARYBUD
MARYSOLE
MARZIPAN
MAS
MASA
MASARID
MASARIDID
MASCAGNINE
MASCAGNITE
MASCALLY
MASCARA
MASCARON
MASCLE
MASCLED
MASCON
MASCOT
MASCOTISM
MASCOTRY
MASCOTTE
MASCULARITY
MASCULATE
MASCULATION
MASCULINE
MASCULINELY
MASCULINENESS
MASCULINISM
MASCULINIST
MASCULINITY
MASCULY
MASDEU
MASER
MASH
MASHA
MASHAK
MASHAL
MASHALLAH
MASHAM
MASHED
MASHELTON
MASHER
MASHGIAH
MASHIE

MASHIER
MASHIES
MASHIEST
MASHING
MASHLOCH
MASHLUM
MASHMAN
MASHMEN
MASHRU
MASHY
MASI
MASJID
MASK
MASKALONGE
MASKED
MASKEG
MASKELYNITE
MASKER
MASKERY
MASKETTE
MASKFLOWER
MASKING
MASKINONGE
MASKOID
MASLIN
MASOCHISM
MASOCHIST
MASOCHISTIC
MASON
MASONED
MASONER
MASONIC
MASONING
MASONITE
MASONRIED
MASONRIES
MASONRY
MASONRYING
MASONS
MASONWORK
MASOOKA
MASOOLA
MASQUE
MASQUER
MASQUERADE
MASQUERADED
MASQUERADER
MASQUERADING
MASS
MASSA
MASSACRE
MASSACRED
MASSACRER
MASSACRING
MASSACROUS
MASSAGE
MASSAGED
MASSAGER
MASSAGEUSE
MASSAGING
MASSAGIST
MASSARANDUBA
MASSASAUGA
MASSE
MASSEBAH
MASSECUITE
MASSED
MASSEL
MASSELGEM
MASSER
MASSES
MASSETER
MASSETERIC
MASSETERINE
MASSEUR
MASSEURS
MASSEUSE

MASSEUSES
MASSICOT
MASSIER
MASSIEST
MASSIF
MASSIG
MASSINESS
MASSIVE
MASSIVELY
MASSIVENESS
MASSIVITY
MASSOTHERAPY
MASSOY
MASSULA
MASSY
MASSYMORE
MAST
MASTABA
MASTABAH
MASTADENITIS
MASTADENOMA
MASTAGE
MASTALGIA
MASTATROPHIA
MASTATROPHY
MASTAUXE
MASTAX
MASTECTOMIES
MASTECTOMY
MASTED
MASTER
MASTERATE
MASTERDOM
MASTERED
MASTERER
MASTERFAST
MASTERFUL
MASTERFULLY
MASTERFULNESS
MASTERHOOD
MASTERIES
MASTERING
MASTERLESS
MASTERLILY
MASTERLINESS
MASTERLY
MASTERMAN
MASTERMEN
MASTERMIND
MASTEROUS
MASTERPIECE
MASTERSHIP
MASTERSINGER
MASTERSINGERS
MASTERSTROKE
MASTERWORK
MASTERWORT
MASTERY
MASTFUL
MASTHEAD
MASTIC
MASTICABLE
MASTICATE
MASTICATED
MASTICATING
MASTICATION
MASTICATOR
MASTICATORIES
MASTICATORY
MASTICIC
MASTICUROUS
MASTIFF
MASTIGATE
MASTIGIA
MASTIGIUM
MASTIGONEME
MASTIGOPOD

MASTIGOTE
MASTIGURE
MASTING
MASTITIS
MASTMAN
MASTMEN
MASTODON
MASTODONT
MASTODONTIC
MASTODONTINE
MASTODONTOID
MASTODYNIA
MASTOID
MASTOIDALE
MASTOIDITIS
MASTOIDOTOMY
MASTOLOGICAL
MASTOLOGIST
MASTOLOGY
MASTOMENIA
MASTOPATHY
MASTOPEXY
MASTOPLASTIA
MASTORRHAGIA
MASTOTOMY
MASTS
MASTURBATE
MASTURBATED
MASTURBATING
MASTURBATION
MASTURBATOR
MASTURBATORY
MASTWOOD
MASTY
MASU
MASURIUM
MAT
MATA
MATACHIN
MATACHINA
MATACHINAS
MATACO
MATADERO
MATADOR
MATAEOLOGUE
MATAEOLOGY
MATAEOTECHNY
MATAGASSE
MATAGORY
MATAI
MATAJUELO
MATALAN
MATAMATA
MATAMORO
MATANZA
MATAPAN
MATAPI
MATARA
MATASANO
MATAX
MATBOARD
MATCH
MATCHABLE
MATCHABLY
MATCHBOARD
MATCHBOARDING
MATCHBOOK
MATCHBOX
MATCHCLOTH
MATCHCOAT
MATCHED
MATCHER
MATCHING
MATCHLESS
MATCHLESSLY
MATCHLESSNESS
MATCHLOCK

MATCHMAKER
MATCHMAKING
MATCHMARK
MATCHSAFE
MATCHSTALK
MATCHSTICK
MATCHWOOD
MATCHY
MATE
MATED
MATEE
MATEGRIFFON
MATELASSE
MATELEY
MATELOT
MATELOTAGE
MATELOTE
MATELOTTE
MATER
MATERFAMILIAS
MATERIA
MATERIABLE
MATERIAL
MATERIALISM
MATERIALIST
MATERIALISTIC
MATERIALITY
MATERIALIZATION
MATERIALIZE
MATERIALIZED
MATERIALIZER
MATERIALIZING
MATERIALLY
MATERIALMAN
MATERIALMEN
MATERIALNESS
MATERIALS
MATERIATE
MATERIATION
MATERIEL
MATERNAL
MATERNALITY
MATERNALIZE
MATERNALLY
MATERNALNESS
MATERNITIES
MATERNITY
MATERNOLOGY
MATEY
MATEZITE
MATFELLON
MATFELON
MATGRASS
MATH
MATHE
MATHEMATIC
MATHEMATICAL
MATHEMATICALLY
MATHEMATICALS
MATHEMATICIAN
MATHEMATICS
MATHEMATIZE
MATHEMEG
MATHER
MATHES
MATHESIS
MATHETIC
MATHS
MATICO
MATIE
MATIES
MATILDITE
MATIN
MATINA
MATINAL
MATINEE
MATING

MATINS
MATIPO
MATKA
MATKAH
MATLOCKITE
MATLOW
MATMAKER
MATMAKING
MATMAN
MATRA
MATRACE
MATRAH
MATRAL
MATRANEE
MATRASS
MATREED
MATRIARCH
MATRIARCHAL
MATRIARCHATE
MATRIARCHIC
MATRIARCHIES
MATRIARCHIST
MATRIARCHY
MATRIC
MATRICAL
MATRICE
MATRICES
MATRICIDAL
MATRICIDE
MATRICULA
MATRICULABLE
MATRICULAE
MATRICULANT
MATRICULAR
MATRICULATE
MATRICULATED
MATRICULATING
MATRICULATION
MATRICULATOR
MATRICULATORY
MATRIHERITAGE
MATRIHERITAL
MATRILINEAL
MATRILINEAR
MATRILINY
MATRILOCAL
MATRIMONIAL
MATRIMONIES
MATRIMONIOUS
MATRIMONY
MATRIOTISM
MATRIS
MATRIX
MATRIXES
MATROCLINAL
MATROCLINIC
MATROCLINOUS
MATROCLINY
MATRON
MATRONAGE
MATRONAL
MATRONIZE
MATRONIZED
MATRONIZING
MATRONLIKE
MATRONLINESS
MATRONLY
MATRONYMIC
MATROSS
MATSTER
MATSU
MATSUE
MATSURI
MATTA
MATTAMORE
MATTARO
MATTE

MATTED
MATTEDLY
MATTEDNESS
MATTER
MATTERED
MATTERING
MATTERS
MATTERY
MATTI
MATTIN
MATTING
MATTO
MATTOCK
MATTOID
MATTOIR
MATTRASS
MATTRESS
MATTULLA
MATURABLE
MATURATE
MATURATED
MATURATING
MATURATION
MATURATIVE
MATURE
MATURED
MATURELY
MATURENESS
MATURER
MATURESCENCE
MATURESCENT
MATUREST
MATURING
MATURITY
MATUTINAL
MATUTINALLY
MATUTINARY
MATUTINE
MATUTINELY
MATWEED
MATY
MATZO
MATZOH
MATZOON
MATZOS
MATZOT
MATZOTH
MAU
MAUCACO
MAUCHERITE
MAUD
MAUDELINE
MAUDLE
MAUDLIN
MAUDLINISM
MAUDLINLY
MAUGER
MAUGH
MAUGHT
MAUGRE
MAUKA
MAUKIN
MAUL
MAULA
MAULANA
MAULED
MAULER
MAULEY
MAULING
MAULSTICK
MAULVI
MAUM
MAUMET
MAUMETRY
MAUN
MAUNA
MAUNCHE

MAUND
MAUNDER
MAUNDERED
MAUNDERER
MAUNDERING
MAUNDFUL
MAUNDY
MAUNGE
MAUNNA
MAURICIO
MAUSOLE
MAUSOLEA
MAUSOLEAL
MAUSOLEAN
MAUSOLEUM
MAUSOLEUMS
MAUT
MAUTHER
MAUVE
MAUVEIN
MAUVETTE
MAUVINE
MAUX
MAVERICK
MAVIE
MAVIS
MAVOURNEEN
MAVOURNIN
MAVRODAPHNE
MAW
MAWALI
MAWBOUND
MAWK
MAWKIN
MAWKISH
MAWKISHLY
MAWKISHNESS
MAWKS
MAWKY
MAWMISH
MAWP
MAWTHER
MAWWORM
MAX
MAXILLA
MAXILLAE
MAXILLARIES
MAXILLARY
MAXILLIFORM
MAXILLIPED
MAXILLIPEDARY
MAXILLIPEDE
MAXILLOJUGAL
MAXILLOLABIAL
MAXIM
MAXIMA
MAXIMAL
MAXIMALLY
MAXIMATE
MAXIMATION
MAXIMED
MAXIMIST
MAXIMISTIC
MAXIMITE
MAXIMIZATION
MAXIMIZE
MAXIMIZED
MAXIMIZER
MAXIMIZING
MAXIMUM
MAXIMUMS
MAXIMUS
MAXIXE
MAXWELL
MAY
MAYA
MAYACACEOUS

MAYAPIS
MAYAPPLE
MAYBE
MAYBERRY
MAYBUSH
MAYCOCK
MAYDAY
MAYDUKE
MAYENCE
MAYEST
MAYFISH
MAYFISHES
MAYFLOWER
MAYFLY
MAYHAP
MAYHAPPEN
MAYHAPS
MAYHEM
MAYNE
MAYONNAISE
MAYOR
MAYORAL
MAYORALTY
MAYORESS
MAYORSHIP
MAYPOLE
MAYPOP
MAYSIN
MAYST
MAYTEN
MAYTHE
MAYTHES
MAYWEED
MAZA
MAZAGRAN
MAZALGIA
MAZAME
MAZAPILITE
MAZAR
MAZARD
MAZARINE
MAZDOOR
MAZE
MAZED
MAZEDLY
MAZEDNESS
MAZEFUL
MAZER
MAZIC
MAZIER
MAZIEST
MAZILY
MAZINESS
MAZING
MAZODYNIA
MAZOLYSIS
MAZOLYTIC
MAZOPATHIA
MAZOPATHIC
MAZOPEXY
MAZOURKA
MAZUCA
MAZUMA
MAZURKA
MAZUT
MAZY
MAZZARD
MBORI
ME
MEABLE
MEACHING
MEACOCK
MEAD
MEADER
MEADOW
MEADOWED
MEADOWER

MEADOWING
MEADOWINK
MEADOWLAND
MEADOWLARK
MEADOWS
MEADOWSWEET
MEADOWY
MEADSMAN
MEADWORT
MEAGER
MEAGERLY
MEAGERNESS
MEAGRE
MEAGRELY
MEAGRENESS
MEAK
MEAL
MEALABLE
MEALED
MEALER
MEALIE
MEALIER
MEALIES
MEALIEST
MEALILY
MEALINESS
MEALING
MEALMAN
MEALMEN
MEALMONGER
MEALMOUTH
MEALMOUTHED
MEALOCK
MEALS
MEALTIDE
MEALTIME
MEALY
MEALYBUG
MEALYMOUTH
MEALYMOUTHED
MEALYWING
MEAN
MEANDER
MEANDERED
MEANDERER
MEANDERING
MEANDRITE
MEANDROUS
MEANED
MEANER
MEANEST
MEANIE
MEANING
MEANINGFUL
MEANINGFULLY
MEANINGFULNESS
MEANINGLESS
MEANINGLY
MEANINGNESS
MEANLESS
MEANLY
MEANNESS
MEANS
MEANT
MEANTIME
MEANTONE
MEANWHILE
MEANY
MEAR
MEARE
MEARSTONE
MEASE
MEASLE
MEASLED
MEASLEDNESS
MEASLES
MEASLIER

MEASLIEST
MEASLY
MEASONDUE
MEASURABILITY
MEASURABLE
MEASURABLY
MEASURAGE
MEASURATION
MEASURE
MEASURED
MEASUREDLY
MEASUREDNESS
MEASURELESS
MEASURELY
MEASUREMENT
MEASURER
MEASURES
MEASURING
MEAT
MEATAL
MEATBALL
MEATBIRD
MEATCUTTER
MEATED
MEATH
MEATHE
MEATHOOK
MEATIC
MEATIER
MEATIEST
MEATINESS
MEATLESS
MEATMAN
MEATMEN
MEATOMETER
MEATORRHAPHY
MEATOSCOPE
MEATOSCOPY
MEATOTOME
MEATOTOMY
MEATURE
MEATUS
MEATUSES
MEATWORKS
MEATY
MEBBE
MEBOS
MECATE
MECCA
MECHANALITY
MECHANALIZE
MECHANIC
MECHANICAL
MECHANICALLY
MECHANICIAN
MECHANICS
MECHANISM
MECHANIST
MECHANISTIC
MECHANIZATION
MECHANIZE
MECHANIZER
MECHANOLATER
MECHANOLOGY
MECHOACAN
MECKELECTOMY
MECODONT
MECOMETER
MECOMETRY
MECON
MECONIC
MECONIDIUM
MECONIN
MECONIOID
MECONIUM
MECONOLOGY
MECOPTERAN

MECOPTERON
MECOPTEROUS
MEDA
MEDAL
MEDALED
MEDALET
MEDALING
MEDALIST
MEDALIZE
MEDALLARY
MEDALLED
MEDALLIC
MEDALLICALLY
MEDALLING
MEDALLION
MEDALLIONED
MEDALLIONING
MEDALLIONIST
MEDDLE
MEDDLECOME
MEDDLED
MEDDLER
MEDDLESOME
MEDDLESOMELY
MEDDLING
MEDENAGAN
MEDIA
MEDIACID
MEDIACY
MEDIAD
MEDIAE
MEDIAEVAL
MEDIAEVALISM
MEDIAEVALIST
MEDIAL
MEDIALIZE
MEDIALKALINE
MEDIALLY
MEDIAN
MEDIANIC
MEDIANIMIC
MEDIANIMITY
MEDIANISM
MEDIANITY
MEDIANLY
MEDIANT
MEDIASTINA
MEDIASTINAL
MEDIASTINE
MEDIASTINUM
MEDIATE
MEDIATED
MEDIATELY
MEDIATING
MEDIATINGLY
MEDIATION
MEDIATIVE
MEDIATIZE
MEDIATIZED
MEDIATIZING
MEDIATOR
MEDIATORIAL
MEDIATORIOUS
MEDIATORY
MEDIATRESS
MEDIATRICE
MEDIATRIX
MEDIC
MEDICABLE
MEDICAL
MEDICALLY
MEDICAMENT
MEDICAMENTAL
MEDICARE
MEDICASTER
MEDICATE
MEDICATED

MEDICATING
MEDICATION
MEDICATIVE
MEDICATOR
MEDICATORY
MEDICINABLE
MEDICINAL
MEDICINARY
MEDICINE
MEDICINED
MEDICINER
MEDICINING
MEDICK
MEDICO
MEDICODENTAL
MEDICOLEGAL
MEDICOMORAL
MEDICOS
MEDIETY
MEDIEVAL
MEDIEVALISM
MEDIEVALIST
MEDIEVALLY
MEDIFIXED
MEDIGLACIAL
MEDILLE
MEDIMNO
MEDIMNOS
MEDIMNUS
MEDIN
MEDINE
MEDINO
MEDIO
MEDIOCARPAL
MEDIOCRAL
MEDIOCRE
MEDIOCRITIES
MEDIOCRITY
MEDIOCUBITAL
MEDIODIGITAL
MEDIODORSAL
MEDIOFRONTAL
MEDIOLATERAL
MEDIOPALATAL
MEDIOPASSIVE
MEDIOPONTINE
MEDIOSILICIC
MEDIOTARSAL
MEDIOVENTRAL
MEDISANCE
MEDISECT
MEDISECTION
MEDITABUND
MEDITANCE
MEDITANT
MEDITATE
MEDITATED
MEDITATER
MEDITATING
MEDITATION
MEDITATIST
MEDITATIVE
MEDITATIVELY
MEDITATOR
MEDITERRANE
MEDITERRANEAN
MEDITHORAX
MEDITULLIUM
MEDIUM
MEDIUMISTIC
MEDIUMIZE
MEDIUMS
MEDIUS
MEDJIDIE
MEDJIDIEH
MEDLAR
MEDLEY

MEDLEYED	MEGALITH	MEHARIS	MELANOBLAST	MELIORATED
MEDLEYING	MEGALITHIC	MEHARIST	MELANOCERITE	MELIORATER
MEDLEYS	MEGALOBLAST	MEHMANDAR	MELANOCHROIC	MELIORATING
MEDLIED	MEGALOBLASTIC	MEHTAR	MELANOCOMOUS	MELIORATION
MEDREGAL	MEGALOCARDIA	MEHTARSHIP	MELANOCRATE	MELIORATIVE
MEDRICK	MEGALOCORNEA	MEILE	MELANOCRATIC	MELIORATOR
MEDRINACKS	MEGALOCYTE	MEILER	MELANODERMA	MELIORISM
MEDRINACLES	MEGALOGRAPH	MEIN	MELANODERMIA	MELIORIST
MEDRINAQUE	MEGALOGRAPHY	MEINIE	MELANODERMIC	MELIORISTIC
MEDULLA	MEGALOMANIA	MEINIES	MELANOGEN	MELIORITY
MEDULLAE	MEGALOMANIAC	MEINY	MELANOID	MELIPHAGOUS
MEDULLAR	MEGALOMELIA	MEIO	MELANOMA	MELIPHANITE
MEDULLARY	MEGALOPENIS	MEIOBAR	MELANOMAS	MELIPONINE
MEDULLAS	MEGALOPHONIC	MEIONITE	MELANOMATA	MELIS
MEDULLATE	MEGALOPIC	MEIOPHYLLY	MELANOPATHIA	MELISMA
MEDULLATED	MEGALOPINE	MEIOSIS	MELANOPATHY	MELISMATA
MEDULLATION	MEGALOPOLIS	MEIOTAXY	MELANOPHORE	MELISMATIC
MEDULLITIS	MEGALOPORE	MEIOTIC	MELANOPLAKIA	MELISMATICS
MEDULLOSE	MEGALOPS	MEISJE	MELANORRHEA	MELITAEMIA
MEDULLOUS	MEGALOPSYCHY	MEITH	MELANOSCOPE	MELITEMIA
MEDUSA	MEGALOSAUR	MEIZOSEISMAL	MELANOSE	MELITHAEMIA
MEDUSAE	MEGALOSCOPE	MEIZOSEISMIC	MELANOSED	MELITHEMIA
MEDUSAL	MEGALOSCOPY	MEJORANA	MELANOSITY	MELITIS
MEDUSAN	MEGALOSPHERE	MEKE	MELANOTEKITE	MELITTOLOGIST
MEDUSAS	MEGAMETER	MEKIL	MELANOTIC	MELITTOLOGY
MEDUSIFEROUS	MEGAMETRE	MEKILTA	MELANOUS	MELITURIA
MEDUSIFORM	MEGAMPERE	MEKOMETER	MELANTERITE	MELITURIC
MEDUSOID	MEGAPHONE	MEL	MELANTHY	MELKHOUT
MEEBOS	MEGAPHONED	MELA	MELANURE	MELL
MEECH	MEGAPHONIC	MELACONITE	MELANURENIC	MELLAGINOUS
MEECHER	MEGAPHONING	MELADA	MELANURESIS	MELLAH
MEECHING	MEGAPOD	MELADIORITE	MELANURIA	MELLATE
MEED	MEGAPODE	MELAENA	MELANURIC	MELLAY
MEEDLESS	MEGAPOLIS	MELAENIC	MELAPHYRE	MELLEOUS
MEEK	MEGAPROSOPOUS	MELAGABBRO	MELASMA	MELLER
MEEKEN	MEGAPTERINE	MELAGRA	MELASMIC	MELLIFEROUS
MEEKER	MEGARON	MELAGRANITE	MELASSIGENIC	MELLIFICATE
MEEKEST	MEGASCLERE	MELALGIA	MELASTOMAD	MELLIFICATION
MEEKHEARTED	MEGASCLERIC	MELAM	MELASTOME	MELLIFLUATE
MEEKLY	MEGASCLEROUS	MELAMED	MELATOPE	MELLIFLUENCE
MEEKNESS	MEGASCLERUM	MELAMIN	MELAXUMA	MELLIFLUENT
MEER	MEGASCOPE	MELAMINE	MELCH	MELLIFLUENTLY
MEERED	MEGASCOPIC	MELAMMED	MELD	MELLIFLUOUS
MEERKAT	MEGASCOPICAL	MELAMPOD	MELDER	MELLILOT
MEERSCHAUM	MEGASEISM	MELAMPODE	MELDOMETER	MELLISONANT
MEES	MEGASEISMIC	MELAMPODIUM	MELDROP	MELLISUGENT
MEESE	MEGASPORANGE	MELAMPYRIN	MELE	MELLIT
MEET	MEGASPORE	MELAMPYRITE	MELEAGRINE	MELLITATE
MEETEN	MEGASPORIC	MELAMPYRITOL	MELEE	MELLITE
MEETER	MEGASS	MELANAEMIA	MELENA	MELLITIC
MEETERLY	MEGASSE	MELANAEMIC	MELENE	MELLIVOROUS
MEETHELP	MEGATHERE	MELANAGOGAL	MELENIC	MELLON
MEETHELPER	MEGATHERIAN	MELANAGOGUE	MELEZITASE	MELLONE
MEETING	MEGATHERINE	MELANCHOLIA	MELEZITOSE	MELLONIDES
MEETINGER	MEGATHERIOID	MELANCHOLIAC	MELIACEOUS	MELLOPHONE
MEETINGHOUSE	MEGATHERIUM	MELANCHOLIC	MELIATIN	MELLOW
MEETINGS	MEGATHERM	MELANCHOLIES	MELIBIOSE	MELLOWED
MEETLY	MEGATHERMIC	MELANCHOLIOUS	MELIC	MELLOWER
MEG	MEGATHEROID	MELANCHOLIST	MELICERA	MELLOWEST
MEGABAR	MEGATON	MELANCHOLIZE	MELICERIC	MELLOWING
MEGACEPHALIA	MEGATYPE	MELANCHOLY	MELICERIS	MELLOWLY
MEGACEPHALIC	MEGATYPY	MELANEMIA	MELICEROUS	MELLOWNESS
MEGACEPHALY	MEGAVOLT	MELANEMIC	MELICHROUS	MELLOWY
MEGACERINE	MEGAZOOID	MELANGE	MELICITOSE	MELLSMAN
MEGACEROTINE	MEGAZOOSPORE	MELANGER	MELICRATE	MELOCOTON
MEGACHILID	MEGILP	MELANGES	MELICRATON	MELOCOTOON
MEGACOLON	MEGILPH	MELANGEUR	MELICRATORY	MELODEON
MEGACURIE	MEGOHM	MELANIAN	MELICRATUM	MELODIA
MEGACYCLE	MEGOHMIT	MELANIC	MELILITE	MELODIAL
MEGADONT	MEGOHMMETER	MELANIFEROUS	MELILITITE	MELODIALLY
MEGADYNAMICS	MEGOMIT	MELANIN	MELILOT	MELODIC
MEGADYNE	MEGOTALC	MELANISM	MELINE	MELODICA
MEGAFARAD	MEGRIM	MELANISTIC	MELINITE	MELODICAL
MEGAFOG	MEGRIMS	MELANITE	MELIORABILITY	MELODICALLY
MEGAGAMETE	MEGUILP	MELANITIC	MELIORABLE	MELODICS
MEGALEME	MEHALLA	MELANIZE	MELIORANT	MELODIED
MEGALESTHETE	MEHARI	MELANO	MELIORATE	MELODIES

MELODION	MEMBRACID	MEND	MENOPAUSE	MENTIFORM
MELODIOUS	MEMBRACINE	MENDACIOUS	MENOPAUSIC	MENTIGEROUS
MELODIOUSLY	MEMBRAL	MENDACIOUSLY	MENOPHANIA	MENTIMETER
MELODIOUSNESS	MEMBRALLY	MENDACITIES	MENOPLANIA	MENTION
MELODISM	MEMBRANA	MENDACITY	MENORRHAGIA	MENTIONABLE
MELODIST	MEMBRANATE	MENDED	MENORRHAGIC	MENTIONED
MELODIZE	MEMBRANE	MENDEE	MENORRHAGY	MENTIONER
MELODIZED	MEMBRANED	MENDELEVIUM	MENORRHEA	MENTIONING
MELODIZER	MEMBRANELLA	MENDER	MENORRHEIC	MENTOHYOID
MELODIZING	MEMBRANELLE	MENDICANCY	MENORRHOEA	MENTOLABIAL
MELODRAMA	MEMBRANIFORM	MENDICANT	MENORRHOEIC	MENTONIERE
MELODRAMATIC	MEMBRANIN	MENDICATE	MENOSCHESIS	MENTONNIERE
MELODRAMATICAL	MEMBRANOID	MENDICATED	MENOSCHETIC	MENTOR
MELODRACTICALLY	MEMBRANOLOGY	MENDICATING	MENOSEPSIS	MENTORIAL
MELODRAMATICS	MEMBRANOSIS	MENDICATION	MENOSTASIA	MENTUM
MELODRAMATIST	MEMBRANOUS	MENDICITY	MENOSTASIS	MENU
MELODRAMATIZE	MEMBRANOUSLY	MENDIGO	MENOSTATIC	MENUS
MELODY	MEMBRANULA	MENDING	MENOSTAXIS	MEOW
MELODYING	MEMBRANULE	MENDINGS	MENOTYPHLIC	MEPHITIC
MELOE	MEMBRETTE	MENDIPITE	MENOXENIA	MEPHITICAL
MELOGRAM	MEMBRETTO	MENDOLE	MENSA	MEPHITINE
MELOGRAPH	MEMEL	MENDOZITE	MENSAE	MEPHITIS
MELOGRAPHIC	MEMENTO	MENDY	MENSAL	MEPHITISM
MELOID	MEMENTOES	MENE	MENSALIZE	MEPROBAMATE
MELOLOGUE	MEMENTOS	MENEGHINITE	MENSE	MER
MELOLONTHINE	MEMINNA	MENEHUNE	MENSEFUL	MERAI
MELOMAME	MEMO	MENEL	MENSELESS	MERALGIA
MELOMANIA	MEMOIR	MENFOLK	MENSERVANTS	MERALINE
MELOMANIAC	MEMOIRISM	MENFOLKS	MENSES	MERBABY
MELOMANIC	MEMOIRIST	MENG	MENSHEVIK	MERCANTILE
MELON	MEMOIRS	MENHADEN	MENSK	MERCANTILELY
MELONCUS	MEMORABILE	MENHADENS	MENSTRUA	MERCANTILISM
MELONGENA	MEMORABILIA	MENHIR	MENSTRUAL	MERCANTILIST
MELONGROWER	MEMORABILITY	MENIAL	MENSTRUANT	MERCANTILISTIC
MELONIST	MEMORABLE	MENIALISM	MENSTRUATE	MERCANTILITY
MELONITE	MEMORABLY	MENIALITY	MENSTRUATED	MERCAPTAL
MELONLIKE	MEMORANDA	MENIALLY	MENSTRUATING	MERCAPTAN
MELONMONGER	MEMORANDIST	MENIALTY	MENSTRUATION	MERCAPTIDES
MELONRY	MEMORANDIZE	MENILITE	MENSTRUOSITY	MERCAPTIDS
MELOPHONE	MEMORANDUM	MENINGEAL	MENSTRUOUS	MERCAPTO
MELOPHONIC	MEMORANDUMS	MENINGES	MENSTRUUM	MERCAPTOL
MELOPHONIST	MEMORATE	MENINGIC	MENSTRUUMS	MERCAPTOLE
MELOPIANO	MEMORATION	MENINGINA	MENSUAL	MERCATORIAL
MELOPIANOS	MEMORATIVE	MENINGISM	MENSURABLE	MERCATURE
MELOPLAST	MEMORIA	MENINGISMUS	MENSURABLY	MERCE
MELOPLASTIC	MEMORIAL	MENINGITIC	MENSURAL	MERCEMENT
MELOPLASTY	MEMORIALIST	MENINGITIDES	MENSURALIST	MERCENARIAN
MELOPOEIA	MEMORIALIZE	MENINGITIS	MENSURATE	MERCENARIES
MELOPOEIC	MEMORIALIZED	MENINGOCELE	MENSURATION	MERCENARILY
MELOS	MEMORIALIZER	MENINGORRHEA	MENSURATIVE	MERCENARY
MELOTE	MEMORIALIZING	MENINGOSIS	MENT	MERCER
MELOTRAGEDY	MEMORIALLY	MENINTING	MENTA	MERCERESS
MELOTRAGIC	MEMORIED	MENINX	MENTAGRA	MERCERIES
MELOTROPE	MEMORIES	MENISCAL	MENTAL	MERCERIZE
MELPELL	MEMORIOUS	MENISCATE	MENTALIS	MERCERIZED
MELSH	MEMORIST	MENISCI	MENTALISM	MERCERIZER
MELT	MEMORITER	MENISCIFORM	MENTALIST	MERCERIZING
MELTABILITY	MEMORIZATION	MENISCITIS	MENTALISTIC	MERCERY
MELTABLE	MEMORIZE	MENISCOID	MENTALITIES	MERCH
MELTAGE	MEMORIZED	MENISCOIDAL	MENTALITY	MERCHANDISABLE
MELTED	MEMORIZER	MENISCUS	MENTALLY	MERCHANDISE
MELTEIGITE	MEMORIZING	MENISCUSES	MENTATION	MERCHANDISED
MELTER	MEMORY	MENISE	MENTERY	MERCHANDISER
MELTERS	MEMOS	MENISON	MENTHACEOUS	MERCHANDIZE
MELTETH	MEN	MENISPERM	MENTHADIENE	MERCHANDRISE
MELTING	MENACE	MENISPERMIN	MENTHAN	MERCHANDRY
MELTINGLY	MENACED	MENISPERMINE	MENTHANE	MERCHANDY
MELTINGNESS	MENACER	MENKIND	MENTHE	MERCHANT
MELTITH	MENACING	MENNOM	MENTHENE	MERCHANTABLE
MELTON	MENACINGLY	MENNON	MENTHENOL	MERCHANTEER
MELTWATER	MENACME	MENNUET	MENTHENONE	MERCHANTER
MELVIE	MENAGE	MENO	MENTHOL	MERCHANTLIKE
MEM	MENAGERIE	MENOGNATH	MENTHOLATED	MERCHANTLY
MEMBER	MENAGERIST	MENOGNATHOUS	MENTHONE	MERCHANTMAN
MEMBERED	MENALD	MENOLOGIES	MENTHYL	MERCHANTMEN
MEMBERS	MENARCHE	MENOLOGY	MENTICULTURE	MERCHANTRY
MEMBERSHIP	MENAT	MENOMINEE	MENTIFEROUS	MERCHANTSHIP

MERCHET	MERISMOID	MERRILY	MESETHMOID	MESOCRATIC
MERCI	MERIST	MERRIMENT	MESETHMOIDAL	MESODE
MERCIABLE	MERISTELE	MERRINESS	MESH	MESODERM
MERCIABLELY	MERISTEM	MERROW	MESHED	MESODERMAL
MERCIABLY	MERISTEMATIC	MERROWES	MESHING	MESODERMIC
MERCIES	MERISTIC	MERRY	MESHRABIYEH	MESODIC
MERCIFUL	MERISTICALLY	MERRYMAKE	MESHREBEEYEH	MESODONT
MERCIFULLY	MERIT	MERRYMAKER	MESHUGGA	MESOFURCA
MERCIFULNESS	MERITABLE	MERRYMAKING	MESHUMMAD	MESOFURCAL
MERCIFY	MERITED	MERRYMAN	MESHWORK	MESOGASTER
MERCILESS	MERITEDLY	MERRYMEETING	MESHY	MESOGASTRAL
MERCILESSLY	MERITER	MERRYMEN	MESIAD	MESOGASTRIC
MERCILESSNESS	MERITING	MERRYTHOUGHT	MESIAL	MESOGASTRIUM
MERCIMENT	MERITMONGER	MERRYTROTTER	MESIALLY	MESOGLOEA
MERCURATE	MERITMONGERY	MERRYWING	MESIAN	MESOGLOEAL
MERCURATION	MERITORIOUS	MERSE	MESIC	MESOGNATHIC
MERCURIAL	MERITORY	MERSION	MESILLA	MESOGNATHION
MERCURIALISM	MERKHET	MERULIOID	MESIODISTAL	MESOGNATHISM
MERCURIALIST	MERKIN	MERVEILLEUX	MESIOINCISAL	MESOGNATHOUS
MERCURIALITY	MERL	MERWINITE	MESIOLABIAL	MESOGNATHY
MERCURIALIZE	MERLE	MERWOMAN	MESIOLINGUAL	MESOGYRATE
MERCURIALLY	MERLETTE	MERYCISM	MESIOPULPAL	MESOHEPAR
MERCURIATE	MERLIGO	MES	MESITINE	MESOLABE
MERCURIC	MERLIN	MESA	MESITITE	MESOLE
MERCURID	MERLON	MESABITE	MESITYL	MESOLECITHAL
MERCURIDE	MERMAID	MESACONATE	MESITYLENE	MESOLIMNION
MERCURIES	MERMAIDEN	MESACONIC	MESKED	MESOLITE
MERCURIFIED	MERMAN	MESADENIA	MESMERIAN	MESOLITHIC
MERCURIFY	MERMEN	MESAIL	MESMERIC	MESOLOGIC
MERCURIFYING	MERMITHANER	MESAL	MESMERICAL	MESOLOGY
MERCURIZE	MERMITHIZED	MESALLIANCE	MESMERICALLY	MESOMERE
MERCURIZED	MERMITHOGYNE	MESALLY	MESMERISE	MESOMETRAL
MERCURIZING	MERMOTHER	MESAMEBOID	MESMERISM	MESOMETRIC
MERCUROUS	MERO	MESANGE	MESMERIST	MESOMETRIUM
MERCURY	MEROBLASTIC	MESAORTITIS	MESMERITE	MESOMORPH
MERCY	MEROCELE	MESARAIC	MESMERIZATION	MESOMORPHIC
MERD	MEROCELIC	MESARAICAL	MESMERIZE	MESOMORPHOUS
MERDA	MEROCERITE	MESARCH	MESMERIZED	MESOMORPHY
MERDIVOROUS	MEROCERITIC	MESARTERITIC	MESMERIZEE	MESOMYODIAN
MERDURINOUS	MEROCYTE	MESARTERITIS	MESMERIZER	MESOMYODOUS
MERE	MEROGAMY	MESATICEPHAL	MESMERIZING	MESON
MERED	MEROGASTRULA	MESATISKELIC	MESNALITY	MESONASAL
MEREL	MEROGENESIS	MESAXONIC	MESNALTIES	MESONEPHRIC
MERELS	MEROGENETIC	MESCAL	MESNALTY	MESONEPHROS
MERELY	MEROGENIC	MESCALISM	MESNE	MESONOTAL
MERENCHYMA	MEROGNATHITE	MESCHANT	MESO	MESONOTUM
MERESMAN	MEROGONIC	MESCHANTLY	MESOAPPENDIX	MESOPAUSE
MERESMEN	MEROGONY	MESDAMES	MESOARIAL	MESOPETALUM
MEREST	MEROHEDRAL	MESE	MESOARIUM	MESOPHIL
MERESTONE	MEROHEDRIC	MESECTODERM	MESOBAR	MESOPHILE
MERESWINE	MEROHEDRISM	MESEEMS	MESOBENTHOS	MESOPHILIC
MERETRICES	MEROISTIC	MESEL	MESOBLAST	MESOPHILOUS
MERETRICIOUS	MEROMORPHIC	MESELED	MESOBLASTEM	MESOPHRAGMA
MERETRIX	MEROP	MESELEDNESS	MESOBLASTEMA	MESOPHRAGMAL
MERFOLD	MEROPIA	MESELRY	MESOBLASTIC	MESOPHRYON
MERFOLK	MEROPIC	MESELY	MESOBREGMATE	MESOPHYL
MERGANSER	MEROPIDAN	MESEM	MESOCAECAL	MESOPHYLL
MERGE	MEROPLANKTON	MESEMBRYO	MESOCAECUM	MESOPHYLLUM
MERGED	MEROPODITE	MESEMBRYONIC	MESOCARDIA	MESOPHYTE
MERGENCE	MEROPODITIC	MESENCHYMA	MESOCARDIUM	MESOPHYTIC
MERGER	MERORGANIZE	MESENCHYMAL	MESOCARP	MESOPHYTISM
MERGH	MEROS	MESENCHYME	MESOCENTROUS	MESOPIC
MERGING	MEROSOMAL	MESENDODERM	MESOCEPHAL	MESOPLANKTON
MERIAH	MEROSOMATOUS	MESENNA	MESOCEPHALIC	MESOPLAST
MERICARP	MEROSOME	MESENTERA	MESOCEPHALON	MESOPLASTIC
MERICE	MEROSTHENIC	MESENTERIAL	MESOCEPHALOUS	MESOPLASTRA
MERIDIAN	MEROSTOME	MESENTERIC	MESOCEPHALY	MESOPLASTRAL
MERIDIONAL	MEROTOMIZE	MESENTERICAL	MESOCHILIUM	MESOPLASTRON
MERIDIONALLY	MEROTOMY	MESENTERIES	MESOCHROIC	MESOPLEURA
MERINGUE	MEROTROPISM	MESENTERITIC	MESOCOELE	MESOPLEURAL
MERINGUED	MEROTROPY	MESENTERITIS	MESOCOELIA	MESOPLEURON
MERINO	MEROXENE	MESENTERIUM	MESOCOELIAN	MESOPLODONT
MERINOS	MEROZOITE	MESENTERON	MESOCOELIC	MESOPODIA
MERIQUINONE	MERPEOPLE	MESENTERONIC	MESOCOLIC	MESOPODIAL
MERIQUINONIC	MERRIER	MESENTERY	MESOCOLON	MESOPODIALE
MERISM	MERRIEST	MESEPIMERAL	MESOCORACOID	MESOPODIALIA
MERISMATIC	MERRILESS	MESEPIMERON	MESOCRANIAL	MESOPODIUM

MESOPOTAMIA	MESSAGE	METACHEMIC	METALLICS	METAPHRAGM
MESOPROSOPIC	MESSAGED	METACHEMICAL	METALLIDE	METAPHRAGMA
MESORCHIAL	MESSAGERY	METACHEMISTRY	METALLIFORM	METAPHRAGMAL
MESORCHIUM	MESSAGING	METACHROME	METALLIFY	METAPHRASE
MESORECTAL	MESSALINE	METACHRONISM	METALLIK	METAPHRASED
MESORECTUM	MESSAN	METACHROSIS	METALLINE	METAPHRASING
MESORHIN	MESSE	METACISM	METALLING	METAPHRAST
MESORHINAL	MESSED	METACLASE	METALLISH	METAPHRASTIC
MESORHINE	MESSELITE	METACNEME	METALLIST	METAPHYSEAL
MESORHINIAN	MESSENGER	METACOELE	METALLIZATION	METAPHYSIC
MESORHINISM	MESSER	METACONAL	METALLIZE	METAPHYSICAL
MESORHINIUM	MESSET	METACONE	METALLOGENIC	METAPHYSICALLY
MESORHINY	MESSIER	METACONID	METALLOGENY	METAPHYSICIAN
MESORRHIN	MESSIEST	METACONULE	METALLOGRAPH	METAPHYSICIST
MESORRHINAL	MESSIEURS	METACORACOID	METALLOID	METAPHYSICS
MESORRHINIAN	MESSILY	METACRASIS	METALLOIDAL	METAPHYSIS
MESORRHINISM	MESSIN	METACROMIAL	METALLOMETER	METAPHYTE
MESORRHINIUM	MESSINESS	METACROMION	METALLOPHONE	METAPLASIA
MESORRHINY	MESSING	METACRYST	METALLURGIC	METAPLASIS
MESOSALPINX	MESSIRE	METACYCLIC	METALLURGICAL	METAPLASM
MESOSAUR	MESSMAN	METAD	METALLURGIST	METAPLASMIC
MESOSCAPULA	MESSMATE	METADROMOUS	METALLURGY	METAPLAST
MESOSCAPULAR	MESSMEN	METAE	METALOGIC	METAPLASTIC
MESOSCUTAL	MESSOR	METAFLUIDAL	METALOGICAL	METAPLEUR
MESOSCUTUM	MESSROOM	METAGALACTIC	METALOPH	METAPLEURA
MESOSEISMAL	MESSTIN	METAGALAXIES	METALORGANIC	METAPLEURAL
MESOSEME	MESSUAGE	METAGALAXY	METALOSCOPE	METAPLEURE
MESOSIGMOID	MESSY	METAGASTER	METALOSCOPY	METAPLEURON
MESOSOMA	MESTA	METAGASTRIC	METALS	METAPNEUSTIC
MESOSOMATA	MESTEE	METAGASTRULA	METALUMINATE	METAPODIA
MESOSOMATIC	MESTENO	METAGE	METALWARE	METAPODIAL
MESOSPERM	MESTESO	METAGELATIN	METALWORK	METAPODIALE
MESOSPHERE	MESTFULL	METAGELATINE	METALWORKER	METAPODIUM
MESOSPHERIC	MESTINO	METAGENESIS	METALWORKING	METAPOLITIC
MESOSPORE	MESTIZA	METAGENETIC	METALWORKS	METAPOLITICAL
MESOSPORIC	MESTIZO	METAGENIC	METAMER	METAPOLITICIAN
MESOSTASIS	MESTIZOES	METAGEOMETER	METAMERAL	METAPOLITICS
MESOSTERNA	MESTIZOS	METAGEOMETRY	METAMERE	METAPOPHYSIS
MESOSTERNAL	MESTLEN	METAGNATH	METAMERIC	METAPORE
MESOSTERNUM	MESTO	METAGNATHISM	METAMERIDE	METAPROTEIN
MESOSTETHIUM	MESTOME	METAGNATHOUS	METAMERISM	METAPSYCHIC
MESOSTOMID	MESYMNION	METAGNOMY	METAMERIZED	METAPSYCHICAL
MESOSTYLOUS	MET	METAGNOSTIC	METAMEROUS	METAPSYCHICS
MESOSUCHIAN	META	METAGRAM	METAMERY	METAPSYCHISM
MESOTARSAL	METABASES	METAGRAPHIC	METAMORPHIC	METAPSYCHIST
MESOTHELIAL	METABASIS	METAGRAPHY	METAMORPHISM	METAPSYCHOLOGY
MESOTHELIUM	METABASITE	METAIGNEOUS	METAMORPHIZE	METAROSSITE
MESOTHERM	METABATIC	METAIRIE	METAMORPHOSE	METASCUTUM
MESOTHERMAL	METABIOLOGICAL	METAKINESIS	METAMORPHOSED	METASOMA
MESOTHESIS	METABIOLOGY	METAKINETIC	METAMORPHOSING	METASOMASIS
MESOTHETIC	METABIOSIS	METAL	METAMORPHOSIS	METASOMATA
MESOTHETICAL	METABIOTIC	METALCRAFT	METAMORPHOSY	METASOMATIC
MESOTHORACIC	METABLETIC	METALDEHYDE	METAMORPHOUS	METASOMATISM
MESOTHORAX	METABOLE	METALED	METAMORPHY	METASPERM
MESOTHORIUM	METABOLIAN	METALEPSES	METANALYSIS	METASPERMIC
MESOTONIC	METABOLIC	METALEPSIS	METANAUPLIUS	METASPERMOUS
MESOTROCH	METABOLICAL	METALEPTIC	METANEPHRIC	METASTABLE
MESOTROCHA	METABOLISM	METALEPTICAL	METANEPHRITIC	METASTANNATE
MESOTROCHAL	METABOLITE	METALER	METANEPHRON	METASTASES
MESOTROCHOUS	METABOLIZE	METALINE	METANEPHROS	METASTASIS
MESOTRON	METABOLIZED	METALINED	METANEPIONIC	METASTASIZE
MESOTROPIC	METABOLIZING	METALING	METANILINE	METASTASIZED
MESOTYPE	METABOLON	METALISE	METANOMEN	METASTATIC
MESOVARIA	METABOLOUS	METALIST	METANOTAL	METASTATICAL
MESOVARIAN	METABOLY	METALIZATION	METANOTUM	METASTATICALLY
MESOVARIUM	METABORATE	METALIZE	METANYM	METASTERNAL
MESOVENTRAL	METABORIC	METALIZED	METAPEPTONE	METASTERNUM
MESOVENTRALLY	METABRANCHIAL	METALIZING	METAPHASE	METASTHENIC
MESOXALATE	METABRUSHITE	METALLARY	METAPHLOEM	METASTIBNITE
MESOXALIC	METABULAR	METALLED	METAPHONICAL	METASTOMA
MESOXALYL	METACARPAL	METALLEITY	METAPHONIZE	METASTOMATA
MESOZOAN	METACARPALE	METALLER	METAPHONY	METASTROPHE
MESPIL	METACARPUS	METALLIC	METAPHOR	METASTROPHIC
MESQUIN	METACENTER	METALLICAL	METAPHORIC	METATARSAL
MESQUITA	METACENTRAL	METALLICALLY	METAPHORICAL	METATARSALE
MESQUITE	METACENTRE	METALLICITY	METAPHORICALLY	METATARSE
MESS	METACENTRIC	METALLICLY	METAPHORIST	METATARSI

METATARSUS
METATATIC
METATATICAL
METATAXIC
METATAXIS
METATE
METATHALAMUS
METATHESES
METATHESIS
METATHETIC
METATHETICAL
METATHORACIC
METATHORAX
METATHORAXES
METATITANATE
METATROPHIC
METATYPE
METATYPIC
METAVANADATE
METAVAUXITE
METAVOLTINE
METAXITE
METAXYLEM
METAYAGE
METAYER
METAZOAL
METAZOAN
METAZOEA
METAZOIC
METAZOON
METE
METED
METEL
METEMPIRIC
METEMPIRICAL
METEMPIRICS
METEMPSYCHIC
METEMPSYCHOSIS
METEMPTOSIS
METENTERON
METENTERONIC
METEOR
METEORGRAPH
METEORIC
METEORICAL
METEORICALLY
METEORISM
METEORIST
METEORISTIC
METEORITAL
METEORITE
METEORITICS
METEORIZE
METEORLIKE
METEOROGRAM
METEOROGRAPH
METEOROID
METEOROIDAL
METEOROLITE
METEOROLITIC
METEOROLOGIC
METEOROLOGICAL
METEOROLOGICALLY
METEOROLOGIST
METEOROLOGY
METEOROMETER
METEOROSCOPY
METEOROUS
METEORSCOPE
METEPIMERON
METER
METERAGE
METERED
METERER
METERGRAM
METERING
METERMAN

METESTICK
METEWAND
METEYARD
METHACRYLATE
METHACRYLIC
METHADONE
METHANAL
METHANATE
METHANATED
METHANATING
METHANE
METHANOIC
METHANOL
METHANOMETER
METHE
METHEGLIN
METHENAMINE
METHENE
METHENYL
METHER
METHIDE
METHINE
METHINKS
METHIODIDE
METHIONIC
METHIONINE
METHOD
METHODIC
METHODICAL
METHODICALLY
METHODICALNESS
METHODICS
METHODISM
METHODIST
METHODIZE
METHODIZED
METHODIZER
METHODIZING
METHODLESS
METHODOLOGICAL
METHODOLOGICALLY
METHODOLOGIST
METHODOLOGY
METHODS
METHONE
METHOUGHT
METHOXY
METHOXYL
METHRONIC
METHYL
METHYLAL
METHYLAMINE
METHYLATE
METHYLATED
METHYLATING
METHYLATION
METHYLATOR
METHYLENE
METHYLENITAN
METHYLIC
METHYLOSIS
METHYLOTIC
METIC
METICULOSITY
METICULOUS
METICULOUSLY
METIER
METIF
METING
METIS
METISSE
METOCHOUS
METOCHY
METOESTROUS
METOESTRUM
METONYM
METONYMIC

METONYMICAL
METONYMOUS
METONYMOUSLY
METONYMY
METOPE
METOPIC
METOPION
METOPISM
METOPOMANCY
METOPON
METOPOSCOPIC
METOPOSCOPY
METORGANISM
METOSTEAL
METOSTEON
METRA
METRALGIA
METRAN
METRANEMIA
METRATONIA
METRAZOL
METRE
METRECTASIA
METRECTATIC
METRECTOMY
METRECTOPIA
METRECTOPIC
METRECTOPY
METREGRAM
METREME
METRETA
METRETES
METREZA
METRIA
METRIC
METRICAL
METRICALLY
METRICIAN
METRICISM
METRICIST
METRICIZE
METRICS
METRIFIED
METRIFIER
METRIFY
METRIFYING
METRIST
METRITIS
METRO
METROLOGICAL
METROLOGIST
METROLOGUE
METROLOGY
METROMANIA
METROMANIAC
METRONOME
METRONOMIC
METRONOMICAL
METRONYM
METRONYMIC
METRONYMY
METROPOLE
METROPOLEIS
METROPOLIC
METROPOLIS
METROPOLISES
METROPOLITAN
METROPOLITE
METRORRHAGIA
METRORRHAGIC
METRORTHOSIS
METROSTYLE
METTAR
METTLE
METTLED
METTLESOME
METTLESOMELY

METUMP
METUSIA
METWAND
METZE
MEUBLES
MEUM
MEURE
MEUSE
MEUTE
MEW
MEWED
MEWER
MEWING
MEWL
MEWLED
MEWLER
MEWLING
MEWS
MEXICAL
MEZCAL
MEZCALINE
MEZEREON
MEZEREUM
MEZQUIT
MEZQUITE
MEZUZA
MEZUZAH
MEZUZAHS
MEZUZOTH
MEZZA
MEZZANINE
MEZZO
MEZZOGRAPH
MEZZOS
MEZZOTINT
MEZZOTINTED
MEZZOTINTER
MEZZOTINTING
MEZZOTINTO
MHO
MHOMETER
MHORR
MI
MIAMIA
MIAN
MIANG
MIAOU
MIAOW
MIAOWER
MIARGYRITE
MIAROLITIC
MIAS
MIASCITE
MIASKITE
MIASM
MIASMA
MIASMAL
MIASMAS
MIASMATA
MIASMATIC
MIASMATICAL
MIASMATOLOGY
MIASMATOUS
MIASMIC
MIASMOLOGY
MIASMOUS
MIAUER
MIAUL
MIAULED
MIAULER
MIAULING
MIAUW
MIB
MICA
MICACEOUS
MICACIOUS
MICACITE

MICASIZATION
MICASIZE
MICATE
MICATION
MICE
MICELL
MICELLA
MICELLAR
MICELLE
MICH
MICHE
MICHED
MICHER
MICHERY
MICHING
MICK
MICKERY
MICKEY
MICKEYS
MICKLE
MICKLENESS
MICO
MICONCAVE
MICRA
MICRACOUSTIC
MICRAESTHETE
MICRAMOCK
MICRANDER
MICRANDROUS
MICRANER
MICRESTHETE
MICRIFIED
MICRIFY
MICRIFYING
MICRO
MICROAMMETER
MICROANALYSIS
MICROANALYST
MICROBAL
MICROBALANCE
MICROBATTERY
MICROBE
MICROBEPROOF
MICROBIAL
MICROBIAN
MICROBIC
MICROBICIDE
MICROBIOSIS
MICROBIOTA
MICROBIOTIC
MICROBIOUS
MICROBISM
MICROBOTANY
MICROBURNER
MICROCARPOUS
MICROCENTRUM
MICROCEPHAL
MICROCEPHALI
MICROCEPHALY
MICROCHAETA
MICROCHAETAE
MICROCIRCUIT
MICROCLASTIC
MICROCLIMATE
MICROCLINE
MICROCOAT
MICROCOCCAL
MICROCOCCI
MICROCOCCUS
MICROCOPIED
MICROCOPIES
MICROCOPY
MICROCOPYING
MICROCOSM
MICROCOSMAL
MICROCOSMIAN
MICROCOSMIC

MICROCOSMOS	MICROPIPET	MICRURGICAL	MIDTARSAL	MIKE
MICROCRANOUS	MICROPIPETTE	MICRURGIST	MIDTERM	MIKER
MICROCRITH	MICROPLAKITE	MICRURGY	MIDTOWN	MIKRA
MICROCYST	MICROPODAL	MICTION	MIDVEIN	MIKRON
MICROCYTE	MICROPODOUS	MICTURATE	MIDVENTRAL	MIKVAH
MICROCYTOSIS	MICROPORE	MICTURATED	MIDWARD	MIL
MICRODONT	MICROPRINT	MICTURATING	MIDWATCH	MILA
MICRODONTISM	MICROPSIA	MICTURITION	MIDWAY	MILACRE
MICRODONTOUS	MICROPSY	MID	MIDWEEK	MILADI
MICRODRAWING	MICROPTERISM	MIDAFTERNOON	MIDWEEKLY	MILADIES
MICRODRIVE	MICROPTEROUS	MIDAIR	MIDWIFE	MILADY
MICROFELSITE	MICROPYLAR	MIDBRAIN	MIDWIFED	MILAGE
MICROFICHE	MICROPYLE	MIDCARPAL	MIDWIFERY	MILAN
MICROFILARIA	MICRORHABDUS	MIDDAY	MIDWIFING	MILARITE
MICROFILM	MICROSAURIAN	MIDDEN	MIDWINTER	MILCH
MICROFLUIDAL	MICROSCLERE	MIDDENSTEAD	MIDWINTERLY	MILCHER
MICROFORM	MICROSCLEROUS	MIDDES	MIDWINTRY	MILCHIGS
MICROGAMETE	MICROSCLERUM	MIDDIES	MIDWISE	MILCHY
MICROGAMY	MICROSCOPE	MIDDLE	MIDWIVED	MILD
MICROGLIA	MICROSCOPIC	MIDDLEBROW	MIDWIVES	MILDEN
MICROGRAM	MICROSCOPICAL	MIDDLECLASS	MIDWIVING	MILDENED
MICROGRAMME	MICROSCOPICS	MIDDLED	MIDYEAR	MILDENING
MICROGRANITE	MICROSCOPIST	MIDDLELAND	MIEN	MILDER
MICROGRAPH	MICROSCOPIZE	MIDDLEMAN	MIERSITE	MILDEST
MICROGRAPHER	MICROSCOPY	MIDDLEMEN	MIFF	MILDEW
MICROGRAPHIC	MICROSECOND	MIDDLEMOST	MIFFED	MILDEWER
MICROGRAPHY	MICROSEISM	MIDDLER	MIFFIER	MILDEWY
MICROGRAVER	MICROSEISMIC	MIDDLES	MIFFIEST	MILDFUL
MICROGROOVE	MICROSEPTUM	MIDDLETONE	MIFFINESS	MILDFULNESS
MICROHMMETER	MICROSMATIC	MIDDLEWAY	MIFFY	MILDHEARTED
MICROINCH	MICROSMATISM	MIDDLEWEIGHT	MIG	MILDLY
MICROLEVEL	MICROSOMA	MIDDLEWOMAN	MIGALE	MILDNESS
MICROLITE	MICROSOME	MIDDLEWOMEN	MIGGLE	MILE
MICROLITH	MICROSOMMITE	MIDDLING	MIGGLES	MILEAGE
MICROLITHIC	MICROSPECIES	MIDDLINGLY	MIGHT	MILEPOST
MICROLITIC	MICROSPHERE	MIDDLINGNESS	MIGHTED	MILER
MICROLOGIC	MICROSPHERIC	MIDDY	MIGHTFUL	MILES
MICROLOGICAL	MICROSPORE	MIDE	MIGHTFULLY	MILESIMA
MICROLOGUE	MICROSPORIC	MIDEWIN	MIGHTFULNESS	MILESTONE
MICROLOGY	MICROSPOROUS	MIDEWIWIN	MIGHTIER	MILEWAY
MICROMANIA	MICROSTAT	MIDGE	MIGHTIEST	MILFOIL
MICROMANIAC	MICROSTHENE	MIDGET	MIGHTILY	MILHA
MICROMELIA	MICROSTOME	MIDGETY	MIGHTINESS	MILIA
MICROMELIC	MICROSTOMOUS	MIDGUT	MIGHTLESS	MILIACEOUS
MICROMELUS	MICROSTYLOUS	MIDGY	MIGHTLY	MILIARENSES
MICROMERAL	MICROTECHNIC	MIDHEAVEN	MIGHTS	MILIARENSIS
MICROMERE	MICROTHEOS	MIDINETTE	MIGHTY	MILIARIA
MICROMERIC	MICROTHERM	MIDIRON	MIGLIO	MILIARIUM
MICROMERISM	MICROTHERMIC	MIDLAND	MIGMATITE	MILIARY
MICROMERITIC	MICROTHORAX	MIDMAIN	MIGNIARD	MILICE
MICROMETER	MICROTIA	MIDMORN	MIGNIARDISE	MILIÉU
MICROMETHOD	MICROTOME	MIDMOST	MIGNIARDIZE	MILIOLIFORM
MICROMETRIC	MICROTOMIC	MIDNIGHT	MIGNON	MILIOLINE
MICROMETRY	MICROTOMICAL	MIDNIGHTLY	MIGNONETTE	MILIOLITE
MICROMHO	MICROTOMIST	MIDNOON	MIGNONNE	MILIOLITIC
MICROMICRON	MICROTOMY	MIDPARENT	MIGRAINE	MILITANCY
MICROMODULE	MICROTONE	MIDPARENTAGE	MIGRAINOID	MILITANT
MICROMOTION	MICROTYPAL	MIDPARENTAL	MIGRAINOUS	MILITANTLY
MICRON	MICROTYPE	MIDPOINT	MIGRANS	MILITANTNESS
MICRONOMETER	MICROTYPICAL	MIDRASH	MIGRANT	MILITAR
MICRONUCLEAR	MICROVOLUME	MIDRASHIC	MIGRATE	MILITARILY
MICRONUCLEI	MICROWATT	MIDRASHIM	MIGRATED	MILITARISM
MICRONUCLEUS	MICROWAVE	MIDRASHOTH	MIGRATING	MILITARIST
MICROORGANIC	MICROZOA	MIDRIB	MIGRATION	MILITARISTIC
MICROORGANISM	MICROZOAL	MIDRIBBED	MIGRATIONAL	MILITARISTICAL
MICROORGANISMS	MICROZOAN	MIDRIFF	MIGRATIONIST	MILITARIZATION
MICROPHAGE	MICROZOARIA	MIDS	MIGRATIVE	MILITARIZE
MICROPHAGOUS	MICROZOARIAN	MIDSHIP	MIGRATOR	MILITARIZED
MICROPHAGY	MICROZOARY	MIDSHIPMAN	MIGRATORIAL	MILITARIZING
MICROPHONE	MICROZOIC	MIDSHIPMEN	MIGRATORY	MILITARY
MICROPHONIC	MICROZONE	MIDSHIPMITE	MIHARAITE	MILITARYISM
MICROPHONICS	MICROZOOID	MIDSHIPS	MIHRAB	MILITARYMENT
MICROPHYSICS	MICROZOON	MIDST	MIJAKITE	MILITASTER
MICROPHYTAL	MICROZYMA	MIDSTEAD	MIJNHEER	MILITATE
MICROPHYTE	MICROZYME	MIDSTYLED	MIKADO	MILITATED
MICROPHYTIC	MICROZYMIAN	MIDSUMMER	MIKADOATE	MILITATING
MICROPIN	MICRURGIC	MIDSUMMERY	MIKADOS	MILITATION

MILITIA
MILITIAMAN
MILITIAMEN
MILITIATE
MILIUM
MILJEE
MILK
MILKBUSH
MILKED
MILKEN
MILKER
MILKERESS
MILKFISH
MILKFISHES
MILKGRASS
MILKIER
MILKIEST
MILKILY
MILKINESS
MILKING
MILKLESS
MILKMAID
MILKMAN
MILKMEN
MILKNESS
MILKSHED
MILKSICK
MILKSOP
MILKSOPPING
MILKSOPPISH
MILKSOPPY
MILKSTONE
MILKTOAST
MILKWEED
MILKWOOD
MILKWORT
MILKY
MILL
MILLA
MILLAGE
MILLANARE
MILLBOARD
MILLCLAPPER
MILLCOURSE
MILLDAM
MILLDOLL
MILLE
MILLED
MILLEFIORE
MILLEFIORI
MILLEFLEURS
MILLEFLOROUS
MILLEFOLIATE
MILLENARIAN
MILLENARIES
MILLENARIST
MILLENARY
MILLENIUM
MILLENNIA
MILLENNIAL
MILLENNIALLY
MILLENNIAN
MILLENNIARY
MILLENNIUMS
MILLEPED
MILLEPEDE
MILLEPORE
MILLEPORINE
MILLEPORITE
MILLEPOROUS
MILLER
MILLERESS
MILLERING
MILLERITE
MILLESIMAL
MILLET
MILLFEED

MILLHOUSE
MILLIAD
MILLIAMMETER
MILLIAMPERE
MILLIARD
MILLIARDAIRE
MILLIARY
MILLIBAR
MILLICRON
MILLICURIE
MILLIEME
MILLIER
MILLIFARAD
MILLIFOLD
MILLIFORM
MILLIGRADE
MILLIGRAM
MILLIGRAMAGE
MILLIGRAMME
MILLIHENRY
MILLILAMBERT
MILLILE
MILLILITER
MILLILITRE
MILLILUX
MILLIMETER
MILLIMETRE
MILLIMICRON
MILLIMOL
MILLIMOLAR
MILLIMOLE
MILLINCOST
MILLINE
MILLINER
MILLINERIAL
MILLINERING
MILLINERY
MILLING
MILLINORMAL
MILLIOCTAVE
MILLIOERSTED
MILLION
MILLIONAIRE
MILLIONAIRESS
MILLIONARY
MILLIONED
MILLIONER
MILLIONFOLD
MILLIONISM
MILLIONIST
MILLIONIZE
MILLIONNAIRE
MILLIONS
MILLIONTH
MILLIPED
MILLIPEDE
MILLIPHOT
MILLIPOISE
MILLISECOND
MILLISTERE
MILLITHRUM
MILLIVOLT
MILLIWATT
MILLIWEBER
MILLKEN
MILLMAN
MILLMEN
MILLOCRACY
MILLOCRAT
MILLOCRATISM
MILLOWNER
MILLPOND
MILLPOOL
MILLPOST
MILLRACE
MILLRIND
MILLRYND

MILLS
MILLSITE
MILLSTOCK
MILLSTONE
MILLSTONES
MILLSTREAM
MILLTAIL
MILLWARD
MILLWORK
MILLWORKER
MILLWRIGHT
MILLY
MILN
MILNER
MILO
MILORD
MILPA
MILQUETOAST
MILREIS
MILRIND
MILSEY
MILSIE
MILT
MILTED
MILTER
MILTING
MILTSICK
MILTY
MILVINE
MILVINOUS
MILWELL
MIM
MIMA
MIMAE
MIMAMSA
MIMBAR
MIMBLE
MIME
MIMED
MIMEOGRAPH
MIMEOGRAPHED
MIMEOGRAPHIC
MIMEOGRAPHING
MIMER
MIMESIS
MIMESTER
MIMETENE
MIMETESITE
MIMETIC
MIMETICALLY
MIMETISM
MIMETITE
MIMIAMBI
MIMIAMBIC
MIMIAMBICS
MIMIC
MIMICAL
MIMICALLY
MIMICISM
MIMICKED
MIMICKER
MIMICKING
MIMICRIES
MIMICRY
MIMINE
MIMING
MIMINYPIMINY
MIMMATION
MIMMED
MIMMING
MIMMOCK
MIMMOCKING
MIMMOCKY
MIMMOUTHED
MIMODRAMA
MIMOGRAPHER
MIMOGRAPHY

MIMOLOGIST
MIMOSA
MIMOSACEOUS
MIMOSITE
MIMOTYPE
MIMOTYPIC
MIMP
MIMSEY
MIMZY
MIN
MINA
MINACIOUS
MINACIOUSLY
MINACIOUSNESS
MINACITY
MINAE
MINAL
MINAR
MINARET
MINARETED
MINARGENT
MINAS
MINASRAGRITE
MINATORIAL
MINATORIALLY
MINATORIES
MINATORILY
MINATORY
MINAUDERIE
MINAWAY
MINBAR
MINBU
MINCE
MINCED
MINCEMEAT
MINCER
MINCHAH
MINCHEN
MINCHERY
MINCHIATE
MINCING
MINCINGLY
MINCINGNESS
MINCIO
MIND
MINDED
MINDEDNESS
MINDER
MINDFUL
MINDFULLY
MINDFULNESS
MINDING
MINDLESS
MINDLESSLY
MINDLESSNESS
MINDLY
MINDSIGHT
MINE
MINED
MINEFIELD
MINELAYER
MINEOWNER
MINER
MINERAL
MINERALIZATION
MINERALIZE
MINERALIZED
MINERALIZER
MINERALIZING
MINERALOGIC
MINERALOGIES
MINERALOGIST
MINERALOGIZE
MINERALOGY
MINERALS
MINERS
MINERVAL

MINERY
MINES
MINESTRA
MINESTRONE
MINESWEEPER
MINETTE
MINEWORKER
MING
MINGE
MINGIE
MINGLE
MINGLED
MINGLER
MINGLING
MINGUETITE
MINGWORT
MINGY
MINHAG
MINHAH
MINIACEOUS
MINIATE
MINIATED
MINIATING
MINIATOR
MINIATOUS
MINIATURE
MINIATURED
MINIATURING
MINIATURIST
MINIATURIZE
MINIATURIZED
MINIBUS
MINICAM
MINIFICATION
MINIFIED
MINIFY
MINIFYING
MINIKEN
MINIKIN
MINIKINLY
MINIM
MINIMA
MINIMACID
MINIMAL
MINIMALIST
MINIMALLY
MINIMETRIC
MINIMI
MINIMIFIDIAN
MINIMISE
MINIMISM
MINIMISTIC
MINIMIZATION
MINIMIZE
MINIMIZED
MINIMIZER
MINIMIZING
MINIMUM
MINIMUMS
MINIMUS
MINIMUSCULAR
MINING
MINION
MINIONETTE
MINIONLY
MINISH
MINISHED
MINISHER
MINISHING
MINISHMENT
MINISKIRT
MINISTER
MINISTERED
MINISTERIAL
MINISTERING
MINISTERIUM
MINISTERSHIP

MINISTRABLE	MINX	MIRYACHIT	MISCASTING	MISDEAL
MINISTRANT	MINXES	MIRZA	MISCASUALTY	MISDEALER
MINISTRATE	MINY	MIS	MISCE	MISDEALING
MINISTRATION	MINYAN	MISACCEPT	MISCEABILITY	MISDEALT
MINISTRATIVE	MIOCARDIA	MISACCEPTION	MISCEGENATE	MISDEED
MINISTRATOR	MIOMBO	MISADVENTURE	MISCEGENATION	MISDEEM
MINISTRER	MIOPLASMIA	MISADVISE	MISCEGENATOR	MISDEEMED
MINISTRIES	MIOSIS	MISADVISED	MISCEGENETIC	MISDEEMFUL
MINISTRY	MIOTHERMIC	MISADVISEDLY	MISCEGENIST	MISDEEMING
MINITANT	MIOTIC	MISADVISING	MISCEGINE	MISDEMEAN
MINITRACK	MIQRA	MISAFFECT	MISCELLANE	MISDEMEANANT
MINIUM	MIQUELET	MISALLIANCE	MISCELLANEA	MISDEMEANED
MINIVER	MIR	MISALLIED	MISCELLANEAL	MISDEMEANING
MINIVET	MIRABILIA	MISALLY	MISCELLANEOUS	MISDEMEANIST
MINK	MIRABILIARY	MISALLYING	MISCELLANIES	MISDEMEANOR
MINKERY	MIRABILITE	MISANDRY	MISCELLANIST	MISDEMEANOUR
MINKS	MIRABLE	MISANTHROPE	MISCELLANY	MISDERIVE
MINNESINGER	MIRAC	MISANTHROPI	MISCHANCE	MISDERIVED
MINNESONG	MIRACH	MISANTHROPIC	MISCHANCY	MISDERIVING
MINNIE	MIRACIDIUM	MISANTHROPOS	MISCHIEF	MISDESCRIBE
MINNIEBUSH	MIRACLE	MISANTHROPY	MISCHIEFFUL	MISDESCRIBED
MINNING	MIRACLED	MISAPPLIED	MISCHIEVE	MISDESCRIBER
MINNOW	MIRACLING	MISAPPLIER	MISCHIEVOUS	MISDESERT
MINNOWS	MIRACLIST	MISAPPLY	MISCHIEVOUSLY	MISDESERVE
MINNY	MIRACULAR	MISAPPLYING	MISCHIEVOUSNESS	MISDID
MINO	MIRACULIST	MISAPPREHEND	MISCHIO	MISDIRECT
MINOIZE	MIRACULIZE	MISAPPREHENSION	MISCHOICE	MISDIRECTED
MINOR	MIRACULOSITY	MISAPPREHENSIVE	MISCHOOSE	MISDIRECTING
MINORAGE	MIRACULOUS	MISARCHISM	MISCHOOSING	MISDIRECTION
MINORATE	MIRACULOUSLY	MISARCHIST	MISCHOSE	MISDIVISION
MINORATION	MIRADOR	MISARRANGE	MISCHOSEN	MISDO
MINORESS	MIRAGE	MISARRANGED	MISCIBILITY	MISDOER
MINORITY	MIRAGY	MISARRANGEMENT	MISCIBLE	MISDOING
MINOT	MIRANDOUS	MISARRANGING	MISCOGNIZANT	MISDONE
MINSITIVE	MIRATE	MISATTEND	MISCOLOR	MISDOUBT
MINSTER	MIRCROBICIDAL	MISAUNTER	MISCOLOUR	MISDOUBTED
MINSTERYARD	MIRD	MISBAPTIZE	MISCONCEIVE	MISDOUBTING
MINSTREL	MIRDAHA	MISBEAR	MISCONCEIVED	MISDREAD
MINSTRELESS	MIRDHA	MISBECAME	MISCONCEIVER	MISE
MINSTRELSY	MIRE	MISBECOME	MISCONCEIVING	MISEASE
MINT	MIRED	MISBECOMING	MISCONCEPTION	MISEASED
MINTAGE	MIREPOIS	MISBEDE	MISCONDUCT	MISEMPHASIS
MINTBUSH	MIREPOIX	MISBEFALL	MISCONDUCTED	MISEMPHASIZE
MINTED	MIRESNIPE	MISBEFALLEN	MISCONDUCTING	MISEMPLOY
MINTER	MIRID	MISBEGET	MISCONSTRUCT	MISEMPLOYED
MINTING	MIRIER	MISBEGOT	MISCONSTRUCTIO	MISEMPLOYING
MINTMAN	MIRIEST	MISBEGOTTEN	MISCONSTRUE	MISENITE
MINTMASTER	MIRIFIC	MISBEHAVE	MISCONSTRUED	MISENTREAT
MINTWEED	MIRIFICAL	MISBEHAVED	MISCONSTRUER	MISER
MINTY	MIRIKI	MISBEHAVING	MISCONVEY	MISERABILISM
MINUEND	MIRING	MISBEHAVIOR	MISCORRECT	MISERABILIST
MINUET	MIRISH	MISBEHAVIOUR	MISCORRECTED	MISERABILITY
MINUETIC	MIRK	MISBEHOLDEN	MISCORRECTING	MISERABLE
MINUETISH	MIRKILY	MISBELIEF	MISCOUNSEL	MISERABLY
MINUS	MIRKINESS	MISBELIEVE	MISCOUNSELED	MISERE
MINUSCULAR	MIRKISH	MISBELIEVED	MISCOUNSELING	MISERERE
MINUSCULE	MIRKLY	MISBELIEVER	MISCOUNSELLED	MISERICORD
MINUTARY	MIRKNESS	MISBELIEVING	MISCOUNSELLING	MISERICORDE
MINUTATION	MIRKSOME	MISBIRTH	MISCOUNT	MISERICORDIA
MINUTE	MIRKY	MISBODE	MISCREANCE	MISERIES
MINUTED	MIRLED	MISBORN	MISCREANCY	MISERISM
MINUTELY	MIRLIGO	MISBRAND	MISCREANT	MISERLINESS
MINUTEMAN	MIRLITON	MISCAL	MISCREATE	MISERLY
MINUTEMEN	MIRLY	MISCALCULATE	MISCREATED	MISERY
MINUTENESS	MIRO	MISCALCULATED	MISCREATING	MISES
MINUTER	MIRROR	MISCALCULATING	MISCREATION	MISESTEEM
MINUTES	MIRRORED	MISCALCULATION	MISCREATIVE	MISESTEEMED
MINUTHESIS	MIRRORING	MISCALCULATOR	MISCREATOR	MISESTEEMING
MINUTIA	MIRRORSCOPE	MISCALL	MISCREED	MISESTIMATE
MINUTIAE	MIRRORY	MISCALLED	MISCROP	MISESTIMATED
MINUTIAL	MIRTH	MISCALLER	MISCUE	MISFAITH
MINUTING	MIRTHFUL	MISCALLING	MISCUED	MISFALL
MINUTIOSE	MIRTHFULLY	MISCARRIAGE	MISCUING	MISFARE
MINUTIOUS	MIRTHFULNESS	MISCARRIED	MISDATE	MISFATE
MINUTIOUSLY	MIRTHLESS	MISCARRY	MISDATED	MISFEASANCE
MINUTISSIMIC	MIRTHLESSLY	MISCARRYING	MISDATEFUL	MISFEASOR
MINVERITE	MIRY	MISCAST	MISDATING	MISFEATURE

MISFEIGN
MISFIELD
MISFIGURE
MISFIRE
MISFIRED
MISFIRING
MISFIT
MISFITTED
MISFITTING
MISFORGIVE
MISFORTUNATE
MISFORTUNE
MISFORTUNED
MISFORTUNER
MISGAVE
MISGIVE
MISGIVEN
MISGIVING
MISGIVINGLY
MISGO
MISGOTTEN
MISGOVERN
MISGOVERNED
MISGOVERNING
MISGOVERNOR
MISGRAFF
MISGROWTH
MISGUGGLE
MISGUIDANCE
MISGUIDE
MISGUIDED
MISGUIDEDLY
MISGUIDER
MISGUIDING
MISGUIDINGLY
MISGUISE
MISHANDLE
MISHANDLED
MISHANDLING
MISHANTER
MISHAP
MISHAPPEN
MISHARA
MISHAVE
MISHEAR
MISHEARD
MISHEARING
MISHIT
MISHMASH
MISHMEE
MISHMI
MISIMPROVE
MISIMPROVED
MISIMPROVING
MISINFORM
MISINFORMANT
MISINFORMED
MISINFORMER
MISINFORMING
MISINTERPRET
MISINTERPRETATION
MISIONES
MISJOINDER
MISJUDGE
MISJUDGED
MISJUDGEMENT
MISJUDGER
MISJUDGING
MISJUDGINGLY
MISJUDGMENT
MISKAL
MISKEN
MISKENNING
MISKNEW
MISKNOW
MISKNOWLEDGE
MISKNOWN

MISKY
MISLAID
MISLAY
MISLAYER
MISLAYING
MISLE
MISLEAD
MISLEADER
MISLEADING
MISLEADINGLY
MISLEAR
MISLEARED
MISLED
MISLEERED
MISLEST
MISLIKE
MISLIKED
MISLIKEN
MISLIKER
MISLIKING
MISLIKINGLY
MISLIPPEN
MISLUCK
MISMADE
MISMAKE
MISMANAGE
MISMANAGEABLE
MISMANAGED
MISMANAGEMENT
MISMANAGER
MISMANAGING
MISMANNERED
MISMANNERS
MISMARRIAGE
MISMARRY
MISMATCH
MISMATCHMENT
MISMATE
MISMATED
MISMATING
MISMAZE
MISMEAN
MISMOVE
MISNAME
MISNAMED
MISNAMING
MISNOMED
MISNOMER
MISO
MISOCAPNIC
MISOCAPNIST
MISOGALLIC
MISOGAMIC
MISOGAMIST
MISOGAMY
MISOGYNE
MISOGYNIC
MISOGYNICAL
MISOGYNISM
MISOGYNIST
MISOGYNISTIC
MISOGYNOUS
MISOGYNY
MISOHELLENE
MISOLOGIST
MISOLOGY
MISOMATH
MISONEISM
MISONEIST
MISONEISTIC
MISOPAEDIA
MISOPAEDISM
MISOPAEDIST
MISOPATERIST
MISOPEDIA
MISOPEDISM
MISOPEDIST

MISORDER
MISOSCOPIST
MISOSOPHER
MISOSOPHIST
MISOSOPHY
MISOTHEISM
MISOTHEIST
MISOTHEISTIC
MISOTYRANNY
MISOXENE
MISOXENY
MISPAID
MISPAY
MISPAYING
MISPICK
MISPICKEL
MISPLACE
MISPLACED
MISPLACEMENT
MISPLACING
MISPLANT
MISPLAY
MISPLEAD
MISPLEADED
MISPLEADING
MISPLED
MISPRAISE
MISPRINT
MISPRISAL
MISPRISE
MISPRISION
MISPRIZE
MISPRIZED
MISPRIZER
MISPRIZING
MISPROFESS
MISPRONOUNCE
MISPRONOUNCED
MISPRONUNCIATI
MISPROUD
MISPUT
MISQUOTATION
MISQUOTE
MISQUOTED
MISQUOTER
MISQUOTING
MISREAD
MISREADER
MISREADING
MISRECKON
MISRECKONED
MISRECKONING
MISREMEMBER
MISREPORT
MISREPORTER
MISREPRESENT
MISREPRESENTATION
MISRULE
MISRULED
MISRULING
MISRUN
MISS
MISSAID
MISSAL
MISSARY
MISSATICAL
MISSAY
MISSAYING
MISSCRIPT
MISSED
MISSEEM
MISSEL
MISSERVE
MISSERVICE
MISSES
MISSET
MISSETTING

MISSHAPE
MISSHAPED
MISSHAPEN
MISSHAPENLY
MISSHAPING
MISSI
MISSIBLE
MISSIES
MISSILE
MISSILEMAN
MISSILEMEN
MISSILERY
MISSILES
MISSILRY
MISSING
MISSINGLY
MISSION
MISSIONAL
MISSIONARIES
MISSIONARIZE
MISSIONARY
MISSIONER
MISSIONIZER
MISSIS
MISSISH
MISSIT
MISSIVE
MISSMARK
MISSMENT
MISSOURITE
MISSOUT
MISSPEAK
MISSPEAKING
MISSPEECH
MISSPEED
MISSPELL
MISSPELLED
MISSPELLING
MISSPEND
MISSPENDER
MISSPENDING
MISSPENT
MISSPOKE
MISSTATE
MISSTATED
MISSTATEMENT
MISSTATER
MISSTATING
MISSTAY
MISSTEP
MISSUADE
MISSUS
MISSY
MIST
MISTAKABLE
MISTAKABLY
MISTAKE
MISTAKEN
MISTAKENLY
MISTAKENNESS
MISTAKER
MISTAKING
MISTAKINGLY
MISTAL
MISTASSINI
MISTASTE
MISTAUGHT
MISTBOW
MISTEACH
MISTEACHER
MISTED
MISTELL
MISTELLING
MISTEMPER
MISTEMPERED
MISTER
MISTERED

MISTERING
MISTERS
MISTETCH
MISTEUK
MISTFALL
MISTFLOWER
MISTHINK
MISTHINKING
MISTHOUGHT
MISTIC
MISTICO
MISTIDE
MISTIER
MISTIEST
MISTIFY
MISTIGRI
MISTIGRIS
MISTILY
MISTIME
MISTIMED
MISTIMING
MISTINESS
MISTING
MISTION
MISTLE
MISTLETOE
MISTOLD
MISTONE
MISTONUSK
MISTOOK
MISTRADITION
MISTRAIN
MISTRAL
MISTRANSLATE
MISTREAT
MISTREATMENT
MISTRESS
MISTRESSLY
MISTRIAL
MISTRIST
MISTROW
MISTRUST
MISTRUSTER
MISTRUSTFUL
MISTRUSTFULLY
MISTRUSTFULNESS
MISTRUSTING
MISTRUSTINGLY
MISTRY
MISTRYST
MISTURE
MISTURN
MISTY
MISUNDERSTAND
MISUNDERSTANDI
MISUNDERSTOOD
MISURA
MISUSAGE
MISUSE
MISUSED
MISUSING
MISVALUATION
MISVALUE
MISVALUED
MISVALUING
MISVENTURE
MISVENTUROUS
MISVOUCH
MISWED
MISWEND
MISWERN
MISWISH
MISWOMAN
MISWORD
MISWORDED
MISWORDING
MISWORSHIP

MISWORSHIPER
MISWREST
MISWRITE
MISWRITING
MISWRITTEN
MISWROTE
MISY
MISZEALOUS
MIT
MITAPSIS
MITCHBOARD
MITE
MITER
MITERED
MITERER
MITERFLOWER
MITERING
MITERWORT
MITHAN
MITHER
MITHRIDATE
MITHRIDATIC
MITHRIDATISM
MITHRIDATIZE
MITIGABLE
MITIGANT
MITIGATE
MITIGATED
MITIGATING
MITIGATION
MITIGATIVE
MITIGATOR
MITIGATORY
MITING
MITIS
MITOCHONDRIA
MITOGENETIC
MITOME
MITOSIS
MITOSOME
MITOTIC
MITOTICALLY
MITRA
MITRAILLE
MITRAILLEUR
MITRAILLEUSE
MITRAL
MITRATE
MITRE
MITRED
MITREFLOWER
MITRER
MITREWORT
MITRIFORM
MITRING
MITSUMATA
MITSVAH
MITSVOTH
MITT
MITTELHAND
MITTEN
MITTENED
MITTIMUS
MITTLE
MITTY
MITY
MITZVAH
MITZVAHS
MITZVOTH
MIURUS
MIX
MIXABLE
MIXBLOOD
MIXED
MIXEN
MIXER
MIXERESS

MIXHILL
MIXIBLE
MIXILINEAL
MIXING
MIXITE
MIXOBARBARIC
MIXOTROPHIC
MIXT
MIXTIFORM
MIXTILINEAR
MIXTION
MIXTURE
MIXUP
MIXY
MIZENMAST
MIZMAZE
MIZRACH
MIZZEN
MIZZENMAST
MIZZENTOPMAN
MIZZENTOPMEN
MIZZLE
MIZZLED
MIZZLING
MIZZLY
MIZZONITE
MIZZY
MKS
MLECHCHHA
MNEME
MNEMONIC
MNEMONICAL
MNEMONICALLY
MNEMONICON
MNEMONICS
MNEMONISM
MNEMONIST
MNEMONIZE
MNEMONIZED
MNEMONIZING
MNEMOTECHNY
MNESIC
MNESTIC
MNIACEOUS
MNIOID
MO
MOA
MOAB
MOALA
MOAN
MOANED
MOANFUL
MOANFULLY
MOANING
MOANO
MOAT
MOATHILL
MOB
MOBBED
MOBBER
MOBBIE
MOBBING
MOBBISH
MOBBISHLY
MOBBISHNESS
MOBBISM
MOBBIST
MOBBY
MOBCAP
MOBED
MOBILE
MOBILIANER
MOBILIARY
MOBILISE
MOBILITIES
MOBILITY
MOBILIZATION

MOBILIZE
MOBILIZED
MOBILIZING
MOBILOMETER
MOBLE
MOBOCRACIES
MOBOCRACY
MOBOCRAT
MOBOCRATIC
MOBOCRATICAL
MOBOLATRY
MOBSMAN
MOBSMEN
MOBSTER
MOCCASIN
MOCCENIGO
MOCH
MOCHA
MOCHILA
MOCHRAS
MOCHUDI
MOCHY
MOCK
MOCKADO
MOCKAGE
MOCKBIRD
MOCKED
MOCKER
MOCKERIES
MOCKERNUT
MOCKERY
MOCKETER
MOCKGROUND
MOCKING
MOCKINGBIRD
MOCKINGLY
MOCKINGSTOCK
MOCKISH
MOCKUP
MOCMAIN
MOCO
MOCOCK
MOCOMOCO
MOCUCK
MODAL
MODALIST
MODALISTIC
MODALITIES
MODALITY
MODALIZE
MODALLY
MODDER
MODE
MODEL
MODELED
MODELER
MODELESS
MODELESSNESS
MODELING
MODELIST
MODELIZE
MODELLED
MODELLER
MODELLING
MODELMAKER
MODELMAKING
MODENA
MODER
MODERANT
MODERANTISM
MODERANTIST
MODERATE
MODERATED
MODERATELY
MODERATENESS
MODERATING
MODERATION

MODERATISM
MODERATIST
MODERATO
MODERATOR
MODERN
MODERNER
MODERNISM
MODERNIST
MODERNISTIC
MODERNITIES
MODERNITY
MODERNIZATION
MODERNIZE
MODERNIZED
MODERNIZER
MODERNIZING
MODERNLY
MODERNNESS
MODEST
MODESTIES
MODESTLY
MODESTNESS
MODESTY
MODIATION
MODICA
MODICITY
MODICUM
MODICUMS
MODIFIABLE
MODIFIABLY
MODIFICABLE
MODIFICATION
MODIFICATIVE
MODIFICATOR
MODIFICATORY
MODIFIED
MODIFIER
MODIFY
MODIFYING
MODILLION
MODIOLAR
MODIOLI
MODIOLUS
MODISH
MODISHLY
MODISHNESS
MODIST
MODISTE
MODISTRY
MODS
MODULABILITY
MODULANT
MODULAR
MODULATE
MODULATED
MODULATING
MODULATION
MODULATIVE
MODULATOR
MODULATORY
MODULE
MODULET
MODULI
MODULIZE
MODULO
MODULUS
MODUR
MODUS
MODY
MOE
MOELLON
MOERITHERE
MOERITHERIAN
MOEURS
MOFETTE
MOFF
MOFFETTE

MOFFLE
MOFUSSIL
MOFUSSILITE
MOG
MOGADORE
MOGGAN
MOGGED
MOGGI
MOGGIES
MOGGING
MOGGIO
MOGGY
MOGIGRAPHIC
MOGIGRAPHY
MOGILALIA
MOGILALISM
MOGIPHONIA
MOGITOCIA
MOGO
MOGOTE
MOGUEY
MOGUL
MOHA
MOHABAT
MOHAIR
MOHAR
MOHATRA
MOHAWKITE
MOHEL
MOHNSEED
MOHO
MOHOE
MOHOS
MOHR
MOHUR
MOHWA
MOIDER
MOIDORE
MOIETER
MOIETIES
MOIETY
MOIL
MOILED
MOILER
MOILES
MOILING
MOILINGLY
MOILSOME
MOINE
MOINEAU
MOIO
MOIRE
MOIREED
MOIREING
MOIRETTE
MOISE
MOISON
MOISSANITE
MOIST
MOISTEN
MOISTENED
MOISTENER
MOISTENING
MOISTFUL
MOISTIFY
MOISTLESS
MOISTLY
MOISTNESS
MOISTURE
MOIST'
MOIT
MOITY
MOJARRA
MOJO
MOJOS
MOKADDAM
MOKAMOKA

MOKE	MOLLESCENCE	MOMENTANEITY	MONARDA	MONEYSAVING
MOKI	MOLLESCENT	MOMENTANEOUS	MONARTICULAR	MONEYWORT
MOKIHANA	MOLLETON	MOMENTANEOUSLY	MONAS	MONG
MOKIHI	MOLLICHOP	MOMENTARILY	MONASCIDIAN	MONGER
MOKO	MOLLICRUSH	MOMENTARY	MONASE	MONGERING
MOKSHA	MOLLIE	MOMENTLY	MONASTER	MONGERY
MOKUM	MOLLIENISIA	MOMENTOUS	MONASTERIAL	MONGLER
MOKY	MOLLIENT	MOMENTOUSLY	MONASTERIES	MONGO
MOL	MOLLIFIABLE	MOMENTOUSNESS	MONASTERY	MONGOE
MOLA	MOLLIFIED	MOMENTUM	MONASTIC	MONGOOSE
MOLAL	MOLLIFIER	MOMENTUMS	MONASTICAL	MONGOOSES
MOLALITY	MOLLIFY	MOMI	MONASTICALLY	MONGREL
MOLAR	MOLLIFYING	MOMIOLOGY	MONASTICISM	MONGRELDOM
MOLARIFORM	MOLLIFYINGLY	MOMISH	MONATOMIC	MONGRELISH
MOLARIMETER	MOLLIGRANT	MOMISM	MONATOMICITY	MONGRELISM
MOLARITY	MOLLIPILOSE	MOMIST	MONATOMISM	MONGRELITY
MOLARY	MOLLISIOSE	MOMMA	MONAUL	MONGRELIZE
MOLASSES	MOLLISOL	MOMME	MONAULI	MONGRELLY
MOLASSIED	MOLLITIES	MOMMY	MONAULOS	MONGRELNESS
MOLASSY	MOLLITIOUS	MOMO	MONAURAL	MONHEIMITE
MOLAVE	MOLLITUDE	MOMUS	MONAX	MONIAL
MOLD	MOLLUSC	MOMUSES	MONAXIAL	MONICA
MOLDABLE	MOLLUSCAN	MON	MONAXON	MONICKER
MOLDAVITE	MOLLUSCOID	MONA	MONAXONIAL	MONIE
MOLDBOARD	MOLLUSCOIDAL	MONACANTHID	MONAXONIC	MONIER
MOLDED	MOLLUSCOUS	MONACANTHINE	MONAZITE	MONIES
MOLDER	MOLLUSCUM	MONACANTHOUS	MONCHIQUITE	MONIKER
MOLDERED	MOLLUSK	MONACH	MONDAINE	MONILATED
MOLDERING	MOLLY	MONACHAL	MONDE	MONILETHRIX
MOLDERY	MOLLYCODDLE	MONACHATE	MONDEGO	MONILIACEOUS
MOLDINESS	MOLLYCODDLED	MONACHISM	MONDIAL	MONILICORN
MOLDING	MOLLYCODDLER	MONACHIST	MONDO	MONILIFORM
MOLDINGS	MOLLYCOSSET	MONACHIZE	MONDSEE	MONILIFORMLY
MOLDMADE	MOLLYCOT	MONACID	MONE	MONILIOID
MOLDWARP	MOLMAN	MONACT	MONECIOUS	MONIMENT
MOLDY	MOLMEN	MONACTIN	MONEMBRYONIC	MONIMIACEOUS
MOLE	MOLOCH	MONACTINAL	MONEMBRYONY	MONIMOLITE
MOLECAST	MOLOCKER	MONACTINE	MONEPIC	MONIMOSTYLIC
MOLECULA	MOLOID	MONAD	MONEPISCOPAL	MONISH
MOLECULAR	MOLOKER	MONADELPH	MONEPISCOPUS	MONISHER
MOLECULARIST	MOLOMPI	MONADELPHIAN	MONER	MONISHMENT
MOLECULARITY	MOLOSSIC	MONADELPHOUS	MONERA	MONISM
MOLECULE	MOLOSSINE	MONADES	MONERAL	MONIST
MOLED	MOLOSSOID	MONADIC	MONERAN	MONISTIC
MOLEHEAD	MOLOSSUS	MONADICAL	MONERGIC	MONISTICAL
MOLEHEAP	MOLPE	MONADICALLY	MONERGISM	MONISTICALLY
MOLEHILL	MOLROOKEN	MONADIFORM	MONERGIST	MONITION
MOLEHILLISH	MOLT	MONADIGEROUS	MONERGISTIC	MONITIVE
MOLEHILLY	MOLTED	MONADISM	MONERIC	MONITOR
MOLEISM	MOLTEN	MONADISTIC	MONERON	MONITORIAL
MOLENDINAR	MOLTENLY	MONADNOCK	MONERONS	MONITORIALLY
MOLENDINARY	MOLTER	MONADOLOGY	MONERULA	MONITORSHIP
MOLESKIN	MOLTING	MONAL	MONESIA	MONITORY
MOLEST	MOLTO	MONAMNIOTIC	MONETARILY	MONITRESS
MOLESTATION	MOLY	MONANDER	MONETARY	MONK
MOLESTED	MOLYBDATE	MONANDRIAN	MONETITE	MONKBIRD
MOLESTER	MOLYBDENA	MONANDRIC	MONETIZATION	MONKCRAFT
MOLESTFUL	MOLYBDENIC	MONANDROUS	MONETIZE	MONKERIES
MOLESTFULLY	MOLYBDENITE	MONANDRY	MONETIZED	MONKERY
MOLESTIE	MOLYBDENOUS	MONANTHOUS	MONETIZING	MONKESS
MOLESTING	MOLYBDENUM	MONAPHASE	MONEY	MONKEY
MOLESTIOUS	MOLYBDIC	MONAPSAL	MONEYAGE	MONKEYBOARD
MOLET	MOLYBDITE	MONARCH	MONEYBAG	MONKEYFIED
MOLIES	MOLYBDOCOLIC	MONARCHAL	MONEYBAGS	MONKEYFY
MOLIMEN	MOLYBDOMANCY	MONARCHALLY	MONEYCHANGER	MONKEYFYING
MOLIMINOUS	MOLYBDONOSUS	MONARCHIAN	MONEYED	MONKEYING
MOLINARY	MOLYBDOSIS	MONARCHIC	MONEYER	MONKEYNUT
MOLINE	MOLYBDOUS	MONARCHICAL	MONEYGRUB	MONKEYPOD
MOLINET	MOLYSITE	MONARCHIES	MONEYGRUBBER	MONKEYPOT
MOLING	MOM	MONARCHISM	MONEYING	MONKEYRY
MOLITION	MOMBIN	MONARCHIST	MONEYLENDER	MONKEYS
MOLKA	MOMBLE	MONARCHISTIC	MONEYLENDING	MONKEYSHINE
MOLLA	MOME	MONARCHIZE	MONEYMAKER	MONKEYTAIL
MOLLAH	MOMENT	MONARCHIZED	MONEYMAKING	MONKFISH
MOLLAND	MOMENTA	MONARCHIZER	MONEYMAN	MONKFISHES
MOLLE	MOMENTAL	MONARCHIZING	MONEYMONGER	MONKFLOWER
MOLLES	MOMENTALLY	MONARCHY	MONEYS	MONKHOOD

MONKISH	MONOCOTYL	MONOGRAMMING	MONONYCHOUS	MONORGANIC
MONKISHLY	MONOCRACY	MONOGRAPH	MONONYM	MONORHYME
MONKISHNESS	MONOCRAT	MONOGRAPHED	MONONYMIC	MONORHYMED
MONKISM	MONOCRATIC	MONOGRAPHER	MONONYMIZE	MONORHYTHMIC
MONKLINESS	MONOCROTIC	MONOGRAPHIC	MONONYMY	MONOSACCHARIDE
MONKLY	MONOCROTISM	MONOGRAPHING	MONOOUSIAN	MONOSCHEMIC
MONKMONGER	MONOCULAR	MONOGRAPHIST	MONOOUSIOUS	MONOSE
MONKS	MONOCULARITY	MONOGRAPHY	MONOPARENTAL	MONOSEMIC
MONKSHOOD	MONOCULARLY	MONOGRAPTID	MONOPARESIS	MONOSEPALOUS
MONMOUTHITE	MONOCULE	MONOGYNIC	MONOPERSONAL	MONOSERVICE
MONNIKER	MONOCULOUS	MONOGYNIOUS	MONOPETALOUS	MONOSILANE
MONO	MONOCULTURE	MONOGYNIST	MONOPHAGIA	MONOSIPHONIC
MONOACETATE	MONOCULUS	MONOGYNOUS	MONOPHAGISM	MONOSKI
MONOACID	MONOCYCLE	MONOGYNY	MONOPHAGOUS	MONOSPERM
MONOACIDIC	MONOCYCLIC	MONOHYBRID	MONOPHAGY	MONOSPERMAL
MONOAMID	MONOCYSTIC	MONOHYDRATE	MONOPHASIC	MONOSPERMIC
MONOAMIDE	MONOCYTE	MONOHYDRATED	MONOPHOBIA	MONOSPERMOUS
MONOAMIN	MONOCYTIC	MONOHYDRIC	MONOPHONE	MONOSPORE
MONOAMINE	MONODACTYL	MONOHYDROGEN	MONOPHONIC	MONOSPORED
MONOAMINO	MONODACTYLE	MONOICOUS	MONOPHONOUS	MONOSPOROUS
MONOAZO	MONODACTYLY	MONOID	MONOPHOTAL	MONOSTELE
MONOBASE	MONODELPHIAN	MONOLATER	MONOPHOTE	MONOSTELIC
MONOBASIC	MONODELPHIC	MONOLATRIST	MONOPHTHONG	MONOSTELOUS
MONOBASICITY	MONODELPHOUS	MONOLATROUS	MONOPHTHONGAL	MONOSTELY
MONOBLASTIC	MONODERMIC	MONOLATRY	MONOPHTHONGIZE	MONOSTICH
MONOBLEPSIA	MONODIC	MONOLAYER	MONOPHYLETIC	MONOSTICHOUS
MONOBLEPSIS	MONODICAL	MONOLINE	MONOPHYLITE	MONOSTOME
MONOBLOC	MONODICALLY	MONOLINGUAL	MONOPHYLLOUS	MONOSTOMOUS
MONOBROMATED	MONODIES	MONOLINGUIST	MONOPHYODONT	MONOSTROPHE
MONOBROMIDE	MONODIMETRIC	MONOLITERAL	MONOPLACULA	MONOSTROPHIC
MONOCARBONIC	MONODIST	MONOLITH	MONOPLACULAR	MONOSTYLOUS
MONOCARDIAN	MONODIZE	MONOLITHIC	MONOPLANE	MONOSULPHIDE
MONOCARP	MONODOMOUS	MONOLITHS	MONOPLANIST	MONOSYLLABIC
MONOCARPAL	MONODONT	MONOLOBULAR	MONOPLAST	MONOSYLLABLE
MONOCARPELLARY	MONODONTAL	MONOLOCULAR	MONOPLASTIC	MONOSYMMETRY
MONOCARPIAN	MONODRAM	MONOLOG	MONOPLEGIA	MONOTHALAMAN
MONOCARPIC	MONODRAMA	MONOLOGIAN	MONOPLEGIC	MONOTHECAL
MONOCARPOUS	MONODRAME	MONOLOGIC	MONOPODE	MONOTHEISM
MONOCELLULAR	MONODROMIC	MONOLOGICAL	MONOPODIA	MONOTHEIST
MONOCENTRIC	MONODROMY	MONOLOGIST	MONOPODIAL	MONOTHEISTIC
MONOCERCOUS	MONODY	MONOLOGIZE	MONOPODIALLY	MONOTHELIOUS
MONOCEROS	MONODYNAMIC	MONOLOGIZED	MONOPODIC	MONOTHETIC
MONOCEROUS	MONODYNAMISM	MONOLOGIZING	MONOPODIES	MONOTIC
MONOCHASIAL	MONOECIAN	MONOLOGUE	MONOPODIUM	MONOTINT
MONOCHASIUM	MONOECIOUS	MONOLOGUIST	MONOPODOUS	MONOTOCOUS
MONOCHLOR	MONOECIOUSLY	MONOLOGY	MONOPODY	MONOTOMOUS
MONOCHLORIDE	MONOECISM	MONOMACHIST	MONOPOLAR	MONOTONE
MONOCHLORO	MONOEIDIC	MONOMACHY	MONOPOLARIC	MONOTONIC
MONOCHORD	MONOESTROUS	MONOMANIA	MONOPOLARITY	MONOTONICAL
MONOCHORDIST	MONOGAMIAN	MONOMANIAC	MONOPOLE	MONOTONIST
MONOCHORDIZE	MONOGAMIC	MONOMANIACAL	MONOPOLIES	MONOTONIZE
MONOCHROIC	MONOGAMIST	MONOMER	MONOPOLISE	MONOTONOUS
MONOCHROMASY	MONOGAMISTIC	MONOMERIC	MONOPOLISM	MONOTONOUSLY
MONOCHROMAT	MONOGAMOUS	MONOMEROUS	MONOPOLIST	MONOTONY
MONOCHROMATE	MONOGAMOUSLY	MONOMETALISM	MONOPOLISTIC	MONOTREMAL
MONOCHROME	MONOGAMY	MONOMETALIST	MONOPOLIZE	MONOTREMATE
MONOCHROMIC	MONOGASTRIC	MONOMETALLIC	MONOPOLIZED	MONOTREME
MONOCHROMIST	MONOGENE	MONOMETER	MONOPOLIZER	MONOTREMOUS
MONOCHROMOUS	MONOGENEITY	MONOMETHYL	MONOPOLIZING	MONOTRICHIC
MONOCHROMY	MONOGENEOUS	MONOMETHYLIC	MONOPOLOUS	MONOTRICHOUS
MONOCHRONIC	MONOGENESIS	MONOMETRIC	MONOPOLY	MONOTRIGLYPH
MONOCILIATED	MONOGENESIST	MONOMETRICAL	MONOPRIONID	MONOTROCHAL
MONOCLE	MONOGENESY	MONOMIAL	MONOPSYCHISM	MONOTROCHIAN
MONOCLED	MONOGENETIC	MONOMICT	MONOPTERAL	MONOTROCHOUS
MONOCLEID	MONOGENIC	MONOMINERAL	MONOPTEROUS	MONOTROPHIC
MONOCLEIDE	MONOGENISM	MONOMORPHIC	MONOPTIC	MONOTROPIC
MONOCLINAL	MONOGENIST	MONOMORPHISM	MONOPTICAL	MONOTROPY
MONOCLINALLY	MONOGENISTIC	MONOMORPHOUS	MONOPTOTE	MONOTYPAL
MONOCLINE	MONOGENOUS	MONOMYARIAN	MONOPTOTIC	MONOTYPE
MONCCLINIAN	MONOGENY	MONONCH	MONOPYRENOUS	MONOTYPIC
MONOCLINIC	MONOGLOT	MONONEURAL	MONORAIL	MONOTYPICAL
MONOCLINISM	MONOGONEUTIC	MONONITRATE	MONORAILROAD	MONOTYPOUS
MONOCLINOUS	MONOGONY	MONONITRATED	MONORAILWAY	MONOVALENCE
MONOCONDYLAR	MONOGRAM	MONONOMIAL	MONORCHID	MONOVALENCY
MONOCOQUE	MONOGRAMING	MONONOMIAN	MONORCHIDISM	MONOVALENT
MONOCORMIC	MONOGRAMMED	MONONT	MONORCHIS	MONOVARIANT
MONOCOT	MONOGRAMMIC	MONONUCLEAR	MONORCHISM	MONOVOLTINE

MONOVULAR	MONY	MOONRAKER	MOOTWORTHY	MORBIDNESS
MONOXENOUS	MONZODIORITE	MOONRAKING	MOP	MORBIFERAL
MONOXIDE	MONZOGABBRO	MOONRAT	MOPANE	MORBIFEROUS
MONOXYLA	MONZONITE	MOONRISE	MOPANI	MORBIFIC
MONOXYLE	MONZONITIC	MOONSAIL	MOPBOARD	MORBIFICAL
MONOXYLIC	MOO	MOONSEED	MOPE	MORBIFICALLY
MONOXYLON	MOOCAH	MOONSET	MOPED	MORBIFY
MONOXYLOUS	MOOCH	MOONSHADE	MOPEHAWK	MORBILLARY
MONOZOAN	MOOCHA	MOONSHEE	MOPER	MORBILLI
MONOZOIC	MOOCHER	MOONSHINE	MOPERY	MORBILLIFORM
MONOZYGOTIC	MOOD	MOONSHINER	MOPES	MORBILLOUS
MONROLITE	MOODER	MOONSHINING	MOPH	MORBLEU
MONS	MOODIER	MOONSHINY	MOPHEAD	MORBOSE
MONSEIGNEUR	MOODIEST	MOONSHOT	MOPHEADED	MORBUS
MONSIEUR	MOODILY	MOONSICK	MOPING	MORCEAU
MONSIGNOR	MOODINESS	MOONSICKNESS	MOPISH	MORCEAUX
MONSIGNORE	MOODIR	MOONSTONE	MOPISHLY	MORCELLATE
MONSIGNORIAL	MOODISH	MOONSTRICKEN	MOPISHNESS	MORCELLATED
MONSOON	MOODISHLY	MOONSTRUCK	MOPLA	MORCELLATING
MONSOONAL	MOODISHNESS	MOONTIDE	MOPLAH	MORCELLATION
MONSPERMY	MOODS	MOONWORT	MOPOKE	MORDACIOUS
MONSTER	MOODY	MOONY	MOPPED	MORDACIOUSLY
MONSTRANCE	MOOED	MOOP	MOPPER	MORDACITY
MONSTRICIDE	MOOING	MOOR	MOPPET	MORDANCY
MONSTRIFY	MOOKHTAR	MOORAGE	MOPPY	MORDANT
MONSTROSITIES	MOOKTAR	MOORBALL	MOPS	MORDANTED
MONSTROSITY	MOOL	MOORBAND	MOPSEY	MORDANTING
MONSTROUS	MOOLAH	MOORBERRIES	MOPSTICK	MORDELLID
MONSTROUSLY	MOOLEY	MOORBERRY	MOPSY	MORDELLOID
MONT	MOOLINGS	MOORBIRD	MOPUS	MORDENITE
MONTABYN	MOOLS	MOORBURN	MOPUSES	MORDENT
MONTAGE	MOOLUM	MOORBURNER	MOPUSSES	MORDICATE
MONTANAS	MOON	MOORBURNING	MOQUETTE	MORDICATION
MONTANE	MOONACK	MOORED	MORA	MORDICATIVE
MONTANITE	MOONAL	MOORFLOWER	MORABIT	MORDIEU
MONTANT	MOONBEAM	MOORFOWL	MORACEOUS	MORDISHEEN
MONTANTO	MOONBILL	MOORHEN	MORADA	MORDORE
MONTBRETIA	MOONBLIND	MOORIER	MORAE	MORDU
MONTE	MOONBLINK	MOORIEST	MORAINAL	MORE
MONTEGRE	MOONCALF	MOORING	MORAINE	MOREEN
MONTEITH	MOONCREEPER	MOORISH	MORAINIC	MOREISH
MONTEM	MOONDOG	MOORLAND	MORAL	MOREL
MONTERA	MOONDOWN	MOORLANDER	MORALE	MORELLA
MONTERO	MOONDROP	MOORMAN	MORALER	MORELLE
MONTEROS	MOONED	MOORMEN	MORALISE	MORELLO
MONTES	MOONER	MOORPAN	MORALISM	MORENA
MONTGOLFIER	MOONERY	MOORPUNKY	MORALIST	MORENCITE
MONTH	MOONET	MOORS	MORALISTIC	MORENDO
MONTHLIES	MOONEYE	MOORSTONE	MORALITIES	MORENESS
MONTHLY	MOONFACE	MOORTETTER	MORALITY	MORENITA
MONTHON	MOONFACED	MOORUP	MORALIZATION	MORENOSITE
MONTHS	MOONFALL	MOORWORT	MORALIZE	MOREOVER
MONTICELLITE	MOONFISH	MOORY	MORALIZED	MOREPEON
MONTICLE	MOONFISHES	MOOS	MORALIZER	MOREPORK
MONTICOLINE	MOONFLOWER	MOOSA	MORALIZING	MORES
MONTICULATE	MOONGLADE	MOOSE	MORALLER	MORFOND
MONTICULE	MOONGLOW	MOOSEBERRIES	MORALLY	MORFOUND
MONTICULOSE	MOONHEAD	MOOSEBERRY	MORALS	MORFOUNDER
MONTICULOUS	MOONIE	MOOSEBIRD	MORAS	MORFREY
MONTICULUS	MOONIER	MOOSEBUSH	MORASS	MORG
MONTIFORM	MOONIEST	MOOSECALL	MORASSIC	MORGA
MONTIGENEOUS	MOONING	MOOSEFLOWER	MORASSWEED	MORGANATIC
MONTILLA	MOONISH	MOOSEMILK	MORASSY	MORGANATICAL
MONTJOY	MOONITE	MOOSETONGUE	MORAT	MORGANIC
MONTJOYE	MOONJA	MOOSEWOOD	MORATE	MORGANITE
MONTMARTRITE	MOONLET	MOOSEY	MORATION	MORGANIZE
MONTON	MOONLIGHT	MOOST	MORATORIA	MORGAY
MONTRE	MOONLIGHTED	MOOT	MORATORIUM	MORGEN
MONTROYDITE	MOONLIGHTER	MOOTCH	MORATORY	MORGENS
MONTURE	MOONLIGHTING	MOOTED	MORAVITE	MORGLAY
MONTUVIO	MOONLING	MOOTER	MORAY	MORGUE
MONUMENT	MOONLIT	MOOTH	MORB	MORIBUND
MONUMENTAL	MOONLITTEN	MOOTING	MORBID	MORIBUNDITY
MONUMENTALLY	MOONMAN	MOOTMAN	MORBIDEZZA	MORIBUNDLY
MONUMENTARY	MOONMEN	MOOTMEN	MORBIDITIES	MORICHE
MONUMENTED	MOONPATH	MOOTSTEAD	MORBIDITY	MORIFORM
MONUMENTING	MOONPENNY	MOOTSUDDY	MORBIDLY	MORIGERATE

MORIGERATION	MORPHIC	MORTGAGEE	MOSSBACK	MOTIONS
MORIGEROUS	MORPHICALLY	MORTGAGER	MOSSBACKED	MOTITATION
MORIGEROUSLY	MORPHIN	MORTGAGING	MOSSBANKER	MOTIVATE
MORIGLIO	MORPHINE	MORTGAGOR	MOSSBERRY	MOTIVATED
MORILLON	MORPHINIC	MORTH	MOSSBUNKER	MOTIVATING
MORIN	MORPHINISM	MORTHWYRTHA	MOSSED	MOTIVATION
MORIND!N	MORPHINIST	MORTICE	MOSSER	MOTIVATIONAL
MORINDONE	MORPHINIZE	MORTICED	MOSSERY	MOTIVE
MORINEL	MORPHIOMANIA	MORTICER	MOSSES	MOTIVED
MORINGACEOUS	MORPHOGENIC	MORTICIAN	MOSSHEAD	MOTIVENESS
MORINGAD	MORPHOGENY	MORTICING	MOSSHORN	MOTIVING
MORINGUID	MORPHOGRAPHY	MORTIER	MOSSIER	MOTIVITY
MORINGUOID	MORPHOLIN	MORTIFEROUS	MOSSIEST	MOTLEY
MORION	MORPHOLINE	MORTIFIC	MOSSINESS	MOTLEYER
MORKIN	MORPHOLOGIC	MORTIFICATION	MOSSING	MOTLEYEST
MORLING	MORPHOLOGICAL	MORTIFIED	MOSSO	MOTLEYNESS
MORLOP	MORPHOLOGIES	MORTIFIEDLY	MOSSTROOPER	MOTMOT
MORMAER	MORPHOLOGIST	MORTIFY	MOSSTROOPERY	MOTO
MORMAL	MORPHOLOGY	MORTIFYING	MOSSWORT	MOTOFACIENT
MORMAORDOM	MORPHOMETRY	MORTIFYINGLY	MOSSY	MOTOGRAPH
MORMAORSHIP	MORPHON	MORTISE	MOST	MOTOGRAPHIC
MORMO	MORPHONOMIC	MORTISED	MOSTDEAL	MOTOMAGNETIC
MORMON	MORPHONOMY	MORTISER	MOSTLIKE	MOTONEURON
MORMORANDO	MORPHOPHYLY	MORTISING	MOSTLINGS	MOTOPHONE
MORMYR	MORPHOPLASM	MORTLAKE	MOSTLY	MOTOR
MORMYRE	MORPHOSIS	MORTLING	MOSTRA	MOTORABLE
MORMYRIAN	MORPHOTIC	MORTMAIN	MOSTWHAT	MOTORBIKE
MORMYRID	MORPHOTROPIC	MORTMAINER	MOT	MOTORBOAT
MORMYROID	MORPHOTROPY	MORTORIO	MOTACIL	MOTORBOATMAN
MORN	MORPHOUS	MORTREUX	MOTACILLID	MOTORBUS
MORNE	MORPHREY	MORTREWES	MOTACILLINE	MOTORCAB
MORNED	MORPION	MORTUARIES	MOTATORIOUS	MOTORCADE
MORNETTE	MORPUNKEE	MORTUARY	MOTATORY	MOTORCAR
MORNING	MORRAL	MORTUOUS	MOTE	MOTORCYCLE
MORNINGLY	MORRHUATE	MORULA	MOTED	MOTORCYCLED
MORNINGS	MORRHUIN	MORULAE	MOTEL	MOTORCYCLING
MORNINGTIDE	MORRICER	MORULAR	MOTER	MOTORCYCLIST
MORNTIME	MORRION	MORULATION	MOTET	MOTORDROME
MORO	MORRIS	MORULOID	MOTETTIST	MOTORED
MOROC	MORRO	MORVIN	MOTETUS	MOTORING
MOROÇAIN	MORROS	MORWONG	MOTEY	MOTORISM
MOROCCO	MORROW	MOS	MOTH	MOTORIST
MOROCOTA	MORROWING	MOSAIC	MOTHBALL	MOTORIUM
MOROLOGICAL	MORROWMASS	MOSAICAL	MOTHED	MOTORIZATION
MOROLOGIST	MORROWSPEECH	MOSAICALLY	MOTHER	MOTORIZE
MOROLOGY	MORSAL	MOSAICIST	MOTHERED	MOTORIZED
MOROMANCY	MORSE	MOSAICKED	MOTHERER	MOTORIZING
MORON	MORSEL	MOSAICKING	MOTHERGATE	MOTORMAN
MORONCY	MORSELED	MOSAIST	MOTHERHOOD	MOTORMEN
MORONES	MORSELING	MOSANDRITE	MOTHERING	MOTORNEER
MORONG	MORSELIZE	MOSASAUR	MOTHERLAND	MOTORPHOBE
MORONIC	MORSELLED	MOSASAURIAN	MOTHERLESS	MOTORPHOBIA
MORONICALLY	MORSELLING	MOSASAURID	MOTHERLINESS	MOTORPHOBIAC
MORONISM	MORSING	MOSASAUROID	MOTHERLY	MOTORSHIP
MORONITY	MORSURE	MOSCH	MOTHERWORT	MOTORTRUCK
MORONRY	MORT	MOSCHATE	MOTHERY	MOTORWAY
MOROR	MORTACIOUS	MOSCHATEL	MOTHIER	MOTRE
MOROSAURIAN	MORTAL	MOSCHIFEROUS	MOTHIEST	MOTRICITY
MOROSAUROID	MORTALISM	MOSCHINE	MOTHPROOF	MOTT
MOROSE	MORTALIST	MOSE	MOTHPROOFED	MOTTE
MOROSELY	MORTALITIES	MOSESITE	MOTHPROOFING	MOTTLE
MOROSENESS	MORTALITY	MOSEY	MOTHS	MOTTLED
MOROSIS	MORTALIZE	MOSEYED	MOTHWORM	MOTTLEDNESS
MOROSITY	MORTALIZED	MOSEYING	MOTHY	MOTTLEMENT
MOROSOPH	MORTALIZING	MOSHAV	MOTIF	MOTTLER
MOROXITE	MORTALLY	MOSK	MOTIFIC	MOTTLING
MORPH	MORTAR	MOSKENEER	MOTILE	MOTTO
MORPHALLAXIS	MORTARBOARD	MOSKER	MOTILITY	MOTTOED
MORPHEA	MORTARED	MOSLINGS	MOTION	MOTTOES
MORPHEME	MORTARING	MOSQUE	MOTIONABLE	MOTTOS
MORPHEMES	MORTARWARE	MOSQUITAL	MOTIONAL	MOTTRAMITE
MORPHEMIC	MORTARY	MOSQUITO	MOTIONED	MOTTY
MORPHETIC	MORTBELL	MOSQUITOBILL	MOTIONER	MOTU
MORPHEW	MORTCLOTH	MOSQUITOES	MOTIONING	MOTYKA
MORPHIA	MORTERSHEEN	MOSQUITOEY	MOTIONIST	MOU
MORPHIATE	MORTGAGE	MOSQUITOS	MOTIONLESS	MOUCH
	MORTGAGED	MOSS	MOTIONLESSLY	MOUCHARABIES

MOUCHARABY	MOURNE	MOVABLENESS	MUCHWHAT	MUCULENT
MOUCHARD	MOURNED	MOVABLY	MUCID	MUCUS
MOUCHARDISM	MOURNER	MOVANT	MUCIDITY	MUCUSIN
MOUCHE	MOURNFUL	MOVE	MUCIDNESS	MUD
MOUCHOIR	MOURNFULLY	MOVEABILITY	MUCIFEROUS	MUDAR
MOUDIE	MOURNFULNESS	MOVEABLE	MUCIFIC	MUDBANK
MOUDIEMAN	MOURNING	MOVEABLENESS	MUCIFORM	MUDCAP
MOUDY	MOURNINGLY	MOVEABLY	MUCIGEN	MUDCAPPED
MOUE	MOURNIVAL	MOVED	MUCIGENOUS	MUDCAPPING
MOUFFLON	MOUSE	MOVELESS	MUCILAGE	MUDCAT
MOUFLON	MOUSEBANE	MOVELESSLY	MUCILAGINOUS	MUDDEN
MOUFLONS	MOUSEBIRD	MOVELESSNESS	MUCIN	MUDDER
MOUILLATION	MOUSED	MOVEMENT	MUCINOGEN	MUDDIED
MOUILLE	MOUSEFISH	MOVEMENTS	MUCINOID	MUDDIER
MOUILLURE	MOUSEFISHES	MOVENT	MUCINOUS	MUDDIEST
MOUJIK	MOUSEHAWK	MOVER	MUCIPAROUS	MUDDIFY
MOUL	MOUSEHOLE	MOVES	MUCIVORE	MUDDILY
MOULAGE	MOUSEHOUND	MOVIE	MUCIVOROUS	MUDDINESS
MOULD	MOUSELET	MOVIEGOER	MUCK	MUDDISH
MOULDBOARD	MOUSELING	MOVIEGOING	MUCKAMUCK	MUDDLE
MOULDED	MOUSEMILL	MOVIELAND	MUCKED	MUDDLED
MOULDER	MOUSEPROOF	MOVING	MUCKENDER	MUDDLEDOM
MOULDERED	MOUSER	MOVINGLY	MUCKER	MUDDLEHEAD
MOULDERING	MOUSERIES	MOW	MUCKERER	MUDDLEHEADED
MOULDERY	MOUSERY	MOWABLE	MUCKET	MUDDLER
MOULDIER	MOUSETAIL	MOWANA	MUCKHILL	MUDDLESOME
MOULDIEST	MOUSETRAP	MOWBURN	MUCKIBUS	MUDDLING
MOULDING	MOUSETRAPPED	MOWBURNT	MUCKIER	MUDDY
MOULDMADE	MOUSEWEB	MOWE	MUCKIEST	MUDDYBRAINED
MOULDWARP	MOUSEY	MOWED	MUCKILY	MUDDYBREAST
MOULDY	MOUSIER	MOWER	MUCKINESS	MUDDYHEADED
MOULE	MOUSIEST	MOWHA	MUCKING	MUDDYING
MOULIN	MOUSILY	MOWHAY	MUCKITE	MUDFISH
MOULINAGE	MOUSINESS	MOWIE	MUCKLE	MUDFISHES
MOULINET	MOUSING	MOWING	MUCKMAN	MUDFLOW
MOULLEEN	MOUSLE	MOWLAND	MUCKMENT	MUDGE
MOULRUSH	MOUSLINGLY	MOWN	MUCKMIDDEN	MUDGUARD
MOULS	MOUSME	MOWRA	MUCKNA	MUDHEAD
MOULT	MOUSMEE	MOWS	MUCKRAKE	MUDHOLE
MOULTED	MOUSQUETAIRE	MOWSTEAD	MUCKRAKED	MUDHOOK
MOULTER	MOUSSE	MOWTH	MUCKRAKER	MUDIR
MOULTING	MOUSSELINE	MOXA	MUCKRAKING	MUDIRIA
MOULY	MOUSSEUX	MOXIE	MUCKSWEAT	MUDIRIEH
MOUND	MOUSTACHE	MOXIEBERRY	MUCKSY	MUDLAND
MOUNDED	MOUSTACHED	MOY	MUCKTHRIFT	MUDLARK
MOUNDING	MOUSTACHIAL	MOYEN	MUCKWEED	MUDLARKER
MOUNDSMAN	MOUSTACHIO	MOYENANT	MUCKWORM	MUDRA
MOUNDWORK	MOUSTOC	MOYENER	MUCKY	MUDROCK
MOUNT	MOUSY	MOYENNE	MUCOCELE	MUDSILL
MOUNTABLE	MOUTAN	MOYITE	MUCODERMAL	MUDSKIPPER
MOUNTAIN	MOUTH	MOYLE	MUCOFIBROUS	MUDSLINGER
MOUNTAINED	MOUTHABLE	MOYO	MUCOID	MUDSLINGING
MOUNTAINEER	MOUTHBREEDER	MOZAMBIQUE	MUCOIDAL	MUDSPATE
MOUNTAINEERING	MOUTHED	MOZEMIZE	MUCOPROTEIN	MUDSTAIN
MOUNTAINET	MOUTHER	MOZETTA	MUCOPURULENT	MUDSTONE
MOUNTAINETTE	MOUTHFUL	MOZING	MUCOPUS	MUDSUCKER
MOUNTAINOUS	MOUTHFULS	MOZO	MUCOR	MUDTRACK
MOUNTAINS	MOUTHIER	MOZZARELLA	MUCORACEOUS	MUDWEED
MOUNTAINSIDE	MOUTHIEST	MOZZETTA	MUCORINE	MUDWORT
MOUNTAINTOP	MOUTHILY	MPRET	MUCORIOID	MUEDDIN
MOUNTAINY	MOUTHINESS	MU	MUCORMYCOSIS	MUERMO
MOUNTANCE	MOUTHING	MUABLE	MUCORRHEA	MUET
MOUNTANT	MOUTHISHLY	MUANCE	MUCORRHOEA	MUETTE
MOUNTEBANK	MOUTHLIKE	MUANG	MUCOSA	MUEZZIN
MOUNTEBANKED	MOUTHPART	MUBARAT	MUCOSAL	MUFASAL
MOUNTEBANKLY	MOUTHPIECE	MUCAGO	MUCOSE	MUFF
MOUNTED	MOUTHPIPE	MUCARO	MUCOSEROUS	MUFFED
MOUNTEE	MOUTHS	MUCEDIN	MUCOSITY	MUFFET
MOUNTER	MOUTHWASH	MUCEDINE	MUCOUS	MUFFETEE
MOUNTIE	MOUTHY	MUCEDINEOUS	MUCRO	MUFFIN
MOUNTING	MOUTON	MUCEDINOUS	MUCRONATE	MUFFINEER
MOUNTINGLY	MOUTONEED	MUCH	MUCRONATED	MUFFING
MOUNTS	MOUTONNEE	MUCHACHA	MUCRONATELY	MUFFLE
MOUNTURE	MOUZAH	MUCHACHO	MUCRONATION	MUFFLED
MOUNTY	MOUZOUNA	MUCHACHOS	MUCRONES	MUFFLEMAN
MOUP	MOVABILITY	MUCHLY	MUCRONIFORM	MUFFLEMEN
MOURN	MOVABLE	MUCHNESS	MUCRONULATE	MUFFLER

MUFFLIN	MULCTED	MULTIFIDUS	MULTOCULAR	MUNGCORN
MUFFLING	MULCTUARY	MULTIFLOW	MULTUM	MUNGE
MUFFY	MULE	MULTIFOIL	MULTUNGULATE	MUNGER
MUFTI	MULEBACK	MULTIFOILED	MULTURE	MUNGEY
MUFTIS	MULEFOOT	MULTIFOLD	MULTURER	MUNGO
MUFTY	MULEFOOTED	MULTIFORM	MULVEL	MUNGOFA
MUG	MULEMAN	MULTIFORMED	MUM	MUNGOOSE
MUGA	MULEMEN	MULTIFORMITY	MUMBLE	MUNGOOSES
MUGEARITE	MULES	MULTIGAP	MUMBLEBEE	MUNGUBA
MUGG	MULET	MULTIGRAPH	MUMBLED	MUNGY
MUGGA	MULETA	MULTIGRAPHER	MUMBLEMENT	MUNI
MUGGAR	MULETEER	MULTILATERAL	MUMBLER	MUNICIPAL
MUGGED	MULETRESS	MULTILINGUAL	MUMBLING	MUNICIPALISM
MUGGER	MULETTA	MULTILITERAL	MUMBLINGLY	MUNICIPALIST
MUGGET	MULEWORT	MULTILITH	MUMBUDGET	MUNICIPALITIES
MUGGIER	MULEY	MULTILOCATION	MUMCHANCE	MUNICIPALITY
MUGGIEST	MULGA	MULTILOQUENT	MUME	MUNICIPALIZE
MUGGINESS	MULIEBRAL	MULTILOQUOUS	MUMHOUSE	MUNICIPALIZED
MUGGING	MULIEBRIA	MULTILOQUY	MUMJUMA	MUNICIPALIZING
MUGGINS	MULIEBRILE	MULTIMARBLE	MUMM	MUNICIPALLY
MUGGISH	MULIEBRITY.	MULTIMEDIA	MUMMED	MUNICIPIA
MUGGLES	MULIEBROUS	MULTIMODAL	MUMMER	MUNICIPIUM
MUGGS	MULIER	MULTINOMIAL	MUMMERIES	MUNIFIC
MUGGUR	MULIERINE	MULTIPARA	MUMMERY	MUNIFICENCE
MUGGY	MULIERLY	MULTIPARAE	MUMMIA	MUNIFICENCY
MUGHOPINE	MULIEROSE	MULTIPARITY	MUMMICHOG	MUNIFICENT
MUGHOUSE	MULIEROSITY	MULTIPAROUS	MUMMICK	MUNIFICENTLY
MUGIENCE	MULISH	MULTIPARTITE	MUMMIED	MUNIFY
MUGIENCY	MULISHLY	MULTIPED	MUMMIES	MUNIMENT
MUGIENT	MULISHNESS	MULTIPEDE	MUMMIFIED	MUNIMENTS
MUGILIFORM	MULITA	MULTIPHASE	MUMMIFORM	MUNITE
MUGILOID	MULK	MULTIPHASER	MUMMIFY	MUNITION
MUGS	MULL	MULTIPLANE	MUMMIFYING	MUNITIONARY
MUGUET	MULLA	MULTIPLE	MUMMING	MUNITIONEER
MUGWEED	MULLAH	MULTIPLET	MUMMY	MUNITIONER
MUGWET	MULLAR	MULTIPLEX	MUMMYING	MUNITY
MUGWORT	MULLED	MULTIPLIABLE	MUMMYLIKE	MUNJ
MUGWUMP	MULLEIN	MULTIPLICAND	MUMP	MUNJEET
MUGWUMPERY	MULLEN	MULTIPLICATE	MUMPED	MUNJISTIN
MUGWUMPIAN	MULLENIZE	MULTIPLICATION	MUMPER	MUNK
MUGWUMPISM	MULLER	MULTIPLICITY	MUMPHEAD	MUNNION
MUHAMMADI	MULLET	MULTIPLIED	MUMPING	MUNSHI
MUHLIES	MULLETRY	MULTIPLIER	MUMPISH	MUNSIFF
MUHLY	MULLETS	MULTIPLY	MUMPISHLY	MUNTIN
MUID	MULLEY	MULTIPLYING	MUMPISHNESS	MUNTING
MUIR	MULLID	MULTIPOLAR	MUMPS	MUNTJAC
MUIRBURN	MULLIGAN	MULTIPOLE	MUMPSIMUS	MUNTJAK
MUIRCOCK	MULLIGATAWNY	MULTIPOTENT	MUMRUFFIN	MUON
MUIRFOWL	MULLIGRUBS	MULTIPRESENT	MUMU	MUR
MUISHOND	MULLING	MULTISCIENCE	MUN	MURA
MUJER	MULLION	MULTISECT	MUNA	MURAENOID
MUJERES	MULLIONED	MULTISECTOR	MUNCH	MURAGE
MUJIK	MULLIONING	MULTISENSUAL	MUNCHED	MURAL
MUJTAHID	MULLOCK	MULTISONANT	MUNCHEE	MURALED
MUKHTAR	MULLOCKER	MULTISONOUS	MUNCHEEL	MURALIST
MUKLUK	MULLOCKY	MULTISTAGE	MUNCHER	MURARIUM
MUKTAR	MULLOID	MULTITARIAN	MUNCHET	MURASAKITE
MUKTATMA	MULLOWAY	MULTITHEISM	MUNCHING	MURCHY
MUKTEAR	MULM	MULTITUBE	MUND	MURCIANA
MUKTI	MULMUL	MULTITUDE	MUNDAL	MURDER
MUKTUK	MULSE	MULTITUDINAL	MUNDANE	MURDERED
MULADA	MULT	MULTITUDINOUS	MUNDANELY	MURDERER
MULADI	MULTANGLE	MULTITURN	MUNDANENESS	MURDERESS
MULAPRAKRITI	MULTANGULAR	MULTIVAGANT	MUNDANISM	MURDERING
MULATTO	MULTANGULOUS	MULTIVALENCE	MUNDANITY	MURDERINGLY
MULATTOES	MULTANGULUM	MULTIVALENCY	MUNDATORY	MURDEROUS
MULBERRIES	MULTANIMOUS	MULTIVALENT	MUNDIC	MURDEROUSLY
MULBERRY	MULTEITY	MULTIVALVE	MUNDIFICANT	MURDRUM
MULCH	MULTIBREAK	MULTIVARIANT	MUNDIFIER	MURE
MULCHED	MULTICOLORED	MULTIVARIOUS	MUNDIFY	MURED
MULCHING	MULTICYCLE	MULTIVERSANT	MUNDIL	MURENGER
MULCT	MULTIFARIOUS	MULTIVERSE	MUNDIVAGANT	MURES
MULCTABLE	MULTIFARIOUSNE	MULTIVIOUS	MUNDLE	MUREX
MULCTARY	MULTIFEROUS	MULTIVOCAL	MUNDUNGO	MUREXAN
MULCTATION	MULTIFID	MULTIVOLENT	MUNDUNGUS	MUREXES
MULCTATIVE	MULTIFIDLY	MULTIVOLTINE	MUNG	MUREXID
MULCTATORY	MULTIFIDOUS	MULTIWALL	MUNGA	MUREXIDE

MURGEON	MUSACEOUS	MUSHED	MUSLIN	MUTAGEN
MURIATE	MUSAF	MUSHER	MUSLINED	MUTANT
MURIATED	MUSAL	MUSHHEAD	MUSLINET	MUTAROTATE
MURIATIC	MUSANG	MUSHHEADED	MUSLINETTE	MUTAROTATION
MURICATE	MUSAR	MUSHIER	MUSNUD	MUTASE
MURICATED	MUSARD	MUSHIEST	MUSOPHAGINE	MUTATE
MURICES	MUSARDRY	MUSHILY	MUSPIKE	MUTATED
MURICID	MUSCA	MUSHINESS	MUSQUASH	MUTATING
MURICIFORM	MUSCADE	MUSHING	MUSQUASHROOT	MUTATION
MURICINE	MUSCADEL	MUSHLA	MUSQUASHWEED	MUTATIONAL
MURICOID	MUSCADIN	MUSHMELON	MUSQUASPEN	MUTATIONALLY
MURICULATE	MUSCADINE	MUSHROOM	MUSQUAW	MUTATIONISM
MURID	MUSCAE	MUSHROOMER	MUSROL	MUTATIONIST
MURIE	MUSCARDINE	MUSHROOMIC	MUSROOMED	MUTATIVE
MURIFORM	MUSCARIFORM	MUSHROOMING	MUSS	MUTATORY
MURIFORMLY	MUSCARINE	MUSHROOMY	MUSSACK	MUTAWALLI
MURINE	MUSCAT	MUSHRU	MUSSAL	MUTAWALLIS
MURING	MUSCATEL	MUSHRUMP	MUSSALCHEE	MUTCH
MURINUS	MUSCAVADA	MUSHY	MUSSED	MUTCHKIN
MURIONITRIC	MUSCICAPINE	MUSIC	MUSSEL	MUTE
MURIUM	MUSCICIDE	MUSICA	MUSSELCRACKER	MUTED
MURK	MUSCICOLE	MUSICAL	MUSSELED	MUTELY
MURKIER	MUSCICOLINE	MUSICALE	MUSSELER	MUTENESS
MURKIEST	MUSCICOLOUS	MUSICALITY	MUSSICK	MUTER
MURKILY	MUSCID	MUSICALIZE	MUSSIER	MUTESCENCE
MURKINESS	MUSCIFORM	MUSICALLY	MUSSIEST	MUTESSARIF
MURKISH	MUSCLE	MUSICALNESS	MUSSILY	MUTESSARIFAT
MURKLY	MUSCLED	MUSICATE	MUSSINESS	MUTH
MURKNESS	MUSCLEMAN	MUSICIAN	MUSSING	MUTHMANNITE
MURKSOME	MUSCLES	MUSICIANER	MUSSITATE	MUTI
MURKY	MUSCLING	MUSICIANLY	MUSSITATION	MUTIC
MURL	MUSCLY	MUSICIANS	MUSSUCK	MUTICOUS
MURLACK	MUSCOID	MUSICIANSHIP	MUSSUK	MUTILATE
MURLAIN	MUSCOLOGIC	MUSICKER	MUSSURANA	MUTILATED
MURLEMEWES	MUSCOLOGIST	MUSICLESS	MUSSY	MUTILATING
MURLIN	MUSCOLOGY	MUSICMONGER	MUST	MUTILATION
MURLOCK	MUSCONE	MUSICO	MUSTACHE	MUTILATIVE
MURLY	MUSCOSE	MUSICOGRAPHY	MUSTACHED	MUTILATOR
MURMUR	MUSCOSENESS	MUSICOLOGIES	MUSTACHIAL	MUTILATORY
MURMURATION	MUSCOSITY	MUSICOLOGIST	MUSTACHIO	MUTILLID
MURMURATOR	MUSCOVADE	MUSICOLOGY	MUSTACHIOED	MUTILOUS
MURMURED	MUSCOVADITE	MUSICOMANIA	MUSTAFINA	MUTINADO
MURMURER	MUSCOVADO	MUSICOPHOBIA	MUSTAFUZ	MUTINE
MURMURING	MUSCOVITE	MUSICOPOETIC	MUSTANG	MUTINEER
MURMURINGLY	MUSCOVITIZE	MUSICRY	MUSTANGER	MUTINEERS
MURMURISH	MUSCOVITIZED	MUSIMON	MUSTARD	MUTING
MURMUROUS	MUSCOVY	MUSING	MUSTARDER	MUTINIED
MURMUROUSLY	MUSCULAR	MUSINGLY	MUSTED	MUTINIES
MURNIVAL	MUSCULARITY	MUSION	MUSTEE	MUTINOUS
MUROID	MUSCULARIZE	MUSIVE	MUSTELID	MUTINOUSLY
MUROMONTITE	MUSCULARLY	MUSJID	MUSTELIN	MUTINOUSNESS
MURON	MUSCULATION	MUSK	MUSTELINE	MUTINY
MURPHIES	MUSCULATURE	MUSKALLUNGE	MUSTELINOUS	MUTINYING
MURPHY	MUSCULE	MUSKEG	MUSTELOID	MUTISM
MURR	MUSCULI	MUSKEGGY	MUSTER	MUTIST
MURRA	MUSCULIN	MUSKELLUNGE	MUSTERED	MUTISTIC
MURRAH	MUSCULUS	MUSKELLUNGES	MUSTERER	MUTIVE
MURRAIN	MUSE	MUSKET	MUSTERING	MUTIVITY
MURRAL	MUSED	MUSKETADE	MUSTERMASTER	MUTOSCOPE
MURRAY	MUSEE	MUSKETEER	MUSTERS	MUTOSCOPIC
MURRE	MUSEFUL	MUSKETOON	MUSTH	MUTSJE
MURRELET	MUSEFULLY	MUSKETRY	MUSTIER	MUTSUDDY
MURRES	MUSELESS	MUSKGRASS	MUSTIEST	MUTT
MURREY	MUSELESSNESS	MUSKIE	MUSTIFY	MUTTER
MURRHA	MUSEOGRAPHER	MUSKIER	MUSTILY	MUTTERED
MURRHINE	MUSEOGRAPHY	MUSKIEST	MUSTINESS	MUTTERER
MURRHUINE	MUSEOLOGIST	MUSKIFIED	MUSTING	MUTTERING
MURRINA	MUSEOLOGY	MUSKILY	MUSTULENT	MUTTERINGLY
MURRNONG	MUSER	MUSKINESS	MUSTY	MUTTON
MURRY	MUSERY	MUSKISH	MUSUMEE	MUTTONBIRD
MURSHID	MUSES	MUSKIT	MUT	MUTTONCHOP
MURTHER	MUSET	MUSKMELON	MUTA	MUTTONCHOPS
MURTHERER	MUSETTE	MUSKRAT	MUTABILITY	MUTTONFISH
MURUMURU	MUSEUM	MUSKRATS	MUTABLE	MUTTONFISHES
MURUP	MUSH	MUSKROOT	MUTABLENESS	MUTTONHEAD
MURVA	MUSHA	MUSKWOOD	MUTABLY	MUTTONHEADED
MURZA	MUSHAA	MUSKY	MUTAGE	MUTTONMONGER

MUTTONWOOD
MUTUA
MUTUAL
MUTUALISM
MUTUALIST
MUTUALISTIC
MUTUALITY
MUTUALIZE
MUTUALIZED
MUTUALIZING
MUTUALLY
MUTUARY
MUTUATE
MUTUATITIOUS
MUTUEL
MUTULE
MUTUUM
MUTWALLI
MUUMUU
MUVULE
MUX
MUY
MUYUSA
MUZHIK
MUZJIK
MUZOONA
MUZZ
MUZZIER
MUZZIEST
MUZZLE
MUZZLED
MUZZLELOADER
MUZZLELOADING
MUZZLER
MUZZLEWOOD
MUZZLING
MUZZY
MWAMI
MY
MYAL
MYALGIA
MYALGIC
MYALISM
MYALL
MYARIAN
MYASTHENIA
MYASTHENIC
MYATONIA
MYATONIC
MYATONY
MYATROPHY
MYCELE
MYCELIAL
MYCELIAN
MYCELIOID
MYCELIUM
MYCELOID
MYCETISM
MYCETOCYTE
MYCETOGENIC
MYCETOGENOUS
MYCETOID
MYCETOLOGY
MYCETOMA
MYCETOMATA
MYCETOMATOUS
MYCETOME
MYCETOUS
MYCETOZOAN
MYCETOZOON
MYCOCECIDIUM
MYCODERM
MYCODERMA
MYCODERMIC
MYCODOMATIUM
MYCOID
MYCOLOGIC

MYCOLOGICAL
MYCOLOGIES
MYCOLOGIST
MYCOLOGIZE
MYCOLOGY
MYCOMYCETE
MYCOMYCETOUS
MYCOPHAGIST
MYCOPHAGOUS
MYCOPHAGY
MYCOPLASM
MYCOPLASMA
MYCORHIZA
MYCORHIZAL
MYCORRHIZA
MYCORRHIZAL
MYCORRHIZIC
MYCOSE
MYCOSIN
MYCOSIS
MYCOSTEROL
MYCOTIC
MYCOTROPHIC
MYCTERIC
MYCTERISM
MYCTOPHID
MYDALEINE
MYDATOXINE
MYDINE
MYDRIASINE
MYDRIASIS
MYDRIATIC
MYDRIATINE
MYECTOMIZE
MYECTOMY
MYECTOPIA
MYECTOPY
MYELALGIA
MYELAPOPLEXY
MYELASTHENIA
MYELATROPHY
MYELAUXE
MYELEMIA
MYELIC
MYELIN
MYELINATE
MYELINATED
MYELINATION
MYELINE
MYELINIC
MYELINOGENY
MYELITIC
MYELITIS
MYELOBLAST
MYELOBLASTIC
MYELOCELE
MYELOCOELE
MYELOCYST
MYELOCYSTIC
MYELOCYTE
MYELOCYTIC
MYELOCYTOSIS
MYELOGENESIS
MYELOGENETIC
MYELOGENOUS
MYELOGONIUM
MYELOIC
MYELOID
MYELOMA
MYELOMALACIA
MYELOMAS
MYELOMATA
MYELOMATOID
MYELOMATOSIS
MYELOMENIA
MYELON
MYELONAL

MYELONIC
MYELOPATHIC
MYELOPATHY
MYELOPETAL
MYELOPLAST
MYELOPLASTIC
MYELOPLAX
MYELOPLAXES
MYELOPLEGIA
MYELOPOIESIS
MYELOPOIETIC
MYELORRHAGIA
MYELORRHAPHY
MYELOSARCOMA
MYELOSPASM
MYELOTHERAPY
MYENTASIS
MYENTERIC
MYENTERON
MYGALE
MYGALID
MYGALOID
MYIASIS
MYIODESOPSIA
MYKISS
MYLODONT
MYLOHYOID
MYLOHYOIDEAN
MYLONITE
MYLONITIC
MYMARID
MYNA
MYNAH
MYNHEER
MYNPACHT
MYOALBUMIN
MYOALBUMOSE
MYOATROPHY
MYOBLAST
MYOBLASTIC
MYOCARDIAC
MYOCARDIAL
MYOCARDITIC
MYOCARDITIS
MYOCARDIUM
MYOCLONIC
MYOCLONUS
MYOCOEL
MYOCOELE
MYOCOELOM
MYOCOLPITIS
MYOCOMMA
MYOCOMMATA
MYOCYTE
MYODIASTASIS
MYODYNAMIA
MYODYNAMIC
MYODYNAMICS
MYOEDEMA
MYOELECTRIC
MYOENOTOMY
MYOFIBRIL
MYOFIBRILLA
MYOFIBROMA
MYOGEN
MYOGENESIS
MYOGENETIC
MYOGENIC
MYOGENOUS
MYOGLOBIN
MYOGLOBULIN
MYOGRAM
MYOGRAPH
MYOGRAPHER
MYOGRAPHIC
MYOGRAPHICAL
MYOGRAPHIST

MYOGRAPHY
MYOHAEMATIN
MYOHEMATIN
MYOID
MYOKINESIS
MYOLEMMA
MYOLIPOMA
MYOLIPOSIS
MYOLOGIC
MYOLOGICAL
MYOLOGIST
MYOLOGY
MYOLYSIS
MYOMA
MYOMALACIA
MYOMANCY
MYOMANTIC
MYOMATA
MYOMATOUS
MYOMECTOMIES
MYOMECTOMY
MYOMELANOSIS
MYOMERE
MYOMETRITIS
MYOMETRIUM
MYOMORPH
MYOMORPHIC
MYOMOTOMY
MYONEMA
MYONEME
MYONEURAL
MYONEURALGIA
MYONEURE
MYONEUROMA
MYONEUROSIS
MYONOSUS
MYOPACHYNSIS
MYOPARALYSIS
MYOPARESIS
MYOPATHIA
MYOPATHIC
MYOPATHY
MYOPE
MYOPHAN
MYOPHORE
MYOPHOROUS
MYOPHYSICAL
MYOPHYSICS
MYOPIA
MYOPIC
MYOPICAL
MYOPICALLY
MYOPLASM
MYOPLASTIC
MYOPLASTY
MYOPOLAR
MYOPORACEOUS
MYOPORAD
MYOPROTEID
MYOPROTEIN
MYOPROTEOSE
MYOPS
MYOPY
MYORRHAPHY
MYORRHEXIS
MYOSARCOMA
MYOSCLEROSIS
MYOSCOPE
MYOSEPTUM
MYOSIN
MYOSIS
MYOSITIC
MYOSITIS
MYOSOTE
MYOSOTIS
MYOSPASM
MYOSPASMIA

MYOSUTURE
MYOSYNIZESIS
MYOTASIS
MYOTHERMIC
MYOTIC
MYOTOME
MYOTOMIC
MYOTOMY
MYOTONIA
MYOTROPHY
MYOWUN
MYOXINE
MYRCENE
MYRIACOULOMB
MYRIAD
MYRIADED
MYRIADLY
MYRIAGRAM
MYRIAGRAMME
MYRIALITER
MYRIALITRE
MYRIAMETER
MYRIAMETRE
MYRIAPOD
MYRIAPODAN
MYRIAPODOUS
MYRIARCH
MYRIARCHY
MYRIARE
MYRICA
MYRICACEOUS
MYRICETIN
MYRICIN
MYRICYL
MYRICYLIC
MYRINGA
MYRINGECTOMY
MYRINGITIS
MYRINGOTOME
MYRINGOTOMY
MYRIOLOGIST
MYRIOLOGUE
MYRIORAMA
MYRIOSCOPE
MYRIOSPOROUS
MYRIOTHEISM
MYRISTATE
MYRISTIC
MYRISTIN
MYRISTONE
MYRMECOBIINE
MYRMECOCHORY
MYRMECOID
MYRMECOIDY
MYRMECOLOGY
MYRMECOPHILE
MYRMECOPHILY
MYRMECOPHYTE
MYRMEKITE
MYRMICID
MYRMICINE
MYRMICOID
MYRMIDON
MYRMOTHERINE
MYROBALAN
MYRONATE
MYROPOLIST
MYROSIN
MYRRH
MYRRHED
MYRRHIC
MYRRHINE
MYRRHOL
MYRRHOPHORE
MYRRHY
MYRSINACEOUS
MYRSINAD

MYRT
MYRTACEOUS
MYRTAL
MYRTIFORM
MYRTLE
MYRTLEBERRY
MYRTOL
MYSELF
MYSEN
MYSID
MYSIDEAN
MYSOID
MYSOPHOBIA
MYSOST
MYST
MYSTACAL
MYSTACIAL
MYSTACINE
MYSTACINOUS
MYSTAGOG
MYSTAGOGIC
MYSTAGOGICAL
MYSTAGOGUE
MYSTAGOGY
MYSTAX
MYSTERIAL
MYSTERIARCH
MYSTERIES
MYSTERIOUS
MYSTERIOUSLY
MYSTERIZE
MYSTERY
MYSTES
MYSTIC
MYSTICAL
MYSTICALITY
MYSTICALLY
MYSTICALNESS
MYSTICETE
MYSTICISM
MYSTICITY
MYSTIFICALLY
MYSTIFICATOR
MYSTIFIED
MYSTIFIER
MYSTIFY
MYSTIFYING
MYSTIFYINGLY
MYSTIQUE
MYTACISM
MYTH
MYTHE
MYTHIC
MYTHICAL
MYTHICALISM
MYTHICALITY
MYTHICALLY
MYTHICALNESS
MYTHICISM
MYTHICIST
MYTHICIZE
MYTHICIZED
MYTHICIZER
MYTHICIZING
MYTHIFY
MYTHIST
MYTHOCLAST
MYTHOCLASTIC
MYTHOGENESIS
MYTHOGENY
MYTHOGONIC
MYTHOGONY
MYTHOGRAPHER
MYTHOGRAPHY
MYTHOGREEN
MYTHOHEROIC
MYTHOLOGEMA

MYTHOLOGER
MYTHOLOGIAN
MYTHOLOGIC
MYTHOLOGICAL
MYTHOLOGIES
MYTHOLOGISE
MYTHOLOGIST
MYTHOLOGIZE
MYTHOLOGIZED
MYTHOLOGIZER
MYTHOLOGIZING
MYTHOLOGUE
MYTHOLOGY
MYTHOMANIA
MYTHOMANIAC
MYTHOMETER
MYTHONOMY
MYTHOPEIC
MYTHOPEIST
MYTHOPOEIA
MYTHOPOEIC
MYTHOPOEISM
MYTHOPOEIST
MYTHOPOEM
MYTHOPOESIS
MYTHOPOESY
MYTHOPOET
MYTHOPOETIC
MYTHOPOETIZE
MYTHOPOETRY
MYTHOS
MYTILACEAN
MYTILACEOUS
MYTILID
MYTILIFORM
MYTILOID
MYTILOTOXINE
MYXA
MYXADENITIS
MYXADENOMA
MYXAEMIA
MYXAMOEBA
MYXANGITIS
MYXASTHENIA
MYXEDEMA
MYXEDEMATOUS
MYXEDEMIC
MYXEMIA
MYXINOID
MYXO
MYXOBLASTOMA
MYXOCYSTOMA
MYXOCYTE
MYXOEDEMA
MYXOEDEMIC
MYXOFIBROMA
MYXOGASTER
MYXOGLIOMA
MYXOID
MYXOINOMA
MYXOLIPOMA
MYXOMA
MYXOMAS
MYXOMATA
MYXOMATOSIS
MYXOMATOUS
MYXOMYCETE
MYXOMYCETOUS
MYXOMYOMA
MYXONEUROMA
MYXOPODIA
MYXOPODIUM
MYXORRHEA
MYXOSARCOMA
MYXOSPORE
MYXOSPOROUS
MYXOTHECA

MYZONT
MYZOSTOMID
MYZOSTOMIDAN
MYZOSTOMOUS

NA
NAAM
NAARTJE
NAB
NABAK
NABAM
NABBED
NABBER
NABBING
NABBUK
NABBY
NABCHEAT
NABEE
NABK
NABLA
NABLE
NABLUS
NABO
NABOB
NABOBERY
NABOBESS
NABOBICAL
NABOBISH
NABOBISHLY
NABOBISM
NABOBRY
NABS
NACARAT
NACARINE
NACE
NACELLE
NACHTMAAL
NACK
NACKET
NACRE
NACRED
NACREOUS
NACRINE
NACROUS
NACRY
NADA
NADDER
NADIR
NADIRAL
NADORITE
NAE
NAEGAIT
NAEGATE
NAEGATES
NAEL
NAEVE
NAEVOID
NAEVUS
NAG
NAGA
NAGAIKA
NAGAMI
NAGANA
NAGARA
NAGATELITE
NAGGAR
NAGGED
NAGGER
NAGGIN
NAGGING
NAGGINGLY
NAGGINGNESS

NAGGISH
NAGGLE
NAGGLY
NAGGY
NAGHT
NAGID
NAGKASSAR
NAGMAAL
NAGMAN
NAGOR
NAGSMAN
NAGSTER
NAGUAL
NAGUALISM
NAGUALIST
NAGYAGITE
NAHIE
NAHOOR
NAIAD
NAIANT
NAIB
NAID
NAIF
NAIFLY
NAIG
NAIGUE
NAIK
NAIL
NAILED
NAILER
NAILERY
NAILHEAD
NAILING
NAILLESS
NAILROD
NAILS
NAILSICK
NAILWORT
NAILY
NAINSEL
NAINSELL
NAINSOOK
NAIO
NAIQUE
NAIRY
NAIS
NAISH
NAISSANCE
NAISSANT
NAIT
NAITLY
NAIVE
NAIVELY
NAIVENESS
NAIVETE
NAIVETY
NAK
NAKE
NAKED
NAKEDIZE
NAKEDLY
NAKEDNESS
NAKEDWOOD
NAKER
NAKHLITE
NAKHOD
NAKHODA
NAKONG
NAKOO
NAL
NALL
NALLAH
NALLE
NAMABILITY
NAMABLE
NAMAQUA
NAMAYCUSH

NAMAZ
NAMAZLIK
NAMBY
NAMDA
NAME
NAMEABILITY
NAMEABLE
NAMEBOARD
NAMED
NAMELESS
NAMELESSLY
NAMELESSNESS
NAMELING
NAMELY
NAMEPLATE
NAMER
NAMESAKE
NAMING
NAMMAD
NAN
NANA
NANANDER
NANAWOOD
NANCA
NANCY
NANDIN
NANDINE
NANDOW
NANDU
NANDUTI
NANE
NANES
NANGA
NANGCA
NANGER
NANGKA
NANIGO
NANISM
NANITIC
NANIZATION
NANKEEN
NANKEENS
NANKIN
NANKINS
NANMU
NANNANDER
NANNIE
NANNIES
NANNINOSE
NANNY
NANOCEPHALIA
NANOCEPHALIC
NANOCEPHALUS
NANOCEPHALY
NANOID
NANOMELIA
NANOMELOUS
NANOMELUS
NANOPLANKTON
NANOSOMA
NANOSOMUS
NANPIE
NANSOMIA
NANT
NANTLE
NANTOKITE
NANTS
NAO
NAOLOGICAL
NAOLOGY
NAOMETRY
NAOS
NAP
NAPA
NAPAL
NAPALM
NAPE

NAPEAD
NAPECREST
NAPELLUS
NAPERER
NAPERIES
NAPERY
NAPHTHA
NAPHTHACENE
NAPHTHALATE
NAPHTHALENE
NAPHTHALENIC
NAPHTHALIC
NAPHTHALIZE
NAPHTHAMINE
NAPHTHENE
NAPHTHENIC
NAPHTHIONATE
NAPHTHOIC
NAPHTHOL
NAPHTHOLATE
NAPHTHOUS
NAPHTHYL
NAPHTHYLENE
NAPHTHYLIC
NAPIFORM
NAPKIN
NAPKINED
NAPKINING
NAPKINS
NAPLESS
NAPLESSNESS
NAPOLEON
NAPOO
NAPOOH
NAPPE
NAPPED
NAPPER
NAPPIE
NAPPINESS
NAPPING
NAPPISHNESS
NAPPY
NAPRAPATHY
NAPRON
NAPU
NAR
NARCEIN
NARCEINE
NARCISM
NARCISSISM
NARCISSIST
NARCISSISTIC
NARCISSUS
NARCIST
NARCISTIC
NARCOHYPNIA
NARCOLEPSY
NARCOLEPTIC
NARCOMA
NARCOMANIA
NARCOMANIAC
NARCOMANIACAL
NARCOMAS
NARCOMATA
NARCOMEDUSAN
NARCOSE
NARCOSIS
NARCOTIA
NARCOTIC
NARCOTICAL
NARCOTICALLY
NARCOTICISM
NARCOTICS
NARCOTIN
NARCOTINA
NARCOTINE
NARCOTINIC

NARCOTISM
NARCOTIST
NARCOTIZE
NARCOTIZED
NARCOTIZING
NARD
NARDINE
NARDO
NARDOO
NARDU
NARE
NARES
NARGHILE
NARGIL
NARGILE
NARGILEH
NARIAL
NARICA
NARICORN
NARIFORM
NARINE
NARINGENIN
NARINGIN
NARIS
NARK
NARKY
NARR
NARRA
NARRANTE
NARRAS
NARRATABLE
NARRATE
NARRATION
NARRATIONAL
NARRATIVE
NARRATIVELY
NARRATOR
NARRATORY
NARRATRESS
NARRAWOOD
NARROW
NARROWED
NARROWER
NARROWEST
NARROWING
NARROWLY
NARROWNESS
NARROWY
NARSARSUKITE
NARSINGA
NARTHECAL
NARTHEX
NARWAL
NARWHAL
NARWHALE
NARY
NAS
NASAB
NASAL
NASALIS
NASALISM
NASALITY
NASALIZATION
NASALIZE
NASALIZED
NASALIZING
NASALLY
NASARD
NASAT
NASAUMP
NASCENCE
NASCENCY
NASCENT
NASCH
NASE
NASEBERRY
NASETHMOID

NASH
NASHGAB
NASHGOB
NASI
NASIAL
NASICORN
NASICORNOUS
NASIFORM
NASILABIAL
NASILLATE
NASILLATION
NASION
NASITIS
NASOANTRAL
NASOBASILAR
NASOBUCCAL
NASOCILIARY
NASOFRONTAL
NASOLABIAL
NASOLOGICAL
NASOLOGIST
NASOLOGY
NASOMALAR
NASONITE
NASOORBITAL
NASOPALATAL
NASOPALATINE
NASOPHARYNX
NASOROSTRAL
NASOSCOPE
NASOSEPTAL
NASOSINUITIS
NASOSUBNASAL
NASROL
NASSOLOGY
NAST
NASTALIQ
NASTIC
NASTIER
NASTIEST
NASTIKA
NASTILY
NASTINESS
NASTURTIUM
NASTY
NASUS
NASUTE
NASUTENESS
NASUTIFORM
NAT
NATA
NATABILITY
NATAKA
NATAL
NATALITIAL
NATALITY
NATANT
NATANTLY
NATATION
NATATOR
NATATORIAL
NATATORIOUS
NATATORIUM
NATATORY
NATCH
NATCHBONE
NATCHNEE
NATE
NATED
NATES
NATHE
NATHER
NATHLESS
NATICIFORM
NATICINE
NATICOID
NATIFORM

NATION
NATIONAL
NATIONALISM
NATIONALIST
NATIONALISTIC
NATIONALISTICALLY
NATIONALITY
NATIONALIZATION
NATIONALIZE
NATIONALIZED
NATIONALIZER
NATIONALIZING
NATIONALLY
NATIONALNESS
NATIONS
NATIVE
NATIVELY
NATIVISM
NATIVIST
NATIVISTIC
NATIVITIES
NATIVITY
NATR
NATRIUM
NATROCHALCITE
NATROJAROSITE
NATROLITE
NATRON
NATTE
NATTER
NATTERED
NATTEREDNESS
NATTERJACK
NATTIER
NATTIEST
NATTILY
NATTLE
NATTOCK
NATTY
NATUARY
NATURA
NATURAL
NATURALESQUE
NATURALIA
NATURALISE
NATURALISM
NATURALIST
NATURALISTIC
NATURALITY
NATURALIZE
NATURALIZED
NATURALIZER
NATURALIZING
NATURALLY
NATURALNESS
NATURATA
NATURE
NATURECRAFT
NATURED
NATURING
NATURISM
NATURIST
NATURISTIC
NATURIZE
NATUROPATH
NATUROPATHIC
NATUROPATHY
NATYA
NAU
NAUCORID
NAUCRAR
NAUCRARY
NAUFRAGE
NAUFRAGOUS
NAUGER
NAUGHT
NAUGHTIER

NAUGHTIEST
NAUGHTILY
NAUGHTINESS
NAUGHTY
NAUJAITE
NAUKRAR
NAULUM
NAUMACHIA
NAUMACHIAE
NAUMACHIAS
NAUMACHIES
NAUMACHY
NAUMANNITE
NAUMK
NAUMKEAG
NAUMKEAGER
NAUNT
NAUNTLE
NAUPATHIA
NAUPLIAL
NAUPLIIFORM
NAUPLIOID
NAUPLIUS
NAUROPOMETER
NAUSCOPY
NAUSEA
NAUSEANT
NAUSEATE
NAUSEATED
NAUSEATING
NAUSEATION
NAUSEOUS
NAUSEOUSLY
NAUSEOUSNESS
NAUSITY
NAUT
NAUTCH
NAUTHER
NAUTIC
NAUTICAL
NAUTICALITY
NAUTICALLY
NAUTICS
NAUTIFORM
NAUTILACEAN
NAUTILI
NAUTILICONE
NAUTILIFORM
NAUTILITE
NAUTILOID
NAUTILOIDEAN
NAUTILUS
NAUTILUSES
NAVAL
NAVALISM
NAVALIST
NAVALISTIC
NAVARCH
NAVARCHY
NAVARHO
NAVARIN
NAVE
NAVEL
NAVELED
NAVELWORT
NAVET
NAVETA
NAVETTE
NAVEW
NAVIA
NAVICELLA
NAVICERT
NAVICULA
NAVICULAR
NAVICULARE
NAVICULOID
NAVIES

NAVIFORM
NAVIGABILITY
NAVIGABLE
NAVIGABLENESS
NAVIGABLY
NAVIGANT
NAVIGATE
NAVIGATED
NAVIGATING
NAVIGATION
NAVIGATIONAL
NAVIGATOR
NAVIGEROUS
NAVIPENDULAR
NAVIPENDULUM
NAVITE
NAVVIE
NAVVIES
NAVVY
NAVY
NAW
NAWAB
NAWOB
NAWT
NAY
NAYAK
NAYAUR
NAYSAY
NAYWARD
NAYWORD
NAZARD
NAZE
NAZI
NAZIFICATION
NAZIFIED
NAZIFY
NAZIFYING
NAZIM
NAZIR
NAZIS
NE
NEAKES
NEAL
NEALLOTYPE
NEANIC
NEAP
NEAPED
NEAR
NEARABOUT
NEARABOUTS
NEARAWAY
NEARAWAYS
NEARBY
NEARED
NEARER
NEAREST
NEARING
NEARISH
NEARLIER
NEARLIEST
NEARLY
NEARMOST
NEARNESS
NEARSIGHT
NEARSIGHTED
NEARSIGHTEDLY
NEARSIGHTEDNESS
NEARTHROSIS
NEASCUS
NEAT
NEATEN
NEATER
NEATEST
NEATH
NEATHERD
NEATHERDESS
NEATHMOST

NEATIFY
NEATLY
NEATNESS
NEAVIL
NEB
NEBACK
NEBALIOID
NEBBED
NEBBUCK
NEBBUK
NEBBY
NEBENKERN
NEBRIS
NEBRODI
NEBUK
NEBULA
NEBULAE
NEBULAR
NEBULARIZATION
NEBULARIZE
NEBULAS
NEBULATED
NEBULATION
NEBULE
NEBULESCENT
NEBULIFEROUS
NEBULITE
NEBULIUM
NEBULIZATION
NEBULIZE
NEBULIZED
NEBULIZER
NEBULIZING
NEBULON
NEBULOSE
NEBULOSITY
NEBULOUS
NEBULOUSLY
NEBULOUSNESS
NECESSAR
NECESSARIES
NECESSARILY
NECESSARY
NECESSE
NECESSISM
NECESSIST
NECESSITARIAN
NECESSITATE
NECESSITATED
NECESSITATING
NECESSITATIVE
NECESSITIES
NECESSITOUS
NECESSITUDE
NECESSITY
NECK
NECKAR
NECKATEE
NECKBAND
NECKCLOTH
NECKED
NECKENGER
NECKER
NECKERCHER
NECKERCHIEF
NECKGUARD
NECKING
NECKINGER
NECKLACE
NECKLACED
NECKLACEWEED
NECKLET
NECKLINE
NECKMOLD
NECKMOULD
NECKPIECE
NECKTIE

NECKWEAR
NECKWEED
NECRAEMIA
NECRECTOMY
NECREMIA
NECROBIOSIS
NECROBIOTIC
NECROGENIC
NECROGENOUS
NECROLATRY
NECROLOGICAL
NECROLOGIST
NECROLOGUE
NECROLOGY
NECROMANCER
NECROMANCING
NECROMANCY
NECROMANIA
NECROMANTIC
NECRONITE
NECROPATHY
NECROPHAGOUS
NECROPHIL
NECROPHILE
NECROPHILIA
NECROPHILIC
NECROPHILOUS
NECROPHOBIA
NECROPHOBIC
NECROPOLEIS
NECROPOLIS
NECROPOLISES
NECROPOLITAN
NECROPSIES
NECROPSY
NECROSCOPIC
NECROSCOPY
NECROSE
NECROSED
NECROSES
NECROSING
NECROSIS
NECROTIC
NECROTIZE
NECROTOMIC
NECROTOMIES
NECROTOMIST
NECROTOMY
NECROTYPE
NECROTYPIC
NECTAR
NECTAREAL
NECTAREAN
NECTARED
NECTAREOUS
NECTAREOUSLY
NECTARIAL
NECTARIAN
NECTARIED
NECTARIES
NECTARIFEROUS
NECTARIN
NECTARINE
NECTARIOUS
NECTARIUM
NECTARIZE
NECTAROUS
NECTARY
NECTIFEROUS
NECTOCALYCES
NECTOCALYCINE
NECTOCALYX
NECTON
NECTOPHORE
NECTOPOD
NECTRON
NEDDER

NEDDIES
NEDDY
NEE
NEED
NEEDER
NEEDFIRE
NEEDFUL
NEEDFULLY
NEEDFULNESS
NEEDGATES
NEEDIER
NEEDIEST
NEEDINESS
NEEDING
NEEDLE
NEEDLEBILL
NEEDLEBOOK
NEEDLEBUSH
NEEDLECASE
NEEDLED
NEEDLEFISH
NEEDLEFISHES
NEEDLEFUL
NEEDLELIKE
NEEDLEMAKER
NEEDLEMAKING
NEEDLEMAN
NEEDLEMEN
NEEDLEMONGER
NEEDLEPOINT
NEEDLEPROOF
NEEDLER
NEEDLES
NEEDLESS
NEEDLESSLY
NEEDLESSNESS
NEEDLESTONE
NEEDLEWOMAN
NEEDLEWOOD
NEEDLEWORK
NEEDLEWORKER
NEEDLING
NEEDLY
NEEDMENTS
NEEDS
NEEDSOME
NEEDY
NEELE
NEEM
NEEMBA
NEEN
NEENCEPHALIC
NEENCEPHALON
NEEP
NEER
NEESE
NEEZE
NEF
NEFANDOUS
NEFARIOUS
NEFARIOUSLY
NEFAS
NEFAST
NEFFY
NEFTE
NEFTGIL
NEGARA
NEGATE
NEGATED
NEGATING
NEGATION
NEGATIONAL
NEGATIONIST
NEGATIVE
NEGATIVED
NEGATIVELY
NEGATIVENESS

NEGATIVER
NEGATIVING
NEGATIVISM
NEGATIVIST
NEGATIVISTIC
NEGATIVITY
NEGATOR
NEGATORY
NEGER
NEGINOTH
NEGLECT
NEGLECTABLE
NEGLECTED
NEGLECTER
NEGLECTFUL
NEGLECTFULLY
NEGLECTFULNESS
NEGLECTING
NEGLECTION
NEGLECTIVE
NEGLECTOR
NEGLIGEE
NEGLIGENCE
NEGLIGENCY
NEGLIGENT
NEGLIGENTLY
NEGLIGIBILITY
NEGLIGIBLE
NEGLIGIBLY
NEGOCE
NEGOTIABLE
NEGOTIANT
NEGOTIATE
NEGOTIATED
NEGOTIATING
NEGOTIATION
NEGOTIATOR
NEGOTIATORY
NEGOTIATRESS
NEGOTIATRIX
NEGRILLO
NEGRINE
NEGRITA
NEGRITUDE
NEGRO
NEGROHEAD
NEGROS
NEGUS
NEHILOTH
NEHU
NEI
NEIF
NEIFE
NEIGH
NEIGHBOR
NEIGHBORED
NEIGHBORER
NEIGHBORESS
NEIGHBORHOOD
NEIGHBORHOODS
NEIGHBORING
NEIGHBORLY
NEIGHBORS
NEIGHBOUR
NEIGHBOURED
NEIGHBOURER
NEIGHBOURESS
NEIGHBOURHOOD
NEIGHBOURING
NEIGHBOURLY
NEIGHED
NEIGHER
NEIGHING
NEILAH
NEIPER
NEIST
NEITHER

NEKTON
NELLY
NELMA
NELSONITE
NELUMBIAN
NELUMBO
NEMA
NEMALINE
NEMALITE
NEMATHECE
NEMATHECIAL
NEMATHECIUM
NEMATOBLAST
NEMATOCERAN
NEMATOCIDE
NEMATOCYST
NEMATOCYSTIC
NEMATODE
NEMATODIASIS
NEMATOGEN
NEMATOGENE
NEMATOGENIC
NEMATOGONE
NEMATOIDEAN
NEMATOLOGIST
NEMATOLOGY
NEMATOPHYTON
NEMATOZOOID
NEMBUTSU
NEMEA
NEMERTEAN
NEMERTIAN
NEMERTINE
NEMERTINEAN
NEMERTOID
NEMESIC
NEMESIS
NEMME
NEMN
NEMOPHILIST
NEMOPHILOUS
NEMOPHILY
NEMORAL
NEMORICOLE
NEMORICOLINE
NEMORICOLOUS
NEMPNE
NENE
NENTA
NENUPHAR
NEO
NEOBLASTIC
NEOCEROTIC
NEOCLASSIC
NEOCLASSICISM
NEOCOSMIC
NEOCRACY
NEOCRITICISM
NEOCYANINE
NEOCYTE
NEOCYTOSIS
NEODAMODE
NEODIDYMIUM
NEODYMIUM
NEOFETAL
NEOFETUS
NEOFORMATION
NEOFORMATIVE
NEOGAMOUS
NEOGAMY
NEOGENESIS
NEOGENETIC
NEOGNATHIC
NEOGNATHOUS
NEOGRAPHIC
NEOIMPRESSIONISM
NEOLATER

NEOLATRY
NEOLITH
NEOLITHIC
NEOLOGIAN
NEOLOGIC
NEOLOGICAL
NEOLOGICALLY
NEOLOGISM
NEOLOGIST
NEOLOGISTIC
NEOLOGISTICAL
NEOLOGIZE
NEOLOGIZED
NEOLOGIZING
NEOLOGY
NEOMENIA
NEOMENIAN
NEOMIRACLE
NEOMODAL
NEOMORPH
NEOMORPHIC
NEOMORPHISM
NEOMYCIN
NEON
NEONATAL
NEONATUS
NEONOMIAN
NEONOMIANISM
NEONYCHIUM
NEOORTHODOXY
NEOPAGAN
NEOPAGANISM
NEOPAGANIZE
NEOPALLIAL
NEOPALLIUM
NEOPHILISM
NEOPHOBIA
NEOPHOBIC
NEOPHRASTIC
NEOPHYTE
NEOPHYTIC
NEOPHYTISH
NEOPHYTISM
NEOPINE
NEOPLASIA
NEOPLASM
NEOPLASMS
NEOPLASTIC
NEOPLASTIES
NEOPLASTY
NEOPRENE
NEORAMA
NEOSSIN
NEOSSOLOGY
NEOSSOPTILE
NEOSTRIATUM
NEOSTYLE
NEOTEINIA
NEOTENIA
NEOTENY
NEOTERIC
NEOTERICAL
NEOTERICALLY
NEOTERISM
NEOTERIST
NEOTERISTIC
NEOTERIZE
NEOTHALAMUS
NEOTYPE
NEOVITALISM
NEOVOLCANIC
NEOYTTERBIUM
NEP
NEPAL
NEPE
NEPENTHE
NEPENTHEAN

NEPENTHES
NEPER
NEPHALISM
NEPHALIST
NEPHELINE
NEPHELINIC
NEPHELINITE
NEPHELINITIC
NEPHELITE
NEPHELOGNOSY
NEPHELOID
NEPHELOMETER
NEPHELOSCOPE
NEPHESH
NEPHEW
NEPHIONIC
NEPHOGRAM
NEPHOGRAPH
NEPHOLOGICAL
NEPHOLOGIST
NEPHOLOGY
NEPHOSCOPE
NEPHRALGIA
NEPHRALGIC
NEPHRATONIA
NEPHRAUXE
NEPHRECTASIA
NEPHRECTASIS
NEPHRECTOMIES
NEPHRECTOMY
NEPHRELCOSIS
NEPHREMIA
NEPHRIA
NEPHRIC
NEPHRIDIA
NEPHRIDIAL
NEPHRIDIUM
NEPHRISM
NEPHRITE
NEPHRITIC
NEPHRITICAL
NEPHRITIS
NEPHROCELE
NEPHROCOELE
NEPHROCOLIC
NEPHROCYTE
NEPHRODINIC
NEPHROGENIC
NEPHROGENOUS
NEPHROID
NEPHROLITH
NEPHROLITHIC
NEPHROLOGY
NEPHROLYSIN
NEPHROLYSIS
NEPHROLYTIC
NEPHROMERE
NEPHRON
NEPHRONCUS
NEPHROPATHY
NEPHROPEXY
NEPHROPORE
NEPHROPTOSIA
NEPHROPTOSIS
NEPHROPYOSIS
NEPHROS
NEPHROSIS
NEPHROSTOME
NEPHROTIC
NEPHROTOME
NEPHROTOMY
NEPHROTOXIC
NEPHROTOXIN
NEPHROTYPHUS
NEPID
NEPIONIC
NEPMAN

NEPMEN
NEPOTAL
NEPOTE
NEPOTIC
NEPOTIOUS
NEPOTISM
NEPOTIST
NEPOTISTICAL
NEPOUITE
NEPTUNISM
NEPTUNIUM
NER
NERAL
NERE
NEREITE
NERITE
NERITIC
NERITOID
NERKA
NEROL
NEROLI
NERTEROLOGY
NERVAL
NERVATE
NERVATION
NERVATURE
NERVE
NERVED
NERVELESS
NERVELESSLY
NERVELESSNESS
NERVELET
NERVER
NERVEROOT
NERVES
NERVI
NERVID
NERVIDUCT
NERVIER
NERVIEST
NERVIMOTION
NERVIMOTOR
NERVINE
NERVING
NERVISH
NERVISM
NERVOSE
NERVOSISM
NERVOSITY
NERVOUS
NERVOUSLY
NERVOUSNESS
NERVULAR
NERVULE
NERVULET
NERVULOSE
NERVURATION
NERVURE
NERVUS
NERVY
NESCIENCE
NESCIENT
NESE
NESH
NESIOTE
NESLAVE
NESLE
NESLIA
NESQUEHONITE
NESS
NESSBERRY
NESSLERIZE
NESSLERIZED
NEST
NESTABLE
NESTAGE
NESTED

NESTER
NESTIATRIA
NESTING
NESTITHERAPY
NESTLE
NESTLED
NESTLER
NESTLING
NESTORINE
NESTY
NET
NETBALL
NETBRAIDER
NETBUSH
NETCHA
NETER
NETHE
NETHEIST
NETHER
NETHERMORE
NETHERMOST
NETHERSTOCK
NETHERSTONE
NETHERWARD
NETHERWORLD
NETI
NETLEAF
NETLIKE
NETMAKER
NETMAKING
NETMAN
NETMONGER
NETOP
NETS
NETSMAN
NETSUKE
NETTABLE
NETTED
NETTER
NETTING
NETTLE
NETTLEBIRD
NETTLED
NETTLEFIRE
NETTLEFOOT
NETTLEMONGER
NETTLER
NETTLESOME
NETTLEWORT
NETTLING
NETTLY
NETTY
NETWORK
NEU
NEUCK
NEUGROSCHEN
NEUM
NEUMATIC
NEUMATIZE
NEUME
NEUMIC
NEURAD
NEURAL
NEURALGIA
NEURALGIAC
NEURALGIC
NEURALGIFORM
NEURALGY
NEURALIST
NEURASTHENIA
NEURASTHENIC
NEURASTHENICAL
NEURATAXIA
NEURATAXY
NEURATION
NEURATROPHIA
NEURATROPHIC

NEURATROPHY
NEURAXIS
NEURAXON
NEURAXONE
NEURECTASIA
NEURECTASIS
NEURECTASY
NEURECTOME
NEURECTOMIC
NEURECTOMY
NEURECTOPIA
NEURECTOPY
NEURENTERIC
NEURERGIC
NEURHYPNOTIST
NEURIC
NEURILEMMA
NEURILEMMAL
NEURILITY
NEURIN
NEURINE
NEURINOMA
NEURINOMAS
NEURINOMATA
NEURISM
NEURITE
NEURITIC
NEURITIDES
NEURITIS
NEUROBLAST
NEUROCANAL
NEUROCARDIAC
NEUROCENTRAL
NEUROCENTRUM
NEUROCHITIN
NEUROCHORD
NEUROCITY
NEUROCLONIC
NEUROCOELE
NEUROCYTE
NEUROCYTOMA
NEURODYNIA
NEUROFIBRIL
NEUROFIBROMA
NEUROFIL
NEUROGASTRIC
NEUROGENESIS
NEUROGENETIC
NEUROGENIC
NEUROGENOUS
NEUROGLIA
NEUROGLIAC
NEUROGLIAL
NEUROGLIAR
NEUROGLIOMA
NEUROGLIOSIS
NEUROGRAM
NEUROGRAPHY
NEUROID
NEUROKERATIN
NEUROKYME
NEUROLOGICAL
NEUROLOGIST
NEUROLOGIZE
NEUROLOGY
NEUROLYMPH
NEUROLYSIS
NEUROMA
NEUROMALACIA
NEUROMALAKIA
NEUROMATOSIS
NEUROMATOUS
NEUROMERE
NEUROMERISM
NEUROMEROUS
NEUROMOTOR
NEURON

NEURONIC
NEURONISM
NEURONYM
NEURONYMY
NEUROPATH
NEUROPATHIC
NEUROPATHIST
NEUROPATHY
NEUROPHILE
NEUROPHILIC
NEUROPIL
NEUROPILE
NEUROPILEM
NEUROPLASM
NEUROPLASMIC
NEUROPLASTY
NEUROPLEXUS
NEUROPODIUM
NEUROPODOUS
NEUROPORE
NEUROPSYCHIC
NEUROPTERIST
NEUROPTEROID
NEUROPTERON
NEUROSAL
NEUROSES
NEUROSIS
NEUROSKELETAL
NEUROSOME
NEUROSPASM
NEUROSPAST
NEUROSTHENIA
NEUROSURGEON
NEUROSURGERY
NEUROSUTURE
NEUROSYNAPSE
NEUROTENSION
NEUROTHERAPY
NEUROTIC
NEUROTICALLY
NEUROTICISM
NEUROTOME
NEUROTOMICAL
NEUROTOMIST
NEUROTOMIZE
NEUROTOMY
NEUROTONIC
NEUROTOXIA
NEUROTOXIC
NEUROTOXIN
NEUROTRIPSY
NEUROTROPHIC
NEUROTROPHY
NEUROTROPIC
NEUROTROPISM
NEUROTROPY
NEUROVACCINE
NEURULA
NEURYPNOLOGY
NEUSTON
NEUTER
NEUTERDOM
NEUTERED
NEUTERING
NEUTERLY
NEUTERNESS
NEUTRAL
NEUTRALISE
NEUTRALISM
NEUTRALIST
NEUTRALITIES
NEUTRALITY
NEUTRALIZE
NEUTRALIZED
NEUTRALIZER
NEUTRALIZING
NEUTRALLY

NEUTRALNESS	NEWSTELLER	NICKNAMED	NIDUSES	NIGHTINGALE
NEUTRIA	NEWSWORTHY	NICKNAMEE	NIE	NIGHTINGALIZE
NEUTRINO	NEWSY	NICKNAMER	NIECE	NIGHTISH
NEUTRON	NEWT	NICKNAMING	NIEF	NIGHTJAR
NEUTROPHIL	NEWTAKE	NICKPOT	NIELLATED	NIGHTLONG
NEUTROPHILE	NEWTON	NICKSTICK	NIELLED	NIGHTLY
NEUTROPHILIA	NEWTONITE	NICKUM	NIELLI	NIGHTMAN
NEVADITE	NEXAL	NICKY	NIELLIST	NIGHTMARE
NEVAT	NEXT	NICOLAYITE	NIELLO	NIGHTMARISH
NEVE	NEXTLY	NICOLO	NIELLOED	NIGHTMARISHLY
NEVEL	NEXTNESS	NICOTIA	NIELLOING	NIGHTMARY
NEVELL	NEXUM	NICOTIAN	NIELLOS	NIGHTMEN
NEVEN	NEXUS	NICOTIANIN	NIEPA	NIGHTRIDER
NEVER	NEXUSES	NICOTIN	NIESHOUT	NIGHTS
NEVERMASS	NEY	NICOTINA	NIEVE	NIGHTSHADE
NEVERMORE	NEYANDA	NICOTINE	NIEVETA	NIGHTSHIRT
NEVERTHELESS	NGAI	NICOTINEAN	NIEVLING	NIGHTSPOT
NEVES	NGAIO	NICOTINED	NIF	NIGHTSTICK
NEVOID	NGAN	NICOTINIAN	NIFE	NIGHTTIDE
NEVOY	NGAPI	NICOTINIC	NIFESIMA	NIGHTTIME
NEVUS	NGU	NICOTINISM	NIFFER	NIGHTWAKE
NEVYANSKITE	NI	NICOTINIZE	NIFIC	NIGHTWALKER
NEW	NIACIN	NICOTISM	NIFLE	NIGHTWALKING
NEWBERYITE	NIATA	NICOTIZE	NIFLING	NIGHTWARD
NEWBORN	NIB	NICTATE	NIFTIER	NIGHTWEAR
NEWCAL	NIBBED	NICTATED	NIFTIEST	NIGHTWORK
NEWCOME	NIBBER	NICTATING	NIFTY	NIGHTWORKER
NEWCOMER	NIBBLE	NICTATION	NIG	NIGHTY
NEWEL	NIBBLED	NICTITANT	NIGGARD	NIGNAY
NEWELTY	NIBBLER	NICTITATE	NIGGARDLY	NIGNYE
NEWER	NIBBLING	NICTITATED	NIGGER	NIGON
NEWEST	NIBBY	NICTITATING	NIGGERED	NIGORI
NEWFANGLE	NIBLIC	NICTITATION	NIGGERFISH	NIGRE
NEWFANGLED	NIBLICK	NID	NIGGERFISHES	NIGRESCENCE
NEWFISH	NIBONG	NIDAL	NIGGERGOOSE	NIGRESCENT
NEWING	NIBS	NIDAMENTAL	NIGGERHEAD	NIGRESCITE
NEWISH	NIBSOME	NIDANA	NIGGERISH	NIGRICANT
NEWLANDITE	NIBUNG	NIDARY	NIGGERISM	NIGRIFICATION
NEWLIGHT	NICCOLIC	NIDATION	NIGGERLING	NIGRIFIED
NEWLINGS	NICCOLITE	NIDATORY	NIGGERTOE	NIGRIFY
NEWLINS	NICCOLO	NIDDER	NIGGERWEED	NIGRIFYING
NEWLY	NICCOLOUS	NIDDERING	NIGGERY	NIGRINE
NEWLYWED	NICE	NIDDICK	NIGGET	NIGRITIES
NEWMARKET	NICELING	NIDDICOCK	NIGGLE	NIGRITUDE
NEWMOWN	NICELY	NIDDLE	NIGGLED	NIGROSIN
NEWNESS	NICENESS	NIDE	NIGGLER	NIGROSINE
NEWS	NICER	NIDERING	NIGGLING	NIGROUS
NEWSAGENT	NICEST	NIDGE	NIGGLINGLY	NIGS
NEWSBILL	NICETIES	NIDGET	NIGGLY	NIGUA
NEWSBOARD	NICETISH	NIDGETY	NIGGOT	NIGUN
NEWSBOAT	NICETY	NIDI	NIGGUN	NIHIL
NEWSBOY	NICHE	NIDICOLOUS	NIGH	NIHILIANISM
NEWSCAST	NICHED	NIDIFICANT	NIGHED	NIHILIFICATION
NEWSCASTER	NICHELINO	NIDIFICATE	NIGHER	NIHILIFY
NEWSDEALER	NICHEVO	NIDIFICATED	NIGHEST	NIHILISM
NEWSIER	NICHIL	NIDIFICATING	NIGHING	NIHILIST
NEWSIEST	NICHING	NIDIFICATION	NIGHLY	NIHILISTIC
NEWSINESS	NICHT	NIDIFICATIONAL	NIGHT	NIHILITIC
NEWSLETTER	NICK	NIDIFIED	NIGHTCAP	NIHILITIES
NEWSMAGAZINE	NICKED	NIDIFUGOUS	NIGHTCAPPED	NIHILITY
NEWSMAN	NICKEL	NIDIFY	NIGHTCAPS	NIHILOBSTAT
NEWSMEN	NICKELBLOOM	NIDIFYING	NIGHTCLOTHES	NIHILUM
NEWSMONGER	NICKELIC	NIDING	NIGHTCLUB	NIKAU
NEWSMONGERING	NICKELIFEROUS	NIDIOT	NIGHTDRESS	NIKENO
NEWSMONGERY	NICKELINE	NIDOLOGIST	NIGHTED	NIKLESITE
NEWSPAPER	NICKELIZE	NIDOLOGY	NIGHTERY	NIL
NEWSPAPERMAN	NICKELODEON	NIDOR	NIGHTFALL	NILGAI
NEWSPAPERMEN	NICKELOUS	NIDOROSE	NIGHTFISH	NILGAIS
NEWSPAPERWOMAN	NICKELTYPE	NIDOROSITY	NIGHTFLIT	NILGAU
NEWSPAPERWOMEN	NICKER	NIDOROUS	NIGHTFOWL	NILL
NEWSPAPERY	NICKERPECKER	NIDORULENT	NIGHTGALE	NILPOTENT
NEWSPRINT	NICKERY	NIDULANT	NIGHTGLASS	NIM
NEWSREADER	NICKEY	NIDULATE	NIGHTGOWN	NIMB
NEWSREEL	NICKING	NIDULATION	NIGHTHAWK	NIMBATED
NEWSROOM	NICKLE	NIDULI	NIGHTIE	NIMBI
NEWSSHEET	NICKNACK	NIDULUS	NIGHTIES	NIMBIFEROUS
NEWSSTAND	NICKNAME	NIDUS	NIGHTING	NIMBIFICATION

NIMBLE	NIPPITATE	NITROANILIN	NJAVE	NOCTUOID
NIMBLEBRAINED	NIPPITATO	NITROANILINE	NO	NOCTURIA
NIMBLENESS	NIPPITATUM	NITROBACTERIA	NOA	NOCTURN
NIMBLER	NIPPITATY	NITROBARITE	NOANCE	NOCTURNAL
NIMBLEST	NIPPLE	NITROBENZENE	NOB	NOCTURNALLY
NIMBLY	NIPPLED	NITROCALCITE	NOBBER	NOCTURNE
NIMBOSE	NIPPLEWORT	NITROCOTTON	NOBBIER	NOCUMENT
NIMBOSTRATUS	NIPPLING	NITROFORM	NOBBIEST	NOCUOUS
NIMBUS	NIPPONIUM	NITROGELATIN	NOBBLE	NOCUOUSLY
NIMBUSED	NIPPY	NITROGELATINE	NOBBLED	NOCUOUSNESS
NIMBUSES	NIPS	NITROGEN	NOBBLER	NOD
NIMIETY	NIPTER	NITROGENATE	NOBBLING	NODAL
NIMINY	NIRIS	NITROGENATION	NOBBUT	NODALITY
NIMIOUS	NIRLES	NITROGENIZATION	NOBBY	NODALLY
NIMMED	NIRLS	NITROGENIZE	NOBELIUM	NODATED
NIMMER	NIRMANAKAYA	NITROGENIZED	NOBILIARY	NODDED
NIMMING	NIRVANA	NITROGENIZING	NOBILITATE	NODDER
NIMSHI	NIRVANIC	NITROGENOUS	NOBILITIES	NODDIES
NINCOM	NIS	NITROGLYCERIN	NOBILITY	NODDING
NINCOMPOOP	NISBERRY	NITROGLYCERINE	NOBLE	NODDLE
NINCOMPOOPERY	NISHIKI	NITROLAMINE	NOBLED	NODDLEBONE
NINCOMPOOPHOOD	NISI	NITROLIC	NOBLEHEARTED	NODDLED
NINCOMPOOPISH	NISNAS	NITROMAGNESITE	NOBLEMAN	NODDLING
NINCUM	NISPERO	NITROMETER	NOBLEMANLY	NODDY
NINE	NISSE	NITROMURIATE	NOBLEMEN	NODE
NINEBARK	NISUS	NITROPARAFFIN	NOBLENESS	NODED
NINEFOLD	NIT	NITROPHENOL	NOBLER	NODIAK
NINEHOLES	NITCH	NITROPHILOUS	NOBLESSE	NODICAL
NINEPEGS	NITCHEVO	NITROPHYTE	NOBLEST	NODICORN
NINEPENCE	NITCHIE	NITROPHYTIC	NOBLEWOMAN	NODIFEROUS
NINEPENCES	NITE	NITROPRUSSIC	NOBLEWOMEN	NODIFLOROUS
NINEPENNIES	NITENCY	NITROSAMIN	NOBLEY	NODIFORM
NINEPENNY	NITENT	NITROSAMINE	NOBLIFY	NODOSARIAN
NINEPIN	NITER	NITROSATE	NOBLING	NODOSARIFORM
NINEPINS	NITERED	NITROSIFY	NOBLY	NODOSARINE
NINESCORE	NITERING	NITROSITE	NOBOB	NODOSAUR
NINETED	NITHER	NITROSTARCH	NOBODIES	NODOSE
NINETEEN	NITHING	NITROSULPHATE	NOBODY	NODOSITIES
NINETEENTH	NITID	NITROSYL	NOBODYNESS	NODOSITY
NINETEENTHLY	NITIDOUS	NITROTOLUENE	NOBS	NODOUS
NINETIETH	NITO	NITROTOLUOL	NOBUT	NODULAR
NINETY	NITON	NITROUS	NOCAKE	NODULATE
NINGLE	NITOR	NITROXYL	NOCENCE	NODULATED
NINNIES	NITOS	NITRYL	NOCENT	NODULATION
NINNY	NITRAMIN	NITTE	NOCERITE	NODULE
NINNYHAMMER	NITRAMINE	NITTER	NOCHT	NODULED
NINNYISH	NITRANILIC	NITTY	NOCICEPTIVE	NODULES
NINNYISM	NITRATE	NITWIT	NOCICEPTOR	NODULIZE
NINNYSHIP	NITRATED	NIVAL	NOCIVE	NODULIZED
NINNYWATCH	NITRATINE	NIVATION	NOCK	NODULIZING
NINO	NITRATING	NIVEAU	NOCKED	NODULOSE
NINOS	NITRATION	NIVELLATE	NOCKERL	NODUS
NINTH	NITRATOR	NIVELLATION	NOCKET	NOED
NINTHLY	NITRE	NIVELLATOR	NOCKING	NOEGENESIS
NINTU	NITRED	NIVELLIZATION	NOCKTAT	NOEGENETIC
NINUT	NITRIARIES	NIVENITE	NOCTAMBULANT	NOEL
NIOBATE	NITRIARY	NIVEOUS	NOCTAMBULE	NOEMATICAL
NIOBIC	NITRIC	NIVER	NOCTIDIAL	NOESIS
NIOBITE	NITRID	NIVERNAISE	NOCTIDIURNAL	NOETIC
NIOBIUM	NITRIDATION	NIVICOLOUS	NOCTILUCA	NOETICS
NIOBOUS	NITRIDE	NIVOSITY	NOCTILUCAN	NOEUD
NIOG	NITRIDING	NIX	NOCTILUCENCE	NOG
NIOTA	NITRIDIZATION	NIXE	NOCTILUCENT	NOGADA
NIP	NITRIDIZE	NIXEN	NOCTILUCIN	NOGAI
NIPA	NITRIFACTION	NIXES	NOCTILUCINE	NOGAKU
NIPCHEESE	NITRIFEROUS	NIXIE	NOCTILUCOUS	NOGAL
NIPE	NITRIFIABLE	NIXTAMAL	NOCTIMANIA	NOGG
NIPMUCK	NITRIFICATION	NIXY	NOCTIVAGANT	NOGGED
NIPPED	NITRIFIED	NIYANDA	NOCTIVAGATION	NOGGEN
NIPPER	NITRIFIER	NIYO	NOCTIVAGOUS	NOGGIN
NIPPERKIN	NITRIFY	NIYOGA	NOCTOGRAPH	NOGGING
NIPPERS	NITRIFYING	NIZ	NOCTOVISION	NOGHEAD
NIPPIER	NITRIL	NIZAMAT	NOCTUID	NOGHEADED
NIPPIEST	NITRILE	NIZAMATE	NOCTUIDEOUS	NOH
NIPPING	NITRITE	NIZAMUT	NOCTUIDOUS	NOHOW
NIPPINGLY	NITRO	NIZEY	NOCTUIFORM	NOI
	NITROAMINE	NIZY	NOCTULE	NOIBWOOD

NOIL
NOILAGE
NOILER
NOILY
NOING
NOINT
NOIO
NOIR
NOISANCE
NOISE
NOISED
NOISEFUL
NOISEFULLY
NOISELESS
NOISELESSLY
NOISELESSNESS
NOISEMAKER
NOISEMAKING
NOISES
NOISETTE
NOISIER
NOISIEST
NOISILY
NOISINESS
NOISING
NOISOME
NOISOMELY
NOISOMENESS
NOISY
NOIT
NOIX
NOKI
NOKIN
NOKTA
NOLA
NOLD
NOLITION
NOLL
NOLLEITY
NOLO
NOM
NOMA
NOMAD
NOMADE
NOMADIAN
NOMADIC
NOMADICAL
NOMADICALLY
NOMADISM
NOMAN
NOMANCY
NOMARCH
NOMARCHIES
NOMARCHY
NOMARTHRAL
NOMBLES
NOMBRIL
NOME
NOMEN
NOMENCLATE
NOMENCLATIVE
NOMENCLATOR
NOMENCLATORIAL
NOMENCLATORY
NOMENCLATURAL
NOMENCLATURE
NOMENCLATURIST
NOMEUS
NOMIAL
NOMIC
NOMINA
NOMINABLE
NOMINAL
NOMINALISM
NOMINALIST
NOMINALISTIC
NOMINALITY

NOMINALLY
NOMINATE
NOMINATED
NOMINATELY
NOMINATING
NOMINATION
NOMINATIVE
NOMINATOR
NOMINATRIX
NOMINATURE
NOMINEE
NOMINEEISM
NOMINY
NOMISM
NOMISMA
NOMISMATA
NOMISTIC
NOMOCANON
NOMOCRACY
NOMOGENIST
NOMOGENOUS
NOMOGENY
NOMOGRAM
NOMOGRAPH
NOMOGRAPHER
NOMOGRAPHIC
NOMOGRAPHICAL
NOMOGRAPHIES
NOMOGRAPHY
NOMOLOGICAL
NOMOLOGIST
NOMOLOGY
NOMOPELMOUS
NOMOPHYLAX
NOMOPHYLLOUS
NOMOS
NOMOTHETE
NOMOTHETES
NOMOTHETIC
NOMOTHETICAL
NON
NONA
NONABILITY
NONABJURER
NONACCESS
NONACOSANE
NONACT
NONADDRESS
NONADDRESSER
NONADECANE
NONADJUSTIVE
NONAGE
NONAGENARIAN
NONAGENARIES
NONAGENARY
NONAGESIMAL
NONAGON
NONAGREEMENT
NONAHYDRATE
NONAMINO
NONAN
NONANE
NONAPPEARANCE
NONARCHING
NONARCKING
NONARY
NONASPIRATE
NONBEING
NONBELIEVER
NONBEVERAGE
NONCALLABLE
NONCASTE
NONCE
NONCERTAIN
NONCHALANCE
NONCHALANT
NONCHALANTLY

NONCHALANTNESS
NONCITIZEN
NONCLAIM
NONCLERICAL
NONCOMBATANT
NONCOMBUSTIBLE
NONCOME
NONCOMMISSIONED
NONCOMMITALLY
NONCOMMITTAL
NONCOMMITTALNESS
NONCOMMUNION
NONCOMMUTATIVE
NONCOMPEARANCE
NONCOMPLIANCE
NONCOMPOS
NONCOMPOSES
NONCOMPOUNDER
NONCON
NONCONDENSING
NONCONDUCTING
NCNCONDUCTOR
NONCONFORM
NONCONFORMABLE
NONCONFORMABLY
NONCONFORMER
NONCONFORMING
NONCONFORMISM
NONCONFORMIST
NONCONFORMITY
NONCONTENT
NONCONTINUOUS
NONCONTRADICTION
NONCOOPERATION
NONCURANTIST
NONDA
NONDECIDUATE
NONDENUMERABLE
NONDEPENDENT
NONDESCRIPT
NONDETINET
NONDISCLOSURE
NONDISJUNCT
NONDISJUNCTION
NONDISTINCTIVE
NONDO
NONDUALISM
NONDUMPING
NONE
NONEFFECTIVE
NONEGO
NONELASTIC
NONENE
NONENT
NONENTITIES
NONENTITIVE
NONENTITIZE
NONENTITY
NONENTITYISM
NONENTRES
NONENTRESSE
NONENTRY
NONES
NONESSENTIAL
NONESUCH
NONET
NONETHELESS
NONETTO
NONEXISTENCE
NONEXISTENT
NONFEASANCE
NONFEASOR
NONFERROUS
NONFICTION
NONFICTIONALLY
NONFLAMMABLE
NONGYPSY

NONHARMONIC
NONHEARER
NONIC
NONILLION
NONINCREASING
NONINDUCTIVE
NONINDUCTIVELY
NONINDUCTIVITY
NONINJURY
NONINTRUSION
NONION
NONISOBARIC
NONISSUABLE
NONIUS
NONJOINDER
NONJURANCY
NONJURANT
NONJURANTISM
NONJURING
NONJUROR
NONLEGAL
NONLEGATO
NONLICET
NONMAGNETIC
NONMETAL
NONMETALLIC
NONMODAL
NONMORAL
NONMORALITY
NONNAT
NONNATURAL
NONNATURALISM
NONNATURALITY
NONNATURALS
NONNY
NONOBJECTIVE
NONOBJECTIVITY
NONOIC
NONOPENING
NONPAREIL
NONPAROUS
NONPARTICIPATING
NONPARTISAN
NONPARTIZAN
NONPASSERINE
NONPAYMENT
NONPERMANENT
NONPHENOMENAL
NONPLACET
NONPLANE
NONPLUS
NONPLUSATION
NONPLUSED
NONPLUSING
NONPLUSSATION
NONPLUSSED
NONPLUSSING
NONPOISONOUS
NONPOLAR
NONPOSITIVE
NONPRODUCTIVE
NONPRODUCTIVELY
NONPRODUCTIVENESS
NONPROFESSIONAL
NONPROFIT
NONPROTEIN
NONQUOTA
NONREACTIVE
NONREDUCING
NONREGENT
NONREGULATION
NONRESIDENCE
NONRESIDENCY
NONRESIDENT
NONRESIDENTER
NONRESIDENTIARY
NONRESIDENTOR

NONRESISTANCE
NONRESISTANT
NONRESTRAINT
NONRESTRICTIVE
NONRIGID
NONROTATING
NONSCRIPTURAL
NONSECTARIAN
NONSENSE
NONSENSICAL
NONSENSICALITY
NONSENSICALLY
NONSENSICALNESS
NONSENSIFICATION
NONSENSIFY
NONSENTENCE
NONSEPARATIST
NONSIPHONAGE
NONSKED
NONSKID
NONSKIDDING
NONSPORED
NONSTANDARD
NONSTELLAR
NONSTOP
NONSTRIATED
NONSUBSCRIBER
NONSUBSTANTIALISM
NONSUBSTANTIALIST
NONSUCH
NONSUGAR
NONSUIT
NONSUPPORT
NONSWEARER
NONSWEARING
NONSYLLABIC
NONSYLLABICNESS
NONSYMBIOTIC
NONSYMBIOTICALLY
NONSYNC
NONTENURE
NONTERM
NONTERMINATING
NONTHEMATIC
NONTRONITE
NONUMBILICATE
NONUNIFORM
NONUNIFORMIST
NONUNIFORMLY
NONUNION
NONUNIONISM
NONUNIONIST
NONUPLE
NONUPLET
NONUPLICATE
NONUSER
NONVALENT
NONVIBRATORY
NONVIOLENCE
NONVOLUNTARY
NONVORTICAL
NONVORTICALLY
NONWHITE
NONYA
NONYL
NONYLENE
NONYLIC
NOO
NOODLE
NOOK
NOOKED
NOOKERY
NOOKIER
NOOKIEST
NOOKING
NOOKY
NOOLOGICAL

NOOLOGIST
NOOLOGY
NOOMETRY
NOON
NOONDAY
NOONED
NOONFLOWER
NOONING
NOONLIGHT
NOONLIT
NOONMEAT
NOONSTEAD
NOONTIDE
NOONTIME
NOOP
NOOSCOPIC
NOOSE
NOOSED
NOOSER
NOOSING
NOOT
NOPAL
NOPALRY
NOPE
NOPINENE
NOR
NORATE
NORATION
NORBERGITE
NORCAMPHANE
NORDCAPER
NORDMARKITE
NORGINE
NORI
NORIA
NORICE
NORIE
NORIMON
NORIT
NORITE
NORITO
NORKYN
NORLAND
NORLANDER
NORLANDISM
NORLEUCINE
NORM
NORMA
NORMAL
NORMALCY
NORMALISM
NORMALIST
NORMALITY
NORMALIZATION
NORMALIZE
NORMALIZED
NORMALIZER
NORMALIZING
NORMALLY
NORMALNESS
NORMATED
NORMATIVE
NORMATIVENESS
NORMOCYTE
NORRY
NORSEL
NORSELED
NORSELING
NORSELLED
NORSELLING
NORSH
NORTELRY
NORTH
NORTHBOUND
NORTHEAST
NORTHEASTER
NORTHEASTERLY

NORTHEASTERN
NORTHEASTWARD
NORTHEASTWARDLY
NORTHEASTWARDS
NORTHEN
NORTHER
NORTHERED
NORTHERING
NORTHERLINESS
NORTHERLY
NORTHERN
NORTHERNER
NORTHERNLY
NORTHEST
NORTHING
NORTHLAND
NORTHLANDER
NORTHLIGHT
NORTHMOST
NORTHNESS
NORTHUPITE
NORTHWARD
NORTHWARDLY
NORTHWARDS
NORTHWEST
NORTHWESTER
NORTHWESTERLY
NORTHWESTERN
NORTHWESTWARD
NORTHWESTWARDLY
NORTHWESTWARDS
NORWARD
NORWARDS
NORWESTER
NOSARIAN
NOSE
NOSEAN
NOSEANITE
NOSEBAG
NOSEBAND
NOSEBLEED
NOSEBONE
NOSEBURN
NOSED
NOSEGAY
NOSEHOLE
NOSELITE
NOSEPIECE
NOSEPINCH
NOSER
NOSESMART
NOSETHIRL
NOSETIOLOGY
NOSEWING
NOSEWISE
NOSEWORT
NOSEY
NOSIER
NOSIEST
NOSILY
NOSINE
NOSINESS
NOSING
NOSISM
NOSITE
NOSOCOMIUM
NOSOGENESIS
NOSOGENETIC
NOSOGENIC
NOSOGENY
NOSOGRAPHER
NOSOGRAPHIC
NOSOGRAPHIES
NOSOGRAPHY
NOSOHAEMIA
NOSOHEMIA
NOSOLOGICAL

NOSOLOGICALLY
NOSOLOGIES
NOSOLOGIST
NOSOLOGY
NOSOMANIA
NOSOMYCOSIS
NOSONOMY
NOSOPHOBIA
NOSOPHYTE
NOSOPOETIC
NOSOPOIETIC
NOSOTAXY
NOSOTROPHY
NOSSEL
NOSTALGIA
NOSTALGIC
NOSTIC
NOSTOC
NOSTOCACEOUS
NOSTOLOGY
NOSTOMANIA
NOSTRIFICATE
NOSTRIFICATION
NOSTRIL
NOSTRILED
NOSTRILITY
NOSTRILLED
NOSTRUM
NOSTRUMS
NOSY
NOT
NOTA
NOTABILIA
NOTABILITIES
NOTABILITY
NOTABLE
NOTABLENESS
NOTABLY
NOTACANTHID
NOTACANTHOID
NOTACANTHOUS
NOTAEAL
NOTAEUM
NOTAL
NOTALGIA
NOTALGIC
NOTALIA
NOTAM
NOTAN
NOTANDUDA
NOTANDUM
NOTANDUMS
NOTAR
NOTARIAL
NOTARIALLY
NOTARIATE
NOTARIES
NOTARIKON
NOTARIZATION
NOTARIZE
NOTARIZED
NOTARIZING
NOTARY
NOTATE
NOTATION
NOTATIONAL
NOTATIVE
NOTATOR
NOTAULIX
NOTCH
NOTCHBOARD
NOTCHED
NOTCHEL
NOTCHER
NOTCHES
NOTCHING
NOTCHWEED

NOTCHWING
NOTCHWORT
NOTCHY
NOTE
NOTEBOOK
NOTECASE
NOTED
NOTEDLY
NOTEDNESS
NOTEHEAD
NOTEHOLDER
NOTELESS
NOTELESSLY
NOTELESSNESS
NOTEMAN
NOTEMIGGE
NOTEMUGGE
NOTER
NOTES
NOTEWORTHILY
NOTEWORTHY
NOTHAL
NOTHARCTID
NOTHER
NOTHING
NOTHINGARIAN
NOTHINGISM
NOTHINGIST
NOTHINGIZE
NOTHINGLESS
NOTHINGLY
NOTHINGNESS
NOTHOSAUR
NOTHOSAURIAN
NOTHOUS
NOTICE
NOTICEABILITY
NOTICEABLE
NOTICEABLY
NOTICED
NOTICER
NOTICING
NOTIDANIAN
NOTIFIABLE
NOTIFICATION
NOTIFIED
NOTIFIER
NOTIFY
NOTIFYING
NOTING
NOTION
NOTIONABLE
NOTIONAL
NOTIONALIST
NOTIONALITY
NOTIONALLY
NOTIONALNESS
NOTIONARY
NOTIONATE
NOTIONED
NOTIONIST
NOTIONS
NOTIST
NOTITIA
NOTITION
NOTOCENTRUM
NOTOCHORD
NOTODONTIAN
NOTODONTID
NOTODONTOID
NOTOIRE
NOTONECTID
NOTOPODIAL
NOTOPODIUM
NOTOPTERID
NOTOPTEROID
NOTORHIZAL

NOTORIETIES
NOTORIETY
NOTORIOUS
NOTORIOUSLY
NOTORIOUSNESS
NOTORNIS
NOTOTRIBE
NOTOUNGULATE
NOTOUR
NOTOURLY
NOTSELF
NOTT
NOTUM
NOTUNGULATE
NOTWITHSTANDING
NOUCH
NOUCHE
NOUE
NOUGAT
NOUGATINE
NOUGHT
NOUGHTILY
NOUGHTINESS
NOUGHTLY
NOUGHTY
NOUILLE
NOUILLES
NOUMEA
NOUMEAITE
NOUMEITE
NOUMENAL
NOUMENALISM
NOUMENALIST
NOUMENALITY
NOUMENALLY
NOUMENISM
NOUMENON
NOUMMOS
NOUN
NOUNAL
NOUNALLY
NOUNIZE
NOUNS
NOUP
NOURISH
NOURISHABLE
NOURISHED
NOURISHER
NOURISHING
NOURISHINGLY
NOURISHMENT
NOURITURE
NOUS
NOUTHER
NOUVEAU
NOUVEAUTE
NOUVELLE
NOUVELLES
NOVA
NOVACULITE
NOVAE
NOVALE
NOVALIA
NOVANTIQUE
NOVAS
NOVATE
NOVATIVE
NOVATOR
NOVATORY
NOVATRIX
NOVCIC
NOVEL
NOVELA
NOVELANT
NOVELCRAFT
NOVELET
NOVELETIST

NOVELETTE	NOYAU	NUCLEOPLASM	NULLIPARAE	NUMMULOIDAL
NOVELETTER	NOYFUL	NUCLEOPLASMIC	NULLIPARITY	NUMMUS
NOVELISM	NOYOUS	NUCLEOPROTEIN	NULLIPAROUS	NUMNAH
NOVELIST	NOZZLE	NUCLEOSID	NULLIPENNATE	NUMPS
NOVELISTIC	NOZZLER	NUCLEOSIDE	NULLIPLEX	NUMSKULL
NOVELISTICALLY	NRITTA	NUCLEOTIDE	NULLIPORE	NUMSKULLED
NOVELIZATION	NTH	NUCLEUS	NULLIPOROUS	NUMSKULLISM
NOVELIZE	NU	NUCLEUSES	NULLITIES	NUN
NOVELIZED	NUADU	NUCULANE	NULLITY	NUNATAK
NOVELIZING	NUANCE	NUCULANIA	NULLIVERSE	NUNATAKS
NOVELLA	NUANCED	NUCULANIUM	NULLO	NUNBIRD
NOVELLAE	NUANCES	NUCULE	NUMB	NUNCE
NOVELLAS	NUANCING	NUCULIFORM	NUMBAT	NUNCHEON
NOVELLE	NUB	NUCULOID	NUMBED	NUNCHION
NOVELRY	NUBBIN	NUD	NUMBEDNESS	NUNCIATE
NOVELTIES	NUBBLE	NUDATE	NUMBER	NUNCIATIVE
NOVELTY	NUBBLING	NUDDLE	NUMBERED	NUNCIATORY
NOVELWRIGHT	NUBBLY	NUDE	NUMBERER	NUNCIATURE
NOVENA	NUBECULA	NUDELY	NUMBERFUL	NUNCIO
NOVENAE	NUBECULAE	NUDENESS	NUMBERING	NUNCIOS
NOVENARY	NUBIA	NUDGE	NUMBERLESS	NUNCLE
NOVENDIAL	NUBILATE	NUDGED	NUMBEROUS	NUNCUPATE
NOVENE	NUBILATION	NUDGING	NUMBERS	NUNCUPATION
NOVENNIAL	NUBILE	NUDIBRANCH	NUMBERSOME	NUNCUPATIVE
NOVERCAL	NUBILITY	NUDICAUDATE	NUMBFISH	NUNCUPATIVELY
NOVERINT	NUBILOSE	NUDICAUL	NUMBFISHES	NUNDINAL
NOVICE	NUBILOUS	NUDICAULOUS	NUMBING	NUNDINATION
NOVICEHOOD	NUBK	NUDIFIER	NUMBINGLY	NUNDINE
NOVICERY	NUCAL	NUDIFLOROUS	NUMBLE	NUNKY
NOVICIATE	NUCAMENT	NUDIPED	NUMBLES	NUNLET
NOVILLADA	NUCELLAR	NUDISM	NUMBLY	NUNNARI
NOVILLO	NUCELLI	NUDIST	NUMBNESS	NUNNATION
NOVILUNAR	NUCELLUS	NUDITARIAN	NUMDA	NUNNED
NOVITIAL	NUCHA	NUDITY	NUMDAH	NUNNERIES
NOVITIATE	NUCHAE	NUDNICK	NUMEN	NUNNERY
NOVITIATION	NUCHAL	NUE	NUMERABLE	NUNNI
NOVITY	NUCHALE	NUGACIOUS	NUMERABLY	NUNNIFY
NOVOCAIN	NUCHALGIA	NUGACIOUSNESS	NUMERAL	NUNNING
NOVOCAINE	NUCHE	NUGACITIES	NUMERALLY	NUNNISH
NOVODAMUS	NUCICULTURE	NUGACITY	NUMERALS	NUNNISHNESS
NOVUM	NUCIFEROUS	NUGAE	NUMERANT	NUNRY
NOW	NUCIFORM	NUGAMENT	NUMERARY	NUNTING
NOWADAYS	NUCIN	NUGATOR	NUMERATE	NUNTIUS
NOWANIGHTS	NUCIVOROUS	NUGATORILY	NUMERATED	NUPSON
NOWAY	NUCK	NUGATORINESS	NUMERATING	NUPTIAL
NOWAYS	NUCLEAL	NUGATORY	NUMERATION	NUPTIALITY
NOWDER	NUCLEAR	NUGGAR	NUMERATIVE	NUPTIALIZE
NOWED	NUCLEARY	NUGGET	NUMERATOR	NUPTIALLY
NOWEL	NUCLEASE	NUGGETY	NUMERIC	NUQUE
NOWHAT	NUCLEATE	NUGIFY	NUMERICAL	NUR
NOWHEN	NUCLEATED	NUGILOGUE	NUMERICALLY	NURAGH
NOWHENCE	NUCLEATING	NUIK	NUMERICALNESS	NURAGHE
NOWHERE	NUCLEATION	NUISANCE	NUMERIST	NURL
NOWHERES	NUCLEATOR	NUISANCER	NUMERO	NURLY
NOWHIT	NUCLEI	NUISOME	NUMEROLOGY	NURRY
NOWHITHER	NUCLEIFORM	NUIT	NUMEROS	NURSE
NOWISE	NUCLEIN	NUKE	NUMEROSITY	NURSED
NOWN	NUCLEINASE	NUL	NUMEROUS	NURSEGIRL
NOWNESS	NUCLEOALBUMIN	NULL	NUMEROUSLY	NURSEHOUND
NOWT	NUCLEOFUGAL	NULLA	NUMEROUSNESS	NURSEMAID
NOWTHE	NUCLEOHISTONE	NULLABLE	NUMINA	NURSER
NOWTHER	NUCLEOID	NULLAH	NUMINISM	NURSERIES
NOWTHERD	NUCLEOLAR	NULLED	NUMINOUS	NURSERY
NOWY	NUCLEOLATE	NULLIBICITY	NUMINOUSLY	NURSERYMAID
NOXA	NUCLEOLATED	NULLIBIETY	NUMISMATIC	NURSERYMAN
NOXAE	NUCLEOLE	NULLIBILITY	NUMISMATICAL	NURSERYMEN
NOXAL	NUCLEOLI	NULLIBIQUITOUS	NUMISMATICALLY	NURSETENDER
NOXIAL	NUCLEOLINI	NULLIBIST	NUMISMATICS	NURSING
NOXIOUS	NUCLEOLINUS	NULLIFICATION	NUMISMATIST	NURSINGLY
NOXIOUSLY	NUCLEOLOID	NULLIFICATOR	NUMMARY	NURSLE
NOXIOUSNESS	NUCLEOLUS	NULLIFIDIAN	NUMMIFORM	NURSLING
NOY	NUCLEOLYSIS	NULLIFIED	NUMMULAR	NURSY
NOYADE	NUCLEON	NULLIFIER	NUMMULARY	NURTURAL
NOYADED	NUCLEONE	NULLIFY	NUMMULATION	NURTURE
NOYADING	NUCLEONIC	NULLIFYING	NUMMULINE	NURTURED
NOYANCE	NUCLEONICS	NULLING	NUMMULITE	NURTURER
NOYANT	NUCLEONS	NULLIPARA	NUMMULITIC	NURTURING

NUSFIAH
NUSS
NUSUB
NUT
NUTANT
NUTARIAN
NUTATE
NUTATED
NUTATING
NUTATION
NUTATIONAL
NUTBREAKER
NUTBROWN
NUTCAKE
NUTCRACK
NUTCRACKER
NUTCRACKERS
NUTCRACKERY
NUTGALL
NUTGRASS
NUTHATCH
NUTHOOK
NUTJOBBER
NUTLET
NUTLIKE
NUTMEG
NUTMEGGED
NUTMEGGY
NUTPECKER
NUTPICK
NUTRAMIN
NUTRIA
NUTRICE
NUTRICIAL
NUTRICISM
NUTRIENT
NUTRIFY
NUTRIMENT
NUTRIMENTAL
NUTRITION
NUTRITIONAL
NUTRITIONALLY
NUTRITIONARY
NUTRITIONIST
NUTRITIOUS
NUTRITIOUSLY
NUTRITIVE
NUTRITIVELY
NUTRITIVENESS
NUTRITORY
NUTS
NUTSHELL
NUTTED
NUTTER
NUTTERY
NUTTIER
NUTTIEST
NUTTILY
NUTTINESS
NUTTING
NUTTY
NUTWOOD
NUWAB
NUZZER
NUZZLE
NUZZLED
NUZZLING
NYALA
NYANZA
NYAS
NYASA
NYCE
NYCHTHEMERON
NYCTALOPE
NYCTALOPIA
NYCTALOPIC
NYCTALOPS

NYCTERIBIID
NYCTIPELAGIC
NYCTITROPIC
NYCTITROPISM
NYCTOPHOBIA
NYCTURIA
NYE
NYET
NYLAST
NYLGAU
NYLON
NYMIL
NYMPH
NYMPHA
NYMPHAE
NYMPHAEA
NYMPHAEUM
NYMPHAL
NYMPHALINE
NYMPHEAL
NYMPHEAN
NYMPHET
NYMPHEUM
NYMPHIC
NYMPHICAL
NYMPHID
NYMPHINE
NYMPHITIS
NYMPHLIN
NYMPHOLEPSIA
NYMPHOLEPSY
NYMPHOLEPT
NYMPHOLEPTIC
NYMPHOMANIA
NYMPHOMANIAC
NYMPHOSIS
NYMPHOTOMY
NYMSS
NYSTAGMIC
NYSTAGMUS
NYSTATIN
NYTRIL
NYXIS

OADAL
OADE
OAF
OAFDOM
OAFISH
OAFISHLY
OAFISHNESS
OAFS
OAK
OAKBERRY
OAKEN
OAKENSHAW
OAKER
OAKMOSS
OAKS
OAKUM
OAKWEB
OAKWOOD
OAKY
OAM
OAR
OARAGE
OARCOCK
OARED
OARFISH
OARFISHES
OARIALGIA
OARING
OARIOCELE
OARIOPATHIC
OARIOPATHY
OARIOTOMY
OARITIC
OARITIS
OARIUM
OARLOCK
OARLOP
OARS
OARSMAN
OARSMANSHIP
OARSMEN
OARSWOMAN
OARSWOMEN
OARWEED
OARY
OASAL
OASEAN
OASES
OASIS
OASITIC
OAST
OASTHOUSE
OASY
OAT
OATCAKE
OATEAR
OATEN
OATENMEAL
OATFOWL
OATH
OATHAY
OATHED
OATHS
OATLAND
OATMEAL
OATS
OATSEED

OATY
OAVES
OB
OBA
OBAMBULATE
OBAMBULATION
OBAMBULATORY
OBAN
OBANG
OBARNE
OBARNI
OBBA
OBBLIGATI
OBBLIGATO
OBBLIGATOS
OBCLAVATE
OBCLUDE
OBCOMPRESSED
OBCONIC
OBCONICAL
OBCORDATE
OBCORDIFORM
OBCUNEATE
OBDELTOID
OBDORMITION
OBDUCTION
OBDURACY
OBDURATE
OBDURATELY
OBDURATENESS
OBDURATION
OBDURE
OBE
OBEAHISM
OBECHE
OBEDIENCE
OBEDIENCY
OBEDIENT
OBEDIENTIAL
OBEDIENTIALLY
OBEDIENTIAR
OBEDIENTIARIES
OBEDIENTIARY
OBEDIENTLY
OBEISANCE
OBEISANT
OBEISANTLY
OBEISH
OBEISM
OBELI
OBELIA
OBELIAC
OBELIAL
OBELION
OBELISCAL
OBELISCAR
OBELISK
OBELISKED
OBELISKING
OBELISKOID
OBELISM
OBELIZE
OBELIZED
OBELIZING
OBELUS
OBESE
OBESELY
OBESENESS
OBESITY
OBEX
OBEY
OBEYED
OBEYER
OBEYING
OBFUSCABLE
OBFUSCATE
OBFUSCATED

OBFUSCATING
OBFUSCATION
OBFUSCATOR
OBFUSCITY
OBFUSCOUS
OBFUSK
OBI
OBIA
OBIAH
OBIISM
OBISPO
OBIT
OBITAL
OBITER
OBITUAL
OBITUARIAN
OBITUARIES
OBITUARIST
OBITUARIZE
OBITUARY
OBJECT
OBJECTABLE
OBJECTATION
OBJECTATIVE
OBJECTED
OBJECTEE
OBJECTIFICATION
OBJECTIFIED
OBJECTIFY
OBJECTIFYING
OBJECTING
OBJECTION
OBJECTIONABILITY
OBJECTIONABLE
OBJECTIONABLY
OBJECTIONAL
OBJECTIONER
OBJECTIONIST
OBJECTIONS
OBJECTIVAL
OBJECTIVATE
OBJECTIVATED
OBJECTIVATING
OBJECTIVATION
OBJECTIVE
OBJECTIVELY
OBJECTIVENESS
OBJECTIVISM
OBJECTIVIST
OBJECTIVISTIC
OBJECTIVITY
OBJECTIVIZE
OBJECTIVIZED
OBJECTIVIZING
OBJECTIZATION
OBJECTIZE
OBJECTIZED
OBJECTIZING
OBJECTLESS
OBJECTOR
OBJECTS
OBJICIENT
OBJURATION
OBJURE
OBJURGATE
OBJURGATED
OBJURGATING
OBJURGATION
OBJURGATIVE
OBJURGATIVELY
OBJURGATOR
OBJURGATORILY
OBJURGATORY
OBJURGATRIX
OBLANCEOLATE
OBLAST

OBLAT
OBLATA
OBLATE
OBLATED
OBLATELY
OBLATENESS
OBLATING
OBLATIO
OBLATION
OBLATIONAL
OBLATIONARY
OBLATORY
OBLECTATE
OBLECTATION
OBLEY
OBLICQUE
OBLIGABLE
OBLIGANCY
OBLIGANT
OBLIGATE
OBLIGATED
OBLIGATING
OBLIGATION
OBLIGATIONAL
OBLIGATIONARY
OBLIGATIVE
OBLIGATIVENESS
OBLIGATO
OBLIGATOR
OBLIGATORILY
OBLIGATORINESS
OBLIGATORY
OBLIGATUM
OBLIGE
OBLIGED
OBLIGEDLY
OBLIGEDNESS
OBLIGEE
OBLIGEMENT
OBLIGER
OBLIGING
OBLIGINGLY
OBLIGINGNESS
OBLIGISTIC
OBLIGOR
OBLIQUATE
OBLIQUATION
OBLIQUE
OBLIQUED
OBLIQUELY
OBLIQUENESS
OBLIQUING
OBLIQUITIES
OBLIQUITOUS
OBLIQUITY
OBLIQUUS
OBLITERABLE
OBLITERATE
OBLITERATED
OBLITERATING
OBLITERATION
OBLITERATIVE
OBLITERATOR
OBLIVESCENCE
OBLIVIAL
OBLIVIALITY
OBLIVION
OBLIVIONATE
OBLIVIONIZE
OBLIVIOUS
OBLIVIOUSLY
OBLIVIOUSNESS
OBLIVISCENCE
OBLIVISCIBLE
OBLOCUTOR
OBLONG
OBLONGATA

OBLONGATAL
OBLONGATED
OBLONGITUDE
OBLONGITUDINAL
OBLONGLY
OBLONGNESS
OBLOQUIAL
OBLOQUIES
OBLOQUIOUS
OBLOQUY
OBMIT
OBMUTESCENCE
OBMUTESCENT
OBNEBULATE
OBNOUNCE
OBNOXIETY
OBNOXIOUS
OBNOXIOUSLY
OBNOXIOUSNESS
OBNUBILATE
OBNUBILATION
OBOE
OBOIST
OBOL
OBOLARY
OBOLE
OBOLI
OBOLOS
OBOLUS
OBOMEGOID
OBOVAL
OBOVATE
OBOVOID
OBPYRAMIDAL
OBPYRIFORM
OBREPTION
OBREPTITIOUS
OBREPTITIOUSLY
OBRIZE
OBROGATE
OBROGATION
OBROK
OBROTUND
OBSCENE
OBSCENELY
OBSCENENESS
OBSCENITIES
OBSCENITY
OBSCURANCY
OBSCURANT
OBSCURANTIC
OBSCURANTISM
OBSCURANTIST
OBSCURATION
OBSCURATIVE
OBSCURE
OBSCURED
OBSCURELY
OBSCUREMENT
OBSCURENESS
OBSCURER
OBSCUREST
OBSCURING
OBSCURITIES
OBSCURITY
OBSECRATE
OBSECRATED
OBSECRATING
OBSECRATION
OBSECRATIONARY
OBSECRATORY
OBSEDE
OBSEQUENCE
OBSEQUENT
OBSEQUIAL
OBSEQUIES
OBSEQUIOUS

OBSEQUIOUSLY	OBSTIPANT	OBTUSITY	OCCUPANCE	OCHRING
OBSEQUITY	OBSTIPATION	OBUMBRANT	OCCUPANCIES	OCHRO
OBSEQUY	OBSTREPERATE	OBUMBRATE	OCCUPANCY	OCHROCARPOUS
OBSERVABILITY	OBSTREPEROUS	OBUMBRATION	OCCUPANT	OCHROID
OBSERVABLE	OBSTREPEROUSLY	OBUS	OCCUPATION	OCHROLEUCOUS
OBSERVABLENESS	OBSTRICTION	OBVALLATE	OCCUPATIONAL	OCHROLITE
OBSERVABLY	OBSTRINGE	OBVELATION	OCCUPATIONALIST	OCHRONOSIS
OBSERVANCE	OBSTRUCT	OBVENTION	OCCUPATIONALLY	OCHRONOTIC
OBSERVANDA	OBSTRUCTANT	OBVERSE	OCCUPATIVE	OCHROUS
OBSERVANDUM	OBSTRUCTED	OBVERSELY	OCCUPIED	OCHRY
OBSERVANT	OBSTRUCTER	OBVERSION	OCCUPIER	OCK
OBSERVANTLY	OBSTRUCTING	OBVERT	OCCUPY	OCKER
OBSERVANTNESS	OBSTRUCTION	OBVERTED	OCCUPYING	OCKSTER
OBSERVATION	OBSTRUCTIONISM	OBVERTEND	OCCUR	OCOTE
OBSERVATIONAL	OBSTRUCTIONIST	OBVERTING	OCCURRED	OCOTILLO
OBSERVATIONALLY	OBSTRUCTIVE	OBVIABLE	OCCURRENCE	OCQUE
OBSERVATIVE	OBSTRUCTIVELY	OBVIATE	OCCURRENT	OCRACY
OBSERVATORIAL	OBSTRUCTIVENESS	OBVIATED	OCCURRING	OCREA
OBSERVATORIES	OBSTRUCTIVITY	OBVIATING	OCCURSE	OCREACEOUS
OBSERVATORY	OBSTRUCTOR	OBVIATION	OCEAN	OCREAE
OBSERVE	OBSTRUENT	OBVIATOR	OCEANED	OCREATE
OBSERVED	OBSTRUSE	OBVIOUS	OCEANET	OCREATED
OBSERVER	OBTAIN	OBVIOUSLY	OCEANIC	OCTACHLORIDE
OBSERVING	OBTAINABLE	OBVIOUSNESS	OCEANITY	OCTACHORD
OBSERVINGLY	OBTAINAL	OBVOLUTE	OCEANOGRAPHER	OCTACHORDAL
OBSESS	OBTAINANCE	OBVOLUTED	OCEANOGRAPHIC	OCTACOLIC
OBSESSED	OBTAINED	OBVOLUTION	OCEANOGRAPHICAL	OCTACTINAL
OBSESSING	OBTAINER	OBVOLUTIVE	OCEANOGRAPHICALLY	OCTACTINE
OBSESSION	OBTAINING	OBVOLVE	OCEANOGRAPHIST	OCTAD
OBSESSIONAL	OBTAINMENT	OBVOLVENT	OCEANOGRAPHY	OCTADECANE
OBSESSIVE	OBTECT	OC	OCEANOUS	OCTADECYL
OBSESSOR	OBTECTED	OCA	OCEANSIDE	OCTADIC
OBSIDE	OBTEMPER	OCARINA	OCELLANA	OCTADRACHM
OBSIDIAN	OBTEND	OCCAMY	OCELLAR	OCTADRACHMA
OBSIDIANITE	OBTENEBRATE	OCCASION	OCELLATE	OCTAECHOS
OBSIDIONAL	OBTENEBRATION	OCCASIONAL	OCELLATED	OCTAEMERA
OBSIDIONARY	OBTENT	OCCASIONALISM	OCELLATION	OCTAEMERON
OBSIDIOUS	OBTENTION	OCCASIONALIST	OCELLI	OCTAETERIC
OBSIGN	OBTEST	OCCASIONALISTIC	OCELLICYST	OCTAETERID
OBSIGNATE	OBTESTATION	OCCASIONALITY	OCELLICYSTIC	OCTAETERIS
OBSIGNATION	OBTESTED	OCCASIONALLY	OCELLIFEROUS	OCTAGON
OBSIGNATORY	OBTESTING	OCCASIONARY	OCELLIFORM	OCTAGONAL
OBSOLESCE	OBTRECT	OCCASIONED	OCELLIGEROUS	OCTAGONALLY
OBSOLESCED	OBTRIANGULAR	OCCASIONER	OCELLUS	OCTAHEDRA
OBSOLESCENCE	OBTRUDE	OCCASIONING	OCELOID	OCTAHEDRAL
OBSOLESCENT	OBTRUDED	OCCASIVE	OCELOT	OCTAHEDRIC
OBSOLESCENTLY	OBTRUDER	OCCIDENT	OCELOTS	OCTAHEDRICAL
OBSOLESCING	OBTRUDING	OCCIDENTAL	OCH	OCTAHEDRITE
OBSOLETE	OBTRUNCATE	OCCIDENTALITY	OCHAVA	OCTAHEDROID
OBSOLETELY	OBTRUNCATION	OCCIDENTALLY	OCHAVO	OCTAHEDRON
OBSOLETENESS	OBTRUNCATOR	OCCIPITA	OCHE	OCTAHEDROUS
OBSOLETION	OBTRUSION	OCCIPITAL	OCHER	OCTAHYDRATE
OBSOLETISM	OBTRUSIONIST	OCCIPITALIS	OCHERED	OCTAHYDRATED
OBSTACLE	OBTRUSIVE	OCCIPITOOTIC	OCHERING	OCTAMERISM
OBSTANCY	OBTRUSIVELY	OCCIPUT	OCHERISH	OCTAMEROUS
OBSTANT	OBTRUSIVENESS	OCCISION	OCHEROUS	OCTAMETER
OBSTETRIC	OBTUND	OCCITONE	OCHERY	OCTAN
OBSTETRICAL	OBTUNDED	OCCLUDE	OCHIDORE	OCTANDRIAN
OBSTETRICALLY	OBTUNDENT	OCCLUDED	OCHLESIS	OCTANDRIOUS
OBSTETRICATE	OBTUNDER	OCCLUDENT	OCHLESITIC	OCTANE
OBSTETRICATED	OBTUNDING	OCCLUDING	OCHLETIC	OCTANGLE
OBSTETRICATING	OBTUNDITY	OCCLUSAL	OCHLOCRACY	OCTANGULAR
OBSTETRICIAN	OBTURATE	OCCLUSE	OCHLOCRAT	OCTANGULARNESS
OBSTETRICS	OBTURATED	OCCLUSION	OCHLOCRATIC	OCTANT
OBSTETRICY	OBTURATING	OCCLUSIVE	OCHLOCRATICAL	OCTANTAL
OBSTETRIST	OBTURATION	OCCLUSOMETER	OCHLOMANIA	OCTAPLA
OBSTETRIX	OBTURATOR	OCCLUSOR	OCHLOPHOBIA	OCTAPLOID
OBSTINACIES	OBTURATORY	OCCULT	OCHLOPHOBIST	OCTAPLOIDIC
OBSTINACIOUS	OBTURBINATE	OCCULTATE	OCHNACEOUS	OCTAPLOIDY
OBSTINACY	OBTUSE	OCCULTATION	OCHONE	OCTAPODIC
OBSTINANCE	OBTUSELY	OCCULTED	OCHRA	OCTAPODY
OBSTINANCY	OBTUSENESS	OCCULTER	OCHRACEOUS	OCTARCH
OBSTINATE	OBTUSER	OCCULTING	OCHRE	OCTARCHIES
OBSTINATELY	OBTUSEST	OCCULTISM	OCHREA	OCTARCHY
OBSTINATENESS	OBTUSIFID	OCCULTIST	OCHRED	OCTARIUS
OBSTINATION	OBTUSILOBOUS	OCCULTLY	OCHREISH	OCTASEMIC
OBSTINATIVE	OBTUSION	OCCULTNESS	OCHREOUS	OCTASTICH

OCTASTICHON
OCTASTROPHIC
OCTASTYLOS
OCTATEUCH
OCTAVAL
OCTAVALENT
OCTAVARIA
OCTAVARIUM
OCTAVE
OCTAVIC
OCTAVINA
OCTAVO
OCTAVOS
OCTENE
OCTENNIAL
OCTENNIALLY
OCTET
OCTETTE
OCTIC
OCTILLION
OCTILLIONTH
OCTINE
OCTOAD
OCTOALLOY
OCTOATE
OCTOBASS
OCTOCOTYLOID
OCTODACTYL
OCTODACTYLE
OCTODE
OCTODECIMAL
OCTODECIMO
OCTODECIMOS
OCTODENTATE
OCTODIANOME
OCTODONT
OCTOECHOS
OCTOFID
OCTOFOIL
OCTOFOILED
OCTOGAMY
OCTOGENARIAN
OCTOGENARIES
OCTOGENARY
OCTOGILD
OCTOGLOT
OCTOGYNIAN
OCTOGYNIOUS
OCTOGYNOUS
OCTOHEDRAL
OCTOIC
OCTOID
OCTOLATERAL
OCTOLOCULAR
OCTOMERAL
OCTOMEROUS
OCTONAL
OCTONARE
OCTONARIAN
OCTONARIES
OCTONARIUS
OCTONARY
OCTONEMATOUS
OCTONION
OCTONOCULAR
OCTOON
OCTOPARTITE
OCTOPEAN
OCTOPED
OCTOPEDE
OCTOPETALOUS
OCTOPHYLLOUS
OCTOPI
OCTOPINE
OCTOPOD
OCTOPODAN
OCTOPODES

OCTOPODOUS
OCTOPOLAR
OCTOPUS
OCTOPUSES
OCTORADIAL
OCTORADIATE
OCTORADIATED
OCTOREME
OCTOROON
OCTOSE
OCTOSEPALOUS
OCTOSPERMOUS
OCTOSPORE
OCTOSPOROUS
OCTOSTICHOUS
OCTOSYLLABIC
OCTOSYLLABLE
OCTOVALENT
OCTOYL
OCTROI
OCTROY
OCTUOR
OCTUPLE
OCTUPLED
OCTUPLET
OCTUPLEX
OCTUPLICATE
OCTUPLICATION
OCTUPLING
OCTUPLY
OCTYL
OCTYLENE
OCTYNE
OCUBY
OCULAR
OCULARIST
OCULARLY
OCULARY
OCULATE
OCULATED
OCULAUDITORY
OCULI
OCULIFEROUS
OCULIFORM
OCULIGEROUS
OCULINID
OCULINOID
OCULIST
OCULISTIC
OCULOFACIAL
OCULOFRONTAL
OCULOMOTOR
OCULOMOTORY
OCULONASAL
OCULOSPINAL
OCULUS
OCYDROME
OCYDROMINE
OCYME
OCYPODAN
OCYPODIAN
OCYPODOID
OD
ODA
ODACOID
ODAL
ODALBORN
ODALISK
ODALISQUE
ODALLER
ODD
ODDBALL
ODDER
ODDEST
ODDITIES
ODDITY
ODDLEGS

ODDLY
ODDMAN
ODDMENT
ODDMENTS
ODDNESS
ODDS
ODDSMAN
ODE
ODEA
ODEL
ODELET
ODEON
ODEUM
ODHAL
ODIBLE
ODIC
ODICALLY
ODINISM
ODINITE
ODIOMETER
ODIOUS
ODIOUSLY
ODIOUSNESS
ODIST
ODIUM
ODLING
ODOGRAPH
ODOLOGY
ODOMETER
ODOMETRICAL
ODOMETRY
ODONTOTRIPSIS
ODONTAGRA
ODONTALGIA
ODONTALGIC
ODONTATROPHY
ODONTEXESIS
ODONTIASIS
ODONTIC
ODONTIST
ODONTITIS
ODONTOBLAST
ODONTOBLASTIC
ODONTOCELE
ODONTOCETE
ODONTOCETOUS
ODONTOCLASIS
ODONTOCLAST
ODONTODYNIA
ODONTOGEN
ODONTOGENESIS
ODONTOGENIC
ODONTOGENY
ODONTOGRAPH
ODONTOGRAPHIC
ODONTOGRAPHY
ODONTOID
ODONTOLCATE
ODONTOLCOUS
ODONTOLITE
ODONTOLITH
ODONTOLOGICAL
ODONTOLOGIST
ODONTOLOGY
ODONTOLOXIA
ODONTOMA
ODONTOMOUS
ODONTOPATHY
ODONTOPHORAL
ODONTOPHORE
ODONTOSCOPE
ODONTOTECHNY
ODOOM
ODOPHONE
ODOR
ODORABLE
ODORANT

ODORATE
ODORATOR
ODORED
ODORIFERANT
ODORIFEROUS
ODORIFEROUSLY
ODORIFIC
ODORIPHOR
ODORIPHORE
ODORIVECTOR
ODORIZE
ODORLESS
ODORLESSLY
ODORLESSNESS
ODOROMETER
ODOROSITY
ODOROUS
ODOROUSLY
ODOROUSNESS
ODORS
ODOUR
ODOURED
ODSO
ODUM
ODYL
ODYLE
ODYLIC
ODYLISM
ODYLIST
ODYLIZATION
ODYLIZE
ODYSSEYS
OE
OECIST
OECODOMIC
OECOID
OECONOMUS
OECOPARASITE
OECOPARASITISM
OECUMENIAN
OECUMENIC
OECUMENICAL
OECUMENICITY
OECUS
OEDEMA
OEDEMERID
OEDICNEMINE
OEILLADE
OEKIST
OELET
OENANTHATE
OENANTHIC
OENANTHYL
OENANTHYLATE
OENIN
OENOCHOAE
OENOCHOE
OENOCYTE
OENOCYTIC
OENOLIN
OENOLOGICAL
OENOLOGIES
OENOLOGIST
OENOLOGY
OENOMANCY
OENOMEL
OENOMETER
OENOPHILIST
OENOPHOBIST
OENOPOETIC
OERSTED
OESOPHAGAL
OESOPHAGEAL
OESOPHAGEAN
OESOPHAGISM
OESOPHAGITIS
OESOPHAGUS

OESTRIAN
OESTRIASIS
OESTRID
OESTRIN
OESTRIOL
OESTROGEN
OESTROID
OESTRONE
OESTROUS
OESTRUAL
OESTRUATE
OESTRUATION
OESTRUM
OESTRUS
OEUVRE
OEUVRES
OF
OFAY
OFF
OFFAL
OFFALING
OFFBEAT
OFFBREAK
OFFCAST
OFFCOME
OFFCUT
OFFED
OFFENCE
OFFENCELESS
OFFENCELESSLY
OFFEND
OFFENDANT
OFFENDED
OFFENDEDLY
OFFENDEDNESS
OFFENDER
OFFENDERS
OFFENDING
OFFENDRESS
OFFENSE
OFFENSELESS
OFFENSELESSLY
OFFENSIBLE
OFFENSIVE
OFFENSIVELY
OFFENSIVENESS
OFFER
OFFERED
OFFERER
OFFERING
OFFERINGS
OFFEROR
OFFERTORIAL
OFFERTORIES
OFFERTORY
OFFGOING
OFFGRADE
OFFHAND
OFFHANDED
OFFHANDEDLY
OFFHANDEDNESS
OFFICARIES
OFFICE
OFFICEHOLDER
OFFICER
OFFICERAGE
OFFICERED
OFFICERESS
OFFICERIAL
OFFICERING
OFFICERS
OFFICIAL
OFFICIALDOM
OFFICIALISM
OFFICIALITIES
OFFICIALITY
OFFICIALIZE

OFFICIALLY
OFFICIANT
OFFICIARY
OFFICIATE
OFFICIATED
OFFICIATING
OFFICIATION
OFFICIATOR
OFFICINA
OFFICINAL
OFFICINALLY
OFFICIOUS
OFFICIOUSLY
OFFICIOUSNESS
OFFING
OFFISH
OFFISHLY
OFFISHNESS
OFFLAP
OFFLET
OFFLOOK
OFFPRINT
OFFSADDLE
OFFSCAPE
OFFSCOUR
OFFSCOURER
OFFSCOURING
OFFSCOURINGS
OFFSCUM
OFFSET
OFFSHOOT
OFFSHORE
OFFSIDE
OFFSIDER
OFFSPRING
OFFTAKE
OFFTYPE
OFFUSCATE
OFFUSCATION
OFFWARD
OFFWARDS
OFICINA
OFLAG
OFLETE
OFT
OFTEN
OFTENNESS
OFTENS
OFTENTIME
OFTENTIMES
OFTHINK
OFTLY
OFTNESS
OFTTIME
OFTTIMES
OFTWHILES
OGAM
OGAMIC
OGDOAD
OGDOAS
OGEE
OGEED
OGGANITION
OGHAM
OGHAMIC
OGIVAL
OGIVE
OGIVED
OGLE
OGLED
OGLER
OGLING
OGLIO
OGRE
OGREISH
OGRESS
OGRISH

OGTIERN
OGUM
OH
OHED
OHELO
OHIA
OHING
OHM
OHMAGE
OHMIC
OHMMETER
OHNE
OHO
OHONE
OIDIA
OIDIOID
OIDIOMYCOSIS
OIDIOMYCOTIC
OII
OIKOLOGY
OIKOMANIA
OIKOPLAST
OIL
OILBERRIES
OILBERRY
OILBIRD
OILCAN
OILCASE
OILCLOTH
OILCOAT
OILDOM
OILED
OILER
OILERY
OILFISH
OILFISHES
OILHOLE
OILIER
OILIEST
OILILY
OILINESS
OILISH
OILLESS
OILLESSNESS
OILLET
OILMAN
OILMEN
OILMONGER
OILMONGERY
OILOMETER
OILPAPER
OILPROOF
OILPROOFING
OILSEED
OILSKIN
OILSKINNED
OILSTOCK
OILSTONE
OILSTONED
OILSTONING
OILSTOVE
OILTIGHT
OILTIGHTNESS
OILWAY
OILWELL
OILY
OIME
OIMEE
OINOCHOE
OINOLOGY
OINOMANCY
OINOMANIA
OINOMEL
OINT
OINTMENT
OISIVITY
OITA

OITAVA
OJO
OK
OKA
OKAPI
OKAPIS
OKAY
OKE
OKEE
OKEH
OKENITE
OKET
OKEYDOKE
OKI
OKIA
OKIE
OKIEH
OKOLEHAO
OKONITE
OKOUME
OKOW
OKRA
OKRO
OKROOG
OKRUG
OKRUZI
OKSHOOFD
OKTHABAH
OLA
OLACACEOUS
OLACAD
OLAM
OLAY
OLD
OLDEN
OLDENED
OLDENING
OLDER
OLDERMOST
OLDERS
OLDEST
OLDFANGLED
OLDFANGLEDNESS
OLDHAMITE
OLDHEARTED
OLDISH
OLDLAND
OLDNESS
OLDS
OLDSTER
OLDWENCH
OLDWIFE
OLDWIVES
OLE
OLEACEOUS
OLEAGINOUS
OLEAGINOUSLY
OLEANA
OLEANDER
OLEANDRIN
OLEASE
OLEASTER
OLEATE
OLECRANAL
OLECRANON
OLEFIANT
OLEFIN
OLEFINE
OLEFINIC
OLEIC
OLEIFEROUS
OLEIN
OLEINE
OLEN
OLENA
OLENELLIDIAN
OLENID

OLENIDIAN
OLENT
OLEO
OLEOCELLOSIS
OLEOCYST
OLEODUCT
OLEOGRAPH
OLEOGRAPHER
OLEOGRAPHIC
OLEOGRAPHY
OLEOMARGARIN
OLEOMARGARINE
OLEOMETER
OLEOPTENE
OLEORESIN
OLEORESINOUS
OLEOSE
OLEOSITY
OLEOSTEARATE
OLEOSTEARIN
OLEOSTEARINE
OLEOTHORAX
OLEOUS
OLEPI
OLEPY
OLER
OLERACEOUS
OLERICULTURE
OLETHREUTID
OLEUM
OLFACT
OLFACTABLE
OLFACTIBLE
OLFACTION
OLFACTOLOGY
OLFACTOMETER
OLFACTOMETRIC
OLFACTOMETRY
OLFACTOR
OLFACTORIES
OLFACTORILY
OLFACTORY
OLFACTY
OLIBAN
OLIBANUM
OLID
OLIGAEMIA
OLIGANDROUS
OLIGANTHOUS
OLIGARCH
OLIGARCHAL
OLIGARCHIC
OLIGARCHICAL
OLIGARCHIES
OLIGARCHISM
OLIGARCHIST
OLIGARCHIZE
OLIGARCHY
OLIGEMIA
OLIGIDRIA
OLIGIST
OLIGISTIC
OLIGISTICAL
OLIGOCARPOUS
OLIGOCHAETE
OLIGOCHETE
OLIGOCHOLIA
OLIGOCHROME
OLIGOCHYLIA
OLIGOCLASE
OLIGOCLASITE
OLIGOCYSTIC
OLIGODIPSIA
OLIGODONTOUS
OLIGODYNAMIC
OLIGOHEMIA
OLIGOLACTIA

OLIGOMEROUS
OLIGOMERY
OLIGOMYODIAN
OLIGOMYOID
OLIGONEPHRIC
OLIGONITE
OLIGOPEPSIA
OLIGOPHAGOUS
OLIGOPHRENIA
OLIGOPHRENIC
OLIGOPLASMIA
OLIGOPNEA
OLIGOPOLIST
OLIGOPOLY
OLIGOPSYCHIA
OLIGOPYRENE
OLIGORHIZOUS
OLIGOSIALIA
OLIGOSITE
OLIGOSPERMIA
OLIGOTOKEUS
OLIGOTRICHIA
OLIGOTROPHIC
OLIGOTROPHY
OLIGURESIA
OLIGURESIS
OLIGURETIC
OLIGURIA
OLIO
OLIOS
OLIPHANT
OLIPRANCE
OLITORY
OLIVA
OLIVACEOUS
OLIVARY
OLIVASTER
OLIVE
OLIVED
OLIVENESS
OLIVENITE
OLIVERMAN
OLIVERMEN
OLIVERSMITH
OLIVES
OLIVESCENT
OLIVET
OLIVETTE
OLIVEWOOD
OLIVIFEROUS
OLIVIFORM
OLIVIL
OLIVILE
OLIVILIN
OLIVINE
OLIVINEFELS
OLIVINIC
OLIVINITE
OLIVINITIC
OLLA
OLLAE
OLLAMH
OLLAPOD
OLLAV
OLLENITE
OLLOCK
OLLUCK
OLM
OLOGICAL
OLOGIST
OLOGISTIC
OLOGY
OLOMAO
OLONA
OLOROSO
OLP
OLPAE

OLPE
OLPH
OLTONDE
OLTUNNA
OLYCOOK
OLYKOEK
OM
OMADAWN
OMADHAUN
OMAGRA
OMALGIA
OMAO
OMARTHRITIS
OMASA
OMASUM
OMBER
OMBRE
OMBRETTE
OMBRIFUGE
OMBROGRAPH
OMBROLOGICAL
OMBROLOGY
OMBROMETER
OMBROPHIL
OMBROPHILE
OMBROPHILIC
OMBROPHILOUS
OMBROPHILY
OMBROPHOBE
OMBROPHOBOUS
OMBROPHOBY
OMBROPHYTE
OMBUDSMAN
OMBUDSMEN
OMDA
OMDEH
OMEGA
OMEGOID
OMEL
OMELET
OMELETTE
OMELIE
OMEN
OMENED
OMENOLOGY
OMENTA
OMENTAL
OMENTECTOMY
OMENTITIS
OMENTOCELE
OMENTOPEXY
OMENTOPLASTY
OMENTOTOMY
OMENTULUM
OMENTUM
OMER
OMICRON
OMIKRON
OMINATE
OMINOUS
OMINOUSLY
OMINOUSNESS
OMISSIBLE
OMISSION
OMISSIVE
OMISSIVELY
OMIT
OMITIS
OMITTED
OMITTER
OMITTING
OMLAH
OMMATEA
OMMATEAL
OMMATEUM
OMMATIDIA
OMMATIDIAL

OMMATIDIUM
OMMATOPHORE
OMNEITY
OMNES
OMNIACTIVE
OMNIANA
OMNIARCH
OMNIBUS
OMNIBUSES
OMNIBUSMAN
OMNIERUDITE
OMNIESSENCE
OMNIFACIAL
OMNIFARIOUS
OMNIFEROUS
OMNIFIC
OMNIFICENT
OMNIFIDEL
OMNIFIED
OMNIFORM
OMNIFORMAL
OMNIFORMITY
OMNIFY
OMNIFYING
OMNIGENOUS
OMNIGERENT
OMNIGRAPH
OMNIHUMAN
OMNIHUMANITY
OMNILEGENT
OMNILINGUAL
OMNILOQUENT
OMNILUCENT
OMNIMENTAL
OMNIMETER
OMNIMODE
OMNIMODOUS
OMNINESCIENT
OMNIPARENT
OMNIPARIENT
OMNIPARITY
OMNIPAROUS
OMNIPATIENT
OMNIPERFECT
OMNIPOTENCE
OMNIPOTENCY
OMNIPOTENT
OMNIPOTENTLY
OMNIPRESENCE
OMNIPRESENT
OMNIPRUDENCE
OMNIPRUDENT
OMNIRANGE
OMNIREGENCY
OMNIREGENT
OMNISCIENCE
OMNISCIENCY
OMNISCIENT
OMNISCIENTLY
OMNISCOPE
OMNISCRIBENT
OMNISENTIENT
OMNISPECTIVE
OMNIST
OMNITEMPORAL
OMNITENENT
OMNITOLERANT
OMNITONAL
OMNITONALITY
OMNITONIC
OMNITUDE
OMNIUM
OMNIVAGANT
OMNIVALENCE
OMNIVALENT
OMNIVALOUS
OMNIVARIOUS

OMNIVIDENCE
OMNIVIDENT
OMNIVISION
OMNIVOLENT
OMNIVORACITY
OMNIVORE
OMNIVOROUS
OMNIVOROUSLY
OMODYNIA
OMOHYOID
OMOIDEUM
OMOPHAGIA
OMOPHAGIC
OMOPHAGIST
OMOPHAGOUS
OMOPHAGY
OMOPHORIA
OMOPHORION
OMOPLATE
OMOSTEGITE
OMOSTERNAL
OMOSTERNUM
OMPHACINE
OMPHACITE
OMPHACY
OMPHALECTOMY
OMPHALI
OMPHALIC
OMPHALISM
OMPHALITIS
OMPHALOCELE
OMPHALODE
OMPHALODIA
OMPHALODIUM
OMPHALOID
OMPHALOMA
OMPHALONCUS
OMPHALORRHEA
OMPHALOS
OMPHALOSITE
OMPHALOTOMY
OMPHALUS
OMRAH
ON
ONA
ONAGER
ONAGERS
ONAGRA
ONAGRACEOUS
ONAGRI
ONANISM
ONANIST
ONANISTIC
ONCA
ONCE
ONCET
ONCETTA
ONCIA
ONCIN
ONCOGRAPH
ONCOGRAPHY
ONCOLOGIC
ONCOLOGICAL
ONCOLOGY
ONCOME
ONCOMETER
ONCOMETRIC
ONCOMETRY
ONCOMING
ONCOSIMETER
ONCOSIS
ONCOSPHERE
ONCOST
ONCOSTMAN
ONCOTOMY
ONDAGRAM
ONDAGRAPH

ONDAMETER
ONDASCOPE
ONDATRA
ONDE
ONDINE
ONDOGRAM
ONDOGRAPH
ONDOMETER
ONDOSCOPE
ONDOYANT
ONDULE
ONE
ONEBERRY
ONEFOLD
ONEFOLDNESS
ONEGITE
ONEHOOD
ONEHOW
ONEIRIC
ONEIROCRITIC
ONEIROCRITICS
ONEIRODYNIA
ONEIROLOGIST
ONEIROLOGY
ONEIROMANCER
ONEIROMANCY
ONEIROSCOPIC
ONEIROSCOPY
ONEIROTIC
ONEISM
ONEMENT
ONENESS
ONER
ONERARY
ONERATE
ONERATIVE
ONEROSE
ONEROSITY
ONEROUS
ONEROUSLY
ONEROUSNESS
ONERY
ONESELF
ONETHE
ONETIME
ONEWHERE
ONEYER
ONFALL
ONFLEMED
ONFLOW
ONFLOWING
ONGARO
ONGLE
ONGOING
ONHANGER
ONI
ONIOMANIA
ONIOMANIAC
ONION
ONIONET
ONIONIZED
ONIONPEEL
ONIONS
ONIONSKIN
ONIONY
ONIROTIC
ONISCIFORM
ONISCOID
ONISCOIDEAN
ONKILONITE
ONKOS
ONLAP
ONLAY
ONLEPY
ONLESS
ONLINESS
ONLOOK

ONLOOKER
ONLOOKING
ONLY
ONMARCH
ONOCENTAUR
ONOCROTAL
ONOFRITE
ONOLATRY
ONOMANCY
ONOMASTIC
ONOMASTICAL
ONOMASTICON
ONOMASTICS
ONOMATOLOGY
ONOMATOPE
ONOMATOPLASM
ONOMATOPOEIA
ONOMATOPOEIC
ONOMATOPOESY
ONOMATOPY
ONOMATOUS
ONON
ONOTOGENIC
ONRUSH
ONRUSHING
ONS
ONSET
ONSETTER
ONSHORE
ONSIDE
ONSIGHT
ONSLAUGHT
ONSTAND
ONSTANDING
ONSTEAD
ONSWEEP
ONSWEEPING
ONTAL
ONTIC
ONTO
ONTOCYCLE
ONTOCYCLIC
ONTOGENAL
ONTOGENESIS
ONTOGENETIC
ONTOGENIST
ONTOGENY
ONTOGRAPHY
ONTOLOGIC
ONTOLOGICAL
ONTOLOGICALLY
ONTOLOGIES
ONTOLOGISM
ONTOLOGIST
ONTOLOGISTIC
ONTOLOGIZE
ONTOLOGY
ONUS
ONWAITING
ONWARD
ONWARDLY
ONWARDNESS
ONWARDS
ONY
ONYCHA
ONYCHAUXIS
ONYCHIA
ONYCHIN
ONYCHITE
ONYCHITIS
ONYCHIUM
ONYCHOID
ONYCHOLYSIS
ONYCHOPATHIC
ONYCHOPATHY
ONYCHOPHAGIA
ONYCHOPHAGY

ONYCHOPHORAN	OOMIAC	OPACITY	OPERATIVENESS	OPHTHALMY
ONYCHOPHYMA	OOMIAK	OPACOUS	OPERATIVITY	OPIANE
ONYCHOPTOSIS	OOMPAH	OPACOUSNESS	OPERATIZE	OPIANIC
ONYCHOSIS	OOMPH	OPAH	OPERATOR	OPIANYL
ONYCHOTROPHY	OOMYCETE	OPAL	OPERATORY	OPIATE
ONYM	OOMYCETES	OPALED	OPERATRICES	OPIATED
ONYMAL	OOMYCETOUS	OPALESCE	OPERATRIX	OPIATIC
ONYMATIC	OON	OPALESCED	OPERCELE	OPIATING
ONYMITY	OONS	OPALESCENCE	OPERCLE	OPIE
ONYMIZE	OONT	OPALESCENT	OPERCLED	OPIFEX
ONYMOUS	OOP	OPALESCING	OPERCULA	OPIFICE
ONYMY	OOPACK	OPALEYE	OPERCULAR	OPIFICER
ONYX	OOPAK	OPALINE	OPERCULATE	OPIHI
ONYXES	OOPHORALGIA	OPALINID	OPERCULATED	OPIISM
ONYXIS	OOPHORAUXE	OPALININE	OPERCULE	OPILIACEOUS
ONZA	OOPHORE	OPALIZE	OPERCULIFORM	OPIME
OO	OOPHORECTOMY	OPALIZED	OPERCULUM	OPINABILITY
OOANGIUM	OOPHORIC	OPALIZING	OPERETTIST	OPINABLE
OOBLAST	OOPHORIDIA	OPALOID	OPERETTA	OPINABLY
OOBLASTIC	OOPHORIDIUM	OPAQUE	OPERETTAS	OPINANT
OOCYESIS	OOPHORIDIUMS	OPAQUED	OPERETTE	OPINATIVE
OOCYST	OOPHORITIS	OPAQUELY	OPEROSE	OPINATIVELY
OOCYSTACEOUS	OOPHOROCELE	OPAQUENESS	OPEROSELY	OPINATOR
OOCYSTIC	OOPHOROMA	OPAQUING	OPEROSENESS	OPINE
OOCYTE	OOPHOROMANIA	OPDALITE	OPHELIMITY	OPINED
OODLES	OOPHORON	OPE	OPHIASIS	OPINER
OODLINS	OOPHOROPEXY	OPED	OPHIC	OPING
OOECIA	OOPHOROSTOMY	OPEIDOSCOPE	OPHICALCITE	OPINIATE
OOECIAL	OOPHOROTOMY	OPELET	OPHICHTHYOID	OPINIATED
OOECIUM	OOPHYTE	OPELU	OPHICLEIDE	OPINIATEDLY
OOF	OOPHYTIC	OPEN	OPHICLEIDEAN	OPINIATER
OOFBIRD	OOPLASM	OPENBAND	OPHICLEIDIST	OPINIATIVE
OOFIER	OOPLASMIC	OPENBEAK	OPHIDIAN	OPINIATIVELY
OOFIEST	OOPLAST	OPENBILL	OPHIDIOID	OPINIATRE
OOFTISH	OOPOD	OPENCAST	OPHIDIOMANIA	OPINIATRETY
OOFY	OOPODAL	OPENCUT	OPHIDIOUS	OPINICUS
OOGAMETE	OOPORPHYRIN	OPENED	OPHIOGRAPHY	OPINING
OOGAMOUS	OOPUHUE	OPENER	OPHIOID	OPINION
OOGAMY	OORALI	OPENEST	OPHIOLATER	OPINIONABLE
OOGENESIS	OORD	OPENHANDED	OPHIOLATROUS	OPINIONAL
OOGENETIC	OORIAL	OPENHANDEDLY	OPHIOLATRY	OPINIONATE
OOGENY	OORIE	OPENHEAD	OPHIOLITE	OPINIONATED
OOGLEA	OOSCOPE	OPENHEARTED	OPHIOLITIC	OPINIONATEDLY
OOGLOEA	OOSCOPY	OPENHEARTEDLY	OPHIOLOGIC	OPINIONATELY
OOGONE	OOSPERM	OPENING	OPHIOLOGICAL	OPINIONATIVE
OOGONIA	OOSPHERE	OPENINGS	OPHIOLOGIST	OPINIONED
OOGONIAL	OOSPORANGIA	OPENLY	OPHIOLOGY	OPINIONIST
OOGONIOPHORE	OOSPORANGIUM	OPENMOUTHED	OPHIOMANCY	OPINIONS
OOGONIUM	OOSPORE	OPENNESS	OPHIOMORPHIC	OPIOMANIA
OOGONIUMS	OOSPORIC	OPENSIDE	OPHIONID	OPIOMANIAC
OOGRAPH	OOSPOROUS	OPENWORK	OPHIONINE	OPIOPHAGISM
OOID	OOSTEGITE	OPERA	OPHIOPHAGOUS	OPIOPHAGY
OOIDAL	OOSTEGITIC	OPERABILITY	OPHIOPHILISM	OPISOMETER
OOK	OOT	OPERABLE	OPHIOPHILIST	OPISTHENAR
OOKINESIS	OOTHECA	OPERABLY	OPHIOPHOBE	OPISTHION
OOKINETE	OOTHECAL	OPERAGOER	OPHIOPHOBIA	OPISTHOCOME
OOKINETIC	OOTID	OPERALOGUE	OPHIOPHOBY	OPISTHODETIC
OOLACHAN	OOTOCOID	OPERAMETER	OPHIOPLUTEUS	OPISTHODOME
OOLAK	OOTOCOIDEAN	OPERANCE	OPHIOURIDE	OPISTHODONT
OOLEMMA	OOTOCOUS	OPERANCY	OPHITE	OPISTHOGRAPH
OOLITE	OOTWITH	OPERAND	OPHITIC	OPISTHOSOMAL
OOLITIC	OOTYPE	OPERANT	OPHIURAN	OPISTHOTIC
OOLLIES	OOZE	OPERARY	OPHIURID	OPISTHOTONIC
OOLLY	OOZED	OPERAS	OPHIUROID	OPISTHOTONOS
OOLOGIC	OOZEL	OPERATABLE	OPHIUROIDEAN	OPIUM
OOLOGICAL	OOZIER	OPERATE	OPHRYON	OPIUMISM
OOLOGICALLY	OOZIEST	OPERATED	OPHTHALMAGRA	OPOBALSAM
OOLOGIST	OOZILY	OPERATEE	OPHTHALMIA	OPOBALSAMUM
OOLOGIZE	OOZINESS	OPERATIC	OPHTHALMIAC	OPODELDOC
OOLOGY	OOZING	OPERATICAL	OPHTHALMIATER	OPODIDYMUS
OOLONG	OOZOID	OPERATICALLY	OPHTHALMIC	OPOPANAX
OOM	OOZY	OPERATING	OPHTHALMIOUS	OPOSSUM
OOMANCY	OPACATE	OPERATION	OPHTHALMIST	OPOSSUMS
OOMANTIA	OPACIFIER	OPERATIONAL	OPHTHALMITE	OPPIDA
OOMETER	OPACIFY	OPERATIONS	OPHTHALMITIC	OPPIDAN
OOMETRIC	OPACITE	OPERATIVE	OPHTHALMITIS	OPPIDUM
OOMETRY	OPACITIES	OPERATIVELY	OPHTHALMOPOD	OPPIGNERATE

OPPIGNORATE	OPSONOGEN	OPUSCULUM	ORATORIOS	ORCHIDALGIA
OPPILANT	OPSONOID	OQUASSA	ORATORIZE	ORCHIDECTOMY
OPPILATE	OPSONOMETRY	OQUE	ORATORY	ORCHIDIST
OPPILATED	OPSONOPHILIA	OQUI	ORATRESS	ORCHIDITIS
OPPILATING	OPSONOPHILIC	OR	ORATRICES	ORCHIDOCELE
OPPILATION	OPSONOPHORIC	ORA	ORATRIX	ORCHIDOLOGIST
OPPILATIVE	OPSONOTHERAPY	ORABASSU	ORB	ORCHIDOLOGY
OPPLETE	OPT	ORACH	ORBAL	ORCHIDOPEXY
OPPLETION	OPTABLE	ORACHE	ORBATE	ORCHIDOTOMY
OPPO	OPTABLENESS	ORACLE	ORBED	ORCHIDS
OPPONENCY	OPTABLY	ORACLER	ORBELL	ORCHIECTOMY
OPPONENS	OPTANT	ORACULA	ORBIC	ORCHIL
OPPONENT	OPTATE	ORACULAR	ORBICAL	ORCHILLA
OPPORTUNE	OPTATION	ORACULARITY	ORBICLE	ORCHILYTIC
OPPORTUNELY	OPTATIVE	ORACULARLY	ORBICULAR	ORCHIOCELE
OPPORTUNISM	OPTATIVELY	ORACULARNESS	ORBICULARIS	ORCHIODYNIA
OPPORTUNIST	OPTED	ORACULATE	ORBICULARITY	ORCHIONCUS
OPPORTUNISTIC	OPTIC	ORACULOUS	ORBICULARLY	ORCHIOPEXY
OPPORTUNITIES	OPTICAL	ORACULOUSLY	ORBICULATE	ORCHIOPLASTY
OPPORTUNITY	OPTICALLY	ORACULOUSNESS	ORBICULATED	ORCHIOTOMY
OPPOSABILITY	OPTICIAN	ORACULUM	ORBICULATELY	ORCHIS
OPPOSABLE	OPTICIST	ORAD	ORBICULATION	ORCHISES
OPPOSAL	OPTICITY	ORAGE	ORBIFIC	ORCHITIC
OPPOSE	OPTICS	ORAGIOUS	ORBING	ORCHITIS
OPPOSED	OPTIGRAPH	ORAL	ORBIT	ORCHOTOMY
OPPOSELESS	OPTIMA	ORALE	ORBITAL	ORCIN
OPPOSER	OPTIMACY	ORALER	ORBITALE	ORCINE
OPPOSING	OPTIMAL	ORALISM	ORBITARY	ORCINOL
OPPOSINGLY	OPTIMATE	ORALIST	ORBITE	ORDAIN
OPPOSIT	OPTIMATES	ORALITY	ORBITELAR	ORDAINABLE
OPPOSITE	OPTIME	ORALLY	ORBITELARIAN	ORDAINED
OPPOSITELY	OPTIMISM	ORALOGIST	ORBITELE	ORDAINER
OPPOSITENESS	OPTIMIST	ORALOGY	ORBITELOUS	ORDAINING
OPPOSITION	OPTIMISTIC	ORANG	ORBITER	ORDAINMENT
OPPOSITIONAL	OPTIMISTICAL	ORANGE	ORBITOLITE	ORDALIAN
OPPOSITIOUS	OPTIMISTICALLY	ORANGEADE	ORBITOMALAR	ORDALIUM
OPPOSITIVE	OPTIMITY	ORANGEADO	ORBITONASAL	ORDANCHITE
OPPOSITIVELY	OPTIMIZATION	ORANGEAT	ORBITOSTAT	ORDEAL
OPPOSURE	OPTIMIZE	ORANGEBERRIES	ORBITOTOMY	ORDENE
OPPRESS	OPTIMIZED	ORANGEBERRY	ORBITUDE	ORDER
OPPRESSED	OPTIMIZING	ORANGEBIRD	ORBITY	ORDERABLE
OPPRESSING	OPTIMUM	ORANGELEAF	ORBY	ORDERED
OPPRESSION	OPTIMUMS	ORANGER	ORC	ORDEREDNESS
OPPRESSIVE	OPTING	ORANGEROOT	ORCANET	ORDERER
OPPRESSIVELY	OPTION	ORANGERY	ORCANETTE	ORDERING
OPPRESSIVENESS	OPTIONAL	ORANGEWOMAN	ORCEIN	ORDERLESS
OPPRESSOR	OPTIONALITY	ORANGEWOOD	ORCHAMUS	ORDERLIES
OPPROBRIATE	OPTIONALIZE	ORANGEY	ORCHANET	ORDERLINESS
OPPROBRIOUS	OPTIONALLY	ORANGIST	ORCHARD	ORDERLY
OPPROBRIUM	OPTIONARY	ORANGITE	ORCHARDING	ORDERS
OPPROBRY	OPTIONEE	ORANGIZE	ORCHARDIST	ORDINABILITY
OPPUGN	OPTIONOR	ORANGOUTANG	ORCHARDMAN	ORDINABLE
OPPUGNACY	OPTIVE	ORANGUTAN	ORCHARDMEN	ORDINAL
OPPUGNANCE	OPTOBLAST	ORANS	ORCHEITIS	ORDINANCE
OPPUGNANCY	OPTOGRAM	ORANT	ORCHEN	ORDINAND
OPPUGNANT	OPTOGRAPHY	ORANTE	ORCHESIS	ORDINANT
OPPUGNATE	OPTOLOGICAL	ORANTES	ORCHESTIAN	ORDINAR
OPPUGNATION	OPTOLOGIST	ORARIA	ORCHESTIC	ORDINARIES
OPPUGNED	OPTOLOGY	ORARIAN	ORCHESTIID	ORDINARILY
OPPUGNER	OPTOMENINX	ORARION	ORCHESTRA	ORDINARINESS
OPPUGNING	OPTOMETER	ORARY	ORCHESTRAL	ORDINARY
OPSIGAMY	OPTOMETRICAL	ORAS	ORCHESTRALLY	ORDINATE
OPSIMATH	OPTOMETRIST	ORATE	ORCHESTRATE	ORDINATED
OPSIMATHY	OPTOMETRY	ORATED	ORCHESTRATED	ORDINATING
OPSISFORM	OPTOPHONE	ORATING	ORCHESTRATER	ORDINATION
OPSISTYPE	OPTOTYPE	ORATION	ORCHESTRATING	ORDINATIVE
OPSONIA	OPULENCE	ORATIONAL	ORCHESTRATION	ORDINATOR
OPSONIC	OPULENCY	ORATIONER	ORCHESTRATOR	ORDINEE
OPSONIFEROUS	OPULENT	ORATOR	ORCHESTRIC	ORDINES
OPSONIFIED	OPULENTLY	ORATORIAL	ORCHESTRION	ORDNANCE
OPSONIFY	OPULUS	ORATORIALLY	ORCHIALGIA	ORDO
OPSONIFYING	OPUNTIA	ORATORIAN	ORCHIC	ORDONNANCE
OPSONIN	OPUNTIOID	ORATORIC	ORCHICHOREA	ORDONNANT
OPSONIST	OPUS	ORATORICAL	ORCHID	ORDOS
OPSONIUM	OPUSCLE	ORATORICALLY	ORCHIDACEAN	ORDOSITE
OPSONIZATION	OPUSCULAR	ORATORIES	ORCHIDACEOUS	ORDU
OPSONIZE	OPUSCULE	ORATORIO		ORDURE

ORDUROUS
ORE
OREAD
ORECCHION
ORECTIC
ORECTIVE
OREGANO
OREIDE
OREILET
OREILLER
OREILLETTE
OREJON
ORELLIN
OREMUS
ORENDA
ORENDITE
OREOPHASINE
OREOPITHECUS
OREOTRAGINE
ORES
OREWEED
OREWOOD
OREXIS
ORF
ORFE
ORFEVRERIE
ORFGILD
ORFRAY
ORGAMENT
ORGAMY
ORGAN
ORGANA
ORGANAL
ORGANBIRD
ORGANDIE
ORGANDIES
ORGANDY
ORGANELLA
ORGANELLAE
ORGANELLE
ORGANER
ORGANETTE
ORGANIC
ORGANICAL
ORGANICALLY
ORGANICISM
ORGANICISMAL
ORGANICIST
ORGANICISTIC
ORGANICITY
ORGANIFIC
ORGANIFIER
ORGANIFY
ORGANING
ORGANISATION
ORGANISE
ORGANISM
ORGANISMAL
ORGANISMIC
ORGANISMS
ORGANIST
ORGANISTIC
ORGANISTRUM
ORGANITY
ORGANIZABLE
ORGANIZATION
ORGANIZATIONAL
ORGANIZATORY
ORGANIZE
ORGANIZED
ORGANIZER
ORGANIZING
ORGANOGEL
ORGANOGEN
ORGANOGENIC
ORGANOGENIST
ORGANOGENY

ORGANOGRAPHY
ORGANOID
ORGANOLEPTIC
ORGANOLOGIC
ORGANOLOGIST
ORGANOLOGY
ORGANON
ORGANONOMIC
ORGANONOMY
ORGANONYMAL
ORGANONYMIC
ORGANONYMY
ORGANONYN
ORGANOPATHY
ORGANOPHONE
ORGANOPHONIC
ORGANOPHYLY
ORGANOSCOPY
ORGANOSOL
ORGANOTROPY
ORGANRY
ORGANULE
ORGANUM
ORGANUMS
ORGANY
ORGANZA
ORGANZINE
ORGANZINED
ORGANZINING
ORGASM
ORGASMIC
ORGASTIC
ORGEAT
ORGIA
ORGIAC
ORGIACS
ORGIASM
ORGIAST
ORGIASTIC
ORGIASTICAL
ORGIC
ORGIES
ORGONE
ORGUE
ORGUEIL
ORGUIL
ORGUINETTE
ORGUL
ORGULOUS
ORGULOUSLY
ORGY
ORGYIA
ORHAMWOOD
ORIBATID
ORIBI
ORIBIS
ORICHALC
ORICHALCEOUS
ORICHALCH
ORICHALCUM
ORIEL
ORIENCY
ORIENT
ORIENTAL
ORIENTALISM
ORIENTALIST
ORIENTALITY
ORIENTALIZE
ORIENTALIZED
ORIENTALIZING
ORIENTALLY
ORIENTATE
ORIENTATED
ORIENTATING
ORIENTATION
ORIENTATIVE

ORIENTATOR
ORIENTED
ORIENTING
ORIENTITE
ORIENTIZE
ORIENTNESS
ORIFACIAL
ORIFICE
ORIFICIAL
ORIFLAMB
ORIFLAMME
ORIFORM
ORIGAMI
ORIGAN
ORIGANIZED
ORIGIN
ORIGINABLE
ORIGINAL
ORIGINALIST
ORIGINALITIES
ORIGINALITY
ORIGINALLY
ORIGINANT
ORIGINARILY
ORIGINARY
ORIGINATE
ORIGINATED
ORIGINATING
ORIGINATION
ORIGINATIVE
ORIGINATIVELY
ORIGINATOR
ORIGINATRESS
ORIGINES
ORIGINIST
ORIGNAL
ORIHON
ORILLON
ORINASAL
ORINASALITY
ORIOLE
ORISHA
ORISMOLOGIC
ORISMOLOGY
ORISON
ORISTIC
ORKEY
ORKYN
ORLAGE
ORLE
ORLEAN
ORLET
ORLO
ORLOP
ORMER
ORMOLU
ORMUZINE
ORN
ORNA
ORNAMENT
ORNAMENTAL
ORNAMENTALLY
ORNAMENTARY
ORNAMENTATION
ORNAMENTED
ORNAMENTER
ORNAMENTING
ORNAMENTIST
ORNAMENTS
ORNARY
ORNATE
ORNATELY
ORNATENESS
ORNATION
ORNATURE
ORNE
ORNERINESS

ORNERY
ORNES
ORNIFY
ORNIS
ORNISCOPIC
ORNISCOPIST
ORNISCOPY
ORNITHIC
ORNITHICHNITE
ORNITHINE
ORNITHOGAL
ORNITHOID
ORNITHOLITE
ORNITHOLITIC
ORNITHOLOGIC
ORNITHOLOGIST
ORNITHOLOGY
ORNITHOMANCY
ORNITHOMANIA
ORNITHON
ORNITHOPHILE
ORNITHOPHILY
ORNITHOPOD
ORNITHOPTER
ORNITHOSCOPY
ORNITHOSIS
ORNITHOTOMY
ORNITHURIC
ORNITHUROUS
ORNOITE
ORO
OROANAL
OROBANCHEOUS
OROCRATIC
OROGEN
OROGENESIS
OROGENESY
OROGENETIC
OROGENIC
OROGENY
OROGRAPH
OROGRAPHIC
OROGRAPHICAL
OROGRAPHY
OROIDE
OROLOGICAL
OROLOGIST
OROLOGY
OROMETER
OROMETRIC
OROMETRY
ORONOCO
ORONOKO
ORONOOKO
OROPHARYNGES
OROPHARYNX
OROPHARYNXES
OROTUND
OROTUNDITY
ORP
ORPED
ORPHAN
ORPHANAGE
ORPHANED
ORPHANHOOD
ORPHANING
ORPHANRY
ORPHARION
ORPHEON
ORPHEONIST
ORPHEUM
ORPHIC
ORPHICAL
ORPHICALLY
ORPHREY
ORPHREYED
ORPHREYS

ORPIMENT
ORPIN
ORPINE
ORPIT
ORRA
ORRERIES
ORRERY
ORRHOID
ORRHOLOGY
ORRHOTHERAPY
ORRICE
ORRIS
ORRISROOT
ORROW
ORSEDE
ORSEDUE
ORSEILLE
ORSEILLINE
ORSEL
ORSELLER
ORSELLINATE
ORSELLINIC
ORT
ORTALID
ORTALIDIAN
ORTERDE
ORTHAL
ORTHIAN
ORTHICON
ORTHID
ORTHITE
ORTHITIC
ORTHO
ORTHOBIOSIS
ORTHOBORATE
ORTHOCARPOUS
ORTHOCENTER
ORTHOCENTRE
ORTHOCENTRIC
ORTHOCLASE
ORTHOCLASITE
ORTHOCLASTIC
ORTHOCYMENE
ORTHODIAGRAM
ORTHODONTIA
ORTHODONTIC
ORTHODONTICS
ORTHODONTIST
ORTHODOX
ORTHODOXAL
ORTHODOXALLY
ORTHODOXIAN
ORTHODOXICAL
ORTHODOXIES
ORTHODOXISM
ORTHODOXIST
ORTHODOXLY
ORTHODOXNESS
ORTHODOXY
ORTHODROMIC
ORTHODROMICS
ORTHODROMY
ORTHOEPIC
ORTHOEPICAL
ORTHOEPIST
ORTHOEPISTIC
ORTHOEPY
ORTHOGENESIS
ORTHOGENETIC
ORTHOGENIC
ORTHOGNATHIC
ORTHOGNATHUS
ORTHOGNATHY
ORTHOGONAL
ORTHOGONALLY
ORTHOGONIAL
ORTHOGRADE

ORTHOGRANITE
ORTHOGRAPH
ORTHOGRAPHER
ORTHOGRAPHIC
ORTHOGRAPHIES
ORTHOGRAPHY
ORTHOLOGER
ORTHOLOGIAN
ORTHOLOGICAL
ORTHOLOGY
ORTHOMETOPIC
ORTHOMETRIC
ORTHOMETRY
ORTHOPAEDIA
ORTHOPAEDIC
ORTHOPAEDICS
ORTHOPAEDIST
ORTHOPAEDY
ORTHOPATH
ORTHOPATHIC
ORTHOPATHY
ORTHOPEDIA
ORTHOPEDIC
ORTHOPEDICS
ORTHOPEDIST
ORTHOPEDY
ORTHOPHONIC
ORTHOPHONY
ORTHOPHORIA
ORTHOPHORIC
ORTHOPHYRE
ORTHOPHYRIC
ORTHOPLASTIC
ORTHOPLASY
ORTHOPNEA
ORTHOPNEIC
ORTHOPNOEA
ORTHOPNOEIC
ORTHOPRAXY
ORTHOPRISM
ORTHOPTER
ORTHOPTERAL
ORTHOPTERAN
ORTHOPTERIST
ORTHOPTEROID
ORTHOPTERON
ORTHOPTEROUS
ORTHOPTIC
ORTHOPTICS
ORTHORHOMBIC
ORTHORRHAPHY
ORTHOSCOPE
ORTHOSCOPIC
ORTHOSE
ORTHOSILICIC
ORTHOSIS
ORTHOSITE
ORTHOSOMATIC
ORTHOSTATIC
ORTHOSTICHIES
ORTHOSTICHY
ORTHOSTYLE
ORTHOTACTIC
ORTHOTECTIC
ORTHOTIC
ORTHOTOMIC
ORTHOTONE
ORTHOTONESIS
ORTHOTONIC
ORTHOTONUS
ORTHOTROPAL
ORTHOTROPIC
ORTHOTROPISM
ORTHOTROPOUS
ORTHOTROPY
ORTHOTYPE
ORTHOTYPOUS

ORTHRON
ORTHROS
ORTIGA
ORTIVE
ORTOLAN
ORTS
ORTSTALER
ORTSTEIN
ORTYGAN
ORTYGINE
ORVET
ORVIETAN
ORVIETITE
ORY
ORYCTICS
ORYCTOGNOSY
ORYCTOLOGIC
ORYCTOLOGIST
ORYCTOLOGY
ORYSSID
ORYX
ORYXES
ORYZANIN
ORYZANINE
ORYZENIN
ORYZIVOROUS
OS
OSAMINE
OSAR
OSAZONE
OSCELLA
OSCHEITIS
OSCHEOCELE
OSCHEOLITH
OSCHEOMA
OSCHEONCUS
OSCHEOPLASTY
OSCILLANCE
OSCILLANCY
OSCILLANT
OSCILLATE
OSCILLATED
OSCILLATING
OSCILLATION
OSCILLATIVE
OSCILLATOR
OSCILLATORY
OSCILLOGRAM
OSCILLOGRAPH
OSCILLOMETER
OSCILLOMETRY
OSCILLOSCOPE
OSCIN
OSCINE
OSCINIAN
OSCININE
OSCITANCE
OSCITANCIES
OSCITANCY
OSCITANT
OSCITANTLY
OSCITATE
OSCITATION
OSCNODE
OSCULA
OSCULABLE
OSCULANT
OSCULAR
OSCULARITY
OSCULATE
OSCULATED
OSCULATING
OSCULATION
OSCULATORIES
OSCULATORY
OSCULATRIX
OSCULATRIXES

OSCULE
OSCULIFEROUS
OSCULUM
OSCURANTIST
OSE
OSELA
OSELE
OSELLA
OSELLE
OSHAC
OSID
OSIDE
OSIER
OSIERED
OSIERIES
OSIERS
OSIERY
OSITE
OSKEN
OSMATE
OSMATIC
OSMATISM
OSMAZOMATIC
OSMAZOMATOUS
OSMAZOME
OSMESIS
OSMETERIA
OSMETERIUM
OSMIC
OSMICS
OSMIDROSIS
OSMIN
OSMIOUS
OSMIRIDIUM
OSMIUM
OSMOGENE
OSMOGRAPH
OSMOLAGNIA
OSMOLOGY
OSMOMETER
OSMOMETRIC
OSMOMETRY
OSMOND
OSMONDITE
OSMOSCOPE
OSMOSE
OSMOSED
OSMOSING
OSMOSIS
OSMOTACTIC
OSMOTAXIS
OSMOTHERAPY
OSMOTIC
OSMOTICALLY
OSMOUS
OSMUND
OSMUNDACEOUS
OSMUNDINE
OSNABURG
OSOBERRIES
OSOBERRY
OSONE
OSOPHIES
OSOPHY
OSPHRADIA
OSPHRADIAL
OSPHRADIUM
OSPHRESIS
OSPHRETIC
OSPHYALGIA
OSPHYALGIC
OSPHYITIS
OSPHYOCELE
OSPREY
OSPREYS
OSS
OSSA

OSSAL
OSSARIUM
OSSATURE
OSSE
OSSEIN
OSSELET
OSSEMENTS
OSSEOMUCOID
OSSEOUS
OSSEOUSLY
OSSIA
OSSICLE
OSSICULA
OSSICULAR
OSSICULATE
OSSICULATED
OSSICULE
OSSICULOTOMY
OSSICULUM
OSSIFEROUS
OSSIFIC
OSSIFICATION
OSSIFIED
OSSIFIER
OSSIFLUENCE
OSSIFLUENT
OSSIFORM
OSSIFRAGE
OSSIFRANGENT
OSSIFY
OSSIFYING
OSSIVOROUS
OSSUARIES
OSSUARIUM
OSSUARY
OSSYPITE
OSTALGIA
OSTARTHRITIS
OSTE
OSTEAL
OSTEALGIA
OSTECTOMY
OSTEECTOMY
OSTEECTOPIA
OSTEECTOPY
OSTEIN
OSTEITIC
OSTEITIS
OSTEMIA
OSTEMPYESIS
OSTEND
OSTENSIBLE
OSTENSIBLY
OSTENSION
OSTENSIVE
OSTENSIVELY
OSTENSORIA
OSTENSORIES
OSTENSORIUM
OSTENSORY
OSTENT
OSTENTATE
OSTENTATION
OSTENTATIOUS
OSTENTATIOUSLY
OSTEOBLAST
OSTEOBLASTIC
OSTEOCELE
OSTEOCLASIA
OSTEOCLASIS
OSTEOCLAST
OSTEOCLASTIC
OSTEOCLASTY
OSTEOCOLLA
OSTEOCOMMA
OSTEOCRANIUM
OSTEOCYSTOMA

OSTEODENTINE
OSTEODERM
OSTEODERMAL
OSTEODERMIA
OSTEODERMIS
OSTEODERMOUS
OSTEODYNIA
OSTEOFIBROUS
OSTEOGEN
OSTEOGENESIS
OSTEOGENETIC
OSTEOGENIC
OSTEOGENIST
OSTEOGENOUS
OSTEOGENY
OSTEOGLOSSID
OSTEOGRAPHER
OSTEOGRAPHY
OSTEOID
OSTEOLITE
OSTEOLOGIC
OSTEOLOGICAL
OSTEOLOGIST
OSTEOLOGY
OSTEOLYSIS
OSTEOLYTIC
OSTEOMA
OSTEOMALACIA
OSTEOMALACIC
OSTEOMANCY
OSTEOMANTY
OSTEOMAS
OSTEOMATA
OSTEOMATOID
OSTEOME
OSTEOMERE
OSTEOMETRIC
OSTEOMETRY
OSTEONCUS
OSTEOPATH
OSTEOPATHIC
OSTEOPATHIST
OSTEOPATHY
OSTEOPHAGIA
OSTEOPHONE
OSTEOPHONY
OSTEOPHORE
OSTEOPHYMA
OSTEOPHYTE
OSTEOPHYTIC
OSTEOPLAQUE
OSTEOPLAST
OSTEOPLASTIC
OSTEOPLASTIES
OSTEOPLASTY
OSTEOPOROSIS
OSTEOPOROTIC
OSTEORRHAPHY
OSTEOSARCOMA
OSTEOSCOPE
OSTEOSTIXIS
OSTEOSTOMOUS
OSTEOTOME
OSTEOTOMIES
OSTEOTOMIST
OSTEOTOMY
OSTEOTRIBE
OSTEOTRITE
OSTEOTROPHY
OSTERIA
OSTIA
OSTIAL
OSTIARIES
OSTIARY
OSTIATE
OSTINATO
OSTIOLAR

OSTIOLATE
OSTIOLE
OSTITIS
OSTIUM
OSTLER
OSTLERESS
OSTMARK
OSTOMATID
OSTOSIS
OSTRACA
OSTRACEAN
OSTRACEOUS
OSTRACINE
OSTRACIOID
OSTRACISE
OSTRACISM
OSTRACITE
OSTRACIZATION
OSTRACIZE
OSTRACIZED
OSTRACIZER
OSTRACIZING
OSTRACOD
OSTRACODE
OSTRACODERM
OSTRACODOUS
OSTRACON
OSTRACOPHORE
OSTRACUM
OSTRAITE
OSTREACEOUS
OSTREGER
OSTREIFORM
OSTREOID
OSTREOPHAGE
OSTRICH
OSTRICHES
OSTRICHLIKE
OTACOUSTIC
OTACOUSTICON
OTACUST
OTALGIA
OTALGIC
OTALGY
OTARIAN
OTARIES
OTARIINE
OTARINE
OTARIOID
OTARY
OTATE
OTECTOMY
OTELCOSIS
OTHAEMATOMA
OTHELCOSIS
OTHEMATOMA
OTHEMATOMATA
OTHEMORRHEA
OTHEOSCOPE
OTHER
OTHEREST
OTHERGATES
OTHERGUESS
OTHERGUISE
OTHERHOW
OTHERISM
OTHERIST
OTHERNESS
OTHERS
OTHERSOME
OTHERTIME
OTHERTIMES
OTHERWHENCE
OTHERWHERE
OTHERWHERES
OTHERWHILE
OTHERWHILES

OTHERWHITHER
OTHERWISE
OTHERWORLDLY
OTHMANY
OTHYGROMA
OTIANT
OTIATRIC
OTIATRICS
OTIATRY
OTIC
OTICODINIA
OTIDIA
OTIDIFORM
OTIDINE
OTIDIUM
OTIORHYNCHID
OTIOSE
OTIOSELY
OTIOSENESS
OTIOSITY
OTITIC
OTITIS
OTIUM
OTKON
OTOANTRITIS
OTOCARIASIS
OTOCLEISIS
OTOCONIA
OTOCONIAL
OTOCONITE
OTOCONIUM
OTOCRANIAL
OTOCRANIC
OTOCRANIUM
OTOCYST
OTOCYSTIC
OTODYNIA
OTODYNIC
OTOGENIC
OTOGENOUS
OTOGRAPHICAL
OTOGRAPHY
OTOLITE
OTOLITH
OTOLITIC
OTOLOGICAL
OTOLOGIST
OTOLOGY
OTOMASSAGE
OTOMYCES
OTOMYCOSIS
OTONEURALGIA
OTOPATHIC
OTOPATHY
OTOPHONE
OTOPIESIS
OTOPLASTIC
OTOPLASTY
OTOPOLYPUS
OTOPYORRHEA
OTOPYOSIS
OTORRHAGIA
OTORRHEA
OTORRHOEA
OTOSCLEROSIS
OTOSCOPE
OTOSCOPIC
OTOSCOPY
OTOSIS
OTOSTEAL
OTOSTEON
OTOTOI
OTOTOMY
OTTAJANITE
OTTAR
OTTAVA
OTTAVARIMA

OTTAVE
OTTAVINO
OTTER
OTTERER
OTTERHOUND
OTTETTO
OTTINGER
OTTO
OTTOMAN
OTTRELITE
OTTROYE
OU
OUABAIN
OUABAIO
OUABE
OUACHITITE
OUAKARI
OUANANICHE
OUANGA
OUBLIANCE
OUBLIET
OUBLIETTE
OUCH
OUD
OUDENARDE
OUED
OUENITE
OUF
OUGH
OUGHT
OUGHTLINGS
OUGHTLINS
OUGLE
OUIJA
OUISTITI
OUK
OUKIA
OULAP
OULK
OUNCE
OUNDING
OUNDY
OUPH
OUPHE
OUR
OURANG
OURARI
OURE
OUREBI
OURICURY
OURIE
OUROUB
OURS
OURSEL
OURSELF
OURSELS
OURSELVES
OUSEL
OUSIA
OUST
OUSTED
OUSTEE
OUSTER
OUSTING
OUT
OUTACT
OUTADMIRAL
OUTAGE
OUTAMBUSH
OUTARDE
OUTARGUE
OUTAS
OUTASK
OUTBABBLE
OUTBACK
OUTBACKER
OUTBADE

OUTBAKE
OUTBALANCE
OUTBANTER
OUTBARGAIN
OUTBARK
OUTBAWL
OUTBEAM
OUTBEAR
OUTBEARING
OUTBEG
OUTBEGGAR
OUTBELCH
OUTBELLOW
OUTBETTER
OUTBID
OUTBIDDEN
OUTBIDDER
OUTBIDDING
OUTBIRTH
OUTBLACKEN
OUTBLAZE
OUTBLEAT
OUTBLESS
OUTBLOOM
OUTBLOSSOM
OUTBLOWN
OUTBLUFF
OUTBLUNDER
OUTBLUSH
OUTBLUSTER
OUTBOARD
OUTBOAST
OUTBOND
OUTBOOK
OUTBORE
OUTBORN
OUTBORNE
OUTBOUND
OUTBOWL
OUTBOX
OUTBRAG
OUTBRAID
OUTBRAVE
OUTBRAVED
OUTBRAVING
OUTBRAZEN
OUTBREAK
OUTBREAKING
OUTBREATHE
OUTBREATHER
OUTBRED
OUTBREED
OUTBREEDING
OUTBRIBE
OUTBUILD
OUTBUILDING
OUTBULK
OUTBULLY
OUTBURN
OUTBURST
OUTBUY
OUTBUZZ
OUTBY
OUTBYE
OUTCAME
OUTCANT
OUTCAPER
OUTCAROL
OUTCARRY
OUTCASE
OUTCAST
OUTCASTE
OUTCASTED
OUTCASTING
OUTCASTS
OUTCAVIL
OUTCEPT

OUTCHAMBER
OUTCHARM
OUTCHATTER
OUTCHEAT
OUTCHIDE
OUTCLASS
OUTCLIMB
OUTCOME
OUTCOMER
OUTCOMING
OUTCOMPASS
OUTCOMPLETE
OUTCOUNTRY
OUTCRAWL
OUTCRICKET
OUTCRIED
OUTCRIER
OUTCRIES
OUTCROP
OUTCROPPED
OUTCROPPER
OUTCROPPING
OUTCROSS
OUTCROSSING
OUTCROW
OUTCRY
OUTCRYING
OUTCURE
OUTCURSE
OUTCURVE
OUTCURVED
OUTCURVING
OUTDANCE
OUTDARE
OUTDATE
OUTDATED
OUTDATING
OUTDAZZLE
OUTDEVIL
OUTDID
OUTDISPATCH
OUTDISTANCE
OUTDISTANCED
OUTDISTANCING
OUTDO
OUTDODGE
OUTDOER
OUTDOING
OUTDONE
OUTDOOR
OUTDOORS
OUTDOORSMAN
OUTDOORSMEN
OUTDRAFT
OUTDRAGON
OUTDRAUGHT
OUTDREAM
OUTDRESS
OUTDRINK
OUTDRIVE
OUTDURE
OUTDWELLER
OUTE
OUTEAT
OUTECHO
OUTED
OUTEN
OUTER
OUTERLY
OUTERMOST
OUTERWEAR
OUTFABLE
OUTFACE
OUTFACED
OUTFACING
OUTFALL
OUTFAME

OUTFAST
OUTFAWN
OUTFEAST
OUTFEAT
OUTFERRET
OUTFICTION
OUTFIELD
OUTFIELDER
OUTFIELDSMAN
OUTFIELDSMEN
OUTFIGHT
OUTFIGHTER
OUTFIGHTING
OUTFISH
OUTFIT
OUTFITTED
OUTFITTER
OUTFITTING
OUTFLANK
OUTFLANKER
OUTFLANKING
OUTFLATTER
OUTFLING
OUTFLOAT
OUTFLOW
OUTFLUNKY
OUTFLUSH
OUTFLUX
OUTFLY
OUTFOOL
OUTFOOT
OUTFORM
OUTFORT
OUTFORTH
OUTFOX
OUTFRONT
OUTFROWN
OUTGABBLE
OUTGAIN
OUTGALLOP
OUTGAMBLE
OUTGAME
OUTGANG
OUTGARTH
OUTGATE
OUTGAUGE
OUTGAZE
OUTGENERAL
OUTGENERALED
OUTGENERALING
OUTGENERALLED
OUTGENERALLING
OUTGIVE
OUTGIVING
OUTGLAD
OUTGLARE
OUTGLITTER
OUTGLOW
OUTGNAW
OUTGO
OUTGOER
OUTGOES
OUTGOING
OUTGONE
OUTGREEN
OUTGREW
OUTGRIN
OUTGROWING
OUTGROWN
OUTGROWTH
OUTGUARD
OUTGUESS
OUTGUN
OUTGUSH
OUTHAMMER
OUTHASTEN
OUTHAUL

OUTHAULER
OUTHEAR
OUTHECTOR
OUTHEEL
OUTHER
OUTHIT
OUTHOLD
OUTHORN
OUTHORROR
OUTHOUSE
OUTHOUSING
OUTHOWL
OUTHUE
OUTHUMOR
OUTHUNT
OUTHUT
OUTHYMN
OUTIMAGE
OUTING
OUTINVENT
OUTISH
OUTJAZZ
OUTJINX
OUTJOCKEY
OUTJOURNEY
OUTJUGGLE
OUTJUMP
OUTJUT
OUTKEEPER
OUTKICK
OUTKILL
OUTKING
OUTKISS
OUTKNAVE
OUTKNEE
OUTLABOR
OUTLAND
OUTLANDER
OUTLANDISH
OUTLANDISHLY
OUTLASH
OUTLAST
OUTLAUGH
OUTLAW
OUTLAWED
OUTLAWING
OUTLAWRIES
OUTLAWRY
OUTLAY
OUTLEAP
OUTLEARN
OUTLEGEND
OUTLER
OUTLET
OUTLIE
OUTLIER
OUTLIGHTEN
OUTLIMN
OUTLINE
OUTLINEAR
OUTLINED
OUTLINER
OUTLINGER
OUTLINING
OUTLIVE
OUTLIVED
OUTLIVER
OUTLIVING
OUTLODGING
OUTLOOK
OUTLOOKER
OUTLOPE
OUTLORD
OUTLOVE
OUTLUNG
OUTLUSTER
OUTLY

OUTLYING
OUTMAGIC
OUTMALAPROP
OUTMAN
OUTMANEUVER
OUTMANNED
OUTMANNING
OUTMANTLE
OUTMARCH
OUTMARRIAGE
OUTMARRY
OUTMASTER
OUTMATCH
OUTMATE
OUTMEASURE
OUTMIRACLE
OUTMODE
OUTMODED
OUTMOST
OUTMOUNT
OUTMOUTH
OUTMOVE
OUTNAME
OUTNESS
OUTNIGHT
OUTNOISE
OUTNUMBER
OUTPAGE
OUTPAINT
OUTPARAGON
OUTPARAMOUR
OUTPARISH
OUTPART
OUTPARTS
OUTPASS
OUTPASSION
OUTPATIENT
OUTPAYMENT
OUTPEER
OUTPENSION
OUTPENSIONER
OUTPERFORM
OUTPICK
OUTPICKET
OUTPIPE
OUTPITCH
OUTPITY
OUTPLACE
OUTPLAN
OUTPLAY
OUTPLAYED
OUTPLEASE
OUTPLOD
OUTPLOT
OUTPOCKETING
OUTPOINT
OUTPOISE
OUTPOISON
OUTPOLL
OUTPOMP
OUTPOPULATE
OUTPORT
OUTPORTER
OUTPORTION
OUTPOST
OUTPOUR
OUTPOURED
OUTPOURER
OUTPOURING
OUTPRACTICE
OUTPRAISE
OUTPRAY
OUTPREACH
OUTPREEN
OUTPRICE
OUTPRODIGY
OUTPRODUCE

OUTPROMISE
OUTPRY
OUTPULL
OUTPURL
OUTPURSE
OUTPUSH
OUTPUT
OUTPUTTER
OUTQUEEN
OUTQUESTION
OUTQUIBBLE
OUTQUOTE
OUTRACE
OUTRAGE
OUTRAGED
OUTRAGELY
OUTRAGEOUS
OUTRAGEOUSLY
OUTRAGER
OUTRAGING
OUTRAIL
OUTRAKE
OUTRAN
OUTRANCE
OUTRANGE
OUTRANK
OUTRANT
OUTRAP
OUTRATE
OUTRAVE
OUTRAY
OUTRAZE
OUTRE
OUTREACH
OUTREASON
OUTRECKON
OUTREDDEN
OUTREIGN
OUTRELIEF
OUTREMER
OUTRHYME
OUTRIDDEN
OUTRIDE
OUTRIDER
OUTRIDING
OUTRIG
OUTRIGGED
OUTRIGGER
OUTRIGGERED
OUTRIGGING
OUTRIGHT
OUTRIGHTLY
OUTRIGHTNESS
OUTRIVAL
OUTRIVE
OUTROAD
OUTROAR
OUTRODE
OUTROGUE
OUTROLL
OUTROMANCE
OUTROOP
OUTROOPER
OUTROOT
OUTROVE
OUTROW
OUTROYAL
OUTRUN
OUTRUNNER
OUTRUNNING
OUTRUSH
OUTS
OUTSAIL
OUTSAINT
OUTSAT
OUTSATISFY
OUTSAVOR

OUTSCAPE
OUTSCENT
OUTSCOLD
OUTSCORE
OUTSCORN
OUTSCOUR
OUTSCOURING
OUTSCOUT
OUTSCREAM
OUTSEA
OUTSEE
OUTSELL
OUTSELLING
OUTSEND
OUTSENTINEL
OUTSENTRY
OUTSERT
OUTSET
OUTSETTING
OUTSHADOW
OUTSHAKE
OUTSHAME
OUTSHARP
OUTSHARPEN
OUTSHEATHE
OUTSHIFTS
OUTSHINE
OUTSHINER
OUTSHINING
OUTSHONE
OUTSHOOT
OUTSHOOTING
OUTSHOT
OUTSHOUT
OUTSHOWER
OUTSHRIEK
OUTSHUT
OUTSIDE
OUTSIDED
OUTSIDER
OUTSIDES
OUTSIGHT
OUTSIN
OUTSING
OUTSIT
OUTSITTING
OUTSIZE
OUTSIZED
OUTSKILL
OUTSKIP
OUTSKIRMISH
OUTSKIRT
OUTSKIRTER
OUTSKIRTS
OUTSLANDER
OUTSLANG
OUTSLEEP
OUTSLING
OUTSLIP
OUTSMART
OUTSMILE
OUTSNORE
OUTSOAR
OUTSOLD
OUTSOLE
OUTSOLER
OUTSONNET
OUTSOUND
OUTSPAN
OUTSPANNED
OUTSPANNING
OUTSPARKLE
OUTSPEAK
OUTSPEAKER
OUTSPEAKING
OUTSPEECH
OUTSPEED

OUTSPEND
OUTSPENT
OUTSPIT
OUTSPLENDOR
OUTSPOKE
OUTSPOKEN
OUTSPOKENLY
OUTSPORT
OUTSPOUT
OUTSPREAD
OUTSPREADING
OUTSPRINT
OUTSTAGGER
OUTSTAID
OUTSTAND
OUTSTANDER
OUTSTANDING
OUTSTANDINGLY
OUTSTARE
OUTSTART
OUTSTARTER
OUTSTATE
OUTSTATION
OUTSTATURE
OUTSTAY
OUTSTAYED
OUTSTAYING
OUTSTEP
OUTSTING
OUTSTINK
OUTSTOOD
OUTSTORM
OUTSTRETCH
OUTSTRETCHED
OUTSTRETCHER
OUTSTRETCHING
OUTSTRIDE
OUTSTRIP
OUTSTRIPPED
OUTSTRIPPING
OUTSTRIVE
OUTSTROKE
OUTSTRUT
OUTSTUDY
OUTSTUNT
OUTSUBTLE
OUTSUCKEN
OUTSUFFER
OUTSUITOR
OUTSULK
OUTSUM
OUTSWAGGER
OUTSWEAR
OUTSWEEPING
OUTSWEETEN
OUTSWELL
OUTSWIFT
OUTSWIM
OUTSWINDLE
OUTTAKE
OUTTAKEN
OUTTALENT
OUTTALK
OUTTASK
OUTTASTE
OUTTEASE
OUTTELL
OUTTELLING
OUTTHIEVE
OUTTHINK
OUTTHREATEN
OUTTHROB
OUTTHROUGH
OUTTHROW
OUTTHRUST
OUTTHWACK
OUTTOIL

OUTTOLD
OUTTONGUE
OUTTOP
OUTTOPPED
OUTTOPPING
OUTTOWER
OUTTRADE
OUTTRAIL
OUTTRAVEL
OUTTRICK
OUTTROT
OUTTRUMP
OUTTURN
OUTTURNED
OUTTWINE
OUTTYRANNIZE
OUTUSURE
OUTVALUE
OUTVAUNT
OUTVELVET
OUTVENOM
OUTVICTOR
OUTVIE
OUTVILLAIN
OUTVOICE
OUTVOTE
OUTVOTER
OUTWAIT
OUTWAKE
OUTWALE
OUTWALK
OUTWALL
OUTWALLOP
OUTWAR
OUTWARBLE
OUTWARD
OUTWARDLY
OUTWARDS
OUTWASH
OUTWASTE
OUTWATCH
OUTWAY
OUTWEALTH
OUTWEAPON
OUTWEAR
OUTWEARING
OUTWEARY
OUTWEIGH
OUTWEIGHT
OUTWENT
OUTWHIRL
OUTWICK
OUTWILE
OUTWILL
OUTWIN
OUTWIND
OUTWING
OUTWISH
OUTWIT
OUTWITH
OUTWITTAL
OUTWITTED
OUTWITTER
OUTWITTING
OUTWOE
OUTWOMAN
OUTWORD
OUTWORE
OUTWORK
OUTWORKED
OUTWORKING
OUTWORLD
OUTWORN
OUTWORTH
OUTWRANGLE
OUTWREST
OUTWRESTLE

OUTWRIGGLE
OUTWRITE
OUTWRITING
OUTWRITTEN
OUTWROTE
OUTWROUGHT
OUTYELP
OUTYIELD
OUTZANY
OUVERT
OUVERTE
OUVRAGE
OUVRIER
OUVRIERE
OUYEZD
OUZEL
OUZO
OVA
OVAL
OVALBUMIN
OVALIFORM
OVALIZATION
OVALIZE
OVALNESS
OVALOID
OVALWISE
OVANT
OVARIA
OVARIAL
OVARIAN
OVARIECTOMY
OVARIES
OVARIN
OVARIOCELE
OVARIOCYESIS
OVARIOLE
OVARIOSTOMY
OVARIOTOMIES
OVARIOTOMIST
OVARIOTOMIZE
OVARIOTOMY
OVARIOUS
OVARITIS
OVARIUM
OVARY
OVATE
OVATECONICAL
OVATED
OVATELY
OVATION
OVATIONAL
OVATOCONICAL
OVATOCORDATE
OVATODELTOID
OVATOGLOBOSE
OVATOOBLONG
OVATOSERRATE
OVEN
OVENBIRD
OVENDRY
OVENED
OVENING
OVENLY
OVENMAN
OVENMEN
OVENPEEL
OVENS
OVENSMAN
OVENSTONE
OVENWARE
OVENWISE
OVER
OVERABUNDANCE
OVERABUNDANT
OVERACT
OVERAGE
OVERALL

OVERALLED
OVERALLS
OVERARCH
OVERARM
OVERATE
OVERAWE
OVERAWED
OVERAWING
OVERBADE
OVERBALANCE
OVERBANK
OVERBARISH
OVERBEAR
OVERBEARANCE
OVERBEARER
OVERBEARING
OVERBEARINGLY
OVERBEND
OVERBERG
OVERBID
OVERBIDDEN
OVERBIDDING
OVERBIDE
OVERBIT
OVERBITE
OVERBLEW
OVERBLOUSE
OVERBLOW
OVERBLOWING
OVERBLOWN
OVERBOARD
OVERBODY
OVERBOIL
OVERBOOK
OVERBORE
OVERBORNE
OVERBOUGHT
OVERBOWED
OVERBOWL
OVERBREATHE
OVERBRIBE
OVERBRIDGE
OVERBRIM
OVERBRIMMED
OVERBRIMMING
OVERBROOD
OVERBROW
OVERBUILD
OVERBUILDING
OVERBUILT
OVERBURDEN
OVERBURN
OVERBURST
OVERBUSY
OVERBUY
OVERBUYING
OVERBY
OVERCALL
OVERCAME
OVERCARRY
OVERCAST
OVERCASTING
OVERCATCH
OVERCERTIFY
OVERCHARGE
OVERCHARGED
OVERCHARGER
OVERCHARGING
OVERCHECK
OVERCLOTHES
OVERCLOUD
OVERCOAT
OVERCOATED
OVERCOATING
OVERCOIL
OVERCOME
OVERCOMER

OVERCOMING
OVERCOMPOUND
OVERCONFIDENT
OVERCOOK
OVERCORRECT
OVERCOUNT
OVERCOVER
OVERCROP
OVERCROW
OVERCROWD
OVERCURRENT
OVERCUT
OVERDARE
OVERDATED
OVERDECK
OVERDECORATED
OVERDEN
OVERDEVELOP
OVERDEVELOPED
OVERDID
OVERDO
OVERDOER
OVERDOING
OVERDONE
OVERDOOR
OVERDOSAGE
OVERDOSE
OVERDRAFT
OVERDRAPE
OVERDRAPERY
OVERDRAUGHT
OVERDRAW
OVERDRAWER
OVERDRAWING
OVERDRAWN
OVERDRESS
OVERDREW
OVERDRIED
OVERDRIVE
OVERDRIVEN
OVERDRIVING
OVERDROVE
OVERDUE
OVERDYE
OVERDYED
OVERDYEING
OVEREAGER
OVEREAT
OVEREATEN
OVEREATING
OVERED
OVEREDUCATED
OVERELABORATE
OVERENTER
OVERENTRY
OVEREST
OVERESTIMATE
OVERESTIMATED
OVERESTIMATING
OVEREXERT
OVEREXPOSE
OVEREXPOSED
OVEREXPOSING
OVEREXPOSURE
OVEREYE
OVERFACE
OVERFALL
OVERFALLEN
OVERFALLING
OVERFASTIDIOUS
OVERFED
OVERFEED
OVERFELL
OVERFINE
OVERFISH
OVERFLEW
OVERFLIGHT

OVERFLOAT
OVERFLOOD
OVERFLOURISH
OVERFLOW
OVERFLOWED
OVERFLOWER
OVERFLOWING
OVERFLOWN
OVERFLUSH
OVERFLUTTER
OVERFLY
OVERFLYING
OVERFOLD
OVERFOOT
OVERFREIGHT
OVERFRET
OVERFRIEZE
OVERFULL
OVERGANG
OVERGARMENT
OVERGAZE
OVERGET
OVERGETTING
OVERGILD
OVERGIVE
OVERGLANCE
OVERGLAZE
OVERGLAZED
OVERGLAZING
OVERGLIDE
OVERGLOOM
OVERGO
OVERGOING
OVERGONE
OVERGOT
OVERGOTTEN
OVERGOVERN
OVERGRAIN
OVERGRAINER
OVERGRAZE
OVERGREW
OVERGROUND
OVERGROW
OVERGROWING
OVERGROWN
OVERGROWTH
OVERHAIL
OVERHAIR
OVERHALE
OVERHAND
OVERHANDED
OVERHANG
OVERHANGING
OVERHAUL
OVERHAULED
OVERHAULER
OVERHAULING
OVERHEAD
OVERHEAP
OVERHEAR
OVERHEARD
OVERHEARER
OVERHEARING
OVERHEAT
OVERHEAVE
OVERHIE
OVERHIP
OVERHIT
OVERHUNG
OVERINFORM
OVERING
OVERINSURE
OVERISSUE
OVERISSUED
OVERISSUING
OVERJOY
OVERJUDGE

OVERJUMP
OVERKEEP
OVERKILL
OVERKING
OVERKNEE
OVERKNOW
OVERLABOR
OVERLABORED
OVERLABORING
OVERLABOUR
OVERLABOURED
OVERLABOURING
OVERLADE
OVERLADED
OVERLADEN
OVERLADING
OVERLAID
OVERLAIN
OVERLAND
OVERLANDER
OVERLAP
OVERLAPPED
OVERLAPPING
OVERLASH
OVERLAUNCH
OVERLAVE
OVERLAY
OVERLAYER
OVERLAYING
OVERLEAD
OVERLEAF
OVERLEAP
OVERLEAPED
OVERLEAPING
OVERLEAPT
OVERLEATHER
OVERLEAVE
OVERLEAVEN
OVERLICK
OVERLIE
OVERLIER
OVERLIFT
OVERLINE
OVERLING
OVERLIP
OVERLISTEN
OVERLIVE
OVERLIVER
OVERLOAD
OVERLOADED
OVERLOCK
OVERLOCKER
OVERLONG
OVERLOOK
OVERLOOKED
OVERLOOKER
OVERLOOKING
OVERLORD
OVERLOUP
OVERLOVE
OVERLOVER
OVERLY
OVERLYING
OVERMAN
OVERMANTLE
OVERMARCH
OVERMARK
OVERMARKING
OVERMASK
OVERMAST
OVERMASTER
OVERMATCH
OVERMATURITY
OVERMEASURE
OVERMEN
OVERMICKLE
OVERMIND

OVERMODEST
OVERMORE
OVERMOST
OVERMOUNT
OVERMOUNTS
OVERMUCH
OVERMUSE
OVERNAME
OVERNET
OVERNICE
OVERNICELY
OVERNICETY
OVERNIGHT
OVERNOISE
OVERNUMBER
OVERPAID
OVERPAINT
OVERPART
OVERPARTED
OVERPARTY
OVERPASS
OVERPASSED
OVERPASSING
OVERPAY
OVERPAYING
OVERPAYMENT
OVERPEER
OVERPENDING
OVERPEOPLE
OVERPERSUADE
OVERPERSUADED
OVERPERSUADING
OVERPICK
OVERPICTURE
OVERPITCH
OVERPITCHED
OVERPLAY
OVERPLIED
OVERPLUS
OVERPLY
OVERPLYING
OVERPOLE
OVERPOPULATE
OVERPOPULATED
OVERPOPULATING
OVERPOST
OVERPOT
OVERPOUR
OVERPOWER
OVERPOWERED
OVERPOWERING
OVERPREACH
OVERPRECISE
OVERPRESS
OVERPRICE
OVERPRICED
OVERPRICING
OVERPRINT
OVERPRIZE
OVERPRIZED
OVERPRIZER
OVERPRIZING
OVERPRODUCE
OVERPRODUCED
OVERPRODUCING
OVERPROOF
OVERPROTECT
OVERPURCHASE
OVERPUT
OVERQUELL
OVERRACK
OVERRAKE
OVERRAKED
OVERRAKING
OVERRAN
OVERRATE
OVERRATED

OVERRATING
OVERRAUGHT
OVERREACH
OVERREACHED
OVERREACHER
OVERREACHING
OVERREAD
OVERREADER
OVERREADING
OVERREADY
OVERRECKON
OVERREFINED
OVERREGISTER
OVERRENT
OVERRID
OVERRIDDEN
OVERRIDE
OVERRIDER
OVERRIDING
OVERRIGHT
OVERRIM
OVERRIOT
OVERRIPE
OVERRIPENESS
OVERRISE
OVERRISEN
OVERRISING
OVERRODE
OVERROLL
OVERROOF
OVERROSE
OVERRUFF
OVERRULE
OVERRULED
OVERRULER
OVERRULING
OVERRUN
OVERRUNNER
OVERRUNNING
OVERS
OVERSAID
OVERSAIL
OVERSANDED
OVERSAW
OVERSAY
OVERSCENTED
OVERSCORE
OVERSCORED
OVERSCORING
OVERSCURF
OVERSCUTCHED
OVERSEA
OVERSEAM
OVERSEAMER
OVERSEARCH
OVERSEAS
OVERSEE
OVERSEEING
OVERSEEN
OVERSEER
OVERSELL
OVERSELLING
OVERSENSITIVE
OVERSENTIMENTAL
OVERSET
OVERSETTER
OVERSETTING
OVERSEW
OVERSEWED
OVERSEWING
OVERSEWN
OVERSEXED
OVERSHADE
OVERSHADED
OVERSHADING
OVERSHADOW
OVERSHADOWED

OVERSHADOWER
OVERSHADOWING
OVERSHAVE
OVERSHINE
OVERSHINING
OVERSHIRT
OVERSHOE
OVERSHOES
OVERSHONE
OVERSHOOT
OVERSHOOTING
OVERSHOT
OVERSIDE
OVERSIGHT
OVERSIGNED
OVERSILE
OVERSIZE
OVERSIZED
OVERSKIP
OVERSKIPPER
OVERSKIRT
OVERSLAUGH
OVERSLAUGHED
OVERSLAUGHING
OVERSLEEP
OVERSLEEPING
OVERSLEPT
OVERSLID
OVERSLIDDEN
OVERSLIDE
OVERSLIDING
OVERSLIP
OVERSLIPPED
OVERSLIPPING
OVERSLOP
OVERSMOKE
OVERSNOW
OVERSOFT
OVERSOLD
OVERSOUL
OVERSOUND
OVERSOW
OVERSOWED
OVERSOWING
OVERSOWN
OVERSPAN
OVERSPANNED
OVERSPANNING
OVERSPARRED
OVERSPEAK
OVERSPEAKING
OVERSPEND
OVERSPENDING
OVERSPENT
OVERSPILL
OVERSPIN
OVERSPOKE
OVERSPOKEN
OVERSPREAD
OVERSPREADING
OVERSPRING
OVERSPRUNG
OVERSPUN
OVERSTAID
OVERSTAND
OVERSTANDING
OVERSTATE
OVERSTATED
OVERSTATEMENT
OVERSTATING
OVERSTAY
OVERSTAYAL
OVERSTAYED
OVERSTAYING
OVERSTEP
OVERSTEPPED
OVERSTEPPING

OVERSTITCH	OVERTOWER	OVERWRITE	OVULARY	OXANILIDE
OVERSTOCK	OVERTRACE	OVERWRITING	OVULATE	OXAZIN
OVERSTOOD	OVERTRACK	OVERWRITTEN	OVULATED	OXAZINE
OVERSTOPING	OVERTRADE	OVERWROTE	OVULATING	OXAZOLE
OVERSTORY	OVERTRADED	OVERWROUGHT	OVULATION	OXBANE
OVERSTRAIN	OVERTRADER	OVERYEAR	OVULE	OXBERRIES
OVERSTRAINED	OVERTRADING	OVERZEALOUS	OVULIFEROUS	OXBERRY
OVERSTRAINING	OVERTRAIN	OVEST	OVULIGEROUS	OXBIRD
OVERSTRAITEN	OVERTRAINED	OVEY	OVULITE	OXBITER
OVERSTRETCH	OVERTRAINING	OVIBOS	OVULUM	OXBLOOD
OVERSTREW	OVERTRAVEL	OVIBOVINE	OVUM	OXBOW
OVERSTREWED	OVERTREAD	OVICAPSULAR	OW	OXBOY
OVERSTREWING	OVERTREADING	OVICAPSULE	OWE	OXBRAKE
OVERSTREWN	OVERTRICK	OVICELL	OWED	OXCART
OVERSTRICKEN	OVERTROD	OVICELLULAR	OWELTY	OXCHEEK
OVERSTRIDDEN	OVERTRODDEN	OVICIDAL	OWER	OXDIAZOLE
OVERSTRIDE	OVERTRUMP	OVICIDE	OWERANCE	OXEA
OVERSTRIDING	OVERTUMBLE	OVICULAR	OWHERE	OXEATE
OVERSTRIKE	OVERTURE	OVICULATED	OWING	OXEN
OVERSTRIKING	OVERTURED	OVICULUM	OWL	OXEOTE
OVERSTRING	OVERTURING	OVICYST	OWLER	OXER
OVERSTRINGING	OVERTURN	OVICYSTIC	OWLERIES	OXEYE
OVERSTRODE	OVERTURNED	OVIDUCAL	OWLERY	OXFLY
OVERSTRUCK	OVERTURNING	OVIDUCT	OWLET	OXFORD
OVERSTRUNG	OVERTYPE	OVIDUCTAL	OWLHEAD	OXGALL
OVERSTUDIED	OVERUSE	OVIFEROUS	OWLING	OXGANG
OVERSTUDY	OVERVAULT	OVIFICATION	OWLISH	OXGATE
OVERSTUFF	OVERVEIL	OVIFORM	OWLISHLY	OXGOAD
OVERSUM	OVERVIEW	OVIGENESIS	OWLISHNESS	OXHARROW
OVERSUPPLIED	OVERVOLTAGE	OVIGENETIC	OWLLIGHT	OXHEAD
OVERSUPPLY	OVERVOTE	OVIGENIC	OWLY	OXHEAL
OVERSUPPLYING	OVERWADE	OVIGENOUS	OWN	OXHEART
OVERSWARM	OVERWAGES	OVIGER	OWNABLE	OXHIDE
OVERSWAY	OVERWAKE	OVIGERM	OWNED	OXHOFT
OVERSWELL	OVERWALK	OVIGEROUS	OWNER	OXHORN
OVERSWELLED	OVERWART	OVILE	OWNERLESS	OXHOUSE
OVERSWELLING	OVERWASH	OVIN	OWNERSHIP	OXHUVUD
OVERSWOLLEN	OVERWATCH	OVINE	OWNHOOD	OXID
OVERT	OVERWATCHER	OVINIA	OWNING	OXIDABILITY
OVERTAKE	OVERWEAR	OVIPARA	OWNNESS	OXIDABLE
OVERTAKEN	OVERWEARIED	OVIPARAL	OWNWAYISH	OXIDANT
OVERTAKER	OVERWEARING	OVIPARITY	OWRE	OXIDASE
OVERTAKING	OVERWEARY	OVIPAROUS	OWRECOME	OXIDASIC
OVERTASK	OVERWEARYING	OVIPAROUSLY	OWREHIP	OXIDATE
OVERTAX	OVERWEATHER	OVIPOSIT	OWRELAY	OXIDATED
OVERTAXATION	OVERWEEN	OVIPOSITED	OWSE	OXIDATING
OVERTAXED	OVERWEENED	OVIPOSITING	OWSEN	OXIDATION
OVERTAXING	OVERWEENER	OVIPOSITION	OWTCHAH	OXIDATIONAL
OVERTEEM	OVERWEENING	OVIPOSITOR	OWYHEEITE	OXIDATIVE
OVERTELL	OVERWEEP	OVISAC	OWZEL	OXIDATOR
OVERTELLING	OVERWEIGH	OVISM	OX	OXIDE
OVERTEST	OVERWEIGHT	OVIST	OXADIAZOLE	OXIDIMETRIC
OVERTHINK	OVERWELT	OVISTIC	OXALACETIC	OXIDIMETRY
OVERTHREW	OVERWEND	OVIVOROUS	OXALAEMIA	OXIDISE
OVERTHROW	OVERWENT	OVOCYTE	OXALATE	OXIDIZABLE
OVERTHROWAL	OVERWHELM	OVOELLIPTIC	OXALATO	OXIDIZE
OVERTHROWER	OVERWHELMER	OVOGENESIS	OXALEMIA	OXIDIZED
OVERTHROWING	OVERWHELMING	OVOGENETIC	OXALIC	OXIDIZER
OVERTHROWN	OVERWHELMINGLY	OVOGENOUS	OXALIS	OXIDIZING
OVERTHRUST	OVERWIN	OVOGONIUM	OXALURAMID	OXIDO
OVERTHWART	OVERWIND	OVOID	OXALURAMIDE	OXIDULATED
OVERTHWARTLY	OVERWINDING	OVOIDAL	OXALURATE	OXIM
OVERTIDE	OVERWING	OVOLI	OXALURIA	OXIMATE
OVERTILT	OVERWINNING	OVOLO	OXALURIC	OXIMATION
OVERTIME	OVERWINTER	OVOLOGICAL	OXALYL	OXIME
OVERTIMED	OVERWIPED	OVOLOGIST	OXALYLUREA	OXLAND
OVERTIMER	OVERWOMAN	OVOLOGY	OXAMATE	OXLIKE
OVERTIMING	OVERWON	OVOLYTIC	OXAMETHANE	OXLIP
OVERTITLE	OVERWOOD	OVOMUCOID	OXAMIC	OXMAN
OVERTLY	OVERWORD	OVOPLASM	OXAMIDE	OXMANSHIP
OVERTOE	OVERWORE	OVOPLASMIC	OXAMIDIN	OXMEN
OVERTOIL	OVERWORK	OVOPYRIFORM	OXAMIDINE	OXO
OVERTOISE	OVERWORKED	OVORHOMBOID	OXAMMITE	OXONIUM
OVERTOLD	OVERWORKING	OVOTESTIS	OXAN	OXOZONE
OVERTONE	OVERWORN	OVULA	OXANE	OXOZONIDES
OVERTOOK	OVERWOUND	OVULAR	OXANILATE	OXPECKER
OVERTOP	OVERWREST	OVULARIAN	OXANILIC	OXREIM

OXSHOE
OXSKIN
OXTAIL
OXTER
OXTONGUE
OXWORT
OXY
OXYACANTHIN
OXYACANTHINE
OXYACANTHOUS
OXYACETYLENE
OXYACID
OXYALDEHYDE
OXYAMINE
OXYAPHIA
OXYASTER
OXYAZO
OXYBAPHA
OXYBENZYL
OXYBERBERINE
OXYBLEPSIA
OXYBROMIDE
OXYBUTYRIA
OXYCALCIUM
OXYCAMPHOR
OXYCAPROIC
OXYCARBONATE
OXYCELLULOSE
OXYCEPHALIC
OXYCEPHALISM
OXYCEPHALOUS
OXYCEPHALY
OXYCHLORATE
OXYCHLORIC
OXYCHLORID
OXYCHLORIDE
OXYCHLORINE
OXYCHROMATIC
OXYCHROMATIN
OXYCINNAMIC
OXYCOPAIVIC
OXYCOUMARIN
OXYCRATE
OXYCYANIDE
OXYDACTYL
OXYDIACT
OXYESTHESIA
OXYETHER
OXYETHYL
OXYGEN
OXYGENANT
OXYGENATE
OXYGENATED
OXYGENATING
OXYGENATOR
OXYGENERATOR
OXYGENIC
OXYGENICITY
OXYGENIUM
OXYGENIZABLE
OXYGENIZE
OXYGENIZED
OXYGENIZER
OXYGENIZING
OXYGENOUS
OXYGEUSIA
OXYGNATHOUS
OXYGON
OXYGONAL
OXYGONIAL
OXYHAEMATIN
OXYHALIDE
OXYHALOID
OXYHEMATIN
OXYHEXACTINE
OXYHEXASTER
OXYHYDRATE

OXYHYDRIC
OXYHYDROGEN
OXYIODIDE
OXYKETONE
OXYL
OXYLUCIFERIN
OXYMEL
OXYMETHYLENE
OXYMORA
OXYMORON
OXYMURIATE
OXYMURIATIC
OXYNEURIN
OXYNEURINE
OXYNITRATE
OXYNTIC
OXYOPHITIC
OXYOPIA
OXYOPY
OXYOSPHRESIA
OXYPETALOUS
OXYPHENOL
OXYPHENYL
OXYPHIL
OXYPHILE
OXYPHILIC
OXYPHILOUS
OXYPHONIA
OXYPHONY
OXYPHOSPHATE
OXYPHTHALIC
OXYPHYLLOUS
OXYPHYTE
OXYPICRIC
OXYPROLINE
OXYPROPIONIC
OXYPURINE
OXYPYCNOS
OXYQUINOLINE
OXYQUINONE
OXYRHINE
OXYRHINOUS
OXYRHYNCH
OXYRHYNCHID
OXYRHYNCHOUS
OXYRRHYNCHID
OXYSALICYLIC
OXYSALT
OXYSTEARIC
OXYSTOMATOUS
OXYSTOME
OXYSULFID
OXYSULFIDE
OXYSULPHATE
OXYSULPHID
OXYSULPHIDE
OXYTERPENE
OXYTOCIA
OXYTOCIC
OXYTOCIN
OXYTOCOUS
OXYTOLUENE
OXYTOLUIC
OXYTONE
OXYTONESIS
OXYTONICAL
OXYTONIZE
OXYTYLOTATE
OXYTYLOTE
OXYURIASIS
OXYURICIDE
OXYURID
OXYUROUS
OXYWELDING
OY
OYAPOCK
OYE

OYER
OYES
OYEZ
OYSTER
OYSTERAGE
OYSTERBIRD
OYSTERER
OYSTERFISH
OYSTERFISHES
OYSTERGREEN
OYSTERHOUSE
OYSTERING
OYSTERLING
OYSTERMAN
OYSTERMEN
OYSTEROUS
OYSTERROOT
OYSTERS
OYSTERSEED
OYSTERSHELL
OYSTERWIFE
OYSTERWOMAN
OZAENA
OZARKITE
OZENA
OZOBROME
OZOCERITE
OZOENA
OZONATE
OZONATION
OZONE
OZONED
OZONER
OZONIC
OZONID
OZONIDE
OZONIFEROUS
OZONIFY
OZONIZATION
OZONIZE
OZONIZED
OZONIZER
OZONIZING
OZONOMETER
OZONOMETRY
OZONOSCOPE
OZONOSCOPIC
OZONOSPHERE
OZONOSPHERIC
OZONOUS
OZOSTOMIA
OZOTYPE

PA
PAAGE
PAAL
PAAR
PAAUW
PAB
PABBLE
PABLO
PABULAR
PABULARY
PABULATION
PABULATORY
PABULOUS
PABULUM
PAC
PACA
PACABLE
PACANE
PACATE
PACATELY
PACATION
PACATIVE
PACAY
PACAYA
PACCIOLI
PACE
PACEBOARD
PACED
PACEMAKER
PACEMAKING
PACER
PACHA
PACHAK
PACHALIC
PACHINKO
PACHISI
PACHNOLITE
PACHOULI
PACHUCO
PACHYDACTYL
PACHYDACTYLY
PACHYDERM
PACHYDERMA
PACHYDERMAL
PACHYDERMIA
PACHYDERMIAL
PACHYDERMIC
PACHYDERMOID
PACHYDERMOUS
PACHYGLOSSAL
PACHYLOSIS
PACHYMENIA
PACHYMENIC
PACHYMENINX
PACHYMETER
PACHYNEMA
PACHYNSIS
PACHYNTIC
PACHYSANDRA
PACHYTENE
PACIFIABLE
PACIFIC
PACIFICAL
PACIFICALLY
PACIFICATE
PACIFICATED
PACIFICATING

PACIFICATION
PACIFICATOR
PACIFICATORY
PACIFICITY
PACIFICO
PACIFICOS
PACIFIED
PACIFIER
PACIFISM
PACIFIST
PACIFISTIC
PACIFY
PACIFYING
PACING
PACK
PACKAGE
PACKAGED
PACKAGING
PACKALL
PACKBUILDER
PACKCLOTH
PACKED
PACKER
PACKERIES
PACKERY
PACKET
PACKETED
PACKETING
PACKHORSE
PACKHOUSE
PACKING
PACKINGHOUSE
PACKLESS
PACKLY
PACKMAN
PACKMEN
PACKNESS
PACKSACK
PACKSADDLE
PACKSTAFF
PACKSTAVES
PACKTHREAD
PACKTONG
PACKWARE
PACKWAX
PACKWAY
PACO
PACOS
PACOTA
PACOURYUVA
PACT
PACTA
PACTION
PACTIONAL
PACTIONALLY
PACTUM
PAD
PADANG
PADASHA
PADAUK
PADCLOTH
PADDED
PADDER
PADDING
PADDLE
PADDLED
PADDLEFISH
PADDLEFISHES
PADDLER
PADDLEWOOD
PADDLING
PADDO
PADDOCK
PADDOCKED
PADDOCKING
PADDOCKRIDE
PADDOCKSTONE

PADDOCKSTOOL
PADDY
PADDYBIRD
PADDYMELON
PADDYWACK
PADDYWATCH
PADDYWHACK
PADELION
PADELLA
PADEMELON
PADFOOT
PADGE
PADI
PADISHAH
PADLE
PADLOCK
PADLOCKED
PADLOCKING
PADMASANA
PADMELON
PADNAG
PADOU
PADRE
PADRES
PADRI
PADRINO
PADROADIST
PADROADO
PADRONA
PADRONE
PADRONES
PADRONI
PADRONISM
PADS
PADSHAH
PADSTONE
PADTREE
PADUASOY
PAEAN
PAEANISM
PAEANIZE
PAEANIZED
PAEANIZING
PAEDARCHY
PAEDATROPHIA
PAEDATROPHY
PAEDERAST
PAEDERASTIC
PAEDERASTY
PAEDIATRIC
PAEDIATRICS
PAEDOBAPTISM
PAEDOBAPTIST
PAEDOGENESIS
PAEDOGENETIC
PAEDOLOGICAL
PAEDOLOGIST
PAEDOLOGY
PAEDOMETER
PAEDOMORPHIC
PAEDONYMIC
PAEDONYMY
PAEDOTRIBE
PAEDOTROPHIC
PAEDOTROPHY
PAEGEL
PAEGL
PAEGLE
PAELLA
PAENULA
PAENULAE
PAEON
PAEONIC
PAEPAE
PAGA
PAGADOR
PAGAN

PAGANDOM
PAGANIC
PAGANICAL
PAGANICALLY
PAGANISH
PAGANISM
PAGANIST
PAGANISTIC
PAGANITY
PAGANIZATION
PAGANIZE
PAGANIZED
PAGANIZER
PAGANIZING
PAGANRY
PAGE
PAGEANT
PAGEANTED
PAGEANTEER
PAGEANTIC
PAGEANTRIES
PAGEANTRY
PAGEBOY
PAGED
PAGER
PAGES
PAGGLE
PAGINA
PAGINAE
PAGINAL
PAGINARY
PAGINATE
PAGINATED
PAGINATING
PAGINATION
PAGINE
PAGING
PAGLE
PAGNE
PAGODA
PAGODAS
PAGOSCOPE
PAGRUS
PAGURIAN
PAGURID
PAGURINE
PAGUROID
PAGUS
PAH
PAHA
PAHAUTEA
PAHI
PAHLAVI
PAHLEVI
PAHMI
PAHO
PAHOEHOE
PAHUA
PAHUTAN
PAI
PAICHE
PAID
PAIDEIA
PAIDEUTIC
PAIDEUTICS
PAIDLE
PAIDOLOGICAL
PAIDOLOGIST
PAIDOLOGY
PAIK
PAIL
PAILETTE
PAILFUL
PAILLASSE
PAILLES
PAILLETTE
PAILLETTED

PAILLETTES
PAILLON
PAILLONS
PAILOLO
PAILOO
PAILOU
PAILOW
PAIN
PAINCH
PAINDEMAINE
PAINED
PAINFUL
PAINFULLY
PAINFULNESS
PAINING
PAININGLY
PAINKILLER
PAINLESS
PAINLESSLY
PAINLESSNESS
PAINS
PAINSTAKER
PAINSTAKING
PAINSWORTHY
PAINT
PAINTBOX
PAINTBRUSH
PAINTED
PAINTER
PAINTERLY
PAINTIER
PAINTIEST
PAINTINESS
PAINTING
PAINTINGNESS
PAINTINGS
PAINTLESS
PAINTPOT
PAINTRESS
PAINTRY
PAINTS
PAINTURE
PAINTY
PAIOCK
PAIOCKE
PAIP
PAIR
PAIRED
PAIREDNESS
PAIRER
PAIRIAL
PAIRING
PAIRMENT
PAIRS
PAIRT
PAIS
PAISA
PAISANITE
PAISANO
PAISE
PAIWARI
PAJAHUELLO
PAJAK
PAJAMA
PAJAMAED
PAJAMAS
PAJAROELLO
PAJERO
PAJOCK
PAKCHOI
PAKE
PAKEHA
PAKKA
PAKTONG
PAL
PALA
PALABRA

PALACE	PALATIVE	PALERON	PALLE	PALMICOLEUS
PALACED	PALATIZATION	PALEST	PALLED	PALMIER
PALACEOUS	PALATIZE	PALESTRA	PALLESCENCE	PALMIEST
PALACH	PALATODENTAL	PALESTRAE	PALLESCENT	PALMIFEROUS
PALADIN	PALATOGRAM	PALESTRAL	PALLESTHESIA	PALMIFORM
PALAEOBOTANY	PALATOGRAPH	PALESTRIAN	PALLET	PALMIGRADE
PALAEOCYCLIC	PALATOGRAPHY	PALESTRIC	PALLETING	PALMILLA
PALAEOETHNIC	PALATOMETER	PALET	PALLETIZE	PALMILLO
PALAEOGLYPH	PALAVER	PALETIOLOGY	PALLETIZED	PALMILOBATE
PALAEOGRAPH	PALAVERED	PALETOT	PALLETIZING	PALMILOBATED
PALAEOGRAPHY	PALAVERER	PALETTE	PALLETTE	PALMILOBED
PALAEOLATRY	PALAVERING	PALETZ	PALLHOLDER	PALMINERVATE
PALAEOLITH	PALAVERIST	PALEW	PALLI	PALMINERVED
PALAEOLITHIC	PALAVERMENT	PALEWISE	PALLIA	PALMING
PALAEOLITHY	PALAVEROUS	PALFRENIER	PALLIAL	PALMIPED
PALAEOLOGIST	PALAY	PALFREY	PALLIARD	PALMIRA
PALAEOLOGY	PALAYAN	PALFREYED	PALLIASSE	PALMIST
PALAEOPHYTIC	PALAZZI	PALFREYS	PALLIATA	PALMISTRY
PALAEOPLAIN	PALAZZO	PALFRY	PALLIATE	PALMITATE
PALAEOSOPHY	PALBERRY	PALGAT	PALLIATED	PALMITE
PALAEOSTYLIC	PALCH	PALI	PALLIATING	PALMITIC
PALAEOSTYLY	PALE	PALIER	PALLIATION	PALMITIN
PALAEOTYPE	PALEA	PALIEST	PALLIATIVE	PALMITINE
PALAESTRA	PALEACEOUS	PALIFICATION	PALLIATIVELY	PALMITO
PALAESTRAE	PALEAE	PALIFORM	PALLIATOR	PALMITONE
PALAESTRAL	PALEANTHROPIC	PALIKAR	PALLIATORY	PALMITOS
PALAESTRIAN	PALEATE	PALIKINESIA	PALLID	PALMIVEINED
PALAESTRIC	PALEBELLY	PALILA	PALLIDITY	PALMIVOROUS
PALAESTRICS	PALEBREAST	PALILALIA	PALLIDLY	PALMO
PALAETIOLOGY	PALEBUCK	PALILOGETIC	PALLIDNESS	PALMODIC
PALAFITTE	PALED	PALILOGY	PALLIER	PALMOSCOPY
PALAGONITE	PALEDNESS	PALIMBACCHIC	PALLIES	PALMOSPASMUS
PALAGONITIC	PALEFACE	PALIMPSEST	PALLIEST	PALMS
PALAIOTYPE	PALEGOLD	PALINAL	PALLINESS	PALMULA
PALAIS	PALEHEARTED	PALINDROME	PALLING	PALMUS
PALAISTE	PALEIFORM	PALINDROMIC	PALLION	PALMWISE
PALAITE	PALELY	PALINDROMIST	PALLIOPEDAL	PALMWOOD
PALAKA	PALENESS	PALING	PALLISER	PALMY
PALAMA	PALEOATAVISM	PALINGENESIS	PALLIUM	PALMYRA
PALAMAE	PALEOBIOLOGY	PALINGENETIC	PALLIUMS	PALO
PALAMATE	PALEOBOTANIC	PALINGENIST	PALLOGRAPH	PALOLO
PALAME	PALEOBOTANY	PALINGENY	PALLOGRAPHIC	PALOMA
PALAMPORE	PALEOCOSMIC	PALINODE	PALLOMETRIC	PALOMBINO
PALANDER	PALEOCRYSTAL	PALINODED	PALLONE	PALOMETA
PALANKA	PALEOCRYSTIC	PALINODIAL	PALLOR	PALOMINO
PALANKEEN	PALEOCYCLIC	PALINODIC	PALLY	PALOMINOS
PALANKEENED	PALEOECOLOGY	PALINODIST	PALM	PALOOKA
PALANKEENING	PALEOETHNIC	PALINODY	PALMA	PALOSAPIS
PALANQUIN	PALEOFAUNA	PALIPHRASIA	PALMACEOUS	PALOUR
PALANQUINED	PALEOGENETIC	PALIRRHEA	PALMAD	PALOUSER
PALANQUINING	PALEOGLYPH	PALIS	PALMAR	PALOVERDE
PALAPALA	PALEOGRAPH	PALISADE	PALMARIAN	PALP
PALAPALAI	PALEOGRAPHER	PALISADED	PALMARIS	PALPABILITY
PALAR	PALEOGRAPHY	PALISADING	PALMARY	PALPABLE
PALAS	PALEOKINETIC	PALISADO	PALMATE	PALPABLENESS
PALATABILITY	PALEOLA	PALISADOES	PALMATED	PALPABLY
PALATABLE	PALEOLATE	PALISADOING	PALMATELY	PALPACLE
PALATABLY	PALEOLATRY	PALISH	PALMATIFID	PALPAL
PALATAL	PALEOLITH	PALISANDER	PALMATIFORM	PALPATE
PALATALISM	PALEOLITHIC	PALISTROPHIA	PALMATILOBED	PALPATED
PALATALITY	PALEOLITHIST	PALKEE	PALMATION	PALPATING
PALATALIZE	PALEOLITHOID	PALKI	PALMATISECT	PALPATION
PALATE	PALEOLITHY	PALL	PALMATURE	PALPATORY
PALATED	PALEOLOGIST	PALLA	PALMCRIST	PALPEBRA
PALATEFUL	PALEOLOGY	PALLADAMMIN	PALMED	PALPEBRAE
PALATIAL	PALEONTOLOGY	PALLADAMMINE	PALMELLOID	PALPEBRAL
PALATIALLY	PALEOPHYTIC	PALLADIC	PALMER	PALPEBRATE
PALATIALNESS	PALEOPICRITE	PALLADIUM	PALMERIES	PALPEBRATION
PALATIAN	PALEOPLAIN	PALLADIUMIZE	PALMERITE	PALPEBRITIS
PALATIC	PALEOPSYCHIC	PALLADIZE	PALMERY	PALPED
PALATINAL	PALEOSTYLIC	PALLADOUS	PALMETTE	PALPI
PALATINATE	PALEOSTYLY	PALLAE	PALMETTO	PALPIFER
PALATINE	PALEOTECHNIC	PALLAH	PALMETTOES	PALPIFEROUS
PALATINITE	PALEOTHERMAL	PALLALL	PALMETTOS	PALPIFORM
PALATION	PALEOTHERMIC	PALLAR	PALMETUM	PALPIGER
PALATIST	PALEOZOOLOGY	PALLASITE	PALMFUL	PALPIGEROUS
PALATITIS	PALER	PALLBEARER	PALMI	PALPITANT

PALPITATE
PALPITATED
PALPITATING
PALPITATION
PALPOCIL
PALPON
PALPULUS
PALPUS
PALSGRAVE
PALSGRAVINE
PALSIED
PALSIES
PALSIFY
PALSTAFF
PALSTAVE
PALSTER
PALSY
PALSYING
PALT
PALTER
PALTERED
PALTERER
PALTERING
PALTERLY
PALTOCK
PALTRIER
PALTRIEST
PALTRILY
PALTRINESS
PALTRY
PALU
PALUDAL
PALUDAMENT
PALUDE
PALUDIAL
PALUDIC
PALUDICOLE
PALUDICOLINE
PALUDICOLOUS
PALUDIFEROUS
PALUDINAL
PALUDINE
PALUDINOUS
PALUDISM
PALUDOSE
PALUDOUS
PALULE
PALULI
PALULUS
PALUS
PALUSTRAL
PALUSTRIAN
PALUSTRINE
PALY
PALYNOLOGY
PAM
PAMBANMANCHE
PAMBY
PAMENT
PAMMENT
PAMPA
PAMPANITO
PAMPAS
PAMPEAN
PAMPER
PAMPERED
PAMPEREDLY
PAMPEREDNESS
PAMPERER
PAMPERING
PAMPERIZE
PAMPERO
PAMPEROS
PAMPHAGOUS
PAMPHARMACON
PAMPHLET
PAMPHLETAGE

PAMPHLETARY
PAMPHLETEER
PAMPHLETER
PAMPHLETIC
PAMPHLETICAL
PAMPHLETIZE
PAMPHYSIC
PAMPHYSICAL
PAMPHYSICISM
PAMPILION
PAMPINIFORM
PAMPINOCELE
PAMPLEGIA
PAMPOOTEE
PAMPOOTIE
PAMPRE
PAMPRODACTYL
PAMPSYCHISM
PAMPSYCHIST
PAN
PANABASE
PANACE
PANACEA
PANACEAN
PANACEIST
PANACHE
PANACHED
PANACHURE
PANADA
PANADE
PANAESTHESIA
PANAESTHETIC
PANAGIARION
PANAMA
PANAPOSPORY
PANARCHIC
PANARCHY
PANARIS
PANARITIUM
PANARTERITIS
PANARTHRITIS
PANARY
PANATELA
PANATROPHY
PANAX
PANCAKE
PANCAKED
PANCAKING
PANCARDITIS
PANCHAMA
PANCHART
PANCHAX
PANCHAYAT
PANCHAYET
PANCHEON
PANCHION
PANCHRESTON
PANCHROMATIC
PANCHWAY
PANCOSMIC
PANCOSMISM
PANCOSMIST
PANCRATIAN
PANCRATIAST
PANCRATIC
PANCRATICAL
PANCRATISM
PANCRATIST
PANCRATIUM
PANCREAS
PANCREATIC
PANCREATIN
PANCREATISM
PANCREATITIC
PANCREATITIS
PANCREATIZE
PANCREATOID

PANCREATOMY
PAND
PANDA
PANDAL
PANDAN
PANDAR
PANDARAM
PANDAS
PANDATION
PANDAVA
PANDECT
PANDEMIA
PANDEMIC
PANDEMICITY
PANDEMONIAC
PANDEMONIC
PANDEMONISM
PANDEMONIUM
PANDEMY
PANDER
PANDERAGE
PANDERED
PANDERER
PANDERESS
PANDERING
PANDERISM
PANDERIZE
PANDERLY
PANDERMITE
PANDEROUS
PANDIED
PANDIES
PANDIT
PANDITA
PANDLE
PANDLEWHEW
PANDOOR
PANDORA
PANDORE
PANDOUR
PANDOWDY
PANDROP
PANDURA
PANDURATE
PANDURIFORM
PANDY
PANDYING
PANE
PANED
PANEE
PANEGOISM
PANEGOIST
PANEGYRE
PANEGYRIC
PANEGYRICA
PANEGYRICAL
PANEGYRICIZE
PANEGYRICON
PANEGYRICUM
PANEGYRIS
PANEGYRIST
PANEGYRIZE
PANEGYRIZED
PANEGYRIZER
PANEGYRIZING
PANEITY
PANEL
PANELA
PANELATION
PANELED
PANELER
PANELING
PANELIST
PANELLATION
PANELLING
PANELWORK
PANENTHEISM

PANESTHESIA
PANESTHETIC
PANETELA
PANETELLA
PANETIERE
PANFIL
PANFISH
PANFRY
PANG
PANGA
PANGAMIC
PANGAMOUS
PANGAMOUSLY
PANGAMY
PANGANE
PANGARA
PANGASI
PANGEN
PANGENE
PANGENESIS
PANGENETIC
PANGENIC
PANGENS
PANGERANG
PANGLESS
PANGLESSLY
PANGLIMA
PANGOLIN
PANGUINGUI
PANHANDLE
PANHANDLED
PANHANDLER
PANHANDLING
PANHARMONIC
PANHAS
PANHEAD
PANHEADED
PANHIDROSIS
PANHUMAN
PANHYGROUS
PANHYPEREMIA
PANIC
PANICKED
PANICKING
PANICKY
PANICLE
PANICLED
PANICMONGER
PANICULATE
PANICULATED
PANICULATELY
PANIDROSIS
PANIER
PANIFICATION
PANIME
PANIMMUNITY
PANINI
PANIOLO
PANION
PANISC
PANISCUS
PANISK
PANIVOROUS
PANJANDRUM
PANK
PANKIN
PANLOGICAL
PANLOGISM
PANMAN
PANMELODION
PANMERISM
PANMERISTIC
PANMIXIA
PANMIXY
PANMNESIA
PANMUG
PANNADE

PANNAG
PANNAGE
PANNAM
PANNE
PANNED
PANNEL
PANNER
PANNERY
PANNEURITIC
PANNEURITIS
PANNICLE
PANNICULAR
PANNICULITIS
PANNICULUS
PANNIER
PANNIERED
PANNIERMAN
PANNIKIN
PANNING
PANNOSE
PANNOSELY
PANNUM
PANNUS
PANOCHA
PANOCHE
PANOCOCO
PANOISTIC
PANOMPHAEAN
PANOMPHAIC
PANOMPHEAN
PANOMPHIC
PANOPLIED
PANOPLIES
PANOPLIST
PANOPLY
PANOPLYING
PANOPTIC
PANOPTICAL
PANOPTICON
PANORAM
PANORAMA
PANORAMIC
PANORAMICAL
PANORAMIST
PANORPID
PANOSTEITIS
PANOSTITIS
PANOTITIS
PANOWIE
PANPHARMACON
PANPLEGIA
PANPOLISM
PANPSYCHIC
PANPSYCHISM
PANPSYCHIST
PANS
PANSCIENTIST
PANSCLEROSIS
PANSCLEROTIC
PANSE
PANSEXUAL
PANSEXUALISM
PANSEXUALIST
PANSEXUALITY
PANSEXUALIZE
PANSHARD
PANSIDE
PANSIDEMAN
PANSIED
PANSIERE
PANSIES
PANSIL
PANSINUITIS
PANSINUSITIS
PANSIT
PANSMITH
PANSOPHIC

PANSOPHICAL
PANSOPHISM
PANSOPHIST
PANSOPHY
PANSPERMIA
PANSPERMY
PANSY
PANT
PANTACOSM
PANTAGAMY
PANTAGOGUE
PANTAGRAPH
PANTAGRAPHIC
PANTALAN
PANTALEON
PANTALET
PANTALETS
PANTALETTE
PANTALETTED
PANTALETTES
PANTALGIA
PANTALON
PANTALOON
PANTALOONED
PANTALOONERY
PANTALOONS
PANTAMETER
PANTAMORPH
PANTAMORPHIA
PANTAMORPHIC
PANTANEMONE
PANTAPHOBIA
PANTARBE
PANTARCHY
PANTAS
PANTASCOPE
PANTASCOPIC
PANTATROPHIA
PANTATROPHY
PANTATYPE
PANTECHNIC
PANTECHNICON
PANTED
PANTELEPHONE
PANTELLERITE
PANTER
PANTERER
PANTH
PANTHEA
PANTHEIC
PANTHEISM
PANTHEIST
PANTHEISTIC
PANTHELISM
PANTHEOLOGY
PANTHEON
PANTHEONIC
PANTHEONIZE
PANTHER
PANTHERESS
PANTHERINE
PANTHERS
PANTHERWOOD
PANTHEUM
PANTIES
PANTILE
PANTILED
PANTILING
PANTINE
PANTING
PANTINGLY
PANTISOCRACY
PANTISOCRAT
PANTLE
PANTLER
PANTO
PANTOCHROME

PANTOCHROMIC
PANTOFFLE
PANTOFLE
PANTOGLOT
PANTOGRAPH
PANTOGRAPHER
PANTOGRAPHIC
PANTOGRAPHY
PANTOLOGIC
PANTOLOGICAL
PANTOLOGIST
PANTOLOGY
PANTOMANCER
PANTOMANIA
PANTOMETER
PANTOMETRY
PANTOMIME
PANTOMIMIC
PANTOMIMICAL
PANTOMIMICRY
PANTOMIMIST
PANTOMNESIA
PANTOMNESIC
PANTOMORPH
PANTOMORPHIA
PANTOMORPHIC
PANTON
PANTOON
PANTOPHAGIC
PANTOPHAGIST
PANTOPHAGY
PANTOPHILE
PANTOPHOBIA
PANTOPHOBIC
PANTOPHOBOUS
PANTOPTEROUS
PANTOSCOPE
PANTOSCOPIC
PANTOTACTIC
PANTOTHENATE
PANTOTYPE
PANTOUM
PANTRIES
PANTRY
PANTRYMAN
PANTRYWOMAN
PANTS
PANTSUIT
PANTUN
PANTYWAIST
PANUELO
PANUELOS
PANUNG
PANURE
PANURGIC
PANURGY
PANYAR
PANZER
PANZOISM
PANZOOTIA
PANZOOTIC
PANZOOTY
PAOLI
PAOLO
PAON
PAOPAO
PAP
PAPA
PAPABILITY
PAPABLE
PAPABOT
PAPABOTE
PAPACIES
PAPACY
PAPAGALLO
PAPAGAYO
PAPAIN

PAPAIO
PAPAL
PAPALISM
PAPALIST
PAPALISTIC
PAPALIZATION
PAPALIZE
PAPALIZER
PAPALOI
PAPALTY
PAPANE
PAPAPHOBIA
PAPAPHOBIST
PAPARCHICAL
PAPARCHY
PAPAVERIN
PAPAVERINE
PAPAVEROUS
PAPAW
PAPAYA
PAPAYOTIN
PAPBOAT
PAPE
PAPELON
PAPELONNE
PAPER
PAPERBACK
PAPERBARK
PAPERBOARD
PAPERED
PAPERER
PAPERHANGER
PAPERHANGING
PAPERING
PAPERKNIFE
PAPERKNIVES
PAPERMAKER
PAPERMAKING
PAPERMOUTH
PAPERN
PAPERS
PAPERSHELL
PAPERWEIGHT
PAPERWORK
PAPERY
PAPETERIE
PAPEY
PAPICOLAR
PAPICOLIST
PAPIER
PAPILLA
PAPILLAE
PAPILLAR
PAPILLARY
PAPILLATE
PAPILLECTOMY
PAPILLEDEMA
PAPILLIFORM
PAPILLITIS
PAPILLOEDEMA
PAPILLOMA
PAPILLOMAS
PAPILLOMATA
PAPILLON
PAPILLOSE
PAPILLOSITY
PAPILLOTE
PAPILLOUS
PAPILLULATE
PAPILLULE
PAPINGO
PAPION
PAPIOPIO
PAPISH
PAPISHER
PAPISM
PAPIST

PAPISTIC
PAPISTICAL
PAPISTICALLY
PAPISTRY
PAPIZE
PAPLESS
PAPMEAT
PAPOLATER
PAPOLATROUS
PAPOLATRY
PAPOOSE
PAPOOSEROOT
PAPOULA
PAPPESCENT
PAPPI
PAPPIER
PAPPIES
PAPPIEST
PAPPIFEROUS
PAPPIFORM
PAPPOOSE
PAPPOSE
PAPPOUS
PAPPOX
PAPPUS
PAPPY
PAPREG
PAPRICA
PAPRIKA
PAPULA
PAPULAE
PAPULAN
PAPULAR
PAPULATE
PAPULATED
PAPULATION
PAPULE
PAPULIFEROUS
PAPULOSE
PAPULOUS
PAPYRACEOUS
PAPYRAL
PAPYRI
PAPYRIAN
PAPYRIN
PAPYRINE
PAPYRITIOUS
PAPYROCRACY
PAPYROGRAPH
PAPYROLOGIST
PAPYROLOGY
PAPYROPHOBIA
PAPYROTAMIA
PAPYROTINT
PAPYROTYPE
PAPYRUS
PAR
PARA
PARABANATE
PARABANIC
PARABAPTISM
PARABASIC
PARABASIS
PARABEMA
PARABEMATA
PARABEMATIC
PARABIEN
PARABIOSIS
PARABIOTIC
PARABLAST
PARABLASTIC
PARABLE
PARABLED
PARABLEPSIA
PARABLEPSIS
PARABLEPSY
PARABLEPTIC

PARABLING
PARABOLA
PARABOLANUS
PARABOLAS
PARABOLIC
PARABOLICAL
PARABOLIFORM
PARABOLIST
PARABOLIZE
PARABOLIZED
PARABOLIZER
PARABOLIZING
PARABOLOID
PARABOLOIDAL
PARABOTULISM
PARABRANCHIA
PARABULIA
PARABULIC
PARACARMINE
PARACENTESIS
PARACENTRAL
PARACENTRIC
PARACEPHALUS
PARACHOLIA
PARACHOR
PARACHORDAL
PARACHROMA
PARACHRONISM
PARACHROSE
PARACHUTE
PARACHUTED
PARACHUTIC
PARACHUTING
PARACHUTISM
PARACHUTIST
PARACHUTISTS
PARACLETE
PARACME
PARACOELE
PARACOELIAN
PARACOLPITIS
PARACOLPIUM
PARACONE
PARACONID
PARACOROLLA
PARACROSTIC
PARACUSIA
PARACUSIC
PARACUSIS
PARACYANOGEN
PARACYESIS
PARACYSTIC
PARACYSTITIS
PARACYSTIUM
PARADE
PARADED
PARADENTAL
PARADENTIUM
PARADER
PARADERM
PARADIASTOLE
PARADIDYMAL
PARADIDYMIS
PARADIGM
PARADIGMATIC
PARADING
PARADINGLY
PARADISAIC
PARADISAICAL
PARADISAL
PARADISE
PARADISEAN
PARADISIAC
PARADISIACAL
PARADISIAL
PARADISIAN
PARADISIC

PARADISICAL
PARADO
PARADOS
PARADOSES
PARADOX
PARADOXAL
PARADOXER
PARADOXIAL
PARADOXIC
PARADOXICAL
PARADOXICIAN
PARADOXIDIAN
PARADOXIST
PARADOXOLOGY
PARADOXURE
PARADOXY
PARADROMIC
PARADROP
PARAENESIS
PARAENESIZE
PARAENETIC
PARAENETICAL
PARAESTHESIA
PARAESTHETIC
PARAFFIN
PARAFFINE
PARAFFINED
PARAFFINER
PARAFFINIC
PARAFFINING
PARAFFINOID
PARAFFLE
PARAFLE
PARAFORM
PARAFRONT
PARAGANGLION
PARAGASTER
PARAGASTRAL
PARAGASTRIC
PARAGASTRULA
PARAGE
PARAGENESIA
PARAGENESIS
PARAGENETIC
PARAGENIC
PARAGERONTIC
PARAGEUSIA
PARAGEUSIC
PARAGEUSIS
PARAGLENAL
PARAGLOSSA
PARAGLOSSAE
PARAGLOSSAL
PARAGLOSSATE
PARAGLOSSIA
PARAGNATH
PARAGNATHISM
PARAGNATHOUS
PARAGNATHS
PARAGNATHUS
PARAGNOSIA
PARAGOGE
PARAGOGIC
PARAGOGICAL
PARAGOGIZE
PARAGON
PARAGONED
PARAGONING
PARAGONITE
PARAGONITIC
PARAGRAM
PARAGRAPH
PARAGRAPHED
PARAGRAPHER
PARAGRAPHIA
PARAGRAPHIC
PARAGRAPHING

PARAGRAPHIST
PARAH
PARAHEMATIN
PARAHEPATIC
PARAHOPEITE
PARAHORMONE
PARAHYPNOSIS
PARAIBA
PARAKEET
PARAKILYA
PARAKINESIA
PARAKINESIS
PARAKINETIC
PARALALIA
PARALDEHYDE
PARALEIPSIS
PARALEPSIS
PARALEXIA
PARALEXIC
PARALGESIA
PARALGESIC
PARALIAN
PARALININ
PARALIPOMENA
PARALIPSIS
PARALITICAL
PARALLACTIC
PARALLAX
PARALLEL
PARALLELED
PARALLELER
PARALLELING
PARALLELISM
PARALLELIST
PARALLELITH
PARALLELIZE
PARALLELIZED
PARALLELIZER
PARALLELLED
PARALLELLING
PARALLELLY
PARALLELOGRAM
PARALLELS
PARALOGIC
PARALOGICAL
PARALOGISM
PARALOGIST
PARALOGISTIC
PARALOGIZE
PARALOGY
PARALUMINITE
PARALYSES
PARALYSIS
PARALYTIC
PARALYTICAL
PARALYZANT
PARALYZATION
PARALYZE
PARALYZED
PARALYZER
PARALYZING
PARAMAGNET
PARAMAGNETIC
PARAMASTITIS
PARAMASTOID
PARAMATTA
PARAMECIUM
PARAMEDIAN
PARAMENIA
PARAMENT
PARAMERE
PARAMERIC
PARAMESE
PARAMESIAL
PARAMETER
PARAMETRAL
PARAMETRIC

PARAMETRICAL
PARAMETRITIC
PARAMETRITIS
PARAMID
PARAMIDE
PARAMILITARY
PARAMIMIA
PARAMITA
PARAMITOM
PARAMITOME
PARAMNESIA
PARAMO
PARAMORPH
PARAMORPHIC
PARAMORPHISM
PARAMORPHOUS
PARAMOS
PARAMOUNT
PARAMOUNTCY
PARAMOUNTLY
PARAMOUR
PARAMOURS
PARAMUTHETIC
PARAMYELIN
PARAMYOTONE
PARAMYOTONIA
PARANASAL
PARANATELLON
PARANEMA
PARANEMATIC
PARANEPHROS
PARANEPIONIC
PARANETE
PARANG
PARANGI
PARANJA
PARANOEAC
PARANOIA
PARANOIAC
PARANOID
PARANOIDAL
PARANOIDISM
PARANOMIA
PARANOSIC
PARANTHELION
PARANUCLEAR
PARANUCLEATE
PARANUCLEI
PARANUCLEIC
PARANUCLEIN
PARANUCLEUS
PARANYMPH
PARANYMPHAL
PARAO
PARAPARESIS
PARAPARETIC
PARAPEGM
PARAPEGMA
PARAPEGMATA
PARAPET
PARAPETALOUS
PARAPETED
PARAPH
PARAPHASIA
PARAPHASIC
PARAPHED
PARAPHEMIA
PARAPHERNA
PARAPHERNAL
PARAPHIA
PARAPHIMOSIS
PARAPHING
PARAPHONIA
PARAPHONIC
PARAPHRASE
PARAPHRASED
PARAPHRASER

PARAPHRASIA
PARAPHRASING
PARAPHRAST
PARAPHRASTIC
PARAPHRENIA
PARAPHRENIC
PARAPHYLLIA
PARAPHYLLIUM
PARAPHYSATE
PARAPHYSICAL
PARAPHYSIS
PARAPLASM
PARAPLASMIC
PARAPLASTIC
PARAPLASTIN
PARAPLECTIC
PARAPLEGIA
PARAPLEGIC
PARAPLEGY
PARAPLEURUM
PARAPOD
PARAPODIAL
PARAPODIUM
PARAPRAXES
PARAPRAXIA
PARAPRAXIS
PARAPROCTIUM
PARAPSIDAL
PARAPSIS
PARAPSYCHISM
PARAPTERA
PARAPTERAL
PARAPTERON
PARAPTERUM
PARAQUADRATE
PARAQUET
PARAREKA
PARARTHRIA
PARASANG
PARASCENIUM
PARASCEVE
PARASELENAE
PARASELENE
PARASELENIC
PARASHAH
PARASHIOTH
PARASHOTH
PARASITAL
PARASITARY
PARASITE
PARASITES
PARASITIC
PARASITICAL
PARASITICIDE
PARASITISM
PARASITIZE
PARASITOID
PARASITOLOGY
PARASITOSIS
PARASOL
PARASOLED
PARASOLETTE
PARASPECIFIC
PARASPHENOID
PARASTADES
PARASTAS
PARASTATIC
PARASTEMON
PARASTEMONAL
PARASTERNAL
PARASTERNUM
PARASTICHIES
PARASTICHY
PARASTYLE
PARASYNAPSIS
PARASYNAPTIC
PARASYNDESIS

PARASYNESIS
PARASYNETIC
PARASYPHILIS
PARASYSTOLE
PARATACTIC
PARATACTICAL
PARATAXIS
PARATE
PARATERMINAL
PARATHESIS
PARATHETIC
PARATHORMONE
PARATHYROID
PARATITLA
PARATITLES
PARATITLON
PARATOMIAL
PARATOMIUM
PARATONIC
PARATONNERRE
PARATORIUM
PARATORY
PARATRIPTIC
PARATROOPER
PARATROOPS
PARATROPHIC
PARATROPHY
PARATYPE
PARATYPHOID
PARATYPIC
PARATYPICAL
PARAVAIL
PARAVANE
PARAVANT
PARAVAUXITE
PARAVENT
PARAVESICAL
PARAXIAL
PARAXIALLY
PARAXON
PARAXONIC
PARAZONIUM
PARBAKE
PARBOIL
PARBOILED
PARBOILING
PARBREAK
PARBUCKLE
PARBUCKLED
PARBUCKLING
PARCEL
PARCELED
PARCELING
PARCELLED
PARCELLING
PARCELS
PARCENARY
PARCENER
PARCH
PARCHED
PARCHEESI
PARCHEMIN
PARCHER
PARCHESI
PARCHING
PARCHINGLY
PARCHISI
PARCHMENT
PARCHMENTIZE
PARCHY
PARCIDENTATE
PARCILOQUY
PARCITY
PARCLOSE
PARCOOK
PARD
PARDAL

PARDALE	PAREUNIA	PARKY	PAROMOEON	PARROTED
PARDALOTE	PAREVE	PARLANCE	PAROMOLOGIA	PARROTER
PARDAO	PARFAIT	PARLANDO	PAROMOLOGY	PARROTING
PARDAOS	PARFEY	PARLATORY	PARONOMASIA	PARROTLET
PARDE	PARFILAGE	PARLAY	PARONOMASIAN	PARROTRY
PARDED	PARFLECHE	PARLE	PARONOMASTIC	PARROTY
PARDEE	PARFLESH	PARLEMENT	PARONYCHIA	PARRS
PARDESI	PARFOCAL	PARLESIE	PARONYCHIAL	PARRY
PARDHAN	PARGANA	PARLEY	PARONYCHIUM	PARRYING
PARDI	PARGANNA	PARLEYED	PARONYM	PARS
PARDIE	PARGASITE	PARLEYER	PARONYMIC	PARSE
PARDIEU	PARGE	PARLEYING	PARONYMIZE	PARSEC
PARDINE	PARGET	PARLEYS	PARONYMOUS	PARSED
PARDNER	PARGETED	PARLIAMENT	PARONYMY	PARSER
PARDO	PARGETER	PARLIAMENTAL	PAROO	PARSIMONIOUS
PARDON	PARGETING	PARLIAMENTARIAN	PAROOPHORON	PARSIMONY
PARDONABLE	PARGETTED	PARLIAMENTARY	PAROPSIS	PARSING
PARDONABLY	PARGETTING	PARLIAMENTER	PAROPTESIS	PARSLEY
PARDONED	PARGO	PARLING	PAROPTIC	PARSLEYWORT
PARDONEE	PARGOS	PARLISH	PAROQUET	PARSNIP
PARDONER	PARHELIA	PARLOR	PAROREXIA	PARSON
PARDONING	PARHELIACAL	PARLORMAID	PAROSMIA	PARSONAGE
PARDONMONGER	PARHELIC	PARLOUR	PAROSMIC	PARSONARCHY
PARDY	PARHELION	PARLOUS	PAROSTEAL	PARSONED
PARE	PARHELIUM	PARLOUSLY	PAROSTEITIS	PARSONESE
PAREA	PARHOMOLOGY	PARLOUSNESS	PAROSTEOSIS	PARSONESS
PARECIOUS	PARHYPATE	PARLY	PAROSTOSIS	PARSONET
PARED	PARI	PARMA	PAROSTOTIC	PARSONIC
PAREGAL	PARIAH	PARMACETY	PAROTIC	PARSONICAL
PAREGORIC	PARIAL	PARMACK	PAROTID	PARSONICALLY
PAREGORICAL	PARIAN	PARMAK	PAROTIDITIS	PARSONING
PAREIRA	PARICA	PARMENTIER	PAROTIS	PARSONITY
PAREJA	PARIDIGITATE	PARNAS	PAROTITIC	PARSONLY
PAREL	PARIDROSIS	PARNEL	PAROTITIS	PARSONOLATRY
PARELL	PARIES	PARO	PAROTOID	PARSONOLOGY
PARELLA	PARIET	PAROARION	PAROUS	PARSONRY
PARELLE	PARIETAL	PAROARIUM	PAROUSIA	PARSONS
PAREN	PARIETARY	PAROCCIPITAL	PAROVARIAN	PARSONSITE
PARENCHYM	PARIETES	PAROCH	PAROVARIUM	PART
PARENCHYMA	PARIETOJUGAL	PAROCHIAL	PAROXYSM	PARTABLE
PARENCHYMAL	PARIFY	PAROCHIALISM	PAROXYSMAL	PARTAGE
PARENCHYME	PARIGENIN	PAROCHIALIST	PAROXYSMALLY	PARTAKE
PARENCHYMOUS	PARIGLIN	PAROCHIAN	PAROXYSMIC	PARTAKEN
PARENESIS	PARILLIN	PAROCHIN	PAROXYTONE	PARTAKER
PARENESIZE	PARIMUTUEL	PAROCHINE	PAROXYTONIC	PARTAKING
PARENETIC	PARINE	PARODE	PARPAL	PARTAN
PARENETICAL	PARING	PARODI	PARPEN	PARTANFULL
PARENT	PARINGS	PARODIABLE	PARQUET	PARTED
PARENTAGE	PARIPINNATE	PARODIAL	PARQUETED	PARTEN
PARENTAL	PARISH	PARODIC	PARQUETING	PARTER
PARENTALISM	PARISHED	PARODICAL	PARQUETRY	PARTERRE
PARENTALITY	PARISHEN	PARODIED	PARR	PARTERRED
PARENTALLY	PARISHIONAL	PARODIES	PARRAH	PARTES
PARENTATE	PARISHIONATE	PARODINIA	PARRAKEET	PARTHENIAD
PARENTATION	PARISHIONER	PARODIST	PARRAL	PARTHENIAN
PARENTELA	PARISIA	PARODISTIC	PARRALL	PARTHENIC
PARENTELIC	PARISIS	PARODONTITIS	PARRAMATTA	PARTHENOGENY
PARENTERAL	PARISOLOGY	PARODOS	PARRED	PARTHENOLOGY
PARENTERALLY	PARISON	PARODUS	PARREL	PARTI
PARENTHESES	PARISONIC	PARODY	PARRHESIA	PARTIAL
PARENTHESIS	PARISTHMIC	PARODYING	PARRICIDAL	PARTIALIST
PARENTHESIZE	PARISTHMION	PAROECIOUS	PARRICIDALLY	PARTIALITIES
PARENTHETIC	PARISYLLABIC	PAROECIOUSLY	PARRIC!DE	PARTIALITY
PARENTHOOD	PARITIES	PAROECISM	PARRICIDED	PARTIALLY
PARENTICIDE	PARITOR	PAROECY	PARRICIDIAL	PARTIALNESS
PARER	PARITY	PAROEMIA	PARRIDGE	PARTIARY
PARERETHESIS	PARIVINCULAR	PAROEMIAC	PARRIED	PARTIBILITY
PARERGAL	PARK	PAROEMIOLOGY	PARRIER	PARTIBLE
PARERGIC	PARKA	PAROICOUS	PARRIES	PARTICIPABLE
PARERGON	PARKED	PAROL	PARRING	PARTICIPANCE
PARESES	PARKEE	PAROLABLE	PARRITCH	PARTICIPANCY
PARESIS	PARKER	PAROLE	PARROCK	PARTICIPANT
PARESTHESIA	PARKIN	PAROLED	PARROKET	PARTICIPATE
PARESTHETIC	PARKING	PAROLEE	PARROQUET	PARTICIPATED
PARETIC	PARKLAND	PAROLI	PARROT	PARTICIPATOR
PARETICALLY	PARKLEAVES	PAROLING	PARROTBEAK	PARTICIPIAL
PAREU	PARKWAY	PAROLIST	PARROTBILL	PARTICIPLE

PARTICLE
PARTICLES
PARTICULAR
PARTICULARLY
PARTICULATE
PARTICULE
PARTIES
PARTIGEN
PARTILE
PARTIM
PARTIMEN
PARTIMENTO
PARTING
PARTINIUM
PARTISAN
PARTISANSHIP
PARTITA
PARTITE
PARTITION
PARTITIONAL
PARTITIONARY
PARTITIONED
PARTITIONER
PARTITIONING
PARTITIONIST
PARTITIVE
PARTITURA
PARTIVERSAL
PARTIVITY
PARTIZAN
PARTLESS
PARTLET
PARTLY
PARTNER
PARTNERSHIP
PARTOOK
PARTRIDGE
PARTRIDGES
PARTRIDGING
PARTS
PARTSCHINITE
PARTURE
PARTURIATE
PARTURIENCE
PARTURIENCY
PARTURIENT
PARTURITION
PARTURITIVE
PARTY
PARTYISM
PARTYIST
PARTYMONGER
PARULIS
PARUMBILICAL
PARURA
PARURE
PARURIA
PARVANIMITY
PARVE
PARVENU
PARVENUISM
PARVIFLOROUS
PARVIFOLIATE
PARVIFOLIOUS
PARVIPOTENT
PARVIS
PARVISCIENT
PARVITUDE
PARVOLIN
PARVOLINE
PARVULE
PARYPHODROME
PAS
PASA
PASAN
PASANG
PASAR

PASCHAL
PASCHALIST
PASCHFLOWER
PASCOITE
PASCOLA
PASCUAGE
PASCUAL
PASCUOUS
PASEAR
PASENG
PASEO
PASEWA
PASH
PASHA
PASHALIC
PASHALIK
PASHED
PASHIM
PASHING
PASHM
PASHMINA
PASI
PASIG
PASIGRAPHIC
PASIGRAPHY
PASILALY
PASILLO
PASIN
PASIS
PASMO
PASO
PASQUEFLOWER
PASQUIL
PASQUILANT
PASQUILER
PASQUILIC
PASQUILLANT
PASQUILLER
PASQUILLIC
PASQUIN
PASQUINADE
PASQUINADED
PASQUINADER
PASQUINADING
PASS
PASSABLE
PASSABLENESS
PASSABLY
PASSACAGLIA
PASSACAGLIO
PASSADE
PASSADO
PASSADOES
PASSADOS
PASSAGE
PASSAGEABLE
PASSAGED
PASSAGER
PASSAGEWAY
PASSAGGI
PASSAGGIO
PASSAGING
PASSAGGIO
PASSAMENT
PASSANGRAHAN
PASSANT
PASSAREE
PASSATA
PASSAY
PASSBACK
PASSBOOK
PASSE
PASSED
PASSEE
PASSEGARDE
PASSEL
PASSEMEASURE

PASSEMENT
PASSEMENTED
PASSEMENTING
PASSEMEZZO
PASSEN
PASSENGER
PASSEPIED
PASSER
PASSERBY
PASSERINE
PASSERS
PASSES
PASSEWA
PASSGANG
PASSIBILITY
PASSIBLE
PASSIBLENESS
PASSIM
PASSING
PASSINGLY
PASSION
PASSIONAL
PASSIONATE
PASSIONATELY
PASSIONATIVE
PASSIONATO
PASSIONED
PASSIONFLOWER
PASSIONLESS
PASSIONWORT
PASSIR
PASSIVAL
PASSIVATE
PASSIVATION
PASSIVE
PASSIVELY
PASSIVENESS
PASSIVISM
PASSIVIST
PASSIVITY
PASSKEY
PASSLESS
PASSMAN
PASSOMETER
PASSOUT
PASSOVER
PASSPENNY
PASSPORT
PASSULATE
PASSULATION
PASSUS
PASSWAY
PASSWORD
PAST
PASTA
PASTE
PASTEBOARD
PASTEBOARDY
PASTED
PASTEDOWN
PASTEL
PASTELIST
PASTELLIST
PASTER
PASTERER
PASTERN
PASTERNED
PASTEURELLA
PASTEURISE
PASTEURISM
PASTEURIZE
PASTEURIZED
PASTEURIZER
PASTEURIZING
PASTICCIO
PASTICHE
PASTICHEUR

PASTIER
PASTIES
PASTIEST
PASTIL
PASTILE
PASTILED
PASTILING
PASTILLE
PASTILLED
PASTILLING
PASTIME
PASTIMER
PASTINESS
PASTING
PASTLER
PASTNESS
PASTOPHOR
PASTOPHORION
PASTOPHORIUM
PASTOPHORUS
PASTOR
PASTORA
PASTORAL
PASTORALE
PASTORALES
PASTORALI
PASTORALIST
PASTORALITY
PASTORALIZE
PASTORALLY
PASTORALNESS
PASTORATE
PASTORITA
PASTORIUM
PASTORIUMS
PASTORIZE
PASTORLY
PASTORSHIP
PASTOSE
PASTOSITY
PASTOUR
PASTOURELLE
PASTRAMI
PASTRIES
PASTRY
PASTRYMAN
PASTURABLE
PASTURAGE
PASTURAL
PASTURE
PASTURED
PASTURELAND
PASTURER
PASTURES
PASTURING
PASTY
PASUL
PAT
PATA
PATACA
PATACAO
PATACHE
PATACO
PATACOON
PATAGIA
PATAGIAL
PATAGIATE
PATAGIUM
PATAGON
PATAGONIA
PATAKA
PATAMAR
PATANA
PATAND
PATAO
PATAPAT
PATAQUE

PATART
PATAS
PATASHTE
PATATA
PATAVINITY
PATBALL
PATBALLER
PATCH
PATCHABLE
PATCHCOCK
PATCHED
PATCHER
PATCHERIES
PATCHERY
PATCHES
PATCHHEAD
PATCHIER
PATCHIEST
PATCHILY
PATCHINESS
PATCHING
PATCHLEAF
PATCHOULI
PATCHOULY
PATCHWORD
PATCHWORK
PATCHY
PATE
PATEFY
PATEL
PATELLA
PATELLAE
PATELLAR
PATELLAROID
PATELLATE
PATELLIFORM
PATELLINE
PATELLOID
PATELLULA
PATELLULAE
PATELLULATE
PATEN
PATENCY
PATENER
PATENT
PATENTABLE
PATENTABLY
PATENTE
PATENTED
PATENTEE
PATENTING
PATENTLY
PATENTOR
PATER
PATERA
PATERAE
PATERERO
PATERIFORM
PATERISSA
PATERNAL
PATERNALISM
PATERNALIST
PATERNALITY
PATERNALIZE
PATERNALLY
PATERNITY
PATERNOSTER
PATESI
PATESIATE
PATETICO
PATH
PATHBREAKER
PATHED
PATHEMA
PATHEMATIC
PATHETIC
PATHETICAL

PATHETICALLY	PATRIARCH	PATTE	PAUPER	PAWNBROKER
PATHETICATE	PATRIARCHAL	PATTED	PAUPERAGE	PAWNBROKERY
PATHFARER	PATRIARCHATE	PATTEE	PAUPERATE	PAWNBROKING
PATHFINDER	PATRIARCHESS	PATTEN	PAUPERED	PAWNE
PATHFINDING	PATRIARCHIC	PATTENED	PAUPERESS	PAWNED
PATHIC	PATRIARCHIST	PATTENER	PAUPERISM	PAWNEE
PATHLESS	PATRIARCHY	PATTER	PAUPERITIC	PAWNER
PATHLESSNESS	PATRICIAN	PATTERED	PAUPERIZE	PAWNIE
PATHMENT	PATRICIANLY	PATTERER	PAUPERIZED	PAWNING
PATHOANATOMY	PATRICIATE	PATTERING	PAUPERIZING	PAWNOR
PATHOBIOLOGY	PATRICIDAL	PATTERIST	PAURAQUE	PAWNS
PATHOCHEMISTRY	PATRICIDE	PATTERN	PAUROPOD	PAWNSHOP
PATHODONTIA	PATRICK	PATTERNED	PAUSABLY	PAWPAW
PATHOGEN	PATRICO	PATTERNER	PAUSAL	PAX
PATHOGENE	PATRIDGE	PATTERNING	PAUSATION	PAXILLA
PATHOGENESIS	PATRILINEAL	PATTERNIZE	PAUSE	PAXILLAE
PATHOGENESY	PATRILINEAR	PATTERNMAKER	PAUSED	PAXILLAR
PATHOGENETIC	PATRILINY	PATTERNS	PAUSEMENT	PAXILLARY
PATHOGENIC	PATRILOCAL	PATTERNY	PAUSER	PAXILLATE
PATHOGENOUS	PATRIMONIAL	PATTI	PAUSING	PAXILLI
PATHOGENY	PATRIMONIES	PATTIDARI	PAUSSID	PAXILLIFORM
PATHOGERM	PATRIMONY	PATTIE	PAUT	PAXILLOSE
PATHOGERMIC	PATRIN	PATTIES	PAUXI	PAXILLUS
PATHOGNOMIC	PATRIOLATRY	PATTING	PAVADE	PAXIUBA
PATHOGNOMY	PATRIOT	PATTOO	PAVAGE	PAXWAX
PATHOGNOSTIC	PATRIOTEER	PATTU	PAVAN	PAY
PATHOGRAPHY	PATRIOTIC	PATTY	PAVANE	PAYABILITY
PATHOLOGIC	PATRIOTICAL	PATTYPAN	PAVE	PAYABLE
PATHOLOGICAL	PATRIOTICS	PATU	PAVED	PAYABLY
PATHOLOGIST	PATRIOTISM	PATUCA	PAVEED	PAYBOX
PATHOLOGY	PATRIST	PATULENT	PAVEMENT	PAYCHECK
PATHOLYSIS	PATRISTIC	PATULIN	PAVEMENTAL	PAYDAY
PATHOLYTIC	PATRISTICAL	PATULOUS	PAVEN	PAYED
PATHOMANIA	PATRISTICISM	PATULOUSLY	PAVER	PAYEE
PATHOMIMESIS	PATRISTICS	PATULOUSNESS	PAVESTONE	PAYER
PATHOMIMICRY	PATRIX	PATWARI	PAVID	PAYING
PATHONOMIA	PATRIZATE	PATY	PAVIDITY	PAYLOAD
PATHONOMY	PATRIZATION	PAU	PAVIE	PAYMASTER
PATHOPHOBIA	PATROCINIUM	PAUA	PAVIES	PAYMENT
PATHOPHORIC	PATROCLINIC	PAUCIDENTATE	PAVILION	PAYMISTRESS
PATHOPLASTIC	PATROCLINOUS	PAUCIFLOROUS	PAVILLON	PAYNIM
PATHOPOEIA	PATROCLINY	PAUCIFOLIATE	PAVING	PAYNIMHOOD
PATHOPOIESIS	PATROGENESIS	PAUCIFOLIOUS	PAVIOR	PAYNIMRIE
PATHOPOIETIC	PATROL	PAUCIFY	PAVIOUR	PAYNIMRY
PATHOS	PATROLE	PAUCIJUGATE	PAVIS	PAYOFF
PATHOSOCIAL	PATROLLED	PAUCILOCULAR	PAVISADE	PAYOLA
PATHS	PATROLLER	PAUCILOQUENT	PAVISADO	PAYONG
PATHWAY	PATROLLING	PAUCILOQUY	PAVISE	PAYROLL
PATHY	PATROLMAN	PAUCINERVATE	PAVISER	PAYSAGE
PATIBLE	PATROLOGIC	PAUCIPINNATE	PAVISOR	PAYSAGIST
PATIBULARY	PATROLOGICAL	PAUCIPLICATE	PAVISSE	PAYSANNE
PATIBULATE	PATROLOGIST	PAUCIRADIATE	PAVOIS	PAYYETAN
PATIENCE	PATROLOGY	PAUCISPIRAL	PAVONATED	PAZAREE
PATIENCY	PATRON	PAUCITIES	PAVONAZZO	PE
PATIENT	PATRONAGE	PAUCITY	PAVONE	PEA
PATIENTLY	PATRONAL	PAUGHTY	PAVONIAN	PEABERRY
PATIENTNESS	PATRONATE	PAUK	PAVONINE	PEABIRD
PATIN	PATRONESS	PAUKPAN	PAVONIZE	PEABUSH
PATINA	PATRONITE	PAUKY	PAVY	PEACE
PATINAE	PATRONIZE	PAUL	PAW	PEACEABLE
PATINATE	PATRONIZED	PAULAR	PAWAW	PEACEABLY
PATINATION	PATRONIZER	PAULDRON	PAWDITE	PEACEBREAKER
PATINE	PATRONIZING	PAULIE	PAWED	PEACEFUL
PATINED	PATRONLY	PAULIN	PAWER	PEACEFULLY
PATINIZE	PATRONNE	PAULOPAST	PAWING	PEACEFULNESS
PATINOUS	PATRONYM	PAULOPOST	PAWK	PEACELESS
PATIO	PATRONYMIC	PAULOSPORE	PAWKERY	PEACEMAKER
PATIOS	PATRONYMY	PAUN	PAWKIER	PEACEMAKING
PATISE	PATROON	PAUNCH	PAWKIEST	PEACEMAN
PATISSERIE	PATROONRY	PAUNCHE	PAWKILY	PEACEMONGER
PATNIDAR	PATROULLART	PAUNCHED	PAWKINESS	PEACETIME
PATO	PATRUITY	PAUNCHFUL	PAWKRIE	PEACH
PATOIS	PATSY	PAUNCHILY	PAWKY	PEACHBERRY
PATOLA	PATT	PAUNCHINESS	PAWL	PEACHBLOOM
PATONCE	PATTA	PAUNCHY	PAWN	PEACHBLOSSOM
PATRIA	PATTAMAR	PAUNE	PAWNABLE	PEACHBLOW
PATRIAL	PATTARA	PAUP	PAWNAGE	PEACHEN

PEACHER
PEACHERY
PEACHICK
PEACHIER
PEACHIEST
PEACHIFY
PEACHINESS
PEACHLET
PEACHWOOD
PEACHWORT
PEACHY
PEACK
PEACOAT
PEACOCK
PEACOCKERY
PEACOCKISH
PEACOCKISHLY
PEACOCKS
PEACOCKY
PEACOD
PEAFOWL
PEAFOWLS
PEAG
PEAGE
PEAGOOSE
PEAHEN
PEAI
PEAIISM
PEAK
PEAKED
PEAKEDLY
PEAKEDNESS
PEAKER
PEAKGOOSE
PEAKILY
PEAKINESS
PEAKING
PEAKISH
PEAKISHLY
PEAKISHNESS
PEAKY
PEAL
PEALED
PEALER
PEALIKE
PEALING
PEAN
PEANE
PEANUT
PEAPOD
PEAR
PEARCE
PEARCEITE
PEARCH
PEARL
PEARLASH
PEARLBERRY
PEARLBIRD
PEARLBUSH
PEARLED
PEARLER
PEARLET
PEARLFISH
PEARLIER
PEARLIEST
PEARLIN
PEARLING
PEARLINGS
PEARLISH
PEARLITE
PEARLITIC
PEARLSIDES
PEARLSPAR
PEARLWEED
PEARLWORT
PEARLY
PEARMAIN

PEARMONGER
PEARS
PEART
PEARTEN
PEARWOOD
PEAS
PEASANT
PEASANTIZE
PEASANTLIKE
PEASANTLY
PEASANTRY
PEASCOD
PEASE
PEASECOD
PEASEWEEP
PEASHOOTER
PEASOUPER
PEASTAKE
PEASTAKING
PEASTICK
PEASTICKING
PEASTONE
PEASY
PEAT
PEATERY
PEATHOUSE
PEATIER
PEATIEST
PEATMAN
PEATMEN
PEATSHIP
PEATSTACK
PEATWEED
PEATWOOD
PEATY
PEAU
PEAUDER
PEAVEY
PEAVIE
PEAVINE
PEAVY
PEBA
PEBBLE
PEBBLED
PEBBLES
PEBBLESTONE
PEBBLEWARE
PEBBLIER
PEBBLIEST
PEBBLING
PEBBLY
PEBRINE
PEBRINOUS
PECA
PECAN
PECCABILITY
PECCABLE
PECCADILLO
PECCADILLOES
PECCADILLOS
PECCANCIES
PECCANCY
PECCANT
PECCANTLY
PECCANTNESS
PECCARIES
PECCARY
PECCATION
PECCAVI
PECE
PECH
PECHAN
PECHAY
PECHILI
PECHT
PECHYS
PECIFY

PECITE
PECK
PECKAGE
PECKED
PECKER
PECKERWOOD
PECKET
PECKHAMITE
PECKIER
PECKIEST
PECKINESS
PECKING
PECKISH
PECKISHLY
PECKISHNESS
PECKLE
PECKLED
PECKLY
PECKY
PECORINO
PECTASE
PECTATE
PECTEN
PECTIC
PECTIN
PECTINACEOUS
PECTINAL
PECTINASE
PECTINATE
PECTINATED
PECTINATELY
PECTINEAL
PECTINEUS
PECTINID
PECTINIFORM
PECTINITE
PECTINOUS
PECTIZABLE
PECTIZATION
PECTIZE
PECTIZED
PECTIZING
PECTOLITE
PECTORAL
PECTORALGIA
PECTORALIS
PECTORALIST
PECTORILOQUE
PECTORILOQUY
PECTOUS
PECTRON
PECTUNCULATE
PECTUS
PECUL
PECULATE
PECULATED
PECULATING
PECULATION
PECULATOR
PECULIAR
PECULIARISM
PECULIARITY
PECULIARIZE
PECULIARIZED
PECULIARLY
PECULIUM
PECUNIARY
PECUNIOSITY
PECUNIOUS
PED
PEDA
PEDAGE
PEDAGESE
PEDAGOG
PEDAGOGIC

PEDAGOGICAL
PEDAGOGICS
PEDAGOGISM
PEDAGOGIST
PEDAGOGUE
PEDAGOGUERY
PEDAGOGUISH
PEDAGOGY
PEDAL
PEDALED
PEDALER
PEDALFER
PEDALIAN
PEDALIER
PEDALING
PEDALIST
PEDALITER
PEDALITY
PEDALLED
PEDALLER
PEDANT
PEDANTESS
PEDANTIC
PEDANTICAL
PEDANTICALLY
PEDANTICISM
PEDANTISM
PEDANTIZE
PEDANTOCRACY
PEDANTOCRAT
PEDANTRY
PEDARY
PEDATE
PEDATED
PEDATELY
PEDATIFID
PEDATIFORM
PEDATILOBATE
PEDATILOBED
PEDATINERVED
PEDATISECT
PEDATISECTED
PEDATROPHIA
PEDATROPHY
PEDDER
PEDDLE
PEDDLED
PEDDLER
PEDDLERY
PEDDLING
PEDDLINGLY
PEDEE
PEDELION
PEDERAST
PEDERASTIC
PEDERASTY
PEDERERO
PEDES
PEDESIS
PEDESTAL
PEDESTALED
PEDESTALING
PEDESTALLED
PEDESTALLING
PEDESTRIAL
PEDESTRIALLY
PEDESTRIAN
PEDETENTOUS
PEDIAL
PEDIALGIA
PEDIATRIC
PEDIATRICIAN
PEDIATRICS
PEDIATRIST
PEDIATRY
PEDICAB
PEDICEL

PEDICELED
PEDICELLAR
PEDICELLARIA
PEDICELLATE
PEDICELLATED
PEDICELLED
PEDICLE
PEDICULAR
PEDICULATE
PEDICULATED
PEDICULE
PEDICULICIDE
PEDICULOSIS
PEDICULOUS
PEDICURE
PEDICURED
PEDICURING
PEDICURISM
PEDICURIST
PEDIFORM
PEDIGEROUS
PEDIGRAIC
PEDIGREE
PEDIGREED
PEDILUVIUM
PEDIMENT
PEDIMENTAL
PEDIMENTED
PEDIMENTUM
PEDION
PEDIONOMITE
PEDIPALP
PEDIPALPAL
PEDIPALPATE
PEDIPALPUS
PEDIPULATE
PEDIPULATION
PEDIPULATOR
PEDIWAK
PEDLAR
PEDLARY
PEDLER
PEDOBAPTISM
PEDOBAPTIST
PEDODONTIA
PEDODONTIC
PEDODONTIST
PEDOGRAPH
PEDOLOGICAL
PEDOLOGIST
PEDOLOGY
PEDOMANCY
PEDOMANIA
PEDOMETER
PEDOMETRICAL
PEDOMETRIST
PEDOMORPHIC
PEDOMORPHISM
PEDOMOTIVE
PEDOMOTOR
PEDOPHILIA
PEDOPHILIC
PEDOSPHERE
PEDOSPHERIC
PEDOTRIBE
PEDOTROPHIC
PEDOTROPHIST
PEDOTROPHY
PEDRAIL
PEDREGAL
PEDRERO
PEDRO
PEDROS
PEDULE
PEDUM
PEDUNCLE
PEDUNCLED

PEDUNCULAR
PEDUNCULATE
PEDUNCULATED
PEDUNCULI
PEDUNCULUS
PEE
PEEBEEN
PEEBLES
PEED
PEEING
PEEK
PEEKABOO
PEEKED
PEEKING
PEEL
PEELCROW
PEELE
PEELED
PEELEDNESS
PEELER
PEELHOUSE
PEELING
PEELMAN
PEELS
PEEN
PEENED
PEENGE
PEENING
PEEOY
PEEP
PEEPED
PEEPER
PEEPEYE
PEEPHOLE
PEEPING
PEEPUL
PEEPY
PEER
PEERAGE
PEERDOM
PEERED
PEERESS
PEERIE
PEERING
PEERLESS
PEERLESSLY
PEERLESSNESS
PEERLING
PEERLY
PEERT
PEERY
PEES
PEESASH
PEESEWEEP
PEESOREH
PEESWEEP
PEETWEET
PEEVE
PEEVED
PEEVEDLY
PEEVEDNESS
PEEVER
PEEVERS
PEEVING
PEEVISH
PEEVISHLY
PEEVISHNESS
PEEWEE
PEEWEEP
PEG
PEGA
PEGADOR
PEGALL
PEGANITE
PEGBOARD
PEGBOX
PEGGED

PEGGER
PEGGING
PEGGLE
PEGGY
PEGGYMAST
PEGH
PEGMA
PEGMAN
PEGMATITE
PEGMATITIC
PEGMATIZE
PEGMATOID
PEGMATOPHYRE
PEGME
PEGMEN
PEGOLOGY
PEGOMANCY
PEGROOTS
PEGWOOD
PEHO
PEIGNOIR
PEIKTHA
PEINE
PEIRAMETER
PEIRASTIC
PEIS
PEISAGE
PEISANT
PEISE
PEISER
PEIXERE
PEIXEREY
PEIZE
PEJERREY
PEJORATE
PEJORATION
PEJORATIVE
PEJORATIVELY
PEJORISM
PEJORIST
PEJORITY
PEKAN
PEKIN
PEKOE
PEKOK
PEL
PELA
PELADE
PELADIC
PELADO
PELADORE
PELAGE
PELAGIAL
PELAGIAN
PELAGIC
PELAGRA
PELAMYD
PELANOS
PELARGIC
PELARGONATE
PELARGONIC
PELARGONIDIN
PELARGONIN
PELARGONIUM
PELEAN
PELECAN
PELELITH
PELELIU
PELENG
PELERIN
PELERINE
PELETRE
PELF
PELICAN
PELICANRY
PELICK
PELICOMETER

PELIKE
PELIOM
PELIOMA
PELIOSIS
PELISSE
PELITE
PELITIC
PELL
PELLAGE
PELLAGRA
PELLAGRIN
PELLAGROSE
PELLAGROUS
PELLAR
PELLARD
PELLAS
PELLATE
PELLATION
PELLER
PELLET
PELLETED
PELLETIERINE
PELLETING
PELLETS
PELLETY
PELLICLE
PELLICULAR
PELLICULATE
PELLILE
PELLITORIES
PELLITORY
PELLMELL
PELLOCK
PELLOTIN
PELLOTINE
PELLUCID
PELLUCIDLY
PELLUCIDNESS
PELMA
PELMATA
PELMATIC
PELMATOGRAM
PELMET
PELOG
PELOID
PELOK
PELON
PELOPEA
PELORIA
PELORIAN
PELORIATE
PELORIC
PELORISM
PELORIZATION
PELORIZE
PELORUS
PELOTA
PELOTAS
PELOTHERAPY
PELOTON
PELT
PELTA
PELTAE
PELTAST
PELTATE
PELTATED
PELTATELY
PELTATION
PELTER
PELTERER
PELTIFEROUS
PELTIFOLIOUS
PELTIFORM
PELTIGERINE
PELTIGEROUS
PELTINERVATE
PELTINERVED

PELTING
PELTINGLY
PELTISH
PELTMONGER
PELTRIES
PELTRY
PELU
PELUDO
PELURE
PELVES
PELVIC
PELVIFORM
PELVIGRAPH
PELVIGRAPHY
PELVIMETER
PELVIMETRIC
PELVIMETRY
PELVIOPLASTY
PELVIOSCOPY
PELVIOTOMY
PELVIRECTAL
PELVIS
PELVISES
PELVISTERNAL
PELVISTERNUM
PELYCOGRAM
PELYCOGRAPHY
PELYCOLOGY
PELYCOMETER
PELYCOMETRY
PEMBINA
PEMBROKE
PEMICAN
PEMMICAN
PEMMICANIZE
PEMPHIGOID
PEMPHIGOUS
PEMPHIGUS
PEMPHIX
PEN
PENACUTE
PENAL
PENALISE
PENALIST
PENALITY
PENALIZATION
PENALIZE
PENALIZED
PENALIZING
PENALLY
PENALTIES
PENALTY
PENANCE
PENANCED
PENANCER
PENANCING
PENANCY
PENANG
PENANNULAR
PENATES
PENBARD
PENCATITE
PENCE
PENCEL
PENCEY
PENCH
PENCHANT
PENCHE
PENCHUTE
PENCIL
PENCILED
PENCILER
PENCILIFORM
PENCILING
PENCILLED
PENCILLER
PENCILLIKE

PENCILLING
PENCILRY
PENCILWOOD
PENCLERK
PENCRAFT
PEND
PENDA
PENDANT
PENDANTED
PENDANTING
PENDELOQUE
PENDENCY
PENDENT
PENDENTIVE
PENDENTLY
PENDICLE
PENDICLER
PENDING
PENDLE
PENDOM
PENDRAGON
PENDRAGONISH
PENDULANT
PENDULAR
PENDULATE
PENDULE
PENDULINE
PENDULOSITY
PENDULOUS
PENDULOUSLY
PENDULUM
PENDULUMS
PENE
PENEID
PENEPLAIN
PENEPLANE
PENES
PENESEISMIC
PENEST
PENETRABLE
PENETRABLY
PENETRAL
PENETRALIA
PENETRALIAN
PENETRANCE
PENETRANCY
PENETRANT
PENETRATE
PENETRATED
PENETRATING
PENETRATION
PENETRATIVE
PENETRATOR
PENETROLOGY
PENETROMETER
PENFIELDITE
PENFUL
PENGHULU
PENGO
PENGOS
PENGUIN
PENGUINERY
PENGUN
PENHEAD
PENHOLDER
PENIAL
PENIBLE
PENICILLATE
PENICILLATED
PENICILLIN
PENICILLIUM
PENIDE
PENILE
PENINSULA
PENINSULAR
PENINSULATE
PENINTIME

PENINVARIANT
PENIS
PENISES
PENISTONE
PENITENCE
PENITENCER
PENITENT
PENITENTIAL
PENITENTIARIES
PENITENTIARY
PENITENTLY
PENK
PENKEEPER
PENKNIFE
PENKNIVES
PENLITE
PENLOP
PENMAKER
PENMAKING
PENMAN
PENMANSHIP
PENMASTER
PENMEN
PENNA
PENNACEOUS
PENNAE
PENNAGE
PENNANT
PENNATE
PENNATED
PENNATULID
PENNATULOID
PENNED
PENNEECH
PENNEECK
PENNER
PENNI
PENNIA
PENNIED
PENNIES
PENNIFEROUS
PENNIFORM
PENNIGEROUS
PENNILESS
PENNILESSLY
PENNILL
PENNINE
PENNINERVATE
PENNINERVED
PENNING
PENNINITE
PENNIPOTENT
PENNIS
PENNIVEINED
PENNON
PENNONCEL
PENNONCELLE
PENNONED
PENNOPLUMA
PENNOPLUME
PENNORTH
PENNY
PENNYBIRD
PENNYCRESS
PENNYEARTH
PENNYFLOWER
PENNYHOLE
PENNYLAND
PENNYLEAF
PENNYROT
PENNYROYAL
PENNYSILLER
PENNYSTONE
PENNYWEIGHT
PENNYWINKLE
PENNYWORT
PENNYWORTH

PENOCHI
PENOLOGIC
PENOLOGICAL
PENOLOGIES
PENOLOGIST
PENOLOGY
PENONCEL
PENORCON
PENOUN
PENRACK
PENROSEITE
PENS
PENSCRIPT
PENSE
PENSEE
PENSEFUL
PENSEFULNESS
PENSEROSO
PENSHIP
PENSIL
PENSILE
PENSILENESS
PENSILITY
PENSION
PENSIONABLE
PENSIONARIES
PENSIONARY
PENSIONED
PENSIONER
PENSIONING
PENSIONNAIRE
PENSIONNAT
PENSIVE
PENSIVED
PENSIVELY
PENSIVENESS
PENSTEMON
PENSTER
PENSTICK
PENSTOCK
PENSUM
PENSY
PENT
PENTABASIC
PENTABROMIDE
PENTACAPSULAR
PENTACARBON
PENTACE
PENTACETATE
PENTACHENIUM
PENTACHLORIDE
PENTACHORD
PENTACHROMIC
PENTACID
PENTACLE
PENTACOCCOUS
PENTACONTANE
PENTACOSANE
PENTACRINITE
PENTACRINOID
PENTACRON
PENTACROSTIC
PENTACTINAL
PENTACTINE
PENTACULAR
PENTACYCLIC
PENTAD
PENTADACTYL
PENTADACTYLE
PENTADECAGON
PENTADECANE
PENTADECOIC
PENTADECYL
PENTADICITY
PENTADRACHM
PENTADRACHMA
PENTAFID

PENTAGAMIST
PENTAGLOSSAL
PENTAGLOT
PENTAGON
PENTAGONAL
PENTAGONALLY
PENTAGONOID
PENTAGONON
PENTAGRAM
PENTAGYN
PENTAGYNIAN
PENTAGYNOUS
PENTAHALIDE
PENTAHEDRA
PENTAHEDRAL
PENTAHEDROID
PENTAHEDRON
PENTAHEDROUS
PENTAHYDRATE
PENTAHYDRIC
PENTAIL
PENTAIODIDE
PENTALOBATE
PENTALOGUE
PENTALOGY
PENTALPHA
PENTAMERAL
PENTAMERAN
PENTAMERID
PENTAMERISM
PENTAMEROID
PENTAMEROUS
PENTAMERY
PENTAMETER
PENTAMETRIST
PENTAMETRIZE
PENTANDER
PENTANDRIAN
PENTANDROUS
PENTANE
PENTANGLE
PENTANGULAR
PENTANITRATE
PENTANOLIDE
PENTANONE
PENTAPLOID
PENTAPLOIDIC
PENTAPLOIDY
PENTAPODY
PENTAPOLIS
PENTAPOLITAN
PENTAPTEROUS
PENTAPTOTE
PENTAPTYCH
PENTARCH
PENTARCHICAL
PENTARCHIES
PENTARCHY
PENTASILICATE
PENTASPHERIC
PENTASTICH
PENTASTICHY
PENTASTYLE
PENTASTYLOS
PENTATEUCHAL
PENTATHIONIC
PENTATHLETE
PENTATHLON
PENTATHLOS
PENTATOMIC
PENTATOMID
PENTATONE
PENTATONIC
PENTAVALENCE
PENTAVALENCY
PENTAVALENT
PENTECONTER

PENTECOSTAL
PENTECOSTYS
PENTENE
PENTETERIC
PENTHEMIMER
PENTHIOPHENE
PENTHOUSE
PENTHOUSED
PENTHOUSING
PENTICLE
PENTILE
PENTIMENTO
PENTINE
PENTIT
PENTITOL
PENTLANDITE
PENTODE
PENTOIC
PENTOMIC
PENTOSAN
PENTOSANE
PENTOSE
PENTOSID
PENTOSIDE
PENTOSURIA
PENTOXIDE
PENTREMITAL
PENTREMITE
PENTROUGH
PENTSTEMON
PENTSTOCK
PENTYL
PENTYLENE
PENTYLIC
PENTYNE
PENUCHE
PENUCHI
PENUCHLE
PENUCKLE
PENULT
PENULTIMA
PENULTIMATE
PENUMBRA
PENUMBRAE
PENUMBRAL
PENUMBRAS
PENUMBROUS
PENURIOUS
PENURIOUSLY
PENURY
PENWIPER
PENWOMAN
PENWOMANSHIP
PENWOMEN
PENWORK
PENWORKER
PENWRIGHT
PEON
PEONAGE
PEONES
PEONIES
PEONISM
PEONY
PEOPLE
PEOPLED
PEOPLEIZE
PEOPLER
PEOPLES
PEOPLET
PEOPLING
PEOPLISH
PEOTOMY
PEP
PEPEREK
PEPERINE
PEPERINO
PEPERONI

PEPINELLA
PEPINO
PEPLOS
PEPLOSED
PEPLUM
PEPLUMS
PEPLUS
PEPO
PEPON
PEPONIDA
PEPONIUM
PEPOS
PEPPED
PEPPER
PEPPERBOX
PEPPERCORN
PEPPERED
PEPPERER
PEPPERGRASS
PEPPERIDGE
PEPPERING
PEPPERMINT
PEPPERONI
PEPPERROOT
PEPPERS
PEPPERWEED
PEPPERWOOD
PEPPERWORT
PEPPERY
PEPPILY
PEPPIN
PEPPINESS
PEPPING
PEPPY
PEPSIN
PEPSINATE
PEPSINATED
PEPSINATING
PEPSINE
PEPSINOGEN
PEPSIS
PEPTIC
PEPTICAL
PEPTICITY
PEPTIDASE
PEPTIDE
PEPTIZABLE
PEPTIZATION
PEPTIZE
PEPTIZED
PEPTIZER
PEPTIZING
PEPTOGASTER
PEPTONATE
PEPTONE
PEPTONIC
PEPTONIZE
PEPTONIZED
PEPTONIZER
PEPTONIZING
PEPTONOID
PEPTOTOXINE
PER
PERACEPHALUS
PERACID
PERACIDITE
PERACIDITY
PERACT
PERACUTE
PERADVENTURE
PERAGRATE
PERAGRATION
PERAMBLE
PERAMBULANT
PERAMBULATE
PERAMBULATED
PERAMBULATION

PERAMBULATOR
PERAMELINE
PERAMELOID
PERAU
PERBORATE
PERBROMIDE
PERCALE
PERCALINE
PERCARBONIC
PERCASE
PERCEANT
PERCEIVABLE
PERCEIVABLY
PERCEIVANCE
PERCEIVE
PERCEIVED
PERCEIVER
PERCEIVING
PERCENTABLE
PERCENTABLY
PERCENTAGE
PERCENTAGED
PERCENTAL
PERCENTILE
PERCENTS
PERCENTUAL
PERCENTUM
PERCEPT
PERCEPTIBLE
PERCEPTIBLY
PERCEPTION
PERCEPTIONAL
PERCEPTIVE
PERCEPTIVELY
PERCEPTIVITY
PERCEPTUAL
PERCEPTUALLY
PERCEPTUM
PERCESOCINE
PERCH
PERCHANCE
PERCHE
PERCHED
PERCHER
PERCHES
PERCHING
PERCHLORATE
PERCHLORIC
PERCHLORIDE
PERCHROMATE
PERCHROMIC
PERCID
PERCIFORM
PERCIPI
PERCIPIENCE
PERCIPIENCY
PERCIPIENT
PERCLOSE
PERCNOSOME
PERCOCT
PERCOID
PERCOIDEAN
PERCOLATE
PERCOLATION
PERCOLATIVE
PERCOLATOR
PERCOMORPH
PERCONTATION
PERCONTATORIAL
PERCRIBRATE
PERCRIBRATION
PERCULSION
PERCULSIVE
PERCUR
PERCURRATION
PERCURRENT
PERCURSORY

PERCUSS
PERCUSSION
PERCUSSIONAL
PERCUSSIONER
PERCUSSIVE
PERCUSSIVELY
PERCUSSOR
PERCUTANEOUS
PERCUTIENT
PERCYLITE
PERDENDO
PERDENDOSI
PERDIE
PERDILIGENCE
PERDILIGENT
PERDIT
PERDITION
PERDRICIDE
PERDRIGON
PERDU
PERDUE
PERDUELLION
PERDURABLE
PERDURABLY
PERDURANCE
PERDURANT
PERDURE
PERDURED
PERDURING
PERDURINGLY
PERDY
PERE
PEREGRIN
PEREGRINA
PEREGRINATE
PEREGRINATED
PEREGRINATOR
PEREGRINE
PEREGRINITY
PEREGRINOID
PEREGRINUS
PEREION
PEREIOPOD
PEREIRA
PEREIRINE
PEREJONET
PEREJONETTE
PEREMPT
PEREMPTION
PEREMPTORILY
PEREMPTORY
PERENDINANT
PERENDINATE
PERENDURE
PERENNATE
PERENNATION
PERENNIAL
PERENNIALITY
PERENNIALIZE
PERENNIALLY
PERENNIBRANCH
PEREQUITATE
PERES
PEREUNDEM
PEREZONE
PERFAY
PERFECT
PERFECTATION
PERFECTED
PERFECTER
PERFECTI
PERFECTIBLE
PERFECTING
PERFECTION
PERFECTIONER
PERFECTIONIST
PERFECTISM

PERFECTIST
PERFECTIVE
PERFECTIVELY
PERFECTIVIZE
PERFECTLY
PERFECTNESS
PERFECTO
PERFECTOR
PERFECTOS
PERFERVENT
PERFERVID
PERFERVIDLY
PERFICIENT
PERFIDIES
PERFIDIOUS
PERFIDIOUSLY
PERFIDY
PERFILOGRAPH
PERFINS
PERFIX
PERFLATE
PERFLATION
PERFLUENT
PERFOLIATE
PERFOLIATION
PERFORABLE
PERFORANT
PERFORATE
PERFORATED
PERFORATING
PERFORATION
PERFORATIONS
PERFORATIVE
PERFORATOR
PERFORATORY
PERFORCE
PERFORM
PERFORMABLE
PERFORMANCE
PERFORMANCES
PERFORMANT
PERFORMATIVE
PERFORMED
PERFORMER
PERFORMING
PERFRICATION
PERFUMATORY
PERFUME
PERFUMED
PERFUMER
PERFUMERY
PERFUMES
PERFUMING
PERFUMY
PERFUNCTORY
PERFUSATE
PERFUSE
PERFUSED
PERFUSING
PERFUSION
PERFUSIVE
PERGAMENEOUS
PERGAMYN
PERGE
PERGOLA
PERGOLAS
PERHALIDE
PERHALOGEN
PERHAPS
PERHAZARD
PERHORRESCE
PERI
PERIACINAL
PERIACTUS
PERIADENITIS
PERIANAL
PERIANGIOMA

PERIANGITIS
PERIANTH
PERIANTHIAL
PERIANTHIUM
PERIAORTIC
PERIAORTITIS
PERIAPICAL
PERIAPT
PERIAREUM
PERIARTERIAL
PERIARTERITIS
PERIARTHRIC
PERIARTHRITIS
PERIARTICULAR
PERIASTRAL
PERIASTRON
PERIASTRUM
PERIATRIAL
PERIAXIAL
PERIAXILLARY
PERIAXONAL
PERIBLASTIC
PERIBLASTULA
PERIBLEM
PERIBOLOS
PERIBOLUS
PERIBULBAR
PERIBURSAL
PERICAECAL
PERICAECITIS
PERICAPSULAR
PERICARDIA
PERICARDIAC
PERICARDIAL
PERICARDIAN
PERICARDITIS
PERICARDIUM
PERICARP
PERICARPIAL
PERICARPIC
PERICECAL
PERICECITIS
PERICELLULAR
PERICEMENTAL
PERICEMENTUM
PERICENTER
PERICENTRAL
PERICENTRE
PERICENTRIC
PERICEPHALIC
PERICEREBRAL
PERICHAETE
PERICHAETIAL
PERICHAETIUM
PERICHETE
PERICHONDRAL
PERICHORD
PERICHORDAL
PERICHORESIS
PERICHYLOUS
PERICLADIUM
PERICLASE
PERICLASITE
PERICLINAL
PERICLINALLY
PERICLINE
PERICLINIUM
PERICLITATE
PERICOLITIS
PERICOLPITIS
PERICONCHAL
PERICOPAL
PERICOPE
PERICOPE
PERICOPIC
PERICORNEAL
PERICOXITIS

PERICRANIA
PERICRANIAL
PERICRANITIS
PERICRANIUM
PERICRISTATE
PERICULANT
PERICULUM
PERICYCLE
PERICYCLIC
PERICYCLOID
PERICYCLONE
PERICYCLONIC
PERICYSTIC
PERICYSTITIS
PERICYSTIUM
PERICYTIAL
PERIDERM
PERIDERMAL
PERIDERMIC
PERIDESM
PERIDESMIC
PERIDESMITIS
PERIDESMIUM
PERIDIA
PERIDIAL
PERIDIASTOLE
PERIDIDYMIS
PERIDIIFORM
PERIDINIAL
PERIDINIAN
PERIDINID
PERIDIOLE
PERIDIOLUM
PERIDIUM
PERIDOT
PERIDOTIC
PERIDOTITE
PERIDOTITIC
PERIDUCTAL
PERIEGESIS
PERIEGETIC
PERIELESIS
PERIENTERIC
PERIENTERON
PERIERGY
PERIFISTULAR
PERIFOLIARY
PERIGASTRIC
PERIGASTRULA
PERIGEAL
PERIGEAN
PERIGEE
PERIGEMMAL
PERIGENESIS
PERIGENITAL
PERIGEUM
PERIGLIAL
PERIGLOEA
PERIGLOTTIC
PERIGLOTTIS
PERIGNATHIC
PERIGON
PERIGONADIAL
PERIGONE
PERIGONIAL
PERIGONIUM
PERIGRAPH
PERIGRAPHIC
PERIGYNIAL
PERIGYNIUM
PERIGYNOUS
PERIGYNY
PERIHELIA
PERIHELIAL
PERIHELIAN
PERIHELION
PERIHEPATIC

PERIHERNIAL
PERIHYSTERIC
PERIJOVE
PERIKARYA
PERIKARYON
PERIL
PERILED
PERILING
PERILLED
PERILLING
PERILOBAR
PERILOUS
PERILOUSLY
PERILOUSNESS
PERILUNE
PERILYMPH
PERIMASTITIS
PERIMETER
PERIMETRIC
PERIMETRICAL
PERIMETRITIC
PERIMETRITIS
PERIMETRIUM
PERIMETRY
PERIMORPH
PERIMORPHIC
PERIMORPHISM
PERIMORPHOUS
PERIMYELITIS
PERIMYSIAL
PERIMYSIUM
PERINAEUM
PERINE
PERINEAL
PERINEOCELE
PERINEOSTOMY
PERINEOTOMY
PERINEPHRAL
PERINEPHRIAL
PERINEPHRIC
PERINEPHRIUM
PERINEUM
PERINEURAL
PERINEURIA
PERINEURIAL
PERINEURITIS
PERINEURIUM
PERINIUM
PERINUCLEAR
PERIOCULAR
PERIOD
PERIODATE
PERIODIC
PERIODICAL
PERIODICALLY
PERIODICALNESS
PERIODICITY
PERIODID
PERIODIDE
PERIODOGRAM
PERIODOLOGY
PERIODONTAL
PERIODONTIA
PERIODONTIC
PERIODONTICS
PERIODONTIST
PERIODONTIUM
PERIODOSCOPE
PERIOECI
PERIOECIC
PERIOECID
PERIOMPHALIC
PERIONYCHIA
PERIONYCHIUM
PERIOPLE
PERIOPLIC
PERIOQUE

PERIORAL
PERIORBIT
PERIORBITA
PERIORBITAL
PERIORCHITIS
PERIOSTEAL
PERIOSTEOMA
PERIOSTEOUS
PERIOSTEUM
PERIOSTITIC
PERIOSTITIS
PERIOSTOSIS
PERIOSTRACAL
PERIOSTRACUM
PERIOTIC
PERIOVULAR
PERIPATETIC
PERIPATIZE
PERIPATOID
PERIPENIAL
PERIPETALOUS
PERIPETASMA
PERIPETEIA
PERIPETIA
PERIPETY
PERIPHACITIS
PERIPHERAD
PERIPHERAL
PERIPHERALLY
PERIPHERIAL
PERIPHERIC
PERIPHERICAL
PERIPHERIES
PERIPHERY
PERIPHRACTIC
PERIPHRASE
PERIPHRASED
PERIPHRASES
PERIPHRASING
PERIPHRASIS
PERIPHRASTIC
PERIPHRAXY
PERIPHYLLUM
PERIPHYSIS
PERIPLASM
PERIPLAST
PERIPLASTIC
PERIPLEURAL
PERIPLUS
PERIPNEUSTIC
PERIPOLAR
PERIPORTAL
PERIPROCT
PERIPROCTAL
PERIPROCTOUS
PERIPTER
PERIPTERAL
PERIPTEROI
PERIPTEROS
PERIPTEROUS
PERIPTERY
PERIPYLORIC
PERIQUE
PERIRECTAL
PERIRECTITIS
PERIRENAL
PERIRHINAL
PERIS
PERISARC
PERISARCAL
PERISARCOUS
PERISCIANS
PERISCII
PERISCOPAL
PERISCOPE
PERISCOPIC
PERISCOPICAL

PERISH
PERISHABLE
PERISHABLY
PERISHED
PERISHING
PERISHINGLY
PERISINUITIS
PERISINUOUS
PERISOMA
PERISOMAL
PERISOMATIC
PERISOME
PERISOMIAL
PERISPERM
PERISPERMAL
PERISPERMIC
PERISPHERE
PERISPHERIC
PERISPLENIC
PERISPOMENA
PERISPOMENON
PERISPORE
PERISSAD
PERISSOLOGIC
PERISSOLOGY
PERISTALITH
PERISTALSIS
PERISTALTIC
PERISTELE
PERISTERITE
PERISTERONIC
PERISTEROPOD
PERISTETHIUM
PERISTOLE
PERISTOMA
PERISTOMAL
PERISTOMATIC
PERISTOME
PERISTOMIAL
PERISTOMIUM
PERISTREPHIC
PERISTYLAR
PERISTYLE
PERISTYLOS
PERISYNOVIAL
PERISYSTOLE
PERISYSTOLIC
PERIT
PERITE
PERITECTIC
PERITHECE
PERITHECIAL
PERITHECIUM
PERITHELIAL
PERITHELIOMA
PERITHELIUM
PERITHORACIC
PERITOMIZE
PERITOMOUS
PERITOMY
PERITONAEA
PERITONAEAL
PERITONAEUM
PERITONEA
PERITONEAL
PERITONEALLY
PERITONEUM
PERITONISM
PERITONITAL
PERITONITIC
PERITONITIS
PERITRACHEAL
PERITREMA
PERITREME
PERITRICH
PERITRICHA
PERITRICHAN

PERITRICHIC
PERITRICHOUS
PERITROCH
PERITROCHAL
PERITROPAL
PERITROPHIC
PERITROPOUS
PERITYPHLIC
PERIUNGUAL
PERIURETERIC
PERIURETHRAL
PERIUTERINE
PERIUVULAR
PERIVAGINAL
PERIVASCULAR
PERIVENOUS
PERIVESICAL
PERIVISCERAL
PERIVITELLIN
PERIWIG
PERIWIGPATED
PERIWINKLE
PERIWINKLED
PERIWINKLER
PERIZONIUM
PERJINK
PERJINKETY
PERJINKITIES
PERJINKLY
PERJURE
PERJURED
PERJUREDLY
PERJUREDNESS
PERJURER
PERJURIES
PERJURING
PERJURIOUS
PERJURIOUSLY
PERJURY
PERK
PERKIER
PERKIEST
PERKILY
PERKIN
PERKINESS
PERKING
PERKISH
PERKNITE
PERKY
PERLACEOUS
PERLE
PERLECHE
PERLECTION
PERLID
PERLIGENOUS
PERLINGUAL
PERLINGUALLY
PERLITE
PERLITIC
PERLOIR
PERLUSTRATE
PERLUSTRATOR
PERMAFROST
PERMALLOY
PERMANENCE
PERMANENCY
PERMANENT
PERMANENTLY
PERMANGANATE
PERMANGANIC
PERMANSIVE
PERMEABILITY
PERMEABLE
PERMEABLY
PERMEAMETER
PERMEANCE
PERMEANT

PERMEATE
PERMEATED
PERMEATING
PERMEATION
PERMEATIVE
PERMEATOR
PERMILLAGE
PERMIRIFIC
PERMISS
PERMISSIBLE
PERMISSIBLY
PERMISSION
PERMISSIONED
PERMISSIVE
PERMISSIVELY
PERMISSORY
PERMIT
PERMITTABLE
PERMITTED
PERMITTEDLY
PERMITTEE
PERMITTER
PERMITTIVITY
PERMIX
PERMIXABLE
PERMIXTION
PERMIXTIVE
PERMIXTURE
PERMORALIZE
PERMUTABLE
PERMUTABLY
PERMUTATE
PERMUTATION
PERMUTATOR
PERMUTATORY
PERMUTE
PERMUTED
PERMUTER
PERMUTING
PERN
PERNANCY
PERNASAL
PERNAVIGATE
PERNICIOUS
PERNICIOUSLY
PERNICKETTY
PERNICKETY
PERNICKITY
PERNINE
PERNIO
PERNOCTATE
PERNOCTATION
PERNOR
PERO
PEROBA
PEROCHIRUS
PERODACTYLUS
PEROMELOUS
PEROMELUS
PERONATE
PERONEAL
PERONEUS
PERONIAL
PERONIUM
PEROPOD
PEROPODOUS
PEROPUS
PERORAL
PERORALLY
PERORATE
PERORATED
PERORATING
PERORATION
PERORATIONAL
PERORATIVE
PERORATOR
PERORATORY

PEROSMATE
PEROSOMUS
PEROVSKITE
PEROXIDASE
PEROXIDE
PEROXIDED
PEROXIDIC
PEROXIDING
PEROXIDIZE
PEROXY
PEROXYL
PERPEND
PERPENDICLE
PERPENDICULAR
PERPENDICULARITY
PERPENDICULARLY
PERPENSE
PERPENT
PERPERA
PERPET
PERPETRABLE
PERPETRATE
PERPETRATED
PERPETRATING
PERPETRATION
PERPETRATOR
PERPETUABLE
PERPETUAL
PERPETUALIST
PERPETUALLY
PERPETUANA
PERPETUANCE
PERPETUANT
PERPETUATE
PERPETUATED
PERPETUATING
PERPETUATION
PERPETUATOR
PERPETUITY
PERPLANTAR
PERPLEX
PERPLEXED
PERPLEXEDLY
PERPLEXER
PERPLEXING
PERPLEXINGLY
PERPLEXITIES
PERPLEXITY
PERPLICATION
PERQUADRAT
PERQUEER
PERQUEERLY
PERQUEIR
PERQUEST
PERQUISITE
PERQUISITION
PERQUISITOR
PERRADIAL
PERRADIALLY
PERRADIATE
PERRADIUS
PERRIE
PERRIER
PERRON
PERRUCHE
PERRUQUIER
PERRUTHENATE
PERRY
PERRYMAN
PERSALT
PERSCRIBE
PERSCRUTATE
PERSCRUTATOR
PERSE
PERSECUTE
PERSECUTED
PERSECUTEE

PERSECUTING
PERSECUTION
PERSECUTIVE
PERSECUTOR
PERSECUTORY
PERSEITE
PERSEITOL
PERSEITY
PERSEVERANCE
PERSEVERANT
PERSEVERATE
PERSEVERE
PERSEVERED
PERSEVERING
PERSICARIA
PERSICARY
PERSICO
PERSICOT
PERSIENNE
PERSIENNES
PERSIFLAGE
PERSIFLATE
PERSIFLEUR
PERSILICIC
PERSILLADE
PERSIMMON
PERSIO
PERSIS
PERSIST
PERSISTENCE
PERSISTENCY
PERSISTENT
PERSISTENTLY
PERSISTER
PERSISTINGLY
PERSISTIVE
PERSISTIVELY
PERSNICKETY
PERSOLVE
PERSON
PERSONA
PERSONABLE
PERSONABLY
PERSONAE
PERSONAGE
PERSONAL
PERSONALIA
PERSONALISM
PERSONALIST
PERSONALITY
PERSONALIZE
PERSONALIZED
PERSONALLY
PERSONALTIES
PERSONALTY
PERSONATE
PERSONATED
PERSONATING
PERSONATION
PERSONATIVE
PERSONATOR
PERSONED
PERSONEITY
PERSONIFIANT
PERSONIFICATION
PERSONIFY
PERSONIFYING
PERSONIZE
PERSONNEL
PERSONS
PERSPECTIVE
PERSPECTIVED
PERSPICACIOUS
PERSPICACITY
PERSPICUITY
PERSPICUOUS
PERSPIRABLE

PERSPIRANT
PERSPIRATION
PERSPIRATIVE
PERSPIRATORY
PERSPIRE
PERSPIRED
PERSPIRING
PERSPIRY
PERSTAND
PERSTRINGE
PERSTRINGED
PERSUADABLE
PERSUADABLY
PERSUADE
PERSUADED
PERSUADER
PERSUADING
PERSUASIBLE
PERSUASIBLY
PERSUASION
PERSUASIVE
PERSUASIVELY
PERSUASORY
PERSUE
PERSULFATE
PERSULPHATE
PERSULPHIDE
PERSULPHURIC
PERT
PERTAIN
PERTAINING
PERTEN
PERTENENCIA
PERTHITE
PERTHOSITE
PERTINACIOUS
PERTINACITY
PERTINENCE
PERTINENCY
PERTINENT
PERTINENTIA
PERTINENTLY
PERTLY
PERTNESS
PERTURB
PERTURBABLE
PERTURBANCE
PERTURBANCY
PERTURBANT
PERTURBATE
PERTURBATION
PERTURBATIVE
PERTURBATOR
PERTURBATORY
PERTURBED
PERTURBEDLY
PERTURBER
PERTURBING
PERTUSE
PERTUSED
PERTUSION
PERTUSSAL
PERTUSSIS
PERUKE
PERUKER
PERUKERY
PERUKIER
PERULA
PERULATE
PERULE
PERUSABLE
PERUSAL
PERUSE
PERUSED
PERUSER
PERUSING
PERVADE

PERVADED
PERVADENCE
PERVADER
PERVADING
PERVADINGLY
PERVAGATE
PERVAGATION
PERVALVAR
PERVASION
PERVASIVE
PERVASIVELY
PERVENCHE
PERVERSE
PERVERSELY
PERVERSENESS
PERVERSION
PERVERSITIES
PERVERSITY
PERVERSIVE
PERVERT
PERVERTED
PERVERTEDLY
PERVERTER
PERVERTIBLE
PERVERTIBLY
PERVERTING
PERVERTIVE
PERVIAL
PERVICACIOUS
PERVICACITY
PERVIGILIUM
PERVIOUS
PERVIOUSLY
PERVIOUSNESS
PERVULGATE
PERWICK
PERWITSKY
PERY
PES
PESA
PESADE
PESAGE
PESANTE
PESCOD
PESETA
PESHKAR
PESHKASH
PESHWA
PESKIER
PESKIEST
PESKILY
PESKINESS
PESKY
PESO
PESOS
PESS
PESSA
PESSARIES
PESSARY
PESSIMISM
PESSIMIST
PESSIMISTIC
PESSIMIZE
PESSONER
PESSULAR
PESSULUS
PEST
PESTE
PESTER
PESTERED
PESTERER
PESTERING
PESTEROUS
PESTFUL
PESTHOLE
PESTHOUSE
PESTICIDAL

PESTICIDE
PESTIDUCT
PESTIFEROUS
PESTIFUGOUS
PESTIFY
PESTILENCE
PESTILENT
PESTILENTIAL
PESTILENTLY
PESTIS
PESTLE
PESTLED
PESTLING
PESTO
PESTOLOGICAL
PESTOLOGIST
PESTOLOGY
PET
PETA
PETAL
PETALAGE
PETALED
PETALIFEROUS
PETALINE
PETALING
PETALISM
PETALITE
PETALLED
PETALLING
PETALOCEROUS
PETALODIC
PETALODONT
PETALODONTID
PETALODY
PETALOID
PETALOIDEOUS
PETALON
PETALOUS
PETALY
PETARA
PETARD
PETARDING
PETASMA
PETASOS
PETASUS
PETATE
PETAURINE
PETAURIST
PETCHARY
PETCOCK
PETE
PETECA
PETECHIA
PETECHIAE
PETECHIAL
PETECHIATE
PETEGREU
PETEMAN
PETER
PETERED
PETERERO
PETERING
PETERMAN
PETERMEN
PETERNET
PETERSHAM
PETFUL
PETHER
PETIOLAR
PETIOLATE
PETIOLATED
PETIOLE
PETIOLED
PETIOLI
PETIOLULAR
PETIOLULATE
PETIOLULE

PETIOLUS
PETIT
PETITE
PETITGRAIN
PETITION
PETITIONAL
PETITIONARY
PETITIONED
PETITIONEE
PETITIONER
PETITIONING
PETITIONIST
PETITOR
PETITORY
PETKIN
PETLING
PETO
PETRARY
PETRE
PETREAN
PETREITY
PETREL
PETRESCENCE
PETRESCENCY
PETRESCENT
PETRICOLOUS
PETRIE
PETRIFACTION
PETRIFACTIVE
PETRIFIABLE
PETRIFIC
PETRIFIED
PETRIFIER
PETRIFY
PETRIFYING
PETRISSAGE
PETROGENESIS
PETROGENIC
PETROGENY
PETROGLYPH
PETROGLYPHIC
PETROGLYPHY
PETROGRAPH
PETROGRAPHER
PETROGRAPHIC
PETROGRAPHY
PETROHYOID
PETROL
PETROLAGE
PETROLATUM
PETROLEAN
PETROLENE
PETROLEOUS
PETROLEUM
PETROLEUR
PETROLEUSE
PETROLIC
PETROLIFIC
PETROLIST
PETROLITHIC
PETROLIZE
PETROLIZED
PETROLIZING
PETROLOGIC
PETROLOGICAL
PETROLOGIST
PETROLOGY
PETROMASTOID
PETRONEL
PETRONELLA
PETRONELLIER
PETROSA
PETROSAL
PETROSILEX
PETROSTEARIN
PETROUS
PETROXOLIN

PETTABLE
PETTAH
PETTED
PETTEDLY
PETTEDNESS
PETTER
PETTI
PETTIAGUA
PETTICHAPS
PETTICOAT
PETTICOATED
PETTICOATERY
PETTICOATING
PETTICOATISM
PETTIER
PETTIEST
PETTIFOG
PETTIFOGGED
PETTIFOGGER
PETTIFOGGERY
PETTIFOGGING
PETTILY
PETTINESS
PETTING
PETTISH
PETTISHLY
PETTISHNESS
PETTITOES
PETTLE
PETTLED
PETTLING
PETTO
PETTY
PETTYFOG
PETTYGOD
PETULANCE
PETULANCY
PETULANT
PETULANTLY
PETUN
PETUNE
PETUNIA
PETUNSE
PETUNTZE
PETWOOD
PETZITE
PEUCITES
PEUGH
PEULVAN
PEVA
PEW
PEWAGE
PEWEE
PEWFELLOW
PEWHOLDER
PEWING
PEWIT
PEWKE
PEWMATE
PEWTER
PEWTERER
PEWTERWORT
PEWTERY
PEWY
PEY
PEYOTE
PEYOTISM
PEYOTL
PEYTON
PEZANTIC
PEZIZACEOUS
PEZIZAEFORM
PEZIZIFORM
PEZIZOID
PEZOGRAPH
PEZZO
PFEFFERNUSS

PFENNIG
PFENNIGE
PFENNIGS
PFIFF
PFUI
PFUND
PFUNDE
PHACELITE
PHACELLA
PHACELLITE
PHACELLUS
PHACITIS
PHACOCELE
PHACOCHERE
PHACOCHOERE
PHACOCYST
PHACOID
PHACOIDAL
PHACOLITE
PHACOLITH
PHACOLYSIS
PHACOMETER
PHACOPID
PHACOSCOPE
PHAEISM
PHAENANTHERY
PHAENOLOGY
PHAEOCHROUS
PHAEOPHORE
PHAEOPHYL
PHAEOPHYLL
PHAEOPHYTIN
PHAEOPLAST
PHAEOSPORE
PHAEOSPOROUS
PHAET
PHAETON
PHAGEDAENA
PHAGEDAENIC
PHAGEDAENICAL
PHAGEDAENOUS
PHAGEDENA
PHAGEDENIC
PHAGEDENICAL
PHAGEDENOUS
PHAGOCYTABLE
PHAGOCYTAL
PHAGOCYTE
PHAGOCYTER
PHAGOCYTIC
PHAGOCYTISM
PHAGOCYTIZE
PHAGOCYTOSE
PHAGOCYTOSED
PHAGOCYTOSIS
PHAGOLYSIS
PHAGOMANIA
PHALACROSIS
PHALAENOPSID
PHALANGAL
PHALANGE
PHALANGEAL
PHALANGEAN
PHALANGER
PHALANGES
PHALANGETTE
PHALANGIAN
PHALANGID
PHALANGIDAN
PHALANGIDEAN
PHALANGIFORM
PHALANGIST
PHALANGITE
PHALANSTERIC
PHALANSTERY
PHALANX
PHALANXED

PHALANXES
PHALARICA
PHALAROPE
PHALERA
PHALERAE
PHALERATE
PHALERATED
PHALLACEOUS
PHALLALGIA
PHALLEPHORIC
PHALLIC
PHALLICAL
PHALLICISM
PHALLICIST
PHALLIN
PHALLISM
PHALLIST
PHALLITIS
PHALLODYNIA
PHALLOID
PHALLONCUS
PHALLOPLASTY
PHALLUS
PHAN
PHANERIC
PHANERITE
PHANEROCRYST
PHANEROGAM
PHANEROGAMY
PHANEROGENIC
PHANEROMERE
PHANEROSCOPE
PHANEROSIS
PHANEROZOIC
PHANIC
PHANO
PHANSIGAR
PHANTASCOPE
PHANTASIA
PHANTASIES
PHANTASIZE
PHANTASM
PHANTASMA
PHANTASMAL
PHANTASMALLY
PHANTASMATA
PHANTASMATIC
PHANTASMIC
PHANTAST
PHANTASY
PHANTIC
PHANTOM
PHANTOMATIC
PHANTOMIC
PHANTOMIZE
PHANTOMIZER
PHANTOMRY
PHANTOMY
PHANTOSCOPE
PHARE
PHARISAICAL
PHARISAISM
PHARISEE
PHARMACAL
PHARMACEUTIC
PHARMACIC
PHARMACIES
PHARMACIST
PHARMACITE
PHARMACOLITE
PHARMACOLOGY
PHARMACON
PHARMACY
PHARMAKOI
PHARMAKOS
PHARMIC
PHARO

PHAROLOGY
PHAROS
PHARYNGAL
PHARYNGEAL
PHARYNGES
PHARYNGIC
PHARYNGISMUS
PHARYNGITIS
PHARYNGOCELE
PHARYNGOLITH
PHARYNGOLOGY
PHARYNGOTOME
PHARYNGOTOMY
PHARYNX
PHARYNXES
PHASCACEOUS
PHASCOLOME
PHASE
PHASEAL
PHASED
PHASELIN
PHASEMETER
PHASEMY
PHASEOLIN
PHASEOLOUS
PHASES
PHASIANIC
PHASIANID
PHASIANINE
PHASIANOID
PHASIC
PHASING
PHASIS
PHASM
PHASMA
PHASMATID
PHASMATOID
PHASMATROPE
PHASOGENEOUS
PHASOR
PHASOTROPY
PHAT
PHEAL
PHEALE
PHEARSE
PHEASANT
PHEASANTRY
PHEASANTS
PHEBE
PHEEAL
PHEER
PHELLANDRENE
PHELLEM
PHELLODERM
PHELLODERMAL
PHELLOGEN
PHELLOGENIC
PHELLOPLASTIC
PHEMIC
PHENACAINE
PHENACETIN
PHENACETINE
PHENACETURIC
PHENACITE
PHENACYL
PHENAKISM
PHENANTHRENE
PHENANTHROL
PHENARSINE
PHENAZIN
PHENAZINE
PHENAZONE
PHENE
PHENENE
PHENETHYL
PHENETIDINE
PHENETOL

PHENETOLE
PHENGITE
PHENGITICAL
PHENIC
PHENICATE
PHENICIOUS
PHENICOPTER
PHENIN
PHENINE
PHENIX
PHENMIAZINE
PHENOBARBITOL
PHENOCOLL
PHENOCOPY
PHENOCRYST
PHENOGENESIS
PHENOGENETIC
PHENOL
PHENOLATE
PHENOLIC
PHENOLIZE
PHENOLOGIC
PHENOLOGICAL
PHENOLOGIST
PHENOLOGY
PHENOMENA
PHENOMENAL
PHENOMENALLY
PHENOMENON
PHENOQUINONE
PHENOSAL
PHENOSOL
PHENOSPERMY
PHENOTYPE
PHENOTYPIC
PHENOTYPICAL
PHENOXAZINE
PHENOXIDE
PHENYL
PHENYLACETIC
PHENYLAMIDE
PHENYLAMINE
PHENYLATE
PHENYLATED
PHENYLATION
PHENYLENE
PHENYLIC
PHEON
PHEOPHYTIN
PHERETRER
PHEW
PHI
PHIAL
PHIALE
PHIALED
PHIALINE
PHIALING
PHIALLED
PHIALLING
PHILABEG
PHILADELPHITE
PHILADELPHY
PHILALETHIST
PHILAMOT
PHILANDER
PHILANDERED
PHILANDERER
PHILANDERING
PHILANTHID
PHILANTHROPE
PHILANTHROPIC
PHILANTHROPIST
PHILANTHROPY
PHILANTOMBA
PHILARCHAIST
PHILATELIC
PHILATELIST

PHILATELY
PHILATHLETIC
PHILAUTY
PHILHARMONIC
PHILHELLENE
PHILHELLENIC
PHILHIPPIC
PHILHYMNIC
PHILIA
PHILIATER
PHILIBEG
PHILINE
PHILIPPICIZE
PHILIPPIZE
PHILIPPIZER
PHILIPPUS
PHILLILEW
PHILLILOO
PHILLIPEENER
PHILLIPSINE
PHILLIPSITE
PHILLYRIN
PHILOBIBLIAN
PHILOBIBLIC
PHILOBIBLICAL
PHILOBIBLIST
PHILOBOTANIC
PHILOBRUTISH
PHILOCALIC
PHILOCALIST
PHILOCALY
PHILOCOMAL
PHILOCUBIST
PHILOCYNIC
PHILOCYNICAL
PHILOCYNY
PHILODEMIC
PHILODENDRON
PHILODESPOT
PHILODOX
PHILODOXER
PHILODOXICAL
PHILOFELIST
PHILOFELON
PHILOGARLIC
PHILOGASTRIC
PHILOGEANT
PHILOGRAPH
PHILOGRAPHIC
PHILOGYNIST
PHILOGYNOUS
PHILOGYNY
PHILOKLEPTIC
PHILOLOGER
PHILOLOGIC
PHILOLOGICAL
PHILOLOGIST
PHILOLOGIZE
PHILOLOGUE
PHILOLOGY
PHILOMATH
PHILOMATHIC
PHILOMATHY
PHILOME
PHILOMEL
PHILOMELIAN
PHILOMUSE
PHILOMUSICAL
PHILOMYSTIC
PHILOMYTHIA
PHILOMYTHIC
PHILONATURAL
PHILONEISM
PHILONIST
PHILONIUM
PHILONOIST
PHILOPAGAN

PHILOPATER
PHILOPATRIAN
PHILOPENA
PHILOPIG
PHILOPOET
PHILOPOGON
PHILOPOLEMIC
PHILOPORNIST
PHILORADICAL
PHILORNITHIC
PHILOSOPH
PHILOSOPHE
PHILOSOPHEME
PHILOSOPHER
PHILOSOPHERESS
PHILOSOPHESS
PHILOSOPHIC
PHILOSOPHICAL
PHILOSOPHIES
PHILOSOPHISM
PHILOSOPHIST
PHILOSOPHIZE
PHILOSOPHY
PHILOTADPOLE
PHILOTECHNIC
PHILOTHEISM
PHILOTHEIST
PHILOTHERIAN
PHILOZOIC
PHILOZOIST
PHILOZOONIST
PHILP
PHILTER
PHILTERED
PHILTERER
PHILTERING
PHILTRE
PHILTRED
PHILTRING
PHILTRUM
PHIMOSED
PHIMOSIS
PHIMOTIC
PHIP
PHIPPE
PHIT
PHITONES
PHIZ
PHIZOG
PHLEBALGIA
PHLEBECTASIA
PHLEBECTASIS
PHLEBECTASY
PHLEBECTOMY
PHLEBECTOPIA
PHLEBECTOPY
PHLEBENTERIC
PHLEBITIS
PHLEBOGRAM
PHLEBOGRAPH
PHLEBOGRAPHY
PHLEBOID
PHLEBOIDAL
PHLEBOLITE
PHLEBOLITH
PHLEBOLITHIC
PHLEBOLITIC
PHLEBOLOGY
PHLEBOPEXY
PHLEBOPLASTY
PHLEBORRHAGE
PHLEBORRHEXIS
PHLEBOSTASIA
PHLEBOSTASIS
PHLEBOTOME
PHLEBOTOMIC
PHLEBOTOMIST

PHLEBOTOMIZE
PHLEBOTOMY
PHLEGM
PHLEGMA
PHLEGMAGOGUE
PHLEGMASIA
PHLEGMATIC
PHLEGMATICAL
PHLEGMATICLY
PHLEGMATISM
PHLEGMATIST
PHLEGMATOUS
PHLEGMON
PHLEGMONIC
PHLEGMONOID
PHLEGMONOUS
PHLEGMY
PHLOBAPHENE
PHLOBATANNIN
PHLOEM
PHLOEOTERMA
PHLOEUM
PHLOGISTIAN
PHLOGISTIC
PHLOGISTON
PHLOGOGENIC
PHLOGOPITE
PHLOGOSED
PHLOGOSIN
PHLOGOSIS
PHLOGOTIC
PHLORETIN
PHLORHIZIN
PHLORIDZIN
PHLORINA
PHLORIZIN
PHLOROL
PHLYCTAENA
PHLYCTAENULA
PHLYCTENA
PHLYCTENAE
PHLYCTENOID
PHLYCTENULA
PHLYCTENULE
PHLYZACIOUS
PHLYZACIUM
PHO
PHOBIA
PHOBIAC
PHOBIC
PHOBIES
PHOBISM
PHOBIST
PHOBIST
PHOBY
PHOCA
PHOCACEAN
PHOCACEOUS
PHOCAENINE
PHOCAL
PHOCENIN
PHOCID
PHOCIFORM
PHOCINE
PHOCODONT
PHOCOID
PHOCOMELIA
PHOCOMELUS
PHOEBADS
PHOEBE
PHOENICEAN
PHOENICOPTER
PHOENICUROUS
PHOENIGM
PHOENIX
PHOENIXES
PHOENIXITY

PHOLAD
PHOLADIAN
PHOLADID
PHOLADOID
PHOLCID
PHOLCOID
PHOLIDOLITE
PHOLIDOTE
PHON
PHONAL
PHONATE
PHONATED
PHONATING
PHONATION
PHONATORY
PHONAUTOGRAM
PHONE
PHONED
PHONEME
PHONEMIC
PHONEMICALLY
PHONEMICS
PHONES
PHONESIS
PHONETIC
PHONETICAL
PHONETICALLY
PHONETICIAN
PHONETICISM
PHONETICIST
PHONETICIZE
PHONETICS
PHONETISM
PHONETIST
PHONETIZATION
PHONETIZE
PHONEY
PHONGHI
PHONIATRICS
PHONIATRY
PHONIC
PHONICS
PHONIER
PHONIES
PHONIEST
PHONIKON
PHONING
PHONO
PHONOCAMPTIC
PHONODEIK
PHONOGLYPH
PHONOGRAM
PHONOGRAMIC
PHONOGRAMMIC
PHONOGRAPH
PHONOGRAPHER
PHONOGRAPHIC
PHONOGRAPHY
PHONOLITE
PHONOLITIC
PHONOLOGER
PHONOLOGIC
PHONOLOGICAL
PHONOLOGIST
PHONOLOGY
PHONOMANIA
PHONOMETER
PHONOMETRY
PHONOMIMIC
PHONOMOTOR
PHONON
PHONOPATHY
PHONOPHONE
PHONOPHORE
PHONOPHORIC
PHONOPHOROUS
PHONOPHOTE

PHONOPLEX
PHONOSCOPE
PHONOTYPE
PHONOTYPER
PHONOTYPIC
PHONOTYPIST
PHONOTYPY
PHONY
PHOO
PHOOEY
PHOOKA
PHORANTHIUM
PHORBIN
PHORESIS
PHORESY
PHORIA
PHORID
PHORMINX
PHOROMETER
PHOROMETRIC
PHOROMETRY
PHORONE
PHORONID
PHORONOMIA
PHORONOMIC
PHORONOMICS
PHORONOMY
PHOROSCOPE
PHOROZOOID
PHORRHEA
PHOS
PHOSE
PHOSGENE
PHOSGENITE
PHOSIS
PHOSPHAGEN
PHOSPHAM
PHOSPHAMIDE
PHOSPHATASE
PHOSPHATE
PHOSPHATED
PHOSPHATEMIA
PHOSPHATESE
PHOSPHATIC
PHOSPHATIDE
PHOSPHATION
PHOSPHATIZE
PHOSPHATIZED
PHOSPHATIZING
PHOSPHATURIA
PHOSPHATURIC
PHOSPHENE
PHOSPHENYL
PHOSPHID
PHOSPHIDE
PHOSPHINATE
PHOSPHINE
PHOSPHINIC
PHOSPHITE
PHOSPHOLIPID
PHOSPHONATE
PHOSPHONIC
PHOSPHONIUM
PHOSPHOR
PHOSPHORATE
PHOSPHORE
PHOSPHOREAL
PHOSPHORENT
PHOSPHOREOUS
PHOSPHORESCE
PHOSPHORESCENCE
PHOSPHORESCENT
PHOSPHORETED
PHOSPHORI
PHOSPHORIC
PHOSPHORICAL
PHOSPHORISM

PHOSPHORITE
PHOSPHORITIC
PHOSPHORIZE
PHOSPHOROGEN
PHOSPHOROGENE
PHOSPHOROUS
PHOSPHORUS
PHOSPHORYL
PHOSPHURIA
PHOSPHYL
PHOSS
PHOSSY
PHOT
PHOTA
PHOTAL
PHOTALGIA
PHOTECHY
PHOTEOLIC
PHOTIC
PHOTICS
PHOTISM
PHOTISTIC
PHOTO
PHOTOACTINIC
PHOTOBATHIC
PHOTOBIOTIC
PHOTOBROMIDE
PHOTOCAMPSIS
PHOTOCATHODE
PHOTOCHEMIST
PHOTOCHLORIDE
PHOTOCHROME
PHOTOCHROMY
PHOTOCOMPOSE
PHOTOCOPIER
PHOTOCOPY
PHOTOCRAYON
PHOTOCURRENT
PHOTODRAMA
PHOTODROME
PHOTODROMY
PHOTODYNAMIC
PHOTOELECTRIC
PHOTOENGRAVE
PHOTOENGRAVED
PHOTOENGRAVER
PHOTOENGRAVING
PHOTOETCH
PHOTOETCHED
PHOTOETCHER
PHOTOETCHING
PHOTOGELATIN
PHOTOGEN
PHOTOGENE
PHOTOGENIC
PHOTOGENY
PHOTOGEOLOGY
PHOTOGLYPH
PHOTOGLYPHIC
PHOTOGLYPHY
PHOTOGRAM
PHOTOGRAPH
PHOTOGRAPHEE
PHOTOGRAPHER
PHOTOGRAPHIC
PHOTOGRAPHY
PHOTOGRAVURE
PHOTOGYRIC
PHOTOHALIDE
PHOTOKINESIS
PHOTOLITH
PHOTOLOGIC
PHOTOLOGICAL
PHOTOLOGIST
PHOTOLOGY
PHOTOLYSIS
PHOTOLYTIC

PHOTOMA
PHOTOMAP
PHOTOMAPPER
PHOTOMETEOR
PHOTOMETER
PHOTOMETRIC
PHOTOMETRY
PHOTOMONTAGE
PHOTOMURAL
PHOTON
PHOTONASTY
PHOTONIC
PHOTONOSUS
PHOTONUCLEAR
PHOTOPATHIC
PHOTOPATHY
PHOTOPERIOD
PHOTOPHANE
PHOTOPHILE
PHOTOPHILIC
PHOTOPHILOUS
PHOTOPHILY
PHOTOPHOBE
PHOTOPHOBIA
PHOTOPHOBIC
PHOTOPHOBOUS
PHOTOPHONE
PHOTOPHONIC
PHOTOPHONY
PHOTOPHORE
PHOTOPHYGOUS
PHOTOPIA
PHOTOPIC
PHOTOPILE
PHOTOPLAY
PHOTOPLAYER
PHOTOPRINT
PHOTOPRINTER
PHOTORADIO
PHOTORELIEF
PHOTOSALT
PHOTOSCOPE
PHOTOSCOPIC
PHOTOSCOPY
PHOTOSPHERE
PHOTOSPHERIC
PHOTOSTABLE
PHOTOSTAT
PHOTOSTATED
PHOTOSTATIC
PHOTOSTATING
PHOTOSTATTED
PHOTOSTATTING
PHOTOSYNTAX
PHOTOTACTIC
PHOTOTACTISM
PHOTOTAXIS
PHOTOTAXY
PHOTOTHERAPY
PHOTOTHERMIC
PHOTOTIMER
PHOTOTONIC
PHOTOTONUS
PHOTOTROPE
PHOTOTROPIC
PHOTOTROPISM
PHOTOTUBE
PHOTOTYPE
PHOTOTYPIC
PHOTOTYPY
PHOTOVISUAL
PHOTOVOLTAIC
PHOTURIA
PHOUSDAR
PHRAGMA
PHRAGMOID
PHRAGMOSIS

PHRAMPEL
PHRASABLE
PHRASAL
PHRASALLY
PHRASE
PHRASEABLE
PHRASED
PHRASELESS
PHRASEMAKER
PHRASEMAKING
PHRASEMAN
PHRASEMONGER
PHRASEOGRAM
PHRASEOGRAPH
PHRASEOLOGIES
PHRASEOLOGY
PHRASER
PHRASINESS
PHRASING
PHRASY
PHRATOR
PHRATRAL
PHRATRIAC
PHRATRIAL
PHRATRIC
PHRATRIES
PHRATRY
PHREATIC
PHREATOPHYTE
PHREN
PHRENESIA
PHRENESIAC
PHRENESIS
PHRENETIC
PHRENETICAL
PHRENIC
PHRENICOTOMY
PHRENICS
PHRENITIC
PHRENITIS
PHRENOCARDIA
PHRENOGRAM
PHRENOGRAPH
PHRENOGRAPHY
PHRENOLOGER
PHRENOLOGIST
PHRENOLOGIZE
PHRENOLOGY
PHRENOPATHIC
PHRENOPATHY
PHRENOPLEGIA
PHRENOSIN
PHRENOSINIC
PHRENOTROPIC
PHRENSY
PHRONESIS
PHRYGANEID
PHRYGANEOID
PHRYGIA
PHRYGIUM
PHRYNID
PHRYNIN
PHTHALACENE
PHTHALAN
PHTHALATE
PHTHALEIN
PHTHALEINE
PHTHALIC
PHTHALIDE
PHTHALIMIDE
PHTHALIN
PHTHALYL
PHTHANITE
PHTHINOID
PHTHIRIASIS
PHTHISIC
PHTHISICAL

PHTHISICKY
PHTHISIS
PHTHONGAL
PHTHOR
PHTHORIC
PHTOR
PHU
PHUGOID
PHUL
PHULKARI
PHULWARA
PHUT
PHYCITE
PHYCITID
PHYCITOL
PHYCOCHROM
PHYCOCHROME
PHYCOCYANIN
PHYCOGRAPHY
PHYCOLOGICAL
PHYCOLOGIST
PHYCOLOGY
PHYCOMYCETE
PHYCOMYCETES
PHYCOPHAEIN
PHYLA
PHYLACTERIC
PHYLACTERIED
PHYLACTERIES
PHYLACTERIZE
PHYLACTERY
PHYLACTIC
PHYLARCH
PHYLARCHIC
PHYLARCHICAL
PHYLARCHY
PHYLE
PHYLEPHEBIC
PHYLESIS
PHYLETIC
PHYLETICALLY
PHYLETISM
PHYLIC
PHYLLADE
PHYLLARY
PHYLLIFORM
PHYLLIN
PHYLLINE
PHYLLITE
PHYLLITIC
PHYLLOCARID
PHYLLOCERATE
PHYLLOCLAD
PHYLLOCLADE
PHYLLOCYST
PHYLLOCYSTIC
PHYLLODE
PHYLLODIA
PHYLLODIAL
PHYLLODINOUS
PHYLLODIUM
PHYLLODY
PHYLLOGENOUS
PHYLLOID
PHYLLOIDAL
PHYLLOMANCY
PHYLLOMANIA
PHYLLOME
PHYLLOMIC
PHYLLOMORPH
PHYLLOMORPHY
PHYLLOPHORE
PHYLLOPOD
PHYLLOPODAN
PHYLLOPODE
PHYLLOPODOUS
PHYLLOPTOSIS

PHYLLORHINE
PHYLLOSOMA
PHYLLOSOME
PHYLLOTACTIC
PHYLLOTAXIS
PHYLLOTAXY
PHYLLOUS
PHYLLOXERA
PHYLLOXERAN
PHYLLOXERIC
PHYLLOZOOID
PHYLOGENESIS
PHYLOGENETIC
PHYLOGENY
PHYLON
PHYLUM
PHYMA
PHYMATA
PHYMATIC
PHYMATOID
PHYMATOSIS
PHYSAGOGUE
PHYSALIAN
PHYSALITE
PHYSCIOID
PHYSETEROID
PHYSIATRIC
PHYSIATRICS
PHYSIC
PHYSICAL
PHYSICALIST
PHYSICALITY
PHYSICALLY
PHYSICALNESS
PHYSICIAN
PHYSICIANCY
PHYSICIANED
PHYSICIANER
PHYSICIANING
PHYSICIANLY
PHYSICISM
PHYSICIST
PHYSICKED
PHYSICKER
PHYSICKING
PHYSICKY
PHYSICOLOGIC
PHYSICOMORPH
PHYSICS
PHYSID
PHYSIFORM
PHYSIOCRACY
PHYSIOCRAT
PHYSIOCRATIC
PHYSIOGENIC
PHYSIOGENY
PHYSIOGNOMIC
PHYSIOGNOMY
PHYSIOGONY
PHYSIOGRAPHY
PHYSIOLATER
PHYSIOLATRY
PHYSIOLOGER
PHYSIOLOGIAN
PHYSIOLOGIC
PHYSIOLOGICAL
PHYSIOLOGIST
PHYSIOLOGIZE
PHYSIOLOGUE
PHYSIOLOGUS
PHYSIOLOGY
PHYSIOSOPHIC
PHYSIOSOPHY
PHYSIQUE
PHYSIQUED
PHYSIS
PHYSITHEISM

PHYSITISM
PHYSIURGIC
PHYSIURGY
PHYSOCARPOUS
PHYSOCELE
PHYSOCLIST
PHYSOCLISTIC
PHYSOGASTRIC
PHYSOGASTRY
PHYSOMETRA
PHYSONECTOUS
PHYSOPOD
PHYSOSTIGMINE
PHYSOSTOME
PHYSOSTOMOUS
PHYTASE
PHYTATE
PHYTIC
PHYTIN
PHYTIVOROUS
PHYTOBEZOAR
PHYTOCHLORE
PHYTOCHLORIN
PHYTOGAMY
PHYTOGENESIS
PHYTOGENETIC
PHYTOGENIC
PHYTOGENY
PHYTOGNOMY
PHYTOGRAPH
PHYTOGRAPHER
PHYTOGRAPHIC
PHYTOGRAPHY
PHYTOID
PHYTOKININ
PHYTOL
PHYTOLOGIC
PHYTOLOGICAL
PHYTOLOGIST
PHYTOLOGY
PHYTOMA
PHYTOME
PHYTOMER
PHYTOMERA
PHYTOMETER
PHYTOMONAD
PHYTON
PHYTONIC
PHYTOPHAGAN
PHYTOPHAGIC
PHYTOPHAGOUS
PHYTOPHAGY
PHYTOPHILOUS
PHYTOPSYCHE
PHYTOPTID
PHYTOPTOSE
PHYTOPTOSIS
PHYTORHODIN
PHYTOSAUR
PHYTOSAURIAN
PHYTOSIS
PHYTOSTEROL
PHYTOSTROTE
PHYTOTOMIST
PHYTOTOMY
PHYTOTOXIC
PHYTOTOXIN
PHYTOTRON
PHYTOZOAN
PHYTOZOON
PHYTYL
PI
PIA
PIABA
PIACABA
PIACEVOLE
PIACHE

PIACLE
PIACULA
PIACULAR
PIACULARITY
PIACULARLY
PIACULUM
PIAFFE
PIAFFED
PIAFFER
PIAFFING
PIALYN
PIAN
PIANET
PIANETA
PIANETTE
PIANGENDO
PIANI
PIANIC
PIANINO
PIANISM
PIANISSIMO
PIANISSIMOS
PIANIST
PIANISTE
PIANISTIC
PIANNET
PIANO
PIANOFORTE
PIANOGRAPH
PIANOLA
PIANOLIST
PIANOLOGUE
PIANOS
PIANOSA
PIARHAEMIC
PIARHEMIC
PIASABA
PIASAVA
PIASSABA
PIASSAVA
PIASTER
PIASTRE
PIAT
PIATION
PIATTI
PIAY
PIAZIN
PIAZZA
PIAZZAED
PIAZZETTA
PIAZZIAN
PIBCORN
PIBGORN
PIBLOCKTO
PIBLOKTO
PIBROCH
PIC
PICA
PICACHO
PICACHOS
PICADOR
PICADURA
PICAL
PICAMAR
PICARA
PICARD
PICAREL
PICARESQUE
PICARIAN
PICARO
PICAROON
PICAYUNE
PICAYUNISH
PICAYUNISHLY
PICCADILL
PICCADILLY
PICCAGE

PICCALILLI
PICCANINNY
PICCIOTTO
PICCOLO
PICCOLOIST
PICCOLOS
PICE
PICEIN
PICENE
PICEOUS
PICEWORTH
PICHI
PICHICIAGO
PICHICIAGOS
PICHICIEGO
PICHURIC
PICHURIM
PICIFORM
PICINE
PICK
PICKABACK
PICKADIL
PICKAGE
PICKANINNIES
PICKANINNY
PICKAROON
PICKAX
PICKAXE
PICKBACK
PICKED
PICKEDEVANT
PICKEDLY
PICKEDNESS
PICKEER
PICKEERED
PICKEERING
PICKEL
PICKER
PICKEREL
PICKERELS
PICKERELWEED
PICKERING
PICKERINGITE
PICKERY
PICKET
PICKETEER
PICKETER
PICKI
PICKING
PICKLE
PICKLED
PICKLEMAN
PICKLER
PICKLES
PICKLEWEED
PICKLEWORM
PICKLING
PICKLOCK
PICKMAN
PICKMAW
PICKMEN
PICKOFF
PICKOUT
PICKOVER
PICKPENNY
PICKPOCKET
PICKPOCKETRY
PICKPOLE
PICKPURSE
PICKSMAN
PICKSMITH
PICKSOME
PICKSOMENESS
PICKTHANK
PICKTHATCH
PICKTOOTH
PICKUP

PICKWICK
PICKY
PICNIC
PICNICKED
PICNICKER
PICNICKERY
PICNICKING
PICNICKY
PICO
PICOID
PICOLINE
PICOLINIC
PICORY
PICOT
PICOTAH
PICOTE
PICOTEE
PICOTITE
PICOTS
PICOTTAH
PICQUET
PICQUETER
PICRA
PICRASMIN
PICRATE
PICRATED
PICRIC
PICRITE
PICROCARMINE
PICROL
PICROLITE
PICROMERITE
PICRORHIZA
PICRORHIZIN
PICROTIN
PICROTOXIC
PICROTOXIN
PICRY
PICRYL
PICT
PICTARNIE
PICTOGRAM
PICTOGRAPH
PICTOGRAPHIC
PICTOGRAPHY
PICTORIAL
PICTORIALLY
PICTORIC
PICTORICAL
PICTORICALLY
PICTUN
PICTURABLE
PICTURABLY
PICTURAL
PICTURE
PICTURED
PICTUREDOM
PICTUREDROME
PICTURELY
PICTURER
PICTURESQUE
PICTURING
PICTURIZE
PICTURY
PICUCULE
PICUDA
PICUDILLA
PICUDO
PICUL
PICULE
PICULET
PICULS
PICULULE
PIDAN
PIDDLE
PIDDLED
PIDDLER

PIDDLING	PIEWOMAN	PIGROOT	PILEORHIZA	PILLORYING
PIDDOCK	PIEZO	PIGROOTS	PILEORHIZE	PILLOW
PIDGIN	PIEZOMETER	PIGS	PILEOUS	PILLOWBEER
PIE	PIEZOMETRIC	PIGSKIN	PILER	PILLOWBER
PIEBALD	PIEZOMETRY	PIGSNEY	PILES	PILLOWBERE
PIEBALDLY	PIFERO	PIGSNIES	PILEUM	PILLOWCASE
PIEBALDNESS	PIFF	PIGSTICK	PILEUS	PILLOWING
PIECE	PIFFERO	PIGSTICKER	PILEWEED	PILLOWMADE
PIECEABLE	PIFFLE	PIGSTICKING	PILEWORK	PILLOWWORK
PIECED	PIFFLED	PIGSTIES	PILEWORM	PILLOWY
PIECEMEAL	PIFFLING	PIGSTY	PILEWORT	PILLS
PIECEN	PIG	PIGTAIL	PILFER	PILLULE
PIECENER	PIGBELLY	PIGTAILED	PILFERAGE	PILLWORM
PIECER	PIGBOAT	PIGWASH	PILFERER	PILLWORT
PIECES	PIGDAN	PIGWEED	PILFERING	PILM
PIECETTE	PIGEON	PIGWIDGEON	PILFERY	PILMY
PIECEWORK	PIGEONABLE	PIGWIDGIN	PILFRE	PILOCARPIN
PIECEWORKER	PIGEONBERRY	PIGWIGEON	PILGARLIC	PILOCARPINE
PIECING	PIGEONEER	PIGYARD	PILGARLICKY	PILOCYSTIC
PIECRUST	PIGEONER	PIITIS	PILGER	PILOERECTION
PIED	PIGEONFOOT	PIJA	PILGRIM	PILOMOTOR
PIEDE	PIGEONGRAM	PIK	PILGRIMAGE	PILON
PIEDFORT	PIGEONHOLE	PIKA	PILGRIMAGER	PILONCILLO
PIEDLY	PIGEONRY	PIKAKE	PILGRIMATIC	PILONIDAL
PIEDMONT	PIGEONS	PIKE	PILGRIMER	PILORI
PIEDMONTITE	PIGEONTAIL	PIKED	PILGRIMESS	PILOSE
PIEDNESS	PIGEONWEED	PIKEL	PILGRIMIZE	PILOSIN
PIEDRA	PIGEONWING	PIKELET	PILI	PILOSINE
PIEDROIT	PIGEONWOOD	PIKEMAN	PILIDIUM	PILOSIS
PIEHOUSE	PIGFACE	PIKEMEN	PILIFER	PILOSISM
PIEING	PIGFISH	PIKEMONGER	PILIFEROUS	PILOSITY
PIEMAG	PIGFISHES	PIKER	PILIFORM	PILOT
PIEMAN	PIGFLOWER	PIKES	PILIGAN	PILOTAGE
PIEMARKER	PIGFOOT	PIKESTAFF	PILIGANIN	PILOTAXITIC
PIEN	PIGGED	PIKESTAVES	PILIGANINE	PILOTED
PIENA	PIGGERIES	PIKETAIL	PILIKAI	PILOTHOUSE
PIENANNY	PIGGERY	PIKEY	PILIKIA	PILOTING
PIEND	PIGGIE	PIKI	PILILLOO	PILOTISM
PIENO	PIGGIN	PIKING	PILIMICTION	PILOTMAN
PIENTAO	PIGGING	PIKLE	PILINE	PILOTRY
PIEPAN	PIGGISH	PIKOL	PILING	PILOTWEED
PIEPLANT	PIGGISHLY	PIKY	PILITICO	PILOUS
PIEPOUDRE	PIGGISHNESS	PIL	PILK	PILPUL
PIEPOWDER	PIGGLE	PILA	PILKINS	PILPULIST
PIEPRINT	PIGGY	PILAF	PILL	PILPULISTIC
PIER	PIGGYBACK	PILAFF	PILLAGE	PILSENER
PIERCE	PIGGYBACKING	PILAGE	PILLAGED	PILSNER
PIERCED	PIGHEAD	PILANDITE	PILLAGER	PILT
PIERCEL	PIGHEADED	PILAPIL	PILLAGERS	PILTOCK
PIERCER	PIGHEADEDLY	PILAR	PILLAGING	PILULA
PIERCING	PIGHERD	PILARY	PILLAR	PILULAR
PIERCINGLY	PIGHTEL	PILASTER	PILLARED	PILULE
PIERCINGNESS	PIGHTLE	PILASTERED	PILLARET	PILULIST
PIERDROP	PIGLET	PILASTERING	PILLARING	PILULOUS
PIERHEAD	PIGLIKE	PILASTRADE	PILLARIST	PILUM
PIERID	PIGLING	PILASTRADED	PILLARLET	PILUS
PIERIDINE	PIGLY	PILASTRIC	PILLARLIKE	PILWILLET
PIERINE	PIGMAKER	PILAU	PILLARY	PILY
PIERRETTE	PIGMAKING	PILAUED	PILLAS	PIMA
PIERROT	PIGMAN	PILAW	PILLBOX	PIMBINA
PIERROTIC	PIGMENT	PILCH	PILLED	PIMELATE
PIERT	PIGMENTARY	PILCHARD	PILLEDNESS	PIMELIC
PIESHOP	PIGMENTATION	PILCHER	PILLER	PIMELITE
PIET	PIGMENTIZE	PILCHERD	PILLERY	PIMELITIS
PIETAS	PIGMENTOSE	PILCORN	PILLET	PIMENT
PIETIC	PIGMEW	PILCROW	PILLEUS	PIMENTO
PIETIES	PIGMY	PILE	PILLICOCK	PIMENTON
PIETISM	PIGNOLIA	PILEA	PILLION	PIMENTOS
PIETIST	PIGNON	PILEATA	PILLIVER	PIMGENET
PIETISTIC	PIGNORA	PILEATE	PILLIWINKS	PIMIENTA
PIETISTICAL	PIGNORATE	PILEATED	PILLMAKER	PIMIENTO
PIETON	PIGNORATION	PILED	PILLMAKING	PIMIENTOS
PIETOSE	PIGNORATIVE	PILEIFORM	PILLMONGER	PIMLICO
PIETOSO	PIGNUS	PILELESS	PILLORIED	PIMOLA
PIETY	PIGNUT	PILEOLATED	PILLORIES	PIMP
PIEWIFE	PIGPEN	PILEOLI	PILLORIZE	PIMPED
PIEWIPE	PIGRITIA	PILEOLUS	PILLORY	PIMPERNEL

PIMPERY
PIMPING
PIMPLE
PIMPLEBACK
PIMPLED
PIMPLIER
PIMPLIEST
PIMPLINESS
PIMPLING
PIMPLO
PIMPLY
PIN
PINA
PINABETE
PINACEOUS
PINACHROME
PINACLE
PINACOCYTAL
PINACOCYTE
PINACOID
PINACOIDAL
PINACOL
PINACOLATE
PINACOLIN
PINACOLINE
PINACULUM
PINAFORE
PINAG
PINAKIOLITE
PINAKOID
PINAKOIDAL
PINAKOTHEKE
PINANG
PINAS
PINASTER
PINATA
PINAVERDOL
PINAX
PINAYUSA
PINBALL
PINBEFORE
PINBONE
PINBUSH
PINCASE
PINCEMENT
PINCER
PINCERLIKE
PINCERS
PINCETTE
PINCH
PINCHBACK
PINCHBECK
PINCHBUG
PINCHCOCK
PINCHE
PINCHED
PINCHEDLY
PINCHEDNESS
PINCHEM
PINCHER
PINCHFIST
PINCHFISTED
PINCHGUT
PINCHING
PINCHPENNY
PINCPINC
PINCUSHION
PINCUSHIONY
PIND
PINDA
PINDAL
PINDARICAL
PINDARICALLY
PINDARICS
PINDER
PINDJAJAP
PINDLING

PINDY
PINE
PINEAL
PINEALISM
PINEALOMA
PINEAPPLE
PINEBANK
PINECONE
PINED
PINEDROPS
PINELAND
PINENE
PINER
PINERIES
PINERY
PINES
PINESAP
PINETA
PINETUM
PINEWEED
PINEWOODS
PINEY
PINFALL
PINFEATHER
PINFEATHERED
PINFEATHERER
PINFEATHERY
PINFIRE
PINFISH
PINFISHES
PINFOLD
PING
PINGE
PINGED
PINGING
PINGLE
PINGLER
PINGO
PINGRASS
PINGSTER
PINGUE
PINGUECULA
PINGUEDINOUS
PINGUEFACTION
PINGUEFY
PINGUESCENCE
PINGUESCENT
PINGUICULA
PINGUID
PINGUIDITY
PINGUIN
PINGUITE
PINGUITUDE
PINHEAD
PINHEADED
PINHOLD
PINHOLE
PINHOOK
PINIC
PINIER
PINIEST
PINING
PININGLY
PININGS
PINION
PINIONED
PINIONING
PINIPICRIN
PINITE
PINITOL
PINJANE
PINJRA
PINK
PINKANY
PINKBERRY
PINKED
PINKEEN

PINKEN
PINKENY
PINKER
PINKEYE
PINKFISH
PINKFISHES
PINKIE
PINKIFIED
PINKIFY
PINKIFYING
PINKING
PINKISH
PINKROOT
PINKSOME
PINKWEED
PINKWOOD
PINKWORT
PINKY
PINLOCK
PINMAKER
PINMAKING
PINMAN
PINNA
PINNACE
PINNACLE
PINNACLED
PINNACLING
PINNAE
PINNAGE
PINNAGLOBIN
PINNAL
PINNAS
PINNATE
PINNATED
PINNATELY
PINNATIFID
PINNATIFIDLY
PINNATION
PINNATIPED
PINNATISECT
PINNATULATE
PINNED
PINNEL
PINNER
PINNET
PINNIGRADE
PINNING
PINNIPED
PINNIPEDIAN
PINNOCK
PINNOITE
PINNOTERE
PINNOTHERE
PINNOTHERIAN
PINNULA
PINNULAE
PINNULAR
PINNULATE
PINNULATED
PINNULE
PINNULET
PINNY
PINNYWINKLE
PINO
PINOCHLE
PINOCLE
PINOLE
PINOLEUM
PINOLIA
PINOLIN
PINON
PINOT
PINPATCH
PINPILLOW
PINPOINT
PINPRICK
PINPROOF

PINRAIL
PINROWED
PINS
PINSCHER
PINSETTER
PINSON
PINSONS
PINT
PINTA
PINTADERA
PINTADO
PINTADOES
PINTADOITE
PINTADOS
PINTAIL
PINTAILS
PINTANO
PINTANOS
PINTE
PINTID
PINTLE
PINTO
PINTURA
PINUELA
PINULUS
PINUP
PINWEED
PINWHEEL
PINWORK
PINWORM
PINXIT
PINY
PINYL
PINYON
PIOLET
PION
PIONED
PIONEER
PIONEERED
PIONEERING
PIONERY
PIONNOTES
PIOSCOPE
PIOTED
PIOTINE
PIOTTY
PIOUPIOU
PIOURY
PIOUS
PIOUSLY
PIOUSNESS
PIP
PIPA
PIPAGE
PIPAL
PIPE
PIPEAGE
PIPECOLIN
PIPECOLINE
PIPECOLINIC
PIPED
PIPEFISH
PIPEFISHES
PIPEFITTER
PIPEFITTING
PIPEFUL
PIPEFULS
PIPELAYER
PIPELAYING
PIPELESS
PIPELIKE
PIPELINE
PIPEMAN
PIPEMOUTH
PIPER
PIPERACEOUS
PIPERATE

PIPERAZINE
PIPERIDE
PIPERIDEINE
PIPERIDGE
PIPERIDID
PIPERIDIDE
PIPERIDIN
PIPERIDINE
PIPERINE
PIPERITIOUS
PIPERITONE
PIPERLY
PIPERONAL
PIPERONYL
PIPERY
PIPERYLENE
PIPES
PIPESTAPPLE
PIPESTEM
PIPESTONE
PIPET
PIPETTE
PIPEWALKER
PIPEWOOD
PIPEWORK
PIPEWORT
PIPEY
PIPI
PIPID
PIPIER
PIPIEST
PIPIKAULA
PIPING
PIPINGLY
PIPINGNESS
PIPIRI
PIPISTREL
PIPISTRELLE
PIPIT
PIPKIN
PIPPED
PIPPEN
PIPPER
PIPPIER
PIPPIEST
PIPPIN
PIPPINER
PIPPINFACE
PIPPING
PIPPLE
PIPPY
PIPRINE
PIPROID
PIPSISSEWA
PIPUNCULID
PIPY
PIQUABLE
PIQUANCY
PIQUANT
PIQUANTLY
PIQUANTNESS
PIQUE
PIQUED
PIQUERO
PIQUET
PIQUETTE
PIQUEUR
PIQUIA
PIQUIERE
PIQUING
PIQURE
PIR
PIRACIES
PIRACY
PIRAGUA
PIRAI
PIRANA

PIRANHA	PISHPASH	PITCHFIELD	PITTER	PLACENTAE
PIRARUCU	PISHU	PITCHFORK	PITTICITE	PLACENTAL
PIRATE	PISIFORM	PITCHHOLE	PITTINE	PLACENTALIAN
PIRATED	PISK	PITCHI	PITTING	PLACENTARY
PIRATERY	PISKUN	PITCHIER	PITTITE	PLACENTAS
PIRATIC	PISKY	PITCHIEST	PITTO	PLACENTATE
PIRATICAL	PISMIRE	PITCHILY	PITTOID	PLACENTATION
PIRATICALLY	PISMIRISM	PITCHINESS	PITTOSPORE	PLACENTIFORM
PIRATING	PISO	PITCHING	PITUITAL	PLACENTITIS
PIRATISM	PISOLITE	PITCHMAN	PITUITARIES	PLACENTOID
PIRATRY	PISOLITIC	PITCHOMETER	PITUITARY	PLACENTOMA
PIRATY	PISOTE	PITCHPIKE	PITUITE	PLACER
PIRAYA	PISS	PITCHSTONE	PITUITOUS	PLACET
PIRCA	PISSABED	PITCHWORK	PITURI	PLACID
PIRE	PISSANT	PITCHY	PITWOOD	PLACIDAMENTE
PIRIJIRI	PISSED	PITE	PITWORK	PLACIDITY
PIRIPIRI	PISSING	PITEIRA	PITWRIGHT	PLACIDLY
PIRIRIGUA	PIST	PITEOUS	PITY	PLACIDNESS
PIRL	PISTACHE	PITEOUSLY	PITYING	PLACING
PIRLIE	PISTACHIO	PITEOUSNESS	PITYINGLY	PLACIT
PIRN	PISTACHIOS	PITFALL	PITYOCAMPA	PLACITUM
PIRNED	PISTACITE	PITFOLD	PITYOCAMPE	PLACK
PIRNER	PISTAREEN	PITH	PITYRIASIC	PLACKET
PIRNIE	PISTE	PITHANOLOGY	PITYRIASIS	PLACKLESS
PIRNY	PISTEOLOGY	PITHEAD	PITYROID	PLACODE
PIROGEN	PISTIC	PITHECAN	PIU	PLACODERM
PIROGUE	PISTICK	PITHECIAN	PIUI	PLACODERMAL
PIROJKI	PISTIL	PITHECIINE	PIUPIU	PLACODERMOID
PIROL	PISTILLAR	PITHECISM	PIURA	PLACODONT
PIROOT	PISTILLARY	PITHECOID	PIURI	PLACOID
PIROPLASM	PISTILLATE	PITHECOLOGY	PIVA	PLACOIDAL
PIROPLASMOSIS	PISTILLID	PITHECUS	PIVOT	PLACOIDEAN
PIROSHKI	PISTILLIDIUM	PITHED	PIVOTAL	PLACOPLAST
PIROT	PISTILLINE	PITHIER	PIVOTALLY	PLACULA
PIROUETTE	PISTILLODE	PITHIEST	PIVOTED	PLADAROMA
PIROUETTED	PISTILLODY	PITHILY	PIVOTER	PLAFOND
PIROUETTER	PISTILLOID	PITHINESS	PIVOTING	PLAGA
PIROUETTIST	PISTILS	PITHING	PIX	PLAGAL
PIRR	PISTIOLOGY	PITHLESS	PIXIE	PLAGATE
PIRRAURA	PISTLE	PITHOI	PIXIES	PLAGE
PIRRAURU	PISTLER	PITHOLE	PIXILATED	PLAGIAPLITE
PIRRMAW	PISTOL	PITHOS	PIXY	PLAGIARICAL
PIRSSONITE	PISTOLADE	PITHSOME	PIYYUT	PLAGIARIES
PIRY	PISTOLE	PITHY	PIZE	PLAGIARISE
PISACA	PISTOLED	PITIABILITY	PIZZA	PLAGIARISM
PISACHA	PISTOLEER	PITIABLE	PIZZERIA	PLAGIARIST
PISACHEE	PISTOLET	PITIABLENESS	PIZZICATO	PLAGIARISTIC
PISACHI	PISTOLETER	PITIABLY	PIZZLE	PLAGIARIZE
PISANG	PISTOLETIER	PITIED	PLACABILITY	PLAGIARIZED
PISANITE	PISTOLGRAM	PITIER	PLACABLE	PLAGIARIZER
PISAY	PISTOLGRAPH	PITIES	PLACABLENESS	PLAGIARIZING
PISCARIES	PISTOLIER	PITIFUL	PLACABLY	PLAGIARY
PISCARY	PISTOLING	PITIFULLY	PLACARD	PLAGIHEDRAL
PISCATION	PISTOLLED	PITIFULNESS	PLACARDED	PLAGIOCLASE
PISCATOLOGY	PISTOLLING	PITIKINS	PLACARDER	PLAGIOCLINAL
PISCATOR	PISTOLOGY	PITILESS	PLACARDING	PLAGIODONT
PISCATORIAL	PISTOLPROOF	PITILESSLY	PLACATE	PLAGIOGRAPH
PISCATORIAN	PISTON	PITILESSNESS	PLACATED	PLAGIONITE
PISCATORIOUS	PISTONHEAD	PITIRRI	PLACATER	PLAGIOPHYRE
PISCATORY	PISTRICES	PITMAN	PLACATING	PLAGIOSTOME
PISCIAN	PISTRIX	PITMANS	PLACATION	PLAGIOTROPIC
PISCICAPTURE	PIT	PITMEN	PLACATIVE	PLAGIUM
PISCICOLOUS	PITA	PITMIRK	PLACATORY	PLAGOSE
PISCICULTURE	PITAHAYA	PITO	PLACCATE	PLAGOSITY
PISCIFAUNA	PITANGA	PITOMETER	PLACE	PLAGUE
PISCIFEROUS	PITANGUA	PITOMIE	PLACEBO	PLAGUED
PISCIFORM	PITAPAT	PITON	PLACEBOES	PLAGUER
PISCINA	PITAPATATION	PITPAN	PLACEBOS	PLAGUESOME
PISCINAL	PITARAH	PITPIT	PLACED	PLAGUEY
PISCINE	PITAU	PITPROP	PLACEHOLDER	PLAGUILY
PISCINITY	PITBIRD	PITSAW	PLACEMAKER	PLAGUING
PISCIVOROUS	PITCH	PITSIDE	PLACEMAN	PLAGULA
PISCO	PITCHBLENDE	PITTACAL	PLACEMEN	PLAGUY
PISE	PITCHED	PITTANCE	PLACEMENT	PLAICE
PISH	PITCHER	PITTANCER	PLACEMONGER	PLAID
PISHAUG	PITCHERED	PITTARD	PLACENT	PLAIDED
PISHOGUE	PITCHERY	PITTED	PLACENTA	PLAIDMAN

PLAIDOYER
PLAIK
PLAIN
PLAINBACK
PLAINBACKS
PLAINED
PLAINER
PLAINEST
PLAINFUL
PLAINING
PLAINLY
PLAINNESS
PLAINS
PLAINSCRAFT
PLAINSFOLK
PLAINSMAN
PLAINSMEN
PLAINSOLED
PLAINSONG
PLAINSTONES
PLAINSWOMAN
PLAINSWOMEN
PLAINT
PLAINTAIL
PLAINTEXT
PLAINTIFF
PLAINTILE
PLAINTIVE
PLAINTIVELY
PLAINWARD
PLAINY
PLAISTER
PLAIT
PLAITED
PLAITER
PLAITING
PLAITWORK
PLAKAT
PLAN
PLANAEA
PLANAR
PLANARIAN
PLANARIFORM
PLANARIOID
PLANARITY
PLANATE
PLANATION
PLANCH
PLANCHE
PLANCHEITE
PLANCHER
PLANCHET
PLANCHETTE
PLANCHING
PLANCIER
PLANDOK
PLANE
PLANED
PLANER
PLANES
PLANET
PLANETA
PLANETABLE
PLANETABLER
PLANETAL
PLANETARIA
PLANETARIAN
PLANETARIES
PLANETARIUM
PLANETARIUMS
PLANETARY
PLANETED
PLANETESIMAL
PLANETFALL
PLANETIC
PLANETICOSE
PLANETING

PLANETOGENY
PLANETOID
PLANETOIDAL
PLANETOLOGIC
PLANETOLOGY
PLANETS
PLANFORM
PLANFUL
PLANFULLY
PLANFULNESS
PLANG
PLANGENCY
PLANGENT
PLANGENTLY
PLANGI
PLANGOR
PLANGOROUS
PLANICIPITAL
PLANIFOLIOUS
PLANIFORM
PLANIGRAPH
PLANILLA
PLANIMETER
PLANIMETRIC
PLANIMETRY
PLANING
PLANIPENNATE
PLANIPENNINE
PLANIROSTAL
PLANISCOPE
PLANISCOPIC
PLANISH
PLANISHED
PLANISHER
PLANISHING
PLANISPHERAL
PLANISPHERE
PLANISPHERIC
PLANISPIRAL
PLANK
PLANKAGE
PLANKED
PLANKER
PLANKING
PLANKS
PLANKTER
PLANKTOLOGY
PLANKTON
PLANKTONIC
PLANKTONT
PLANKWAYS
PLANKWISE
PLANLESS
PLANLESSLY
PLANLESSNESS
PLANNED
PLANNER
PLANNING
PLANOBLAST
PLANOBLASTIC
PLANOFERRITE
PLANOGAMETE
PLANOGRAPH
PLANOGRAPHIC
PLANOGRAPHY
PLANOMETER
PLANOMETRY
PLANOMILLER
PLANONT
PLANORBIFORM
PLANORBINE
PLANORBOID
PLANOSOME
PLANOSPORE
PLANT
PLANTA
PLANTAD

PLANTAGE
PLANTAIN
PLANTAL
PLANTANO
PLANTAR
PLANTARIS
PLANTARIUM
PLANTATION
PLANTATOR
PLANTED
PLANTER
PLANTERLY
PLANTIGRADE
PLANTIGRADY
PLANTING
PLANTIVOROUS
PLANTLET
PLANTLING
PLANTOCRACY
PLANTS
PLANTSMAN
PLANTULAE
PLANTULAR
PLANTULE
PLANULA
PLANULAE
PLANULAN
PLANULAR
PLANULATE
PLANULIFORM
PLANULOID
PLANUM
PLANURIA
PLANXTY
PLAP
PLAPPERT
PLAQUE
PLAQUETTE
PLASH
PLASHED
PLASHER
PLASHET
PLASHING
PLASHY
PLASM
PLASMA
PLASMASE
PLASMATIC
PLASMATICAL
PLASMATION
PLASMIC
PLASMOCHIN
PLASMOCYTE
PLASMODESM
PLASMODESMUS
PLASMODIA
PLASMODIAL
PLASMODIATE
PLASMODIUM
PLASMOGEN
PLASMOID
PLASMOLYSIS
PLASMOLYTIC
PLASMOLYZE
PLASMOMA
PLASMOMATA
PLASMON
PLASMOPHAGY
PLASMOPTYSIS
PLASMOQUIN
PLASMOQUINE
PLASMOSOMA
PLASMOSOMATA
PLASMOSOME
PLASMOTOMY
PLASOME
PLASS

PLASSON
PLASTEIN
PLASTER
PLASTERBILL
PLASTERBOARD
PLASTERED
PLASTERER
PLASTERINESS
PLASTERING
PLASTERWORK
PLASTERY
PLASTIC
PLASTICALLY
PLASTICINE
PLASTICISM
PLASTICITY
PLASTICIZE
PLASTICIZED
PLASTICIZER
PLASTICIZING
PLASTICLY
PLASTICS
PLASTID
PLASTIDIUM
PLASTIDOME
PLASTIDULAR
PLASTIDULE
PLASTIFY
PLASTIN
PLASTINOID
PLASTIQUE
PLASTOGAMIC
PLASTOGAMY
PLASTOMERE
PLASTOMETER
PLASTOSOME
PLASTOTYPE
PLASTRAL
PLASTRON
PLASTRUM
PLAT
PLATALEIFORM
PLATALEINE
PLATAN
PLATANE
PLATANIST
PLATANNA
PLATANO
PLATBAND
PLATCH
PLATE
PLATEA
PLATEASM
PLATEAU
PLATEAUS
PLATEAUX
PLATED
PLATEFUL
PLATEFULS
PLATEHOLDER
PLATEIASMUS
PLATELAYER
PLATELET
PLATEMAKER
PLATEMAKING
PLATEMAN
PLATEMEN
PLATEN
PLATER
PLATERER
PLATERESQUE
PLATERY
PLATES
PLATEWAY
PLATEWORK
PLATFORM
PLATFORMALLY

PLATFORMIST
PLATIC
PLATICLY
PLATIE
PLATILLA
PLATINA
PLATINAMIN
PLATINAMINE
PLATINAMMIN
PLATINAMMINE
PLATINATE
PLATINE
PLATING
PLATINIC
PLATINIZE
PLATINIZED
PLATINIZING
PLATINOID
PLATINOTYPE
PLATINOUS
PLATINUM
PLATITUDE
PLATITUDINAL
PLATLY
PLATODE
PLATOID
PLATONICALLY
PLATOON
PLATOPIC
PLATTED
PLATTEN
PLATTER
PLATTERFACE
PLATTING
PLATTNERITE
PLATTY
PLATUROUS
PLATY
PLATYBASIC
PLATYCARPOUS
PLATYCELIAN
PLATYCELOUS
PLATYCEPHALY
PLATYCHEIRIA
PLATYCNEMIA
PLATYCNEMIC
PLATYCOELIAN
PLATYCOELOUS
PLATYCORIA
PLATYCRANIA
PLATYCRANIAL
PLATYDACTYL
PLATYDACTYLE
PLATYFISH
PLATYGLOSSAL
PLATYGLOSSIA
PLATYHIERIC
PLATYLOBATE
PLATYMERIA
PLATYMETER
PLATYMYOID
PLATYNITE
PLATYNOTAL
PLATYODONT
PLATYOPE
PLATYOPIA
PLATYOPIC
PLATYPELLIC
PLATYPOD
PLATYPODIA
PLATYPODOUS
PLATYPUS
PLATYPUSES
PLATYPYGOUS
PLATYRRHIN
PLATYRRHINE
PLATYRRHINY

PLATYSMA	PLEACHER	PLEDGEE	PLEROMATIC	PLICAE
PLATYSOMID	PLEACHING	PLEDGEOR	PLEROME	PLICAL
PLATYSTERNAL	PLEAD	PLEDGER	PLEROMORPH	PLICATE
PLATYTROPE	PLEADABLE	PLEDGESHOP	PLEROPHORIC	PLICATED
PLAUD	PLEADED	PLEDGET	PLEROPHORY	PLICATELY
PLAUDATION	PLEADER	PLEDGING	PLEROSIS	PLICATENESS
PLAUDIT	PLEADING	PLEDGOR	PLEROTIC	PLICATINE
PLAUDITE	PLEADINGLY	PLEE	PLESIOBIOSIS	PLICATION
PLAUDITOR	PLEADINGNESS	PLEGAPHONIA	PLESIOSAUR	PLICATOR
PLAUDITORY	PLEASANCE	PLEGOMETER	PLESIOSAURUS	PLICATULATE
PLAUENITE	PLEASANT	PLEIN	PLESIOTYPE	PLICATURE
PLAUSIBILITY	PLEASANTLY	PLEIOBAR	PLESSIGRAPH	PLICIFEROUS
PLAUSIBLE	PLEASANTNESS	PLEIOCHROMIA	PLESSOR	PLICIFORM
PLAUSIBLY	PLEASANTRY	PLEIOCHROMIC	PLET	PLIED
PLAUSIVE	PLEASANTSOME	PLEIOMEROUS	PLETE	PLIER
PLAUSTRAL	PLEASAUNCE	PLEIOMERY	PLETHORA	PLIERS
PLAY	PLEASE	PLEION	PLETHORIC	PLIES
PLAYA	PLEASED	PLEIONIAN	PLETHORICAL	PLIGHT
PLAYABILITY	PLEASEDLY	PLEIOPHYLLY	PLETHOROUS	PLIGHTED
PLAYABLE	PLEASEDNESS	PLEIOTAXIS	PLETHORY	PLIGHTER
PLAYAS	PLEASEMAN	PLEISTOSEIST	PLETHRON	PLIGHTING
PLAYBACK	PLEASEMEN	PLEMOCHOE	PLETHRUM	PLIM
PLAYBILL	PLEASER	PLENA	PLEURA	PLIMSOLL
PLAYBOOK	PLEASHIP	PLENAL	PLEURAE	PLINTH
PLAYBOX	PLEASING	PLENARILY	PLEURAL	PLINTHER
PLAYBOY	PLEASINGLY	PLENARINESS	PLEURIC	PLINTHIFORM
PLAYBROKER	PLEASINGNESS	PLENARIUM	PLEURISY	PLIOSAUR
PLAYDAY	PLEASURABLE	PLENARTY	PLEURITIC	PLIOSAURIAN
PLAYDOWN	PLEASURABLY	PLENARY	PLEURITIS	PLIOTHERMIC
PLAYED	PLEASURE	PLENICORN	PLEUROBRANCH	PLISKIE
PLAYER	PLEASURED	PLENILUNAL	PLEUROCARP	PLISKY
PLAYERESS	PLEASUREFUL	PLENILUNE	PLEUROCELE	PLISSE
PLAYFELLOW	PLEASUREMAN	PLENIPO	PLEUROCEROID	PLITCH
PLAYFERE	PLEASUREMENT	PLENIPOTENCE	PLEURODONT	PLOAT
PLAYFIELD	PLEASURER	PLENIPOTENT	PLEUROGENIC	PLOCE
PLAYFUL	PLEASURING	PLENISH	PLEUROLITH	PLOCEIFORM
PLAYFULLY	PLEASURIST	PLENISHING	PLEURON	PLOCK
PLAYFULNESS	PLEASUROUS	PLENISHMENT	PLEURONECTID	PLOD
PLAYGOER	PLEAT	PLENISM	PLEUROPEDAL	PLODDED
PLAYGOING	PLEATED	PLENIST	PLEUROPODIUM	PLODDER
PLAYGROUND	PLEATER	PLENITUDE	PLEUROSTEAL	PLODDERLY
PLAYHOUSE	PLEATS	PLENITY	PLEUROSTICT	PLODDING
PLAYING	PLEB	PLENTEOUS	PLEUROTOMIES	PLODDINGLY
PLAYINGLY	PLEBE	PLENTEOUSLY	PLEUROTOMY	PLODDINGNESS
PLAYLET	PLEBEIAN	PLENTIES	PLEUROTRIBE	PLODGE
PLAYMAKER	PLEBEIANISM	PLENTIFUL	PLEURUM	PLOESTI
PLAYMAKING	PLEBEIANIZE	PLENTIFULLY	PLEUSTON	PLOIMATE
PLAYMAN	PLEBEIANIZED	PLENTIFULNESS	PLEVIN	PLOMB
PLAYMARE	PLEBEIANLY	PLENTY	PLEW	PLONK
PLAYMATE	PLEBEIANNESS	PLENUM	PLEWCH	PLOOK
PLAYMONGER	PLEBEITY	PLENUMS	PLEWE	PLOP
PLAYOCK	PLEBES	PLENY	PLEWGH	PLOPPED
PLAYOFF	PLEBICOLAR	PLEOCHROIC	PLEX	PLOPPING
PLAYPEN	PLEBICOLIST	PLEOCHROISM	PLEXAL	PLORATION
PLAYREADER	PLEBICOLOUS	PLEOCHROOUS	PLEXICOSE	PLORATORY
PLAYROOM	PLEBIFY	PLEODONT	PLEXIFORM	PLOSH
PLAYSCRIPT	PLEBISCITARY	PLEOMASTIA	PLEXIGLAS	PLOSION
PLAYSOME	PLEBISCITE	PLEOMASTIC	PLEXIGLASS	PLOSIVE
PLAYSOMELY	PLEBISCITIC	PLEOMETROSIS	PLEXIMETER	PLOT
PLAYSOMENESS	PLEBISCITUM	PLEOMETROTIC	PLEXIMETRIC	PLOTCH
PLAYSTEAD	PLEBS	PLEOMORPHIC	PLEXIMETRY	PLOTCOCK
PLAYSTOW	PLECK	PLEOMORPHIST	PLEXIPPUS	PLOTFUL
PLAYTE	PLECOPTERAN	PLEOMORPHY	PLEXODONT	PLOTOSID
PLAYTHING	PLECOPTERID	PLEON	PLEXOR	PLOTPROOF
PLAYTIME	PLECOPTEROUS	PLEONASM	PLEXURE	PLOTT
PLAYWARD	PLECOTINE	PLEONAST	PLEXUS	PLOTTAGE
PLAYWOMAN	PLECTOGNATH	PLEONASTE	PLEXUSES	PLOTTED
PLAYWOMEN	PLECTRA	PLEONASTIC	PLIABILITY	PLOTTER
PLAYWORK	PLECTRE	PLEONASTICAL	PLIABLE	PLOTTERY
PLAYWRIGHT	PLECTRIDIAL	PLEONECTIC	PLIABLENESS	PLOTTING
PLAYWRITER	PLECTRIDIUM	PLEONEXIA	PLIABLY	PLOTTINGLY
PLAYWRITING	PLECTRON	PLEONIC	PLIANCY	PLOTTON
PLAZA	PLECTRUM	PLEOPOD	PLIANT	PLOTTY
PLAZOLITE	PLECTRUMS	PLEOPODITE	PLIANTLY	PLOUGH
PLEA	PLED	PLERERGATE	PLIANTNESS	PLOUGHBOY
PLEACH	PLEDGE	PLEROCERCOID	PLICA	PLOUGHED
PLEACHED	PLEDGED	PLEROMA	PLICABLE	PLOUGHFISH

PLOUGHFOOT	PLUGGED	PLUMOSE	PLURIPOTENT	PNEUMATIZE
PLOUGHGANG	PLUGGER	PLUMOSELY	PLURISEPTATE	PNEUMATIZED
PLOUGHGATE	PLUGGING	PLUMOSENESS	PLURISERIAL	PNEUMATOCELE
PLOUGHHEAD	PLUGGINGLY	PLUMOSITY	PLURISERIATE	PNEUMATOCYST
PLOUGHING	PLUGGY	PLUMOUS	PLURISETOSE	PNEUMATOGRAM
PLOUGHJOGGER	PLUGHOLE	PLUMP	PLURISPIRAL	PNEUMATOLOGY
PLOUGHLAND	PLUGMAN	PLUMPEN	PLURISPOROUS	PNEUMATOSIS
PLOUGHLINE	PLUGMEN	PLUMPER	PLURISY	PNEUMATURIA
PLOUGHMAN	PLUGS	PLUMPEST	PLURIVALENT	PNEUME
PLOUGHMELL	PLUGTRAY	PLUMPING	PLURIVALVE	PNEUMECTOMY
PLOUGHPOINT	PLUKE	PLUMPLY	PLURIVOROUS	PNEUMOCELE
PLOUGHSHARE	PLUM	PLUMPNESS	PLURIVORY	PNEUMOCOCCUS
PLOUGHSHOE	PLUMA	PLUMPS	PLUS	PNEUMODERMA
PLOUGHSTAFF	PLUMACEOUS	PLUMPY	PLUSES	PNEUMOGASTRIC
PLOUGHSTILT	PLUMACH	PLUMROCK	PLUSH	PNEUMOGRAM
PLOUGHTAIL	PLUMADE	PLUMULA	PLUSHED	PNEUMOGRAPH
PLOUGHWISE	PLUMAGE	PLUMULACEOUS	PLUSHETTE	PNEUMOLITH
PLOUGHWRIGHT	PLUMAGED	PLUMULAR	PLUSHIER	PNEUMOLOGY
PLOUK	PLUMAGERY	PLUMULARIAN	PLUSHIEST	PNEUMOLYSIS
PLOUNCE	PLUMASITE	PLUMULATE	PLUSHILY	PNEUMONALGIA
PLOUSIOCRACY	PLUMASSIER	PLUMULE	PLUSHINESS	PNEUMONIA
PLOUT	PLUMATE	PLUMULIFORM	PLUSHY	PNEUMONIC
PLOUTER	PLUMATELLID	PLUMULOSE	PLUSQUAM	PNEUMONITIC
PLOVER	PLUMATELLOID	PLUMY	PLUSSAGE	PNEUMONOCACE
PLOVERS	PLUMB	PLUNDER	PLUTEAL	PNEUMONOCELE
PLOVERY	PLUMBAGE	PLUNDERAGE	PLUTEAN	PNEUMONOLITH
PLOW	PLUMBAGINE	PLUNDERBUND	PLUTEI	PNEUMONOPEXY
PLOWABLE	PLUMBAGINOUS	PLUNDERED	PLUTEIFORM	PNEUMONOSIS
PLOWBOTE	PLUMBAGO	PLUNDERER	PLUTEUS	PNEUMOPEXY
PLOWBOY	PLUMBAGOS	PLUNDERESS	PLUTEUSES	PNEUMOTHORAX
PLOWED	PLUMBATE	PLUNDERING	PLUTOCRACIES	PNEUMOTOMY
PLOWER	PLUMBEAN	PLUNDERINGLY	PLUTOCRACY	PNEUMOTOXIN
PLOWFISH	PLUMBED	PLUNDEROUS	PLUTOCRAT	PO
PLOWFOOT	PLUMBEOUS	PLUNDERPROOF	PLUTOCRATIC	POACEOUS
PLOWGANG	PLUMBER	PLUNGE	PLUTOCRATICAL	POACH
PLOWGATE	PLUMBERIES	PLUNGED	PLUTOLATRY	POACHED
PLOWGRAITH	PLUMBERY	PLUNGEON	PLUTOLOGICAL	POACHER
PLOWHEAD	PLUMBET	PLUNGER	PLUTOLOGIST	POACHIER
PLOWING	PLUMBIC	PLUNGING	PLUTOLOGY	POACHIEST
PLOWJOGGER	PLUMBING	PLUNGY	PLUTOMANIA	POACHINESS
PLOWLAND	PLUMBISM	PLUNK	PLUTONIAN	POACHING
PLOWLIGHT	PLUMBITE	PLUNKED	PLUTONIC	POACHY
PLOWLINE	PLUMBLESS	PLUNKING	PLUTONISM	POAK
PLOWMAKER	PLUMBNESS	PLUNTHER	PLUTONIST	POAKE
PLOWMAKING	PLUMBOG	PLUPATRIOTIC	PLUTONITE	POALI
PLOWMAN	PLUMBOUS	PLUPERFECT	PLUTONIUM	POALO
PLOWMELL	PLUMBUM	PLUPERFECTLY	PLUTONOMIC	POAP
PLOWMEN	PLUMCOT	PLURAL	PLUTONOMIST	POB
PLOWPOINT	PLUME	PLURALISM	PLUTONOMY	POBBIES
PLOWSHARE	PLUMED	PLURALIST	PLUTTER	POBBY
PLOWSHOE	PLUMELET	PLURALISTIC	PLUVIAL	POBEDY
PLOWSTAFF	PLUMEMAKER	PLURALITIES	PLUVIALINE	POBLACION
PLOWSTILT	PLUMEMAKING	PLURALITY	PLUVINE	POBS
PLOWTAIL	PLUMEOUS	PLURALIZE	PLUVIOGRAPH	POCAN
PLOWTER	PLUMER	PLURALIZED	PLUVIOGRAPHY	POCHADE
PLOWWISE	PLUMERY	PLURALIZER	PLUVIOMETER	POCHARD
PLOWWOMAN	PLUMET	PLURALIZING	PLUVIOMETRIC	POCHAY
PLOWWRIGHT	PLUMETE	PLURALLY	PLUVIOMETRY	POCHE
PLOY	PLUMETIS	PLURATIVE	PLUVIOSCOPE	POCHETTE
PLOYMENT	PLUMETTE	PLUREL	PLUVIOSITY	POCHETTINO
PLUCK	PLUMICORN	PLURENNIAL	PLUVIOUS	POCHISMO
PLUCKED	PLUMIER	PLURIAXIAL	PLY	POCHOIR
PLUCKER	PLUMIERIDE	PLURICIPITAL	PLYFR	POCHOTE
PLUCKIER	PLUMIEST	PLURICUSPID	PLYGAIN	POCILLIFORM
PLUCKIEST	PLUMING	PLURIES	PLYING	POCK
PLUCKILY	PLUMIPED	PLURIFACIAL	PLYWOOD	POCKET
PLUCKINESS	PLUMIPEDE	PLURIFOLIATE	PNEOGRAPH	POCKETABLE
PLUCKING	PLUMIST	PLURIFY	PNEOMETER	POCKETBOOK
PLUCKY	PLUMLIKE	PLURILATERAL	PNEOMETRY	POCKETED
PLUD	PLUMMER	PLURILINGUAL	PNEOSCOPE	POCKETER
PLUFF	PLUMMET	PLURILOCULAR	PNEUMA	POCKETFUL
PLUFFER	PLUMMETED	PLURINOMINAL	PNEUMATIC	POCKETFULS
PLUFFY	PLUMMETLESS	PLURIPARA	PNEUMATICAL	POCKETING
PLUG	PLUMMIER	PLURIPARITY	PNEUMATICITY	POCKETKNIFE
PLUGBOARD	PLUMMIEST	PLURIPAROUS	PNEUMATICS	POCKETKNIVES
PLUGDRAWER	PLUMMING	PLURIPARTITE	PNEUMATISM	POCKETS
PLUGGABLE	PLUMMY	PLURIPOTENCE	PNEUMATIST	POCKETY

POCKHOUSE	PODOMERE	POGONOLOGIST	POISER	POLEAXE
POCKIER	PODOPHYLLIC	POGONOLOGY	POISING	POLEAXER
POCKIEST	PODOPHYLLIN	POGONOTOMY	POISON	POLEBURN
POCKMANKY	PODOPHYLLOUS	POGONOTROPHY	POISONABLE	POLECAT
POCKMARK	PODOS	POGROM	POISONBERRY	POLECATS
POCKWEED	PODOSCAPH	POGROMIST	POISONBUSH	POLED
POCKWOOD	PODOSCAPHER	POGUE	POISONED	POLEHEAD
POCKY	PODOSCOPY	POGY	POISONER	POLEMAN
POCO	PODOSPERM	POH	POISONING	POLEMARCH
POCOCURANTE	PODOTHECA	POHA	POISONMAKER	POLEMIC
POCOSIN	PODOTHECAL	POHICKORY	POISONOUS	POLEMICAL
POCULARY	PODS	POHUTUKAWA	POISONOUSLY	POLEMICALLY
POCULATION	PODSOL	POI	POISONWEED	POLEMICIAN
POCULENT	PODURAN	POIESIS	POISONWOOD	POLEMICIST
POCULIFORM	PODURID	POIETIC	POISSARDE	POLEMICS
POD	PODWARE	POIGNADO	POISSON	POLEMIST
PODAGRA	PODZOL	POIGNANCE	POISTER	POLEMIZE
PODAGRAL	PODZOLIC	POIGNANCIES	POISURE	POLEMOSCOPE
PODAGRIC	POE	POIGNANCY	POIT	POLENTA
PODAGRICAL	POEBIRD	POIGNANT	POITRAIL	POLER
PODAGROUS	POECHORE	POIGNANTLY	POITREL	POLES
PODAGRY	POECHORIC	POIGNET	POITRINAIRE	POLESAW
PODAL	POECILITIC	POIKILE	POIVRADE	POLESETTER
PODALGIA	POECILOGONY	POIKILITIC	POIZE	POLESTAR
PODALIC	POECILOMERE	POIKILOBLAST	POKAL	POLEWARD
PODANGER	POECILONYM	POIKILOCYTE	POKE	POLEWARDS
PODARGUE	POECILONYMIC	POIKILOTHERM	POKEBERRY	POLEY
PODARTHRITIS	POECILONYMY	POIKILOTHERMAL	POKED	POLEYN
PODARTHRUM	POECILOPOD	POIL	POKEFUL	POLEYNE
PODATUS	POEM	POILU	POKELOKEN	POLI
PODDED	POEMATIC	POIMENIC	POKER	POLIAD
PODDER	POEMS	POIMENICS	POKERISH	POLIADIC
PODDIDGE	POENOLOGY	POINADO	POKERISHLY	POLIANITE
PODDIGE	POEPHAGOUS	POINARD	POKERISHNESS	POLICE
PODDING	POESIS	POINCIANA	POKEROOT	POLICED
PODDISH	POESY	POIND	POKEWEED	POLICEMAN
PODDLE	POET	POINDABLE	POKEY	POLICEMEN
PODDOCK	POETASTER	POINDER	POKIES	POLICEWOMAN
PODDY	POETASTERING	POINDING	POKING	POLICEWOMEN
PODE	POETASTERY	POING	POKKE	POLICIAL
PODELCOMA	POETASTRIC	POINT	POKOMOO	POLICIES
PODEON	POETASTRICAL	POINTABLE	POKUNT	POLICING
PODESTA	POETASTRY	POINTAGE	POKY	POLICIZE
PODESTERATE	POETESQUE	POINTAL	POLACCA	POLICIZER
PODETIIFORM	POETESS	POINTBLANK	POLACRE	POLICLINIC
PODETIUM	POETIC	POINTE	POLAK	POLICY
PODEX	POETICAL	POINTED	POLAR	POLICYHOLDER
PODGE	POETICALITY	POINTEDLY	POLARIC	POLIES
PODGER	POETICALLY	POINTEDNESS	POLARIMETER	POLIGAR
PODGIER	POETICIZE	POINTEL	POLARIMETRIC	POLIGARSHIP
PODGIEST	POETICS	POINTER	POLARIMETRY	POLILLA
PODGILY	POETICULE	POINTES	POLARISCOPE	POLING
PODGINESS	POETITO	POINTIER	POLARISCOPY	POLIO
PODGY	POETIZATION	POINTIEST	POLARISE	POLIORCETIC
PODIA	POETIZE	POINTILLE	POLARISTIC	POLIOSIS
PODIAL	POETIZED	POINTILLISM	POLARITY	POLIS
PODIATRIST	POETIZER	POINTILLIST	POLARIZABLE	POLISH
PODIATRY	POETIZING	POINTING	POLARIZATION	POLISHED
PODICAL	POETLING	POINTINGLY	POLARIZE	POLISHER
PODILEGOUS	POETLY	POINTLESS	POLARIZED	POLISHING
PODITE	POETOMACHIA	POINTLESSLY	POLARIZER	POLISHINGS
PODITIC	POETRY	POINTLET	POLARIZING	POLISHMENT
PODITTI	POFFLE	POINTLETED	POLARON	POLISSOIR
PODIUM	POGAMOGGAN	POINTMAKER	POLARY	POLISTA
PODLER	POGEY	POINTMAKING	POLATOUCHE	POLITARCH
PODLEY	POGGE	POINTMAN	POLAXIS	POLITARCHIC
PODO	POGGIES	POINTMEN	POLDAVIS	POLITE
PODOBRANCH	POGGY	POINTMENT	POLDAVY	POLITEFUL
PODOCARP	POGIE	POINTS	POLDER	POLITEIA
PODODERM	POGIES	POINTSMAN	POLDERBOY	POLITELY
PODODYNIA	POGO	POINTURE	POLDERLAND	POLITENESS
PODOGYN	POGONIA	POINTWAYS	POLDERMAN	POLITER
PODOGYNE	POGONIASIS	POINTWISE	POLDOODY	POLITESSE
PODOGYNIUM	POGONIATE	POINTY	POLDRON	POLITEST
PODOLITE	POGONION	POIS	POLE	POLITIC
PODOLOGY	POGONIP	POISE	POLEARM	POLITICAL
PODOMANCY	POGONITE	POISED	POLEAX	POLITICALISM

POLITICALIZE
POLITICALLY
POLITICIAN
POLITICIOUS
POLITICIST
POLITICIZE
POLITICIZED
POLITICIZER
POLITICIZING
POLITICK
POLITICLY
POLITICOS
POLITICS
POLITIED
POLITIES
POLITIST
POLITIZE
POLITURE
POLITY
POLITZERIZE
POLJE
POLK
POLKA
POLKAED
POLKAING
POLL
POLLABLE
POLLACK
POLLAGE
POLLAKIURIA
POLLAM
POLLAN
POLLARCHY
POLLARD
POLLARDED
POLLARDING
POLLBOOK
POLLE
POLLED
POLLEE
POLLEN
POLLENATE
POLLENATION
POLLENED
POLLENITE
POLLENT
POLLER
POLLERA
POLLET
POLLETEN
POLLETTE
POLLEX
POLLICAL
POLLICAR
POLLICES
POLLICITATION
POLLINAR
POLLINARIUM
POLLINATE
POLLINATED
POLLINATING
POLLINATION
POLLINATOR
POLLINCTOR
POLLINCTURE
POLLING
POLLINIC
POLLINIUM
POLLINIZE
POLLINIZER
POLLINODIAL
POLLINODIUM
POLLINOID
POLLINOSE
POLLINOSIS
POLLIWOG
POLLOCK

POLLSTER
POLLUCITE
POLLUTANT
POLLUTE
POLLUTED
POLLUTER
POLLUTING
POLLUTION
POLLYWOG
POLO
POLOCONIC
POLOIST
POLONAISE
POLONICK
POLONIUM
POLONY
POLOS
POLSKA
POLSTER
POLT
POLTERGEIST
POLTFOOT
POLTFOOTED
POLTINA
POLTINIK
POLTOPHAGIC
POLTOPHAGIST
POLTOPHAGY
POLTROON
POLTROONERY
POLTROONISH
POLTROONISM
POLVERINE
POLY
POLYACID
POLYACOUSTIC
POLYACT
POLYACTINAL
POLYACTINE
POLYAD
POLYADELPH
POLYADENIA
POLYADIC
POLYAEMIA
POLYAEMIC
POLYALCOHOL
POLYAMIDE
POLYAMYLOSE
POLYANDRIA
POLYANDRIAN
POLYANDRIC
POLYANDRISM
POLYANDRIST
POLYANDRIUM
POLYANDROUS
POLYANDRY
POLYANTHA
POLYANTHUS
POLYARCH
POLYARCHAL
POLYARCHICAL
POLYARCHIST
POLYARCHY
POLYAXON
POLYAXONE
POLYBASIC
POLYBASICITY
POLYBASITE
POLYBLAST
POLYBORINE
POLYBUNOUS
POLYBUNY
POLYCARPIC
POLYCARPOUS
POLYCARPY
POLYCENTRISM

POLYCENTRIST
POLYCHAETAL
POLYCHAETAN
POLYCHAETE
POLYCHAETOUS
POLYCHASIAL
POLYCHASIUM
POLYCHLORIDE
POLYCHOERANY
POLYCHORD
POLYCHREST
POLYCHRESTIC
POLYCHRESTY
POLYCHROIC
POLYCHROMATE
POLYCHROME
POLYCHROMIA
POLYCHROMIC
POLYCHROMISM
POLYCHROMIZE
POLYCHROMOUS
POLYCHROMY
POLYCLAD
POLYCLADINE
POLYCLINIC
POLYCONIC
POLYCOTYL
POLYCRACY
POLYCRASE
POLYCRATIC
POLYCROTIC
POLYCROTISM
POLYCYCLIC
POLYCYESIS
POLYDACTYL
POLYDACTYLE
POLYDACTYLY
POLYDEMIC
POLYDIPSIA
POLYDISPERSE
POLYDOMOUS
POLYDYMITE
POLYDYNAMIC
POLYEIDIC
POLYEIDISM
POLYEMIA
POLYEMIC
POLYERGIC
POLYESTHESIA
POLYETHNIC
POLYETHYLENE
POLYGALIN
POLYGAM
POLYGAMIAN
POLYGAMIC
POLYGAMICAL
POLYGAMIST
POLYGAMIZE
POLYGAMOUS
POLYGAMY
POLYGAR
POLYGENE
POLYGENESIC
POLYGENESIS
POLYGENESIST
POLYGENETIC
POLYGENIC
POLYGENISM
POLYGENIST
POLYGENOUS
POLYGENY
POLYGLOSSARY
POLYGLOT
POLYGLOTRY
POLYGLOTTAL
POLYGLOTTED
POLYGLOTTER

POLYGLOTTERY
POLYGLOTTIC
POLYGLOTTING
POLYGLOTTISM
POLYGLOTTIST
POLYGLYCEROL
POLYGON
POLYGONAL
POLYGONALLY
POLYGONEUTIC
POLYGONIC
POLYGONOID
POLYGONOUS
POLYGONUM
POLYGONY
POLYGRAM
POLYGRAPH
POLYGRAPHER
POLYGRAPHIC
POLYGRAPHY
POLYGYN
POLYGYNAIKY
POLYGYNIAN
POLYGYNIST
POLYGYNOUS
POLYGYNY
POLYGYRAL
POLYGYRIA
POLYHAEMIA
POLYHAEMIC
POLYHALIDE
POLYHALITE
POLYHARMONIC
POLYHARMONY
POLYHEDRA
POLYHEDRAL
POLYHEDRIC
POLYHEDRICAL
POLYHEDROID
POLYHEDRON
POLYHEDRONS
POLYHEDROUS
POLYHEMIA
POLYHEMIC
POLYHIDROSIS
POLYHISTOR
POLYHISTORIC
POLYHISTORY
POLYHYBRID
POLYHYDRIC
POLYHYDROXY
POLYIDEIC
POLYIDEISM
POLYIDROSIS
POLYLEMMA
POLYLEPIDOUS
POLYLITH
POLYLITHIC
POLYLOGY
POLYLOQUENT
POLYMAGNET
POLYMANIA
POLYMASTIA
POLYMASTIC
POLYMASTISM
POLYMASTY
POLYMATH
POLYMATHIC
POLYMATHIST
POLYMATHY
POLYMAZIA
POLYMELIA
POLYMELIAN
POLYMELY
POLYMER
POLYMERE
POLYMERIA

POLYMERIC
POLYMERISE
POLYMERISM
POLYMERIZE
POLYMEROUS
POLYMETER
POLYMETOCHIC
POLYMICRIAN
POLYMICROBIC
POLYMIGNITE
POLYMIXIID
POLYMNITE
POLYMNY
POLYMORPH
POLYMORPHIC
POLYMORPHISM
POLYMORPHOUS
POLYMORPHY
POLYMYARIAN
POLYMYODIAN
POLYMYODOUS
POLYMYOID
POLYMYOSITIS
POLYMYTHIC
POLYMYTHY
POLYNEE
POLYNEMID
POLYNEMOID
POLYNESIC
POLYNEURITIC
POLYNEURITIS
POLYNICES
POLYNOID
POLYNOMIAL
POLYNOMIC
POLYNUCLEAR
POLYNUCLEATE
POLYNYA
POLYODON
POLYODONT
POLYODONTAL
POLYODONTIA
POLYODONTOID
POLYOECIOUS
POLYOECISM
POLYOICOUS
POLYOL
POLYONOMOUS
POLYONOMY
POLYONYCHIA
POLYONYM
POLYONYMAL
POLYONYMIC
POLYONYMIST
POLYONYMOUS
POLYONYMY
POLYOPIA
POLYORAMA
POLYORGANIC
POLYOSE
POLYOXIDE
POLYP
POLYPARIA
POLYPARIAN
POLYPARIES
POLYPARIUM
POLYPAROUS
POLYPARY
POLYPEAN
POLYPED
POLYPEPTIDE
POLYPETAL
POLYPETALOUS
POLYPETALY
POLYPHAGE
POLYPHAGIA
POLYPHAGIAN

POLYPHAGIC
POLYPHAGIST
POLYPHAGOUS
POLYPHAGY
POLYPHARMACY
POLYPHARMIC
POLYPHASAL
POLYPHASE
POLYPHASER
POLYPHEMIAN
POLYPHEMIC
POLYPHEMUS
POLYPHENOL
POLYPHOBIA
POLYPHONE
POLYPHONED
POLYPHONIC
POLYPHONICAL
POLYPHONIES
POLYPHONISM
POLYPHONIST
POLYPHONIUM
POLYPHONOUS
POLYPHONY
POLYPHORE
POLYPHOTAL
POLYPHOTE
POLYPHYLESIS
POLYPHYLETIC
POLYPHYLLINE
POLYPHYLY
POLYPHYODONT
POLYPIAN
POLYPIDE
POLYPIDOM
POLYPIFEROUS
POLYPIGEROUS
POLYPITE
POLYPLASTIC
POLYPLOID
POLYPLOIDIC
POLYPLOIDY
POLYPNOEA
POLYPOD
POLYPODIA
POLYPODIES
POLYPODY
POLYPOID
POLYPOIDAL
POLYPORE
POLYPORITE
POLYPOROID
POLYPOSE
POLYPOSIS
POLYPOTOME
POLYPOUS
POLYPRAGMACY
POLYPRAGMATY
POLYPRAGMON
POLYPRENE
POLYPRISM
POLYPSYCHIC
POLYPSYCHISM
POLYPTERID
POLYPTEROID
POLYPTOTON
POLYPTYCH
POLYPUS
POLYRHYTHMIC
POLYSACCHARIDE
POLYSARCIA
POLYSARCOUS
POLYSCOPE
POLYSCOPIC
POLYSEMANT
POLYSEMANTIC

POLYSEMEIA
POLYSEMIA
POLYSEMY
POLYSENSUOUS
POLYSIPHONIC
POLYSOMIA
POLYSOMITIC
POLYSPAST
POLYSPASTON
POLYSPERMIA
POLYSPERMIC
POLYSPERMY
POLYSPONDYLY
POLYSPORE
POLYSPORED
POLYSPORIC
POLYSPOROUS
POLYSTAURION
POLYSTELE
POLYSTELLIC
POLYSTICHOID
POLYSTOME
POLYSTOMIUM
POLYSTYLE
POLYSTYLOUS
POLYSTYRENE
POLYSULFIDE
POLYSULPHID
POLYSULPHIDE
POLYSYLLABIC
POLYSYLLABLE
POLYSYNDETIC
POLYSYNDETON
POLYTECHNIC
POLYTECHNICS
POLYTECHNIST
POLYTHEISM
POLYTHEIST
POLYTHEISTIC
POLYTHEIZE
POLYTHELIA
POLYTHIONIC
POLYTOCOUS
POLYTOMOUS
POLYTOMY
POLYTONAL
POLYTONALISM
POLYTONALITY
POLYTONE
POLYTONIC
POLYTONY
POLYTOPE
POLYTOPIC
POLYTOPICAL
POLYTRICHIA
POLYTRICHOUS
POLYTROCHAL
POLYTROCHOUS
POLYTROPE
POLYTROPHIC
POLYTYPE
POLYTYPED
POLYTYPIC
POLYTYPICAL
POLYTYPING
POLYTYPY
POLYURESIS
POLYURETHANE
POLYURIA
POLYURIC
POLYVALENCE
POLYVALENT
POLYVE
POLYVINYL
POLYVIRULENT
POLYVOLTINE
POLYZOAN

POLYZOARIA
POLYZOARIAL
POLYZOARIUM
POLYZOARY
POLYZOIC
POLYZOISM
POLYZONAL
POLYZOOID
POLYZOON
POLZENITE
POM
POMACE
POMACENTRID
POMACENTROID
POMACEOUS
POMADA
POMADE
POMADED
POMADING
POMANDER
POMANE
POMARINE
POMARIUM
POMARY
POMATE
POMATO
POMATOES
POMATOMID
POMATORHINE
POMATUM
POMBE
POMBO
POME
POMEGRANATE
POMELO
POMELY
POMERIA
POMERIUM
POMEROY
POMESHCHIK
POMEWATER
POMEY
POMEYS
POMFRET
POMICULTURE
POMIFEROUS
POMIFORM
POMIVOROUS
POMMADO
POMMAGE
POMME
POMMEE
POMMEL
POMMELED
POMMELER
POMMELING
POMMELION
POMMELLED
POMMELLER
POMMELLING
POMMELO
POMMER
POMMIES
POMMY
POMOERIUM
POMOLO
POMOLOGICAL
POMOLOGIST
POMOLOGY
POMONAL
POMONIC
POMP
POMPA
POMPADOUR
POMPAL
POMPANO
POMPANOS

POMPELMOOSE
POMPELMOUS
POMPERKIN
POMPHOLIX
POMPHOLYX
POMPHUS
POMPIER
POMPILID
POMPILOID
POMPION
POMPIST
POMPLESS
POMPON
POMPOON
POMPOSITY
POMPOSO
POMPOUS
POMPOUSLY
POMPOUSNESS
POMSTER
PON
PONCE
PONCEAU
PONCELET
PONCHO
PONCHOED
PONCHOS
POND
PONDAGE
PONDBUSH
PONDER
PONDERABILITY
PONDERABLE
PONDERAL
PONDERANCE
PONDERANCY
PONDERANT
PONDERARY
PONDERATE
PONDERATION
PONDERATIVE
PONDERED
PONDERER
PONDERING
PONDERINGLY
PONDERLING
PONDEROSITY
PONDEROUS
PONDEROUSLY
PONDEROUSNESS
PONDFISH
PONDFISHES
PONDGRASS
PONDMAN
PONDOK
PONDOKKIE
PONDUS
PONDWEED
PONDWORT
PONDY
PONE
PONENT
PONERID
PONERINE
PONEROID
PONEROLOGY
PONEY
PONG
PONGA
PONGEE
PONGID
PONGO
PONHAWS
PONIARD
PONIARDED
PONIARDING
PONICA

PONIER
PONIES
PONJA
PONOR
PONS
PONT
PONTAGE
PONTAL
PONTEE
PONTES
PONTIC
PONTICELLO
PONTICULAR
PONTICULUS
PONTIFEX
PONTIFF
PONTIFIC
PONTIFICAL
PONTIFICALLY
PONTIFICATE
PONTIFICATED
PONTIFICES
PONTIFICIAL
PONTIFY
PONTIL
PONTILE
PONTIN
PONTINE
PONTIST
PONTLEVIS
PONTON
PONTONIER
PONTOON
PONTUS
PONTVOLANT
PONY
PONYTAIL
PONZITE
POO
POOA
POOAH
POOCH
POOD
POODLE
POODLER
POOGYE
POOH
POOJA
POOJAH
POOK
POOKA
POOKAUN
POOKAWN
POOKHAUN
POOKOO
POOL
POOLER
POOLI
POOLROOM
POOLROOT
POOLWORT
POOLY
POON
POONA
POONAC
POONGEE
POONGHEE
POONGHIE
POOP
POOPED
POOPHYTE
POOPHYTIC
POOR
POORER
POOREST
POORHOUSE
POORISH

POORLINESS	POPPYWORT	PORISTIC	PORRACEOUS	PORTIONED
POORLING	POPSHOP	PORISTICAL	PORRECT	PORTIONER
POORLY	POPSICLE	PORITE	PORRET	PORTIONING
POORLYISH	POPSKULL	PORITOID	PORRIDGE	PORTIONIST
POORMASTER	POPULACE	PORK	PORRIDGY	PORTIONLESS
POORNESS	POPULACY	PORKEATER	PORRIGINOUS	PORTITOR
POORT	POPULAR	PORKER	PORRIGO	PORTLAST
POORTITH	POPULARES	PORKERY	PORRINGER	PORTLET
POORWILL	POPULARISE	PORKET	PORRY	PORTLIGATURE
POOSE	POPULARISM	PORKFISH	PORT	PORTLIGHT
POOT	POPULARITY	PORKFISHES	PORTA	PORTLILY
POOTHER	POPULARIZE	PORKIER	PORTABILITY	PORTLINESS
POOTY	POPULARIZED	PORKIES	PORTABLE	PORTLY
POP	POPULARIZER	PORKIEST	PORTABLENESS	PORTMAN
POPADAM	POPULARIZING	PORKIN	PORTABLY	PORTMANMOTE
POPAL	POPULARLY	PORKISH	PORTAGE	PORTMANTEAU
POPCORN	POPULARNESS	PORKLING	PORTAGUE	PORTMANTLE
POPDOCK	POPULATE	PORKMAN	PORTAL	PORTMENT
POPE	POPULATED	PORKPEN	PORTALED	PORTMOOT
POPEDOM	POPULATING	PORKPIE	PORTALLED	PORTMOTE
POPEHOLY	POPULATION	PORKWOOD	PORTAMENTI	PORTO
POPEHOOD	POPULATIONAL	PORKY	PORTAMENTO	PORTOISE
POPEISM	POPULATOR	PORNERASTIC	PORTANCE	PORTOLANO
POPEL	POPULEON	PORNO	PORTAS	PORTPAYNE
POPELER	POPULICIDE	PORNOCRACY	PORTASS	PORTRAIT
POPELINE	POPULIN	PORNOCRAT	PORTATILE	PORTRAITIST
POPELING	POPULOUS	PORNOGRAPHER	PORTATIVE	PORTRAITURE
POPELY	POPULOUSLY	PORNOGRAPHIC	PORTATO	PORTRAY
POPERY	POPULOUSNESS	PORNOGRAPHIES	PORTATOR	PORTRAYABLE
POPEYE	POPWEED	PORNOGRAPHY	PORTCRAYON	PORTRAYAL
POPEYED	PORAIL	PORNOLOGICAL	PORTCULLIS	PORTRAYED
POPGLOVE	PORAL	PORO	PORTCULLISED	PORTRAYER
POPGUN	PORBEAGLE	PORODINE	PORTCULLISING	PORTRAYING
POPGUNNER	PORCATE	PORODITE	PORTEACID	PORTRAYIST
POPGUNNERY	PORCATED	POROGAM	PORTED	PORTRAYMENT
POPINAC	PORCELAIN	POROGAMIC	PORTEND	PORTREEVE
POPINJAY	PORCELAINIZE	POROGAMOUS	PORTENDANCE	PORTRESS
POPISH	PORCELAINLIKE	POROGAMY	PORTENDED	PORTSALE
POPISHLY	PORCELAINOUS	POROMA	PORTENDING	PORTSIDE
POPISHNESS	PORCELANEOUS	POROMAS	PORTENSION	PORTSIDER
POPJOY	PORCELANIC	POROMATA	PORTENT	PORTSMAN
POPLAR	PORCELANITE	POROMETER	PORTENTION	PORTSOKEN
POPLARED	PORCELANOUS	POROPLASTIC	PORTENTIVE	PORTUGAIS
POPLEMAN	PORCELLANIAN	POROPORO	PORTENTOSITY	PORTULACA
POPLESIE	PORCELLANIC	POROROCA	PORTENTOUS	PORTUNIAN
POPLET	PORCELLANID	POROS	PORTENTOUSLY	PORTUNID
POPLIN	PORCELLANITE	POROSCOPE	PORTEOUS	PORTURE
POPLINETTE	PORCELLANIZE	POROSCOPIC	PORTER	PORTY
POPLITAEAL	PORCELLANOUS	POROSCOPY	PORTERAGE	PORULE
POPLITEAL	PORCH	POROSE	PORTERESS	PORULOSE
POPLITEUS	PORCHED	POROSENESS	PORTERHOUSE	PORULOUS
POPLITIC	PORCHING	POROSIMETER	PORTERLY	PORUS
POPLOLLY	PORCINE	POROSIS	PORTESSE	PORWIGLE
POPOMASTIC	PORCUPINE	POROSITIES	PORTFIRE	PORY
POPOVER	PORCUPINISH	POROSITY	PORTFOLIO	POS
POPPA	PORE	POROTIC	PORTFOLIOS	POSADA
POPPABILITY	PORED	POROTYPE	PORTGLAIVE	POSADAS
POPPABLE	PORER	POROUS	PORTGLAVE	POSCA
POPPEAN	PORES	POROUSLY	PORTGRAVE	POSCHAY
POPPED	PORET	POROUSNESS	PORTGREVE	POSE
POPPER	PORETT	PORPENTINE	PORTHOLE	POSED
POPPET	PORGE	PORPHYRATIN	PORTHOOK	POSEMENT
POPPETHEAD	PORGER	PORPHYRIAN	PORTHORS	POSER
POPPIED	PORGIES	PORPHYRIES	PORTHOUSE	POSEUR
POPPIES	PORGY	PORPHYRIN	PORTICO	POSEUSE
POPPIN	PORI	PORPHYRINE	PORTICOED	POSEY
POPPING	PORICIDAL	PORPHYRION	PORTICOES	POSH
POPPLE	PORIFERAL	PORPHYRITE	PORTICOS	POSIED
POPPLED	PORIFERAN	PORPHYRITIC	PORTICUS	POSIES
POPPLING	PORIFEROUS	PORPHYROID	PORTIERE	POSING
POPPLY	PORIFORM	PORPHYROUS	PORTIERED	POSIT
POPPY	PORINA	PORPHYRY	PORTIFY	POSITED
POPPYCOCK	PORINESS	PORPITOID	PORTING	POSITING
POPPYCOCKISH	PORING	PORPOISE	PORTIO	POSITION
POPPYFISH	PORION	PORPOISES	PORTION	POSITIONAL
POPPYFISHES	PORISM	PORPORATE	PORTIONAL	POSITIONED
POPPYHEAD	PORISMATIC	PORR	PORTIONALLY	POSITIONER

POSITIONING	POSTCENTRAL	POSTICUM	POSTREMOTE	POTBOIL
POSITIVAL	POSTCENTRUM	POSTICUS	POSTRIDER	POTBOILER
POSITIVE	POSTCIBAL	POSTIL	POSTRORSE	POTBOY
POSITIVELY	POSTCLASSIC	POSTILER	POSTS	POTBOYDOM
POSITIVENESS	POSTCLAVICLE	POSTILION	POSTSCAPULA	POTCH
POSITIVISM	POSTCLIVAL	POSTILIONED	POSTSCAPULAR	POTCHER
POSITIVIST	POSTCOENAL	POSTILLATE	POSTSCENIUM	POTCHERMAN
POSITIVISTIC	POSTCOLONIAL	POSTILLATION	POSTSCHOOL	POTCHERMEN
POSITIVITY	POSTCOMITIAL	POSTILLATOR	POSTSCRIBE	POTDAR
POSITIVIZE	POSTCONTACT	POSTILLER	POSTSCRIPT	POTE
POSITOR	POSTCORNU	POSTILLION	POSTSCRIPTUM	POTECARY
POSITRINO	POSTCOSMIC	POSTILLIONED	POSTSPHENOID	POTEEN
POSITRON	POSTCRIBRATE	POSTILS	POSTSYNAPTIC	POTENCE
POSITRONIUM	POSTDATE	POSTIN	POSTSYSTOLIC	POTENCIES
POSITUM	POSTDATED	POSTING	POSTTEMPORAL	POTENCY
POSITURE	POSTDATING	POSTINGLY	POSTTONIC	POTENT
POSNET	POSTDENTAL	POSTIQUE	POSTTYMPANIC	POTENTACY
POSOL	POSTDICROTIC	POSTJACENT	POSTULANCY	POTENTATE
POSOLE	POSTDILUVIAL	POSTLIMINARY	POSTULANT	POTENTIAL
POSOLOGIC	POSTDILUVIAN	POSTLIMINIUM	POSTULATE	POTENTIALITY
POSOLOGICAL	POSTE	POSTLIMINOUS	POSTULATED	POTENTIALIZE
POSOLOGIST	POSTEA	POSTLIMINY	POSTULATING	POTENTIALLY
POSOLOGY	POSTED	POSTLUDE	POSTULATION	POTENTIATE
POSOSTEMAD	POSTEEN	POSTLUDIUM	POSTULATOR	POTENTIATION
POSPOLITE	POSTEL	POSTMAN	POSTULATORY	POTENTILLA
POSS	POSTENTRIES	POSTMARITAL	POSTULATUM	POTENTIZE
POSSE	POSTENTRY	POSTMARK	POSTURAL	POTENTLY
POSSEMAN	POSTER	POSTMARRIAGE	POSTURE	POTENTNESS
POSSEMEN	POSTERIAD	POSTMASTER	POSTURED	POTER
POSSESS	POSTERIAL	POSTMATURITY	POSTURER	POTESTAL
POSSESSED	POSTERIOR	POSTMEDIA	POSTURING	POTESTAS
POSSESSEDLY	POSTERIORI	POSTMEDIAL	POSTURIST	POTESTATE
POSSESSING	POSTERIORIC	POSTMEDIAN	POSTURIZE	POTESTATIVE
POSSESSION	POSTERIORITY	POSTMEN	POSTURIZED	POTEYE
POSSESSIONAL	POSTERIORLY	POSTMERIDIAN	POSTURIZING	POTFUL
POSSESSIONED	POSTERIORS	POSTMINERAL	POSTVELAR	POTGUN
POSSESSIONER	POSTERIORUMS	POSTMISTRESS	POSTVERBAL	POTHANGER
POSSESSIONS	POSTERIST	POSTMORTAL	POSTVIDE	POTHEAD
POSSESSIVE	POSTERITY	POSTMORTEM	POSTVOCALIC	POTHECARIES
POSSESSOR	POSTERIZE	POSTMORTUARY	POSTWAR	POTHECARY
POSSESSORIAL	POSTERN	POSTMUNDANE	POSTWARD	POTHEEN
POSSESSORY	POSTETERNITY	POSTMUTATIVE	POSTWISE	POTHER
POSSET	POSTEXILIAN	POSTNARIAL	POSTWOMAN	POTHERB
POSSIBILE	POSTEXILIC	POSTNARIS	POSTWOMEN	POTHERED
POSSIBILIST	POSTEXIST	POSTNASAL	POSTYARD	POTHERING
POSSIBILITY	POSTEXISTENT	POSTNATAL	POSY	POTHERMENT
POSSIBLE	POSTFACE	POSTNATE	POT	POTHERY
POSSIBLENESS	POSTFACT	POSTNATI	POTABILITY	POTHOLE
POSSIBLY	POSTFIX	POSTNATUS	POTABLE	POTHOOK
POSSIE	POSTFIXED	POSTNUPTIAL	POTABLENESS	POTHOOKERY
POSSODIE	POSTFLECTION	POSTOCULAR	POTAGE	POTHOOKS
POSSUM	POSTFLEXION	POSTORBITAL	POTAGER	POTHOUSE
POSSUMHAW	POSTFRONTAL	POSTOTIC	POTAGERE	POTHOUSEY
POST	POSTFURCA	POSTPAGAN	POTAGERIE	POTHUNT
POSTABDOMEN	POSTFURCAL	POSTPAID	POTAGERY	POTHUNTED
POSTABLE	POSTGEMINUM	POSTPALATAL	POTAIL	POTHUNTER
POSTADJUNCT	POSTGENITURE	POSTPALATINE	POTAMIC	POTHUNTING
POSTAGE	POSTGLACIAL	POSTPARIETAL	POTAMOLOGIST	POTICHE
POSTAL	POSTGLENOID	POSTPARTUM	POTAMOLOGY	POTICHES
POSTALVEOLAR	POSTGRACILE	POSTPHRAGMA	POTAMOMETER	POTIFER
POSTAMENT	POSTGRADUATE	POSTPLACE	POTASH	POTIN
POSTANTENNAL	POSTHABIT	POSTPONABLE	POTASHERY	POTION
POSTASPIRATE	POSTHASTE	POSTPONE	POTASS	POTLACH
POSTAXIAD	POSTHITIS	POSTPONED	POTASSA	POTLACHE
POSTAXIAL	POSTHOLDER	POSTPONEMENT	POTASSAMIDE	POTLATCH
POSTAXIALLY	POSTHOLE	POSTPONENCE	POTASSIC	POTLEG
POSTBAG	POSTHOUSE	POSTPONER	POTASSIUM	POTLICKER
POSTBOOK	POSTHUMA	POSTPONING	POTATE	POTLID
POSTBOX	POSTHUME	POSTPOSE	POTATION	POTLIKKER
POSTBOY	POSTHUMOUS	POSTPOSITED	POTATIVE	POTLINE
POSTCARD	POSTHUMOUSLY	POSTPOSITION	POTATO	POTLING
POSTCARDINAL	POSTHYPNOTIC	POSTPOSITIVE	POTATOES	POTLUCK
POSTCARNATE	POSTIC	POSTPRANDIAL	POTATOR	POTMAN
POSTCART	POSTICAL	POSTPROPHESY	POTATORY	POTMEN
POSTCAVA	POSTICALLY	POSTPUBIC	POTBANK	POTOMANIA
POSTCAVAL	POSTICHE	POSTPUBIS	POTBELLIED	POTOMATO
POSTCENAL	POSTICOUS	POSTRAMUS	POTBELLY	POTOMETER

POTONG	POULTRY	POWERFULLY	PRAEDIUM	PRANCER
POTOO	POULTRYMAN	POWERFULNESS	PRAEFECT	PRANCING
POTOROO	POUNAMU	POWERHOUSE	PRAEPECTORIAL	PRANCINGLY
POTPIE	POUNCE	POWERLESS	PRAEFECTUS	PRANCOME
POTPOURRI	POUNCED	POWERLESSLY	PRAEFERVID	PRANDIAL
POTRACK	POUNCER	POWERMONGER	PRAEHALLUX	PRANG
POTRERO	POUNCET	POWERS	PRAELABRUM	PRANK
POTRO	POUNCING	POWHEAD	PRAELECT	PRANKED
POTS	POUNCY	POWITCH	PRAELECTION	PRANKER
POTSHARD	POUND	POWLDOODY	PRAELECTOR	PRANKIER
POTSHAW	POUNDAGE	POWNIE	PRAELECTRESS	PRANKIEST
POTSHERD	POUNDAL	POWNY	PRAELUDIUM	PRANKING
POTSHOOT	POUNDCAKE	POWSODDY	PRAEMAXILLA	PRANKINGLY
POTSHOOTER	POUNDER	POWSOWDY	PRAEMOLAR	PRANKISH
POTSHOT	POUNDING	POWT	PRAEMUNIRE	PRANKISHLY
POTSIE	POUNDKEEPER	POWWOW	PRAENARIAL	PRANKISHNESS
POTSTICK	POUNDMAN	POWWOWER	PRAENEURAL	PRANKLE
POTSTONE	POUNDMASTER	POWWOWISM	PRAENOMEN	PRANKS
POTSY	POUNDMEAL	POX	PRAENOMINA	PRANKSOME
POTT	POUNDS	POXY	PRAENOMINAL	PRANKSTER
POTTAGE	POUNDSTONE	POY	PRAEPOSITOR	PRANKT
POTTAH	POUNDWORTH	POYBIRD	PRAEPOSITURE	PRANKY
POTTARO	POUNE	POYOU	PRAEPOSITUS	PRASE
POTTED	POUR	POZ	PRAEPOSTER	PRASEOLITE
POTTER	POURBOIRE	POZZOLANA	PRAEPUBIS	PRASINE
POTTERED	POURED	POZZOLANIC	PRAEPUCE	PRASKEEN
POTTERER	POURER	POZZUOLANA	PRAESCUTUM	PRASOID
POTTERIES	POURIE	POZZUOLANIC	PRAESERTIM	PRASOPHAGOUS
POTTERING	POURING	PRAAM	PRAESES	PRASOPHAGY
POTTERINGLY	POURPARLER	PRABBLE	PRAESIDIUM	PRASTHA
POTTERN	POURPARLEY	PRABHU	PRAESPHENOID	PRAT
POTTERY	POURPOINT	PRACTIC	PRAESTERNAL	PRATAL
POTTIES	POURPOINTER	PRACTICABLE	PRAESTERNUM	PRATE
POTTING	POURPRISE	PRACTICABLY	PRAESTOMIUM	PRATED
POTTINGER	POURVETE	PRACTICAL	PRAESYSTOLIC	PRATEMENT
POTTLE	POUS	PRACTICALISM	PRAETAXATION	PRATENSIAN
POTTLED	POUSE	PRACTICALIST	PRAETEXTA	PRATER
POTTO	POUSER	PRACTICALITY	PRAETOR	PRATEY
POTTOS	POUSSE	PRACTICALIZE	PRAETORIAL	PRATFALL
POTTUR	POUSSETTE	PRACTICALIZED	PRAETORIAN	PRATILOMA
POTTY	POUSSETTED	PRACTICALLY	PRAETORIUM	PRATINCOLE
POTWALLER	POUSSETTING	PRACTICALNESS	PRAETORSHIP	PRATINCOLINE
POTWALLING	POUSSIE	PRACTICANT	PRAGMATIC	PRATINCOLOUS
POTWARE	POUSSIN	PRACTICE	PRAGMATICA	PRATING
POTWHISKY	POUSTIE	PRACTICED	PRAGMATICAL	PRATINGLY
POTWORK	POUSY	PRACTICER	PRAGMATICISM	PRATIQUE
POTWORT	POUT	PRACTICIAN	PRAGMATISM	PRATTLE
POTYCARY	POUTED	PRACTICING	PRAGMATIST	PRATTLED
POU	POUTER	PRACTICO	PRAGMATISTIC	PRATTLEMENT
POUAH	POUTFUL	PRACTICUM	PRAGMATIZE	PRATTLER
POUCE	POUTING	PRACTISANT	PRAGMATIZER	PRATTLING
POUCER	POUTINGLY	PRACTISE	PRAHAM	PRATTLINGLY
POUCEY	POUTY	PRACTISED	PRAHU	PRATTLY
POUCH	POVERISH	PRACTISER	PRAIRIE	PRATTY
POUCHED	POVERISHMENT	PRACTISING	PRAIRIED	PRAU
POUCHING	POVERTY	PRACTITIONAL	PRAIRIEWEED	PRAVE
POUCY	POVERTYWEED	PRACTITIONER	PRAIRILLON	PRAVILEGE
POUDRET	POVIE	PRACTIVE	PRAISABLE	PRAVITY
POUDRETTE	POW	PRAD	PRAISABLY	PRAVOUS
POUF	POWAN	PRADHANA	PRAISE	PRAWN
POUFFE	POWCAT	PRAEABDOMEN	PRAISED	PRAWNER
POUL	POWDER	PRAEANAL	PRAISEFUL	PRAWNY
POULAINE	POWDERED	PRAECAVA	PRAISEFULLY	PRAXINOSCOPE
POULARD	POWDERER	PRAECIPE	PRAISER	PRAXIOLOGY
POULARDIZE	POWDERING	PRAECIPUUM	PRAISES	PRAXIS
POULDRON	POWDERIZE	PRAECOCES	PRAISEWORTHY	PRAXITHEA
POULE	POWDERIZER	PRAECOCIAL	PRAISING	PRAY
POULET	POWDERMAN	PRAECORACOID	PRAISINGLY	PRAYA
POULETTE	POWDERY	PRAECORDIA	PRAISS	PRAYABLE
POULP	POWDIKE	PRAECORDIAL	PRAJNA	PRAYED
POULPE	POWELLITE	PRAECORDIUM	PRAKRITI	PRAYER
POULT	POWER	PRAECORNU	PRALINE	PRAYERFUL
POULTER	POWERABLE	PRAECOX	PRALLTRILLER	PRAYERFULLY
POULTERER	POWERABLY	PRAECUNEUS	PRAM	PRAYERMAKER
POULTICE	POWERBOAT	PRAEDIAL	PRANA	PRAYERMAKING
POULTICED	POWERED	PRAEDIALIST	PRANCE	PRAYERS
POULTICING	POWERFUL	PRAEDIALITY	PRANCED	PRAYFUL

PRAYING
PREACE
PREACH
PREACHED
PREACHER
PREACHERESS
PREACHERIZE
PREACHIER
PREACHIEST
PREACHIFIED
PREACHIFY
PREACHIFYING
PREACHILY
PREACHING
PREACHMAN
PREACHMENT
PREACHY
PREADAMIC
PREADAMITE
PREADAMITIC
PREADAMITISM
PREADJUNCT
PREADMISSION
PREAGONAL
PREAGONY
PREALLABLE
PREALLABLY
PREALVEOLAR
PREAMBLE
PREAMBLED
PREAMBLING
PREAMBULARY
PREAMBULATE
PREAMP
PREAMPLIFIER
PREANIMISM
PREANTERIOR
PREARRANGE
PREARRANGED
PREASEPTIC
PREATAXIC
PREAUDIENCE
PREAXIAL
PREAXIALLY
PREBACILLARY
PREBELLUM
PREBEND
PREBENDAL
PREBENDARIES
PREBENDARY
PREBENDATE
PREBRACHIAL
PREBRACHIUM
PREBRONCHIAL
PRECANCEL
PRECANCELED
PRECANCELING
PRECANCELLED
PRECANCELLING
PRECANCEROUS
PRECANONICAL
PRECANT
PRECANTATION
PRECARIOUS
PRECARIOUSLY
PRECARIUM
PRECARTILAGE
PRECARY
PRECAST
PRECATION
PRECATIVE
PRECATIVELY
PRECATORY
PRECAUSATION
PRECAUTION
PRECAUTIONAL
PRECAUTIOUS

PRECAVA
PRECEDABLE
PRECEDANEOUS
PRECEDE
PRECEDED
PRECEDENCE
PRECEDENCIES
PRECEDENCY
PRECEDENT
PRECEDENTARY
PRECEDENTED
PRECEDENTIAL
PRECEDER
PRECEDING
PRECEL
PRECENT
PRECENTOR
PRECENTORIAL
PRECENTORY
PRECENTRAL
PRECENTRESS
PRECENTRUM
PRECEPT
PRECEPTION
PRECEPTIST
PRECEPTIVE
PRECEPTIVELY
PRECEPTOR
PRECEPTORAL
PRECEPTORATE
PRECEPTORIAL
PRECEPTORY
PRECEPTRESS
PRECEPTUAL
PRECEPTUALLY
PRECERAMIC
PRECES
PRECESS
PRECESSED
PRECESSING
PRECESSION
PRECESSIONAL
PRECHORDAL
PRECIATION
PRECIDE
PRECIEUSE
PRECIEUX
PRECINCT
PRECINCTION
PRECINCTIVE
PRECIOSITIES
PRECIOSITY
PRECIOUS
PRECIOUSLY
PRECIOUSNESS
PRECIPE
PRECIPICE
PRECIPICED
PRECIPITABLE
PRECIPITANCE
PRECIPITANCY
PRECIPITANT
PRECIPITATE
PRECIPITATED
PRECIPITATELY
PRECIPITATION
PRECIPITATOR
PRECIPITIN
PRECIPITOUS
PRECIPITOUSLY
PRECIS
PRECISE
PRECISELY
PRECISENESS
PRECISIAN
PRECISIANISM
PRECISIANIST

PRECISION
PRECISIONAL
PRECISIONER
PRECISIONIST
PRECISIVE
PRECISO
PRECLARE
PRECLINICAL
PRECLIVAL
PRECLUDE
PRECLUDED
PRECLUDING
PRECLUSION
PRECLUSIVE
PRECOCIAL
PRECOCIOUS
PRECOCIOUSLY
PRECOCITY
PRECOGITATE
PRECOGNITION
PRECOGNITIVE
PRECOGNIZE
PRECOGNOSCE
PRECOMPOSE
PRECONCEIVE
PRECONCEIVED
PRECONCEIVING
PRECONCEPT
PRECONCERT
PRECONCERTED
PRECONDITION
PRECONIZE
PRECONIZED
PRECONIZER
PRECONIZING
PRECONQUEST
PRECONSCIOUS
PRECONSIGN
PRECONTACT
PRECONY
PRECOOK
PRECOOL
PRECOOLER
PRECOOLING
PRECORACOID
PRECORDIA
PRECORDIAL
PRECORDIALLY
PRECORNU
PRECOSTAL
PRECOURSE
PRECOX
PRECRITICAL
PRECRURAL
PRECULE
PRECUNEATE
PRECUNEUS
PRECURRENT
PRECURRER
PRECURSAL
PRECURSE
PRECURSIVE
PRECURSOR
PRECURSORY
PREDABLE
PREDACEAN
PREDACEOUS
PREDACIOUS
PREDACITY
PREDATE
PREDATED
PREDATING
PREDATION
PREDATISM
PREDATIVE
PREDATOR
PREDATORILY

PREDATORY
PREDAZZITE
PREDE
PREDECAY
PREDECEASE
PREDECEASER
PREDECESS
PREDECESSOR
PREDEFINE
PREDEFINITE
PREDELLA
PREDENTARY
PREDENTATE
PREDESIGNATE
PREDESTINATE
PREDESTINATION
PREDESTINE
PREDESTINED
PREDESTINING
PREDESTINY
PREDETERMINE
PREDETERMINED
PREDEVOTE
PREDIAL
PREDIALIST
PREDIALITY
PREDIASTOLIC
PREDIATORY
PREDICABLE
PREDICABLY
PREDICAMENT
PREDICANT
PREDICATE
PREDICATED
PREDICATING
PREDICATION
PREDICATIVE
PREDICATOR
PREDICATORY
PREDICROTIC
PREDICT
PREDICTABLE
PREDICTABLY
PREDICTED
PREDICTING
PREDICTION
PREDICTIONAL
PREDICTIVE
PREDICTIVELY
PREDICTOR
PREDICTORY
PREDIGEST
PREDIGESTION
PREDIKANT
PREDILECT
PREDILECTED
PREDILECTION
PREDISPONENT
PREDISPOSE
PREDISPOSED
PREDISPOSITION
PREDOMINANCE
PREDOMINANT
PREDOMINATE
PREDOMINATING
PREDOMINATOR
PREDOOM
PREDY
PREDYNASTIC
PREE
PREED
PREEING
PREEMINENCE
PREEMINENT
PREEMINENTLY
PREEMPT
PREEMPTION

PREEMPTIVE
PREEMPTOR
PREEMPTORY
PREEN
PREENED
PREENER
PREENING
PREEXILIAN
PREEXILIC
PREEXIST
PREEXISTENCE
PREEXISTENT
PREFABRICATE
PREFABRICATED
PREFABRICATING
PREFACE
PREFACED
PREFACER
PREFACIAL
PREFACING
PREFACIST
PREFACTOR
PREFATOR
PREFATORIAL
PREFATORILY
PREFATORY
PREFECT
PREFECTLY
PREFECTORAL
PREFECTORIAL
PREFECTORIAN
PREFECTUAL
PREFECTURAL
PREFECTURE
PREFER
PREFERABLE
PREFERABLY
PREFERENCE
PREFERENT
PREFERENTIAL
PREFERMENT
PREFERRED
PREFERREDLY
PREFERRER
PREFERRING
PREFERVID
PREFET
PREFIGURATE
PREFIGURE
PREFIGURED
PREFIGURING
PREFILTER
PREFINAL
PREFINE
PREFIX
PREFIXAL
PREFIXALLY
PREFIXATION
PREFIXED
PREFIXEDLY
PREFIXION
PREFIXTURE
PREFLECTION
PREFLEXION
PREFLIGHT
PREFORM
PREFORMATION
PREFORMATIVE
PREFORMED
PREFORMISM
PREFORMIST
PREFORMISTIC
PREFORMULATE
PREFRACT
PREFRONTAL
PREFULGENCE
PREFULGENCY

PREFULGENT
PREGEMINUM
PREGENIAL
PREGENICULUM
PREGENITAL
PREGHIERA
PREGLACIAL
PREGLOBULIN
PREGNABILITY
PREGNABLE
PREGNANCE
PREGNANCIES
PREGNANCY
PREGNANT
PREGNANTLY
PREGNANTNESS
PREGRACILE
PREGUST
PREGUSTANT
PREGUSTATION
PREGUSTATOR
PREGUSTIC
PREHALLUX
PREHALTER
PREHALTERES
PREHEND
PREHENSIBLE
PREHENSILE
PREHENSILITY
PREHENSION
PREHENSIVE
PREHENSOR
PREHENSORIAL
PREHENSORY
PREHEPATIC
PREHEPATICUS
PREHISTORIAN
PREHISTORIC
PREHISTORICS
PREHISTORY
PREHNITE
PREHUMAN
PREHYDRATION
PREIGNITION
PREINCARNATE
PREINDICANT
PREINDICATE
PREINSTRUCT
PREINSULA
PREINSULAR
PREINTONE
PREIOTIZE
PREJACENT
PREJUDGE
PREJUDGED
PREJUDGEMENT
PREJUDGER
PREJUDGING
PREJUDGMENT
PREJUDICATE
PREJUDICATOR
PREJUDICE
PREJUDICED
PREJUDICEDLY
PREJUDICIAL
PREJUDICING
PREJUDICIOUS
PREKE
PRELABRUM
PRELACHRYMAL
PRELACIES
PRELACTEAL
PRELACY
PRELAPSARIAN
PRELATE
PRELATEITY
PRELATESHIP

PRELATESS
PRELATIAL
PRELATIC
PRELATICAL
PRELATICALLY
PRELATION
PRELATISH
PRELATISM
PRELATIST
PRELATIZE
PRELATRY
PRELATURE
PRELE
PRELECT
PRELECTION
PRELECTOR
PRELECTRESS
PRELEGACY
PRELEGATE
PRELEGATEE
PRELIBATION
PRELIM
PRELIMINARY
PRELIMIT
PRELIMITATE
PRELINGUAL
PRELITERATE
PRELITHIC
PRELOGIC
PRELOGICAL
PRELORAL
PRELOREAL
PRELUDE
PRELUDED
PRELUDER
PRELUDIAL
PRELUDING
PRELUDIO
PRELUDIOUS
PRELUDIOUSLY
PRELUDIUM
PRELUDIZE
PRELUMBAR
PRELUSION
PRELUSIVE
PRELUSIVELY
PRELUSORILY
PRELUSORY
PREMAN
PREMATERNITY
PREMATURE
PREMATURELY
PREMATURITY
PREMAXILLA
PREMAXILLARY
PREMED
PREMEDIA
PREMEDIAL
PREMEDIAN
PREMEDIC
PREMEDICAL
PREMEDITATE
PREMEDITATED
PREMEDITATOR
PREMENSTRUAL
PREMERIDIAN
PREMETALLIC
PREMIAL
PREMIANT
PREMIATED
PREMIATING
PREMIE
PREMIER
PREMIERAL
PREMIERE
PREMIERED
PREMIERESS

PREMIERING
PREMIERSHIP
PREMIO
PREMIOUS
PREMISAL
PREMISE
PREMISED
PREMISING
PREMISORY
PREMISS
PREMIUM
PREMIUMS
PREMIXED
PREMOLAR
PREMONISH
PREMONITION
PREMONITIVE
PREMONITOR
PREMONITORY
PREMORSE
PREMOTION
PREMOVE
PREMOVEMENT
PREMOVER
PREMULTIPLY
PREMUNDANE
PREMUNE
PREMUNITORY
PREMUTATIVE
PRENAME
PRENARIAL
PRENASAL
PRENATAL
PRENATALIST
PRENDER
PRENDRE
PRENEPHRITIC
PRENEURAL
PRENOBLE
PRENODAL
PRENOMEN
PRENOMINATE
PRENOMINATED
PRENOTATION
PRENOTE
PRENOTICE
PRENOTIFY
PRENOTION
PRENTICE
PRENTICESHIP
PRENUNCIAL
PRENUPTIAL
PRENZIE
PREOCCUPANCY
PREOCCUPATE
PREOCCUPATION
PREOCCUPIED
PREOCCUPIER
PREOCCUPY
PREOCCUPYING
PREOCULAR
PREOPERATIVE
PREOPERCLE
PREOPERCULAR
PREOPERCULUM
PREOPINION
PREOPTION
PREORAL
PREORBITAL
PREORDAIN
PREORDER
PREORGANIC
PREP
PREPACKAGE
PREPACKAGED
PREPACKAGING
PREPAID

PREPALATAL
PREPARATEUR
PREPARATION
PREPARATIVE
PREPARATOR
PREPARATORY
PREPARDON
PREPARE
PREPARED
PREPAREDLY
PREPAREDNESS
PREPAREMENT
PREPARENTAL
PREPARER
PREPARIETAL
PREPARING
PREPARINGLY
PREPATELLAR
PREPAY
PREPAYING
PREPAYMENT
PREPEND
PREPENIAL
PREPENSE
PREPENSELY
PREPERCEIVE
PREPERFECT
PREPHRAGMA
PREPLACENTAL
PREPOLLENCE
PREPOLLENCY
PREPOLLENT
PREPOLLEX
PREPONDER
PREPONDERANCE
PREPONDERANT
PREPONDERATE
PREPONDERATING
PREPONDEROUS
PREPONTINE
PREPOSE
PREPOSED
PREPOSING
PREPOSITION
PREPOSITIVE
PREPOSITOR
PREPOSITURE
PREPOSSESS
PREPOSSESSED
PREPOSSESSION
PREPOSTER
PREPOSTEROUS
PREPOSTOR
PREPOTENCE
PREPOTENCY
PREPOTENT
PREPOTENTIAL
PREPOTENTLY
PREPRINT
PREPUBERTAL
PREPUBERTY
PREPUBESCENT
PREPUBIC
PREPUBIS
PREPUCE
PREPUPA
PREPUPAL
PREPUTIAL
PREPUTIUM
PRERAMUS
PREREDUCTION
PREREGAL
PREREGNANT
PRERELEASE
PREREMOTE
PREREPTION
PREREQUISITE

PREROGATIVAL
PREROGATIVE
PREROGATIVED
PRERUPT
PRES
PRESA
PRESAGE
PRESAGED
PRESAGEFUL
PRESAGEFULLY
PRESAGEMENT
PRESAGER
PRESAGIENT
PRESAGING
PRESAID
PRESANCTIFY
PRESAY
PRESAYING
PRESBYOPE
PRESBYOPIA
PRESBYOPIC
PRESBYTE
PRESBYTER
PRESBYTERAL
PRESBYTERATE
PRESBYTERE
PRESBYTERESS
PRESBYTERIAL
PRESBYTERIAN
PRESBYTERY
PRESBYTIA
PRESBYTIC
PRESCAPULA
PRESCAPULAR
PRESCHOOL
PRESCIENCE
PRESCIENT
PRESCIENTLY
PRESCIND
PRESCINDENT
PRESCISSION
PRESCRIBE
PRESCRIBED
PRESCRIBER
PRESCRIBING
PRESCRIPT
PRESCRIPTION
PRESCRIPTIVE
PRESCUTAL
PRESCUTUM
PRESE
PRESEMINAL
PRESEMINARY
PRESENCE
PRESENCED
PRESENCELESS
PRESENILE
PRESENILITY
PRESENSION
PRESENT
PRESENTABLE
PRESENTABLY
PRESENTAL
PRESENTATION
PRESENTATIVE
PRESENTED
PRESENTEE
PRESENTER
PRESENTIAL
PRESENTIENT
PRESENTIMENT
PRESENTING
PRESENTIST
PRESENTIVE
PRESENTIVELY
PRESENTLY
PRESENTMENT

PRESERVABLE
PRESERVAL
PRESERVATION
PRESERVATIVE
PRESERVATIZE
PRESERVATORY
PRESERVE
PRESERVED
PRESERVER
PRESERVING
PRESES
PRESEXUAL
PRESHOW
PRESIDE
PRESIDED
PRESIDENCE
PRESIDENCIA
PRESIDENCY
PRESIDENT
PRESIDENTE
PRESIDENTES
PRESIDENTIAL
PRESIDENTS
PRESIDER
PRESIDIAL
PRESIDIARY
PRESIDING
PRESIDIO
PRESIDIOS
PRESIDIUM
PRESIDY
PRESIGNIFIED
PRESIGNIFY
PRESIGNIFYING
PRESIMIAN
PRESOCIAL
PRESPHENOID
PRESPHYGMIC
PRESS
PRESSBOARD
PRESSED
PRESSEL
PRESSER
PRESSFAT
PRESSGANG
PRESSING
PRESSINGLY
PRESSION
PRESSIROSTRAL
PRESSIVE
PRESSLY
PRESSMAN
PRESSMARK
PRESSMASTER
PRESSMEN
PRESSOR
PRESSPACK
PRESSROOM
PRESSURAGE
PRESSURAL
PRESSURE
PRESSURIZE
PRESSURIZED
PRESSURIZING
PRESSWOMAN
PRESSWOMEN
PRESSWORK
PRESSWORKER
PREST
PRESTABILISM
PRESTABLE
PRESTANT
PRESTATE
PRESTATED
PRESTATING
PRESTATION
PRESTER

PRESTERNAL
PRESTERNUM
PRESTEZZA
PRESTIDIGITATOR
PRESTIGE
PRESTIGIATE
PRESTIGIATOR
PRESTIGIOUS
PRESTISSIMO
PRESTLY
PRESTO
PRESTOMIAL
PRESTOMIUM
PRESUBICULUM
PRESUL
PRESUMABLE
PRESUMABLY
PRESUME
PRESUMED
PRESUMEDLY
PRESUMER
PRESUMING
PRESUMPTION
PRESUMPTIVE
PRESUMPTUOUS
PRESUMPTUOUSLY
PRESUPPOSAL
PRESUPPOSE
PRESURMISE
PRESYLVIAN
PRESYNAPSIS
PRESYNAPTIC
PRESYSTOLE
PRESYSTOLIC
PRET
PRETA
PRETAN
PRETANNAGE
PRETANNED
PRETANNING
PRETEMPORAL
PRETENCE
PRETEND
PRETENDANT
PRETENDED
PRETENDEDLY
PRETENDER
PRETENDING
PRETENSE
PRETENSES
PRETENSION
PRETENSIONAL
PRETENSIVE
PRETENSIVELY
PRETENTIOUS
PRETENTIOUSNESS
PRETER
PRETERCANINE
PRETEREQUINE
PRETERGRESS
PRETERHUMAN
PRETERIENCE
PRETERIENT
PRETERIST
PRETERIT
PRETERITE
PRETERITION
PRETERITIVE
PRETERLEGAL
PRETERLETHAL
PRETERMIT
PRETERMITTED
PRETERMITTER
PRETERMITTING
PRETERNATIVE
PRETERNATURAL
PRETERROYAL

PRETERVECTION
PRETEST
PRETEXT
PRETEXTED
PRETEXTUOUS
PRETHORACIC
PRETIL
PRETIUM
PRETONE
PRETONIC
PRETOR
PRETORIAL
PRETORIAN
PRETORIUM
PRETREAT
PRETREATMENT
PRETREATY
PRETREMATIC
PRETTIER
PRETTIES
PRETTIEST
PRETTIFIED
PRETTIFIER
PRETTIFY
PRETTIFYING
PRETTIKIN
PRETTILY
PRETTINESS
PRETTY
PRETTYFACE
PRETTYISM
PRETYMPANIC
PRETYPIFY
PRETZEL
PREU
PREUX
PREVAIL
PREVAILED
PREVAILING
PREVAILINGLY
PREVAILMENT
PREVALENCE
PREVALENCIES
PREVALENCY
PREVALENT
PREVALENTLY
PREVALESCENT
PREVARICATE
PREVARICATED
PREVARICATOR
PREVASCULAR
PREVE
PREVELAR
PREVENANCE
PREVENANT
PREVENE
PREVENED
PREVENIENCE
PREVENIENT
PREVENING
PREVENT
PREVENTABLE
PREVENTATIVE
PREVENTED
PREVENTER
PREVENTIBLE
PREVENTING
PREVENTION
PREVENTIVE
PREVENTIVELY
PREVENTORIUM
PREVERNAL
PREVESICAL
PREVIDE
PREVIDENCE
PREVIEW
PREVIOUS

PREVIOUSLY
PREVIOUSNESS
PREVISE
PREVISED
PREVISING
PREVISION
PREVISIONAL
PREVISIVE
PREVISOR
PREVOCALIC
PREVOMER
PREVOST
PREVOT
PREVOTAL
PREVOYANCE
PREVOYANT
PREVUE
PREWAR
PREWARN
PREWE
PREX
PREXIES
PREXY
PREY
PREYED
PREYER
PREYFUL
PREYING
PREYINGLY
PREZONAL
PREZONE
PRIACANTHID
PRIAPISM
PRIAPUS
PRIBBLE
PRICE
PRICED
PRICEITE
PRICELESS
PRICER
PRICES
PRICING
PRICK
PRICKADO
PRICKANT
PRICKED
PRICKER
PRICKET
PRICKFOOT
PRICKING
PRICKISH
PRICKLE
PRICKLED
PRICKLIER
PRICKLIEST
PRICKLING
PRICKLINGLY
PRICKLOUSE
PRICKLY
PRICKMADAM
PRICKSEAM
PRICKSHOT
PRICKSPUR
PRICKTIMBER
PRICKWOOD
PRICKY
PRIDE
PRIDED
PRIDEFUL
PRIDEFULLY
PRIDEFULNESS
PRIDELING
PRIDIAN
PRIDING
PRIDY
PRIE
PRIED

PRIER
PRIES
PRIEST
PRIESTAL
PRIESTCAP
PRIESTCRAFT
PRIESTEEN
PRIESTERY
PRIESTESS
PRIESTFISH
PRIESTHOOD
PRIESTIANITY
PRIESTISM
PRIESTLIER
PRIESTLIEST
PRIESTLIKE
PRIESTLINESS
PRIESTLING
PRIESTLY
PRIESTS
PRIESTSHIRE
PRIG
PRIGGED
PRIGGER
PRIGGERY
PRIGGING
PRIGGISH
PRIGGISHLY
PRIGGISHNESS
PRIGGISM
PRIGMAN
PRIGSTER
PRILL
PRILLION
PRIM
PRIMA
PRIMACY
PRIMAGE
PRIMAL
PRIMALITY
PRIMAR
PRIMARIAN
PRIMARIED
PRIMARIES
PRIMARILY
PRIMARY
PRIMATAL
PRIMATE
PRIMATESHIP
PRIMATIAL
PRIMATIC
PRIMATICAL
PRIMATOLOGY
PRIMAVERA
PRIMAVERAL
PRIME
PRIMED
PRIMELY
PRIMENESS
PRIMER
PRIMERO
PRIMEROLE
PRIMEUR
PRIMEVAL
PRIMEVALLY
PRIMEVERIN
PRIMEVEROSE
PRIMEVITY
PRIMEVOUS
PRIMI
PRIMICES
PRIMIGENE
PRIMIGENIAL
PRIMIGENIAN
PRIMIGRAVIDA
PRIMINE
PRIMING

PRIMIPARA
PRIMIPARAE
PRIMIPARITY
PRIMIPAROUS
PRIMIPILAR
PRIMITIAE
PRIMITIAL
PRIMITIVE
PRIMITIVELY
PRIMITIVENESS
PRIMITIVISM
PRIMITIVITY
PRIMITY
PRIMLY
PRIMMED
PRIMMER
PRIMMEST
PRIMMING
PRIMNESS
PRIMO
PRIMOGENIAL
PRIMOGENITOR
PRIMOGENOUS
PRIMOMO
PRIMOPRIME
PRIMORDIAL
PRIMORDIALLY
PRIMORDIATE
PRIMORDIUM
PRIMOSITY
PRIMOST
PRIMP
PRIMPED
PRIMPING
PRIMPRINT
PRIMROSE
PRIMROSED
PRIMROSETIDE
PRIMROSETIME
PRIMROSY
PRIMSIE
PRIMULACEOUS
PRIMULAVERIN
PRIMULINE
PRIMUS
PRIMWORT
PRIMY
PRIN
PRINCE
PRINCEAGE
PRINCECRAFT
PRINCEDOM
PRINCEHOOD
PRINCEKIN
PRINCELET
PRINCELIER
PRINCELIEST
PRINCELIKE
PRINCELINESS
PRINCELING
PRINCELY
PRINCEPS
PRINCES
PRINCESS
PRINCESSE
PRINCESSLY
PRINCEWOOD
PRINCIFIED
PRINCIFY
PRINCIPAL
PRINCIPALITY
PRINCIPALLY
PRINCIPATE
PRINCIPE
PRINCIPES
PRINCIPIA
PRINCIPIANT

PRINCIPIUM
PRINCIPLE
PRINCIPLED
PRINCIPLES
PRINCIPLING
PRINCOCK
PRINCOD
PRINCOX
PRINE
PRINGLE
PRINK
PRINKED
PRINKER
PRINKING
PRINKLE
PRINKY
PRINOS
PRINT
PRINTABILITY
PRINTABLE
PRINTED
PRINTER
PRINTERIES
PRINTERY
PRINTING
PRINTLESS
PRINTLINE
PRINTSCRIPT
PRINTWORKS
PRIODONT
PRION
PRIONID
PRIONINE
PRIONODONT
PRIONOPINE
PRIOR
PRIORACY
PRIORAL
PRIORATE
PRIORESS
PRIORIES
PRIORISTIC
PRIORITE
PRIORITIES
PRIORITY
PRIORLY
PRIORSHIP
PRIORY
PRISABLE
PRISAGE
PRISAL
PRISCAN
PRISE
PRISM
PRISMAL
PRISMATIC
PRISMATICAL
PRISMATIZE
PRISMATOID
PRISMATOIDAL
PRISMED
PRISMOID
PRISMOIDAL
PRISMY
PRISOMETER
PRISON
PRISONER
PRISONERS
PRISONMENT
PRISONOUS
PRISS
PRISSIER
PRISSIES
PRISSIEST
PRISSILY
PRISSINESS
PRISSY

PRISTANE
PRISTAV
PRISTAW
PRISTINE
PRITCH
PRITCHEL
PRITHEE
PRITTLE
PRIUS
PRIVACIES
PRIVACITY
PRIVACY
PRIVADO
PRIVANT
PRIVATE
PRIVATEER
PRIVATEERED
PRIVATEERING
PRIVATELY
PRIVATENESS
PRIVATION
PRIVATIVE
PRIVATIVELY
PRIVE
PRIVET
PRIVIES
PRIVILEGE
PRIVILEGED
PRIVILEGER
PRIVILEGING
PRIVILY
PRIVITIES
PRIVITY
PRIVY
PRIX
PRIZABLE
PRIZE
PRIZEABLE
PRIZED
PRIZEFIGHT
PRIZEFIGHTER
PRIZEHOLDER
PRIZEMAN
PRIZEMEN
PRIZER
PRIZERY
PRIZES
PRIZETAKER
PRIZING
PRO
PROA
PROACH
PROAERESIS
PROAIRESIS
PROAL
PROAMBIENT
PROAMNION
PROAMNIOTIC
PROANAPHORA
PROANAPHORAL
PROANTHROPOS
PROATLAS
PROAULION
PROAVIAN
PROB
PROBABILISM
PROBABILIST
PROBABILITY
PROBABILIZE
PROBABLE
PROBABLY
PROBAL
PROBANG
PROBANT
PROBATE
PROBATED
PROBATING

PROBATION
PROBATIONAL
PROBATIONARY
PROBATIONER
PROBATIONISM
PROBATIONIST
PROBATIVE
PROBATOR
PROBATORY
PROBE
PROBEABLE
PROBED
PROBER
PROBING
PROBITY
PROBLEM
PROBLEMATIC
PROBLEMATICAL
PROBLEMATIST
PROBLEMATIZE
PROBLEMIST
PROBLEMISTIC
PROBLEMIZE
PROBOSCIDAL
PROBOSCIDATE
PROBOSCIDEAN
PROBOSCIDES
PROBOSCIDIAL
PROBOSCIDIAN
PROBOSCIFORM
PROBOSCIS
PROBOSCISES
PROBOULEUTIC
PROCACCIA
PROCACCIO
PROCACIOUS
PROCACIOUSLY
PROCACITY
PROCAINE
PROCAMBIAL
PROCAMBIUM
PROCARP
PROCARPIUM
PROCATARCTIC
PROCATARXIS
PROCATHEDRAL
PROCEDENDO
PROCEDURAL
PROCEDURE
PROCEED
PROCEEDED
PROCEEDER
PROCEEDING
PROCEEDINGS
PROCEEDS
PROCELLAS
PROCELLOSE
PROCELLOUS
PROCEPHALIC
PROCERCOID
PROCERE
PROCEREBRAL
PROCEREBRUM
PROCERES
PROCERITE
PROCERITY
PROCERUS
PROCESS
PROCESSAL
PROCESSED
PROCESSER
PROCESSING
PROCESSION
PROCESSIONAL
PROCESSIONER
PROCESSIVE
PROCESSOR

PROCESSUAL
PROCESSUS
PROCHAIN
PROCHEIN
PROCHLORITE
PROCHONDRAL
PROCHOOS
PROCHORDAL
PROCHORION
PROCHRONIC
PROCHRONISM
PROCHRONIZE
PROCIDENCE
PROCIDENT
PROCINCT
PROCK
PROCLAIM
PROCLAIMANT
PROCLAIMED
PROCLAIMER
PROCLAIMING
PROCLAMATION
PROCLAMATOR
PROCLINE
PROCLISIS
PROCLITIC
PROCLIVE
PROCLIVITIES
PROCLIVITOUS
PROCLIVITY
PROCLIVOUS
PROCNEMIAL
PROCOELIA
PROCOELIAN
PROCOELOUS
PROCONSUL
PROCONSULAR
PROCONSULATE
PROCRASTINATE
PROCRASTINATION
PROCREANT
PROCREATE
PROCREATED
PROCREATING
PROCREATION
PROCREATIVE
PROCREATOR
PROCREATORY
PROCTALGIA
PROCTALGY
PROCTATRESIA
PROCTATRESY
PROCTECTASIA
PROCTECTOMY
PROCTITIS
PROCTOCELE
PROCTOCLYSIS
PROCTOCOLITIS
PROCTODAEAL
PROCTODAEUM
PROCTODYNIA
PROCTOLOGIC
PROCTOLOGICAL
PROCTOLOGIST
PROCTOLOGY
PROCTOPLASTY
PROCTOPLEGIA
PROCTOPTOSIS
PROCTOR
PROCTORAGE
PROCTORAL
PROCTORIAL
PROCTORIALLY
PROCTORICAL
PROCTORIZE
PROCTORRHEA
PROCTORSHIP

PROCTOSCOPE	PRODUCTIVE	PROFITLESS	PROGRAMMING	PROLETARY
PROCTOSCOPIC	PRODUCTIVELY	PROFITMONGER	PROGRAMMIST	PROLETCULT
PROCTOSCOPY	PRODUCTIVITY	PROFITS	PROGREDE	PROLETKULT
PROCTOSPASM	PRODUCTOID	PROFLATED	PROGREDIENCY	PROLICIDAL
PROCTOSTOMY	PRODUCTOR	PROFLAVINE	PROGREDIENT	PROLICIDE
PROCTOTOME	PRODUCTORY	PROFLIGACIES	PROGRESS	PROLIFERANT
PROCTOTOMY	PRODUCTS	PROFLIGACY	PROGRESSED	PROLIFERATE
PROCTOTRESIA	PROEGUMENAL	PROFLIGATE	PROGRESSER	PROLIFEROUS
PROCULCATE	PROEM	PROFLIGATED	PROGRESSING	PROLIFIC
PROCULCATION	PROEMBRYO	PROFLIGATELY	PROGRESSION	PROLIFICACY
PROCUMBENT	PROEMBRYONIC	PROFLUENCE	PROGRESSISM	PROLIFICAL
PROCURABLE	PROEMIAL	PROFLUENT	PROGRESSIST	PROLIFICALLY
PROCURACIES	PROEMIUM	PROFLUVIOUS	PROGRESSIVE	PROLIFICATE
PROCURACY	PROEMPTOSIS	PROFLUVIUM	PROGRESSIVELY	PROLIFICATED
PROCURAL	PROEPIMERON	PROFONDE	PROGRESSOR	PROLIFICATING
PROCURANCE	PROETHICAL	PROFOUND	PROHEIM	PROLIFICITY
PROCURATE	PROETHNIC	PROFOUNDLY	PROHIBIT	PROLIFICNESS
PROCURATION	PROETID	PROFOUNDNESS	PROHIBITED	PROLIFY
PROCURATIVE	PROETTE	PROFRE	PROHIBITER	PROLIGEROUS
PROCURATOR	PROF	PROFUGATE	PROHIBITING	PROLIN
PROCURATORY	PROFACE	PROFULGENT	PROHIBITION	PROLINE
PROCURATRIX	PROFANATION	PROFUNDA	PROHIBITIONIST	PROLIX
PROCURE	PROFANATORY	PROFUNDITY	PROHIBITIVE	PROLIXITY
PROCURED	PROFANE	PROFUSE	PROHIBITOR	PROLIXLY
PROCUREMENT	PROFANED	PROFUSELY	PROHIBITORY	PROLIXNESS
PROCURER	PROFANELY	PROFUSENESS	PROJACIENT	PROLLER
PROCURESS	PROFANEMENT	PROFUSER	PROJECT	PROLOCUTION
PROCUREUR	PROFANENESS	PROFUSION	PROJECTEDLY	PROLOCUTOR
PROCURING	PROFANER	PROFUSIVELY	PROJECTILE	PROLOCUTRIX
PROCURRENT	PROFANING	PROG	PROJECTING	PROLOG
PROCURSIVE	PROFANISM	PROGAMETE	PROJECTINGLY	PROLOGIST
PROCURVATION	PROFANITIES	PROGAMIC	PROJECTION	PROLOGIZE
PROCURVED	PROFANITY	PROGANOSAUR	PROJECTIONAL	PROLOGIZER
PROCYONINE	PROFANIZE	PROGENERATE	PROJECTIVE	PROLOGUE
PROD	PROFECTION	PROGENIES	PROJECTIVITY	PROLOGUIST
PRODATARY	PROFECTIONAL	PROGENITAL	PROJECTOR	PROLOGUIZE
PRODD	PROFER	PROGENITIVE	PROJECTRIX	PROLOGUIZER
PRODDED	PROFERMENT	PROGENITOR	PROJECTURE	PROLONG
PRODDER	PROFERT	PROGENITRIX	PROJET	PROLONGATE
PRODDING	PROFESS	PROGENITURE	PROJICIENCE	PROLONGATION
PRODDLE	PROFESSED	PROGENITY	PROJICIENT	PROLONGE
PRODELISION	PROFESSEDLY	PROGENY	PROJICIENTLY	PROLONGED
PRODENTINE	PROFESSION	PROGERIA	PROKE	PROLONGER
PRODIALOGUE	PROFESSIONAL	PROGESTIN	PROKEIMENON	PROLONGING
PRODIGAL	PROFESSIONALLY	PROGG	PROKER	PROLONGMENT
PRODIGALISH	PROFESSIVE	PROGGED	PROLABIUM	PROLUSION
PRODIGALISM	PROFESSIVELY	PROGGER	PROLACTIN	PROLUSIONIZE
PRODIGALITY	PROFESSOR	PROGGING	PROLAMIN	PROLUSORY
PRODIGALIZE	PROFESSORATE	PROGLOTTIC	PROLAMINE	PROLYL
PRODIGALLY	PROFESSORIAL	PROGLOTTID	PROLAPSE	PROM
PRODIGIOSITY	PROFESSORSHIP	PROGLOTTIDES	PROLAPSED	PROMACHOS
PRODIGIOUS	PROFESSORY	PROGLOTTIS	PROLAPSING	PROMENADE
PRODIGIOUSLY	PROFFER	PROGNATHI	PROLAPSION	PROMENADED
PRODIGUS	PROFFERED	PROGNATHIC	PROLAPSUS	PROMENADER
PRODIGY	PROFFERER	PROGNATHISM	PROLATE	PROMENADING
PRODITION	PROFFERING	PROGNATHOUS	PROLATELY	PROMERISTEM
PRODITOR	PROFICHI	PROGNATHY	PROLATENESS	PROMERIT
PRODITORIOUS	PROFICIENCE	PROGNE	PROLATION	PROMETHIUM
PRODROMAL	PROFICIENCY	PROGNOSE	PROLATIVE	PROMIC
PRODROME	PROFICIENT	PROGNOSIS	PROLEAGUE	PROMINENCE
PRODROMOUS	PROFICIENTLY	PROGNOSTIC	PROLEAGUER	PROMINENCY
PRODROMUS	PROFICUOUS	PROGNOSTICAL	PROLEG	PROMINENT
PRODUCE	PROFICUOUSLY	PROGNOSTICATE	PROLEGATE	PROMINENTLY
PRODUCEABLE	PROFILE	PROGNOSTICATION	PROLEGOMENAL	PROMISCUITY
PRODUCED	PROFILED	PROGNOSTICATOR	PROLEGOMENON	PROMISCUOUS
PRODUCEMENT	PROFILER	PROGONEATE	PROLEPSES	PROMISCUOUSLY
PRODUCENT	PROFILING	PROGRAM	PROLEPSIS	PROMISE
PRODUCER	PROFILIST	PROGRAMATIC	PROLEPTIC	PROMISED
PRODUCIBLE	PROFILOGRAPH	PROGRAMED	PROLEPTICAL	PROMISEE
PRODUCING	PROFIT	PROGRAMER	PROLEPTICS	PROMISER
PRODUCT	PROFITABLE	PROGRAMING	PROLES	PROMISING
PRODUCTED	PROFITABLY	PROGRAMIST	PROLETAIRE	PROMISINGLY
PRODUCTIBLE	PROFITED	PROGRAMMATIC	PROLETAIRISM	PROMISOR
PRODUCTID	PROFITEER	PROGRAMMA	PROLETARIAN	PROMISS
PRODUCTILE	PROFITEERING	PROGRAMMATIC	PROLETARIAT	PROMISSIVE
PRODUCTION	PROFITER	PROGRAMMED	PROLETARIATE	PROMISSOR
PRODUCTIONAL	PROFITING	PROGRAMMER	PROLETARIZE	PROMISSORY

PROMIT
PROMITOSIS
PROMITTOR
PROMNESIA
PROMONTORIES
PROMONTORY
PROMORPH
PROMOTE
PROMOTED
PROMOTER
PROMOTING
PROMOTION
PROMOTIONAL
PROMOTIVE
PROMOTORIAL
PROMOVAL
PROMOVE
PROMOVENT
PROMPT
PROMPTBOOK
PROMPTER
PROMPTING
PROMPTITUDE
PROMPTIVE
PROMPTLY
PROMPTNESS
PROMPTUARY
PROMPTURE
PROMULGATE
PROMULGATED
PROMULGATING
PROMULGATION
PROMULGE
PROMULGED
PROMULGER
PROMULGING
PROMUSCIDATE
PROMUSCIS
PROMYCELIAL
PROMYCELIUM
PRONAOS
PRONATE
PRONATED
PRONATING
PRONATION
PRONATOR
PRONE
PRONELY
PRONENESS
PRONEPHRIC
PRONEPHROS
PRONEUR
PRONG
PRONGBUCK
PRONGED
PRONGER
PRONGHORN
PRONGHORNS
PRONGY
PRONIC
PRONITY
PRONOGRADE
PRONOMINAL
PRONOMINALLY
PRONONCE
PRONOTUM
PRONOUN
PRONOUNAL
PRONOUNCE
PRONOUNCEABLE
PRONOUNCED
PRONOUNCEDLY
PRONOUNCEMENT
PRONOUNCER
PRONOUNCING
PRONTO
PRONUBA

PRONUBIAL
PRONUCLEAR
PRONUCLEI
PRONUCLEUS
PRONUNCIABLE
PRONUNCIAL
PRONUNCIATION
PRONUNCIATOR
PRONYMPH
PRONYMPHAL
PROO
PROODE
PROOEMIAC
PROOEMION
PROOEMIUM
PROOF
PROOFER
PROOFFUL
PROOFING
PROOFLESS
PROOFLESSLY
PROOFREAD
PROOFREADER
PROOFREADING
PROOFROOM
PROOFY
PROP
PROPAEDEUTIC
PROPAGABLE
PROPAGANDA
PROPAGANDIC
PROPAGANDISM
PROPAGANDIST
PROPAGANDIZE
PROPAGATE
PROPAGATED
PROPAGATING
PROPAGATION
PROPAGATIVE
PROPAGATOR
PROPAGATORY
PROPAGINES
PROPAGO
PROPAGULE
PROPAGULUM
PROPALE
PROPALINAL
PROPANE
PROPANEDIOL
PROPARENT
PROPARGYL
PROPARGYLIC
PROPARIAN
PROPASSION
PROPATAGIAL
PROPATAGIAN
PROPATAGIUM
PROPEL
PROPELLANT
PROPELLED
PROPELLENT
PROPELLER
PROPELLING
PROPELMENT
PROPEND
PROPENDENT
PROPENE
PROPENSE
PROPENSELY
PROPENSENESS
PROPENSION
PROPENSITIES
PROPENSITY
PROPENYL
PROPENYLIC
PROPER
PROPERISPOME

PROPERLY
PROPERNESS
PROPERTIED
PROPERTIES
PROPERTY
PROPERTYSHIP
PROPHASE
PROPHASIS
PROPHECIES
PROPHECY
PROPHESIED
PROPHESIER
PROPHESY
PROPHESYING
PROPHET
PROPHETESS
PROPHETHOOD
PROPHETIC
PROPHETICAL
PROPHETICISM
PROPHETICLY
PROPHETISM
PROPHETIZE
PROPHETRY
PROPHLOEM
PROPHORIC
PROPHYLACTIC
PROPHYLAXIS
PROPHYLL
PROPHYLLUM
PROPINATION
PROPINE
PROPINED
PROPINING
PROPINQUANT
PROPINQUE
PROPINQUITY
PROPINQUOUS
PROPIO
PROPIOLATE
PROPIOLIC
PROPIONATE
PROPIONE
PROPIONIC
PROPIONYL
PROPITIABLE
PROPITIAL
PROPITIATE
PROPITIATED
PROPITIATING
PROPITIATION
PROPITIATIVE
PROPITIATOR
PROPITIATORY
PROPITIOUS
PROPITIOUSLY
PROPJET
PROPLASM
PROPLASTIC
PROPLEURON
PROPLEX
PROPLEXUS
PROPODEAL
PROPODEUM
PROPODIAL
PROPODIALE
PROPODITE
PROPODITIC
PROPODIUM
PROPOLIS
PROPOLIZE
PROPOMA
PROPOMATA
PROPONE
PROPONED
PROPONEMENT
PROPONENT

PROPONER
PROPONING
PROPONS
PROPORT
PROPORTION
PROPORTIONAL
PROPORTIONATENESS
PROPORTIONED
PROPORTIONER
PROPOSAL
PROPOSANT
PROPOSE
PROPOSED
PROPOSEDLY
PROPOSER
PROPOSING
PROPOSITIO
PROPOSITION
PROPOSITUS
PROPOUND
PROPOUNDED
PROPOUNDER
PROPOUNDING
PROPOUNDMENT
PROPOXY
PROPPAGE
PROPPED
PROPPER
PROPPING
PROPRAETOR
PROPRETOR
PROPRIATION
PROPRIATORY
PROPRIETAGE
PROPRIETARY
PROPRIETIES
PROPRIETOR
PROPRIETORY
PROPRIETOUS
PROPRIETRESS
PROPRIETY
PROPRIUM
PROPROCTOR
PROPS
PROPTERYGIAL
PROPTERYGIUM
PROPTOSED
PROPTOSES
PROPTOSIS
PROPUGN
PROPUGNACLED
PROPUGNATION
PROPUGNATOR
PROPULSATION
PROPULSATORY
PROPULSE
PROPULSION
PROPULSITY
PROPULSIVE
PROPULSOR
PROPULSORY
PROPUPA
PROPUPAL
PROPWOOD
PROPYGIDIUM
PROPYL
PROPYLAEA
PROPYLAEUM
PROPYLAMINE
PROPYLATION
PROPYLENE
PROPYLIC
PROPYLIDENE
PROPYLITE
PROPYLON
PROPYNE
PROQUAESTOR

PRORATA
PRORATABLE
PRORATE
PRORATED
PRORATING
PRORATION
PRORE
PROREAN
PRORECTOR
PRORECTORATE
PROREPTION
PROREX
PRORHINAL
PROROGATE
PROROGATION
PROROGATOR
PROROGUE
PROROGUED
PROROGUER
PROROGUING
PRORRHESIS
PRORSA
PRORSAL
PRORUMP
PRORUPTION
PROS
PROSAIC
PROSAICAL
PROSAICALLY
PROSAICISM
PROSAICNESS
PROSAISM
PROSAIST
PROSAL
PROSAPY
PROSAR
PROSCAPULA
PROSCAPULAR
PROSCENIA
PROSCENIUM
PROSCIND
PROSCIUTTO
PROSCOLECINE
PROSCOLEX
PROSCOLICES
PROSCRIBE
PROSCRIBED
PROSCRIBER
PROSCRIBING
PROSCRIPT
PROSCRIPTION
PROSCRIPTIVE
PROSE
PROSECT
PROSECTION
PROSECTOR
PROSECUTE
PROSECUTED
PROSECUTING
PROSECUTION
PROSECUTOR
PROSED
PROSELENIC
PROSELYTE
PROSELYTED
PROSELYTER
PROSELYTICAL
PROSELYTING
PROSELYTISM
PROSELYTIST
PROSELYTIZE
PROSELYTIZED
PROSELYTIZER
PROSEMAN
PROSEMINAR
PROSEMINARY
PROSEMINATE

PROSENCHYMA	PROSTERNAL	PROTEIDE	PROTOCOLAR	PROTOPLAST
PROSER	PROSTERNUM	PROTEIFORM	PROTOCOLARY	PROTOPLASTIC
PROSETHMOID	PROSTHECA	PROTEIN	PROTOCOLED	PROTOPOD
PROSEUCHA	PROSTHENIC	PROTEINASE	PROTOCOLING	PROTOPODIAL
PROSEUCHE	PROSTHESES	PROTEINOUS	PROTOCOLIST	PROTOPODITE
PROSIER	PROSTHESIS	PROTEINS	PROTOCOLIZE	PROTOPODITIC
PROSIEST	PROSTHETIC	PROTEINURIA	PROTOCOLLED	PROTOPOPE
PROSIFY	PROSTHETICS	PROTEND	PROTOCOLLING	PROTOPRISM
PROSILIENCY	PROSTHETIST	PROTENDED	PROTOCONCH	PROTORE
PROSILIENT	PROSTHION	PROTENDING	PROTOCONCHAL	PROTOREBEL
PROSILIENTLY	PROSTHIONIC	PROTENSE	PROTOCONE	PROTOSALT
PROSILY	PROSTITUTE	PROTENSION	PROTOCONID	PROTOSINNER
PROSIMIAN	PROSTITUTED	PROTENSITY	PROTOCONULE	PROTOSOCIAL
PROSINESS	PROSTITUTING	PROTENSIVE	PROTOCORM	PROTOSPASM
PROSING	PROSTITUTION	PROTENSIVELY	PROTODEACON	PROTOSPORE
PROSIPHON	PROSTITUTOR	PROTEOLYSIS	PROTODERM	PROTOSTELE
PROSIPHONAL	PROSTOMIAL	PROTEOLYTIC	PROTODEVIL	PROTOSTELIC
PROSIPHONATE	PROSTOMIATE	PROTEOPECTIC	PROTODONATAN	PROTOSTOME
PROSISH	PROSTOMIUM	PROTEOPEXIC	PROTODONATE	PROTOTHECA
PROSIT	PROSTRATE	PROTEOPEXIS	PROTODONT	PROTOTHECAL
PROSLAVER	PROSTRATED	PROTEOPEXY	PROTOGENAL	PROTOTHEME
PROSLAVERY	PROSTRATING	PROTEOSE	PROTOGENES	PROTOTHERE
PROSNEUSIS	PROSTRATION	PROTEOSOMAL	PROTOGENESIS	PROTOTRAITOR
PROSO	PROSTRATIVE	PROTEOSOME	PROTOGENETIC	PROTOTROCH
PROSOBRANCH	PROSTRATOR	PROTEOSURIA	PROTOGENIC	PROTOTROPHIC
PROSOCELE	PROSTYLE	PROTERANDRY	PROTOGENIST	PROTOTYPAL
PROSOCOELE	PROSTYLOS	PROTEROBASE	PROTOGINE	PROTOTYPE
PROSODE	PROSY	PROTEROGLYPH	PROTOGOD	PROTOTYPIC
PROSODEMIC	PROSYLLOGISM	PROTEROGYNY	PROTOGONOUS	PROTOTYPICAL
PROSODETIC	PROTACTIC	PROTEROTYPE	PROTOGRAPH	PROTOVILLAIN
PROSODIAC	PROTACTINIUM	PROTERVE	PROTOGYNOUS	PROTOVUM
PROSODIAL	PROTAGON	PROTERVITY	PROTOGYNY	PROTOXID
PROSODIAN	PROTAGONISM	PROTEST	PROTOHOMO	PROTOXIDE
PROSODIC	PROTAGONIST	PROTESTANCY	PROTOHUMAN	PROTOXIDIZE
PROSODICAL	PROTAMIN	PROTESTANT	PROTOLITHIC	PROTOXIDIZED
PROSODICALLY	PROTAMINE	PROTESTATION	PROTOLOG	PROTOXYLEM
PROSODION	PROTANDRIC	PROTESTATOR	PROTOLOGIST	PROTOZOAL
PROSODIST	PROTANDRISM	PROTESTATORY	PROTOMA	PROTOZOAN
PROSODUS	PROTANDROUS	PROTESTED	PROTOMALA	PROTOZOEA
PROSODY	PROTANDRY	PROTESTER	PROTOMALAL	PROTOZOEAN
PROSOGASTER	PROTANOMAL	PROTESTING	PROTOMALAR	PROTOZOIASIS
PROSOGYRATE	PROTANOPE	PROTESTINGLY	PROTOMARTYR	PROTOZOIC
PROSOMA	PROTANOPIA	PROTESTIVE	PROTOME	PROTOZOON
PROSOMAL	PROTANOPIC	PROTEXT	PROTOMERITE	PROTOZOONAL
PROSOMATIC	PROTARSAL	PROTHALAMION	PROTOMERITIC	PROTRACT
PROSONCMASIA	PROTARSUS	PROTHALAMIUM	PROTOMETALS	PROTRACTED
PROSOPIC	PROTASIS	PROTHALLIAL	PROTOMORPH	PROTRACTEDLY
PROSOPICALLY	PROTASPIS	PROTHALLINE	PROTOMORPHIC	PROTRACTER
PROSOPITE	PROTATIC	PROTHALLIUM	PROTON	PROTRACTILE
PROSOPLASIA	PROTATICALLY	PROTHALLOID	PROTONE	PROTRACTING
PROSOPOLEPSY	PROTAXIAL	PROTHALLUS	PROTONEGROID	PROTRACTION
PROSOPON	PROTAXIS	PROTHECA	PROTONEMA	PROTRACTIVE
PROSOPYLE	PROTE	PROTHESES	PROTONEMAL	PROTRACTOR
PROSORUS	PROTEAD	PROTHESIS	PROTONEMATA	PROTREPTIC
PROSPECT	PROTEAN	PROTHETIC	PROTONEMATAL	PROTREPTICAL
PROSPECTED	PROTEASE	PROTHETICAL	PROTONEME	PROTRIAENE
PROSPECTING	PROTECT	PROTHONOTARY	PROTONEPHROS	PROTRUDE
PROSPECTIVE	PROTECTED	PROTHORACES	PROTONEUTRON	PROTRUDED
PROSPECTOR	PROTECTIBLE	PROTHORACIC	PROTONIC	PROTRUDENT
PROSPECTUS	PROTECTING	PROTHORAX	PROTONOTARY	PROTRUDING
PROSPER	PROTECTINGLY	PROTHORAXES	PROTONOTATER	PROTRUSIBLE
PROSPERED	PROTECTION	PROTHROMBIN	PROTONYM	PROTRUSILE
PROSPERER	PROTECTIONAL	PROTHYSTERON	PROTONYMPH	PROTRUSION
PROSPERING	PROTECTIVE	PROTID	PROTONYMPHAL	PROTRUSIVE
PROSPERITY	PROTECTIVELY	PROTIDE	PROTOPAPAS	PROTRUSIVELY
PROSPEROUS	PROTECTOR	PROTIST	PROTOPARENT	PROTUBERANCE
PROSPEROUSLY	PROTECTORAL	PROTISTAN	PROTOPATHIC	PROTUBERANCES
PROSPICE	PROTECTORATE	PROTISTIC	PROTOPATHY	PROTUBERANT
PROSPICIENCE	PROTECTORIAN	PROTISTOLOGY	PROTOPECTIN	PROTUBERATE
PROSS	PROTECTORIES	PROTISTON	PROTOPEPSIA	PROTUBERATED
PROSSY	PROTECTORY	PROTOBLAST	PROTOPHLOEM	PROTUBEROUS
PROSTATE	PROTECTRESS	PROTOBLASTIC	PROTOPHYTE	PROTURAN
PROSTATIC	PROTEGE	PROTOCITIZEN	PROTOPHYTIC	PROTUTOR
PROSTATISM	PROTEGEE	PROTOCLASTIC	PROTOPINE	PROTUTORY
PROSTATOLITH	PROTEGULUM	PROTOCNEME	PROTOPLASM	PROTYL
PROSTATOTOMY	PROTEIC	PROTOCOCCOID	PROTOPLASMAL	PROTYLE
PROSTERN	PROTEID	PROTOCOL	PROTOPLASMIC	PROTYPE

PROUD
PROUDER
PROUDEST
PROUDFUL
PROUDHEARTED
PROUDISH
PROUDISHLY
PROUDLING
PROUDLY
PROUSTITE
PROVABILITY
PROVABLE
PROVABLENESS
PROVABLY
PROVAND
PROVANT
PROVE
PROVECT
PROVECTION
PROVED
PROVEDITOR
PROVEDOR
PROVEDORE
PROVEN
PROVENANCE
PROVEND
PROVENDER
PROVENE
PROVENIENCE
PROVENIENT
PROVENLY
PROVENT
PROVER
PROVERB
PROVERBIAL
PROVERBIALLY
PROVERBIC
PROVERBIZE
PROVES
PROVIANT
PROVICAR
PROVICARIATE
PROVIDANCE
PROVIDE
PROVIDED
PROVIDENCE
PROVIDENT
PROVIDENTIAL
PROVIDENTLY
PROVIDER
PROVIDING
PROVIDORE
PROVINCE
PROVINCES
PROVINCIAL
PROVINCIALLY
PROVINCIATE
PROVINCULUM
PROVINE
PROVING
PROVINGLY
PROVISION
PROVISIONAL
PROVISIONARY
PROVISIONER
PROVISIONS
PROVISIVE
PROVISO
PROVISOES
PROVISOR
PROVISORILY
PROVISORY
PROVISOS
PROVITAMIN
PROVO
PROVOCANT
PROVOCATION

PROVOCATIVE
PROVOCATOR
PROVOCATORY
PROVOKE
PROVOKED
PROVOKEE
PROVOKER
PROVOKING
PROVOKINGLY
PROVOLA
PROVOST
PROVOSTAL
PROVOSTRY
PROVOSTSHIP
PROW
PROWED
PROWER
PROWERSITE
PROWESS
PROWESSED
PROWL
PROWLED
PROWLER
PROWLING
PROWLINGLY
PROX
PROXENET
PROXENETE
PROXENETISM
PROXENOS
PROXENUS
PROXENY
PROXICALLY
PROXIED
PROXIES
PROXIMAD
PROXIMAL
PROXIMATE
PROXIMATELY
PROXIMATION
PROXIME
PROXIMITY
PROXIMO
PROXY
PROXYING
PROXYSM
PROZYMITE
PRUDE
PRUDELY
PRUDENCE
PRUDENT
PRUDENTIAL
PRUDENTIALLY
PRUDENTLY
PRUDERIES
PRUDERY
PRUDISH
PRUDISHLY
PRUDISHNESS
PRUDIST
PRUDITY
PRUINESCENCE
PRUINOSE
PRUINOUS
PRULAURASIN
PRUNABLE
PRUNABLENESS
PRUNABLY
PRUNASE
PRUNASIN
PRUNE
PRUNED
PRUNELL
PRUNELLA
PRUNELLE
PRUNELLO
PRUNER

PRUNING
PRUNITRIN
PRUNT
PRUNTED
PRURIENCE
PRURIENCY
PRURIENT
PRURIENTLY
PRURIGINOUS
PRURIGO
PRURIOUSNESS
PRURITIC
PRURITUS
PRUSIANO
PRUSSIATE
PRUSSIC
PRUSSIN
PRUSSINE
PRUT
PRY
PRYER
PRYING
PRYINGLY
PRYINGNESS
PRYLER
PRYS
PRYSE
PRYTANEUM
PRYTANIS
PRYTANIZE
PRYTANY
PSALIS
PSALLOID
PSALM
PSALMIC
PSALMIST
PSALMISTRY
PSALMODIAL
PSALMODIC
PSALMODICAL
PSALMODIES
PSALMODIST
PSALMODIZE
PSALMODY
PSALMOGRAPH
PSALMY
PSALOID
PSALTER
PSALTERER
PSALTERIA
PSALTERIAL
PSALTERIAN
PSALTERIST
PSALTERIUM
PSALTERY
PSAMMITE
PSAMMITIC
PSAMMOLITHIC
PSAMMOLOGY
PSAMMOMA
PSAMMOPHILE
PSAMMOUS
PSCHENT
PSELLISM
PSELLISMUS
PSEPHISM
PSEPHISMA
PSEPHITE
PSEPHITIC
PSEPHOLOGIST
PSEPHOLOGY
PSEPHOMANCY
PSEUDACONIN
PSEUDACONINE
PSEUDACUSIS
PSEUDANDRY
PSEUDAPHIA

PSEUDAPOSTLE
PSEUDATOLL
PSEUDAXIS
PSEUDHAEMAL
PSEUDHEMAL
PSEUDIMAGO
PSEUDO
PSEUDOACACIA
PSEUDOALUM
PSEUDOANGINA
PSEUDOAQUATIC
PSEUDOBRANCH
PSEUDOBULB
PSEUDOBULBAR
PSEUDOBULBIL
PSEUDOCARP
PSEUDOCHINA
PSEUDOCLASSIC
PSEUDOCONE
PSEUDOCORTEX
PSEUDOCUMYL
PSEUDOCYST
PSEUDODERM
PSEUDODONT
PSEUDODOX
PSEUDODOXAL
PSEUDOFARCY
PSEUDOGALENA
PSEUDOGLIOMA
PSEUDOGRAPH
PSEUDOGRAPHY
PSEUDOGYNE
PSEUDOGYNY
PSEUDOISM
PSEUDOLALIA
PSEUDOLATRY
PSEUDOLICHEN
PSEUDOLOGICAL
PSEUDOLOGIST
PSEUDOLOGUE
PSEUDOLOGY
PSEUDOMANCY
PSEUDOMANIA
PSEUDOMANTIC
PSEUDOMITOTIC
PSEUDOMORPH
PSEUDOMUCIN
PSEUDONITROL
PSEUDONYM
PSEUDONYMAL
PSEUDONYMIC
PSEUDONYMITY
PSEUDONYMOUS
PSEUDOPLASM
PSEUDOPOD
PSEUDOPODAL
PSEUDOPODE
PSEUDOPODIAL
PSEUDOPODIUM
PSEUDOPORE
PSEUDOPSIA
PSEUDOPTICS
PSEUDOPTOSIS
PSEUDOPUPA
PSEUDOPUPAL
PSEUDORABIES
PSEUDORAMOSE
PSEUDOSALT
PSEUDOSCININE
PSEUDOSCOPE
PSEUDOSCOPIC
PSEUDOSCOPY
PSEUDOSMIA
PSEUDOSOPH
PSEUDOSOPHER
PSEUDOSPERM
PSEUDOSPHERE

PSEUDOSPORE
PSEUDOSTOMA
PSEUDOSUCHIAN
PSEUDOTABES
PSEUDOVUM
PSHA
PSHAW
PSHAWED
PSHAWING
PSHEM
PSI
PSILANTHROPIC
PSILANTHROPY
PSILATRO
PSILOCERAN
PSILOCERATAN
PSILOCERATID
PSILOI
PSILOLOGY
PSILOMELANE
PSILOMELANIC
PSILOPHYTE
PSILOSIS
PSILOSOPHER
PSILOSOPHY
PSILOTACEOUS
PSILOTHRUM
PSILOTIC
PSITHURISM
PSITTACEOUS
PSITTACINE
PSITTACINITE
PSITTACISM
PSITTACISTIC
PSITTACOSIS
PSOAS
PSOATIC
PSOCID
PSOCINE
PSOITIS
PSOMOPHAGIST
PSOMOPHAGY
PSORA
PSORIASIFORM
PSORIASIS
PSORIATIC
PSOROID
PSOROPTIC
PSOROSIS
PSOROSPERM
PSOROSPERMIC
PSOROUS
PSOVIE
PST
PSYCHAGOGIC
PSYCHAGOGOS
PSYCHAGOGUE
PSYCHAGOGY
PSYCHAL
PSYCHALGIA
PSYCHE
PSYCHEDELIC
PSYCHEOMETRY
PSYCHIASIS
PSYCHIATER
PSYCHIATRIC
PSYCHIATRIST
PSYCHIATRIZE
PSYCHIATRY
PSYCHIC
PSYCHICAL
PSYCHICALLY
PSYCHICISM
PSYCHICIST
PSYCHICS
PSYCHID
PSYCHISM

PSYCHO
PSYCHOANALYST
PSYCHOCLINIC
PSYCHODRAMA
PSYCHOFUGAL
PSYCHOGENESIS
PSYCHOGENETIC
PSYCHOGENIC
PSYCHOGENY
PSYCHOGNOSIS
PSYCHOGNOSY
PSYCHOGRAM
PSYCHOGRAPH
PSYCHOGRAPHY
PSYCHOID
PSYCHOKINESIA
PSYCHOKYME
PSYCHOLEPSY
PSYCHOLEPTIC
PSYCHOLOGER
PSYCHOLOGIC
PSYCHOLOGICAL
PSYCHOLOGICS
PSYCHOLOGISM
PSYCHOLOGIST
PSYCHOLOGIZE
PSYCHOLOGUE
PSYCHOLOGY
PSYCHOMACHY
PSYCHOMANCY
PSYCHOMETER
PSYCHOMETRIC
PSYCHOMETRY
PSYCHOMOTOR
PSYCHON
PSYCHONOMIC
PSYCHONOMICS
PSYCHOPATH
PSYCHOPATHIC
PSYCHOPATHY
PSYCHOPETAL
PSYCHOPHOBIA
PSYCHOPLASM
PSYCHOPOMP
PSYCHOPOMPOS
PSYCHOREFLEX
PSYCHOSES
PSYCHOSEXUAL
PSYCHOSIS
PSYCHOSOCIAL
PSYCHOSOME
PSYCHOSOPHY
PSYCHOSTATIC
PSYCHOTAXIS
PSYCHOTHEISM
PSYCHOTIC
PSYCHOTRINE
PSYCHOTROPIC
PSYCHROGRAPH
PSYCHROMETER
PSYCHROMETRY
PSYCHROPHILE
PSYCHROPHOBIA
PSYCHROPHORE
PSYCHROPHYTE
PSYCHURGY
PSYKTER
PSYLLID
PSYLLIUM
PSYWAR
PTARMIC
PTARMICAL
PTARMIGAN
PTARMIGANS
PTERANODONT
PTERASPID
PTERERGATE

PTERIC
PTERIDEOUS
PTERIDIUM
PTERIDOID
PTERIDOLOGY
PTERIDOPHYTE
PTERIDOSPERM
PTERIN
PTERION
PTERNA
PTEROCARPOUS
PTERODACTYL
PTEROGRAPHY
PTEROID
PTEROMA
PTEROMALID
PTERON
PTEROPAEDES
PTEROPEGAL
PTEROPEGOUS
PTEROPEGUM
PTEROPID
PTEROPINE
PTEROPOD
PTEROPODAL
PTEROPODAN
PTEROPODIAL
PTEROPODIUM
PTEROPODOUS
PTEROSAUR
PTEROSAURIAN
PTEROSTIGMA
PTEROSTIGMAL
PTEROTHECA
PTEROTHORAX
PTEROTIC
PTERYGIAL
PTERYGIUM
PTERYGIUMS
PTERYGODE
PTERYGODUM
PTERYGOID
PTERYGOIDAL
PTERYGOIDEAN
PTERYGOPHORE
PTERYGOTE
PTERYGOTOUS
PTERYLA
PTERYLAE
PTERYLOGRAPHY
PTERYLOLOGY
PTERYLOSIS
PTILINAL
PTILINUM
PTILOPAEDES
PTILOPAEDIC
PTILOSIS
PTINID
PTINOID
PTISAN
PTOCHOCRACY
PTOCHOGONY
PTOCHOLOGY
PTOMAIN
PTOMAINE
PTOMAINIC
PTOMATROPINE
PTOSIS
PTOTIC
PTYALAGOGUE
PTYALIN
PTYALISM
PTYALIZE
PTYALIZED
PTYALIZING
PTYALOCELE
PTYALOGENIC

PTYALOLITH
PTYALORRHEA
PTYXIS
PU
PUAN
PUB
PUBAL
PUBBLE
PUBERAL
PUBERTAL
PUBERTIC
PUBERTY
PUBERULENT
PUBES
PUBESCENCE
PUBESCENCY
PUBESCENT
PUBIAN
PUBIGEROUS
PUBIOTOMY
PUBIS
PUBLIC
PUBLICAN
PUBLICANISM
PUBLICATE
PUBLICATION
PUBLICE
PUBLICISM
PUBLICIST
PUBLICITY
PUBLICIZE
PUBLICIZED
PUBLICIZING
PUBLICLY
PUBLICNESS
PUBLISH
PUBLISHABLE
PUBLISHED
PUBLISHER
PUBLISHING
PUBLISHMENT
PUBOFEMORAL
PUBOILIAC
PUBOISCHIAC
PUBOISCHIAL
PUBORECTALIS
PUBOTIBIAL
PUCCA
PUCCOON
PUCE
PUCELAGE
PUCELLAGE
PUCELLE
PUCERON
PUCHERA
PUCHERITE
PUCHERO
PUCK
PUCKA
PUCKBALL
PUCKER
PUCKERBUSH
PUCKERED
PUCKEREL
PUCKERER
PUCKERIER
PUCKERIEST
PUCKERING
PUCKERMOUTH
PUCKERY
PUCKFIST
PUCKFOIST
PUCKISH
PUCKISHLY
PUCKISHNESS
PUCKNEEDLE
PUCKREL

PUCKSEY
PUCKSTER
PUD
PUDDEE
PUDDENING
PUDDER
PUDDING
PUDDINGBERRY
PUDDINGHEAD
PUDDINGHEADED
PUDDINGHOUSE
PUDDINGWIFE
PUDDINGWIVES
PUDDINGY
PUDDLE
PUDDLEBALL
PUDDLEBAR
PUDDLED
PUDDLER
PUDDLING
PUDDLY
PUDDOCK
PUDDY
PUDENCY
PUDENDAL
PUDENDOUS
PUDENDUM
PUDENT
PUDER
PUDGE
PUDGIER
PUDGIEST
PUDGILY
PUDGINESS
PUDGY
PUDIANO
PUDIBUND
PUDIBUNDITY
PUDIC
PUDICAL
PUDICITIA
PUDICITY
PUDOR
PUDU
PUE
PUEBLITO
PUEBLO
PUEBLOS
PUER
PUERARIA
PUERICULTURE
PUERILE
PUERILELY
PUERILENESS
PUERILISM
PUERILITIES
PUERILITY
PUERPERA
PUERPERAL
PUERPERALISM
PUERPERANT
PUERPERIUM
PUERPEROUS
PUFF
PUFFBACK
PUFFBALL
PUFFBIRD
PUFFED
PUFFER
PUFFERIES
PUFFERY
PUFFIER
PUFFIEST
PUFFIN
PUFFINESS
PUFFINET
PUFFING

PUFFS
PUFFWIG
PUFFY
PUG
PUGENELLO
PUGGAREE
PUGGED
PUGGER
PUGGI
PUGGING
PUGGISH
PUGGLE
PUGGREE
PUGGRY
PUGGY
PUGH
PUGIL
PUGILANT
PUGILISM
PUGILIST
PUGILISTIC
PUGILISTICAL
PUGLIANITE
PUGMARK
PUGMILL
PUGMILLER
PUGNACIOUS
PUGNACIOUSLY
PUGNACITY
PUGREE
PUGUA
PUHA
PUIRTITH
PUISNE
PUISNY
PUISSANCE
PUISSANT
PUISSANTLY
PUISSANTNESS
PUIST
PUIT
PUJA
PUKA
PUKATEA
PUKATEINE
PUKE
PUKED
PUKEKA
PUKEKO
PUKER
PUKEWEED
PUKING
PUKISH
PUKISHNESS
PUKKA
PUKRAS
PUKU
PUKY
PUL
PULAHAN
PULAHANES
PULAHANISM
PULAJAN
PULAS
PULASAN
PULASKITE
PULCHRIFY
PULCHRITUDE
PULE
PULED
PULEGOL
PULEGONE
PULER
PULEYN
PULGADA
PULI
PULICARIOUS

PULICAT	PULPIFY	PULVILLUS	PUNCTILIO	PUNKA
PULICATE	PULPIFYING	PULVINAR	PUNCTILIOS	PUNKAH
PULICENE	PULPILY	PULVINARIAN	PUNCTILIOUS	PUNKER
PULICID	PULPINESS	PULVINATE	PUNCTION	PUNKETTO
PULICIDAL	PULPING	PULVINATED	PUNCTIST	PUNKIE
PULICIDE	PULPIT	PULVINATION	PUNCTUAL	PUNKIES
PULICINE	PULPITAL	PULVINIFORM	PUNCTUALIST	PUNKISH
PULICOID	PULPITARIAN	PULVINO	PUNCTUALITY	PUNKLING
PULICOSE	PULPITEER	PULVINULUS	PUNCTUALLY	PUNKT
PULICOSITY	PULPITER	PULVINUS	PUNCTUATE	PUNKWOOD
PULICOUS	PULPITIC	PULVIPLUME	PUNCTUATED	PUNKY
PULIJAN	PULPITICAL	PULWAR	PUNCTUATING	PUNNABLE
PULING	PULPITICALLY	PULY	PUNCTUATION	PUNNAGE
PULINGLY	PULPITIS	PUMA	PUNCTUATIVE	PUNNED
PULIOL	PULPITLESS	PUMEX	PUNCTUATOR	PUNNER
PULISH	PULPITLY	PUMICATE	PUNCTUIST	PUNNET
PULK	PULPITRY	PUMICATED	PUNCTULATE	PUNNIC
PULKA	PULPOTOMY	PUMICATING	PUNCTULATED	PUNNICAL
PULL	PULPOUS	PUMICE	PUNCTULATION	PUNNIGRAM
PULLABLE	PULPOUSNESS	PUMICED	PUNCTULE	PUNNING
PULLAILE	PULPSTONE	PUMICEOUS	PUNCTULUM	PUNNINGLY
PULLALUE	PULPWOOD	PUMICER	PUNCTUM	PUNNOLOGY
PULLBACK	PULPY	PUMICIFORM	PUNCTURATION	PUNSTER
PULLBOAT	PULQUE	PUMICITE	PUNCTURE	PUNT
PULLDEVIL	PULSANT	PUMICOSE	PUNCTURER	PUNTA
PULLDOO	PULSAR	PUMIE	PUNCTURING	PUNTABOUT
PULLDOWN	PULSATE	PUMMEL	PUNCTUS	PUNTAL
PULLED	PULSATED	PUMMELED	PUND	PUNTELLO
PULLEN	PULSATILE	PUMMELING	PUNDIGRION	PUNTER
PULLER	PULSATING	PUMMELLED	PUNDIT	PUNTI
PULLERIES	PULSATION	PUMMELLING	PUNDITA	PUNTIES
PULLERY	PULSATIONAL	PUMMICE	PUNDITIC	PUNTILLA
PULLET	PULSATIVE	PUMP	PUNDITICALLY	PUNTIST
PULLEY	PULSATIVELY	PUMPAGE	PUNDITRY	PUNTO
PULLEYS	PULSATOR	PUMPELLYITE	PUNDONOR	PUNTOUT
PULLICAT	PULSATORY	PUMPER	PUNDUM	PUNTSMAN
PULLING	PULSE	PUMPERNICKEL	PUNECA	PUNTY
PULLISEE	PULSED	PUMPET	PUNEE	PUNY
PULLOCK	PULSEJET	PUMPHANDLE	PUNESE	PUNYISM
PULLOUT	PULSELESS	PUMPING	PUNG	PUNYSHIP
PULLOVER	PULSELESSLY	PUMPKIN	PUNGAPUNG	PUP
PULLSHOVEL	PULSELLUM	PUMPKINIFY	PUNGAR	PUPA
PULLULANT	PULSIDGE	PUMPKINITY	PUNGE	PUPAE
PULLULATE	PULSIFIC	PUMPKINSEED	PUNGENCE	PUPAL
PULLULATED	PULSIMETER	PUMPKNOT	PUNGENCY	PUPARIAL
PULLULATING	PULSING	PUMPMAN	PUNGENT	PUPARIUM
PULLULATION	PULSION	PUMPS	PUNGENTLY	PUPAS
PULLULATIVE	PULSIVE	PUMPWRIGHT	PUNGER	PUPATE
PULLUS	PULSOMETER	PUN	PUNGEY	PUPATED
PULMENT	PULSUS	PUNA	PUNGI	PUPATING
PULMOGASTRIC	PULTACEOUS	PUNAISE	PUNGLE	PUPATION
PULMOMETER	PULTON	PUNALUA	PUNGLED	PUPELO
PULMOMETRY	PULTUN	PUNALUAN	PUNGY	PUPIFEROUS
PULMONAR	PULTURE	PUNAMU	PUNGYI	PUPIFORM
PULMONARIAN	PULU	PUNATOO	PUNICACEOUS	PUPIGENOUS
PULMONARY	PULVERABLE	PUNCH	PUNICEOUS	PUPIL
PULMONATE	PULVERACEOUS	PUNCHABLE	PUNICIAL	PUPILABILITY
PULMONIC	PULVERANT	PUNCHAYET	PUNICIN	PUPILAGE
PULMONICAL	PULVERATE	PUNCHBOARD	PUNIER	PUPILAR
PULMONITIS	PULVERATED	PUNCHED	PUNIEST	PUPILARITY
PULMOTOR	PULVERATING	PUNCHEON	PUNILY	PUPILARY
PULP	PULVEREOUS	PUNCHER	PUNINESS	PUPILATE
PULPACEOUS	PULVERIN	PUNCHINELLO	PUNISH	PUPILED
PULPAL	PULVERINE	PUNCHINESS	PUNISHABLE	PUPILIZE
PULPALGIA	PULVERIZATE	PUNCHING	PUNISHED	PUPILLAGE
PULPATONE	PULVERIZATOR	PUNCHY	PUNISHER	PUPILLAR
PULPATOON	PULVERIZE	PUNCT	PUNISHING	PUPILLARITY
PULPBOARD	PULVERIZED	PUNCTAL	PUNISHMENT	PUPILLARY
PULPECTOMY	PULVERIZER	PUNCTATE	PUNITION	PUPILLATE
PULPED	PULVERIZING	PUNCTATED	PUNITIONAL	PUPILLED
PULPEFACTION	PULVEROUS	PUNCTATIM	PUNITIONALLY	PUPILLIZE
PULPER	PULVERULENCE	PUNCTATION	PUNITIVE	PUPILLONIAN
PULPERIA	PULVERULENT	PUNCTATOR	PUNITIVELY	PUPILMONGER
PULPIER	PULVIL	PUNCTICULAR	PUNITIVENESS	PUPIPAROUS
PULPIEST	PULVILLAR	PUNCTICULOSE	PUNITORY	PUPIVORE
PULPIFIED	PULVILLI	PUNCTIFORM	PUNJUM	PUPIVOROUS
PULPIFIER	PULVILLIFORM	PUNCTILIAR	PUNK	PUPPED

PUPPET
PUPPETEER
PUPPETHEAD
PUPPETISM
PUPPETIZE
PUPPETMAN
PUPPETMASTER
PUPPETRY
PUPPIED
PUPPIES
PUPPIFY
PUPPILY
PUPPING
PUPPY
PUPPYDOM
PUPPYFISH
PUPPYFOOT
PUPPYHOOD
PUPPYING
PUPPYISM
PUPULO
PUPUNHA
PUR
PURAQUE
PURAU
PURBLIND
PURBLINDLY
PURBLINDNESS
PURCHASABLE
PURCHASE
PURCHASED
PURCHASER
PURCHASERY
PURCHASING
PURDAH
PURDY
PURE
PUREAYN
PUREBLOOD
PUREBRED
PURED
PUREDEE
PUREE
PURELY
PURENESS
PURER
PUREST
PUREY
PURFLE
PURFLED
PURFLER
PURFLING
PURFLY
PURGA
PURGAMENT
PURGATION
PURGATIVE
PURGATORIAL
PURGATORIAN
PURGATORY
PURGE
PURGED
PURGER
PURGERY
PURGING
PURIFICANT
PURIFICATION
PURIFICATOR
PURIFICATORY
PURIFIED
PURIFIER
PURIFORM
PURIFY
PURIFYING
PURIN
PURINE
PURIRI

PURISM
PURIST
PURISTIC
PURISTICAL
PURITAN
PURITANIC
PURITANICAL
PURITANISM
PURITANO
PURITY
PURL
PURLED
PURLER
PURLHOUSE
PURLICUE
PURLICUES
PURLIEU
PURLIEUMAN
PURLIEUMEN
PURLIEUS
PURLIN
PURLINE
PURLING
PURLMAN
PURLOIN
PURLOINER
PURO
PURPARTY
PURPENSE
PURPIE
PURPLE
PURPLED
PURPLEHEART
PURPLELY
PURPLES
PURPLESCENT
PURPLEWORT
PURPLING
PURPLISH
PURPLISHNESS
PURPLY
PURPORT
PURPORTED
PURPORTEDLY
PURPORTING
PURPOSE
PURPOSED
PURPOSEDLY
PURPOSEFUL
PURPOSEFULLY
PURPOSELESS
PURPOSELIKE
PURPOSELY
PURPOSER
PURPOSES
PURPOSING
PURPOSIVE
PURPOSIVELY
PURPOSIVISM
PURPRESTURE
PURPRISE
PURPRISION
PURPURA
PURPURACEOUS
PURPURATE
PURPURE
PURPUREAL
PURPUREAN
PURPURESCENT
PURPURIC
PURPURIN
PURPURINE
PURPURITE
PURPURIZE
PURPUROID
PURR
PURRAH

PURRE
PURRED
PURREE
PURREL
PURRER
PURRING
PURRONE
PURRY
PURSE
PURSED
PURSEFUL
PURSELIKE
PURSER
PURSES
PURSET
PURSIER
PURSIEST
PURSINESS
PURSING
PURSIVE
PURSLANE
PURSLEY
PURSUABLE
PURSUAL
PURSUANCE
PURSUANT
PURSUANTLY
PURSUE
PURSUED
PURSUER
PURSUING
PURSUIT
PURSUITMETER
PURSUIVANT
PURSY
PURTENANCE
PURTY
PURULENCE
PURULENCY
PURULENT
PURULENTLY
PURULOID
PURUSHA
PURUSHARTHA
PURVEY
PURVEYABLE
PURVEYAL
PURVEYANCE
PURVEYANCER
PURVEYED
PURVEYING
PURVEYOR
PURVIEW
PURVOE
PURWANNAH
PUS
PUSH
PUSHBALL
PUSHCARD
PUSHCART
PUSHED
PUSHER
PUSHFUL
PUSHFULLY
PUSHFULNESS
PUSHIER
PUSHIEST
PUSHILY
PUSHINESS
PUSHING
PUSHINGLY
PUSHINGNESS
PUSHMOBILE
PUSHOVER
PUSHPIN
PUSHUM
PUSHWAINLING

PUSHY
PUSIL
PUSILL
PUSILLANIMOUS
PUSS
PUSSCAT
PUSSIER
PUSSIES
PUSSIEST
PUSSLEY
PUSSLY
PUSSY
PUSSYCAT
PUSSYFOOT
PUSSYFOOTED
PUSSYFOOTER
PUSSYFOOTING
PUSSYFOOTISM
PUSSYTOE
PUSTULANT
PUSTULAR
PUSTULATE
PUSTULATED
PUSTULATING
PUSTULATION
PUSTULATOUS
PUSTULE
PUSTULED
PUSTULIFORM
PUSTULOSE
PUSTULOUS
PUSZTA
PUT
PUTAGE
PUTAIN
PUTAMEN
PUTAMINOUS
PUTANISM
PUTATION
PUTATIONARY
PUTATIVE
PUTATIVELY
PUTBACK
PUTCHEN
PUTCHER
PUTE
PUTEAL
PUTELEE
PUTELI
PUTHERY
PUTID
PUTIDLY
PUTIDNESS
PUTING
PUTLOCK
PUTLOG
PUTOIS
PUTREDINOUS
PUTREFACIENT
PUTREFACTION
PUTREFACTIVE
PUTREFIED
PUTREFIER
PUTREFY
PUTREFYING
PUTRESCE
PUTRESCENCE
PUTRESCENCY
PUTRESCENT
PUTRESCIBLE
PUTRESCINE
PUTRICIDE
PUTRID
PUTRIDITY
PUTRIDLY
PUTRIDNESS
PUTRIFACTED

PUTRIFORM
PUTRILAGE
PUTSCHISM
PUTSCHIST
PUTT
PUTTAN
PUTTEE
PUTTER
PUTTERER
PUTTERINGLY
PUTTI
PUTTIED
PUTTIER
PUTTING
PUTTO
PUTTOCK
PUTTOO
PUTTY
PUTTYBLOWER
PUTTYHEARTED
PUTTYING
PUTTYROOT
PUTURE
PUTZ
PUUD
PUXY
PUY
PUZZLE
PUZZLEATION
PUZZLED
PUZZLEDLY
PUZZLEDNESS
PUZZLEHEAD
PUZZLEHEADED
PUZZLEMAN
PUZZLEMENT
PUZZLEPATE
PUZZLEPATED
PUZZLER
PUZZLING
PUZZLINGLY
PUZZLINGNESS
PYAEMIA
PYAEMIC
PYAL
PYARTHROSIS
PYAT
PYCHE
PYCNIAL
PYCNIC
PYCNID
PYCNIDIOSPORE
PYCNIDIUM
PYCNIOSPORE
PYCNITE
PYCNIUM
PYCNODONT
PYCNOGONID
PYCNOGONOID
PYCNOMETER
PYCNOSIS
PYCNOSPORE
PYCNOSPORIC
PYCNOSTYLE
PYCNOTIC
PYE
PYELECTASIS
PYELIC
PYELITIC
PYELITIS
PYELOGRAM
PYELOGRAPHIC
PYELOGRAPHY
PYEMESIS
PYEMIA
PYEMIC
PYENGADU

PYGAL
PYGARG
PYGARGUS
PYGIDID
PYGIDIUM
PYGMAEAN
PYGMEAN
PYGMIES
PYGMOID
PYGMY
PYGMYWEED
PYGOFER
PYGON
PYGOPAGUS
PYGOPOD
PYGOPODINE
PYGOPODOUS
PYGOSTYLE
PYGOSTYLED
PYGOSTYLOUS
PYIC
PYIN
PYJAMA
PYJAMAED
PYJAMAS
PYKAR
PYKE
PYKNATOM
PYKNIC
PYLA
PYLAGORE
PYLANGIAL
PYLANGIUM
PYLAR
PYLIC
PYLON
PYLORALGIA
PYLORIC
PYLORITIS
PYLOROPLASTY
PYLOROPTOSIS
PYLOROSCOPY
PYLOROSPASM
PYLORUS
PYNE
PYNOT
PYNUNG
PYOCELE
PYOCTANIN
PYOCTANINE
PYOCYANASE
PYOCYANIN
PYOCYST
PYOCYTE
PYODERMIA
PYODERMIC
PYOGENESIS
PYOGENETIC
PYOGENIC
PYOGENIN
PYOGENOUS
PYOID
PYOLYMPH
PYOMETRA
PYOMETRITIS
PYONEPHRITIS
PYONEPHROTIC
PYOPHAGIA
PYOPHTHALMIA
PYOPLANIA
PYOPOIESIS
PYOPOIETIC
PYOPTYSIS
PYORRHEAL
PYORRHOEAL
PYOSALPINX
PYOSIS

PYOSPERMIA
PYOT
PYOTHERAPY
PYOTHORAX
PYOURETER
PYOXANTHOSE
PYR
PYRACANTH
PYRACANTHA
PYRACENE
PYRAL
PYRALIDAN
PYRALIDID
PYRALIDIFORM
PYRALIS
PYRALOID
PYRAMID
PYRAMIDAIRE
PYRAMIDAL
PYRAMIDALE
PYRAMIDALIS
PYRAMIDALLY
PYRAMIDATE
PYRAMIDED
PYRAMIDELLID
PYRAMIDER
PYRAMIDIA
PYRAMIDIC
PYRAMIDICAL
PYRAMIDING
PYRAMIDION
PYRAMIDOIDAL
PYRAMIDS
PYRAMOIDAL
PYRAN
PYRANOMETER
PYRANOSE
PYRANYL
PYRARGYRITE
PYRAZIN
PYRAZINE
PYRAZOLE
PYRAZOLINE
PYRAZOLONE
PYRAZOLYL
PYRE
PYRECTIC
PYRENA
PYRENE
PYRENIN
PYRENOCARP
PYRENODEAN
PYRENODEOUS
PYRENOID
PYRENOLICHEN
PYRETHRIN
PYRETHRUM
PYRETIC
PYRETICOSIS
PYRETOGENIC
PYRETOGENOUS
PYRETOGRAPHY
PYRETOLOGY
PYRETOLYSIS
PYREX
PYREXIA
PYREXIAL
PYREXIC
PYREXICAL
PYRGEOMETER
PYRGOIDAL
PYRGOLOGIST
PYRGOM
PYRIBOLE
PYRIDAZINE
PYRIDIC
PYRIDINE

PYRIDINIUM
PYRIDINIZE
PYRIDONE
PYRIDOXINE
PYRIDYL
PYRIFORM
PYRIFORMIS
PYRIMIDIN
PYRIMIDINE
PYRIMIDYL
PYRITACEOUS
PYRITE
PYRITES
PYRITIC
PYRITICAL
PYRITIFEROUS
PYRITIZE
PYRITOHEDRAL
PYRITOHEDRON
PYRITOID
PYRITOLOGY
PYRITOUS
PYROACETIC
PYROARSENATE
PYROARSENIC
PYROARSENITE
PYROBALLOGY
PYROBELONITE
PYROBORATE
PYROBORIC
PYROCATECHIN
PYROCATECHOL
PYROCHEMICAL
PYROCHLORE
PYROCITRIC
PYROCLASTIC
PYROCOLL
PYROCOTTON
PYROELECTRIC
PYROGALLATE
PYROGALLIC
PYROGALLOL
PYROGEN
PYROGENATION
PYROGENESIA
PYROGENESIS
PYROGENIC
PYROGENOUS
PYROGNOMIC
PYROGNOSTIC
PYROGNOSTICS
PYROGRAPH
PYROGRAPHER
PYROGRAPHIC
PYROGRAPHY
PYROGRAVURE
PYROGUAIACIN
PYROID
PYROLACEOUS
PYROLATER
PYROLATRY
PYROLIGNEOUS
PYROLIGNIC
PYROLIGNITE
PYROLIGNOUS
PYROLITE
PYROLOGICAL
PYROLOGIST
PYROLOGY
PYROLUSITE
PYROLYSIS
PYROLYTIC
PYROMACHY
PYROMAGNETIC
PYROMANCER
PYROMANCY
PYROMANIA

PYROMANIACAL
PYROMANTIC
PYROMELLITIC
PYROMETER
PYROMETRIC
PYROMETRICAL
PYROMETRY
PYROMORPHITE
PYROMORPHOUS
PYROMOTOR
PYROMUCATE
PYROMUCIC
PYROMUCYL
PYRONAPHTHA
PYRONE
PYRONOMICS
PYRONYXIS
PYROPE
PYROPEN
PYROPHANITE
PYROPHANOUS
PYROPHILE
PYROPHILOUS
PYROPHOBIA
PYROPHONE
PYROPHORIC
PYROPHOROUS
PYROPHORUS
PYROPHYLLITE
PYROPUNCTURE
PYROPUS
PYROSCOPE
PYROSCOPY
PYROSIS
PYROSMALITE
PYROSPHERE
PYROSTAT
PYROSTILPNITE
PYROSULPHATE
PYROSULPHITE
PYROTARTARIC
PYROTARTRATE
PYROTECHNIAN
PYROTECHNIC
PYROTECHNICS
PYROTECHNIST
PYROTECHNY
PYROTEREBIC
PYROTIC
PYROTOXIN
PYROTRITARIC
PYROURIC
PYROVANADIC
PYROXANTHIN
PYROXENE
PYROXENIC
PYROXENITE
PYROXMANGITE
PYROXYLIC
PYROXYLIN
PYROXYLINE
PYRRHIC
PYRRHICHIAN
PYRRHICHIUS
PYRRHICIST
PYRRHOTINE
PYRRHOTISM
PYRRHOTITE
PYRRHOUS
PYRRHULOXIA
PYRRHUS
PYRRODIAZOLE
PYRROL
PYRROLE
PYRROLIC
PYRROLIDINE
PYRROLIDONE

PYRROLIDYL
PYRROLINE
PYRROPHYLLIN
PYRROYL
PYRRYL
PYRRYLENE
PYRUVATE
PYRUVIC
PYRUVYL
PYRYLIUM
PYSE
PYTHOGENIC
PYTHON
PYTHONESS
PYTHONIC
PYTHONICAL
PYTHONID
PYTHONIFORM
PYTHONINE
PYTHONISM
PYTHONIST
PYTHONIZE
PYTHONOID
PYTHONOMORPH
PYURIA
PYX
PYXIDATE
PYXIDES
PYXIDIUM
PYXIE
PYXIS

QABBALA
QABBALAH
QADARITE
QADI
QAID
QAIMAQAM
QANEH
QANTAR
QASAB
QAT
QAZAQ
QERI
QIBLA
QINAH
QIYAS
QOBAR
QRI
QU
QUA
QUAA
QUAB
QUABIRD
QUACHIL
QUACK
QUACKED
QUACKERIES
QUACKERY
QUACKHOOD
QUACKING
QUACKISH
QUACKISHLY
QUACKISHNESS
QUACKISM
QUACKLE
QUACKSALVER
QUACKSTER
QUACKY
QUAD
QUADDED
QUADDLE
QUADE
QUADER
QUADLE
QUADRA
QUADRABLE
QUADRAE
QUADRAGESIMAL
QUADRAL
QUADRANGLE
QUADRANGLED
QUADRANGULAR
QUADRANGULED
QUADRANS
QUADRANT
QUADRANTAL
QUADRANTILE
QUADRAPHONIC
QUADRAT
QUADRATE
QUADRATED
QUADRATIC
QUADRATICAL
QUADRATICS
QUADRATING
QUADRATRIX
QUADRATUM
QUADRATURE

QUADRATUS
QUADREL
QUADRENNIA
QUADRENNIAL
QUADRENNIUM
QUADRENNIUMS
QUADRIAD
QUADRIC
QUADRICEPS
QUADRICINIUM
QUADRICIPITAL
QUADRICONE
QUADRICYCLE
QUADRICYCLER
QUADRIENNIUM
QUADRIFID
QUADRIFILAR
QUADRIFOCAL
QUADRIFOLIUM
QUADRIFORM
QUADRIFRONS
QUADRIGA
QUADRIGAE
QUADRIGAMIST
QUADRIGATE
QUADRIGATUS
QUADRIHYBRID
QUADRIJUGAL
QUADRILATERAL
QUADRILLE
QUADRILLED
QUADRILLES
QUADRILLING
QUADRILLION
QUADRILOGY
QUADRIMUM
QUADRIN
QUADRINE
QUADRINOMIAL
QUADRIPAROUS
QUADRIPLANAR
QUADRISECT
QUADRIURATE
QUADRIVALENT
QUADRIVIA
QUADRIVIAL
QUADRIVIOUS
QUADRIVIUM
QUADROON
QUADRUAL
QUADRUM
QUADRUMANAL
QUADRUMANE
QUADRUMANOUS
QUADRUPED
QUADRUPEDAL
QUADRUPEDAN
QUADRUPEDANT
QUADRUPEDATE
QUADRUPEDOUS
QUADRUPLANE
QUADRUPLATE
QUADRUPLATOR
QUADRUPLE
QUADRUPLED
QUADRUPLET
QUADRUPLEX
QUADRUPLING
QUAEDAM
QUAERE
QUAESITA
QUAESITUM
QUAESTIO
QUAESTIONES
QUAESTOR
QUAESTORIAL
QUAESTORIAN

QUAESTORSHIP
QUAESTUARY
QUAFF
QUAFFED
QUAFFER
QUAFFING
QUAG
QUAGGA
QUAGGAS
QUAGGIER
QUAGGIEST
QUAGGLE
QUAGGY
QUAGMIRE
QUAGMIRED
QUAGMIRY
QUAHAUG
QUAHOG
QUAI
QUAICH
QUAIFE
QUAIGH
QUAIL
QUAILED
QUAILERIES
QUAILERY
QUAILHEAD
QUAILING
QUAILY
QUAINT
QUAINTANCE
QUAINTER
QUAINTEST
QUAINTISE
QUAINTLY
QUAINTNESS
QUAIR
QUAIS
QUAKE
QUAKED
QUAKER
QUAKERBIRD
QUAKETAIL
QUAKIER
QUAKIEST
QUAKILY
QUAKINESS
QUAKING
QUAKINGLY
QUAKY
QUALE
QUALIA
QUALIFIABLE
QUALIFICATION
QUALIFICATOR
QUALIFIED
QUALIFIEDLY
QUALIFIER
QUALIFY
QUALIFYING
QUALIMETER
QUALITATIVE
QUALITIED
QUALITIES
QUALITY
QUALLY
QUALM
QUALMISH
QUALMISHLY
QUALMISHNESS
QUALMY
QUALTAGH
QUAMASH
QUAN
QUANDANG
QUANDARIES
QUANDARY

QUANDONG
QUANDY
QUANNET
QUANT
QUANTA
QUANTIC
QUANTICAL
QUANTIFIED
QUANTIFIER
QUANTIFY
QUANTIFYING
QUANTIMETER
QUANTITATE
QUANTITATIVE
QUANTITIED
QUANTITIES
QUANTITIVE
QUANTITIVELY
QUANTITY
QUANTIVALENT
QUANTIZATION
QUANTIZE
QUANTIZED
QUANTIZING
QUANTOMETER
QUANTONG
QUANTULUM
QUANTUM
QUAP
QUAQUAVERSAL
QUAR
QUARANTINE
QUARANTINED
QUARANTINER
QUARANTINING
QUARANTY
QUARDEEL
QUARE
QUARENDEN
QUARENDER
QUARENTENE
QUARESMA
QUARION
QUARK
QUARL
QUARLE
QUARLES
QUARRED
QUARREL
QUARRELED
QUARRELING
QUARRELLED
QUARRELLING
QUARRELLOUS
QUARRELOUS
QUARRELOUSLY
QUARRELSOME
QUARRELSOMENESS
QUARRIED
QUARRIER
QUARRIES
QUARRION
QUARROME
QUARRY
QUARRYING
QUARRYMAN
QUARRYMEN
QUARRYSTONE
QUART
QUARTA
QUARTAN
QUARTANE
QUARTANO
QUARTATION
QUARTAUT
QUARTE
QUARTER

QUARTERAGE
QUARTERBACK
QUARTERED
QUARTERER
QUARTERFOIL
QUARTERING
QUARTERLAND
QUARTERLIES
QUARTERLY
QUARTERMAN
QUARTERMASTER
QUARTERMEN
QUARTERN
QUARTERNIGHT
QUARTERNION
QUARTERON
QUARTERPACE
QUARTERS
QUARTERSAW
QUARTERSAWED
QUARTERSAWING
QUARTERSAWN
QUARTERSTAFF
QUARTERSTAVES
QUARTET
QUARTETTE
QUARTIC
QUARTILE
QUARTIN
QUARTINE
QUARTINHO
QUARTIPAROUS
QUARTO
QUARTOLE
QUARTOS
QUARTZ
QUARTZIC
QUARTZITE
QUARTZITIC
QUARTZOID
QUARTZOSE
QUARTZOUS
QUARTZY
QUAS
QUASAR
QUASH
QUASHED
QUASHEY
QUASHING
QUASHY
QUASI
QUASKIES
QUASKY
QUASS
QUASSATION
QUASSATIVE
QUASSIA
QUASSIIN
QUASSIN
QUAT
QUATCH
QUATE
QUATENUS
QUATERN
QUATERNARIES
QUATERNARIUS
QUATERNARY
QUATERNATE
QUATERNION
QUATERNIONIC
QUATERNITIES
QUATERNITY
QUATERON
QUATERS
QUATERTENSES
QUATORZAIN
QUATORZE

QUATRAIN
QUATRAL
QUATRAYLE
QUATRE
QUATREBLE
QUATREFOIL
QUATREFOILED
QUATRIBLE
QUATRIN
QUATTIE
QUATTRINI
QUATTRINO
QUATTROCENTO
QUATTY
QUATUOR
QUAVER
QUAVERED
QUAVERER
QUAVERING
QUAVERINGLY
QUAVEROUS
QUAVERY
QUAVIVER
QUAW
QUAWK
QUAX
QUAY
QUAYAGE
QUAYED
QUAYING
QUAYSIDE
QUAYSIDER
QUEACH
QUEACHIER
QUEACHIEST
QUEACHY
QUEAK
QUEAL
QUEAN
QUEANISH
QUEASE
QUEASIER
QUEASIEST
QUEASILY
QUEASINESS
QUEASOM
QUEASY
QUEAZEN
QUEBRACHITE
QUEBRACHITOL
QUEBRACHO
QUEBRADA
QUEBRADILLA
QUEBRITH
QUECH
QUED
QUEDE
QUEDLY
QUEDNESS
QUEDSHIP
QUEE
QUEECHY
QUEED
QUEEL
QUEEN
QUEENCAKE
QUEENCRAFT
QUEENCUP
QUEENFISH
QUEENFISHES
QUEENING
QUEENITE
QUEENLET
QUEENLIER
QUEENLIEST
QUEENLIKE
QUEENLINESS

QUEENLY
QUEENRIGHT
QUEENROOT
QUEENS
QUEENSBERRIES
QUEENSBERRY
QUEENWEED
QUEENWOOD
QUEER
QUEERER
QUEEREST
QUEERITY
QUEERLY
QUEERNESS
QUEERSOME
QUEERY
QUEEST
QUEET
QUEEVE
QUEI
QUEINTISE
QUELCH
QUELITE
QUELL
QUELLED
QUELLER
QUELLING
QUELLIO
QUELLUNG
QUELME
QUELT
QUEMADO
QUEME
QUEMEFUL
QUEMELY
QUENA
QUENCH
QUENCHABLE
QUENCHED
QUENCHER
QUENCHING
QUENCHLESS
QUENCHLESSLY
QUENDA
QUENELLE
QUENSELITE
QUENT
QUENTISE
QUERCETIC
QUERCETIN
QUERCETUM
QUERCIC
QUERCIN
QUERCINE
QUERCITANNIN
QUERCITE
QUERCITOL
QUERCITRIN
QUERCITRON
QUERCIVOROUS
QUERELA
QUERELAE
QUERELE
QUERENCIA
QUERENT
QUERIDA
QUERIDAS
QUERIDO
QUERIDOS
QUERIED
QUERIER
QUERIES
QUERIMAN
QUERIMANS
QUERIMONIES
QUERIMONIOUS
QUERIMONY

QUERIST
QUERKEN
QUERL
QUERN
QUERNAL
QUERNSTONE
QUERRE
QUERULENT
QUERULENTIAL
QUERULIST
QUERULITY
QUERULOSITY
QUERULOUS
QUERULOUSLY
QUERY
QUERYING
QUERYINGLY
QUESAL
QUESITED
QUESITIVE
QUEST
QUESTED
QUESTER
QUESTEUR
QUESTHOUSE
QUESTING
QUESTION
QUESTIONABLE
QUESTIONABLY
QUESTIONARIES
QUESTIONARY
QUESTIONED
QUESTIONEE
QUESTIONER
QUESTIONING
QUESTIONIST
QUESTIONLESS
QUESTIONNAIRE
QUESTIONS
QUESTMAN
QUESTMEN
QUESTMONGER
QUESTOR
QUESTORIAL
QUESTRIST
QUET
QUETCH
QUETENITE
QUETHE
QUETSCH
QUETZAL
QUEUE
QUEY
QUEZAL
QUEZALES
QUI
QUIAPO
QUIAQUIA
QUIB
QUIBBLE
QUIBBLED
QUIBBLER
QUIBBLING
QUIBLET
QUICA
QUICK
QUICKBEAM
QUICKBORN
QUICKED
QUICKEN
QUICKENANCE
QUICKENBEAM
QUICKENED
QUICKENER
QUICKENING
QUICKER
QUICKEST

QUICKFOOT
QUICKHATCH
QUICKIE
QUICKING
QUICKLIME
QUICKLY
QUICKNESS
QUICKSAND
QUICKSANDY
QUICKSET
QUICKSIDE
QUICKSILVER
QUICKSILVERY
QUICKSTEP
QUICKTHORN
QUICKWATER
QUICKWORK
QUID
QUIDAM
QUIDDANY
QUIDDATIVE
QUIDDER
QUIDDIT
QUIDDITATIVE
QUIDDITIES
QUIDDITY
QUIDDLE
QUIDDLED
QUIDDLER
QUIDDLING
QUIDNUNC
QUIENAL
QUIESCE
QUIESCED
QUIESCENCE
QUIESCENCY
QUIESCENT
QUIESCENTLY
QUIESCING
QUIET
QUIETAGE
QUIETED
QUIETEN
QUIETENER
QUIETER
QUIETEST
QUIETING
QUIETISM
QUIETIST
QUIETISTIC
QUIETIVE
QUIETLIKE
QUIETLY
QUIETNESS
QUIETSOME
QUIETUDE
QUIETUS
QUIFF
QUIINACEOUS
QUILA
QUILATE
QUILE
QUILECES
QUILES
QUILESES
QUILEZ
QUILISMA
QUILK
QUILKIN
QUILL
QUILLAI
QUILLAIC
QUILLAJIC
QUILLBACK
QUILLED
QUILLER
QUILLET

QUILLETED
QUILLFISH
QUILLFISHES
QUILLING
QUILLITY
QUILLON
QUILLTAIL
QUILLWORK
QUILLWORT
QUILLY
QUILT
QUILTED
QUILTER
QUILTING
QUIM
QUIN
QUINA
QUINACRINE
QUINALDIC
QUINALDIN
QUINALDINE
QUINALDINIC
QUINALDINIUM
QUINALDYL
QUINAMICIN
QUINAMICINE
QUINAMIDIN
QUINAMIDINE
QUINAMIN
QUINAMINE
QUINANISOLE
QUINAQUINA
QUINARIAN
QUINARIES
QUINARIUS
QUINARY
QUINAS
QUINATE
QUINATOXIN
QUINATOXINE
QUINAZOLIN
QUINAZOLINE
QUINAZOLYL
QUINCE
QUINCEWORT
QUINCH
QUINCUNCIAL
QUINCUNX
QUINCUNXES
QUINCUNXIAL
QUINDECAD
QUINDECAGON
QUINDECEMVIR
QUINDECEMVIRI
QUINDECIM
QUINDECIMA
QUINDECIMVIR
QUINDENE
QUINE
QUINELLA
QUINET
QUINETUM
QUINHYDRONE
QUINIA
QUINIBLE
QUINIC
QUINICIN
QUINICINE
QUINIDIN
QUINIDINE
QUINIELA
QUININ
QUININA
QUININE
QUININISM
QUININIZE
QUINIRETIN

QUINISEXT
QUINISEXTINE
QUINITE
QUINITOL
QUINIZARIN
QUINK
QUINNAT
QUINNET
QUINOA
QUINOFORM
QUINOGEN
QUINOID
QUINOIDAL
QUINOIDATION
QUINOIDIN
QUINOIDINE
QUINOL
QUINOLAS
QUINOLIN
QUINOLINE
QUINOLINIUM
QUINOLINYL
QUINOLOGIST
QUINOLOGY
QUINOLYL
QUINOMETRY
QUINON
QUINONE
QUINONIC
QUINONIMIN
QUINONIMINE
QUINONIZE
QUINONOID
QUINONYL
QUINOPYRIN
QUINOVATE
QUINOVIN
QUINOVOSE
QUINOXALIN
QUINOXALINE
QUINOXALYL
QUINOYL
QUINQUENNIA
QUINQUENNIAD
QUINQUENNIAL
QUINQUENNIUM
QUINQUENNIUMS
QUINQUERTIUM
QUINQUEVIR
QUINQUEVIRS
QUINQUINA
QUINQUINO
QUINSE
QUINSIED
QUINSY
QUINSYBERRIES
QUINSYBERRY
QUINSYWORT
QUINT
QUINTA
QUINTAD
QUINTADENA
QUINTADENE
QUINTAIN
QUINTAL
QUINTAN
QUINTANT
QUINTARY
QUINTE
QUINTELEMENT
QUINTERNION
QUINTESSENCE
QUINTET
QUINTETTE
QUINTETTO
QUINTFOIL
QUINTIC

QUINTILE
QUINTILLION
QUINTIN
QUINTIPED
QUINTO
QUINTOLE
QUINTON
QUINTROON
QUINTUPLE
QUINTUPLED
QUINTUPLET
QUINTUPLING
QUINTUS
QUINUCLIDINE
QUINYIE
QUINYL
QUINZAINE
QUINZE
QUINZIEME
QUIP
QUIPO
QUIPPE
QUIPPED
QUIPPER
QUIPPING
QUIPPISH
QUIPPISHNESS
QUIPPU
QUIPPY
QUIPSOME
QUIPSTER
QUIPU
QUIPUS
QUIRA
QUIRCAL
QUIRE
QUIRED
QUIREWISE
QUIRING
QUIRITARIAN
QUIRK
QUIRKED
QUIRKIER
QUIRKIEST
QUIRKING
QUIRKSEY
QUIRKSOME
QUIRKY
QUIRL
QUIRQUINCHO
QUIRT
QUIS
QUISBY
QUISCOS
QUISLING
QUISLINGISM
QUISQUEITE
QUISQUILIAN
QUISQUILIARY
QUISQUILIOUS
QUISQUOUS
QUIST
QUISTRON
QUISUTSCH
QUIT
QUITANTIE
QUITCH
QUITCLAIM
QUITCLAIMED
QUITCLAIMING
QUITE
QUITELY
QUITEVE
QUITRENT
QUITS
QUITTANCE
QUITTED

QUITTER
QUITTERBONE
QUITTING
QUITTOR
QUIVER
QUIVERED
QUIVERER
QUIVERFUL
QUIVERING
QUIVERLEAF
QUIVERY
QUIXOTIC
QUIXOTICAL
QUIXOTISM
QUIXOTIZE
QUIXOTRY
QUIZ
QUIZZACIOUS
QUIZZATORIAL
QUIZZED
QUIZZEE
QUIZZER
QUIZZERY
QUIZZICAL
QUIZZICALITY
QUIZZICALLY
QUIZZIFY
QUIZZING
QUIZZISH
QUIZZISM
QUIZZITY
QUIZZY
QUO
QUOAD
QUOCK
QUOD
QUODDED
QUODDIES
QUODDING
QUODDITY
QUODLIBET
QUODLIBETARY
QUODLIBETIC
QUODLING
QUOG
QUOILERS
QUOIN
QUOINED
QUOINING
QUOIT
QUOITER
QUOITS
QUOKKA
QUOMINUS
QUOMODO
QUONDAM
QUONIAM
QUONK
QUONKING
QUOP
QUORUM
QUORUMS
QUOT
QUOTA
QUOTABILITY
QUOTABLE
QUOTABLENESS
QUOTABLY
QUOTAS
QUOTATION
QUOTATIONAL
QUOTATIONIST
QUOTATIVE
QUOTE
QUOTED
QUOTEE
QUOTELESS

QUOTENNIAL
QUOTER
QUOTEWORTHY
QUOTH
QUOTHA
QUOTIDIAN
QUOTIDIANLY
QUOTIENT
QUOTIETIES
QUOTIETY
QUOTING
QUOTINGLY
QUOTITY
QUOTT
QUOTUM
QUOY
QUOZ
QUYTE

RA
RAAD
RAADZAAL
RAAN
RAASCH
RAASH
RAB
RABAND
RABANNA
RABAT
RABATINE
RABATO
RABATTE
RABATTED
RABATTEMENT
RABATTING
RABBAN
RABBET
RABBETED
RABBETING
RABBI
RABBIES
RABBIN
RABBINATE
RABBINIC
RABBINICAL
RABBINICALLY
RABBINISM
RABBINIST
RABBINISTIC
RABBINISTICAL
RABBINITE
RABBINITIC
RABBINIZE
RABBIS
RABBISH
RABBIT
RABBITBERRIES
RABBITBERRY
RABBITER
RABBITEYE
RABBITFISH
RABBITMOUTH
RABBITRIES
RABBITROOT
RABBITRY
RABBITS
RABBITSKIN
RABBITWEED
RABBITWOOD
RABBITY
RABBLE
RABBLED
RABBLEMENT
RABBLEPROOF
RABBLER
RABBLESOME
RABBLING
RABBONI
RABDOMANCY
RABFAK
RABI
RABIATOR
RABIC
RABID
RABIDITY
RABIDLY

RABIDNESS
RABIES
RABIETIC
RABIFIC
RABIFORM
RABIGENIC
RABINET
RABIOUS
RABIRUBIA
RABITIC
RABLIN
RABULISTIC
RABULOUS
RACA
RACAHOUT
RACALLABLE
RACCHE
RACCOON
RACCOONBERRY
RACCOONS
RACE
RACEABOUT
RACECOURSE
RACED
RACEGOER
RACEGOING
RACEHORSE
RACEHORSES
RACELIKE
RACELINE
RACEMASE
RACEMATE
RACEMATION
RACEME
RACEMED
RACEMIC
RACEMIFEROUS
RACEMIFORM
RACEMISM
RACEMIZATION
RACEMIZE
RACEMIZED
RACEMIZING
RACEMOID
RACEMOSE
RACEMOSELY
RACEMOUS
RACEMULE
RACEMULOSE
RACER
RACES
RACETRACK
RACETTE
RACEWAY
RACH
RACHE
RACHES
RACHIAL
RACHIALGIA
RACHIALGIC
RACHICENTESIS
RACHIDES
RACHIDIAN
RACHIFORM
RACHIGRAPH
RACHILLA
RACHILLAE
RACHIODONT
RACHIODYNIA
RACHIOMETER
RACHIOPLEGIA
RACHIOTOME
RACHIOTOMY
RACHIPAGUS
RACHIS
RACHISCHISIS
RACHISES

RACHITIC
RACHITIS
RACHITISM
RACHITOGENIC
RACHITOME
RACHITOMOUS
RACHITOMY
RACIAL
RACIALISM
RACIALIST
RACIALITY
RACIALIZATION
RACIALIZE
RACIALLY
RACILY
RACINESS
RACING
RACION
RACISM
RACIST
RACK
RACKABONES
RACKAN
RACKAPEE
RACKBONE
RACKED
RACKER
RACKET
RACKETEER
RACKETEERING
RACKETER
RACKETRY
RACKETT
RACKETY
RACKING
RACKLE
RACKMAN
RACKWAY
RACKWORK
RACLOIR
RACON
RACONTEUR
RACOON
RACQUET
RACY
RAD
RADA
RADAR
RADARSCOPE
RADDLE
RADDLED
RADDLEMAN
RADDLEMEN
RADDLING
RADDLINGS
RADE
RADEAU
RADECTOMY
RADEUR
RADEVORE
RADFORD
RADIABILITY
RADIABLE
RADIAL
RADIALE
RADIALITY
RADIALIZATION
RADIALIZE
RADIALLY
RADIAN
RADIANCE
RADIANCY
RADIANT
RADIANTLY
RADIANTNESS
RADIATE
RADIATED

RADIATIFORM
RADIATING
RADIATION
RADIATIONAL
RADIATIVE
RADIATOR
RADIATORS
RADIATORY
RADIATURE
RADICAL
RADICALISM
RADICALITY
RADICALIZATION
RADICALIZE
RADICALLY
RADICALNESS
RADICAND
RADICANT
RADICATE
RADICATED
RADICATING
RADICATION
RADICEL
RADICES
RADICICOLA
RADICLE
RADICOLOUS
RADICOSE
RADICULA
RADICULAR
RADICULE
RADICULECTOMY
RADICULITIS
RADICULOSE
RADIENT
RADIESCENT
RADIFEROUS
RADII
RADIO
RADIOACOUSTICS
RADIOACTINIUM
RADIOACTIVATE
RADIOACTIVE
RADIOACTIVITY
RADIOBIOLOGY
RADIOBSERVER
RADIOCARBON
RADIOCARPAL
RADIOCHEMICAL
RADIOCHEMISTRY
RADIOCONDUCTOR
RADIODATING
RADIODE
RADIODETECTOR
RADIODIGITAL
RADIODONTIA
RADIODONTIC
RADIODONTIST
RADIODYNAMIC
RADIODYNAMICS
RAD!OED
RADIOELEMENT
RADIOGRAM
RADIOGRAPH
RADIOGRAPHER
RADIOGRAPHIC
RADIOGRAPHICAL
RADIOGRAPHICALLY
RADIOGRAPHY
RADIOHUMERAL
RADIOING
RADIOISOTOPE
RADIOLARIAN
RADIOLEAD
RADIOLITE
RADIOLITIC
RADIOLOCATION

RADIOLOGIC
RADIOLOGICAL
RADIOLOGIST
RADIOLOGY
RADIOLUCENCY
RADIOLUCENT
RADIOMAN
RADIOMEN
RADIOMETER
RADIOMETRIC
RADIOMETRICALLY
RADIOMETRY
RADIOMICROMETER
RADIOMOVIES
RADIONIC
RADIOPACITY
RADIOPALMAR
RADIOPAQUE
RADIOPHARE
RADIOPHONE
RADIOPHONIC
RADIOPHONY
RADIOPHOTOGRAPH
RADIOPHOTOGRAPHY
RADIOPRAXIS
RADIOS
RADIOSCOPE
RADIOSCOPIC
RADIOSCOPICAL
RADIOSCOPY
RADIOSENSIBILITY
RADIOSENSITIVE
RADIOSENSITIVITY
RADIOSONDE
RADIOSONIC
RADIOSYMMETRICAL
RADIOTECHNOLOGY
RADIOTELEGRAM
RADIOTELEGRAPH
RADIOTELEGRAPHY
RADIOTELEPHONE
RADIOTELEPHONIC
RADIOTELEPHONY
RADIOTHALLIUM
RADIOTHERAPEUTIC
RADIOTHERAPEUTICS
RADIOTHERAPEUTIST
RADIOTHERAPIST
RADIOTHERAPY
RADIOTHERMY
RADIOTHORIUM
RADIOTOXIC
RADIOTRANSPARENCY
RADIOTRANSPARENT
RADIOTRICIAN
RADIOTROPIC
RADIOTROPISM
RADIOUS
RADIOVISION
RADISH
RADIUM
RADIUMIZATION
RADIUMIZE
RADIUS
RADIUSES
RADIX
RADKNIGHT
RADLY
RADMAN
RADOME
RADON
RADULA
RADULAE
RADULAR
RADULATE
RADULIFEROUS
RADULIFORM

RADZIMIR
RAE
RAFALE
RAFF
RAFFE
RAFFEE
RAFFIA
RAFFINASE
RAFFING
RAFFINOSE
RAFFISH
RAFFISHLY
RAFFISHNESS
RAFFLE
RAFFLED
RAFFLER
RAFFLESIA
RAFFLESIACEOUS
RAFFLING
RAFFMAN
RAFT
RAFTAGE
RAFTER
RAFTINESS
RAFTMAN
RAFTSMAN
RAFTSMEN
RAFTY
RAG
RAGA
RAGABASH
RAGABRASH
RAGAMUFFIN
RAGAMUFFINLY
RAGBAG
RAGE
RAGED
RAGEOUS
RAGEOUSLY
RAGEOUSNESS
RAGERY
RAGFISH
RAGGED
RAGGEDLY
RAGGEDNESS
RAGGEE
RAGGER
RAGGERY
RAGGETY
RAGGI
RAGGIL
RAGGILY
RAGGING
RAGGLE
RAGGLED
RAGGY
RAGHOUSE
RAGI
RAGING
RAGINGLY
RAGLAN
RAGLANITE
RAGLET
RAGLIN
RAGMAN
RAGMEN
RAGONDIN
RAGOUT
RAGOUTED
RAGOUTING
RAGPICKER
RAGS
RAGSELLER
RAGSHAG
RAGSORTER
RAGSTONE
RAGTAG

RAGTIME
RAGTIMER
RAGTIMEY
RAGULE
RAGULY
RAGUSYE
RAGWEED
RAGWORT
RAH
RAHDAR
RAHDAREE
RAHDARI
RAIA
RAID
RAIDER
RAIK
RAIL
RAILAGE
RAILBIRD
RAILED
RAILER
RAILHEAD
RAILING
RAILLERY
RAILLEUR
RAILLY
RAILMAN
RAILMEN
RAILROAD
RAILROADER
RAILROADING
RAILWAY
RAIM
RAIMENT
RAIN
RAINBAND
RAINBIRD
RAINBOUND
RAINBOW
RAINBOWY
RAINBURST
RAINCOAT
RAINDROP
RAINER
RAINES
RAINFALL
RAINFOWL
RAINIER
RAINIEST
RAINILY
RAININESS
RAINLESS
RAINLIGHT
RAINMAKER
RAINMAKING
RAINOUT
RAINPROOF
RAINPROOFER
RAINSPOUT
RAINSTORM
RAINTIGHT
RAINWASH
RAINWATER
RAINWORM
RAINY
RAIOID
RAIR
RAIS
RAISE
RAISED
RAISER
RAISIN
RAISINE
RAISING
RAISINS
RAISINY
RAISONNE

RAIT
RAITH
RAIYAT
RAJ
RAJA
RAJAH
RAJAS
RAJBANSI
RAJOGUNA
RAK
RAKA
RAKAH
RAKAN
RAKE
RAKEAGE
RAKED
RAKEE
RAKEHELL
RAKEHELLISH
RAKEHELLY
RAKELY
RAKEOFF
RAKER
RAKERY
RAKESTEEL
RAKESTELE
RAKH
RAKI
RAKIA
RAKIJA
RAKILY
RAKING
RAKING
RAKISH
RAKISHLY
RAKISHNESS
RAKIT
RAKSHASA
RALE
RALISH
RALLENTANDO
RALLERY
RALLIANCE
RALLIER
RALLIES
RALLIFORM
RALLINE
RALLY
RALLYING
RALO
RALPH
RALSTONITE
RAM
RAMACK
RAMADA
RAMAGE
RAMARAMA
RAMARK
RAMASS
RAMATE
RAMBARRE
RAMBEH
RAMBERGE
RAMBLA
RAMBLE
RAMBLED
RAMBLER
RAMBLING
RAMBLINGLY
RAMBONG
RAMBOOZE
RAMBUNCTIOUS
RAMBURE
RAMBUTAN
RAME
RAMEAL
RAMEE

RAMEKIN
RAMELLOSE
RAMENT
RAMENTA
RAMENTACEOUS
RAMENTAL
RAMENTUM
RAMEOUS
RAMEQUIN
RAMEX
RAMFEEZLED
RAMFORCE
RAMGUNSHOCH
RAMHEAD
RAMI
RAMICORN
RAMIE
RAMIFICATE
RAMIFICATION
RAMIFIED
RAMIFORM
RAMIFY
RAMIFYING
RAMILLIE
RAMISECTION
RAMISECTOMY
RAMLINE
RAMMACK
RAMMAGE
RAMMASS
RAMMED
RAMMEL
RAMMELSBERGITE
RAMMER
RAMMERMAN
RAMMERMEN
RAMMING
RAMMISH
RAMMISHNESS
RAMMY
RAMON
RAMONEUR
RAMOSE
RAMOUS
RAMP
RAMPACIOUS
RAMPACIOUSLY
RAMPAGE
RAMPAGED
RAMPAGEOUS
RAMPAGEOUSLY
RAMPAGEOUSNESS
RAMPAGER
RAMPAGING
RAMPAGIOUS
RAMPANCY
RAMPANT
RAMPANTLY
RAMPART
RAMPARTED
RAMPARTING
RAMPER
RAMPICK
RAMPIER
RAMPIKE
RAMPION
RAMPIRE
RAMPISH
RAMPLER
RAMPLOR
RAMPOLE
RAMRACE
RAMROD
RAMRODDY
RAMSCALLION
RAMSCH
RAMSHACKLE

RAMSHACKLENESS
RAMSON
RAMSTAM
RAMSTEAD
RAMTIL
RAMULAR
RAMULIFEROUS
RAMULOSE
RAMULOUS
RAMULUS
RAMUS
RAMVERSE
RAN
RANA
RANAL
RANARIA
RANARIAN
RANARIUM
RANCE
RANCEL
RANCELLOR
RANCELMAN
RANCELMEN
RANCER
RANCESCENT
RANCH
RANCHE
RANCHER
RANCHERIA
RANCHERO
RANCHEROS
RANCHMAN
RANCHMEN
RANCHO
RANCHOS
RANCHWOMAN
RANCID
RANCIDIFICATION
RANCIDIFY
RANCIDITY
RANCIDLY
RANCIDNESS
RANCIO
RANCOR
RANCOROUS
RANCOROUSLY
RANCOUR
RAND
RANDALL
RANDAN
RANDANNITE
RANDEM
RANDER
RANDERS
RANDIE
RANDING
RANDIR
RANDOM
RANDOMIZE
RANDOMIZED
RANDOMIZING
RANDOMLY
RANDOMNESS
RANDOMWISE
RANDON
RANDORI
RANDY
RANE
RANEE
RANFORCE
RANG
RANGALE
RANGDOODLES
RANGE
RANGED
RANGEHEADS
RANGEMAN

RANGEMEN
RANGER
RANGERSHIP
RANGEWORK
RANGIER
RANGIEST
RANGING
RANGLE
RANGY
RANI
RANINE
RANINIAN
RANK
RANKER
RANKET
RANKING
RANKISH
RANKLE
RANKLED
RANKLING
RANKLY
RANKNESS
RANKS
RANKSMAN
RANKSMEN
RANN
RANNEL
RANNIGAL
RANNY
RANPIKE
RANSACK
RANSACKER
RANSEL
RANSELMEN
RANSES
RANSOM
RANSOMER
RANSOMLESS
RANSTEAD
RANT
RANTAN
RANTANKEROUS
RANTEPOLE
RANTER
RANTING
RANTIPOLE
RANTISM
RANTIZE
RANTOCK
RANTOON
RANTREE
RANTY
RANULA
RANUNCULI
RANUNCULUS
RANUNCULUSES
RAOB
RAP
RAPACEUS
RAPACIOUS
RAPACIOUSLY
RAPACITY
RAPAKIVI
RAPATEACEOUS
RAPE
RAPED
RAPEFUL
RAPELY
RAPER
RAPESEED
RAPEYE
RAPHAE
RAPHANIA
RAPHANUS
RAPHANY
RAPHE
RAPHIA

RAPHIDE
RAPHIDES
RAPHIDIFEROUS
RAPHIS
RAPHUS
RAPIC
RAPID
RAPIDAMENTE
RAPIDE
RAPIDITY
RAPIDLY
RAPIDNESS
RAPIDO
RAPIDS
RAPIER
RAPIERED
RAPILLO
RAPIN
RAPINE
RAPING
RAPINIC
RAPIST
RAPLOCH
RAPORT
RAPPAGE
RAPPAREE
RAPPE
RAPPED
RAPPEE
RAPPEL
RAPPELLED
RAPPELLING
RAPPEN
RAPPER
RAPPING
RAPPINI
RAPPIST
RAPPORT
RAPSCALLION
RAPSCALLIONISM
RAPSCALLIONLY
RAPSCALLIONRY
RAPT
RAPTATORIAL
RAPTER
RAPTLY
RAPTNESS
RAPTOR
RAPTORIAL
RAPTORIOUS
RAPTRIL
RAPTURE
RAPTURED
RAPTURIST
RAPTURIZE
RAPTUROUS
RAPTUROUSLY
RAPTUROUSNESS
RAPTUS
RAQUET
RARE
RAREBIT
RAREFACTION
RAREFACTIONAL
RAREFACTIVE
RAREFIABLE
RAREFICATION
RAREFIED
RAREFIER
RAREFY
RAREFYING
RARELY
RARENESS
RARER
RARERIPE
RAREST
RARICONSTANT

RARIETY
RARING
RARIORA
RARISH
RARITIES
RARITY
RAS
RASA
RASAMALA
RASANT
RASBORA
RASCACIO
RASCAL
RASCALITIES
RASCALITY
RASCALLY
RASCALRY
RASCETA
RASE
RASED
RASEE
RASEN
RASER
RASGADO
RASH
RASHBUSS
RASHER
RASHFUL
RASHING
RASHLY
RASHNESS
RASING
RASION
RASOIR
RASON
RASOR
RASORIAL
RASOUR
RASP
RASPATORY
RASPBERRY
RASPED
RASPER
RASPIER
RASPIEST
RASPING
RASPINGLY
RASPINGNESS
RASPIS
RASPISH
RASPITE
RASPY
RASSASY
RASSE
RASSLE
RASTIK
RASTY
RASURE
RAT
RATA
RATABLE
RATABLENESS
RATABLY
RATAFEE
RATAFIA
RATAL
RATAN
RATANY
RATAPLAN
RATAPLANNED
RATAPLANNING
RATBAG
RATBITE
RATCATCHER
RATCH
RATCHEL
RATCHER

RATCHET
RATCHETY
RATE
RATEABILITY
RATEABLE
RATED
RATEL
RATEPAYER
RATEPAYING
RATER
RATERO
RATES
RATFISH
RATH
RATHA
RATHE
RATHELY
RATHENESS
RATHER
RATHERIPE
RATHERISH
RATHERLY
RATHEST
RATHITE
RATHOLE
RATHRIPE
RATHSKELLER
RATI
RATIFIA
RATIFICATION
RATIFICATIONIST
RATIFIED
RATIFY
RATIFYING
RATIHABITION
RATINE
RATING
RATIO
RATIOCINANT
RATIOCINATE
RATIOCINATED
RATIOCINATING
RATIOCINATION
RATIOCINATIVE
RATIOCINATOR
RATIOCINATORY
RATIOMETER
RATION
RATIONABLE
RATIONAL
RATIONALE
RATIONALISM
RATIONALIST
RATIONALISTIC
RATIONALITIES
RATIONALITY
RATIONALIZE
RATIONALIZED
RATIONALIZER
RATIONALLY
RATIONALNESS
RATIONATE
RATIONING
RATIONS
RATIOS
RATITE
RATIUNCLE
RATLINE
RATLINER
RATO
RATON
RATOON
RATS
RATSBANE
RATTAIL
RATTAN
RATTAREE

RATTATTOO
RATTED
RATTEEN
RATTEL
RATTEN
RATTENED
RATTENER
RATTENING
RATTER
RATTERY
RATTI
RATTINET
RATTING
RATTINGLY
RATTISH
RATTLE
RATTLEBAG
RATTLEBONES
RATTLEBOX
RATTLEBRAIN
RATTLEBRAINED
RATTLEBUSH
RATTLED
RATTLEHEAD
RATTLEHEADED
RATTLEJACK
RATTLEMOUSE
RATTLENUT
RATTLEPATE
RATTLEPATED
RATTLER
RATTLERAN
RATTLEROOT
RATTLERTREE
RATTLES
RATTLESKULL
RATTLESKULLED
RATTLESNAKE
RATTLESOME
RATTLETRAP
RATTLEWEED
RATTLEWORT
RATTLING
RATTLINGNESS
RATTLY
RATTON
RATTONER
RATTOON
RATTRAP
RATTY
RATWA
RATWOOD
RAUCID
RAUCIDITY
RAUCITY
RAUCOUS
RAUCOUSLY
RAUCOUSNESS
RAUGRAVE
RAUK
RAULI
RAUN
RAUNCHY
RAUNGE
RAUNPICK
RAUPO
RAURACI
RAURIKI
RAVAGE
RAVAGED
RAVAGEMENT
RAVAGER
RAVAGING
RAVE
RAVED
RAVEHOOK
RAVEL

RAVELED
RAVELER
RAVELIN
RAVELING
RAVELLED
RAVELLER
RAVELLING
RAVELLY
RAVELMENT
RAVEN
RAVENER
RAVENING
RAVENINGLY
RAVENLING
RAVENOUS
RAVENOUSLY
RAVENOUSNESS
RAVENRY
RAVENSTONE
RAVER
RAVERY
RAVIGOTE
RAVIN
RAVINATE
RAVINE
RAVINED
RAVINEMENT
RAVINEY
RAVING
RAVIOLI
RAVISH
RAVISHED
RAVISHER
RAVISHING
RAVISHINGLY
RAVISHMENT
RAVISON
RAVISSANT
RAW
RAWBONE
RAWBONED
RAWBONES
RAWED
RAWHEAD
RAWHIDE
RAWHIDER
RAWIN
RAWING
RAWISH
RAWISHNESS
RAWKY
RAWLY
RAWNESS
RAWNIE
RAX
RAY
RAYA
RAYAGE
RAYAH
RAYAT
RAYED
RAYGRASS
RAYING
RAYLESS
RAYLESSLY
RAYLESSNESS
RAYNE
RAYON
RAYONNANCE
RAYONNANT
RAYS
RAZE
RAZED
RAZEE
RAZEED
RAZEEING
RAZING

RAZON
RAZOO
RAZOR
RAZORBACK
RAZORBILL
RAZOREDGE
RAZORMAKER
RAZORMAKING
RAZORMAN
RAZORSTROP
RAZOUR
RAZZ
RAZZBERRIES
RAZZBERRY
RAZZIA
RAZZING
RAZZLY
RE
REA
REAAL
REABLE
REACCESS
REACH
REACHED
REACHER
REACHING
REACHLESS
REACHY
REACQUIRE
REACT
REACTANCE
REACTANT
REACTION
REACTIONAL
REACTIONALLY
REACTIONARIES
REACTIONARINESS
REACTIONARISM
REACTIONARIST
REACTIONARY
REACTIONARYISM
REACTIONISM
REACTIONIST
REACTIVATE
REACTIVATED
REACTIVATING
REACTIVATION
REACTIVATOR
REACTIVE
REACTIVELY
REACTIVENESS
REACTIVITY
REACTOLOGICAL
REACTOLOGY
REACTOR
REACTUALIZATION
REACTUALIZE
REACTUATE
READ
READABILITY
READABLE
READABLENESS
READABLY
READDRESS
READEPT
READER
READERSHIP
READIED
READIER
READIEST
READILY
READINESS
READING
READINGDOM
READJUST
READJUSTABLE
READJUSTER

READJUSTMENT
READMISSION
READMIT
READMITTANCE
READMITTED
READMITTING
READS
READVERTENCY
READY
READYING
REAFFIRM
REAFFIRMANCE
REAFFIRMER
REAGENCY
REAGENT
REAGGRAVATE
REAGGRAVATION
REAGIN
REAK
REAKS
REAL
REALES
REALEST
REALGAR
REALIA
REALIGN
REALIGNMENT
REALISM
REALIST
REALISTIC
REALISTICALLY
REALISTICIZE
REALITIES
REALITY
REALIZABLE
REALIZATION
REALIZE
REALIZED
REALIZER
REALIZING
REALLY
REALM
REALNESS
REALS
REALTIES
REALTOR
REALTY
REAM
REAMAGE
REAME
REAMER
REAMERER
REAMY
REAN
REANIMATE
REANIMATED
REANIMATING
REANIMATION
REANSWER
REAP
REAPABLE
REAPDOLE
REAPER
REAPERS
REAPING
REAPPEAR
REAPPEARANCE
REAR
REARDOSS
REARED
REARER
REARHORSE
REARING
REARLING
REARLY
REARM
REARMAMENT

REARMED
REARMOST
REARMOUSE
REARRANGE
REARRANGED
REARRANGEMENT
REARRANGING
REARWARD
REARWARDS
REASINESS
REASON
REASONABILITY
REASONABLE
REASONABLENESS
REASONABLY
REASONAL
REASONED
REASONER
REASONING
REASONLESS
REASONLESSLY
REASONLESSNESS
REASONS
REASSEMBLE
REASSERT
REASSERTION
REASSERTOR
REASSIGN
REASSOCIATION
REASSUME
REASSUMPTION
REASSURANCE
REASSURE
REASSURED
REASSUREDLY
REASSUREMENT
REASSURER
REASSURING
REASSURINGLY
REASTINESS
REASTY
REASY
REATUS
REAUTE
REAVE
REAVED
REAVER
REAVERY
REAVING
REB
REBAB
REBACK
REBAIT
REBAN
REBAPTISM
REBAPTISMAL
REBAPTIZATION
REBAPTIZE
REBAPTIZER
REBAR
REBARBATIVE
REBATE
REBATED
REBATEMENT
REBATER
REBATING
REBATO
REBBE
REBEAT
REBEC
REBECK
REBEL
REBELDOM
REBELLED
REBELLING
REBELLION
REBELLIOUS

REBELLIOUSLY
REBELLIOUSNESS
REBELLY
REBIA
REBID
REBILLING
REBIND
REBIRTH
REBOANT
REBOANTIC
REBOATION
REBOIL
REBOISE
REBOISEMENT
REBOKE
REBOLERA
REBOLT
REBORN
REBOTE
REBOUND
REBOUNDER
REBOUNDING
REBOZO
REBROADCAST
REBUFF
REBUILD
REBUILDER
REBUILT
REBUKABLE
REBUKE
REBUKED
REBUKER
REBUKING
REBUN
REBURSE
REBUS
REBUSED
REBUSES
REBUSING
REBUT
REBUTE
REBUTTAL
REBUTTED
REBUTTER
REBUTTING
RECADENCY
RECADO
RECALCITRANCE
RECALCITRANCY
RECALCITRANT
RECALCITRATE
RECALCITRATION
RECALESCE
RECALESCED
RECALESCENCE
RECALESCENT
RECALESCING
RECALL
RECALLED
RECALLING
RECALLIST
RECALLMENT
RECAMERA
RECANT
RECANTATION
RECANTED
RECANTER
RECANTING
RECAP
RECAPITALIZATION
RECAPITALIZE
RECAPITALIZED
RECAPITALIZING
RECAPITULATE
RECAPITULATED
RECAPITULATING
RECAPITULATION

RECAPPED
RECAPPER
RECAPPING
RECAPTION
RECAPTOR
RECAPTURE
RECAPTURED
RECAPTURING
RECARBON
RECARBONIZE
RECARBONIZER
RECARBURIZATION
RECARBURIZE
RECARBURIZER
RECAST
RECASTER
RECASTING
RECAULESCENCE
RECCE
RECCHE
RECCO
RECCY
RECEDE
RECEDED
RECEDENCE
RECEDENT
RECEDER
RECEDING
RECEIPT
RECEIPTED
RECEIPTER
RECEIPTING
RECEIPTMENT
RECEIPTOR
RECEIVABILITY
RECEIVABLE
RECEIVABLENESS
RECEIVABLES
RECEIVAL
RECEIVE
RECEIVED
RECEIVEDNESS
RECEIVER
RECEIVERSHIP
RECEIVING
RECENCY
RECENSE
RECENSION
RECENSURE
RECENT
RECENTLY
RECENTNESS
RECEPT
RECEPTACLE
RECEPTACULAR
RECEPTANT
RECEPTIBILITY
RECEPTIBLE
RECEPTION
RECEPTIONISM
RECEPTIONIST
RECEPTITIOUS
RECEPTIVE
RECEPTIVELY
RECEPTIVENESS
RECEPTIVITY
RECEPTOR
RECEPTORAL
RECEPTORIAL
RECEPTUAL
RECEPTUALLY
RECERCELEE
RECESS
RECESSED
RECESSER
RECESSION
RECESSIONAL

RECESSIONARY
RECESSIVE
RECESSIVELY
RECHANGE
RECHARGE
RECHARTER
RECHASE
RECHASER
RECHATE
RECHAUFFE
RECHE
RECHERCHE
RECIDE
RECIDIVATE
RECIDIVATION
RECIDIVE
RECIDIVISM
RECIDIVIST
RECIDIVISTIC
RECIDIVITY
RECIDIVOUS
RECIPE
RECIPIANGLE
RECIPIENCE
RECIPIENCY
RECIPIEND
RECIPIENDARY
RECIPIENT
RECIPIOMOTOR
RECIPROCABLE
RECIPROCAL
RECIPROCALITY
RECIPROCALIZE
RECIPROCALLY
RECIPROCANT
RECIPROCANTIVE
RECIPROCATE
RECIPROCATED
RECIPROCATING
RECIPROCATION
RECIPROCATIVE
RECIPROCATOR
RECIPROCATORY
RECIPROCITY
RECISION
RECIT
RECITAL
RECITALIST
RECITANDO
RECITATION
RECITATIONIST
RECITATIVE
RECITE
RECITED
RECITEMENT
RECITER
RECITING
RECK
RECKLA
RECKLESS
RECKLESSLY
RECKLESSNESS
RECKLING
RECKON
RECKONED
RECKONER
RECKONING
RECLAIM
RECLAIMABLE
RECLAIMABLENES
RECLAIMABLY
RECLAIMANT
RECLAIMED
RECLAIMER
RECLAIMLESS
RECLAIMMENT

RECLAMA
RECLAMATION
RECLAME
RECLINABLE
RECLINATE
RECLINATED
RECLINATION
RECLINE
RECLINED
RECLINER
RECLINING
RECLOSE
RECLUDE
RECLUSE
RECLUSELY
RECLUSENESS
RECLUSERY
RECLUSION
RECLUSIVE
RECLUSIVENESS
RECOCT
RECOCTION
RECOGITATE
RECOGITATION
RECOGNITA
RECOGNITION
RECOGNITIVE
RECOGNITOR
RECOGNITORY
RECOGNIZABLE
RECOGNIZABLY
RECOGNIZANCE
RECOGNIZANT
RECOGNIZE
RECOGNIZED
RECOGNIZEE
RECOGNIZER
RECOGNIZING
RECOGNIZOR
RECOGNOSCE
RECOIL
RECOILED
RECOILING
RECOILLESS
RECOILMENT
RECOIN
RECOINAGE
RECOLLECT
RECOLLECTED
RECOLLECTEDLY
RECOLLECTEDNESS
RECOLLECTION
RECOLLECTIVE
RECOLLECTIVELY
RECOLLECTIVENESS
RECOLLET
RECOMBINATION
RECOMEMBER
RECOMFORT
RECOMMAND
RECOMMENCE
RECOMMENCEMENT
RECOMMENCER
RECOMMEND
RECOMMENDABILITY
RECOMMENDABLE
RECOMMENDABLENESS
RECOMMENDABLY
RECOMMENDATION
RECOMMENDATORY
RECOMMENDEE
RECOMMENDER
RECOMMIT
RECOMMITING
RECOMMITMENT
RECOMMITTAL
RECOMMITTED

RECOMPENSABLE
RECOMPENSATION
RECOMPENSE
RECOMPENSED
RECOMPENSER
RECOMPENSING
RECOMPENSIVE
RECOMPOSE
RECOMPOSED
RECOMPOSER
RECOMPOSING
RECOMPOSITION
RECOMPRESS
RECOMPRESSION
RECONCENTRADO
RECONCENTRATE
RECONCENTRATION
RECONCILABILITY
RECONCILABLE
RECONCILABLENESS
RECONCILABLY
RECONCILE
RECONCILED
RECONCILEE
RECONCILELESS
RECONCILEMENT
RECONCILER
RECONCILIABILITY
RECONCILIABLE
RECONCILIATE
RECONCILIATION
RECONCILIATIVE
RECONCILIATOR
RECONCILIATORY
RECONCILING
RECONCILINGLY
RECOND
RECONDITE
RECONDITELY
RECONDITENESS
RECONDITION
RECONDUCT
RECONDUCTION
RECONNAISSANCE
RECONNOITER
RECONNOITERED
RECONNOITERER
RECONNOITERING
RECONSIDER
RECONSIDERATIO
RECONSIGN
RECONSIGNMENT
RECONSTITUENT
RECONSTITUTE
RECONSTITUTION
RECONSTRUCT
RECONSTRUCTED
RECONSTRUCTION
RECONSTRUCTIONAL
RECONSTRUCTIONARY
RECONSTRUCTIONIST
RECONSTRUCTIVE
RECONSTRUCTIVENESS
RECONSTRUCTOR
RECONTER
RECONVENTION
RECONVENTIONAL
RECONVERT
RECONVERTIBLE
RECONVEY
RECONVEYANCE
RECOPILATION
RECORD
RECORDANT
RECORDATION
RECORDATIVE
RECORDATIVELY

RECORDATORY
RECORDED
RECORDER
RECORDING
RECORDIST
RECORDS
RECOUNT
RECOUNTAL
RECOUNTED
RECOUNTER
RECOUNTING
RECOUNTMENT
RECOUP
RECOUPABLE
RECOUPE
RECOUPED
RECOUPER
RECOUPING
RECOUPLING
RECOUPMENT
RECOUR
RECOURSE
RECOVER
RECOVERABILITY
RECOVERABLE
RECOVERABLENESS
RECOVERANCE
RECOVERED
RECOVEREE
RECOVERER
RECOVERIES
RECOVERY
RECRAYED
RECREANCE
RECREANCY
RECREANT
RECREANTLY
RECREANTNESS
RECREATE
RECREATED
RECREATING
RECREATION
RECREATIONAL
RECREATIONIST
RECREATIVE
RECREATIVELY
RECREATIVENESS
RECREATOR
RECREDENTIAL
RECREMENT
RECREMENTAL
RECREMENTITIAL
RECREMENTITIOUS
RECRESCENCE
RECREW
RECRIMINATE
RECRIMINATOR
RECRUDENCY
RECRUDESCE
RECRUDESCED
RECRUDESCENCE
RECRUDESCENCY
RECRUDESCENT
RECRUDESCING
RECRUIT
RECRUITAGE
RECRUITAL
RECRUITEE
RECRUITER
RECRUITING
RECRUITMENT
RECRUSHER
RECRYSTALLIZE
RECT
RECTAL
RECTANGLE
RECTANGLED

RECTANGULAR
RECTANGULARLY
RECTANGULARNESS
RECTANGULATE
RECTIFIABLE
RECTIFICATION
RECTIFICATIVE
RECTIFICATOR
RECTIFIED
RECTIFIER
RECTIFY
RECTIFYING
RECTIGRADE
RECTILINEAL
RECTILINEALLY
RECTILINEAR
RECTILINEAR
RECTILINEARITY
RECTILINEARNESS
RECTINERVED
RECTION
RECTIROSTRAL
RECTISERIAL
RECTITUDE
RECTITUDINOUS
RECTO
RECTOCELE
RECTOCLYSIS
RECTOCOLITIC
RECTOCOLONIC
RECTOGENITAL
RECTOPEXY
RECTOPLASTY
RECTOR
RECTORAL
RECTORATE
RECTORIAL
RECTORRHAPHY
RECTORY
RECTOS
RECTOSCOPE
RECTOSCOPY
RECTOSIGMOID
RECTOSTOMY
RECTOTOME
RECTOTOMY
RECTOVESICAL
RECTRESS
RECTRICES
RECTRICIAL
RECTRIX
RECTUM
RECTUS
RECU
RECUBANT
RECUBATE
RECUBATION
RECUEIL
RECUEILLEMENT
RECULADE
RECULE
RECUMB
RECUMBENCE
RECUMBENCY
RECUMBENT
RECUMBENTLY
RECUPERANCE
RECUPERATE
RECUPERATED
RECUPERATING
RECUPERATION
RECUPERATIVE
RECUPERATOR
RECUPERATORY
RECUR
RECURE
RECURRED

RECURRENCE
RECURRENCY
RECURRENT
RECURRENTLY
RECURRER
RECURRING
RECURRINGLY
RECURSE
RECURSION
RECURSIVE
RECURVANT
RECURVATE
RECURVATION
RECURVATURE
RECURVE
RECURVED
RECURVING
RECURVOUS
RECUSANCE
RECUSANCY
RECUSANT
RECUSATION
RECUSATIVE
RECUSATOR
RECUSE
RECUSED
RECUSING
RECUSSION
RECUTTING
RECYCLE
RED
REDACT
REDACTED
REDACTEUR
REDACTING
REDACTION
REDACTIONAL
REDACTOR
REDACTORIAL
REDAMATION
REDAME
REDAN
REDARGUE
REDARGUED
REDARGUING
REDARGUTION
REDARGUTIVE
REDARGUTORY
REDBACK
REDBAITING
REDBAY
REDBEARD
REDBELLY
REDBERRY
REDBILL
REDBIRD
REDBONE
REDBREAST
REDBRUSH
REDBUCK
REDBUD
REDCAP
REDCOAT
REDCOLL
REDD
REDDE
REDDED
REDDEN
REDDENDA
REDDENDO
REDDENDUM
REDDER
REDDEST
REDDING
REDDINGITE
REDDISH
REDDISHLY

REDDISHNESS
REDDITION
REDDITIVE
REDDLE
REDDLED
REDDLEMEN
REDDLING
REDDOCK
REDDSMAN
REDDY
REDE
REDEAR
REDECORATE
REDECORATED
REDECORATING
REDECORATION
REDECUSSATE
REDEEM
REDEEMABLE
REDEEMABLY
REDEEMER
REDEEMING
REDEEMLESS
REDELESS
REDELIVER
REDELIVERANCE
REDELIVERER
REDELIVERY
REDELY
REDEMAND
REDEMANDABLE
REDEMPTIBLE
REDEMPTION
REDEMPTIONAL
REDEMPTIONER
REDEMPTIVE
REDEMPTIVELY
REDEMPTOR
REDEMPTORIAL
REDEMPTORY
REDEMPTRESS
REDEMPTRICE
REDESMAN
REDETERMINE
REDEVELOP
REDEVELOPER
REDEYE
REDFIN
REDFINCH
REDFISH
REDHEAD
REDHEADEDLY
REDHEARTED
REDHIBITION
REDHIBITORY
REDHOOP
REDHORSE
REDIA
REDIENT
REDIF
REDINGOTE
REDINTEGRATE
REDINTEGRATED
REDINTEGRATION
REDINTEGRATIVE
REDINTEGRATOR
REDIRECT
REDIRECTION
REDISCOUNT
REDISSEIZE
REDISTILL
REDISTRIBUTE
REDISTRICT
REDITION
REDIVIVE
REDIVIVOUS
REDIVIVUS

REDJACKET
REDKNEES
REDLEG
REDLEGS
REDLINE
REDLY
REDMOUTH
REDNECK
REDNESS
REDO
REDOLENCE
REDOLENCY
REDOLENT
REDOLENTLY
REDONDILLA
REDOUBLE
REDOUBLED
REDOUBLEMENT
REDOUBLER
REDOUBLING
REDOUBT
REDOUBTABLE
REDOUBTABLENESS
REDOUBTABLY
REDOUBTED
REDOUBTING
REDOUND
REDOUNDED
REDOUNDING
REDOUTE
REDOWA
REDPOLL
REDRAFT
REDRAW
REDRAWER
REDRESS
REDRESSAL
REDRESSED
REDRESSER
REDRESSING
REDRESSIVE
REDRESSOR
REDROOT
REDSEAR
REDSHANK
REDSHIRT
REDSKIN
REDSTART
REDSTREAK
REDTAB
REDTAIL
REDTOP
REDUB
REDUBBER
REDUCCION
REDUCE
REDUCED
REDUCED
REDUCEMENT
REDUCENT
REDUCER
REDUCIBILITY
REDUCIBLE
REDUCIBLENESS
REDUCIBLY
REDUCING
REDUCT
REDUCTANT
REDUCTASE
REDUCTIBILITY
REDUCTIO
REDUCTION
REDUCTIONAL
REDUCTIONIST
REDUCTIVE
REDUCTIVELY
REDUCTOR

REDUCTORIAL
REDUE
REDUIT
REDUNDANCE
REDUNDANCIES
REDUNDANCY
REDUNDANT
REDUNDANTLY
REDUPLICATE
REDUPLICATED
REDUPLICATING
REDUPLICATION
REDUPLICATIVE
REDUPLICATIVELY
REDUPLICATORY
REDUPLICATURE
REDUX
REDWARD
REDWARE
REDWEED
REDWING
REDWITHE
REDWOOD
REDYE
REE
REECH
REECHO
REECHY
REED
REEDBIRD
REEDBUCK
REEDBUSH
REEDED
REEDEN
REEDER
REEDIER
REEDIEST
REEDINESS
REEDING
REEDISH
REEDLESS
REEDLIKE
REEDLING
REEDMAKER
REEDMAKING
REEDPLOT
REEDS
REEDWORK
REEDY
REEF
REEFABLE
REEFED
REEFER
REEFING
REEFY
REEK
REEKED
REEKER
REEKIER
REEKIEST
REEKING
REEKY
REEL
REELABLE
REELED
REELER
REELING
REELRALL
REEM
REEMISH
REENFORCE
REENFORCEMENT
REENLISTMENT
REENTER
REENTERING
REENTRANT
REENTRY

REEPER
REERE
REESE
REESHIE
REESHLE
REESK
REESLE
REEST
REESTER
REESTLE
REESTY
REET
REEVALUATE
REEVALUATED
REEVALUATING
REEVALUATION
REEVE
REEVED
REEVELAND
REEVING
REEVOKE
REEXAMINE
REEXPORT
REF
REFACE
REFAIT
REFATHERED
REFECT
REFECTION
REFECTIONARY
REFECTIONER
REFECTIVE
REFECTORER
REFECTORIAL
REFECTORIAN
REFECTORY
REFEL
REFER
REFERABLE
REFEREE
REFEREED
REFEREEING
REFERENCE
REFERENDAL
REFERENDARIES
REFERENDARY
REFERENDUM
REFERENT
REFERENTIAL
REFERENTLY
REFERRABLE
REFERRAL
REFERRED
REFERRER
REFERRIBLE
REFERRING
REFETE
REFFO
REFIGURE
REFILL
REFILTER
REFINAGE
REFINANCE
REFINE
REFINED
REFINEDLY
REFINEDNESS
REFINEMENT
REFINER
REFINERIES
REFINERY
REFINING
REFININGLY
REFINISH
REFIT
REFITMENT
REFITTED

REFITTING
REFLAIR
REFLATE
REFLATED
REFLATING
REFLATION
REFLECT
REFLECTANCE
REFLECTED
REFLECTEDLY
REFLECTENT
REFLECTER
REFLECTING
REFLECTINGLY
REFLECTION
REFLECTIONAL
REFLECTIONING
REFLECTIVE
REFLECTIVELY
REFLECTIVITY
REFLECTOR
REFLET
REFLEX
REFLEXED
REFLEXIBLE
REFLEXIONAL
REFLEXISM
REFLEXIVE
REFLEXIVELY
REFLEXIVITY
REFLEXOLOGY
REFLORESCENT
REFLOURISH
REFLOW
REFLUENCE
REFLUENCY
REFLUENT
REFLUOUS
REFLUX
REFLUXED
REFOCILLATE
REFONT
REFOREST
REFORESTIZE
REFORGE
REFORGER
REFORM
REFORMADO
REFORMANDA
REFORMANDUM
REFORMATION
REFORMATIVE
REFORMATORY
REFORMED
REFORMER
REFORMING
REFORMISM
REFORMIST
REFORMISTIC
REFOUND
REFOUNDER
REFRACT
REFRACTED
REFRACTEDLY
REFRACTILE
REFRACTILITY
REFRACTING
REFRACTION
REFRACTIONAL
REFRACTIVE
REFRACTIVELY
REFRACTIVITY
REFRACTOR
REFRACTORIES
REFRACTORILY
REFRACTORY
REFRACTURE

REFRAGABLE
REFRAIN
REFRAINER
REFRAINMENT
REFRANGENT
REFRANGIBLE
REFREID
REFREIT
REFRENATION
REFRESCO
REFRESH
REFRESHANT
REFRESHED
REFRESHER
REFRESHFUL
REFRESHFULLY
REFRESHING
REFRESHINGLY
REFRESHMENT
REFRIGERANT
REFRIGERATE
REFRIGERATED
REFRIGERATION
REFRIGERATOR
REFRINGE
REFRINGENCE
REFRINGENCY
REFRINGENT
REFROID
REFT
REFUEL
REFUELED
REFUELING
REFUELLED
REFUELLING
REFUGE
REFUGED
REFUGEE
REFUGEEISM
REFUGING
REFULGE
REFULGENCE
REFULGENCY
REFULGENT
REFULGENTLY
REFULGENTNESS
REFUND
REFUNDED
REFUNDER
REFUNDING
REFURBISH
REFURBISHMENT
REFUSABLE
REFUSAL
REFUSE
REFUSED
REFUSER
REFUSING
REFUSION
REFUSIVE
REFUTABILITY
REFUTABLE
REFUTABLY
REFUTAL
REFUTATION
REFUTATIVE
REFUTATORY
REFUTE
REFUTED
REFUTER
REFUTING
REG
REGAIN
REGAINER
REGAL
REGALADO
REGALD

REGALE
REGALED
REGALEMENT
REGALER
REGALIA
REGALIAN
REGALING
REGALIO
REGALISM
REGALIST
REGALITIES
REGALITY
REGALIZE
REGALLY
REGALO
REGARD
REGARDANCE
REGARDANCY
REGARDANT
REGARDED
REGARDER
REGARDFUL
REGARDFULLY
REGARDING
REGARDLESS
REGARDLESSLY
REGATTA
REGELATE
REGELATED
REGELATING
REGELATION
REGENCE
REGENCIES
REGENCY
REGENERABLE
REGENERACY
REGENERANCE
REGENERANT
REGENERATE
REGENERATED
REGENERATING
REGENERATION
REGENERATIVE
REGENERATOR
REGENESIS
REGENT
REGENTAL
REGES
REGEST
REGIA
REGIAN
REGICIDAL
REGICIDE
REGICIDISM
REGIDOR
REGIE
REGIFUGE
REGIME
REGIMEN
REGIMENAL
REGIMENT
REGIMENTAL
REGIMENTALED
REGIMENTALLED
REGIMENTALS
REGIMENTARY
REGIMENTATION
REGIMENTED
REGIMENTING
REGIMINAL
REGIN
REGINA
REGINAL
REGION
REGIONAL
REGIONALISM
REGIONALIST

REGIONALISTIC
REGIONALIZE
REGIONALLY
REGIONARY
REGIONED
REGIONS
REGISSEUR
REGISTER
REGISTERED
REGISTERER
REGISTERING
REGISTRABILITY
REGISTRABLE
REGISTRAL
REGISTRANT
REGISTRAR
REGISTRARSHIP
REGISTRARY
REGISTRATE
REGISTRATION
REGISTRATOR
REGISTRER
REGISTRY
REGITIVE
REGIUS
REGLE
REGLEMENTARY
REGLEMENTIST
REGLET
REGLOW
REGMA
REGMACARP
REGMATA
REGNAL
REGNANCY
REGNANT
REGNUM
REGOLITH
REGORGE
REGORGED
REGORGING
REGOSOL
REGRACY
REGRADATION
REGRADE
REGRADED
REGRADING
REGRANT
REGRASS
REGRATE
REGRATED
REGRATER
REGRATING
REGREDE
REGREET
REGRESS
REGRESSED
REGRESSING
REGRESSION
REGRESSIVE
REGRESSIVELY
REGRESSIVITY
REGRESSOR
REGRET
REGRETFUL
REGRETFULLY
REGRETTABLE
REGRETTABLY
REGRETTED
REGRETTER
REGRETTING
REGULA
REGULABLE
REGULAR
REGULARISE
REGULARITIES
REGULARITY

REGULARIZATION
REGULARIZE
REGULARIZED
REGULARIZER
REGULARLY
REGULARNESS
REGULATE
REGULATED
REGULATES
REGULATING
REGULATION
REGULATIVE
REGULATOR
REGULATORY
REGULI
REGULINE
REGULIZE
REGULUS
REGUR
REGURGITANT
REGURGITATE
REGURGITATED
REH
REHABILITATE
REHABILITATION
REHAIR
REHANDLING
REHARMONIZE
REHASH
REHAYTE
REHBOC
REHEARD
REHEARING
REHEARSAL
REHEARSE
REHEARSED
REHEARSER
REHEARSING
REHEAT
REHEATED
REHEATER
REHETE
REHOUSE
REI
REICHSGULDEN
REICHSMARK
REICHSPFENNIG
REICHSTALER
REIF
REIFICATION
REIFIED
REIFIER
REIFY
REIFYING
REIGN
REIGNED
REIGNER
REIGNING
REIK
REIMBURSABLE
REIMBURSE
REIMBURSED
REIMBURSEMENT
REIMBURSER
REIMBURSING
REIMBUSH
REIMBUSHMENT
REIMKENNAR
REIMMIGRANT
REIMPEL
REIMPLANT
REIMPORT
REIMPOSE
REIMPOSITION
REIMPOSURE
REIMPRESSION
REIN

REINA
REINCARNATE
REINCARNATED
REINCENSE
REINCIDENCE
REINCIDENCY
REINCRUDATE
REINDEER
REINDICTMENT
REINETTE
REINFECT
REINFECTION
REINFECTIOUS
REINFORCE
REINFORCED
REINFORCEMENT
REINFORCER
REINLESS
REINS
REINSMAN
REINSTALL
REINSTALMENT
REINSTATE
REINSTATED
REINSTATING
REINSTATION
REINSTATOR
REINSURANCE
REINSURE
REINSURED
REINSURER
REINSURING
REINTEGRATE
REINTHRONE
REINVERSION
REINVEST
REINVESTMENT
REINVIGORATE
REIS
REISE
REISSUE
REISSUING
REISTER
REIT
REITBOK
REITER
REITERABLE
REITERANCE
REITERANT
REITERATE
REITERATED
REITERATING
REITERATION
REITERATIVE
REIVE
REIVER
REJA
REJECT
REJECTAGE
REJECTAMENTA
REJECTED
REJECTER
REJECTING
REJECTION
REJECTIVE
REJECTOR
REJOICE
REJOICED
REJOICEFUL
REJOICEMENT
REJOICER
REJOICING
REJOIN
REJOINDER
REJOINED
REJOINING
REJOLT

REJON
REJONEADOR
REJONEO
REJOUNCE
REJOURN
REJUDGE
REJUNCTION
REJUVENANT
REJUVENATE
REJUVENATED
REJUVENATING
REJUVENATION
REJUVENATIVE
REJUVENATOR
REJUVENESCE
REJUVENIZE
REKE
REKHTI
REKINDLE
REKINDLER
REL
RELACHE
RELAIS
RELAPSE
RELAPSED
RELAPSER
RELAPSING
RELAST
RELASTER
RELATA
RELATABILITY
RELATABLE
RELATE
RELATED
RELATEDNESS
RELATER
RELATING
RELATION
RELATIONAL
RELATIONALLY
RELATIONARY
RELATIONISM
RELATIONIST
RELATIONS
RELATIONSHIP
RELATIONSHIPS
RELATIVAL
RELATIVE
RELATIVELY
RELATIVENESS
RELATIVES
RELATIVISM
RELATIVIST
RELATIVISTIC
RELATIVITY
RELATOR
RELATRIX
RELATUM
RELAX
RELAXABLE
RELAXANT
RELAXATION
RELAXATIVE
RELAXATORY
RELAXED
RELAXEDLY
RELAXEDNESS
RELAXER
RELAXIN
RELAXING
RELAY
RELAYER
RELAYMAN
RELBUN
RELEARN
RELEASE
RELEASED

RELEASEE
RELEASEMENT
RELEASER
RELEASING
RELEASOR
RELECTION
RELEGABLE
RELEGATE
RELEGATED
RELEGATING
RELEGATION
RELENT
RELENTED
RELENTING
RELENTINGLY
RELENTLESS
RELENTLESSLY
RELENTMENT
RELES
RELESSEE
RELESSOR
RELEVANCE
RELEVANCY
RELEVANT
RELEVANTLY
RELEVATE
RELEVATION
RELEVATOR
RELEVE
RELIABILITY
RELIABLE
RELIABLENESS
RELIABLY
RELIANCE
RELIANT
RELIANTLY
RELIC
RELICARY
RELICMONGER
RELICS
RELICT
RELICTED
RELICTION
RELIDE
RELIED
RELIEF
RELIER
RELIEVABLE
RELIEVE
RELIEVED
RELIEVEDLY
RELIEVER
RELIEVING
RELIEVINGLY
RELIEVO
RELIGATE
RELIGATION
RELIGIEUSE
RELIGIEUSES
RELIGIO
RELIGION
RELIGIONARY
RELIGIONATE
RELIGIONER
RELIGIONISM
RELIGIONIST
RELIGIONIZE
RELIGIOSE
RELIGIOSITY
RELIGIOSO
RELIGIOUS
RELIGIOUSLY
RELINQUENT
RELINQUISH
RELINQUISHED
RELINQUISHER
RELIQUAIRE

RELIQUARIES
RELIQUARY
RELIQUE
RELIQUIAE
RELIQUIAN
RELIQUISM
RELISH
RELISHABLE
RELISHED
RELISHER
RELISHING
RELISHINGLY
RELISHY
RELIVE
RELIVED
RELIVING
RELOCABLE
RELOCATE
RELOCATION
RELOCATOR
RELONG
RELUCE
RELUCENT
RELUCT
RELUCTANCE
RELUCTANCY
RELUCTANT
RELUCTANTLY
RELUCTATE
RELUCTATION
RELUCTIVITY
RELUME
RELUMED
RELUMINE
RELUMING
RELY
RELYING
REM
REMAIN
REMAINDER
REMAINDERMAN
REMAINDERMEN
REMAINED
REMAINER
REMAINING
REMAINS
REMAN
REMANATION
REMANCIPATE
REMAND
REMANDMENT
REMANENCE
REMANENCY
REMANENT
REMANET
REMANIE
REMANNED
REMANNING
REMARGIN
REMARK
REMARKABILITY
REMARKABLE
REMARKABLENESS
REMARKABLY
REMARKED
REMARKER
REMARKING
REMARQUE
REMARRIAGE
REMARRIED
REMARRY
REMARRYING
REMATCH
REMBLAI
REMBLE
REMBLERE
REME

REMEANT
REMEDE
REMEDIABLE
REMEDIABLENESS
REMEDIABLY
REMEDIAL
REMEDIALLY
REMEDIATION
REMEDIED
REMEDIES
REMEDILESS
REMEDILESSLY
REMEDILESSNESS
REMEDY
REMEDYING
REMEMBER
REMEMBERABLE
REMEMBERED
REMEMBERER
REMEMBERING
REMEMBRANCE
REMEMBRANCER
REMEMORATE
REMEMORATION
REMEMORATIVE
REMENE
REMERCY
REMEX
REMICLE
REMIGATE
REMIGES
REMIGIAL
REMIGRANT
REMIGRATE
REMIGRATION
REMIND
REMINDAL
REMINDER
REMINDFUL
REMINISCE
REMINISCED
REMINISCENCE
REMINISCENT
REMINISCENTLY
REMINISCING
REMIPED
REMISE
REMISED
REMISING
REMISS
REMISSFUL
REMISSIBLE
REMISSION
REMISSIVE
REMISSIVELY
REMISSNESS
REMISSORY
REMIT
REMITMENT
REMITTABLE
REMITTAL
REMITTANCE
REMITTANCER
REMITTED
REMITTEE
REMITTENCE
REMITTENCY
REMITTENT
REMITTENTLY
REMITTER
REMITTING
REMITTITUR
REMITTOR
REMNANT
REMNANTAL
REMNANTS
REMODEL

REMODELED
REMODELER
REMODELING
REMODELLED
REMODELLER
REMODELLING
REMODELMENT
REMOLADE
REMONETIZATION
REMONETIZE
REMONSTRANCE
REMONSTRANT
REMONSTRATE
REMONSTRATED
REMONSTRATING
REMONSTRATOR
REMONTADO
REMONTANT
REMONTOIR
REMORA
REMORD
REMORE
REMORSE
REMORSEFUL
REMORSEFULLY
REMORSEFULNESS
REMORSELESS
REMOTE
REMOTELY
REMOTENESS
REMOTER
REMOTEST
REMOTION
REMOTIVE
REMOULADE
REMOUNT
REMOVABILITY
REMOVABLE
REMOVABLY
REMOVAL
REMOVE
REMOVED
REMOVEDLY
REMOVEDNESS
REMOVELESS
REMOVEMENT
REMOVER
REMOVES
REMOVING
REMUABLE
REMUDA
REMUE
REMUNERABLE
REMUNERABLY
REMUNERATE
REMUNERATED
REMUNERATING
REMUNERATION
REMUNERATIVE
REMUNERATOR
REMUNERATORY
REMURMUR
REMUTATION
RENA
RENABLE
RENABLY
RENAIL
RENAISSANCE
RENAL
RENAME
RENASCENCE
RENASCENCY
RENASCENT
RENASCIBLE
RENATURE
RENAY
RENCH

RENCONTRE
RENCOUNTER
RENCOUNTERED
RENCOUNTERING
REND
RENDEMENT
RENDER
RENDERABLE
RENDERED
RENDERER
RENDERING
RENDERSET
RENDEZVOUS
RENDING
RENDITION
RENDLEWOOD
RENDOUN
RENDROCK
RENDU
RENDZINA
RENEGADE
RENEGADO
RENEGATION
RENEGE
RENEGED
RENEGER
RENEGING
RENERVE
RENES
RENETTE
RENEW
RENEWABLE
RENEWAL
RENEWED
RENEWING
RENEWMENT
RENGE
RENGUE
RENGUERA
RENICULUS
RENIFORM
RENIG
RENIN
RENIPORTAL
RENISH
RENISHLY
RENITENCE
RENITENCY
RENITENT
RENK
RENKY
RENNE
RENNER
RENNET
RENNIN
RENNINOGEN
RENOGASTRIC
RENOGRAPHY
RENOMEE
RENOMINATE
RENOMME
RENOMMEE
RENONE
RENOUNCE
RENOUNCED
RENOUNCEMENT
RENOUNCER
RENOUNCING
RENOVATE
RENOVATED
RENOVATER
RENOVATING
RENOVATION
RENOVATIVE
RENOVATOR
RENOVATORY
RENOVE

RENOVIZE
RENOWN
RENOWNED
RENOWNEDLY
RENOWNEDNESS
RENOWNER
RENOWNFUL
RENSH
RENT
RENTABLE
RENTAGE
RENTAL
RENTE
RENTED
RENTEE
RENTER
RENTIER
RENTING
RENTLESS
RENTRANT
RENTREE
RENUMERATE
RENUMERATION
RENUNCIABLE
RENUNCIANCE
RENUNCIANT
RENUNCIATE
RENUNCIATION
RENUNCIATIVE
RENUNCIATOR
RENUNCIATORY
RENVERSE
RENVERSEMENT
RENVOI
RENVOY
REOCCUPY
REOCCUR
REOIL
REOMETER
REOPEN
REOPHORE
REORDER
REORDINATION
REORGANISE
REORGANIZATION
REORGANIZE
REORGANIZED
REORGANIZER
REORGANIZING
REORIENT
REP
REPACE
REPAID
REPAINT
REPAIR
REPAIRABLE
REPAIRED
REPAIRER
REPAIRING
REPAIRMAN
REPAIRMEN
REPAIRS
REPAND
REPANDLY
REPANDOUS
REPARABILITY
REPARABLE
REPARABLY
REPARATE
REPARATION
REPARATIVE
REPARATORY
REPAREL
REPART
REPARTABLE
REPARTEE
REPARTITION

REPASS
REPASSAGE
REPASSER
REPAST
REPASTURE
REPATENCY
REPATRIATE
REPATRIATED
REPATRIATING
REPATRIATION
REPAY
REPAYABLE
REPAYAL
REPAYING
REPAYMENT
REPEAL
REPEALABLE
REPEALED
REPEALER
REPEALING
REPEALIST
REPEAT
REPEATABLE
REPEATAL
REPEATED
REPEATEDLY
REPEATER
REPEATING
REPEL
REPELLED
REPELLENCE
REPELLENCY
REPELLENT
REPELLER
REPELLING
REPENT
REPENTANCE
REPENTANT
REPENTANTLY
REPENTED
REPENTER
REPENTING
REPEOPLE
REPERCEPT
REPERCUSS
REPERCUSSION
REPERCUSSIVE
REPERCUSSOR
REPERCUTIENT
REPERIBLE
REPERTOIRE
REPERTORIAL
REPERTORILY
REPERTORIUM
REPERTORY
REPETEND
REPETITION
REPETITIONAL
REPETITIOUS
REPETITIOUSLY
REPETITIVE
REPETITIVELY
REPETITORY
REPHRASE
REPHRASED
REPHRASING
REPINE
REPINED
REPINEMENT
REPINER
REPINING
REPIQUE
REPIQUED
REPIQUING
REPKIE
REPLACE
REPLACEABLE

REPLACED
REPLACEMENT
REPLACER
REPLACING
REPLANT
REPLANTATION
REPLANTER
REPLEADER
REPLEDGE
REPLEDGER
REPLENISH
REPLENISHED
REPLENISHER
REPLENISHING
REPLETE
REPLETION
REPLETIVE
REPLETIVELY
REPLETORY
REPLEVIABLE
REPLEVIED
REPLEVIN
REPLEVISABLE
REPLEVISOR
REPLEVY
REPLEVYING
REPLIAL
REPLIANT
REPLICA
REPLICATE
REPLICATED
REPLICATILE
REPLICATION
REPLICATIVE
REPLICATIVELY
REPLICATORY
REPLIED
REPLIER
REPLIES
REPLIQUE
REPLOT
REPLOTMENT
REPLOTTER
REPLUM
REPLUME
REPLY
REPLYING
REPOLON
REPONE
REPOPE
REPORT
REPORTABLE
REPORTAGE
REPORTED
REPORTEDLY
REPORTER
REPORTING
REPORTINGLY
REPORTORIAL
REPORTORIALLY
REPORTS
REPOSAL
REPOSE
REPOSED
REPOSEDLY
REPOSEDNESS
REPOSEFUL
REPOSEFULLY
REPOSER
REPOSING
REPOSIT
REPOSITION
REPOSITOR
REPOSITORY
REPOSOIR
REPOSSESS
REPOSSESSION

REPOSSESSOR
REPOST
REPOSTPONE
REPOSURE
REPOUSSAGE
REPOUSSE
REPP
REPPED
REPREHEND
REPREHENDED
REPREHENDER
REPREHENDING
REPREHENSIBLE
REPREHENSION
REPREHENSORY
REPRESENT
REPRESENTAMEN
REPRESENTANT
REPRESENTATION
REPRESENTATIVE
REPRESENTED
REPRESENTER
REPRESENTING
REPRESENTMENT
REPRESENTS
REPRESS
REPRESSED
REPRESSEDLY
REPRESSER
REPRESSIBLE
REPRESSIBLY
REPRESSING
REPRESSION
REPRESSIVE
REPRESSIVELY
REPRESSOR
REPRESSORY
REPRESSURE
REPRIEVABLE
REPRIEVAL
REPRIEVE
REPRIEVED
REPRIEVER
REPRIEVING
REPRIMAND
REPRIMANDED
REPRIMANDER
REPRIMANDING
REPRIME
REPRIMER
REPRINT
REPRINTER
REPRISAL
REPRISE
REPRISTINATE
REPROACH
REPROACHABLE
REPROACHABLY
REPROACHED
REPROACHER
REPROACHES
REPROACHFUL
REPROACHING
REPROBACY
REPROBANCE
REPROBATE
REPROBATED
REPROBATER
REPROBATING
REPROBATION
REPROBATIVE
REPROBATOR
REPROBATORY
REPRODUCE
REPRODUCEABLE
REPRODUCED
REPRODUCER

REPRODUCIBLE
REPRODUCING
REPRODUCTION
REPRODUCTIVE
REPRODUCTORY
REPROFFER
REPROOF
REPROVABLE
REPROVABLY
REPROVAL
REPROVE
REPROVED
REPROVER
REPROVING
REPROVINGLY
REPRY
REPTANT
REPTATION
REPTATORIAL
REPTATORY
REPTILE
REPTILIAN
REPTILIARY
REPTILIOUS
REPTILISM
REPTILITY
REPTILOID
REPUBLIC
REPUBLICAL
REPUBLICAN
REPUBLISH
REPUBLISHER
REPUDIABLE
REPUDIATE
REPUDIATED
REPUDIATING
REPUDIATION
REPUDIATIVE
REPUDIATOR
REPUDIATORY
REPUGN
REPUGNABLE
REPUGNANCE
REPUGNANCY
REPUGNANT
REPUGNATE
REPUGNER
REPULLULATE
REPULPIT
REPULSE
REPULSED
REPULSELESS
REPULSER
REPULSING
REPULSION
REPULSIVE
REPULSIVELY
REPULSORY
REPURCHASE
REPURCHASER
REPUTABILITY
REPUTABLE
REPUTABLY
REPUTATION
REPUTATIVE
REPUTATIVELY
REPUTE
REPUTED
REPUTEDLY
REPUTELESS
REPUTING
REQUEEN
REQUEST
REQUESTER
REQUIEM
REQUIESCAT
REQUIESCENCE

REQUIN
REQUINS
REQUIRABLE
REQUIRE
REQUIRED
REQUIREMENT
REQUIRER
REQUIRING
REQUISITE
REQUISITELY
REQUISITION
REQUISITOR
REQUISITORY
REQUITABLE
REQUITAL
REQUITATIVE
REQUITE
REQUITED
REQUITELESS
REQUITEMENT
REQUITER
REQUITING
RERADIATION
RERAILER
RERD
RERDE
REREAD
REREBRACE
RERECORD
REREDOS
REREE
REREFIEF
REREMOUSE
RERESUPPER
REROLL
RERUN
RERUNNING
RES
RESACA
RESAI
RESAIL
RESAK
RESALABLE
RESALE
RESAW
RESAWER
RESAWYER
RESAY
RESCIND
RESCINDABLE
RESCINDED
RESCINDER
RESCINDING
RESCISSIBLE
RESCISSION
RESCISSORY
RESCORE
RESCRIBE
RESCRIPT
RESCRIPTION
RESCRIPTIVE
RESCUABLE
RESCUE
RESCUED
RESCUER
RESCUING
RESE
RESEAL
RESEARCH
RESEARCHER
RESEARCHFUL
RESEARCHIST
RESEAT
RESEAU
RESEAUX
RESECATE
RESECT

RESECTION
RESECTIONAL
RESEDA
RESEDACEOUS
RESEISER
RESEIZE
RESEIZER
RESEIZURE
RESELL
RESELLING
RESEMBLANCE
RESEMBLANT
RESEMBLE
RESEMBLED
RESEMBLER
RESEMBLING
RESEMINATE
RESEND
RESENDING
RESENE
RESENT
RESENTED
RESENTER
RESENTFUL
RESENTFULLY
RESENTIENCE
RESENTING
RESENTIVE
RESENTLESS
RESENTMENT
RESERATE
RESERPINE
RESERVABLE
RESERVAL
RESERVATION
RESERVATIVE
RESERVATORY
RESERVE
RESERVED
RESERVEDLY
RESERVEDNESS
RESERVEE
RESERVER
RESERVERY
RESERVING
RESERVIST
RESERVOIR
RESERVOIRED
RESET
RESETTER
RESETTING
RESGAT
RESH
RESHIP
RESHIPMENT
RESHIPPED
RESHIPPER
RESHIPPING
RESIANCE
RESIANCY
RESIANT
RESICCATE
RESIDE
RESIDENCE
RESIDENCER
RESIDENCIA
RESIDENCIES
RESIDENCY
RESIDENT
RESIDENTAL
RESIDENTER
RESIDENTIAL
RESIDENTIARY
RESIDER
RESIDING
RESIDUA
RESIDUAL

RESIDUARY	RESIZER	RESPECTLESS	RESTIVE	RESUSCITABLE
RESIDUATION	RESIZING	RESPECTUOUS	RESTIVELY	RESUSCITANT
RESIDUE	RESKEW	RESPELL	RESTIVENESS	RESUSCITATE
RESIDUENT	RESNATRON	RESPERSIVE	RESTLESS	RESUSCITATED
RESIDUOUS	RESOJET	RESPIRABLE	RESTLESSLY	RESUSCITATION
RESIDUUM	RESOLE	RESPIRATION	RESTLESSNESS	RESUSCITATOR
RESIGN	RESOLED	RESPIRATIVE	RESTOCK	RESYNTHESIS
RESIGNATARY	RESOLING	RESPIRATOR	RESTORAL	RET
RESIGNATION	RESOLUBILITY	RESPIRATORY	RESTORATION	RETABLE
RESIGNED	RESOLUBLE	RESPIRE	RESTORATIVE	RETABLO
RESIGNEDLY	RESOLUTE	RESPIRED	RESTORATOR	RETAIL
RESIGNEDNESS	RESOLUTELY	RESPIRING	RESTORATORY	RETAILER
RESIGNEE	RESOLUTENESS	RESPIRIT	RESTORE	RETAIN
RESIGNER	RESOLUTION	RESPIROMETER	RESTORED	RETAINABLE
RESIGNFUL	RESOLUTIONER	RESPITE	RESTORER	RETAINAL
RESIGNMENT	RESOLUTIVE	RESPITED	RESTORING	RETAINED
RESILE	RESOLUTORY	RESPITING	RESTRAIN	RETAINER
RESILED	RESOLVABLE	RESPLEND	RESTRAINABLE	RETAINING
RESILEMENT	RESOLVANCY	RESPLENDENCE	RESTRAINED	RETAKE
RESILIA	RESOLVE	RESPLENDENCY	RESTRAINEDLY	RETAKEN
RESILIAL	RESOLVED	RESPLENDENT	RESTRAINER	RETAKER
RESILIATE	RESOLVEDLY	RESPOND	RESTRAINING	RETAKING
RESILIENCE	RESOLVEDNESS	RESPONDE	RESTRAINT	RETALIATE
RESILIENCY	RESOLVENT	RESPONDENCE	RESTRESS	RETALIATED
RESILIENT	RESOLVER	RESPONDENCY	RESTRICT	RETALIATING
RESILIENTLY	RESOLVIBLE	RESPONDENT	RESTRICTED	RETALIATION
RESILIFER	RESOLVING	RESPONDENTIA	RESTRICTING	RETALIATIVE
RESILING	RESON	RESPONDER	RESTRICTION	RETALIATOR
RESILIOMETER	RESONANCE	RESPONSABLE	RESTRICTIVE	RETALIATORY
RESILITION	RESONANCIES	RESPONSAL	RESTRICTIVELY	RETAMA
RESILIUM	RESONANCY	RESPONSARY	RESTRIKE	RETAN
RESILVER	RESONANT	RESPONSE	RESTRINGE	RETARD
RESIN	RESONANTLY	RESPONSER	RESTRINGENCY	RETARDANCE
RESINA	RESONATE	RESPONSIBILITY	RESTRINGENT	RETARDANT
RESINACEOUS	RESONATED	RESPONSIBLE	RESTY	RETARDATE
RESINATE	RESONATING	RESPONSIBLY	RESTYLE	RETARDATION
RESINATED	RESONATOR	RESPONSION	RESUDATION	RETARDATIVE
RESINATING	RESONATORY	RESPONSIVE	RESUE	RETARDED
RESINBUSH	RESORB	RESPONSIVELY	RESUING	RETARDER
RESINER	RESORBENCE	RESPONSIVENESS	RESULT	RETARDING
RESINIC	RESORBENT	RESPONSIVITY	RESULTANCE	RETARDIVE
RESINIFEROUS	RESORCIN	RESPONSORIAL	RESULTANCY	RETARDMENT
RESINIFLUOUS	RESORCINAL	RESPONSORY	RESULTANT	RETARDURE
RESINIFORM	RESORCINISM	RESPUE	RESULTATIVE	RETCH
RESINIFY	RESORCINOL	RESSAIDAR	RESULTED	RETE
RESINIZE	RESORCINUM	RESSALA	RESULTING	RETECIOUS
RESINOGENOUS	RESORCYLIC	RESSAUT	RESULTIVE	RETELL
RESINOID	RESORPTION	RESSORT	RESUMABLE	RETELLING
RESINOL	RESORPTIVE	REST	RESUME	RETEM
RESINOPHORE	RESORT	RESTANT	RESUMED	RETENE
RESINOSIS	RESORTED	RESTATE	RESUMEING	RETENT
RESINOUS	RESORTER	RESTATEMENT	RESUMER	RETENTION
RESINOUSLY	RESORUFIN	RESTAUR	RESUMING	RETENTIVE
RESINOUSNESS	RESOUND	RESTAURANT	RESUMMON	RETENTIVELY
RESINY	RESOUNDER	RESTAURATE	RESUMMONS	RETENTIVITIES
RESIPISCENCE	RESOUNDING	RESTAURATEUR	RESUMPTION	RETENTIVITY
RESIPISCENT	RESOURCE	RESTAURATION	RESUMPTIVE	RETENTOR
RESIST	RESOURCEFUL	RESTBALK	RESUMPTIVELY	RETENUE
RESISTABLE	RESOURCEFULLY	RESTED	RESUPINATE	RETEPORE
RESISTANCE	RESOURCEFULNESS	RESTER	RESUPINATED	RETEXTURE
RESISTANT	RESOURCES	RESTERILIZE	RESUPINATION	RETHE
RESISTED	RESOWN	RESTES	RESUPINE	RETHENESS
RESISTER	RESP	RESTFUL	RESURFACE	RETHER
RESISTFUL	RESPASSE	RESTFULLY	RESURFACED	RETIA
RESISTIBLE	RESPEAK	RESTFULNESS	RESURFACING	RETIARIAN
RESISTIBLY	RESPECT	RESTHARROW	RESURGAM	RETIARII
RESISTING	RESPECTABILITY	RESTHOUSE	RESURGE	RETIARIUS
RESISTINGLY	RESPECTABLE	RESTIAD	RESURGED	RETIARY
RESISTIVE	RESPECTABLY	RESTIFORM	RESURGENCE	RETICELLA
RESISTIVELY	RESPECTANT	RESTING	RESURGENCY	RETICENCE
RESISTIVITY	RESPECTED	RESTIS	RESURGENT	RETICENCIES
RESISTLESS	RESPECTER	RESTITUE	RESURGING	RETICENCY
RESISTLESSLY	RESPECTFUL	RESTITUTE	RESURRECT	RETICENT
RESISTOR	RESPECTFULLY	RESTITUTION	RESURRECTION	RETICENTLY
RESITTING	RESPECTING	RESTITUTIVE	RESURRECTIVE	RETICLE
RESIZE	RESPECTIVE	RESTITUTOR	RESURRECTOR	RETICULA
RESIZED	RESPECTIVELY	RESTITUTORY	RESURVEY	RETICULAR

RETICULARIAN
RETICULARY
RETICULATE
RETICULATED
RETICULATING
RETICULATION
RETICULE
RETICULED
RETICULIN
RETICULITIS
RETICULOCYTE
RETICULOSE
RETICULUM
RETIFORM
RETINA
RETINACULA
RETINACULAR
RETINACULATE
RETINACULUM
RETINAL
RETINASPHALT
RETINENE
RETINERVED
RETINIAN
RETINISPORA
RETINITE
RETINITIS
RETINIZE
RETINOID
RETINOL
RETINOPHORAL
RETINOPHORE
RETINOSCOPE
RETINOSCOPIC
RETINOSCOPIST
RETINOSCOPY
RETINUE
RETINULA
RETINULAE
RETINULE
RETIP
RETIRACIED
RETIRACY
RETIRADE
RETIRAL
RETIRE
RETIRED
RETIREMENT
RETIRING
RETIRINGLY
RETIRINGNESS
RETOLD
RETOLERATE
RETOLERATION
RETOMB
RETONATION
RETOOK
RETORSION
RETORT
RETORTED
RETORTER
RETORTING
RETORTION
RETORTIVE
RETORTS
RETOUCH
RETOUCHER
RETOUCHING
RETOUCHMENT
RETOUR
RETRACE
RETRACEABLE
RETRACED
RETRACEMENT
RETRACT
RETRACTABLE
RETRACTATION

RETRACTED
RETRACTIBLE
RETRACTILE
RETRACTILITY
RETRACTING
RETRACTION
RETRACTIVE
RETRACTIVELY
RETRACTOR
RETRAD
RETRADITION
RETRAHENT
RETRAIT
RETRAL
RETRALLY
RETRAXIT
RETREAD
RETREADED
RETREADING
RETREAT
RETREATED
RETREATER
RETREATFUL
RETREATING
RETREATIVE
RETREATMENT
RETREE
RETRENCH
RETRENCHED
RETRENCHER
RETRENCHING
RETRENCHMENT
RETRIAL
RETRIBUTE
RETRIBUTION
RETRIBUTIVE
RETRIBUTOR
RETRIBUTORY
RETRICKED
RETRIED
RETRIEVABLE
RETRIEVABLY
RETRIEVAL
RETRIEVE
RETRIEVED
RETRIEVELESS
RETRIEVEMENT
RETRIEVER
RETRIEVING
RETRIM
RETRIMMER
RETROACT
RETROACTION
RETROACTIVE
RETROBUCCAL
RETROBULBAR
RETROCAECAL
RETROCEDE
RETROCEDENCE
RETROCEDENT
RETROCESSION
RETROCESSIVE
RETROCHOIR
RETROCLUSION
RETROCOLIC
RETROCOSTAL
RETROCURVED
RETRODATE
RETRODUCTION
RETRODURAL
RETROFIRE
RETROFLECTED
RETROFLEX
RETROFLEXED
RETROFLEXION
RETROFRACT
RETROFRACTED

RETROFRONTAL
RETROGASTRIC
RETROGRADE
RETROGRADED
RETROGRADELY
RETROGRADING
RETROGRADISM
RETROGRADIST
RETROGRESS
RETROGRESSION
RETROHEPATIC
RETROINSULAR
RETROIRIDIAN
RETROJECT
RETROJECTION
RETROJUGULAR
RETROLENTAL
RETROLINGUAL
RETROMINGENT
RETRONASAL
RETROPOSED
RETROPUBIC
RETROPULSION
RETROPULSIVE
RETRORECTAL
RETRORENAL
RETROROCKET
RETRORSE
RETRORSELY
RETROSERRATE
RETROSPECT
RETROSPLENIC
RETROSTALSIS
RETROSTALTIC
RETROSTERNAL
RETROTARSAL
RETROTHYROID
RETROUSSAGE
RETROUSSE
RETROVACCINE
RETROVERSE
RETROVERSION
RETROVERT
RETROXIPHOID
RETRUDE
RETRUSIBLE
RETRUSION
RETRY
RETRYING
RETTE
RETTED
RETTER
RETTERIES
RETTERY
RETTI
RETTING
RETTORY
RETUND
RETUNDED
RETUNDING
RETURN
RETURNABLE
RETURNED
RETURNER
RETURNING
RETURNLESS
RETURNLESSLY
RETURNS
RETUSE
RETZIAN
REUNE
REUNIFY
REUNION
REUNIONISM
REUNIONIST
REUNIONISTIC
REUNITE

REUNITED
REUNITER
REUNITING
REUNITION
REUNITIVE
REUS
REUT
REUTE
REV
REVACCINATE
REVALENTA
REVALESCENCE
REVALESCENT
REVALIDATE
REVALIDATION
REVALORIZE
REVALUATE
REVALUATED
REVALUATING
REVALUATION
REVALUE
REVALUED
REVALUING
REVAMP
REVAMPER
REVAMPMENT
REVANCHE
REVANCHISM
REVANCHIST
REVAY
REVE
REVEAL
REVEALABLE
REVEALED
REVEALER
REVEALING
REVEALMENT
REVEILLE
REVEL
REVELABILITY
REVELANT
REVELATION
REVELATIONAL
REVELATIONER
REVELATIVE
REVELATOR
REVELATORY
REVELED
REVELER
REVELING
REVELLED
REVELLENT
REVELLER
REVELLER
REVELLING
REVELLY
REVELMENT
REVELOUS
REVELROUS
REVELROUT
REVELRY
REVELS
REVENANT
REVENDICATE
REVENEER
REVENGE
REVENGEABLE
REVENGED
REVENGEFUL
REVENGEFULLY
REVENGEMENT
REVENGER
REVENGING
REVENUAL
REVENUE
REVENUED
REVENUER

REVENUES
REVERB
REVERBATORY
REVERBERANT
REVERBERATE
REVERBERATING
REVERBERATION
REVERBERATIONS
REVERBERATIVE
REVERBERATOR
REVERBRATE
REVERDI
REVERDURE
REVERE
REVERED
REVEREE
REVERENCE
REVERENCED
REVERENCER
REVERENCING
REVEREND
REVERENDLY
REVERENT
REVERENTIAL
REVERENTLY
REVERER
REVERIE
REVERIES
REVERIFY
REVERING
REVERIST
REVERS
REVERSAL
REVERSE
REVERSED
REVERSEDLY
REVERSEFUL
REVERSELESS
REVERSELY
REVERSEMENT
REVERSER
REVERSI
REVERSIBLE
REVERSIBLY
REVERSING
REVERSINGLY
REVERSION
REVERSIONABLE
REVERSIONAL
REVERSIONARY
REVERSIONER
REVERSIONIST
REVERSIST
REVERSIVE
REVERSO
REVERT
REVERTAL
REVERTED
REVERTER
REVERTIBLE
REVERTING
REVERTIVE
REVERTIVELY
REVERY
REVEST
REVESTIARY
REVESTRY
REVET
REVETMENT
REVETTED
REVETTING
REVICTUAL
REVICTUALED
REVICTUALING
REVICTUALLED
REVICTUALLING
REVIE

REVIEW
REVIEWAGE
REVIEWAL
REVIEWED
REVIEWER
REVIEWING
REVIGOR
REVIGORATE
REVIGORATION
REVIGOUR
REVILE
REVILED
REVILEMENT
REVILER
REVILING
REVILING
REVILINGLY
REVINCE
REVINDICATE
REVIRADO
REVIRESCENCE
REVIRESCENT
REVISAL
REVISE
REVISED
REVISER
REVISING
REVISION
REVISIONAL
REVISIONARY
REVISIONISM
REVISIONIST
REVISIT
REVISITANT
REVISITATION
REVITALIZE
REVITALIZED
REVITALIZER
REVITALIZING
REVIVAL
REVIVALISM
REVIVALIST
REVIVALISTIC
REVIVATORY
REVIVE
REVIVED
REVIVEMENT
REVIVER
REVIVIFIED
REVIVIFIER
REVIVIFY
REVIVIFYING
REVIVING
REVIVINGLY
REVIVISCENCE
REVIVISCENCY
REVIVISCENT
REVIVISCIBLE
REVIVOR
REVOCABILITY
REVOCABLE
REVOCABLY
REVOCATE
REVOCATION
REVOCATIVE
REVOCATORY
REVOICE
REVOICED
REVOICING
REVOKABLE
REVOKE
REVOKED
REVOKEMENT
REVOKER
REVOKING
REVOLANT
REVOLT

REVOLTED
REVOLTER
REVOLTING
REVOLTINGLY
REVOLUBILITY
REVOLUBLE
REVOLUBLY
REVOLUTE
REVOLUTION
REVOLUTIONAL
REVOLUTIONARY
REVOLUTIONER
REVOLUTIONIST
REVOLVABLE
REVOLVE
REVOLVED
REVOLVENCY
REVOLVER
REVOLVES
REVOLVING
REVOLVINGLY
REVS
REVUE
REVUETTE
REVUIST
REVULSANT
REVULSE
REVULSED
REVULSION
REVULSIONARY
REVULSIVE
REVULSIVELY
REVVED
REVVING
REW
REWARD
REWARDED
REWARDER
REWARDING
REWARDINGLY
REWCH
REWE
REWED
REWEIGHT
REWET
REWIND
REWINDER
REWIRE
REWIRED
REWIRING
REWME
REWORD
REWORKED
REWRITE
REWRITER
REWRITTEN
REWROTE
REX
REXEN
REXINE
REY
REYLE
REYOUTH
REYSON
REZAI
REZBANYITE
RH
RHABDITE
RHABDITIFORM
RHABDIUM
RHABDOID
RHABDOLITH
RHABDOM
RHABDOMAL
RHABDOMANCER
RHABDOMANCY

RHABDOMANTIC
RHABDOME
RHABDOMYOMA
RHABDOPHANE
RHABDOPOD
RHABDOS
RHABDOSOME
RHABDOSOPHY
RHABDOSPHERE
RHABDUS
RHACHIS
RHAEBOSIS
RHAGADES
RHAGADIFORM
RHAGIONID
RHAGITE
RHAGON
RHAGONATE
RHAGOSE
RHAMN
RHAMNACEOUS
RHAMNAL
RHAMNETIN
RHAMNINASE
RHAMNINOSE
RHAMNITE
RHAMNITOL
RHAMNOHEXITE
RHAMNOHEXOSE
RHAMNONIC
RHAMNOSE
RHAMNOSIDE
RHAMPHOID
RHAMPHOTHECA
RHAPHE
RHAPONTIC
RHAPONTICIN
RHAPONTIN
RHAPSODE
RHAPSODIC
RHAPSODICAL
RHAPSODIES
RHAPSODISM
RHAPSODIST
RHAPSODISTIC
RHAPSODIZE
RHAPSODIZED
RHAPSODIZING
RHAPSODY
RHASON
RHASOPHORE
RHATANIA
RHATANY
RHATIKON
RHE
RHEA
RHEADINE
RHEBOK
RHEBOSIS
RHEEBOK
RHEEN
RHEGMATYPE
RHEGMATYPY
RHEIM
RHEINBERRY
RHEINGOLD
RHEMA
RHEMATIC
RHEMATOLOGY
RHEME
RHENEA
RHENIUM
RHEOBASE
RHEOCRAT
RHEOLOGIST
RHEOLOGY
RHEOMETER

RHEOMETRIC
RHEOMETRY
RHEOPHILE
RHEOPHORE
RHEOPHORIC
RHEOPLANKTON
RHEOSCOPE
RHEOSCOPIC
RHEOSTAT
RHEOSTATIC
RHEOSTATICS
RHEOTACTIC
RHEOTAN
RHEOTAXIS
RHEOTOME
RHEOTROPE
RHEOTROPIC
RHEOTROPISM
RHESIAN
RHESIS
RHESUS
RHETOR
RHETORIC
RHETORICAL
RHETORICALLY
RHETORICALS
RHETORICIAN
RHETORIZE
RHEUM
RHEUMATALGIA
RHEUMATIC
RHEUMATICAL
RHEUMATICKY
RHEUMATISM
RHEUMATISMAL
RHEUMATIVE
RHEUMATIZ
RHEUMATIZE
RHEUMATOID
RHEUMATOIDAL
RHEUMED
RHEUMIC
RHEUMILY
RHEUMINESS
RHEUMY
RHEXIS
RHIGOLENE
RHIGOSIS
RHIGOTIC
RHINAL
RHINALGIA
RHINARIUM
RHINCOSPASM
RHIND
RHINESTONE
RHINEURYNTER
RHINION
RHINITIS
RHINO
RHINOBYON
RHINOCAUL
RHINOCELE
RHINOCELIAN
RHINOCERINE
RHINOCEROID
RHINOCEROS
RHINOCEROSES
RHINOCEROTIC
RHINOCOELE
RHINOCOELIAN
RHINODYNIA
RHINOGENOUS
RHINOLALIA
RHINOLITH
RHINOLITHIC
RHINOLOGIST
RHINOLOGY

RHINOPHARYNX
RHINOPHORE
RHINOPHYMA
RHINOPLASTIC
RHINOPLASTY
RHINOPOLYPUS
RHINORRHAGIA
RHINORRHEA
RHINORRHEAL
RHINORRHOEA
RHINOS
RHINOSCOPE
RHINOSCOPIC
RHINOSCOPY
RHINOTHECA
RHINOTHECAL
RHIPIDATE
RHIPIDION
RHIPIDISTIAN
RHIPIDIUM
RHIPIPHORID
RHIZANTHOUS
RHIZINE
RHIZINOUS
RHIZOBIA
RHIZOBIUM
RHIZOCARP
RHIZOCARPIC
RHIZOCARPOUS
RHIZOCAUL
RHIZOCAULUS
RHIZOCORM
RHIZODERMIS
RHIZOGEN
RHIZOGENETIC
RHIZOGENIC
RHIZOGENOUS
RHIZOID
RHIZOIDAL
RHIZOMA
RHIZOMATIC
RHIZOMATOUS
RHIZOME
RHIZOMELIC
RHIZOMIC
RHIZOMORPH
RHIZOMORPHIC
RHIZONEURE
RHIZOPHAGOUS
RHIZOPHILOUS
RHIZOPHORE
RHIZOPHYTE
RHIZOPLAST
RHIZOPOD
RHIZOPODAL
RHIZOPODAN
RHIZOPODIST
RHIZOPODOUS
RHIZOSTOME
RHIZOSTOMOUS
RHIZOTAXIS
RHIZOTAXY
RHIZOTE
RHIZOTIC
RHIZOTOMI
RHIZOTOMY
RHO
RHODA
RHODAMIN
RHODAMINE
RHODANATE
RHODANINE
RHODANTHE
RHODEOSE
RHODESWOOD
RHODIC
RHODING

RHODINOL
RHODITE
RHODIUM
RHODIZITE
RHODIZONIC
RHODOCYTE
RHODODAPHNE
RHODODENDRON
RHODOLITE
RHODONITE
RHODOPHANE
RHODOPHYLL
RHODOPLAST
RHODOPSIN
RHODORA
RHODOSPERM
RHODOSPERMIN
RHOMB
RHOMBI
RHOMBIC
RHOMBICAL
RHOMBIFORM
RHOMBOCLASE
RHOMBOGANOID
RHOMBOGENE
RHOMBOGENIC
RHOMBOGENOUS
RHOMBOHEDRA
RHOMBOHEDRAL
RHOMBOHEDRIC
RHOMBOHEDRON
RHOMBOID
RHOMBOIDAL
RHOMBOIDALLY
RHOMBOIDES
RHOMBOIDEUS
RHOMBOIDLY
RHOMBOS
RHOMBOVATE
RHOMBUS
RHOMBUSES
RHONCHAL
RHONCHIAL
RHONCHUS
RHOPALIC
RHOPALISM
RHOPALIUM
RHOTACISM
RHOTACISMUS
RHOTACIST
RHUBARB
RHUBARBY
RHUM
RHUMB
RHUMBA
RHYACOLITE
RHYME
RHYMED
RHYMEMAKER
RHYMEMAKING
RHYMER
RHYMERY
RHYMESTER
RHYMIC
RHYMING
RHYMY
RHYNCHODONT
RHYNCHOLITE
RHYNIA
RHYOBASALT
RHYODACITE
RHYOLITE
RHYOLITIC
RHYOTAXITIC
RHYPOGRAPHY
RHYPTIC
RHYPTICAL

RHYSIMETER
RHYTHM
RHYTHMAL
RHYTHMIC
RHYTHMICAL
RHYTHMICALLY
RHYTHMICITY
RHYTHMICIZE
RHYTHMICS
RHYTHMIST
RHYTHMIZABLE
RHYTHMIZE
RHYTHMOMETER
RHYTHMUS
RHYTIDOME
RHYTINA
RHYTON
RI
RIA
RIAL
RIALTY
RIANT
RIANTLY
RIATA
RIB
RIBALD
RIBALDISH
RIBALDRIES
RIBALDROUS
RIBALDRY
RIBAND
RIBANDMAKER
RIBANDRY
RIBAT
RIBAUDEQUIN
RIBAUDRED
RIBAZUBA
RIBBAND
RIBBED
RIBBER
RIBBET
RIBBING
RIBBLE
RIBBON
RIBBONBACK
RIBBONER
RIBBONFISH
RIBBONFISHES
RIBBONLIKE
RIBBONMAKER
RIBBONS
RIBBONWOOD
RIBBONY
RIBBY
RIBE
RIBGRASS
RIBIBE
RIBLESS
RIBOFLAVIN
RIBONIC
RIBONUCLEASE
RIBOSE
RIBOSOMAL
RIBOSOME
RIBROAST
RIBROASTER
RIBROASTING
RIBS
RIBSKIN
RIBWORT
RIBZUBA
RICASSO
RICE
RICEBIRD
RICEGRASS
RICER
RICERCARE

RICERCATA
RICEY
RICH
RICHARD
RICHDOM
RICHE
RICHELLITE
RICHEN
RICHER
RICHES
RICHESSE
RICHEST
RICHLING
RICHLY
RICHNESS
RICHT
RICHTERITE
RICHWEED
RICIN
RICINELAIDIC
RICININE
RICINIUM
RICINOLEATE
RICINOLEIC
RICINOLEIN
RICK
RICKARDITE
RICKER
RICKETIER
RICKETIEST
RICKETILY
RICKETINESS
RICKETISH
RICKETS
RICKETTSIA
RICKETTSIAE
RICKETTSIAL
RICKETY
RICKEYS
RICKLE
RICKMATIC
RICKRACK
RICKSHAW
RICKSTADDLE
RICKSTAND
RICKSTICK
RICKYARD
RICO
RICOCHET
RICOCHETED
RICOCHETING
RICOCHETTED
RICOLETTAITE
RICOTTA
RICRAC
RICTAL
RICTUS
RID
RIDABLE
RIDDAM
RIDDANCE
RIDDED
RIDDEL
RIDDEN
RIDDER
RIDDING
RIDDLE
RIDDLED
RIDDLEMEREE
RIDDLER
RIDDLING
RIDDLINGLY
RIDDLINGS
RIDE
RIDEN
RIDENT
RIDER

RIDERED
RIDGE
RIDGEBAND
RIDGEBONE
RIDGED
RIDGELING
RIDGEPOLE
RIDGEPOLED
RIDGER
RIDGEROPE
RIDGEROPE
RIDGES
RIDGIER
RIDGIEST
RIDGIL
RIDGING
RIDGLING
RIDGY
RIDIBUND
RIDICULE
RIDICULED
RIDICULER
RIDICULING
RIDICULOSITY
RIDICULOUS
RIDICULOUSLY
RIDING
RIDINGMAN
RIDINGMEN
RIDOTTO
RIDOTTOS
RIE
RIEBECKITE
RIEL
RIEM
RIEMPIE
RIER
RIEVER
RIFACIMENTO
RIFART
RIFE
RIFELY
RIFENESS
RIFER
RIFEST
RIFF
RIFFLE
RIFFLED
RIFFLER
RIFFRAFF
RIFLE
RIFLEBIRD
RIFLED
RIFLEMAN
RIFLEMANSHIP
RIFLEMEN
RIFLEPROOF
RIFLER
RIFLERY
RIFLESHOT
RIFLING
RIFT
RIFTER
RIFTY
RIG
RIGADIG
RIGADON
RIGADOON
RIGAMAJIG
RIGAMAROLE
RIGAUDON
RIGBANE
RIGESCENCE
RIGESCENT
RIGGAL
RIGGED
RIGGER

RIGGING
RIGGISH
RIGGOT
RIGHT
RIGHTABOUT
RIGHTEN
RIGHTEOUS
RIGHTEOUSLY
RIGHTEOUSNESS
RIGHTER
RIGHTEST
RIGHTFORTH
RIGHTFUL
RIGHTFULLY
RIGHTFULNESS
RIGHTHAND
RIGHTHEADED
RIGHTHEARTED
RIGHTIST
RIGHTLE
RIGHTLESS
RIGHTLY
RIGHTMOST
RIGHTNESS
RIGHTO
RIGHTS
RIGHTSHIP
RIGHTWARD
RIGHTWARDLY
RIGHTWARDS
RIGHTY
RIGID
RIGIDIFIED
RIGIDIFY
RIGIDIFYING
RIGIDIST
RIGIDITIES
RIGIDITY
RIGIDLY
RIGIDNESS
RIGIDULOUS
RIGINAL
RIGLET
RIGLING
RIGMAREE
RIGMAROLE
RIGMAROLERY
RIGNUM
RIGO
RIGODON
RIGOL
RIGOLE
RIGOLETTE
RIGOR
RIGORISM
RIGORIST
RIGORISTIC
RIGOROUS
RIGOROUSLY
RIGOROUSNESS
RIGOUR
RIGOURISM
RIGOURISTIC
RIGSBY
RIGSDALER
RIGWIDDIE
RIGWIDDY
RIGWOODIE
RIKK
RIKSDAALDER
RILAWA
RILE
RILED
RILEY
RILIEVO
RILING
RILL

RILLE
RILLET
RILLETT
RILLETTE
RILLOCK
RILLOW
RILLS
RILLSTONE
RILY
RIM
RIMA
RIMAL
RIMAS
RIMATE
RIMBASE
RIME
RIMED
RIMER
RIMERY
RIMESTER
RIMFIRE
RIMIC
RIMIER
RIMIEST
RIMIFORM
RIMING
RIMLESS
RIMMAKER
RIMMAKING
RIMMED
RIMMER
RIMOSE
RIMOSELY
RIMOSITY
RIMOUS
RIMPI
RIMPLE
RIMPLED
RIMPLING
RIMPTION
RIMROCK
RIMU
RIMULA
RIMULOSE
RIMUR
RIMY
RIN
RINCEAU
RINCON
RIND
RINDED
RINDERPEST
RINDLE
RINDS
RINDY
RINE
RINFORZANDO
RING
RINGBILL
RINGBIRD
RINGBOLT
RINGBONE
RINGBONED
RINGCRAFT
RINGDOVE
RINGE
RINGED
RINGENT
RINGER
RINGEYE
RINGGIVER
RINGGIVING
RINGGOER
RINGHALS
RINGHALSES
RINGHEAD
RINGINESS

RINGING
RINGINGLY
RINGITE
RINGLE
RINGLEAD
RINGLEADER
RINGLET
RINGLETED
RINGLETS
RINGLETY
RINGLIKE
RINGMAKER
RINGMAKING
RINGMAN
RINGMASTER
RINGNECK
RINGS
RINGSAIL
RINGSIDE
RINGSIDER
RINGSTER
RINGSTICK
RINGSTRAKED
RINGTAIL
RINGTAW
RINGTIME
RINGTOSS
RINGWALK
RINGWALL
RINGWISE
RINGWORM
RINGY
RINK
RINKA
RINKER
RINKITE
RINN
RINNEITE
RINNER
RINNING
RINSE
RINSED
RINSER
RINSING
RINTHEREOUT
RIO
RIOT
RIOTED
RIOTER
RIOTING
RIOTINGLY
RIOTISE
RIOTIST
RIOTISTIC
RIOTOCRACY
RIOTOUS
RIOTOUSLY
RIOTOUSNESS
RIOTRY
RIP
RIPA
RIPAL
RIPARIAL
RIPARIAN
RIPARIOUS
RIPCORD
RIPE
RIPED
RIPELY
RIPEN
RIPENED
RIPENER
RIPENESS
RIPENING
RIPENINGLY
RIPER
RIPEST

RIPGUT
RIPICOLOUS
RIPIDOLITE
RIPIENIST
RIPIENO
RIPIER
RIPON
RIPOST
RIPOSTE
RIPOSTED
RIPOSTING
RIPPABLE
RIPPED
RIPPER
RIPPERMAN
RIPPERMEN
RIPPET
RIPPIER
RIPPING
RIPPINGLY
RIPPINGNESS
RIPPIT
RIPPLE
RIPPLED
RIPPLER
RIPPLES
RIPPLET
RIPPLING
RIPPLINGLY
RIPPLY
RIPPON
RIPRAP
RIPRAPPED
RIPRAPPING
RIPSACK
RIPSAW
RIPSNORTER
RIPSNORTING
RIPTIDE
RIPUP
RIRORIRO
RISALA
RISALDAR
RISBERM
RISCO
RISDALER
RISE
RISEN
RISER
RISH
RISHI
RISHTADAR
RISIBILITIES
RISIBILITY
RISIBLE
RISIBLENESS
RISIBLES
RISIBLY
RISING
RISK
RISKED
RISKER
RISKFUL
RISKFULNESS
RISKIER
RISKIEST
RISKILY
RISKINESS
RISKING
RISKISH
RISKLESS
RISKY
RISOM
RISORGIMENTO
RISORIAL
RISORIUS
RISORSE

RISOTTO
RISP
RISPER
RISPETTO
RISPOSTA
RISQUE
RISSER
RISSLE
RISSOID
RISSOLE
RISSOM
RIST
RISTORI
RISUS
RIT
RITARD
RITARDANDO
RITARDANDOS
RITE
RITELY
RITENUTO
RITES
RITHE
RITMASTER
RITORNEL
RITORNELLE
RITORNELLO
RITRATTO
RITSU
RITTINGERITE
RITTOCK
RITUAL
RITUALISM
RITUALIST
RITUALISTIC
RITUALITIES
RITUALITY
RITUALLY
RITUS
RITZ
RITZIER
RITZIEST
RITZY
RIVA
RIVAGE
RIVAL
RIVALED
RIVALING
RIVALISM
RIVALITY
RIVALIZE
RIVALLED
RIVALLING
RIVALRIES
RIVALROUS
RIVALRY
RIVE
RIVED
RIVEL
RIVELED
RIVELING
RIVELL
RIVEN
RIVER
RIVERAIN
RIVERBANK
RIVERBED
RIVERBOAT
RIVERDAMP
RIVERED
RIVERET
RIVERHEAD
RIVERINE
RIVERISH
RIVERLET
RIVERLING
RIVERLY

RIVERMAN
RIVERMEN
RIVERS
RIVERSIDE
RIVERSIDER
RIVERWASH
RIVERWAY
RIVERWEED
RIVERY
RIVET
RIVETED
RIVETER
RIVETING
RIVETS
RIVIERE
RIVING
RIVO
RIVOSE
RIVULATION
RIVULET
RIVULETS
RIVULOSE
RIX
RIXATRIX
RIXDALER
RIXY
RIYAL
RIZIFORM
RIZZAR
RIZZER
RIZZLE
RIZZOM
RIZZOMED
RO
ROACH
ROACHBACK
ROACHED
ROACHING
ROAD
ROADABILITY
ROADBED
ROADBLOCK
ROADBOOK
ROADCRAFT
ROADED
ROADER
ROADFELLOW
ROADHEAD
ROADHOUSE
ROADING
ROADITE
ROADMAN
ROADMASTER
ROADRUNNER
ROADS
ROADSIDE
ROADSIDER
ROADSTEAD
ROADSTER
ROADSTONE
ROADWAY
ROADWEED
ROADWISE
ROADWORK
ROADWORTHY
ROAG
ROAM
ROAMAGE
ROAMED
ROAMER
ROAMING
ROAMINGLY
ROAN
ROAR
ROARED
ROARER
ROARING

ROARINGLY
ROAST
ROASTABLE
ROASTED
ROASTER
ROASTING
ROASTINGLY
ROB
ROBALITO
ROBALO
ROBAND
ROBBED
ROBBER
ROBBERY
ROBBIN
ROBBING
ROBE
ROBED
ROBER
ROBERD
ROBERT
ROBHAH
ROBIN
ROBINET
ROBING
ROBININ
ROBLE
ROBORANT
ROBORATE
ROBORATION
ROBORATIVE
ROBOREAN
ROBOREOUS
ROBOT
ROBOTESQUE
ROBOTIAN
ROBOTISM
ROBOTISTIC
ROBOTIZATION
ROBOTIZE
ROBOTRY
ROBUR
ROBURITE
ROBUST
ROBUSTFUL
ROBUSTFULLY
ROBUSTIC
ROBUSTICITY
ROBUSTIOUS
ROBUSTIOUSLY
ROBUSTITY
ROBUSTLY
ROBUSTNESS
ROC
ROCAILLE
ROCAMBOLE
ROCCA
ROCCELLIN
ROCCELLINE
ROCHE
ROCHELIME
ROCHER
ROCHET
ROCK
ROCKABLE
ROCKABLY
ROCKABY
ROCKABYE
ROCKALLITE
ROCKAT
ROCKBELL
ROCKBIRD
ROCKBORN
ROCKBRUSH
ROCKCIST
ROCKCRAFT
ROCKELAY

ROCKER
ROCKERTHON
ROCKERY
ROCKET
ROCKETED
ROCKETER
ROCKETING
ROCKETRY
ROCKETS
ROCKETSONDE
ROCKETY
ROCKFALL
ROCKFISH
ROCKFISHES
ROCKFOIL
ROCKHAIR
ROCKHEARTED
ROCKIER
ROCKIEST
ROCKINESS
ROCKING
ROCKINGLY
ROCKISH
ROCKLAY
ROCKLING
ROCKLINGS
ROCKMAN
ROCKOON
ROCKRIBBED
ROCKROSE
ROCKS
ROCKSHAFT
ROCKSLIDE
ROCKSTAFF
ROCKTREE
ROCKWEED
ROCKWOOD
ROCKWORK
ROCKY
ROCOCO
ROCOLO
ROCTA
ROD
RODD
RODDEN
RODDIKIN
RODDIN
RODDING
RODE
RODENT
RODENTIAL
RODENTIALLY
RODENTIAN
RODEO
RODGE
RODHAM
RODING
RODINGITE
RODLESS
RODLIKE
RODMAKER
RODMAN
RODNEY
RODOMONTADE
RODOMONTADOR
RODS
RODSMAN
RODSTER
RODWOOD
ROEBLINGITE
ROEBUCK
ROED
ROEDE
ROENENG
ROENTGEN
ROENTGENISM
ROENTGENIZE

ROER
ROESTONE
ROEY
ROG
ROGAN
ROGATION
ROGATIVE
ROGATORY
ROGER
ROGERIAN
ROGERSITE
ROGGLE
ROGNON
ROGNONS
ROGUE
ROGUED
ROGUERIES
ROGUERY
ROGUING
ROGUISH
ROGUISHLY
ROGUISHNESS
ROGUY
ROHAN
ROHOB
ROHU
ROHUN
ROHUNA
ROI
ROID
ROIL
ROILED
ROILIER
ROILIEST
ROILING
ROILY
ROIN
ROINISH
ROIS
ROIST
ROISTER
ROISTERER
ROISTERING
ROISTERLY
ROISTEROUS
ROISTEROUSLY
ROIT
ROITELET
ROJO
ROKA
ROKE
ROKEAGE
ROKEE
ROKELAY
ROKER
ROKEY
ROKY
ROLA
ROLE
ROLEO
ROLL
ROLLABLE
ROLLAWAY
ROLLBACK
ROLLED
ROLLEJEE
ROLLER
ROLLERMAKER
ROLLERMAKING
ROLLERMAN
ROLLEY
ROLLEYWAY
ROLLEYWAYMAN
ROLLICHE
ROLLICHIE
ROLLICK
ROLLICKED

ROLLICKER
ROLLICKING
ROLLICKINGLY
ROLLICKSOME
ROLLICKY
ROLLING
ROLLIX
ROLLMOP
ROLLTOP
ROLLWAY
ROLOWAY
ROLP
ROLPENS
ROM
ROMAIKA
ROMAINE
ROMAL
ROMAN
ROMANCE
ROMANCEALIST
ROMANCEAN
ROMANCED
ROMANCER
ROMANCES
ROMANCICAL
ROMANCING
ROMANCIST
ROMANCY
ROMANESQUE
ROMANIUM
ROMANTIC
ROMANTICAL
ROMANTICALLY
ROMANTICISM
ROMANTICIST
ROMANTICITY
ROMANTICIZE
ROMANTICLY
ROMANTICNESS
ROMANTISM
ROMANTIST
ROMANZA
ROMAUNT
ROMBLE
ROMBOS
ROMBOWLINE
ROMEITE
ROMERILLO
ROMERO
ROMI
ROMMACK
ROMNI
ROMP
ROMPED
ROMPER
ROMPERS
ROMPING
ROMPINGLY
ROMPISH
ROMPISHLY
ROMPISHNESS
ROMPU
ROMPY
RON
RONCADOR
RONCET
RONCHO
RONCO
ROND
RONDACHE
RONDACHER
RONDAWEL
RONDE
RONDEAU
RONDEAUX
RONDEL
RONDELET

RONDELIER
RONDELLE
RONDELLIER
RONDINO
RONDLE
RONDO
RONDOLETTO
RONDOS
RONDURE
RONE
RONEO
RONG
RONGEUR
RONIER
RONIN
RONION
RONQUIL
RONTGENISM
RONYON
ROO
ROOD
ROODEBOK
ROODLES
ROODSTONE
ROOF
ROOFAGE
ROOFED
ROOFER
ROOFING
ROOFLESS
ROOFLET
ROOFMAN
ROOFMEN
ROOFTREE
ROOFWARD
ROOFY
ROOIBOK
ROOINEK
ROOK
ROOKED
ROOKER
ROOKERIED
ROOKERY
ROOKIE
ROOKING
ROOKS
ROOKUS
ROOKY
ROOL
ROOM
ROOMAGE
ROOMER
ROOMETTE
ROOMFUL
ROOMIE
ROOMIER
ROOMIEST
ROOMILY
ROOMINESS
ROOMING
ROOMKEEPER
ROOMMATE
ROOMS
ROOMSOME
ROOMSTEAD
ROOMTH
ROOMTHILY
ROOMTHINESS
ROOMTHY
ROOMWARD
ROOMY
ROON
ROOP
ROORBACK
ROOSA
ROOSE
ROOSEVELT

ROOST
ROOSTED
ROOSTER
ROOSTERFISH
ROOSTERS
ROOSTY
ROOT
ROOTAGE
ROOTCAP
ROOTED
ROOTEDLY
ROOTEDNESS
ROOTER
ROOTERY
ROOTFAST
ROOTFASTNESS
ROOTHOLD
ROOTIER
ROOTIEST
ROOTINESS
ROOTLE
ROOTLESS
ROOTLESSNESS
ROOTLET
ROOTLIKE
ROOTLING
ROOTS
ROOTSTALK
ROOTSTOCK
ROOTWALT
ROOTWORM
ROOTY
ROOVE
ROOYEBOK
ROPABLE
ROPAND
ROPANI
ROPE
ROPEBAND
ROPEBARK
ROPED
ROPEDANCE
ROPEDANCER
ROPEDANCING
ROPELAYER
ROPELAYING
ROPEMAKER
ROPEMAKING
ROPEMAN
ROPEMEN
ROPER
ROPERIPE
ROPERY
ROPES
ROPESMITH
ROPEWALK
ROPEWALKER
ROPEWAY
ROPEWORK
ROPEY
ROPIER
ROPIEST
ROPILY
ROPINESS
ROPING
ROPISH
ROPISHNESS
ROPLOCH
ROPY
ROQUE
ROQUELAURE
ROQUET
ROQUETED
ROQUETING
ROQUETTE
ROQUILLE
ROQUIST

RORAL
RORATORIO
RORIC
RORID
RORIFEROUS
RORIFLUENT
RORITORIOUS
RORQUAL
RORT
RORTY
RORULENT
ROSACE
ROSACEAN
ROSACEOUS
ROSAKER
ROSANILINE
ROSARIAN
ROSARIES
ROSARIUM
ROSARUBY
ROSARY
ROSATED
ROSCHERITE
ROSCID
ROSCOELITE
ROSE
ROSEAL
ROSEATE
ROSEATELY
ROSEBAY
ROSEBUD
ROSEBUSH
ROSED
ROSEDROP
ROSEFISH
ROSEFISHES
ROSEHEAD
ROSEHILL
ROSEHILLER
ROSEI
ROSEINE
ROSEL
ROSELET
ROSELITE
ROSELLA
ROSELLATE
ROSELLE
ROSEMARIES
ROSEMARY
ROSEN
ROSENBUSCHITE
ROSEOLA
ROSEOLAR
ROSEOLIFORM
ROSEOLOUS
ROSEOUS
ROSER
ROSEROOT
ROSES
ROSET
ROSETAN
ROSETANGLE
ROSETIME
ROSETTE
ROSETTED
ROSETTY
ROSETTY
ROSETUM
ROSETY
ROSEWAYS
ROSEWISE
ROSEWOOD
ROSEWORT
ROSIED
ROSIER
ROSIERESITE
ROSIEST

ROSILLA
ROSILLO
ROSILY
ROSIN
ROSINESS
ROSING
ROSINOUS
ROSINWEED
ROSINY
ROSLAND
ROSMARINE
ROSOLIC
ROSOLIO
ROSOLITE
ROSORIAL
ROSSER
ROSSITE
ROSTEL
ROSTELLA
ROSTELLAR
ROSTELLATE
ROSTELLIFORM
ROSTELLUM
ROSTER
ROSTRA
ROSTRAL
ROSTRALLY
ROSTRATE
ROSTRATED
ROSTRIFEROUS
ROSTRIFORM
ROSTROID
ROSTRULAR
ROSTRULATE
ROSTRULUM
ROSTRUM
ROSTRUMS
ROSULAR
ROSULATE
ROSY
ROT
ROTA
ROTACISM
ROTAL
ROTALIAN
ROTALIFORM
ROTAMAN
ROTAMEN
ROTAMETER
ROTAN
ROTANG
ROTARIANIZE
ROTARY
ROTATABLE
ROTATE
ROTATED
ROTATING
ROTATION
ROTATIONAL
ROTATIVE
ROTATIVELY
ROTATIVISM
ROTATOPLANE
ROTATOR
ROTATORES
ROTATORY
ROTCH
ROTCHE
ROTE
ROTELLA
ROTENONE
ROTGE
ROTGUT
ROTHER
ROTHERMUCK
ROTI
ROTIFER

ROTIFERAL
ROTIFEROUS
ROTIFORM
ROTISSERIE
ROTL
ROTN
ROTO
ROTOGRAPH
ROTOGRAVURE
ROTONDE
ROTOR
ROTTA
ROTTAN
ROTTE
ROTTED
ROTTEN
ROTTENLY
ROTTENNESS
ROTTENSTONE
ROTTER
ROTTING
ROTTLE
ROTTLERA
ROTTLERIN
ROTTOCK
ROTTOLO
ROTULA
ROTULAD
ROTULAR
ROTULET
ROTULIAN
ROTULIFORM
ROTULUS
ROTUND
ROTUNDA
ROTUNDATE
ROTUNDITIES
ROTUNDITY
ROTUNDLY
ROTUNDNESS
ROTURIER
ROTURIERS
ROUB
ROUBLE
ROUBOUH
ROUCH
ROUCHE
ROUCOU
ROUDAS
ROUE
ROUERIE
ROUGE
ROUGEAU
ROUGED
ROUGEMONTITE
ROUGEOT
ROUGH
ROUGHAGE
ROUGHCAST
ROUGHCASTER
ROUGHCASTING
ROUGHDRAFT
ROUGHDRAW
ROUGHDRESS
ROUGHDRIED
ROUGHDRY
ROUGHDRYING
ROUGHEN
ROUGHENED
ROUGHENER
ROUGHER
ROUGHET
ROUGHHEW
ROUGHHEWED
ROUGHHEWER
ROUGHHEWING
ROUGHHEWN

ROUGHHOUSE
ROUGHHOUSER
ROUGHHOUSING
ROUGHHOUSY
ROUGHIE
ROUGHINGS
ROUGHISH
ROUGHISHLY
ROUGHISHNESS
ROUGHLEG
ROUGHLY
ROUGHNECK
ROUGHNESS
ROUGHOMETER
ROUGHRIDE
ROUGHRIDER
ROUGHROOT
ROUGHSCUFF
ROUGHSETTER
ROUGHSHOD
ROUGHSLANT
ROUGHSOME
ROUGHSTRING
ROUGHSTUFF
ROUGHT
ROUGHTAILED
ROUGHWORK
ROUGHWROUGHT
ROUGHY
ROUGING
ROUKY
ROULADE
ROULEAU
ROULEAUS
ROULEAUX
ROULETTE
ROUN
ROUNCE
ROUNCEVAL
ROUNCY
ROUND
ROUNDABOUT
ROUNDABOUTLY
ROUNDED
ROUNDEL
ROUNDELAY
ROUNDELEER
ROUNDER
ROUNDERS
ROUNDHEADED
ROUNDHOUSE
ROUNDING
ROUNDISH
ROUNDISHNESS
ROUNDLET
ROUNDLINE
ROUNDLY
ROUNDNESS
ROUNDNOSE
ROUNDNOSED
ROUNDS
ROUNDSMAN
ROUNDTAIL
ROUNDTOP
ROUNDUP
ROUNDWORM
ROUNDY
ROUNGE
ROUNSPIK
ROUNTREE
ROUP
ROUPET
ROUPIE
ROUPIT
ROUPY
ROUSE
ROUSEABOUT

ROUSED	ROWTY	RUBERYTHRIC	RUDDIEST	RUGOSITY
ROUSEMENT	ROWY	RUBESCENCE	RUDDINESS	RUGOUS
ROUSER	ROX	RUBESCENT	RUDDISH	RUIN
ROUSETTE	ROXY	RUBIACEOUS	RUDDLE	RUINABLE
ROUSING	ROY	RUBIANIC	RUDDLED	RUINATE
ROUSINGLY	ROYAL	RUBIATE	RUDDLEMAN	RUINATED
ROUSSEAU	ROYALE	RUBIATOR	RUDDLEMEN	RUINATING
ROUST	ROYALET	RUBIBLE	RUDDLING	RUINATION
ROUSTABOUT	ROYALISM	RUBICAN	RUDDOCK	RUINATIOUS
ROUSTING	ROYALIST	RUBICUND	RUDDY	RUINATOR
ROUT	ROYALISTIC	RUBICUNDITY	RUDE	RUINED
ROUTE	ROYALIZATION	RUBIDIC	RUDELY	RUINER
ROUTED	ROYALIZE	RUBIDINE	RUDENESS	RUING
ROUTER	ROYALLY	RUBIDIUM	RUDENTED	RUINIFORM
ROUTH	ROYALMAST	RUBIED	RUDER	RUINOUS
ROUTHERCOCK	ROYALME	RUBIES	RUDERA	RUINOUSLY
ROUTHY	ROYALTIES	RUBIFIC	RUDERAL	RUINOUSNESS
ROUTIER	ROYALTY	RUBIFICATION	RUDERATE	RUINPROOF
ROUTINARY	ROYD	RUBIFICATIVE	RUDESBY	RUINS
ROUTINE	ROYET	RUBIFY	RUDEST	RUKH
ROUTINEER	ROYETNESS	RUBIGINOUS	RUDGE	RULE
ROUTINELY	ROYETOUS	RUBIGO	RUDIMENT	RULED
ROUTING	ROYETOUSLY	RUBIJERVINE	RUDIMENTAL	RULEMONGER
ROUTINISH	ROYLE	RUBIN	RUDIMENTARY	RULER
ROUTINISM	ROYNOUS	RUBINE	RUDISH	RULERS
ROUTINIST	ROYT	RUBINEOUS	RUDITY	RULERSHIP
ROUTINIZE	ROZUM	RUBIOUS	RUDLOFF	RULES
ROUTINIZED	RSI	RUBLE	RUDOUS	RULING
ROUTINIZING	RUACH	RUBLIS	RUE	RULINGLY
ROUTIVARITE	RUADE	RUBOR	RUED	RULL
ROUTOUS	RUANA	RUBRIC	RUEFUL	RULLER
ROUTOUSLY	RUAY	RUBRICAL	RUEFULLY	RULLION
ROUVILLITE	RUB	RUBRICALITY	RUEFULNESS	RULLOCK
ROUX	RUBABOO	RUBRICALLY	RUELLE	RUM
ROVE	RUBACE	RUBRICATE	RUELY	RUMAL
ROVED	RUBAIYAT	RUBRICATED	RUEN	RUMBA
ROVER	RUBAN	RUBRICATING	RUER	RUMBARGE
ROVESCIO	RUBASSE	RUBRICATION	RUESOME	RUMBELOW
ROVET	RUBATO	RUBRICATOR	RUESOMENESS	RUMBLE
ROVETTO	RUBBABOO	RUBRICIAN	RUEWORT	RUMBLED
ROVING	RUBBED	RUBRICISM	RUF	RUMBLEGARIE
ROVINGLY	RUBBEE	RUBRICIST	RUFESCENCE	RUMBLEGUMPTION
ROVINGNESS	RUBBER	RUBRICITY	RUFESCENT	RUMBLEMENT
ROW	RUBBERIZE	RUBRICIZE	RUFF	RUMBLER
ROWABLE	RUBBERIZED	RUBRICOSE	RUFFE	RUMBLING
ROWAN	RUBBERIZING	RUBRIFIC	RUFFED	RUMBLINGLY
ROWANBERRIES	RUBBERNECK	RUBRIFY	RUFFER	RUMBLY
ROWANBERRY	RUBBERNOSE	RUBROSPINAL	RUFFIAN	RUMBO
ROWBOAT	RUBBERS	RUBSTONE	RUFFIANAGE	RUMBOOZE
ROWDILY	RUBBERSTONE	RUBY	RUFFIANISH	RUMBOWLINE
ROWDINESS	RUBBERY	RUBYING	RUFFIANISM	RUMBOWLING
ROWDY	RUBBING	RUBYTAIL	RUFFIANIZE	RUMBULLION
ROWDYDOW	RUBBIO	RUCERVINE	RUFFIANLY	RUMBUMPTIOUS
ROWDYISH	RUBBISHING	RUCERVUS	RUFFING	RUMBUSTICAL
ROWDYISHLY	RUBBISHINGLY	RUCHE	RUFFLE	RUMBUSTIOUS
ROWDYISM	RUBBISHLY	RUCHING	RUFFLED	RUMCHUNDER
ROWED	RUBBISHRY	RUCK	RUFFLER	RUMEN
ROWEL	RUBBISHY	RUCKLE	RUFFLINESS	RUMENITIS
ROWELED	RUBBLE	RUCKSACK	RUFFLING	RUMENOTOMY
ROWELHEAD	RUBBLER	RUCKSEY	RUFFLY	RUMFUSTIAN
ROWELING	RUBBLES	RUCKUS	RUFFMANS	RUMGUMPTION
ROWELLED	RUBBLESTONE	RUCKY	RUFOUS	RUMGUMPTIOUS
ROWELLING	RUBBLEWORK	RUCTION	RUFULOUS	RUMINA
ROWEN	RUBBLY	RUCTIOUS	RUFUS	RUMINAL
ROWER	RUBDOWN	RUD	RUG	RUMINANT
ROWET	RUBEDINOUS	RUDAS	RUGA	RUMINANTLY
ROWINESS	RUBEDITY	RUDBECKIA	RUGAE	RUMINANTS
ROWING	RUBEFACIENCE	RUDD	RUGATE	RUMINATE
ROWK	RUBEFACIENT	RUDDER	RUGG	RUMINATED
ROWLANDITE	RUBEFACTION	RUDDERFISH	RUGGED	RUMINATING
ROWLET	RUBELET	RUDDERHEAD	RUGGEDLY	RUMINATINGLY
ROWLOCK	RUBELLA	RUDDERHOLE	RUGGEDNESS	RUMINATION
ROWN	RUBELLE	RUDDERLESS	RUGGING	RUMINATIVE
ROWP	RUBELLITE	RUDDERPOST	RUGGLE	RUMINATIVELY
ROWPORT	RUBEOLA	RUDDERSTOCK	RUGGY	RUMINATOR
ROWS	RUBEOLAR	RUDDIED	RUGINE	RUMKIN
ROWTH	RUBEOLOID	RUDDIER	RUGOSE	RUMMAGE

RUMMAGED
RUMMAGER
RUMMAGING
RUMMAGY
RUMMER
RUMMES
RUMMIER
RUMMIEST
RUMMILY
RUMMINESS
RUMMLE
RUMMY
RUMNESS
RUMNEY
RUMOR
RUMORED
RUMORER
RUMORING
RUMORMONGER
RUMOROUS
RUMOUR
RUMOURED
RUMOURER
RUMOURING
RUMP
RUMPAD
RUMPADE
RUMPLE
RUMPLED
RUMPLING
RUMPUS
RUMPY
RUMRUNNER
RUMSHOP
RUMTYTOO
RUN
RUNABOUT
RUNAGADO
RUNAGATE
RUNAROUND
RUNAWAY
RUNBACK
RUNBY
RUNCH
RUNCHWEED
RUNCINATE
RUND
RUNDALE
RUNDEL
RUNDLE
RUNDLET
RUNDOWN
RUNE
RUNECRAFT
RUNEFOLK
RUNER
RUNES
RUNESMITH
RUNESTAFF
RUNEWORD
RUNFISH
RUNG
RUNGHEAD
RUNHOLDER
RUNIC
RUNIFORM
RUNITE
RUNKEEPER
RUNKLE
RUNLET
RUNMAN
RUNN
RUNNEL
RUNNER
RUNNERS
RUNNET
RUNNING

RUNNY
RUNOFF
RUNOLOGIST
RUNOLOGY
RUNOUT
RUNOVER
RUNRIG
RUNROUND
RUNS
RUNSY
RUNT
RUNTED
RUNTEE
RUNTIER
RUNTIEST
RUNTINESS
RUNTISH
RUNTISHLY
RUNTISHNESS
RUNTY
RUNWAY
RUPA
RUPEE
RUPELLARY
RUPESTRAL
RUPESTRIAN
RUPESTRINE
RUPIA
RUPIAH
RUPICOLINE
RUPICOLOUS
RUPIE
RUPITIC
RUPTILE
RUPTION
RUPTIVE
RUPTUARY
RUPTURABLE
RUPTURE
RUPTURED
RUPTUREWORT
RUPTURING
RURAL
RURALISM
RURALIST
RURALITE
RURALITIES
RURALITY
RURALIZATION
RURALIZE
RURALIZED
RURALIZING
RURALLY
RURIC
RURIDECANAL
RURIGENOUS
RURU
RUSE
RUSH
RUSHBUSH
RUSHED
RUSHEN
RUSHER
RUSHES
RUSHIER
RUSHIEST
RUSHINESS
RUSHING
RUSHLAND
RUSHLIGHT
RUSHLIGHTED
RUSHLIKE
RUSHY
RUSINE
RUSK
RUSKY
RUSMA

RUSOT
RUSPONE
RUSSEL
RUSSELET
RUSSET
RUSSETING
RUSSETISH
RUSSUD
RUST
RUSTIC
RUSTICAL
RUSTICALLY
RUSTICALNESS
RUSTICATE
RUSTICATED
RUSTICATING
RUSTICATION
RUSTICATOR
RUSTICIAL
RUSTICISM
RUSTICITIES
RUSTICITY
RUSTICIZE
RUSTICOAT
RUSTICWORK
RUSTIER
RUSTIEST
RUSTINESS
RUSTLE
RUSTLED
RUSTLER
RUSTLING
RUSTLINGLY
RUSTLY
RUSTRE
RUSTRED
RUSTY
RUSTYISH
RUSWUT
RUT
RUTAB
RUTABAGA
RUTACEOUS
RUTE
RUTELIAN
RUTH
RUTHE
RUTHENATE
RUTHENIC
RUTHENIOUS
RUTHENIUM
RUTHENOUS
RUTHER
RUTHERFORD
RUTHFUL
RUTHFULLY
RUTHFULNESS
RUTHLESS
RUTHLESSLY
RUTHLESSNESS
RUTIC
RUTIDOSIS
RUTILANT
RUTILATE
RUTILATED
RUTILATION
RUTILE
RUTILOUS
RUTIN
RUTINOSE
RUTTEE
RUTTER
RUTTIER
RUTTIEST
RUTTINESS
RUTTING
RUTTISH

RUTTISHNESS
RUTTLE
RUTTY
RUTYL
RUTYLENE
RUVID
RUX
RYAL
RYBAT
RYDER
RYE
RYEGRASS
RYEL
RYEN
RYFT
RYG
RYKE
RYKED
RYKING
RYME
RYND
RYNT
RYOT
RYOTWAR
RYOTWARI
RYPE
RYPECK
RYTIDOSIS

SA
SAA
SAAH
SAAME
SAB
SABA
SABADILLA
SABADIN
SABADINE
SABAKHA
SABALO
SABALOTE
SABANA
SABATON
SABAYON
SABBAT
SABBATICAL
SABBATINE
SABBATISM
SABBATON
SABBEKA
SABBITHA
SABBY
SABDARIFFA
SABE
SABECA
SABED
SABEING
SABELLAN
SABELLID
SABELLOID
SABER
SABERBILL
SABERED
SABERING
SABERTOOTH
SABHA
SABIACEOUS
SABICU
SABIN
SABINA
SABINE
SABINO
SABIO
SABLA
SABLE
SABLEFISH
SABLEFISHES
SABLENESS
SABLES
SABLY
SABORA
SABORAIM
SABOT
SABOTAGE
SABOTAGED
SABOTAGING
SABOTED
SABOTEUR
SABOTIER
SABOTINE
SABRE
SABREBILL
SABRETACHE
SABRETOOTH
SABREUR
SABRING

SABULINE
SABULITE
SABULOSE
SABULOSITY
SABULOUS
SABULUM
SABURRA
SABURRAL
SABURRATE
SABURRATION
SABUTAN
SABZI
SAC
SACALAIT
SACALINE
SACATE
SACATON
SACATRA
SACBROOD
SACCADE
SACCADGE
SACCADIC
SACCAGE
SACCATE
SACCATED
SACCHARATE
SACCHARATED
SACCHARIC
SACCHARIDE
SACCHARIFIED
SACCHARIFIER
SACCHARIFY
SACCHARIFYING
SACCHARILLA
SACCHARIN
SACCHARINATE
SACCHARINE
SACCHARINELY
SACCHARINIC
SACCHARINITY
SACCHARIZE
SACCHARIZED
SACCHARIZING
SACCHAROID
SACCHAROIDAL
SACCHARONATE
SACCHARONE
SACCHARONIC
SACCHAROSE
SACCHAROSURIA
SACCODERM
SACCOON
SACCOS
SACCULAR
SACCULATE
SACCULATED
SACCULATION
SACCULE
SACCULUS
SACCUS
SACE
SACELLA
SACELLUM
SACER
SACERDOCY
SACERDOS
SACERDOTAGE
SACERDOTAL
SACERDOTALLY
SACERDOTICAL
SACERDOTISM
SACERDOTIUM
SACHEM
SACHEMDOM
SACHEMIC
SACHET
SACK

SACKAGE
SACKBAG
SACKBUT
SACKBUTT
SACKCLOTH
SACKCLOTHED
SACKDOUDLE
SACKED
SACKEN
SACKER
SACKET
SACKFUL
SACKING
SACKLESS
SACKMAKER
SACKMAKING
SACKS
SACO
SACOPE
SACQUE
SACRA
SACRAD
SACRAL
SACRALGIA
SACRAMENT
SACRAMENTAL
SACRAMENTALISM
SACRAMENTALIST
SACRAMENTALITY
SACRAMENTALLY
SACRAMENTARIAN
SACRAMENTARY
SACRAMENTER
SACRAMENTIZE
SACRAMENTUM
SACRARIA
SACRARIAL
SACRARIUM
SACRARY
SACRATE
SACRE
SACRECTOMY
SACRED
SACREDLY
SACREDNESS
SACRI
SACRIFICATION
SACRIFICATOR
SACRIFICATORY
SACRIFICATURE
SACRIFICE
SACRIFICED
SACRIFICER
SACRIFICES
SACRIFICIAL
SACRIFICIALLY
SACRIFICING
SACRIFICINGLY
SACRILEGE
SACRILEGER
SACRILEGIOUS
SACRILEGIOUSLY
SACRILEGIST
SACRING
SACRIST
SACRISTAN
SACRISTIES
SACRISTY
SACRO
SACROCOCCYX
SACROCOXITIS
SACRODORSAL
SACRODYNIA
SACROILIAC
SACROSANCT
SACROSCIATIC
SACROSPINOUS

SACROTUBEROUS
SACRUM
SACRY
SAD
SADD
SADDEN
SADDENED
SADDENING
SADDER
SADDEST
SADDHU
SADDIK
SADDISH
SADDLE
SADDLEBACK
SADDLEBAG
SADDLEBOW
SADDLECLOTH
SADDLED
SADDLELEAF
SADDLELESS
SADDLELIKE
SADDLEMAKER
SADDLENOSE
SADDLER
SADDLERIES
SADDLERY
SADDLES
SADDLESICK
SADDLESORE
SADDLETREE
SADDLETREES
SADDLING
SADE
SADH
SADHANA
SADHE
SADHEARTED
SADHU
SADIC
SADIRON
SADISM
SADIST
SADISTIC
SADISTICALLY
SADLY
SADNESS
SADO
SADOO
SADR
SADWARE
SAE
SAEBEINS
SAECULAR
SAECULUM
SAER
SAERNAITE
SAETER
SAEX
SAFARI
SAFE
SAFEBLOWER
SAFEBLOWING
SAFEBREAKER
SAFEBREAKING
SAFECRACKER
SAFECRACKING
SAFEGUARD
SAFEGUARDER
SAFEHOLD
SAFEKEEPER
SAFEKEEPING
SAFELIGHT
SAFELY
SAFEMAKER
SAFENER
SAFENESS

SAFER
SAFEST
SAFETIES
SAFETY
SAFFI
SAFFIAN
SAFFIOR
SAFFLOR
SAFFLORITE
SAFFLOW
SAFFLOWER
SAFFO
SAFFRON
SAFFRONED
SAFFRONWOOD
SAFFRONY
SAFIE
SAFIR
SAFRANIN
SAFRANINE
SAFRANOPHIL
SAFRANOPHILE
SAFROL
SAFROLE
SAFTLY
SAG
SAGA
SAGACIATE
SAGACIOUS
SAGACIOUSLY
SAGACIOUSNESS
SAGACITY
SAGAIE
SAGAMAN
SAGAMITE
SAGAMORE
SAGANASH
SAGAPEN
SAGAPENUM
SAGATHY
SAGE
SAGEBRUSH
SAGEBRUSHER
SAGEER
SAGELEAF
SAGELY
SAGENE
SAGENESS
SAGENITE
SAGENITIC
SAGER
SAGEROSE
SAGESHIP
SAGESSE
SAGEST
SAGEWOOD
SAGGAR
SAGGARD
SAGGED
SAGGER
SAGGING
SAGGON
SAGGY
SAGHAVART
SAGIER
SAGIEST
SAGINATE
SAGINATION
SAGING
SAGITTA
SAGITTAE
SAGITTAL
SAGITTALLY
SAGITTARII
SAGITTARIUS
SAGITTARY
SAGITTATE

SAGITTIFORM
SAGITTOCYST
SAGITTOID
SAGO
SAGOIN
SAGOS
SAGOWEER
SAGUARO
SAGUAROS
SAGUING
SAGUM
SAGURAN
SAGURANES
SAGVANDITE
SAGWIRE
SAGY
SAH
SAHEB
SAHH
SAHIB
SAHLITE
SAHME
SAHRAS
SAHU
SAI
SAIBLING
SAIC
SAICE
SAID
SAIDE
SAIF
SAIGA
SAIL
SAILABLE
SAILAGE
SAILBOAT
SAILCLOTH
SAILED
SAILER
SAILFIN
SAILFISH
SAILFISHES
SAILING
SAILMAKER
SAILMAKING
SAILOR
SAILORING
SAILORIZING
SAILORLY
SAILORMAN
SAILOUR
SAILPLANE
SAILS
SAILSHIP
SAILSMAN
SAILY
SAILYE
SAIM
SAIMIRI
SAIMY
SAIN
SAINDOUX
SAINFOIN
SAINT
SAINTE
SAINTED
SAINTHOOD
SAINTING
SAINTISH
SAINTISM
SAINTLIER
SAINTLIEST
SAINTLIKE
SAINTLINESS
SAINTLY
SAINTS
SAINTSHIP

SAIR
SAIRVE
SAIS
SAITHE
SAIYID
SAJ
SAJOU
SAKE
SAKEBER
SAKEEN
SAKER
SAKHA
SAKI
SAKIA
SAKIEH
SAKIYEH
SAKKOS
SAKULYA
SAL
SALA
SALAAM
SALABILITY
SALABLE
SALABLENESS
SALABLY
SALACIOUS
SALACIOUSLY
SALACIOUSNESS
SALACITY
SALACOT
SALAD
SALADA
SALADANG
SALADE
SALADERO
SALADIN
SALADING
SALAGO
SALAGRAMA
SALAL
SALAM
SALAMANDARIN
SALAMANDER
SALAMANDRA
SALAMANDRINE
SALAMANDROID
SALAMAT
SALAMBAO
SALAME
SALAMI
SALAMO
SALAMPORE
SALANGANE
SALANGID
SALAR
SALARIAT
SALARIED
SALARIEGO
SALARIES
SALARY
SALARYING
SALAT
SALAY
SALBAND
SALCHOW
SALDID
SALE
SALEABLE
SALEB
SALEEITE
SALEGOER
SALELE
SALEM
SALEMA
SALEP
SALERATUS
SALEROOM

SALES
SALESCLERK
SALESGIRL
SALESITE
SALESLADIES
SALESLADY
SALESMAN
SALESMANSHIP
SALESMEN
SALESPEOPLE
SALESPERSON
SALESROOM
SALESWOMAN
SALESWOMEN
SALEW
SALEWARE
SALEWORK
SALEYARD
SALFERN
SALIANT
SALIC
SALICACEOUS
SALICETUM
SALICIN
SALICIONAL
SALICORN
SALICYL
SALICYLAL
SALICYLATE
SALICYLIC
SALICYLIDE
SALICYLISM
SALICYLIZE
SALICYLURIC
SALICYLYL
SALIENCE
SALIENCY
SALIENT
SALIENTIAN
SALIENTLY
SALIENTNESS
SALIFEROUS
SALIFIABLE
SALIFICATION
SALIFIED
SALIFY
SALIFYING
SALIGENIN
SALIGENOL
SALIGOT
SALIGRAM
SALINA
SALINAS
SALINATION
SALINE
SALINELLE
SALINIFORM
SALINITY
SALINIZE
SALINOMETER
SALINOMETRY
SALITE
SALITED
SALIVA
SALIVANT
SALIVARY
SALIVATE
SALIVATED
SALIVATING
SALIVATION
SALIVATOR
SALIVATORY
SALIVOUS
SALL
SALLE
SALLEE
SALLEEMAN

SALLEEMEN
SALLENDERS
SALLET
SALLIED
SALLIER
SALLIES
SALLO
SALLOO
SALLOW
SALLOWED
SALLOWER
SALLOWING
SALLOWISH
SALLOWNESS
SALLOWY
SALLY
SALLYING
SALLYMAN
SALLYMEN
SALLYWOOD
SALM
SALMA
SALMAGUNDI
SALMARY
SALMI
SALMIAC
SALMIN
SALMINE
SALMIS
SALMON
SALMONBERRIES
SALMONBERRY
SALMONELLOSIS
SALMONET
SALMONID
SALMONIFORM
SALMONOID
SALMONSITE
SALMWOOD
SALNATRON
SALOL
SALOMETER
SALOMETRY
SALOMON
SALON
SALONIKA
SALONS
SALOON
SALOONIST
SALOONKEEPER
SALOOP
SALOP
SALOPIAN
SALP
SALPACEAN
SALPIAN
SALPICON
SALPID
SALPIFORM
SALPINGES
SALPINGIAN
SALPINGION
SALPINGITIS
SALPINGOCELE
SALPINX
SALPOID
SALSE
SALSIFIES
SALSIFY
SALSILLA
SALSO
SALSODA
SALSUGINOSE
SALSUGINOUS
SALT
SALTA
SALTANDO

SALTANT
SALTARELLO
SALTARY
SALTATE
SALTATION
SALTATIVENESS
SALTATO
SALTATORIAL
SALTATORIC
SALTATORY
SALTATRAS
SALTBOX
SALTBRUSH
SALTBUSH
SALTCAT
SALTCATCH
SALTCELLAR
SALTEAUX
SALTED
SALTEE
SALTEN
SALTER
SALTERETTO
SALTERN
SALTERY
SALTEST
SALTFAT
SALTFOOT
SALTHOUSE
SALTICID
SALTIE
SALTIER
SALTIERRA
SALTIERWISE
SALTIEST
SALTIGRADE
SALTILY
SALTIMBANCO
SALTINE
SALTINESS
SALTING
SALTIRE
SALTIREWISE
SALTISH
SALTMAKING
SALTMAN
SALTMOUTH
SALTNESS
SALTO
SALTOMETER
SALTOREL
SALTPAN
SALTPANS
SALTPETER
SALTPETRE
SALTS
SALTSHAKER
SALTSPOONFUL
SALTSPRINKLER
SALTUS
SALTWEED
SALTWORK
SALTWORKER
SALTWORKS
SALTWORT
SALTY
SALUBRIFY
SALUBRIOUS
SALUBRIOUSLY
SALUBRITY
SALUDA
SALUE
SALUKI
SALUNG
SALUS
SALUTARILY
SALUTARINESS

SALUTARY	SAMECH	SANCTIFYING	SANDMITE	SANITARIES
SALUTATION	SAMEK	SANCTILOGY	SANDNATTER	SANITARIST
SALUTATIONAL	SAMEKH	SANCTILOQUENT	SANDPAPER	SANITARIUM
SALUTATIOUS	SAMEL	SANCTIMONIAL	SANDPAPERER	SANITARIUMS
SALUTATORIAN	SAMELY	SANCTIMONIOUS	SANDPEEP	SANITARY
SALUTATORIES	SAMEN	SANCTIMONIOUSLY	SANDPILE	SANITATE
SALUTATORY	SAMENESS	SANCTIMONIOUSNESS	SANDPIPER	SANITATED
SALUTE	SAMESOME	SANCTIMONY	SANDPIPERS	SANITATING
SALUTER	SAMGHA	SANCTION	SANDRA	SANITATION
SALUTES	SAMH	SANCTIONARY	SANDROCK	SANITIZE
SALVABILITY	SAMHITA	SANCTIONATIVE	SANDSHOE	SANITIZED
SALVABLE	SAMIEL	SANCTIONED	SANDSOAP	SANITY
SALVABLY	SAMIRESITE	SANCTIONER	SANDSPIT	SANJAK
SALVAGE	SAMIRI	SANCTITIES	SANDSPUR	SANJAKBEG
SALVAGEABLE	SAMISEN	SANCTITUDE	SANDSTAY	SANK
SALVAGED	SAMITE	SANCTITY	SANDSTONE	SANKH
SALVAGEE	SAMKARA	SANCTOLOGIST	SANDSTORM	SANKHA
SALVAGER	SAMKHYA	SANCTORIUM	SANDUNGA	SANN
SALVAGING	SAMLET	SANCTUARIED	SANDUST	SANNA
SALVARSAN	SAMM	SANCTUARIES	SANDWEED	SANNAITE
SALVATELLA	SAMMEL	SANCTUARIZE	SANDWICH	SANNHEMP
SALVATION	SAMMER	SANCTUARY	SANDWICHED	SANNUP
SALVATIONAL	SAMMIER	SANCTUM	SANDWICHING	SANNYASI
SALVATIONISM	SAMMY	SANCTUMS	SANDWOOD	SANNYASIN
SALVATIONIST	SAMNANI	SANCYITE	SANDWORM	SANS
SALVATOR	SAMOGON	SAND	SANDWORT	SANSAR
SALVATORY	SAMOGONKA	SANDAK	SANDY	SANSARA
SALVE	SAMOHU	SANDAL	SANDYISH	SANSCULOT
SALVED	SAMORY	SANDALED	SANDYX	SANSERIF
SALVER	SAMOTHERE	SANDALIFORM	SANE	SANSHACH
SALVERFORM	SAMOVAR	SANDALING	SANELY	SANSI
SALVIA	SAMP	SANDALLED	SANENESS	SANT
SALVIANIN	SAMPAGUITA	SANDALLING	SANER	SANTA
SALVIFIC	SAMPALOC	SANDALWOOD	SANEST	SANTAL
SALVIFICAL	SAMPAN	SANDALWORT	SANG	SANTALACEOUS
SALVING	SAMPHIRE	SANDAN	SANGA	SANTALIN
SALVIOL	SAMPI	SANDARAC	SANGAH	SANTALOL
SALVO	SAMPLE	SANDARACIN	SANGAMON	SANTAPEE
SALVOES	SAMPLED	SANDASTRA	SANGAR	SANTAR
SALVOR	SAMPLEMAN	SANDASTROS	SANGAREE	SANTENE
SALVOS	SAMPLEMEN	SANDBAG	SANGFROID	SANTIMS
SALVY	SAMPLER	SANDBAGGED	SANGGAU	SANTIR
SALWE	SAMPLERY	SANDBAGGER	SANGH	SANTO
SALWIN	SAMPLES	SANDBAGGING	SANGHA	SANTOL
SAM	SAMPLING	SANDBANK	SANGIL	SANTON
SAMA	SAMSARA	SANDBAR	SANGLANT	SANTONICA
SAMADH	SAMSHU	SANDBLAST	SANGLEY	SANTONIN
SAMADHI	SAMSKARA	SANDBLASTER	SANGLIER	SANTONINE
SAMAJ	SAMSONITE	SANDBLIND	SANGREEROOT	SANTORINITE
SAMAN	SAMUIN	SANDBOARD	SANGREL	SANTOS
SAMARA	SAMUM	SANDBOX	SANGU	SANTOUR
SAMARIA	SAMURAI	SANDBOY	SANGUICOLOUS	SANTY
SAMARIFORM	SAMVAT	SANDBUR	SANGUIFEROUS	SANUKITE
SAMARIUM	SAN	SANDBURR	SANGUIFIER	SAO
SAMAROID	SANA	SANDCLUB	SANGUIMOTOR	SAORA
SAMARSKITE	SANABILITY	SANDED	SANGUIMOTORY	SAP
SAMBA	SANABLE	SANDER	SANGUINARY	SAPA
SAMBAL	SANAD	SANDERLING	SANGUINE	SAPAJOU
SAMBAQUI	SANAI	SANDERS	SANGUINELESS	SAPAN
SAMBAQUIS	SANATION	SANDERSWOOD	SANGUINELY	SAPANWOOD
SAMBAR	SANATIVE	SANDFISH	SANGUINENESS	SAPBUSH
SAMBARS	SANATIVENESS	SANDGOBY	SANGUINEOUS	SAPE
SAMBAS	SANATORIUM	SANDHEAT	SANGUINITY	SAPEC
SAMBEL	SANATORIUMS	SANDHI	SANGUINOLENT	SAPEK
SAMBHAR	SANATORY	SANDHOG	SANGUINOUS	SAPFUL
SAMBHUR	SANBENITO	SANDIA	SANGUISUGE	SAPHEAD
SAMBO	SANCHO	SANDIER	SANGUISUGENT	SAPHEADED
SAMBOS	SANCORD	SANDIES	SANGUISUGOUS	SAPHEADEDNESS
SAMBOUK	SANCT	SANDIEST	SANICLE	SAPHENA
SAMBOUSE	SANCTA	SANDING	SANIDINE	SAPHENAE
SAMBUCA	SANCTANIMITY	SANDIVER	SANIDINITE	SAPHENAL
SAMBUK	SANCTIFICATE	SANDIX	SANIES	SAPHENOUS
SAMBUKE	SANCTIFICATION	SANDKEY	SANIFICATION	SAPHIE
SAMBUL	SANCTIFIED	SANDLAPPER	SANIFY	SAPIAO
SAMBUNIGRIN	SANCTIFIEDLY	SANDLING	SANIOUS	SAPID
SAMBUR	SANCTIFIER	SANDLOT	SANITARIA	SAPIDITY
SAME	SANCTIFY	SANDMAN	SANITARIAN	SAPIDNESS

SAPIENCE
SAPIENCY
SAPIENT
SAPIENTIAL
SAPIENTIALLY
SAPIENTIZE
SAPIENTLY
SAPIN
SAPINDA
SAPINDACEOUS
SAPINDASHIP
SAPINDUS
SAPIT
SAPIUTAN
SAPLE
SAPLESS
SAPLESSNESS
SAPLING
SAPO
SAPODILLA
SAPODILLO
SAPOGENIN
SAPONACEOUS
SAPONACITY
SAPONARIN
SAPONARY
SAPONIFIABLE
SAPONIFIED
SAPONIFIER
SAPONIFY
SAPONIFYING
SAPONIN
SAPONINE
SAPONITE
SAPONUL
SAPONULE
SAPOPHORIC
SAPOR
SAPORIFIC
SAPOROSITY
SAPOROUS
SAPOTACEOUS
SAPOTE
SAPOTOXIN
SAPPANWOOD
SAPPARE
SAPPED
SAPPER
SAPPHIRE
SAPPHIRED
SAPPHIRINE
SAPPIER
SAPPIEST
SAPPILY
SAPPING
SAPPLES
SAPPY
SAPRAEMIA
SAPREMIA
SAPREMIC
SAPRIN
SAPRINE
SAPROCOLL
SAPRODIL
SAPRODONTIA
SAPROGEN
SAPROGENIC
SAPROGENOUS
SAPROLITE
SAPROLITIC
SAPROPEL
SAPROPELIC
SAPROPELITE
SAPROPHAGAN
SAPROPHAGOUS
SAPROPHILOUS
SAPROPHYTE

SAPROPHYTIC
SAPROPHYTISM
SAPROPLANKTON
SAPROSTOMOUS
SAPROZOIC
SAPS
SAPSAGO
SAPSAP
SAPSUCK
SAPSUCKER
SAPUCAIA
SAPUCAINHA
SAPWOOD
SAPWORT
SARAAD
SARABAND
SARAF
SARAFAN
SARAN
SARANGI
SARANGOUSTY
SARAPE
SARAVAN
SARAWAKITE
SARBACANE
SARCASM
SARCAST
SARCASTIC
SARCASTICAL
SARCASTICALLY
SARCASTICNESS
SARCEL
SARCELLE
SARCELLY
SARCENET
SARCILIS
SARCITIS
SARCLE
SARCLER
SARCOBLAST
SARCOCARP
SARCOCELE
SARCOCOL
SARCOCOLLIN
SARCOCYTE
SARCODE
SARCODERM
SARCODERMA
SARCODES
SARCODIC
SARCOGENIC
SARCOGENOUS
SARCOGLIA
SARCOID
SARCOLEMMA
SARCOLEMMIC
SARCOLEMMOUS
SARCOLINE
SARCOLITE
SARCOLOGIC
SARCOLOGICAL
SARCOLOGIST
SARCOLOGY
SARCOLYSIS
SARCOLYTE
SARCOLYTIC
SARCOMA
SARCOMATA
SARCOMATOID
SARCOMATOSIS
SARCOMATOUS
SARCOMERE
SARCOPHAGAL
SARCOPHAGI
SARCOPHAGIC
SARCOPHAGID
SARCOPHAGIZE

SARCOPHAGOUS
SARCOPHAGUS
SARCOPHAGY
SARCOPHILE
SARCOPHILOUS
SARCOPLASM
SARCOPLASMA
SARCOPLASMIC
SARCOPLAST
SARCOPLASTIC
SARCOPTIC
SARCOPTID
SARCOSEPSIS
SARCOSINE
SARCOSIS
SARCOSOMA
SARCOSOME
SARCOSPERM
SARCOSPORID
SARCOSTOSIS
SARCOSTYLE
SARCOTHECA
SARCOTIC
SARCOUS
SARD
SARDACHATE
SARDANA
SARDAR
SARDEL
SARDELLE
SARDINE
SARDINES
SARDIUS
SARDONIC
SARDONICALLY
SARDONICISM
SARDONYX
SAREE
SARGASSO
SARGASSUM
SARGE
SARGO
SARGOS
SARGUS
SARI
SARIGUE
SARIN
SARINDA
SARIP
SARIS
SARK
SARKFUL
SARKICAL
SARKING
SARKINITE
SARKIT
SARKLESS
SARLAK
SARLYK
SARMATIER
SARMENT
SARMENTA
SARMENTOSE
SARMENTOUS
SARMENTUM
SARNA
SAROD
SARON
SARONG
SARONIC
SARONIDE
SAROS
SAROTHRUM
SARPE
SARPLER
SARPO
SARRA

SARRAZIN
SARRE
SARROW
SARRUSOPHONE
SARSA
SARSAPARILLA
SARSAR
SARSEN
SARSENET
SARSNET
SARSON
SARTOR
SARTORIAD
SARTORIAL
SARTORIALLY
SARTORIAN
SARTORITE
SARTORIUS
SARUS
SARWAN
SASAN
SASANI
SASANQUA
SASARARA
SASH
SASHAY
SASHED
SASHERIES
SASHERY
SASHES
SASHIMI
SASHING
SASHOON
SASIN
SASINE
SASKATOON
SASS
SASSABIES
SASSABY
SASSAFRAS
SASSAGUM
SASSANDRA
SASSE
SASSIER
SASSIEST
SASSOLIN
SASSOLINE
SASSWOOD
SASSY
SASSYBARK
SASSYWOOD
SASTRA
SASTRUGA
SASTRUGI
SAT
SATANG
SATANIC
SATANICAL
SATANICALLY
SATANIST
SATANIZE
SATARA
SATCHEL
SATCHELED
SATE
SATED
SATEEN
SATEENWOOD
SATELLES
SATELLITE
SATELLITED
SATELLITIAN
SATELLITIC
SATELLITIOUS
SATELLITIUM
SATELLITOID
SATELLITORY

SATELLOID
SATI
SATIABILITY
SATIABLE
SATIABLENESS
SATIABLY
SATIATE
SATIATED
SATIATING
SATIATION
SATIENT
SATIETIES
SATIETY
SATIN
SATINAY
SATINBUSH
SATINE
SATINED
SATINET
SATINETTE
SATINFIN
SATINFLOWER
SATING
SATINING
SATINITE
SATINITY
SATINIZE
SATINLEAF
SATINPOD
SATINWOOD
SATINY
SATION
SATIRE
SATIRIC
SATIRICAL
SATIRICALLY
SATIRICALNESS
SATIRIST
SATIRIZABLE
SATIRIZE
SATIRIZED
SATIRIZER
SATIRIZING
SATISDATION
SATISDICTION
SATISFACTION
SATISFACTIONAL
SATISFACTIVE
SATISFACTORILY
SATISFACTORY
SATISFIED
SATISFIEDLY
SATISFIEDNESS
SATISFIER
SATISFY
SATISFYING
SATISFYINGLY
SATISPASSION
SATIVE
SATLIJK
SATORI
SATRAP
SATRAPATE
SATRAPESS
SATRAPIC
SATRAPICAL
SATRAPIES
SATRAPY
SATRON
SATSOP
SATTAR
SATTIE
SATTVA
SATURA
SATURABILITY
SATURABLE
SATURANT

SATURATE
SATURATED
SATURATER
SATURATING
SATURATION
SATURATOR
SATURITY
SATURNIID
SATURNINE
SATURNINELY
SATURNINITY
SATURNISM
SATURNIST
SATURNIZE
SATURY
SATYAGRAHA
SATYASHODAK
SATYR
SATYRESQUE
SATYRESS
SATYRIASIS
SATYRIC
SATYRICAL
SATYRID
SATYRINE
SATYRION
SATYRISM
SATYROMANIAC
SAUCE
SAUCEBOAT
SAUCEBOX
SAUCEDISH
SAUCEMAN
SAUCEMEN
SAUCEPAN
SAUCEPOT
SAUCER
SAUCERLEAF
SAUCERLIKE
SAUCERY
SAUCH
SAUCIER
SAUCIEST
SAUCILY
SAUCINESS
SAUCISSE
SAUCY
SAUERBRATEN
SAUERKRAUT
SAUGER
SAUGH
SAUGHEN
SAUGHT
SAUK
SAUL
SAULGE
SAULIE
SAULT
SAUM
SAUMON
SAUMONT
SAUNA
SAUNDERS
SAUNT
SAUNTER
SAUNTERED
SAUNTERER
SAUNTERING
SAUQUI
SAUR
SAUREL
SAURIAN
SAURIOSIS
SAURISCHIAN
SAURLESS
SAURODONT
SAUROID

SAUROPOD
SAUROPSID
SAUROPSIDAN
SAURY
SAUSAGE
SAUSINGER
SAUSSURITE
SAUTE
SAUTEED
SAUTEING
SAUTER
SAUTEREAU
SAUTERELLE
SAUTERNE
SAUTERNES
SAUTEUR
SAUTOIR
SAUTREE
SAUVE
SAVABLE
SAVABLENESS
SAVAGE
SAVAGED
SAVAGEDOM
SAVAGELY
SAVAGENESS
SAVAGER
SAVAGERIES
SAVAGEROUS
SAVAGERY
SAVAGESS
SAVAGEST
SAVAGING
SAVAGISM
SAVAGIZE
SAVANILLA
SAVANNA
SAVANNAH
SAVANT
SAVARIN
SAVATE
SAVATION
SAVE
SAVED
SAVELHA
SAVELOY
SAVEMENT
SAVER
SAVEY
SAVILE
SAVIN
SAVINE
SAVING
SAVINGLY
SAVINGNESS
SAVINGS
SAVIOR
SAVIORESS
SAVIOUR
SAVIOURESS
SAVOLA
SAVOR
SAVORED
SAVORER
SAVORILY
SAVORINESS
SAVORING
SAVORLESS
SAVORLY
SAVOROUS
SAVORY
SAVOUR
SAVOURIER
SAVOURIEST
SAVOURY
SAVOY
SAVOYED

SAVOYING
SAVSSAT
SAVVIED
SAVVY
SAVVYING
SAW
SAWAH
SAWALI
SAWBACK
SAWBELLY
SAWBILL
SAWBONES
SAWBUCK
SAWBWA
SAWDER
SAWDUST
SAWDUSTISH
SAWDUSTY
SAWED
SAWER
SAWFISH
SAWFISHES
SAWFLIES
SAWFLOM
SAWFLY
SAWHORSE
SAWING
SAWINGS
SAWLIKE
SAWLOG
SAWLSHOT
SAWMAN
SAWMILL
SAWMONT
SAWN
SAWNEB
SAWNEY
SAWNIE
SAWNY
SAWSETTER
SAWSMITH
SAWT
SAWTOOTH
SAWWAY
SAWWORT
SAWYER
SAX
SAXATILE
SAXAUL
SAXBOARD
SAXCORNET
SAXHORN
SAXICOLE
SAXICOLINE
SAXICOLOUS
SAXIFRAGANT
SAXIFRAGOUS
SAXIFRAX
SAXIGENOUS
SAXON
SAXONITE
SAXOPHONE
SAXOPHONIC
SAXOPHONIST
SAXOTROMBA
SAXTUBA
SAY
SAYA
SAYER
SAYETTE
SAYID
SAYING
SAYINGS
SAYNAY
SAYNETE
SAYON
SAYONARA

SAYYID
SAZEN
SAZERAC
SBIRRO
SCAB
SCABBADO
SCABBARD
SCABBED
SCABBEDNESS
SCABBERY
SCABBIER
SCABBIEST
SCABBILY
SCABBINESS
SCABBING
SCABBLE
SCABBLED
SCABBLER
SCABBLING
SCABBY
SCABELLUM
SCABERULOUS
SCABETIC
SCABIA
SCABIES
SCABIETIC
SCABINE
SCABINUS
SCABIOSA
SCABIOSITY
SCABIOUS
SCABISH
SCABLAND
SCABRATE
SCABRESCENT
SCABRID
SCABRIDITY
SCABRIDULOUS
SCABRIN
SCABRITIES
SCABROCK
SCABROUS
SCABROUSLY
SCABROUSNESS
SCABWORT
SCACCHIC
SCAD
SCADDLE
SCADS
SCAENA
SCAFF
SCAFFER
SCAFFERY
SCAFFIE
SCAFFLE
SCAFFOLD
SCAFFOLDAGE
SCAFFOLDED
SCAFFOLDER
SCAFFOLDING
SCAFFY
SCAGLIA
SCAGLIOLA
SCAGLIOLIST
SCAIFE
SCALA
SCALABLE
SCALADE
SCALADO
SCALAE
SCALAGE
SCALAR
SCALARE
SCALARIFORM
SCALARWISE
SCALARY
SCALAWAG

SCALAWAGGERY
SCALAWAGGY
SCALD
SCALDBERRY
SCALDED
SCALDER
SCALDFISH
SCALDIC
SCALDING
SCALDINI
SCALDINO
SCALDWEED
SCALDY
SCALE
SCALEBACK
SCALEBARK
SCALEBOARD
SCALED
SCALEDRAKE
SCALEFISH
SCALEFUL
SCALEMAN
SCALEMEN
SCALENE
SCALENON
SCALENOUS
SCALENUM
SCALENUS
SCALEPAN
SCALER
SCALES
SCALESMITH
SCALET
SCALETAIL
SCALEWING
SCALEWORK
SCALFE
SCALIER
SCALIEST
SCALIGER
SCALINESS
SCALING
SCALL
SCALLAGE
SCALLAWAG
SCALLED
SCALLION
SCALLOM
SCALLOP
SCALLOPED
SCALLOPER
SCALLOPING
SCALLYWAG
SCALMA
SCALOPPINE
SCALP
SCALPED
SCALPEEN
SCALPEL
SCALPELLAR
SCALPELLIC
SCALPELLUM
SCALPER
SCALPING
SCALPLESS
SCALPRA
SCALPRIFORM
SCALPRUM
SCULPTURE
SCALY
SCAM
SCAMBLE
SCAMBLED
SCAMBLER
SCAMBLING
SCAMILLUS
SCAMMEL

SCAMMONIATE
SCAMMONY
SCAMP
SCAMPAVIA
SCAMPER
SCAMPERED
SCAMPERER
SCAMPERING
SCAMPI
SCAMPING
SCAMPISH
SCAMPISHLY
SCAMPISHNESS
SCAN
SCANCE
SCANDAL
SCANDALED
SCANDALING
SCANDALIZATION
SCANDALIZE
SCANDALIZED
SCANDALIZING
SCANDALLED
SCANDALLING
SCANDALMONGER
SCANDALOUS
SCANDALOUSLY
SCANDALOUSNESS
SCANDAROON
SCANDENT
SCANDIA
SCANDIC
SCANDICUS
SCANDIUM
SCANMAG
SCANNABLE
SCANNED
SCANNER
SCANNING
SCANNINGLY
SCANSION
SCANSIONIST
SCANSORIAL
SCANSORIOUS
SCANSORY
SCANT
SCANTED
SCANTER
SCANTEST
SCANTIER
SCANTIES
SCANTIEST
SCANTILY
SCANTINESS
SCANTING
SCANTITY
SCANTLE
SCANTLET
SCANTLING
SCANTLINGED
SCANTLY
SCANTNESS
SCANTY
SCAPE
SCAPEGOAT
SCAPEGRACE
SCAPEL
SCAPELESS
SCAPETHRIFT
SCAPHA
SCAPHE
SCAPHION
SCAPHISM
SCAPHITE
SCAPHITOID
SCAPHOCERITE
SCAPHOCERITIC

SCAPHOID
SCAPHOLUNAR
SCAPHOPOD
SCAPHOPODOUS
SCAPI
SCAPIFORM
SCAPIGEROUS
SCAPOID
SCAPOLITE
SCAPOSE
SCAPPLE
SCAPPLER
SCAPULA
SCAPULAR
SCAPULARE
SCAPULARY
SCAPULATED
SCAPULET
SCAPULETTE
SCAPULIMANCY
SCAPULOPEXY
SCAPUS
SCAR
SCARAB
SCARABAEAN
SCARABAEI
SCARABAEID
SCARABAEOID
SCARABAEUS
SCARABAEUSES
SCARABEE
SCARABOID
SCARCE
SCARCELINS
SCARCELY
SCARCEMENT
SCARCEN
SCARCENESS
SCARCER
SCARCEST
SCARCITY
SCARCY
SCARE
SCAREBABE
SCAREBUG
SCARECROW
SCARECROWISH
SCARECROWY
SCARED
SCAREFUL
SCAREHEAD
SCAREMONGER
SCAREMONGERING
SCARER
SCAREY
SCARF
SCARFE
SCARFED
SCARFER
SCARFING
SCARFPIN
SCARFS
SCARFSKIN
SCARID
SCARIER
SCARIEST
SCARIFICATION
SCARIFICATOR
SCARIFIED
SCARIFIER
SCARIFY
SCARIFYING
SCARING
SCARINGLY
SCARIOLE
SCARIOSE
SCARIOUS

SCARLATINA
SCARLATINAL
SCARLATINOID
SCARLET
SCARLETBERRY
SCARLETSEED
SCARLETY
SCARN
SCAROID
SCAROLA
SCARP
SCARPA
SCARPE
SCARPED
SCARPER
SCARPETTI
SCARPH
SCARPINES
SCARPING
SCARPLET
SCARR
SCARRED
SCARRER
SCARRING
SCARROW
SCARRY
SCARS
SCART
SCARTH
SCARUS
SCARVED
SCARVES
SCARY
SCAT
SCATBACK
SCATCH
SCATH
SCATHE
SCATHED
SCATHEFUL
SCATHELESS
SCATHELESSLY
SCATHFUL
SCATHING
SCATHINGLY
SCATHY
SCATLAND
SCATOLOGIA
SCATOLOGIC
SCATOLOGICAL
SCATOLOGIST
SCATOLOGY
SCATOPHAGOUS
SCATOPHAGY
SCATOSCOPY
SCATT
SCATTED
SCATTER
SCATTERATION
SCATTERAWAY
SCATTERBRAIN
SCATTERBRAINED
SCATTERBRAINS
SCATTERED
SCATTERER
SCATTERGOOD
SCATTERING
SCATTERINGLY
SCATTERLING
SCATTERMOUCH
SCATTERY
SCATTIER
SCATTIEST
SCATTING
SCATTY
SCATULA
SCATURIENT

SCAUD
SCAUM
SCAUP
SCAUPER
SCAUPS
SCAUR
SCAURIE
SCAUT
SCAVAGE
SCAVAGER
SCAVAGERY
SCAVENAGE
SCAVENGE
SCAVENGED
SCAVENGER
SCAVENGERY
SCAVENGING
SCAW
SCAWTITE
SCAZON
SCAZONTIC
SCEAR
SCEAT
SCEGGER
SCELERAT
SCELOTYRBE
SCENA
SCENARIO
SCENARIOS
SCENARIST
SCENARIZE
SCENARIZING
SCENARY
SCEND
SCENE
SCENECRAFT
SCENERY
SCENES
SCENESHIFTER
SCENEWRIGHT
SCENIC
SCENICAL
SCENIST
SCENITE
SCENOGRAPH
SCENOGRAPHER
SCENOGRAPHIC
SCENOGRAPHY
SCENSION
SCENT
SCENTED
SCENTER
SCENTFUL
SCENTING
SCENTLESS
SCENTWOOD
SCEPSIS
SCEPTER
SCEPTERDOM
SCEPTERED
SCEPTERING
SCEPTERLESS
SCEPTIC
SCEPTICAL
SCEPTICISM
SCEPTICIZE
SCEPTICIZED
SCEPTICIZING
SCEPTRAL
SCEPTRE
SCEPTRED
SCEPTREDOM
SCEPTRELESS
SCEPTRING
SCEPTROSOPHY
SCEPTRY
SCERNE

SCETE
SCEUOPHYLAX
SCEWING
SCHADCHAN
SCHAIRERITE
SCHAL
SCHALMEI
SCHALMEY
SCHALSTEIN
SCHANZ
SCHAPPE
SCHAPPING
SCHAPSKA
SCHARF
SCHATCHEN
SCHEAT
SCHEDIASM
SCHEDULAR
SCHEDULATE
SCHEDULE
SCHEDULED
SCHEDULING
SCHEDULIZE
SCHEELIN
SCHEELITE
SCHEFFEL
SCHEFFERITE
SCHEL
SCHELLING
SCHELLY
SCHELM
SCHELTOPUSIK
SCHEMA
SCHEMATA
SCHEMATIC
SCHEMATICAL
SCHEMATICALLY
SCHEMATISM
SCHEMATIST
SCHEMATIZE
SCHEMATOGRAM
SCHEMATOGRAPH
SCHEMATONICS
SCHEME
SCHEMED
SCHEMER
SCHEMERY
SCHEMING
SCHEMIST
SCHEMOZZLE
SCHEMY
SCHENE
SCHEPEL
SCHEPEN
SCHERM
SCHERZANDO
SCHERZI
SCHERZO
SCHERZOS
SCHESIS
SCHIAVONE
SCHIFFLI
SCHIH
SCHILLER
SCHILLERFELS
SCHILLERIZE
SCHILLERIZED
SCHILLERIZING
SCHILLING
SCHILLU
SCHIMMEL
SCHIPPERKE
SCHISM
SCHISMA
SCHISMATIC
SCHISMATICAL
SCHISMATICALLY

SCHISMATISM
SCHISMATIST
SCHISMATIZE
SCHISMATIZED
SCHISMATIZING
SCHISMIC
SCHIST
SCHISTACEOUS
SCHISTIC
SCHISTOCYTE
SCHISTOID
SCHISTOSCOPE
SCHISTOSE
SCHISTOSITY
SCHISTOSOME
SCHISTOUS
SCHIZAXON
SCHIZOCARP
SCHIZOCARPIC
SCHIZOCHROAL
SCHIZOCOELE
SCHIZODINIC
SCHIZOGAMY
SCHIZOGENESIS
SCHIZOGENETIC
SCHIZOGENIC
SCHIZOGENOUS
SCHIZOGNATH
SCHIZOGONIC
SCHIZOGONY
SCHIZOID
SCHIZOIDISM
SCHIZOLITE
SCHIZOMYCETE
SCHIZOMYCETES
SCHIZONT
SCHIZOPELMOUS
SCHIZOPHASIA
SCHIZOPHRENE
SCHIZOPHRENIA
SCHIZOPHYTE
SCHIZOPOD
SCHIZOPODAL
SCHIZOPODOUS
SCHIZORHINAL
SCHIZOSPORE
SCHIZOSTELE
SCHIZOSTELIC
SCHIZOSTELY
SCHIZOTHECAL
SCHIZOTHYME
SCHIZOTHYMIA
SCHIZOTHYMIC
SCHIZOTRICHIA
SCHIZTIC
SCHIZZO
SCHLEMIEL
SCHLENTER
SCHLEPP
SCHLIEREN
SCHLOCK
SCHLOOP
SCHMALTZ
SCHMALZ
SCHMALZY
SCHMEISS
SCHMELZ
SCHMO
SCHMOOSE
SCHMOOZE
SCHMUCK
SCHNAPPER
SCHNAPPS
SCHNAUZER
SCHNEIDER
SCHNELL
SCHNITZ

SCHNITZEL
SCHNOOK
SCHNORRER
SCHNOZZLE
SCHO
SCHOCHE
SCHOENANTH
SCHOENOBATIC
SCHOKKER
SCHOLA
SCHOLAPTITUDE
SCHOLAR
SCHOLARCH
SCHOLARIAN
SCHOLARISM
SCHOLARLIKE
SCHOLARLY
SCHOLARS
SCHOLARSHIP
SCHOLASM
SCHOLASTIC
SCHOLASTICAL
SCHOLASTICALLY
SCHOLASTICATE
SCHOLASTICISM
SCHOLASTICLY
SCHOLASTICUS
SCHOLIA
SCHOLIAST
SCHOLIASTIC
SCHOLION
SCHOLIUM
SCHOLIUMS
SCHONE
SCHONFELSITE
SCHOOL
SCHOOLABLE
SCHOOLAGE
SCHOOLBOOK
SCHOOLBOOKISH
SCHOOLBOY
SCHOOLBOYDOM
SCHOOLBOYISH
SCHOOLBOYISHLY
SCHOOLBOYISM
SCHOOLCRAFT
SCHOOLDAME
SCHOOLED
SCHOOLER
SCHOOLERY
SCHOOLFELLOW
SCHOOLGIRL
SCHOOLGIRLHOOD
SCHOOLGIRLISH
SCHOOLGIRLISHLY
SCHOOLGIRLISM
SCHOOLGIRLY
SCHOOLHOUSE
SCHOOLING
SCHOOLINGLY
SCHOOLISH
SCHOOLKEEPER
SCHOOLMAN
SCHOOLMARM
SCHOOLMASTER
SCHOOLMASTERING
SCHOOLMASTERISM
SCHOOLMASTERLY
SCHOOLMASTERY
SCHOOLMATE
SCHOOLMEN
SCHOOLMISTRESS
SCHOOLMISTRESSY
SCHOOLROOM
SCHOOLTEACHER
SCHOOLTIME
SCHOOLWARD

SCHOOLWARDS
SCHOOLWORK
SCHOOLYARD
SCHOON
SCHOONER
SCHOPPEN
SCHORL
SCHORLACEOUS
SCHORLOMITE
SCHORLOUS
SCHORLY
SCHOTTISCHE
SCHOUT
SCHOUW
SCHRADAN
SCHREINER
SCHRIK
SCHROTHER
SCHRUND
SCHTICK
SCHUH
SCHUIT
SCHUL
SCHULE
SCHULTENITE
SCHUNGITE
SCHUSS
SCHUYT
SCHWA
SCHWABACHER
SCHWANPAN
SCHWARZ
SCHYL
SCIAENID
SCIAENIFORM
SCIAENOID
SCIAGRAPH
SCIAGRAPHED
SCIAGRAPHIC
SCIAGRAPHING
SCIALYTIC
SCIAMACHIES
SCIAMACHY
SCIAMETRY
SCIAPOD
SCIAPODOUS
SCIARID
SCIASCOPE
SCIASCOPY
SCIATH
SCIATHERIC
SCIATHERICAL
SCIATIC
SCIATICA
SCIATICAL
SCIATICALLY
SCIATICKY
SCIBILE
SCIENCE
SCIENCED
SCIENT
SCIENTER
SCIENTIA
SCIENTIAL
SCIENTIARUM
SCIENTIFIC
SCIENTIFICAL
SCIENTIFICALLY
SCIENTISM
SCIENTIST
SCIENTISTIC
SCIENTIZE
SCIENTOLISM
SCILICET
SCILLAIN
SCILLIPICRIN
SCILLITIN

SCILLITINE
SCILLITOXIN
SCIMETAR
SCIMITAR
SCIMITARED
SCIMITARPOD
SCIMITER
SCIMITERED
SCIMITERPOD
SCINCID
SCINCIDOID
SCINCIFORM
SCINCOID
SCINCOIDIAN
SCIND
SCINIPH
SCINK
SCINTIL
SCINTILLA
SCINTILLANT
SCINTILLANTLY
SCINTILLATE
SCINTILLATED
SCINTILLATING
SCINTILLATINGLY
SCINTILLATION
SCINTILLATOR
SCINTILLESCENT
SCINTILLOMETER
SCINTILLOSCOPE
SCINTILLOSE
SCINTILLOUS
SCINTILLOUSLY
SCINTLE
SCINTLED
SCINTLER
SCINTLING
SCIOLISM
SCIOLIST
SCIOLISTIC
SCIOLOUS
SCIOLTO
SCIOMACHY
SCIOMANCY
SCION
SCIOPHILOUS
SCIOPHYTE
SCIOPTIC
SCIOPTICON
SCIOPTICS
SCIOPTRIC
SCIOSOPHIST
SCIOSOPHY
SCIOTHEISM
SCIOUS
SCIRENGA
SCIRRHI
SCIRRHOID
SCIRRHOSIS
SCIRRHOSITIES
SCIRRHOSITY
SCIRRHOUS
SCIRRHUS
SCIRRHUSES
SCIRTOPOD
SCIRTOPODOUS
SCISCITATION
SCISSEL
SCISSIBLE
SCISSIL
SCISSILE
SCISSION
SCISSOR
SCISSORBILL
SCISSORBIRD
SCISSORED
SCISSORER

SCISSORIA
SCISSORING
SCISSORIUM
SCISSORS
SCISSORTAIL
SCISSURA
SCISSURE
SCITUATE
SCIURID
SCIURINE
SCIUROID
SCLAFF
SCLAFFED
SCLAFFER
SCLAFFERT
SCLAFFING
SCLAT
SCLATCH
SCLAW
SCLERA
SCLERAL
SCLERANTH
SCLERE
SCLEREDEMA
SCLEREID
SCLEREMA
SCLERENCHYMA
SCLERENCHYME
SCLERERYTHRIN
SCLERETINITE
SCLERIASIS
SCLERIFY
SCLERITE
SCLERITIC
SCLERITIS
SCLERIZED
SCLEROBASE
SCLEROBASIC
SCLEROBLAST
SCLEROBLASTIC
SCLEROCAULY
SCLERODERM
SCLERODERMA
SCLERODERMIA
SCLERODERMIC
SCLERODERMITE
SCLEROGEN
SCLEROGENIC
SCLEROGENOUS
SCLEROID
SCLEROMA
SCLEROMATA
SCLEROMERE
SCLEROMETER
SCLERONYCHIA
SCLERONYXIS
SCLEROPHYLL
SCLEROPHYLLY
SCLEROPROTEIN
SCLEROSAL
SCLEROSE
SCLEROSED
SCLEROSEPTUM
SCLEROSES
SCLEROSIS
SCLEROTAL
SCLEROTE
SCLEROTIA
SCLEROTIAL
SCLEROTIC
SCLEROTICA
SCLEROTICAL
SCLEROTINIAL
SCLEROTIOID
SCLEROTITIC
SCLEROTITIS
SCLEROTIUM

SCLEROTIZED
SCLEROTOID
SCLEROTOME
SCLEROTOMIC
SCLEROTOMIES
SCLEROTOMY
SCLEROUS
SCLIFF
SCLIMB
SCLUM
SCLY
SCOAD
SCOB
SCOBBY
SCOBE
SCOBICULAR
SCOBIFORM
SCOBS
SCODGY
SCOFF
SCOFFED
SCOFFER
SCOFFERY
SCOFFING
SCOFFLAW
SCOG
SCOGGAN
SCOGGER
SCOGGIN
SCOGIE
SCOKE
SCOLD
SCOLDED
SCOLDENORE
SCOLDER
SCOLDING
SCOLDINGLY
SCOLECES
SCOLECIASIS
SCOLECID
SCOLECIFORM
SCOLECITE
SCOLECOID
SCOLERYNG
SCOLEX
SCOLEY
SCOLIA
SCOLICES
SCOLIID
SCOLIOGRAPTIC
SCOLIOMETER
SCOLION
SCOLIOSIS
SCOLIOTIC
SCOLIOTONE
SCOLITE
SCOLLOP
SCOLLOPER
SCOLOC
SCOLOG
SCOLOPENDRID
SCOLOPHORE
SCOLYTID
SCOLYTOID
SCOLYTUS
SCOMBRID
SCOMBRIFORM
SCOMBRINE
SCOMBROID
SCOMBRONE
SCOMFIT
SCOMM
SCON
SCONCE
SCONCED
SCONCER
SCONCHEON

SCONCIBLE
SCONCING
SCONE
SCOOCH
SCOON
SCOOP
SCOOPED
SCOOPER
SCOOPFUL
SCOOPING
SCOOR
SCOOT
SCOOTER
SCOOTERS
SCOOTS
SCOP
SCOPA
SCOPARIN
SCOPARIUS
SCOPATE
SCOPE
SCOPELISM
SCOPHONY
SCOPIC
SCOPINE
SCOPIOUS
SCOPIPED
SCOPOLA
SCOPOLAMIN
SCOPOLAMINE
SCOPOLEINE
SCOPOLETIN
SCOPOLINE
SCOPONE
SCOPPERIL
SCOPS
SCOPTICAL
SCOPULA
SCOPULARIAN
SCOPULATE
SCOPULIPED
SCOPULITE
SCORBUCH
SCORBUTE
SCORBUTIC
SCORBUTICAL
SCORBUTIZE
SCORBUTUS
SCORCE
SCORCH
SCORCHED
SCORCHER
SCORCHING
SCORCHINGLY
SCORCHINGNESS
SCORDATO
SCORDATURA
SCORDIUM
SCORE
SCORED
SCOREKEEPER
SCORELESS
SCORER
SCORES
SCORIA
SCORIAC
SCORIACEOUS
SCORIAE
SCORIFICATION
SCORIFIED
SCORIFIER
SCORIFORM
SCORIFY
SCORIFYING
SCORING
SCORIOUS
SCORKLE

SCORN
SCORNED
SCORNER
SCORNFUL
SCORNFULLY
SCORNFULNESS
SCORNING
SCORNY
SCORODITE
SCORPAENID
SCORPAENOID
SCORPENE
SCORPER
SCORPIOID
SCORPIOIDAL
SCORPION
SCORPIONIC
SCORPIONID
SCORPIONWORT
SCORSE
SCORSER
SCORTATION
SCORTATORY
SCORZA
SCOT
SCOTAL
SCOTALE
SCOTCH
SCOTCHED
SCOTCHER
SCOTCHING
SCOTCHMAN
SCOTE
SCOTER
SCOTERS
SCOTIA
SCOTINO
SCOTODINIA
SCOTOGRAM
SCOTOGRAPH
SCOTOGRAPHIC
SCOTOGRAPHY
SCOTOMA
SCOTOMATOUS
SCOTOMIA
SCOTOMIC
SCOTOMY
SCOTOPHOBIA
SCOTOPIA
SCOTOPIC
SCOTOSCOPE
SCOTOSIS
SCOTT
SCOUCH
SCOUNDREL
SCOUNDRELISH
SCOUNDRELLY
SCOUP
SCOUR
SCOURAGE
SCOURED
SCOURER
SCOURFISH
SCOURFISHES
SCOURGE
SCOURGED
SCOURGER
SCOURGING
SCOURGINGLY
SCOURING
SCOURINGS
SCOURWAY
SCOURWEED
SCOURWORT
SCOURY
SCOUSE
SCOUT

SCOUTCRAFT
SCOUTED
SCOUTER
SCOUTH
SCOUTHER
SCOUTHOOD
SCOUTING
SCOUTMASTER
SCOUTS
SCOUTWATCH
SCOVE
SCOVEL
SCOVY
SCOW
SCOWBANK
SCOWBANKER
SCOWDER
SCOWL
SCOWLED
SCOWLER
SCOWLING
SCOWLINGLY
SCOWMAN
SCOWMEN
SCOWTHER
SCRAB
SCRABBLE
SCRABBLED
SCRABBLER
SCRABBLING
SCRABBLY
SCRABE
SCRABER
SCRAE
SCRAFFLE
SCRAG
SCRAGGED
SCRAGGEDLY
SCRAGGEDNESS
SCRAGGER
SCRAGGIER
SCRAGGIEST
SCRAGGINESS
SCRAGGING
SCRAGGLE
SCRAGGLED
SCRAGGLING
SCRAGGLY
SCRAGGY
SCRAICH
SCRAIGH
SCRAILY
SCRAM
SCRAMASAX
SCRAMBLE
SCRAMBLED
SCRAMBLER
SCRAMBLING
SCRAMBLINGLY
SCRAMBLY
SCRAMMED
SCRAMMING
SCRAMPUM
SCRAN
SCRANCH
SCRANK
SCRANKY
SCRANNEL
SCRANNIER
SCRANNIEST
SCRANNING
SCRANNY
SCRAP
SCRAPABLE
SCRAPBOOK
SCRAPE
SCRAPED

SCRAPEPENNY
SCRAPER
SCRAPIE
SCRAPING
SCRAPINGLY
SCRAPMAN
SCRAPMONGER
SCRAPPAGE
SCRAPPER
SCRAPPET
SCRAPPIER
SCRAPPIEST
SCRAPPILY
SCRAPPINESS
SCRAPPLE
SCRAPPY
SCRAPS
SCRAPY
SCRAT
SCRATCH
SCRATCHBOARD
SCRATCHBRUSH
SCRATCHCARDING
SCRATCHCAT
SCRATCHED
SCRATCHER
SCRATCHES
SCRATCHIER
SCRATCHIEST
SCRATCHING
SCRATCHWEED
SCRATCHY
SCRATTER
SCRATTLE
SCRATTLING
SCRAUCHLE
SCRAW
SCRAWK
SCRAWL
SCRAWLED
SCRAWLER
SCRAWLIER
SCRAWLIEST
SCRAWLINESS
SCRAWLING
SCRAWLY
SCRAWM
SCRAWNIER
SCRAWNIEST
SCRAWNILY
SCRAWNINESS
SCRAWNY
SCRAY
SCRAYE
SCRAZE
SCREAK
SCREAKED
SCREAKING
SCREAKY
SCREAM
SCREAMED
SCREAMER
SCREAMINESS
SCREAMING
SCREAMINGLY
SCREAMY
SCREAR
SCREE
SCREECH
SCREECHBIRD
SCREECHED
SCREECHER
SCREECHIER
SCREECHIEST
SCREECHING
SCREECHY
SCREED

SCREEK	SCRIMPIT	SCROLAR	SCRUTO	SCUNDER
SCREEL	SCRIMPTION	SCROLL	SCRUTOIRE	SCUNGILI
SCREEMAN	SCRIMPY	SCROLLED	SCRUZE	SCUNGILLI
SCREEN	SCRIMSHANK	SCROLLERY	SCRY	SCUNNER
SCREENABLE	SCRIMSHAW	SCROLLHEAD	SCRYER	SCUP
SCREENAGE	SCRIMY	SCROLLING	SCRYING	SCUPPAUG
SCREENED	SCRIN	SCROLLWORK	SCUBA	SCUPPER
SCREENER	SCRINCH	SCROLLY	SCUD	SCUPPERNONG
SCREENING	SCRINE	SCRONACH	SCUDDALER	SCUPPERS
SCREENINGS	SCRINGE	SCROO	SCUDDAWN	SCUPPET
SCREENMAN	SCRINIARY	SCROOCH	SCUDDED	SCUPPIT
SCREENO	SCRIP	SCROOP	SCUDDER	SCUPPLER
SCREENPLAY	SCRIPEE	SCROTAL	SCUDDICK	SCUR
SCREENSMAN	SCRIPPAGE	SCROTIFORM	SCUDDING	SCURDY
SCREENY	SCRIPSIT	SCROTUM	SCUDDLE	SCURF
SCREEVE	SCRIPT	SCROUGE	SCUDDY	SCURFER
SCREEVED	SCRIPTER	SCROUGER	SCUDI	SCURFIER
SCREEVER	SCRIPTION	SCROUNGE	SCUDO	SCURFIEST
SCREEVING	SCRIPTITIOUS	SCROUNGED	SCUDS	SCURFINESS
SCREW	SCRIPTITORY	SCROUNGING	SCUFE	SCURFY
SCREWBALL	SCRIPTIVE	SCROUT	SCUFF	SCURLING
SCREWBARREL	SCRIPTOR	SCROW	SCUFFED	SCURRIED
SCREWDRIVER	SCRIPTORIAL	SCROYLE	SCUFFER	SCURRIER
SCREWED	SCRIPTORIUM	SCRUB	SCUFFING	SCURRIL
SCREWER	SCRIPTORY	SCRUBBED	SCUFFLE	SCURRILE
SCREWING	SCRIPTURAL	SCRUBBER	SCUFFLED	SCURRILITY
SCREWLESS	SCRIPTURALLY	SCRUBBING	SCUFFLER	SCURRILOUS
SCREWMAN	SCRIPTURE	SCRUBBIRD	SCUFFLING	SCURRILOUSLY
SCREWPILE	SCRIPTURIENT	SCRUBBLY	SCUFFY	SCURRY
SCREWPOD	SCRIPTWRITER	SCRUBBOARD	SCUFT	SCURRYING
SCREWSMAN	SCRIPULUM	SCRUBBY	SCUFTER	SCURVIED
SCREWSTOCK	SCRIT	SCRUBGRASS	SCUG	SCURVILY
SCREWWORM	SCRITCH	SCRUBLAND	SCUGGERY	SCURVINESS
SCREWY	SCRITE	SCRUFF	SCULCH	SCURVISH
SCRIB	SCRITHE	SCRUFFLE	SCULDUDDERIES	SCURVY
SCRIBABLE	SCRIVAN	SCRUFFMAN	SCULDUDDERY	SCUSE
SCRIBACIOUS	SCRIVANO	SCRUFFY	SCULL	SCUSIN
SCRIBAL	SCRIVE	SCRUM	SCULLED	SCUT
SCRIBATIOUS	SCRIVED	SCRUMMAGE	SCULLER	SCUTA
SCRIBBET	SCRIVELLO	SCRUMMAGED	SCULLERIES	SCUTAGE
SCRIBBLAGE	SCRIVELLOES	SCRUMMAGER	SCULLERY	SCUTAL
SCRIBBLATIVE	SCRIVELLOS	SCRUMMAGING	SCULLING	SCUTATE
SCRIBBLATORY	SCRIVEN	SCRUMP	SCULLION	SCUTATED
SCRIBBLE	SCRIVENER	SCRUMPLE	SCULLOG	SCUTATIFORM
SCRIBBLED	SCRIVENERY	SCRUMPTIOUS	SCULLOGUE	SCUTATION
SCRIBBLEMENT	SCRIVENING	SCRUMPTIOUSLY	SCULLS	SCUTCH
SCRIBBLER	SCRIVER	SCRUNCH	SCULP	SCUTCHEON
SCRIBBLING	SCRIVING	SCRUNCHY	SCULPIN	SCUTCHER
SCRIBBLINGLY	SCROB	SCRUNGE	SCULPINS	SCUTCHING
SCRIBBLY	SCROBBLE	SCRUNT	SCULPSIT	SCUTE
SCRIBE	SCROBE	SCRUNTY	SCULPT	SCUTELLA
SCRIBED	SCROBICULA	SCRUPLE	SCULPTILE	SCUTELLAE
SCRIBER	SCROBICULAR	SCRUPLED	SCULPTITORY	SCUTELLAR
SCRIBING	SCROBICULATE	SCRUPLER	SCULPTOGRAPH	SCUTELLARIN
SCRIBISM	SCROBICULE	SCRUPLING	SCULPTOR	SCUTELLATE
SCRIDE	SCROBICULUS	SCRUPULAR	SCULPTRESS	SCUTELLATED
SCRIEVE	SCROBIS	SCRUPULIST	SCULPTURAL	SCUTELLATION
SCRIEVED	SCROD	SCRUPULOSITY	SCULPTURE	SCUTELLIFORM
SCRIEVER	SCRODGILL	SCRUPULOUS	SCULPTURED	SCUTELLUM
SCRIEVING	SCROFF	SCRUPULOUSLY	SCULPTURER	SCUTIFER
SCRIGGLE	SCROFULA	SCRUSH	SCULPTURESQUE	SCUTIFEROUS
SCRIGGLY	SCROFULAROOT	SCRUTABILITY	SCULPTURING	SCUTIFORM
SCRIKE	SCROFULAWEED	SCRUTABLE	SCULT	SCUTIGER
SCRIM	SCROFULISM	SCRUTATE	SCUM	SCUTIGERAL
SCRIME	SCROFULITIC	SCRUTATION	SCUMBER	SCUTIGEROUS
SCRIMER	SCROFULODERM	SCRUTATOR	SCUMBLE	SCUTIPED
SCRIMMAGE	SCROFULOSIS	SCRUTATORY	SCUMBLED	SCUTTER
SCRIMMAGED	SCROFULOUS	SCRUTINANT	SCUMBLING	SCUTTLE
SCRIMMAGER	SCROFULOUSLY	SCRUTINATE	SCUMBOARD	SCUTTLEBUTT
SCRIMMAGING	SCROG	SCRUTINEER	SCUMFISH	SCUTTLED
SCRIMP	SCROGGED	SCRUTINIZE	SCUMMED	SCUTTLEMAN
SCRIMPED	SCROGGIE	SCRUTINIZED	SCUMMER	SCUTTLER
SCRIMPER	SCROGGY	SCRUTINIZER	SCUMMIER	SCUTTLING
SCRIMPIER	SCROGIE	SCRUTINIZING	SCUMMIEST	SCUTTOCK
SCRIMPIEST	SCROGS	SCRUTINOUS	SCUMMING	SCUTTY
SCRIMPINESS	SCROINOCH	SCRUTINOUSLY	SCUMMY	SCUTULA
SCRIMPING	SCROINOGH	SCRUTINY	SCUN	SCUTULAR

SCUTULATE
SCUTULUM
SCUTUM
SCYBALUM
SCYE
SCYELITE
SCYLD
SCYLLITE
SCYLLITOL
SCYPHA
SCYPHATE
SCYPHIFORM
SCYPHISTOMA
SCYPHOPHORE
SCYPHOSE
SCYPHOZOAN
SCYPHULA
SCYPHULUS
SCYPHUS
SCYTALE
SCYTHE
SCYTHED
SCYTHEMAN
SCYTHESMITH
SCYTHESTONE
SCYTHING
SDAIN
SDEIGN
SDRUCCIOLA
SE
SEA
SEABAG
SEABEACH
SEABEARD
SEABED
SEABERRY
SEABIRD
SEABOARD
SEABOOT
SEABORDERER
SEACANNIE
SEACATCH
SEACOAST
SEACONNY
SEACRAFT
SEACRAFTY
SEACROSS
SEACUNNY
SEADOG
SEADROME
SEAFARE
SEAFARER
SEAFARING
SEAFLOOD
SEAFLOWER
SEAFOAM
SEAFOLK
SEAFOOD
SEAFOWL
SEAGIRT
SEAGOER
SEAGOING
SEAH
SEAHOUND
SEAK
SEAL
SEALABLE
SEALCH
SEALED
SEALER
SEALERIES
SEALERY
SEALET
SEALIKE
SEALINE
SEALING
SEALKIE

SEALLESS
SEALS
SEALSKIN
SEALSKINS
SEALWORT
SEAM
SEAMAN
SEAMANITE
SEAMANLIKE
SEAMANLY
SEAMANSHIP
SEAMARK
SEAMBITER
SEAMED
SEAMEN
SEAMER
SEAMIER
SEAMIEST
SEAMINESS
SEAMING
SEAMLESS
SEAMLET
SEAMLIKE
SEAMOST
SEAMOUNT
SEAMREND
SEAMROG
SEAMS
SEAMSTER
SEAMSTRESS
SEAMY
SEANCE
SEAPIECE
SEAPLANE
SEAPOOSE
SEAPORT
SEAPOST
SEAQUAKE
SEAR
SEARCE
SEARCER
SEARCH
SEARCHABLE
SEARCHANT
SEARCHER
SEARCHFUL
SEARCHING
SEARCHINGLY
SEARCHINGNESS
SEARCHLESS
SEARCHLIGHT
SEARED
SEARER
SEARING
SEARY
SEAS
SEASCAPE
SEASCOUTING
SEASHELL
SEASHINE
SEASHORE
SEASICK
SEASICKNESS
SEASIDE
SEASIDER
SEASON
SEASONABLE
SEASONABLY
SEASONAL
SEASONALITY
SEASONALLY
SEASONED
SEASONER
SEASONING
SEAT
SEATANG
SEATED

SEATER
SEATING
SEATRAIN
SEATRON
SEATS
SEATSTONE
SEAVE
SEAVY
SEAWALL
SEAWAN
SEAWARD
SEAWARDLY
SEAWARDS
SEAWARE
SEAWATER
SEAWAY
SEAWEED
SEAWIFE
SEAWORN
SEAWORTHINESS
SEAWORTHY
SEAX
SEBACATE
SEBACEOUS
SEBACIC
SEBAGO
SEBAIT
SEBASTIANITE
SEBAT
SEBEL
SEBESTEN
SEBIC
SEBIFEROUS
SEBIFIC
SEBILLA
SEBKA
SEBKHA
SEBOLITH
SEBORRHAGIA
SEBORRHEA
SEBORRHEAL
SEBORRHOEA
SEBUM
SEBUNDY
SEC
SECABLE
SECALIN
SECALINE
SECALOSE
SECANCY
SECANT
SECANTLY
SECATEUR
SECCHIO
SECCO
SECEDE
SECEDED
SECEDER
SECEDING
SECERN
SECERNED
SECERNING
SECERNMENT
SECESH
SECESHER
SECESS
SECESSION
SECESSIONAL
SECESSIONALIST
SECESSIONISM
SECESSIONIST
SECK
SECLE
SECLUDE
SECLUDED
SECLUDEDLY
SECLUDEDNESS

SECLUDING
SECLUSE
SECLUSION
SECLUSIONIST
SECLUSIVE
SECLUSIVELY
SECODONT
SECOHM
SECOND
SECONDAR
SECONDARILY
SECONDARY
SECONDE
SECONDER
SECONDHAND
SECONDINE
SECONDLY
SECONDO
SECONDS
SECOURS
SECQUE
SECRECY
SECRET
SECRETA
SECRETAGE
SECRETAIRE
SECRETAR
SECRETARIAL
SECRETARIAN
SECRETARIAT
SECRETARIES
SECRETARY
SECRETE
SECRETED
SECRETIN
SECRETING
SECRETION
SECRETIONAL
SECRETIONARY
SECRETITIOUS
SECRETIVE
SECRETIVELY
SECRETIVENESS
SECRETLY
SECRETOR
SECRETORY
SECRETS
SECRETUM
SECT
SECTA
SECTARIAL
SECTARIAN
SECTARIANISM
SECTARIANIZE
SECTARIANIZED
SECTARIANIZING
SECTARIANLY
SECTARIES
SECTARISM
SECTARIST
SECTARY
SECTATOR
SECTILE
SECTILITY
SECTION
SECTIONAL
SECTIONALISM
SECTIONALIST
SECTIONALIZE
SECTIONALIZED
SECTIONALIZING
SECTIONALLY
SECTIONARY
SECTIONIZE
SECTISM
SECTIST
SECTOR

SECTORAL
SECTORIAL
SECTUARY
SECULAR
SECULARISM
SECULARIST
SECULARISTIC
SECULARITIES
SECULARITY
SECULARIZE
SECULARIZED
SECULARIZING
SECULUM
SECUND
SECUNDINE
SECUNDIPARA
SECUNDLY
SECUNDUM
SECURABLE
SECURE
SECURED
SECUREFUL
SECURELY
SECUREMENT
SECURENESS
SECURER
SECURING
SECURITIES
SECURITY
SECUS
SECUTOR
SEDAN
SEDANIER
SEDATE
SEDATELY
SEDATENESS
SEDATION
SEDATIVE
SEDENT
SEDENTARILY
SEDENTARINESS
SEDENTARY
SEDENTATION
SEDERUNT
SEDGE
SEDGELIKE
SEDGY
SEDILE
SEDILIA
SEDILIUM
SEDIMENT
SEDIMENTAL
SEDIMENTARIES
SEDIMENTARY
SEDIMENTATE
SEDIMENTATION
SEDIMENTOUS
SEDIMETRIC
SEDITION
SEDITIONARY
SEDITIONIST
SEDITIOUS
SEDITIOUSLY
SEDITIOUSNESS
SEDJADEH
SEDUCE
SEDUCEABLE
SEDUCED
SEDUCEE
SEDUCEMENT
SEDUCER
SEDUCIBLE
SEDUCING
SEDUCIVE
SEDUCT
SEDUCTION
SEDUCTIONIST

SEDUCTIVE	SEEP	SEIGNIORAGE	SELAGITE	SELICTAR
SEDUCTIVELY	SEEPAGE	SEIGNIORAL	SELAH	SELIGMANNITE
SEDUCTIVENESS	SEEPED	SEIGNIORALTY	SELAMIN	SELIHOTH
SEDUCTRESS	SEEPWEED	SEIGNIORIES	SELAMLIK	SELING
SEDULITY	SEEPY	SEIGNIORY	SELBERGITE	SELION
SEDULOUS	SEER	SEIGNORAGE	SELCOUTH	SELL
SEDULOUSLY	SEERBAND	SEIGNORAL	SELD	SELLA
SEDULOUSNESS	SEERESS	SEIGNORIAL	SELDEN	SELLABLE
SEDUM	SEERFISH	SEIGNORIZE	SELDOM	SELLAITE
SEE	SEERHAND	SEIGNORY	SELDOMCY	SELLAR
SEECATCH	SEERPAW	SEIL	SELDOMLY	SELLARY
SEECATCHIE	SEERSUCKER	SEIMAS	SELDSEEN	SELLATE
SEECAWK	SEESAW	SEIN	SELE	SELLE
SEECHELT	SEESAWINESS	SEINE	SELECT	SELLER
SEED	SEESEE	SEINED	SELECTED	SELLING
SEEDAGE	SEET	SEINER	SELECTEDLY	SELLOUT
SEEDBALL	SEETHE	SEINING	SELECTEE	SELLY
SEEDBED	SEETHED	SEIROSPORE	SELECTING	SELSOVIET
SEEDBIRD	SEETHER	SEIROSPORIC	SELECTION	SELT
SEEDBOX	SEETHING	SEISE	SELECTIONISM	SELTZER
SEEDCAKE	SEETHINGLY	SEISM	SELECTIONIST	SELTZOGENE
SEEDCASE	SEEWEE	SEISMAL	SELECTIVE	SELVA
SEEDEATER	SEG	SEISMATICAL	SELECTIVITY	SELVAGE
SEEDED	SEGA	SEISMETIC	SELECTMAN	SELVAGED
SEEDER	SEGAR	SEISMIC	SELECTMEN	SELVAGEE
SEEDFUL	SEGATHY	SEISMICAL	SELECTNESS	SELVEDGE
SEEDGALL	SEGE	SEISMICALLY	SELECTOR	SELVEDGED
SEEDIER	SEGETAL	SEISMICITY	SELENATE	SELVES
SEEDIEST	SEGG	SEISMISM	SELENIAN	SELY
SEEDILY	SEGGE	SEISMOGRAM	SELENIATE	SEMANG
SEEDINESS	SEGGED	SEISMOGRAPH	SELENIC	SEMANTEME
SEEDING	SEGGIO	SEISMOGRAPHER	SELENIDE	SEMANTIC
SEEDKIN	SEGGIOLA	SEISMOGRAPHY	SELENIFEROUS	SEMANTICALLY
SEEDLEAF	SEGGROM	SEISMOLOGIC	SELENION	SEMANTICIST
SEEDLESS	SEGGY	SEISMOLOGICAL	SELENIOUS	SEMANTICS
SEEDLET	SEGHOL	SEISMOLOGIST	SELENITE	SEMANTOLOGY
SEEDLING	SEGHOLATE	SEISMOLOGUE	SELENITIC	SEMANTRON
SEEDLINGS	SEGMENT	SEISMOLOGY	SELENITICAL	SEMAPHORE
SEEDLIP	SEGMENTAL	SEISMOMETER	SELENIUM	SEMAPHORIST
SEEDMAN	SEGMENTALLY	SEISMOMETRIC	SELENODONT	SEMAR
SEEDNESS	SEGMENTARY	SEISMOMETRY	SELENODONTY	SEMARUM
SEEDS	SEGMENTATE	SEISMOSCOPE	SELENOGRAPH	SEMASIOLOGIST
SEEDSMAN	SEGMENTATION	SEISMOTECTONIC	SELENOGRAPHER	SEMASIOLOGY
SEEDSMEN	SEGMENTED	SEISMOTHERAPY	SELENOGRAPHIC	SEMATEME
SEEDSTALK	SEGMENTS	SEISMOTIC	SELENOGRAPHY	SEMATOGRAPHY
SEEDSTER	SEGNI	SEISOR	SELENOLOGICAL	SEMATOLOGY
SEEDTIME	SEGNO	SEIT	SELENOLOGIST	SEMATROPE
SEEDY	SEGO	SEITH	SELENOLOGY	SEMBE
SEEGE	SEGOL	SEITY	SELENOMANCY	SEMBLABLE
SEEING	SEGOLATE	SEIZABLE	SELENOSCOPE	SEMBLABLY
SEEINGLY	SEGOS	SEIZE	SELENOTROPISM	SEMBLANCE
SEEINGNESS	SEGOU	SEIZED	SELENOTROPY	SEMBLANT
SEEK	SEGRA	SEIZER	SELENSILVER	SEMBLATIVE
SEEKER	SEGREANT	SEIZIN	SELENSULPHUR	SEMBLE
SEEKING	SEGREGABLE	SEIZING	SELETAR	SEME
SEEL	SEGREGATE	SEIZOR	SELETY	SEMEE
SEELED	SEGREGATED	SEIZURE	SELEUCIA	SEMEED
SEELFUL	SEGREGATING	SEJANT	SELF	SEMEIA
SEELILY	SEGREGATION	SEJEANT	SELFDOM	SEMEIOGRAPHY
SEELINESS	SEGREGATIONAL	SEJERO	SELFFUL	SEMEIOLOGY
SEELING	SEGREGATIONIST	SEJOIN	SELFHEAL	SEMEION
SEELY	SEGREGATIVE	SEJOINED	SELFHOOD	SEMEIOTIC
SEEM	SEGREGATOR	SEJOUR	SELFISH	SEMEIOTICS
SEEMABLE	SEGUE	SEJUGATE	SELFISHLY	SEMELFACTIVE
SEEMER	SEGUENDO	SEJUGOUS	SELFISHNESS	SEMEME
SEEMING	SEGUIDILLA	SEJUNCT	SELFISM	SEMEN
SEEMINGLY	SEI	SEJUNCTION	SELFIST	SEMENCE
SEEMINGNESS	SEICENTO	SEJUNCTIVE	SELFLESS	SEMENCINAE
SEEMLESS	SEICHE	SEJUNCTIVELY	SELFLESSLY	SEMENCONTRA
SEEMLIER	SEID	SEJUNCTLY	SELFLESSNESS	SEMENTERA
SEEMLIEST	SEIDEL	SEKERE	SELFLIKE	SEMESE
SEEMLIHEAD	SEIF	SEL	SELFLY	SEMESTER
SEEMLILY	SEIGNEUR	SELACHIAN	SELFNESS	SEMESTRAL
SEEMLINESS	SEIGNEURESS	SELACHOID	SELFSAID	SEMESTRIAL
SEEMLY	SEIGNEURIAL	SELACHOSTOME	SELFSAME	SEMI
SEEN	SEIGNEURY	SELADANG	SELFSAMENESS	SEMIAN
SEENIL	SEIGNIOR	SELAGINELLA	SELI	SEMIANNA

SEMIANTHRACITE
SEMIANTIQUE
SEMIAPE
SEMIAQUATIC
SEMIARCH
SEMIBASTION
SEMIBEAM
SEMIBEJAN
SEMIBREVE
SEMIBULL
SEMIC
SEMICADENCE
SEMICELL
SEMICENTENNIAL
SEMICHA
SEMICHORIC
SEMICHORUS
SEMICIRCLE
SEMICIRCLED
SEMICIRCULAR
SEMICIRQUE
SEMICIVILIZED
SEMICLASSIC
SEMICLIMBING
SEMICOKE
SEMICOLON
SEMICOLUMN
SEMICOMA
SEMICONDUCTOR
SEMICONSCIOUS
SEMICOPE
SEMICUBICAL
SEMICUPE
SEMICURSIVE
SEMICYCLIC
SEMIDARKNESS
SEMIDEPONENT
SEMIDETACHED
SEMIDIAMETER
SEMIDIAPASON
SEMIDIAPENTE
SEMIDINE
SEMIDITONE
SEMIDIURNAL
SEMIDIVINE
SEMIDOLE
SEMIDOME
SEMIDOMED
SEMIDOUBLE
SEMIDRESS
SEMIDRYING
SEMIEDUCATED
SEMIEFFIGY
SEMIELISION
SEMIFIGURE
SEMIFINAL
SEMIFINALIST
SEMIFINISHED
SEMIFLEXIBLE
SEMIFLORET
SEMIFLOSCULE
SEMIFLUID
SEMIFLUIDIC
SEMIFORM
SEMIFORMAL
SEMIFRATER
SEMIFY
SEMIGIRDER
SEMIGLOSS
SEMIHIATUS
SEMIHORAL
SEMIJUBILEE
SEMIKAH
SEMILIQUID
SEMILOCULAR
SEMILOR
SEMILUNAR

SEMILUNATE
SEMILUNE
SEMIMACHINE
SEMIMEMBER
SEMIMETAL
SEMIMETALLIC
SEMIMINIM
SEMIMONTHLY
SEMIMUTE
SEMINAL
SEMINALITY
SEMINALLY
SEMINAR
SEMINARIAL
SEMINARIAN
SEMINARIST
SEMINARISTIC
SEMINARIZE
SEMINARY
SEMINASE
SEMINATE
SEMINATED
SEMINATING
SEMINATION
SEMINATIVE
SEMINIFERAL
SEMINIFEROUS
SEMINIFIC
SEMINIFICAL
SEMINIST
SEMINIUM
SEMINIVOROUS
SEMINOMA
SEMINOMAS
SEMINOMATA
SEMINOSE
SEMINULE
SEMINURIA
SEMINVARIANT
SEMIOFFICIAL
SEMIOFFICIALLY
SEMIOGRAPHY
SEMIOLOGIST
SEMIOLOGY
SEMIOPAL
SEMIOPAQUE
SEMIOTIC
SEMIOTICAL
SEMIOTICS
SEMIOVIPAROUS
SEMIPALMATE
SEMIPALMATION
SEMIPED
SEMIPEDAL
SEMIPERMEABLE
SEMIPLUME
SEMIPORCELAIN
SEMIPORTABLE
SEMIPOSTAL
SEMIPRECIOUS
SEMIPRIVATE
SEMIPRO
SEMIPROOF
SEMIPUPA
SEMIQUARTILE
SEMIQUAVER
SEMIQUIETIST
SEMIQUOTE
SEMIREGULAR
SEMIRIGID
SEMIRING
SEMIROTARY
SEMIROTATING
SEMIROUND
SEMIS
SEMISAGITTATE
SEMISERIOUS

SEMISERVILE
SEMISEVERE
SEMISEVERELY
SEMISEXTILE
SEMISHRUB
SEMISHRUBBY
SEMISKILLED
SEMISOFT
SEMISOLEMN
SEMISOLID
SEMISOUN
SEMISPINALIS
SEMISQUARE
SEMISTEEL
SEMISTOCK
SEMISUCCESSFUL
SEMITA
SEMITAL
SEMITANDEM
SEMITANGENT
SEMITAUR
SEMITERTIAN
SEMITONAL
SEMITONE
SEMITONIC
SEMITRAILER
SEMIUNCIAL
SEMIVOCAL
SEMIVOCALIC
SEMIVOWEL
SEMIWEEKLY
SEMIYEARLY
SEMMEL
SEMMET
SEMMIT
SEMOIS
SEMOLA
SEMOLELLA
SEMOLINA
SEMOLOGY
SEMOTED
SEMOULE
SEMPER
SEMPERIDEM
SEMPERVIRENT
SEMPERVIRID
SEMPITERN
SEMPITERNAL
SEMPITERNITY
SEMPITERNIZE
SEMPITERNOUS
SEMPLE
SEMPLICE
SEMPRE
SEMPSTER
SEMPSTRESS
SEMPSTRY
SEMSEM
SEMUL
SEMUNCIA
SEMUNCIAL
SEMY
SEN
SENACHIE
SENAGE
SENAITE
SENAL
SENAM
SENARIAN
SENARIUS
SENARMONTITE
SENARY
SENATE
SENATOR
SENATORIAL
SENATORIAN
SENATORSHIP

SENATORY
SENATRESS
SENATRIX
SENATUS
SENCIO
SENCION
SEND
SENDA
SENDAL
SENDER
SENDING
SENDLE
SENDOFF
SENE
SENECIOID
SENECIONINE
SENECTITUDE
SENECTUDE
SENECTUOUS
SENEGA
SENEGIN
SENESCE
SENESCENCE
SENESCENCY
SENESCENT
SENESCHAL
SENGE
SENGREEN
SENHOR
SENHORA
SENHORITA
SENICIDE
SENILE
SENILISM
SENILITY
SENIOR
SENIORITY
SENIORY
SENIT
SENIUM
SENN
SENNA
SENNE
SENNET
SENNETT
SENNIGHT
SENNIT
SENNITE
SENOCULAR
SENOR
SENORA
SENORES
SENORITA
SENOUFO
SENS
SENSABLE
SENSAL
SENSATE
SENSATED
SENSATING
SENSATION
SENSATIONAL
SENSATIONALISM
SENSATIONALIST
SENSATIONALISTIC
SENSATIONARY
SENSATIONISM
SENSATIONIST
SENSATIONISTIC
SENSATORIAL
SENSATORY
SENSE
SENSED
SENSEFUL
SENSELESS
SENSELESSLY
SENSELESSNESS

SENSES
SENSIBILITIES
SENSIBILITIST
SENSIBILITOUS
SENSIBILITY
SENSIBILIZATION
SENSIBILIZE
SENSIBLE
SENSIBLENESS
SENSIBLY
SENSICAL
SENSIFACIENT
SENSIFIC
SENSIFICATORY
SENSIFICS
SENSIFY
SENSILE
SENSILLA
SENSILLAE
SENSING
SENSION
SENSISM
SENSIST
SENSISTIC
SENSITIVE
SENSITIVELY
SENSITIVENESS
SENSITIVITY
SENSITIZATION
SENSITIZE
SENSITIZED
SENSITIZER
SENSITIZING
SENSITOMETER
SENSITORY
SENSIVE
SENSO
SENSOR
SENSORIA
SENSORIAL
SENSORIES
SENSORIMOTOR
SENSORIUM
SENSORIUMS
SENSORY
SENSUAL
SENSUALISE
SENSUALISM
SENSUALIST
SENSUALISTIC
SENSUALITIES
SENSUALITY
SENSUALIZE
SENSUALIZED
SENSUALIZING
SENSUALLY
SENSUALNESS
SENSUISM
SENSUIST
SENSUM
SENSUOSITY
SENSUOUS
SENSUOUSLY
SENSUOUSNESS
SENSUS
SENT
SENTENCE
SENTENCED
SENTENCER
SENTENCING
SENTENTIAL
SENTENTIALLY
SENTENTIARIST
SENTENTIARY
SENTENTIOSITY
SENTENTIOUS
SENTENTIOUSLY

SENTIENCE
SENTIENCY
SENTIENDUM
SENTIENT
SENTIMENT
SENTIMENTAL
SENTIMENTALISM
SENTIMENTALIST
SENTIMENTALITIES
SENTIMENTALITY
SENTIMENTALIZE
SENTIMENTALIZED
SENTIMENTALIZER
SENTIMENTALIZING
SENTIMENTALLY
SENTIMENTER
SENTIMENTO
SENTINE
SENTINEL
SENTINELED
SENTINELING
SENTINELLED
SENTINELLING
SENTISECTION
SENTITION
SENTRIES
SENTRY
SENUFO
SENVY
SENYE
SEPAD
SEPAL
SEPALED
SEPALINE
SEPALODY
SEPALOID
SEPALOUS
SEPARABILITY
SEPARABLE
SEPARABLENESS
SEPARABLY
SEPARATE
SEPARATED
SEPARATELY
SEPARATENESS
SEPARATICAL
SEPARATING
SEPARATION
SEPARATISM
SEPARATIST
SEPARATISTIC
SEPARATIVE
SEPARATIVELY
SEPARATIVENESS
SEPARATOR
SEPARATORY
SEPARATRIX
SEPARTE
SEPAWN
SEPHEN
SEPHIRA
SEPHIRAH
SEPIA
SEPIACEOUS
SEPIAE
SEPIAN
SEPIARIAN
SEPIARY
SEPIAS
SEPICOLOUS
SEPIMENT
SEPIOLITE
SEPION
SEPIOSTAIRE
SEPIUM
SEPON
SEPONE

SEPOSE
SEPOY
SEPPUKU
SEPS
SEPSID
SEPSIN
SEPSINE
SEPSIS
SEPT
SEPTA
SEPTAL
SEPTAN
SEPTANE
SEPTANGLE
SEPTANGLED
SEPTARIA
SEPTARIAN
SEPTARIATE
SEPTARIUM
SEPTATE
SEPTATED
SEPTATION
SEPTAVE
SEPTECTOMY
SEPTEMVIOUS
SEPTEMVIR
SEPTENAR
SEPTENARIES
SEPTENARIUS
SEPTENARY
SEPTENATE
SEPTENNATE
SEPTENNIAL
SEPTENNIUM
SEPTENTRION
SEPTET
SEPTETTE
SEPTFOIL
SEPTIC
SEPTICAL
SEPTICALLY
SEPTICEMIA
SEPTICEMIC
SEPTICIDAL
SEPTICIDE
SEPTICITY
SEPTICIZATION
SEPTIER
SEPTIFOLIOUS
SEPTIFRAGAL
SEPTILATERAL
SEPTILE
SEPTILLION
SEPTILLIONTH
SEPTIMAL
SEPTIME
SEPTIMOLE
SEPTINSULAR
SEPTIVALENT
SEPTLEVA
SEPTOCOSTA
SEPTOIC
SEPTONASAL
SEPTOTOMY
SEPTUAGENARY
SEPTULA
SEPTULATE
SEPTULUM
SEPTUM
SEPTUNCIAL
SEPTUOR
SEPTUPLE
SEPTUPLET
SEPTUPLICATE
SEPULCHER
SEPULCHERED
SEPULCHERING

SEPULCHRAL
SEPULCHRALLY
SEPULCHRE
SEPULCHRED
SEPULCHRING
SEPULCHROUS
SEPULT
SEPULTURAL
SEPULTURE
SEQUA
SEQUACES
SEQUACIOUS
SEQUACIOUSLY
SEQUACITY
SEQUEL
SEQUELA
SEQUELAE
SEQUELANT
SEQUENCE
SEQUENCER
SEQUENT
SEQUENTIAL
SEQUENTIALITY
SEQUEST
SEQUESTER
SEQUESTERED
SEQUESTERING
SEQUESTERMENT
SEQUESTRA
SEQUESTRABLE
SEQUESTRAL
SEQUESTRANT
SEQUESTRATE
SEQUESTRATED
SEQUESTRATING
SEQUESTRATION
SEQUESTRATOR
SEQUESTRUM
SEQUIN
SEQUITUR
SEQUOIA
SER
SERA
SERAB
SERAC
SERAGLI
SERAGLIO
SERAHULI
SERAI
SERAIL
SERAING
SERAL
SERAPE
SERAPH
SERAPHIC
SERAPHICAL
SERAPHICALLY
SERAPHICISM
SERAPHICNESS
SERAPHIM
SERAPHINE
SERAPHISM
SERAPHS
SERAPHTIDE
SERASKER
SERASKIER
SERASKIERAT
SERAU
SERAYA
SERCIAL
SERDAB
SERE
SEREH
SEREIN
SEREMENT
SERENA
SERENADE

SERENADED
SERENADER
SERENADING
SERENATA
SERENATAS
SERENATE
SERENDIBITE
SERENDIPITY
SERENDITE
SERENE
SERENED
SERENELY
SERENENESS
SERENIFY
SERENISSIMO
SERENITIES
SERENITY
SERENIZE
SERENO
SERF
SERFAGE
SERFDOM
SERFHOOD
SERFISM
SERFS
SERFSHIP
SERGE
SERGEANCY
SERGEANT
SERGEANTRY
SERGEANTSHIP
SERGEANTY
SERGEDESOY
SERGEDUSOY
SERGELIM
SERGER
SERGETTE
SERGING
SERGIPE
SERGLOBULIN
SERIAL
SERIALISM
SERIALITY
SERIALIZATION
SERIALIZE
SERIALIZED
SERIALIZING
SERIALLY
SERIARY
SERIATE
SERIATELY
SERIATIM
SERIATION
SERIAUNT
SERICATE
SERICATED
SERICEA
SERICEOUS
SERICICULTURE
SERICIN
SERICON
SERICTERIES
SERICTERY
SERICULTURE
SERIEMA
SERIES
SERIF
SERIFIC
SERIFORM
SERIGRAPH
SERIGRAPHER
SERIGRAPHIC
SERIGRAPHY
SERIMETER
SERIMPI
SERIN
SERINE

SERINETTE
SERINGA
SERINGAL
SERINGHI
SERIO
SERIOCOMIC
SERIOLINE
SERIOSITIES
SERIOSITY
SERIOSO
SERIOUS
SERIOUSLY
SERIOUSNESS
SERIPOSITOR
SERIR
SERJEANCY
SERJEANT
SERJEANTRY
SERJEANTY
SERMENT
SERMO
SERMON
SERMONEER
SERMONER
SERMONET
SERMONIC
SERMONICAL
SERMONICALLY
SERMONICS
SERMONISH
SERMONISM
SERMONIST
SERMONIZE
SERMONIZED
SERMONIZER
SERMONIZING
SERMONOID
SERMONOLOGY
SERMUNCLE
SERNAMBY
SERO
SEROLEMMA
SEROLIN
SEROLOGIC
SEROLOGICAL
SEROLOGIST
SEROLOGY
SERON
SERONEGATIVE
SEROON
SEROOT
SEROPOSITIVE
SEROPURULENT
SEROSA
SEROSE
SEROSITIES
SEROSITIS
SEROSITY
SEROTINAL
SEROTINE
SEROTINOUS
SEROTONIN
SEROTYPE
SEROUS
SEROUSNESS
SEROVACCINE
SEROW
SEROZEM
SERPEDINOUS
SERPENT
SERPENTARIA
SERPENTARIUM
SERPENTARY
SERPENTEAU
SERPENTESS
SERPENTILE
SERPENTIN

SERPENTINE	SERVANT	SESSA	SETULA	SEXCENTENARY
SERPENTINIC	SERVANTS	SESSILE	SETULE	SEXDIGITAL
SERPENTINIZE	SERVATION	SESSILITY	SETULIFORM	SEXDIGITATE
SERPENTINOID	SERVE	SESSION	SETULOSE	SEXDIGITATED
SERPENTINOUS	SERVED	SESSIONAL	SETULOUS	SEXDIGITISM
SERPENTIZE	SERVENTE	SESSIONALLY	SETUP	SEXED
SERPENTLIKE	SERVER	SESSIONARY	SETWALL	SEXENARY
SERPENTLY	SERVERY	SESSIONS	SETWISE	SEXENNIAL
SERPENTOID	SERVES	SESSPOOL	SETWORK	SEXENNIUM
SERPENTRY	SERVET	SESTERCE	SETWORKS	SEXERN
SERPENTWOOD	SERVETTE	SESTERCES	SEUCH	SEXIER
SERPETTE	SERVIABLE	SESTERTIA	SEUDAH	SEXIEST
SERPHID	SERVICE	SESTERTIUM	SEUGH	SEXISM
SERPHOID	SERVICEABLE	SESTERTIUS	SEVE	SEXIST
SERPIERITE	SERVICEABLY	SESTET	SEVEN	SEXISYLLABLE
SERPIGINOUS	SERVICEBERRIES	SESTETTO	SEVENBARK	SEXLESS
SERPIGO	SERVICEBERRY	SESTI	SEVENER	SEXLESSLY
SERPIVOLANT	SERVICED	SESTIAD	SEVENFOLD	SEXLESSNESS
SERPOLET	SERVICELESS	SESTINA	SEVENFOLDED	SEXLIKE
SERPULAN	SERVICEMAN	SESTINE	SEVENSCORE	SEXLY
SERPULID	SERVICEMEN	SESTOLE	SEVENTEEN	SEXOLOGIC
SERPULIDAN	SERVICING	SESTOLET	SEVENTEENTH	SEXOLOGICAL
SERPULINE	SERVIENT	SESTON	SEVENTH	SEXOLOGIST
SERPULITE	SERVIETTE	SESTUOR	SEVENTHLY	SEXOLOGY
SERPULOID	SERVILE	SET	SEVENTIES	SEXPARTITE
SERR	SERVILELY	SETA	SEVENTIETH	SEXPLOITATION
SERRA	SERVILENESS	SETACEOUS	SEVENTY	SEXT
SERRADELLA	SERVILISM	SETACEOUSLY	SEVER	SEXTACTIC
SERRAE	SERVILITIES	SETAE	SEVERABLE	SEXTAIN
SERRAGE	SERVILITY	SETAL	SEVERAL	SEXTAN
SERRAI	SERVING	SETARID	SEVERALITY	SEXTANS
SERRAN	SERVINGMAN	SETARIOUS	SEVERALIZE	SEXTANT
SERRANA	SERVIST	SETATION	SEVERALLY	SEXTANTAL
SERRANID	SERVITEUR	SETBACK	SEVERALTY	SEXTARIUS
SERRANO	SERVITIAL	SETBOLT	SEVERANCE	SEXTENNIAL
SERRANOID	SERVITIUM	SETDOWN	SEVERATE	SEXTERN
SERRANOS	SERVITOR	SETE	SEVERATION	SEXTET
SERRATE	SERVITORIAL	SETER	SEVERE	SEXTETTE
SERRATED	SERVITRIX	SETH	SEVERED	SEXTIC
SERRATIA	SERVITUDE	SETHEAD	SEVERELY	SEXTILE
SERRATIC	SERVITURE	SETIER	SEVERENESS	SEXTILLION
SERRATILE	SERVO	SETIFEROUS	SEVERER	SEXTILLIONTH
SERRATION	SERVOMECHANISM	SETIFORM	SEVEREST	SEXTIPARA
SERRATURE	SERVOMOTOR	SETIGER	SEVERING	SEXTIPARTITE
SERRATUS	SERVOS	SETLINE	SEVERISH	SEXTIPLY
SERRICORN	SERVOTAB	SETLING	SEVERITY	SEXTIPOLAR
SERRIED	SERVULATE	SETNESS	SEVERIZE	SEXTO
SERRIEDLY	SERVUS	SETNET	SEVERY	SEXTOLE
SERRIEDNESS	SERWAMBY	SETOFF	SEVIER	SEXTOLET
SERRIFEROUS	SESAME	SETON	SEVILLANAS	SEXTON
SERRIFORM	SESAMIN	SETOSE	SEVUM	SEXTRY
SERRING	SESAMINE	SETOUS	SEW	SEXTUOR
SERRIPED	SESAMOID	SETOUT	SEWAGE	SEXTUPLE
SERRULA	SESAMOIDAL	SETOVER	SEWAN	SEXTUPLED
SERRULATE	SESAMOIDITIS	SETSCREW	SEWED	SEXTUPLET
SERRULATED	SESAMOL	SETSMAN	SEWELLEL	SEXTUPLICATE
SERRULATION	SESCUPLE	SETT	SEWEN	SEXTUPLICATED
SERRURERIE	SESI	SETTAINE	SEWER	SEXTUPLICATING
SERRY	SESKIN	SETTE	SEWERAGE	SEXTUPLING
SERRYING	SESMA	SETTECENTO	SEWERED	SEXTUPLY
SERT	SESPERAL	SETTEE	SEWERMAN	SEXTUR
SERTA	SESQUI	SETTER	SEWERY	SEXUAL
SERTO	SESQUIALTER	SETTERGRASS	SEWIN	SEXUALE
SERTULARIAN	SESQUIALTERA	SETTERS	SEWING	SEXUALISM
SERTULARIOID	SESQUIALTERAL	SETTERWORT	SEWLESS	SEXUALIST
SERTULAROID	SESQUICENTENNIAL	SETTIMA	SEWN	SEXUALITY
SERTULE	SESQUINONA	SETTIMO	SEWROUND	SEXUALIZE
SERTULUM	SESQUINONAL	SETTING	SEWSTER	SEXUALLY
SERTUM	SESQUIOCTAVA	SETTLE	SEX	SEXUOUS
SERULE	SESQUIPEDAL	SETTLED	SEXADECIMAL	SEXUPARA
SERUM	SESQUIPLICATE	SETTLEMENT	SEXAGENARIAN	SEXUPAROUS
SERUMAL	SESQUIQUARTA	SETTLEMENTS	SEXAGENARY	SEXY
SERUMS	SESQUIQUINTA	SETTLER	SEXAGESIMAL	SEY
SERVABLE	SESQUISEXTAL	SETTLERS	SEXANGLE	SEYBERTITE
SERVAGE	SESQUITERPENE	SETTLING	SEXANGLED	SEYID
SERVAL	SESQUITERTIA	SETTLOR	SEXANGULAR	SFERICS
SERVALINE	SESS	SETTSMAN	SEXANGULARLY	SFOGATO

SFORZANDO
SFORZANDOS
SFORZATO
SFUMATO
SGABELLO
SGRAFFIATO
SGRAFFITO
SHA
SHAATNEZ
SHAB
SHABANDAR
SHABASH
SHABBAT
SHABBED
SHABBIER
SHABBIEST
SHABBIFY
SHABBILY
SHABBINESS
SHABBLE
SHABBOS
SHABBY
SHABEQUE
SHABRACK
SHABROON
SHABUNDER
SHACHLE
SHACK
SHACKANITE
SHACKATORY
SHACKBOLT
SHACKLE
SHACKLEBONE
SHACKLED
SHACKLER
SHACKLING
SHACKLY
SHACKY
SHAD
SHADBELLY
SHADBERRIES
SHADBERRY
SHADBIRD
SHADBLOW
SHADBUSH
SHADCHAN
SHADDOCK
SHADE
SHADED
SHADER
SHADES
SHADETAIL
SHADFLOWER
SHADIER
SHADIEST
SHADILY
SHADINE
SHADINESS
SHADING
SHADKAN
SHADOOF
SHADOW
SHADOWBOX
SHADOWED
SHADOWER
SHADOWGRAM
SHADOWGRAPH
SHADOWINESS
SHADOWING
SHADOWIST
SHADOWLAND
SHADOWLESS
SHADOWLY
SHADOWS
SHADOWY
SHADRACH
SHADS

SHADUF
SHADY
SHAFFLE
SHAFII
SHAFT
SHAFTED
SHAFTER
SHAFTING
SHAFTMAN
SHAFTMENT
SHAFTSMAN
SHAFTWAY
SHAFTY
SHAG
SHAGANAPPI
SHAGANAPPY
SHAGBARK
SHAGBUSH
SHAGGED
SHAGGEDNESS
SHAGGIER
SHAGGIEST
SHAGGILY
SHAGGINESS
SHAGGING
SHAGGY
SHAGLET
SHAGRAG
SHAGREEN
SHAGREENED
SHAGROON
SHAGTAIL
SHAH
SHAHARIT
SHAHARITH
SHAHDOM
SHAHEE
SHAHEEN
SHAHI
SHAHIDI
SHAHIN
SHAHZADA
SHAHZADAH
SHAIKH
SHAIKHI
SHAIRD
SHAIRN
SHAITAN
SHAKABLE
SHAKE
SHAKEABLE
SHAKEDOWN
SHAKEFORK
SHAKEN
SHAKEOUT
SHAKEPROOF
SHAKER
SHAKES
SHAKESCENE
SHAKEUP
SHAKHA
SHAKIER
SHAKIEST
SHAKILY
SHAKINESS
SHAKING
SHAKINGS
SHAKO
SHAKOS
SHAKSHEER
SHAKTIS
SHAKU
SHAKY
SHAL
SHALDER
SHALE
SHALED

SHALEE
SHALEMAN
SHALL
SHALLAL
SHALLON
SHALLOON
SHALLOP
SHALLOT
SHALLOW
SHALLOWER
SHALLOWEST
SHALLOWLY
SHALLOWNESS
SHALLOWPATE
SHALLOWPATED
SHALLU
SHALLY
SHALM
SHALOM
SHALWAR
SHALY
SHAM
SHAMA
SHAMAL
SHAMAN
SHAMANESS
SHAMANIC
SHAMANISM
SHAMANIST
SHAMANISTIC
SHAMATEUR
SHAMATEURISM
SHAMBA
SHAMBLE
SHAMBLED
SHAMBLES
SHAMBLING
SHAMBRIER
SHAME
SHAMED
SHAMEFACE
SHAMEFACED
SHAMEFACEDLY
SHAMEFACEDNESS
SHAMEFAST
SHAMEFASTLY
SHAMEFASTNESS
SHAMEFUL
SHAMEFULLY
SHAMEFULNESS
SHAMELESS
SHAMELESSLY
SHAMELESSNESS
SHAMER
SHAMES
SHAMIANAH
SHAMING
SHAMMAS
SHAMMASH
SHAMMED
SHAMMER
SHAMMING
SHAMMISH
SHAMMOCK
SHAMMOCKING
SHAMMOS
SHAMMY
SHAMPOO
SHAMPOOED
SHAMPOOER
SHAMPOOING
SHAMROCK
SHAMROOT
SHAMSHEER
SHAMUS
SHANACHAS
SHANACHIE

SHANACHUS
SHAND
SHANDITE
SHANDRY
SHANDRYDAN
SHANDY
SHANDYGAFF
SHANGAN
SHANGHAI
SHANGHAIED
SHANGHAIING
SHANGY
SHANK
SHANKED
SHANKER
SHANKING
SHANKINGS
SHANKPIECE
SHANKS
SHANNA
SHANNY
SHANT
SHANTEY
SHANTIES
SHANTUNG
SHANTY
SHANTYMAN
SHANTYMEN
SHANTYTOWN
SHAPABLE
SHAPE
SHAPED
SHAPEFUL
SHAPELESS
SHAPELESSLY
SHAPELESSNESS
SHAPELIER
SHAPELIEST
SHAPELINESS
SHAPELY
SHAPEN
SHAPER
SHAPEUP
SHAPIER
SHAPIEST
SHAPING
SHAPINGLY
SHAPOMETER
SHAPOO
SHAPY
SHAR
SHARD
SHARDY
SHARE
SHAREBONE
SHAREBROKER
SHARECROPPER
SHARED
SHAREEF
SHAREHOLDER
SHAREMAN
SHAREPENNY
SHARER
SHARES
SHAREWORT
SHARGAR
SHARGER
SHARGOSS
SHARIAT
SHARING
SHARK
SHARKED
SHARKER
SHARKI
SHARKING
SHARKISH
SHARKLET

SHARKSKIN
SHARKY
SHARN
SHARNBUD
SHARNBUG
SHARNY
SHARON
SHARP
SHARPED
SHARPEN
SHARPENED
SHARPENER
SHARPENING
SHARPER
SHARPERS
SHARPEST
SHARPIE
SHARPING
SHARPISH
SHARPITE
SHARPLING
SHARPLY
SHARPNESS
SHARPS
SHARPSAW
SHARPSHOD
SHARPSHOOTER
SHARPTAIL
SHARPWARE
SHARPY
SHARRY
SHASLIK
SHASTAITE
SHASTRA
SHASTRAIK
SHASTRAS
SHASTRI
SHASTRIK
SHAT
SHATHMONT
SHATTER
SHATTERBRAIN
SHATTERED
SHATTERER
SHATTERING
SHATTERPATED
SHATTERPROOF
SHATTERWIT
SHATTERY
SHATTUCKITE
SHAUCHLE
SHAUGH
SHAUL
SHAUP
SHAURI
SHAVE
SHAVED
SHAVEE
SHAVELING
SHAVEN
SHAVER
SHAVERY
SHAVESTER
SHAVETAIL
SHAVIE
SHAVING
SHAVINGS
SHAW
SHAWABTI
SHAWFOWL
SHAWL
SHAWLED
SHAWLING
SHAWM
SHAWNEEWOOD
SHAWNY
SHAY

SHAYED	SHEEPHERDER	SHELLAPPLE	SHERBET	SHIFTS
SHAYKH	SHEEPHERDING	SHELLBACK	SHERBETLEE	SHIFTY
SHCHI	SHEEPHOOK	SHELLBARK	SHERBETZIDE	SHIGGAION
SHE	SHEEPIFIED	SHELLBLOW	SHERD	SHIGIONOTH
SHEA	SHEEPIFY	SHELLBOUND	SHERE	SHIGRAM
SHEADING	SHEEPIFYING	SHELLBURST	SHEREEF	SHIH
SHEAF	SHEEPISH	SHELLEATER	SHERIAT	SHIKAR
SHEAFAGE	SHEEPISHLY	SHELLED	SHERIF	SHIKARA
SHEAFY	SHEEPISHNESS	SHELLER	SHERIFATE	SHIKAREE
SHEAL	SHEEPKILL	SHELLFIRE	SHERIFF	SHIKARGAH
SHEALING	SHEEPLIKE	SHELLFISH	SHERIFFDOM	SHIKARI
SHEAR	SHEEPMAN	SHELLFISHERIES	SHERIFFESS	SHIKASTA
SHEARBILL	SHEEPMASTER	SHELLFISHERY	SHERIFFRY	SHIKII
SHEARED	SHEEPMEN	SHELLFISHES	SHERIFFWICK	SHIKIMI
SHEARER	SHEEPMINT	SHELLFLOWER	SHERIFIAN	SHIKIMOL
SHEARERS	SHEEPNOSE	SHELLHEAD	SHERISTADAR	SHIKIMOTOXIN
SHEARGRASS	SHEEPNUT	SHELLIER	SHERLOCK	SHIKKEN
SHEARHOG	SHEEPPEN	SHELLING	SHEROOT	SHIKO
SHEARING	SHEEPSHEAD	SHELLMAN	SHERRIES	SHIKRA
SHEARLING	SHEEPSHEADS	SHELLMEN	SHERRIS	SHIKSE
SHEARMAN	SHEEPSHEAR	SHELLMONGER	SHERRY	SHILF
SHEARMOUSE	SHEEPSHEARER	SHELLPAD	SHERRYVALLIES	SHILFA
SHEARS	SHEEPSHEARING	SHELLPOT	SHERWANI	SHILL
SHEARTAIL	SHEEPSKIN	SHELLPROOF	SHETH	SHILLA
SHEARWATER	SHEEPSKINS	SHELLS	SHEUCH	SHILLABER
SHEARWATERS	SHEEPSPLIT	SHELLUM	SHEUGH	SHILLALA
SHEATFISH	SHEEPSTEAL	SHELLWORK	SHEVEL	SHILLALAH
SHEATFISHES	SHEEPWALK	SHELLY	SHEVELED	SHILLELAGH
SHEATH	SHEEPWALKER	SHELLYCOAT	SHEVRI	SHILLER
SHEATHBILL	SHEEPWEED	SHELM	SHEW	SHILLET
SHEATHE	SHEEPY	SHELTA	SHEWBREAD	SHILLETY
SHEATHED	SHEER	SHELTER	SHEWEL	SHILLIBEER
SHEATHER	SHEERING	SHELTERAGE	SHEWER	SHILLING
SHEATHERY	SHEERLY	SHELTERED	SHEYLE	SHILLOO
SHEATHING	SHEERNESS	SHELTERER	SHI	SHILLY
SHEATHS	SHEERS	SHELTERING	SHIBAH	SHILP
SHEAVE	SHEET	SHELTERLESS	SHIBAR	SHILPIT
SHEAVED	SHEETAGE	SHELTERWOOD	SHIBBOLETH	SHIM
SHEAVEMAN	SHEETED	SHELTERY	SHIBUICHI	SHIMAL
SHEAVES	SHEETER	SHELTIE	SHICE	SHIMMED
SHEAVING	SHEETFLOOD	SHELTIES	SHICER	SHIMMER
SHEBANG	SHEETING	SHELTRON	SHICK	SHIMMERED
SHEBAR	SHEETLET	SHELTY	SHICKER	SHIMMERING
SHEBEEN	SHEETS	SHELVE	SHICKERED	SHIMMERY
SHEBEENER	SHEETWASH	SHELVED	SHICKSA	SHIMMEY
SHECHITA	SHEETWAYS	SHELVER	SHIDE	SHIMMIED
SHED	SHEETWISE	SHELVES	SHIED	SHIMMING
SHEDDED	SHEETWORK	SHELVING	SHIEL	SHIMMY
SHEDDER	SHEETY	SHELVY	SHIELD	SHIMMYING
SHEDDING	SHEEVE	SHENANIGAN	SHIELDED	SHIMOSE
SHEDER	SHEGETZ	SHEND	SHIELDER	SHIMPER
SHEDHAND	SHEHITA	SHENDFUL	SHIELDFERN	SHIN
SHEDIM	SHEIK	SHENDING	SHIELDFLOWER	SHINARUMP
SHEDMAN	SHEIKDOM	SHENG	SHIELDING	SHINBONE
SHEDU	SHEIKH	SHENT	SHIELDLESS	SHINDIG
SHEE	SHEIKHDOM	SHEOGUE	SHIELDLESSLY	SHINDLE
SHEEFISH	SHEIKHLY	SHEOL	SHIELDLESSNESS	SHINDY
SHEELING	SHEIKLY	SHEOLIC	SHIELDMAY	SHINE
SHEEN	SHEILING	SHEP	SHIELDS	SHINED
SHEENLY	SHEITAN	SHEPE	SHIELDTAIL	SHINER
SHEENY	SHEITEL	SHEPHERD	SHIELING	SHING
SHEEP	SHEKEL	SHEPHERDESS	SHIER	SHINGLE
SHEEPBACK	SHELA	SHEPHERDISM	SHIEST	SHINGLED
SHEEPBACKS	SHELAH	SHEPHERDS	SHIFT	SHINGLER
SHEEPBERRY	SHELD	SHEPHERDY	SHIFTED	SHINGLES
SHEEPBINE	SHELDER	SHEPPECK	SHIFTER	SHINGLEWOOD
SHEEPBITER	SHELDFOWL	SHEPPERDING	SHIFTFUL	SHINGLING
SHEEPBITING	SHELDRAKE	SHEPPEY	SHIFTFULNESS	SHINGLY
SHEEPCOT	SHELDRAKES	SHEPPHERDED	SHIFTIER	SHINGON
SHEEPCOTE	SHELDUCK	SHEPPICK	SHIFTIEST	SHINIER
SHEEPCROOK	SHELF	SHEPSTARE	SHIFTINESS	SHINIEST
SHEEPFACED	SHELL	SHEPSTER	SHIFTING	SHININESS
SHEEPFOLD	SHELLAC	SHER	SHIFTINGLY	SHINING
SHEEPFOOT	SHELLACK	SHERARDIZE	SHIFTLESS	SHININGLY
SHEEPFOOTS	SHELLACKED	SHERARDIZED	SHIFTLESSLY	SHININGNESS
SHEEPGATE	SHELLACKING	SHERARDIZING	SHIFTLESSNESS	SHINLEAF
SHEEPHEADED	SHELLAK	SHERBACHA	SHIFTMAN	SHINNER

SHINNERIES
SHINNERY
SHINNIED
SHINNY
SHINNYING
SHINPLASTER
SHINS
SHINTAI
SHINTIYAN
SHINTY
SHINTYAN
SHINWOOD
SHINY
SHINZA
SHIP
SHIPBOARD
SHIPBOY
SHIPBUILDER
SHIPBUILDING
SHIPFERD
SHIPFITTER
SHIPFUL
SHIPFULS
SHIPHIRE
SHIPHOLDER
SHIPKEEPER
SHIPLAP
SHIPLET
SHIPLOAD
SHIPMAN
SHIPMANSHIP
SHIPMAST
SHIPMASTER
SHIPMATE
SHIPMEN
SHIPMENT
SHIPOWNER
SHIPPABLE
SHIPPAGE
SHIPPED
SHIPPEN
SHIPPER
SHIPPING
SHIPPLANE
SHIPPO
SHIPPON
SHIPPY
SHIPRADE
SHIPS
SHIPSHAPE
SHIPSIDE
SHIPWAY
SHIPWORM
SHIPWRECK
SHIPWRECKY
SHIPWRIGHT
SHIPYARD
SHIR
SHIRALEE
SHIRE
SHIREHOUSE
SHIREMAN
SHIREMEN
SHIRK
SHIRKER
SHIRL
SHIRPIT
SHIRR
SHIRRA
SHIRRED
SHIRREL
SHIRRER
SHIRRING
SHIRT
SHIRTBAND
SHIRTING
SHIRTLESS

SHIRTLESSNESS
SHIRTMAKER
SHIRTMAKING
SHIRTMAN
SHIRTMEN
SHIRTS
SHIRTTAIL
SHIRTWAIST
SHIRTY
SHISH
SHISHAM
SHISN
SHIST
SHITA
SHITHER
SHITTAH
SHITTEN
SHITTIMWOOD
SHITTLE
SHIV
SHIVA
SHIVAREE
SHIVE
SHIVER
SHIVERED
SHIVEREENS
SHIVERING
SHIVERINGLY
SHIVERS
SHIVERWEED
SHIVERY
SHIVEY
SHIVOO
SHIVVY
SHIZOKU
SHLEMIEL
SHO
SHOADER
SHOAL
SHOALBRAIN
SHOALER
SHOALIER
SHOALIEST
SHOALINESS
SHOALNESS
SHOALY
SHOAR
SHOAT
SHOCHET
SHOCK
SHOCKABLE
SHOCKED
SHOCKER
SHOCKHEAD
SHOCKHEADED
SHOCKING
SHOCKINGLY
SHOCKINGNESS
SHOCKS
SHOD
SHODDIED
SHODDIER
SHODDIES
SHODDIEST
SHODDY
SHODDYING
SHODE
SHODER
SHOE
SHOEBILL
SHOEBINDER
SHOEBINDERY
SHOEBINDING
SHOEBIRD
SHOEBLACK
SHOEBOY
SHOECRAFT

SHOEFLOWER
SHOEHORN
SHOEING
SHOEINGSMITH
SHOELACE
SHOEMAKE
SHOEMAKER
SHOEMAKING
SHOEMAN
SHOEPAC
SHOEPACK
SHOER
SHOES
SHOESHINE
SHOESTRING
SHOETREE
SHOFAR
SHOFUL
SHOG
SHOGGIE
SHOGGLE
SHOGGLY
SHOGI
SHOGUN
SHOHET
SHOJI
SHOLA
SHOLE
SHOMA
SHONDE
SHONE
SHONEEN
SHONEENS
SHONKINITE
SHOO
SHOOD
SHOOFA
SHOOFLIES
SHOOFLY
SHOOGLE
SHOOH
SHOOI
SHOOK
SHOOL
SHOON
SHOOP
SHOOT
SHOOTER
SHOOTING
SHOOTIST
SHOOTMAN
SHOP
SHOPBOARD
SHOPBOOK
SHOPBOY
SHOPBREAKER
SHOPBREAKING
SHOPGIRL
SHOPHAR
SHOPKEEPER
SHOPKEEPERY
SHOPKEEPING
SHOPLIFT
SHOPLIFTER
SHOPLIFTING
SHOPLIKE
SHOPMAID
SHOPMAN
SHOPMARK
SHOPMATE
SHOPOCRACY
SHOPOCRAT
SHOPPE
SHOPPED
SHOPPER
SHOPPIER
SHOPPIEST

SHOPPING
SHOPPINI
SHOPPISH
SHOPPY
SHOPSTER
SHOPTALK
SHOPWALKER
SHOPWEAR
SHOPWINDOW
SHOPWORK
SHOPWORKER
SHOPWORN
SHOQ
SHOR
SHORAN
SHORE
SHOREBERRY
SHOREBIRD
SHORED
SHOREFISH
SHORELAND
SHORELESS
SHORELINE
SHOREMAN
SHORER
SHORESMAN
SHOREWARD
SHOREWARDS
SHOREYER
SHORING
SHORL
SHORN
SHORT
SHORTAGE
SHORTBREAD
SHORTCAKE
SHORTCHANGE
SHORTCHANGED
SHORTCHANGER
SHORTCHANGING
SHORTCOAT
SHORTCOMER
SHORTCOMING
SHORTCUT
SHORTEN
SHORTENED
SHORTENER
SHORTENING
SHORTER
SHORTEST
SHORTFALL
SHORTHAND
SHORTHANDED
SHORTHEAD
SHORTHEELS
SHORTHORN
SHORTIA
SHORTIE
SHORTISH
SHORTITE
SHORTLY
SHORTNESS
SHORTS
SHORTSIGHTED
SHORTSIGHTEDLY
SHORTSOME
SHORTSTAFF
SHORTSTOP
SHORTY
SHOSHONITE
SHOT
SHOTBUSH
SHOTCRETE
SHOTE
SHOTGUN
SHOTMAKER
SHOTMAN

SHOTS
SHOTSHELL
SHOTSTAR
SHOTT
SHOTTED
SHOTTEN
SHOTTY
SHOU
SHOUGH
SHOULD
SHOULDER
SHOULDERED
SHOULDERER
SHOULDERETTE
SHOULDERING
SHOULDERS
SHOULDEST
SHOULDNA
SHOULDST
SHOULERD
SHOUT
SHOUTED
SHOUTER
SHOUTHER
SHOUTING
SHOUTS
SHOVAL
SHOVE
SHOVED
SHOVEL
SHOVELBILL
SHOVELBOARD
SHOVELED
SHOVELER
SHOVELFISH
SHOVELHEAD
SHOVELLED
SHOVELLING
SHOVELNOSE
SHOVELWEED
SHOVER
SHOVING
SHOW
SHOWABLE
SHOWANCE
SHOWBIRD
SHOWBOARD
SHOWBOAT
SHOWBREAD
SHOWCASE
SHOWD
SHOWDOWN
SHOWED
SHOWER
SHOWERED
SHOWERER
SHOWERIER
SHOWERIEST
SHOWERING
SHOWERY
SHOWFUL
SHOWIER
SHOWIEST
SHOWILY
SHOWINESS
SHOWING
SHOWISH
SHOWMAN
SHOWMANSHIP
SHOWN
SHOWOFF
SHOWPIECE
SHOWROOM
SHOWSHOP
SHOWUP
SHOWY
SHOYA

SHOYU	SHRIVEL	SHUNNED	SIBYLIC	SIDEBONE
SHRAB	SHRIVELED	SHUNNER	SIBYLLA	SIDEBONES
SHRADD	SHRIVELING	SHUNNING	SIBYLLAE	SIDEBOX
SHRADDHA	SHRIVELLED	SHUNPIKE	SIBYLLIC	SIDEBURNS
SHRAG	SHRIVELLING	SHUNT	SIBYLLINE	SIDECAR
SHRAM	SHRIVEN	SHUNTED	SIBYLLISM	SIDECHECK
SHRAME	SHRIVER	SHUNTER	SIBYLLIST	SIDED
SHRAMMED	SHRIVING	SHUNTING	SIC	SIDEFLASH
SHRANK	SHROFF	SHURE	SICARIAN	SIDEHEAD
SHRAP	SHROG	SHURF	SICARII	SIDEHILL
SHRAPE	SHROGS	SHURGEE	SICARIOUS	SIDEHOLD
SHRAPNEL	SHROUD	SHUSH	SICARIUS	SIDEKICK
SHRAVE	SHROUDED	SHUT	SICCA	SIDELANG
SHRAVEY	SHROUDING	SHUTDOWN	SICCANEOUS	SIDELIGHT
SHRED	SHROUDS	SHUTE	SICCANT	SIDELINE
SHREDCOCK	SHROUDY	SHUTEYE	SICCAR	SIDELINED
SHREDDED	SHROVE	SHUTOFF	SICCATE	SIDELING
SHREDDER	SHROVED	SHUTOUT	SICCATED	SIDELINGS
SHREDDING	SHROVER	SHUTTER	SICCATING	SIDELINING
SHREDDY	SHROVING	SHUTTERBUG	SICCATION	SIDELINS
SHREDS	SHROVY	SHUTTERING	SICCATIVE	SIDELOCK
SHREE	SHRUB	SHUTTING	SICCIMETER	SIDELONG
SHREEVE	SHRUBBED	SHUTTLE	SICCITY	SIDEMAN
SHREND	SHRUBBERIES	SHUTTLECOCK	SICE	SIDENESS
SHREW	SHRUBBERY	SHUTTLECOCKED	SICER	SIDENOTE
SHREWD	SHRUBBIER	SHUTTLECOCKING	SICHT	SIDEPIECE
SHREWDER	SHRUBBIEST	SHUTTLER	SICILIENNE	SIDER
SHREWDEST	SHRUBBINESS	SHUTTLEWISE	SICINNIAN	SIDERAL
SHREWDLY	SHRUBBY	SHWA	SICK	SIDERATE
SHREWDNESS	SHRUBLET	SHWANPAN	SICKBAY	SIDERATED
SHREWDY	SHRUBS	SHWEBO	SICKBED	SIDERATION
SHREWISH	SHRUBWOOD	SHY	SICKED	SIDEREAL
SHREWISHLY	SHRUFF	SHYER	SICKEN	SIDEREALIZE
SHREWISHNESS	SHRUG	SHYING	SICKENED	SIDEREALLY
SHREWMOUSE	SHRUGGED	SHYISH	SICKENER	SIDEREAN
SHREWSTRUCK	SHRUGGING	SHYLY	SICKENING	SIDERISM
SHRI	SHRUNK	SHYNESS	SICKENINGLY	SIDERITE
SHRIDE	SHRUNKEN	SHYSTER	SICKER	SIDERITIC
SHRIEK	SHRUPS	SI	SICKEST	SIDEROGNOST
SHRIEKED	SHRUTI	SIACALLE	SICKET	SIDEROGRAPHY
SHRIEKER	SHTCHEE	SIAFU	SICKING	SIDEROLITE
SHRIEKERY	SHTETEL	SIAK	SICKISH	SIDEROLOGY
SHRIEKING	SHTETL	SIAL	SICKISHLY	SIDEROMANCY
SHRIEKY	SHTICK	SIALAGOGIC	SICKISHNESS	SIDEROMELANE
SHRIEVAL	SHUBA	SIALAGOGUE	SICKLE	SIDERONATRITE
SHRIEVALTIES	SHUBUNKIN	SIALIC	SICKLEBILL	SIDERONYM
SHRIEVALTY	SHUCK	SIALID	SICKLED	SIDEROSCOPE
SHRIEVE	SHUCKED	SIALIDAN	SICKLEMAN	SIDEROSE
SHRIFT	SHUCKER	SIALOID	SICKLEMEN	SIDEROSIS
SHRIKE	SHUCKING	SIAMANG	SICKLEMIA	SIDEROSTAT
SHRILL	SHUCKS	SIAMESE	SICKLEPOD	SIDEROSTATIC
SHRILLED	SHUD	SIAMOISE	SICKLER	SIDEROUS
SHRILLER	SHUDDER	SIAPO	SICKLERITE	SIDES
SHRILLEST	SHUDDERED	SIAULIAI	SICKLEWORT	SIDESADDLE
SHRILLING	SHUDDERING	SIB	SICKLIED	SIDESHAKE
SHRILLY	SHUDDERSOME	SIBBED	SICKLIER	SIDESHOW
SHRIMP	SHUDDERY	SIBBENDY	SICKLIEST	SIDESLIP
SHRIMPER	SHUDE	SIBBENS	SICKLILY	SIDESMAN
SHRIMPFISH	SHUDNA	SIBBING	SICKLING	SIDESMEN
SHRIMPI	SHUFF	SIBERITE	SICKLY	SIDESPIN
SHRIMPISH	SHUFFLE	SIBILANCE	SICKLYING	SIDESPLITTER
SHRIMPISHNESS	SHUFFLEBOARD	SIBILANCY	SICKNESS	SIDESPLITTING
SHRIMPY	SHUFFLECAP	SIBILANT	SICKROOM	SIDESTEP
SHRINAL	SHUFFLED	SIBILANTLY	SICLIKE	SIDESTEPPED
SHRINE	SHUFFLER	SIBILATE	SICSAC	SIDESTEPPER
SHRINED	SHUFFLEWING	SIBILATOR	SICU	SIDESTEPPING
SHRINING	SHUFFLING	SIBILATORY	SICULA	SIDESWAY
SHRINK	SHUG	SIBILI	SICULAR	SIDESWIPE
SHRINKABLE	SHUILER	SIBILOUS	SIDDER	SIDESWIPED
SHRINKAGE	SHUL	SIBILUS	SIDDOW	SIDESWIPER
SHRINKER	SHULER	SIBLING	SIDDUR	SIDESWIPING
SHRINKING	SHULWAURS	SIBNESS	SIDE	SIDETONE
SHRINKINGLY	SHUMAN	SIBREDE	SIDEAGE	SIDETRACK
SHRIP	SHUN	SIBRIT	SIDEARM	SIDETRACKED
SHRITE	SHUNE	SIBSHIP	SIDEBAND	SIDETRACKING
SHRIVE	SHUNLESS	SIBUCAO	SIDEBAR	SIDEWALK
SHRIVED	SHUNNABLE	SIBYL	SIDEBOARD	SIDEWALL

SIDEWARD	SIGHTFULNESS	SIGNIFICAL	SILGREEN	SILLOGRAPHER
SIDEWARDS	SIGHTHOLE	SIGNIFICANCE	SILHOUETTE	SILLOMETER
SIDEWASH	SIGHTING	SIGNIFICANCY	SILHOUETTED	SILLON
SIDEWAY	SIGHTLESS	SIGNIFICANT	SILHOUETTING	SILLY
SIDEWAYS	SIGHTLESSLY	SIGNIFICANTLY	SILHOUETTIST	SILLYHOW
SIDEWINDER	SIGHTLESSNESS	SIGNIFICATE	SILICA	SILLYTON
SIDEWISE	SIGHTLIER	SIGNIFICATION	SILICAM	SILO
SIDHE	SIGHTLY	SIGNIFICATIVE	SILICATE	SILOED
SIDI	SIGHTPROOF	SIGNIFICATOR	SILICATION	SILOING
SIDING	SIGHTS	SIGNIFICATORY	SILICATIZATION	SILOS
SIDLE	SIGHTSEEING	SIGNIFICATURE	SILICEAN	SILOXANE
SIDLED	SIGHTSMAN	SIGNIFICAVIT	SILICEOUS	SILPHID
SIDLER	SIGHTY	SIGNIFICIAN	SILICIC	SILPHIUM
SIDLING	SIGIL	SIGNIFICS	SILICIDE	SILT
SIDLINGLY	SIGILLARIAN	SIGNIFIE	SILICIDIZE	SILTAGE
SIDLINS	SIGILLARID	SIGNIFIED	SILICIFEROUS	SILTATION
SIDTH	SIGILLARIOID	SIGNIFIER	SILICIFIED	SILTED
SIDY	SIGILLARIST	SIGNIFY	SILICIFY	SILTING
SIE	SIGILLARY	SIGNIFYING	SILICIFYING	SILTY
SIECLE	SIGILLATE	SIGNING	SILICIOPHITE	SILUNDUM
SIEGE	SIGILLATED	SIGNIOR	SILICIOUS	SILURID
SIEGED	SIGILLATION	SIGNIST	SILICIUM	SILUROID
SIEGENITE	SIGILLATIVE	SIGNITOR	SILICIZE	SILVA
SIEGER	SIGILLISTIC	SIGNLESS	SILICLE	SILVAN
SIEGEWORK	SIGILLOGRAPHY	SIGNMAN	SILICON	SILVANITY
SIEGING	SIGILLUM	SIGNOR	SILICONE	SILVANRY
SIENITE	SIGLA	SIGNORA	SILICONIZE	SILVENDY
SIENITIC	SIGLARIAN	SIGNORE	SILICOSIS	SILVER
SIENNA	SIGLOS	SIGNORIA	SILICOTIC	SILVERBACK
SIER	SIGLUM	SIGNORIAL	SILICULA	SILVERBELLY
SIEROZEM	SIGMA	SIGNORINA	SILICULAR	SILVERBERRIES
SIERRA	SIGMASPIRE	SIGNORINE	SILICULE	SILVERBERRY
SIERRAN	SIGMATE	SIGNORINO	SILICULOSE	SILVERBIDDY
SIESTA	SIGMATIC	SIGNORY	SILICULOUS	SILVERBILL
SIEUR	SIGMATION	SIGNPOST	SILICYL	SILVERBUSH
SIEVE	SIGMODONT	SIGNS	SILIQUA	SILVERED
SIEVED	SIGMOID	SIGNUM	SILIQUE	SILVERER
SIEVEFUL	SIGMOIDAL	SIGNWRITER	SILIQUOSE	SILVERFIN
SIEVELIKE	SIGMOIDALLY	SIGRIM	SILIQUOSE	SILVERFISH
SIEVER	SIGMOIDITIS	SIJIL	SILK	SILVERFISHES
SIEVING	SIGN	SIJILL	SILKALENE	SILVERIER
SIEVINGS	SIGNABLE	SIKA	SILKALINE	SILVERIEST
SIEVY	SIGNACLE	SIKAR	SILKED	SILVERINESS
SIFAC	SIGNAL	SIKARA	SILKEN	SILVERING
SIFAKA	SIGNALED	SIKE	SILKER	SILVERITE
SIFE	SIGNALER	SIKER	SILKFLOWER	SILVERIZE
SIFF	SIGNALETIC	SIKERLY	SILKGROWER	SILVERLEAF
SIFFILATE	SIGNALETICS	SIKHARA	SILKIE	SILVERLING
SIFFLE	SIGNALING	SIKIMI	SILKIER	SILVERLY
SIFFLEMENT	SIGNALIST	SIKSIKA	SILKIEST	SILVERN
SIFFLET	SIGNALITIES	SIKU	SILKILY	SILVERROD
SIFFLEUR	SIGNALITY	SIL	SILKINESS	SILVERSIDE
SIFFLEURS	SIGNALIZE	SILAGE	SILKMAN	SILVERSIDES
SIFFLEUSE	SIGNALIZED	SILANE	SILKMEN	SILVERSKIN
SIFFLEUSES	SIGNALIZING	SILANGA	SILKNESS	SILVERSMITH
SIFFLOT	SIGNALLER	SILCRETE	SILKSMAN	SILVERSMITHING
SIFT	SIGNALLING	SILD	SILKTAIL	SILVERSMITHS
SIFTAGE	SIGNALLY	SILE	SILKWEED	SILVERSPOT
SIFTED	SIGNALMAN	SILEN	SILKWOMAN	SILVERTAIL
SIFTER	SIGNALMENT	SILENACEOUS	SILKWOOD	SILVERTIP
SIFTING	SIGNANCE	SILENCE	SILKWORK	SILVERTOP
SIG	SIGNARY	SILENCED	SILKWORKER	SILVERVINE
SIGATOKA	SIGNATE	SILENCER	SILKWORKS	SILVERWARE
SIGGER	SIGNATION	SILENCING	SILKWORM	SILVERWEED
SIGH	SIGNATOR	SILENIC	SILKY	SILVERWING
SIGHED	SIGNATORY	SILENT	SILL	SILVERWOOD
SIGHER	SIGNATURAL	SILENTIAL	SILLABUB	SILVERWORK
SIGHFUL	SIGNATURE	SILENTIARY	SILLADAR	SILVERY
SIGHING	SIGNATURIST	SILENTIOUS	SILLANDAR	SILVICAL
SIGHINGLY	SIGNBOARD	SILENTIUM	SILLAR	SILVICOLOUS
SIGHINGNESS	SIGNED	SILENTLY	SILLER	SILVICS
SIGHT	SIGNEE	SILENTNESS	SILLIER	SILVICULTURE
SIGHTED	SIGNER	SILENTS	SILLIES	SIM
SIGHTEN	SIGNET	SILENUS	SILLIEST	SIMA
SIGHTENING	SIGNEURY	SILESIA	SILLILY	SIMAGRE
SIGHTER	SIGNIFER	SILEX	SILLINESS	SIMAL
SIGHTFUL	SIGNIFIABLE	SILEXITE	SILLOCK	SIMAR
			SILLOGRAPH	

SIMARA	SIMPLICITY	SINECURE	SINISTRATION	SIPHONOGAM
SIMARRE	SIMPLICIZE	SINECURED	SINISTRIN	SIPHONOGAMIC
SIMARUBA	SIMPLIFICATION	SINECURING	SINISTRORSAL	SIPHONOGLYPH
SIMBA	SIMPLIFICATIVE	SINECURISM	SINISTRORSE	SIPHONOPHORAN
SIMBALL	SIMPLIFICATOR	SINECURIST	SINISTROUS	SIPHONOPHORE
SIMBIL	SIMPLIFIED	SINEW	SINISTROUSLY	SIPHONOPLAX
SIMBLIN	SIMPLIFIEDLY	SINEWED	SINJER	SIPHONOSOME
SIMBLING	SIMPLIFIER	SINEWING	SINK	SIPHONOSTELE
SIMBLOT	SIMPLIFY	SINEWLESS	SINKAGE	SIPHONOSTELIC
SIME	SIMPLIFYING	SINEWOUS	SINKBOAT	SIPHONOSTELY
SIMIAD	SIMPLING	SINEWY	SINKBOX	SIPHONOSTOME
SIMIAL	SIMPLISM	SINFONIA	SINKER	SIPHONOZOOID
SIMIAN	SIMPLIST	SINFUL	SINKHEAD	SIPHONULA
SIMIANITY	SIMPLISTIC	SINFULLY	SINKHOLE	SIPHORHINAL
SIMIESQUE	SIMPLUM	SINFULNESS	SINKING	SIPHUNCLE
SIMIID	SIMPLY	SING	SINKLESS	SIPHUNCLED
SIMILAR	SIMPSON	SINGABLE	SINKROOM	SIPHUNCULAR
SIMILARITY	SIMRI	SINGALLY	SINKSTONE	SIPID
SIMILARLY	SIMSON	SINGARIP	SINKY	SIPIDITY
SIMILATE	SIMULACRA	SINGE	SINLESS	SIPING
SIMILATIVE	SIMULACRAL	SINGED	SINLESSLY	SIPLING
SIMILE	SIMULACRE	SINGEING	SINLESSNESS	SIPO
SIMILIMUM	SIMULACRIZE	SINGEINGLY	SINNED	SIPPED
SIMILITER	SIMULACRUM	SINGER	SINNER	SIPPER
SIMILITIVE	SIMULANCE	SINGERESS	SINNET	SIPPET
SIMILITUDE	SIMULANT	SINGERIE	SINNING	SIPPING
SIMILITUDINIZE	SIMULAR	SINGERS	SINNOWED	SIPPIO
SIMILIZE	SIMULATE	SINGH	SINOMENINE	SIPPLE
SIMILOR	SIMULATED	SINGILLATIM	SINOPIA	SIPUNCULID
SIMIOID	SIMULATING	SINGING	SINOPITE	SIPUNCULOID
SIMIOUS	SIMULATION	SINGKAMAS	SINOPLE	SIPYLITE
SIMIOUSNESS	SIMULATIVE	SINGLE	SINSRING	SIR
SIMIR	SIMULATIVELY	SINGLEBAR	SINSYNE	SIRCAR
SIMITAR	SIMULATOR	SINGLED	SINTER	SIRDAR
SIMITY	SIMULATORY	SINGLEHANDED	SINTOC	SIRE
SIMKIN	SIMULCAST	SINGLEHANDEDLY	SINUATE	SIRED
SIMLIN	SIMULE	SINGLEHANDEDNESS	SINUATED	SIRELESS
SIMLING	SIMULIID	SINGLEHEARTED	SINUATEDENTATE	SIREN
SIMMER	SIMULIZE	SINGLEHEARTEDLY	SINUATELY	SIRENE
SIMMERED	SIMULTANEOUS	SINGLEHEARTEDNESS	SINUATING	SIRENIAN
SIMMERING	SIMULTANEOUSLY	SINGLEHOOD	SINUATION	SIRENIC
SIMMON	SIMULTY	SINGLENESS	SINUITIS	SIRENICAL
SIMMONS	SIMURG	SINGLER	SINUOSE	SIRENICALLY
SIMNEL	SIMURGH	SINGLES	SINUOSITIES	SIRENING
SIMOLEON	SIN	SINGLESTICK	SINUOSITY	SIRENIZE
SIMONIAC	SINA	SINGLET	SINUOUS	SIRENOID
SIMONIACAL	SINAITE	SINGLETON	SINUOUSLY	SIRENOMELUS
SIMONIOUS	SINAL	SINGLETREE	SINUOUSNESS	SIRENY
SIMONISM	SINALBIN	SINGLING	SINUPALLIAL	SIREX
SIMONIST	SINAMAY	SINGLY	SINUPALLIATE	SIRGANG
SIMONIZE	SINAMIN	SINGSONG	SINUS	SIRI
SIMONY	SINAMINE	SINGSPIEL	SINUSAL	SIRIAN
SIMOOM	SINAPATE	SINGSTRESS	SINUSITIS	SIRICID
SIMOON	SINAPIC	SINGULAR	SINUSOID	SIRIH
SIMOUS	SINAPIN	SINGULARISM	SINUSOIDAL	SIRING
SIMP	SINAPINE	SINGULARIST	SINUSOIDALLY	SIRIOMETER
SIMPAI	SINAPISM	SINGULARITIES	SINZER	SIRKAR
SIMPATICO	SINAPIZE	SINGULARITY	SIOL	SIRKEER
SIMPER	SINAPOLINE	SINGULARIZATION	SION	SIRKI
SIMPERED	SINAWA	SINGULARIZE	SIP	SIRKY
SIMPERER	SINCALINE	SINGULARIZED	SIPAGE	SIRLOIN
SIMPERING	SINCAMAS	SINGULARIZING	SIPAPU	SIRLOINY
SIMPERINGLY	SINCE	SINGULARLY	SIPE	SIRMARK
SIMPLE	SINCERE	SINGULARNESS	SIPER	SIROCCO
SIMPLED	SINCERELY	SINGULT	SIPERS	SIROS
SIMPLER	SINCERENESS	SINGULTOUS	SIPHAC	SIRPEA
SIMPLES	SINCERER	SINGULTUS	SIPHON	SIRPLE
SIMPLEST	SINCEREST	SINHASAN	SIPHONACEOUS	SIRPOON
SIMPLETON	SINCERITY	SINIGRIN	SIPHONAGE	SIRRAH
SIMPLETONIAN	SINCIPITAL	SINISTER	SIPHONAL	SIRREE
SIMPLETONIC	SINCIPUT	SINISTERLY	SIPHONATED	SIRS
SIMPLEX	SINDER	SINISTERNESS	SIPHONEOUS	SIRSE
SIMPLEXED	SINDLE	SINISTRA	SIPHONET	SIRUABALLI
SIMPLEXITY	SINDON	SINISTRAD	SIPHONIA	SIRUELAS
SIMPLICIST	SINE	SINISTRAL	SIPHONIC	SIRUP
SIMPLICITER	SINEBADA	SINISTRALITY	SIPHONIFORM	SIRUPED
SIMPLICITIES	SINECURAL	SINISTRALLY	SIPHONIUM	SIRUPER

SIRUPY	SIWASHED	SKATING	SKEP	SKIDPROOF
SIRVENT	SIWASHING	SKATIST	SKEPFUL	SKIDS
SIS	SIX	SKATOL	SKEPPE	SKIDWAY
SISAL	SIXAIN	SKATOLE	SKEPPIST	SKIED
SISALANA	SIXER	SKATOLOGY	SKEPPUND	SKIEGH
SISCOWET	SIXFOLD	SKATOSINE	SKEPSIS	SKIEPPE
SISE	SIXMO	SKATOXYL	SKEPTIC	SKIER
SISEL	SIXPENCE	SKEAN	SKEPTICAL	SKIES
SISERARA	SIXPENCES	SKEANOCKLE	SKEPTICALLY	SKIEUR
SISERARY	SIXPENNY	SKEAT	SKEPTICALNESS	SKIFF
SISH	SIXPENNYWORTH	SKED	SKEPTICISM	SKIFFLE
SISI	SIXSCORE	SKEDADDLE	SKEPTICIZE	SKIFFLED
SISITH	SIXSOME	SKEDADDLED	SKEPTICIZED	SKIFFLING
SISKIN	SIXTE	SKEDADDLER	SKEPTICIZING	SKIFT
SISS	SIXTEEN	SKEDADDLING	SKERM	SKIING
SISSIES	SIXTEENER	SKEDGE	SKERRICK	SKIJORE
SISSIFICATION	SIXTEENMO	SKEDLOCK	SKERRIES	SKIJORER
SISSIFIED	SIXTEENTH	SKEE	SKERRY	SKIJORING
SISSONE	SIXTH	SKEED	SKETCH	SKIL
SISSONNE	SIXTIES	SKEEG	SKETCHABLE	SKILDER
SISSOO	SIXTIETH	SKEEING	SKETCHBOOK	SKILDFEL
SISSU	SIXTY	SKEEL	SKETCHED	SKILFISH
SISSY	SIZABLE	SKEELING	SKETCHER	SKILFUL
SIST	SIZABLENESS	SKEENYIE	SKETCHIER	SKILFULLY
SISTEN	SIZABLY	SKEER	SKETCHIEST	SKILL
SISTER	SIZAR	SKEERED	SKETCHILY	SKILLAGALEE
SISTERHOOD	SIZARSHIP	SKEERY	SKETCHINESS	SKILLED
SISTERING	SIZE	SKEES	SKETCHING	SKILLET
SISTERIZE	SIZEABLE	SKEESICKS	SKETCHIST	SKILLFUL
SISTERLINESS	SIZED	SKEET	SKETCHY	SKILLFULLY
SISTERLY	SIZEINE	SKEETER	SKETE	SKILLFULNESS
SISTERN	SIZEMAN	SKEEZIX	SKETIOTAI	SKILLING
SISTERS	SIZER	SKEG	SKEUOMORPH	SKILLION
SISTERSHIP	SIZES	SKEGGER	SKEVISH	SKILLO
SISTLE	SIZIER	SKEICH	SKEW	SKILLS
SISTOMENSIN	SIZIEST	SKEIF	SKEWBACK	SKILLY
SISTREN	SIZINESS	SKEIGH	SKEWBACKED	SKILPOT
SISTROID	SIZING	SKEIN	SKEWBALD	SKILTS
SISTRUM	SIZINGS	SKEINER	SKEWED	SKILTY
SIT	SIZY	SKELB	SKEWER	SKIM
SITAO	SIZYGIUM	SKELDER	SKEWERED	SKIMBACK
SITAR	SIZZ	SKELDOCK	SKEWERER	SKIME
SITATUNGA	SIZZARD	SKELDRAKE	SKEWERING	SKIMMED
SITATUNGAS	SIZZING	SKELET	SKEWERWOOD	SKIMMER
SITE	SIZZLE	SKELETAL	SKEWING	SKIMMING
SITFAST	SIZZLED	SKELETIN	SKEWINGS	SKIMMINGS
SITH	SIZZLER	SKELETON	SKEWL	SKIMMINGTON
SITHE	SIZZLING	SKELETONIAN	SKEWNESS	SKIMMITY
SITHENCE	SIZZLINGLY	SKELETONIC	SKEWWISE	SKIMP
SITHENS	SJAMBOK	SKELETONIZATION	SKEWY	SKIMPIER
SITHES	SJOMIL	SKELETONIZE	SKEY	SKIMPIEST
SITIENT	SJOMILA	SKELETONIZED	SKEYTING	SKIMPILY
SITIO	SKAALPUND	SKELETONIZER	SKHIAN	SKIMPINESS
SITOLOGY	SKAAMOOG	SKELETONIZING	SKI	SKIMPY
SITOMANIA	SKADDLE	SKELETONY	SKIAGRAM	SKIN
SITOSTERIN	SKAFF	SKELF	SKIAGRAPH	SKINBALL
SITOSTEROL	SKAFFIE	SKELGOOSE	SKIAGRAPHED	SKINBOUND
SITOTOXISM	SKAG	SKELL	SKIAGRAPHIC	SKINCH
SITREP	SKAIF	SKELLAT	SKIAGRAPHING	SKINFLICK
SITTER	SKAIL	SKELLER	SKIAMETER	SKINFLINT
SITTINE	SKAILLIE	SKELLOCH	SKIAMETRY	SKINFLINTILY
SITTING	SKAINSMATE	SKELLUM	SKIAPOD	SKINFLINTINESS
SITTRINGY	SKAIR	SKELLY	SKIAPODOUS	SKINFLINTY
SITU	SKAITBIRD	SKELP	SKIASCOPE	SKINFUL
SITUAL	SKAITHY	SKELPED	SKIASCOPY	SKINFULS
SITUATE	SKALAWAG	SKELPER	SKIBBET	SKINHEAD
SITUATED	SKALD	SKELPIN	SKIBBY	SKINK
SITUATION	SKALDIC	SKELPING	SKICE	SKINKED
SITUATIONAL	SKALPUND	SKELTER	SKID	SKINKER
SITULA	SKANDHAS	SKELVY	SKIDDED	SKINKING
SITUS	SKARN	SKEMMEL	SKIDDER	SKINKLE
SITZ	SKAT	SKEMP	SKIDDING	SKINLESS
SITZMARK	SKATE	SKEN	SKIDDOO	SKINNED
SIVE	SKATED	SKENAI	SKIDDY	SKINNER
SIVER	SKATER	SKENE	SKIDDYCOCK	SKINNERS
SIVVENS	SKATES	SKEO	SKIDOO	SKINNERY
SIWASH	SKATIKAS	SKEOUGH	SKIDPAN	SKINNIER

SKINNIEST	SKLINTER	SKYT	SLANGIEST	SLAUGHTERDOM
SKINNING	SKOAL	SKYUGLE	SLANGILY	SLAUGHTERED
SKINNY	SKOGBOLITE	SKYWARD	SLANGINESS	SLAUGHTERER
SKINS	SKOKIAAN	SKYWARDS	SLANGING	SLAUGHTERHOUSE
SKINTIGHT	SKOLLY	SKYWAY	SLANGISH	SLAUGHTERING
SKINWORM	SKOMERITE	SKYWRITE	SLANGISHLY	SLAUGHTERMAN
SKIOGRAM	SKOOKUM	SKYWRITER	SLANGISM	SLAUGHTEROUS
SKIOGRAPH	SKOOT	SKYWRITING	SLANGKOP	SLAUGHTEROUSLY
SKIP	SKOUT	SLA	SLANGOUS	SLAUM
SKIPBRAIN	SKRAELLING	SLAB	SLANGRELL	SLAVE
SKIPDENT	SKREEL	SLABBED	SLANGSTER	SLAVED
SKIPJACK	SKREIGH	SLABBER	SLANGUAGE	SLAVEHOLDER
SKIPJACKLY	SKRIKE	SLABBERED	SLANGULAR	SLAVEHOLDING
SKIPJACKS	SKRUPUL	SLABBERER	SLANGY	SLAVELET
SKIPKENNEL	SKRYER	SLABBERING	SLANK	SLAVELING
SKIPMAN	SKUA	SLABBERY	SLANT	SLAVER
SKIPPED	SKUG	SLABBINESS	SLANTED	SLAVERED
SKIPPER	SKULDUGGERY	SLABBING	SLANTER	SLAVERER
SKIPPERED	SKULK	SLABBY	SLANTING	SLAVERING
SKIPPERSHIP	SKULKED	SLABMAN	SLANTINGLY	SLAVERY
SKIPPERY	SKULKER	SLABS	SLANTLY	SLAVES
SKIPPET	SKULKING	SLABSTONE	SLANTWAYS	SLAVEY
SKIPPING	SKULL	SLABWOOD	SLANTWISE	SLAVIKITE
SKIPPLE	SKULLBANKER	SLACK	SLAP	SLAVIN
SKIPPUND	SKULLCAP	SLACKAGE	SLAPDAB	SLAVING
SKIPPY	SKULLERY	SLACKED	SLAPDASH	SLAVISH
SKIPS	SKULLFISH	SLACKEN	SLAPDASHERIES	SLAVOCRACY
SKIPTAIL	SKULLY	SLACKENED	SLAPDASHERY	SLAVOCRAT
SKIRL	SKUNK	SLACKENING	SLAPE	SLAVOCRATIC
SKIRLCOCK	SKUNKBILL	SLACKER	SLAPHAPPIER	SLAW
SKIRLING	SKUNKBUSH	SLACKEST	SLAPHAPPIEST	SLAWBANK
SKIRM	SKUNKERY	SLACKIE	SLAPHAPPY	SLAY
SKIRMISH	SKUNKISH	SLACKING	SLAPJACK	SLAYER
SKIRMISHED	SKUNKTOP	SLACKLY	SLAPPED	SLEATHY
SKIRMISHER	SKUNKWEED	SLACKNESS	SLAPPER	SLEAVE
SKIRMISHING	SKUNKY	SLACKS	SLAPPING	SLEAVED
SKIRP	SKURRY	SLAD	SLAPPY	SLEAVING
SKIRR	SKUTTERUDITE	SLADE	SLAPSTICK	SLEAZINESS
SKIRREH	SKY	SLAG	SLARE	SLEAZY
SKIRRET	SKYBAL	SLAGGED	SLART	SLED
SKIRT	SKYBALD	SLAGGING	SLARTH	SLEDDED
SKIRTBOARD	SKYCOACH	SLAGGY	SLASH	SLEDDER
SKIRTED	SKYCRAFT	SLAIN	SLASHED	SLEDDING
SKIRTER	SKYED	SLAINTE	SLASHER	SLEDGE
SKIRTING	SKYER	SLAISTER	SLASHERS	SLEDGED
SKIRTS	SKYEY	SLAISTERY	SLASHING	SLEDGEHAMMER
SKIRTY	SKYFTE	SLAIT	SLASHINGLY	SLEDGEMETER
SKIS	SKYHOOK	SLAKE	SLASHY	SLEDGER
SKISE	SKYHOOT	SLAKED	SLAT	SLEDGING
SKISH	SKYING	SLAKELESS	SLATCH	SLEE
SKIT	SKYISH	SLAKER	SLATE	SLEECH
SKITE	SKYJACK	SLAKIER	SLATED	SLEECHY
SKITER	SKYJACKING	SLAKIEST	SLATELIKE	SLEEK
SKITHER	SKYLARK	SLAKIN	SLATER	SLEEKED
SKITTER	SKYLARKED	SLAKING	SLATES	SLEEKEN
SKITTERY	SKYLARKER	SLAKY	SLATH	SLEEKENED
SKITTISH	SKYLARKING	SLALOM	SLATHER	SLEEKENING
SKITTISHLY	SKYLESS	SLAM	SLATIER	SLEEKER
SKITTISHNESS	SKYLIGHT	SLAMBANG	SLATIEST	SLEEKIER
SKITTLE	SKYLINE	SLAMMED	SLATIFIED	SLEEKING
SKITTLED	SKYLOOK	SLAMMING	SLATIFY	SLEEKIT
SKITTLES	SKYMAN	SLAMMOCK	SLATIFYING	SLEEKLY
SKITTLING	SKYME	SLAMMOCKING	SLATING	SLEEKNESS
SKITTY	SKYPHOS	SLAMMOCKY	SLATISH	SLEEKY
SKITTYBOOT	SKYPORT	SLAMP	SLATS	SLEEP
SKIV	SKYR	SLAMPAMP	SLATTED	SLEEPER
SKIVE	SKYRE	SLAMPANT	SLATTER	SLEEPERED
SKIVED	SKYRGALIARD	SLANDER	SLATTERED	SLEEPIER
SKIVER	SKYRIN	SLANDERER	SLATTERING	SLEEPIEST
SKIVERWOOD	SKYROCKET	SLANDERING	SLATTERN	SLEEPIFY
SKIVIE	SKYROCKETY	SLANDEROUS	SLATTERNISH	SLEEPING
SKIVING	SKYSAIL	SLANDEROUSLY	SLATTERNLINESS	SLEEPISH
SKIVVIES	SKYSCAPE	SLANDEROUSNESS	SLATTERNLY	SLEEPLESS
SKIVVY	SKYSCRAPER	SLANE	SLATTERY	SLEEPLESSLY
SKLENT	SKYSCRAPING	SLANG	SLATTING	SLEEPLESSNESS
SKLEROPELITE	SKYSHINE	SLANGED	SLATY	SLEEPMARKEN
SKLIM	SKYSTONE	SLANGIER	SLAUGHTER	SLEEPRY

SLEEPWALK	SLIDDERY	SLIPCASE	SLIVOVITZ	SLOPSTONE
SLEEPWALKER	SLIDDRY	SLIPCOAT	SLIVVER	SLOPWORK
SLEEPWALKING	SLIDE	SLIPCOTE	SLO	SLOPWORKER
SLEEPWORT	SLIDEGROAT	SLIPCOVER	SLOAK	SLOPY
SLEEPY	SLIDEHEAD	SLIPE	SLOAN	SLORP
SLEEPYHEAD	SLIDEKNOT	SLIPES	SLOAT	SLOSH
SLEER	SLIDEMAN	SLIPHALTER	SLOB	SLOSHED
SLEET	SLIDER	SLIPHORN	SLOBBER	SLOSHER
SLEETED	SLIDEWAY	SLIPHOUSE	SLOBBERCHOPS	SLOSHILY
SLEETIER	SLIDING	SLIPKNOT	SLOBBERER	SLOSHINESS
SLEETIEST	SLIDOMETER	SLIPMAN	SLOBBERS	SLOSHING
SLEETING	SLIER	SLIPOVER	SLOBBERY	SLOSHY
SLEETY	SLIEST	SLIPPAGE	SLOBBY	SLOT
SLEEVE	SLIFTER	SLIPPED	SLOCK	SLOTE
SLEEVED	SLIGGEEN	SLIPPER	SLOCKEN	SLOTH
SLEEVEEN	SLIGHT	SLIPPERED	SLOCKER	SLOTHFUL
SLEEVEFISH	SLIGHTED	SLIPPERFLOWER	SLOCKINGSTONE	SLOTHFULLY
SLEEVELESS	SLIGHTER	SLIPPERIER	SLOCKSTER	SLOTHFULNESS
SLEEVELET	SLIGHTEST	SLIPPERIEST	SLOD	SLOTTED
SLEEVER	SLIGHTIER	SLIPPERILY	SLODDER	SLOTTEN
SLEEVES	SLIGHTIEST	SLIPPERINESS	SLODGE	SLOTTER
SLEEVING	SLIGHTING	SLIPPERWEED	SLODGER	SLOTTERY
SLEEZY	SLIGHTINGLY	SLIPPERWORT	SLOE	SLOTTING
SLEIDED	SLIGHTLY	SLIPPERY	SLOEBERRIES	SLOUBBIE
SLEIGH	SLIGHTNESS	SLIPPERYBACK	SLOEBERRY	SLOUCH
SLEIGHER	SLIGHTY	SLIPPERYROOT	SLOEBUSH	SLOUCHED
SLEIGHING	SLIKE	SLIPPIER	SLOETREE	SLOUCHER
SLEIGHT	SLILY	SLIPPIEST	SLOG	SLOUCHIER
SLEIGHTNESS	SLIM	SLIPPINESS	SLOGAN	SLOUCHIEST
SLEIGHTY	SLIME	SLIPPING	SLOGANEER	SLOUCHILY
SLENDANG	SLIMED	SLIPPINGLY	SLOGGED	SLOUCHINESS
SLENDER	SLIMEMAN	SLIPPROOF	SLOGGER	SLOUCHING
SLENDERER	SLIMEMEN	SLIPPY	SLOGGING	SLOUCHINGLY
SLENDEREST	SLIMER	SLIPRAIL	SLOGWOOD	SLOUCHY
SLENDERISH	SLIMIER	SLIPS	SLOID	SLOUGH
SLENDERIZE	SLIMIEST	SLIPSHEET	SLOJD	SLOUGHED
SLENDERIZED	SLIMILY	SLIPSHOD	SLOKA	SLOUGHING
SLENDERIZING	SLIMINESS	SLIPSHOE	SLOKE	SLOUGHY
SLENDERLY	SLIMING	SLIPSKIN	SLOKED	SLOUM
SLENDERNESS	SLIMISH	SLIPSLAP	SLOKEN	SLOUNGE
SLENT	SLIMISHNESS	SLIPSLOP	SLOKING	SLOUNGER
SLEPEZ	SLIMLY	SLIPSLOPPISH	SLOMMACK	SLOUR
SLEUTH	SLIMMED	SLIPSLOPPISM	SLON	SLOVEN
SLEUTHED	SLIMMER	SLIPSOLE	SLONE	SLOVENLIER
SLEUTHHOUND	SLIMMEST	SLIPSTICK	SLONK	SLOVENLIEST
SLEUTHING	SLIMMING	SLIPSTREAM	SLOO	SLOVENLINESS
SLEW	SLIMMISH	SLIPSTRING	SLOOM	SLOVENLY
SLEWED	SLIMNESS	SLIPT	SLOOMY	SLOW
SLEWER	SLIMPSY	SLIPTOPPED	SLOOP	SLOWBACK
SLEWING	SLIMSIER	SLIPUP	SLOOPMAN	SLOWBELLIED
SLEWTH	SLIMSIEST	SLIPWARE	SLOOPMEN	SLOWBELLIES
SLEY	SLIMSY	SLIPWAY	SLOOSH	SLOWBELLY
SLEYED	SLIMY	SLIRT	SLOOT	SLOWDOWN
SLEYING	SLINE	SLISH	SLOP	SLOWED
SLIBBERSAUCE	SLING	SLIT	SLOPE	SLOWER
SLICE	SLINGE	SLITE	SLOPED	SLOWEST
SLICED	SLINGER	SLITHER	SLOPER	SLOWFUL
SLICER	SLINGING	SLITHERING	SLOPEWAYS	SLOWGOING
SLICES	SLINGSHOT	SLITHEROO	SLOPING	SLOWHEADED
SLICING	SLINGSMAN	SLITHERS	SLOPINGLY	SLOWHEARTED
SLICINGLY	SLINGSMEN	SLITHERY	SLOPINGNESS	SLOWING
SLICK	SLINGSTONE	SLITING	SLOPMAKER	SLOWISH
SLICKED	SLINK	SLITSHELL	SLOPMAKING	SLOWLY
SLICKENS	SLINKER	SLITTED	SLOPPAGE	SLOWMOUTHED
SLICKENSIDE	SLINKIER	SLITTER	SLOPPED	SLOWNESS
SLICKENSIDED	SLINKIEST	SLITTING	SLOPPERIES	SLOWPOKE
SLICKER	SLINKING	SLITTY	SLOPPERY	SLOWRIE
SLICKERED	SLINKINGLY	SLITWORK	SLOPPIER	SLOWS
SLICKERY	SLINKSKIN	SLIVE	SLOPPIEST	SLOWWITTED
SLICKEST	SLINKWEED	SLIVER	SLOPPILY	SLOWWITTEDLY
SLICKING	SLINKY	SLIVERED	SLOPPINESS	SLOWWORM
SLICKLY	SLIP	SLIVERER	SLOPPING	SLOYD
SLID	SLIPBACK	SLIVERING	SLOPPY	SLUB
SLIDAGE	SLIPBAND	SLIVERS	SLOPS	SLUBBED
SLIDDEN	SLIPBOARD	SLIVERY	SLOPSELLER	SLUBBER
SLIDDER	SLIPBODIES	SLIVING	SLOPSELLING	SLUBBERED
SLIDDERNESS	SLIPBODY	SLIVOVIC	SLOPSHOP	SLUBBERER

SLUBBERING	SLUNGBODY	SMALLS	SMELLAGE	SMITHERY
SLUBBERINGLY	SLUNGE	SMALLSWORD	SMELLED	SMITHIED
SLUBBERY	SLUNGSHOT	SMALLTIME	SMELLER	SMITHIER
SLUBBING	SLUNK	SMALLWARE	SMELLFUL	SMITHIES
SLUBBY	SLUNKEN	SMALLY	SMELLIE	SMITHING
SLUD	SLUP	SMALM	SMELLIER	SMITHITE
SLUDDER	SLUR	SMALMED	SMELLIEST	SMITHSONITE
SLUDDERY	SLURBOW	SMALMING	SMELLING	SMITHUM
SLUDE	SLURP	SMALT	SMELLY	SMITHWORK
SLUDGE	SLURRED	SMALTER	SMELT	SMITHY
SLUDGED	SLURRIED	SMALTI	SMELTED	SMITHYDANDER
SLUDGER	SLURRIES	SMALTINE	SMELTER	SMITHYING
SLUDGING	SLURRING	SMALTITE	SMELTERIES	SMITING
SLUDGY	SLURRY	SMALTO	SMELTERY	SMITTEN
SLUE	SLURRYING	SMALTZ	SMELTING	SMITTER
SLUED	SLUSH	SMARAGD	SMELTS	SMITTING
SLUER	SLUSHED	SMARAGDE	SMERK	SMITTLE
SLUFF	SLUSHER	SMARAGDINE	SMERVY	SMITTLEISH
SLUG	SLUSHIER	SMARAGDITE	SMETHE	SMITTLISH
SLUGABED	SLUSHIEST	SMARM	SMEU	SMOCK
SLUGFEST	SLUSHING	SMARMIER	SMEUSE	SMOCKED
SLUGGARD	SLUSHPIT	SMARMIEST	SMEUTH	SMOCKER
SLUGGARDING	SLUSHY	SMARMY	SMEW	SMOCKFACE
SLUGGARDIZE	SLUT	SMART	SMICH	SMOCKING
SLUGGARDLY	SLUTCH	SMARTED	SMICKER	SMOCKLESS
SLUGGED	SLUTCHY	SMARTEN	SMICKET	SMOG
SLUGGER	SLUTE	SMARTER	SMICKLY	SMOKABLES
SLUGGING	SLUTHER	SMARTEST	SMIDDY	SMOKE
SLUGGINGLY	SLUTTED	SMARTIES	SMIDGE	SMOKEBOX
SLUGGISH	SLUTTER	SMARTING	SMIDGEN	SMOKEBUSH
SLUGGISHLY	SLUTTERED	SMARTINGLY	SMIDGEON	SMOKED
SLUGGISHNESS	SLUTTERING	SMARTISM	SMIDGIN	SMOKEHOUSE
SLUGGY	SLUTTERY	SMARTLESS	SMIFT	SMOKEJACK
SLUGHORN	SLUTTING	SMARTLY	SMIGGINS	SMOKEJUMPER
SLUICE	SLUTTISH	SMARTNESS	SMILACACEOUS	SMOKELESS
SLUICED	SLUTTISHLY	SMARTWEED	SMILAX	SMOKELESSLY
SLUICER	SLUTTISHNESS	SMARTY	SMILE	SMOKELESSNESS
SLUICEWAY	SLUTTY	SMASH	SMILED	SMOKEPOT
SLUICING	SLY	SMASHAGE	SMILEFUL	SMOKEPROOF
SLUICY	SLYBOOTS	SMASHED	SMILEFULNESS	SMOKER
SLUIG	SLYER	SMASHER	SMILEMAKER	SMOKERY
SLUING	SLYEST	SMASHERY	SMILEMAKING	SMOKES
SLUIT	SLYISH	SMASHING	SMILER	SMOKESTACK
SLUM	SLYLY	SMASHINGLY	SMILEY	SMOKESTONE
SLUMBER	SLYNESS	SMASHUP	SMILING	SMOKETIGHT
SLUMBERED	SLYPE	SMATCH	SMILINGLY	SMOKEWOOD
SLUMBERER	SMA	SMATCHET	SMILINGNESS	SMOKEY
SLUMBERING	SMACH	SMATTER	SMILO	SMOKIER
SLUMBERINGLY	SMACHRIE	SMATTERED	SMILY	SMOKIEST
SLUMBERLAND	SMACK	SMATTERER	SMINTHURID	SMOKILY
SLUMBERLESS	SMACKED	SMATTERING	SMIRCH	SMOKINESS
SLUMBEROUS	SMACKEE	SMATTERINGLY	SMIRCHED	SMOKING
SLUMBEROUSLY	SMACKER	SMATTERY	SMIRCHER	SMOKISH
SLUMBERY	SMACKING	SMAZE	SMIRCHING	SMOKO
SLUMBROUS	SMACKINGLY	SMEAR	SMIRCHY	SMOKY
SLUMDOM	SMACKSMAN	SMEARCASE	SMIRIS	SMOKYSEEMING
SLUMGULLION	SMACKSMEN	SMEARED	SMIRK	SMOLDER
SLUMGUM	SMAD	SMEARER	SMIRKED	SMOLDERED
SLUMLAND	SMAIK	SMEARIER	SMIRKER	SMOLDERING
SLUMLORD	SMAIL	SMEARIEST	SMIRKING	SMOLT
SLUMMAGE	SMAK	SMEARINESS	SMIRKINGLY	SMOOCH
SLUMMED	SMALL	SMEARING	SMIRKISH	SMOOCHY
SLUMMER	SMALLAGE	SMEARLESS	SMIRKLE	SMOODGE
SLUMMIER	SMALLCLOTHES	SMEARY	SMIRKY	SMOODGER
SLUMMIEST	SMALLCOAL	SMECTIC	SMIRR	SMOOGE
SLUMMING	SMALLEN	SMECTITE	SMIRTLE	SMOOR
SLUMMOCK	SMALLER	SMEDDUM	SMIT	SMOORICH
SLUMMOCKY	SMALLEST	SMEE	SMITABLE	SMOOT
SLUMMY	SMALLHEARTED	SMEECH	SMITCH	SMOOTH
SLUMP	SMALLHOLDER	SMEEK	SMITE	SMOOTHBOOTS
SLUMPED	SMALLING	SMEEKY	SMITER	SMOOTHBORE
SLUMPING	SMALLISH	SMEER	SMITH	SMOOTHBORED
SLUMPWORK	SMALLMOUTH	SMEETH	SMITHCRAFT	SMOOTHCOAT
SLUMPY	SMALLMOUTHED	SMEGMA	SMITHER	SMOOTHED
SLUMS	SMALLNESS	SMEGMATIC	SMITHEREENS	SMOOTHEN
SLUNG	SMALLNESSES	SMEIR	SMITHERIES	SMOOTHER
SLUNGBODIES	SMALLPOX	SMELL	SMITHERS	SMOOTHEST

SMOOTHIE	SMUTTILY	SNAKIEST	SNEAD	SNIDERY
SMOOTHIFY	SMUTTINESS	SNAKILY	SNEAK	SNIFF
SMOOTHING	SMUTTING	SNAKINESS	SNEAKED	SNIFFED
SMOOTHINGLY	SMUTTY	SNAKING	SNEAKER	SNIFFER
SMOOTHLY	SMY	SNAKISH	SNEAKIER	SNIFFIER
SMOOTHNESS	SMYTH	SNAKY	SNEAKIEST	SNIFFIEST
SMOOTHPATE	SMYTRIE	SNAP	SNEAKILY	SNIFFILY
SMOOTHY	SNA	SNAPBACK	SNEAKINESS	SNIFFINESS
SMOPPLE	SNAB	SNAPBAG	SNEAKING	SNIFFING
SMORE	SNABBIE	SNAPBERRY	SNEAKINGLY	SNIFFINGLY
SMORGASBORD	SNABBLE	SNAPDRAGON	SNEAKINGNESS	SNIFFISH
SMORZANDO	SNABBY	SNAPE	SNEAKISH	SNIFFISHNESS
SMORZATO	SNACK	SNAPER	SNEAKISHLY	SNIFFLE
SMOT	SNACKLE	SNAPHAAN	SNEAKISHNESS	SNIFFLED
SMOTE	SNACKY	SNAPHANCE	SNEAKSBY	SNIFFLER
SMOTHER	SNAFF	SNAPHEAD	SNEAKY	SNIFFLES
SMOTHERATION	SNAFFLE	SNAPHOLDER	SNEAP	SNIFFLING
SMOTHERED	SNAFFLEBIT	SNAPJACK	SNEATH	SNIFFY
SMOTHERER	SNAFFLED	SNAPLESS	SNEB	SNIFT
SMOTHERINESS	SNAFFLES	SNAPPAGE	SNECK	SNIFTED
SMOTHERING	SNAFFLING	SNAPPED	SNECKDRAW	SNIFTER
SMOTHERINGLY	SNAFU	SNAPPER	SNECKDRAWING	SNIFTERS
SMOTHERY	SNAFUED	SNAPPIER	SNECKDRAWN	SNIFTING
SMOTTER	SNAFUING	SNAPPIEST	SNECKED	SNIFTY
SMOUCH	SNAFUS	SNAPPILY	SNECKER	SNIG
SMOUCHER	SNAG	SNAPPINESS	SNECKET	SNIGGER
SMOULDER	SNAGBUSH	SNAPPING	SNECKING	SNIGGERER
SMOULDERED	SNAGGED	SNAPPINGLY	SNED	SNIGGERING
SMOULDERING	SNAGGER	SNAPPISH	SNEDDED	SNIGGERS
SMOUS	SNAGGIER	SNAPPISHLY	SNEDDING	SNIGGLE
SMOUSE	SNAGGIEST	SNAPPISHNESS	SNEE	SNIGGLED
SMOUSER	SNAGGING	SNAPPY	SNEER	SNIGGLER
SMOUT	SNAGGLE	SNAPS	SNEERED	SNIGGLING
SMRITI	SNAGGLED	SNAPSACK	SNEERER	SNIGGORINGLY
SMRTI	SNAGGLETEETH	SNAPSHARE	SNEERFUL	SNIGHT
SMUDDER	SNAGGLETOOTH	SNAPSHOT	SNEERFULNESS	SNIGS
SMUDGE	SNAGGLETOOTHED	SNAPSHOTTED	SNEERING	SNIP
SMUDGED	SNAGGY	SNAPSHOTTER	SNEERINGLY	SNIPE
SMUDGEDLY	SNAGLINE	SNAPSHOTTING	SNEERY	SNIPEBILL
SMUDGER	SNAGREL	SNAPWEED	SNEESH	SNIPED
SMUDGIER	SNAIL	SNAPWOOD	SNEESHIN	SNIPEFISH
SMUDGIEST	SNAILEATER	SNAPWORT	SNEESHING	SNIPEFISHES
SMUDGILY	SNAILERY	SNAPY	SNEEST	SNIPER
SMUDGINESS	SNAILFLOWER	SNARE	SNEESTY	SNIPERSCOPE
SMUDGING	SNAILISH	SNARED	SNEEZE	SNIPES
SMUDGY	SNAILISHLY	SNARER	SNEEZED	SNIPING
SMUG	SNAILY	SNARING	SNEEZER	SNIPISH
SMUGGER	SNAKE	SNARK	SNEEZEWEED	SNIPJACK
SMUGGERY	SNAKEBARK	SNARL	SNEEZEWOOD	SNIPOCRACY
SMUGGEST	SNAKEBERRY	SNARLED	SNEEZEWORT	SNIPPED
SMUGGISH	SNAKEBIRD	SNARLER	SNEEZING	SNIPPER
SMUGGISHLY	SNAKEBITE	SNARLEYOW	SNEEZY	SNIPPERADO
SMUGGISHNESS	SNAKED	SNARLEYYOW	SNEG	SNIPPERTY
SMUGGLE	SNAKEFISH	SNARLING	SNELL	SNIPPET
SMUGGLED	SNAKEFISHES	SNARLINGLY	SNELLY	SNIPPETY
SMUGGLER	SNAKEFLOWER	SNARLISH	SNERP	SNIPPIER
SMUGGLERY	SNAKEHEAD	SNARLY	SNEW	SNIPPIEST
SMUGGLING	SNAKEHOLING	SNARY	SNIB	SNIPPING
SMUGLY	SNAKELET	SNASH	SNIBBLE	SNIPPY
SMUGNESS	SNAKELIKE	SNAST	SNIBBLED	SNIPS
SMUISTY	SNAKEMOUTH	SNASTE	SNIBBLER	SNIPTIOUS
SMUR	SNAKENECK	SNASTY	SNIBEL	SNIPY
SMURR	SNAKEOLOGY	SNATCH	SNICK	SNIRL
SMURRY	SNAKEPIECE	SNATCHED	SNICKDRAW	SNIRT
SMURTLE	SNAKEPIPE	SNATCHER	SNICKED	SNIRTLE
SMUSE	SNAKER	SNATCHIER	SNICKER	SNIT
SMUSH	SNAKEROOT	SNATCHIEST	SNICKERED	SNITCH
SMUT	SNAKERY	SNATCHING	SNICKERING	SNITCHER
SMUTCH	SNAKES	SNATCHINGLY	SNICKERINGLY	SNITE
SMUTCHED	SNAKESKIN	SNATCHY	SNICKERSNEE	SNITHE
SMUTCHIN	SNAKESTONE	SNATH	SNICKET	SNITHY
SMUTCHING	SNAKEWEED	SNATHE	SNICKEY	SNITS
SMUTCHY	SNAKEWOOD	SNATTOCK	SNICKING	SNITTLE
SMUTTED	SNAKEWORM	SNAVEL	SNICKLE	SNITZ
SMUTTER	SNAKEWORT	SNAVVLE	SNIDDLE	SNIVEL
SMUTTIER	SNAKEY	SNAW	SNIDE	SNIVELED
SMUTTIEST	SNAKIER	SNAZZY	SNIDENESS	SNIVELER

SNIVELING	SNORTINGLY	SNOWWORM	SOAKEN	SOBRALITE
SNIVELLED	SNORTLE	SNOWY	SOAKER	SOBREVEST
SNIVELLER	SNORTY	SNOZZLE	SOAKERS	SOBRIETIES
SNIVELLING	SNOT	SNUB	SOAKING	SOBRIETY
SNIVELLY	SNOTTER	SNUBBED	SOAKINGLY	SOBRIQUET
SNIVELS	SNOTTERY	SNUBBEE	SOAKY	SOC
SNIVELY	SNOTTIE	SNUBBER	SOAL	SOCAGE
SNIVEY	SNOTTIER	SNUBBING	SOALLIES	SOCAGER
SNIVY	SNOTTIEST	SNUBBINGLY	SOALLY	SOCCAGE
SNOB	SNOTTY	SNUBBISH	SOAM	SOCCER
SNOBBER	SNOUCH	SNUBBISHLY	SOAP	SOCCERIST
SNOBBERY	SNOUT	SNUBBISHNESS	SOAPBARK	SOCCERITE
SNOBBING	SNOUTED	SNUBBY	SOAPBERRIES	SOCE
SNOBBISH	SNOUTER	SNUCK	SOAPBERRY	SOCIABILITIES
SNOBBISHLY	SNOUTFAIR	SNUDGE	SOAPBOX	SOCIABILITY
SNOBBISHNESS	SNOUTISH	SNUDGERY	SOAPBOXER	SOCIABLE
SNOBBISM	SNOUTY	SNUFF	SOAPBUBBLY	SOCIABLENESS
SNOBBY	SNOVE	SNUFFBOX	SOAPBUSH	SOCIABLY
SNOBISM	SNOW	SNUFFBOXER	SOAPED	SOCIAL
SNOBOCRACY	SNOWBALL	SNUFFCOLORED	SOAPER	SOCIALISM
SNOBOCRAT	SNOWBALLED	SNUFFED	SOAPERIES	SOCIALIST
SNOBOGRAPHER	SNOWBALLING	SNUFFER	SOAPERY	SOCIALISTIC
SNOBOGRAPHY	SNOWBANK	SNUFFERS	SOAPFISH	SOCIALITE
SNOBOLOGIST	SNOWBELL	SNUFFIER	SOAPFISHES	SOCIALITIES
SNOBONOMER	SNOWBERG	SNUFFIEST	SOAPIER	SOCIALITY
SNOBS	SNOWBERRIES	SNUFFILY	SOAPIEST	SOCIALIZATION
SNOBSCAT	SNOWBERRY	SNUFFINESS	SOAPING	SOCIALIZE
SNOCAT	SNOWBIRD	SNUFFING	SOAPLEES	SOCIALIZED
SNOCHER	SNOWBLINK	SNUFFINGLY	SOAPLESS	SOCIALIZER
SNOCK	SNOWBLOWER	SNUFFISH	SOAPMAKER	SOCIALIZING
SNOCKER	SNOWBOUND	SNUFFKIN	SOAPMAKING	SOCIALLY
SNOD	SNOWBREAK	SNUFFLE	SOAPROCK	SOCIATE
SNODE	SNOWBROTH	SNUFFLED	SOAPROOT	SOCIATION
SNODLY	SNOWBUSH	SNUFFLER	SOAPSTONE	SOCIATIVE
SNOEK	SNOWCAP	SNUFFLES	SOAPSTONER	SOCIES
SNOEKING	SNOWCRAFT	SNUFFLESS	SOAPSUDDY	SOCIETAL
SNOGA	SNOWDRIFT	SNUFFLINESS	SOAPSUDS	SOCIETALLY
SNOOD	SNOWDROP	SNUFFLING	SOAPSUDSY	SOCIETARIAN
SNOODED	SNOWED	SNUFFLINGLY	SOAPWEED	SOCIETARY
SNOODING	SNOWFALL	SNUFFLY	SOAPWOOD	SOCIETAS
SNOOK	SNOWFLAKE	SNUFFMAN	SOAPWORT	SOCIETE
SNOOKER	SNOWFLIGHT	SNUFFY	SOAPY	SOCIETEIT
SNOOKERED	SNOWFLOWER	SNUG	SOAR	SOCIETIES
SNOOKS	SNOWFOWL	SNUGGED	SOARABILITY	SOCIETIFIED
SNOOL	SNOWHAMMER	SNUGGER	SOARABLE	SOCIETISM
SNOOP	SNOWHOUSE	SNUGGERIES	SOARED	SOCIETIST
SNOOPER	SNOWIER	SNUGGERY	SOARER	SOCIETOLOGIST
SNOOPIER	SNOWIEST	SNUGGEST	SOARING	SOCIETOLOGY
SNOOPIEST	SNOWILY	SNUGGIES	SOARINGLY	SOCIETY
SNOOPY	SNOWINESS	SNUGGING	SOARY	SOCIETYISH
SNOOT	SNOWING	SNUGGISH	SOAVE	SOCII
SNOOTFUL	SNOWK	SNUGGLE	SOAVEMENTE	SOCIOCENTRIC
SNOOTIER	SNOWL	SNUGGLED	SOB	SOCIOCRACY
SNOOTIEST	SNOWLAND	SNUGGLING	SOBBED	SOCIOCRAT
SNOOTY	SNOWLESS	SNUGIFY	SOBBER	SOCIOCRATIC
SNOOVE	SNOWLIKE	SNUGLY	SOBBING	SOCIOCULTURAL
SNOOZE	SNOWMAN	SNUGNESS	SOBBINGLY	SOCIOECONOMIC
SNOOZED	SNOWMELT	SNUM	SOBBY	SOCIOECONOMICALLY
SNOOZER	SNOWMEN	SNUP	SOBEIT	SOCIOEDUCATIONAL
SNOOZING	SNOWMOBILE	SNUPPER	SOBER	SOCIOGENESIS
SNOOZLE	SNOWPACK	SNUR	SOBERED	SOCIOGENETIC
SNOOZY	SNOWPLOUGH	SNURL	SOBERER	SOCIOGENY
SNOP	SNOWPLOW	SNURLY	SOBEREST	SOCIOGRAPHY
SNORE	SNOWS	SNURP	SOBERING	SOCIOLATRY
SNORED	SNOWSCAPE	SNURT	SOBERINGLY	SOCIOLEGAL
SNORER	SNOWSHADE	SNUSH	SOBERIZE	SOCIOLOGIAN
SNORING	SNOWSHED	SNUZZLE	SOBERLY	SOCIOLOGIC
SNORINGLY	SNOWSHINE	SNY	SOBERNESS	SOCIOLOGICAL
SNORK	SNOWSHOE	SNYE	SOBERSIDED	SOCIOLOGICALLY
SNORKEL	SNOWSHOED	SNYED	SOBERSIDES	SOCIOLOGIST
SNORKELED	SNOWSHOEING	SNYING	SOBFUL	SOCIOLOGISTIC
SNORKELING	SNOWSHOER	SO	SOBOL	SOCIOLOGY
SNORKER	SNOWSLIDE	SOA	SOBOLE	SOCIOMEDICAL
SNORT	SNOWSLIP	SOAK	SOBOLES	SOCIOMETRIC
SNORTED	SNOWSTORM	SOAKAGE	SOBOLIFEROUS	SOCIOMETRY
SNORTER	SNOWSUIT	SOAKAWAY	SOBOR	SOCIONOMIC
SNORTING	SNOWTHROWER	SOAKED	SOBPROOF	SOCIONOMY

SOCIOPHAGOUS	SOFTBALL	SOLAND	SOLECIZED	SOLID
SOCIOPOLITICAL	SOFTCOAL	SOLANDER	SOLECIZER	SOLIDAGO
SOCIORELIGIOUS	SOFTEN	SOLANDRA	SOLECIZING	SOLIDAGOS
SOCIOROMANTIC	SOFTENED	SOLANEIN	SOLED	SOLIDARE
SOCIOSTATIC	SOFTENER	SOLANEINE	SOLEIFORM	SOLIDARIC
SOCIOTECHNICAL	SOFTENING	SOLANEOUS	SOLEIL	SOLIDARISM
SOCIUS	SOFTER	SOLANIDIN	SOLEIN	SOLIDARIST
SOCK	SOFTEST	SOLANIDINE	SOLELESS	SOLIDARISTIC
SOCKDOLAGER	SOFTHEAD	SOLANIN	SOLELY	SOLIDARITIES
SOCKDOLOGER	SOFTHEARTED	SOLANINE	SOLEMN	SOLIDARITY
SOCKER	SOFTHEARTEDLY	SOLANO	SOLEMNCHOLY	SOLIDARIZE
SOCKEROO	SOFTHEARTEDNESS	SOLANOS	SOLEMNESS	SOLIDARIZED
SOCKET	SOFTHORN	SOLANUM	SOLEMNIFIED	SOLIDARIZING
SOCKETED	SOFTIE	SOLAR	SOLEMNIFY	SOLIDARY
SOCKETING	SOFTIES	SOLARIA	SOLEMNIFYING	SOLIDATE
SOCKEYE	SOFTISH	SOLARIEGO	SOLEMNISE	SOLIDATED
SOCKHEAD	SOFTLING	SOLARIMETER	SOLEMNITIES	SOLIDATING
SOCKMAKER	SOFTLY	SOLARISM	SOLEMNITUDE	SOLIDEO
SOCKMAKING	SOFTNESS	SOLARIST	SOLEMNITY	SOLIDER
SOCKMAN	SOFTS	SOLARISTIC	SOLEMNIZATION	SOLIDEST
SOCKO	SOFTTACK	SOLARISTICALLY	SOLEMNIZE	SOLIDI
SOCKS	SOFTWARE	SOLARISTICS	SOLEMNIZED	SOLIDIFICATION
SOCKY	SOFTWOOD	SOLARIUM	SOLEMNIZER	SOLIDIFIED
SOCLE	SOFTY	SOLARIUMS	SOLEMNIZING	SOLIDIFIER
SOCMAN	SOG	SOLARIZATION	SOLEMNLY	SOLIDIFORM
SOCMANRY	SOGA	SOLARIZE	SOLEMNNESS	SOLIDIFY
SOCMEN	SOGGARTH	SOLARIZED	SOLENACEAN	SOLIDIFYING
SOCO	SOGGED	SOLARIZING	SOLENACEOUS	SOLIDISM
SOD	SOGGENDALITE	SOLAROMETER	SOLENETTE	SOLIDIST
SODA	SOGGIER	SOLARY	SOLENIAL	SOLIDISTIC
SODACLASE	SOGGIEST	SOLATE	SOLENITE	SOLIDITIES
SODAIC	SOGGILY	SOLATIA	SOLENITIS	SOLIDITY
SODALIST	SOGGINESS	SOLATION	SOLENIUM	SOLIDLY
SODALITE	SOGGING	SOLATIUM	SOLENNE	SOLIDNESS
SODALITHITE	SOGGY	SOLAY	SOLENNEMENTE	SOLIDUM
SODALITIES	SOH	SOLD	SOLENOCYTE	SOLIDUNGULAR
SODALITY	SOHO	SOLDADO	SOLENODONT	SOLIDUS
SODAMID	SOIGNE	SOLDADOES	SOLENOGASTER	SOLIFIDIAN
SODAMIDE	SOIGNEE	SOLDADOS	SOLENOGLYPH	SOLIFIDIANISM
SODAR	SOIL	SOLDAN	SOLENOID	SOLIFLUCTION
SODBUSTER	SOILAGE	SOLDANEL	SOLENOIDAL	SOLIFORM
SODDED	SOILED	SOLDANELLE	SOLENOIDALLY	SOLIFUGE
SODDEN	SOILIER	SOLDANRIE	SOLENOSTELE	SOLILOQUACIOUS
SODDENLY	SOILIEST	SOLDAT	SOLENOSTELIC	SOLILOQUIES
SODDENNESS	SOILING	SOLDATESQUE	SOLENOSTOMID	SOLILOQUISE
SODDIER	SOILS	SOLDER	SOLENTINE	SOLILOQUIST
SODDIES	SOILURE	SOLDERED	SOLEPIECE	SOLILOQUIZE
SODDIEST	SOILY	SOLDERER	SOLEPLATE	SOLILOQUIZED
SODDING	SOIREE	SOLDERING	SOLEPRINT	SOLILOQUIZER
SODDITE	SOIXANTINE	SOLDI	SOLER	SOLILOQUIZING
SODDY	SOJA	SOLDIER	SOLERET	SOLILOQUIZINGLY
SODIC	SOJOURN	SOLDIERBIRD	SOLERT	SOLILOQUY
SODIOAUROUS	SOJOURNED	SOLDIERBUSH	SOLES	SOLILUNAR
SODIOCITRATE	SOJOURNER	SOLDIERED	SOLEUS	SOLING
SODIOHYDRIC	SOJOURNING	SOLDIERFARE	SOLEYN	SOLION
SODIUM	SOJOURNMENT	SOLDIERFISH	SOLEYNE	SOLIPED
SODOKU	SOK	SOLDIERFISHES	SOLFATARA	SOLIPEDAL
SODOMITE	SOKA	SOLDIERHEARTED	SOLFATARIC	SOLIPEDOUS
SODOMITIC	SOKE	SOLDIERIES	SOLFEGE	SOLIPSISM
SODOMITICAL	SOKEMAN	SOLDIERING	SOLFEGGI	SOLIPSISMAL
SODOMITICALLY	SOKEMANEMOT	SOLDIERLIKE	SOLFEGGIARE	SOLIPSIST
SODOMY	SOKEMANRIES	SOLDIERLINESS	SOLFEGGIO	SOLIPSISTIC
SODS	SOKEMANRY	SOLDIERLY	SOLFEGGIOS	SOLIQUID
SODWORK	SOKEN	SOLDIERPROOF	SOLFERINO	SOLISTE
SOE	SOL	SOLDIERS	SOLI	SOLITAIRE
SOEVER	SOLA	SOLDIERWOOD	SOLICIT	SOLITARIAN
SOFA	SOLACE	SOLDIERY	SOLICITANT	SOLITARIES
SOFANE	SOLACED	SOLDO	SOLICITATION	SOLITARILY
SOFAR	SOLACEMENT	SOLE	SOLICITED	SOLITARINESS
SOFFARID	SOLACER	SOLEA	SOLICITEE	SOLITARY
SOFFIONE	SOLACH	SOLECISE	SOLICITER	SOLITIDAL
SOFFIONI	SOLACING	SOLECISM	SOLICITING	SOLITUDE
SOFFIT	SOLAH	SOLECIST	SOLICITOR	SOLITUDINIZE
SOFI	SOLAK	SOLECISTIC	SOLICITOUS	SOLITUDINIZED
SOFKEE	SOLAN	SOLECISTICAL	SOLICITOUSLY	SOLITUDINIZING
SOFT	SOLANACEOUS	SOLECISTICALLY	SOLICITOUSNESS	SOLITUDINOUS
SOFTA	SOLANAL	SOLECIZE	SOLICITUDE	SOLIVAGANT

SOLIVAGOUS
SOLLAR
SOLLER
SOLLERET
SOLMIZATE
SOLMIZATION
SOLO
SOLOED
SOLOING
SOLOIST
SOLONETZ
SOLONIST
SOLOS
SOLOTH
SOLPUGID
SOLS
SOLSTICE
SOLSTICION
SOLSTITIAL
SOLSTITIALLY
SOLUBILITIES
SOLUBILITY
SOLUBILIZE
SOLUBLE
SOLUBLENESS
SOLUBLY
SOLUM
SOLUS
SOLUTE
SOLUTIO
SOLUTION
SOLUTIONAL
SOLUTIONER
SOLUTIONIST
SOLUTIONS
SOLUTIVE
SOLUTORY
SOLVABILITY
SOLVABLE
SOLVABLENESS
SOLVATE
SOLVATION
SOLVE
SOLVED
SOLVENCIES
SOLVENCY
SOLVEND
SOLVENT
SOLVENTLY
SOLVER
SOLVING
SOLVOLYSIS
SOLVOLYTIC
SOLVOLYZE
SOLVOLYZED
SOLVOLYZING
SOLVSBERGITE
SOLVUS
SOMA
SOMACULE
SOMAL
SOMALO
SOMAPLASM
SOMATA
SOMATEN
SOMATENES
SOMATIC
SOMATICAL
SOMATICALLY
SOMATISM
SOMATIST
SOMATOCHROME
SOMATOCYST
SOMATOCYSTIC
SOMATODERM
SOMATOGENIC
SOMATOGNOSIS

SOMATOLOGIC
SOMATOLOGIST
SOMATOLOGY
SOMATOME
SOMATOMIC
SOMATOPHYTE
SOMATOPHYTIC
SOMATOPLASM
SOMATOPLEURE
SOMATOTROPIC
SOMBER
SOMBERISH
SOMBERLY
SOMBERNESS
SOMBRE
SOMBREISH
SOMBREITE
SOMBRELY
SOMBRENESS
SOMBRERO
SOMBREROED
SOMBREROS
SOMBROUS
SOMBROUSLY
SOMBROUSNESS
SOMDEL
SOMDIEL
SOME
SOMEBODIES
SOMEBODY
SOMEDAY
SOMEDEAL
SOMEGATE
SOMEHOW
SOMEONE
SOMEPART
SOMEPLACE
SOMER
SOMERS
SOMERSAULT
SOMERSET
SOMERVILLITE
SOMESTHESIA
SOMESTHESIS
SOMESTHETIC
SOMETHING
SOMETIME
SOMETIMES
SOMEWAY
SOMEWAYS
SOMEWHAT
SOMEWHATLY
SOMEWHATNESS
SOMEWHEN
SOMEWHENCE
SOMEWHERE
SOMEWHERES
SOMEWHILE
SOMEWHILES
SOMEWHITHER
SOMEWHY
SOMEWISE
SOMITAL
SOMITE
SOMITIC
SOMLER
SOMMA
SOMMAITE
SOMME
SOMMELIER
SOMMITE
SOMNAMBULANCE
SOMNAMBULANCY
SOMNAMBULANT
SOMNAMBULAR
SOMNAMBULARY
SOMNAMBULATE

SOMNAMBULATED
SOMNAMBULATING
SOMNAMBULATION
SOMNAMBULATOR
SOMNAMBULE
SOMNAMBULENCY
SOMNAMBULIC
SOMNAMBULICALLY
SOMNAMBULISM
SOMNAMBULIST
SOMNAMBULISTIC
SOMNAMBULIZE
SOMNAMBULOUS
SOMNIAL
SOMNIATE
SOMNIATIVE
SOMNIFACIENT
SOMNIFEROUS
SOMNIFIC
SOMNIFUGE
SOMNIFUGOUS
SOMNIFY
SOMNILOQUENCE
SOMNILOQUENT
SOMNILOQUISM
SOMNILOQUIST
SOMNILOQUOUS
SOMNILOQUY
SOMNIPATHIST
SOMNIPATHY
SOMNIVOLENCY
SOMNIVOLENT
SOMNO
SOMNOLENCE
SOMNOLENCY
SOMNOLENT
SOMNOLENTLY
SOMNOLESCENT
SOMNOLISM
SOMNORIFIC
SOMNUS
SOMPAY
SOMPNE
SOMPNER
SON
SONABLE
SONANCE
SONANT
SONANTAL
SONANTIC
SONAR
SONARMAN
SONATA
SONATINA
SONATINAS
SONATINE
SONATION
SONCY
SONDAGE
SONDATION
SONDE
SONDELI
SONDER
SONDERCLASS
SONE
SONED
SONERI
SONG
SONGBIRD
SONGBOOK
SONGCRAFT
SONGER
SONGFUL
SONGFULLY
SONGFULNESS
SONGISH
SONGLAND

SONGLE
SONGLESS
SONGLET
SONGMAN
SONGS
SONGSTER
SONGSTRESS
SONGWRIGHT
SONGWRITER
SONGY
SONIC
SONICA
SONICS
SONIFEROUS
SONIFICATION
SONING
SONIOU
SONK
SONLY
SONNET
SONNETARY
SONNETED
SONNETEER
SONNETIC
SONNETING
SONNETIST
SONNETIZE
SONNETRY
SONNETTED
SONNETTING
SONNY
SONOBUOY
SONORANT
SONORESCENCE
SONORESCENT
SONORIC
SONORIFEROUS
SONORIFIC
SONORITIES
SONORITY
SONORIZE
SONOROPHONE
SONOROUS
SONOROUSLY
SONOROUSNESS
SONOVOX
SONS
SONSE
SONSHIP
SONSIE
SONSY
SONTAG
SOO
SOOCHONG
SOODLE
SOODLED
SOODLING
SOODLY
SOOEY
SOOGAN
SOOGEE
SOOK
SOOKIE
SOOKY
SOOL
SOOLOOS
SOOM
SOON
SOOND
SOONER
SOONEST
SOONISH
SOOP
SOOPER
SOOR
SOORAWN
SOOREYN

SOORKEE
SOORKI
SOORKY
SOORMA
SOOSOO
SOOT
SOOTED
SOOTER
SOOTERKIN
SOOTH
SOOTHE
SOOTHED
SOOTHER
SOOTHERER
SOOTHEST
SOOTHFAST
SOOTHFASTLY
SOOTHFUL
SOOTHING
SOOTHINGLY
SOOTHINGNESS
SOOTHLY
SOOTHSAID
SOOTHSAW
SOOTHSAY
SOOTHSAYER
SOOTHSAYING
SOOTIED
SOOTIER
SOOTIEST
SOOTILY
SOOTINESS
SOOTING
SOOTISH
SOOTY
SOOTYING
SOP
SOPE
SOPH
SOPHEME
SOPHENE
SOPHER
SOPHIC
SOPHICAL
SOPHICALLY
SOPHIOLOGIC
SOPHIOLOGY
SOPHISM
SOPHIST
SOPHISTER
SOPHISTIC
SOPHISTICAL
SOPHISTICALLY
SOPHISTICALNESS
SOPHISTICANT
SOPHISTICATE
SOPHISTICATED
SOPHISTICATING
SOPHISTICATION
SOPHISTICATIVE
SOPHISTICATOR
SOPHISTICISM
SOPHISTRIES
SOPHISTRY
SOPHOMORE
SOPHOMORIC
SOPHOMORICAL
SOPHOMORICALLY
SOPHORIA
SOPHRONIZE
SOPHRONIZED
SOPHRONIZING
SOPHTA
SOPHY
SOPIE
SOPITE
SOPITED

SOPITING
SOPITION
SOPOR
SOPORATE
SOPORIFEROUS
SOPORIFIC
SOPORIFICAL
SOPOROSE
SOPPED
SOPPER
SOPPIER
SOPPIEST
SOPPING
SOPPY
SOPRA
SOPRANI
SOPRANINO
SOPRANIST
SOPRANO
SOPRANOS
SOPT
SORA
SORAGE
SORAL
SORANCE
SORB
SORBATE
SORBEFACIENT
SORBENT
SORBET
SORBIC
SORBILE
SORBITAN
SORBITE
SORBITIC
SORBITIZE
SORBITOL
SORBOSE
SORBOSID
SORBOSIDE
SORCER
SORCERER
SORCERESS
SORCERIES
SORCERING
SORCEROUS
SORCEROUSLY
SORCERY
SORD
SORDA
SORDAVALITE
SORDAWALITE
SORDELLINA
SORDES
SORDID
SORDIDITY
SORDIDLY
SORDIDNESS
SORDINE
SORDINO
SORDO
SORDOR
SORE
SOREDIA
SOREDIAL
SOREDIATE
SOREDIFEROUS
SOREDIFORM
SOREDIOID
SOREDIUM
SOREFALCON
SOREFOOT
SOREHAWK
SOREHEAD
SOREHEADED
SOREHEADEDLY
SOREHEADEDNESS

SOREHEARTED
SOREHON
SOREL
SORELY
SOREMA
SORENESS
SORER
SOREST
SORGE
SORGHE
SORGHO
SORGHUM
SORGO
SORGOS
SORI
SORICID
SORICIDENT
SORICINE
SORICOID
SORIFEROUS
SORITE
SORITES
SORITIC
SORITICAL
SORN
SORNARI
SORNER
SOROBAN
SOROCHE
SORORAL
SORORATE
SORORIAL
SORORIALLY
SORORICIDAL
SORORICIDE
SORORITIES
SORORITY
SORORIZE
SOROSE
SOROSES
SOROSIS
SOROSPHERE
SORPTION
SORRA
SORRANCE
SORREL
SORREN
SORRENTO
SORRIER
SORRIEST
SORRILY
SORRINESS
SORROW
SORROWED
SORROWER
SORROWFUL
SORROWFULLY
SORROWFULNESS
SORROWING
SORROWINGLY
SORRY
SORRYHEARTED
SORRYISH
SORS
SORT
SORTABLE
SORTABLY
SORTAL
SORTANCE
SORTATION
SORTED
SORTER
SORTES
SORTIARY
SORTIE
SORTILEGE
SORTILEGER

SORTILEGI
SORTILEGIC
SORTILEGIOUS
SORTILEGUS
SORTIMENT
SORTING
SORTITA
SORTITION
SORTLY
SORTMENT
SORTS
SORTY
SORUS
SORVA
SORY
SOSH
SOSHED
SOSIE
SOSO
SOSOISH
SOSPIRO
SOSQUIL
SOSS
SOSSIEGO
SOSSLE
SOSTENENDO
SOSTENENTE
SOSTENUTI
SOSTENUTO
SOSTENUTOS
SOSTINENTE
SOSTINENTO
SOT
SOTERIOLOGIC
SOTERIOLOGY
SOTH
SOTIE
SOTNIA
SOTNIK
SOTOL
SOTS
SOTTAGE
SOTTED
SOTTER
SOTTERY
SOTTING
SOTTISE
SOTTISH
SOTTISHLY
SOTTISHNESS
SOTTO
SOTWEED
SOU
SOUARI
SOUBISE
SOUBRETTE
SOUBRETTISH
SOUBRIQUET
SOUCAR
SOUCE
SOUCH
SOUCHIE
SOUCHONG
SOUD
SOUDAGUR
SOUDAN
SOUFFLE
SOUFFLEED
SOUFFLEUR
SOUGAN
SOUGH
SOUGHED
SOUGHER
SOUGHING
SOUGHT
SOUK
SOUL

SOULACK
SOULCAKE
SOULDIE
SOULE
SOULED
SOULFUL
SOULFULLY
SOULFULNESS
SOULHEAL
SOULHEALTH
SOULICAL
SOULISH
SOULLESS
SOULLESSLY
SOULLESSNESS
SOULPENCE
SOULPENNY
SOULS
SOULTER
SOULTRE
SOULX
SOULY
SOULZ
SOUM
SOUMAK
SOUMANSITE
SOUND
SOUNDABLE
SOUNDAGE
SOUNDBOARD
SOUNDED
SOUNDER
SOUNDFUL
SOUNDHEADED
SOUNDHEADEDNESS
SOUNDHEARTED
SOUNDHEARTEDNESS
SOUNDING
SOUNDINGLY
SOUNDINGNESS
SOUNDLESS
SOUNDLESSLY
SOUNDLESSNESS
SOUNDLY
SOUNDNESS
SOUNDPROOF
SOUNDPROOFING
SOUNDS
SOUNE
SOUP
SOUPBONE
SOUPCON
SOUPER
SOUPFIN
SOUPIER
SOUPIEST
SOUPLE
SOUPLED
SOUPLESS
SOUPLIKE
SOUPLING
SOUPSPOON
SOUPY
SOUR
SOURBALL
SOURBELLIES
SOURBELLY
SOURBERRIES
SOURBERRY
SOURBREAD
SOURBUSH
SOURCE
SOURCROUT
SOURD
SOURDINE
SOURDOOK
SOURDOUGH

SOURDRE
SOURED
SOUREDNESS
SOUREN
SOURER
SOUREST
SOURING
SOURJACK
SOURLING
SOURLY
SOURNESS
SOUROCK
SOURPUSS
SOURSOP
SOURTOP
SOURVELD
SOURWEED
SOURWOOD
SOURY
SOUS
SOUSAPHONE
SOUSAPHONIST
SOUSE
SOUSED
SOUSER
SOUSEWIFE
SOUSING
SOUSLIK
SOUTACHE
SOUTAGE
SOUTANE
SOUTAR
SOUTENU
SOUTER
SOUTERLY
SOUTERRAIN
SOUTH
SOUTHARD
SOUTHBOUND
SOUTHEAST
SOUTHEASTER
SOUTHEASTERLY
SOUTHEASTERN
SOUTHEASTERNMOST
SOUTHEASTWARD
SOUTHEASTWARDLY
SOUTHEASTWARDS
SOUTHED
SOUTHER
SOUTHERLAND
SOUTHERLIES
SOUTHERLINESS
SOUTHERLY
SOUTHERMOST
SOUTHERN
SOUTHERNER
SOUTHERNEST
SOUTHERNISM
SOUTHERNIZE
SOUTHERNLINESS
SOUTHERNLY
SOUTHERNMOST
SOUTHERNWOOD
SOUTHING
SOUTHLAND
SOUTHLANDER
SOUTHMOST
SOUTHNESS
SOUTHPAW
SOUTHRON
SOUTHWARD
SOUTHWARDLY
SOUTHWARDS
SOUTHWEST
SOUTHWESTER
SOUTHWESTERLIES
SOUTHWESTERLY

SOUTHWESTERN	SOZZLED	SPAGYRIC	SPANOPNOEA	SPARRY
SOUTHWESTERNMOST	SOZZLY	SPAGYRICAL	SPANPIECE	SPARRYGRASS
SOUTHWESTWARD	SPA	SPAGYRIST	SPANSPEK	SPARSE
SOUTHWESTWARDLY	SPAAD	SPAHEE	SPANULE	SPARSEDLY
SOUTHWESTWARDS	SPACE	SPAHI	SPANWORM	SPARSELY
SOUVENIR	SPACEBAND	SPAHIS	SPAR	SPARSENESS
SOUVERAIN	SPACECRAFT	SPAIL	SPARABLE	SPARSER
SOV	SPACED	SPAIN	SPARADA	SPARSEST
SOVENEZ	SPACEFUL	SPAIR	SPARADRAP	SPARSILE
SOVEREIGN	SPACELESS	SPAIRGE	SPARAGE	SPARSIM
SOVEREIGNESS	SPACEMAN	SPAIT	SPARASSODONT	SPARSIOPLAST
SOVEREIGNIZE	SPACEMANSHIP	SPAK	SPARCH	SPARSITY
SOVEREIGNLY	SPACEMEN	SPAKE	SPARE	SPART
SOVEREIGNNESS	SPACEPORT	SPAKED	SPARED	SPARTACIST
SOVEREIGNTIES	SPACER	SPALACID	SPAREFUL	SPARTEIN
SOVEREIGNTY	SPACES	SPALACINE	SPARELESS	SPARTEINE
SOVERTY	SPACESHIP	SPALD	SPARELY	SPARTERIE
SOVIET	SPACEWALK	SPALDER	SPARENESS	SPARTH
SOVIETIC	SPACIAL	SPALDING	SPARER	SPARTLE
SOVIETISM	SPACINESS	SPALE	SPARERIB	SPARTLED
SOVIETIST	SPACING	SPALL	SPARESOME	SPARTLING
SOVIETISTIC	SPACIOSITY	SPALLATION	SPAREST	SPARVER
SOVIETIZATION	SPACIOUS	SPALLED	SPARGANUM	SPARY
SOVIETIZE	SPACIOUSLY	SPALLER	SPARGE	SPASM
SOVIETIZED	SPACIOUSNESS	SPALLING	SPARGED	SPASMATIC
SOVIETIZING	SPACK	SPALPEEN	SPARGER	SPASMATICAL
SOVIK	SPACKLE	SPALT	SPARGING	SPASMED
SOVITE	SPACKLED	SPAN	SPARGOSIS	SPASMIC
SOVKHOS	SPACKLING	SPANAEMIA	SPARHAWK	SPASMODIC
SOVKHOSE	SPACY	SPANAEMIC	SPARID	SPASMODICAL
SOVKHOZ	SPAD	SPANCEL	SPARILY	SPASMODICALLY
SOVPRENE	SPADAITE	SPANCELED	SPARING	SPASMODICALNESS
SOVRAN	SPADASSIN	SPANCELING	SPARINGLY	SPASMODISM
SOVRANLY	SPADDLE	SPANCELLED	SPARINGNESS	SPASMODIST
SOVRANTY	SPADE	SPANCELLING	SPARK	SPASMOPHILIA
SOW	SPADEBONE	SPANDEX	SPARKBACK	SPASMOPHILIC
SOWAN	SPADED	SPANDLE	SPARKED	SPASMOTIN
SOWAR	SPADEFISH	SPANDREL	SPARKER	SPASMOTOXIN
SOWARREE	SPADEFOOT	SPANDRIL	SPARKIER	SPASMOTOXINE
SOWARRY	SPADEFUL	SPANDY	SPARKIEST	SPASMOUS
SOWBACK	SPADEMAN	SPANE	SPARKINESS	SPASMUS
SOWBACKED	SPADEMEN	SPANED	SPARKING	SPASTIC
SOWBANE	SPADER	SPANEMIA	SPARKINGLY	SPASTICALLY
SOWBELLY	SPADES	SPANEMIC	SPARKISH	SPASTICITY
SOWBREAD	SPADESMAN	SPANEMY	SPARKISHLY	SPAT
SOWCAR	SPADEWORK	SPANG	SPARKISHNESS	SPATALAMANCY
SOWCE	SPADGER	SPANGED	SPARKLE	SPATANGOID
SOWD	SPADIARD	SPANGHEW	SPARKLEBERRY	SPATCHCOCK
SOWDER	SPADICEOUS	SPANGING	SPARKLED	SPATE
SOWDONES	SPADICES	SPANGLE	SPARKLER	SPATED
SOWED	SPADICIFORM	SPANGLED	SPARKLET	SPATH
SOWEL	SPADICOSE	SPANGLER	SPARKLINESS	SPATHA
SOWENS	SPADILLA	SPANGLET	SPARKLING	SPATHACEOUS
SOWER	SPADILLE	SPANGLIER	SPARKLINGNESS	SPATHAE
SOWF	SPADILLO	SPANGLIEST	SPARKLY	SPATHAL
SOWFF	SPADING	SPANGLING	SPARKPLUG	SPATHE
SOWFOOT	SPADISH	SPANGLY	SPARKPLUGGED	SPATHED
SOWING	SPADIX	SPANGOLITE	SPARKPLUGGING	SPATHIC
SOWISH	SPADO	SPANIEL	SPARKS	SPATHILLA
SOWL	SPADONES	SPANING	SPARKY	SPATHILLAE
SOWLE	SPADONIC	SPANIPELAGIC	SPARLING	SPATHOSE
SOWLTH	SPADONISM	SPANK	SPAROID	SPATHOUS
SOWN	SPADROON	SPANKED	SPARPLE	SPATHULATE
SOWP	SPAE	SPANKER	SPARPLED	SPATIAL
SOWSE	SPAEBOOK	SPANKILY	SPARPLING	SPATIALITY
SOWTH	SPAECRAFT	SPANKING	SPARRED	SPATIALIZATION
SOX	SPAED	SPANKINGLY	SPARRER	SPATIALIZE
SOY	SPAEDOM	SPANKLED	SPARRIER	SPATIALLY
SOYA	SPAEING	SPANKY	SPARRIEST	SPATIATE
SOYATE	SPAEMAN	SPANLESS	SPARRING	SPATIATION
SOYBEAN	SPAER	SPANN	SPARRINGLY	SPATILOMANCY
SOYL	SPAEWIFE	SPANNED	SPARROW	SPATING
SOYLE	SPAEWOMAN	SPANNER	SPARROWCIDE	SPATIUM
SOYLED	SPAEWORK	SPANNERMAN	SPARROWGRASS	SPATTANIA
SOZIN	SPAEWRIGHT	SPANNERMEN	SPARROWISH	SPATTED
SOZOLIC	SPAGHETTI	SPANNING	SPARROWWORT	SPATTER
SOZZLE	SPAGNUOLO	SPANOPNEA	SPARROWY	SPATTERDASH

SPATTERDOCK
SPATTERED
SPATTERING
SPATTERINGLY
SPATTERWORK
SPATTING
SPATTLE
SPATTLED
SPATTLEHOE
SPATTLING
SPATULA
SPATULAMANCY
SPATULAR
SPATULATE
SPATULATION
SPATULE
SPATULIFORM
SPATULOSE
SPATULOUS
SPATZLE
SPAUGHT
SPAUL
SPAULD
SPAULDROCHY
SPAVER
SPAVIE
SPAVIED
SPAVIET
SPAVIN
SPAVINE
SPAVINED
SPAVIT
SPAWL
SPAWLER
SPAWN
SPAWNEATER
SPAWNED
SPAWNER
SPAWNING
SPAWNY
SPAY
SPAYAD
SPAYARD
SPAYED
SPAYING
SPEAK
SPEAKABLE
SPEAKABLENESS
SPEAKABLY
SPEAKEASIES
SPEAKEASY
SPEAKER
SPEAKERESS
SPEAKERSHIP
SPEAKHOUSE
SPEAKIES
SPEAKING
SPEAKINGLY
SPEAKINGNESS
SPEAKLESS
SPEAKLESSLY
SPEAL
SPEALBONE
SPEAN
SPEAR
SPEARED
SPEARER
SPEAREYE
SPEARFISH
SPEARFISHES
SPEARFLOWER
SPEARHEAD
SPEARING
SPEARMAN
SPEARMANSHIP
SPEARMEN
SPEARMINT

SPEARPROOF
SPEARSMAN
SPEARSMEN
SPEARWOOD
SPEARWORT
SPEARY
SPEAVE
SPEC
SPECCHIE
SPECE
SPECH
SPECIAL
SPECIALISE
SPECIALISM
SPECIALIST
SPECIALISTIC
SPECIALITIES
SPECIALITY
SPECIALIZATION
SPECIALIZE
SPECIALIZED
SPECIALIZER
SPECIALIZING
SPECIALLY
SPECIALNESS
SPECIALTIES
SPECIALTY
SPECIATE
SPECIATION
SPECIE
SPECIES
SPECIFIABLE
SPECIFIC
SPECIFICAL
SPECIFICALITY
SPECIFICALLY
SPECIFICATE
SPECIFICATION
SPECIFICATIVE
SPECIFICATIVELY
SPECIFICITY
SPECIFICIZE
SPECIFICLY
SPECIFIED
SPECIFIER
SPECIFIST
SPECIFY
SPECIFYING
SPECIMEN
SPECIMENIZE
SPECIMENIZED
SPECIMENS
SPECIOLOGY
SPECIOSITIES
SPECIOSITY
SPECIOUS
SPECIOUSLY
SPECIOUSNESS
SPECK
SPECKED
SPECKEDNESS
SPECKFALL
SPECKIER
SPECKIEST
SPECKING
SPECKLE
SPECKLEBELLY
SPECKLEBREAST
SPECKLED
SPECKLEDBILL
SPECKLEDY
SPECKLEHEAD
SPECKLESS
SPECKLESSLY
SPECKLESSNESS
SPECKLING
SPECKLY

SPECKS
SPECKSIONEER
SPECKY
SPECS
SPECTACLE
SPECTACLED
SPECTACLES
SPECTACULAR
SPECTACULARISM
SPECTACULARITY
SPECTACULARLY
SPECTATE
SPECTATOR
SPECTATORIAL
SPECTATORY
SPECTATRESS
SPECTATRIX
SPECTER
SPECTERED
SPECTERLIKE
SPECTRA
SPECTRAL
SPECTRALISM
SPECTRALITY
SPECTRALLY
SPECTRALNESS
SPECTRE
SPECTRED
SPECTROGRAM
SPECTROGRAPH
SPECTROLOGY
SPECTROMETER
SPECTROMETRIC
SPECTROMETRY
SPECTROPHOBY
SPECTROPHONE
SPECTROSCOPE
SPECTROSCOPY
SPECTRUM
SPECTRUMS
SPECTRY
SPECULA
SPECULAR
SPECULARLY
SPECULATE
SPECULATED
SPECULATING
SPECULATION
SPECULATIST
SPECULATIVE
SPECULATIVELY
SPECULATIVENESS
SPECULATOR
SPECULATORY
SPECULATRICES
SPECULATRIX
SPECULIST
SPECULUM
SPECULUMS
SPECUS
SPED
SPEECE
SPEECH
SPEECHCRAFT
SPEECHER
SPEECHFUL
SPEECHFULNESS
SPEECHIFICATION
SPEECHIFIED
SPEECHIFIER
SPEECHIFY
SPEECHIFYING
SPEECHING
SPEECHLESS
SPEECHLESSLY
SPEECHLESSNESS
SPEECHLORE

SPEECHMAKER
SPEECHMAKING
SPEECHMENT
SPEED
SPEEDBALL
SPEEDBOAT
SPEEDBOATING
SPEEDBOATMAN
SPEEDED
SPEEDER
SPEEDFUL
SPEEDFULLY
SPEEDFULNESS
SPEEDGUN
SPEEDIER
SPEEDIEST
SPEEDILY
SPEEDINESS
SPEEDING
SPEEDINGLY
SPEEDLY
SPEEDOMETER
SPEEDSTER
SPEEDUP
SPEEDWAY
SPEEDWELL
SPEEDY
SPEEL
SPEELLESS
SPEER
SPEERED
SPEERING
SPEERINGS
SPEIGHT
SPEIR
SPEISE
SPEISKOBALT
SPEISS
SPEISSCOBALT
SPEKBOOM
SPEKT
SPELAEAN
SPELD
SPELDER
SPELDING
SPELDRIN
SPELDRING
SPELDRON
SPELE
SPELEAN
SPELEOLOGIST
SPELEOLOGY
SPELK
SPELL
SPELLBIND
SPELLBINDER
SPELLBINDING
SPELLBOUND
SPELLCRAFT
SPELLDOWN
SPELLED
SPELLER
SPELLFUL
SPELLING
SPELLINGDOWN
SPELLINGLY
SPELLKEN
SPELLMONGER
SPELLPROOF
SPELLWORD
SPELLWORK
SPELMAN
SPELT
SPELTER
SPELTERMAN
SPELTERMEN
SPELTOID

SPELTZ
SPELUNCAR
SPELUNCEAN
SPELUNK
SPELUNKER
SPELUNKING
SPENCE
SPENCER
SPENCERITE
SPENCIE
SPENCY
SPEND
SPENDER
SPENDFUL
SPENDIBLE
SPENDING
SPENDLESS
SPENDTHRIFT
SPENDTHRIFTY
SPENSE
SPENT
SPEOS
SPERAGE
SPERATE
SPERE
SPERK
SPERKET
SPERLING
SPERM
SPERMA
SPERMACETI
SPERMADUCT
SPERMALIST
SPERMAPHYTE
SPERMAPHYTIC
SPERMARIES
SPERMARIUM
SPERMARY
SPERMATA
SPERMATHECA
SPERMATHECAE
SPERMATHECAL
SPERMATIA
SPERMATIC
SPERMATID
SPERMATIN
SPERMATISM
SPERMATIST
SPERMATITIS
SPERMATIUM
SPERMATIZE
SPERMATOCELE
SPERMATOCYST
SPERMATOCYTE
SPERMATOGENY
SPERMATOID
SPERMATOVA
SPERMATOVUM
SPERMATOZOA
SPERMATOZOAL
SPERMATOZOAN
SPERMATOZOIC
SPERMATOZOID
SPERMATOZOON
SPERMATURIA
SPERMIC
SPERMIDIN
SPERMIDINE
SPERMIDUCAL
SPERMIDUCT
SPERMIGEROUS
SPERMIN
SPERMINE
SPERMISM
SPERMIST
SPERMOBLAST
SPERMOCARP

SPERMODERM	SPHENE	SPHINX	SPIDERY	SPIN
SPERMODUCT	SPHENETHMOID	SPHINXES	SPIDGER	SPINA
SPERMOGENOUS	SPHENIC	SPHINXIAN	SPIED	SPINACEOUS
SPERMOGONE	SPHENION	SPHINXINE	SPIEGEL	SPINACH
SPERMOGONIA	SPHENISCINE	SPHINXLIKE	SPIEGELEISEN	SPINACHLIKE
SPERMOGONIUM	SPHENODON	SPHRAGIDE	SPIEL	SPINAE
SPERMOGONOUS	SPHENODONT	SPHRAGISTIC	SPIELER	SPINAGE
SPERMOLOGER	SPHENOGRAM	SPHRAGISTICS	SPIER	SPINAL
SPERMOLOGIST	SPHENOGRAPHY	SPHYGMIA	SPIES	SPINALES
SPERMOLOGY	SPHENOID	SPHYGMIC	SPIFF	SPINALIS
SPERMOPHILE	SPHENOIDAL	SPHYGMODIC	SPIFFED	SPINALLY
SPERMOPHORE	SPHENOIDITIS	SPHYGMOGRAM	SPIFFIER	SPINATE
SPERMOSPHERE	SPHENOLITH	SPHYGMOGRAPH	SPIFFIEST	SPINDER
SPERMOTHECA	SPHENOMALAR	SPHYGMOID	SPIFFILY	SPINDLAGE
SPERMOTOXIN	SPHENOTIC	SPHYGMOLOGY	SPIFFINESS	SPINDLE
SPERMOUS	SPHENOTRIBE	SPHYGMOMETER	SPIFFING	SPINDLEAGE
SPERMULE	SPHENOTRIPSY	SPHYGMOPHONE	SPIFFLICATE	SPINDLED
SPERMY	SPHERABLE	SPHYGMUS	SPIFFLICATED	SPINDLEHEAD
SPERON	SPHERADIAN	SPIAL	SPIFFLICATION	SPINDLELEGS
SPERONARA	SPHERAL	SPICA	SPIFFY	SPINDLER
SPERONARAS	SPHERALITY	SPICAE	SPIFLICATE	SPINDLETAIL
SPERONARES	SPHERASTER	SPICANT	SPIFLICATED	SPINDLEWOOD
SPERONARO	SPHERATION	SPICATE	SPIFLICATION	SPINDLIER
SPERONAROES	SPHERE	SPICATED	SPIG	SPINDLIEST
SPERONAROS	SPHERED	SPICCATO	SPIGGOTY	SPINDLINESS
SPERONE	SPHERELESS	SPICE	SPIGNEL	SPINDLING
SPERPLE	SPHERIC	SPICEBERRIES	SPIGNET	SPINDLY
SPERRYLITE	SPHERICAL	SPICEBERRY	SPIGNUT	SPINDRIFT
SPERSE	SPHERICALITY	SPICEBUSH	SPIGOT	SPINE
SPES	SPHERICALLY	SPICECAKE	SPIKE	SPINEBILL
SPESSARTINE	SPHERICALNESS	SPICED	SPIKEBILL	SPINEBONE
SPESSARTITE	SPHERICIST	SPICEFUL	SPIKED	SPINED
SPET	SPHERICITIES	SPICEHOUSE	SPIKEDNESS	SPINEFINNED
SPETCH	SPHERICITY	SPICELAND	SPIKEFISH	SPINEL
SPETCHES	SPHERICLE	SPICER	SPIKEFISHES	SPINELESS
SPEUCHAN	SPHERICS	SPICERIES	SPIKEHOLE	SPINELESSLY
SPEW	SPHERIER	SPICERY	SPIKEHORN	SPINELESSNESS
SPEWED	SPHERIEST	SPICES	SPIKELET	SPINELET
SPEWER	SPHERIFORM	SPICEWOOD	SPIKELIKE	SPINELLE
SPEWIER	SPHERIFY	SPICIER	SPIKENARD	SPINES
SPEWIEST	SPHERING	SPICIEST	SPIKER	SPINESCENCE
SPEWINESS	SPHEROGRAPH	SPICIFEROUS	SPIKES	SPINESCENT
SPEWING	SPHEROID	SPICIFORM	SPIKETAIL	SPINET
SPEWY	SPHEROIDAL	SPICIGEROUS	SPIKETOP	SPINETAIL
SPEX	SPHEROIDALLY	SPICILEGE	SPIKEWEED	SPINGEL
SPEY	SPHEROIDIC	SPICILY	SPIKIER	SPINIBULBAR
SPEYERIA	SPHEROIDICAL	SPICINESS	SPIKIEST	SPINICARPOUS
SPHACEL	SPHEROIDISM	SPICING	SPIKILY	SPINIDENTATE
SPHACELATE	SPHEROIDITY	SPICK	SPIKINESS	SPINIER
SPHACELATED	SPHEROIDIZE	SPICKET	SPIKING	SPINIEST
SPHACELATING	SPHEROME	SPICKLE	SPIKY	SPINIFEROUS
SPHACELATION	SPHEROMERE	SPICKNEL	SPILE	SPINIFEX
SPHACELIA	SPHEROMETER	SPICOSE	SPILED	SPINIFORM
SPHACELIAL	SPHERULA	SPICOSITY	SPILEHOLE	SPINIFUGAL
SPHACELISM	SPHERULAR	SPICOUS	SPILER	SPINIGEROUS
SPHACELOUS	SPHERULATE	SPICOUSNESS	SPILEWORM	SPINIGRADE
SPHACELUS	SPHERULE	SPICULA	SPILI	SPININESS
SPHAERIDIA	SPHERULITE	SPICULAR	SPILIKIN	SPINIPETAL
SPHAERIDIAL	SPHERULITIC	SPICULATE	SPILING	SPINITIS
SPHAERIDIUM	SPHERULITIZE	SPICULATED	SPILITE	SPINK
SPHAERITE	SPHERY	SPICULATION	SPILITIC	SPINNABLE
SPHAEROBLAST	SPHETERIZE	SPICULE	SPILL	SPINNAKER
SPHAEROSOME	SPHEXIDE	SPICULIFORM	SPILLAGE	SPINNEL
SPHAEROSPORE	SPHINCTER	SPICULOFIBER	SPILLED	SPINNER
SPHAGIA	SPHINCTERAL	SPICULOSE	SPILLER	SPINNERET
SPHAGION	SPHINCTERATE	SPICULOUS	SPILLET	SPINNERETTE
SPHAGNACEOUS	SPHINCTERIAL	SPICULUM	SPILLIKIN	SPINNERIES
SPHAGNOLOGY	SPHINCTERIC	SPICY	SPILLING	SPINNERS
SPHAGNOUS	SPHINDID	SPIDER	SPILLOVER	SPINNERULAR
SPHAGNUM	SPHINGAL	SPIDERED	SPILLWAY	SPINNERULE
SPHALERITE	SPHINGES	SPIDERFLOWER	SPILLY	SPINNERY
SPHALM	SPHINGID	SPIDERISH	SPILOMA	SPINNEY
SPHALMA	SPHINGIFORM	SPIDERLING	SPILOMAS	SPINNEYS
SPHECID	SPHINGINE	SPIDERLY	SPILOSITE	SPINNIES
SPHECIUS	SPHINGOMETER	SPIDERWEB	SPILT	SPINNING
SPHECOID	SPHINGOSIN	SPIDERWORK	SPILTH	SPINNINGLY
SPHENDONE	SPHINGOSINE	SPIDERWORT	SPILUS	SPINNY

SPINOBULBAR
SPINODE
SPINOGLENOID
SPINOID
SPINONEURAL
SPINOR
SPINOSE
SPINOSELY
SPINOSENESS
SPINOSITY
SPINOTECTAL
SPINOUS
SPINSTER
SPINSTERHOOD
SPINSTERIAL
SPINSTERISH
SPINSTERISHLY
SPINSTERLY
SPINSTEROUS
SPINSTRESS
SPINSTRY
SPINTEXT
SPINTHERISM
SPINTRY
SPINTURNIX
SPINULA
SPINULATE
SPINULATED
SPINULATION
SPINULE
SPINULESCENT
SPINULIFORM
SPINULOSE
SPINULOSELY
SPINULOUS
SPINY
SPION
SPIONID
SPIRABLE
SPIRACLE
SPIRACULA
SPIRACULAR
SPIRACULATE
SPIRACULUM
SPIRAEA
SPIRAL
SPIRALE
SPIRALED
SPIRALIFORM
SPIRALING
SPIRALISM
SPIRALITY
SPIRALIZATION
SPIRALIZE
SPIRALLED
SPIRALLING
SPIRALLY
SPIRALOID
SPIRALTAIL
SPIRAN
SPIRANE
SPIRANT
SPIRANTHIC
SPIRANTHY
SPIRANTIZE
SPIRASTER
SPIRATE
SPIRATED
SPIRATION
SPIRE
SPIREA
SPIRED
SPIREGRASS
SPIRELET
SPIREM
SPIREME
SPIRICLE

SPIRIFERID
SPIRIFEROID
SPIRIFEROUS
SPIRIFORM
SPIRILLA
SPIRILLAR
SPIRILLOSIS
SPIRILLUM
SPIRING
SPIRIT
SPIRITALLY
SPIRITED
SPIRITEDLY
SPIRITEDNESS
SPIRITER
SPIRITFUL
SPIRITFULLY
SPIRITFULNESS
SPIRITING
SPIRITISM
SPIRITIST
SPIRITISTIC
SPIRITIZE
SPIRITLAND
SPIRITLEAF
SPIRITLESS
SPIRITLESSLY
SPIRITLESSNESS
SPIRITLIKE
SPIRITOSO
SPIRITOUS
SPIRITS
SPIRITSOME
SPIRITUAL
SPIRITUALISE
SPIRITUALISM
SPIRITUALIST
SPIRITUALISTIC
SPIRITUALISTICALLY
SPIRITUALITIES
SPIRITUALITY
SPIRITUALIZATION
SPIRITUALIZE
SPIRITUALIZED
SPIRITUALIZER
SPIRITUALIZING
SPIRITUALLY
SPIRITUALNESS
SPIRITUALTY
SPIRITUEL
SPIRITUELLE
SPIRITUOSITY
SPIRITUOUS
SPIRITUOUSLY
SPIRITUOUSNESS
SPIRITUS
SPIRITWEED
SPIRITY
SPIRIVALVE
SPIRKET
SPIRKETING
SPIRLIE
SPIRO
SPIROCHAETAL
SPIROCHAETE
SPIROCHETAL
SPIROCHETE
SPIROCHETIC
SPIROGRAM
SPIROGRAPH
SPIROGRAPHIC
SPIROGRAPHIN
SPIROGRAPHY
SPIROGYRA
SPIROID
SPIROIDAL
SPIROILIC

SPIROL
SPIROLE
SPIROMETER
SPIROMETRIC
SPIROMETRY
SPIROSCOPE
SPIROUS
SPIRT
SPIRTLE
SPIRULA
SPIRULAE
SPIRULATE
SPIRY
SPISE
SPISS
SPISSATED
SPISSITUDE
SPISSY
SPIT
SPITAL
SPITBALL
SPITBALLER
SPITBOX
SPITCHCOCK
SPITCHCOCKED
SPITCHCOCKING
SPITE
SPITED
SPITEFUL
SPITEFULLY
SPITEFULNESS
SPITFIRE
SPITFROG
SPITFUL
SPITHAME
SPITING
SPITISH
SPITKID
SPITKIT
SPITOUS
SPITPOISON
SPITSCOCKED
SPITSTICK
SPITSTICKER
SPITTED
SPITTER
SPITTING
SPITTLE
SPITTLEFORK
SPITTLEMAN
SPITTLEMEN
SPITTLESTAFF
SPITTOON
SPITZ
SPITZENBERG
SPITZENBURG
SPITZER
SPITZFLUTE
SPITZKOP
SPIV
SPLACHNOID
SPLACKNUCK
SPLAIRGE
SPLAKE
SPLANCHNIC
SPLASH
SPLASHBOARD
SPLASHDOWN
SPLASHED
SPLASHER
SPLASHIER
SPLASHIEST
SPLASHING
SPLASHPROOF
SPLASHWING
SPLASHY
SPLAT

SPLATCH
SPLATCHER
SPLATHER
SPLATHERING
SPLATTER
SPLATTERDASH
SPLATTERER
SPLATTERFACED
SPLATTERWORK
SPLAY
SPLAYED
SPLAYER
SPLAYFEET
SPLAYFOOT
SPLAYFOOTED
SPLAYMOUTH
SPLAYMOUTHED
SPLAYMOUTHS
SPLEEN
SPLEENED
SPLEENFUL
SPLEENFULLY
SPLEENIER
SPLEENIEST
SPLEENING
SPLEENISH
SPLEENISHLY
SPLEENISHNESS
SPLEENLESS
SPLEENWORT
SPLEENY
SPLEET
SPLENADENOMA
SPLENALGIA
SPLENALGIC
SPLENALGY
SPLENATROPHY
SPLENAUXE
SPLENCULI
SPLENCULUS
SPLENDACEOUS
SPLENDACIOUS
SPLENDACIOUSLY
SPLENDATIOUS
SPLENDENT
SPLENDENTLY
SPLENDESCENT
SPLENDID
SPLENDIDER
SPLENDIDEST
SPLENDIDLY
SPLENDIDNESS
SPLENDIFEROUS
SPLENDOR
SPLENDOROUS
SPLENDOUR
SPLENDROUS
SPLENECTAMA
SPLENECTASIS
SPLENECTOMIES
SPLENECTOMY
SPLENECTOPIA
SPLENECTOPY
SPLENELCOSIS
SPLENEMIA
SPLENEOLUS
SPLENETIC
SPLENETICAL
SPLENETIVE
SPLENIA
SPLENIAL
SPLENIC
SPLENICAL
SPLENICTERUS
SPLENIFORM
SPLENII
SPLENITIS

SPLENITIVE
SPLENIUM
SPLENIUS
SPLENIZATION
SPLENOBLAST
SPLENOCELE
SPLENOCLEISIS
SPLENOCOLIC
SPLENOCYTE
SPLENODYNIA
SPLENOGRAPHY
SPLENOHEMIA
SPLENOID
SPLENOLOGY
SPLENOLYMPH
SPLENOLYSIN
SPLENOLYSIS
SPLENOMA
SPLENOMEGALY
SPLENONCUS
SPLENOPATHY
SPLENOPEXIA
SPLENOPEXIS
SPLENOPEXY
SPLENOPTOSIA
SPLENOPTOSIS
SPLENOTOMY
SPLENOTOXIN
SPLENT
SPLENULUS
SPLEUCHAN
SPLICE
SPLICED
SPLICER
SPLICING
SPLINE
SPLINED
SPLINING
SPLINT
SPLINTAGE
SPLINTED
SPLINTER
SPLINTERED
SPLINTERING
SPLINTERNEW
SPLINTERPROOF
SPLINTERY
SPLINTING
SPLINTS
SPLINTWOOD
SPLINTY
SPLIT
SPLITBEAK
SPLITE
SPLITFINGER
SPLITFRUIT
SPLITMOUTH
SPLITNEW
SPLITNUT
SPLITSAW
SPLITTAIL
SPLITTED
SPLITTER
SPLITTERMAN
SPLITTING
SPLITWORM
SPLODGE
SPLOIT
SPLORE
SPLOSH
SPLOSHY
SPLOTCH
SPLOTCHED
SPLOTCHIER
SPLOTCHIEST
SPLOTCHILY
SPLOTCHINESS

SPLOTCHING
SPLOTCHY
SPLOTHER
SPLUNGE
SPLUNT
SPLURGE
SPLURGED
SPLURGILY
SPLURGING
SPLURGY
SPLURT
SPLUTHER
SPLUTTER
SPLUTTERED
SPLUTTERER
SPLUTTERING
SPOACH
SPODE
SPODIOSITE
SPODIUM
SPODOGENIC
SPODOGENOUS
SPODOMANCY
SPODOMANTIC
SPODUMENE
SPOFFISH
SPOFFLE
SPOFFY
SPOGEL
SPOIL
SPOILAGE
SPOILATION
SPOILED
SPOILER
SPOILFIVE
SPOILFUL
SPOILING
SPOILMENT
SPOILS
SPOILSMAN
SPOILSMEN
SPOILSMONGER
SPOILSPORT
SPOILT
SPOKE
SPOKED
SPOKEN
SPOKES
SPOKESHAVE
SPOKESMAN
SPOKESMEN
SPOKESTER
SPOKESWOMAN
SPOKESWOMEN
SPOKING
SPOKY
SPOLIA
SPOLIARIA
SPOLIARIUM
SPOLIARY
SPOLIATE
SPOLIATED
SPOLIATING
SPOLIATION
SPOLIATIVE
SPOLIATOR
SPOLIATORY
SPOLIUM
SPONDAIC
SPONDAICAL
SPONDAIZE
SPONDEAN
SPONDEE
SPONDIL
SPONDULICKS
SPONDULICS
SPONDULIX

SPONDYL
SPONDYLE
SPONDYLIC
SPONDYLIOID
SPONDYLITIC
SPONDYLITIS
SPONDYLIUM
SPONDYLIZEMA
SPONDYLOCACE
SPONDYLOID
SPONDYLOSIS
SPONDYLOTOMY
SPONDYLOUS
SPONDYLUS
SPONE
SPONG
SPONGE
SPONGECAKE
SPONGED
SPONGEOUS
SPONGER
SPONGEWOOD
SPONGIAN
SPONGICOLOUS
SPONGIER
SPONGIEST
SPONGIFEROUS
SPONGIFORM
SPONGILLID
SPONGILLINE
SPONGILY
SPONGIN
SPONGINBLAST
SPONGINESS
SPONGING
SPONGIOBLAST
SPONGIOCYTE
SPONGIOLE
SPONGIOLIN
SPONGIOPILIN
SPONGIOSE
SPONGIOSITY
SPONGIOUS
SPONGIOUSNESS
SPONGOBLAST
SPONGOID
SPONGOLOGY
SPONGOPHORE
SPONGY
SPONK
SPONSAL
SPONSALIA
SPONSION
SPONSIONAL
SPONSON
SPONSOR
SPONSORIAL
SPONSORSHIP
SPONSPECK
SPONTANEITIES
SPONTANEITY
SPONTANEOUS
SPONTANEOUSLY
SPONTANEOUSNESS
SPONTON
SPONTOON
SPOOF
SPOOFED
SPOOFER
SPOOFERIES
SPOOFERY
SPOOFING
SPOOFISH
SPOOK
SPOOKERIES
SPOOKERY
SPOOKIER

SPOOKIES
SPOOKIEST
SPOOKILY
SPOOKINESS
SPOOKISH
SPOOKISM
SPOOKIST
SPOOKOLOGIST
SPOOKOLOGY
SPOOKY
SPOOL
SPOOLED
SPOOLER
SPOOLING
SPOOLWOOD
SPOON
SPOONBILL
SPOONBREAD
SPOONDRIFT
SPOONED
SPOONER
SPOONERISM
SPOONEY
SPOONEYISM
SPOONEYLY
SPOONEYNESS
SPOONEYS
SPOONFUL
SPOONFULS
SPOONHUTCH
SPOONIER
SPOONIES
SPOCNIEST
SPOONILY
SPOONINESS
SPOONING
SPOONISM
SPOONMAKER
SPOONMAKING
SPOONWAYS
SPOONWISE
SPOONWOOD
SPOONY
SPOONYISM
SPOOR
SPOORED
SPOORER
SPOORING
SPOORN
SPORABOLA
SPORACEOUS
SPORADES
SPORADIAL
SPORADIC
SPORADICAL
SPORADICALLY
SPORADICALNESS
SPORADICITY
SPORADIN
SPORADISM
SPORAL
SPORANGE
SPORANGIA
SPORANGIAL
SPORANGIFORM
SPORANGIOID
SPORANGIOLA
SPORANGIOLE
SPORANGIOLUM
SPORANGITE
SPORANGIUM
SPORATION
SPORE
SPORED
SPOREFORMER
SPOREFORMING
SPORELING

SPORES
SPORICIDE
SPORID
SPORIDESM
SPORIDIA
SPORIDIAL
SPORIDIOLE
SPORIDIOLUM
SPORIDIUM
SPORIFEROUS
SPORING
SPORIPARITY
SPORIPAROUS
SPOROBLAST
SPOROCARP
SPOROCARPIA
SPOROCARPIUM
SPOROCYST
SPOROCYSTIC
SPOROCYSTID
SPOROCYTE
SPORODERM
SPORODOCHIA
SPORODOCHIUM
SPORODUCT
SPOROGEN
SPOROGENESIS
SPOROGENIC
SPOROGENOUS
SPOROGENY
SPOROGONE
SPOROGONIA
SPOROGONIAL
SPOROGONIC
SPOROGONIUM
SPOROGONY
SPOROID
SPOROLOGIST
SPOROMYCOSIS
SPORONT
SPOROPHORE
SPOROPHORIC
SPOROPHOROUS
SPOROPHYDIUM
SPOROPHYL
SPOROPHYLL
SPOROPHYLLUM
SPOROPHYTE
SPOROPHYTIC
SPOROPLASM
SPOROSAC
SPOROSTEGIUM
SPOROSTROTE
SPOROUS
SPOROZOAL
SPOROZOAN
SPOROZOIC
SPOROZOID
SPOROZOITE
SPOROZOOID
SPOROZOON
SPORRAN
SPORT
SPORTABILITY
SPORTABLE
SPORTANCE
SPORTED
SPORTER
SPORTFUL
SPORTFULLY
SPORTFULNESS
SPORTIER
SPORTIEST
SPORTILY
SPORTINESS
SPORTING
SPORTIVE

SPORTIVELY
SPORTIVENESS
SPORTLING
SPORTS
SPORTSCAST
SPORTSCASTER
SPORTSMAN
SPORTSMANLIKE
SPORTSMANLY
SPORTSMANSHIP
SPORTSMEN
SPORTSOME
SPORTSWEAR
SPORTSWOMAN
SPORTULA
SPORTULAE
SPORTY
SPORULAR
SPORULATE
SPORULATED
SPORULATING
SPORULATION
SPORULE
SPORULOID
SPOSH
SPOSHY
SPOT
SPOTLESS
SPOTLESSLY
SPOTLESSNESS
SPOTLIGHT
SPOTLIGHTER
SPOTRUMP
SPOTS
SPOTSMAN
SPOTSMEN
SPOTTABLE
SPOTTAIL
SPOTTED
SPOTTELDY
SPOTTER
SPOTTIER
SPOTTIEST
SPOTTILY
SPOTTINESS
SPOTTING
SPOTTLE
SPOTTY
SPOTWELDER
SPOUCHER
SPOUSAGE
SPOUSAL
SPOUSALLY
SPOUSE
SPOUSED
SPOUSEHOOD
SPOUSING
SPOUT
SPOUTED
SPOUTER
SPOUTINESS
SPOUTING
SPOUTLESS
SPOUTY
SPOW
SPOWE
SPRACHLE
SPRACK
SPRACKLY
SPRACKNESS
SPRADDLE
SPRAG
SPRAGGED
SPRAGGER
SPRAGGING
SPRAGGLY
SPRAGMAN

SPRAICH
SPRAIN
SPRAINED
SPRAING
SPRAINING
SPRAINTS
SPRAITH
SPRANG
SPRANGLE
SPRANGLY
SPRANK
SPRAT
SPRATTED
SPRATTER
SPRATTING
SPRATTLE
SPRATTLED
SPRATTLING
SPRATTY
SPRAUCHLE
SPRAWL
SPRAWLED
SPRAWLER
SPRAWLIER
SPRAWLIEST
SPRAWLING
SPRAWLINGLY
SPRAWLY
SPRAY
SPRAYBOARD
SPRAYED
SPRAYER
SPRAYEY
SPRAYING
SPRAYS
SPREAD
SPREADATION
SPREADBOARD
SPREADER
SPREADHEAD
SPREADING
SPREADINGLY
SPREADINGNESS
SPREADOVER
SPREADY
SPREAGH
SPREAGHERY
SPREATH
SPRECKLE
SPREE
SPREED
SPREEING
SPREEUW
SPRENG
SPRENGE
SPRENGING
SPRENT
SPRET
SPRETTY
SPREW
SPRIDHOGUE
SPRIER
SPRIEST
SPRIG
SPRIGGED
SPRIGGER
SPRIGGIER
SPRIGGIEST
SPRIGGING
SPRIGGY
SPRIGHT
SPRIGHTED
SPRIGHTFUL
SPRIGHTFULLY
SPRIGHTFULNESS
SPRIGHTLIER
SPRIGHTLIEST

SPRIGHTLILY
SPRIGHTLINESS
SPRIGHTLY
SPRIGHTY
SPRIGTAIL
SPRINDGE
SPRING
SPRINGAL
SPRINGALD
SPRINGBOARD
SPRINGBOK
SPRINGBOKS
SPRINGBUCK
SPRINGE
SPRINGED
SPRINGEING
SPRINGER
SPRINGERLE
SPRINGFINGER
SPRINGFISH
SPRINGFISHES
SPRINGFUL
SPRINGHAAS
SPRINGHALT
SPRINGHEAD
SPRINGHOUSE
SPRINGIER
SPRINGIEST
SPRINGILY
SPRINGINESS
SPRINGING
SPRINGINGLY
SPRINGLE
SPRINGLED
SPRINGLESS
SPRINGLET
SPRINGLIKE
SPRINGLING
SPRINGLY
SPRINGMAKER
SPRINGMAKING
SPRINGS
SPRINGTAIL
SPRINGTIDE
SPRINGTIME
SPRINGTRAP
SPRINGWOOD
SPRINGWORM
SPRINGWORT
SPRINGY
SPRINK
SPRINKLE
SPRINKLED
SPRINKLER
SPRINKLERED
SPRINKLING
SPRINT
SPRINTED
SPRINTER
SPRINTING
SPRIT
SPRITE
SPRITELY
SPRITISH
SPRITSAIL
SPRITTAIL
SPRITTED
SPRITTING
SPRITTY
SPRITZ
SPRITZER
SPROAT
SPROCKET
SPROD
SPROGUE
SPROIL
SPRONG

SPROSE
SPROT
SPROTTLE
SPROTY
SPROUT
SPROUTAGE
SPROUTED
SPROUTER
SPROUTING
SPROUTLAND
SPROUTLING
SPROUTS
SPROWSY
SPRUCE
SPRUCED
SPRUCELY
SPRUCENESS
SPRUCER
SPRUCERY
SPRUCEST
SPRUCIFICATION
SPRUCIFY
SPRUCING
SPRUE
SPRUER
SPRUG
SPRUIKER
SPRUIT
SPRUNG
SPRUNK
SPRUNNY
SPRUNT
SPRUNTLY
SPRUSADO
SPRUSH
SPRY
SPRYER
SPRYEST
SPRYLY
SPRYNESS
SPUD
SPUDDED
SPUDDER
SPUDDING
SPUDDLE
SPUDDY
SPUDS
SPUE
SPUFFLE
SPUG
SPUILZIE
SPULE
SPULYIEMENT
SPULZIE
SPUME
SPUMED
SPUMESCENCE
SPUMESCENT
SPUMIER
SPUMIEST
SPUMIFEROUS
SPUMIFORM
SPUMING
SPUMOID
SPUMONE
SPUMONI
SPUMOSE
SPUMOUS
SPUMY
SPUN
SPUNG
SPUNGE
SPUNK
SPUNKIE
SPUNKIER
SPUNKIEST
SPUNKILY

SPUNKINESS
SPUNKY
SPUNNIES
SPUNNY
SPUR
SPURDIE
SPURDOG
SPURFLOWER
SPURGALL
SPURGE
SPURIA
SPURIAE
SPURIOUS
SPURIOUSLY
SPURIOUSNESS
SPURL
SPURLESS
SPURLET
SPURLIKE
SPURMAKER
SPURMONEY
SPURN
SPURNED
SPURNER
SPURNING
SPURNPOINT
SPURNWATER
SPURRED
SPURRER
SPURREY
SPURRIER
SPURRIES
SPURRING
SPURRINGS
SPURRITE
SPURRY
SPURS
SPURT
SPURTED
SPURTER
SPURTING
SPURTIVE
SPURTIVELY
SPURTLE
SPURTLEBLADE
SPURTS
SPURWAY
SPURWING
SPURWORT
SPUT
SPUTA
SPUTATIVE
SPUTE
SPUTNIK
SPUTTER
SPUTTERED
SPUTTERER
SPUTTERING
SPUTTERINGLY
SPUTTERY
SPUTUM
SPUTUMARY
SPUTUMOSE
SPUTUMOUS
SPY
SPYBOAT
SPYER
SPYGLASS
SPYING
SQUAB
SQUABASH
SQUABASHER
SQUABBED
SQUABBER
SQUABBIER
SQUABBIEST
SQUABBING

SQUABBISH
SQUABBLE
SQUABBLED
SQUABBLER
SQUABBLING
SQUABBLINGLY
SQUABBLY
SQUABBY
SQUACCO
SQUACCOS
SQUAD
SQUADDED
SQUADDING
SQUADDY
SQUADER
SQUADRATE
SQUADRISM
SQUADROL
SQUADRON
SQUADRONE
SQUADRONED
SQUADRONING
SQUAGGA
SQUAIL
SQUAILER
SQUAILS
SQUALENE
SQUALID
SQUALIDITY
SQUALIDLY
SQUALIDNESS
SQUALIFORM
SQUALL
SQUALLED
SQUALLER
SQUALLERY
SQUALLIER
SQUALLIEST
SQUALLING
SQUALLY
SQUALODONT
SQUALOID
SQUALOR
SQUAM
SQUAMA
SQUAMACEOUS
SQUAMAE
SQUAMATE
SQUAMATED
SQUAMATINE
SQUAMATION
SQUAME
SQUAMELLA
SQUAMELLAE
SQUAMELLATE
SQUAMEOUS
SQUAMIFEROUS
SQUAMIFORM
SQUAMIFY
SQUAMIGEROUS
SQUAMISH
SQUAMOID
SQUAMOSA
SQUAMOSAL
SQUAMOSE
SQUAMOSELY
SQUAMOSENESS
SQUAMOSITY
SQUAMOUS
SQUAMOUSLY
SQUAMOUSNESS
SQUAMULA
SQUAMULAE
SQUAMULATE
SQUAMULATION
SQUAMULE
SQUAMULOSE

SQUAMY
SQUANDER
SQUANDERED
SQUANDERER
SQUANDERING
SQUANDERINGLY
SQUANTUM
SQUAP
SQUARE
SQUAREAGE
SQUARECAP
SQUARED
SQUAREFACE
SQUAREHEAD
SQUARELY
SQUAREMAN
SQUAREMEN
SQUARENESS
SQUARER
SQUARES
SQUARETAIL
SQUARIER
SQUARING
SQUARISH
SQUARISHLY
SQUARK
SQUARROSE
SQUARROSELY
SQUARROUS
SQUARRULOSE
SQUARSON
SQUARSONRY
SQUARY
SQUASH
SQUASHBERRY
SQUASHED
SQUASHER
SQUASHIER
SQUASHIEST
SQUASHILY
SQUASHINESS
SQUASHING
SQUASHY
SQUAT
SQUATAROLE
SQUATEROLE
SQUATINID
SQUATINOID
SQUATLY
SQUATMORE
SQUATNESS
SQUATTAGE
SQUATTED
SQUATTER
SQUATTIER
SQUATTIEST
SQUATTILY
SQUATTINESS
SQUATTING
SQUATTISH
SQUATTLE
SQUATTOCRACY
SQUATTY
SQUAW
SQUAWBERRIES
SQUAWBERRY
SQUAWBUSH
SQUAWFISH
SQUAWFISHES
SQUAWFLOWER
SQUAWK
SQUAWKED
SQUAWKER
SQUAWKIE
SQUAWKIER
SQUAWKIEST
SQUAWKING

SQUAWKINGLY
SQUAWKY
SQUAWL
SQUAWROOT
SQUAWWEED
SQUDGE
SQUDGY
SQUEAK
SQUEAKED
SQUEAKER
SQUEAKERY
SQUEAKILY
SQUEAKINESS
SQUEAKING
SQUEAKINGLY
SQUEAKY
SQUEAL
SQUEALED
SQUEALER
SQUEALING
SQUEAM
SQUEAMISH
SQUEAMISHLY
SQUEAMISHNESS
SQUEEF
SQUEEGE
SQUEEGEE
SQUEEGEED
SQUEEGEEING
SQUEEL
SQUEEZABLE
SQUEEZE
SQUEEZED
SQUEEZEMAN
SQUEEZER
SQUEEZING
SQUEEZINGLY
SQUEEZY
SQUEG
SQUELCH
SQUELCHED
SQUELCHER
SQUELCHIER
SQUELCHIEST
SQUELCHILY
SQUELCHINESS
SQUELCHING
SQUELCHINGLY
SQUELCHINGNESS
SQUELCHY
SQUELETTE
SQUET
SQUETEAGUE
SQUETEE
SQUIB
SQUIBBED
SQUIBBER
SQUIBBERY
SQUIBBING
SQUIBBISH
SQUIBCRACK
SQUIBSTER
SQUID
SQUIDDED
SQUIDDER
SQUIDDING
SQUIDDLE
SQUIDGE
SQUIDGEREEN
SQUIDGIER
SQUIDGIEST
SQUIDGY
SQUIDS
SQUIFFED
SQUIFFER
SQUIFFIER
SQUIFFIEST

SQUIFFY
SQUIGGLE
SQUIGGLIER
SQUIGGLIEST
SQUIGGLY
SQUILGEE
SQUILGEED
SQUILGEEING
SQUILGEER
SQUILL
SQUILLA
SQUILLAGEE
SQUILLGEE
SQUILLIAN
SQUILLID
SQUILLITIC
SQUIN
SQUINACY
SQUINANCE
SQUINANT
SQUINCH
SQUINNY
SQUINT
SQUINTED
SQUINTER
SQUINTING
SQUINTINGLY
SQUINTINGNESS
SQUINTY
SQUIR
SQUIRAGE
SQUIRALTY
SQUIRARCH
SQUIRARCHAL
SQUIRARCHY
SQUIRE
SQUIREARCH
SQUIREARCHAL
SQUIREARCHIES
SQUIREARCHY
SQUIRED
SQUIREEN
SQUIRELING
SQUIRELY
SQUIRESS
SQUIRET
SQUIRING
SQUIRISH
SQUIRK
SQUIRL
SQUIRM
SQUIRMED
SQUIRMER
SQUIRMIER
SQUIRMIEST
SQUIRMINESS
SQUIRMING
SQUIRMINGLY
SQUIRR
SQUIRREL
SQUIRRELFISH
SQUIRRELFISHES
SQUIRRELTAIL
SQUIRRELY
SQUIRT
SQUIRTED
SQUIRTER
SQUIRTINESS
SQUIRTING
SQUIRTINGLY
SQUIRTISH
SQUIRTS
SQUIRTY
SQUISH
SQUISHED
SQUISHING
SQUISHY

SQUISS
SQUIT
SQUITCH
SQUITTER
SQUIZ
SQUSH
SQUSHY
SQUUSH
SQUUSHY
SRADDHA
SRADH
SRADHA
SRAMANA
SRAVAKA
SRI
SRUTI
SSU
STAAB
STAATSRAAD
STAB
STABBED
STABBER
STABBING
STABBINGLY
STABILATE
STABILE
STABILIFY
STABILISE
STABILIST
STABILITATE
STABILITIES
STABILITY
STABILIZATION
STABILIZATOR
STABILIZE
STABILIZED
STABILIZER
STABILIZING
STABLE
STABLEBOY
STABLED
STABLEKEEPER
STABLEMAN
STABLEMEAL
STABLEMEN
STABLENESS
STABLER
STABLES
STABLESTAND
STABLING
STABLISH
STABLY
STABOY
STABWORT
STACCATO
STACCATOS
STACHER
STACHYDRIN
STACHYDRINE
STACHYOSE
STACK
STACKAGE
STACKED
STACKENCLOUD
STACKER
STACKET
STACKFREED
STACKGARTH
STACKING
STACKMAN
STACKMEN
STACKS
STACKSTAND
STACKYARD
STACTE
STACTOMETER
STAD

STADDA
STADDLE
STADDLING
STADE
STADHOLDER
STADHOUSE
STADIA
STADIAL
STADIC
STADIE
STADIMETER
STADIOMETER
STADION
STADIUM
STADTHOLDER
STAFETTE
STAFF
STAFFAGE
STAFFED
STAFFELITE
STAFFER
STAFFIER
STAFFING
STAFFISH
STAFFMAN
STAFFMEN
STAFFS
STAFFSTRIKER
STAG
STAGBUSH
STAGE
STAGECOACH
STAGECOACHING
STAGECRAFT
STAGED
STAGEHAND
STAGEHOUSE
STAGELAND
STAGELIKE
STAGEMAN
STAGEMEN
STAGER
STAGERY
STAGES
STAGEWORTHY
STAGEY
STAGGARD
STAGGART
STAGGED
STAGGER
STAGGERBUSH
STAGGERED
STAGGERER
STAGGERING
STAGGERINGLY
STAGGERS
STAGGERWEED
STAGGERWORT
STAGGERY
STAGGIE
STAGGING
STAGGY
STAGHEAD
STAGHORN
STAGHOUND
STAGHUNT
STAGHUNTER
STAGHUNTING
STAGIARY
STAGIER
STAGIEST
STAGILY
STAGINESS
STAGING
STAGION
STAGMOMETER
STAGNANCY

STAGNANT
STAGNANTLY
STAGNANTNESS
STAGNATE
STAGNATED
STAGNATING
STAGNATION
STAGNATORY
STAGNE
STAGNICOLOUS
STAGNUM
STAGS
STAGSKIN
STAGWORM
STAGY
STAID
STAIDLY
STAIDNESS
STAIG
STAIL
STAIN
STAINABLE
STAINED
STAINER
STAINIERITE
STAINING
STAINLESS
STAINLESSLY
STAIO
STAIR
STAIRBEAK
STAIRBUILDER
STAIRBUILDING
STAIRCASE
STAIRHEAD
STAIRS
STAIRSTEP
STAIRWAY
STAIRWELL
STAIRWORK
STAITH
STAITHMAN
STAITHMEN
STAIVER
STAKE
STAKED
STAKEHEAD
STAKEHOLDER
STAKEMASTER
STAKEOUT
STAKER
STAKING
STALACE
STALACTIC
STALACTICAL
STALACTIFORM
STALACTITAL
STALACTITE
STALACTITES
STALACTITIC
STALACTITIED
STALAG
STALAGMITE
STALAGMITIC
STALDER
STALE
STALED
STALELY
STALEMATE
STALEMATED
STALEMATING
STALENESS
STALER
STALEST
STALING
STALK
STALKED

STALKER
STALKIER
STALKIEST
STALKING
STALKINGLY
STALKLESS
STALKLET
STALKLIKE
STALKO
STALKOES
STALKS
STALKY
STALL
STALLAGE
STALLAND
STALLAR
STALLARY
STALLBOARD
STALLBOAT
STALLED
STALLENGER
STALLER
STALLING
STALLINGER
STALLINGKEN
STALLION
STALLIONIZE
STALLKEEPER
STALLMAN
STALLMEN
STALLMENT
STALLON
STALLS
STALWART
STALWARTISM
STALWARTIZE
STALWARTLY
STALWARTNESS
STALWORTH
STALWORTHLY
STALWORTHNESS
STAM
STAMBHA
STAMBOULINE
STAMEN
STAMENED
STAMENS
STAMIN
STAMINA
STAMINAL
STAMINATE
STAMINEAL
STAMINEOUS
STAMINODE
STAMINODIA
STAMINODIUM
STAMINODY
STAMMEL
STAMMER
STAMMERER
STAMMERING
STAMMERINGLY
STAMMERINGNESS
STAMMERWORT
STAMNOS
STAMP
STAMPAGE
STAMPED
STAMPEDE
STAMPEDED
STAMPEDER
STAMPEDING
STAMPEDO
STAMPEE
STAMPER
STAMPERY
STAMPHEAD

STAMPING
STAMPLE
STAMPMAN
STAMPMEN
STAMPS
STAMPSMAN
STAMPSMEN
STAMPWEED
STANCE
STANCH
STANCHED
STANCHEL
STANCHELED
STANCHER
STANCHEST
STANCHING
STANCHION
STAND
STANDAGE
STANDARD
STANDARDBRED
STANDARDIZABLE
STANDARDIZATION
STANDARDIZE
STANDARDIZED
STANDARDIZER
STANDARDIZING
STANDBY
STANDBYS
STANDEE
STANDEL
STANDELWELKS
STANDELWORT
STANDER
STANDERGRASS
STANDERWORT
STANDFAST
STANDING
STANDISH
STANDOFF
STANDOFFISH
STANDOFFISHNESS
STANDOUT
STANDPAT
STANDPATISM
STANDPATTER
STANDPATTISM
STANDPIPE
STANDPOINT
STANDPOST
STANDSTILL
STANDUP
STANE
STANG
STANHOPE
STANINE
STANITSA
STANITZA
STANJEN
STANK
STANKIE
STANN
STANNANE
STANNARIES
STANNARY
STANNATE
STANNATOR
STANNEL
STANNER
STANNERS
STANNERY
STANNIC
STANNID
STANNIDE
STANNIFEROUS
STANNITE
STANNO

STANNOTYPE
STANNOUS
STANNUM
STANNYL
STANZA
STANZAED
STANZAIC
STANZAICAL
STANZAICALLY
STANZAS
STANZE
STANZO
STAP
STAPEDECTOMY
STAPEDES
STAPEDIAL
STAPEDIFORM
STAPEDIUS
STAPELIA
STAPES
STAPH
STAPHISAGRIA
STAPHYLE
STAPHYLEDEMA
STAPHYLIC
STAPHYLINE
STAPHYLINIC
STAPHYLINID
STAPHYLION
STAPHYLITIS
STAPHYLOMA
STAPHYLONCUS
STAPHYLOSIS
STAPHYLOTOME
STAPHYLOTOMY
STAPLE
STAPLED
STAPLER
STAPLING
STAPP
STAPPLE
STAR
STARBLIND
STARBLOOM
STARBOARD
STARBOLINS
STARBOWLINES
STARBRIGHT
STARCH
STARCHBOARD
STARCHED
STARCHER
STARCHFLOWER
STARCHIER
STARCHIEST
STARCHILY
STARCHINESS
STARCHING
STARCHLY
STARCHMAKER
STARCHMAKING
STARCHMAN
STARCHMEN
STARCHROOT
STARCHWORKS
STARCHWORT
STARCHY
STARCRAFT
STARDOM
STARDUST
STARE
STARED
STAREE
STARER
STARETS
STARFISH
STARFISHES

STARFLOWER
STARFRUIT
STARGAZE
STARGAZED
STARGAZER
STARGAZING
STARIK
STARING
STARK
STARKEN
STARKER
STARKEST
STARKLE
STARKY
STARLESS
STARLESSLY
STARLESSNESS
STARLET
STARLIGHT
STARLIGHTED
STARLIGHTS
STARLIKE
STARLING
STARLIT
STARLITE
STARLITTEN
STARMONGER
STARN
STARNEL
STARNIE
STARNOSE
STARNY
STAROST
STAROSTA
STAROSTI
STAROSTY
STARR
STARRED
STARRIER
STARRIEST
STARRIFY
STARRILY
STARRINESS
STARRING
STARRINGLY
STARRY
STARS
STARSHAKE
STARSHINE
STARSHIP
STARSHOOT
STARSHOT
STARSTONE
STARSTROKE
START
STARTED
STARTER
STARTFUL
STARTFULNESS
STARTHROAT
STARTING
STARTINGLY
STARTISH
STARTLE
STARTLED
STARTLER
STARTLING
STARTLINGLY
STARTLINGNESS
STARTLISH
STARTLISHNESS
STARTLY
STARTS
STARTY
STARVATION
STARVE
STARVEACRE

STARVED	STATISM	STAVESACRE	STEAPSIN	STEENKIRK
STARVEDLY	STATIST	STAVEWOOD	STEARATE	STEEP
STARVELING	STATISTIC	STAVING	STEARIC	STEEPDOWN
STARVEN	STATISTICAL	STAVRITE	STEARIFORM	STEEPED
STARVER	STATISTICALLY	STAW	STEARIN	STEEPEN
STARVING	STATISTICIAN	STAWSOME	STEARINE	STEEPER
STARVY	STATISTICIZE	STAXIS	STEARONE	STEEPEST
STARWISE	STATISTICS	STAY	STEAROPTENE	STEEPGRASS
STARWORM	STATISTOLOGY	STAYED	STEARRHEA	STEEPING
STARWORT	STATIVE	STAYER	STEARRHOEA	STEEPISH
STARY	STATIZE	STAYING	STEARYL	STEEPLE
STASES	STATOBLAST	STAYLACE	STEATIN	STEEPLEBUSH
STASH	STATOCRACY	STAYLESS	STEATITE	STEEPLECHASE
STASHIE	STATOCYST	STAYLESSNESS	STEATITIC	STEEPLECHASER
STASIDIA	STATOHM	STAYMAKER	STEATOCELE	STEEPLECHASING
STASIDION	STATOLATRY	STAYMAKING	STEATOGENOUS	STEEPLED
STASIMA	STATOLITH	STAYNIL	STEATOLYSIS	STEEPLEJACK
STASIMETRIC	STATOLITHIC	STAYPAK	STEATOLYTIC	STEEPLETOP
STASIMON	STATOMETER	STAYS	STEATOMA	STEEPLY
STASIMORPHY	STATOR	STAYSAIL	STEATOMAS	STEEPNESS
STASIPHOBIA	STATORHAB	STAYSHIP	STEATOMATA	STEEPWEED
STASIS	STATOSCOPE	STCHI	STEATOMATOUS	STEEPWORT
STASSFURTITE	STATOSPORE	STEAD	STEATOPATHIC	STEEPY
STATABLE	STATUA	STEADABLE	STEATOPYGA	STEER
STATANT	STATUARIES	STEADFAST	STEATOPYGIA	STEERABLE
STATARY	STATUARISM	STEADFASTLY	STEATOPYGIC	STEERAGE
STATCOULOMB	STATUARIST	STEADFASTNESS	STEATOPYGOUS	STEERAGEWAY
STATE	STATUARY	STEADIED	STEATOPYGY	STEERED
STATECRAFT	STATUE	STEADIER	STEATORRHEA	STEERER
STATED	STATUECRAFT	STEADIEST	STEATORRHOEA	STEERING
STATEDLY	STATUED	STEADILY	STEATOSES	STEERLING
STATEFUL	STATUELIKE	STEADIMENT	STEATOSIS	STEERSMAN
STATEFULLY	STATUES	STEADINESS	STECH	STEERSMATE
STATEFULNESS	STATUESQUE	STEADING	STECHADOS	STEERSMEN
STATELESS	STATUESQUELY	STEADITE	STECHLING	STEERY
STATELET	STATUESQUENESS	STEADMAN	STECKLING	STEEVE
STATELIER	STATUETTE	STEADY	STEDFAST	STEEVED
STATELIEST	STATUING	STEADYING	STEDFASTLY	STEEVELY
STATELINESS	STATURE	STEADYINGLY	STEDFASTNESS	STEEVER
STATELY	STATURED	STEAK	STEE	STEEVING
STATEMENT	STATUS	STEAKHOUSE	STEED	STEFLY
STATEMENTS	STATUSES	STEAL	STEEK	STEG
STATEMONGER	STATUTABLE	STEALAGE	STEEKKAN	STEGANOGRAM
STATEQUAKE	STATUTABLY	STEALER	STEEL	STEGH
STATER	STATUTE	STEALING	STEELBOW	STEGNOSIS
STATERA	STATUTORILY	STEALINGLY	STEELE	STEGNOTIC
STATEROOM	STATUTORY	STEALTH	STEELED	STEGOCARPOUS
STATESBOY	STATUTUM	STEALTHIER	STEELEN	STEGODON
STATESIDE	STATVOLT	STEALTHIEST	STEELER	STEGODONS
STATESMAN	STAUMREL	STEALTHILY	STEELHEAD	STEGODONT
STATESMANLIKE	STAUNCH	STEALTHINESS	STEELHEADS	STEGODONTINE
STATESMANLY	STAUNCHED	STEALTHLIKE	STEELHEARTED	STEGOMYIA
STATESMANSHIP	STAUNCHER	STEALTHY	STEELIER	STEGOSAUR
STATESMEN	STAUNCHEST	STEALY	STEELIEST	STEGOSAURI
STATESMONGER	STAUNCHING	STEAM	STEELIFICATION	STEGOSAURIAN
STATESWOMAN	STAUNCHLY	STEAMBOAT	STEELIFIED	STEGOSAUROID
STATESWOMEN	STAUNCHNESS	STEAMBOATING	STEELIFY	STEGOSAURUS
STATEWAY	STAUP	STEAMBOATMAN	STEELIFYING	STEIN
STATFARAD	STAURACIN	STEAMBOATMEN	STEELINESS	STEINBOK
STATHMOS	STAURAXONIA	STEAMCAR	STEELING	STEINBUCK
STATIC	STAURAXONIAL	STEAMED	STEELMAKER	STEINKIRK
STATICAL	STAURION	STEAMER	STEELMAKING	STELA
STATICALLY	STAUROLATRIES	STEAMERLOAD	STEELPROOF	STELAE
STATICS	STAUROLATRY	STEAMFITTER	STEELWARE	STELAR
STATING	STAUROLITE	STEAMFITTING	STEELWORK	STELE
STATION	STAUROLITIC	STEAMIER	STEELWORKER	STELENE
STATIONAL	STAUROPEGIAL	STEAMIEST	STEELWORKING	STELES
STATIONARIES	STAUROPEGION	STEAMILY	STEELWORKS	STELIC
STATIONARILY	STAUROSCOPE	STEAMINESS	STEELY	STELL
STATIONARINESS	STAUROSCOPIC	STEAMING	STEELYARD	STELLAR
STATIONARY	STAUROTIDE	STEAMPIPE	STEELYARDS	STELLARATOR
STATIONED	STAVE	STEAMROLLER	STEEM	STELLARY
STATIONER	STAVED	STEAMSHIP	STEEN	STELLATE
STATIONERY	STAVER	STEAMTIGHT	STEENBOK	STELLATED
STATIONING	STAVERS	STEAMY	STEENBRAS	STELLATELY
STATIONMAN	STAVERWORT	STEAN	STEENBRASS	STELLATION
STATIONMASTER	STAVES	STEANING	STEENING	STELLATURE

STELLED
STELLERINE
STELLIFEROUS
STELLIFORM
STELLIFY
STELLING
STELLIONATE
STELLISCRIPT
STELLULAR
STELLULARLY
STELLULATE
STELOGRAPHY
STEM
STEMBOK
STEMFORM
STEMHEAD
STEMLESS
STEMLET
STEMMA
STEMMAS
STEMMATA
STEMMATOUS
STEMMED
STEMMER
STEMMERIES
STEMMERY
STEMMIER
STEMMIEST
STEMMING
STEMMY
STEMONACEOUS
STEMPEL
STEMPLE
STEMPOST
STEMSON
STEMWARE
STEN
STENCH
STENCHIER
STENCHIEST
STENCHING
STENCHY
STENCIL
STENCILED
STENCILER
STENCILING
STENCILLED
STENCILLER
STENCILLING
STENCILMAKER
STENCILMAKING
STEND
STENGAH
STENIA
STENION
STENO
STENOBENTHIC
STENOBREGMA
STENOCARDIA
STENOCARDIAC
STENOCEPHALY
STENOCHORIA
STENOCHROME
STENOCHROMY
STENOCRANIAL
STENOGASTRIC
STENOGASTRY
STENOGRAPH
STENOGRAPHED
STENOGRAPHER
STENOGRAPHIC
STENOGRAPHING
STENOGRAPHIST
STENOGRAPHY
STENOHALINE
STENOMETER
STENOPAEIC

STENOPAIC
STENOPEIC
STENOSED
STENOSIS
STENOSPHERE
STENOSTOMIA
STENOTHERMAL
STENOTHORAX
STENOTIC
STENOTROPIC
STENOTYPE
STENOTYPIC
STENOTYPIST
STENOTYPY
STENT
STENTER
STENTERER
STENTING
STENTMASTER
STENTON
STENTOR
STENTORIAN
STENTORIANLY
STENTORINE
STENTORIOUS
STENTORONIC
STENTREL
STEP
STEPAUNT
STEPBAIRN
STEPBROTHER
STEPCHILD
STEPDAME
STEPDAUGHTER
STEPFATHER
STEPFATHERLY
STEPGRANDCHILD
STEPGRANDFATHER
STEPGRANDMOTHER
STEPGRANDSON
STEPHANE
STEPHANIAL
STEPHANIC
STEPHANION
STEPHANITE
STEPHANOME
STEPHANOS
STEPLADDER
STEPMINNIE
STEPMOTHER
STEPMOTHERLINESS
STEPMOTHERLY
STEPNEPHEW
STEPNIECE
STEPONY
STEPPARENT
STEPPE
STEPPED
STEPPER
STEPPING
STEPPINGSTONE
STEPRELATION
STEPS
STEPSIRE
STEPSISTER
STEPSON
STEPSTONE
STEPT
STEPUNCLE
STEPWAY
STEPWISE
STERACLE
STERAD
STERADIAN
STERCOLIN
STERCORAEMIA
STERCORAL

STERCORARIES
STERCORARY
STERCORATE
STERCORATION
STERCOREMIA
STERCORITE
STERCOROL
STERCOROUS
STERCOVOROUS
STERCULIAD
STERE
STEREAGNOSIS
STEREID
STEREO
STEREOBATE
STEREOBATIC
STEREOCAMERA
STEREOCHEMIC
STEREOCHROME
STEREOCHROMY
STEREOED
STEREOGNOSIS
STEREOGRAM
STEREOGRAPH
STEREOGRAPHY
STEREOING
STEREOISOMER
STEREOM
STEREOMATRIX
STEREOME
STEREOMERIC
STEREOMETER
STEREOMETRIC
STEREOMETRY
STEREONEURAL
STEREOPHONE
STEREOPHONIC
STEREOPHONY
STEREOPHYSICS
STEREOPICTURE
STEREOPLASM
STEREOPSIS
STEREOPTICON
STEREOS
STEREOSCOPE
STEREOSCOPIC
STEREOSCOPY
STEREOSTATIC
STEREOSTATICS
STEREOTACTIC
STEREOTAXIS
STEREOTAXY
STEREOTOMIC
STEREOTOMIST
STEREOTOMY
STEREOTROPIC
STEREOTYPE
STEREOTYPED
STEREOTYPER
STEREOTYPERY
STEREOTYPIC
STEREOTYPICAL
STEREOTYPING
STEREOTYPIST
STEREOTYPY
STEREOVISION
STERIC
STERICAL
STERICALLY
STERID
STERIDE
STERIGMA
STERIGMATA
STERIGMATIC
STERILANT
STERILE
STERILELY

STERILENESS
STERILISE
STERILITIES
STERILITY
STERILIZATION
STERILIZE
STERILIZED
STERILIZER
STERILIZING
STERIN
STERLET
STERLING
STERLINGLY
STERLINGNESS
STERN
STERNA
STERNAD
STERNAGE
STERNAL
STERNALIS
STERNBERGITE
STERNCASTLE
STERNEBER
STERNEBRA
STERNEBRAL
STERNER
STERNEST
STERNFOREMOST
STERNFUL
STERNFULLY
STERNITE
STERNKNEE
STERNLY
STERNMAN
STERNMEN
STERNMOST
STERNNESS
STERNOCOSTAL
STERNOFACIAL
STERNOHYOID
STERNOMANCY
STERNONUCHAL
STERNOTHERE
STERNOTRIBE
STERNPOST
STERNSON
STERNUM
STERNUMS
STERNUTATION
STERNUTATIVE
STERNUTATOR
STERNUTATORY
STERNWARD
STERNWARDS
STERNWAY
STERNWAYS
STERNWORKS
STERO
STEROID
STEROL
STERRINCK
STERTOR
STERTORIOUS
STERTOROUS
STERTOROUSLY
STET
STETHAL
STETHOMETER
STETHOMETRIC
STETHOMETRY
STETHOPHONE
STETHOSCOPE
STETHOSCOPIC
STETHOSCOPY
STETHOSPASM
STETHY
STETTED

STETTING
STEVE
STEVEDORAGE
STEVEDORE
STEVEDORED
STEVEDORING
STEVEL
STEVEN
STEW
STEWARD
STEWARDESS
STEWARDLY
STEWARDRY
STEWARDSHIP
STEWART
STEWARTRY
STEWBUM
STEWED
STEWHOUSE
STEWING
STEWISH
STEWPAN
STEWPOND
STEWPOT
STEWY
STEY
STEYN
STEYNING
STHENE
STHENIA
STHENIC
STHENOCHIRE
STIACCIATO
STIB
STIBBLE
STIBBLER
STIBBLERIG
STIBIAL
STIBIALISM
STIBIATE
STIBIATED
STIBICONITE
STIBINE
STIBIUM
STIBNITE
STIBONIUM
STIBOPHEN
STICCADO
STICH
STICHADO
STICHARION
STICHEL
STICHERON
STICHIC
STICHICALLY
STICHID
STICHIDIA
STICHIDIUM
STICHOI
STICHOMANCY
STICHOMETRIC
STICHOMETRY
STICHOMYTHIC
STICHOMYTHY
STICHOS
STICHWORT
STICK
STICKAGE
STICKBALL
STICKED
STICKER
STICKERS
STICKERY
STICKFAST
STICKFUL
STICKFULS
STICKIER

STICKIEST	STIGMEOLOGY	STIMY	STIPULA	STOCKADO
STICKILY	STIGMES	STING	STIPULABLE	STOCKAGE
STICKINESS	STIGMONOSE	STINGAREE	STIPULACEOUS	STOCKANNET
STICKING	STIGONOMANCY	STINGAREEING	STIPULAR	STOCKBOW
STICKIT	STILB	STINGBULL	STIPULARY	STOCKBREEDER
STICKJAW	STILBENE	STINGE	STIPULATE	STOCKBREEDING
STICKLE	STILBESTROL	STINGER	STIPULATED	STOCKBROKER
STICKLEAF	STILBITE	STINGFISH	STIPULATING	STOCKBROKERAGE
STICKLEBACK	STILE	STINGFISHES	STIPULATIO	STOCKBROKING
STICKLED	STILEMAN	STINGIER	STIPULATION	STOCKCAR
STICKLER	STILEMEN	STINGIEST	STIPULATOR	STOCKED
STICKLING	STILET	STINGILY	STIPULATORY	STOCKER
STICKLY	STILETTE	STINGINESS	STIPULE	STOCKFATHER
STICKMAN	STILETTO	STINGING	STIPULED	STOCKFISH
STICKPIN	STILETTOED	STINGINGLY	STIPULIFORM	STOCKFISHES
STICKS	STILETTOES	STINGINGNESS	STIR	STOCKHOLDER
STICKSEED	STILETTOING	STINGLESS	STIRABOUT	STOCKHOLDING
STICKTAIL	STILETTOS	STINGO	STIRIA	STOCKHOUSE
STICKTIGHT	STILL	STINGRAY	STIRK	STOCKIER
STICKUM	STILLAGE	STINGTAIL	STIRLESS	STOCKIEST
STICKUP	STILLATORY	STINGY	STIRLESSLY	STOCKILY
STICKWEED	STILLBIRTH	STINK	STIRLESSNESS	STOCKINESS
STICKWORK	STILLBORN	STINKARD	STIRLING	STOCKINET
STICKY	STILLED	STINKARDLY	STIRP	STOCKINETTE
STICTIFORM	STILLER	STINKBALL	STIRPES	STOCKING
STIDDY	STILLERY	STINKBERRIES	STIRPS	STOCKINGED
STIED	STILLEST	STINKBERRY	STIRRA	STOCKINGER
STIFE	STILLHOUSE	STINKBIRD	STIRRAGE	STOCKINGING
STIFF	STILLICIDE	STINKBUG	STIRRED	STOCKINGLESS
STIFFEN	STILLICIDIUM	STINKBUSH	STIRRER	STOCKINGS
STIFFENED	STILLIER	STINKDAMP	STIRRING	STOCKISH
STIFFENER	STILLIEST	STINKER	STIRRINGLY	STOCKISHLY
STIFFENING	STILLIFORM	STINKHORN	STIRRUP	STOCKISHNESS
STIFFER	STILLING	STINKING	STITCH	STOCKJOBBER
STIFFEST	STILLION	STINKINGLY	STITCHBIRD	STOCKJOBBERY
STIFFHEARTED	STILLISH	STINKINGNESS	STITCHDOWN	STOCKJOBBING
STIFFISH	STILLMAN	STINKO	STITCHED	STOCKJUDGING
STIFFLEG	STILLMEN	STINKPOT	STITCHER	STOCKKEEPER
STIFFLER	STILLNESS	STINKS	STITCHERY	STOCKKEEPING
STIFFLY	STILLROOM	STINKSTONE	STITCHES	STOCKMAKER
STIFFNECK	STILLSTAND	STINKWEED	STITCHING	STOCKMAKING
STIFFNESS	STILLY	STINKWOOD	STITCHWHILE	STOCKMAN
STIFFRUMP	STILO	STINKWORT	STITCHWORK	STOCKMEN
STIFFTAIL	STILT	STINKY	STITCHWORT	STOCKOWNER
STIFLE	STILTED	STINT	STITE	STOCKPILE
STIFLED	STILTEDLY	STINTED	STITH	STOCKPILED
STIFLEDLY	STILTEDNESS	STINTEDLY	STITHE	STOCKPILING
STIFLER	STILTER	STINTEDNESS	STITHIED	STOCKPOT
STIFLING	STILTIER	STINTER	STITHIES	STOCKPROOF
STIFLINGLY	STILTIEST	STINTING	STITHLY	STOCKRIDER
STIGMA	STILTIFIED	STINTS	STITHY	STOCKRIDING
STIGMAI	STILTIFY	STINTY	STITHYING	STOCKROOM
STIGMAL	STILTIFYING	STIPATE	STIVE	STOCKS
STIGMARIA	STILTINESS	STIPE	STIVER	STOCKSTONE
STIGMARIAE	STILTING	STIPED	STIVY	STOCKTAKER
STIGMARIAN	STILTISH	STIPEL	STOA	STOCKTAKING
STIGMARIOID	STILTY	STIPELLATE	STOACH	STOCKWORK
STIGMAS	STIM	STIPEND	STOAE	STOCKWRIGHT
STIGMASTEROL	STIME	STIPENDIA	STOAK	STOCKY
STIGMATA	STIMPART	STIPENDIAL	STOAS	STOCKYARD
STIGMATAL	STIMULABILITY	STIPENDIARIES	STOAT	STOD
STIGMATIC	STIMULABLE	STIPENDIARY	STOATER	STODE
STIGMATICAL	STIMULANCE	STIPENDIATE	STOATING	STODGE
STIGMATICALLY	STIMULANCY	STIPENDIUM	STOATS	STODGED
STIGMATICALNESS	STIMULANT	STIPENDIUMS	STOB	STODGER
STIGMATIFORM	STIMULATE	STIPES	STOBBALL	STODGERY
STIGMATISE	STIMULATED	STIPIFORM	STOBBED	STODGIER
STIGMATISM	STIMULATER	STIPITATE	STOBBING	STODGIEST
STIGMATIST	STIMULATING	STIPITES	STOCAH	STODGILY
STIGMATIZATION	STIMULATION	STIPITIFORM	STOCCADO	STODGINESS
STIGMATIZE	STIMULATIVE	STIPITURE	STOCCATA	STODGING
STIGMATIZED	STIMULATOR	STIPPEN	STOCHASTIC	STODGY
STIGMATIZER	STIMULATORY	STIPPLE	STOCHASTICAL	STODTONE
STIGMATIZING	STIMULATRESS	STIPPLED	STOCK	STOECHIOLOGY
STIGMATOID	STIMULATRIX	STIPPLER	STOCKADE	STOEP
STIGMATOSE	STIMULI	STIPPLING	STOCKADED	STOF
STIGME	STIMULUS	STIPPLY	STOCKADING	STOFF

STOG
STOGA
STOGIE
STOGIES
STOGY
STOIC
STOICAL
STOICALLY
STOICALNESS
STOICHIOLOGY
STOICISM
STOIT
STOITER
STOKE
STOKED
STOKEHOLD
STOKEHOLE
STOKER
STOKES
STOKESITE
STOKING
STOKROOS
STOKVIS
STOLA
STOLAE
STOLE
STOLED
STOLEN
STOLENLY
STOLENNESS
STOLENWISE
STOLID
STOLIDITY
STOLIDLY
STOLIDNESS
STOLIST
STOLKJAERRE
STOLLEN
STOLO
STOLONATE
STOLZITE
STOMA
STOMACACE
STOMACH
STOMACHABLE
STOMACHACHE
STOMACHAL
STOMACHED
STOMACHER
STOMACHFUL
STOMACHFULLY
STOMACHFULNESS
STOMACHIC
STOMACHICAL
STOMACHICALLY
STOMACHING
STOMACHLESS
STOMACHLESSNESS
STOMACHY
STOMATA
STOMATAL
STOMATE
STOMATIC
STOMATITIC
STOMATITIS
STOMATOCACE
STOMATODE
STOMATOGRAPH
STOMATOLOGIC
STOMATOLOGY
STOMATOMENIA
STOMATOMY
STOMATOPATHY
STOMATOPOD
STOMATOSCOPE
STOMATOSCOPY

STOMATOSE
STOMATOTOMY
STOMATOUS
STOMION
STOMIUM
STOMODAEA
STOMODAEAL
STOMODAEUM
STOMODEAL
STOMODEUM
STOMOXYS
STOMP
STOMPER
STONAGE
STONE
STONEBASS
STONEBIRD
STONEBITER
STONEBOAT
STONEBOW
STONEBRASH
STONEBREAK
STONEBROOD
STONECAST
STONECAT
STONECHAT
STONECROP
STONECUTTER
STONECUTTING
STONED
STONEFISH
STONEGALE
STONEGALL
STONEHAND
STONEHATCH
STONEHEAD
STONEHEARTED
STONEITE
STONELAYER
STONELAYING
STONELIKE
STONEMAN
STONEMASON
STONEMASONRY
STONEMEN
STONEMINT
STONEN
STONEPECKER
STONEPUT
STONER
STONEROOT
STONES
STONESHOT
STONESMATCH
STONESMITCH
STONESMITH
STONEWALL
STONEWALLED
STONEWALLER
STONEWALLING
STONEWALLY
STONEWARE
STONEWEED
STONEWISE
STONEWOOD
STONEWORK
STONEWORKER
STONEWORT
STONEY
STONEYARD
STONIER
STONIEST
STONIFIABLE
STONIFY
STONILY
STONINESS
STONING

STONISH
STONISHMENT
STONK
STONKER
STONY
STONYHEARTED
STOOD
STOODED
STOOF
STOOGE
STOOGED
STOOGING
STOOK
STOOKER
STOOKIE
STOOL
STOOLBALL
STOOLED
STOOLIE
STOOLING
STOOP
STOOPED
STOOPER
STOOPGALLANT
STOOPING
STOOPINGLY
STOOR
STOOREY
STOORY
STOOTER
STOOTH
STOOTHING
STOP
STOPA
STOPBACK
STOPBLOCK
STOPBOARD
STOPCOCK
STOPDICE
STOPE
STOPED
STOPEN
STOPER
STOPGAP
STOPHOUND
STOPING
STOPLESS
STOPLESSNESS
STOPLIGHT
STOPOVER
STOPPABILITY
STOPPABLE
STOPPABLY
STOPPAGE
STOPPED
STOPPEL
STOPPER
STOPPERED
STOPPERING
STOPPING
STOPPLE
STOPPLED
STOPPLING
STOPS
STOPSHIP
STOPT
STOPWATCH
STOPWATER
STOPWORK
STOR
STORABLE
STORAGE
STORAX
STORE
STORED
STOREEN
STOREHOUSE

STOREKEEP
STOREKEEPER
STOREKEEPING
STOREMAN
STOREMASTER
STOREMEN
STORER
STOREROOM
STORES
STORESHIP
STOREY
STOREYED
STOREYS
STORGE
STORIAL
STORIATE
STORIATION
STORIED
STORIER
STORIES
STORIETTE
STORIFIED
STORIFY
STORIFYING
STORING
STORIOLOGIST
STORIOLOGY
STORK
STORKEN
STORKLIKE
STORKS
STORKSBILL
STORM
STORMABLE
STORMBELT
STORMBIRD
STORMBOUND
STORMCOCK
STORMED
STORMER
STORMFUL
STORMFULLY
STORMFULNESS
STORMIER
STORMIEST
STORMILY
STORMINESS
STORMING
STORMINGLY
STORMISH
STORMPROOF
STORMS
STORMWIND
STORMY
STORNELLI
STORNELLO
STORY
STORYBOOK
STORYING
STORYMAKER
STORYMONGER
STORYTELLER
STORYTELLING
STORYWORK
STOSH
STOSS
STOSSTON
STOT
STOTER
STOTINKA
STOTINKI
STOTT
STOTTER
STOUN
STOUND
STOUNDMEAL
STOUP

STOUR
STOURE
STOURIE
STOURING
STOURLINESS
STOURLY
STOURNESS
STOURY
STOUSH
STOUT
STOUTEN
STOUTER
STOUTEST
STOUTH
STOUTHEARTED
STOUTHEARTEDLY
STOUTHEARTEDNESS
STOUTHRIEF
STOUTLY
STOUTNESS
STOUTWOOD
STOUTY
STOVE
STOVEBRUSH
STOVED
STOVEHOUSE
STOVEMAKER
STOVEMAKING
STOVEMAN
STOVEMEN
STOVEN
STOVEPIPE
STOVER
STOVEWOOD
STOVIES
STOVING
STOW
STOWAGE
STOWAWAY
STOWBALL
STOWBOARD
STOWBORD
STOWBORDMAN
STOWBORDMEN
STOWCE
STOWDOWN
STOWED
STOWER
STOWING
STOWL
STOWLINS
STOWNET
STOWP
STOWSE
STOWTH
STOWWOOD
STRABISM
STRABISMAL
STRABISMALLY
STRABISMIC
STRABISMICAL
STRABISMUS
STRABOMETER
STRABOMETRY
STRABOTOME
STRABOTOMIES
STRABOTOMY
STRACKLING
STRACT
STRAD
STRADDLE
STRADDLEBACK
STRADDLEBUG
STRADDLED
STRADDLER
STRADDLING
STRADDLINGLY

STRADICO
STRADINE
STRADIOT
STRADLINGS
STRAFE
STRAFED
STRAFER
STRAFING
STRAG
STRAGE
STRAGGLE
STRAGGLED
STRAGGLER
STRAGGLIER
STRAGGLIEST
STRAGGLING
STRAGGLINGLY
STRAGGLY
STRAGULAR
STRAGULUM
STRAIGHT
STRAIGHTAWAY
STRAIGHTEDGE
STRAIGHTEDGED
STRAIGHTEDGING
STRAIGHTEN
STRAIGHTENED
STRAIGHTENER
STRAIGHTENING
STRAIGHTER
STRAIGHTEST
STRAIGHTFORWARD
STRAIGHTFORWARDLY
STRAIGHTFORWARDNESS
STRAIGHTFORWARDS
STRAIGHTHEAD
STRAIGHTLY
STRAIGHTNESS
STRAIGHTWAY
STRAIGHTWAYS
STRAIGHTWISE
STRAIK
STRAIKE
STRAIL
STRAIN
STRAINABLE
STRAINABLY
STRAINED
STRAINEDLY
STRAINEDNESS
STRAINER
STRAINERMAN
STRAINERMEN
STRAINING
STRAININGLY
STRAINSLIP
STRAINT
STRAIT
STRAITEN
STRAITENED
STRAITENING
STRAITER
STRAITEST
STRAITJACKET
STRAITLACED
STRAITLACING
STRAITLY
STRAITNESS
STRAITSMAN
STRAITSMEN
STRAITWORK
STRAKE
STRAKED
STRAKES
STRAKY
STRALET
STRAM

STRAMASH
STRAMAZON
STRAMINEOUS
STRAMMEL
STRAMMER
STRAMONIUM
STRAMONY
STRAMP
STRAN
STRAND
STRANDAGE
STRANDED
STRANDER
STRANDING
STRANDLOOPER
STRANDS
STRANG
STRANGE
STRANGELING
STRANGELY
STRANGENESS
STRANGER
STRANGEST
STRANGLE
STRANGLEABLE
STRANGLED
STRANGLEHOLD
STRANGLEMENT
STRANGLER
STRANGLES
STRANGLETARE
STRANGLEWEED
STRANGLING
STRANGULATE
STRANGULATED
STRANGULATING
STRANGULATION
STRANGULATIVE
STRANGULLION
STRANGURIOUS
STRANGURY
STRANNER
STRANY
STRAP
STRAPHANG
STRAPHANGER
STRAPHEAD
STRAPLESS
STRAPPABLE
STRAPPADO
STRAPPADOES
STRAPPED
STRAPPER
STRAPPING
STRAPPLE
STRAPS
STRAPWORK
STRAPWORT
STRASS
STRATA
STRATAGEM
STRATAGEMS
STRATAL
STRATAMETER
STRATEGE
STRATEGETIC
STRATEGETICAL
STRATEGETICS
STRATEGI
STRATEGIAN
STRATEGIC
STRATEGICAL
STRATEGICALLY
STRATEGICS
STRATEGIES
STRATEGIST
STRATEGIZE

STRATEGOI
STRATEGOS
STRATEGUS
STRATEGY
STRATH
STRATHSPEY
STRATI
STRATIC
STRATICULATE
STRATIFICATION
STRATIFIED
STRATIFORM
STRATIFY
STRATIFYING
STRATIGRAPHER
STRATIGRAPHIC
STRATIGRAPHY
STRATLIN
STRATOCRACIES
STRATOCRACY
STRATOCRAT
STRATOCRATIC
STRATOGRAPHIC
STRATOGRAPHY
STRATONIC
STRATOPAUSE
STRATOSE
STRATOSPHERE
STRATOSPHERIC
STRATOUS
STRATUM
STRATUMS
STRATUS
STRAUGHT
STRAVAGANT
STRAVAGE
STRAVAGED
STRAVAGING
STRAVAGUE
STRAVAIG
STRAVAIGER
STRAW
STRAWBERRIES
STRAWBERRY
STRAWBILL
STRAWBOARD
STRAWBREADTH
STRAWEN
STRAWER
STRAWFLOWER
STRAWFORK
STRAWHAT
STRAWIER
STRAWIEST
STRAWMOTE
STRAWSMEAR
STRAWSTACK
STRAWSTACKER
STRAWWALKER
STRAWWORK
STRAWWORM
STRAWY
STRAWYARD
STRAY
STRAYAWAY
STRAYED
STRAYER
STRAYING
STREAK
STREAKED
STREAKEDLY
STREAKEDNESS
STREAKER
STREAKIER
STREAKIEST
STREAKILY
STREAKINESS

STREAKING
STREAKS
STREAKY
STREAM
STREAMED
STREAMER
STREAMIER
STREAMIEST
STREAMING
STREAMINGLY
STREAMLET
STREAMLINE
STREAMLINED
STREAMLINING
STREAMS
STREAMWAY
STREAMWORT
STREAMY
STRECK
STRECKLY
STREEK
STREEL
STREELER
STREEN
STREEP
STREET
STREETAGE
STREETCAR
STREETS
STREETWALKER
STREETWALKING
STREETWARD
STREETWAY
STREIT
STREITE
STREMMA
STREMMAS
STRENGITE
STRENGTH
STRENGTHEN
STRENGTHENED
STRENGTHENER
STRENGTHENING
STRENGTHENINGLY
STRENGTHILY
STRENGTHLESS
STRENGTHLESSLY
STRENGTHLESSNESS
STRENGTHY
STRENT
STRENUITY
STRENUOSITY
STRENUOUS
STRENUOUSLY
STRENUOUSNESS
STREPENT
STREPERA
STREPEROUS
STREPHONADE
STREPITANT
STREPITANTLY
STREPITATION
STREPITOSO
STREPITOUS
STREPOR
STREPSINEMA
STREPSIPTERAL
STREPSIPTERON
STREPSIS
STREPSITENE
STREPTASTER
STREPTOCOCCI
STREPTOLYSIN
STREPTOMYCIN
STRESS
STRESSED

STRESSER
STRESSFUL
STRESSING
STRESSLESS
STRETCH
STRETCHABLE
STRETCHBERRY
STRETCHED
STRETCHER
STRETCHERMAN
STRETCHINESS
STRETCHING
STRETCHNECK
STRETCHPANTS
STRETCHY
STRETMAN
STRETMEN
STRETTA
STRETTAS
STRETTE
STRETTI
STRETTO
STRETTOS
STREUSEL
STREW
STREWED
STREWER
STREWING
STREWMENT
STREWN
STRIA
STRIAE
STRIAL
STRIATE
STRIATED
STRIATING
STRIATION
STRIATURE
STRICH
STRICK
STRICKEN
STRICKENLY
STRICKENNESS
STRICKER
STRICKLE
STRICKLED
STRICKLER
STRICKLING
STRICT
STRICTER
STRICTEST
STRICTION
STRICTLY
STRICTNESS
STRICTURE
STRICTURED
STRID
STRIDDEN
STRIDDLE
STRIDE
STRIDELEG
STRIDELEGS
STRIDENCE
STRIDENCY
STRIDENT
STRIDENTLY
STRIDER
STRIDES
STRIDEWAYS
STRIDHAN
STRIDHANA
STRIDHANUM
STRIDING
STRIDLING
STRIDLINS
STRIDOR
STRIDULANT

STRIDULATE
STRIDULATED
STRIDULATING
STRIDULATION
STRIDULATOR
STRIDULATORY
STRIDULENT
STRIDULOUS
STRIDULOUSLY
STRIE
STRIFE
STRIFFEN
STRIFT
STRIG
STRIGA
STRIGAE
STRIGAL
STRIGATE
STRIGGLE
STRIGIL
STRIGILATE
STRIGILATION
STRIGILATOR
STRIGILES
STRIGILIS
STRIGILLOSE
STRIGINE
STRIGOSE
STRIGOUS
STRIGOVITE
STRIKE
STRIKEBOUND
STRIKEBREAKER
STRIKEBREAKING
STRIKEOUT
STRIKER
STRIKES
STRIKING
STRIKINGLY
STRIKINGNESS
STRIND
STRING
STRINGBOARD
STRINGCOURSE
STRINGED
STRINGENCIES
STRINGENCY
STRINGENDO
STRINGENDOS
STRINGENT
STRINGENTLY
STRINGENTNESS
STRINGER
STRINGHALT
STRINGHALTED
STRINGHALTY
STRINGIER
STRINGIEST
STRINGILY
STRINGINESS
STRINGING
STRINGMAKER
STRINGMAKING
STRINGMAN
STRINGMEN
STRINGPIECE
STRINGS
STRINGSMAN
STRINGSMEN
STRINGWAYS
STRINGWOOD
STRINGY
STRINGYBARK
STRINKLE
STRIOLA
STRIOLAE
STRIOLATE

STRIOLATED
STRIOLET
STRIP
STRIPE
STRIPED
STRIPER
STRIPES
STRIPIER
STRIPIEST
STRIPING
STRIPLIGHT
STRIPLING
STRIPPAGE
STRIPPED
STRIPPER
STRIPPING
STRIPPLER
STRIPS
STRIPT
STRIPTEASE
STRIPTEASER
STRIPY
STRIT
STRIVE
STRIVED
STRIVEN
STRIVER
STRIVING
STRIX
STROAM
STROBE
STROBIC
STROBIL
STROBILA
STROBILAE
STROBILATE
STROBILATION
STROBILE
STROBILI
STROBILIFORM
STROBILINE
STROBILOID
STROBILUS
STROBOSCOPE
STROBOSCOPIC
STROBOSCOPY
STROCKLE
STROIL
STROKE
STROKED
STROKER
STROKES
STROKESMAN
STROKING
STROKINGS
STROKY
STROLL
STROLLED
STROLLER
STROLLING
STROM
STROMA
STROMAL
STROMATA
STROMATEOID
STROMATIC
STROMATIFORM
STROMATOLOGY
STROMATOUS
STROMB
STROMBIFORM
STROMBITE
STROMBOID
STROMBOLIAN
STROME
STROMEYERITE
STROMMING

STROMUHR
STROND
STRONE
STRONG
STRONGBACK
STRONGBARK
STRONGBOX
STRONGER
STRONGEST
STRONGFULLY
STRONGHAND
STRONGHANDED
STRONGHEADED
STRONGHEARTED
STRONGHOLD
STRONGISH
STRONGLY
STRONGMAN
STRONGMEN
STRONGNESS
STRONGPOINT
STRONGROOM
STRONGYL
STRONGYLATE
STRONGYLE
STRONGYLID
STRONGYLOID
STRONGYLON
STRONGYLOSIS
STRONTIA
STRONTIAN
STRONTIANITE
STRONTIC
STRONTION
STRONTITIC
STRONTIUM
STROOT
STROP
STROPHAIC
STROPHANTHIN
STROPHE
STROPHES
STROPHIC
STROPHICAL
STROPHICALLY
STROPHIOLATE
STROPHIOLE
STROPHOID
STROPHOMENID
STROPHOSIS
STROPHOTAXIS
STROPHULUS
STROPPED
STROPPER
STROPPING
STROPPINGS
STROSSER
STROTH
STROTHER
STROUD
STROUDING
STROUNGE
STROUP
STROUT
STROVE
STROW
STROWD
STROWED
STROWING
STROWN
STROY
STROYER
STROYGOOD
STRUB
STRUBBLY
STRUCION
STRUCK

STRUCKEN
STRUCTURAL
STRUCTURALISM
STRUCTURALIST
STRUCTURALIZATION
STRUCTURALIZE
STRUCTURALLY
STRUCTURATION
STRUCTURE
STRUCTURED
STRUCTURELESS
STRUCTURELESSNESS
STRUCTURELY
STRUCTURES
STRUCTURIST
STRUDE
STRUDEL
STRUE
STRUGGLE
STRUGGLED
STRUGGLER
STRUGGLING
STRUGGLINGLY
STRUIS
STRUISSLE
STRUM
STRUMA
STRUMAE
STRUMATIC
STRUMECTOMY
STRUMIFEROUS
STRUMIFORM
STRUMIPRIVIC
STRUMITIS
STRUMMED
STRUMMER
STRUMMING
STRUMOSE
STRUMOUS
STRUMOUSNESS
STRUMPET
STRUMPETRY
STRUMSTRUM
STRUMULOSE
STRUNG
STRUNT
STRUSE
STRUT
STRUTHIAN
STRUTHIFORM
STRUTHIIFORM
STRUTHIIN
STRUTHIN
STRUTHIOID
STRUTHIONINE
STRUTHIOUS
STRUTTED
STRUTTER
STRUTTING
STRUTTINGLY
STRUVITE
STRY
STRYCH
STRYCHNIA
STRYCHNIC
STRYCHNIN
STRYCHNINE
STRYCHNINISM
STRYCHNINIZE
STRYPE
STUB
STUBACHITE
STUBB
STUBBED
STUBBER
STUBBIER
STUBBIEST

STUBBILY
STUBBINESS
STUBBING
STUBBLE
STUBBLEBERRY
STUBBLED
STUBBLES
STUBBLIER
STUBBLIEST
STUBBLING
STUBBLY
STUBBORN
STUBBORNLY
STUBBORNNESS
STUBBY
STUBCHEN
STUBE
STUBRUNNER
STUCCO
STUCCOED
STUCCOER
STUCCOES
STUCCOING
STUCCOS
STUCCOWORK
STUCCOWORKER
STUCK
STUCKEN
STUCKING
STUCKLING
STUD
STUDBOOK
STUDDED
STUDDER
STUDDERY
STUDDIE
STUDDING
STUDDINGSAIL
STUDDLE
STUDDY
STUDENT
STUDENTRY
STUDENTS
STUDENTSHIP
STUDERITE
STUDFISH
STUDFISHES
STUDHORSE
STUDIA
STUDIED
STUDIEDLY
STUDIEDNESS
STUDIER
STUDIES
STUDIO
STUDIOS
STUDIOUS
STUDIOUSLY
STUDIOUSNESS
STUDIUM
STUDWORK
STUDY
STUDYING
STUE
STUFA
STUFE
STUFF
STUFFAGE
STUFFATA
STUFFED
STUFFENDER
STUFFER
STUFFIER
STUFFIEST
STUFFILY
STUFFINESS
STUFFING

STUFFY
STUG
STUGGY
STUIVER
STULL
STULLER
STULM
STULP
STULTIFIED
STULTIFIER
STULTIFY
STULTIFYING
STULTILOQUY
STULTY
STUM
STUMBLE
STUMBLEBUM
STUMBLED
STUMBLER
STUMBLING
STUMBLINGLY
STUMBLY
STUMER
STUMMED
STUMMEL
STUMMER
STUMMING
STUMMY
STUMOR
STUMOUR
STUMP
STUMPAGE
STUMPED
STUMPER
STUMPIER
STUMPIEST
STUMPINESS
STUMPING
STUMPISH
STUMPLING
STUMPNOSE
STUMPS
STUMPSUCKER
STUMPY
STUN
STUNG
STUNK
STUNKARD
STUNNED
STUNNER
STUNNING
STUNNINGLY
STUNPOLL
STUNSAIL
STUNT
STUNTED
STUNTEDLY
STUNTEDNESS
STUNTER
STUNTINESS
STUNTING
STUNTIST
STUNTNESS
STUNTY
STUP
STUPA
STUPE
STUPED
STUPEFACIENT
STUPEFACTION
STUPEFACTIVE
STUPEFIED
STUPEFIEDNESS
STUPEFIER
STUPEFY
STUPEFYING
STUPEND

STUPENDLY
STUPENDOUS
STUPENDOUSLY
STUPENDOUSNESS
STUPENT
STUPEOUS
STUPEX
STUPHE
STUPID
STUPIDHEAD
STUPIDITIES
STUPIDITY
STUPIDLY
STUPIDNESS
STUPING
STUPOR
STUPORIFIC
STUPOROSE
STUPOROUS
STUPOSE
STUPP
STUPRATE
STUPRATED
STUPRATING
STUPRATION
STUPRUM
STUPULOSE
STURBLE
STURDIED
STURDIER
STURDIEST
STURDILY
STURDINESS
STURDY
STURGEON
STURGEONS
STURIN
STURINE
STURNIFORM
STURNINE
STURNOID
STUROCH
STURSHUM
STURT
STURTAN
STURTE
STURTIN
STURTION
STURTITE
STUSS
STUT
STUTTER
STUTTERER
STUTTERING
STUTTERINGLY
STY
STYAN
STYANY
STYCA
STYCERIN
STYCERINOL
STYCHOMYTHIA
STYE
STYFZIEKTE
STYGIAN
STYING
STYKE
STYLAR
STYLATE
STYLE
STYLEBOOK
STYLED
STYLEDOM
STYLER
STYLET
STYLEWORT
STYLI

STYLIFEROUS
STYLIFORM
STYLINE
STYLING
STYLION
STYLISH
STYLISHLY
STYLISHNESS
STYLIST
STYLISTIC
STYLISTICAL
STYLISTICALLY
STYLISTICS
STYLITE
STYLITISM
STYLIZATION
STYLIZE
STYLIZED
STYLIZER
STYLIZING
STYLO
STYLOBATE
STYLOGLOSSAL
STYLOGLOSSUS
STYLOGRAPH
STYLOGRAPHIC
STYLOGRAPHY
STYLOHYAL
STYLOHYOID
STYLOID
STYLOLITE
STYLOLITIC
STYLOMASTOID
STYLOMETER
STYLOPID
STYLOPIZED
STYLOPOD
STYLOPODIA
STYLOPODIUM
STYLOSPORE
STYLOSPOROUS
STYLOSTEGIUM
STYLOSTEMON
STYLOTYPITE
STYLUS
STYLUSES
STYME
STYMIE
STYMIED
STYMYING
STYPHNATE
STYPHNIC
STYPSIS
STYPTIC
STYPTICAL
STYPTICITY
STYPTICNESS
STYRACACEOUS
STYRACIN
STYRENE
STYROFOAM
STYROGALLOL
STYROL
STYRONE
STYRYL
STYRYLIC
STYTH
STYTHE
SUABILITY
SUABLE
SUABLY
SUADE
SUAHARO
SUANT
SUANTLY
SUASIBLE
SUASION

SUASIONIST
SUASIVE
SUASIVELY
SUASIVENESS
SUASORIA
SUASORY
SUAVE
SUAVELY
SUAVENESS
SUAVEOLENT
SUAVIFY
SUAVILOQUENT
SUAVITIES
SUAVITY
SUB
SUBABDOMINAL
SUBACID
SUBACIDITY
SUBACIDLY
SUBACIDNESS
SUBACT
SUBACTION
SUBACUTE
SUBACUTELY
SUBADAR
SUBADULT
SUBAERIAL
SUBAERIALLY
SUBAGE
SUBAGENCY
SUBAGENT
SUBAH
SUBAHDAR
SUBAHDARY
SUBAHSHIP
SUBAID
SUBALARY
SUBALBID
SUBALKALINE
SUBALMONER
SUBALPINE
SUBALTERN
SUBALTERNANT
SUBALTERNATE
SUBALTERNITY
SUBAMARE
SUBANGLED
SUBANGULAR
SUBANGULATE
SUBANGULATED
SUBANTARCTIC
SUBAPICAL
SUBAPOSTOLIC
SUBAPTEROUS
SUBAQUATIC
SUBAQUEAN
SUBAQUEOUS
SUBARACHNOID
SUBARCH
SUBARCTIC
SUBARCUATE
SUBARCUATED
SUBARCUATION
SUBAREA
SUBAREOLAR
SUBARID
SUBARMALE
SUBARMOR
SUBARRATION
SUBARRHATION
SUBASHI
SUBASSEMBLY
SUBASTRAL
SUBATOM
SUBATOMIC
SUBAUD
SUBAUDIBLE

SUBAUDITION
SUBAUDITUR
SUBAURAL
SUBAURICULAR
SUBBASAL
SUBBASE
SUBBASEMENT
SUBBASS
SUBBASSA
SUBBIFID
SUBBING
SUBBOREAL
SUBBOURDON
SUBBRACHIAL
SUBBRACHIAN
SUBBRACHIATE
SUBBRANCH
SUBBRANCHED
SUBBREED
SUBBRIGADIER
SUBCALCARINE
SUBCALIBER
SUBCALIBRE
SUBCALLOSAL
SUBCANTOR
SUBCAPSULAR
SUBCAPTION
SUBCARBIDE
SUBCARBONATE
SUBCARDINAL
SUBCAST
SUBCASTE
SUBCAUDAL
SUBCAUDATE
SUBCELESTIAL
SUBCELLAR
SUBCENTER
SUBCENTRAL
SUBCENTRALLY
SUBCENTRE
SUBCHAIRMAN
SUBCHANTER
SUBCHASER
SUBCHELA
SUBCHELAE
SUBCHELATE
SUBCHIEF
SUBCHLORIDE
SUBCHONDRAL
SUBCHORDAL
SUBCHORIOID
SUBCHORIONIC
SUBCINCTORIUM
SUBCLAIM
SUBCLASS
SUBCLAUSE
SUBCLAVIAN
SUBCLAVIUS
SUBCLIMACTIC
SUBCLIMAX
SUBCLINICAL
SUBCLONE
SUBCOASTAL
SUBCOAT
SUBCOLUMNAR
SUBCOMMIT
SUBCOMMITTEE
SUBCONSCIOUS
SUBCONSCIOUSLY
SUBCONSCIOUSNESS
SUBCONSTABLE
SUBCONTINENT
SUBCONTRACT
SUBCONTRACTED
SUBCONTRACTOR

SUBCONTRARIES
SUBCONTRARY
SUBCOOL
SUBCORNEOUS
SUBCORTEX
SUBCORTICAL
SUBCORTICES
SUBCOSTA
SUBCOSTAL
SUBCOSTALIS
SUBCREPITANT
SUBCRITICAL
SUBCRUREAL
SUBCRUREUS
SUBCRUST
SUBCRUSTAL
SUBCULTURE
SUBCULTURED
SUBCULTURING
SUBCUTANEOUS
SUBCUTIS
SUBDEACON
SUBDEACONATE
SUBDEACONESS
SUBDEACONRY
SUBDEAN
SUBDEANERY
SUBDEB
SUBDEBUTANTE
SUBDECANAL
SUBDECIMAL
SUBDECUPLE
SUBDELEGATE
SUBDELEGATED
SUBDELIRIUM
SUBDENTED
SUBDERMAL
SUBDIACONAL
SUBDIACONATE
SUBDIAL
SUBDICHOTOMY
SUBDIT
SUBDITITIOUS
SUBDIVERSIFY
SUBDIVIDE
SUBDIVIDED
SUBDIVIDER
SUBDIVIDING
SUBDIVISIBLE
SUBDIVISION
SUBDIVISIVE
SUBDOLOUS
SUBDOLOUSLY
SUBDOMINANT
SUBDORSAL
SUBDORSALLY
SUBDOUBLE
SUBDRAIN
SUBDRAINAGE
SUBDRILL
SUBDUABLE
SUBDUABLY
SUBDUAL
SUBDUCE
SUBDUCED
SUBDUCING
SUBDUCT
SUBDUCTION
SUBDUE
SUBDUED
SUBDUEDLY
SUBDUEDNESS
SUBDUEMENT
SUBDUER
SUBDUING
SUBDUINGLY
SUBDUPLE

SUBDUPLICATE
SUBDURAL
SUBDURALLY
SUBDURE
SUBDWARF
SUBEDIT
SUBEDITOR
SUBEDITORIAL
SUBELAPHINE
SUBELECTRON
SUBENFEOFF
SUBENTITLE
SUBER
SUBERATE
SUBERECT
SUBEREOUS
SUBERIC
SUBERIFEROUS
SUBERIFORM
SUBERIN
SUBERINE
SUBERINIZE
SUBERITE
SUBERIZATION
SUBERIZE
SUBERIZED
SUBERIZING
SUBEROSE
SUBEROUS
SUBETH
SUBEXCITE
SUBFACTORIAL
SUBFAMILIES
SUBFAMILY
SUBFEBRILE
SUBFEU
SUBFEUDATION
SUBFEUDATORY
SUBFIEF
SUBFIX
SUBFLAVOR
SUBFLAVOUR
SUBFLOOR
SUBFLOORING
SUBFLORA
SUBFLUVIAL
SUBFOCAL
SUBFRESHMAN
SUBFUNCTIONAL
SUBFUSC
SUBFUSCOUS
SUBFUSK
SUBGALEA
SUBGALLATE
SUBGENERA
SUBGENERIC
SUBGENERICAL
SUBGENITAL
SUBGENUAL
SUBGENUS
SUBGENUSES
SUBGIANT
SUBGLACIAL
SUBGLACIALLY
SUBGLENOID
SUBGLOSSITIS
SUBGOVERNOR
SUBGRADE
SUBGROUP
SUBHARMONIC
SUBHASTATION
SUBHEAD
SUBHEADING
SUBHEDRAL
SUBHUMAN
SUBHYMENIAL
SUBHYMENIUM

SUBICTERIC
SUBICULAR
SUBICULUM
SUBIMAGINAL
SUBIMAGO
SUBINCIDENT
SUBINCISE
SUBINCISION
SUBINDEX
SUBINDICATE
SUBINDICATED
SUBINDICATING
SUBINDICATION
SUBINDICATIVE
SUBINDICES
SUBINDIVIDUAL
SUBINDUCE
SUBINFEUD
SUBINFEUDATE
SUBINGUINAL
SUBINSPECTOR
SUBINTENT
SUBINVOLUTED
SUBIRRIGATE
SUBIRRIGATED
SUBIRRIGATING
SUBIRRIGATION
SUBITANE
SUBITANEOUS
SUBITANY
SUBITO
SUBITOUS
SUBJACENCY
SUBJACENT
SUBJECT
SUBJECTED
SUBJECTEDLY
SUBJECTEDNESS
SUBJECTIFY
SUBJECTILE
SUBJECTING
SUBJECTION
SUBJECTIONAL
SUBJECTIVE
SUBJECTIVELY
SUBJECTIVENESS
SUBJECTIVISM
SUBJECTIVIST
SUBJECTIVITY
SUBJICIBLE
SUBJOIN
SUBJOINDER
SUBJOINED
SUBJOINING
SUBJOINT
SUBJUGABLE
SUBJUGAL
SUBJUGATE
SUBJUGATED
SUBJUGATING
SUBJUGATION
SUBJUGATOR
SUBJUGULAR
SUBJUNCT
SUBJUNCTION
SUBJUNCTIVE
SUBJUNCTIVELY
SUBKINGDOM
SUBLABIAL
SUBLANGUAGE
SUBLAPSARIAN
SUBLAPSARY
SUBLATE
SUBLATED
SUBLATERAL
SUBLATING
SUBLATION

SUBLATIVE
SUBLEADER
SUBLEASE
SUBLEASED
SUBLEASING
SUBLESSEE
SUBLESSOR
SUBLET
SUBLETHAL
SUBLETTABLE
SUBLETTER
SUBLETTING
SUBLEVATE
SUBLEVATION
SUBLICENSEE
SUBLIEUTENANT
SUBLIGATION
SUBLIMANT
SUBLIMATE
SUBLIMATED
SUBLIMATING
SUBLIMATION
SUBLIMATIONAL
SUBLIMATIONIST
SUBLIMATOR
SUBLIMATORY
SUBLIME
SUBLIMED
SUBLIMELY
SUBLIMENESS
SUBLIMER
SUBLIMEST
SUBLIMIFICATION
SUBLIMINAL
SUBLIMINALLY
SUBLIMING
SUBLIMITIES
SUBLIMITY
SUBLINE
SUBLINEATION
SUBLINGUA
SUBLINGUAE
SUBLINGUAL
SUBLITTORAL
SUBLOBULAR
SUBLUNAR
SUBLUNARY
SUBLUXATE
SUBLUXATION
SUBMAIN
SUBMAN
SUBMARGINAL
SUBMARGINALLY
SUBMARGINATE
SUBMARGINED
SUBMARINE
SUBMARINED
SUBMARINER
SUBMARINING
SUBMARINISM
SUBMARINIST
SUBMAXILLA
SUBMAXILLAE
SUBMAXILLARY
SUBMAXIMAL
SUBMEDIAL
SUBMEDIAN
SUBMEDIANT
SUBMEN
SUBMENTA
SUBMENTAL
SUBMENTUM
SUBMERGE
SUBMERGED
SUBMERGEMENT
SUBMERGENCE
SUBMERGIBILITY

SUBMERGIBLE
SUBMERGING
SUBMERSE
SUBMERSED
SUBMERSIBILITY
SUBMERSIBLE
SUBMERSION
SUBMETER
SUBMETERING
SUBMICRON
SUBMILIARY
SUBMINIATURE
SUBMINIMAL
SUBMINISTER
SUBMISS
SUBMISSIBLE
SUBMISSION
SUBMISSIONIST
SUBMISSIVE
SUBMISSIVELY
SUBMISSIVENESS
SUBMIT
SUBMITTAL
SUBMITTED
SUBMITTER
SUBMITTING
SUBMONTAGNE
SUBMONTANE
SUBMONTANELY
SUBMORPHOUS
SUBMOTIVE
SUBMUCOSA
SUBMUCOSAE
SUBMUCOSAL
SUBMUCOUS
SUBMULTIPLE
SUBNASAL
SUBNASCENT
SUBNATURAL
SUBNECT
SUBNEURAL
SUBNITRATE
SUBNIVEAL
SUBNIVEAN
SUBNORMAL
SUBNORMALITY
SUBNUBILAR
SUBNUCLEUS
SUBNUVOLAR
SUBOCCIPITAL
SUBOCEANIC
SUBOCTAVE
SUBOCTILE
SUBOCTUPLE
SUBOCULAR
SUBOFFICER
SUBOPERCLE
SUBOPERCULAR
SUBOPERCULUM
SUBOPPOSITE
SUBOPTIMAL
SUBORBITAL
SUBORBITAR
SUBORBITARY
SUBORDAIN
SUBORDER
SUBORDINACY
SUBORDINAL
SUBORDINARY
SUBORDINATE
SUBORDINATED
SUBORDINATELY
SUBORDINATENESS
SUBORDINATING
SUBORDINATION
SUBORDINATIVE
SUBORN

SUBORNATION
SUBORNATIVE
SUBORNED
SUBORNER
SUBORNING
SUBOVAL
SUBOXID
SUBOXIDATION
SUBOXIDE
SUBPASSAGE
SUBPENA
SUBPERMANENT
SUBPETIOLAR
SUBPHRENIC
SUBPHYLAR
SUBPHYLUM
SUBPIAL
SUBPLAT
SUBPLATE
SUBPLEURAL
SUBPLINTH
SUBPLOT
SUBPOENA
SUBPOENAED
SUBPOENAING
SUBPOENAL
SUBPOTENCIES
SUBPOTENCY
SUBPOTENT
SUBPRESS
SUBPRINCIPAL
SUBPRIOR
SUBPUNCH
SUBPURCHASER
SUBPURLIN
SUBQUINTUPLE
SUBRACE
SUBRADIAL
SUBRADIUS
SUBRATIONAL
SUBREADER
SUBREGION
SUBREGIONAL
SUBREGULI
SUBREGULUS
SUBRENT
SUBREPTARY
SUBREPTION
SUBRESIN
SUBRIDENT
SUBRIDENTLY
SUBRISION
SUBRISIVE
SUBRISORY
SUBROGATE
SUBROGATED
SUBROGATING
SUBROGATION
SUBROUND
SUBSARTORIAL
SUBSCALE
SUBSCAPULAR
SUBSCAPULARY
SUBSCLERAL
SUBSCLEROTIC
SUBSCRIBE
SUBSCRIBED
SUBSCRIBER
SUBSCRIBING
SUBSCRIPT
SUBSCRIPTION
SUBSCRIPTIONIST
SUBSCRIPTIVE
SUBSCRIVE
SUBSCRIVER
SUBSEA
SUBSECIVE

SUBSECT
SUBSECTION
SUBSECUTE
SUBSECUTIVE
SUBSEGMENT
SUBSELLA
SUBSELLIA
SUBSELLIUM
SUBSEMIFUSA
SUBSEMITONE
SUBSENSIBLE
SUBSEPTUPLE
SUBSEQUENCE
SUBSEQUENCY
SUBSEQUENT
SUBSEQUENTIAL
SUBSEQUENTIALLY
SUBSEQUENTLY
SUBSEQUENTNESS
SUBSEROSA
SUBSEROUS
SUBSERVE
SUBSERVED
SUBSERVIATE
SUBSERVIENCE
SUBSERVIENCY
SUBSERVIENT
SUBSERVIENTLY
SUBSERVIENTNESS
SUBSERVING
SUBSESQUI
SUBSESSILE
SUBSET
SUBSEXTUPLE
SUBSHRUB
SUBSHRUBBY
SUBSICIVE
SUBSIDE
SUBSIDED
SUBSIDENCE
SUBSIDENCY
SUBSIDENT
SUBSIDER
SUBSIDIARIE
SUBSIDIARIES
SUBSIDIARILY
SUBSIDIARINESS
SUBSIDIARY
SUBSIDIES
SUBSIDING
SUBSIDISE
SUBSIDIST
SUBSIDIUM
SUBSIDIZATION
SUBSIDIZE
SUBSIDIZED
SUBSIDIZER
SUBSIDIZING
SUBSIDY
SUBSIGN
SUBSILICIC
SUBSILL
SUBSIMILATION
SUBSIMPLE
SUBSIST
SUBSISTED
SUBSISTENCE
SUBSISTENCY
SUBSISTENT
SUBSISTER
SUBSISTING
SUBSIZAR
SUBSOIL
SUBSOILER
SUBSOLAR
SUBSONIC
SUBSPACE

SUBSPECIES
SUBSPECIFIC
SUBSPECIFICALLY
SUBSPINOUS
SUBSTAGE
SUBSTANCE
SUBSTANCH
SUBSTANDARD
SUBSTANT
SUBSTANTIA
SUBSTANTIAL
SUBSTANTIALISM
SUBSTANTIALIST
SUBSTANTIALITY
SUBSTANTIALIZE
SUBSTANTIALLY
SUBSTANTIALNESS
SUBSTANTIATE
SUBSTANTIATED
SUBSTANTIATING
SUBSTANTIATION
SUBSTANTIATIVE
SUBSTANTIATOR
SUBSTANTIFY
SUBSTANTIOUS
SUBSTANTIVAL
SUBSTANTIVALLY
SUBSTANTIVE
SUBSTANTIVELY
SUBSTANTIVENESS
SUBSTANTIVITY
SUBSTANTIVIZE
SUBSTANTIVIZED
SUBSTANTIVIZING
SUBSTANTIZE
SUBSTATION
SUBSTILE
SUBSTITUENT
SUBSTITUTE
SUBSTITUTED
SUBSTITUTER
SUBSTITUTING
SUBSTITUTION
SUBSTITUTIONAL
SUBSTITUTIONALLY
SUBSTITUTIVE
SUBSTITUTIVELY
SUBSTORY
SUBSTRAT
SUBSTRATA
SUBSTRATAL
SUBSTRATE
SUBSTRATIVE
SUBSTRATOSE
SUBSTRATUM
SUBSTRATUMS
SUBSTREAM
SUBSTRUCT
SUBSTRUCTION
SUBSTRUCTIONAL
SUBSTRUCTURAL
SUBSTRUCTURE
SUBSTYLAR
SUBSTYLE
SUBSULPHATE
SUBSULT
SUBSULTORILY
SUBSULTORY
SUBSULTUS
SUBSUMABLE
SUBSUME
SUBSUMED
SUBSUMING
SUBSUMPTION
SUBSUMPTIVE
SUBSURFACE
SUBTACK

SUBTACKSMAN
SUBTACKSMEN
SUBTANGENT
SUBTARGET
SUBTARTAREAN
SUBTECTACLE
SUBTECTAL
SUBTEEN
SUBTEGMINAL
SUBTEMPERATE
SUBTENANCY
SUBTENANT
SUBTEND
SUBTENDED
SUBTENDING
SUBTENSE
SUBTENURE
SUBTERFLUENT
SUBTERFLUOUS
SUBTERFUGE
SUBTERHUMAN
SUBTERJACENT
SUBTERMARINE
SUBTERPOSE
SUBTERRANE
SUBTERRANEAL
SUBTERRANEAN
SUBTERRENE
SUBTERRESTRIAL
SUBTHALAMIC
SUBTHALAMUS
SUBTHORACIC
SUBTILE
SUBTILELY
SUBTILENESS
SUBTILIATE
SUBTILIATION
SUBTILIN
SUBTILISM
SUBTILIST
SUBTILITIES
SUBTILITY
SUBTILIZATION
SUBTILIZED
SUBTILIZER
SUBTILIZING
SUBTILTIES
SUBTILTY
SUBTITLE
SUBTITULAR
SUBTLE
SUBTLENESS
SUBTLER
SUBTLEST
SUBTLETIES
SUBTLETY
SUBTLIST
SUBTLY
SUBTONE
SUBTONIC
SUBTORRID
SUBTOTAL
SUBTRACT
SUBTRACTED
SUBTRACTER
SUBTRACTING
SUBTRACTION
SUBTRACTIVE
SUBTRAHEND
SUBTRAY
SUBTREASURER
SUBTREASURIES
SUBTREASURY
SUBTRIBE
SUBTRIST
SUBTROPIC
SUBTROPICAL

SUBTROPICS
SUBTRUDE
SUBTUBERANT
SUBTUNIC
SUBTURBARY
SUBTYPE
SUBTYPICAL
SUBUCULA
SUBULATE
SUBULATED
SUBULICORN
SUBULIFORM
SUBUMBONAL
SUBUMBRAL
SUBUMBRELLA
SUBUMBRELLAR
SUBUNGUAL
SUBUNGUIAL
SUBUNGULATE
SUBURB
SUBURBAN
SUBURBANITE
SUBURBANITIES
SUBURBANITY
SUBURBANIZATION
SUBURBANIZE
SUBURBED
SUBURBIA
SUBURBICAN
SUBURBS
SUBVAGINAL
SUBVALUATION
SUBVARIETAL
SUBVARIETY
SUBVENDEE
SUBVENE
SUBVENED
SUBVENING
SUBVENTION
SUBVENTIONED
SUBVENTIVE
SUBVERSAL
SUBVERSION
SUBVERSIONARY
SUBVERSIVE
SUBVERSIVELY
SUBVERT
SUBVERTED
SUBVERTER
SUBVERTIBLE
SUBVERTING
SUBVIRATE
SUBVIRILE
SUBVISIBLE
SUBVITALIZED
SUBVITREOUS
SUBVOCAL
SUBVOLA
SUBWATER
SUBWAY
SUBWEIGHT
SUBZONAL
SUBZONE
SUCCADE
SUCCAH
SUCCEDANEA
SUCCEDANEOUS
SUCCEDANEUM
SUCCEDANEUMS
SUCCEDENT
SUCCEED
SUCCEEDED
SUCCEEDER
SUCCEEDING
SUCCEEDINGLY
SUCCENT
SUCCENTOR

SUCCESS
SUCCESSFUL
SUCCESSFULLY
SUCCESSFULNESS
SUCCESSION
SUCCESSIONAL
SUCCESSIONALLY
SUCCESSIONIST
SUCCESSIVE
SUCCESSIVELY
SUCCESSIVENESS
SUCCESSIVITY
SUCCESSOR
SUCCESSORAL
SUCCIN
SUCCINAMATE
SUCCINAMIC
SUCCINAMIDE
SUCCINANIL
SUCCINATE
SUCCINCT
SUCCINCTLY
SUCCINCTNESS
SUCCINCTORIA
SUCCINCTURE
SUCCINIC
SUCCINIMID
SUCCINIMIDE
SUCCINITE
SUCCINOUS
SUCCINUM
SUCCINYL
SUCCISE
SUCCOR
SUCCORABLE
SUCCORED
SUCCORER
SUCCORING
SUCCORRHEA
SUCCORRHOEA
SUCCORY
SUCCOSE
SUCCOTASH
SUCCOUR
SUCCOURABLE
SUCCOURED
SUCCOURER
SUCCOURING
SUCCOUS
SUCCUBA
SUCCUBAE
SUCCUBI
SUCCUBINE
SUCCUBOUS
SUCCUBUS
SUCCUBUSES
SUCCUDRY
SUCCULA
SUCCULENCE
SUCCULENCIES
SUCCULENCY
SUCCULENT
SUCCULENTLY
SUCCULENTNESS
SUCCULOUS
SUCCUMB
SUCCUMBED
SUCCUMBENCE
SUCCUMBENCY
SUCCUMBENT
SUCCUMBER
SUCCUMBING
SUCCURSAL
SUCCURSALE
SUCCUS
SUCCUSS
SUCCUSSATION

SUCCUSSATORY
SUCCUSSION
SUCCUSSIVE
SUCH
SUCHLIKE
SUCHNESS
SUCHWISE
SUCK
SUCKABOB
SUCKAUHOCK
SUCKED
SUCKEN
SUCKENER
SUCKER
SUCKERED
SUCKEREL
SUCKERFISH
SUCKERFISHES
SUCKERING
SUCKFISH
SUCKFISHES
SUCKHOLE
SUCKING
SUCKLE
SUCKLEBUSH
SUCKLED
SUCKLER
SUCKLING
SUCKSTONE
SUCLAT
SUCRAMIN
SUCRAMINE
SUCRASE
SUCRATE
SUCRE
SUCRIER
SUCROACID
SUCROSE
SUCTION
SUCTIONAL
SUCTORIAL
SUCTORIAN
SUCTORIOUS
SUCUPIRA
SUCURI
SUCURIU
SUCURUJU
SUCURY
SUD
SUDADERO
SUDAMEN
SUDAMINA
SUDAMINAL
SUDARIA
SUDARIUM
SUDARY
SUDATE
SUDATION
SUDATORIA
SUDATORIES
SUDATORIUM
SUDATORY
SUDBURITE
SUDD
SUDDEN
SUDDENLY
SUDDENNESS
SUDDENTY
SUDDER
SUDDLE
SUDIFORM
SUDOR
SUDORAL
SUDORESIS
SUDORIC
SUDORIFEROUS
SUDORIFIC

SUDORIPAROUS
SUDOROUS
SUDS
SUDSIER
SUDSIEST
SUDSMAN
SUDSMEN
SUDSY
SUE
SUED
SUEDE
SUEDINE
SUENT
SUER
SUERTE
SUET
SUETY
SUFF
SUFFARI
SUFFECT
SUFFECTION
SUFFER
SUFFERABLE
SUFFERABLENESS
SUFFERABLY
SUFFERANCE
SUFFERANT
SUFFERED
SUFFERER
SUFFERING
SUFFERINGLY
SUFFETE
SUFFETES
SUFFICE
SUFFICED
SUFFICER
SUFFICIENCIES
SUFFICIENCY
SUFFICIENT
SUFFICIENTLY
SUFFICIENTNESS
SUFFICING
SUFFICINGLY
SUFFICINGNESS
SUFFICTION
SUFFIX
SUFFIXAL
SUFFIXATION
SUFFIXED
SUFFIXING
SUFFIXION
SUFFIXMENT
SUFFLATE
SUFFLATED
SUFFLATING
SUFFLATION
SUFFLUE
SUFFOCATE
SUFFOCATED
SUFFOCATING
SUFFOCATINGLY
SUFFOCATION
SUFFOCATIVE
SUFFRAGAN
SUFFRAGANAL
SUFFRAGANATE
SUFFRAGANCY
SUFFRAGATORY
SUFFRAGE
SUFFRAGETTE
SUFFRAGIAL
SUFFRAGISM
SUFFRAGIST
SUFFRAGISTIC
SUFFRAGO
SUFFRAIN
SUFFRONT

SUFFRUTEX
SUFFRUTICES
SUFFRUTICOSE
SUFFRUTICOUS
SUFFUMIGATE
SUFFUMIGATED
SUFFUSE
SUFFUSED
SUFFUSEDLY
SUFFUSING
SUFFUSION
SUFFUSIVE
SUG
SUGAMO
SUGAN
SUGANN
SUGAR
SUGARBERRIES
SUGARBERRY
SUGARBIRD
SUGARBUSH
SUGARED
SUGARELLY
SUGARER
SUGARHOUSE
SUGARIES
SUGARINESS
SUGARING
SUGARLESS
SUGARPLATE
SUGARPLUM
SUGARSOP
SUGARSWEET
SUGARWORKS
SUGARY
SUGAT
SUGENT
SUGESCENT
SUGGAN
SUGGEST
SUGGESTA
SUGGESTED
SUGGESTER
SUGGESTIBILITY
SUGGESTIBLE
SUGGESTIBLENESS
SUGGESTIBLY
SUGGESTING
SUGGESTINGLY
SUGGESTION
SUGGESTIVE
SUGGESTIVELY
SUGGESTIVENESS
SUGGESTIVITY
SUGGESTUM
SUGGIL
SUGGILLATE
SUGGILLATION
SUGH
SUGI
SUGSLOOT
SUHA
SUICIDAL
SUICIDALLY
SUICIDE
SUICIDED
SUICIDING
SUICIDISM
SUICISM
SUID
SUIDIAN
SUIFORM
SUIKERBOSCH
SUILINE
SUIMATE
SUING
SUINGLY

SUINT
SUISIMILAR
SUISSE
SUIST
SUIT
SUITABILITY
SUITABLE
SUITABLENESS
SUITABLY
SUITCASE
SUITE
SUITED
SUITHOLD
SUITING
SUITLY
SUITOR
SUITORESS
SUITY
SUIVANTE
SUIVEZ
SUJEE
SUJI
SUK
SUKIYAKI
SUKKAH
SUKKENYE
SUL
SULBASUTRA
SULCAL
SULCALIZATION
SULCALIZE
SULCATE
SULCATED
SULCATION
SULCI
SULCIFORM
SULCULAR
SULCULATE
SULCULUS
SULCUS
SULD
SULEA
SULFA
SULFACID
SULFADIAZINE
SULFAMATE
SULFAMIC
SULFAMIDATE
SULFAMIDE
SULFAMIDIC
SULFAMINE
SULFAMINIC
SULFAMYL
SULFANILIC
SULFARSENIDE
SULFARSENITE
SULFATASE
SULFATE
SULFATED
SULFATIC
SULFATING
SULFATIZE
SULFATIZED
SULFATIZING
SULFATO
SULFAZIDE
SULFHYDRATE
SULFHYDRIC
SULFHYDRYL
SULFID
SULFIDE
SULFINATE
SULFINDYLIC
SULFINE
SULFINIC
SULFINIDE
SULFINYL

SULFION	SULLENLY	SULPHONATOR	SUMI	SUMPHISHLY
SULFIONIDE	SULLENNESS	SULPHONE	SUMLESS	SUMPHISHNESS
SULFITE	SULLENS	SULPHONIC	SUMLESSNESS	SUMPHY
SULFITIC	SULLIED	SULPHONIUM	SUMMA	SUMPIT
SULFITO	SULLIES	SULPHONYL	SUMMABILITY	SUMPITAN
SULFOACID	SULLOW	SULPHOPHENYL	SUMMABLE	SUMPLE
SULFOAMIDE	SULLY	SULPHOSOL	SUMMAE	SUMPMAN
SULFOBENZIDE	SULLYING	SULPHOTANNIC	SUMMAGE	SUMPSIMUS
SULFOBENZOIC	SULPHA	SULPHOTOLUIC	SUMMAND	SUMPT
SULFOBORITE	SULPHACID	SULPHOUREA	SUMMAR	SUMPTER
SULFOCYAN	SULPHAMATE	SULPHOVINATE	SUMMARIES	SUMPTION
SULFOCYANIDE	SULPHAMIC	SULPHOVINIC	SUMMARILY	SUMPTUARY
SULFOHALITE	SULPHAMID	SULPHOXID	SUMMARINESS	SUMPTUOSITY
SULFOHYDRATE	SULPHAMIDATE	SULPHOXIDE	SUMMARISE	SUMPTUOUS
SULFOLEIC	SULPHAMIDE	SULPHOXISM	SUMMARIST	SUMPTUOUSLY
SULFOLYSIS	SULPHAMIDIC	SULPHOXYLIC	SUMMARIZATION	SUMPTUOUSNESS
SULFONAL	SULPHAMIN	SULPHUR	SUMMARIZE	SUMPTURE
SULFONAMIC	SULPHAMINE	SULPHURAGE	SUMMARIZED	SUMPWEED
SULFONAMIDE	SULPHAMINIC	SULPHURAN	SUMMARIZER	SUN
SULFONATE	SULPHAMINO	SULPHURATE	SUMMARIZING	SUNBATHER
SULFONATED	SULPHAMYL	SULPHURATED	SUMMARY	SUNBATHING
SULFONATING	SULPHANILIC	SULPHURATING	SUMMAT	SUNBEAM
SULFONATION	SULPHARSENIC	SULPHURATION	SUMMATE	SUNBEAMED
SULFONATOR	SULPHARSENID	SULPHURATOR	SUMMATED	SUNBEAMY
SULFONE	SULPHATASE	SULPHUREA	SUMMATING	SUNBERRY
SULFONIC	SULPHATE	SULPHURED	SUMMATION	SUNBIRD
SULFONIUM	SULPHATED	SULPHUREITY	SUMMATIONAL	SUNBLIND
SULFONYL	SULPHATIC	SULPHUREOUS	SUMMATIVE	SUNBLINK
SULFORICINIC	SULPHATING	SULPHURET	SUMMATORY	SUNBONNET
SULFOUREA	SULPHATION	SULPHURETED	SUMMED	SUNBOW
SULFOVINATE	SULPHATIZE	SULPHURETING	SUMMER	SUNBREAK
SULFOVINIC	SULPHATIZED	SULPHURETTED	SUMMERBIRD	SUNBURN
SULFOXIDE	SULPHATIZING	SULPHURETTING	SUMMERCASTLE	SUNBURNED
SULFOXISM	SULPHATO	SULPHURIC	SUMMERED	SUNBURNING
SULFOXYLATE	SULPHAZID	SULPHURING	SUMMERER	SUNBURNT
SULFOXYLIC	SULPHAZIDE	SULPHURIZE	SUMMERGAME	SUNBURNTNESS
SULFUR	SULPHAZOTIZE	SULPHURIZED	SUMMERHEAD	SUNBURST
SULFURAGE	SULPHETHYLIC	SULPHURIZING	SUMMERHOUSE	SUNCHERCHOR
SULFURAN	SULPHID	SULPHUROSYL	SUMMERING	SUNCK
SULFURATE	SULPHIDATION	SULPHUROUS	SUMMERINGS	SUNCKE
SULFURATION	SULPHIDE	SULPHUROUSLY	SUMMERLAND	SUNCUP
SULFURATOR	SULPHIDIC	SULPHURWEED	SUMMERLAY	SUNDAE
SULFUREA	SULPHIDIZE	SULPHURWORT	SUMMERLINESS	SUNDANG
SULFURED	SULPHIMIDE	SULPHURY	SUMMERLING	SUNDARI
SULFUREOUS	SULPHIN	SULPHURYL	SUMMERLY	SUNDER
SULFUREOUSLY	SULPHINATE	SULPHYDRATE	SUMMERROOM	SUNDERANCE
SULFURET	SULPHINE	SULPHYDRYL	SUMMERSAULT	SUNDERED
SULFURET	SULPHINIC	SULTAM	SUMMERSET	SUNDERER
SULFURETED	SULPHINIDE	SULTAN	SUMMERTIDE	SUNDERING
SULFURETING	SULPHINYL	SULTANA	SUMMERTIME	SUNDERLY
SULFURETTED	SULPHITATION	SULTANATE	SUMMERWARD	SUNDERMENT
SULFURETTING	SULPHITE	SULTANE	SUMMERWOOD	SUNDEW
SULFURIC	SULPHITIC	SULTANESS	SUMMERY	SUNDIAL
SULFURING	SULPHITO	SULTANIC	SUMMING	SUNDIK
SULFURIZE	SULPHO	SULTANIN	SUMMIST	SUNDOG
SULFURIZED	SULPHOBENZID	SULTANISM	SUMMIT	SUNDOWN
SULFURIZING	SULPHOBORITE	SULTANIST	SUMMITAL	SUNDOWNER
SULFUROSYL	SULPHOCYAN	SULTANIZE	SUMMITLESS	SUNDOWNING
SULFUROUS	SULPHOCYANIC	SULTANSHIP	SUMMITRY	SUNDRESS
SULFURY	SULPHOFY	SULTANY	SUMMITY	SUNDRI
SULFURYL	SULPHOGALLIC	SULTONE	SUMMON	SUNDRIES
SULK	SULPHOGEL	SULTRIER	SUMMONED	SUNDRILY
SULKA	SULPHOHALITE	SULTRIEST	SUMMONER	SUNDRINESS
SULKED	SULPHOHALOID	SULTRILY	SUMMONING	SUNDROPS
SULKER	SULPHOLEATE	SULTRINESS	SUMMONS	SUNDRY
SULKIER	SULPHOLIPIN	SULTRY	SUMMONSED	SUNDRYMAN
SULKIES	SULPHOLYSIS	SULUNG	SUMMONSES	SUNDRYMEN
SULKIEST	SULPHONAL	SULVANITE	SUMMONSING	SUNFALL
SULKILY	SULPHONALISM	SULVASUTRA	SUMMULA	SUNFAST
SULKINESS	SULPHONAMID	SUM	SUMMULAE	SUNFISH
SULKING	SULPHONAMIDE	SUMAC	SUMMULIST	SUNFISHER
SULKS	SULPHONAMIDO	SUMACH	SUMNER	SUNFISHERY
SULKY	SULPHONAMINE	SUMAGE	SUMP	SUNFISHES
SULL	SULPHONATE	SUMBAL	SUMPAGE	SUNFLOWER
SULLA	SULPHONATED	SUMBUL	SUMPER	SUNFOIL
SULLAGE	SULPHONATING	SUMBULIC	SUMPH	SUNG
SULLEN	SULPHONATION	SUMEN	SUMPHISH	SUNGAR

SUNGLADE
SUNGLASS
SUNGLASSES
SUNGLO
SUNGLOW
SUNK
SUNKE
SUNKEN
SUNKET
SUNKIE
SUNKLAND
SUNLAMP
SUNLAND
SUNLESS
SUNLESSNESS
SUNLET
SUNLIGHT
SUNLIGHTED
SUNLIT
SUNN
SUNNA
SUNNED
SUNNIER
SUNNIEST
SUNNILY
SUNNINESS
SUNNING
SUNNUD
SUNNY
SUNNYASEE
SUNNYHEARTED
SUNPROOF
SUNQUAKE
SUNRAY
SUNRISE
SUNRISING
SUNROOM
SUNROSE
SUNSCALD
SUNSCORCH
SUNSET
SUNSETTING
SUNSETTY
SUNSHADE
SUNSHINE
SUNSHINY
SUNSMIT
SUNSMITTEN
SUNSPOT
SUNSPOTTED
SUNSPOTTERY
SUNSPOTTY
SUNSQUALL
SUNSTAY
SUNSTEAD
SUNSTONE
SUNSTRICKEN
SUNSTROKE
SUNSTRUCK
SUNT
SUNTAN
SUNTANS
SUNUP
SUNWARD
SUNWARDS
SUNWAYS
SUNWEED
SUNWISE
SUNYATA
SUNYIE
SUP
SUPA
SUPARI
SUPAWN
SUPE
SUPELLECTILE
SUPELLEX

SUPER
SUPERABILITY
SUPERABLE
SUPERABLY
SUPERABOUND
SUPERABUNDANCE
SUPERABUNDANT
SUPERABUNDANTLY
SUPERACID
SUPERADD
SUPERALBAL
SUPERALTAR
SUPERANAL
SUPERANNATE
SUPERANNUATE
SUPERANNUATED
SUPERANNUATING
SUPERARCTIC
SUPERATE
SUPERAURAL
SUPERAVIT
SUPERB
SUPERBIOUS
SUPERBITY
SUPERBLY
SUPERBNESS
SUPERBOMB
SUPERCARGO
SUPERCARGOES
SUPERCARGOS
SUPERCARPAL
SUPERCARRIER
SUPERCENTRAL
SUPERCHARGE
SUPERCHARGED
SUPERCHARGER
SUPERCHARGING
SUPERCILIA
SUPERCILIARY
SUPERCILIOUS
SUPERCILIOUSLY
SUPERCILIOUSNESS
SUPERCILIUM
SUPERCLASS
SUPERCOMBING
SUPERCONSCIOUS
SUPERCONSCIOUSNESS
SUPERCOOL
SUPERCRUST
SUPERDUPER
SUPERDURAL
SUPEREDIFY
SUPEREGO
SUPEREMINENT
SUPEREROGANT
SUPEREROGATE
SUPEREXIST
SUPERFAMILY
SUPERFAT
SUPERFECTA
SUPERFEMALE
SUPERFETATE
SUPERFETATED
SUPERFICIAL
SUPERFICIALISM
SUPERFICIALIST
SUPERFICIALITIES
SUPERFICIALITY
SUPERFICIALIZE
SUPERFICIALLY
SUPERFICIALNESS
SUPERFICIARIES
SUPERFICIARY
SUPERFICIES
SUPERFINE
SUPERFINISH
SUPERFIX

SUPERFLEXION
SUPERFLUENT
SUPERFLUID
SUPERFLUITIES
SUPERFLUITY
SUPERFLUOUS
SUPERFLUOUSLY
SUPERFLUOUSNESS
SUPERFLUX
SUPERFRONTAL
SUPERFUSE
SUPERFUSED
SUPERFUSING
SUPERFUSION
SUPERGENE
SUPERGENERIC
SUPERGENUAL
SUPERGLACIAL
SUPERGLOTTAL
SUPERHEAT
SUPERHEATED
SUPERHEATER
SUPERHEATING
SUPERHIGHWAY
SUPERHUMAN
SUPERHUMANLY
SUPERHUMERAL
SUPERI
SUPERIAL
SUPERIMPOSE
SUPERIMPOSED
SUPERIMPOSING
SUPERIMPOSITION
SUPERIMPOSURE
SUPERINDUCE
SUPERINDUCED
SUPERINDUCING
SUPERINDUCT
SUPERINDUE
SUPERINFUSE
SUPERINTEND
SUPERINTENDED
SUPERINTENDENCE
SUPERINTENDENCY
SUPERINTENDENT
SUPERINTENDING
SUPERIOR
SUPERIORESS
SUPERIORITY
SUPERIORLY
SUPERIUS
SUPERJACENT
SUPERLABIAL
SUPERLATION
SUPERLATIVE
SUPERLATIVELY
SUPERLATIVENESS
SUPERLUNAR
SUPERLUNARY
SUPERMALE
SUPERMAN
SUPERMANLY
SUPERMARINE
SUPERMARKET
SUPERMAXILLA
SUPERMEDIAL
SUPERMEN
SUPERMUSCAN
SUPERNACULAR
SUPERNACULUM
SUPERNAL
SUPERNALLY
SUPERNATANT
SUPERNATURAL
SUPERNATURALIST
SUPERNATURALIZE
SUPERNATURALLY

SUPERNATURALNESS
SUPERNATURE
SUPERNORMAL
SUPERNOVA
SUPERNOVAE
SUPERNOVAS
SUPEROCTAVE
SUPEROCULAR
SUPERODORSAL
SUPERORBITAL
SUPERORDER
SUPERORDINAL
SUPERORDINATE
SUPERORDINATION
SUPERORGANIC
SUPERPARTICULAR
SUPERPHYSICAL
SUPERPLANT
SUPERPLUS
SUPERPOSABLE
SUPERPOSE
SUPERPOSED
SUPERPOSING
SUPERPOSITION
SUPERPOWER
SUPERPOWERED
SUPERRENAL
SUPERROYAL
SUPERSACRAL
SUPERSALIENCY
SUPERSALIENT
SUPERSALT
SUPERSATURATE
SUPERSATURATED
SUPERSATURATING
SUPERSATURATION
SUPERSCRIBE
SUPERSCRIBED
SUPERSCRIBING
SUPERSCRIPT
SUPERSCRIPTION
SUPERSEDE
SUPERSEDEAS
SUPERSEDED
SUPERSEDENCE
SUPERSEDER
SUPERSEDERE
SUPERSEDING
SUPERSEDURE
SUPERSENSIBLE
SUPERSENSIBLY
SUPERSENSORY
SUPERSENSUAL
SUPERSEPTAL
SUPERSESSION
SUPERSESSIVE
SUPERSEX
SUPERSEXUAL
SUPERSISTENT
SUPERSOCIAL
SUPERSOLID
SUPERSONANT
SUPERSONIC
SUPERSONICS
SUPERSTATE
SUPERSTITION
SUPERSTITIONIST
SUPERSTITIOUS
SUPERSTITIOUSLY
SUPERSTITIOUSNESS
SUPERSTRATA
SUPERSTRATUM
SUPERSTRUCT
SUPERSTRUCTED
SUPERSTRUCTING
SUPERSTRUCTION
SUPERSTRUCTIVE

SUPERSTRUCTOR
SUPERSTRUCTORY
SUPERSTRUCTRAL
SUPERSTRUCTURE
SUPERSUBTLE
SUPERTAX
SUPERTERRENE
SUPERTONIC
SUPERTUNIC
SUPERVENE
SUPERVENED
SUPERVENIENT
SUPERVENING
SUPERVENTION
SUPERVISAL
SUPERVISANCE
SUPERVISE
SUPERVISED
SUPERVISING
SUPERVISION
SUPERVISIONARY
SUPERVISIVE
SUPERVISOR
SUPERVISORY
SUPERVISURE
SUPERVOLUTE
SUPERWEENING
SUPINATE
SUPINATED
SUPINATING
SUPINATION
SUPINATOR
SUPINE
SUPINELY
SUPINENESS
SUPPABLE
SUPPAGE
SUPPED
SUPPEDANEA
SUPPEDANEOUS
SUPPEDANEUM
SUPPEDIT
SUPPER
SUPPERING
SUPPERLESS
SUPPERTIME
SUPPERWARD
SUPPERWARDS
SUPPING
SUPPLACE
SUPPLANT
SUPPLANTED
SUPPLANTER
SUPPLANTING
SUPPLE
SUPPLED
SUPPLEJACK
SUPPLELY
SUPPLEMENT
SUPPLEMENTAL
SUPPLEMENTARY
SUPPLEMENTATION
SUPPLEMENTED
SUPPLEMENTER
SUPPLEMENTING
SUPPLENESS
SUPPLER
SUPPLETORIES
SUPPLETORILY
SUPPLETORY
SUPPLIAL
SUPPLIANCE
SUPPLIANCY
SUPPLIANT
SUPPLIANTLY
SUPPLIANTNESS
SUPPLICANCY

SUPPLICANT
SUPPLICANTLY
SUPPLICAT
SUPPLICATE
SUPPLICATED
SUPPLICATING
SUPPLICATION
SUPPLICATOR
SUPPLICATORY
SUPPLICAVIT
SUPPLICE
SUPPLIED
SUPPLIER
SUPPLIES
SUPPLING
SUPPLY
SUPPLYING
SUPPONE
SUPPORT
SUPPORTABILITY
SUPPORTABLE
SUPPORTABLENES
SUPPORTABLY
SUPPORTANCE
SUPPORTASSE
SUPPORTED
SUPPORTER
SUPPORTING
SUPPORTINGLY
SUPPORTIVE
SUPPOSABLE
SUPPOSABLENESS
SUPPOSABLY
SUPPOSAL
SUPPOSE
SUPPOSED
SUPPOSEDLY
SUPPOSER
SUPPOSING
SUPPOSITAL
SUPPOSITION
SUPPOSITIONAL
SUPPOSITITIOUS
SUPPOSITIVE
SUPPOSITIVELY
SUPPOSITORIES
SUPPOSITORY
SUPPOSITUM
SUPPOST
SUPPRESS
SUPPRESSAL
SUPPRESSED
SUPPRESSEDLY
SUPPRESSER
SUPPRESSIBLE
SUPPRESSING
SUPPRESSION
SUPPRESSIVE
SUPPRESSIVELY
SUPPRESSOR
SUPPRIME
SUPPRISE
SUPPURANT
SUPPURATE
SUPPURATED
SUPPURATING
SUPPURATION
SUPPURATIVE
SUPPUTE
SUPRA
SUPRABUCCAL
SUPRACAECAL
SUPRACAUDAL
SUPRACILIARY
SUPRACLAVICLE
SUPRACLUSION
SUPRACOSTAL

SUPRACOXAL
SUPRACRANIAL
SUPRADENTAL
SUPRADORSAL
SUPRADURAL
SUPRAFINE
SUPRAFOLIAR
SUPRAGLACIAL
SUPRAGLENOID
SUPRAGLOTTIC
SUPRAHEPATIC
SUPRAHUMAN
SUPRAHUMANITY
SUPRAILIAC
SUPRAILIUM
SUPRAJURAL
SUPRALABIAL
SUPRALATERAL
SUPRALEGAL
SUPRALIMINAL
SUPRALINEAL
SUPRALINEAR
SUPRALOCAL
SUPRALOCALLY
SUPRALORAL
SUPRALUNAR
SUPRALUNARY
SUPRAMAMMARY
SUPRAMARINE
SUPRAMASTOID
SUPRAMAXILLA
SUPRAMAXIMAL
SUPRAMEATAL
SUPRAMEDIAL
SUPRAMENTAL
SUPRAMORAL
SUPRAMORTAL
SUPRAMUNDANE
SUPRANASAL
SUPRANATIONAL
SUPRANATURAL
SUPRANATURE
SUPRANERVIAN
SUPRANEURAL
SUPRANORMAL
SUPRANUCLEAR
SUPRAOCULAR
SUPRAOPTIMAL
SUPRAOPTIONAL
SUPRAORAL
SUPRAORBITAL
SUPRAORBITAR
SUPRAORDINARY
SUPRAPEDAL
SUPRAPROTEST
SUPRAPUBIAN
SUPRAPUBIC
SUPRAPYGAL
SUPRARATIONAL
SUPRARENAL
SUPRARENALIN
SUPRARENIN
SUPRARENINE
SUPRARIMAL
SUPRASCAPULA
SUPRASCRIPT
SUPRASENSUAL
SUPRASEPTAL
SUPRASOLAR
SUPRASPINAL
SUPRASPINATE
SUPRASPINOUS
SUPRASTATE
SUPRASTERNAL
SUPRASTIGMAL
SUPRASUBTLE
SUPRAVAGINAL

SUPRAVERSION
SUPRAVITAL
SUPRAWORLD
SUPREMACIES
SUPREMACY
SUPREME
SUPREMELY
SUPREMENESS
SUPREMITY
SUPTION
SUQ
SUR
SURA
SURADDITION
SURAH
SURAHEE
SURAHI
SURAL
SURAMIN
SURANAL
SURANGULAR
SURAT
SURBASE
SURBASED
SURBASEMENT
SURBATE
SURBATER
SURBED
SURBEDDED
SURBEDDING
SURCEASE
SURCEASED
SURCEASING
SURCHARGE
SURCHARGED
SURCHARGER
SURCHARGING
SURCINGLE
SURCINGLED
SURCINGLING
SURCLE
SURCLOY
SURCOAT
SURCRUE
SURCULI
SURCULOSE
SURCULOUS
SURCULUS
SURD
SURDATION
SURDENT
SURDIMUTISM
SURDITY
SURDOMUTE
SURE
SUREFIRE
SURELY
SUREMENT
SURENESS
SURER
SURES
SURESBY
SUREST
SURETIES
SURETTE
SURETY
SURETYSHIP
SURF
SURFACE
SURFACED
SURFACEDLY
SURFACELESS
SURFACELY
SURFACEMAN
SURFACEMEN
SURFACER
SURFACING

SURFACTANT
SURFACY
SURFBIRD
SURFBOARD
SURFBOARDING
SURFBOAT
SURFBOATMAN
SURFCASTER
SURFCASTING
SURFEIT
SURFEITED
SURFEITER
SURFEITING
SURFER
SURFICIAL
SURFING
SURFLE
SURFMAN
SURFMANSHIP
SURFMEN
SURFRAPPE
SURFRIDING
SURFUSE
SURFUSION
SURFY
SURGE
SURGED
SURGENCY
SURGENT
SURGEON
SURGEONCIES
SURGEONCY
SURGEONFISH
SURGEONFISHES
SURGER
SURGERIES
SURGERIZE
SURGERY
SURGICAL
SURGICALLY
SURGIER
SURGIEST
SURGING
SURGY
SURHAI
SURICAT
SURICATE
SURIGA
SURINAMINE
SURIQUE
SURLIER
SURLIEST
SURLILY
SURLINESS
SURLY
SURMA
SURMARK
SURMASTER
SURMENAGE
SURMISAL
SURMISANT
SURMISE
SURMISED
SURMISEDLY
SURMISER
SURMISING
SURMIT
SURMOUNT
SURMOUNTABLE
SURMOUNTAL
SURMOUNTED
SURMOUNTER
SURMOUNTING
SURMULLET
SURMULLETS
SURN
SURNAI

SURNAME
SURNAMED
SURNAMER
SURNAMING
SURNAP
SURNAPE
SURNAY
SURNOMINAL
SURNOUN
SURPASS
SURPASSABLE
SURPASSED
SURPASSER
SURPASSING
SURPASSINGLY
SURPASSINGNESS
SURPHUL
SURPLICE
SURPLICED
SURPLICIAN
SURPLUS
SURPLUSAGE
SURPLUSES
SURPOOSE
SURPRINT
SURPRISABLE
SURPRIZAL
SURPRISE
SURPRISED
SURPRISEDLY
SURPRISEMENT
SURPRISER
SURPRISING
SURPRISINGLY
SURPRISINGNESS
SURPRIZAL
SURQUEDRY
SURQUIDRY
SURQUIDY
SURRA
SURRAH
SURREALISM
SURREALIST
SURREALISTIC
SURREALISTICALLY
SURREBOUND
SURREBUT
SURREBUTTAL
SURREBUTTER
SURRECTION
SURREIN
SURREJOIN
SURREJOINDER
SURRENDER
SURRENDERED
SURRENDEREE
SURRENDERER
SURRENDERING
SURRENDEROR
SURREPT
SURREPTION
SURREPTITIOUS
SURREPTITIOUSLY
SURREPTITIOUSNES
SURREVERENCE
SURREY
SURROGATE
SURROGATED
SURROGATING
SURROGATION
SURROSION
SURROUND
SURROUNDED
SURROUNDEDLY
SURROUNDER
SURROUNDING
SURROYAL

SURSISE
SURSIZE
SURSOLID
SURSTYLE
SURTAX
SURTAXED
SURTAXING
SURTOUT
SURTURBRAND
SURUCUCU
SURVEILLANCE
SURVEILLANT
SURVEY
SURVEYAGE
SURVEYAL
SURVEYANCE
SURVEYED
SURVEYING
SURVEYOR
SURVEYORSHIP
SURVIEW
SURVIGROUS
SURVISE
SURVIVAL
SURVIVALISM
SURVIVALIST
SURVIVANCE
SURVIVANCY
SURVIVE
SURVIVED
SURVIVER
SURVIVING
SURVIVOR
SURVIVORSHIP
SUSANEE
SUSCEPT
SUSCEPTANCE
SUSCEPTIBILITY
SUSCEPTIBLE
SUSCEPTIBLENESS
SUSCEPTIBLY
SUSCEPTION
SUSCEPTIVE
SUSCEPTIVENESS
SUSCEPTIVITY
SUSCEPTOR
SUSCITATE
SUSCITATION
SUSCITE
SUSI
SUSLIK
SUSOTOXIN
SUSPECT
SUSPECTED
SUSPECTEDNESS
SUSPECTER
SUSPECTFUL
SUSPECTFULNESS
SUSPECTING
SUSPECTOR
SUSPEND
SUSPENDED
SUSPENDER
SUSPENDIBILITY
SUSPENDIBLE
SUSPENDING
SUSPENSATION
SUSPENSE
SUSPENSION
SUSPENSIVE
SUSPENSIVELY
SUSPENSIVENESS
SUSPENSOID
SUSPENSOR
SUSPENSORIA
SUSPENSORIAL
SUSPENSORIUM

SUSPENSORY
SUSPICION
SUSPICIONAL
SUSPICIOUS
SUSPICIOUSLY
SUSPICIOUSNESS
SUSPIRAL
SUSPIRATION
SUSPIRATIOUS
SUSPIRATIVE
SUSPIRE
SUSPIRED
SUSPIRING
SUSPIRIOUS
SUSS
SUSSEXITE
SUSSULTATORY
SUSSULTORIAL
SUSSY
SUSTAIN
SUSTAINABLE
SUSTAINED
SUSTAINEDLY
SUSTAINER
SUSTAINING
SUSTAININGLY
SUSTAINMENT
SUSTENANCE
SUSTENANT
SUSTENTATE
SUSTENTATION
SUSTENTATIVE
SUSTENTATOR
SUSTENTION
SUSTENTIVE
SUSTENTOR
SUSTINENT
SUSU
SUSURR
SUSURRANT
SUSURRATE
SUSURRATED
SUSURRATING
SUSURRATION
SUSURRINGLY
SUSURROUS
SUSURRUS
SUTE
SUTEL
SUTERBERRIES
SUTERBERRY
SUTHER
SUTILE
SUTLER
SUTLERAGE
SUTLERSHIP
SUTLERY
SUTOR
SUTORIAL
SUTORIAN
SUTORIOUS
SUTRA
SUTRAS
SUTTA
SUTTEE
SUTTEEISM
SUTTER
SUTTLE
SUTURAL
SUTURALLY
SUTURATION
SUTURE
SUTURED
SUTURING
SUUM
SUWAR
SUWARRO

SUZ
SUZERAIN
SUZERAINTY
SUZU
SVABITE
SVAMI
SVAMIN
SVARABHAKTI
SVARABHAKTIC
SVARAJ
SVASTIKA
SVEDBERG
SVELT
SVELTE
SVIATONOSITE
SWAB
SWABBED
SWABBER
SWABBERLY
SWABBING
SWABBLE
SWABBY
SWACK
SWACKED
SWACKEN
SWACKING
SWAD
SWADDER
SWADDISH
SWADDLE
SWADDLEBILL
SWADDLED
SWADDLER
SWADDLING
SWADDY
SWADE
SWAG
SWAGBELLIED
SWAGBELLIES
SWAGBELLY
SWAGE
SWAGED
SWAGER
SWAGGED
SWAGGER
SWAGGERED
SWAGGERER
SWAGGERING
SWAGGERINGLY
SWAGGIE
SWAGGING
SWAGGY
SWAGING
SWAGMAN
SWAGMEN
SWAGSMAN
SWAGSMEN
SWAIL
SWAIMOUS
SWAIN
SWAINISH
SWAINISHNESS
SWAINMOTE
SWAIRD
SWAK
SWALE
SWALER
SWALING
SWALINGLY
SWALLET
SWALLO
SWALLOW
SWALLOWABLE
SWALLOWED
SWALLOWER
SWALLOWING
SWALLOWPIPE

SWALLOWS
SWALLOWTAIL
SWALLOWWORT
SWAM
SWAMI
SWAMIS
SWAMP
SWAMPABLE
SWAMPBERRIES
SWAMPBERRY
SWAMPED
SWAMPER
SWAMPHEN
SWAMPIER
SWAMPIEST
SWAMPINE
SWAMPING
SWAMPISH
SWAMPISHNESS
SWAMPLAND
SWAMPWEED
SWAMPWOOD
SWAMPY
SWAMY
SWAN
SWANFLOWER
SWANG
SWANGY
SWANHERD
SWANIMOTE
SWANK
SWANKER
SWANKEY
SWANKIE
SWANKIER
SWANKIEST
SWANKILY
SWANKINESS
SWANKING
SWANKY
SWANLIKE
SWANMARK
SWANMARKER
SWANMARKING
SWANMOTE
SWANNECK
SWANNECKED
SWANNERIES
SWANNERY
SWANNET
SWANNISH
SWANNY
SWANPAN
SWANS
SWANSDOWN
SWANSKIN
SWANWEED
SWANWORT
SWAP
SWAPE
SWAPPED
SWAPPER
SWAPPING
SWARAJ
SWARAJISM
SWARAJIST
SWARBIE
SWARD
SWARDED
SWARDING
SWARDY
SWARE
SWARF
SWARGA
SWARM
SWARMED
SWARMER

SWARMING
SWARMY
SWART
SWARTBACK
SWARTH
SWARTHIER
SWARTHIEST
SWARTHILY
SWARTHINESS
SWARTHNESS
SWARTHY
SWARTISH
SWARTNESS
SWARTRUTTER
SWARTRUTTING
SWARTY
SWARVE
SWASH
SWASHBUCKLE
SWASHBUCKLER
SWASHBUCKLING
SWASHED
SWASHER
SWASHING
SWASHINGLY
SWASHWAY
SWASHWORK
SWASHY
SWASTICA
SWASTIKA
SWAT
SWATCH
SWATCHER
SWATH
SWATHE
SWATHED
SWATHER
SWATHING
SWATHY
SWATS
SWATTED
SWATTER
SWATTING
SWATTLE
SWAVER
SWAY
SWAYBACK
SWAYED
SWAYER
SWAYING
SWAYINGLY
SWAYLESS
SWEAL
SWEAM
SWEAR
SWEARER
SWEARING
SWEARINGLY
SWEARWORD
SWEAT
SWEATBAND
SWEATBOX
SWEATED
SWEATER
SWEATFUL
SWEATH
SWEATHOUSE
SWEATIER
SWEATIEST
SWEATILY
SWEATINESS
SWEATING
SWEATS
SWEATSHOP
SWEATWEED
SWEATY
SWEB

SWEDE
SWEDGE
SWEDGER
SWEDRU
SWEE
SWEEK
SWEEL
SWEENS
SWEENY
SWEEP
SWEEPAGE
SWEEPBACK
SWEEPBOARD
SWEEPDOM
SWEEPER
SWEEPING
SWEEPINGLY
SWEEPINGNESS
SWEEPSTAKE
SWEEPSTAKES
SWEEPUP
SWEEPWASHER
SWEEPY
SWEER
SWEERT
SWEESWEE
SWEET
SWEETBERRY
SWEETBREAD
SWEETBRIAR
SWEETBRIER
SWEETBRIERY
SWEETCLOVER
SWEETEN
SWEETENED
SWEETENER
SWEETENING
SWEETER
SWEETEST
SWEETFISH
SWEETFUL
SWEETHEART
SWEETHEARTING
SWEETIE
SWEETING
SWEETISH
SWEETISHLY
SWEETISHNESS
SWEETLEAF
SWEETLY
SWEETMAKER
SWEETMEAT
SWEETNESS
SWEETROOT
SWEETS
SWEETSHOP
SWEETSOP
SWEETWATER
SWEETWEED
SWEETWOOD
SWEETWORT
SWEETY
SWEGO
SWELCHIE
SWELL
SWELLAGE
SWELLDOM
SWELLDOODLE
SWELLED
SWELLER
SWELLFISH
SWELLFISHES
SWELLING
SWELLISH
SWELLISHNESS
SWELLMOBSMAN
SWELLNESS

SWELLTOAD
SWELLY
SWELP
SWELT
SWELTER
SWELTERED
SWELTERING
SWELTERINGLY
SWELTH
SWELTRY
SWELTY
SWEPE
SWEPT
SWEPTBACK
SWEPTWING
SWERVE
SWERVED
SWERVER
SWERVILY
SWERVING
SWEVEN
SWEYN
SWICH
SWICK
SWIDDEN
SWIDGE
SWIFT
SWIFTEN
SWIFTER
SWIFTEST
SWIFTFOOT
SWIFTLET
SWIFTLIER
SWIFTLIEST
SWIFTLY
SWIFTNESS
SWIFTY
SWIG
SWIGGED
SWIGGER
SWIGGING
SWIGGLE
SWIKE
SWILE
SWILK
SWILKIE
SWILL
SWILLBOWL
SWILLED
SWILLER
SWILLING
SWILLTUB
SWIM
SWIMBEL
SWIMMER
SWIMMERET
SWIMMING
SWIMMINGLY
SWIMMIST
SWIMMY
SWIMSUIT
SWIMY
SWINDLE
SWINDLED
SWINDLER
SWINDLERS
SWINDLERY
SWINDLING
SWINE
SWINEBREAD
SWINECOTE
SWINEHEAD
SWINEHERD
SWINEHERDSHIP
SWINEHULL
SWINELY
SWINEPIPE

SWINEPOX
SWINERY
SWINESTONE
SWINESTY
SWINEY
SWING
SWINGBACK
SWINGDEVIL
SWINGDINGLE
SWINGE
SWINGED
SWINGEING
SWINGEINGLY
SWINGEL
SWINGEOUR
SWINGER
SWINGING
SWINGINGLY
SWINGKNIFE
SWINGLE
SWINGLEBAR
SWINGLED
SWINGLETAIL
SWINGLETREE
SWINGLING
SWINGMAN
SWINGSTOCK
SWINGTREE
SWINGY
SWINISH
SWINISHLY
SWINISHNESS
SWINK
SWINKER
SWINKING
SWINNEY
SWIP
SWIPE
SWIPED
SWIPES
SWIPING
SWIPLE
SWIPPER
SWIPPLE
SWIPY
SWIRE
SWIRL
SWIRLED
SWIRLING
SWIRLY
SWIRRING
SWISH
SWISHED
SWISHER
SWISHING
SWISHINGLY
SWISHY
SWISS
SWISSING
SWITCH
SWITCHBACK
SWITCHBACKER
SWITCHBOARD
SWITCHED
SWITCHEL
SWITCHER
SWITCHGEAR
SWITCHING
SWITCHKEEPER
SWITCHLIKE
SWITCHMAN
SWITCHMEN
SWITCHTAIL
SWITCHY
SWITCHYARD
SWITH
SWITHE

SWITHEN
SWITHER
SWITHLY
SWIVE
SWIVEL
SWIVELED
SWIVELEYE
SWIVELEYED
SWIVELING
SWIVELLED
SWIVELLIKE
SWIVELLING
SWIVER
SWIVET
SWIVETTY
SWIVVET
SWIZ
SWIZZ
SWIZZLE
SWIZZLER
SWOB
SWOBBER
SWOLLEN
SWONK
SWOON
SWOONED
SWOONING
SWOONINGLY
SWOONY
SWOOP
SWOOPED
SWOOPER
SWOOPING
SWOOSH
SWOP
SWOPE
SWORD
SWORDBILL
SWORDCRAFT
SWORDER
SWORDFISH
SWORDFISHERMAN
SWORDFISHERY
SWORDFISHES
SWORDFISHING
SWORDICK
SWORDING
SWORDKNOT
SWORDMAKER
SWORDMAKING
SWORDMAN
SWORDMANSHIP
SWORDPLAY
SWORDPLAYER
SWORDPROOF
SWORDSLIPPER
SWORDSMAN
SWORDSMANSHIP
SWORDSMEN
SWORDSMITH
SWORDSTICK
SWORDSWOMAN
SWORDTAIL
SWORDWEED
SWORE
SWORL
SWORN
SWOSH
SWOT
SWOTTER
SWOUGH
SWOUN
SWOUND
SWOUNDS
SWOUNS
SWOW
SWUM

SWUNG
SWY
SWYTHE
SY
SYAGUSH
SYBARITICAL
SYBIL
SYBO
SYBOES
SYBOTIC
SYBOTISM
SYBOW
SYCAMINE
SYCAMORE
SYCE
SYCEE
SYCHEE
SYCITE
SYCOCK
SYCOMA
SYCOMANCY
SYCONARIAN
SYCONATE
SYCONES
SYCONIA
SYCONID
SYCONIUM
SYCONOID
SYCONUS
SYCOPHANCIES
SYCOPHANCY
SYCOPHANT
SYCOPHANTIC
SYCOPHANTISH
SYCOPHANTISM
SYCOPHANTIZE
SYCOPHANTRY
SYCOSIFORM
SYCOSIS
SYDDIR
SYE
SYENITE
SYENITIC
SYENODIORITE
SYENOGABBRO
SYKE
SYKER
SYKERLY
SYLE
SYLENE
SYLIB
SYLING
SYLLAB
SYLLABARIES
SYLLABARIUM
SYLLABARY
SYLLABATIM
SYLLABATION
SYLLABE
SYLLABI
SYLLABIC
SYLLABICAL
SYLLABICALLY
SYLLABICATE
SYLLABICATED
SYLLABICATING
SYLLABICNESS
SYLLABIFIED
SYLLABIFY
SYLLABIFYING
SYLLABISM
SYLLABIZE
SYLLABIZED
SYLLABIZING
SYLLABLE
SYLLABLED
SYLLABLES

SYLLABLING
SYLLABUB
SYLLABUS
SYLLABUSES
SYLLEPSES
SYLLEPSIS
SYLLEPTIC
SYLLEPTICAL
SYLLID
SYLLIDIAN
SYLLOGE
SYLLOGISM
SYLLOGIST
SYLLOGISTIC
SYLLOGISTICAL
SYLLOGISTICALL
SYLLOGISTICS
SYLLOGIZE
SYLLOGIZED
SYLLOGIZER
SYLLOGIZING
SYLPH
SYLPHID
SYLPHIDINE
SYLPHISH
SYLPHLIKE
SYLPHY
SYLVA
SYLVAE
SYLVAGE
SYLVAN
SYLVANITE
SYLVANITIC
SYLVANITY
SYLVANRY
SYLVAS
SYLVATE
SYLVATIC
SYLVATICAL
SYLVESTER
SYLVESTRAL
SYLVESTRENE
SYLVESTRIAN
SYLVIID
SYLVIINE
SYLVIN
SYLVINE
SYLVINITE
SYLVITE
SYMAR
SYMBASIC
SYMBASICAL
SYMBASICALLY
SYMBASIS
SYMBION
SYMBIONT
SYMBIONTIC
SYMBIOSIS
SYMBIOT
SYMBIOTE
SYMBIOTIC
SYMBIOTICAL
SYMBIOTICALLY
SYMBIOTICS
SYMBIOTISM
SYMBLEPHARON
SYMBOL
SYMBOLATER
SYMBOLIC
SYMBOLICAL
SYMBOLICALLY
SYMBOLICALNESS
SYMBOLICS
SYMBOLISE
SYMBOLISM
SYMBOLIST
SYMBOLISTIC

SYMBOLISTICAL
SYMBOLISTICALLY
SYMBOLIZATION
SYMBOLIZE
SYMBOLIZED
SYMBOLIZER
SYMBOLIZING
SYMBOLOGICAL
SYMBOLOGIST
SYMBOLOGY
SYMBOLOLATRY
SYMBOLOLOGY
SYMBOLRY
SYMBOLS
SYMBOLUM
SYMBOULEUTIC
SYMBRANCH
SYMBRANCHOID
SYMBRANCHOUS
SYMMACHY
SYMMEDIAN
SYMMELUS
SYMMETALLISM
SYMMETRAL
SYMMETRIAN
SYMMETRIC
SYMMETRICAL
SYMMETRICALITY
SYMMETRICALLY
SYMMETRICALNESS
SYMMETRIES
SYMMETRIST
SYMMETRIZE
SYMMETRIZED
SYMMETRIZING
SYMMETROID
SYMMETRY
SYMMIST
SYMPATHETIC
SYMPATHETICAL
SYMPATHETICALLY
SYMPATHIES
SYMPATHIN
SYMPATHIQUE
SYMPATHISE
SYMPATHISM
SYMPATHIST
SYMPATHIZE
SYMPATHIZED
SYMPATHIZER
SYMPATHIZING
SYMPATHIZINGLY
SYMPATHY
SYMPATRIC
SYMPATRY
SYMPETALOUS
SYMPHILE
SYMPHILIC
SYMPHILOUS
SYMPHILY
SYMPHOGENOUS
SYMPHONETIC
SYMPHONIA
SYMPHONIC
SYMPHONICALLY
SYMPHONIES
SYMPHONION
SYMPHONIOUS
SYMPHONIOUSLY
SYMPHONIST
SYMPHONIZE
SYMPHONIZED
SYMPHONIZING
SYMPHONOUS
SYMPHONY
SYMPHRASE
SYMPHYLAN

SYMPHYLLOUS
SYMPHYLOUS
SYMPHYNOTE
SYMPHYSEAL
SYMPHYSES
SYMPHYSION
SYMPHYSIS
SYMPHYSY
SYMPHYTIC
SYMPHYTISM
SYMPHYTIZE
SYMPLASM
SYMPLAST
SYMPLECTIC
SYMPLESITE
SYMPLOCE
SYMPLOCIUM
SYMPODE
SYMPODIA
SYMPODIAL
SYMPODIALLY
SYMPODIUM
SYMPOSIA
SYMPOSIAC
SYMPOSIACAL
SYMPOSIAL
SYMPOSIARCH
SYMPOSIAST
SYMPOSION
SYMPOSIUM
SYMPOSIUMS
SYMPTOM
SYMPTOMATIC
SYMPTOMATICAL
SYMPTOMATICALLY
SYMPTOMATICS
SYMPTOMATIZE
SYMPTOMS
SYMPTOSIS
SYMPUS
SYN
SYNACME
SYNACMIC
SYNACMY
SYNACTIC
SYNADELPHITE
SYNAERESIS
SYNAESTHESIA
SYNAGOG
SYNAGOGAL
SYNAGOGICAL
SYNAGOGUE
SYNALEPHA
SYNALEPHE
SYNALLACTIC
SYNALOEPHA
SYNALOEPHE
SYNANGE
SYNANGIA
SYNANGIAL
SYNANGIC
SYNANGIUM
SYNANTHEMA
SYNANTHEROUS
SYNANTHESIS
SYNANTHETIC
SYNANTHIC
SYNANTHOUS
SYNANTHROSE
SYNANTHY
SYNAPHEA
SYNAPHEIA
SYNAPSE
SYNAPSES
SYNAPSID
SYNAPSIDAN
SYNAPSIS

SYNAPTAI
SYNAPTASE
SYNAPTE
SYNAPTEROUS
SYNAPTIC
SYNAPTICAL
SYNAPTICALLY
SYNAPTICULA
SYNAPTICULAR
SYNAPTICULUM
SYNAPTID
SYNAPTYCHUS
SYNARCHICAL
SYNARCHY
SYNARMOGOID
SYNARTESIS
SYNARTETE
SYNARTETIC
SYNARTHRODIA
SYNARTHROSES
SYNARTHROSIS
SYNASTRY
SYNAXAR
SYNAXARION
SYNAXARIST
SYNAXARY
SYNAXIS
SYNCARP
SYNCARPIA
SYNCARPIUM
SYNCARPOUS
SYNCARPY
SYNCARYON
SYNCEPHALIC
SYNCEPHALUS
SYNCEREBRAL
SYNCEREBRUM
SYNCHITIC
SYNCHORESIS
SYNCHRO
SYNCHROMESH
SYNCHRONAL
SYNCHRONE
SYNCHRONIC
SYNCHRONICAL
SYNCHRONISM
SYNCHRONIZATION
SYNCHRONIZE
SYNCHRONIZED
SYNCHRONIZER
SYNCHRONIZING
SYNCHRONOUS
SYNCHRONOUSLY
SYNCHRONY
SYNCHROSCOPE
SYNCHROTRON
SYNCHYSIS
SYNCLADOUS
SYNCLASTIC
SYNCLINAL
SYNCLINALLY
SYNCLINE
SYNCLINICAL
SYNCLINORIAL
SYNCLINORIAN
SYNCLINORIUM
SYNCLITIC
SYNCLITICISM
SYNCLITISM
SYNCOELOM
SYNCOPAL
SYNCOPATE
SYNCOPATED
SYNCOPATING
SYNCOPATION
SYNCOPATOR
SYNCOPE

SYNCOPES
SYNCOPIC
SYNCOPISM
SYNCOPIST
SYNCOPIZE
SYNCRANIATE
SYNCRANTERIC
SYNCRASY
SYNCRETIC
SYNCRETICAL
SYNCRETICISM
SYNCRETION
SYNCRETISM
SYNCRETIST
SYNCRETISTIC
SYNCRETIZE
SYNCRETIZED
SYNCRETIZING
SYNCRISIS
SYNCRYPTIC
SYNCYTIA
SYNCYTIAL
SYNCYTIOMA
SYNCYTIOMAS
SYNCYTIOMATA
SYNCYTIUM
SYNDACTYL
SYNDACTYLE
SYNDACTYLIA
SYNDACTYLIC
SYNDACTYLISM
SYNDACTYLOUS
SYNDACTYLY
SYNDERESIS
SYNDESIS
SYNDESMITIS
SYNDESMOLOGY
SYNDESMOMA
SYNDESMOSES
SYNDESMOSIS
SYNDESMOTIC
SYNDESMOTOMY
SYNDET
SYNDETIC
SYNDETICAL
SYNDETICALLY
SYNDIC
SYNDICAL
SYNDICALISM
SYNDICALIST
SYNDICALIZE
SYNDICAT
SYNDICATE
SYNDICATED
SYNDICATEER
SYNDICATING
SYNDICATION
SYNDICATOR
SYNDROME
SYNDROMIC
SYNDYASMIAN
SYNE
SYNECDOCHE
SYNECDOCHIC
SYNECDOCHISM
SYNECHIA
SYNECHIAE
SYNECHIOLOGY
SYNECHOLOGY
SYNECHOTOMY
SYNECHTHRAN
SYNECHTHRY
SYNECIOUS
SYNECOLOGY
SYNECTIC
SYNECTICITY
SYNEDRAL

SYNEDRIAL
SYNEDRIAN
SYNEIDESIS
SYNEMA
SYNEMATA
SYNEMMENON
SYNENTOGNATH
SYNERESIS
SYNERGASTIC
SYNERGETIC
SYNERGIA
SYNERGIC
SYNERGID
SYNERGIDAE
SYNERGIDAL
SYNERGISM
SYNERGIST
SYNERGISTIC
SYNERGIZE
SYNERGY
SYNERIZE
SYNESIS
SYNESTHESIA
SYNESTHETIC
SYNETHNIC
SYNEZISIS
SYNGAMIC
SYNGAMOUS
SYNGAMY
SYNGENESIAN
SYNGENESIOUS
SYNGENESIS
SYNGENETIC
SYNGENISM
SYNGENITE
SYNGNATHID
SYNGNATHOID
SYNGNATHOUS
SYNGRAPH
SYNIZESIS
SYNKARYON
SYNKINESIS
SYNKINETIC
SYNNEMA
SYNNEUROSIS
SYNOCHAL
SYNOCHOUS
SYNOCHUS
SYNOCREATE
SYNOD
SYNODAL
SYNODALIST
SYNODALLY
SYNODIAN
SYNODIC
SYNODICAL
SYNODICALLY
SYNODICON
SYNODIST
SYNODITE
SYNODONTID
SYNODONTOID
SYNODSMAN
SYNODSMEN
SYNOECETE
SYNOECIOSIS
SYNOECIOUS
SYNOECIOUSLY
SYNOECISM
SYNOECIZE
SYNOECY
SYNOEKY
SYNOICOUS
SYNOMOSY
SYNONYM
SYNONYMATIC
SYNONYME

SYNONYMIC
SYNONYMICAL
SYNONYMICON
SYNONYMICS
SYNONYMIES
SYNONYMIST
SYNONYMITY
SYNONYMIZE
SYNONYMIZED
SYNONYMIZING
SYNONYMOUS
SYNONYMOUSLY
SYNONYMY
SYNOPSES
SYNOPSIS
SYNOPSIZE
SYNOPSY
SYNOPTIC
SYNOPTICAL
SYNOPTICALLY
SYNORCHIDISM
SYNORCHISM
SYNOSTEOLOGY
SYNOSTEOSES
SYNOSTEOSIS
SYNOSTOSE
SYNOSTOSES
SYNOSTOSIS
SYNOSTOTIC
SYNOSTOTICAL
SYNOUSIACS
SYNOVECTOMY
SYNOVIA
SYNOVIAL
SYNOVIALLY
SYNOVIPAROUS
SYNOVITIC
SYNOVITIS
SYNPELMOUS
SYNSACRAL
SYNSACRUM
SYNSEPALOUS
SYNSPERMOUS
SYNSPOROUS
SYNTACTIC
SYNTACTICAL
SYNTACTICALLY
SYNTACTICIAN
SYNTAGMA
SYNTAN
SYNTAX
SYNTAXIS
SYNTAXIST
SYNTECHNIC
SYNTECTIC
SYNTECTICAL
SYNTENOSIS
SYNTERESIS
SYNTEXIS
SYNTHEME
SYNTHERMAL
SYNTHESES
SYNTHESIS
SYNTHESISE
SYNTHESISM
SYNTHESIST
SYNTHESIZE
SYNTHESIZED
SYNTHESIZER
SYNTHESIZING
SYNTHETE
SYNTHETIC
SYNTHETICAL
SYNTHETICALLY
SYNTHETICISM
SYNTHETIST
SYNTHETIZATION

SYNTHETIZE
SYNTHETIZER
SYNTHOL
SYNTHRONI
SYNTHRONOI
SYNTHRONOS
SYNTHRONUS
SYNTOMIA
SYNTOMY
SYNTONE
SYNTONIC
SYNTONICAL
SYNTONICALLY
SYNTONIN
SYNTONIZE
SYNTONIZED
SYNTONIZER
SYNTONIZING
SYNTONOUS
SYNTONY
SYNTROPE
SYNTROPHIC
SYNTROPICAL
SYNTROPY
SYNTYPE
SYNTYPIC
SYNTYPICISM
SYNURA
SYNURAE
SYNUSIAST
SYPH
SYPHER
SYPHERED
SYPHERING
SYPHILID
SYPHILIDE
SYPHILIS
SYPHILITIC
SYPHILIZE
SYPHILIZED
SYPHILIZING
SYPHILODERM
SYPHILOGENY
SYPHILOID
SYPHILOLOGY
SYPHILOMA
SYPHILOPHOBE
SYPHILOSIS
SYPHON
SYRETTE
SYRINGA
SYRINGE
SYRINGEAL
SYRINGED
SYRINGES
SYRINGIN
SYRINGING
SYRINGITIS
SYRINGIUM
SYRINGOCELE
SYRINGOCOELE
SYRINGOTOME
SYRINGOTOMY
SYRINX
SYRINXES
SYRMA
SYRPHID
SYRT
SYRTIC
SYRUP
SYRUPED
SYRUPER
SYRUPY
SYRUS
SYSE
SYSSARCOSIC
SYSSARCOSIS

SYSSARCOTIC
SYSSEL
SYSSELMAN
SYSSITIA
SYSSITION
SYSTALTIC
SYSTASIS
SYSTATIC
SYSTEM
SYSTEMATIC
SYSTEMATICAL
SYSTEMATICALITY
SYSTEMATICALLY
SYSTEMATICIAN
SYSTEMATICS
SYSTEMATISE
SYSTEMATISM
SYSTEMATIST
SYSTEMATIZATION
SYSTEMATIZE
SYSTEMATIZED
SYSTEMATIZER
SYSTEMATIZING
SYSTEMIC
SYSTEMICALLY
SYSTEMIZATION
SYSTEMIZE
SYSTEMIZED
SYSTEMIZER
SYSTEMIZING
SYSTILIUS
SYSTOLATED
SYSTOLE
SYSTOLIC
SYSTYLE
SYSTYLOUS
SYZYGAL
SYZYGETIC
SYZYGIA
SYZYGIAL
SYZYGIES
SYZYGIUM
SYZYGY
SZAIBELYITE
SZLACHTA
SZOPELKA

TA
TAA
TAAR
TAB
TABAC
TABACIN
TABACOSIS
TABACUM
TABAGIE
TABANID
TABANUCO
TABARD
TABARDED
TABARDILLO
TABARET
TABASHEER
TABASHIR
TABATIERE
TABBER
TABBIES
TABBINET
TABBY
TABEFACTION
TABEFY
TABELLA
TABELLION
TABER
TABERDAR
TABERNA
TABERNACLE
TABERNACLED
TABERNACLER
TABERNACLING
TABERNACULAR
TABERNAE
TABES
TABESCENCE
TABESCENT
TABET
TABETIC
TABETIFORM
TABETLESS
TABI
TABIA
TABID
TABIDLY
TABIDNESS
TABIFIC
TABIFICAL
TABINET
TABITUDE
TABLA
TABLAS
TABLATURE
TABLE
TABLEAU
TABLEAUS
TABLEAUX
TABLECLOTH
TABLECLOTHY
TABLED
TABLEITY
TABLELAND
TABLEMAID
TABLEMAKER
TABLEMAKING
TABLEMAN

TABLEMATE
TABLER
TABLES
TABLESPOON
TABLESPOONFUL
TABLESPOONFULS
TABLET
TABLETARY
TABLETOP
TABLEWARE
TABLEWISE
TABLIER
TABLINA
TABLING
TABLINUM
TABLITA
TABLOID
TABOG
TABOO
TABOOS
TABOPARALYSIS
TABOPARESIS
TABOPARETIC
TABOPHOBIA
TABOR
TABORED
TABORER
TABORET
TABORIN
TABORINE
TABORING
TABOUR
TABOURED
TABOURER
TABOURET
TABOURINE
TABOURING
TABRET
TABS
TABU
TABULA
TABULABLE
TABULAE
TABULAR
TABULARE
TABULARIA
TABULARIUM
TABULARIZE
TABULARIZED
TABULARIZING
TABULARLY
TABULARY
TABULATE
TABULATED
TABULATING
TABULATION
TABULATOR
TABULATORY
TABULE
TABUN
TABUS
TABUT
TACAHOUT
TACAMAHAC
TACAMAHACA
TACAMAHACK
TACCACEOUS
TACCADA
TACE
TACET
TACH
TACHE
TACHEOGRAPHY
TACHEOMETER
TACHEOMETRIC
TACHEOMETRY
TACHETURE

TACHHYDRITE
TACHIBANA
TACHINA
TACHINARIAN
TACHINID
TACHIOL
TACHOGRAM
TACHOGRAPH
TACHOMETER
TACHOMETRIC
TACHOMETRY
TACHOSCOPE
TACHYCARDIA
TACHYCARDIAC
TACHYGEN
TACHYGENESIS
TACHYGENETIC
TACHYGLOSSAL
TACHYGRAPH
TACHYGRAPHER
TACHYGRAPHIC
TACHYGRAPHY
TACHYLITE
TACHYLYTE
TACHYLYTIC
TACHYMETER
TACHYMETRIC
TACHYMETRY
TACHYSCOPE
TACHYTYPE
TACIT
TACITLY
TACITNESS
TACITURN
TACITURNIST
TACITURNITY
TACITURNLY
TACK
TACKED
TACKER
TACKET
TACKETY
TACKEY
TACKIER
TACKIEST
TACKING
TACKINGLY
TACKLE
TACKLED
TACKLEMAN
TACKLER
TACKLES
TACKLESS
TACKLING
TACKSMAN
TACKSMEN
TACKY
TACLOCUS
TACMAHACK
TACNODE
TACON
TACONITE
TACSO
TACT
TACTFUL
TACTFULLY
TACTFULNESS
TACTIC
TACTICAL
TACTICALLY
TACTICIAN
TACTICS
TACTILE
TACTILIST
TACTILITIES
TACTILITY
TACTION

TACTITE
TACTLESS
TACTLESSLY
TACTLESSNESS
TACTOMETER
TACTOR
TACTUAL
TACTUALITY
TACTUALLY
TACTUS
TACUACINE
TAD
TADBHAVA
TADPOLE
TAE
TAEL
TAENIA
TAENIACIDAL
TAENIACIDE
TAENIAE
TAENIAFUGE
TAENIAL
TAENIAN
TAENIASIS
TAENIATE
TAENICIDE
TAENIDIA
TAENIDIUM
TAENIFORM
TAENIFUGE
TAENIIFORM
TAENIOID
TAENIOSOME
TAENIOSOMOUS
TAENITE
TAENNIN
TAEPO
TAFFAREL
TAFFEREL
TAFFETA
TAFFETY
TAFFIA
TAFFLE
TAFFRAIL
TAFFY
TAFIA
TAFT
TAFWIZ
TAG
TAGASASTE
TAGATOSE
TAGBOARD
TAGETOL
TAGETONE
TAGGE
TAGGED
TAGGER
TAGGERS
TAGGING
TAGGLE
TAGGY
TAGHAIRM
TAGILITE
TAGLIA
TAGLIONI
TAGLOCK
TAGMEME
TAGRAG
TAGRAGGERY
TAGSORE
TAGSTER
TAGTAIL
TAGUA
TAGUAN
TAGWERK
TAHA
TAHALI

TAHANUN
TAHARAH
TAHEEN
TAHGOOK
TAHIN
TAHKHANA
TAHLI
TAHONA
TAHR
TAHSEELDAR
TAHSIL
TAHSILDAR
TAHUA
TAI
TAIAHA
TAIGA
TAIGLE
TAIGLESOME
TAIHOA
TAIKIH
TAIKUN
TAIL
TAILAGE
TAILBAND
TAILBOARD
TAILED
TAILENDER
TAILER
TAILET
TAILFIRST
TAILFLOWER
TAILFOREMOST
TAILGATE
TAILGATED
TAILGATING
TAILGUNNER
TAILHEAD
TAILING
TAILINGS
TAILLE
TAILLESS
TAILLEUR
TAILLIGHT
TAILLOIR
TAILOR
TAILORAGE
TAILORBIRD
TAILORED
TAILORING
TAILORISM
TAILORLY
TAILORS
TAILORY
TAILPIECE
TAILPIN
TAILPIPE
TAILRACE
TAILSKID
TAILSPIN
TAILSTOCK
TAILWISE
TAILY
TAILYE
TAILZEE
TAILZIE
TAILZIED
TAIMEN
TAIMYRITE
TAIN
TAINT
TAINTE
TAINTED
TAINTING
TAINTMENT
TAINTOR
TAINTURE
TAINTWORM

TAIPAN	TALESMAN	TALLOWMAN	TAMBOURINE	TANGA
TAIPO	TALESMEN	TALLOWROOT	TAMBOURING	TANGALUNG
TAIRA	TALETELLER	TALLOWWEED	TAMBOURIST	TANGANTANGAN
TAIRGE	TALETELLING	TALLOWWOOD	TAMBREET	TANGE
TAIS	TALEWISE	TALLOWY	TAMBURA	TANGED
TAISCH	TALI	TALLWOOD	TAMBURAN	TANGEITE
TAISSLE	TALIATION	TALLY	TAMBURELLO	TANGELO
TAISTREL	TALIERA	TALLYHO	TAMBURONE	TANGELOS
TAISTRIL	TALIGRADE	TALLYHOS	TAME	TANGENCE
TAIT	TALION	TALLYING	TAMEABLE	TANGENCIES
TAIVER	TALIONIC	TALLYMAN	TAMED	TANGENCY
TAIVERS	TALIPED	TALLYMEN	TAMEHEARTED	TANGENT
TAIVERT	TALIPEDIC	TALLYWAG	TAMEIN	TANGENTAL
TAJ	TALIPES	TALLYWALKA	TAMELESS	TANGENTALLY
TAJO	TALIPOMANUS	TALLYWOMAN	TAMELESSNESS	TANGENTIAL
TAKABLE	TALIPOT	TALLYWOMEN	TAMELY	TANGENTIALLY
TAKAHE	TALISAY	TALMA	TAMEN	TANGENTLY
TAKAR	TALISMAN	TALMAS	TAMENES	TANGERINE
TAKE	TALISMANIC	TALMOUSE	TAMER	TANGFISH
TAKEDOWN	TALISMANICAL	TALO	TAMEST	TANGFISHES
TAKEFUL	TALISMANNI	TALOFIBULAR	TAMIDINE	TANGHAN
TAKEN	TALISMANS	TALON	TAMIN	TANGHIN
TAKEOFF	TALITE	TALONED	TAMINE	TANGHININ
TAKEOUT	TALITOL	TALONID	TAMING	TANGI
TAKER	TALK	TALOSE	TAMINY	TANGIBILITY
TAKIN	TALKABILITY	TALOTIBIAL	TAMIS	TANGIBLE
TAKING	TALKABLE	TALPACOTI	TAMISE	TANGIBLENESS
TAKINGLY	TALKATHON	TALPATATE	TAMLUNG	TANGIBLY
TAKINGNESS	TALKATIVE	TALPETATE	TAMMAR	TANGIE
TAKKANAH	TALKATIVELY	TALPICIDE	TAMMIE	TANGIER
TAKOSIS	TALKATIVENESS	TALPID	TAMMIES	TANGIEST
TAKROURI	TALKED	TALPIFORM	TAMMY	TANGILIN
TAKT	TALKER	TALPIFY	TAMP	TANGING
TAKY	TALKFEST	TALPINE	TAMPALA	TANGKA
TAKYR	TALKIE	TALPOID	TAMPAN	TANGLAD
TAL	TALKIER	TALSHIDE	TAMPANG	TANGLE
TALA	TALKIEST	TALTER	TAMPED	TANGLEBERRIES
TALABON	TALKING	TALTHIB	TAMPER	TANGLEBERRY
TALAJE	TALKWORTHY	TALUK	TAMPERED	TANGLED
TALAK	TALKY	TALUKA	TAMPERER	TANGLEFISH
TALALGIA	TALL	TALUKDAR	TAMPERING	TANGLEFISHES
TALANTON	TALLAGE	TALUKDARI	TAMPING	TANGLEFOOT
TALAO	TALLAGEABLE	TALUS	TAMPION	TANGLEHEAD
TALAPOIN	TALLAGED	TALUTO	TAMPIONED	TANGLER
TALAR	TALLAGING	TALWOOD	TAMPOE	TANGLEROOT
TALARI	TALLAPOI	TAM	TAMPON	TANGLING
TALARIA	TALLATE	TAMABLE	TAMPONADE	TANGLY
TALARIC	TALLBOY	TAMALE	TAMPONAGE	TANGO
TALAYOT	TALLEGALANE	TAMANDU	TAMPONMENT	TANGOS
TALAYOTI	TALLER	TAMANDUA	TAMPOON	TANGRAM
TALBOT	TALLERO	TAMANOAS	TAMPOY	TANGUE
TALC	TALLEST	TAMANOIR	TAMURE	TANGUILE
TALCED	TALLET	TAMANOWUS	TAN	TANGUIN
TALCER	TALLIABLE	TAMANU	TANA	TANGUM
TALCING	TALLIAR	TAMARA	TANACETIN	TANGUN
TALCKED	TALLIATE	TAMARACK	TANACETYL	TANGY
TALCKING	TALLIATED	TAMARAITE	TANACH	TANHA
TALCKY	TALLIATING	TAMARAO	TANADAR	TANIA
TALCOID	TALLIED	TAMARAU	TANAGER	TANICA
TALCOSE	TALLIER	TAMARIN	TANAGRINE	TANIER
TALCOUS	TALLIES	TAMARIND	TANAK	TANIKO
TALCUM	TALLIS	TAMARISK	TANAN	TANIST
TALE	TALLISH	TAMAS	TANBARK	TANISTIC
TALEBEARER	TALLIT	TAMASHA	TANBUR	TANISTRY
TALEBEARING	TALLITH	TAMBAC	TANCEL	TANISTSHIP
TALEBOOK	TALLNESS	TAMBAROORA	TANDAN	TANJIB
TALECARRIER	TALLOL	TAMBER	TANDAVA	TANJONG
TALECARRYING	TALLOTE	TAMBO	TANDEM	TANK
TALEMASTER	TALLOW	TAMBOOKIE	TANDEMER	TANKA
TALEMONGER	TALLOWBERRIES	TAMBOR	TANDEMIST	TANKAGE
TALENT	TALLOWBERRY	TAMBOUR	TANDEMIZE	TANKAH
TALENTED	TALLOWED	TAMBOURA	TANDEMWISE	TANKARD
TALENTER	TALLOWER	TAMBOURED	TANDLE	TANKED
TALENTING	TALLOWINESS	TAMBOURER	TANDSTICKA	TANKER
TALEPYET	TALLOWING	TAMBOURET	TANEGA	TANKERABOGUS
TALER	TALLOWMAKER	TAMBOURGI	TANEKAHA	TANKETTE
TALES	TALLOWMAKING	TAMBOURIN	TANG	TANKFUL

TANKIE	TAPADERA	TAPS	TAREFITCH	TARRI
TANKING	TAPADERO	TAPSALTEERIE	TARENTE	TARRIANCE
TANKLE	TAPALO	TAPSMAN	TARENTISM	TARRIED
TANKODROME	TAPALOS	TAPSTER	TARES	TARRIER
TANKS	TAPAMAKER	TAPSTRESS	TARFA	TARRIEST
TANLING	TAPAMAKING	TAPT	TARFE	TARRILY
TANNA	TAPAS	TAPU	TARFLOWER	TARRINESS
TANNADAR	TAPASVI	TAPUL	TARGE	TARRING
TANNAGE	TAPE	TAPWORT	TARGED	TARRISH
TANNAIC	TAPED	TAQIYA	TARGEMAN	TARROCK
TANNAIM	TAPELESS	TAQLID	TARGER	TARROW
TANNAITIC	TAPELINE	TAR	TARGET	TARRY
TANNAKIN	TAPEMAN	TARA	TARGETED	TARRYING
TANNASE	TAPEMEN	TARABOOKA	TARGETEER	TARRYINGLY
TANNATE	TAPEN	TARADIDDLE	TARGETIER	TARRYINGNESS
TANNED	TAPER	TARAF	TARGETING	TARS
TANNER	TAPERED	TARAFDAR	TARGING	TARSAL
TANNERIES	TAPERER	TARAGE	TARHOOD	TARSALE
TANNERY	TAPERING	TARAIRI	TARI	TARSALIA
TANNIC	TAPERINGLY	TARAKIHI	TARIE	TARSE
TANNID	TAPERY	TARAMELLITE	TARIFF	TARSECTOMY
TANNIDE	TAPESIUM	TARAN	TARIFFED	TARSI
TANNIFEROUS	TAPESTER	TARAND	TARIFFING	TARSIA
TANNIGEN	TAPESTRIED	TARANTARIZE	TARIFFIST	TARSIER
TANNIN	TAPESTRIES	TARANTAS	TARIFFITE	TARSIOID
TANNINED	TAPESTRY	TARANTASS	TARIFFIZE	TARSO
TANNING	TAPESTRYING	TARANTELLA	TARIN	TARSOME
TANNOGEN	TAPET	TARANTELLE	TARING	TARSOMETATARSUS
TANNOID	TAPETA	TARANTISM	TARIQA	TARSONEMID
TANNOMETER	TAPETAL	TARANTIST	TARIQAT	TARSOTARSAL
TANNY	TAPETI	TARANTULA	TARIRIC	TARSUS
TANNYL	TAPETIS	TARANTULAE	TARIRINIC	TART
TANOA	TAPETUM	TARANTULAR	TARISH	TARTAGO
TANQUAM	TAPEWORM	TARANTULAS	TARKASHI	TARTAN
TANQUEN	TAPHEPHOBIA	TARANTULATED	TARKEEAN	TARTANA
TANREC	TAPHOLE	TARANTULID	TARKHAN	TARTAR
TANSEL	TAPHOUSE	TARANTULITE	TARLATAN	TARTAREOUS
TANSEY	TAPIA	TARANTULOUS	TARLATANED	TARTARET
TANSIES	TAPIDERO	TARASSIS	TARLEATHER	TARTARIC
TANSY	TAPING	TARATA	TARLETAN	TARTARIN
TANTA	TAPINOSIS	TARATAH	TARLIES	TARTARINE
TANTADLIN	TAPIOCA	TARATANTARA	TARLTONIZE	TARTARISH
TANTALATE	TAPIR	TARAU	TARMAC	TARTARIZE
TANTALIC	TAPIRIDIAN	TARAXACUM	TARMOSINED	TARTARIZED
TANTALISE	TAPIRINE	TARBAGAN	TARN	TARTARIZING
TANTALITE	TAPIROID	TARBET	TARNAL	TARTARLY
TANTALIZE	TAPIRS	TARBLE	TARNALLY	TARTAROUS
TANTALIZED	TAPIS	TARBOARD	TARNATION	TARTARUM
TANTALIZER	TAPISER	TARBOOSH	TARNISH	TARTE
TANTALIZING	TAPISM	TARBOY	TARNISHABLE	TARTEN
TANTALUM	TAPISSERIE	TARBRUSH	TARNISHED	TARTINE
TANTAMOUNT	TAPISSIER	TARBUSH	TARNISHER	TARTISH
TANTARA	TAPIST	TARBUTTITE	TARNISHING	TARTISHLY
TANTARARA	TAPIT	TARCEL	TARO	TARTLE
TANTI	TAPLASH	TARCHON	TAROCCO	TARTLET
TANTIEME	TAPLET	TARDAMENTE	TAROGATO	TARTLY
TANTIVIES	TAPLING	TARDANDO	TAROPATCH	TARTNESS
TANTIVY	TAPNET	TARDANT	TAROS	TARTRAMATE
TANTLE	TAPOA	TARDE	TAROT	TARTRAMID
TANTO	TAPOTEMENT	TARDIER	TARP	TARTRAMIDE
TANTRA	TAPOUN	TARDIEST	TARPAN	TARTRATE
TANTRIC	TAPPA	TARDIGRADE	TARPAPER	TARTRATED
TANTRIK	TAPPABLE	TARDILOQUENT	TARPAULIAN	TARTRAZIN
TANTRISM	TAPPABLENESS	TARDILOQUOUS	TARPAULIN	TARTRAZINE
TANTRIST	TAPPALL	TARDILOQUY	TARPON	TARTRAZINIC
TANTRUM	TAPPAUL	TARDILY	TARPONS	TARTRO
TANTUM	TAPPED	TARDINESS	TARPOT	TARTRONATE
TANWOOD	TAPPEN	TARDITY	TARR	TARTRONIC
TANYA	TAPPER	TARDIVE	TARRABA	TARTRONYL
TANYSTOME	TAPPET	TARDLE	TARRACK	TARTROUS
TAO	TAPPING	TARDO	TARRADIDDLE	TARTRYL
TAOS	TAPPISH	TARDY	TARRADIDDLER	TARTRYLIC
TAOTAI	TAPPIT	TARE	TARRAGON	TARTUFE
TAOYIN	TAPPOON	TAREA	TARRAGONA	TARTUFERY
TAP	TAPROOM	TARED	TARRASS	TARTUFFE
TAPA	TAPROOT	TAREFA	TARRED	TARTUFFERY
TAPACULO	TAPROOTED		TARRER	TARTUFFIAN

TARTUFFISH	TATAMI	TAURIN	TAVOY	TAXMAN
TARTUFFISHLY	TATAUPA	TAURINE	TAW	TAXODONT
TARTUFFISM	TATBEB	TAURITE	TAWA	TAXOLOGY
TARTUFIAN	TATCH	TAUROBOLIA	TAWDERED	TAXOMETER
TARTUFISH	TATCHY	TAUROBOLIUM	TAWDRIER	TAXON
TARTUFISHLY	TATE	TAUROCHOLATE	TAWDRIES	TAXONOMER
TARTUFISM	TATER	TAUROCHOLIC	TAWDRIEST	TAXONOMIC
TARTWOMAN	TATH	TAUROCOL	TAWDRILY	TAXONOMICAL
TARTWOMEN	TATHATA	TAUROCOLLA	TAWDRINESS	TAXONOMIST
TARVE	TATINEK	TAURODONT	TAWDRY	TAXONOMY
TARWEED	TATLER	TAUROESQUE	TAWED	TAXOR
TARWHINE	TATMJOLK	TAUROLATRY	TAWER	TAXPAID
TARWOOD	TATOU	TAUROMACHIA	TAWERY	TAXPAYER
TARZAN	TATOUAY	TAUROMACHIAN	TAWHAI	TAXPAYING
TASAJILLO	TATPURUSHA	TAUROMACHIC	TAWHID	TAXY
TASAJO	TATS	TAUROMACHY	TAWIE	TAXYING
TASBIH	TATSMAN	TAUROMORPHIC	TAWING	TAY
TASCAL	TATT	TAUROPHILE	TAWITE	TAYASSUID
TASCO	TATTED	TAUROPHOBE	TAWKEE	TAYER
TASH	TATTER	TAURYL	TAWKIN	TAYIR
TASHERIFF	TATTERED	TAUT	TAWN	TAYLORITE
TASHIE	TATTEREDLY	TAUTAUG	TAWNEY	TAYRA
TASHLIK	TATTEREDNESS	TAUTED	TAWNIE	TAYSAAM
TASHREEF	TATTERING	TAUTEGORICAL	TAWNIER	TAZEEA
TASHRIF	TATTERLY	TAUTEGORY	TAWNIEST	TAZIA
TASIMETER	TATTERSALL	TAUTEN	TAWNINESS	TAZZA
TASIMETRIC	TATTERWAG	TAUTIRITE	TAWNY	TCH
TASIMETRY	TATTERWALLOP	TAUTLY	TAWPIE	TCHA
TASK	TATTERY	TAUTNESS	TAWPY	TCHAI
TASKAGE	TATTIED	TAUTOCHRONE	TAWS	TCHAPAN
TASKED	TATTIES	TAUTOCHRONISM	TAWSE	TCHAST
TASKER	TATTING	TAUTOCHRONOUS	TAX	TCHE
TASKING	TATTLE	TAUTOG	TAXABILITY	TCHEIREK
TASKIT	TATTLED	TAUTOLOGIC	TAXABLE	TCHERVONETS
TASKMASTER	TATTLER	TAUTOLOGIES	TAXABLENESS	TCHERVONETZ
TASKMISTRESS	TATTLERY	TAUTOLOGIUS	TAXABLY	TCHI
TASKSETTER	TATTLETALE	TAUTOLOGIST	TAXACEOUS	TCHICK
TASKSETTING	TATTLING	TAUTOLOGIZE	TAXAMETER	TCHIN
TASKWORK	TATTLINGLY	TAUTOLOGIZED	TAXASPIDEAN	TCHINCOU
TASMANITE	TATTOO	TAUTOLOGIZER	TAXATION	TCHU
TASS	TATTOOAGE	TAUTOLOGIZING	TAXATIONAL	TCK
TASSARD	TATTOOED	TAUTOLOGY	TAXATIVE	TE
TASSE	TATTOOER	TAUTOMER	TAXATIVELY	TEA
TASSEL	TATTOOING	TAUTOMERAL	TAXATOR	TEABERRIES
TASSELED	TATTOOIST	TAUTOMERIC	TAXEATER	TEABERRY
TASSELER	TATTOOMENT	TAUTOMERISM	TAXEATING	TEABOARD
TASSELFISH	TATTOOS	TAUTOMERIZE	TAXED	TEABOX
TASSELING	TATTVA	TAUTOMERS	TAXEL	TEABOY
TASSELLED	TATTY	TAUTOMETER	TAXEME	TEACAKE
TASSELLUS	TATU	TAUTOMETRIC	TAXEOPOD	TEACART
TASSELS	TATUASU	TAUTONYM	TAXEOPODOUS	TEACH
TASSELY	TATUKIRA	TAUTONYMIC	TAXEOPODY	TEACHABILITY
TASSES	TAU	TAUTONYMIES	TAXER	TEACHABLE
TASSET	TAUGA	TAUTONYMY	TAXES	TEACHABLENESS
TASSIE	TAUGHT	TAUTOOUSIAN	TAXGATHERER	TEACHABLY
TASSOO	TAULA	TAUTOPHONIC	TAXGATHERING	TEACHE
TASTABLE	TAULCH	TAUTOPHONY	TAXI	TEACHED
TASTE	TAUM	TAUTOPODIC	TAXIARCH	TEACHER
TASTED	TAUN	TAUTOPODY	TAXIAUTO	TEACHERAGE
TASTEFUL	TAUNT	TAUTOTYPE	TAXIBUS	TEACHERESS
TASTEFULLY	TAUNTED	TAUTOZONAL	TAXICAB	TEACHERLY
TASTEFULNESS	TAUNTER	TAV	TAXIDERMAL	TEACHERY
TASTELESS	TAUNTING	TAVE	TAXIDERMIC	TEACHES
TASTELESSLY	TAUNTINGLY	TAVELL	TAXIDERMIST	TEACHING
TASTEN	TAUNTINGNESS	TAVER	TAXIDERMIZE	TEACHINGLY
TASTER	TAUNTRESS	TAVERN	TAXIDERMY	TEACHLESS
TASTIER	TAUPE	TAVERNER	TAXIED	TEACHY
TASTIEST	TAUPO	TAVERNIZE	TAXIMAN	TEACUP
TASTILY	TAUPOU	TAVERNLY	TAXIMETER	TEACUPFUL
TASTINESS	TAURANGA	TAVERNOUS	TAXIMETERED	TEACUPFULS
TASTING	TAUREAN	TAVERNRY	TAXINE	TEADISH
TASTINGLY	TAURIAN	TAVERS	TAXING	TEAED
TASTO	TAURIC	TAVERT	TAXINGLY	TEAER
TASTY	TAURICIDE	TAVESTOCK	TAXIPLANE	TEAEY
TASU	TAURICORNOUS	TAVISTOCKITE	TAXIS	TEAGARDENY
TAT	TAURIFEROUS	TAVOLA	TAXITE	TEAGLE
TATA	TAURIFORM	TAVOLATITE	TAXITIC	TEAHOUSE

TEAING
TEAK
TEAKETTLE
TEAKWOOD
TEAL
TEALEAFY
TEALLITE
TEALS
TEAM
TEAMAKER
TEAMAKING
TEAMAN
TEAMED
TEAMEO
TEAMING
TEAMLAND
TEAMMAN
TEAMMATE
TEAMSTER
TEAMWORK
TEAN
TEANAL
TEAP
TEAPOT
TEAPOY
TEAR
TEARAGE
TEARCAT
TEARDOWN
TEARDROP
TEARER
TEARFUL
TEARFULLY
TEARFULNESS
TEARIER
TEARIEST
TEARING
TEARLESS
TEARLESSLY
TEARLESSNESS
TEAROOM
TEARPIT
TEARS
TEARSTAIN
TEART
TEARTHUMB
TEARY
TEASE
TEASED
TEASEHOLE
TEASEL
TEASELED
TEASELER
TEASELING
TEASELLED
TEASELLER
TEASELLING
TEASELS
TEASELWORT
TEASER
TEASHOP
TEASING
TEASINGLY
TEASLE
TEASPOON
TEASPOONFUL
TEASPOONFULS
TEASY
TEAT
TEATASTER
TEATED
TEATFISH
TEATIME
TEATLING
TEATMAN
TEATY
TEAVE

TEAZE
TEAZEL
TEAZLE
TEBBAD
TEBELDI
TEC
TECA
TECALI
TECH
TECHIER
TECHIEST
TECHNE
TECHNETIUM
TECHNIC
TECHNICA
TECHNICAL
TECHNICALISM
TECHNICALIST
TECHNICALITIES
TECHNICALITY
TECHNICALIZE
TECHNICALLY
TECHNICIAN
TECHNICISM
TECHNICIST
TECHNICOLOGY
TECHNICOLOR
TECHNICON
TECHNICS
TECHNIPHONE
TECHNIQUE
TECHNISM
TECHNOCAUSIS
TECHNOCRACIES
TECHNOCRACY
TECHNOCRAT
TECHNOCRATIC
TECHNOGRAPHY
TECHNOLITHIC
TECHNOLOGIC
TECHNOLOGICAL
TECHNOLOGIES
TECHNOLOGIST
TECHNOLOGY
TECHNONOMY
TECHOUS
TECHY
TECK
TECOMIN
TECON
TECT
TECTAL
TECTIBRANCH
TECTIFORM
TECTOCEPHALY
TECTOLOGY
TECTONIC
TECTONICS
TECTORIAL
TECTORIUM
TECTOSPHERE
TECTOSPINAL
TECTRICES
TECTRICIAL
TECTRIX
TECTUM
TECTURE
TECUM
TED
TEDDED
TEDDER
TEDDIES
TEDDING
TEDDY
TEDESCA
TEDESCHE
TEDESCHI

TEDESCO
TEDGE
TEDIOSITY
TEDIOUS
TEDIOUSLY
TEDIOUSNESS
TEDIOUSOME
TEDISOME
TEDIUM
TEE
TEECALL
TEED
TEEDLE
TEEING
TEEKA
TEEL
TEEM
TEEMED
TEEMER
TEEMFUL
TEEMFULNESS
TEEMING
TEEMINGLY
TEEMINGNESS
TEEMLESS
TEEMS
TEEN
TEENAGER
TEENET
TEENFUL
TEENFULLY
TEENIER
TEENIEST
TEENS
TEENSY
TEENY
TEENYBOPPER
TEEPEE
TEER
TEES
TEEST
TEET
TEETAN
TEETEE
TEETER
TEETERBOARD
TEETERER
TEETERTAIL
TEETH
TEETHE
TEETHED
TEETHIER
TEETHIEST
TEETHING
TEETHLESS
TEETHRIDGE
TEETHY
TEETING
TEETOTAL
TEETOTALED
TEETOTALER
TEETOTALING
TEETOTALISM
TEETOTALIST
TEETOTALLED
TEETOTALLER
TEETOTALLING
TEETOTALLY
TEETOTUM
TEETOTUMISM
TEETOTUMIZE
TEETSOOK
TEEWHAAP
TEFF
TEFILLIN
TEG
TEGG

TEGMEN
TEGMENT
TEGMENTA
TEGMENTAL
TEGMENTUM
TEGMINA
TEGMINAL
TEGS
TEGU
TEGUA
TEGUEXIN
TEGULA
TEGULAE
TEGULAR
TEGULARLY
TEGULATED
TEGUMEN
TEGUMENT
TEGUMENTAL
TEGUMENTARY
TEGURIA
TEGURIUM
TEHOO
TEHSIL
TEICHER
TEIGLACH
TEIGLECH
TEIHTE
TEIID
TEIL
TEIND
TEINDABLE
TEINDER
TEINLAND
TEINOSCOPE
TEIOID
TEJANO
TEJON
TEJU
TEK
TEKE
TEKIAH
TEKKE
TEKNONYMOUS
TEKNONYMY
TEKTITE
TEKYA
TEL
TELA
TELACOUSTIC
TELAE
TELAESTHESIA
TELAKUCHA
TELAMON
TELAMONES
TELANGIOSIS
TELAR
TELARIAN
TELARLY
TELAUTOGRAM
TELAUTOGRAPH
TELD
TELEBLEM
TELECAST
TELECASTED
TELECASTING
TELECHEMIC
TELECODE
TELEDU
TELEGA
TELEGNOSIS
TELEGNOSTIC
TELEGONIC
TELEGONOUS
TELEGONY
TELEGRAF
TELEGRAM

TELEGRAMMIC
TELEGRAPH
TELEGRAPHED
TELEGRAPHEME
TELEGRAPHER
TELEGRAPHESE
TELEGRAPHIC
TELEGRAPHING
TELEGRAPHIST
TELEGRAPHONE
TELEGRAPHY
TELEIANTHOUS
TELEIOSIS
TELEKINESIS
TELEKINETIC
TELELECTRIC
TELEMARK
TELEMECHANIC
TELEMETER
TELEMETERING
TELEMETRIC
TELEMETRICAL
TELEMETRIST
TELEMETRY
TELEMOTOR
TELENCEPHALON
TELENERGIC
TELENERGY
TELENEURITE
TELENEURON
TELENGISCOPE
TELEODONT
TELEOLOGIC
TELEOLOGICAL
TELEOLOGIES
TELEOLOGISM
TELEOLOGIST
TELEOLOGY
TELEOPHOBIA
TELEOPHORE
TELEOPHYTE
TELEOPTILE
TELEORGANIC
TELEOSAUR
TELEOST
TELEOSTEAN
TELEOSTEOUS
TELEOSTOME
TELEOSTOMOUS
TELEOZOIC
TELEOZOON
TELEPATH
TELEPATHIC
TELEPATHIST
TELEPATHIZE
TELEPATHY
TELEPHEME
TELEPHONE
TELEPHONED
TELEPHONER
TELEPHONIC
TELEPHONING
TELEPHONIST
TELEPHONY
TELEPHOTE
TELEPHOTO
TELEPLASM
TELEPLASMIC
TELEPLASTIC
TELEPOST
TELEPRINTER
TELEPROMPTER
TELERAN
TELERGIC
TELERGICAL
TELERGICALLY
TELERGY

TELESCOPE	TELLIGRAPH	TEMERARIOUS	TEMPT	TENDERFUL
TELESCOPED	TELLINACEAN	TEMERATE	TEMPTABLE	TENDERFULLY
TELESCOPIC	TELLINACEOUS	TEMERITOUS	TEMPTATION	TENDERHEART
TELESCOPICAL	TELLING	TEMERITY	TEMPTATIONAL	TENDERHEARTED
TELESCOPING	TELLINGLY	TEMEROUS	TEMPTATIOUS	TENDERIZE
TELESCOPIST	TELLINOID	TEMEROUSLY	TEMPTATORY	TENDERIZED
TELESCOPY	TELLSOME	TEMEROUSNESS	TEMPTED	TENDERIZER
TELESCRIBE	TELLTALE	TEMESCAL	TEMPTER	TENDERIZING
TELESCRIPT	TELLTALELY	TEMIAK	TEMPTING	TENDERLING
TELESCRIPTOR	TELLTRUTH	TEMIN	TEMPTINGLY	TENDERLOIN
TELESEISM	TELLURAL	TEMP	TEMPTINGNESS	TENDERLY
TELESEISMIC	TELLURATE	TEMPER	TEMPTRESS	TENDERNESS
TELESEME	TELLURETED	TEMPERA	TEMPTSOME	TENDERSOME
TELESIA	TELLURETHYL	TEMPERABLE	TEMPURA	TENDICLE
TELESIS	TELLURETTED	TEMPERABLY	TEMPUS	TENDIDO
TELESIURGIC	TELLURIAN	TEMPERALITY	TEMS	TENDINAL
TELESM	TELLURIC	TEMPERAMENT	TEMSE	TENDINEAL
TELESMATIC	TELLURIDE	TEMPERAMENTAL	TEMSEBREAD	TENDING
TELESMATICAL	TELLURION	TEMPERANCE	TEMSELOAF	TENDINGLY
TELESMETER	TELLURISM	TEMPERATE	TEMULENCE	TENDINOUS
TELESOMATIC	TELLURIST	TEMPERATELY	TEMULENCY	TENDMENT
TELESTERION	TELLURITE	TEMPERATIVE	TEMULENT	TENDO
TELESTHESIA	TELLURIUM	TEMPERATURE	TEMULENTIVE	TENDOMUCOID
TELESTHETIC	TELLURIZE	TEMPERED	TEMULENTLY	TENDON
TELESTIC	TELLURIZED	TEMPEREDLY	TEN	TENDONOUS
TELESTICH	TELLURIZING	TEMPEREDNESS	TENA	TENDONS
TELETACTILE	TELLURONIUM	TEMPERER	TENABILITY	TENDOOR
TELETACTOR	TELLUROUS	TEMPERING	TENABLE	TENDOPLASTY
TELETAPE	TELLY	TEMPERSOME	TENABLENESS	TENDOTOME
TELETHERAPY	TELMATOLOGY	TEMPERY	TENABLY	TENDOTOMY
TELETHON	TELOBLAST	TEMPEST	TENACE	TENDOUR
TELETYPE	TELOBLASTIC	TEMPESTICAL	TENACIOUS	TENDRAC
TELETYPED	TELODENDRIA	TEMPESTIVE	TENACIOUSLY	TENDRE
TELETYPER	TELODENDRION	TEMPESTIVELY	TENACIOUSNESS	TENDREL
TELETYPING	TELODYNAMIC	TEMPESTIVITY	TENACITY	TENDRESSE
TELEUTO	TELOKINESIS	TEMPESTUOUS	TENACLE	TENDRIL
TELEUTOSORUS	TELOLECITHAL	TEMPESTY	TENACULA	TENDRILED
TELEUTOSPORE	TELOLEMMA	TEMPETE	TENACULUM	TENDRILLAR
TELEVIEW	TELOLEMMATA	TEMPI	TENACY	TENDRILLED
TELEVIEWER	TELOMITIC	TEMPLAR	TENAI	TENDRILOUS
TELEVISE	TELONISM	TEMPLARDOM	TENAIL	TENDRON
TELEVISED	TELOPHASE	TEMPLARISM	TENAILLE	TENDRY
TELEVISING	TELOPSIS	TEMPLARY	TENAILLON	TENEBRA
TELEVISION	TELOPTIC	TEMPLATE	TENALGIA	TENEBRES
TELEVISIONAL	TELOS	TEMPLATER	TENANCIES	TENEBRIFIC
TELEVISOR	TELOSYNAPSIS	TEMPLE	TENANCY	TENEBRION
TELEVISUAL	TELOSYNAPTIC	TEMPLED	TENANT	TENEBRIONID
TELEVOCAL	TELOTROCH	TEMPLES	TENANTABLE	TENEBRIOUS
TELEVOX	TELOTROCHA	TEMPLET	TENANTED	TENEBRIOUSLY
TELEX	TELOTROCHAL	TEMPLIZE	TENANTER	TENEBRITY
TELFER	TELOTROCHOUS	TEMPLUM	TENANTING	TENEBROSE
TELFERAGE	TELOTYPE	TEMPO	TENANTLESS	TENEBROSI
TELFORD	TELPHER	TEMPORAL	TENANTLIKE	TENEBROSITY
TELFORDIZE	TELPHERAGE	TEMPORALE	TENANTRIES	TENEBROUS
TELFORDIZED	TELPHERIC	TEMPORALIS	TENANTRY	TENEBROUSLY
TELFORDIZING	TELPHERMAN	TEMPORALISM	TENANTS	TENEMENT
TELHARMONIC	TELPHERMEN	TEMPORALIST	TENANTSHIP	TENEMENTAL
TELHARMONIUM	TELPHERWAY	TEMPORALITIES	TENCH	TENEMENTARY
TELHARMONY	TELSON	TEMPORALITY	TENCHES	TENEMENTER
TELI	TELSONIC	TEMPORALIZE	TENCHWEED	TENEMENTIZE
TELIA	TELURGY	TEMPORALLY	TEND	TENENDA
TELIAL	TELYN	TEMPORALTIES	TENDANCE	TENENDAS
TELIC	TEMA	TEMPORALTY	TENDED	TENENDUM
TELICAL	TEMACHA	TEMPORANEOUS	TENDEJON	TENENT
TELICALLY	TEMADAU	TEMPCRARIES	TENDENCE	TENER
TELIFEROUS	TEMALACATL	TEMPORARILY	TENDENCIES	TENERAL
TELIOSPORE	TEMAN	TEMPORARY	TENDENCIOUS	TENERAMENTE
TELIOSPORIC	TEMBE	TEMPORATOR	TENDENCY	TENERITY
TELIOSTAGE	TEMBEITERA	TEMPORE	TENDENT	TENESMIC
TELIUM	TEMBETA	TEMPORISE	TENDENTIAL	TENESMUS
TELL	TEMBETARA	TEMPORIZE	TENDENTIOUS	TENET
TELLABLE	TEMBLOR	TEMPORIZED	TENDER	TENEZ
TELLACH	TEMBLORES	TEMPORIZER	TENDEREE	TENFOLD
TELLE	TEMBLORS	TEMPORIZING	TENDERER	TENFOLDNESS
TELLER	TEME	TEMPOS	TENDEREST	TENG
TELLERSHIP	TEMENE	TEMPRE	TENDERFEET	TENGERE
TELLIES	TEMENOS	TEMPS	TENDERFOOT	TENGERITE

TENGU
TENIA
TENIACIDAL
TENIACIDE
TENIAFUGE
TENIASIS
TENIENTE
TENIO
TENMANTALE
TENNANTITE
TENNE
TENNER
TENNIS
TENNISY
TENNU
TENON
TENONECTOMY
TENONED
TENONER
TENONING
TENONITIS
TENONTOLOGY
TENONTOTOMY
TENOR
TENORE
TENORINO
TENORIST
TENORITE
TENOROON
TENORRHAPHIES
TENORRHAPHY
TENOSITIS
TENOTOMIES
TENOTOMIST
TENOTOMIZE
TENOTOMY
TENPENCE
TENPENNY
TENPIN
TENPINS
TENPOUNDER
TENREC
TENS
TENSAS
TENSAW
TENSE
TENSED
TENSELY
TENSENESS
TENSER
TENSES
TENSEST
TENSIBILITY
TENSIBLE
TENSIBLENESS
TENSIBLY
TENSIFY
TENSILE
TENSILELY
TENSILENESS
TENSILITY
TENSIMETER
TENSING
TENSIOMETER
TENSION
TENSIONAL
TENSIONED
TENSIONING
TENSITY
TENSIVE
TENSOME
TENSON
TENSOR
TENSORSHIP
TENSURE
TENT
TENTABILITY

TENTACLE
TENTACLED
TENTACULA
TENTACULAR
TENTACULATE
TENTACULATED
TENTACULITE
TENTACULOID
TENTACULUM
TENTAGE
TENTAMEN
TENTATION
TENTATIVE
TENTATIVELY
TENTED
TENTER
TENTERBELLY
TENTERER
TENTERHOOK
TENTFUL
TENTH
TENTHLY
TENTHMETER
TENTHMETRE
TENTHREDINID
TENTICLE
TENTIE
TENTIFORM
TENTIGO
TENTILLA
TENTILLUM
TENTILY
TENTLESS
TENTLET
TENTMAKER
TENTMAKING
TENTMATE
TENTOR
TENTORIAL
TENTORIUM
TENTORY
TENTS
TENTURE
TENTWORK
TENTWORT
TENTY
TENUATE
TENUE
TENUES
TENUIFLOROUS
TENUIFOLIOUS
TENUIROSTER
TENUIROSTRAL
TENUIS
TENUISTRIATE
TENUITY
TENUOUS
TENUOUSLY
TENUOUSNESS
TENURE
TENURIAL
TENURIALLY
TENURY
TENUTO
TENZON
TEOCALLI
TEOCALLIS
TEOPAN
TEOSINTE
TEPACHE
TEPAL
TEPARIES
TEPARY
TEPEE
TEPEFACTION
TEPEFIED
TEPEFY

TEPEFYING
TEPETATE
TEPHILLIN
TEPHRAMANCY
TEPHRITE
TEPHRITIC
TEPHROITE
TEPHROSIS
TEPID
TEPIDARIA
TEPIDARIUM
TEPIDITY
TEPIDLY
TEPIDNESS
TEPONAZTLI
TEPOR
TEQUILA
TEQUILLA
TER
TERA
TERAGLIN
TERAKIHI
TERAMORPHOUS
TERAP
TERAPH
TERAPHIM
TERAS
TERATA
TERATICAL
TERATISM
TERATOGENIC
TERATOGENY
TERATOID
TERATOLOGIC
TERATOLOGIST
TERATOLOGY
TERATOMA
TERATOMAS
TERATOMATA
TERATOMATOUS
TERATOSCOPY
TERATOSIS
TERBIA
TERBIC
TERBIUM
TERCE
TERCEL
TERCELET
TERCENTENARIES
TERCENTENARY
TERCER
TERCERON
TERCET
TERCHLORIDE
TERCIA
TERCINE
TERCIO
TERDIURNAL
TEREBATE
TEREBELLA
TEREBELLID
TEREBELLOID
TEREBELLUM
TEREBENE
TEREBENTHENE
TEREBIC
TEREBINTH
TEREBINTHIC
TEREBINTHINA
TEREBINTHINE
TEREBRA
TEREBRAE
TEREBRAL
TEREBRANT
TEREBRAS
TEREBRATE
TEREBRATION

TEREBRATULAR
TEREBRATULID
TEREDINES
TEREDO
TEREDOS
TEREK
TEREPHAH
TEREPHTHALLIC
TERETE
TERETIAL
TERETISM
TEREU
TERFA
TERFEZ
TERGA
TERGAL
TERGANT
TERGEMINAL
TERGEMINATE
TERGIFEROUS
TERGITE
TERGITIC
TERGIVERSANT
TERGIVERSATE
TERGIVERSATED
TERGIVERSATING
TERGIVERSATION
TERGIVERSE
TERGOLATERAL
TERGUM
TERIN
TERLINGUAITE
TERM
TERMA
TERMAGANCY
TERMAGANT
TERMAGANTISH
TERMAGANTISM
TERMAGANTLY
TERMAGE
TERMAL
TERMATIC
TERMED
TERMEN
TERMER
TERMIN
TERMINABLE
TERMINABLY
TERMINAL
TERMINALLY
TERMINANT
TERMINATE
TERMINATED
TERMINATING
TERMINATION
TERMINATIVE
TERMINATOR
TERMINATORY
TERMINE
TERMINER
TERMING
TERMINI
TERMININE
TERMINISM
TERMINIST
TERMINISTIC
TERMINIZE
TERMINO
TERMINOLOGIES
TERMINOLOGY
TERMINUS
TERMINUSES
TERMITAL
TERMITARIA
TERMITARIUM
TERMITARY
TERMITE

TERMITIC
TERMITOPHILE
TERMLESS
TERMLY
TERMON
TERMOR
TERMS
TERMTIME
TERN
TERNA
TERNAL
TERNAR
TERNARIANT
TERNARIES
TERNARIOUS
TERNARY
TERNATE
TERNATELY
TERNE
TERNED
TERNEPLATE
TERNER
TERNERY
TERNING
TERNION
TERNLET
TERNO
TERP
TERPADIENE
TERPANE
TERPEN
TERPENE
TERPHENYL
TERPILENE
TERPINENE
TERPINEOL
TERPINOL
TERPINOLENE
TERPODION
TERRA
TERRACE
TERRACED
TERRACEOUS
TERRACER
TERRACETTE
TERRACEWORK
TERRACIFORM
TERRACING
TERRAEFILIAL
TERRAEFILIAN
TERRAGE
TERRAIN
TERRAL
TERRAMARA
TERRAMARE
TERRAMYCIN
TERRANE
TERRANEAN
TERRANEOUS
TERRAPIN
TERRAQUEAN
TERRAQUEOUS
TERRAR
TERRARIA
TERRARIUM
TERRARIUMS
TERRAS
TERRASSE
TERRAZZO
TERRE
TERREEN
TERREITY
TERRELLA
TERREMOTIVE
TERRENE
TERRENELY
TERRENENESS

TERRENO	TERVALENT	TESTIFY	TETRACHLORIDE	TETRANE
TERREOUS	TERVARIANT	TESTIFYING	TETRACHLORO	TETRANITRATE
TERREPLEIN	TERVE	TESTIMONIA	TETRACHORD	TETRANITRO
TERRESTRIAL	TERVEE	TESTIMONIAL	TETRACHORDAL	TETRANT
TERRESTRIALLY	TERZET	TESTIMONIES	TETRACHORDON	TETRAODONT
TERRESTRIFY	TERZETTO	TESTIMONIUM	TETRACHORIC	TETRAONID
TERRET	TERZETTOS	TESTIMONY	TETRACID	TETRAONINE
TERRIBLE	TERZINA	TESTINESS	TETRACOCCUS	TETRAPHENOL
TERRIBLENESS	TERZIO	TESTING	TETRACOLIC	TETRAPHONY
TERRIBLY	TERZO	TESTIS	TETRACOLON	TETRAPLA
TERRICOLINE	TESACK	TESTO	TETRACORAL	TETRAPLEGIA
TERRICOLIST	TESCARIA	TESTON	TETRACOSANE	TETRAPLEURON
TERRICOLOUS	TESCHENITE	TESTONE	TETRACT	TETRAPLOID
TERRIE	TESKERIA	TESTOON	TETRACTINAL	TETRAPLOIDIC
TERRIER	TESSARA	TESTOR	TETRACTINOSE	TETRAPLOIDY
TERRIES	TESSARACE	TESTOSTERONE	TETRACTYS	TETRAPLOUS
TERRIFIC	TESSARADECAD	TESTRIL	TETRACYCLIC	TETRAPOD
TERRIFICALLY	TESSARAGLOT	TESTS	TETRACYCLINE	TETRAPODIC
TERRIFICLY	TESSEL	TESTUDINAL	TETRAD	TETRAPODOUS
TERRIFICNESS	TESSELLA	TESTUDINATE	TETRADACTYL	TETRAPODY
TERRIFIED	TESSELLAE	TESTUDINEAL	TETRADACTYLE	TETRAPOLAR
TERRIFIER	TESSELLAR	TESTUDINEOUS	TETRADACTYLY	TETRAPOLIS
TERRIFY	TESSELLATE	TESTUDINES	TETRADARCHY	TETRAPOLITAN
TERRIFYING	TESSELLATED	TESTUDINOUS	TETRADECANE	TETRAPOUS
TERRIFYINGLY	TESSELLATING	TESTUDO	TETRADECYL	TETRAPTERAN
TERRIGENE	TESSELLATION	TESTULE	TETRADIC	TETRAPTERON
TERRIGENOUS	TESSERA	TESTY	TETRADRACHM	TETRAPTEROUS
TERRINE	TESSERACT	TESVINO	TETRADRACHMA	TETRAPTOTE
TERRITORIAL	TESSERAE	TETANIA	TETRADYMITE	TETRAPTYCH
TERRITORIALISM	TESSERAL	TETANIC	TETRAETHYL	TETRAPYLON
TERRITORIAN	TESSERARIAN	TETANICAL	TETRAGAMY	TETRAPYRAMID
TERRITORIED	TESSERATOMIC	TETANICALLY	TETRAGENOUS	TETRARCH
TERRITORIES	TESSERATOMY	TETANIFORM	TETRAGLOT	TETRARCHATE
TERRITORY	TESSITURA	TETANIGENOUS	TETRAGLOTTIC	TETRARCHIC
TERRON	TESSULAR	TETANILLA	TETRAGON	TETRARCHICAL
TERROR	TEST	TETANINE	TETRAGONAL	TETRARCHIES
TERRORFUL	TESTA	TETANISM	TETRAGONALLY	TETRARCHY
TERRORIFIC	TESTABLE	TETANIZATION	TETRAGONOUS	TETRASACCHARIDE
TERRORISE	TESTACEAN	TETANIZE	TETRAGRAM	TETRASEME
TERRORISM	TESTACEOLOGY	TETANIZED	TETRAGYN	TETRASEMIC
TERRORIST	TESTACEOUS	TETANIZING	TETRAGYNIAN	TETRASKELE
TERRORISTIC	TESTACY	TETANOID	TETRAGYNOUS	TETRASKELION
TERRORIZE	TESTAE	TETANOLYSIN	TETRAHEDRA	TETRASPHERIC
TERRORIZED	TESTAMENT	TETANOMOTOR	TETRAHEDRAL	TETRASPORE
TERRORIZER	TESTAMENTA	TETANUS	TETRAHEDRIC	TETRASPORIC
TERRORIZING	TESTAMENTAL	TETANY	TETRAHEDRITE	TETRASPOROUS
TERRORSOME	TESTAMENTARY	TETARD	TETRAHEDROID	TETRASTER
TERRY	TESTAMENTATE	TETARTOCONE	TETRAHEDRON	TETRASTICH
TERSE	TESTAMENTUM	TETARTOCONID	TETRAHEDRONS	TETRASTICHAL
TERSELY	TESTAMUR	TETARTOID	TETRAHEXAHEDRON	TETRASTICHIC
TERSENESS	TESTAO	TETCH	TETRAHYDRATE	TETRASTOON
TERSER	TESTAR	TETCHIER	TETRAHYDRIC	TETRASTYLE
TERSEST	TESTATA	TETCHIEST	TETRAHYDRID	TETRASTYLIC
TERSION	TESTATE	TETCHILY	TETRAHYDRIDE	TETRASTYLOS
TERSULFID	TESTATION	TETCHINESS	TETRAHYDRO	TETRASTYLOUS
TERSULFIDE	TESTATOR	TETCHY	TETRAHYDROXY	TETRASULFID
TERSULPHATE	TESTATORY	TETE	TETRAIODO	TETRASULFIDE
TERSULPHID	TESTATRICES	TETEL	TETRAKETONE	TETRASULPHID
TERSULPHIDE	TESTATRIX	TETH	TETRAKIS	TETRATHEISM
TERSULPHURET	TESTATUM	TETHELIN	TETRAKISAZO	TETRATHEITE
TERTIA	TESTE	TETHER	TETRALEMMA	TETRATHIONIC
TERTIAL	TESTED	TETHERBALL	TETRALOGIC	TETRATOMIC
TERTIAN	TESTEE	TETHERED	TETRALOGIES	TETRATONE
TERTIANA	TESTER	TETHERING	TETRALOGUE	TETRAVALENCE
TERTIANSHIP	TESTES	TETHERY	TETRALOGY	TETRAVALENCY
TERTIARIES	TESTICLE	TETHYDAN	TETRAMASTIA	TETRAVALENT
TERTIARY	TESTICOND	TETOTUM	TETRAMERAL	TETRAXIAL
TERTIATE	TESTICULAR	TETRA	TETRAMERIC	TETRAXILE
TERTIO	TESTICULATE	TETRAAMYLOSE	TETRAMERISM	TETRAXON
TERTON	TESTICULATED	TETRABASIC	TETRAMEROUS	TETRAZANE
TERTULIA	TESTIER	TETRABIBLOS	TETRAMETER	TETRAZENE
TERUAH	TESTIERE	TETRABORATE	TETRAMETHYL	TETRAZIN
TERUNCIUS	TESTIEST	TETRABORIC	TETRAMINE	TETRAZINE
TERUTERO	TESTIFICATE	TETRABRACH	TETRAMORPH	TETRAZO
TERUTERU	TESTIFICATOR	TETRABROMID	TETRAMORPHIC	TETRAZOLE
TERVALENCE	TESTIFIED	TETRABROMIDE	TETRANDER	TETRAZOLIUM
TERVALENCY	TESTIFIER	TETRACHLORID	TETRANDROUS	TETRAZOLYL

TETRAZONE	TEXTURAL	THANAGE	THEATER	THEIST
TETRAZOTIZE	TEXTURALLY	THANAH	THEATERGOER	THEISTIC
TETREMIMERAL	TEXTURE	THANATISM	THEATERGOING	THEISTICAL
TETRIC	TEXTURED	THANATIST	THEATERS	THELION
TETRICAL	TEXTUS	THANATOID	THEATRAL	THELITIS
TETRICALNESS	TEYNE	THANATOLOGY	THEATRE	THELIUM
TETRICITY	TEZ	THANATOMETER	THEATREGOER	THELORRHAGIA
TETRICOUS	TEZKIRAH	THANATOPSIS	THEATREGOING	THELPHUSIAN
TETRIFOL	THA	THANATOSIS	THEATRIC	THELYBLAST
TETRIGID	THACK	THANATOTIC	THEATRICABLE	THELYBLASTIC
TETRIODIDE	THACKER	THANATOUSIA	THEATRICAL	THELYOTOKOUS
TETROBOL	THACKLESS	THANE	THEATRICALITY	THELYOTOKY
TETROBOLON	THACKOOR	THANELAND	THEATRICALS	THEM
TETRODE	THAE	THANESS	THEATRICIAN	THEMA
TETROL	THAG	THANK	THEATRICISM	THEMATA
TETROLE	THAIL	THANKED	THEATRICIZE	THEMATIC
TETROLIC	THAIRM	THANKEE	THEATRICS	THEMATICAL
TETRONIC	THAKUR	THANKER	THEATRIZE	THEMATICALLY
TETRONYMAL	THAKURATE	THANKFUL	THEATROCRACY	THEMATIST
TETROSE	THALAMI	THANKFULLY	THEATRON	THEME
TETROUS	THALAMIA	THANKFULNESS	THEAVE	THEMED
TETROXALATE	THALAMIC	THANKING	THEB	THEMER
TETROXID	THALAMITE	THANKLESS	THEBAIN	THEMING
TETROXIDE	THALAMIUM	THANKLESSLY	THEBAINE	THEMSELVES
TETRYL	THALAMOCELE	THANKS	THEBAISM	THEN
TETTER	THALAMOCOELE	THANKSGIVER	THECA	THENABOUTS
TETTERED	THALAMUS	THANKSGIVING	THECAE	THENADAYS
TETTERING	THALASSA	THANKWORTHY	THECAL	THENAGE
TETTEROUS	THALASSAL	THANNADAR	THECAPHORE	THENAL
TETTERWORT	THALASSIAN	THAPES	THECASPORAL	THENAR
TETTERY	THALASSIARCH	THAR	THECASPORE	THENARDITE
TETTISH	THALASSIC	THARF	THECASPORED	THENCE
TETTIX	THALASSICAL	THARFCAKE	THECASPOROUS	THENCEAFTER
TETTY	THALASSINID	THARGINYAH	THECATE	THENCEFORTH
TETUR	THALASSINOID	THARM	THECIA	THENCEFROM
TEU	THALATTA	THAT	THECITIS	THENCEWARD
TEUCH	THALENITE	THATCH	THECIUM	THENNESS
TEUCHIT	THALER	THATCHED	THECLAN	THEOBROMIN
TEUCRIN	THALIACEAN	THATCHER	THECODONT	THEOBROMINE
TEUGH	THALIDOMIDE	THATCHING	THEDE	THEOCENTRIC
TEUGHLY	THALLI	THATCHWOOD	THEE	THEOCHRISTIC
TEUGHNESS	THALLIC	THATCHY	THEEDOM	THEOCRACIES
TEUK	THALLIFEROUS	THATNESS	THEEK	THEOCRACY
TEVEL	THALLIFORM	THAUGHT	THEEKED	THEOCRASICAL
TEVISS	THALLIN	THAUMASITE	THEEKER	THEOCRASIES
TEW	THALLINE	THAUMATOGENY	THEEKING	THEOCRASY
TEWART	THALLIOUS	THAUMATOLOGIES	THEELIN	THEOCRAT
TEWED	THALLIUM	THAUMATOLOGY	THEELOL	THEOCRATIC
TEWEL	THALLOCHLORE	THAUMATROPE	THEET	THEOCRATICAL
TEWER	THALLODAL	THAUMATURGE	THEETSEE	THEOCRATIST
TEWING	THALLODIC	THAUMATURGI	THEEZAN	THEODICEAN
TEWIT	THALLOGEN	THAUMATURGIA	THEFT	THEODICIES
TEWKE	THALLOGENOUS	THAUMATURGIC	THEFTBOTE	THEODICY
TEWLY	THALLOID	THAUMATURGUS	THEFTDOM	THEODIDACT
TEWSOME	THALLOIDAL	THAUMATURGY	THEFTUOUS	THEODOLITE
TEWTAW	THALLOME	THAUMOSCOPIC	THEFTUOUSLY	THEODOLITIC
TEWTER	THALLOPHYTE	THAW	THEGETHER	THEODY
TEXAS	THALLOPHYTIC	THAWED	THEGIDDER	THEOGAMY
TEXGUINO	THALLOSE	THAWER	THEGITHER	THEOGONAL
TEXT	THALLOUS	THAWIER	THEGN	THEOGONIC
TEXTARIAN	THALLUS	THAWIEST	THEGNDOM	THEOGONICAL
TEXTBOOK	THALLUSES	THAWING	THEGNHOOD	THEOGONIES
TEXTIFEROUS	THALPOSIS	THAWY	THEGNLAND	THEOGONISM
TEXTILE	THALPOTIC	THE	THEGNLIKE	THEOGONIST
TEXTILES	THALTHAN	THEACEOUS	THEGNLY	THEOGONY
TEXTILIST	THALWEG	THEAK	THEGNSHIP	THEOKRASIA
TEXTLET	THAM	THEAL	THEGNWORTHY	THEOKTONIC
TEXTMAN	THAMAKAU	THEAM	THEI	THEOKTONY
TEXTORIAL	THAMENG	THEANDRIC	THEIC	THEOLATROUS
TEXTRINE	THAMIN	THEANTHROPIC	THEIFORM	THEOLATRY
TEXTUAL	THAMNIUM	THEANTHROPOS	THEIN	THEOLOG
TEXTUALISM	THAMNOPHILE	THEANTHROPY	THEINE	THEOLOGASTER
TEXTUALIST	THAMNOPHILINE	THEARCHIC	THEIR	THEOLOGATE
TEXTUALLY	THAMURIA	THEARCHIES	THEIRN	THEOLOGEION
TEXTUARIES	THAN	THEARCHY	THEIRS	THEOLOGER
TEXTUARIST	THANA	THEASUM	THEIRSELVES	THEOLOGI
TEXTUARY	THANADAR	THEAT	THEISM	THEOLOGIAN

THEOLOGIC
THEOLOGICAL
THEOLOGICIAN
THEOLOGICS
THEOLOGIES
THEOLOGISE
THEOLOGISM
THEOLOGIST
THEOLOGIUM
THEOLOGIZE
THEOLOGIZED
THEOLOGIZER
THEOLOGIZING
THEOLOGUE
THEOLOGUS
THEOLOGY
THEOMACHIES
THEOMACHIST
THEOMACHY
THEOMAGIC
THEOMAGICAL
THEOMAGICS
THEOMAGY
THEOMANCY
THEOMANIA
THEOMANIAC
THEOMANTIC
THEOMASTIX
THEOMICRIST
THEOMORPHIC
THEOMORPHISM
THEOMORPHIZE
THEONOMY
THEOPANTISM
THEOPATHETIC
THEOPATHIC
THEOPATHIES
THEOPATHY
THEOPHAGIC
THEOPHAGITE
THEOPHAGOUS
THEOPHAGY
THEOPHANIA
THEOPHANIC
THEOPHANIES
THEOPHANISM
THEOPHANOUS
THEOPHANY
THEOPHILE
THEOPHOBIA
THEOPHORIC
THEOPHOROUS
THEOPHYLLIN
THEOPHYLLINE
THEOPNEUST
THEOPNEUSTED
THEOPNEUSTIC
THEOPNEUSTY
THEORBIST
THEORBO
THEORBOS
THEOREM
THEOREMATIC
THEOREMATIST
THEOREMIC
THEORETIC
THEORETICAL
THEORETICIAN
THEORETICS
THEORIA
THEORIAI
THEORIC
THEORICA
THEORICAL
THEORICALLY
THEORICIAN
THEORICON

THEORICS
THEORIES
THEORISE
THEORISM
THEORIST
THEORIZATION
THEORIZE
THEORIZED
THEORIZER
THEORIZING
THEORUM
THEORY
THEORYLESS
THEOSOPH
THEOSOPHEME
THEOSOPHER
THEOSOPHIC
THEOSOPHICAL
THEOSOPHIES
THEOSOPHISM
THEOSOPHIST
THEOSOPHY
THEOTECHNIC
THEOTECHNIST
THEOTECHNY
THEOTHERAPY
THEOW
THEOWDOM
THEOWMAN
THEOWMEN
THERALITE
THERAPEUSIS
THERAPEUTIC
THERAPEUTICS
THERAPEUTIST
THERAPIA
THERAPIES
THERAPIST
THERAPSID
THERAPY
THERAVADA
THERBLIG
THERE
THEREABOUT
THEREABOUTS
THEREABOVE
THEREACROSS
THEREAFTER
THEREAGAINST
THEREAMONG
THEREAMONGST
THEREANENT
THEREANENTS
THEREAROUND
THEREAS
THEREAT
THEREAWAY
THEREAWAYS
THEREBEFORE
THEREBEN
THEREBESIDE
THEREBIFORN
THEREBY
THEREFOR
THEREFORE
THEREFRO
THEREFROM
THEREIN
THEREINAFTER
THEREINTO
THERENESS
THEREOF
THEREOID
THEREOLOGIST
THEREOLOGY
THEREON
THEREONTO

THEREOUT
THEREOVER
THERERIGHT
THERESE
THERETHROUGH
THERETIL
THERETILL
THERETO
THERETOFORE
THERETOWARD
THEREUNDER
THEREUNTIL
THEREUNTO
THEREUP
THEREUPON
THEREVID
THEREWHILE
THEREWHILES
THEREWHILST
THEREWITH
THEREWITHAL
THEREWITHIN
THERF
THERIAC
THERIACA
THERIACAL
THERIAL
THERIATRICS
THERIDIID
THERIODONT
THERIOMANCY
THERIOMORPH
THERM
THERMAE
THERMAIC
THERMAL
THERMALGESIA
THERMALITY
THERMALLY
THERMANTIC
THERMATOLOGY
THERME
THERMEL
THERMIC
THERMICAL
THERMICALLY
THERMION
THERMIONIC
THERMIONICS
THERMISTOR
THERMIT
THERMITE
THERMOCHROIC
THERMOCHROSY
THERMOCLINE
THERMOCOUPLE
THERMOGEN
THERMOGENIC
THERMOGENOUS
THERMOGRAM
THERMOGRAPH
THERMOGRAPHY
THERMOLABILE
THERMOLOGY
THERMOLYSIS
THERMOLYTIC
THERMOLYZE
THERMOLYZED
THERMOLYZING
THERMOMETER
THERMOMETRIC
THERMOMETRY
THERMOMOTIVE
THERMOMOTOR
THERMONASTIC
THERMONASTY
THERMONOUS

THERMOPAIR
THERMOPHIL
THERMOPHILE
THERMOPHILIC
THERMOPHONE
THERMOPHORE
THERMOPILE
THERMOPLASTIC
THERMOPLEION
THERMOSCOPE
THERMOSCOPIC
THERMOSIPHON
THERMOSPHERE
THERMOSTABLE
THERMOSTAT
THERMOSTATIC
THERMOTACTIC
THERMOTANK
THERMOTAXIC
THERMOTAXIS
THERMOTIC
THERMOTICAL
THERMOTICS
THERMOTROPIC
THERMOTROPY
THERMOTYPE
THERMOTYPIC
THERMOTYPY
THERODONT
THEROID
THEROLOGIC
THEROLOGICAL
THEROLOGIST
THEROLOGY
THEROMORPH
THEROMORPHIA
THEROMORPHIC
THEROPOD
THEROPODAN
THEROPODOUS
THERSITEAN
THERSITICAL
THESAUR
THESAURI
THESAURUS
THESAURY
THESE
THESIAL
THESICLE
THESIS
THESMOTHETE
THESMOTHETES
THESOCYTE
THESTER
THESTREEN
THETA
THETCH
THETIC
THETICAL
THETICALLY
THETICS
THETIN
THETINE
THEURGIC
THEURGICAL
THEURGICALLY
THEURGIES
THEURGIST
THEURGY
THEVETIN
THEW
THEWED
THEWIER
THEWIEST
THEWLESS
THEWLIKE
THEWS

THEWY
THEY
THEYAOU
THIADIAZOLE
THIALDIN
THIALDINE
THIAMID
THIAMIDE
THIAMIN
THIAMINE
THIANTHRENE
THIASI
THIASITE
THIASOI
THIASOS
THIASOTE
THIASUS
THIAZIN
THIAZINE
THIAZOL
THIAZOLE
THIAZOLINE
THIBET
THIBLE
THICK
THICKE
THICKEN
THICKENED
THICKENER
THICKENING
THICKER
THICKEST
THICKET
THICKETED
THICKETY
THICKHEAD
THICKHEADED
THICKISH
THICKLEAF
THICKLIPS
THICKLY
THICKNESS
THICKSET
THICKSKIN
THICKSKULL
THICKSKULLED
THICKWIND
THICKWIT
THICKY
THIEF
THIEFCRAFT
THIEFDOM
THIEFLAND
THIEFLY
THIEFMAKER
THIEFMAKING
THIEFPROOF
THIEFTAKER
THIENONE
THIENYL
THIEVE
THIEVED
THIEVELESS
THIEVER
THIEVERIES
THIEVERY
THIEVES
THIEVING
THIEVISH
THIEVISHLY
THIEVISHNESS
THIG
THIGGER
THIGGING
THIGH
THIGHBONE
THIGHED

THIGHS
THIGHT
THIGHTNESS
THIGMOTACTIC
THIGMOTAXIS
THIGMOTROPIC
THIK
THILK
THILL
THILLER
THILLY
THIMBLE
THIMBLEBERRIES
THIMBLEBERRY
THIMBLED
THIMBLEFUL
THIMBLEFULS
THIMBLEMAKER
THIMBLEMAKING
THIMBLEMAN
THIMBLERIG
THIMBLERIGGED
THIMBLERIGGING
THIMBLES
THIMBLEWEED
THIN
THINDOWN
THINE
THING
THINGAL
THINGAMABOB
THINGAMAJIG
THINGISH
THINGLET
THINGMAN
THINGS
THINGUM
THINGUMABOB
THINGUMAJIG
THINGUMBOB
THINGUT
THINGY
THINK
THINKABLE
THINKABLY
THINKER
THINKING
THINKINGLY
THINLY
THINNED
THINNER
THINNESS
THINNEST
THINNING
THIO
THIOACETIC
THIOALDEHYDE
THIOAMID
THIOAMIDE
THIOARSENATE
THIOARSENIATE
THIOARSENITE
THIOCARBAMIC
THIOCARBONYL
THIOCRESOL
THIOCYANATE
THIOCYANIC
THIOCYANIDE
THIOCYANO
THIOCYANOGEN
THIOHYDRATE
THIOKETONE
THIOL
THIOLACETIC
THIONATE
THIONATION
THIONEINE

THIONIC
THIONIN
THIONINE
THIONITRITE
THIONYL
THIONYLAMINE
THIOPHEN
THIOPHENE
THIOPHENIC
THIOPHENOL
THIOPHOSGENE
THIOPHTHENE
THIOPYRAN
THIOSINAMINE
THIOSTANNIC
THIOSTANNITE
THIOSULFATE
THIOSULPHATE
THIOTOLENE
THIOTUNGSTIC
THIOUREA
THIOURETHAN
THIOXENE
THIOZONE
THIOZONID
THIOZONIDE
THIR
THIRD
THIRDBOROUGH
THIRDENDEAL
THIRDINGS
THIRDLING
THIRDLY
THIRDNESS
THIRDS
THIRDSMAN
THIRL
THIRLAGE
THIRLED
THIRLING
THIRST
THIRSTED
THIRSTER
THIRSTIER
THIRSTIEST
THIRSTILY
THIRSTINESS
THIRSTING
THIRSTINGLY
THIRSTLE
THIRSTY
THIRTEEN
THIRTEENER
THIRTEENTH
THIRTEENTHLY
THIRTIES
THIRTIETH
THIRTY
THIS
THISHOW
THISLIKE
THISNESS
THISSEN
THISTLE
THISTLEBIRD
THISTLED
THISTLEDOWN
THISTLY
THISWISE
THITHER
THITHERTO
THITHERWARD
THITHERWARDS
THITKA
THITSIOL
THIURAM
THIVEL

THIXLE
THIXOLABILE
THIXOTROPIC
THIXOTROPY
THLIPSIS
THO
THOA
THOB
THODE
THOFT
THOFTFELLOW
THOGHT
THOKE
THOKISH
THOLANCE
THOLE
THOLED
THOLEITE
THOLEMOD
THOLING
THOLOI
THOLOS
THOLUS
THOMAN
THOMASING
THOMISID
THOMIST
THOMSENOLITE
THOMSONITE
THON
THONDER
THONE
THONG
THONGED
THONGMAN
THONGS
THONGY
THOOID
THORACECTOMY
THORACES
THORACIC
THORACICAL
THORACIFORM
THORACOGRAPH
THORACOLYSIS
THORACOPAGUS
THORACOSCOPE
THORACOSCOPY
THORAL
THORAX
THORAXES
THORE
THORIA
THORIANITE
THORIATE
THORIC
THORIFEROUS
THORITE
THORIUM
THORN
THORNBACK
THORNBILL
THORNBUSH
THORNED
THORNEN
THORNIER
THORNIEST
THORNING
THORNLESS
THORNLET
THORNTAIL
THORNY
THORO
THOROGUMMITE
THORON
THOROUGH
THOROUGHBRED

THOROUGHFARE
THOROUGHFOOT
THOROUGHFOOTED
THOROUGHFOOTING
THOROUGHGOING
THOROUGHLY
THOROUGHNESS
THOROUGHPIN
THOROUGHSPED
THOROUGHSTEM
THOROUGHWAX
THOROUGHWORT
THORP
THORPE
THORTER
THORTVEITITE
THOSE
THOU
THOUGH
THOUGHT
THOUGHTED
THOUGHTFUL
THOUGHTFULLY
THOUGHTFULNESS
THOUGHTLESS
THOUGHTLESSLY
THOUGHTNESS
THOUGHTS
THOUGHTSICK
THOUGHTY
THOUSAND
THOUSANDFOLD
THOUSANDTH
THOWLESS
THRACK
THRAIL
THRAIN
THRALDOM
THRALL
THRALLBORN
THRALLDOM
THRAM
THRAMMLE
THRANG
THRANGITY
THRANITE
THRAP
THRAPPLE
THRASH
THRASHED
THRASHEL
THRASHER
THRASHERMAN
THRASHING
THRASONIC
THRASONICAL
THRAST
THRATCH
THRAVE
THRAVER
THRAW
THRAWART
THRAWARTLIKE
THRAWARTNESS
THRAWN
THRAWNLY
THRAWNNESS
THREAD
THREADBARE
THREADED
THREADEN
THREADER
THREADFIN
THREADFISH
THREADFISHES
THREADFLOWER
THREADFOOT

THREADIER
THREADIEST
THREADING
THREADLE
THREADLIKE
THREADMAKER
THREADMAKING
THREADS
THREADWAY
THREADWEED
THREADWORM
THREADY
THREAP
THREAPED
THREAPEN
THREAPER
THREAPING
THREAT
THREATEN
THREATENED
THREATENER
THREATENING
THREATENINGLY
THREAVE
THREE
THREEFOLD
THREELING
THREENESS
THREEP
THREEPED
THREEPENCE
THREEPENNY
THREEPING
THREES
THREESCORE
THREESOME
THREIP
THRENE
THRENETIC
THRENETICAL
THRENODE
THRENODIAL
THRENODIAN
THRENODIC
THRENODIES
THRENODIST
THRENODY
THRENOS
THREONINE
THREOSE
THREP
THREPE
THREPSOLOGY
THRESH
THRESHAL
THRESHED
THRESHEL
THRESHER
THRESHERMAN
THRESHING
THRESHOLD
THRESTLE
THREW
THRIBBLE
THRICE
THRICECOCK
THRID
THRIDACE
THRIDACIUM
THRIE
THRIFT
THRIFTBOX
THRIFTIER
THRIFTIEST
THRIFTILY
THRIFTINESS
THRIFTLESS

THRIFTY	THRONE	THUJONE	THURIFY	THYMYL
THRILL	THRONED	THUJYL	THURINGITE	THYMYLIC
THRILLED	THRONELET	THULIA	THURL	THYNNID
THRILLER	THRONES	THULIR	THURLE	THYRATRON
THRILLIER	THRONG	THULITE	THURM	THYREOID
THRILLIEST	THRONGED	THULIUM	THURMUS	THYRIDIA
THRILLING	THRONGER	THULUTH	THURROCK	THYRIDIAL
THRILLINGLY	THRONGING	THUMB	THURSE	THYRIDIUM
THRILLY	THRONING	THUMBED	THURST	THYROCARDIAC
THRIMBLE	THRONIZE	THUMBER	THURT	THYROCELE
THRIMP	THROPE	THUMBING	THUS	THYROCOLLOID
THRING	THROPPLE	THUMBKIN	THUSGATE	THYROGENIC
THRINGING	THROSTLE	THUMBLE	THUSLY	THYROGENOUS
THRINTER	THROTTLE	THUMBLESS	THUSWISE	THYROGLOSSAL
THRIOBOLY	THROTTLED	THUMBLING	THUTTER	THYROHYAL
THRIP	THROTTLER	THUMBMARK	THUYA	THYROHYOID
THRIPEL	THROTTLING	THUMBNAIL	THWACK	THYROID
THRIPID	THROTTLINGLY	THUMBNUT	THWACKED	THYROIDEA
THRIPPLE	THROUGH	THUMBPIECE	THWACKER	THYROIDISM
THRIPS	THROUGHBEAR	THUMBPRINT	THWACKING	THYROIDITIS
THRIST	THROUGHGANG	THUMBROPE	THWACKINGLY	THYROIDLESS
THRIVE	THROUGHGOING	THUMBSCREW	THWACKSTAVE	THYROIDOTOMY
THRIVED	THROUGHGROW	THUMBSTALL	THWAITE	THYROLINGUAL
THRIVELESS	THROUGHLY	THUMBSTRING	THWART	THYRONIN
THRIVEN	THROUGHOUT	THUMBTACK	THWARTED	THYRONINE
THRIVER	THROUGHPUT	THUMBY	THWARTEOUS	THYROPRIVAL
THRIVING	THROUGHWAY	THUMP	THWARTER	THYROPRIVIA
THRIVINGLY	THROVE	THUMPED	THWARTING	THYROPRIVIC
THRIVINGNESS	THROW	THUMPER	THWARTINGLY	THYROPROTEIN
THRO	THROWAWAY	THUMPING	THWARTMAN	THYROSTRACAN
THROAT	THROWBACK	THUMPINGLY	THWARTMEN	THYROTHERAPY
THROATAL	THROWDOWN	THUNBERGILENE	THWARTOVER	THYROTOMY
THROATBAND	THROWER	THUNDER	THWARTSAW	THYROTOXIC
THROATBOLL	THROWING	THUNDERBIRD	THWARTSHIP	THYROXIN
THROATED	THROWN	THUNDERBLAST	THWARTSHIPS	THYROXINE
THROATFUL	THROWOFF	THUNDERBOLT	THWITE	THYROXINIC
THROATIER	THROWOUT	THUNDERBURST	THWITTLE	THYRSE
THROATIEST	THROWST	THUNDERCLAP	THWORL	THYRSI
THROATILY	THROWSTER	THUNDERCLOUD	THY	THYRSOID
THROATINESS	THRU	THUNDERCRACK	THYINE	THYRSOIDAL
THROATING	THRUM	THUNDERED	THYLACINE	THYRSUS
THROATLASH	THRUMBLE	THUNDERER	THYLACITIS	THYSANOPTER
THROATLATCH	THRUMMED	THUNDERFISH	THYMACETIN	THYSANURAN
THROATLET	THRUMMER	THUNDERFISHES	THYME	THYSANUROUS
THROATROOT	THRUMMING	THUNDERHEAD	THYMECTOMY	THYSELF
THROATSTRAP	THRUMMY	THUNDERING	THYMELCOSIS	THYSEN
THROATWORT	THRUMWORT	THUNDERINGLY	THYMELE	TI
THROATY	THRUOUT	THUNDERLIGHT	THYMELIC	TIA
THROB	THRUSH	THUNDEROUS	THYMELICAL	TIAL
THROBBED	THRUSHEL	THUNDEROUSLY	THYMELICI	TIANG
THROBBER	THRUSHER	THUNDERPEAL	THYMENE	TIANGUE
THROBBING	THRUSHLIKE	THUNDERPLUMP	THYMETIC	TIAO
THROBBINGLY	THRUSHY	THUNDERPUMP	THYMIAMA	TIAR
THROBLESS	THRUST	THUNDERSMITE	THYMIC	TIARA
THROCK	THRUSTER	THUNDERSMITING	THYMIER	TIARELLA
THRODDEN	THRUSTING	THUNDERSMOTE	THYMIEST	TIB
THRODDY	THRUSTLE	THUNDERSQUALL	THYMIN	TIBBIT
THROE	THRUTCH	THUNDERSTONE	THYMINE	TIBBY
THROED	THRUTCHINGS	THUNDERSTORM	THYMIOSIS	TIBERT
THROEING	THRUWAY	THUNDERSTROKE	THYMITIS	TIBET
THROM	THRYMSA	THUNDERWOOD	THYMOCYTE	TIBEY
THROMBI	THUD	THUNDERWORM	THYMOGENIC	TIBIA
THROMBIN	THUDDED	THUNDERWORT	THYMOL	TIBIAE
THROMBOCYST	THUDDING	THUNDERY	THYMOLATE	TIBIAL
THROMBOCYTE	THUDDINGLY	THUNDROUS	THYMOLIZE	TIBIALE
THROMBOGEN	THUG	THUNGE	THYMOMA	TIBIALIA
THROMBOGENIC	THUGA	THUNK	THYMOMATA	TIBIALIS
THROMBOID	THUGGED	THUOC	THYMOPATHY	TIBIAS
THROMBOPENIA	THUGGEE	THUR	THYMOPRIVIC	TIBICEN
THROMBOSE	THUGGERIES	THURGI	THYMOPSYCHE	TIBIOFIBULA
THROMBOSED	THUGGERY	THURIBLE	THYMOQUINONE	TIBIOTARSAL
THROMBOSES	THUGGESS	THURIBULER	THYMOTACTIC	TIBIOTARSI
THROMBOSING	THUGGING	THURIBULUM	THYMOTIC	TIBIOTARSUS
THROMBOSIS	THUGGISH	THURIFER	THYMOTINIC	TIBOURBOU
THROMBOTIC	THUGGISM	THURIFEROUS	THYMS	TIBURON
THROMBUS	THUJA	THURIFICATE	THYMUS	TIC
THRONAL	THUJENE	THURIFICATI	THYMY	TICAL

TICCA	TIDEMAKER	TIGEREYE	TILESTONE	TIMBRELLER
TICCHEN	TIDEMAKING	TIGERFLOWER	TILETTE	TIME
TICE	TIDEMARK	TIGERFOOT	TILIACEOUS	TIMECARD
TICEMENT	TIDERACE	TIGERISH	TILICETUM	TIMED
TICER	TIDERIP	TIGERISHLY	TILIKUM	TIMEFUL
TICHEL	TIDES	TIGERISHNESS	TILING	TIMEKEEP
TICHODROME	TIDESMAN	TIGERISM	TILL	TIMEKEEPER
TICHORRHINE	TIDESURVEYOR	TIGERKIN	TILLABLE	TIMEKEEPING
TICK	TIDEWAITER	TIGERLY	TILLAGE	TIMELESS
TICKBEAN	TIDEWATER	TIGERNUT	TILLANDSIA	TIMELESSLY
TICKBIRD	TIDEWAY	TIGERS	TILLED	TIMELESSNESS
TICKED	TIDIED	TIGERWOOD	TILLER	TIMELIER
TICKEN	TIDIER	TIGGER	TILLERED	TIMELIEST
TICKER	TIDIES	TIGH	TILLERING	TIMELILY
TICKET	TIDIEST	TIGHT	TILLERMAN	TIMELINESS
TICKETED	TIDIFE	TIGHTEN	TILLET	TIMELY
TICKETER	TIDILY	TIGHTENED	TILLEY	TIMENOGUY
TICKETING	TIDINESS	TIGHTENER	TILLICUM	TIMEOUS
TICKETMONGER	TIDING	TIGHTENING	TILLING	TIMEOUSLY
TICKEY	TIDINGS	TIGHTER	TILLITE	TIMEPIECE
TICKIE	TIDIOSE	TIGHTEST	TILLMAN	TIMEPLEASER
TICKING	TIDLEY	TIGHTFISTED	TILLODONT	TIMER
TICKLE	TIDLING	TIGHTISH	TILLOT	TIMERAU
TICKLEBACK	TIDOLOGICAL	TIGHTLIER	TILLY	TIMERITY
TICKLEBRAIN	TIDOLOGY	TIGHTLIEST	TILMA	TIMES
TICKLED	TIDY	TIGHTLIPPED	TILMUS	TIMESAVER
TICKLELY	TIDYING	TIGHTLY	TILPAH	TIMESAVING
TICKLENBURG	TIDYTIPS	TIGHTNESS	TILT	TIMESERVER
TICKLENESS	TIE	TIGHTROPE	TILTBOARD	TIMESERVING
TICKLER	TIEBACK	TIGHTS	TILTED	TIMETABLE
TICKLESOME	TIEBOY	TIGHTWAD	TILTER	TIMETAKER
TICKLEWEED	TIED	TIGHTWIRE	TILTH	TIMETAKING
TICKLING	TIEDOG	TIGLALDEHYDE	TILTING	TIMEWORK
TICKLINGLY	TIEGO	TIGLIC	TILTUP	TIMEWORKER
TICKLISH	TIEING	TIGLINIC	TILTURE	TIMEWORN
TICKLISHLY	TIEMANNITE	TIGNON	TILTY	TIMID
TICKLISHNESS	TIEN	TIGNUM	TILTYARD	TIMIDER
TICKLY	TIENDA	TIGRESS	TILYER	TIMIDEST
TICKNEY	TIENS	TIGRINE	TIMALIINE	TIMIDITY
TICKSEED	TIENTA	TIGRISH	TIMALINE	TIMIDLY
TICKSEEDED	TIENTO	TIGROID	TIMAR	TIMIDNESS
TICKTACK	TIEPIN	TIGROLYSIS	TIMARAU	TIMIDOUS
TICKTACKER	TIER	TIGROLYTIC	TIMARIOT	TIMING
TICKTACKTOE	TIERCE	TIGRONE	TIMARRI	TIMISH
TICKTACKTOO	TIERCERON	TIGTAG	TIMAUA	TIMIST
TICKTICK	TIERED	TIKAL	TIMAWA	TIMMER
TICKTOCK	TIERER	TIKE	TIMAZITE	TIMOCRACIES
TICKWEED	TIERRAS	TIKI	TIMBAL	TIMOCRACY
TICKY	TIERSMAN	TIKITIKI	TIMBALE	TIMOCRATIC
TICTACTOE	TIES	TIKKA	TIMBANG	TIMOCRATICAL
TICTIC	TIETICK	TIKKER	TIMBE	TIMON
TICUL	TIEVINE	TIKKUN	TIMBER	TIMONEER
TID	TIEWIG	TIKLIN	TIMBERED	TIMOR
TIDAL	TIFF	TIKOLOSH	TIMBERER	TIMOROSO
TIDBIT	TIFFANIES	TIKOOR	TIMBERHEAD	TIMOROUS
TIDBITS	TIFFANY	TIKOR	TIMBERING	TIMOROUSLY
TIDDER	TIFFANYITE	TIKUG	TIMBERJACK	TIMOROUSNESS
TIDDLE	TIFFED	TIKUR	TIMBERLAND	TIMOTHY
TIDDLEDYWINKS	TIFFIE	TIL	TIMBERLESS	TIMPANI
TIDDLER	TIFFIN	TILAITE	TIMBERLIKE	TIMPANIST
TIDDLEY	TIFFING	TILAK	TIMBERLING	TIMPANO
TIDDLEYWINK	TIFFISH	TILAKA	TIMBERMAN	TIMPANUM
TIDDLING	TIFFLE	TILASITE	TIMBERMEN	TIN
TIDDLY	TIFFY	TILBURIES	TIMBERN	TINA
TIDDLYWINK	TIFINAGH	TILBURY	TIMBERS	TINAGE
TIDDLYWINKER	TIFLE	TILDE	TIMBERSOME	TINAJA
TIDDLYWINKING	TIFT	TILE	TIMBERTUNED	TINAMINE
TIDDLYWINKS	TIFTER	TILED	TIMBERWOOD	TINAMOU
TIDDY	TIG	TILEFISH	TIMBERWORK	TINAMPIPI
TIDE	TIGE	TILEFISHES	TIMBERY	TINCAL
TIDECOACH	TIGELLA	TILER	TIMBESTERE	TINCHEL
TIDED	TIGELLATE	TILERIES	TIMBO	TINCHILL
TIDEFUL	TIGELLE	TILEROOT	TIMBRE	TINCLAD
TIDEHEAD	TIGELLUM	TILERY	TIMBREL	TINCT
TIDELAND	TIGELLUS	TILES	TIMBRELED	TINCTED
TIDELESS	TIGER	TILESEED	TIMBRELER	TINCTING
TIDELY	TIGERBIRD	TILESHERD	TIMBRELLED	TINCTION

TINCTORIAL	TINNER	TIPPIER	TIRRET	TITLEHOLDER
TINCTORIALLY	TINNERY	TIPPIEST	TIRRIT	TITLENE
TINCTURE	TINNET	TIPPING	TIRRIVEE	TITLER
TINCTURED	TINNIENT	TIPPLE	TIRRIVIE	TITLING
TINCTURING	TINNIER	TIPPLED	TIRRLIE	TITLIST
TIND	TINNIEST	TIPPLER	TIRRWIRR	TITMAL
TINDAL	TINNIFIED	TIPPLING	TIRTHANKARA	TITMALL
TINDALO	TINNILY	TIPPY	TIRVE	TITMAN
TINDER	TINNINESS	TIPREE	TIRWIT	TITMEN
TINDERBOX	TINNING	TIPSIER	TIRY	TITMICE
TINDERED	TINNITUS	TIPSIEST	TIS	TITMOUSE
TINDERISH	TINNOCK	TIPSIFIER	TISANE	TITOKI
TINDERY	TINNY	TIPSIFY	TISAR	TITRANT
TINE	TINOSA	TIPSILY	TISSUAL	TITRATABLE
TINEA	TINSEL	TIPSINESS	TISSUE	TITRATE
TINEAL	TINSELED	TIPSTAFF	TISSUED	TITRATED
TINEAN	TINSELING	TIPSTAFFS	TISSUES	TITRATING
TINED	TINSELLED	TIPSTAVES	TISSUEY	TITRATION
TINEGRASS	TINSELLING	TIPSTER	TISSUING	TITRE
TINEID	TINSELLY	TIPSTOCK	TISSWOOD	TITTER
TINEINE	TINSELRY	TIPSY	TISWIN	TITTERATION
TINEMAN	TINSMAN	TIPTAIL	TIT	TITTERED
TINEMEN	TINSMEN	TIPTEERER	TITANATE	TITTEREL
TINEOID	TINSMITH	TIPTILT	TITANAUGITE	TITTERER
TINEOLA	TINSMITHING	TIPTOE	TITANIA	TITTERING
TINES	TINSMITHY	TIPTOED	TITANIC	TITTERINGLY
TINETARE	TINSTONE	TIPTOEING	TITANIFEROUS	TITTERY
TINETY	TINSTUFF	TIPTOEINGLY	TITANITE	TITTIE
TINEWEED	TINSY	TIPTOES	TITANITIC	TITTIVATE
TINFOIL	TINT	TIPTOP	TITANIUM	TITTIVATED
TING	TINTA	TIPTOPPER	TITANOSAUR	TITTIVATING
TINGE	TINTAGE	TIPULID	TITANOTHERE	TITTIVATION
TINGED	TINTAMAR	TIPULOID	TITANOUS	TITTIVATOR
TINGEING	TINTAMARRE	TIPUP	TITANYL	TITTLE
TINGENT	TINTARRON	TIQUEUR	TITAR	TITTLEBAT
TINGER	TINTED	TIR	TITBIT	TITTLER
TINGI	TINTER	TIRADE	TITBITTY	TITTLIN
TINGID	TINTERNELL	TIRAGE	TITE	TITTUP
TINGING	TINTIE	TIRAILLEUR	TITER	TITTUPED
TINGITID	TINTING	TIRALEE	TITFISH	TITTUPING
TINGLASS	TINTIST	TIRASSE	TITHABLE	TITTUPPED
TINGLE	TINTO	TIRAZ	TITHAL	TITTUPPING
TINGLED	TINTOMETER	TIRE	TITHE	TITTUPPY
TINGLER	TINTOMETRIC	TIRED	TITHED	TITTUPY
TINGLING	TINTOMETRY	TIREDER	TITHER	TITTY
TINGLINGLY	TINTY	TIREDEST	TITHES	TITTYMOUSE
TINGLISH	TINTYPE	TIREDLY	TITHING	TITUBANCY
TINGLY	TINTYPER	TIREDNESS	TITHINGMAN	TITUBANT
TINGTANG	TINWALD	TIREHOUSE	TITHINGMEN	TITUBANTLY
TINGUAITE	TINWARE	TIRELESS	TITHINGPENNY	TITUBATE
TINGUAITIC	TINWORK	TIRELESSLY	TITHONIC	TITUBATION
TINGUY	TINWORKER	TIRELESSNESS	TITHONICITY	TITULADO
TINHORN	TINWORKING	TIREMAID	TITHONOMETER	TITULAR
TINHOUSE	TINWORKS	TIREMAN	TITHYMAL	TITULARIES
TINIER	TINY	TIREMEN	TITI	TITULARITY
TINIEST	TINZENITE	TIREMENT	TITIAN	TITULARLY
TINING	TIP	TIRER	TITIEN	TITULARY
TINK	TIPBURN	TIRES	TITILLABILITY	TITULE
TINKER	TIPCART	TIRESMITH	TITILLANT	TITULI
TINKERBIRD	TIPCAT	TIRESOL	TITILLATE	TITULUS
TINKERED	TIPE	TIRESOME	TITILLATED	TIVER
TINKERER	TIPFUL	TIRESOMELY	TITILLATER	TIVOLI
TINKERING	TIPHEAD	TIRESOMENESS	TITILLATING	TIVY
TINKERLY	TIPI	TIREWOMAN	TITILLATINGLY	TIZA
TINKERSHIRE	TIPITI	TIREWOMEN	TITILLATION	TIZEUR
TINKERSHUE	TIPLE	TIRIBA	TITILLATIVE	TIZZIES
TINKLE	TIPLET	TIRING	TITILLATOR	TIZZY
TINKLED	TIPMAN	TIRL	TITILLATORY	TJAELE
TINKLER	TIPMEN	TIRLING	TITIVATE	TJALK
TINKLING	TIPMOST	TIRMA	TITIVATION	TJANDI
TINKLINGLY	TIPOFF	TIRO	TITIVATOR	TJANTING
TINKLY	TIPONI	TIROCINIA	TITIVIL	TJENKAL
TINLET	TIPPABLE	TIROCINIUM	TITIVILLER	TJI
TINMAN	TIPPED	TIROS	TITLARK	TJOSITE
TINMEN	TIPPEE	TIRR	TITLE	TJURUNGA
TINNED	TIPPER	TIRRACKE	TITLEBOARD	TLAC
TINNEN	TIPPET	TIRRALIRRA	TITLED	TLACO

TMEMA	TOCOPHEROL	TOI	TOLLBOOK	TOMCOD
TMEMATA	TOCORORO	TOIL	TOLLBOOTH	TOME
TMESIS	TOCSIN	TOILE	TOLLED	TOMENT
TO	TOCUSSO	TOILED	TOLLER	TOMENTA
TOA	TOD	TOILER	TOLLERY	TOMENTOSE
TOAD	TODAY	TOILET	TOLLGATE	TOMENTULOSE
TOADBACK	TODAYISH	TOILETED	TOLLGATHERER	TOMENTUM
TOADEAT	TODDER	TOILETRIES	TOLLHALL	TOMFOOL
TOADEATER	TODDICK	TOILETRY	TOLLHOUSE	TOMFOOLERIES
TOADFISH	TODDIES	TOILETTE	TOLLHOUSES	TOMFOOLERY
TOADFISHES	TODDITE	TOILETWARE	TOLLIKER	TOMFOOLISH
TOADFLAX	TODDLE	TOILFUL	TOLLING	TOMIA
TOADFLOWER	TODDLED	TOILFULLY	TOLLKEEPER	TOMIAL
TOADHEAD	TODDLER	TOILINET	TOLLMAN	TOMIN
TOADIED	TODDLING	TOILINETTE	TOLLMEN	TOMINES
TOADIER	TODDY	TOILING	TOLLON	TOMISH
TOADIES	TODDYIZE	TOILINGLY	TOLLS	TOMIUM
TOADISH	TODDYMAN	TOILSOME	TOLLWAY	TOMJOHN
TOADO	TODDYMEN	TOILSOMELY	TOLLY	TOMJON
TOADPIPE	TODE	TOILSOMENESS	TOLMEN	TOMKIN
TOADPIPES	TODIES	TOISE	TOLPATCH	TOMME
TOADROOT	TODLOWRIE	TOISECH	TOLPATCHERY	TOMMED
TOADSTONE	TODY	TOISED	TOLSEL	TOMMIES
TOADSTOOL	TOE	TOISING	TOLSESTER	TOMMING
TOADY	TOEBOARD	TOISON	TOLSEY	TOMMY
TOADYING	TOECAP	TOIST	TOLT	TOMMYBAG
TOADYISH	TOED	TOIT	TOLTER	TOMMYCOD
TOADYISM	TOEHOLD	TOITISH	TOLU	TOMMYROT
TOAST	TOEING	TOITOI	TOLUALDEHYDE	TOMNODDY
TOASTED	TOELLITE	TOITY	TOLUATE	TOMNORRY
TOASTEE	TOENAIL	TOKAY	TOLUENE	TOMNOUP
TOASTER	TOEPLATE	TOKE	TOLUIC	TOMOGRAPHY
TOASTINESS	TOETOE	TOKEN	TOLUID	TOMOLO
TOASTING	TOEY	TOKENED	TOLUIDE	TOMORN
TOASTMASTER	TOFF	TOKENWORTH	TOLUIDIN	TOMORROW
TOASTMASTERY	TOFFEE	TOKO	TOLUIDINE	TOMORROWER
TOASTY	TOFFEEMAN	TOKOLOGY	TOLUIDO	TOMORROWING
TOAT	TOFFISH	TOKONOMA	TOLUNITRILE	TOMORROWNESS
TOATOA	TOFFY	TOKOPAT	TOLUOL	TOMOSIS
TOBACCO	TOFFYMAN	TOKTOKJE	TOLUOLE	TOMPION
TOBACCOES	TOFFYMEN	TOL	TOLUTATION	TOMPIPER
TOBACCOFIED	TOFORE	TOLA	TOLUYL	TOMRIG
TOBACCOITE	TOFORN	TOLAN	TOLUYLENE	TOMTATE
TOBACCOMAN	TOFT	TOLANE	TOLYL	TOMTIT
TOBACCOMEN	TOFTER	TOLBOOTH	TOLYLENE	TON
TOBACCONING	TOFTMAN	TOLD	TOLYPEUTINE	TONADA
TOBACCONIZE	TOFTMEN	TOLDERIA	TOLZEY	TONAL
TOBACCOROOT	TOFU	TOLDO	TOM	TONALAMATL
TOBACCOS	TOG	TOLE	TOMAHAWK	TONALIST
TOBACCOSIM	TOGA	TOLED	TOMAHAWKED	TONALITE
TOBACCOY	TOGAE	TOLEDO	TOMAHAWKER	TONALITIES
TOBE	TOGAED	TOLERABILITY	TOMAHAWKING	TONALITIVE
TOBER	TOGAS	TOLERABLE	TOMALLEY	TONALITY
TOBIES	TOGATE	TOLERABLY	TOMAN	TONALLY
TOBINE	TOGATED	TOLERANCE	TOMAND	TONALMATL
TOBIRA	TOGE	TOLERANCY	TOMATILLO	TONANT
TOBOGGAN	TOGEMAN	TOLERANT	TOMATO	TONDE
TOBOGGANED	TOGETHER	TOLERANTLY	TOMATOES	TONDI
TOBOGGANER	TOGETHERNESS	TOLERATE	TOMB	TONDINO
TOBOGGANING	TOGGED	TOLERATED	TOMBAC	TONDO
TOBOGGANIST	TOGGEL	TOLERATING	TOMBACK	TONE
TOBY	TOGGERIES	TOLERATION	TOMBAK	TONED
TOBYMAN	TOGGERY	TOLERATIVE	TOMBAL	TONEDEAFNESS
TOBYMEN	TOGGING	TOLERATOR	TOMBE	TONEE
TOCALOTE	TOGGLE	TOLERISM	TOMBED	TONEL
TOCCATA	TOGGLED	TOLFRAEDIC	TOMBIC	TONELADA
TOCCATINA	TOGGLER	TOLGUACHA	TOMBING	TONELESS
TOCHER	TOGGLING	TOLIDIN	TOMBLET	TONELESSLY
TOCK	TOGLESS	TOLIDINE	TOMBOLA	TONELESSNESS
TOCO	TOGS	TOLING	TOMBOLO	TONEME
TOCOGENETIC	TOGT	TOLIPANE	TOMBOY	TONER
TOCOGONY	TOGUE	TOLITE	TOMBOYFUL	TONES
TOCOKININ	TOHEROA	TOLKE	TOMBOYISH	TONETIC
TOCOLOGICAL	TOHI	TOLL	TOMBOYISHLY	TONETICALLY
TOCOLOGIST	TOHO	TOLLABLE	TOMBS	TONETICIAN
TOCOLOGY	TOHUBOHU	TOLLAGE	TOMBSTONE	TONETICS
TOCOME	TOHUNGA	TOLLBAR	TOMCAT	TONETTE

TONG
TONGA
TONGED
TONGING
TONGKANG
TONGS
TONGSMAN
TONGSMEN
TONGUE
TONGUEBIRD
TONGUED
TONGUEFENCE
TONGUEFENCER
TONGUEFISH
TONGUEFISHES
TONGUEFUL
TONGUEFULS
TONGUELESS
TONGUELET
TONGUEMAN
TONGUEMEN
TONGUER
TONGUEY
TONGUING
TONGUY
TONIC
TONICAL
TONICALLY
TONICITY
TONICIZE
TONICKED
TONICKING
TONIER
TONIES
TONIEST
TONIFY
TONIGHT
TONING
TONISH
TONISHLY
TONISHNESS
TONITE
TONITRUONE
TONITRUOUS
TONJON
TONK
TONKA
TONLET
TONNAGE
TONNE
TONNEAU
TONNEAUS
TONNEAUX
TONNELLE
TONNER
TONNISH
TONNISHLY
TONNISHNESS
TONNLAND
TONOGRAM
TONOGRAPH
TONOLOGICAL
TONOLOGY
TONOMETRIC
TONOMETRY
TONOPHANT
TONOPLAST
TONOSCOPE
TONOTACTIC
TONOTAXIS
TONOUS
TONSBERGITE
TONSIL
TONSILAR
TONSILE
TONSILITIS
TONSILLAR

TONSILLARY
TONSILLITIC
TONSILLOLITH
TONSILLOTOMIES
TONSILLOTOMY
TONSOR
TONSORIAL
TONSURATE
TONSURE
TONSURED
TONSURING
TONTINE
TONTINER
TONUS
TONY
TONYHOOP
TOO
TOOART
TOODLE
TOOK
TOOL
TOOLACH
TOOLBOX
TOOLBUILDER
TOOLBUILDING
TOOLED
TOOLER
TOOLHOLDER
TOOLING
TOOLMAKER
TOOLMAKING
TOOLMAN
TOOLMARK
TCOLMARKING
TOOLMEN
TOOLPLATE
TOOLROOM
TOOLS
TOOLSI
TOOLSLIDE
TOOLSMITH
TOOLSTOCK
TOOLSTONE
TOOLSY
TOOM
TOOMLY
TOON
TOONWOOD
TOOP
TOORIE
TOOROCK
TOOROO
TOOSE
TOOSH
TOOSIE
TOOT
TOOTED
TOOTER
TOOTH
TOOTHACHE
TOOTHACHING
TOOTHACHY
TOOTHBILL
TOOTHBRUSH
TOOTHBRUSHY
TOOTHDRAWER
TOOTHDRAWING
TOOTHED
TOOTHER
TOOTHFLOWER
TOOTHFUL
TOOTHIER
TOOTHIEST
TOOTHILL
TOOTHING
TOOTHLESS
TOOTHLESSLY

TOOTHLET
TOOTHLETED
TOOTHPASTE
TOOTHPICK
TOOTHPLATE
TOOTHPOWDER
TOOTHPROOF
TOOTHSHELL
TOOTHSOME
TOOTHSOMELY
TOOTHSTICK
TOOTHWASH
TOOTHWORK
TOOTHWORT
TOOTHY
TOOTING
TOOTINGHOLE
TOOTLE
TOOTLED
TOOTLER
TOOTLING
TOOTLISH
TOOTMOOT
TOOTS
TOOTSIE
TOOTSIES
TOOTSY
TOOZLE
TOOZOO
TOP
TOPAESTHESIA
TOPARCH
TOPARCHIA
TOPARCHIAE
TOPARCHICAL
TOPARCHIES
TOPARCHY
TOPAS
TOPASS
TOPATO
TOPAU
TOPAZ
TOPAZES
TOPAZFELS
TOPAZINE
TOPAZITE
TOPAZOLITE
TOPAZY
TOPCAP
TOPCAST
TOPCOAT
TOPCOATING
TOPE
TOPECHEE
TOPECTOMIES
TOPECTOMY
TOPED
TOPEE
TOPEEWALLAH
TOPEK
TOPENG
TOPEPO
TOPER
TOPESTHESIA
TOPFILLED
TOPFLIGHT
TOPFUL
TOPFULL
TOPGALLANT
TOPH
TOPHACEOUS
TOPHAIKE
TOPHE
TOPHETIC
TOPHETICAL
TOPHI
TOPHUS

TOPI
TOPIA
TOPIARIA
TOPIARIAN
TOPIARIES
TOPIARIST
TOPIARY
TOPIC
TOPICAL
TOPICALITY
TOPICALLY
TOPINAMBOU
TOPING
TOPIS
TOPIWALA
TOPKICK
TOPKNOT
TOPKNOTTED
TOPLESS
TOPLESSNESS
TOPLIGHTED
TOPLINE
TOPLOFTICAL
TOPLOFTIER
TOPLOFTIEST
TOPLOFTILY
TOPLOFTINESS
TOPLOFTY
TOPMAKER
TOPMAN
TOPMAST
TOPMEN
TOPMINNOW
TOPMOST
TOPMOSTLY
TOPNET
TOPNOTCH
TOPNOTCHER
TOPO
TOPOALGIA
TOPODEME
TOPOGNOSIA
TOPOGNOSIS
TOPOGRAPH
TOPOGRAPHER
TOPOGRAPHIC
TOPOGRAPHICAL
TOPOGRAPHICS
TOPOGRAPHIES
TOPOGRAPHIST
TOPOGRAPHY
TOPOLATRY
TOPOLOGIC
TOPOLOGICAL
TOPOLOGY
TOPONARCOSIS
TOPONEURAL
TOPONEUROSIS
TOPONYM
TOPONYMAL
TOPONYMIC
TOPONYMICAL
TOPONYMICS
TOPONYMIES
TOPONYMY
TOPOPHOBIA
TOPOPHONE
TOPOPOLITAN
TOPOTACTIC
TOPOTAXIS
TOPOTYPE
TOPOTYPIC
TOPOTYPICAL
TOPPED
TOPPER
TOPPIECE
TOPPING

TOPPINGLY
TOPPINGNESS
TOPPLE
TOPPLED
TOPPLER
TOPPLING
TOPPLY
TOPPO
TOPPY
TOPRAIL
TOPROPE
TOPS
TOPSAIL
TOPSAILITE
TOPSIDE
TOPSMAN
TOPSMEN
TOPSOIL
TOPSTONE
TOPSWARM
TOPSYTURN
TOPT
TOPTAIL
TOPWORK
TOQUE
TOQUET
TOQUILLA
TOR
TORA
TORAH
TORAN
TORANA
TORBANITE
TORBANITIC
TORBERNITE
TORC
TORCEL
TORCH
TORCHBEARER
TORCHBEARING
TORCHER
TORCHERE
TORCHET
TORCHLIGHT
TORCHLIGHTED
TORCHLIKE
TORCHLIT
TORCHMAN
TORCHON
TORCHWOOD
TORCHWORT
TORCULAR
TORCULUS
TORDION
TORDRILLITE
TORE
TOREADOR
TORERO
TOREROS
TORET
TOREUTIC
TOREUTICS
TORFACEOUS
TORFEL
TORFLE
TORGOCH
TORI
TORIC
TORIES
TORII
TORIL
TORMA
TORMAE
TORMENT
TORMENTA
TORMENTATIVE
TORMENTED

TORMENTEDLY	TORREFIED	TORTURED	TOTALLY	TOUGH
TORMENTER	TORREFY	TORTUREDLY	TOTANINE	TOUGHEN
TORMENTIL	TORREFYING	TORTURER	TOTAQUINE	TOUGHENED
TORMENTILLA	TORRENT	TORTURING	TOTARA	TOUGHENER
TORMENTING	TORRENTFUL	TORTURINGLY	TOTE	TOUGHENING
TORMENTINGLY	TORRENTIAL	TORTUROUS	TOTED	TOUGHER
TORMENTIVE	TORRENTIALLY	TORTUROUSLY	TOTELOAD	TOUGHEST
TORMENTOR	TORRENTINE	TORU	TOTEM	TOUGHHEAD
TORMENTOUS	TORRENTUOUS	TORULA	TOTEMIC	TOUGHLY
TORMENTRY	TORRET	TORULACEOUS	TOTEMICALLY	TOUGHNESS
TORMENTUM	TORRID	TORULAE	TOTEMISM	TOUGHRA
TORMINA	TORRIDITY	TORULI	TOTEMIST	TOUGHT
TORMINAL	TORRIDLY	TORULIFORM	TOTEMISTIC	TOUMNAH
TORMINOUS	TORRIDNESS	TORULOID	TOTEMIZATION	TOUN
TORMODONT	TORRIFY	TORULOSE	TOTER	TOUP
TORN	TORRONE	TORULOSIS	TOTHER	TOUPEE
TORNADA	TORSADE	TORULOUS	TOTIENT	TOUPEED
TORNADE	TORSALO	TORULUS	TOTING	TOUPET
TORNADIC	TORSE	TORUS	TOTIPALMATE	TOUR
TORNADO	TORSEL	TORVID	TOTIPOTENCE	TOURACO
TORNADOES	TORSI	TORVITY	TOTIPOTENCY	TOURBE
TORNADOS	TORSIGRAPH	TORVOUS	TOTIPOTENT	TOURBILLON
TORNARIA	TORSILE	TORY	TOTITIVE	TOURED
TORNARIAE	TORSIOGRAM	TORYHILLITE	TOTO	TOURELLE
TORNARIAN	TORSIOGRAPH	TORYWEED	TOTOABA	TOURER
TORNESE	TORSION	TOSAPHIST	TOTORA	TOURET
TORNESI	TORSIONAL	TOSAPHOTH	TOTQUOT	TOURETTE
TORNILLA	TORSIONALLY	TOSCA	TOTTED	TOURING
TORNILLO	TORSIONING	TOSE	TOTTER	TOURISM
TORNOTE	TORSIVE	TOSH	TOTTERED	TOURIST
TORNUS	TORSK	TOSHAKHANA	TOTTERER	TOURISTIC
TORO	TORSKS	TOSHER	TOTTERGRASS	TOURISTICAL
TOROID	TORSO	TOSHERY	TOTTERING	TOURISTRY
TOROIDAL	TORSOCLUSION	TOSHLY	TOTTERINGLY	TOURISTY
TOROLILLO	TORSOS	TOSHNAIL	TOTTERISH	TOURMALIN
TORONJA	TORT	TOSHY	TOTTERY	TOURMALINE
TOROROKOMBU	TORTA	TOSIE	TOTTING	TOURMALINIC
TOROS	TORTAYS	TOSS	TOTTLE	TOURMALINIZE
TOROSE	TORTE	TOSSED	TOTTLISH	TOURMALITE
TOROSITY	TORTEAU	TOSSER	TOTTUM	TOURN
TOROTH	TORTEAUS	TOSSICATED	TOTTY	TOURNAI
TOROTORO	TORTEAUX	TOSSING	TOTTYHEAD	TOURNAMENT
TOROUS	TORTEN	TOSSINGLY	TOTUAVA	TOURNAMENTAL
TORP	TORTICOLLAR	TOSSMENT	TOTUM	TOURNASIN
TORPEDINEER	TORTICOLLIS	TOSSPOT	TOTY	TOURNAY
TORPEDINOUS	TORTICONE	TOSSUP	TOTYMAN	TOURNE
TORPEDO	TORTIE	TOSSUT	TOU	TOURNEE
TORPEDOED	TORTIL	TOSSY	TOUART	TOURNEL
TORPEDOER	TORTILE	TOST	TOUCAN	TOURNETTE
TORPEDOES	TORTILITY	TOSTADO	TOUCH	TOURNEUR
TORPEDOING	TORTILLA	TOSTAMENTE	TOUCHABLE	TOURNEY
TORPEDOIST	TORTILLAS	TOSTAO	TOUCHBACK	TOURNEYED
TORPEDOPLANE	TORTILLE	TOSTICATE	TOUCHBELL	TOURNEYER
TORPEDOS	TORTILLON	TOSTICATED	TOUCHBOX	TOURNEYING
TORPENT	TORTIOUS	TOSTICATING	TOUCHDOWN	TOURNEYS
TORPESCENCE	TORTIS	TOSTICATION	TOUCHE	TOURNIQUET
TORPESCENT	TORTIVE	TOSTO	TOUCHED	TOURNOIS
TORPEX	TORTOISE	TOSTON	TOUCHEDNESS	TOURNURE
TORPID	TORTOISES	TOSY	TOUCHER	TOURS
TORPIDITIES	TORTOISESHELL	TOSYL	TOUCHHOLE	TOURT
TORPIDITY	TORTONI	TOT	TOUCHIER	TOURTE
TORPIDLY	TORTOR	TOTA	TOUCHIEST	TOUSCHE
TORPIDNESS	TORTRICES	TOTAL	TOUCHILY	TOUSE
TORPIDS	TORTRICID	TOTALED	TOUCHINESS	TOUSEL
TORPIFIED	TORTRICINE	TOTALING	TOUCHING	TOUSER
TORPIFY	TORTRICOID	TOTALISATOR	TOUCHINGLY	TOUSLE
TORPIFYING	TORTRIX	TOTALITARIAN	TOUCHINGNESS	TOUSLED
TORPITUDE	TORTUE	TOTALITIES	TOUCHLINE	TOUSLING
TORPOR	TORTULA	TOTALITY	TOUCHMARK	TOUSLY
TORPORIFIC	TORTULACEOUS	TOTALIZATION	TOUCHOUS	TOUST
TORQUATE	TORTUOSITIES	TOTALIZATOR	TOUCHPAN	TOUSTIE
TORQUATED	TORTUOSITY	TOTALIZE	TOUCHPIECE	TOUSY
TORQUE	TORTUOUS	TOTALIZED	TOUCHSTONE	TOUT
TORQUED	TORTUOUSLY	TOTALIZER	TOUCHUP	TOUTE
TORQUES	TORTUOUSNESS	TOTALIZING	TOUCHWOOD	TOUTER
TORR	TORTURABLE	TOTALLED	TOUCHY	TOUZLE
TORREFACTION	TORTURE	TOTALLING	TOUG	TOVAR

TOVARIACEOUS	TOWNSITE	TOXOLYSIS	TRACHEATE	TRACTORISM
TOVARICH	TOWNSMAN	TOXON	TRACHEATION	TRACTORIST
TOVARISCH	TOWNSMEN	TOXONE	TRACHEID	TRACTORIZE
TOVARISH	TOWNSPEOPLE	TOXOPHIL	TRACHEIDAL	TRACTRICES
TOVE	TOWNSWOMAN	TOXOPHILE	TRACHEITIS	TRACTRIX
TOVET	TOWNSWOMEN	TOXOPHILISM	TRACHELAGRA	TRACTUS
TOW	TOWNWEAR	TOXOPHILITE	TRACHELATE	TRADAL
TOWAGE	TOWNY	TOXOPHILITIC	TRACHELISMUS	TRADE
TOWAI	TOWPATH	TOXOPHILOUS	TRACHELITIS	TRADECRAFT
TOWAN	TOWROPE	TOXOPHILY	TRACHELIUM	TRADED
TOWARD	TOWSE	TOXOTAE	TRACHELOTOMY	TRADEFUL
TOWARDLINESS	TOWSER	TOY	TRACHENCHYMA	TRADEMARK
TOWARDLY	TOWSON	TOYED	TRACHEOCELE	TRADEMASTER
TOWARDNESS	TOWSY	TOYER	TRACHEOLAR	TRADER
TOWARDS	TOWT	TOYFUL	TRACHEOLE	TRADES
TOWAWAY	TOWY	TOYFULNESS	TRACHEOPHONE	TRADESCANTIA
TOWBOAT	TOWZIE	TOYING	TRACHEOPHYTE	TRADESFOLK
TOWCOCK	TOX	TOYISH	TRACHEOSCOPY	TRADESMAN
TOWDIE	TOXA	TOYISHLY	TRACHEOTOMIES	TRADESMEN
TOWED	TOXAEMIA	TOYISHNESS	TRACHEOTOMY	TRADESPEOPLE
TOWEL	TOXAEMIAS	TOYLE	TRACHINOID	TRADESPERSON
TOWELED	TOXAEMIC	TOYMAN	TRACHITIS	TRADESWOMAN
TOWELETTE	TOXALBUMIC	TOYMEN	TRACHLE	TRADIMENT
TOWELING	TOXALBUMIN	TOYO	TRACHLED	TRADING
TOWELLED	TOXALBUMOSE	TOYON	TRACHLING	TRADITE
TOWELLING	TOXAMIN	TOYOS	TRACHODONT	TRADITION
TOWELRY	TOXANAEMIA	TOYSHOP	TRACHODONTID	TRADITIONAL
TOWER	TOXANEMIA	TOYSOME	TRACHOMA	TRADITIONARIES
TOWERED	TOXEMIA	TOYWORT	TRACHOMATOUS	TRADITIONARY
TOWERING	TOXEMIC	TOZE	TRACHYANDESITE	TRADITIONATE
TOWERINGLY	TOXIC	TOZEE	TRACHYBASALT	TRADITIONER
TOWERLET	TOXICAL	TOZER	TRACHYLINE	TRADITIONIST
TOWERLIKE	TOXICALLY	TOZIE	TRACHYPHONIA	TRADITIONS
TOWERMAN	TOXICANT	TRA	TRACHYTE	TRADITIVE
TOWERMEN	TOXICAROL	TRABACOLI	TRACHYTIC	TRADITOR
TOWERWORT	TOXICATE	TRABACOLO	TRACHYTOID	TRADITORES
TOWERY	TOXICATION	TRABACOLOS	TRACING	TRADUCE
TOWGHT	TOXICITIES	TRABAL	TRACK	TRADUCED
TOWHEAD	TOXICITY	TRABANT	TRACKABLE	TRADUCENT
TOWHEADED	TOXICOGENIC	TRABASCOLO	TRACKAGE	TRADUCER
TOWHEE	TOXICOGNATH	TRABEA	TRACKBARROW	TRADUCIAN
TOWING	TOXICOID	TRABEATE	TRACKED	TRADUCIANISM
TOWKAY	TOXICOLOGIC	TRABEATED	TRACKER	TRADUCIANIST
TOWLINE	TOXICOLOGIST	TRABEATION	TRACKHOUND	TRADUCIBLE
TOWMAST	TOXICOLOGY	TRABECULA	TRACKING	TRADUCING
TOWMOND	TOXICOMANIA	TRABECULAE	TRACKLAYER	TRADUCINGLY
TOWMONT	TOXICON	TRABECULAR	TRACKLESS	TRADUCT
TOWN	TOXICOPATHIC	TRABECULATE	TRACKLESSLY	TRADUCTION
TOWNED	TOXICOPATHY	TRABECULATED	TRACKMAN	TRADY
TOWNEE	TOXICOPHAGY	TRABECULE	TRACKMASTER	TRAFFIC
TOWNER	TOXICOPHIDIA	TRABES	TRACKMEN	TRAFFICABLE
TOWNET	TOXICOSES	TRABU	TRACKPOT	TRAFFICKED
TOWNFARING	TOXICOSIS	TRABUCH	TRACKSHIFTER	TRAFFICKER
TOWNFOLK	TOXICUM	TRABUCHO	TRACKSICK	TRAFFICKING
TOWNFOLKS	TOXIDERMIC	TRABUCO	TRACKSIDE	TRAFFICS
TOWNGATE	TOXIFER	TRABUCOS	TRACKWALKER	TRAFFICWAY
TOWNHOUSE	TOXIFEROUS	TRACASSERIE	TRACKWAY	TRAG
TOWNIE	TOXIFY	TRACASSERIES	TRACT	TRAGACANTH
TOWNIES	TOXIGENIC	TRACE	TRACTABILITIES	TRAGACANTHA
TOWNIFIED	TOXIN	TRACEABILITY	TRACTABILITY	TRAGACANTHIN
TOWNIFY	TOXINAEMIA	TRACEABLE	TRACTABLE	TRAGICOLORED
TOWNIFYING	TOXINE	TRACEABLY	TRACTABLY	TRAGICOMEDY
TOWNINESS	TOXINEMIA	TRACED	TRACTARIAN	TRAGICOMIC
TOWNISH	TOXINFECTION	TRACER	TRACTATE	TRAGICOMICAL
TOWNISHLY	TOXINOSIS	TRACERIED	TRACTATION	TRAGION
TOWNISHNESS	TOXIPHAGI	TRACERIES	TRACTATOR	TRAGOEDIA
TOWNIST	TOXIPHAGUS	TRACERY	TRACTELLATE	TRAGOPAN
TOWNLAND	TOXIPHOBIA	TRACHEA	TRACTELLUM	TRAGULE
TOWNLET	TOXIPHOBIAC	TRACHEAE	TRACTIFEROUS	TRAGUS
TOWNLIKE	TOXIPHORIC	TRACHEAL	TRACTILE	TRAH
TOWNLING	TOXITABELLAE	TRACHEALGIA	TRACTILITY	TRAHEEN
TOWNLY	TOXITY	TRACHEALIS	TRACTION	TRAHISON
TOWNMAN	TOXODONT	TRACHEAN	TRACTIONAL	TRAIK
TOWNMEN	TOXOGENESIS	TRACHEARIAN	TRACTITIAN	TRAIKY
TOWNSBOY	TOXOGLOSSATE	TRACHEARY	TRACTIVE	TRAIL
TOWNSFELLOW	TOXOID	TRACHEAS	TRACTOR	TRAILBASTON
TOWNSHIP	TOXOLOGY		TRACTORATION	TRAILBLAZER

TRAILBLAZING	TRAMMER	TRANSCENDENT	TRANSIENCY	TRANSMUTUAL
TRAILED	TRAMMING	TRANSCENDENTAL	TRANSIENT	TRANSNATURAL
TRAILER	TRAMMON	TRANSCENDING	TRANSIENTLY	TRANSNORMAL
TRAILERY	TRAMONTANA	TRANSCENSION	TRANSIGENCE	TRANSOCEANIC
TRAILING	TRAMONTANE	TRANSCOLOR	TRANSIGENT	TRANSOM
TRAILINGLY	TRAMP	TRANSCREATE	TRANSILIAC	TRANSOMED
TRAILMAN	TRAMPCOCK	TRANSCRIBBLE	TRANSILIENCE	TRANSONIC
TRAILSMAN	TRAMPED	TRANSCRIBE	TRANSILIENCY	TRANSPACIFIC
TRAILSMEN	TRAMPER	TRANSCRIBED	TRANSILIENT	TRANSPADANE
TRAILWAY	TRAMPING	TRANSCRIBER	TRANSIRE	TRANSPARENCE
TRAILY	TRAMPLE	TRANSCRIBING	TRANSISCHIAC	TRANSPARENCIES
TRAIN	TRAMPLED	TRANSCRIPT	TRANSISTOR	TRANSPARENCY
TRAINABLE	TRAMPLER	TRANSCUR	TRANSIT	TRANSPARENT
TRAINAGE	TRAMPLING	TRANSCURRENT	TRANSITABLE	TRANSPASS
TRAINAGRAPH	TRAMPOLIN	TRANSDIALECT	TRANSITER	TRANSPECIATE
TRAINANT	TRAMPOLINE	TRANSDIURNAL	TRANSITION	TRANSPICUITY
TRAINANTE	TRAMPOOSE	TRANSDUCER	TRANSITIONAL	TRANSPICUOUS
TRAINBAND	TRAMPOSO	TRANSDUCTION	TRANSITIVE	TRANSPIERCE
TRAINBEARER	TRAMPOT	TRANSECT	TRANSITIVELY	TRANSPIERCED
TRAINBOLT	TRAMPS	TRANSECTED	TRANSITIVISM	TRANSPIERCING
TRAINBOY	TRAMROAD	TRANSECTING	TRANSITIVITIES	TRANSPIRE
TRAINEAU	TRAMS	TRANSECTION	TRANSITIVITY	TRANSPIRED
TRAINED	TRAMWAY	TRANSELEMENT	TRANSITMAN	TRANSPIRING
TRAINEE	TRAMWAYMAN	TRANSENNA	TRANSITMEN	TRANSPLACE
TRAINEL	TRAMWAYMEN	TRANSENNAE	TRANSITORILY	TRANSPLANT
TRAINER	TRANCE	TRANSEPT	TRANSITORINESS	TRANSPLANTED
TRAINFUL	TRANCED	TRANSEPTAL	TRANSITORY	TRANSPLANTER
TRAINING	TRANCEDLY	TRANSEPTALLY	TRANSITUS	TRANSPLANTING
TRAINLOAD	TRANCHANT	TRANSEUNT	TRANSLADE	TRANSPONDER
TRAINMAN	TRANCHANTE	TRANSFER	TRANSLATABLE	TRANSPONIBLE
TRAINMASTER	TRANCHE	TRANSFERABLE	TRANSLATE	TRANSPONTINE
TRAINMEN	TRANCHEFER	TRANSFERAL	TRANSLATED	TRANSPORT
TRAINS	TRANCHET	TRANSFEREE	TRANSLATING	TRANSPORTAL
TRAINSTER	TRANCHOIR	TRANSFERENCE	TRANSLATION	TRANSPORTATION
TRAINWAY	TRANCING	TRANSFERENT	TRANSLATIVE	TRANSPORTED
TRAINY	TRANEEN	TRANSFEROR	TRANSLATOR	TRANSPORTER
TRAIPSE	TRANGAM	TRANSFERRAL	TRANSLATORY	TRANSPORTING
TRAIPSED	TRANI	TRANSFERRED	TRANSLAY	TRANSPORTIVE
TRAIPSING	TRANK	TRANSFERRER	TRANSLEITHAN	TRANSPOSABLE
TRAIST	TRANKA	TRANSFERRING	TRANSLOCATE	TRANSPOSE
TRAIT	TRANKER	TRANSFIGURE	TRANSLOCATED	TRANSPOSED
TRAITEUR	TRANKUM	TRANSFIGURED	TRANSLOCATING	TRANSPOSER
TRAITEURS	TRANKY	TRANSFIGURING ·	TRANSLUCE	TRANSPOSING
TRAITOR	TRANQUIL	TRANSFINITE	TRANSLUCENCE	TRANSPOSITION
TRAITOROUS	TRANQUILER	TRANSFIX	TRANSLUCENCY	TRANSPOSITOR
TRAITOROUSLY	TRANQUILEST	TRANSFIXED	TRANSLUCENT	TRANSPRINT
TRAITORY	TRANQUILITY	TRANSFIXING	TRANSLUCID	TRANSPROSE
TRAITRESS	TRANQUILIZE	TRANSFIXION	TRANSLUNAR	TRANSPROSER
TRAITS	TRANQUILIZER	TRANSFIXTURE	TRANSLUNARY	TRANSPYLORIC
TRAJECT	TRANQUILIZING	TRANSFLUENT	TRANSMAKE	TRANSRHENANE
TRAJECTED	TRANQUILLER	TRANSFLUX	TRANSMARINE	TRANSSHAPE
TRAJECTILE	TRANQUILLEST	TRANSFORM	TRANSMEDIAN	TRANSSHAPED
TRAJECTING	TRANQUILLISE	TRANSFORMATION	TRANSMEW	TRANSSHAPING
TRAJECTION	TRANQUILLITY	TRANSFORMED	TRANSMIGRANT	TRANSSHIP
TRAJECTORIES	TRANQUILLIZE	TRANSFORMER	TRANSMIGRATE	TRANSSHIPPED
TRAJECTORY	TRANQUILLIZED	TRANSFORMING	TRANSMIGRATED	TRANSSHIPPING
TRAJET	TRANQUILLO	TRANSFORMISM	TRANSMIGRATING	TRANSUBSTANTIATION
TRALATITION	TRANQUILLY	TRANSFORMIST	TRANSMIGRATION	TRANSUDATE
TRALATITIOUS	TRANQUILNESS	TRANSFUGE	TRANSMISSION	TRANSUDATION
TRALIRA	TRANS	TRANSFUSE	TRANSMISSIVE	TRANSUDATIVE
TRAM	TRANSACT	TRANSFUSED	TRANSMISSORY	TRANSUDATORY
TRAMA	TRANSACTED	TRANSFUSER	TRANSMIT	TRANSUDE
TRAMAL	TRANSACTING	TRANSFUSING	TRANSMITTAL	TRANSUDED
TRAMCAR	TRANSACTION	TRANSFUSION	TRANSMITTED	TRANSUDING
TRAME	TRANSACTOR	TRANSFUSIVE	TRANSMITTER	TRANSUME
TRAMFUL	TRANSALPINE	TRANSGRESS	TRANSMITTING	TRANSUMED
TRAMLINE	TRANSANNULAR	TRANSGRESSED	TRANSMOGRIFIED	TRANSUMING
TRAMMED	TRANSAPICAL	TRANSGRESSING	TRANSMOGRIFY	TRANSUMPT
TRAMMEL	TRANSAUDIENT	TRANSGRESSION	TRANSMOGRIFYING	TRANSUMPTION
TRAMMELED	TRANSBAIKAL	TRANSGRESSOR	TRANSMONTANE	TRANSUMPTIVE
TRAMMELER	TRANSBOARD	TRANSHAPE	TRANSMUE	TRANSURANIAN
TRAMMELHEAD	TRANSBORDER	TRANSHIP	TRANSMUTATE	TRANSURANIC
TRAMMELING	TRANSCALENCY	TRANSHIPMENT	TRANSMUTATION	TRANSVAAL
TRAMMELINGLY	TRANSCALENT	TRANSHUMAN	TRANSMUTE	TRANSVALUE
TRAMMELLED	TRANSCEIVER	TRANSHUMANCE	TRANSMUTED	TRANSVALUED
TRAMMELLER	TRANSCEND	TRANSHUMANT	TRANSMUTER	TRANSVALUING
TRAMMELLING ·	TRANSCENDED	TRANSIENCE	TRANSMUTING	TRANSVASE

TRANSVECTANT	TRASHY	TREACHEROUS	TREELING	TRENCHANT
TRANSVECTION	TRASS	TREACHERY	TREEMAKER	TRENCHANTLY
TRANSVENOM	TRASY	TREACLE	TREEMAKING	TRENCHED
TRANSVERBATE	TRATLER	TREACLEWORT	TREEMAN	TRENCHER
TRANSVERSAL	TRATTLE	TREACLINESS	TREEN	TRENCHERING
TRANSVERSALE	TRATTORIA	TREACLY	TREENAIL	TRENCHERMAN
TRANSVERSAN	TRAUCHLE	TREAD	TREES	TRENCHERMEN
TRANSVERSARY	TRAULISM	TREADBOARD	TREESPEELER	TRENCHES
TRANSVERSE	TRAUMA	TREADER	TREETISE	TRENCHING
TRANSVERSELY	TRAUMAS	TREADING	TREETOP	TRENCHLIKE
TRANSVERSER	TRAUMATA	TREADLE	TREEY	TRENCHMASTER
TRANSVERSION	TRAUMATIC	TREADLED	TREF	TRENCHMORE
TRANSVERSIVE	TRAUMATICIN	TREADLER	TREFA	TREND
TRANSVERSUM	TRAUMATICINE	TREADLING	TREFGORDD	TRENDED
TRANSVERSUS	TRAUMATISM	TREADMILL	TREFLE	TRENDEL
TRANSVERT	TRAUMATIZE	TREADWHEEL	TREFLEE	TRENDING
TRANSVERTER	TRAUMATOLOGY	TREAGUE	TREFOIL	TRENDLE
TRANSVEST	TRAUMATOPNEA	TREASON	TREFOILED	TRENDY
TRANSVESTISM	TRAUMATOSIS	TREASONABLE	TREGET	TRENE
TRANSVESTITE	TRAUMATROPIC	TREASONABLY	TREGETOUR	TRENTAL
TRANSWRITTEN	TRAVADO	TREASONIST	TREHALA	TREPAN
TRANT	TRAVAIL	TREASONOUS	TREHALASE	TREPANATION
TRANTER	TRAVAILED	TREASURABLE	TREHALOSE	TREPANG
TRANTLUM	TRAVAILER	TREASURE	TREILLAGE	TREPANNED
TRANVIA	TRAVAILING	TREASURED	TREITOUR	TREPANNER
TRAP	TRAVAILS	TREASURER	TREITRE	TREPANNING
TRAPAN	TRAVALE	TREASURIES	TREK	TREPANNINGLY
TRAPANNER	TRAVALLY	TREASURING	TREKBOER	TREPHINATION
TRAPBALL	TRAVATED	TREASUROUS	TREKKED	TREPHINE
TRAPDOOR	TRAVE	TREASURY	TREKKER	TREPHINED
TRAPES	TRAVEL	TREASURYSHIP	TREKKING	TREPHINER
TRAPEZE	TRAVELED	TREAT	TREKOMETER	TREPHINING
TRAPEZIA	TRAVELER	TREATABLE	TREKPATH	TREPHONE
TRAPEZIAL	TRAVELERS	TREATABLY	TRELLIS	TREPID
TRAPEZIAN	TRAVELING	TREATED	TRELLISED	TREPIDANCY
TRAPEZIFORM	TRAVELLED	TREATEE	TRELLISES	TREPIDANT
TRAPEZING	TRAVELLER	TREATER	TRELLISING	TREPIDATE
TRAPEZIST	TRAVELLING	TREATIES	TRELLISWORK	TREPIDATION
TRAPEZIUM	TRAVELOG	TREATING	TREMATODE	TREPIDATORY
TRAPEZIUMS	TRAVELOGUE	TREATISE	TREMATOID	TREPIDITY
TRAPEZIUS	TRAVELOGUER	TREATISER	TREMBLE	TREPIDLY
TRAPEZOID	TRAVELS	TREATMENT	TREMBLED	TREPIDNESS
TRAPEZOIDAL	TRAVERSABLE	TREATOR	TREMBLEMENT	TREPONEME
TRAPFALL	TRAVERSAL	TREATY	TREMBLER	TREPPE
TRAPHOLE	TRAVERSARY	TREATYIST	TREMBLING	TRES
TRAPICHE	TRAVERSE	TREATYITE	TREMBLINGLY	TRESAIEL
TRAPIFEROUS	TRAVERSED	TREBLE	TREMBLY	TRESANCE
TRAPISH	TRAVERSER	TREBLED	TREMELINE	TRESCHE
TRAPLIGHT	TRAVERSING	TREBLENESS	TREMELLIFORM	TRESILLO
TRAPPEAN	TRAVERSION	TREBLET	TREMELLOID	TRESIS
TRAPPED	TRAVERTIN	TREBLETREE	TREMELLOSE	TRESPASS
TRAPPER	TRAVERTINE	TREBLING	TREMENDOUS	TRESPASSAGE
TRAPPING	TRAVEST	TREBLY	TREMENDOUSLY	TRESPASSED
TRAPPINGLY	TRAVESTIED	TREBUCHET	TREMETOL	TRESPASSER
TRAPPINGS	TRAVESTIER	TREBUCKET	TREMEX	TRESPASSING
TRAPPIST	TRAVESTIES	TRECENTIST	TREMIE	TRESPASSORY
TRAPPOID	TRAVESTY	TRECENTO	TREMOLANDO	TRESS
TRAPPOSE	TRAVESTYING	TRECHMANNITE	TREMOLANT	TRESSED
TRAPPOUS	TRAVIS	TRECK	TREMOLIST	TRESSILATE
TRAPPY	TRAVISS	TRECKPOT	TREMOLITE	TRESSILATION
TRAPROCK	TRAVOIS	TRECKSCHUYT	TREMOLITIC	TRESSON
TRAPS	TRAVOISE	TREDDLE	TREMOLO	TRESSOUR
TRAPSHOOT	TRAVOISES	TREDECILE	TREMOLOS	TRESSURE
TRAPSHOOTER	TRAVOY	TREDEFOWEL	TREMOLOSO	TRESSURED
TRAPSHOOTING	TRAWL	TREDILLE	TREMOR	TRESSY
TRAPSTICK	TRAWLBOAT	TREDRILLE	TREMPLIN	TREST
TRAPT	TRAWLED	TREE	TREMULANDO	TRESTLE
TRASH	TRAWLER	TREEBEARD	TREMULANT	TRESTLETREE
TRASHED	TRAWLERMAN	TREEBINE	TREMULATE	TRESTLEWORK
TRASHERY	TRAWLERMEN	TREED	TREMULATION	TRESTLING
TRASHIER	TRAWLEY	TREEFISH	TREMULENT	TRET
TRASHIEST	TRAWLING	TREEFISHES	TREMULOUS	TRETIS
TRASHIFY	TRAWLNET	TREEHAIR	TREMULOUSLY	TREVALLY
TRASHILY	TRAY	TREEING	TREN	TREVET
TRASHINESS	TRAYNE	TREELESS	TRENAIL	TREVIS
TRASHING	TREACHER	TREELET	TRENCH	TREW
TRASHTRIE	TREACHERIES	TREELIKE	TRENCHANCY	TREWAGE

TREWEL	TRIAZIN	TRICHEVRON	TRICKED	TRICYCLER
TREWS	TRIAZINE	TRICHI	TRICKER	TRICYCLIC
TREWSMAN	TRIAZO	TRICHIA	TRICKERIES	TRICYCLING
TREWSMEN	TRIAZOLE	TRICHIASIS	TRICKERY	TRICYCLIST
TREY	TRIBADE	TRICHINA	TRICKIER	TRIDACTYL
TRIABLE	TRIBADISM	TRICHINAE	TRICKIEST	TRIDAILY
TRIABLENESS	TRIBADY	TRICHINAL	TRICKILY	TRIDDLER
TRIACETATE	TRIBAL	TRICHINIZE	TRICKINESS	TRIDECANE
TRIACHENIUM	TRIBALISM	TRICHINIZED	TRICKING	TRIDECENE
TRIACID	TRIBALIST	TRICHINIZING	TRICKINGLY	TRIDECOIC
TRIACONTANE	TRIBALLY	TRICHINOPOLY	TRICKISH	TRIDECYL
TRIACONTER	TRIBASE	TRICHINOSIS	TRICKISHLY	TRIDECYLENE
TRIACT	TRIBASIC	TRICHINOTIC	TRICKISHNESS	TRIDENT
TRIACTINAL	TRIBBLE	TRICHINOUS	TRICKLE	TRIDENTAL
TRIACTINE	TRIBE	TRICHION	TRICKLED	TRIDENTATE
TRIAD	TRIBELESS	TRICHITE	TRICKLESS	TRIDENTATED
TRIADELPHOUS	TRIBESMAN	TRICHITIC	TRICKLET	TRIDERMIC
TRIADIC	TRIBESMEN	TRICHITIS	TRICKLING	TRIDIAPASON
TRIADICAL	TRIBESPEOPLE	TRICHIURID	TRICKLINGLY	TRIDIGITATE
TRIADICALLY	TRIBLET	TRICHIUROID	TRICKLY	TRIDIURNAL
TRIADISM	TRIBOMETER	TRICHLORID	TRICKMENT	TRIDOMINIUM
TRIADIST	TRIBOROUGH	TRICHLORIDE	TRICKS	TRIDRACHM
TRIAENE	TRIBRACH	TRICHLORO	TRICKSIER	TRIDUAN
TRIAENOSE	TRIBRACHIAL	TRICHOBLAST	TRICKSIEST	TRIDUUM
TRIAGE	TRIBRACHIC	TRICHOCLASIS	TRICKSINESS	TRIDYMITE
TRIAGONAL	TRIBRACTEATE	TRICHOCYST	TRICKSOME	TRIDYNAMOUS
TRIAKID	TRIBROMID	TRICHOCYSTIC	TRICKSTER	TRIECIOUS
TRIAL	TRIBROMIDE	TRICHODE	TRICKSTERING	TRIECIOUSLY
TRIALATE	TRIBROMOETHANOL	TRICHOGEN	TRICKSY	TRIED
TRIALISM	TRIBUAL	TRICHOGENOUS	TRICKTRACK	TRIELAIDIN
TRIALIST	TRIBUALLY	TRICHOGYNE	TRICKY	TRIENE
TRIALITY	TRIBULAR	TRICHOGYNIAL	TRICLAD	TRIENNIA
TRIALOGUE	TRIBULATE	TRICHOGYNIC	TRICLINATE	TRIENNIAL
TRIAMID	TRIBULATION	TRICHOID	TRICLINIA	TRIENNIALITY
TRIAMIDE	TRIBULOID	TRICHOLOGIST	TRICLINIARCH	TRIENNIALLY
TRIAMIN	TRIBUNA	TRICHOLOGY	TRICLINIARY	TRIENNIUM
TRIAMINE	TRIBUNAL	TRICHOMA	TRICLINIC	TRIENNIUMS
TRIAMINO	TRIBUNARY	TRICHOMATOSE	TRICLINIUM	TRIENS
TRIAMMONIUM	TRIBUNATE	TRICHOME	TRICOCCOUS	TRIENTAL
TRIAMORPH	TRIBUNE	TRICHOMIC	TRICOLETTE	TRIENTES
TRIAMORPHOUS	TRIBUNESHIP	TRICHOMONAD	TRICOLIC	TRIER
TRIAMYLOSE	TRIBUNICIAL	TRICHOMONIASIS	TRICOLON	TRIERARCH
TRIANDER	TRIBUNICIAN	TRICHONOSIS	TRICOLOR	TRIERARCHAL
TRIANDRIAN	TRIBUNITIAL	TRICHONOSUS	TRICOLORED	TRIERARCHIES
TRIANDROUS	TRIBUNITIAN	TRICHOPATHIC	TRICOLOUR	TRIERARCHY
TRIANGLE	TRIBUNITIVE	TRICHOPATHY	TRICON	TRIES
TRIANGLED	TRIBUTABLE	TRICHOPHORE	TRICONCH	TRIETERIC
TRIANGLER	TRIBUTARIES	TRICHOPHORIC	TRICONODONT	TRIETERICS
TRIANGULAR	TRIBUTARILY	TRICHOPHYTE	TRICONODONTY	TRIETHYL
TRIANGULARIS	TRIBUTARY	TRICHOPHYTIC	TRICORN	TRIFACIAL
TRIANGULARLY	TRIBUTE	TRICHOPORE	TRICORNE	TRIFARIOUS
TRIANGULATE	TRIBUTED	TRICHOPTER	TRICORNERED	TRIFEROUS
TRIANGULATED	TRIBUTER	TRICHOPTERA	TRICORNUTE	TRIFID
TRIANGULATING	TRIBUTING	TRICHOPTERAN	TRICORPORAL	TRIFISTULARY
TRIANGULATOR	TRIBUTORIAN	TRICHOPTERON	TRICORPORATE	TRIFLE
TRIANGULOID	TRICA	TRICHORD	TRICORYPHEAN	TRIFLED
TRIANNUAL	TRICAE	TRICHOSIS	TRICOSANE	TRIFLER
TRIANNULATE	TRICALCIUM	TRICHOTOMIC	TRICOSANONE	TRIFLES
TRIANON	TRICAR	TRICHOTOMIES	TRICOSTATE	TRIFLET
TRIANTHOUS	TRICARBIMIDE	TRICHOTOMIST	TRICOSYLIC	TRIFLING
TRIAPSIDAL	TRICARBON	TRICHOTOMIZE	TRICOT	TRIFLINGLY
TRIARCH	TRICE	TRICHOTOMOUS	TRICOTEE	TRIFLINGNESS
TRIARCHATE	TRICED	TRICHROIC	TRICOTINE	TRIFLORAL
TRIARCHIES	TRICENARIES	TRICHROISM	TRICOUNI	TRIFLORATE
TRIARCHY	TRICENARIUM	TRICHROMAT	TRICRESOL	TRIFLOROUS
TRIARIAN	TRICENARY	TRICHROMATE	TRICROTIC	TRIFLUORIDE
TRIARII	TRICENNIAL	TRICHROMATIC	TRICROTISM	TRIFOCAL
TRIARY	TRICEPHAL	TRICHROME	TRICROTOUS	TRIFOIL
TRIASTER	TRICEPHALOUS	TRICHROMIC	TRICURVATE	TRIFOLD
TRIATIC	TRICEPHALUS	TRICHRONOUS	TRICUSPID	TRIFOLIATE
TRIATOMIC	TRICEPS	TRICHURIASIS	TRICUSPIDAL	TRIFOLIATED
TRIATOMICITY	TRICEPSES	TRICHY	TRICUSPIDATE	TRIFOLIOLATE
TRIAXAL	TRICERATOPS	TRICING	TRICUSSATE	TRIFOLIOSIS
TRIAXIAL	TRICERIA	TRICINIUM	TRICYANIDE	TRIFOLIUM
TRIAXON	TRICERION	TRICIPITAL	TRICYCLE	TRIFOLY
TRIAXONIAN	TRICHAUXIS	TRICIRCULAR	TRICYCLED	TRIFORIA
TRIAZANE	TRICHECHINE	TRICK	TRICYCLENE	TRIFORIAL

TRIFORIUM
TRIFORM
TRIFORMED
TRIFORMITY
TRIFURCATE
TRIFURCATED
TRIFURCATION
TRIG
TRIGA
TRIGAMIST
TRIGAMOUS
TRIGAMY
TRIGEMINAL
TRIGEMINI
TRIGEMINOUS
TRIGEMINUS
TRIGENERIC
TRIGESIMAL
TRIGGED
TRIGGER
TRIGGERED
TRIGGERFISH
TRIGGERFISHES
TRIGGING
TRIGINTAL
TRIGLANDULAR
TRIGLID
TRIGLOT
TRIGLYPH
TRIGLYPHAL
TRIGLYPHED
TRIGLYPHIC
TRIGLYPHICAL
TRIGNESS
TRIGO
TRIGON
TRIGONAL
TRIGONALLY
TRIGONE
TRIGONELLIN
TRIGONELLINE
TRIGONEUTIC
TRIGONEUTISM
TRIGONIACEAN
TRIGONIC
TRIGONID
TRIGONITE
TRIGONITIS
TRIGONOID
TRIGONOMETER
TRIGONOMETRIES
TRIGONOMETRY
TRIGONON
TRIGONOTYPE
TRIGONOUS
TRIGRAM
TRIGRAMMATIC
TRIGRAPH
TRIGRAPHIC
TRIGYN
TRIGYNIAN
TRIGYNOUS
TRIHALID
TRIHALIDE
TRIHEDRA
TRIHEDRAL
TRIHEDRON
TRIHEDRONS
TRIHEMERAL
TRIHEMIMER
TRIHEMIMERAL
TRIHEMIMERIS
TRIHORAL
TRIHOURLY
TRIHYBRID
TRIHYDRATE
TRIHYDRATED

TRIHYDRIC
TRIHYDRIDE
TRIHYDROXY
TRIJUGATE
TRIJUGOUS
TRIKAYA
TRIKE
TRIKER
TRIKERIA
TRIKERION
TRIKETO
TRIKETONE
TRIKIR
TRILABE
TRILABIATE
TRILAMINAR
TRILATERAL
TRILATERALLY
TRILBIES
TRILEMMA
TRILINEAR
TRILINGUAL
TRILINGUAR
TRILINOLENIN
TRILITERAL
TRILITH
TRILITHIC
TRILITHON
TRILL
TRILLACHAN
TRILLADO
TRILLANDO
TRILLED
TRILLET
TRILLETTO
TRILLI
TRILLIACEOUS
TRILLIBUB
TRILLIIN
TRILLIL
TRILLING
TRILLION
TRILLIONAIRE
TRILLIONIZE
TRILLIONTH
TRILLIUM
TRILLO
TRILLOES
TRILOBAL
TRILOBATE
TRILOBATED
TRILOBATION
TRILOBE
TRILOBED
TRILOBITE
TRILOBITIC
TRILOCULAR
TRILOCULATE
TRILOGIC
TRILOGICAL
TRILOGIES
TRILOGIST
TRILOGY
TRILOPHODONT
TRILUMINAR
TRILUMINOUS
TRIM
TRIMACER
TRIMACULAR
TRIMACULATE
TRIMACULATED
TRIMASTIGATE
TRIME
TRIMELLIC
TRIMELLITIC
TRIMEMBRAL
TRIMENSUAL

TRIMER
TRIMERIC
TRIMERITE
TRIMEROUS
TRIMESIC
TRIMESITIC
TRIMESTER
TRIMESTRAL
TRIMESTRIAL
TRIMESYL
TRIMETALLIC
TRIMETALLISM
TRIMETER
TRIMETHOXY
TRIMETHYL
TRIMETHYLENE
TRIMETRIC
TRIMETRICAL
TRIMETROGON
TRIMLY
TRIMMED
TRIMMER
TRIMMERS
TRIMMEST
TRIMMING
TRIMNESS
TRIMOLECULAR
TRIMONTHLY
TRIMORIC
TRIMORPH
TRIMORPHIC
TRIMORPHISM
TRIMORPHOUS
TRIMSTONE
TRIMTRAM
TRIN
TRINAL
TRINALITY
TRINALIZE
TRINARY
TRINCHERA
TRINDLE
TRINE
TRINED
TRINELY
TRINEURAL
TRINGINE
TRINGLE
TRINGOID
TRINIDADO
TRINING
TRINITIES
TRINITRATE
TRINITRATION
TRINITRID
TRINITRIDE
TRINITRO
TRINITROTOLUENE
TRINITY
TRINK
TRINKERMAN
TRINKERMEN
TRINKET
TRINKETRIES
TRINKETRY
TRINKETY
TRINKLE
TRINKLET
TRINKUMS
TRINOCTIAL
TRINOCTILE
TRINODAL
TRINODE
TRINODINE
TRINOMIAL
TRINOMIALISM
TRINOMIALIST

TRINOMIALITY
TRINOMIALLY
TRINOPTICON
TRINQ
TRINTLE
TRINUCLEATE
TRINUNITY
TRIO
TRIOBOL
TRIOBOLON
TRIOCTILE
TRIODE
TRIODIA
TRIODION
TRIODONTOID
TRIOECIOUS
TRIOECIOUSLY
TRIOECISM
TRIOICOUS
TRIOLE
TRIOLEFIN
TRIOLEFINE
TRIOLET
TRIONFI
TRIONFO
TRIONYCHID
TRIONYCHOID
TRIONYM
TRIONYMAL
TRIOR
TRIORCHIS
TRIOS
TRIOSE
TRIOVULATE
TRIOXID
TRIOXIDE
TRIOZONID
TRIOZONIDE
TRIP
TRIPAL
TRIPALEOLATE
TRIPALMITATE
TRIPALMITIN
TRIPARA
TRIPART
TRIPARTED
TRIPARTEDLY
TRIPARTIBLE
TRIPARTIENT
TRIPARTITE
TRIPARTITELY
TRIPARTITION
TRIPASCHAL
TRIPE
TRIPEDAL
TRIPEL
TRIPEMAN
TRIPEMONGER
TRIPENNATE
TRIPENNY
TRIPERIES
TRIPERSONAL
TRIPERY
TRIPESHOP
TRIPESTONE
TRIPETALOID
TRIPETALOUS
TRIPEWIFE
TRIPEWOMAN
TRIPHAMMER
TRIPHANE
TRIPHASE
TRIPHENYL
TRIPHONY
TRIPHTHONG
TRIPHTHONGAL
TRIPHYLINE

TRIPHYLITE
TRIPHYLLOUS
TRIPINNATE
TRIPINNATED
TRIPINNATELY
TRIPLA
TRIPLANE
TRIPLASIAN
TRIPLASIC
TRIPLE
TRIPLEBACK
TRIPLED
TRIPLEFOLD
TRIPLEGIA
TRIPLET
TRIPLETAIL
TRIPLETREE
TRIPLEX
TRIPLEXITY
TRIPLICATE
TRIPLICATED
TRIPLICATELY
TRIPLICATING
TRIPLICATION
TRIPLICATIVE
TRIPLICATURE
TRIPLICE
TRIPLICITIES
TRIPLICITY
TRIPLING
TRIPLITE
TRIPLOID
TRIPLOIDIC
TRIPLOIDITE
TRIPLOIDY
TRIPLOPIA
TRIPLUM
TRIPLUMBIC
TRIPLY
TRIPOD
TRIPODAL
TRIPODIAL
TRIPODIAN
TRIPODIC
TRIPODIES
TRIPODY
TRIPOINTED
TRIPOLAR
TRIPOLI
TRIPOS
TRIPOSES
TRIPOT
TRIPOTAGE
TRIPOTER
TRIPPANT
TRIPPED
TRIPPER
TRIPPET
TRIPPING
TRIPPINGLY
TRIPPINGNESS
TRIPPLE
TRIPPLER
TRIPSILL
TRIPSIS
TRIPSOME
TRIPSOMELY
TRIPT
TRIPTANE
TRIPTEROUS
TRIPTOTE
TRIPTYCA
TRIPTYCH
TRIPTYQUE
TRIPUDIA
TRIPUDIAL
TRIPUDIANT

TRIPUDIARY	TRISULCATE	TRIUMPHATOR	TROCHISCI	TROMBIDIASIS
TRIPUDIATE	TRISULCATED	TRIUMPHED	TROCHISCUS	TROMBONE
TRIPUDIATION	TRISULFATE	TRIUMPHER	TROCHITE	TROMBONIST
TRIPUDIST	TRISULFID	TRIUMPHING	TROCHITIC	TROMBONY
TRIPUDIUM	TRISULFIDE	TRIUMVIR	TROCHLEA	TROMMEL
TRIPY	TRISULFONE	TRIUMVIRAL	TROCHLEAE	TROMOMETER
TRIPYLAEAN	TRISULFOXID	TRIUMVIRATE	TROCHLEAR	TROMOMETRIC
TRIPYLARIAN	TRISULFOXIDE	TRIUMVIRI	TROCHLEARIS	TROMOMETRY
TRIPYLEAN	TRISULPHATE	TRIUMVIRS	TROCHLEARY	TROMP
TRIPYRENOUS	TRISULPHID	TRIUMVIRSHIP	TROCHLEATE	TROMPE
TRIQUET	TRISULPHIDE	TRIUNE	TROCHLEIFORM	TROMPIL
TRIQUETRA	TRISULPHONE	TRIUNGULIN	TROCHOID	TROMPILLO
TRIQUETRAL	TRISULPHONIC	TRIUNITARIAN	TROCHOIDAL	TRON
TRIQUETRIC	TRISULPHOXID	TRIUNITIES	TROCHOIDALLY	TRONA
TRIQUETROUS	TRISYLLABIC	TRIUNITY	TROCHOIDES	TRONADOR
TRIQUETRUM	TRISYLLABISM	TRIURID	TROCHOMETER	TRONAGE
TRIQUINATE	TRISYLLABLE	TRIVALENCE	TROCHOPHORE	TRONC
TRIQUINOYL	TRITACTIC	TRIVALENCY	TROCHOSPHERE	TRONDHJEMITE
TRIRADIAL	TRITAGONIST	TRIVALENT	TROCHOZOIC	TRONE
TRIRADIALLY	TRITANGENT	TRIVALVE	TROCHOZOON	TRONER
TRIRADIATE	TRITANOPIA	TRIVALVULAR	TROCK	TRONK
TRIRADIATELY	TRITANOPSIA	TRIVANT	TROCKERY	TROODONT
TRIRADIATION	TRITANOPTIC	TRIVARIANT	TROCO	TROOLIE
TRIREGNUM	TRITAPH	TRIVAT	TROCTOLITE	TROOLY
TRIREME	TRITE	TRIVERBIAL	TROD	TROOP
TRISALT	TRITELY	TRIVET	TRODDEN	TROOPED
TRISAZO	TRITENESS	TRIVIA	TRODE	TROOPER
TRISECT	TRITERNATE	TRIVIAL	TROEGERITE	TROOPFOWL
TRISECTED	TRITERNATELY	TRIVIALISM	TROFFER	TROOPIAL
TRISECTING	TRITERPENE	TRIVIALIST	TROFT	TROOPING
TRISECTION	TRITERPENOID	TRIVIALITIES	TROG	TROOPS
TRISECTOR	TRITHEISM	TRIVIALITY	TROGERITE	TROOPSHIP
TRISECTRIX	TRITHEIST	TRIVIALIZE	TROGGER	TROOSHLACH
TRISEME	TRITHEISTIC	TRIVIALLY	TROGGIN	TROOSTITE
TRISEMIC	TRITHEITE	TRIVIALNESS	TROGGS	TROOZ
TRISEPALOUS	TRITHING	TRIVIRGA	TROGLODYTAL	TROP
TRISEPTATE	TRITHIONATES	TRIVIRGATE	TROGLODYTE	TROPACOCAINE
TRISERIAL	TRITICAL	TRIVIUM	TROGLODYTIC	TROPAEOLA
TRISERIALLY	TRITICALITY	TRIVOLTINE	TROGON	TROPAEOLIN
TRISERIATE	TRITICALLY	TRIVVET	TROGONOID	TROPAEOLUM
TRISERIATIM	TRITICALNESS	TRIWEEKLY	TROGS	TROPAEOLUMS
TRISETOSE	TRITICEUM	TRIZOIC	TROGUE	TROPAION
TRISHA	TRITICIN	TRIZOMAL	TROIKA	TROPAL
TRISHNA	TRITICISM	TROAK	TROIL	TROPARIA
TRISKELE	TRITICOID	TROAT	TROILITE	TROPARION
TRISKELIA	TRITICUM	TROBADOR	TROILUS	TROPARY
TRISKELION	TRITISH	TROCA	TROKE	TROPATE
TRISMEGIST	TRITIUM	TROCAR	TROKED	TROPE
TRISMEGISTIC	TRITOCONE	TROCHA	TROKER	TROPEIC
TRISMIC	TRITOCONID	TROCHAIC	TROKING	TROPEIN
TRISMUS	TRITOMITE	TROCHAL	TROLAND	TROPEINE
TRISOME	TRITON	TROCHALOPOD	TROLL	TROPEOLIN
TRISPAST	TRITONE	TROCHANTER	TROLLED	TROPER
TRISPASTON	TRITONOID	TROCHANTERIC	TROLLEITE	TROPESIS
TRISPERMOUS	TRITONYMPH	TROCHANTIN	TROLLER	TROPHAEA
TRISPORIC	TRITONYMPHAL	TROCHANTINE	TROLLEY	TROPHAEUM
TRISPOROUS	TRITOPATORES	TROCHAR	TROLLEYMAN	TROPHALLAXIS
TRIST	TRITOR	TROCHATE	TROLLEYMEN	TROPHEDEMA
TRISTACHYOUS	TRITORAL	TROCHE	TROLLEYS	TROPHEMA
TRISTE	TRITOZOOID	TROCHEAMETER	TROLLFLOWER	TROPHESIAL
TRISTEARATE	TRITTICHAN	TROCHED	TROLLIES	TROPHESY
TRISTESSE	TRITUBERCULY	TROCHEE	TROLLIMOG	TROPHI
TRISTEZA	TRITURABLE	TROCHEEIZE	TROLLING	TROPHIC
TRISTFUL	TRITURAL	TROCHEUS	TROLLMAN	TROPHICAL
TRISTFULLY	TRITURATE	TROCHID	TROLLMEN	TROPHICALLY
TRISTFULNESS	TRITURATED	TROCHIFEROUS	TROLLOL	TROPHICITY
TRISTICH	TRITURATING	TROCHIFORM	TROLLOP	TROPHIED
TRISTICHIC	TRITURATION	TROCHIL	TROLLOPING	TROPHIES
TRISTICHOUS	TRITURATOR	TROCHILI	TROLLOPISH	TROPHISM
TRISTIGMATIC	TRITURATURE	TROCHILIC	TROLLOPS	TROPHOBIONT
TRISTILOQUY	TRITURIUM	TROCHILICS	TROLLOPY	TROPHOBIOSIS
TRISTISONOUS	TRIUMPH	TROCHILIDINE	TROLLY	TROPHOBIOTIC
TRISTIVE	TRIUMPHAL	TROCHILIDIST	TROLLYMAN	TROPHOBLAST
TRISTYLOUS	TRIUMPHANCE	TROCHILINE	TROLLYMEN	TROPHOCYTE
TRISUL	TRIUMPHANCY	TROCHILOS	TROMBA	TROPHODERM
TRISULA	TRIUMPHANT	TROCHILUS	TROMBASH	TROPHODISC
TRISULC	TRIUMPHANTLY	TROCHING	TROMBE	TROPHOGENIC

TROPHOGENY
TROPHOLOGY
TROPHON
TROPHONEMA
TROPHOPATHY
TROPHOPHORE
TROPHOPHYTE
TROPHOPLASM
TROPHOPLAST
TROPHOSOMAL
TROPHOSOME
TROPHOSPERM
TROPHOSPHERE
TROPHOSPORE
TROPHOTAXIS
TROPHOTHYLAX
TROPHOTROPIC
TROPHOZOITE
TROPHOZOOID
TROPHY
TROPIC
TROPICAL
TROPICALITY
TROPICALIZE
TROPICALIZED
TROPICALIZING
TROPICALLY
TROPIDINE
TROPIN
TROPINE
TROPISM
TROPISMATIC
TROPIST
TROPISTIC
TROPOLOGIC
TROPOLOGICAL
TROPOLOGIES
TROPOLOGIZE
TROPOLOGIZED
TROPOLOGIZING
TROPOLOGY
TROPOMETER
TROPOPAUSE
TROPOPHIL
TROPOPHILOUS
TROPOPHYTE
TROPOPHYTIC
TROPOSPHERE
TROPOSPHERIC
TROPOYL
TROPPO
TROPTOMETER
TROPYL
TROSTERA
TROT
TROTCOZY
TROTH
TROTHED
TROTHING
TROTHLESS
TROTHPLIGHT
TROTLINE
TROTTED
TROTTER
TROTTERS
TROTTEUR
TROTTIE
TROTTING
TROTTLES
TROTTOIR
TROTTOIRED
TROTTY
TROTYL
TROUBADOR
TROUBADOURE
TROUBLE
TROUBLED

TROUBLEDLY
TROUBLEDNESS
TROUBLEMAKER
TROUBLER
TROUBLESHOOTER
TROUBLESOME
TROUBLESOMENESS
TROUBLING
TROUBLINGLY
TROUBLOUS
TROUBLOUSLY
TROUBLY
TROUGH
TROUGHING
TROUGHSTER
TROUGHWAY
TROUGHY
TROUNCE
TROUNCED
TROUNCER
TROUNCING
TROUPAND
TROUPE
TROUPED
TROUPER
TROUPIAL
TROUPING
TROUSE
TROUSER
TROUSERED
TROUSERETTES
TROUSERIAN
TROUSERING
TROUSERS
TROUSS
TROUSSE
TROUSSEAU
TROUSSEAUS
TROUSSEAUX
TROUT
TROUTER
TROUTLET
TROUTLING
TROUTY
TROUVAILLE
TROUVERE
TROUVEUR
TROVATORE
TROVE
TROVER
TROW
TROWABLE
TROWANE
TROWEL
TROWELBEAK
TROWELED
TROWELER
TROWELING
TROWELLED
TROWELLING
TROWELMAN
TROWIE
TROWING
TROWMAN
TROWSERS
TROWTH
TROY
TRUANCIES
TRUANCY
TRUANDISE
TRUANT
TRUANTISM
TRUANTLY
TRUANTNESS
TRUANTRY
TRUB
TRUBU

TRUCE
TRUCHA
TRUCHMAN
TRUCIAL
TRUCIDATION
TRUCK
TRUCKAGE
TRUCKED
TRUCKER
TRUCKING
TRUCKLE
TRUCKLED
TRUCKLER
TRUCKLING
TRUCKLINGLY
TRUCKMAN
TRUCKMASTER
TRUCKMEN
TRUCKS
TRUCKSTER
TRUCKWAY
TRUCULENCE
TRUCULENCY
TRUCULENT
TRUCULENTLY
TRUDDO
TRUDELLITE
TRUDGE
TRUDGED
TRUDGEN
TRUDGEON
TRUDGER
TRUDGING
TRUE
TRUEBORN
TRUEBRED
TRUED
TRUELOVE
TRUEMAN
TRUENESS
TRUEPENNY
TRUER
TRUEST
TRUEWOOD
TRUFF
TRUFFES
TRUFFLE
TRUFFLED
TRUFFLER
TRUG
TRUGMALLION
TRUING
TRUISM
TRUISMATIC
TRUISTIC
TRUISTICAL
TRULL
TRULLER
TRULLI
TRULLIZATION
TRULLO
TRULY
TRUMBASH
TRUMEAU
TRUMMEL
TRUMP
TRUMPED
TRUMPER
TRUMPERIES
TRUMPERINESS
TRUMPERY
TRUMPET
TRUMPETBUSH
TRUMPETED
TRUMPETER
TRUMPETING
TRUMPETRY

TRUMPETS
TRUMPETWEED
TRUMPETWOOD
TRUMPETY
TRUMPIE
TRUMPING
TRUMPS
TRUNCAGE
TRUNCAL
TRUNCATE
TRUNCATED
TRUNCATING
TRUNCATION
TRUNCATOR
TRUNCH
TRUNCHED
TRUNCHEON
TRUNCHEONED
TRUNCHEONER
TRUNCUS
TRUNDLE
TRUNDLED
TRUNDLEHEAD
TRUNDLER
TRUNDLESHOT
TRUNDLETAIL
TRUNDLING
TRUNK
TRUNKBACK
TRUNKED
TRUNKFISH
TRUNKFISHES
TRUNKING
TRUNKS
TRUNKWORK
TRUNNEL
TRUNNION
TRUNNIONED
TRUONG
TRUSH
TRUSION
TRUSS
TRUSSED
TRUSSELL
TRUSSER
TRUSSERY
TRUSSING
TRUSSWORK
TRUST
TRUSTBUSTER
TRUSTBUSTING
TRUSTED
TRUSTEE
TRUSTEED
TRUSTEEING
TRUSTEEISM
TRUSTEESHIP
TRUSTER
TRUSTFUL
TRUSTFULLY
TRUSTFULNESS
TRUSTIER
TRUSTIEST
TRUSTIFIED
TRUSTIFY
TRUSTIFYING
TRUSTING
TRUSTINGLY
TRUSTINGNESS
TRUSTLESS
TRUSTLESSLY
TRUSTMAN
TRUSTMEN
TRUSTWOMAN
TRUSTWORTHINESS
TRUSTWORTHY
TRUSTY

TRUTH
TRUTHABLE
TRUTHFUL
TRUTHFULLY
TRUTHFULNESS
TRUTHS
TRUTHSMAN
TRUTHTELLER
TRUTHTELLING
TRUTHY
TRUTINATE
TRUTINATION
TRUTINE
TRUTTACEOUS
TRUXILLIC
TRUXILLIN
TRUXILLINE
TRY
TRYE
TRYGON
TRYHOUSE
TRYING
TRYINGLY
TRYINGNESS
TRYMA
TRYMATA
TRYMS
TRYNE
TRYOUT
TRYP
TRYPA
TRYPANOLYSIN
TRYPANOSOMA
TRYPANOSOME
TRYPETID
TRYPIATE
TRYPOGRAPH
TRYPOGRAPHIC
TRYPSIN
TRYPSINIZE
TRYPSINOGEN
TRYPTASE
TRYPTIC
TRYPTONE
TRYPTONIZE
TRYPTOPHAN
TRYPTOPHANE
TRYSAIL
TRYST
TRYSTE
TRYSTED
TRYSTER
TRYSTING
TRYWORKS
TSADE
TSAMA
TSAMBA
TSANTSA
TSAR
TSARISM
TSARIST
TSATLEE
TSESSEBE
TSETSE
TSIA
TSINE
TSINGTAUITE
TSIOLOGY
TSITSITH
TSUBA
TSUBO
TSUKUPIN
TSUMEBITE
TSUN
TSUNAMI
TSUNGTU
TSWANA

TU
TUA
TUAN
TUANT
TUARN
TUART
TUATARA
TUATERA
TUATH
TUB
TUBA
TUBAE
TUBAGE
TUBAL
TUBAPHONE
TUBAR
TUBARON
TUBAS
TUBATE
TUBBA
TUBBABLE
TUBBAL
TUBBECK
TUBBED
TUBBER
TUBBIE
TUBBIER
TUBBIEST
TUBBING
TUBBISH
TUBBIST
TUBBOE
TUBBY
TUBE
TUBED
TUBEFORM
TUBEHEAD
TUBEHEARTED
TUBELET
TUBEMAN
TUBEMEN
TUBER
TUBERACEOUS
TUBERATION
TUBERCLE
TUBERCLED
TUBERCULA
TUBERCULAR
TUBERCULARLY
TUBERCULATE
TUBERCULATED
TUBERCULE
TUBERCULID
TUBERCULIDE
TUBERCULIN
TUBERCULINE
TUBERCULIZE
TUBERCULOID
TUBERCULOMA
TUBERCULOMAS
TUBERCULOMATA
TUBERCULOSED
TUBERCULOSIS
TUBERCULOUS
TUBERCULUM
TUBERIFEROUS
TUBERIFORM
TUBERIN
TUBERIZATION
TUBERIZE
TUBEROID
TUBEROSE
TUBEROSITIES
TUBEROSITY
TUBEROUS
TUBEROUSLY
TUBEROUSNESS

TUBFISH
TUBFISHES
TUBHUNTER
TUBICEN
TUBICINATE
TUBICINATION
TUBICOLAR
TUBICOLOUS
TUBICORN
TUBICORNOUS
TUBIFACIENT
TUBIFER
TUBIFEROUS
TUBIFEX
TUBIFLOROUS
TUBIFORM
TUBIG
TUBIK
TUBILINGUAL
TUBINARIAL
TUBINARINE
TUBING
TUBIPAROUS
TUBIPORE
TUBIPORID
TUBIPOROID
TUBIPOROUS
TUBMAN
TUBMEN
TUBOCURARINE
TUBORRHEA
TUBOTYMPANAL
TUBS
TUBSTER
TUBTAIL
TUBULAR
TUBULARITY
TUBULATE
TUBULATED
TUBULATING
TUBULATION
TUBULATOR
TUBULATURE
TUBULE
TUBULET
TUBULI
TUBULIFERAN
TUBULIFLORAL
TUBULIFORM
TUBULIPORE
TUBULIPORID
TUBULIPOROID
TUBULIZATION
TUBULOSE
TUBULOUS
TUBULOUSLY
TUBULOUSNESS
TUBULURE
TUBULUS
TUCAN
TUCANDERA
TUCHUN
TUCHUNATE
TUCHUNISM
TUCHUNIZE
TUCK
TUCKAHOE
TUCKED
TUCKER
TUCKERED
TUCKERING
TUCKET
TUCKING
TUCKNER
TUCKSHOP
TUCKTOO
TUCKY

TUCUM
TUCUMA
TUCUMAN
TUEBOR
TUEIRON
TUFA
TUFACEOUS
TUFAN
TUFF
TUFFACEOUS
TUFFET
TUFFING
TUFFOON
TUFT
TUFTAFFETA
TUFTED
TUFTER
TUFTHUNTER
TUFTHUNTING
TUFTING
TUFTS
TUFTY
TUG
TUGBOAT
TUGBOATMAN
TUGBOATMEN
TUGGED
TUGGER
TUGGERY
TUGGING
TUGGINGLY
TUGHRA
TUGUI
TUGURIA
TUGURIUM
TUI
TUILLE
TUILLETTE
TUILYIE
TUILZIE
TUINGA
TUISM
TUITION
TUITIONAL
TUITIONARY
TUITIVE
TUKE
TUKRA
TUKUTUKU
TULADI
TULARAEMIA
TULARE
TULAREMIA
TULASI
TULCAN
TULCE
TULCHAN
TULCHIN
TULE
TULIAC
TULIP
TULIPANT
TULIPFLOWER
TULIPI
TULIPIFEROUS
TULIPIST
TULIPOMANIA
TULIPOMANIAC
TULIPS
TULIPWOOD
TULIPY
TULISAN
TULISANES
TULK
TULLE
TULLIBEE
TULNIC

TULSI
TULWAR
TULWAUR
TULY
TUM
TUMAIN
TUMATAKURU
TUMB
TUMBAK
TUMBAKI
TUMBEK
TUMBEKI
TUMBLE
TUMBLEBUG
TUMBLED
TUMBLER
TUMBLEWEED
TUMBLING
TUMBLINGLY
TUMBLY
TUMBREL
TUMBRIL
TUMEFACIENT
TUMEFACTION
TUMEFIED
TUMEFY
TUMEFYING
TUMESCENCE
TUMESCENT
TUMFIE
TUMID
TUMIDITY
TUMIDLY
TUMIDNESS
TUMMALS
TUMMED
TUMMEL
TUMMELS
TUMMER
TUMMING
TUMMOCK
TUMMY
TUMOR
TUMORED
TUMORLIKE
TUMOROUS
TUMORS
TUMOUR
TUMOURED
TUMP
TUMPHY
TUMPLINE
TUMTUM
TUMULAR
TUMULARY
TUMULATE
TUMULATION
TUMULI
TUMULOSE
TUMULOSITY
TUMULOUS
TUMULT
TUMULTER
TUMULTUARIES
TUMULTUARILY
TUMULTUARY
TUMULTUOSO
TUMULTUOUS
TUMULTUOUSLY
TUMULUS
TUN
TUNA
TUNABLE
TUNABLENESS
TUNABLY
TUNAS
TUNBELLIED

TUNBELLY
TUNCA
TUND
TUNDATION
TUNDISH
TUNDRA
TUNDUN
TUNE
TUNED
TUNEFUL
TUNEFULLY
TUNEFULNESS
TUNELESS
TUNELESSLY
TUNELESSNESS
TUNER
TUNESMITH
TUNESOME
TUNG
TUNGAH
TUNGATE
TUNGO
TUNGSTATE
TUNGSTEN
TUNGSTENIC
TUNGSTENITE
TUNGSTIC
TUNGSTITE
TUNHOOF
TUNIC
TUNICA
TUNICAE
TUNICARY
TUNICATE
TUNICIN
TUNICKED
TUNICLE
TUNING
TUNK
TUNKET
TUNLAND
TUNMOOT
TUNNA
TUNNAGE
TUNNED
TUNNEL
TUNNELED
TUNNELER
TUNNELING
TUNNELITE
TUNNELLED
TUNNELLER
TUNNELLING
TUNNELLITE
TUNNELMAN
TUNNELMEN
TUNNER
TUNNERIES
TUNNERY
TUNNIES
TUNNING
TUNNLAND
TUNNY
TUNO
TUNS
TUNU
TUNY
TUP
TUPAIID
TUPAKIHI
TUPAN
TUPARA
TUPEK
TUPELO
TUPELOS
TUPIK
TUPMAN

TUPMEN	TURFMEN	TURNIPY	TURTLEDOM	TUTORER
TUPPED	TURFS	TURNKEY	TURTLEDOVE	TUTORESS
TUPPENCE	TURFY	TURNKEYS	TURTLEDOVED	TUTORHOOD
TUPPENY	TURGENT	TURNOFF	TURTLEDOVING	TUTORIAL
TUPPING	TURGENTLY	TURNOR	TURTLEHEAD	TUTORIALLY
TUPUNA	TURGESCE	TURNOUT	TURTLEIZE	TUTORIATE
TUQUE	TURGESCED	TURNOVER	TURTLEPEG	TUTORING
TUR	TURGESCENCE	TURNPIKE	TURTLER	TUTORISM
TURACIN	TURGESCENCY	TURNPIKER	TURTLES	TUTORIZATION
TURACOU	TURGESCENT	TURNPIN	TURTLESTONE	TUTORIZE
TURAKOO	TURGESCENTLY	TURNPLATE	TURTLET	TUTORLY
TURANITE	TURGESCING	TURNPLOUGH	TURTLING	TUTORSHIP
TURANOSE	TURGID	TURNPLOW	TURTOSA	TUTORY
TURB	TURGIDITY	TURNPOKE	TURTUR	TUTOYER
TURBAN	TURGIDLY	TURNROW	TURURI	TUTSAN
TURBANED	TURGIDNESS	TURNS	TURUS	TUTSTER
TURBANTO	TURGITE	TURNSCREW	TURVES	TUTTA
TURBANTOP	TURGOID	TURNSHEET	TURWAR	TUTTE
TURBARIES	TURGOR	TURNSKIN	TUSCH	TUTTED
TURBARY	TURGY	TURNSOLE	TUSCHE	TUTTI
TURBEH	TURICATA	TURNSPIT	TUSHE	TUTTIMAN
TURBELLARIAN	TURIO	TURNSTILE	TUSHED	TUTTING
TURBESCENCY	TURION	TURNSTONE	TUSHER	TUTTIS
TURBETH	TURJAITE	TURNTABLE	TUSHERY	TUTTO
TURBID	TURJITE	TURNTAIL	TUSHING	TUTTY
TURBIDIMETER	TURKEN	TURNTALE	TUSK	TUTTYMAN
TURBIDIMETRY	TURKESS	TURNUP	TUSKAR	TUTU
TURBIDITY	TURKEY	TURNVEREIN	TUSKED	TUTUH
TURBIDLY	TURKEYBACK	TURNWAY	TUSKER	TUTULUS
TURBIDNESS	TURKEYBERRY	TURNWREST	TUSKIER	TUTWORK
TURBINACEOUS	TURKEYBUSH	TURNWRIST	TUSKIEST	TUUM
TURBINAGE	TURKEYFOOT	TUROPHILE	TUSKING	TUWI
TURBINAL	TURKEYS	TURP	TUSKLESS	TUX
TURBINATE	TURKIS	TURPENTINE	TUSKY	TUXEDO
TURBINATED	TURKLE	TURPENTINED	TUSSAH	TUXEDOES
TURBINATION	TURKOIS	TURPENTINIC	TUSSAL	TUXEDOS
TURBINE	TURLOUGH	TURPENTINING	TUSSAR	TUYERE
TURBINECTOMY	TURM	TURPENTINOUS	TUSSEH	TUZ
TURBINED	TURMA	TURPENTINY	TUSSER	TUZA
TURBINELLOID	TURMALINE	TURPETH	TUSSICULAR	TUZZ
TURBINER	TURMERIC	TURPETHIN	TUSSIS	TWA
TURBINIFORM	TURMET	TURPID	TUSSIVE	TWADDLE
TURBINOID	TURMIT	TURPIDLY	TUSSLE	TWADDLED
TURBINOTOME	TURMOIL	TURPIFY	TUSSLED	TWADDLEMENT
TURBINOTOMY	TURMOILER	TURPITUDE	TUSSLING	TWADDLER
TURBIT	TURMUT	TURPS	TUSSOCK	TWADDLIER
TURBITH	TURN	TURQUET	TUSSOCKED	TWADDLIEST
TURBITTEEN	TURNABLE	TURQUOIS	TUSSOCKER	TWADDLING
TURBLE	TURNABOUT	TURQUOISE	TUSSOCKY	TWADDLY
TURBOCAR	TURNAGAIN	TURQUOISES	TUSSORE	TWADDY
TURBOFAN	TURNAROUND	TURR	TUSSUCK	TWAG
TURBOJET	TURNAWAY	TURREL	TUSSUR	TWAGGER
TURBOPROP	TURNBACK	TURRELL	TUT	TWAIN
TURBOT	TURNBOUT	TURRET	TUTAMENT	TWAITE
TURBOTS	TURNBROACH	TURRETED	TUTANIA	TWAL
TURBULENCE	TURNBUCKLE	TURRETING	TUTBALL	TWALE
TURBULENCY	TURNCAP	TURRICAL	TUTE	TWALPENNY
TURBULENT	TURNCOAT	TURRICLE	TUTEE	TWALT
TURBULENTLY	TURNCOATISM	TURRICULA	TUTEL	TWANG
TURCO	TURNCOCK	TURRICULAE	TUTELA	TWANGED
TURCOIS	TURNDOWN	TURRICULAR	TUTELAE	TWANGER
TURCOPOLE	TURNDUN	TURRICULATE	TUTELAGE	TWANGING
TURCOPOLIER	TURNED	TURRICULATED	TUTELAR	TWANGLE
TURD	TURNEL	TURRIFEROUS	TUTELARIES	TWANGLED
TURDIFORM	TURNER	TURRIFORM	TUTELARY	TWANGLER
TURDINE	TURNERACEOUS	TURRIGEROUS	TUTELE	TWANGLING
TURDOID	TURNERIES	TURRILITE	TUTENAG	TWANGY
TUREEN	TURNERITE	TURRION	TUTENAGUE	TWANK
TURF	TURNERY	TURRITELLID	TUTIN	TWANKER
TURFED	TURNEY	TURRITELLOID	TUTLER	TWANKING
TURFEN	TURNGATE	TURRUM	TUTLY	TWANKINGLY
TURFIER	TURNHALL	TURSE	TUTMAN	TWANKLE
TURFIEST	TURNICINE	TURSIO	TUTMEN	TWANKY
TURFINESS	TURNING	TURTLE	TUTOIEMENT	TWARLY
TURFING	TURNIP	TURTLEBACK	TUTOR	TWASOME
TURFITE	TURNIPWEED	TURTLEBLOOM	TUTORAGE	TWAT
TURFMAN	TURNIPWOOD	TURTLED	TUTORED	TWATCHEL

TWATTERLIGHT	TWIGGER	TWISTLE	TYLOSTERESIS	TYPHOIDLIKE
TWATTLE	TWIGGIER	TWISTY	TYLOSTYLAR	TYPHOLYSIN
TWATTLED	TWIGGIEST	TWIT	TYLOSTYLE	TYPHOMALARIA
TWATTLER	TWIGGING	TWITCH	TYLOSTYLOTE	TYPHOMANIA
TWATTLING	TWIGGY	TWITCHED	TYLOSTYLUS	TYPHONIC
TWAY	TWIGLESS	TWITCHEL	TYLOTATE	TYPHOON
TWAYBLADE	TWIGLET	TWITCHELING	TYLOTE	TYPHOSE
TWAZZY	TWIGS	TWITCHER	TYLOTIC	TYPHOSIS
TWEAK	TWIGWITHY	TWITCHET	TYLOTOXEA	TYPHOTOXINE
TWEAKED	TWILIGHT	TWITCHETY	TYLOTOXEATE	TYPHOUS
TWEAKER	TWILIGHTY	TWITCHFIRE	TYLUS	TYPHUS
TWEAKING	TWILIT	TWITCHING	TYMBAL	TYPIC
TWEAKY	TWILL	TWITCHINGLY	TYMBALON	TYPICA
TWEE	TWILLED	TWITCHY	TYMP	TYPICAL
TWEED	TWILLER	TWITE	TYMPAN	TYPICALITY
TWEEDED	TWILLING	TWITLARK	TYMPANA	TYPICALLY
TWEEDLE	TWILLY	TWITTED	TYMPANAL	TYPICALNESS
TWEEDLED	TWIN	TWITTEN	TYMPANI	TYPICON
TWEEDLEDEE	TWINBERRIES	TWITTER	TYMPANIC	TYPICUM
TWEEDLEDUM	TWINBERRY	TWITTERATION	TYMPANIES	TYPIFICATION
TWEEDLING	TWINBORN	TWITTERER	TYMPANING	TYPIFIED
TWEEDY	TWIND	TWITTERING	TYMPANISM	TYPIFIER
TWEEG	TWINDLE	TWITTERINGLY	TYMPANIST	TYPIFY
TWEEL	TWINE	TWITTERLY	TYMPANITES	TYPIFYING
TWEEN	TWINEBUSH	TWITTERY	TYMPANITIC	TYPING
TWEENY	TWINED	TWITTING	TYMPANITIS	TYPIST
TWEER	TWINER	TWITTINGLY	TYMPANIZE	TYPO
TWEESE	TWINFLOWER	TWITTLE	TYMPANO	TYPOBAR
TWEESH	TWINFOLD	TWITTY	TYMPANOHYAL	TYPOCOSMY
TWEESHT	TWINGE	TWIXT	TYMPANOSIS	TYPOGRAPHER
TWEEST	TWINGED	TWIZZLE	TYMPANOTOMY	TYPOGRAPHIA
TWEET	TWINGING	TWO	TYMPANUM	TYPOGRAPHIC
TWEETER	TWINGLE	TWOES	TYMPANUMS	TYPOGRAPHIES
TWEEZE	TWINIGHT	TWOFER	TYMPANY	TYPOGRAPHIST
TWEEZED	TWINING	TWOFOLD	TYND	TYPOGRAPHY
TWEEZER	TWINK	TWOFOLDLY	TYPAL	TYPOLOGICAL
TWEEZERED	TWINKLE	TWOFOLDNESS	TYPARCHICAL	TYPOLOGIES
TWEEZERING	TWINKLED	TWOLING	TYPE	TYPOLOGIST
TWEEZERS	TWINKLEDUM	TWONESS	TYPECAST	TYPOLOGY
TWEEZING	TWINKLER	TWOPENCE	TYPECASTING	TYPOMANIA
TWEIL	TWINKLES	TWOPENNY	TYPED	TYPOMETRY
TWELFTH	TWINKLING	TWOS	TYPEFACE	TYPONYM
TWELL	TWINKLINGLY	TWOSOME	TYPEFACES	TYPONYMAL
TWELVE	TWINKLY	TWYER	TYPEHOLDER	TYPONYMIC
TWELVEFOLD	TWINLEAF	TY	TYPER	TYPONYMOUS
TWELVEMO	TWINLING	TYALL	TYPES	TYPOPHILE
TWELVEMONTH	TWINLY	TYAUVE	TYPESCRIPT	TYPORAMA
TWELVEPENCE	TWINNED	TYCHISM	TYPESET	TYPOS
TWELVEPENNY	TWINNER	TYCHITE	TYPESETTER	TYPOTHETAE
TWELVESCORE	TWINNING	TYCHOPOTAMIC	TYPESETTING	TYPP
TWENTIES	TWINS	TYCOON	TYPEWRITE	TYPTOLOGICAL
TWENTIETH	TWINSHIP	TYCOONATE	TYPEWRITER	TYPTOLOGIST
TWENTY	TWINSOMENESS	TYDDEN	TYPEWRITING	TYPTOLOGY
TWENTYFOLD	TWINT	TYDDYN	TYPEWRITTEN	TYPY
TWENTYMO	TWINTER	TYDIE	TYPEWROTE	TYRAMIN
TWERP	TWINY	TYE	TYPHAEMIA	TYRAMINE
TWEYFOLD	TWIRE	TYEE	TYPHEMIA	TYRANNESS
TWIBIL	TWIRK	TYER	TYPHIA	TYRANNIAL
TWIBILL	TWIRL	TYG	TYPHIC	TYRANNIC
TWIBILLED	TWIRLED	TYING	TYPHINIA	TYRANNICAL
TWICE	TWIRLER	TYKE	TYPHIZATION	TYRANNICALLY
TWICER	TWIRLIGIG	TYKEN	TYPHLITIC	TYRANNICIDAL
TWICH	TWIRLING	TYKING	TYPHLITIS	TYRANNICIDE
TWICHILD	TWIRLY	TYLARI	TYPHLOLOGIES	TYRANNICLY
TWICK	TWIRP	TYLARUS	TYPHLOLOGY	TYRANNIES
TWIDDLE	TWISCAR	TYLASTER	TYPHLON	TYRANNINE
TWIDDLED	TWISEL	TYLE	TYPHLOPHILE	TYRANNIS
TWIDDLER	TWIST	TYLER	TYPHLOPID	TYRANNISM
TWIDDLING	TWISTED	TYLI	TYPHLOSIS	TYRANNIZE
TWIDDLY	TWISTEDLY	TYLION	TYPHLOSOLAR	TYRANNIZED
TWIER	TWISTER	TYLOMA	TYPHLOSOLE	TYRANNIZER
TWIFALLOW	TWISTHAND	TYLOPOD	TYPHOAEMIA	TYRANNIZING
TWIFOIL	TWISTICAL	TYLOPODOUS	TYPHOEMIA	TYRANNOSAUR
TWIFOLD	TWISTING	TYLOSE	TYPHOGENIC	TYRANNOUS
TWIG	TWISTINGLY	TYLOSES	TYPHOID	TYRANNOUSLY
TWIGGED	TWISTIWAYS	TYLOSIS	TYPHOIDAL	TYRANNY
TWIGGEN	TWISTIWISE	TYLOSOID	TYPHOIDIN	TYRANT

TYRASOLE
TYRE
TYREMESIS
TYRIASIS
TYRO
TYROGLYPHID
TYROLITE
TYROLOGY
TYROMA
TYROMANCY
TYROMAS
TYROMATA
TYROMATOUS
TYRONE
TYRONIC
TYRONISM
TYROS
TYROSINASE
TYROSINE
TYROSINURIA
TYROSYL
TYROTHRICIN
TYROTOXICON
TYROTOXINE
TYSONITE
TYSTE
TYSTIE
TYT
TYTE
TZAR
TZARDOM
TZARINA
TZEDAKAH
TZETZE
TZIGANE
TZIMMES
TZIRID
TZOLKIN
TZONTLE
TZUT
TZUTE

UAKARI
UALIS
UANG
UAYED
UBE
UBERANT
UBEROUS
UBEROUSLY
UBEROUSNESS
UBERTY
UBI
UBICATION
UBIETY
UBIQUARIAN
UBIQUE
UBIQUIOUS
UBIQUIT
UBIQUITARIAN
UBIQUITARIES
UBIQUITARY
UBIQUITOUS
UBIQUITOUSLY
UBIQUITY
UBUSSU
UCH
UCHE
UCKERS
UCKIA
UCUUBA
UDAD
UDAL
UDALER
UDALLER
UDALMAN
UDASI
UDDER
UDDERED
UDDERFUL
UDDERLESS
UDELL
UDGE
UDO
UDOMETER
UDOMETRIC
UDOMETRY
UDOMOGRAPH
UEBA
UFER
UG
UGGE
UGGLESOME
UGH
UGHTEN
UGLIER
UGLIEST
UGLIFICATION
UGLIFIED
UGLIFIER
UGLIFY
UGLIFYING
UGLILY
UGLINESS
UGLISOME
UGLY
UGRIANIZE
UGRUG
UGSOME
UHLAN

UHLLO
UHTENSANG
UHTSONG
UINAL
UINTAHITE
UINTAITE
UINTATHERE
UINTJIE
UIT
UITLANDER
UITSPAN
UJI
UKASE
UKE
UKIYO
UKIYOYE
UKU
UKULELE
ULA
ULAE
ULAMA
ULAN
ULATROPHIA
ULATROPHY
ULAULA
ULCER
ULCERATE
ULCERATED
ULCERATING
ULCERATION
ULCERATIVE
ULCERED
ULCEROUS
ULCEROUSLY
ULCEROUSNESS
ULCUS
ULCUSCLE
ULCUSCULE
ULE
ULEMA
ULERYTHEMA
ULETIC
ULEXINE
ULEXITE
ULIGINOSE
ULIGINOUS
ULITIS
ULL
ULLAGE
ULLAGED
ULLAGONE
ULLER
ULLING
ULLMANNITE
ULLUCO
ULLUCU
ULMACEOUS
ULME
ULMIC
ULMIN
ULMINIC
ULMO
ULNA
ULNAD
ULNAE
ULNAR
ULNARE
ULNARIA
ULNAS
ULNOCARPAL
ULNOCONDYLAR
ULNORADIAL
ULOBORID
ULOID
ULONCUS
ULOTRICHAN
ULOTRICHOUS
ULOTRICHY

ULPAN
ULRICHITE
ULSTER
ULSTERED
ULSTERETTE
ULSTERING
ULTERIOR
ULTERIORLY
ULTIMA
ULTIMACY
ULTIMATA
ULTIMATE
ULTIMATED
ULTIMATELY
ULTIMATENESS
ULTIMATING
ULTIMATION
ULTIMATUM
ULTIMATUMS
ULTIME
ULTIMITY
ULTIMO
ULTIMUM
ULTION
ULTRA
ULTRABASIC
ULTRABASITE
ULTRACIVIL
ULTRACOMPLEX
ULTRACONSERVATISM
ULTRACONSERVATIVE
ULTRACORDIAL
ULTRAFASHIONABLE
ULTRAFIDIAN
ULTRAFILTER
ULTRAGASEOUS
ULTRAGENTEEL
ULTRAGOOD
ULTRAGRAVE
ULTRAHEROIC
ULTRAISM
ULTRAIST
ULTRAISTIC
ULTRALENIENT
ULTRALIBERAL
ULTRALOGICAL
ULTRALOYAL
ULTRAMARINE
ULTRAMAXIMAL
ULTRAMINUTE
ULTRAMODERN
ULTRAMODEST
ULTRAMONTANE
ULTRAMONTANISM
ULTRAMOROSE
ULTRAMULISH
ULTRAMUNDANE
ULTRANICE
ULTRAOBSCURE
ULTRAORNATE
ULTRAPAPIST
ULTRAPERFECT
ULTRAPIOUS
ULTRAPOPISH
ULTRAPROUD
ULTRAPRUDENT
ULTRARADICAL
ULTRARAPID
ULTRARED
ULTRAREFINED
ULTRASELECT
ULTRASERVILE
ULTRASEVERE
ULTRASHREWD
ULTRASOLEMN
ULTRASONIC
ULTRASONICS

ULTRASPARTAN
ULTRASTELLAR
ULTRASTERILE
ULTRASTRICT
ULTRASUBTLE
ULTRATENSE
ULTRATRIVIAL
ULTRAUGLY
ULTRAURGENT
ULTRAVICIOUS
ULTRAVIOLENT
ULTRAVIOLET
ULTRAVIRUS
ULTRAVISIBLE
ULTRAWEALTHY
ULTRAWISE
ULTRAYOUNG
ULTRAZEALOUS
ULTRONEOUS
ULTRONEOUSLY
ULU
ULUA
ULUHI
ULULANT
ULULATE
ULULATED
ULULATING
ULULATION
ULULATIVE
ULULATORY
ULULU
ULUS
ULVACEOUS
ULYIE
ULZIE
UM
UMANGITE
UMBE
UMBECAST
UMBEL
UMBELAP
UMBELED
UMBELLA
UMBELLAR
UMBELLATE
UMBELLATED
UMBELLATELY
UMBELLED
UMBELLET
UMBELLIC
UMBELLIFER
UMBELLIFERONE
UMBELLIFORM
UMBELLOID
UMBELLULATE
UMBELLULE
UMBELWORT
UMBER
UMBERED
UMBERING
UMBERTY
UMBESET
UMBETHINK
UMBILIC
UMBILICAL
UMBILICALLY
UMBILICAR
UMBILICATE
UMBILICATED
UMBILICATION
UMBILICI
UMBILICIFORM
UMBILICUS
UMBILIFORM
UMBILROOT
UMBLES
UMBO
UMBOLATERAL

UMBONAL
UMBONATE
UMBONATED
UMBONATION
UMBONE
UMBONES
UMBONIAL
UMBONIC
UMBONULATE
UMBONULE
UMBRA
UMBRACLE
UMBRACULATE
UMBRACULUM
UMBRAE
UMBRAGE
UMBRAGEOUS
UMBRAGEOUSLY
UMBRAID
UMBRAL
UMBRALLY
UMBRANA
UMBRATE
UMBRATIC
UMBRATILE
UMBRE
UMBREL
UMBRELLA
UMBRELLAED
UMBRELLAWORT
UMBRET
UMBRETTE
UMBRIFEROUS
UMBRIL
UMBRINE
UMBROSE
UMBROSITY
UMBROUS
UME
UMEST
UMFAAN
UMGANG
UMIACK
UMIAK
UMIRI
UMLAND
UMLAUT
UMMAN
UMP
UMPIRAGE
UMPIRE
UMPIRED
UMPIRESHIP
UMPIRESS
UMPIRING
UMPLE
UMPTEEN
UMPTEENTH
UMPTEKITE
UMPTIETH
UMPTY
UMQUHILE
UMSET
UMSTROKE
UMU
UN
UNABASHED
UNABBREVIATED
UNABLE
UNABLENESS
UNABLY
UNABRIDGED
UNABSOLVABLE
UNACCENTED
UNACCEPTABLE
UNACCEPTED
UNACCOMPANIED
UNACCOUNTABLE

UNACCUSTOMED
UNACQUAINTED
UNACTION
UNACTIVE
UNACTIVELY
UNACTIVITY
UNACTUAL
UNACTUALITY
UNACTUALLY
UNADAPTABLE
UNADAPTABLY
UNADDITIONED
UNADDRESS
UNADEQUATE
UNADEQUATELY
UNADHERENCE
UNADHERENT
UNADHERENTLY
UNADORNED
UNADULTERATED
UNADVANCED
UNADVANCEDLY
UNADVANTAGEOUSLY
UNADVERTENCY
UNADVISABLE
UNADVISABLY
UNADVISED
UNADVISEDLY
UNAFFECTED
UNAFFECTEDLY
UNAFFIED
UNAFRAID
UNAGGRESSIVE
UNAGING
UNAGREEABLE
UNAIDED
UNAIMED
UNAKIN
UNAKITE
UNAL
UNALERT
UNALIENABLE
UNALIENABLY
UNALIKE
UNALIST
UNALLIED
UNALLIEDLY
UNALLOYED
UNALMSED
UNALTERABLE
UNALTERABLY
UNALTERED
UNAMBIGUOUS
UNAMBITION
UNAMBITIOUS
UNAMENABLE
UNAMENABLY
UNAMIABILITY
UNAMIABLE
UNAMIABLY
UNAMO
UNAMUSIVE
UNANCESTORED
UNANCESTRIED
UNANCHOR
UNANELED
UNANIMATE
UNANIMATED
UNANIMATEDLY
UNANIMATELY
UNANIME
UNANIMISM
UNANIMIST
UNANIMISTIC
UNANIMITER
UNANIMITY
UNANIMOUS

UNANIMOUSLY
UNANSWERABLE
UNANSWERABLY
UNANSWERED
UNAPPEALABLE
UNAPPEALABLY
UNAPPROACHABLE
UNAPPROVED
UNAPT
UNAPTLY
UNAPTNESS
UNARGUED
UNARK
UNARM
UNARMED
UNARMEDLY
UNARMEDNESS
UNARMORED
UNARMOURED
UNARRAY
UNARTED
UNARTFUL
UNARTFULLY
UNARTFULNESS
UNARTIFICIAL
UNARTISTIC
UNARTISTICAL
UNARY
UNASINOUS
UNASSAILABLE
UNASSAILABLY
UNASSENTED
UNASSISTED
UNASSOILED
UNASSUETUDE
UNASSUMED
UNASSUMING
UNASSUMINGLY
UNASSURED
UNASSUREDLY
UNATONABLE
UNATTACHED
UNATTAINABLE
UNATTAINTED
UNATTAINTEDLY
UNATTENDED
UNATTIRE
UNATTRACTIVE
UNAU
UNAUDIBLE
UNAUDIBLY
UNAUDIENCED
UNAUSPICIOUS
UNAUTHORIZE
UNAUTHORIZED
UNAUTORITIED
UNAVAILING
UNAVAILINGLY
UNAVOIDABLE
UNAVOIDABLY
UNAVOIDED
UNAVOWED
UNAWARE
UNAWARED
UNAWAREDLY
UNAWARENESS
UNAWARES
UNBACKED
UNBAG
UNBAIN
UNBAITED
UNBAIZED
UNBAKED
UNBALANCE
UNBALANCED
UNBALANCING
UNBALLAST

UNBALLASTED
UNBALLASTING
UNBANE
UNBANK
UNBANKED
UNBAPTIZED
UNBAR
UNBARBED
UNBARE
UNBARK
UNBARRED
UNBARREL
UNBARRING
UNBATED
UNBE
UNBEAR
UNBEARABLE
UNBEARABLY
UNBEARDED
UNBEARED
UNBEARING
UNBEAST
UNBEATEN
UNBEAVERED
UNBECOME
UNBECOMING
UNBECOMINGLY
UNBED
UNBEDDED
UNBEFIT
UNBEFITTING
UNBEFOOL
UNBEFRIEND
UNBEGET
UNBEGILT
UNBEGINNING
UNBEGOT
UNBEGOTTEN
UNBEGOTTENLY
UNBEGUILE
UNBEGUN
UNBEHOVING
UNBEING
UNBEJUGGLED
UNBEKNOWN
UNBEKNOWNST
UNBELIEF
UNBELIEFFUL
UNBELIEVABLE
UNBELIEVABLY
UNBELIEVE
UNBELIEVED
UNBELIEVER
UNBELIEVERS
UNBELIEVING
UNBELT
UNBEND
UNBENDED
UNBENDER
UNBENDING
UNBENDINGLY
UNBENT
UNBEREAVEN
UNBEREFT
UNBERUFEN
UNBESEEM
UNBESEEMING
UNBETHINK
UNBETHOUGHT
UNBETIDE
UNBEWARE
UNBEWILLED
UNBEWITCH
UNBIAS
UNBIASABLE
UNBIASED
UNBIASEDLY

UNBIASEDNESS
UNBIASING
UNBIASSABLE
UNBIASSED
UNBIASSEDLY
UNBIASSING
UNBID
UNBIDABLE
UNBIDDEN
UNBIGGED
UNBIND
UNBINDING
UNBIRDLY
UNBISHOP
UNBITTED
UNBITTING
UNBLAMABLE
UNBLAMABLY
UNBLEACHED
UNBLEMISHED
UNBLENCHED
UNBLESS
UNBLESSED
UNBLEST
UNBLISS
UNBLITHE
UNBLOCK
UNBLOCKED
UNBLOODED
UNBLOODILY
UNBLOODINESS
UNBLOODY
UNBLOOM
UNBLOWN
UNBLUSHING
UNBLUSHINGLY
UNBOAT
UNBODIED
UNBODILINESS
UNBODILY
UNBODKINED
UNBODY
UNBOLD
UNBOLDLY
UNBOLDNESS
UNBOLT
UNBOLTED
UNBOLTING
UNBONE
UNBONED
UNBONNET
UNBONNETED
UNBONNY
UNBOOKED
UNBOOT
UNBORN
UNBOSOM
UNBOSOMED
UNBOSOMER
UNBOSOMING
UNBOTTOMED
UNBOUGHT
UNBOUND
UNBOUNDED
UNBOUNDEDLY
UNBOUNDLESS
UNBOW
UNBOWABLE
UNBOWED
UNBOWEL
UNBOWELED
UNBOWELLED
UNBOWERED
UNBOWSOME
UNBOY
UNBRACE
UNBRACED

UNBRACING
UNBRAID
UNBRAINED
UNBRANDED
UNBREAKABLE
UNBREAST
UNBREATH
UNBREATHED
UNBRED
UNBREECH
UNBRENT
UNBREWED
UNBRICK
UNBRIDLE
UNBRIDLED
UNBRIDLEDLY
UNBROID
UNBROKE
UNBROKEN
UNBROKENLY
UNBROKENNESS
UNBRUTALIZE
UNBRUTE
UNBRUTIFY
UNBRUTIZE
UNBUCKLE
UNBUCKRAMED
UNBUDGEABLE
UNBUDGEABLY
UNBUILD
UNBUILDED
UNBUILDING
UNBUILT
UNBUNDLE
UNBUNG
UNBURDEN
UNBURDENMENT
UNBURIABLE
UNBURIAL
UNBURN
UNBURNISHED
UNBURNT
UNBURROW
UNBURTHEN
UNBURY
UNBUSH
UNBUSIED
UNBUSK
UNBUTTON
UNBUTTONED
UNBUXOM
UNBUXOMLY
UNC
UNCA
UNCAGE
UNCAGED
UNCALLED
UNCALLOW
UNCALLOWER
UNCALM
UNCAMP
UNCANDOR
UNCANDOUR
UNCANNILY
UNCANNINESS
UNCANNY
UNCANONIZE
UNCANONIZED
UNCANONIZING
UNCAP
UNCAPABLE
UNCAPABLY
UNCAPACITATE
UNCAPPED
UNCAPPER
UNCAPPING
UNCAREFUL

UNCAREFULLY
UNCARNATE
UNCART
UNCASE
UNCASTE
UNCASTLE
UNCASTRATED
UNCATE
UNCATHEDRALED
UNCAUGHT
UNCAUSED
UNCAUTELOUS
UNCAUTIOUS
UNCAUTIOUSLY
UNCE
UNCEASABLE
UNCEASING
UNCEASINGLY
UNCELLAR
UNCENTER
UNCENTRE
UNCENTURY
UNCEREMONIOUS
UNCEREMONIOUSLY
UNCERTAIN
UNCERTAINLY
UNCERTAINNESS
UNCERTAINTIES
UNCERTAINTY
UNCERTITUDE
UNCESSANT
UNCESSANTLY
UNCH
UNCHAIN
UNCHALLENGED
UNCHANCE
UNCHANCY
UNCHANGEABLE
UNCHANGEABLENESS
UNCHANGEABLY
UNCHANGING
UNCHARGE
UNCHARGED
UNCHARILY
UNCHARINESS
UNCHARITABLE
UNCHARITABLY
UNCHARITY
UNCHARM
UNCHARNEL
UNCHARTERED
UNCHARY
UNCHASTE
UNCHASTELY
UNCHASTENESS
UNCHASTITY
UNCHECK
UNCHECKED
UNCHEERFUL
UNCHEERFULLY
UNCHILD
UNCHILDISH
UNCHILDISHLY
UNCHRISOM
UNCHRIST
UNCHRISTEN
UNCHRISTENED
UNCHRISTIAN
UNCHURCH
UNCHURCHED
UNCI
UNCIA
UNCIAE
UNCIAL
UNCIALIZE
UNCIALLY
UNCIATIM

UNCIFORM
UNCINAL
UNCINARIASIS
UNCINARIATIC
UNCINATE
UNCINATED
UNCINI
UNCINUS
UNCIPHER
UNCIROSTRATE
UNCITY
UNCIVIL
UNCIVILIZED
UNCIVILLY
UNCLAD
UNCLAMP
UNCLASP
UNCLASSIFY
UNCLE
UNCLEAD
UNCLEAN
UNCLEANLILY
UNCLEANLY
UNCLEANNESS
UNCLEANSE
UNCLEAR
UNCLEARED
UNCLEARLY
UNCLEAVE
UNCLEMENT
UNCLEMENTLY
UNCLENCH
UNCLEVER
UNCLEVERLY
UNCLEW
UNCLIFY
UNCLINCH
UNCLING
UNCLOAK
UNCLOG
UNCLOISTER
UNCLOSE
UNCLOSED
UNCLOSING
UNCLOTHE
UNCLOTHED
UNCLOTHING
UNCLOUD
UNCLOUDED
UNCLUBABLE
UNCLUBBABLE
UNCLUBBY
UNCLUTCH
UNCO
UNCOACH
UNCOACTED
UNCOCK
UNCOFFER
UNCOFFLE
UNCOFT
UNCOGITABLE
UNCOGUIDISM
UNCOHERENT
UNCOHERENTLY
UNCOIF
UNCOIL
UNCOIN
UNCOINED
UNCOLIKE
UNCOLLECTED
UNCOLORED
UNCOLT
UNCOLY
UNCOMBED
UNCOMBINABLE
UNCOMBINABLY
UNCOMBINE

UNCOMBINED
UNCOME
UNCOMELIER
UNCOMELIEST
UNCOMELILY
UNCOMELY
UNCOMFORTABLE
UNCOMFORTABLY
UNCOMMERCIAL
UNCOMMITTED
UNCOMMIXED
UNCOMMODIOUS
UNCOMMON
UNCOMMONER
UNCOMMONEST
UNCOMMONLY
UNCOMMONNESS
UNCOMMUNICATIVE
UNCOMPACT
UNCOMPANIED
UNCOMPASSED
UNCOMPATIBLE
UNCOMPATIBLY
UNCOMPLIABLE
UNCOMPLICATED
UNCOMPLIMENTARY
UNCOMPOSED
UNCOMPOUND
UNCOMPOUNDED
UNCOMPREHEND
UNCOMPROMISING
UNCOMPT
UNCONCEALED
UNCONCEIVING
UNCONCERN
UNCONCERNED
UNCONCERNEDLY
UNCONCERNING
UNCONCLUDENT
UNCONCLUDING
UNCONCLUSIVE
UNCONCOCTED
UNCONDITED
UNCONDITIONAL
UNCONDITIONED
UNCONFINE
UNCONFINED
UNCONFIRMED
UNCONFORMIST
UNCONFORMITIES
UNCONFORMITY
UNCONGENIAL
UNCONNECTED
UNCONQUERED
UNCONQUEST
UNCONSCIOUS
UNCONSCIOUSLY
UNCONSECRATE
UNCONSENT
UNCONSIDERED
UNCONSISTENT
UNCONSONANCY
UNCONSONANT
UNCONSTANCY
UNCONSTANT
UNCONSTANTLY
UNCONSTRAINED
UNCONSTRAINT
UNCONSULT
UNCONTENT
UNCONTENTED
UNCONTROL
UNCONTROLLABLE
UNCONTROLLABLY
UNCONTROLLED
UNCONVENIENT
UNCONVENTIONAL

UNCONVERSING
UNCONVERSION
UNCONVERTED
UNCONVINCING
UNCOOKED
UNCORD
UNCORDED
UNCORDING
UNCORK
UNCORKER
UNCORKING
UNCORPORAL
UNCORRECTED
UNCORRIGIBLE
UNCORRUPT
UNCORRUPTION
UNCORVEN
UNCOS
UNCOST
UNCOUCH
UNCOUCHED
UNCOUCHING
UNCOUNTABLE
UNCOUNTABLY
UNCOUNTED
UNCOUPLE
UNCOUPLED
UNCOUPLER
UNCOUPLING
UNCOURSED
UNCOURTEOUS
UNCOUS
UNCOUTH
UNCOUTHLY
UNCOUTHNESS
UNCOUTHSOME
UNCOVENABLE
UNCOVER
UNCOVERABLE
UNCOVERED
UNCOVEREDLY
UNCOVERING
UNCOW
UNCOWL
UNCRAFTILY
UNCRAFTINESS
UNCRAFTY
UNCRAZED
UNCREATE
UNCREATED
UNCREATING
UNCREATION
UNCREDIBLE
UNCREDIT
UNCREDITABLE
UNCREDITABLY
UNCRINKLE
UNCRINKLED
UNCRINKLING
UNCRITICALLY
UNCRITICISM
UNCROOK
UNCROOKING
UNCROSS
UNCROWN
UNCROWNED
UNCROWNING
UNCRUDDED
UNCRUMPLE
UNCTION
UNCTIONAL
UNCTIONEER
UNCTIONLESS
UNCTIOUS
UNCTIOUSNESS
UNCTORIAN
UNCTUOSITY

UNCTUOUS
UNCTUOUSLY
UNCTUOUSNESS
UNCUBBED
UNCULAR
UNCULTED
UNCULTIVATED
UNCULTURE
UNCULTURED
UNCUMBER
UNCUMBERED
UNCUNNING
UNCUNNINGLY
UNCURABLE
UNCURABLY
UNCURB
UNCURBED
UNCURBING
UNCURED
UNCURL
UNCURLING
UNCURRENT
UNCURRENTLY
UNCURSE
UNCURTAIN
UNCURTAINED
UNCUS
UNCUSTOMED
UNCUT
UNCYA
UNDAMAGED
UNDAMPED
UNDANGERED
UNDARK
UNDARKENED
UNDASHED
UNDATE
UNDATED
UNDATEDNESS
UNDAUGHTERLY
UNDAUNTABLE
UNDAUNTED
UNDAUNTEDLY
UNDAZZLE
UNDE
UNDEADLY
UNDEAF
UNDEAN
UNDEAR
UNDECAGON
UNDECAYED
UNDECEIVABLE
UNDECEIVABLY
UNDECEIVE
UNDECEIVED
UNDECEIVER
UNDECEIVING
UNDECENCY
UNDECENNIAL
UNDECENT
UNDECENTLY
UNDECEPTION
UNDECIDE
UNDECIDED
UNDECIDEDLY
UNDECIDING
UNDECIMAL
UNDECIMAN
UNDECIMOLE
UNDECIPHER
UNDECIPHERED
UNDECISIVE
UNDECISIVELY
UNDECK
UNDECKED
UNDECLARE
UNDECLARED

UNDECLINABLE
UNDECOYED
UNDECREE
UNDECYL
UNDECYLENE
UNDECYLENIC
UNDECYLIC
UNDEE
UNDEEDED
UNDEEMED
UNDEEMOUS
UNDEEMOUSLY
UNDEEP
UNDEFEASIBLE
UNDEFECATED
UNDEFENDED
UNDEFENSIBLE
UNDEFILED
UNDEFINABLE
UNDEFINABLY
UNDEFINE
UNDEFINED
UNDEIFIED
UNDEIFY
UNDEIFYING
UNDELAYEDLY
UNDELIGHT
UNDELIVERABLE
UNDELIVERY
UNDELUDABLE
UNDEMONSTRATIVE
UNDENIABLE
UNDENIABLY
UNDEPENDABLE
UNDEPENDING
UNDEPRIVABLE
UNDER
UNDERACT
UNDERACTED
UNDERACTING
UNDERACTION
UNDERACTOR
UNDERAGE
UNDERAID
UNDERAIR
UNDERARM
UNDERARMING
UNDERBACK
UNDERBARRING
UNDERBEAR
UNDERBEARER
UNDERBEARING
UNDERBEING
UNDERBELLIES
UNDERBELLY
UNDERBID
UNDERBIDDER
UNDERBIDDING
UNDERBILL
UNDERBIND
UNDERBIT
UNDERBITTED
UNDERBITTEN
UNDERBOARD
UNDERBODICE
UNDERBODY
UNDERBORN
UNDERBOUGHT
UNDERBOWED
UNDERBOY
UNDERBRACED
UNDERBRED
UNDERBRIGHT
UNDERBRIM
UNDERBRUSH
UNDERBUILD
UNDERBURN

UNDERBURNED
UNDERBURNT
UNDERBURY
UNDERBUSH
UNDERBUTLER
UNDERBUY
UNDERBUYING
UNDERCANOPY
UNDERCARRIAGE
UNDERCARVED
UNDERCAST
UNDERCHARGE
UNDERCHARGED
UNDERCHARGING
UNDERCLASS
UNDERCLASSMAN
UNDERCLASSMEN
UNDERCLAY
UNDERCLIFF
UNDERCLOTHE
UNDERCLOTHES
UNDERCLUB
UNDERCOAT
UNDERCOATED
UNDERCOATING
UNDERCOLOR
UNDERCOLORED
UNDERCOOL
UNDERCOVER
UNDERCOVERT
UNDERCRAFT
UNDERCREEP
UNDERCREST
UNDERCROFT
UNDERCROP
UNDERCRUST
UNDERCURRENT
UNDERCUT
UNDERCUTTER
UNDERCUTTING
UNDERDEALER
UNDERDEALING
UNDERDECK
UNDERDEVELOPED
UNDERDID
UNDERDITCH
UNDERDO
UNDERDOER
UNDERDOG
UNDERDOING
UNDERDONE
UNDERDOSE
UNDERDRAG
UNDERDRAIN
UNDERDRAINER
UNDERDRAW
UNDERDRAWERS
UNDERDRAWN
UNDERDRESS
UNDERDRIVE
UNDEREARTH
UNDEREATEN
UNDEREDUCATED
UNDERENTER
UNDERER
UNDERESTIMATE
UNDERESTIMATED
UNDERESTIMATING
UNDEREXPOSE
UNDEREXPOSED
UNDEREXPOSING
UNDERFALL
UNDERFED
UNDERFEED
UNDERFEEDING
UNDERFEEL
UNDERFEET

UNDERFELLOW
UNDERFILL
UNDERFILLING
UNDERFIND
UNDERFIRE
UNDERFLEECE
UNDERFLOW
UNDERFO
UNDERFOLD
UNDERFONG
UNDERFOOT
UNDERFRAME
UNDERFRAMING
UNDERFREIGHT
UNDERFUR
UNDERFURROW
UNDERGAGE
UNDERGARMENT
UNDERGAUGE
UNDERGEAR
UNDERGIRD
UNDERGIRDED
UNDERGIRDER
UNDERGIRDING
UNDERGIRDLE
UNDERGIRT
UNDERGIRTH
UNDERGLAZE
UNDERGO
UNDERGOER
UNDERGOES
UNDERGOING
UNDERGONE
UNDERGOWN
UNDERGRADE
UNDERGRADUATE
UNDERGRADUETTE
UNDERGREEN
UNDERGROAN
UNDERGROPE
UNDERGROUND
UNDERGROVE
UNDERGROW
UNDERGROWN
UNDERGROWTH
UNDERHAND
UNDERHANDED
UNDERHANGING
UNDERHEAD
UNDERHEW
UNDERHIVE
UNDERHOLD
UNDERHOLE
UNDERHUNG
UNDERIVED
UNDERJAWED
UNDERKEEP
UNDERLAID
UNDERLAIN
UNDERLAP
UNDERLAY
UNDERLAYER
UNDERLAYING
UNDERLEAF
UNDERLEASE
UNDERLESSEE
UNDERLET
UNDERLETTER
UNDERLETTING
UNDERLEVEL
UNDERLEVER
UNDERLIE
UNDERLIER
UNDERLIFE
UNDERLINE
UNDERLINED
UNDERLINEN

UNDERLINER
UNDERLING
UNDERLINING
UNDERLIP
UNDERLIVE
UNDERLOAD
UNDERLOCK
UNDERLOOK
UNDERLOOKER
UNDERLOUT
UNDERLY
UNDERLYING
UNDERMAN
UNDERMANNED
UNDERMANNING
UNDERMASTED
UNDERMATCH
UNDERMATCHED
UNDERMEAL
UNDERMINE
UNDERMINED
UNDERMINER
UNDERMINING
UNDERMIRTH
UNDERMONEY
UNDERMOST
UNDERMUSLIN
UNDERN
UNDERNAM
UNDERNATURAL
UNDERNEATH
UNDERNESS
UNDERNIM
UNDERNOME
UNDERNOMEN
UNDERNOURISH
UNDERNSONG
UNDERNTIDE
UNDERNTIME
UNDERNUMEN
UNDERPAID
UNDERPAN
UNDERPANTS
UNDERPART
UNDERPASS
UNDERPASSION
UNDERPAY
UNDERPAYING
UNDERPICK
UNDERPICKED
UNDERPIN
UNDERPINNED
UNDERPINNER
UNDERPINNING
UNDERPITCH
UNDERPLANT
UNDERPLANTED
UNDERPLANTING
UNDERPLAY
UNDERPLOT
UNDERPLOTTER
UNDERPOLE
UNDERPOSE
UNDERPOWER
UNDERPRICE
UNDERPRINT
UNDERPROOF
UNDERPROP
UNDERPROPPED
UNDERPROPPER
UNDERPROPPING
UNDERPULL
UNDERPULLER
UNDERPUT
UNDERQUOTE
UNDERQUOTED
UNDERQUOTING

UNDERRAN
UNDERRATE
UNDERRATED
UNDERRATING
UNDERREACH
UNDERREAD
UNDERREAM
UNDERREAMER
UNDERRENT
UNDERRENTED
UNDERRIVER
UNDERROLL
UNDERROOF
UNDERROOT
UNDERRUN
UNDERRUNNING
UNDERSACRISTAN
UNDERSAIL
UNDERSAILED
UNDERSALLY
UNDERSAY
UNDERSCALE
UNDERSCORE
UNDERSCORED
UNDERSCORING
UNDERSCRIBER
UNDERSCRUB
UNDERSEA
UNDERSEAMAN
UNDERSEAS
UNDERSELL
UNDERSELLER
UNDERSELLING
UNDERSENSE
UNDERSERVE
UNDERSET
UNDERSETTER
UNDERSETTING
UNDERSETTLE
UNDERSEXED
UNDERSHAPEN
UNDERSHARP
UNDERSHERIFF
UNDERSHINING
UNDERSHIRT
UNDERSHOOT
UNDERSHOOTING
UNDERSHORE
UNDERSHOT
UNDERSHRUB
UNDERSHRUBBY
UNDERSHUT
UNDERSIDE
UNDERSIGN
UNDERSIGNED
UNDERSIGNER
UNDERSINGING
UNDERSIZE
UNDERSIZED
UNDERSKIRT
UNDERSLEEVE
UNDERSLOPE
UNDERSLUICE
UNDERSLUNG
UNDERSOIL
UNDERSOLD
UNDERSONG
UNDERSPARRED
UNDERSPEND
UNDERSPHERE
UNDERSPIN
UNDERSPORE
UNDERSPREAD
UNDERSPRING
UNDERSTAIRS
UNDERSTAND
UNDERSTANDED

UNDERSTANDER
UNDERSTANDING
UNDERSTATE
UNDERSTATED
UNDERSTATEMENT
UNDERSTATING
UNDERSTOCK
UNDERSTOOD
UNDERSTORY
UNDERSTRATA
UNDERSTRATUM
UNDERSTRATUMS
UNDERSTRIDE
UNDERSTRING
UNDERSTROKE
UNDERSTRUNG
UNDERSTUDIED
UNDERSTUDIES
UNDERSTUDY
UNDERSTUDYING
UNDERSURFACE
UNDERSWEAT
UNDERTAKE
UNDERTAKEN
UNDERTAKER
UNDERTAKING
UNDERTEACHER
UNDERTEAMED
UNDERTENANT
UNDERTHING
UNDERTHINK
UNDERTHRUST
UNDERTIME
UNDERTIMED
UNDERTINT
UNDERTONE
UNDERTONED
UNDERTOOK
UNDERTOW
UNDERTREAD
UNDERTREAT
UNDERTRICK
UNDERTRODDEN
UNDERTRUMP
UNDERTURF
UNDERTURN
UNDERTYPE
UNDERVALUE
UNDERVALUED
UNDERVALUER
UNDERVALUING
UNDERVEST
UNDERVOLTAGE
UNDERWAIST
UNDERWALK
UNDERWARD
UNDERWARP
UNDERWATCH
UNDERWATER
UNDERWAY
UNDERWEAR
UNDERWEIGH
UNDERWEIGHT
UNDERWENT
UNDERWING
UNDERWIT
UNDERWITTED
UNDERWOOD
UNDERWORK
UNDERWORKED
UNDERWORKER
UNDERWORKING
UNDERWORLD
UNDERWRIT
UNDERWRITE
UNDERWRITER
UNDERWRITING

UNDERWRITTEN
UNDERWROTE
UNDERWROUGHT
UNDESCRIPT
UNDESERT
UNDESERVE
UNDESERVED
UNDESERVER
UNDESIGNED
UNDESIGNING
UNDESIRABLE
UNDESIRABLY
UNDESIRE
UNDESIREDLY
UNDETERMINED
UNDEVELOPED
UNDEVIATING
UNDEVIATINGLY
UNDEVIL
UNDEVOTION
UNDID
UNDIES
UNDIFFERENCED
UNDIFFERENTIATED
UNDIG
UNDIGENOUS
UNDIGESTABLE
UNDIGESTED
UNDIGESTIBLE
UNDIGESTION
UNDIGHT
UNDIGHTED
UNDIGNE
UNDIGNIFIED
UNDIGNIFY
UNDILUTED
UNDIMINISHED
UNDIMMED
UNDINE
UNDINED
UNDIOCESED
UNDIRECT
UNDIRECTED
UNDIRECTLY
UNDISCERNING
UNDISCIPLINED
UNDISCLOSE
UNDISCLOSED
UNDISCOURSED
UNDISCREET
UNDISCREETLY
UNDISCRETION
UNDISCRIMINATING
UNDISGUISE
UNDISGUISED
UNDISMAY
UNDISMAYED
UNDISPENSED
UNDISPENSING
UNDISPLAY
UNDISPOSE
UNDISPOSED
UNDISPUTABLE
UNDISPUTABLY
UNDISPUTED
UNDISTINCT
UNDISTINCTLY
UNDISTINGUISHED
UNDISTORTED
UNDISTRESS
UNDISTURBED
UNDIVIDABLE
UNDIVIDABLY
UNDIVIDED
UNDIVIDEDLY
UNDIVIDUAL
UNDIVORCING

UNDO
UNDOCIBLE
UNDOCK
UNDOCTOR
UNDOER
UNDOG
UNDOGMATIC
UNDOING
UNDOMESTICATED
UNDONE
UNDOSE
UNDOUBLE
UNDOUBLED
UNDOUBLING
UNDOUBTABLE
UNDOUBTABLY
UNDOUBTED
UNDOUBTEDLY
UNDRAPE
UNDRAPED
UNDRAW
UNDRAWING
UNDRAWN
UNDREAMED
UNDREAMT
UNDRESS
UNDRESSED
UNDREST
UNDREW
UNDUE
UNDUKE
UNDULANT
UNDULAR
UNDULATANCE
UNDULATE
UNDULATED
UNDULATELY
UNDULATING
UNDULATION
UNDULATIVE
UNDULATORY
UNDULOID
UNDULOSE
UNDULOUS
UNDULY
UNDURE
UNDUST
UNDUSTED
UNDUTIFULNESS
UNDUTY
UNDWELT
UNDY
UNDYED
UNDYING
UNDYINGLY
UNDYINGNESS
UNE
UNEARED
UNEARNED
UNEARTH
UNEARTHED
UNEARTHING
UNEARTHLY
UNEASE
UNEASEFUL
UNEASEFULNESS
UNEASIER
UNEASIEST
UNEASILY
UNEASINESS
UNEASY
UNEATH
UNEATHS
UNEBRIATE
UNEDIBLE
UNEDIBLENESS
UNEDIBLY

UNEDITED
UNEDUCABLE
UNEDUCABLY
UNEDUCATE
UNEDUCATED
UNEFFABLE
UNEFFECTUAL
UNEGAL
UNEGALLY
UNEGALNESS
UNELEGANT
UNELEGANTLY
UNELIGIBLE
UNELIGIBLY
UNEMBELLISHED
UNEMBODIED
UNEMOTIONAL
UNEMOTIONALLY
UNEMOTIONED
UNEMPHATIC
UNEMPLOY
UNEMPLOYABLE
UNEMPLOYED
UNEMPLOYMENT
UNEMPT
UNENCUMBER
UNENCUMBERED
UNENDED
UNENDING
UNENDINGLY
UNENDLY
UNENGAGED
UNENGLISH
UNENJOYABLE
UNENLIGHTENED
UNENTANGLE
UNENTANGLER
UNENTERING
UNENTHUSIASTIC
UNENTRANCE
UNEPISCOPAL
UNEQUABLE
UNEQUABLY
UNEQUAL
UNEQUALED
UNEQUALITY
UNEQUALLED
UNEQUALLY
UNEQUIAXED
UNEQUITABLE
UNEQUITABLY
UNEQUIVOCAL
UNEQUIVOCALLY
UNERECT
UNERRABLE
UNERRABLY
UNERRING
UNERRINGLY
UNESCAPABLE
UNESCAPABLY
UNESSENCE
UNESSENTIAL
UNESTABLISH
UNESTIMABLE
UNETHIC
UNETHICAL
UNETHICALLY
UNEVEN
UNEVENLY
UNEVENNESS
UNEVENTFUL
UNEVENTFULLY
UNEVIDENT
UNEVITABLE
UNEVITABLY
UNEXACT
UNEXACTLY

UNEXACTNESS
UNEXAMPLED
UNEXCEPTIVE
UNEXCITED
UNEXCITING
UNEXCLUSIVE
UNEXCUSABLE
UNEXCUSABLY
UNEXPECT
UNEXPECTED
UNEXPECTEDLY
UNEXPEDIENT
UNEXPENDED
UNEXPENSIVE
UNEXPERIENCE
UNEXPERIENT
UNEXPERT
UNEXPERTLY
UNEXPIRED
UNEXPLAINED
UNEXPLICABLE
UNEXPLOITED
UNEXPOSED
UNEXPRESS
UNEXPRESSIVE
UNEXPURGATED
UNEXTRICABLE
UNEYED
UNFACE
UNFACT
UNFADABLE
UNFADED
UNFADING
UNFADINGLY
UNFAILABLE
UNFAILABLY
UNFAILING
UNFAILINGLY
UNFAIN
UNFAIR
UNFAIRLY
UNFAIRNESS
UNFAITH
UNFAITHFUL
UNFAITHFULLY
UNFALCATED
UNFALLIBLE
UNFALLIBLY
UNFALTERING
UNFAMILIAR
UNFAMILIARLY
UNFAMOUS
UNFARDLE
UNFASHION
UNFASHIONED
UNFAST
UNFASTEN
UNFATHERED
UNFATHOMABLE
UNFATHOMED
UNFAVORABLE
UNFAVORABLY
UNFAVOURABLE
UNFAVOURABLY
UNFEARY
UNFEASABLE
UNFEASABLY
UNFEASIBLE
UNFEASIBLY
UNFEASTLY
UNFEATHER
UNFEATURED
UNFEATY
UNFEEL
UNFEELABLE
UNFEELING
UNFEELINGLY

UNFEELINGNESS	UNFORMALITY	UNGIRDED	UNGULED	UNHENDE
UNFEIGNABLE	UNFORMALLY	UNGIRT	UNGULIGRADE	UNHENT
UNFEIGNABLY	UNFORMALNESS	UNGIRTH	UNGULOUS	UNHEPPEN
UNFEIGNED	UNFORMED	UNGIVE	UNGUM	UNHERD
UNFEIGNEDLY	UNFORTIFIED	UNGKA	UNGUMMED	UNHEROISM
UNFEIGNING	UNFORTUNATE	UNGLAZE	UNGYVE	UNHESITATING
UNFEIGNINGLY	UNFORTUNE	UNGLAZED	UNGYVED	UNHIDABLE
UNFELE	UNFOUND	UNGLE	UNHABILE	UNHIDABLY
UNFELICITOUS	UNFOUNDED	UNGLEE	UNHABIT	UNHIDE
UNFELLOWED	UNFOUNDEDLY	UNGLORIOUS	UNHAD	UNHIDEABLE
UNFERMENTED	UNFOXED	UNGLORIOUSLY	UNHAIR	UNHIDEABLY
UNFERTILE	UNFRAME	UNGLORY	UNHAIRER	UNHINGE
UNFERTILITY	UNFRANGIBLE	UNGLOSSY	UNHAIRING	UNHINGED
UNFESTIVAL	UNFRANK	UNGLOVE	UNHALE	UNHINGING
UNFETTER	UNFRAUGHT	UNGLUE	UNHALLOW	UNHITCH
UNFETTERED	UNFREE	UNGNAW	UNHALLOWED	UNHIVE
UNFEUDALIZE	UNFREEDOM	UNGOD	UNHALSED	UNHOARD
UNFEUED	UNFREELY	UNGODLILY	UNHALTER	UNHOLD
UNFIGURED	UNFREEMAN	UNGODLINESS	UNHAMPERED	UNHOLIER
UNFILIAL	UNFREENESS	UNGODLY	UNHAND	UNHOLIEST
UNFILIALLY	UNFREQUENCY	UNGONE	UNHANDILY	UNHOLILY
UNFILIALNESS	UNFREQUENT	UNGOOD	UNHANDINESS	UNHOLINESS
UNFILLABLE	UNFREQUENTED	UNGOT	UNHANDSOME	UNHOLPEN
UNFILLED	UNFREQUENTLY	UNGOTTEN	UNHANDSOMELY	UNHOLY
UNFILLETED	UNFRET	UNGOVERNABLE	UNHANDY	UNHOME
UNFINANCIAL	UNFRIEND	UNGOVERNABLY	UNHANG	UNHONEST
UNFINE	UNFRIENDED	UNGOWN	UNHAP	UNHONESTLY
UNFINGERED	UNFRIENDING	UNGRACE	UNHAPPIER	UNHONESTY
UNFINISH	UNFRIENDLY	UNGRACEFUL	UNHAPPIEST	UNHONORABLE
UNFINISHED	UNFRIGHTED	UNGRACEFULLY	UNHAPPILY	UNHONORABLY
UNFINISHEDLY	UNFROCK	UNGRACIOUS	UNHAPPINESS	UNHONOURABLE
UNFIRED	UNFROZEN	UNGRACIOUSLY	UNHAPPY	UNHONOURABLY
UNFIRM	UNFRUCTIFY	UNGRADED	UNHARBOR	UNHOOD
UNFIRMLY	UNFRUCTUOUS	UNGRAMMATIC	UNHARBORED	UNHOOK
UNFIRMNESS	UNFRUITFUL	UNGRATEFUL	UNHARBOUR	UNHOOP
UNFIT	UNFRUITFULLY	UNGRATEFULLY	UNHARBOURED	UNHOOPABLE
UNFITLY	UNFULFIL	UNGRAVE	UNHARD	UNHOOPER
UNFITNESS	UNFULFILL	UNGRAVELY	UNHARDILY	UNHOPE
UNFITTED	UNFULFILLMENT	UNGREEABLE	UNHARDINESS	UNHOPED
UNFITTEN	UNFULFILMENT	UNGREEN	UNHARDY	UNHOPEDLY
UNFITTING	UNFUMED	UNGRIPE	UNHARMED	UNHOPEDNESS
UNFITTY	UNFUNDED	UNGROOMED	UNHARMONIOUS	UNHOPEFUL
UNFIX	UNFUR	UNGROUNDED	UNHARNESS	UNHOPEFULLY
UNFIXED	UNFURL	UNGROUNDEDLY	UNHASP	UNHOPPED
UNFLAG	UNFURNISH	UNGUAL	UNHASTE	UNHORSE
UNFLAGGING	UNFURNISHED	UNGUARD	UNHAT	UNHORSED
UNFLAGGINGLY	UNFUSIBLE	UNGUARDED	UNHATTED	UNHORSING
UNFLAME	UNFUSIBLY	UNGUARDEDLY	UNHATTING	UNHOSPITABLE
UNFLAPPABLE	UNGAIN	UNGUEAL	UNHEAD	UNHOSPITABLY
UNFLEDGED	UNGAINLIKE	UNGUENT	UNHEADER	UNHOSPITAL
UNFLEECE	UNGAINLINESS	UNGUENTARIA	UNHEAL	UNHOUSE
UNFLESH	UNGAINLY	UNGUENTARIAN	UNHEALED	UNHOUSED
UNFLESHED	UNGAINNESS	UNGUENTARIUM	UNHEALTH	UNHOUSELED
UNFLESHLY	UNGAITE	UNGUENTARY	UNHEALTHFUL	UNHUMAN
UNFLESHY	UNGALLANT	UNGUENTO	UNHEALTHIER	UNHURRIED
UNFLEXIBLE	UNGALLANTLY	UNGUENTOUS	UNHEALTHIEST	UNHURRIEDLY
UNFLEXIBLY	UNGARO	UNGUENTUM	UNHEALTHILY	UNHURT
UNFLINCHING	UNGEAR	UNGUES	UNHEALTHSOME	UNHUSK
UNFLOWER	UNGENDERED	UNGUICORN	UNHEALTHY	UNHUSKED
UNFLUSH	UNGENEROUS	UNGUICULATE	UNHEARD	UNIAT
UNFOLD	UNGENEROUSLY	UNGUICULE	UNHEARSE	UNIATE
UNFOLDED	UNGENIAL	UNGUIFEROUS	UNHEART	UNIAXIAL
UNFOLDEN	UNGENIALITY	UNGUIFORM	UNHEARTEN	UNIBIVALENT
UNFOLDER	UNGENIALLY	UNGUILED	UNHEARTSOME	UNIBLE
UNFOLDING	UNGENIALNESS	UNGUILEFUL	UNHEARTY	UNIC
UNFOLDMENT	UNGENITURED	UNGUILEFULLY	UNHEATED	UNICAMERAL
UNFOOL	UNGENTEEL	UNGUILTILY	UNHEAVEN	UNICELL
UNFOOTED	UNGENTEELY	UNGUILTINESS	UNHEED	UNICELLATE
UNFORBADE	UNGENTLE	UNGUILTLESS	UNHEEDED	UNICELLED
UNFORCED	UNGENTLEMAN	UNGUILTY	UNHEEDING	UNICELLULAR
UNFORCEDLY	UNGENTLENESS	UNGUINOUS	UNHEEDY	UNICHORD
UNFORCEDNESS	UNGENTLY	UNGUIROSTRAL	UNHEIRED	UNICISM
UNFORESEE	UNGET	UNGUIS	UNHELE	UNICIST
UNFORESEEN	UNGIFTED	UNGULA	UNHELER	UNICITY
UNFORGIVER	UNGILD	UNGULAE	UNHELM	UNICOLOR
UNFORGIVING	UNGILL	UNGULAR	UNHELMET	UNICONSTANT
UNFORMAL	UNGIRD	UNGULATE	UNHELP	UNICORN

UNICORNIC
UNICOSTATE
UNICUM
UNICURSAL
UNICURSALITY
UNICURSALLY
UNICYCLE
UNICYCLIST
UNIDEAED
UNIDEAL
UNIDENTIFIED
UNIDEXTRAL
UNIDIRECT
UNIDLE
UNIDLENESS
UNIDLY
UNIE
UNIFACE
UNIFACED
UNIFACTORIAL
UNIFARIOUS
UNIFIABLE
UNIFIC
UNIFICATION
UNIFIED
UNIFIEDLY
UNIFIEDNESS
UNIFIER
UNIFILAR
UNIFLOROUS
UNIFLOW
UNIFOLIATE
UNIFOLIOLATE
UNIFORM
UNIFORMALIZE
UNIFORMALIZED
UNIFORMALIZING
UNIFORMED
UNIFORMIST
UNIFORMITIES
UNIFORMITY
UNIFORMIZE
UNIFORMLY
UNIFORMNESS
UNIFY
UNIFYING
UNIGENESIS
UNIGENETIC
UNIGENITAL
UNIGENITURE
UNIGENOUS
UNIGRAVIDA
UNIJUGATE
UNILATERAL
UNILATERALLY
UNILINGUAL
UNILITERAL
UNILOBE
UNILOCULAR
UNIMAGINABLE
UNIMAGINATIVE
UNIMANUAL
UNIMBATTLED
UNIMEDIAL
UNIMITABLE
UNIMITABLY
UNIMMERGIBLE
UNIMODAL
UNIMODALITY
UNIMPAIRED
UNIMPASSIONED
UNIMPEDED
UNIMPEDEDLY
UNIMPLICATE
UNIMPORTANCE
UNIMPORTANT
UNIMPRESSED

UNIMPRESSIVE
UNIMPROVABLE
UNIMPROVED
UNIMPROVEDLY
UNINCULCATED
UNINDEBTED
UNINDEBTEDLY
UNINDENTED
UNINFORMED
UNINGENIOUS
UNINGENUOUS
UNINGENUOUSLY
UNINHABITED
UNINHIBITED
UNINJURED
UNINOMINAL
UNINSPIRED
UNINSTRUCTED
UNINTELLIGENT
UNINTELLIGIBLE
UNINTENTIONAL
UNINTENTIONALLY
UNINTERESTED
UNINTERESTING
UNINTERMITTED
UNINTERMITTENT
UNINTERRUPTED
UNINTERRUPTEDLY
UNINTROITIVE
UNINVENTIVE
UNINVITE
UNINVITED
UNIOID
UNION
UNIONED
UNIONIC
UNIONID
UNIONIFORM
UNIONISM
UNIONIST
UNIONISTIC
UNIONIZATION
UNIONIZE
UNIONIZED
UNIONIZING
UNIONOID
UNIOVAL
UNIPARA
UNIPARENTAL
UNIPARIENT
UNIPAROUS
UNIPARTITE
UNIPED
UNIPERIODIC
UNIPERSONAL
UNIPETALOUS
UNIPLANAR
UNIPOLAR
UNIPOLARITY
UNIPOROUS
UNIPOTENCE
UNIPOTENT
UNIPULSE
UNIQUANTIC
UNIQUE
UNIQUELY
UNIQUENESS
UNIQUITY
UNIREME
UNISEPTATE
UNISEX
UNISEXED
UNISEXUAL
UNISEXUALITY
UNISEXUALLY
UNISON
UNISONAL

UNISONANT
UNISONO
UNISONOUS
UNISPARKER
UNISPIRAL
UNISTYLIST
UNIT
UNITABILITY
UNITABLE
UNITABLY
UNITAL
UNITARIAN
UNITARILY
UNITARINESS
UNITARISM
UNITARIST
UNITARY
UNITATION
UNITE
UNITEABLE
UNITEABLY
UNITED
UNITEDLY
UNITEDNESS
UNITELY
UNITEMIZED
UNITENESS
UNITER
UNITIES
UNITING
UNITION
UNITISM
UNITISTIC
UNITIVE
UNITIVELY
UNITIVENESS
UNITIZE
UNITRIVALENT
UNITROPE
UNITS
UNITUDE
UNITY
UNIVALENCE
UNIVALENCY
UNIVALENT
UNIVALID
UNIVALVE
UNIVALVED
UNIVALVULAR
UNIVARIANT
UNIVERSAL
UNIVERSALIA
UNIVERSALITIES
UNIVERSALITY
UNIVERSALIZE
UNIVERSALIZED
UNIVERSALIZING
UNIVERSALLY
UNIVERSE
UNIVERSEFUL
UNIVERSITAS
UNIVERSITIES
UNIVERSITIZE
UNIVERSITY
UNIVERSOLOGY
UNIVOCACY
UNIVOCAL
UNIVOCALLY
UNIVOCATION
UNIVOCITY
UNIVOLTINE
UNIVOROUS
UNJUDICIOUS
UNJUST
UNJUSTIFIED
UNJUSTLY
UNJUSTNESS

UNKAMED
UNKED
UNKEELED
UNKEMBED
UNKEMPT
UNKEMPTLY
UNKEMPTNESS
UNKEN
UNKEND
UNKENNED
UNKENNEL
UNKENNELED
UNKENNELING
UNKENNELLED
UNKENNELLING
UNKENNING
UNKENSOME
UNKENT
UNKEPT
UNKET
UNKID
UNKIND
UNKINDLILY
UNKINDLY
UNKINDNESS
UNKINDRED
UNKINDREDLY
UNKING
UNKINGER
UNKINGSHIP
UNKINK
UNKISS
UNKNIT
UNKNITTED
UNKNITTING
UNKNOW
UNKNOWABLE
UNKNOWABLY
UNKNOWING
UNKNOWINGLY
UNKNOWLEDGED
UNKNOWN
UNKNOWNLY
UNKNOWNNESS
UNKNOWNST
UNKO
UNLABORED
UNLABOURED
UNLACE
UNLACED
UNLACING
UNLADE
UNLADED
UNLADEN
UNLADIFIED
UNLADING
UNLADYFIED
UNLAID
UNLAND
UNLAP
UNLASH
UNLASHER
UNLATCH
UNLATINED
UNLAW
UNLAWED
UNLAWFUL
UNLAWFULLY
UNLAWFULNESS
UNLAY
UNLAYED
UNLAYING
UNLEAD
UNLEADED
UNLEARED
UNLEARN
UNLEARNED

UNLEARNEDLY
UNLEARNING
UNLEARNT
UNLEASH
UNLEAVE
UNLEAVENED
UNLEDE
UNLEEFUL
UNLEESOME
UNLEGITIMATE
UNLEISUM
UNLEISURED
UNLENGTH
UNLERED
UNLESS
UNLETTED
UNLETTERED
UNLETTEREDLY
UNLEVEL
UNLEWTY
UNLICKED
UNLID
UNLIEF
UNLIGHT
UNLIGHTED
UNLIGHTEDLY
UNLIGHTSOME
UNLIKE
UNLIKELIER
UNLIKELIEST
UNLIKELIHOOD
UNLIKELINESS
UNLIKELY
UNLIKEN
UNLIKENESS
UNLIKING
UNLIMB
UNLIMBER
UNLIME
UNLIMITABLE
UNLIMITABLY
UNLIMITED
UNLIMITEDLY
UNLINE
UNLINED
UNLINK
UNLINKED
UNLINKING
UNLIQUIDATED
UNLIQUORED
UNLIST
UNLISTED
UNLISTENED
UNLISTY
UNLIT
UNLITERAL
UNLITERALLY
UNLITTLE
UNLITURGICAL
UNLITURGIZE
UNLIVE
UNLIVED
UNLIVERY
UNLIVING
UNLOAD
UNLOADEN
UNLOADER
UNLOCATED
UNLOCK
UNLOCKER
UNLODGE
UNLOGIC
UNLOGICAL
UNLOGICALLY
UNLOOK
UNLOOKED
UNLOOSE

UNLOOSEN
UNLORD
UNLORDED
UNLORDLY
UNLOUKEN
UNLOUSY
UNLOVE
UNLOVED
UNLOVELIER
UNLOVELIEST
UNLOVELILY
UNLOVELINESS
UNLOVELY
UNLOVERLIKE
UNLOVERLY
UNLOVESOME
UNLOVING
UNLOVINGLY
UNLOVINGNESS
UNLUCK
UNLUCKFUL
UNLUCKIER
UNLUCKIEST
UNLUCKILY
UNLUCKINESS
UNLUCKLY
UNLUCKY
UNLUST
UNLUSTIE
UNLUSTIER
UNLUSTIEST
UNLUSTILY
UNLUSTINESS
UNLUSTY
UNLUTE
UNMACKLY
UNMADE
UNMAGISTRATE
UNMAIDEN
UNMAIL
UNMAILABLE
UNMAKE
UNMAKER
UNMAKING
UNMAN
UNMANACLE
UNMANAGEABLE
UNMANHOOD
UNMANIABLE
UNMANLIER
UNMANLIEST
UNMANLILY
UNMANLINESS
UNMANLY
UNMANNED
UNMANNERED
UNMANNEREDLY
UNMANNERLY
UNMANNING
UNMANTLE
UNMARKED
UNMARRIED
UNMARRY
UNMASK
UNMASKER
UNMASKING
UNMATCHED
UNMATURE
UNMATURELY
UNMATURENESS
UNMATURITY
UNMAZE
UNMEANING
UNMEANINGLY
UNMEANT
UNMEASURABLE
UNMEASURABLY

UNMEASURED
UNMEASUREDLY
UNMEASURELY
UNMECHANIC
UNMECHANICAL
UNMECHANIZE
UNMEDDLE
UNMEDULLATED
UNMEEDFUL
UNMEEDY
UNMEEK
UNMEEKLY
UNMEEKNESS
UNMEET
UNMEETLY
UNMEETNESS
UNMELODIOUS
UNMELT
UNMEMBER
UNMERCHANTABLE
UNMERCIABLE
UNMERCIABLY
UNMERCIED
UNMERCIFUL
UNMERCIFULLY
UNMERCILESS
UNMERITABLE
UNMESH
UNMETE
UNMETH
UNMETHODICAL
UNMEW
UNMIGHT
UNMIGHTY
UNMILD
UNMILDNESS
UNMILITARILY
UNMILITARY
UNMILLED
UNMIND
UNMINDED
UNMINDFUL
UNMINDFULLY
UNMINDING
UNMINGLE
UNMINGLEABLE
UNMINGLED
UNMIST
UNMISTAKABLE
UNMISTAKABLY
UNMITER
UNMITIGATED
UNMITRE
UNMIX
UNMIXED
UNMOBLE
UNMODERATE
UNMODERATELY
UNMODERNIZE
UNMODIFIED
UNMODULATED
UNMOLD
UNMOLEST
UNMOLESTED
UNMONEYED
UNMONOPOLIZE
UNMOOR
UNMOORED
UNMORAL
UNMORALIST
UNMORALITY
UNMORALIZED
UNMORALIZING
UNMORALLY
UNMORALNESS
UNMORRISED
UNMORTALIZE

UNMORTISE
UNMORTISED
UNMORTISING
UNMOTHERED
UNMOTIVED
UNMOULD
UNMOUNT
UNMOUNTED
UNMOVABILITY
UNMOVABLE
UNMOVABLETY
UNMOVABLY
UNMOVED
UNMOVEDLY
UNMOVING
UNMUDDLE
UNMUFFLE
UNMUFFLED
UNMUFFLING
UNMUSICAL
UNMUTABLE
UNMUZZLE
UNMYSTERY
UNNAIL
UNNAPKINED
UNNAPPED
UNNAPT
UNNATURAL
UNNATURALISM
UNNATURALIST
UNNATURALITY
UNNATURALIZE
UNNATURALLY
UNNATURE
UNNEALED
UNNEAR
UNNEATH
UNNECESSARY
UNNEEDED
UNNEIGHBORED
UNNEIGHBORLY
UNNERVE
UNNERVED
UNNERVING
UNNEST
UNNET
UNNETH
UNNETHE
UNNEWSED
UNNIMBED
UNNOBILITY
UNNOBLE
UNNOBLENESS
UNNOBLY
UNNOOKED
UNNOSE
UNNOTED
UNNOTICEABLE
UNNOTICEABLY
UNNOTICED
UNNOTIFY
UNNUMBERABLE
UNNUMBERABLY
UNNUMBERED
UNNUMERABLE
UNNUN
UNOBEDIENCE
UNOBEDIENT
UNOBEDIENTLY
UNOBJECTIONABLE
UNOBLIGING
UNOBLIGINGLY
UNOBSERVANCE
UNOBSERVANT
UNOBSERVED
UNOBSERVEDLY
UNOBSERVING

UNOBSTRUCTED
UNOBTAINABLE
UNOBTAINABLY
UNOBTRUSIVE
UNOCCUPIED
UNOCCUPIEDLY
UNODE
UNOFFENDED
UNOFFENDEDLY
UNOFFENDING
UNOFFENSIVE
UNOFFICIAL
UNOFFICIALLY
UNOFFICINAL
UNOFTEN
UNOIL
UNOLD
UNOPED
UNOPEN
UNOPENED
UNOPENLY
UNOPENNESS
UNOPERATIVE
UNOPERCULATE
UNOPPORTUNE
UNORDAINED
UNORDER
UNORDERED
UNORDERLY
UNORDINARILY
UNORDINARY
UNORDINATE
UNORDINATELY
UNORGANED
UNORGANIC
UNORGANICAL
UNORGANISED
UNORGANIZED
UNORIENTED
UNORIGINAL
UNORIGINATE
UNORIGINATED
UNORN
UNORTHODOX
UNORTHODOXLY
UNORTHODOXY
UNOSTENTATIOUS
UNOWED
UNOWN
UNOWNED
UNPACIFIED
UNPACIFIEDLY
UNPACK
UNPACKER
UNPAGED
UNPAID
UNPAINT
UNPAINTABLE
UNPAINTED
UNPAINTEDLY
UNPAIRED
UNPAISED
UNPALATABLE
UNPALE
UNPALPED
UNPANEL
UNPANNEL
UNPAPER
UNPARADISE
UNPARAGONED
UNPARALLELED
UNPARCH
UNPARDONABLE
UNPARDONABLY
UNPAREGAL
UNPARENTED
UNPARREL

UNPARROTED
UNPARTED
UNPARTIAL
UNPARTIALITY
UNPARTIALLY
UNPASSABLE
UNPASSABLY
UNPASSIONATE
UNPASTOR
UNPATHED
UNPATHWAYED
UNPATIENCE
UNPATIENT
UNPATIENTLY
UNPATRIOTIC
UNPATROLLED
UNPATRONIZED
UNPAVE
UNPAVED
UNPAWN
UNPAY
UNPEACE
UNPEDIGREED
UNPEEL
UNPEELED
UNPEERABLE
UNPEERED
UNPEG
UNPEN
UNPENITENT
UNPENITENTLY
UNPEOPLE
UNPEOPLED
UNPEOPLING
UNPERCEIVED
UNPERCH
UNPERFECT
UNPERFECTED
UNPERFECTION
UNPERFECTLY
UNPERFORATED
UNPERFORMING
UNPERISHABLE
UNPERISHABLY
UNPERMANENCY
UNPERMANENT
UNPERPLEX
UNPERSUASION
UNPERTURBED
UNPERVERT
UNPHRASABLE
UNPHRASED
UNPICK
UNPIECE
UNPIERCED
UNPILE
UNPILLED
UNPIN
UNPINION
UNPINKED
UNPINNED
UNPINNING
UNPITEOUS
UNPITEOUSLY
UNPITIED
UNPITIEDLY
UNPITIEDNESS
UNPITY
UNPITYING
UNPITYINGLY
UNPLACABLE
UNPLACABLY
UNPLACE
UNPLACED
UNPLAID
UNPLAIN
UNPLAINED

UNPLAINLY
UNPLAINNESS
UNPLAIT
UNPLANK
UNPLANNED
UNPLANNEDLY
UNPLANT
UNPLANTED
UNPLAT
UNPLAUSIVE
UNPLAYABLE
UNPLEASANT
UNPLEASANTLY
UNPLEASANTNESS
UNPLEASANTRIES
UNPLEASANTRY
UNPLEASED
UNPLEASING
UNPLEASINGLY
UNPLEASIVE
UNPLEASURE
UNPLEAT
UNPLEDGED
UNPLIGHT
UNPLOWED
UNPLUG
UNPLUMB
UNPLUMBED
UNPLUME
UNPOETIC
UNPOETICAL
UNPOETICALLY
UNPOISED
UNPOISON
UNPOLICED
UNPOLICIED
UNPOLISH
UNPOLISHED
UNPOLITE
UNPOLITELY
UNPOLITENESS
UNPOLITIC
UNPOLITICLY
UNPOLLED
UNPOLLUTED
UNPOLLUTEDLY
UNPOPE
UNPOPULAR
UNPOPULARITY
UNPOPULARIZE
UNPOPULARLY
UNPOPULATE
UNPOPULATED
UNPORTABLE
UNPORTUNATE
UNPORTUOUS
UNPOSSESS
UNPOSSIBLE
UNPOSSIBLY
UNPOWER
UNPOWERFUL
UNPRACTICAL
UNPRACTICED
UNPRACTISED
UNPRAISABLE
UNPRAISE
UNPRAY
UNPRAYABLE
UNPRAYED
UNPREACH
UNPREACHING
UNPREDICT
UNPREDICTABLE
UNPREGNABLE
UNPREJUDICE
UNPREJUDICED
UNPREMEDITATED

UNPREPARE
UNPREPARED
UNPREPAREDLY
UNPREPOSSESSING
UNPREST
UNPRETENDING
UNPRETENTIOUS
UNPREVENTED
UNPRICED
UNPRIEST
UNPRIME
UNPRINCE
UNPRINCIPLE
UNPRINCIPLED
UNPRINTABLE
UNPRINTABLY
UNPRISON
UNPRIVILEGED
UNPRIZABLE
UNPROBABLE
UNPROBABLY
UNPROCLAIMED
UNPROCREATE
UNPRODUCIBLE
UNPRODUCIBLY
UNPRODUCTIVE
UNPRODUCTIVENESS
UNPROFESSIONAL
UNPROFICIENT
UNPROFIT
UNPROFITABLE
UNPROFITABLY
UNPROFITED
UNPROGRESSIVE
UNPROMISE
UNPROMISING
UNPRONOUNCED
UNPROP
UNPROPER
UNPROPERLY
UNPROPERNESS
UNPROPERTIED
UNPROPICE
UNPROPITIOUS
UNPROPORTION
UNPROPRIETY
UNPROSELYTE
UNPROSPERITY
UNPROSPEROUS
UNPROTECTED
UNPROVABLE
UNPROVABLY
UNPROVIDE
UNPROVIDED
UNPROVIDEDLY
UNPROVIDENT
UNPROVISED
UNPROVISEDLY
UNPROVISION
UNPRUDENCE
UNPRUDENT
UNPRUDENTLY
UNPUBLISHED
UNPUCKER
UNPUFF
UNPULLED
UNPUNISHED
UNPUNISHEDLY
UNPUNISHING
UNPURE
UNPURED
UNPURELY
UNPURENESS
UNPURSE
UNPURVEYED
UNPUZZLE
UNQUAILED

UNQUALIFIED
UNQUALIFY
UNQUALITIED
UNQUALITY
UNQUANTIFIED
UNQUEEN
UNQUEME
UNQUEMELY
UNQUERT
UNQUESTIONABLE
UNQUESTIONED
UNQUESTIONING
UNQUICK
UNQUIESCENCE
UNQUIESCENT
UNQUIET
UNQUIETLY
UNQUIETNESS
UNQUIETOUS
UNQUIETUDE
UNQUIT
UNQUOD
UNQUOTE
UNRACED
UNRAKE
UNRAM
UNRANK
UNRATED
UNRATIFIED
UNRATTLED
UNRAVAGED
UNRAVEL
UNRAVELABLE
UNRAVELED
UNRAVELER
UNRAVELING
UNRAVELLABLE
UNRAVELLED
UNRAVELLER
UNRAVELLING
UNRAVELMENT
UNRAY
UNREAD
UNREADABLE
UNREADABLY
UNREADIER
UNREADIEST
UNREADILY
UNREADINESS
UNREADY
UNREAL
UNREALISM
UNREALIST
UNREALISTIC
UNREALITIES
UNREALITY
UNREALIZE
UNREALIZED
UNREALLY
UNREALNESS
UNREASON
UNREASONABLE
UNREASONABLENESS
UNREASONABLY
UNREASONED
UNREASONING
UNREAVE
UNREBUKABLE
UNREBUKABLY
UNREBUKEABLE
UNRECALLING
UNRECKLESS
UNRECOGNIZED
UNRECORDED
UNRECOVERABLE
UNRECOVERED
UNRECTIFIED

UNRECURING
UNRED
UNREDEEMED
UNREDUCT
UNREEL
UNREEVE
UNREEVED
UNREEVING
UNREFINE
UNREFINED
UNREFINEDLY
UNREFINEMENT
UNREFLECTING
UNREFLECTIVE
UNREGARD
UNREGENERACY
UNREGENERATE
UNREGENERATELY
UNREGISTERED
UNREGULAR
UNREGULATED
UNREHEARSED
UNREIN
UNRELATED
UNRELAXED
UNRELENTABLE
UNRELENTANCE
UNRELENTING
UNRELENTLESS
UNRELENTOR
UNRELEVANT
UNRELIABLE
UNRELIABLY
UNRELIANCE
UNRELIEVED
UNRELIGION
UNRELIGIOUS
UNREMEDIABLE
UNREMEMBER
UNREMITTING
UNREMOVED
UNREMUNERATIVE
UNRENOWNED
UNRENOWNEDLY
UNREPAIR
UNREPAIRABLE
UNREPENTABLE
UNREPENTANCE
UNREPLIABLE
UNREPLIABLY
UNREPORTED
UNREPORTEDLY
UNREPROVED
UNREPROVEDLY
UNREPUGNABLE
UNREPUTABLE
UNREQUEST
UNREQUITER
UNRESERVE
UNRESERVED
UNRESERVEDLY
UNRESERVEDNESS
UNRESISTABLE
UNRESISTABLY
UNRESISTANT
UNRESISTED
UNRESISTEDLY
UNRESISTIBLE
UNRESISTIBLY
UNRESISTING
UNRESOLUTE
UNRESOLVE
UNRESPECT
UNRESPECTIVE
UNRESPONSAL
UNRESPONSIVE
UNREST

UNRESTED
UNRESTING
UNRESTRAINED
UNRESTRAINT
UNRESTRICTED
UNRESTY
UNRETURNED
UNREVEALED
UNREVENUED
UNREVERENCE
UNREVEREND
UNREVERENDLY
UNREVERENT
UNREVERENTLY
UNREVOCABLE
UNREVOCABLY
UNREWARDED
UNRICHT
UNRID
UNRIDDLE
UNRIDDLED
UNRIDDLER
UNRIDDLING
UNRIDE
UNRIFLED
UNRIG
UNRIGGED
UNRIGGING
UNRIGHT
UNRIGHTEOUS
UNRIGHTEOUSNESS
UNRIGHTFUL
UNRIGHTFULLY
UNRIGHTLY
UNRIGHTWISE
UNRIND
UNRING
UNRINGED
UNRIP
UNRIPE
UNRIPELY
UNRIPENED
UNRIPENESS
UNRIPPED
UNRIPPING
UNRIVALED
UNRIVALEDLY
UNRIVALLED
UNRIVALLEDLY
UNRIVET
UNRO
UNROADED
UNROAST
UNROBE
UNROLL
UNROLLER
UNROLLMENT
UNROMANTIC
UNROMANTICAL
UNROOF
UNROOST
UNRQOT
UNROPE
UNROUGH
UNROUND
UNROUT
UNROVE
UNROW
UNROYAL
UNROYALIST
UNROYALLY
UNROYALNESS
UNRUDE
UNRUEFULLY
UNRUFE
UNRUFFLE
UNRUFFLED

UNRULE
UNRULED
UNRULEDLY
UNRULEDNESS
UNRULEFUL
UNRULIER
UNRULIEST
UNRULILY
UNRULIMENT
UNRULINESS
UNRULY
UNRUMPLE
UNRUTH
UNSACK
UNSACRAMENT
UNSAD
UNSADDEN
UNSADDLE
UNSADDLED
UNSADDLING
UNSADNESS
UNSAFE
UNSAFELY
UNSAFENESS
UNSAFER
UNSAFEST
UNSAFETY
UNSAID
UNSAINT
UNSAINTLY
UNSAKED
UNSALABILITY
UNSALABLE
UNSALABLY
UNSALEABLE
UNSALEABLY
UNSAME
UNSAMFLED
UNSANCTIFIED
UNSANCTIFY
UNSANCTION
UNSANE
UNSANITARY
UNSANITATION
UNSASH
UNSATIABLE
UNSATIABLY
UNSATIATE
UNSATISFACTORY
UNSATISFY
UNSATISFYING
UNSATURABLE
UNSATURATED
UNSATURATION
UNSAUGHT
UNSAVOR
UNSAVORED
UNSAVORILY
UNSAVORINESS
UNSAVORLY
UNSAVORY
UNSAVOURED
UNSAVOURILY
UNSAVOURY
UNSAY
UNSAYING
UNSCALE
UNSCALED
UNSCALEDNESS
UNSCAPABLE
UNSCATHED
UNSCATHEDLY
UNSCENT
UNSCENTED
UNSCHOLAR
UNSCHOLARLY
UNSCHOOLED

UNSCHOOLEDLY
UNSCIENCE
UNSCIENCED
UNSCIENTIFIC
UNSCOTCH
UNSCOTTIFY
UNSCRAMBLE
UNSCRAMBLED
UNSCRAMBLING
UNSCRAPED
UNSCREEN
UNSCREW
UNSCRUPULOUS
UNSCRUTABLE
UNSEAL
UNSEALER
UNSEAM
UNSEARCHABLE
UNSEARCHABLY
UNSEASON
UNSEASONABLE
UNSEASONABLY
UNSEASONED
UNSEAT
UNSEATED
UNSEAWORTHY
UNSECONDED
UNSECRECY
UNSECRET
UNSECTARIAN
UNSECULARIZE
UNSECURE
UNSECURED
UNSECUREDLY
UNSECURELY
UNSECURENESS
UNSECURITY
UNSEE
UNSEEING
UNSEEL
UNSEELINESS
UNSEELY
UNSEEMING
UNSEEMINGLY
UNSEEMLIER
UNSEEMLIEST
UNSEEMLILY
UNSEEMLINESS
UNSEEMLY
UNSEEN
UNSEIZE
UNSEL
UNSELDOM
UNSELF
UNSELFISH
UNSELFISHLY
UNSELFNESS
UNSELINESS
UNSELTH
UNSELY
UNSEMINARED
UNSENSE
UNSENSED
UNSENSIBLE
UNSENSIBLY
UNSENSUALIZE
UNSENTENCED
UNSEPARABLE
UNSEPARABLY
UNSEPTATE
UNSEPTATED
UNSERRIED
UNSERVED
UNSERVICE
UNSET
UNSETTING
UNSETTLE

UNSETTLED
UNSEVEN
UNSEW
UNSEWERED
UNSEX
UNSEXED
UNSEXING
UNSHACKLE
UNSHACKLED
UNSHACKLING
UNSHADOW
UNSHAKABLE
UNSHAKABLY
UNSHAKEABLE
UNSHAKED
UNSHAKEN
UNSHAKENLY
UNSHAKENNESS
UNSHALE
UNSHAMEFUL
UNSHAMEFULLY
UNSHAPE
UNSHAPED
UNSHAPELY
UNSHAPEN
UNSHAPENLY
UNSHAPENNESS
UNSHARED
UNSHARPEN
UNSHAVE
UNSHAVED
UNSHAVEDLY
UNSHAVEDNESS
UNSHAVEN
UNSHAVENLY
UNSHAVENNESS
UNSHAWL
UNSHEAF
UNSHEATHE
UNSHEATHED
UNSHEATHING
UNSHED
UNSHEET
UNSHELL
UNSHELVE
UNSHENT
UNSHERIFF
UNSHEWED
UNSHIFTABLE
UNSHIFTINESS
UNSHIP
UNSHIPMENT
UNSHIPPED
UNSHIPPING
UNSHOD
UNSHOE
UNSHOOK
UNSHOP
UNSHORN
UNSHOT
UNSHOULDER
UNSHOUT
UNSHRINE
UNSHRINEMENT
UNSHRINK
UNSHROUD
UNSHRUBBED
UNSHUNNING
UNSHUT
UNSHUTTER
UNSIB
UNSICKER
UNSICKERLY
UNSICKERNESS
UNSICKLED
UNSIDED
UNSIEGE

UNSIGHT
UNSIGHTABLE
UNSIGHTED
UNSIGHTEDLY
UNSIGHTING
UNSIGHTLIER
UNSIGHTLIEST
UNSIGHTLY
UNSIGNABLE
UNSIGNED
UNSILENCED
UNSIMILAR
UNSIMILARLY
UNSIMPLICITY
UNSIN
UNSINCERE
UNSINCERELY
UNSINCERITY
UNSINEW
UNSING
UNSINGABLE
UNSISTER
UNSISTERLY
UNSISTING
UNSITTING
UNSITTINGLY
UNSIZED
UNSKAITHED
UNSKILFUL
UNSKILFULLY
UNSKILL
UNSKILLED
UNSKILLEDLY
UNSKILLFUL
UNSKILLFULLY
UNSKIMMED
UNSKIN
UNSKIRMISHED
UNSLAKED
UNSLATE
UNSLAVE
UNSLEEVE
UNSLEPT
UNSLING
UNSLINGING
UNSLIP
UNSLIT
UNSLOCKENED
UNSLOGH
UNSLOT
UNSLOTHFUL
UNSLOTHFULLY
UNSLUICE
UNSLUNG
UNSMART
UNSMARTLY
UNSMARTNESS
UNSMILING
UNSMOOTH
UNSMOTE
UNSNAP
UNSNAPPED
UNSNAPPING
UNSNARE
UNSNARL
UNSNECK
UNSOBER
UNSOBERLY
UNSOBERNESS
UNSOBRIETY
UNSOCIABLE
UNSOCIABLY
UNSOCIAL
UNSOCIALLY
UNSOCIALNESS
UNSOCKET
UNSODDEN

UNSOFT
UNSOIL
UNSOILED
UNSOLDER
UNSOLDIER
UNSOLDIERED
UNSOLDIERLY
UNSOLDIERY
UNSOLEMN
UNSOLEMNESS
UNSOLEMNIZE
UNSOLEMNLY
UNSOLICITED
UNSOLUBILITY
UNSOLUBLE
UNSOLVABLE
UNSOLVABLY
UNSOLVE
UNSOLVED
UNSOME
UNSON
UNSONCY
UNSONSIE
UNSONSY
UNSOOT
UNSOPHISTICATE
UNSOPHISTICATED
UNSORROWED
UNSORTED
UNSOUGHT
UNSOUL
UNSOUND
UNSOUNDLY
UNSOUNDNESS
UNSPAR
UNSPARABLE
UNSPARING
UNSPARINGLY
UNSPEAK
UNSPEAKABLE
UNSPEAKABLY
UNSPEAKING
UNSPECIFIED
UNSPED
UNSPEED
UNSPEEDFUL
UNSPELL
UNSPHERE
UNSPHERED
UNSPHERING
UNSPIABLE
UNSPIKE
UNSPILLABLE
UNSPIN
UNSPIRIT
UNSPIRITUAL
UNSPIT
UNSPLEENED
UNSPOIL
UNSPOILED
UNSPOILT
UNSPOKE
UNSPOKEN
UNSPOKENLY
UNSPORTSMANLIKE
UNSPOT
UNSPOTTED
UNSPOTTEDLY
UNSPOTTEN
UNSPREAD
UNSPRIGHTLY
UNSPRING
UNSPRUNG
UNSQUARE
UNSQUARED
UNSQUIRE
UNSTABILITY

UNSTABLE	UNSTYLISH	UNTANGLED	UNTIE	UNTRIUMPHED
UNSTABLED	UNSTYLISHLY	UNTANGLING	UNTIED	UNTROD
UNSTABLENESS	UNSUBDUED	UNTAP	UNTIGHT	UNTRODDEN
UNSTABLY	UNSUBMISSION	UNTAPPICE	UNTIGHTEN	UNTROTH
UNSTACK	UNSUBSTANTIAL	UNTAR	UNTIGHTENED	UNTROUBLE
UNSTACKER	UNSUBTLE	UNTASTE	UNTIGHTENING	UNTROUBLED
UNSTAID	UNSUBTLENESS	UNTAUGHT	UNTIGHTNESS	UNTROUBLEDLY
UNSTAIDLY	UNSUBTLETY	UNTAX	UNTIL	UNTROWABLE
UNSTAIDNESS	UNSUBTLY	UNTEACH	UNTILE	UNTROWED
UNSTAIN	UNSUCCESS	UNTEACHABLE	UNTILED	UNTRUCED
UNSTAINED	UNSUCCESSFUL	UNTEACHABLY	UNTILLED	UNTRUE
UNSTALKED	UNSUCCESSIVE	UNTEACHING	UNTIME	UNTRUENESS
UNSTAR	UNSUFFERABLE	UNTEAM	UNTIMELESS	UNTRUISM
UNSTARCH	UNSUFFERABLY	UNTECHNICAL	UNTIMELIER	UNTRULY
UNSTATE	UNSUFFERED	UNTEEM	UNTIMELIEST	UNTRUNKED
UNSTAYED	UNSUFFICIENT	UNTELL	UNTIMELINESS	UNTRUSS
UNSTEADFAST	UNSUIT	UNTELLING	UNTIMELY	UNTRUSSER
UNSTEADIER	UNSUITABLE	UNTEMPER	UNTIMEOUS	UNTRUST
UNSTEADIEST	UNSUITABLENESS	UNTEMPERANCE	UNTIMEOUSLY	UNTRUSTFUL
UNSTEADILY	UNSUITABLY	UNTEMPERATE	UNTIMOUS	UNTRUSTWORTHINESS
UNSTEADINESS	UNSUITED	UNTENABLE	UNTIN	UNTRUSTWORTHY
UNSTEADY	UNSULLIED	UNTENABLY	UNTINCT	UNTRUSTY
UNSTECK	UNSULLIEDLY	UNTENANT	UNTINE	UNTRUTH
UNSTEEK	UNSUMMED	UNTENANTED	UNTIRE	UNTRUTHER
UNSTEEL	UNSUMMERED	UNTENDED	UNTIRING	UNTRUTHFUL
UNSTEP	UNSUNG	UNTENDER	UNTITLED	UNTRUTHFULLY
UNSTEPPED	UNSUNNED	UNTENDERLY	UNTO	UNTRUTHS
UNSTEPPING	UNSUPERABLE	UNTENIBLE	UNTOGGLE	UNTUCK
UNSTERILIZED	UNSUPERVISED	UNTENIBLY	UNTOGGLER	UNTUCKERED
UNSTICK	UNSUPPED	UNTENT	UNTOILED	UNTUNE
UNSTIFFEN	UNSUPPLIED	UNTENTED	UNTOLD	UNTURF
UNSTILL	UNSUPPORTED	UNTENTY	UNTOLERABLE	UNTURN
UNSTILLNESS	UNSURE	UNTERMED	UNTOLERABLY	UNTUTORED
UNSTING	UNSURETY	UNTERMINABLE	UNTOLERATED	UNTUTOREDLY
UNSTINTED	UNSURMISED	UNTERMINABLY	UNTOLLED	UNTWILLED
UNSTITCH	UNSURPASSED	UNTERRED	UNTOMB	UNTWIND
UNSTOCK	UNSUSPECT	UNTESTATE	UNTONALITY	UNTWINE
UNSTOIC	UNSUSPECTED	UNTETHER	UNTONE	UNTWINED
UNSTOICIZE	UNSUSPECTING	UNTEWED	UNTONGUE	UNTWINING
UNSTOKEN	UNSUSPICION	UNTHANK	UNTOOTH	UNTWIRL
UNSTONE	UNSUSPICIOUS	UNTHANKFUL	UNTOP	UNTWIST
UNSTOP	UNSWADDLE	UNTHANKFULLY	UNTOPPED	UNTWISTED
UNSTOPPED	UNSWATHE	UNTHATCH	UNTOUCH	UNTWITTEN
UNSTOPPER	UNSWATHED	UNTHENDE	UNTOUCHABLE	UNTYING
UNSTOPPING	UNSWATHING	UNTHEWED	UNTOUCHABLY	UNTZ
UNSTOPPLE	UNSWEAR	UNTHINK	UNTOUCHED	UNUNANIMITY
UNSTORE	UNSWEARING	UNTHINKABLE	UNTOWARD	UNUNANIMOUS
UNSTORED	UNSWEAT	UNTHINKABLY	UNTOWARDLY	UNUNIFORM
UNSTORIED	UNSWEET	UNTHINKER	UNTOWARDNESS	UNUNIFORMITY
UNSTOW	UNSWEETEN	UNTHINKING	UNTOWN	UNUNIFORMLY
UNSTOWED	UNSWEETLY	UNTHINKINGLY	UNTRACE	UNUNITABLE
UNSTRAIN	UNSWEETNESS	UNTHOLEABLE	UNTRACEABLE	UNUNITABLY
UNSTRAINED	UNSWELL	UNTHOLEABLY	UNTRACEABLY	UNUNITED
UNSTRAND	UNSWERVING	UNTHOUGHT	UNTRACTABLE	UNUNIVERSITY
UNSTRAP	UNSWERVINGLY	UNTHOUGHTED	UNTRACTABLY	UNUPRIGHT
UNSTRAPPED	UNSWORE	UNTHOUGHTFUL	UNTRACTED	UNUPRIGHTLY
UNSTRAPPING	UNSWORN	UNTHRALL	UNTRADED	UNURED
UNSTRATIFIED	UNSYLLABIC	UNTHRASHED	UNTRAINED	UNUSABLE
UNSTRENG	UNSYMMETRICAL	UNTHREAD	UNTRAINEDLY	UNUSABLY
UNSTRENGTH	UNSYMMETRY	UNTHRID	UNTRAMMELED	UNUSAGE
UNSTRENGTHEN	UNSYMPATHETIC	UNTHRIDDEN	UNTRAMMELLED	UNUSE
UNSTRESS	UNSYMPATHY	UNTHRIFT	UNTRANCE	UNUSED
UNSTRESSED	UNSYSTEMATIC	UNTHRIFTIER	UNTRAVELED	UNUSEDNESS
UNSTRESSEDLY	UNT	UNTHRIFTIEST	UNTRAVELLED	UNUSUAL
UNSTRETCH	UNTACK	UNTHRIFTILY	UNTREAD	UNUSUALITY
UNSTRIATED	UNTACKLE	UNTHRIFTY	UNTREADING	UNUSUALLY
UNSTRIDE	UNTACTFUL	UNTHRIVE	UNTREASURE	UNUSUALNESS
UNSTRIKE	UNTACTFULLY	UNTHRIVEN	UNTREATABLE	UNUTTERABLE
UNSTRING	UNTAINTED	UNTHRIVING	UNTREATABLY	UNUTTERABLY
UNSTRINGING	UNTAKEN	UNTHRIVINGLY	UNTRENCHED	UNUTTERED
UNSTRIP	UNTALENTED	UNTHRONE	UNTREND	UNVACCINATED
UNSTRIPED	UNTAMED	UNTIDIER	UNTRESSED	UNVALID
UNSTRONG	UNTAMEDLY	UNTIDIEST	UNTRIED	UNVALIDITY
UNSTRUNG	UNTAMEDNESS	UNTIDILY	UNTRIM	UNVALIDLY
UNSTUDIED	UNTANGIBLE	UNTIDINESS	UNTRIMMED	UNVALIDNESS
UNSTUFF	UNTANGIBLY	UNTIDY	UNTRIPE	UNVALUABLE
UNSTY	UNTANGLE		UNTRIST	UNVALUABLY

UNVALUE	UNWARP	UNWIN	UNWROUGHT	UPGRAVE
UNVALUED	UNWARRANT	UNWINCING	UNWRY	UPGROWTH
UNVARIABLE	UNWARRANTED	UNWINCINGLY	UNY	UPHALE
UNVARIABLY	UNWARRAYED	UNWIND	UNYEANED	UPHAND
UNVARIED	UNWARRED	UNWINDING	UNYIELDING	UPHEARTED
UNVARIEDLY	UNWARREN	UNWINDINGLY	UNYIELDINGLY	UPHEAVAL
UNVARNISHED	UNWARY	UNWINK	UNYOKE	UPHEAVALIST
UNVARYING	UNWASHED	UNWINKING	UNYOKED	UPHEAVE
UNVARYINGLY	UNWASHEN	UNWINKINGLY	UNYOKING	UPHEAVED
UNVASSAL	UNWASTEFUL	UNWINLY	UNYOLDEN	UPHEAVING
UNVEIL	UNWATER	UNWINTER	UNZE	UPHELD
UNVEILED	UNWATERED	UNWIRE	UNZEN	UPHELYA
UNVEILEDLY	UNWAVERING	UNWIRED	UNZONED	UPHER
UNVEILEDNESS	UNWAVERINGLY	UNWISDOM	UP	UPHILL
UNVEILER	UNWAX	UNWISE	UPAITHRIC	UPHOLD
UNVEILMENT	UNWAYED	UNWISELY	UPALONG	UPHOLDEN
UNVENGED	UNWEAKENED	UNWISENESS	UPANAYA	UPHOLDER
UNVENOM	UNWEAL	UNWISH	UPANAYANA	UPHOLDING
UNVENUED	UNWEANED	UNWIST	UPANISHADIC	UPHOLSTER
UNVERACITY	UNWEAPON	UNWIT	UPAPURANA	UPHOLSTERED
UNVERBALIZED	UNWEARIABLE	UNWITCH	UPARCHING	UPHOLSTERER
UNVERIFIABLE	UNWEARIABLY	UNWITHHOLDEN	UPARNA	UPHOLSTERIES
UNVERIFIABLY	UNWEARIED	UNWITNESSED	UPAS	UPHOLSTEROUS
UNVERIFIED	UNWEARIEDLY	UNWITTED	UPBAND	UPHOLSTERY
UNVERITY	UNWEARILY	UNWITTILY	UPBANK	UPHOVE
UNVERSED	UNWEARINESS	UNWITTING	UPBAR	UPHROE
UNVERSEDLY	UNWEARY	UNWITTINGLY	UPBEAT	UPKEEP
UNVERSEDNESS	UNWEARYING	UNWITTY	UPBRAID	UPLA
UNVEST	UNWEARYINGLY	UNWIVED	UPBRAIDED	UPLAND
UNVICAR	UNWEATHERED	UNWOMAN	UPBRAIDER	UPLANDER
UNVINCIBLE	UNWEAVE	UNWOMANLY	UPBRAIDING	UPLANDISH
UNVINDICTIVE	UNWEB	UNWONDER	UPBRAIDINGLY	UPLAY
UNVIOLATE	UNWED	UNWONT	UPBRAST	UPLEAN
UNVIRGIN	UNWEDDED	UNWONTED	UPBRAY	UPLEAP
UNVIRILITY	UNWEDDEDLY	UNWONTEDLY	UPBREAK	UPLIFT
UNVIRTUE	UNWEDDEDNESS	UNWONTEDNESS	UPBREATHE	UPLIFTED
UNVIRTUOUS	UNWEDGEABLE	UNWOODED	UPBRING	UPLIFTEDLY
UNVIRTUOUSLY	UNWEEL	UNWOOF	UPBRINGING	UPLIFTEDNESS
UNVISIBLE	UNWEELNESS	UNWORDED	UPBROUGHT	UPLIFTER
UNVISIBLY	UNWEETING	UNWORDY	UPBROW	UPLIFTING
UNVISOR	UNWEETINGLY	UNWORK	UPBUILD	UPLIFTINGLY
UNVITIATED	UNWEFT	UNWORKABLE	UPBUILDER	UPLIMBER
UNVITIATEDLY	UNWELCOME	UNWORKABLY	UPBY	UPLONG
UNVIZARD	UNWELCOMELY	UNWORKER	UPBYE	UPLOOK
UNVOCAL	UNWELDE	UNWORKMANLY	UPCARD	UPLOOKER
UNVOICE	UNWELL	UNWORLD	UPCAST	UPLYING
UNVOICED	UNWELLNESS	UNWORLDLY	UPCHAMBER	UPMAKING
UNVOICING	UNWELTH	UNWORMED	UPCHAUNCE	UPMOST
UNVOLUNTARY	UNWEMMED	UNWORN	UPCHEER	UPON
UNVOTE	UNWEPT	UNWORRIED	UPCHUCK	UPPBAD
UNVOUCHED	UNWHETTED	UNWORRIEDLY	UPCLIMB	UPPER
UNVOUCHEDLY	UNWHIG	UNWORSHIP	UPCLOSE	UPPERCLASSMAN
UNVOWELED	UNWHOLE	UNWORTH	UPCLOSER	UPPERCLASSMEN
UNVOWELLED	UNWHOLESOME	UNWORTHIER	UPCOAST	UPPERCUT
UNVULGARIZE	UNWIELD	UNWORTHIEST	UPCOME	UPPERCUTTING
UNWAGED	UNWIELDIER	UNWORTHILY	UPCOMING	UPPERER
UNWALKABLE	UNWIELDIEST	UNWORTHINESS	UPCOUNTRY	UPPERMORE
UNWALKING	UNWIELDILY	UNWORTHY	UPCUT	UPPERMOST
UNWALLET	UNWIELDINESS	UNWOUND	UPDATE	UPPERS
UNWALLOWED	UNWIELDLY	UNWOUNDED	UPDATED	UPPERSTOCKS
UNWAN	UNWIELDSOME	UNWRAP	UPDATING	UPPING
UNWANDERED	UNWIELDY	UNWRAPPED	UPDIVE	UPPISH
UNWANTED	UNWIFED	UNWRAPPER	UPDRAFT	UPPISHLY
UNWARDED	UNWILD	UNWRAPPERED	UPDRAUGHT	UPPISHNESS
UNWARE	UNWILIER	UNWRAPPING	UPDRESS	UPPITY
UNWARELY	UNWILILY	UNWREAKED	UPEND	UPPOWOC
UNWARENESS	UNWILINESS	UNWREAKEN	UPERIZE	UPRAISAL
UNWARES	UNWILL	UNWREATHE	UPEYGAN	UPRAISE
UNWARILY	UNWILLE	UNWRENCH	UPFEED	UPRAISED
UNWARINESS	UNWILLED	UNWREST	UPFINGERED	UPRAISER
UNWARLIKE	UNWILLFUL	UNWRINKLE	UPFOLD	UPRAISING
UNWARM	UNWILLFULLY	UNWRINKLED	UPGANG	UPRAUGHT
UNWARNED	UNWILLING	UNWRINKLING	UPGIVE	UPREAR
UNWARNEDLY	UNWILLINGLY	UNWRIT	UPGO	UPREARED
UNWARNEDNESS	UNWILLINGNESS	UNWRITE	UPGRADE	UPREARING
UNWARNING	UNWILY	UNWRITTEN	UPGRADED	UPREST
UNWARNISHED	UNWIMPLE	UNWROKEN	UPGRADING	UPRIGHT

UPRIGHTEOUS	UPSWEEP	URANOPHANE	UREDINIA	URIAL
UPRIGHTING	UPSWEEPING	URANOPLASTIC	UREDINIAL	URIC
UPRIGHTLY	UPSWELL	URANOPLASTY	UREDINIUM	URICOLYSIS
UPRIGHTMAN	UPSWELLED	URANOPLEGIA	UREDINOID	URICOLYTIC
UPRIGHTNESS	UPSWELLING	URANORRHAPHY	UREDINOLOGY	URIDROSIS
UPRISAL	UPSWEPT	URANOSCHISIS	UREDINOUS	URIN
UPRISE	UPSWING	URANOSCHISM	UREDIUM	URINAEMIA
UPRISEN	UPSWINGING	URANOSCOPE	UREDO	URINAEMIC
UPRISER	UPSWOLLEN	URANOSCOPIA	UREDOSORUS	URINAL
UPRISING	UPSWUNG	URANOSCOPIC	UREDOSPORE	URINALIST
UPRIST	UPSY	URANOSCOPY	UREDOSPORIC	URINALYSIS
UPRIVER	UPTAKE	URANOSPINITE	UREDOSTAGE	URINANT
UPROAR	UPTAKER	URANOTHORITE	UREIC	URINARIES
UPROARER	UPTEAR	URANOTIL	UREIDE	URINARIUM
UPROARIOUS	UPTHROW	URANOUS	UREIDO	URINARY
UPROARIOUSLY	UPTHRUST	URANYL	UREMIA	URINATE
UPROOT	UPTIGHT	URANYLIC	UREMIC	URINATED
UPROOTAL	UPTILL	URAO	URENT	URINATING
UPROOTED	UPTOWN	URARE	UREOMETER	URINATION
UPROOTER	UPTOWNER	URARI	UREOMETRY	URINATIVE
UPROOTING	UPTRAIN	URASE	URESIS	URINATOR
UPROSE	UPTREND	URATAEMIA	URETAL	URINE
UPROUSE	UPTRILL	URATE	URETER	URINEMIA
UPROUSED	UPTURN	URATEMIA	URETERAL	URINEMIC
UPROUSING	UPTURNED	URATIC	URETERECTOMIES	URINIFEROUS
UPSADDLE	UPTURNING	URATOMA	URETERECTOMY	URINIPAROUS
UPSCUDDLE	UPUPOID	URATOSIS	URETERIC	URINOGENITAL
UPSEDOUN	UPWARD	URATURIA	URETEROCELE	URINOGENOUS
UPSEE	UPWARDLY	URAZIN	URETEROGRAM	URINOLOGIST
UPSEEK	UPWARDS	URAZINE	URETEROGRAPH	URINOLOGY
UPSET	UPWAY	URAZOLE	URETEROLITH	URINOMANCY
UPSETTAL	UPWAYS	URBACITY	URETEROLYSIS	URINOMETER
UPSETTED	UPWIND	URBAINITE	URETEROSTOMA	URINOMETRIC
UPSETTER	UPWITH	URBAN	URETEROSTOMY	URINOMETRY
UPSETTING	UR	URBANE	URETEROTOMY	URINOSCOPIC
UPSETTINGLY	URACHAL	URBANELY	URETHAN	URINOSCOPIES
UPSHOOT	URACHUS	URBANENESS	URETHANE	URINOSCOPIST
UPSHOT	URACIL	URBANISM	URETHRA	URINOSCOPY
UPSIDE	URAEMIA	URBANIST	URETHRAE	URINOSE
UPSIDES	URAEMIC	URBANITE	URETHRAL	URINOUS
UPSIGHTED	URAEUS	URBANITIES	URETHRALGIA	URINOUSNESS
UPSILON	URAL	URBANITY	URETHRAS	URITE
UPSILONISM	URALI	URBANIZATION	URETHRISM	URLAR
UPSITTEN	URALITE	URBANIZE	URETHRITIC	URLED
UPSITTING	URALITIC	URBANIZED	URETHRITIS	URLING
UPSKIP	URALITIZE	URBANIZING	URETHROCELE	URLUCH
UPSLIP	URALITIZED	URBARIAL	URETHROGRAM	URMAN
UPSPEAR	URALITIZING	URBIC	URETHROGRAPH	URN
UPSPIN	URAMIDO	URBICOLOUS	URETHROMETER	URNA
UPSPRANG	URAMIL	URBINATE	URETHROPHYMA	URNAL
UPSPRING	URAMINO	URBS	URETHROPLASTY	URNFIELD
UPSPRINGING	URAN	URCEI	URETHRORRHEA	URNFLOWER
UPSPRUNG	URANALYSIS	URCEIFORM	URETHROSCOPE	URNFUL
UPSTAGE	URANATE	URCEOLAR	URETHROSCOPY	URNFULS
UPSTAGED	URANIC	URCEOLATE	URETHROSPASM	URNING
UPSTAGING	URANIDIN	URCEOLE	URETHROSTOMY	URNINGISM
UPSTAIRS	URANIDINE	URCEOLI	URETHROTOME	UROBILIN
UPSTAND	URANIFEROUS	URCEOLUS	URETHROTOMIC	UROBILINEMIA
UPSTANDER	URANIN	URCEUS	URETHROTOMY	UROBILINOGEN
UPSTANDING	URANINITE	URCHIN	URETHYLAN	UROBILINURIA
UPSTARE	URANION	URCHINESS	URETHYLANE	UROCELE
UPSTART	URANISCUS	URCHINLY	URETIC	UROCHLORALIC
UPSTATE	URANISM	URD	UREYLENE	UROCHORD
UPSTATER	URANIST	URDE	URF	UROCHORDAL
UPSTAY	URANITE	URDEE	URFIRNIS	UROCHORDATE
UPSTIR	URANITIC	URDY	URGE	UROCHROME
UPSTRAIGHT	URANIUM	URE	URGED	UROCHROMOGEN
UPSTREAM	URANOCIRCITE	UREA	URGEFUL	UROCHS
UPSTREET	URANOGRAPHER	UREAL	URGENCE	UROCYANOGEN
UPSTRETCHED	URANOGRAPHIC	UREAMETER	URGENCIES	UROCYST
UPSTROKE	URANOGRAPHY	UREAMETRY	URGENCY	UROCYSTIC
UPSUN	URANOLATRY	UREASE	URGENT	UROCYSTITIS
UPSURGE	URANOLITE	URECHITIN	URGENTLY	URODAEUM
UPSURGED	URANOLOGICAL	URECHITOXIN	URGER	URODELAN
UPSURGENCE	URANOLOGY	UREDEMA	URGING	URODELE
UPSURGING	URANOMETRIA	UREDINEAL	URGINGLY	URODELOUS
UPSWARM	URANOMETRY	UREDINEOUS	URHEEN	URODIALYSIS

URODYNIA
UROEDEMA
UROERYTHRIN
UROGASTER
UROGASTRIC
UROGENIC
UROGENITAL
UROGENOUS
UROGLAUCIN
UROGRAM
UROGRAPHY
UROHAEMATIN
UROHEMATIN
UROHYAL
UROLAGNIA
UROLITH
UROLITHIASIS
UROLITHIC
UROLITHOLOGY
UROLOGIC
UROLOGICAL
UROLOGIST
UROLOGY
UROLUTEIN
UROMANCY
UROMANTIA
UROMANTIST
UROMELANIN
UROMELUS
UROMERE
URONEPHROSIS
URONIC
UROPATAGIUM
UROPHAEIN
UROPHANIC
UROPHANOUS
UROPHEIN
UROPHTHISIS
UROPLANIA
UROPOD
UROPODAL
UROPODOUS
UROPOETIC
UROPOIESIS
UROPOIETIC
UROPORPHYRIN
UROPSILE
UROPTYSIS
UROPYGIAL
UROPYGIUM
UROPYLORIC
UROROSEIN
URORRHAGIA
URORRHEA
URORUBIN
UROSACRAL
UROSCHESIS
UROSCOPIC
UROSCOPIES
UROSCOPIST
UROSCOPY
UROSEPSIS
UROSIS
UROSOMATIC
UROSOME
UROSOMITE
UROSOMITIC
UROSTEALITH
UROSTEGAL
UROSTEGE
UROSTEGITE
UROSTEON
UROSTERNITE
UROSTHENE
UROSTHENIC
UROSTYLAR
UROSTYLE

UROTOXIC
UROTOXICITY
UROTOXIES
UROTOXIN
UROTOXY
UROX
UROXANATE
UROXANTHIN
UROXIN
URRHODIN
URRHODINIC
URSICIDAL
URSICIDE
URSIFORM
URSIGRAM
URSINE
URSOID
URSON
URSONE
URSUK
URTICACEOUS
URTICAL
URTICANT
URTICARIA
URTICARIAL
URTICARIOUS
URTICATE
URTICATED
URTICATING
URTICATION
URTICOSE
URTITE
URUBU
URUCA
URUCU
URUCUM
URUCURI
URUCURY
URUISG
URUNDAY
URUS
URUSHI
URUSHIOL
URUSHIYE
URVA
URVED
US
USABILITY
USABLE
USABLENESS
USABLY
USAGE
USAGER
USANCE
USANT
USAR
USARON
USATION
USAUNCE
USE
USEABLE
USED
USEDLY
USEDNESS
USEE
USEFUL
USEFULLISH
USEFULLY
USEFULNESS
USEHOLD
USELESS
USELESSLY
USELESSNESS
USER
USES
USHABTI
USHABTIU

USHER
USHERANCE
USHERED
USHERER
USHERETTE
USHERIAN
USHERING
USING
USINGS
USITATE
USITATIVE
USNEACEOUS
USNEOID
USQUABAE
USQUE
USQUEBAE
USQUEBAUGH
USSELF
USSELS
USSELVEN
USSINGITE
USTION
USTORIOUS
USTULATE
USTULATION
USUAL
USUALISM
USUALLY
USUALNESS
USUARY
USUCAPIENT
USUCAPION
USUCAPIONARY
USUCAPT
USUCAPTABLE
USUCAPTIBLE
USUFRUCT
USUFRUCTUARIES
USUFRUCTUARY
USURA
USURE
USURER
USURIES
USURIOUS
USURIOUSLY
USURIOUSNESS
USURP
USURPATION
USURPATIVE
USURPATIVELY
USURPATORY
USURPATURE
USURPED
USURPER
USURPING
USURPINGLY
USURY
USUS
UT
UTAC
UTAHITE
UTAI
UTAS
UTCH
UTCHY
UTENSIL
UTENSILE
UTENSILS
UTERALGIA
UTERECTOMY
UTERI
UTERINE
UTEROCELE
UTEROGRAM
UTEROGRAPHY
UTEROLITH
UTEROLOGY

UTEROMETER
UTEROPELVIC
UTEROPLASTY
UTEROSACRAL
UTEROSCOPE
UTEROTOMY
UTEROTONIC
UTEROTUBAL
UTEROVAGINAL
UTEROVENTRAL
UTEROVESICAL
UTERUS
UTIA
UTIBLE
UTICK
UTILE
UTILIDOR
UTILITARIAN
UTILITIES
UTILITY
UTILIZABLE
UTILIZATION
UTILIZE
UTILIZED
UTILIZER
UTILIZING
UTINAM
UTIS
UTLAGARY
UTMOST
UTOPIA
UTOPIAN
UTOPIANISM
UTOPIANIST
UTOPIAST
UTOPISM
UTOPIST
UTOPISTIC
UTOPOGRAPHER
UTRAQUIST
UTRAQUISTIC
UTRECHT
UTRICLE
UTRICULAR
UTRICULATE
UTRICULIFORM
UTRICULITIS
UTRICULOID
UTRICULOSE
UTRICULUS
UTRIFORM
UTRUBI
UTRUM
UTTER
UTTERABILITY
UTTERABLE
UTTERANCE
UTTERED
UTTERER
UTTEREST
UTTERING
UTTERLESS
UTTERLY
UTTERMOST
UTTERNESS
UTU
UTUM
UTURUNCU
UVA
UVAL
UVALA
UVALHA
UVANITE
UVAROVITE
UVATE
UVEA
UVEAL

UVEITIC
UVEITIS
UVEOUS
UVID
UVITIC
UVITO
UVULA
UVULAE
UVULAR
UVULARLY
UVULAS
UVULE
UVULITIS
UVULOPTOSIS
UVULOTOME
UVULOTOMIES
UVULOTOMY
UXORIAL
UXORIALITY
UXORIALLY
UXORICIDAL
UXORICIDE
UXORIOUS
UXORIOUSLY
UYEZD
UZAN
UZARIN
UZARON

VA
VAAD
VAAGMAER
VAAGMAR
VAALITE
VACANCE
VACANCIES
VACANCY
VACANT
VACANTIA
VACANTLY
VACATE
VACATED
VACATING
VACATION
VACATIONAL
VACATIONER
VACATIONIST
VACATUR
VACCARY
VACCICIDE
VACCIGENOUS
VACCINA
VACCINABLE
VACCINAL
VACCINATE
VACCINATED
VACCINATING
VACCINATION
VACCINATOR
VACCINATORY
VACCINE
VACCINEE
VACCINELLA
VACCINIA
VACCINIAL
VACCINIFER
VACCINIFORM
VACCINIOLA
VACCINIST
VACCINIZATION
VACHE
VACILLANCY
VACILLANT
VACILLATE
VACILLATED
VACILLATING
VACILLATION
VACILLATOR
VACILLATORY
VACOA
VACONA
VACOUA
VACOUF
VACUA
VACUAL
VACUATE
VACUATION
VACUEFY
VACUIST
VACUIT
VACUITIES
VACUITY
VACUO
VACUOLAR
VACUOLATED
VACUOLATION

VACUOLE
VACUOME
VACUOMETER
VACUOUS
VACUOUSLY
VACUUM
VACUUMIZE
VACUUMS
VADE
VADELECT
VADER
VADIMONIUM
VADIMONY
VADIUM
VADOSE
VADY
VAE
VAFROUS
VAG
VAGABOND
VAGABONDAGE
VAGABONDIA
VAGABONDISM
VAGABONDIZE
VAGABONDIZED
VAGABONDIZER
VAGABONDIZING
VAGABONDRY
VAGAL
VAGANCY
VAGANT
VAGARIAN
VAGARIES
VAGARIOUS
VAGARISH
VAGARISOME
VAGARIST
VAGARITY
VAGARY
VAGAS
VAGATION
VAGI
VAGIENT
VAGIFORM
VAGILE
VAGINA
VAGINAL
VAGINALITIS
VAGINANT
VAGINATE
VAGINECTOMY
VAGINERVOSE
VAGINICOLOUS
VAGINIFEROUS
VAGINISMUS
VAGINITIS
VAGINULA
VAGINULATE
VAGINULE
VAGITUS
VAGOGRAM
VAGOLYSIS
VAGOTOMIZE
VAGOTOMY
VAGOTONIA
VAGOTONIC
VAGOTONY
VAGOTROPIC
VAGOTROPISM
VAGOUS
VAGRANCE
VAGRANCY
VAGRANT
VAGRANTISM
VAGRANTIZE
VAGRANTLY
VAGRANTNESS

VAGRATE
VAGROM
VAGUE
VAGUELY
VAGUENESS
VAGUER
VAGUEST
VAGUITY
VAGULOUS
VAGUS
VAH
VAHINE
VAIL
VAILABLE
VAILE
VAIN
VAINER
VAINEST
VAINFUL
VAINGLORIOUS
VAINGLORY
VAINLY
VAIR
VAIRAGI
VAIRE
VAIREE
VAIVODE
VAJRA
VAJRASANA
VAKASS
VAKEEL
VAKIA
VAKIL
VAKKALIGA
VAKUF
VALANCE
VALANCED
VALANCHE
VALBELLITE
VALE
VALEDICTION
VALEDICTORIES
VALEDICTORY
VALENCE
VALENCIA
VALENCIANITE
VALENCIES
VALENCY
VALENT
VALENTINE
VALERAMID
VALERAMIDE
VALERATE
VALERIAN
VALERIANATE
VALERIANIC
VALERIC
VALERIN
VALERONE
VALERYL
VALERYLENE
VALET
VALETA
VALETED
VALETING
VALETRY
VALETUDE
VALETUDINARY
VALEUR
VALEW
VALEWE
VALGOID
VALGUS
VALI
VALIANCE
VALIANCY
VALIANT

VALIANTLY
VALIANTNESS
VALID
VALIDATE
VALIDATED
VALIDATING
VALIDATION
VALIDATORY
VALIDITY
VALIDOUS
VALINCH
VALINE
VALISE
VALISES
VALLA
VALLANCY
VALLAR
VALLARY
VALLATE
VALLATED
VALLATION
VALLECULA
VALLECULAR
VALLECULATE
VALLEVARITE
VALLEY
VALLEYS
VALLICULA
VALLICULAE
VALLICULAR
VALLIDOM
VALLIES
VALLIS
VALLUM
VALLUMS
VALONIA
VALONIACEOUS
VALOP
VALOR
VALORIZATION
VALORIZE
VALOROUS
VALOROUSLY
VALOROUSNESS
VALOUR
VALOUWE
VALSE
VALSOID
VALUABLE
VALUABLY
VALUATE
VALUATION
VALUATIONAL
VALUATOR
VALUE
VALUED
VALUELESS
VALUER
VALUES
VALUING
VALURE
VALUTA
VALVA
VALVAE
VALVAL
VALVAR
VALVATE
VALVE
VALVELESS
VALVELET
VALVEMAN
VALVEMEN
VALVIFEROUS
VALVIFORM
VALVOTOMY
VALVULA
VALVULAE

VALVULAR
VALVULATE
VALVULE
VALVULITIS
VALVULOTOME
VALVULOTOMY
VALYL
VALYLENE
VAMBRACE
VAMBRACED
VAMBRASH
VAMFONT
VAMMAZSA
VAMOOSE
VAMOS
VAMOSE
VAMP
VAMPED
VAMPER
VAMPEY
VAMPHORN
VAMPING
VAMPIRE
VAMPIRIC
VAMPIRISH
VAMPIRISM
VAMPIRIZE
VAMPLATE
VAMPYRE
VAMURE
VAN
VANADATE
VANADIATE
VANADIC
VANADINITE
VANADIOUS
VANADIUM
VANADOUS
VANADYL
VANCOURIER
VANDAL
VANDALISH
VANDALISM
VANDALISTIC
VANDALIZE
VANDELAS
VANE
VANED
VANESSIAN
VANFOSS
VANG
VANGEE
VANGELI
VANGLO
VANGLOE
VANGUARD
VANILLA
VANILLAL
VANILLAS
VANILLATE
VANILLE
VANILLERY
VANILLIC
VANILLIN
VANILLINE
VANILLISM
VANILLON
VANILLOYL
VANILLYL
VANISH
VANISHED
VANISHER
VANISHING
VANISHINGLY
VANISHMENT
VANITARIANISM
VANITIED

VANITIES	VAR	VARIOLATE	VASEFUL	VAUDEVILLIST
VANITORY	VARA	VARIOLATED	VASHEGYITE	VAUDY
VANITOUS	VARAN	VARIOLATING	VASICENTRIC	VAUGNERITE
VANITY	VARAS	VARIOLATION	VASICINE	VAULT
VANLAY	VARDAPET	VARIOLE	VASIFEROUS	VAULTAGE
VANMAN	VARDI	VARIOLIC	VASIFORM	VAULTED
VANMEN	VARDY	VARIOLIFORM	VASO	VAULTEDLY
VANMOST	VARE	VARIOLITE	VASOCORONA	VAULTER
VANNED	VAREC	VARIOLITIC	VASODENTINE	VAULTING
VANNER	VARECH	VARIOLOID	VASODILATIN	VAULTY
VANNERMAN	VAREHEADED	VARIOLOUS	VASODILATING	VAUMURE
VANNERMEN	VARELLA	VARIOMETER	VASODILATION	VAUNCE
VANNET	VAREUSE	VARIORUM	VASODILATOR	VAUNT
VANNING	VARGE	VARIOTINTED	VASOFACTIVE	VAUNTAGE
VANNUS	VARGUENO	VARIOUS	VASOGANGLION	VAUNTED
VANQUISH	VARI	VARIOUSLY	VASOLIGATION	VAUNTER
VANQUISHED	VARIA	VARIOUSNESS	VASOMOTION	VAUNTERY
VANQUISHER	VARIABILITY	VARISCITE	VASOMOTOR	VAUNTFUL
VANQUISHING	VARIABLE	VARISSE	VASOPARESIS	VAUNTIE
VANS	VARIABLENESS	VARITYPE	VASOREFLEX	VAUNTINESS
VANSIRE	VARIANCE	VARITYPED	VASOSPASM	VAUNTING
VANT	VARIANCY	VARITYPING	VASOTONIC	VAUNTINGLY
VANTAGE	VARIANT	VARITYPIST	VASOTROPHIC	VAUNTLAY
VANTERIE	VARIATE	VARIX	VASQUINE	VAUNTMURE
VANWARD	VARIATED	VARKAS	VASSAL	VAUNTY
VAPID	VARIATING	VARLET	VASSALAGE	VAURIEN
VAPIDISM	VARIATION	VARLETAILLE	VASSALED	VAUXITE
VAPIDITY	VARIATIONAL	VARLETESS	VASSALESS	VAVASOR
VAPIDLY	VARIATIONIST	VARLETRY	VASSALIC	VAVASORY
VAPIDNESS	VARIATIONS	VARLETTO	VASSALING	VAVASOUR
VAPOGRAPHY	VARIATIVE	VARMENT	VASSALISM	VAWARD
VAPOR	VARIATIVELY	VARMINT	VASSALITY	VAY
VAPORABILITY	VARIATOR	VARNA	VASSALIZE	VAZA
VAPORABLE	VARICATED	VARNASHRAMA	VASSALIZED	VEADORE
VAPORARIUM	VARICATION	VARNISH	VASSALIZING	VEAL
VAPORATE	VARICELLA	VARNISHED	VASSALLING	VEALER
VAPORED	VARICELLAR	VARNISHER	VASSALRY	VEALINESS
VAPORER	VARICELLATE	VARNISHING	VASSALS	VEALSKIN
VAPORETTI	VARICELLATION	VARNISHMENT	VAST	VEALY
VAPORETTO	VARICELLOID	VARNISHY	VASTATE	VEAU
VAPORIFORM	VARICELLOUS	VARNPLIKTIGE	VASTATION	VECKE
VAPORIMETER	VARICES	VARNSINGITE	VASTIDITY	VECTIGAL
VAPORING	VARICIFORM	VARSHA	VASTITIES	VECTION
VAPORINGLY	VARICOCELE	VARSITY	VASTITUDE	VECTIS
VAPORISH	VARICOID	VARSOVIANA	VASTITY	VECTOR
VAPORIZATION	VARICOLORED	VARSOVIENNE	VASTLY	VECTORIAL
VAPORIZE	VARICOLOROUS	VARTABED	VASTNESS	VECTORIALLY
VAPORIZER	VARICOLOURED	VARUS	VASTY	VECTURE
VAPOROGRAPH	VARICOSE	VARVE	VASU	VEDANA
VAPOROSE	VARICOSED	VARVED	VAT	VEDET
VAPOROSITY	VARICOSIS	VARY	VATES	VEDETTE
VAPOROUS	VARICOSITIES	VARYING	VATFUL	VEDIKA
VAPOROUSLY	VARICOSITY	VAS	VATFULS	VEDRO
VAPORS	VARICOTOMY	VASA	VATIC	VEE
VAPORY	VARICULA	VASAL	VATICAL	VEEN
VAPOUR	VARIED	VASALLED	VATICANAL	VEER
VAPOURABILITY	VARIEGATE	VASCON	VATICANIC	VEERABLE
VAPOURABLE	VARIEGATED	VASCULA	VATICANICAL	VEERIES
VAPOURED	VARIEGATING	VASCULAR	VATICIDE	VEERING
VAPOURER	VARIEGATION	VASCULARITIES	VATICINAL	VEERY
VAPOURING	VARIEGATOR	VASCULARITY	VATICINANT	VEGA
VAPOURINGLY	VARIER	VASCULARIZE	VATICINATE	VEGASITE
VAPOURISH	VARIETAL	VASCULARIZED	VATICINATED	VEGECULTURE
VAPOURIZE	VARIETAS	VASCULARIZING	VATICINATING	VEGETABILITY
VAPOURIZED	VARIETIES	VASCULARLY	VATICINATION	VEGETABLE
VAPOURIZER	VARIETIST	VASCULATED	VATICINATOR	VEGETABLES
VAPOURIZING	VARIETY	VASCULATURE	VATICINE	VEGETABLIZE
VAPOUROSE	VARIFORM	VASCULIFEROUS	VATMAKER	VEGETABLY
VAPOUROUS	VARIFORMED	VASCULIFORM	VATMAKING	VEGETAL
VAPOUROUSLY	VARIFORMITY	VASCULITIS	VATMAN	VEGETALCULE
VAPOURS	VARIFORMLY	VASCULOMOTOR	VATS	VEGETALITY
VAPOURY	VARIFY	VASCULOSE	VATTED	VEGETANT
VAPULATE	VARIGRADATION	VASCULUM	VATTER	VEGETARIAN
VAPULATION	VARIOCOUPLER	VASE	VATTING	VEGETATE
VAPULATORY	VARIOLA	VASECTOMIES	VAU	VEGETATED
VAQUERO	VARIOLAR	VASECTOMIZE	VAUDEVILLE	VEGETATING
VAQUEROS	VARIOLATE	VASECTOMY	VAUDEVILLIAN	VEGETATION

VEGETATIVE
VEGETE
VEGETENESS
VEGETISM
VEGETIVE
VEGETOUS
VEHEMENCE
VEHEMENCY
VEHEMENT
VEHEMENTLY
VEHICLE
VEHICLES
VEHICULAR
VEHICULARY
VEHICULATE
VEHICULATION
VEI
VEIGLE
VEIL
VEILED
VEILEDLY
VEILEDNESS
VEILER
VEILING
VEILLESS
VEILLEUSE
VEILY
VEIN
VEINAGE
VEINAL
VEINED
VEINER
VEINERY
VEINING
VEINLET
VEINOUS
VEINS
VEINSTONE
VEINULE
VEINULET
VEINY
VELA
VELAMEN
VELAMENTOUS
VELAMENTUM
VELAMINA
VELAR
VELARIC
VELARIUM
VELARIZE
VELARY
VELATE
VELATED
VELATION
VELATURA
VELD
VELDE
VELDMAN
VELDSCHOEN
VELDSCHOENEN
VELDSCHOENS
VELDT
VELDTSCHOEN
VELDTSMAN
VELIC
VELIFEROUS
VELIFORM
VELIGER
VELITATION
VELITES
VELL
VELLALA
VELLEITIES
VELLEITY
VELLICATE
VELLICATED
VELLICATING

VELLICATION
VELLICATIVE
VELLINCH
VELLINCHER
VELLON
VELLOSIN
VELLOSINE
VELLUM
VELLUMY
VELLUTE
VELO
VELOCE
VELOCIMAN
VELOCIMETER
VELOCIOUS
VELOCIOUSLY
VELOCIPEDAL
VELOCIPEDE
VELOCIPEDED
VELOCIPEDIC
VELOCIPEDING
VELOCITIES
VELOCITOUS
VELOCITY
VELODROME
VELOMETER
VELOUR
VELOURS
VELOUTE
VELOUTINE
VELT
VELTE
VELTFARE
VELUM
VELUMEN
VELUMINA
VELUNGE
VELURE
VELURED
VELURING
VELUTINOUS
VELVERET
VELVET
VELVETBREAST
VELVETED
VELVETEEN
VELVETEENED
VELVETINESS
VELVETING
VELVETLEAF
VELVETMAKER
VELVETMAKING
VELVETRY
VELVETSEED
VELVETWEED
VELVETWORK
VELVETY
VELYARDE
VENA
VENADA
VENAE
VENAL
VENALITIES
VENALITY
VENALIZATION
VENALIZE
VENANZITE
VENATIC
VENATICAL
VENATICALLY
VENATION
VENATIONAL
VENATOR
VENATORIAL
VENATORIOUS
VENATORY
VENCOLA

VEND
VENDACE
VENDAGE
VENDAVAL
VENDED
VENDEE
VENDER
VENDETTA
VENDETTAS
VENDETTIST
VENDEUSE
VENDIBILITIES
VENDIBILITY
VENDIBLE
VENDIBLENESS
VENDIBLY
VENDICATE
VENDING
VENDIS
VENDITATE
VENDITION
VENDITOR
VENDOR
VENDUE
VENE
VENEER
VENEERED
VENEERER
VENEERING
VENEERS
VENEFIC
VENEFICAL
VENEFICIOUS
VENENATE
VENENATION
VENENE
VENENIFEROUS
VENENIFIC
VENENOSE
VENENOSITY
VENENOUS
VENEPUNCTURE
VENERABILITY
VENERABLE
VENERABLY
VENERAL
VENERANCE
VENERANT
VENERATE
VENERATED
VENERATING
VENERATION
VENERATIVE
VENERATIVELY
VENERATOR
VENERE
VENEREAL
VENEREAN
VENERER
VENERIAL
VENERIAN
VENERIFORM
VENERO
VENEROS
VENERY
VENESECT
VENESECTION
VENESECTOR
VENESIA
VENEUR
VENEZOLANO
VENGEABLE
VENGEANCE
VENGEANCELY
VENGEANT
VENGEFUL
VENGEFULLY

VENGEOUSLY
VENGER
VENIABLE
VENIAL
VENIALITIES
VENIALITY
VENIALLY
VENIALNESS
VENIE
VENIN
VENIPLEX
VENIPUNCTURE
VENIRE
VENIREMAN
VENIREMEN
VENISE
VENISON
VENKISEN
VENLIN
VENNEL
VENNER
VENOM
VENOMED
VENOMER
VENOMIZE
VENOMOUS
VENOMOUSLY
VENOMSOME
VENOMY
VENOSAL
VENOSE
VENOSITY
VENOSTASIS
VENOUS
VENOUSLY
VENOUSNESS
VENT
VENTA
VENTAGE
VENTAIL
VENTANA
VENTED
VENTER
VENTHOLE
VENTIDUCT
VENTIFACT
VENTIL
VENTILABLE
VENTILAGIN
VENTILATE
VENTILATED
VENTILATING
VENTILATION
VENTILATIVE
VENTILATOR
VENTILATORY
VENTIN
VENTING
VENTOMETER
VENTOSE
VENTOSENESS
VENTOSITY
VENTOY
VENTPIECE
VENTRAD
VENTRAL
VENTRALLY
VENTRIC
VENTRICLE
VENTRICOSE
VENTRICOSITY
VENTRICULAR
VENTRICULI
VENTRICULUS
VENTRIDUCT
VENTRILOQUAL
VENTRILOQUE

VENTRILOQUIST
VENTRILOQUY
VENTRIMESAL
VENTRIMESON
VENTRINE
VENTRIPOTENT
VENTROMYEL
VENTROSITY
VENTS
VENTURE
VENTURED
VENTURER
VENTURESOME
VENTURESOMELY
VENTURI
VENTURINE
VENTURING
VENTUROUS
VENTUROUSLY
VENUE
VENULA
VENULAE
VENULAR
VENULE
VENULOSE
VENULOUS
VENUST
VENUSTY
VENVILLE
VENY
VER
VERA
VERACIOUS
VERACIOUSLY
VERACITIES
VERACITY
VERAMENT
VERANDA
VERANDAED
VERANDAH
VERANDAHED
VERASCOPE
VERATRAL
VERATRALBIN
VERATRALBINE
VERATRATE
VERATRIA
VERATRIC
VERATRIDIN
VERATRIDINE
VERATRIN
VERATRINA
VERATRINE
VERATRINIZE
VERATRINIZED
VERATRINIZING
VERATRIZED
VERATRIZING
VERATROL
VERATROLE
VERATROYL
VERATRYL
VERAY
VERB
VERBAL
VERBALISM
VERBALIST
VERBALITY
VERBALIZE
VERBALIZED
VERBALIZER
VERBALIZING
VERBARIAN
VERBARIUM
VERBASCO
VERBASCOSE
VERBATE

VERBATIM
VERBENA
VERBENACEOUS
VERBENALIKE
VERBENALIN
VERBENATE
VERBENATED
VERBENATING
VERBENE
VERBENONE
VERBERATE
VERBERATION
VERBERATIVE
VERBIAGE
VERBICIDE
VERBICULTURE
VERBID
VERBIFIED
VERBIFYING
VERBIGERATE
VERBIGERATED
VERBIGERATING
VERBILE
VERBOMANIAC
VERBOMOTOR
VERBOSE
VERBOSELY
VERBOSENESS
VERBOSITIES
VERBOSITY
VERBOTEN
VERBY
VERCHOC
VERD
VERDANCIES
VERDANCY
VERDANT
VERDEA
VERDELHO
VERDERER
VERDEROR
VERDET
VERDETTO
VERDICT
VERDIGRIS
VERDIGRISY
VERDIN
VERDITER
VERDOY
VERDUGO
VERDUN
VERDURE
VERDURED
VERDURER
VERDUROUS
VERECUND
VERECUNDITY
VERECUNDNESS
VEREDICT
VEREK
VERENDA
VERGE
VERGED
VERGENCE
VERGENCY
VERGENT
VERGENTNESS
VERGER
VERGERISM
VERGERY
VERGI
VERGIFORM
VERGING
VERGLAS
VERGOBRET
VERGOYNE
VERGUNNING

VERI
VERIDIC
VERIDICAL
VERIDICALITIES
VERIDICALITY
VERIDICALLY
VERIDICOUS
VERIDITY
VERIER
VERIEST
VERIFIABLE
VERIFIABLY
VERIFICATE
VERIFICATION
VERIFICATIVE
VERIFIED
VERIFIER
VERIFY
VERIFYING
VERILY
VERIMENT
VERIN
VERINE
VERISCOPE
VERISIMILAR
VERISIMILITY
VERISM
VERISMO
VERIST
VERISTIC
VERITABLE
VERITABLY
VERITAS
VERITE
VERITIES
VERITISM
VERITIST
VERITISTIC
VERITY
VERJUICE
VERMEIL
VERMENGING
VERMEOLOGIST
VERMEOLOGY
VERMETID
VERMIAN
VERMICELLI
VERMICEOUS
VERMICIDAL
VERMICIDE
VERMICIOUS
VERMICLE
VERMICULAR
VERMICULARLY
VERMICULATE
VERMICULATED
VERMICULATING
VERMICULATION
VERMICULE
VERMICULITE
VERMICULOSE
VERMICULOUS
VERMIFORM
VERMIFORMITY
VERMIFUGAL
VERMIFUGE
VERMIFUGOUS
VERMIGEROUS
VERMIGRADE
VERMIL
VERMILION
VERMILIONETTE
VERMILIONIZE
VERMILY
VERMIN
VERMINAL
VERMINATE

VERMINATION
VERMINER
VERMINLY
VERMINOSIS
VERMINOUS
VERMINOUSLY
VERMINY
VERMIPAROUS
VERMIS
VERMIVOROUS
VERMIX
VERMOREL
VERMOULU
VERMOULUE
VERMOUTH
VERNACCIA
VERNACLE
VERNACULAR
VERNACULARLY
VERNACULATE
VERNAGE
VERNAL
VERNALITY
VERNALIZE
VERNANT
VERNATION
VERNEUK
VERNEUKER
VERNEUKERY
VERNICLE
VERNICOSE
VERNIER
VERNILE
VERNILITY
VERNISSAGE
VERNITION
VERNIX
VERNONIN
VERONALISM
VERQUERE
VERRA
VERRAY
VERRE
VERREL
VERRELL
VERRICULATE
VERRICULATED
VERRICULE
VERRUCA
VERRUCAE
VERRUCANO
VERRUCATED
VERRUCOSE
VERRUCOSIS
VERRUCOSITIES
VERRUCOSITY
VERRUCOUS
VERRUCULOSE
VERRUGA
VERRUGAS
VERS
VERSABILITY
VERSABLE
VERSABLENESS
VERSAL
VERSANT
VERSATE
VERSATILE
VERSATILITIES
VERSATILITY
VERSATION
VERSATIVE
VERSE
VERSED
VERSEMAN
VERSEMANSHIP
VERSEMEN

VERSEMONGER
VERSER
VERSES
VERSET
VERSETTE
VERSEWRIGHT
VERSICLE
VERSICLER
VERSICOLOR
VERSICOLOUR
VERSICULAR
VERSICULE
VERSICULI
VERSICULUS
VERSIERA
VERSIFIABLE
VERSIFIASTER
VERSIFICATION
VERSIFICATOR
VERSIFIED
VERSIFIER
VERSIFORM
VERSIFY
VERSIFYING
VERSILOQUY
VERSION
VERSIONAL
VERSIONER
VERSIONIST
VERSIONIZE
VERSIPEL
VERSO
VERSOR
VERST
VERSTA
VERSTE
VERSUAL
VERSUS
VERSUTE
VERTEBRA
VERTEBRAE
VERTEBRAL
VERTEBRALESS
VERTEBRALLY
VERTEBRAS
VERTEBRATE
VERTEBRATED
VERTEBRATION
VERTEBRIFORM
VERTEP
VERTEX
VERTEXES
VERTIBILITY
VERTIBLE
VERTIBLENESS
VERTICAL
VERTICALED
VERTICALING
VERTICALISM
VERTICALITY
VERTICALLED
VERTICALLING
VERTICALLY
VERTICES
VERTICIL
VERTICILLARY
VERTICILLATE
VERTICILLI
VERTICILLUS
VERTICITY
VERTICOMENTAL
VERTIGINATE
VERTIGINES
VERTIGINOUS
VERTIGO
VERTIGOES
VERTILINEAR

VERTIMETER
VERTU
VERTUGAL
VERTY
VERULED
VERUMONTANUM
VERUTA
VERUTUM
VERVAIN
VERVE
VERVECEAN
VERVECINE
VERVEL
VERVELED
VERVELLE
VERVELLED
VERVENIA
VERVER
VERVET
VERVINE
VERY
VERZINI
VERZINO
VES
VESANIA
VESANIC
VESBITE
VESI
VESICA
VESICAE
VESICAL
VESICANT
VESICATE
VESICATED
VESICATING
VESICATION
VESICATORY
VESICLE
VESICOCELE
VESICOCLYSIS
VESICOTOMY
VESICULA
VESICULAE
VESICULAR
VESICULARLY
VESICULASE
VESICULATE
VESICULATED
VESICULATING
VESICULATION
VESICULE
VESICULOSE
VESICULOUS
VESICULUS
VESKIT
VESPACIDE
VESPAL
VESPER
VESPERAL
VESPERIAN
VESPERING
VESPERS
VESPERTIDE
VESPERTILIAN
VESPERTINAL
VESPERTINE
VESPETRO
VESPIARIES
VESPIARY
VESPID
VESPIFORM
VESPINE
VESPOID
VESSEL
VESSELED
VESSELLED
VESSELS

VESSES
VESSETS
VESSICNON
VESSIGNON
VEST
VESTAL
VESTED
VESTEE
VESTER
VESTIARIAN
VESTIARIES
VESTIARIUM
VESTIARY
VESTIBLE
VESTIBULA
VESTIBULAR
VESTIBULATE
VESTIBULE
VESTIBULED
VESTIBULING
VESTIBULUM
VESTIGE
VESTIGIA
VESTIGIAL
VESTIGIALLY
VESTIGIARY
VESTIGIUM
VESTIMENT
VESTIMENTAL
VESTING
VESTITURE
VESTLET
VESTMENT
VESTMENTAL
VESTMENTED
VESTRAL
VESTRICAL
VESTRIES
VESTRIFY
VESTRY
VESTRYMAN
VESTRYMANLY
VESTRYMEN
VESTUARY
VESTURAL
VESTURE
VESTURED
VESTURER
VESTURING
VESUVIAN
VESUVIANITE
VESUVIATE
VESUVIN
VESUVITE
VESZELYITE
VET
VETA
VETANDA
VETCH
VETCHIER
VETCHIEST
VETCHLING
VETCHY
VETERAN
VETERANIZE
VETERANS
VETERINARIAN
VETERINARIES
VETERINARY
VETITIVE
VETIVENE
VETIVENOL
VETIVER
VETO
VETOED
VETOER
VETOES

VETOING
VETOISM
VETOIST
VETOISTIC
VETOISTICAL
VETTED
VETTING
VETTURA
VETTURE
VETTURINO
VETUST
VETUSTY
VEUGLAIRE
VEUVE
VEX
VEXATION
VEXATIOUS
VEXATIOUSLY
VEXATORY
VEXED
VEXEDLY
VEXEDNESS
VEXER
VEXFUL
VEXIL
VEXILLA
VEXILLARIOUS
VEXILLARY
VEXILLATE
VEXILLATION
VEXILLUM
VEXING
VEYN
VIA
VIABILITY
VIABLE
VIADUCT
VIAE
VIAGE
VIAGGIATORY
VIAGRAM
VIAGRAPH
VIAJACA
VIAL
VIALED
VIALING
VIALLED
VIALLING
VIAMETER
VIAND
VIANDEN
VIANDER
VIANDRY
VIANDS
VIATIC
VIATICA
VIATICAL
VIATICALS
VIATICUM
VIATOR
VIATORES
VIATORIAL
VIATORIALLY
VIBES
VIBETOITE
VIBEX
VIBGYOR
VIBICES
VIBRACULA
VIBRACULAR
VIBRACULOID
VIBRACULUM
VIBRANCIES
VIBRANCY
VIBRANT
VIBRANTLY
VIBRAPHONE

VIBRATE
VIBRATED
VIBRATILE
VIBRATILITY
VIBRATING
VIBRATION
VIBRATIONAL
VIBRATIUNCLE
VIBRATIVE
VIBRATO
VIBRATOR
VIBRATORY
VIBRIOID
VIBRION
VIBRIONIC
VIBRISSA
VIBRISSAE
VIBRISSAL
VIBROGRAPH
VIBROMETER
VIBROMOTIVE
VIBROPHONE
VIBROSCOPE
VIBURNIC
VIBURNIN
VIC
VICAIRE
VICAR
VICARAGE
VICARATE
VICARESS
VICARIAL
VICARIAN
VICARIANISM
VICARIATE
VICARII
VICARIOUS
VICARIOUSLY
VICARIUS
VICARLY
VICARSHIP
VICE
VICECOMES
VICECOMITAL
VICECOMITES
VICED
VICEGERAL
VICEGERENCY
VICEGERENT
VICENARY
VICENNIAL
VICEREGAL
VICEREGALLY
VICEREINE
VICEROY
VICEROYAL
VICEROYALTY
VICETY
VICHY
VICHYSSOISE
VICI
VICIANIN
VICIANOSE
VICILIN
VICIN
VICINAGE
VICINAL
VICINE
VICING
VICINITIES
VICINITY
VICIOUS
VICIOUSLY
VICIOUSNESS
VICISSITOUS
VICISSITUDE
VICOITE

VICONTIEL
VICONTIELS
VICTIM
VICTIMIZABLE
VICTIMIZATION
VICTIMIZE
VICTIMIZED
VICTIMIZER
VICTIMIZING
VICTLESS
VICTOR
VICTORDOM
VICTORESS
VICTORFISH
VICTORFISHES
VICTORIATE
VICTORIATUS
VICTORIES
VICTORINE
VICTORIOUS
VICTORIOUSLY
VICTORIUM
VICTORY
VICTRESS
VICTRIX
VICTUAL
VICTUALAGE
VICTUALED
VICTUALER
VICTUALING
VICTUALLED
VICTUALLER
VICTUALLING
VICTUALS
VICTUS
VICUDA
VICUNA
VICUNAS
VICUS
VID
VIDAME
VIDAN
VIDDUI
VIDDUY
VIDE
VIDELICET
VIDENDA
VIDENDUM
VIDEO
VIDERUFF
VIDETTE
VIDETUR
VIDICON
VIDIMUS
VIDONIA
VIDRY
VIDUAGE
VIDUAL
VIDUALLY
VIDUATE
VIDUATED
VIDUATION
VIDUITY
VIDUOUS
VIDYA
VIE
VIED
VIEJA
VIELLE
VIER
VIERKLEUR
VIERLING
VIERTEL
VIEW
VIEWED
VIEWER
VIEWING

VIEWLESS
VIEWLESSLY
VIEWLY
VIEWPOINT
VIEWSTER
VIEWY
VIF
VIFDA
VIGA
VIGAS
VIGENTENNIAL
VIGESIMAL
VIGESIMATION
VIGGLE
VIGIA
VIGIL
VIGILANCE
VIGILANCY
VIGILANT
VIGILANTE
VIGILANTLY
VIGILATE
VIGILATION
VIGNERON
VIGNERONS
VIGNETTE
VIGNETTED
VIGNETTER
VIGNETTING
VIGNETTIST
VIGNIN
VIGOGNE
VIGONE
VIGONIA
VIGOR
VIGORISH
VIGORIST
VIGOROSO
VIGOROUS
VIGOROUSLY
VIGOROUSNESS
VIGOUR
VIHARA
VIHUELA
VIJAO
VIKING
VIKINGISM
VILA
VILAYET
VILD
VILDLY
VILDNESS
VILE
VILELY
VILENESS
VILER
VILEST
VILEYNS
VILIACO
VILIFICATION
VILIFIED
VILIFIER
VILIFY
VILIFYING
VILIPEND
VILIPENDED
VILIPENDER
VILIPENDING
VILIPENDIOUS
VILITIES
VILITY
VILL
VILLA
VILLACHE
VILLADOM
VILLAETTE
VILLAGE

VILLAGELET
VILLAGEOUS
VILLAGER
VILLAGERY
VILLAGET
VILLAGEY
VILLAGISM
VILLAIN
VILLAINESS
VILLAINIES
VILLAINIST
VILLAINOUS
VILLAINOUSLY
VILLAINY
VILLAKIN
VILLANAGE
VILLANCICO
VILLANELLA
VILLANELLE
VILLANETTE
VILLAR
VILLATE
VILLATIC
VILLAYET
VILLE
VILLEGIATURE
VILLEIN
VILLEINAGE
VILLEINHOLD
VILLENAGE
VILLI
VILLIAUMITE
VILLICUS
VILLIFORM
VILLITIS
VILLOID
VILLOSE
VILLOSITY
VILLOTA
VILLOTE
VILLOUS
VILLUS
VILY
VIM
VIMANA
VIMEN
VIMINA
VIMINAL
VIMINEOUS
VIMPA
VIN
VINA
VINACEOUS
VINAGE
VINAGRON
VINAIGRE
VINAIGRETTE
VINAIGRETTED
VINAIGRIER
VINAIGROUS
VINAL
VINASSE
VINATA
VINCENT
VINCETOXIN
VINCHUCA
VINCIBILITY
VINCIBLE
VINCIBLENESS
VINCIBLY
VINCULA
VINCULAR
VINCULATE
VINCULATION
VINCULUM
VINDEMIAL
VINDEMIATE

VINDEMIATION
VINDEMIATORY
VINDEX
VINDICABLE
VINDICABLY
VINDICATE
VINDICATED
VINDICATING
VINDICATION
VINDICATIVE
VINDICATOR
VINDICATORY
VINDICATRESS
VINDICES
VINDICT
VINDICTA
VINDICTIVE
VINDICTIVELY
VINE
VINEA
VINEAE
VINEAL
VINEATIC
VINED
VINEDRESSER
VINEGAR
VINEGARER
VINEGARETTE
VINEGARIST
VINEGARROON
VINEGARWEED
VINEGARY
VINEGROWER
VINEITY
VINELAND
VINELET
VINER
VINERIES
VINERY
VINESTALK
VINETTA
VINEW
VINEYARD
VINEYARDING
VINEYARDIST
VINEYARDS
VINGT
VINGTIEME
VINGTUN
VINHATICO
VINIA
VINIC
VINICULTURAL
VINICULTURE
VINIFERA
VINIFEROUS
VINIFICATION
VINIFICATOR
VINING
VINITOR
VINNY
VINO
VINOLENT
VINOLOGIST
VINOLOGY
VINOMETER
VINOSE
VINOSITY
VINOUS
VINOUSLY
VINOUSNESS
VINT
VINTA
VINTAGE
VINTAGER
VINTAGING
VINTEM

VINTENER
VINTLITE
VINTNER
VINTNERESS
VINTNERY
VINTRESS
VINTRY
VINUM
VINY
VINYL
VINYLENE
VINYLIC
VINYLIDENE
VINYON
VIOL
VIOLA
VIOLABILITY
VIOLABLE
VIOLABLENESS
VIOLABLY
VIOLACEOUS
VIOLACEOUSLY
VIOLAL
VIOLAN
VIOLAND
VIOLANIN
VIOLATE
VIOLATED
VIOLATER
VIOLATING
VIOLATION
VIOLATIONAL
VIOLATIVE
VIOLATOR
VIOLATURE
VIOLE
VIOLENCE
VIOLENT
VIOLENTLY
VIOLENTNESS
VIOLER
VIOLESCENT
VIOLET
VIOLETTE
VIOLETY
VIOLIN
VIOLINA
VIOLINE
VIOLINED
VIOLINETTE
VIOLINING
VIOLINIST
VIOLINISTIC
VIOLINO
VIOLIST
VIOLON
VIOLONCELLIST
VIOLONCELLO
VIOLONCELLOS
VIOLONE
VIOLOTTA
VIOLOUS
VIOLURIC
VIOSTEROL
VIPER
VIPERESS
VIPERFISH
VIPERFISHES
VIPERID
VIPERIFORM
VIPERINE
VIPEROID
VIPEROUS
VIPEROUSLY
VIPEROUSNESS
VIPERY
VIR

VIRAGIN
VIRAGINIAN
VIRAGINITY
VIRAGO
VIRAGOES
VIRAL
VIRASON
VIRE
VIRELAI
VIRELAY
VIREMENT
VIRENT
VIREO
VIREONINE
VIREOS
VIRES
VIRESCENCE
VIRESCENT
VIRGA
VIRGAL
VIRGATE
VIRGATER
VIRGATION
VIRGE
VIRGIN
VIRGINAL
VIRGINALIST
VIRGINALITY
VIRGINALLY
VIRGINEOUS
VIRGINHEAD
VIRGINITY
VIRGINIUM
VIRGINLY
VIRGULA
VIRGULAR
VIRGULATE
VIRGULE
VIRGULTUM
VIRIAL
VIRICIDE
VIRID
VIRIDARIA
VIRIDARIUM
VIRIDESCENCE
VIRIDESCENT
VIRIDIAN
VIRIDIGENOUS
VIRIDIN
VIRIDINE
VIRIDITE
VIRIDITY
VIRIFIC
VIRIFY
VIRILE
VIRILELY
VIRILENESS
VIRILESCENCE
VIRILIA
VIRILIFY
VIRILIOUSLY
VIRILISM
VIRILIST
VIRILITIES
VIRILITY
VIRIPOTENT
VIRITOOT
VIRITRATE
VIRL
VIROLE
VIROLED
VIROLOGIST
VIROLOGY
VIRON
VIROSE
VIROSES
VIROSIS

VIROUS
VIRTU
VIRTUAL
VIRTUALISM
VIRTUALIST
VIRTUALITY
VIRTUALLY
VIRTUE
VIRTUED
VIRTUEFY
VIRTUOSA
VIRTUOSE
VIRTUOSI
VIRTUOSIC
VIRTUOSITY
VIRTUOSO
VIRTUOSOS
VIRTUOUS
VIRTUOUSLY
VIRTUS
VIRTUTI
VIRTUTIS
VIRUCIDAL
VIRUCIDE
VIRUELA
VIRULENCE
VIRULENCY
VIRULENT
VIRULENTED
VIRULENTLY
VIRUS
VIS
VISA
VISAED
VISAGE
VISAGED
VISAGRAPH
VISAING
VISAMMIN
VISARD
VISARGA
VISCACHA
VISCERA
VISCERAL
VISCERATE
VISCERATED
VISCERATING
VISCERATION
VISCEROUS
VISCID
VISCIDITY
VISCIDIZE
VISCIDLY
VISCIDNESS
VISCIDULOUS
VISCIN
VISCOID
VISCOIDAL
VISCOMETER
VISCOMETRY
VISCONTAL
VISCONTIAL
VISCOSCOPE
VISCOSE
VISCOSIMETER
VISCOSITIES
VISCOSITY
VISCOUNT
VISCOUNTCIES
VISCOUNTCY
VISCOUNTESS
VISCOUNTY
VISCOUS
VISCOUSLY
VISCOUSNESS
VISCUS
VISE

VISED
VISEED
VISEING
VISEMENT
VISENOMY
VISIBILITIES
VISIBILITY
VISIBILIZE
VISIBLE
VISIBLENESS
VISIBLY
VISIE
VISIER
VISILE
VISING
VISION
VISIONAL
VISIONALLY
VISIONARILY
VISIONARY
VISIONED
VISIONER
VISIONIZE
VISIONS
VISIT
VISITA
VISITABLE
VISITADOR
VISITANT
VISITATION
VISITATIONAL
VISITATIVE
VISITATOR
VISITATORIAL
VISITE
VISITED
VISITING
VISITOR
VISITORIAL
VISITRESS
VISITS
VISIVE
VISNE
VISNEY
VISON
VISOR
VISORED
VISORING
VISORY
VISS
VISTA
VISTAED
VISTAL
VISTAMENTE
VISTO
VISUAL
VISUALIST
VISUALITIES
VISUALITY
VISUALIZE
VISUALIZED
VISUALIZER
VISUALIZING
VISUOMETER
VITA
VITAE
VITAGRAPH
VITAL
VITALISM
VITALIST
VITALISTIC
VITALITY
VITALIZATION
VITALIZE
VITALIZED
VITALIZER
VITALIZING

VITALIZINGLY
VITALLY
VITALNESS
VITALS
VITAMIN
VITAMINE
VITAMINIC
VITAMINIZE
VITAMINOLOGY
VITAMINS
VITAPATH
VITAPATHY
VITAPHONE
VITASCOPE
VITASCOPIC
VITASTI
VITATIVENESS
VITE
VITELLARIUM
VITELLARY
VITELLIN
VITELLINE
VITELLOSE
VITELLUS
VITERBITE
VITESSE
VITIABLE
VITIAL
VITIATE
VITIATED
VITIATING
VITIATION
VITIATOR
VITICETUM
VITICULTURE
VITICULTURIST
VITIFEROUS
VITILIGINOUS
VITILIGO
VITILITIGATE
VITIOSITIES
VITIOSITY
VITIUM
VITRAGE
VITRAIL
VITRAILED
VITRAILLIST
VITRAIN
VITRAUX
VITRE
VITREAL
VITREAN
VITRELLA
VITREMYTE
VITREOSITY
VITREOUS
VITREOUSLY
VITREOUSNESS
VITRESCENCE
VITRESCENCY
VITRESCENT
VITRESCIBLE
VITREUM
VITRIAL
VITRIC
VITRICS
VITRIFACTION
VITRIFACTURE
VITRIFIABLE
VITRIFICATE
VITRIFICATION
VITRIFIED
VITRIFORM
VITRIFY
VITRIFYING
VITRINE
VITRINOID

VITRIOL
VITRIOLATE
VITRIOLATED
VITRIOLATING
VITRIOLATION
VITRIOLED
VITRIOLIC
VITRIOLINE
VITRIOLING
VITRIOLIZE
VITRIOLIZED
VITRIOLIZING
VITRIOLLED
VITRIOLLING
VITRITE
VITRO
VITROBASALT
VITROPHYRE
VITROPHYRIC
VITROTYPE
VITROUS
VITRUM
VITRY
VITTA
VITTAE
VITTATE
VITTLE
VITTLES
VITULAR
VITULARY
VITULINE
VITUPER
VITUPERABLE
VITUPERATE
VITUPERATED
VITUPERATING
VITUPERATION
VITUPERATIVE
VITUPERATOR
VITUPERATORY
VITUPERY
VIUVA
VIVA
VIVACE
VIVACIOUS
VIVACIOUSLY
VIVACISSIMO
VIVACITIES
VIVACITY
VIVAMENTE
VIVANDIER
VIVANDIERE
VIVANT
VIVARIA
VIVARIES
VIVARIUM
VIVARIUMS
VIVARY
VIVAT
VIVAX
VIVDA
VIVE
VIVELY
VIVENCY
VIVER
VIVERRIFORM
VIVERRINE
VIVERS
VIVES
VIVEUR
VIVIANITE
VIVID
VIVIDER
VIVIDEST
VIVIDITY
VIVIDLY
VIVIDNESS

VIVIFIC
VIVIFICAL
VIVIFICANT
VIVIFICATE
VIVIFICATED
VIVIFICATING
VIVIFICATION
VIVIFICATIVE
VIVIFICATOR
VIVIFIED
VIVIFIER
VIVIFY
VIVIFYING
VIVIPARISM
VIVIPARITY
VIVIPAROUS
VIVIPARY
VIVIPERFUSE
VIVISECT
VIVISECTED
VIVISECTING
VIVISECTION
VIVISECTIVE
VIVISECTOR
VIVO
VIVRE
VIVRES
VIX
VIXEN
VIXENISH
VIXENISHLY
VIXENLY
VIZARD
VIZARDED
VIZARDING
VIZCACHA
VIZIER
VIZIERATE
VIZIERIAL
VIZIR
VIZIRATE
VIZIRIAL
VIZNOMY
VIZOR
VIZORED
VIZORING
VIZSLA
VIZY
VIZZY
VLEI
VLEY
VLOKA
VLY
VOAR
VOCABILITY
VOCABLE
VOCABLY
VOCABULAR
VOCABULARIAN
VOCABULARIED
VOCABULARIES
VOCABULARY
VOCABULATION
VOCABULIST
VOCAL
VOCALIC
VOCALION
VOCALISATION
VOCALISE
VOCALISM
VOCALIST
VOCALITY
VOCALIZATION
VOCALIZE
VOCALIZED
VOCALIZER
VOCALIZING

VOCALLER
VOCALLY
VOCALNESS
VOCATE
VOCATION
VOCATIONAL
VOCATIONALLY
VOCATIVE
VOCATIVELY
VOCE
VOCES
VOCI
VOCICULTURAL
VOCIFERANCE
VOCIFERANT
VOCIFERATE
VOCIFERATED
VOCIFERATING
VOCIFERATION
VOCIFERATIVE
VOCIFERATOR
VOCIFERIZE
VOCIFEROSITY
VOCIFEROUS
VOCIFEROUSLY
VOCIFICATION
VOCIMOTOR
VOCODER
VOCOID
VOCULAR
VOCULE
VODKA
VODUN
VOE
VOET
VOETGANGER
VOETSAK
VOEU
VOG
VOGER
VOGESITE
VOGIE
VOGLITE
VOGUE
VOGUISH
VOICE
VOICED
VOICEFUL
VOICEFULNESS
VOICELESS
VOICELESSLY
VOICER
VOICES
VOICING
VOID
VOIDABLE
VOIDANCE
VOIDED
VOIDEE
VOIDER
VOIDING
VOIDLY
VOIDNESS
VOIDS
VOILA
VOILE
VOILIER
VOISINAGE
VOITURE
VOITURETTE
VOITURIER
VOIVOD
VOIVODE
VOKIE
VOL
VOLA
VOLABLE

VOLACIOUS	VOLSELLA	VOLUTION	VOTATION	VULCANIZATE
VOLADOR	VOLT	VOLUTOID	VOTE	VULCANIZATION
VOLAGE	VOLTA	VOLVA	VOTEABLE	VULCANIZE
VOLAILLE	VOLTAGE	VOLVATE	VOTED	VULCANIZED
VOLANT	VOLTAGRAPHY	VOLVE	VOTEEN	VULCANIZER
VOLANTE	VOLTAIC	VOLVELL	VOTER	VULCANIZING
VOLANTLY	VOLTAISM	VOLVELLE	VOTES	VULCANO
VOLAPIE	VOLTAITE	VOLVENT	VOTING	VULCANOLOGY
VOLAR	VOLTAMETER	VOLVOCACEOUS	VOTIST	VULGAR
VOLARY	VOLTAMETRIC	VOLVULUS	VOTIVE	VULGARE
VOLATA	VOLTAMMETER	VOLYER	VOTIVELY	VULGARER
VOLATIC	VOLTAPLAST	VOMBATID	VOTIVENESS	VULGAREST
VOLATILE	VOLTATYPE	VOME	VOTOMETER	VULGARIAN
VOLATILELY	VOLTE	VOMER	VOTRESS	VULGARISM
VOLATILENESS	VOLTEADOR	VOMERINE	VOUCH	VULGARIST
VOLATILITIES	VOLTEADORES	VOMICA	VOUCHABLE	VULGARITIES
VOLATILITY	VOLTI	VOMICIN	VOUCHED	VULGARITY
VOLATILIZATION	VOLTIGEUR	VOMICINE	VOUCHEE	VULGARIZATION
VOLATILIZE	VOLTINISM	VOMIT	VOUCHER	VULGARIZE
VOLATILIZED	VOLTIVITY	VOMITED	VOUCHING	VULGARIZED
VOLATILIZER	VOLTIZE	VOMITER	VOUCHMENT	VULGARIZER
VOLATILIZING	VOLTMETER	VOMITING	VOUCHSAFE	VULGARIZING
VOLATION	VOLTO	VOMITINGLY	VOUCHSAFED	VULGARLY
VOLATIONAL	VOLTZINE	VOMITION	VOUCHSAFING	VULGARNESS
VOLBORTHITE	VOLTZITE	VOMITIVE	VOUGE	VULGO
VOLCANIAN	VOLUBILITY	VOMITO	VOULGE	VULGUS
VOLCANIC	VOLUBLE	VOMITORIES	VOUR	VULGUSES
VOLCANICALLY	VOLUBLENESS	VOMITORY	VOUSSOIR	VULN
VOLCANICITY	VOLUBLY	VOMITURE	VOUST	VULNED
VOLCANIST	VOLUCRINE	VOMITUS	VOUSTER	VULNERABILITY
VOLCANITE	VOLUME	VON	VOUSTY	VULNERABLE
VOLCANITY	VOLUMED	VONSENITE	VOW	VULNERABLY
VOLCANIZE	VOLUMEN	VOODOO	VOWED	VULNERAL
VOLCANIZED	VOLUMETER	VOODOOED	VOWEL	VULNERARY
VOLCANIZING	VOLUMETRIC	VOODOOING	VOWELISM	VULNERATE
VOLCANO	VOLUMETRY	VOODOOISM	VOWELIST	VULNERATIVE
VOLCANOES	VOLUMINA	VOODOOIST	VOWELIZE	VULNIFIC
VOLCANOLOGY	VOLUMINAL	VOODOOISTIC	VOWELLIKE	VULNIFICAL
VOLCANOS	VOLUMINOSITY	VOOG	VOWELLY	VULNOSE
VOLE	VOLUMINOUS	VOORHUIS	VOWELS	VULPECULAR
VOLEE	VOLUMINOUSLY	VOORTREKKER	VOWELY	VULPIC
VOLEMITE	VOLUMIST	VORACIOUS	VOWER	VULPICIDAL
VOLEMITOL	VOLUMOMETER	VORACIOUSLY	VOWESS	VULPICIDE
VOLENCY	VOLUNTARIATE	VORACITY	VOWING	VULPICIDISM
VOLENT	VOLUNTARIES	VORAGE	VOX	VULPINE
VOLENTLY	VOLUNTARILY	VORAGINOUS	VOYAGE	VULPINIC
VOLERIES	VOLUNTARIOUS	VORAGO	VOYAGEABLE	VULPINISM
VOLERY	VOLUNTARISM	VORANT	VOYAGED	VULPINITE
VOLET	VOLUNTARIST	VORAZ	VOYAGER	VULSELLA
VOLGE	VOLUNTARITY	VORHAND	VOYAGEUR	VULSELLUM
VOLHYNITE	VOLUNTARY	VORLAGE	VOYAGING	VULSINITE
VOLITANT	VOLUNTARYISM	VORONDREO	VOYAL	VULT
VOLITATE	VOLUNTARYIST	VORPAL	VOYANCE	VULTURE
VOLITATION	VOLUNTATIVE	VORTEX	VOYEUR	VULTURINE
VOLITATIONAL	VOLUNTEER	VORTEXES	VOYEURISM	VULTURISH
VOLITIENCY	VOLUNTEERED	VORTICAL	VOYEUSE	VULTURISM
VOLITIENT	VOLUNTEERING	VORTICALLY	VOYOL	VULTURN
VOLITION	VOLUNTEERLY	VORTICEL	VRAI	VULTUROUS
VOLITIONAL	VOLUNTY	VORTICELLID	VRAIC	VULVA
VOLITIONARY	VOLUPER	VORTICES	VRAICKER	VULVAL
VOLITIONATE	VOLUPT	VORTICIFORM	VRAICKING	VULVAR
VOLITIVE	VOLUPTAS	VORTICISM	VRBAITE	VULVATE
VOLITORIAL	VOLUPTUARIES	VORTICIST	VRIDDHI	VULVIFORM
VOLK	VOLUPTUARY	VORTICITY	VRILLE	VULVITIS
VOLKSRAAD	VOLUPTUATE	VORTICOSE	VROCHT	VULVOCRURAL
VOLLENGE	VOLUPTUOSITY	VORTICOSELY	VROTHER	VULVOUTERINE
VOLLEY	VOLUPTUOUS	VORTICULAR	VROUW	VULVOVAGINAL
VOLLEYBALL	VOLUPTUOUSNESS	VORTICULARLY	VUE	VULVOVAGINITIS
VOLLEYED	VOLUPTY	VORTIGINOUS	VUG	VUM
VOLLEYER	VOLUTA	VOTA	VUGG	VYINGLY
VOLLEYING	VOLUTAE	VOTABLE	VUGGY	VYT
VOLLEYINGLY	VOLUTATE	VOTAL	VUGH	
VOLLEYS	VOLUTATION	VOTALLY	VUIDE	
VOLOST	VOLUTE	VOTARESS	VULCANICITY	
VOLOW	VOLUTED	VOTARIES	VULCANISM	
VOLPLANE	VOLUTIFORM	VOTARIST	VULCANIST	
VOLPLANIST	VOLUTIN	VOTARY	VULCANITE	

WA
WAAG
WAAPA
WAB
WABAYO
WABBER
WABBLE
WABBLED
WABBLER
WABBLINESS
WABBLING
WABBLINGLY
WABBLY
WABBY
WABE
WABENO
WABI
WABRON
WABUR
WACADASH
WACAPOU
WACE
WACHNA
WACK
WACKE
WACKER
WACKIER
WACKIEST
WACKY
WAD
WADCUTTER
WADD
WADDED
WADDENT
WADDER
WADDIE
WADDIED
WADDIES
WADDING
WADDLE
WADDLED
WADDLER
WADDLESOME
WADDLING
WADDLY
WADDY
WADDYING
WADDYWOOD
WADE
WADED
WADER
WADGE
WADI
WADIES
WADING
WADINGLY
WADMAAL
WADMAKER
WADMAKING
WADMAL
WADMOL
WADMOLL
WADNA
WADSET
WADSETTED
WADSETTING
WADY

WAEFU
WAEFUL
WAEG
WAENESS
WAESUCK
WAESUCKS
WAF
WAFER
WAFERED
WAFERER
WAFERING
WAFERMAKER
WAFERWOMAN
WAFERWORK
WAFERY
WAFF
WAFFIE
WAFFLE
WAFFLIKE
WAFFLY
WAFFNESS
WAFT
WAFTAGE
WAFTED
WAFTER
WAFTING
WAFTURE
WAFTY
WAG
WAGANG
WAGATI
WAGBEARD
WAGE
WAGED
WAGELESS
WAGELING
WAGER
WAGERED
WAGERER
WAGERING
WAGES
WAGET
WAGEWORK
WAGEWORKER
WAGEWORKING
WAGGED
WAGGEL
WAGGER
WAGGERIES
WAGGERY
WAGGIE
WAGGING
WAGGISH
WAGGISHLY
WAGGISHNESS
WAGGLE
WAGGLED
WAGGLING
WAGGLINGLY
WAGGLY
WAGGON
WAGGONABLE
WAGGONAGE
WAGGONED
WAGGONER
WAGGONETTE
WAGGONING
WAGGONLOAD
WAGGONRY
WAGGONSMITH
WAGGONWAY
WAGGONWAYMAN
WAGGONWRIGHT
WAGGY
WAGH
WAGING
WAGNERITE

WAGON
WAGONABLE
WAGONAGE
WAGONED
WAGONER
WAGONETTE
WAGONING
WAGONLOAD
WAGONMAKER
WAGONMAKING
WAGONMAN
WAGONRY
WAGONSMITH
WAGONWAY
WAGONWAYMAN
WAGONWRIGHT
WAGSOME
WAGTAIL
WAGWAG
WAGWANTS
WAGWIT
WAH
WAHAHE
WAHCONDA
WAHINE
WAHOO
WAHWAH
WAIATA
WAIF
WAIK
WAIKLY
WAIKNESS
WAIL
WAILED
WAILER
WAILFUL
WAILFULLY
WAILING
WAILMENT
WAILSOME
WAILY
WAIN
WAINAGE
WAINBOTE
WAINER
WAINMAN
WAINMEN
WAINROPE
WAINSCOT
WAINSCOTED
WAINSCOTING
WAINSCOTTED
WAINSCOTTING
WAINWRIGHT
WAIPIRO
WAIR
WAIRCH
WAIRD
WAIREPO
WAIRSH
WAISE
WAIST
WAISTBAND
WAISTCLOTH
WAISTCOAT
WAISTCOATED
WAISTCOATEER
WAISTED
WAISTER
WAISTING
WAISTLESS
WAISTLINE
WAIT
WAITED
WAITER
WAITERAGE
WAITERING

WAITING
WAITINGLY
WAITRESS
WAITSMEN
WAIVATUA
WAIVE
WAIVED
WAIVER
WAIVERY
WAIVING
WAJANG
WAK
WAKA
WAKAN
WAKANDA
WAKE
WAKEA
WAKED
WAKEFUL
WAKEFULLY
WAKEFULNESS
WAKELESS
WAKEMAN
WAKEMEN
WAKEN
WAKENED
WAKENER
WAKENING
WAKER
WAKERIFE
WAKERIFENESS
WAKES
WAKETIME
WAKF
WAKIF
WAKIKI
WAKING
WAKINGLY
WAKIUP
WAKON
WAKONDA
WAKY
WAL
WALAHEE
WALD
WALDFLUTE
WALDGRAVE
WALDGRAVINE
WALDHORN
WALDMEISTER
WALE
WALED
WALEPIECE
WALER
WALI
WALING
WALK
WALKAWAY
WALKED
WALKENE
WALKER
WALKERS
WALKING
WALKIST
WALKMILL
WALKMILLER
WALKOUT
WALKOVER
WALKRIFE
WALKSMAN
WALKSMEN
WALKUP
WALKWAY
WALKYRIE
WALL
WALLA
WALLABA

WALLABIES
WALLABY
WALLAGO
WALLAH
WALLAROO
WALLBIRD
WALLBOARD
WALLED
WALLER
WALLET
WALLEYE
WALLEYED
WALLFLOWER
WALLHICK
WALLIE
WALLING
WALLOCH
WALLOON
WALLOP
WALLOPER
WALLOPING
WALLOW
WALLOWED
WALLOWER
WALLOWING
WALLOWISH
WALLOWISHLY
WALLPAPER
WALLPAPERING
WALLPIECE
WALLS
WALLWORT
WALLY
WALLYDRAG
WALLYDRAIGLE
WALM
WALNUT
WALPURGITE
WALRUS
WALRUSES
WALSH
WALSPERE
WALT
WALTER
WALTRON
WALTROT
WALTY
WALTZ
WALTZED
WALTZER
WALTZING
WALWE
WALY
WALYCOAT
WAMARA
WAMB
WAMBAIS
WAMBLE
WAMBLED
WAMBLINESS
WAMBLING
WAMBLINGLY
WAMBLY
WAME
WAMED
WAMEFOU
WAMEFU
WAMEFUL
WAMEL
WAMFLE
WAMMUS
WAMP
WAMPEE
WAMPISH
WAMPLE
WAMPUM
WAMPUMPEAG

WAMPUS
WAMUS
WAN
WANA
WANCHANCY
WAND
WANDE
WANDER
WANDERER
WANDERING
WANDERINGLY
WANDERLUST
WANDERLUSTER
WANDEROO
WANDERY
WANDERYEAR
WANDFLOWER
WANDLE
WANDOO
WANDOUGHT
WANDRETH
WANDSMAN
WANDY
WANE
WANED
WANELESS
WANEY
WANG
WANGA
WANGALA
WANGAN
WANGATEUR
WANGER
WANGHEE
WANGLE
WANGLED
WANGLER
WANGLING
WANGO
WANGRACE
WANGTOOTH
WANGUN
WANHAP
WANHAPPY
WANHOPE
WANHORN
WANIAND
WANIGAN
WANING
WANION
WANKAPIN
WANKLE
WANKLINESS
WANKLY
WANKY
WANLAS
WANLE
WANLY
WANMOL
WANNED
WANNER
WANNESS
WANNEST
WANNIGAN
WANNING
WANNY
WANREST
WANRESTFUL
WANRUFE
WANRULY
WANSHAPE
WANSITH
WANSOME
WANSONSY
WANT
WANTAGE
WANTED

WANTER
WANTFUL
WANTHILL
WANTHRIFT
WANTHRIVEN
WANTING
WANTINGLY
WANTINGNESS
WANTON
WANTONED
WANTONER
WANTONING
WANTONIZE
WANTONLY
WANTONNESS
WANTROKE
WANTRUST
WANTWIT
WANTY
WANWEIRD
WANWIT
WANWORDY
WANWORTH
WANY
WANZE
WAP
WAPACUT
WAPATA
WAPATOO
WAPED
WAPENTAKE
WAPIN
WAPITI
WAPITIS
WAPP
WAPPED
WAPPENED
WAPPENSCHAW
WAPPER
WAPPET
WAPPING
WAQF
WAR
WARABI
WARAL
WARATAH
WARBIRD
WARBITE
WARBLE
WARBLED
WARBLELIKE
WARBLER
WARBLERLIKE
WARBLET
WARBLING
WARBLINGLY
WARBLY
WARCH
WARCRAFT
WARD
WARDABLE
WARDAGE
WARDATOUR
WARDAY
WARDCORS
WARDED
WARDEN
WARDENCY
WARDENRIES
WARDENRY
WARDENSHIP
WARDER
WARDHOLDING
WARDIAN
WARDING
WARDITE
WARDMAID

WARDMAN
WARDMEN
WARDMOTE
WARDRESS
WARDROBE
WARDROBER
WARDROOM
WARDSHIP
WARDSMAID
WARDSMAN
WARDSWOMAN
WARDWITE
WARDWOMAN
WARDWOMEN
WARDWORD
WARE
WARED
WAREFUL
WAREHOU
WAREHOUSE
WAREHOUSED
WAREHOUSEMAN
WAREHOUSEMEN
WAREHOUSING
WARELESS
WARELY
WARENTMENT
WAREROOM
WARES
WARESHIP
WARF
WARFA
WARFARE
WARFARED
WARFARER
WARFARING
WARFUL
WARGUS
WARHEAD
WARI
WARIANCE
WARIANGLE
WARIED
WARIER
WARIEST
WARILY
WARIMENT
WARINE
WARINESS
WARINGIN
WARISH
WARISON
WARK
WARKAMOOWEE
WARKLOOM
WARKLUME
WARLIKE
WARLIKELY
WARLIKENESS
WARLING
WARLOCK
WARLOCKRY
WARLORD
WARLOW
WARLUCK
WARLY
WARM
WARMAKER
WARMAKING
WARMAN
WARMED
WARMEDLY
WARMEN
WARMER
WARMEST
WARMFUL
WARMHEARTED

WARMHOUSE
WARMING
WARMLY
WARMMESS
WARMONGER
WARMONGERING
WARMOUTH
WARMTH
WARMUP
WARMUS
WARN
WARNAGE
WARND
WARNED
WARNEL
WARNER
WARNING
WARNINGLY
WARNISH
WARNISON
WARNISS
WARNOTH
WARP
WARPAGE
WARPATH
WARPED
WARPER
WARPING
WARPLANE
WARPLE
WARPOWER
WARPROOF
WARRAGAL
WARRAMBOOL
WARRANDICE
WARRANT
WARRANTABLE
WARRANTABLY
WARRANTED
WARRANTEE
WARRANTER
WARRANTIES
WARRANTING
WARRANTISE
WARRANTIZE
WARRANTOR
WARRANTY
WARRAY
WARRE
WARRED
WARREE
WARREN
WARRENER
WARRER
WARRIGAL
WARRIN
WARRING
WARRIOR
WARRISH
WARROK
WARRYN
WARSAW
WARSHIP
WARSLE
WARSLED
WARSLER
WARSLING
WARSTLE
WARSTLER
WART
WARTED
WARTFLOWER
WARTH
WARTIER
WARTIEST
WARTIME
WARTLIKE

WARTWEED
WARTWORT
WARTY
WARTYBACK
WARVE
WARWARDS
WARWICKITE
WARWOLF
WARWORK
WARWORKER
WARWORN
WARY
WARYTREE
WAS
WASABI
WASE
WASEL
WASH
WASHABILITY
WASHABLE
WASHBASIN
WASHBASKET
WASHBOARD
WASHBOWL
WASHBREW
WASHCLOTH
WASHDAY
WASHDISH
WASHDOWN
WASHED
WASHER
WASHERIES
WASHERLESS
WASHERMAN
WASHERMEN
WASHERWIFE
WASHERWOMAN
WASHERWOMEN
WASHERY
WASHERYMAN
WASHERYMEN
WASHHAND
WASHHOUSE
WASHIER
WASHIEST
WASHIN
WASHINESS
WASHING
WASHINGS
WASHLAND
WASHLEATHER
WASHMAID
WASHMAN
WASHMEN
WASHOFF
WASHOUT
WASHPOT
WASHRAG
WASHROOM
WASHSHED
WASHSTAND
WASHTAIL
WASHTRAY
WASHTROUGH
WASHTUB
WASHWAY
WASHWOMAN
WASHWOMEN
WASHWORK
WASHY
WASP
WASPEN
WASPIER
WASPIEST
WASPISH
WASPISHLY
WASPISHNESS

WASPLING
WASPNESTING
WASPS
WASPY
WASSAIL
WASSAILED
WASSAILER
WASSAILING
WASSAILOUS
WASSIE
WAST
WASTABLE
WASTAGE
WASTE
WASTEBASKET
WASTED
WASTEFUL
WASTEFULLY
WASTEFULNESS
WASTEL
WASTELAND
WASTELBREAD
WASTELESS
WASTELOT
WASTELY
WASTEMAN
WASTEMEN
WASTEMENT
WASTENESS
WASTEPAPER
WASTER
WASTERFUL
WASTERIE
WASTERN
WASTERY
WASTETHRIFT
WASTEWAY
WASTEWEIR
WASTEWORD
WASTEYARD
WASTIER
WASTIEST
WASTINE
WASTING
WASTINGLY
WASTINGNESS
WASTME
WASTREL
WASTRIE
WASTRIFE
WASTRY
WASTY
WAT
WATAP
WATAPE
WATAPEH
WATCH
WATCHBAND
WATCHBILL
WATCHBOAT
WATCHCASE
WATCHCRY
WATCHDOG
WATCHED
WATCHER
WATCHERS
WATCHES
WATCHET
WATCHEYE
WATCHFREE
WATCHFUL
WATCHFULLY
WATCHFULNESS
WATCHGLASS
WATCHHOUSE
WATCHING
WATCHINGLY

WATCHKEEPER
WATCHLESS
WATCHMAKER
WATCHMAKING
WATCHMAN
WATCHMANLY
WATCHMATE
WATCHMEN
WATCHMENT
WATCHOUT
WATCHTOWER
WATCHWORD
WATCHWORK
WATE
WATER
WATERAGE
WATERBAILAGE
WATERBANK
WATERBEAR
WATERBELLY
WATERBLINK
WATERBLOOM
WATERBOARD
WATERBOK
WATERBORNE
WATERBOSH
WATERBOUND
WATERBRAIN
WATERBROO
WATERBROSE
WATERBUCK
WATERBUCKS
WATERBUSH
WATERCASTER
WATERCHAT
WATERCOLOR
WATERCOURSE
WATERCRAFT
WATERCRESS
WATERCUP
WATERDOE
WATERDROP
WATERED
WATERER
WATERFALL
WATERFINDER
WATERFLOOD
WATERFOWL
WATERFOWLS
WATERFREE
WATERFRONT
WATERGLASS
WATERHEAD
WATERHEAP
WATERHORSE
WATERIE
WATERILY
WATERINESS
WATERING
WATERINGLY
WATERINGMAN
WATERISH
WATERISHLY
WATERISHNESS
WATERLEAF
WATERLEAVE
WATERLESS
WATERLESSLY
WATERLINE
WATERLOG
WATERLOGGED
WATERLOGGER
WATERMAN
WATERMANSHIP
WATERMARK
WATERMARKED
WATERMASTER

WATERMELON
WATERMEN
WATERMONGER
WATERPIT
WATERPLANE
WATERPOT
WATERPOWER
WATERPROOF
WATERPROOFED
WATERPROOFER
WATERRUG
WATERSCAPE
WATERSHAKE
WATERSHED
WATERSHOOT
WATERSHUT
WATERSIDE
WATERSIDER
WATERSKIN
WATERSMEET
WATERSPOUT
WATERSTOUP
WATERTIGHT
WATERTIGHTAL
WATERWALL
WATERWAY
WATERWEED
WATERWHEEL
WATERWISE
WATERWOOD
WATERWORK
WATERWORKER
WATERWORKS
WATERWORM
WATERWORN
WATERWORT
WATERY
WATH
WATHE
WATHER
WATHSTEAD
WATO
WATT
WATTAGE
WATTAPE
WATTER
WATTEST
WATTIS
WATTLE
WATTLEBIRD
WATTLEBOY
WATTLED
WATTLES
WATTLESS
WATTLEWORK
WATTLING
WATTMAN
WATTMEN
WATTMETER
WAUBEEN
WAUBLE
WAUCH
WAUCHLE
WAUCHT
WAUF
WAUFF
WAUGH
WAUGHT
WAUGHY
WAUK
WAUKE
WAUKIT
WAUKRIFE
WAUL
WAUNS
WAUR
WAUREGAN

WAUVE
WAVABLE
WAVABLY
WAVE
WAVED
WAVELENGTH
WAVELESS
WAVELET
WAVELLITE
WAVEMARK
WAVEMENT
WAVEMETER
WAVEOFF
WAVER
WAVERED
WAVERER
WAVERING
WAVERINGLY
WAVERINGNESS
WAVEROUS
WAVERY
WAVESON
WAVEY
WAVEYS
WAVIER
WAVIES
WAVIEST
WAVILY
WAVINESS
WAVING
WAVINGLY
WAVY
WAW
WAWA
WAWAH
WAWASKEESH
WAWE
WAWL
WAX
WAXAND
WAXBERRIES
WAXBERRY
WAXBILL
WAXBIRD
WAXBUSH
WAXCHANDLER
WAXCHANDLERY
WAXCOMB
WAXED
WAXEN
WAXER
WAXES
WAXFLOWER
WAXHEARTED
WAXIER
WAXIEST
WAXINESS
WAXING
WAXINGLY
WAXMAKER
WAXMAKING
WAXMAN
WAXWEED
WAXWING
WAXWORK
WAXWORKER
WAXWORKING
WAXWORM
WAXY
WAY
WAYAKA
WAYANG
WAYBACK
WAYBERRY
WAYBILL
WAYBIRD
WAYBOOK

WAYBREAD
WAYBUNG
WAYER
WAYFARE
WAYFARER
WAYFARING
WAYFARINGLY
WAYFELLOW
WAYGANG
WAYGATE
WAYGOER
WAYGOING
WAYGONE
WAYGOOSE
WAYHOUSE
WAYING
WAYLAID
WAYLAY
WAYLAYER
WAYLAYING
WAYLEAVE
WAYMAKER
WAYMAN
WAYMARK
WAYMATE
WAYMEN
WAYMENT
WAYNE
WAYPOST
WAYS
WAYSIDE
WAYSIDER
WAYSLIDING
WAYTE
WAYTHORN
WAYWARD
WAYWARDEN
WAYWARDLY
WAYWARDNESS
WAYWISER
WAYWORN
WAYWORT
WAYZGOOSE
WAZIR
WAZIRATE
WAZIRSHIP
WE
WEA
WEAK
WEAKBRAINED
WEAKEN
WEAKENED
WEAKENER
WEAKENING
WEAKER
WEAKEST
WEAKFISH
WEAKFISHES
WEAKHANDED
WEAKHEARTED
WEAKISH
WEAKISHLY
WEAKISHNESS
WEAKLIER
WEAKLIEST
WEAKLINESS
WEAKLING
WEAKLY
WEAKMOUTHED
WEAKNESS
WEAKY
WEAL
WEALD
WEALDISH
WEALDSMAN
WEALDSMEN
WEALFUL

WEALSMAN	WEATHERCOCKY	WEEDED	WEIGHBAR	WELLADAY
WEALSOME	WEATHERED	WEEDER	WEIGHBAUK	WELLAT
WEALTH	WEATHERER	WEEDERY	WEIGHBRIDGE	WELLAWAY
WEALTHFUL	WEATHERGLASS	WEEDHOOK	WEIGHED	WELLBORN
WEALTHFULLY	WEATHERGLEAM	WEEDIER	WEIGHER	WELLCURB
WEALTHIER	WEATHERHEAD	WEEDIEST	WEIGHHOUSE	WELLED
WEALTHIEST	WEATHERING	WEEDILY	WEIGHIN	WELLER
WEALTHILY	WEATHERLY	WEEDINESS	WEIGHING	WELLHEAD
WEALTHINESS	WEATHERMAKER	WEEDING	WEIGHLOCK	WELLHOLE
WEALTHMAKER	WEATHERMAN	WEEDLESS	WEIGHMAN	WELLING
WEALTHMAKING	WEATHERMEN	WEEDS	WEIGHMASTER	WELLINGTON
WEALTHMONGER	WEATHERMOST	WEEDY	WEIGHMEN	WELLISH
WEALTHY	WEATHEROLOGY	WEEK	WEIGHSHAFT	WELLMAKER
WEAM	WEATHERPROOF	WEEKDAY	WEIGHT	WELLMAKING
WEAN	WEATHERSICK	WEEKEND	WEIGHTCHASER	WELLMAN
WEANED	WEATHERTIGHT	WEEKENDER	WEIGHTED	WELLMEN
WEANEDNESS	WEATHERWORN	WEEKLIES	WEIGHTEDLY	WELLMOST
WEANEL	WEATHERY	WEEKLONG	WEIGHTEDNESS	WELLNEAR
WEANER	WEATINGS	WEEKLY	WEIGHTER	WELLQUEME
WEANIE	WEAVE	WEEKS	WEIGHTIER	WELLRING
WEANING	WEAVED	WEEKWAM	WEIGHTIEST	WELLS
WEANLING	WEAVER	WEEL	WEIGHTILY	WELLSIDE
WEANLY	WEAVERBIRD	WEELFARD	WEIGHTINESS	WELLSITE
WEANYER	WEAVERESS	WEEM	WEIGHTING	WELLSPRING
WEAPON	WEAVING	WEEN	WEIGHTLESS	WELLSTEAD
WEAPONED	WEAZEN	WEENIE	WEIGHTLESSLY	WELLSTRAND
WEAPONEER	WEAZENED	WEENIER	WEIGHTOMETER	WELLY
WEAPONLESS	WEAZENY	WEENIEST	WEIGHTS	WELLYARD
WEAPONMAKER	WEB	WEENING	WEIGHTY	WELME
WEAPONMAKING	WEBB	WEENONG	WEIHE	WELOO
WEAPONPROOF	WEBBE	WEENSY	WEILANG	WELS
WEAPONRY	WEBBED	WEENT	WEIN	WELSH
WEAPONS	WEBBER	WEENTY	WEIR	WELSHED
WEAR	WEBBING	WEENY	WEIRD	WELSHER
WEARABILITY	WEBBY	WEEP	WEIRDFUL	WELSHING
WEARABLE	WEBELOS	WEEPER	WEIRDIE	WELSIUM
WEARED	WEBER	WEEPERED	WEIRDIES	WELSOM
WEARER	WEBEYE	WEEPIER	WEIRDLESS	WELT
WEARIED	WEBFEET	WEEPIEST	WEIRDLINESS	WELTED
WEARIEDLY	WEBFOOT	WEEPING	WEIRDLY	WELTER
WEARIEDNESS	WEBMAKER	WEEPLY	WEIRDNESS	WELTERED
WEARIER	WEBMAKING	WEEPS	WEIRDSOME	WELTERING
WEARIEST	WEBSTER	WEEPY	WEIRDWOMAN	WELTERWEIGHT
WEARIFUL	WEBSTERITE	WEER	WEIRDWOMEN	WELTING
WEARIFULLY	WEBWORK	WEERISH	WEIRING	WELY
WEARIFULNESS	WEBWORM	WEESHEE	WEISBACHITE	WEM
WEARILESS	WECCHE	WEESHY	WEISE	WEME
WEARILESSLY	WECHT	WEEST	WEISSITE	WEMLESS
WEARILY	WED	WEET	WEIZE	WEMMY
WEARINESS	WEDANA	WEETBIRD	WEJACK	WEMOD
WEARING	WEDBED	WEETLESS	WEKA	WEMODNESS
WEARINGLY	WEDBEDRIP	WEETY	WEKAU	WEN
WEARISH	WEDDED	WEEVER	WEKEEN	WENCH
WEARISHLY	WEDDEDLY	WEEVIL	WEKI	WENCHED
WEARISHNESS	WEDDEDNESS	WEEVILED	WEL	WENCHEL
WEARISOME	WEDDEED	WEEVILLED	WELCH	WENCHER
WEARISOMELY	WEDDER	WEEVILLY	WELCHER	WENCHING
WEARISOMENESS	WEDDING	WEEVILY	WELCOME	WEND
WEARY	WEDDINGER	WEEWAW	WELCOMED	WENDE
WEARYING	WEDE	WEEWOW	WELCOMELY	WENDED
WEARYINGLY	WEDFEE	WEEZE	WELCOMENESS	WENDIGO
WEASAND	WEDGE	WEEZLE	WELCOMER	WENDIGOS
WEASEL	WEDGEBILL	WEFT	WELCOMING	WENDING
WEASELED	WEDGED	WEFTAGE	WELCOMINGLY	WENE
WEASELING	WEDGER	WEFTED	WELD	WENETH
WEASELLY	WEDGIE	WEFTWISE	WELDABILITY	WENLICHE
WEASELS	WEDGIER	WEFTY	WELDABLE	WENNEBERGITE
WEASELSKIN	WEDGIEST	WEGENERIAN	WELDED	WENNISH
WEASELSNOUT	WEDGING	WEGOTISM	WELDER	WENNY
WEASER	WEDGWOOD	WEHRLITE	WELDING	WENRO
WEASON	WEDGY	WEIBYEITE	WELE	WENT
WEATHER	WEDLOCK	WEICHSELWOOD	WELFARE	WENTLE
WEATHERBEATEN	WEE	WEID	WELFARING	WENTLETRAP
WEATHERBOARD	WEEBLE	WEIGELA	WELI	WENZEL
WEATHERBREAK	WEED	WEIGELITE	WELK	WEPMAN
WEATHERCAST	WEEDA	WEIGH	WELKIN	WEPMANKIN
WEATHERCOCK	WEEDAGE	WEIGHAGE	WELL	WEPT

WER	WETBIRD	WHARF	WHEELMAKING	WHEREFORE
WERD	WETE	WHARFAGE	WHEELMAN	WHEREFORTH
WERE	WETHE	WHARFED	WHEELMEN	WHEREFROM
WEREBEAR	WETHER	WHARFHEAD	WHEELRACE	WHEREHENCE
WERECALF	WETHERHOG	WHARFHOLDER	WHEELROAD	WHEREIN
WERED	WETHERTEG	WHARFIE	WHEELS	WHEREINTO
WEREFOLK	WETLANDS	WHARFING	WHEELSMAN	WHERENESS
WEREFOX	WETLY	WHARFINGER	WHEELSMEN	WHEREOF
WEREGILD	WETNESS	WHARFLAND	WHEELSMITH	WHEREON
WEREHYENA	WETTABILITY	WHARFMAN	WHEELSPIN	WHEREOUT
WEREJAGUAR	WETTABLE	WHARFMASTER	WHEELWAY	WHEREOVER
WERELEOPARD	WETTED	WHARFMEN	WHEELWORK	WHERESO
WERETIGER	WETTER	WHARFRAE	WHEELWRIGHT	WHERESOEVER
WEREWALL	WETTEST	WHARFS	WHEELY	WHERESOMEVER
WEREWOLF	WETTING	WHARFSIDE	WHEEN	WHERETHROUGH
WEREWOLFISH	WETTISH	WHARL	WHEENCAT	WHERETILL
WEREWOLFISM	WEVE	WHARP	WHEEP	WHERETO
WEREWOLVES	WEVED	WHARROW	WHEEPLE	WHERETOEVER
WERF	WEVET	WHART	WHEEPLED	WHEREUNDER
WERGELD	WEY	WHARVE	WHEEPLING	WHEREUNTIL
WERGELT	WEYNE	WHARVES	WHEERIKINS	WHEREUNTO
WERGILD	WHA	WHAT	WHEESHT	WHEREUP
WERI	WHAAP	WHATA	WHEETLE	WHEREUPON
WERING	WHABBY	WHATABOUTS	WHEEZE	WHEREVER
WERK	WHACK	WHATE	WHEEZED	WHEREWITH
WERMETHE	WHACKED	WHATEVER	WHEEZER	WHEREWITHAL
WERN	WHACKER	WHATKIN	WHEEZIER	WHERRET
WERNARD	WHACKING	WHATLIKE	WHEEZIEST	WHERRIED
WERNE	WHACKY	WHATMAN	WHEEZILY	WHERRIES
WERNERITE	WHADDIE	WHATNESS	WHEEZINESS	WHERRIT
WEROOLE	WHALE	WHATNOT	WHEEZING	WHERRY
WEROWANCE	WHALEBACK	WHATRECK	WHEEZINGLY	WHERRYING
WERP	WHALEBIRD	WHATSO	WHEEZLE	WHERRYMAN
WERSE	WHALEBOAT	WHATSOEVER	WHEEZY	WHERVE
WERSH	WHALEBONE	WHATTEN	WHEFT	WHET
WERSLETE	WHALEBONED	WHAU	WHEKAU	WHETHER
WERT	WHALED	WHAUP	WHEKI	WHETILE
WERTE	WHALEHEAD	WHAUVE	WHELK	WHETROCK
WESKIT	WHALELIKE	WHAWL	WHELKED	WHETSTONE
WESSEL	WHALEMAN	WHEAL	WHELKER	WHETTED
WESSELTON	WHALEMEN	WHEALED	WHELKIER	WHETTER
WEST	WHALER	WHEALING	WHELKIEST	WHETTING
WESTAWAY	WHALERIES	WHEALWORM	WHELKY	WHEW
WESTBOUND	WHALEROAD	WHEAM	WHELM	WHEWELLITE
WESTE	WHALERS	WHEAT	WHELMED	WHEWER
WESTEN	WHALERY	WHEATBIRD	WHELMING	WHEWL
WESTER	WHALES	WHEATEAR	WHELP	WHEWT
WESTERING	WHALESHIP	WHEATEARED	WHELPED	WHEY
WESTERLIES	WHALING	WHEATEN	WHELPING	WHEYBEARD
WESTERLINESS	WHALISH	WHEATGRASS	WHELPLESS	WHEYBIRD
WESTERLING	WHALL	WHEATGROWER	WHELPLING	WHEYEY
WESTERLY	WHALLY	WHEATLAND	WHELVE	WHEYEYNESS
WESTERN	WHALM	WHEATLIKE	WHEMMEL	WHEYFACE
WESTERNER	WHALY	WHEATWORM	WHEMMLE	WHEYFACED
WESTERNISM	WHAM	WHEATY	WHEN	WHEYISH
WESTERNIZE	WHAMBLE	WHEE	WHENABOUTS	WHEYISNESS
WESTERNIZED	WHAME	WHEEDLE	WHENAS	WHEYNESS
WESTERNIZING	WHAMMED	WHEEDLED	WHENCE	WHEYWORM
WESTERNMOST	WHAMMIES	WHEEDLER	WHENCEFORTH	WHEYWORMED
WESTERWARDS	WHAMMING	WHEEDLING	WHENCESOEVER	WHI
WESTFALITE	WHAMMY	WHEEDLINGLY	WHENCEVER	WHIBA
WESTING	WHAMP	WHEEL	WHENEVER	WHICH
WESTLAN	WHAMPLE	WHEELAGE	WHENNESS	WHICHEVER
WESTLAND	WHANG	WHEELBAND	WHENSO	WHICHSOEVER
WESTLANDWAYS	WHANGAM	WHEELBARROW	WHENSOEVER	WHICHWAY
WESTLINS	WHANGDOODLE	WHEELBASE	WHENSOMEVER	WHICHWAYS
WESTME	WHANGEE	WHEELBIRD	WHERE	WHICK
WESTMELESS	WHANK	WHEELBOX	WHEREABOUT	WHICKER
WESTMOST	WHAP	WHEELCHAIR	WHEREABOUTS	WHID
WESTNESS	WHAPPER	WHEELED	WHEREAFTER	WHIDAH
WESTWARD	WHAPPET	WHEELER	WHEREANENT	WHIFF
WESTWARDLY	WHAPPING	WHEELERY	WHEREAS	WHIFFED
WESTWARDS	WHAPUKA	WHEELHOUSE	WHEREASES	WHIFFER
WESTY	WHAPUKEE	WHEELING	WHEREAT	WHIFFET
WET	WHAPUKU	WHEELINGLY	WHEREAWAY	WHIFFING
WETA	WHAR	WHEELLESS	WHEREBY	WHIFFLE
WETBACK	WHARE	WHEELMAKER	WHEREFOR	WHIFFLED

WHIFFLER
WHIFFLERIES
WHIFFLERY
WHIFFLETREE
WHIFFLING
WHIFFLINGLY
WHIFFY
WHIFT
WHIG
WHIGMALEERIE
WHIGMALEERY
WHIGMELEERIE
WHILE
WHILEAS
WHILEEN
WHILEND
WHILES
WHILEY
WHILIE
WHILK
WHILLABALLOO
WHILLALOO
WHILLILEW
WHILLY
WHILLYWHA
WHILOCK
WHILOM
WHILST
WHILTER
WHIM
WHIMBREL
WHIMLING
WHIMMED
WHIMMIER
WHIMMIEST
WHIMMING
WHIMMY
WHIMPER
WHIMPERED
WHIMPERER
WHIMPERING
WHIMPERINGLY
WHIMSEY
WHIMSEYS
WHIMSIC
WHIMSICAL
WHIMSICALITY
WHIMSICALLY
WHIMSIED
WHIMSIES
WHIMSY
WHIMWHAM
WHIN
WHINBERRIES
WHINBERRY
WHINCHACKER
WHINCHAT
WHINCHECK
WHINCOW
WHINDLE
WHINE
WHINED
WHINER
WHINESTONE
WHING
WHINGE
WHINGER
WHINING
WHININGLY
WHINNEL
WHINNER
WHINNIED
WHINNIES
WHINNOCK
WHINNY
WHINNYING
WHINSTONE

WHINY
WHINYARD
WHIP
WHIPBELLY
WHIPBIRD
WHIPCAT
WHIPCORD
WHIPCORDY
WHIPCRACK
WHIPCRACKER
WHIPCRAFT
WHIPGRAFT
WHIPJACK
WHIPKING
WHIPLASH
WHIPMAKER
WHIPMAKING
WHIPMAN
WHIPMANSHIP
WHIPMASTER
WHIPPA
WHIPPABLE
WHIPPAREE
WHIPPED
WHIPPER
WHIPPERGINNY
WHIPPERSNAPPER
WHIPPERTAIL
WHIPPET
WHIPPETER
WHIPPING
WHIPPINGLY
WHIPPLETREE
WHIPPOORWILL
WHIPPOST
WHIPPY
WHIPS
WHIPSAW
WHIPSAWED
WHIPSAWING
WHIPSAWN
WHIPSAWYER
WHIPSOCKET
WHIPSTAFF
WHIPSTALK
WHIPSTALL
WHIPSTER
WHIPSTICK
WHIPSTITCH
WHIPSTOCK
WHIPT
WHIPTAIL
WHIPTREE
WHIPWORM
WHIR
WHIRL
WHIRLABOUT
WHIRLBAT
WHIRLBLAST
WHIRLBONE
WHIRLBRAIN
WHIRLED
WHIRLER
WHIRLGIG
WHIRLICANE
WHIRLICOTE
WHIRLIGIG
WHIRLING
WHIRLPOOL
WHIRLPUFF
WHIRLS
WHIRLWIG
WHIRLWIND
WHIRLWINDISH
WHIRLWINDY
WHIRLY
WHIRLYBIRD

WHIRR
WHIRRED
WHIRREY
WHIRRICK
WHIRRIED
WHIRRING
WHIRRY
WHIRRYING
WHIRTLE
WHISH
WHISHT
WHISK
WHISKBROOM
WHISKED
WHISKER
WHISKERAGE
WHISKERANDO
WHISKERANDOS
WHISKERED
WHISKERER
WHISKERS
WHISKERY
WHISKET
WHISKEY
WHISKEYS
WHISKIED
WHISKIES
WHISKIFIED
WHISKIN
WHISKING
WHISKINGLY
WHISKY
WHISP
WHISPER
WHISPERATION
WHISPERED
WHISPERER
WHISPERING
WHISPERINGLY
WHISPEROUS
WHISPEROUSLY
WHISPERY
WHISS
WHIST
WHISTER
WHISTERPOOP
WHISTLE
WHISTLEBELLY
WHISTLED
WHISTLEFISH
WHISTLEFISHES
WHISTLER
WHISTLERISM
WHISTLEWING
WHISTLEWOOD
WHISTLING
WHISTLINGLY
WHIT
WHITBLOW
WHITE
WHITEBAIT
WHITEBARK
WHITEBEAM
WHITEBEARD
WHITEBELLY
WHITEBERRY
WHITEBILL
WHITEBLAZE
WHITEBLOW
WHITEBOY
WHITECAP
WHITECAPPER
WHITECOAT
WHITECOMB
WHITECORN
WHITECUP
WHITED

WHITEFACE
WHITEFEET
WHITEFISH
WHITEFISHER
WHITEFISHERY
WHITEFISHES
WHITEFLY
WHITEFOOT
WHITEFOOTISM
WHITEHANDED
WHITEHASS
WHITEHAWSE
WHITEHEAD
WHITEHEARTED
WHITELIKE
WHITELY
WHITEN
WHITENED
WHITENER
WHITENESS
WHITENING
WHITENOSE
WHITEOUT
WHITEPOT
WHITER
WHITEROOT
WHITERUMP
WHITES
WHITESARK
WHITESHANK
WHITESIDE
WHITESMITH
WHITEST
WHITESTONE
WHITESTRAITS
WHITETAIL
WHITETHORN
WHITETHROAT
WHITETIP
WHITETOP
WHITEVEIN
WHITEVEINS
WHITEWALL
WHITEWARE
WHITEWASH
WHITEWASHED
WHITEWASHER
WHITEWASHING
WHITEWEED
WHITEWING
WHITEWOOD
WHITEWORT
WHITEY
WHITHER
WHITHERWARD
WHITHERWARDS
WHITING
WHITINGS
WHITISH
WHITISHNESS
WHITLEATHER
WHITLING
WHITLOW
WHITLOWWORT
WHITNEY
WHITNEYITE
WHITRACK
WHITS
WHITSTER
WHITTAW
WHITTAWER
WHITTEN
WHITTER
WHITTERICK
WHITTLE
WHITTLED
WHITTLER

WHITTLING
WHITTLINGS
WHITTRET
WHITY
WHIZ
WHIZBANG
WHIZGIG
WHIZZ
WHIZZED
WHIZZER
WHIZZERMAN
WHIZZES
WHIZZING
WHIZZINGLY
WHIZZLE
WHO
WHOA
WHODUNIT
WHOEVER
WHOLE
WHOLEHEARTED
WHOLENESS
WHOLESALE
WHOLESALED
WHOLESALER
WHOLESALING
WHOLESOME
WHOLESOMELY
WHOLESOMER
WHOLESOMEST
WHOLEWISE
WHOLLY
WHOM
WHOMP
WHOMSO
WHOMSOEVER
WHON
WHONE
WHOO
WHOOF
WHOOP
WHOOPE
WHOOPED
WHOOPEE
WHOOPER
WHOOPING
WHOOPINGLY
WHOOSH
WHOOT
WHOP
WHOPPED
WHOPPER
WHOPPING
WHORAGE
WHORE
WHORED
WHOREDOM
WHOREHOUSE
WHOREMASTER
WHOREMASTERY
WHOREMONGER
WHOREMONGING
WHORESON
WHORING
WHORISH
WHORISHLY
WHORISHNESS
WHORL
WHORLE
WHORLED
WHORLFLOWER
WHORLY
WHORLYWORT
WHORRY
WHORT
WHORTLE
WHORTLEBERRY

WHOSE
WHOSESOEVER
WHOSO
WHOSOEVER
WHUD
WHUFF
WHUFFLE
WHULE
WHULTER
WHUMP
WHUP
WHURL
WHUSH
WHUTE
WHUTTER
WHUTTERING
WHY
WHYDAH
WHYEVER
WHYFOR
WHYO
WIBBLE
WICH
WICHTISITE
WICHTJE
WICK
WICKAWEE
WICKED
WICKEDLY
WICKEDNESS
WICKEN
WICKER
WICKERWARE
WICKERWORK
WICKERWORKED
WICKERWORKER
WICKET
WICKETKEEPER
WICKETS
WICKING
WICKIUP
WICKY
WICOPIES
WICOPY
WID
WIDBIN
WIDDERSHINS
WIDDIES
WIDDIFOW
WIDDLE
WIDDLED
WIDDLING
WIDDRIM
WIDDY
WIDE
WIDEGAB
WIDEGAP
WIDEHEARTED
WIDELY
WIDEMOUTHED
WIDEN
WIDENED
WIDENER
WIDENESS
WIDENING
WIDER
WIDERSHINS
WIDESPREAD
WIDESPREADLY
WIDEST
WIDEWHERE
WIDEWORK
WIDGE
WIDGEON
WIDGEONS
WIDGET
WIDOW

WIDOWED
WIDOWER
WIDOWERED
WIDOWERY
WIDOWHOOD
WIDOWLY
WIDOWMAN
WIDOWMEN
WIDOWY
WIDTH
WIDTHLESS
WIDTHWAY
WIDTHWAYS
WIDTHWISE
WIDU
WIEL
WIELARE
WIELD
WIELDED
WIELDER
WIELDING
WIELDY
WIENER
WIENERWURST
WIENIE
WIES
WIFE
WIFECARL
WIFED
WIFEHOOD
WIFELESS
WIFELESSNESS
WIFELIER
WIFELIEST
WIFELY
WIFETHING
WIFEWARD
WIFING
WIFLE
WIFT
WIG
WIGAN
WIGELING
WIGEON
WIGG
WIGGED
WIGGEN
WIGGER
WIGGERIES
WIGGERY
WIGGING
WIGGISM
WIGGLE
WIGGLER
WIGGLY
WIGGY
WIGHER
WIGHT
WIGHTLY
WIGHTNESS
WIGMAKER
WIGMAKING
WIGTAIL
WIGWAG
WIGWAGGED
WIGWAGGER
WIGWAGGING
WIGWAM
WIIKITE
WIKE
WIKEN
WIKING
WIKIUP
WIKIWIKI
WILCWEME
WILD
WILDBORE

WILDCAT
WILDCATS
WILDCATTED
WILDCATTER
WILDCATTING
WILDE
WILDEBEEST
WILDED
WILDER
WILDERED
WILDERING
WILDERMENT
WILDERN
WILDERNESS
WILDEST
WILDFIRE
WILDFLOWER
WILDFOWL
WILDFOWLS
WILDGRAVE
WILDING
WILDISH
WILDISHLY
WILDISHNESS
WILDLIFE
WILDLING
WILDLY
WILDNESS
WILDWIND
WILDWOOD
WILE
WILED
WILFUL
WILFULLY
WILFULNESS
WILGA
WILGERS
WILIER
WILIEST
WILILY
WILINESS
WILING
WILIWILI
WILK
WILKEITE
WILL
WILLABLE
WILLAWA
WILLE
WILLED
WILLEDNESS
WILLEMITE
WILLER
WILLES
WILLET
WILLETS
WILLEY
WILLFUL
WILLFULLY
WILLFULNESS
WILLIAMSITE
WILLICHE
WILLIED
WILLIER
WILLIES
WILLIEWAUCHT
WILLING
WILLINGHOOD
WILLINGLY
WILLINGNESS
WILLIWAW
WILLMAKER
WILLMAKING
WILLNESS
WILLOCK
WILLOW
WILLOWBITER

WILLOWED
WILLOWER
WILLOWISH
WILLOWLIKE
WILLOWWARE
WILLOWWEED
WILLOWWORM
WILLOWWORT
WILLOWY
WILLY
WILLYARD
WILLYART
WILLYER
WILLYING
WILN
WILNE
WILNING
WILRONE
WILROUN
WILSOME
WILSOMELY
WILSOMENESS
WILT
WILTED
WILTER
WILTING
WILY
WILYCOAT
WIM
WIMBLE
WIMBLED
WIMBLING
WIMICK
WIMLUNGE
WIMPLE
WIMPLED
WIMPLER
WIMPLING
WIN
WINARE
WINBROW
WINCE
WINCED
WINCER
WINCEY
WINCH
WINCHER
WINCHMAN
WINCHMEN
WINCING
WINCOPIPE
WIND
WINDABLE
WINDAGE
WINDAS
WINDBAG
WINDBAGGED
WINDBAGGERY
WINDBALL
WINDBERRY
WINDBIBBER
WINDBRACING
WINDBREAK
WINDBREAKER
WINDBROACH
WINDBURN
WINDBURNED
WINDBURNT
WINDCLOTHES
WINDCUFFER
WINDDOG
WINDED
WINDEDLY
WINDEDNESS
WINDEL
WINDER
WINDFALL

WINDFALLEN
WINDFANNER
WINDFIRM
WINDFISH
WINDFISHES
WINDFLAW
WINDFLOWER
WINDGALL
WINDGALLED
WINDHOLE
WINDHOVER
WINDIER
WINDIEST
WINDIGO
WINDIGOS
WINDILL
WINDILY
WINDINESS
WINDING
WINDINGLY
WINDINGNESS
WINDJAM
WINDJAMMER
WINDJAMMING
WINDLASS
WINDLASSED
WINDLASSER
WINDLASSING
WINDLE
WINDLES
WINDLESS
WINDLESTRAE
WINDLESTRAW
WINDLIN
WINDLING
WINDMILL
WINDMILLY
WINDORE
WINDOW
WINDOWED
WINDOWING
WINDOWLIKE
WINDOWMAKER
WINDOWMAKING
WINDOWMAN
WINDOWPANE
WINDOWPEEPER
WINDOWS
WINDOWSILL
WINDOWY
WINDPIPE
WINDPROOF
WINDRING
WINDROAD
WINDROOT
WINDROW
WINDROWED
WINDROWER
WINDROWING
WINDS
WINDSAIL
WINDSCREEN
WINDSHAKE
WINDSHIELD
WINDSHOCK
WINDSLAB
WINDSOCK
WINDSORITE
WINDSTORM
WINDSUCKER
WINDTIGHT
WINDUP
WINDWARD
WINDWARDLY
WINDWARDNESS
WINDWAY
WINDWAYWARD

WINDY	WINKLEHOLE	WIREDANCING	WISH	WITELESS
WINE	WINKLOT	WIREDRAW	WISHA	WITENAGEMOT
WINEBALL	WINLY	WIREDRAWER	WISHBONE	WITENAGEMOTE
WINEBERRIES	WINNA	WIREDRAWING	WISHED	WITEPENNY
WINEBERRY	WINNABLE	WIREDRAWN	WISHEDLY	WITESS
WINEBIBBER	WINNARD	WIREDREW	WISHER	WITFUL
WINEBIBBERY	WINNEL	WIREGRASS	WISHFUL	WITH
WINEBIBBING	WINNER	WIREHAIR	WISHFULLY	WITHAL
WINECONNER	WINNING	WIRELESS	WISHFULNESS	WITHAM
WINED	WINNINGLY	WIRELESSLY	WISHING	WITHAMITE
WINEDRAF	WINNINGNESS	WIRELESSNESS	WISHINGLY	WITHBEG
WINEGLASS	WINNINISH	WIREMAKER	WISHLY	WITHCALL
WINEGLASSFUL	WINNLE	WIREMAKING	WISHMAY	WITHDRAUGHT
WINEGLASSFULS	WINNOCK	WIREMAN	WISHNESS	WITHDRAW
WINEGROWER	WINNONISH	WIREMEN	WISHT	WITHDRAWAL
WINEGROWING	WINNOW	WIREMONGER	WISHTONWISH	WITHDRAWER
WINEHOUSE	WINNOWED	WIREPHOTO	WISKET	WITHDRAWING
WINELIKE	WINNOWER	WIREPULL	WISKINKIE	WITHDRAWMENT
WINEMAY	WINNOWING	WIREPULLER	WISKINKY	WITHDRAWN
WINEPOT	WINOES	WIREPULLING	WISMUTH	WITHDREW
WINEPRESS	WINOS	WIRER	WISP	WITHE
WINEPRESSER	WINSOME	WIRES	WISPED	WITHED
WINER	WINSOMELY	WIRESMITH	WISPIER	WITHEN
WINERIES	WINSOMENESS	WIRESPUN	WISPIEST	WITHER
WINERY	WINSOMER	WIRESTITCHED	WISPING	WITHERBAND
WINES	WINSOMEST	WIRETAIL	WISPISH	WITHERBLENCH
WINESHOP	WINSTER	WIRETAP	WISPY	WITHERCRAFT
WINESKIN	WINTER	WIRETAPPED	WISS	WITHERDEED
WINESOP	WINTERBERRY	WIRETAPPER	WISSE	WITHERED
WINETASTER	WINTERBLOOM	WIRETAPPING	WISSEL	WITHEREDLY
WINETREE	WINTERBOURNE	WIREWALKER	WISSHE	WITHEREDNESS
WINEVAT	WINTERDYKES	WIREWAY	WISSING	WITHERER
WINEYARD	WINTERED	WIREWEED	WISSLE	WITHERING
WINFREE	WINTERER	WIREWORK	WIST	WITHERINGLY
WING	WINTERFEED	WIREWORKER	WISTED	WITHERITE
WINGBACK	WINTERGREEN	WIREWORKING	WISTENED	WITHERLING
WINGBEAT	WINTERHAIN	WIREWORKS	WISTER	WITHERLY
WINGBOW	WINTERING	WIREWORM	WISTERIA	WITHERNAM
WINGCUT	WINTERIZE	WIRIER	WISTFUL	WITHERS
WINGDING	WINTERIZED	WIRIEST	WISTFULLY	WITHERSHINS
WINGED	WINTERIZING	WIRILY	WISTFULNESS	WITHERTIP
WINGER	WINTERKILL	WIRINESS	WISTING	WITHERWEIGHT
WINGFISH	WINTERKILLED	WIRING	WISTIT	WITHERY
WINGFISHES	WINTERLESS	WIRL	WISTITI	WITHGANG
WINGHANDED	WINTERLIKE	WIRLING	WISTLESS	WITHGATE
WINGIER	WINTERLINESS	WIRR	WISTLESSNESS	WITHHELD
WINGIEST	WINTERLY	WIRRA	WISURE	WITHHELE
WINGING	WINTERTIDE	WIRRAH	WIT	WITHHIE
WINGLE	WINTERTIME	WIRRASTHRU	WITAN	WITHHOLD
WINGLESS	WINTERWEED	WIRTH	WITCH	WITHHOLDAL
WINGLESSNESS	WINTERY	WIRY	WITCHBELLS	WITHHOLDEN
WINGLET	WINTLE	WIS	WITCHBROOM	WITHHOLDER
WINGLIKE	WINTRIER	WISDOM	WITCHCRAFT	WITHHOLDING
WINGMAN	WINTRIEST	WISE	WITCHED	WITHHOLDMENT
WINGMANSHIP	WINTRIFY	WISEACRE	WITCHEDLY	WITHIES
WINGOVER	WINTRILY	WISEACRED	WITCHEN	WITHIN
WINGPIECE	WINTRINESS	WISECRACK	WITCHERCULLY	WITHINDOORS
WINGPOST	WINTRY	WISECRACKER	WITCHERIES	WITHINFORTH
WINGS	WINY	WISECRACKERY	WITCHERING	WITHING
WINGSEED	WINZE	WISEHEAD	WITCHERY	WITHINWARD
WINGSPREAD	WINZEMAN	WISEHEARTED	WITCHET	WITHINWARDS
WINGSTEM	WINZEMEN	WISEHEIMER	WITCHETTY	WITHNAY
WINGY	WIO	WISELIER	WITCHGRASS	WITHNESS
WINIER	WIP	WISELIEST	WITCHING	WITHNIM
WINIEST	WIPE	WISELIKE	WITCHINGLY	WITHOUT
WINISH	WIPED	WISELING	WITCHLEAF	WITHOUTDOORS
WINK	WIPER	WISELY	WITCHMAN	WITHOUTEN
WINKED	WIPING	WISEMAN	WITCHMONGER	WITHOUTFORTH
WINKEL	WIPPEN	WISEN	WITCHUCK	WITHOUTSIDE
WINKELMAN	WIR	WISENESS	WITCHWEED	WITHOUTWARDS
WINKER	WIRABLE	WISENHEIMER	WITCHWIFE	WITHSAVE
WINKERED	WIRBLE	WISENT	WITCHWOMAN	WITHSAW
WINKERS	WIRE	WISER	WITCHWOOD	WITHSAY
WINKING	WIREBAR	WISEST	WITCHWORK	WITHSAYER
WINKINGLY	WIREBIRD	WISEWEED	WITCHY	WITHSET
WINKLE	WIRED	WISEWOMAN	WITCRAFT	WITHSLIP
WINKLEHAWK	WIREDANCER	WISEWOMEN	WITE	WITHSPAR

WITHSTAND	WLATFUL	WOLDY	WOMP	WOODENLY
WITHSTANDER	WLATSOME	WOLE	WOMPLIT	WOODENNESS
WITHSTANDING	WLECCHE	WOLEAI	WON	WOODENWARE
WITHSTAY	WLECH	WOLF	WOND	WOODENWEARY
WITHSTOOD	WLENCH	WOLFACHITE	WONDE	WOODFALL
WITHSTRAIN	WLITE	WOLFBERRIES	WONDER	WOODFISH
WITHTAKE	WLITY	WOLFBERRY	WONDERBERRY	WOODGELD
WITHTEE	WLO	WOLFED	WONDERDEED	WOODGRUB
WITHTURN	WLOKA	WOLFEN	WONDERED	WOODHACK
WITHVINE	WLONK	WOLFER	WONDERER	WOODHACKER
WITHY	WLONKHEDE	WOLFFISH	WONDERFUL	WOODHEN
WITHYPOT	WO	WOLFHOUND	WONDERFULLER	WOODHEWER
WITHYWIND	WOAD	WOLFING	WONDERFULLY	WOODHOLE
WITIE	WOADED	WOLFISH	WONDERING	WOODHORSE
WITJAR	WOADER	WOLFISHLY	WONDERINGLY	WOODHOUSE
WITLESS	WOADMAN	WOLFISHNESS	WONDERLAND	WOODHUNG
WITLESSLY	WOADWAXEN	WOLFKIN	WONDERMENT	WOODIE
WITLESSNESS	WOALD	WOLFLIKE	WONDERSMITH	WOODIER
WITLET	WOB	WOLFLING	WONDERSOME	WOODIEST
WITLING	WOBBEGONG	WOLFRAM	WONDERWORK	WOODINE
WITLOOF	WOBBLE	WOLFRAMITE	WONDERWORTHY	WOODINESS
WITLOSEN	WOBBLED	WOLFRAMIUM	WONDIE	WOODING
WITMONGER	WOBBLER	WOLFSBANE	WONDROUS	WOODISH
WITNESS	WOBBLIES	WOLFSBERGITE	WONDROUSLY	WOODJOBBER
WITNESSED	WOBBLINESS	WOLFSKIN	WONDROUSNESS	WOODKERN
WITNESSER	WOBBLING	WOLLASTONITE	WONE	WOODKNACKER
WITNESSING	WOBBLINGLY	WOLLOCK	WONG	WOODLAND
WITNEY	WOBBLY	WOLLOMAI	WONGA	WOODLANDER
WITNEYER	WOBEGONE	WOLVE	WONGAH	WOODLARK
WITS	WOBEGONENESS	WOLVEBOON	WONGSHY	WOODLESS
WITSAFE	WOBEGONISH	WOLVER	WONGSKY	WOODLIND
WITSHIP	WOBSTER	WOLVERENE	WONING	WOODLOCKED
WITTALL	WOCAS	WOLVERINE	WONKIER	WOODMAID
WITTED	WOCHEINITE	WOLVERINES	WONKIEST	WOODMAN
WITTEN	WOD	WOLVES	WONKY	WOODMANCRAFT
WITTER	WODE	WOMAN	WONNA	WOODMANSHIP
WITTERING	WODELEIE	WOMANBODIES	WONNED	WOODMEN
WITTERLY	WODGE	WOMANBODY	WONNER	WOODMONGER
WITTERNESS	WODGY	WOMANED	WONNING	WOODMOTE
WITTICASTER	WOE	WOMANFOLK	WONNOT	WOODNESS
WITTICHENITE	WOEBEGONE	WOMANFULLY	WONT	WOODNOTE
WITTICISM	WOEBEGONISH	WOMANHEAD	WONTED	WOODPECK
WITTICIZE	WOEFARE	WOMANHEARTED	WONTEDLY	WOODPECKER
WITTIER	WOEFUL	WOMANHOOD	WONTEDNESS	WOODPECKERS
WITTIEST	WOEFULLY	WOMANHOUSE	WONTING	WOODPENNY
WITTIFIED	WOEFULNESS	WOMANING	WONTLESS	WOODPILE
WITTILY	WOEHLERITE	WOMANISH	WOO	WOODPRINT
WITTINESS	WOESOME	WOMANISHLY	WOOABLE	WOODREED
WITTING	WOEVINE	WOMANISM	WOOD	WOODREEVE
WITTINGLY	WOEWORN	WOMANIST	WOODBARK	WOODRICK
WITTOL	WOFFLER	WOMANITY	WOODBIN	WOODRIME
WITTOME	WOFUL	WOMANIZE	WOODBIND	WOODRIS
WITTY	WOFULLY	WOMANIZED	WOODBINE	WOODROCK
WITWALL	WOFULNESS	WOMANIZER	WOODBINED	WOODROW
WITWANTON	WOG	WOMANIZING	WOODBLOCK	WOODRUFF
WITWORD	WOGE	WOMANKIND	WOODBORER	WOODS
WITWORM	WOGGLE	WOMANLIER	WOODBOUND	WOODSCREW
WITZCHOURA	WOGH	WOMANLIEST	WOODBUSH	WOODSERE
WIVE	WOGHE	WOMANLIKE	WOODCARVER	WOODSHED
WIVED	WOGHNESS	WOMANLINESS	WOODCARVING	WOODSHIP
WIVER	WOGIET	WOMANLY	WOODCHAT	WOODSHOP
WIVERN	WOHLAC	WOMANMUCKLE	WOODCHUCK	WOODSIDE
WIVES	WOHLERITE	WOMANPOST	WOODCOCK	WOODSIER
WIVING	WOIBE	WOMB	WOODCOCKIZE	WOODSIEST
WIWI	WOID	WOMBAT	WOODCOCKS	WOODSILVER
WIZ	WOIDRE	WOMBED	WOODCRACKER	WOODSKIN
WIZARD	WOIK	WOMBSIDE	WOODCRAFT	WOODSMAN
WIZARDLY	WOILIE	WOMBSTONE	WOODCRAFTER	WOODSMEN
WIZARDRY	WOK	WOMBY	WOODCRAFTY	WOODSPITE
WIZEN	WOKAS	WOMEN	WOODCUT	WOODSTONE
WIZENED	WOKE	WOMENFOLK	WOODCUTTER	WOODSY
WIZENEDNESS	WOKEN	WOMENFOLKS	WOODCUTTING	WOODTURNER
WIZZEN	WOKIE	WOMERA	WOODED	WOODTURNING
WLACH	WOKOWI	WOMERAH	WOODEN	WOODWALE
WLAFF	WOLD	WOMMALA	WOODENDITE	WOODWALL
WLANK	WOLDES	WOMMERA	WOODENHEAD	WOODWARD
WLATE	WOLDSMAN	WOMMERAH	WOODENHEADED	WOODWAX

WOODWAXEN	WOOMERANG	WORKDAY	WORMSEED	WOULDEST
WOODWIND	WOON	WORKED	WORMWEED	WOULDING
WOODWINDS	WOONE	WORKER	WORMWOOD	WOULDST
WOODWISE	WOONS	WORKFELLOW	WORMY	WOUND
WOODWORK	WOORALI	WORKFOLK	WORN	WOUNDED
WOODWORKER	WOORARI	WORKFOLKS	WORNNESS	WOUNDEDLY
WOODWORKING	WOOSH	WORKFUL	WORRAL	WOUNDER
WOODWORM	WOOSTER	WORKGIRL	WORREL	WOUNDILY
WOODWOSE	WOOT	WORKHAND	WORRIABLE	WOUNDING
WOODY	WOOTZ	WORKHORSE	WORRICOW	WOUNDINGLY
WOODYARD	WOOZIER	WORKHOUSE	WORRIECOW	WOUNDLESS
WOOED	WOOZIEST	WORKHOUSED	WORRIED	WOUNDLY
WOOER	WOOZILY	WORKING	WORRIEDLY	WOUNDS
WOOF	WOOZINESS	WORKINGLY	WORRIEDNESS	WOUNDWORT
WOOFED	WOOZLE	WORKINGMAN	WORRIER	WOUNDWORTH
WOOFELL	WOOZY	WORKINGMEN	WORRIES	WOUNDY
WOOFER	WOP	WORKINGWOMAN	WORRIMENT	WOURNIL
WOOFY	WOPPISH	WORKLESS	WORRISOME	WOUSTOUR
WOOHOO	WOPS	WORKLESSNESS	WORRISOMELY	WOVE
WOOING	WOPSE	WORKLOAD	WORRIT	WOVEN
WOOINGLY	WOPSY	WORKLOOM	WORRITER	WOW
WOOL	WOPY	WORKMAN	WORRY	WOWENING
WOOLD	WORBLE	WORKMANLIKE	WORRYING	WOWER
WOOLDED	WORCESTER	WORKMANLY	WORRYINGLY	WOWF
WOOLDER	WORD	WORKMANSHIP	WORRYWART	WOWL
WOOLDING	WORDABLE	WORKMASTER	WORSE	WOWSER
WOOLED	WORDABLY	WORKMEN	WORSEMENT	WOWSERIAN
WOOLEN	WORDAGE	WORKOUT	WORSEN	WOWSERISH
WOOLENET	WORDBOOK	WORKPEOPLE	WORSENED	WOWSERISM
WOOLENETTE	WORDBUILDING	WORKPIECE	WORSENESS	WOWSERY
WOOLENIZE	WORDCRAFT	WORKPLACE	WORSENING	WOWT
WOOLER	WORDED	WORKROOM	WORSER	WOX
WOOLERT	WORDER	WORKS	WORSET	WOXE
WOOLFELL	WORDIER	WORKSHEET	WORSHIP	WRABBE
WOOLGATHERER	WORDIEST	WORKSHIP	WORSHIPED	WRABILL
WOOLGROWER	WORDILY	WORKSHOP	WORSHIPER	WRACK
WOOLGROWING	WORDINESS	WORKSOME	WORSHIPERS	WRACKFUL
WOOLHEAD	WORDING	WORKSTAND	WORSHIPFUL	WRAGER
WOOLIE	WORDISH	WORKTABLE	WORSHIPFULLY	WRAGGLE
WOOLLED	WORDISHLY	WORKTIME	WORSHIPING	WRAIST
WOOLLEN	WORDISHNESS	WORKWAYS	WORSHIPPED	WRAITH
WOOLLENIZE	WORDLE	WORKWISE	WORSHIPPER	WRAITHE
WOOLLENS	WORDLESS	WORKWOMAN	WORSHIPPING	WRAITHY
WOOLLIER	WORDLESSLY	WORKWOMANLY	WORST	WRAKE
WOOLLIES	WORDLESSNESS	WORKWOMEN	WORSTED	WRAKER
WOOLLIEST	WORDLIER	WORKY	WORSTING	WRALL
WOOLLINESS	WORDLORIST	WORKYARD	WORSUM	WRAMP
WOOLLY	WORDMAKER	WORLD	WORT	WRANG
WOOLLYHEAD	WORDMAKING	WORLDAUGHT	WORTH	WRANGLE
WOOLLYISH	WORDMAN	WORLDED	WORTHFUL	WRANGLED
WOOLMAN	WORDMANSHIP	WORLDISH	WORTHIER	WRANGLER
WOOLMEN	WORDMEN	WORLDLIEST	WORTHIES	WRANGLESOME
WOOLPACK	WORDMONGER	WORLDLINESS	WORTHIEST	WRANGLING
WOOLPRESS	WORDMONGERY	WORLDLING	WORTHILY	WRANNOCK
WOOLSACK	WORDNESS	WORLDLY	WORTHINESS	WRANNY
WOOLSEY	WORDPLAY	WORLDMAKER	WORTHING	WRAP
WOOLSHEARER	WORDS	WORLDMAKING	WORTHLESS	WRAPAROUND
WOOLSHEARING	WORDSMAN	WORLDMAN	WORTHLESSLY	WRAPLE
WOOLSHEARS	WORDSMANSHIP	WORLDPROOF	WORTHLESSNESS	WRAPPAGE
WOOLSHED	WORDSMEN	WORLDQUAKE	WORTHWHILE	WRAPPED
WOOLSKIN	WORDSMITH	WORLDS	WORTHY	WRAPPER
WOOLSORTER	WORDSPITE	WORLDWAY	WORTS	WRAPPERER
WOOLSORTING	WORDSTER	WORLDWIDE	WORTWORM	WRAPPERING
WOOLSOWER	WORDY	WORM	WORY	WRAPPING
WOOLSTOCK	WORE	WORMED	WOSBIRD	WRAPRASCAL
WOOLULOSE	WORK	WORMER	WOSITH	WRAPS
WOOLWASHER	WORKABILITY	WORMHOLE	WOSOME	WRAPT
WOOLWEED	WORKABLE	WORMHOLED	WOST	WRASE
WOOLWHEEL	WORKABLENESS	WORMIER	WOT	WRASSE
WOOLWINDER	WORKADAY	WORMIEST	WOTH	WRAST
WOOLWORK	WORKAWAY	WORMIL	WOTLINK	WRASTLE
WOOLWORKER	WORKBAG	WORMINESS	WOTTE	WRASTLER
WOOLWORKING	WORKBASKET	WORMING	WOU	WRAT
WOOLY	WORKBENCH	WORMLIKE	WOUBIT	WRATACK
WOOM	WORKBOOK	WORMLING	WOUGH	WRATE
WOOMERA	WORKBOX	WORMROOT	WOUHLECHE	WRATH
WOOMERAH	WORKBRITTLE	WORMS	WOULD	WRATHFUL

WRATHFULLY
WRATHFULNESS
WRATHIER
WRATHIEST
WRATHILY
WRATHINESS
WRATHY
WRAW
WRAWL
WRAWLER
WRAXLE
WRAXLED
WRAXLING
WRAY
WRAYFUL
WREAK
WREAKED
WREAKER
WREAKFUL
WREAKING
WREAKLESS
WREATH
WREATHAGE
WREATHE
WREATHED
WREATHEN
WREATHER
WREATHING
WREATHMAKER
WREATHMAKING
WREATHS
WREATHWORK
WREATHWORT
WREATHY
WRECK
WRECKAGE
WRECKED
WRECKER
WRECKFISH
WRECKFISHES
WRECKFUL
WRECKING
WRECKY
WREIL
WRELE
WREN
WRENCH
WRENCHED
WRENCHER
WRENCHING
WRENCHINGLY
WRENLET
WRENTAIL
WREST
WRESTED
WRESTER
WRESTING
WRESTINGLY
WRESTLE
WRESTLED
WRESTLER
WRESTLING
WRETCH
WRETCHED
WRETCHEDLY
WRETCHEDNESS
WRETCHLESS
WRETCHLESSLY
WRETCHOCK
WRIBLE
WRICK
WRIDE
WRIED
WRIEL
WRIER
WRIEST
WRIG

WRIGGLE
WRIGGLED
WRIGGLER
WRIGGLESOME
WRIGGLING
WRIGGLY
WRIGHT
WRIGHTRY
WRIHTE
WRIMPLE
WRINE
WRING
WRINGBOLT
WRINGED
WRINGER
WRINGING
WRINGLE
WRINGSTAFF
WRINGSTAVES
WRINK
WRINKLE
WRINKLED
WRINKLEDY
WRINKLEFUL
WRINKLES
WRINKLET
WRINKLIER
WRINKLIEST
WRINKLING
WRINKLY
WRIST
WRISTBAND
WRISTBONE
WRISTED
WRISTER
WRISTFALL
WRISTIKIN
WRISTLET
WRISTLOCK
WRISTS
WRISTWATCH
WRISTWORK
WRIT
WRITABILITY
WRITABLE
WRITATION
WRITATIVE
WRITE
WRITEABLE
WRITEE
WRITER
WRITHE
WRITHED
WRITHEDLY
WRITHEDNESS
WRITHEN
WRITHENECK
WRITHER
WRITHING
WRITHINGLY
WRITHLED
WRITHY
WRITING
WRITINGER
WRITINGS
WRITTEN
WRITTER
WRIXLE
WRIZZLED
WRO
WROIK
WRONG
WRONGDOER
WRONGDOING
WRONGED
WRONGER
WRONGFUL

WRONGFULLY
WRONGFULNESS
WRONGHEAD
WRONGHEADED
WRONGHEARTED
WRONGING
WRONGLESS
WRONGLESSLY
WRONGLY
WRONGNESS
WRONGOUS
WRONGOUSLY
WRONGOUSNESS
WROOT
WROT
WROTE
WROTH
WROTHE
WROTHFUL
WROTHLY
WROTHSOME
WROUGHT
WROX
WRUNG
WRUNGNESS
WRY
WRYBILL
WRYER
WRYEST
WRYING
WRYLY
WRYMOUTH
WRYNECK
WRYNECKED
WRYNESS
WUD
WUDDIE
WUDGE
WUDU
WUGG
WULDER
WULFENITE
WUMMEL
WUN
WUND
WUNGEE
WUNNA
WUNTEE
WURD
WURLEY
WURLEYS
WURLIES
WURLY
WURP
WURRALUH
WURRUNG
WURRUP
WURRUS
WURST
WURTH
WURTZITE
WUSP
WUTHER
WUTHERING
WUYEN
WUZ
WUZU
WUZZER
WUZZLE
WUZZLED
WUZZLING
WY
WYCH
WYDE
WYE
WYES
WYF

WYLE
WYLED
WYLIECOAT
WYLING
WYLW
WYME
WYMOTE
WYN
WYND
WYNE
WYNKERNEL
WYNN
WYNRIS
WYPE
WYRE
WYROCK
WYROK
WYS
WYSTY
WYTHE

XALLE
XANTHALINE
XANTHAMID
XANTHAMIDE
XANTHANE
XANTHATE
XANTHATION
XANTHEIN
XANTHELASMA
XANTHENE
XANTHIC
XANTHID
XANTHIDE
XANTHIN
XANTHINE
XANTHINURIA
XANTHIONE
XANTHITE
XANTHIURIA
XANTHOCHROIA
XANTHOCHROID
XANTHOCONE
XANTHOCONITE
XANTHODERM
XANTHODERMA
XANTHOGEN
XANTHOGENATE
XANTHOGENIC
XANTHOMA
XANTHOMAS
XANTHOMATA
XANTHOMATOUS
XANTHOMETER
XANTHONE
XANTHOPHANE
XANTHOPHORE
XANTHOPHYL
XANTHOPHYLL
XANTHOPIA
XANTHOPSIA
XANTHOPSIN
XANTHOPTERIN
XANTHOSIS
XANTHOUS
XANTHOXENITE
XANTHOXYLIN
XANTHURIA
XANTHYDROL
XANTHYL
XARQUE
XAT
XEBEC
XEME
XENACANTHINE
XENAGOGUE
XENAGOGY
XENARTHRAL
XENARTHROUS
XENELASIA
XENELASY
XENIA
XENIAL
XENIAN
XENIUM
XENOBIOSIS
XENOBLAST
XENOCYST

XENODERM
XENODOCHIUM
XENODOCHY
XENOGAMOUS
XENOGAMY
XENOGENESIS
XENOGENOUS
XENOLITE
XENOLITH
XENOMANIA
XENOMORPHIC
XENON
XENOPARASITE
XENOPELTID
XENOPHOBE
XENOPHOBIA
XENOPHOBIC
XENOPHYA
XENOPODID
XENOPODOID
XENOPTERAN
XENOSAURID
XENOSAUROID
XENOTIME
XENYL
XENYLAMINE
XERAFIN
XERANSIS
XERANTIC
XERAPHIN
XERARCH
XERASIA
XERIC
XERIF
XERIFF
XERODERMA
XEROGRAPHER
XEROGRAPHIC
XEROGRAPHY
XEROMA
XEROMORPH
XEROMORPHIC
XEROMORPHOUS
XEROMORPHY
XEROMYRON
XERONATE
XERONIC
XEROPHAGY
XEROPHIL
XEROPHILE
XEROPHILOUS
XEROPHILY
XEROPHOBOUS
XEROPHYTE
XEROPHYTIC
XEROPHYTISM
XEROSERE
XEROSIS
XEROSTOMA
XEROTES
XEROTHERM
XEROTIC
XEROTRIPSIS
XEROX
XIBALBA
XIFOID
XIPHIIFORM
XIPHIOID
XIPHISTERNAL
XIPHISTERNUM
XIPHOCOSTAL
XIPHODYNIA
XIPHOID
XIPHOIDAL
XIPHOIDIAN
XIPHOPAGIC
XIPHOPAGOUS

XIPHOPAGUS
XIPHOSURAN
XIPHOSURE
XIPHOSUROUS
XIPHYDRIID
XOANA
XOANON
XUREL
XYLAN
XYLANTHRAX
XYLATE
XYLEM
XYLENE
XYLENOL
XYLENYL
XYLIC
XYLIDIN
XYLIDINE
XYLINDEIN
XYLITE
XYLITOL
XYLITONE
XYLOCARP
XYLOCARPOUS
XYLOCOPID
XYLOGEN
XYLOGLYPHY
XYLOGRAPH
XYLOGRAPHER
XYLOGRAPHIC
XYLOGRAPHY
XYLOID
XYLOIDIN
XYLOIDINE
XYLOL
XYLOLOGY
XYLOMA
XYLOMANCY
XYLOMAS
XYLOMATA
XYLOMETER
XYLON
XYLOPHAGAN
XYLOPHAGE
XYLOPHAGID
XYLOPHAGOUS
XYLOPHILOUS
XYLOPHONE
XYLOPHONIC
XYLOPHONIST
XYLOPLASTIC
XYLOPOLIST
XYLOQUINONE
XYLORCIN
XYLORCINOL
XYLOSE
XYLOSID
XYLOSIDE
XYLOSTROMA
XYLOSTROMATA
XYLOTILE
XYLOTOMIST
XYLOTOMOUS
XYLOTOMY
XYLOYL
XYLYL
XYLYLENE
XYRID
XYRIDACEOUS
XYST
XYSTA
XYSTER
XYSTUS

YA
YABBER
YABBI
YABBIE
YABBLE
YABBY
YABOA
YABOO
YABU
YACAL
YACARE
YACATA
YACCA
YACH
YACHAN
YACHT
YACHTER
YACHTING
YACHTIST
YACHTMAN
YACHTSMAN
YACHTSMEN
YACHTY
YAD
YADAYIM
YADE
YAE
YAF
YAFE
YAFF
YAFFIL
YAFFLE
YAFFLER
YAGER
YAGUA
YAGUARUNDI
YAGUAS
YAGUAZA
YAH
YAHAN
YAHOO
YAHRZEIT
YAIR
YAIRD
YAJE
YAJEIN
YAJEINE
YAJENIN
YAJENINE
YAJNOPAVITA
YAK
YAKALO
YAKAMIK
YAKATTALO
YAKIN
YAKKA
YAKMAK
YAKS
YAKSA
YAKSHA
YAKSHI
YAL
YALD
YALI
YALLOCK
YAM
YAMAMAI

YAMASKITE
YAMEN
YAMILKE
YAMMADJI
YAMMER
YAMMERLY
YAMP
YAMPEE
YAMPH
YAMSHIK
YAMSTCHIK
YAN
YANACONA
YANCE
YANE
YANG
YANGGONA
YANGTAO
YANK
YANKED
YANKER
YANKING
YANKY
YANNAM
YANOLITE
YANQUI
YANTRA
YAP
YAPA
YAPNESS
YAPOCK
YAPOK
YAPON
YAPP
YAPPED
YAPPER
YAPPINESS
YAPPING
YAPPINGLY
YAPPISH
YAPPY
YAPSTER
YAQONA
YAR
YARAGE
YARAK
YARAY
YARB
YARD
YARDAGE
YARDANG
YARDARM
YARDBIRD
YARDED
YARDER
YARDGRASS
YARDING
YARDKEEP
YARDLAND
YARDMAN
YARDMASTER
YARDMEN
YARDS
YARDSMAN
YARDSTICK
YARDWAND
YARE
YARELY
YARETA
YARIYARI
YARK
YARKE
YARKEE
YARM
YARMULKE
YARN
YARNEN

YARNER
YARNS
YARNWINDLE
YAROVIZE
YARPHA
YARR
YARRAMAN
YARRAN
YARROW
YARRY
YARTHEN
YARWHELP
YARWHIP
YAS
YASHIRO
YASHMAC
YASHMAK
YAT
YATAGAN
YATAGHAN
YATALITE
YATCH
YATE
YATI
YATTER
YAUD
YAULD
YAUP
YAUPER
YAUPON
YAUTIA
YAVA
YAW
YAWD
YAWED
YAWING
YAWL
YAWLER
YAWMETER
YAWN
YAWNED
YAWNER
YAWNILY
YAWNINESS
YAWNING
YAWNINGLY
YAWNY
YAWP
YAWPER
YAWROOT
YAWS
YAWSHRUB
YAWWEED
YAWY
YAXCHE
YAY
YAYA
YCIE
YCLEPED
YCLEPT
YDRIADES
YE
YEA
YEAD
YEAGHE
YEAH
YEALING
YEAN
YEANED
YEANING
YEANLING
YEAR
YEARA
YEARBIRD
YEARBOOK
YEARDAY
YEARED

YEARLING
YEARLONG
YEARLY
YEARN
YEARNED
YEARNFUL
YEARNFULLY
YEARNFULNESS
YEARNING
YEARNINGLY
YEARNINGS
YEARNLING
YEAROCK
YEARS
YEAST
YEASTIER
YEASTIEST
YEASTING
YEASTY
YEAT
YED
YEDDA
YEDDE
YEDDING
YEDE
YEDER
YEDERLY
YEELIN
YEGG
YEGGMAN
YEGUITA
YEILD
YEKE
YELD
YELDE
YELDRIN
YELDRINE
YELDRING
YELDROCK
YELK
YELL
YELLED
YELLER
YELLING
YELLOCH
YELLOW
YELLOWBACK
YELLOWBARK
YELLOWBELLY
YELLOWBERRIES
YELLOWBERRY
YELLOWBILL
YELLOWBIRD
YELLOWER
YELLOWEST
YELLOWFIN
YELLOWFISH
YELLOWHAMMER
YELLOWHEAD
YELLOWISH
YELLOWLEGS
YELLOWLY
YELLOWMAN
YELLOWNESS
YELLOWROOT
YELLOWS
YELLOWSEED
YELLOWSHANK
YELLOWSHANKS
YELLOWSHiNS
YELLOWTAIL
YELLOWTAILS
YELLOWTHROAT
YELLOWTOP
YELLOWWARE
YELLOWWEED
YELLOWWOOD

YELLOWWORT
YELLOWY
YELM
YELMER
YELP
YELPED
YELPER
YELPING
YELVER
YELWE
YEME
YEMELESS
YEMER
YEMING
YEMSCHIK
YEMSEL
YEN
YEND
YENI
YENITE
YENNED
YENNING
YENTNITE
YEOMAN
YEOMANLY
YEOMANRY
YEOMEN
YEORLING
YEOWOMAN
YEOWOMEN
YEP
YEPE
YEPELEIC
YEPELY
YEPHEDE
YEPLY
YER
YERBA
YERBAL
YERBALES
YERCUM
YERGA
YERK
YERN
YERNE
YERRA
YERTCHUK
YES
YESES
YESO
YESSO
YESTER
YESTERDAY
YESTEREVE
YESTEREVEN
YESTERMORN
YESTERN
YESTERNIGHT
YESTERNOON
YESTERWEEK
YESTERYEAR
YESTREEN
YET
YETAPA
YETER
YETH
YETHHOUNDS
YETI
YETLIN
YETLING
YETT
YETTE
YETTER
YETZER
YEUK
YEUKIENESS
YEUKY

YEW	YOGHURT	YOUNKER	YUSDRUM
YEWEN	YOGI	YOUPON	YUTU
YEWK	YOGIN	YOUR	YUZLIK
YEX	YOGISM	YOURN	YUZLUK
YEZ	YOGIST	YOURS	YWIS
YEZZY	YOGOITE	YOURSELF	
YFACKS	YOGURT	YOURSELVES	
YFERRE	YOHIMBI	YOURT	
YGOE	YOHIMBIN	YOUSE	
YGONE	YOHIMBINE	YOUSTIR	
YHTE	YOHO	YOUT	
YIELD	YOHOURT	YOUTH	
YIELDANCE	YOICK	YOUTHEN	
YIELDED	YOICKS	YOUTHFUL	
YIELDER	YOJAN	YOUTHFULLY	
YIELDING	YOJANA	YOUTHFULNESS	
YIELDINGLY	YOK	YOUTHILY	
YIGH	YOKAGE	YOUTHINESS	
YILL	YOKE	YOUTHLESS	
YILT	YOKEAGE	YOUTHLIKE	
YIN	YOKED	YOUTHS	
YINCE	YOKEFELLOW	YOUTHSOME	
YIP	YOKEL	YOUTHWORT	
YIPE	YOKELESS	YOUTHY	
YIPPIE	YOKELISH	YOUWARD	
YIRD	YOKELRY	YOUWARDS	
YIRM	YOKEMATE	YOUZE	
YIRMILIK	YOKEMATING	YOW	
YIRN	YOKER	YOWDEN	
YIRR	YOKEWOOD	YOWE	
YIS	YOKING	YOWIE	
YISSE	YOKY	YOWL	
YISSER	YOLDRING	YOWLED	
YISSING	YOLE	YOWLER	
YIT	YOLK	YOWLEY	
YITE	YOLKED	YOWLING	
YIVER	YOLKIER	YOWT	
YIVERLY	YOLKIEST	YOX	
YIVERNESS	YOLKY	YOY	
YIZKOR	YOLL	YPERITE	
YLAHAYLL	YOLPE	YPSILIFORM	
YLE	YOM	YPSILOID	
YLEM	YOMER	YSOWNDIR	
YLESPIL	YON	YTHE	
YLICHE	YONCOPIN	YTTERBIA	
YMAGE	YOND	YTTERBIC	
YMMOTE	YONDER	YTTERBIUM	
YMPET	YONDWARD	YTTRIA	
YMPNE	YONGE	YTTRIALITE	
YMUR	YONI	YTTRIC	
YNAMBU	YONKER	YTTRIFEROUS	
YNGOODLY	YONSIDE	YTTRIUM	
YNKELL	YOOP	YTTROCERITE	
YNPRIDID	YORA	YTTROCRASITE	
YO	YORE	YTTROGUMMITE	
YOB	YORETIME	YTWYN	
YOBI	YORK	YUCA	
YOCCO	YORKER	YUCCA	
YOCKEL	YORLIN	YUCK	
YOCKERNUT	YOT	YUCKER	
YOD	YOTACISM	YUCKLE	
YODEL	YOTACIZE	YUFT	
YODELED	YOTE	YUGADA	
YODELER	YOU	YUH	
YODELING	YOUDITH	YUK	
YODELIST	YOUFF	YUKKEL	
YODELLED	YOUNG	YULAN	
YODELLER	YOUNGBERRIES	YULE	
YODELLING	YOUNGBERRY	YULETIDE	
YODH	YOUNGER	YULOH	
YODLE	YOUNGEST	YUMMY	
YODLED	YOUNGISH	YUNGAN	
YODLER	YOUNGLET	YUNKER	
YOE	YOUNGLING	YUPON	
YOGA	YOUNGLY	YURT	
YOGH	YOUNGSTER	YURTA	
YOGHOURT	YOUNGTH	YUS	

Z

ZA
ZABAGLIONE
ZABETA
ZABRA
ZABTI
ZABURRO
ZAC
ZACATE
ZACATON
ZACHUN
ZAD
ZADDIK
ZADRUGA
ZAFFAR
ZAFFER
ZAFFIR
ZAFFRE
ZAFFREE
ZAG
ZAGGED
ZAGGING
ZAGUAN
ZAIBATSU
ZAIN
ZAK
ZAKAH
ZAKAT
ZAKUSKA
ZALAMBDODONT
ZAMAN
ZAMANG
ZAMARRA
ZAMARRO
ZAMBO
ZAMBOMBA
ZAMINDAR
ZAMINDARI
ZAMINDARY
ZAMORIN
ZAMORINE
ZAMOUSE
ZAMPOGNA
ZANANA
ZANDER
ZANDMOLE
ZANELLA
ZANIES
ZANJA
ZANJERO
ZANJON
ZANJONA
ZANT
ZANTE
ZANTHOXYLUM
ZANY
ZANYISH
ZANYISM
ZANZE
ZAPAS
ZAPATEADO
ZAPATERO
ZAPHARA
ZAPHRENTID
ZAPHRENTOID
ZAPOTE
ZAPTIAH
ZAPTIEH

ZAPUPE
ZAR
ZARAH
ZARATITE
ZAREBA
ZAREEBA
ZARF
ZARNEC
ZARNICH
ZARP
ZART
ZARZUELA
ZASTRUGA
ZASTRUGI
ZATI
ZATTARE
ZAX
ZAYAT
ZAYIN
ZEAL
ZEALED
ZEALOT
ZEALOTIC
ZEALOTICAL
ZEALOTISM
ZEALOTIST
ZEALOTRY
ZEALOUS
ZEALOUSLY
ZEALOUSNESS
ZEALOUSY
ZEAXANTHIN
ZEBEC
ZEBECK
ZEBRA
ZEBRAIC
ZEBRALIKE
ZEBRAS
ZEBRASS
ZEBRAWOOD
ZEBRINE
ZEBRINNIES
ZEBRINNY
ZEBROID
ZEBRULA
ZEBRULE
ZEBU
ZEBUB
ZEBURRO
ZEBUS
ZECCHINO
ZECHIN
ZED
ZEDOARY
ZEDS
ZEE
ZEEKOE
ZEES
ZEHNER
ZEIN
ZEINE
ZEISM
ZEIST
ZEL
ZELANT
ZELATOR
ZELATRICE
ZELATRIX
ZELOTYPIA
ZELOTYPIE
ZEME
ZEMEISM
ZEMI
ZEMIISM
ZEMINDAR
ZEMINDARI
ZEMMI

ZEMNI
ZEMSTVO
ZEMSTVOS
ZENANA
ZENDICIAN
ZENDIK
ZENDIKITE
ZENICK
ZENIK
ZENITH
ZENITHAL
ZENOCENTRIC
ZENOGRAPHIC
ZENOGRAPHY
ZENTNER
ZENU
ZENZIC
ZEOLITE
ZEOLITIC
ZEOLITIZE
ZEOLITIZED
ZEOLITIZING
ZEOSCOPE
ZEPHYR
ZEPHYREAN
ZEPHYRIAN
ZEPHYROUS
ZEPHYRUS
ZEPHYRY
ZEPP
ZEPPELIN
ZEQUIN
ZER
ZERDA
ZEREBA
ZERMAHBUB
ZERO
ZEROAXIAL
ZEROES
ZEROIZE
ZEROS
ZERUMBET
ZEST
ZESTED
ZESTFUL
ZESTING
ZESTY
ZETA
ZETACISM
ZETETIC
ZEUGITE
ZEUGLODONT
ZEUGMA
ZEUGMATIC
ZEUNERITE
ZHO
ZIAMET
ZIARA
ZIARAT
ZIBEB
ZIBELINE
ZIBELLINE
ZIBETH
ZIBETUM
ZIEGA
ZIEGER
ZIFFS
ZIG
ZIGANKA
ZIGGER
ZIGGURAT
ZIGZAG
ZIGZAGGEDLY
ZIGZAGGER
ZIGZAGGERY
ZIGZAGGY
ZIHAR

ZIIM
ZIKURAT
ZILLAH
ZIMARRA
ZIMB
ZIMBABWE
ZIMBALON
ZIMBI
ZIMENTWATER
ZIMME
ZIMMI
ZIMMIS
ZIMMY
ZIMOCCA
ZINC
ZINCALISM
ZINCATE
ZINCED
ZINCIC
ZINCID
ZINCIDE
ZINCIFEROUS
ZINCIFIED
ZINCIFY
ZINCIFYING
ZINCING
ZINCITE
ZINCKE
ZINCKED
ZINCKING
ZINCKY
ZINCO
ZINCOGRAPH
ZINCOGRAPHER
ZINCOGRAPHIC
ZINCOGRAPHY
ZINCOID
ZINCOLYSIS
ZINCOUS
ZINCUM
ZINCURET
ZINCY
ZINDIQ
ZINEB
ZINFANDEL
ZING
ZINGANA
ZINGANO
ZINGARA
ZINGARESCA
ZINGARI
ZINGARO
ZINGEL
ZINGERONE
ZINGIBERENE
ZINGIBEROL
ZINK
ZINKE
ZINKENITE
ZINKY
ZINNIA
ZINNWALDITE
ZINOBER
ZINSANG
ZIP
ZIPHIAN
ZIPHIOID
ZIPPER
ZIPPIER
ZIPPIEST
ZIPPING
ZIPPINGLY
ZIPPY
ZIRA
ZIRAI
ZIRAM
ZIRCITE

ZIRCON
ZIRCONATE
ZIRCONIA
ZIRCONIC
ZIRCONIUM
ZIRCONOID
ZIRCONYL
ZIRKELITE
ZIRKITE
ZITHER
ZITHERIST
ZITTERN
ZIZANY
ZIZEL
ZIZITH
ZIZZ
ZIZZLE
ZIZZLED
ZIZZLING
ZLOTY
ZLOTYS
ZNAK
ZO
ZOA
ZOACUM
ZOANTHID
ZOANTHODEME
ZOANTHODEMIC
ZOANTHOID
ZOANTHROPY
ZOARIA
ZOARIAL
ZOARIUM
ZOBO
ZOBTENITE
ZOBU
ZOCALO
ZOCCO
ZOCCOLO
ZODIAC
ZODIACAL
ZODIOPHILOUS
ZOEA
ZOEAFORM
ZOEAL
ZOEHEMERA
ZOETIC
ZOETROPE
ZOETROPIC
ZOGAN
ZOGO
ZOH
ZOIATRIA
ZOIC
ZOID
ZOIDOGAMOUS
ZOILUS
ZOISITE
ZOISITIZATION
ZOISM
ZOIST
ZOISTIC
ZOKOR
ZOLL
ZOLOTNIK
ZOMBI
ZOMBIE
ZOMBIES
ZOMBIISM
ZOMBIS
ZOMOTHERAPY
ZONA
ZONAE
ZONAESTHESIA
ZONAL
ZONALITY
ZONALLY

ZONAR
ZONARY
ZONATE
ZONATED
ZONATION
ZONDA
ZONE
ZONED
ZONELESS
ZONELET
ZONESTHESIA
ZONIC
ZONIFEROUS
ZONING
ZONITE
ZONITID
ZONNAR
ZONOCHLORITE
ZONOCILIATE
ZONOID
ZONOLIMNETIC
ZONOSKELETON
ZONULA
ZONULAR
ZONULE
ZONULET
ZONURE
ZONURID
ZONUROID
ZOO
ZOOBENTHOS
ZOOBLAST
ZOOCARP
ZOOCECIDIUM
ZOOCHEMY
ZOOCHORE
ZOOCULTURAL
ZOOCULTURE
ZOOCURRENT
ZOOCYST
ZOOCYTIAL
ZOOCYTIUM
ZOODENDRIUM
ZOODYNAMICS
ZOOECIA
ZOOECIAL
ZOOECIUM
ZOOERYTHRIN
ZOOFULVIN
ZOOGAMETE
ZOOGAMOUS
ZOOGAMY
ZOOGENE
ZOOGENOUS
ZOOGEOGRAPHY
ZOOGLER
ZOOGLOEA
ZOOGLOEAL
ZOOGLOEIC
ZOOGONIDIUM
ZOOGONOUS
ZOOGRAFT
ZOOGRAFTING
ZOOGRAPHER
ZOOGRAPHIC
ZOOGRAPHY
ZOOID
ZOOIDAL
ZOOLATER
ZOOLATRIES
ZOOLATROUS
ZOOLATRY
ZOOLITE
ZOOLITH
ZOOLITHIC
ZOOLITIC
ZOOLOGIC

ZOOLOGICAL
ZOOLOGIES
ZOOLOGIST
ZOOLOGIZE
ZOOLOGIZED
ZOOLOGIZING
ZOOLOGY
ZOOM
ZOOMAGNETIC
ZOOMAGNETISM
ZOOMANIA
ZOOMELANIN
ZOOMETRIC
ZOOMETRY
ZOOMIMETIC
ZOOMIMIC
ZOOMORPH
ZOOMORPHIC
ZOOMORPHISM
ZOOMORPHIZE
ZOOMORPHY
ZOON
ZOONAL
ZOONIC
ZOONIST
ZOONITE
ZOONITIC
ZOONOMY
ZOONOSES
ZOONOSIS
ZOONOSOLOGY
ZOONOTIC
ZOONS
ZOONULE
ZOOPANTHEON
ZOOPARASITE
ZOOPATHOLOGY
ZOOPERAL
ZOOPERIST
ZOOPERY
ZOOPHAGAN
ZOOPHAGOUS
ZOOPHARMACY
ZOOPHILE
ZOOPHILIA
ZOOPHILIC
ZOOPHILISM
ZOOPHILIST
ZOOPHILITE
ZOOPHILOUS
ZOOPHILY
ZOOPHOBIA
ZOOPHOBOUS
ZOOPHORI
ZOOPHORIC
ZOOPHORUS
ZOOPHYSICAL
ZOOPHYSICS
ZOOPHYTAL
ZOOPHYTE
ZOOPHYTIC
ZOOPHYTICAL
ZOOPHYTISH
ZOOPHYTOID
ZOOPHYTOLOGY
ZOOPLANKTON
ZOOPLASTIC
ZOOPLASTY
ZOOPRAXISCOPE
ZOOSCOPIC
ZOOSCOPY
ZOOSIS
ZOOSPERM
ZOOSPHERE
ZOOSPORANGE
ZOOSPORE
ZOOSPORIC

ZOOSPOROUS
ZOOTAXY
ZOOTECHNIC
ZOOTECHNY
ZOOTHECIA
ZOOTHECIAL
ZOOTHECIUM
ZOOTHEISM
ZOOTHEIST
ZOOTHEISTIC
ZOOTHERAPY
ZOOTHOME
ZOOTIC
ZOOTOMIC
ZOOTOMICAL
ZOOTOMIST
ZOOTOXIN
ZOOTROPHIC
ZOOTROPHY
ZOOTYPE
ZOOXANTHELLA
ZOOXANTHIN
ZOOZOO
ZOPE
ZOPILOTE
ZOPPA
ZOPPO
ZORGITE
ZORIL
ZORILLA
ZORILLE
ZORRA
ZORRILLO
ZORRO
ZORTZICO
ZOSTER
ZOSTERIFORM
ZOUNDS
ZOWIE
ZOYSIA
ZUCCARINO
ZUCCHETTO
ZUCCHINI
ZUCHE
ZUDDA
ZUFFOLO
ZUFOLO
ZUGZWANG
ZUISIN
ZULU
ZUMATIC
ZUMBOORUK
ZUNYITE
ZUPA
ZUPAN
ZUPANATE
ZUURVELDT
ZUZA
ZWANZIGER
ZWIEBACK
ZWITTER
ZWITTERION
ZYGA
ZYGADENIN
ZYGADENINE
ZYGAENID
ZYGAL
ZYGANTRUM
ZYGAPOPHYSIS
ZYGENID
ZYGION
ZYGITE
ZYGOBRANCH
ZYGODACTYL
ZYGODACTYLE
ZYGODACTYLIC
ZYGODONT

ZYGOLABIALIS
ZYGOMA
ZYGOMATA
ZYGOMATIC
ZYGOMATICUM
ZYGOMATICUS
ZYGOMORPHIC
ZYGOMORPHOUS
ZYGOMYCETE
ZYGOMYCETES
ZYGOMYCETOUS
ZYGON
ZYGONEURE
ZYGOPHORE
ZYGOPHORIC
ZYGOPHYCEOUS
ZYGOPHYTE
ZYGOPLEURAL
ZYGOPTERAN
ZYGOPTERID
ZYGOPTEROUS
ZYGOSE
ZYGOSIS
ZYGOSPERM
ZYGOSPHENAL
ZYGOSPHENE
ZYGOSPHERE
ZYGOSPORE
ZYGOSPORIC
ZYGOSTYLE
ZYGOTACTIC
ZYGOTAXIS
ZYGOTE
ZYGOTENE
ZYGOTOID
ZYGOUS
ZYGOZOOSPORE
ZYMASE
ZYME
ZYMIC
ZYMIN
ZYMITE
ZYMOGEN
ZYMOGENE
ZYMOGENESIS
ZYMOGENIC
ZYMOGENOUS
ZYMOID
ZYMOLOGIC
ZYMOLOGICAL
ZYMOLOGIST
ZYMOLOGY
ZYMOLYSIS
ZYMOLYTIC
ZYMOME
ZYMOMETER
ZYMOMIN
ZYMOPHORE
ZYMOPHORIC
ZYMOPLASTIC
ZYMOSCOPE
ZYMOSIMETER
ZYMOSIS
ZYMOSTEROL
ZYMOSTHENIC
ZYMOTECHNIC
ZYMOTECHNICS
ZYMOTIC
ZYMOTICALLY
ZYMURGY
ZYTHUM

PART II

High-Scoring Word Lists

Words Containing

High-Point Letters

J, Q, X and Z

High-Scoring Words Containing

J

2-3 LETTER WORDS

ALPHABETICAL ORDER		POSITIONAL ORDER		SCORING ORDER	
AJI	JOT	JA	JUD	**19**	JOD
AJO	JOW	JAB	JUG	JIZ	JOG
DJO	JOY	JAD	JUM		JUD
HAJ	JUB	JAG	JUR		JUG
JA	JUD	JAK	JUS	**14**	
JAB	JUG	JAM	JUT	JAK	**10**
JAD	JUM	JAN			AJI
JAG	JUR	JAP	AJI	**13**	AJO
JAK	JUS	JAR	AJO	HAJ	JAN
JAM	JUT	JAW	DJO	JAW	JAR
JAN	OJO	JAY	OJO	JAY	JEE
JAP	RAJ	JED	TJI	JEW	JEN
JAR	SAJ	JEE	UJI	JOW	JES
JAW	TAJ	JEN		JOY	JET
JAY	TJI	JES	HAJ		JEU
JED	UJI	JET	RAJ	**12**	JOE
JEE		JEU	SAJ	JAB	JOT
JEN		JEW	TAJ	JAM	JUR
JES		JIB		JAP	JUS
JET		JIG		JIB	JUT
JEU		JIZ		JOB	OJO
JEW		JO		JUB	RAJ
JIB		JOB		JUM	SAJ
JIG		JOD			TAJ
JIZ		JOE		**11**	TJI
JO		JOG		DJO	
JOB		JOT		JAD	
JOD		JOW		JAG	**9**
JOE		JOY		JED	JA
JOG		JUB		JIG	JO

501

ALPHABETICAL LIST OF 4-LETTER WORDS

AJAR	JAMB	JERK	JOCU	JUJU
AJAX	JAMI	JERL	JOES	JUKE
AJEE	JANE	JERM	JOEY	JUMP
AJOG	JANG	JERT	JOGI	JUNE
BAJU	JANK	JESS	JOHN	JUNK
BENJ	JANN	JEST	JOIN	JUNT
BIJA	JAOB	JETE	JOKE	JUPE
CAJA	JAPE	JEUX	JOKY	JURA
CAJI	JARA	JHIL	JOLE	JURE
CAJU	JARG	JHOW	JOLI	JURM
DJIN	JARK	JHUM	JOLL	JURR
DOJO	JARL	JIBE	JOLT	JURT
EJOO	JASK	JIBI	JONG	JURY
FAJA	JASM	JIFF	JONK	JUSI
GAJO	JASS	JILL	JOOM	JUST
GUNJ	JATI	JILT	JOPY	JUTE
HADJ	JATO	JIMP	JOSH	JYNX
HAJE	JAUD	JINA	JOSS	KOJI
HAJI	JAUG	JING	JOTA	LIJA
HAJJ	JAUK	JINK	JOTI	LOJA
HOJA	JAUN	JINN	JOUG	MAJA
IJMA	JAUP	JINX	JOUK	MAJO
JACA	JAVA	JIRD	JOVY	MOJO
JACK	JAWS	JIRT	JOWL	MUNJ
JACU	JAWY	JITI	JUBA	PUJA
JADE	JAZZ	JIVA	JUBE	RAJA
JADU	JEAN	JIVE	JUBO	REJA
JADY	JEEL	JOBE	JUCK	ROJO
JAGG	JEEP	JOBO	JUDD	SOJA
JAGS	JEER	JOBS	JUDO	SUJI
JAIL	JEEZ	JOCH	JUEY	TAJO
JAKE	JEFE	JOCK	JUEZ	TEJU
JAKO	JEFF	JOCO	JUGA	YAJE
JAMA	JELL			

POSITIONAL ORDER LIST OF 4-LETTER WORDS

JACA	JAWS	JIRT	JUBA	BAJU
JACK	JAWY	JITI	JUBE	BIJA
JACU	JAZZ	JIVA	JUBO	CAJA
JADE	JEAN	JIVE	JUCK	CAJI
JADU	JEEL	JOBE	JUDD	CAJU
JADY	JEEP	JOBO	JUDO	DOJO
JAGG	JEER	JOBS	JUEY	FAJA
JAGS	JEEZ	JOCH	JUEZ	GAJO
JAIL	JEFE	JOCK	JUGA	HAJE
JAKE	JEFF	JOCO	JUJU	HAJI
JAKO	JELL	JOCU	JUKE	HAJJ
JAMA	JERK	JOES	JUMP	HOJA
JAMB	JERL	JOEY	JUNE	JUJU
JAMI	JERM	JOGI	JUNK	KOJI
JANE	JERT	JOHN	JUNT	LIJA
JANG	JESS	JOIN	JUPE	LOJA
JANK	JEST	JOKE	JURA	MAJA
JANN	JETE	JOKY	JURE	MAJO
JAOB	JEUX	JOLE	JURM	MOJO
JAPE	JHIL	JOLI	JURR	PUJA
JARA	JHOW	JOLL	JURT	RAJA
JARG	JHUM	JOLT	JURY	REJA
JARK	JIBE	JONG	JUSI	ROJO
JARL	JIBI	JONK	JUST	SOJA
JASK	JIFF	JOOM	JUTE	SUJI
JASM	JILL	JOPY	JYNX	TAJO
JASS	JILT	JOSH		TEJU
JATI	JIMP	JOSS	AJAR	YAJE
JATO	JINA	JOTA	AJAX	
JAUD	JING	JOTI	AJEE	BENJ
JAUG	JINK	JOUG	AJOG	GUNJ
JAUK	JINN	JOUK	DJIN	HADJ
JAUN	JINX	JOVY	EJOO	HAJJ
JAUP	JIRD	JOWL	IJMA	MUNJ
JAVA				

SCORING ORDER LIST OF 4-LETTER WORDS

21	JARK	CAJI	DOJO	JEST
JYNX	JASK	CAJU	GAJO	JETE
	JAUK	HAJJ	GUNJ	JILL
20	JERK	IJMA	JADE	JILT
JEEZ	JIMP	JACA	JADU	JINA
JUEZ	JINK	JACU	JAGS	JINN
	JOKE	JAGG	JANG	JIRT
19	JONK	JAMA	JARG	JITI
JAZZ	JOUK	JAMI	JAUD	JOES
	JUKE	JAOB	JAUG	JOIN
18	JUMP	JAPE	JING	JOLE
AJAX	JUNK	JASM	JIRD	JOLI
JEUX	KOJI	JAUP	JOGI	JOLL
JINX		JEEP	JONG	JOLT
JOKY	**14**	JERM	JOUG	JOSS
	FAJA	JIBE	JUDO	JOTA
17	HAJE	JIBI	JUGA	JOTI
JACK	HAJI	JOBE		JUNE
JAWY	HOJA	JOBO	**11**	JUNT
JEFF	JAVA	JOBS	AJAR	JURA
JHOW	JAWS	JOCO	AJEE	JURE
JIFF	JEFE	JOCU	EJOO	JURR
JOCK	JHIL	JOOM	JAIL	JURT
JOVY	JIVA	JUBA	JANE	JUSI
JUCK	JIVE	JUBE	JANN	JUST
	JOEY	JUBO	JARA	JUTE
16	JOHN	JUDD	JARL	LIJA
JHUM	JOSH	JUPE	JASS	LOJA
JOCH	JOWL	JURM	JATI	RAJA
JOPY	JUEY	MAJA	JATO	REJA
	JURY	MAJO	JAUN	ROJO
15	YAJE	MOJO	JEAN	SOJA
HADJ		MUNJ	JEEL	SUJI
JADY	**13**	PUJA	JEER	TAJO
JAKE	BAJU		JELL	TEJU
JAKO	BENJ	**12**	JERL	
JAMB	BIJA	AJOG	JERT	**10**
JANK	CAJA	DJIN	JESS	JUJU

ALPHABETICAL LIST OF 5-LETTER WORDS

ADJAB	COOJA	JACKS	JAMON	JEBEL
ADJAG	DJATI	JACKY	JANTU	JEDGE
AGUJA	DJINN	JADED	JANTY	JEERS
AJAJA	DORJE	JADOO	JANUA	JEERY
AJARI	DUJAN	JAELA	JAOUR	JEHAD
AJAVA	EJECT	JAGAT	JAPAN	JEHUP
AJHAR	EJIDO	JAGER	JAPED	JELAB
AJIVA	ENJOY	JAGGY	JAPER	JELLO
AJOUR	FJALL	JAGIR	JARDE	JELLY
ANJAN	FJELD	JAGLA	JARRA	JEMMY
ARJAN	FJORD	JAGRA	JARRY	JENNA
ARJUN	GANJA	JAGUA	JASEY	JENNY
ATAJO	GJOLL	JAKES	JASPE	JEREZ
BADJU	GUIJO	JAKEY	JATHA	JERIB
BAJRA	GUNJA	JAKOS	JAUNE	JERKS
BANJO	HADJI	JALAP	JAUNT	JERKY
BEJAN	HAJIB	JALEO	JAUPS	JERRY
BEJEL	HAJJI	JALET	JAVEL	JETEE
BENJY	HODJA	JALOP	JAVER	JETON
BIJOU	IJMAA	JAMAH	JAWAB	JETTO
BRUJO	INAJA	JAMAN	JAWED	JETTY
CAJON	JABIA	JAMBA	JAZEL	JEWEL
CAJOU	JABOT	JAMBE	JAZZY	JEZIA
CAJUN	JACAL	JAMBO	JEANS	JHANA
CHAJA	JACKO	JAMMY	JEBAT	JHEEL

JHOOL	JODEL	JOWEL	JUMPY	MAJOR
JHOOM	JOINT	JOWER	JUNCO	MAJOS
JIBBA	JOISE	JOWLY	JUNDY	MOJOS
JIBED	JOIST	JOWPY	JUNKY	MUJER
JIBER	JOKED	JOYED	JUNTA	MUJIK
JIBOA	JOKER	JUBBE	JUNTO	NJAVE
JIFFY	JOKEY	JUBUS	JUPES	OUIJA
JIGGY	JOKUL	JUDEX	JUPON	PAJAK
JIGUA	JOLIE	JUDGE	JURAL	POLJE
JIHAD	JOLLY	JUDKA	JURAT	PONJA
JIMMY	JOLTY	JUFTI	JUREL	POOJA
JIMPY	JOOLA	JUFTS	JUROR	RAJAH
JINGO	JORAM	JUGAL	JUSTO	RAJAS
JINJA	JOREE	JUGER	JUTES	REJON
JINKS	JORUM	JUGUM	JUTIA	SAJOU
JINNI	JOSEF	JUICE	JUTKA	SAMAJ
JINNY	JOSEY	JUICY	JUTTY	SHOJI
JIPPO	JOSHI	JUISE	JUVIA	SIJIL
JIQUE	JOSIE	JUKES	JUXTA	SLOJD
JIQUI	JOSSA	JULEP	KALIJ	SUJEE
JIRGA	JOSUP	JULID	KHAJA	TEJON
JIXIE	JOTTY	JULIO	KHOJA	THUJA
JIZYA	JOUGH	JULOL	KOPJE	TJALK
JNANA	JOUGS	JUMBA	LINJA	VAJRA
JNANI	JOULE	JUMBO	LINJE	VIEJA
JOCKO	JOURS	JUMBY	MAJAS	VIJAO
JOCKS	JOUST	JUMMA	MAJID	YOJAN
JOCUM	JOWAR	JUMPS	MAJOE	ZANJA

POSITIONAL ORDER LIST OF 5-LETTER WORDS

JABIA	JAUNE	JIGGY	JOUGH	JURAT
JABOT	JAUNT	JIGUA	JOUGS	JUREL
JACAL	JAUPS	JIHAD	JOULE	JUROR
JACKO	JAVEL	JIMMY	JOURS	JUSTO
JACKS	JAVER	JIMPY	JOUST	JUTES
JACKY	JAWAB	JINGO	JOWAR	JUTIA
JADED	JAWED	JINJA	JOWEL	JUTKA
JADOO	JAZEL	JINKS	JOWER	JUTTY
JAELA	JAZZY	JINNI	JOWLY	JUVIA
JAGAT	JEANS	JINNY	JOWPY	JUXTA
JAGER	JEBAT	JIPPO	JOYED	
JAGGY	JEBEL	JIQUE	JUBBE	AJAJA
JAGIR	JEDGE	JIQUI	JUBUS	AJARI
JAGLA	JEERS	JIRGA	JUDEX	AJAVA
JAGRA	JEERY	JIXIE	JUDGE	AJHAR
JAGUA	JEHAD	JIZYA	JUDKA	AJIVA
JAKES	JEHUP	JNANA	JUFTI	AJOUR
JAKEY	JELAB	JNANI	JUFTS	DJATI
JAKOS	JELLO	JOCKO	JUGAL	DJINN
JALAP	JELLY	JOCKS	JUGER	EJECT
JALEO	JEMMY	JOCUM	JUGUM	EJIDO
JALET	JENNA	JODEL	JUICE	FJALL
JALOP	JENNY	JOINT	JUICY	FJELD
JAMAH	JEREZ	JOISE	JUISE	FJORD
JAMAN	JERIB	JOIST	JUKES	GJOLL
JAMBA	JERKS	JOKED	JULEP	IJMAA
JAMBE	JERKY	JOKER	JULID	NJAVE
JAMBO	JERRY	JOKEY	JULIO	TJALK
JAMMY	JETEE	JOKUL	JULOL	
JAMON	JETON	JOLIE	JUMBA	ADJAB
JANTU	JETTO	JOLLY	JUMBO	ADJAG
JANTY	JETTY	JOLTY	JUMBY	ANJAN
JANUA	JEWEL	JOOLA	JUMMA	ARJAN
JAOUR	JEZIA	JORAM	JUMPS	ARJUN
JAPAN	JHANA	JOREE	JUMPY	BAJRA
JAPED	JHEEL	JORUM	JUNCO	BEJAN
JAPER	JHOOL	JOSEF	JUNDY	BEJEL
JARDE	JHOOM	JOSEY	JUNKY	BIJOU
JARRA	JIBBA	JOSHI	JUNTA	CAJON
JARRY	JIBED	JOSIE	JUNTO	CAJOU
JASEY	JIBER	JOSSA	JUPES	CAJUN
JASPE	JIBOA	JOSUP	JUPON	DUJAN
JATHA	JIFFY	JOTTY	JURAL	ENJOY

HAJIB	RAJAS	ATAJO	HADJI	POLJE
HAJJI	REJON	BADJU	HAJJI	PONJA
MAJAS	SAJOU	BANJO	HODJA	POOJA
MAJID	SIJIL	BENJY	INAJA	SHOJI
MAJOE	SUJEE	BRUJO	JINJA	SLOJD
MAJOR	TEJON	CHAJA	KHAJA	THUJA
MAJOS	VAJRA	COOJA	KHOJA	VIEJA
MOJOS	VIJAO	DORJE	KOPJE	ZANJA
MUJER	YOJAN	GANJA	LINJA	
MUJIK		GUIJO	LINJE	KALIJ
PAJAK	AGUJA	GUNJA	OUIJA	SAMAJ
RAJAH	AJAJA			

SCORING ORDER LIST OF 5-LETTER WORDS

24	JUICY	JHOOL	JERIB	ARJUN
JIZYA		JIBED	JIBER	ATAJO
	16	JINNY	JIBOA	INAJA
23	FJELD	JOLLY	JORAM	JAELA
JAZZY	FJORD	JOLTY	JORUM	JALEO
	HADJI	JOSEF	JOSUP	JALET
21	HODJA	JOSEY	JUBUS	JANTU
JACKY	JAKES	JOSHI	JUDGE	JANUA
JAZEL	JAKOS	JOTTY	JUICE	JAOUR
JEREZ	JAMBA	JOWAR	JULEP	JARRA
JEZIA	JAMBE	JOWEL	JUNCO	JAUNE
JIFFY	JAMBO	JOWER	JUPES	JAUNT
JIQUE	JAWED	JUFTI	JUPON	JEANS
JIQUI	JEHAD	JUFTS	MAJAS	JEERS
ZANJA	JERKS	JUGUM	MAJOE	JELLO
	JIBBA	JUTTY	MAJOR	JENNA
20	JIHAD	JUVIA	MAJOS	JETEE
JOWPY	JINKS	MAJID	MOJOS	JETON
JUDEX	JIPPO	NJAVE	MUJER	JETTO
	JOCUM	RAJAH	POLJE	JINNI
19	JOKER	SHOJI	PONJA	JNANA
JAKEY	JOKUL	THUJA	POOJA	JNANI
JAMMY	JOUGH	VAJRA	SAMAJ	JOINT
JEMMY	JOYED	VIEJA		JOISE
JERKY	JUBBE	VIJAO	**13**	JOIST
JIMMY	JUKES	YOJAN	AGUJA	JOLIE
JIMPY	JUMBA		DJATI	JOOLA
JIXIE	JUMBO	**14**	DJINN	JOREE
JOKEY	JUMMA	ADJAG	DORJE	JOSIE
JUMBY	JUMPS	BAJRA	DUJAN	JOSSA
JUMPY	JUNDY	BANJO	EJIDO	JOULE
JUNKY	JUTKA	BEJAN	GANJA	JOURS
JUXTA	KALIJ	BEJEL	GJOLL	JOUST
KHAJA	TJALK	BIJOU	GUIJO	JUISE
KHOJA		BRUJO	GUNJA	JULIO
	15	CAJON	JADOO	JULOL
18	ADJAB	CAJOU	JAGAT	JUNTA
JACKO	AJAVA	CAJUN	JAGER	JUNTO
JACKS	AJHAR	COOJA	JAGIR	JURAL
JOCKO	AJIVA	EJECT	JAGLA	JURAT
JOCKS	BADJU	HAJJI	JAGRA	JUREL
JOWLY	ENJOY	IJMAA	JAGUA	JUROR
KOPJE	FJALL	JABIA	JARDE	JUSTO
MUJIK	JANTY	JABOT	JIGUA	JUTES
PAJAK	JAPED	JACAL	JINGO	JUTIA
	JARRY	JADED	JIRGA	LINJA
17	JASEY	JALAP	JODEL	LINJE
BENJY	JATHA	JALOP	JOUGS	OUIJA
CHAJA	JAVEL	JAMAN	JUGAL	RAJAS
HAJIB	JAVER	JAMON	JUGER	REJON
JAGGY	JEERY	JAPAN	JULID	SAJOU
JAMAH	JELLY	JAPER	SLOJD	SIJIL
JAWAB	JENNY	JASPE		SUJEE
JEHUP	JERRY	JAUPS	**12**	TEJON
JHOOM	JETTY	JEBAT	AJARI	
JIGGY	JEWEL	JEBEL	AJOUR	**11**
JOKED	JHANA	JEDGE	ANJAN	AJAJA
JUDKA	JHEEL	JELAB	ARJAN	JINJA

ALPHABETICAL LIST OF 6-LETTER WORDS

ABJECT	JABBED	JASSID	JILTED	JOWERY
ABJURE	JABBER	JATACO	JILTEE	JOWLER
ACAJOU	JABBLE	JATOBA	JILTER	JOWLOP
ADJECT	JABERS	JAUDIE	JIMJAM	JOWSER
ADJIGA	JABIRU	JAUNCE	JIMMER	JOWTER
ADJOIN	JABOTS	JAUNER	JIMPLY	JOYANT
ADJURE	JABULS	JAUNTY	JIMSON	JOYFUL
ADJUST	JACANA	JAVALI	JINETE	JOYHOP
AGUAJI	JACARE	JAVVER	JINGAL	JOYING
AGUJON	JACATE	JAWING	JINGLE	JOYOUS
AJENJO	JACENT	JAYGEE	JINGLY	JUBARB
AJIMEZ	JACKAL	JAYPIE	JINKED	JUBATE
AJOINT	JACKED	JAYVEE	JINKER	JUBBAH
AJOURE	JACKER	JAZZER	JINKET	JUBHAH
AJOWAN	JACKET	JEERED	JINKLE	JUBILE
ALFAJE	JACOBY	JEERER	JINNEE	JUDDER
ALJAMA	JADDED	JEETEE	JINSHA	JUDGED
ANTJAR	JADDER	JEJUNA	JIPPER	JUDGER
AVIJJA	JADERY	JEJUNE	JIRBLE	JUECES
BAJADA	JADING	JELICK	JIRGAH	JUFFER
BAJREE	JADISH	JELLAB	JITNEY	JUGALE
BANJAK	JAEGER	JEMBLE	JITTER	JUGATE
BANJOS	JAGEER	JENKIN	JIZYAH	JUGFUL
BEJADE	JAGGAR	JENNET	JIZZEN	JUGGED
BEJANT	JAGGED	JENOAR	JOBADE	JUGGER
BEJAPE	JAGGER	JERBOA	JOBBED	JUGGLE
BEJUCO	JAGHIR	JEREED	JOBBER	JUGLAR
BIJOUX	JAGONG	JERKED	JOBBLE	JUGULA
BOJITE	JAGUAR	JERKER	JOBMAN	JUGUMS
BOOJUM	JAGUEY	JERKIN	JOBMEN	JUICER
CABUJA	JAILED	JERNIE	JOBSON	JUJUBE
CADJAN	JAILER	JERQUE	JOCANT	JULOID
CAJAVA	JAILOR	JERRID	JOCKER	JULOLE
CAJETA	JALAPA	JERSEY	JOCKEY	JUMART
CAJOLE	JALKAR	JERVIA	JOCKOS	JUMBIE
CARAJO	JALOPY	JERVIN	JOCOSE	JUMBLE
CONJEE	JAMBEE	JESSED	JOCOTE	JUMBLY
CONJON	JAMBER	JESSUR	JOCUMA	JUMBOS
COROJO	JAMBON	JESTED	JOCUND	JUMENT
CROJIK	JAMBUL	JESTEE	JOGGED	JUMFRU
CUNJAH	JAMMED	JESTER	JOGGER	JUMPED
CUNJER	JAMMER	JETSAM	JOGGLE	JUMPER
DEEJAY	JAMNUT	JETTED	JOGGLY	JUNCOS
DEJECT	JAMOKE	JETTER	JOHNIN	JUNCUS
DJEBEL	JAMPAN	JETTON	JOINED	JUNDIE
DJELFA	JANAPA	JETTRU	JOINER	JUNGLE
DJERIB	JANGAR	JEWELS	JOINTS	JUNGLI
DJERSA	JANGLE	JEWELY	JOINTY	JUNGLY
DJINNI	JANGLY	JEWING	JOJOBA	JUNIOR
DONJON	JANKER	JEZAIL	JOKIER	JUNKER
EJECTA	JANNER	JEZIAH	JOKING	JUNKET
EJIDAL	JANTEE	JHARAL	JOKISH	JUNKIE
ELCAJA	JAPERY	JIBBAH	JOKIST	JUNTAS
ENJAIL	JAPING	JIBBED	JOLLOP	JUNTOS
ENJAMB	JAPISH	JIBBEH	JOLTED	JUPATI
ENJOIN	JARABE	JIBBER	JOLTER	JURANT
EVEJAR	JARANA	JIBING	JONDLA	JURARA
FANJET	JARBLE	JIBMAN	JORDAN	JURATA
FINJAN	JARBOT	JIBMEN	JORDEN	JURIES
FREIJO	JAREED	JIBOYA	JOROPO	JURING
FYLGJA	JARFLY	JICAMA	JORRAM	JURIST
GIDJEE	JARFUL	JICARA	JOSEPH	JURORS
GOUJAT	JARGON	JIFFLE	JOSHER	JUSLIK
GOUJON	JARINA	JIGGED	JOSKIN	JUSSAL
GUNJAH	JARNUT	JIGGER	JOSSER	JUSSEL
GURJAN	JAROOL	JIGGET	JOSTLE	JUSTEN
GURJUN	JARRAH	JIGGIT	JOTISI	JUSTER
GYTTJA	JARRED	JIGGLE	JOTTED	JUSTLE
HEJIRA	JARRET	JIGGLY	JOTTER	JUSTLY
HIJACK	JARVEY	JIGMAN	JOUNCE	JUTTED
INJECT	JASEYS	JIGMEN	JOUSTS	JUVENT
INJURE	JASMIN	JIGOTE	JOUTES	JUVITE
INJURY	JASPER	JIGSAW	JOVIAL	JUWISE
INJUST	JASPIS	JILLET	JOWARI	JUZAIL

KHAJUR	MILJEE	PAREJA	SEJERO	TINAJA
KHARAJ	MOONJA	PINJRA	SEJOIN	TJAELE
KHOJAH	MOUJIK	POOJAH	SEJOUR	TJANDI
KONJAK	MUSJID	POPJOY	SIJILL	TOMJON
KURUNJ	MUTSJE	PRAJNA	SINJER	TONJON
LOGJAM	MUZJIK	PUNJUM	SJOMIL	TRAJET
LUJULA	OBJECT	PYJAMA	SVARAJ	UNJUST
MAATJE	OBJURE	RAKIJA	SWARAJ	WAJANG
MAJOON	OREJON	REJECT	TALAJE	WEJACK
MANJAK	OUTJUT	REJOIN	TANJIB	WITJAR
MANJEL	PAJAMA	REJOLT	TASAJO	YAJEIN
MASJID	PAJERO	SANJAK	TEJANO	YOJANA
MEISJE	PAJOCK	SEJANT	THUJYL	ZANJON

POSITIONAL ORDER LIST OF 6-LETTER WORDS

JABBED	JARBLE	JESTER	JIZYAH	JOYFUL
JABBER	JARBOT	JETSAM	JIZZEN	JOYHOP
JABBLE	JAREED	JETTED	JOBADE	JOYING
JABERS	JARFLY	JETTER	JOBBED	JOYOUS
JABIRU	JARFUL	JETTON	JOBBER	JUBARB
JABOTS	JARGON	JETTRU	JOBBLE	JUBATE
JABULS	JARINA	JEWELS	JOBMAN	JUBBAH
JACANA	JARNUT	JEWELY	JOBMEN	JUBHAH
JACARE	JAROOL	JEWING	JOBSON	JUBILE
JACATE	JARRAH	JEZAIL	JOCANT	JUDDER
JACENT	JARRED	JEZIAH	JOCKER	JUDGED
JACKAL	JARRET	JHARAL	JOCKEY	JUDGER
JACKED	JARVEY	JIBBAH	JOCKOS	JUECES
JACKER	JASEYS	JIBBED	JOCOSE	JUFFER
JACKET	JASMIN	JIBBEH	JOCOTE	JUGALE
JACOBY	JASPER	JIBBER	JOCUMA	JUGATE
JADDED	JASPIS	JIBING	JOCUND	JUGFUL
JADDER	JASSID	JIBMAN	JOGGED	JUGGED
JADERY	JATACO	JIBMEN	JOGGER	JUGGER
JADING	JATOBA	JIBOYA	JOGGLE	JUGGLE
JADISH	JAUDIE	JICAMA	JOGGLY	JUGLAR
JAEGER	JAUNCE	JICARA	JOHNIN	JUGULA
JAGEER	JAUNER	JIFFLE	JOINED	JUGUMS
JAGGAR	JAUNTY	JIGGED	JOINER	JUICER
JAGGED	JAVALI	JIGGER	JOINTS	JUJUBE
JAGGER	JAVVER	JIGGET	JOINTY	JULOID
JAGHIR	JAWING	JIGGIT	JOKIER	JULOLE
JAGONG	JAYGEE	JIGGLE	JOKING	JUMART
JAGUAR	JAYPIE	JIGGLY	JOKISH	JUMBIE
JAGUEY	JAYVEE	JIGMAN	JOKIST	JUMBLE
JAILED	JAZZER	JIGMEN	JOLLOP	JUMBLY
JAILER	JEERED	JIGOTE	JOLTED	JUMBOS
JAILOR	JEERER	JIGSAW	JOLTER	JUMENT
JALAPA	JEETEE	JILLET	JONDLA	JUMFRU
JALKAR	JEJUNA	JILTED	JORDAN	JUMPED
JALOPY	JEJUNE	JILTEE	JORDEN	JUMPER
JAMBEE	JELICK	JILTER	JOROPO	JUNCOS
JAMBER	JELLAB	JIMJAM	JORRAM	JUNCUS
JAMBON	JEMBLE	JIMJAM	JOSEPH	JUNDIE
JAMBUL	JENKIN	JIMMER	JOSHER	JUNGLE
JAMMED	JENNET	JIMPLY	JOSKIN	JUNGLI
JAMMER	JENOAR	JIMSON	JOSSER	JUNGLY
JAMNUT	JERBOA	JINETE	JOSTLE	JUNIOR
JAMOKE	JEREED	JINGAL	JOTISI	JUNKER
JAMPAN	JERKED	JINGLE	JOTTED	JUNKET
JANAPA	JERKER	JINGLY	JOTTER	JUNKIE
JANGAR	JERKIN	JINKED	JOUNCE	JUNTAS
JANGLE	JERNIE	JINKER	JOUSTS	JUNTOS
JANGLY	JERQUE	JINKET	JOUTES	JUPATI
JANKER	JERRID	JINKLE	JOVIAL	JURANT
JANNER	JERSEY	JINNEE	JOWARI	JURARA
JANTEE	JERVIA	JINSHA	JOWERY	JURATA
JAPERY	JERVIN	JIPPER	JOWLER	JURIES
JAPING	JESSED	JIRBLE	JOWLOP	JURING
JAPISH	JESSUR	JIRGAH	JOWSER	JURIST
JARABE	JESTED	JITNEY	JOWTER	JURORS
JARANA	JESTEE	JITTER	JOYANT	JUSLIK

JUSSAL	ADJOIN	PAJAMA	DEEJAY	THUJYL
JUSSEL	ADJURE	PAJERO	DONJON	TOMJON
JUSTEN	ADJUST	PAJOCK	EVEJAR	TONJON
JUSTER	ALJAMA	PYJAMA	FANJET	TRAJET
JUSTLE	BAJADA	REJECT	FINJAN	WITJAR
JUSTLY	BAJREE	REJOIN	GIDJEE	ZANJON
JUTTED	BEJADE	REJOLT	GOUJAT	
JUVENT	BEJANT	SEJANT	GOUJON	AGUAJI
JUVITE	BEJAPE	SEJERO	GUNJAH	AJENJO
JUWISE	BEJUCO	SEJOIN	GURJAN	ALFAJE
JUZAIL	BIJOUX	SEJOUR	GURJUN	AVIJJA
	BOJITE	SIJILL	KHAJUR	CABUJA
AJENJO	CAJAVA	TEJANO	KHOJAH	CARAJO
AJIMEZ	CAJETA	UNJUST	KONJAK	COROJO
AJOINT	CAJOLE	WAJANG	LOGJAM	ELCAJA
AJOURE	DEJECT	WEJACK	MANJAK	FREIJO
AJOWAN	ENJAIL	YAJEIN	MANJEL	FYLGJA
DJEBEL	ENJAMB	YOJANA	MASJID	GYTTJA
DJELFA	ENJOIN		MILJEE	MAATJE
DJERIB	HEJIRA	ACAJOU	MOUJIK	MEISJE
DJERSA	HIJACK	AGUJON	MUSJID	MOONJA
DJINNI	INJECT	ANTJAR	MUZJIK	MUTSJE
EJECTA	INJURE	AVIJJA	OREJON	PAREJA
EJIDAL	INJURY	BANJAK	OUTJUT	RAKIJA
SJOMIL	INJUST	BANJOS	PINJRA	TALAJE
TJAELE	JEJUNA	BOOJUM	POOJAH	TASAJO
TJANDI	JEJUNE	CROJIK	POPJOY	TINAJA
	JUJUBE	CADJAN ·	PRAJNA	
ABJECT	LUJULA	CONJEE	PUNJUM	KHARAJ
ABJURE	MAJOON	CONJON	SANJAK	KURUNJ
ADJECT	OBJECT	CUNJAH	SINJER	SVARAJ
ADJIGA	OBJURE	CUNJER	TANJIB	SWARAJ

SCORING ORDER LIST OF 6-LETTER WORDS

28	JUBBAH	JAYPIE	JAMPAN	JUNKER
JIZYAH	JUMBLY	JERKED	JANGLY	JUNKET
MUZJIK	KHAJUR	JIBBED	JANKER	JUNKIE
	KHARAJ	JIBOYA	JAWING	JUSLIK
25	POPJOY	JIGGLY	JAYGEE	KURUNJ
JEZIAH	PYJAMA	JINKED	JEMBLE	OBJECT
		JOBBED	JENKIN	PAJAMA
24	**19**	JOGGLY	JERKER	PUNJUM
AJIMEZ	BANJAK	JOKING	JERKIN	RAKIJA
	CROJIK	JOSEPH	JEWING	SANJAK
23	JACKAL	JOWLOP	JIBBER	WAJANG
KHOJAH	JACKER	JUMFRU	JIBMAN	
	JACKET	JUMPED	JIBMEN	**16**
22	JAMOKE	POOJAH	JICAMA	ADJECT
BIJOUX	JARFLY		JIGSAW	AJOWAN
HIJACK	JARVEY	**17**	JIMMER	ALFAJE
JERQUE	JAVVER	ABJECT	JINGLY	BAJADA
JEZAIL	JAYVEE	BEJAPE	JINKER	BEJADE
JOCKEY	JELICK	BEJUCO	JINKET	CADJAN
JUZAIL	JEWELY	BOOJUM	JINKLE	DEJECT
WEJACK	JIFFLE	CABUJA	JIPPER	DJEBEL
ZANJON	JOCKER	DEEJAY	JIRGAH	DJERIB
	JOCKOS	DJELFA	JOBBER	EVEJAR
21	JOWERY	ENJAMB	JOBBLE	FANJET
JAZZER	JOYFUL	GUNJAH	JOBMAN	FINJAN
JIZZEN	JUFFER	GYTTJA	JOBMEN	FREIJO
JOYHOP	MANJAK	JABBER	JOCUMA	HEJIRA
JUBHAH	MOUJIK	JABBLE	JOKIER	INJURY
PAJOCK	THUJYL	JADERY	JOKIST	JADDED
		JADISH	JOSKIN	JAGGED
20	**18**	JAGHIR	JOYING	JAPING
FYLGJA	CAJAVA	JAGUEY	JUBARB	JARFUL
JACKED	CUNJAH	JALKAR	JUGFUL	JARRAH
JACOBY	JABBED	JAMBEE	JUMBIE	JASEYS
JIBBAH	JALOPY	JAMBER	JUMBLE	JAUNTY
JIBBEH	JAMMED	JAMBON	JUMBOS	JAVALI
JIMPLY	JAPERY	JAMBUL	JUMPER	JERSEY
JOKISH	JAPISH	JAMMER	JUNGLY	JERVIA

JERVIN
JEWELS
JHARAL
JIBING
JIGGED
JIGMAN
JIGMEN
JIMJAM
JINSHA
JITNEY
JOBADE
JOCUND
JOGGED
JOINTY
JOSHER
JOVIAL
JOWARI
JOWLER
JOWSER
JOWTER
JOYANT
JOYOUS
JUDGED
JUGGED
JUGUMS
JUSTLY
JUVENT
JUVITE
JUWISE
KONJAK
LOGJAM
MASJID
MUSJID
SVARAJ
SWARAJ
WITJAR
YAJEIN
YOJANA

15
ABJURE
ACAJOU
ADJIGA
ALJAMA
AVIJJA
BAJREE
BANJOS
BEJANT
BOJITE
CAJETA
CAJOLE
CARAJO
CONJEE
CONJON
COROJO

CUNJER
EJECTA
ELCAJA
GIDJEE
INJECT
JABERS
JABIRU
JABOTS
JABULS
JACANA
JACARE
JACATE
JACENT
JADDER
JADING
JAGGAR
JAGGER
JAGONG
JALAPA
JAMNUT
JANAPA
JARABE
JARBLE
JARBOT
JASMIN
JASPER
JASPIS
JATACO
JATOBA
JAUNCE
JELLAB
JERBOA
JETSAM
JICARA
JIGGER
JIGGET
JIGGIT
JIGGLE
JIMSON
JIRBLE
JOBSON
JOCANT
JOCOSE
JOCOTE
JOGGER
JOGGLE
JOLLOP
JOROPO
JORRAM
JOUNCE
JUBATE
JUBILE
JUDDER
JUDGER
JUECES

JUGGER
JUGGLE
JUICER
JUMART
JUMENT
JUNCOS
JUNCUS
JUPATI
MAATJE
MAJOON
MANJEL
MEISJE
MILJEE
MOONJA
MUTSJE
OBJURE
PAJERO
PAREJA
PINJRA
PRAJNA
REJECT
SJOMIL
TANJIB
TOMJON

14
ADJOIN
ADJURE
ADJUST
AGUAJI
AGUJON
DJERSA
DJINNI
DONJON
EJIDAL
GOUJAT
GOUJON
GURJAN
GURJUN
JAEGER
JAGEER
JAGUAR
JAILED
JANGAR
JANGLE
JAREED
JARGON
JARRED
JASSID
JAUDIE
JEERED
JEREED
JERRID
JESSED
JESTED

JETTED
JIGOTE
JILTED
JINGAL
JINGLE
JOINED
JOJOBA
JOLTED
JONDLA
JORDAN
JORDEN
JOTTED
JUGALE
JUGATE
JUGLAR
JUGULA
JUJUBE
JULOID
JUNDIE
JUNGLE
JUNGLI
JURING
JUTTED
TJANDI

13
AJOINT
AJOURE
ANTJAR
ENJAIL
ENJOIN
INJURE
INJUST
JAILER
JAILOR
JANNER
JANTEE
JARANA
JARINA
JARNUT
JAROOL
JARRET
JAUNER
JEERER
JEETEE
JENNET
JENOAR
JERNIE
JESSUR
JESTEE
JESTER
JETTER
JETTON
JETTRU

JILLET
JILTEE
JILTER
JINETE
JINNEE
JITTER
JOINER
JOINTS
JOLTER
JOSSER
JOSTLE
JOTISI
JOTTER
JOUSTS
JOUTES
JULOLE
JUNIOR
JUNTAS
JUNTOS
JURANT
JURARA
JURATA
JURIES
JURIST
JURORS
JUSSAL
JUSSEL
JUSTEN
JUSTER
JUSTLE
LUJULA
OREJON
OUTJUT
REJOIN
REJOLT
SEJANT
SEJERO
SEJOIN
SEJOUR
SIJILL
SINJER
TALAJE
TASAJO
TEJANO
TINAJA
TJAELE
TONJON
TRAJET
UNJUST

12
AJENJO
JEJUNA
JEJUNE

ALPHABETICAL LIST OF 7-LETTER WORDS

ABADEJO
ABJOINT
ABJUDGE
ABJURED
ABJURER
ADJIGER
ADJOINT
ADJOURN
ADJOUST
ADJUDGE
ADJUNCT

ADJURED
ADJURER
ADJUROR
ADJUTOR
AJANGLE
AJITTER
AJIVIKA
ALFORJA
ALJAMIA
APAREJO
APOJOVE

ARVEJON
AZUELJO
BACKJAW
BAJOCCO
BAJOCHI
BAJOIRE
BANJARA
BANJOES
BANJORE
BASENJI
BEJESUS

BEJEWEL
BENJOIN
BIJASAL
BLIJVER
BRINJAL
CAJAPUT
CAJEPUT
CAJOLED
CAJOLER
CAJUELA
CAJUPUT

CATJANG
COJUROR
COMITJE
CONJECT
CONJOIN
CONJURE
CONJURY
DEJECTA
DEJEUNE
DISJECT
DISJOIN

DISJUNE	JALOUSE	JEOPARD	JOEWOOD	JUNCITE
DJIBBAH	JAMBEAU	JERICAN	JOGGING	JUNCOUS
EJECTED	JAMBONE	JERKIER	JOGGLED	JUNCTLY
EJECTOR	JAMBOOL	JERKILY	JOGGLER	JUNGLED
EJULATE	JAMBOSA	JERKING	JOINANT	JUNIATA
EJURATE	JAMDANI	JERKISH	JOINDER	JUNIPER
ENJEWEL	JAMMING	JERQUED	JOINERY	JUNKING
ENJOYED	JAMPANI	JERQUER	JOINING	JUNKMAN
ENJOYER	JAMWOOD	JERRIES	JOINTED	JUNKMEN
FAUJDAR	JANAPAN	JERSEYS	JOINTER	JURALLY
FERIDJI	JANAPUM	JERVINA	JOINTLY	JURATOR
FERIJEE	JANDERS	JERVINE	JOISTED	JURIDIC
FINDJAN	JANGADA	JESSAMY	JOKELET	JURYMAN
FJORDED	JANGKAR	JESSANT	JOKIEST	JURYMEN
FOUJDAR	JANGLED	JESSING	JOLLIED	JUSSION
GALJOEN	JANGLER	JESTING	JOLLIER	JUSSIVE
GEITJIE	JANITOR	JETBEAD	JOLLIES	JUSSORY
GIOJOSO	JANKERS	JETPORT	JOLLIFY	JUSTICE
GJEDOST	JANNOCK	JETTAGE	JOLLILY	JUSTICO
GOTRAJA	JAPYGID	JETTEAU	JOLLITY	JUSTIFY
GUAJIRA	JAQUIMA	JETTIED	JOLTING	JUSTLER
HAJILIJ	JARAGUA	JETTIES	JONQUIL	JUTTIES
HANDJAR	JARBIRD	JETTING	JORNADA	JUTTING
HIJINKS	JARGOON	JETWARE	JOSEITE	JUVENAL
IJOLITE	JARHEAD	JEWBIRD	JOSTLED	JYNGINE
INJELLY	JARKMAN	JEWBUSH	JOSTLER	KAJAWAH
INJOINT	JARLESS	JEWELED	JOTTING	KAJEPUT
INJUNCT	JARLITE	JEWELER	JOUBARB	KANDJAR
INJURED	JARRING	JEWELLY	JOUKERY	KANKREJ
INJURER	JARVEYS	JEWELRY	JOULEAN	KEDJAVE
INJURIA	JASEYED	JEWFISH	JOUNCED	KHANJAR
JABBING	JASMINE	JIBBING	JOURNAL	KHANJEE
JABORIN	JASMONE	JIBBOOM	JOURNEY	KILADJA
JABULES	JASPERY	JIBHEAD	JOUSTER	KILLJOY
JACALES	JASPOID	JIBSTAY	JOYANCE	KORADJI
JACAMAR	JAUNDER	JIFFIES	JOYANCY	LOCKJAW
JACAMIN	JAUNTED	JIGGERS	JOYLEAF	LONGJAW
JACATOO	JAUNTIE	JIGGETY	JOYLESS	MAHAJAN
JACCHUS	JAVELIN	JIGGING	JOYRIDE	MAHAJUN
JACINTH	JAVELOT	JIGGISH	JOYSOME	MAHJONG
JACKALS	JAWBONE	JIGGLED	JOYWEED	MAJAGUA
JACKASH	JAWFALL	JIKUNGU	JUAMAVE	MAJESTY
JACKASS	JAWFEET	JILLING	JUBILEE	MAJORAT
JACKBOX	JAWFISH	JILLION	JUBILUS	MANJACK
JACKBOY	JAWFOOT	JILTING	JUCHART	MANJEET
JACKDAW	JAWHOLE	JIMBANG	JUCKIES	MOJARRA
JACKEEN	JAYHAWK	JIMJAMS	JUDCOCK	MONTJOY
JACKETY	JAYPIET	JIMMIED	JUDDOCK	MUJERES
JACKING	JAYWALK	JIMMIES	JUDGING	MUMJUMA
JACKLEG	JAZERAN	JINGALL	JUDICES	MUNJEET
JACKMAN	JAZZBOW	JINGLED	JUGATED	MUNTJAC
JACKMEN	JAZZIER	JINGLER	JUGGING	MUNTJAK
JACKPOT	JAZZILY	JINGLET	JUGGINS	NAARTJE
JACKROD	JEALOUS	JINGOED	JUGGLED	OBJECTS
JACKSAW	JECORAL	JINGOES	JUGGLER	OUTJAZZ
JACKTAN	JECORIN	JINJILI	JUGHEAD	OUTJINX
JACOBIN	JEDCOCK	JINKING	JUGLONE	OUTJUMP
JACOBUS	JEDDOCK	JINNIES	JUGULAR	OVERJOY
JACONET	JEEPERS	JINRIKI	JUGULUM	PAJAMAS
JACTANT	JEEPNEY	JINSING	JUICIER	PARANJA
JACTURE	JEERING	JITNEUR	JUICILY	PERJINK
JACUARU	JEJUNAL	JITNEYS	JUJUIST	PERJURE
JADDING	JEJUNUM	JITTERS	JUJITSU	PERJURY
JADEDLY	JELLICA	JITTERY	JUJUISM	PINJANE
JADEITE	JELLICO	JIVATMA	JUJUTSU	PIROJKI
JAGGARY	JELLIED	JOANNES	JUKEBOX	PROJECT
JAGGERY	JELLIES	JOBARBE	JULIDAN	PROPJET
JAGGIER	JELLIFY	JOBBERY	JULIETT	PULAJAN
JAGGING	JELLILY	JOBBING	JULOLIN	PULIJAN
JAGHEER	JELLOID	JOBBISH	JUMBLED	PYJAMAS
JAGHIRE	JEMADAR	JOBLESS	JUMBLER	REJOICE
JAGRATA	JEMIDAR	JOBSITE	JUMBUCK	REJONEO
JAGUARS	JEMMIES	JOCKEYS	JUMELLE	REJOURN
JAILAGE	JEMMILY	JOCOQUE	JUMPERS	REJUDGE
JALAPIC	JENNIER	JOCOQUI	JUMPIER	SAPAJOU
JALAPIN	JENNIES	JOCULAR	JUMPING	SATLIJK
JALOPPY	JEOFAIL	JOEBUSH	JUMPOFF	SEJEANT

SEJUNCT	STANJEN	TJENKAL	TURJITE	WINDJAM
SJAMBOK	SUBJECT	TJOSITE	UINTJIE	YAJEINE
SJOMILA	SUBJOIN	TOMJOHN	VANJOHN	YAJENIN
SKIJORE	TANJONG	TORONJA	VIAJACA	ZANJERO
SKYJACK	THUJENE	TRAJECT	WICHTJE	ZANJONA
SOJOURN	THUJONE			

POSITIONAL ORDER LIST OF 7-LETTER WORDS

JABBING	JAPYGID	JERQUER	JOCKEYS	JUICILY
JABORIN	JAQUIMA	JERRIES	JOCOQUE	JUJUIST
JABULES	JARAGUA	JERSEYS	JOCOQUI	JUJITSU
JACALES	JARBIRD	JERVINA	JOCULAR	JUJUISM
JACAMAR	JARGOON	JERVINE	JOEBUSH	JUJUTSU
JACAMIN	JARHEAD	JESSAMY	JOEWOOD	JUKEBOX
JACATOO	JARKMAN	JESSANT	JOGGING	JULIDAN
JACCHUS	JARLESS	JESSING	JOGGLED	JULIETT
JACINTH	JARLITE	JESTING	JOGGLER	JULOLIN
JACKALS	JARRING	JETBEAD	JOINANT	JUMBLED
JACKASH	JARVEYS	JETPORT	JOINDER	JUMBLER
JACKASS	JASEYED	JETTAGE	JOINERY	JUMBUCK
JACKBOX	JASMINE	JETTEAU	JOINING	JUMELLE
JACKBOY	JASMONE	JETTIED	JOINTED	JUMPERS
JACKDAW	JASPERY	JETTIES	JOINTER	JUMPIER
JACKEEN	JASPOID	JETTING	JOINTLY	JUMPING
JACKETY	JAUNDER	JETWARE	JOISTED	JUMPOFF
JACKING	JAUNTED	JEWBIRD	JOKELET	JUNCITE
JACKLEG	JAUNTIE	JEWBUSH	JOKIEST	JUNCOUS
JACKMAN	JAVELIN	JEWELED	JOLLIED	JUNCTLY
JACKMEN	JAVELOT	JEWELER	JOLLIER	JUNGLED
JACKPOT	JAWBONE	JEWELLY	JOLLIES	JUNIATA
JACKROD	JAWFALL	JEWELRY	JOLLIFY	JUNIPER
JACKSAW	JAWFEET	JEWFISH	JOLLILY	JUNKING
JACKTAN	JAWFISH	JIBBING	JOLLITY	JUNKMAN
JACOBIN	JAWFOOT	JIBBOOM	JOLTING	JUNKMEN
JACOBUS	JAWHOLE	JIBHEAD	JONQUIL	JURALLY
JACONET	JAYHAWK	JIBSTAY	JORNADA	JURATOR
JACTANT	JAYPIET	JIFFIES	JOSEITE	JURIDIC
JACTURE	JAYWALK	JIGGERS	JOSTLED	JURYMAN
JACUARU	JAZERAN	JIGGETY	JOSTLER	JURYMEN
JADDING	JAZZBOW	JIGGING	JOTTING	JUSSION
JADEDLY	JAZZIER	JIGGISH	JOUBARB	JUSSIVE
JADEITE	JAZZILY	JIGGLED	JOUKERY	JUSSORY
JAGGARY	JEALOUS	JIKUNGU	JOULEAN	JUSTICE
JAGGERY	JECORAL	JILLING	JOUNCED	JUSTICO
JAGGIER	JECORIN	JILLION	JOUNCES	JUSTIFY
JAGGING	JEDCOCK	JILTING	JOURNAL	JUSTLER
JAGHEER	JEDDOCK	JIMBANG	JOURNEY	JUTTIES
JAGHIRE	JEEPERS	JIMJAMS	JOUSTER	JUTTING
JAGRATA	JEEPNEY	JIMMIED	JOYANCE	JUVENAL
JAGUARS	JEERING	JIMMIES	JOYANCY	JYNGINE
JAILAGE	JEJUNAL	JINGALL	JOYLEAF	
JALAPIC	JEJUNUM	JINGLED	JOYLESS	AJANGLE
JALAPIN	JELLICA	JINGLER	JOYRIDE	AJITTER
JALOPPY	JELLICO	JINGLET	JOYSOME	AJIVIKA
JALOUSE	JELLIED	JINGOED	JOYWEED	DJIBBAH
JAMBEAU	JELLIES	JINGOES	JUAMAVE	EJECTED
JAMBONE	JELLIFY	JINJILI	JUBILEE	EJECTOR
JAMBOOL	JELLILY	JINKING	JUBILUS	EJULATE
JAMBOSA	JELLOID	JINNIES	JUCHART	EJURATE
JAMDANI	JEMADAR	JINRIKI	JUCKIES	FJORDED
JAMMING	JEMIDAR	JINSING	JUDCOCK	GJEDOST
JAMPANI	JEMMIES	JITNEUR	JUDDOCK	IJOLITE
JAMWOOD	JEMMILY	JITNEYS	JUDGING	SJAMBOK
JANAPAN	JENNIER	JITTERS	JUDICES	SJOMILA
JANAPUM	JENNIES	JITTERY	JUGATED	TJENKAL
JANDERS	JEOFAIL	JIVATMA	JUGGING	TJOSITE
JANGADA	JEOPARD	JOANNES	JUGGINS	
JANGKAR	JERICAN	JOBARBE	JUGGLED	ABJOINT
JANGLED	JERKIER	JOBBERY	JUGGLER	ABJUDGE
JANGLER	JERKILY	JOBBING	JUGHEAD	ABJURED
JANITOR	JERKING	JOBBISH	JUGLONE	ABJURER
JANKERS	JERKISH	JOBLESS	JUGULAR	ADJIGER
JANNOCK	JERQUED	JOBSITE	JUGULUM	ADJOINT
			JUICIER	

ADJOURN	INJURED	BANJORE	PROJECT	MONTJOY
ADJOUST	INJURER	BENJOIN	SKIJORE	MUNTJAC
ADJUDGE	INJURIA	BLIJVER	SKYJACK	MUNTJAK
ADJUNCT	JEJUNAL	CATJANG	SUBJECT	OVERJOY
ADJURED	JEJUNUM	CONJECT	SUBJOIN	PIROJKI
ADJURER	JUJUIST	CONJOIN	TANJONG	PROPJET
ADJUROR	JUJITSU	CONJURE	THUJENE	PULAJAN
ADJUTOR	JUJUISM	CONJURY	THUJONE	PULIJAN
ALJAMIA	JUJUTSU	DISJECT	TOMJOHN	SAPAJOU
BAJOCCO	KAJAWAH	DISJOIN	TRAJECT	STANJEN
BAJOCHI	KAJEPUT	DISJUNE	TURJITE	UINTJIE
BAJOIRE	MAJAGUA	FAUJDAR	VANJOHN	WINDJAM
BEJESUS	MAJESTY	FOUJDAR	VIAJACA	
BEJEWEL	MAJORAT	GALJOEN	ZANJERO	
BIJASAL	MOJARRA	GIOJOSO	ZANJONA	ABADEJO
CAJAPUT	MUJERES	GUAJIRA		ALFORJA
CAJEPUT	OBJECTS	JIMJAMS		APAREJO
CAJOLED	PAJAMAS	JINJILI	ARVEJON	AZUELJO
CAJOLER	PYJAMAS	KEDJAVE	BACKJAW	BASENJI
CAJUELA	REJOICE	MAHJONG	BRINJAL	COMITJE
CAJUPUT	REJONEO	MANJACK	FERIJEE	FERIDJI
COJUROR	REJOURN	MANJEET	FINDJAN	GOTRAJA
DEJECTA	REJUDGE	MUMJUMA	GEITJIE	KILADJA
DEJEUNE	SEJEANT	MUNJEET	HANDJAR	KORADJI
ENJEWEL	SEJUNCT	OUTJAZZ	KANDJAR	NAARTJE
ENJOYED	SOJOURN	OUTJINX	KHANJAR	PARANJA
ENJOYER	YAJEINE	OUTJUMP	KHANJEE	SATLIJK
HAJILIJ	YAJENIN	PERJINK	KILLJOY	TORONJA
HIJINKS		PERJURE	LOCKJAW	WICHTJE
INJELLY	APOJOVE	PERJURY	LONGJAW	
INJOINT	BANJARA	PINJANE	MAHAJAN	HAJILIJ
INJUNCT	BANJOES		MAHAJUN	KANKREJ

SCORING ORDER LIST OF 7-LETTER WORDS

29	ZANJERO	KILLJOY	**19**	JUNKING
JACKBOX	ZANJONA	OUTJINX	APOJOVE	JURYMAN
		PYJAMAS	BEJEWEL	JURYMEN
27	**22**		BLIJVER	KANDJAR
JAYHAWK	DJIBBAH	**20**	CONJURY	KILADJA
JAZZBOW	JACKMAN	BAJOCCO	FJORDED	KORADJI
JUKEBOX	JACKMEN	JACKALS	JABBING	MAHAJAN
	JACKPOT	JACKASS	JACINTH	MAHAJUN
25	JAZZIER	JACKEEN	JADEDLY	MAJESTY
BACKJAW	JEDDOCK	JACKTAN	JAGGARY	MONTJOY
JACKBOY	JEWBUSH	JAMWOOD	JAGGERY	PERJURY
JAQUIMA	JOYANCY	JANNOCK	JAMMING	TOMJOHN
JAZZILY	JUDDOCK	JARKMAN	JANGKAR	VIAJACA
JOCOQUE	KEDJAVE	JARVEYS	JASPERY	
JOCOQUI	MANJACK	JAWFALL	JAWBONE	**18**
	OUTJAZZ	JAWFEET	JAYPIET	ABJUDGE
24	SJAMBOK	JAWFOOT	JEEPNEY	CAJAPUT
JACKDAW	SKYJACK	JAWHOLE	JERKING	CAJEPUT
JAYWALK	WICHTJE	JELLIFY	JESSAMY	CAJUPUT
JERQUED		JEWBIRD	JIBBING	COMITJE
JUMBUCK	**21**	JEWELLY	JIBSTAY	CONJECT
JUMPOFF	AJIVIKA	JEWELRY	JIGGETY	ENJOYED
KAJAWAH	BAJOCHI	JIBBOOM	JIGGISH	FAUJDAR
	HIJINKS	JIBHEAD	JIKUNGU	FERIDJI
23	JACCHUS	JIFFIES	JIMBANG	FINDJAN
AZUELJO	JACKING	JOLLIFY	JIMMIED	FOUJDAR
JACKASH	JACKLEG	JOYLEAF	JINKING	HANDJAR
JACKETY	JACKROD	JUCKIES	JIVATMA	JACAMAR
JACKSAW	JALOPPY	JUNKMAN	JOBBING	JACAMIN
JAWFISH	JAPYGID	JUNKMEN	JOEBUSH	JACOBIN
JAZERAN	JEMMILY	JUSTIFY	JOYANCE	JACOBUS
JEDCOCK	JERKILY	KAJEPUT	JOYSOME	JAGHEER
JERQUER	JERKISH	MAHJONG	JUAMAVE	JAGHIRE
JEWFISH	JOBBERY	MUNTJAK	JUCHART	JALAPIC
JOCKEYS	JOBBISH	OVERJOY	JUGHEAD	JAMBEAU
JONQUIL	JOUKERY	PERJINK	JUICILY	JAMBONE
JUDCOCK	JOYWEED	PIROJKI	JUMBLED	JAMBOOL
LOCKJAW	KHANJAR	VANJOHN	JUMPING	JAMBOSA
	KHANJEE	WINDJAM	JUNCTLY	JAMPANI

			15	**14**
JANAPUM	JERVINA	HAJILIJ	ADJOINT	AJITTER
JANKERS	JERVINE	INJUNCT	ADJOURN	EJULATE
JARHEAD	JETBEAD	JABORIN	ADJOUST	EJURATE
JASEYED	JETWARE	JABULES	ADJURER	IJOLITE
JEMMIES	JEWELER	JACALES	ADJUROR	INJOINT
JERKIER	JIGGING	JACATOO	ADJUTOR	INJURER
JEWELED	JIGGLED	JACONET	AJANGLE	INJURIA
JIMMIES	JIMJAMS	JACTANT	DEJEUNE	JALOUSE
JINRIKI	JITNEYS	JACTURE	DISJOIN	JANITOR
JOBARBE	JITTERY	JACUARU	DISJUNE	JARLESS
JOEWOOD	JOGGING	JAGGIER	GALJOEN	JARLITE
JOKELET	JOGGLED	JALAPIN	GEITJIE	JAUNTIE
JOKIEST	JOINERY	JANAPAN	GIOJOSO	JEALOUS
JOUBARB	JOINTLY	JANGADA	GOTRAJA	JELLIES
JOYRIDE	JOLLILY	JANGLED	GUAJIRA	JENNIER
JUMBLER	JOLLITY	JASMINE	INJURED	JENNIES
JUMPERS	JOUNCED	JASMONE	JADEITE	JERRIES
JUMPIER	JOURNEY	JECORAL	JAGRATA	JESSANT
JYNGINE	JOYLESS	JECORIN	JAGUARS	JETTEAU
LONGJAW	JUDGING	JEEPERS	JAILAGE	JETTIES
MUNTJAC	JUDICES	JELLICA	JANDERS	JILLION
OBJECTS	JUGGING	JELLICO	JANGLER	JINNIES
OUTJUMP	JUGGLED	JERICAN	JARAGUA	JITNEUR
PAJAMAS	JUGULUM	JETPORT	JARGOON	JITTERS
PROJECT	JURALLY	JIGGERS	JARRING	JOANNES
PROPJET	JURIDIC	JINGLED	JAUNDER	JOINANT
SATLIJK	JUSSIVE	JINGOED	JAUNTED	JOINTER
SKIJORE	JUSSORY	JOBLESS	JEERING	JOLLIER
SUBJECT	JUVENAL	JOBSITE	JEJUNUM	JOLLIES
TJENKAL	KANKREJ	JOCULAR	JELLIED	JOSEITE
	MAJAGUA	JOGGLER	JELLOID	JOSTLER
17	MUMJUMA	JUBILEE	JESSING	JOULEAN
ABADEJO	THUJENE	JUBILUS	JESTING	JOURNAL
ABJURED	THUJONE	JUGATED	JETTAGE	JOUSTER
ADJUDGE	YAJEINE	JUGGINS	JETTIED	JULIETT
ADJUNCT	YAJENIN	JUGGLER	JETTING	JULOLIN
ALFORJA		JUICIER	JILLING	JUNIATA
ARVEJON	**16**	JUMELLE	JILTING	JURATOR
CAJOLED	ABJOINT	JUNCITE	JINGALL	JUSSION
CATJANG	ABJURER	JUNCOUS	JINGLER	JUSTLER
DEJECTA	ADJIGER	JUNGLED	JINGLET	JUTTIES
DISJECT	ADJURED	JUNIPER	JINGOES	NAARTJE
EJECTED	ALJAMIA	JUSTICE	JINSING	REJONEO
ENJEWEL	APAREJO	JUSTICO	JOINDER	REJOURN
ENJOYER	BAJOIRE	MAJORAT	JOINING	SEJEANT
FERIJEE	BANJARA	MANJEET	JOINTED	SOJOURN
INJELLY	BANJOES	MOJARRA	JOISTED	STANJEN
JADDING	BANJORE	MUJERES	JOLLIED	TJOSITE
JAGGING	BASENJI	MUNJEET	JOLTING	TORONJA
JAMDANI	BEJESUS	PARANJA	JORNADA	TURJITE
JARBIRD	BENJOIN	PERJURE	JOSTLED	UINTJIE
JASPOID	BIJASAL	PINJANE	JOTTING	
JAVELIN	BRINJAL	PULAJAN	JUGLONE	**13**
JAVELOT	CAJOLER	PULIJAN	JUGULAR	JEJUNAL
JELLILY	CAJUELA	REJOICE	JUJUISM	JINJILI
JEMADAR	COJUROR	REJUDGE	JULIDAN	JUJUIST
JEMIDAR	CONJOIN	SAPAJOU	JUTTING	JUJITSU
JEOFAIL	CONJURE	SEJUNCT	TANJONG	JUJUTSU
JEOPARD	EJECTOR	SJOMILA		
JERSEYS	GJEDOST	SUBJOIN		
		TRAJECT		

ALPHABETICAL LIST OF 8-LETTER WORDS

ABJECTLY	ADJUDGER	ADJUSTER	ADJUTRIX	AJUTMENT
ABJURING	ADJUGATE	ADJUSTOR	ADJUVANT	ALJAMADO
ADJACENT	ADJUMENT	ADJUTAGE	ADJUVATE	ALJAMIAH
ADJOINED	ADJURING	ADJUTANT	AJONJOLI	ALLELUJA
ADJUDGED	ADJUSTED	ADJUTORY	AJOURISE	APAREJOS

BABAJAGA	JACCONOT	JAZERANT	JOLLITRY	MAHARAJA
BAJONADO	JACINTHE	JAZZIEST	JOLLOPED	MAHJONGG
BAJULATE	JACITARA	JEALOUSE	JOLLYING	MAJESTIC
BEJABERS	JACKAROO	JEALOUSY	JOLTHEAD	MAJIDIEH
BEJUGGLE	JACKBIRD	JECORIZE	JONGLERY	MAJOLICA
BENJAMIN	JACKBOOT	JEJUNELY	JONGLEUR	MAJOLIST
BIAJAIBA	JACKEROO	JEJUNITY	JOOKERIE	MAJORATE
BIJUGATE	JACKETED	JELERANG	JORDANON	MAJORITY
BIJUGOUS	JACKFISH	JELLYING	JOSEFITE	MAJORIZE
BIJWONER	JACKHEAD	JELOTONG	JOSTLING	MARJORAM
BLATJANG	JACKPOTS	JELUTONG	JOTATION	MEDJIDIE
BLUEJACK	JACKROLL	JEOPARDY	JOTISARU	MEJORANA
BOBJEROM	JACKSHAY	JEREMIAD	JOUNCING	MIJAKITE
BOOTJACK	JACKSHEA	JERKIEST	JOURNEYS	MIJNHEER
BOSTANJI	JACKSTAY	JERKINED	JOUSTING	MISJUDGE
BRINJAUL	JACKWEED	JERKSOME	JOVIALLY	MONTJOYE
BRUJERIA	JACKWOOD	JERMONAL	JOVIALTY	MUJTAHID
BUCKJUMP	JACOBAEA	JEROBOAM	JOVILABE	NAUJAITE
CAJOLERY	JACOLATT	JERQUING	JOYFULLY	NIGHTJAR
CAJOLING	JACOUNCE	JERRICAN	JOYHOUSE	NONJUROR
CANAJONG	JACQUARD	JERRYISM	JOYOUSLY	OBJECTED
CARAJURA	JACTANCE	JERSEYED	JUBARTAS	OBJECTEE
CARCAJOU	JACTANCY	JESTBOOK	JUBARTES	OBJECTOR
COADJUST	JACULATE	JESTWORD	JUBEROUS	OVERJUMP
COADJUTE	JADISHLY	JETLINER	JUBILANT	PAJAMAED
CONJOINT	JAGGEDLY	JETTISON	JUBILATE	PEJERREY
CONJUGAL	JAGGHERY	JEUNESSE	JUBILEAN	PEJORATE
CONJUNCT	JAGGIEST	JEWELING	JUBILIST	PEJORISM
CONJURED	JAGIRDAR	JEWELLED	JUBILIZE	PEJORIST
CONJURER	JAILBIRD	JEWELLER	JUDAIZER	PEJORITY
CONJUROR	JAILMATE	JEZEKITE	JUDGMENT	PEJORITY
CRACKJAW	JAILYARD	JIBBINGS	JUDICATE	PERIJOVE
CUNJEVOI	JAKFRUIT	JIGGERED	JUDICIAL	PERJURED
DEJECTED	JALAPENO	JIGGERER	JUDICIUM	PERJURER
DEJERATE	JALLOPED	JIGGLING	JUGATION	POPINJAY
DEJEUNER	JALOPIES	JIMCRACK	JUGGLERY	PREJUDGE
DEMIJOHN	JALOUSED	JIMMYING	JUGGLING	PULSEJET
DEVARAJA	JALOUSIE	JIMPNESS	JUGULATE	PYJAMAED
DISJEUNE	JALPAITE	JIMSEDGE	JUICIEST	RAJBANSI
DISJOINT	JAMBEAUX	JINGBANG	JULIENNE	RAJOGUNA
DISJUNCT	JAMBOLAN	JINGLING	JULOLINE	READJUST
DJAGOONG	JAMBOREE	JINGOISH	JUMBLING	REJECTED
DOORJAMB	JAMDANEE	JINGOISM	JUMBOISM	REJECTER
EARJEWEL	JAMPANEE	JINGOIST	JUMPIEST	REJECTOR
EJECTING	JAMTLAND	JINNIYEH	JUMPROCK	REJOICED
EJECTION	JANGLING	JINSHANG	JUMPSEED	REJOICER
EJECTIVE	JANICEPS	JIPIJAPA	JUMPSOME	REJOINED
EJICIENT	JANISARY	JIRKINET	JUNCTION	REJOUNCE
EMAJAGUA	JANITRIX	JITNEUSE	JUNCTIVE	SEDJADEH
ENJAMBED	JANIZARY	JIUJITSU	JUNCTURE	SEJOINED
ENJOINED	JAPANNED	JIUJUTSU	JUNEFISH	SEJUGATE
ENJOINER	JAPANNER	JOBATION	JUNGLIER	SEJUGOUS
ENJOYING	JAPERIES	JOBSMITH	JUNKETED	SERJEANT
FERIDJEE	JAPISHLY	JOCATORY	JUNKETER	SKIJORER
FLAPJACK	JAPONICA	JOCKEYED	JUNKYARD	SKIPJACK
FLIPJACK	JAPYGOID	JOCOSELY	JURAMENT	SLAPJACK
FORJUDGE	JAQUETTE	JOCOSITY	JURATION	SNAPJACK
FOUJDARY	JARARACA	JOCTELEG	JURATIVE	SNIPJACK
FRABJOUS	JARGONAL	JOCUNDLY	JURATORY	SOURJACK
GALIONJI	JARGONED	JOCUNDRY	JURISTIC	STICKJAW
GRANJENO	JARGONEL	JODHPURS	JUSSHELL	SUBJOINT
GUAJILLO	JARGONER	JOGGLETY	JUSTICED	SUBJUGAL
HAMINGJA	JARGONIC	JOGGLING	JUSTICER	SUBJUNCT
HIGHJACK	JAROSITE	JOHANNES	JUSTITIA	SUCURUJU
HIJACKER	JAROVIZE	JOHNBOAT	JUSTMENT	TATMJOLK
HUAJILLO	JASMINED	JOINERED	JUSTNESS	TENDEJON
IJUSSITE	JASPERED	JOINHAND	JUVENATE	TJANTING
INJECTED	JASPONYX	JOINTAGE	JUVENILE	TJURUNGA
INJECTOR	JASPOPAL	JOINTING	KABELJOU	TOKTOKJE
INJURIES	JAUNDERS	JOINTIST	KAJUGARU	TURBOJET
INJURING	JAUNDICE	JOINTURE	KINKAJOU	TURJAITE
INJUSTLY	JAUNTIER	JOISTING	KOMITAJI	UNJUSTLY
JABBERED	JAUNTILY	JOKESOME	KOMMETJE	VERJUICE
JABBERER	JAUNTING	JOKESTER	KUJAWIAK	YAJENINE
JABORINE	JAVELINA	JOKINGLY	LONGJAWS	YAMMADJI
JACCONET	JAWSMITH	JOLLIEST	LUTJANID	

POSITIONAL ORDER LIST OF 8-LETTER WORDS

JABBERED	JAUNDICE	JOINTING	JUVENATE	OBJECTEE
JABBERER	JAUNTIER	JOINTIST	JUVENILE	OBJECTOR
JABORINE	JAUNTILY	JOINTURE		PAJAMAED
JACCONET	JAUNTING	JOISTING	AJONJOLI	PEJERREY
JACCONOT	JAVELINA	JOKESOME	AJONJOLI	PEJORATE
JACINTHE	JAWSMITH	JOKESTER	AJOURISE	PEJORISM
JACITARA	JAZERANT	JOKINGLY	AJUTMENT	PEJORIST
JACKAROO	JAZZIEST	JOLLIEST	DJAGOONG	PEJORITY
JACKBIRD	JEALOUSE	JOLLITRY	EJECTING	PYJAMAED
JACKBOOT	JEALOUSY	JOLLOPED	EJECTION	RAJBANSI
JACKEROO	JECORIZE	JOLLYING	EJECTIVE	RAJOGUNA
JACKETED	JEJUNELY	JOLTHEAD	EJICIENT	REJECTED
JACKFISH	JEJUNITY	JONGLERY	IJUSSITE	REJECTER
JACKHEAD	JELERANG	JONGLEUR	TJANTING	REJECTOR
JACKPOTS	JELLYING	JOOKERIE	TJURUNGA	REJOICED
JACKROLL	JELOTONG	JORDANON		REJOICER
JACKSHAY	JELUTONG	JOSEFITE	ABJECTLY	REJOINED
JACKSHEA	JEOPARDY	JOSTLING	ABJURING	REJOUNCE
JACKSTAY	JEREMIAD	JOTATION	ADJACENT	SEJOINED
JACKWEED	JERKIEST	JOTISARU	ADJOINED	SEJUGATE
JACKWOOD	JERKINED	JOUNCING	ADJUDGED	SEJUGOUS
JACOBAEA	JERKSOME	JOURNEYS	ADJUDGER	UNJUSTLY
JACOLATT	JERMONAL	JOUSTING	ADJUGATE	YAJENINE
JACOUNCE	JEROBOAM	JOVIALLY	ADJUMENT	
JACQUARD	JERQUING	JOVIALTY	ADJURING	BENJAMIN
JACTANCE	JERRICAN	JOVILABE	ADJUSTED	BIAJAIBA
JACTANCY	JERRYISM	JOYFULLY	ADJUSTER	BOBJEROM
JACULATE	JERSEYED	JOYHOUSE	ADJUSTOR	BRUJERIA
JADISHLY	JESTBOOK	JOYOUSLY	ADJUTAGE	CONJOINT
JAGGEDLY	JESTWORD	JUBARTAS	ADJUTANT	CONJUGAL
JAGGHERY	JETLINER	JUBARTES	ADJUTORY	CONJUNCT
JAGGIEST	JETTISON	JUBEROUS	ADJUTRIX	CONJURED
JAGIRDAR	JEUNESSE	JUBILANT	ADJUVANT	CONJURER
JAILBIRD	JEWELING	JUBILATE	ADJUVATE	CONJUROR
JAILMATE	JEWELLED	JUBILEAN	ALJAMADO	CUNJEVOI
JAILYARD	JEWELLER	JUBILIST	ALJAMIAH	DISJEUNE
JAKFRUIT	JEZEKITE	JUBILIZE	BAJONADO	DISJOINT
JALAPENO	JIBBINGS	JUDAIZER	BAJULATE	DISJUNCT
JALLOPED	JIGGERED	JUDGMENT	BEJABERS	EARJEWEL
JALOPIES	JIGGERER	JUDICATE	BEJUGGLE	EMAJAGUA
JALOUSED	JIGGLING	JUDICIAL	BIJUGATE	FORJUDGE
JALOUSIE	JIMCRACK	JUDICIUM	BIJUGOUS	FOUJDARY
JALPAITE	JIMMYING	JUGATION	BIJWONER	GUAJILLO
JAMBEAUX	JIMPNESS	JUGGLERY	CAJOLERY	HUAJILLO
JAMBOLAN	JIMSEDGE	JUGGLING	CAJOLING	JIUJITSU
JAMBOREE	JINGBANG	JUGULATE	DEJECTED	JIUJUTSU
JAMDANEE	JINGLING	JUICIEST	DEJERATE	LUTJANID
JAMPANEE	JINGOISH	JULIENNE	DEJEUNER	MAHJONGG
JAMTLAND	JINGOISM	JULOLINE	ENJAMBED	MARJORAM
JANGLING	JINGOIST	JUMBLING	ENJOINED	MEDJIDIE
JANICEPS	JINNIYEH	JUMBOISM	ENJOINER	MISJUDGE
JANISARY	JINSHANG	JUMPIEST	ENJOYING	NAUJAITE
JANITRIX	JIPIJAPA	JUMPROCK	HIJACKER	NONJUROR
JANIZARY	JIRKINET	JUMPSEED	INJECTED	PERJURED
JAPANNED	JITNEUSE	JUMPSOME	INJECTOR	PERJURER
JAPANNER	JIUJITSU	JUNCTION	INJURIES	PREJUDGE
JAPERIES	JIUJUTSU	JUNCTIVE	INJURING	SEDJADEH
JAPISHLY	JOBATION	JUNCTURE	INJUSTLY	SERJEANT
JAPONICA	JOBSMITH	JUNEFISH	JEJUNELY	SKIJORER
JAPYGOID	JOCATORY	JUNGLIER	JEJUNITY	SUBJOINT
JAQUETTE	JOCKEYED	JUNKETED	KAJUGARU	SUBJUGAL
JARARACA	JOCOSELY	JUNKETER	KUJAWIAK	SUBJUNCT
JARGONAL	JOCOSITY	JUNKYARD	MAJESTIC	TURJAITE
JARGONED	JOCTELEG	JURAMENT	MAJIDIEH	VERJUICE
JARGONEL	JOCUNDLY	JURATION	MAJOLICA	
JARGONER	JOCUNDRY	JURATIVE	MAJOLIST	BABAJAGA
JARGONIC	JODHPURS	JURATORY	MAJORATE	BLATJANG
JAROSITE	JOGGLETY	JURISTIC	MAJORITY	BLUEJACK
JAROVIZE	JOGGLING	JUSSHELL	MAJORIZE	BOOTJACK
JASMINED	JOHANNES	JUSTICED	MEJORANA	BRINJAUL
JASPERED	JOHNBOAT	JUSTICER	MIJAKITE	BUCKJUMP
JASPONYX	JOINERED	JUSTITIA	MIJNHEER	CANAJONG
JASPOPAL	JOINHAND	JUSTMENT	MUJTAHID	CARAJURA
JAUNDERS	JOINTAGE	JUSTNESS	OBJECTED	COADJUST

COADJUTE	LONGJAWS	SOURJACK	NIGHTJAR	DEVARAJA
DEMIJOHN	MONTJOYE	TATMJOLK	POPINJAY	GALIONJI
DOORJAMB	OVERJUMP		PULSEJET	HAMINGJA
FLAPJACK	PERIJOVE	APAREJOS	STICKJAW	KOMITAJI
FLIPJACK	READJUST	CARCAJOU	TENDEJON	KOMMETJE
FRABJOUS	SKIPJACK	CRACKJAW	TURBOJET	MAHARAJA
GRANJENO	SLAPJACK	FERIDJEE		SUCURUJU
HIGHJACK	SNAPJACK	KABELJOU	ALLELUJA	TOKTOKJE
JIPIJAPA	SNIPJACK	KINKAJOU	BOSTANJI	YAMMADJI

SCORING ORDER LIST OF 8-LETTER WORDS

28
HIGHJACK
JEZEKITE

27
BUCKJUMP
JACKFISH
JACKSHAY
JACQUARD
JANIZARY
JAROVIZE
JASPONYX

26
CRACKJAW
FLAPJACK
FLIPJACK
JAMBEAUX
JECORIZE
JUBILIZE
MAJORIZE

25
JACKHEAD
JACKWEED
JACKWOOD
JERQUING
JIMCRACK
JOCKEYED
JUDAIZER
JUMPROCK

24
HIJACKER
JACKBIRD
JACKSHEA
JACKSTAY
JAQUETTE
JAZERANT
JOYFULLY
STICKJAW

23
ADJUTRIX
BLUEJACK
BOOTJACK
JACKBOOT
JACKPOTS
JAGGHERY
JAPISHLY
JAWSMITH
JAZZIEST
JIMMYING
JOKINGLY
JUNKYARD
KOMMETJE
PYJAMAED
SLAPJACK
SNAPJACK
SNIPJACK
YAMMADJI

22
ABJECTLY
FOUJDARY
JACKETED
JACTANCY
JADISHLY
JAKFRUIT
JANITRIX
JAPYGOID
JOBSMITH
MAHJONGG
OVERJUMP
POPINJAY
SKIPJACK

21
BOBJEROM
DEMIJOHN
HAMINGJA
JACKAROO
JACKEROO
JACKROLL
JAGGEDLY
JEOPARDY
JERKSOME
JESTBOOK
JINNIYEH
JOCUNDLY
JOCUNDRY
JODHPURS
JOKESOME
JOVIALLY
JOVIALTY
JOYHOUSE
JUMBOISM
JUMPSOME
JUNEFISH
KABELJOU
KOMITAJI
KUJAWIAK
MAJIDIEH
MIJAKITE
MUJTAHID
SOURJACK
TATMJOLK

20
ALJAMIAH
BABAJAGA
BIJWONER
CAJOLERY
CUNJEVOI
DOORJAMB
EJECTIVE
ENJAMBED
FORJUDGE
FRABJOUS
JABBERED
JACINTHE
JERKINED
JERRYISM

JIBBINGS
JOCATORY
JOCOSELY
JOCOSITY
JOGGLETY
JOHNBOAT
JOVILABE
JUDICIUM
JUGGLERY
JUMBLING
JUMPSEED
JUNCTIVE
JUNKETED
KAJUGARU
MAHARAJA
MAJORITY
MIJNHEER
MONTJOYE
OBJECTED
PAJAMAED
PEJERREY
PERIJOVE
SEDJADEH
VERJUICE

19
ADJUDGED
ADJUTORY
ADJUVANT
ADJUVATE
BEJABERS
BEJUGGLE
BENJAMIN
BIAJAIBA
CARCAJOU
CONJUNCT
DEJECTED
DEVARAJA
ENJOYING
FERIDJEE
JABBERER
JACCONET
JACCONOT
JACOBAEA
JACOUNCE
JACTANCE
JAILYARD
JAMBOLAN
JAMBOREE
JAMPANEE
JANICEPS
JAPONICA
JASPOPAL
JELLYING
JERKIEST
JEROBOAM
JERSEYED
JESTWORD
JEWELING
JEWELLED
JIMPNESS
JIMSEDGE

JINGBANG
JINGOISH
JINSHANG
JIRKINET
JOINHAND
JOKESTER
JOLLYING
JOLTHEAD
JONGLERY
JOOKERIE
JUDGMENT
JUMPIEST
JUNKETER
LONGJAWS
MAJESTIC
MAJOLICA
MARJORAM
MEDJIDIE
MISJUDGE
NIGHTJAR
OBJECTEE
OBJECTOR
PEJORISM
PREJUDGE
SKIJORER
SUBJUNCT

18
ABJURING
ADJACENT
ADJUDGER
ADJUMENT
ALJAMADO
BAJONADO
BIJUGATE
BIJUGOUS
BLATJANG
CAJOLING
CANAJONG
COADJUST
COADJUTE
CONJUGAL
CONJURED
DISJUNCT
DJAGOONG
EARJEWEL
EJECTING
EMAJAGUA
HUAJILLO
INJECTED
INJUSTLY
JAILBIRD
JALLOPED
JAMDANEE
JAMTLAND
JANISARY
JAPANNED
JARGONIC
JASMINED
JASPERED
JAUNDICE
JAUNTILY

JAVELINA
JEALOUSY
JEREMIAD
JEWELLER
JIGGERED
JIGGLING
JINGOISM
JIPIJAPA
JOCTELEG
JOGGLING
JOHANNES
JOLLITRY
JOLLOPED
JOSEFITE
JOUNCING
JOURNEYS
JUDICATE
JUDICIAL
JUGGLING
JURATIVE
JURATORY
JUSSHELL
JUSTICED
JUVENATE
JUVENILE
KINKAJOU
PERJURED
REJECTED
REJOICED
SUBJUGAL
TOKTOKJE
UNJUSTLY
YAJENINE

17
ADJOINED
ADJUGATE
ADJURING
ADJUSTED
ADJUTAGE
AJUTMENT
APAREJOS
BAJULATE
BOSTANJI
BRINJAUL
BRUJERIA
CARAJURA
CONJOINT
CONJURER
CONJUROR
EJECTION
EJICIENT
INJECTOR
JABORINE
JACITARA
JACOLATT
JACULATE
JAGGIEST
JAGIRDAR
JAILMATE
JALAPENO
JALOPIES

JALPAITE
JANGLING
JAPANNER
JAPERIES
JARARACA
JARGONED
JEJUNELY
JEJUNITY
JERMONAL
JERRICAN
JIGGERER
JINGLING
JOBATION
JUBARTAS
JUBARTES
JUBEROUS
JUBILANT
JUBILATE
JUBILEAN
JUBILIST
JUICIEST
JUNCTION
JUNCTURE
JURAMENT
JURISTIC

JUSTICER
JUSTMENT
MAJOLIST
MAJORATE
MEJORANA
PEJORATE
PEJORIST
PERJURER
PULSEJET
RAJBANSI
REJECTER
REJECTOR
REJOICER
REJOUNCE
SUBJOINT
SUCURUJU
TURBOJET

16
ADJUSTER
ADJUSTOR
ADJUTANT
DEJERATE
DEJEUNER
DISJEUNE

DISJOINT
ENJOINED
GALIONJI
GRANJENO
GUAJILLO
INJURING
JALOUSED
JARGONAL
JARGONEL
JARGONER
JAUNDERS
JAUNTING
JELERANG
JELOTONG
JELUTONG
JINGOIST
JOINERED
JOINTAGE
JOINTING
JOISTING
JONGLEUR
JORDANON
JOSTLING
JOUSTING

JUGATION
JUGULATE
JUNGLIER
LUTJANID
RAJOGUNA
READJUST
REJOINED
SEJOINED
SEJUGATE
SEJUGOUS
TENDEJON
TJANTING
TJURUNGA

15
AJOURISE
ALLELUJA
ENJOINER
IJUSSITE
INJURIES
JALOUSIE
JAROSITE
JAUNTIER
JEALOUSE

JETLINER
JETTISON
JEUNESSE
JITNEUSE
JOINTIST
JOINTURE
JOLLIEST
JOTATION
JOTISARU
JULIENNE
JULOLINE
JURATION
JUSTITIA
JUSTNESS
NAUJAITE
NONJUROR
SERJEANT
TURJAITE

14
AJONJOLI
JIUJITSU
JIUJUTSU

ALPHABETICAL LIST OF 9-LETTER WORDS

ABJECTION
ABJECTIVE
ADJACENCY
ADJECTION
ADJECTIVE
ADJOINING
ADJOURNAL
ADJUDGING
ADJUNCTLY
ADJUSTAGE
ADJUSTIVE
ADJUTANCY
ADJUTRICE
ALJAMIADO
ALJOFAINA
AMBERJACK
ANKLEJACK
APJOHNITE
APPLEJACK
APPLEJOHN
BACKJOINT
BANJORINE
BARAJILLO
BEJABBERS
BEJEWELED
BIJUGULAR
BLACKJACK
BLUEJOINT
BOOTJACKS
BRINJAREE
BRINJARRY
CAJUPUTOL
CISJURANE
COADJUTOR
CONJOINED
CONJOINER
CONJOBBLE
CONJUGACY

CONJUGANT
CONJUGATA
CONJUGATE
CONJUGIAL
CONJUGIUM
CONJURING
CROSSJACK
DEJECTILE
DEJECTION
DEJECTORY
DEJECTURE
DEMIJAMBE
DISJASKED
DISJASKIT
DISJECTED
DISJOINED
DJALMAITE
EJACULATE
EJECTMENT
ENJEOPARD
ENJOINDER
ENJOINING
ENJOYABLE
ENJOYABLY
ENJOYMENT
FAUJASITE
FOREJUDGE
FORJASKIT
FORJESKET
FORJUDGED
FORJUDGER
FOUJDARRY
FRAILEJON
GUEJARITE
INJECTING
INJECTION
INJUREDLY
INJURIOUS

INJUSTICE
INTERJECT
INTERJOIN
JABBERING
JABORANDI
JACARANDA
JACKEROOS
JACKETING
JACKFRUIT
JACKKNIFE
JACKLIGHT
JACKPLANE
JACKSCREW
JACKSHAFT
JACKSLAVE
JACKSMELT
JACKSMITH
JACKSNIPE
JACKSTOCK
JACKSTONE
JACKSTRAW
JACOBSITE
JACQUERIE
JACTATION
JACTITATE
JACULATED
JACULATOR
JACUTINGA
JADEDNESS
JAGHIRDAR
JAGUARETE
JAILERESS
JAILERING
JAILHOUSE
JAILORING
JALOUSIED
JALOUSING
JAMBALAYA

JAMBOLANA
JAMBSTONE
JAMROSADE
JANISSARY
JANITRESS
JAPACONIN
JAPANNERY
JAPANNING
JARGONING
JARGONISH
JARGONIST
JARGONIUM
JARGONIZE
JAROVIZED
JASPAGATE
JASPERITE
JASPERIZE
JASPEROID
JASPIDEAN
JASPILITE
JASPILYTE
JATAMANSI
JATROPHIC
JAUNDICED
JAUNTIEST
JAWBATION
JAWFALLEN
JAWFISHES
JAWFOOTED
JAYHAWKER
JAYWALKER
JAZZINESS
JEALOUSLY
JEERINGLY
JEJUNATOR
JEJUNITIS
JELLIFIED
JELLYBEAN

JELLYFISH
JELLYLEAF
JELLYLIKE
JEMMINESS
JENNERIZE
JENNETING
JEOPARDED
JEOPARDER
JEQUERITY
JEQUIRITY
JERKINESS
JERKWATER
JERMOONAL
JESSAKEED
JESSAMIES
JESSAMINE
JESTINGLY
JETTATORE
JETTATURA
JETTINESS
JETTYHEAD
JEWELLERY
JEWELLING
JEWELWEED
JEWFISHES
JIGAMAREE
JIGGERMAN
JIGGINESS
JIGGUMBOB
JILLFLIRT
JIMBERJAW
JIMMYWEED
JINGLEBOB
JINNESTAN
JINNIWINK
JINNYWINK
JITNEYMAN
JITTERBUG

JNANAYOGA
JOBBERIES
JOBHOLDER
JOBMASTER
JOBMONGER
JOCKEYING
JOCKEYISM
JOCKSTRAP
JOCKTELEG
JOCULARLY
JOCULATOR
JOCUNDITY
JOHANNITE
JOINERING
JOININGLY
JOINTEDLY
JOINTRESS
JOINTURED
JOINTWEED
JOINTWOOD
JOINTWORM
JOKESMITH
JOLLIFIED
JOLLIMENT
JOLLINESS
JOLLITIES
JOLLYHEAD
JOLTINESS
JONQUILLE
JORDANITE
JOURNALED
JOURNEYED

JOURNEYER
JOVIALIST
JOVIALITY
JOVIALIZE
JOYLESSLY
JOYPOPPER
JUBILANCE
JUBILANCY
JUBILATED
JUBILATIO
JUCUNDITY
JUDGEMENT
JUDGMATIC
JUDGMENTS
JUDICABLE
JUDICATOR
JUDICIARY
JUDICIOUS
JUGLANDIN
JUGULATED
JUICINESS
JULIENITE
JULOIDIAN
JULOLIDIN
JUMENTOUS
JUMILLITE
JUMPINESS
JUMPROCKS
JUNCIFORM
JUNECTOMY
JUNGLIEST
JUNIORATE

JUNIORITY
JUNKBOARD
JUNKERDOM
JUNKERISM
JUNKETING
JURAMENTA
JURIDICAL
JURUPAITE
JURYWOMAN
JUSTICIAL
JUSTICIAR
JUSTICIER
JUSTICIES
JUSTICING
JUSTIFIED
JUSTIFIER
JUSTMENTS
JUTTINGLY
JUVENILIA
JUVENTUDE
JUXTAPOSE
KILOJOULE
KOMITADJI
KOORAJONG
KURRAJONG
LUJAURITE
LUJAVRITE
MAHARAJAH
MAJESTIES
MAJORDOMO
MAJORETTE
MAJUSCULE

MARIJUANA
MATAJUELO
MEDJIDIEH
MISJUDGED
MISJUDGER
MUNJISTIN
NONINJURY
NONJURANT
NONJURING
NUTJOBBER
OBJECTIFY
OBJECTING
OBJECTION
OBJECTIVE
OBJECTIZE
OBJICIENT
OBJURGATE
OUTJOCKEY
OUTJUGGLE
OVERJUDGE
PEREJONET
PERJINKLY
PERJURIES
PERJURING
PREJACENT
PREJUDGED
PREJUDGER
PREJUDICE
PROJECTOR
QUILLAJIC
REDJACKET
REJECTAGE

REJECTING
REJECTION
REJECTIVE
REJOICING
REJOINDER
REJOINING
RETROJECT
SANJAKBEG
SEJUNCTLY
SEMIBEJAN
SERJEANCY
SERJEANTY
SKIJORING
SKIPJACKS
SMOKEJACK
SOJOURNED
SOJOURNER
SUBJACENT
SUBJECTED
SUBJOINED
SUBJUGATE
SURREJOIN
SWARAJISM
SWARAJIST
TASAJILLO
TRAJECTED
TRIJUGATE
TRIJUGOUS
UNIJUGATE
UNINJURED
VAJRASANA

POSITIONAL ORDER LIST OF 9-LETTER WORDS

JABBERING
JABORANDI
JACARANDA
JACKEROOS
JACKETING
JACKFRUIT
JACKKNIFE
JACKLIGHT
JACKPLANE
JACKSCREW
JACKSHAFT
JACKSLAVE
JACKSMELT
JACKSMITH
JACKSNIPE
JACKSTOCK
JACKSTONE
JACKSTRAW
JACOBSITE
JACQUERIE
JACTATION
JACTITATE
JACULATED
JACULATOR
JACUTINGA
JADEDNESS
JAGHIRDAR
JAGUARETE
JAILERESS
JAILERING
JAILHOUSE
JAILORING
JALOUSIED
JALOUSING
JAMBALAYA
JAMBOLANA
JAMBSTONE
JAMROSADE
JANISSARY

JANITRESS
JAPACONIN
JAPANNERY
JAPANNING
JARGONING
JARGONISH
JARGONIST
JARGONIUM
JARGONIZE
JAROVIZED
JASPAGATE
JASPERITE
JASPERIZE
JASPEROID
JASPIDEAN
JASPILITE
JASPILYTE
JATAMANSI
JATROPHIC
JAUNDICED
JAUNTIEST
JAWBATION
JAWFALLEN
JAWFISHES
JAWFOOTED
JAYHAWKER
JAYWALKER
JAZZINESS
JEALOUSLY
JEERINGLY
JEJUNATOR
JEJUNITIS
JELLIFIED
JELLYBEAN
JELLYFISH
JELLYLEAF
JELLYLIKE
JEMMINESS
JENNERIZE

JENNETING
JEOPARDED
JEOPARDER
JEQUERITY
JEQUIRITY
JERKINESS
JERKWATER
JERMOONAL
JESSAKEED
JESSAMIES
JESSAMINE
JESTINGLY
JETTATORE
JETTATURA
JETTINESS
JETTYHEAD
JEWELLERY
JEWELLING
JEWELWEED
JEWFISHES
JIGAMAREE
JIGGERMAN
JIGGINESS
JIGGUMBOB
JILLFLIRT
JIMBERJAW
JIMMYWEED
JINGLEBOB
JINNESTAN
JINNIWINK
JINNYWINK
JITNEYMAN
JITTERBUG
JNANAYOGA
JOBBERIES
JOBHOLDER
JOBMASTER
JOBMONGER
JOCKEYING

JOCKEYISM
JOCKSTRAP
JOCKTELEG
JOCULARLY
JOCULATOR
JOCUNDITY
JOHANNITE
JOINERING
JOININGLY
JOINTEDLY
JOINTRESS
JOINTURED
JOINTWEED
JOINTWOOD
JOINTWORM
JOKESMITH
JOLLIFIED
JOLLIMENT
JOLLINESS
JOLLITIES
JOLLYHEA
JOLTINESS
JONQUILLE
JORDANITE
JOURNALED
JOURNEYED
JOURNEYER
JOVIALIST
JOVIALITY
JOVIALIZE
JOYLESSLY
JOYPOPPER
JUBILANCE
JUBILANCY
JUBILATED
JUBILATIO
JUCUNDITY
JUDGEMENT
JUDGMATIC

JUDGMENTS
JUDICABLE
JUDICATOR
JUDICIARY
JUDICIOUS
JUGLANDIN
JUGULATED
JUICINESS
JULIENITE
JULOIDIAN
JULOLIDIN
JUMENTOUS
JUMILLITE
JUMPINESS
JUMPROCKS
JUNCIFORM
JUNECTOMY
JUNGLIEST
JUNIORATE
JUNIORITY
JUNKBOARD
JUNKERDOM
JUNKERISM
JUNKETING
JURAMENTA
JURIDICAL
JURUPAITE
JURYWOMAN
JUSTICIAL
JUSTICIAR
JUSTICIER
JUSTICIES
JUSTICING
JUSTIFIED
JUSTIFIER
JUSTMENTS
JUTTINGLY
JUVENILIA
JUVENTUDE

JUXTAPOSE

DJALMAITE
EJACULATE
EJECTMENT

ABJECTION
ABJECTIVE
ADJACENCY
ADJECTION
ADJECTIVE
ADJOINING
ADJOURNAL
ADJUDGING
ADJUNCTLY
ADJUSTAGE
ADJUSTIVE
ADJUTANCY
ADJUTRICE
ALJAMIADO
ALJOFAINA
APJOHNITE
BEJABBERS
BEJEWELED
BIJUGULAR
CAJUPUTOL
DEJECTILE
DEJECTION
DEJECTORY
DEJECTURE
ENJEOPARD
ENJOINDER
ENJOINING

ENJOYABLE
ENJOYABLY
ENJOYMENT
INJECTING
INJECTION
INJUREDLY
INJURIOUS
INJUSTICE
JEJUNATOR
JEJUNITIS
LUJAURITE
LUJAVRITE
MAJESTIES
MAJORDOMO
MAJORETTE
MAJUSCULE
OBJECTIFY
OBJECTING
OBJECTION
OBJECTIVE
OBJECTIZE
OBJICIENT
OBJURGATE
REJECTAGE
REJECTING
REJECTION
REJECTIVE
REJOICING
REJOINDER
REJOINING
SEJUNCTLY
SOJOURNED
SOJOURNER

VAJRASANA

BANJORINE
CISJURANE
CONJOINED
CONJOINER
CONJOBBLE
CONJUGACY
CONJUGANT
CONJUGATA
CONJUGATE
CONJUGIAL
CONJUGIUM
CONJURING
DISJASKED
DISJASKIT
DISJECTED
DISJOINED
FAUJASITE
FORJASKIT
FORJESKET
FORJUDGED
FORJUDGER
FOUJDARRY
GUEJARITE
MEDJIDIEH
MISJUDGED
MISJUDGER
MUNJISTIN
NONJURANT
NONJURING
NUTJOBBER
OUTJOCKEY

OUTJUGGLE
PERJINKLY
PERJURIES
PERJURING
PREJACENT
PREJUDGED
PREJUDGER
PREJUDICE
PROJECTOR
REDJACKET
SANJAKBEG
SERJEANCY
SERJEANTY
SKIJORING
SUBJACENT
SUBJECTED
SUBJOINED
SUBJUGATE
TRAJECTED
TRIJUGATE
TRIJUGOUS
UNIJUGATE

BACKJOINT
BARAJILLO
BLUEJOINT
BOOTJACKS
BRINJAREE
BRINJARRY
COADJUTANT
COADJUTOR
DEMIJAMBE
FOREJUDGE

KILOJOULE
MARIJUANA
MATAJUELO
OVERJUDGE
PEREJONET
SKIPJACKS
TASAJILLO
UNINJURED

AMBERJACK
ANKLEJACK
APPLEJACK
APPLEJOHN
BLACKJACK
CROSSJACK
INTERJECT
INTERJOIN
KOORAJONG
KURRAJONG
NONINJURY
RETROJECT
SMOKEJACK
SURREJOIN
SWARAJISM
SWARAJIST

FRAILEJON
JIMBERJAW
MAHARAJAH
QUILLAJIC
SEMIBEJAN

KOMITADJI

SCORING ORDER LIST OF 9-LETTER WORDS

29
JAROVIZED
JAYHAWKER
OBJECTIZE

28
JACKSHAFT
JEQUERITY
JEQUIRITY
JOVIALIZE

27
JACKSCREW
JACKSMITH
JACQUERIE
JASPERIZE
JIMMYWEED
JOCKEYISM
QUILLAJIC

26
AMBERJACK
APPLEJACK
JACKLIGHT
JARGONIZE
JAYWALKER
JINNYWINK
JOCKEYING
JUMPROCKS
OBJECTIFY

25
BLACKJACK
JACKFRUIT
JACKSLAVE
JACKSTRAW
JAWFISHES
JELLYFISH

JENNERIZE
JEWFISHES
JOKESMITH
JONQUILLE
JUXTAPOSE
OUTJOCKEY
PERJINKLY

24
ADJACENCY
BACKJOINT
BOOTJACKS
CONJUGACY
CROSSJACK
ENJOYABLY
JACKKNIFE
JACKPLANE
JACKSMELT
JACKSNIPE
JAZZINESS
JIGGUMBOB
JOCKSTRAP
JURYWOMAN
MAHARAJAH

23
ABJECTIVE
APPLEJOHN
DEMIJAMBE
FORJASKIT
FORJESKET
FOUJDARRY
JACKETING
JACKSTOCK
JAMBALAYA
JATROPHIC
JAWFOOTED
JELLYLIKE

JERKWATER
JETTYHEAD
JEWELWEED
JINNIWINK
JOCKTELEG
JOLLYHEAD
JUBILANCY
JUNCIFORM
JUNECTOMY
JUNKBOARD
JUNKERDOM
KOMITADJI
MEDJIDIEH
OBJECTIVE
REDJACKET
SANJAKBEG
SKIPJACKS
SMOKEJACK

22
ADJECTIVE
ADJUNCTLY
ADJUTANCY
BEJEWELED
CONJOBBLE
DEJECTORY
DISJASKED
FORJUDGED
JACKEROOS
JACKSTONE
JAWFALLEN
JELLYLEAF
JEWELLERY
JIMBERJAW
JOBHOLDER
JOCUNDITY
JOVIALITY
JOYLESSLY

JOYPOPPER
JUCUNDITY
JUDGMATIC
JUDICIARY
JUNKERISM

21
ANKLEJACK
APJOHNITE
BRINJARRY
CONJUGIUM
DISJASKIT
ENJOYABLE
ENJOYMENT
FOREJUDGE
FORJUDGER
JABBERING
JAGHIRDAR
JAPANNERY
JASPILYTE
JAWBATION
JELLYBEAN
JESSAKEED
JINGLEBOB
JITNEYMAN
JOBMONGER
JOCULARLY
JOINTWORM
JUDICABLE
JUNKETING
KOORAJONG
KURRAJONG
MAJORDOMO
MISJUDGED
OBJECTING
OVERJUDGE
PREJUDGED
PREJUDICE

REJECTIVE
SEJUNCTLY
SERJEANCY
SKIJORING
SUBJECTED
SWARAJISM

20
ABJECTION
ADJUDGING
ADJUSTIVE
CAJUPUTOL
DISJECTED
EJECTMENT
INJUREDLY
JACOBSITE
JAMBOLANA
JAMBSTONE
JAPACONIN
JARGONISH
JAUNDICED
JEERINGLY
JELLIFIED
JEMMINESS
JEOPARDED
JERKINESS
JESTINGLY
JEWELLING
JIGGERMAN
JNANAYOGA
JOBBERIES
JOBMASTER
JOININGLY
JOINTEDLY
JOINTWEED
JOINTWOOD
JOLLIFIED
JOURNEYED

JUBILANCE
JUDGEMENT
JUDGMENTS
JUMPINESS
JUSTIFIED
JUTTINGLY
JUVENTUDE
KILOJOULE
MAJUSCULE
MISJUDGER
NUTJOBBER
OBJECTION
OBJICIENT
PREJACENT
PREJUDGER
PROJECTOR
SEMIBEJAN
SUBJACENT

19
ADJECTION
ADJUTRICE
ALJAMIADO
ALJOFAINA
BEJABBERS
BIJUGŪLAR
COADJUTOR
CONJOINED
CONJUGANT
CONJUGATA
CONJUGATE
CONJUGIAL
CONJURING
DEJECTILE
DEJECTION
DEJECTURE
DJALMAITE
ENJEOPARD

FAUJASITE
FRAILEJON
INJECTING
JABORANDI
JACARANDA
JACULATED
JACUTINGA
JAILHOUSE
JAMROSADE
JANISSARY
JAPANNING
JARGONIUM
JASPAGATE
JASPEROID
JASPIDEAN
JEALOUSLY
JEOPARDER
JIGAMAREE
JILLFLIRT
JITTERBUG
JOHANNITE
JOURNEYER
JOVIALIST
JUBILATED
JUDICATOR
JUDICIOUS
JUNIORITY
JURIDICAL
JUSTICING
JUSTIFIER
JUVENILIA
LUJAVRITE
NONINJURY
OBJURGATE
PERJURING
REJECTAGE
REJECTING
REJOICING

SERJEANTY
SUBJOINED
SUBJUGATE
SWARAJIST
TRAJECTED
VAJRASANA

18
ADJOINING
ADJUSTAGE
BANJORINE
BARAJILLO
BLUEJOINT
BRINJAREE
CISJURANE
CONJOINER
DISJOINED
EJACULATE
INJECTION
INJUSTICE
INTERJECT
JACTATION
JACTITATE
JACULATOR
JADEDNESS
JARGONING
JASPERITE
JASPILITE
JATAMANSI
JERMOONAL
JESSAMIES
JESSAMINE
JIGGINESS
JOCULATOR
JOLLIMENT
JUBILATIO
JUGLANDIN
JUGULATED

JUICINESS
JUMENTOUS
JUMILLITE
JURAMENTA
JURUPAITE
JUSTICIAL
JUSTICIAR
JUSTICIER
JUSTICIES
JUSTMENTS
MAJESTIES
MAJORETTE
MARIJUANA
MATAJUELO
MUNJISTIN
OUTJUGGLE
PEREJONET
PERJURIES
REJECTION
RETROJECT

17
ADJOURNAL
ENJOINDER
ENJOINING
GUEJARITE
JAGUARETE
JAILERING
JAILORING
JALOUSIED
JALOUSING
JARGONIST
JENNETING
JOINERING
JOINTURED
JORDANITE
JOURNALED
JULOIDIAN

JULOLIDIN
JUNGLIEST
NONJURING
REJOINDER
REJOINING
SOJOURNED
TRIJUGATE
TRIJUGOUS
UNIJUGATE
UNINJURED

16
INJURIOUS
INTERJOIN
JAILERESS
JANITRESS
JAUNTIEST
JETTATORE
JETTATURA
JETTINESS
JINNESTAN
JOINTRESS
JOLLINESS
JOLLITIES
JOLTINESS
JULIENITE
JUNIORATE
LUJAURITE
NONJURANT
SOJOURNER
SURREJOIN
TASAJILLO

15
JEJUNATOR
JEJUNITIS

ALPHABETICAL LIST OF 10-LETTER WORDS

ABJECTNESS
ABJUDICATE
ABJUNCTIVE
ABJURATION
ABJURATORY
ABJUREMENT
ADJACENTLY
ADJECTIVAL
ADJOINEDLY
ADJUDICATE
ADJUNCTION
ADJUNCTIVE
ADJURATION
ADJURATORY
ADJUSTABLE
ADJUSTMENT
ARROJADITE
BEJEWELING
BEJEWELLED
BIJOUTERIE
BLUEJACKET
BUTTERJAGS
CAJOLEMENT
CAJOLERIES
CAJOLINGLY
CAJUPUTENE
CAODJACENCY
CHAPARAJOS

CHAPAREJOS
CLAMJAMFRY
COADJACENT
COADJUMENT
COADJUTANT
COADJUTIVE
COADJUTRIX
COADJUVANT
CONJECTIVE
CONJECTURE
CONJOINING
CONJOINTLY
CONJUGABLE
CONJUGALLY
CONJUGATED
CONJUGATOR
CONJUNCTLY
CONJUNCTUR
CONJURATOR
CRACKAJACK
DEJECTEDLY
DIJUDICATE
DISJECTING
DISJECTION
DISJOINING
DISJOINTED
DISJOINTLY
DISJUNCTOR

EJACULATED
EJACULATOR
EJECTIVELY
EJECTIVITY
ENJAMBMENT
ENJEOPARDY
ENJOINMENT
EQUIJACENT
FIDEJUSSOR
FOREJUDGED
FOREJUDGER
FORJUDGING
FRABJOUSLY
HIGHJACKER
INCONJUNCT
INJUDICIAL
INJUNCTION
INJUNCTIVE
INTERJOIST
JABBERMENT
JABOTICABA
JACKANAPES
JACKASSERY
JACKFISHES
JACKHAMMER
JACKKNIVES
JACKSNIPES
JACTITATED

JACULATING
JACULATION
JACULATIVE
JACULATORY
JADISHNESS
JAGGEDNESS
JAGHEERDAR
JAGHIREDAR
JAGUARONDI
JAGUARUNDI
JAILKEEPER
JAMESONITE
JANITORIAL
JANIZARIES
JAPACONINE
JAPISHNESS
JARDINIERE
JARGONELLE
JARGONIZED
JAROVIZING
JASPACHATE
JASPERATED
JASPERIZED
JASPIDEOUS
JAUNDICING
JAUNTINESS
JAVELINEER
JAWBREAKER

JAWCRUSHER
JAYWALKING
JEALOUSIES
JEJUNENESS
JEJUNOTOMY
JELLIFYING
JENTACULAR
JEOPARDIED
JEOPARDING
JEOPARDIZE
JEOPARDOUS
JERRYBUILD
JERRYBUILT
JEWELHOUSE
JEWELSMITH
JIMPRICUTE
JINGLINGLY
JINGOISTIC
JINRICKSHA
JINRIKIMAN
JINRIKIMEN
JINRIKISHA
JNANAMARGA
JOAQUINITE
JOBBERNOWL
JOCOSENESS
JOCOSITIES
JOCULARITY

JOCULATORY
JOCUNDNESS
JOGGLEWORK
JOHNNYCAKE
JOINTURESS
JOINTURING
JOLLIFYING
JOLTERHEAD
JOLTHEADED
JOSTLEMENT
JOUISSANCE
JOULEMETER
JOURNALESE
JOURNALING
JOURNALISE
JOURNALISM
JOURNALIST
JOURNALIZE
JOURNALLED
JOURNEYING
JOURNEYMAN
JOURNEYMEN
JOVIALIZED
JOYFULNESS
JOYOUSNESS
JUBILANTLY
JUBILARIAN
JUBILATING
JUBILATION
JUBILATORY

JUDICATION
JUDICATIVE
JUDICATORY
JUDICATURE
JUDICIABLE
JUDICIALLY
JUDOPHOBIA
JUGGERNAUT
JUGGLEMENT
JUGGLERIES
JUGGLINGLY
JUGULATING
JUGULATION
JULOLIDINE
JUMBLEMENT
JUMPSCRAPE
JUNCACEOUS
JUNCTIONAL
JUNGLESIDE
JUNGLEWOOD
JUNKDEALER
JURAMENTAL
JURAMENTUM
JURATORIAL
JURIDICIAL
JURISTICAL
JUSTICIARY
JUSTIFYING
JUVENILELY

JUVENILIFY
JUVENILISM
JUVENILITY
JUXTAPOSED
JUXTAPOSIT
LUMBERJACK
MAJESTICAL
MAJESTIOUS
MAJORATION
MAJORITIES
MAJUSCULAE
MAJUSCULAR
MISJOINDER
MISJUDGING
NATTERJACK
NONABJURER
NONJOINDER
NONJURANCY
OBJECTABLE
OBJECTIONS
OBJECTIVAL
OBJECTIZED
OBJECTLESS
OBJURATION
OBJURGATED
OBJURGATOR
OTTAJANITE
OUTJOURNEY
PAJAHUELLO

PAJAROELLO
PANJANDRUM
PEJORATION
PEJORATIVE
PERJINKETY
PERJUREDLY
PERJURIOUS
POSTJACENT
PREADJUNCT
PREJUDGING
PREJUDICED
PROJACIENT
PROJECTILE
PROJECTING
PROJECTION
PROJECTIVE
PROJECTRIX
PROJECTURE
PROJICIENT
RATTLEJACK
READJUSTER
REJOICEFUL
REJONEADOR
REJUNCTION
REJUVENANT
REJUVENATE
REJUVENIZE
SEJUNCTION
SEJUNCTIVE

SERJEANTRY
SKIPJACKLY
SKYJACKING
SOJOURNING
SUBJACENCY
SUBJECTIFY
SUBJECTILE
SUBJECTING
SUBJECTION
SUBJECTIVE
SUBJICIBLE
SUBJOINDER
SUBJOINING
SUBJUGABLE
SUBJUGATED
SUBJUGATOR
SUBJUGULAR
SUPPLEJACK
SUPRAJURAL
TIMBERJACK
TRAJECTILE
TRAJECTING
TRAJECTION
TRAJECTORY
UNDERJAWED
UNJUSTNESS
WEREJAGUAR
WINDJAMMER
WOODJOBBER

POSITIONAL ORDER LIST OF 10-LETTER WORDS

JABBERMENT
JABOTICABA
JACKANAPES
JACKASSERY
JACKFISHES
JACKHAMMER
JACKKNIVES
JACKSNIPES
JACTITATED
JACULATING
JACULATION
JACULATIVE
JACULATORY
JADISHNESS
JAGGEDNESS
JAGHEERDAR
JAGHIREDAR
JAGUARONDI
JAGUARUNDI
JAILKEEPER
JAMESONITE
JANITORIAL
JANIZARIES
JAPACONINE
JAPISHNESS
JARDINIERE
JARGONELLE
JARGONIZED
JAROVIZING
JASPACHATE
JASPERATED
JASPERIZED
JASPIDEOUS
JAUNDICING
JAUNTINESS
JAVELINEER
JAWBREAKER
JAWCRUSHER
JAYWALKING
JEALOUSIES
JEJUNENESS

JEJUNOTOMY
JELLIFYING
JENTACULAR
JEOPARDIED
JEOPARDING
JEOPARDIZE
JEOPARDOUS
JERRYBUILD
JERRYBUILT
JEWELHOUSE
JEWELSMITH
JIMPRICUTE
JINGLINGLY
JINGOISTIC
JINRICKSHA
JINRIKIMAN
JINRIKIMEN
JINRIKISHA
JNANAMARGA
JOAQUINITE
JOBBERNOWL
JOCOSENESS
JOCOSITIES
JOCULARITY
JOCULATORY
JOCUNDNESS
JOGGLEWORK
JOHNNYCAKE
JOINTURESS
JOINTURING
JOLLIFYING
JOLTERHEAD
JOLTHEADED
JOSTLEMENT
JOUISSANCE
JOULEMETER
JOURNALESE
JOURNALING
JOURNALISE
JOURNALISM
JOURNALIST

JOURNALIZE
JOURNALLED
JOURNEYING
JOURNEYMAN
JOURNEYMEN
JOVIALIZED
JOYFULNESS
JOYOUSNESS
JUBILANTLY
JUBILARIAN
JUBILATING
JUBILATION
JUBILATORY
JUDICATION
JUDICATIVE
JUDICATORY
JUDICATURE
JUDICIABLE
JUDICIALLY
JUDOPHOBIA
JUGGERNAUT
JUGGLEMENT
JUGGLERIES
JUGGLINGLY
JUGULATING
JUGULATION
JULOLIDINE
JUMBLEMENT
JUMPSCRAPE
JUNCACEOUS
JUNCTIONAL
JUNGLESIDE
JUNGLEWOOD
JUNKDEALER
JURAMENTAL
JURAMENTUM
JURATORIAL
JURIDICIAL
JURISTICAL
JUSTICIARY
JUSTIFYING

JUVENILELY
JUVENILIFY
JUVENILISM
JUVENILITY
JUXTAPOSED
JUXTAPOSIT

EJACULATED
EJACULATOR
EJECTIVELY
EJECTIVITY

ABJECTNESS
ABJUDICATE
ABJUNCTIVE
ABJURATION
ABJURATORY
ABJUREMENT
ADJACENTLY
ADJECTIVAL
ADJOINEDLY
ADJUDICATE
ADJUNCTION
ADJUNCTIVE
ADJURATION
ADJURATORY
ADJUSTABLE
ADJUSTMENT
BEJEWELING
BEJEWELLED
BIJOUTERIE
CAJOLEMENT
CAJOLERIES
CAJOLINGLY
CAJUPUTENE
DEJECTEDLY
DIJUDICATE
ENJAMBMENT
ENJEOPARDY
ENJOINMENT
INJUDICIAL

INJUNCTION
INJUNCTIVE
JEJUNENESS
JEJUNOTOMY
MAJESTICAL
MAJESTIOUS
MAJORATION
MAJORITIES
MAJUSCULAE
MAJUSCULAR
OBJECTABLE
OBJECTIONS
OBJECTIVAL
OBJECTIZED
OBJECTLESS
OBJURATION
OBJURGATED
OBJURGATOR
PAJAHUELLO
PAJAROELLO
PEJORATION
PEJORATIVE
REJOICEFUL
REJONEADOR
REJUNCTION
REJUVENANT
REJUVENATE
REJUVENIZE
SEJUNCTION
SEJUNCTIVE
SOJOURNING
UNJUSTNESS

CONJECTIVE
CONJOINING
CONJOINTLY
CONJUGABLE
CONJUGALLY
CONJUGATED
CONJUGATOR
CONJUNCTLY

CONJUNCTUR
CONJURATOR
DISJECTING
DISJECTION
DISJOINING
DISJOINTED
DISJOINTLY
DISJUNCTOR
FORJUDGING
MISJOINDER
MISJUDGING
NONJOINDER
NONJURANCY
OUTJOURNEY
PANJANDRUM
PERJUREDLY
PERJURIOUS
PREJUDGING

PREJUDICED
PROJACIENT
PROJECTILE
PROJECTING
PROJECTION
PROJECTIVE
PROJECTRIX
PROJECTURE
PROJICIENT
SERJEANTRY
SKYJACKING
SUBJACENCY
SUBJECTIFY
SUBJECTILE
SUBJECTING
SUBJECTION
SUBJECTIVE

SUBJICIBLE
SUBJOINDER
SUBJOINING
SUBJUGABLE
SUBJUGATED
SUBJUGATOR
SUBJUGULAR
TRAJECTILE
TRAJECTING
TRAJECTION
TRAJECTORY

ARROJADITE
BLUEJACKET
CLAMJAMFRY
COADJACENT
COADJUMENT

COADJUTIVE
COADJUTRIX
COADJUVANT
EQUIJACENT
FIDEJUSSOR
FOREJUDGED
FOREJUDGER
FRABJOUSLY
HIGHJACKER
OTTAJANITE
POSTJACENT
READJUSTER
SKIPJACKLY
WEREJAGUAR
WINDJAMMER
WOODJOBBER

INCONJUNCT
INTERJOIST
NONABJURER
PREADJUNCT
SUPRAJURAL
UNDERJAWED

BUTTERJAGS
CRACKAJACK
LUMBERJACK
NATTERJACK
RATTLEJACK
SUPPLEJACK
TIMBERJACK

CHAPARAJOS
CHAPAREJOS

SCORING ORDER LIST OF 10-LETTER WORDS

31
OBJECTIZED

30
HIGHJACKER
JACKHAMMER
JAROVIZING
JOVIALIZED

29
CLAMJAMFRY
JACKFISHES
JASPERIZED
JEOPARDIZE
JOHNNYCAKE
REJUVENIZE

28
EQUIJACENT
JARGONIZED
JAYWALKING
PROJECTRIX

27
JUXTAPOSED
LUMBERJACK
SKIPJACKLY
SUBJECTIFY
SUPPLEJACK
TIMBERJACK

26
JACKASSERY
JANIZARIES
JAWBREAKER
JINRICKSHA
JOAQUINITE
JOGGLEWORK
JOURNALIZE
JUVENILIFY
JUXTAPOSIT
PERJINKETY
SKYJACKING
SUBJACENCY

25
BLUEJACKET
EJECTIVELY
EJECTIVITY
FRABJOUSLY
JACKANAPES
JACKKNIVES

JACKSNIPES
JAWCRUSHER
JEWELSMITH
JUDOPHOBIA
JUMPSCRAPE
WINDJAMMER
WOODJOBBER

24
ABJUNCTIVE
CHAPARAJOS
CHAPAREJOS
CONJECTIVE
CONJUNCTLY
DEJECTEDLY
JASPACHATE
JELLIFYING
JINRIKISHA
JOBBERNOWL
JOLLIFYING
JUSTIFYING
OBJECTIVAL
PROJECTIVE
SUBJECTIVE

23
ADJACENTLY
ADJECTIVAL
ADJUNCTIVE
BEJEWELING
BEJEWELLED
CAJOLINGLY
COADJUTIVE
COADJUVANT
CONJUGALLY
CRACKAJACK
ENJAMBMENT
ENJEOPARDY
FOREJUDGED
FORJUDGING
JABBERMENT
JABOTICABA
JAILKEEPER
JERRYBUILD
JEWELHOUSE
JIMPRICUTE
JINRIKIMAN
JINRIKIMEN
JOYFULNESS
JUDICATIVE
JUDICATORY
JUDICIALLY

JUGGLINGLY
JUMBLEMENT
JUVENILELY
JUVENILITY
NATTERJACK
OBJECTABLE
PERJUREDLY
PREJUDICED
RATTLEJACK
SUBJICIBLE

22
ABJUDICATE
ABJURATORY
ADJOINEDLY
COADJACENT
COADJUMENT
CONJOINTLY
CONJUGABLE
FOREJUDGER
INJUNCTIVE
JACULATIVE
JACULATORY
JAGHEERDAR
JAGHIREDAR
JAPISHNESS
JERRYBUILT
JINGLINGLY
JOCULARITY
JOCULATORY
JOLTHEADED
JOURNEYMAN
JOURNEYMEN
JUBILANTLY
JUBILATORY
JUDICIABLE
JUNGLEWOOD
JUNKDEALER
JUSTICIARY
JUVENILISM
MISJUDGING
NONJURANCY
PAJAHUELLO
PANJANDRUM
PEJORATIVE
PREADJUNCT
PREJUDGING
PROJECTING
REJOICEFUL
SEJUNCTIVE
SUBJECTING
SUBJUGABLE

TRAJECTORY
UNDERJAWED

21
ABJECTNESS
ABJUREMENT
ADJUDICATE
ADJURATORY
CAJOLEMENT
CAJUPUTENE
CONJECTURE
CONJUGATED
CONJUNCTUR
DIJUDICATE
DISJECTING
DISJOINTLY
FIDEJUSSOR
INCONJUNCT
JADISHNESS
JAPACONINE
JAUNDICING
JEJUNOTOMY
JEOPARDIED
JEOPARDING
JOLTERHEAD
JOURNEYING
JUGGLEMENT
JUNCACEOUS
JURAMENTUM
MAJESTICAL
MAJUSCULAE
MAJUSCULAR
OBJECTIONS
OBJECTLESS
OBJURGATED
POSTJACENT
PROJACIENT
PROJECTILE
PROJECTION
PROJECTURE
PROJICIENT
SUBJECTILE
SUBJECTION
SUBJUGATED
WEREJAGUAR

20
ADJUNCTION
ADJUSTABLE
ADJUSTMENT
BUTTERJAGS
COADJUTANT

CONJOINING
CONJUGATOR
DISJECTION
DISJUNCTOR
EJACULATED
INJUDICIAL
JACTITATED
JACULATING
JAGGEDNESS
JASPERATED
JASPIDEOUS
JAVELINEER
JEOPARDOUS
JINGOISTIC
JNANAMARGA
JOCUNDNESS
JOYOUSNESS
JUBILATING
JUDICATION
JUDICATURE
JURIDICIAL
MISJOINDER
OBJURGATOR
OUTJOURNEY
REJUVENANT
REJUVENATE
SERJEANTRY
SUBJOINDER
SUBJOINING
SUBJUGATOR
SUBJUGULAR
TRAJECTING

19
ABJURATION
BIJOUTERIE
CAJOLERIES
CONJURATOR
DISJOINING
DISJOINTED
EJACULATOR
ENJOINMENT
INJUNCTION
JACULATION
JAGUARONDI
JAGUARUNDI
JAMESONITE
JENTACULAR
JOCOSENESS
JOCOSITIES
JOSTLEMENT
JOUISSANCE

JOULEMETER
JOURNALISM
JUBILARIAN
JUBILATION
JUGGERNAUT
JUGGLERIES
JUGULATING
JUNCTIONAL
JUNGLESIDE
JURAMENTAL
JURISTICAL

MAJESTIOUS
MAJORATION
MAJORITIES
NONABJURER
OBJURATION
PAJAROELLO
PEJORATION
PERJURIOUS
REJUNCTION
SEJUNCTION
SUPRAJURAL

TRAJECTILE
TRAJECTION

18
ADJURATION
ARROJADITE
JARDINIERE
JARGONELLE
JOINTURING
JOURNALING
JOURNALLED

JUGULATION
JULOLIDINE
NONJOINDER
READJUSTER
REJONEADOR
SOJOURNING

17
INTERJOIST
JANITORIAL
JAUNTINESS

JEALOUSIES
JOINTURESS
JOURNALESE
JOURNALISE
JOURNALIST
JURATORIAL
OTTAJANITE
UNJUSTNESS

16
JEJUNENESS

ALPHABETICAL LIST OF WORDS OVER 10 LETTERS

ABJECTEDNESS
ABJUDICATION
ABJUDICATOR
ADJECTIONAL
ADJECTIVALLY
ADJECTIVELY
ADJOURNMENT
ADJUDICATED
ADJUDICATING
ADJUDICATION
ADJUDICATIVE
ADJUDICATOR
ADJUDICATURE
ADJUNCTIVELY
ADJUTANCIES
ADJUTANTSHIP
ADJUTORIOUS
BEJEWELLING
BENJAMINITE
BICONJUGATE
BRINJARRIES
CIRCUMJACENT
CLAMJAMFERY
CLAMJAMPHRIE
COADDJUVANCY
COADJACENCE
COADJACENTLY
COADJUTATOR
COADJUTEMENT
COADJUTRESS
COADJUTRICE
COADJUTRICES
CONJECTURAL
CONJECTURALLY
CONJECTURED
CONJECTURER
CONJECTURING
CONJOINTNESS
CONJUBILANT
CONJUGALITY
CONJUGATING
CONJUGATION
CONJUGATIVE
CONJUNCTION
CONJUNCTIVAE
CONJUNCTIVAL
CONJUNCTIVAS
CONJUNCTIVE
CONJUNCTIVELY
CONJUNCTURAL
CONJUNCTURE
CONJURATION
COPALJOCOTE
DEJECTEDNESS
DEJUNKERIZE
DIJUDICATION
DISJOINTEDLY
DISJOINTING
DISJOINTURE

DISJUNCTION
DISJUNCTIVE
DISJUNCTIVELY
DISJUNCTURE
EJACULATING
EJACULATION
EJACULATIVE
EJACULATORY
EJECTAMENTA
ENJAMBEMENT
ENJOYABLENESS
EXCONJUGANT
EXTRAJUDICIAL
FIDEJUSSION
FIDEJUSSORY
FOREJUDGING
GIMBALJAWED
GIMBERJAWED
GUANAJUATITE
IMPREJUDICE
INCONJOINABLE
INJUDICIALLY
INJUDICIOUS
INJUDICIOUSLY
INJUNCTIVELY
INJUREDNESS
INJURIOUSLY
INSUBJECTION
INTERJACENCE
INTERJACENT
INTERJECTED
INTERJECTING
INTERJECTION
INTERJECTOR
INTERJECTORY
INTERJUNCTION
INTROJECTION
JABBERINGLY
JACAMEROPINE
JACKPUDDING
JACTITATING
JACTITATION
JACULATORIAL
JACULIFEROUS
JAPACONITIN
JAPACONITINE
JARARACUSSU
JARGONIZING
JARGONNELLE
JAROVIZATION
JASMINEWOOD
JASPERIZING
JATEORHIZIN
JATEORHIZINE
JAUNDICEROOT
JAWBREAKING
JAWBREAKINGLY
JEALOUSNESS
JEFFERISITE

JEFFERSONITE
JEJUNOSTOMY
JELLIEDNESS
JELLIFICATION
JELLYFISHES
JEOPARDIOUS
JEOPARDIZED
JEOPARDIZING
JEOPARDOUSLY
JEOPARDYING
JEQUIRITIES
JERRYBUILDING
JESTINGSTOCK
JIMBERJAWED
JINGLEJANGLE
JNANASHAKTI
JNANENDRIYA
JOBLESSNESS
JOBMISTRESS
JOCOSERIOUS
JOCULARNESS
JOCUNDITIES
JOGTROTTISM
JOHNSTRUPITE
JOINTEDNESS
JOKESOMENESS
JOLLIFICATION
JOLTERHEADED
JOSEPHINITE
JOURNALISTIC
JOURNALIZED
JOURNALIZER
JOURNALIZING
JOURNALLING
JOURNEYCAKE
JOURNEYWOMAN
JOURNEYWOMEN
JOURNEYWORK
JOVIALISTIC
JOVIALIZING
JOVIALNESS
JOYLESSNESS
JUBILIZATION
JUDGMATICAL
JUDICATORIAL
JUDICATORIES
JUDICIALITY
JUDICIALIZE
JUDICIARIES
JUDICIARILY
JUDICIOUSLY
JUDICIOUSNESS
JURAMENTADO
JURAMENTALLY
JURIDICALLY
JURISCONSULT
JURISDICTION
JURISDICTIVE
JURISPRUDENCE

JURISPRUDENT
JURISTICALLY
JUSTAUCORPS
JUSTICEHOOD
JUSTICESHIP
JUSTICEWEED
JUSTICIABLE
JUSTIFIABLE
JUSTIFIABLY
JUSTIFICATION
JUSTIFICATIVE
JUSTIFICATOR
JUSTIFYINGLY
JUVENESCENCE
JUVENESCENT
JUVENILENESS
JUVENILITIES
JUXTAMARINE
JUXTAPOSING
JUXTAPOSITION
JUXTAPYLORIC
JUXTASPINAL
KATJEPIERING
KATZENJAMMER
KJELDAHLIZE
LEATHERJACKET
LUMBERJACKET
MAHARAJRANA
MAJESTICALLY
MALADJUSTED
MALADJUSTMENT
MISJUDGEMENT
MISJUDGINGLY
MISJUDGMENT
NATROJAROSITE
NONADJUSTIVE
NONDISJUNCT
NONJURANTISM
NONOBJECTIVE
OBJECTATION
OBJECTATIVE
OBJECTIFIED
OBJECTIFYING
OBJECTIONABLE
OBJECTIONABLY
OBJECTIONAL
OBJECTIONER
OBJECTIONIST
OBJECTIVATE
OBJECTIVATED
OBJECTIVATING
OBJECTIVATION
OBJECTIVELY
OBJECTIVENESS
OBJECTIVISM
OBJECTIVIST
OBJECTIVISTIC
OBJECTIVITY
OBJECTIVIZE

OBJECTIVIZED
OBJECTIVIZING
OBJECTIZATION
OBJECTIZING
OBJURGATING
OBJURGATION
OBJURGATIVE
OBJURGATIVELY
OBJURGATORILY
OBJURGATORY
OBJURGATRIX
PARIETOJUGAL
PAUCIJUGATE
PEJORATIVELY
PEREJONETTE
PERJINKITIES
PERJUREDNESS
PERJURIOUSLY
POSTADJUNCT
PREJUDGEMENT
PREJUDGMENT
PREJUDICATE
PREJUDICATOR
PREJUDICEDLY
PREJUDICIAL
PREJUDICING
PREJUDICIOUS
PROJECTEDLY
PROJECTINGLY
PROJECTIONAL
PROJECTIVITY
PROJICIENCE
PROJICIENTLY
READJUSTABLE
READJUSTMENT
REJECTAMENTA
REJOICEMENT
REJUVENATED
REJUVENATING
REJUVENATION
REJUVENATIVE
REJUVENATOR
REJUVENESCE
RETROJECTION
RETROJUGULAR
RUBIJERVINE
SEJUNCTIVELY
SEMIJUBILEE
SMOKEJUMPER
SOJOURNMENT
STEEPLEJACK
STOCKJOBBER
STOCKJOBBERY
STOCKJOBBING
STOCKJUDGING
STOLKJAERRE
STRAITJACKET
SUBJECTEDLY
SUBJECTEDNESS

SUBJECTIONAL SUBJUGATING SUBTERJACENT TRAJECTORIES UNPREJUDICE
SUBJECTIVELY SUBJUGATION SUPERJACENT TRONDHJEMITE UNPREJUDICED
SUBJECTIVISM SUBJUNCTION SURREJOINDER UNBEJUGGLED WINDJAMMING
SUBJECTIVIST SUBJUNCTIVE THINGAMAJIG UNJUDICIOUS YAJNOPAVITA
SUBJECTIVITY SUBJUNCTIVELY THINGUMAJIG UNJUSTIFIED

POSITIONAL ORDER LIST OF WORDS OVER 10 LETTERS

JABBERINGLY JUDICATORIES ENJOYABLENESS CONJUGATIVE READJUSTABLE
JACAMEROPINE JUDICIALITY INJUDICIALLY CONJUNCTION READJUSTMENT
JACKPUDDING JUDICIALIZE INJUDICIOUS CONJUNCTIVAE SEMIJUBILEE
JACTITATING JUDICIARIES INJUDICIOUSLY CONJUNCTIVAL UNBEJUGGLED
JACTITATION JUDICIARILY INJUNCTIVELY CONJUNCTIVAS
JACULATORIAL JUDICIOUSLY INJUREDNESS CONJUNCTIVE WINDJAMMING
JACULIFEROUS JUDICIOUSNESS INJURIOUSLY CONJUNCTIVELY
JAPACONITIN JURAMENTADO MAJESTICALLY CONJUNCTURAL BICONJUGATE
JAPACONITINE JURAMENTALLY OBJECTATION CONJUNCTURE COADDJUVANCY
JARARACUSSU JURIDICALLY OBJECTATIVE CONJURATION COPALJOCOTE
JARGONIZING JURISCONSULT OBJECTIFIED DISJOINTEDLY EXCONJUGANT
JARGONNELLE JURISDICTION OBJECTIFYING DISJOINTING EXTRAJUDICIAL
JAROVIZATION JURISDICTIVE OBJECTIONABLE DISJOINTURE GUANAJUATITE
JASMINEWOOD JURISPRUDENCE OBJECTIONABLY DISJUNCTION IMPREJUDICE
JASPERIZING JURISPRUDENT OBJECTIONAL DISJUNCTIVE INCONJOINABLE
JATEORHIZIN JURISTICALLY OBJECTIONER DISJUNCTIVELY INSUBJECTION
JATEORHIZINE JUSTAUCORPS OBJECTIONIST DISJUNCTURE INTERJACENCE
JAUNDICEROOT JUSTICEHOOD OBJECTIVATE KATJEPIERING INTERJACENT
JAWBREAKING JUSTICESHIP OBJECTIVATED MISJUDGEMENT INTERJECTED
JAWBREAKINGLY JUSTICEWEED OBJECTIVATING MISJUDGINGLY INTERJECTING
JEALOUSNESS JUSTICIABLE OBJECTIVATION MISJUDGMENT INTERJECTION
JEFFERISITE JUSTIFIABLE OBJECTIVELY NONJURANTISM INTERJECTOR
JEFFERSONITE JUSTIFIABLY OBJECTIVENESS PERJINKITIES INTERJECTORY
JEJUNOSTOMY JUSTIFICATION OBJECTIVISM PERJUREDNESS INTERJUNCTION
JELLIEDNESS JUSTIFICATIVE OBJECTIVIST PERJURIOUSLY INTROJECTION
JELLIFICATION JUSTIFICATOR OBJECTIVISTIC PREJUDGEMENT MALADJUSTED
JELLYFISHES JUSTIFYINGLY OBJECTIVITY PREJUDGMENT MALADJUSTMENT
JEOPARDIOUS JUVENESCENCE OBJECTIVIZE PREJUDICATE NATROJAROSITE
JEOPARDIZED JUVENESCENT OBJECTIVIZED PREJUDICATOR NONADJUSTIVE
JEOPARDIZING JUVENILENESS OBJECTIVIZING PREJUDICEDLY NONOBJECTIVE
JEOPARDOUSLY JUVENILITIES OBJECTIZATION PREJUDICIAL PAUCIJUGATE
JEOPARDYING JUXTAMARINE OBJECTIZING PREJUDICING RETROJECTION
JEQUIRITIES JUXTAPOSING OBJURGATING PREJUDICIOUS RETROJUGULAR
JERRYBUILDING JUXTAPOSITION OBJURGATION PROJECTEDLY RUBIJERVINE
JESTINGSTOCK JUXTAPYLORIC OBJURGATIVE PROJECTINGLY SMOKEJUMPER
JIMBERJAWED JUXTASPINAL OBJURGATIVELY PROJECTIONAL STOCKJOBBER
JINGLEJANGLE OBJURGATORILY PROJECTIVITY STOCKJOBBERY
JNANASHAKTI EJACULATING OBJURGATORY PROJICIENCE STOCKJOBBING
JNANENDRIYA EJACULATION OBJURGATRIX PROJICIENTLY STOCKJUDGING
JOBLESSNESS EJACULATIVE PEJORATIVELY SUBJECTEDLY STOLKJAERRE
JOBMISTRESS EJACULATORY REJECTAMENTA SUBJECTEDNESS SUPERJACENT
JOCOSERIOUS EJECTAMENTA REJOICEMENT SUBJECTIONAL SURREJOINDER
JOCULARNESS JEJUNOSTOMY REJUVENATED SUBJECTIVELY UNPREJUDICE
JOCUNDITIES KJELDAHLIZE REJUVENATING SUBJECTIVISM UNPREJUDICED
JOGTROTTISM REJUVENATION SUBJECTIVIST
JOHNSTRUPITE ABJECTEDNESS REJUVENATIVE SUBJECTIVITY CIRCUMJACENT
JOINTEDNESS ABJUDICATION REJUVENATOR SUBJUGATING GIMBALJAWED
JOKESOMENESS ABJUDICATOR REJUVENESCE SUBJUGATION GIMBERJAWED
JOLLIFICATION ADJECTIONAL SEJUNCTIVELY SUBJUNCTION JIMBERJAWED
JOLTERHEADED ADJECTIVALLY SOJOURNMENT SUBJUNCTIVE JINGLEJANGLE
JOSEPHINITE ADJECTIVELY UNJUDICIOUS SUBJUNCTIVELY KATZENJAMMER
JOURNALISTIC ADJOURNMENT UNJUSTIFIED TRAJECTORIES LUMBERJACKET
JOURNALIZED ADJUDICATED YAJNOPAVITA MAHARAJRANA
JOURNALIZER ADJUDICATING BRINJARRIES NONDISJUNCT
JOURNALIZING ADJUDICATION BENJAMINITE CLAMJAMFERY POSTADJUNCT
JOURNALLING ADJUDICATIVE CAODJACENCY CLAMJAMPHRIE STRAITJACKET
JOURNEYCAKE ADJUDICATOR CONJECTURAL COADJACENCE SUBTERJACENT
JOURNEYWOMAN ADJUDICATURE CONJECTURALLY COADJACENTLY TRONDHJEMITE
JOURNEYWOMEN ADJUNCTIVELY CONJECTURE COADJUTATOR
JOURNEYWORK ADJUTANCIES CONJECTURED COADJUTEMENT LEATHERJACKET
JOVIALISTIC ADJUTANTSHIP CONJECTURER COADJUTRESS PARIETOJUGAL
JOVIALIZING ADJUTORIUS CONJECTURING COADJUTRICE STEEPLEJACK
JOVIALNESS BEJEWELLING CONJOINTNESS COADJUTRICES
JOYLESSNESS DEJECTEDNESS CONJUBILANT FIDEJUSSION THINGAMAJIG
JUBILIZATION DEJUNKERIZE CONJUGALITY FIDEJUSSORY THINGUMAJIG
JUDGMATICAL DIJUDICATION CONJUGATING FOREJUDGING
JUDICATORIAL ENJAMBEMENT CONJUGATION PEREJONETTE

SCORING ORDER LIST OF WORDS OVER 10 LETTERS

37
OBJECTIVIZING

36
KATZENJAMMER
OBJECTIVIZED

35
KJELDAHLIZE

34
OBJECTIVIZE

33
JAWBREAKINGLY
JUXTAPYLORIC
OBJECTIZATION

32
DEJUNKERIZE
JEOPARDIZING
OBJECTIZING
STOCKJOBBERY

31
COADDJUVANCY
JAROVIZATION
JATEORHIZINE
JEOPARDIZED
JOVIALIZING

30
CLAMJAMFERY
CLAMJAMPHRIE
CONJUNCTIVELY
EXTRAJUDICIAL
JASPERIZING
JATEORHIZIN
JUBILIZATION
JUDICIALIZE
OBJECTIFYING
STOCKJOBBING
SUBJUNCTIVELY

29
DISJUNCTIVELY
JACKPUDDING
JARGONIZING
JOURNALIZING
JUSTIFYINGLY
JUXTAPOSITION
LEATHERJACKET
LUMBERJACKET
OBJECTIONABLY
OBJECTIVISTIC
OBJURGATIVELY
PROJECTIVITY
SUBJECTIVELY
SUBJECTIVITY

28
ADJECTIVALLY
ADJUNCTIVELY
EXCONJUGANT
JAWBREAKING
JOURNALIZED
JOURNEYWORK
JUSTIFICATIVE
JUXTAPOSING
OBJECTIVATING
OBJECTIVELY

OBJECTIVITY
OBJURGATRIX
PREJUDICEDLY
SMOKEJUMPER
STOCKJOBBER
STOCKJUDGING
SUBJECTIVISM

27
ADJECTIVELY
COADJACENTLY
CONJECTURALLY
GIMBALJAWED
GIMBERJAWED
INJUNCTIVELY
JELLYFISHES
JEQUIRITIES
JERRYBUILDING
JOURNALIZER
JOURNEYCAKE
JOURNEYWOMAN
JOURNEYWOMEN
JUXTASPINAL
MISJUDGINGLY
OBJECTIVATED
OBJECTIVATION
OBJECTIVENESS
OBJECTIVISM
PEJORATIVELY
PROJECTINGLY
SEJUNCTIVELY
WINDJAMMING

26
ADJUDICATIVE
CONJUNCTIVAE
CONJUNCTIVAL
CONJUNCTIVAS
INJUDICIOUSLY
JABBERINGLY
JESTINGSTOCK
JUSTIFIABLY
JUVENESCENCE
KATJEPIERING
MAJESTICALLY
NONOBJECTIVE
OBJECTIFIED
OBJECTIONABLE
OBJURGATORILY
PROJECTEDLY
PROJICIENTLY
STEEPLEJACK
SUBJECTEDLY
SUBJECTIVIST
YAJNOPAVITA

25
ADJUTANTSHIP
CAODJACENCY
CONJUNCTIVE
ENJOYABLENESS
FIDEJUSSORY
IMPREJUDICE
INJUDICIALLY
JACAMEROPINE
JEFFERSONITE
JELLIFICATION
JEOPARDOUSLY
JEOPARDYING
JIMBERJAWED
JNANASHAKTI

JOKESOMENESS
JOLLIFICATION
JURISDICTIVE
JURISPRUDENCE
JUSTICESHIP
JUSTIFICATION
MALADJUSTMENT
MISJUDGEMENT
OBJECTATIVE
OBJECTIVATE
OBJECTIVIST
PERJINKITIES
PREJUDGEMENT
REJUVENATIVE
STRAITJACKET
SUBJECTEDNESS
SUBJUNCTIVE
THINGAMAJIG
THINGUMAJIG
TRONDHJEMITE
UNPREJUDICED

24
ABJECTEDNESS
ABJUDICATION
ADJUDICATING
BEJEWELLING
CIRCUMJACENT
COADJUTEMENT
COADJUTRICES
CONJECTURING
CONJUGALITY
CONJUGATIVE
COPALJOCOTE
DISJOINTEDLY
DISJUNCTIVE
ENJAMBEMENT
FOREJUDGING
INCONJOINABLE
INTERJECTORY
JACULIFEROUS
JASMINEWOOD
JEFFERISITE
JOHNSTRUPITE
JOLTERHEADED
JUDGMATICAL
JUDICIALITY
JUDICIARILY
JUDICIOUSLY
JURAMENTALLY
JURIDICALLY
JURISTICALLY
JUSTICEHOOD
JUSTICEWEED
JUSTIFICATOR
MISJUDGMENT
OBJURGATIVE
OBJURGATORY
PERJURIOUSLY
PREJUDGMENT
PREJUDICATOR
PREJUDICING
PREJUDICIOUS
PROJICIENCE

23
ABJUDICATOR
ADJUDICATED
ADJUDICATION
ADJUDICATURE
BICONJUGATE

COADJUTRICE
CONJECTURED
CONJUNCTURAL
DEJECTEDNESS
DIJUDICATION
EJACULATIVE
EJACULATORY
INSUBJECTION
INTERJACENCE
JAPACONITINE
JOSEPHINITE
JOVIALISTIC
JUDICIOUSNESS
JUSTIFIABLE
JUVENESCENT
MAHARAJRANA
NONADJUSTIVE
OBJECTIONIST
PAUCIJUGATE
POSTADJUNCT
PREJUDICATE
PREJUDICIAL
PROJECTIONAL
REJECTAMENTA
REJUVENATING
REJUVENESCE
RUBIJERVINE
SUBJECTIONAL
SUBTERJACENT
UNBEJUGGLED
UNPREJUDICE

22
ADJUDICATOR
BENJAMINITE
COADJACENCE
CONJECTURAL
CONJECTURER
CONJUBILANT
CONJUGATING
CONJUNCTION
CONJUNCTURE
EJECTAMENTA
FIDEJUSSION
INTERJECTING
INTERJUNCTION
JAPACONITIN
JAUNDICEROOT
JEJUNOSTOMY
JNANENDRIYA
JOBMISTRESS
JUDICATORIAL
JUDICATORIES
JURISDICTION
JURISPRUDENT
JUSTAUCORPS
JUSTICIABLE
JUVENILENESS
JUVENILITIES
MALADJUSTED
OBJECTATION
OBJECTIONAL
OBJECTIONER
OBJURGATING
PARIETOJUGAL
PERJUREDNESS
READJUSTABLE
READJUSTMENT
REJOICEMENT
REJUVENATED
REJUVENATION
SEMIJUBILEE

STOLKJAERRE
SUBJUGATING
SUBJUNCTION
SUPERJACENT
UNJUSTIFIED

21
ADJECTIONAL
ADJOURNMENT
ADJUTANCIES
COADJUTATOR
COADJUTRESS
CONJOINTNESS
CONJUGATION
DISJUNCTION
DISJUNCTURE
EJACULATING
INJUDICIOUS
INJURIOUSLY
INTERJECTED
INTERJECTION
INTRODUCTION
JACTITATING
JACULATORIAL
JEOPARDIOUS
JOCUNDITIES
JOGTROTTISM
JOURNALISTIC
JOYLESSNESS
JUDICIARIES
JURAMENTADO
JURISCONSULT
NONDISJUNCT
NONJURANTISM
OBJURGATION
REJUVENATOR
RETROJECTION
SUBJUGATION
TRAJECTORIES
UNJUDICIOUS

20
BRINJARRIES
CONJURATION
DISJOINTING
EJACULATION
GUANAJUATITE
INTERJACENT
INTERJECTOR
JACTITATION
JARARACUSSU
JINGLEJANGLE
JOBLESSNESS
JOCOSERIOUS
JOCULARNESS
JOVIALNESS
NATROJAROSITE
PEREJONETTE
RETROJUGULAR
SOJOURNMENT
SURREJOINDER

19
ADJUTORIOUS
DISJOINTURE
INJUREDNESS
JARGONNELLE
JELLIEDNESS
JOINTEDNESS
JOURNALLING

18
JEALOUSNESS

High-Scoring Words Containing

2-3 LETTER WORDS

ALPHABETICAL LIST OF 4-LETTER WORDS

AQUA	QUAB	QUAW	QUIB	QUOD
AQUO	QUAD	QUAX	QUID	QUOG
CINQ	QUAG	QUAY	QUIM	QUOP
OQUE	QUAI	QUED	QUIN	QUOT
OQUI	QUAN	QUEE	QUIP	QUOY
QADI	QUAP	QUEI	QUIS	QUOZ
QAID	QUAR	QUET	QUIT	SHOQ
QERI	QUAS	QUEY	QUIZ	WAQF
QUAA	QUAT			

POSITIONAL ORDER LIST OF 4-LETTER WORDS

QADI	QUAP	QUEI	QUIT	AQUA
QAID	QUAR	QUET	QUIZ	AQUO
QERI	QUAS	QUEY	QUOD	OQUE
QUAA	QUAT	QUIB	QUOG	OQUI
QUAB	QUAW	QUID	QUOP	
QUAD	QUAX	QUIM	QUOT	WAQF
QUAG	QUAY	QUIN	QUOY	
QUAI	QUED	QUIP	QUOZ	CINQ
QUAN	QUEE	QUIS		SHOQ

SCORING ORDER LIST OF 4-LETTER WORDS

22	QUAY	QUOP	**13**	QUEE
QUIZ	QUEY		AQUA	QUEI
QUOZ	QUOY		AQUO	QUET
	SHOQ	**14**	OQUE	QUIN
20		QADI	OQUI	QUIS
QUAX	**15**	QAID	QERI	QUIT
	CINQ	QUAD	QUAA	QUOT
19	QUAB	QUAG	QUAI	
WAQF	QUAP	QUED	QUAN	
	QUIB	QUID	QUAR	
16	QUIM	QUOD	QUAS	
QUAW	QUIP	QUOG	QUAT	

ALPHABETICAL LIST OF 5-LETTER WORDS

AQUAE	QIBLA	QUASS	QUEST	QUIRT
AQUAS	QINAH	QUATE	QUEUE	QUIST
BEQAA	QIYAS	QUAWK	QUICA	QUITE
BULAQ	QOBAR	QUEAK	QUICK	QUITS
CEQUI	QUACK	QUEAL	QUIET	QUOAD
COQUE	QUADE	QUEAN	QUIFF	QUOCK
EQUAL	QUAFF	QUECH	QUILA	QUOIN
EQUES	QUAIL	QUEDE	QUILE	QUOIT
EQUID	QUAIR	QUEED	QUILK	QUONK
EQUIP	QUAIS	QUEEL	QUILL	QUOTA
FAQIH	QUAKE	QUEEN	QUILT	QUOTE
JIQUE	QUAKY	QUEER	QUINA	QUOTH
JIQUI	QUALE	QUEET	QUINE	QUOTT
MAQUI	QUALM	QUELL	QUINK	QUYTE
MIQRA	QUANT	QUELT	QUINT	ROQUE
NUQUE	QUARE	QUEME	QUIPO	SEQUA
OCQUE	QUARK	QUENA	QUIPU	SQUAB
PIQUE	QUARL	QUENT	QUIRA	SQUAD
QANEH	QUART	QUERL	QUIRE	SQUAM
QASAB	QUASH	QUERN	QUIRK	SQUAP
QAZAQ	QUASI	QUERY	QUIRL	SQUAT

SQUAW	SQUIB	SQUIR	SQUSH	TUQUE
SQUEG	SQUID	SQUIT	TOQUE	USQUE
SQUET	SQUIN	SQUIZ	TRINQ	

POSITIONAL ORDER LIST OF 5-LETTER WORDS

QANEH	QUATE	QUIFF	QUOTA	SQUIT
QASAB	QUAWK	QUILA	QUOTE	SQUIZ
QAZAQ	QUEAK	QUILE	QUOTH	SQUSH
QIBLA	QUEAL	QUILK	QUOTT	
QINAH	QUEAN	QUILL	QUYTE	BEQAA
QIYAS	QUECH	QUILT		CEQUI
QOBAR	QUEDE	QUINA	AQUAE	COQUE
QUACK	QUEED	QUINE	AQUAS	FAQIH
QUADE	QUEEL	QUINK	EQUAL	JIQUE
QUAFF	QUEEN	QUINT	EQUES	JIQUI
QUAIL	QUEER	QUIPO	EQUID	MAQUI
QUAIR	QUEET	QUIPU	EQUIP	MIQRA
QUAIS	QUELL	QUIRA	SQUAB	NUQUE
QUAKE	QUELT	QUIRE	SQUAD	OCQUE
QUAKY	QUEME	QUIRK	SQUAM	PIQUE
QUALE	QUENA	QUIRL	SQUAP	ROQUE
QUALM	QUENT	QUIRT	SQUAT	SEQUA
QUANT	QUERL	QUIST	SQUAW	TOQUE
QUARE	QUERN	QUITE	SQUEG	TUQUE
QUARK	QUERY	QUITS	SQUET	USQUE
QUARL	QUEST	QUOAD	SQUIB	
QUART	QUEUE	QUOCK	SQUID	BULAQ
QUASH	QUICA	QUOIN	SQUIN	QAZAQ
QUASI	QUICK	QUOIT	SQUIR	TRINQ
QUASS	QUIET	QUONK		

SCORING ORDER LIST OF 5-LETTER WORDS

23	QUINK	QUALM	QUAIS	QUINA
SQUIZ	QUIRK	QUEME	QUALE	QUINE
	QUONK	QUICA	QUANT	QUINT
22		QUIPO	QUARE	QUIRA
QAZAQ	**17**	QUIPU	QUARL	QUIRE
	QANEH	SQUAB	QUART	QUIRL
21	QINAH	SQUAM	QUASI	QUIRT
JIQUE	QIYAS	SQUAP	QUASS	QUIST
JIQUI	QUASH	SQUIB	QUATE	QUITE
QUAKY	QUERY		QUEAL	QUITS
QUAWK	QUOTH	**15**	QUEAN	QUOIN
	QUYTE	EQUID	QUEEL	QUOIT
20	SQUAW	QUADE	QUEEN	QUOTA
FAQIH	SQUSH	QUEDE	QUEER	QUOTE
QUACK		QUEED	QUEET	QUOTT
QUAFF	**16**	QUOAD	QUELL	ROQUE
QUICK	BEQAA	SQUAD	QUELT	SEQUA
QUIFF	BULAQ	SQUEG	QUENA	SQUAT
QUOCK	CEQUI	SQUID	QUENT	SQUET
	COQUE		QUERL	SQUIN
19	EQUIP	**14**	QUERN	SQUIR
QUECH	MAQUI	AQUAE	QUEST	SQUIT
	MIQRA	AQUAS	QUEUE	TOQUE
18	OCQUE	EQUAL	QUIET	TRINQ
QUAKE	PIQUE	EQUES	QUILA	TUQUE
QUARK	QASAB	NUQUE	QUILE	USQUE
QUEAK	QIBLA	QUAIL	QUILL	
QUILK	QOBAR	QUAIR	QUILT	

ALPHABETICAL LIST OF 6-LETTER WORDS

ACQUIT	MAQUIS	QUASHY	QUINSY	SQUARE
AEQUOR	MARQUE	QUASKY	QUINTA	SQUARK
ANAQUA	MASQUE	QUATCH	QUINTE	SQUARY
AQUAGE	MOSQUE	QUATRE	QUINTO	SQUASH
AQUATE	NAIQUE	QUATTY	QUINYL	SQUAWK
AQUILA	OPAQUE	QUAVER	QUINZE	SQUAWL
AQUOSE	PIQUED	QUAYED	QUIPPE	SQUDGE
ASQUAT	PIQUET	QUEACH	QUIPPU	SQUDGY
BANQUE	PIQUIA	QUEASE	QUIPPY	SQUEAK
BARQUE	PIQURE	QUEASY	QUIPUS	SQUEAL
BASQUE	PLAQUE	QUEDLY	QUIRED	SQUEAM
BISQUE	PULQUE	QUEENS	QUIRKY	SQUEEF
BOSQUE	QANTAR	QUEERY	QUISBY	SQUEEL
BRIQUE	QUACKY	QUEEST	QUITCH	SQUIDS
CAIQUE	QUADER	QUEEVE	QUIVER	SQUILL
CALQUE	QUADLE	QUELCH	QUIZZY	SQUINT
CASQUE	QUADRA	QUELME	QUOITS	SQUIRE
CHEQUE	QUAERE	QUENCH	QUOKKA	SQUIRK
CINQUE	QUAGGA	QUENDA	QUORUM	SQUIRL
CIRQUE	QUAGGY	QUERRE	QUOTAS	SQUIRM
CLAQUE	QUAHOG	QUESAL	QUOTED	SQUIRR
CLIQUE	QUAICH	QUETCH	QUOTEE	SQUIRT
CLIQUY	QUAIFE	QUETHE	QUOTER	SQUISH
COQUET	QUAIGH	QUEZAL	QUOTHA	SQUISS
COQUIN	QUAILY	QUIAPO	QUOTUM	SQUSHY
EQUANT	QUAINT	QUIDAM	RAQUET	SQUUSH
EQUATE	QUAKED	QUILES	REQUIN	TAQIYA
EQUINE	QUAKER	QUILEZ	RISQUE	TAQLID
EQUIPT	QUALIA	QUILLY	ROQUET	TARIQA
EQUITY	QUALLY	QUINAS	SACQUE	TOQUET
EQUOID	QUALMY	QUINCE	SAUQUI	TORQUE
EVEQUE	QUANDY	QUINCH	SECQUE	UBIQUE
EXEQUY	QUANTA	QUINET	SEQUEL	UNIQUE
FAQUIR	QUARLE	QUINIA	SEQUIN	UNQUIT
JERQUE	QUARRY	QUINIC	SESQUI	UNQUOD
LASQUE	QUARTA	QUININ	SQUAIL	XARQUE
LIQUET	QUARTE	QUINOA	SQUALL	YANQUI
LIQUID	QUARTO	QUINOL	SQUAMA	YAQONA
LIQUOR	QUARTZ	QUINON	SQUAME	ZEQUIN
LOQUAT	QUASAR	QUINSE	SQUAMY	ZINDIQ
MANQUE				

POSITIONAL ORDER LIST OF 6-LETTER WORDS

QANTAR	QUASAR	QUILES	QUITCH	SQUAMY
QUACKY	QUASHY	QUILEZ	QUIZZY	SQUARE
QUADER	QUASKY	QUILLY	QUIVER	SQUARK
QUADLE	QUATCH	QUINAS	QUOITS	SQUARY
QUADRA	QUATRE	QUINCE	QUOKKA	SQUASH
QUAERE	QUATTY	QUINCH	QUORUM	SQUAWK
QUAGGA	QUAVER	QUINET	QUOTAS	SQUAWL
QUAGGY	QUAYED	QUINIA	QUOTED	SQUDGE
QUAHOG	QUEACH	QUINIC	QUOTEE	SQUDGY
QUAICH	QUEASE	QUININ	QUOTER	SQUEAK
QUAIFE	QUEASY	QUINOA	QUOTHA	SQUEAL
QUAIGH	QUEDLY	QUINOL	QUOTUM	SQUEAM
QUAILY	QUEENS	QUINON		SQUEEF
QUAINT	QUEERY	QUINSE		SQUEEL
QUAKED	QUEEST	QUINSY	AQUAGE	SQUIDS
QUAKER	QUEEVE	QUINTA	AQUATE	SQUILL
QUALIA	QUELCH	QUINTE	AQUILA	SQUINT
QUALLY	QUELME	QUINTO	AQUOSE	SQUIRE
QUALMY	QUENCH	QUINYL	EQUANT	SQUIRK
QUANDY	QUENDA	QUINZE	EQUATE	SQUIRL
QUANTA	QUERRE	QUIPPE	EQUINE	SQUIRM
QUARLE	QUESAL	QUIPPU	EQUIPT	SQUIRR
QUARRY	QUETCH	QUIPPY	EQUITY	SQUIRT
QUARTA	QUETHE	QUIPUS	EQUOID	SQUISH
QUARTE	QUEZAL	QUIRED	SQUAIL	SQUISS
QUARTO	QUIAPO	QUIRKY	SQUALL	SQUSHY
QUARTZ	QUIDAM	QUISBY	SQUAMA	SQUUSH
			SQUAME	

ACQUIT	PIQURE	ANAQUA	CLIQUE	RISQUE
AEQUOR	RAQUET	BANQUE	CLIQUY	SACQUE
ASQUAT	REQUIN	BARQUE	EVEQUE	SAUQUI
COQUET	ROQUET	BASQUE	EXEQUY	SECQUE
COQUIN	SEQUEL	BISQUE	JERQUE	SESQUI
FAQUIR	SEQUIN	BOSQUE	LASQUE	TORQUE
LIQUET	TAQIYA	BRIQUE	MANQUE	UBIQUE
LIQUID	TAQLID	CAIQUE	MARQUE	UNIQUE
LIQUOR	TOQUET	CALQUE	MASQUE	XARQUE
LOQUAT	UNQUIT	CASQUE	MOSQUE	YANQUI
MAQUIS	UNQUOD	CHEQUE	NAIQUE	
PIQUED	YAQONA	CINQUE	OPAQUE	TARIQA
PIQUET	ZEQUIN	CIRQUE	PLAQUE	
PIQUIA		CLAQUE	PULQUE	ZINDIQ

SCORING ORDER LIST OF 6-LETTER WORDS

26	**19**	**17**	UBIQUE	QUEEST
QUIZZY	QUAHOG	ACQUIT		QUERRE
	QUAIGH	BANQUE	**16**	QUESAL
25	QUAKER	BARQUE	AQUAGE	QUILES
EXEQUY	QUANDY	BASQUE	EQUOID	QUINAS
ZINDIQ	QUAYED	BISQUE	LIQUID	QUINET
	QUEDLY	BOSQUE	QUADER	QUINIA
24	QUIPPE	BRIQUE	QUADLE	QUININ
QUACKY	QUIPPU	CAIQUE	QUADRA	QU!NOA
QUARTZ	SQUARK	CALQUE	QUENDA	QUINOL
QUEZAL	SQUEAK	CASQUE	QUIRED	QUINON
QUILEZ	SQUIRK	CINQUE	QUOTED	QUINSE
QUINZE		CIRQUE	SQUIDS	QUINTA
ZEQUIN	**18**	CLAQUE	TAQLID	QUINTE
	EQUITY	CLIQUE	UNQUOD	QUINTO
22	EVEQUE	COQUET		QUOITS
JERQUE	FAQUIR	COQUIN	**15**	QUOTAS
QUASKY	PIQUED	EQUIPT	AEQUOR	QUOTEE
QUIPPY	QUAIFE	MANQUE	ANAQUA	QUOTER
QUIRKY	QUAILY	MAQUIS	AQUATE	RAQUET
SQUAWK	QUALLY	MARQUE	AQUILA	REQUIN
XARQUE	QUARRY	MASQUE	AQUOSE	RISQUE
	QUATTY	MOSQUE	ASQUAT	ROQUET
21	QUAVER	OPAQUE	EQUANT	SAUQUI
QUASHY	QUEASY	PIQUET	EQUATE	SEQUEL
SQUSHY	QUEERY	PIQUIA	EQUINE	SEQUIN
	QUEEVE	PIQURE	LASQUE	SESQUI
20	QUETHE	PLAQUE	LIQUET	SQUAIL
CHEQUE	QUIDAM	PULQUE	LIQUOR	SQUALL
CLIQUY	QUILLY	QUAGGA	LOQUAT	SQUARE
QUAGGY	QUINSY	QUELME	NAIQUE	SQUEAL
QUAICH	QUINYL	QUIAPO	QANTAR	SQUEEL
QUAKED	QUIVER	QUINCE	QUAERE	SQUILL
QUALMY	QUOKKA	QUINIC	QUAINT	SQUINT
QUATCH	QUOTHA	QUIPUS	QUALIA	SQUIRE
QUEACH	SQUARY	QUORUM	QUANTA	SQUIRL
QUELCH	SQUASH	QUOTUM	QUARLE	SQUIRR
QUENCH	SQUAWL	SACQUE	QUARTA	SQUIRT
QUETCH	SQUEEF	SECQUE	QUARTE	SQUISS
QUINCH	SQUISH	SQUAMA	QUARTO	TARIQA
QUISBY	SQUUSH	SQUAME	QUASAR	TOQUET
QUITCH	TAQIYA	SQUDGE	QUATRE	TORQUE
SQUAMY	YANQUI	SQUEAM	QUEASE	UNIQUE
SQUDGY	YAQONA	SQUIRM	QUEENS	UNQUIT

ALPHABETICAL LIST OF 7-LETTER WORDS

ACEQUIA	ACQUIRE	ALIQUID	ANQUERA	AQUABIB
ACQUENT	ACQUIST	ALIQUOT	ANTIQUA	AQUAFER
ACQUEST	ALFAQUI	ALQUIER	ANTIQUE	AQUARIA

AQUATIC	INQUIRY	QUAKILY	QUICKLY	REQUIRE
AQUAVIT	JAQUIMA	QUAKING	QUIDDER	REQUITE
AQUEITY	JERQUED	QUALIFY	QUIDDIT	RONQUIL
AQUEOUS	JERQUER	QUALITY	QUIDDLE	ROQUIST
AQUIFER	JOCOQUE	QUAMASH	QUIENAL	RORQUAL
AQUIVER	JOCOQUI	QUANNET	QUIESCE	SEQUELA
ASQUARE	JONQUIL	QUANTIC	QUIETED	SEQUENT
ASQUEAL	KUMQUAT	QUANTUM	QUIETEN	SEQUEST
ASQUINT	LACQUER	QUARION	QUIETER	SEQUOIA
ASQUIRM	LACQUEY	QUARLES	QUIETLY	SILIQUA
BANQUET	LAQUEAR	QUARRED	QUIETUS	SILIQUE
BAROQUE	LAQUEUS	QUARREL	QUILATE	SOSQUIL
BASQUED	LIQUATE	QUARTAN	QUILKIN	SQUABBY
BATUQUE	LIQUEFY	QUARTER	QUILLAI	SQUACCO
BEQUEST	LIQUEUR	QUARTET	QUILLED	SQUADDY
BEZIQUE	LIQUIDS	QUARTIC	QUILLER	SQUADER
BOSQUET	LIQUIDY	QUARTIN	QUILLET	SQUAGGA
BOUQUET	LIQUIFY	QUARTOS	QUILLON	SQUAILS
BRASQUE	LIQUORS	QUARTZY	QUILTED	SQUALID
BRIQUET	LIQUORY	QUASHED	QUILTER	SQUALLY
BRISQUE	LOQUENT	QUASHEY	QUINARY	SQUALOR
BRUSQUE	MACAQUE	QUASSIA	QUINATE	SQUAMAE
CACIQUE	MADOQUA	QUASSIN	QUININA	SQUARED
CASAQUE	MANQUEE	QUATERN	QUININE	SQUARER
CASQUED	MARQUEE	QUATERS	QUINITE	SQUARES
CASQUET	MARQUIS	QUATRAL	QUINNAT	SQUASHY
CAWQUAW	MASQUER	QUATRIN	QUINNET	SQUATLY
CAZIQUE	MESQUIN	QUATTIE	QUINOID	SQUATTY
CHALQUE	MEZQUIT	QUATUOR	QUINONE	SQUAWKY
CHARQUI	MUSQUAW	QUAVERY	QUINOYL	SQUEAKY
CHEQUER	NAMAQUA	QUAYAGE	QUINTAD	SQUEEGE
CLIQUED	OBLIQUE	QUAYING	QUINTAL	SQUEEZE
COEQUAL	OBLOQUY	QUEACHY	QUINTAN	SQUEEZY
COMIQUE	OBSEQUY	QUEASOM	QUINTET	SQUELCH
CONQUER	OPAQUED	QUEAZEN	QUINTIC	SQUETEE
COQUINA	OQUASSA	QUEECHY	QUINTIN	SQUIDGE
COQUITA	PARQUET	QUEENLY	QUINTON	SQUIDGY
COQUITO	PASQUIL	QUEERER	QUINTUS	SQUIFFY
COSAQUE	PASQUIN	QUEERLY	QUINYIE	SQUILLA
CROQUET	PATAQUE	QUELITE	QUIPPED	SQUINCH
CROQUIS	PERIQUE	QUELLED	QUIPPER	SQUINNY
CUMQUAT	PICQUET	QUELLER	QUIRCAL	SQUINTY
DEQUEEN	PIQUANT	QUELLIO	QUIRING	SQUIRED
ENQUIRE	PIQUERO	QUEMADO	QUIRKED	SQUIRET
ENQUIRY	PIQUEUR	QUEMELY	QUIRKED	SQUIRTS
EQUABLE	PIQUING	QUERCIC	QUISCOS	SQUIRTY
EQUABLY	PURAQUE	QUERCIN	QUITELY	SQUISHY
EQUALED	QABBALA	QUERELA	QUITEVE	SQUITCH
EQUALLY	QUABIRD	QUERELE	QUITTED	SQUUSHY
EQUATED	QUACHIL	QUERENT	QUITTER	SURIQUE
EQUATOR	QUACKED	QUERIDA	QUITTOR	TANQUAM
EQUERRY	QUACKLE	QUERIDO	QUIVERY	TANQUEN
EQUILIN	QUADDED	QUERIED	QUIZZED	TARIQAT
EQUINAL	QUADDLE	QUERIER	QUIZZEE	TEQUILA
EQUINIA	QUADRAE	QUERIES	QUIZZER	TORQUED
EQUINOX	QUADRAL	QUERIST	QUODDED	TORQUES
EQUINUS	QUADRAT	QUERKEN	QUOINED	TOTQUOT
EQUISON	QUADREL	QUERNAL	QUOITER	TRIQUET
EQUITES	QUADRIC	QUESTED	QUOMODO	TURQUET
EQUULEI	QUADRIN	QUESTER	QUONDAM	UBIQUIT
ESQUIRE	QUADRUM	QUESTOR	QUONIAM	UNEQUAL
ESTOQUE	QUAEDAM	QUETSCH	QUORUMS	UNQUEEN
ETIQUET	QUAFFED	QUETZAL	QUOTING	UNQUEME
EXQUIRE	QUAFFER	QUIBBLE	QUOTITY	UNQUERT
FLASQUE	QUAGGAS	QUIBLET	RACQUET	UNQUICK
GRECQUE	QUAGGLE	QUICKED	RELIQUE	UNQUIET
INEQUAL	QUAHAUG	QUICKEN	REQUEEN	UNQUOTE
INQUEST	QUAILED	QUICKER	REQUEST	VAQUERO
INQUIET	QUAKIER	QUICKIE	REQUIEM	VAQUITA
INQUIRE			REQUINS	

POSITIONAL ORDER LIST OF 7-LETTER WORDS

QABBALA	QUACKED	QUADDLE	QUADRAT	QUADRIN
QUABIRD	QUACKLE	QUADRAE	QUADREL	QUADRUM
QUACHIL	QUADDED	QUADRAL	QUADRIC	QUAEDAM

QUAFFED	QUIBLET	AQUAFER	ASQUINT	ETIQUET
QUAFFER	QUICKED	AQUARIA	ASQUIRM	INEQUAL
QUAGGAS	QUICKEN	AQUATIC	BEQUEST	JERQUED
QUAGGLE	QUICKER	AQUAVIT	COQUINA	JERQUER
QUAHAUG	QUICKIE	AQUEITY	COQUITA	JONQUIL
QUAILED	QUICKLY	AQUEOUS	COQUITO	KUMQUAT
QUAKIER	QUIDDER	AQUIFER	DEQUEEN	LACQUER
QUAKILY	QUIDDIT	AQUIVER	ENQUIRE	LACQUEY
QUAKING	QUIDDLE	EQUABLE	ENQUIRY	MANQUEE
QUALIFY	QUIENAL	EQUABLY	ESQUIRE	MARQUEE
QUALITY	QUIESCE	EQUALED	EXQUIRE	MARQUIS
QUAMASH	QUIETED	EQUALLY	INQUEST	MASQUER
QUANNET	QUIETEN	EQUATED	INQUIET	MESQUIN
QUANTIC	QUIETER	EQUATOR	INQUIRE	MEZQUIT
QUANTUM	QUIETLY	EQUERRY	INQUIRY	MUSQUAW
QUARION	QUIETUS	EQUILIN	JAQUIMA	OPAQUED
QUARLES	QUILATE	EQUINAL	LAQUEAR	PARQUET
QUARRED	QUILKIN	EQUINIA	LAQUEUS	PASQUIL
QUARREL	QUILLAI	EQUINOX	LIQUATE	PASQUIN
QUARTAN	QUILLED	EQUINUS	LIQUEFY	PICQUET
QUARTER	QUILLER	EQUISON	LIQUEUR	RACQUET
QUARTET	QUILLET	EQUITES	LIQUIDS	RONQUIL
QUARTIC	QUILLON	EQUULEI	LIQUIDY	RORQUAL
QUARTIN	QUILTED	OQUASSA	LIQUIFY	SOSQUIL
QUARTOS	QUILTER	SQUABBY	LIQUORS	TANQUAM
QUARTZY	QUINARY	SQUACCO	LIQUORY	TANQUEN
QUASHED	QUINATE	SQUADDY	LOQUENT	TORQUED
QUASHEY	QUININA	SQUADER	PIQUANT	TORQUES
QUASSIA	QUININE	SQUAGGA	PIQUERO	TOTQUOT
QUASSIN	QUINITE	SQUAILS	PIQUEUR	TRIQUET
QUATERN	QUINNAT	SQUALID	PIQUING	TURQUET
QUATERS	QUINNET	SQUALLY	REQUEEN	UBIQUIT
QUATRAL	QUINOID	SQUALOR	REQUEST	UNEQUAL
QUATRIN	QUINONE	SQUAMAE	REQUIEM	
QUATTIE	QUINOYL	SQUARED	REQUINS	
QUATUOR	QUINTAD	SQUARER	REQUIRE	ALFAQUI
QUAVERY	QUINTAL	SQUARES	REQUITE	ANTIQUA
QUAYAGE	QUINTAN	SQUASHY	ROQUIST	ANTIQUE
QUAYING	QUINTET	SQUATLY	SEQUELA	BAROQUE
QUEACHY	QUINTIC	SQUATTY	SEQUENT	BATUQUE
QUEASOM	QUINTIN	SQUAWKY	SEQUEST	BEZIQUE
QUEAZEN	QUINTON	SQUEAKY	SEQUOIA	BRASQUE
QUEECHY	QUINTUS	SQUEEGE	TEQUILA	BRISQUE
QUEENLY	QUINYIE	SQUEEZE	UNQUEEN	BRUSQUE
QUEERER	QUIPPED	SQUEEZY	UNQUEME	CACIQUE
QUEERLY	QUIPPER	SQUELCH	UNQUERT	CASAQUE
QUELITE	QUIRCAL	SQUETEE	UNQUICK	CAZIQUE
QUELLED	QUIRING	SQUIDGE	UNQUIET	CHALQUE
QUELLER	QUIRKED	SQUIDGY	UNQUOTE	CHARQUI
QUELLIO	QUISCOS	SQUIFFY	VAQUERO	COMIQUE
QUEMADO	QUITELY	SQUILLA	VAQUITA	COSAQUE
QUEMELY	QUITEVE	SQUINCH		ESTOQUE
QUERCIC	QUITTED	SQUINNY	ACEQUIA	FLASQUE
QUERCIN	QUITTER	SQUINTY	ALIQUID	GRECQUE
QUERELA	QUITTOR	SQUIRED	ALIQUOT	JOCOQUE
QUERELE	QUIVERY	SQUIRET	BANQUET	JOCOQUI
QUERENT	QUIZZED	SQUIRTS	BASQUED	MACAQUE
QUERIDA	QUIZZEE	SQUIRTY	BOSQUET	MADOQUA
QUERIDO	QUIZZER	SQUISHY	BOUQUET	NAMAQUA
QUERIED	QUODDED	SQUITCH	BRIQUET	OBLIQUE
QUERIER	QUOINED	SQUUSHY	CASQUED	OBLOQUY
QUERIES	QUOITER		CASQUET	OBSEQUY
QUERIST	QUOMODO	ACQUENT	CAWQUAW	PATAQUE
QUERKEN	QUONDAM	ACQUEST	CHEQUER	PERIQUE
QUERNAL	QUONIAM	ACQUIRE	CLIQUED	PURAQUE
QUESTED	QUORUMS	ACQUIST	COEQUAL	RELIQUE
QUESTER	QUOTING	ALQUIER	CONQUER	SILIQUA
QUESTOR	QUOTITY	ANQUERA	CROQUET	SILIQUE
QUETSCH		ASQUARE	CROQUIS	SURIQUE
QUETZAL	AQUABIB	ASQUEAL	CUMQUAT	TARIQAT
QUIBBLE				

SCORING ORDER LIST OF 7-LETTER WORDS

28	QUIPPED	VAQUERO	UNQUEME	QUARTAN
QUARTZY	QUIRKED	VAQUITA		QUARTER
SQUEEZY	SQUADDY		**17**	QUARTET
	SQUELCH	**18**	ALIQUID	QUARTIN
27	SQUIDGY	ACEQUIA	DEQUEEN	QUARTOS
BEZIQUE	SQUINCH	ACQUENT	EQUALED	QUASSIA
MEZQUIT	SQUITCH	ACQUEST	EQUATED	QUASSIN
		ACQUIRE	LIQUIDS	QUATERN
26	**20**	ACQUIST	QUADRAE	QUATERS
SQUAWKY	AQUABIB	AQUATIC	QUADRAL	QUATRAL
	CACIQUE	ASQUIRM	QUADRAT	QUATRIN
25	COMIQUE	BANQUET	QUADREL	QUATTIE
JAQUIMA	CUMQUAT	BAROQUE	QUADRIN	QUATUOR
JOCOQUE	LIQUIDY	BATUQUE	QUAILED	QUEERER
JOCOQUI	MACAQUE	BEQUEST	QUARRED	QUELITE
QUEAZEN	PICQUET	BOSQUET	QUELLED	QUELLER
QUETZAL	QABBALA	BOUQUET	QUERIDA	QUELLIO
QUICKLY	QUAHAUG	BRASQUE	QUERIDO	QUERELA
QUIZZED	QUAKIER	BRIQUET	QUERIED	QUERELE
SQUEEZE	QUASHED	BRISQUE	QUESTED	QUERENT
SQUIFFY	QUAYAGE	BRUSQUE	QUIETED	QUERIER
	QUAYING	CASAQUE	QUILLED	QUERIES
24	QUERCIC	CASQUET	QUILTED	QUERIST
CAWQUAW	QUERKEN	COEQUAL	QUINOID	QUERNAL
JERQUED	QUIBBLE	CONQUER	QUINTAD	QUESTER
QUEACHY	QUILKIN	COQUINA	QUIRING	QUESTOR
QUEECHY	QUIPPER	COQUITA	QUITTED	QUIENAL
QUIZZEE	SQUACCO	COQUITO	QUOINED	QUIETEN
QUIZZER		COSAQUE	QUOTING	QUIETER
	19	CROQUET	SQUADER	QUIETUS
23	ALFAQUI	CROQUIS	SQUALID	QUILATE
EQUINOX	AQUAFER	EQUABLE	SQUARED	QUILLAI
EXQUIRE	AQUAVIT	LACQUER	SQUEEGE	QUILLER
JERQUER	AQUEITY	MANQUEE	SQUIRED	QUILLET
JONQUIL	AQUIFER	MARQUEE	TORQUED	QUILLON
QUACKED	AQUIVER	MARQUIS		QUILTER
QUAFFED	BASQUED	MASQUER	**16**	QUINATE
QUAKILY	CASQUED	MESQUIN	ALIQUOT	QUININA
QUICKED	CLIQUED	NAMAQUA	ALQUIER	QUININE
SQUABBY	ENQUIRY	OBLIQUE	ANQUERA	QUINITE
SQUEAKY	EQUALLY	PARQUET	ANTIQUA	QUINNAT
	EQUERRY	PASQUIL	ANTIQUE	QUINNET
22	FLASQUE	PASQUIN	AQUARIA	QUINONE
KUMQUAT	GRECQUE	PATAQUE	AQUEOUS	QUINTAL
LIQUEFY	INQUIRY	PERIQUE	ASQUARE	QUINTAN
LIQUIFY	LIQUORY	PIQUANT	ASQUEAL	QUINTET
QUACKLE	MADOQUA	PIQUERO	ASQUINT	QUINTIN
QUAFFER	OPAQUED	PIQUEUR	ENQUIRE	QUINTON
QUALIFY	PIQUING	PURAQUE	EQUATOR	QUINTUS
QUASHEY	QUABIRD	QUADDLE	EQUILIN	QUITTER
QUAVERY	QUADDED	QUAGGAS	EQUINAL	QUITTOR
QUICKEN	QUADRIC	QUAGGLE	EQUINIA	QUOITER
QUICKER	QUADRUM	QUANTIC	EQUINUS	RELIQUE
QUICKIE	QUAEDAM	QUANTUM	EQUISON	REQUEEN
QUIVERY	QUALITY	QUARTIC	EQUITES	REQUEST
SQUASHY	QUEENLY	QUEASOM	EQUULEI	REQUINS
SQUISHY	QUEERLY	QUERCIN	ESQUIRE	REQUIRE
SQUUSHY	QUEMADO	QUIBLET	ESTOQUE	REQUITE
UNQUICK	QUIETLY	QUIDDER	ETIQUET	RONQUIL
	QUINARY	QUIDDIT	INEQUAL	ROQUIST
21	QUINOYL	QUIDDLE	INQUEST	RORQUAL
CHALQUE	QUINYIE	QUIESCE	INQUIET	SEQUELA
CHARQUI	QUITELY	QUINTIC	INQUIRE	SEQUENT
CHEQUER	QUITEVE	QUIRCAL	LAQUEAR	SEQUEST
EQUABLY	QUODDED	QUISCOS	LAQUEUS	SEQUOIA
LACQUEY	QUOMODO	QUONIAM	LIQUATE	SILIQUA
MUSQUAW	QUONDAM	QUORUMS	LIQUEUR	SILIQUE
OBLOQUY	QUOTITY	RACQUET	LIQUORS	SOSQUIL
OBSEQUY	SQUALLY	REQUIEM	LOQUENT	SQUAILS
QUACHIL	SQUATLY	SQUAGGA	OQUASSA	SQUALOR
QUAKING	SQUATTY	SQUAMAE	QUANNET	SQUARER
QUAMASH	SQUINNY	SQUIDGE	QUARION	SQUARES
QUEMELY	SQUINTY	TANQUAM	QUARLES	SQUETEE
QUETSCH	SQUIRTY	UBIQUIT	QUARREL	SQUILLA

SQUIRET	TANQUEN	TORQUES	TURQUET	UNQUERT
SQUIRTS	TARIQAT	TOTQUOT	UNEQUAL	UNQUIET
SURIQUE	TEQUILA	TRIQUET	UNQUEEN	UNQUOTE

ALPHABETICAL LIST OF 8-LETTER WORDS

ACQUAINT	CLIQUING	JAQUETTE	QUADROON	QUEERITY
ACQUIRED	CLIQUISH	JERQUING	QUADRUAL	QUELLING
ACQUIRER	CLIQUISM	LIMEQUAT	QUAESITA	QUELLUNG
ACQUITAL	COEQUATE	LINQUISH	QUAESTIO	QUEMEFUL
ADEQUACY	COLLOQUE	LIQUABLE	QUAESTOR	QUENCHED
ADEQUATE	COLLOQUY	LIQUAMEN	QUAFFING	QUENCHER
ALAMIQUI	CONQUEST	LIQUATED	QUAGGIER	QUENELLE
ALFAQUIN	CONQUIAN	LIQUESCE	QUAGMIRE	QUENTISE
ALIQUANT	COQUETRY	LIQUIDLY	QUAGMIRY	QUERCINE
ALQUEIRE	COQUETTE	LIQUIDUS	QUAILERY	QUERCITE
ALQUIFOU	COQUILLE	LIQUORED	QUAILING	QUERELAE
ANTIQUED	CORSEQUE	LIQUORER	QUAINTER	QUERIDAS
ANTIQUER	COTQUEAN	LOQUENCE	QUAINTLY	QUERIDOS
APPLIQUE	CRITIQUE	LOQUENCY	QUAKIEST	QUERIMAN
AQUACADE	DAIQUIRI	LOQUITUR	QUALMISH	QUERYING
AQUALUNG	DETRAQUE	MAQUETTE	QUALTAGH	QUESITED
AQUANAUT	DISQUIET	MAROQUIN	QUANDANG	QUESTEUR
AQUARIAL	ELIQUATE	MARQUESS	QUANDARY	QUESTING
AQUARIAN	ELOQUENT	MARQUISE	QUANDONG	QUESTION
AQUARIST	EMBUSQUE	MARQUITO	QUANTIFY	QUESTMAN
AQUARIUM	ENQUIRER	MESQUITA	QUANTITY	QUESTMEN
AQUARTER	EQUACITY	MESQUITE	QUANTIZE	QUEZALES
AQUATICS	EQUAEVAL	MEZQUITE	QUANTONG	QUIAQUIA
AQUATILE	EQUALING	MIQUELET	QUARANTY	QUIBBLED
AQUATINT	EQUALISE	MISQUOTE	QUARDEEL	QUIBBLER
AQUATION	EQUALIST	MOQUETTE	QUARESMA	QUICKEST
AQUATONE	EQUALITY	MOSQUITO	QUARRIED	QUICKING
AQUEDUCT	EQUALIZE	MUSQUASH	QUARRIER	QUICKSET
AQUIFORM	EQUALLED	MYSTIQUE	QUARRIES	QUIDDANY
AQUIFUGE	EQUATING	NASTALIQ	QUARRION	QUIDDITY
AQUILEGE	EQUATION	NONQUOTA	QUARROME	QUIDDLED
AQUILINE	EQUATIVE	OBLICQUE	QUARTANE	QUIDDLER
AQUILINO	EQUAIXED	OBLIQUED	QUARTANO	QUIDNUNC
AQUOSITY	EQUIFORM	OBLIQUUS	QUARTAUT	QUIESCED
AQUOTIZE	EQUINATE	OPAQUELY	QUARTERN	QUIETAGE
ARQUEBUS	EQUINITY	OPAQUING	QUARTERS	QUIETEST
ASPIQUEE	EQUIPAGA	OUTQUEEN	QUARTILE	QUIETING
BARBEQUE	EQUIPAGE	OUTQUOTE	QUARTINE	QUIETISM
BARQUEST	EQUIPPED	PARAQUET	QUARTOLE	QUIETIST
BASQUINE	EQUIPPER	PAROQUET	QUARTZIC	QUIETIVE
BEDQUILT	EQUISETA	PAURAQUE	QUASHING	QUIETUDE
BELDUQUE	EQUITANT	PERIOQUE	QUASKIES	QUILECES
BEQUEATH	EQUITIES	PERQUEER	QUASSIIN	QUILESES
BERLOQUE	EQUITIST	PERQUEIR	QUATENUS	QUILISMA
BIQUARTZ	EQUIVOKE	PERQUEST	QUATERON	QUILLAIC
BORASQUE	EQUULEUS	PHYSIQUE	QUATORZE	QUILLING
BOUTIQUE	ESQUIRED	PIQUABLE	QUATRAIN	QUILLITY
BRASQUED	ESQUISSE	PIQUANCY	QUAVERED	QUILTING
BRELOQUE	EXEQUIES	PIQUETTE	QUAVERER	QUINAMIN
BROQUERY	FABRIQUE	PIQUIERE	QUAVIVER	QUINCUNX
CALANQUE	FILIOQUE	QABBALAH	QUAYSIDE	QUINDENE
CASAQUIN	FREQUENT	QADARITE	QUEANISH	QUINELLA
CHAQUETA	HAQUETON	QAIMAQAM	QUEASIER	QUINETUM
CHEQUEEN	HENEQUEN	QUACKERY	QUEASILY	QUINIBLE
CHEQUERS	HUISQUIL	QUACKING	QUEBRADA	QUINICIN
CHICQUED	ICEQUAKE	QUACKISH	QUEBRITH	QUINIDIN
CHICQUER	ILLIQUID	QUACKISM	QUEDNESS	QUINIELA
CHIQUEST	INEQUITY	QUADRANS	QUEDSHIP	QUINITOL
CINQFOIL	INIQUITY	QUADRANT	QUEENCUP	QUINOGEN
CINQUAIN	INQUIRED	QUADRATE	QUEENING	QUINOLAS
CLAQUEUR	INQUIRER	QUADRIAD	QUEENITE	QUINOLIN
CLINIQUE	INQUISIT	QUADRIGA	QUEENLET	QUINOLYL
CLIQUIER	JACQUARD	QUADRINE	QUEEREST	QUINONIC

QUINONYL	QUODDITY	SQUABBED	SQUATTED	SQUIREEN
QUINOVIN	QUODLING	SQUABBER	SQUATTER	SQUIRELY
QUINSIED	QUOILERS	SQUABBLE	SQUATTLE	SQUIRESS
QUINTAIN	QUOINING	SQUABBLY	SQUAWKED	SQUIRING
QUINTANT	QUOMINUS	SQUACCOS	SQUAWKER	SQUIRISH
QUINTARY	QUONKING	SQUADDED	SQUAWKIE	SQUIRMED
QUINTILE	QUOTABLE	SQUADROL	SQUEAKED	SQUIRMER
QUINTOLE	QUOTABLY	SQUADRON	SQUEAKER	SQUIRREL
QUIPPING	QUOTIENT	SQUAILER	SQUEALED	SQUIRTED
QUIPPISH	QUOTIETY	SQUALENE	SQUEALER	SQUIRTER
QUIPSOME	RAMEQUIN	SQUALLED	SQUEEGEE	SQUISHED
QUIPSTER	REMARQUE	SQUALLER	SQUEEZED	SQUITTER
QUIRKIER	REPIQUED	SQUALOID	SQUEEZER	SUNQUAKE
QUIRKING	REPLIQUE	SQUAMATE	SQUELCHY	SURQUIDY
QUIRKSEY	REQUIRED	SQUAMIFY	SQUIBBED	TEQUILLA
QUISLING	REQUIRER	SQUAMISH	SQUIBBER	TORQUATE
QUISTRON	REQUITAL	SQUAMOID	SQUIDDED	TRANQUIL
QUITRENT	REQUITED	SQUAMOSA	SQUIDDER	TURQUOIS
QUITTING	REQUITER	SQUAMOSE	SQUIDDLE	UBIQUITY
QUIVERED	ROQUETED	SQUAMOUS	SQUIFFED	UMQUHILE
QUIVERER	ROQUETTE	SQUAMULA	SQUIFFER	UNIQUELY
QUIXOTIC	ROQUILLE	SQUAMULE	SQUIGGLE	UNIQUITY
QUIXOTRY	SAMBAQUI	SQUANDER	SQUIGGLY	UNSQUARE
QUIZZERY	SASANQUA	SQUANTUM	SQUILGEE	UNSQUIRE
QUIZZIFY	SEAQUAKE	SQUARELY	SQUILLID	USQUABAE
QUIZZING	SEQUACES	SQUARIER	SQUINACY	USQUEBAE
QUIZZISH	SEQUELAE	SQUARING	SQUINANT	VANQUISH
QUIZZISM	SEQUENCE	SQUARISH	SQUINTED	VAQUEROS
QUIZZITY	SEQUITUR	SQUARSON	SQUINTER	VASQUINE
QUODDIES	SHABEQUE	SQUASHED	SQUIRAGE	VERQUERE
QUODDING	SOLIQUID	SQUASHER		

POSITIONAL ORDER LIST OF 8-LETTER WORDS

QABBALAH	QUARRIER	QUENCHED	QUILLAIC	QUIXOTIC
QADARITE	QUARRIES	QUENCHER	QUILLING	QUIXOTRY
QAIMAQAM	QUARRION	QUENELLE	QUILLITY	QUODDIES
QUACKERY	QUARROME	QUENTISE	QUILTING	QUIZZERY
QUACKING	QUARTANE	QUERCINE	QUINAMIN	QUIZZIFY
QUACKISH	QUARTANO	QUERCITE	QUINCUNX	QUIZZING
QUACKISM	QUARTAUT	QUERELAE	QUINDENE	QUIZZISH
QUADRANS	QUARTERN	QUERIDAS	QUINELLA	QUIZZISM
QUADRANT	QUARTERS	QUERIDOS	QUINETUM	QUIZZITY
QUADRATE	QUARTILE	QUERIMAN	QUINIBLE	QUODDING
QUADRIAD	QUARTINE	QUERYING	QUINICIN	QUODDITY
QUADRIGA	QUARTOLE	QUESITED	QUINIDIN	QUODLING
QUADRINE	QUARTZIC	QUESTEUR	QUINIELA	QUOILERS
QUADROON	QUASHING	QUESTING	QUINITOL	QUOINING
QUADRUAL	QUASKIES	QUESTION	QUINOGEN	QUOMINUS
QUAESITA	QUASSIIN	QUESTMAN	QUINOLAS	QUONKING
QUAESTIO	QUATENUS	QUESTMEN	QUINOLIN	QUOTABLE
QUAESTOR	QUATERON	QUEZALES	QUINOLYL	QUOTABLY
QUAFFING	QUATORZE	QUIAQUIA	QUINONIC	QUOTIENT
QUAGGIER	QUATRAIN	QUIBBLED	QUINONYL	QUOTIETY
QUAGMIRE	QUAVERED	QUIBBLER	QUINOVIN	
QUAGMIRY	QUAVERER	QUICKEST	QUINSIED	AQUACADE
QUAILERY	QUAVIVER	QUICKING	QUINTAIN	AQUALUNG
QUAILING	QUAYSIDE	QUICKSET	QUINTANT	AQUANAUT
QUAINTER	QUEANISH	QUIDDANY	QUINTARY	AQUARIAL
QUAINTLY	QUEASIER	QUIDDITY	QUINTILE	AQUARIAN
QUAKIEST	QUEASILY	QUIDDLED	QUINTOLE	AQUARIST
QUALMISH	QUEBRADA	QUIDDLER	QUIPPING	AQUARIUM
QUALTAGH	QUEBRITH	QUIDNUNC	QUIPPISH	AQUARTER
QUANDANG	QUEDNESS	QUIESCED	QUIPSOME	AQUATICS
QUANDARY	QUEDSHIP	QUIETAGE	QUIPSTER	AQUATILE
QUANDONG	QUEENCUP	QUIETEST	QUIRKIER	AQUATINT
QUANTIFY	QUEENING	QUIETING	QUIRKING	AQUATION
QUANTITY	QUEENITE	QUIETISM	QUIRKSEY	AQUATONE
QUANTIZE	QUEENLET	QUIETIST	QUISLING	AQUEDUCT
QUANTONG	QUEEREST	QUIETIVE	QUISTRON	AQUIFORM
QUARANTY	QUEERITY	QUIETUDE	QUITRENT	AQUIFUGE
QUARDEEL	QUELLING	QUILECES	QUITTING	AQUILEGE
QUARESMA	QUELLUNG	QUILESES	QUIVERED	AQUILINE
QUARRIED	QUEMEFUL	QUILISMA	QUIVERER	AQUILINO

AQUOSITY	SQUASHED	COQUETTE	CHEQUERS	ALFAQUIN
AQUOTIZE	SQUASHER	COQUILLE	CHIQUEST	ANTIQUED
EQUACITY	SQUATTED	ENQUIRER	CINQFOIL	ANTIQUER
EQUAEVAL	SQUATTER	ESQUIRED	CINQUAIN	ASPIQUEE
EQUALING	SQUATTLE	ESQUISSE	CLAQUEUR	BRASQUED
EQUALISE	SQUAWKED	HAQUETON	CLIQUIER	CASAQUIN
EQUALIST	SQUAWKER	INQUIRED	CLIQUING	CHICQUED
EQUALITY	SQUAWKIE	INQUIRER	CLIQUISH	CHICQUER
EQUALIZE	SQUEAKED	INQUISIT	CLIQUISM	HENEQUEN
EQUALLED	SQUEAKER	JAQUETTE	COEQUATE	HUISQUIL
EQUATING	SQUEALED	LIQUABLE	CONQUEST	ILLIQUID
EQUATION	SQUEALER	LIQUAMEN	CONQUIAN	LIMEQUAT
EQUATIVE	SQUEEGEE	LIQUATED	COTQUEAN	MAROQUIN
EQUAIXED	SQUEEZED	LIQUESCE	DAIQUIRI	OBLIQUED
EQUIFORM	SQUEEZER	LIQUIDLY	DISQUIET	OBLIQUUS
EQUINATE	SQUELCHY	LIQUIDUS	ELIQUATE	PARAQUET
EQUINITY	SQUIBBED	LIQUORED	ELOQUENT	PAROQUET
EQUIPAGA	SQUIBBER	LIQUORER	EXEQUIES	QUIAQUIA
EQUIPAGE	SQUIDDED	LOQUENCE	FREQUENT	RAMEQUIN
EQUIPPED	SQUIDDER	LOQUENCY	ICEQUAKE	REPIQUED
EQUIPPER	SQUIDDLE	LOQUITUR	INEQUITY	SOLIQUID
EQUISETA	SQUIFFED	MAQUETTE	INIQUITY	TRANQUIL
EQUITANT	SQUIFFER	MIQUELET	JACQUARD	
EQUITIES	SQUIGGLE	MOQUETTE	JERQUING	ALAMIQUI
EQUITIST	SQUIGGLY	PIQUABLE	LINQUISH	APPLIQUE
EQUIVOKE	SQUILGEE	PIQUANCY	MARQUESS	BARBEQUE
EQUULEUS	SQUILLID	PIQUETTE	MARQUISE	BELDUQUE
SQUABBED	SQUINACY	PIQUIERE	MARQUITO	BERLOQUE
SQUABBER	SQUINANT	REQUIRED	MESQUITA	BORASQUE
SQUABBLE	SQUINTED	REQUIRER	MESQUITE	BOUTIQUE
SQUABBLY	SQUINTER	REQUITAL	MEZQUITE	BRELOQUE
SQUACCOS	SQUIRAGE	REQUITED	MISQUOTE	CALANQUE
SQUADDED	SQUIREEN	REQUITER	MOSQUITO	CLINIQUE
SQUADROL	SQUIRELY	ROQUETED	MUSQUASH	COLLOQUE
SQUADRON	SQUIRESS	ROQUETTE	NONQUOTA	COLLOQUY
SQUAILER	SQUIRING	ROQUILLE	OPAQUELY	CORSEQUE
SQUALENE	SQUIRISH	SEQUACES	OPAQUING	CRITIQUE
SQUALLED	SQUIRMED	SEQUELAE	OUTQUEEN	DETRAQUE
SQUALLER	SQUIRMER	SEQUENCE	OUTQUOTE	EMBUSQUE
SQUALOID	SQUIRREL	SEQUITUR	PERQUEER	FABRIQUE
SQUAMATE	SQUIRTED	TEQUILLA	PERQUEIR	FILIOQUE
SQUAMIFY	SQUIRTER	UMQUHILE	PERQUEST	MYSTIQUE
SQUAMISH	SQUISHED	USQUABAE	SEAQUAKE	OBLICQUE
SQUAMOID	SQUITTER	USQUEBAE	SUNQUAKE	PAURAQUE
SQUAMOSA		VAQUEROS	SURQUIDY	PERIOQUE
SQUAMOSE	ACQUAINT		TORQUATE	PHYSIQUE
SQUAMOUS	ACQUIRED	ADEQUACY	TURQUOIS	QAIMAQAM
SQUAMULA	ACQUIRER	ADEQUATE	UBIQUITY	REMARQUE
SQUAMULE	ACQUITAL	ALIQUANT	UNIQUELY	REPLIQUE
SQUANDER	ALQUEIRE	BARQUEST	UNIQUITY	SAMBAQUI
SQUANTUM	ALQUIFOU	BASQUINE	UNSQUARE	SASANQUA
SQUARELY	ARQUEBUS	BEDQUILT	UNSQUIRE	SHABEQUE
SQUARIER	BEQUEATH	BROQUERY	VANQUISH	
SQUARING	BIQUARTZ	CHAQUETA	VASQUINE	NASTALIQ
SQUARISH	COQUETRY	CHEQUEEN	VERQUERE	
SQUARSON				

SCORING ORDER LIST OF 8-LETTER WORDS

31	SQUEEZED	**25**	PIQUANCY	QUAGMIRY
QUIZZIFY		CHICQUED	QABBALAH	QUANTIFY
		EQUAIXED	QUACKING	QUAVIVER
28	**26**	JERQUING	QUAFFING	QUEDSHIP
BIQUARTZ	AQUOTIZE	PHYSIQUE	QUICKING	QUENCHED
MEZQUITE	EQUALIZE	QUACKISM	QUIPPISH	QUICKEST
QUARTZIC	QUACKERY	SQUAMIFY	QUIRKSEY	QUICKSET
QUIZZERY	QUACKISH	SQUAWKED	SQUABBLY	SQUIFFER
QUIZZISH	QUANTIZE	SQUELCHY	SQUAWKER	VANQUISH
QUIZZITY	QUATORZE		SQUAWKIE	
	QUEZALES	**24**	SQUIFFED	**22**
27	QUINCUNX	CHICQUER		AQUIFORM
JACQUARD	QUIXOTIC	EQUIVOKE	**23**	BEQUEATH
QUIXOTRY	QUIZZING	EXEQUIES	ADEQUACY	BROQUERY
QUIZZISM	SQUEEZER	JAQUETTE	ICEQUAKE	CHAQUETA

CHEQUEEN	AQUEDUCT	CASAQUIN	SQUAMULE	ALQUEIRE
CHEQUERS	AQUOSITY	CINQUAIN	SQUANTUM	ANTIQUER
CHIQUEST	BEDQUILT	CLAQUEUR	SQUIDDER	AQUANAUT
CINQFOIL	BELDUQUE	CLINIQUE	SQUIDDLE	AQUARIAL
CLIQUISH	BRASQUED	CLIQUIER	SQUIGGLE	AQUARIAN
COLLOQUY	CLIQUING	COEQUATE	SQUIRMER	AQUARIST
COQUETRY	EQUAEVAL	COLLOQUE	USQUABAE	AQUARTER
EQUACITY	EQUALITY	CONQUEST		AQUATILE
EQUIFORM	EQUATIVE	CONQUIAN	**18**	AQUATINT
EQUIPPED	EQUINITY	COQUETTE	ADEQUATE	AQUATION
FABRIQUE	EQUIPAGA	COQUILLE	ANTIQUED	AQUATONE
LOQUENCY	EQUIPAGE	CORSEQUE	AQUALUNG	AQUILINE
MUSQUASH	FILIOQUE	COTQUEAN	AQUILEGE	AQUILINO
MYSTIQUE	FREQUENT	CRITIQUE	DAIQUIRI	ELIQUATE
OPAQUELY	HAQUETON	LIMEQUAT	DETRAQUE	ELOQUENT
QUALMISH	HENEQUEN	LIQUABLE	DISQUIET	ENQUIRER
QUEBRITH	HUISQUIL	LIQUAMEN	EQUALING	EQUALISE
QUEMEFUL	INEQUITY	LIQUESCE	EQUALLED	EQUALIST
QUENCHER	INIQUITY	LOQUENCE	EQUATING	EQUATION
QUIBBLED	LINQUISH	MAQUETTE	ESQUIRED	EQUINATE
QUIDDANY	OBLIQUED	MAROQUIN	ILLIQUID	EQUISETA
QUIDDITY	OPAQUING	MARQUESS	INQUIRED	EQUITANT
QUIPPING	QAIMAQAM	MARQUISE	LIQUATED	EQUITIES
QUIRKING	QUAGMIRE	MARQUITO	LIQUIDUS	EQUITIST
QUODDITY	QUAILERY	MESQUITA	LIQUORED	EQUULEUS
QUONKING	QUAINTLY	MESQUITE	QUADRANS	ESQUISSE
QUOTABLY	QUANTITY	MIQUELET	QUADRANT	INQUIRER
SHABEQUE	QUARANTY	MISQUOTE	QUADRATE	INQUISIT
SQUABBED	QUAVERER	MOQUETTE	QUADRINE	LIQUORER
SQUAMISH	QUEANISH	MOSQUITO	QUADROON	LOQUITUR
SQUEAKED	QUEASILY	OBLIQUUS	QUADRUAL	NASTALIQ
SQUIBBED	QUEBRADA	PARAQUET	QUAILING	NONQUOTA
SQUIGGLY	QUEERITY	PAROQUET	QUANTONG	OUTQUEEN
SQUINACY	QUIDDLED	PAURAQUE	QUARDEEL	OUTQUOTE
UBIQUITY	QUIDNUNC	PERIOQUE	QUARRIED	QUAESITA
UMQUHILE	QUIESCED	PERQUEER	QUEDNESS	QUAESTIO
	QUIETIVE	PERQUEIR	QUEENING	QUAESTOR
21	QUILLITY	PERQUEST	QUELLING	QUAINTER
APPLIQUE	QUINOLYL	PIQUETTE	QUELLUNG	QUARRIER
AQUIFUGE	QUINONYL	PIQUIERE	QUERIDAS	QUARRIES
BARBEQUE	QUINOVIN	QUADRIAD	QUERIDOS	QUARRION
CLIQUISM	QUINTARY	QUADRIGA	QUESITED	QUARTANE
EMBUSQUE	QUIVERER	QUAGGIER	QUESTING	QUARTANO
EQUIPPER	QUODDING	QUANDANG	QUIETAGE	QUARTAUT
LIQUIDLY	QUOTIETY	QUANDONG	QUIETING	QUARTERN
OBLICQUE	REPIQUED	QUARESMA	QUIETUDE	QUARTERS
PIQUABLE	SQUADDED	QUARROME	QUILLING	QUARTILE
QUAKIEST	SQUAMOID	QUERCINE	QUILTING	QUARTINE
QUALTAGH	SQUARELY	QUERCITE	QUINDENE	QUARTOLE
QUANDARY	SQUARISH	QUERIMAN	QUINIDIN	QUASSIIN
QUASHING	SQUASHER	QUESTMAN	QUINOGEN	QUATENUS
QUASKIES	SQUIDDED	QUESTMEN	QUINSIED	QUATERON
QUAVERED	SQUIRELY	QUIDDLER	QUISLING	QUATRAIN
QUAYSIDE	SQUIRISH	QUIETISM	QUITTING	QUEASIER
QUEENCUP	SQUIRMED	QUILECES	QUOINING	QUEENITE
QUERYING	UNIQUELY	QUILISMA	REQUIRED	QUEENLET
QUIBBLER	UNIQUITY	QUILLAIC	REQUITED	QUEEREST
QUIPSOME	VAQUEROS	QUINAMIN	ROQUETED	QUENELLE
QUIRKIER	VASQUINE	QUINETUM	SOLIQUID	QUENTISE
QUIVERED	VERQUERE	QUINIBLE	SQUADROL	QUERELAE
SAMBAQUI		QUINICIN	SQUADRON	QUESTEUR
SEAQUAKE	**19**	QUINONIC	SQUALLED	QUESTION
SQUABBER	ACQUAINT	QUIPSTER	SQUALOID	QUIETEST
SQUABBLE	ACQUIRER	QUODDIES	SQUANDER	QUIETIST
SQUACCOS	ACQUITAL	QUODLING	SQUARING	QUILESES
SQUASHED	ALAMIQUI	QUOMINUS	SQUATTED	QUINELLA
SQUEAKER	AQUARIUM	QUOTABLE	SQUEALED	QUINIELA
SQUIBBER	AQUATICS	RAMEQUIN	SQUEEGEE	QUINITOL
SQUISHED	ARQUEBUS	REMARQUE	SQUILGEE	QUINOLAS
SUNQUAKE	ASPIQUEE	REPLIQUE	SQUILLID	QUINOLIN
SURQUIDY	BARQUEST	SEQUACES	SQUINTED	QUINTAIN
	BASQUINE	SEQUENCE	SQUIRAGE	QUINTANT
20	BERLOQUE	SQUAMATE	SQUIRING	QUINTILE
ACQUIRED	BORASQUE	SQUAMOSA	SQUIRTED	QUINTOLE
ALFAQUIN	BOUTIQUE	SQUAMOSE		QUISTRON
ALQUIFOU	BRELOQUE	SQUAMOUS	**17**	QUITRENT
AQUACADE	CALANQUE	SQUAMULA	ALIQUANT	QUOILERS

QUOTIENT	SEQUELAE	SQUATTER	SQUIRREL	TURQUOIS
REQUIRER	SEQUITUR	SQUATTLE	SQUIRTER	UNSQUARE
REQUITAL	SQUAILER	SQUEALER	SQUITTER	UNSQUIRE
REQUITER	SQUALENE	SQUINANT	TEQUILLA	
ROQUETTE	SQUALLER	SQUINTER	TORQUATE	**16**
ROQUILLE	SQUARIER	SQUIREEN	TORQUATE	QUIAQUIA
SASANQUA	SQUARSON	SQUIRESS	TRANQUIL	

ALPHABETICAL LIST OF 9-LETTER WORDS

ACQUEREUR	COQUETOON	JONQUILLE	QUADRIFID	QUEINTISE
ACQUIESCE	COQUETTED	LACQUERED	QUADRIGAE	QUENCHING
ACQUIRING	CROQUETED	LACQUERER	QUADRILLE	QUERCETIC
ACQUISITA	CROQUETTE	LAQUEARIA	QUADRIMUM	QUERCETIN
ACQUISITE	CUCKQUEAN	LIQUATING	QUADRIVIA	QUERCETUM
ACQUITTAL	DELIQUIUM	LIQUATION	QUADRUPED	QUERCITOL
ACQUITTED	DEMIPIQUE	LIQUEFIED	QUADRUPLE	QUERENCIA
ACQUITTER	DISQUISIT	LIQUEFIER	QUAESITUM	QUERIMANS
AEQUOREAL	DURAQUARA	LIQUEURED	QUAGGIEST	QUERIMONY
ALAMBIQUE	ELIQUATED	LIQUIDATE	QUAGMIRED	QUERULENT
ANGELIQUE	ELOQUENCE	LIQUIDITY	QUAILHEAD	QUERULIST
ANTILOQUY	ENCHEQUER	LIQUIDIZE	QUAINTEST	QUERULITY
ANTIQUARY	EQUALIZED	LIQUIFORM	QUAINTISE	QUERULOUS
ANTIQUATE	EQUALIZER	LIQUORICE	QUAKETAIL	QUESITIVE
ANTIQUELY	EQUALLING	LIQUORING	QUAKINESS	QUESTIONS
ANTIQUING	EQUALNESS	LIQUORISH	QUAKINGLY	QUESTRIST
ANTIQUIST	EQUERRIES	LIQUORIST	QUALIFIED	QUETENITE
ANTIQUITY	EQUIMODAL	LONQUHARD	QUALIFIER	QUIBBLING
APPLIQUED	EQUIMOLAR	LOQUACITY	QUALITIED	QUICKBEAM
AQUAGREEN	EQUIPEDAL	LOQUENTLY	QUALITIES	QUICKBORN
AQUAMETER	EQUIPLUVE	MANNEQUIN	QUANTICAL	QUICKENED
AQUAPLANE	EQUIPMENT	MARQUETRY	QUANTIZED	QUICKENER
AQUARELLE	EQUIPOISE	MARQUISAL	QUANTULUM	QUICKFOOT
AQUARIIST	EQUIPPING	MISQUOTED	QUARENDEN	QUICKLIME
AQUARIUMS	EQUISETIC	MISQUOTER	QUARENDER	QUICKNESS
AQUATICAL	EQUISETUM	MONOCOQUE	QUARRELED	QUICKSAND
AQUEOUSLY	EQUITABLE	MOSQUITAL	QUARRYING	QUICKSIDE
AQUILEGIA	EQUITABLY	MOSQUITOS	QUARRYMAN	QUICKSTEP
ARABESQUE	EQUIVALVE	OBLIQUATE	QUARRYMEN	QUICKWORK
ARQUERITE	EQUIVOCAL	OBLIQUELY	QUARTERED	QUIDDLING
BALDAQUIN	EQUIVOQUE	OBLIQUING	QUARTERER	QUIESCENT
BANQUETED	ESQUAMATE	OBLIQUITY	QUARTERLY	QUIESCING
BANQUETER	ESQUIRING	OBLOQUIAL	QUARTERON	QUIETENER
BANQUETTE	ETIQUETTE	OBLOQUIES	QUARTETTE	QUIETLIKE
BEQUIRTLE	EXCHEQUER	OBSEQUENT	QUARTINHO	QUIETNESS
BILBOQUET	EXEQUATUR	OBSEQUIAL	QUARTZITE	QUIETSOME
BISQUETTE	EXQUISITE	OBSEQUIES	QUARTZOID	QUILLAJIC
BOURASQUE	FANTASQUE	OBSEQUITY	QUARTZOSE	QUILLBACK
BRASQUING	FOURQUINE	ODALISQUE	QUARTZOUS	QUILLETED
BRIQUETTE	FREQUENCE	OVERQUELL	QUATRAYLE	QUILLFISH
BRODEQUIN	FREQUENCY	PALANQUIN	QUATREBLE	QUILLTAIL
BRUSQUELY	GRASSQUIT	PARQUETED	QUATRIBLE	QUILLWORK
BURLESQUE	GRIQUAITE	PARQUETRY	QUATTRINI	QUILLWORT
CACIQUISM	GROTESQUE	PARROQUET	QUATTRINO	QUINALDIC
CAIQUEJEE	HALOESQUE	PASQUILER	QUAVERING	QUINALDIN
CANNEQUIN	HARLEQUIN	PASQUILIC	QUAVEROUS	QUINALDYL
CARQUAISE	HARQUEBUS	PHYSIQUED	QUAYSIDER	QUINAMINE
CASQUETEL	INEQUALLY	PICQUETER	QUEACHIER	QUINARIAN
CASQUETTE	INQUIETLY	PIQUANTLY	QUEASIEST	QUINARIES
CHIBOUQUE	INQUILINE	PLAQUETTE	QUEBRACHO	QUINARIUS
CHICQUING	INQUINATE	PLASTIQUE	QUEENCAKE	QUINDECAD
CLINQUANT	INQUIRENT	PROPINQUE	QUEENFISH	QUINDECIM
CLIQUIEST	INQUIRIES	QUACKHOOD	QUEENLIER	QUINICINE
COEQUALLY	INQUIRING	QUACKSTER	QUEENLIKE	QUINIDINE
COEQUATED	INQUISITE	QUADRABLE	QUEENROOT	QUININISM
COLOQUIES	INSEQUENT	QUADRATED	QUEENWEED	QUININIZE
CONQUEDLE	JACQUERIE	QUADRATIC	QUEENWOOD	QUINISEXT
CONQUERED	JEQUERITY	QUADRATUM	QUEERNESS	QUINOFORM
CONQUEROR	JEQUIRITY	QUADRATUS	QUEERSOME	QUINOIDAL

QUINOIDIN	QUOTATION	SQUABBLED	SQUATTISH	SQUIRARCH
QUINOLINE	QUOTATIVE	SQUABBLER	SQUAWBUSH	SQUIRMIER
QUINOLOGY	QUOTELESS	SQUADDING	SQUAWFISH	SQUIRMING
QUINONIZE	QUOTIDIAN	SQUADRATE	SQUAWKIER	SQUIRRELY
QUINONOID	QUOTINGLY	SQUADRISM	SQUAWKING	SQUIRTING
QUINOVATE	REACQUIRE	SQUADRONE	SQUAWROOT	SQUIRTISH
QUINOVOSE	RELIQUARY	SQUALIDLY	SQUAWWEED	SQUISHING
QUINQUINA	RELIQUIAE	SQUALLERY	SQUEAKERY	SUBAQUEAN
QUINQUINO	RELIQUIAN	SQUALLIER	SQUEAKILY	SUBSESQUI
QUINTETTE	RELIQUISM	SQUALLING	SQUEAKING	SURQUEDRY
QUINTETTO	REPIQUING	SQUAMATED	SQUEALING	SURQUIDRY
QUINTFOIL	REQUESTER	SQUAMELLA	SQUEAMISH	TECHNIQUE
QUINTIPED	REQUIRING	SQUAMEOUS	SQUEEGEED	TORQUATED
QUINTROON	REQUISITE	SQUAMOSAL	SQUEEZING	TOTAQUINE
QUINTUPLE	REQUITING	SQUAMULAE	SQUELCHED	TRIPTYQUE
QUINZAINE	ROQUETING	SQUAREAGE	SQUELCHER	TRIQUETRA
QUINZIEME	SAMBAQUIS	SQUARECAP	SQUELETTE	TURQUOISE
QUIREWISE	SEMIQUOTE	SQUAREMAN	SQUIBBERY	UBIQUIOUS
QUIRKIEST	SEQUACITY	SQUAREMEN	SQUIBBING	UNEQUABLE
QUIRKSOME	SEQUELANT	SQUARROSE	SQUIBBISH	UNEQUABLY
QUISQUOUS	SEQUENCER	SQUARROUS	SQUIBSTER	UNEQUALED
QUISUTSCH	SEQUESTER	SQUASHIER	SQUIDDING	UNEQUALLY
QUITANTIE	SEQUESTRA	SQUASHILY	SQUIDGIER	UNQUAILED
QUITCLAIM	SILIQUOSE	SQUASHING	SQUIFFIER	UNQUALIFY
QUITTANCE	SIMIESQUE	SQUATINID	SQUILGEED	UNQUALITY
QUIVERFUL	SOBRIQUET	SQUATMORE	SQUILGEER	UNQUEMELY
QUIVERING	SOLILOQUY	SQUATNESS	SQUILLGEE	UNQUIETLY
QUIXOTISM	SQUABBASH	SQUATTAGE	SQUILLIAN	UNREQUEST
QUIXOTIZE	SQUABBIER	SQUATTIER	SQUINANCE	UNSQUARED
QUIZZICAL	SQUABBING	SQUATTILY	SQUINTING	UTRAQUIST
QUODLIBET	SQUABBISH	SQUATTING	SQUIRALTY	WELLQUEME

POSITIONAL ORDER LIST OF 9-LETTER WORDS

QUACKHOOD	QUARTETTE	QUESTIONS	QUININISM	QUOTINGLY
QUACKSTER	QUARTINHO	QUESTRIST	QUININIZE	
QUADRABLE	QUARTZITE	QUETENITE	QUINISEXT	AQUAGREEN
QUADRATED	QUARTZOID	QUIBBLING	QUINOFORM	AQUAMETER
QUADRATIC	QUARTZOSE	QUICKBEAM	QUINOIDAL	AQUAPLANE
QUADRATUM	QUARTZOUS	QUICKBORN	QUINOIDIN	AQUARELLE
QUADRATUS	QUATRAYLE	QUICKENED	QUINOLINE	AQUARIIST
QUADRIFID	QUATREBLE	QUICKENER	QUINOLOGY	AQUARIUMS
QUADRIGAE	QUATRIBLE	QUICKFOOT	QUINONIZE	AQUATICAL
QUADRILLE	QUATTRINI	QUICKLIME	QUINONOID	AQUEOUSLY
QUADRIMUM	QUATTRINO	QUICKNESS	QUINOVATE	AQUILEGIA
QUADRIVIA	QUAVERING	QUICKSAND	QUINOVOSE	EQUALIZED
QUADRUPED	QUAVEROUS	QUICKSIDE	QUINQUINA	EQUALIZER
QUADRUPLE	QUAYSIDER	QUICKSTEP	QUINQUINO	EQUALLING
QUAESITUM	QUEACHIER	QUICKWORK	QUINTETTE	EQUALNESS
QUAGGIEST	QUEASIEST	QUIDDLING	QUINTETTO	EQUERRIES
QUAGMIRED	QUEBRACHO	QUIESCENT	QUINTFOIL	EQUIMODAL
QUAILHEAD	QUEENCAKE	QUIESCING	QUINTIPED	EQUIMOLAR
QUAINTEST	QUEENFISH	QUIETENER	QUINTROON	EQUIPEDAL
QUAINTISE	QUEENLIER	QUIETLIKE	QUINTUPLE	EQUIPLUVE
QUAKETAIL	QUEENLIKE	QUIETNESS	QUINZAINE	EQUIPMENT
QUAKINESS	QUEENROOT	QUIETSOME	QUINZIEME	EQUIPOISE
QUAKINGLY	QUEENWEED	QUILLAJIC	QUIREWISE	EQUIPPING
QUALIFIED	QUEENWOOD	QUILLBACK	QUIRKIEST	EQUISETIC
QUALIFIER	QUEERNESS	QUILLETED	QUIRKSOME	EQUISETUM
QUALITIED	QUEERSOME	QUILLFISH	QUISQUOUS	EQUITABLE
QUALITIES	QUEINTISE	QUILLTAIL	QUISUTSCH	EQUITABLY
QUANTICAL	QUENCHING	QUILLWORK	QUITANTIE	EQUIVALVE
QUANTIZED	QUERCETIC	QUILLWORT	QUITCLAIM	EQUIVOCAL
QUANTULUM	QUERCETIN	QUINALDIC	QUITTANCE	EQUIVOQUE
QUARENDEN	QUERCETUM	QUINALDIN	QUIVERFUL	SQUABBASH
QUARENDER	QUERCITOL	QUINALDYL	QUIVERING	SQUABBIER
QUARRELED	QUERENCIA	QUINAMINE	QUIXOTISM	SQUABBING
QUARRYING	QUERIMANS	QUINARIAN	QUIXOTIZE	SQUABBISH
QUARRYMAN	QUERIMONY	QUINARIES	QUIZZICAL	SQUABBLED
QUARRYMEN	QUERULENT	QUINARIUS	QUODLIBET	SQUABBLER
QUARTERED	QUERULIST	QUINDECAD	QUOTATION	SQUADDING
QUARTERER	QUERULITY	QUINDECIM	QUOTATIVE	SQUADRATE
QUARTERLY	QUERULOUS	QUINICINE	QUOTELESS	SQUADRISM
QUARTERON	QUESITIVE	QUINIDINE	QUOTIDIAN	SQUADRONE

SQUALIDLY	SQUINANCE	REQUIRING	PARQUETED	RELIQUARY
SQUALLERY	SQUINTING	REQUISITE	PARQUETRY	RELIQUIAE
SQUALLIER	SQUIRALTY	REQUITING	PASQUILER	RELIQUIAN
SQUALLING	SQUIRARCH	ROQUETING	PASQUILIC	RELIQUISM
SQUAMATED	SQUIRMIER	SEQUACITY	PICQUETER	REPIQUING
SQUAMELLA	SQUIRMING	SEQUELANT	PLAQUETTE	SEMIQUOTE
SQUAMEOUS	SQUIRRELY	SEQUENCER	SURQUEDRY	SILIQUOSE
SQUAMOSAL	SQUIRTING	SEQUESTER	SURQUIDRY	SUBAQUEAN
SQUAMULAE	SQUIRTISH	SEQUESTRA	TORQUATED	TOTAQUINE
SQUAREAGE		UNQUAILED	TRIQUETRA	UNREQUEST
SQUARECAP	ACQUEREUR	UNQUALIFY	TURQUOISE	UTRAQUIST
SQUAREMAN	ACQUIESCE	UNQUALITY	UBIQUIOUS	WELLQUEME
SQUAREMEN	ACQUIRING	UNQUEMELY	UNEQUABLE	
SQUARROSE	ACQUISITA	UNQUIETLY	UNEQUABLY	APPLIQUED
SQUARROUS	ACQUISITE		UNEQUALED	BALDAQUIN
SQUASHIER	ACQUITTAL	BANQUETED	UNEQUALLY	BILBOQUET
SQUASHILY	ACQUITTED	BANQUETER	UNSQUARED	BRODEQUIN
SQUASHING	ACQUITTER	BANQUETTE	VANQUISHER	CANNEQUIN
SQUATINID	AEQUOREAL	BISQUETTE	VANQUISHED	ENCHEQUER
SQUATMORE	ARQUERITE	BRIQUETTE		EXCHEQUER
SQUATNESS	BEQUIRTLE	CAIQUEJEE	ANTIQUARY	GRASSQUIT
SQUATTAGE	COQUETOON	CARQUAISE	ANTIQUATE	HARLEQUIN
SQUATTIER	COQUETTED	CASQUETEL	ANTIQUELY	MANNEQUIN
SQUATTILY	ESQUAMATE	CASQUETTE	ANTIQUING	PALANQUIN
SQUATTING	ESQUIRING	CLIQUIEST	ANTIQUIST	PARROQUET
SQUATTISH	EXQUISITE	COEQUALLY	ANTIQUITY	PHYSIQUED
SQUAWBUSH	INQUIETLY	COEQUATED	BRASQUING	SAMBAQUIS
SQUAWFISH	INQUILINE	CONQUEDLE	BRUSQUELY	SOBRIQUET
SQUAWKIER	INQUINATE	CONQUERED	CACIQUISM	
SQUAWKING	INQUIRENT	CONQUEROR	CHICQUING	ALAMBIQUE
SQUAWROOT	INQUIRIES	CROQUETED	CLINQUANT	ANGELIQUE
SQUAWWEED	INQUIRING	CROQUETTE	COLOQUIES	ANTILOQUY
SQUEAKERY	INQUISITE	DISQUISIT	CUCKQUEAN	ARABESQUE
SQUEAKILY	JEQUERITY	ELIQUATED	DELIQUIUM	BOURASQUE
SQUEAKING	JEQUIRITY	ELOQUENCE	DURAQUARA	BURLESQUE
SQUEALING	LAQUEARIA	ETIQUETTE	FOURQUINE	CHIBOUQUE
SQUEAMISH	LIQUATING	EXEQUATUR	INSEQUENT	DEMIPIQUE
SQUEEGEED	LIQUATION	FREQUENCE	OBLIQUATE	EQUIVOQUE
SQUEEZING	LIQUEFIED	FREQUENCY	OBLIQUELY	FANTASQUE
SQUELCHED	LIQUEFIER	GRIQUAITE	OBLIQUING	GROTESQUE
SQUELCHER	LIQUEURED	HARQUEBUS	OBLIQUITY	HALOESQUE
SQUELETTE	LIQUIDATE	INEQUALLY	OBLOQUIAL	MONOCOQUE
SQUIBBERY	LIQUIDITY	JACQUERIE	OBLOQUIES	ODALISQUE
SQUIBBING	LIQUIDIZE	JONQUILLE	OBSEQUENT	PLASTIQUE
SQUIBBISH	LIQUIFORM	LACQUERED	OBSEQUIAL	PROPINQUE
SQUIBSTER	LIQUORICE	LACQUERER	OBSEQUIES	SIMIESQUE
SQUIDDING	LIQUORING	LONQUHARD	OBSEQUITY	SOLILOQUY
SQUIDGIER	LIQUORISH	MARQUETRY	OVERQUELL	SUBSESQUI
SQUIFFIER	LIQUORIST	MARQUISAL	QUINQUINA	TECHNIQUE
SQUILGEED	LOQUACITY	MISQUOTED	QUINQUINO	TRIPTYQUE
SQUILGEER	LOQUENTLY	MISQUOTER	QUISQUOUS	
SQUILLGEE	PIQUANTLY	MOSQUITAL	REACQUIRE	
SQUILLIAN	REQUESTER	MOSQUITOS		

SCORING ORDER LIST OF 9-LETTER WORDS

34	QUIZZICAL	**26**	QUEBRACHO	QUACKSTER
QUIXOTIZE	SQUEEZING	CHICQUING	QUICKENED	QUEENCAKE
		CUCKQUEAN	QUICKSAND	QUEENFISH
30	**27**	FREQUENCY	QUICKSIDE	QUENCHING
EXCHEQUER	CAIQUEJEE	QUAKINGLY	QUILLWORK	QUICKENER
	EQUALIZER	QUICKBORN	QUINISEXT	QUICKNESS
29	JACQUERIE	QUICKLIME	SQUABBASH	QUILLFISH
QUINZIEME	PHYSIQUED	QUICKSTEP	SQUABBISH	QUIRKSOME
	QUARTZITE	QUICKWORK	SQUAWKIER	QUIVERFUL
28	QUARTZOSE	QUILLBACK	SQUAWWEED	SQUASHILY
EQUALIZED	QUARTZOUS	SQUAWBUSH	SQUEAKERY	SQUELCHED
JEQUERITY	QUICKFOOT	SQUAWKING	SQUEAKILY	SQUIFFIER
JEQUIRITY	QUILLAJIC		SQUIBBERY	UNQUALIFY
LIQUIDIZE	QUININIZE	**25**	SQUIBBISH	
QUACKHOOD	QUINZAINE	CHIBOUQUE		**23**
QUANTIZED	QUIXOTISM	EXEQUATUR	**24**	APPLIQUED
QUARTZOID	SQUAWFISH	EXQUISITE	CACIQUISM	BRUSQUELY
QUICKBEAM		JONQUILLE	EQUIVALVE	COEQUALLY

DEMIPIQUE
ENCHEQUER
EQUIPLUVE
EQUIPPING
EQUITABLY
EQUIVOCAL
FREQUENCE
HARQUEBUS
LIQUIFORM
LOQUACITY
MARQUETRY
OBLIQUELY
OBLIQUITY
OBSEQUITY
PARQUETRY
PIQUANTLY
QUADRIFID
QUADRIMUM
QUARRYMAN
QUARRYMEN
QUEACHIER
QUERIMONY
QUIBBLING
QUINDECIM
QUINOFORM
QUISUTSCH
SEQUACITY
SQUABBING
SQUABBLED
SQUEAKING
SQUEAMISH
SQUELCHER
SQUIBBING
SQUIRARCH
TECHNIQUE
TRIPTYQUE
UNEQUABLY
UNQUEMELY
WELLQUEME

22
ACQUIESCE
ALAMBIQUE
BILBOQUET
EQUIPMENT
LIQUEFIED
LIQUIDITY
LONQUHARD
MONOCOQUE
PASQUILIC
PICQUETER
PROPINQUE
QUADRIVIA
QUADRUPED
QUAGMIRED
QUAILHEAD
QUAKETAIL
QUAKINESS
QUALIFIED
QUARRYING
QUAVERING
QUAYSIDER
QUEENLIKE
QUEENWEED
QUEENWOOD
QUERCETIC
QUERCETUM
QUIETLIKE
QUINALDYL
QUINDECAD
QUINOLOGY
QUIRKIEST
QUITCLAIM
QUIVERING
QUOTINGLY
SAMBAQUIS
SQUABBIER
SQUABBLER

SQUALIDLY
SQUARECAP
SQUASHING
SQUISHING
SURQUEDRY
SURQUIDRY

21
ACQUIRING
ACQUITTED
ANTILOQUY
ANTIQUARY
ANTIQUELY
ANTIQUITY
AQUEOUSLY
BALDAQUIN
BANQUETED
BRASQUING
BRODEQUIN
COEQUATED
CONQUEDLE
CONQUERED
COQUETTED
CROQUETED
DELIQUIUM
EQUIMODAL
EQUIPEDAL
FANTASQUE
FOURQUINE
HALOESQUE
HARLEQUIN
INEQUALLY
INQUIETLY
LACQUERED
LIQUEFIER
LIQUORISH
LOQUENTLY
MISQUOTED
OBLIQUING
OVERQUELL
PARQUETED
QUADRABLE
QUADRATIC
QUADRATUM
QUADRUPLE
QUALIFIER
QUARTERLY
QUARTINHO
QUATRAYLE
QUAVEROUS
QUERULITY
QUESITIVE
QUIDDLING
QUIESCING
QUILLWORT
QUINALDIC
QUINOVATE
QUINOVOSE
QUINTFOIL
QUINTIPED
QUIREWISE
QUODLIBET
QUOTATIVE
RELIQUARY
REPIQUING
SOLILOQUY
SQUADDING
SQUADRISM
SQUALLERY
SQUAMATED
SQUASHIER
SQUATTILY
SQUATTISH
SQUAWROOT
SQUIDDING
SQUIRALTY
SQUIRMING
SQUIRRELY

SQUIRTISH
UNEQUALLY
UNQUALITY
UNQUIETLY

20
ACQUEREUR
ACQUISITA
ACQUISITE
ACQUITTAL
ACQUITTER
AQUAMETER
AQUAPLANE
AQUARIUMS
AQUATICAL
ARABESQUE
BANQUETER
BANQUETTE
BEQUIRTLE
BISQUETTE
BOURASQUE
BRIQUETTE
BURLESQUE
CANNEQUIN
CARQUAISE
CASQUETEL
CASQUETTE
CLINQUANT
CLIQUIEST
COLOQUIES
CONQUEROR
COQUETOON
CROQUETTE
ELOQUENCE
EQUIMOLAR
EQUIPOISE
EQUISETIC
EQUISETUM
EQUITABLE
EQUIVOQUE
ESQUAMATE
LACQUERER
LIQUORICE
MANNEQUIN
MARQUISAL
MISQUOTER
MOSQUITAL
MOSQUITOS
OBLIQUATE
OBLOQUIAL
OBLOQUIES
OBSEQUENT
OBSEQUIAL
OBSEQUIES
PALANQUIN
PARROQUET
PASQUILER
PLAQUETTE
PLASTIQUE
QUADRATED
QUADRIGAE
QUAESITUM
QUAGGIEST
QUANTICAL
QUANTULUM
QUATREBLE
QUATRIBLE
QUEERSOME
QUERCETIN
QUERCITOL
QUERENCIA
QUERIMANS
QUIESCENT
QUIETSOME
QUINAMINE
QUINICINE
QUININISM
QUINTUPLE

QUITTANCE
REACQUIRE
RELIQUISM
SEMIQUOTE
SEQUENCER
SIMIESQUE
SOBRIQUET
SQUAMELLA
SQUAMEOUS
SQUAMOSAL
SQUAMULAE
SQUAREMAN
SQUAREMEN
SQUATMORE
SQUEEGEED
SQUIBSTER
SQUIDGIER
SQUILGEED
SQUINANCE
SQUIRMIER
SUBAQUEAN
SUBSESQUI
UBIQUIOUS
UNEQUABLE

19
ANGELIQUE
ANTIQUING
AQUAGREEN
AQUILEGIA
DISQUISIT
DURAQUARA
ELIQUATED
EQUALLING
ESQUIRING
GRASSQUIT
GRIQUAITE
GROTESQUE
INQUIRING
LIQUATING
LIQUEURED
LIQUIDATE
LIQUORING
ODALISQUE
QUADRATUS
QUADRILLE
QUALITIED
QUARENDEN
QUARENDER
QUARRELED
QUARTERED
QUILLETED
QUINALDIN
QUINIDINE
QUINOIDAL
QUINOIDIN
QUINONOID
QUOTIDIAN
REQUIRING
REQUITING
ROQUETING
SQUADRATE
SQUADRONE
SQUALLING
SQUAREAGE
SQUATINID
SQUATTAGE
SQUATTING
SQUEALING
SQUILGEER
SQUILLGEE
SQUINTING
SQUIRTING
TORQUATED
UNEQUALED
UNQUAILED
UNSQUARED

18
AEQUOREAL
ANTIQUATE
ANTIQUIST
AQUARELLE
AQUARIIST
ARQUERITE
EQUALNESS
EQUERRIES
ETIQUETTE
INQUILINE
INQUINATE
INQUIRENT
INQUIRIES
INQUISITE
INSEQUENT
LAQUEARIA
LIQUATION
LIQUORIST
QUAINTEST
QUAINTISE
QUALITIES
QUARTERER
QUARTERON
QUARTETTE
QUATTRINI
QUATTRINO
QUEASIEST
QUEENLIER
QUEENROOT
QUEERNESS
QUEINTISE
QUERULENT
QUERULIST
QUERULOUS
QUESTIONS
QUESTRIST
QUETENITE
QUIETENER
QUIETNESS
QUILLTAIL
QUINARIAN
QUINARIES
QUINARIUS
QUINOLINE
QUINTETTE
QUINTETTO
QUINTROON
QUITANTIE
QUOTATION
QUOTELESS
RELIQUIAE
RELIQUIAN
REQUESTER
REQUISITE
SEQUELANT
SEQUESTER
SEQUESTRA
SILIQUOSE
SQUALLIER
SQUARROSE
SQUARROUS
SQUATNESS
SQUATTIER
SQUELETTE
SQUILLIAN
TOTAQUINE
TRIQUETRA
TURQUOISE
UNREQUEST
UTRAQUIST

17
QUINQUINA
QUINQUINO
QUISQUOUS

ALPHABETICAL LIST OF 10-LETTER WORDS

ACEQUIADOR	DEMIQUAVER	LIQUIDABLE	QUANTITIED	QUINTUPLED
ACQUAINTED	DESQUAMATE	LIQUIDATED	QUANTITIES	QUINTUPLET
ACQUIESCED	DISQUALIFY	LIQUIDATOR	QUANTITIVE	QUISQUEITE
ACQUIESCER	DISQUIETED	LIQUIDIZED	QUARANTINE	QUIVERLEAF
ACQUIRABLE	DISQUIETER	LIQUIDNESS	QUARENTENE	QUIXOTICAL
ACQUIRENDA	DISQUIETLY	LOQUACIOUS	QUARRELING	QUOTENNIAL
ACQUISIBLE	DISQUISITE	MAGNIFIQUE	QUARRELLED	QUOTIETIES
ACQUISITED	DISQUIXOTE	MAQUAHUITL	QUARRELOUS	RADIOPAQUE
ACQUISITOR	DULCILOQUY	MARQUISATE	QUARTATION	RELINQUENT
ACQUISITUM	EARTHQUAKE	MARQUISDOM	QUARTERAGE	RELINQUISH
ACQUITMENT	EARTHQUAVE	MARQUISESS	QUARTERING	RELIQUAIRE
ACQUITTING	ELIQUATING	MARQUISINA	QUARTERMAN	REQUIESCAT
ADEQUATELY	ELIQUATION	MASQUERADE	QUARTERMEN	REQUIRABLE
ADEQUATION	EQUABILITY	MEDRINAQUE	QUARTERSAW	REQUISITOR
ADEQUATIVE	EQUALITIES	MISQUOTING	QUARTZITIC	REQUITABLE
ALCORNOQUE	EQUALIZING	MOSQUITOES	QUASSATION	ROBOTESQUE
ANTIMASQUE	EQUANGULAR	MOSQUITOEY	QUASSATIVE	ROQUELAURE
ANTIQUATED	EQUANIMITY	MULTILOQUY	QUATERNARY	SATYRESQUE
ANTISQUAMA	EQUANIMOUS	MUSQUASPEN	QUATERNATE	SEMICIRQUE
APOQUININE	EQUATIONAL	NOVANTIQUE	QUATERNION	SEMIQUAVER
AQUAFORTIS	EQUATOREAL	OBLOQUIOUS	QUATERNITY	SEMISQUARE
AQUAMARINE	EQUATORIAL	OBSEQUENCE	QUATORZAIN	SEQUACIOUS
AQUAPLANED	EQUESTRIAN	OBSEQUIOUS	QUATREFOIL	SEQUENTIAL
AQUASCUTUM	EQUIFORMAL	OPAQUENESS	QUEACHIEST	SEQUESTRAL
AQUATINTER	EQUIJACENT	OUTQUIBBLE	QUEASINESS	SEQUESTRUM
AQUAVALENT	EQUILIBRIA	OXYQUINONE	QUEENCRAFT	SESQUINONA
AQUICOLOUS	EQUIPARANT	PARCILOQUY	QUEENLIEST	SOMNILOQUY
AQUIFEROUS	EQUIPARATE	PARQUETING	QUEENRIGHT	SOUBRIQUET
AQUILAWOOD	EQUIPOISED	PASQUILANT	QUENCHABLE	SQUABASHER
AQUIPAROUS	EQUISETUMS	PASQUILLER	QUENCHLESS	SQUABBIEST
ARBORESQUE	EQUISIGNAL	PASQUILLIC	QUENSELITE	SQUABBLING
BANQUETEER	EQUISONANT	PASQUINADE	QUERCITRIN	SQUADRONED
BANQUETING	EQUITATION	PAUCILOQUY	QUERCITRON	SQUALIDITY
BEQUEATHAL	EQUITATIVE	PENDELOQUE	QUERNSTONE	SQUALIFORM
BEQUEATHER	EQUIVALENT	PERQUADRAT	QUERYINGLY	SQUALLIEST
BIQUADRATE	EQUIVOCACY	PERQUEERLY	QUESTHOUSE	SQUALODONT
BIQUINTILE	EQUIVOCATE	PERQUISITE	QUESTIONED	SQUAMATINE
BLANQUETTE	EQUIVOROUS	PERRUQUIER	QUESTIONEE	SQUAMATION
BLANQUILLO	EUMOLPIQUE	PLASMOQUIN	QUESTIONER	SQUAMELLAE
BLOTTESQUE	FOURSQUARE	QUACKERIES	QUESTORIAL	SQUAMIFORM
BROQUINEER	FREQUENTED	QUACKISHLY	QUICKENING	SQUAMOSELY
BRUSQUERIE	FREQUENTER	QUADRANGLE	QUICKHATCH	SQUAMOSITY
BURLESQUED	FREQUENTLY	QUADRANTAL	QUICKSANDY	SQUAMOUSLY
BURLESQUER	GRANDESQUE	QUADRATICS	QUICKTHORN	SQUAMULATE
CATAFALQUE	HARLEQUINA	QUADRATING	QUICKWATER	SQUAMULOSE
CHAUTAUQUA	HARQUEBUSS	QUADRATRIX	QUIDDATIVE	SQUANDERED
CHEQUERING	HEARTQUAKE	QUADRATURE	QUIDDITIES	SQUANDERER
CHERQUERED	HUMORESQUE	QUADRENNIA	QUIESCENCE	SQUAREFACE
CHINQUAPIN	ILLAQUEATE	QUADRICEPS	QUIESCENCY	SQUAREHEAD
CHOUQUETTE	ILLIQUIDLY	QUADRICONE	QUIETISTIC	SQUARENESS
CIGARESQUE	INADEQUACY	QUADRIFORM	QUINACRINE	SQUARETAIL
CINQUEFOIL	INADEQUATE	QUADRIGATE	QUINALDINE	SQUARISHLY
CINQUEPACE	INELOQUENT	QUADRILLED	QUINAMICIN	SQUARSONRY
CLIQUISHLY	INEQUALITY	QUADRILLES	QUINAMIDIN	SQUASHIEST
COEQUALITY	INEQUATION	QUADRILOGY	QUINAQUINA	SQUATAROLE
COEQUATION	INEQUITIES	QUADRISECT	QUINATOXIN	SQUATEROLE
COLLIQUATE	INFREQUENT	QUADRIVIAL	QUINAZOLIN	SQUATINOID
COLLOQUIAL	INIQUITIES	QUADRIVIUM	QUINAZOLYL	SQUATTIEST
COLLOQUIST	INIQUITOUS	QUADRUMANE	QUINCEWORT	SQUAWBERRY
COLLOQUIUM	INQUESTUAL	QUADRUPLED	QUINCUNXES	SQUAWKIEST
COLLOQUIZE	INQUIETUDE	QUADRUPLET	QUINDECIMA	SQUEEZABLE
CONQUERING	INQUINATED	QUADRUPLEX	QUINIRETIN	SQUEEZEMAN
CONQUININE	INQUIRABLE	QUAESTUARY	QUINIZARIN	SQUELCHIER
CONSEQUENT	INQUIRENDO	QUAILERIES	QUINOIDINE	SQUELCHILY
COQUELICOT	INQUISITOR	QUAINTANCE	QUINOLINYL	SQUELCHING
COQUELUCHE	JOAQUINITE	QUAINTNESS	QUINOMETRY	SQUETEAGUE
COQUETRIES	LACQUERING	QUAKERBIRD	QUINONIMIN	SQUIBCRACK
COQUETTING	LACQUERIST	QUALIFYING	QUINOPYRIN	SQUIDGIEST
COQUETTISH	LAMBREQUIN	QUALIMETER	QUINOXALIN	SQUIFFIEST
COQUIMBITE	LANSQUENET	QUALMISHLY	QUINOXALYL	SQUIGGLIER
CRAQUELURE	LAQUEARIAN	QUANDARIES	QUINQUEVIR	SQUILLAGEE
CROQUETING	LIQUEFYING	QUANTIFIED	QUINSYWORT	SQUILLITIC
DELINQUENT	LIQUESCENT	QUANTIFIER	QUINTADENA	SQUIRARCHY
DELIQUESCE	LIQUEURING	QUANTITATE	QUINTADENE	SQUIREARCH

SQUIRELING
SQUIRMIEST
STATEQUAKE
STATUESQUE
SUBAQUATIC
SUBAQUEOUS
SUBSEQUENT
TAUROESQUE

TERRAQUEAN
TOURNIQUET
TRANQUILER
TRANQUILLO
TRANQUILLY
TRIQUETRAL
TRIQUETRIC
TRIQUETRUM

TRIQUINATE
TRIQUINOYL
TURQUOISES
UBIQUARIAN
UBIQUITARY
UBIQUITOUS
UNADEQUATE
UNCONQUEST

UNDERQUOTE
UNEQUALITY
UNEQUALLED
UNEQUIAXED
UNFREQUENT
UNIQUANTIC
UNIQUENESS
UNLIQUORED

UNQUIETOUS
UNQUIETUDE
UNREQUITER
USQUEBAUGH
VANQUISHED
VANQUISHER
VERSILOQUY
WORLDQUAKE

POSITIONAL ORDER LIST OF 10-LETTER WORDS

QUACKERIES
QUACKISHLY
QUADRANGLE
QUADRANTAL
QUADRATICS
QUADRATING
QUADRATRIX
QUADRATURE
QUADRENNIA
QUADRICEPS
QUADRICONE
QUADRIFORM
QUADRIGATE
QUADRILLED
QUADRILLES
QUADRILOGY
QUADRISECT
QUADRIVIAL
QUADRIVIUM
QUADRUMANE
QUADRUPLED
QUADRUPLET
QUADRUPLEX
QUAESTUARY
QUAILERIES
QUAINTANCE
QUAINTNESS
QUAKERBIRD
QUALIFYING
QUALIMETER
QUALMISHLY
QUANDARIES
QUANTIFIED
QUANTIFIER
QUANTITATE
QUANTITIED
QUANTITIES
QUANTITIVE
QUARANTINE
QUARENTENE
QUARRELING
QUARRELLED
QUARRELOUS
QUARTATION
QUARTERAGE
QUARTERING
QUARTERMAN
QUARTERMEN
QUARTERSAW
QUARTZITIC
QUASSATION
QUASSATIVE
QUATERNARY
QUATERNATE
QUATERNION
QUATERNITY
QUATORZAIN
QUATREFOIL
QUEACHIEST
QUEASINESS
QUEENCRAFT
QUEENLIEST
QUEENRIGHT

QUENCHABLE
QUENCHLESS
QUENSELITE
QUERCITRIN
QUERCITRON
QUERNSTONE
QUERYINGLY
QUESTHOUSE
QUESTIONED
QUESTIONEE
QUESTIONER
QUESTORIAL
QUICKENING
QUICKHATCH
QUICKSANDY
QUICKTHORN
QUICKWATER
QUIDDATIVE
QUIDDITIES
QUIESCENCE
QUIESCENCY
QUIETISTIC
QUINACRINE
QUINALDINE
QUINAMICIN
QUINAMIDIN
QUINAQUINA
QUINATOXIN
QUINAZOLIN
QUINAZOLYL
QUINCEWORT
QUINCUNXES
QUINDECIMA
QUINIRETIN
QUINIZARIN
QUINOIDINE
QUINOLINYL
QUINOMETRY
QUINONIMIN
QUINOPYRIN
QUINOXALIN
QUINOXALYL
QUINQUEVIR
QUINSYWORT
QUINTADENA
QUINTADENE
QUINTUPLED
QUINTUPLET
QUISQUEITE
QUIVERLEAF
QUIXOTICAL
QUOTENNIAL
QUOTIETIES

AQUAFORTIS
AQUAMARINE
AQUAPLANED
AQUASCUTUM
AQUATINTER
AQUAVALENT
AQUICOLOUS
AQUIFEROUS
AQUILAWOOD

AQUIPAROUS
EQUABILITY
EQUALITIES
EQUALIZING
EQUANGULAR
EQUANIMITY
EQUANIMOUS
EQUATIONAL
EQUATOREAL
EQUATORIAL
EQUESTRIAN
EQUIFORMAL
EQUIJACENT
EQUILIBRIA
EQUIPARANT
EQUIPARATE
EQUIPOISED
EQUISETUMS
EQUISIGNAL
EQUISONANT
EQUITATION
EQUITATIVE
EQUIVALENT
EQUIVOCACY
EQUIVOCATE
EQUIVOROUS
SQUABASHER
SQUABBIEST
SQUABBLING
SQUADRONED
SQUALIDITY
SQUALIFORM
SQUALLIEST
SQUALODONT
SQUAMATINE
SQUAMATION
SQUAMELLAE
SQUAMIFORM
SQUAMOSELY
SQUAMOSITY
SQUAMOUSLY
SQUAMULATE
SQUAMULOSE
SQUANDERED
SQUANDERER
SQUAREFACE
SQUAREHEAD
SQUARENESS
SQUARETAIL
SQUARISHLY
SQUARSONRY
SQUASHIEST
SQUATAROLE
SQUATEROLE
SQUATINOID
SQUATTIEST
SQUAWBERRY
SQUAWKIEST
SQUEEZABLE
SQUEEZEMAN
SQUELCHIER
SQUELCHILY
SQUELCHING

SQUETEAGUE
SQUIBCRACK
SQUIDGIEST
SQUIFFIEST
SQUIGGLIER
SQUILLAGEE
SQUILLITIC
SQUIRARCHY
SQUIREARCH
SQUIRELING
SQUIRMIEST

ACQUAINTED
ACQUIESCED
ACQUIESCER
ACQUIRABLE
ACQUIRENDA
ACQUISIBLE
ACQUISITED
ACQUISITOR
ACQUISITUM
ACQUITMENT
ACQUITTING
BEQUEATHAL
BEQUEATHER
BIQUADRATE
BIQUINTILE
COQUELICOT
COQUELUCHE
COQUETRIES
COQUETTING
COQUETTISH
COQUIMBITE
INQUESTUAL
INQUIETUDE
INQUINATED
INQUIRABLE
INQUIRENDO
INQUISITOR
LAQUEARIAN
LIQUEFYING
LIQUESCENT
LIQUEURING
LIQUIDABLE
LIQUIDATED
LIQUIDATOR
LIQUIDIZED
LIQUIDNESS
LOQUACIOUS
MAQUAHUITL
REQUIESCAT
REQUIRABLE
REQUISITOR
REQUITABLE
ROQUELAURE
SEQUACIOUS
SEQUENTIAL
SEQUESTRAL
SEQUESTRUM
UNQUIETOUS
UNQUIETUDE
USQUEBAUGH

ACEQUIADOR
ADEQUATELY
ADEQUATION
ADEQUATIVE
APOQUININE
BANQUETEER
BANQUETING
BROQUINEER
CHEQUERING
CINQUEFOIL
CINQUEPACE
CLIQUISHLY
COEQUALITY
COEQUATION
CONQUERING
CONQUININE
CRAQUELURE
CROQUETING
DESQUAMATE
DISQUALIFY
DISQUIETED
DISQUIETER
DISQUIETLY
DISQUISITE
DISQUIXOTE
ELIQUATING
ELIQUATION
FREQUENTED
FREQUENTER
FREQUENTLY
HARQUEBUSS
INEQUALITY
INEQUATION
INEQUITIES
INIQUITIES
INIQUITOUS
JOAQUINITE
LACQUERING
LACQUERIST
MARQUISATE
MARQUISDOM
MARQUISESS
MARQUISINA
MASQUERADE
MISQUOTING
MOSQUITOES
MOSQUITOEY
MUSQUASPEN
OPAQUENESS
OUTQUIBBLE
OXYQUINONE
PARQUETING
PASQUILANT
PASQUILLER
PASQUILLIC
PASQUINADE
PERQUADRAT
PERQUEERLY
PERQUISITE
SESQUINONA
TRIQUETRAL
TRIQUETRIC
TRIQUETRUM

TRIQUINATE	ILLAQUEATE	COLLOQUIST	SUBSEQUENT	CHAUTAUQUA
TRIQUINOYL	ILLIQUIDLY	COLLOQUIUM	TERRAQUEAN	CIGARESQUE
TURQUOISES	LANSQUENET	COLLOQUIZE	UNADEQUATE	DULCILOQUY
UBIQUARIAN	OBLOQUIOUS	CONSEQUENT	UNCONQUEST	EUMOLPIQUE
UBIQUITARY	OBSEQUENCE	DELINQUENT	UNDERQUOTE	GRANDESQUE
UBIQUITOUS	OBSEQUIOUS	EARTHQUAKE	UNFREQUENT	HUMORESQUE
UNEQUALITY	QUINQUEVIR	EARTHQUAVE	WORLDQUAKE	MAGNIFIQUE
UNEQUALLED	QUISQUEITE	FOURSQUARE		MEDRINAQUE
UNEQUIAXED	RELIQUAIRE	HARLEQUINA	BURLESQUED	MULTILOQUY
UNIQUANTIC	SEMIQUAVER	HEARTQUAKE	BURLESQUER	NOVANTIQUE
UNIQUENESS	SUBAQUATIC	INADEQUACY	LAMBREQUIN	PARCILOQUY
	SUBAQUEOUS	INADEQUATE	PLASMOQUIN	PAUCILOQUY
ANTIQUATED	TRANQUILER	INELOQUENT	SOUBRIQUET	PENDELOQUE
BLANQUETTE	TRANQUILLO	INFREQUENT	TOURNIQUET	RADIOPAQUE
BLANQUILLO	TRANQUILLY	PERRUQUIER		ROBOTESQUE
BRUSQUERIE	UNLIQUORED	QUINAQUINA	ALCORNOQUE	SATYRESQUE
CHERQUERED	UNREQUITER	RELINQUENT	ANTIMASQUE	SEMICIRQUE
CHINQUAPIN		RELINQUISH	ARBORESQUE	SOMNILOQUY
CHOUQUETTE	ANTISQUAMA	SEMISQUARE	BLOTTESQUE	STATUESQUE
DELIQUESCE	COLLIQUATE	STATEQUAKE	CATAFALQUE	TAUROESQUE
DEMIQUAVER	COLLOQUIAL			

SCORING ORDER LIST OF 10-LETTER WORDS

33	HEARTQUAKE	EQUANIMITY	MUSQUASPEN	MISQUOTING
QUICKHATCH	JOAQUINITE	EQUIFORMAL	OBSEQUENCE	NOVANTIQUE
	LIQUEFYING	EQUIVOCATE	OUTQUIBBLE	PARQUETING
31	PARCILOQUY	HARQUEBUSS	PASQUILLIC	PASQUINADE
QUACKISHLY	PAUCILOQUY	HUMORESQUE	PLASMOQUIN	PENDELOQUE
QUINAZOLYL	QUAKERBIRD	MAQUAHUITL	QUADRIVIAL	PERQUADRAT
	QUALIFYING	MARQUISDOM	QUADRUPLED	QUADRATICS
30	QUENCHABLE	MOSQUITOEY	QUANTIFIED	QUADRICONE
LIQUIDIZED	QUERYINGLY	MULTILOQUY	QUEENRIGHT	QUADRISECT
QUARTZITIC	QUICKENING	PERQUEERLY	QUIESCENCE	QUADRUMANE
SQUEEZABLE	QUIESCENCY	QUADRICEPS	QUINAMICIN	QUADRUPLET
SQUEEZEMAN	QUINATOXIN	QUADRILOGY	SEMICIRQUE	QUAESTUARY
	QUINOXALIN	QUEACHIEST	SQUABBIEST	QUANTIFIER
29	SQUAMIFORM	QUEENCRAFT	SQUALIDITY	QUANTITIVE
EQUALIZING	SQUAWKIEST	QUENCHLESS	SQUAREHEAD	QUARTERSAW
EQUIVOCACY	VANQUISHED	QUIDDATIVE	STATEQUAKE	QUASSATIVE
OXYQUINONE		QUINCEWORT	SUBAQUATIC	QUATERNARY
QUADRUPLEX	**25**	QUINDECIMA	SUBSEQUENT	QUATERNITY
QUICKSANDY	CHEQUERING	QUINOMETRY		QUATREFOIL
QUINOXALYL	CHERQUERED	QUINOPYRIN	**22**	QUESTHOUSE
SQUIBCRACK	CINQUEPACE	SEMIQUAVER	ACEQUIADOR	QUINAMIDIN
	COQUIMBITE	SOMNILOQUY	ACQUAINTED	QUINOLINYL
28	DULCILOQUY	SQUABASHER	ACQUIRENDA	QUINTUPLED
EQUIJACENT	EARTHQUAVE	SQUABBLING	ACQUISITED	RADIOPAQUE
QUATORZAIN	FREQUENTLY	SQUALIFORM	ACQUITTING	SATYRESQUE
QUICKTHORN	INADEQUACY	SQUAMOSELY	AQUAFORTIS	SQUARSONRY
QUICKWATER	MAGNIFIQUE	SQUAMOSITY	AQUAPLANED	SQUASHIEST
QUINAZOLIN	QUACKERIES	SQUAMOUSLY	AQUAVALENT	TRANQUILLY
QUINCUNXES	QUADRIFORM	SQUAREFACE	AQUIFEROUS	TRIQUINOYL
QUINIZARIN	QUADRIVIUM	SQUELCHIER	BANQUETING	UNEQUALITY
QUIXOTICAL	QUINSYWORT	SQUIREARCH	BIQUADRATE	UNFREQUENT
	QUIVERLEAF	UBIQUITARY	BURLESQUED	
27	SQUARISHLY		CIGARESQUE	**21**
CLIQUISHLY	SQUELCHING	**23**	CONQUERING	ACQUISITOR
DISQUIXOTE	SQUIFFIEST	ACQUIESCER	COQUETTING	ALCORNOQUE
QUADRATRIX	USQUEBAUGH	ACQUIRABLE	CROQUETING	ANTIMASQUE
QUALMISHLY	VANQUISHER	ACQUISIBLE	DELIQUESCE	ANTISQUAMA
SQUAWBERRY	VERSILOQUY	ACQUISITUM	EQUIPOISED	APOQUININE
SQUELCHILY		ACQUITMENT	EQUITATIVE	AQUAMARINE
SQUILLAGEE	**24**	ADEQUATELY	EQUIVALENT	AQUICOLOUS
SQUIRARCHY	ACQUIESCED	ADEQUATIVE	EQUIVOROUS	AQUIPAROUS
UNEQUIAXED	BEQUEATHAL	AQUASCUTUM	FOURSQUARE	ARBORESQUE
WORLDQUAKE	BEQUEATHER	AQUILAWOOD	FREQUENTER	BANQUETEER
	CATAFALQUE	COLLOQUIUM	HARLEQUINA	BIQUINTILE
26	CHAUTAUQUA	COQUELICOT	INEQUALITY	BLANQUETTE
CHINQUAPIN	CHOUQUETTE	DISQUIETLY	INFREQUENT	BLANQUILLO
COQUELUCHE	CINQUEFOIL	EUMOLPIQUE	LACQUERING	BLOTTESQUE
DISQUALIFY	COEQUALITY	FREQUENTED	LIQUIDABLE	BROQUINEER
EARTHQUAKE	COQUETTISH	ILLIQUIDLY	MASQUERADE	BRUSQUERIE
ELIQUATING	EQUABILITY	LAMBREQUIN	MEDRINAQUE	BURLESQUER

COEQUATION
COLLIQUATE
COLLOQUIAL
COLLOQUIST
CONQUININE
CONSEQUENT
COQUETRIES
CRAQUELURE
DISQUIETED
EQUANIMOUS
EQUIPARANT
EQUIPARATE
EQUISETUMS
GRANDESQUE
INQUIRABLE
LACQUERIST
LIQUESCENT
LIQUIDATED
LOQUACIOUS
MARQUISATE
MARQUISESS
MARQUISINA
MOSQUITOES
OBLOQUIOUS
OBSEQUIOUS
OPAQUENESS
PASQUILANT
PASQUILLER
PERQUISITE
PERRUQUIER
QUADRANGLE
QUADRATING
QUADRIGATE
QUADRILLED
QUAINTANCE
QUALIMETER
QUARTERMAN

QUARTERMEN
QUERCITRIN
QUERCITRON
QUIDDITIES
QUIETISTIC
QUINACRINE
QUINONIMIN
QUINQUEVIR
QUINTUPLET
REQUIESCAT
REQUIRABLE
REQUITABLE
ROBOTESQUE
SEMISQUARE
SEQUACIOUS
SEQUESTRUM
SOUBRIQUET
SQUADRONED
SQUAMATINE
SQUAMATION
SQUAMELLAE
SQUAMULATE
SQUAMULOSE
SQUANDERED
SQUIGGLIER
SQUILLITIC
SQUIRMIEST
TRIQUETRIC
TRIQUETRUM
UBIQUARIAN
UBIQUITOUS
UNCONQUEST
UNIQUANTIC

20
ADEQUATION

ANTIQUATED
DELINQUENT
DISQUIETER
DISQUISITE
EQUISIGNAL
INADEQUATE
INQUIETUDE
INQUINATED
INQUIRENDO
LIQUEURING
LIQUIDATOR
LIQUIDNESS
QUADRANTAL
QUADRATURE
QUADRENNIA
QUADRILLES
QUANDARIES
QUANTITIED
QUARRELING
QUARTERAGE
QUARTERING
QUESTIONED
QUINALDINE
QUINOIDINE
QUINTADENA
QUINTADENE
SQUALODONT
SQUANDERER
SQUATINOID
SQUETEAGUE
UNADEQUATE
UNDERQUOTE
UNEQUALLED
UNLIQUORED
UNQUIETUDE

19
AQUATINTER
ELIQUATION
EQUALITIES
EQUANGULAR
EQUATIONAL
EQUATOREAL
EQUATORIAL
EQUESTRIAN
EQUILIBRIA
EQUISONANT
EQUITATION
ILLAQUEATE
INELOQUENT
INEQUATION
INEQUITIES
INIQUITIES
INIQUITOUS
INQUESTUAL
INQUISITOR
LANSQUENET
LAQUEARIAN
QUAILERIES
QUAINTNESS
QUANTITATE
QUANTITIES
QUARANTINE
QUARENTENE
QUARRELOUS
QUARTATION
QUASSATION
QUATERNATE
QUATERNION
QUEASINESS
QUEENLIEST
QUENSELITE

QUERNSTONE
QUESTIONEE
QUESTIONER
QUESTORIAL
QUINIRETIN
QUOTENNIAL
QUOTIETIES
RELINQUENT
RELIQUAIRE
REQUISITOR
ROQUELAURE
SEQUENTIAL
SEQUESTRAL
SESQUINONA
SQUALLIEST
SQUARENESS
SQUARETAIL
SQUATAROLE
SQUATEROLE
SQUATTIEST
STATUESQUE
TAUROESQUE
TERRAQUEAN
TOURNIQUET
TRANQUILER
TRANQUILLO
TRIQUETRAL
TRIQUINATE
TURQUOISES
UNIQUENESS
UNQUIETOUS
UNREQUITER

18
QUINAQUINA
QUISQUEITE

ALPHABETICAL LIST OF WORDS OVER 10 LETTERS

ABSQUATULATE
ACQUAINTANCE
ACQUAINTANT
ACQUIESCENCE
ACQUIESCENT
ACQUIESCING
ACQUIREMENT
ACQUISITION
ACQUISITIVE
ACQUISITIVELY
ACQUITTANCE
ADEQUATENESS
ALTILOQUENCE
ALTILOQUENT
AMPHORILOQUY
ANTHRAQUINOL
ANTIMASQUER
ANTIQUARIAN
ANTIQUARIES
ANTIQUARISM
ANTIQUATING
ANTIQUATION
ANTIQUENESS
ANTIQUITIES
APPLIQUEING
AQUACULTURAL
AQUACULTURE
AQUAEMANALE
AQUAEMANALIA

AQUAFORTIST
AQUAPLANING
AQUAPUNCTURE
AQUARELLIST
AQUATICALLY
AQUATIVENESS
AQUEOGLACIAL
AQUEOIGNEOUS
AQUEOUSNESS
AQUICULTURAL
AQUICULTURE
AQUOTIZATION
ARABESQUELY
ARABESQUERIE
BANQUETEERING
BARBARESQUE
BARQUENTINE
BECQUERELITE
BIQUADRANTAL
BIQUADRATIC
BIQUARTERLY
BLOTTESQUELY
BOUDOIRESQUE
BOUQUETIERE
BOUQUINISTE
BREVILOQUENT
BRONCHILOQUY
BRUSQUENESS
BURLESQUELY

BURLESQUING
CHEQUERBOARD
CHEQUERWISE
CHEQUERWORK
CHIVALRESQUE
CHYMAQUEOUS
CINQUECENTO
CLIQUISHNESS
COEQUALNESS
COLLIQUATION
COLLIQUATIVE
COLLOQUIALLY
COLLOQUIZED
COLLOQUIZING
COLOQUINTIDA
CONQUERABLE
CONQUERINGLY
CONQUINAMINE
CONQUISTADOR
CONSEQUENCE
CONSEQUENTIAL
CONSEQUENTLY
CONTRAMARQUE
COQUECIGRUE
COQUETTISHLY
CROQUIGNOLE
DELINQUENCIES
DELINQUENCY
DELINQUENTLY

DELIQUESCED
DELIQUESCENT
DELIQUESCING
DENTILOQUIST
DESQUAMATED
DESQUAMATION
DESQUAMATIVE
DESQUAMATORY
DISACQUAINT
DISCOTHEQUE
DISEQUALIZE
DISQUALIFIED
DISQUIETEDLY
DISQUIETING
DISQUIETUDE
DISQUIPARANT
DISQUISITED
DISQUISITING
DISQUISITION
DISQUISITIVE
DISQUISITOR
DISQUISITORY
DULCILOQUENT
DUROQUINONE
EARTHQUAKED
EARTHQUAKEN
EARTHQUAKING
ELOQUENTIAL

EQUABLENESS
EQUALITARIAN
EQUALIZATION
EQUANIMOUSLY
EQUATIONALLY
EQUATIONISM
EQUATIONIST
EQUATORIALLY
EQUESTRIENNE
EQUIDISTANCE
EQUIDISTANT
EQUIDISTANTLY
EQUIDIURNAL
EQUIFORMITY
EQUIGRANULAR
EQUILATERAL
EQUILIBRANT
EQUILIBRATE
EQUILIBRATED
EQUILIBRATING
EQUILIBRATION
EQUILIBRATIVE
EQUILIBRATOR
EQUILIBRATORY
EQUILIBRIAL
EQUILIBRIATE
EQUILIBRIOUS
EQUILIBRIST

EQUILIBRISTAT	INCONSEQUENT	PASQUEFLOWER	QUALIFIEDLY	QUINAMIDINE
EQUILIBRISTIC	INELOQUENCE	PASQUILLANT	QUALITATIVE	QUINANISOLE
EQUILIBRITY	INEQUALITIES	PASQUINADED	QUALMISHNESS	QUINATOXINE
EQUILIBRIUM	INEQUALNESS	PASQUINADER	QUANTIFYING	QUINAZOLINE
EQUILIBRIUMS	INEQUITABLE	PASQUINADING	QUANTIMETER	QUINCUNCIAL
EQUILIBRIZE	INEQUITABLY	PAUCILOQUENT	QUANTITATIVE	QUINCUNXIAL
EQUIMOLECULAR	INEQUIVALVE	PECTORILOQUE	QUANTITIVELY	QUINDECAGON
EQUIMOMENTAL	INFREQUENCE	PECTORILOQUY	QUANTIVALENT	QUINDECEMVIR
EQUIMULTIPLE	INFREQUENCY	PEREQUITATE	QUANTIZATION	QUINDECEMVIR
EQUINANGULAR	INIQUITABLE	PERQUISITION	QUANTIZING	QUINDECIMVIR
EQUINOCTIAL	INIQUITOUSLY	PERQUISITOR	QUANTOMETER	QUINHYDRONE
EQUINOCTIAL	INQUAINTANCE	PHENOQUINONE	QUAQUAVERSAL	QUINISEXTINE
EQUINOCTIALLY	INQUARTATION	PICTURESQUE	QUARANTINED	QUINOIDATION
EQUINOVARUS	INQUIETNESS	PIQUANTNESS	QUARANTINER	QUINOLINIUM
EQUIPARATION	INQUILINISM	PLASMOQUINE	QUARANTINING	QUINOLOGIST
EQUIPARTILE	INQUILINITY	PLATERESQUE	QUARRELLING	QUINONIMINE
EQUIPARTITION	INQUILINOUS	POLYLOQUENT	QUARRELLOUS	QUINOXALINE
EQUIPOISING	INQUINATING	PRECONQUEST	QUARRELOUSLY	QUINQUENNIAD
EQUIPOISING	INQUINATION	PREREQUISITE	QUARRELSOME	QUINQUENNIA
EQUIPOLLENCE	INQUIRATION	PRETEREQUINE	QUARRYSTONE	QUINQUENNIAL
EQUIPOLLENCY	INQUIRINGLY	PROPINQUANT	QUARTERBACK	QUINQUENNIUM
EQUIPOLLENT	INQUISITION	PROPINQUITY	QUARTERFOIL	QUINQUENNIUMS
EQUIPOLLENTLY	INQUISITIONAL	PROPINQUOUS	QUARTERLAND	QUINQUERTIUM
EQUIPONDERANT	INQUISITIVE	PROQUAESTOR	QUARTERLIES	QUINQUEVIRS
EQUIPONDERATE	INQUISITORIAL	PSEUDOAQUATIC	QUARTERMASTER	QUINSYBERRIES
EQUIPOSTILE	INQUISITORY	QUACKISHNESS	QUARTERNIGHT	QUINSYBERRY
EQUIPOTENTIAL	ISOQUINOLINE	QUACKSALVER	QUARTERNION	QUINTELEMENT
EQUIPROBABLE	JEQUIRITIES	QUADRAGESIMAL	QUARTERPACE	QUINTERNION
EQUISETACEOUS	LACQUERWORK	QUADRANGLED	QUARTERSAWED	QUINTESSENCE
EQUISONANCE	LIQUEFACIENT	QUADRANGULAR	QUARTERSAWING	QUINTILLION
EQUIVALENCE	LIQUEFACTION	QUADRANGULED	QUARTERSAWN	QUINTUPLING
EQUIVALENCED	LIQUEFACTIVE	QUADRANTILE	QUARTERSTAFF	QUINUCLIDINE
EQUIVALENCY	LIQUEFIABLE	QUADRAPHONIC	QUARTERSTAVES	QUIPPISHNESS
EQUIVALENTLY	LIQUESCENCE	QUADRATICAL	QUARTIPAROUS	QUIRITARIAN
EQUIVOCALITY	LIQUESCENCY	QUADRENNIAL	QUATERNARIES	QUIRQUINCHO
EQUIVOCATED	LIQUIDAMBAR	QUADRENNIUM	QUATERNARIUS	QUISLINGISM
EQUIVOCATING	LIQUIDAMBER	QUADRENNIUMS	QUATERNIONIC	QUISQUILIAN
EQUIVOCATION	LIQUIDATING	QUADRICINIUM	QUATERNITIES	QUISQUILIARY
EQUIVOCATOR	LIQUIDATION	QUADRICIPITAL	QUATERTENSES	QUISQUILIOUS
EQUIVOCATORY	LIQUIDIZING	QUADRICYCLE	QUATREFOILED	QUITCLAIMED
EQUIVOLUMINAL	LIQUIDOGENIC	QUADRICYCLER	QUATTROCENTO	QUITCLAIMING
ESQUAMULOSE	LIQUORISHLY	QUADRENNIUM	QUAVERINGLY	QUITTERBONE
ETIQUETTICAL	LIQUORISHNESS	QUADRIFILAR	QUEBRACHITE	QUIZZACIOUS
EXQUISITELY	LONGINQUITY	QUADRIFOCAL	QUEBRACHITOL	QUIZZATORIAL
EXQUISITENESS	LOQUACIOUSLY	QUADRIFOLIUM	QUEBRADILLA	QUIZZICALITY
EXQUISITISM	MAGNILOQUENT	QUADRIFRONS	QUEENFISHES	QUIZZICALLY
EXQUISITIVELY	MARQUETERIE	QUADRIGAMIST	QUEENLINESS	QUODLIBETARY
FATILOQUENT	MARQUISETTE	QUADRIGATUS	QUEENSBERRIES	QUODLIBETIC
FOREQUARTER	MARQUISOTTE	QUADRIHYBRID	QUEENSBERRY	QUOTABILITY
FORMALESQUE	MASQUERADED	QUADRIJUGAL	QUENCHLESSLY	QUOTABLENESS
FOURSQUARELY	MASQUERADER	QUADRILATERAL	QUERCITANNIN	QUOTATIONAL
FREQUENCIES	MASQUERADING	QUADRILLING	QUERCIVOROUS	QUOTATIONIST
FREQUENTABLE	MERIQUINONE	QUADRILLION	QUERIMONIES	QUOTEWORTHY
FREQUENTAGE	MERIQUINONIC	QUADRINOMIAL	QUERIMONIOUS	QUOTIDIANLY
FREQUENTATION	MILQUETOAST	QUADRIPAROUS	QUERULENTIAL	RELINQUISHED
FREQUENTATIVE	MISQUOTATION	QUADRIPLANAR	QUERULOSITY	RELINQUISHER
FREQUENTING	MONCHIQUITE	QUADRIURATE	QUERULOUSLY	RELIQUARIES
FREQUENTNESS	MOSQUITOBILL	QUADRIVALENT	QUESTIONABLE	REQUIESCENCE
GIGANTESQUE	MOUSQUETAIRE	QUADRIVIOUS	QUESTIONABLY	REQUIREMENT
GORGONESQUE	MULTILOQUENT	QUADRUMANAL	QUESTIONARIES	REQUISITELY
GRANDILOQUENT	MULTILOQUOUS	QUADRUMANOUS	QUESTIONARY	REQUISITION
GROTESQUELY	MUSQUASHROOT	QUADRUPEDAL	QUESTIONING	REQUISITORY
GROTESQUERIE	MUSQUASHWEED	QUADRUPEDAN	QUESTIONIST	REQUITATIVE
GROTESQUERY	NATURALESQUE	QUADRUPEDANT	QUESTIONLESS	REQUITELESS
HARLEQUINADE	NESQUEHONITE	QUADRUPEDATE	QUESTIONNAIRE	REQUITEMENT
HARLEQUINIC	OBLIQUATION	QUADRUPEDOUS	QUESTMONGER	RIBAUDEQUIN
HARLEQUINIZE	OBLIQUENESS	QUADRUPLANE	QUICKENANCE	SANCTILOQUENT
HEADQUARTER	OBLIQUITIES	QUADRUPLATE	QUICKENBEAM	SCULPTURESQUE
HEADQUARTERS	OBLIQUITOUS	QUADRUPLATOR	QUICKSILVER	SEMIANTIQUE
HINDQUARTER	OBSEQUIOUSLY	QUADRUPLING	QUICKSILVERY	SEMIAQUATIC
HINDQUARTERS	OMNILOQUENT	QUAESTIONES	QUIDDITATIVE	SEMIQUARTILE
HYDROQUININE	OSTEOPLAQUE	QUAESTORIAL	QUIESCENTLY	SEMIQUIETIST
HYDROQUINONE	OUTQUESTION	QUAESTORIAN	QUIINACEOUS	SEQUACIOUSLY
ILLIQUATION	OXYQUINOLINE	QUAESTORSHIP	QUILLFISHES	SEQUENTIALITY
INADEQUATELY	PALANQUINED	QUALIFIABLE	QUINALDINIC	SEQUESTERED
INADEQUATION	PALANQUINING	QUALIFICATION	QUINALDINIUM	SEQUESTERING
INCONSEQUENCE	PARAQUADRATE	QUALIFICATOR	QUINAMICINE	SEQUESTERMENT

SEQUESTRABLE
SEQUESTRANT
SEQUESTRATE
SEQUESTRATED
SEQUESTRATING
SEQUESTRATION
SEQUESTRATOR
SESQUIALTER
SESQUIALTERA
SESQUIALTERAL
SESQUINONAL
SESQUIOCTAVA
SESQUIPEDAL
SESQUIPLICATE
SESQUIQUARTA
SESQUIQUINTA
SESQUISEXTAL
SESQUITERPENE
SESQUITERTIA
SOLDATESQUE
SOLILOQUIES
SOLILOQUISE
SOLILOQUIST
SOLILOQUIZE
SOLILOQUIZED
SOLILOQUIZER
SOLILOQUIZING
SOMNILOQUENCE

SOMNILOQUENT
SOMNILOQUISM
SOMNILOQUIST
SOMNILOQUOUS
SQUABBLINGLY
SQUADRONING
SQUALIDNESS
SQUAMACEOUS
SQUAMELLATE
SQUAMIFEROUS
SQUAMIGEROUS
SQUAMOSENESS
SQUAMOUSNESS
SQUAMULATION
SQUANDERING
SQUANDERINGLY
SQUARROSELY
SQUARRULOSE
SQUASHBERRY
SQUASHINESS
SQUATTINESS
SQUATTOCRACY
SQUAWBERRIES
SQUAWFISHES
SQUAWFLOWER
SQUAWKINGLY
SQUEAKINESS

SQUEAKINGLY
SQUEAMISHLY
SQUEAMISHNESS
SQUEEGEEING
SQUEEZINGLY
SQUELCHIEST
SQUELCHINESS
SQUELCHINGLY
SQUIDGEREEN
SQUIGGLIEST
SQUILGEEING
SQUINTINGLY
SQUINTINGNESS
SQUIRARCHAL
SQUIREARCHAL
SQUIREARCHIES
SQUIREARCHY
SQUIRMINESS
SQUIRMINGLY
SQUIRRELFISH
SQUIRRELTAIL
SQUIRTINESS
SQUIRTINGLY
STATUESQUELY
STULTILOQUY
SUAVILOQUENT
SUBQUINTUPLE

SUBSEQUENCE
SUBSEQUENCY
SUBSEQUENTIAL
SUBSEQUENTLY
SYMPATHIQUE
TERLINQUAITE
TERRAQUEOUS
THUNDERSQUALL
THYMOQUINONE
TRANQUILEST
TRANQUILITY
TRANQUILIZE
TRANQUILIZER
TRANQUILIZING
TRANQUILLER
TRANQUILLEST
TRANQUILLISE
TRANQUILLITY
TRANQUILLIZE
TRANQUILLIZED
TRANQUILNESS
TRIQUETROUS
TRISTILOQUY
UBIQUITARIAN
UBIQUITARIES
UBIQUITOUSLY
UNACQUAINTED

UNADEQUATELY
UNCONQUERED
UNDERQUOTED
UNDERQUOTING
UNEQUITABLE
UNEQUITABLY
UNEQUIVOCAL
UNEQUIVOCALLY
UNFREQUENCY
UNFREQUENTED
UNFREQUENTLY
UNLIQUIDATED
UNQUALIFIED
UNQUALITIED
UNQUANTIFIED
UNQUESTIONED
UNQUESTIONING
UNQUIESCENCE
UNQUIESCENT
UNQUIETNESS
UTRAQUISTIC
VANQUISHING
VENTRILOQUAL
VENTRILOQUE
VENTRILOQUIST
VENTRILOQUY
XYLOQUINONE

POSITIONAL ORDER LIST OF WORDS OVER 10 LETTERS

QUACKISHNESS
QUACKSALVER
QUADRAGESIMAL
QUADRANGLED
QUADRANGULAR
QUADRANGULED
QUADRANTILE
QUADRAPHONIC
QUADRATICAL
QUADRENNIAL
QUADRENNIUM
QUADRENNIUMS
QUADRICINIUM
QUADRICIPITAL
QUADRICYCLE
QUADRICYCLER
QUADRIENNIUM
QUADRIFILAR
QUADRIFOCAL
QUADRIFOLIUM
QUADRIFRONS
QUADRIGAMIST
QUADRIGATUS
QUADRIHYBRID
QUADRIJUGAL
QUADRILATERAL
QUADRILLING
QUADRILLION
QUADRINOMIAL
QUADRIPAROUS
QUADRIPLANAR
QUADRIURATE
QUADRIVALENT
QUADRIVIOUS
QUADRUMANAL
QUADRUMANOUS
QUADRUPEDAL
QUADRUPEDAN
QUADRUPEDANT
QUADRUPEDATE
QUADRUPEDOUS
QUADRUPLANE
QUADRUPLATE

QUADRUPLATOR
QUADRUPLING
QUAESTIONES
QUAESTORIAL
QUAESTORIAN
QUAESTORSHIP
QUALIFIABLE
QUALIFICATION
QUALIFICATOR
QUALIFIEDLY
QUALITATIVE
QUALMISHNESS
QUANTIFYING
QUANTIMETER
QUANTITATIVE
QUANTITIVELY
QUANTIVALENT
QUANTIZATION
QUANTIZING
QUANTOMETER
QUAQUAVERSAL
QUARANTINED
QUARANTINER
QUARANTINING
QUARRELLING
QUARRELLOUS
QUARRELOUSLY
QUARRELSOME
QUARRYSTONE
QUARTERBACK
QUARTERFOIL
QUARTERLAND
QUARTERLIES
QUARTERMASTER
QUARTERNIGHT
QUARTERNION
QUARTERPACE
QUARTERSAWED
QUARTERSAWING
QUARTERSAWN
QUARTERSTAFF
QUARTERSTAVES
QUARTIPAROUS

QUATERNARIES
QUATERNARIUS
QUATERNIONIC
QUATERNITIES
QUATERTENSES
QUATREFOILED
QUATTROCENTO
QUAVERINGLY
QUEBRACHITE
QUEBRACHITOL
QUEBRADILLA
QUEENFISHES
QUEENLINESS
QUEENSBERRIES
QUEENSBERRY
QUENCHLESSLY
QUERCITANNIN
QUERCIVOROUS
QUERIMONIES
QUERIMONIOUS
QUERULENTIAL
QUERULOSITY
QUERULOUSLY
QUESTIONABLE
QUESTIONABLY
QUESTIONARIES
QUESTIONARY
QUESTIONING
QUESTIONIST
QUESTIONLESS
QUESTIONNAIRE
QUESTMONGER
QUICKENANCE
QUICKENBEAM
QUICKSILVER
QUICKSILVERY
QUIDDITATIVE
QUIESCENTLY
QUIINACEOUS
QUILLFISHES
QUINALDINIC
QUINALDINIUM
QUINAMICINE

QUINAMIDINE
QUINANISOLE
QUINATOXINE
QUINAZOLINE
QUINCUNCIAL
QUINCUNXIAL
QUINDECAGON
QUINDECEMVIR
QUINDECEMVIRI
QUINDECIMVIR
QUINHYDRONE
QUINISEXTINE
QUINOIDATION
QUINOLINUM
QUINOLOGIST
QUINONIMINE
QUINOXALINE
QUINQUENNIA
QUINQUENNIAD
QUINQUENNIAL
QUINQUENNIUM
QUINQUENNIUMS
QUINQUERTIUM
QUINQUEVIRS
QUINSYBERRIES
QUINSYBERRY
QUINTELEMENT
QUINTERNION
QUINTESSENCE
QUINTILLION
QUINTUPLING
QUINUCLIDINE
QUIPPISHNESS
QUIRITARIAN
QUIRQUINCHO
QUISLINGISM
QUISQUILIAN
QUISQUILIARY
QUISQUILIOUS
QUITCLAIMED
QUITCLAIMING
QUITTERBONE
QUIZZACIOUS

QUIZZATORIAL
QUIZZICALITY
QUIZZICALLY
QUODLIBETARY
QUODLIBETIC
QUOTABILITY
QUOTABLENESS
QUOTATIONAL
QUOTATIONIST
QUOTEWORTHY
QUOTIDIANLY

AQUACULTURAL
AQUACULTURE
AQUAEMANALE
AQUAEMANALIA
AQUAFORTIST
AQUAPLANING
AQUAPUNCTURE
AQUARELLIST
AQUATICALLY
AQUATIVENESS
AQUEOGLACIAL
AQUEOIGNEOUS
AQUEOUSNESS
AQUICULTURAL
AQUICULTURE
AQUOTIZATION
EQUABLENESS
EQUALITARIAN
EQUALIZATION
EQUANIMOUSLY
EQUATIONALLY
EQUATIONISM
EQUATIONIST
EQUATORIALLY
EQUESTRIENNE
EQUIDISTANCE
EQUIDISTANT
EQUIDISTANTLY
EQUIDIURNAL
EQUIFORMITY
EQUIGRANULAR

EQUILATERAL	SQUEAMISHLY	REQUISITELY	INIQUITOUSLY	PARAQUADRATE
EQUILIBRANT	SQUEAMISHNESS	REQUISITION	ISOQUINOLINE	PEREQUITATE
EQUILIBRATE	SQUEEGEEING	REQUISITORY	LACQUERWORK	QUINQUENNIA
EQUILIBRATED	SQUEEZINGLY	REQUITATIVE	MARQUETERIE	QUINQUENNIAD
EQUILIBRATING	SQUELCHIEST	REQUITELESS	MARQUISETTE	QUINQUENNIAL
EQUILIBRATION	SQUELCHINESS	REQUITEMENT	MARQUISOTTE	QUINQUENNIUM
EQUILIBRATIVE	SQUELCHINGLY	SEQUACIOUSLY	MASQUERADED	QUINQUENNIUMS
EQUILIBRATOR	SQUIDGEREEN	SEQUENTIALITY	MASQUERADER	QUINQUERTIUM
EQUILIBRATORY	SQUIGGLIEST	SEQUESTERED	MASQUERADING	QUINQUEVIRS
EQUILIBRIAL	SQUILGEEING	SEQUESTERING	MILQUETOAST	QUIRQUINCHO
EQUILIBRIATE	SQUINTINGLY	SEQUESTERMENT	MISQUOTATION	QUISQUILIAN
EQUILIBRIOUS	SQUINTINGNESS	SEQUESTRABLE	MOSQUITOBILL	QUISQUILIARY
EQUILIBRIST	SQUIRARCHAL	SEQUESTRANT	MUSQUASHROOT	QUISQUILIOUS
EQUILIBRISTAT	SQUIREARCHAL	SEQUESTRATE	MUSQUASHWEED	RELIQUARIES
EQUILIBRISTIC	SQUIREARCHIES	SEQUESTRATED	NESQUEHONITE	SEMIQUARTILE
EQUILIBRITY	SQUIREARCHY	SEQUESTRATING	OUTQUESTION	SEMIQUIETIST
EQUILIBRIUM	SQUIRMINESS	SEQUESTRATION	OXYQUINOLINE	TRANQUILEST
EQUILIBRIUMS	SQUIRMINGLY	SEQUESTRATOR	PASQUEFLOWER	TRANQUILITY
EQUILIBRIZE	SQUIRRELFISH	UNQUALIFIED	PASQUILLANT	TRANQUILIZE
EQUIMOLECULAR	SQUIRRELTAIL	UNQUALITIED	PASQUINADED	TRANQUILIZER
EQUIMOMENTAL	SQUIRTINESS	UNQUANTIFIED	PASQUINADER	TRANQUILIZING
EQUIMULTIPLE	SQUIRTINGLY	UNQUESTIONED	PASQUINADING	TRANQUILLER
EQUINANGULAR		UNQUESTIONING	PERQUISITION	TRANQUILLEST
EQUINOCTIAL	ACQUAINTANCE	UNQUIESCENCE	PERQUISITOR	TRANQUILLISE
EQUINOCTIAL	ACQUAINTANT	UNQUIESCENT	PROQUAESTOR	TRANQUILLITY
EQUINOCTIALLY	ACQUIESCENCE	UNQUIETNESS	QUAQUAVERSAL	TRANQUILLIZE
EQUINOVARUS	ACQUIESCENT		SESQUIALTER	TRANQUILLIZED
EQUIPARATION	ACQUIESCING	ABSQUATULATE	SESQUIALTERA	TRANQUILNESS
EQUIPARTILE	ACQUIREMENT	ADEQUATENESS	SESQUIALTERAL	UNACQUAINTED
EQUIPARTITION	ACQUISITION	BANQUETEERING	SESQUINONAL	UNLIQUIDATED
EQUIPOISING	ACQUISITIVE	BARQUENTINE	SESQUIOCTAVA	UTRAQUISTIC
EQUIPOLLENCE	ACQUISITIVELY	BECQUERELITE	SESQUIPEDAL	XYLOQUINONE
EQUIPOLLENCY	ACQUITTANCE	BOUQUETIERE	SESQUIPLICATE	
EQUIPOLLENT	BIQUADRANTAL	BOUQUINISTE	SESQUIQUARTA	APPLIQUEING
EQUIPOLLENTLY	BIQUADRATIC	CHEQUERBOARD	SESQUIQUINTA	CHYMAQUEOUS
EQUIPONDERANT	BIQUARTERLY	CHEQUERWISE	SESQUISEXTAL	COLLIQUATION
EQUIPONDERAT	COQUECIGRUE	CHEQUERWORK	SESQUITERPENE	COLLIQUATIVE
EQUIPOSTILE	COQUETTISHLY	CINQUECENTO	SESQUITERTIA	COLLOQUIALLY
EQUIPOTENTIAL	ESQUAMULOSE	CLIQUISHNESS	SUBQUINTUPLE	COLLOQUIZED
EQUIPROBABLE	EXQUISITELY	COEQUALNESS	TRIQUETROUS	COLLOQUIZING
EQUISETACEOUS	EXQUISITENESS	CONQUERABLE	UBIQUITARIAN	CONSEQUENCE
EQUISONANCE	EXQUISITISM	CONQUERINGLY	UBIQUITARIES	CONSEQUENTIAL
EQUIVALENCE	EXQUISITIVELY	CONQUINAMINE	UBIQUITOUSLY	CONSEQUENTLY
EQUIVALENCED	INQUAINTANCE	CONQUISTADOR	UNEQUITABLE	DELINQUENCIES
EQUIVALENCY	INQUARTATION	CONQUISTADORES	UNEQUITABLY	DELINQUENCY
EQUIVALENTLY	INQUIETNESS	CROQUIGNOLE	UNEQUIVOCAL	DELINQUENTLY
EQUIVOCALITY	INQUILINISM	DESQUAMATED	UNEQUIVOCALLY	DISACQUAINT
EQUIVOCATED	INQUILINITY	DESQUAMATING	VANQUISHING	EARTHQUAKED
EQUIVOCATING	INQUILINOUS	DESQUAMATION		EARTHQUAKEN
EQUIVOCATION	INQUINATING	DESQUAMATIVE	ANTIQUARIAN	EARTHQUAKING
EQUIVOCATOR	INQUINATION	DESQUAMATORY	ANTIQUARIES	FOURSQUARELY
EQUIVOCATORY	INQUIRATION	DISQUALIFIED	ANTIQUARISM	HARLEQUINADE
EQUIVOLUMINAL	INQUIRINGLY	DISQUIETEDLY	ANTIQUATING	HARLEQUINIC
SQUABBLINGLY	INQUISITION	DISQUIETING	ANTIQUATION	HARLEQUINIZE
SQUADRONING	INQUISITIONAL	DISQUIETUDE	ANTIQUENESS	HYDROQUININE
SQUALIDNESS	INQUISITIVE	DISQUIPARANT	ANTIQUITIES	HYDROQUINONE
SQUAMACEOUS	INQUISITORIAL	DISQUISITED	BRUSQUENESS	INADEQUATELY
SQUAMELLATE	INQUISITORY	DISQUISITING	COLOQUINTIDA	INADEQUATION
SQUAMIFEROUS	JEQUIRITIES	DISQUISITION	DELIQUESCED	INELOQUENCE
SQUAMIGEROUS	LIQUEFACIENT	DISQUISITIVE	DELIQUESCENT	INFREQUENCE
SQUAMOSENESS	LIQUEFACTION	DISQUISITOR	DELIQUESCING	INFREQUENCY
SQUAMOUSNESS	LIQUEFACTIVE	DISQUISITORY	DISEQUALIZE	PALANQUINED
SQUAMULATION	LIQUEFIABLE	ELOQUENTIAL	DUROQUINONE	PALANQUINING
SQUANDERING	LIQUESCENCE	ETIQUETTICAL	FOREQUARTER	PHENOQUINONE
SQUANDERINGLY	LIQUESCENCY	FREQUENCIES	HEADQUARTER	PREREQUISITE
SQUARROSELY	LIQUIDAMBAR	FREQUENTABLE	HEADQUARTERS	RELINQUISHED
SQUARRULOSE	LIQUIDAMBER	FREQUENTAGE	HINDQUARTER	RELINQUISHER
SQUASHBERRY	LIQUIDATING	FREQUENTATION	HINDQUARTERS	SEMIAQUATIC
SQUASHINESS	LIQUIDATION	FREQUENTATIVE	ILLIQUATION	SUBSEQUENCE
SQUATTINESS	LIQUIDIZING	FREQUENTING	MERIQUINONE	SUBSEQUENCY
SQUATTOCRACY	LIQUIDOGENIC	FREQUENTNESS	MERIQUINONIC	SUBSEQUENTIAL
SQUAWBERRIES	LIQUORISHLY	INEQUALITIES	MOUSQUETAIRE	SUBSEQUENTLY
SQUAWFISHES	LIQUORISHNESS	INEQUALNESS	OBLIQUATION	TERRAQUEOUS
SQUAWFLOWER	LOQUACIOUSLY	INEQUITABLE	OBLIQUENESS	THYMOQUINONE
SQUAWKINGLY	PIQUANTNESS	INEQUITABLY	OBLIQUITIES	UNADEQUATELY
SQUEAKINESS	REQUIESCENCE	INEQUIVALVE	OBLIQUITOUS	UNCONQUERED
SQUEAKINGLY	REQUIREMENT	INIQUITABLE	OBSEQUIOUSLY	UNDERQUOTED

UNDERQUOTING
UNFREQUENCY
UNFREQUENTED
UNFREQUENTLY

ALTILOQUENCE
ALTILOQUENT
ANTHRAQUINOL
ARABESQUELY
ARABESQUERIE
BURLESQUELY
BURLESQUING
FATILOQUENT
GROTESQUELY
GROTESQUERIE
GROTESQUERY
LONGINQUITY
MONCHIQUITE

OMNILOQUENT
PLASMOQUINE
POLYLOQUENT
PRECONQUEST
PROPINQUANT
PROPINQUITY
PROPINQUOUS
SESQUIQUARTA
SESQUIQUINTA
SOLILOQUIES
SOLILOQUISE
SOLILOQUIST
SOLILOQUIZE
SOLILOQUIZED
SOLILOQUIZER
SOLILOQUIZING
TERLINQUAITE

ANTIMASQUER
BLOTTESQUELY
BREVILOQUENT
DENTILOQUIST
DULCILOQUENT
INCONSEQUENCE
INCONSEQUENT
MAGNILOQUENT
MULTILOQUENT
MULTILOQUOUS
PAUCILOQUENT
PRETEREQUINE
PSEUDOAQUATIC
RIBAUDEQUIN
SOMNILOQUENCE
SOMNILOQUENT
SOMNILOQUISM
SOMNILOQUIST

SOMNILOQUOUS
STATUESQUELY
SUAVILOQUENT

BARBARESQUE
DISCOTHEQUE
FORMALESQUE
GIGANTESQUE
GORGONESQUE
GRANDILOQUENT
OSTEOPLAQUE
PICTURESQUE
PLATERESQUE
SANCTILOQUENT
SEMIANTIQUE
SOLDATESQUE
STULTILOQUY
SYMPATHIQUE

THUNDERSQUALL
TRISTILOQUY
VENTRILOQUAL
VENTRILOQUE
VENTRILOQUIST
VENTRILOQUY

AMPHORILOQUY
BOUDOIRESQUE
BRONCHILOQUY
CHIVALRESQUE
CONTRAMARQUE
NATURALESQUE
PECTORILOQUE
PECTORILOQUY

SCULPTURESQUE

SCORING ORDER LIST OF WORDS OVER 10 LETTERS

35
EXQUISITIVELY

34
QUIZZICALITY

33
HARLEQUINIZE
QUICKSILVERY
QUIZZICALLY
SQUEEZINGLY

32
CHEQUERWORK
SOLILOQUIZING
TRANQUILIZING

31
AMPHORILOQUY
BRONCHILOQUY
LIQUIDIZING
SOLILOQUIZED
SQUAWKINGLY

30
ACQUISITIVELY
AQUOTIZATION
CHYMAQUEOUS
DISEQUALIZE
EQUALIZATION
EXQUISITELY
MUSQUASHWEED
QUACKISHNESS
QUANTIZATION
QUICKENBEAM
QUINDECEMVIRI
QUIZZACIOUS
SOLILOQUIZER
SQUELCHINGLY
SYMPATHIQUE
TRANQUILIZER
TRANQUILLIZE
UNEQUIVOCALLY
XYLOQUINONE

29
CHEQUERBOARD
CHIVALRESQUE
COQUETTISHLY
EARTHQUAKING
EQUIVOCATORY
EXQUISITENESS
EXQUISITISM

LACQUERWORK
LIQUEFACTIVE
PASQUEFLOWER
QUACKSALVER
QUADRAPHONIC
QUADRICYCLER
QUADRIJUGAL
QUANTIZING
QUENCHLESSLY
QUICKSILVER
QUINAZOLINE
QUINCUNXIAL
QUINDECEMVIR
QUINDECIMVIR
QUIZZATORIAL
QUOTEWORTHY
SOLILOQUIZE
SQUABBLINGLY
SQUAWFISHES
SQUAWFLOWER
THYMOQUINONE
TRANQUILIZE

28
CHEQUERWISE
EARTHQUAKED
EQUIFORMITY
EQUIPOLLENCY
FREQUENTATIVE
HYDROQUININE
HYDROQUINONE
PECTORILOQUY
QUADRICYCLE
QUARTERBACK
QUEBRACHITOL
QUICKENANCE
QUINISEXTINE
QUINSYBERRY
QUIPPISHNESS
SESQUISEXTAL
SQUASHBERRY
SQUATTOCRACY
SQUEAKINGLY
SQUEAMISHLY
SQUIREARCHY
UNFREQUENCY

27
CONQUERINGLY
DESQUAMATIVE
DESQUAMATORY
EARTHQUAKEN
EQUILIBRATIVE

EQUILIBRATORY
EQUINOCTIALLY
EQUIPOLLENTLY
EQUIPROBABLE
EQUIVALENCED
EQUIVOCATING
EQUIVOLUMINAL
FOURSQUARELY
JEQUIRITIES
LIQUESCENCY
MONCHIQUITE
PROPINQUITY
PSEUDOAQUATIC
QUADRICIPITAL
QUADRIFOLIUM
QUALIFICATION
QUALIFIEDLY
QUANTIFYING
QUANTITIVELY
QUARTERSTAFF
QUAVERINGLY
QUEBRACHITE
QUINATOXINE
QUINHYDRONE
QUINOXALINE
QUINSYBERRIES
QUODLIBETARY
SQUANDERINGLY
SQUEAMISHNESS
SQUIREARCHIES
SQUIRRELFISH
SUBSEQUENCY
UNFREQUENTLY
VANQUISHING

26
BLOTTESQUELY
BREVILOQUENT
CLIQUISHNESS
COLLIQUATIVE
COLLOQUIALLY
CONSEQUENTLY
DELINQUENCY
DISCOTHEQUE
DISQUALIFIED
DISQUIETEDLY
EQUANIMOUSLY
EQUIDISTANTLY
EQUILIBRISTIC
EQUIMOLECULAR
EQUIVOCATED
EQUIVOCATION
FREQUENTABLE

LIQUEFACIENT
LIQUEFACTION
LIQUORISHLY
LOQUACIOUSLY
MUSQUASHROOT
OBSEQUIOUSLY
PHENOQUINONE
QUADRAGESIMAL
QUADRICINIUM
QUADRIFOCAL
QUAESTORSHIP
QUALIFICATOR
QUALMISHNESS
QUARTERSAWING
QUEENFISHES
QUERCIVOROUS
QUESTIONABLY
QUIDDITATIVE
QUILLFISHES
QUITCLAIMING
SCULPTURESQUE
SEQUACIOUSLY
SESQUIOCTAVA
SESQUIPLICATE
SOMNILOQUENCE
SQUAMIFEROUS
SQUAWBERRIES
SQUELCHINESS
SQUIREARCHAL
SQUIRMINGLY
SUBSEQUENTLY
THUNDERSQUALL
UBIQUITOUSLY
VENTRILOQUY

25
ACQUAINTANCE
ACQUIESCING
ACQUISITIVE
APPLIQUEING
AQUAPUNCTURE
AQUATICALLY
ARABESQUELY
BANQUETEERING
BECQUERELITE
BIQUADRATIC
BIQUARTERLY
BURLESQUELY
CONQUINAMINE
CONTRAMARQUE
COQUECIGRUE
DELINQUENCIES
DELINQUENTLY

DELIQUESCING
DESQUAMATING
DISQUISITIVE
DISQUISITORY
EQUILIBRITY
EQUILIBRIUMS
EQUIMOMENTAL
EQUIMULTIPLE
EQUIPOLLENCE
EQUIPONDERANT
EQUIVALENCE
EQUIVOCATOR
FORMALESQUE
FREQUENCIES
FREQUENTATION
HARLEQUINADE
HARLEQUINIC
HEADQUARTERS
HINDQUARTERS
LIQUEFIABLE
LIQUIDAMBAR
LIQUIDAMBER
LIQUIDOGENIC
LIQUORISHNESS
MASQUERADING
MERIQUINONIC
MOSQUITOBILL
PASQUINADING
PAUCILOQUENT
PECTORILOQUE
POLYLOQUENT
QUADRIGAMIST
QUADRIVALENT
QUADRUPEDANT
QUADRUPEDATE
QUADRUPEDOUS
QUALIFIABLE
QUARTERNIGHT
QUARTERSAWED
QUARTERSTAVES
QUATREFOILED
QUEENSBERRY
QUIESCENTLY
QUITCLAIMED
QUODLIBETIC
QUOTABILITY
RELINQUISHED
REQUIESCENCE
SEQUENTIALITY
SOMNILOQUISM
SQUELCHIEST
SQUIRARCHAL
SUBQUINTUPLE

UNADEQUATELY
UNEQUITABLY
UNEQUIVOCAL
UNFREQUENTED
UNQUANTIFIED
UNQUIESCENCE
VENTRILOQUIST

24
ACQUIESCENCE
ACQUIESCENT
ACQUIREMENT
ACQUITTANCE
ANTHRAQUINOL
AQUATIVENESS
AQUEOGLACIAL
BARBARESQUE
BIQUADRANTAL
BOUDOIRESQUE
CINQUECENTO
COLOQUINTIDA
CONQUERABLE
CONQUISTADOR
CONSEQUENCE
CONSEQUENTIAL
DELIQUESCED
DELIQUESCENT
DESQUAMATED
DESQUAMATION
DISQUIPARANT
DULCILOQUENT
EQUATIONALLY
EQUATORIALLY
EQUIDISTANCE
EQUILIBRATED
EQUILIBRATION
EQUILIBRISTAT
EQUILIBRIUM
EQUIPARTITION
EQUIPONDERAT
EQUIPOTENTIAL
EQUISETACEOUS
FREQUENTAGE
FREQUENTING
FREQUENTNESS
GRANDILOQUENT
GROTESQUELY
GROTESQUERY
HEADQUARTER
HINDQUARTER
INQUIRINGLY
LIQUESCENCE
LONGINQUITY
MAGNILOQUENT
MASQUERADED
NESQUEHONITE
PALANQUINING
PARAQUADRATE
PASQUINADED
PICTURESQUE
PLASMOQUINE
PRECONQUEST
PROPINQUANT
PROPINQUOUS
QUADRANGULED
QUADRENNIUMS
QUADRIENNIUM
QUADRIFILAR
QUADRIFRONS
QUADRINOMIAL
QUADRIPAROUS
QUADRIPLANAR
QUADRIVIOUS
QUADRUMANOUS
QUADRUPEDAL
QUADRUPEDAN
QUADRUPLATOR
QUADRUPLING
QUANTITATIVE
QUANTIVALENT

QUARRELOUSLY
QUARTERMASTER
QUARTERPACE
QUEENSBERRIES
QUINALDINIUM
QUINAMICINE
QUINCUNCIAL
QUINDECAGON
QUINUCLIDINE
QUIRQUINCHO
QUOTIDIANLY
RELINQUISHER
SANCTILOQUENT
SEMIAQUATIC
SEQUESTERMENT
SESQUITERPENE
SQUAMACEOUS
SQUAMIGEROUS
SQUEAKINESS
SQUINTINGLY
SQUIRTINGLY
STATUESQUELY
SUAVILOQUENT
SUBSEQUENCE
SUBSEQUENTIAL
TRANQUILLITY
UNACQUAINTED
UNQUALIFIED
VENTRILOQUAL

23
ABSQUATULATE
ALTILOQUENCE
AQUACULTURAL
AQUAEMANALIA
AQUAFORTIST
AQUAPLANING
AQUICULTURAL
ARABESQUERIE
BURLESQUING
COLLIQUATION
CROQUIGNOLE
DISACQUAINT
DISQUISITING
EQUILIBRATOR
EQUILIBRIATE
EQUILIBRIOUS
EQUINOVARUS
EQUIPARATION
ETIQUETTICAL
FATILOQUENT
FOREQUARTER
INELOQUENCE
INQUISITIVE
INQUISITORY
MASQUERADER
MISQUOTATION
MOUSQUETAIRE
MULTILOQUENT
MULTILOQUOUS
PALANQUINED
PASQUINADER
PERQUISITION
PREREQUISITE
PRETEREQUINE
QUADRANGLED
QUADRANGULAR
QUADRATICAL
QUADRENNIUM
QUADRILATERAL
QUADRUMANAL
QUADRUPLANE
QUADRUPLATE
QUALITATIVE
QUAQUAVERSAL
QUARRYSTONE
QUARTERFOIL
QUARTERSAWN
QUARTIPAROUS

QUATERNIONIC
QUATTROCENTO
QUEBRADILLA
QUERCITANNIN
QUERIMONIOUS
QUERULOSITY
QUERULOUSLY
QUESTIONABLE
QUESTIONARY
QUESTMONGER
QUINALDINIC
QUINAMIDINE
QUINQUENNIUMS
QUINTELEMENT
QUINTESSENCE
QUINTUPLING
QUISLINGISM
QUISQUILIARY
QUOTABLENESS
REQUISITELY
REQUISITORY
REQUITATIVE
RIBAUDEQUIN
SEMIQUARTILE
SEMIQUIETIST
SEQUESTRABLE
SEQUESTRATING
SESQUIPEDAL
SOMNILOQUENT
SOMNILOQUISM
SOMNILOQUOUS
SQUAMOSENESS
SQUAMOUSNESS
SQUAMULATION
SQUARROSELY
SQUASHINESS
SQUINTINGNESS
STULTILOQUY
TRANQUILITY
TRISTILOQUY
UBIQUITARIAN
UBIQUITARIES
UNCONQUERED
UNDERQUOTING
UNLIQUIDATED
UNQUESTIONING
VENTRILOQUE

22
ACQUAINTANT
ACQUISITION
ADEQUATENESS
ANTIMASQUER
ANTIQUARISM
AQUACULTURE
AQUAEMANALE
AQUEOIGNEOUS
AQUICULTURE
BARQUENTINE
BOUQUETIERE
BOUQUINISTE
BRUSQUENESS
COEQUALNESS
DENTILOQUIST
DISQUIETING
DISQUIETUDE
DISQUISITED
DISQUISITION
EQUABLENESS
EQUATIONISM
EQUINANGULAR
EQUIGRANULAR
EQUILIBRANT
EQUILIBRATE
EQUILIBRIAL
EQUILIBRIST
EQUINOCTIAL
EQUINOCTIAL
EQUIPARTILE

EQUIPOLLENT
EQUIPOSTILE
EQUISONANCE
ESQUAMULOSE
GIGANTESQUE
GORGONESQUE
GROTESQUERIE
LIQUIDATING
MARQUETERIE
MARQUISETTE
MARQUISOTTE
MERIQUINONE
MILQUETOAST
OBLIQUATION
OBLIQUENESS
OBLIQUITIES
OBLIQUITOUS
OMNILOQUENT
OSTEOPLAQUE
PASQUILLANT
PEREQUITATE
PERQUISITOR
PIQUANTNESS
PLATERESQUE
PROQUAESTOR
QUADRIGATUS
QUADRILLING
QUANTIMETER
QUANTOMETER
QUARANTINING
QUARRELSOME
QUERIMONIES
QUESTIONARIES
QUESTIONNAIRE
QUIINACEOUS
QUINOIDATION
QUINOLINIUM
QUINONIMINE
QUINQUENNIUM
QUINQUERTIUM
QUINQUEVIRS
QUITTERBONE
REQUIREMENT
REQUITEMENT
SEMIANTIQUE
SEQUESTERING
SEQUESTRATED
SEQUESTRATION
SESQUIALTERAL
SQUADRONING
SQUAMELLATE
SQUANDERING
SQUEEGEEING
SQUIDGEREEN
SQUIGGLIEST
SQUILGEEING
SQUIRMINESS
UNDERQUOTED
UNEQUITABLE
UNQUESTIONED
UNQUIESCENT
UTRAQUISTIC

21
ANTIQUATING
DISQUISITOR
DUROQUINONE
EQUALITARIAN
EQUESTRIENNE
EQUIDISTANT
EQUIDIURNAL
ISOQUINOLINE
LIQUIDATION
NATURALESQUE
QUADRANTILE
QUADRENNIAL
QUADRILLION
QUADRIURATE
QUARANTINED

QUARRELLING
QUARTERLAND
QUATERNARIES
QUATERNARIUS
QUATERNITIES
QUATERTENSES
QUERULENTIAL
QUESTIONING
QUESTIONLESS
QUINOLOGIST
QUINQUENNIAD
QUOTATIONIST
SEQUESTERED
SEQUESTRATOR
SESQUIALTERA
SOLDATESQUE
SESQUITERTIA
SQUALIDNESS
SQUIRRELTAIL
TERLINQUAITE
TRANQUILLEST
TRANQUILLISE
TRANQUILNESS
UNQUALITIED

20
ALTILOQUENT
ANTIQUARIAN
ANTIQUARIES
ANTIQUATION
ANTIQUENESS
ANTIQUITIES
AQUARELLIST
AQUEOUSNESS
ELOQUENTIAL
EQUATIONIST
EQUILATERAL
ILLIQUATION
INQUIRATION
OUTQUESTION
QUAESTIONES
QUAESTORIAL
QUAESTORIAN
QUARANTINER
QUARRELLOUS
QUARTERLIES
QUARTERNION
QUEENLINESS
QUESTIONIST
QUINANISOLE
QUINQUENNIAL
QUINTERNION
QUINTILLION
QUIRITARIAN
QUISQUILIOUS
QUOTATIONAL
RELIQUARIES
REQUISITION
REQUITELESS
SEQUESTRANT
SEQUESTRATE
SESQUIALTER
SESQUIQUARTA
SESQUIQUINTA
SESQUINONAL
SOLILOQUIES
SOLILOQUISE
SOLILOQUIST
SQUATTINESS
SQUIRTINESS
TERRAQUEOUS
TRANQUILEST
TRANQUILLER
TRIQUETROUS
UNQUIETNESS

19
QUINQUENNIA
QUISQUILIAN

High-Scoring Words Containing

2-3 LETTER WORDS

ALPHABETICAL ORDER		POSITIONAL ORDER		SCORING ORDER	
ARX	ROX	XAT	PYX	**19**	**11**
AUX	RUX		RAX	ZAX	DIX
AX	SAX	AX	REX		DUX
AXE	SEX	AXE	RIX	**15**	
BOX	SIX	EX	ROX	PYX	**10**
COX	SOX	EXUL	RUX		ARX
DIX	TAX	OX	SAX	**14**	AUX
DUX	TOX	OXO	SEX	KEX	AXE
EX	TUX	OXY	SIX		LAX
FAX	VEX		SOX	**13**	LEX
FIX	VIX	ARX	TAX	FAX	LOX
FOX	VOX	AUX	TOX	FIX	LUX
HEX	WAX	BOX	TUX	FOX	NIX
HOX	WOX	DIX	VEX	HEX	OXO
KEX	XAT	DUX	VIX	HOX	RAX
LAX	YEX	COX	VOX	OXY	REX
LEX	YOX	FAX	WAX	VEX	RIX
LOX	ZAX	FIX	WOX	VIX	ROX
LUX		FOX	YEX	VOX	RUX
MAX		HEX	YOX	WAX	SAX
MIX		HOX	ZAX	WOX	SEX
MUX		KEX		YEX	SIX
NIX		LAX		YOX	SOX
OX		LEX			TAX
OXO		LOX		**12**	TOX
OXY		LUX		BOX	TUX
PAX		MAX		COX	XAT
PIX		MIX		MAX	
POX		MUX		MIX	**9**
PYX		NIX		MUX	AX
RAX		PAX		PAX	EX
REX		PIX		PIX	OX
RIX		POX		POX	

ALPHABETICAL LIST OF 4-LETTER WORDS

ABOX	DIXY	FOXY	NEXT	PUXY
APEX	DOUX	GREX	NIXE	QUAX
AXAL	DOXY	HEXT	NIXY	RIXY
AXAN	EAUX	HOAX	NOIX	ROUX
AXED	ELIX	IBEX	NOXA	ROXY
AXEL	ESOX	ILEX	OBEX	SAEX
AXES	EXAM	JEUX	ONYX	SEAX
AXIL	EXEC	JINX	ORYX	SEXT
AXIS	EXES	JYNX	OXAN	SEXY
AXLE	EXIT	KEXY	OXEA	SPEX
AXON	EXON	KREX	OXEN	TAXI
BAXA	EXUL	LANX	OXER	TAXY
BOXY	FAEX	LUXE	OXID	TEXT
CALX	FALX	LYNX	OXIM	TOXA
CAXI	FAUX	MAUX	OXYL	UROX
COAX	FIXT	MINX	PIXY	WAXY
COIX	FIXY	MIXT	PLEX	WOXE
COXA	FLAX	MIXY	POXY	WROX
COXY	FLEX	MOXA	PREX	XEME
CRUX	FLIX	MYXA	PRIX	XYST
DIXI	FLUX	MYXO	PROX	

POSITIONAL ORDER LIST OF 4-LETTER WORDS

XEME	OXIM	MYXO	CALX	JYNX
XYST	OXYL	NEXT	COAX	KREX
		NIXE	COIX	LANX
AXAL	BAXA	NIXY	CRUX	LYNX
AXAN	BOXY	NOXA	DOUX	MAUX
AXED	CAXI	PIXY	EAUX	MINX
AXEL	COXA	POXY	ELIX	NOIX
AXES	COXY	PUXY	ESOX	OBEX
AXIL	DIXI	RIXY	FAEX	ONYX
AXIS	DIXY	ROXY	FALX	ORYX
AXLE	DOXY	SEXT	FAUX	PLEX
AXON	FIXT	SEXY	FLAX	PREX
EXAM	FIXY	TAXI	FLEX	PRIX
EXEC	FOXY	TAXY	FLIX	PROX
EXES	HEXT	TEXT	FLUX	QUAX
EXIT	KEXY	TOXA	GREX	ROUX
EXON	LUXE	WAXY	HOAX	SAEX
OXAN	MIXT	WOXE	IBEX	SEAX
OXEA	MIXY		ILEX	SPEX
OXEN	MOXA	ABOX	JEUX	UROX
OXER	MYXA	APEX	JINX	WROX
OXID				

SCORING ORDER LIST OF 4-LETTER WORDS

21	MIXY	FLIX	APEX	PRIX
JYNX	MYXA	FLUX	BAXA	PROX
	MYXO	HEXT	CALX	SPEX
20	PIXY	HOAX	CAXI	XEME
QUAX	POXY	LYNX	COAX	
	PUXY	NIXY	COIX	**12**
18		ONYX	COXA	AXED
JEUX	**15**	ORYX	CRUX	DIXI
JINX	DIXY	OXYL	EXAM	DOUX
KEXY	DOXY	RIXY	EXEC	GREX
	KREX	ROXY	IBEX	OXID
17		SEXY	MAUX	
FIXY	**14**	TAXY	MINX	**11**
FOXY	FAEX	WOXE	MIXT	AXAL
WAXY	FALX	WROX	MOXA	AXAN
	FAUX	XYST	OBEX	AXEL
16	FIXT		OXIM	AXES
BOXY	FLAX	**13**	PLEX	AXIL
COXY	FLEX	ABOX	PREX	AXIS

AXLE	EXIT	NEXT	OXEN	SEXT
AXON	EXON	NIXE	OXER	TAXI
EAUX	EXUL	NOIX	ROUX	TEXT
ELIX	ILEX	NOXA	SAEX	TOXA
ESOX	LANX	OXAN	SEAX	UROX
EXES	LUXE	OXEA		

ALPHABETICAL LIST OF 5-LETTER WORDS

ADDAX	DIOXY	FOXER	NOXAL	TAXEL
ADFIX	DIXIE	FOXES	NYXIS	TAXER
ADMIX	DIXIT	GULIX	OXANE	TAXES
ADNEX	DONAX	HELIX	OXBOW	TAXIS
ADOXY	DOXIE	HEXAD	OXBOY	TAXON
AFFIX	DRUXY	HEXER	OXEYE	TAXOR
ALPAX	DURAX	HEXIS	OXFLY	TELEX
AMPYX	DUXES	HEXYL	OXIDE	TEXAS
ANNEX	EMBOX	HUXEN	OXIDO	TOXIC
ATAXY	EPOXY	HYRAX	OXIME	TOXIN
AUXIN	EXACT	IMMIX	OXLIP	TOXON
AXIAL	EXALT	INDEX	OXMAN	TWIXT
AXILE	EXCEL	INFIX	OXMEN	UNFIX
AXINE	EXCUR	IXTLE	OXTER	UNMIX
AXIOM	EXEAT	JIXIE	PANAX	UNSEX
AXION	EXEDE	JUDEX	PAUXI	UNTAX
AXITE	EXEEM	JUXTA	PINAX	UNWAX
AXLED	EXEME	KYLIX	PIXIE	VARIX
AXMAN	EXERT	LARIX	PODEX	VEXED
AXMEN	EXIDO	LATEX	PREXY	VEXER
AXOID	EXIES	LAXER	PROXY	VEXIL
AXONE	EXILE	LAXLY	PUMEX	VIBEX
AZOXY	EXINE	LEXIA	PYREX	VIVAX
BERYX	EXIST	LEXIC	PYXIE	VIXEN
BIXIN	EXITE	LOXIA	PYXIS	WAXED
BORAX	EXLEX	LUXES	RADIX	WAXEN
BOXEN	EXODE	LUXUR	RAMEX	WAXER
BOXER	EXODY	LUXUS	REDUX	WAXES
BOXES	EXORN	MALAX	RELAX	XALLE
BOXTY	EXPEL	MATAX	REMEX	XEBEC
BRAXY	EXTER	MAXIM	REXEN	XENIA
BUXOM	EXTOL	MIXED	SAXON	XENON
CAPAX	EXTRA	MIXEN	SEXED	XENYL
CAREX	EXTRE	MIXER	SEXLY	XERIC
CAXON	EXUDE	MIXUP	SEXTO	XERIF
CHOUX	EXULT	MONAX	SILEX	XEROX
CIMEX	EXURB	MOXIE	SIREX	XOANA
COAXY	EXUST	MUREX	SIXER	XUREL
CODEX	EXUTE	NEXAL	SIXMO	XYLAN
COXAE	FAULX	NEXUM	SIXTE	XYLEM
COXAL	FAXED	NEXUS	SIXTH	XYLIC
CYLIX	FIXED	NIXEN	SIXTY	XYLON
DEFIX	FIXER	NIXES	SOULX	XYLYL
DESEX	FLAXY	NIXIE	STRIX	XYRID
DEVEX	FOXED	NOXAE	TAXED	XYSTA
DEWAX				

POSITIONAL ORDER LIST OF 5-LETTER WORDS

XALLE	XOANA	XYSTA	AXLED	EXCUR
XEBEC	XUREL		AXMAN	EXEAT
XENIA	XYLAN	AXIAL	AXMEN	EXEDE
XENON	XYLEM	AXILE	AXOID	EXEEM
XENYL	XYLIC	AXINE	AXONE	EXEME
XERIC	XYLON	AXIOM	EXACT	EXERT
XERIF	XYLYL	AXION	EXALT	EXIDO
XEROX	XYRID	AXITE	EXCEL	EXIES

EXILE	BUXOM	NIXEN	ADOXY	GULIX
EXINE	CAXON	NIXES	ATAXY	HELIX
EXIST	COXAE	NIXIE	AZOXY	HYRAX
EXITE	COXAL	NOXAE	BRAXY	IMMIX
EXLEX	DIXIE	NOXAL	COAXY	INDEX
EXODE	DIXIT	NYXIS	DIOXY	INFIX
EXODY	DOXIE	PIXIE	DRUXY	JUDEX
EXORN	DUXES	PYXIE	EPOXY	KYLIX
EXPEL	FAXED	PYXIS	FLAXY	LARIX
EXTER	FIXED	REXEN	PAUXI	LATEX
EXTOL	FIXER	SAXON	PREXY	MALAX
EXTRA	FOXED	SEXED	PROXY	MATAX
EXTRE	FOXER	SEXLY	TWIXT	MONAX
EXUDE	FOXES	SEXTO		MUREX
EXULT	HEXAD	SIXER	ADDAX	PANAX
EXURB	HEXER	SIXMO	ADFIX	PINAX
EXUST	HEXIS	SIXTE	ADMIX	PODEX
EXUTE	HEXYL	SIXTH	ADNEX	PUMEX
IXTLE	HUXEN	SIXTY	AFFIX	PYREX
OXANE	JIXIE	TAXED	ALPAX	RADIX
OXBOW	JUXTA	TAXEL	AMPYX	RAMEX
OXBOY	LAXER	TAXER	ANNEX	REDUX
OXEYE	LAXLY	TAXES	BERYX	RELAX
OXFLY	LEXIA	TAXIS	BORAX	REMEX
OXIDE	LEXIC	TAXON	CAPAX	SILEX
OXIDO	LOXIA	TAXOR	CAREX	SIREX
OXIME	LUXES	TEXAS	CHOUX	SOULX
OXLIP	LUXUR	TOXIC	CIMEX	STRIX
OXMAN	LUXUS	TOXIN	CODEX	TELEX
OXMEN	MAXIM	TOXON	CYLIX	UNFIX
OXTER	MIXED	VEXED	DEFIX	UNMIX
	MIXEN	VEXER	DESEX	UNSEX
AUXIN	MIXER	VEXIL	DEVEX	UNTAX
BIXIN	MIXUP	VIXEN	DEWAX	UNWAX
BOXEN	MOXiE	WAXED	DONAX	VARIX
BOXER	NEXAL	WAXEN	DURAX	VIBEX
BOXES	NEXUM	WAXER	EMBOX	VIVAX
BOXTY	NEXUS	WAXES	FAULX	XEROX

SCORING ORDER LIST OF 5-LETTER WORDS

24	PROXY	XYRID	WAXES	MIXEN
AZOXY	PYREX		XENYL	MIXER
	PYXIE	**15**	XERIF	MONAX
20	PYXIS	ADMIX	XYLAN	MOXIE
JUDEX	VIBEX	ATAXY	XYLON	MUREX
	XYLEM	CODEX	XYSTA	NEXUM
19	XYLIC	FAULX		OXIME
AMPYX		FIXER	**14**	OXLIP
JIXIE	**16**	FOXER	ADDAX	OXMAN
JUXTA	ADFIX	FOXES	ALPAX	OXMEN
KYLIX	ADOXY	HELIX	AXIOM	PANAX
	BUXOM	HEXER	AXMAN	PAUXI
18	CAPAX	HEXIS	AXMEN	PINAX
AFFIX	CIMEX	HUXEN	BIXIN	PIXIE
FLAXY	DEFIX	INFIX	BORAX	RAMEX
HEXYL	DEVEX	LAXLY	BOXEN	REMEX
HYRAX	DEWAX	MIXED	BOXER	SIXMO
OXFLY	DIOXY	NYXIS	BOXES	TOXIC
VIVAX	DRUXY	OXEYE	CAREX	UNMIX
XYLYL	EMBOX	PODEX	CAXON	XERIC
	EXODY	SEXLY	COXAE	
17	FAXED	SIXTH	COXAL	**13**
BERYX	FIXED	SIXTY	EXACT	ADNEX
BOXTY	FOXED	TWIXT	EXCEL	AXLED
BRAXY	HEXAD	UNFIX	EXCUR	AXOID
CHOUX	IMMIX	UNWAX	EXEEM	DESEX
COAXY	MAXIM	VARIX	EXEME	DIXIE
CYLIX	MIXUP	VEXER	EXPEL	DIXIT
EPOXY	PUMEX	VEXIL	EXURB	DONAX
OXBOW	VEXED	VIXEN	LEXIC	DOXIE
OXBOY	WAXED	WAXEN	MALAX	DURAX
PREXY	XEBEC	WAXER	MATAX	DUXES

EXEDE	AXINE	EXULT	NOXAE	TAXIS
EXIDO	AXION	EXUST	NOXAL	TAXON
EXODE	AXITE	EXUTE	OXANE	TAXOR
EXUDE	AXONE	IXTLE	OXTER	TELEX
GULIX	EXALT	LARIX	RELAX	TEXAS
INDEX	EXEAT	LATEX	REXEN	TOXIN
OXIDE	EXERT	LAXER	SAXON	TOXON
OXIDO	EXIES	LEXIA	SEXTO	UNSEX
RADIX	EXILE	LOXIA	SILEX	UNTAX
REDUX	EXINE	LUXES	SIREX	XALLE
SEXED	EXIST	LUXUR	SIXER	XENIA
TAXED	EXITE	LUXUS	SIXTE	XENON
	EXORN	NEXAL	SOULX	XOANA
12	EXTER	NEXUS	STRIX	XUREL
ANNEX	EXTOL	NIXEN	TAXEL	
AUXIN	EXTRA	NIXES	TAXER	**11**
AXIAL	EXTRE	NIXIE	TAXES	EXLEX
AXILE				XEROX

ALPHABETICAL LIST OF 6-LETTER WORDS

ADIEUX	CALXES	EXCAVE	EXTANT	HOTBOX
ADMIXT	CARANX	EXCEED	EXTEND	IBEXES
ADNEXA	CARFAX	EXCELS	EXTENT	ICEBOX
AFFIXT	CAUDEX	EXCEPT	EXTERN	ILEXES
AFFLUX	CAXIRI	EXCERN	EXTILL	IMBREX
ALEXIA	CERVIX	EXCESS	EXTIMA	IMMIXT
ALEXIN	CIXIID	EXCIDE	EXTIME	IMPLEX
ALKOXY	CLIMAX	EXCISE	EXTINE	INAXON
ALLOXY	COAXAL	EXCITE	EXTIRP	INFLEX
AMIXIA	COAXED	EXCOCT	EXTOLL	INFLUX
AMPLEX	COAXER	EXCUSE	EXTORT	INTEXT
ANAXON	COCCYX	EXCUSS	EXTUND	IODOXY
ANNEXA	COMMIX	EXCYST	EXTURB	IXODIC
ANNEXE	CONFIX	EXEDRA	EXUDED	IXODID
ANOXIA	CONNEX	EXEMPT	FIXAGE	KLAXON
ANOXIC	CONVEX	EXEQUY	FIXATE	KORDAX
APEXED	CORDAX	EXERCE	FIXING	LARNAX
APEXES	CORTEX	EXEUNT	FIXITY	LARYNX
AROXYL	COUXIA	EXHALE	FIXURE	LASTEX
ATAXIA	COUXIO	EXHORT	FLAXEN	LAXATE
ATAXIC	COXIER	EXHUME	FLEXED	LAXEST
ATWIXT	COXITE	EXILED	FLEXOR	LAXISM
AUSPEX	CRUXES	EXILER	FLUXED	LAXIST
AXEMAN	DARNEX	EXILIC	FLUXER	LAXITY
AXENIC	DEFLEX	EXITUS	FORFEX	LUMMOX
AXIATE	DEFLUX	EXODIC	FORNIX	LUXATE
AXILLA	DELUXE	EXODUS	FOXERY	LUXIVE
AXLIKE	DENTEX	EXOGEN	FOXIER	LUXURY
AXONAL	DEXTER	EXOLVE	FOXILY	LYNXES
AXSEED	DEXTRO	EXOMIS	FOXING	LYXOSE
AXTREE	DIAXON	EXONER	FOXISH	MASTAX
AXUNGE	DIOXAN	EXOPOD	FRAXIN	MATRIX
AXWEED	DIPLEX	EXOTIC	FRUTEX	MAXIMA
BADAXE	DIXAIN	EXPAND	GALAXY	MAXIXE
BAXTER	DOXIES	EXPECT	HALLUX	MENINX
BIAXAL	DRUXEY	EXPEDE	HATBOX	MINXES
BIFLEX	DUPLEX	EXPEND	HEXADE	MIXING
BIJOUX	EARWAX	EXPERT	HEXANE	MIXITE
BISEXT	EFFLUX	EXPIRE	HEXENE	MYSTAX
BOLLIX	ELIXIR	EXPIRY	HEXINE	MYXOID
BOMBYX	EMPEXA	EXPLAT	HEXODE	MYXOMA
BONXIE	EUTAXY	EXPONE	HEXOIC	NEXTLY
BOXCAR	EXACTA	EXPORT	HEXONE	NOXIAL
BOXING	EXALTE	EXPOSE	HEXOSE	ONYXES
BOXMAN	EXAMEN	EXPUGN	HEXYNE	ONYXIS
BOYAUX	EXARCH	EXSECT	HOAXEE	OPIFEX
BUTOXY	EXCAMB	EXSERT	HOAXER	OREXIS

OUTBOX	OXYAZO	REFLUX	SURTAX	VEXFUL
OUTFOX	OXYGEN	REXINE	SYNTAX	VEXING
OXALIC	OXYGON	RHEXIS	SYRINX	VINDEX
OXALIS	OXYMEL	ROLLIX	TARBOX	VORTEX
OXALYL	OXYOPY	SANDIX	TAXEME	WAXAND
OXAMIC	PAPPOX	SANDYX	TAXIED	WAXIER
OXAZIN	PATRIX	SAXAUL	TAXINE	WAXING
OXBANE	PAXWAX	SCOLEX	TAXING	WAXMAN
OXBIRD	PEGBOX	SEXERN	TAXITE	WRAXLE
OXCART	PERFIX	SEXIER	TAXMAN	WRIXLE
OXEATE	PERMIX	SEXISM	TEABOX	XARQUE
OXEOTE	PEROXY	SEXIST	TETTIX	XENIAL
OXFORD	PHENIX	SEXTAN	TEXTUS	XENIAN
OXGALL	PICKAX	SEXTET	THIXLE	XENIUM
OXGANG	PINXIT	SEXTIC	THORAX	XERIFF
OXGATE	PIXIES	SEXTON	TORPEX	XEROMA
OXGOAD	PLEXAL	SEXTRY	TOXIFY	XIFOID
OXHEAD	PLEXOR	SEXTUR	TOXINE	XOANON
OXHEAL	PLEXUS	SEXUAL	TOXITY	XYLATE
OXHIDE	POLEAX	SIXAIN	TOXOID	XYLENE
OXHOFT	POLLEX	SMILAX	TOXONE	XYLITE
OXHORN	PRAXIS	SPADIX	TREMEX	XYLOID
OXLAND	PRECOX	SPHINX	TUXEDO	XYLOMA
OXLIKE	PREFIX	STAXIS	UNISEX	XYLOSE
OXREIM	PROLIX	STORAX	UROXIN	XYLOYL
OXSHOE	PROREX	STUPEX	VERMIX	XYSTER
OXSKIN	PTYXIS	SUBFIX	VERNIX	XYSTUS
OXTAIL	REFLEX	SUFFIX	VERTEX	YAXCHE
OXWORT				

POSITIONAL ORDER LIST OF 6-LETTER WORDS

XARQUE	EXCITE	EXTENT	OXYAZO	LAXITY
XENIAL	EXCOCT	EXTERN	OXYGEN	LUXATE
XENIAN	EXCUSE	EXTILL	OXYGON	LUXIVE
XENIUM	EXCUSS	EXTIMA	OXYMEL	LUXURY
XERIFF	EXCYST	EXTIME	OXYOPY	LYXOSE
XEROMA	EXEDRA	EXTINE		MAXIMA
XIFOID	EXEMPT	EXTIRP	BAXTER	MAXIXE
XOANON	EXEQUY	EXTOLL	BOXCAR	MIXING
XYLATE	EXERCE	EXTORT	BOXING	MIXITE
XYLENE	EXEUNT	EXTUND	BOXMAN	MYXOID
XYLITE	EXHALE	EXTURB	CAXIRI	MYXOMA
XYLOID	EXHORT	EXUDED	CIXIID	NEXTLY
XYLOMA	EXHUME	IXODIC	COXIER	NOXIAL
XYLOSE	EXILED	IXODID	COXITE	PAXWAX
XYLOYL	EXILER	OXALIC	DEXTER	PIXIES
XYSTER	EXILIC	OXALIS	DEXTRO	REXINE
XYSTUS	EXITUS	OXALYL	DIXAIN	SAXAUL
	EXODIC	OXAMIC	DOXIES	SEXERN
AXEMAN	EXODUS	OXAZIN	FIXAGE	SEXIER
AXENIC	EXOGEN	OXBANE	FIXATE	SEXISM
AXIATE	EXOLVE	OXBIRD	FIXING	SEXIST
AXILLA	EXOMIS	OXCART	FIXITY	SEXTAN
AXLIKE	EXONER	OXEATE	FIXURE	SEXTET
AXONAL	EXOPOD	OXEOTE	FOXERY	SEXTIC
AXSEED	EXOTIC	OXFORD	FOXIER	SEXTON
AXTREE	EXPAND	OXGALL	FOXILY	SEXTRY
AXUNGE	EXPECT	OXGANG	FOXING	SEXTUR
AXWEED	EXPEDE	OXGATE	FOXISH	SEXUAL
EXACTA	EXPEND	OXGOAD	HEXADE	SIXAIN
EXALTE	EXPERT	OXHEAD	HEXANE	TAXEME
EXAMEN	EXPIRE	OXHEAL	HEXENE	TAXIED
EXARCH	EXPIRY	OXHIDE	HEXINE	TAXINE
EXCAMB	EXPLAT	OXHOFT	HEXODE	TAXING
EXCAVE	EXPONE	OXHORN	HEXOIC	TAXITE
EXCEED	EXPORT	OXLAND	HEXONE	TAXMAN
EXCELS	EXPOSE	OXLIKE	HEXOSE	TEXTUS
EXCEPT	EXPUGN	OXREIM	HEXYNE	TOXIFY
EXCERN	EXSECT	OXSHOE	LAXATE	TOXINE
EXCESS	EXSERT	OXSKIN	LAXEST	TOXITY
EXCIDE	EXTANT	OXTAIL	LAXISM	TOXOID
EXCISE	EXTEND	OXWORT	LAXIST	TOXONE

TUXEDO	FLUXED	BISEXT	DENTEX	PICKAX
VEXFUL	FLUXER	BUTOXY	DIPLEX	POLEAX
VEXING	FRAXIN	DELUXE	DUPLEX	POLLEX
WAXAND	HOAXEE	EMPEXA	EARWAX	PRECOX
WAXIER	HOAXER	EUTAXY	EFFLUX	PREFIX
WAXING	IBEXES	GALAXY	FORFEX	PROLIX
WAXMAN	ILEXES	IMMIXT	FORNIX	PROREX
YAXCHE	INAXON	INTEXT	FRUTEX	REFLEX
	KLAXON	IODOXY	HALLUX	REFLUX
ALEXIA	LYNXES	MAXIXE	HATBOX	ROLLIX
ALEXIN	MINXES	PEROXY	HOTBOX	SANDIX
AMIXIA	ONYXES		ICEBOX	SANDYX
ANAXON	ONYXIS		IMBREX	SCOLEX
ANOXIA	OREXIS	ADIEUX	IMPLEX	SMILAX
ANOXIC	PINXIT	AFFLUX	INFLEX	SPADIX
APEXED	PLEXAL	AMPLEX	INFLUX	SPHINX
APEXES	PLEXOR	AUSPEX	KORDAX	STORAX
AROXYL	PLEXUS	BIFLEX	LARNAX	STUPEX
ATAXIA	PRAXIS	BIJOUX	LARYNX	SUBFIX
ATAXIC	PTYXIS	BOLLIX	LASTEX	SUFFIX
BIAXAL	RHEXIS	BOMBYX	LUMMOX	SURTAX
BONXIE	STAXIS	BOYAUX	MASTAX	SYNTAX
CALXES	THIXLE	CARANX	MATRIX	SYRINX
COAXAL	UROXIN	CARFAX	MENINX	TARBOX
COAXED	WRAXLE	CAUDEX	MYSTAX	TEABOX
COAXER	WRIXLE	CERVIX	OPIFEX	TETTIX
COUXIA		CLIMAX	OUTBOX	THORAX
COUXIO	ADMIXT	COCCYX	OUTFOX	TORPEX
CRUXES	ADNEXA	COMMIX	PAPPOX	TREMEX
DIAXON	AFFIXT	CONFIX	PATRIX	UNISEX
DIOXAN	ALKOXY	CONNEX	PAXWAX	VERMIX
DRUXEY	ALLOXY	CONVEX	PEGBOX	VERNIX
ELIXIR	ANNEXA	CORDAX	PERFIX	VERTEX
FLAXEN	ANNEXE	CORTEX	PERMIX	VINDEX
FLEXED	ATWIXT	DARNEX	PHENIX	VORTEX
FLEXOR	BADAXE	DEFLEX		
		DEFLUX		

SCORING ORDER LIST OF 6-LETTER WORDS

25	TOXIFY	XYLOMA	OXHEAD	EXHALE
EXEQUY	VEXFUL		OXHIDE	EXHORT
OXYAZO	XERIFF	**17**	OXLIKE	EXODIC
	XYLOYL	AMPLEX	OXSKIN	EXOLVE
22		AXLIKE	OXYGEN	EXOPOD
BIJOUX	**18**	AXWEED	OXYGON	EXPAND
BOMBYX	BIFLEX	BOXCAR	PAXWAX	EXPEDE
OXAZIN	BOYAUX	BOXMAN	PERMIX	EXPEND
XARQUE	BUTOXY	CLIMAX	PRECOX	EXPUGN
	CARFAX	DEFLEX	SANDYX	FIXATE
21	CERVIX	DEFLUX	VEXING	FIXURE
OXYOPY	CONFIX	DRUXEY	VINDEX	FLAXEN
PICKAX	CONVEX	EMPEXA	WAXAND	FLEXOR
YAXCHE	EXARCH	EXCEPT	WAXING	FLUXER
	EXCAVE	EXCOCT	XIFOID	FORNIX
20	EXCYST	EXEMPT	XYLOID	FOXIER
ALKOXY	EXHUME	EXPECT		FRAXIN
MYXOMA	EXPIRY	FIXAGE	**16**	FRUTEX
	HATBOX	FIXING	ADMIXT	HALLUX
19	HEXOIC	FLEXED	ALLOXY	HEXANE
AFFIXT	HOTBOX	FLUXED	APEXED	HEXENE
AFFLUX	KORDAX	FOXING	AROXYL	HEXINE
COCCYX	MYSTAX	GALAXY	ATWIXT	HEXONE
COMMIX	OPIFEX	HEXADE	BADAXE	HEXOSE
EFFLUX	OXYMEL	HEXODE	BOXING	HOAXEE
EXCAMB	PEGBOX	ICEBOX	CAUDEX	HOAXER
FIXITY	PERFIX	IMBREX	CIXIID	INFLEX
FORFEX	PEROXY	IMMIXT	COAXED	INFLUX
FOXERY	PHENIX	IMPLEX	CORDAX	IXODIC
FOXILY	PREFIX	IODOXY	DIPLEX	LARYNX
FOXISH	PTYXIS	KLAXON	DUPLEX	LAXITY
HEXYNE	SPHINX	LUMMOX	EARWAX	LUXIVE
MYXOID	SUBFIX	MAXIMA	EUTAXY	LUXURY
OXHOFT	VERMIX	OXAMIC	EXCEED	LYNXES
SUFFIX	WAXMAN	OXFORD	EXCIDE	LYXOSE

MIXING	BISEXT	MENINX	DEXTRO	EXTINE
NEXTLY	BOLLIX	MINXES	DIAXON	EXTOLL
ONYXES	BONXIE	MIXITE	DIOXAN	EXTORT
ONYXIS	CALXES	OUTBOX	DIXAIN	ILEXES
OUTFOX	CARANX	OXALIC	DOXIES	INAXON
OXALYL	CAXIRI	OXBANE	EXEDRA	INTEXT
OXBIRD	COAXAL	OXCART	EXILED	LARNAX
OXHEAL	COAXER	OXGANG	EXODUS	LASTEX
OXHORN	CONNEX	OXGOAD	EXOGEN	LAXATE
OXSHOE	CORTEX	OXREIM	EXTEND	LAXEST
OXWORT	COUXIA	PATRIX	EXTUND	LAXIST
PAPPOX	COUXIO	PINXIT	MAXIXE	LUXATE
REFLEX	COXIER	PIXIES	OXGALL	NOXIAL
REFLUX	COXITE	PLEXAL	OXGATE	OREXIS
RHEXIS	CRUXES	PLEXOR	OXLAND	OXALIS
SEXTRY	EXACTA	PLEXUS	SANDIX	OXEATE
SPADIX	EXAMEN	POLEAX	TAXIED	OXEOTE
SYNTAX	EXCELS	POLLEX	TAXING	OXTAIL
SYRINX	EXCERN	PRAXIS	TOXOID	REXINE
THIXLE	EXCESS	PROLIX	TUXEDO	ROLLIX
THORAX	EXCISE	PROREX		SAXAUL
TOXITY	EXCITE	SCOLEX	**13**	SEXERN
VERNIX	EXCUSE	SEXISM	ALEXIA	SEXIER
VERTEX	EXCUSS	SEXTIC	ALEXIN	SEXIST
VORTEX	EXERCE	SMILAX	ANAXON	SEXTAN
WAXIER	EXILIC	STUPEX	ANNEXA	SEXTET
WRAXLE	EXOMIS	TARBOX	ANNEXE	SEXTON
WRIXLE	EXOTIC	TAXEME	ANOXIA	SEXTUR
XYLATE	EXPERT	TAXMAN	ATAXIA	SEXUAL
XYLENE	EXPIRE	TEABOX	AXIATE	SIXAIN
XYLITE	EXPLAT	TORPEX	AXILLA	STAXIS
XYLOSE	EXPONE	TREMEX	AXONAL	STORAX
XYSTER	EXPORT	XENIUM	AXTREE	SURTAX
XYSTUS	EXPOSE	XEROMA	ELIXIR	TAXINE
	EXSECT		EXALTE	TAXITE
15	EXTIMA	**14**	EXEUNT	TETTIX
AMIXIA	EXTIME	ADIEUX	EXILER	TEXTUS
ANOXIC	EXTIRP	ADNEXA	EXITUS	TOXINE
APEXES	EXTURB	AXSEED	EXONER	TOXONE
ATAXIC	EXUDED	AXUNGE	EXSERT	UNISEX
AUSPEX	IBEXES	DARNEX	EXTANT	UROXIN
AXEMAN	IXODID	DELUXE	EXTENT	XENIAL
AXENIC	LAXISM	DENTEX	EXTERN	XENIAN
BAXTER	MASTAX	DEXTER	EXTILL	XOANON
BIAXAL	MATRIX			

ALPHABETICAL LIST OF 7-LETTER WORDS

ABACAXI	ALLOXAN	ASPHYXY	BATEAUX	BOXWORK
ABAXIAL	AMPYXES	ATARAXY	BAUXITE	BRAXIES
ABAXILE	ANAXIAL	ATAXITE	BEESWAX	BREAKAX
ABRASAX	ANAXONE	AURIFEX	BENZOXY	BROADAX
ABRAXAS	ANNEXED	AUXESIS	BETWIXT	BRUXISM
ACRONYX	ANNEXER	AUXETIC	BIAXIAL	BUREAUX
ADAXIAL	ANOREXY	AUXOTOX	BIOTAXY	BUTOXYL
ADMIXED	ANTAPEX	AXIALLY	BISEXED	BUXERRY
ADNEXAL	ANTEFIX	AXIFORM	BISSEXT	BUXOMLY
ADNEXED	ANTHRAX	AXILLAE	BOSTRYX	CACHEXY
ADOXIES	ANXIETY	AXILLAR	BOXBUSH	CAKEBOX
AFFIXAL	ANXIOUS	AXINITE	BOXCARS	CARAPAX
AFFIXED	APEXING	AXMAKER	BOXFISH	CAREFOX
AFFIXER	APOPLEX	AXOGAMY	BOXHAUL	CASEBOX
AFFREUX	APRAXIA	AXOLOTL	BOXHEAD	CASHBOX
AGALAXY	APTERYX	AXONEME	BOXINGS	CHOENIX
AGNEAUX	APYREXY	AXONOST	BOXLIKE	COALBOX
ALEXINE	ARTIFEX	AXSTONE	BOXROOM	COAXIAL
ALKOXID	ARUSPEX	AZOXINE	BOXTREE	COAXING
ALKOXYL	ASEXUAL	BANDBOX	BOXWOOD	COEXIST

COLAUXE	EXHAUST	FIXABLE	LEXICAL	PHALANX
COMMIXT	EXHEDRA	FIXATED	LEXICON	PHARYNX
COMPLEX	EXHIBIT	FIXATIF	LOCKBOX	PHOENIX
CONFLUX	EXHUMED	FIXATOR	LOXOTIC	PICKAXE
CONTEXT	EXHUMER	FIXEDLY	LUXATED	PILLBOX
COXALGY	EXIGENT	FIXINGS	MAILBOX	PISTRIX
COXCOMB	EXILIAN	FIXTURE	MALAXED	PLANXTY
COXIEST	EXILING	FLAXIER	MARTEXT	PLAYBOX
COXITIS	EXILITY	FLAXMAN	MARTRIX	PLEXURE
CURTAXE	EXINITE	FLEXILE	MAXILLA	POLAXIS
CURTLAX	EXISTED	FLEXING	MAXIMAL	POLEAXE
DEEDBOX	EXISTER	FLEXION	MAXIMED	POSTBOX
DEXTRAD	EXITIAL	FLEXIVE	MAXIMUM	POSTFIX
DEXTRAL	EXITION	FLEXURA	MAXIMUS	PRAECOX
DEXTRAN	EXITURE	FLEXURE	MAXWELL	PRETEXT
DEXTRIN	EXOCARP	FLUMMOX	METHOXY	PREXIES
DIAXIAL	EXOCONE	FLUXILE	MEXICAL	PRINCOX
DIAXONE	EXODERM	FLUXING	MIXABLE	PROPLEX
DICEBOX	EXODIST	FLUXION	MIXHILL	PROPOXY
DIGOXIN	EXODIUM	FLUXIVE	MIXIBLE	PROTEXT
DIOXANE	EXOGAMY	FLUXURE	MIXTION	PROXENY
DIOXIDE	EXOLETE	FOXBANE	MIXTURE	PROXIED
DIOXIME	EXOMION	FOXCHOP	MONAXON	PROXIES
DUSTBOX	EXORATE	FOXFEET	MUREXAN	PROXIME
ELIXATE	EXORMIA	FOXFIRE	MUREXES	PROXIMO
EPAXIAL	EXOSMIC	FOXFISH	MUREXID	PROXYSM
EPOXIDE	EXOSTRA	FOXHOLE	MYOXINE	PYREXIA
EQUINOX	EXOTISM	FOXIEST	MYXEMIA	PYREXIC
ESEXUAL	EXPANSE	FOXLIKE	MYXOMAS	PYXIDES
ETHOXYL	EXPEDED	FOXSKIN	NARTHEX	RECTRIX
EUTAXIC	EXPENSE	FOXTAIL	NEXUSES	RELAXED
EUTAXIE	EXPIATE	FOXTROT	NOXIOUS	RELAXER
EUTEXIA	EXPIRED	GEARBOX	ORATRIX	RELAXIN
EXACTED	EXPIREE	GEOTAXY	OUTFLUX	RESEAUX
EXACTER	EXPIRER	GITOXIN	OUTJINX	SALPINX
EXACTLY	EXPLAIN	GLOMMOX	OVERTAX	SALTBOX
EXACTOR	EXPLANT	GLYOXAL	OXALATE	SANDBOX
EXALATE	EXPLETE	GLYOXYL	OXALATO	SAXHORN
EXALTED	EXPLODE	GUAXIMA	OXAMATE	SAXTUBA
EXALTEE	EXPLOIT	HEADBOX	OXAMIDE	SEEDBOX
EXALTER	EXPLORE	HELIXIN	OXAZINE	SEXIEST
EXAMINE	EXPOSAL	HELLBOX	OXAZOLE	SEXLESS
EXAMPLE	EXPOSED	HEMIXIS	OXBERRY	SEXLIKE
EXARATE	EXPOSER	HEXACID	OXBITER	SEXTAIN
EXARCHY	EXPOSIT	HEXADIC	OXBLOOD	SEXTANS
EXASPER	EXPOUND	HEXAGON	OXBRAKE	SEXTANT
EXCELSE	EXPREME	HEXAGYN	OXCHEEK	SEXTERN
EXCERPT	EXPRESS	HEXAMER	OXHEART	SEXTILE
EXCHEAT	EXPULSE	HEXANAL	OXHOUSE	SEXTOLE
EXCIDED	EXPUNGE	HEXAPED	OXHUVUD	SEXTUOR
EXCIPLE	EXPURGE	HEXAPLA	OXIDANT	SEXUALE
EXCISED	EXQUIRE	HEXAPOD	OXIDASE	SEXUOUS
EXCISOR	EXRADIO	HEXAXON	OXIDATE	SIDEBOX
EXCITED	EXSCIND	HEXEREI	OXIDISE	SIMPLEX
EXCITER	EXSOLVE	HEXERIS	OXIDIZE	SINKBOX
EXCITON	EXSURGE	HEXITOL	OXIMATE	SIXFOLD
EXCITOR	EXTANCY	HEXONIC	OXONIUM	SIXSOME
EXCLAIM	EXTENSE	HEXOSAN	OXOZONE	SIXTEEN
EXCLAVE	EXTERNA	HEXYLIC	OXYACID	SIXTIES
EXCLUDE	EXTERNE	HOMODOX	OXYMORA	SKEEZIX
EXCRETA	EXTINCT	INDEXED	OXYNTIC	SOAPBOX
EXCRETE	EXTRACT	INDEXER	OXYOPIA	SONOVOX
EXCUDIT	EXTREAT	INDEXES	OXYPHIL	SPANDEX
EXCURSE	EXTREME	INDOXYL	OXYTONE	SPITBOX
EXCUSAL	EXTRUCT	INEXACT	OXYURID	SUBOXID
EXCUSED	EXTRUDE	INEXIST	PACKWAX	SYNAXAR
EXCUSER	EXUDATE	INFIXED	PANCHAX	SYNAXIS
EXECUTE	EXUDING	INFIXES	PANMIXY	TAXABLE
EXEDENT	EXULATE	IXODIAN	PARADOX	TAXABLY
EXEGETE	EXULTED	JACKBOX	PARAXON	TAXATOR
EXEMPLA	EXULTET	JUKEBOX	PAXILLA	TAXIBUS
EXERGUE	EXURBIA	KICKXIA	PAXILLI	TAXICAB
EXERTED	EXUVIAE	KINEPOX	PAXIUBA	TAXIMAN
EXESION	EXUVIAL	KLEENEX	PEIXERE	TAXITIC
EXFLECT	FACTRIX	LARIXIN	PEMPHIX	TAXPAID
EXHALED	FEEDBOX	LATEXES	PEROXYL	TAXYING
EXHANCE	FIREBOX	LAXNESS	PERPLEX	TECTRIX

TELEVOX	TOXOTAE	UROTOXY	WAXWING	XERONIC
TEXTILE	TRIAXAL	UXORIAL	WAXWORK	XEROSIS
TEXTLET	TRIAXON	VAUXITE	WAXWORM	XEROTES
TEXTMAN	TRIOXID	VEXEDLY	WEREFOX	XEROTIC
TEXTUAL	TRIPLEX	VEXILLA	WOODWAX	XIBAL3A
TEXTURE	TUBIFEX	VICTRIX	WORKBOX	XIPHOID
TOOLBOX	TUXEDOS	VITRAUX	WRAXLED	XYLENOL
TORTRIX	ULEXINE	VIXENLY	XANTHIC	XYLENYL
TOXAMIN	ULEXITE	WAXBILL	XANTHID	XYLIDIN
TOXEMIA	UNBUXOM	WAXBIRD	XANTHIN	XYLITOL
TOXEMIC	UNEXACT	WAXBUSH	XANTHYL	XYLOGEN
TOXICAL	UNFIXED	WAXCOMB	XERAFIN	XYLOMAS
TOXICON	UNFOXED	WAXIEST	XERARCH	XYLOSID
TOXICUM	UNSEXED	WAXWEED	XERASIA	ZOOTAXY
TOXIFER				

POSITIONAL ORDER LIST OF 7-LETTER WORDS

XANTHIC	EXCLAIM	EXPLANT	OXIDISE	FOXLIKE
XANTHID	EXCLAVE	EXPLETE	OXIDIZE	FOXSKIN
XANTHIN	EXCLUDE	EXPLODE	OXIMATE	FOXTAIL
XANTHYL	EXCRETA	EXPLOIT	OXONIUM	FOXTROT
XERAFIN	EXCRETE	EXPLORE	OXOZONE	HEXACID
XERARCH	EXCUDIT	EXPOSAL	OXYACID	HEXADIC
XERASIA	EXCURSE	EXPOSED	OXYMORA	HEXAGON
XERONIC	EXCUSAL	EXPOSER	OXYNTIC	HEXAGYN
XEROSIS	EXCUSED	EXPOSIT	OXYOPIA	HEXAMER
XEROTES	EXCUSER	EXPOUND	OXYPHIL	HEXANAL
XEROTIC	EXECUTE	EXPREME	OXYSALT	HEXAPED
XIBALBA	EXEDENT	EXPRESS	OXYTONE	HEXAPLA
XIPHOID	EXEGETE	EXPULSE	OXYURID	HEXAPOD
XYLENOL	EXEMPLA	EXPUNGE	UXORIAL	HEXAXON
XYLENYL	EXERGUE	EXPURGE		HEXEREI
XYLIDIN	EXERTED	EXQUIRE	ANXIETY	HEXERIS
XYLITOL	EXESION	EXRADIO	ANXIOUS	HEXITOL
XYLOGEN	EXFLECT	EXSCIND	AUXESIS	HEXONIC
XYLOMAS	EXHALED	EXSOLVE	AUXETIC	HEXOSAN
XYLOSID	EXHANCE	EXSURGE	AUXOTOX	HEXYLIC
	EXHAUST	EXTANCY	AUXOTOX	LAXNESS
AXIALLY	EXHEDRA	EXTENSE	BOXBUSH	LEXICAL
AXIFORM	EXHIBIT	EXTERNA	BOXCARS	LEXICON
AXILLAE	EXHUMED	EXTERNE	BOXFISH	LOXOTIC
AXILLAR	EXHUMER	EXTINCT	BOXHAUL	LUXATED
AXINITE	EXIGENT	EXTRACT	BOXHEAD	MAXILLA
AXMAKER	EXILIAN	EXTREAT	BOXINGS	MAXIMAL
AXOGAMY	EXILING	EXTREME	BOXLIKE	MAXIMED
AXOLOTL	EXILITY	EXTRUCT	BOXROOM	MAXIMUM
AXONEME	EXINITE	EXTRUDE	BOXTREE	MAXIMUS
AXONOST	EXISTED	EXUDATE	BOXWOOD	MAXWELL
AXSTONE	EXISTER	EXUDING	BOXWORK	MEXICAL
EXACTED	EXITIAL	EXULATE	BUXERRY	MIXABLE
EXACTER	EXITION	EXULTED	BUXOMLY	MIXHILL
EXACTLY	EXITURE	EXULTET	COXALGY	MIXIBLE
EXACTOR	EXOCARP	EXURBIA	COXCOMB	MIXTION
EXALATE	EXOCONE	EXUVIAE	COXIEST	MIXTURE
EXALTED	EXODERM	EXUVIAL	COXITIS	MYXEMIA
EXALTEE	EXODIST	IXODIAN	DEXTRAD	MYXOMAS
EXALTER	EXODIUM	OXALATE	DEXTRAL	NEXUSES
EXAMINE	EXOGAMY	OXALATO	DEXTRAN	NOXIOUS
EXAMPLE	EXOLETE	OXAMATE	DEXTRIN	PAXILLA
EXARATE	EXOMION	OXAMIDE	FIXABLE	PAXILLI
EXARCHY	EXORATE	OXAZINE	FIXATED	PAXIUBA
EXASPER	EXORMIA	OXAZOLE	FIXATIF	PYXIDES
EXCELSE	EXOSMIC	OXBERRY	FIXATOR	SAXHORN
EXCERPT	EXOSTRA	OXBITER	FIXEDLY	SAXTUBA
EXCHEAT	EXOTISM	OXBLOOD	FIXINGS	SEXIEST
EXCIDED	EXPANSE	OXBRAKE	FIXTURE	SEXLESS
EXCIPLE	EXPEDED	OXCHEEK	FOXBANE	SEXLIKE
EXCISED	EXPENSE	OXHEART	FOXCHOP	SEXTAIN
EXCISOR	EXPIATE	OXHOUSE	FOXFEET	SEXTANS
EXCITED	EXPIRED	OXHUVUD	FOXFIRE	SEXTANT
EXCITER	EXPIREE	OXIDANT	FOXFISH	SEXTERN
EXCITON	EXPIRER	OXIDASE	FOXHOLE	SEXTILE
EXCITOR	EXPLAIN	OXIDATE	FOXIEST	SEXTOLE

SEXTUOR	BRUXISM	ANNEXER	BIOTAXY	GLOMMOX
SEXUALE	COAXIAL	APRAXIA	BISSEXT	HEADBOX
SEXUOUS	COAXING	BISEXED	CACHEXY	HELLBOX
SIXFOLD	COEXIST	BUTOXYL	COLAUXE	HOMODOX
SIXSOME	DIAXIAL	DIGOXIN	COMMIXT	JACKBOX
SIXTEEN	DIAXONE	ETHOXYL	CONTEXT	JUKEBOX
SIXTIES	DIOXANE	EUTAXIC	CURTAXE	KINEPOX
TAXABLE	DIOXIDE	EUTAXIE	GEOTAXY	KLEENEX
TAXABLY	DIOXIME	EUTEXIA	MARTEXT	LOCKBOX
TAXATOR	ELIXATE	GITOXIN	METHOXY	MAILBOX
TAXIBUS	EPAXIAL	GLYOXAL	PANMIXY	MARTRIX
TAXICAB	EPOXIDE	GLYOXYL	PICKAXE	NARTHEX
TAXIMAN	ESEXUAL	HELIXIN	POLEAXE	ORATRIX
TAXITIC	FLAXIER	HEMIXIS	PRETEXT	OUTFLUX
TAXPAID	FLAXMAN	HEXAXON	PROPOXY	OUTJINX
TAXYING	FLEXILE	INDEXED	PROTEXT	OVERTAX
TEXTILE	FLEXING	INDEXER	UROTOXY	PACKWAX
TEXTLET	FLEXION	INDEXES	ZOOTAXY	PANCHAX
TEXTMAN	FLEXIVE	INDOXYL		PARADOX
TEXTUAL	FLEXURA	INFIXED		PEMPHIX
TEXTURE	FLEXURE	INFIXES	ABRASAX	PERPLEX
TOXAMIN	FLUXILE	KICKXIA	ACRONYX	PHALANX
TOXEMIA	FLUXING	LARIXIN	AFFREUX	PHARYNX
TOXEMIC	FLUXION	LATEXES	AGNEAUX	PHOENIX
TOXICAL	FLUXIVE	MALAXED	ANTAPEX	PILLBOX
TOXICON	FLUXURE	MONAXON	ANTEFIX	PISTRIX
TOXICUM	GUAXIMA	MUREXAN	ANTHRAX	PLAYBOX
TOXIFER	INEXACT	MUREXES	APOPLEX	POSTBOX
TOXOTAE	INEXIST	MUREXID	APTERYX	POSTFIX
TUXEDOS	MYOXINE	PARAXON	ARTIFEX	PRAECOX
VEXEDLY	PEIXERE	PEROXYL	ARUSPEX	PRINCOX
VEXILLA	PLEXURE	PLANXTY	AURIFEX	PROPLEX
VIXENLY	PREXIES	POLAXIS	BANDBOX	RECTRIX
WAXBILL	PROXENY	PYREXIA	BATEAUX	RESEAUX
WAXBIRD	PROXIED	PYREXIC	BEESWAX	SALPINX
WAXBUSH	PROXIES	RELAXED	BOSTRYX	SALTBOX
WAXCOMB	PROXIME	RELAXER	BREAKAX	SANDBOX
WAXIEST	PROXIMO	RELAXIN	BROADAX	SEEDBOX
WAXWEED	PROXYSM	SUBOXID	BUREAUX	SIDEBOX
WAXWING	ULEXINE	SYNAXAR	CAKEBOX	SIMPLEX
WAXWORK	ULEXITE	SYNAXIS	CARAPAX	SINKBOX
WAXWORM	UNEXACT	TRIAXAL	CAREFOX	SKEEZIX
	VAUXITE	TRIAXON	CASEBOX	SOAPBOX
ABAXIAL	WRAXLED	TRIOXID	CASHBOX	SONOVOX
ABAXILE		UNBUXOM	CHOENIX	SPANDEX
ADAXIAL	ABRAXAS	UNFIXED	COALBOX	SPITBOX
ADOXIES	ADMIXED	UNFOXED	COMPLEX	TECTRIX
ALEXINE	ADNEXAL	UNSEXED	CONFLUX	TELEVOX
ANAXIAL	ADNEXED		CURTLAX	TOOLBOX
ANAXONE	AFFIXAL	ABACAXI	DEEDBOX	TORTRIX
APEXING	AFFIXED	AGALAXY	DICEBOX	TRIPLEX
ASEXUAL	AFFIXER	ANOREXY	DUSTBOX	TUBIFEX
ATAXITE	ALKOXID	APYREXY	EQUINOX	VICTRIX
AZOXINE	ALKOXYL	ASPHYXY	FACTRIX	VITRAUX
BAUXITE	ALLOXAN	ATARAXY	FEEDBOX	WEREFOX
BIAXIAL	AMPYXES	BENZOXY	FIREBOX	WOODWAX
BRAXIES	ANNEXED	BETWIXT	FLUMMOX	WORKBOX
			GEARBOX	

SCORING ORDER LIST OF 7-LETTER WORDS

29	**25**	EQUINOX	BOXFISH	**21**
JACKBOX	ASPHYXY	EXQUIRE	CAKEBOX	AFFIXED
	PACKWAX	FOXFISH	COXCOMB	ALKOXYL
28		OXAZINE	EXARCHY	AMPYXES
BENZOXY	**24**	OXAZOLE	HEXYLIC	BOXBUSH
	CACHEXY	OXCHEEK	LOCKBOX	BUXOMLY
27	FOXCHOP	OXOZONE	METHOXY	CASHBOX
JUKEBOX	OXIDIZE	PEMPHIX	OXYPHIL	FIXEDLY
SKEEZIX	WAXWORK	WAXCOMB	PHARYNX	FLUMMOX
		WORKBOX	PICKAXE	FOXLIKE
26	**23**		WAXBUSH	FOXSKIN
ZOOTAXY	AZOXINE	**22**	WAXWORM	GLYOXYL
	BOXWORK	APYREXY		

HEXAGYN	EXFLECT	MEXICAL	FLUXION	DIOXIDE
MYXEMIA	EXHANCE	MIXABLE	FLUXURE	EPAXIAL
MYXOMAS	EXHIBIT	MIXIBLE	FOXIEST	EUTAXIC
OUTJINX	EXHUMER	OXYURID	FOXTAIL	EXACTER
OXHUVUD	EXTANCY	PAXIUBA	FOXTROT	EXACTOR
PANCHAX	FACTRIX	PERPLEX	GEARBOX	EXAMINE
PANMIXY	FIREBOX	PILLBOX	GUAXIMA	EXASPER
PLAYBOX	FIXABLE	POSTBOX	HELIXIN	EXCELSE
PROPOXY	FLAXMAN	PRAECOX	HEXANAL	EXCISOR
PROXYSM	FOXBANE	PRINCOX	HEXEREI	EXCITER
PYREXIC	GLOMMOX	PROPLEX	HEXERIS	EXCITON
VEXEDLY	HELLBOX	PROXIME	HEXITOL	EXCITOR
WAXWEED	HEMIXIS	PROXIMO	HEXOSAN	EXCRETA
WAXWING	HEXAMER	SEXLIKE	INFIXES	EXCRETE
WOODWAX	HEXAPLA	SIMPLEX	MALAXED	EXCURSE
	HEXONIC	SIXFOLD	MAXIMUM	EXCUSAL
20	KICKXIA	SOAPBOX	MUREXID	EXCUSER
AFFIXAL	MAXIMED	SPITBOX	NARTHEX	EXECUTE
AFFIXER	MAXWELL	TAXICAB	OUTFLUX	EXOCONE
AFFREUX	MIXHILL	TAXYING	OVERTAX	EXOMION
AXMAKER	MYOXINE	TOXEMIC	OXAMIDE	EXORMIA
AXOGAMY	OXBERRY	TOXICUM	OXBLOOD	EXOTISM
BOXHEAD	OXYMORA	UNBUXOM	OXHEART	EXPANSE
BOXLIKE	OXYNTIC	UNFIXED	OXHOUSE	EXPENSE
BOXWOOD	OXYOPIA	UNFOXED	OXYTONE	EXPIATE
BREAKAX	PEROXYL	WRAXLED	PARADOX	EXPIREE
COMMIXT	PHALANX	XANTHID	PROXIED	EXPIRER
COMPLEX	PHOENIX	XIBALBA	SANDBOX	EXPLAIN
COXALGY	PLANXTY	XYLIDIN	SAXHORN	EXPLANT
ETHOXYL	POSTFIX	XYLOGEN	SEEDBOX	EXPLETE
EXHUMED	PROXENY	XYLOSID	SIDEBOX	EXPLOIT
EXOGAMY	PYREXIA		SONOVOX	EXPLORE
FEEDBOX	TAXABLY	**17**	SPANDEX	EXPOSAL
FIXATIF	TUBIFEX	ANOREXY	SUBOXID	EXPOSER
FLEXIVE	VICTRIX	ANTEFIX	SYNAXAR	EXPOSIT
FLUXIVE	WAXBILL	ANTHRAX	SYNAXIS	EXPRESS
FOXFEET	XANTHIC	ANXIETY	TAXPAID	EXPULSE
FOXFIRE	XERARCH	APEXING	TELEVOX	EXTINCT
FOXHOLE	XYLOMAS	ARTIFEX	TOXIFER	EXTRACT
HEADBOX		ATARAXY	UROTOXY	EXTREME
HEXACID	**18**	AURIFEX	VAUXITE	EXTRUCT
HEXADIC	ABACAXI	AXIALLY	VEXILLA	EXUDING
HEXAPED	ADMIXED	BISEXED	VITRAUX	EXURBIA
HEXAPOD	AGALAXY	BOXINGS	WAXIEST	HEXAXON
HOMODOX	APOPLEX	BROADAX	XANTHIN	INDEXED
KINEPOX	BOXCARS	COAXING	XERAFIN	INEXACT
OXBRAKE	BOXROOM	DIOXIME	XYLENOL	LEXICAL
OXYACID	BRUXISM	DUSTBOX	XYLITOL	LEXICON
PYXIDES	CARAPAX	EPOXIDE		LOXOTIC
SINKBOX	CASEBOX	EXACTED	**16**	MARTEXT
VIXENLY	COALBOX	EXCISED	ABAXIAL	MARTRIX
WAXBIRD	DEEDBOX	EXCITED	ABAXILE	MAXILLA
WEREFOX	EXAMPLE	EXCLUDE	ABRASAX	MIXTION
XANTHYL	EXCERPT	EXCUDIT	ABRAXAS	MIXTURE
XIPHOID	EXCIDED	EXCUSED	ADNEXED	MONAXON
XYLENYL	EXCIPLE	EXHAUST	ANTAPEX	MUREXAN
	EXCLAIM	EXILITY	APRAXIA	MUREXES
19	EXEMPLA	EXODERM	ARUSPEX	OXAMATE
ACRONYX	EXHALED	EXODIUM	AUXETIC	OXBITER
ALKOXID	EXHEDRA	EXPIRED	AXONEME	OXIMATE
APTERYX	EXOCARP	EXPLODE	BATEAUX	OXONIUM
AXIFORM	EXOSMIC	EXPOSED	BAUXITE	PARAXON
BANDBOX	EXPEDED	EXPOUND	BIAXIAL	PAXILLA
BEESWAX	EXPREME	EXPUNGE	BISSEXT	PAXILLI
BETWIXT	FIXATED	EXPURGE	BOXTREE	PEIXERE
BIOTAXY	FIXINGS	EXSCIND	BRAXIES	PISTRIX
BOSTRYX	FLEXING	EXSOLVE	BUREAUX	PLEXURE
BOXHAUL	FLUXING	EXUVIAE	COAXIAL	POLAXIS
BUTOXYL	GEOTAXY	EXUVIAL	COEXIST	POLEAXE
BUXERRY	GLYOXAL	FIXATOR	COLAUXE	PRETEXT
CAREFOX	HEXAGON	FIXTURE	CONTEXT	PREXIES
CHOENIX	INDOXYL	FLAXIER	COXIEST	PROTEXT
CONFLUX	INFIXED	FLEXILE	COXITIS	PROXIES
DICEBOX	KLEENEX	FLEXION	CURTAXE	RECTRIX
EXACTLY	MAILBOX	FLEXURA	CURTLAX	SALPINX
EXCHEAT	MAXIMAL	FLEXURE	DEXTRAD	SALTBOX
EXCLAVE	MAXIMUS	FLUXILE	DIGOXIN	SAXTUBA

SIXSOME	DIOXANE	**14**	EXITIAL	SEXTANT
TAXABLE	EXALTED	ALEXINE	EXITION	SEXTERN
TAXIBUS	EXEDENT	ALLOXAN	EXITURE	SEXTILE
TAXIMAN	EXEGETE	ANAXIAL	EXOLETE	SEXTOLE
TAXITIC	EXERGUE	ANAXONE	EXORATE	SEXTUOR
TECTRIX	EXERTED	ANNEXER	EXOSTRA	SEXUALE
TEXTMAN	EXIGENT	ANXIOUS	EXTENSE	SEXUOUS
TOOLBOX	EXILING	ASEXUAL	EXTERNA	SIXTEEN
TOXAMIN	EXISTED	ATAXITE	EXTERNE	SIXTIES
TOXEMIA	EXODIST	AUXESIS	EXTREAT	TAXATOR
TOXICAL	EXRADIO	AXILLAE	EXULATE	TEXTILE
TOXICON	EXSURGE	AXILLAR	EXULTET	TEXTLET
TRIPLEX	EXTRUDE	AXINITE	INEXIST	TEXTUAL
UNEXACT	EXUDATE	AXOLOTL	LARIXIN	TEXTURE
XERONIC	EXULTED	AXONOST	LATEXES	TORTRIX
XEROTIC	GITOXIN	AXSTONE	LAXNESS	TOXOTAE
	INDEXER	ELIXATE	NEXUSES	TRIAXAL
15	INDEXES	ESEXUAL	NOXIOUS	TRIAXON
ADAXIAL	IXODIAN	EUTAXIE	ORATRIX	ULEXINE
ADNEXAL	LUXATED	EUTEXIA	OXALATE	ULEXITE
ADOXIES	OXIDANT	EXALATE	OXALATO	UXORIAL
AGNEAUX	OXIDASE	EXALTEE	RELAXER	XERASIA
ANNEXED	OXIDATE	EXALTER	RELAXIN	XEROSIS
DEXTRAL	OXIDISE	EXARATE	RESEAUX	XEROTES
DEXTRAN	RELAXED	EXESION	SEXIEST	
DEXTRIN	TRIOXID	EXILIAN	SEXLESS	**13**
DIAXIAL	TUXEDOS	EXINITE	SEXTAIN	AUXOTOX
DIAXONE	UNSEXED	EXISTER	SEXTANS	

ALPHABETICAL LIST OF 8-LETTER WORDS

ACETOXIM	AUXOBODY	BREAKAXE	DEFLEXED	EXCALATE
ACETOXYL	AUXOCYTE	BROADAXE	DETOXIFY	EXCAMBER
ACXOYATL	AUXOLOGY	CACHEXIA	DEXTRANE	EXCAVATE
ADJUTRIX	AVIATRIX	CACHEXIC	DEXTRINE	EXCECATE
ADMIXING	AXHAMMER	CACODOXY	DEXTROSE	EXCEDENT
AFFIXING	AXIALITY	CACOMIXL	DEXTROUS	EXCEEDED
AFFIXION	AXIFUGAL	CARBOXYL	DIAXONIC	EXCELLED
AGALAXIA	AXILEMMA	CARNIFEX	DIPLEXER	EXCELSIN
ALDOXIME	AXILLANT	CATHEXIS	DISANNEX	EXCEPTED
ALEXINIC	AXILLARY	CAUDEXES	DIXENITE	EXCEPTER
ALKOXIDE	AXIOLITE	CEROXYLE	DOXASTIC	EXCEPTIO
AMIDOXYL	AXIOLOGY	CERVIXES	DOXOLOGY	EXCERPTA
AMPLEXUS	AXLETREE	CHAFEWAX	DUPLEXED	EXCHANGE
ANATEXIS	AXMAKING	CHAFFWAX	DUPLEXER	EXCIDING
ANATOXIN	AXMASTER	CHAPEAUX	DUPLEXES	EXCIPULE
ANAUXITE	AXOFUGAL	CHATEAUX	DUXELLES	EXCIRCLE
ANNEXING	AXOIDEAN	CHRONAXY	DYSOREXY	EXCISING
ANNEXION	AXOLYSIS	CICATRIX	DYSTAXIA	EXCISION
ANNEXIVE	AXOMETER	CLAVILUX	EFFLUXES	EXCITANT
ANNEXURE	AXONEURE	CLIMAXED	EPICALYX	EXCITATE
ANOREXIA	AXOPETAL	COEXTEND	EQUAIXED	EXCITING
ANOXEMIA	AXOPHYTE	COLOPEXY	ESSEXITE	EXCITIVE
ANOXEMIC	AXOPLASM	COLTPIXY	ETHOXIDE	EXCITORY
ANTEFIXA	AXOSTYLE	COMMIXED	EUPRAXIA	EXCITRON
ANTHELIX	BANDBOXY	CONFIXED	EUTAXIE	EXCLUDED
APODIXIS	BANDEAUX	CONNEXES	EUXENITE	EXCLUDER
APOMIXIS	BAROTAXY	CONNEXUS	EXACTING	EXCRESCE
APOPLEXY	BETWIXEN	CONTUMAX	EXACTION	EXCRETAL
APOXESIS	BICONVEX	CONVEXED	EXACTIVE	EXCRETED
APPENDIX	BILLYWIX	CONVEXLY	EXACUATE	EXCRETER
APPRAXIC	BINOXIDE	COUTEAUX	EXALTATE	EXCRETES
APYREXIA	BISEXUAL	COXALGIA	EXALTING	EXCUBANT
ASPHYXIA	BIXBYITE	COXALGIC	EXAMINED	EXCUDATE
ATARAXIA	BOLLIXED	COXBONES	EXAMINEE	EXCURSED
ATARAXIC	BOXBERRY	COXCOMBY	EXAMINER	EXCURSUS
AUXILIAR	BOXBOARD	COXSWAIN	EXAMPLED	EXCURVED
AUXILIUM	BOXTHORN	CRESOXID	EXANTHEM	EXCUSING
AUXIMONE	BREADBOX	CRUCIFIX	EXARCHAL	EXCUSIVE

EXCUSSED	EXPENSES	FLEXIBLE	MATCHBOX	OXYSALT
EXCYSTED	EXPERTLY	FLEXIBLY	MATRIXES	OXYSTOME
EXECRATE	EXPIABLE	FLEXUOSE	MAXILLAE	OXYTOCIA
EXECUTED	EXPIATED	FLEXUOUS	MAXIMATE	OXYTOCIC
EXECUTER	EXPIATOR	FLEXURAL	MAXIMIST	OXYTOCIN
EXECUTOR	EXPILATE	FLEXURED	MAXIMITE	OXYUROUS
EXECUTRY	EXPIRANT	FLUXIBLE	MAXIMIZE	PAINTBOX
EXEGESES	EXPIRATE	FLUXIBLY	MAXIMUMS	PANMIXIA
EXEGESIS	EXPIRIES	FLUXROOT	MAZOPEXY	PARADOXY
EXEGETIC	EXPIRING	FLUXWEED	MEIOTAXY	PARALLAX
EXEMPLAR	EXPLICIT	FORNAXID	MELAXUMA	PARAXIAL
EXEMPLUM	EXPLODED	FOXBERRY	MERETRIX	PAROXYSM
EXEQUIAL	EXPLODER	FOXGLOVE	MEROXENE	PAXILLAE
EXEQUIES	EXPLORED	FOXHOUND	METAXITE	PAXILLAR
EXERCENT	EXPLORER	FOXINESS	METHOXYL	PAXILLUS
EXERCISE	EXPONENT	FRAXETIN	MILLILUX	PEIXEREY
EXERESIS	EXPORTED	GALAXIAN	MIREPOIX	PEROXIDE
EXERGUAL	EXPORTER	GALAXIAS	MISOXENE	PHILODOX
EXERTING	EXPOSING	GENETRIX	MISOXENY	PHORMINX
EXERTION	EXPOSURE	GEOTAXIS	MIXBLOOD	PLATEAUX
EXERTIVE	EXPULSER	GLYOXIME	MIXERESS	PLEXUSES
EXFIGURE	EXPUNGED	GREENWAX	MONAXIAL	POLEAXER
EXHALANT	EXPUNGER	HARUSPEX	MONOXIDE	POLYAXON
EXHALATE	EXRADIUS	HERITRIX	MONOXYLA	PONTIFEX
EXHALING	EXRUPEAL	HEXAFOIL	MONOXYLE	PREAXIAL
EXHIBITS	EXSCRIBE	HEXAFOOS	MORCEAUX	PRECIEUX
EXHORTED	EXSCRIPT	HEXAGLOT	MOROXITE	PREEXIST
EXHORTER	EXSECANT	HEXAGRAM	MORTREUX	PREFIXAL
EXHUMATE	EXSECTOR	HEXAMINE	MOUSSEUX	PREFIXED
EXHUMING	EXSERTED	HEXAMMIN	MUREXIDE	PREMIXED
EXIGEANT	EXSHEATH	HEXANDRY	MYELAUXE	PROLIXLY
EXIGENCE	EXTENDED	HEXAPLAR	MYXAEMIA	PROTAXIS
EXIGENCY	EXTENDER	HEXAPODY	MYXEDEMA	PROTOXID
EXIGIBLE	EXTENSOR	HEXARCHY	MYXINOID	PROXENET
EXIGUITY	EXTENSUM	HEXASEME	MYXOCYTE	PROXENOS
EXIGUOUS	EXTERIOR	HEXASTER	MYXOMATA	PROXENUS
EXILARCH	EXTERNAL	HEXYLENE	NEURAXIS	PROXIMAD
EXIMIOUS	EXTERNAT	HOMAXIAL	NEURAXON	PROXIMAL
EXISTENT	EXTERNUM	HOMOTAXY	NEXTNESS	PROXYING
EXISTING	EXTISPEX	HORSEPOX	NITROXYL	PYREXIAL
EXITIOUS	EXTOLLED	HYPAXIAL	NIXTAMAL	PYXIDATE
EXOCLINE	EXTOLLER	INDEXING	NOSOTAXY	PYXIDIUM
EXOCOELE	EXTORTED	INEXPERT	NOTAULIX	QUINCUNX
EXODROMY	EXTORTER	INFIXING	NOVATRIX	QUIXOTIC
EXOGAMIC	EXTRACTS	INFIXION	OCTUPLEX	QUIXOTRY
EXOGENIC	EXTRADOS	INFLEXED	OPOPANAX	REEXPORT
EXOGRAPH	EXTRARED	INTERMIX	ORTHODOX	REFLEXED
EXOLEMMA	EXTREMER	INTERREX	OXALEMIA	REFLUXED
EXOPHAGY	EXTREMES	INTERSEX	OXALURIA	RELATRIX
EXORABLE	EXTREMUM	INTERTEX	OXALURIC	RELAXANT
EXORCISE	EXTRORSE	INTEXINE	OXAMIDIN	RELAXING
EXORCISM	EXTRUDED	JAMBEAUX	OXAMMITE	RETRAXIT
EXORCIST	EXTRUDER	JANITRIX	OXANILIC	RIXATRIX
EXORCIZE	EXTUBATE	JASPONYX	OXHARROW	RIXDALER
EXORDIAL	EXTUSION	KETOXIME	OXIDABLE	RONDEAUX
EXORDIUM	EXUDENCE	LARYNXES	OXIDASIC	ROULEAUX
EXORDIZE	EXULTANT	LAXATION	OXIDATED	SARDONYX
EXOSPERM	EXULTING	LAXATIVE	OXIDATOR	SAXATILE
EXOSPORE	EXUMBRAL	LEUCORYX	OXIDIZED	SAXBOARD
EXOSTOME	EXUNDATE	LIPOXENY	OXIDIZER	SAXICOLE
EXOSTRAE	EXUVIATE	LITHOXYL	OXPECKER	SAXIFRAX
EXOTERIC	FABLIAUX	LIXIVIAL	OXTONGUE	SAXONITE
EXOTHECA	FIXATING	LIXIVIUM	OXYAMINE	SENATRIX
EXOTOXIC	FIXATION	LOXOCOSM	OXYAPHIA	SEXANGLE
EXOTOXIN	FIXATIVE	LOXODONT	OXYASTER	SEXENARY
EXPANDED	FIXATURE	LOXOSOMA	OXYBAPHA	SEXOLOGY
EXPANDER	FIXIDITY	LOXOTOMY	OXYCRATE	SEXTETTE
EXPANSUM	FIXITIES	LUXATING	OXYDIACT	SEXTIPLY
EXPECTED	FLAXBIRD	LUXATION	OXYETHER	SEXTOLET
EXPECTER	FLAXBUSH	LUXURIES	OXYETHYL	SEXTUPLE
EXPEDING	FLAXDROP	LUXURIST	OXYGENIC	SEXTUPLY
EXPEDITE	FLAXIEST	LUXURITY	OXYGONAL	SEXUALLY
EXPELLED	FLAXSEED	MALAXAGE	OXYMORON	SEXUPARA
EXPELLEE	FLAXTAIL	MALAXATE	OXYPHILE	SILEXITE
EXPELLER	FLAXWEED	MALAXING	OXYPHONY	SILOXANE
EXPENDED	FLAXWIFE	MANTEAUX	OXYPHYTE	SIXPENCE
EXPENDER	FLAXWORT	MASTAUXE	OXYRHINE	SIXPENNY

SIXSCORE	TAXATION	TORTEAUX	VEXATION	XENOGAMY
SIXTIETH	TAXATIVE	TOUCHBOX	VEXATORY	XENOLITE
SKATOXYL	TAXEATER	TOXAEMIA	VEXILLUM	XENOLITH
SMALLPOX	TAXEOPOD	TOXAEMIC	VIXENISH	XENOPHYA
SMOKEBOX	TAXIARCH	TOXICANT	VORTEXES	XENOTIME
SNUFFBOX	TAXIAUTO	TOXICATE	WAXBERRY	XERANSIS
SPHEXIDE	TAXINGLY	TOXICITY	WAXINESS	XERANTIC
SPHINXES	TAXODONT	TOXICOID	WAXINGLY	XERAPHIN
SPINIFEX	TAXOLOGY	TOXODONT	WAXMAKER	XERONATE
SPINTEXT	TAXONOMY	TOXOLOGY	WHEELBOX	XEROPHIL
SUBINDEX	TAXPAYER	TOXOPHIL	WRAXLING	XEROSERE
SUBOXIDE	TEGUEXIN	TRACTRIX	XANTHANE	XIPHIOID
SUFFIXAL	TETRAXON	TRANSFIX	XANTHATE	XYLIDINE
SUFFIXED	TETROXID	TRIAXIAL	XANTHEIN	XYLITONE
SUPELLEX	TEXGUINO	TRIOXIDE	XANTHENE	XYLOCARP
SUPERFIX	TEXTBOOK	TUXEDOES	XANTHIDE	XYLOIDIN
SUPERSEX	TEXTILES	UNEXPECT	XANTHINE	XYLOLOGY
SUPERTAX	TEXTRINE	UNEXPERT	XANTHITE	XYLOMATA
SURTAXED	TEXTUARY	UNIAXIAL	XANTHOMA	XYLORCIN
SWEATBOX	TEXTURAL	UNISEXED	XANTHONE	XYLOSIDE
SWINEPOX	TEXTURED	UNSEXING	XANTHOUS	XYLOTILE
SYNAXARY	THIOXENE	UROTOXIC	XENAGOGY	XYLOTOMY
SYNTAXIS	THORAXES	UROTOXIN	XENELASY	XYLYLENE
SYNTEXIS	THYROXIN	UXORIOUS	XENOCYST	ZELATRIX
SYRINXES	TOADFLAX	VENIPLEX	XENODERM	ZOOTOXIN
TABLEAUX	TONNEAUX	VERTEXES		

POSITIONAL ORDER LIST OF 8-LETTER WORDS

XANTHANE	AXIOLOGY	EXCITING	EXHORTER	EXPELLED
XANTHATE	AXLETREE	EXCITIVE	EXHUMATE	EXPELLEE
XANTHEIN	AXMAKING	EXCITORY	EXHUMING	EXPELLER
XANTHENE	AXMASTER	EXCITRON	EXIGEANT	EXPENDED
XANTHIDE	AXOFUGAL	EXCLUDED	EXIGENCE	EXPENDER
XANTHINE	AXOIDEAN	EXCLUDER	EXIGENCY	EXPENSES
XANTHITE	AXOLYSIS	EXCRESCE	EXIGIBLE	EXPERTLY
XANTHOMA	AXOMETER	EXCRETAL	EXIGUITY	EXPIABLE
XANTHONE	AXONEURE	EXCRETED	EXIGUOUS	EXPIATED
XANTHOUS	AXOPETAL	EXCRETER	EXILARCH	EXPIATOR
XENAGOGY	AXOPHYTE	EXCRETES	EXIMIOUS	EXPILATE
XENELASY	AXOPLASM	EXCUBANT	EXISTENT	EXPIRANT
XENOCYST	AXOSTYLE	EXCUDATE	EXISTING	EXPIRATE
XENODERM	EXACTING	EXCURSED	EXITIOUS	EXPIRIES
XENOGAMY	EXACTION	EXCURSUS	EXOCLINE	EXPIRING
XENOLITE	EXACTIVE	EXCURVED	EXOCOELE	EXPLICIT
XENOLITH	EXACUATE	EXCUSING	EXODROMY	EXPLODED
XENOPHYA	EXALTATE	EXCUSIVE	EXOGAMIC	EXPLODER
XENOTIME	EXALTING	EXCUSSED	EXOGENIC	EXPLORED
XERANSIS	EXAMINED	EXCYSTED	EXOGRAPH	EXPLORER
XERANTIC	EXAMINEE	EXECRATE	EXOLEMMA	EXPONENT
XERAPHIN	EXAMINER	EXECUTED	EXOPHAGY	EXPORTED
XERONATE	EXAMPLED	EXECUTER	EXORABLE	EXPORTER
XEROPHIL	EXANTHEM	EXECUTOR	EXORCISE	EXPOSING
XEROSERE	EXARCHAL	EXECUTRY	EXORCISM	EXPOSURE
XIPHIOID	EXCALATE	EXEGESES	EXORCIST	EXPULSER
XYLIDINE	EXCAMBER	EXEGESIS	EXORCIZE	EXPUNGED
XYLITONE	EXCAVATE	EXEGETIC	EXORDIAL	EXPUNGER
XYLOCARP	EXCECATE	EXEMPLAR	EXORDIUM	EXRADIUS
XYLOIDIN	EXCEDENT	EXEMPLUM	EXORDIZE	EXRUPEAL
XYLOLOGY	EXCEEDED	EXEQUIAL	EXOSPERM	EXSCRIBE
XYLOMATA	EXCELLED	EXEQUIES	EXOSPORE	EXSCRIPT
XYLORCIN	EXCELSIN	EXERCENT	EXOSTOME	EXSECANT
XYLOSIDE	EXCEPTED	EXERCISE	EXOSTRAE	EXSECTOR
XYLOTILE	EXCEPTER	EXERESIS	EXOTERIC	EXSERTED
XYLOTOMY	EXCEPTIO	EXERGUAL	EXOTHECA	EXSHEATH
XYLYLENE	EXCERPTA	EXERTING	EXOTOXIC	EXTENDED
	EXCHANGE	EXERTION	EXOTOXIN	EXTENDER
AXHAMMER	EXCIDING	EXERTIVE	EXPANDED	EXTENSOR
AXIALITY	EXCIPULE	EXFIGURE	EXPANDER	EXTENSUM
AXIFUGAL	EXCIRCLE	EXHALANT	EXPANSUM	EXTERIOR
AXILEMMA	EXCISING	EXHALATE	EXPECTED	EXTERNAL
AXILLANT	EXCISION	EXHALING	EXPECTER	EXTERNAT
AXILLARY	EXCITANT	EXHIBITS	EXPEDING	EXTERNUM
AXIOLITE	EXCITATE	EXHORTED	EXPEDITE	EXTISPEX

EXTOLLED	DEXTROSE	SEXTUPLY	PROXIMAL	ANATOXIN
EXTOLLER	DEXTROUS	SEXUALLY	PROXYING	ANOREXIA
EXTORTED	DIXENITE	SEXUPARA	QUIXOTIC	APODIXIS
EXTORTER	DOXASTIC	SIXPENCE	QUIXOTRY	APOMIXIS
EXTRACTS	DOXOLOGY	SIXPENNY	REEXPORT	APPRAXIC
EXTRADOS	DUXELLES	SIXSCORE	UNEXPECT	APYREXIA
EXTRARED	EUXENITE	SIXTIETH	UNEXPERT	ASPHYXIA
EXTREMER	FIXATING	TAXATION	WRAXLING	ATARAXIA
EXTREMES	FIXATION	TAXATIVE		ATARAXIC
EXTREMUM	FIXATIVE	TAXEATER	ADMIXING	BETWIXEN
EXTRORSE	FIXATURE	TAXEOPOD	AFFIXING	BOLLIXED
EXTRUDED	FIXIDITY	TAXIARCH	AFFIXION	CACHEXIA
EXTRUDER	FIXITIES	TAXIAUTO	ALDOXIME	CACHEXIC
EXTUBATE	FOXBERRY	TAXINGLY	ALKOXIDE	CARBOXYL
EXTUSION	FOXGLOVE	TAXODONT	ANAUXITE	CATHEXIS
EXUDENCE	FOXHOUND	TAXOLOGY	ANNEXING	CAUDEXES
EXULTANT	FOXINESS	TAXONOMY	ANNEXION	CERVIXES
EXULTING	HEXAFOIL	TAXPAYER	ANNEXIVE	CLIMAXED
EXUMBRAL	HEXAFOOS	TEXGUINO	ANNEXURE	COMMIXED
EXUNDATE	HEXAGLOT	TEXTBOOK	BINOXIDE	CONFIXED
EXUVIATE	HEXAGRAM	TEXTILES	BISEXUAL	CONNEXES
OXALEMIA	HEXAMINE	TEXTRINE	CACOXENE	CONNEXUS
OXALURIA	HEXAMMIN	TEXTUARY	CEROXYLE	CONVEXED
OXALURIC	HEXANDRY	TEXTURAL	DETOXIFY	CONVEXLY
OXAMIDIN	HEXAPLAR	TEXTURED	ESSEXITE	CRESOXID
OXAMMITE	HEXAPODY	TOXAEMIA	ETHOXIDE	DEFLEXED
OXANILIC	HEXARCHY	TOXAEMIC	EUTAXITE	DIPLEXER
OXHARROW	HEXASEME	TOXICANT	GALAXIAN	DUPLEXED
OXIDABLE	HEXASTER	TOXICATE	GALAXIAS	DUPLEXER
OXIDASIC	HEXYLENE	TOXICITY	GLYOXIME	DUPLEXES
OXIDATED	LAXATION	TOXICOID	HOMAXIAL	DYSTAXIA
OXIDATOR	LAXATIVE	TOXODONT	HYPAXIAL	EFFLUXES
OXIDIZED	LIXIVIAL	TOXOLOGY	INDEXING	EQUAIXED
OXIDIZER	LIXIVIUM	TOXOPHIL	INFIXING	EUPRAXIA
OXPECKER	LOXOCOSM	TUXEDOES	INFIXION	EXOTOXIC
OXTONGUE	LOXODONT	VEXATION	INTEXINE	EXOTOXIN
OXYAMINE	LOXOSOMA	VEXATORY	KETOXIME	FORNAXID
OXYAPHIA	LOXOTOMY	VEXILLUM	LIPOXENY	GEOTAXIS
OXYASTER	LUXATING	VIXENISH	MALAXAGE	INFLEXED
OXYBAPHA	LUXATION	WAXBERRY	MALAXATE	LARYNXES
OXYCRATE	LUXURIES	WAXINESS	MALAXING	LITHOXYL
OXYDIACT	LUXURIST	WAXINGLY	MELAXUMA	MATRIXES
OXYETHER	LUXURITY	WAXMAKER	MEROXENE	METHOXYL
OXYETHYL	MAXILLAE		METAXITE	NEURAXIS
OXYGENIC	MAXIMATE	ALEXINIC	MISOXENE	NEURAXON
OXYGONAL	MAXIMIST	ANOXEMIA	MISOXENY	NITROXYL
OXYMORON	MAXIMITE	ANOXEMIC	MONAXIAL	PANMIXIA
OXYPHILE	MAXIMIZE	APOXESIS	MONOXIDE	POLEAXER
OXYPHONY	MAXIMUMS	COEXTEND	MONOXYLA	POLYAXON
OXYPHYTE	MIXBLOOD	DIAXONIC	MONOXYLE	PREFIXAL
OXYRHINE	MIXERESS	FLAXBIRD	MOROXITE	PREFIXED
OXYSALT	MYXAEMIA	FLAXBUSH	MUREXIDE	PREMIXED
OXYSTOME	MYXEDEMA	FLAXDROP	PARAXIAL	PROLIXLY
OXYTOCIA	MYXINOID	FLAXIEST	PAROXYSM	PROTAXIS
OXYTOCIC	MYXOCYTE	FLAXSEED	PEROXIDE	PROTOXID
OXYTOCIN	MYXOMATA	FLAXTAIL	PREAXIAL	REFLEXED
OXYUROUS	NEXTNESS	FLAXWEED	PREEXIST	REFLUXED
UXORIOUS	NIXTAMAL	FLAXWIFE	PYREXIAL	RETRAXIT
	PAXILLAE	FLAXWORT	RELAXANT	SKATOXYL
ACXOYATL	PAXILLAR	FLEXIBLE	RELAXING	SPHINXES
AUXILIAR	PAXILLUS	FLEXIBLY	SILEXITE	SUFFIXAL
AUXILIUM	PYXIDATE	FLEXUOSE	SILOXANE	SUFFIXED
AUXIMONE	PYXIDIUM	FLEXUOUS	SPHEXIDE	SURTAXED
AUXOBODY	RIXATRIX	FLEXURAL	SUBOXIDE	SYNTAXIS
AUXOCYTE	RIXDALER	FLEXURED	SYNAXARY	SYNTEXIS
AUXOLOGY	SAXATILE	FLUXIBLE	THIOXENE	SYRINXES
BIXBYITE	SAXBOARD	FLUXIBLY	TRIAXIAL	TEGUEXIN
BOXBERRY	SAXICOLE	FLUXROOT	TRIOXIDE	TETRAXON
BOXBOARD	SAXIFRAX	FLUXWEED	UNIAXIAL	TETROXID
BOXTHORN	SAXONITE	FRAXETIN	UNSEXING	THORAXES
COXALGIA	SEXANGLE	INEXPERT		THYROXIN
COXALGIC	SEXENARY	PEIXEREY	ACETOXIM	UNISEXED
COXBONES	SEXOLOGY	PLEXUSES	ACETOXYL	UROTOXIC
COXCOMBY	SEXTETTE	PROXENET	AGALAXIA	UROTOXIN
COXSWAIN	SEXTIPLY	PROXENOS	AMIDOXYL	VERTEXES
DEXTRANE	SEXTOLET	PROXENUS	AMPLEXUS	VORTEXES
DEXTRINE	SEXTUPLE	PROXIMAD	ANATEXIS	ZOOTOXIN

ANTEFIXA	ADJUTRIX	FABLIAUX	MOUSSEUX	SMALLPOX
APOPLEXY	ANTHELIX	GENETRIX	NOTAULIX	SMOKEBOX
BANDBOXY	APPENDIX	GREENWAX	NOVATRIX	SNUFFBOX
BAROTAXY	AVIATRIX	HARUSPEX	OCTUPLEX	SPINIFEX
BREAKAXE	BANDEAUX	HERITRIX	OPOPANAX	SUBINDEX
BROADAXE	BICONVEX	HORSEPOX	ORTHODOX	SUPELLEX
CACODOXY	BILLYWIX	INTERMIX	PAINTBOX	SUPERFIX
CACOMIXL	BREADBOX	INTERREX	PARALLAX	SUPERSEX
CHRONAXY	CARNIFEX	INTERSEX	PHILODOX	SUPERTAX
COLOPEXY	CHAFEWAX	INTERTEX	PHORMINX	SWEATBOX
COLTPIXY	CHAFFWAX	JAMBEAUX	PLATEAUX	SWINEPOX
DYSOREXY	CHAPEAUX	JANITRIX	PONTIFEX	TABLEAUX
HOMOTAXY	CHATEAUX	JASPONYX	PRECIEUX	TOADFLAX
MASTAUXE	CICATRIX	LEUCORYX	QUINCUNX	TONNEAUX
MAZOPEXY	CLAVILUX	MANTEAUX	RELATRIX	TORTEAUX
MEIOTAXY	CONTUMAX	MATCHBOX	RIXATRIX	TOUCHBOX
MYELAUXE	COUTEAUX	MERETRIX	RONDEAUX	TRACTRIX
NOSOTAXY	CRUCIFIX	MILLILUX	ROULEAUX	TRANSFIX
PARADOXY	DISANNEX	MIREPOIX	SARDONYX	VENIPLEX
SPINTEXT	EPICALYX	MORCEAUX	SAXIFRAX	WHEELBOX
	EXTISPEX	MORTREUX	SENATRIX	ZELATRIX

SCORING ORDER LIST OF 8-LETTER WORDS

31	CACODOXY	OXYTOCIC	PREFIXED	EXOGAMIC
MAZOPEXY	CHRONAXY	PAROXYSM	PROXYING	EXOTHECA
	CONVEXLY	PHORMINX	PYXIDATE	EXPECTED
29	FLAXBUSH	SKATOXYL	SPHEXIDE	EXPERTLY
CHAFFWAX	FLEXIBLY	SUFFIXED	SUFFIXAL	FABLIAUX
	FLUXIBLY	TOUCHBOX	SYNAXARY	FLEXIBLE
28	FOXBERRY	WAXINGLY	TEXTBOOK	FLUXIBLE
MAXIMIZE	HOMOTAXY	XYLOCARP	THYROXIN	HARUSPEX
	HYPAXIAL	XYLOLOGY	VEXATORY	HEXAMINE
27	METHOXYL		VIXENISH	HEXAPLAR
JASPONYX	MYXEDEMA	**21**	XENOGAMY	HEXASEME
QUIXOTRY	OXPECKER	AFFIXION	XIPHIOID	HOMAXIAL
	OXYAPHIA	AMIDOXYL	XYLYLENE	HORSEPOX
26	OXYPHILE	APPRAXIC		LEUCORYX
CHAFEWAX	PYXIDIUM	AUXOBODY	**20**	LIPOXENY
COXCOMBY	SMOKEBOX	BREAKAXE	ACETOXYL	LIXIVIUM
EXORCIZE	SNUFFBOX	CACHEXIC	ACXOYATL	LOXOTOMY
HEXARCHY	WAXBERRY	CACOMIXL	ALKOXIDE	MEIOTAXY
JAMBEAUX	WHEELBOX	CONFIXED	APPENDIX	MISOXENY
OXIDIZED	XENOPHYA	CONVEXED	APYREXIA	MIXBLOOD
OXYPHONY	XYLOTOMY	EFFLUXES	AUXOCYTE	MONOXYLA
OXYPHYTE		EXCAMBER	BAROTAXY	MONOXYLE
QUINCUNX	**22**	EXCHANGE	BETWIXEN	MYELAUXE
QUIXOTIC	AFFIXING	EXCURVED	BOXBOARD	OXYAMINE
	APOPLEXY	EXCYSTED	BOXTHORN	OXYCRATE
25	AXHAMMER	EXEMPLUM	BREADBOX	OXYMORON
EQUAIXED	AXMAKING	EXHUMING	CARNIFEX	OXYSTOME
EXORDIZE	BICONVEX	EXIGENCY	CATHEXIS	OXYTOCIA
MYXOCYTE	BIXBYITE	EXODROMY	CEROXYLE	OXYTOCIN
OXIDIZER	BOXBERRY	EXOGRAPH	CERVIXES	PEIXEREY
OXYBAPHA	BOXBERRY	EXSHEATH	CHATEAUX	POLYAXON
	CACHEXIA	FIXATIVE	CLAVILUX	PONTIFEX
24	CARBOXYL	FLAXBIRD	CLIMAXED	PREFIXAL
EXEQUIAL	CHAPEAUX	FLAXDROP	COXALGIC	PREMIXED
EXEQUIES	COLOPEXY	FLAXWORT	COXSWAIN	PROLIXLY
EXOPHAGY	COLTPIXY	GLYOXIME	DEFLEXED	PROXIMAD
FLAXWIFE	COMMIXED	HEXAFOIL	DOXOLOGY	PYREXIAL
HEXAPODY	CRUCIFIX	HEXAFOOS	EXACTIVE	SEXTIPLY
MATCHBOX	DETOXIFY	HEXAGRAM	EXAMPLED	SEXTUPLY
OXYETHYL	DYSOREXY	HEXYLENE	EXANTHEM	SIXPENNY
WAXMAKER	EPICALYX	KETOXIME	EXARCHAL	SPHINXES
ZELATRIX	FIXIDITY	LITHOXYL	EXCAVATE	SPINIFEX
ZOOTOXIN	FLAXWEED	MYXINOID	EXCEPTED	SUPERFIX
	FLUXWEED	OXHARROW	EXCITIVE	SWEATBOX
23	FOXGLOVE	OXYDIACT	EXCITORY	SWINEPOX
ADJUTRIX	FOXHOUND	OXYETHER	EXCUSIVE	TAXIARCH
ASPHYXIA	HEXAMMIN	OXYGENIC	EXECUTRY	TAXONOMY
AXOPHYTE	HEXANDRY	OXYRHINE	EXHIBITS	TAXPAYER
BANDBOXY	JANITRIX	PARADOXY	EXHUMATE	TOXICITY
BILLYWIX	MYXAEMIA	PHILODOX	EXILARCH	TOXOPHIL
	MYXOMATA			

VENIPLEX
VEXILLUM
XANTHOMA
XENAGOGY
XENOCYST
XERAPHIN
XEROPHIL
XYLOMATA
XYLORCIN

19
ACETOXIM
ADMIXING
AMPLEXUS
ANOXEMIC
APOMIXIS
AUXOLOGY
AXIFUGAL
AXILEMMA
AXIOLOGY
AXOFUGAL
AXOPLASM
CACOXENE
CICATRIX
CONTUMAX
COXBONES
DUPLEXED
DYSTAXIA
ETHOXIDE
EXCECATE
EXCEEDED
EXCEPTER
EXCEPTIO
EXCERPTA
EXCIDING
EXCIPULE
EXCIRCLE
EXCLUDED
EXCRESCE
EXCUBANT
EXEMPLAR
EXFIGURE
EXHALING
EXHORTED
EXIGUITY
EXOLEMMA
EXORCISM
EXOSPERM
EXPANDED
EXPANSUM
EXPECTER
EXPEDING
EXPENDED
EXPIABLE
EXPLICIT
EXPLODED
EXPUNGED
EXSCRIBE
EXSCRIPT
EXTREMUM
EXUMBRAL
FIXATING
FLAXSEED
FLEXURED
FORNAXID
GREENWAX
HEXAGLOT
INFIXING
INFLEXED
LOXOCOSM
MAXIMATE
MAXIMIST
MAXIMITE
MELAXUMA
MIREPOIX
MORCEAUX

OCTUPLEX
OPOPANAX
ORTHODOX
OXAMMITE
OXYGONAL
PAINTBOX
PANMIXIA
PRECIEUX
PROXIMAL
REFLEXED
REFLUXED
SARDONYX
SEXOLOGY
SIXPENCE
SMALLPOX
TAXINGLY
TAXOLOGY
TOADFLAX
TOXAEMIC
TOXOLOGY
UNEXPECT
WRAXLING
XANTHIDE
XYLIDINE
XYLOIDIN
XYLOSIDE

18
ALDOXIME
ANNEXIVE
ANTEFIXA
ANTHELIX
APODIXIS
AVIATRIX
AXIALITY
AXILLARY
AXOLYSIS
AXOSTYLE
BANDEAUX
BINOXIDE
BOLLIXED
BROADAXE
CAUDEXES
COEXTEND
COXALGIA
CRESOXID
DIAXONIC
DIPLEXER
DOXASTIC
DUPLEXER
DUPLEXES
EXACTING
EXAMINED
EXCEDENT
EXCELLED
EXCISING
EXCITING
EXCLUDER
EXCRETED
EXCUDATE
EXCURSED
EXCUSING
EXCUSSED
EXECUTED
EXEGETIC
EXERTIVE
EXHALANT
EXHALATE
EXHORTER
EXIGENCE
EXIGIBLE
EXOGENIC
EXORDIUM
EXPANDER
EXPEDITE
EXPELLED

EXPENDER
EXPIATED
EXPIRING
EXPLODER
EXPLORED
EXPORTED
EXPOSING
EXPUNGER
EXUDENCE
EXUVIATE
FIXATION
FIXATURE
FIXITIES
FLAXIEST
FLAXTAIL
FLEXUOSE
FLEXUOUS
FLEXURAL
FLUXROOT
FOXINESS
FRAXETIN
HERITRIX
HEXASTER
INFIXION
LARYNXES
LAXATIVE
LIXIVIAL
LUXURITY
MALAXAGE
MALAXING
MAXIMUMS
MONOXIDE
MUREXIDE
NITROXYL
NOSOTAXY
NOVATRIX
OXAMIDIN
OXIDABLE
OXIDASIC
OXYASTER
OXYUROUS
PEROXIDE
PROTOXID
SAXBOARD
SEXENARY
SEXUALLY
SIXTIETH
SUBINDEX
SUBOXIDE
SYNTAXIS
SYNTEXIS
SYRINXES
TAXATIVE
TAXEOPOD
TEXTUARY
THIOXENE
THORAXES
TOXICOID
TRANSFIX
VERTEXES
VEXATION
VORTEXES
WAXINESS
XANTHANE
XANTHATE
XANTHEIN
XANTHENE
XANTHINE
XANTHITE
XANTHONE
XANTHOUS
XENELASY
XENODERM
XENOLITH
XYLITONE
XYLOTILE

17
ALEXINIC
ANOXEMIA
APOXESIS
ATARAXIC
AUXILIUM
AUXIMONE
AXMASTER
AXOMETER
AXOPETAL
BISEXUAL
CONNEXES
CONNEXUS
COUTEAUX
EUPRAXIA
EXACTION
EXACUATE
EXAMINEE
EXAMINER
EXCALATE
EXCELSIN
EXCISION
EXCITANT
EXCITATE
EXCITRON
EXCRETAL
EXCRETER
EXCRETES
EXCURSUS
EXECRATE
EXECUTER
EXECUTOR
EXERCENT
EXERCISE
EXIMIOUS
EXOCLINE
EXOCOELE
EXORABLE
EXORCISE
EXORCIST
EXOSPORE
EXOSTOME
EXOTERIC
EXPELLEE
EXPELLER
EXPENSES
EXPIATOR
EXPILATE
EXPIRANT
EXPIRATE
EXPIRIES
EXPLORER
EXPONENT
EXPORTER
EXPOSURE
EXPULSER
EXRUPEAL
EXSECANT
EXSECTOR
EXTENDED
EXTENSUM
EXTERNUM
EXTRACTS
EXTREMER
EXTREMES
EXTRUDED
EXTUBATE
INDEXING
INEXPERT
INTERMIX
LOXOSOMA
MALAXATE
MANTEAUX
MASTAUXE
MATRIXES
MAXILLAE

MERETRIX
MEROXENE
METAXITE
MILLILUX
MISOXENE
MIXERESS
MONAXIAL
MOROXITE
MORTREUX
MOUSSEUX
NIXTAMAL
OXALEMIA
OXALURIC
OXANILIC
OXIDATED
OXYSALT
PARALLAX
PARAXIAL
PAXILLAE
PAXILLAR
PAXILLUS
PLATEAUX
PLEXUSES
POLEAXER
PREAXIAL
PREEXIST
PROTAXIS
PROXENET
PROXENOS
PROXENUS
REEXPORT
SAXICOLE
SAXIFRAX
SEXTUPLE
SEXUPARA
SIXSCORE
SPINTEXT
SUPELLEX
SUPERSEX
SUPERTAX
TABLEAUX
TOXAEMIA
TOXICANT
TOXICATE
TRACTRIX
UNEXPERT
UROTOXIC
XENOTIME
XERANTIC

16
AGALAXIA
ANNEXING
AXOIDEAN
DEXTRANE
DEXTRINE
DEXTROSE
DEXTROUS
DISANNEX
DIXENITE
DUXELLES
EXALTING
EXEGESES
EXEGESIS
EXERGUAL
EXERTING
EXIGEANT
EXIGUOUS
EXISTING
EXORDIAL
EXOTOXIC
EXRADIUS
EXSERTED
EXTENDER
EXTISPEX
EXTOLLED

EXTORTED	TEXGUINO	ESSEXITE	INTEXINE	SILOXANE
EXTRADOS	TEXTURED	EUTAXITE	LAXATION	TAXATION
EXTRARED	TOXODONT	EUXENITE	LUXATION	TAXEATER
EXTRUDER	TRIOXIDE	EXALTATE	LUXURIES	TAXIAUTO
EXULTING	TUXEDOES	EXERESIS	LUXURIST	TETRAXON
EXUNDATE	UNISEXED	EXERTION	NEURAXIS	TEXTILES
GALAXIAN	UNSEXING	EXISTENT	NEURAXON	TEXTRINE
GALAXIAS		EXITIOUS	NEXTNESS	TEXTURAL
GENETRIX	**15**	EXOSTRAE	NOTAULIX	TONNEAUX
GEOTAXIS	ANATEXIS	EXTENSOR	OXALURIA	TORTEAUX
LOXODONT	ANATOXIN	EXTERIOR	RELATRIX	TRIAXIAL
LUXATING	ANAUXITE	EXTERNAL	RELAXANT	UNIAXIAL
OXIDATOR	ANNEXION	EXTERNAT	RETRAXIT	UROTOXIN
OXTONGUE	ANNEXURE	EXTOLLER	RIXATRIX	UXORIOUS
RELAXING	ANOREXIA	EXTORTER	ROULEAUX	XENOLITE
RIXDALER	ATARAXIA	EXTRORSE	SAXATILE	XERANSIS
RONDEAUX	AUXILIAR	EXTUSION	SAXONITE	XERONATE
SEXANGLE	AXILLANT	EXULTANT	SENATRIX	XEROSERE
SURTAXED	AXIOLITE	INTERREX	SEXTETTE	
TAXODONT	AXLETREE	INTERSEX	SEXTOLET	**14**
TEGUEXIN	AXONEURE	INTERTEX	SILEXITE	EXOTOXIN
TETROXID				

ALPHABETICAL LIST OF 9-LETTER WORDS

ABOIDEAUX	AUXOFLUOR	CHRONAXIE	DUPLEXITY	EXCEPTANT
ACETOXIME	AUXOGRAPH	CICUTOXIN	ELIXATION	EXCEPTING
ADMIXTION	AUXOMETER	CLIMAXING	EMPHRAXIS	EXCEPTION
ADMIXTURE	AUXOSPORE	COAXATION	ENDOMIXIS	EXCEPTIVE
ADNEXITIS	AUXOTONIC	COAXIALLY	ENDOTOXIC	EXCERPTED
AEROTAXIS	AXBREAKER	COAXINGLY	ENDOTOXIN	EXCERPTOR
AFFIXTURE	AXEMASTER	COLOPEXIA	ENTERAUXE	EXCESSIVE
AFFLUXION	AXILEMMAS	COMMIXING	ENTREDEUX	EXCESSMAN
AGITATRIX	AXIOLITIC	COMPLEXLY	EPAXIALLY	EXCESSMEN
ALLOXANIC	AXIOMATIC	COMPLEXUS	EPIPLEXIS	EXCHANGED
ALLOXURIC	AXIOPISTY	CONFIXING	EPISTAXIS	EXCHANGER
AMIDOXIME	AXLESMITH	CONNEXION	EPITOXOID	EXCHEQUER
AMPHIOXUS	AXMANSHIP	CONNEXITY	EPIZEUXIS	EXCIPIENT
AMYOTAXIA	AXONEURON	CONNEXIVA	EUTAXITIC	EXCIPULAR
ANAPTYXIS	AXOPODIUM	CONNEXIVE	EXACTABLE	EXCIPULUM
ANNEXABLE	AZOXONIUM	CONVEXITY	EXACTMENT	EXCISABLE
ANNEXMENT	BAROTAXIS	COXCOMBRY	EXACTNESS	EXCISEMAN
ANOXAEMIA	BAROXYTON	COXODYNIA	EXADVERSO	EXCISEMEN
ANOXAEMIC	BASIFIXED	CRESOXIDE	EXAGITATE	EXCITABLE
ANTECOXAL	BAUXITITE	CYTOTAXIS	EXAIRESIS	EXCITABLY
ANTEFIXAL	BIAXIALLY	CYTOTOXIC	EXALTEDLY	EXCITANCY
ANTEFIXES	BISECTRIX	CYTOTOXIN	EXAMINANT	EXCITATOR
ANTHOTAXY	BISEXUOUS	DECOMPLEX	EXAMINATE	EXCITEDLY
ANTHROXAN	BIXACEOUS	DEFLEXING	EXAMINING	EXCLAIMED
ANTIHELIX	BOISSEAUX	DEFLEXION	EXAMPLING	EXCLAIMER
ANXIETIES	BOLLIXING	DEFLEXURE	EXANIMATE	EXCLUDING
ANXIETUDE	BOXHOLDER	DEFLUXION	EXANTHEMA	EXCLUSION
ANXIOUSLY	BOXKEEPER	DENDRAXON	EXANTLATE	EXCLUSIVE
APOSTAXIS	BOXWALLAH	DEOXIDIZE	EXARATION	EXCLUSORY
APROSEXIA	BUTTERBOX	DEXTERITY	EXARCHATE	EXCOCTION
APYREXIAL	BUXACEOUS	DEXTEROUS	EXARCHIST	EXCORIATE
ASEXUALLY	BUXERRIES	DEXTRALLY	EXCAMBION	EXCREMENT
ASPHYXIAL	BUXOMNESS	DEXTRORSE	EXCARNATE	EXCRETING
ASPHYXIED	CACOMIXLE	DIAPLEXUS	EXCAUDATE	EXCRETION
ASSERTRIX	CALCIPEXY	DIAZEUXIS	EXCAVATED	EXCRETIVE
ATLOAXOID	CANDLEBOX	DICTATRIX	EXCAVATOR	EXCRETORY
AUTOTOXIC	CARBOXIDE	DIGITOXIN	EXCEEDING	EXCULPATE
AUTOTOXIN	CARDIAUXE	DIHYDROXY	EXCELENTE	EXCURRENT
AUXETICAL	CATALEXIS	DIMETHOXY	EXCELLENT	EXCURSING
AUXILIARY	CATAPLEXY	DIRECTRIX	EXCELLING	EXCURSION
AUXILIATE	CAULOTAXY	DORSIFLEX	EXCELSIOR	EXCURSIVE
AUXOBLAST	CHEMOTAXY	DRUXINESS	EXCENTRAL	EXCURVATE
AUXOFLORE	CHRONAXIA	DUPLEXING	EXCENTRIC	EXCUSABLE

EXCUSABLY	EXOTERICS	EXSTROPHY	HEXABASIC	MEDIATRIX
EXCUSATOR	EXOTHECAL	EXSUCCOUS	HEXABIOSE	MEDIFIXED
EXCUSSING	EXOTICISM	EXSUCTION	HEXACHORD	MENOXENIA
EXECRABLE	EXOTICIST	EXSURGENT	HEXACOLIC	MESAXONIC
EXECRABLY	EXOTICITY	EXTEMPORE	HEXADECYL	MESOXALIC
EXECRATED	EXOTROPIA	EXTENDING	HEXADIENE	MESOXALYL
EXECRATOR	EXPALPATE	EXTENSILE	HEXADIINE	METATAXIC
EXECUTANT	EXPANDING	EXTENSION	HEXADIYNE	METATAXIS
EXECUTING	EXPANSILE	EXTENSITY	HEXAGONAL	METAXYLEM
EXECUTION	EXPANSION	EXTENSIVE	HEXAHEDRA	MIXTIFORM
EXECUTIVE	EXPANSIVE	EXTENUATE	HEXAMERAL	MONAXONIC
EXECUTORY	EXPANSURE	EXTERMINE	HEXAMERON	MONOXYLIC
EXECUTRIX	EXPATIATE	EXTERNATE	HEXAMETER	MONOXYLON
EXEGETICS	EXPECTANT	EXTERNIZE	HEXAMMINE	MULTIPLEX
EXEGETIST	EXPECTING	EXTERNIZE	HEXANDRIC	MYELOPLAX
EXEMPLARY	EXPECTIVE	EXTINCTOR	HEXAPLOID	MYXAMOEBA
EXEMPLIFY	EXPEDIATE	EXTIRPATE	HEXASEMIC	MYXEDEMIC
EXEMPTILE	EXPEDIENT	EXTISPICY	HEXASTICH	MYXOEDEMA
EXEMPTION	EXPEDITED	EXTOLLING	HEXASTIGM	MYXOINOMA
EXEMPTIVE	EXPEDITER	EXTOLMENT	HEXATHLON	MYXOMYOMA
EXEQUATUR	EXPEDITOR	EXTORSIVE	HEXATOMIC	MYXOPODIA
EXERCISED	EXPELLANT	EXTORTING	HOAXPROOF	MYXORRHEA
EXERCISER	EXPELLENT	EXTORTION	HOMOTAXIS	MYXOSPORE
EXERCISES	EXPELLING	EXTORTIVE	HYDROXIDE	MYXOTHECA
EXERCITOR	EXPENDING	EXTRABOLD	HYPOTAXIA	NEPHRAUXE
EXFODIATE	EXPENSIVE	EXTRACTED	HYPOTAXIC	NEURATAXY
EXFOLIATE	EXPERIENT	EXTRACTOR	HYPOTAXIS	NEURAXONE
EXHALABLE	EXPERTISE	EXTRADITE	IMMIXTURE	NOXIOUSLY
EXHAUSTED	EXPIATING	EXTRALITE	IMPERMIXT	NULLIPLEX
EXHAUSTER	EXPIATION	EXTRALITY	IMPOSTRIX	OBNOXIETY
EXHIBITED	EXPIATIST	EXTRANEAN	INCOMPLEX	OBNOXIOUS
EXHIBITOR	EXPIATIVE	EXTRAVERT	INDEXICAL	OBSTETRIX
EXHORTING	EXPIATORY	EXTREMELY	INDOXYLIC	OPERATRIX
EXHUMATED	EXPILATOR	EXTREMEST	INEXACTLY	ORTHODOXY
EXHUMATOR	EXPIRATOR	EXTREMISM	INEXPIATE	OVEREXERT
EXIGEANTE	EXPISCATE	EXTREMIST	INEXPRESS	OVERSEXED
EXIGENTER	EXPLAINED	EXTREMITY	INFLEXION	OVERTAXED
EXIGENTLY	EXPLAINER	EXTRICATE	INFLEXIVE	OXALAEMIA
EXINANITE	EXPLANATE	EXTRINSIC	INFLUXION	OXALURATE
EXISTENCE	EXPLEMENT	EXTRORSAL	INFLUXIVE	OXAMIDINE
EXOCARDIA	EXPLETIVE	EXTROVERT	INMIXTURE	OXANILATE
EXOCLINAL	EXPLETORY	EXTRUDING	INNOXIOUS	OXANILIDE
EXOCOELAR	EXPLICATE	EXTRUSILE	INOXIDIZE	OXBERRIES
EXOCOELIC	EXPLODENT	EXTRUSION	INTERAXAL	OXDIAZOLE
EXOCOELOM	EXPLODING	EXTRUSIVE	INTERAXIS	OXIDATING
EXOCOELUM	EXPLOITED	EXTRUSORY	INTERMIXT	OXIDATION
EXOCULATE	EXPLOITER	EXUBERANT	INTEXTINE	OXIDATIVE
EXOCYCLIC	EXPLORING	EXUBERATE	INTEXTURE	OXIDIZING
EXODERMIS	EXPLOSION	EXUDATION	INTROFLEX	OXIMATION
EXODONTIA	EXPLOSIVE	EXUDATIVE	ISOXAZOLE	OXMANSHIP
EXODROMIC	EXPONENCE	EXUDATORY	JUXTAPOSE	OXYBENZYL
EXOENZYME	EXPONENTS	EXULTANCY	KATAPLEXY	OXYDACTYL
EXOGAMOUS	EXPONIBLE	EXULULATE	KENOTOXIN	OXYGENANT
EXOGENOUS	EXPORTING	EXUVIABLE	KOSOTOXIN	OXYGENATE
EXONERATE	EXPOSITOR	EXUVIATED	LATEXOSIS	OXYGENIUM
EXONEURAL	EXPOUNDED	FIXEDNESS	LEPOTHRIX	OXYGENIZE
EXOPATHIC	EXPOUNDER	FLAMBEAUX	LEUCOXENE	OXYGENOUS
EXOPHORIA	EXPRESSED	FLAXBOARD	LEXICALIC	OXYGEUSIA
EXOPHORIA	EXPRESSER	FLAXWENCH	LIPOPEXIA	OXYHALIDE
EXOPHORIC	EXPRESSLY	FLAXWOMAN	LITHOXYLE	OXYHALOID
EXOPODITE	EXPROBATE	FLEXILITY	LIXIVIATE	OXYHYDRIC
EXORBITAL	EXPUITION	FLEXIONAL	LIXIVIOUS	OXYIODIDE
EXORCISED	EXPULSION	FLUMMOXED	LOOMFIXER	OXYKETONE
EXORCISER	EXPULSIVE	FLUXATION	LOXOCLASE	OXYNEURIN
EXORCIZED	EXPULSORY	FLUXILITY	LOXODROME	OXYPHENOL
EXORCIZER	EXPUNGING	FLUXIONAL	LOXODROMY	OXYPHENYL
EXORDIUMS	EXPURGATE	FLUXMETER	LUXURIANT	OXYPHILIC
EXORGANIC	EXQUISITE	FOXTAILED	LUXURIATE	OXYPHONIA
EXOSEPSIS	EXSCINDED	FUNDATRIX	LUXURIOUS	OXYPICRIC
EXOSMOSIS	EXSECTILE	GLYOXALIC	MALAXABLE	OXYPURINE
EXOSMOTIC	EXSECTION	GLYOXYLIC	MALAXATOR	OXYPYCNOS
EXOSPHERE	EXSERTILE	GONOCALYX	MALPRAXIS	OXYRHYNCH
EXOSPORAL	EXSERTING	HEMIAUXIN	MASTOPEXY	OXYSULFID
EXOSTOSED	EXSERTION	HEMOTOXIC	MAXILLARY	OXYTOCOUS
EXOSTOSES	EXSICCATE	HEMOTOXIN	MAXIMALLY	OXYTOLUIC
EXOSTOSIS	EXSOMATIC	HEPTOXIDE	MAXIMIZED	OXYTONIZE
EXOSTOTIC	EXSPUTORY	HETERODOX	MAXIMIZER	

OXYTYLOTE	PREEXILIC	SEXENNIUM	TAXIMETER	UXORIALLY
PANSEXUAL	PREFIXION	SEXLESSLY	TAXIPLANE	UXORICIDE
PARADOXAL	PREHALLUX	SEXOLOGIC	TAXOMETER	VEXATIOUS
PARADOXER	PREPOLLEX	SEXTACTIC	TAXONOMER	VEXEDNESS
PARADOXIC	PRESEXUAL	SEXTANTAL	TAXONOMIC	VEXILLARY
PARALEXIA	PRETEXTED	SEXTARIUS	TAXPAYING	VEXILLATE
PARALEXIC	PROLIXITY	SEXTIPARA	TESTATRIX	WAXFLOWER
PARATAXIS	PROPLEXUS	SEXTUPLED	TETRAXILE	WAXMAKING
PARAXONIC	PROSCOLEX	SEXTUPLET	TETROXIDE	WAXWORKER
PAROREXIA	PROTAXIAL	SEXUALISM	TEXTARIAN	WOADWAXEN
PAXILLARY	PROTHORAX	SEXUALIST	TEXTILIST	WOODWAXEN
PAXILLATE	PROTOXIDE	SEXUALITY	TEXTORIAL	XANTHAMID
PAXILLOSE	PROXENETE	SEXUALIZE	TEXTUALLY	XANTHIONE
PENTOXIDE	PROXIMATE	SHADOWBOX	THRIFTBOX	XANTHOGEN
PEPPERBOX	PROXIMITY	SIMPLEXED	THYROXINE	XANTHOMAS
PERIAXIAL	PSEUDAXIS	SIXPENCES	TINDERBOX	XANTHOPIA
PEROXIDED	PSEUDODOX	SIXTEENER	TONOTAXIS	XANTHOSIS
PEROXIDIC	PYOTHORAX	SIXTEENMO	TOPOTAXIS	XANTHURIA
PERPLEXED	PYREXICAL	SIXTEENTH	TOXAEMIAS	XENAGOGUE
PERPLEXER	PYRONYXIS	SOAPBOXER	TOXANEMIA	XENELASIA
PHALANXED	PYROTOXIN	SPHINXIAN	TOXICALLY	XENOBLAST
PHALANXES	PYROXENIC	SPHINXINE	TOXICAROL	XENODOCHY
PHARYNXES	PYROXYLIC	SPLENAUXE	TOXICOSES	XENOMANIA
PHENOXIDE	PYROXYLIN	SPONDULIX	TOXICOSIS	XENOPODID
PHOENIXES	QUINISEXT	STRONGBOX	TOXIGENIC	XERODERMA
PHONOPLEX	QUIXOTISM	SUBCLIMAX	TOXINEMIA	XEROMORPH
PHOTOTAXY	QUIXOTIZE	SUBCORTEX	TOXINOSIS	XEROMYRON
PIXILATED	RATTLEBOX	SUBEXCITE	TOXIPHAGI	XEROPHAGY
PLAINTEXT	RECTOPEXY	SUBLUXATE	TOXOLYSIS	XEROPHILE
PLEONEXIA	REEXAMINE	SUFFIXING	TOXOPHILE	XEROPHILY
PLEXICOSE	REFLEXISM	SUFFIXION	TOXOPHILY	XEROPHYTE
PLEXIFORM	REFLEXIVE	SUFFRUTEX	TRANSFLUX	XEROSTOMA
PLEXIGLAS	RELAXABLE	SULFOXIDE	TRUXILLIC	XEROTHERM
PLEXIPPUS	RELAXEDLY	SULFOXISM	TRUXILLIN	XIPHOIDAL
PLEXODONT	RETEXTURE	SULPHOXID	TYLOTOXEA	XIPHOSURE
POLYAXONE	RETROFLEX	SUPERFLUX	UNBUXOMLY	XYLINDEIN
POLYOXIDE	RHEOTAXIS	SURTAXING	UNEXACTLY	XYLOCOPID
POMPHOLIX	RHIZOTAXY	SUSOTOXIN	UNEXCITED	XYLOGRAPH
POMPHOLYX	SAPOTOXIN	SUSSEXITE	UNEXPIRED	XYLOIDINE
POSTAXIAD	SAXCORNET	SYNTAXIST	UNEXPOSED	XYLOMANCY
POSTAXIAL	SAXOPHONE	TARAXACUM	UNEXPRESS	XYLOMETER
POSTEXIST	SCHIZAXON	TAXACEOUS	UNISEXUAL	XYLOPHAGE
POSTFIXED	SCRAMASAX	TAXAMETER	UNPERPLEX	XYLOPHONE
PRAETEXTA	SERVITRIX	TAXEATING	UNRELAXED	ZEROAXIAL
PRAXITHEA	SEXANGLED	TAXEOPODY	UROTOXIES	ZYGOTAXIS
PREATAXIC	SEXENNIAL	TAXIDERMY	UROXANATE	

POSITIONAL ORDER LIST OF 9-LETTER WORDS

XANTHAMID	XYLOCOPID	EXAMINANT	EXCEPTIVE	EXCLUSORY
XANTHIONE	XYLOGRAPH	EXAMINATE	EXCERPTED	EXCULPATE
XANTHOGEN	XYLOIDINE	EXAMINING	EXCERPTOR	EXCOCTION
XANTHOMAS	XYLOMANCY	EXAMPLING	EXCESSIVE	EXCORIATE
XANTHOPIA	XYLOMETER	EXANIMATE	EXCESSMAN	EXCREMENT
XANTHOSIS	XYLOPHAGE	EXANTHEMA	EXCESSMEN	EXCRETING
XANTHURIA	XYLOPHONE	EXANTLATE	EXCHANGED	EXCRETION
XENAGOGUE		EXARATION	EXCHANGER	EXCRETIVE
XENELASIA	AXBREAKER	EXARCHATE	EXCHEQUER	EXCRETORY
XENOBLAST	AXEMASTER	EXARCHIST	EXCIPIENT	EXCURRENT
XENODOCHY	AXILEMMAS	EXCAMBION	EXCIPULAR	EXCURSING
XENOMANIA	AXIOLITIC	EXCARNATE	EXCIPULUM	EXCURSION
XENOPODID	AXIOMATIC	EXCAUDATE	EXCISABLE	EXCURSIVE
XERODERMA	AXIOPISTY	EXCAVATED	EXCISEMAN	EXCURVATE
XEROMORPH	AXLESMITH	EXCAVATOR	EXCISEMEN	EXCUSABLE
XEROMYRON	AXMANSHIP	EXCEEDING	EXCITABLE	EXCUSABLY
XEROPHAGY	AXONEURON	EXCELENTE	EXCITABLY	EXCUSATOR
XEROPHILE	AXOPODIUM	EXCELLENT	EXCITANCY	EXCUSSING
XEROPHILY	EXACTABLE	EXCELLING	EXCITATOR	EXECRABLE
XEROPHYTE	EXACTMENT	EXCELSIOR	EXCITEDLY	EXECRABLY
XEROSTOMA	EXACTNESS	EXCENTRAL	EXCLAIMED	EXECRATED
XEROTHERM	EXADVERSO	EXCENTRIC	EXCLAIMER	EXECRATOR
XIPHOIDAL	EXAGITATE	EXCEPTANT	EXCLUDING	EXECUTANT
XIPHOSURE	EXAIRESIS	EXCEPTING	EXCLUSION	EXECUTING
XYLINDEIN	EXALTEDLY	EXCEPTION	EXCLUSIVE	EXECUTION

EXECUTIVE	EXPANSURE	EXTERMINE	OXYPURINE	MYXOEDEMA
EXECUTORY	EXPATIATE	EXTERNATE	OXYPYCNOS	MYXOINOMA
EXECUTRIX	EXPECTANT	EXTERNIZE	OXYRHYNCH	MYXOMYOMA
EXEGETICS	EXPECTING	EXTERNIZE	OXYSULFID	MYXOPODIA
EXEGETIST	EXPECTIVE	EXTINCTOR	OXYTOCOUS	MYXORRHEA
EXEMPLARY	EXPEDIATE	EXTIRPATE	OXYTOLUIC	MYXOSPORE
EXEMPLIFY	EXPEDIENT	EXTISPICY	OXYTONIZE	MYXOTHECA
EXEMPTILE	EXPEDITED	EXTOLLING	OXYTYLOTE	NOXIOUSLY
EXEMPTION	EXPEDITER	EXTOLMENT	UXORIALLY	PAXILLARY
EXEMPTIVE	EXPEDITOR	EXTORSIVE	UXORICIDE	PAXILLATE
EXEQUATUR	EXPELLANT	EXTORTING		PAXILLOSE
EXERCISED	EXPELLENT	EXTORTION	ANXIETIES	PIXILATED
EXERCISER	EXPELLING	EXTORTIVE	ANXIETUDE	SAXCORNET
EXERCISES	EXPENDING	EXTRABOLD	ANXIOUSLY	SAXOPHONE
EXERCITOR	EXPENSIVE	EXTRACTED	AUXETICAL	SEXANGLED
EXFODIATE	EXPERIENT	EXTRACTOR	AUXILIARY	SEXENNIAL
EXFOLIATE	EXPERTISE	EXTRADITE	AUXILIATE	SEXENNIUM
EXHALABLE	EXPIATING	EXTRALITE	AUXOBLAST	SEXLESSLY
EXHAUSTED	EXPIATION	EXTRALITY	AUXOFLORE	SEXOLOGIC
EXHAUSTER	EXPIATIST	EXTRANEAN	AUXOFLUOR	SEXTACTIC
EXHIBITED	EXPIATIVE	EXTRAVERT	AUXOGRAPH	SEXTANTAL
EXHIBITOR	EXPIATORY	EXTREMELY	AUXOMETER	SEXTARIUS
EXHORTING	EXPILATOR	EXTREMEST	AUXOSPORE	SEXTIPARA
EXHUMATED	EXPIRATOR	EXTREMISM	AUXOTONIC	SEXTUPLED
EXHUMATOR	EXPISCATE	EXTREMIST	BIXACEOUS	SEXTUPLET
EXIGEANTE	EXPLAINED	EXTREMITY	BOXHOLDER	SEXUALISM
EXIGENTER	EXPLAINER	EXTRICATE	BOXKEEPER	SEXUALIST
EXIGENTLY	EXPLANATE	EXTRINSIC	BOXWALLAH	SEXUALITY
EXINANITE	EXPLEMENT	EXTRORSAL	BUXACEOUS	SEXUALIZE
EXISTENCE	EXPLETIVE	EXTROVERT	BUXERRIES	SIXPENCES
EXOCARDIA	EXPLETORY	EXTRUDING	BUXOMNESS	SIXTEENER
EXOCLINAL	EXPLICATE	EXTRUSILE	COXCOMBRY	SIXTEENMO
EXOCOELAR	EXPLODENT	EXTRUSION	COXODYNIA	SIXTEENTH
EXOCOELIC	EXPLODING	EXTRUSIVE	DEXTERITY	TAXACEOUS
EXOCOELOM	EXPLOITED	EXTRUSORY	DEXTEROUS	TAXAMETER
EXOCOELUM	EXPLOITER	EXUBERANT	DEXTRALLY	TAXEATING
EXOCULATE	EXPLORING	EXUBERATE	DEXTRORSE	TAXEOPODY
EXOCYCLIC	EXPLOSION	EXUDATION	FIXEDNESS	TAXIDERMY
EXODERMIS	EXPLOSIVE	EXUDATIVE	FOXTAILED	TAXIMETER
EXODONTIA	EXPONENCE	EXUDATORY	HEXABASIC	TAXIPLANE
EXODROMIC	EXPONENTS	EXULTANCY	HEXABIOSE	TAXOMETER
EXOENZYME	EXPONIBLE	EXULULATE	HEXACHORD	TAXONOMER
EXOGAMOUS	EXPORTING	EXUVIABLE	HEXACOLIC	TAXONOMIC
EXOGENOUS	EXPOSITOR	EXUVIATED	HEXADECYL	TAXPAYING
EXONERATE	EXPOUNDED	OXALAEMIA	HEXADIENE	TEXTARIAN
EXONEURAL	EXPOUNDER	OXALURATE	HEXADIINE	TEXTILIST
EXOPATHIC	EXPRESSED	OXAMIDINE	HEXADIYNE	TEXTORIAL
EXOPHORIA	EXPRESSER	OXANILATE	HEXAGONAL	TEXTUALLY
EXOPHORIC	EXPRESSLY	OXANILIDE	HEXAHEDRA	TOXAEMIAS
EXOPODITE	EXPROBATE	OXBERRIES	HEXAMERAL	TOXANEMIA
EXORBITAL	EXPUITION	OXDIAZOLE	HEXAMERON	TOXICALLY
EXORCISED	EXPULSION	OXIDATING	HEXAMETER	TOXICAROL
EXORCISER	EXPULSIVE	OXIDATION	HEXAMMINE	TOXICOSES
EXORCIZED	EXPULSORY	OXIDATIVE	HEXANDRIC	TOXICOSIS
EXORCIZER	EXPUNGING	OXIDIZING	HEXAPLOID	TOXIGENIC
EXORDIUMS	EXPURGATE	OXIMATION	HEXASEMIC	TOXINEMIA
EXORGANIC	EXQUISITE	OXMANSHIP	HEXASTICH	TOXINOSIS
EXOSEPSIS	EXSCINDED	OXYBENZYL	HEXASTIGM	TOXIPHAGI
EXOSMOSIS	EXSECTILE	OXYDACTYL	HEXATHLON	TOXOLYSIS
EXOSMOTIC	EXSECTION	OXYGENANT	HEXATOMIC	TOXOPHILE
EXOSPHERE	EXSERTILE	OXYGENATE	JUXTAPOSE	TOXOPHILY
EXOSPORAL	EXSERTING	OXYGENIUM	LEXICALIC	VEXATIOUS
EXOSTOSED	EXSERTION	OXYGENIZE	LIXIVIATE	VEXEDNESS
EXOSTOSES	EXSICCATE	OXYGENOUS	LIXIVIOUS	VEXILLARY
EXOSTOSIS	EXSOMATIC	OXYGEUSIA	LOXOCLASE	VEXILLATE
EXOSTOTIC	EXSPUTORY	OXYGONIAL	LOXODROME	WAXFLOWER
EXOTERICS	EXSTROPHY	OXYHALIDE	LOXODROMY	WAXMAKING
EXOTHECAL	EXSUCCOUS	OXYHALOID	LUXURIANT	WAXWORKER
EXOTICISM	EXSUCTION	OXYHYDRIC	LUXURIATE	
EXOTICIST	EXSURGENT	OXYIODIDE	LUXURIOUS	ANOXAEMIA
EXOTICITY	EXTEMPORE	OXYKETONE	MAXILLARY	ANOXAEMIC
EXOTROPIA	EXTENDING	OXYNEURIN	MAXIMALLY	ASEXUALLY
EXPALPATE	EXTENSILE	OXYPHENOL	MAXIMIZED	AZOXONIUM
EXPANDING	EXTENSION	OXYPHENYL	MAXIMIZER	BAUXITITE
EXPANSILE	EXTENSITY	OXYPHILIC	MIXTIFORM	BIAXIALLY
EXPANSION	EXTENSIVE	OXYPHONIA	MYXAMOEBA	COAXATION
EXPANSIVE	EXTENUATE	OXYPICRIC	MYXEDEMIC	COAXIALLY

COAXINGLY	MESOXALIC	POSTEXIST	HEMOTOXIN	MASTOPEXY
DEOXIDIZE	MESOXALYL	PREFIXION	HOMOTAXIS	NEPHRAUXE
DRUXINESS	METAXYLEM	PRESEXUAL	HYPOTAXIA	NEURATAXY
ELIXATION	MONAXONIC	PRETEXTED	HYPOTAXIC	ORTHODOXY
EPAXIALLY	MONOXYLIC	PROLIXITY	HYPOTAXIS	PHOTOTAXY
FLAXBOARD	MONOXYLON	PROTAXIAL	INTERAXAL	PLAINTEXT
FLAXWENCH	OBNOXIETY	PROTOXIDE	INTERAXIS	QUINISEXT
FLAXWOMAN	OBNOXIOUS	REFLEXISM	KENOTOXIN	RECTOPEXY
FLEXILITY	PARAXONIC	REFLEXIVE	KOSOTOXIN	RHIZOTAXY
FLEXIONAL	PEROXIDED	SPHINXIAN	LIPOPEXIA	SPLENAUXE
FLUXATION	PEROXIDIC	SPHINXINE	LOOMFIXER	
FLUXILITY	PREEXILIC	SUBLUXATE	MALPRAXIS	ABOIDEAUX
FLUXIONAL	PYREXICAL	SUFFIXING	MEDIFIXED	AGITATRIX
FLUXMETER	PYROXENIC	SUFFIXION	METATAXIC	ANTIHELIX
HOAXPROOF	PYROXYLIC	SULFOXIDE	METATAXIS	ASSERTRIX
INEXACTLY	PYROXYLIN	SULFOXISM	OVERSEXED	BISECTRIX
INEXPIATE	RELAXABLE	SURTAXING	OVERTAXED	BOISSEAUX
INEXPRESS	RELAXEDLY	SUSSEXITE	PARADOXAL	BUTTERBOX
INOXIDIZE	RETEXTURE	SYNTAXIST	PARADOXER	CANDLEBOX
ISOXAZOLE	SUBEXCITE	TETRAXILE	PARADOXIC	DECOMPLEX
PLEXICOSE	TARAXACUM	TETROXIDE	PARALEXIA	DICTATRIX
PLEXIFORM	UNBUXOMLY	THYROXINE	PARALEXIC	DIRECTRIX
PLEXIGLAS		UNISEXUAL	PARATAXIS	DORSIFLEX
PLEXIPPUS	ACETOXIME	UROTOXIES	PAROREXIA	ENTREDEUX
PLEXODONT	AFFLUXION	ZEROAXIAL	PERPLEXED	EXECUTRIX
PRAXITHEA	AMIDOXIME		PERPLEXER	FLAMBEAUX
PROXENETE	APYREXIAL	AEROTAXIS	PHALANXED	FUNDATRIX
PROXIMATE	ASPHYXIAL	AMPHIOXUS	PHALANXES	GONOCALYX
PROXIMITY	ASPHYXIED	AMYOTAXIA	PHARYNXES	HETERODOX
QUIXOTISM	ATLOAXOID	ANAPTYXIS	PHOENIXES	IMPOSTRIX
QUIXOTIZE	BOLLIXING	ANTECOXAL	PLEONEXIA	INCOMPLEX
REEXAMINE	CARBOXIDE	ANTEFIXAL	POSTFIXED	INTROFLEX
TRUXILLIC	CLIMAXING	ANTEFIXES	PRAETEXTA	LEPOTHRIX
TRUXILLIN	COMMIXING	ANTHROXAN	PREATAXIC	MEDIATRIX
UNEXACTLY	CONFIXING	APOSTAXIS	PROPLEXUS	MULTIPLEX
UNEXCITED	CONNEXION	APROSEXIA	PSEUDAXIS	MYELOPLAX
UNEXPIRED	CONNEXITY	AUTOTOXIC	PYRONYXIS	NULLIPLEX
UNEXPOSED	CONNEXIVA	AUTOTOXIN	PYROTOXIN	OBSTETRIX
UNEXPRESS	CONNEXIVE	BAROTAXIS	RHEOTAXIS	OPERATRIX
UROXANATE	CONVEXITY	BASIFIXED	SAPOTOXIN	PEPPERBOX
	CRESOXIDE	CACOMIXLE	SCHIZAXON	PHONOPLEX
ADMIXTION	DEFLEXING	CATALEXIS	SIMPLEXED	POMPHOLIX
ADMIXTURE	DEFLEXION	CHRONAXIA	SOAPBOXER	POMPHOLYX
ADNEXITIS	DEFLEXURE	CHRONAXIE	SULPHOXID	PREHALLUX
AFFIXTURE	DEFLUXION	CICUTOXIN	SUSOTOXIN	PREPOLLEX
ALLOXANIC	DUPLEXING	COLOPEXIA	TONOTAXIS	PROSCOLEX
ALLOXURIC	DUPLEXITY	COMPLEXLY	TOPOTAXIS	PROTHORAX
ANNEXABLE	EPITOXOID	COMPLEXUS	TYLOTOXEA	PSEUDODOX
ANNEXMENT	HEPTOXIDE	CYTOTAXIS	UNRELAXED	PYOTHORAX
BAROXYTON	HYDROXIDE	CYTOTOXIC	WOADWAXEN	RATTLEBOX
BISEXUOUS	INFLEXION	CYTOTOXIN	WOODWAXEN	RETROFLEX
EUTAXITIC	INFLEXIVE	DENDRAXON	ZYGOTAXIS	SCRAMASAX
GLYOXALIC	INFLUXION	DIAPLEXUS		SERVITRIX
GLYOXYLIC	INFLUXIVE	DIAZEUXIS	ANTHOTAXY	SHADOWBOX
IMMIXTURE	LEUCOXENE	DIGITOXIN	CALCIPEXY	SPONDULIX
INDEXICAL	LITHOXYLE	EMPHRAXIS	CARDIAUXE	STRONGBOX
INDOXYLIC	NEURAXONE	ENDOMIXIS	CATAPLEXY	SUBCLIMAX
INMIXTURE	OVEREXERT	ENDOTOXIC	CAULOTAXY	SUBCORTEX
INNOXIOUS	PANSEXUAL	ENDOTOXIN	CHEMOTAXY	SUFFRUTEX
INTEXTINE	PENTOXIDE	EPIPLEXIS	DIHYDROXY	SUPERFLUX
INTEXTURE	PERIAXIAL	EPISTAXIS	DIMETHOXY	TESTATRIX
LATEXOSIS	PHENOXIDE	EPIZEUXIS	ENTERAUXE	THRIFTBOX
MALAXABLE	POLYAXONE	FLUMMOXED	IMPERMIXT	TINDERBOX
MALAXATOR	POLYOXIDE	HEMIAUXIN	INTERMIXT	TRANSFLUX
MENOXENIA	POSTAXIAD	HEMOTOXIC	KATAPLEXY	UNPERPLEX
MESAXONIC	POSTAXIAL			

SCORING ORDER LIST OF 9-LETTER WORDS

34	**31**	EXOENZYME	**29**	**28**
QUIXOTIZE	RHIZOTAXY	MAXIMIZED	MAXIMIZER	EXORCIZED
		OXYRHYNCH	OXYGENIZE	OXYHYDRIC
33	**30**	SCHIZAXON	ZYGOTAXIS	OXYTONIZE
OXYBENZYL	EXCHEQUER			POMPHOLYX

27
AZOXONIUM
COXCOMBRY
DEOXIDIZE
DIHYDROXY
DUPLEXITY
EPIZEUXIS
EXORCIZER
FLAXWENCH
OXIDIZING
OXYPHENYL
QUIXOTISM

26
CHEMOTAXY
DIAZEUXIS
EXEMPLIFY
HYPOTAXIC
INOXIDIZE
MYXEDEMIC
MYXOTHECA
OXDIAZOLE
OXYPHILIC
OXYPYCNOS
PYROXYLIC
WAXMAKING
WAXWORKER
XYLOMANCY

25
ASPHYXIED
CALCIPEXY
COMPLEXLY
DIMETHOXY
EXEQUATUR
EXQUISITE
EXTERNIZE
GLYOXYLIC
HEXACHORD
HEXADECYL
ISOXAZOLE
JUXTAPOSE
KATAPLEXY
MYXAMOEBA
MYXOMYOMA
OXYDACTYL
OXYPICRIC
POMPHOLIX
QUINISEXT
SEXUALIZE
SHADOWBOX
WAXFLOWER
XENODOCHY
XEROPHAGY
XYLOGRAPH
XYLOPHAGE
ZEROAXIAL

24
ASPHYXIAL
BOXKEEPER
BOXWALLAH
CONVEXITY
EXSTROPHY
FLAXWOMAN
FLUMMOXED
HEXASTICH
HOAXPROOF
HYDROXIDE
HYPOTAXIA
HYPOTAXIS
MYXOEDEMA
MYXOPODIA
MYXORRHEA
OXYPHENOL
OXYPHONIA
PHARYNXES

PHOTOTAXY
PYOTHORAX
PYRONYXIS
PYROXYLIN
THRIFTBOX
TOXOPHILY
XEROPHILY
XEROPHYTE
XYLOCOPID
XYLOPHONE

23
AMPHIOXUS
AXMANSHIP
CATAPLEXY
COMMIXING
CYTOTOXIC
DECOMPLEX
EMPHRAXIS
EXCEPTIVE
EXCHANGED
EXCITABLY
EXCITANCY
EXCUSABLY
EXECRABLY
EXEMPLARY
EXEMPTIVE
EXOPATHIC
EXOPHORIC
EXPECTIVE
EXTISPICY
FLAMBEAUX
HEMOTOXIC
HEXABASIC
HEXACOLIC
HEXADIYNE
HEXAHEDRA
HEXAMMINE
HEXASEMIC
HEXATOMIC
MASTOPEXY
MAXIMALLY
MEDIFIXED
METAXYLEM
MIXTIFORM
MONOXYLIC
MYELOPLAX
MYXOINOMA
MYXOSPORE
ORTHODOXY
OXMANSHIP
OXYHALIDE
OXYHALOID
OXYKETONE
OXYSULFID
PHONOPLEX
PLEXIFORM
PROXIMITY
PYREXICAL
PYROXENIC
RECTOPEXY
SUFFIXING
UNBUXOMLY
WOADWAXEN
WOODWAXEN
XEROMORPH

22
AFFIXTURE
AFFLUXION
ANTHOTAXY
AUXOGRAPH
AXBREAKER
BASIFIXED
BOXHOLDER
CACOMIXLE
COAXINGLY

COMPLEXUS
CONFIXING
COXODYNIA
EXCAMBION
EXCAVATED
EXCHANGER
EXCIPULUM
EXCITEDLY
EXHIBITED
EXHUMATED
EXOCYCLIC
FLAXBOARD
FLEXILITY
FLUXILITY
GLYOXALIC
GONOCALYX
HEPTOXIDE
HEXANDRIC
HEXAPLOID
HEXASTIGM
HEXATHLON
IMPERMIXT
INCOMPLEX
INDOXYLIC
INFLEXIVE
INFLUXIVE
LITHOXYLE
LOXODROMY
OXYGENIUM
OXYTYLOTE
PHALANXED
PHENOXIDE
POLYOXIDE
POSTFIXED
REFLEXIVE
SUBCLIMAX
SUFFIXION
SUFFRUTEX
SULPHOXID
TAXEOPODY
TAXIDERMY
TAXPAYING
THYROXINE
TOXIPHAGI
VEXILLARY
XANTHAMID
XIPHOIDAL

21
AMIDOXIME
AMYOTAXIA
ANAPTYXIS
APYREXIAL
AXIOPISTY
AXLESMITH
AXOPODIUM
BAROXYTON
BIAXIALLY
CANDLEBOX
CARBOXIDE
CAULOTAXY
CHRONAXIA
CHRONAXIE
CLIMAXING
COAXIALLY
CONNEXITY
CONNEXIVA
CONNEXIVE
CYTOTAXIS
CYTOTOXIN
DEFLEXING
EPAXIALLY
EXAMPLING
EXANTHEMA
EXARCHATE
EXARCHIST
EXCAVATOR

EXCEPTING
EXCERPTED
EXCESSIVE
EXCLAIMED
EXCLUSIVE
EXCLUSORY
EXCRETIVE
EXCRETORY
EXCURSIVE
EXCURVATE
EXECUTIVE
EXECUTORY
EXHALABLE
EXHIBITOR
EXHUMATOR
EXODROMIC
EXOSPHERE
EXOTHECAL
EXOTICITY
EXPANSIVE
EXPECTING
EXPENSIVE
EXPIATIVE
EXPIATORY
EXPLETIVE
EXPLETORY
EXPLOSIVE
EXPRESSLY
EXPULSIVE
EXPULSORY
EXSPUTORY
EXTREMELY
EXTREMITY
EXULTANCY
EXUVIABLE
FLUXMETER
HEMIAUXIN
HEMOTOXIN
HEXABIOSE
HEXAMERAL
HEXAMERON
HEXAMETER
HOMOTAXIS
INEXACTLY
LEPOTHRIX
LOOMFIXER
MAXILLARY
MESOXALYL
MONOXYLON
NEPHRAUXE
OBNOXIETY
OXYIODIDE
OXYPURINE
OXYTOCOUS
OXYTOLUIC
PARADOXIC
PAXILLARY
PEPPERBOX
PEROXIDIC
PERPLEXED
PHALANXES
PHOENIXES
POLYAXONE
PRAXITHEA
PREFIXION
PREHALLUX
PROLIXITY
PROTHORAX
PYROTOXIN
REFLEXISM
SAXOPHONE
SIMPLEXED
SPHINXIAN
SPHINXINE
SULFOXISM
SUPERFLUX
TOXICALLY

TOXOPHILE
UNEXACTLY
XANTHOMAS
XANTHOPIA
XEROMYRON
XEROPHILE
XEROTHERM
XIPHOSURE
XYLOMETER

20
ACETOXIME
ANOXAEMIC
AXILEMMAS
AXIOMATIC
BISECTRIX
BIXACEOUS
BUTTERBOX
BUXACEOUS
BUXOMNESS
CICUTOXIN
COLOPEXIA
DEFLEXION
DEFLEXURE
DEFLUXION
DEXTERITY
DEXTRALLY
DORSIFLEX
DUPLEXING
EPIPLEXIS
EXACTABLE
EXACTMENT
EXADVERSO
EXALTEDLY
EXCEEDING
EXCENTRIC
EXCEPTANT
EXCEPTION
EXCERPTOR
EXCESSMAN
EXCESSMEN
EXCIPIENT
EXCIPULAR
EXCISABLE
EXCISEMAN
EXCISEMEN
EXCITABLE
EXCLAIMER
EXCLUDING
EXCOCTION
EXCREMENT
EXCULPATE
EXCUSABLE
EXECRABLE
EXEMPTILE
EXEMPTION
EXFODIATE
EXHAUSTED
EXHORTING
EXIGENTLY
EXOCOELIC
EXOCOELOM
EXOCOELUM
EXOSMOTIC
EXOTICISM
EXPALPATE
EXPANDING
EXPECTANT
EXPEDITED
EXPENDING
EXPISCATE
EXPLEMENT
EXPLICATE
EXPLODING
EXPONENCE
EXPONIBLE
EXPOUNDED

EXPROBATE
EXPUNGING
EXSCINDED
EXSICCATE
EXSOMATIC
EXSUCCOUS
EXTEMPORE
EXTREMISM
EXUDATIVE
EXUDATORY
EXUVIATED
FIXEDNESS
FOXTAILED
FUNDATRIX
HETERODOX
HEXADIENE
HEXADIINE
HEXAGONAL
IMMIXTURE
IMPOSTRIX
KENOTOXIN
KOSOTOXIN
LEXICALIC
LIPOPEXIA
MALAXABLE
MALPRAXIS
MESAXONIC
MESOXALIC
METATAXIC
MONAXONIC
MULTIPLEX
OVERSEXED
OVERTAXED
OXIDATIVE
OXYGENANT
OXYGENATE
OXYGENOUS
OXYGEUSIA
OXYGONIAL
PARALEXIC
PARAXONIC
PEROXIDED
PERPLEXER
PLEXICOSE
PREATAXIC
PREEXILIC
PREPOLLEX
PROPLEXUS
PROSCOLEX
PROXIMATE
PSEUDODOX
RELAXEDLY
SCRAMASAX
SEXTACTIC
SIXPENCES
SOAPBOXER
SUBCORTEX
SUBEXCITE
SULFOXIDE
TARAXACUM
TAXONOMIC
UNPERPLEX
VEXEDNESS
XANTHOGEN
XENOPODID
XYLINDEIN
XYLOIDINE

19
ABOIDEAUX
ADMIXTION
ADMIXTURE
ANTEFIXAL
ANTEFIXES
ANTHROXAN
ANTIHELIX
ANXIOUSLY

ASEXUALLY
AUXILIARY
AUXOFLORE
AUXOFLUOR
BOLLIXING
CARDIAUXE
CRESOXIDE
DIAPLEXUS
DICTATRIX
DIRECTRIX
ENDOMIXIS
EPITOXOID
EXAMINING
EXCAUDATE
EXCELLING
EXCRETING
EXCURSING
EXCUSSING
EXECRATED
EXECUTING
EXEGETICS
EXERCISED
EXFOLIATE
EXHAUSTER
EXOCARDIA
EXODERMIS
EXOGAMOUS
EXOPODITE
EXORCISED
EXORDIUMS
EXORGANIC
EXPEDIATE
EXPEDIENT
EXPEDITER
EXPEDITOR
EXPELLING
EXPIATING
EXPLAINED
EXPLODENT
EXPLOITED
EXPLORING
EXPORTING
EXPOUNDER
EXPRESSED
EXPURGATE
EXTENSITY
EXTENSIVE
EXTORSIVE
EXTORTIVE
EXTRABOLD
EXTRACTED
EXTRALITY
EXTRAVERT
EXTROVERT
EXTRUSIVE
EXTRUSORY
FLEXIONAL
FLUXATION
FLUXIONAL
INDEXICAL
INFLEXION
INFLUXION
INTROFLEX
LIXIVIATE
LIXIVIOUS
LOXODROME
MEDIATRIX
NEURATAXY
NOXIOUSLY
OVEREXERT
OXAMIDINE
OXYNEURIN
PARADOXAL
PARADOXER
PENTOXIDE
PIXILATED
PLEXIGLAS

PLEXIPPUS
PLEXODONT
POSTAXIAD
PRETEXTED
PROTOXIDE
PSEUDAXIS
RETROFLEX
RHEOTAXIS
SERVITRIX
SEXLESSLY
SEXOLOGIC
SEXTUPLED
SEXUALITY
SIXTEENTH
SPONDULIX
STRONGBOX
SYNTAXIST
TEXTUALLY
TINDERBOX
TOXIGENIC
TOXOLYSIS
TRANSFLUX
TYLOTOXEA
UNEXCITED
UNEXPIRED
UNEXPOSED
UXORIALLY
UXORICIDE
VEXATIOUS
VEXILLATE
XANTHIONE
XANTHOSIS
XANTHURIA
XERODERMA

18
ALLOXANIC
ALLOXURIC
ANNEXABLE
ANNEXMENT
ANOXAEMIA
ANTECOXAL
APOSTAXIS
APROSEXIA
AUTOTOXIC
AUXETICAL
AUXOBLAST
AUXOMETER
AUXOSPORE
AUXOTONIC
AXEMASTER
AXIOLITIC
BAROTAXIS
BAUXITITE
BISEXUOUS
BOISSEAUX
BUXERRIES
CATALEXIS
COAXATION
CONNEXION
DENDRAXON
DIGITOXIN
EPISTAXIS
EUTAXITIC
EXACTNESS
EXAMINANT
EXAMINATE
EXANIMATE
EXCARNATE
EXCELENTE
EXCELLENT
EXCELSIOR
EXCENTRAL
EXCITATOR
EXCLUSION
EXCORIATE
EXCRETION

EXCURRENT
EXCURSION
EXCUSATOR
EXECRATOR
EXECUTANT
EXECUTION
EXERCISER
EXERCISES
EXERCITOR
EXISTENCE
EXOCLINAL
EXOCOELAR
EXOCULATE
EXORBITAL
EXORCISER
EXOSEPSIS
EXOSMOSIS
EXOSPORAL
EXOSTOTIC
EXOTERICS
EXOTICIST
EXOTROPIA
EXPANSILE
EXPANSION
EXPANSURE
EXPATIATE
EXPELLANT
EXPELLENT
EXPERIENT
EXPERTISE
EXPIATION
EXPIATIST
EXPILATOR
EXPIRATOR
EXPLAINER
EXPLANATE
EXPLOITER
EXPLOSION
EXPONENTS
EXPOSITOR
EXPRESSER
EXPUITION
EXPULSION
EXSECTILE
EXSECTION
EXSUCTION
EXTENDING
EXTERMINE
EXTINCTOR
EXTIRPATE
EXTOLMENT
EXTRACTOR
EXTREMEST
EXTREMIST
EXTRICATE
EXTRINSIC
EXTRUDING
EXUBERANT
EXUBERATE
INEXPIATE
INEXPRESS
INMIXTURE
INTERMIXT
LEUCOXENE
LOXOCLASE
MALAXATOR
MENOXENIA
METATAXIS
NULLIPLEX
OBNOXIOUS
OBSTETRIX
OPERATRIX
OXALAEMIA
OXBERRIES
OXIDATING
OXIMATION
PANSEXUAL

PARALEXIA
PARATAXIS
PAROREXIA
PAXILLATE
PAXILLOSE
PERIAXIAL
PLAINTEXT
PLEONEXIA
POSTAXIAL
POSTEXIST
PRAETEXTA
PRESEXUAL
PROTAXIAL
PROXENETE
RATTLEBOX
REEXAMINE
RELAXABLE
SAPOTOXIN
SAXCORNET
SEXANGLED
SEXENNIUM
SEXTIPARA
SEXTUPLET
SEXUALISM
SIXTEENMO
SPLENAUXE
SUBLUXATE
TAXACEOUS
TAXAMETER
TAXIMETER
TAXIPLANE
TAXOMETER
TAXONOMER
TOPOTAXIS
TOXAEMIAS
TOXANEMIA
TOXICAROL
TOXICOSES
TOXICOSIS
TOXINEMIA
TRUXILLIC
UNEXPRESS
XENAGOGUE
XENOBLAST
XENOMANIA
XEROSTOMA

17
ADNEXITIS
AGITATRIX
ANXIETUDE
ATLOAXOID
DEXTEROUS
DEXTRORSE
DRUXINESS
ENDOTOXIN
ENTREDEUX
EXAGITATE
EXECUTRIX
EXEGETIST
EXIGEANTE
EXIGENTER
EXODONTIA
EXOGENOUS
EXOSTOSED
EXSERTING
EXSURGENT
EXTOLLING
EXTORTING
EXTRADITE
EXUDATION
OXANILIDE
OXIDATION
SURTAXING
TAXEATING
TETROXIDE
UNRELAXED

16

AEROTAXIS	EXONEURAL	EXTRORSAL	LUXURIOUS	TESTATRIX
ANXIETIES	EXOSTOSES	EXTRUSILE	NEURAXONE	TETRAXILE
ASSERTRIX	EXOSTOSIS	EXTRUSION	OXALURATE	TEXTARIAN
AUTOTOXIN	EXSERTILE	EXULULATE	OXANILATE	TEXTILIST
AUXILIATE	EXSERTION	INNOXIOUS	RETEXTURE	TEXTORIAL
AXONEURON	EXTENSILE	INTERAXAL	SEXENNIAL	TONOTAXIS
ELIXATION	EXTENSION	INTERAXIS	SEXTANTAL	TOXINOSIS
ENTERAUXE	EXTENUATE	INTEXTINE	SEXTARIUS	TRUXILLIN
EXAIRESIS	EXTERNATE	INTEXTURE	SEXUALIST	UNISEXUAL
EXARATION	EXTORTION	LATEXOSIS	SIXTEENER	UROTOXIES
EXINANITE	EXTRALITE	LUXURIANT	SUSOTOXIN	UROXANATE
EXONERATE	EXTRANEAN	LUXURIATE	SUSSEXITE	XENELASIA

ALPHABETICAL LIST OF 10-LETTER WORDS

ACAROTOXIC	AXIOMATIZE	DEXTRINATE	EXCHANGING	EXINGUINAL
ACCUSATRIX	AXONOMETRY	DEXTRINIZE	EXCITATION	EXISTENTLY
ACROATAXIA	BIAXIALITY	DEXTRINOUS	EXCITATIVE	EXOCARDIAC
ADIPOPEXIA	BINOXALATE	DEXTROGYRE	EXCITATORY	EXOCARDIAL
ADIPOPEXIS	BISEXUALLY	DEXTRORSAL	EXCITEMENT	EXOCENTRIC
ADNEXOPEXY	BISSEXTILE	DEXTROUSLY	EXCITINGLY	EXOCHORION
ADOXACEOUS	BOBBYSOXER	DIASTATAXY	EXCLAIMING	EXOCOLITIS
AFFIXATION	BORDEREAUX	DIETOTOXIC	EXCOGITATE	EXOCULATED
ALEXANDERS	BOXBERRIES	DIGITOXOSE	EXCORIABLE	EXOGASTRIC
ALEXITERIC	BRACHYAXIS	DISQUIXOTE	EXCORIATED	EXOGENETIC
ALLOXANATE	CACODOXIAN	DISULFOXID	EXCORIATOR	EXOMORPHIC
ALLOXANTIN	CACOXENITE	DORSIFIXED	EXCRESCENT	EXOMPHALOS
AMAXOMANIA	CARBOXYLIC	DOXASTICON	EXCRUCIATE	EXOMPHALUS
AMBIDEXTER	CARNIFEXES	DOXOGRAPHY	EXCUDERUNT	EXONARTHEX
AMBOSEXOUS	CHAETOTAXY	DOXOLOGIES	EXCULPABLE	EXONERATED
AMINOXYLOL	CHALUMEAUX	DOXOLOGIZE	EXCULPATED	EXONERATOR
AMPHIMIXIS	CHATTERBOX	DYSOXIDIZE	EXCURVATED	EXONERETUR
ANEMOTAXIS	CHEMOTAXIS	ECHOPRAXIA	EXCUSATIVE	EXOPHAGOUS
ANNEXATION	CHRONAXIES	ENDOTHORAX	EXCUSATORY	EXOPODITIC
ANOXYSCOPE	CICATRIXES	ENTOMOTAXY	EXCYSTMENT	EXORBITANT
ANTEFLEXED	CIRCUMFLEX	EPEXEGESIS	EXECRATING	EXORBITATE
ANTHOTAXIS	COADJUTRIX	EPEXEGETIC	EXECRATION	EXORCISING
ANTICLIMAX	COEXISTENT	EPICALYXES	EXECRATIVE	EXORCISMAL
ANTIOXYGEN	COLLOXYLIN	EPIPHARYNX	EXECRATORY	EXORCISORY
ANTISPADIX	COLONOPEXY	EPIPLOPEXY	EXECUTABLE	EXORCISTIC
ANTITOXINE	COMMIXTION	ERGOTOXINE	EXECUTANCY	EXORCIZING
APICIFIXED	COMMIXTURE	ESONARTHEX	EXECUTIONS	EXORNATION
APLOTAXENE	COMPLEXIFY	EUXANTHATE	EXECUTRESS	EXOSPHERIC
APPENDIXED	COMPLEXION	EUXANTHONE	EXEGETICAL	EXOSPORIUM
APPENDIXES	COMPLEXITY	EXACERBATE	EXEMPLARIC	EXOSPOROUS
APPROXIMAL	CONNEXIVUM	EXACTINGLY	EXEMPTIBLE	EXOTERICAL
ARSENOXIDE	CONTEXTUAL	EXACTITUDE	EXENTERATE	EXOTHECATE
ASEXUALITY	CONTEXTURE	EXADVERSUM	EXERCISING	EXOTHECIUM
ASEXUALIZE	CONTRAPLEX	EXAGGERATE	EXERCITANT	EXOTHERMAL
ASPHYXIANT	CONVEXEDLY	EXALTATION	EXFOLIATED	EXOTHERMIC
ASPHYXIATE	CONVEXNESS	EXALTATIVE	EXHALATION	EXOTICALLY
ATAXIAGRAM	COXCOMBESS	EXAMINABLE	EXHALATORY	EXOTICNESS
ATAXINOMIC	COXCOMICAL	EXAMINATOR	EXHAUSTING	EXOTOSPORE
ATAXONOMIC	COXOCERITE	EXANTHEMAS	EXHAUSTION	EXOTROPISM
AUTOXIDIZE	COXOPODITE	EXASPERATE	EXHAUSTIVE	EXPANDEDLY
AUXANOGRAM	CRIOSPHINX	EXASPIDEAN	EXHIBITANT	EXPANSIBLE
AUXANOLOGY	CYCLOHEXYL	EXAUGURATE	EXHIBITING	EXPANSIBLY
AUXILIARLY	DEOXIDIZED	EXCALATION	EXHIBITION	EXPATIATED
AUXILIATOR	DEOXIDIZER	EXCALCEATE	EXHIBITIVE	EXPATIATER
AUXOACTION	DERMATAUXE	EXCAVATING	EXHIBITORY	EXPATIATOR
AUXOCARDIA	DESOXALATE	EXCAVATION	EXHILARANT	EXPATRIATE
AUXOCHROME	DETOXICANT	EXCECATION	EXHILARATE	EXPECTABLE
AXEBREAKER	DETOXICATE	EXCELLENCE	EXHUMATING	EXPECTANCE
AXHAMMERED	DEXIOTROPE	EXCELLENCY	EXHUMATION	EXPECTANCY
AXILEMMATA	DEXTERICAL	EXCEPTIOUS	EXHUMATORY	EXPEDIENCE
AXILLARIES	DEXTRALITY	EXCERPTING	EXIGENCIES	EXPEDIENCY
AXINOMANCY	DEXTRAURAL	EXCERPTION	EXIGUOUSLY	EXPEDIENTE
AXIOLOGIST	DEXTRINASE	EXCERPTIVE	EXIMIOUSLY	EXPEDITATE

EXPEDITELY	EXTRAPOLAR	INEXORABLE	OXIDIZABLE	PERPLEXITY
EXPEDITING	EXTRASOLAR	INEXORABLY	OLEOTHORAX	PETROSILEX
EXPEDITION	EXTRATUBAL	INEXPECTED	OMENTOPEXY	PETROXOLIN
EXPELLABLE	EXTREMITAL	INEXPERTLY	ONYCHAUXIS	PHILODOXER
EXPENDABLE	EXTRICABLE	INEXPIABLE	OOPHORAUXE	PHLEBOPEXY
EXPENDITOR	EXTRICABLY	INEXPIABLY	OPTOMENINX	PHOENIXITY
EXPENSEFUL	EXTRICATED	INEXPLICIT	ORCHIOPEXY	PHOTOTAXIS
EXPERIENCE	EXTROITIVE	INFLEXIBLE	OROPHARYNX	PHYLLOTAXY
EXPERIMENT	EXTROPICAL	INFLEXIBLY	ORTHODOXAL	PHYLLOXERA
EXPERTNESS	EXTRORSELY	INOXIDIZED	ORTHODOXLY	PHYTOTOXIC
EXPILATION	EXTROSPECT	INSPECTRIX	ORTHOPRAXY	PHYTOTOXIN
EXPIRATION	EXTUBATION	INSPEXIMUS	OSCULATRIX	PICROTOXIC
EXPIRATORY	EXUBERANCE	INTERAXIAL	OVEREXPOSE	PICROTOXIN
EXPISCATED	EXUBERANCY	INTERMIXED	OVERTAXING	PLEIOTAXIS
EXPISCATOR	EXUBERATED	INTOXATION	OXADIAZOLE	PLEXIGLASS
EXPLAINING	EXULCERATE	INTOXICANT	OXALACETIC	PLEXIMETER
EXPLANATOR	EXULTANTLY	INTOXICATE	OXALURAMID	PLEXIMETRY
EXPLICABLE	EXULTATION	JUXTAPOSED	OXALYLUREA	PLURIAXIAL
EXPLICATED	EXULTINGLY	JUXTAPOSIT	OXAMETHANE	PNEUMOPEXY
EXPLICATOR	EXUMBRELLA	KERFLUMMOX	OXIDIMETRY	POLYMIXIID
EXPLICITLY	EXUNDATION	LACROIXITE	OXIDIZABLE	POSTEXILIC
EXPLOITAGE	EXURBANITE	LACTOTOXIN	OXIDULATED	PRAEHALLUX
EXPLOITING	EXUVIATING	LAXATIVELY	OXOZONIDES	PRAXIOLOGY
EXPLOITIVE	EXUVIATION	LEUCOTOXIC	OXYBLEPSIA	PREAXIALLY
EXPLOITURE	EXZODIACAL	LEXICALITY	OXYBROMIDE	PREEXILIAN
EXPLORATOR	FLEXUOSITY	LEXICOLOGY	OXYBUTYRIA	PREFIXALLY
EXPLOSIBLE	FLEXUOUSLY	LEXICONIST	OXYCALCIUM	PREFIXEDLY
EXPLOSIVES	FLUMMOXING	LEXICONIZE	OXYCAMPHOR	PREFIXTURE
EXPORTABLE	FLUXIONARY	LEXIGRAPHY	OXYCAPROIC	PREFLEXION
EXPOSITION	FLUXIONIST	LEXIPHANIC	OXYCEPHALY	PREMAXILLA
EXPOSITIVE	FOXBERRIES	LIBERATRIX	OXYCHLORIC	PROJECTRIX
EXPOSITORY	FRAXINELLA	LIENOTOXIN	OXYCHLORID	PROLIXNESS
EXPOUNDING	GASTROPEXY	LIPOMYXOMA	OXYCYANIDE	PROTEOPEXY
EXPRESSAGE	GENERATRIX	LIPOXENOUS	OXYGENATED	PROTOXYLEM
EXPRESSING	GERONTOXON	LIXIVIATED	OXYGENATOR	PROXICALLY
EXPRESSIVE	GLYOXALASE	LIXIVIATOR	OXYGENIZED	PYOSALPINX
EXPRESSMAN	GLYOXALINE	LOXODROMIC	OXYGENIZER	PYRIDOXINE
EXPRESSWAY	GOOGOLPLEX	LUXURIANCE	OXYHEMATIN	PYROXENITE
EXPUGNABLE	HELIOTAXIS	LUXURIANCY	OXYHYDRATE	PYROXYLINE
EXPUNCTION	HEMOTHORAX	LUXURIATED	OXYMURIATE	QUADRATRIX
EXPURGATED	HETERODOXY	MALAXATION	OXYNEURINE	QUADRUPLEX
EXPURGATOR	HEXABROMID	MALAXERMAN	OXYNITRATE	QUINATOXIN
EXSANGUINE	HEXACOSANE	MALAXERMEN	OXYOPHITIC	QUINCUNXES
EXSCINDING	HEXACTINAL	MAXILLIPED	OXYPHILOUS	QUINOXALIN
EXSIBILATE	HEXACYCLIC	MAXIMATION	OXYPROLINE	QUINOXALYL
EXSICCATAE	HEXADECANE	MAXIMISTIC	OXYQUINONE	QUIXOTICAL
EXSICCATED	HEXAEMERIC	MAXIMIZING	OXYRHINOUS	RADIOTOXIC
EXSILIENCY	HEXAEMERON	MEDITHORAX	OXYSTEARIC	REFLEXIBLE
EXSPUITION	HEXAGYNOUS	MENOSTAXIS	OXYSULFIDE	RELAXATION
EXSUFFLATE	HEXAHEDRAL	MESOTHORAX	OXYSULPHID	RELAXATIVE
EXTEMPORAL	HEXAHEDRON	MESOXALATE	OXYTERPENE	RELAXATORY
EXTENDEDLY	HEXAHYDRIC	METAGALAXY	OXYTOLUENE	RHIZOTAXIS
EXTENDIBLE	HEXAMERISM	METATHORAX	OXYTONESIS	SAXICOLINE
EXTENSIBLE	HEXAMEROUS	MIXILINEAL	OXYTONICAL	SAXICOLOUS
EXTENUATED	HEXAMETRAL	MONAXONIAL	OXYURIASIS	SAXIGENOUS
EXTENUATOR	HEXAMETRIC	MONOXENOUS	OXYURICIDE	SAXOPHONIC
EXTERIORLY	HEXANDROUS	MONOXYLOUS	OXYWELDING	SAXOTROMBA
EXTERNALLY	HEXANGULAR	MOXIEBERRY	PARADOXIAL	SEPARATRIX
EXTINCTEUR	HEXAPLARIC	MYDATOXINE	PARADOXIST	SEXAGENARY
EXTINCTION	HEXAPODIES	MYORRHEXIS	PARADOXURE	SEXANGULAR
EXTINCTIVE	HEXARADIAL	MYXADENOMA	PARAPRAXIA	SEXDIGITAL
EXTINGUISH	HEXARCHIES	MYXANGITIS	PARAPRAXES	SEXOLOGIST
EXTIRPATED	HEXASTICHY	MYXOEDEMIC	PARAPRAXIS	SEXPARTITE
EXTIRPATOR	HEXASTYLOS	MYXOGASTER	PARAXIALLY	SEXTENNIAL
EXTISPICES	HEXATRIOSE	MYXOGLIOMA	PAROXYSMAL	SEXTILLION
EXTOGENOUS	HEXAVALENT	MYXOLIPOMA	PAROXYSMIC	SEXTIPOLAR
EXTOLLMENT	HEXPARTITE	MYXOMATOUS	PAROXYTONE	SEXTUPLING
EXTOOLITIC	HOLOPLEXIA	MYXOMYCETE	PERIAXONAL	SEXUPAROUS
EXTRACTING	HOMOSEXUAL	MYXOPODIUM	PERIPHRAXY	SIMPLEXITY
EXTRACTION	HYDROTAXIS	NECTOCALYX	PERMIXABLE	SITOTOXISM
EXTRACTIVE	HYPEROXIDE	NEPHROPEXY	PERMIXTION	SNUFFBOXER
EXTRADITED	HYPOPRAXIA	NEURATAXIA	PERMIXTIVE	SOIXANTINE
EXTRADOSED	HYPOZEUXIS	NEUROTOXIA	PERMIXTURE	SPECTATRIX
EXTRADOTAL	IMPERATRIX	NEUROTOXIC	PEROXIDASE	SPHINXLIKE
EXTRAMURAL	INDICATRIX	NEUROTOXIN	PEROXIDING	SPINTURNIX
EXTRANEITY	INEXERTION	NOMINATRIX	PEROXIDIZE	SPLENOPEXY
EXTRANEOUS	INEXISTENT	NOMOPHYLAX	PERPLEXING	STEREOTAXY

SUBAXILLAR	THIXOTROPY	TRUXILLINE	WAXWORKING	XEROGRAPHY
SUBMAXILLA	THYROTOXIC	TYROTOXINE	XANTHALINE	XEROMORPHY
SUBMAXIMAL	TOXALBUMIC	UNCOMMIXED	XANTHAMIDE	XEROPHYTIC
SUFFIXMENT	TOXALBUMIN	UNDERSEXED	XANTHATION	XIPHIIFORM
SULFOXYLIC	TOXANAEMIA	UNEQUIAXED	XANTHIURIA	XIPHODYNIA
SULPHOXIDE	TOXICATION	UNEXAMPLED	XANTHOCONE	XIP'HOIDIAN
SULPHOXISM	TOXICITIES	UNEXCITING	XANTHODERM	XIPHOPAGIC
SUPEREXIST	TOXICOLOGY	UNEXPECTED	XANTHOMATA	XIPHOPAGUS
SUPRACOXAL	TOXIDERMIC	UNEXPENDED	XANTHOPHYL	XIPHOSURAN
SYNAXARION	TOXIFEROUS	UNEXPERTLY	XANTHOPSIA	XIPHYDRIID
SYNAXARIST	TOXINAEMIA	UNFLEXIBLE	XANTHOPSIN	XYLANTHRAX
TAXABILITY	TOXIPHAGUS	UNFLEXIBLY	XANTHYDROL	XYLOGLYPHY
TAXATIONAL	TOXIPHOBIA	UNIDEXTRAL	XENARTHRAL	XYLOGRAPHY
TAXATIVELY	TOXIPHORIC	UNORTHODOX	XENOBIOSIS	XYLOPHAGAN
TAXIDERMAL	TRANSFIXED	UROXANTHIN	XENOGAMOUS	XYLOPHAGID
TAXIDERMIC	TRIAXONIAN	UXORIALITY	XENOGENOUS	XYLOPHONIC
TAXONOMIST	TRICHAUXIS	UXORICIDAL	XENOPELTID	XYLOPOLIST
TEXTUALISM	TRIHYDROXY	UXORIOUSLY	XENOPHOBIA	XYLORCINOL
TEXTUALIST	TRIMETHOXY	VINCETOXIN	XENOPHOBIC	XYLOSTROMA
TEXTUARIES	TRIPLEXITY	VIXENISHLY	XENOPODOID	XYLOTOMIST
TEXTUARIST	TRISECTRIX	WAXBERRIES	XENOPTERAN	XYLOTOMOUS
TEXTURALLY	TROUSSEAUX	WAXHEARTED	XENOSAURID	ZOOXANTHIN
THEOMASTIX				

POSITIONAL ORDER LIST OF 10-LETTER WORDS

XANTHALINE	AXIOLOGIST	EXECRATION	EXONERETUR	EXPIRATION
XANTHAMIDE	AXIOMATIZE	EXECRATIVE	EXOPHAGOUS	EXPIRATORY
XANTHATION	AXONOMETRY	EXECRATORY	EXOPODITIC	EXPISCATED
XANTHIURIA	EXACERBATE	EXECUTABLE	EXORBITANT	EXPISCATOR
XANTHOCONE	EXACTINGLY	EXECUTANCY	EXORBITATE	EXPLAINING
XANTHODERM	EXACTITUDE	EXECUTIONS	EXORCISING	EXPLANATOR
XANTHOMATA	EXADVERSUM	EXECUTRESS	EXORCISMAL	EXPLICABLE
XANTHOPHYL	EXAGGERATE	EXEGETICAL	EXORCISORY	EXPLICATED
XANTHOPSIA	EXALTATION	EXEMPLARIC	EXORCISTIC	EXPLICATOR
XANTHOPSIN	EXALTATIVE	EXEMPTIBLE	EXORCIZING	EXPLICITLY
XANTHYDROL	EXAMINABLE	EXENTERATE	EXORNATION	EXPLOITAGE
XENARTHRAL	EXAMINATOR	EXERCISING	EXOSPHERIC	EXPLOITING
XENOBIOSIS	EXANTHEMAS	EXERCITANT	EXOSPORIUM	EXPLOITIVE
XENOGAMOUS	EXASPERATE	EXFOLIATED	EXOSPOROUS	EXPLOITURE
XENOGENOUS	EXASPIDEAN	EXHALATION	EXOTERICAL	EXPLORATOR
XENOPELTID	EXAUGURATE	EXHALATORY	EXOTHECATE	EXPLOSIBLE
XENOPHOBIA	EXCALATION	EXHAUSTING	EXOTHECIUM	EXPLOSIVES
XENOPHOBIC	EXCALCEATE	EXHAUSTION	EXOTHERMAL	EXPORTABLE
XENOPODOID	EXCAVATING	EXHAUSTIVE	EXOTHERMIC	EXPOSITION
XENOPTERAN	EXCAVATION	EXHIBITANT	EXOTICALLY	EXPOSITIVE
XENOSAURID	EXCECATION	EXHIBITING	EXOTICNESS	EXPOSITORY
XEROGRAPHY	EXCELLENCE	EXHIBITION	EXOTOSPORE	EXPOUNDING
XEROMORPHY	EXCELLENCY	EXHIBITIVE	EXOTROPISM	EXPRESSAGE
XEROPHYTIC	EXCEPTIOUS	EXHIBITORY	EXPANDEDLY	EXPRESSING
XIPHIIFORM	EXCERPTING	EXHILARANT	EXPANSIBLE	EXPRESSIVE
XIPHODYNIA	EXCERPTION	EXHILARATE	EXPANSIBLY	EXPRESSMAN
XIPHOIDIAN	EXCERPTIVE	EXHUMATING	EXPATIATED	EXPRESSWAY
XIPHOPAGIC	EXCHANGING	EXHUMATION	EXPATIATER	EXPUGNABLE
XIPHOPAGUS	EXCITATION	EXHUMATORY	EXPATIATOR	EXPUNCTION
XIPHOSURAN	EXCITATIVE	EXIGENCIES	EXPATRIATE	EXPURGATED
XIPHYDRIID	EXCITATORY	EXIGUOUSLY	EXPECTABLE	EXPURGATOR
XYLANTHRAX	EXCITEMENT	EXIMIOUSLY	EXPECTANCE	EXSANGUINE
XYLOGLYPHY	EXCITINGLY	EXINGUINAL	EXPECTANCY	EXSCINDING
XYLOGRAPHY	EXCLAIMING	EXISTENTLY	EXPEDIENCE	EXSIBILATE
XYLOPHAGAN	EXCOGITATE	EXOCARDIAC	EXPEDIENCY	EXSICCATAE
XYLOPHAGID	EXCORIABLE	EXOCARDIAL	EXPEDIENTE	EXSICCATED
XYLOPHONIC	EXCORIATED	EXOCENTRIC	EXPEDITATE	EXSILIENCY
XYLOPOLIST	EXCORIATOR	EXOCHORION	EXPEDITELY	EXSPUITION
XYLORCINOL	EXCRESCENT	EXOCOLITIS	EXPEDITING	EXSUFFLATE
XYLOSTROMA	EXCRUCIATE	EXOCULATED	EXPEDITION	EXTEMPORAL
XYLOTOMIST	EXCUDERUNT	EXOGASTRIC	EXPELLABLE	EXTENDEDLY
XYLOTOMOUS	EXCULPABLE	EXOGENETIC	EXPENDABLE	EXTENDIBLE
	EXCULPATED	EXOMORPHIC	EXPENDITOR	EXTENSIBLE
AXEBREAKER	EXCURVATED	EXOMPHALOS	EXPENSEFUL	EXTENUATED
AXHAMMERED	EXCUSATIVE	EXOMPHALUS	EXPERIENCE	EXTENUATOR
AXILEMMATA	EXCUSATORY	EXONARTHEX	EXPERIMENT	EXTERIORLY
AXILLARIES	EXCYSTMENT	EXONERATED	EXPERTNESS	EXTERNALLY
AXINOMANCY	EXECRATING	EXONERATOR	EXPILATION	EXTINCTEUR

EXTINCTION
EXTINCTIVE
EXTINGUISH
EXTIRPATED
EXTIRPATOR
EXTISPICES
EXTOGENOUS
EXTOLLMENT
EXTOOLITIC
EXTRACTING
EXTRACTION
EXTRACTIVE
EXTRADITED
EXTRADOSED
EXTRADOTAL
EXTRAMURAL
EXTRANEITY
EXTRANEOUS
EXTRAPOLAR
EXTRASOLAR
EXTRATUBAL
EXTREMITAL
EXTRICABLE
EXTRICABLY
EXTRICATED
EXTROITIVE
EXTROPICAL
EXTRORSELY
EXTROSPECT
EXTUBATION
EXUBERANCE
EXUBERANCY
EXUBERATED
EXULCERATE
EXULTANTLY
EXULTATION
EXULTINGLY
EXUMBRELLA
EXUNDATION
EXURBANITE
EXUVIATING
EXUVIATION
EXZODIACAL
OXIDIZABLE
OXADIAZOLE
OXALACETIC
OXALURAMID
OXALYLUREA
OXAMETHANE
OXIDIMETRY
OXIDIZABLE
OXIDULATED
OXOZONIDES
OXYBLEPSIA
OXYBROMIDE
OXYBUTYRIA
OXYCALCIUM
OXYCAMPHOR
OXYCAPROIC
OXYCEPHALY
OXYCHLORIC
OXYCHLORID
OXYCYANIDE
OXYGENATED
OXYGENATOR
OXYGENIZED
OXYGENIZER
OXYHEMATIN
OXYHYDRATE
OXYMURIATE
OXYNEURINE
OXYNITRATE
OXYOPHITIC
OXYPHILOUS
OXYPROLINE
OXYQUINONE
OXYRHINOUS

OXYSTEARIC
OXYSULFIDE
OXYSULPHID
OXYTERPENE
OXYTOLUENE
OXYTONESIS
OXYTONICAL
OXYURIASIS
OXYURICIDE
OXYWELDING
UXORIALITY
UXORICIDAL
UXORIOUSLY

AUXANOGRAM
AUXANOLOGY
AUXILIARLY
AUXILIATOR
AUXOACTION
AUXOCARDIA
AUXOCHROME
BOXBERRIES
COXCOMBESS
COXCOMICAL
COXOCERITE
COXOPODITE
DEXIOTROPE
DEXTERICAL
DEXTRALITY
DEXTRAURAL
DEXTRINASE
DEXTRINATE
DEXTRINIZE
DEXTRINOUS
DEXTROGYRE
DEXTRORSAL
DEXTROUSLY
DOXASTICON
DOXOGRAPHY
DOXOLOGIES
DOXOLOGIZE
EUXANTHATE
EUXANTHONE
FOXBERRIES
HEXABROMID
HEXACOSANE
HEXACTINAL
HEXACYCLIC
HEXADECANE
HEXAEMERIC
HEXAEMERON
HEXAGYNOUS
HEXAHEDRAL
HEXAHEDRON
HEXAHYDRIC
HEXAMERISM
HEXAMEROUS
HEXAMETRAL
HEXAMETRIC
HEXANDROUS
HEXANGULAR
HEXAPLARIC
HEXAPODIES
HEXARADIAL
HEXARCHIES
HEXASTICHY
HEXASTYLOS
HEXATRIOSE
HEXAVALENT
HEXPARTITE
JUXTAPOSED
JUXTAPOSIT
LAXATIVELY
LEXICALITY
LEXICOLOGY
LEXICONIST
LEXICONIZE

LEXIGRAPHY
LEXIPHANIC
LIXIVIATED
LIXIVIATOR
LOXODROMIC
LUXURIANCE
LUXURIANCY
LUXURIATED
MAXILLIPED
MAXIMATION
MAXIMISTIC
MAXIMIZING
MIXILINEAL
MOXIEBERRY
MYXADENOMA
MYXANGITIS
MYXOEDEMIC
MYXOGASTER
MYXOGLIOMA
MYXOLIPOMA
MYXOMATOUS
MYXOMYCETE
MYXOPODIUM
SAXICOLINE
SAXICOLOUS
SAXIGENOUS
SAXOPHONIC
SAXOTROMBA
SEXAGENARY
SEXANGULAR
SEXDIGITAL
SEXOLOGIST
SEXPARTITE
SEXTENNIAL
SEXTILLION
SEXTIPOLAR
SEXTUPLING
SEXUPAROUS
TAXABILITY
TAXATIONAL
TAXATIVELY
TAXIDERMAL
TAXIDERMIC
TAXONOMIST
TEXTUALISM
TEXTUALIST
TEXTUARIES
TEXTUARIST
TEXTURALLY
TOXALBUMIC
TOXALBUMIN
TOXANAEMIA
TOXICATION
TOXICITIES
TOXICOLOGY
TOXIDERMIC
TOXIFEROUS
TOXINAEMIA
TOXIPHAGUS
TOXIPHOBIA
TOXIPHORIC
VIXENISHLY
WAXBERRIES
WAXHEARTED
WAXWORKING

ADOXACEOUS
ALEXANDERS
ALEXITERIC
AMAXOMANIA
ANOXYSCOPE
ASEXUALITY
ASEXUALIZE
ATAXIAGRAM
ATAXINOMIC
ATAXONOMIC
BIAXIALITY

COEXISTENT
DEOXIDIZED
DEOXIDIZER
EPEXEGESIS
EPEXEGETIC
FLEXUOSITY
FLEXUOUSLY
FLUXIONARY
FLUXIONIST
FRAXINELLA
INEXERTION
INEXISTENT
INEXORABLE
INEXORABLY
INEXPECTED
INEXPERTLY
INEXPIABLE
INEXPIABLY
INEXPLICIT
INOXIDIZED
PLEXIGLASS
PLEXIMETER
PLEXIMETRY
PRAXIOLOGY
PROXICALLY
QUIXOTICAL
SOIXANTINE
THIXOTROPY
TRUXILLINE
UNEXAMPLED
UNEXCITING
UNEXPECTED
UNEXPENDED
UNEXPERTLY
UROXANTHIN
ZOOXANTHIN

AFFIXATION
ALLOXANATE
ALLOXANTIN
ANNEXATION
AUTOXIDIZE
BINOXALATE
BISEXUALLY
CACOXENITE
DESOXALATE
DETOXICANT
DETOXICATE
DYSOXIDIZE
GLYOXALASE
GLYOXALINE
INTOXATION
INTOXICANT
INTOXICATE
LIPOXENOUS
MALAXATION
MALAXERMAN
MALAXERMEN
MESOXALATE
MONAXONIAL
MONOXENOUS
MONOXYLOUS
PARAXIALLY
PAROXYSMAL
PAROXYSMIC
PAROXYTONE
PEROXIDASE
PEROXIDING
PEROXIDIZE
PREAXIALLY
PREEXILIAN
PYROXENITE
PYROXYLINE
RELAXATION
RELAXATIVE
RELAXATORY
SUBAXILLAR

SYNAXARION
SYNAXARIST
TRIAXONIAN

AMINOXYLOL
ANTIOXYGEN
APPROXIMAL
ASPHYXIANT
ASPHYXIATE
BISSEXTILE
CARBOXYLIC
COLLOXYLIN
COMMIXTION
COMMIXTURE
CONNEXIVUM
CONTEXTUAL
CONTEXTURE
CONVEXEDLY
CONVEXNESS
INFLEXIBLE
INFLEXIBLY
INSPEXIMUS
OVEREXPOSE
PERIAXONAL
PERMIXABLE
PERMIXTION
PERMIXTIVE
PERMIXTURE
PETROXOLIN
POSTEXILIC
PREFIXALLY
PREFIXEDLY
PREFIXTURE
PREMAXILLA
PROLIXNESS
PROTOXYLEM
QUINOXALIN
QUINOXALYL
REFLEXIBLE
SPHINXLIKE
SUBMAXILLA
SUBMAXIMAL
SUFFIXMENT
SULFOXYLIC
UNFLEXIBLE
UNFLEXIBLY
UNIDEXTRAL

AMBIDEXTER
AMBOSEXOUS
ANTITOXINE
APLOTAXENE
ARSENOXIDE
CACODOXIAN
CHRONAXIES
COMPLEXIFY
COMPLEXION
COMPLEXITY
DIGITOXOSE
DISQUIXOTE
ERGOTOXINE
FLUMMOXING
HOMOSEXUAL
HYPEROXIDE
INTERAXIAL
LACROIXITE
LIPOMYXOMA
MYDATOXINE
OVERTAXING
PARADOXIAL
PARADOXIST
PARADOXURE
PERPLEXING
PERPLEXITY
PHOENIXITY
PHYLLOXERA
PLURıAXIAL

POLYMIXIID	DORSIFIXED	PICROTOXIC	ORCHIOPEXY	IMPERATRIX
PREFLEXION	ECHOPRAXIA	PICROTOXIN	ORTHOPRAXY	INDICATRIX
PYRIDOXINE	EPICALYXES	PLEIOTAXIS	PERIPHRAXY	INSPECTRIX
SIMPLEXITY	GERONTOXON	QUINATOXIN	PHLEBOPEXY	KERFLUMMOX
SITOTOXISM	HELIOTAXIS	QUINCUNXES	PHYLLOTAXY	LIBERATRIX
SULPHOXIDE	HOLOPLEXIA	RADIOTOXIC	PNEUMOPEXY	MEDITHORAX
SULPHOXISM	HYDROTAXIS	RHIZOTAXIS	PROTEOPEXY	MESOTHORAX
SUPEREXIST	HYPOPRAXIA	SNUFFBOXER	SPLENOPEXY	METATHORAX
TRIPLEXITY	HYPOZEUXIS	SUPRACOXAL	STEREOTAXY	NECTOCALYX
TYROTOXINE	INTERMIXED	THYROTOXIC	TRIHYDROXY	NOMINATRIX
	LACTOTOXIN	TRANSFIXED	TRIMETHOXY	NOMOPHYLAX
ACAROTOXIC	LEUCOTOXIC	TRICHAUXIS		OLEOTHORAX
ACROATAXIA	LIENOTOXIN	UNCOMMIXED	ACCUSATRIX	OPTOMENINX
ADIPOPEXIA	MENOSTAXIS	UNDERSEXED	ANTICLIMAX	OROPHARYNX
ADIPOPEXIS	MYORRHEXIS	UNEQUIAXED	ANTISPADIX	OSCULATRIX
AMPHIMIXIS	NEURATAXIA	VINCETOXIN	BORDEREAUX	PETROSILEX
ANEMOTAXIS	NEUROTOXIA		CHALUMEAUX	PRAEHALLUX
ANTEFLEXED	NEUROTOXIC	ADNEXOPEXY	CHATTERBOX	PROJECTRIX
ANTHOTAXIS	NEUROTOXIN	CHAETOTAXY	CIRCUMFLEX	PYOSALPINX
APICIFIXED	ONYCHAUXIS	DERMATAUXE	COADJUTRIX	QUADRATRIX
APPENDIXED	ORTHODOXAL	DIASTATAXY	CONTRAPLEX	QUADRUPLEX
APPENDIXES	ORTHODOXLY	ENTOMOTAXY	CRIOSPHINX	SEPARATRIX
BOBBYSOXER	PARAPRAXIA	EPIPLOPEXY	ENDOTHORAX	SPECTATRIX
BRACHYAXIS	PARAPRAXES	GASTROPEXY	EPIPHARYNX	SPINTURNIX
CARNIFEXES	PARAPRAXIS	HETERODOXY	ESONARTHEX	THEOMASTIX
CHEMOTAXIS	PHILODOXER	METAGALAXY	EXONARTHEX	TRISECTRIX
CICATRIXES	PHOTOTAXIS	NEPHROPEXY	GENERATRIX	TROUSSEAUX
CYCLOHEXYL	PHYTOTOXIC	OMENTOPEXY	GOOGOLPLEX	UNORTHODOX
DIETOTOXIC	PHYTOTOXIN	OOPHORAUXE	HEMOTHORAX	XYLANTHRAX
DISULFOXID				

SCORING ORDER LIST OF 10-LETTER WORDS

34	QUINCUNXES	CARBOXYLIC	FLUMMOXING	ECHOPRAXIA
HYPOZEUXIS	QUIXOTICAL	CIRCUMFLEX	HEMOTHORAX	EPICALYXES
	WAXWORKING	COMPLEXITY	HEXABROMID	EXCELLENCY
31	XANTHOPHYL	CONVEXEDLY	HEXARCHIES	EXCERPTIVE
DYSOXIDIZE	XYLOGLYPHY	EXOMORPHIC	INFLEXIBLY	EXCHANGING
MAXIMIZING		EXPECTANCY	MYORRHEXIS	EXCYSTMENT
OXYGENIZED	**27**	HEXACYCLIC	MYXADENOMA	EXECUTANCY
	AUTOXIDIZE	HYPEROXIDE	MYXOGLIOMA	EXOMPHALOS
30	BRACHYAXIS	JUXTAPOSIT	ONYCHAUXIS	EXOMPHALUS
CYCLOHEXYL	DEXTRINIZE	LEXIGRAPHY	OROPHARYNX	EXOSPHERIC
OXYCEPHALY	DISQUIXOTE	LIPOMYXOMA	ORTHOPRAXY	EXOTHECIUM
OXYGENIZER	DOXOGRAPHY	MYXOLIPOMA	OXYBROMIDE	EXOTHERMIC
	EPIPHARYNX	OXYCALCIUM	OXYBUTYRIA	EXPANDEDLY
29	HYPOPRAXIA	OXYCAPROIC	OXYHEMATIN	EXPANSIBLY
COMPLEXIFY	JUXTAPOSED	OXYCHLORID	OXYPHILOUS	EXPLICITLY
DEOXIDIZED	MYXOEDEMIC	OXYCYANIDE	OXYWELDING	EXTRICABLY
EXORCIZING	MYXOPODIUM	OXYSULPHID	PHOENIXITY	EXUBERANCY
EXZODIACAL	NEPHROPEXY	PAROXYSMIC	PHYLLOXERA	HETERODOXY
HEXAHYDRIC	NOMOPHYLAX	PNEUMOPEXY	PHYTOTOXIN	HEXAEMERIC
MYXOMYCETE	ORCHIOPEXY	PREFIXEDLY	POLYMIXIID	HEXAGYNOUS
OXIDIZABLE	OXADIAZOLE	QUINATOXIN	PREFIXALLY	HEXAHEDRAL
OXYCAMPHOR	OXOZONIDES	QUINOXALIN	PYROXYLINE	HEXAHEDRON
OXYQUINONE	OXYCHLORIC	SPHINXLIKE	SNUFFBOXER	HEXAMERISM
PEROXIDIZE	OXYHYDRATE	VIXENSHIP	SUFFIXMENT	HEXAMETRIC
PHLEBOPEXY	OXYOPHITIC	XENOPHOBIC	SULFOXYLIC	HEXAPLARIC
QUADRUPLEX	PERIPHRAXY	XEROGRAPHY	THIXOTROPY	HYDROTAXIS
QUINOXALYL	PHYTOTOXIC	XIPHODYNIA	THYROTOXIC	INEXPIABLY
RHIZOTAXIS	QUADRATRIX	XYLOPHAGAN	TRIMETHOXY	LEXIPHANIC
XYLOGRAPHY	TRIHYDROXY		UNFLEXIBLY	MOXIEBERRY
ZOOXANTHIN	UNEQUIAXED	**25**	XIPHOPAGUS	MYXOMATOUS
	XEROMORPHY	APICIFIXED		NECTOCALYX
28	XEROPHYTIC	ASPHYXIANT	**24**	OMENTOPEXY
AXIOMATIZE	XIPHIIFORM	ASPHYXIATE	ANOXYSCOPE	ORTHODOXLY
DEOXIDIZER	XIPHOPAGIC	AXHAMMERED	AUXOCHROME	OXYBLEPSIA
DOXOLOGIZE	XIPHYDRIID	CHAETOTAXY	AXINOMANCY	OXYSULFIDE
HEXASTICHY	XYLOPHAGID	COXCOMBESS	CHALUMEAUX	PAROXYSMAL
INOXIDIZED	XYLOPHONIC	EXHIBITIVE	CHATTERBOX	PERMIXTIVE
KERFLUMMOX		EXHIBITORY	CHEMOTAXIS	PERPLEXITY
LEXICONIZE	**26**	EXHUMATORY	COLONOPEXY	PLEXIMETRY
PHYLLOTAXY	AMPHIMIXIS	EXPEDIENCY	CONNEXIVUM	PROTEOPEXY
PROJECTRIX	ASEXUALIZE	EXPRESSWAY	CRIOSPHINX	PROTOXYLEM

PROXICALLY
PYOSALPINX
SAXOPHONIC
SIMPLEXITY
SPLENOPEXY
SULPHOXISM
TOXIPHOBIA
TOXIPHORIC
UNCOMMIXED
WAXHEARTED
XANTHYDROL
XENOPHOBIA

23
AFFIXATION
APPENDIXED
APPROXIMAL
AXEBREAKER
BOBBYSOXER
COMMIXTION
COMMIXTURE
COMPLEXION
EPIPLOPEXY
EXACTINGLY
EXADVERSUM
EXCAVATING
EXCITINGLY
EXCULPABLE
EXCURVATED
EXEMPLARIC
EXEMPTIBLE
EXHALATORY
EXHAUSTIVE
EXHIBITING
EXHUMATING
EXOPHAGOUS
EXPECTABLE
EXPECTANCE
EXPEDITELY
EXPLICABLE
EXSUFFLATE
FLEXUOSITY
FLEXUOUSLY
FLUXIONARY
GASTROPEXY
HEXADECANE
HEXAPODIES
HEXASTYLOS
HEXAVALENT
LAXATIVELY
LEXICOLOGY
MAXIMISTIC
MEDITHORAX
METAGALAXY
MYDATOXINE
MYXANGITIS
MYXOGASTER
OXIDIMETRY
OXYRHINOUS
OXYURICIDE
PERMIXABLE
PHILODOXER
PICROTOXIC
PRAXIOLOGY
PYRIDOXINE
SUBMAXIMAL
SULPHOXIDE
TAXATIVELY
TOXALBUMIC
TOXICOLOGY
TOXIPHAGUS
XANTHAMIDE
XANTHODERM
XIPHOIDIAN

22
ADIPOPEXIA

ADIPOPEXIS
ADNEXOPEXY
AMBIDEXTER
AMINOXYLOL
APPENDIXES
AXONOMETRY
BIAXIALITY
BISEXUALLY
CACODOXIAN
CARNIFEXES
CHRONAXIES
COLLOXYLIN
CONVEXNESS
COXCOMICAL
COXOPODITE
DEXTROGYRE
DISULFOXID
DORSIFIXED
ENTOMOTAXY
EPEXEGETIC
EXANTHEMAS
EXCAVATION
EXCERPTING
EXCITATIVE
EXCITATORY
EXCLAIMING
EXCULPATED
EXCUSATIVE
EXCUSATORY
EXECRATIVE
EXECRATORY
EXHIBITANT
EXHIBITION
EXHUMATION
EXIMIOUSLY
EXOCARDIAC
EXOCHORION
EXOPODITIC
EXORCISORY
EXOTHECATE
EXOTHERMAL
EXOTICALLY
EXPEDIENCE
EXPENDABLE
EXPENSEFUL
EXPIRATORY
EXPISCATED
EXPLICATED
EXPLOITIVE
EXPLOSIVES
EXPOSITIVE
EXPOSITORY
EXPRESSIVE
EXPUGNABLE
EXSICCATED
EXSILIENCY
EXTENDEDLY
EXTINCTIVE
EXTRACTIVE
FOXBERRIES
HEXACOSANE
HEXACTINAL
HEXAEMERON
HEXAMEROUS
HEXAMETRAL
HEXPARTITE
HOLOPLEXIA
HOMOSEXUAL
INEXORABLY
INEXPECTED
INEXPERTLY
INFLEXIBLE
LEXICALITY
LOXODROMIC
LUXURIANCY
MAXILLIPED
MESOTHORAX

METATHORAX
MONOXYLOUS
OOPHORAUXE
OVEREXPOSE
OXAMETHANE
OXYGENATED
OXYMURIATE
OXYPROLINE
OXYSTEARIC
OXYTERPENE
OXYTONICAL
PARAXIALLY
PAROXYTONE
PERPLEXING
PHOTOTAXIS
PRAEHALLUX
PREAXIALLY
PREFIXTURE
PREFLEXION
PYROXENITE
REFLEXIBLE
TAXABILITY
TAXIDERMIC
THEOMASTIX
TOXIDERMIC
TRICHAUXIS
TRIPLEXITY
UNEXAMPLED
UNEXPECTED
UNEXPERTLY
UNFLEXIBLE
VINCETOXIN
WAXBERRIES
XANTHOCONE
XANTHOMATA
XANTHOPSIA
XANTHOPSIN
XIPHOSURAN
XYLANTHRAX
XYLOPOLIST
XYLORCINOL
XYLOSTROMA
XYLOTOMIST
XYLOTOMOUS

21
ACAROTOXIC
ACCUSATRIX
AMAXOMANIA
AMBOSEXOUS
ANTEFLEXED
ANTICLIMAX
ANTIOXYGEN
ATAXINOMIC
ATAXONOMIC
AUXANOLOGY
AXILEMMATA
BOXBERRIES
CACOXENITE
CICATRIXES
CONTRAPLEX
COXOCERITE
DEXTRALITY
DEXTROUSLY
DIASTATAXY
ENDOTHORAX
EXACERBATE
EXAMINABLE
EXCALCEATE
EXCECATION
EXCELLENCE
EXCEPTIOUS
EXCERPTION
EXCITEMENT
EXECUTABLE
EXFOLIATED
EXHAUSTING

EXIGUOUSLY
EXOCENTRIC
EXORCISMAL
EXORCISTIC
EXOSPORIUM
EXOTROPISM
EXPANSIBLE
EXPEDITING
EXPELLABLE
EXPERIENCE
EXPERIMENT
EXPISCATOR
EXPLICATOR
EXPLOSIBLE
EXPORTABLE
EXPOUNDING
EXPRESSMAN
EXPUNCTION
EXPURGATED
EXSCINDING
EXSICCATAE
EXTEMPORAL
EXTINGUISH
EXTISPICES
EXTRICABLE
EXTROPICAL
EXTROSPECT
EXUBERANCE
EXULTINGLY
EXUMBRELLA
EXUVIATING
GLYOXALASE
GLYOXALINE
GOOGOLPLEX
HEXANDROUS
HEXANGULAR
HEXARADIAL
IMPERATRIX
INEXPIABLE
INEXPLICIT
INSPECTRIX
INSPEXIMUS
LEUCOTOXIC
LIXIVIATED
MALAXERMAN
MALAXERMEN
MAXIMATION
OPTOMENINX
ORTHODOXAL
OVERTAXING
OXALACETIC
OXYGENATOR
PARAPRAXIA
PARAPRAXES
PARAPRAXIS
PERMIXTION
PERMIXTURE
PEROXIDING
PICROTOXIN
PLEXIMETER
POSTEXILIC
PREMAXILLA
SAXOTROMBA
SEXAGENARY
SPECTATRIX
SUBMAXILLA
SUPRACOXAL
TOXALBUMIN
TRANSFIXED
UNEXPENDED
UNORTHODOX
XENOPODOID

20
ADOXACEOUS
ANTHOTAXIS
ANTISPADIX

ASEXUALITY
ATAXIAGRAM
AUXANOGRAM
AUXILIARLY
AUXOCARDIA
BORDEREAUX
DERMATAUXE
DETOXICANT
DETOXICATE
DEXIOTROPE
DEXTERICAL
DIETOTOXIC
DOXASTICON
EPEXEGESIS
ESONARTHEX
EUXANTHATE
EUXANTHONE
EXACTITUDE
EXALTATIVE
EXASPIDEAN
EXCUDERUNT
EXECRATING
EXEGETICAL
EXERCISING
EXHALATION
EXHAUSTION
EXHILARANT
EXHILARATE
EXIGENCIES
EXISTENTLY
EXOCARDIAL
EXOCULATED
EXOGASTRIC
EXOGENETIC
EXORCISING
EXPATIATED
EXPEDIENTE
EXPEDITATE
EXPEDITION
EXPENDITOR
EXPLAINING
EXPLOITAGE
EXPLOITING
EXPRESSAGE
EXPRESSING
EXPURGATOR
EXTENDIBLE
EXTERIORLY
EXTERNALLY
EXTIRPATED
EXTRACTING
EXTRANEITY
EXTRICATED
EXTROITIVE
EXTRORSELY
EXUBERATED
EXULTANTLY
EXUVIATION
FLUXIONIST
FRAXINELLA
HELIOTAXIS
HEXATRIOSE
INDICATRIX
INTERMIXED
LIXIVIATOR
OLEOTHORAX
OXALURAMID
OXALYLUREA
OXYNEURINE
OXYNITRATE
OXYTOLUENE
OXYTONESIS
OXYURIASIS
PARADOXIAL
PARADOXIST
PARADOXURE
PEROXIDASE

PLEXIGLASS
RADIOTOXIC
RELAXATIVE
RELAXATORY
SEXTUPLING
STEREOTAXY
SYNAXARION
SYNAXARIST
TAXIDERMAL
TEXTURALLY
TOXIFEROUS
TYROTOXINE
UNEXCITING
UROXANTHIN
UXORIALITY
UXORICIDAL
UXORIOUSLY
XANTHALINE
XANTHATION
XANTHIURIA
XENARTHRAL
XENOGAMOUS
XENOPELTID

19
ACROATAXIA
ALEXITERIC
ANEMOTAXIS
APLOTAXENE
AUXOACTION
BINOXALATE
BISSEXTILE
COEXISTENT
CONTEXTUAL
CONTEXTURE
DIGITOXOSE
DOXOLOGIES
EXAGGERATE
EXAMINATOR

EXASPERATE
EXCALATION
EXCITATION
EXECRATION
EXECUTIONS
EXECUTRESS
EXERCITANT
EXOCOLITIS
EXONARTHEX
EXORBITANT
EXORBITATE
EXOSPOROUS
EXOTERICAL
EXOTICNESS
EXOTOSPORE
EXPATIATER
EXPATIATOR
EXPATRIATE
EXPERTNESS
EXPILATION
EXPIRATION
EXPLANATOR
EXPLOITURE
EXPLORATOR
EXPOSITION
EXSIBILATE
EXSPUITION
EXTENSIBLE
EXTINCTEUR
EXTINCTION
EXTIRPATOR
EXTOLLMENT
EXTOOLITIC
EXTRACTION
EXTRADITED
EXTRADOSED
EXTRAMURAL
EXTRAPOLAR
EXTRATUBAL

EXTREMITAL
EXTUBATION
EXULCERATE
EXURBANITE
INEXORABLE
INTOXICANT
INTOXICATE
LACROIXITE
LACTOTOXIN
LEXICONIST
LIBERATRIX
LIPOXENOUS
LUXURIANCE
MALAXATION
MENOSTAXIS
MESOXALATE
MIXILINEAL
MONAXONIAL
MONOXENOUS
NEUROTOXIC
NOMINATRIX
OSCULATRIX
OXIDULATED
PERIAXONAL
PETROSILEX
PETROXOLIN
PLEIOTAXIS
PLURIAXIAL
PREEXILIAN
PROLIXNESS
SAXICOLINE
SAXICOLOUS
SEPARATRIX
SEXDIGITAL
SEXPARTITE
SEXTIPOLAR
SEXUPAROUS
SITOTOXISM
SPINTURNIX

SUBAXILLAR
SUPEREXIST
TAXONOMIST
TEXTUALISM
TOXANAEMIA
TOXICATION
TOXICITIES
TOXINAEMIA
TRISECTRIX
UNDERSEXED
XENOBIOSIS
XENOPTERAN

18
ALEXANDERS
ARSENOXIDE
AXIOLOGIST
DESOXALATE
DEXTRAURAL
DEXTRINASE
DEXTRINATE
DEXTRINOUS
DEXTRORSAL
ERGOTOXINE
EXAUGURATE
EXINGUINAL
EXONERATED
EXSANGUINE
EXTENUATED
EXTOGENOUS
EXTRADOTAL
EXUNDATION
GENERATRIX
GERONTOXON
LUXURIATED
SAXIGENOUS
SEXANGULAR
SEXOLOGIST
UNIDEXTRAL

XENOGENOUS
XENOSAURID

17
ALLOXANATE
ALLOXANTIN
ANNEXATION
ANTITOXINE
AUXILIATOR
AXILLARIES
EXALTATION
EXENTERATE
EXONERATOR
EXONERETUR
EXORNATION
EXTENUATOR
EXTRANEOUS
EXTRASOLAR
EXULTATION
INEXERTION
INEXISTENT
INTERAXIAL
INTOXATION
LIENOTOXIN
NEURATAXIA
NEUROTOXIA
NEUROTOXIN
RELAXATION
SEXTENNIAL
SEXTILLION
SOIXANTINE
TAXATIONAL
TEXTUALIST
TEXTUARIES
TEXTUARIST
TRIAXONIAN
TROUSSEAUX
TRUXILLINE

ALPHABETICAL LIST OF WORDS OVER 10 LETTERS

ACROASPHYXIA
ACTINOPRAXIS
ADENOMYXOMA
ADMAXILLARY
ADOXOGRAPHY
ALEXANDRITE
ALEXIPHARMIC
ALEXIPYRETIC
AMBIDEXTERITY
AMBIDEXTRAL
AMBIDEXTROUS
AMIDOHEXOSE
AMPLEXATION
AMPLEXICAUL
AMYLODEXTRIN
ANAPHYLAXIS
ANDROSPHINX
ANGIOATAXIA
ANGIORRHEXIS
ANHYDROXIME
ANILIDOXIME
ANISALDOXIME
ANNEXATIONAL
ANNEXATIONIST
ANNEXIONIST
ANOXIDATIVE
ANOXYBIOSIS

ANOXYBIOTIC
ANTEFLEXION
ANTHEXIMETER
ANTHOXANTHIN
ANTHRAXOLITE
ANTHRAXYLON
ANTHROXANIC
ANTIOXIDANT
ANTIOXYGENIC
ANXIOUSNESS
AORTOMALAXIS
APHOTOTAXIS
APOPHYLAXIS
APOPLEXIOUS
APPENDIXING
APPROXIMATE
APPROXIMATED
APPROXIMATELY
APPROXIMATING
APPROXIMATION
APPROXIMATIVE
APPROXIMATOR
ARCHEOPTERYX
ARCHOSYRINX
ARTHROSYRINX
ASEXUALIZED
ASEXUALIZING

ASPHYXIATED
ASPHYXIATING
ASPHYXIATION
ASPHYXIATOR
ATAXAPHASIA
ATAXIAGRAPH
ATAXIAMETER
ATAXIAPHASIA
ATAXOPHEMIA
ATLANTOAXIAL
ATLOIDOAXOID
AUTOCRATRIX
AUTOTOXAEMIA
AUTOTOXEMIA
AUTOXIDATION
AUTOXIDATOR
AUXANOMETER
AUXETICALLY
AUXILIARIES
AUXILIATION
AUXILIATORY
AUXOAMYLASE
AUXOCHROMIC
AUXOCHROMISM
AUXOCHROMOUS
AUXOGRAPHIC
AUXOHORMONE

AXIOLOGICAL
AXIOMATICAL
AXISYMMETRIC
AXODENDRITE
AXONOLIPOUS
AXONOMETRIC
AXONOPHOROUS
AXOSPERMOUS
BACTERIOTOXIC
BANDBOXICAL
BENZALDOXIME
BIMAXILLARY
BISAXILLARY
BISEXUALISM
BISEXUALITY
CARBETHOXYL
CARBOLXYLOL
CARBOXYLASE
CARBOXYLATE
CARBOXYLATED
CARDIATAXIA
CARDIOTOXIC
CHALCEDONYX
CHARTOPHYLAX
CHEMIOTAXIC
CHEMIOTAXIS
CHEMOREFLEX

CHIROPRAXIS
CHYLOTHORAX
CIRCUMAXIAL
CIRCUMAXILE
CLITORIDAUXE
COEXISTENCE
COEXISTENCY
COEXTENSION
COEXTENSIVE
COLOPEXOTOMY
COLPORRHEXIS
COMPETITRIX
COMPLEXIONAL
COMPLEXIONARY
COMPLEXIONED
COMPLEXITIES
COMPLEXNESS
CONFLUXIBLE
CONNEXITIES
CONSOLATRIX
CONTEXTUALLY
CONTEXTURAL
CONTEXTURED
CONVEXEDNESS
CONVEXITIES
COSTOXIPHOID
COXARTHRITIS

COXCOMBICAL
COXOCERITIC
COXOFEMORAL
CREATOTOXISM
CRUCIFIXION
CYCLOHEXANE
CYCLOHEXANOL
CYCLOHEXENE
CYSTOMYXOMA
CYSTOSYRINX
CYTOPHARYNX
DECIMOSEXTO
DEOXIDIZING
DEOXYGENATE
DEOXYGENATED
DEOXYGENIZE
DESEXUALIZE
DESEXUALIZED
DETOXICATED
DETOXICATING
DETOXICATION
DETOXICATOR
DEXIOTROPIC
DEXIOTROPISM
DEXIOTROPOUS
DEXTEROUSLY
DEXTROCARDIA
DEXTROCULAR
DEXTROGYRATE
DEXTROSAZONE
DEXTROSURIA
DEXTROUSNESS
DIASTATAXIC
DICARBOXYLIC
DICATALEXIS
DIHEXAHEDRAL
DIHEXAHEDRON
DIRECTRIXES
DISOXYGENATE
DISPENSATRIX
DISULPHOXID
DISULPHOXIDE
DOPAOXIDASE
DORSIFLEXION
DORSIFLEXOR
DOXOGRAPHER
DOXOLOGICAL
DOXOLOGIZED
DOXOLOGIZING
DYSOXIDATION
ELECTROTAXIS
ENTEROPEXIA
ENTEROTOXEMIA
EPEXEGETICAL
ESOTHYROPEXY
EXACERBATED
EXACERBATING
EXACERBATION
EXACTINGNESS
EXACTIVENESS
EXAGGERATED
EXAGGERATING
EXAGGERATION
EXAGGERATIVE
EXAGGERATOR
EXAGGERATORY
EXALBUMINOSE
EXALBUMINOUS
EXALLOTRIOTE
EXALTEDNESS
EXAMINATION
EXAMINATIONAL
EXAMINATIVE
EXAMINATORY
EXANIMATION
EXANTHEMATIC
EXANTLATION

EXARTERITIS
EXARTICULATE
EXASPERATED
EXASPERATING
EXASPERATION
EXASPERATER
EXASPERATIVE
EXAUCTORATE
EXAUGURATION
EXAUTHORIZE
EXCALCARATE
EXCANDESCENT
EXCANTATION
EXCARNATION
EXCATHEDRAL
EXCAVATIONS
EXCEEDINGLY
EXCELLENCIES
EXCELLENTLY
EXCEPTIONAL
EXCEPTIONALLY
EXCEPTIONARY
EXCEPTIONER
EXCEPTIVELY
EXCERPTIBLE
EXCESSIVELY
EXCESSIVENESS
EXCHANGEABLE
EXCHANGEABLY
EXCIPULIFORM
EXCITABILITY
EXCITABLENESS
EXCITEDNESS
EXCITOMOTOR
EXCITOMOTORY
EXCLAMATION
EXCLAMATIONAL
EXCLAMATIVE
EXCLAMATIVELY
EXCLAMATORILY
EXCLAMATORY
EXCLUSIONARY
EXCLUSIONER
EXCLUSIONISM
EXCLUSIONIST
EXCLUSIVELY
EXCLUSIVENESS
EXCLUSIVISM
EXCLUSIVITY
EXCOGITABLE
EXCOGITATED
EXCOGITATING
EXCOGITATION
EXCOGITATIVE
EXCOGITATOR
EXCOMMUNICANT
EXCOMMUNICATE
EXCOMMUNION
EXCONJUGANT
EXCORIATING
EXCORIATION
EXCORTICATE
EXCORTICATED
EXCORTICATING
EXCORTICATION
EXCREMENTAL
EXCREMENTARY
EXCREMENTIVE
EXCRESCENCE
EXCRESCENCES
EXCRESCENCIES
EXCRESCENCY
EXCRESCENTIAL
EXCRETIONARY
EXCRIMINATE
EXCRUCIABLE
EXCRUCIATED

EXCRUCIATING
EXCRUCIATION
EXCRUCIATOR
EXCULPATING
EXCULPATION
EXCULPATIVE
EXCULPATORY
EXCURSIONAL
EXCURSIONARY
EXCURSIONER
EXCURSIONISM
EXCURSIONIST
EXCURSIONIZE
EXCURSIVELY
EXCURVATURE
EXCUSABILITY
EXCUSABLENESS
EXCYSTATION
EXECRABLENESS
EXECUTIONAL
EXECUTIONER
EXECUTIVELY
EXECUTIVENESS
EXECUTORIAL
EXECUTRICES
EXECUTRIXES
EXEGETICALLY
EXEMPLARILY
EXEMPLARINESS
EXEMPLARISM
EXEMPLARITY
EXEMPLIFIED
EXEMPLIFIER
EXEMPLIFYING
EXENCEPHALIA
EXENCEPHALIC
EXENCEPHALUS
EXENTERATED
EXENTERATING
EXENTERATION
EXERCISABLE
EXERCITATION
EXERCITORIAL
EXFIGURATION
EXFILTRATION
EXFLAGELLATE
EXFODIATION
EXFOLIATING
EXFOLIATION
EXFOLIATIVE
EXFOLIATORY
EXHAUSTEDLY
EXHAUSTEDNESS
EXHAUSTIBLE
EXHAUSTINGLY
EXHAUSTIVELY
EXHAUSTLESS
EXHAUSTLESSLY
EXHIBITIONAL
EXHIBITIONER
EXHIBITIONISM
EXHIBITIONIST
EXHIBITIVELY
EXHIBITORSHIP
EXHILARATED
EXHILARATING
EXHILARATION
EXHILARATIVE
EXHILARATOR
EXHILARATORY
EXHORTATIVE
EXHORTATIVELY
EXHORTATORY
EXIGUOUSNESS
EXILARCHATE
EXIMIOUSNESS
EXINANITION

EXISTENTIAL
EXISTENTIALLY
EXISTLESSNESS
EXOARTERITIS
EXOCCIPITAL
EXOCULATING
EXOGASTRITIS
EXOGENOUSLY
EXOGNATHION
EXOGNATHITE
EXOMETRITIS
EXOMOLOGESIS
EXOMORPHISM
EXOMPHALOUS
EXONERATING
EXONERATION
EXONERATIVE
EXOPERIDIUM
EXOPHTHALMIA
EXOPHTHALMIC
EXOPHTHALMOS
EXOPHTHALMUS
EXORABILITY
EXORABLENESS
EXORBITANCE
EXORBITANCY
EXORBITANTLY
EXORBITATION
EXORCISATION
EXORCISEMENT
EXORCISTICAL
EXORCIZATION
EXORCIZEMENT
EXOSKELETAL
EXOSKELETON
EXOSTRACISM
EXOSTRACIZE
EXOTERICALLY
EXOTERICISM
EXOTHERMOUS
EXOTICALNESS
EXPANDEDNESS
EXPANDINGLY
EXPANSIBILITY
EXPANSIONAL
EXPANSIONISM
EXPANSIONIST
EXPANSIVELY
EXPANSIVENESS
EXPANSIVITY
EXPATIATING
EXPATIATION
EXPATIATIVE
EXPATIATORY
EXPATRIATED
EXPATRIATING
EXPATRIATION
EXPECTANCIES
EXPECTANTLY
EXPECTATION
EXPECTATIVE
EXPECTORANT
EXPECTORATE
EXPECTORATED
EXPECTORATING
EXPECTORATION
EXPECTORATOR
EXPEDIENCIES
EXPEDIENTIAL
EXPEDIENTIST
EXPEDIENTLY
EXPEDITATED
EXPEDITATING
EXPEDITATION
EXPEDITENESS
EXPEDITIONARY
EXPEDITIONIST

EXPEDITIOUS
EXPEDITIOUSLY
EXPENDABILITY
EXPENDITRIX
EXPENDITURE
EXPENSILATION
EXPENSIVELY
EXPENSIVENESS
EXPENTHESIS
EXPERIENCED
EXPERIENCER
EXPERIENCES
EXPERIENCING
EXPERIENTIAL
EXPERIMENTAL
EXPERIMENTED
EXPERIMENTEE
EXPERIMENTER
EXPERIMENTING
EXPERIMENTIST
EXPERIMENTIZE
EXPERMENTIZED
EXPERIMENTLY
EXPIATIONAL
EXPIATORINESS
EXPISCATING
EXPISCATION
EXPISCATORY
EXPLAINABLE
EXPLANATION
EXPLANATIVE
EXPLANATIVELY
EXPLANATORILY
EXPLANATORY
EXPLANTATION
EXPLEMENTAL
EXPLETIVELY
EXPLETIVENESS
EXPLICATING
EXPLICATION
EXPLICATIVE
EXPLICATORY
EXPLICITNESS
EXPLOITABLE
EXPLOITATION
EXPLOITATIVE
EXPLORATION
EXPLORATIONAL
EXPLORATIVE
EXPLORATIVELY
EXPLORATORY
EXPLOREMENT
EXPLOSIBILITY
EXPLOSIONIST
EXPLOSIVELY
EXPLOSIVENESS
EXPONENTIAL
EXPONENTIALLY
EXPORTABILITY
EXPORTATION
EXPOSITIONAL
EXPOSITIONARY
EXPOSITIVELY
EXPOSITORIAL
EXPOSITORILY
EXPOSTULATE
EXPOSTULATED
EXPOSTULATING
EXPOSTULATION
EXPOSTULATIVE
EXPOSTULATOR
EXPOSTULATORY
EXPRESSIBLE
EXPRESSION
EXPRESSIONAL
EXPRESSIONISM
EXPRESSIONIST

EXPRESSIVELY	EXTERRANEOUS	EXTROSPECTION	INEXPLICABLY	MICROTHORAX
EXPRESSLESS	EXTERRESTRIAL	EXTROSPECTIVE	INEXPLICITLY	MIXOBARBARIC
EXPROBRATORY	EXTERRITORIAL	EXTROVERSION	INEXPRESSIBLE	MIXOTROPHIC
EXPROMISSION	EXTINGUISHED	EXTROVERSIVE	INEXPRESSIVE	MIXTILINEAR
EXPROPRIATE	EXTINGUISHER	EXTUMESCENCE	INEXTENSIVE	MONILETHRIX
EXPROPRIATED	EXTIRPATING	EXUBERANTLY	INEXTIRPABLE	MORPHALLAXIS
EXPROPRIATING	EXTIRPATION	EXUBERANTNESS	INEXTRICABLE	MYELAPOPLEXY
EXPROPRIATION	EXTIRPATIVE	EXUBERATING	INEXTRICABLY	MYELOPLAXES
EXPROPRIATOR	EXTIRPATORY	EXUBERATION	INFLEXIBILITY	MYTILOTOXINE
EXPULSATORY	EXTISPICIOUS	EXULCERATED	INFLUXIONISM	MYXADENITIS
EXPURGATING	EXTOLLATION	EXULCERATING	INNOXIOUSLY	MYXASTHENIA
EXPURGATION	EXTORSIVELY	EXULCERATION	INOBNOXIOUS	MYXEDEMATOUS
EXPURGATIVE	EXTORTIONARY	EXULCERATIVE	INOXIDIZING	MYXOBLASTOMA
EXPURGATORIAL	EXTORTIONATE	EXULCERATORY	INTERMIXEDLY	MYXOCYSTOMA
EXPURGATORY	EXTORTIONER	EXUMBRELLAR	INTERMIXING	MYXOFIBROMA
EXQUISITELY	EXTORTIONIST	EXUVIABILITY	INTERMIXTLY	MYXOMATOSIS
EXQUISITENESS	EXTRABULBAR	FIBROMYXOMA	INTERMIXTURE	MYXOMYCETOUS
EXQUISITISM	EXTRACAPSULAR	FLEXANIMOUS	INTERSEXUAL	MYXONEUROMA
EXQUISITIVELY	EXTRACARPAL	FLEXIBILITY	INTERTEXTURE	MYXOSARCOMA
EXSANGUINATE	EXTRACOSTAL	FLEXIBLENESS	INTERXYLARY	MYXOSPOROUS
EXSANGUINOUS	EXTRACTABLE	FLEXUOSITIES	INTOXICABLE	NASOPHARYNX
EXSANGUIOUS	EXTRACTIBLE	FLEXUOUSNESS	INTOXICATED	NEGOTIATRIX
EXSCRIPTURAL	EXTRACTIFORM	FLUXIBILITY	INTOXICATING	NEOORTHODOXY
EXSCULPTATE	EXTRACYSTIC	FLUXIBLENESS	INTOXICATION	NEPHROTOXIC
EXSCUTELLATE	EXTRADITABLE	FLUXIONALLY	INTOXICATIVE	NEPHROTOXIN
EXSICCATING	EXTRADITING	FORMALDOXIME	INTOXICATOR	NEUROPLEXUS
EXSICCATION	EXTRADITION	FORNICATRIX	INTRAXYLARY	NONEXISTENCE
EXSICCATIVE	EXTRADUCTION	FRICANDEAUX	INTROFLEXION	NONEXISTENT
EXSTIPULATE	EXTRAENTERIC	FUCOXANTHIN	IRREFLEXIVE	NOXIOUSNESS
EXSUFFLATION	EXTRAFORMAL	GALVANOTAXIS	JUXTAMARINE	OBJURGATRIX
EXSUFFLICATE	EXTRAGALACTIC	GASTROTAXIS	JUXTAPOSING	OBNOXIOUSLY
EXTEMPORALLY	EXTRAJUDICIAL	GASTROXYNSIS	JUXTAPOSITION	OBNOXIOUSNESS
EXTEMPORARY	EXTRALATERAL	GENUFLEXION	JUXTAPYLORIC	ODONTEXESIS
EXTEMPORARILY	EXTRAMUNDANE	GENUFLEXUOUS	JUXTASPINAL	ODONTOLOXIA
EXTEMPORIZE	EXTRAMURALLY	GITOXIGENIN	KARYORRHEXIS	OOPHOROPEXY
EXTEMPORIZED	EXTRANEOUSLY	GRIPPOTOXIN	KERATONYXIS	ORCHIDOPEXY
EXTEMPORIZER	EXTRAORDINARY	GUBERNATRIX	LAURINOXYLON	OROPHARYNXES
EXTEMPORIZING	EXTRAPHYSICAL	HETERODOXIES	LAXATIVENESS	ORTHODOXALLY
EXTENDEDNESS	EXTRAPOLATE	HETEROSEXUAL	LAXIFLOROUS	ORTHODOXIAN
EXTENDIBILITY	EXTRAPOLATED	HETEROTAXIA	LAXIFOLIATE	ORTHODOXICAL
EXTENSIBILITY	EXTRAPOLATING	HETEROTAXIC	LAXIFOLIOUS	ORTHODOXIES
EXTENSIMETER	EXTRAPOLATION	HETEROTAXIS	LEGISLATRIX	ORTHODOXISM
EXTENSIONAL	EXTRAPOLATIVE	HETEROXENOUS	LEXICOGRAPHY	ORTHODOXIST
EXTENSIONIST	EXTRAPOLATOR	HEXABROMIDE	LEXICOLOGIC	ORTHODOXNESS
EXTENSIVELY	EXTRAREGULAR	HEXAGONALLY	LEXICOLOGICAL	OSCULATRIXES
EXTENSIVENESS	EXTRARETINAL	HEXASTICHIC	LEXICOLOGIST	OSTEOSTIXIS
EXTENSOMETER	EXTRASENSORY	HEXOBARBITAL	LEXIGRAPHIC	OVEREXPOSED
EXTENUATING	EXTRASEROUS	HOMOSEXUALITY	LEXIGRAPHICAL	OVEREXPOSING
EXTENUATINGLY	EXTRASYSTOLE	HYDROEXTRACT	LIFERENTRIX	OVEREXPOSURE
EXTENUATION	EXTRATARSAL	HYDROTHORAX	LITHANTHRAX	OVERTAXATION
EXTENUATIVE	EXTRATRIBAL	HYPOPHARYNX	LITHOLAPAXY	OXALURAMIDE
EXTENUATORY	EXTRAUTERINE	HYPOTOXICITY	LITHOXYLITE	OXIDABILITY
EXTERIORATE	EXTRAVAGANCE	HYPOXANTHINE	LIXIVIATING	OXIDATIONAL
EXTERIORATION	EXTRAVAGANCY	ICHTHYOTOXIN	LIXIVIATION	OXIDIMETRIC
EXTERIORITY	EXTRAVAGANT	IDEOPRAXIST	LOXODOGRAPH	OXYACANTHIN
EXTERIORIZE	EXTRAVAGANTLY	IMMUNOTOXIN	LOXODROMICS	OXYACANTHINE
EXTERIORIZED	EXTRAVAGANZA	IMPROPRIATRIX	LOXODROMISM	OXYACANTHOUS
EXTERIORIZING	EXTRAVAGATE	INDEXICALLY	LUXULLIANITE	OXYACETYLENE
EXTERIORNESS	EXTRAVAGATED	INDEXTERITY	LUXURIANTLY	OXYALDEHYDE
EXTERMINATE	EXTRAVAGATING	INEXACTITUDE	LUXURIANTNESS	OXYBERBERINE
EXTERMINATED	EXTRAVAGATION	INEXACTNESS	LUXURIATING	OXYCARBONATE
EXTERMINATING	EXTRAVAGINAL	INEXCUSABLE	LUXURIATION	OXYCELLULOSE
EXTERMINATION	EXTRAVASATE	INEXCUSABLY	LUXURIOUSLY	OXYCEPHALIC
EXTERMINATIVE	EXTRAVASATED	INEXECUTION	LUXURIOUSNESS	OXYCEPHALISM
EXTERMINATOR	EXTRAVASATING	INEXHAUSTIBLE	LYMPHOTOXIN	OXYCEPHALOUS
EXTERMINATORY	EXTRAVASATION	INEXHAUSTIVE	MAXILLARIES	OXYCHLORATE
EXTERNALISM	EXTRAVASCULAR	INEXISTENCE	MAXILLIFORM	OXYCHLORIDE
EXTERNALIST	EXTRAVERSION	INEXISTENCY	MAXILLIPEDARY	OXYCHLORINE
EXTERNALISTIC	EXTRAVIOLET	INEXPECTEDLY	MAXILLIPEDE	OXYCHROMATIC
EXTERNALITIES	EXTREMENESS	INEXPEDIENCY	MAXILLOJUGAL	OXYCHROMATIN
EXTERNALITY	EXTREMISTIC	INEXPEDIENT	MAXILLOLABIAL	OXYCINNAMIC
EXTERNALIZE	EXTREMITIES	INEXPENSIVE	MAXIMIZATION	OXYCOPAIVIC
EXTERNATION	EXTRICATING	INEXPERIENCE	MERVEILLEUX	OXYCOUMARIN
EXTERNIZATION	EXTRICATION	INEXPERIENCED	MESOAPPENDIX	OXYESTHESIA
EXTEROCEPTIST	EXTRINSICAL	INEXPERTNESS	MESOSALPINX	OXYGENATING
EXTEROCEPTIVE	EXTRINSICALLY	INEXPLICABLE	METAGALAXIES	OXYGENERATOR
EXTEROCEPTOR	EXTRINSICATE	INEXPLICABLES	METAVAUXITE	OXYGENICITY

OXYGENIZABLE	POSTFLEXION	SESQUISEXTAL	THERMOTAXIC	UNORTHODOXY
OXYGENIZING	PRAEMAXILLA	SEXADECIMAL	THERMOTAXIS	URECHITOXIN
OXYGNATHOUS	PRAETAXATION	SEXAGENARIAN	THIGMOTAXIS	UROTOXICITY
OXYHAEMATIN	PRAXINOSCOPE	SEXAGESIMAL	THIXOLABILE	VASOREFLEX
OXYHEXACTINE	PREEXISTENCE	SEXANGULARLY	THIXOTROPIC	VEXATIOUSLY
OXYHEXASTER	PREEXISTENT	SEXCENTENARY	THOROUGHWAX	VEXILLARIOUS
OXYHYDROGEN	PREFIXATION	SEXDIGITATE	TOXALBUMOSE	VEXILLATION
OXYLUCIFERIN	PREMAXILLARY	SEXDIGITATED	TOXICOGENIC	WAXCHANDLER
OXYMETHYLENE	PRETEXTUOUS	SEXDIGITISM	TOXICOGNATH	WAXCHANDLERY
OXYMURIATIC	PROCATARXIS	SEXISYLLABLE	TOXICOLOGIC	XANTHELASMA
OXYOSPHRESIA	PROCURATRIX	SEXLESSNESS	TOXICOLOGIST	XANTHINURIA
OXYPETALOUS	PROGENITRIX	SEXOLOGICAL	TOXICOMANIA	XANTHOCHROIA
OXYPHOSPHATE	PROLOCUTRIX	SEXPLOITATION	TOXICOPATHIC	XANTHOCHROID
OXYPHTHALIC	PROPHYLAXIS	SEXTILLIONTH	TOXICOPATHY	XANTHOCONITE
OXYPHYLLOUS	PROTEOPEXIC	SEXTIPARTITE	TOXICOPHAGY	XANTHODERMA
OXYPROPIONIC	PROTEOPEXIS	SEXTUPLICATE	TOXICOPHIDIA	XANTHOGENATE
OXYQUINOLINE	PROTHORAXES	SEXTUPLICATED	TOXINFECTION	XANTHOGENIC
OXYRHYNCHID	PROTOXIDIZE	SHIKIMOTOXIN	TOXIPHOBIAC	XANTHOMATOUS
OXYRHYNCHOUS	PROTOXIDIZED	SIPHONOPLAX	TOXITABELLAE	XANTHOMETER
OXYRRHYNCHID	PROXENETISM	SPASMOTOXIN	TOXOGENESIS	XANTHOPHANE
OXYSALICYLIC	PROXIMATELY	SPASMOTOXINE	TOXOGLOSSATE	XANTHOPHORE
OXYSTOMATOUS	PROXIMATION	SPECULATRIX	TOXOPHILISM	XANTHOPHYLL
OXYSULPHATE	PSEUDOCORTEX	SPERMOTOXIN	TOXOPHILITIC	XANTHOPTERIN
OXYSULPHIDE	PSEUDODOXAL	SPLENOPEXIA	TOXOPHILOUS	XANTHOXENITE
OXYTYLOTATE	PSYCHOREFLEX	SPLENOPEXIS	TRANSFIXING	XANTHOXYLIN
PACHYMENINX	PSYCHOSEXUAL	SPLENOTOXIN	TRANSFIXION	XENACANTHINE
PANSEXUALISM	PSYCHOTAXIS	STAURAXONIA	TRANSFIXTURE	XENARTHROUS
PANSEXUALIST	PTEROTHORAX	STAURAXONIAL	TRISULFOXID	XENODOCHIUM
PANSEXUALITY	PYOXANTHOSE	STENOTHORAX	TRISULPHOXID	XENOGENESIS
PANSEXUALIZE	PYROXMANGITE	STEREOMATRIX	TROPHALLAXIS	XENOMORPHIC
PARADOXICAL	PYRRHULOXIA	STEREOTAXIS	TROPHOTAXIS	XENOPARASITE
PARADOXICIAN	QUINATOXINE	STIMULATRIX	TROPHOTHYLAX	XENOSAUROID
PARADOXIDIAN	QUINCUNXIAL	STROPHOTAXIS	TYLOTOXEATE	XENYLAMINE
PARADOXOLOGY	QUINISEXTINE	SUBAXILLARY	TYPHOTOXINE	XEROGRAPHER
PARAVAUXITE	QUINOXALINE	SUBLUXATION	TYROTOXICON	XEROGRAPHIC
PAROXYSMALLY	RADIOPRAXIS	SUBMAXILLAE	ULTRACOMPLEX	XEROMORPHIC
PAROXYTONIC	REFLEXIONAL	SUBMAXILLARY	ULTRAMAXIMAL	XEROMORPHOUS
PAXILLIFORM	REFLEXIVELY	SUBOXIDATION	UNDEREXPOSE	XEROPHILOUS
PEPTOTOXINE	REFLEXIVITY	SUBSEXTUPLE	UNDEREXPOSED	XEROPHOBOUS
PERIAXILLARY	REFLEXOLOGY	SUFFIXATION	UNDEREXPOSING	XEROPHYTISM
PERICOXITIS	RELAXEDNESS	SULFOXYLATE	UNEXACTNESS	XEROTRIPSIS
PERPLEXEDLY	RETROFLEXED	SULPHOXYLIC	UNEXCEPTIVE	XIPHISTERNAL
PERPLEXINGLY	RETROFLEXION	SUPERFLEXION	UNEXCLUSIVE	XIPHISTERNUM
PERPLEXITIES	RETROXIPHOID	SUPERMAXILLA	UNEXCUSABLE	XIPHOCOSTAL
PHENOXAZINE	RHAMNOHEXOSE	SUPERSEXUAL	UNEXCUSABLY	XIPHOPAGOUS
PHILODOXICAL	RHAMNOHEXITE	SUPRAMAXILLA	UNEXPECTEDLY	XIPHOSUROUS
PHLEBORRHEXIS	RHINOPHARYNX	SUPRAMAXIMAL	UNEXPEDIENT	XYLOCARPOUS
PHOTOSYNTAX	RHYOTAXITIC	TAXABLENESS	UNEXPENSIVE	XYLOGRAPHER
PHYLLOTAXIS	SACROCOCCYX	TAXASPIDEAN	UNEXPERIENCE	XYLOGRAPHIC
PHYLLOXERAN	SACROCOXITIS	TAXEOPODOUS	UNEXPERIENT	XYLOPHAGOUS
PHYLLOXERIC	SAXIFRAGANT	TAXGATHERER	UNEXPLAINED	XYLOPHILOUS
PILOTAXITIC	SAXIFRAGOUS	TAXGATHERING	UNEXPLICABLE	XYLOPHONIST
PLEXIMETRIC	SAXOPHONIST	TAXIDERMIST	UNEXPLOITED	XYLOPLASTIC
PNEUMONOPEX	SCAPULOPEXY	TAXIDERMIZE	UNEXPRESSIVE	XYLOQUINONE
PNEUMOTHORAX	SCEUOPHYLAX	TAXIMETERED	UNEXPURGATED	XYLOSTROMATA
PNEUMOTOXIN	SCILLITOXIN	TAXONOMICAL	UNEXTRICABLE	XYRIDACEOUS
POLYHYDROXY	SCLERONYXIS	TETRAHYDROXY	UNISEXUALITY	ZANTHOXYLUM
POSTAXIALLY	SEMIFLEXIBLE	TETROXALATE	UNISEXUALLY	ZOOPRAXISCOPE
POSTEXILIAN	SEMISEXTILE	TEXTIFEROUS	UNORTHODOXLY	ZOOXANTHELLA
POSTEXISTENT				

POSITIONAL ORDER LIST OF WORDS OVER 10 LETTERS

XANTHELASMA	XANTHOPHORE	XENOSAUROID	XIPHISTERNUM	XYLOQUINONE
XANTHINURIA	XANTHOPHYLL	XENYLAMINE	XIPHOCOSTAL	XYLOSTROMATA
XANTHOCHROIA	XANTHOPTERIN	XEROGRAPHER	XIPHOPAGOUS	XYRIDACEOUS
XANTHOCHROID	XANTHOXENITE	XEROGRAPHIC	XIPHOSUROUS	
XANTHOCONITE	XANTHOXYLIN	XEROMORPHIC	XYLOCARPOUS	AXIOLOGICAL
XANTHODERMA	XENACANTHINE	XEROMORPHOUS	XYLOGRAPHER	AXIOMATICAL
XANTHOGENATE	XENARTHROUS	XEROPHILOUS	XYLOGRAPHIC	AXISYMMETRIC
XANTHOGENIC	XENODOCHIUM	XEROPHOBOUS	XYLOPHAGOUS	AXODENDRITE
XANTHOMATOUS	XENOGENESIS	XEROPHYTISM	XYLOPHILOUS	AXONOLIPOUS
XANTHOMETER	XENOMORPHIC	XEROTRIPSIS	XYLOPHONIST	AXONOMETRIC
XANTHOPHANE	XENOPARASITE	XIPHISTERNAL	XYLOPLASTIC	AXONOPHOROUS

AXOSPERMOUS	EXCOMMUNICANT	EXHAUSTIVELY	EXPATRIATING	EXPLOSIVENESS
EXACERBATED	EXCOMMUNICATE	EXHAUSTLESS	EXPATRIATION	EXPONENTIAL
EXACERBATING	EXCOMMUNION	EXHAUSTLESSLY	EXPECTANCIES	EXPONENTIALLY
EXACERBATION	EXCONJUGANT	EXHIBITIONAL	EXPECTANTLY	EXPORTABILITY
EXACTINGNESS	EXCORIATING	EXHIBITIONER	EXPECTATION	EXPORTATION
EXACTIVENESS	EXCORIATION	EXHIBITIONISM	EXPECTATIVE	EXPOSITIONAL
EXAGGERATED	EXCORTICATE	EXHIBITIONIST	EXPECTORANT	EXPOSITIONARY
EXAGGERATING	EXCORTICATED	EXHIBITIVELY	EXPECTORATE	EXPOSITIVELY
EXAGGERATION	EXCORTICATING	EXHIBITORSHIP	EXPECTORATED	EXPOSITORIAL
EXAGGERATIVE	EXCORTICATION	EXHILARATED	EXPECTORATING	EXPOSITORILY
EXAGGERATOR	EXCREMENTAL	EXHILARATING	EXPECTORATION	EXPOSTULATE
EXAGGERATORY	EXCREMENTARY	EXHILARATION	EXPECTORATOR	EXPOSTULATED
EXALBUMINOSE	EXCREMENTIVE	EXHILARATIVE	EXPEDIENCIES	EXPOSTULATING
EXALBUMINOUS	EXCRESCENCE	EXHILARATOR	EXPEDIENTIAL	EXPOSTULATION
EXALLOTRIOTE	EXCRESCENCES	EXHILARATORY	EXPEDIENTIST	EXPOSTULATIVE
EXALTEDNESS	EXCRESCENCIES	EXHORTATIVE	EXPEDIENTLY	EXPOSTULATOR
EXAMINATION	EXCRESCENCY	EXHORTATIVELY	EXPEDITATED	EXPOSTULATORY
EXAMINATIONAL	EXCRESCENTIAL	EXHORTATORY	EXPEDITATING	EXPRESSIBLE
EXAMINATIVE	EXCRETIONARY	EXIGUOUSNESS	EXPEDITATION	EXPRESSION
EXAMINATORY	EXCRIMINATE	EXILARCHATE	EXPEDITENESS	EXPRESSIONAL
EXANIMATION	EXCRUCIABLE	EXIMIOUSNESS	EXPEDITIONARY	EXPRESSIONISM
EXANTHEMATIC	EXCRUCIATED	EXINANITION	EXPEDITIONIST	EXPRESSIONIST
EXARTERITIS	EXCRUCIATING	EXISTENTIAL	EXPEDITIOUS	EXPRESSIVELY
EXARTICULATE	EXCRUCIATION	EXISTENTIALLY	EXPEDITIOUSLY	EXPRESSLESS
EXASPERATED	EXCRUCIATOR	EXISTLESSNESS	EXPENDABILITY	EXPROBRATORY
EXASPERATER	EXCULPATING	EXOARTERITIS	EXPENDITRIX	EXPROMISSION
EXASPERATING	EXCULPATION	EXOCCIPITAL	EXPENDITURE	EXPROPRIATE
EXASPERATION	EXCULPATIVE	EXOCULATING	EXPENSILATION	EXPROPRIATED
EXASPERATIVE	EXCULPATORY	EXOGASTRITIS	EXPENSIVELY	EXPROPRIATING
EXAUCTORATE	EXCURSIONAL	EXOGENOUSLY	EXPENSIVENESS	EXPROPRIATION
EXAUGURATION	EXCURSIONARY	EXOGNATHION	EXPENTHESIS	EXPROPRIATOR
EXAUTHORIZE	EXCURSIONER	EXOGNATHITE	EXPERIENCED	EXPULSATORY
EXCALCARATE	EXCURSIONISM	EXOMETRITIS	EXPERIENCER	EXPURGATING
EXCANDESCENT	EXCURSIONIST	EXOMOLOGESIS	EXPERIENCES	EXPURGATION
EXCANTATION	EXCURSIONIZE	EXOMORPHISM	EXPERIENCING	EXPURGATIVE
EXCARNATION	EXCURSIVELY	EXOMPHALOUS	EXPERIENTIAL	EXPURGATORIAL
EXCATHEDRAL	EXCURVATURE	EXONERATING	EXPERIMENTAL	EXPURGATORY
EXCAVATIONS	EXCUSABILITY	EXONERATION	EXPERIMENTED	EXQUISITELY
EXCEEDINGLY	EXCUSABLENESS	EXONERATIVE	EXPERIMENTEE	EXQUISITENESS
EXCELLENCIES	EXCYSTATION	EXOPERIDIUM	EXPERIMENTER	EXQUISITISM
EXCELLENTLY	EXECRABLENESS	EXOPHTHALMIA	EXPERIMENTING	EXQUISITIVELY
EXCEPTIONAL	EXECUTIONAL	EXOPHTHALMIC	EXPERIMENTIST	EXSANGUINATE
EXCEPTIONALLY	EXECUTIONER	EXOPHTHALMOS	EXPERIMENTIZE	EXSANGUINOUS
EXCEPTIONARY	EXECUTIVELY	EXOPHTHALMUS	EXPERMENTIZED	EXSANGUIOUS
EXCEPTIONER	EXECUTIVENESS	EXORABILITY	EXPERIMENTLY	EXSCRIPTURAL
EXCEPTIVELY	EXECUTORIAL	EXORABLENESS	EXPIATIONAL	EXSCULPTATE
EXCERPTIBLE	EXECUTRICES	EXORBITANCE	EXPIATORINESS	EXSCUTELLATE
EXCESSIVELY	EXECUTRIXES	EXORBITANCY	EXPISCATING	EXSICCATING
EXCESSIVENESS	EXEGETICALLY	EXORBITANTLY	EXPISCATION	EXSICCATION
EXCHANGEABLE	EXEMPLARILY	EXORBITATION	EXPISCATORY	EXSICCATIVE
EXCHANGEABLY	EXEMPLARINESS	EXORCISATION	EXPLAINABLE	EXSTIPULATE
EXCIPULIFORM	EXEMPLARISM	EXORCISEMENT	EXPLANATION	EXSUFFLATION
EXCITABILITY	EXEMPLARITY	EXORCISTICAL	EXPLANATIVE	EXSUFFLICATE
EXCITABLENESS	EXEMPLIFIED	EXORCIZATION	EXPLANATIVELY	EXTEMPORALLY
EXCITEDNESS	EXEMPLIFIER	EXORCIZEMENT	EXPLANATORILY	EXTEMPORARY
EXCITOMOTOR	EXEMPLIFYING	EXOSKELETAL	EXPLANATORY	EXTEMPORARILY
EXCITOMOTORY	EXENCEPHALIA	EXOSKELETON	EXPLANTATION	EXTEMPORIZE
EXCLAMATION	EXENCEPHALIC	EXOSTRACISM	EXPLEMENTAL	EXTEMPORIZED
EXCLAMATIONAL	EXENCEPHALUS	EXOSTRACIZE	EXPLETIVELY	EXTEMPORIZER
EXCLAMATIVE	EXENTERATED	EXOTERICALLY	EXPLETIVENESS	EXTEMPORIZING
EXCLAMATIVELY	EXENTERATING	EXOTERICISM	EXPLICATING	EXTENDEDNESS
EXCLAMATORILY	EXENTERATION	EXOTHERMOUS	EXPLICATION	EXTENDIBILITY
EXCLAMATORY	EXERCISABLE	EXOTICALNESS	EXPLICATIVE	EXTENSIBILITY
EXCLUSIONARY	EXERCITATION	EXPANDEDNESS	EXPLICATORY	EXTENSIMETER
EXCLUSIONER	EXERCITORIAL	EXPANDINGLY	EXPLICITNESS	EXTENSIONAL
EXCLUSIONISM	EXFIGURATION	EXPANSIBILITY	EXPLOITABLE	EXTENSIONIST
EXCLUSIONIST	EXFILTRATION	EXPANSIONAL	EXPLOITATION	EXTENSIVELY
EXCLUSIVELY	EXFLAGELLATE	EXPANSIONISM	EXPLOITATIVE	EXTENSIVENESS
EXCLUSIVENESS	EXFODIATION	EXPANSIONIST	EXPLORATION	EXTENSOMETER
EXCLUSIVISM	EXFOLIATING	EXPANSIVELY	EXPLORATIONAL	EXTENUATING
EXCLUSIVITY	EXFOLIATION	EXPANSIVENESS	EXPLORATIVE	EXTENUATINGLY
EXCOGITABLE	EXFOLIATIVE	EXPANSIVITY	EXPLORATIVELY	EXTENUATION
EXCOGITATED	EXFOLIATORY	EXPATIATING	EXPLORATORY	EXTENUATIVE
EXCOGITATING	EXHAUSTEDLY	EXPATIATION	EXPLOREMENT	EXTENUATORY
EXCOGITATION	EXHAUSTEDNESS	EXPATIATIVE	EXPLOSIBILITY	EXTERIORATE
EXCOGITATIVE	EXHAUSTIBLE	EXPATIATORY	EXPLOSIONIST	EXTERIORATION
EXCOGITATOR	EXHAUSTINGLY	EXPATRIATED	EXPLOSIVELY	EXTERIORITY

EXTERIORIZE
EXTERIORIZED
EXTERIORIZING
EXTERIORNESS
EXTERMINATE
EXTERMINATED
EXTERMINATING
EXTERMINATION
EXTERMINATIVE
EXTERMINATOR
EXTERMINATORY
EXTERNALISM
EXTERNALIST
EXTERNALISTIC
EXTERNALITIES
EXTERNALITY
EXTERNALIZE
EXTERNATION
EXTERNIZATION
EXTEROCEPTIST
EXTEROCEPTIVE
EXTEROCEPTOR
EXTERRANEOUS
EXTERRESTRIAL
EXTERRITORIAL
EXTINGUISHED
EXTINGUISHER
EXTIRPATING
EXTIRPATION
EXTIRPATIVE
EXTIRPATORY
EXTISPICIOUS
EXTOLLATION
EXTORSIVELY
EXTORTIONARY
EXTORTIONATE
EXTORTIONER
EXTORTIONIST
EXTRABULBAR
EXTRACAPSULAR
EXTRACARPAL
EXTRACOSTAL
EXTRACTABLE
EXTRACTIBLE
EXTRACTIFORM
EXTRACYSTIC
EXTRADITABLE
EXTRADITING
EXTRADITION
EXTRADUCTION
EXTRAENTERIC
EXTRAFORMAL
EXTRAGALACTIC
EXTRAJUDICIAL
EXTRALATERAL
EXTRAMUNDANE
EXTRAMURALLY
EXTRANEOUSLY
EXTRAORDINARY
EXTRAPHYSICAL
EXTRAPOLATE
EXTRAPOLATED
EXTRAPOLATING
EXTRAPOLATION
EXTRAPOLATIVE
EXTRAPOLATOR
EXTRAREGULAR
EXTRARETINAL
EXTRASENSORY
EXTRASEROUS
EXTRASYSTOLE
EXTRATARSAL
EXTRATRIBAL
EXTRAUTERINE
EXTRAVAGANCE
EXTRAVAGANCY
EXTRAVAGANT

EXTRAVAGANTLY
EXTRAVAGANZA
EXTRAVAGATE
EXTRAVAGATED
EXTRAVAGATING
EXTRAVAGATION
EXTRAVAGINAL
EXTRAVASATE
EXTRAVASATED
EXTRAVASATING
EXTRAVASATION
EXTRAVASCULAR
EXTRAVERSION
EXTRAVIOLET
EXTREMENESS
EXTREMISTIC
EXTREMITIES
EXTRICATING
EXTRICATION
EXTRINSICAL
EXTRINSICALLY
EXTRINSICATE
EXTROSPECTION
EXTROSPECTIVE
EXTROVERSION
EXTROVERSIVE
EXTUMESCENCE
EXUBERANTLY
EXUBERANTNESS
EXUBERATING
EXUBERATION
EXULCERATED
EXULCERATING
EXULCERATION
EXULCERATIVE
EXULCERATORY
EXUMBRELLAR
EXUVIABILITY
OXALURAMIDE
OXIDABILITY
OXIDATIONAL
OXIDIMETRIC
OXYACANTHIN
OXYACANTHINE
OXYACANTHOUS
OXYACETYLENE
OXYALDEHYDE
OXYBERBERINE
OXYCARBONATE
OXYCELLULOSE
OXYCEPHALIC
OXYCEPHALISM
OXYCEPHALOUS
OXYCHLORATE
OXYCHLORIDE
OXYCHLORINE
OXYCHROMATIC
OXYCHROMATIN
OXYCINNAMIC
OXYCOPAIVIC
OXYCOUMARIN
OXYESTHESIA
OXYGENATING
OXYGENERATOR
OXYGENICITY
OXYGENIZABLE
OXYGENIZING
OXYGNATHOUS
OXYHAEMATIN
OXYHEXACTINE
OXYHEXASTER
OXYHYDROGEN
OXYLUCIFERIN
OXYMETHYLENE
OXYMURIATIC
OXYOSPHRESIA
OXYPETALOUS

OXYPHOSPHATE
OXYPHTHALIC
OXYPHYLLOUS
OXYPROPIONIC
OXYQUINOLINE
OXYRHYNCHID
OXYRHYNCHOUS
OXYRRHYNCHID
OXYSALICYLIC
OXYSTOMATOUS
OXYSULPHATE
OXYSULPHIDE
OXYTYLOTATE

ANXIOUSNESS
AUXANOMETER
AUXETICALLY
AUXILIARIES
AUXILIATION
AUXILIATORY
AUXOAMYLASE
AUXOCHROMIC
AUXOCHROMISM
AUXOCHROMOUS
AUXOGRAPHIC
AUXOHORMONE
COXARTHRITIS
COXCOMBICAL
COXOCERITIC
COXOFEMORAL
DEXIOTROPIC
DEXIOTROPISM
DEXIOTROPOUS
DEXTEROUSLY
DEXTROCARDIA
DEXTROCULAR
DEXTROGYRATE
DEXTROSAZONE
DEXTROSURIA
DEXTROUSNESS
DOXOGRAPHER
DOXOLOGICAL
DOXOLOGIZED
DOXOLOGIZING
HEXABROMIDE
HEXAGONALLY
HEXASTICHIC
HEXOBARBITAL
JUXTAMARINE
JUXTAPOSING
JUXTAPOSITION
JUXTAPYLORIC
JUXTASPINAL
LAXATIVENESS
LAXIFLOROUS
LAXIFOLIATE
LAXIFOLIOUS
LEXICOGRAPHY
LEXICOLOGIC
LEXICOLOGICAL
LEXICOLOGIST
LEXIGRAPHIC
LEXIGRAPHICAL
LIXIVIATING
LIXIVIATION
LOXODOGRAPH
LOXODROMICS
LOXODROMISM
LUXULLIANITE
LUXURIANTLY
LUXURIANTNESS
LUXURIATING
LUXURIATION
LUXURIOUSLY
LUXURIOUSNESS
MAXILLARIES
MAXILLIFORM

MAXILLIPEDARY
MAXILLIPEDE
MAXILLOJUGAL
MAXILLOLABIAL
MAXIMIZATION
MIXOBARBARIC
MIXOTROPHIC
MIXTILINEAR
MYXADENITIS
MYXASTHENIA
MYXEDEMATOUS
MYXOBLASTOMA
MYXOCYSTOMA
MYXOFIBROMA
MYXOMATOSIS
MYXOMYCETOUS
MYXONEUROMA
MYXOSARCOMA
MYXOSPOROUS
NOXIOUSNESS
PAXILLIFORM
SAXIFRAGANT
SAXIFRAGOUS
SAXOPHONIST
SEXADECIMAL
SEXAGENARIAN
SEXAGESIMAL
SEXANGULARLY
SEXCENTENARY
SEXDIGITATE
SEXDIGITATED
SEXDIGITISM
SEXISYLLABLE
SEXLESSNESS
SEXOLOGICAL
SEXPLOITATION
SEXTILLIONTH
SEXTIPARTITE
SEXTUPLICATE
SEXTUPLICATED
TAXABLENESS
TAXASPIDEAN
TAXEOPODOUS
TAXGATHERER
TAXGATHERING
TAXIDERMIST
TAXIDERMIZE
TAXIMETERED
TAXONOMICAL
TEXTIFEROUS
TOXALBUMOSE
TOXICOGENIC
TOXICOGNATH
TOXICOLOGIC
TOXICOLOGIST
TOXICOMANIA
TOXICOPATHIC
TOXICOPATHY
TOXICOPHAGY
TOXICOPHIDIA
TOXINFECTION
TOXIPHOBIAC
TOXITABELLAE
TOXOGENESIS
TOXOGLOSSATE
TOXOPHILISM
TOXOPHILITIC
TOXOPHILOUS
VEXATIOUSLY
VEXILLARIOUS
VEXILLATION
WAXCHANDLER
WAXCHANDLERY

ADOXOGRAPHY
ALEXANDRITE
ALEXIPHARMIC

ALEXIPYRETIC
ANOXIDATIVE
ANOXYBIOSIS
ANOXYBIOTIC
ASEXUALIZED
ASEXUALIZING
ATAXAPHASIA
ATAXIAGRAPH
ATAXIAMETER
ATAXIAPHASIA
ATAXOPHEMIA
COEXISTENCE
COEXISTENCY
COEXTENSION
COEXTENSIVE
DEOXIDIZING
DEOXYGENATE
DEOXYGENATED
DEOXYGENIZE
EPEXEGETICAL
FLEXANIMOUS
FLEXIBILITY
FLEXIBLENESS
FLEXUOSITIES
FLEXUOUSNESS
FLUXIBILITY
FLUXIBLENESS
FLUXIONALLY
INEXACTITUDE
INEXACTNESS
INEXCUSABLE
INEXCUSABLY
INEXECUTION
INEXHAUSTIBLE
INEXHAUSTIVE
INEXISTENCE
INEXISTENCY
INEXPECTEDLY
INEXPEDIENCY
INEXPEDIENT
INEXPENSIVE
INEXPERIENCE
INEXPERIENCED
INEXPERTNESS
INEXPLICABLE
INEXPLICABLES
INEXPLICABLY
INEXPLICITLY
INEXPRESSIBLE
INEXPRESSIVE
INEXTENSIVE
INEXTIRPABLE
INEXTRICABLE
INEXTRICABLY
INOXIDIZING
PLEXIMETRIC
PRAXINOSCOPE
PROXENETISM
PROXIMETALLY
PROXIMATION
PYOXANTHOSE
THIXOLABILE
THIXOTROPIC
UNEXACTNESS
UNEXCEPTIVE
UNEXCLUSIVE
UNEXCUSABLE
UNEXCUSABLY
UNEXPECTEDLY
UNEXPEDIENT
UNEXPENSIVE
UNEXPERIENCE
UNEXPERIENT
UNEXPLAINED
UNEXPLICABLE
UNEXPLOITED
UNEXPRESSIVE

UNEXPURGATED	DOPAOXIDASE	PHYLLOXERAN	ANISALDOXIME	TROPHOTAXIS
UNEXTRICABLE	INFLEXIBILITY	PHYLLOXERIC	APHOTOTAXIS	URECHITOXIN
ZOOXANTHELLA	INFLUXIONISM	PILOTAXITIC	APOPHYLAXIS	
	INTERXYLARY	PRAEMAXILLA	ATLANTOAXIAL	ACROASPHYXIA
ADMAXILLARY	INTRAXYLARY	PRAETAXATION	ATLOIDOAXOID	ACTINOPRAXIS
ANNEXATIONAL	LITHOXYLITE	RHYOTAXITIC	BENZALDOXIME	ANGIORRHEXIS
ANNEXATIONIST	OVEREXPOSED	SEMISEXTILE	CARBETHOXYL	AORTOMALAXIS
AUTOXIDATION	OVEREXPOSING	STAURAXONIA	CARDIATAXIA	COLPORRHEXIS
AUTOXIDATOR	OVEREXPOSURE	STAURAXONIAL	CARDIOTOXIC	ELECTROTAXIS
BIMAXILLARY	OXYHEXACTINE	SULPHOXYLIC	CHEMIOTAXIC	GALVANOTAXIS
BISAXILLARY	OXYHEXASTER	TYLOTOXEATE	CHEMIOTAXIS	ICHTHYOTOXIN
BISEXUALISM	PANSEXUALISM	TYROTOXICON	CHIROPRAXIS	KARYORRHEXIS
BISEXUALITY	PANSEXUALIST	UNDEREXPOSE	COLONOPEXY	LITHOLAPAXY
DESEXUALIZE	PANSEXUALITY	UNDEREXPOSED	CREATOTOXISM	MORPHALLAXIS
DESEXUALIZED	PANSEXUALIZE	UNDEREXPOSING	DECIMOSEXTO	OOPHOROPEXY
DETOXICATED	PERIAXILLARY	XANTHOXENITE	DIASTATAXIC	ORCHIDOPEXY
DETOXICATING	PHENOXAZINE	XANTHOXYLIN	DICATALEXIS	OROPHARYNXES
DETOXICATION	POSTAXIALLY	ZANTHOXYLUM	DIRECTRIXES	OSCULATRIXES
DETOXICATOR	POSTEXILIAN	ZOOPRAXISCOPE	DISULPHOXID	POLYHYDROXY
DIHEXAHEDRAL	POSTEXISTENT		DISULPHOXIDE	SCAPULOPEXY
DIHEXAHEDRON	PREFIXATION	ADENOMYXOMA	DORSIFLEXION	SHIKIMOTOXIN
DISOXYGENATE	PREMAXILLARY	AMIDOHEXOSE	DORSIFLEXOR	STROPHOTAXIS
DYSOXIDATION	PRETEXTUOUS	AMYLODEXTRIN	ENTEROPEXIA	TRISULPHOXID
FUCOXANTHIN	PROTOXIDIZE	ANHYDROXIME	ENTEROTOXEMIA	TROPHALLAXIS
GITOXIGENIN	PROTOXIDIZED	ANILIDOXIME	EXECUTRIXES	UNORTHODOXLY
HYPOXANTHINE	QUINOXALINE	ANTEFLEXION	FORMALDOXIME	UNORTHODOXY
INDEXICALLY	REFLEXIVELY	APPENDIXING	GASTROTAXIS	VASOREFLEX
INDEXTERITY	REFLEXIVITY	CIRCUMAXIAL	GRIPPOTOXIN	
INNOXIOUSLY	REFLEXOLOGY	CIRCUMAXILE	HETERODOXIES	ANDROSPHINX
INTOXICABLE	RETROXIPHOID	CRUCIFIXION	HETEROSEXUAL	ARCHOSYRINX
INTOXICATED	SUBLUXATION	CYCLOHEXANE	HETEROTAXIA	AUTOCRATRIX
INTOXICATING	SUBMAXILLAE	CYCLOHEXANOL	HETEROTAXIC	BACTERIOTOXIC
INTOXICATION	SUBMAXILLARY	CYCLOHEXENE	HETEROTAXIS	CHALCEDONYX
INTOXICATIVE	SUBSEXTUPLE	CYSTOMYXOMA	IMMUNOTOXIN	CHEMOREFLEX
INTOXICATOR	SUFFIXATION	DICARBOXYLIC	INTROFLEXION	CHYLOTHORAX
NONEXISTENCE	SULFOXYLATE	FIBROMYXOMA	KERATONYXIS	CLITORIDAUXE
NONEXISTENT	TETROXALATE	GENUFLEXION	LYMPHOTOXIN	COMPETITRIX
OBNOXIOUSLY	UNISEXUALITY	GENUFLEXUOUS	METAGALAXIES	CONSOLATRIX
OBNOXIOUSNESS	UNISEXUALLY	IDEOPRAXIST	MYELOPLAXES	CYSTOSYRINX
PAROXYSMALLY	UROTOXICITY	INTERMIXEDLY	MYTILOTOXINE	CYTOPHARYNX
PAROXYTONIC		INTERMIXING	NEPHROTOXIC	ESOTHYROPEXY
PREEXISTENCE	AMBIDEXTERITY	INTERMIXTLY	NEPHROTOXIN	EXPENDITRIX
PREEXISTENT	AMBIDEXTRAL	INTERMIXTURE	NEUROPLEXUS	FORNICATRIX
PYROXMANGITE	AMBIDEXTROUS	INTERSEXUAL	ODONTOLOXIA	FRICANDEAUX
RELAXEDNESS	ANTHRAXOLITE	INTERTEXTURE	OSTEOSTIXIS	GUBERNATRIX
SUBAXILLARY	ANTHRAXYLON	IRREFLEXIVE	PHYLLOTAXIS	HYDROTHORAX
SUBOXIDATION	ANTHROXANIC	LAURINOXYLON	PNEUMOTOXIN	HYPOPHARYNX
	APOPLEXIOUS	METAVAUXITE	PROCATARXIS	LEGISLATRIX
AMPLEXATION	AUTOTOXAEMIA	ORTHODOXALLY	PROPHYLAXIS	LIFERENTRIX
AMPLEXICAUL	AUTOTOXEMIA	ORTHODOXIAN	PROTEOPEXIC	LITHANTHRAX
ANTHEXIMETER	BANDBOXICAL	ORTHODOXICAL	PROTEOPEXIS	MERVEILLEUX
ANTHOXANTHIN	CARBOLXYLOL	ORTHODOXIES	PROTHORAXES	MESOSALPINX
ANTIOXIDANT	COLOPEXOTOMY	ORTHODOXISM	PSEUDODOXAL	MICROTHORAX
ANTIOXYGENIC	COMPLEXIONAL	ORTHODOXIST	PSYCHOSEXUAL	MONILETHRIX
APPROXIMATE	COMPLEXIONARY	ORTHODOXNESS	PSYCHOTAXIS	MYELAPOPLEXY
APPROXIMATED	COMPLEXIONED	PARAVAUXITE	PYRRHULOXIA	NASOPHARYNX
APPROXIMATELY	COMPLEXITIES	PEPTOTOXINE	RADIOPRAXIS	NEGOTIATRIX
APPROXIMATING	COMPLEXNESS	PHILODOXICAL	RETROFLEXED	NEOORTHODOXY
APPROXIMATION	CONFLUXIBLE	POSTFLEXION	RETROFLEXION	OBJURGATRIX
APPROXIMATIVE	GASTROXYNSIS	QUINATOXINE	RHAMNOHEXOSE	PACHYMENINX
APPROXIMATOR	HETEROXENOUS	QUINCUNXIAL	RHAMNOHEXITE	PHLEBORRHEXIS
ASPHYXIATED	HOMOSEXUALITY	QUINISEXTINE	SCILLITOXIN	PHOTOSYNTAX
ASPHYXIATING	HYDROEXTRACT	SACROCOXITIS	SCLERONYXIS	PNEUMONOPEXY
ASPHYXIATION	HYPOTOXICITY	SEMIFLEXIBLE	SESQUISEXTAL	PROCURATRIX
ASPHYXIATOR	INOBNOXIOUS	SUPERMAXILLA	SPASMOTOXIN	PROGENITRIX
CARBOXYLASE	ODONTEXESIS	SUPERSEXUAL	SPASMOTOXINE	PROLOCUTRIX
CARBOXYLATE	OVERTAXATION	SUPRAMAXILLA	SPERMATOXIN	PTEROTHORAX
CARBOXYLATED	PARADOXICAL	SUPRAMAXIMAL	SPLENOPEXIA	SACROCOCCYX
CONNEXITIES	PARADOXICIAN	TRANSFIXING	SPLENOPEXIS	SCEUOPHYLAX
CONTEXTUALLY	PARADOXIDIAN	TRANSFIXION	SPLENOTOXIN	SIPHONOPLAX
CONTEXTUAL	PARADOXOLOGY	TRANSFIXTURE	STEREOTAXIS	SPECULATRIX
CONTEXTURED	PERICOXITIS	TYPHOTOXINE	SUPERFLEXION	STENOTHORAX
CONVEXEDNESS	PERPLEXEDLY	ULTRAMAXIMAL	THERMOTAXIC	STIMULATRIX
CONVEXITIES	PERPLEXINGLY		THERMOTAXIS	TETRAHYDROXY
COSTOXIPHOID	PERPLEXITIES	ANAPHYLAXIS	THIGMOTAXIS	THOROUGHWAX
		ANGIOATAXIA	TRISULFOXID	

ARCHEOPTERYX	DISPENSATRIX	PSEUDOCORTEX	STEREOMATRIX	IMPROPRIATRIX
ARTHROSYRINX	MESOAPPENDIX	PSYCHOREFLEX	TROPHOTHYLAX	
CHARTOPHYLAX	PNEUMOTHORAX	RHINOPHARYNX	ULTRACOMPLEX	

SCORING ORDER LIST OF WORDS OVER 10 LETTERS

35
EXQUISITIVELY
ZANTHOXYLUM
ZOOPRAXISCOPE

34
EXPERMENTIZED
EXTEMPORIZING
HYPOPHARYNX
OXYGENIZABLE
OXYRRHYNCHID

33
BENZALDOXIME
EXPERIMENTIZE
EXTEMPORIZED
JUXTAPYLORIC
OXYRHYNCHID
OXYRHYNCHOUS

32
CHARTOPHYLAX
DEOXYGENIZE
EXORCIZEMENT
EXTEMPORIZER
EXTRAVAGANZA
HYPOTOXICITY
MAXIMIZATION
OXYGENIZING
OXYPHOSPHATE
PHENOXAZINE
PROTOXIDIZED
PSYCHOREFLEX

31
CYTOPHARYNX
DOXOLOGIZING
EXOPHTHALMIC
EXTEMPORIZE
MYELAPOPLEXY
MYXOMYCETOUS
OXYCEPHALISM
OXYCHROMATIC
OXYPHTHALIC
OXYQUINOLINE
WAXCHANDLERY
ZOOXANTHELLA

30
CYSTOMYXOMA
DEOXIDIZING
DESEXUALIZED
DOXOLOGIZED
ESOTHYROPEXY
EXAUTHORIZE
EXCHANGEABLY
EXCLAMATIVELY
EXCURSIONIZE
EXEMPLIFYING
EXHIBITIVELY
EXHIBITORSHIP
EXORCIZATION
EXQUISITELY
EXTERIORIZING
EXTRAPHYSICAL
HYPOXANTHINE
ICHTHYOTOXIN

LEXICOGRAPHY
MYXOCYSTOMA
MYXOFIBROMA
OXYCEPHALIC
OXYCOPAIVIC
OXYMETHYLENE
PACHYMENINX
PANSEXUALIZE
PHLEBORRHEXIS
PROTOXIDIZE
RHINOPHARYNX
TAXIDERMIZE
TROPHOTHYLAX
XYLOQUINONE

29
ACROASPHYXIA
APPROXIMATELY
APPROXIMATIVE
ARCHEOPTERYX
ASEXUALIZING
CHALCEDONYX
CHYLOTHORAX
COMPLEXIONARY
CYCLOHEXANOL
DEXTROSAZONE
DICARBOXYLIC
EXHORTATIVELY
EXOPHTHALMIA
EXOPHTHALMOS
EXOPHTHALMUS
EXOSTRACIZE
EXQUISITENESS
EXQUISITISM
EXTERIORIZED
EXTERNIZATION
INOXIDIZING
JUXTAPOSITION
KARYORRHEXIS
MAXILLOJUGAL
ORCHIDOPEXY
OXYALDEHYDE
OXYCEPHALOUS
OXYCHROMATIN
OXYHYDROGEN
OXYPHYLLOUS
OXYSALICYLIC
PAROXYSMALLY
POLYHYDROXY
PSYCHOSEXUAL
QUINCUNXIAL
TETRAHYDROXY
XANTHOPHYLL
XYLOGRAPHIC

28
ADOXOGRAPHY
ALEXIPHARMIC
AMBIDEXTERITY
APOPHYLAXIS
ASEXUALIZED
ASPHYXIATING
AUXOCHROMISM
AXISYMMETRIC
CARBETHOXYL
CHEMOREFLEX

COLOPEXOTOMY
CYCLOHEXANE
CYCLOHEXENE
DESEXUALIZE
EXCEPTIVELY
EXCIPULIFORM
EXCOMMUNICANT
EXCOMMUNICATE
EXCONJUGANT
EXENCEPHALIC
EXHAUSTIVELY
EXPENDABILITY
EXPLANATIVELY
EXPLORATIVELY
EXTRAVAGANCY
HEXASTICHIC
HOMOSEXUALITY
HYDROEXTRACT
HYDROTHORAX
INEXPLICABLY
INFLEXIBILITY
JUXTAPOSING
LEXIGRAPHICAL
LYMPHOTOXIN
MAXILLIPEDARY
MYXOBLASTOMA
OBJURGATRIX
OOPHOROPEXY
OXYPROPIONIC
PHYLLOXERIC
PNEUMONOPEXY
PROPHYLAXIS
PSYCHOTAXIS
QUINISEXTINE
SCEUOPHYLAX
SESQUISEXTAL
SHIKIMOTOXIN
SULPHOXYLIC
THOROUGHWAX
TOXICOPATHIC
TOXICOPATHY
XANTHOCHROID
XEROPHYTISM

27
ANHYDROXIME
APPROXIMATING
ASPHYXIATED
ASPHYXIATION
AUXOCHROMIC
CARBOXYLATED
CHEMIOTAXIC
COSTOXIPHOID
DIHEXAHEDRAL
DIHEXAHEDRON
EXCEPTIONALLY
EXCHANGEABLE
EXCLAMATORILY
EXHIBITIONISM
EXOMORPHISM
EXPANSIBILITY
EXPLOSIBILITY
EXPORTABILITY
EXPOSITIVELY
EXPRESSIVELY
EXSUFFLICATE
EXTEMPORARILY

EXTERIORIZE
EXTERNALIZE
EXTEROCEPTIVE
EXTRAVAGANTLY
EXTROSPECTIVE
EXUVIABILITY
FORMALDOXIME
INEXPECTEDLY
INEXPEDIENCY
JUXTASPINAL
MIXOBARBARIC
MIXOTROPHIC
MYXEDEMATOUS
MYXOSARCOMA
OROPHARYNXES
OXYACANTHINE
OXYACANTHOUS
OXYACETYLENE
OXYCHLORIDE
OXYCINNAMIC
OXYGENICITY
OXYLUCIFERIN
OXYOSPHRESIA
OXYSULPHIDE
PERPLEXINGLY
PHILODOXICAL
PYROXMANGITE
QUINATOXINE
QUINOXALINE
REFLEXIVELY
REFLEXIVITY
RHAMNOHEXOSE
RHAMNOHEXITE
SCAPULOPEXY
TOXICOPHIDIA
TOXIPHOBIAC
UNEXPECTEDLY
WAXCHANDLER
XANTHOCHROIA
XENOMORPHIC
XEROMORPHIC
XYLOGRAPHER
XYLOPHAGOUS

26
ADENOMYXOMA
ALEXIPYRETIC
ANAPHYLAXIS
APPROXIMATED
APPROXIMATION
ARCHOSYRINX
ASPHYXIATOR
AUXOCHROMOUS
AUXOGRAPHIC
BACTERIOTOXIC
COLPORRHEXIS
COMPLEXIONED
CYSTOSYRINX
DISULPHOXIDE
EXANTHEMATIC
EXCEPTIONARY
EXCESSIVELY
EXCITABILITY
EXCITOMOTORY
EXCLUSIVELY
EXCLUSIVITY
EXCREMENTARY

EXCREMENTIVE
EXCURSIVELY
EXCUSABILITY
EXECUTIVELY
EXEMPLIFIED
EXENCEPHALIA
EXENCEPHALUS
EXHAUSTINGLY
EXHAUSTLESSLY
EXPANSIVELY
EXPANSIVITY
EXPEDITIONARY
EXPEDITIOUSLY
EXPENSIVELY
EXPERIMENTLY
EXPLETIVELY
EXPLOSIVELY
EXPROBRATORY
EXTEMPORALLY
EXTENDIBILITY
EXTRACTIFORM
FLEXIBILITY
FLUXIBILITY
FUCOXANTHIN
HEXABROMIDE
HEXOBARBITAL
IMPROPRIATRIX
INEXPLICABLES
INEXPLICITLY
INEXTRICABLY
LEXIGRAPHIC
LITHOLAPAXY
MESOAPPENDIX
MORPHALLAXIS
MYXASTHENIA
NASOPHARYNX
NEOORTHODOXY
ORTHODOXALLY
OXYACANTHIN
OXYBERBERINE
OXYCARBONATE
OXYCHLORATE
OXYCHLORINE
OXYHAEMATIN
OXYHEXACTINE
OXYSULPHATE
PARADOXOLOGY
PERPLEXEDLY
PHOTOSYNTAX
PHYLLOTAXIS
PHYLLOXERAN
PNEUMOTHORAX
PREMAXILLARY
PYOXANTHOSE
PYRRHULOXIA
RHYOTAXITIC
SEMIFLEXIBLE
SUBMAXILLARY
TOXOPHILITIC
TYPHOTOXINE
UNORTHODOXLY
XANTHOPHANE
XANTHOPHORE
XENODOCHIUM
XEROGRAPHIC
XEROMORPHOUS
XIPHISTERNUM

XIPHOPAGOUS
XYLOPHILOUS
XYLOPHONIST

25
AMYLODEXTRIN
ANOXYBIOTIC
ANTHOXANTHIN
ANTIOXYGENIC
APPROXIMATOR
ARTHROSYRINX
ATAXOPHEMIA
BANDBOXICAL
BIMAXILLARY
CARBOLXYLOL
CARBOXYLASE
CARBOXYLATE
CHEMIOTAXIS
CHIROPRAXIS
COEXISTENCY
COMPLEXIONAL
COMPLEXITIES
CONFLUXIBLE
CONVEXEDNESS
COXCOMBICAL
COXOFEMORAL
CRUCIFIXION
DEOXYGENATED
DISULPHOXID
DOXOGRAPHER
EXCEEDINGLY
EXCESSIVENESS
EXCLAMATIVE
EXCLAMATORY
EXCLUSIVENESS
EXCLUSIVISM
EXCOGITATIVE
EXCORTICATING
EXCULPATIVE
EXCULPATORY
EXECUTIVENESS
EXEGETICALLY
EXEMPLARILY
EXEMPLARITY
EXEMPLIFIER
EXHAUSTEDLY
EXHIBITIONIST
EXHILARATIVE
EXHILARATORY
EXOMPHALOUS
EXORBITANCY
EXPANDINGLY
EXPANSIVENESS
EXPECTANCIES
EXPECTANTLY
EXPECTATIVE
EXPECTORATING
EXPENSIVENESS
EXPERIMENTING
EXPISCATORY
EXPLANATORILY
EXPLETIVENESS
EXPLICATIVE
EXPLICATORY
EXPLOSIVENESS
EXPONENTIALLY
EXPOSITIONAL
EXPOSTULATIVE
EXPOSTULATORY
EXPROPRIATING
EXSICCATIVE
EXSUFFLATION
EXTEMPORARY
EXTENSIBILITY
EXTERMINATIVE
EXTERMINATORY
EXTRACYSTIC

EXTRAGALACTIC
EXTRAPOLATIVE
EXTRAVAGANCE
EXTRAVAGATING
EXTRAVASCULAR
EXTRINSICALLY
EXTROVERSIVE
EXTUMESCENCE
HEXAGONALLY
INEXCUSABLY
INEXHAUSTIBLE
INEXHAUSTIVE
INEXPERIENCED
INEXPLICABLE
INTERMIXEDLY
KERATONYXIS
LEXICOLOGICAL
LOXODOGRAPH
MAXILLIFORM
MICROTHORAX
MYELOPLAXES
MYXOMATOSIS
MYXONEUROMA
MYXOSPOROUS
NEPHROTOXIC
ORTHODOXICAL
OVEREXPOSING
OXYCOUMARIN
OXYGNATHOUS
OXYMURIATIC
PAROXYTONIC
PAXILLIFORM
PRAXINOSCOPE
PROXIMATELY
REFLEXOLOGY
RETROXIPHOID
SEXTUPLICATED
SIPHONOPLAX
SUPRAMAXIMAL
THERMOTAXIC
THIXOTROPIC
TOXOPHILISM
TRISULPHOXID
ULTRACOMPLEX
UNEXCEPTIVE
UNEXCUSABLY
UNEXPLICABLE
UNORTHODOXY
XEROPHOBOUS
XIPHOCOSTAL
XYLOCARPOUS
XYLOPLASTIC

24
ADMAXILLARY
AMBIDEXTROUS
AMIDOHEXOSE
AMPLEXICAUL
ANDROSPHINX
ANTHEXIMETER
ANTHRAXYLON
APPENDIXING
APPROXIMATE
ATAXIAGRAPH
ATAXIAPHASIA
AXONOPHOROUS
CIRCUMAXIAL
CIRCUMAXILE
COMPETITRIX
COMPLEXNESS
CONTEXTUALLY
COXARTHRITIS
DEXIOTROPISM
DEXTROGYRATE
DISOXYGENATE
DYSOXIDATION
EPEXEGETICAL

EXACERBATING
EXACTIVENESS
EXAGGERATIVE
EXAGGERATORY
EXASPERATIVE
EXCANDESCENT
EXCATHEDRAL
EXCERPTIBLE
EXCITABLENESS
EXCLAMATIONAL
EXCLUSIONARY
EXCOMMUNION
EXCORTICATED
EXCORTICATION
EXCRESCENCY
EXCRESCENTIAL
EXCRETIONARY
EXCRUCIABLE
EXCRUCIATING
EXCURSIONARY
EXCUSABLENESS
EXECRABLENESS
EXEMPLARINESS
EXEMPLARISM
EXFOLIATIVE
EXFOLIATORY
EXHAUSTEDNESS
EXHIBITIONAL
EXHIBITIONER
EXHORTATIVE
EXHORTATORY
EXOCCIPITAL
EXORBITANTLY
EXOTERICALLY
EXPECTORATED
EXPECTORATION
EXPEDIENCIES
EXPEDIENTLY
EXPERIENCING
EXPERIMENTED
EXPERIMENTIST
EXPLOITATIVE
EXPOSITORILY
EXPRESSIONISM
EXPROPRIATED
EXPROPRIATION
EXPURGATIVE
EXPURGATORY
EXTENSIVELY
EXTENUATINGLY
EXTEROCEPTIST
EXTINGUISHED
EXTORSIVELY
EXTRACAPSULAR
EXTRAMURALLY
EXTRAORDINARY
EXTRAVAGATED
EXTRAVAGATION
EXTRAVASATING
EXTROSPECTION
EXULCERATIVE
EXULCERATORY
FLEXIBLENESS
FLUXIBLENESS
FLUXIONALLY
FRICANDEAUX
INDEXICALLY
INEXPRESSIBLE
INEXPRESSIVE
INFLUXIONISM
INTERXYLARY
INTOXICATIVE
INTRAXYLARY
IRREFLEXIVE
LITHANTHRAX
LITHOXYLITE
MAXILLOLABIAL

MYTILOTOXINE
MYXADENITIS
ORTHODOXISM
OVEREXPOSED
OVEREXPOSURE
OXIDABILITY
OXYCELLULOSE
OXYESTHESIA
OXYSTOMATOUS
OXYTYLOTATE
PANSEXUALITY
PARADOXICIAN
PERIAXILLARY
PLEXIMETRIC
PROTEOPEXIC
PSEUDOCORTEX
SEXCENTENARY
SEXISYLLABLE
STROPHOTAXIS
SUFFIXATION
SULFOXYLATE
SUPERFLEXION
TAXGATHERING
THIGMOTAXIS
TOXICOGNATH
TOXINFECTION
TROPHALLAXIS
UNDEREXPOSING
UNEXPRESSIVE
VEXATIOUSLY
XANTHOCONITE
XANTHODERMA
XANTHOGENIC
XANTHOMATOUS
XANTHOPTERIN
XENACANTHINE
XEROGRAPHER
XIPHISTERNAL
XYLOSTROMATA
XYRIDACEOUS

23
ACTINOPRAXIS
AMBIDEXTRAL
ANGIORRHEXIS
ANOXYBIOSIS
ANTHROXANIC
APHOTOTAXIS
ATAXAPHASIA
AUXETICALLY
AUXOAMYLASE
AUXOHORMONE
BISAXILLARY
BISEXUALITY
CARDIOTOXIC
COEXTENSIVE
CONVEXITIES
CREATOTOXISM
DECIMOSEXTO
DEOXYGENATE
DETOXICATING
DEXIOTROPIC
DEXTROCARDIA
DORSIFLEXION
EXACERBATED
EXACERBATION
EXALBUMINOSE
EXALBUMINOUS
EXAMINATIVE
EXAMINATORY
EXCAVATIONS
EXCELLENCIES
EXCELLENTLY
EXCLUSIONISM
EXCOGITABLE
EXCOGITATING
EXCRESCENCIES

EXCRUCIATED
EXCRUCIATION
EXCULPATING
EXCURSIONISM
EXCURVATURE
EXCYSTATION
EXFIGURATION
EXFLAGELLATE
EXHAUSTIBLE
EXHILARATING
EXILARCHATE
EXISTENTIALLY
EXOPERIDIUM
EXORABILITY
EXORCISEMENT
EXORCISTICAL
EXOTHERMOUS
EXPANDEDNESS
EXPANSIONISM
EXPATIATIVE
EXPATIATORY
EXPECTORATOR
EXPEDITATING
EXPEDITIONIST
EXPENTHESIS
EXPERIENCED
EXPERIMENTAL
EXPERIMENTEE
EXPERIMENTER
EXPISCATING
EXPLANATIVE
EXPLANATORY
EXPLICATING
EXPLICITNESS
EXPLORATIVE
EXPLORATORY
EXPOSTULATING
EXPROMISSION
EXPROPRIATOR
EXPULSATORY
EXPURGATORIAL
EXSCRIPTURAL
EXSICCATING
EXTENSIVENESS
EXTERMINATING
EXTEROCEPTOR
EXTINGUISHER
EXTIRPATIVE
EXTIRPATORY
EXTISPICIOUS
EXTRAFORMAL
EXTRAPOLATING
EXTRAVAGINAL
EXTRAVASATED
EXTRAVASATION
EXUBERANTLY
FLEXANIMOUS
FORNICATRIX
GALVANOTAXIS
GASTROXYNSIS
GENUFLEXUOUS
GRIPPOTOXIN
HETERODOXIES
HETEROTAXIC
INEXISTENCY
INEXPENSIVE
INEXPERIENCE
INEXTIRPABLE
INEXTRICABLE
INTERMIXTLY
LEXICOLOGIC
LOXODROMICS
LOXODROMISM
MAXILLIPEDE
MERVEILLEUX
METAVAUXITE
MONILETHRIX

NEPHROTOXIN
OBNOXIOUSLY
ORTHODOXNESS
OXIDIMETRIC
OXYGENATING
OXYGENERATOR
OXYHEXASTER
OXYPETALOUS
PANSEXUALISM
PARADOXICAL
PARADOXIDIAN
PARAVAUXITE
PERPLEXITIES
POSTAXIALLY
POSTFLEXION
PREEXISTENCE
PREFIXATION
PROTHORAXES
PTEROTHORAX
SACROCOCCYX
SACROCOXITIS
SAXOPHONIST
SCLERONYXIS
SEXADECIMAL
SEXANGULARLY
SEXTUPLICATE
SPASMOTOXINE
SUBAXILLARY
SUPERMAXILLA
SUPRAMAXILLA
THERMOTAXIS
THIXOLABILE
TOXICOGENIC
TOXICOLOGIC
TOXOPHILOUS
TROPHOTAXIS
TYROTOXICON
ULTRAMAXIMAL
UNDEREXPOSED
UNEXCLUSIVE
UNEXPENSIVE
UNEXPERIENCE
UNEXPURGATED
UNEXTRICABLE
URECHITOXIN
UROTOXICITY
VASOREFLEX
XANTHELASMA
XANTHOGENATE
XANTHOMETER
XANTHOXYLIN
XEROPHILOUS
XIPHOSUROUS

22
AMPLEXATION
ANISALDOXIME
ANOXIDATIVE
ANTHRAXOLITE
APOPLEXIOUS
AXIOMATICAL
AXONOMETRIC
AXOSPERMOUS
BISEXUALISM
CLITORIDAUXE
COEXISTENCE
DETOXICATED
DETOXICATION
DEXIOTROPOUS
DEXTEROUSLY
DISPENSATRIX
DOPAOXIDASE
DORSIFLEXOR
DOXOLOGICAL
EXACTINGNESS
EXAGGERATING
EXAMINATIONAL

EXASPERATING
EXCALCARATE
EXCEPTIONAL
EXCEPTIONER
EXCITOMOTOR
EXCLAMATION
EXCOGITATED
EXCOGITATION
EXCORTICATE
EXCREMENTAL
EXCRESCENCES
EXCRUCIATOR
EXCULPATION
EXECUTRICES
EXERCISABLE
EXFILTRATION
EXFODIATION
EXFOLIATING
EXHILARATED
EXHILARATION
EXOGENOUSLY
EXOGNATHION
EXOGNATHITE
EXOMOLOGESIS
EXORBITANCE
EXOSKELETAL
EXOSKELETON
EXOSTRACISM
EXOTERICISM
EXPATRIATING
EXPECTATION
EXPECTORANT
EXPECTORATE
EXPEDIENTIAL
EXPEDIENTIST
EXPEDITATED
EXPEDITATION
EXPEDITENESS
EXPENSILATION
EXPERIENCER
EXPERIENCES
EXPIATORINESS
EXPISCATION
EXPLAINABLE
EXPLEMENTAL
EXPLICATION
EXPLOITABLE
EXPLORATIONAL
EXPLOREMENT
EXPOSTULATED
EXPOSTULATION
EXPRESSIBLE
EXPRESSIONIST
EXPROPRIATE
EXPURGATING
EXSCULPTATE
EXSICCATION
EXTERMINATED
EXTERMINATION
EXTERNALISTIC
EXTORTIONARY
EXTRABULBAR
EXTRACARPAL
EXTRACTABLE
EXTRACTIBLE
EXTRADITABLE
EXTRADUCTION
EXTRAMUNDANE
EXTRANEOUSLY
EXTRAPOLATED
EXTRAPOLATION
EXTRASENSORY
EXTRASYSTOLE
EXTRAVAGANT
EXTRAVAGATE
EXTRAVERSION
EXTREMISTIC

EXTROVERSION
EXUBERANTNESS
EXULCERATING
EXUMBRELLAR
FLEXUOSITIES
FLEXUOUSNESS
GENUFLEXION
HETEROSEXUAL
HETEROXENOUS
INDEXTERITY
INEXACTITUDE
INEXCUSABLE
INTOXICABLE
INTOXICATING
INTROFLEXION
LAURINOXYLON
LAXATIVENESS
LEXICOLOGIST
LIXIVIATING
MESOSALPINX
METAGALAXIES
OBNOXIOUSNESS
ORTHODOXIAN
ORTHODOXIES
ORTHODOXIST
OVERTAXATION
PEPTOTOXINE
PERICOXITIS
PILOTAXITIC
PNEUMOTOXIN
PRAEMAXILLA
PROCATARXIS
PROCURATRIX
PROLOCUTRIX
PROTEOPEXIS
PROXENETISM
PROXIMATION
PSEUDODOXAL
RETROFLEXED
RETROFLEXION
SAXIFRAGANT
SAXIFRAGOUS
SEXDIGITATED
SEXDIGITISM
SEXPLOITATION
SEXTILLIONTH
SPASMOTOXIN
SPECULATRIX
SPERMOTOXIN
SPLENOPEXIA
SPLENOPEXIS
SUBMAXILLAE
SUBOXIDATION
SUBSEXTUPLE
TAXGATHERER
TAXONOMICAL
TOXALBUMOSE
TOXICOLOGIST
TOXICOMANIA
TRANSFIXING
TRANSFIXTURE
TRISULFOXID
UNEXCUSABLE
UNISEXUALITY
VEXILLARIOUS
XENYLAMINE

21
ANILIDOXIME
ANTEFLEXION
AORTOMALAXIS
ATLOIDOAXOID
AUTOTOXAEMIA
AUXILIATORY
AXIOLOGICAL
CARDIATAXIA
CONTEXTURED

COXOCERITIC
DETOXICATOR
DEXTROCULAR
DIASTATAXIC
DICATALEXIS
DIRECTRIXES
ELECTROTAXIS
EXAGGERATED
EXAGGERATION
EXARTICULATE
EXASPERATED
EXASPERATION
EXCITEDNESS
EXCLUSIONIST
EXCOGITATOR
EXCORIATING
EXCRESCENCE
EXCURSIONIST
EXERCITATION
EXERCITORIAL
EXFOLIATION
EXHAUSTLESS
EXHILARATOR
EXIMIOUSNESS
EXOCULATING
EXONERATIVE
EXORABLENESS
EXORBITATION
EXORCISATION
EXOTICALNESS
EXPANSIONIST
EXPATIATING
EXPATRIATED
EXPATRIATION
EXPEDITIOUS
EXPENDITURE
EXPERIENTIAL
EXPLANTATION
EXPLOITATION
EXPLOSIONIST
EXPOSITIONAL
EXPOSITORIAL
EXPOSTULATOR
EXPRESSIONAL
EXPURGATION
EXSCUTELLATE
EXTENDEDNESS
EXTENSIMETER
EXTENSOMETER
EXTENUATIVE
EXTENUATORY
EXTERIORITY
EXTERMINATOR
EXTERNALITY
EXTIRPATING
EXTRAENTERIC
EXTRAPOLATOR
EXTRAVASATE
EXTRAVIOLET
EXTRICATING
EXTRINSICATE
EXUBERATING
EXULCERATED
EXULCERATION
GUBERNATRIX
HETEROTAXIA
HETEROTAXIS
IDEOPRAXIST
INEXPEDIENT
INEXPERTNESS
INEXTENSIVE
INNOXIOUSLY
INTERMIXING
INTERMIXTURE
INTOXICATED
INTOXICATION
LAXIFLOROUS

LAXIFOLIATE
LAXIFOLIOUS
LIFERENTRIX
LIXIVIATION
LUXURIANTLY
LUXURIOUSLY
NONEXISTENCE
OSCULATRIXES
OXALURAMIDE
PANSEXUALIST
POSTEXISTENT
PRAETAXATION
PROGENITRIX
RADIOPRAXIS
REFLEXIONAL
SEXAGESIMAL
SEXOLOGICAL
SEXTIPARTITE
STENOTHORAX
STEREOMATRIX
TAXASPIDEAN
TAXEOPODOUS
TAXIDERMIST
TAXIMETERED
TEXTIFEROUS
TOXITABELLAE
TRANSFIXION
TYLOTOXEATE
UNDEREXPOSE
UNEXPEDIENT
UNEXPLAINED
UNEXPLOITED
UNISEXUALLY
VEXILLATION
XANTHINURIA
XANTHOXENITE
XENARTHROUS
XENOPARASITE

20
ANNEXATIONIST
ATAXIAMETER
AUTOCRATRIX
AUTOTOXEMIA
AUTOXIDATION
AUXANOMETER
AXODENDRITE
AXONOLIPOUS
COEXTENSION
CONNEXITIES
CONSOLATRIX
CONTEXTUAL
DEXTROUSNESS
ENTEROPEXIA
EXAGGERATOR
EXAMINATION
EXANIMATION
EXASPERATER
EXAUCTORATE
EXAUGURATION
EXCANTATION
EXCARNATION
EXCLUSIONER
EXCORIATION
EXCURSIONAL
EXCURSIONER
EXECUTIONAL
EXECUTIONER
EXECUTORIAL
EXENTERATING
EXIGUOUSNESS
EXISTLESSNESS
EXOGASTRITIS
EXOMETRITIS
EXPANSIONAL
EXPATIATION
EXPENDITRIX

EXPLANATION
EXPLORATION
EXPONENTIAL
EXPORTATION
EXPOSTULATE
EXPRESSLESS
EXSANGUINATE
EXSANGUINOUS
EXSTIPULATE
EXTERIORATION
EXTERMINATE
EXTERNALISM
EXTERNALITIES
EXTERRESTRIAL
EXTERRITORIAL
EXTIRPATION
EXTRACOSTAL
EXTRADITING
EXTRAPOLATE
EXTRAREGULAR
EXTRATRIBAL
EXTREMENESS
EXTREMITIES
EXTRICATION
EXTRINSICAL

EXUBERATION
GITOXIGENIN
INEXACTNESS
INEXECUTION
INEXISTENCE
INOBNOXIOUS
INTOXICATOR
LUXURIANTNESS
LUXURIOUSNESS
MAXILLARIES
MIXTILINEAR
NEUROPLEXUS
POSTEXILIAN
PREEXISTENT
PRETEXTUOUS
SCILLITOXIN
SEMISEXTILE
SEXAGENARIAN
SEXDIGITATE
SPLENOTOXIN
STIMULATRIX
SUBLUXATION
SUPERSEXUAL
TAXABLENESS
TOXOGLOSSATE

UNEXACTNESS
UNEXPERIENT
XEROTRIPSIS

19
ALEXANDRITE
ANGIOATAXIA
ANNEXATIONAL
ANTIOXIDANT
ATLANTOAXIAL
AUTOXIDATOR
DEXTROSURIA
EXALLOTRIOTE
EXALTEDNESS
EXECUTRIXES
EXENTERATED
EXENTERATION
EXOARTERITIS
EXONERATING
EXPIATIONA
EXPRESSION
EXSANGUIOUS
EXTENSIONIST
EXTENUATING
EXTERIORNESS

EXTERRANEOUS
EXTORTIONATE
EXTORTIONIST
EXTRADITION
EXTRALATERAL
EXTRARETINAL
EXTRAUTERINE
GASTROTAXIS
INTERTEXTURE
LEGISLATRIX
LUXULLIANITE
LUXURIATING
NEGOTIATRIX
ODONTEXESIS
ODONTOLOXIA
OXIDATIONAL
RELAXEDNESS
STAURAXONIAL
TOXOGENESIS
XENOGENESIS
XENOSAUROID

18
ANNEXIONIST
ANXIOUSNESS

AUXILIARIES
AUXILIATION
EXANTLATION
EXARTERITIS
EXINANITION
EXISTENTIAL
EXONERATION
EXTENSIONAL
EXTENUATION
EXTERIORATE
EXTERNALIST
EXTERNATION
EXTOLLATION
EXTORTIONER
EXTRASEROUS
EXTRATARSAL
INTERSEXUAL
LUXURIATION
NONEXISTENT
NOXIOUSNESS
OSTEOSTIXIS
SEXLESSNESS
STAURAXONIA
STEREOTAXIS
TETROXALATE

High-Scoring Words Containing

Z

2-3 LETTER WORDS

ALPHABETICAL ORDER		POSITIONAL ORDER		SCORING ORDER	
ADZ	ZAX	ZA	GEZ	**19**	DZO
AZO	ZED	ZAC	GUZ	JIZ	GAZ
BIZ	ZEE	ZAD	HIZ	ZAX	GEZ
DZO	ZEL	ZAG	HUZ		GUZ
FEZ	ZER	ZAK	JIZ	**16**	ZAD
FIZ	ZHO	ZAR	NIZ	ZAK	ZAG
GAZ	ZIG	ZAX	POZ		ZED
GEZ	ZIP	ZED	SUZ	**15**	ZIG
GUZ	ZO	ZEE	TEZ	FEZ	
HIZ	ZOA	ZEL	TUZ	FIZ	
HUZ	ZOH	ZER	VIZ	HIZ	**12**
JIZ	ZOO	ZHO	WIZ	HUZ	AZO
NIZ		ZIG	WUZ	VIZ	NIZ
POZ		ZIP	YEZ	WIZ	SUZ
SUZ		ZO		WUZ	TEZ
TEZ		ZOA		YEZ	TUZ
TUZ		ZOH		ZHO	ZAR
VIZ		ZOO		ZOH	ZEE
WIZ					ZEL
WUZ		AZO		**14**	ZER
YEZ		DZO		BIZ	ZOA
ZA				POZ	ZOO
ZAC		ADZ		ZAC	
ZAD		BIZ		ZIP	
ZAG		FEZ			**11**
ZAK		FIZ		**13**	ZA
ZAR		GAZ		ADZ	ZO

595

ALPHABETICAL LIST OF 4-LETTER WORDS

ADZE	FUZE	LUTZ	TOZE	ZERO
AZAM	FUZZ	MAZA	TUZA	ZEST
AZAN	GAZE	MAZE	TUZZ	ZETA
AZEW	GAZI	MAZY	TZAR	ZIIM
AZON	GAZY	MOZO	TZUT	ZIMB
AZYM	GIZZ	MUZZ	UNTZ	ZINC
BATZ	GUZE	NAZE	UNZE	ZING
BAZE	HAYZ	NAZI	UZAN	ZINK
BIZE	HAZE	NIZY	VAZA	ZIRA
BOZA	HAZY	ONZA	VIZY	ZIZZ
BOZO	HIZZ	OOZE	WHIZ	ZNAK
BUZZ	HUZZ	OOZY	WUZU	ZOBO
CAZA	IZAR	OUZO	ZAIN	ZOBU
CAZY	IZBA	OYEZ	ZANT	ZOEA
CHEZ	IZLE	PIZE	ZANY	ZOGO
COZE	JAZZ	PUTZ	ZARF	ZOIC
COZY	JEEZ	QUIZ	ZARP	ZOID
CZAR	JUEZ	QUOZ	ZART	ZOLL
DAZE	KAZI	RAZE	ZATI	ZONA
DAZY	KAZY	RAZZ	ZEAL	ZONE
DOZE	KNEZ	RITZ	ZEBU	ZOOM
DOZY	KOZO	SITZ	ZEDS	ZOON
EZBA	LAZE	SIZE	ZEES	ZOPE
FAZE	LAZO	SIZY	ZEIN	ZULU
FIZZ	LAZY	SIZZ	ZEME	ZUPA
FOZE	LEZA	SUZU	ZEMI	ZUZA
FOZY	LITZ	SWIZ	ZENU	ZYME
FRIZ	LIZA	TIZA	ZEPP	

POSITIONAL ORDER LIST OF 4-LETTER WORDS

ZAIN	ZOIC	BOZA	LAZY	BATZ
ZANT	ZOID	BOZO	LEZA	BUZZ
ZANY	ZOLL	BUZZ	LIZA	CHEZ
ZARF	ZONA	CAZA	MAZA	FIZZ
ZARP	ZONE	CAZY	MAZE	FRIZ
ZART	ZOOM	COZE	MAZY	FUZZ
ZATI	ZOON	COZY	MOZO	GIZZ
ZEAL	ZOPE	DAZE	MUZZ	HAYZ
ZEBU	ZULU	DAZY	NAZE	HIZZ
ZEDS	ZUPA	DOZE	NAZI	HUZZ
ZEES	ZUZA	DOZY	NIZY	JAZZ
ZEIN	ZYGA	FAZE	ONZA	JEEZ
ZEME	ZYME	FIZZ	OOZE	JUEZ
ZEMI		FOZE	OOZY	KNEZ
ZENU	AZAM	FOZY	OUZO	LITZ
ZEPP	AZAN	FUZE	PIZE	LUTZ
ZERO	AZEW	FUZZ	RAZE	MUZZ
ZEST	AZON	GAZE	RAZZ	OYEZ
ZETA	AZYM	GAZY	SIZE	PUTZ
ZIIM	CZAR	GIZZ	SIZY	QUIZ
ZIMB	EZBA	GUZE	SIZZ	QUOZ
ZINC	IZAR	HAZE	SUZU	RAZZ
ZING	IZBA	HAZY	TIZA	RITZ
ZINK	IZLE	HIZZ	TOZE	SITZ
ZIRA	TZAR	HUZZ	TUZA	SIZZ
ZIZZ	TZUT	JAZZ	TUZZ	SWIZ
ZNAK	UZAN	KAZI	UNZE	TUZZ
ZOBO		KAZY	VAZA	UNTZ
ZOBU	ADZE	KOZO	VIZY	WHIZ
ZOEA	BAZE	LAZE	WUZU	ZIZZ
ZOGO	BIZE	LAZO	ZIZZ	
			ZUZA	

SCORING ORDER LIST OF 4-LETTER WORDS

22	20	19	JAZZ	18
QUIZ	JEEZ	FOZY	VIZY	AZYM
QUOZ	JUEZ	HAYZ	WHIZ	CAZY
	KAZY	HAZY		CHEZ

COZY	SWIZ	ZARP	**13**	UZAN
MAZY	VAZA	ZEBU	AZAN	ZAIN
ZYME	WUZU	ZEME	AZON	ZANT
	ZANY	ZEMI	GIZZ	ZART
17	ZARF	ZIIM	IZAR	ZATI
DAZY		ZINC	IZLE	ZEAL
DOZY		ZOBO	LAZE	ZEES
GAZY	**15**	ZOBU	LAZO	ZEIN
KAZI	AZAM	ZOIC	LEZA	ZENU
KNEZ	BATZ	ZOOM	LITZ	ZERO
KOZO	BAZE	ZOPE	LIZA	ZEST
ZEPP	BIZE	ZUPA	LUTZ	ZETA
ZIMB	BOZA		NAZE	ZIRA
ZINK	BOZO		NAZI	ZOEA
ZNAK	CAZA	**14**	ONZA	ZOLL
	COZE	ADZE	OOZE	ZONA
16	CZAR	BUZZ	OUZO	ZONE
AZEW	EZBA	DAZE	RAZE	ZOON
FAZE	FIZZ	DOZE	RITZ	ZULU
FOZE	FUZZ	GAZE	SITZ	
FRIZ	HIZZ	GAZI	SIZE	
FUZE	HUZZ	GUZE	SUZU	**12**
HAZE	IZBA	MUZZ	TIZA	RAZZ
LAZY	MAZA	ZEDS	TOZE	SIZZ
NIZY	MAZE	ZING	TUZA	TUZZ
OOZY	MOZO	ZOGO	TZAR	ZUZA
OYEZ	PIZE	ZOID	TZUT	
SIZY	PUTZ		UNTZ	**11**
			UNZE	ZIZZ

ALPHABETICAL LIST OF 5-LETTER WORDS

ABAZE	BLIZZ	DOZEN	GLAZE	KNYAZ
ABUZZ	BONZA	DOZER	GLAZY	KONZE
ADOZE	BONZE	DROZE	GLOZE	KOUZA
ADZER	BORTZ	ECIZE	GRAZE	KUDZU
ADZES	BOZAH	ENZYM	GROSZ	LANAZ
AGAZE	BOZAL	ERIZO	GUAZA	LAZAR
AIZLE	BOZZE	FAIZE	HAFIZ	LAZED
ALEZE	BRAZA	FAZED	HAMZA	LAZZO
AMAZE	BRAZE	FEAZE	HAZAN	LEAZE
AMUZE	BRIZE	FEEZE	HAZEL	LOZEN
ARROZ	BRIZZ	FELZE	HAZEN	MAINZ
ARZUN	BRUZZ	FEZZY	HAZER	MAIZE
AZIDE	BUAZE	FIZZY	HAZLE	MATZO
AZINE	BUZZY	FRAZE	HEAZY	MAZAR
AZLON	BWAZI	FRIZE	HEEZE	MAZED
AZOCH	BYZEN	FRIZZ	HERTZ	MAZER
AZOFY	CAFIZ	FROZE	HOOZE	MAZIC
AZOIC	CAHIZ	FURZE	HUZZA	MAZUT
AZOLE	CHOZA	FURZY	HUZZY	METZE
AZOTE	CLIZA	FUZEE	IZARD	MEZZA
AZOTH	COLZA	FUZIL	IZOTE	MEZZO
AZOXY	COZED	FUZZY	IZTLE	MIMZY
AZURE	COZEN	GAIZE	IZTLI	MIRZA
AZURY	COZEY	GANZA	IZZAT	MIZZY
AZYME	COZIE	GAUZE	JAZEL	MURZA
BAIZA	CRAZE	GAUZY	JAZZY	MUZZY
BAIZE	CRAZY	GAZED	JEREZ	NAMAZ
BAZAR	CROZE	GAZEL	JEZIA	NAZIM
BAZOO	DANZA	GAZER	JIZYA	NAZIR
BEZEL	DARZI	GAZET	KAFIZ	NAZIS
BEZIL	DAZED	GAZON	KANZU	NEEZE
BEZZO	DIAZO	GAZOO	KAREZ	N:ZEY
BIZLE	DIZEN	GAZOZ	KAZAK	OOZED
BLAZE	DIZZY	GEYZE	KAZOO	OOZEL
BLAZY	DOOZY	GHAZI	KNEZI	OUZEL
BLITZ	DOZED	GIZMO	KNIAZ	OWZEL

OZENA	SOZIN	WEIZE	ZEMMI	ZOISM
OZONE	SPITZ	WHIZZ	ZEMNI	ZOIST
PEIZE	SQUIZ	WINZE	ZENIK	ZOKOR
PEZZO	SWIZZ	WIZEN	ZERDA	ZOMBI
PIEZO	TAZIA	WOOTZ	ZEROS	ZONAE
PIZZA	TAZZA	WOOZY	ZESTY	ZONAL
PLAZA	TEAZE	YEZZY	ZIARA	ZONAR
POIZE	TENEZ	YOUZE	ZIBEB	ZONDA
PRIZE	TERZO	ZABRA	ZIEGA	ZONED
QAZAQ	TIRAZ	ZABTI	ZIFFS	ZONIC
RAZEE	TIZZY	ZAKAH	ZIHAR	ZOOID
RAZED	TOPAZ	ZAKAT	ZIMBI	ZOONS
RAZON	TOZEE	ZAMAN	ZIMME	ZOPPA
RAZOO	TOZER	ZAMBO	ZIMMI	ZOPPO
RAZOR	TOZIE	ZANJA	ZIMMY	ZORIL
REZAI	TROOZ	ZANTE	ZINCO	ZORRA
RITZY	TZUTE	ZANZE	ZINCY	ZORRO
ROZUM	ULZIE	ZAPAS	ZINEB	ZOWIE
SABZI	UNZEN	ZARAH	ZINKE	ZUCHE
SAZEN	UYEZD	ZAYAT	ZINKY	ZUDDA
SEIZE	VIZIR	ZAYIN	ZIPPY	ZUPAN
SIZAR	VIZOR	ZEBEC	ZIRAI	ZYGAL
SIZED	VIZZY	ZEBRA	ZIRAM	ZYGON
SIZER	VORAZ	ZEBUB	ZIZEL	ZYMIC
SIZES	WALTZ	ZEBUS	ZLOTY	ZYMIN
SMAZE	WANZE	ZEINE	ZOCCO	
SNITZ	WAZIR	ZEISM	ZOEAL	
SOULZ	WEEZE	ZEIST	ZOGAN	

POSITIONAL ORDER LIST OF 5-LETTER WORDS

ZABRA	ZIZEL	AZYME	GAZEL	PEZZO
ZABTI	ZLOTY	IZARD	GAZER	PIZZA
ZAKAH	ZOCCO	IZOTE	GAZET	QAZAQ
ZAKAT	ZOEAL	IZTLE	GAZI	RAZEE
ZAMAN	ZOGAN	IZTLI	GAZON	RAZED
ZAMBO	ZOISM	IZZAT	GAZOO	RAZON
ZANJA	ZOIST	OZENA	GAZOZ	RAZOO
ZANTE	ZOKOR	OZONE	GIZMO	RAZOR
ZANZE	ZOMBI	TZUTE	HAZAN	REZAI
ZAPAS	ZONAE		HAZEL	ROZUM
ZARAH	ZONAL	ADZER	HAZEN	SAZEN
ZAYAT	ZONAR	ADZES	HAZER	SIZAR
ZAYIN	ZONDA	AIZLE	HAZLE	SIZED
ZEBEC	ZONED	ARZUN	HUZZA	SIZER
ZEBRA	ZONIC	BAZAR	HUZZY	SIZES
ZEBUB	ZOOID	BAZOO	IZZAT	SOZIN
ZEBUS	ZOONS	BEZEL	JAZEL	TAZIA
ZEINE	ZOPPA	BEZIL	JAZZY	TAZZA
ZEISM	ZOPPO	BEZZO	JEZIA	TIZZY
ZEIST	ZORIL	BIZLE	JIZYA	TOZEE
ZEMMI	ZORRA	BOZAH	KAZAK	TOZER
ZEMNI	ZORRO	BOZAL	KAZOO	TOZIE
ZENIK	ZOWIE	BOZZE	LAZAR	ULZIE
ZERDA	ZUCHE	BUZZY	LAZED	UNZEN
ZEROS	ZUDDA	BYZEN	LAZZO	VIZIR
ZESTY	ZUPAN	COZED	LOZEN	VIZOR
ZIARA	ZYGAL	COZEN	MAZAR	VIZZY
ZIBEB	ZYGON	COZEY	MAZED	WAZIR
ZIEGA	ZYMIC	COZIE	MAZER	WIZEN
ZIFFS	ZYMIN	DAZED	MAZIC	YEZZY
ZIHAR		DIZEN	MAZUT	ZIZEL
ZIMBI	AZIDE	DIZZY	MEZZA	ABAZE
ZIMME	AZINE	DOZED	MEZZO	ABUZZ
ZIMMI	AZLON	DOZEN	MIZZY	ADOZE
ZIMMY	AZOCH	DOZER	MUZZY	AGAZE
ZINCO	AZOFY	ENZYM	NAZIM	ALEZE
ZINCY	AZOIC	FAZED	NAZIR	AMAZE
ZINEB	AZOLE	FEZZY	NAZIS	AMUZE
ZINKE	AZOTE	FIZZY	NIZEY	BAIZA
ZINKY	AZOTH	FUZEE	OOZED	BAIZE
ZIPPY	AZOXY	FUZIL	OOZEL	BEZZO
ZIRAI	AZURE	FUZZY	OUZEL	BLAZE
ZIRAM	AZURY	GAZED	OWZEL	BLAZY

BLIZZ	FEEZE	JAZZY	SEIZE	CAHIZ
BONZA	FELZE	KANZU	SMAZE	FRIZZ
BONZE	FEZZY	KNEZI	SWIZZ	GAZOZ
BOZZE	FIZZY	KONZE	TAZZA	GROSZ
BRAZA	FRAZE	KOUZA	TEAZE	HAFIZ
BRAZE	FRIZE	KUDZU	TERZO	HERTZ
BRIZE	FRIZZ	LAZZO	TIZZY	JEREZ
BRIZZ	FROZE	LEAZE	UYEZD	KAFIZ
BRUZZ	FURZE	MAIZE	VIZZY	KAREZ
BUAZE	FURZY	MATZO	WANZE	KNIAZ
BUZZY	FUZZY	METZE	WEEZE	KNYAZ
BWAZI	GAIZE	MEZZA	WEIZE	LANAZ
CHOZA	GANZA	MEZZO	WHIZZ	MAINZ
CLIZA	GAUZE	MIMZY	WINZE	NAMAZ
COLZA	GAUZY	MIRZA	WOOZY	SNITZ
CRAZE	GEYZE	MIZZY	YEZZY	SOULZ
CRAZY	GHAZI	MURZA	YOUZE	SPITZ
CROZE	GLAZE	MUZZY	ZANZE	SQUIZ
DANZA	GLAZY	NEEZE		SWIZZ
DARZI	GLOZE	PEIZE		TENEZ
DIAZO	GRAZE	PEZZO	ABUZZ	TIRAZ
DIZZY	GUAZA	PIEZO	ARROZ	TOPAZ
DOOZY	HAMZA	PIZZA	BLITZ	TROOZ
DROZE	HEAZY	PLAZA	BLIZZ	VORAZ
ECIZE	HEEZE	POIZE	BORTZ	WALTZ
ERIZO	HOOZE	PRIZE	BRIZZ	WHIZZ
FAIZE	HUZZA	RITZY	BRUZZ	WOOTZ
FEAZE	HUZZY	SABZI	CAFIZ	

SCORING ORDER LIST OF 5-LETTER WORDS

24	COZEY	ZIMME	WALTZ	CRAZE
AZOXY	CRAZY	ZIMMI	WANZE	CROZE
JIZYA	ENZYM	ZINKE	WAZIR	DAZED
	FEZZY	ZOCCO	WEEZE	DOZED
23	FIZZY	ZOKOR	WEIZE	ECIZE
JAZZY	FUZZY	ZOMBI	WINZE	FRIZZ
SQUIZ	HAMZA	ZOPPA	WIZEN	GAZED
	HUZZY	ZOPPO	WOOTZ	HUZZA
22	KUDZU	ZYGAL	YOUZE	MAINZ
QAZAQ	VIZZY	ZYGON	ZARAH	MAIZE
	WHIZZ		ZAYAT	MATZO
21	YEZZY	**17**	ZAYIN	MAZAR
JAZEL	ZINCY	AZOTH	ZESTY	MAZER
JEREZ	ZUCHE	AZURY	ZIHAR	MAZUT
JEZIA	ZYMIN	COZED	ZLOTY	METZE
KAFIZ		DIZZY	ZOWIE	MIRZA
KNYAZ	**18**	FAIZE		MURZA
MIMZY	BUZZY	FEAZE	**16**	NAMAZ
ZAKAH	DOOZY	FEEZE	ABAZE	NAZIM
ZANJA	FAZED	FELZE	AMAZE	PEIZE
ZIMMY	GAUZY	FRAZE	AMUZE	PIEZO
ZINKY	GEYZE	FRIZE	AZOIC	PLAZA
ZIPPY	GHAZI	FROZE	BAIZA	POIZE
ZYMIC	GLAZY	FURZE	BAIZE	PRIZE
	KANZU	FUZEE	BAZAR	ROZUM
20	KAREZ	FUZIL.	BAZOO	SABZI
AZOFY	KAZOO	GIZMO	BEZEL	SMAZE
FURZY	KNEZI	HAZAN	BEZIL	SPITZ
HAFIZ	KNIAZ	HAZEL	BIZLE	SWIZZ
HEAZY	KONZE	HAZEN	BLAZE	TIZZY
WOOZY	KOUZA	HAZER	BLITZ	TOPAZ
ZIFFS	MAZIC	HAZLE	BONZA	ZABRA
	MIZZY	HEEZE	BONZE	ZABTI
19	MUZZY	HERTZ	BORTZ	ZAMAN
AZOCH	UYEZD	HOOZE	BOZAL	ZAPAS
AZYME	ZAKAT	KAZAK	BRAZA	ZEBRA
BLAZY	ZAMBO	MAZED	BRAZE	ZEBUS
BOZAH	ZEBEC	NIZEY	BRIZE	ZEISM
BWAZI	ZEBUB	OWZEL	BUAZE	ZEMNI
BYZEN	ZEMMI	RITZY	CLIZA	ZINCO
CAFIZ	ZENIK	VIZIR	COLZA	ZINEB
CAHIZ	ZIBEB	VIZOR	COZEN	ZIRAM
CHOZA	ZIMBI	VORAZ	COZIE	ZOISM

ZONIC	GAUZE	ZOOID	OUZEL	TZUTE
ZUDDA	GAZEL		OZENA	ULZIE
ZUPAN	GAZER	**14**	OZONE	UNZEN
	GAZET	AIZLE	RAZEE	ZANTE
15	GAZON	ALEZE	RAZON	ZEINE
ABUZZ	GAZOO	ARROZ	RAZOO	ZEIST
ADOZE	GLAZE	ARZUN	RAZOR	ZEROS
ADZER	GLOZE	AZINE	REZAI	ZIARA
ADZES	GRAZE	AZLON	SAZEN	ZIRAI
AGAZE	GROSZ	AZOLE	SEIZE	ZOEAL
AZIDE	GUAZA	AZOTE	SIZAR	ZOIST
BEZZO	IZARD	AZURE	SIZER	ZONAE
BLIZZ	LAZED	ERIZO	SIZES	ZONAL
BOZZE	MEZZA	GAZOZ	SNITZ	ZONAR
BRIZZ	MEZZO	IZOTE	SOULZ	ZOONS
BRUZZ	OOZED	IZTLE	SOZIN	ZORIL
DANZA	PEZZO	IZTLI	TAZIA	ZORRA
DARZI	PIZZA	LANAZ	TEAZE	ZORRO
DIAZO	RAZED	LAZAR	TENEZ	
DIZEN	SIZED	LEAZE	TERZO	**13**
DOZEN	ZERDA	LOZEN	TIRAZ	IZZAT
DOZER	ZIEGA	NAZIR	TOZEE	LAZZO
DROZE	ZOGAN	NAZIS	TOZER	TAZZA
GAIZE	ZONDA	NEEZE	TOZIE	ZANZE
GANZA	ZONED	OOZEL	TROOZ	

ALPHABETICAL LIST OF 6-LETTER WORDS

ABLAZE	BEZANT	CHAZAN	ENDAZE	GEEZER
ABRAZO	BEZOAR	CHINTZ	ENGAZE	GHAZAL
ACRAZE	BEZZLE	COROZO	ENTREZ	GHAZEL
AGAZED	BLAZED	CORYZA	ENZYME	GIZZEN
AGNIZE	BLAZER	COZIER	EOZOON	GLAZED
AJIMEZ	BLAZES	COZILY	EPIZOA	GLAZEN
AKAZGA	BLAZON	COZING	ERSATZ	GLAZER
ALAZOR	BLEEZE	CRAZED	ETHIZE	GLOZED
ALEZAN	BLEEZY	CROZED	FAZING	GLOZER
ALTEZA	BLINTZ	CROZER	FEAZED	GOOZLE
AMAZED	BLOWZE	CROZLE	FEZZED	GOZELL
AMAZON	BLOWZY	CUNZIE	FEZZES	GOZILL
APOZEM	BONNAZ	DANZON	FIZGIG	GOZZAN
ASSIZE	BONZER	DARZEE	FIZZED	GRANZA
ATAZIR	BORIZE	DAZING	FIZZER	GRAZED
AVELOZ	BORZOI	DAZZLE	FIZZLE	GROSZY
AZALEA	BOZINE	DENIZE	FLOOZY	GROUZE
AZILUT	BRAIZE	DESIZE	FOOZLE	GROWZE
AZIMIN	BRAZED	DEUZAN	FRAZER	GROZER
AZIOLA	BRAZEN	DEZINC	FRAZIL	GUZZLE
AZONAL	BRAZER	DIAZID	FREEZE	HALERZ
AZONIC	BRAZIL	DIAZIN	FREEZY	HALUTZ
AZOTEA	BREEZE	DIZDAR	FRENZY	HAMETZ
AZOTED	BREEZY	DIZZEN	FRIEZE	HAMZAH
AZOTIC	BRONZE	DONZEL	FRIEZY	HAZARD
AZOTIN	BRONZY	DOZENS	FRIZEL	HAZIER
AZTECA	BROUZE	DOZENT	FRIZER	HAZILY
AZURED	BRYNZA	DOZIER	FRIZZY	HAZING
AZYGOS	BUDZAT	DOZILY	FROUZE	HAZZAN
BAIZED	BUZANE	DOZING	FROUZY	HELZEL
BANZAI	BUZZED	DOZZLE	FROWZE	HIZZIE
BATZEN	BUZZER	DRAZEL	FROWZY	HOWITZ
BAZAAR	BUZZLE	DRAZIL	FROZEN	HUZOOR
BEDAZE	BYZANT	DURZEE	FURZED	HUZZAH
BEEZER	CABEZA	DZEREN	FUZZLE	IODIZE
BENZAL	CANZON	DZERIN	GANZIE	IONIZE
BENZIL	CAZIBI	DZERON	GAZABO	IOTIZE
BENZIN	CAZIMI	ECZEMA	GAZEBO	ITZEBU
BENZOL	CENIZO	EGOIZE	GAZING	IZAFAT
BENZYL	CEREZA		GAZOOK	IZZARD

JAZZER	OBRIZE	SIZING	WIZZEN	ZINCED
JEZAIL	OKRUZI	SIZZLE	WOOZLE	ZINCIC
JEZIAH	OOZIER	SLEAZY	WUZZER	ZINCID
JIZYAH	OOZILY	SLEEZY	WUZZLE	ZINCKE
JUZAIL	OOZING	SLEPEZ	YETZER	ZINCKY
KHAZEN	OOZOID	SMALTZ	YIZKOR	ZINCUM
KIBITZ	OUYEZD	SNAZZY	YUZLIK	ZINDIQ
KOLKOZ	OXAZIN	SNEEZE	YUZLUK	ZINGEL
KORZEC	OZAENA	SNEEZY	ZABETA	ZINNIA
KRANTZ	OZOENA	SNOOZE	ZACATE	ZIPPER
KUDIZE	OZONED	SNOOZY	ZACHUN	ZIRCON
KUVASZ	OZONER	SOZZLE	ZADDIK	ZITHER
KVUTZA	OZONIC	SOZZLY	ZAFFAR	ZIZANY
LANZON	OZONID	SPELTZ	ZAFFER	ZIZITH
LAZARY	PALETZ	SPRITZ	ZAFFIR	ZIZZLE
LAZIER	PANZER	STANZA	ZAFFRE	ZLOTYS
LAZILY	PAPIZE	STANZE	ZAGGED	ZOACUM
LAZING	PHIZOG	STANZO	ZAGUAN	ZOARIA
LAZULE	PIAZIN	SUIVEZ	ZAMANG	ZOCALO
LAZULI	PIAZZA	SYZYGY	ZANANA	ZODIAC
LIZARD	PIZZLE	TAFWIZ	ZANDER	ZOETIC
LIZARY	PRIZED	TARZAN	ZANIES	ZOILUS
MAHZOR	PRIZER	TAZEEA	ZANJON	ZOMBIE
MAIZER	PRIZES	TEAZEL	ZAPOTE	ZOMBIS
MAMZER	PUSZTA	TEAZLE	ZAPUPE	ZONARY
MANZIL	PUZZLE	TENZON	ZAREBA	ZONATE
MARKAZ	QUARTZ	TERFEZ	ZARNEC	ZONING
MATZOH	QUEZAL	TERZET	ZEALED	ZONITE
MATZOS	QUILEZ	TERZIO	ZEALOT	ZONNAR
MATZOT	QUINZE	TIZEUR	ZEBECK	ZONOID
MAZAME	QUIZZY	TOLZEY	ZEBRAS	ZONULA
MAZARD	RAZEED	TOOZLE	ZECHIN	ZONULE
MAZIER	RAZING	TOOZOO	ZEEKOE	ZONURE
MAZILY	RAZOUR	TOPAZY	ZEHNER	ZOONAL
MAZING	RAZZIA	TOUZLE	ZELANT	ZOONIC
MAZUCA	RAZZLY	TOWZIE	ZENANA	ZOOSIS
MAZUMA	REBOZO	TRIAZO	ZENDIK	ZOOTIC
MEZCAL	RESIZE	TWAZZY	ZENICK	ZOOZOO
MEZUZA	RIZZAR	TWEEZE	ZENITH	ZOSTER
MEZZOS	RIZZER	TZETZE	ZENZIC	ZOUNDS
MIZZEN	RIZZLE	TZIRID	ZEPHYR	ZOYSIA
MIZZLE	RIZZOM	UNMAZE	ZEQUIN	ZUFOLO
MIZZLY	SCAZON	URAZIN	ZEREBA	ZUISIN
MOUZAH	SCHANZ	UZARIN	ZEROES	ZYGION
MOZING	SCORZA	UZARON	ZESTED	ZYGITE
MUZHIK	SCRAZE	VIZARD	ZEUGMA	ZYGOMA
MUZJIK	SCRUZE	VIZIER	ZIAMET	ZYGOSE
MUZZLE	SEIZED	VIZSLA	ZIARAT	ZYGOTE
MYZONT	SEIZER	WEAZEN	ZIBETH	ZYGOUS
NAZARD	SEIZIN	WEEZLE	ZIEGER	ZYMASE
NAZIFY	SEIZOR	WENZEL	ZIGGER	ZYMITE
NOZZLE	SHINZA	WHEEZE	ZIGZAG	ZYMOID
NUZZER	SINZER	WHEEZY	ZILLAH	ZYMOME
NUZZLE	SIZIER	WIZARD	ZIMMIS	ZYTHUM

POSITIONAL ORDER LIST OF 6-LETTER WORDS

ZABETA	ZAPUPE	ZEPHYR	ZINCID	ZOCALO
ZACATE	ZAREBA	ZEQUIN	ZINCKE	ZODIAC
ZACHUN	ZARNEC	ZEREBA	ZINCKY	ZOETIC
ZADDIK	ZEALED	ZEROES	ZINCUM	ZOILUS
ZAFFAR	ZEALOT	ZESTED	ZINDIQ	ZOMBIE
ZAFFER	ZEBECK	ZEUGMA	ZINGEL	ZOMBIS
ZAFFIR	ZEBRAS	ZIAMET	ZINNIA	ZONARY
ZAFFRE	ZECHIN	ZIARAT	ZIPPER	ZONATE
ZAGGED	ZEEKOE	ZIBETH	ZIRCON	ZONING
ZAGUAN	ZEHNER	ZIEGER	ZITHER	ZONITE
ZAMANG	ZELANT	ZIGGER	ZIZANY	ZONNAR
ZANANA	ZENANA	ZIGZAG	ZIZITH	ZONOID
ZANDER	ZENDIK	ZILLAH	ZIZZLE	ZONULA
ZANIES	ZENICK	ZIMMIS	ZLOTYS	ZONULE
ZANJON	ZENITH	ZINCED	ZOACUM	ZONURE
ZAPOTE	ZENZIC	ZINCIC	ZOARIA	ZOONAL

ZOONIC	ECZEMA	RIZZAR	EPIZOA	SEIZER
ZOOSIS	ENZYME	RIZZER	FEAZED	SEIZIN
ZOOTIC	EOZOON	RIZZLE	FEEZED	SEIZOR
ZOOZOO	FAZING	RIZZOM	FEZZES	SINZER
ZOSTER	FEZZED	SIZIER	FIZZED	SIZZLE
ZOUNDS	FEZZES	SIZING	FIZZER	SNAZZY
ZOYSIA	FIZGIG	SIZZLE	FIZZLE	SOZZLE
ZUFOLO	FIZZED	SOZZLE	FOOZLE	SOZZLY
ZUISIN	FIZZER	SOZZLY	FRAZER	TARZAN
ZYGION	FIZZLE	SYZYGY	FRAZIL	TEAZEL
ZYGITE	FUZZLE	TAZEEA	FRIZEL	TEAZLE
ZYGOMA	GAZABO	TIZEUR	FRIZER	TENZON
ZYGOSE	GAZEBO	VIZARD	FRIZZY	TERZET
ZYGOTE	GAZING	VIZIER	FROZEN	TERZIO
ZYGOUS	GAZOOK	VIZSLA	FURZED	TOLZEY
ZYMASE	GIZZEN	WIZARD	FUZZLE	TOOZLE
ZYMITE	GOZELL	WIZZEN	GANZIE	TOOZOO
ZYMOID	GOZILL	WUZZER	GEEZER	TOUZLE
ZYMOME	GOZZAN	WUZZLE	GHAZAL	TOWZIE
ZYTHUM	GUZZLE	YIZKOR	GHAZEL	TWAZZY
	HAZARD	YUZLIK	GIZZEN	URAZIN
AZALEA	HAZIER	YUZLUK	GLAZED	WEAZEN
AZILUT	HAZILY	ZIZANY	GLAZEN	WEEZLE
AZIMIN	HAZING	ZIZITH	GLAZER	WENZEL
AZIOLA	HAZZAN	ZIZZLE	GLOZED	WIZZEN
AZONAL	HIZZIE		GLOZER	WOOZLE
AZONIC	HUZOOR	AGAZED	GOOZLE	WUZZER
AZOTEA	HUZZAH	AKAZGA	GOZZAN	WUZZLE
AZOTED	ITZEBU	ALAZOR	GRAZED	YETZER
AZOTIC	IZZARD	ALEZAN	GROZER	ZENZIC
AZOTIN	JAZZER	AMAZED	GUZZLE	ZIGZAG
AZTECA	JEZAIL	AMAZON	HAMZAH	ZIZZLE
AZURED	JEZIAH	APOZEM	HAZZAN	ZOOZOO
AZYGOS	JIZYAH	ATAZIR	HELZEL	
DZEREN	JUZAIL	BAIZED	HIZZIE	ABLAZE
DZERIN	LAZARY	BANZAI	HUZZAH	ABRAZO
DZERON	LAZIER	BATZEN	JAZZER	ACRAZE
IZAFAT	LAZILY	BEEZER	KHAZEN	AGNIZE
IZZARD	LAZING	BENZAL	KORZEC	ALTEZA
OZAENA	LAZULE	BENZIL	LANZON	ASSIZE
OZOENA	LAZULI	BENZIN	MAHZOR	BEDAZE
OZONED	LIZARD	BENZOL	MAIZER	BLEEZE
OZONER	LIZARY	BENZYL	MAMZER	BLEEZY
OZONIC	MAZAME	BEZZLE	MANZIL	BLOWZE
OZONID	MAZARD	BLAZED	MATZOH	BLOWZY
TZETZE	MAZIER	BLAZER	MATZOS	BORIZE
TZIRID	MAZILY	BLAZES	MATZOT	BRAIZE
UZARIN	MAZING	BLAZON	MEZZOS	BREEZE
UZARON	MAZUCA	BONZER	MIZZEN	BREEZY
	MAZUMA	BORZOI	MIZZLE	BRONZE
BAZAAR	MEZCAL	BRAZED	MIZZLY	BRONZY
BEZANT	MEZUZA	BRAZEN	MOUZAH	BROUZE
BEZOAR	MEZZOS	BRAZER	MUZZLE	BRYNZA
BEZZLE	MIZZEN	BRAZIL	NOZZLE	CABEZA
BOZINE	MIZZLE	BUDZAT	NUZZER	CENIZO
BUZANE	MIZZLY	BUZZED	NUZZLE	CEREZA
BUZZED	MOZING	BUZZER	OXAZIN	COROZO
BUZZER	MUZHIK	BUZZLE	PANZER	CORYZA
BUZZLE	MUZJIK	CANZON	PHIZOG	DENIZE
BYZANT	MUZZLE	CHAZAN	PIAZIN	DESIZE
CAZIBI	MYZONT	CRAZED	PIAZZA	EGOIZE
CAZIMI	NAZARD	CROZED	PIZZLE	ENDAZE
COZIER	NAZIFY	CROZER	PRIZED	ENGAZE
COZILY	NOZZLE	CROZLE	PRIZER	ETHIZE
COZING	NUZZER	CUNZIE	PRIZES	FLOOZY
DAZING	NUZZLE	DANZON	PUSZTA	FREEZE
DAZZLE	OOZIER	DARZEE	PUZZLE	FREEZY
DEZINC	OOZILY	DAZZLE	QUEZAL	FRENZY
DIZAIN	OOZING	DEUZAN	QUIZZY	FRIEZE
DIZDAR	OOZOID	DIAZID	RAZZIA	FRIEZY
DIZZEN	PIZZLE	DIAZIN	RAZZLY	FRIZZY
DOZENS	PUZZLE	DIZZEN	RIZZAR	FROUZE
DOZENT	RAZEED	DONZEL	RIZZER	FROUZY
DOZIER	RAZING	DOZZLE	RIZZLE	FROWZE
DOZILY	RAZOUR	DRAZEL	RIZZOM	FROWZY
DOZING	RAZZIA	DRAZIL	SCAZON	GRANZA
DOZZLE	RAZZLY	DURZEE	SEIZED	GROSZY

GROUZE	QUIZZY	STANZA	AVELOZ	KUVASZ
GROWZE	REBOZO	STANZE	BLINTZ	MARKAZ
IODIZE	RESIZE	STANZO	BONNAZ	PALETZ
IONIZE	SCORZA	TOPAZY	CHINTZ	QUARTZ
IOTIZE	SCRAZE	TRIAZO	ENTREZ	QUILEZ
KUDIZE	SCRUZE	TWAZZY	ERSATZ	SCHANZ
KVUTZA	SHINZA	TWEEZE	HALERZ	SLEPEZ
MEZUZA	SLEAZY	TZETZE	HALUTZ	SMALTZ
OBRIZE	SLEEZY	UNMAZE	HAMETZ	SPELTZ
OKRUZI	SNAZZY	WHEEZE	HOWITZ	SPRITZ
OUYEZD	SNEEZE	WHEEZY	KIBITZ	SUIVEZ
PAPIZE	SNEEZY		KOLKOZ	TAFWIZ
PIAZZA	SNOOZE		KRANTZ	TERFEZ
QUINZE	SNOOZY	AJIMEZ		

SCORING ORDER LIST OF 6-LETTER WORDS

28	SYZYGY	FURZED	GAZEBO	AZTECA
JIZYAH	TAFWIZ	GHAZAL	HALERZ	BANZAI
MUZJIK	WHEEZE	GHAZEL	HALUTZ	BATZEN
	ZADDIK	GROSZY	HAZIER	BAZAAR
26	ZAFFAR	GROWZE	HELZEL	BEEZER
QUIZZY	ZAFFER	HAZARD	HUZOOR	BENZAL
	ZAFFIR	HAZING	IZAFAT	BENZIL
25	ZAFFRE	KRANTZ	KOLKOZ	BENZIN
JEZIAH	ZENICK	MAMZER	LAZARY	BENZOL
ZINDIQ	ZINCKE	MAZAME	LAZILY	BEZANT
	ZYGOMA	MAZUCA	LIZARY	BEZOAR
24	ZYMOID	MAZUMA	MAZARD	BLAZER
AJIMEZ		MEZCAL	MAZING	BLAZES
FROWZY	**20**	MIZZLY	MOZING	BLAZON
MUZHIK	AKAZGA	OKRUZI	OOZILY	BLEEZE
QUARTZ	BENZYL	OUYEZD	OOZING	BLINTZ
QUEZAL	BLEEZY	PAPIZE	PRIZED	BONNAZ
QUILEZ	BLOWZE	VIZARD	SHINZA	BONZER
QUINZE	BREEZY	WIZARD	SLEAZY	BORIZE
WHEEZY	BRONZY	ZAPUPE	SLEEZY	BORZOI
ZEQUIN	BRYNZA	ZEEKOE	SNEEZY	BOZINE
ZINCKY	BYZANT	ZIMMIS	SNOOZY	BRAIZE
	CHAZAN	ZINCIC	SUIVEZ	BRAZEN
23	CHINTZ	ZINCUM	TERFEZ	BRAZER
BLOWZY	CORYZA	ZIPPER	TOLZEY	BRAZIL
HAMZAH	COZILY	ZOACUM	TOWZIE	BREEZE
ZEBECK	ENZYME	ZOMBIE	TWEEZE	BRONZE
ZEPHYR	FIZGIG	ZOMBIS	VIZIER	BROUZE
ZYTHUM	FRIZZY	ZYGION	VIZSLA	BUZANE
	GAZOOK	ZYGITE	WEAZEN	BUZZED
22	HAMETZ	ZYGOSE	WEEZLE	CANZON
JEZAIL	HUZZAH	ZYGOTE	WENZEL	CENIZO
JUZAIL	KUDIZE	ZYGOUS	WOOZLE	CEREZA
KHAZEN	MAHZOR		YETZER	COROZO
KUVASZ	MATZOH	**18**	ZAGGED	COZIER
KVUTZA	MAZILY	AMAZED	ZAMANG	CROZER
OXAZIN	MOUZAH	AVELOZ	ZEHNER	CROZLE
YIZKOR	MYZONT	BAIZED	ZENITH	CUNZIE
YUZLIK	SCHANZ	BEDAZE	ZEUGMA	DAZING
YUZLUK	TOPAZY	BLAZED	ZILLAH	DIAZID
ZANJON	TWAZZY	BRAZED	ZINCED	DIZDAR
ZYMOME	ZACHUN	BUDZAT	ZINCID	DOZING
	ZECHIN	COZING	ZITHER	EPIZOA
21	ZENDIK	CRAZED	ZLOTYS	FEZZES
FLOOZY	ZIBETH	CROZED	ZODIAC	FIZZER
FREEZY	ZYMASE	DEZINC	ZONARY	FIZZLE
FRENZY	ZYMITE	ETHIZE	ZOYSIA	FUZZLE
FRIEZY		FEZZED	ZUFOLO	GAZING
FROUZY	**19**	FIZZED		GLAZED
FROWZE	APOZEM	FOOZLE	**17**	GLOZED
HAZILY	AZYGOS	FRAZER	ABLAZE	GRAZED
HOWITZ	CABEZA	FRAZIL	ABRAZO	HAZZAN
JAZZER	CAZIBI	FREEZE	ACRAZE	HIZZIE
KIBITZ	CAZIMI	FRIEZE	AGAZED	ITZEBU
KORZEC	DOZILY	FRIZEL	AMAZON	MAIZER
MARKAZ	ECZEMA	FRIZER	AZIMIN	MANZIL
NAZIFY	FAZING	FROZEN	AZONIC	MATZOS
PHIZOG	FEAZED	GAZABO	AZOTIC	MATZOT

MAZIER
OBRIZE
OZONIC
PALETZ
PANZER
PIAZIN
PRIZER
PRIZES
PUSZTA
RAZZLY
REBOZO
SCAZON
SCORZA
SCRAZE
SCRUZE
SLEPEZ
SMALTZ
SNAZZY
SOZZLY
SPELTZ
SPRITZ
UNMAZE
WIZZEN
WUZZER
WUZZLE
ZABETA
ZACATE
ZAPOTE
ZAREBA
ZARNEC
ZEBRAS
ZEREBA
ZIAMET
ZIGGER
ZIRCON
ZIZANY
ZIZITH
ZOCALO
ZOETIC
ZOONIC
ZOOTIC

16
AGNIZE
AZOTED
AZURED
BEZZLE
BUZZER
BUZZLE
DANZON
DARZEE
DENIZE
DESIZE
DEUZAN
DIAZIN
DIZAIN
DONZEL
DOZENS
DOZENT
DOZIER
DRAZEL
DRAZIL
DURZEE
DZEREN
DZERIN
DZERON
EGOIZE
ENDAZE
ENGAZE
GANZIE
GEEZER
GLAZEN
GLAZER
GLOZER
GOOZLE
GOZELL
GOZILL
GRANZA
GROUZE
GROZER
IODIZE
LAZING
LIZARD

MEZUZA
MEZZOS
MIZZEN
MIZZLE
MUZZLE
NAZARD
OOZOID
OZONED
OZONID
PIAZZA
PIZZLE
PUZZLE
RAZEED
RAZING
RIZZOM
SEIZED
SIZING
TZIRID
ZAGUAN
ZANDER
ZEALED
ZENZIC
ZESTED
ZIEGER
ZIGZAG
ZINGEL
ZONING
ZONOID
ZOUNDS

15
ALAZOR
ALEZAN
ALTEZA
ASSIZE
ATAZIR
AZALEA
AZILUT
AZIOLA
AZONAL
AZOTEA
AZOTIN

DAZZLE
DIZZEN
DOZZLE
ENTREZ
EOZOON
ERSATZ
GIZZEN
GOZZAN
GUZZLE
IONIZE
IOTIZE
IZZARD
LANZON
LAZIER
LAZULE
LAZULI
OOZIER
OZAENA
OZOENA
OZONER
RAZOUR
RESIZE
SEIZER
SEIZIN
SEIZOR
SINZER
SIZIER
SNEEZE
SNOOZE
STANZA
STANZE
STANZO
TARZAN
TAZEEA
TEAZEL
TEAZLE
TENZON
TERZET
TERZIO
TIZEUR
TOOZLE
TOOZOO

TOUZLE
TRIAZO
URAZIN
UZARIN
UZARON
ZANANA
ZANIES
ZEALOT
ZELANT
ZENANA
ZEROES
ZIARAT
ZINNIA
ZOARIA
ZOILUS
ZONATE
ZONITE
ZONNAR
ZONULA
ZONULE
ZONURE
ZOONAL
ZOOSIS
ZOSTER
ZUISIN

14
NOZZLE
NUZZER
NUZZLE
RAZZIA
RIZZAR
RIZZER
RIZZLE
SIZZLE
SOZZLE
TZETZE
ZOOZOO

13
ZIZZLE

ALPHABETICAL LIST OF 7-LETTER WORDS

ABBOZZO
ABLEEZE
ACIDIZE
ADAZZLE
ADONIZE
AGATIZE
AGENIZE
AGNIZED
AGONIZE
AKAZGIN
ALCAZAR
ALECIZE
ALFEREZ
ALGAZEL
ALIZARI
ALTEZZA
ALVELOZ
AMAZING
ANALYZE
ANIMIZE
ANODIZE
APOZEMA
APPRIZE

ARIENZO
ARMSIZE
ASSEIZE
ASSIZED
ASSIZER
ASSIZES
ATHEIZE
ATOMIZE
AZAFRAN
AZAFRIN
AZAROLE
AZELAIC
AZELATE
AZIMENE
AZIMINE
AZIMINO
AZIMUTH
AZOFIER
AZONIUM
AZOPHEN
AZORITE
AZOTATE
AZOTINE

AZOTITE
AZOTOUS
AZOXINE
AZUELJO
AZULENE
AZULITE
AZUMBRE
AZUREAN
AZURINE
AZURITE
AZUROUS
AZYGOTE
AZYGOUS
AZYMITE
AZYMOUS
BAIZING
BAPTIZE
BAZOOKA
BAZZITE
BEDIZEN
BEMAZED
BENZEIN
BENZENE

BENZINE
BENZOIC
BENZOIN
BENZOLE
BENZOXY
BENZOYL
BEZANTE
BEZANTY
BEZETTA
BEZETTE
BEZIQUE
BEZZANT
BEZZLED
BIOZONE
BIZARRE
BLAZING
BLINTZE
BLOWZED
BONANZA
BONZERY
BONZIAN
BOOZING
BORAZON

BRAZERA
BRAZIER
BRAZING
BREEZED
BRITZKA
BROMIZE
BRONZED
BRONZEN
BRONZER
BROWZER
BRULZIE
BUDZART
BUMBAZE
BUZZARD
BUZZIER
BUZZIES
BUZZING
BUZZWIG
CABEZON
CACHAZA
CADENZA
CALZADA
CANEZOU

CANZONA	EMBLAZE	HAZIEST	ONYMIZE	SIZEMAN
CANZONE	EMERIZE	HOATZIN	OOZIEST	SIZIEST
CANZONI	EMPRIZE	HORIZON	OPALIZE	SIZINGS
CAPATAZ	ENOLIZE	HUARIZO	ORGANZA	SIZZARD
CAPSIZE	ENTOZOA	HUMBUZZ	OSAZONE	SIZZING
CARRIZO	EPIZOAL	HUTZPAH	OUTBUZZ	SIZZLED
CAZIQUE	EPIZOAN	HUZZARD	OUTGAZE	SIZZLER
CHALAZA	EPIZOIC	IAMBIZE	OUTJAZZ	SKEEZIX
CHALAZE	EPIZOON	IDOLIZE	OUTRAZE	SNEEZED
CHAZZAN	FAHLERZ	IMBLAZE	OUTSIZE	SNEEZER
CHEMIZO	FANZINE	INDAZOL	OUTZANY	SNOOZED
CHINTZE	FAZENDA	IODIZED	OVALIZE	SNOOZER
CHINTZY	FEAZING	IODIZER	OXAZINE	SNOOZLE
CHIZZEL	FILAZER	IONIZER	OXAZOLE	SNOZZLE
CITIZEN	FILMIZE	IOTIZED	OXIDIZE	SNUZZLE
COALIZE	FIZZIER	IRIDIZE	OXOZONE	SOVENEZ
COCUIZA	FIZZING	IRONIZE	OZONATE	SOVKHOZ
COGNIZE	FIZZLED	ITEMIZE	OZONIDE	SOZOLIC
COROZOS	FOOZLED	JAZERAN	OZONIFY	SOZZLED
COZENER	FOOZLER	JAZZBOW	OZONIZE	SPATZLE
COZIEST	FRAZZLE	JAZZIER	OZONOUS	SPITZER
CRAZIER	FREEZER	JAZZILY	OZOTYPE	SPULZIE
CRAZIES	FRIEZED	KIBBUTZ	PALAZZI	SQUEEZE
CRAZILY	FRIEZER	KLEZMER	PALAZZO	SQUEEZY
CRAZING	FRISZKA	KOLKHOZ	PAZAREE	STANZAS
CRITIZE	FRIZADO	KREUZER	PECTIZE	STATIZE
CRIZZLE	FRIZZES	KUNZITE	PEPTIZE	STYLIZE
CRIZZEL	FRIZZED	KVUTZAH	PETZITE	SUBZONE
CROZIER	FRIZZEN	KWAZOKU	POETIZE	SURSIZE
CROZING	FRIZZER	KYANIZE	PONZITE	SWIZZLE
CROZZLE	FRIZZLE	LAICIZE	PRENZIE	SYZYGAL
CROZZLY	FRIZZLY	LAZARET	PRETZEL	SYZYGIA
CRUZADO	FURZERY	LAZARLY	PREZONE	TAILZEE
CYANIZE	FUZZIER	LAZIEST	PRIZERY	TAILZIE
CYCLIZE	FUZZILY	LAZYBED	PRIZING	TERZINA
CZARDOM	GALLIZE	LIONIZE	PUZZLED	TETRAZO
CZARINA	GARNETZ	LOZENGE	PUZZLER	THEEZAN
CZARISH	GAUZIER	LOZENGY	PYRAZIN	THIAZIN
CZARISM	GAUZILY	MAGHZEN	QUARTZY	THIAZOL
CZARIST	GAZABOS	MAKHZAN	QUEAZEN	TIZZIES
CZIGANY	GAZEBOS	MAKHZEN	QUETZAL	TOPAZES
DAMOZEL	GAZELLE	MANZANA	QUIZZED	TRAPEZE
DAZEDLY	GAZETTE	MATANZA	QUIZZEE	TRIAZIN
DAZZLED	GENIZAH	MATZOON	QUIZZER	TRISAZO
DAZZLED	GEZERAH	MATZOTH	RANTIZE	TRIZOIC
DAZZLER	GHAWAZI	MAZDOOR	RAZZING	TUILZIE
DEGLAZE	GHAZIES	MAZEDLY	REALIZE	TWEEZED
DENIZEN	GHIZITE	MAZEFUL	RESEIZE	TWEEZER
DIALYZE	GIZZARD	MAZIEST	RESIZED	TWIZZLE
DIARIZE	GIZZERN	MAZURKA	RESIZER	TZARDOM
DIAZIDE	GLAIZIE	MAZZARD	RETZIAN	TZARINA
DIAZINE	GLAZIER	MESTIZA	RHIZINE	TZIGANE
DIAZOIC	GLAZILY	MESTIZO	RHIZOID	TZIMMES
DIAZOLE	GLAZING	METREZA	RHIZOMA	TZOLKIN
DIAZOMA	GLOZING	MEZQUIT	RHIZOME	TZONTLE
DIZAINE	GODDIZE	MEZUZAH	RHIZOTE	UNGLAZE
DIZENED	GONZALO	MINOIZE	RIBZUBA	UNITIZE
DIZZARD	GOZZARD	MISMAZE	RITZIER	UNSEIZE
DIZZIED	GRAZIER	MITZVAH	ROMANZA	UNSIZED
DIZZIER	GRAZING	MIZMAZE	SAZERAC	UNZONED
DIZZILY	GRIZARD	MIZRACH	SCHERZI	UPERIZE
DOCKIZE	GRIZZLE	MIZZLED	SCHERZO	URAZINE
DOZENED	GRIZZLY	MONOAZO	SCHIZZO	URAZOLE
DOZENER	GROTZEN	MOZETTA	SCHMALZ	UTILIZE
DOZENTH	GROZART	MUZOONA	SCHMELZ	VERZINI
DOZIEST	GRUNZIE	MUZZIER	SCHNITZ	VERZINO
DOZZLED	GUANIZE	MUZZLED	SCHWARZ	VIZNOMY
DRIZZLE	GUAZUTI	MUZZLER	SEIZING	VIZORED
DRIZZLY	GUEREZA	NIZAMAT	SEIZURE	VOLTIZE
DUALIZE	GUZERAT	NIZAMUT	SELTZER	WALTZED
DUREZZA	GUZZLED	NOUNIZE	SEROZEM	WALTZER
EBONIZE	GUZZLER	NOZZLER	SHEGETZ	WEAZENY
ECHOIZE	HAMOTZI	NUZZLED	SHIZOKU	WHEEZED
ECTOZOA	HAZANUT	OBELIZE	SIZABLE	WHEEZER
EGOTIZE	HAZELED	ODORIZE	SIZABLY	WHEEZLE
ELEGIZE	HAZELLY	ODYLIZE	SIZEINE	WHIZGIG

WHIZZED	ZAPHARA	ZEUGITE	ZIRCITE	ZOOLITE
WHIZZER	ZAPTIAH	ZIBETUM	ZIRKITE	ZOOLITH
WHIZZES	ZAPTIEH	ZIGANKA	ZITTERN	ZOOLOGY
WHIZZLE	ZAREEBA	ZIKURAT	ZIZZLED	ZOONIST
WIZENED	ZARNICH	ZIMARRA	ZOARIAL	ZOONITE
WOOZIER	ZATTARE	ZIMOCCA	ZOARIUM	ZOONOMY
WOOZILY	ZEALOUS	ZINCATE	ZOCCOLO	ZOONULE
WUZZLED	ZEBRAIC	ZINCIDE	ZOISITE	ZOOPERY
YAGUAZA	ZEBRINE	ZINCIFY	ZOISTIC	ZOOTAXY
ZABURRO	ZEBROID	ZINCING	ZOMBIES	ZOOTYPE
ZACATON	ZEBRULE	ZINCITE	ZONALLY	ZORGITE
ZADRUGA	ZEBURRO	ZINCKED	ZONATED	ZORILLA
ZAFFREE	ZEDOARY	ZINCOID	ZONELET	ZORILLE
ZAGGING	ZELATOR	ZINCOUS	ZONITID	ZUFFOLO
ZAKUSKA	ZEMEISM	ZINGANA	ZONULAR	ZUMATIC
ZAMARRA	ZEMIISM	ZINGANO	ZONULET	ZUNYITE
ZAMARRO	ZEMSTVO	ZINGARA	ZONURID	ZWITTER
ZAMORIN	ZENTNER	ZINGARI	ZOOCARP	ZYGENID
ZAMOUSE	ZEOLITE	ZINGARO	ZOOCYST	ZYGOSIS
ZANELLA	ZEPHYRY	ZINOBER	ZOOECIA	ZYMOGEN
ZANJERO	ZEROIZE	ZINSANG	ZOOGAMY	ZYMOMIN
ZANJONA	ZESTFUL	ZIPHIAN	ZOOGENE	ZYMOSIS
ZANYISH	ZESTING	ZIPPIER	ZOOGLER	ZYMOTIC
ZANYISM	ZETETIC	ZIPPING	ZOOIDAL	ZYMURGY

POSITIONAL ORDER LIST OF 7-LETTER WORDS

ZABURRO	ZINCIDE	ZOONOMY	AZYGOTE	DIZZIED
ZACATON	ZINCIFY	ZOONULE	AZYGOUS	DIZZIER
ZADRUGA	ZINCING	ZOOPERY	AZYMITE	DIZZILY
ZAFFREE	ZINCITE	ZOOTAXY	AZYMOUS	DOZENED
ZAGGING	ZINCKED	ZOOTYPE	CZARDOM	DOZENER
ZAKUSKA	ZINCOID	ZORGITE	CZARINA	DOZENTH
ZAMARRA	ZINCOUS	ZORILLA	CZARISH	DOZIEST
ZAMARRO	ZINGANA	ZORILLE	CZARISM	DOZZLED
ZAMORIN	ZINGANO	ZUFFOLO	CZARIST	FAZENDA
ZAMOUSE	ZINGARA	ZUMATIC	CZIGANY	FIZZIER
ZANELLA	ZINGARI	ZUNYITE	OZONATE	FIZZING
ZANJERO	ZINGARO	ZWITTER	OZONIDE	FIZZLED
ZANJONA	ZINOBER	ZYGENID	OZONIFY	FUZZIER
ZANYISH	ZINSANG	ZYGOSIS	OZONIZE	FUZZILY
ZANYISM	ZIPHIAN	ZYMOGEN	OZONOUS	GAZABOS
ZAPHARA	ZIPPIER	ZYMOMIN	OZOTYPE	GAZEBOS
ZAPTIAH	ZIPPING	ZYMOSIS	TZARDOM	GAZELLE
ZAPTIEH	ZIRCITE	ZYMOTIC	TZARINA	GAZETTE
ZAREEBA	ZIRKITE	ZYMURGY	TZIGANE	GEZERAH
ZARNICH	ZITTERN		TZIMMES	GIZZARD
ZATTARE	ZIZZLED	AZAFRAN	TZOLKIN	GIZZERN
ZEALOUS	ZOARIAL	AZAFRIN	TZONTLE	GOZZARD
ZEBRAIC	ZOARIUM	AZAROLE		GUZERAT
ZEBRINE	ZOCCOLO	AZELAIC	BAZOOKA	GUZZLED
ZEBROID	ZOISITE	AZELATE	BAZZITE	GUZZLER
ZEBRULE	ZOISTIC	AZIMENE	BEZANTE	HAZANUT
ZEBURRO	ZOMBIES	AZIMINE	BEZANTY	HAZELED
ZEDOARY	ZONALLY	AZIMINO	BEZETTA	HAZELLY
ZELATOR	ZONATED	AZIMUTH	BEZETTE	HAZIEST
ZEMEISM	ZONELET	AZOFIER	BEZIQUE	HUZZARD
ZEMIISM	ZONITID	AZONIUM	BEZZANT	JAZERAN
ZEMSTVO	ZONULAR	AZOPHEN	BEZZLED	JAZZBOW
ZENTNER	ZONULET	AZORITE	BIZARRE	JAZZIER
ZEOLITE	ZONURID	AZOTATE	BUZZARD	JAZZILY
ZEPHYRY	ZOOCARP	AZOTINE	BUZZIER	LAZARET
ZEROIZE	ZOOCYST	AZOTITE	BUZZIES	LAZARLY
ZESTFUL	ZOOECIA	AZOTOUS	BUZZING	LAZIEST
ZESTING	ZOOGAMY	AZOXINE	BUZZWIG	LAZYBED
ZETETIC	ZOOGENE	AZUELJO	COZENER	LOZENGE
ZEUGITE	ZOOGLER	AZULENE	COZIEST	LOZENGY
ZIBETUM	ZOOIDAL	AZULITE	DAZEDLY	MAZDOOR
ZIGANKA	ZOOLITE	AZUMBRE	DAZZLED	MAZEDLY
ZIKURAT	ZOOLITH	AZUREAN	DAZZLER	MAZEFUL
ZIMARRA	ZOOLOGY	AZURINE	DIZAINE	MAZIEST
ZIMOCCA	ZOONIST	AZURITE	DIZENED	MAZURKA
ZINCATE	ZOONITE	AZUROUS	DIZZARD	MAZZARD

MEZQUIT	CHAZZAN	KWAZOKU	BLOWZED	SNOOZLE
MEZUZAH	CHIZZEL	MANZANA	BORAZON	SNOZZLE
MIZMAZE	CRAZIER	MATZOON	BREEZED	SNUZZLE
MIZRACH	CRAZIES	MATZOTH	BRITZKA	SPATZLE
MIZZLED	CRAZILY	MAZZARD	BRONZED	SPITZER
MOZETTA	CRAZING	MITZVAH	BRONZEN	SPULZIE
MUZOONA	CRIZZLE	MIZZLED	BRONZER	STANZAS
MUZZIER	CRIZZEL	MUZZIER	BROWZER	SWIZZLE
MUZZLED	CROZIER	MUZZLED	BRULZIE	TAILZEE
MUZZLER	CROZING	MUZZLER	CABEZON	TAILZIE
NIZAMAT	CROZZLE	NOZZLER	CANEZOU	THEEZAN
NIZAMUT	CROZZLY	NUZZLED	CHAZZAN	THIAZIN
NOZZLER	CRUZADO	OSAZONE	CHIZZEL	THIAZOL
NUZZLED	DAZZLED	OUTZANY	CITIZEN	TOPAZES
OOZIEST	DAZZLER	OXAZINE	COROZOS	TRIAZIN
PAZAREE	DIAZIDE	OXAZOLE	CRIZZLE	TUILZIE
PUZZLED	DIAZINE	OXOZONE	CRIZZEL	TWEEZED
PUZZLER	DIAZOIC	PETZITE	CROZZLE	TWEEZER
RAZZING	DIAZOLE	PONZITE	CROZZLY	TWIZZLE
SAZERAC	DIAZOMA	PREZONE	DAMOZEL	UNSIZED
SIZABLE	DIZZARD	PRIZERY	DENIZEN	WALTZED
SIZABLY	DIZZIED	PRIZING	DRIZZLE	WALTZER
SIZEINE	DIZZIER	PUZZLED	DRIZZLY	WHEEZED
SIZEMAN	DIZZILY	PUZZLER	DUREZZA	WHEEZER
SIZIEST	DOZZLED	QUIZZED	ECTOZOA	WHEEZLE
SIZINGS	DRIZZLE	QUIZZEE	ENTOZOA	WHIZZED
SIZZARD	DRIZZLY	QUIZZER	FILAZER	WHIZZER
SIZZING	EPIZOAL	RAZZING	FRAZZLE	WHIZZES
SIZZLED	EPIZOAN	RETZIAN	FREEZER	WHIZZLE
SIZZLER	EPIZOIC	RHIZINE	FRIEZED	
SOZOLIC	EPIZOON	RHIZOID	FRIEZER	ABBOZZO
SOZZLED	FANZINE	RHIZOMA	FRISZKA	ABLEEZE
SYZYGAL	FEAZING	RHIZOME	FRIZZES	ACIDIZE
SYZYGIA	FIZZIER	RHIZOTE	FRIZZED	ADONIZE
TIZZIES	FIZZING	RIBZUBA	FRIZZEN	AGATIZE
UNZONED	FIZZLED	RITZIER	FRIZZER	AGENIZE
VIZNOMY	FOOZLED	SEIZURE	FRIZZLE	AGONIZE
VIZORED	FOOZLER	SHIZOKU	FRIZZLY	ALECIZE
WIZENED	FRAZZLE	SIZZARD	GENIZAH	ALTEZZA
WUZZLED	FRIZADO	SIZZING	GLAIZIE	ANALYZE
ZIZZLED	FRIZZES	SIZZLED	GRIZZLE	ANIMIZE
	FRIZZED	SIZZLER	GRIZZLY	ANODIZE
ADAZZLE	FRIZZEN	SNOZZLE	GROTZEN	APPRIZE
AKAZGIN	FRIZZER	SNUZZLE	GRUNZIE	ARIENZO
ALIZARI	FRIZZLE	SOZZLED	HOATZIN	ARMSIZE
AMAZING	FRIZZLY	SWIZZLE	HORIZON	ASSEIZE
APOZEMA	FURZERY	TERZINA	INDAZOL	ATHEIZE
BAIZING	FUZZIER	TIZZIES	IODIZED	ATOMIZE
BAZZITE	FUZZILY	TRIZOIC	IODIZER	BAPTIZE
BENZEIN	GAUZIER	TWIZZLE	IONIZER	BLINTZE
BENZENE	GAUZILY	URAZINE	IOTIZED	BONANZA
BENZINE	GHAZIES	URAZOLE	KREUZER	BROMIZE
BENZOIC	GHIZITE	VERZINI	KVUTZAH	BUMBAZE
BENZOIN	GIZZARD	VERZINO	MAGHZEN	CACHAZA
BENZOLE	GIZZERN	WEAZENY	MAKHZAN	CAPSIZE
BENZOXY	GLAZIER	WHIZGIG	MAKHZEN	CARRIZO
BENZOYL	GLAZILY	WHIZZED	MEZUZAH	CHALAZA
BEZZANT	GLAZING	WHIZZER	PALAZZI	CHALAZE
BEZZLED	GLOZING	WHIZZES	PALAZZO	CHEMIZO
BIOZONE	GONZALO	WHIZZLE	PRENZIE	CHINTZE
BLAZING	GOZZARD	WOOZIER	PRETZEL	CHINTZY
BONZERY	GRAZIER	WOOZILY	PYRAZIN	COALIZE
BONZIAN	GRAZING	WUZZLED	QUEAZEN	COCUIZA
BOOZING	GRIZARD	ZIZZLED	QUETZAL	COGNIZE
BRAZERA	GRIZZLE		QUIZZED	CRITIZE
BRAZIER	GRIZZLY	ABBOZZO	QUIZZEE	CYANIZE
BRAZING	GROZART	ADAZZLE	QUIZZER	CYCLIZE
BUDZART	GUAZUTI	AGNIZED	RESIZED	DEGLAZE
BUZZARD	GUZZLED	ALCAZAR	RESIZER	DIALYZE
BUZZIER	GUZZLER	ALGAZEL	SCHIZZO	DIARIZE
BUZZIES	HUTZPAH	ALTEZZA	SELTZER	DOCKIZE
BUZZING	HUZZARD	ASSIZED	SEROZEM	DUALIZE
BUZZWIG	JAZZBOW	ASSIZER	SKEEZIX	DUREZZA
CALZADA	JAZZIER	ASSIZES	SNEEZED	EBONIZE
CANZONA	JAZZILY	BEDIZEN	SNEEZER	ECHOIZE
CANZONE	KLEZMER	BEMAZED	SNOOZED	EGOTIZE
CANZONI	KUNZITE		SNOOZER	ELEGIZE

EMBLAZE	KYANIZE	OUTGAZE	SCHERZO	ALFEREZ
EMERIZE	LAICIZE	OUTJAZZ	SCHIZZO	ALVELOZ
EMPRIZE	LIONIZE	OUTRAZE	SQUEEZE	CAPATAZ
ENOLIZE	MATANZA	OUTSIZE	SQUEEZY	FAHLERZ
FILMIZE	MESTIZA	OVALIZE	STATIZE	GARNETZ
GALLIZE	MESTIZO	OXIDIZE	STYLIZE	HUMBUZZ
GHAWAZI	METREZA	OZONIZE	SURSIZE	KIBBUTZ
GODDIZE	MINOIZE	PALAZZI	TETRAZO	KOLKHOZ
GUANIZE	MISMAZE	PALAZZO	TRAPEZE	OUTBUZZ
GUEREZA	MIZMAZE	PECTIZE	TRISAZO	OUTJAZZ
HAMOTZI	MONOAZO	PEPTIZE	UNGLAZE	SCHMALZ
HUARIZO	NOUNIZE	POETIZE	UNITIZE	SCHMELZ
HUMBUZZ	OBELIZE	QUARTZY	UNSEIZE	SCHNITZ
IAMBIZE	ODORIZE	RANTIZE	UPERIZE	SCHWARZ
IDOLIZE	ODYLIZE	REALIZE	UTILIZE	SHEGETZ
IMBLAZE	ONYMIZE	RESEIZE	VOLTIZE	SOVENEZ
IRIDIZE	OPALIZE	ROMANZA	YAGUAZA	SOVKHOZ
IRONIZE	ORGANZA	SCHERZI	ZEROIZE	
ITEMIZE	OUTBUZZ			

SCORING ORDER LIST OF 7-LETTER WORDS

28	OXAZOLE	BENZOYL	AZYGOTE	ZEMIISM
BENZOXY	OXOZONE	BEZANTY	AZYGOUS	ZIBETUM
QUARTZY	SCHMALZ	BONZERY	BAPTIZE	ZIKURAT
SQUEEZY	SCHMELZ	BROWZER	BENZOIC	ZIPPIER
	SHIZOKU	BUZZWIG	BROMIZE	ZIRKITE
27	SYZYGAL	CHALAZA	CABEZON	ZOCCOLO
BEZIQUE	SYZYGIA	CHALAZE	CAPATAZ	ZOMBIES
JAZZBOW	WHEEZED	CHINTZE	CAPSIZE	ZOOCARP
MEZQUIT	ZANJERO	CRAZILY	COCUIZA	ZOOLOGY
SKEEZIX	ZANJONA	CYANIZE	COZENAGE	ZUMATIC
ZEPHYRY	ZINCKED	CZARDOM	CROZZLY	ZYGOSIS
	ZYMOMIN	CZARISH	CZARISM	
26	ZYMOTIC	DAZEDLY	DIALYZE	**19**
KVUTZAH		ECHOIZE	DOZENTH	ABBOZZO
SOVKHOZ	**22**	FILMIZE	EMBLAZE	ACIDIZE
ZOOTAXY	BAZOOKA	FRIZZLY	EMPRIZE	ALFEREZ
	BLOWZED	FUZZILY	EPIZOIC	ALVELOZ
25	BRITZKA	HAMOTZI	FAZENDA	AMAZING
JAZZILY	BUMBAZE	MATZOTH	FEAZING	ANALYZE
MAKHZAN	CZIGANY	MAZEFUL	FOOZLED	ATHEIZE
MAKHZEN	FAHLERZ	ONYMIZE	FRIEZED	AZAFRAN
QUEAZEN	FURZERY	OZOTYPE	FRIZADO	AZAFRIN
QUETZAL	HAZELLY	PRIZERY	GAUZILY	AZOFIER
QUIZZED	HUMBUZZ	PYRAZIN	GENIZAH	BAIZING
SQUEEZE	JAZZIER	RHIZOMA	GEZERAH	BEDIZEN
ZYMURGY	KLEZMER	RHIZOME	GHAZIES	BLAZING
	KOLKHOZ	SCHERZI	GHIZITE	BOOZING
24	KWAZOKU	SCHERZO	GLAZILY	BRAZING
CHINTZY	LAZYBED	SCHNITZ	HAZELED	BREEZED
HUTZPAH	MAGHZEN	SIZABLY	IAMBIZE	BRONZED
KIBBUTZ	MAZEDLY	WHIZZER	IMBLAZE	BUDZART
MITZVAH	MAZURKA	WHIZZES	KREUZER	CADENZA
OXIDIZE	OUTJAZZ	WHIZZLE	KUNZITE	CALZADA
QUIZZEE	OZONIFY	ZANYISM	LOZENGY	COGNIZE
QUIZZER	WEAZENY	ZAPHARA	MEZUZAH	CRAZING
SCHWARZ	WHEEZER	ZAPTIAH	MISMAZE	CROZING
VIZNOMY	WHEEZLE	ZAPTIEH	ODYLIZE	CRUZADO
WHIZGIG	WHIZZED	ZARNICH	PECTIZE	DAMOZEL
ZINCIFY	WOOZILY	ZEMSTVO	PEPTIZE	DIAZOIC
	ZAFFREE	ZIGANKA	RHIZOID	DIAZOMA
23	ZANYISH	ZIPHIAN	RIBZUBA	DIZZILY
AZOXINE	ZIMOCCA	ZIPPING	SCHIZZO	DRIZZLY
AZUELJO	ZOOGAMY	ZOOCYST	SHEGETZ	FANZINE
CACHAZA	ZUFFOLO	ZOONOMY	TWEEZED	FILAZER
CHEMIZO	ZYMOGEN	ZOOPERY	TZIMMES	FIZZING
CYCLIZE		ZOOTYPE	TZOLKIN	FIZZLED
DOCKIZE	**21**	ZYGENID	VIZORED	FOOZLER
FRISZKA	AKAZGIN	ZYMOSIS	WALTZED	FREEZER
GHAWAZI	AZIMUTH		WIZENED	FRIEZER
JAZERAN	AZOPHEN	**20**	YAGUAZA	FRIZZED
KYANIZE	AZYMITE	APOZEMA	ZEBRAIC	GAZABOS
MIZRACH	AZYMOUS	APPRIZE	ZEDOARY	GAZEBOS
OXAZINE	BEMAZED	AZUMBRE	ZEMEISM	GODDIZE

GRIZZLY	CANEZOU	SUBZONE	GUZERAT	LAZIEST
HAZANUT	CANZONA	SWIZZLE	GUZZLED	LIONIZE
HAZIEST	CANZONE	TOPAZES	IDOLIZE	NOUNIZE
HOATZIN	CANZONI	TRAPEZE	INDAZOL	NUZZLED
HORIZON	CARRIZO	TRIZOIC	IODIZER	OOZIEST
HUARIZO	CITIZEN	TWIZZLE	IOTIZED	OSAZONE
HUZZARD	COALIZE	UPERIZE	IRIDIZE	OUTRAZE
LAZARLY	COROZOS	ZABURRO	LOZENGE	OUTSIZE
MAZDOOR	COZENER	ZACATON	MUZZIER	OZONATE
MIZMAZE	COZIEST	ZADRUGA	MUZZLER	OZONOUS
OUTZANY	CRAZIER	ZAMARRA	ODORIZE	RANTIZE
OVALIZE	CRAZIES	ZAMARRO	ORGANZA	RAZZING
PRIZING	CRITIZE	ZAMORIN	OUTBUZZ	REALIZE
RHIZINE	CROZIER	ZAMOUSE	OUTGAZE	RESEIZE
RHIZOTE	CZARINA	ZAREEBA	OZONIDE	RESIZER
SOVENEZ	CZARIST	ZEBRINE	PALAZZI	RETZIAN
STYLIZE	DEGLAZE	ZEBRULE	PALAZZO	RITZIER
THEEZAN	DIAZIDE	ZEBURRO	PUZZLER	SEIZURE
THIAZIN	DIZENED	ZETETIC	RESIZED	SELTZER
THIAZOL	DOZENED	ZIMARRA	SEIZING	SIZEINE
TWEEZER	EBONIZE	ZINCATE	SIZINGS	SIZIEST
TZARDOM	ECTOZOA	ZINCITE	SNEEZED	SIZZARD
VERZINI	EMERIZE	ZINCOUS	SNOOZED	SIZZING
VERZINO	EPIZOAL	ZINOBER	TZIGANE	SIZZLED
VOLTIZE	EPIZOAN	ZIRCITE	UNGLAZE	SNEEZER
WALTZER	EPIZOON	ZOARIUM	UNSIZED	SNOOZER
WOOZIER	FIZZIER	ZOISTIC	UNZONED	SNOOZLE
WUZZLED	FRAZZLE	ZOOECIA	ZESTING	SOZZLED
ZAGGING	FRIZZES		ZEUGITE	STANZAS
ZAKUSKA	FRIZZEN	**17**	ZINGANA	STATIZE
ZEBROID	FRIZZER	ADONIZE	ZINGANO	SURSIZE
ZESTFUL	FRIZZLE	AGATIZE	ZINGARA	TAILZEE
ZINCIDE	FUZZIER	AGENIZE	ZINGARI	TAILZIE
ZINCING	GLAZING	AGONIZE	ZINGARO	TERZINA
ZINCOID	GLOZING	ALGAZEL	ZINSANG	TETRAZO
ZONALLY	GRAZING	ANODIZE	ZONATED	TRIAZIN
ZOOLITH	GRIZARD	ASSIZED	ZONITID	TRISAZO
ZUNYITE	IODIZED	BAZZITE	ZONURID	TUILZIE
ZWITTER	ITEMIZE	BEZZANT	ZOOGENE	TZARINA
	LAICIZE	BUZZIER	ZOOGLER	TZONTLE
18	MANZANA	BUZZIES	ZOOIDAL	UNITIZE
ABLEEZE	MATANZA	CRIZZLE	ZORGITE	UNSEIZE
AGNIZED	MATZOON	CRIZZEL		URAZINE
ALCAZAR	MAZIEST	CROZZLE	**16**	URAZOLE
ALECIZE	MAZZARD	DAZZLED	ADAZZLE	UTILIZE
ANIMIZE	MESTIZA	DENIZEN	ALIZARI	ZANELLA
ARMSIZE	MESTIZO	DIARIZE	ARIENZO	ZATTARE
ATOMIZE	METREZA	DIAZINE	ASSEIZE	ZEALOUS
AZELAIC	MINOIZE	DIAZOLE	ASSIZER	ZELATOR
AZIMENE	MIZZLED	DIZAINE	ASSIZES	ZENTNER
AZIMINE	MONOAZO	DIZZARD	AZAROLE	ZEOLITE
AZIMINO	MOZETTA	DIZZIED	AZELATE	ZITTERN
AZONIUM	MUZOONA	DOZENER	AZORITE	ZOARIAL
BENZEIN	MUZZLED	DOZIEST	AZOTATE	ZOISITE
BENZENE	NIZAMAT	DOZZLED	AZOTINE	ZONELET
BENZINE	NIZAMUT	DUALIZE	AZOTITE	ZONULAR
BENZOIN	OBELIZE	EGOTIZE	AZOTOUS	ZONULET
BENZOLE	OPALIZE	ELEGIZE	AZULENE	ZOOLITE
BEZANTE	PAZAREE	GALLIZE	AZULITE	ZOONIST
BEZETTA	PETZITE	GARNETZ	AZUREAN	ZOONITE
BEZETTE	POETIZE	GAUZIER	AZURINE	ZOONULE
BEZZLED	PONZITE	GAZELLE	AZURITE	ZORILLA
BIOZONE	PRENZIE	GAZETTE	AZUROUS	ZORILLE
BIZARRE	PRETZEL	GIZZARD	DAZZLER	
BLINTZE	PREZONE	GLAIZIE	DIZZIER	**15**
BONANZA	PUZZLED	GLAZIER	DRIZZLE	ALTEZZA
BONZIAN	ROMANZA	GONZALO	DUREZZA	NOZZLER
BORAZON	SAZERAC	GOZZARD	ENOLIZE	OZONIZE
BRAZERA	SEROZEM	GRAZIER	ENTOZOA	SIZZLER
BRAZIER	SIZABLE	GROTZEN	GIZZERN	SNOZZLE
BRONZEN	SIZEMAN	GROZART	GRIZZLE	SNUZZLE
BRONZER	SOZOLIC	GRUNZIE	GUZZLER	TIZZIES
BRULZIE	SPATZLE	GUANIZE	IONIZER	ZEROIZE
BUZZARD	SPITZER	GUAZUTI	IRONIZE	ZIZZLED
BUZZING	SPULZIE	GUEREZA	LAZARET	

ALPHABETICAL LIST OF 8-LETTER WORDS

ACTIVIZE	BEZANTEE	CRAZIEST	EULOGIZE	HAZARDER
ADONIZED	BEZONIAN	CRAZYCAT	EUPHUIZE	HAZARDRY
AGATIZED	BEZZLING	CREOLIZE	EXORCIZE	HAZELNUT
AGNIZING	BIBENZYL	CRUELIZE	EXORDIZE	HAZINESS
AGONIZED	BIGAMIZE	CRUZEIRO	FABULIZE	HAZNADAR
AGONIZER	BIQUARTZ	CURARIZE	FARADIZE	HAZZANUT
AKAZGINE	BIZZARRO	CUTINIZE	FATALIZE	HEMOZOON
ALBIZZIA	BLAZONED	CYANIZED	FEAZINGS	HEPATIZE
ALBRONZE	BLAZONER	CYTOZOIC	FEMINIZE	HEREZELD
ALCAZABA	BLAZONRY	CYTOZOON	FIBERIZE	HERTZIAN
ALCAZAVA	BLIZZARD	CYTOZYME	FIGURIZE	HETERIZE
ALDOLIZE	BLOWZIER	CZAREVNA	FILMIZED	HOACTZIN
ALGUAZIL	BLOWZING	CZARITZA	FINALIZE	HOLOZOIC
ALIZARIN	BOMBAZET	DANDYIZE	FIZZIEST	HOMILIZE
ALKALIZE	BOTANIZE	DAZZLING	FIZZLING	HOWITZER
ALKYLIZE	BRACOZZO	DECATIZE	FLOOZIES	HUMANIZE
ALMUERZO	BRAGOZZO	DEGLAZED	FLUIDIZE	HUMORIZE
AMAZEFUL	BOZZETTO	DEIONIZE	FOCALIZE	HYDRAZIN
AMINOAZO	BRAZENED	DEMONIZE	FOOZLING	HYLOZOIC
AMORTIZE	BRAZENLY	DENAZIFY	FORMAZAN	HYPOZOAN
ANALGIZE	BRAZIERY	DENIZATE	FORMAZYL	HYPOZOIC
ANALYZED	BREEZIER	DEPUTIZE	FORUMIZE	IDEALIZE
ANALYZER	BREEZING	DETONIZE	FOZINESS	IDIOZOME
ANGELIZE	BREEZILY	DEVILIZE	FRAZZLED	IDOLIZED
ANNALIZE	BRITZSKA	DIALYZED	FREEZING	IDOLIZER
ANODIZED	BROMIZER	DIALYZER	FRENZIED	IMIDAZOL
ANTICIZE	BRONZIFY	DIAZOATE	FRENZIES	IMMUNIZE
ANTIZOEA	BRONZING	DIAZOTIC	FRENZILY	INDAZOLE
APHETIZE	BRONZINE	DIBENZYL	FRIEZING	INDENIZE
APHORIZE	BRONZITE	DIGITIZE	FRIZETTE	INFAMIZE
APPETIZE	BROOZLED	DISDIAZO	FRIZZIER	INSULIZE
APPRIZAL	BRUNIZEM	DISPRIZE	FRIZZILY	IODIZING
APPRIZER	BRYOZOAN	DISSEIZE	FRIZZING	IOTIZING
APRENDIZ	BRYOZOON	DIVINIZE	FRIZZLED	IRIDIZED
ARANZADA	BRYOZOUM	DIZENING	FRIZZLER	ISOZOOID
ARBORIZE	BULLDOZE	DIZZIEST	FROWZIER	ITEMIZED
ARCHAIZE	BUZZIEST	DIZZYING	FROWZILY	ITEMIZER
ARMOZEEN	CACOZEAL	DONZELLA	FROWZLED	JANIZARY
ARMOZINE	CACOZYME	DOUZAINE	FROZENLY	JAROVIZE
ARRHIZAL	CALABAZA	DOUZEPER	FUELIZER	JAZERANT
ASSIZING	CALABOZO	DOZINESS	FURZETOP	JAZZIEST
ASTATIZE	CALORIZE	DRIZZLED	FUZZBALL	JECORIZE
ATHEIZER	CALZOONS	DUALIZED	FUZZIEST	JEZEKITE
ATHETIZE	CANALIZE	DUELLIZE	FUZZTAIL	JUBILIZE
ATMOLYZE	CANONIZE	DYNAMIZE	GARBANZO	JUDAIZER
ATOMIZED	CANZONET	EBONIZED	GARVANZO	KAMIKAZE
ATOMIZER	CAPONIZE	ECHOIZED	GAUZIEST	KATALYZE
ATTICIZE	CAPSIZAL	ECTOZOAN	GAZABOES	KETONIZE
AUTOLYZE	CAPSIZED	ECTOZOIC	GAZEBOES	KEVUTZAH
AVESTRUZ	CARBAZIC	EGOTIZED	GAZELESS	KIBITZER
AVIANIZE	CARBAZIN	ELEGIZED	GAZELLES	KREUTZER
AZOBLACK	CARROZZA	EMBEZZLE	GAZEMENT	LABILIZE
AZOGREEN	CATALYZE	EMBLAZED	GAZETTAL	LACONIZE
AZOHUMIC	CATZERIE	EMBLAZER	GAZETTED	LAICIZED
AZOIMIDE	CHALAZAE	EMBLAZON	GAZINGLY	LAICIZER
AZOTEMIA	CHALAZAL	EMBOLIZE	GAZOGENE	LATINIZE
AZOTIZED	CHALAZAS	EMBRONZE	GAZPACHO	LAZAROLE
AZOTURIA	CHINTZES	ENERGIZE	GAZZETTA	LAZARONE
BACONIZE	CHUTZPAH	ENFRENZY	GHAWAZEE	LAZAROUS
BAETZNER	CINEMIZE	ENTOZOAL	GIANTIZE	LAZINESS
BAKELIZE	CIVILIZE	ENTOZOAN	GIZZENED	LAZULITE
BAPTIZED	COALIZED	ENTOZOIC	GLAZIERS	LAZURITE
BAPTIZEE	COENZYME	ENTOZOON	GLAZIERY	LAZYBACK
BAPTIZER	COGNIZED	ENZOOTIC	GLAZIEST	LAZYBIRD
BAROMETZ	COGNIZEE	EOZOONAL	GOYAZITE	LAZYBONE
BARTIZAN	COGNIZER	EPIZOOTY	GRANDEZA	LAZYLEGS
BARUKHZY	COGNIZOR	EQUALIZE	GRAZIERY	LEGALIZE
BEDAZZLE	COLONIZE	ERGOTIZE	GRAZIOSO	LHERZITE
BENZENYL	COMPRIZE	ERZAHLER	GRIZZLED	LINENIZE
BENZIDIN	CORONIZE	ESTERIZE	GRIZZLER	LIONIZED
BENZILIC	COZENAGE	ETERNIZE	GUZZLING	LIONIZER
BENZOATE	COZENING	ETHERIZE	GWERZIOU	LOCALIZE
BENZOBIS	COZINESS	ETHICIZE	HALAZONE	LOGICIZE
BENZYLIC	CRAZEDLY	ETIOLIZE	HALUTZIM	LOZENGED

LOZENGER	ORANGIZE	REALIZER	SUBERIZE	WINZEMAN
LUNATIZE	ORGANIZE	REGALIZE	SUBSIZAR	WINZEMEN
MACARIZE	ORMUZINE	REGULIZE	SUBZONAL	WIZARDLY
MAGADIZE	ORYZANIN	RENDZINA	SUZERAIN	WIZARDRY
MAGAZINE	ORYZENIN	RENOVIZE	SWIZZLER	WOOZIEST
MAGAZINY	OSMAZOME	RESEIZER	SYNERIZE	WRIZZLED
MAJORIZE	OUTBLAZE	RESINIZE	SYZYGIAL	WOMANIZE
MALGUZAR	OUTSIZED	RESIZING	SYZYGIES	WURTZITE
MARKAZES	OVERGAZE	RETINIZE	SYZYGIUM	WUZZLING
MARZIPAN	OVERSIZE	RHIZOBIA	SZLACHTA	YAHRZEIT
MATEZITE	OXIDIZED	RHIZOGEN	SZOPELKA	YAROVIZE
MAXIMIZE	OXIDIZER	RHIZOIDAL	TAILZIED	YOTACIZE
MAZAGRAN	OZARKITE	RHIZOMIC	TEMPLIZE	ZAIBATSU
MAZALGIA	OZOBROME	RHIZOPOD	TERRAZZO	ZAMBOMBA
MAZARINE	OZONIZED	RHIZOTIC	TERZETTO	ZAMINDAR
MAZINESS	OZONIZER	RIBAZUBA	TETANIZE	ZAMORINE
MAZOPEXY	PAEANIZE	RITZIEST	TETRAZIN	ZAMPOGNA
MAZOURKA	PAGANIZE	RIVALIZE	TEZKIRAH	ZANDMOLE
MEDALIZE	PALATIZE	RIZIFORM	THEORIZE	ZAPATERO
MELANIZE	PANZOISM	RIZZOMED	THIAZINE	ZARATITE
MELODIZE	PANZOOTY	ROBOTIZE	THIAZOLE	ZARZUELA
MEMORIZE	PAPALIZE	ROYALIZE	THIOZONE	ZASTRUGA
MESOZOAN	PARALYZE	RUMBOOZE	THRONIZE	ZASTRUGI
MESTIZOS	PARTIZAN	RURALIZE	TIMAZITE	ZEALOTIC
METALIZE	PATINIZE	SALINIZE	TODDYIZE	ZEALOTRY
METAZOAL	PAVONIZE	SANITIZE	TONICIZE	ZEALOUSY
METAZOAN	PECTIZED	SARRAZIN	TOPAZINE	ZEBRINNY
METAZOEA	PELORIZE	SATANIZE	TOPAZITE	ZECCHINO
METAZOIC	PENALIZE	SATINIZE	TOTALIZE	ZELATRIX
METAZOON	PEPTIZED	SATIRIZE	TRAPEZIA	ZEMINDAR
METRAZOL	PEPTIZER	SAVAGIZE	TRIAZANE	ZEMSTVOS
MEZEREON	PEREZONE	SCHERZOS	TRIAZINE	ZENITHAL
MEZEREUM	PETUNTZE	SCHIZOID	TRIAZOLE	ZEOLITIC
MEZQUITE	PEZANTIC	SCHIZONT	TRISTEZA	ZEOSCOPE
MEZUZAHS	PEZIZOID	SCHIZTIC	TRIZOMAL	ZEPHYRUS
MEZUZOTH	PHENAZIN	SCHMALTZ	TROTCOZY	ZEPPELIN
MICASIZE	PIAZZAED	SCHMALZY	TUBERIZE	ZERUMBET
MICROZOA	PIAZZIAN	SCHMOOZE	TUTORIZE	ZETACISM
MINIMIZE	PIZZERIA	SEIZABLE	TWEEZERS	ZIBELINE
MISPRIZE	POETIZED	SERENIZE	TWEEZING	ZIGGURAT
MITZVAHS	POETIZER	SEVERIZE	TZEDAKAH	ZIGZAGGY
MITZVOTH	POLARIZE	SFORZATO	UNBAIZED	ZIMBABWE
MIZZLING	POLEMIZE	SHAATNEZ	UNCRAZED	ZIMBALON
MOBILIZE	POLICIZE	SHAHZADA	UNDAZZLE	ZINCKING
MODALIZE	POLITIZE	SIEROZEM	UNFROZEN	ZINCURET
MODELIZE	POLYZOAN	SILICIZE	UNGLAZED	ZIPHIOID
MODULIZE	POLYZOIC	SIMILIZE	UNIONIZE	ZIPPIEST
MONAZITE	POLYZOON	SIMONIZE	UNMUZZLE	ZIRCONIA
MONETIZE	PREZONAL	SIMULIZE	UNPUZZLE	ZIRCONIC
MONODIZE	PRIZABLE	SINAPIZE	UNVIZARD	ZIRCONYL
MONOZOAN	PRIZEMAN	SIRENIZE	URBANIZE	ZIZZLING
MONOZOIC	PRIZEMEN	SITZMARK	VALORIZE	ZOANTHID
MORALIZE	PROTOZOA	SIZEABLE	VAMMAZSA	ZODIACAL
MOTORIZE	PTYALIZE	SIZINESS	VAPORIZE	ZOEAFORM
MOUZOUNA	PUPILIZE	SIZYGIUM	VELARIZE	ZOETROPE
MOZEMIZE	PUZZLING	SIZZLING	VENALIZE	ZOIATRIA
MUSTAFUZ	PYRAZINE	SMORZATO	VENOMIZE	ZOLOTNIK
MUZZIEST	PYRAZOLE	SNEEZING	VITALIZE	ZOMBIISM
MUZZLING	PYRITIZE	SNOOZING	VIZARDED	ZONALITY
NAKEDIZE	QUANTIZE	SOBERIZE	VIZCACHA	ZONATION
NAMAZLIK	QUARTZIC	SOLARIZE	VIZIRATE	ZONELESS
NASALIZE	QUATORZE	SOLECIZE	VIZIRIAL	ZONUROID
NATURIZE	QUEZALES	SOLONETZ	VIZORING	ZOOBLAST
NAZIFIED	QUIZZERY	SONORIZE	VOCALIZE	ZOOCHEMY
NEBULIZE	QUIZZIFY	SORORIZE	VOLTZINE	ZOOCHORE
NICOTIZE	QUIZZING	SPITZKOP	VOLTZITE	ZOOECIAL
NIZAMATE	QUIZZISH	SPRITZER	VOWELIZE	ZOOECIUM
NODULIZE	QUIZZISM	SPUILZIE	UTILIZED	ZOOGLOEA
NOTARIZE	QUIZZITY	SQUEEZED	UTILIZER	ZOOGRAFT
NOVELIZE	RAADZAAL	SQUEEZER	WALTZING	ZOOLATER
NUZZLING	RACEMIZE	STANITZA	WAZIRATE	ZOOLATRY
OBELIZED	RADZIMIR	STANZAED	WEAZENED	ZOOLITIC
OOLOGIZE	RAMBOOZE	STANZAIC	WHEEZIER	ZOOLOGIC
OOZINESS	RAZBOOCH	STARGAZE	WHEEZILY	ZOOMANIA
OPALIZED	RAZEEING	STOLZITE	WHEEZING	ZOOMETRY
OPSONIZE	RAZORMAN	STYLIZED	WHIZBANG	ZOOMIMIC
OPTIMIZE	REALIZED	STYLIZER	WHIZZING	ZOOMORPH

ZOONITIC	ZOOPHILY	ZOOTOMIC	ZUGZWANG	ZYGOMATA
ZOONOSES	ZOOPHORI	ZOOTOXIN	ZUPANATE	ZYGOTENE
ZOONOSIS	ZOOPHYTE	ZOPILOTE	ZWIEBACK	ZYGOTOID
ZOONOTIC	ZOOSCOPY	ZORRILLO	ZYGAENID	ZYMOGENE
ZOOPERAL	ZOOSPORE	ZORTZICO	ZYGODONT	ZYMOLOGY
ZOOPHILE	ZOOTHOME	ZUCCHINI		

POSITIONAL ORDER LIST OF 8-LETTER WORDS

ZAIBATSU	ZOONITIC	FIZZIEST	RAZEEING	FOOZLING
ZAMBOMBA	ZOONOSES	FIZZLING	RAZORMAN	FRAZZLED
ZAMINDAR	ZOONOSIS	FOZINESS	RIZIFORM	FRIZETTE
ZAMORINE	ZOONOTIC	FUZZBALL	RIZZOMED	FRIZZIER
ZAMPOGNA	ZOOPERAL	FUZZIEST	SIZEABLE	FRIZZILY
ZANDMOLE	ZOOPHILE	FUZZTAIL	SIZINESS	FRIZZING
ZAPATERO	ZOOPHILY	GAZABOES	SIZYGIUM	FRIZZLED
ZARATITE	ZOOPHORI	GAZEBOES	SIZZLING	FRIZZLER
ZARZUELA	ZOOPHYTE	GAZELESS	SUZERAIN	FROZENLY
ZASTRUGA	ZOOSCOPY	GAZELLES	SYZYGIAL	FURZETOP
ZASTRUGI	ZOOSPERM	GAZEMENT	SYZYGIES	FUZZBALL
ZEALOTIC	ZOOSPORE	GAZETTAL	SYZYGIUM	FUZZIEST
ZEALOTRY	ZOOTHOME	GAZETTED	TEZKIRAH	FUZZTAIL
ZEALOUSY	ZOOTOMIC	GAZINGLY	VIZARDED	GAUZIEST
ZEBRINNY	ZOOTOXIN	GAZOGENE	VIZCACHA	GAZZETTA
ZECCHINO	ZOPILOTE	GAZPACHO	VIZIRATE	GIZZENED
ZELATRIX	ZORRILLO	GAZZETTA	VIZIRIAL	GLAZIERS
ZEMINDAR	ZORTZICO	GIZZENED	VIZORING	GLAZIERY
ZEMSTVOS	ZUCCHINI	GUZZLING	WAZIRATE	GLAZIEST
ZENITHAL	ZUGZWANG	HAZARDER	WIZARDLY	GRAZIERY
ZEOLITIC	ZUPANATE	HAZARDRY	WIZARDRY	GRAZIOSO
ZEOSCOPE	ZWIEBACK	HAZELNUT	WUZZLING	GRIZZLED
ZEPHYRUS	ZYGAENID	HAZINESS	ZIZZLING	GRIZZLER
ZEPPELIN	ZYGODONT	HAZNADAR	ZYZYPHUS	GUZZLING
ZERUMBET	ZYGOMATA	HAZZANUT		HAZZANUT
ZETACISM	ZYGOTENE	JAZERANT	AKAZGINE	ISOZOOID
ZIBELINE	ZYGOTOID	JAZZIEST	ALIZARIN	JAZZIEST
ZIGGURAT	ZYMOGENE	JEZEKITE	AMAZEFUL	MARZIPAN
ZIGZAGGY	ZYMOLOGY	LAZAROLE	BENZENYL	MITZVAHS
ZIMBABWE		LAZARONE	BENZIDIN	MITZVOTH
ZIMBALON	AZOBLACK	LAZAROUS	BENZILIC	MIZZLING
ZINCKING	AZOGREEN	LAZINESS	BENZOATE	MOUZOUNA
ZINCURET	AZOHUMIC	LAZULITE	BENZOBIS	MUZZIEST
ZIPHIOID	AZOIMIDE	LAZURITE	BENZYLIC	MUZZLING
ZIPPIEST	AZOTEMIA	LAZYBACK	BEZZLING	NUZZLING
ZIRCONIA	AZOTIZED	LAZYBIRD	BIZZARRO	ORYZANIN
ZIRCONIC	AZOTURIA	LAZYBONE	BLAZONED	ORYZENIN
ZIRCONYL	CZAREVNA	LAZYLEGS	BLAZONER	PANZOISM
ZIZZLING	CZARITZA	LOZENGED	BLAZONRY	PANZOOTY
ZOANTHID	OZARKITE	LOZENGER	BLIZZARD	PIAZZAED
ZODIACAL	OZOBROME	MAZAGRAN	BOZZETTO	PIAZZIAN
ZOEAFORM	OZONIZED	MAZALGIA	BRAZENED	PIZZERIA
ZOETROPE	OZONIZER	MAZARINE	BRAZENLY	PREZONAL
ZOIATRIA	SZLACHTA	MAZINESS	BRAZIERY	PRIZABLE
ZOLOTNIK	SZOPELKA	MAZOPEXY	BUZZIEST	PRIZEMAN
ZOMBIISM	TZEDAKAH	MAZOURKA	CALZOONS	PRIZEMEN
ZONALITY		MEZEREON	CANZONET	PUZZLING
ZONATION	BEZANTEE	MEZEREUM	CATZERIE	QUEZALES
ZONELESS	BEZONIAN	MEZQUITE	CRAZEDLY	QUIZZERY
ZONUROID	BEZZLING	MEZUZAHS	CRAZIEST	QUIZZIFY
ZOOBLAST	BIZZARRO	MEZUZOTH	CRAZYCAT	QUIZZING
ZOOCHEMY	BOZZETTO	MIZZLING	CRUZEIRO	QUIZZISH
ZOOCHORE	BUZZIEST	MOZEMIZE	DAZZLING	QUIZZISM
ZOOECIAL	CAZIQUE	MOZEMIZE	DIAZOATE	QUIZZITY
ZOOECIUM	COZENAGE	MUZZIEST	DIAZOTIC	RADZIMIR
ZOOGLOEA	COZENING	MUZZLING	DIZZIEST	RHIZOBIA
ZOOGRAFT	COZINESS	NAZIFIED	DIZZYING	RHIZOGEN
ZOOLATER	DAZZLING	NIZAMATE	DONZELLA	RHIZOIDAL
ZOOLATRY	DIZENING	NUZZLING	DOUZAINE	RHIZOMIC
ZOOLITIC	DIZZIEST	OOZINESS	DOUZEPER	RHIZOPOD
ZOOLOGIC	DIZZYING	PEZANTIC	DRIZZLED	RHIZOTIC
ZOOMANIA	DOZINESS	PEZIZOID	EPIZOOTY	RITZIEST
ZOOMETRY	ENZOOTIC	PIZZERIA	FEAZINGS	RIZZOMED
ZOOMIMIC	EOZOONAL	PUZZLING	FIZZIEST	SEIZABLE
ZOOMORPH	ERZAHLER	RAZBOOCH	FIZZLING	SITZMARK

SIZZLING	GRIZZLED	TWEEZING	HALUTZIM	ANTICIZE
SUBZONAL	GRIZZLER	UNDAZZLE	HOACTZIN	APHETIZE
SWIZZLER	GWERZIOU	UNMUZZLE	HOWITZER	APHORIZE
TERZETTO	HALAZONE	UNPUZZLE	HYDRAZIN	APPETIZE
TRIZOMAL	HEMOZOON	UNVIZARD	IDOLIZED	ARBORIZE
WEAZENED	HEREZELD	VOLTZINE	IDOLIZER	ARCHAIZE
WHIZBANG	HERTZIAN	VOLTZITE	IMIDAZOL	ASTATIZE
WHIZZING	HOLOZOIC	WALTZING	IRIDIZED	ATHETIZE
WINZEMAN	HYLOZOIC	WHEEZIER	ITEMIZED	ATMOLYZE
WINZEMEN	HYPOZOAN	WHEEZILY	ITEMIZER	ATTICIZE
WOOZIEST	HYPOZOIC	WHEEZING	JUDAIZER	AUTOLYZE
WRIZZLED	IDIOZOME	WHIZZING	KEVUTZAH	AVIANIZE
WUZZLING	INDAZOLE	WRIZZLED	KIBITZER	BACONIZE
ZARZUELA	IODIZING	WURTZITE	KREUTZER	BAKELIZE
ZIGZAGGY	IOTIZING	YAHRZEIT	LAICIZED	BARUKHZY
ZIZZLING	JANIZARY	ZORTZICO	LAICIZER	BIGAMIZE
ZUGZWANG	LHERZITE		LIONIZED	BOTANIZE
	MAGAZINE	ADONIZED	LIONIZER	BRACOZZO
AGNIZING	MAGAZINY	AGATIZED	MALGUZAR	BRAGOZZO
ALBIZZIA	MATEZITE	AGONIZED	MARKAZES	BULLDOZE
ALCAZABA	MESOZOAN	AGONIZER	MESTIZOS	CALABAZA
ALCAZAVA	METAZOAL	ALBIZZIA	METRAZOL	CALABOZO
ANTIZOEA	METAZOAN	ALGUAZIL	MICROZOA	CALORIZE
ARANZADA	METAZOEA	ANALYZED	OBELIZED	CANALIZE
ARMOZEEN	METAZOIC	ANALYZER	OPALIZED	CANONIZE
ARMOZINE	METAZOON	ANODIZED	OUTSIZED	CAPONIZE
ASSIZING	MEZUZAHS	APPRIZAL	OXIDIZED	CARROZZA
BAETZNER	MEZUZOTH	APPRIZER	OXIDIZER	CATALYZE
BEDAZZLE	MONAZITE	ARRHIZAL	OZONIZED	CINEMIZE
BLIZZARD	MONOZOAN	ATHEIZER	OZONIZER	CIVILIZE
BLOWZIER	MONOZOIC	ATOMIZED	PARTIZAN	COLONIZE
BLOWZING	NAMAZLIK	ATOMIZER	PECTIZED	COMPRIZE
BREEZIER	ORMUZINE	AZOTIZED	PEPTIZED	CORONIZE
BREEZING	OSMAZOME	BAPTIZED	PEPTIZER	CREOLIZE
BREEZILY	PEREZONE	BAPTIZEE	PHENAZIN	CRUELIZE
BRITZSKA	PEZIZOID	BAPTIZER	POETIZED	CURARIZE
BRONZIFY	PIAZZAED	BARTIZAN	POETIZER	CUTINIZE
BRONZING	PIAZZIAN	BEDAZZLE	PROTOZOA	CZARITZA
BRONZINE	POLYZOAN	BIBENZYL	QUARTZIC	DANDYIZE
BRONZITE	POLYZOIC	BOMBAZET	REALIZED	DECATIZE
BROOZLED	POLYZOON	BRACOZZO	REALIZER	DEIONIZE
BRYOZOAN	PYRAZINE	BRAGOZZO	RESEIZER	DEMONIZE
BRYOZOON	PYRAZOLE	BROMIZER	SARRAZIN	DEPUTIZE
BRYOZOUM	QUIZZERY	BRUNIZEM	SCHERZOS	DETONIZE
CACOZEAL	QUIZZIFY	CADENZA	SIEROZEM	DEVILIZE
CACOZYME	QUIZZING	CAPSIZAL	SPRITZER	DIGITIZE
CHUTZPAH	QUIZZISH	CARBAZIC	SPUILZIE	DISDIAZO
COENZYME	QUIZZISM	CARBAZIN	SQUEEZED	DISPRIZE
CYTOZOIC	QUIZZITY	CARROZZA	SQUEEZER	DISSEIZE
CYTOZOON	RAADZAAL	CHALAZAE	STYLIZED	DIVINIZE
CYTOZYME	RENDZINA	CHALAZAL	STYLIZER	DUELLIZE
DENAZIFY	RESIZING	CHALAZAS	SUBSIZAR	DYNAMIZE
DENIZATE	RIBAZUBA	CHINTZES	TERRAZZO	EMBOLIZE
DRIZZLED	SCHIZOID	COALIZED	TETRAZIN	EMBRONZE
ECTOZOAN	SCHIZONT	COGNIZED	TRAPEZIA	ENERGIZE
ECTOZOIC	SCHIZTIC	COGNIZEE	UNBAIZED	ENFRENZY
EMBEZZLE	SFORZATO	COGNIZER	UNCRAZED	EQUALIZE
ENTOZOAL	SHAHZADA	COGNIZOR	UNDAZZLE	ERGOTIZE
ENTOZOAN	SMORZATO	CYANIZED	UNFROZEN	ESTERIZE
ENTOZOIC	SNEEZING	DEGLAZED	UNGLAZED	ETERNIZE
ENTOZOON	SNOOZING	DIALYZED	UNMUZZLE	ETHERIZE
FLOOZIES	SPITZKOP	DIALYZER	UNPUZZLE	ETHICIZE
FRAZZLED	STANZAED	DIBENZYL	UTILIZED	ETIOLIZE
FREEZING	STANZAIC	DUALIZED	UTILIZER	EULOGIZE
FRENZIED	STOLZITE	EBONIZED	VAMMAZSA	EUPHUIZE
FRENZIES	SWIZZLER	ECHOIZED		EXORCIZE
FRENZILY	TAILZIED	EGOTIZED		EXORDIZE
FRIEZING	THIAZINE	ELEGIZED	ACTIVIZE	FABULIZE
FRIZZIER	THIAZOLE	EMBEZZLE	ALBRONZE	FARADIZE
FRIZZILY	THIOZONE	EMBLAZED	ALDOLIZE	FATALIZE
FRIZZING	TIMAZITE	EMBLAZER	ALKALIZE	FEMINIZE
FRIZZLED	TOPAZINE	EMBLAZON	ALKYLIZE	FIBERIZE
FRIZZLER	TOPAZITE	FILMIZED	ALMUERZO	FIGURIZE
FROWZIER	TRIAZANE	FORMAZAN	AMINOAZO	FINALIZE
FROWZILY	TRIAZINE	FORMAZYL	AMORTIZE	FLUIDIZE
FROWZLED	TRIAZOLE	FUELIZER	ANALGIZE	FOCALIZE
GOYAZITE	TWEEZERS	GHAWAZEE	ANGELIZE	FORUMIZE
			ANNALIZE	

GARBANZO	MAXIMIZE	OVERGAZE	RUMBOOZE	THRONIZE
GARVANZO	MEDALIZE	OVERSIZE	RURALIZE	TODDYIZE
GIANTIZE	MELANIZE	PAEANIZE	SALINIZE	TONICIZE
GRANDEZA	MELODIZE	PAGANIZE	SANITIZE	TOTALIZE
HEPATIZE	MEMORIZE	PALATIZE	SATANIZE	TRISTEZA
HETERIZE	METALIZE	PAPALIZE	SATINIZE	TROTCOZY
HOMILIZE	MICASIZE	PARALYZE	SATIRIZE	TUBERIZE
HUMANIZE	MINIMIZE	PATINIZE	SAVAGIZE	TUTORIZE
HUMORIZE	MISPRIZE	PAVONIZE	SCHMALZY	UNIONIZE
IDEALIZE	MOBILIZE	PELORIZE	SCHMOOZE	URBANIZE
IMMUNIZE	MODALIZE	PENALIZE	SERENIZE	VALORIZE
INDENIZE	MODELIZE	PETUNTZE	SEVERIZE	VAPORIZE
INFAMIZE	MODULIZE	POLARIZE	SILICIZE	VELARIZE
INSULIZE	MONETIZE	POLEMIZE	SIMILIZE	VENALIZE
JAROVIZE	MONODIZE	POLICIZE	SIMONIZE	VENOMIZE
JECORIZE	MORALIZE	POLITIZE	SIMULIZE	VITALIZE
JUBILIZE	MOTORIZE	PTYALIZE	SINAPIZE	VOCALIZE
KAMIKAZE	NAKEDIZE	PUPILIZE	SIRENIZE	VOWELIZE
KATALYZE	NASALIZE	PYRITIZE	SOBERIZE	WOMANIZE
KETONIZE	NATURIZE	QUANTIZE	SOLARIZE	YAROVIZE
LABILIZE	NEBULIZE	QUATORZE	SOLECIZE	YOTACIZE
LACONIZE	NICOTIZE	RACEMIZE	SONORIZE	
LATINIZE	NODULIZE	RAMBOOZE	SORORIZE	APRENDIZ
LEGALIZE	NOTARIZE	REGALIZE	STANITZA	AVESTRUZ
LINENIZE	NOVELIZE	REGULIZE	STARGAZE	BAROMETZ
LOCALIZE	OOLOGIZE	RENOVIZE	SUBERIZE	BIQUARTZ
LOGICIZE	OPSONIZE	RESINIZE	SYNERIZE	MUSTAFUZ
LUNATIZE	OPTIMIZE	RETINIZE	TEMPLIZE	SCHMALTZ
MACARIZE	ORANGIZE	RIVALIZE	TERRAZZO	SHAATNEZ
MAGADIZE	ORGANIZE	ROBOTIZE	TETANIZE	SOLONETZ
MAJORIZE	OUTBLAZE	ROYALIZE	THEORIZE	

SCORING ORDER LIST OF 8-LETTER WORDS

31	OXIDIZED	DENAZIFY	DYNAMIZE	BAPTIZED
MAZOPEXY	QUANTIZE	FROWZLED	ECHOIZED	BENZENYL
QUIZZIFY	QUATORZE	GHAWAZEE	ENFRENZY	BIGAMIZE
	QUEZALES	HAZARDRY	FILMIZED	BLAZONRY
29	QUIZZING	HYDRAZIN	FRENZILY	BLOWZIER
BARUKHZY	SQUEEZER	JAZERANT	FROWZIER	BRAZENLY
	SYZYGIUM	KATALYZE	FROZENLY	BRAZIERY
28	WHEEZILY	POLYZOIC	HOWITZER	BREEZILY
BIQUARTZ	WHIZBANG	RAZBOOCH	JAZZIEST	BRYOZOAN
JEZEKITE	ZIMBABWE	RHIZOMIC	KIBITZER	BRYOZOON
LAZYBACK	ZYMOLOGY	SCHIZTIC	LAZYBIRD	CAPSIZED
MAXIMIZE		SCHMALTZ	MAGAZINY	CATALYZE
MEZQUITE	**25**	SCHMOOZE	MARKAZES	CHALAZAE
QUARTZIC	AZOBLACK	SHAHZADA	MAZOURKA	CHALAZAL
QUIZZERY	BRONZIFY	SYZYGIAL	NAMAZLIK	CHALAZAS
QUIZZISH	EXORDIZE	SYZYGIES	RHIZOPOD	CHINTZES
QUIZZITY	FORMAZYL	TEZKIRAH	SCHIZOID	CIVILIZE
ZWIEBACK	GAZPACHO	VAMMAZSA	SITZMARK	CYTOZOON
	HYLOZOIC	WHEEZING	SIZYGIUM	CZAREVNA
27	HYPOZOAN	WIZARDLY	SZOPELKA	DANDYIZE
CHUTZPAH	JUDAIZER	WIZARDRY	VOWELIZE	DIALYZED
CYTOZYME	MITZVAHS	ZECCHINO	WHEEZIER	EMBLAZED
HYPOZOIC	MITZVOTH	ZELATRIX	WHIZZING	EPIZOOTY
JANIZARY	OXIDIZER	ZINCKING	YAHRZEIT	ETHICIZE
JAROVIZE	SPITZKOP	ZOOMORPH	YAROVIZE	EUPHUIZE
KEVUTZAH	TZEDAKAH	ZOOSCOPY	ZIPHIOID	FABULIZE
QUIZZISM	ZAMBOMBA	ZOOTOXIN	ZOMBIISM	FEMINIZE
SCHMALZY	ZEPHYRUS	ZUCCHINI	ZOOMIMIC	FIBERIZE
SQUEEZED	ZOOPHILY		ZYGOMATA	FOCALIZE
VIZCACHA	ZOOPHYTE	**23**	ZYMOGENE	FORMAZAN
ZOOCHEMY		BAKELIZE		FORUMIZE
	24	BLOWZING	**22**	FRIZZILY
26	ALKYLIZE	BOMBAZET	ACTIVIZE	FURZETOP
CACOZYME	AZOHUMIC	BRITZSKA	AKAZGINE	GAZINGLY
EQUALIZE	BENZYLIC	CARBAZIC	ALCAZAVA	HALUTZIM
EXORCIZE	BIBENZYL	CARBAZIDE	AMAZEFUL	HEMOZOON
FROWZILY	BRYOZOUM	COMPRIZE	APHETIZE	HEPATIZE
JECORIZE	COENZYME	CRAZEDLY	APHORIZE	HOACTZIN
JUBILIZE	CRAZYCAT	CYANIZED	ARCHAIZE	HOLOZOIC
MAJORIZE	CYTOZOIC	DIBENZYL	ATMOLYZE	HOMILIZE

HUMANIZE
HUMORIZE
INFAMIZE
KAMIKAZE
LAZYBONE
MUSTAFUZ
NAKEDIZE
PANZOOTY
PARALYZE
PAVONIZE
PECTIZED
PEPTIZED
PHENAZIN
POLYZOAN
POLYZOON
PTYALIZE
PYRAZINE
PYRAZOLE
PYRITIZE
RHIZOBIA
RHIZOIDAL
RHIZOTIC
RIZIFORM
SCHERZOS
SCHIZONT
SZLACHTA
TODDYIZE
TROTCOZY
VAPORIZE
VENOMIZE
VIZARDED
VOCALIZE
WINZEMAN
WINZEMEN
WOMANIZE
YOTACIZE
ZAMPOGNA
ZEBRINNY
ZEMSTVOS
ZIGZAGGY
ZIRCONYL
ZOEAFORM
ZOOCHORE
ZOOMETRY
ZOOPHILE
ZOOPHORI
ZOOTHOME
ZYGAENID
ZYGODONT
ZYGOTOID

21
ALCAZABA
ALKALIZE
ANALYZED
APPETIZE
APPRIZAL
APPRIZER
BACONIZE
BAPTIZEE
BAPTIZER
BAROMETZ
BENZILIC
BENZOBIS
BROMIZER
BRUNIZEM
CACOZEAL
CALABAZA
CALABOZO
CAPONIZE
CAPSIZAL
CARBAZIN
CINEMIZE
COGNIZED
DEVILIZE
DIALYZER
DIVINIZE

DIZZYING
ECTOZOIC
EMBLAZER
EMBLAZON
EMBOLIZE
EMBRONZE
FARADIZE
FEAZINGS
FIGURIZE
FLUIDIZE
FOOZLING
FREEZING
FRENZIED
FRIEZING
FUZZBALL
GARVANZO
GLAZIERY
GOYAZITE
GRAZIERY
GWERZIOU
HAZARDER
HAZNADAR
HEREZELD
IMMUNIZE
KETONIZE
KREUTZER
LAZYLEGS
MACARIZE
MAGADIZE
MARZIPAN
MEMORIZE
METAZOIC
MEZEREUM
MEZUZAHS
MEZUZOTH
MICASIZE
MICROZOA
MINIMIZE
MISPRIZE
MOBILIZE
MONOZOIC
NAZIFIED
OPTIMIZE
OSMAZOME
OVERGAZE
OZARKITE
OZOBROME
PANZOISM
PAPALIZE
PEPTIZER
PEZANTIC
POLEMIZE
POLICIZE
PRIZABLE
PRIZEMAN
PRIZEMEN
PUPILIZE
RACEMIZE
RAMBOOZE
RHIZOGEN
RIBAZUBA
RUMBOOZE
SAVAGIZE
STYLIZED
TEMPLIZE
TWEEZING
UNVIZARD
VIZORING
WALTZING
WEAZENED
ZEOSCOPE
ZEPPELIN
ZERUMBET
ZETACISM
ZIMBALON
ZIPPIEST
ZIRCONIC

ZOANTHID
ZOLOTNIK
ZOOECIUM
ZOOGRAFT
ZOOTOMIC
ZUGZWANG
ZYGOTENE

20
ANALYZER
APRENDIZ
ARRHIZAL
ATHEIZER
ATHETIZE
ATOMIZED
AUTOLYZE
AVESTRUZ
AVIANIZE
AZOIMIDE
BENZIDIN
BLAZONED
BRACOZZO
BRAZENED
BREEZING
BRONZING
BROOZLED
BULLDOZE
COALIZED
COGNIZEE
COGNIZER
COGNIZOR
COZENING
DECATIZE
DEGLAZED
DEMONIZE
DEPUTIZE
DIAZOTIC
DISPRIZE
DOUZEPER
EBONIZED
EMBEZZLE
ERZAHLER
ETHERIZE
FATALIZE
FINALIZE
FIZZLING
FLOOZIES
FOZINESS
FRAZZLED
FRENZIES
FRIZETTE
FRIZZING
FRIZZLED
FUELIZER
GARBANZO
GAZABOES
GAZEBOES
GAZEMENT
HALAZONE
HAZELNUT
HAZINESS
HERTZIAN
HETERIZE
IDIOZOME
IMIDAZOL
ITEMIZED
LAICIZED
LHERZITE
LOGICIZE
MAGAZINE
MALGUZAR
MAZAGRAN
MAZALGIA
MEDALIZE
MELODIZE
MODALIZE
MODELIZE

MODULIZE
MONODIZE
MOZEMIZE
NOVELIZE
OBELIZED
OPALIZED
ORYZANIN
ORYZENIN
OVERSIZE
PAGANIZE
POETIZED
RADZIMIR
RENOVIZE
RIVALIZE
ROYALIZE
SEVERIZE
SFORZATO
SHAATNEZ
STYLIZER
SYNERIZE
THEORIZE
THIAZINE
THIAZOLE
THIOZONE
THRONIZE
TWEEZERS
UNBAIZED
UNCRAZED
UNFROZEN
VALORIZE
VELARIZE
VENALIZE
VITALIZE
VIZIRATE
VIZIRIAL
VOLTZINE
VOLTZITE
WAZIRATE
WOOZIEST
WRIZZLED
WURTZITE
WUZZLING
ZAMINDAR
ZANDMOLE
ZEALOTRY
ZEALOUSY
ZEMINDAR
ZENITHAL
ZODIACAL
ZONALITY
ZOOLATRY
ZOOLOGIC

19
ADONIZED
AGATIZED
AGNIZING
AGONIZED
ALBRONZE
ALMUERZO
AMINOAZO
AMORTIZE
ANODIZED
ANTICIZE
ARBORIZE
ARMOZEEN
ARMOZINE
ATOMIZER
ATTICIZE
AZOTEMIA
BAETZNER
BARTIZAN
BEDAZZLE
BENZOATE
BEZANTEE
BEZONIAN
BEZZLING

BLAZONER
BLIZZARD
BOTANIZE
BRAGOZZO
BREEZIER
BRONZINE
BRONZITE
CALORIZE
CALZOONS
CANALIZE
CANONIZE
CANZONET
CATZERIE
COLONIZE
CORONIZE
COZINESS
CRAZIEST
CREOLIZE
CRUELIZE
CRUZEIRO
CURARIZE
CUTINIZE
DIGITIZE
DISDIAZO
DIZENING
DUALIZED
ECTOZOAN
EGOTIZED
ELEGIZED
ENTOZOIC
ENZOOTIC
FIZZIEST
FRIZZIER
FRIZZLER
FUZZIEST
FUZZTAIL
GAZETTED
GAZOGENE
GRANDEZA
HAZZANUT
IDOLIZED
IODIZING
IRIDIZED
ITEMIZER
LABILIZE
LACONIZE
LAICIZER
LOCALIZE
LOZENGED
MATEZITE
MAZARINE
MAZINESS
MELANIZE
MESOZOAN
MESTIZOS
METALIZE
METAZOAL
METAZOAN
METAZOEA
METAZOON
METRAZOL
MEZEREON
MIZZLING
MONAZITE
MONETIZE
MONOZOAN
MORALIZE
MOTORIZE
MOUZOUNA
MUZZLING
NEBULIZE
NICOTIZE
NIZAMATE
OPSONIZE
ORMUZINE
OUTBLAZE
PAEANIZE

PALATIZE	ZAIBATSU	ENERGIZE	UNPUZZLE	RITZIEST
PARTIZAN	ZAMORINE	ERGOTIZE	UTILIZED	RURALIZE
PATINIZE	ZAPATERO	EULOGIZE	ZASTRUGA	SALINIZE
PELORIZE	ZEALOTIC	GAUZIEST	ZASTRUGI	SANITIZE
PENALIZE	ZEOLITIC	GAZELESS	ZONUROID	SARRAZIN
PEREZONE	ZIBELINE	GAZELLES	ZOOGLOEA	SATANIZE
PETUNTZE	ZIGGURAT	GAZETTAL	ZORTZICO	SATINIZE
PEZIZOID	ZINCURET	GIANTIZE		SATIRIZE
PIAZZAED	ZIRCONIA	GIZZENED		SERENIZE
POETIZER	ZOETROPE	GLAZIERS	**17**	SIRENIZE
POLARIZE	ZOOBLAST	GLAZIEST	ALIZARIN	SIZINESS
POLITIZE	ZOOECIAL	GRAZIOSO	ANNALIZE	SIZZLING
PREZONAL	ZOOLITIC	GRIZZLED	ANTIZOEA	SOLARIZE
PROTOZOA	ZOOMANIA	GUZZLING	ASTATIZE	SOLONETZ
PUZZLING	ZOONITIC	IDEALIZE	AZOTIZED	SONORIZE
RAZORMAN	ZOONOTIC	IDOLIZER	AZOTURIA	SORORIZE
RIZZOMED	ZOOPERAL	INDAZOLE	DIZZIEST	STANITZA
ROBOTIZE	ZOOSPORE	INDENIZE	ENTOZOAL	STOLZITE
SEIZABLE	ZOPILOTE	IOTIZING	ENTOZOAN	SUZERAIN
SIEROZEM	ZUPANATE	ISOZOOID	ENTOZOON	TERZETTO
SILICIZE		LEGALIZE	EOZOONAL	TETANIZE
SIMILIZE	**18**	LIONIZED	ESTERIZE	TETRAZIN
SIMONIZE	AGONIZER	LOZENGER	ETERNIZE	TOTALIZE
SIMULIZE	ALBIZZIA	MUZZIEST	ETIOLIZE	TRIAZANE
SINAPIZE	ALDOLIZE	NODULIZE	GAZZETTA	TRIAZINE
SIZEABLE	ALGUAZIL	OOLOGIZE	GRIZZLER	TRIAZOLE
SMORZATO	ANALGIZE	ORANGIZE	INSULIZE	TRISTEZA
SOBERIZE	ANGELIZE	ORGANIZE	LATINIZE	TUTORIZE
SOLECIZE	ARANZADA	OUTSIZED	LAZAROLE	UNDAZZLE
SPRITZER	ASSIZING	PIAZZIAN	LAZARONE	UNIONIZE
SPUILZIE	AZOGREEN	PIZZERIA	LAZAROUS	UTILIZER
STANZAIC	BIZZARRO	RAADZAAL	LAZINESS	ZARATITE
SUBERIZE	BUZZIEST	RAZEEING	LAZULITE	ZOIATRIA
SUBSIZAR	CZARITZA	REALIZED	LAZURITE	ZONATION
SUBZONAL	DAZZLING	REALIZER	LINENIZE	ZONELESS
SWIZZLER	DEIONIZE	REGALIZE	LIONIZER	ZOOLATER
TIMAZITE	DENIZATE	REGULIZE	LUNATIZE	ZOONOSES
TONICIZE	DETONIZE	RENDZINA	NASALIZE	ZOONOSIS
TOPAZINE	DIAZOATE	RESIZING	NATURIZE	ZORRILLO
TOPAZITE	DISSEIZE	SNEEZING	NOTARIZE	
TRAPEZIA	DONZELLA	SNOOZING	NUZZLING	
TRIZOMAL	DOUZAINE	STANZAED	OOZINESS	**16**
TUBERIZE	DOZINESS	STARGAZE	OZONIZED	OZONIZER
UNGLAZED	DRIZZLED	TAILZIED	RESEIZER	TERRAZZO
URBANIZE	DUELLIZE	UNMUZZLE	RESINIZE	ZARZUELA
			RETINIZE	ZIZZLING

ALPHABETICAL LIST OF 9-LETTER WORDS

ABURABOZU	ALUMINIZE	APHRIZITE	AUTHORIZE	BALSAMIZE
ACADEMIZE	AMAZEMENT	APOLOGIZE	AUTOZOOID	BALZARINE
ACETALIZE	AMAZONITE	APPETIZED	AVIZANDUM	BAMBOOZLE
ACETONIZE	AMORTIZED	APPETIZER	AZALEAMUM	BANTAMIZE
ACETYLIZE	ANABOLIZE	APPRIZING	AZEDARACH	BAPTIZING
ACTIONIZE	ANALOGIZE	ARBORIZED	AZEOTROPE	BARBARIZE
ACTUALIZE	ANALYZING	ARCHAIZED	AZEOTROPY	BEAVERIZE
ADONIZING	ANARCHIZE	ARCHAIZER	AZIETHANE	BEDAZZLED
ADVERTIZE	ANATOMIZE	ARCHIZOIC	AZIMUTHAL	BEDIZENED
AGATIZING	ANGELIZED	ARCTICIZE	AZLACTONE	BEDLAMIZE
AGOMYZID	ANGLICIZE	ARIZONITE	AZOBENZIL	BENZAMIDE
AGONIZING	ANHYDRIZE	AROMATIZE	AZOBENZOL	BENZAMIDO
ALCARRAZA	ANIMALIZE	ARRHIZOUS	AZOCYCLIC	BENZENOID
ALCHEMIZE	ANNUALIZE	ARZRUNITE	AZOFORMIC	BENZIDINE
ALDOLIZED	ANODIZING	ASSOILZIE	AZOLITMIN	BENZIDINO
ALIZARATE	ANTHOZOAN	ASTATIZED	AZOPHENOL	BENZOATED
ALIZARINE	ANTHOZOIC	ASTATIZER	AZOPHENYL	BENZOLATE
ALKALIZER	ANTHOZOON	ATHETIZED	AZOTIZING	BENZOLINE
ALLOZOOID	APHIDOZER	ATMOLYZER	AZOXONIUM	BENZOLIZE
ALTERNIZE	APHORIZED	ATOMIZING	BACTERIZE	BERGINIZE
ALUMETIZE	APHORIZER	ATTICIZED	BALKANIZE	BEZESTEEN

BEZOARDIC	COPROZOIC	EMBEZZLER	GERMANIZE	LAMZIEKTE
BILHARZIC	COSMOZOIC	EMBLAZING	GIGANTIZE	LAZARETTE
BIOLOGIZE	COTTONIZE	EMBLEMIZE	GLAMORIZE	LAZARETTO
BIZARDITE	COURTEZAN	EMPHASIZE	GLAZEWORK	LAZULITIC
BIZARRELY	CRAZINESS	ENDENIZEN	GLAZINESS	LAZYBONES
BLAZONING	CRAZYWEED	ENERGIZED	GLUTINIZE	LAZYBOOTS
BLIZZARDY	CREOLEIZE	ENERGIZER	GLYCERIZE	LAZZARONE
BLOWZIEST	CREOLIZED	ENZYMATIC	GONOZOOID	LAZZARONI
BOMBAZINE	CRITICIZE	ENZYMOSIS	GORGONIZE	LEGALIZED
BOOZINESS	CURARIZED	ENZYMOTIC	GOSPELIZE	LICHENIZE
BOTANIZED	CUTINIZED	EPILOGIZE	GRANITIZE	LIGNITIZE
BOTANIZER	CYANIZING	EPIPOLIZE	GRANULIZE	LINEARIZE
BRAZENING	CZARINIAN	EPITOMIZE	GRAZINGLY	LINENIZER
BRAZILEIN	CZARISTIC	EPIZEUXIS	GRIZZLIER	LIONIZING
BRAZILITE	DAZEDNESS	EPIZOOTIC	GRIZZLIES	LIQUIDIZE
BREEZEWAY	DECADENZA	EQUALIZED	GRIZZLING	LITURGIZE
BREEZIEST	DECATIZER	EQUALIZER	GUACONIZE	LOCALIZED.
BRUTALIZE	DEEPFROZE	ERGOTIZED	HAMLETIZE	LOCALIZER
BULLDOZED	DEFERRIZE	ESOTERIZE	HAPHAZARD	MACARIZED
BULLDOZER	DEGLAZING	ETERNIZED	HARMONIZE	MAGAZINED
BURKUNDAZ	DEMONIZED	ETHERIZED	HAZARDOUS	MAGAZINER
BURTONIZE	DENITRIZE	ETHERIZER	HELIOZOAN	MAGNETIZE
BUZZARDLY	DENTALIZE	ETHICIZED	HERALDIZE	MAINPRIZE
BUZZGLOAK	DEODORIZE	EULOGIZED	HERBALIZE	MAIZEBIRD
CALORIZER	DEOXIDIZE	EULOGIZER	HERBARIZE	MALGUZARI
CANALIZED	DEOZONIZE	EUPHEMIZE	HERBORIZE	MAMMONIZE
CANONIZED	DEPUTIZED	EUPHONIZE	HISTORIZE	MANGANIZE
CANONIZER	DESPOTIZE	EUPHUIZED	HUMANIZER	MANGONIZE
CAPONIZER	DEVILIZED	EVAPORIZE	HUMOURIZE	MANNERIZE
CAPRIZANT	DEZINCIFY	EXOENZYME	HYALINIZE	MANZANITA
CAPSIZING	DEZINKIFY	EXORCIZED	HYBRIDIZE	MARBELIZE
CARBAZIDE	DIABOLIZE	EXORCIZER	HYDRAZINE	MARBLEIZE
CARBAZINE	DIALOGIZE	FACTORIZE	HYDRAZOIC	MARMARIZE
CARBAZOLE	DIALYZATE	FACULTIZE	HYDRAZONE	MARRANIZE
CARBOLIZE	DIALYZING	FANTASIZE	HYDROLYZE	MARTYRIZE
CARBONIZE	DIAZEUTIC	FARADIZED	HYDROZOAL	MATRONIZE
CARBURIZE	DIAZEUXIS	FARADIZER	HYDROZOAN	MAXIMIZED
CARNALIZE	DIAZOAMIN	FAUCALIZE	HYDROZOIC	MAXIMIZER
CARTELIZE	DIAZONIUM	FECUNDIZE	HYDROZOON	MAZEDNESS
CATALYZED	DIAZOTATE	FERTILIZE	HYGIENIZE	MAZODYNIA
CATALYZER	DIAZOTIZE	FETICHIZE	HYLOZOISM	MAZOLYSIS
CATECHIZE	DIAZOTYPE	FEUDALIZE	HYLOZOIST	MAZOLYTIC
CATHARIZE	DIBENZOYL	FIBERIZER	HYPNOTIZE	MECHANIZE
CAUPONIZE	DIESELIZE	FILMIZING	HYPOCRIZE	MEDIALIZE
CAUTERIZE	DIETZEITE	FINALIZED	IDEALIZED	MEDIATIZE
CEREBRIZE	DIGITIZED	FISCALIZE	IDEALIZER	MEDIUMIZE
CHABAZITE	DIGITIZER	FISTULIZE	IDOLIZING	MEGAZOOID
CHALAZIAN	DISPRIZED	FIZELYITE	IMIDAZOLE	MELODIZED
CHALAZION	DISSEIZED	FLORIZINE	IMMUNIZED	MELODIZER
CHALAZIUM	DISSEIZEE	FLUIDIZED	INFAMIZED	MEMORIZED
CHEMOLYZE	DISSEIZOR	FOCALIZED	INFLUENZA	MEMORIZER
CHERNOZEM	DIVINIZED	FOREPRIZE	INOXIDIZE	MENDOZITE
CHINTZIER	DIZENMENT	FORMALIZE	IONIZABLE	MENSALIZE
CHORIZONT	DIZYGOTIC	FORMULIZE	IRIDIZING	MERCERIZE
CHRYSAZIN	DIZZARDLY	FORTHGAZE	ISOMERIZE	MERCURIZE
CHRYSAZOL	DIZZINESS	FOSSILIZE	ISONIAZID	MESMERIZE
CICATRIZE	DOCTORIZE	FRAZZLING	ISOXAZOLE	MESTIZOES
CITIZENLY	DOGMATIZE	FREEZABLE	ITALICIZE	METALIZED
CITIZENRY	DOUZEPERS	FRENZYING	ITEMIZING	METALLIZE
CITRONIZE	DRAGONIZE	FRIVOLIZE	IZVOZCHIK	METEORIZE
CIVILIZEE	DRAMATIZE	FRIZZIEST	JARGONIZE	METHODIZE
CIVILIZED	DRIZZLING	FRIZZLING	JAROVIZED	METRICIZE
CIVILIZER	DUALIZING	FROWZIEST	JASPERIZE	MEZCALINE
CLAVELIZE	DUCTILIZE	FURZECHAT	JAZZINESS	MEZZANINE
CLIMATIZE	DUNZIEKTE	FUZZINESS	JENNERIZE	MEZZOTINT
COALIZING	DZIGGETAI	GALLINAZO	JOVIALIZE	MICROZOAL
COCAINIZE	EBONIZING	GALVANIZE	KAOLINIZE	MICROZOAN
COELOZOIC	ECHOIZING	GARDENIZE	KEVAZINGO	MICROZOIC
COGNIZANT	ECONOMIZE	GAUZELIKE	KEVUTZOTH	MICROZONE
COGNIZING	ECPHORIZE	GAUZEWING	KIBBUTZIM	MICROZOON
COLAZIONE	ECTOENZYM	GAUZINESS	KRANTZITE	MICROZYMA
COLONIZED	EGOTIZING	GAZEHOUND	LABIALIZE	MICROZYME
COLONIZER	EKPHORIZE	GAZETTEER	LACONIZED	MINIMIZED
COMMUNIZE	ELECTRIZE	GAZETTING	LACONIZER	MINIMIZER
COMPRIZAL	ELEGIZING	GENIALIZE	LACTONIZE	MISPRIZED
COMPRIZED	ELENCHIZE	GENTILIZE	LADRONIZE	MISPRIZER
COPPERIZE	EMBEZZLED	GEOLOGIZE	LAICIZING	MIZENMAST

MIZZONITE	PAUPERIZE	QUINZIEME	SPOROZOON	UNCIALIZE
MNEMONIZE	PAVONAZZO	QUIZZICAL	SQUEEZING	UNDERSIZE
MOBILIZED	PECTIZING	RABBINIZE	STABILIZE	UNIONIZED
MODERNIZE	PEDANTIZE	RACEMIZED	STARGAZED	UNREALIZE
MONACHIZE	PEGMATIZE	RACIALIZE	STARGAZER	URALITIZE
MONETIZED	PENALIZED	RADIALIZE	STERILIZE	URBANIZED
MONZONITE	PEOPLEIZE	RADIUMIZE	STRAMAZON	UTILIZING
MORALIZED	PEPTIZING	RANDOMIZE	STYLIZING	VACUUMIZE
MORALIZER	PEPTONIZE	RAPTURIZE	SUBERIZED	VAMPIRIZE
MORGANIZE	PERHAZARD	RAZORBACK	SUBSIDIZE	VANDALIZE
MORSELIZE	PERSONIZE	RAZORBILL	SULCALIZE	VAPORIZER
MORTALIZE	PESSIMIZE	RAZOREDGE	SULFATIZE	VAPOURIZE
MOTORIZED	PETROLIZE	RAZZBERRY	SULFAZIDE	VASSALIZE
MULLENIZE	PEZOGRAPH	REALIZING	SULFURIZE	VERBALIZE
MUTUALIZE	PHENAZINE	REBAPTIZE	SULPHAZID	VERNALIZE
MYCORHIZA	PHENAZONE	RECOGNIZE	SULTANIZE	VICTIMIZE
MYSTERIZE	PHENOLIZE	RESEIZURE	SUMMARIZE	VISCIDIZE
MYTHICIZE	PHILOZOIC	RHETORIZE	SURGERIZE	VISIONIZE
NARCOTIZE	PHLORIZIN	RHEUMATIZ	SURPRIZAL	VISUALIZE
NASALIZED	PHONETIZE	RHIZINOUS	SYLLABIZE	VITALIZED
NAZIFYING	PHYTOZOAN	RHIZOBIUM	SYLLOGIZE	VITALIZER
NEBULIZED	PHYTOZOON	RHIZOCARP	SYMBOLIZE	VIZARDING
NEBULIZER	PIAZZETTA	RHIZOCAUL	SYNCOPIZE	VIZIERATE
NECROTIZE	PICTURIZE	RHIZOCORM	SYNERGIZE	VIZIERIAL
NECTARIZE	PILLORIZE	RHIZOTAXY	SYNEZISIS	VOCALIZED
NEOLOGIZE	PIZZICATO	RHIZOTOMI	SYNIZESIS	VOCALIZER
NEOTERIZE	PLATINIZE	RHIZOTOMY	SYNOECIZE	VOLCANIZE
NEUMATIZE	PLURALIZE	RHODIZITE	SYNOPSIZE	VULCANIZE
NICKELIZE	POETICIZE	RHYTHMIZE	SYNTONIZE	VULGARIZE
NITRIDIZE	POETIZING	ROUTINIZE	SYPHILIZE	WANTONIZE
NODULIZED	POLARIZED	RUBBERIZE	SYSTEMIZE	WAYZGOOSE
NORMALIZE	POLARIZER	RUBRICIZE	SYZYGETIC	WAZIRSHIP
NOTARIZED	POLICIZER	RURALIZED	TANDEMIZE	WHEEZIEST
NOVELIZED	POLYZOARY	RUSTICIZE	TANTALIZE	WINTERIZE
OBELIZING	POLYZOISM	SANITIZED	TARIFFIZE	WITTICIZE
OBJECTIZE	POLYZONAL	SAPROZOIC	TARTARIZE	WOMANIZED
ONIONIZED	POLYZOOID	SATIRIZED	TARTRAZIN	WOMANIZER
OPALIZING	POLZENITE	SATIRIZER	TAVERNIZE	WOOLENIZE
OPERATIZE	POSTERIZE	SATURNIZE	TELEOZOIC	WOOZINESS
OPTIMIZED	POSTURIZE	SCAZONTIC	TELEOZOON	ZAMINDARI
ORATORIZE	POTENTIZE	SCENARIZE	TELLURIZE	ZAMINDARY
ORGANIZED	POWDERIZE	SCHIZAXON	TEMPORIZE	ZAPATEADO
ORGANIZER	POZZOLANA	SCHIZOPOD	TENDERIZE	ZEALOTISM
ORGANZINE	PRECONIZE	SCHNAUZER	TERMINIZE	ZEALOTIST
ORIENTIZE	PREIOTIZE	SCHNITZEL	TERRORIZE	ZEALOUSLY
ORYZANINE	PRELATIZE	SCHNOZZLE	TERZETTOS	ZEBRALIKE
OSTRACIZE	PRELUDIZE	SCIENTIZE	TETANIZED	ZEBRAWOOD
OUTBRAZEN	PRESTEZZA	SCLERIZED	TETRAZANE	ZELATRICE
OUTDAZZLE	PRIZEABLE	SENSITIZE	TETRAZENE	ZELOTYPIA
OVERGLAZE	PROFANIZE	SERIALIZE	TETRAZINE	ZELOTYPIE
OVERGRAZE	PROLOGIZE	SERMONIZE	TETRAZOLE	ZEMINDARI
OVERPRIZE	PROPOLIZE	SEXUALIZE	TETRAZONE	ZENDICIAN
OVERSIZED	PROTOZOAL	SFORZANDO	THEATRIZE	ZENDIKITE
OXDIAZOLE	PROTOZOAN	SHAHZADAH	THEORIZED	ZEOLITIZE
OXIDIZING	PROTOZOEA	SIGNALIZE	THEORIZER	ZEPHYREAN
OXYBENZYL	PROTOZOIC	SILVERIZE	THIOZONID	ZEPHYRIAN
OXYGENIZE	PROTOZOON	SISTERIZE	THYMOLIZE	ZEPHYROUS
OXYTONIZE	PROZYMITE	SIZARSHIP	TINZENITE	ZERMAHBUB
OZOCERITE	PRYTANIZE	SLIVOVITZ	TOPAZFELS	ZEROAXIAL
OZONATION	PTYALIZED	SMORZANDO	TOTALIZED	ZEUGMATIC
OZONIZING	PUBLICIZE	SOCIALIZE	TOTALIZER	ZEUNERITE
OZOSTOMIA	PULVERIZE	SOLARIZED	TRAPEZIAL	ZIBELLINE
PAEANIZED	PUPILLIZE	SOLECIZED	TRAPEZIAN	ZINCALISM
PAGANIZED	PUPPETIZE	SOLECIZER	TRAPEZING	ZINCIFIED
PAGANIZER	PURPURIZE	SOLEMNIZE	TRAPEZIST	ZINFANDEL
PALLADIZE	PUZZLEDLY	SOLMIZATE	TRAPEZIUM	ZINGERONE
PALLETIZE	PUZZLEMAN	SOLVOLYZE	TRAPEZIUS	ZINKENITE
PAMPERIZE	PYRAZOLYL	SONNETIZE	TRAPEZOID	ZIPPINGLY
PANDERIZE	PYTHONIZE	SORBITIZE	TRINALIZE	ZIRCONATE
PANZOOTIA	QUANTIZED	SOVIETIZE	TRIOZONID	ZIRCONIUM
PANZOOTIC	QUARTZITE	SPIRALIZE	TUCHUNIZE	ZIRCONOID
PAPALIZER	QUARTZOID	SPIRITIZE	TURTLEIZE	ZIRKELITE
PARALYZED	QUARTZOSE	SPONDAIZE	TWEEZERED	ZITHERIST
PARALYZER	QUARTZOUS	SPOROZOAL	TYMPANIZE	ZOANTHOID
PASTORIZE	QUININIZE	SPOROZOAN	TYRANNIZE	ZOBTENITE
PATRIZATE	QUINONIZE	SPOROZOIC	UGRIANIZE	ZOEHEMERA
PATRONIZE	QUINZAINE	SPOROZOID	UNBRUTIZE	ZOETROPIC

ZOOCYTIAL	ZOOLOGIST	ZOOPHYTIC	ZUCCARINO	ZYGOSPERM
ZOOCYTIUM	ZOOLOGIZE	ZOOPLASTY	ZUCCHETTO	ZYGOSPORE
ZOOFULVIN	ZOOMETRIC	ZOOSCOPIC	ZUMBOORUK	ZYGOSTYLE
ZOOGAMETE	ZOOMORPHY	ZOOSPHERE	ZUURVELDT	ZYGOTAXIS
ZOOGAMOUS	ZOOPERIST	ZOOSPORIC	ZWANZIGER	ZYMOGENIC
ZOOGENOUS	ZOOPHAGAN	ZOOTECHNY	ZYGADENIN	ZYMOLOGIC
ZOOGLOEAL	ZOOPHILIA	ZOOTHECIA	ZYGANTRUM	ZYMOLYSIS
ZOOGLOEIC	ZOOPHILIC	ZOOTHEISM	ZYGOMATIC	ZYMOLYTIC
ZOOGONOUS	ZOOPHOBIA	ZOOTHEIST	ZYGONEURE	ZYMOMETER
ZOOGRAPHY	ZOOPHORIC	ZOOTOMIST	ZYGOPHORE	ZYMOPHORE
ZOOLITHIC	ZOOPHORUS	ZOOTROPHY	ZYGOPHYTE	ZYMOSCOPE
ZOOLOGIES	ZOOPHYTAL			

POSITIONAL ORDER LIST OF 9-LETTER WORDS

ZAMINDARI	ZOOPHORIC	OZONIZING	ALIZARATE	MANZANITA
ZAMINDARY	ZOOPHORUS	OZOSTOMIA	ALIZARINE	MEZZANINE
ZAPATEADO	ZOOPHYTAL		AMAZEMENT	MEZZOTINT
ZEALOTISM	ZOOPHYTIC	ARZRUNITE	AMAZONITE	MIZZONITE
ZEALOTIST	ZOOPLASTY	BEZESTEEN	ARIZONITE	MONZONITE
ZEALOUSLY	ZOOSCOPIC	BEZOARDIC	AVIZANDUM	ORYZANINE
ZEBRALIKE	ZOOSPHERE	BIZARDITE	BALZARINE	PANZOOTIA
ZEBRAWOOD	ZOOSPORIC	BIZARRELY	BENZAMIDE	PANZOOTIC
ZELATRICE	ZOOTECHNY	BUZZARDLY	BENZAMIDO	PIAZZETTA
ZELOTYPIA	ZOOTHECIA	BUZZGLOAK	BENZENOID	PIZZICATO
ZELOTYPIE	ZOOTHEISM	DAZEDNESS	BENZIDINE	POLZENITE
ZEMINDARI	ZOOTHEIST	DEZINCIFY	BENZIDINO	POZZOLANA
ZENDICIAN	ZOOTOMIST	DEZINKIFY	BENZOATED	PRIZEABLE
ZENDIKITE	ZOOTROPHY	DIZENMENT	BENZOLATE	PROZYMITE
ZEOLITIZE	ZUCCARINO	DIZYGOTIC	BENZOLINE	PUZZLEDLY
ZEPHYREAN	ZUCCHETTO	DIZZARDLY	BENZOLIZE	PUZZLEMAN
ZEPHYRIAN	ZUMBOORUK	DIZZINESS	BLAZONING	QUIZZICAL
ZEPHYROUS	ZUURVELDT	ENZYMATIC	BLIZZARDY	RAZZBERRY
ZERMAHBUB	ZWANZIGER	ENZYMOSIS	BOOZINESS	RHIZINOUS
ZEROAXIAL	ZYGADENIN	ENZYMOTIC	BRAZENING	RHIZOBIUM
ZEUGMATIC	ZYGANTRUM	FIZELYITE	BRAZILEIN	RHIZOCARP
ZEUNERITE	ZYGOMATIC	FUZZINESS	BRAZILITE	RHIZOCAUL
ZIBELLINE	ZYGONEURE	GAZEHOUND	BUZZARDLY	RHIZOCORM
ZINCALISM	ZYGOPHORE	GAZETTEER	BUZZGLOAK	RHIZOTAXY
ZINCIFIED	ZYGOPHYTE	GAZETTING	CRAZINESS	RHIZOTOMI
ZINFANDEL	ZYGOSPERM	HAZARDOUS	CRAZYWEED	RHIZOTOMY
ZINGERONE	ZYGOSPORE	JAZZINESS	DIAZEUTIC	SCAZONTIC
ZINKENITE	ZYGOSTYLE	LAZARETTE	DIAZEUXIS	TERZETTOS
ZIPPINGLY	ZYGOTAXIS	LAZARETTO	DIAZOAMIN	TINZENITE
ZIRCONATE	ZYMOGENIC	LAZULITIC	DIAZONIUM	WAYZGOOSE
ZIRCONIUM	ZYMOLOGIC	LAZYBONES	DIAZOTATE	WOOZINESS
ZIRCONOID	ZYMOLYSIS	LAZYBOOTS	DIAZOTIZE	
ZIRKELITE	ZYMOLYTIC	LAZZARONE	DIAZOTYPE	ALLOZOOID
ZITHERIST	ZYMOMETER	LAZZARONI	DIZZARDLY	AUTOZOOID
ZOANTHOID	ZYMOPHORE	MAZEDNESS	DIZZINESS	BEDAZZLED
ZOBTENITE	ZYMOSCOPE	MAZODYNIA	DOUZEPERS	BEDIZENED
ZOEHEMERA		MAZOLYSIS	DRIZZLING	BLIZZARDY
ZOETROPIC	AZALEAMUM	MAZOLYTIC	DUNZIEKTE	BLOWZIEST
ZOOCYTIAL	AZEDARACH	MEZCALINE	EPIZEUXIS	BREEZEWAY
ZOOCYTIUM	AZEOTROPE	MEZZANINE	EPIZOOTIC	BREEZIEST
ZOOFULVIN	AZEOTROPY	MEZZOTINT	FRAZZLING	CITIZENLY
ZOOGAMETE	AZIETHANE	MIZENMAST	FRIZZIEST	CITIZENRY
ZOOGAMOUS	AZIMUTHAL	MIZZONITE	FRIZZLING	COLAZIONE
ZOOGENOUS	AZLACTONE	NAZIFYING	FURZECHAT	DIETZEITE
ZOOGLOEAL	AZOBENZIL	PEZOGRAPH	FUZZINESS	DRIZZLING
ZOOGLOEIC	AZOBENZOL	PIZZICATO	GAUZELIKE	EMBEZZLED
ZOOGONOUS	AZOCYCLIC	POZZOLANA	GAUZEWING	EMBEZZLER
ZOOGRAPHY	AZOFORMIC	PUZZLEDLY	GAUZINESS	FRAZZLING
ZOOLITHIC	AZOLITMIN	PUZZLEMAN	GLAZEWORK	FREEZABLE
ZOOLOGIES	AZOPHENOL	RAZORBACK	GLAZINESS	FRENZYING
ZOOLOGIST	AZOPHENYL	RAZORBILL	GRAZINGLY	FRIZZIEST
ZOOLOGIZE	AZOTIZING	RAZOREDGE	GRIZZLIER	FRIZZLING
ZOOMETRIC	AZOXONIUM	RAZZBERRY	GRIZZLIES	FROWZIEST
ZOOMORPHY	CZARINIAN	SIZARSHIP	GRIZZLING	GONOZOOID
ZOOPERIST	CZARISTIC	SYZYGETIC	JAZZINESS	GRIZZLIER
ZOOPHAGAN	DZIGGETAI	VIZARDING	LAMZIEKTE	GRIZZLIES
ZOOPHILIA	IZVOZCHIK	VIZIERATE	LAZZARONE	GRIZZLING
ZOOPHILIC	OZOCERITE	VIZIERIAL	LAZZARONI	HYLOZOISM
ZOOPHOBIA	OZONATION	WAZIRSHIP	MAIZEBIRD	HYLOZOIST

IONIZABLE	EXOENZYME	TETRAZONE	ETHERIZED	SATIRIZER
IZVOZCHIK	FILMIZING	TRAPEZIAL	ETHERIZER	SCHNAUZER
KEVAZINGO	FLORIZINE	TRAPEZIAN	ETHICIZED	SCHNITZEL
MAGAZINED	HAPHAZARD	TRAPEZING	EULOGIZED	SCHNOZZLE
MAGAZINER	HELIOZOAN	TRAPEZIST	EULOGIZER	SCLERIZED
MEGAZOOID	HYDRAZINE	TRAPEZIUM	EUPHUIZED	SOLARIZED
PIAZZETTA	HYDRAZOIC	TRAPEZIUS	EXORCIZED	SOLARIZED
POLYZOARY	HYDRAZONE	TRAPEZOID	EXORCIZER	SOLECIZED
POLYZOISM	HYDROZOAL	UTILIZING	FARADIZED	SOLECIZER
POLYZONAL	HYDROZOAN		FARADIZER	STARGAZED
POLYZOOID	HYDROZOIC	AGROMYZID	FIBERIZER	STARGAZER
PYRAZOLYL	HYDROZOON	ALDOLIZED	FINALIZED	STRAMAZON
QUINZAINE	IDOLIZING	ALKALIZER	FLUIDIZED	SUBERIZED
QUINZIEME	IMIDAZOLE	AMORTIZED	FOCALIZED	SULPHAZID
QUIZZICAL	IRIDIZING	ANGELIZED	HUMANIZER	SURPRIZAL
SCHIZAXON	ISOXAZOLE	APHIDOZER	IDEALIZED	TARTRAZIN
SCHIZOPOD	ITEMIZING	APHORIZED	IDEALIZER	TETANIZED
SFORZANDO	KEVUTZOTH	APHORIZER	IMMUNIZED	THEORIZED
SHAHZADAH	KRANTZITE	APPETIZED	INFAMIZED	THEORIZER
SMORZANDO	LAICIZING	APPETIZER	ISONIAZID	TOTALIZED
SYNEZISIS	LIONIZING	ARBORIZED	JAROVIZED	TOTALIZER
SYNIZESIS	MALGUZARI	ARCHAIZED	KIBBUTZIM	UNIONIZED
THIOZONID	MENDOZITE	ARCHAIZER	LACONIZED	URBANIZED
TOPAZFELS	MESTIZOES	ASSOILZIE	LACONIZER	VAPORIZER
TRIOZONID	MICROZOAL	ASTATIZED	LEGALIZED	VITALIZED
TWEEZERED	MICROZOAN	ASTATIZER	LINENIZER	VITALIZER
WHEEZIEST	MICROZOIC	ATHETIZED	LOCALIZED	VOCALIZED
ZWANZIGER	MICROZONE	ATMOLYZER	LOCALIZER	VOCALIZER
	MICROZOON	ATTICIZED	MACARIZED	WOMANIZED
ADONIZING	MICROZYMA	AZOBENZIL	MAXIMIZED	WOMANIZER
AGATIZING	MICROZYME	AZOBENZOL	MAXIMIZER	
AGONIZING	OBELIZING	BAMBOOZLE	MELODIZED	ABURABOZU
ANALYZING	OPALIZING	BILHARZIC	MELODIZER	ACADEMIZE
ANODIZING	ORGANZINE	BOTANIZED	MEMORIZER	ACETONIZE
ANTHOZOAN	OUTDAZZLE	BOTANIZER	METALIZED	ACETYLIZE
ANTHOZOIC	OXDIAZOLE	BULLDOZED	MINIMIZED	ACTIONIZE
ANTHOZOON	OXIDIZING	BULLDOZER	MINIMIZER	ACTUALIZE
APHRIZITE	OZONIZING	CALORIZER	MISPRIZED	ADVERTIZE
APPRIZING	PATRIZATE	CANALIZED	MISPRIZER	ALCARRAZA
ARCHIZOIC	PECTIZING	CANONIZED	MOBILIZED	ALCHEMIZE
ARRHIZOUS	PEPTIZING	CANONIZER	MONETIZED	ALTERNIZE
ATOMIZING	PERHAZARD	CAPONIZER	MORALIZED	ALUMETIZE
AZOTIZING	PHENAZINE	CATALYZED	MORALIZER	ALUMINIZE
BAPTIZING	PHENAZONE	CATALYZER	MOTORIZED	ANABOLIZE
BEDAZZLED	PHILOZOIC	CHERNOZEM	NASALIZED	ANALOGIZE
BOMBAZINE	PHYTOZOAN	CHRYSAZIN	NEBULIZED	ANARCHIZE
CAPRIZANT	PHYTOZOON	CHRYSAZOL	NEBULIZER	ANATOMIZE
CAPSIZED	POETIZING	CIVILIZEE	NODULIZED	ANGLICIZE
CAPSIZING	PROTOZOAL	CIVILIZED	NOTARIZED	ANHYDRIZE
CARBAZIDE	PROTOZOAN	CIVILIZER	NOVELIZED	ANIMALIZE
CARBAZINE	PROTOZOEA	COLONIZED	ONIONIZED	ANNUALIZE
CARBAZOLE	PROTOZOIC	COLONIZER	OPTIMIZED	APOLOGIZE
CHABAZITE	PROTOZOON	COMPRIZAL	ORGANIZED	ARCTICIZE
CHALAZIAN	QUARTZITE	COMPRIZED	ORGANIZER	AROMATIZE
CHALAZION	QUARTZOID	COURTEZAN	OUTBRAZEN	AUTHORIZE
CHALAZIUM	QUARTZOSE	CREOLIZED	OUTDAZZLE	BACTERIZE
CHINTZIER	QUARTZOUS	CURARIZED	OVERSIZED	BALKANIZE
CHORIZONT	REALIZING	CUTINIZED	OXYBENZYL	BALSAMIZE
COALIZING	RESEIZURE	DECATIZER	PAEANIZED	BANTAMIZE
COELOZOIC	RHODIZITE	DEMONIZED	PAGANIZED	BARBARIZE
COGNIZANT	SAPROZOIC	DEPUTIZED	PAGANIZER	BEAVERIZE
COGNIZING	SCHNOZZLE	DEVILIZED	PAPALIZER	BEDLAMIZE
COPROZOIC	SOLMIZATE	DIGITIZED	PARALYZED	BERGINIZE
COSMOZOIC	SPOROZOAL	DIGITIZER	PARALYZER	BIOLOGIZE
CYANIZING	SPOROZOAN	DISPRIZED	PAVONAZZO	BRUTALIZE
DEGLAZING	SPOROZOIC	DISSEIZED	PENALIZED	BURTONIZE
DIALYZATE	SPOROZOID	DISSEIZEE	PHLORIZIN	CARBOLIZE
DIALYZING	SPOROZOON	DISSEIZOR	POLARIZED	CARBONIZE
DIBENZOYL	SQUEEZING	DIVINIZED	POLARIZER	CARBURIZE
DUALIZING	STYLIZING	ECTOENZYM	POLICIZER	CARNALIZE
EBONIZING	SULFAZIDE	ENDENIZEN	PRESTEZZA	CARTELIZE
ECHOIZING	TELEOZOIC	ENERGIZED	PTYALIZED	CATECHIZE
EGOTIZING	TELEOZOON	ENERGIZER	QUANTIZED	CATHARIZE
ELEGIZING	TETRAZANE	EQUALIZED	RACEMIZED	CAUPONIZE
EMBEZZLED	TETRAZENE	EQUALIZER	RURALIZED	CAUTERIZE
EMBEZZLER	TETRAZINE	ERGOTIZED	SANITIZED	CEREBRIZE
EMBLAZING	TETRAZOLE	ETERNIZED	SATIRIZED	CHEMOLYZE

CICATRIZE	GENIALIZE	MEMORIZED	POETICIZE	SULFURIZE
CITRONIZE	GENTILIZE	MENSALIZE	POSTERIZE	SULTANIZE
CLAVELIZE	GEOLOGIZE	MERCERIZE	POSTURIZE	SUMMARIZE
CLIMATIZE	GERMANIZE	MERCURIZE	POTENTIZE	SURGERIZE
COCAINIZE	GIGANTIZE	MESMERIZE	POWDERIZE	SYLLABIZE
COMMUNIZE	GLAMORIZE	METALLIZE	PRECONIZE	SYLLOGIZE
COPPERIZE	GLUTINIZE	METEORIZE	PREIOTIZE	SYMBOLIZE
COTTONIZE	GLYCERIZE	METHODIZE	PRELATIZE	SYNCOPIZE
CREOLEIZE	GORGONIZE	METRICIZE	PRELUDIZE	SYNERGIZE
CRITICIZE	GOSPELIZE	MNEMONIZE	PRESTEZZA	SYNOECIZE
DECADENZA	GRANITIZE	MODERNIZE	PROFANIZE	SYNOPSIZE
DEEPFROZE	GRANULIZE	MONACHIZE	PROLOGIZE	SYNTONIZE
DEFERRIZE	GUACONIZE	MORGANIZE	PROPOLIZE	SYPHILIZE
DENITRIZE	HAMLETIZE	MORSELIZE	PRYTANIZE	SYSTEMIZE
DENTALIZE	HARMONIZE	MORTALIZE	PUBLICIZE	TANDEMIZE
DEODORIZE	HERALDIZE	MULLENIZE	PULVERIZE	TANTALIZE
DEOXIDIZE	HERBALIZE	MUTUALIZE	PUPILLIZE	TARIFFIZE
DEOZONIZE	HERBARIZE	MYCORHIZA	PUPPETIZE	TARTARIZE
DESPOTIZE	HERBORIZE	MYSTERIZE	PURPURIZE	TAVERNIZE
DIABOLIZE	HISTORIZE	MYTHICIZE	PYTHONIZE	TELLURIZE
DIALOGIZE	HUMOURIZE	NARCOTIZE	QUININIZE	TEMPORIZE
DIAZOTIZE	HYALINIZE	NECROTIZE	QUINONIZE	TENDERIZE
DIESELIZE	HYBRIDIZE	NECTARIZE	RABBINIZE	TERMINIZE
DOCTORIZE	HYDROLYZE	NEOLOGIZE	RACIALIZE	TERRORIZE
DOGMATIZE	HYGIENIZE	NEOTERIZE	RADIALIZE	THEATRIZE
DRAGONIZE	HYPNOTIZE	NEUMATIZE	RADIUMIZE	THYMOLIZE
DRAMATIZE	HYPOCRIZE	NICKELIZE	RANDOMIZE	TRINALIZE
DUCTILIZE	INFLUENZA	NITRIDIZE	RAPTURIZE	TUCHUNIZE
ECONOMIZE	INOXIDIZE	NORMALIZE	REBAPTIZE	TURTLEIZE
ECPHORIZE	ISOMERIZE	OBJECTIZE	RECOGNIZE	TYMPANIZE
EKPHORIZE	ITALICIZE	OPERATIZE	RHETORIZE	TYRANNIZE
ELECTRIZE	JARGONIZE	ORATORIZE	RHYTHMIZE	UGRIANIZE
ELENCHIZE	JASPERIZE	ORIENTIZE	ROUTINIZE	UNBRUTIZE
EMBLEMIZE	JENNERIZE	OSTRACIZE	RUBBERIZE	UNCIALIZE
EMPHASIZE	JOVIALIZE	OVERGLAZE	RUBRICIZE	UNDERSIZE
EPILOGIZE	KAOLINIZE	OVERGRAZE	RUSTICIZE	UNREALIZE
EPIPOLIZE	LABIALIZE	OVERPRIZE	SATURNIZE	URALITIZE
EPITOMIZE	LACTONIZE	OXYGENIZE	SCENARIZE	VACUUMIZE
ESOTERIZE	LADRONIZE	OXYTONIZE	SCIENTIZE	VAMPIRIZE
EUPHEMIZE	LICHENIZE	PALLADIZE	SENSITIZE	VANDALIZE
EUPHONIZE	LIGNITIZE	PALLETIZE	SERIALIZE	VAPOURIZE
EVAPORIZE	LINEARIZE	PAMPERIZE	SERMONIZE	VASSALIZE
FACTORIZE	LIQUIDIZE	PANDERIZE	SEXUALIZE	VERBALIZE
FACULTIZE	LITURGIZE	PASTORIZE	SIGNALIZE	VERNALIZE
FANTASIZE	MAGNETIZE	PATRONIZE	SILVERIZE	VICTIMIZE
FAUCALIZE	MAINPRIZE	PAUPERIZE	SISTERIZE	VISCIDIZE
FECUNDIZE	MAMMONIZE	PAVONAZZO	SOCIALIZE	VISIONIZE
FERTILIZE	MANGANIZE	PEDANTIZE	SOLEMNIZE	VISUALIZE
FETICHIZE	MANGONIZE	PEGMATIZE	SOLVOLYZE	VOLCANIZE
FEUDALIZE	MANNERIZE	PEOPLEIZE	SONNETIZE	VULCANIZE
FISCALIZE	MARBELIZE	PEPTONIZE	SORBITIZE	VULGARIZE
FISTULIZE	MARBLEIZE	PERSONIZE	SOVIETIZE	WANTONIZE
FOREPRIZE	MARMARIZE	PESSIMIZE	SPIRALIZE	WINTERIZE
FORMALIZE	MARRANIZE	PETROLIZE	SPIRITIZE	WITTICIZE
FORMULIZE	MARTYRIZE	PHENOLIZE	SPONDAIZE	WOOLENIZE
FORTHGAZE	MATRONIZE	PHONETIZE	STABILIZE	ZOOLOGIZE
FOSSILIZE	MECHANIZE	PICTURIZE	STERILIZE	
FRIVOLIZE	MEDIALIZE	PILLORIZE	SUBSIDIZE	BURKUNDAZ
GALLINAZO	MEDIATIZE	PLATINIZE	SULCALIZE	RHEUMATIZ
GALVANIZE	MEDIUMIZE	PLURALIZE	SULFATIZE	SLIVOVITZ
GARDENIZE				

SCORING ORDER LIST OF 9-LETTER WORDS

33	ZYGOPHYTE	ZYGOTAXIS	KIBBUTZIM	ZOOPHYTIC
OXYBENZYL			LIQUIDIZE	ZYMOLYTIC
	29	**28**	MYCORHIZA	ZYMOPHORE
31	DEZINKIFY	CHEMOLYZE	MYTHICIZE	
RHIZOTAXY	IZVOZCHIK	EQUALIZED	OXYTONIZE	**27**
	JAROVIZED	EXORCIZED	QUANTIZED	AZOXONIUM
30	MAXIMIZER	HYDROLYZE	QUARTZOID	CRAZYWEED
EXOENZYME	OBJECTIZE	HYPOCRIZE	QUIZZICAL	DEOXIDIZE
MAXIMIZED	OXYGENIZE	JOVIALIZE	SQUEEZING	DEZINCIFY
SCHIZAXON	QUINZIEME	KEVUTZOTH	ZOOMORPHY	EKPHORIZE

EPIZEUXIS
EQUALIZER
EXORCIZER
HAPHAZARD
HYBRIDIZE
HYDRAZOIC
HYDROZOIC
JASPERIZE
MICROZYMA
MICROZYME
OXIDIZING
QUARTZITE
QUARTZOSE
QUARTZOUS
QUININIZE
QUINONIZE
QUINZAINE
SYZYGETIC
ZERMAHBUB
ZOOGRAPHY
ZYGOPHORE
ZYMOSCOPE

26
AZOPHENYL
BREEZEWAY
CHRYSAZIN
CHRYSAZOL
DIAZEUXIS
FETICHIZE
FURZECHAT
GLAZEWORK
HYLOZOISM
HYPNOTIZE
INOXIDIZE
JARGONIZE
KEVAZINGO
OXDIAZOLE
PEZOGRAPH
PHYTOZOAN
PHYTOZOON
POLYZOARY
PYRAZOLYL
PYTHONIZE
RAZORBACK
RHIZOTOMY
SCHIZOPOD
SYPHILIZE
THYMOLIZE
WAZIRSHIP
ZEPHYREAN
ZEPHYRIAN
ZEPHYROUS
ZIPPINGLY
ZOOPHYTAL
ZOOTECHNY
ZOOTROPHY
ZUMBOORUK
ZYGOMATIC
ZYGOSPERM
ZYMOGENIC
ZYMOLOGIC
ZYMOLYSIS

25
AGROMYZID
ALCHEMIZE
ANHYDRIZE
ARCHIZOIC
AZOFORMIC
BILHARZIC
BURKUNDAZ
CATECHIZE
CHABAZITE
CHALAZIUM
CHERNOZEM
COMPRIZED

DIZYGOTIC
ECPHORIZE
ECTOENZYM
EMPHASIZE
ENZYMATIC
ENZYMOTIC
EUPHEMIZE
FORTHGAZE
FRENZYING
HYDRAZINE
HYDRAZONE
HYDROZOAL
HYDROZOAN
HYDROZOON
HYGIENIZE
ISOXAZOLE
JENNERIZE
MAZOLYTIC
MECHANIZE
MONACHIZE
NAZIFYING
PHILOZOIC
POLYZOISM
PROZYMITE
RHIZOBIUM
RHIZOCARP
RHIZOCORM
SEXUALIZE
SYMBOLIZE
SYNCOPIZE
TYMPANIZE
VACUUMIZE
VAMPIRIZE
VICTIMIZE
WAYZGOOSE
ZEROAXIAL
ZOOCYTIUM
ZOOPHILIC
ZOOPHOBIA
ZOOPHORIC
ZUCCHETTO
ZYGOSTYLE
ZYMOMETER

24
APHIDOZER
APHORIZED
ARCHAIZED
AVIZANDUM
AZEDARACH
AZOCYCLIC
BALKANIZE
BAMBOOZLE
BOMBAZINE
BUZZGLOAK
CATALYZED
CIVILIZED
COMMUNIZE
COMPRIZAL
COPPERIZE
COPROZOIC
COSMOZOIC
CYANIZING
DEEPFROZE
DIAZOTYPE
DIBENZOYL
ECHOIZING
EMBLEMIZE
ETHICIZED
EUPHUIZED
FECUNDIZE
FILMIZING
FIZELYITE
FOCALIZED
FRIVOLIZE
FROWZIEST
GLYCERIZE

HYALINIZE
HYLOZOIST
INFAMIZED
JAZZINESS
LAMZIEKTE
MAZODYNIA
METHODIZE
MICROZOIC
NICKELIZE
PAMPERIZE
PARALYZED
PERHAZARD
POLYZOOID
POWDERIZE
PTYALIZED
PUBLICIZE
SHAHZADAH
SLIVOVITZ
SOLVOLYZE
SULPHAZID
TARIFFIZE
VISCIDIZE
VOCALIZED
WHEEZIEST
WOMANIZED
ZAMINDARY
ZEBRALIKE
ZEBRAWOOD
ZINCIFIED
ZOOFULVIN
ZOOPHAGAN
ZOOSCOPIC
ZYGANTRUM
ZYGOSPORE

23
ACADEMIZE
ACETYLIZE
ANARCHIZE
ANTHOZOIC
APHORIZER
APHRIZITE
APPETIZED
APPRIZING
ARCHAIZER
ATMOLYZER
AZEOTROPY
AZIMUTHAL
AZOPHENOL
BAPTIZING
BEAVERIZE
BEDLAMIZE
BENZAMIDE
BENZAMIDO
BEZOARDIC
BIZARRELY
BLIZZARDY
BLOWZIEST
BUZZARDLY
CAPSIZING
CATALYZER
CATHARIZE
CHALAZIAN
CHALAZION
CHINTZIER
CHORIZONT
CITIZENLY
CITIZENRY
CIVILIZEE
CIVILIZER
CLAVELIZE
FACTORIZE
DEVILIZED
DIALYZING
DIVINIZED
DUNZIEKTE
ELENCHIZE

EMBLAZING
ENZYMOSIS
EUPHONIZE
EVAPORIZE
FACULTIZE
FARADIZED
FAUCALIZE
FIBERIZER
FISCALIZE
FLUIDIZED
FOREPRIZE
FORMALIZE
FORMULIZE
FREEZABLE
GAUZELIKE
GAUZEWING
GAZEHOUND
GRAZINGLY
GRIZZLIER
HAMLETIZE
HARMONIZE
HERBALIZE
HERBARIZE
HERBORIZE
HUMANIZER
HUMOURIZE
IMMUNIZED
LAZYBONES
LAZYBOOTS
LICHENIZE
MACARIZED
MAIZEBIRD
MARTYRIZE
MAZOLYSIS
MEDIUMIZE
MEMORIZED
MINIMIZED
MISPRIZED
MOBILIZED
MYSTERIZE
OPTIMIZED
OVERPRIZE
PARALYZER
PECTIZING
PEGMATIZE
PEPTIZING
PHENAZINE
PHENAZONE
PHENOLIZE
PHLORIZIN
PHONETIZE
POLYZONAL
PROFANIZE
PRYTANIZE
PULVERIZE
PUZZLEDLY
RACEMIZED
RHEUMATIZ
RHIZOCAUL
RHIZOTOMI
SCHNAUZER
SCHNITZEL
SIZARSHIP
SYLLABIZE
SYNOECIZE
SYNOPSIZE
SYSTEMIZE
TOPAZFELS
TUCHUNIZE
VAPORIZER
VAPOURIZE
VERBALIZE
VIZARDING
VOCALIZER
VOLCANIZE
VULCANIZE
WITTICIZE

WOMANIZER
ZELOTYPIA
ZELOTYPIE
ZENDIKITE
ZEUGMATIC
ZOEHEMERA
ZOOCYTIAL
ZOOLITHIC
ZOOPHILIA
ZOOPHORUS
ZOOPLASTY
ZOOSPHERE
ZOOTHECIA
ZOOTHEISM
ZYGADENIN

22
ABURABOZU
ADVERTIZE
ALKALIZER
AMAZEMENT
ANALYZING
APPETIZER
ARCTICIZE
ATHETIZED
AZALEAMUM
BACTERIZE
BALSAMIZE
BANTAMIZE
BARBARIZE
BEDIZENED
BULLDOZED
CAPONIZER
CAPRIZANT
CARBAZINE
CARBAZOLE
CARBOLIZE
CARBONIZE
CARBURIZE
CAUPONIZE
CEREBRIZE
CICATRIZE
CLIMATIZE
COCAINIZE
COELOZOIC
COGNIZING
CRITICIZE
CZARISTIC
DECADENZA
DEFERRIZE
DEMONIZED
DEPUTIZED
DIALYZATE
DISPRIZED
DIZZARDLY
DOGMATIZE
ECONOMIZE
EMBEZZLED
EPIPOLIZE
EPITOMIZE
EPIZOOTIC
ETHERIZED
FARADIZER
FEUDALIZE
FINALIZED
GALVANIZE
HAZARDOUS
HERALDIZE
KAOLINIZE
KRANTZITE
MAGAZINED
MAINPRIZE
MARBELIZE
MARBLEIZE
MARMARIZE
MEGAZOOID
MELODIZED

MEMORIZER	ARBORIZED	MORALIZED	AGATIZING	MESTIZOES
MERCERIZE	ARRHIZOUS	MORGANIZE	AGONIZING	METALLIZE
MERCURIZE	ATOMIZING	MOTORIZED	ALCARRAZA	METEORIZE
MESMERIZE	ATTICIZED	NEBULIZED	ALDOLIZED	MONZONITE
METRICIZE	AUTHORIZE	OBELIZING	ALUMETIZE	MORALIZER
MEZCALINE	AZIETHANE	OPALIZING	ALUMINIZE	MORSELIZE
MICROZOAL	BEDAZZLED	ORYZANINE	AMAZONITE	MORTALIZE
MICROZOAN	BENZENOID	PAEANIZED	ANABOLIZE	MULLENIZE
MICROZONE	BENZIDINE	PAGANIZER	ANATOMIZE	MUTUALIZE
MICROZOON	BENZIDINO	PALLADIZE	ANGELIZED	NARCOTIZE
MINIMIZER	BENZOATED	PANDERIZE	ANIMALIZE	NEBULIZER
MISPRIZER	BERGINIZE	PEDANTIZE	ANODIZING	NECROTIZE
MIZENMAST	BIOLOGIZE	PENALIZED	AROMATIZE	NECTARIZE
MNEMONIZE	BIZARDITE	PIZZICATO	AZEOTROPE	NEUMATIZE
NOVELIZED	BLAZONING	POETIZING	AZLACTONE	NODULIZED
OVERGLAZE	BOTANIZED	POLARIZED	AZOLITMIN	NORMALIZE
OVERGRAZE	BRAZENING	PRELUDIZE	BALZARINE	OPERATIZE
OVERSIZED	BULLDOZER	PROLOGIZE	BENZOLATE	ORGANIZED
PAGANIZED	CANALIZED	PUPPETIZE	BENZOLINE	OSTRACIZE
PANZOOTIC	CANONIZED	PUZZLEMAN	BEZESTEEN	OUTBRAZEN
PAPALIZER	COALIZING	RADIUMIZE	BOOZINESS	OZOCERITE
PAUPERIZE	COGNIZANT	RANDOMIZE	BOTANIZER	OZOSTOMIA
PAVONAZZO	COLONIZED	RECOGNIZE	BRAZILEIN	PALLETIZE
PEOPLEIZE	CREOLIZED	RHETORIZE	BRAZILITE	PANZOOTIA
PEPTONIZE	CURARIZED	RHIZINOUS	BRUTALIZE	PASTORIZE
PESSIMIZE	CUTINIZED	SCLERIZED	BURTONIZE	PATRIZATE
POETICIZE	DECATIZER	SILVERIZE	CALORIZER	PATRONIZE
POLICIZER	DEGLAZING	SMORZANDO	CANONIZER	PERSONIZE
PRECONIZE	DESPOTIZE	SOLECIZED	CARNALIZE	PETROLIZE
PRIZEABLE	DIABOLIZE	SOVIETIZE	CARTELIZE	PILLORIZE
PROPOLIZE	DIAZEUTIC	SPONDAIZE	CAUTERIZE	PLATINIZE
PROTOZOIC	DIAZOAMIN	SPOROZOID	CITRONIZE	PLURALIZE
PUPILLIZE	DIAZONIUM	SUBERIZED	COLAZIONE	POLARIZER
PURPURIZE	DIGITIZED	SUBSIDIZE	COLONIZER	POLZENITE
RABBINIZE	DIZENMENT	SULFATIZE	COTTONIZE	POSTERIZE
RAZZBERRY	DOCTORIZE	SULFURIZE	COURTEZAN	POSTURIZE
REBAPTIZE	DOUZEPERS	SYNEZISIS	CRAZINESS	POTENTIZE
RHODIZITE	DRAMATIZE	SYNIZESIS	CREOLEIZE	PREIOTIZE
RUBBERIZE	DUCTILIZE	SYNTONIZE	CZARINIAN	PRELATIZE
RUBRICIZE	DZIGGETAI	TANDEMIZE	DAZEDNESS	PROTOZOAL
SAPROZOIC	EBONIZING	TAVERNIZE	DEODORIZE	PROTOZOAN
SCAZONTIC	EMBEZZLER	THEATRIZE	DIALOGIZE	PROTOZOEA
SCHNOZZLE	EPILOGIZE	THEORIZER	DIGITIZER	PROTOZOON
SFORZANDO	ETHERIZER	TRAPEZING	DISSEIZED	RACIALIZE
SPOROZOIC	FANTASIZE	TRAPEZOID	DRAGONIZE	RAPTURIZE
STYLIZING	FERTILIZE	TYRANNIZE	DUALIZING	RAZORBILL
SULFAZIDE	FISTULIZE	URBANIZED	EGOTIZING	RAZOREDGE
SUMMARIZE	FLORIZINE	VASSALIZE	ELECTRIZE	RUSTICIZE
SYLLOGIZE	FOSSILIZE	VERNALIZE	ELEGIZING	SCENARIZE
SYNERGIZE	FRAZZLING	VISIONIZE	ENERGIZED	SCIENTIZE
TEMPORIZE	FRIZZLING	VISUALIZE	ERGOTIZED	SERMONIZE
THEORIZED	GERMANIZE	VITALIZER	EULOGIZED	SOCIALIZE
THIOZONID	GLAMORIZE	VIZIERATE	FRIZZIEST	SOLECIZER
TRAPEZIUM	GOSPELIZE	VIZIERIAL	FUZZINESS	SOLEMNIZE
TWEEZERED	GUACONIZE	WANTONIZE	GARDENIZE	SOLMIZATE
VANDALIZE	HELIOZOAN	WINTERIZE	GAZETTING	SORBITIZE
VITALIZED	HISTORIZE	WOOLENIZE	GEOLOGIZE	SPIRALIZE
VULGARIZE	IMIDAZOLE	WOOZINESS	GIGANTIZE	SPIRITIZE
ZINCALISM	INFLUENZA	ZAMINDARI	GONOZOOID	SPOROZOAL
ZINFANDEL	ITEMIZING	ZAPATEADO	GORGONIZE	SPOROZOAN
ZINKENITE	LACONIZED	ZEALOUSLY	IDEALIZED	SPOROZOON
ZIRCONIUM	LAICIZING	ZEMINDARI	IDOLIZING	STABILIZE
ZIRKELITE	LOCALIZED	ZENDICIAN	IONIZABLE	STARGAZED
ZOANTHOID	MAGAZINER	ZIRCONOID	IRIDIZING	STRAMAZON
ZOETROPIC	MAGNETIZE	ZITHERIST	ISOMERIZE	SULCALIZE
ZOOMETRIC	MALGUZARI	ZOOGAMETE	ITALICIZE	SURPRIZAL
ZOOSPORIC	MAMMONIZE	ZOOGAMOUS	LABIALIZE	TELEOZOIC
ZUCCARINO	MANGANIZE	ZOOGLOEIC	LACONIZER	TERMINIZE
ZUURVELDT	MANGONIZE	ZOOTHEIST	LACTONIZE	TRAPEZIAL
ZYGONEURE	MAZEDNESS	ZWANZIGER	LAZULITIC	TRAPEZIAN
	MEDIALIZE		LEGALIZED	TRAPEZIST
21	MEDIATIZE	**20**	LOCALIZER	TRAPEZIUS
AMORTIZED	MELODIZER	ACETALIZE	MANNERIZE	UNBRUTIZE
ANGLICIZE	MENDOZITE	ACETONIZE	MANZANITA	UNCIALIZE
ANTHOZOAN	METALIZED	ACTIONIZE	MARRANIZE	ZEALOTISM
ANTHOZOON	MODERNIZE	ACTUALIZE	MATRONIZE	ZELATRICE
APOLOGIZE	MONETIZED	ADONIZING	MENSALIZE	ZIBELLINE

ZIRLONATE
ZOOPERIST
ZOOTOMIST

19
ALLOZOOID
ANALOGIZE
ASTATIZED
AUTOZOOID
AZOBENZIL
AZOBENZOL
BENZOLIZE
DENITRIZE
DENTALIZE
DIAZOTATE
DIESELIZE
DIETZEITE
DISSEIZOR
DRIZZLING
ENDENIZEN
ENERGIZER
ETERNIZED
EULOGIZER
GALLINAZO
GAUZINESS
GAZETTEER
GENIALIZE
GENTILIZE

GLAZINESS
GLUTINIZE
GRANITIZE
GRANULIZE
GRIZZLING
IDEALIZER
ISONIAZID
LADRONIZE
LIGNITIZE
LIONIZING
LITURGIZE
MEZZANINE
MEZZOTINT
MIZZONITE
NASALIZED
NEOLOGIZE
NITRIDIZE
NOTARIZED
ONIONIZED
ORGANIZER
ORGANZINE
PIAZZETTA
POZZOLANA
PRESTEZZA
RADIALIZE
REALIZING
RURALIZED
SANITIZED

SATIRIZED
SIGNALIZE
SOLARIZED
STARGAZER
SURGERIZE
TENDERIZE
TETANIZED
TOTALIZED
TRIOZONID
UNDERSIZE
UNIONIZED
UTILIZING
ZINGERONE
ZOOGENOUS
ZOOGLOEAL
ZOOGONOUS
ZOOLOGIES
ZOOLOGIST

18
ALIZARATE
ALIZARINE
ALTERNIZE
ANNUALIZE
ARIZONITE
ARZRUNITE
ASSOILZIE

ASTATIZER
AZOTIZING
DEOZONIZE
DIAZOTIZE
DIZZINESS
ESOTERIZE
GRIZZLIES
LAZARETTE
LAZARETTO
LINEARIZE
LINENIZER
NEOTERIZE
ORATORIZE
ORIENTIZE
OUTDAZZLE
OZONATION
OZONIZING
RESEIZURE
ROUTINIZE
SATIRIZER
SATURNIZE
SENSITIZE
SERIALIZE
SISTERIZE
SONNETIZE
STERILIZE
SULTANIZE

TANTALIZE
TARTARIZE
TARTRAZIN
TELEOZOON
TELLURIZE
TERRORIZE
TERZETTOS
TETRAZANE
TETRAZENE
TETRAZINE
TETRAZOLE
TETRAZONE
TINZENITE
TOTALIZER
TRINALIZE
TURTLEIZE
UNREALIZE
URALITIZE
ZEALOTIST
ZEUNERITE
ZOOLOGIZE

17
LAZZARONE
LAZZARONI
ZEOLITIZE

ALPHABETICAL LIST OF 10-LETTER WORDS

ACADEMIZED
ACETYLIZER
ACTINOZOAL
ACTINOZOAN
ACTIONIZED
ACTUALIZED
ADRENALIZE
ADULTERIZE
AGGRANDIZE
AGLAOZONIA
AIZOACEOUS
AKHUNDZADA
ALBUMENIZE
ALBUMINIZE
ALCALIZATE
ALCHEMIZED
ALCOHOLIZE
ALDOLIZING
ALGEBRAIZE
ALKALINIZE
ALKALIZATE
ALLEGORIZE
ALLOCHEZIA
ALTAZIMUTH
ALUMINIZED
AMALGAMIZE
AMIDRAZONE
AMMONOLYZE
AMORTIZING
ANABIBAZON
ANALOGIZED
ANALYZABLE
ANATHEMIZE
ANATOMIZED
ANATOMIZER
ANAZOTURIA
ANGELICIZE
ANGELIZING

ANGLICIZED
ANGULARIZE
ANIMALIZED
ANTAGONIZE
ANTHOZOOID
ANTIFREEZE
APHORIZING
APOLOGIZED
APOLOGIZER
APOSTATIZE
APOSTOLIZE
APOZEMICAL
APPETIZING
ARBORIZING
ARCHAIZING
ARCTICIZED
AROMATIZED
AROMATIZER
ARSENICIZE
ARTHROZOAN
ARTHROZOIC
ASEPTICIZE
ASEXUALIZE
ASSIZEMENT
ASTATIZING
ASYZYGETIC
ATHETIZING
ATROPINIZE
ATTICIZING
AUTHORIZED
AUTHORIZER
AUTOLYZATE
AUTOMATIZE
AUTONOMIZE
AUTOTOMIZE
AUTOXIDIZE
AXIOMATIZE
AZEOTROPIC

AZOBENZENE
AZOBENZOIC
AZOCORINTH
AZOCYANIDE
AZOGALLEIN
AZOMETHINE
AZOPHENINE
AZOPROTEIN
AZOTENESIS
AZOTOLUENE
AZOTOMETER
AZOTORRHEA
AZOVERNINE
AZTHIONIUM
AZYGOSPERM
AZYGOSPORE
BACTERIZED
BALKANIZED
BAMBOOZLED
BAMBOOZLER
BANTINGIZE
BARBARIZED
BARTIZANED
BASTARDIZE
BEBIZATION
BEDAZZLING
BEDIZENING
BENZEDRINE
BENZOCAINE
BENZOPYRAN
BENZOYLATE
BERZELIITE
BESTIALIZE
BILHARZIAL
BITUMINIZE
BIZARRERIE
BLAZONMENT
BLIZZARDLY

BOBIZATION
BOLSHEVIZE
BOMBAZETTE
BOTANIZING
BOUCHERIZE
BOURBONIZE
BOWDLERIZE
BRAZENFACE
BRAZENNESS
BRAZILETTE
BRAZILWOOD
BREEZINESS
BRONZEWING
BRONZITITE
BRUTALIZED
BULLDOZING
BURGLARIZE
BURNETTIZE
CALZONERAS
CANALIZING
CANONIZANT
CANONIZING
CAPITALIZE
CARAMELIZE
CARBAZYLIC
CARBOLIZED
CARBONIZED
CARBONIZER
CARBURIZED
CARBURIZER
CARNALIZED
CASTORIZED
CATABOLIZE
CATALYZING
CATECHIZED
CATECHIZER
CATEGORIZE
CATHARIZED

CAUSTICIZE
CAUTERIZED
CENTRALIZE
CHALAZOGAM
CHANNELIZE
CHATTELIZE
CHERVONETZ
CHIMPANZEE
CHINTZIEST
CHITINIZED
CHLORALIZE
CHLORAZIDE
CHLORIDIZE
CHLORITIZE
CHLORODIZE
CHRIZONTAL
CHROMATIZE
CHROMICIZE
CICATRIZED
CICATRIZER
CICERONIZE
CINCHONIZE
CITIZENESS
CITIZENISM
CITIZENIZE
CIVILIZING
CLASSICIZE
COAZERVATE
COCAINIZED
COCKNEYIZE
COGNIZABLE
COGNIZABLY
COGNIZANCE
COLEORHIZA
COLLOQUIZE
COLONIZING
COMMUNIZED
COMPRIZING

CONCERTIZE	DOGGRELIZE	FLUIDIZING	LACONIZING	MONONYMIZE
CONCRETIZE	DOGMATIZED	FOCALIZING	LATERALIZE	MONOPOLIZE
COSMOZOANS	DOGMATIZER	FORMALIZED	LATIBULIZE	MONOTONIZE
COSMOZOISM	DOLOMITIZE	FORMULIZED	LAZARETTOS	MONZONITIC
COZENINGLY	DOUZAINIER	FORMULIZER	LEGALIZING	MORALIZING
CRAZEDNESS	DOXOLOGIZE	FOSSILIZED	LEGITIMIZE	MORPHINIZE
CREOLIZING	DRAMATIZED	FRATERNIZE	LETHARGIZE	MORTALIZED
CRITICIZED	DRAMATIZER	FRENZIEDLY	LEXICONIZE	MOTORIZING
CRITICIZER	DUCTILIZED	FRIVOLIZED	LIBERALIZE	MOZZARELLA
CROFTERIZE	DYSOXIDIZE	FRIZZINESS	LINGUALIZE	MUSICALIZE
CRYPTOZOIC	ECONOMIZED	FROWZINESS	LIONIZABLE	MUTUALIZED
CUCKOLDIZE	ECONOMIZER	FROZENNESS	LIQUIDIZED	MUZZLEWOOD
CURARIZING	ECTOENZYME	GALLICIZER	LITERALIZE	MYCETOZOAN
CUTINIZING	ECZEMATOID	GALVANIZED	LIZARDTAIL	MYCETOZOON
CUTIZATION	ECZEMATOUS	GALVANIZER	LOCALIZING	MYCOLOGIZE
CYTOZYMASE	EFFEMINIZE	GAZANGABIN	LOGICALIZE	MYCORHIZAL
CZAREVITCH	ELASTICIZE	GELATINIZE	MACADAMIZE	MYCORRHIZA
DANDIZETTE	ELECTRIZED	GENERALIZE	MACARIZING	MYECTOMIZE
DASTARDIZE	ELECTRIZER	GEOLOGIZED	MAGAZINAGE	MYTHICIZED
DAZZLINGLY	EMBEZZLING	GEOMETRIZE	MAGAZINING	MYTHICIZER
DEALKALIZE	EMBLAZONED	GLAMORIZED	MAGAZINISM	MYZOSTOMID
DECIMALIZE	EMBLAZONER	GLOTTALIZE	MAGAZINIST	NANIZATION
DECIVILIZE	EMBLAZONRY	GLUTTONIZE	MAGNETIZED	NARCOTIZED
DECOLORIZE	EMBLEMIZED	GNATHONIZE	MAGNETIZER	NASALIZING
DEEPFREEZE	EMOTIONIZE	GOLANDAUZE	MAHOGANIZE	NATURALIZE
DEEPFROZEN	EMPATHIZED	GOLUNDAUZE	MAINPRIZER	NEBULARIZE
DEFEMINIZE	EMPHASIZED	GORGONIZED	MALLEINIZE	NEBULIZING
DEFERRIZED	EMPHATHIZE	GRANGERIZE	MANZANILLA	NEOLOGIZED
DEFINITIZE	ENDOENZYME	GRAPHITIZE	MANZANILLO	NESSLERIZE
DEHEMATIZE	ENERGIZING	GRIZZLIEST	MARBLEIZED	NEUTRALIZE
DEHEPATIZE	ENGRANDIZE	GRIZZLYMAN	MARBLEIZER	NICOTINIZE
DEHUMANIZE	ENIGMATIZE	HARMONIZER	MARMARIZED	NONCITIZEN
DELEGALIZE	ENOLIZABLE	HEMATOZOON	MARTIALIZE	NORMALIZED
DELIMITIZE	ENTHRONIZE	HERETICIZE	MARTYRIZED	NORMALIZER
DELOCALIZE	ENZYMOLOGY	HOMOGENIZE	MARTYRIZER	NOTARIZING
DELUMINIZE	EPILOGIZED	HOMOLOGIZE	MATRONIZED	NOTHINGIZE
DEMOBILIZE	EPIRHIZOUS	HOMOZYGOTE	MAXIMIZING	NOTORHIZAL
DEMONIZING	EPISCOPIZE	HOMOZYGOUS	MAZAPILITE	NOVELIZING
DEMORALIZE	EPISTOLIZE	HORIZONTAL	MAZOPATHIA	OBITUARIZE
DENATURIZE	EPITAPHIZE	HYBRIDIZER	MAZOPATHIC	OBJECTIZED
DENAZIFIED	EPITHELIZE	HYDRAZOATE	MECHANIZER	ONTOLOGIZE
DENIZATION	EPITOMIZED	HYDRORHIZA	MEDIATIZED	ORGANIZING
DENIZENIZE	EPITOMIZER	HYPNOIDIZE	MELEZITASE	ORGANZINED
DEODORIZED	EQUALIZING	HYPOZEUGMA	MELEZITOSE	ORIGANIZED
DEODORIZER	ERGOTIZING	HYPOZEUXIS	MELODIZING	OSTRACIZED
DEOXIDIZED	ESTERIZING	ICHTHYIZED	MEMORIZING	OSTRACIZER
DEOXIDIZER	ETERNALIZE	IDEALIZING	MERCERIZED	OVERFRIEZE
DEOZONIZER	ETERNIZING	IDOLATRIZE	MERCERIZER	OVERGLAZED
DEPETALIZE	ETHERIZING	ILLEGALIZE	MERCURIZED	OVERPRIZED
DEPOLARIZE	ETHICIZING	IMIDAZOLYL	MEROTOMIZE	OVERPRIZER
DEPRIORIZE	EUHEMERIZE	IMMOBILIZE	MESMERIZED	OXADIAZOLE
DEPUTIZING	EULOGIZING	INFAMIZING	MESMERIZEE	OXIDIZABLE
DERESINIZE	EUPHEMIZED	INFAMONIZE	MESMERIZER	OXOZONIDES
DEVILIZING	EUPHEMIZER	INFLUENZAL	METABOLIZE	OXYGENIZED
DEVIRILIZE	EUPHONIZED	INFLUENZIC	METALIZING	OXYGENIZER
DEVITALIZE	EUPHUIZING	INGRANDIZE	METHODIZED	OZONOMETER
DEVOCALIZE	EUPOLYZOAN	INKHORNIZE	METHODIZER	OZONOMETRY
DEXTRINIZE	EURYZYGOUS	INOXIDIZED	MEZZOGRAPH	OZONOSCOPE
DEZYMOTIZE	EVANGELIZE	INTERMEZZI	MEZZOTINTO	PAEANIZING
DIABOLIZED	EXORCIZING	INTERMEZZO	MICROZOARY	PAGANIZING
DIALOGIZED	EXZODIACAL	INTERZONAL	MICROZOOID	PALATALIZE
DIALYZABLE	FACKELTANZ	INTHRONIZE	MILITARIZE	PALLETIZED
DIALYZATOR	FACTORIZED	IODIZATION	MILLIONIZE	PANEGYRIZE
DIAMONDIZE	FANATICIZE	IONIZATION	MINERALIZE	PARABOLIZE
DIAZOAMINE	FANTASIZED	IOTIZATION	MINIMIZING	PARAGOGIZE
DIAZOIMIDE	FARCIALIZE	ITALICIZED	MIRACULIZE	PARALOGIZE
DIAZOTIZED	FASCISTIZE	JANIZARIES	MISBAPTIZE	PARALYZANT
DIGITALIZE	FASHIONIZE	JARGONIZED	MISPRIZING	PARALYZING
DIGITIZING	FAZENDEIRO	JAROVIZING	MIZZENMAST	PARASITIZE
DIPLOIDIZE	FEDERALIZE	JASPERIZED	MNEMONIZED	PARAZONIUM
DIPOLARIZE	FERTILIZED	JEOPARDIZE	MOBILIZING	PARENESIZE
DISASINIZE	FERTILIZER	JOURNALIZE	MODERNIZED	PARONYMIZE
DISPRIZING	FERTILIZIN	JOVIALIZED	MODERNIZER	PASSEMEZZO
DISREALIZE	FEUDALIZED	KAMAREZITE	MONARCHIZE	PASTEURIZE
DISSEIZURE	FICTIONIZE	KATABOLIZE	MONETIZING	PATRONIZED
DIVINIZING	FINALIZING	KERATINIZE	MONGRELIZE	PATRONIZER
DOCTRINIZE	FISCALIZED	LABIALIZED	MONOLOGIZE	PATTERNIZE

PAUPERIZED	QUINAZOLYL	SILICIDIZE	TANTALIZER	VOLATILIZE
PEASANTIZE	QUINIZARIN	SILICONIZE	TARLTONIZE	VOLCANIZED
PECTIZABLE	QUARTZITIC	SIMPLICIZE	TARTARIZED	VULCANIZED
PENALIZING	QUATORZAIN	SIZZLINGLY	TARTRAZINE	VULCANIZER
PEPTIZABLE	RACEMIZING	SKEPTICIZE	TAUTOZONAL	VULGARIZED
PEPTONIZED	RADICALIZE	SLEAZINESS	TELFORDIZE	VULGARIZER
PEPTONIZER	RAMFEEZLED	SLENDERIZE	TELLURIZED	WESTERNIZE
PERIPATIZE	RANDOMIZED	SNEEZEWEED	TEMPORIZED	WHEEZINESS
PERITOMIZE	RAZORMAKER	SNEEZEWOOD	TEMPORIZER	WHEEZINGLY
PERIZONIUM	RAZORSTROP	SNEEZEWORT	TENDERIZED	WHITEBLAZE
PEROXIDIZE	REALIZABLE	SOCIALIZED	TENDERIZER	WHIZZERMAN
PETROLIZED	REBAPTIZER	SOCIALIZER	TENOTOMIZE	WHIZZINGLY
PEZIZIFORM	RECOGNIZEE	SOLARIZING	TEPONAZTLI	WINTERIZED
PHANTASIZE	RECOGNIZED	SOLECIZING	TERRORIZED	WITZCHOURA
PHANTOMIZE	RECOGNIZER	SOLEMNIZED	TERRORIZER	WOMANIZING
PHILIPPIZE	RECOGNIZOR	SOLEMNIZER	TETANIZING	WOOLLENIZE
PHILOZOIST	REDISSEIZE	SOLIDARIZE	TETRAZOLYL	ZABAGLIONE
PHLORHIZIN	REGULARIZE	SOLUBILIZE	THEOLOGIZE	ZAPHRENTID
PHLORIDZIN	REJUVENIZE	SOLVOLYZED	THEORIZING	ZEALOTICAL
PHLYZACIUM	REMONETIZE	SOPHRONIZE	THERMOLYZE	ZEBRINNIES
PICRORHIZA	RENDEZVOUS	SOVIETIZED	THIAZOLINE	ZENOGRAPHY
PIEZOMETER	REORGANIZE	SPATIALIZE	THIOZONIDE	ZEOLITIZED
PIEZOMETRY	REVALORIZE	SPECIALIZE	TOPAZOLITE	ZEUGLODONT
PIGMENTIZE	REVITALIZE	SPERMATIZE	TOTALIZING	ZIGZAGGERY
PILEORHIZA	REZBANYITE	SPHETERIZE	TRACTORIZE	ZINCIFYING
PILEORHIZE	RHAPSODIZE	SPIRANTIZE	TRAPEZIUMS	ZINCOGRAPH
PILGRIMIZE	RHEUMATIZE	SPITZFLUTE	TRAUMATIZE	ZINCOLYSIS
PIPERAZINE	RHIZOGENIC	SPOROZOITE	TRICHINIZE	ZINGARESCA
PLAGIARIZE	RHIZOMATIC	SPOROZOOID	TRIOZONIDE	ZINGIBEROL
PLASMOLYZE	RHIZOMELIC	SQUEEZABLE	TRITOZOOID	ZOANTHROPY
PLASTICIZE	RHIZOMORPH	SQUEEZEMAN	TRIVIALIZE	ZONIFEROUS
PLATINIZED	RHIZONEURE	STABILIZED	TROCHEEIZE	ZOOBENTHOS
PLURALIZED	RHIZOPHORE	STABILIZER	TROCHOZOIC	ZOOCULTURE
PLURALIZER	RHIZOPHYTE	STANZAICAL	TROCHOZOON	ZOOCURRENT
PNEUMATIZE	RHIZOPLAST	STARGAZING	TRYPSINIZE	ZOOGRAPHER
POLARIZING	RHIZOPODAL	STERILIZED	TRYPTONIZE	ZOOGRAPHIC
POLITICIZE	RHIZOPODAN	STERILIZER	TWEEZERING	ZOOLATRIES
POLYGAMIZE	RHIZOSTOME	STIGMATIZE	TYRANNIZED	ZOOLATROUS
POLYMERIZE	RHIZOTAXIS	STRATEGIZE	TYRANNIZER	ZOOLOGICAL
POLYTHEIZE	RHODIZONIC	STYFZIEKTE	WARRANTIZE	ZOOLOGIZED
POLYZOARIA	ROUTINIZED	STYLOPIZED	UNBAPTIZED	ZOOMELANIN
POPULARIZE	RUBBERIZED	SUBERINIZE	UNCANONIZE	ZOOMIMETIC
POSITIVIZE	RUFFIANIZE	SUBERIZING	UNDERGLAZE	ZOOMORPHIC
POSTURIZED	RURALIZING	SUBSIDIZED	UNDERSIZED	ZOOPHAGOUS
POULARDIZE	SACCHARIZE	SUBSIDIZER	UNIFORMIZE	ZOOPHILISM
POWDERIZER	SALICYLIZE	SUBTILIZED	UNIONIZING	ZOOPHILIST
POZZOLANIC	SAPIENTIZE	SUBTILIZER	UNITEMIZED	ZOOPHILITE
POZZUOLANA	SATIRIZING	SULFATIZED	UNPRIZABLE	ZOOPHILOUS
PRAGMATIZE	SCANDALIZE	SULFURIZED	UNREALIZED	ZOOPHOBOUS
PRECOGNIZE	SCEPTICIZE	SULPHATIZE	UNSTOICIZE	ZOOPHYSICS
PRECONIZED	SCHEDULIZE	SULPHAZIDE	URALITIZED	ZOOPHYTISH
PRECONIZER	SCHEMATIZE	SULPHIDIZE	URBANIZING	ZOOPHYTOID
PREDAZZITE	SCHEMOZZLE	SULPHURIZE	UTILIZABLE	ZOOPLASTIC
PRESSURIZE	SCHERZANDO	SUMMARIZED	VAGOTOMIZE	ZOOSPOROUS
PRISMATIZE	SCHIZOCARP	SUMMARIZER	VAGRANTIZE	ZOOTECHNIC
PRIZEFIGHT	SCHIZOGAMY	SUZERAINTY	VAPOURIZED	ZOOTHECIAL
PRIZETAKER	SCHIZOGONY	SYLLABIZED	VAPOURIZER	ZOOTHECIUM
PROBLEMIZE	SCHIZOLITE	SYLLOGIZED	VASSALIZED	ZOOTHERAPY
PROCTORIZE	SCORBUTIZE	SYLLOGIZER	VENEZOLANO	ZOOTOMICAL
PROLOGUIZE	SCRUTINIZE	SYMBOLIZED	VERATRIZED	ZOOTROPHIC
PROPHETIZE	SCYPHOZOAN	SYMBOLIZER	VERBALIZED	ZOOXANTHIN
PROVERBIZE	SECTIONIZE	SYMMETRIZE	VERBALIZER	ZWITTERION
PSALMODIZE	SECULARIZE	SYMPATHIZE	VERSIONIZE	ZYGADENINE
PTYALIZING	SELTZOGENE	SYMPHONIZE	VESZELYITE	ZYGOBRANCH
PUBLICIZED	SEMINARIZE	SYMPHYTIZE	VETERANIZE	ZYGODACTYL
PULVERIZED	SENSITIZED	SYNCRETIZE	VICTIMIZED	ZYGOMYCETE
PULVERIZER	SENSITIZER	SYNONYMIZE	VICTIMIZER	ZYGOPHORIC
PUZZLEHEAD	SENSUALIZE	SYNTHESIZE	VISIBILIZE	ZYGOSPHENE
PUZZLEMENT	SERIALIZED	SYNTHETIZE	VISUALIZED	ZYGOSPHERE
PUZZLEPATE	SERMONIZED	SYNTONIZED	VISUALIZER	ZYGOSPORIC
PUZZLINGLY	SERMONIZER	SYNTONIZER	VITALIZING	ZYGOTACTIC
PYRAZOLINE	SERPENTIZE	SYPHILIZED	VITAMINIZE	ZYMOGENOUS
PYRAZOLONE	SEVERALIZE	SYSTEMIZED	VITRIOLIZE	ZYMOLOGIST
PYRIDAZINE	SFORZANDOS	SYSTEMIZER	VOCALIZING	ZYMOPHORIC
PYRIDINIZE	SHERARDIZE	TABULARIZE	VOCIFERIZE	ZYMOSTEROL
QUINAZOLIN	SIGNALIZED	TANTALIZED		

POSITIONAL ORDER LIST OF 10-LETTER WORDS

ZABAGLIONE	AZTHIONIUM	MIZZENMAST	MELEZITOSE	SCHERZANDO
ZAPHRENTID	AZYGOSPERM	MONZONITIC	NANIZATION	SPOROZOITE
ZEALOTICAL	AZYGOSPORE	MOZZARELLA	PARAZONIUM	SPOROZOOID
ZEBRINNIES	CZAREVITCH	MUZZLEWOOD	PERIZONIUM	SQUEEZABLE
ZENOGRAPHY	OZONOMETER	OXOZONIDES	PEZIZIFORM	SQUEEZEMAN
ZEOLITIZED	OZONOMETRY	PIEZOMETER	PHLYZACIUM	TAUTOZONAL
ZEUGLODONT	OZONOSCOPE	PIEZOMETRY	POLYZOARIA	TETRAZOLYL
ZIGZAGGERY		POZZOLANIC	PYRAZOLINE	TRAPEZIUMS
ZINCIFYING	AIZOACEOUS	POZZUOLANA	PYRAZOLONE	TRITOZOOID
ZINCOGRAPH	BIZARRERIE	PRIZEFIGHT	SCHIZOCARP	UNPRIZABLE
ZINCOLYSIS	COZENINGLY	PRIZETAKER	SCHIZOGAMY	UTILIZABLE
ZINGARESCA	DAZZLINGLY	PUZZLEHEAD	SCHIZOGONY	
ZINGIBEROL	DEZYMOTIZE	PUZZLEMENT	SCHIZOLITE	ACTINOZOAL
ZOANTHROPY	ECZEMATOID	PUZZLEPATE	SELTZOGENE	ACTINOZOAN
ZONIFEROUS	ECZEMATOUS	PUZZLINGLY	SFORZANDOS	AKHUNDZADA
ZOOBENTHOS	ENZYMOLOGY	RHIZOGENIC	SLEAZINESS	ALCALIZATE
ZOOCULTURE	EXZODIACAL	RHIZOMATIC	SNEEZEWEED	ALDOLIZING
ZOOCURRENT	FAZENDEIRO	RHIZOMELIC	SNEEZEWOOD	ALKALIZATE
ZOOGRAPHER	GAZANGABIN	RHIZOMORPH	SNEEZEWORT	AMIDRAZONE
ZOOGRAPHIC	LAZARETTOS	RHIZONEURE	SPITZFLUTE	AMORTIZING
ZOOLATRIES	LIZARDTAIL	RHIZOPHORE	STANZAICAL	ANGELIZING
ZOOLATROUS	MAZAPILITE	RHIZOPHYTE	STYFZIEKTE	APHORIZING
ZOOLOGICAL	MAZOPATHIA	RHIZOPLAST	THIAZOLINE	APPETIZING
ZOOLOGIZED	MAZOPATHIC	RHIZOPODAL	THIOZONIDE	ARBORIZING
ZOOMELANIN	MEZZOGRAPH	RHIZOPODAN	TOPAZOLITE	ARCHAIZING
ZOOMIMETIC	MEZZOTINTO	RHIZOSTOME	TRIOZONIDE	ARTHROZOAN
ZOOMORPHIC	MIZZENMAST	RHIZOTAXIS	TWEEZERING	ARTHROZOIC
ZOOPHAGOUS	MOZZARELLA	SIZZLINGLY	VENEZOLANO	ASTATIZING
ZOOPHILISM	MUZZLEWOOD	VESZELYITE	WHEEZINESS	ATHETIZING
ZOOPHILIST	MYZOSTOMID	WHIZZERMAN	WHEEZINGLY	ATTICIZING
ZOOPHILITE	PEZIZIFORM	WHIZZINGLY	WHIZZERMAN	AUTOLYZATE
ZOOPHILOUS	POZZOLANIC	WITZCHOURA	WHIZZINGLY	AZOBENZENE
ZOOPHOBOUS	POZZUOLANA	ZIGZAGGERY		AZOBENZOIC
ZOOPHYSICS	PUZZLEHEAD		AGLAOZONIA	BAMBOOZLED
ZOOPHYTISH	PUZZLEMENT	ALTAZIMUTH	ANALYZABLE	BAMBOOZLER
ZOOPHYTOID	PUZZLEPATE	ASSIZEMENT	ANTHOZOOID	BILHARZIAL
ZOOPLASTIC	PUZZLINGLY	BEBIZATION	BARTIZANED	BOTANIZING
ZOOSPOROUS	RAZORMAKER	BEDAZZLING	BEDAZZLING	BULLDOZING
ZOOTECHNIC	RAZORSTROP	BEDIZENING	BOMBAZETTE	CANALIZING
ZOOTHECIAL	REZBANYITE	BLIZZARDLY	CARBAZYLIC	CANONIZANT
ZOOTHECIUM	SIZZLINGLY	BOBIZATION	CHALAZOGAM	CANONIZING
ZOOTHERAPY	SUZERAINTY	BREEZINESS	CHINTZIEST	CATALYZING
ZOOTOMICAL		BRONZEWING	COGNIZABLE	CHLORAZIDE
ZOOTROPHIC	ANAZOTURIA	BRONZITITE	COGNIZABLY	CIVILIZING
ZOOXANTHIN	APOZEMICAL	CHRIZONTAL	COGNIZANCE	COLONIZING
ZWITTERION	ASYZYGETIC	CITIZENESS	COSMOZOANS	COMPRIZING
ZYGADENINE	BENZEDRINE	CITIZENISM	COSMOZOISM	CREOLIZING
ZYGOBRANCH	BENZOCAINE	CITIZENIZE	DANDIZETTE	CRYPTOZOIC
ZYGODACTYL	BENZOPYRAN	CUTIZATION	DIALYZABLE	CURARIZING
ZYGOMYCETE	BENZOYLATE	CYTOZYMASE	DIALYZATOR	CUTINIZING
ZYGOPHORIC	BERZELIITE	DENAZIFIED	EMBEZZLING	DEMONIZING
ZYGOSPHENE	BLAZONMENT	DENIZATION	EMBLAZONED	DEPUTIZING
ZYGOSPHERE	BLIZZARDLY	DENIZENIZE	EMBLAZONER	DEVILIZING
ZYGOSPORIC	BRAZENFACE	EMBEZZLING	EMBLAZONRY	DIGITIZING
ZYGOTACTIC	BRAZENNESS	EURYZYGOUS	ENOLIZABLE	DISPRIZING
ZYMOGENOUS	BRAZILETTE	FRENZIEDLY	HYDRAZOATE	DISSEIZURE
ZYMOLOGIST	BRAZILWOOD	FRIZZINESS	IMIDAZOLYL	DIVINIZING
ZYMOPHORIC	CALZONERAS	FROWZINESS	INTERZONAL	ECTOENZYME
ZYMOSTEROL	COAZERVATE	GRIZZLIEST	LIONIZABLE	ENDOENZYME
	CRAZEDNESS	GRIZZLYMAN	MICROZOARY	ENERGIZING
AZEOTROPIC	DAZZLINGLY	HOMOZYGOTE	MICROZOOID	EPIRHIZOUS
AZOBENZENE	DEOZONIZER	HOMOZYGOUS	ORGANZINED	EQUALIZING
AZOBENZOIC	DIAZOAMINE	HORIZONTAL	OXIDIZABLE	ERGOTIZING
AZOCORINTH	DIAZOIMIDE	HYPOZEUGMA	PECTIZABLE	ESTERIZING
AZOCYANIDE	DIAZOTIZED	HYPOZEUXIS	PEPTIZABLE	ETERNIZING
AZOGALLEIN	DOUZAINIER	IODIZATION	PHILOZOIST	ETHERIZING
AZOMETHINE	FRIZZINESS	IONIZATION	PREDAZZITE	ETHICIZING
AZOPHENINE	FROZENNESS	IOTIZATION	QUARTZITIC	EULOGIZING
AZOPROTEIN	GRIZZLIEST	JANIZARIES	QUINAZOLIN	EUPHUIZING
AZOTENESIS	GRIZZLYMAN	MAGAZINAGE	QUINAZOLYL	EUPOLYZOAN
AZOTOLUENE	MANZANILLA	MAGAZINING	QUINIZARIN	EXORCIZING
AZOTOMETER	MANZANILLO	MAGAZINISM	REALIZABLE	FINALIZING
AZOTORRHEA	MEZZOGRAPH	MAGAZINIST	RENDEZVOUS	FLUIDIZING
AZOVERNINE	MEZZOTINTO	MELEZITASE	RHODIZONIC	FOCALIZING

HEMATOZOON	AUTHORIZED	INTERMEZZI	RUBBERIZED	ALCOHOLIZE
IDEALIZING	AUTHORIZER	INTERMEZZO	SCHEMOZZLE	ALGEBRAIZE
INFAMIZING	BACTERIZED	ITALICIZED	SENSITIZED	ALKALINIZE
JAROVIZING	BALKANIZED	JARGONIZED	SENSITIZER	ALLEGORIZE
KAMAREZITE	BARBARIZED	JASPERIZED	SERIALIZED	AMALGAMIZE
LACONIZING	BRUTALIZED	JOVIALIZED	SERMONIZED	AMMONOLYZE
LEGALIZING	CARBOLIZED	LABIALIZED	SERMONIZER	ANATHEMIZE
LOCALIZING	CARBONIZED	LIQUIDIZED	SIGNALIZED	ANGELICIZE
MACARIZING	CARBONIZER	MAGNETIZED	SOCIALIZED	ANGULARIZE
MAXIMIZING	CARBURIZED	MAGNETIZER	SOCIALIZER	ANTAGONIZE
MELODIZING	CARBURIZER	MAINPRIZER	SOLEMNIZED	ANTIFREEZE
MEMORIZING	CARNALIZED	MARBLEIZED	SOLEMNIZER	APOSTATIZE
METALIZING	CASTORIZED	MARBLEIZER	SOLVOLYZED	APOSTOLIZE
MINIMIZING	CATECHIZED	MARMARIZED	SOVIETIZED	ARSENICIZE
MISFRIZING	CATECHIZER	MARTYRIZED	STABILIZED	ASEPTICIZE
MOBILIZING	CATHARIZED	MARTYRIZER	STABILIZER	ASEXUALIZE
MONETIZING	CAUTERIZED	MATRONIZED	STERILIZED	ATROPINIZE
MORALIZING	CHIMPANZEE	MECHANIZER	STERILIZER	AUTOMATIZE
MOTORIZING	CHITINIZED	MEDIATIZED	STYLOPIZED	AUTONOMIZE
MYCETOZOAN	CICATRIZED	MERCERIZED	SUBSIDIZED	AUTOTOMIZE
MYCETOZOON	CICATRIZER	MERCERIZER	SUBSIDIZER	AUTOXIDIZE
NASALIZING	COCAINIZED	MERCURIZED	SUBTILIZED	AXIOMATIZE
NEBULIZING	COMMUNIZED	MESMERIZED	SUBTILIZER	BANTINGIZE
NOTARIZING	CRITICIZED	MESMERIZEE	SULFATIZED	BASTARDIZE
NOVELIZING	CRITICIZER	MESMERIZER	SULFURIZED	BESTIALIZE
ORGANIZING	DEEPFROZEN	METHODIZED	SUMMARIZED	BITUMINIZE
OXADIAZOLE	DEFERRIZED	METHODIZER	SUMMARIZER	BOLSHEVIZE
PAEANIZING	DEODORIZED	MNEMONIZED	SYLLABIZED	BOUCHERIZE
PAGANIZING	DEODORIZER	MODERNIZED	SYLLOGIZED	BOURBONIZE
PARALYZANT	DEOXIDIZED	MODERNIZER	SYLLOGIZER	BOWDLERIZE
PARALYZING	DEOXIDIZER	MORTALIZED	SYMBOLIZED	BURGLARIZE
PENALIZING	DEOZONIZER	MUTUALIZED	SYMBOLIZER	BURNETTIZE
PIPERAZINE	DIABOLIZED	MYCORHIZAL	SYNTONIZED	CAPITALIZE
POLARIZING	DIALOGIZED	MYTHICIZED	SYNTONIZER	CARAMELIZE
PREDAZZITE	DIAZOTIZED	MYTHICIZER	SYPHILIZED	CATABOLIZE
PTYALIZING	DOGMATIZED	NARCOTIZED	SYSTEMIZED	CATEGORIZE
PYRIDAZINE	DOGMATIZER	NEOLOGIZED	SYSTEMIZER	CAUSTICIZE
QUATORZAIN	DRAMATIZED	NONCITIZEN	TANTALIZED	CENTRALIZE
RACEMIZING	DRAMATIZER	NORMALIZED	TANTALIZER	CHANNELIZE
RAMFEEZLED	DUCTILIZED	NORMALIZER	TARTARIZED	CHATTELIZE
RURALIZING	ECONOMIZED	NOTORHIZAL	TELLURIZED	CHLORALIZE
SATIRIZING	ECONOMIZER	OBJECTIZED	TEMPORIZED	CHLORIDIZE
SCHEMOZZLE	ELECTRIZED	ORIGANIZED	TEMPORIZER	CHLORITIZE
SCYPHOZOAN	ELECTRIZER	OSTRACIZED	TENDERIZED	CHLORODIZE
SOLARIZING	EMBLEMIZED	OSTRACIZER	TENDERIZER	CHROMATIZE
SOLECIZING	EMPATHIZED	OVERGLAZED	TERRORIZED	CHROMICIZE
STARGAZING	EMPHASIZED	OVERPRIZED	TERRORIZER	CICERONIZE
SUBERIZING	EPILOGIZED	OVERPRIZER	TYRANNIZED	CINCHONIZE
SULPHAZIDE	EPITOMIZED	OXYGENIZED	TYRANNIZER	CITIZENIZE
TARTRAZINE	EPITOMIZER	OXYGENIZER	UNBAPTIZED	CLASSICIZE
TEPONAZTLI	EUPHEMIZED	PALLETIZED	UNDERSIZED	COCKNEYIZE
TETANIZING	EUPHEMIZER	PASSEMEZZO	UNITEMIZED	COLEORHIZA
THEORIZING	EUPHONIZED	PATRONIZED	UNREALIZED	COLLOQUIZE
TOTALIZING	FACTORIZING	PATRONIZER	URALITIZED	CONCERTIZE
TROCHOZOIC	FANTASIZED	PAUPERIZED	VAPOURIZED	CROFTERIZE
TROCHOZOON	FERTILIZED	PEPTONIZED	VAPOURIZER	CUCKOLDIZE
UNIONIZING	FERTILIZER	PEPTONIZER	VASSALIZED	DASTARDIZE
URBANIZING	FERTILIZIN	PETROLIZED	VERATRIZED	DEALKALIZE
VITALIZING	FEUDALIZED	PHLORHIZIN	VERBALIZED	DECIMALIZE
VOCALIZING	FISCALIZED	PHLORIDZIN	VERBALIZER	DECIVILIZE
	FORMALIZED	PLATINIZED	VICTIMIZED	DECOLORIZE
ACADEMIZED	FORMULIZED	PLURALIZED	VICTIMIZER	DEEPFREEZE
ACETYLIZER	FORMULIZER	PLURALIZER	VISUALIZED	DEFEMINIZE
ACTIONIZED	FOSSILIZED	POSTURIZED	VISUALIZER	DEFINITIZE
ACTUALIZED	FRIVOLIZED	POWDERIZER	VOLCANIZED	DEHEMATIZE
ALCHEMIZED	GALLICIZER	PRECONIZED	VULCANIZED	DEHEPATIZE
ALLOCHEZIA	GALVANIZED	PRECONIZER	VULCANIZER	DEHUMANIZE
ALUMINIZED	GALVANIZER	PUBLICIZED	VULGARIZED	DELEGALIZE
ANABIBAZON	GEOLOGIZED	PULVERIZED	VULGARIZER	DELIMITIZE
ANALOGIZED	GLAMORIZED	PULVERIZER	WINTERIZED	DELOCALIZE
ANGLICIZED	GORGONIZED	RANDOMIZED	ZOOLOGIZED	DELUMINIZE
ANIMALIZED	HARMONIZER	REBAPTIZER		DEMOBILIZE
APOLOGIZED	HYBRIDIZER	RECOGNIZEE	ADRENALIZE	DEMORALIZE
APOLOGIZER	ICHTHYIZED	RECOGNIZED	ADULTERIZE	DENATURIZE
ARCTICIZED	INFLUENZAL	RECOGNIZER	AGGRANDIZE	DENIZENIZE
AROMATIZED	INFLUENZIC	RECOGNIZOR	ALBUMENIZE	DEPETALIZE
AROMATIZER	INOXIDIZED	ROUTINIZED	ALBUMINIZE	DEPOLARIZE

DEPRIORIZE	GRANGERIZE	MYCOLOGIZE	PRESSURIZE	SPIRANTIZE
DERESINIZE	GRAPHITIZE	MYCORRHIZA	PRISMATIZE	STIGMATIZE
DEVIRILIZE	HERETICIZE	MYECTOMIZE	PROBLEMIZE	STRATEGIZE
DEVITALIZE	HOMOGENIZE	NATURALIZE	PROCTORIZE	SUBERINIZE
DEVOCALIZE	HOMOLOGIZE	NEBULARIZE	PROLOGUIZE	SULPHATIZE
DEXTRINIZE	HYDRORHIZA	NESSLERIZE	PROPHETIZE	SULPHIDIZE
DEZYMOTIZE	HYPNOIDIZE	NEUTRALIZE	PROVERBIZE	SULPHURIZE
DIAMONDIZE	IDOLATRIZE	NICOTINIZE	PSALMODIZE	SYMMETRIZE
DIGITALIZE	ILLEGALIZE	NOTHINGIZE	PYRIDINIZE	SYMPATHIZE
DIPLOIDIZE	IMMOBILIZE	OBITUARIZE	RADICALIZE	SYMPHONIZE
DIPOLARIZE	INFAMONIZE	ONTOLOGIZE	REDISSEIZE	SYMPHYTIZE
DISASINIZE	INGRANDIZE	OVERFRIEZE	REGULARIZE	SYNCRETIZE
DISREALIZE	INKHORNIZE	PALATALIZE	REJUVENIZE	SYNONYMIZE
DOCTRINIZE	INTERMEZZI	PANEGYRIZE	REMONETIZE	SYNTHESIZE
DOGGRELIZE	INTERMEZZO	PARABOLIZE	REORGANIZE	SYNTHETIZE
DOLOMITIZE	INTHRONIZE	PARAGOGIZE	REVALORIZE	TABULARIZE
DOXOLOGIZE	JEOPARDIZE	PARALOGIZE	REVITALIZE	TARLTONIZE
DYSOXIDIZE	JOURNALIZE	PARASITIZE	RHAPSODIZE	TELFORDIZE
EFFEMINIZE	KATABOLIZE	PARENESIZE	RHEUMATIZE	TENOTOMIZE
ELASTICIZE	KERATINIZE	PARONYMIZE	RUFFIANIZE	THEOLOGIZE
EMOTIONIZE	LATERALIZE	PASSEMEZZO	SACCHARIZE	THERMOLYZE
EMPHATHIZE	LATIBULIZE	PASTEURIZE	SALICYLIZE	TRACTORIZE
ENGRANDIZE	LEGITIMIZE	PATTERNIZE	SAPIENTIZE	TRAUMATIZE
ENIGMATIZE	LETHARGIZE	PEASANTIZE	SCANDALIZE	TRICHINIZE
ENTHRONIZE	LEXICONIZE	PERIPATIZE	SCEPTICIZE	TRIVIALIZE
EPISCOPIZE	LIBERALIZE	PERITOMIZE	SCHEDULIZE	TROCHEEIZE
EPISTOLIZE	LINGUALIZE	PEROXIDIZE	SCHEMATIZE	TRYPSINIZE
EPITAPHIZE	LITERALIZE	PHANTASIZE	SCORBUTIZE	TRYPTONIZE
EPITHELIZE	LOGICALIZE	PHANTOMIZE	SCRUTINIZE	UNCANONIZE
ETERNALIZE	MACADAMIZE	PHILIPPIZE	SECTIONIZE	UNDERGLAZE
EUHEMERIZE	MAHOGANIZE	PICRORHIZA	SECULARIZE	UNIFORMIZE
EVANGELIZE	MALLEINIZE	PIGMENTIZE	SEMINARIZE	UNSTOICIZE
FANATICIZE	MARTIALIZE	PILEORHIZA	SENSUALIZE	VAGOTOMIZE
FARCIALIZE	MEROTOMIZE	PILEORHIZE	SERPENTIZE	VAGRANTIZE
FASCISTIZE	METABOLIZE	PILGRIMIZE	SEVERALIZE	VERSIONIZE
FASHIONIZE	MILITARIZE	PLAGIARIZE	SHERARDIZE	VETERANIZE
FEDERALIZE	MILLIONIZE	PLASMOLYZE	SILICIDIZE	VISIBILIZE
FICTIONIZE	MINERALIZE	PLASTICIZE	SILICONIZE	VITAMINIZE
FRATERNIZE	MIRACULIZE	PNEUMATIZE	SIMPLICIZE	VITRIOLIZE
GELATINIZE	MISBAPTIZE	POLITICIZE	SKEPTICIZE	VOCIFERIZE
GENERALIZE	MONARCHIZE	POLYGAMIZE	SLENDERIZE	VOLATILIZE
GEOMETRIZE	MONGRELIZE	POLYMERIZE	SOLIDARIZE	WARRANTIZE
GLOTTALIZE	MONOLOGIZE	POLYTHEIZE	SOLUBILIZE	WESTERNIZE
GLUTTONIZE	MONONYMIZE	POPULARIZE	SOPHRONIZE	WHITEBLAZE
GNATHONIZE	MONOPOLIZE	POSITIVIZE	SPATIALIZE	WOOLLENIZE
GOLANDAUZE	MONOTONIZE	POULARDIZE	SPECIALIZE	
GOLUNDAUZE	MORPHINIZE	PRAGMATIZE	SPERMATIZE	CHERVONETZ
GORMANDIZE	MUSICALIZE	PRECOGNIZE	SPHETERIZE	FACKELTANZ

SCORING ORDER LIST OF 10-LETTER WORDS

34	OXYGENIZER	MYCORRHIZA	CRYPTOZOIC	ZENOGRAPHY
HYPOZEUXIS	QUARTZITIC	MYTHICIZER	CUCKOLDIZE	ZINCIFYING
	RHIZOPHYTE	OXIDIZABLE	DEOXIDIZER	ZOOMORPHIC
32	SCHIZOGAMY	PEROXIDIZE	DOXOLOGIZE	ZOOPHYTOID
SYMPHYTIZE	SQUEEZABLE	REJUVENIZE	ENZYMOLOGY	ZYGOSPHENE
	SQUEEZEMAN	RHIZOMORPH	FACKELTANZ	ZYGOSPHERE
31	ZOOPHYTISH	RHIZOTAXIS	HOMOZYGOTE	
DYSOXIDIZE	ZYGOBRANCH	SCYPHOZOAN	HOMOZYGOUS	**27**
ICHTHYIZED	ZYGOMYCETE	STYFZIEKTE	HYBRIDIZER	ALCHEMIZED
MAXIMIZING	ZYGOPHORIC	SYMPATHIZE	HYPNOIDIZE	AUTOXIDIZE
OBJECTIZED		SYMPHONIZE	INOXIDIZED	AZYGOSPERM
OXYGENIZED	**29**	WHEEZINGLY	JARGONIZED	BOLSHEVIZE
PHLYZACIUM	CYTOZYMASE	ZOOPHYSICS	LEXICONIZE	CATECHIZED
QUINAZOLYL	CZAREVITCH	ZOOXANTHIN	MAZOPATHIC	CHALAZOGAM
ZYMOPHORIC	DEOXIDIZED	ZYGODACTYL	MYECTOMIZE	CHERVONETZ
	EMPHATHIZE		PRIZEFIGHT	COGNIZABLY
30	EQUALIZING	**28**	QUATORZAIN	DEXTRINIZE
COCKNEYIZE	EXORCIZING	AKHUNDZADA	QUINAZOLIN	EFFEMINIZE
HYPOZEUGMA	EXZODIACAL	ASYZYGETIC	QUINIZARIN	EMPATHIZED
JAROVIZING	HYDRORHIZA	AXIOMATIZE	SCHIZOCARP	EMPHASIZED
JOVIALIZED	JASPERIZED	CARBAZYLIC	SCHIZOGONY	EUPHEMIZED
LIQUIDIZED	JEOPARDIZE	CHIMPANZEE	SYPHILIZED	MYCOLOGIZE
MYTHICIZED	MYCORHIZAL	CHROMICIZE	WHIZZINGLY	MYZOSTOMID

OXADIAZOLE
OXOZONIDES
PHLORHIZIN
POLYGAMIZE
POLYTHEIZE
RHIZOPHORE
SKEPTICIZE
SYMBOLIZED
SYNONYMIZE
THERMOLYZE
VICTIMIZED
VOCIFERIZE
WHITEBLAZE
WITZCHOURA
ZINCOGRAPH
ZOANTHROPY
ZOOGRAPHIC
ZOOTHERAPY
ZYGOSPORIC
ZYGOTACTIC

26
AMMONOLYZE
ASEXUALIZE
BALKANIZED
BAMBOOZLED
BENZOPYRAN
BOUCHERIZE
BRAZENFACE
CATECHIZER
CHROMATIZE
CINCHONIZE
COMMUNIZED
COMPRIZING
ECTOENZYME
EMBLAZONRY
EMBLEMIZED
EPITAPHIZE
EUPHEMIZER
EURYZYGOUS
FRENZIEDLY
FRIVOLIZED
HYDRAZOATE
INKHORNIZE
JANIZARIES
JOURNALIZE
MACADAMIZE
MAZOPATHIA
MECHANIZER
METHODIZED
MEZZOGRAPH
MICROZOARY
MONARCHIZE
MONONYMIZE
MORPHINIZE
MYCETOZOAN
MYCETOZOON
PARONYMIZE
PHANTOMIZE
PICRORHIZA
PIEZOMETRY
PLASMOLYZE
POLYMERIZE
PROPHETIZE
PROVERBIZE
PUBLICIZED
RHIZOMATIC
RHIZOMELIC
SACCHARIZE
SCHEMATIZE
SOLVOLYZED
SYMBOLIZER
SYMMETRIZE
TANTALIZED
TROCHOZOIC
VICTIMIZER
WHIZZERMAN

ZOOPHILISM
ZOOPHOBOUS
ZOOTECHNIC
ZOOTHECIUM
ZOOTROPHIC

25
ACADEMIZED
APHORIZING
APOZEMICAL
ARCHAIZING
AZOCYANIDE
AZYGOSPORE
BAMBOOZLER
BOMBAZETTE
BOWDLERIZE
BRAZILWOOD
BRONZEWING
CATALYZING
CATHARIZED
CHITINIZED
CHLORAZIDE
CHLORIDIZE
CHLORODIZE
CIVILIZING
COSMOZOISM
COZENINGLY
DECIVILIZE
DEEPFREEZE
DEEPFROZEN
DEFEMINIZE
DEHEMATIZE
DEHEPATIZE
DEHUMANIZE
DEVOCALIZE
DIALYZABLE
ENDOENZYME
EPISCOPIZE
ETHICIZING
EUPHONIZED
EUPHUIZING
FACTORIZED
FASHIONIZE
FISCALIZED
FOCALIZING
FORMALIZED
FORMULIZED
FROWZINESS
GRAPHITIZE
HOMOGENIZE
HOMOLOGIZE
IMIDAZOLYL
IMMOBILIZE
INFAMIZING
KAMAREZITE
KATABOLIZE
MAHOGANIZE
MARTYRIZED
METHODIZER
MISBAPTIZE
OVERFRIEZE
OVERPRIZED
PANEGYRIZE
PARALYZING
PECTIZABLE
PEPTIZABLE
PEZIZIFORM
PHILIPPIZE
PHLORIDZIN
POWDERIZE
PRIZETAKER
PROBLEMIZE
PTYALIZING
PULVERIZED
PYRIDAZINE
PYRIDINIZE
RAMFEEZLED

RAZORMAKER
RHAPSODIZE
RHIZOGENIC
RHIZOPODAL
RHIZOPODAN
RHODIZONIC
RUFFIANIZE
SCEPTICIZE
SCHEDULIZE
SCHEMOZZLE
SCHERZANDO
SIMPLICIZE
STYLOPIZED
SULPHAZIDE
SULPHIDIZE
SYLLABIZED
SYNTHESIZE
SYNTHETIZE
SYSTEMIZED
VAGOTOMIZE
VAPOURIZED
VERBALIZED
VESZELYITE
VOCALIZING
VOLCANIZED
VULCANIZED
WHEEZINESS
WOMANIZING
ZAPHRENTID
ZOOGRAPHER
ZOOMIMETIC
ZOOPHAGOUS
ZYMOGENOUS
ZYMOLOGIST

24
ACETYLIZER
ALCOHOLIZE
ALLOCHEZIA
ALTAZIMUTH
AMALGAMIZE
ANALYZABLE
ANATHEMIZE
APPETIZING
ARCTICIZED
ARTHROZOIC
AZOCORINTH
AZOMETHINE
AZOPHENINE
AZTHIONIUM
BACTERIZED
BARBARIZED
BENZOYLATE
BILHARZIAL
BLIZZARDLY
CARBOLIZED
CARBONIZED
CARBURIZED
CHANNELIZE
CHATTELIZE
CHINTZIEST
CHLORALIZE
CHLORITIZE
CHRIZONTAL
CICATRIZED
COAZERVATE
COCAINIZED
COGNIZABLE
COGNIZANCE
COLEORHIZA
CRITICIZED
CROFTERIZE
DEALKALIZE
DECIMALIZE
DEFERRIZED
DEMOBILIZE
DENAZIFIED

DEVILIZING
DEZYMOTIZE
DIVINIZING
DOGMATIZED
ECONOMIZED
ECZEMATOID
EMBLAZONED
EPIRHIZOUS
EPITHELIZE
EPITOMIZED
EUHEMERIZE
EUPOLYZOAN
FANATICIZE
FARCIALIZE
FASCISTIZE
FEUDALIZED
FICTIONIZE
FLUIDIZING
FORMULIZER
GALVANIZED
GRIZZLYMAN
HARMONIZER
HEMATOZOON
HERETICIZE
INFAMONIZE
INFLUENZIC
MACARIZING
MAGAZINISM
MARBLEIZED
MARMARIZED
MARTYRIZER
MEMORIZING
MERCERIZED
MERCURIZED
MESMERIZED
MICROZOOID
MINIMIZING
MISPRIZING
MNEMONIZED
MOBILIZING
MUZZLEWOOD
OVERGLAZED
OVERPRIZER
OZONOMETRY
PARALYZANT
PAUPERIZED
PEPTONIZED
PHANTASIZE
PHILOZOIST
PIGMENTIZE
PILEORHIZA
PILEORHIZE
PILGRIMIZE
POLYZOARIA
POSITIVIZE
PRAGMATIZE
PRECOGNIZE
PRECONIZED
PSALMODIZE
PULVERIZER
PUZZLEHEAD
PUZZLINGLY
PYRAZOLINE
PYRAZOLONE
RACEMIZING
REZBANYITE
RHEUMATIZE
RHIZOPLAST
RHIZOSTOME
RUBBERIZED
SALICYLIZE
SCHIZOLITE
SOPHRONIZE
SPHETERIZE
SPITZFLUTE
SULPHATIZE
SULPHURIZE

SUMMARIZED
SYLLOGIZED
SYNCRETIZE
SYSTEMIZER
TEMPORIZED
TRICHINIZE
TROCHEEIZE
TROCHOZOON
TRYPSINIZE
TRYPTONIZE
UNBAPTIZED
UNIFORMIZE
VAPOURIZER
VERBALIZER
VISIBILIZE
VITAMINIZE
VULCANIZER
VULGARIZED
ZIGZAGGERY
ZINCOLYSIS
ZOOBENTHOS
ZOOPHILIST
ZOOPHILITE
ZOOPHILOUS
ZOOTHECIAL
ZYGADENINE
ZYMOSTEROL

23
ALBUMENIZE
ALBUMINIZE
ALKALINIZE
ALKALIZATE
ANABIBAZON
ANGLICIZED
ANTHOZOOID
APOLOGIZED
ASEPTICIZE
ATHETIZING
AUTHORIZED
AZEOTROPIC
BEBIZATION
BEDIZENING
BENZOCAINE
BITUMINIZE
BLAZONMENT
BOBIZATION
BOURBONIZE
BULLDOZING
CAPITALIZE
CARAMELIZE
CARBONIZER
CARBURIZER
CATABOLIZE
CAUSTICIZE
CICATRIZER
CICERONIZE
CITIZENISM
CLASSICIZE
CONCERTIZE
CONCRETIZE
COSMOZOANS
CRITICIZER
DAZZLINGLY
DEFINITIZE
DEMONIZING
DEPUTIZING
DEVIRILIZE
DEVITALIZE
DIABOLIZED
DIALYZATOR
DIAMONDIZE
DIAZOIMIDE
DIPLOIDIZE
DISPRIZING
DOGMATIZER
DRAMATIZED

DUCTILIZED
ECONOMIZER
ECZEMATOUS
EMBEZZLING
EMBLAZONER
EPILOGIZED
EPITOMIZER
ETHERIZING
EVANGELIZE
FANTASIZED
FAZENDEIRO
FEDERALIZE
FERTILIZED
FINALIZING
FOSSILIZED
GALVANIZER
GAZANGABIN
GLAMORIZED
GNATHONIZE
GORMANDIZE
KERATINIZE
LETHARGIZE
MAGAZINAGE
MAGAZINING
MAGNETIZED
MAINPRIZER
MARBLEIZER
MAZAPILITE
MEDIATIZED
MELODIZING
MERCERIZER
MEROTOMIZE
MESMERIZEE
MESMERIZER
METABOLIZE
MIRACULIZE
MODERNIZED
MONOPOLIZE
MONZONITIC
MUSICALIZE
NOTHINGIZE
NOVELIZING
OZONOSCOPE
PAGANIZING
PARABOLIZE
PARAGOGIZE
PARAZONIUM
PEPTONIZER
PERIPATIZE
PERITOMIZE
PERIZONIUM
PIEZOMETER
PIPERAZINE
PLASTICIZE
PNEUMATIZE
POLITICIZE
POPULARIZE
PRECONIZER
PRISMATIZE
PROCTORIZE
RANDOMIZED
REBAPTIZER
RECOGNIZED
RENDEZVOUS
SCORBUTIZE
SFORZANDOS
SHERARDIZE
SNEEZEWEED
SNEEZEWOOD
SOVIETIZED
SPECIALIZE
SPERMATIZE
SUBSIDIZED
SULFATIZED
SULFURIZED
SUMMARIZER
SYLLOGIZER

SYNTONIZED
TELFORDIZE
TEMPORIZER
THEOLOGIZE
THEORIZING
THIOZONIDE
TRAPEZIUMS
TWEEZERING
TYRANNIZED
UNPRIZABLE
VAGRANTIZE
VASSALIZED
VERATRIZED
VISUALIZED
VITALIZING
VULGARIZER
WINTERIZED
ZOOPLASTIC
ZOOTOMICAL

22
ACTIONIZED
ACTUALIZED
AGGRANDIZE
ALGEBRAIZE
ALUMINIZED
AMIDRAZONE
AMORTIZING
ANATOMIZED
ANGELICIZE
ANIMALIZED
ANTIFREEZE
APOLOGIZER
ARBORIZING
AROMATIZED
ARTHROZOAN
ATTICIZING
AUTHORIZER
AUTOLYZATE
AZOBENZOIC
AZOTORRHEA
AZOVERNINE
BANTINGIZE
BARTIZANED
BASTARDIZE
BEDAZZLING
BENZEDRINE
BOTANIZING
BRUTALIZED
BURGLARIZE
CANALIZING
CANONIZING
CARNALIZED
CASTORIZED
CATEGORIZE
CAUTERIZED
COLONIZING
CRAZEDNESS
CREOLIZING
CURARIZING
CUTINIZING
DECOLORIZE
DELIMITIZE
DELOCALIZE
DELUMINIZE
DEMORALIZE
DEODORIZED
DEPETALIZE
DEPOLARIZE
DEPRIORIZE
DIALOGIZED
DIAZOAMINE
DIGITIZING
DIPOLARIZE
DOCTRINIZE
DOGGRELIZE
DOLOMITIZE

DRAMATIZER
ELECTRIZED
ENIGMATIZE
ENTHRONIZE
FERTILIZER
FERTILIZIN
FRATERNIZE
FROZENNESS
GALLICIZER
GEOLOGIZED
GEOMETRIZE
GORGONIZED
HORIZONTAL
INFLUENZAL
INTHRONIZE
ITALICIZED
LABIALIZED
LACONIZING
LEGITIMIZE
LOCALIZING
LOGICALIZE
MAGAZINIST
MAGNETIZER
MATRONIZED
METALIZING
MIZZENMAST
MODERNIZER
MONETIZING
MONGRELIZE
MONOLOGIZE
MORALIZING
MORTALIZED
MOTORIZING
MUTUALIZED
NARCOTIZED
NEBULIZING
NORMALIZED
NOTORHIZAL
OSTRACIZED
PAEANIZING
PALLETIZED
PARALOGIZE
PASSEMEZZO
PATRONIZED
PENALIZING
PETROLIZED
PLAGIARIZE
PLATINIZED
PLURALIZED
POLARIZING
POSTURIZED
POULARDIZE
POZZOLANIC
PROLOGUIZE
PUZZLEMENT
PUZZLEPATE
RADICALIZE
RECOGNIZEE
RECOGNIZER
RECOGNIZOR
REVALORIZE
REVITALIZE
RHIZONEURE
SCANDALIZE
SERMONIZED
SEVERALIZE
SILICIDIZE
SIZZLINGLY
SNEEZEWORT
SOCIALIZED
SOLECIZING
SOLEMNIZED
SPOROZOOID
STABILIZED
STIGMATIZE
SUBERIZING
SUBSIDIZER

SUBTILIZED
SUZERAINTY
SYNTONIZER
TETRAZOLYL
THIAZOLINE
TRIVIALIZE
TYRANNIZER
UNITEMIZED
URBANIZING
VENEZOLANO
VERSIONIZE
VETERANIZE
VISUALIZER
VITRIOLIZE
VOLATILIZE
WARRANTIZE
WESTERNIZE
WOOLLENIZE
ZABAGLIONE
ZINGARESCA
ZINGIBEROL
ZONIFEROUS
ZOOLOGICAL
ZWITTERION

21
ACTINOZOAL
ACTINOZOAN
AIZOACEOUS
ALCALIZATE
ALDOLIZING
ANALOGIZED
ANATOMIZER
ANGELIZING
APOSTATIZE
APOSTOLIZE
AROMATIZER
ARSENICIZE
ASSIZEMENT
ATROPINIZE
AUTOMATIZE
AUTONOMIZE
AUTOTOMIZE
AZOPROTEIN
AZOTOMETER
BERZELIITE
BESTIALIZE
BIZARRERIE
BRAZENNESS
BRAZILETTE
BREEZINESS
BRONZITITE
BURNETTIZE
CALZONERAS
CANONIZANT
CENTRALIZE
CITIZENESS
CUTIZATION
DASTARDIZE
DELEGALIZE
DEODORIZER
DIGITALIZE
ELASTICIZE
ELECTRIZER
EMOTIONIZE
ENERGIZING
ENGRANDIZE
ENOLIZABLE
EPISTOLIZE
ERGOTIZING
EULOGIZING
FRIZZINESS
GOLANDAUZE
GOLUNDAUZE
GRANGERIZE
IDEALIZING
INGRANDIZE

LATIBULIZE
LEGALIZING
LIBERALIZE
LIONIZABLE
MALLEINIZE
MANZANILLA
MANZANILLO
MARTIALIZE
MELEZITASE
MELEZITOSE
MILITARIZE
MILLIONIZE
MINERALIZE
MONOTONIZE
NEBULARIZE
NEOLOGIZED
NICOTINIZE
NONCITIZEN
NORMALIZER
OBITUARIZE
ORGANIZING
ORGANZINED
ORIGANIZED
OSTRACIZER
OZONOMETER
PALATALIZE
PARASITIZE
PARENESIZE
PASTEURIZE
PATRONIZER
PATTERNIZE
PEASANTIZE
PLURALIZER
PREDAZZITE
PRESSURIZE
RAZORSTROP
REALIZABLE
REMONETIZE
SAPIENTIZE
SCRUTINIZE
SECTIONIZE
SECULARIZE
SEMINARIZE
SERMONIZER
SERPENTIZE
SIGNALIZED
SILICONIZE
SOCIALIZER
SOLEMNIZER
SOLUBILIZE
SPATIALIZE
SPIRANTIZE
SPOROZOITE
STABILIZER
STANZAICAL
STARGAZING
SUBERINIZE
SUBTILIZER
TABULARIZE
TENDERIZED
TENOTOMIZE
TEPONAZTLI
TOPAZOLITE
TRACTORIZE
TRAUMATIZE
UNCANONIZE
UNDERGLAZE
UNDERSIZED
UTILIZABLE
ZEALOTICAL
ZEBRINNIES
ZEUGLODONT
ZOOCULTURE
ZOOCURRENT
ZOOMELANIN
ZOOSPOROUS

20

ADRENALIZE
ADULTERIZE
AGLAOZONIA
ALLEGORIZE
ANGULARIZE
ANTAGONIZE
ASTATIZING
AZOBENZENE
AZOGALLEIN
CITIZENIZE
DENATURIZE
DENIZATION
DERESINIZE
DIAZOTIZED
DISASINIZE
DISREALIZE
DISSEIZURE
DOUZAINIER
ESTERIZING

ETERNIZING
GELATINIZE
GENERALIZE
GLOTTALIZE
GLUTTONIZE
IDOLATRIZE
ILLEGALIZE
INTERMEZZI
INTERMEZZO
IODIZATION
LINGUALIZE
LIZARDTAIL
MEZZOTINTO
MOZZARELLA
NASALIZING
NOTARIZING
ONTOLOGIZE
POZZUOLANA
REDISSEIZE

REGULARIZE
REORGANIZE
ROUTINIZED
RURALIZING
SATIRIZING
SELTZOGENE
SENSITIZED
SERIALIZED
SLENDERIZE
SOLARIZING
SOLIDARIZE
STERILIZED
STRATEGIZE
TARTARIZED
TELLURIZED
TENDERIZER
TERRORIZED
TETANIZING
TOTALIZING

TRIOZONIDE
TRITOZOOID
UNIONIZING
UNREALIZED
URALITIZED
ZOOLOGIZED

19

ANAZOTURIA
AZOTENESIS
AZOTOLUENE
DENIZENIZE
DEOZONIZER
ETERNALIZE
GRIZZLIEST
INTERZONAL
IONIZATION
IOTIZATION
LATERALIZE

LAZARETTOS
LITERALIZE
NANIZATION
NATURALIZE
NESSLERIZE
NEUTRALIZE
SENSITIZER
SENSUALIZE
SLEAZINESS
STERILIZER
TANTALIZER
TARLTONIZE
TARTRAZINE
TAUTOZONAL
TERRORIZER
UGRIANIZE
ZEOLITIZED
ZOOLATRIES
ZOOLATROUS

ALPHABETICAL LIST OF WORDS OVER 10 LETTERS

ABASTARDIZE
ABNORMALIZE
ABOLITIONIZE
ACADEMIZING
ACCLIMATIZE
ACCLIMATIZED
ACCLIMATIZER
ACCLIMATIZING
ACCULTURIZE
ACCUSTOMIZE
ACCUSTOMIZED
ACCUSTOMIZING
ACETOBENZOIC
ACETONIZATION
ACETYLIZABLE
ACETYLIZATION
ACHROMATIZE
ACHROMATIZED
ACTIONIZING
ACTUALIZATION
ACTUALIZING
ADENIZATION
ADVERBIALIZE
ADVERTIZEMENT
ADVERTIZING
AESTHETICIZE
AGGUTINIZE
AGGRANDIZED
AGGRANDIZER
AGGRANDIZING
AGRARIANIZE
ALBITIZATION
ALBUMENIZED
ALBUMENIZER
ALBUMENIZING
ALBUMINIZED
ALBUMINIZING
ALCHEMIZING
ALCOHOLIZED
ALCOHOLIZING
ALDOLIZATION
ALGEBRAIZED
ALGEBRIZATION
ALGEBRAIZING
ALKALINIZED
ALKALINIZING

ALKALIZABLE
ALKALIZATION
ALLEGORIZED
ALLEGORIZER
ALLEGORIZING
ALLOTROPIZE
ALPHABETIZE
ALPHABETIZED
ALPHABETIZER
ALPHABETIZING
ALUMINIZING
AMMONIZATION
AMORTIZABLE
AMORTIZATION
AMORTIZEMENT
ANABAPTIZED
ANABAPTIZING
ANACEPHALIZE
ANACHRONIZE
ANAESTHETIZE
ANAESTHETIZED
ANAESTHETIZER
ANALOGIZING
ANALYZATION
ANATHEMATIZE
ANATOMIZING
ANESTHETIZE
ANESTHETIZER
ANGIOSTOMIZE
ANGLICIZING
ANHYDRIDIZE
ANIMALIZATION
ANIMALIZING
ANTAGONIZED
ANTAGONIZER
ANTAGONIZING
ANTHEROZOID
ANTHEROZOOID
ANTHOLOGIZE
ANTHOLOGIZED
ANTHOLOGIZING
ANTHROPOZOIC
ANTIFREEZING
ANTIPATHIZE
ANTISEPTICIZE
ANTITHESIZE

APAESTHETIZE
APESTHETIZE
APOLOGIZING
APOSTATIZED
APOSTATIZING
APOSTROPHIZE
APOTHEOSIZE
APOTHEOSIZED
APPETIZINGLY
APPRIZEMENT
ARBORIZATION
ARCTICIZING
ARITHMETIZE
AROMATIZING
ARSENIZATION
ARTERIALIZE
ARTERIALIZED
ASBESTINIZE
ASCIDIOZOOID
ASEPTICIZED
ASEPTICIZING
ASEXUALIZED
ASEXUALIZING
ASPHETERIZE
ASTIGMATIZER
ASTROLOGIZE
ASTRONOMIZE
ATMOLYZATION
ATOMIZATION
ATTITUDINIZE
AUTHORIZATION
AUTHORIZING
AUTOCATALYZE
AZADIRACHTA
AZEOTROPISM
AZIMETHYLENE
AZIMUTHALLY
AZOCOCHINEAL
AZOCORALLINE
AZODIPHENYL
AZOERYTHRIN
AZOFICATION
AZOOSPERMIA
AZOPARAFFIN
AZOPHENETOLE
AZOPHENYLENE

AZOPHOSPHIN
AZOPHOSPHORE
AZOSULPHINE
AZOSULPHONIC
AZOTETRAZOLE
AZOTHIONIUM
AZOTOBACTER
AZOTORRHOEA
AZYGOMATOUS
BACCHANALIZE
BACHELORIZE
BACTERIOLYZE
BACTERIZING
BALKANIZING
BAMBOOZLEMENT
BAMBOOZLING
BAPTIZEMENT
BARBARIZING
BASTARDIZED
BASTARDIZING
BATTOLOGIZE
BEDAZZLINGLY
BEDIZENMENT
BENZALDEHYDE
BENZALDOXIME
BENZINDULINE
BENZOHYDROL
BENZOINATED
BENZONITRILE
BENZONITROL
BENZOPHENONE
BENZOYLATION
BENZYLAMINE
BERGINIZATION
BERZELIANITE
BESSEMERIZE
BESSEMERIZED
BESSEMERIZING
BESTIALIZED
BESTIALIZING
BILHARZIASIS
BILHARZIOSIS
BIOGRAPHIZE
BISTETRAZOLE
BISTRIAZOLE
BITUMINIZED

BIVOCALIZED
BIZARRENESS
BIZYGOMATIC
BLIZZARDOUS
BOLSHEVIZED
BOLSHEVIZING
BOWDLERIZED
BOWDLERIZING
BRAZENFACED
BROMIZATION
BROMOBENZENE
BROMOIODIZED
BRONZESMITH
BRUTALIZING
BURGLARIZED
BURGLARIZING
BURKUNDAUZE
BURNETTIZED
BURNETTIZING
BURTONIZATION
BUZZERPHONE
CACOPHONIZE
CACOZEALOUS
CALABAZILLA
CANALIZATION
CANNIBALIZE
CANNIBALIZED
CANNIBALIZING
CANONIZATION
CANTHARIDIZE
CAPERCAILZIE
CAPITALIZED
CAPITALIZING
CARAMELIZED
CARAMELIZING
CARBOAZOTINE
CARBOLIZING
CARBONIZING
CARBURIZING
CARNALIZING
CATABIBAZON
CATABOLIZED
CATABOLIZING
CATALEPTIZE
CATALOGUIZE
CATALYZATOR

CATECHIZATION
CATECHIZING
CATEGORIZED
CATEGORIZING
CATHARIZING
CATHETERIZE
CATHETERIZED
CATHOLICIZE
CATHOLICIZED
CATHOLICIZING
CAUSTICIZED
CAUSTICIZER
CAUSTICIZING
CAUTERIZATION
CAUTERIZING
CELESTIALIZE
CELESTIALIZED
CENOZOOLOGY
CENTRALIZED
CENTRALIZER
CENTRALIZING
CHALAZOGAMIC
CHALAZOGAMY
CHALAZOIDITE
CHAMELEONIZE
CHAMPAGNIZE
CHAMPAGNIZED
CHAMPAGNIZING
CHANNELIZED
CHANNELIZING
CHARACTERIZE
CHARACTERIZED
CHARACTERIZER
CHEERFULIZE
CHEMICALIZE
CHITINIZATION
CHLAMYDOZOAN
CHLORALIZED
CHLORALIZING
CHLORIDIZED
CHLORIDIZING
CHLORODIZED
CHLORODIZING
CHORIAMBIZE
CHORIZATION
CHORIZONTES
CHORIZONTIC
CHORIZONTIST
CHROMICIZING
CHRONOLOGIZE
CHRONOLOGIZED
CICATRIZANT
CICATRIZATE
CICATRIZING
CINCHONIZED
CINCHONIZING
CIRCULARIZE
CIRCULARIZED
CIRCULARIZING
CITIZENIZED
CITIZENIZING
CITIZENRIES
CITIZENSHIP
CIVILIZABLE
CIVILIZATION
CIVILIZATORY
CLASSICIZED
CLASSICIZING
COAZERVATION
COCAINIZING
COLLECTIVIZE
COLLECTIVIZED
COLLODIONIZE
COLLOQUIZED
COLLOQUIZING
COLONIZATION
COMMEMORIZE

COMMEMORIZED
COMMEMORIZING
COMMERCIALIZE
COMMUNALIZE
COMMUNALIZED
COMMUNALIZER
COMMUNIZATION
COMMUNIZING
COMPANIONIZE
COMPANIONIZED
CONCERTIZED
CONCERTIZER
CONCERTIZING
CONCRETIZED
CONCRETIZING
CONSERVATIZE
CONSONANTIZE
CONTEMPORIZE
CONTEMPORIZED
COPOLYMERIZE
COPOLYMERIZED
COPPERIZATION
CORPOREALIZE
COSMOGONIZE
CREOLIZATION
CRITICIZABLE
CRITICIZING
CRYPTOZONATE
CRYPTOZYGOUS
CRYSTALLIZE
CRYSTALLIZED
CRYSTALLIZER
CRYSTALLIZING
CURARIZATION
CUTICULARIZE
CUTINIZATION
CYCLIZATION
DACTYLOZOOID
DAMENIZATION
DEBENZOLIZE
DECAFFEINIZE
DECARBONIZE
DECARBONIZED
DECARBONIZER
DECARBURIZE
DECARBURIZED
DECENTRALIZE
DECEREBRIZE
DECHORALIZE
DECICERONIZE
DECIMALIZED
DECIMALIZING
DECOLORIZED
DECOLORIZER
DECOLORIZING
DECOLOURIZE
DEEPFREEZED
DEEPFREEZING
DEFERRIZING
DEFIBRINIZE
DEFINITIZED
DEFINITIZING
DEHUMANIZED
DEHUMANIZING
DEHYPNOTIZE
DEHYPNOTIZED
DEJUNKERIZE
DELIMITIZED
DELIMITIZING
DELOCALIZED
DELOCALIZING
DEMAGNETIZE
DEMAGNETIZED
DEMAGNETIZER
DEMANGANIZE
DEMENTHOLIZE
DEMEPHITIZE

DEMICIVILIZED
DEMILITARIZE
DEMILITARIZED
DEMINERALIZE
DEMOBILIZED
DEMOBILIZING
DEMOCRATIZE
DEMOCRATIZED
DEMONETIZED
DEMONETIZING
DEMORALIZED
DEMORALIZER
DEMORALIZING
DEMUTIZATION
DENATURALIZE
DENATURIZER
DENAZIFYING
DENICOTINIZE
DENIZENATION
DEODORIZING
DEOXIDIZING
DEOXYGENIZE
DEPAUPERIZE
DEPAUPERIZED
DEPERSONIZE
DEPIGMENTIZE
DEPOLARIZED
DEPOLARIZER
DEPOLARIZING
DEPOLYMERIZE
DERACIALIZE
DERATIZATION
DERMATOZOON
DESACRALIZE
DESCLOIZITE
DESENSITIZE
DESENSITIZER
DESEXUALIZE
DESEXUALIZED
DESILICONIZE
DESILVERIZE
DESILVERIZER
DESTERILIZE
DESTINEZITE
DESULFURIZE
DESULFURIZED
DESULFURIZER
DESULPHURIZE
DESYNONYMIZE
DETRIBALIZE
DEUTEROZOOID
DEVITALIZED
DEVITALIZING
DEVITAMINIZE
DEVOCALIZED
DEVOCALIZING
DEVULGARIZE
DEXTROSAZONE
DEZINCATION
DEZINCIFIED
DEZINCIFYING
DIABOLIZING
DIAGONALIZE
DIALECTALIZE
DIALECTICIZE
DIALOGIZING
DIALYZATION
DIAMONDIZED
DIAMONDIZING
DIAZENTITHAL
DIAZOBENZENE
DIAZOMETHANE
DIAZOTIZING
DICHOTOMIZE
DICHOTOMIZED
DIEZEUGMENON
DIMERIZATION

DIPHTHONGIZE
DIPHTHONGIZED
DIPHYOZOOID
DIPLOMATIZE
DIPLOMATIZED
DISCANONIZE
DISCANONIZED
DISEQUALIZE
DISGOSPELIZE
DISHARMONIZE
DISORGANIZE
DISORGANIZED
DISORGANIZER
DISPAUPERIZE
DISSEIZORESS
DISSOCIALIZE
DISSYLLABIZE
DIVINIZATION
DOCKIZATION
DOCTRINIZED
DOCTRINIZING
DOCUMENTIZE
DOGGERELIZE
DOGGERELIZED
DOGGERELIZING
DOGMATIZING
DOMESTICIZE
DOMESTICIZED
DOXOLOGIZED
DOXOLOGIZING
DRAMATIZATION
DRAMATIZING
DUALIZATION
DUCTILIZING
DYNAMIZATION
ECONOMIZATION
ECONOMIZING
ECZEMATOSIS
EDITORIALIZE
EDITORIALIZED
EFFECTUALIZE
EFFEMINATIZE
EFFEMINIZED
EFFEMINIZING
ELASTICIZER
ELECTRALIZE
ELECTRICALIZE
ELECTRICIZE
ELECTRIZING
ELECTROLYZE
ELECTROLYZED
ELECTROLYZER
ELECTROLYZING
ELECTROTONIZE
EMBEZZLEMENT
EMBLEMATICIZE
EMBLEMATIZE
EMBLEMATIZED
EMBLEMATIZING
EMBLEMIZING
EMOTIONALIZE
EMOTIONALIZED
EMPATHIZING
EMPHASIZING
EMULSIONIZE
ENCARNALIZE
ENCARNALIZED
ENCARNALIZING
ENCYCLOPEDIZE
ENHYPOSTATIZE
ENIGMATIZED
ENIGMATIZING
ENOLIZATION
ENSORCELIZE
ENSORCERIZE
ENTHRONIZED
ENTHRONIZING

ENTOMOLOGIZE
ENTOMOLOGIZED
ENTOZOOLOGY
ENZYMICALLY
ENZYMOLYSIS
ENZYMOLYTIC
EPENTHESIZE
EPIDOTIZATION
EPIGRAMMATIZE
EPILOGIZING
EPISCOPIZED
EPISCOPIZING
EPISTOLIZABLE
EPITHALAMIZE
EPITOMIZATION
EPITOMIZING
EPIZOOTIOLOGY
EQUALIZATION
EQUILIBRIZE
ERGOTIZATION
ERYTHROZYME
ESTERIZATION
ETERNIZATION
ETHEREALIZE
ETHEREALIZED
ETHEREALIZING
ETHERIZATION
ETHNOZOOLOGY
ETYMOLOGIZE
ETYMOLOGIZED
ETYMOLOGIZING
EUCHARISTIZE
EUCHARISTIZED
EUDAEMONIZE
EUHEMERIZED
EUHEMERIZING
EULOGIZATION
EUPHEMIZING
EUPHONIZING
EVANGELIZED
EVANGELIZER
EVANGELIZING
EVENTUALIZE
EVOLUTIONIZE
EXAUTHORIZE
EXCURSIONIZE
EXORCIZATION
EXORCIZEMENT
EXOSTRACIZE
EXPERIMENTIZE
EXPERMENTIZED
EXTEMPORIZE
EXTEMPORIZED
EXTEMPORIZER
EXTEMPORIZING
EXTERIORIZE
EXTERIORIZED
EXTERIORIZING
EXTERNALIZE
EXTERNIZATION
EXTRAVAGANZA
FACSIMILIZE
FACTORIZATION
FACTORIZING
FAMILIARIZE
FAMILIARIZED
FAMILIARIZER
FAMILIARIZING
FANATICIZED
FANATICIZING
FANTASIZING
FARADIZATION
FASCISTICIZE
FEDERALIZED
FEDERALIZING
FEMINIZATION
FERTILIZABLE

FERTILIZATION	HIERARCHIZE	KYANIZATION	MERORGANIZE	NAPHTHALIZE
FERTILIZING	HOMOGENIZER	LABIALIZING	MESMERIZATION	NARCOTIZING
FEUDALIZATION	HOPPERDOZER	LABILIZATION	MESMERIZING	NASALIZATION
FEUDALIZING	HORIZOMETER	LAICIZATION	METABOLIZED	NATIONALIZE
FICTIONALIZED	HORIZONTALITY	LALAPALOOZA	METABOLIZING	NATIONALIZED
FICTIONIZED	HORIZONTALIZE	LALLAPALOOZA	METALIZATION	NATIONALIZER
FICTIONIZING	HORIZONTALLY	LAPAROTOMIZE	METALLIZATION	NATIONALIZING
FISCALIZATION	HORIZONTICAL	LATERALIZED	METAMERIZED	NATURALIZED
FISCALIZING	HOSPITALIZE	LATERALIZING	METAMORPHIZE	NATURALIZER
FLAMBOYANTIZE	HURRICANIZE	LATERIZATION	METAPHONIZE	NATURALIZING
FLUIDIZATION	HYBRIDIZABLE	LEGALIZATION	METASTASIZE	NAZIFICATION
FOCALIZATION	HYBRIDIZATION	LEGITIMATIZE	METASTASIZED	NEBULIZATION
FORMALIZATION	HYDROBENZOIN	LEGITIMATIZED	METHODIZING	NEMATOZOOID
FORMALIZING	HYDROGENIZE	LEGITIMIZED	MEZZOTINTED	NEOLOGIZING
FORMULARIZE	HYDROLYZATE	LEGITIMIZING	MEZZOTINTER	NEOPAGANIZE
FORMULARIZED	HYDRORHIZAL	LETHARGIZED	MEZZOTINTING	NESSLERIZED
FORMULARIZING	HYDROZINCITE	LETHARGIZING	MICASIZATION	NEUROLOGIZE
FORMULIZATION	HYPERBOLIZE	LIBERALIZED	MICROSCOPIZE	NEUROTOMIZE
FORMULIZING	HYPERBOLIZED	LIBERALIZER	MICROZOARIA	NEUTRALIZED
FOSSILIZATION	HYPOSTATIZE	LIBERALIZING	MICROZOARIAN	NEUTRALIZER
FOSSILIZING	ICHTHYIZATION	LICHENIZATION	MICROZYMIAN	NEUTRALIZING
FRACTIONALIZE	IDEALIZATION	LIEDERKRANZ	MIGNIARDIZE	NEWSMAGAZINE
FRACTIONIZE	IDOLATRIZED	LINEARIZATION	MILITARIZED	NIGHTINGALIZE
FRACTIONIZING	IDOLATRIZER	LIONIZATION	MILITARIZING	NITRIDIZATION
FRATERNIZED	IDOLATRIZING	LIQUIDIZING	MINERALIZED	NITROBENZENE
FRATERNIZER	IDOLIZATION	LITERALIZED	MINERALIZER	NITROGENIZE
FRATERNIZING	ILLEGALIZED	LITERALIZER	MINERALIZING	NITROGENIZED
FRICTIONIZE	ILLEGALIZING	LITERALIZING	MINERALOGIZE	NITROGENIZING
FRICTIONIZED	IMBASTARDIZE	LITHOTOMIZE	MINIATURIZE	NIVELLIZATION
FRICTIONIZING	IMMATERIALIZE	LOCALIZABLE	MINIATURIZED	NODULIZING
FRIVOLIZING	IMMETHODIZE	LOCALIZATION	MINIMIZATION	NONENTITIZE
FUNCTIONIZE	IMMOBILIZED	LOGOMACHIZE	MISCOGNIZANT	NONPARTIZAN
FUROMONAZOLE	IMMOBILIZING	LORENZENITE	MISEMPHASIZE	NORMALIZATION
GABERLUNZIE	IMMORTALIZE	MACADAMIZED	MISSIONARIZE	NORMALIZING
GALVANIZATION	IMMORTALIZED	MACADAMIZER	MISSIONIZER	NOTARIZATION
GALVANIZING	IMMORTALIZING	MACADAMIZING	MITHRIDATIZE	NOVELIZATION
GASTEROZOOID	IMPACTIONIZE	MAGAZINABLE	MIZZENTOPMAN	NUPTIALIZE
GASTROZOOID	IMPATRONIZE	MAGNETIZABLE	MIZZENTOPMEN	OBJECTIVIZE
GAZETTEERAGE	IMPERIALIZE	MAGNETIZATION	MNEMONIZING	OBJECTIVIZED
GAZINGSTOCK	IMPERIALIZED	MAGNETIZING	MOBILIZATION	OBJECTIVIZING
GELATINIZED	IMPERIALIZING	MALLEABLEIZE	MODERNIZATION	OBJECTIZATION
GELATINIZER	IMPERSONALIZE	MALLEABLEIZED	MODERNIZING	OBJECTIZING
GELATINIZING	IMPROBABILIZE	MALLEABLIZE	MONARCHIZED	OBLIVIONIZE
GENEALOGIZE	INDIVIDUALIZE	MAMMONIZATION	MONARCHIZER	ODYLIZATION
GENEALOGIZER	INDOCTRINIZE	MANORIALIZE	MONARCHIZING	OFFICIALIZE
GENERALIZABLE	INFORMALIZE	MARBLEIZING	MONETIZATION	OLIGARCHIZE
GENERALIZED	INOXIDIZING	MARGINALIZE	MONOCHORDIZE	OLIGORHIZOUS
GENERALIZER	INTELLIGIZE	MARMARIZING	MONOLOGIZED	OPSONIZATION
GEOGRAPHIZE	INTERMEZZOS	MARSUPIALIZE	MONOLOGIZING	OPTIMIZATION
GEOGRAPHIZED	INTERNALIZE	MARTYRIZING	MONOPOLIZED	OPTIMIZING
GEOLOGIZING	IODOBENZENE	MATERIALIZE	MONOPOLIZER	OPTIONALIZE
GEOMETRICIZE	IRIDIZATION	MATERIALIZED	MONOPOLIZING	ORGANIZABLE
GEOMETRIZED	IRREALIZABLE	MATERIALIZER	MONOZYGOTIC	ORGANIZATION
GEOMETRIZING	IRREGULARIZE	MATERIALIZING	MONZODIORITE	ORGANIZATORY
GLAMORIZING	ISOCHRONIZE	MATERNALIZE	MONZOGABBRO	ORGANZINING
GLUCOSAZONE	ISOCHRONIZED	MATHEMATIZE	MORALIZATION	ORIENTALIZE
GLUTTONIZED	ISOCHRONIZING	MATRONIZING	MORTALIZING	ORIENTALIZED
GLUTTONIZING	ITALICIZING	MAXIMIZATION	MOTORIZATION	ORIENTALIZING
GLYCERINIZE	ITEMIZATION	MECHANALIZE	MUNICIPALIZE	ORYZIVOROUS
GLYCYRRHIZIN	JARGONIZING	MECHANIZATION	MUNICIPALIZED	OSMAZOMATIC
GORMANDIZER	JAROVIZATION	MEDIATIZING	MUSCOVITIZE	OSMAZOMATOUS
GRAMMATICIZE	JASPERIZING	MEGAZOOSPORE	MUSCOVITIZED	OSTRACIZATION
GRANULITIZE	JATEORHIZIN	MEIZOSEISMAL	MUSCULARIZE	OSTRACIZING
GRAPHITIZED	JATEORHIZINE	MEIZOSEISMIC	MUTUALIZING	OUTTYRANNIZE
GUTTURALIZE	JEOPARDIZED	MELANCHOLIZE	MUZZLELOADER	OVALIZATION
GUTTURALIZING	JEOPARDIZING	MELODRAMATIZE	MUZZLELOADING	OVARIOTOMIZE
GYNECOMAZIA	JOURNALIZED	MEMORANDIZE	MYCORRHIZAL	OVERGLAZING
GYROHORIZON	JOURNALIZER	MEMORIALIZE	MYCORRHIZIC	OVERPRIZING
HAPHAZARDLY	JOURNALIZING	MEMORIALIZED	MYOSYNIZESIS	OVERZEALOUS
HAPHAZARDNESS	JOVIALIZING	MEMORIALIZER	MYTHICIZING	OXYGENIZABLE
HARLEQUINIZE	JUBILIZATION	MEMORIALIZING	MYTHOLOGIZE	OXYGENIZING
HARMONIZING	JUDICIALIZE	MEMORIZATION	MYTHOLOGIZED	OZONIFEROUS
HARZBURGITE	KATZENJAMMER	MERCERIZING	MYTHOLOGIZER	OZONIZATION
HAZARDOUSLY	KETONIZATION	MERCHANDIZE	MYTHOLOGIZING	OZONOSCOPIC
HAZARDOUSNESS	KJELDAHLIZE	MERCURIALIZE	MYTHOPOETIZE	OZONOSPHERE
HETEROZYGOTE		MERCURIZING	MYZOSTOMIDAN	OZONOSPHERIC
HETEROZYGOUS		MERMITHIZED	MYZOSTOMOUS	PAGANIZATION

PALATIZATION	PLURALIZING	RECAPITALIZE	SCHIZOGENIC	SOLITUDINIZE
PALEOZOOLOGY	PNEUMATIZED	RECAPITALIZED	SCHIZOGENOUS	SOLITUDINIZED
PALLADIUMIZE	POETIZATION	RECARBONIZE	SCHIZOGNATH	SOLMIZATION
PALLETIZING	POLARIZABLE	RECARBONIZER	SCHIZOGONIC	SOLVOLYZING
PAMPHLETIZE	POLARIZATION	RECARBURIZE	SCHIZOIDISM	SOMNAMBULIZE
PANCREATIZE	POLITICALIZE	RECARBURIZER	SCHIZOMYCETE	SOPHRONIZED
PANEGYRICIZE	POLITICIZED	RECIPROCALIZE	SCHIZOMYCETES	SOPHRONIZING
PANEGYRIZED	POLITICIZER	RECOGNIZABLE	SCHIZOPELMOUS	SOUTHERNIZE
PANEGYRIZER	POLITICIZING	RECOGNIZABLY	SCHIZOPHASIA	SOVEREIGNIZE
PANEGYRIZING	POLITZERIZE	RECOGNIZANCE	SCHIZOPHRENE	SOVIETIZATION
PANSEXUALIZE	POLYCHROMIZE	RECOGNIZANT	SCHIZOPHRENIA	SOVIETIZING
PANTHEONIZE	POLYZOARIAL	RECOGNIZING	SCHIZOPHYTE	SPECIALIZED
PAPALIZATION	POLYZOARIUM	RECRYSTALLIZE	SCHIZOPODAL	SPECIALIZER
PARABOLIZED	POPULARIZED	REFORESTIZE	SCHIZOPODOUS	SPECIALIZING
PARABOLIZER	POPULARIZER	REGIONALIZE	SCHIZORHINAL	SPECIFICIZE
PARABOLIZING	POPULARIZING	REGULARIZED	SCHIZOSPORE	SPECIMENIZE
PARAENESIZE	PORCELAINIZE	REGULARIZER	SCHIZOSTELE	SPECIMENIZED
PARALYZATION	PORCELLANIZE	REHARMONIZE	SCHIZOSTELIC	SPERMATOZOA
PARCHMENTIZE	POSTURIZING	RELIGIONIZE	SCHIZOSTELY	SPERMATOZOAL
PARENTHESIZE	POTENTIALIZE	REORGANIZED	SCHIZOTHECAL	SPERMATOZOAN
PASTEURIZED	POZZUOLANIC	REORGANIZER	SCHIZOTHYME	SPERMATOZOIC
PASTEURIZER	PRACTICALIZE	REORGANIZING	SCHIZOTHYMIA	SPERMATOZOID
PASTEURIZING	PRACTICALIZED	RESTERILIZE	SCHIZOTHYMIC	SPERMATOZOON
PASTORALIZE	PRAGMATIZER	REVITALIZED	SCHIZOTRICHIA	SPHEROIDIZE
PATERNALIZE	PREACHERIZE	REVITALIZER	SCLEROTIZED	SPHERULITIZE
PATRIZATION	PRESERVATIZE	REVITALIZING	SCRUTINIZED	SPIRALIZATION
PATRONIZING	PRESSURIZED	RHAPSODIZED	SCRUTINIZER	SPIRITUALIZE
PAUPERIZING	PRESSURIZING	RHAPSODIZING	SCRUTINIZING	SPIRITUALIZED
PECTIZATION	PRIZEFIGHTER	RHIZANTHOUS	SECTARIANIZE	SPIRITUALIZER
PECULIARIZE	PRIZEHOLDER	RHIZOCARPIC	SECTARIANIZED	SPITZENBERG
PECULIARIZED	PROBABILIZE	RHIZOCARPOUS	SECTIONALIZE	SPITZENBURG
PELORIZATION	PROBLEMATIZE	RHIZOCAULUS	SECTIONALIZED	SPLENIZATION
PEMMICANIZE	PRODIGALIZE	RHIZODERMIS	SECULARIZED	SPONDYLIZEMA
PENALIZATION	PROLETARIZE	RHIZOGENETIC	SECULARIZING	SQUEEZINGLY
PENTAMETRIZE	PROLOGUIZER	RHIZOGENOUS	SEMICIVILIZED	STABILIZATION
PEPTIZATION	PROPAGANDIZE	RHIZOMATOUS	SEMPITERNIZE	STABILIZATOR
PEPTONIZING	PROSELYTIZE	RHIZOMORPHIC	SENSIBILIZE	STABILIZING
PERFECTIVIZE	PROSELYTIZED	RHIZOPHAGOUS	SENSITIZATION	STALLIONIZE
PERMORALIZE	PROSELYTIZER	RHIZOPHILOUS	SENSITIZING	STALWARTIZE
PERSONALIZE	PROTOCITIZEN	RHIZOPODIST	SENSUALIZED	STANDARDIZE
PERSONALIZED	PROTOCOLIZE	RHIZOPODOUS	SENSUALIZING	STANDARDIZED
PETROLIZING	PROTOXIDIZE	RHIZOSTOMOUS	SEPTICIZATION	STANDARDIZER
PEZIZACEOUS	PROTOXIDIZED	RHYTHMICIZE	SERIALIZATION	STANDARDIZING
PEZIZAEFORM	PROTOZOEAN	RHYTHMIZABLE	SERIALIZING	STANZAICALLY
PHAGOCYTIZE	PROTOZOIASIS	RINFORZANDO	SERMONIZING	STATISTICIZE
PHANEROZOIC	PROTOZOONAL	ROBOTIZATION	SERPENTINIZE	STERILIZATION
PHANTOMIZER	PSYCHIATRIZE	ROENTGENIZE	SHERARDIZED	STERILIZING
PHENMIAZINE	PSYCHOLOGIZE	ROMANTICIZE	SHERARDIZING	STIGMATIZED
PHENOXAZINE	PUBLICIZING	ROTARIANIZE	SHERBETZIDE	STIGMATIZER
PHILIPPICIZE	PULVERIZATE	ROUTINIZING	SIDEREALIZE	STIGMATIZING
PHILIPPIZER	PULVERIZATOR	ROYALIZATION	SIGNALIZING	STRUCTURALIZE
PHILOLOGIZE	PULVERIZING	RUBBERIZING	SIMULACRIZE	STRYCHNINIZE
PHILOSOPHIZE	PUZZLEATION	RURALIZATION	SINGULARIZE	STYLIZATION
PHILOZOONIST	PUZZLEDNESS	SACCHARIZED	SINGULARIZED	SUBERIZATION
PHLEBOTOMIZE	PUZZLEHEADED	SACCHARIZING	SINGULARIZING	SUBSIDIZATION
PHLYZACIOUS	PUZZLEPATED	SACRAMENTIZE	SIPHONOZOOID	SUBSIDIZING
PHONETICIZE	PUZZLINGNESS	SAILORIZING	SIZABLENESS	SUBSTANTIVIZE
PHONETIZATION	PYRRODIAZOLE	SANCTUARIZE	SKELETONIZE	SUBSTANTIZE
PHOSPHATIZE	QUANTIZATION	SARCOPHAGIZE	SKELETONIZED	SUBTILIZATION
PHOSPHATIZED	QUIZZICALITY	SATIRIZABLE	SKELETONIZER	SUBTILIZING
PHOSPHORIZE	QUIZZICALLY	SCANDALIZED	SKELETONIZING	SUBURBANIZE
PHRENOLOGIZE	QUIZZACIOUS	SCANDALIZING	SKEPTICIZED	SUBVITALIZED
PHYLACTERIZE	QUIZZATORIAL	SCENARIZING	SKEPTICIZING	SULCALIZATION
PHYLLOZOOID	RACEMIZATION	SCEPTICIZED	SLENDERIZED	SULFADIAZINE
PHYSIOLOGIZE	RACIALIZATION	SCEPTICIZING	SLENDERIZING	SULFATIZING
PHYTOBEZOAR	RADIALIZATION	SCHILLERIZE	SLUGGARDIZE	SULFOBENZIDE
PICRORHIZIN	RADIUMIZATION	SCHILLERIZED	SOCIALIZATION	SULFOBENZOIC
PIEZOMETRIC	RANDOMIZING	SCHILLERIZING	SOCIALIZING	SULFURIZING
PLAGIARIZED	RATIONALIZE	SCHISMATIZE	SOLARIZATION	SULPHATIZED
PLAGIARIZER	RATIONALIZED	SCHISMATIZED	SOLEMNIZATION	SULPHATIZING
PLAGIARIZING	RATIONALIZER	SCHISMATIZING	SOLEMNIZING	SULPHAZOTIZE
PLASTICIZED	RAZORMAKING	SCHIZOCARPIC	SOLIDARIZED	SULPHOBENZID
PLASTICIZER	RAZZBERRIES	SCHIZOCARPY	SOLIDARIZING	SULPHURIZED
PLASTICIZING	REACTUALIZE	SCHIZOCHROAL	SOLILOQUIZE	SULPHURIZING
PLATINIZING	REALISTICIZE	SCHIZOCOELE	SOLILOQUIZED	SUMMARIZATION
PLEBEIANIZE	REALIZATION	SCHIZODINIC	SOLILOQUIZER	SUMMARIZING
PLEBEIANIZED	REBAPTIZATION	SCHIZOGENESIS	SOLILOQUIZING	SYCOPHANTIZE
		SCHIZOGENETIC		

SYLLABIZING	TEMPORALIZE	ULTRAZEALOUS	VERBALIZING	ZOOCECIDIUM
SYLLOGIZING	TEMPORIZING	UNAUTHORIZE	VERMILIONIZE	ZOOCULTURAL
SYMBOLIZATION	TENDERIZING	UNAUTHORIZED	VICTIMIZABLE	ZOODENDRIUM
SYMBOLIZING	TENEMENTIZE	UNBRUTALIZE	VICTIMIZATION	ZOODYNAMICS
SYMMETRIZED	TERRORIZING	UNCANONIZED	VICTIMIZING	ZOOERYTHRIN
SYMMETRIZING	TETANIZATION	UNCANONIZING	VISUALIZING	ZOOGEOGRAPHY
SYMPATHIZED	TETRAKISAZO	UNCIVILIZED	VITALIZATION	ZOOGONIDIUM
SYMPATHIZER	TETRAZOLIUM	UNFEUDALIZE	VITALIZINGLY	ZOOGRAFTING
SYMPATHIZING	TETRAZOTIZE	UNIFORMALIZE	VITRIOLIZED	ZOOLOGIZING
SYMPHONIZED	THEATRICIZE	UNIFORMALIZED	VITRIOLIZING	ZOOMAGNETIC
SYMPHONIZING	THEOLOGIZED	UNIONIZATION	VOCALIZATION	ZOOMAGNETISM
SYMPTOMATIZE	THEOLOGIZER	UNIVERSALIZED	VOLATILIZED	ZOOMORPHISM
SYNCHRONIZE	THEOLOGIZING	UNIVERSITIZE	VOLATILIZER	ZOOMORPHIZE
SYNCHRONIZED	THEOMORPHIZE	UNLITURGIZE	VOLATILIZING	ZOONOSOLOGY
SYNCHRONIZER	THEORIZATION	UNMECHANIZE	VOLCANIZING	ZOOPANTHEON
SYNCHRONIZING	THERMOLYZED	UNMODERNIZE	VULCANIZATE	ZOOPARASITE
SYNCRETIZED	THERMOLYZING	UNMORALIZED	VULCANIZATION	ZOOPATHOLOGY
SYNCRETIZING	THIADIAZOLE	UNMORALIZING	VULCANIZING	ZOOPHARMACY
SYNDICALIZE	TOBACCONIZE	UNMORTALIZE	VULGARIZATION	ZOOPHYSICAL
SYNONYMIZED	TOTALIZATION	UNNATURALIZE	VULGARIZING	ZOOPHYTICAL
SYNONYMIZING	TOTALIZATOR	UNNATURALIZE	WESTERNIZED	ZOOPHYTOLOGY
SYNTHESIZED	TOTEMIZATION	UNORGANIZED	WESTERNIZING	ZOOPLANKTON
SYNTHESIZER	TOURMALINIZE	UNPATRONIZED	WINTERIZING	ZOOPRAXISCOPE
SYNTHESIZING	TRAILBLAZER	UNPOPULARIZE	WIZENEDNESS	ZOOSPORANGE
SYNTHETIZER	TRAILBLAZING	UNRECOGNIZED	WOODCOCKIZE	ZOOTHEISTIC
SYNTONIZING	TRANQUILIZE	UNSECULARIZE	ZANTHOXYLUM	ZOOXANTHELLA
SYPHILIZING	TRANQUILIZER	UNSOLEMNIZE	ZAPHRENTOID	ZOSTERIFORM
SYSTEMATIZE	TRANQUILIZING	UNSTERILIZED	ZEALOUSNESS	ZYGAPOPHYSIS
SYSTEMATIZED	TRANQUILLIZE	UNVERBALIZED	ZENOCENTRIC	ZYGODACTYLE
SYSTEMATIZER	TRANQUILLIZED	UNVULGARIZE	ZENOGRAPHIC	ZYGODACTYLIC
SYSTEMATIZING	TRAPEZIFORM	URALITIZING	ZEOLITIZING	ZYGOLABIALIS
SYSTEMIZATION	TRAPEZOIDAL	URBANIZATION	ZIGZAGGEDLY	ZYGOMATICUM
SYSTEMIZING	TRICHINIZED	UTILIZATION	ZIMENTWATER	ZYGOMATICUS
SZAIBELYITE	TRICHINIZING	VACCINIZATION	ZINCIFEROUS	ZYGOMORPHIC
TABULARIZED	TRICHOTOMIZE	VAGABONDIZE	ZINCOGRAPHER	ZYGOMORPHOUS
TABULARIZING	TRILLIONIZE	VAGABONDIZED	ZINCOGRAPHIC	ZYGOMYCETES
TANTALIZING	TROPHOZOITE	VAGABONDIZER	ZINCOGRAPHY	ZYGOMYCETOUS
TARANTARIZE	TROPHOZOOID	VAGABONDIZING	ZINGIBERENE	ZYGOPHYCEOUS
TARTARIZING	TROPICALIZE	VALORIZATION	ZINNWALDITE	ZYGOPLEURAL
TARTRAZINIC	TROPICALIZED	VAPORIZATION	ZOANTHODEME	ZYGOPTERAN
TAUTOLOGIZE	TROPICALIZING	VAPOURIZING	ZOANTHODEMIC	ZYGOPTERID
TAUTOLOGIZED	TROPOLOGIZE	VASCULARIZE	ZODIOPHILOUS	ZYGOPTEROUS
TAUTOLOGIZER	TROPOLOGIZED	VASCULARIZED	ZOIDOGAMOUS	ZYGOSPHENAL
TAXIDERMIZE	TROPOLOGIZING	VASCULARIZING	ZOISITIZATION	ZYMOGENESIS
TCHERVONETZ	TRULLIZATION	VASECTOMIZE	ZOMOTHERAPY	ZYMOLOGICAL
TECHNICALIZE	TUBERCULIZE	VASSALIZING	ZONAESTHESIA	ZYMOPLASTIC
TEETOTUMIZE	TUBERIZATION	VEGETABLIZE	ZONESTHESIA	ZYMOSIMETER
TELEPATHIZE	TUBULIZATION	VENALIZATION	ZONOCHLORITE	ZYMOSTHENIC
TELFORDIZED	TUTORIZATION	VERATRINIZE	ZONOCILIATE	ZYMOTECHNIC
TELFORDIZING	TYPHIZATION	VERATRINIZED	ZONOLIMNETIC	ZYMOTECHNICS
TELLURIZING	TYRANNIZING	VERATRINIZING	ZONOSKELETON	ZYMOTICALLY
		VERATRIZING		

POSITIONAL ORDER LIST OF WORDS OVER 10 LETTERS

ZANTHOXYLUM	ZONAESTHESIA	ZOOPANTHEON	ZYGOMORPHOUS	AZIMETHYLENE
ZAPHRENTOID	ZONESTHESIA	ZOOPARASITE	ZYGOMYCETES	AZIMUTHALLY
ZEALOUSNESS	ZONOCHLORITE	ZOOPATHOLOGY	ZYGOMYCETOUS	AZOCOCHINEAL
ZENOCENTRIC	ZONOCILIATE	ZOOPHARMACY	ZYGOPHYCEOUS	AZOCORALLINE
ZENOGRAPHIC	ZONOLIMNETIC	ZOOPHYSICAL	ZYGOPLEURAL	AZODIPHENYL
ZEOLITIZING	ZONOSKELETON	ZOOPHYTICAL	ZYGOPTERAN	AZOERYTHRIN
ZIGZAGGEDLY	ZOOCECIDIUM	ZOOPHYTOLOGY	ZYGOPTERID	AZOFICATION
ZIMENTWATER	ZOOCULTURAL	ZOOPLANKTON	ZYGOPTEROUS	AZOOSPERMIA
ZINCIFEROUS	ZOODENDRIUM	ZOOPRAXISCOPE	ZYGOSPHENAL	AZOPARAFFIN
ZINCOGRAPHER	ZOODYNAMICS	ZOOSPORANGE	ZYMOGENESIS	AZOPHENETOLE
ZINCOGRAPHIC	ZOOERYTHRIN	ZOOTHEISTIC	ZYMOLOGICAL	AZOPHENYLENE
ZINCOGRAPHY	ZOOGEOGRAPHY	ZOOXANTHELLA	ZYMOPLASTIC	AZOPHOSPHIN
ZINGIBERENE	ZOOGONIDIUM	ZOSTERIFORM	ZYMOSIMETER	AZOPHOSPHORE
ZINNWALDITE	ZOOGRAFTING	ZYGAPOPHYSIS	ZYMOSTHENIC	AZOSULPHINE
ZOANTHODEME	ZOOLOGIZING	ZYGODACTYLE	ZYMOTECHNIC	AZOSULPHONIC
ZOANTHODEMIC	ZOOMAGNETIC	ZYGODACTYLIC	ZYMOTECHNICS	AZOTETRAZOLE
ZODIOPHILOUS	ZOOMAGNETISM	ZYGOLABIALIS	ZYMOTICALLY	AZOTHIONIUM
ZOIDOGAMOUS	ZOOMORPHISM	ZYGOMATICUM		AZOTOBACTER
ZOISITIZATION	ZOOMORPHIZE	ZYGOMATICUS	AZADIRACHTA	AZOTORRHOEA
ZOMOTHERAPY	ZOONOSOLOGY	ZYGOMORPHIC	AZEOTROPISM	AZYGOMATOUS

OZONIFEROUS
OZONIZATION
OZONOSCOPIC
OZONOSPHERE
OZONOSPHERIC
SZAIBELYITE

BIZARRENESS
BIZYGOMATIC
BUZZERPHONE
DEZINCATION
DEZINCIFIED
DEZINCIFYING
ECZEMATOSIS
ENZYMICALLY
ENZYMOLYSIS
ENZYMOLYTIC
GAZETTEERAGE
GAZINGSTOCK
HAZARDOUSLY
HAZARDOUSNESS
MEZZOTINTED
MEZZOTINTER
MEZZOTINTING
MIZZENTOPMAN
MIZZENTOPMEN
MUZZLELOADER
MUZZLELOADING
MYZOSTOMIDAN
MYZOSTOMOUS
NAZIFICATION
PEZIZACEOUS
PEZIZAEFORM
POZZUOLANIC
PUZZLEATION
PUZZLEDNESS
PUZZLEHEADED
PUZZLEPATED
PUZZLINGNESS
RAZORMAKING
RAZZBERRIES
SIZABLENESS
WIZENEDNESS

BENZALDEHYDE
BENZALDOXIME
BENZINDULINE
BENZOHYDROL
BENZOINATED
BENZONITRILE
BENZONITROL
BENZOPHENONE
BENZOYLATION
BENZYLAMINE
BERZELIANITE
BLIZZARDOUS
BRAZENFACED
BUZZERPHONE
COAZERVATION
DIAZENITHAL
DIAZOBENZENE
DIAZOMETHANE
DIAZOTIZING
DIEZEUGMENON
EPIZOOTIOLOGY
HARZBURGITE
KATZENJAMMER
MEIZOSEISMAL
MEIZOSEISMIC
MEZZOTINTED
MEZZOTINTER
MEZZOTINTING
MIZZENTOPMAN
MIZZENTOPMEN
MONZODIORITE
MONZOGABBRO
MUZZLELOADER

MUZZLELOADING
ORYZIVOROUS
PIEZOMETRIC
POZZUOLANIC
PRIZEFIGHTER
PRIZEHOLDER
PUZZLEATION
PUZZLEDNESS
PUZZLEHEADED
PUZZLEPATED
PUZZLINGNESS
QUIZZACIOUS
QUIZZATORIAL
QUIZZICALITY
QUIZZICALLY
RAZZBERRIES
RHIZANTHOUS
RHIZOCARPIC
RHIZOCARPOUS
RHIZOCAULUS
RHIZODERMIS
RHIZOGENETIC
RHIZOGENOUS
RHIZOMATOUS
RHIZOMORPHIC
RHIZOPHAGOUS
RHIZOPHILOUS
RHIZOPODIST
RHIZOPODOUS
RHIZOSTOMOUS
ZIGZAGGEDLY

BEDAZZLINGLY
BEDIZENMENT
BLIZZARDOUS
BRONZESMITH
CACOZEALOUS
CENOZOOLOGY
CITIZENIZED
CITIZENIZING
CITIZENRIES
CITIZENSHIP
DENAZIFYING
DENIZENATION
EMBEZZLEMENT
ENTOZOOLOGY
HORIZOMETER
HORIZONTALITY
HORIZONTALIZE
HORIZONTALLY
HORIZONTICAL
MAGAZINABLE
MEGAZOOSPORE
MONOZYGOTIC
OSMAZOMATIC
OSMAZOMATOUS
OVERZEALOUS
PEZIZACEOUS
PEZIZAEFORM
PHLYZACIOUS
POLYZOARIAL
POLYZOARIUM
QUIZZACIOUS
QUIZZATORIAL
QUIZZICALITY
QUIZZICALLY
SCHIZOCARPIC
SCHIZOCHROAL
SCHIZOCOELE
SCHIZODINIC
SCHIZOGENESIS
SCHIZOGENETIC
SCHIZOGENIC
SCHIZOGENOUS
SCHIZOGNATH
SCHIZOGONIC
SCHIZOIDISM

SCHIZOMYCETE
SCHIZOMYCETES
SCHIZOPELMOUS
SCHIZOPHASIA
SCHIZOPHRENE
SCHIZOPHRENIA
SCHIZOPHYTE
SCHIZOPODAL
SCHIZOPODOUS
SCHIZORHINAL
SCHIZOSPORE
SCHIZOSTELE
SCHIZOSTELIC
SCHIZOSTELY
SCHIZOTHECAL
SCHIZOTHYME
SCHIZOTHYMIA
SCHIZOTHYMIC
SCHIZOTRICHIA
SPITZENBERG
SPITZENBURG
STANZAICALLY

ADENIZATION
ANALYZATION
APPRIZEMENT
ATOMIZATION
BAPTIZEMENT
BEDAZZLINGLY
BROMIZATION
CHALAZOGAMIC
CHALAZOGAMY
CHALAZOIDITE
CHORIZATION
CHORIZONTES
CHORIZONTIC
CHORIZONTIST
CYCLIZATION
DEBENZOLIZE
DIALYZATION
DOCKIZATION
DUALIZATION
EMBEZZLEMENT
ENOLIZATION
ETHNOZOOLOGY
HAPHAZARDLY
HAPHAZARDNESS
HYDROZINCITE
IDOLIZATION
IRIDIZATION
ITEMIZATION
KYANIZATION
LAICIZATION
LIONIZATION
LORENZENITE
MICROZOARIA
MICROZOARIAN
MICROZYMIAN
ODYLIZATION
ORGANZINING
OVALIZATION
OZONIZATION
PALEOZOOLOGY
PATRIZATION
PECTIZATION
PEPTIZATION
PHILOZOONIST
POETIZATION
PROTOZOEAN
PROTOZOIASIS
PROTOZOONAL
QUINAZOLINE
QUINAZOLINE
REALIZATION
SOLMIZATION
SQUEEZINGLY
STYLIZATION

TETRAZOLIUM
TETRAZOTIZE
TRAPEZIFORM
TRAPEZOIDAL
TYPHIZATION
ULTRAZEALOUS
UTILIZATION

ALBITIZATION
ALDOLIZATION
ALKALIZABLE
ALKALIZATION
AMMONIZATION
AMORTIZABLE
AMORTIZATION
AMORTIZEMENT
APPETIZINGLY
ARBORIZATION
ARSENIZATION
ATMOLYZATION
BAMBOOZLEMENT
BAMBOOZLING
BILHARZIASIS
BILHARZIOSIS
CALABAZILLA
CANALIZATION
CANONIZATION
CARBOAZOTINE
CATALYZATOR
CIVILIZABLE
CIVILIZATION
CIVILIZATORY
COLONIZATION
CREOLIZATION
CRYPTOZONATE
CRYPTOZYGOUS
CURARIZATION
CUTINIZATION
DAMENIZATION
DEMUTIZATION
DERATIZATION
DIMERIZATION
DIPHYOZOOID
DISSEIZORESS
DIVINIZATION
DYNAMIZATION
EQUALIZATION
ERGOTIZATION
ESTERIZATION
ETERNIZATION
ETHERIZATION
EULOGIZATION
EXORCIZATION
EXORCIZEMENT
FARADIZATION
FEMINIZATION
FLUIDIZATION
FOCALIZATION
GASTROZOOID
HETEROZYGOTE
HETEROZYGOUS
IDEALIZATION
JAROVIZATION
JUBILIZATION
KETONIZATION
LABILIZATION
LATERIZATION
LEGALIZATION
LOCALIZABLE
LOCALIZATION
MAXIMIZATION
MEMORIZATION
METALIZATION
MICASIZATION
MINIMIZATION
MOBILIZATION
MONETIZATION

MORALIZATION
MOTORIZATION
NASALIZATION
NEBULIZATION
NEMATOZOOID
NODULIZING
NOTARIZATION
NOVELIZATION
OPSONIZATION
OPTIMIZATION
OPTIMIZING
ORGANIZABLE
ORGANIZATION
ORGANIZATORY
PAGANIZATION
PALATIZATION
PAPALIZATION
PARALYZATION
PELORIZATION
PENALIZATION
PHYLLOZOOID
POLARIZABLE
POLARIZATION
QUANTIZATION
QUANTIZING
QUANTIZING
RACEMIZATION
RINFORZANDO
ROBOTIZATION
ROYALIZATION
RURALIZATION
SATIRIZABLE
SOLARIZATION
SPLENIZATION
SUBERIZATION
TARTRAZINIC
TETANIZATION
THEORIZATION
TOTALIZATION
TOTALIZATOR
TOTEMIZATION
TROPHOZOITE
TROPHOZOOID
TRULLIZATION
TUBERIZATION
TUBULIZATION
TUTORIZATION
UNIONIZATION
URBANIZATION
VALORIZATION
VAPORIZATION
VENALIZATION
VITALIZATION
VITALIZINGLY
VOCALIZATION

ACADEMIZING
ACETONIZATION
ACETYLIZABLE
ACETYLIZATION
ACTIONIZING
ACTUALIZATION
ACTUALIZING
ADVERTIZEMENT
ADVERTIZING
ALCHEMIZING
ALGEBRIZATION
ALUMINIZING
ANALOGIZING
ANATOMIZING
ANGLICIZING
ANIMALIZATION
ANIMALIZING
ANTHEROZOID
ANTHEROZOOID
APOLOGIZING
ARCTICIZING

AROMATIZING
ASCIDIOZOOID
AUTHORIZATION
AUTHORIZING
BACTERIZING
BALKANIZING
BARBARIZING
BERGINIZATION
BISTRIAZOLE
BRUTALIZING
BURTONIZATION
CARBOLIZING
CARBONIZING
CARBURIZING
CARNALIZING
CATECHIZATION
CATECHIZING
CATHARIZING
CAUTERIZATION
CAUTERIZING
CHITINIZATION
CICATRIZANT
CICATRIZATE
CICATRIZING
COCAINIZING
COMMUNIZATION
COMMUNIZING
COPPERIZATION
CRITICIZABLE
CRITICIZING
DACTYLOZOOID
DEFERRIZING
DEODORIZING
DEOXIDIZING
DERMATOZOON
DESCLOIZITE
DESTINEZITE
DEUTEROZOOID
DIABOLIZING
DIALOGIZING
DIAZOTIZING
DOGMATIZING
DRAMATIZATION
DRAMATIZING
DUCTILIZING
ECONOMIZATION
ECONOMIZING
ELECTRIZING
EMBLEMIZING
EMPATHIZING
EMPHASIZING
EPIDOTIZATION
EPILOGIZING
EPITOMIZATION
EPITOMIZING
ERYTHROZYME
EUPHEMIZING
EUPHONIZING
EXTERNIZATION
FACTORIZATION
FANTASIZING
FERTILIZABLE
FERTILIZATION
FERTILIZING
FEUDALIZATION
FEUDALIZING
FISCALIZATION
FISCALIZING
FORMALIZATION
FORMALIZING
FORMULIZATION
FORMULIZING
FOSSILIZATION
FOSSILIZING
FRIVOLIZING
GALVANIZATION
GALVANIZING

GASTEROZOOID
GEOLOGIZING
GLAMORIZING
GLUCOSAZONE
HARMONIZING
HYBRIDIZABLE
HYBRIDIZATION
HYDROLYZATE
ICHTHYIZATION
INOXIDIZING
INTERMEZZOS
IODOBENZENE
IRREALIZABLE
ITALICIZING
JARGONIZING
JASPERIZING
JOVIALIZING
LABIALIZING
LICHENIZATION
LINEARIZATION
LIQUIDIZING
MAGNETIZABLE
MAGNETIZATION
MAGNETIZING
MAMMONIZATION
MARBLEIZING
MARMARIZING
MARTYRIZING
MATRONIZING
MECHANIZATION
MEDIATIZING
MERCERIZING
MERCURIZING
MESMERIZATION
MESMERIZING
METALLIZATION
METHODIZING
MNEMONIZING
MODERNIZATION
MODERNIZING
MORTALIZING
MUTUALIZING
MYOSYNIZESIS
MYTHICIZING
NARCOTIZING
NEOLOGIZING
NITRIDIZATION
NIVELLIZATION
NORMALIZATION
NORMALIZING
OBJECTIZATION
OBJECTIZING
OSTRACIZATION
OSTRACIZING
OVERGLAZING
OVERPRIZING
OXYGENIZABLE
OXYGENIZING
PALLETIZING
PATRONIZING
PAUPERIZING
PEPTONIZING
PETROLIZING
PHANEROZOIC
PHENMIAZINE
PHENOXAZINE
PHONETIZATION
PHYTOBEZOAR
PLATINIZING
PLURALIZING
POSTURIZING
PUBLICIZING
PULVERIZATE
PULVERIZATOR
PULVERIZING
RACIALIZATION
RADIALIZATION

RADIUMIZATION
RANDOMIZING
REBAPTIZATION
RECOGNIZABLE
RECOGNIZABLY
RECOGNIZANCE
RECOGNIZANT
RECOGNIZING
RHYTHMIZABLE
ROUTINIZING
RUBBERIZING
SAILORIZING
SCENARIZING
SENSITIZATION
SENSITIZING
SEPTICIZATION
SERIALIZATION
SERIALIZING
SERMONIZING
SHERBETZIDE
SIGNALIZING
SIPHONOZOOID
SOCIALIZATION
SOCIALIZING
SOLEMNIZATION
SOLEMNIZING
SOLVOLYZING
SOVIETIZATION
SOVIETIZING
SPIRALIZATION
STABILIZATION
STABILIZATOR
STABILIZING
STERILIZATION
STERILIZING
SUBSIDIZATION
SUBSIDIZING
SUBTILIZING
SULCALIZATION
SULFATIZING
SULFURIZING
SUMMARIZATION
SUMMARIZING
SYLLABIZING
SYLLOGIZING
SYMBOLIZATION
SYMBOLIZING
SYNTONIZING
SYPHILIZING
SYSTEMIZATION
SYSTEMIZING
TANTALIZING
TARTARIZING
TELLURIZING
TEMPORIZING
TENDERIZING
TERRORIZING
THIADIAZOLE
TYRANNIZING
URALIZATION
VACCINIZATION
VAPOURIZING
VASSALIZING
VERATRIZING
VERBALIZING
VICTIMIZABLE
VICTIMIZATION
VICTIMIZING
VISUALIZING
VOLCANIZING
VULCANIZATE
VULCANIZATION
VULCANIZING
VULGARIZATION
VULGARIZING
WINTERIZING

ZEOLITIZING
ZOISITIZATION
ZOOLOGIZING

ACETOBENZOIC
AGGUTINIZE
AGGRANDIZED
AGGRANDIZER
AGGRANDIZING
ALBUMENIZED
ALBUMENIZER
ALBUMENIZING
ALBUMINIZED
ALBUMINIZING
ALCOHOLIZED
ALCOHOLIZING
ALGEBRAIZED
ALKALINIZED
ALKALINIZING
ALLEGORIZED
ALLEGORIZER
ALLEGORIZING
ANABAPTIZED
ANABAPTIZING
ANTAGONIZED
ANTAGONIZER
ANTAGONIZING
ANTHROPOZOIC
ANTIFREEZING
APOSTATIZED
APOSTATIZING
ASEPTICIZED
ASEPTICIZING
ASEXUALIZED
ASEXUALIZING
AZOTETRAZOLE
BASTARDIZED
BASTARDIZING
BESTIALIZED
BESTIALIZING
BISTETRAZOLE
BITUMINIZED
BIVOCALIZED
BOLSHEVIZED
BOLSHEVIZING
BOWDLERIZED
BOWDLERIZING
BROMOBENZENE
BURGLARIZED
BURGLARIZING
BURNETTIZED
BURNETTIZING
CAPITALIZED
CAPITALIZING
CARAMELIZED
CARAMELIZING
CATABIBAZON
CATABOLIZED
CATABOLIZING
CATEGORIZED
CATEGORIZING
CAUSTICIZED
CAUSTICIZER
CAUSTICIZING
CENTRALIZED
CENTRALIZER
CENTRALIZING
CHANNELIZED
CHANNELIZING
CHLAMYDOZOAN
CHLORALIZED
CHLORALIZING
CHLORIDIZED
CHLORIDIZING
CHLORODIZED
CHLORODIZING
CHROMICIZING

CINCHONIZED
CINCHONIZING
CITIZENIZED
CITIZENIZING
CLASSICIZED
CLASSICIZING
COLLOQUIZED
COLLOQUIZING
CONCERTIZED
CONCERTIZER
CONCERTIZING
CONCRETIZE
CONCRETIZED
CONCRETIZING
DECIMALIZED
DECIMALIZING
DECOLORIZED
DECOLORIZER
DECOLORIZING
DEEPFREEZED
DEEPFREEZING
DEFINITIZED
DEFINITIZING
DEHUMANIZED
DEHUMANIZING
DELIMITIZED
DELIMITIZING
DELOCALIZED
DELOCALIZING
DEMOBILIZED
DEMOBILIZING
DEMONETIZED
DEMONETIZING
DEMORALIZED
DEMORALIZER
DEMORALIZING
DENATURIZER
DEPOLARIZED
DEPOLARIZER
DEPOLARIZING
DEVITALIZED
DEVITALIZING
DEVOCALIZED
DEVOCALIZING
DEXTROSAZONE
DIAMONDIZED
DIAMONDIZING
DIAZOBENZENE
DOCTRINIZED
DOCTRINIZING
DOXOLOGIZED
DOXOLOGIZING
EFFEMINIZED
EFFEMINIZING
ELASTICIZER
ENIGMATIZED
ENIGMATIZING
ENTHRONIZED
ENTHRONIZING
EPISCOPIZED
EPISCOPIZING
EPISTOLIZABLE
EUHEMERIZED
EUHEMERIZING
EVANGELIZED
EVANGELIZER
EVANGELIZING
FANATICIZED
FANATICIZING
FEDERALIZED
FEDERALIZING
FICTIONIZED
FICTIONIZING
FRATERNIZED
FRATERNIZER
FRATERNIZING
FUROMONAZOLE

GABERLUNZIE	NEUTRALIZING	SPERMATOZOID	ANHYDRIDIZE	DEOXYGENIZE
GELATINIZED	NEWSMAGAZINE	SPERMATOZOON	ANTHOLOGIZE	DEPAUPERIZE
GELATINIZER	NITROBENZENE	SPONDYLIZEMA	ANTHOLOGIZED	DEPAUPERIZED
GELATINIZING	NONPARTIZAN	STIGMATIZED	ANTHOLOGIZING	DEPERSONIZE
GENERALIZABLE	NUPTIALIZE	STIGMATIZER	ANTIPATHIZE	DERACIALIZE
GENERALIZED	OLIGORHIZOUS	STIGMATIZING	ANTITHESIZE	DESACRALIZE
GENERALIZER	PANEGYRIZED	SULFADIAZINE	APESTHETIZE	DESENSITIZE
GEOMETRIZED	PANEGYRIZER	SULFOBENZIDE	APOTHEOSIZE	DESENSITIZER
GEOMETRIZING	PANEGYRIZING	SULFOBENZOIC	APOTHEOSIZED	DESEXUALIZE
GLUTTONIZED	PARABOLIZED	SULPHATIZED	ARITHMETIZE	DESEXUALIZED
GLUTTONIZING	PARABOLIZER	SULPHATIZING	ARTERIALIZE	DESILVERIZE
GORMANDIZER	PARABOLIZING	SULPHURIZED	ARTERIALIZED	DESILVERIZER
GRAPHITIZED	PASTEURIZED	SULPHURIZING	ASBESTINIZE	DESTERILIZE
GYNECOMAZIA	PASTEURIZER	SYMMETRIZED	ASPHETERIZE	DESULFURIZE
GYROHORIZON	PASTEURIZING	SYMMETRIZING	ASTIGMATIZER	DESULFURIZED
HOMOGENIZER	PHANTOMIZER	SYMPATHIZED	ASTROLOGIZE	DESULFURIZER
HOPPERDOZER	PHILIPPIZER	SYMPATHIZER	ASTRONOMIZE	DETRIBALIZE
HYDROBENZOIN	PICRORHIZIN	SYMPATHIZING	BACHELORIZE	DEVULGARIZE
HYDRORHIZAL	PLAGIARIZED	SYMPHONIZED	BATTOLOGIZE	DIAGONALIZE
IDOLATRIZED	PLAGIARIZER	SYMPHONIZING	BESSEMERIZE	DICHOTOMIZE
IDOLATRIZER	PLAGIARIZING	SYNCRETIZED	BESSEMERIZED	DICHOTOMIZED
IDOLATRIZING	PLASTICIZED	SYNCRETIZING	BESSEMERIZING	DIPLOMATIZE
ILLEGALIZED	PLASTICIZER	SYNONYMIZED	BIOGRAPHIZE	DIPLOMATIZED
ILLEGALIZING	PLASTICIZING	SYNONYMIZING	BROMOIODIZED	DISCANONIZE
IMMOBILIZED	PNEUMATIZED	SYNTHESIZED	BURKUNDAUZE	DISCANONIZED
IMMOBILIZING	POLITICIZED	SYNTHESIZER	CACOPHONIZE	DISEQUALIZE
INTERMEZZOS	POLITICIZER	SYNTHESIZING	CANNIBALIZE	DISORGANIZE
INTHRONIZATE	POLITICIZING	SYNTHETIZER	CANNIBALIZED	DISORGANIZED
JATEORHIZIN	POPULARIZED	TABULARIZED	CANNIBALIZING	DISORGANIZER
JATEORHIZINE	POPULARIZER	TABULARIZING	CAPERCAILZIE	DOCUMENTIZE
JEOPARDIZED	POPULARIZING	TELFORDIZED	CATALEPTIZE	DOGGERELIZE
JEOPARDIZING	PRAGMATIZER	TELFORDIZING	CATALOGUIZE	DOGGERELIZER
JOURNALIZED	PRESSURIZED	THEOLOGIZED	CATHETERIZE	DOGGERELIZING
JOURNALIZER	PRESSURIZING	THEOLOGIZER	CATHETERIZED	DOMESTICIZE
JOURNALIZING	PROLOGUIZER	THEOLOGIZING	CATHOLICIZE	DOMESTICIZED
LATERALIZED	PYRRODIAZOLE	THERMOLYZED	CATHOLICIZED	ELECTRALIZE
LATERALIZING	REGULARIZED	THERMOLYZING	CATHOLICIZING	ELECTRICIZE
LEGITIMIZED	REGULARIZER	TRAILBLAZER	CHAMPAGNIZE	ELECTROLYZE
LEGITIMIZING	REORGANIZED	TRAILBLAZING	CHAMPAGNIZED	ELECTROLYZED
LETHARGIZED	REORGANIZER	TRICHINIZED	CHAMPAGNIZING	ELECTROLYZER
LETHARGIZING	REORGANIZING	TRICHINIZING	CHEERFULIZE	ELECTROLYZING
LIBERALIZED	REVITALIZED	UNCANONIZED	CHEMICALIZE	EMBLEMATIZE
LIBERALIZER	REVITALIZER	UNCANONIZED	CHORIAMBIZE	EMBLEMATIZED
LIBERALIZING	REVITALIZING	UNCIVILIZED	CIRCULARIZE	EMBLEMATIZING
LITERALIZED	RHAPSODIZED	UNMORALIZED	CIRCULARIZED	EMULSIONIZE
LITERALIZER	RHAPSODIZING	UNMORALIZING	CIRCULARIZING	ENCARNALIZE
LITERALIZING	SACCHARIZED	UNORGANIZED	COMMEMORIZE	ENCARNALIZED
MACADAMIZED	SACCHARIZING	VITRIOLIZED	COMMEMORIZED	ENCARNALIZING
MACADAMIZER	SCANDALIZED	VITRIOLIZING	COMMEMORIZING	ENSORCELIZE
MACADAMIZING	SCANDALIZING	VOLATILIZED	COMMUNALIZE	ENSORCERIZE
MERMITHIZED	SCEPTICIZED	VOLATILIZER	COMMUNALIZED	EPENTHESIZE
METABOLIZED	SCEPTICIZING	VOLATILIZING	COMMUNALIZER	EQUILIBRIZE
METABOLIZING	SCLEROTIZED	WESTERNIZED	COSMOGONIZE	ETHEREALIZE
METAMERIZED	SCRUTINIZED	WESTERNIZING	CRYSTALLIZE	ETHEREALIZED
MILITARIZED	SCRUTINIZER		CRYSTALLIZED	ETHEREALIZING
MILITARIZING	SCRUTINIZING	ABASTARDIZE	CRYSTALLIZER	ETYMOLOGIZE
MINERALIZED	SECULARIZED	ABNORMALIZE	CRYSTALLIZING	ETYMOLOGIZED
MINERALIZER	SECULARIZING	ACCLIMATIZE	DEBENZOLIZE	ETYMOLOGIZING
MINERALIZING	SENSUALIZED	ACCLIMATIZED	DECARBONIZE	EUDAEMONIZE
MISCOGNIZANT	SENSUALIZING	ACCLIMATIZER	DECARBONIZED	EVENTUALIZE
MISSIONIZER	SHERARDIZED	ACCLIMATIZING	DECARBONIZER	EXAUTHORIZE
MONARCHIZED	SHERARDIZING	ACCULTURIZE	DECARBURIZE	EXOSTRACIZE
MONARCHIZER	SKEPTICIZED	ACCUSTOMIZE	DECARBURIZED	EXTEMPORIZE
MONARCHIZING	SKEPTICIZING	ACCUSTOMIZED	DECEREBRIZE	EXTEMPORIZED
MONOLOGIZED	SLENDERIZED	ACCUSTOMIZING	DECHORALIZE	EXTEMPORIZER
MONOLOGIZING	SLENDERIZING	ACHROMATIZE	DECOLOURIZE	EXTEMPORIZING
MONOPOLIZED	SOLIDARIZED	ACHROMATIZED	DEFIBRINIZE	EXTERIORIZE
MONOPOLIZER	SOLIDARIZING	AGRARIANIZE	DEHYPNOTIZE	EXTERIORIZED
MONOPOLIZING	SOPHRONIZED	ALGEBRAIZING	DEHYPNOTIZED	EXTERIORIZING
MYCORRHIZAL	SOPHRONIZING	ALLOTROPIZE	DEJUNKERIZE	EXTERNALIZE
MYCORRHIZIC	SPECIALIZED	ALPHABETIZE	DEMAGNETIZE	FACSIMILIZE
NATURALIZED	SPECIALIZER	ALPHABETIZED	DEMAGNETIZED	FAMILIARIZE
NATURALIZER	SPECIALIZING	ALPHABETIZER	DEMAGNETIZER	FAMILIARIZED
NATURALIZING	SPERMATOZOA	ALPHABETIZING	DEMANGANIZE	FAMILIARIZER
NESSLERIZED	SPERMATOZOAL	ANACHRONIZE	DEMEPHITIZE	FAMILIARIZING
NEUTRALIZED	SPERMATOZOAN	ANESTHETIZE	DEMOCRATIZE	FORMULARIZE
NEUTRALIZER	SPERMATOZOIC	ANESTHETIZER	DEMOCRATIZED	FORMULARIZED

FORMULARIZING
FRACTIONIZATIO
FRACTIONIZE
FRACTIONIZING
FRICTIONIZE
FRICTIONIZED
FRICTIONIZING
FUNCTIONIZE
GENEALOGIZE
GENEALOGIZER
GEOGRAPHIZE
GEOGRAPHIZED
GLYCERINIZE
GLYCYRRHIZIN
GRANULITIZE
GUTTURALIZE
GUTTURALIZING
HIERARCHIZE
HOSPITALIZE
HURRICANIZE
HYDROGENIZE
HYPERBOLIZE
HYPERBOLIZED
HYPOSTATIZE
IMMETHODIZE
IMMORTALIZE
IMMORTALIZED
IMMORTALIZER
IMMORTALIZING
IMPATRONIZE
IMPERIALIZE
IMPERIALIZED
IMPERIALIZING
INFORMALIZE
INTELLIGIZE
INTERNALIZE
ISOCHRONIZE
ISOCHRONIZED
ISOCHRONIZING
JUDICIALIZE
KJELDAHLIZE
LALAPALOOZA
LITHOTOMIZE
LOGOMACHIZE
MALLEABLIZE
MANORIALIZE
MARGINALIZE
MATERIALIZE
MATERIALIZED
MATERIALIZER
MATERIALIZING
MATERNALIZE
MATHEMATIZE
MECHANALIZE
MEMORANDIZE
MEMORIALIZE
MEMORIALIZED
MEMORIALIZER
MEMORIALIZING
MERCHANDIZE
MERORGANIZE
METAPHONIZE
METASTASIZE
METASTASIZED
MIGNIARDIZE
MINIATURIZE
MINIATURIZED
MUSCOVITIZE
MUSCOVITIZED
MUSCULARIZE
MYTHOLOGIZE
MYTHOLOGIZED
MYTHOLOGIZER
MYTHOLOGIZING
NAPHTHALIZE
NATIONALIZE
NATIONALIZED

NATIONALIZER
NATIONALIZING
NEOPAGANIZE
NEUROLOGIZE
NEUROTOMIZE
NITROGENIZE
NITROGENIZED
NITROGENIZING
NONENTITIZE
OBJECTIVIZE
OBJECTIVIZED
OBJECTIVIZING
OBLIVIONIZE
OFFICIALIZE
OLIGARCHIZE
OPTIONALIZE
ORIENTALIZE
ORIENTALIZED
ORIENTALIZING
PAMPHLETIZE
PANCREATIZE
PANTHEONIZE
PARAENESIZE
PASTORALIZE
PATERNALIZE
PECULIARIZE
PECULIARIZED
PEMMICANIZE
PERMORALIZE
PERSONALIZE
PERSONALIZED
PHAGOCYTIZE
PHILOLOGIZE
PHONETICIZE
PHOSPHATIZE
PHOSPHATIZED
PHOSPHORIZE
PLEBEIANIZE
PLEBEIANIZED
POLITZERIZE
PREACHERIZE
PROBABILIZE
PRODIGALIZE
PROLETARIZE
PROSELYTIZE
PROSELYTIZED
PROSELYTIZER
PROTOCITIZEN
PROTOCOLIZE
PROTOXIDIZE
PROTOXIDIZED
RATIONALIZE
RATIONALIZED
RATIONALIZER
REACTUALIZE
RECARBONIZE
RECARBONIZER
RECARBURIZE
RECARBURIZER
REFORESTIZE
REGIONALIZE
REHARMONIZE
RELIGIONIZE
RESTERILIZE
RHYTHMICIZE
ROENTGENIZE
ROMANTICIZE
ROTARIANIZE
SANCTUARIZE
SCHILLERIZE
SCHILLERIZED
SCHILLERIZING
SCHISMATIZE
SCHISMATIZED
SCHISMATIZING
SENSIBILIZE
SIDEREALIZE

SIMULACRIZE
SINGULARIZE
SINGULARIZED
SINGULARIZING
SKELETONIZE
SKELETONIZED
SKELETONIZER
SKELETONIZING
SLUGGARDIZE
SOLILOQUIZE
SOLILOQUIZED
SOLILOQUIZER
SOLILOQUIZING
SOUTHERNIZE
SPECIFICIZE
SPECIMENIZE
SPECIMENIZED
SPHEROIDIZE
STALLIONIZE
STALWARTIZE
STANDARDIZE
STANDARDIZED
STANDARDIZER
STANDARDIZING
SUBSTANTIZE
SUBURBANIZE
SUBVITALIZED
SULPHOBENZID
SYNCHRONIZE
SYNCHRONIZED
SYNCHRONIZER
SYNCHRONIZING
SYNDICALIZE
SYSTEMATIZE
SYSTEMATIZED
SYSTEMATIZER
SYSTEMATIZING
TARANTARIZE
TAUTOLOGIZE
TAUTOLOGIZED
TAUTOLOGIZER
TAXIDERMIZE
TEETOTUMIZE
TELEPATHIZE
TEMPORALIZE
TENEMENTIZE
TETRAKISAZO
TETRAZOTIZE
THEATRICIZE
TOBACCONIZE
TRANQUILIZE
TRANQUILIZER
TRANQUILIZING
TRILLIONIZE
TROPICALIZE
TROPICALIZED
TROPICALIZING
TROPOLOGIZE
TROPOLOGIZED
TROPOLOGIZING
TUBERCULIZE
UNAUTHORIZE
UNAUTHORIZED
UNBRUTALIZE
UNFEUDALIZE
UNLITURGIZE
UNMECHANIZE
UNMODERNIZE
UNMORTALIZE
UNPATRONIZED
UNRECOGNIZED
UNSOLEMNIZE
UNSTERILIZED
UNVERBALIZED
UNVULGARIZE
VAGABONDIZE
VAGABONDIZED

VAGABONDIZER
VAGABONDIZING
VASCULARIZE
VASCULARIZED
VASCULARIZING
VASECTOMIZE
VEGETABLIZE
VERATRINIZE
VERATRINIZED
VERATRINIZING
WOODCOCKIZE
ZOOMORPHIZE

ABOLITIONIZE
ADVERBIALIZE
AESTHETICIZE
ANACEPHALIZE
ANAESTHETIZE
ANAESTHETIZED
ANAESTHETIZER
ANATHEMATIZE
ANGIOSTOMIZE
APAESTHETIZE
APOSTROPHIZE
ATTITUDINIZE
AUTOCATALYZE
BACCHANALIZE
BACTERIOLYZE
CANTHARIDIZE
CELESTIALIZE
CELESTIALIZED
CHAMELEONIZE
CHARACTERIZE
CHARACTERIZED
CHARACTERIZER
CHRONOLOGIZE
CHRONOLOGIZED
COLLECTIVIZE
COLLECTIVIZED
COLLODIONIZE
COMPANIONIZE
COMPANIONIZED
CONSERVATIZE
CONSONANTIZE
CONTEMPORIZE
CONTEMPORIZED
COPOLYMERIZE
COPOLYMERIZED
CORPOREALIZE
CUTICULARIZE
DECAFFEINIZE
DECENTRALIZE
DECICERONIZE
DEMENTHOLIZE
DEMICIVILIZED
DEMILITARIZE
DEMILITARIZED
DEMINERALIZE
DENATURALIZE
DENICOTINIZE
DEPIGMENTIZE
DEPOLYMERIZE
DESILICONIZE
DESULPHURIZE
DESYNONYMIZE
DEVITAMINIZE
DIALECTALIZE
DIALECTICIZE
DIPHTHONGIZE
DIPHTHONGIZED
DISGOSPELIZE
DISHARMONIZE
DISPAUPERIZE
DISSOCIALIZE
DISSYLLABIZE
EDITORIALIZE
EDITORIALIZED

EFFECTUALIZE
EFFEMINATIZE
EMOTIONALIZE
EMOTIONALIZED
ENTOMOLOGIZE
ENTOMOLOGIZED
EPITHALAMIZE
EUCHARISTIZE
EUCHARISTIZED
EVOLUTIONIZE
EXCURSIONIZE
EXPERMENTIZED
EXTRAVAGANZA
FASCISTICIZE
FICTIONALIZE
GEOMETRICIZE
GRAMMATICIZE
HARLEQUINIZE
IMBASTARDIZE
IMPACTIONIZE
INDOCTRINIZE
IRREGULARIZE
LALLAPALOOZA
LAPAROTOMIZE
LEGITIMATIZE
LEGITIMATIZED
LIEDERKRANZ
MALLEABLEIZE
MALLEABLEIZED
MARSUPIALIZE
MELANCHOLIZE
MERCURIALIZE
METAMORPHIZE
MICROSCOPIZE
MINERALOGIZE
MISEMPHASIZE
MISSIONARIZE
MITHRIDATIZE
MONOCHORDIZE
MUNICIPALIZE
MUNICIPALIZED
MYTHOPOETIZE
OUTTYRANNIZE
OVARIOTOMIZE
PALLADIUMIZE
PANEGYRICIZE
PANSEXUALIZE
PARCHMENTIZE
PARENTHESIZE
PENTAMETRIZE
PERFECTIVIZE
PHILIPPICIZE
PHILOSOPHIZE
PHLEBOTOMIZE
PHRENOLOGIZE
PHYLACTERIZE
PHYSIOLOGIZE
POLITICALIZE
POLYCHROMIZE
PORCELAINIZE
PORCELLANIZE
POTENTIALIZE
PRACTICALIZE
PRACTICALIZED
PRESERVATIZE
PROBLEMATIZE
PROPAGANDIZE
PSYCHIATRIZE
PSYCHOLOGIZE
REALISTICIZE
RECAPITALIZE
RECAPITALIZED
SACRAMENTIZE
SARCOPHAGIZE
SECTARIANIZE
SECTARIANIZED
SECTIONALIZE

SECTIONALIZED	SPIRITUALIZER	TRANQUILLIZE	ANTISEPTICIZE	HORIZONTALIZE
SEMICIVILIZED	STATISTICIZE	TRANQUILLIZED	COMMERCIALIZE.	IMMATERIALIZE
SEMPITERNIZE	STRYCHNINIZE	TRICHOTOMIZE	ELECTRICALIZE	IMPERSONALIZE
SERPENTINIZE	SULPHAZOTIZE	UNIFORMALIZE	ELECTROTONIZE	IMPROBABILIZE
SOLITUDINIZE	SULPHAZOTIZE	UNIFORMALIZED	EMBLEMATICIZE	INDIVIDUALIZE
SOLITUDINIZED	SYCOPHANTIZE	UNIVERSALIZED	ENCYCLOPEDIZE	MELODRAMATIZE
SOMNAMBULIZE	SYMPTOMATIZE	UNIVERSITIZE	ENHYPOSTATIZE	NIGHTINGALIZE
SOVEREIGNIZE	TCHERVONETZ	UNNATURALIZE	EPIGRAMMATIZE	RECIPROCALIZE
SPHERULITIZE	TECHNICALIZE	UNPOPULARIZE	EXPERIMENTIZE	RECRYSTALLIZE
SPIRITUALIZE	THEOMORPHIZE	UNSECULARIZE	FLAMBOYANTIZE	STRUCTURALIZE
SPIRITUALIZED	TOURMALINIZE	VERMILIONIZE	FRACTIONALIZE	SUBSTANTIVIZE

SCORING ORDER LIST OF WORDS OVER 10 LETTERS

37
OBJECTIVIZING

36
KATZENJAMMER
OBJECTIVIZED
SCHIZOTHYMIC

35
KJELDAHLIZE
ZANTHOXYLUM
ZOOPRAXISCOPE
ZYGAPOPHYSIS
ZYGOPHYCEOUS

34
EXPERMENTIZED
EXTEMPORIZING
OBJECTIVIZE
OXYGENIZABLE
QUIZZICALITY
RHYTHMIZABLE
SCHIZOMYCETES
SCHIZOTHYMIA

33
BENZALDOXIME
CHAMPAGNIZING
DIPHTHONGIZED
EXPERIMENTIZE
EXTEMPORIZED
GLYCYRRHIZIN
HARLEQUINIZE
ICHTHYIZATION
OBJECTIZATION
POLYCHROMIZE
QUIZZICALLY
RHIZOMORPHIC
SCHIZOMYCETE
SCHIZOPHYTE
SCHIZOTHYME
SQUEEZINGLY
ZOOPHYTOLOGY
ZYGODACTYLIC
ZYGOMORPHIC
ZYMOTECHNICS

32
CHAMPAGNIZED
CHLAMYDOZOAN
COPOLYMERIZED
CRYPTOZYGOUS
DEJUNKERIZE
DEOXYGENIZE
ENCYCLOPEDIZE
EXORCIZEMENT
EXTEMPORIZER
EXTRAVAGANZA
FLAMBOYANTIZE
HAPHAZARDLY

HYBRIDIZABLE
HYPERBOLIZED
JEOPARDIZING
MAXIMIZATION
MYCORRHIZIC
MYTHOLOGIZING
OBJECTIZING
OXYGENIZING
PHENOXAZINE
PHOSPHATIZED
PROTOXIDIZED
PSYCHOLOGIZE
SCHIZOPHRENIA
SCHIZOTRICHIA
SOLILOQUIZING
SYMPATHIZING
SYMPHONIZING
TRANQUILIZING
TRANQUILLIZED
WOODCOCKIZE
ZOOPHARMACY
ZYGOMORPHOUS
ZYGOMYCETOUS
ZYMOTECHNIC

31
AZOPHOSPHORE
BENZALDEHYDE
CHALAZOGAMIC
CHALAZOGAMY
CHROMICIZING
DEHYPNOTIZED
DEMICIVILIZED
DEZINCIFYING
DIPHTHONGIZE
DOXOLOGIZING
EQUILIBRIZE
ERYTHROZYME
EXTEMPORIZE
HAPHAZARDNESS
HYBRIDIZATION
JAROVIZATION
JATEORHIZINE
JEOPARDIZED
JOVIALIZING
LIQUIDIZING
MYTHICIZING
MYTHOLOGIZED
MYTHOPOETIZE
PERFECTIVIZE
PHAGOCYTIZE
PHILOSOPHIZE
PHYLACTERIZE
PSYCHIATRIZE
SCHIZOCHROAL
SCHIZOPELMOUS
SCHIZOPHASIA
SCHIZOPHRENE
SCHIZOTHECAL
SOLILOQUIZED

SYCOPHANTIZE
SYMPATHIZED
SYMPHONIZED
SYNCHRONIZING
THEOMORPHIZE
ZINCOGRAPHIC
ZINCOGRAPHY
ZOOGEOGRAPHY
ZOOXANTHELLA
ZYGOMYCETES

30
ALPHABETIZING
AZOPHOSPHIN
BACCHANALIZE
BAMBOOZLEMENT
BIZYGOMATIC
BOLSHEVIZING
CATHOLICIZING
CHAMPAGNIZE
CHARACTERIZED
COLLECTIVIZED
COMMERCIALIZE
COPOLYMERIZE
DECAFFEINIZE
DEOXIDIZING
DESEXUALIZED
DESYNONYMIZE
DICHOTOMIZED
DIPHYOZOOID
DISEQUALIZE
DOXOLOGIZED
EFFEMINIZING
EMBLEMATICIZE
ENHYPOSTATIZE
ENZYMICALLY
ENZYMOLYTIC
EQUALIZATION
EXAUTHORIZE
EXCURSIONIZE
EXORCIZATION
EXTERIORIZING
HYDROBENZOIN
HYDROLYZATE
HYDRORHIZAL
HYDROZINCITE
HYPERBOLIZE
IMPROBABILIZE
JASPERIZING
JATEORHIZIN
JUBILIZATION
JUDICIALIZE
METAMORPHIZE
MISEMPHASIZE
MYCORRHIZAL
MYTHOLOGIZER
PANSEXUALIZE
PARCHMENTIZE
PHLEBOTOMIZE
PHLYZACIOUS

PHOSPHATIZE
PHOSPHORIZE
PHYSIOLOGIZE
PHYTOBEZOAR
PRIZEFIGHTER
PROTOXIDIZE
QUANTIZATION
QUIZZACIOUS
RHIZOPHAGOUS
SCHISMATIZING
SCHIZOGENETIC
SEMICIVILIZED
SKEPTICIZING
SOLILOQUIZER
SYMPATHIZER
SYMPTOMATIZE
SYNCHRONIZED
SYNONYMIZING
TAXIDERMIZE
THERMOLYZING
TRANQUILIZER
TRANQUILLIZE
VAGABONDIZING
VICTIMIZABLE
ZOMOTHERAPY
ZOOPATHOLOGY
ZOOPHYSICAL
ZOOPHYTICAL
ZYGODACTYLE
ZYGOMATICUM
ZYMOSTHENIC
ZYMOTICALLY

29
ACCLIMATIZING
ACCUSTOMIZING
ACHROMATIZED
ALPHABETIZED
APPETIZINGLY
ASEXUALIZING
AZIMETHYLENE
AZODIPHENYL
AZOPHENYLENE
BENZOHYDROL
BOLSHEVIZED
CACOPHONIZE
CATECHIZATION
CATHOLICIZED
CHARACTERIZER
CHEMICALIZE
CHORIAMBIZE
CHRONOLOGIZED
CINCHONIZING
CIVILIZATORY
COMPANIONIZED
CONTEMPORIZED
DEHYPNOTIZE
DEPOLYMERIZE
DEXTROSAZONE
EFFECTUALIZE

EFFEMINATIZE
EFFEMINIZED
EMBLEMATIZING
EPIGRAMMATIZE
ETYMOLOGIZING
EXOSTRACIZE
EXTERIORIZED
EXTERNIZATION
GEOGRAPHIZED
INOXIDIZING
JARGONIZING
JOURNALIZING
MACADAMIZING
MECHANIZATION
MICROSCOPIZE
MICROZYMIAN
MONARCHIZING
MONOCHORDIZE
MUNICIPALIZED
MUSCOVITIZED
MYOSYNIZESIS
MYTHOLOGIZE
MYZOSTOMIDAN
PAMPHLETIZE
PANEGYRICIZE
PHILIPPICIZE
PHYLLOZOOID
PRACTICALIZED
QUANTIZING
QUINAZOLINE
QUIZZATORIAL
RECOGNIZABLY
RHIZOCARPIC
RHIZOPHILOUS
SACCHARIZING
SARCOPHAGIZE
SCHISMATIZED
SCHIZOCARPIC
SCHIZOGNATH
SCHIZOPODOUS
SCHIZORHINAL
SKEPTICIZED
SOLILOQUIZE
SPECIFICIZE
SPONDYLIZEMA
STRYCHNINIZE
SULPHOBENZID
SYMBOLIZATION
SYMMETRIZING
SYNCHRONIZER
SYNONYMIZED
SYPHILIZING
THERMOLYZED
TRANQUILIZE
VACCINIZATION
VAGABONDIZED
VICTIMIZATION
ZINCOGRAPHER
ZOANTHODEMIC
ZOOMORPHISM

ZYGOSPHENAL
ZYMOPLASTIC

28
ACCLIMATIZED
ACCUSTOMIZED
ACETYLIZABLE
ADVERTIZEMENT
ALCHEMIZING
ALPHABETIZER
ANACEPHALIZE
ANHYDRIDIZE
ANTHROPOZOIC
APOSTROPHIZE
ASEXUALIZED
AZIMUTHALLY
AZOCOCHINEAL
AZOPARAFFIN
AZOSULPHONIC
BACTERIOLYZE
BENZOPHENONE
BIOGRAPHIZE
BIVOCALIZED
BOWDLERIZING
BRAZENFACED
CATECHIZING
CHAMELEONIZE
CHARACTERIZE
CHEERFULIZE
CHLORIDIZING
CHLORODIZING
CINCHONIZED
COLLECTIVIZE
COMMEMORIZING
COMMUNALIZED
COMMUNIZATION
COPPERIZATION
CRYPTOZONATE
CRYSTALLIZING
DACTYLOZOOID
DEEPFREEZING
DEHUMANIZING
DEMEPHITIZE
DESEXUALIZE
DEVOCALIZING
DICHOTOMIZE
ELECTROLYZING
EMBLEMATIZED
EMPATHIZING
EMPHASIZING
ENZYMOLYSIS
EPISCOPIZING
EPITHALAMIZE
EPIZOOTIOLOGY
ETHNOZOOLOGY
ETYMOLOGIZED
EUCHARISTIZED
EUPHEMIZING
FAMILIARIZING
FASCISTICIZE
FICTIONALIZED
FORMULARIZING
FRACTIONIZING
FRICTIONIZING
GAZINGSTOCK
GRAMMATICIZE
GYNECOMAZIA
HETEROZYGOTE
HETEROZYGOUS
HIERARCHIZE
HOPPERDOZER
HORIZONTALITY
HYDROGENIZE
HYPOSTATIZE
IMMETHODIZE
IMMOBILIZING
ISOCHRONIZING

JOURNALIZED
LOGOMACHIZE
MACADAMIZED
MELANCHOLIZE
MERCHANDIZE
MERMITHIZED
MONARCHIZED
MONOZYGOTIC
NAPHTHALIZE
OFFICIALIZE
OZONOSPHERIC
PANEGYRIZING
PEMMICANIZE
RECIPROCALIZE
RHAPSODIZING
RHIZOCARPOUS
SACCHARIZED
SCEPTICIZING
SCHILLERIZING
SCHIZODINIC
SCHIZOGENESIS
SCHIZOGENIC
SCHIZOGONIC
SCHIZOIDISM
SCHIZOPODAL
SCHIZOSTELIC
SCHIZOSTELY
SPECIMENIZED
SULFOBENZOIC
SYMBOLIZING
SYMMETRIZED
SYNCHRONIZE
SYNTHESIZING
SYSTEMATIZING
TCHERVONETZ
TECHNICALIZE
TRICHOTOMIZE
TYPHIZATION
UNIFORMALIZED
VAGABONDIZER
VASCULARIZING
VICTIMIZING
VITALIZINGLY
ZENOGRAPHIC
ZOODYNAMICS
ZYGOMATICUS
ZYMOLOGICAL

27
ACCLIMATIZER
ACETOBENZOIC
ACETYLIZATION
ACHROMATIZE
ADVERBIALIZE
ALCOHOLIZING
ALPHABETIZE
ANTHOLOGIZING
APOTHEOSIZED
BACHELORIZE
BALKANIZING
BAMBOOZLING
BEDAZZLINGLY
BENZYLAMINE
BESSEMERIZING
BOWDLERIZED
BROMOBENZENE
BROMOIODIZED
BRONZESMITH
BURKUNDAUZE
CANNIBALIZING
CANTHARIDIZE
CAPERCAILZIE
CATHETERIZE
CATHOLICIZE
CHALAZOIDITE
CHANNELIZING
CHITINIZATION

CHLORALIZING
CHLORIDIZED
CHLORODIZED
CHORIZONTIC
CHRONOLOGIZE
CIRCULARIZING
CITIZENSHIP
CIVILIZABLE
COMMEMORIZED
COMMUNALIZER
COMMUNIZING
COMPANIONIZE
CONTEMPORIZE
CRITICIZABLE
CRYSTALLIZED
CYCLIZATION
DECARBONIZED
DECARBURIZED
DECIMALIZING
DEEPFREEZED
DEHUMANIZED
DEMENTHOLIZE
DEMOBILIZING
DEMOCRATIZED
DEPAUPERIZED
DEPIGMENTIZE
DESULPHURIZE
DEVITAMINIZE
DEVOCALIZED
DEZINCIFIED
DIAZOMETHANE
DIPLOMATIZED
DISHARMONIZE
DISSYLLABIZE
DOCKIZATION
DOMESTICIZED
DYNAMIZATION
ELECTROLYZED
EMBLEMIZING
EPISCOPIZED
EUHEMERIZING
EXTERIORIZE
EXTERNALIZE
FACSIMILIZE
FACTORIZATION
FAMILIARIZED
FANATICIZING
FICTIONIZING
FISCALIZATION
FORMALIZATION
FORMULARIZED
FORMULIZATION
FRACTIONALIZE
FRICTIONIZED
FRIVOLIZING
GEOGRAPHIZE
GRAPHITIZED
GYROHORIZON
HAZARDOUSLY
HORIZONTALLY
IMMOBILIZED
IMMORTALIZING
IMPACTIONIZE
IMPERIALIZING
INDIVIDUALIZE
ISOCHRONIZED
JOURNALIZER
KYANIZATION
LICHENIZATION
MACADAMIZER
MALLEABLEIZED
MATHEMATIZE
MECHANALIZE
MEIZOSEISMIC
MELODRAMATIZE
MEMORIALIZING
METAPHONIZE

METHODIZING
MITHRIDATIZE
MONARCHIZER
MONZOGABBRO
MUNICIPALIZE
MUSCOVITIZE
MYZOSTOMOUS
NEWSMAGAZINE
NIGHTINGALIZE
PALEOZOOLOGY
PANEGYRIZED
PHANEROZOIC
PHANTOMIZER
PHENMIAZINE
PHONETICIZE
PHONETIZATION
PHRENOLOGIZE
PICRORHIZIN
POLYZOARIUM
PRACTICALIZE
PREACHERIZE
PROBLEMATIZE
PROPAGANDIZE
PROSELYTIZED
PUBLICIZING
PUZZLEHEADED
PYRRODIAZOLE
RAZORMAKING
RECAPITALIZED
RECRYSTALLIZE
RHAPSODIZED
RHIZOGENETIC
SCEPTICIZED
SCHILLERIZED
SCHISMATIZE
SCHIZOCOELE
SCHIZOGENOUS
SCHIZOSPORE
SIPHONOZOOID
SKELETONIZING
SOLVOLYZING
SOMNAMBULIZE
SOPHRONIZING
SPERMATOZOIC
SUBSTANTIVIZE
SUBVITALIZED
SULFOBENZIDE
SULPHATIZING
SULPHURIZING
SYNCRETIZING
SYNTHESIZED
SYSTEMATIZED
SYSTEMIZATION
TRAPEZIFORM
TRICHINIZING
TROPICALIZING
UNMECHANIZE
UNVERBALIZED
VAGABONDIZE
VASCULARIZED
VASECTOMIZE
VULCANIZATION
ZODIOPHILOUS
ZOOCECIDIUM
ZYGOLABIALIS
ZYMOSIMETER

26
ACADEMIZING
ACCLIMATIZE
ACCUSTOMIZE
AESTHETICIZE
ALBUMENIZING
ALBUMINIZING
ALCOHOLIZED
ALKALINIZING
ALKALIZABLE

ANABAPTIZING
ANAESTHETIZED
ANATHEMATIZE
ANTHOLOGIZED
ANTISEPTICIZE
APAESTHETIZE
APPRIZEMENT
ASEPTICIZING
ATMOLYZATION
AUTOCATALYZE
AZADIRACHTA
AZOERYTHRIN
AZOPHENETOLE
AZYGOMATOUS
BAPTIZEMENT
BENZOYLATION
BESSEMERIZED
BILHARZIASIS
BILHARZIOSIS
BUZZERPHONE
CANNIBALIZED
CAPITALIZING
CARAMELIZING
CATABIBAZON
CATABOLIZING
CATHARIZING
CAUSTICIZING
CENOZOOLOGY
CHANNELIZED
CHLORALIZED
CHORIZONTIST
CIRCULARIZED
CIVILIZATION
CLASSICIZING
COAZERVATION
COMMUNALIZE
CONCERTIZING
CONCRETIZING
CONSERVATIZE
CRYSTALLIZER
DECARBONIZER
DECHORALIZE
DECICERONIZE
DECIMALIZED
DEFIBRINIZE
DEFINITIZING
DEMAGNETIZED
DEMILITARIZED
DEMOBILIZED
DESULFURIZED
DEVITALIZING
DIALECTICIZE
DIAMONDIZING
DISPAUPERIZE
DOGGERELIZING
ECONOMIZATION
ELECTROLYZER
EMBEZZLEMENT
EMBLEMATIZE
ENTOMOLOGIZED
EPISTOLIZABLE
EPITOMIZATION
ETHEREALIZING
ETYMOLOGIZE
EUCHARISTIZE
EUHEMERIZED
EUPHONIZING
EVANGELIZING
FACTORIZING
FAMILIARIZER
FANATICIZED
FEDERALIZING
FEMINIZATION
FERTILIZABLE
FEUDALIZATION
FICTIONIZED
FISCALIZING

FOCALIZATION
FORMALIZING
FORMULIZING
FUROMONAZOLE
GALVANIZATION
GEOMETRICIZE
GLYCERINIZE
HARMONIZING
HARZBURGITE
HAZARDOUSNESS
HOMOGENIZER
HORIZONTICAL
IMBASTARDIZE
IMMATERIALIZE
IMMORTALIZED
IMPERIALIZED
IMPERSONALIZE
LEGITIMATIZED
LETHARGIZING
MAGNETIZABLE
MARTYRIZING
MEGAZOOSPORE
MEMORIALIZED
MESMERIZATION
METABOLIZING
MISCOGNIZANT
MIZZENTOPMAN
MIZZENTOPMEN
MONOPOLIZING
NAZIFICATION
OLIGARCHIZE
ORYZIVOROUS
OSMAZOMATIC
OVARIOTOMIZE
OVERPRIZING
OZONOSCOPIC
PALLADIUMIZE
PANEGYRIZER
PARABOLIZING
PARALYZATION
PARENTHESIZE
PECULIARIZED
PEZIZAEFORM
PHILIPPIZER
PHILOLOGIZE
PHILOZOONIST
PIEZOMETRIC
PLASTICIZING
PLEBEIANIZED
POLITICIZING
POPULARIZING
PRESERVATIZE
PRIZEHOLDER
PROBABILIZE
PROSELYTIZER
PULVERIZATOR
PULVERIZING
REBAPTIZATION
RECOGNIZABLE
RECOGNIZANCE
RHIZANTHOUS
RHIZODERMIS
RHIZOPODIST
RHIZOPODOUS
RHIZOSTOMOUS
SEPTICIZATION
SHERARDIZING
SHERBETZIDE
SKELETONIZED
SOPHRONIZED
SPECIALIZING
SPECIMENIZE
SPERMATOZOID
SPHEROIDIZE
SPHERULITIZE
STANZAICALLY
SULPHATIZED

SULPHURIZED
SUMMARIZATION
SYLLABIZING
SYNCRETIZED
SYNDICALIZE
SYNTHESIZER
SYNTHETIZER
SYSTEMATIZER
SYSTEMIZING
TELFORDIZING
THEOLOGIZING
TOBACCONIZE
TRICHINIZED
TROPHOZOOID
TROPICALIZED
TROPOLOGIZING
UNCIVILIZED
UNIFORMALIZE
UNIVERSALIZED
VAPORIZATION
VAPOURIZING
VEGETABLIZE
VERATRINIZING
VERBALIZING
VERMILIONIZE
VOCALIZATION
VOLCANIZING
VULCANIZING
VULGARIZATION
ZAPHRENTOID
ZIGZAGGEDLY
ZOANTHODEME
ZONOCHLORITE
ZOOERYTHRIN
ZOOMAGNETISM
ZOOMORPHIZE
ZOOPLANKTON
ZYGOPLEURAL
ZYGOPTERID
ZYGOPTEROUS
ZYMOGENESIS

25
ADVERTIZING
AGGRANDIZING
ALBUMENIZED
ALBUMINIZED
ALGEBRIZATION
ALKALINIZED
ALKALIZATION
AMMONIZATION
AMORTIZEMENT
ANABAPTIZED
ANACHRONIZE
ANAESTHETIZER
ANTHEROZOOID
ANTIFREEZING
ANTIPATHIZE
APESTHETIZE
APOTHEOSIZE
ARCTICIZING
ARITHMETIZE
ASCIDIOZOOID
ASEPTICIZED
ASPHETERIZE
AUTHORIZATION
AZOFICATION
AZOSULPHINE
AZOTHIONIUM
BACTERIZING
BARBARIZING
BASTARDIZING
BEDIZENMENT
BERGINIZATION
BITUMINIZED
BURGLARIZING
CAPITALIZED

CARAMELIZED
CARBOAZOTINE
CARBOLIZING
CARBONIZING
CARBURIZING
CATABOLIZED
CATALYZATOR
CATEGORIZING
CATHETERIZE
CAUSTICIZED
CELESTIALIZED
CHORIZATION
CHORIZONTES
CICATRIZING
CLASSICIZED
COCAINIZING
COMMEMORIZE
CONCERTIZED
CONCRETIZED
CORPOREALIZE
COSMOGONIZE
CRITICIZING
CRYSTALLIZE
CUTICULARIZE
DECARBONIZE
DECARBURIZE
DECEREBRIZE
DECOLORIZING
DEFERRIZING
DEFINITIZED
DELIMITIZING
DELOCALIZING
DEMAGNETIZER
DEMOCRATIZE
DEMORALIZING
DEPAUPERIZE
DEPOLARIZING
DESILVERIZER
DESULFURIZER
DEVITALIZED
DEVULGARIZE
DIAMONDIZED
DIAZENTITHAL
DIEZEUGMENON
DIPLOMATIZE
DISCANONIZED
DISGOSPELIZE
DIVINIZATION
DOCTRINIZING
DOCUMENTIZE
DOGMATIZING
DOMESTICIZE
DRAMATIZATION
ECONOMIZING
ELECTROLYZE
EMOTIONALIZED
ENCARNALIZING
ENIGMATIZING
ENTHRONIZING
EPENTHESIZE
EPIDOTIZATION
EPITOMIZING
ETHEREALIZED
EVANGELIZED
FAMILIARIZE
FARADIZATION
FEDERALIZED
FERTILIZATION
FEUDALIZING
FLUIDIZATION
FORMULARIZE
FOSSILIZATION
FRACTIONIZE
FRATERNIZING
FRICTIONIZE
FUNCTIONIZE
GALVANIZING

GENERALIZABLE
GEOMETRIZING
HORIZOMETER
HOSPITALIZE
HURRICANIZE
IMMORTALIZER
INFORMALIZE
ISOCHRONIZE
KETONIZATION
LAPAROTOMIZE
LEGITIMIZING
LETHARGIZED
LIEDERKRANZ
LITHOTOMIZE
MAGAZINABLE
MAGNETIZATION
MALLEABLEIZE
MAMMONIZATION
MARBLEIZING
MARMARIZING
MARSUPIALIZE
MATERIALIZING
MEIZOSEISMAL
MEMORANDIZE
MEMORIALIZER
MEMORIZATION
MERCERIZING
MERCURIALIZE
MERCURIZING
MESMERIZING
METABOLIZED
METAMERIZED
MICASIZATION
MICROZOARIAN
MINIMIZATION
MNEMONIZING
MOBILIZATION
MODERNIZATION
MONOLOGIZING
MONOPOLIZED
MUZZLELOADING
NIVELLIZATION
OBLIVIONIZE
OLIGORHIZOUS
OPTIMIZATION
ORGANIZATORY
OSMAZOMATOUS
OVERGLAZING
OZONOSPHERE
PANTHEONIZE
PAPALIZATION
PARABOLIZED
PAUPERIZING
PENTAMETRIZE
PEPTONIZING
PLAGIARIZING
PLASTICIZED
PNEUMATIZED
POLITICALIZE
POLITICIZED
POLYZOARIAL
POPULARIZED
PORCELAINIZE
PORCELLANIZE
PRAGMATIZER
PROSELYTIZE
PROTOCITIZEN
PULVERIZATE
RACEMIZATION
RADIUMIZATION
RECAPITALIZE
RECARBONIZER
RECARBURIZER
REHARMONIZE
REVITALIZING
RHIZOCAULUS
RHIZOMATOUS

RUBBERIZING
SACRAMENTIZE
SCANDALIZING
SCHILLERIZE
SCHIZOSTELE
SECTARIANIZED
SECTIONALIZED
SEMPITERNIZE
SHERARDIZED
SKELETONIZER
SOVEREIGNIZE
SOVIETIZATION
SPECIALIZED
SPERMATOZOAL
SPERMATOZOAN
SPERMATOZOON
SPIRITUALIZED
SPITZENBERG
SPITZENBURG
STANDARDIZING
STIGMATIZING
SUBSIDIZATION
SULFADIAZINE
SULPHAZOTIZE
SUMMARIZING
SYLLOGIZING
SYSTEMATIZE
SZAIBELYITE
TELEPATHIZE
TELFORDIZED
TEMPORIZING
THEATRICIZE
THEOLOGIZED
TROPHOZOITE
TROPOLOGIZED
UNAUTHORIZED
UNPOPULARIZE
UNRECOGNIZED
VASCULARIZE
VERATRINIZED
VITRIOLIZING
VOLATILIZING
VULCANIZATE
VULGARIZING
WESTERNIZING
ZIMENTWATER
ZINCIFEROUS
ZONOLIMNETIC
ZONOSKELETON
ZOOGRAFTING
ZOOMAGNETIC
ZOOPANTHEON
ZOOTHEISTIC
ZOSTERIFORM
ZYGOPTERAN

24
ABNORMALIZE
ACCULTURIZE
ACETONIZATION
ACTUALIZATION
AGGRANDIZED
ALBUMENIZER
ALGEBRAIZED
AMORTIZABLE
ANAESTHETIZE
ANESTHETIZER
ANGIOSTOMIZE
ANGLICIZING
ANIMALIZATION
ANTHEROZOID
ANTHOLOGIZE
APOLOGIZING
APOSTATIZING
ASTIGMATIZER
AUTHORIZING
AZEOTROPISM

AZOOSPERMIA
AZOTOBACTER
BASTARDIZED
BENZINDULINE
BESSEMERIZE
BESTIALIZING
BROMIZATION
BURGLARIZED
BURNETTIZING
BURTONIZATION
CACOZEALOUS
CALABAZILLA
CANNIBALIZE
CATALEPTIZE
CATEGORIZED
CAUSTICIZER
CAUTERIZATION
CENTRALIZING
CICATRIZANT
CICATRIZATE
CIRCULARIZE
COLLODIONIZE
CONCERTIZER
DAMENIZATION
DECENTRALIZE
DECOLORIZED
DELIMITIZED
DELOCALIZED
DEMAGNETIZE
DEMANGANIZE
DEMILITARIZE
DEMINERALIZE
DEMONETIZED
DEMORALIZER
DENICOTINIZE
DEPOLARIZED
DESILICONIZE
DESILVERIZE
DESULFURIZE
DIABOLIZING
DIALECTALIZE
DIALYZATION
DIMERIZATION
DISORGANIZED
DISSOCIALIZE
DOCTRINIZED
DOGGERELIZER
DRAMATIZING
DUCTILIZING
ECZEMATOSIS
EDITORIALIZED
ELECTRICIZE
ELECTROTONIZE
ENCARNALIZED
ENIGMATIZED
ENTHRONIZED
ENTOMOLOGIZE
ENTOZOOLOGY
EPILOGIZING
ETHERIZATION
EVANGELIZER
EVOLUTIONIZE
FANTASIZING
FERTILIZING
FOSSILIZING
FRATERNIZED
GEOMETRIZED
GLAMORIZING
GORMANDIZER
GUTTURALIZING
HORIZONTALIZE
IMMORTALIZE
IMPATRONIZE
IMPERIALIZE
INDOCTRINIZE
INTHRONIZATE
LEGITIMATIZE

LEGITIMIZED
LIBERALIZING
LOCALIZABLE
MAGNETIZING
MALLEABLIZE
MATERIALIZED
MEDIATIZING
MEMORIALIZE
METALLIZATION
METASTASIZED
MICROZOARIA
MIGNIARDIZE
MILITARIZING
MINERALIZING
MINERALOGIZE
MINIATURIZED
MODERNIZING
MONOLOGIZED
MONOPOLIZER
MONZODIORITE
MUSCULARIZE
NITROGENIZING
NORMALIZATION
NOVELIZATION
ODYLIZATION
OPTIMIZING
OSTRACIZATION
OUTTYRANNIZE
PAGANIZATION
PANCREATIZE
PARABOLIZER
PASTEURIZING
PECTIZATION
PECULIARIZE
PEPTIZATION
PERMORALIZE
PERSONALIZED
PLAGIARIZED
PLASTICIZER
PLEBEIANIZE
POLARIZABLE
POLITICIZER
POPULARIZER
PRESSURIZING
PRODIGALIZE
PROTOCOLIZE
PUZZLEPATED
RACIALIZATION
RANDOMIZING
RECARBONIZE
RECARBURIZE
RECOGNIZING
REVITALIZED
RHIZOGENOUS
RINFORZANDO
ROMANTICIZE
ROYALIZATION
SCANDALIZED
SCRUTINIZING
SECULARIZING
SIMULACRIZE
SINGULARIZING
SKELETONIZE
SOCIALIZATION
SOLEMNIZATION
SOLITUDINIZED
SOVIETIZING
SPECIALIZER
SPERMATOZOA
SPIRALIZATION
SPIRITUALIZER
STABILIZATION
STANDARDIZED
STIGMATIZED
STRUCTURALIZE
SUBSIDIZING
SUBTILIZATION

SUBURBANIZE
SULCALIZATION
SULFATIZING
SULFURIZING
SYNTONIZING
TABULARIZING
TEMPORALIZE
TETRAKISAZO
THEOLOGIZER
THEORIZATION
THIADIAZOLE
TRAILBLAZING
TROPICALIZE
TUBERCULIZE
TYRANNIZING
UNCANONIZING
UNFEUDALIZE
UNIVERSITIZE
UNMORALIZING
UNPATRONIZED
UNVULGARIZE
VALORIZATION
VASSALIZING
VENALIZATION
VERATRIZING
VISUALIZING
VITALIZATION
VITRIOLIZED
VOLATILIZED
WESTERNIZED
WINTERIZING
WIZENEDNESS
ZENOCENTRIC
ZINNWALDITE
ZOIDOGAMOUS
ZONAESTHESIA
ZOODENDRIUM
ZOOGONIDIUM

23

ABASTARDIZE
ABOLITIONIZE
ACTIONIZING
ACTUALIZING
AGGRANDIZER
ALBITIZATION
ALLEGORIZING
ALUMINIZING
AMORTIZATION
ANALYZATION
ANATOMIZING
ANESTHETIZE
ANIMALIZING
ANTAGONIZING
ANTITHESIZE
APOSTATIZED
ARBORIZATION
AROMATIZING
AZOCORALLINE
AZOTORRHOEA
BATTOLOGIZE
BENZOINATED
BENZONITRILE
BERZELIANITE
BESTIALIZED
BISTETRAZOLE
BRUTALIZING
BURNETTIZED
CANALIZATION
CANONIZATION
CARNALIZING
CATALOGUIZE
CAUTERIZING
CELESTIALIZE
CENTRALIZED
CITIZENIZING
COLONIZATION

CONSONANTIZE
CREOLIZATION
CURARIZATION
CUTINIZATION
DECOLORIZER
DECOLOURIZE
DEMONTETIZE
DEMORALIZER
DENAZIFYING
DEODORIZING
DEPERSONIZE
DEPOLARIZER
DERACIALIZE
DERMATOZOON
DESACRALIZE
DESCLOIZITE
DETRIBALIZE
DEUTEROZOOID
DEZINCATION
DIALOGIZING
DIAZOBENZENE
DISCANONIZE
DISORGANIZER
DOGGERELIZE
ELECTRIZING
EMOTIONALIZE
ETHEREALIZE
EUDAEMONIZE
EVENTUALIZE
FRATERNIZER
GABERLUNZIE
GASTEROZOOID
GAZETTEERAGE
GELATINIZING
GENEALOGIZER
GEOLOGIZING
GLUCOSAZONE
GLUTTONIZING
IDOLATRIZING
ILLEGALIZING
IODOBENZENE
IRREALIZABLE
ITALICIZING
LABIALIZING
LABILIZATION
LALLAPALOOZA
LIBERALIZED
LOCALIZATION
MARGINALIZE
MATERIALIZER
MATRONIZING
MERORGANIZE
METALIZATION
MEZZOTINTING
MILITARIZED
MINERALIZED
MISSIONARIZE
MONETIZATION
MORALIZATION
MORTALIZING
MOTORIZATION
MUTUALIZING
MUZZLELOADER
NARCOTIZING
NATIONALIZING
NEBULIZATION
NEMATOZOOID
NEOPAGANIZE
NITRIDIZATION
NITROBENZENE
NITROGENIZED
NORMALIZING
OPSONIZATION
ORGANIZABLE
ORIENTALIZING
OSTRACIZING
OVALIZATION

OVERZEALOUS
OZONIFEROUS
PALATIZATION
PALLETIZING
PASTEURIZED
PATRONIZING
PELORIZATION
PENALIZATION
PETROLIZING
PEZIZACEOUS
PLAGIARIZER
PLATINIZING
PLURALIZING
POLARIZATION
POSTURIZING
POTENTIALIZE
POZZUOLANIC
PRESSURIZED
PROLOGUIZER
PROTOZOIASIS
PUZZLINGNESS
RADIALIZATION
REALISTICIZE
RECOGNIZANT
REFORESTIZE
REORGANIZING
REVITALIZER
RHYTHMICIZE
ROBOTIZATION
SCENARIZING
SCLEROTIZED
SCRUTINIZED
SECTARIANIZE
SECTIONALIZE
SECULARIZED
SERMONIZING
SERPENTINIZE
SINGULARIZED
SLENDERIZING
SLUGGARDIZE
SOCIALIZING
SOLEMNIZING
SOLIDARIZING
SOUTHERNIZE
SPIRITUALIZE
SPLENIZATION
STABILIZATOR
STABILIZING
STALWARTIZE
STANDARDIZER
STATISTICIZE
STIGMATIZER
STYLIZATION
SUBERIZATION
SUBTILIZING
TABULARIZED
TAUTOLOGIZED
TOTEMIZATION
TOURMALINIZE
TRAPEZOIDAL
TROPOLOGIZE
TUBERIZATION
TUBULIZATION
UNAUTHORIZE
UNCANONIZED
UNMODERNIZE
UNMORALIZED
UNSECULARIZE
URBANIZATION
VERATRINIZE
VOLATILIZER
ZINGIBERENE
ZONESTHESIA
ZOOSPORANGE

22
ALDOLIZATION

ALLEGORIZED
ALLOTROPIZE
ANALOGIZING
ANTAGONIZED
ARTERIALIZED
ASBESTINIZE
ASTRONOMIZE
ATOMIZATION
ATTITUDINIZE
BENZONITROL
BISTRIAZOLE
BIZARRENESS
BLIZZARDOUS
CENTRALIZER
CITIZENIZED
CITIZENRIES
DEBENZOLIZE
DENATURALIZE
DENIZENATION
DERATIZATION
DESENSITIZER
DIAGONALIZE
DISORGANIZE
DISSEIZORESS
EDITORIALIZE
ELASTICIZER
ELECTRALIZE
ELECTRICALIZE
EMULSIONIZE
ENCARNALIZE
ENSORCELIZE
ENSORCERIZE
ERGOTIZATION
EULOGIZATION
GASTROZOOID
GELATINIZED
GENEALOGIZE
GENERALIZED
GLUTTONIZED
IDEALIZATION
IDOLATRIZED
ILLEGALIZED
IRREGULARIZE
ITEMIZATION

LAICIZATION
LALAPALOOZA
LATERALIZING
LEGALIZATION
LIBERALIZER
LINEARIZATION
LITERALIZING
MANORIALIZE
MATERIALIZE
MATERNALIZE
METASTASIZE
MEZZOTINTED
MINERALIZER
MINIATURIZE
MISSIONIZER
NATIONALIZED
NATURALIZING
NEOLOGIZING
NEUROTOMIZE
NEUTRALIZING
NONPARTIZAN
OPTIONALIZE
ORGANIZATION
ORGANZINING
ORIENTALIZED
PARAENESIZE
PASTEURIZER
PASTORALIZE
PATERNALIZE
PATRIZATION
PERSONALIZE
POETIZATION
PROLETARIZE
PROTOZOONAL
PUZZLEDNESS
RATIONALIZED
REACTUALIZE
REGULARIZED
REORGANIZED
SANCTUARIZE
SATIRIZABLE
SCRUTINIZER
SENSIBILIZE
SENSITIZATION

SENSUALIZING
SERIALIZATION
SIGNALIZING
SIZABLENESS
SLENDERIZED
SOLIDARIZED
SOLITUDINIZE
SOLMIZATION
STANDARDIZE
STERILIZATION
SUBSTANTIZE
TARTRAZINIC
TAUTOLOGIZER
TEETOTUMIZE
TENDERIZING
TENEMENTIZE
TETRAZOLIUM
TRAILBLAZER
UNBRUTALIZE
UNMORTALIZE
UNORGANIZED
UNSOLEMNIZE
UNSTERILIZED
ZONOCILIATE
ZOOCULTURAL
ZOOPARASITE

21
ADENIZATION
AGGUTINIZE
AGRARIANIZE
ALLEGORIZER
ANTAGONIZER
ARSENIZATION
ASTROLOGIZE
DENATURIZER
DESENSITIZE
DESTERILIZE
DESTINEZITE
DIAZOTIZING
DUALIZATION
ESTERIZATION
ETERNIZATION
GELATINIZER

GENERALIZER
GRANULITIZE
GUTTURALIZE
IDOLATRIZER
IDOLIZATION
INTELLIGIZE
INTERMEZZOS
IRIDIZATION
LATERALIZED
LATERIZATION
LITERALIZED
MEZZOTINTER
NASALIZATION
NATIONALIZER
NATURALIZED
NESSLERIZED
NEUROLOGIZE
NEUTRALIZED
NITROGENIZE
NODULIZING
NOTARIZATION
NUPTIALIZE
POLITZERIZE
PROTOZOEAN
PUZZLEATION
RATIONALIZER
RAZZBERRIES
REGIONALIZE
REGULARIZER
RELIGIONIZE
REORGANIZER
ROENTGENIZE
ROUTINIZING
RURALIZATION
SAILORIZING
SENSITIZING
SENSUALIZED
SERIALIZING
SIDEREALIZE
SINGULARIZE
SOLARIZATION
STERILIZING
TANTALIZING
TARTARIZING

TAUTOLOGIZE
TELLURIZING
TERRORIZING
TETANIZATION
TOTALIZATION
TRULLIZATION
TUTORIZATION
ULTRAZEALOUS
UNIONIZATION
UNLITURGIZE
UNNATURALIZE
URALITIZING
ZOISITIZATION
ZOOLOGIZING

20
ARTERIALIZE
AZOTETRAZOLE
ENOLIZATION
INTERNALIZE
LIONIZATION
LITERALIZER
LORENZENITE
NATIONALIZE
NATURALIZER
NEUTRALIZER
NONENTITIZE
ORIENTALIZE
RATIONALIZE
REALIZATION
RESTERILIZE
ROTARIANIZE
STALLIONIZE
TARANTARIZE
TOTALIZATOR
TRILLIONIZE
UTILIZATION
ZEALOUSNESS
ZEOLITIZING

19
OZONIZATION
TETRAZOTIZE